SEPTUAGINT BIBLE IN ENGLISH

The Complete Translation of the Greek Old Testament.
Including the Apocrypha

Table of Contents

DISCLAIMER

In the text that follows, you may notice the absence of certain verses. This is due to differences in translations and editions of the original Biblical text. The Septuagint, a Greek translation of the Old Testament, may present variations compared to other versions, such as the Masoretic Text or the Vulgate. These differences can include omissions, additions, or relocations of verses.

In particular, the translation by Sir Lancelot Benton may have discrepancies compared to other editions of the Septuagint. These discrepancies result from different manuscripts used for the translations and various editorial decisions made by the translators.

We apologize for any inconvenience caused by these omissions and encourage you to consult multiple translations and commentaries for a more comprehensive and accurate understanding of the Biblical text.

GENESIS

Gen.1 1 In the beginning God made the heaven and the earth. 2 But the earth was unsightly and unfurnished, and darkness was over the deep, and the Spirit of God moved over the water. 3 And God said, Let there be light, and there was light. 4 And God saw the light that it was good, and God divided between the light and the darkness. 5 And God called the light Day, and the darkness he called Night, and there was evening and there was morning, the first day. 6 And God said, Let there be a firmament in the midst of the water, and let it be a division between water and water, and it was so. 7 And God made the firmament, and God divided between the water which was under the firmament and the water which was above the firmament. 8 And God called the firmament Heaven, and God saw that it was good, and there was evening and there was morning, the second day. 9 And God said, Let the water which is under the heaven be collected into one place, and let the dry land appear, and it was so. And the water which was under the heaven was collected into its places, and the dry land appeared. 10 And God called the dry land Earth, and the gatherings of the waters he called Seas, and God saw that it was good. 11 And God said, Let the earth bring forth the herb of grass bearing seed according to its kind and according to its likeness, and the fruit-tree bearing fruit whose seed is in it, according to its kind on the earth, and it was so. 12 And the earth brought forth the herb of grass bearing seed according to its kind and according to its likeness, and the fruit tree bearing fruit whose seed is in it, according to its kind on the earth, and God saw that it was good. 13 And there was evening and there was morning, the third day. 14 And God said, Let there be lights in the firmament of the heaven to give light upon the earth, to divide between day and night, and let them be for signs and for seasons and for days and for years. 15 And let them be for light in the firmament of the heaven, so as to shine upon the earth, and it was so. 16 And God made the two great lights, the greater light for regulating the day and the lesser light for regulating the night, the stars also. 17 And God placed them in the firmament of the heaven, so as to shine upon the earth, 18 and to regulate day and night, and to divide between the light and the darkness. And God saw that it was good. 19 And there was evening and there was morning, the fourth day. 20 And God said, Let the waters bring forth reptiles having life, and winged creatures flying above the earth in the firmament of heaven, and it was so. 21 And God made great whales, and every living reptile, which the waters brought forth according to their kinds, and every creature that flies with wings according to its kind, and God saw that they were good. 22 And God blessed them saying, Increase and multiply and fill the waters in the seas, and let the creatures that fly be multiplied on the earth. 23 And there was evening and there was morning, the fifth day. 24 And God said, Let the earth bring forth the living creature according to its kind, quadrupeds and reptiles and wild beasts of the earth according to their kind, and it was so. 25 And God made the wild beasts of the earth according to their kind, and cattle according to their kind, and all the reptiles of the earth according to their kind, and God saw that they were good. 26 And God said, Let us make man according to our image and likeness, and let them have dominion over the fish of the sea, and over the flying creatures of heaven, and over the cattle and all the earth, and over all the reptiles that creep on the earth. 27 And God made man, according to the image of God he made him, male and female he made them. 28 And God blessed them, saying, Increase and multiply, and fill the earth and subdue it, and have dominion over the fish of the seas and flying creatures of heaven, and all the cattle and all the earth, and all the reptiles that creep on the earth. 29 And God said, Behold I have given to you every seed-bearing herb sowing seed which is upon all the earth, and every tree which has in itself the fruit of seed that is sown, to you it shall be for food. 30 And to all the wild beasts of the earth, and to all the flying creatures of heaven, and to every reptile creeping on the earth, which has in itself the breath of life, even every green plant for food; and it was so. 31 And God saw all the things that he had made, and, behold, they were very good. And there was evening and there was morning, the sixth day.

Gen.2 1 And the heavens and the earth were finished, and the whole world of them. 2 And God finished on the sixth day his works which he made, and he ceased on the seventh day from all his works which he made. 3 And God blessed the seventh day and sanctified it, because in it he ceased from all his works which God began to do. 4 This *is* the book of the generation of heaven and earth, when they were made, in the day in which the Lord God made the heaven and the earth, 5 and every herb of the field before it was on the earth, and all the grass of the field before it sprang up, for God had not rained on the earth, and there was not a man to cultivate it. 6 But there rose a fountain out of the earth, and watered the whole face of the earth. 7 And God formed the man *of* dust of the earth, and breathed upon his face the breath of life, and the man became a living soul. 8 And God planted a garden eastward in Edem, and placed there the man whom he had formed. 9 And God made to spring up also out of the earth every tree beautiful to the eye and good for food, and the tree of life in the midst of the garden, and the tree of learning the knowledge of good and evil. 10 And a river proceeds out of Edem to water the garden, thence it divides itself into four heads. 11 The name of the one, Phisom, this it is which encircles the whole land of Evilat, where there is gold. 12 And the gold of that land is good, there also is carbuncle and emerald. 13 And the name of the second river is Geon, this it is which encircles the whole land of Ethiopia. 14 And the third river is Tigris, this is that which flows forth over against the Assyrians. And the fourth river is Euphrates. 15 And the Lord God took the man whom he had formed, and placed him in the garden of Delight, to cultivate and keep it. 16 And the Lord God gave a charge to Adam, saying, Of every tree which is in the garden thou mayest freely eat, 17 but of the tree of the knowledge of good and evil—of it ye shall not eat, but in whatsoever day ye eat of it, ye shall surely die. 18 And the Lord God said, *It is* not good that the man should be alone, let us make for him a help suitable to him. 19 And God formed yet farther out of the earth all the wild beasts of the field, and all the birds of the sky, and he brought them to Adam, to see what he would call them, and whatever Adam called any living creature, that was the name of it. 20 And Adam gave names to all the cattle and to all the birds of the sky, and to all the wild beasts of the field, but for Adam there was not found a help like to himself. 21 And God brought a trance upon Adam, and he slept, and he took one of his ribs, and filled up the flesh instead thereof. 22 And God formed the rib which he took from Adam into a woman, and brought her to Adam. 23 And Adam said, This now is bone of my bones, and flesh of my flesh; she shall be called woman, because she was taken out of her husband. 24 Therefore shall a man leave his father and his mother and shall cleave to his wife, and they two shall be one flesh.

Gen.3 1 And the two were naked, both Adam and his wife, and were not ashamed. 2 Now the serpent was the most crafty of all the brutes on the earth, which the Lord God made, and the serpent said to the woman, Wherefore has God said, Eat not of every tree of the garden? 3 And the woman said to the serpent, We may eat of the fruit of the trees of the garden, 4 but of the fruit of the tree which is in the midst of the garden, God said, Ye shall not eat of it, neither shall ye touch it, lest ye die. 5 And the serpent said to the woman, Ye shall not surely die. 6 For God knew that in whatever day ye should eat of it your eyes would be opened, and ye would be as gods, knowing good and evil. 7 And the woman saw that the tree was good for food, and that it was pleasant to the eyes to look upon and beautiful to contemplate, and having taken of its fruit she ate, and she gave to her husband also with her, and they ate. 8 And the eyes of both were opened, and they perceived that they were naked, and they sewed fig leaves together, and made themselves aprons to go round them. 9 And they heard the voice of the Lord God walking in the garden in the afternoon; and both Adam and his wife hid themselves from the face of the Lord God in the midst of the trees of the garden. 10 And the Lord God called Adam and said to him, Adam, where art thou? 11 And he said to him, I heard thy voice as thou walkedst in the garden, and I feared because I was naked and I hid myself. 12 And God said to him, Who told thee that thou wast naked, unless thou hast eaten of the tree concerning which I charged thee of it alone not to eat? 13 And Adam said, The woman whom thou gavest to be with me—she gave me of the tree and I ate. 14 And the Lord God said to the woman, Why hast thou done this? And the woman said, The serpent deceived me and I ate. 15 And the Lord God said to the serpent, Because thou hast done this thou art cursed above all cattle and all the brutes of the earth, on thy breast and belly thou shalt go, and thou shalt eat earth all the days of thy life. 16 And I will put enmity between thee and the woman and between thy seed and her seed, he shall watch against thy head, and thou shalt watch against his heel. 17 And to the woman he said, I will greatly multiply thy pains and thy groanings; in pain thou shalt bring forth children, and thy submission shall be to thy husband, and he shall rule over thee. 18 And to Adam he said, Because thou hast hearkened to the voice of thy wife, and eaten of the tree concerning which I charged thee of it only not to eat—of that thou hast eaten, cursed *is* the ground in thy labours, in pain shalt thou eat of it all the days of thy life. 19 Thorns and thistles shall it bring forth to thee, and thou shalt eat the herb of the field. 20 In the sweat of thy face shalt thou eat thy bread until thou return to the earth out of which thou wast taken, for earth thou art and to earth thou shalt return. 21 And Adam called the name of his wife Life, because she was the mother of all living. 22 And the Lord God made for Adam and his wife garments of skin, and clothed them. 23 And God said, Behold, Adam is become as one of us, to know good and evil, and now lest at any time he stretch forth his hand, and take of the tree of life and eat, and *so* he shall live forever— 24 So the Lord God sent him forth out of the garden of Delight to cultivate the ground out of which he was taken. 25 And he cast out Adam and caused him to dwell over against the garden of Delight, and stationed the cherubs and the fiery sword that turns about to keep the way of the tree of life.

Gen.4 1 And Adam knew Eve his wife, and she conceived and brought forth Cain and said, I have gained a man through God. 2 And she again bore his brother Abel. And Abel was a keeper of sheep, but Cain was a tiller of the ground. 3 And it was so after some time that Cain brought of the fruits of the earth a sacrifice to the Lord. 4 And Abel also brought of the first born of his sheep and of his fatlings, and God looked upon Abel and his gifts, 5 but Cain and his sacrifices he regarded not, and Cain was exceedingly sorrowful and his countenance fell. 6 And the Lord God said to Cain, Why art thou become very sorrowful and why is thy countenance fallen? 7 Hast thou not sinned if thou hast brought it rightly, but not rightly divided it? be still, to thee shall be his submission, and thou shalt rule over him. 8 And Cain said to Abel his brother, Let us go out into the plain; and it came to pass that when they were in the plain Cain rose up against Abel his brother, and slew him. 9 And the Lord God said to Cain, Where is Abel thy brother? and he said, I know not, am I my brother's keeper? 10 And the Lord said, What hast thou done? the voice of thy brother's blood cries to me out of the ground. 11 And now thou *art* cursed from the earth which has opened her mouth to receive thy brother's blood from thy hand. 12 When thou tillest the earth, then it shall not continue to give its strength to thee: thou shalt be groaning and trembling on the earth. 13 And Cain said to the Lord God, My crime *is* too great for me to be forgiven. 14 If thou castest me out this day from the face of the earth, and I shall be hidden from thy presence, and I shall be groaning and trembling upon the earth, then it will be that any one that finds me shall slay me. 15 And the Lord God said to him, Not so, any one that slays Cain shall suffer seven-fold vengeance; and the Lord

God set a mark upon Cain that no one that found him might slay him. 16 So Cain went forth from the presence of God and dwelt in the land of Nod over against Edem. 17 And Cain knew his wife, and having conceived she bore Enoch; and he built a city; and he named the city after the name of his son, Enoch. 18 And to Enoch was born Gaidad; and Gaidad begot Maleleel; and Maleleel begot Mathusala; and Mathusala begot Lamech. 19 And Lamech took to himself two wives; the name of the one was Ada, and the name of the second Sella. 20 And Ada bore Jobel; he was the father of those that dwell in tents, feeding cattle. 21 And the name of his brother was Jubal; he it was who invented the psaltery and harp. 22 And Sella also bore Thobel; he was a smith, a manufacturer both of brass and iron; and the sister of Thobel was Noema. 23 And Lamech said to his wives, Ada and Sella, Hear my voice, ye wives of Lamech, consider my words, because I have slain a man to my sorrow and a youth to my grief. 24 Because vengeance has been exacted seven times on Cain's behalf, on Lamech's *it shall be* seventy times seven. 25 And Adam knew Eve his wife, and she conceived and bore a son, and called his name Seth, saying, For God has raised up to me another seed instead of Abel, whom Cain slew. 26 And Seth had a son, and he called his name Enos: he hoped to call on the name of the Lord God.

Gen.5 1 This *is* the genealogy of men in the day in which God made Adam; in the image of God he made him: 2 male and female he made them, and blessed them; and he called his name Adam, in the day in which he made them. 3 And Adam lived two hundred and thirty years, and begot *a son* after his *own* form, and after his *own* image, and he called his name Seth. 4 And the days of Adam, which he lived after his begetting Seth, were seven hundred years; and he begot sons and daughters. 5 And all the days of Adam which he lived were nine hundred and thirty years, and he died. 6 Now Seth lived two hundred and five years, and begot Enos. 7 And Seth lived after his begetting Enos, seven hundred and seven years, and he begot sons and daughters. 8 And all the days of Seth were nine hundred and twelve years, and he died. 9 And Enos lived an hundred and ninety years, and begot Cainan. 10 And Enos lived after his begetting Cainan, seven hundred and fifteen years, and he begot sons and daughters. 11 And all the days of Enos were nine hundred and five years, and he died. 12 And Cainan lived an hundred and seventy years, and he begot Maleleel. 13 And Cainan lived after his begetting Maleleel, seven hundred and forty years, and he begot sons and daughters. 14 And all the days of Cainan were nine hundred and ten years, and he died. 15 And Maleleel lived an hundred and sixty and five years, and he begot Jared. 16 And Maleleel lived after his begetting Jared, seven hundred and thirty years, and he begot sons and daughters. 17 And all the days of Maleleel were eight hundred and ninety and five years, and he died. 18 And Jared lived an hundred and sixty and two years, and begot Enoch: 19 and Jared lived after his begetting Enoch, eight hundred years, and he begot sons and daughters. 20 And all the days of Jared were nine hundred and sixty and two years, and he died. 21 And

Enoch lived an hundred and sixty and five years, and begat Mathusala. 22 And Enoch was well-pleasing to God after his begetting Mathusala, two hundred years, and he begot sons and daughters. 23 And all the days of Enoch were three hundred and sixty and five years. 24 And Enoch was well-pleasing to God, and was not found, because God translated him. 25 And Mathusala lived an hundred and sixty and seven years, and begot Lamech. 26 And Mathusala lived after his begetting Lamech eight hundred and two years, and begot sons and daughters. 27 And all the days of Mathusala which he lived, were nine hundred and sixty and nine years, and he died. 28 And Lamech lived an hundred and eighty and eight years, and begot a son. 29 And he called his name Noe, saying, This one will cause us to cease from our works, and from the toils of our hands, and from the earth, which the Lord God has cursed. 30 And Lamech lived after his begetting Noe, five hundred and sixty and five years, and begot sons and daughters. 31 And all the days of Lamech were seven hundred and fifty-three years, and he died.

Gen.6 1 And Noe was five hundred years old, and he begot three sons, Sem, Cham, and Japheth. 2 And it came to pass when men began to be numerous upon the earth, and daughters were born to them, 3 that the sons of God having seen the daughters of men that they were beautiful, took to themselves wives of all whom they chose. 4 And the Lord God said, My Spirit shall certainly not remain among these men for ever, because they are flesh, but their days shall be an hundred and twenty years. 5 Now the giants were upon the earth in those days; and after that when the sons of God were wont to go in to the daughters of men, they bore *children* to them, those were the giants of old, the men of renown. 6 And the Lord God, having seen that the wicked actions of men were multiplied upon the earth, and that every one in his heart was intently brooding over evil continually, 7 then God laid it to heart that he had made man upon the earth, and he pondered *it* deeply. 8 And God said, I will blot out man whom I have made from the face of the earth, even man with cattle, and reptiles with flying creatures of the sky, for I am grieved that I have made them. 9 But Noe found grace before the Lord God. 10 And these *are* the generations of Noe. Noe was a just man; being perfect in his generation, Noe was well-pleasing to God. 11 And Noe begot three sons, Sem, Cham, Japheth. 12 But the earth was corrupted before God, and the earth was filled with iniquity. 13 And the Lord God saw the earth, and it was corrupted; because all flesh had corrupted its way upon the earth. 14 And the Lord God said to Noe, A period of all men is come before me; because the earth has been filled with iniquity by them, and, behold, I destroy them and the earth. 15 Make therefore for thyself an ark of square timber; thou shalt make the ark in compartments, and thou shalt pitch it within and without with pitch. 16 And thus shalt thou make the ark; three hundred cubits the length of the ark, and fifty cubits the breadth, and thirty cubits the height of it. 17 Thou shalt narrow the ark in making it, and in a cubit above thou shalt finish it, and the door of the ark thou shalt make on the side; with lower, second, and third stories thou shalt make it. 18 And behold I bring a flood of water upon the earth, to destroy all flesh in which is the breath of life under heaven, and whatsoever things are upon the earth shall die. 19 And I will establish my covenant with thee, and thou shalt enter into the ark, and thy sons and thy wife, and thy sons' wives with thee. 20 And of all cattle and of all reptiles and of all wild beasts, even of all flesh, thou shalt bring by pairs of all, into the ark, that thou mayest feed them with thyself: male and female they shall be. 21 Of all winged birds after their kind, and of all cattle after their kind, and of all reptiles creeping upon the earth after their kind, pairs of all shall come in to thee, male and female to be fed with thee. 22 And thou shalt take to thyself of all kinds of food which ye eat, and thou shalt gather them to thyself, and it shall be for thee and themtoeat.23 And Noe did all things whatever the Lord God commanded him, so did he.

Gen.7 1 And the Lord God said to Noe, Enter thou and all thy family into the ark, for thee have I seen righteous before me in this generation. 2 And of the clean cattle take in to thee sevens, male and female, and of the unclean cattle pairs male and female. 3 And of clean flying creatures of the sky sevens, male and female, and of all unclean flying creatures pairs, male and female, to maintain seed on all the earth. 4 For yet seven days *having passed* I bring rain upon the earth forty days and forty nights, and I will blot out every offspring which I have made from the face of all the earth. 5 And Noe *did* all things whatever the Lord God commanded him. 6 And Noe was six hundred years old when the flood of water was upon the earth. 7 And then went in Noe and his sons and his wife, and his sons' wives with him into the ark, because of the water of the flood. 8 And of clean flying creatures and of unclean flying creatures, and of clean cattle and of unclean cattle, and of all things that creep upon the earth, 9 pairs went in to Noe into the ark, male and female, as God commanded Noe. 10 And it came to pass after the seven days that the water of the flood came upon the earth. 11 In the six hundredth year of the life of Noe, in the second month, on the twenty-seventh day of the month, on this day all the fountains of the abyss were broken up, and the flood-gates of heaven were opened. 12 And the rain was upon the earth forty days and forty nights. 13 On that very day entered Noe, Sem, Cham, Japheth, the sons of Noe, and the wife of Noe, and the three wives of his sons with him into the ark. 14 And all the wild beasts after their kind, and all cattle after their kind, and every reptile moving itself on the earth after its kind, and every flying bird after its kind, 15 went in to Noe into the ark, pairs, male and female of all flesh in which is the breath of life. 16 And they that entered went in male and female of all flesh, as God commanded Noe, and the Lord God shut the ark outside of him. 17 And the flood was upon the earth forty days and forty nights, and the water abounded greatly and bore up the ark, and it was lifted on high from off the earth. 18 And the water prevailed and abounded exceedingly upon the earth, and the ark was borne upon the water. 19 And the water prevailed exceedingly upon the earth, and covered all the high

mountains which were under heaven. 20 Fifteen cubits upwards was the water raised, and it covered all the high mountains. 21 And there died all flesh that moved upon the earth, of flying creatures and cattle, and of wild beasts, and every reptile moving upon the earth, and every man. 22 And all things which have the breath of life, and whatever was on the dry land, died. 23 And *God* blotted out every offspring which was upon the face of the earth, both man and beast, and reptiles, and birds of the sky, and they were blotted out from the earth, and Noe was left alone, and those with him in the ark. 24 And the water was raised over the earth an hundred and fifty days.

Gen.8 1 And God remembered Noe, and all the wild beasts, and all the cattle, and all the birds, and all the reptiles that creep, as many as were with him in the ark, and God brought a wind upon the earth, and the water stayed. 2 And the fountains of the deep were closed up, and the flood-gates of heaven, and the rain from heaven was withheld. 3 And the water subsided, and went off the earth, and after an hundred and fifty days the water was diminished, and the ark rested in the seventh month, on the twenty-seventh day of the month, on the mountains of Ararat. 4 And the water continued to decrease until the tenth month. 5 And in the tenth month, on the first day of the month, the heads of the mountains were seen. 6 And it came to pass after forty days Noe opened the window of the ark which he had made. 7 And he sent forth a raven; and it went forth and returned not until the water was dried from off the earth. 8 And he sent a dove after it to see if the water had ceased from off the earth. 9 And the dove not having found rest for her feet, returned to him into the ark, because the water was on all the face of the earth, and he stretched out his hand and took her, and brought her to himself into the ark. 10 And having waited yet seven other days, he again sent forth the dove from the ark. 11 And the dove returned to him in the evening, and had a leaf of olive, a sprig in her mouth; and Noe knew that the water had ceased from off the earth. 12 And having waited yet seven other days, he again sent forth the dove, and she did not return to him again any more. 13 And it came to pass in the six hundred and first year of the life of Noe, in the first month, on the first day of the month, the water subsided from off the earth, and Noe opened the covering of the ark which he had made, and he saw that the water had subsided from the face of the earth. 14 And in the second month the earth was dried, on the twenty-seventh day of the month. 15 And the Lord God spoke to Noe, saying, 16 Come out from the ark, thou and thy wife and thy sons, and thy sons' wives with thee. 17 And all the wild beasts as many as are with thee, and all flesh both of birds and beasts, and every reptile moving upon the earth, bring forth with thee: and increase ye and multiply upon the earth. 18 And Noe came forth, and his wife and his sons, and his sons' wives with him. 19 And all the wild beasts and all the cattle and every bird, and every reptile creeping upon the earth after their kind, came forth out of the ark. 20 And Noe built an altar to the Lord, and took of all clean beasts, and of all clean birds, and offered a whole burnt-offering upon the altar. 21 And the Lord God smelled a smell of sweetness, and the Lord God having considered, said, I will not any more curse the earth, because of the works of men, because the imagination of man is intently bent upon evil things from his youth, I will not therefore any more smite all living flesh as I have done. 22 All the days of the earth, seed and harvest, cold and heat, summer and spring, shall not cease by day or night.

Gen.9 1 And God blessed Noe and his sons, and said to them, Increase and multiply, and fill the earth and have dominion over it. 2 And the dread and the fear of you shall be upon all the wild beasts of the earth, on all the birds of the sky, and on all things moving upon the earth, and upon all the fishes of the sea, I have placed them under you power. 3 And every reptile which is living shall be to you for meat, I have given all things to you as the green herbs. 4 But flesh with blood of life ye shall not eat. 5 For your blood of your lives will I require at the hand of all wild beasts, and I will require the life of man at the hand of *his* brother man. 6 He that sheds man's blood, instead of that blood shall his own be shed, for in the image of God I made man. 7 But do ye increase and multiply, and fill the earth, and have dominion over it. 8 And God spoke to Noe, and to his sons with him, saying, 9 And behold I establish my covenant with you, and with your seed after you, 10 and with every living creature with you, of birds and of beasts, and with all the wild beasts of the earth, as many as are with you, of all that come out of the ark. 11 And I will establish my covenant with you and all flesh shall not any more die by the water of the flood, and there shall no more be a flood of water to destroy all the earth. 12 And the Lord God said to Noe, This *is* the sign of the covenant which I set between me and you, and between every living creature which is with you for perpetual generations. 13 I set my bow in the cloud, and it shall be for a sign of covenant between me and the earth. 14 And it shall be when I gather clouds upon the earth, that my bow shall be seen in the cloud. 15 And I will remember my covenant, which is between me and you, and between every living soul in all flesh, and there shall no longer be water for a deluge, so as to blot out all flesh. 16 And my bow shall be in the cloud, and I will look to remember the everlasting covenant between me and the earth, and between *every* living soul in all flesh, which is upon the earth. 17 And God said to Noe, This *is* the sign of the covenant, which I have made between me and all flesh, which is upon the earth. 18 Now the sons of Noe which came out of the ark, were Sem, Cham, Japheth. And Cham was father of Chanaan. 19 These three are the sons of Noe, of these were men scattered over all the earth. 20 And Noe began to be a husbandman, and he planted a vineyard. 21 And he drank of the wine, and was drunk, and was naked in his house. 22 And Cham the father of Chanaan saw the nakedness of his father, and he went out and told his two brothers without. 23 And Sem and Japheth having taken a garment, put it on both their backs and went backwards, and covered the nakedness of their father; and their face *was* backward, and they saw not the nakedness of their father. 24 And Noe recovered from the wine, and knew all that his younger son had done to him. 25 And he said, Cursed be the servant Chanaan, a slave shall he be to his brethren. 26 And he said, Blessed *be* the Lord God of Sem, and Chanaan shall be his bond-servant. 27 May God make room for Japheth, and let him dwell in the habitations of Sem, and let Chanaan be his servant. 28 And Noe lived after the flood three hundred and fifty years. 29 And all the days of Noe were nine hundred and fifty years, and he died.

Gen.10 1 Now these *are* the generations of the sons of Noe, Sem, Cham, Japheth; and sons were born to them after the flood. 2 The sons of Japheth, Gamer, and Magog, and Madoi, and Jovan, and Elisa, and Thobel, and Mosoch, and Thiras. 3 And the sons of Gamer, Aschanaz, and Riphath, and Thorgama. 4 And the sons of Jovan, Elisa, and Tharseis, Cetians, Rhodians. 5 From these were the islands of the Gentiles divided in their land, each according to his tongue, in their tribes and in their nations. 6 And the sons of Cham, Chus, and Mesrain, Phud, and Chanaan. 7 And the sons of Chus, Saba, and Evila, and Sabatha, and Rhegma, and Sabathaca. And the sons of Rhegma, Saba, and Dadan. 8 And Chus begot Nebrod: he began to be a giant upon the earth. 9 He was a giant hunter before the Lord God; therefore they say, As Nebrod the giant hunter before the Lord. 10 And the beginning of his kingdom was Babylon, and Orech, and Archad, and Chalanne, in the land of Senaar. 11 Out of that land came Assur, and built Ninevi, and the city Rhooboth, and Chalach, 12 and Dase between Ninevi and Chalach: this is the great city. 13 And Mesrain begot the Ludiim, and the Nephthalim, and the Enemetiim, and the Labiim, 14 and the Patrosoniim, and the Chasmoniim (whence came forth Phylistiim) and the Gaphthoriim. 15 And Chanaan begot Sidon his fist-born, and the Chettite, 16 and the Jebusite, and the Amorite, and the Girgashite, 17 and the Evite, and the Arukite, and the Asennite, 18 and the Aradian, and the Samarean, and the Amathite; and after this the tribes of the Chananites were dispersed. 19 And the boundaries of the Chananites were from Sidon till one comes to Gerara and Gaza, till one comes to Sodom and Gomorrha, Adama and Seboim, as far as Dasa. 20 There *were* the sons of Cham in their tribes according to their tongues, in their countries, and in their nations. 21 And to Sem himself also were children born, the father of all the sons of Heber, the brother of Japheth the elder. 22 Sons of Sem, Elam, and Assur, and Arphaxad, and Lud, and Aram, and Cainan. 23 And sons of Aram, Uz, and Ul, and Gater, and Mosoch. 24 And Arphaxad begot Cainan, and Cainan begot Sala. And Sala begot Heber. 25 And to Heber were born two sons, the name of the one, Phaleg, because in his days the earth was divided, and the name of his brother Jektan. 26 And Jektan begot Elmodad, and Saleth, and Sarmoth, and Jarach, 27 and Odorrha, and Aibel, and Decla, 28 Eval, and Abimael, and Saba, 29 and Uphir, and Evila, and Jobab, all these were the sons of Jektan. 30 And their dwelling was from Masse, till one comes to Saphera, a mountain of the east. 31 These were the sons of Sem in their tribes, according to their tongues, in their countries, and in their nations. 32 These are the tribes of the sons of Noe, according to their generations, according to their nations: of them were the islands of the Gentiles scattered over the earth after the flood.

Gen.11 1 And all the earth was one lip, and there was one language to all. 2 And it came to pass as they moved from the east, they found a plain in the land of Senaar, and they dwelt there. 3 And a man said to his neighbour, Come, let us make bricks and bake them with fire. And the brick was to them for stone, and their mortar was bitumen. 4 And they said, Come, let us build to ourselves a city and tower, whose top shall be to heaven, and let us make to ourselves a name, before we are scattered abroad upon the face of all the earth. 5 And the Lord came down to see the city and the tower, which the sons of men built. 6 And the Lord said, Behold, *there is* one race, and one lip of all, and they have begun to do this, and now nothing shall fail from them of all that they may have undertaken to do. 7 Come, and having gone down let us there confound their tongue, that they may not understand each the voice of his neighbour. 8 And the Lord scattered them thence over the face of all the earth, and they left off building the city and the tower. 9 On this account its name was called Confusion, because there the Lord confounded the languages of all the earth, and thence the Lord scattered them upon the face of all the earth. 10 And these *are* the generations of Sem: and Sem was a hundred years old when he begot Arphaxad, the second year after the flood. 11 And Sem lived, after he had begotten Arphaxad, five hundred years, and begot sons and daughters, and died. 12 And Arphaxad lived a hundred and thirty-five years, and begot Cainan. 13 And Arphaxad lived after he had begotten Cainan, four hundred years, and begot sons and daughters, and died. And Cainan lived a hundred and thirty years and begot Sala; and Canaan lived after he had begotten Sala, three hundred and thirty years, and begot sons and daughters, and died. 14 And Sala lived an hundred and thirty years, and begot Heber. 15 And Sala lived after he had begotten Heber, three hundred and thirty years, and begot sons and daughters, and died. 16 And Heber lived an hundred and thirty-four years, and begot Phaleg. 17 And Heber lived after he had begotten Phaleg two hundred and seventy years, and begot sons and daughters, and died. 18 And Phaleg lived and hundred and thirty years, and begot Ragau. 19 And Phaleg lived after he had begotten Ragau, two hundred and nine years, and begot sons and daughters, and died. 20 And Ragau lived and hundred thirty and two years, and begot Seruch. 21 And Raau lived after he had begotten Seruch, two hundred and seven years, and begot sons and daughters, and died. 22 And Seruch lived a hundred and thirty years, and begot Nachor. 23 And Seruch lived after he had begotten Nachor, two hundred years, and begot sons and daughters, and died. 24 And Nachor lived a hundred and seventy-nine years, and begot Tharrha. 25 And Nachor lived after he had begotten Tharrha, an hundred and twenty-five years, and begot sons and daughters, and he died. 26 And Tharrha lived seventy years, and begot Abram, and Nachor, and Arrhan. 27 And these *are* the generations of Tharrha. Tharrha begot Abram and Nachor, and Arrhan; and Arrhan begot Lot. 28 And Arrhan died in the presence of Tharrha his father, in the land in which he was born, in the country of the Chaldees. 29 And Abram and Nachor took to themselves wives, the name of the wife of Abram was Sara, and the name of the wife of Nachor, Malcha, daughter of Arrhan, and he was the father of Malcha, the father of Jescha. 30 And Sara was barren, and did not bear children. 31 And Tharrha took Abram his son, and Lot the son Arrhan, the son of his son, and Sara his daughter-in-law, the wife of Abram his son, and led them forth out of the land of the Chaldees, to go into the land of Chanaan, and they came as far as Charrhan, and he dwelt there. 32 And all the days of Tharrha in the land of Charrhan were two hundred and five years, and Tharrha died in Charrhan.

Gen.12 1 And the Lord said to Abram, Go forth out of thy land and out of thy kindred, and out of the house of thy father, and come into the land which I will shew thee. 2 And I will make thee a great nation, and I will bless thee and magnify thy name, and thou shalt be blessed. 3 And I will bless those that bless thee, and curse those that curse thee, and in thee shall all the tribes of the earth be blessed. 4 And Abram went as the Lord spoke to him, and Lot departed with him, and Abram was seventy-five years old, when he went out of Charrhan. 5 And Abram took Sara his wife, and Lot the son of his brother, and all their possessions, as many as they had got, and every soul which they had got in Charrhan, and they went forth to go into the land of Chanaan. 6 And Abram traversed the land lengthwise as far as the place Sychem, to the high oak, and the Chananites then inhabited the land. 7 And the Lord appeared to Abram, and said to him, I will give this land to thy seed. And Abram built an altar there to the Lord who appeared to him. 8 And he departed thence to the mountain eastward of Baethel, and there he pitched his tent in Baethel near the sea, and Aggai toward the east, and there he built an altar to the Lord, and called on the name of the Lord. 9 And Abram departed and went and encamped in the wilderness. 10 And there was a famine in the land, and Abram went down to Egypt to sojourn there, because the famine prevailed in the land. 11 And it came to pass when Abram drew nigh to enter into Egypt, Abram said to Sara his wife, I know that thou art a fair woman. 12 It shall come to pass then that when the Egyptians shall see thee, they shall say, This is his wife, and they shall slay me, but they shall save thee alive. 13 Say, therefore, I am his sister, that it may be well with me on account of thee, and my soul shall live because of thee. 14 And it came to pass when Abram entered into Egypt—the Egyptians having seen his wife that she was very beautiful— 15 that the princes of Pharao saw her, and praised her to Pharao and brought her into the house of Pharao. 16 And they treated Abram well on her account, and he had sheep, and calves, and asses, and men-servants, and women-servants, and mules, and camels. 17 And God afflicted Pharao with great and severe afflictions, and his house, because of Sara, Abram's wife. 18 And Pharao having called Abram, said, What is this thou hast done to me, that thou didst not tell me that she was thy wife? 19 Wherefore didst thou say, She is my sister? and I took her for a wife to myself; and now, behold, thy wife is before thee, take her and go quickly away. 20 And Pharao gave charge to men concerning Abram, to join in sending him forward, and his wife, and all that he had.

Gen.13 1 And Abram went up out of Egypt, he and his wife, and all that he had, and Lot with him, into the wilderness. 2 And Abram was very rich in cattle, and silver, and gold. 3 And he went *to the place* whence he came, into the wilderness as far as Baethel, as far as the place where his tent was before, between Baethel and Aggai, 4 to the place of the altar, which he built there at first, and Abram there called on the name of the Lord. 5 And Lot who went out with Abram had sheep, and oxen, and tents. 6 And the land was not large enough for them to live together, because their possessions were great; and the land was not large enough for them to live together. 7 And there was a strife between the herdmen of Abram's cattle, and the herdmen of Lot's cattle, and the Chananites and the Pherezites then inhabited the land. 8 And Abram said to Lot, Let there not be a strife between me and thee, and between my herdmen and thy herdmen, for we are brethren. 9 Lo! is not the whole land before thee? Separate thyself from me; if thou *goest* to the left, I will go to the right, and if thou goest to the right, I will go to the left. 10 And Lot having lifted up his eyes, observed all the country round about Jordan, that it was all watered, before God overthrew Sodom and Gomorrha, as the garden of the Lord, and as the land of Egypt, until thou come to Zogora. 11 And Lot chose for himself all the country round Jordan, and Lot went from the east, and they were separated each from his brother. And Abram dwelt in the land of Chanaan. 12 And Lot dwelt in a city of the neighbouring people, and pitched his tent in Sodom. 13 But the men of Sodom were evil, and exceedingly sinful before God. 14 And God said to Abram after Lot was separated from him, Look up with thine eyes, and behold from the place where thou now art northward and southward, and eastward and seaward; 15 for all the land which thou seest, I will give it to thee and to thy seed for ever. 16 And I will make thy seed like the dust of the earth; if any one is able to number the dust of the earth, then shall thy seed be numbered. 17 Arise and traverse the land, both in the length of it and in the breadth; for to thee will I give it, and to thy seed for ever. 18 And Abram having removed his tent, came and dwelt by the oak of Mambre, which was in Chebrom, and he there built an altar to the Lord.

Gen.14 1 And it came to pass in the reign of Amarphal king of Sennaar, and Arioch king of Ellasar, that Chodollogomor king of Elam, and Thargal king of nations, 2 made war with Balla king of Sodom, and with Barsa king of Gomorrha, and with Sennaar, king of Adama, and with Symobor king of Seboim and the king of Balac, this is Segor. 3 All these met with one consent at the salt valley; this is *now* the sea of salt. 4 Twelve years they served Chodollogomor, and the thirteenth year they revolted. 5 And in the fourteenth year came Chodollogomor, and the kings with him, and cut to pieces the giants in Astaroth, and Carnain, and strong nations with them, and the Ommaeans in the city Save. 6 And the Chorrhaeans in the mountains of Seir, to the turpentine tree of Pharan, which is in the desert. 7 And having turned back they came to the well of judgment; this is Cades, and they cut in pieces all the princes of Amalec, and the Amorites dwelling in Asasonthamar. 8 And the king of Sodom went out, and the king of Gomorrha, and king of Adama, and king of Seboim, and king of Balac, this is Segor, and they set themselves in array against them for war in the salt valley, 9 against Chodollogomor king of Elam, and Thargal king of nations, and Amarphal king of Sennaar, and Arioch king of Ellasar, the four kings against the five. 10 Now the salt valley *consists of* slime-pits. And the king of Sodom fled and the king of Gomorrha, and they fell in there: and they that were left fled to the mountain country. 11 And they took all the cavalry of Sodom and Gomorrha, and all their provisions, and departed. 12 And they took also Lot the son of Abram's brother, and his baggage, and departed, for he dwelt in Sodom. 13 And one of them that had been rescued came and told Abram the Hebrew; and he dwelt by the oak of Mamre the Amorite the brother of Eschol, and the brother of Aunan, who were confederates with Abram. 14 And Abram having heard that Lot his nephew had been taken captive, numbered his own home-born *servants* three hundred and eighteen, and pursued after them to Dan. 15 And he came upon them by night, he and his servants, and he smote them and pursued them as far as Choba, which is on the left of Damascus. 16 And he recovered all the cavalry of Sodom, and he recovered Lot his nephew, and all his possessions, and the women and the people. 17 And the king of Sodom went out to meet him, after he returned from the slaughter of Chodollogomor, and the kings with him, to the valley of Saby; this was the plain of the kings. 18 And Melchisedec king of Salem brought forth loaves and wine, and he was the priest of the most high God. 19 And he blessed Abram, and said, Blessed be Abram of the most high God, who made heaven and earth, 20 and blessed be the most high God who delivered thine enemies into thy power. And Abram gave him the tithe of all. 21 And the king of Sodom said to Abram, Give me the men, and take the horses to thyself. 22 And Abram said to the king of Sodom, I will stretch out my hand to the Lord the most high God, who made the heaven and the earth, 23 *that* I will not take from all thy goods from a string to a shoe-latchet, lest thou shouldest say, I have made Abram rich. 24 Except what things the young men have eaten, and the portion of the men that went with me, Eschol, Aunan, Mambre, these shall take a portion.

Gen.15 1 And after these things the word of the Lord came to Abram in a vision, saying, Fear not, Abram, I shield thee, thy reward shall be very great. 2 And Abram said, Master *and* Lord, what wilt thou give me? whereas I am departing without a child, but the son of Masek my home-born female slave, this Eliezer of Damascus *is mine heir.* 3 And Abram said, *I am grieved* since thou hast given me no seed, but my home-born *servant* shall succeed me. 4 And immediately there was a voice of the Lord to him, saying, This shall not be thine heir; but he that shall come out of thee shall be thine heir. 5 And he brought him out and said to him, Look up now to heaven, and count the stars, if thou shalt be able to number them fully, and he said, Thus shall thy seed be. 6 And Abram believed God, and it was counted to him for righteousness. 7 And he said to him, I am God that brought thee out of the land of the Chaldeans, so as to give thee this land to inherit. 8 And he said, Master *and* Lord, how shall I know that I shall inherit it? 9 And he said to him, Take for me an heifer in her third year, and a she-goat in her third year, and a ram in his third year, and a dove and a pigeon. 10 So he took to him all these, and divided them in the midst, and set them opposite to each other, but the birds he did not divide. 11 And birds came down upon the bodies, *even* upon the divided parts of them, and Abram sat down by them. 12 And about sunset a trance fell upon Abram, and lo! a great gloomy terror falls upon him. 13 And it was said to Abram, Thou shalt surely know that thy seed shall be a sojourner in a land not their won, and they shall enslave them, and afflict them, and humble them four hundred years. 14 And the nation whomsoever they shall serve I will judge; and after this, they shall come forth hither with much property. 15 But thou shalt depart to thy fathers in peace, nourished in a good old age. 16 And in the fourth generation they shall return hither, for the sins of the Amorites are not yet filled up, even until now. 17 And when the sun was about to set, there was a flame, and behold a smoking furnace and lamps of fire, which passed between these divided pieces. 18 In that day the Lord made a covenant with Abram, saying, To thy seed I will give this land, from the river of Egypt to the great river Euphrates. 19 The Kenites, and the Kenezites, and the Kedmoneans, 20 and the Chettites, and the Pherezites, and the Raphaim, 21 and the Amorites, and the Chananites, and the Evites, and the Gergesites, and the Jebusites.

Gen.16 1 And Sara the wife of Abram bore him no children; and she had an Egyptian maid, whose name was Agar. 2 And Sara said to Abram, Behold, the Lord has restrained me from bearing, go therefore in to my maid, that I may get children for myself through her. And Abram hearkened to the voice of Sara. 3 So Sara the wife of Abram having taken Agar the Egyptian her handmaid, after Abram had dwelt ten years in the land of Chanaan, gave her to Abram her husband as a wife to him. 4 And he went in to Agar, and she conceived, and saw that she was with child, and her mistress was dishonoured before her. 5 And Sara said to Abram, I am injured by thee; I gave my handmaid into thy bosom, and when I saw that she was with child, I was dishonoured before her. The Lord judge between me and thee. 6 And Abram said to Sara, Behold thy handmaid is in thy hands, use her as it may seem good to thee. And Sara afflicted her, and she fled from her face. 7 And an angel of the Lord found her by the fountain of water in the wilderness, by the fountain in the way to Sur. 8 And the angel of the Lord said to her, Agar, Sara's maid, whence comest thou, and wither goest thou? and she said, I am fleeing from the face of my mistress Sara. 9 And the angel of the Lord said to her, Return to thy mistress, and submit thyself under her hands. 10 And the angel of the Lord said to her, I will surely multiply thy seed, and it shall not be numbered for multitude. 11 And the angel of the Lord said to her, Behold thou art with child, and shalt bear a son, and shalt call his name Ismael, for the Lord hath hearkened to thy humiliation. 12 He shall be a wild man, his hands against all, and the hands of all against him, and he shall dwell in the presence of all his brethren. 13 And she called the name of the Lord God who spoke to her, Thou art God who seest me; for she said, For I have openly seen him that appeared to me. 14 Therefore she called the well, The well of him whom I have openly seen; behold it is between Cades and Barad. 15 And Agar bore a son to Abram; and Abram called the name of his son which Agar bore to him, Ismael. 16 And Abram was eighty-six years old, when Agar bore Ismael to Abram.

Gen.17 1 And Abram was ninety-nine years old, and the Lord appeared to Abram and said to him, I am thy God, be well-pleasing before me, and be blameless. 2 And I will establish my covenant between me and thee, and I will multiply thee exceedingly. 3 And Abram fell upon his face, and God spoke to him, saying, 4 And I, behold! my covenant *is* with thee, and thou shalt be a father of a multitude of nations. 5 And thy name shall no more be called Abram, but thy name shall be Abraam, for I have made thee a father of many nations. 6 And I will increase thee very exceedingly, and I will make nations of thee, and kings shall come out of thee. 7 And I will establish my covenant between thee and thy seed after thee, to their generations, for an everlasting covenant, to be thy God, and *the God* of thy seed after thee. 8 And I will give to thee and to thy seed after thee the land wherein thou sojournest, even all the land of Chanaan for an everlasting possession, and I will be to them a God. 9 And God said to Abraam, Thou also shalt fully keep my covenant, thou and thy seed after thee for their generations. 10 And this *is* the covenant which thou shalt fully keep between me and you, and between thy seed after thee for their generations; every male of you shall be circumcised. 11 And ye shall be circumcised in the flesh of your foreskin, and it shall be for a sign of a covenant between me and you. 12 And the child of eight days *old* shall be circumcised by you, every male throughout your generations, and *the servant* born in the house and he that is bought with money, of every son of a stranger, who is not of thy seed. 13 He that is born in thy house, and he that is bought with money shall be surely circumcised, and my covenant shall be on your flesh for an everlasting covenant. 14 And the uncircumcised male, who shall not be circumcised in the flesh of his foreskin on the eighth day, that soul shall be utterly destroyed from its family, for he has broken my covenant. 15 And God said to Abraam, Sara thy wife—her name shall not be called Sara, Sarrha shall be her name. 16 And I will bless her, and give thee a son of her, and I will bless him, and he shall become nations, and kings of nations shall be of him. 17 And Abraam fell upon his face, and laughed; and spoke in his heart, saying, Shall there be a child to one who is a hundred years old, and shall Sarrha who is ninety years old, bear? 18 And Abraam said to God, Let this Ismael live before thee. 19 And God said to Abraam, Yea, behold, Sarrha thy wife shall bear thee a son, and thou shalt call his name Isaac; and I will establish my covenant with him, for an everlasting covenant, to be a God to him and to his seed after him. 20 And concerning Ismael, behold, I have heard thee, and, behold, I have blessed him, and will increase him and multiply him exceedingly; twelve nations shall he beget, and I will make him a great nation. 21 But I will establish my covenant with Isaac, whom Sarrha shall bear to thee at this time, in the next year. 22 And he left off speaking with him, and God went up from Abraam. 23 And Abraam took Ismael his son, and all his home-born *servants*, and all those bought with money, and every male of the men in the house of Abraam, and he circumcised their foreskins in the time of that day, according as God spoke to him. 24 And Abraam was ninety-nine years old, when he was circumcised in the flesh of his foreskin. 25 And Ismael his son was thirteen years old when he was circumcised in the flesh of his foreskin. 26 And at the period of that day, Abraam was circumcised, and Ismael his son, 27 and all the men of his house, both those born in the house, and those bought with money of foreign nations.

Gen.18 1 And God appeared to him by the oak of Mambre, as he sat by the door of his tent at noon. 2 And he lifted up his eyes and beheld, and lo! three men stood before him; and having seen them he ran to meet them from the door of his tent, and did obeisance to the ground. 3 And he said, Lord, if indeed I have found grace in thy sight, pass not by thy servant. 4 Let water now be brought, and let them wash your feet, and do ye refresh *yourselves* under the tree. 5 And I will bring bread, and ye shall eat, and after this ye shall depart on your journey, on account of which *refreshment* ye have turned aside to your servant. And he said, So do, as thou hast said. 6 And Abraam hasted to the tent to Sarrha, and said to her, Hasten, and knead three measures of fine flour, and make cakes. 7 And Abraam ran to the kine, and took a young calf, tender and good, and gave it to his servant, and he hasted to dress it. 8 And he took butter and milk, and the calf which he had dressed; and he set them before them, and they did eat, and he stood by them under the tree. 9 And he said to him, Where is Sarrha thy wife? And he answered and said, Behold! in the tent. 10 And he said, I will return and come to thee according to this period seasonably, and Sarrha thy wife shall have a son; and Sarrha heard at the door of the tent, being behind him. 11 And Abraam and Sarrha were old, advanced in days, and the custom of women ceased with Sarrha. 12 And Sarrha laughed in herself, saying, The thing has not as yet happened to me, even until now, and my lord is old. 13 And the Lord said to Abraam, Why is it that Sarrha has laughed in herself, saying, Shall I then indeed bear? but I am grown old. 14 Shall anything be impossible with the Lord? At this time I will return to thee seasonably, and Sarrha shall have a son. 15 But Sarrha denied, saying, I did not laugh, for she was afraid. And he said to her, Nay, but thou didst laugh. 16 And the men having risen up from thence looked towards Sodom and Gomorrha. And Abraam went with them, attending them on their journey. 17 And the Lord said, Shall I hide from Abraam my servant what things I intend to do? 18 But Abraam shall become a great and populous nation, and in him shall all the nations of the earth be blest. 19 For I know that he will order his sons, and his house after him, and they will keep the ways of the Lord, to do justice and judgment, that the Lord may bring upon Abraam all things whatsoever he has spoken to him. 20 And the Lord said, The cry of Sodom and Gomorrha has been increased towards me, and their sins are very great. 21 I will therefore go down and see, if they completely correspond with the cry which comes to me, and if not, that I may know. 22 And the men having departed thence, came to Sodom; and Abraam was still standing before the Lord. 23 And Abraam drew nigh and said, Wouldest thou destroy the righteous with the wicked, and shall the righteous be as the wicked? 24 Should there be fifty righteous in the city, wilt thou destroy them? wilt thou not spare the whole place for the sake of the fifty righteous, if they be in it? 25 By no means shalt thou do as this thing *is* so as to destroy the righteous with the wicked, so the righteous shall be as the wicked: by no means. Thou that judgest the whole earth, shalt thou not do right? 26 And the Lord said, If there should be in Sodom fifty righteous in the city, I will spare the whole city, and the whole place for their sakes. 27 And Abraam answered and said, Now I have begun to speak to my Lord, and I am earth and ashes. 28 But if the fifty righteous should be diminished to forty-five, wilt thou destroy the whole city because of the five *wanting*? And he said, I will not destroy it, if I should find there forty-five. 29 And he continued to speak to him still, and said, But if there should be found there forty? And he said, I will not destroy it for the forty's sake. 30 And he said, Will there be anything *against me*, Lord, if I shall speak? but if there be found there thirty? And he said, I will not destroy it for the thirty's sake. 31 And he said, Since I am able to speak to the Lord, what if there should be found there twenty? And he said, I will not destroy it, if I should find there twenty. 32 And he said, Will there be anything *against me*, Lord, if I speak yet once? but if there should be found there ten? And he said, I will not destroy it for the ten's sake. 33 And the Lord departed, when he left off speaking to Abraam, and Abraam returned to his place.

Gen.19 1 And the two angels came to Sodom at evening. And Lot sat by the gate of Sodom, and Lot having seen them, rose up to meet them, and he worshipped with his face to the ground, and said, 2 Lo! *my* lords, turn aside to the house of your servant, and rest from your journey, and wash your feet, and having risen early in the morning ye shall depart on your journey. And they said, Nay, but we will lodge in the street. 3 And he constrained them, and they turned aside to him, and they entered into his house, and he made a feast for them, and baked unleavened cakes for them, and they did eat. 4 But before they went to sleep, the men of the city, the Sodomites, compassed the house, both young and old, all the people together. 5 And they called out Lot, and said to him, Where are the men that went in to thee this night? bring them out to us that we may be with them. 6 And Lot went out to them to the porch, and he shut the door after him, 7 and said to them, By no means, brethren, do not act villanously. 8 But I have two daughters, who have not known a man. I will bring them out to you, and do ye use them as it may please you, only do not injury to these men, to avoid which they came under the shelter of my roof. 9 And they said to him, Stand back there, thou camest in to sojourn, was it also to judge? Now then we would harm thee more than them. And they pressed hard on the man, even Lot, and they drew nigh to break the door. 10 And the men stretched forth their hands and drew Lot in to them into the house, and shut the door of the house. 11 And they smote the men that were at the door of the house with blindness, both small and great, and they were wearied with seeking the door. 12 And the men said to Lot, Hast thou here sons-in-law, or sons or daughters, or if thou hast any other friend in the city, bring them out of this place. 13 For we are going to destroy this place; for their cry has been raised up before the Lord, and the Lord has sent us to destroy it. 14 And Lot went out, and spoke to his sons-in-law who had married his daughters, and said, Rise up, and depart out of this place, for the Lord is about to destroy the city; but he seemed to be speaking absurdly before his sons-in-law. 15 But when it was morning, the angels hastened Lot, saying, Arise and take thy wife, and thy two daughters whom thou hast, and go forth; lest thou also be destroyed with the iniquities of the city. 16 And they were troubled, and the angels laid hold on his hand, and the hand of his wife, and the hands of his two daughters, in that the Lord spared him. 17 And it came to pass when they brought them out, that they said, Save thine own life by all means; look not round to that which is behind, nor stay in all the country round about, escape to the mountain, lest perhaps thou be overtaken together with them. 18 And Lot said to them, I pray, Lord, 19 since thy servant has found mercy before thee, and thou hast magnified thy righteousness, in what thou doest towards me that my soul may live, —but I shall not be able to escape to the mountain, lest perhaps the calamity overtake me and I die. 20 Behold this city is near for me to escape thither, which is a small one, and there shall I be preserved, is it not little? and my soul shall live because of thee. 21 And he said to him, Behold, I have had respect to thee also about this thing, that I should not overthrow the city about which thou hast spoken. 22 Hasten therefore to escape thither, for I shall not be able to do anything until thou art come thither; therefore he called the name of that city, Segor. 23 The sun was risen upon the earth, when Lot entered into Segor. 24 And the Lord rained on Sodom and Gomorrha brimstone and fire from the Lord out of heaven. 25 And he overthrew these cities, and all the country round about, and all that dwelt in the cities, and the plants springing out of the ground. 26 And his wife looked back, and she became a pillar of salt. 27 And Abraam rose up early to go to the place, where he had stood before the Lord. 28 And he looked towards Sodom and Gomorrha, and towards the surrounding country, and saw, and behold a flame went up from the earth, as the smoke of a furnace. 29 And it came to pass that when God destroyed all the cities of the region round about, God remembered Abraam, and sent Lot out of the midst of the overthrow, when the Lord overthrew those cities in which Lot dwelt.

30 And Lot went up out of Segor, and dwelt in the mountain, he and his two daughters with him, for he feared to dwell in Segor; and he dwelt in a cave, he and his two daughters with him. 31 And the elder said to the younger, Our father is old, and there is no one on the earth who shall come in to us, as it is fit in all the earth. 32 Come and let us make our father drink wine, and let us sleep with him, and let us raise up seed from our father. 33 So they made their father drink wine in that night, and the elder went in and lay with her father that night, and he knew not when he slept and when he rose up. 34 And it came to pass on the morrow, that the elder said to the younger, Behold, I slept yesternight with our father, let us make him drink wine in this night also, and do thou go in and sleep with him, and let us raise up seed of our father. 35 So they made their father drink wine in that night also, and the younger went in and slept with her father, and he knew not when he slept, nor when he arose. 36 And the two daughters of Lot conceived by their father. 37 And the elder bore a son and called his name Moab, saying, *He is* of my father. This is the father of the Moabites to this present day. 38 And the younger also bore a son, and called his name Amman, saying, The son of my family. This is the father of the Ammanites to this present day.

Gen.20 1 And Abraam removed thence to the southern country, and dwelt between Cades and Sur, and sojourned in Gerara. 2 And Abraam said concerning Sarrha his wife, She is my sister, for he feared to say, She is my wife, lest at any time the men of the city should kill him for her sake. So Abimelech king of Gerara sent and took Sarrha. 3 And God came to Abimelech by night in sleep, and said, Behold, thou diest for the woman, whom thou hast taken, whereas she has lived with a husband. 4 But Abimelech had not touched her, and he said, Lord, wilt thou destroy an ignorantly *sinning* and just nation? 5 Said he not to me, She is my sister, and said she not to me, He is my brother? with a pure heart and in the righteousness of my hands have I done this. 6 And God said to him in sleep, Yea, I knew that thou didst this with a pure heart, and I spared thee, so that thou shouldest not sin against me, therefore I suffered thee not to touch her. 7 But now return the man his wife; for he is a prophet, and shall pray for thee, and thou shalt live; but if thou restore her not, know that thou shalt die and all thine. 8 And Abimelech rose early in the morning, and called all his servants, and he spoke all these words in their ears, and all the men feared exceedingly. 9 And Abimelech called Abraam and said to him, What is this that thou hast done to us? Have we sinned against thee, that thou hast brought upon me and upon my kingdom a great sin? Thou hast done to me a deed, which no one ought to do. 10 And Abimelech said to Abraam, What hast thou seen in *me* that thou hast done this? 11 And Abraam said, Why I said, Surely there is not the worship of God in this place, and they will slay me because of my wife. 12 For truly she is my sister by my father, but not by my mother, and she became my wife. 13 And it came to pass when God brought me forth out of the house of my father, that I said to her, This righteousness thou shalt perform to me, in every place into which we may enter, say of me, He is my brother. 14 And Abimelech took a thousand pieces of silver, and sheep, and calves, and servants, and maid-servants, and gave them to Abraam, and he returned him Sarrha his wife. 15 And Abimelech said to Abraam, Behold, my land is before thee, dwell wheresoever it may please thee. 16 And to Sarrha he said, Behold, I have given thy brother a thousand pieces of silver, those shall be to thee for the price of thy countenance, and to all the women with thee, and speak the truth in all things. 17 And Abraam prayed to God, and God healed Abimelech, and his wife, and his women servants, and they bore children. 18 Because the Lord had fast closed from without every womb in the house of Abimelech, because of Sarrha Abraam's wife.

Gen.21 1 And the Lord visited Sarrha, as he said, and the Lord did to Sarrha, as he spoke. 2 And she conceived and bore to Abraam a son in old age, at the set time according as the Lord spoke to him. 3 And Abraam called the name of his son that was born to him, whom Sarrha bore to him, Isaac. 4 And Abraam circumcised Isaac on the eighth day, as God commanded him. 5 And Abraam was a hundred years old when Isaac his son was born to him. 6 And Sarrha said, The Lord has made laughter for me, for whoever shall hear shall rejoice with me. 7 And she said, Who shall say to Abraam that Sarrha suckles a child? for I have born a child in my old age. 8 And the child grew and was weaned, and Abraam made a great feast the day that his son Isaac was weaned. 9 And Sarrha having seen the son of Agar the Egyptian who was born to Abraam, sporting with Isaac her son, 10 then she said to Abraam, Cast out this bondwoman and her son, for the son of this bondwoman shall not inherit with my son Isaac. 11 But the word appeared very hard before Abraam concerning his son. 12 But God said to Abraam, Let it not be hard before thee concerning the child, and concerning the bondwoman; in all things whatsoever Sarrha shall say to thee, hear her voice, for in Isaac shall thy seed be called. 13 And moreover I will make the son of this bondwoman a great nation, because he is thy seed. 14 And Abraam rose up in the morning and took loaves and a skin of water, and gave *them* to Agar, and he put the child on her shoulder, and sent her away, and she having departed wandered in the wilderness near the well of the oath. 15 And the water failed out of the skin, and she cast the child under a fir tree. 16 And she departed and sat down opposite him at a distance, as it were a bow-shot, for she said, Surely I cannot see the death of my child: and she sat opposite him, and the child cried aloud and wept. 17 And God heard the voice of the child from the place where he was, and an angel of God called Agar out of heaven, and said to her, What is it, Agar? fear not, for God has heard the voice of the child from the place where he is. 18 Rise up, and take the child, and hold him in thine hand, for I will make him a great nation. 19 And God opened her eyes, and she saw a well of springing water; and she went and filled the skin with water, and gave the child drink. 20 And God was with the child, and he grew and dwelt in the wilderness, and became an archer. 21 And he dwelt in the wilderness, and his mother took him a wife out of Pharan of Egypt. 22

And it came to pass at that time that Abimelech spoke, and Ochozath his friend, and Phichol the chief captain of his host, to Abraam, saying, God is with thee in all things, whatsoever thou mayest do. 23 Now therefore swear to me by God that thou wilt not injure me, nor my seed, nor my name, but according to the righteousness which I have performed with thee thou shalt deal with me, and with the land in which thou hast sojourned. 24 And Abraam said, I will swear. 25 And Abraam reproved Abimelech because of the wells of water, which the servants of Abimelech took away. 26 And Abimelech said to him, I know not who has done this thing to thee, neither didst thou tell it me, neither heard I it but only to-day. 27 And Abraam took sheep and calves, and gave them to Abimelech, and both made a covenant. 28 And Abraam set seven ewe-lambs by themselves. 29 And Abimelech said to Abraam, What are these seven ewe-lambs which thou hast set alone? 30 And Abraam said, Thou shalt receive the seven ewe-lambs of me, that they may be for me as a witness, that I dug this well. 31 Therefore he named the name of that place, The Well of the Oath, for there they both swore. 32 And they made a covenant at the well of the oath. And there rose up Abimelech, Ochozath his friend, and Phichol the commander-in-chief of his army, and they returned to the land of the Phylistines. 33 And Abraam planted a field at the well of the oath, and called there on the name of the Lord, the everlasting God. 34 And Abraam sojourned in the land of the Phylistines many days.

Gen.22 1 And it came to pass after these things that God tempted Abraam, and said to him, Abraam, Abraam; and he said, Lo! I *am here.* 2 And he said, Take thy son, the beloved one, whom thou hast loved—Isaac, and go into the high land, and offer him there for a whole-burnt-offering on one of the mountains which I will tell thee of. 3 And Abraam rose up in the morning and saddled his ass, and he took with him two servants, and Isaac his son, and having split wood for a whole-burnt-offering, he arose and departed, and came to the place of which God spoke to him, 4 on the third day; and Abraam having lifted up his eyes, saw the place afar off. 5 And Abraam said to his servants, Sit ye here with the ass, and I and the lad will proceed thus far, and having worshipped we will return to you. 6 And Abraam took the wood of the whole-burnt-offering, and laid it on Isaac his son, and he took into his hands both the fire and the knife, and the two went together. 7 And Isaac said to Abraam his father, Father. And he said, What is it, son? And he said, Behold the fire and the wood, where is the sheep for a whole-burnt-offering? 8 And Abraam said, God will provide himself a sheep for a whole-burnt-offering, *my* son. And both having gone together, 9 came to the place which God spoke of to him; and there Abraam built the altar, and laid the wood on it, and having bound the feet of Isaac his son together, he laid him on the altar upon the wood. 10 And Abraam stretched forth his hand to take the knife to slay his son. 11 And an angel of the Lord called him out of heaven, and said, Abraam, Abraam. And he said, Behold, I *am here.* 12 And he said, Lay not thine hand upon the child, neither do anything to him, for now I know that thou fearest God, and for my sake thou hast not spared thy beloved son. 13 And Abraam lifted up his eyes and beheld, and lo! a ram caught by his horns in a plant of Sabec; and Abraam went and took the ram, and offered him up for a whole- burnt-offering in the place of Isaac his son. 14 And Abraam called the name of that place, The Lord hath seen; that they might say to-day, In the mount the Lord was seen. 15 And an angel of the Lord called Abraam the second time out of heaven, saying, 16 I have sworn by myself, says the Lord, because thou hast done this thing, and on my account hast not spared thy beloved son, 17 surely blessing I will bless thee, and multiplying I will multiply thy seed as the stars of heaven, and as the sand which is by the shore of the sea, and thy seed shall inherit the cities of their enemies. 18 And in thy seed shall all the nations of the earth be blessed, because thou hast hearkened to my voice. 19 And Abraam returned to his servants, and they arose and went together to the well of the oath; and Abraam dwelt at the well of the oath. 20 And it came to pass after these things, that it was reported to Abraam, saying, Behold, Melcha herself too has born sons to Nachor thy brother, 21 Uz the first-born, and Baux his brother, and Camuel the father of the Syrians, and Chazad, and 22 Azav and Phaldes, and Jeldaph, and Bathuel, and Bathuel begot Rebecca; 23 these are eight sons, which Melcha bore to Nachor the brother of Abraam. 24 And his concubine whose name was Rheuma, she also bore Tabec, and Taam, and Tochos, and Mocha.

Gen.23 1 And the life of Sarrha was an hundred and twenty-seven years. 2 And Sarrha died in the city of Arboc, which is in the valley, this is Chebron in the land of Chanaan; and Abraam came to lament for Sarrha and to mourn. 3 And Abraam stood up from before his dead; and Abraam spoke to the sons of Chet, saying, 4 I am a sojourner and a stranger among you, give me therefore possession of a burying-place among you, and I will bury my dead away from me. 5 And the sons of Chet answered to Abraam, saying, Not so, Sir, 6 but hear us; thou art in the midst of us a king from God; bury thy dead in our choice sepulchres, for not one of us will by any means withhold his sepulchre from thee, so that thou shouldest not bury thy dead there. 7 And Abraam rose up and did obeisance to the people of the land, to the sons of Chet. 8 And Abraam spoke to them, saying, If ye have it in your mind that I should bury my dead out of my sight, hearken to me, and speak for me to Ephron the son Saar. 9 And let him give me the double cave which he has, which is in a part of his field, let him give it me for the money it is worth for possession of a burying-place among you. 10 Now Ephron was sitting in the midst of the children of Chet, and Ephron the Chettite answered Abraam and spoke in the hearing of the sons of Chet, and of all who entered the city, saying, 11 Attend to me, my lord, and hear me, I give to thee the field and the cave which is in it; I have given it thee before all my country men; bury thy dead. 12 And Abraam did obeisance before the people of the land. 13 And he said in the ears of Ephron before the people of the land, Since thou art on my side, hear me; take the price of the field

from me, and I will bury my dead there. 14 But Ephron answered Abraam, saying, 15 Nay, my lord, I have heard indeed, the land *is worth* four hundred silver didrachms, but what can this be between me and thee? nay, do thou bury thy dead. 16 And Abraam hearkened to Ephron, and Abraam rendered to Ephron the money, which he mentioned in the ears of the sons of Chet, four hundred didrachms of silver approved with merchants. 17 And the field of Ephron, which was in Double Cave, which is opposite Mambre, the field and the cave, which was in it, and every tree which was in the field, and whatever is in its borders round about, were made sure in its borders round about, were made sure 18 to Abraam for a possession, before the sons of Chet, and all that entered into the city. 19 After this Abraam buried Sarrha his wife in the Double Cave of the field, which is opposite Mambre, this is Chebron in the land of Chanaan. 20 So the field and the cave which was in it were made sure to Abraam for possession of a burying place, by the sons of Chet.

Gen.24 1 And Abraam was old, advanced in days, and the Lord blessed Abraam in all things. 2 And Abraam said to his servant the elder of his house, who had rule over all his possessions, Put thy hand under my thigh, 3 and I will adjure thee by the Lord the God of heaven, and the God of the earth, that thou take not a wife for my son Isaac from the daughters of the Chananites, with whom I dwell, in the midst of them. 4 But thou shalt go instead to my country, where I was born, and to my tribe, and thou shalt take from thence a wife for my son Isaac. 5 And the servant said to him, Shall I carry back thy son to the land whence thou camest forth, if haply the woman should not be willing to return with me to this land? 6 And Abraam said to him, Take heed to thyself that thou carry not my son back thither. 7 The Lord the God of heaven, and the God of the earth, who took me out of my father's house, and out of the land whence I sprang, who spoke to me, and who swore to me, saying, I will give this land to thee and to thy seed, he shall send his angel before thee, and thou shalt take a wife to my son from thence. 8 And if the woman should not be willing to come with thee into this land, thou shalt be clear from my oath, only carry not my son thither again. 9 And the servant put his hand under the thigh of his master Abraam, and swore to him concerning this matter. 10 And the servant took ten camels of his master's camels, and *he took* of all the goods of his master with him, and he arose and went into Mesopotamia to the city of Nachor. 11 And he rested his camels without the city by the well of water towards evening, when damsels go forth to draw water. 12 And he said, O Lord God of my master Abraam, prosper my way before me to day, and deal mercifully with my master Abraam. 13 Lo! I stand by the well of water, and the daughters of them that inhabit the city come forth to draw water. 14 And it shall be, the virgin to whomsoever I shall say, Incline thy water-pot, that I may drink, and she shall say, Drink thou, and I will give thy camels drink, until they shall have done drinking—even this one thou hast prepared for thy servant Isaac, and hereby shall I know that thou hast dealt mercifully with my master Abraam. 15 And it came to pass before he had done speaking in his mind, that behold, Rebecca the daughter of Bathuel, the son of Melcha, the wife of Nachor, and *the same* the brother of Abraam, came forth, having a water-pot on her shoulders. 16 And the virgin was very beautiful in appearance, she was a virgin, a man had not known her; and she went down to the well, and filled her water-pot, and came up. 17 And the servant ran up to meet her, and said, Give me a little water to drink out of thy pitcher; 18 and she said, Drink, Sir; and she hasted, and let down the pitcher upon her arm, and gave him to drink, till he ceased drinking. 19 And she said, I will also draw water for thy camels, till they shall all have drunk. 20 And she hasted, and emptied the water-pot into the trough, and ran to the well to draw again, and drew water for all the camels. 21 And the man took great notice of her, and remained silent to know whether the Lord had made his way prosperous or not. 22 And it came to pass when all the camels ceased drinking, that the man took golden ear-rings, each of a drachm weight, and he *put* two bracelets on her hands, their weight was ten pieces of gold. 23 And he asked her, and said, Whose daughter art thou? Tell me if there is room for us to lodge with thy father. 24 And she said to him, I am the daughter of Bathuel the son of Melcha, whom she bore to Nachor. 25 And she said to him, We have both straw and much provender, and a place for resting. 26 And the man being well pleased, worshipped the Lord, 27 and said, Blessed be the Lord the God of my master Abraam, who has not suffered his righteousness to fail, nor his truth from my master, and the Lord has brought me prosperously to the house of the brother of my lord. 28 And the damsel ran and reported to the house of her mother according to these words. 29 And Rebecca had a brother whose name was Laban; and Laban ran out to meet the man, to the well. 30 And it came to pass when he saw the ear-rings and the bracelets on the hands of his sister, and when he heard the words of Rebecca his sister, saying, Thus the man spoke to me, that he went to the man, as he stood by the camels at the well. 31 And he said to him, Come in hither, thou blessed of the Lord, why standest thou without, whereas I have prepared the house and a place for the camels? 32 And the man entered into the house, and unloaded the camels, and gave the camels straw and provender, and water to wash his feet, and the feet of the men that were with him. 33 And he set before them loaves to eat; but he said, I will not eat, until I have told my errand. And he said, Speak on. 34 And he said, I am a servant of Abraam; 35 and the Lord has blessed my master greatly, and he is exalted, and he has given him sheep, and calves, and silver, and gold, servants and servant- maids, camels, and asses. 36 And Sarrha my master's wife bore one son to my master after he had grown old; and he gave him whatever he had. 37 And my master caused me to swear, saying, Thou shalt not take a wife to my son of the daughters of the Chananites, among whom I sojourn in their land. 38 But thou shalt go to the house of my father, and to my tribe, and thou shalt take thence a wife for my son. 39 And I said to my master, Haply the woman will not go with me. 40 And he said to me, The Lord God to whom I have been acceptable in his presence, himself shall send

out his angel with thee, and shall prosper thy journey, and thou shalt take a wife for my son of my tribe, and of the house of my father. 41 Then shalt thou be clear from my curse, for whensoever thou shalt have come to my tribe, and they shall not give her to thee, then shalt thou be clear from my oath. 42 And having come this day to the well, I said, Lord God of my master Abraam, if thou prosperest my journey on which I am now going, 43 behold, I stand by the well of water, and the daughters of the men of the city come forth to draw water, and it shall be *that* the damsel to whom I shall say, Give me a little water to drink out of thy pitcher, 44 and she shall say to me, Both drink thou, and I will draw water for thy camels, this *shall be* the wife whom the Lord has prepared for his own servant Isaac; and hereby shall I know that thou hast wrought mercy with my master Abraam. 45 And it came to pass before I had done speaking in my mind, straightway Rebecca came forth, having her pitcher on her shoulders; and she went down to the well, and drew water; and I said to her, Give me to drink. 46 And she hasted and let down her pitcher on her arm from her head, and said, Drink thou, and I will give thy camels drink; and I drank, and she gave the camels drink. 47 And I asked her, and said, Whose daughter art thou? tell me; and she said, I am daughter of Bathuel the son of Nachor, whom Melcha bore to him; and I put on her the ear-rings, and the bracelets on her hands. 48 And being well-pleased I worshipped the Lord, and I blessed the Lord the God of my master Abraam, who has prospered me in a true way, so that I should take the daughter of my master's brother for his son. 49 If then ye *will* deal mercifully and justly with my lord, *tell me*, and if not, tell me, that I may turn to the right hand or to the left. 50 And Laban and Bathuel answered and said, This matter has come forth from the Lord, we shall not be able to answer thee bad or good. 51 Behold, Rebecca is before thee, take her and go away, and let her be wife to the son of thy master, as the Lord has said. 52 And it came to pass when the servant of Abraam heard these words, he bowed himself to the Lord down to the earth. 53 And the servant having brought forth jewels of silver and gold and raiment, gave them to Rebecca, and gave gifts to her brother, and to her mother. 54 And both he and the men with him ate and drank and went to sleep. And he arose in the morning and said, Send me away, that I may go to my master. 55 And her brethren and her mother said, Let the virgin remain with us about ten days, and after that she shall depart. 56 But he said to them, Hinder me not, for the Lord has prospered my journey for me; send me away, that I may depart to my master. 57 And they said, Let us call the damsel, and enquire at her mouth. 58 And they called Rebecca, and said to her, Wilt thou go with this man? and she said, I will go. 59 So they sent forth Rebecca their sister, and her goods, and the servant of Abraam, and his attendants. 60 And they blessed Rebecca, and said to her, Thou art our sister; become thou thousands of myriads, and let thy seed possess the cities of their enemies. 61 And Rebecca rose up and her maidens, and they mounted the camels and went with the man; and the servant having taken up Rebecca, departed. 62 And Isaac went through the wilderness to the well of the vision, and he dwelt in the land toward the south. 63 And Isaac went forth into the plain toward evening to meditate; and having lifted up his eyes, he saw camels coming. 64 And Rebecca lifted up her eyes, and saw Isaac; and she alighted briskly from the camel, 65 and said to the servant, Who is that man that walks in the plain to meet us? And the servant said, This is my master; and she took her veil and covered herself. 66 And the servant told Isaac all that he had done. 67 And Isaac went into the house of his mother, and took Rebecca, and she became his wife, and he loved her; and Isaac was comforted for Sarrha his mother.

Gen.25 1 And Abraam again took a wife, whose name was Chettura. 2 And she bore to him Zombran, and Jezan, and Madal, and Madiam, and Jesboc, and Soie. 3 And Jezan begot Saba and Dedan. And the sons of Dedan were the Assurians and the Latusians, and Laomim. 4 And the sons of Madiam *were* Gephar and Aphir, and Enoch, and Abeida, and Eldaga; all these were sons of Chettura. 5 But Abraam gave all his possessions to Isaac his son. 6 But to the sons of his concubines Abraam gave gifts, and he sent them away from his son Isaac, while he was yet living, to the east into the country of the east. 7 And these *were* the years of the days of the life of Abraam as many as he lived, a hundred and seventy-five years. 8 And Abraam failing died in a good old age, an old man and full of days, and was added to his people. 9 And Isaac and Ismael his sons buried him in the double cave, in the field of Ephron the son of Saar the Chettite, which is over against Mambre: 10 *even* the field and the cave which Abraam bought of the sons of Chet; there they buried Abraam and Sarrha his wife. 11 And it came to pass after Abraam was dead, that God blessed Isaac his son, and Isaac dwelt by the well of the vision. 12 And these *are* the generations of Ismael the son of Abraam, whom Agar the Egyptian the hand- maid of Sarrha bore to Abraam. 13 And these *are* the names of the sons of Ismael, according to the names of their generations. The firstborn of Ismael, Nabaioth, and Kedar, and Nabdeel, and Massam, 14 and Masma, and Duma, and Masse, 15 and Choddan, and Thaeman, and Jetur, and Naphes, and Kedma. 16 These *are* the sons of Ismael, and these are their names in their tents and in their dwellings, twelve princes according to their nations. 17 And these *are* the years of the life of Ismael, a hundred and thirty-seven years; and he failed and died, and was added to his fathers. 18 And he dwelt from Evilat to Sur, which is opposite Egypt, until one comes to the Assyrians; he dwelt in the presence of all his brethren. 19 And these *are* the generations of Isaac the son of Abraam. 20 Abraam begot Isaac. And Isaac was forty years old when he took to wife Rebecca, daughter of Bathuel the Syrian, out of Syrian Mesopotamia, sister of Laban the Syrian. 21 And Isaac prayed the Lord concerning Rebecca his wife, because she was barren; and the Lord heard him, and his wife Rebecca conceived in her womb. 22 And the babes leaped within her; and she said, If it will be so with me, why is this to me? And she went to enquire of the Lord. 23 And the Lord said to her, There are two nations in thy womb, and two peoples shall be separated from thy belly, and one people shall excel the other, and the elder shall serve the younger. 24 And the days were fulfilled that she should be delivered, and she had twins in her womb. 25 And the first came out red, hairy all over like a skin; and she called his name Esau. 26 And after this came forth his brother, and his hand took hold of the heel of Esau; and she called his name Jacob. And Isaac was sixty years old when Rebecca bore them. 27 And the lads grew, and Esau was a man skilled in hunting, dwelling in the country, and Jacob a simple man, dwelling in a house. 28 And Isaac loved Esau, because his venison was his food, but Rebecca loved Jacob. 29 And Jacob cooked pottage, and Esau came from the plain, fainting. 30 And Esau said to Jacob, Let me taste of that red pottage, because I am fainting; therefore his name was called Edom. 31 And Jacob said to Esau, Sell me this day thy birthright. 32 And Esau said, Behold, I am going to die, and for what good does this birthright *belong* to me? 33 And Jacob said to him, Swear to me this day; and he swore to him; and Esau sold his birthright to Jacob. 34 And Jacob gave bread to Esau, and pottage of lentiles; and he ate and drank, and he arose and departed; so Esau slighted his birthright.

Gen.26 1 And there was a famine in the land, besides the former famine, which was in the time of Abraam; and Isaac went to Abimelech the king of the Phylistines to Gerara. 2 And the Lord appeared to him and said, Go not down to Egypt, but dwell in the land, which I shall tell thee of. 3 And sojourn in this land; and I will be with thee, and bless thee, for I will give to thee and to thy seed all this land; and I will establish my oath which I swore to thy father Abraam. 4 And I will multiply thy seed as the stars of heaven; and I will give to thy seed all this land, and all the nations of the earth shall be blest in thy seed. 5 Because Abraam thy father hearkened to my voice, and kept my injunctions, and my commandments, and my ordinances, and my statutes. 6 And Isaac dwelt in Gerara. 7 And the men of the place questioned him concerning Rebecca his wife, and he said, She is my sister, for he feared to say, She is my wife, lest at any time the men of the place should slay him because of Rebecca, because she was fair. 8 And he remained there a long time, and Abimelech the king of Gerara leaned to look through the window, and saw Isaac sporting with Rebecca his wife. 9 And Abimelech called Isaac, and said to him, Is she then thy wife? why hast thou said, She is my sister? And Isaac said to him, *I did so*, for I said, Lest at any time I die on her account. 10 And Abimelech said to him, Why hast thou done this to us? one of my kindred within a little had lain with thy wife, and thou wouldest have brought *a sin of* ignorance upon us. 11 And Abimelech charged all his people, saying Every man that touches this man and his wife shall be liable to death. 12 And Isaac sowed in that land, and he found in that year barley and hundred-fold, and the Lord blessed him. 13 And the man was exalted, and advancing he increased, till he became very great. 14 And he had cattle of sheep, and cattle of oxen, and many tilled lands, and the Phylistines envied him. 15 And all the wells which the servants of his father had dug in the time of his father, the Phylistines stopped them, and filled them with earth. 16 And Abimelech said to Isaac, Depart from us, for thou art become much mightier than we. 17 And Isaac departed thence, and rested in the valley of Gerara, and dwelt there. 18 And Isaac dug again the wells of water, which the servants of his father Abraam had dug, and the Phylistines had stopped them, after the death of his father Abraam; and he gave them names, according to the names by which his father named them. 19 And the servants of Isaac dug in the valley of Gerara, and they found there a well of living water. 20 And the shepherds of Gerara strove with the shepherds of Isaac, saying that the water was theirs; and they called the name of the well, Injury, for they injured him. 21 And having departed thence he dug another well, and they strove also for that; and he named the name of it, Enmity. 22 And he departed thence and dug another well; and they did not strive about that; and he named the name of it, Room, saying, Because now the Lord has made room for us, and has increased us upon the earth. 23 And he went up thence to the well of the oath. 24 And the Lord appeared to him in that night, and said, I am the God of Abraam thy father; fear not, for I am with thee, and I will bless thee, and multiply thy seed for the sake of Abraam thy father. 25 And he built there an altar, and called on the name of the Lord, and there he pitched his tent, and there the servants of Isaac dug a well in the valley of Gerara. 26 And Abimelech came to him from Gerara, and so did Ochozath his friend, and Phichol the commander-in-chief of his army. 27 And Isaac said to them, Wherefore have ye come to me? whereas ye hated me, and sent me away from you. 28 And they said, We have surely seen that the Lord was with thee, and we said, Let there be an oath between us and thee, and we will make a covenant with thee, 29 that thou shalt do no wrong by us, as we have not abhorred thee, and according as we have treated thee well, and have sent thee forth peaceably; and now thou art blessed of the Lord. 30 And he made a feast for them, and they ate and drank. 31 And they arose in the morning, and swore each to his neighbour; and Isaac sent them forth, and they departed from him in safety. 32 And it came to pass in that day, that the servants of Isaac came and told him of the well which they had dug; and they said, We have not found water. 33 And he called it, Oath: therefore he called the name of that city, the Well of Oath, until this day. 34 And Esau was forty years old; and he took to wife Judith the daughter of Beoch the Chettite, and Basemath, daughter of Helon the Chettite. 35 And they were provoking to Isaac and Rebecca.

Gen.27 1 And it came to pass after Isaac was old, that his eyes were dimmed so that he could not see; and he called Esau, his elder son, and said to him, My son; and he said, Behold, I *am here*. 2 And he said, Behold, I am grown old, and know not the day of my death. 3 Now then take the weapons, both thy quiver and thy bow, and go into the plain, and get me venison, 4 and make me meats, as I like them, and bring them to me that I may eat, that my soul may bless thee, before I die. 5 And Rebecca heard Isaac speaking to Esau his son; and Esau went to the plain to procure venison for his father. 6 And Rebecca said to Jacob her younger son, Behold, I heard thy father speaking to Esau thy brother, saying, 7 Bring me venison, and prepare me meats, that I may eat and bless thee before the Lord before I die. 8 Now then, my son, hearken to me, as I command thee. 9 And go to the cattle and take for me thence two kids, tender and good, and I will make them meats for thy father, as he likes. 10 And thou shalt bring them in to thy father, and he shall eat, that thy father may bless thee before he dies. 11 And Jacob said to his mother Rebecca, Esau my brother is a hairy man, and I a smooth man. 12 Peradventure my father may feel me, and I shall be before him as one ill-intentioned, and I shall bring upon me a curse, and not a blessing. 13 And his mother said to him, On me be thy curse, son; only hearken to my voice, and go and bring *them* me. 14 So he went and took and brought them to his mother; and his mother made meats, as his father liked *them*. 15 And Rebecca having taken the fine raiment of her elder son Esau which was with her in the house, put it on Jacob her younger son. 16 And she put on his arms the skins of the kids, and on the bare parts of his neck. 17 And she gave the meats, and the loaves which she had prepared, into the hands of Jacob her son. 18 And he brought *them* to his father, and said, Father; and he said, Behold I *am here*; who art thou, son? 19 And Jacob said to his father, I, Esau thy first- born, have done as thou toldest me; rise, sit, and eat of my venison, that thy soul may bless me. 20 And Isaac said to his son, What is this which thou hast quickly found? And he said, That which the Lord thy God presented before me. 21 And Isaac said to Jacob, Draw night to me, and I will feel thee, son, if thou art my son Esau or not. 22 And Jacob drew night to his father Isaac, and he felt him, and said, The voice *is* Jacob's voice, but the hands *are* the hands of Esau. 23 And he knew him not, for his hands were as the hands of his brother Esau, hairy; and he blessed him, 24 and he said, Art thou my son Esau? and he said, I *am*. 25 And he said, Bring hither, and I will eat of thy venison, son, that my soul may bless thee; and he brought *it* near to him, and he ate, and he brought him wine, and he drank. 26 And Isaac his father said to him, Draw nigh to me, and kiss me, son. 27 And he drew nigh and kissed him, and smelled the smell of his garments, and blessed him, and said, Behold, the smell of my son is as the smell of an abundant field, which the Lord has blessed. 28 And may God give thee of the dew of heaven, and of the fatness of the earth, and abundance of corn and wine. 29 And let nations serve thee, and princes bow down to thee, and be thou lord of thy brother, and the sons of thy father shall do thee reverence; accursed is he that curses thee, and blessed is he that blesses thee. 30 And it came to pass after Isaac had ceased blessing his son Jacob, it even came to pass, just when Jacob had gone out from the presence of Isaac his father, that Esau his brother came in from his hunting. 31 And he also had made meats and brought them to his father; and he said to his father, Let my father arise and eat of his son's venison, that thy soul may bless me. 32 And Isaac his father said to him, Who art thou? And he said, I am thy first-born son Esau. 33 And Isaac was amazed with very great amazement, and said, Who then is it that has procured venison for me and brought it to me? and I have eaten of all before thou camest, and I have blessed him, and he shall be blessed. 34 And it came to pass when

Esau heard the words of his father Isaac, he cried out with a great and very bitter cry, and said, Bless, I pray thee, me also, father. 35 And he said to him, Thy brother has come with subtlety, and taken thy blessing. 36 And he said, Rightly was his name called Jacob, for lo! this second time has he supplanted me; he has both taken my birthright, and now he has taken my blessing; and Esau said to his father, Hast thou not left a blessing for me, father? 37 And Isaac answered and said to Esau, If I have made him thy lord, and have made all his brethren his servants, and have strengthened him with corn and wine, what then shall I do for thee, son? 38 And Esau said to his father, Hast thou *only* one blessing, father? Bless, I pray thee, me also, father. And Isaac being troubled, Esau cried aloud and wept. 39 And Isaac his father answered and said to him, Behold, thy dwelling shall be of the fatness of the earth, and of the dew of heaven from above. 40 And thou shalt live by thy sword, and shalt serve thy brother; and there shall be *a time* when thou shalt break and loosen his yoke from off thy neck. 41 And Esau was angry with Jacob because of the blessing, with which his father blessed him; and Esau said in his mind, Let the days of my father's mourning draw nigh, that I may slay my brother Jacob. 42 And the words of Esau her elder son were reported to Rebecca, and she sent and called Jacob her younger son, and said to him, Behold, Esau thy brother threatens thee to kill thee. 43 Now then, my son, hear my voice, and rise and depart quickly into Mesopotamia to Laban my brother into Charran. 44 And dwell with him certain days, until thy brother's anger 45 and rage depart from thee, and he forget what thou hast done to him; and I will send and fetch thee thence, lest at any time I should be bereaved of you both in one day. 46 And Rebecca said to Isaac, I am weary of my life, because of the daughters of the sons of Chet; if Jacob shall take a wife of the daughters of this land, wherefore should I live?

Gen.28 1 And Isaac having called for Jacob, blessed him, and charged him, saying, Thou shalt not take a wife of the daughters of the Chananites. 2 Rise and depart quickly into Mesopotamia, to the house of Bathuel the father of thy mother, and take to thyself thence a wife of the daughters of Laban thy mother's brother. 3 And may my God bless thee, and increase thee, and multiply thee, and thou shalt become gatherings of nations. 4 And may he give thee the blessing of my father Abraam, even to thee and to thy seed after thee, to inherit the land of thy sojourning, which God gave to Abraam. 5 So Isaac sent away Jacob, and he went into Mesopotamia to Laban the son of Bethuel the Syrian, the brother of Rebecca the mother of Jacob and Esau. 6 And Esau saw that Isaac blessed Jacob, and sent him away to Mesopotamia of Syria as he blessed him, to take to himself a wife thence, and *that* he charged him, saying, Thou shalt not take a wife of the daughters of the Chananites; 7 and *that* Jacob hearkened to his father and his mother, and went to Mesopotamia of Syria. 8 And Esau also having seen that the daughters of Chanaan were evil before his father Isaac, 9 Esau went to Ismael, and took Maeleth the daughter of Ismael, the son of Abraam, the sister of Nabeoth, a wife in addition to his *other* wives. 10 And Jacob

went forth from the well of the oath, and departed into Charrhan. 11 And came to a certain place and slept there, for the sun had gone down; and he took *one* of the stones of the place, and put it at his head, and lay down to sleep in that place, 12 and dreamed, and behold a ladder fixed on the earth, whose top reached to heaven, and the angels of God ascended and descended on it. 13 And the Lord stood upon it, and said, I am the God of thy father Abraam, and the God of Isaac; fear not, the land on which thou liest, to thee will I give it, and to thy seed. 14 And thy seed shall be as the sand of the earth; and it shall spread abroad to the sea, and the south, and the north, and to the east; and in thee and in thy seed shall all the tribes of the earth be blessed. 15 And behold I am with thee to preserve thee continually in all the way wherein thou shalt go; and I will bring thee back to this land; for I will not desert thee, until I have done all that I have said to thee. 16 And Jacob awaked out of his sleep, and said, The Lord is in this place, and I knew it not. 17 And he was afraid, and said, How fearful is this place! this is none other than the house of God, and this is the gate of heaven. 18 And Jacob rose up in the morning, and took the stone he *had* laid there by his head, and he set it up *as* a pillar, and poured oil on the top of it. 19 And he called the name of that place, the House of God; and the name of the city before was Ulam-luz. 20 And Jacob vowed a vow, saying, If the Lord God will be with me, and guard me throughout on this journey, on which I am going, and give me bread to eat, and raiment to put on, 21 and bring me back in safety to the house of my father, then shall the Lord be for a God to me. 22 And this stone, which I have set up for a pillar, shall be to me a house of God; and of all whatsoever thou shalt give me, I will tithe a tenth for thee.

Gen.29 1 And Jacob started and went to the land of the east to Laban, the son of Bathuel the Syrian, and the brother of Rebecca, mother of Jacob and Esau. 2 And he looks, and behold! a well in the plain; and there were there three flocks of sheep resting at it, for out of that well they watered the flocks, but there was a great stone at the mouth of the well. 3 And there were all the flocks gathered, and they used to roll away the stone from the mouth of the well, and water the flocks, and set the stone again in its place on the mouth of the well. 4 And Jacob said to them, Brethren, whence are ye? and they said, We are of Charrhan. 5 And he said to them, Know ye Laban, the son of Nachor? and they said, We do know *him*. 6 And he said to them, Is he well? And they said, He is well. And behold Rachel his daughter came with the sheep. 7 And Jacob said, it is yet high day, it is not yet time that the flocks be gathered together; water ye the flocks, and depart and feed them. 8 And they said, We shall not be able, until all the shepherds be gathered together, and they shall roll away the stone from the mouth of the well, then we will water the flocks. 9 While he was yet speaking to them, behold, Rachel the daughter of Laban came with her father's sheep, for she fed the sheep of her father. 10 And it came to pass when Jacob saw Rachel the daughter of Laban, his mother's brother, and the sheep of Laban, his mother's brother, that Jacob came and rolled away the stone from the mouth of the well, and watered the sheep of Laban, his mother's brother. 11 And Jacob kissed Rachel, and cried with a loud voice and wept. 12 And he told Rachel that he was the near relative of her father, and the son of Rebecca; and she ran and reported to her father according to these words. 13 And it came to pass when Laban heard the name of Jacob, his sister's son, he ran to meet him, and embraced and kissed him, and brought him into his house; and he told Laban all these sayings. 14 And Laban said to him, Thou art of my bones and of my flesh; and he was with him a full month. 15 And Laban said to Jacob, Surely thou shalt not serve me for nothing, because thou art my brother; tell me what thy reward is to be. 16 Now Laban had two daughters, the name of the elder was Lea, and the name of the younger, Rachel. 17 And the eyes of Lea were weak. But Rachel was beautiful in appearance, and exceedingly fair in countenance. 18 And Jacob loved Rachel, and said, I will serve thee seven years for thy younger daughter Rachel. 19 And Laban said to him, *It is* better that I should give her to thee, than that I should give her to another man; dwell with me. 20 And Jacob served for Rachel seven years, and they were before him as a few days, by reason of his loving her. 21 And Jacob said to Laban, Give me my wife, for my days are fulfilled, that I may go in to her. 22 And Laban gathered together all the men of the place, and made a marriage-feast. 23 And it was even, and he took his daughter Lea, and brought her in to Jacob, and Jacob went in to her. 24 And Laban gave to his daughter Lea, Zelpha his handmaid, as a handmaid for her. 25 And it was morning, and behold it was Lea; and Jacob said to Laban, What is this that thou hast done to me? did I not serve thee for Rachel? and wherefore hast thou deceived me? 26 And Laban answered, It is not done thus in our country, to give the younger before the elder. 27 Fulfil then her sevens, and I will give to thee her also in return for thy labour, which thou labourest with me, yet seven other years. 28 And Jacob did so, and fulfilled her sevens; and Laban gave him his daughter Rachel to wife. 29 And Laban gave to his daughter his handmaid Balla, for a handmaid to her. 30 And he went in to Rachel; and he loved Rachel more than Lea; and he served him seven other years. 31 And when the Lord God saw that Lea was hated, he opened her womb; but Rachel was barren. 32 And Lea conceived and bore a son to Jacob; and she called his name, Ruben; saying, Because the Lord has looked on my humiliation, and has given me a son, now then my husband will love me. 33 And she conceived again, and bore a second son to Jacob; and she said, Because the Lord has heard that I am hated, he has given to me this one also; and she called his name, Simeon. 34 And she conceived yet again, and bore a son, and said, In the present time my husband will be with me, for I have born him three sons; therefore she called his name, Levi. 35 And having conceived yet again, she bore a son, and said, Now yet again this time will I give thanks to the Lord; therefore she called his name, Juda; and ceased bearing.

Gen.30 1 And Rachel having perceived that she bore Jacob no children, was jealous of her sister; and said to Jacob, Give me children; and if not, I shall die. 2 And Jacob was angry with Rachel, and said to her, Am I in the place of God, who has deprived thee of the fruit of the womb? 3 And Rachel said to Jacob, Behold my handmaid Balla, go in to her, and she shall bear upon my knees, and I also shall have children by her. 4 And she gave him Balla her maid, for a wife to him; and Jacob went in to her. 5 And Balla, Rachel's maid, conceived, and bore Jacob a son. 6 And Rachel said, God has given judgment for me, and hearkened to my voice, and has given me a son; therefore she called his name, Dan. 7 And Balla, Rachel's maid, conceived yet again, and bore a second son to Jacob. 8 And Rachel said, God has helped me, and I contended with my sister and prevailed; and she called his name, Nephthalim. 9 And Lea saw that she ceased from bearing, and she took Zelpha her maid, and gave her to Jacob for a wife; and he went in to her. 10 And Zelpha the maid of Lea conceived, and bore Jacob a son. 11 And Lea said, *It is* happily: and she called his name, Gad. 12 And Zelpha the maid of Lea conceived yet again, and bore Jacob a second son. 13 And Lea said, I am blessed, for the women will pronounce me blessed; and she called his name, Aser. 14 And Ruben went in the day of barley-harvest, and found apples of mandrakes in the field, and brought them to his mother Lea; and Rachel said to Lea her sister, Give me of thy son's mandrakes. 15 And Lea said, *Is it* not enough for thee that thou hast taken my husband, wilt thou also take my son's mandrakes? And Rachel said, Not so: let him lie with thee to-night for thy son's mandrakes. 16 And Jacob came in out of the field at even; and Lea went forth to meet him, and said, Thou shalt come in to me this day, for I have hired thee for my son's mandrakes; and he lay with her that night. 17 And God hearkened to Lea, and she conceived, and bore Jacob a fifth son. 18 And Lea said, God has given me my reward, because I gave my maid to my husband; and she called his name Issachar, which is, Reward. 19 And Lea conceived again, and bore Jacob a sixth son. 20 And Lea said, God has given me a good gift in this time; my husband will choose me, for I have born him six sons: and she called his name, Zabulon. 21 And after this she bore a daughter; and she called her name, Dina. 22 And God remembered Rachel, and God hearkened to her, and he opened her womb. 23 And she conceived, and bore Jacob a son; and Rachel said, God has taken away my reproach. 24 And she called his name Joseph, saying, Let God add to me another son. 25 And it came to pass when Rachel had born Joseph, Jacob said to Laban, Send me away, that I may go to my place and to my land. 26 Restore my wives and my children, for whom I have served thee, that I may depart, for thou knowest the service wherewith I have served thee. 27 And Laban said to him, If I have found grace in thy sight, I would augur *well*, for the Lord has blessed me at thy coming in. 28 Appoint me thy wages, and I will give *them*. 29 And Jacob said, Thou knowest in what things I have served thee, and how many cattle of thine are with me. 30 For it was little thou hadst before my time, and it is increased to a multitude, and the Lord God has blessed thee since my coming; now then, when shall I set up also my own house? 31 And Laban said to him, What shall I give thee? and Jacob said to him, Thou shalt not give me anything; if thou wilt do this thing for me, I will again tend thy flocks and keep them. 32 Let all thy sheep pass by to-day, and separate thence every grey sheep among the rams, and every one that is speckled and spotted among the goats—*this* shall be my reward. 33 And my righteousness shall answer for me on the morrow, for it is my reward before thee: whatever shall not be spotted and speckled among the goats, and grey among the rams, shall be stolen with me. 34 And Laban said to him, Let it be according to thy word. 35 And he separated in that day the spotted and speckled he-goats, and all the spotted and speckled she-goats, and all that was grey among the rams, and every one that was white among them, and he gave them into the hand of his sons. 36 And he set a distance of a three days' journey between them and Jacob. And Jacob tended the cattle of Laban that were left behind. 37 And Jacob took to himself green rods of storax tree and walnut and plane-tree; and Jacob peeled in them white stripes; and as he drew off the green, the white stripe which he had made appeared alternate on the rods. 38 And he laid the rods which he had peeled, in the hollows of the watering-troughs, that whensoever the cattle should come to drink, as they should have come to drink before the rods, the cattle might conceive at the rods. 39 So the cattle conceived at the rods, and the cattle brought forth *young* speckled, and streaked and spotted with ash-coloured *spots*. 40 And Jacob separated the lambs, and set before the sheep a speckled ram, and every variegated one among the lambs, and he separated flocks for himself alone, and did not mingle them with the sheep of Laban. 41 And it came to pass in the time wherein the cattle became pregnant, conceiving in the belly, Jacob put the rods before the cattle in the troughs, that they might conceive by the rods. 42 But he did not put them in *indiscriminately* whenever the cattle happened to bring forth, but the unmarked ones were Laban's, and the marked ones were Jacob's. 43 And the man became very rich, and he had many cattle, and oxen, and servants, and maid-servants, and camels, and asses.

Gen.31 1 And Jacob heard the words of the sons of Laban, saying, Jacob has taken all that was our father's, and of our father's property has he gotten all this glory. 2 And Jacob saw the countenance of Laban, and behold it was not toward him as before. 3 And the Lord said to Jacob, Return to the land of thy father, and to thy family, and I will be with thee. 4 And Jacob sent and called Lea and Rachel to the plain where the flocks were. 5 And he said to them, I see the face of your father, that it is not toward me as before, but the God of my father was with me. 6 And ye too know that with all my might I have served your father. 7 But your father deceived me, and changed my wages for the ten lambs, yet God gave him not *power* to hurt me. 8 If he should say thus, The speckled shall be thy reward, then all the cattle would bear speckled; and if he should say, The white shall be thy reward, then would all the cattle bear white. 9 So God has taken away all the cattle of your father, and given them to me. 10 And it came to pass when the cattle conceived and were with young, that I beheld with mine eyes in sleep, and behold the he-goats and the rams leaping on the sheep and the she-goats, speckled and variegated and spotted with ash-coloured spots. 11 And the angel of God said to me in a dream, Jacob; and I said, What is it? 12 And he said, Look up with thine eyes, and behold the he -goats and the rams leaping on the sheep and the she-goats, speckled and variegated and spotted with ash-coloured spots; for I have seen all things that Laban does to thee. 13 I am God that appeared to thee in the place of God where thou anointedst a pillar to me, and vowedst to me there a vow; now then arise and depart out of this land, depart into the land of thy nativity, and I will be with thee. 14 And Rachel and Lea answered and said to him, Have we yet a part or inheritance in the house of our father? 15 Are we not considered strangers by him? for he has sold us, and quite devoured our money. 16 All the wealth and the glory which God has taken from our father, it shall be our's and our children's; now then do whatsoever God has said to thee. 17 And Jacob arose and took his wives and his children up on the camels; 18 and he took away all his possessions and all his store, which he had gotten in Mesopotamia, and all that belonged to him, to depart to Isaac his father in the land of Chanaan. 19 And Laban went to shear his sheep; and Rachel stole her father's images. 20 And Jacob hid *the matter from* Laban the Syrian, so as not to tell him that he ran away. 21 And he departed himself and all that belonged to him, and passed over the river, and went into the mountain Galaad. 22 But it was told Laban the Syrian on the third day, that Jacob was fled. 23 And having taken his brethren with him, he pursued after him seven days' journey, and overtook him on Mount Galaad. 24 And God came to Laban the Syrian in sleep by night, and said to him, Take heed to thyself that thou speak not at any time to Jacob evil things. 25 And Laban overtook Jacob; and Jacob pitched his tent in the mountain; and Laban stationed his brothers in the mount Galaad. 26 And Laban said to Jacob, What hast thou done? wherefore didst thou run away secretly, and pillage me, and lead away my daughters as captives taken with the sword? 27 Whereas if thou hadst told me, I would have sent thee away with mirth, and with songs, and timbrels, and harp. 28 And I was not counted worthy to embrace my children and my daughters; now then thou hast wrought foolishly. 29 And now my hand has power to hurt thee; but the God of thy father spoke to me yesterday, saying, Take heed to thyself that thou speak not evil words to Jacob. 30 Now then go on thy way, for thou hast earnestly desired to depart to the house of thy father; wherefore hast thou stolen my gods? 31 And Jacob answered and said to Laban, Because I was afraid; for I said, Lest at any time thou shouldest take away thy daughters from me, and all my possessions. 32 And Jacob said, With whomsoever thou shalt find thy gods, he shall not live in the presence of our brethren; take notice of what I have of thy property, and take it; and he observed nothing with him, but Jacob knew not that his wife Rachel had stolen them. 33 And Laban went in and searched in the house of Lea, and found *them* not; and he went out of the house of Lea, and searched in the house of Jacob, and in the house of the two maid-servants, and found them not; and he went also into the house of Rachel. 34 And Rachel took the idols, and cast them among the camel's packs, and sat upon them. 35 And she said to her father, Be not indignant, Sir; I cannot rise up before thee, for it is with me according to the manner of women. Laban searched in all the house, and found not the images. 36 And Jacob was angry, and strove with Laban; and Jacob answered and said to Laban, What is my injustice, and what my sin, that thou hast pursued after me, 37 and that thou hast searched all the furniture of my house? what hast thou found of all the furniture of thine house? set it here between thy relations and my relations, and let them decide between us two. 38 These twenty years have I been with thee; thy sheep, and thy she-goats have not failed in bearing; I devoured not the rams of thy cattle. 39 That which was taken of beasts I brought not to thee; I made good of myself the thefts of the day, and the thefts of the night. 40 I was parched with heat by day, and *chilled* with frost by night, and my sleep departed from my eyes. 41 These twenty years have I been in thy house; I served thee fourteen years for thy two daughters, and six years among thy sheep, and thou didst falsely rate my wages for ten lambs. 42 Unless I had the God of my father Abraam, and the fear of Isaac, now thou wouldest have sent me away empty; God saw my humiliation, and the labour of my hands, and rebuked thee yesterday. 43 And Laban answered and said to Jacob, The daughters are my daughters, and the sons my sons, and the cattle are my cattle, and all things which thou seest are mine, and *the property* of my daughters; what shall I do to them to-day, or their children which they bore? 44 Now then come, let me make a covenant, both I and thou, and it shall be for a witness between me and thee; and he said to him, Behold, there is no one with us; behold, God is witness between me and thee. 45 And Jacob having taken a stone, set it up for a pillar. 46 And Jacob said to his brethren, Gather stones; and they gathered stones and made a heap, and ate there upon the heap; and Laban said to him, This heap witnesses between me and thee to-day. 47 And Laban called it, the Heap of Testimony; and Jacob called it, the Witness Heap. 48 And Laban said to Jacob, Behold this heap, and the pillar, which I have set between me and thee; this heap witnesses, and this pillar witnesses; therefore its name was called, the Heap witnesses. 49 And the vision of which he said—Let God look to it between me and thee, because we are about to depart from each other, — 50 If thou shalt humble my daughters, if thou shouldest take wives in addition to my daughters, see, there is no one with us looking on. God *is* witness between me and thee. 51 And Laban said to Jacob, Behold, this heap, and this pillar are a witness. 52 For if I should not cross over unto thee, neither shouldest thou cross over to me, for mischief beyond this heap and this pillar. 53 The God of Abraam and the God of Nachor judge between us; and Jacob swore by the Fear of his father Isaac. 54 And he offered a sacrifice in the mountain, and called his brethren, and they ate and drank, and slept in the mountain. 55 And Laban rose up in the morning, and kissed his sons and his daughters, and blessed them; and Laban having turned back, departed to his place.

Gen.32 1 And Jacob departed for his journey; and having looked up, he saw the host of God encamped; and the angels of God met him. 2 And Jacob said, when he saw them, This is the Camp of God; and he called the name of that place, Encampments. 3 And Jacob sent messengers before him to Esau his brother to the land of Seir, to the country of Edom. 4 And he charged them, saying, Thus shall ye say to my lord Esau: Thus saith thy servant Jacob; I have sojourned with Laban and tarried until now. 5 And there were born to me oxen, and asses, and sheep, and men-servants and women-servants; and I sent to tell my lord Esau, that thy servant might find grace in thy sight. 6 And the messengers returned to Jacob, saying, We came to thy brother Esau, and lo! he comes to meet thee, and four hundred men with him. 7 And Jacob was greatly terrified, and was perplexed; and he divided the people that was with him, and the cows, and the camels, and the sheep, into two camps. 8 And Jacob said, If Esau should come to one camp, and smite it, the other camp shall be in safety. 9 And Jacob said, God of my father Abraam, and God of my father Isaac, O Lord, thou *art* he that said to me, Depart quickly to the land of thy birth, and I will do thee good. 10 Let there be to me a sufficiency of all the justice and all the truth which thou hast wrought with thy servant; for with this my staff I passed over this Jordan, and now I am become two camps. 11 Deliver me from the hand of my brother, from the hand of Esau, for I am afraid of him, lest haply he should come and smite me, and the mother upon the children. 12 But thou saidst, I will do thee good, and will make thy seed as the sand of the sea, which shall not be numbered for multitude. 13 And he slept there that night, and took of the gifts which he carried *with him*, and sent out to Esau his brother, 14 two hundred she-goats, twenty he-goats, two hundred sheep, twenty rams, 15 milch camels, and their foals, thirty, forty kine, ten bulls, twenty asses, and ten colts. 16 And he gave them to his servants *each* drove apart; and he said to his servants, Go on before me, and put a space between drove and drove. 17 And he charged the first, saying, If Esau my brother meet thee, and he ask thee, saying, Whose art thou? and whither wouldest thou go, and whose are these possessions advancing before thee? 18 Thou shalt say, Thy servant Jacob's; he hath sent gifts to my lord Esau, and lo! he is behind us. 19 And he charged the first and the second and the third, and all that went before him after these flocks, saying, Thus shall ye speak to Esau when ye find him; 20 and ye shall say, Behold thy servant Jacob comes after us. For he said, I will propitiate his countenance with the gifts going before his presence, and afterwards I will behold his face, for peradventure he will accept me. 21 So the presents went on before him, but he himself lodged that night in the camp. 22 And he rose up in that night, and took his two wives and his two servant-maids, and his eleven children, and crossed over the ford of Jaboch. 23 And he took them, and passed over the torrent, and brought over all his possessions. 24 And Jacob was left alone; and a man wrestled with him till the morning. 25 And he saw that he prevailed not against him; and he touched the broad part of his thigh, and the broad part of Jacob's thigh was benumbed in his wrestling with him. 26 And he said to him, Let me go, for the day has dawned; but he said, I will not let thee go, except thou bless me. 27 And he said to him, What is thy name? and he answered, Jacob. 28 And he said to him, Thy name shall no longer be called Jacob, but Israel shall be thy name; for thou hast prevailed with God, and shalt be mighty with men. 29 And Jacob asked and said, Tell me thy name; and he said, Wherefore dost thou ask after my name? and he blessed him there. 30 And Jacob called the name of that place, the Face of God; for, *said he,* I have seen God face to face, and my life was preserved. 31 And the sun rose upon him, when he passed the Face of God; and he halted upon his thigh. 32 Therefore the children of Israel will by no means eat of the sinew which was benumbed, which is on the broad part of the thigh, until this day, because *the angel* touched the broad part of the thigh of Jacob—*even* the sinew which was benumbed.

Gen.33 1 And Jacob lifted up his eyes, and beheld, and lo! Esau his brother coming, and four hundred men with him; and Jacob divided the children to Lea and to Rachel, and the two handmaidens. 2 And he put the two handmaidens and their children with the first, and Lea and her children behind, and Rachel and Joseph last. 3 But he advanced himself before them, and did reverence to the ground seven times, until he drew near to his brother. 4 And Esau ran on to meet him, and embraced him, and fell on his neck, and kissed him; and they both wept. 5 And Esau looked up and saw the women and the children, and said, What are these to thee? And he said, The children with which God has mercifully blessed thy servant. 6 And the maid-servants and their children drew near and did reverence. 7 And Lea and her children drew near and did reverence; and after this drew near Rachel and Joseph, and did reverence. 8 And he said, What are these things to thee, all these companies that I have met? And he said, That thy servant might find grace in thy sight, my lord. 9 And Esau said, I have much, my brother; keep thine own. 10 And Jacob said, If I have found grace in thy sight, receive the gifts through my hands; therefore have I seen thy face, as if any one should see the face of God, and thou shalt be well- pleased with me. 11 Receive my blessings, which I have brought thee, because God has had mercy on me, and I have all things; and he constrained him, and he took *them.* 12 And he said, Let us depart, and proceed right onward. 13 And he said to him, My lord knows, that the children are very tender, and the flocks and the herds with me are with young; if then I shall drive them hard one day, all the cattle will die. 14 Let my lord go on before his servant, and I shall have strength on the road according to the ease of the journey before me, and according to the strength of the children, until I come to my lord to Seir. 15 And Esau said, I will leave with thee some of the people who are with me. And he said, Why so? it is enough that I have found favour before thee, *my* lord. 16 And Esau returned on that day on his journey to Seir. 17 And Jacob departs to his tents; and he made for himself there habitations, and for his cattle he made booths; therefore he called the name of that place, Booths. 18 And Jacob came to Salem, a city of Secima, which is in the land of Chanaan, when he departed out of Mesopotamia of Syria, and took up a position in front of the city. 19 And he bought the portion of the field, where he pitched his tent, of Emmor the father of Sychem, for a hundred lambs. 20 And he set up there an alter, and called on the God of Israel.

Gen.34 1 And Dina, the daughter of Lea, whom she bore to Jacob, went forth to observe the daughters of the inhabitants. 2 And Sychem the son of Emmor the Evite, the ruler of the land, saw her, and took her and lay with her, and humbled her. 3 And he was attached to the soul of Dina the daughter of Jacob, and he loved the damsel, and he spoke kindly to the damsel. 4 Sychem spoke to Emmor his father, saying, Take for me this damsel to wife. 5 And Jacob heard that the son of Emmor had defiled Dina his daughter (now his sons were with his cattle in the plain). And Jacob was silent until they came. 6 And Emmor the father of Sychem went forth to Jacob, to speak to him. 7 And the sons of Jacob came from the plain; and when they heard, the men were deeply pained, and it was very grievous to them, because *the man* wrought folly in Israel, having lain with the daughter of Jacob, and so it must not be. 8 And Emmor spoke to them, saying, Sychem my son has chosen in his heart your daughter; give her therefore to him for a wife, 9 and intermarry with us. Give us your daughters, and take our daughters for your sons. 10 And dwell in the midst of us; and, behold, the land is spacious before you, dwell in it, and trade, and get possessions in it. 11 And Sychem said to her father and to her brothers, I would find grace before you, and we will give whatever ye shall name. 12 Multiply *your demand of* dowry very much, and I will give accordingly as ye shall say to me, only ye shall give me this damsel for a wife. 13 And the sons of Jacob answered to Sychem and Emmor his father craftily, and spoke to them, because they had defiled Dina their sister. 14 And Symeon and Levi, the brothers of Dina, said to them, We shall not be able to do this thing, to give our sister to a man who is uncircumcised, for it is a reproach to us. 15 Only on these terms will we conform to you, and dwell among you, if ye also will be as we are, in that every male of you be circumcised. 16 And we will give our daughters to you, and we will take of your daughters for wives to us, and we will dwell with you, and we will be as one race. 17 But if ye will not hearken to us to be circumcised, we will take our daughter and depart. 18 And the words pleased Emmor, and Sychem the son of Emmor. 19 And the young man delayed not to do this thing, for he was much attached to Jacob's daughter, and he was the most honourable of all in his father's house. 20 And Emmor and Sychem his son came to the gate of their city, and spoke to the men of their city, saying, 21 These men are peaceable, let them dwell with us upon the land, and let them trade in it, and behold the land is extensive before them; we will take their daughters to us for wives, and we will give them our daughters. 22 Only on these terms will the men conform to us to dwell with us so as to be one people, if every male of us be circumcised, as they also are circumcised. 23 And shall not their cattle and their herds, and their possessions, be ours? only in this let us conform to them, and they will dwell with us. 24 And all that went in at the gate of their city hearkened to Emmor and Sychem his son, and they were circumcised in the flesh of their foreskin every male. 25 And it came to pass on the third day, when they were in pain, the two sons of Jacob, Symeon and Levi, Dina's brethren, took each man his sword, and came upon the city securely, and slew every male. 26 And they slew Emmor and Sychem his son with the edge of the sword, and took Dina out of the house of Sychem, and went forth. 27 But the sons of Jacob came upon the wounded, and ravaged the city wherein they had defiled Dina their sister. 28 And their sheep, and their oxen, and their asses they took, and all things whatsoever were in the city, and whatsoever were in the plain. 29 And they took captive all the persons of them, and all their store, and their wives, and plundered both whatever things there were in the city, and whatever things there were in the houses. 30 And Jacob said to Symeon and Levi, Ye have made me hateful so that I should be evil to all the inhabitants of the land, both among the Chananites and the Pherezites, and I am few in number; they will gather themselves against me and cut me in pieces, and I shall be utterly destroyed, and my house. 31 And they said, Nay, but shall they treat our sister as an harlot?

Gen.35 1 And God said to Jacob, Arise, go up to the place, Baethel, and dwell there; and make there an altar to the God that appeared to thee, when thou fleddest from the face of Esau thy brother. 2 And Jacob said to his house, and to all that were with him, Remove the strange gods that are with you from the midst of you, and purify yourselves, and change your clothes. 3 And let us rise and go up to Baethel, and let us there make an alter to God who hearkened to me in the day of calamity, who was with me, and preserved me throughout in the journey, by which I went. 4 And they gave to Jacob the strange gods, which were in their hands, and the ear-rings which were in their ears, and Jacob hid them under the turpentine tree which is in Secima, and destroyed them to this day. 5 So Israel departed from Secima, and the fear of God was upon the cities round about them, and they did not pursue after the children of Israel. 6 And Jacob came to Luza, which is in the land of Chanaan, which is Baethel, he and all the people that were with him. 7 And he built there an altar, and called the name of the place Baethel; for there God appeared to him, when he fled from the face of his brother Esau. 8 And Deborrha, Rebecca's nurse, died, and was buried below Baethel under the oak; and Jacob called its name, The Oak of Mourning. 9 And God appeared to Jacob once more in Luza, when he came out of Mesopotamia of Syria, and God blessed him. 10 And God said to him, Thy name shall not be called Jacob, but Israel shall be thy name; and he called his name Israel. 11 And God said to him, I am thy God; increase and multiply; for nations and gatherings of nations shall be of thee, and kings shall come out of thy loins. 12 And the land which I gave to Abraam and Isaac, I have given it to thee; and it shall come to pass that I will give this land also to thy seed after thee. 13 And God went up from him from the place where he spoke with him. 14 And Jacob set up a pillar in the place where God spoke with him, *even* a pillar of stone; and offered a libation upon it, and poured oil upon it. 15 And Jacob called the name of the place in which God spoke with him, Baethel. 16 [[And Jacob removed from Baethel, and pitched his tent beyond the tower of Gader,]]and it came to pass when he drew nigh to Chabratha, to enter into Ephratha, Rachel travailed; and in her travail she was in hard labour. 17 And it came to pass in her hard labour, that the midwife said to her, Be of good courage, for thou shalt also have this son. 18 And it came to pass in her giving up the ghost (for she was dying), that she called his name, The son of my pain; but his father called his name Benjamin. 19 So Rachel died, and was buried in the way of the course of Ephratha, this is Bethleem. 20 And Jacob set up a pillar on her tomb; this is the pillar on the tomb of Rachel, until this day. 21 And it came to pass when Israel dwelt in that land, that Ruben went and lay with Balla, the concubine of his father Jacob; and Israel heard, and the thing appeared grievous before him. 22 And the sons of Jacob were twelve. 23 The sons of Lea, the first-born of Jacob; Ruben, Symeon, Levi, Judas, Issachar, Zabulon. 24 And the sons of Rachel; Joseph and Benjamin. 25 And the sons of Balla, the hand-maid of Rachel; Dan and Nephthalim. 26 And the sons of Zelpha, the hand-maid of Lea; Gad and Aser. These *are* the sons of Jacob, which were born to him in Mesopotamia of Syria. 27 And Jacob came to Isaac his father to Mambre, to a city of the plain; this is Chebron in the land of Chanaan, where Abraam and Isaac sojourned. 28 And the days of Isaac which he lived were an hundred and eighty years. 29 And Isaac gave up the ghost and died, and was laid to his family, old and full of days; and Esau and Jacob his sons buried him.

Gen.36 1 And these *are* the generations of Esau; this is Edom. 2 And Esau took to himself wives of the daughters of the Chananites; Ada, the daughter of Ælom the Chettite; and Olibema, daughter of Ana the son of Sebegon, the Evite; 3 and Basemath, daughter of Ismael, sister of Nabaioth. 4 And Ada bore to him Eliphas; and Basemath bore Raguel. 5 And Olibema bore Jeus, and Jeglom, and Core; these *are* the sons of Esau, which were born to him in the land of Chanaan. 6 And Esau took his wives, and his sons, and his daughters, and all the persons of his house, and all his possessions, and all his cattle, and all that he had got, and all things whatsoever he had acquired in the land of Chanaan; and Esau went forth from the land of Chanaan, from the face of his brother Jacob. 7 For their substance was too great for them to dwell together; and the land of their sojourning could not bear them, because of the abundance of their possessions. 8 And Esau dwelt in mount Seir; Esau, he is Edom. 9 And these *are* the generations of Esau, the father of Edom in the mount Seir. 10 And these *are* the names of the sons of Esau. Eliphas, the son of Ada, the wife of Esau; and Raguel, the son of Basemath, wife of Esau. 11 And the sons of Eliphas were Thaeman, Omar, Sophar, Gothom, and Kenez. 12 And Thamna was a concubine of Eliphaz, the son of Esau; and she bore Amalec to Eliphas. These *are* the sons of Ada, the wife of Esau. 13 And these *are* the sons of Raguel; Nachoth, Zare, Some, and Moze. These were the sons of Basemath, wife of Esau. 14 And these *are* the sons of Olibema, the daughter of Ana, the son of Sebegon, the wife of Esau; and she bore to Esau, Jeus, and Jeglom, and Core. 15 These *are* the chiefs of the son of Esau, *even* the sons of Eliphas, the first-born of Esau; chief Thaeman, chief Omar, chief Sophar, chief Kenez, 16 chief Core, chief Gothom, chief Amalec. These *are* the chiefs of Eliphas, in the land of Edom; these are the sons of Ada. 17 And these *are* the sons of Raguel, the son of Esau; chief Nachoth, chief Zare, chief Some, chief Moze. These *are* the chiefs of Raguel, in the land of Edom; these are the sons of Basemath, wife of Esau. 18 And these *are* the sons of Olibema, wife of Esau; chief Jeus, chief Jeglom, chief Core. These *are* the chiefs of Olibema, daughter of Ana, wife of Esau. 19 These *are* the sons of Esau, and these are the chiefs; these are the sons of Edom. 20 And these *are* the sons of Seir, the Chorrhite, who inhabited the land; Lotan, Sobal, Sebegon, Ana, 21 and Deson, and Asar, and Rison. These *are* the chiefs of the Chorrhite, the son of Seir, in the land of Edom. 22 And the sons of Lotan *were* Chorrhi and Haeman; and the sister of Lotan, Thamna. 23 And these *are* the sons of Sobal; Golam, and Manachath, and Gaebel, and Sophar, and Omar. 24 And these *are* the sons of Sebegon; Aie, and Ana; this is the Ana who found Jamin in the wilderness, when he tended the beasts of his father Sebegon. 25 And these *are* the sons of Ana; Deson—and Olibema *was* daughter of Ana. 26 And these *are* the sons of Deson; Amada, and Asban, and Ithran, and Charrhan. 27 And these *are* the sons of Asar; Balaam, and Zucam, and Jucam. 28 And these *are* the sons of Rison; Hos, and Aran. 29 And these *are* the chiefs of Chorri; chief Lotan, chief Sobal, chief Sebegon, chief Ana, 30 chief Deson, chief Asar, chief Rison. These *are* the chiefs of Chorri, in their principalities in the land of Edom. 31 these *are* the kings which reigned in Edom, before a king reigned in Israel. 32 And Balac, son of Beor, reigned in Edom; and the name of his city *was* Dennaba. 33 And Balac died; and Jobab, son of Zara, from Bosorrha reigned in his stead. 34 And Jobab died; and Asom, from the land of the Thaemanites, reigned in his stead. 35 And Asom died; and Adad son of Barad, who cut off Madiam in the plain of Moab, ruled in his stead; and the name of his city was Getthaim. 36 And Adad died; and Samada of Massecca reigned in his stead. 37 Samada died; and Saul of Rhooboth by the river reigned in his stead. 38 And Saul died; and Ballenon the son of Achobor reigned in his stead. 39 And Ballenon the son of Achobor died; and Arad the son of Barad reigned in his stead; and the name of his city was Phogor; and the name of his wife was Metebeel, daughter of Matraith, son of Maizoob. 40 These *are* the names of the chiefs of Esau, in their tribes, according to their place, in their countries, and in their nations; chief Thamna, chief Gola, chief Jether, 41 chief Olibema, chief Helas, chief Phinon, 42 chief Kenez, chief Thaeman, chief Mazar, 43 chief Magediel, chief Zaphoin. These are the chiefs of Edom in their dwelling-places in the land of their possession; this is Esau, the father of Edom. 44 And Jacob dwelt in the land where his father sojourned, in the land of Chanaan.

Gen.37 1 And these are the generations of Jacob. And Joseph was seventeen years old, feeding the sheep of his father with his brethren, being young; with the sons of Balla, and with the sons of Zelpha, the wives of his father; and Joseph brought to Israel their father their evil reproach. 3 And Jacob loved Joseph more than all his sons, because he was to him the son of old age; and he made for him a coat of many colours. 4 And his brethren having seen that his father loved him more than all his sons, hated him, and could not speak anything peaceable to him. 5 And Joseph dreamed a dream, and reported it to his brethren. 6 And he said to them, Hear this dream which I have dreamed. 7 I thought ye were binding sheaves in the middle of the field, and my sheaf stood up and was erected, and your sheaves turned round, and did obeisance to my sheaf. 8 And his brethren said to him, Shalt thou indeed reign over us, or shalt thou indeed be lord over us? And they hated him still more for his dreams and for his words. 9 And he dreamed another dream, and related it to his father, and to his brethren, and said, Behold, I have dreamed another dream: as it were the sun, and the moon, and the eleven stars did me reverence. 10 And his father rebuked him, and said to him, What is this dream which thou hast dreamed? shall indeed both I and thy mother and thy brethren come and bow before thee to the earth? 11 And his brethren envied him; but his father observed the saying. 12 And his brethren went to feed the sheep of their father to Sychem. 13 And Israel said to Joseph, Do not thy brethren feed their flock in Sychem? Come, I will send thee to them; and he said to him, Behold, I *am here*. 14 And Israel said to him, Go and see if thy brethren and the sheep are well, and bring me word; and he sent him out of the valley of Chebron, and he came to Sychem. 15 And a man found him wandering in the field; and the man asked him, saying, What seekest thou? 16 And he said, I am seeking my brethren; tell me where they feed *their flocks*. 17 And the man said to him, They have departed hence, for I heard them saying, Let us go to Dothaim; and Joseph went after his brethren, and found them in Dothaim. 18 And they spied him from a distance before he drew nigh to them, and they wickedly took counsel to slay him. 19 And each said to his brother, Behold, that dreamer comes. 20 Now then come, let us kill him, and cast him into one of the pits; and we will say, An evil wild beast has devoured him; and we shall see what his dreams will be. 21 And Ruben having heard it, rescued him out of their hands, and said, Let us not kill him. 22 And Ruben said to them, Shed not blood; cast him into one of these pits in the wilderness, but do not lay *your* hands upon him; that he might rescue him out of their hands, and restore him to his father. 23 And it came to pass, when Joseph came to his brethren, that they stripped Joseph of his many-coloured coat that was upon him. 24 And they took him and cast him into the pit; and the pit was empty, it had not water. 25 And they sat down to eat bread; and having lifted up their eyes they beheld, and lo, Ismaelitish travellers came from Galaad, and their camels were heavily loaded with spices, and resin, and myrrh; and they went to bring them to Egypt. 26 And Judas said to his brethren, What profit is it if we slay our brother, and conceal his blood? 27 Come, let us sell him to these Ismaelites, but let not our hands be upon him, because he is our brother and our flesh; and his brethren hearkened. 28 And the men, the merchants of Madian, went by, and they drew and lifted Joseph out of the pit, and sold Joseph to the Ismaelites for twenty pieces of gold; and they brought Joseph down into Egypt. 29 And Ruben returned to the pit, and sees not Joseph in the pit; and he rent his garments. 30 And he returned to his brethren and said, The boy is not; and I, whither am I yet to go? 31 And having taken the coat of Joseph, they slew a kid of the goats, and stained the coat with the blood. 32 And they sent the coat of many colours; and they brought it to their father, and said, This have we found; know if it be thy son's coat or no. And he recognised it, and said, It is my son's coat, an evil wild beast has devoured him; a wild beast has carried off Joseph. 33 And Jacob rent his clothes, and put sackcloth on his loins, and mourned for his son many days. 34 And all his sons and his daughters gathered themselves together, and came to comfort him; but he would not be comforted, saying, I will go down to my son mourning to Hades; and his father wept for him. 35 And the Madianites sold Joseph into Egypt; to Petephres, the eunuch of Pharao, captain of the guard.

Gen.38 1 And it came to pass at that time that Judas went down from his brethren, and came as far as to a certain man of Odollam, whose name was Iras. 2 And Judas saw there the daughter of a Chananitish man, whose name was Sava; and he took her, and went in to her. 3 And she conceived and bore a son, and called his name, Er. 4 And she conceived and bore a son again; and called his name, Aunan. 5 And she again bore a son; and called his name, Selom: and she was in Chasbi when she bore them. 6 And Judas took a wife for Er his first-born, whose name was Thamar. 7 And Er, the first-born of Judas, was wicked before the Lord; and God killed him. 8 And Judas said to Aunan, Go in to thy brother's wife, and marry her as her brother-in- law, and raise up seed to thy brother. 9 And Aunan, knowing that the seed should not be his—it came to pass when he went in to his brother's wife, that he spilled *it* upon the ground, so that he should not give seed to his brother's wife. 10 And his doing this appeared evil before God; and he slew him also. 11 And Judas said to Thamar, his daughter-in-law, Sit thou a widow in the house of thy father- in-law, until Selom my son be grown; for he said, lest he also die as his brethren; and Thamar departed, and sat in the house of her father. 12 And the days were fulfilled, and Sava the wife of Judas died; and Judas, being comforted, went to them that sheared his sheep, himself and Iras his Shepherd the Odollamite, to Thamna. 13 And it was told Thamar his daughter-in-law, saying, Behold, thy father-in-law goeth up to Thamna, to shear his sheep. 14 And having taken off the garments of her widowhood from her, she put on a veil, and ornamented her face, and sat by the gates of Ænan, which is in the way to Thamna, for she saw that Selom was grown; but he gave her not to him for a wife. 15 And when Judas saw her, he thought her to be a harlot; for she covered her face, and he knew her not. 16 And he went out of his way to her, and said to her, Let me

come in to thee; for he knew not that she was his daughter-in-law; and she said, What wilt thou give me if thou shouldest come in to me? 17 And he said, I will send thee a kid of the goats from my flock; and she said, *Well,* if thou wilt give me an earnest, until thou send it. 18 And he said, What is the earnest that I shall give thee? and she said, Thy ring, and thy bracelet, and the staff in thy hand; and he gave them to her, and went in to her, and she conceived by him. 19 And she arose and departed, and took her veil from off her, and put on the garments of her widowhood. 20 And Judas sent the kid of the goats by the hand of his shepherd the Odollamite, to receive the pledge from the woman; and he found her not. 21 And he asked the men of the place, Where is the harlot who was in Ænan by the way-side? and they said, There was no harlot here. 22 And he returned to Judas, and said, I have not found her; and the men of the place say, There is no harlot here. 23 And Judas said, Let her have them, but let us not be ridiculed; I sent this kid, but thou hast not found her. 24 And it came to pass after three months, that it was told Judas, saying, Thamar thy daughter-in-law has grievously played the harlot, and behold she is with child by whoredom; and Judas said, Bring her out, and let her be burnt. 25 And as they were bringing her, she sent to her father-in-law, saying, I am with child by the man whose these things are; and she said, See whose is this ring and bracelet and staff. 26 And Judas knew *them,* and said, Thamar is cleared rather than I, forasmuch as I gave her not to Selom my son: and he knew her not again. 27 And it came to pass when she was in labour, that she also had twins in her womb. 28 And it came to pass as she was bringing forth, one thrust forth his hand, and the midwife having taken hold of it, bound upon hid hand a scarlet *thread,* saying, This one shall come out first. 29 And when he drew back his hand, then immediately came forth his brother; and she said, Why has the barrier been cut through because of thee? and she called his name, Phares. 30 And after this came forth his brother, on whose hand was the scarlet thread; and she called his name, Zara.

Gen.39 1 And Joseph was brought down to Egypt; and Petephres the eunuch of Pharao, the captain of the guard, an Egyptian, bought him of the hands of the Ismaelites, who brought him down thither. 2 And the Lord was with Joseph, and he was a prosperous man; and he was in the house with his lord the Egyptian. 3 And his master knew that the Lord was with him, and the Lord prospers in his hands whatsoever he happens to do. 4 And Joseph found grace in the presence of his lord, and was well-pleasing to him; and he set him over his house, and all that he had he gave into the hand of Joseph. 5 And it came to pass after that he was set over his house, and over all that he had, that the Lord blessed the house of the Egyptian for Joseph's sake; and the blessing of the Lord was on all his possessions in the house, and in his field. 6 And he committed all that he had into the hands of Joseph; and he knew not of anything that belonged to him, save the bread which he himself ate. And Joseph was handsome in form, and exceedingly beautiful in countenance. 7 And it came to pass after these things, that his master's wife cast her eyes upon

Joseph, and said, Lie with me. 8 But he would not; but said to his master's wife, If because of me my master knows nothing in his house, and has given into my hands all things that belong to him: 9 and in this house there is nothing above me, nor has anything been kept back from me, but thou, because thou art his wife—how then shall I do this wicked thing, and sin against God? 10 And when she talked with Joseph day by day, and he hearkened not to her to sleep with her, so as to be with her, 11 it came to pass on a certain day, that Joseph went into the house to do his business, and there was no one of the household within. 12 And she caught hold of him by his clothes, and said, Lie with me; and having left his clothes in her hands, he fled, and went forth. 13 And it came to pass, when she saw that he had left his clothes in her hands, and fled, and gone forth, 14 that she called those that were in the house, and spoke to them, saying, See, he has brought in to us a Hebrew servant to mock us— he came in to me, saying, Lie with me, and I cried with a loud voice. 15 And when he heard that I lifted up my voice and cried, having left his clothes with me, he fled, and went forth out. 16 So she leaves the clothes by her, until the master came to his house. 17 And she spoke to him according to these words, saying, The Hebrew servant, whom thou broughtest in to us, came in to me to mock me, and said to me, I will lie with thee. 18 And when he heard that I lifted up my voice and cried, having left his clothes with me, he fled and departed forth. 19 And it came to pass, when his master heard all the words of his wife, that she spoke to him, saying, Thus did thy servant to me, that he was very angry. 20 And his master took Joseph, and cast him into the prison, into the place where the king's prisoners are kept, there in the prison. 21 And the Lord was with Joseph, and poured down mercy upon him; and he gave him favour in the sight of the chief keeper of the prison. 22 And the chief keeper of the prison gave the prison into the hand of Joseph, and all the prisoners as many as were in the prison; and all things whatsoever they do there, he did them. 23 Because of him the chief keeper of the prison knew nothing, for all things were in the hand of Joseph, because the Lord was with him; and whatever things he did, the Lord made them to prosper in his hands.

Gen.40 1 And it came to pass after these things, that the chief cupbearer of the king of Egypt and the chief baker trespassed against their lord the king of Egypt. 2 And Pharao was wroth with his two eunuchs, with his chief cupbearer, and with his chief baker. 3 And he put them in ward, into the prison, into the place whereinto Joseph had been led. 4 And the chief keeper of the prison committed them to Joseph, and he stood by them; and they were *some* days in the prison. 5 And they both had a dream in one night; and the vision of the dream of the chief cupbearer and chief baker, who belonged to the king of Egypt, who were in the prison, was this. 6 Joseph went in to them in the morning, and saw them, and they had been troubled. 7 And he asked the eunuchs of Pharao who were with him in the prison with his master, saying, Why is it that your countenances are sad to-day? 8 And they said to him, We

have seen a dream, and there is no interpreter of it. And Joseph said to them, Is not the interpretation of them through god? tell *them* than to me. 9 And the chief cupbearer related his dream to Joseph, and said, In my dream a vine was before me. 10 And in the vine *were* three stems; and it budding shot forth blossoms; the clusters of grapes were ripe. 11 And the cup of Pharao was in my hand; and I took the bunch of grapes, and squeezed it into the cup, and gave the cup into Pharao's hand. 12 And Joseph said to him, This is the interpretation of it. The three stems are three days. 13 Yet three days and Pharao shall remember thy office, and he shall restore thee to thy place of chief cupbearer, and thou shalt give the cup of Pharao into his hand, according to thy former high place, as thou wast wont to be cupbearer. 14 But remember me of thyself, when it shall be well with thee, and thou shalt deal mercifully with me, and thou shalt make mention of me to Pharao, and thou shalt bring me forth out of this dungeon. 15 For surely I was stolen away out of the land of the Hebrews, and here I have done nothing, but they have cast me into this pit. 16 And the chief baker saw that he interpreted aright; and he said to Joseph, I also saw a dream, and methought I took up on my head three baskets of mealy food. 17 And in the upper basket there was the work of the baker of every kind which Pharao eats; and the fowls of the air ate them out of the basket that was on my head. 18 And Joseph answered and said to him, This is the interpretation of it; The three baskets are three days. 19 Yet three days, and Pharao shall take away thy head from off thee, and shall hang thee on a tree, and the birds of the sky shall eat thy flesh from off thee. 20 And it came to pass on the third day that it was Pharao's birth-day, and he made a banquet for all his servants, and he remembered the office of the cupbearer and the office of the baker in the midst of his servants. 21 And he restored the chief cupbearer to his office, and he gave the cup into Pharao's hand. 22 And he hanged the chief baker, as Joseph, interpreted to them. 23 Yet did not the chief cupbearer remember Joseph, but forgot him.

Gen.41 1 And it came to pass after two full years that Pharao had a dream. He thought he stood upon *the bank of* the river. 2 And lo, there came up as it were out of the river seven cows, fair in appearance, and choice of flesh, and they fed on the sedge. 3 And other seven cows came up after these out of the river, ill-favoured and lean-fleshed, and fed by the *other* cows on the bank of the river. 4 And the seven ill-favoured and lean cows devoured the seven well-favoured and choice-fleshed cows; and Pharao awoke. 5 And he dreamed again. And, behold, seven ears came up on one stalk, choice and good. 6 And, behold, seven ears thin and blasted with the wind, grew up after them. 7 And the seven thin ears and blasted with the wind devoured the seven choice and full ears; and Pharao awoke, and it was a dream. 8 And it was morning, and his soul was troubled; and he sent and called all the interpreters of Egypt, and all her wise men; and Pharao related to them his dream, and there was no one to interpret it to Pharao. 9 And the chief cupbearer spoke to Pharao, saying, I this day remember my fault: 10 Pharao was angry with his servants, and put us in prison in the house of the captain of the guard, both me and the chief baker. 11 And we had a dream both in one night, I and he; we saw, each according to his dream. 12 And there was there with us a young man, a Hebrew servant of the captain of the guard; and we related to him *our dreams*, and he interpreted *them* to us. 13 And it came to pass, as he interpreted them to us, so also it happened, both that I was restored to my office, and that he was hanged. 14 And Pharao having sent, called Joseph; and they brought him out from the prison, and shaved him, and changed his dress, and he came to Pharao. 15 And Pharao said to Joseph, I have seen a vision, and there is no one to interpret it; but I have heard say concerning thee that thou didst hear dreams and interpret them. 16 And Joseph answered Pharao and said, Without God an answer of safety shall not be given to Pharao. 17 And Pharao spoke to Joseph, saying, In my dream methought I stood by the bank of the river; 18 and there came up as it were out of the river, seven cows well-favoured and choice-fleshed, and they fed on the sedge. 19 And behold seven other cows came up after them out of the river, evil and ill-favoured and lean-fleshed, such that I never saw worse in all the land of Egypt. 20 And the seven ill-favoured and thin cows ate up the seven first good and choice cows. 21 And they went into their bellies; and it was not perceptible that they had gone into their bellies, and their appearance was ill- favoured, as also at the beginning; and after I awoke I slept, 22 and saw again in my sleep, and as it were seven ears came up on one stem, full and good. 23 And other seven ears, thin and blasted with the wind, sprang up close to them. 24 And the seven thin and blasted ears devoured the seven fine and full ears: so I spoke to the interpreters, and there was no one to explain it to me. 25 And Joseph said to Pharao, The dream of Pharao is one; whatever God does, he has shewn to Pharao. 26 The seven good cows are seven years, and the seven good ears are seven years; the dream of Pharao is one. 27 And the seven thin kine that came up after them are seven years; and the seven thin and blasted ears are seven years; there shall be seven years of famine. 28 And as for the word which I have told Pharao, whatsoever God intends to do, he has shewn to Pharao: 29 behold, for seven years there is coming great plenty in all the land of Egypt. 30 But there shall come seven years of famine after these, and they shall forget the plenty that shall be in all Egypt, and the famine shall consume the land. 31 And the plenty shall not be known in the land by reason of the famine that shall be after this, for it shall be very grievous. 32 And concerning the repetition of the dream to Pharao twice, *it is* because the saying which is from God shall be true, and God will hasten to accomplish it. 33 Now then, look out a wise and prudent man, and set him over the land of Egypt. 34 And let Pharao make and appoint local governors over the land; and let them take up a fifth part of all the produce of the land of Egypt for the seven years of the plenty. 35 And let them gather all the food of these seven good years that are coming, and let the corn be gathered under the hand of Pharao; let food be kept in the cities. 36 And the stored food shall be for the land against the seven years of famine, which shall be in the land of Egypt; and the land shall not be utterly destroyed by the famine. 37 And the word was pleasing in the sight of Pharao, and in the sight of all his servants. 38 And Pharao said to all his servants, Shall we find such a man as this, who has the Spirit of God in him? 39 And Pharao said to Joseph, Since God has shewed thee all these things, there is not a wiser or more prudent man than thou. 40 Thou shalt be over my house, and all my people shall be obedient to thy word; only in the throne will I excel thee. 41 And Pharao said to Joseph, Behold, I set thee this day over all the land of Egypt. 42 And Pharao took his ring off his hand, and put it on the hand of Joseph, and put on him a robe of fine linen, and put a necklace of gold about his neck. 43 And he mounted him on the second of his chariots, and a herald made proclamation before him; and he set him over all the land of Egypt. 44 And Pharao said to Joseph, I am Pharao; without thee no one shall lift up his hand on all the land of Egypt. 45 And Pharao called the name of Joseph, Psonthomphanech; and he gave him Aseneth, the daughter of Petephres, priest of Heliopolis, to wife. 46 And Joseph was thirty years old when he stood before Pharao, king of Egypt. And Joseph went out from the presence of Pharao, and went through all the land of Egypt. 47 And the land produced, in the seven years of plenty, *whole* handfuls *of corn*. 48 And he gathered all the food of the seven years, in which was the plenty in the land of Egypt; and he laid up the food in the cities; the food of the fields of a city round about it he laid up in it. 49 And Joseph gathered very much corn as the sand of the sea, until it could not be numbered, for there was no number *of it*. 50 And to Joseph were born two sons, before the seven years of famine came, which Aseneth, the daughter of Petephres, priest of Heliopolis, bore to him. 51 And Joseph called the name of the first-born, Manasse; for God, *said he*, has made me forget all my toils, and all my father's house. 52 And he called the name of the second, Ephraim; for God, *said he*, has increased me in the land of my humiliation. 53 And the seven years of plenty passed away, which were in the land of Egypt. 54 And the seven years of famine began to come, as Joseph said; and there was a famine in all the land; but in all the land of Egypt there was bread. 55 And all the land of Egypt was hungry; and the people cried to Pharao for bread. And Pharao said to all the Egyptians, Go to Joseph, and do whatsoever he shall tell you. 56 And the famine was on the face of all the earth; and Joseph opened all the granaries, and sold to all the Egyptians. 57 And all countries came to Egypt to buy of Joseph, for the famine prevailed in all the earth.

Gen.42 1 And Jacob having seen that there was a sale *of corn* in Egypt, said to his sons, Why are ye indolent? 2 Behold, I have heard that there is corn in Egypt; go down thither, and buy for us a little food, that we may live, and not die. 3 And the ten brethren of Joseph went down to buy corn out of Egypt. 4 But *Jacob* sent not Benjamin, the brother of Joseph, with his brethren; for he said, Lest, haply, disease befall him. 5 And the sons of Israel came to buy with those that came, for the famine was in the land of Chanaan. 6 And Joseph was ruler of the land; he sold to all the people of the land. And the brethren of Joseph, having come, did reverence to him, *bowing* with the face to the ground. 7 And when Joseph saw his brethren, he knew them, and estranged himself from them, and spoke hard words to them; and said to them, Whence are ye come? And they said, Out of the land of Chanaan, to buy food. 8 And Joseph knew his brethren, but they knew not him. 9 And Joseph remembered his dream, which he saw; and he said to them, Ye are spies; to observe the marks of the land are ye come. 10 But they said, Nay, Sir, we thy servants are come to buy food; 11 we are all sons of one man; we are peaceable, thy servants are not spies. 12 And he said to them, Nay, but ye are come to observe the marks of the land. 13 And they said, We thy servants are twelve brethren, in the land of Chanaan; and, behold, the youngest is with our father to-day, but the other one is not. 14 And Joseph said to them, This is it that I spoke to you, saying, ye are spies; 15 herein shall ye be manifested; by the health of Pharao, ye shall not depart hence, unless your younger brother come hither. 16 Send one of you, and take your brother; and go ye to prison, till your words be clear, whether ye speak the truth or not; but, if not, by the health of Pharao, verily ye are spies. 17 And he put them in prison three days. 18 And he said to them on the third day, This do, and ye shall live, for I fear God. 19 If ye be peaceable, let one of your brethren be detained in prison; but go ye, and carry back the corn ye have purchased. 20 And bring your younger brother to me, and your words shall be believed; but, if not, ye shall die. And they did so. 21 And each said to his brother, Yes, indeed, for we are in fault concerning our brother, when we disregarded the anguish of his soul, when he besought us, and we hearkened not to him; and therefore has this affliction come upon us. 22 And Ruben answered them, saying, Did I not speak to you, saying, Hurt not the boy, and ye heard me not? and, behold, his blood is required. 23 But they knew not that Joseph understood them; for there was an interpreter between them. 24 And Joseph turned away from them, and wept; and again he came to them, and spoke to them; and he took Symeon from them, and bound him before their eyes. 25 And Joseph gave orders to fill their vessels with corn, and to return their money to each into his sack, and to give them provision for the way; and it was so done to them. 26 And having put the corn on the asses, they departed thence. 27 And one having opened his sack to give his asses fodder, at the place where they rested, saw also his bundle of money, for it was on the mouth of his sack. 28 And he said to his brethren, My money has been restored to me, and behold this is in my sack. And their heart was wonder-struck, and they were troubled, saying one to another, What is this that God has done to us? 29 And they came to their father, Jacob, into the land of Chanaan, and reported to him all that had happened to them, saying, 30 The man, the lord of the land, spoke harsh words to us, and put us in prison as spies of the land. 31 And we said to him, We are men of peace, we are not spies. 32 We are twelve brethren, sons of our father; one is not, and the youngest is with his father to-day in the land of Chanaan. 33 And the man, the lord of the land, said to us, Herein shall I know that ye are peaceable; leave one brother here with me, and having taken the corn ye have purchased

for your family, depart. 34 And bring to me your younger brother; then I shall know that ye are not spies, but that ye are men of peace: and I will restore you your brother, and ye shall trade in the land. 35 And it came to pass as they were emptying their sacks, there was each man's bundle of money in his sack; and they and their father saw their bundles of money, and they were afraid. 36 And their father Jacob said to them, Ye have bereaved me. Joseph is not, Symeon is not, and will ye take Benjamin? all these things have come upon me. 37 And Ruben spoke to his father, saying, Slay my two sons, if I bring him not to thee; give him into my hand, and I will bring him back to thee. 38 But he said, My son shall not go down with you, because his brother is dead, and he only has been left; and *suppose* it shall come to pass that he is afflicted by the way by which ye go, then ye shall bring down my old age with sorrow to Hades.

Gen. 43 1 But the famine prevailed in the land. 2 And it came to pass, when they had finished eating the corn which they had brought out of Egypt, that their father said to them, Go again; buy us a little food. 3 And Judas spoke to him, saying, The man, the lord of the country, positively testified to us, saying, Ye shall not see my face, unless your younger brother be with you. 4 If, then, thou send our brother with us, we will go down, and buy thee food; 5 but if thou send not our brother with us, we will not go: for the man spoke to us, saying, Ye shall not see my face, unless your younger brother be with you. 6 And Israel said, Why did ye harm me, inasmuch as ye told the man that ye had a brother? 7 And they said, The man closely questioned us about our family also, saying, Does your father yet live, and have ye a brother? and we answered him according to this question: did we know that he would say to us, Bring your brother? 8 And Judas said to his father Israel, Send the boy with me, and we will arise and go, that we may live and not die, both we and thou, and our store. 9 And I engage for him; at my hand do thou require him; if I bring him not to thee, and place him before thee, I shall be guilty toward thee for ever. 10 For if we had not tarried, we should now have returned twice. 11 And Israel, their father, said to them, If it be so, do this; take of the fruits of the earth in your vessels, and carry down to the man presents of gum and honey, and frankincense, and stacte, and turpentine, and walnuts. 12 And take double money in your hands, and the money that was returned in your sacks, carry back with you, lest peradventure it is a mistake. 13 And take your brother; and arise, go down to the man. 14 And my God give you favour in the sight of the man, and send away your other brother, and Benjamin, for I accordingly as I have been bereaved, am bereaved. 15 And the men having taken these presents, and the double money, took in their hands also Benjamin; and they rose up and went down to Egypt, and stood before Joseph. 16 And Joseph saw them and his brother Benjamin, born of the same mother; and he said to the steward of his household, Bring the men into the house, and slay beasts and make ready, for the men are to eat bread with me at noon. 17 And the man did as Joseph said; and he brought the men into the house of Joseph. 18 And the men, when they perceived that they were brought into the house of Joseph, said, We are brought in because of the money that was returned in our sacks at the first; even in order to inform against us, and lay it to our charge; to take us for servants, and our asses. 19 And having approached the man who was over the house of Joseph, they spoke to him in the porch of the house, 20 saying, We pray *thee*, Sir; we came down at first to buy food. 21 And it came to pass, when we came to unlade, and opened our sacks, *there was* also this money of each in his sack; we have now brought back our money by weight in our hands. 22 And we have brought other money with us to buy food; we know not who put the money into our sacks. 23 And he said to them, *God deal* mercifully with you; be not afraid; your God, and the God of your fathers, has given you treasures in your sacks, and I have enough of your good money. And he brought Symeon out to them. 24 And he brought water to wash their feet; and gave provender to their asses. 25 And they prepared their gifts, until Joseph came at noon, for they heard that he was going to dine there. 26 And Joseph entered into the house, and they brought him the gifts which they had in their hands, into the house; and they did him reverence with their face to the ground. 27 And he asked them, How are ye? and he said to them, Is your father, the old man of whom ye spoke, well? Does he yet live? 28 And they said, Thy servant our father is well; he is yet alive. And he said, Blessed be that man by God; —and they bowed, and did him reverence. 29 And Joseph lifted up his eyes, and saw his brother Benjamin, born of the same mother; and he said, Is this your younger brother, whom ye spoke of bringing to me? and he said, God have mercy on thee, my son. 30 And Joseph was troubled, for his bowels yearned over his brother, and he sought to weep; and he went into his chamber, and wept there. 31 And he washed his face and came out, and refrained himself, and said, Set on bread. 32 And they set on *bread* for him alone, and for them by themselves, and for the Egyptians feasting with him by themselves, for the Egyptians could not eat bread with the Hebrews, for it is an abomination to the Egyptians. 33 And they sat before him, the first-born according to his seniority, and the younger according to his youth; and the men looked with amazement every one at his brother. 34 And they took their portions from him to themselves; but Benjamin's portion was five times as much as the portions of *the others*. And they drank and were filled with drink with him.

Gen.44 1 And Joseph charged the steward of his house, saying, Fill the men's sacks with food, as much as they can carry, and put the money of each in the mouth of his sack. 2 And put my silver cup into the sack of the youngest, and the price of his corn. And it was done according to the word of Joseph, as he said. 3 The morning dawned, and the men were sent away, they and their asses. 4 And when they had gone out of the city, *and* were not far off, then Joseph said to his steward, Arise, and pursue after the men; and thou shalt overtake them, and say to them, Why have ye returned evil for good? 5 Why have ye stolen my silver cup? is it not this out of which my lord drinks? and he divines augury with it; ye have accomplished evil in that which ye

have done. 6 And he found them, and spoke to them according to these words. 7 And they said to him, Why does our lord speak according to these words? far be it from thy servants to do according to this word. 8 If we brought back to thee out of the land of Chanaan the money which we found in our sacks, how should we steal silver or gold out of the house of thy lord? 9 With whomsoever of thy servants thou shalt find the cup, let him die; and, moreover, we will be servants to our lord. 10 And he said, Now then it shall be as ye say; with whomsoever the cup shall be found, he shall be my servant, and ye shall be clear. 11 And they hasted, and took down every man his sack on the ground, and they opened every man his sack. 12 And he searched, beginning from the eldest, until he came to the youngest; and he found the cup in Benjamin's sack. 13 And they rent their garments, and laid each man his sack on his ass, and returned to the city. 14 And Judas and his brethren came in to Joseph, while he was yet there, and fell on the ground before him. 15 And Joseph said to them, What is this thing that ye have done? know ye not that a man such as I can surely divine? 16 And Judas said, What shall we answer to our lord, or what shall we say, or wherein should we be justified? whereas God has discovered the unrighteousness of thy servants; behold, we are slaves to our lord, both we and he with whom the cup has been found. 17 And Joseph said, Far be it from me to do this thing; the man with whom the cup has been found, he shall be my servant; but do ye go up with safety to your father. 18 And Judas drew near him, and said, I pray, Sir, let thy servant speak a word before thee, and be not angry with thy servant, for thou art next to Pharao. 19 Sir, thou askedst thy servants, saying, Have ye a father or a brother? 20 And we said to *my* lord, We have a father, an old man, and he has a son of his old age, a young one, and his brother is dead, and he alone has been left behind to his mother, and his father loves him. 21 And thou saidst to they servants, Bring him down to me, and I will take care of him. 22 And we said to *my* lord, The child will not be able to leave his father; but if he should leave his father, he will die. 23 But thou saidst to they servants, Except your younger brother come down with you, ye shall not see my face again. 24 And it came to pass, when we went up to thy servant our father, we reported to him the words of our lord. 25 And our father said, Go again, and buy us a little food. 26 And we said, We shall not be able to go down; but if our younger brother go down with us, we will go down; for we shall not be able to see the man's face, our younger brother not being with us. 27 And thy servant our father said to us, Ye know that my wife bore me two *sons*; 28 and one is departed from me; and ye said that he was devoured of wild beasts, and I have not seen him until now. 29 If then ye take this one also from my presence, and an affliction happen to him by the way, then shall ye bring down my old age with sorrow to the grave. 30 Now then, if I should go in to they servant, and our father, and the boy should not be with us, (and his life depends on this *lad's* life) 31 —it shall even come to pass, when he sees the boy is not with us, *that* he will die, and thy servants will bring down the old age of thy servant, and our father, with sorrow to the grave. 32 For thy servant has received the boy *in charge* from his father, saying, If I bring him not to thee, and place him before thee, I shall be guilty towards my father for ever. 33 Now then I will remain a servant with thee instead of the lad, a domestic of my lord; but let the lad go up with his brethren. 34 For how shall I go up to my father, the lad not being with us? lest I behold the evils which will befall my father.

Gen.45 1 And Joseph could not refrain himself when all were standing by him, but said, Dismiss all from me; and no one stood near Joseph, when he made himself known to his brethren. 2 And he uttered his voice with weeping; and all the Egyptians heard, and it was reported to the house of Pharao. 3 And Joseph said to his brethren, I am Joseph; doth my father yet live? And his brethren could not answer him, for they were troubled. 4 And Joseph said to his brethren, Draw nigh to me; and they drew nigh; and he said, I am your brother Joseph, whom ye sold into Egypt. 5 Now then be not grieved, and let it not seem hard to you that ye sold me hither, for God sent me before you for life. 6 For this second year there is famine on the earth, and there are yet five years remaining, in which there is to be neither ploughing, nor mowing. 7 For God sent me before you, that there might be left to you a remnant upon the earth, even to nourish a great remnant of you. 8 Now then ye did not send me hither, but God; and he hath made me as a father of Pharao, and lord of all his house, and ruler of all the land of Egypt. 9 Hasten, therefore, and go up to my father, and say to him, These things saith thy son Joseph; God has made me lord of all the land of Egypt; come down therefore to me, and tarry not. 10 And thou shalt dwell in the land of Gesem of Arabia; and thou shalt be near me, thou and thy sons, and thy sons' sons, thy sheep and thine oxen, and whatsoever things are thine. 11 And I will nourish thee there: for the famine is yet for five years; lest thou be consumed, and thy sons, and all thy possessions. 12 Behold, your eyes see, and the eyes of my brother Benjamin, that it is my mouth that speaks to you. 13 Report, therefore, to my father all my glory in Egypt, and all things that ye have seen, and make haste and bring down my father hither. 14 And he fell on his brother Benjamin's neck, and wept on him; and Benjamin wept on his neck. 15 And he kissed all his brethren, and wept on them; and after these things his brethren spoke to him. 16 And the report was carried into the house of Pharao, saying, Joseph's brethren are come; and Pharao was glad, and his household. 17 And Pharao said to Joseph, Say to thy brethren, Do this; fill your waggons, and depart into the land of Chanaan. 18 And take up your father, and your possessions, and come to me; and I will give you of all the goods of Egypt, and ye shall eat the marrow of the land. 19 And do thou charge them thus; that they should take for them waggons out of the land of Egypt, for your little ones, and for your wives; and take up your father, and come. 20 And be not sparing in regard to your property, for all the good of Egypt shall be yours. 21 And the children of Israel did so; and Joseph gave to them waggons, according to the words spoken by king Pharao; and he gave them provision for the journey. 22 And he gave to them all two sets of raiment apiece; but to Benjamin he gave three hundred pieces of gold, and five changes of raiment. 23 And to his father he sent *presents* at the same rate, and ten asses, bearing some of all the good things of Egypt, and ten mules, bearing bread for his father for thy journey. 24 And he sent away his brethren, and they went; and he said to them, Be not angry by the way. 25 And they went up out of Egypt, and came into the land of Chanaan, to Jacob their father. 26 And they reported to him, saying, Thy son Joseph is living, and he is ruler over all the land of Egypt; and Jacob was amazed, for he did not believe them. 27 But they spoke to him all the words uttered by Joseph, whatsoever he said to them; and having seen the chariots which Joseph sent to take him up, the spirit of Jacob their father revived. 28 And Israel said, It is a great thing for me if Joseph my son is yet alive. I will go and see him before I die.

Gen.46 1 And Israel departed, he and all that he had, and came to the well of the oath; and he offered sacrifice to the God of his father Isaac. 2 And God spoke to Israel in a night vision, saying, Jacob, Jacob; and he said, What is it? 3 And he says to him, I am the God of thy fathers; fear not to go down into Egypt, for I will make thee there a great nation. 4 And I will go down with thee into Egypt, and I will bring thee up at the end; and Joseph shall put his hands on thine eyes. 5 And Jacob rose up from the well of the oath; and the sons of Israel took up their father, and the baggage, and their wives on the waggons, which Joseph sent to take them. 6 And they took up their goods, and all their property, which they had gotten in the land of Chanaan; they came into the land of Egypt, Jacob, and all his seed with him. 7 The sons, and the sons of his sons with him; *his* daughters, and the daughters of his daughters; and he brought all his seed into Egypt. 8 And these are the names of the sons of Israel that went into Egypt with their father Jacob—Jacob and his sons. The first-born of Jacob, Ruben. 9 And the sons of Ruben; Enoch, and Phallus, Asron, and Charmi. 10 and the sons of Symeon; Jemuel, and Jamin, and Aod, and Achin, and Saar, and Saul, the son of a Chananitish woman. 11 And the sons of Levi; Gerson, Cath, and Merari. 12 And the sons of Judas; Er, and Aunan, and Selom, and Phares, and Zara: and Er and Aunan died in the land of Chanaan. 13 And the sons of Phares *were* Esron, and Jemuel. And the sons of Issachar; Thola, and Phua, and Asum, and Sambran. 14 And the sons of Zabulun, Sered, and Allon, and Achoel. 15 These *are* the sons of Lea, which she bore to Jacob in Mesopotamia of Syria, and Dina his daughter; all the souls, sons and daughters, thirty-three. 16 And the sons of Gad; Saphon, and Angis, and Sannis, and Thasoban, and Aedis, and Aroedis, and Areelis. 17 And the sons of Aser; Jemna, Jessua, and Jeul, and Baria, and Sara their sister. And the sons of Baria; Chobor, and Melchiil. 18 These *are* the sons of Zelpha, which Laban gave to his daughter Lea, who bore these to Jacob, sixteen souls. 19 And the sons of Rachel, the wife of Jacob; Joseph, and Benjamin. 20 And there were sons born to Joseph in the land of Egypt, whom Aseneth, the daughter of Petephres, priest of Heliopolis, bore to him, *even* Manasses and Ephraim. And there were sons born to Manasses, which the Syrian concubine bore to him, *even* Machir. And Machir begot Galaad. And the sons of Ephraim, the brother of Manasses; Sutalaam, and Taam. And the sons of Sutalaam; Edom. 21 and the sons of Benjamin; Bala, and Bochor, and Asbel. And the sons of Bala were Gera, and Noeman, and Anchis, and Ros, and Mamphim. And Gera begot Arad. 22 These *are* the sons of Rachel, which she bore to Jacob; all the souls eighteen. 23 And the sons of Dan; Asom. 24 And the sons of Nephthalim; Asiel, and Goni, and Issaar, and Sollem. 25 These *are* the sons of Balla, whom Laban gave to his daughter Rachel, who bore these to Jacob; all the souls, seven. 26 And all the souls that came with Jacob into Egypt, who came out of his loins, besides the wives of the sons of Jacob, *even* all the souls were sixty-six. 27 And the sons of Joseph, who were born to him in the land of Egypt, were nine souls; all the souls of the house of Jacob who came with Joseph into Egypt, were seventy-five souls. 28 And he sent Judas before him to Joseph, to meet him to the city of Heroes, into the land of Ramesses. 29 And Joseph having made ready his chariots, went up to meet Israel his father, at the city of Heroes; and having appeared to him, fell on his neck, and wept with abundant weeping. 30 And Israel said to Joseph, After this I will *gladly* die, since I have seen thy face, for thou art yet living. 31 And Joseph said to his brethren, I will go up and tell Pharao, and will say to him, My brethren, and my father's house, who were in the land of Chanaan, are come to me. 32 And the men are shepherds; for they have been feeders of cattle, and they have brought with them their cattle, and their kine, and all their property. 33 If then Pharao call you, and say to you, What is you occupation? 34 Ye shall say, We thy servants are herdsmen from our youth until now, both we and our fathers: that ye may dwell in the land of Gesem of Arabia, for every shepherd is an abomination to the Egyptians.

Gen.47 1 And Joseph came and told Pharao, *saying*, My father, and my brethren, and their cattle, and their oxen, and all their possessions, are come out of the land of Chanaan, and behold, they are in the land of Gesem. 2 And he took of his brethren five men, and set them before Pharao. 3 And Pharao said to the brethren of Joseph, What is your occupation? and they said to Pharao, Thy servants are shepherds, both we and our father. 4 And they said to Pharao, We are come to sojourn in the land, for there is no pasture for the flocks of thy servants, for the famine has prevailed in the land of Chanaan; now then, we will dwell in the land of Gesem. And Pharao said to Joseph, Let them dwell in the land of Gesem; and if thou knowest that there are among them able men, make them overseers of my cattle. So Jacob and his sons came into Egypt, to Joseph; and Pharao, king of Egypt, heard *of it.* 5 And Pharao spoke to Joseph, saying, Thy father, and thy brethren, are come to thee. 6 Behold, the land of Egypt is before thee; settle thy father and thy brethren in the best land. 7 And Joseph brought in Jacob his father, and set him before Pharao; and Jacob blessed Pharao. 8 And Pharao said to Jacob, How many are the years of the days of thy life? 9 And Jacob said to Pharao, The days of the years of my life, wherein I

sojourn, are a hundred and thirty years; few and evil have been the days of the years of my life, they have not attained to the days of the life of my fathers, in which days they sojourned. 10 And Jacob blessed Pharao, and departed from him. 11 And Joseph settled his father and his brethren, and gave them a possession in the land of Egypt, in the best land, in the land of Ramesses, as Pharao commanded. 12 And Joseph gave provision to his father, and his brethren, and to all the house of his father, corn for each person. 13 And there was no corn in all the land, for the famine prevailed greatly; and the land of Egypt, and the land of Chanaan, fainted for the famine. 14 And Joseph gathered all the money that was found in the land of Egypt, and the land of Chanaan, *in return for* the corn which they bought, and he distributed corn to them; and Joseph brought all the money into the house of Pharao. 15 And all the money failed out of the land of Egypt, and out of the land of Chanaan; and all the Egyptians came to Joseph, saying, Give us bread, and why do we die in thy presence? for our money is spent. 16 And Joseph said to them, Bring your cattle, and I will give you bread for your cattle, if your money is spent. 17 And they brought their cattle to Joseph; and Joseph gave them bread in return for their horses, and for their sheep, and for their oxen, and for their asses; and Joseph maintained them with bread for all their cattle in that year. 18 And that year passed, and they came to him in the second year, and said to him, Must we then be consumed from before our lord? for if our money has failed, and our possessions, and our cattle, *brought* to thee our lord, and there has not been left to us before our lord more than our own bodies and our land, *we are indeed destitute.* 19 In order, then, that we die not before thee, and the land be made desolate, buy us and our land for bread, and we and our land will be servants to Pharao: give seed that we may sow, and live and not die, so our land shall not be made desolate. 20 And Joseph bought all the land of the Egyptians, for Pharao; for the Egyptians sold their land to Pharao; for the famine prevailed against them, and the land became Pharao's. 21 And he brought the people into bondage to him, for servants, from one extremity of Egypt to the other, 22 except only the land of the priests; Joseph bought not this, for Pharao gave a portion in the way of gift to the priests; and they ate their portion which Pharao gave them; therefore they sold not their land. 23 And Joseph said to all the Egyptians, Behold, I have bought you and your land this day for Pharao; take seed for you, and sow the land. 24 And there shall be the fruits of it; and ye shall give the fifth part to Pharao, and the four *remaining* parts shall be for yourselves, for seed for the earth, and for food for you, and all that are in your houses. 25 And they said, Thou hast saved us; we have found favour before our lord, and we will be servants to Pharao. 26 And Joseph appointed it to them for an ordinance until this day; to reserve a fifth part for Pharao, on the land of Egypt, except only the land of the priests, that was not Pharao's. 27 And Israel dwelt in Egypt, in the land of Gesem, and they gained an inheritance upon it; and they increased and multiplied very greatly. 28 And Jacob survived seventeen years in the land of Egypt; and Jacob's days of the years of his life were a hundred and forty-seven years. 29 and the days of Israel drew nigh for him to die: and he called his son Joseph, and said to him, If I have found favour before thee, put thy hand under my thigh, and thou shalt execute mercy and truth toward me, so as not to bury me in Egypt. 30 But I will sleep with my fathers, and thou shalt carry me up out of Egypt, and bury me in their sepulchre. And he said, I will do according to thy word. 31 And he said, Swear to me; and he swore to him. And Israel did reverence, leaning on the top of his staff.

Gen.48 1 And it came to pass after these things, that it was reported to Joseph, Behold, thy father is ill; and, having taken his two sons, Manasse and Ephraim, he came to Jacob. 2 And it was reported to Jacob, saying, Behold, thy son Joseph cometh to thee; and Israel having strengthened himself, sat upon the bed. 3 And Jacob said to Joseph, My God appeared to me in Luza, in the land of Chanaan, and blessed me, 4 and said to me, Behold, I will increase thee, and multiply thee, and will make of thee multitudes of nations; and I will give this land to thee, and to thy seed after thee, for an everlasting possession. 5 Now then thy two sons, who were born to thee in the land of Egypt, before I came to thee into Egypt, are mine; Ephraim and Manasse, as Ruben and Symeon they shall be mine. 6 And the children which thou shalt beget hereafter, shall be in the name of their brethren; they shall be named after their inheritances. 7 And as for me, when I came out of Mesopotamia of Syria, Rachel, thy mother, died in the land of Chanaan, as I drew night to the horse-course of Chabratha of the land *of Chanaan*, so as to come to Ephratha; and I buried her in the road of the course; this is Bethlehem. 8 And when Israel saw the sons of Joseph, he said, Who are these to thee? 9 And Joseph said to his father, They are my sons, whom God gave me here; and Jacob said, Bring me them, that I may bless them. 10 Now the eyes of Israel were dim through age, and he could not see; and he brought them near to him, and he kissed them, and embraced them. 11 And Israel said to Joseph, Behold, I have not been deprived of *seeing* thy face, and lo! God has showed me thy seed also. 12 And Joseph brought them out from *between* his knees, and they did reverence to him, with their face to the ground. 13 And Joseph took his two sons, both Ephraim in his right hand, but on the left of Israel, and Manasse on his left hand, but on the right of Israel, and brought them near to him. 14 But Israel having stretched out his right hand, laid it on the head of Ephraim, and he was the younger; and his left hand on the head of Manasse, *guiding* his hands crosswise. 15 And he blessed them and said, The God in whose sight my fathers were well pleasing, *even* Abraam and Isaac, the God who continues to feed me from my youth until this day; 16 the angel who delivers me from all evils, bless these boys, and my name shall be called upon them, and the name of my fathers, Abraam and Isaac; and let them be increased to a great multitude on the earth. 17 And Joseph having seen that his father put his right hand on the head of Ephraim— it seemed grievous to him; and Joseph took hold of the hand of his father, to remove it from the head of Ephraim to the head of Manasse. 18 And Joseph said to his father, Not so, father; for this is the first-born; lay thy right-hand upon his head. 19 And he would not, but said, I know it, son, I know it; he also shall be a people, and he shall be exalted, but his younger brother shall be greater than he, and his seed shall become a multitude of nations. 20 And he blessed them in that day, saying, In you shall Israel be blessed, saying, God make thee as Ephraim and Manasse; and he set Ephraim before Manasse. 21 And Israel said to Joseph, Behold, I die; and God shall be with you, and restore you to the land of your fathers. 22 And I give to thee Sicima, a select portion above thy brethren, which I took out of the hand of the Amorites with my sword and bow.

Gen.49 1 And Jacob called his sons, and said to them, 2 Assemble yourselves, that I may tell you what shall happen to you in the last days. Gather yourselves together, and hear me, sons of Jacob; hear Israel, hear your father. 3 Ruben, thou *art* my first-born, thou my strength, and the first of my children, hard to be endured, *hard and* self-willed. 4 Thou wast insolent like water, burst not forth with violence, for thou wentest up to the bed of thy father; then thou defiledst the couch, whereupon thou wentest up. 5 Symeon and Levi, brethren, accomplished the injustice of their cutting off. 6 Let not my soul come into their counsel, and let not mine inward parts contend in their conspiracy, for in their wrath they slew men, and in their passion they houghed a bull. 7 Cursed be their wrath, for it was willful, and their anger, for it was cruel: I will divide them in Jacob, and scatter them in Israel. 8 Juda, thy brethren have praised thee, and thy hands shall be on the back of thine enemies; thy father's sons shall do thee reverence. 9 Juda is a lion's whelp: from the tender plant, my son, thou art gone up, having couched thou liest as a lion, and as a whelp; who shall stir him up? 10 A ruler shall not fail from Juda, nor a prince from his loins, until there come the things stored up for him; and he is the expectation of nations. 11 Binding his foal to the vine, and the foal of his ass to the branch *of it*, he shall wash his robe in wine, and his garment in the blood of the grape. 12 His eyes shall be more cheering than wine, and his teeth whiter than milk. 13 Zabulon shall dwell on the coast, and he *shall be* by a haven of ships, and shall extend to Sidon. 14 Issachar has desired that which is good; resting between the inheritances. 15 And having seen the resting place that it was good, and the land that it was fertile, he subjected his shoulder to labour, and became a husbandman. 16 Dan shall judge his people, as one tribe too in Israel. 17 And let Dan be a serpent in the way, besetting the path, biting the heel of the horse (and the rider shall fall backward), 18 waiting for the salvation of the Lord. 19 Gad, a plundering troop shall plunder him; but he shall plunder him, *pursuing him* closely. 20 Aser, his bread *shall be* fat; and he shall yield dainties to princes. 21 Nephthalim is a spreading stem, bestowing beauty on its fruit. 22 Joseph is a son increased; my dearly loved son is increased; my youngest son, turn to me. 23 Against whom men taking evil counsel reproached *him*, and the archers pressed hard upon him. 24 But their bow and arrows were mightily consumed, and the sinews of their arms were slackened by the hand of the mighty one of Jacob; thence is he that strengthened Israel from the

God of thy father; 25 and my God helped thee, and he blessed thee with the blessing of heaven from above, and the blessing of the earth possessing all things, because of the blessing of the breasts and of the womb, 26 the blessings of thy father and thy mother—it has prevailed above the blessing of the lasting mountains, and beyond the blessings of the everlasting hills; they ·shall be upon the head of Joseph, and upon the head of the brothers of whom he took the lead. 27 Benjamin, as a ravening wolf, shall eat still in the morning, and at evening he gives food. 28 All these *are* the twelve sons of Jacob; and their father spoke these words to them, and he blessed them; he blessed each of them according to his blessing. 29 And he said to them, I am added to my people; ye shall bury me with my fathers in the cave, which is in the field of Ephron the Chettite, 30 in the double cave which is opposite Mambre, in the land of Chanaan, the cave which Abraam bought of Ephron the Chettite, for a possession of a sepulchre. 31 There they buried Abraam and Sarrha his wife; there they buried Isaac, and Rebecca his wife; there they buried Lea; 32 in the portion of the field, and of the cave that was in it, *purchased* of the sons of Chet. 33 And Jacob ceased giving charges to his sons; and having lifted up his feet on the bed, he died, and was gathered to his people.

Gen.50 1 And Joseph fell upon his father's face, and wept on him, and kissed him. 2 And Joseph commanded his servants the embalmers to embalm his father; and the embalmers embalmed Israel. 3 And they fulfilled forty days for him, for so are the days of embalming numbered; and Egypt mourned for him seventy days. 4 And when the days of mourning were past, Joseph spoke to the princes of Pharao, saying, If I have found favour in your sight, speak concerning me in the ears of Pharao, saying, 5 My father adjured me, saying, In the sepulchre which I dug for myself in the land of Chanaan, there thou shalt bury me; now then I will go up and bury my father, and return again. 6 And Pharao said to Joseph, Go up, bury thy father, as he constrained thee to swear. 7 So Joseph went up to bury his father; and all the servants of Pharao went up with him, and the elders of his house, and all the elders of the land of Egypt. 8 And all the household of Joseph, and his brethren, and all the house of his father, and his kindred; and they left behind the sheep and the oxen in the land of Gesem. 9 And there went up with him also chariots and horsemen; and there was a very great company. 10 And they came to the threshing- floor of Atad, which is beyond Jordan; and they bewailed him with a great and very sore lamentation; and he made a mourning for his father seven days. 11 And the inhabitants of the land of Chanaan saw the mourning at the floor of Atad, and said, This is a great mourning to the Egyptians; therefore he called its name, The mourning of Egypt, which is beyond Jordan. 12 And thus his sons did to him. 13 So his sons carried him up into the land of Chanaan, and buried him in the double cave, which cave Abraam bought for possession of a burying place, of Ephrom the Chettite, before Mambre. 14 And Joseph returned to Egypt, he and his brethren, and those that had gone up with him to bury his father. 15 And when the

brethren of Joseph saw that their father was dead, they said, *Let us take heed*, lest at any time Joseph remember evil against us, and recompense to us all the evils which we have done against him. 16 And they came to Joseph, and said, Thy father adjured *us* before his death, saying, 17 Thus say ye to Joseph, Forgive them their injustice and their sin, forasmuch as they have done thee evil; and now pardon the injustice of the servants of the God of thy father. And Joseph wept while they spoke to him. 18 And they came to him and said, We, these *persons*, are thy servants. 19 And Joseph said to them, Fear not, for I am God's. 20 Ye took counsel against me for evil, but God took counsel for me for good, that *the matter* might be as *it is* to-day, and much people might be fed. 21 And he said to them, Fear not, I will maintain you, and your families: and he comforted them, and spoke kindly to them. 22 And Joseph dwelt in Egypt, he and his brethren, and all the family of his father; and Joseph lived a hundred and ten years. 23 And Joseph saw the children of Ephraim to the third generation; and the sons of Machir the son of Manasse were borne on the sides of Joseph. 24 And Joseph spoke to his brethren, saying, I die, and God will surely visit you, and will bring you out of this land to the land concerning which God sware to our fathers, Abraam, Isaac, and Jacob. 25 And Joseph adjured the sons of Israel, saying, At the visitation with which God shall visit you, then ye shall carry up my bones hence with you. 26 And Joseph died, aged an hundred and ten years; and they prepared his corpse, and put him in a coffin in Egypt.

EXODUS

Ex.1 1 These are the names of the sons of Israel that came into Egypt together with Jacob their father; they came in each with their whole family. 2 Ruben, Simeon, Levi, Judas, 3 Issachar, Zabulon, Benjamin, 4 Dan and Nephthalim, Gad and Aser. 5 But Joseph was in Egypt. And all the souls *born* of Jacob were seventy-five. 6 And Joseph died, and all his brethren, and all that generation. 7 And the children of Israel increased and multiplied, and became numerous and grew exceedingly strong, and the land multiplied them. 8 And there arose up another king over Egypt, who knew not Joseph. 9 And he said to his nation, Behold, the race of the children of Israel is a great multitude, and is stronger than we: 10 come then, let us deal craftily with them, lest at any time they be increased, and whensoever war shall happen to us, these also shall be added to our enemies, and having prevailed against us in war, they will depart out of the land. 11 And he set over them task-masters, who should afflict them in their works; and they built strong cities for Pharao, both Pitho, and Ramesses, and On, which is Heliopolis. 12 But as they humbled them, by so much they multiplied, and grew exceedingly strong; and the Egyptians greatly abhorred the children of Israel. 13 And the Egyptians tyrannised over the children of Israel by force. 14 And they embittered their life by hard labours, in the clay and in brick- making, and all the works in the plains, according to all the works, wherein they caused them to serve with violence. 15 And the king of the Egyptians spoke to the midwives of the Hebrews; the name of the one was,

Sepphora; and the name of the second, Phua. 16 And he said, When ye do the office of midwives to the Hebrew women, and they are about to be delivered, if it be a male, kill it; but if a female, save it. 17 But the midwives feared God, and did not as the king of Egypt appointed them; and they saved the male children alive. 18 And the king of Egypt called the midwives, and said to them, Why is it that ye have done this thing, and saved the male children alive? 19 And the midwives said to Pharao, The Hebrew women are not as the women of Egypt, for they are delivered before the midwives go in to them. So they bore children. 20 And God did well to the midwives, and the people multiplied, and grew very strong. 21 And as the midwives feared God, they established for themselves families. 22 And Pharao charged all his people, saying, Whatever male *child* shall be born to the Hebrews, cast into the river; and every female, save it alive.

Ex.2 1 And there was a certain man of the tribe of Levi, who took to wife one of the daughters of Levi. 2 And she conceived, and bore a male child; and having seen that he was fair, they hid him three months. 3 And when they could no longer hide him, his mother took for him an ark, and besmeared it with bitumen, and cast the child into it, and put it in the ooze by the river. 4 And his sister was watching from a distance, to learn what would happen to him. 5 And the daughter of Pharao came down to the river to bathe; and her maids walked by the river's side, and having seen the ark in the ooze, she sent her maid, and took it up. 6 And having opened it, she sees the babe weeping in the ark: and the daughter of Pharao had compassion on it, and said, This *is one* of the Hebrew's children. 7 And his sister said to the daughter of Pharao, Wilt thou that I call to thee a nurse of the Hebrews, and shall she suckle the child for thee? 8 And the daughter of Pharao said, Go: and the young woman went, and called the mother of the child. 9 And the daughter of Pharao said to her, Take care of this child, and suckled it for me, and I will give thee the wages; and the woman took the child, and suckled it. 10 And when the boy was grown, she brought him to the daughter of Pharao, and he became her son; and she called his name, Moses, saying, I took him out of the water. 11 And it came to pass in that length of time, that Moses having grown, went out to his brethren the sons of Israel: and having noticed their distress, he sees an Egyptian smiting a certain Hebrew of his brethren the children of Israel. 12 And having looked round this way and that way, he sees no one; and he smote the Egyptian, and hid him in the sand. 13 And having gone out the second day he sees two Hebrew men fighting; and he says to the injurer, Wherefore smitest thou thy neighbour? 14 And he said, Who made thee a ruler and a judge over us? wilt thou slay me as thou yesterday slewest the Egyptian? Then Moses was alarmed, and said, If *it be* thus, this matter has become known. 15 And Pharao heard this matter, and sought to slay Moses; and Moses departed from the presence of Pharao, and dwelt in the land of Madiam; and having come into the land of Madiam, he sat on the well. 16 And the priest of Madiam had seven daughters, feeding the flock of their father Jothor; and they came and drew water until they filled their pitchers, to water the flock of their father Jothor. 17 And the shepherds came, and were driving them away; and Moses rose up and rescued them, and drew water for them, and watered their sheep. 18 And they came to Raguel their father; and he said to them, Why have ye come so quickly to-day? 19 And they said, An Egyptian delivered us from the shepherds, and drew water for us and watered our sheep. 20 And he said to his daughters, And where is he? and why have ye left the man? call him therefore, that he may eat bread. 21 And Moses was established with the man, and he gave Sepphora his daughter to Moses to wife. 22 And the woman conceived and bore a son, and Moses called his name Gersam, saying, I am a sojourner in a strange land. 23 And in those days after a length of time, the king of Egypt died; and the children of Israel groaned because of their tasks, and cried, and their cry because of their tasks went up to God. 24 And God heard their groanings, and God remembered his covenant made with Abraam and Isaac and Jacob. 25 And God looked upon the children of Israel, and was made known to them.

Ex.3 1 And Moses was feeding the flock of Jothor his father-in-law, the priest of Madiam; and he brought the sheep nigh to the wilderness, and came to the mount of Choreb. 2 And an angel of the Lord appeared to him in flaming fire out of the bush, and he sees that the bush burns with fire, —but the bush was not consumed. 3 And Moses said, I will go near and see this great sight, why the bush is not consumed. 4 And when the Lord saw that he drew nigh to see, the Lord called him out of the bush, saying, Moses, Moses; and he said, What is it? 5 And he said, Draw not nigh hither: loose thy sandals from off thy feet, for the place whereon thou standest is holy ground. 6 And he said, I am the God of thy father, the God of Abraam, and the God of Isaac, and the God of Jacob; and Moses turned away his face, for he was afraid to gaze at God. 7 And the Lord said to Moses, I have surely seen the affliction of my people that is in Egypt, and I have heard their cry *caused* by their task-masters; for I know their affliction. 8 And I have come down to deliver them out of the hand of the Egyptians, and to bring them out of that land, and to bring them into a good and wide land, into a land flowing with milk and honey, into the place of the Chananites, and the Chettites, and Amorites, and Pherezites, and Gergesites, and Evites, and Jebusites. 9 And now, behold, the cry of the children of Israel is come to me, and I have seen the affliction with which the Egyptians afflict them. 10 And now come, I will send thee to Pharao king of Egypt, and thou shalt bring out my people the children of Israel from the land of Egypt. 11 And Moses said to God, Who am I, that I should go to Pharao king of Egypt, and that I should bring out the children of Israel from the land of Egypt? 12 And God spoke to Moses, saying, I will be with thee, and this shall be the sign to thee that I shall send thee forth, —when thou bringest out my people out of Egypt, then ye shall serve God in this mountain. 13 And Moses said to God, Behold, I shall go forth to the children of Israel, and shall say to them, The God of our fathers has sent me to you; and they will ask me, What is his name? What shall I say to them? 14 And God spoke to Moses, saying, I am THE BEING; and he said, Thus shall ye say to the children of Israel, THE BEING has sent me to you. 15 And God said again to Moses, Thus shalt thou say to the sons of Israel, The Lord God of our fathers, the God of Abraam, and God of Isaac, and God of Jacob, has sent me to you: this is my name for ever, and my memorial to generations of generations. 16 Go then and gather the elders of the children of Israel, and thou shalt say to them, The Lord God of our fathers has appeared to me, the God of Abraam, and God of Isaac, and God of Jacob, saying, I have surely looked upon you, and upon all the things which have happened to you in Egypt. 17 And he said, I will bring you up out of the affliction of the Egyptians to the land of the Chananites and the Chettites, and Amorites and Pherezites, and Gergesites, and Evites, and Jebusites, to a land flowing with milk and honey. 18 And they shall hearken to thy voice, and thou and the elders of Israel shall go in to Pharao king of Egypt, and thou shalt say to him, The God of the Hebrews has called us; we will go then a journey of three days into the wilderness, that we may sacrifice to our God. 19 But I know that Pharao king of Egypt will not let you go, save with a mighty hand; 20 and I will stretch out my hand, and smite the Egyptians with all my wonders, which I shall work among them, and after that he will send you forth. 21 And I will give this people favour in the sight of the Egyptians, and whenever ye shall escape, ye shall not depart empty. 22 But *every* woman shall ask of her neighbour and fellow lodger, articles of gold and silver, and apparel; and ye shall put them upon your sons and upon your daughters, —and spoil ye the Egyptians.

Ex.4 1 And Moses answered and said, If they believe me not, and do not hearken to my voice (for they will say, God has not appeared to thee), what shall I say to them? 2 And the Lord said to him, What is this thing that is in thine hand? and he said, A rod. 3 And he said, Cast it on the ground: and he cast it on the ground, and it became a serpent, and Moses fled from it. 4 And the Lord said to Moses, Stretch forth thine hand, and take hold of its tail: so he stretched forth his hand and took hold of the tail, 5 and it became a rod in his hand, —that they may believe thee, that the God of thy fathers has appeared to thee, the God of Abraam, and God of Isaac, and God of Jacob. 6 And the Lord said again to him, Put thine hand into thy bosom; and he put his hand into his bosom, and brought his hand out of his bosom, and his hand became as snow. 7 And he said again, Put thy hand into thy bosom; and he put his hand into his bosom, and brought his hand out of his bosom, and it was again restored to the complexion of his *other* flesh. 8 And if they will not believe thee, nor hearken to the voice of the first sign, they will believe thee *because* of the voice of the second sign. 9 And it shall come to pass if they will not believe thee for these two signs, and will not hearken to thy voice, that thou shalt take of the water of the river and pour it upon the dry land, and the water which thou shalt take from the river shall be blood upon the dry land. 10 And Moses said to the Lord, I pray, Lord, I have

not been sufficient in former times, neither from the time that thou hast begun to speak to thy servant: I am weak in speech, and slow-tongued. 11 And the Lord said to Moses, Who has given a mouth to man, and who has made the very hard of hearing, and the deaf, the seeing and the blind? have not I, God? 12 And now go and I will open thy mouth, and will instruct thee in what thou shalt say. 13 And Moses said, I pray thee, Lord, appoint another able *person* whom thou shalt send. 14 And the Lord was greatly angered against Moses, and said, Lo! is not Aaron the Levite thy brother? I know that he will surely speak to thee; and, behold, he will come forth to meet thee, and beholding thee he will rejoice within himself. 15 And thou shalt speak to him; and thou shalt put my words into his mouth, and I will open thy mouth and his mouth, and I will instruct you in what ye shall do. 16 And he shall speak for thee to the people, and he shall be thy mouth, and thou shalt be for him in things pertaining to God. 17 And this rod that was turned into a serpent thou shalt take in thine hand, wherewith thou shalt work miracles. 18 And Moses went and returned to Jothor his father-in-law, and says, I will go and return to my brethren in Egypt, and will see if they are yet living. And Jothor said to Moses, Go in health. And in those days after some time, the king of Egypt died. 19 And the Lord said to Moses in Madiam, Go, depart into Egypt, for all that sought thy life are dead. 20 And Moses took his wife and his children, and mounted them on the beasts, and returned to Egypt; and Moses took the rod *which he had* from God in his hand. 21 And the Lord said to Moses, When thou goest and returnest to Egypt, see—all the miracles I have charged thee with, thou shalt work before Pharao: and I will harden his heart, and he shall certainly not send away the people. 22 And thou shalt say to Pharao, These things saith the Lord, Israel *is* my first-born. 23 And I said to thee, Send away my people, that they may serve me: now if thou wilt not send them away, see, I will slay thy fir-born son. 24 And it came to pass *that* the angel of the Lord met him by the way in the inn, and sought to slay him. 25 and Sepphora having taken a stone cut off the foreskin of her son, and fell at his feet and said, The blood of the circumcision of my son is staunched: 26 and he departed from him, because she said, The blood of the circumcision of my son is staunched. 27 And the Lord said to Aaron, Go into the wilderness to meet Moses; and he went and met him in the mount of God, and they kissed each other. 28 And Moses reported to Aaron all the words of the Lord, which he sent, and all the things which he charged him. 29 And Moses and Aaron went and gathered the elders of the children of Israel. 30 And Aaron spoke all these words, which God spoke to Moses, and wrought the miracles before the people. 31 and the people believed and rejoiced, because God visited the children of Israel, and because he saw their affliction: and the people bowed and worshipped.

Ex.5 1 And after this went in Moses and Aaron to Pharao, and they said to him, These things says the Lord God of Israel, Send my people away, that they may keep a feast to me in the wilderness. 2 And Pharao said, Who is he that I should hearken to his voice, so that I should send away the children of Israel? I do not know the Lord, and I will not let Israel go. 3 And they say to him, The God of the Hebrews has called us to him: we will go therefore a three days' journey into the wilderness, that we may sacrifice to the Lord our God, lest at any time death or slaughter happen to us. 4 And the king of Egypt said to them, Why do ye, Moses and Aaron, turn the people from their works? depart each of you to your works. 5 And Pharao said, Behold now, the people is very numerous; let us not then give them rest from their work. 6 And Pharao gave orders to the task-masters of the people and the accountants, saying, 7 Ye shall no longer give straw to the people for brick-making as yesterday and the third day; but let them go themselves, and collect straw for themselves. 8 And thou shalt impose on them daily the rate of brick-making which they perform: thou shalt not abate anything, for they are idle; therefore have they cried, saying, Let us arise and do sacrifice to our God. 9 Let the works of these men be made grievous, and let them care for these things, and not care for vain words. 10 And the taskmasters and the accountants hastened them, and they spoke to the people, saying, thus says Pharao, I *will* give you straw no longer. 11 Go ye, yourselves, get for yourselves straw whencesoever ye can find it, for nothing is diminished from your rate. 12 So the people were dispersed in all the land of Egypt, to gather stubble for straw. 13 and the taskmasters hastened them, saying, Fulfil your regular daily tasks, even as when straw was given you. 14 And the accountants of the race of the children of Israel, who were set over them by the masters of Pharao, were scourged, [[and questioned,]]*men* saying, Why have ye not fulfilled your rates of brick-work as yesterday and the third day, to-day also? 15 And the accountants of the children of Israel went in and cried to Pharao, saying, Why dost thou act thus to thy servants? 16 Straw is not given to thy servants, and they tell us to make brick; and behold thy servants have been scourged: thou wilt therefore injure thy people. 17 And he said to them, Ye are idle, ye are idlers: therefore ye say, Let us go *and* do sacrifice to our God. 18 Now then go and work, for straw shall not be given to you, yet ye shall return the rate of bricks. 19 And the accountants of the children of Israel saw themselves in an evil plight, *men* saying, Ye shall not fail to deliver the daily rate of the brick-making. 20 And they met Moses and Aaron coming forth to meet them, as they came forth from Pharao. 21 And they said to them, The Lord look upon you and judge you, for ye have made our savour abominable before Pharao, and before his servants, to put a sword into his hands to slay us. 22 And Moses turned to the Lord, and said, I pray, Lord, why hast thou afflicted this people? and wherefore hast thou sent me? 23 For from the time that I went to Pharao to speak in thy name, he has afflicted this people, and thou hast not delivered thy people.

Ex.6 1 And the Lord said to Moses, Now thou shalt see what I will do to Pharao; for he shall send them forth with a mighty hand, and with a high arm shall he cast them out of his land. 2 And God spoke to Moses and said to him, I *am* the Lord. 3 And I appeared to Abraam and Isaac and Jacob, being their God, but I did not manifest to them my name Lord. 4 And I established my covenant with them, to give them the land of the Chananites, the land wherein they sojourned, in which also they dwelt as strangers. 5 And I hearkened to the groaning of the children of Israel (the affliction with which the Egyptians enslave them) and I remembered the covenant with you. 6 Go, speak to the children of Israel, saying, I *am* the Lord; and I will lead you forth from the tyranny of the Egyptians, and I will deliver you from bondage, and I will ransom you with a high arm, and great judgment. 7 And I will take you to me a people for myself, and will be your God; and ye shall know that I am the Lord your God, who brought you out from the tyranny of the Egyptians. 8 And I will bring you into the land concerning which I stretched out my hand to give it to Abraam and Isaac and Jacob, and I will give it you for an inheritance: I *am* the Lord. 9 And Moses spoke thus to the sons of Israel, and they hearkened not to Moses for faint-heartedness, and for their hard tasks. 10 And the Lord spoke to Moses, saying, 11 Go in, speak to Pharao king of Egypt, that he send forth the children of Israel out of his land. 12 And Moses spoke before the Lord, saying, Behold, the children of Israel hearkened not to me, and how shall Pharao hearken to me? and I am not eloquent. 13 And the Lord spoke to Moses and Aaron, and gave them a charge to Pharao king of Egypt, that he should send forth the children of Israel out of the land of Egypt. 14 And these are the heads of the houses of their families: the sons of Ruben the first-born of Israel; Enoch and Phallus, Asron, and Charmi, this is the kindred of Ruben. 15 And the sons of Symeon, Jemuel and Jamin, and Aod, and Jachin and Saar, and Saul the son of a Phoenician woman, these are the families of the sons of Symeon. 16 And these are the names of the sons of Levi according to their kindreds, Gedson, Caath, and Merari; and the years of the life of Levi were a hundred and thirty-seven. 17 And these are the sons of Gedson, Lobeni and Semei, the houses of their family. And the sons of Caath, 18 Ambram and Issaar, Chebron, and Oziel; and the years of the life of Caath were a hundred and thirty-three years. 19 And the sons of Merari, Mooli, and Omusi, these are the houses of the families of Levi, according to their kindreds. 20 And Ambram took to wife Jochabed the daughter of his father's brother, and she bore to him both Aaron and Moses, and Mariam their sister: and the years of the life of Ambram were a hundred and thirty-two years. 21 And the sons of Issaar, Core, and Naphec, and Zechri. 22 And the sons of Oziel, Misael, and Elisaphan, and Segri. 23 And Aaron took to himself to wife Elisabeth daughter of Aminadab sister of Naasson, and she bore to him both Nadab and Abiud, and Eleazar and Ithamar. 24 And the sons of Core, Asir, and Elkana, and Abiasar, these are the generations of Core. 25 And Eleazar the son of Aaron took to himself for a wife *one* of the daughters of Phutiel, and she bore to him Phinees. These are the heads of the family of the Levites, according to their generations. 26 This is Aaron and Moses, whom God told to bring out the children of Israel out of the land of Egypt with their forces. 27 These are they that spoke with Pharao king of Egypt, and Aaron himself and Moses brought out the children of Israel from the land of Egypt, 28 in the day in which the Lord spoke to Moses in the land of Egypt; 29 then the Lord spoke to Moses, saying, I am the Lord: speak to Pharao king of Egypt whatsoever I say to thee. 30 And Moses said before the Lord, Behold, I am not able in speech, and how shall Pharao hearken to me?

Ex.7 1 And the Lord spoke to Moses, saying, Behold, I have made thee a god to Pharao, and Aaron thy brother shall be thy prophet. 2 And thou shalt say to him all things that I charge thee, and Aaron thy brother shall speak to Pharao, that he should send forth the children of Israel out of his land. 3 And I will harden the heart of Pharao, and I will multiply my signs and wonders in the land of Egypt. 4 And Pharao will not hearken to you, and I will lay my hand upon Egypt; and will bring out my people the children of Israel with my power out of the land of Egypt with great vengeance. 5 And all the Egyptians shall know that I am the Lord, stretching out my hand upon Egypt, and I will bring out the children of Israel out of the midst of them. 6 And Moses and Aaron did as the Lord commanded them, so did they. 7 And Moses was eighty years old, and Aaron his brother was eighty-three years old, when he spoke to Pharao. 8 And the Lord spoke to Moses and Aaron, saying, 9 Now if Pharao should speak to you, saying, Give us a sign or a wonder, then shalt thou say to thy brother Aaron, Take thy rod and cast it upon the ground before Pharao, and before his servants, and it shall become a serpent. 10 And Moses and Aaron went in before Pharao, and *before* his servants, and they did so, as the Lord commanded them; and Aaron cast down his rod before Pharao, and before his servants, and it became a serpent. 11 But Pharao called together the wise men of Egypt, and the sorcerers, and the charmers also of the Egyptians did likewise with their sorceries. 12 And they cast down each his rod, and they became serpents, but the rod of Aaron swallowed up their rods. 13 and the heart of Pharao was hardened, and he hearkened not to them, as the Lord charged them. 14 and the Lord said to Moses, The heart of Pharao is made hard, so that he should not let the people go. 15 Go to Pharao early in the morning: behold, he goes forth to the water; and thou shalt meet him on the bank of the river, and thou shalt take in thine hand the rod that was turned into a serpent. 16 And thou shalt say to him, The Lord God of the Hebrews has sent me to thee, saying,

Send my people away, that they may serve me in the wilderness, and, behold, hitherto thou hast not hearkened. 17 These things saith the Lord: Hereby shalt thou know that I am the Lord: behold, I strike with the rod that is in my hand on the water which is in the river, and it shall change it into blood. 18 And the fish that are in the river shall die, and the river shall stink thereupon, and the Egyptians shall not be able to drink water from the river. 19 And the Lord said to Moses, Say to thy brother Aaron, Take thy rod in thy hand, and stretch forth thy hand over the waters of Egypt, and over their rivers, and over their canals, and over their ponds, and over all their standing water, and it shall become blood: and there was blood in all the land of Egypt, both in vessels of wood and of stone. 20 and Moses and

Aaron did so, as the Lord commanded them; and *Aaron* having lifted up *his hand* with his rod, smote the water in the river before Pharao, and before his servants, and changed all the water in the river into blood. 21 And the fish in the river died, and the river stank thereupon; and the Egyptians could not drink water from the river, and the blood was in all the land of Egypt. 22 And the charmers also of the Egyptians did so with their sorceries; and the heart of Pharao was hardened, and he did not hearken to them, even as the Lord said. 23 And Pharao turned and entered into his house, nor did he fix his attention even on this thing. 24 And all the Egyptians dug round about the river, so as to drink water, for they could not drink water from the river. 25 and seven days were fulfilled after the Lord has smitten the river.

Ex.8 1 And the Lord said to Moses, Go in to Pharao, and thou shalt say to him, These things says the Lord: send forth my people, that they may serve me. 2 And if thou wilt not send them forth, behold, I afflict all thy borders with frogs: 3 and the river shall teem with frogs, and they shall go up and enter into thy houses, and into thy bed-chambers, and upon thy beds, and upon the houses of thy servants, and of thy people and on thy dough, and on thine ovens. 4 And upon thee, and upon thy servants, and upon thy people, shall the frogs come up. 5 And the Lord said to Moses, Say to Aaron thy brother, Stretch forth with the hand thy rod over the rivers, and over the canals, and over the pools, and bring up the frogs. 6 And Aaron stretched forth his hand over the waters of Egypt, and brought up the frogs: and the frog was brought up, and covered the land of Egypt. 7 And the charmers of the Egyptians also did likewise with their sorceries, and brought up the frogs on the land of Egypt. 8 And Pharao called Moses and Aaron, and said, Pray for me to the Lord, and let him take away the frogs from me and from my people; and I will send them away, and they shall sacrifice to the Lord. 9 And Moses said to Pharao, Appoint me *a time* when I shall pray for thee, and for thy servants, and for thy people, to cause the frogs to disappear from thee, and from thy people, and from your houses, only in the river shall they be left behind. 10 And he said, On the morrow: he said therefore, As thou has said; that thou mayest know, that there is no other *God* but the Lord. 11 And the frogs shall be removed away from thee, and from your houses and from the villages, and from thy servants, and from thy people, only in the river they shall be left. 12 And Moses and Aaron went forth from Pharao, and Moses cried to the Lord concerning the restriction of the frogs, as Pharao appointed him. 13 And the Lord did as Moses said, and the frogs died out of the houses, and out of the villages, and out of the fields. 14 And they gathered them together in heaps, and the land stank. 15 And when Pharao saw that there was relief, his heart was hardened, and he did not hearken to them, as the Lord spoke. 16 And the Lord said to Moses, Say to Aaron, Stretch forth thy rod with thy hand and smite the dust of the earth; and there shall be lice both upon man, and upon quadrupeds, and in all the land of Egypt. 17 So Aaron stretched out his rod with his hand, and smote the dust of the earth; and the lice were on men and on quadrupeds, and in all the dust of the earth there were lice. 18 And the charmers also did so with their sorceries, to bring forth the louse, and they could not. And the lice were both on the men and on the quadrupeds. 19 So the charmers said to Pharao, This is the finger of God. But the heart of Pharao was hardened, and he hearkened not to them, as the Lord said. 20 And the Lord said to Moses, Rise up early in the morning, and stand before Pharao: and behold, he will go forth to the water, and thou shalt say to him, These things says the Lord: Send away my people, that they may serve me in the wilderness. 21 And if thou wilt not let my people go, behold, I send upon thee, and upon thy servants, and upon thy people, and upon your houses, the dog-fly; and the houses of the Egyptians shall be filled with the dog-fly, even throughout the land upon which they are. 22 and I will distinguish marvellously in that day the land of Gesem, on which my people dwell, in which the dog-fly shall not be: that thou mayest know that I am the Lord the God of all the earth. 23 And I will put a difference between my people and thy people, and on the morrow shall this be on the land. And the Lord did thus. 24 And the dog-fly came in abundance into the houses of Pharao, and into the houses of his servants, and into all the land of Egypt; and the land was destroyed by the dog-fly. 25 And Pharao called Moses and Aaron, saying, Go and sacrifice to the Lord your God in the land. 26 And Moses said, It cannot be so, for we shall sacrifice to the Lord our God the abominations of the Egyptians; for if we sacrifice the abominations of the Egyptians before them, we shall be stoned. 27 We will go a journey of three days into the wilderness, and we will sacrifice to the Lord our God, as the Lord said to us. 28 And Pharao said, I *will* let you go, and do ye sacrifice to your God in the wilderness, but do not go very far away: pray then for me to the Lord. 29 And Moses said, I then will go forth from thee and pray to God, and the dog-fly shall depart both from thy servants, and from thy people to-morrow. Do not thou, Pharao, deceive again, so as not to send the people away to do sacrifice to the Lord. 30 And Moses went out from Pharao, and prayed to God. 31 And the Lord did as Moses said, and removed the dog- fly from Pharao, and from his servants, and from his people, and there was not one left. 32 And Pharao hardened his heart, even on this occasion, and he would not send the people away.

Ex.9 1 And the Lord said to Moses, Go in to Pharao, and thou shalt say to him, These things saith the Lord God of the Hebrews; Send my people away that they may serve me. 2 If however thou wilt not send my people away, but yet detainest them: 3 behold, the hand of the Lord shall be upon thy cattle in the fields, both on the horses, and on the asses, and on the camels and oxen and sheep, a very great mortality. 4 And I will make a marvellous distinction in that time between the cattle of the Egyptians, and the cattle of the children of Israel: nothing shall die of all that is of the children's of Israel. 5 And God fixed a limit, saying, To-morrow the Lord will do this thing on the land. 6 And the Lord did this thing on the next day, and all the cattle of the Egyptians died, but of the cattle of the children of Israel there died not one. 7 And when Pharao saw, that of all the cattle of the children of Israel there died not one, the heart of Pharao was hardened, and he did not let the people go. 8 And the Lord spoke to Moses and Aaron, saying, Take you handfuls of ashes of the furnace, and let Moses scatter it toward heaven before Pharao, and before his servants. 9 And let it become dust over all the land of Egypt, and there shall be upon men and upon beasts sore blains breaking forth both on men and on beasts, in all the land of Egypt. 10 So he took of the ashes of the furnace before Pharao, and Moses scattered it toward heaven, and it became sore blains breaking forth both on men and on beasts. 11 And the sorcerers could not stand before Moses because of the sores, for the sores were on the sorcerers, and in all the land of Egypt. 12 And the Lord hardened Pharao's heart, and he hearkened not to them, as the Lord appointed. 13 And the Lord said to Moses, Rise up early in the morning, and stand before Pharao; and thou shalt say to him, These things saith the Lord God of the Hebrews, Send away my people that they may serve me. 14 For at this present time do I send forth all my plagues into thine heart, and the heart of thy servants and of thy people; that thou mayest know that there is not another such as I in all the earth. 15 For now I will stretch forth my hand and smite thee and kill thy people, and thou shalt be consumed from off the earth. 16 And for this purpose hast thou been preserved, that I might display in thee my strength, and that my name might be published in all the earth. 17 Dost thou then yet exert thyself to hinder my people, so as not to let them go? 18 Behold, to-morrow at this hour I will rain a very great hail, such as has not been in Egypt, from the time it was created until this day. 19 Now then hasten to gather thy cattle, and all that thou hast in the fields; for all the men and cattle as many as shall be found in the fields, and shall not enter into a house, (but the hail shall fall upon them,) shall die. 20 He of the servants of Pharao that feared the word of the Lord, gathered his cattle into the houses. 21 And he that did not attend in his mind to the word of the Lord, left the cattle in the fields. 22 And the Lord said to Moses, Stretch out thine hand to heaven, and there shall be hail on all the land of Egypt, both on the men and on the cattle, and on all the herbage on the land. 23 And Moses stretched forth his hand to heaven, and the Lord sent thunderings and hail; and the fire ran along upon the ground, and the Lord rained hail on all the land of Egypt. 24 So there was hail and flaming fire mingled with hail; and the hail was very great, such as was not in Egypt, from the time there was a nation upon it. 25 And the hail smote in all the land of Egypt both man and beast, and the hail smote all the grass in the field, and the hail broke in pieces all the trees in the field. 26 Only in the land of Gesem where the children of Israel were, the hail was not. 27 And Pharao sent and called Moses and Aaron, and said to them, I have sinned this time: the Lord *is* righteous, and I and my people are wicked. 28 Pray then for me to the Lord, and let him cause the thunderings of God to cease, and the hail and the fire, and I will send you forth and ye shall remain no longer. 29 And Moses said to him, When I shall have departed from the city, I will stretch out my hands to the Lord, and the thunderings shall cease, and the hail and the rain shall be no longer, that thou mayest know that the earth *is* the Lord's. 30 But as for thee and thy servants, I know that ye have not yet feared the Lord. 31 And the flax and the barley were smitten, for the barley was advanced, and the flax was seeding. 32 But the wheat and the rye were not smitten, for they were late. 33 And Moses went forth from Pharao out of the city, and stretched out his hands to the Lord, and the thunders ceased and the hail, and the rain did not drop on the earth. 34 And when Pharao saw that the rain and the hail and the thunders ceased, he continued to sin; and *he* hardened his heart, and the heart of his servants. 35 And the heart of Pharao was hardened, and he did not send forth the children of Israel, as the Lord said to Moses.

Ex.10 1 And the Lord spoke to Moses, saying, Go in to Pharao: for I have hardened his heart and the heart of his servants, that these signs may come upon them; in order 2 that ye may relate in the ears of your children, and to your children's children, in how many things I have mocked the Egyptians, and my wonders which I wrought among them; and ye shall know that I *am* the Lord. 3 And Moses and Aaron went in before Pharao, and they said to him, These things saith the Lord God of the Hebrews, How long dost thou refuse to reverence me? Send my people away, that they may serve me. 4 But if thou wilt not send my people away, behold, at this hour to-morrow I will bring an abundance of locusts upon all thy coasts. 5 And they shall cover the face of the earth, and thou shalt not be able to see the earth; and they shall devour all that is left of the abundance of the earth, which the hail has left you, and shall devour every tree that grows for you on the land. 6 And thy houses shall be filled, and the houses of thy servants, and all the houses in all the land of the Egyptians; things which thy fathers have never seen, nor their forefathers, from the day that they were upon the earth until this day. And Moses turned away and departed from Pharao. 7 And the servants of Pharao say to him, How long shall this be a snare to us? send away the men, that they may serve their God; wilt thou know that Egypt is destroyed? 8 And they brought back both Moses and Aaron to Pharao; and he said to them, Go and serve the Lord your God; but who are they that are going with you? 9 And Moses said, We will go with the young and the old, with our sons, and daughters, and sheep, and oxen, for it is a feast of the Lord. 10 And he said to them, So let the Lord be with you: as I *will* send you away, *must I send away* you store also? see that evil is attached to you. 11 Not so, but let the men go and serve God, for this ye yourselves seek; and they cast them out from the presence of Pharao. 12 And the Lord said to Moses, Stretch out thine hand over the land of Egypt, and let the locust come up on the land, and it shall devour every herb of the land, and all the fruit of the trees, which the hail left. 13 And Moses lifted up his rod towards heaven, and the Lord brought a south wind upon the earth, all that day and all that night: the morning dawned, and the south wind brought up the locusts, 14 and brought them up over all the land of Egypt. And they rested in very great

abundance over all the borders of Egypt. Before them there were not such locusts, neither after them shall there be. 15 And they covered the face of the earth, and the land was wasted, and they devoured all the herbage of the land, and all the fruit of the trees, which was left by the hail: there was no green thing left on the trees, nor on all the herbage of the field, in all the land of Egypt. 16 And Pharao hasted to call Moses and Aaron, saying, I have sinned before the Lord your God, and against you; 17 pardon therefore my sin yet this time, and pray to the Lord your God, and let him take away from me this death. 18 And Moses went forth from Pharao, and prayed to God. 19 And the Lord brought in the opposite direction a strong wind from the sea, and took up the locusts and cast them into the Red Sea, and there was not one locust left in all the land of Egypt. 20 And the Lord hardened the heart of Pharao, and he did not send away the children of Israel. 21 And the Lord said to Moses, Stretch out thy hand to heaven, and let there be darkness over the land of Egypt—darkness that may be felt. 22 And Moses stretched out his hand to heaven, and there was darkness very black, even a storm over all the land of Egypt three days. 23 And for three days no man saw his brother, and no man rose up from his bed for three days: but all the children of Israel had light in all the places where they were. 24 And Pharao called Moses and Aaron, saying, Go, serve the Lord your God, only leave your sheep and your oxen, and let your store depart with you. 25 And Moses said, Nay, but thou shalt give to us whole burnt-offerings and sacrifices, which we will sacrifice to the Lord our God. 26 And our cattle shall go with us, and we will not leave a hoof behind, for of them we will take to serve the Lord our God: but we know not in what manner we shall serve the Lord our God, until we arrive there. 27 But the Lord hardened the heart of Pharao, and he would not let them go. 28 And Pharao says, Depart from me, beware of seeing my face again, for in what day thou shalt appear before me, thou shalt die. 29 And Moses says, Thou hast said, I will not appear in thy presence again.

Ex.11 1 And the Lord said to Moses, I will yet bring one plague upon Pharao and upon Egypt, and after that he will send you forth thence; and whenever he sends you forth with every thing, he will indeed drive you out. 2 Speak therefore secretly in the ears of the people, and let every one ask of his neighbour jewels of silver and gold, and raiment. 3 And the Lord gave his people favour in the sight of the Egyptians, and they lent to them; and the man Moses was very great before the Egyptians, and before Pharao, and before his servants. 4 And Moses said, These things saith the Lord, About midnight I go forth into the midst of Egypt. 5 And every first-born in the land of Egypt shall die, from the first-born of Pharao that sits on the throne, even to the first-born of the woman-servant that is by the mill, and to the first-born of all cattle. 6 And there shall be a great cry through all the land of Egypt, such as has not been, and such shall not be repeated any more. 7 But among all the children of Israel shall not a dog snarl with his tongue, either at man or beast; that thou mayest know how wide a distinction the Lord will make between the Egyptians and

Israel. 8 And all these thy servants shall come down to me, and do me reverence, saying, Go forth, thou and all the people over whom thou presidest, and afterwards I will go forth. 9 And Moses went forth from Pharao with wrath. And the Lord said to Moses, Pharao will not hearken to you, that I may greatly multiply my signs and wonders in the land *of* Egypt. 10 And Moses and Aaron wrought all these signs and wonders in the land *of* Egypt before Pharao; and the Lord hardened the heart of Pharao, and he did not hearken to send forth the children of Israel out of the land of Egypt.

Ex.12 1 And the Lord spoke to Moses and Aaron in the land of Egypt, saying, 2 This month *shall be* to you the beginning of months: it is the first to you among the months of the year. 3 Speak to all the congregation of the children of Israel, saying, On the tenth of this month let them take each man a lamb according to the houses of their families, every man a lamb for his household. 4 And if they be few in a household, so that there are not enough for the lamb, he shall take with himself his neighbour that lives near to him, —as to the number of souls, every one according to that which suffices him shall make a reckoning for the lamb. 5 It shall be to you a lamb unblemished, a male of a year old: ye shall take it of the lambs and the kids. 6 And it shall be kept by you till the fourteenth of this month, and all the multitude of the congregation of the children of Israel shall kill it toward evening. 7 And they shall take of the blood, and shall put it on the two door-posts, and on the lintel, in the houses in which soever they shall eat them. 8 And they shall eat the flesh in this night roast with fire, and they shall eat unleavened *bread* with bitter herbs. 9 Ye shall not eat of it raw nor sodden in water, but only roast with fire, the head with the feet and the appurtenances. 10 Nothing shall be left of it till the morning, and a bone of it ye shall not break; but that which is left of it till the morning ye shall burn with fire. 11 And thus shall ye eat it: your loins girded, and your sandals on your feet, and your staves in your hands, and ye shall eat it in haste. It is a passover to the Lord. 12 and I will go throughout the land of Egypt in that night, and will smite every first-born in the land of Egypt both man and beast, and on all the gods of Egypt will I execute vengeance: I *am* the Lord. 13 And the blood shall be for a sign to you on the houses in which ye are, and I will see the blood, and will protect you, and there shall not be on you the plague of destruction, when I smite in the land of Egypt. 14 And this day shall be to you a memorial, and ye shall keep it a feast to the Lord through all your generations; ye shall keep it a feast for a perpetual ordinance. 15 Seven days ye shall eat unleavened bread, and from the first day ye shall utterly remove leaven from your houses: whoever shall eat leaven, that soul shall be utterly destroyed from Israel, from the first day until the seventh day. 16 And the first day shall be called holy, and the seventh day shall be a holy convocation to you: ye shall do no servile work on them, only as many things as will *necessarily* be done by every soul, this only shall be done by you. 17 And ye shall keep this commandment, for on this day will I bring out your force out of the land of Egypt; and ye shall make this day a perpetual ordinance for you throughout your generations. 18 Beginning the fourteenth day of the first month, ye shall eat unleavened bread from evening, till the twenty- first day of the month, till evening. 19 Seven days leaven shall not be found in your houses; whosoever shall eat anything leavened, that soul shall be cut off from the congregation of Israel, both among the occupiers of the land and the original inhabitants. 20 Ye shall eat nothing leavened, but in every habitation of your ye shall eat unleavened bread. 21 And Moses called all the elders of the children of Israel, and said to them, Go away and take to yourselves a lamb according to your kindreds, and slay the passover. 22 And ye shall take a bunch of hyssop, and having dipped it into some of the blood that is by the door, ye shall touch the lintel, and *shall put it* upon both door-posts, even of the blood which is by the door; but ye shall not go out every one from the door of his house till the morning. 23 And the Lord shall pass by to smite the Egyptians, and shall see the blood upon the lintel, and upon both the door- posts; and the Lord shall pass by the door, and shall not suffer the destroyer to enter into your houses to smite *you*. 24 And keep ye this thing as an ordinance for thyself and for thy children for ever. 25 And if ye should enter into the land, which the Lord shall give you, as he has spoken, keep this service. 26 And it shall come to pass, if your sons say to you, What is this service? 27 that ye shall say to them, This passover is a sacrifice to the Lord, as he defended the houses of the children of Israel in Egypt, when he smote the Egyptians, but delivered our houses. 28 And the people bowed and worshipped. And the children of Israel departed and did as the Lord commanded Moses and Aaron, so did they. 29 And it came to pass at midnight that the Lord smote all the first-born in the land of Egypt, from the first-born of Pharao that sat on the throne, to the first-born of the captive-maid in the dungeon, and the first-born of all cattle. 30 And Pharao rose up by night, and his servants, and all the Egyptians; and there was a great cry in all the land of Egypt, for there was not a house in which there was not one dead. 31 And Pharao called Moses and Aaron by night, and said to them, Rise and depart from my people, both ye and the children of Israel. Go and serve the Lord your God, even as ye say. 32 And take with you your sheep, and your oxen: bless me also, I pray you. 33 And the Egyptians constrained the people, so that they cast them out of the land with haste, for they said, We all shall die. 34 And the people took their dough before their meal was leavened, bound up *as it was* in their garments, on their shoulders. 35 And the children of Israel did as Moses commanded them, and they asked of the Egyptians articles of silver and gold and apparel. 36 And the Lord gave his people favour in the sight of the Egyptians, and they lent to them; and they spoiled the Egyptians. 37 And the children Israel departed from Ramesses to Socchoth, to *the full number of* six hundred thousand footmen, even men, besides the baggage. 38 And a great mixed *company* went up with them, and sheep and oxen and very much cattle. 39 And they baked the dough which they brought out of Egypt, unleavened cakes, for it had not been leavened; for the Egyptians cast them out, and they could not remain, neither did they prepare provision for themselves for the journey. 40 And the sojourning of the children of Israel, while they sojourned in the land of Egypt and the land of Chanaan, *was* four hundred and thirty years. 41 And it came to pass after the four hundred and thirty *years*, all the forces of the Lord came forth out of the land of Egypt by night. 42 It is a watch kept to the Lord, so that he should bring them out of the land of Egypt; that very night is a watch kept to the Lord, so that it should be to all the children of Israel to their generations. 43 And the Lord said to Moses and Aaron, This is the law of the passover: no stranger shall eat of it. 44 And every slave or servant bought with money—him thou shalt circumcise, and then shall he eat of it. 45 A sojourner or hireling shall not eat of it. 46 In one house shall it be eaten, and ye shall not carry of the flesh out from the house; and a bone of it ye shall not break. 47 All the congregation of the children of Israel shall keep it. 48 And if any proselyte shall come to you to keep the passover to the Lord, thou shalt circumcise every male of him, and then shall he approach to sacrifice it, and he shall be even as the original inhabitant of the land; no uncircumcised person shall eat of it. 49 There shall be one law to the native, and to the proselyte coming among you. 50 And the children of Israel did as the Lord commanded Moses and Aaron for them, so they did. 51 And it came to pass in that day that the Lord brought out the children of Israel from the land of Egypt with their forces.

Ex.13 1 And the Lord spoke to Moses, saying, 2 Sanctify to me every first-born, first produced, opening every womb among the children of Israel both of man and beast: it is mine. 3 And Moses said to the people, Remember this day, in which ye came forth out of the land of Egypt, out of the house of bondage, for with a strong hand the Lord brought you forth thence; and leaven shall not be eaten. 4 For on this day ye go forth in the month of new *corn*. 5 And it shall come to pass when the Lord thy God shall have brought thee into the land of the Chananites, and the Chettites, and Amorites, and Evites, and Jebusites, and Gergesites, and Pherezites, which he sware to thy fathers to give thee, a land flowing with milk and honey, that thou shalt perform this service in this month. 6 Six days ye shall eat unleavened bread, and on the seventh day is a feast to the Lord. 7 Seven days shall ye eat unleavened bread; nothing leavened shall be seen with thee, neither shalt thou have leaven in all thy borders. 8 And thou shalt tell thy son in that day, saying, Therefore the Lord dealt thus with me, as I was going out of Egypt. 9 And it shall be to thee a sign upon thy hand and a memorial before thine eyes, that the law of the Lord may be in thy mouth, for with a strong hand the Lord God brought thee out of Egypt. 10 And preserve ye this law according to the times of the seasons, from year to year. 11 And it shall come to pass when the Lord thy God shall bring thee into the land of the Chananites, as he sware to thy fathers, and shall give it thee, 12 that thou shalt set apart every *offspring* opening the womb, the males to the Lord, every one that opens the womb out of the herds or among thy cattle, as many as thou shalt have: thou shalt sanctify the males to the Lord. 13 Every *offspring* opening the womb

of the ass thou shalt change for a sheep; and if thou wilt not change it, thou shalt redeem it: every first-born of man of thy sons shalt thou redeem. 14 And if thy son should ask thee hereafter, saying, What is this? then thou shalt say to him, With a strong hand the Lord brought us out of Egypt, out of the house of bondage. 15 And when Pharao hardened *his heart so as not* to send us away, he slew every first-born in the land of Egypt, both the first-born of man and the first-born of beast; therefore do I sacrifice every *offspring* that opens the womb, the males to the Lord, and every first-born of my sons I will redeem. 16 And it shall be for a sign upon thy hand, and immovable before thine eyes, for with a strong hand the Lord brought thee out of Egypt. 17 And when Pharao sent forth the people, God led them not by the way of the land of the Phylistines, because it was near; for God said, Lest at any time the people repent when they see war, and return to Egypt. 18 And God led the people round by the way to the wilderness, to the Red Sea: and in the fifth generation the children of Israel went up out of the land of Egypt. 19 And Moses took the bones of Joseph with him, for he had solemnly adjured the children of Israel, saying, God will surely visit you, and ye shall carry up my bones hence with you. 20 And the children of Israel departed from Socchoth, and encamped in Othom by the wilderness. 21 And God led them, in the day by a pillar of cloud, to show them the way, and in the night by a pillar of fire. 22 And the pillar of cloud failed not by day, nor the pillar of fire by night, before all the people.

Ex.14 1 And the Lord spoke to Moses, saying, 2 Speak to the children of Israel, and let them turn and encamp before the village, between Magdol and the sea, opposite Beel-sepphon: before them shalt thou encamp by the sea. 3 And Pharao will say to his people, As for these children of Israel, they are wandering in the land, for the wilderness has shut them in. 4 And I will harden the heart of Pharao, and he shall pursue after them; and I will be glorified in Pharao, and in all his host, and all the Egyptians shall know that I am the Lord. And they did so. 5 And it was reported to the king of the Egyptians that the people had fled: and the heart of Pharao was turned, and that of his servants against the people; and they said, What is this that we have done, to let the children of Israel go, so that they should not serve us? 6 So Pharao yoked his chariots, and led off all his people with himself: 7 having also taken six hundred chosen chariots, and all the cavalry of the Egyptians, and rulers over all. 8 And the Lord hardened the heart of Pharao king of Egypt, and of his servants, and he pursued after the children of Israel; and the children of Israel went forth with a high hand. 9 And the Egyptians pursued after them, and found them encamped by the sea; and all the cavalry and the chariots of Pharao, and the horsemen, and his host *were* before the village, over against Beel-sepphon. 10 And Pharao approached, and the children of Israel having looked up, beheld, and the Egyptians encamped behind them: and they were very greatly terrified, and the children of Israel cried to the Lord; 11 and said to Moses, Because there were no graves in the land of Egypt, hast thou brought us forth to slay *us* in the wilderness? What is this that thou hast done to us, having brought us out of Egypt? 12 Is not this the word which we spoke to thee in Egypt, saying, Let us alone that we may serve the Egyptians? for it is better for us to serve the Egyptians than to die in this wilderness. 13 And Moses said to the people, Be of good courage: stand and see the salvation which is from the Lord, which he will work for us this day; for as ye have seen the Egyptians to-day, ye shall see them again no more for ever. 14 The Lord shall fight for you, and ye shall hold your peace. 15 and the Lord said to Moses, Why criest thou to me? speak to the children of Israel, and let them proceed. 16 And do thou lift up thy rod, and stretch forth thy hand over the sea, and divide it, and let the children of Israel enter into the midst of the sea on the dry land. 17 And lo! I will harden the heart of Pharao and of all the Egyptians, and they shall go in after them; and I will be glorified upon Pharao, and on all his host, and on his chariots and his horses. 18 And all the Egyptians shall know that I am the Lord, when I am glorified upon Pharao and upon his chariots and his horses. 19 And the angel of God that went before the camp of the children of Israel removed and went behind, and the pillar of the cloud also removed from before them and stood behind them. 20 And it went between the camp of the Egyptians and the camp of Israel, and stood; and there was darkness and blackness; and the night passed, and they came not near to one another during the whole night. 21 And Moses stretched forth his hand over the sea, and the Lord carried back the sea with a strong south wind all the night, and made the sea dry, and the water was divided. 22 And the children of Israel went into the midst of the sea on the dry land, and the water of it was a wall on the right hand and a wall on the left. 23 And the Egyptians pursued them and went in after them, and every horse of Pharao, and his chariots, and his horsemen, into the midst of the sea. 24 And it came to pass in the morning watch that the Lord looked forth on the camp of the Egyptians through the pillar of fire and cloud, and troubled the camp of the Egyptians, 25 and bound the axle-trees of their chariots, and caused them to go with difficulty; and the Egyptians said, Let us flee from the face of Israel, for the Lord fights for them against the Egyptians. 26 And the Lord said to Moses, Stretch forth tine hand over the sea, and let the water be turned back to its place, and let it cover the Egyptians *coming* both upon the chariots and the riders. 27 And Moses stretched forth his hand over the sea, and the water returned to its place toward day; and the Egyptians fled from the water, and the Lord shook off the Egyptians in the midst of the sea. 28 and the water returned and covered the chariots and the riders, and all the forces of Pharao, who entered after them into the sea: and there was not left of them even one. 29 But the children of Israel went along dry land in the midst of the sea, and the water was to them a wall on the right hand, and a wall on the left. 30 So the Lord delivered Israel in that day from the hand of the Egyptians, and Israel saw the Egyptians dead by the shore of the sea. 31 And Israel saw the mighty hand, the *things* which the Lord did to the Egyptians; and the people feared the Lord, and they believed God and Moses his servant.

Ex.15 1 Then sang Moses and the children of Israel this song to God, and spoke, saying, Let us sing to the Lord, for he is very greatly glorified: horse and rider he has thrown into the sea. 2 He was to me a helper and protector for salvation: this is my God and I will glorify him; my father's God, and I will exalt him. 3 The Lord bringing wars to nought, the Lord *is* his name. 4 He has cast the chariots of Pharao and his host into the sea, the chosen mounted captains: they were swallowed up in the Red Sea. 5 He covered them with the sea: they sank to the depth like a stone. 6 Thy right hand, O God, has been glorified in strength; thy right hand, O God, has broken the enemies. 7 And in the abundance of thy glory thou hast broken the adversaries to pieces: thou sentest forth thy wrath, it devoured them as stubble. 8 And by the breath of thine anger the water parted asunder; the waters were congealed as a wall, the waves were congealed in the midst of the sea. 9 The enemy said, I will pursue, I will overtake, I will divide the spoils; I will satisfy my soul, I will destroy with my sword, my hand shall have dominion. 10 Thou sentest forth thy wind, the sea covered them; they sank like lead in the mighty water. 11 Who is like to thee among the gods, O Lord? who is like to thee? glorified in holiness, marvellous in glories, doing wonders. 12 Thou stretchedst forth thy right hand, the earth swallowed them up. 13 Thou hast guided in thy righteousness this thy people whom thou hast redeemed, by thy strength thou hast called them into thy holy resting-place. 14 The nations heard and were angry, pangs have seized on the dwellers among the Phylistines. 15 Then the princes of Edom, and the chiefs of the Moabites hasted; trembling took hold upon them, all the inhabitants of Chanaan melted away. 16 Let trembling and fear fall upon them; by the greatness of thine arm, let them become as stone; till thy people pass over, O Lord, till this thy people pass over, whom thou hast purchased. 17 Bring them in and plant them in the mountain of their inheritance, in thy prepared habitation, which thou, O Lord, hast prepared; the sanctuary, O Lord, which thine hands have made ready. 18 The Lord reigns for ever and ever and ever. 19 For the horse of Pharao went in with the chariots and horsemen into the sea, and the Lord brought upon them the water of the sea, but the children of Israel walked through dry land in the midst of the sea. 20 And Mariam the prophetess, the sister of Aaron, having taken a timbrel in her hand—then there went forth all the women after her with timbrels and dances. 21 And Mariam led them, saying, Let us sing to the Lord, for he has been very greatly glorified: the horse and rider has he cast into the sea. 22 So Moses brought up the children of Israel from the Red Sea, and brought them into the wilderness of Sur; and they went three days in the wilderness, and found no water to drink. 23 and they came to Merrha, and could not drink of Merrha, for it was bitter; therefore he named the name of that place, Bitterness. 24 And the people murmured against Moses, saying, What shall we drink? 25 And Moses cried to the Lord, and the Lord shewed him a tree, and he cast it into the water, and the water was sweetened: there he established to him ordinances and judgments, and there he proved him, 26 and said, If thou wilt indeed hear the voice of the Lord thy God, and do things pleasing before him, and wilt hearken to his commands, and keep all his ordinances, no disease which I have brought upon the Egyptians will I bring upon thee, for I am the Lord thy God that heals thee. 27 And they came to Ælim, and there were there twelve fountains of water, and seventy stems of palm-trees; and they encamped there by the waters.

Ex.16 1 And they departed from Ælim, and all the congregation of the children of Israel came to the wilderness of Sin, which is between Ælim and Sina; and on the fifteenth day, in the second month after their departure from the land of Egypt, 2 all the congregation of the children of Israel murmured against Moses and Aaron. 3 And the children of Israel said to them, Would we had died smitten by the Lord in the land of Egypt, when we sat by the flesh-pots, and ate bread to satiety! for ye have brought us out into this wilderness, to slay all this congregation with hunger. 4 And the Lord said to Moses, Behold, I *will* rain bread upon you out of heaven: and the people shall go forth, and they shall gather their daily portion for the day, that I may try them whether they will walk in my law or not. 5 And it shall come to pass on the sixth day that they shall prepare whatsoever they have brought in, and it shall be double of what they shall have gathered for the day, daily. 6 And Moses and Aaron said to all the congregation of the children of Israel, At even ye shall know that the Lord has brought you out of the land of Egypt; 7 and in the morning ye shall see the glory of the Lord, inasmuch as he hears your murmuring against God; and who are we, that ye continue to murmur against us? 8 And Moses said, *This shall be* when the Lord gives you in the evening flesh to eat, and bread in the morning to satiety, because the Lord has heard your murmuring, which ye murmur against us: and what are we? for your murmuring is not against us, but against God. 9 And Moses said to Aaron, Say to all the congregation of the children of Israel, Come near before God; for he has heard your murmuring. 10 And when Aaron spoke to all the congregation of the children of Israel, and they turned toward the wilderness, then the glory of the Lord appeared in a cloud. 11 And the Lord spoke to Moses, saying, 12 I have heard the murmuring of the children of Israel: speak to them, saying, Towards evening ye shall eat flesh, and in the morning ye shall be satisfied with bread; and ye shall know that I am the Lord your God. 13 And it was evening, and quails came up and covered the camp: 14 in the morning it came to pass as the dew ceased round about the camp, that, behold, on the face of the wilderness *was* a small thing like white coriander seed, as frost upon the earth. 15 And when the children of Israel saw it, they said one to another, What is this? for they knew not what it was; and Moses said to them, 16 This *is* the bread which the Lord has given you to eat. This is that which the Lord has appointed: gather of it each man for his family, a homer for each person, according to the number of your souls, gather each of you with his fellow-lodgers. 17 And the children of Israel did so, and gathered some much and some less. 18 And having measured the homer *full*, he that gathered much had nothing over, and he that had gathered less had no lack;

each gathered according to the need of those who belonged to him. 19 And Moses said to them, Let no man leave of it till the morning. 20 But they did not hearken to Moses, but some left of it till the morning; and it bred worms and stank: and Moses was irritated with them. 21 And they gathered it every morning, each man what he needed, and when the sun waxed hot it melted. 22 And it came to pass on the sixth day, they gathered double what was needed, two homers for one *man*; and all the chiefs of the synagogue went in and reported it to Moses. 23 And Moses said to them, Is not this the word which the Lord spoke? To-morrow *is* the sabbath, a holy rest to the Lord: bake that ye will bake, and seethe that ye will seethe, and all that is over leave to be laid by for the morrow. 24 And they left of it till the morning, as Moses commanded them; and it stank not, neither was there a worm in it. 25 And Moses said, Eat *that* to-day, for to-day is a sabbath to the Lord: *it* shall not be found in the plain. 26 Six days ye shall gather it, and on the seventh day is a sabbath, for there shall be none on that *day*. 27 And it came to pass on the seventh day *that* some of the people went forth to gather, and found none. 28 And the Lord said to Moses, How long are ye unwilling to hearken to my commands and my law? 29 See, for the Lord has given you this day *as* the sabbath, therefore he has given you on the sixth day the bread of two days: ye shall sit each of you in your houses; let no one go forth from his place on the seventh day. 30 And the people kept sabbath on the seventh day. 31 And the children of Israel called the name of it Man; and it was as white coriander seed, and the taste of it as a wafer with honey. 32 And Moses said, This *is* the thing which the Lord hath commanded, Fill an homer with manna, to be laid up for your generations; that they may see the bread which ye ate in the wilderness, when the Lord led you forth out of the land of Egypt. 33 And Moses said to Aaron, Take a golden pot, and cast into it one full homer of manna; and thou shalt lay it up before God, to be kept for your generations, 34 as the Lord commanded Moses: and Aaron laid it up before the testimony to be kept. 35 And the children of Israel ate manna forty years, until they came to the land they ate the manna, until they came to the region of Phoenicia. 36 Now the homer was the tenth part of three measures.

Ex.17 1 And all the congregation of the children of Israel departed from the wilderness of Sin, according to their encampments, by the word of the Lord; and they encamped in Raphidin: and there was no water for the people to drink. 2 And the people reviled Moses, saying, Give us water, that we may drink; and Moses said to them, Why do ye revile me, and why tempt ye the Lord? 3 And the people thirsted there for water, and there the people murmured against Moses, saying, Why is this? hast thou brought us up out of Egypt to slay us and our children and our cattle with thirst? 4 And Moses cried to the Lord, saying, What shall I do to this people? yet a little while and they will stone me. 5 And the Lord said to Moses, Go before this people, and take to thyself of the elders of the people; and the rod with which thou smotest the river, take in thine hand, and thou shalt go. 6 Behold, I stand there before thou *come*, on the rock in Choreb, and thou shalt smite the rock, and water shall come out from it, and the people shall drink. And Moses did so before the sons of Israel. 7 And he called the name of that place, Temptation, and Reviling, because of the reviling of the children of Israel, and because they tempted the Lord, saying, Is the Lord among us or not? 8 And Amalec came and fought with Israel in Raphidin. 9 And Moses said to Joshua, Choose out for thyself mighty men, and go forth and set the army in array against Amalec to-morrow; and, behold, I *shall* stand on the top of the hill, and the rod of God *will be* in my hand. 10 And Joshua did as Moses said to him, and he went out and set the army in array against Amalec, and Moses and Aaron and Or went up to the top of the hill. 11 And it came to pass, when Moses lifted up his hands, Israel prevailed; and when he let down his hands, Amalec prevailed. 12 But the hands of Moses were heavy, and they took a stone and put it under him, and he sat upon it; and Aaron and Or supported his hands one on this side and the other on that, and the hands of Moses were supported till the going down of the sun. 13 And Joshua routed Amalec and all his people with the slaughter of the sword. 14 And the Lord said to Moses, Write this for a memorial in a book, and speak *this* in the ears of Joshua; for I will utterly blot out the memorial of Amalec from under heaven. 15 And Moses built an altar to the Lord, and called the name of it, The Lord my Refuge. 16 For with a secret hand the Lord wages war upon Amalec to all generations.

Ex.18 1 And Jothor the priest of Madiam, the father-in-law of Moses, heard of all that the Lord did to his people Israel; for the Lord brought Israel out of Egypt. 2 And Jothor the father-in-law of Moses, took Sepphora the wife of Moses after she had been sent away, 3 and her two sons: the name of the one was Gersam, *his father* saying, I was a sojourner in a strange land; — 4 and the name of the second Eliezer, saying, For the God of my father *is* my helper, and he has rescued me out of the hand of Pharao. 5 And Jothor the father-in-law of Moses, and his sons and his wife, went forth to Moses into the wilderness, where he encamped on the mount of God. 6 And it was told Moses, saying, Behold, thy father-in-law Jothor is coming to thee, and thy wife and two sons with him. 7 And Moses went forth to meet his father-in-law, and did him reverence, and kissed him, and they embraced each other, and he brought them into the tent. 8 And Moses related to his father-in-law all things that the Lord did to Pharao and all the Egyptians for Israel's sake, and all the labour that had befallen them in the way, and that the Lord had rescued them out of the hand of Pharao, and out of the hand of the Egyptians. 9 And Jothor was amazed at all the good things which the Lord did to them, forasmuch as he rescued them out of the hand of the Egyptians and out of the hand of Pharao. 10 And Jothor said, Blessed be the Lord, because he has rescued them out of the hand of the Egyptians and out of the hand of Pharao. 11 Now know I that the Lord is great above all gods, because of this, wherein they attacked them. 12 And Jothor the father-in-law of Moses took whole burnt-offerings and sacrifices for God, for Aaron and all the elders of Israel

came to eat bread with the father-in- law of Moses before God. 13 And it came to pass after the morrow that Moses sat to judge the people, and all the people stood by Moses from morning till evening. 14 And Jothor having seen all that *Moses* did to the people, says, What is this that thou doest to the people? wherefore sittest thou alone, and all the people stand by thee from morning till evening? 15 And Moses says to his father-in-law, Because the people come to me to seek judgment from God. 16 For whenever there is a dispute among them, and they come to me, I give judgment upon each, and I teach them the ordinances of God and his law. 17 And the father-in-law of Moses said to him, Thou dost not this thing rightly, 18 thou wilt wear away with intolerable weariness, both those and all this people which is with thee: this thing is hard, thou wilt not be able to endure it thyself alone. 19 Now then hearken to me, and I will advise thee, and God shall be with thee: be thou to the people in the things pertaining to God, and thou shalt bring their matters to God. 20 And thou shalt testify to them the ordinances of God and his law, and thou shalt shew to them the ways in which they shall walk, and the works which they shall do. 21 And do thou look out for thyself out of all the people able men, fearing God, righteous men, hating pride, and thou shalt set over the people captains of thousands and captains of hundreds, and captains of fifties, and captains of tens. 22 And they shall judge the people at all times, and the too burdensome matter they shall bring to thee, but they shall judge the smaller cases; so they shall relieve thee and help thee. 23 If thou wilt do this thing, God shall strengthen thee, and thou shalt be able to attend, and all this people shall come with peace into their own place. 24 And Moses hearkened to the voice of his father- in-law, and did whatsoever he said to him. 25 And Moses chose out able men out of all Israel, and he made them captains of thousands and captains of hundreds, and captains of fifties and captains of tens over the people. 26 And they judged the people at all times; and every too burdensome matter they brought to Moses, but every light matter they judged themselves. 27 And Moses dismissed his father-in-law, and he returned to his own land.

Ex.19 1 And in the third month of the departure of the children of Israel out of the land of Egypt, on the same day, they came into the wilderness of Sina. 2 And they departed from Raphidin, and came into the wilderness of Sina, and there Israel encamped before the mountain. 3 And Moses went up to the mount of God, and God called him out of the mountain, saying, These things shalt thou say to the house of Jacob, and thou shalt report them to the children of Israel. 4 Ye have seen all that I have done to the Egyptians, and I took you up as upon eagles' wings, and I brought you near to myself. 5 And now if ye will indeed hear my voice, and keep my covenant, ye shall be to me a peculiar people above all nations; for the whole earth is mine. 6 And ye shall be to me a royal priesthood and a holy nation: these words shalt thou speak to the children of Israel. 7 And Moses came and called the elders of the people, and he set before them all these words, which God appointed them. 8 And all the people answered with one accord, and said, All things that God has spoken, we will do and hearken to: and Moses reported these words to God. 9 And the Lord said to Moses, Lo! I come to thee in a pillar of a cloud, that the people may hear me speaking to thee, and may believe thee for ever: and Moses reported the words of the people to the Lord. 10 And the Lord said to Moses, Go down and solemnly charge the people, and sanctify them to-day and to-morrow, and let them wash their garments. 11 And let them be ready against the third day, for on the third day the Lord will descend upon mount Sina before all the people. 12 And thou shalt separate the people round about, saying, Take heed to yourselves that ye go not up into the mountain, nor touch any part of it: every one that touches the mountain shall surely die. 13 A hand shall not touch it, for *every one that touches* shall be stoned with stones or shot through with a dart, whether beast or whether man, it shall not live: when the voices and trumpets and cloud depart from off the mountain, they shall come up on the mountain. 14 And Moses went down from the mountain to the people, and sanctified them, and they washed their clothes. 15 And he said to the people, Be ready: for three days come not near to a woman. 16 And it came to pass on the third day, as the morning drew nigh, there were voices and lightnings and a dark cloud on mount Sina: the voice of the trumpet sounded loud, and all the people in the camp trembled. 17 And Moses led the people forth out of the camp to meet God, and they stood by under the camp. 18 The mount of Sina was altogether on a smoke, because God had descended upon it in fire; and the smoke went up as the smoke of a furnace, and the people were exceedingly amazed. 19 And the sounds of the trumpet were waxing very much louder. Moses spoke, and God answered him with a voice. 20 And the Lord came down upon mount Sina on the top of the mountain; and the Lord called Moses to the top of the mountain, and Moses went up. 21 And God spoke to Moses, saying, Go down, and solemnly charge the people, lest at any time they draw nigh to God to gaze, and a multitude of them fall. 22 And let the priests that draw nigh to the Lord God sanctify themselves, lest he destroy some of them. 23 And Moses said to God, The people will not be able to approach to the mount of Sina, for thou hast solemnly charged us, saying, Set bounds to the mountain and sanctify it. 24 And the Lord said to him, Go, descend, and come up thou and Aaron with thee; but let not the priests and the people force their way to come up to God, lest the Lord destroy some of them. 25 And Moses went down to the people, and spoke to them.

Ex.20 1 And the Lord spoke all these words, saying: 2 I am the Lord thy God, who brought thee out of the land of Egypt, out of the house of bondage. 3 Thou shalt have no other gods beside me. 4 Thou shalt not make to thyself an idol, nor likeness of anything, whatever things are in the heaven above, and whatever are in the earth beneath, and whatever are in the waters under the earth. 5 Thou shalt not bow down to them, nor serve them; for I am the Lord thy God, a jealous God, recompensing the sins of the fathers upon the children, to the third and fourth generation to them that hate me, 6 and bestowing mercy on them that love me to thousands *of them*, and on them that keep my commandments. 7 Thou shalt not take the name of the Lord thy God in vain; for the Lord thy God will not acquit him that takes his name in vain. 8 Remember the sabbath day to keep it holy. 9 Six days thou shalt labour, and shalt perform all thy work. 10 But on the seventh day is the sabbath of the Lord thy God; on it thou shalt do no work, thou, nor thy son, nor thy daughter, thy servant nor thy maidservant, thine ox nor thine ass, nor any cattle of thine, nor the stranger that sojourns with thee. 11 For in six days the Lord made the heaven and the earth, and the sea and all things in them, and rested on the seventh day; therefore the Lord blessed the seventh day, and hallowed it. 12 Honour thy father and thy mother, that it may be well with thee, and that thou mayest live long on the good land, which the Lord thy God gives to thee. 13 Thou shalt not commit adultery. 14 Thou shalt not steal. 15 Thou shalt not kill. 16 Thou shalt not bear false witness against thy neighbour. 17 Thou shalt not covet thy neighbour's wife; thou shalt not covet thy neighbour's house; nor his field, nor his servant, nor his maid, nor his ox, nor his ass, nor any of his cattle, nor whatever belongs to thy neighbour. 18 And all the people perceived the thundering, and the flashes, and the voice of the trumpet, and the mountain smoking; and all the people feared and stood afar off, 19 and said to Moses, Speak thou to us, and let not God speak to us, lest we die. 20 And Moses says to them, Be of good courage, for God is come to you to try you, that his fear may be among you, that ye sin not. 21 And the people stood afar off, and Moses went into the darkness where God was. 22 And the Lord said to Moses, Thus shalt thou say to the house of Jacob, and thou shalt report it to the children of Israel, Ye have seen that I have spoken to you from heaven. 23 Ye shall not make to yourselves gods of silver, and gods of gold ye shall not make to yourselves. 24 Ye shall make to me an altar of earth; and upon it ye shall sacrifice your whole burnt-offerings, and your peace- offerings, and your sheep and your calves in every place, where I shall record my name; and I will come to thee and bless thee. 25 And if thou wilt make to me an altar of stones, thou shalt not build them hewn *stones*; for thou hast lifted up thy tool upon them, and they are defiled. 26 Thou shalt not go up to my altar by steps, that thou mayest not uncover thy nakedness upon it.

Ex.21 1 And these *are* the ordinances which thou shalt set before them. 2 If thou buy a Hebrew servant, six years shall he serve thee, and in the seventh year he shall go forth free for nothing. 3 If he should have come in alone, he shall also go forth alone; and if his wife should have gone in together with him, his wife also shall go out. 4 Moreover, if his master give him a wife, and she have *born* him sons or daughters, the wife and the children shall be his master's; and he shall go forth alone. 5 And if the servant should answer and say, I love my master and wife and children, I will not go away free; 6 his master shall bring him to the judgment-seat of God, and then shall he bring him to the door, —to the door-post, and his master shall bore his ear through with an awl, and he shall serve him for ever. 7 And if any one sell his daughter as a domestic, she shall not depart as the maid-servants depart. 8 If she be not pleasing to her master, after she has betrothed herself to him, he shall let her go free; but he is not at liberty to sell her to a foreign nation, because he has trifled with her. 9 And if he should have betrothed her to his son, he shall do to her according to the right of daughters. 10 And if he take another to himself, he shall not deprive her of necessaries and her apparel, and her companionship *with him*. 11 And if he will not do these three things to her, she shall go out free without money. 12 And if any man smite another and he die, let him be certainly put to death. 13 But as for him that did it not willingly, but God delivered him into his hands, I will give thee a place whither the slayer may flee. 14 And if any one lie in wait for his neighbour to slay him by craft, and he go for refuge, thou shalt take him from my altar to put him to death. 15 Whoever smites his father or his mother, let him be certainly put to death. 16 Whosoever shall steal one of the children of Israel, and prevail over him and sell him, and he be found with him, let him certainly die. 17 He that reviles his father or his mother shall surely die. 18 And if two men revile each other and smite the one the other with a stone or his fist, and he die not, but be laid upon his bed; 19 if the man arise and walk abroad on his staff, he that smote him shall be clear; only he shall pay for his loss of time, and for his healing. 20 And if a man smite his man-servant or his maid-servant, with a rod, and *the party* die under his hands, he shall be surely punished. 21 But if *the servant* continue to live a day or two, let not *the master* be punished; for he is his money. 22 And if two men strive and smite a woman with child, and her child be born imperfectly formed, he shall be forced to pay a penalty: as the woman's husband may lay upon him, he shall pay with a valuation. 23 But if it be perfectly formed, he shall give life for life, 24 eye for eye, tooth for tooth, hand for hand, foot for foot, 25 burning for burning, wound for wound, stripe for stripe. 26 And if one smite the eye of his man- servant, or the eye of his maid-servant, and put it out, he shall let them go free for their eye's sake. 27 And if he should smite out the tooth of his man-servant, or the tooth of his maid-servant, he shall send them away free for their tooth's sake. 28 And if a bull gore a man or woman and they die, the bull shall be stoned with stones, and his flesh shall not be eaten; but the owner of the bull shall be clear. 29 But if the bull should have been given to goring in former time, and men should have told his owner, and he have not removed him, but he should have slain a man or woman, the bull shall be stoned, and his owner shall die also. 30 And if a ransom should be imposed on him, he shall pay for the ransom of his soul as much as they shall lay upon him. 31 And if *the bull* gore a son or daughter, let them do to him according to this ordinance. 32 And if the bull gore a man-servant or maid-servant, he shall pay to their master thirty silver didrachms, and the bull shall be stoned. 33 And if any one open a pit or dig a cavity in stone, and cover it not, and an ox or an ass fall in there, 34 the owner of the pit shall make compensation; he shall give money to their owner, and the dead shall be his own. 35 And if any man's bull gore the bull of his neighbour, and it die, they shall sell the living bull and divide the money, and they shall divide the dead bull. 36 But if the bull be known to have been given to goring in time past, and they have testified to his owner, and he have not removed him, he shall repay bull for bull, but the dead shall be his own.

Ex.22 1 And if one steal an ox or a sheep, and kill it or sell it, he shall pay five calves for a calf, and four sheep for a sheep. 2 And if the thief be found in the breach *made by himself* and be smitten and die, there shall not be blood shed for him. 3 But if the sun be risen upon him, he is guilty, he shall die instead; and if a thief have nothing, let him be sold in compensation for what he has stolen. 4 And if the thing stolen be left and be in his hand alive, whether ox or sheep, he shall restore them two-fold. 5 And if any one should feed down a field or a vineyard, and should send in his beast to feed down another field, he shall make compensation of his own field according to his produce; and if he shall have fed down the whole field, he shall pay for compensation the best of his own field and the best of his vineyard. 6 And if fire have gone forth and caught thorns, and should also set on fire threshing-floors or ears of corn or a field, he that kindled the fire shall make compensation. 7 And if any one give to his neighbour money r goods to keep, and they be stolen out of the man's house, if the thief be found he shall repay double. 8 But if the thief be not found, the master of the house shall come forward before God, and shall swear that surely he has not wrought wickedly in regard of any part of his neighbour's deposit, 9 according to every injury alleged, both concerning a calf, and an ass, and a sheep, and a garment, and every alleged loss, whatsoever in fact it may be, —the judgment of both shall proceed before God, and he that is convicted by God shall repay to his neighbour double. 10 And if any one give to his neighbour to keep a calf or sheep or any beast, and it be wounded or die or be taken, and no one know, 11 an oath of God shall be between both, *each swearing* that he has surely not at all been guilty in the matter of his neighbour's deposit; and so his master shall hold him guiltless, and he shall not make compensation. 12 And if it be stolen from him, he shall make compensation to the owner. 13 And if it be seized of beasts, he shall bring him to *witness* the prey, and he shall not make compensation. 14 And if any one borrow *ought* of his neighbour, and it be wounded or die or be carried away, and the owner of it be not with it, he shall make compensation. 15 But if the owner be with it, he shall not make compensation: but if it be a hired thing, there shall be *a compensation* to him instead of his hire. 16 And if any one deceive a virgin that is not betrothed, and lie with her, he shall surely endow her for a wife to himself. 17 And if her father positively refuse, and will not consent to give her to him for a wife, he shall pay compensation to her father according to the amount of the dowry of virgins. 18 Ye shall not save the lives of sorcerers. 19 Every one that lies with a beast ye shall surely put to death. 20 He that sacrifices to any gods but to the Lord alone, shall be destroyed by death. 21 And ye shall not hurt a stranger, nor afflict him; for ye were strangers in the land of Egypt. 22 Ye shall hurt no widow or orphan. 23 And if ye should afflict them by ill-treatment, and they should cry aloud to me, I will surely hear their voice. 24 And I will be very angry, and will slay you with the sword, and your wives shall be widows and your children orphans. 25 And if thou shouldest lend money to thy poor brother who is by thee, thou shalt not be hard upon him thou shalt not exact usury of him. 26 And if thou take thy neighbour's garment for a pledge, thou shalt restore it to him before sunset. 27 For this is his clothing, this is the only covering of his nakedness; wherein shall he sleep? If then he shall cry to me, I will hearken to him, for I am merciful. 28 Thou shalt not revile the gods, nor speak ill of the ruler of thy people. 29 Thou shalt not keep back the first-fruits of thy threshing floor and press. The first-born of thy sons thou shalt give to me. 30 So shalt thou do with thy calf and thy sheep and thine ass; seven days shall it be under the mother, and the eighth day thou shalt give it to me. 31 And ye shall be holy men to me; and ye shall not eat flesh taken of beasts, ye shall cast it to the dog.

Ex.23 1 Thou shalt not receive a vain report: thou shalt not agree with the unjust *man* to become an unjust witness. 2 Thou shalt not associate with the multitude for evil; thou shalt not join thyself with a multitude to turn aside with the majority so as to shut out judgment. 3 And thou shalt not spare a poor man in judgment. 4 And if thou meet thine enemy's ox or his ass going astray, thou shalt turn them back and restore them to him. 5 And if thou see thine enemy's ass fallen under its burden, thou shalt not pass by it, but shalt help to raise it with him. 6 Thou shalt not wrest the sentence of the poor in his judgment. 7 Thou shalt abstain from every unjust thing: thou shalt not slay the innocent and just, and thou shalt not justify the wicked for gifts. 8 And thou shalt not receive gifts; for gifts blind the eyes of the seeing, and corrupt just words. 9 And ye shall not afflict a stranger, for ye know the heart of a stranger; for ye were yourselves strangers in the land of Egypt. 10 Six years thou shalt sow thy land, and gather in the fruits of it. 11 But in the seventh year thou shalt let it rest, and leave it, and the poor of thy nation shall feed; and the wild beasts of the field shall eat that which remains: thus shalt thou do to thy vineyard and to thine oliveyard. 12 Six days shalt thou do thy works, and on the seventh day there shall be rest, that thine ox and thine ass may rest, and that the son of thy maid-servant and the stranger may be refreshed. 13 Observe all things whatsoever I have commanded you; and ye shall make no mention of the name of other gods, neither shall they be heard out of your mouth. 14 Keep ye a feast to me three times in the year. 15 Take heed to keep the feast of unleavened bread: seven days ye shall eat unleavened bread, as I charged thee at the season of the month of new *corn*, for in it thou camest out of Egypt: thou shalt not appear before me empty. 16 And thou shalt keep the feast of the harvest of first-fruits of thy labours, whatsoever thou shalt have sown in thy field, and the feast of completion at the end of the year in the gathering in of thy fruits out of thy field. 17 Three times in the year shall all thy males appear before the Lord thy God. 18 For when I shall have cast out the nations from before thee, and shall have widened thy borders, thou shalt not offer the blood of my sacrifice with leaven, neither must the fat of my feast abide till the morning. 19 Thou shalt bring the first-offerings of the first-fruits of thy land into the house of the Lord thy God. Thou shalt not seethe a lamb in its mother's milk. 20 And, behold, I send my angel before thy face, that he may keep thee in the way, that he may bring thee into the land which I have prepared for thee. 21 Take heed to thyself and hearken to him, and disobey him not; for he will not give way to thee, for my name is on him. 22 If ye will indeed hear my voice, and if thou wilt do all the things I shall charge thee with, and keep my covenant, ye shall be to me a peculiar people above all nations, for the whole earth is mine; and ye shall be to me a royal priesthood, and a holy nation: these words shall ye speak to the children of Israel, If ye shall indeed hear my voice, and do all the things I shall tell thee, I will be an enemy to thine enemies, and an adversary to thine adversaries. 23 For my angel shall go as thy leader, and shall bring thee to the Amorite, and Chettite, and Pherezite, and Chananite, and Gergesite, and Evite, and Jebusite, and I will destroy them. 24 Thou shalt not worship their gods, nor serve them: thou shalt not do according to their works, but shalt utterly destroy them, and break to pieces their pillars. 25 And thou shalt serve the Lord thy God, and I will bless thy bread and thy wine and thy water, and I will turn away sickness from you. 26 There shall not be on thy land one that is impotent or barren. I will surely fulfil the number of thy days. 27 And I will send terror before thee, and I will strike with amazement all the nations to which thou shalt come, and I will make all thine enemies to flee. 28 And I will send hornets before thee, and thou shalt cast out the Amorites and the Evites, and the Chananites and the Chettites from thee. 29 I will not cast them out in one year, lest the land become desolate, and the beasts of the field multiply against thee. 30 By little *and little* I will cast them out from before thee, until thou shalt be increased and inherit the earth. 31 And I will set thy borders from the Red Sea, to the sea of the Phylistines, and from the wilderness to the great river Euphrates; and I will give into your hand those that dwell in the land, and will cast them out from thee. 32 Thou shalt make no covenant with them and their gods. 33 And they shall not dwell in thy land, lest they cause thee to sin against me; for if thou shouldest serve their gods, these will be an offence to thee.

Ex.24 1 And to Moses he said, Go up to the Lord, thou and Aaron and Nadab and Abiud, and seventy of the elders of Israel: and they shall worship the Lord from a distance. 2 And Moses alone shall draw nigh to God; and they shall not draw nigh, and the people shall not come up with them. 3 And Moses went in and related to the people all the words of God and the ordinances; and all the people answered with one voice, saying, All the words which the Lord has spoken, we will do and be obedient. 4 And Moses wrote all the words of the Lord; and Moses rose up early in the morning, and built an altar under the mountain, and *set up* twelve stones for the twelve tribes of Israel. 5 And he sent forth the young men of the children of Israel, and they offered whole burnt-offerings, and they sacrificed young calves as a peace- offering to God. 6 And Moses took half the blood and poured it into bowls, and half the blood he poured out upon the altar. 7 And he took the book of the covenant and read it in the ears of the people, and they said, All things whatsoever the Lord has spoken we will do and hearken therein. 8 And Moses took the blood and sprinkled it upon the people, and said, Behold the blood of the covenant, which the Lord has made with you concerning all these words. 9 And Moses went up, and Aaron, and Nadab and Abiud, and seventy of the elders of Israel. 10 And they saw the place where the God of Israel stood; and under his feet was as it were a work of sapphire slabs, and as it were the appearance of the firmament of heaven in its purity. 11 And of the chosen ones of Israel there was not even one missing, and they appeared in the place of God, and did eat and drink. 12 And the Lord said to Moses, Come up to me into the mountain, and be there; and I will give thee the tables of stone, the law and the commandments, which I have written to give them laws. 13 And Moses rose up and Joshua his attendant, and they went up into the mount of God. 14 And to the elders they said, Rest there till we return to you; and behold, Aaron and Or are with you: if any man have a cause to be tried, let them go to them. 15 And Moses and Joshua went up to the mountain, and the cloud covered the mountain. 16 And the glory of God came down upon the mount Sina, and the cloud covered it six days; and the Lord called Moses on the seventh day out of the midst of the cloud. 17 And the appearance of the glory of the Lord was as burning fire on the top of the mountain, before the children of Israel. 18 And Moses went into the midst of the cloud, and went up to the mountain, and was there in the mountain forty days and forty nights.

Ex.25 1 And the Lord spoke to Moses, saying, 2 Speak to the children of Israel, and take first-fruits of all, who may be disposed in their heart to give; and ye shall take my first-fruits. 3 And this is the offering which ye shall take of them; gold and silver and brass, 4 and blue, and purple, and double scarlet, and fine spun linen, and goats' hair, 5 and rams' skins dyed red, and blue skins, and incorruptible wood, 6 and oil for the light, incense for anointing oil, and for the composition of incense, 7 and sardius stones, and stones for the carved work of the breast-plate, and the full-length robe. 8 And thou shalt make me a sanctuary, and I will appear among you. 9 And thou shalt make for me according to all things which I shew thee in the mountain; even the pattern of the tabernacle, and the pattern of all its furniture: so shalt thou make it. 10 And thou shalt make the ark of testimony of incorruptible wood; the length of two cubits and a half, and the breadth of a cubit and a half, and the height of a cubit and a half. 11 And thou shalt gild it with pure gold, thou shalt gild it within and without; and thou shalt make for it golden wreaths twisted round about. 12 And thou shalt cast for it four golden rings, and shalt put them on the four sides; two rings on the one side, and two rings on the other side. 13 And thou shalt make staves *of* incorruptible wood, and shalt gild them with gold. 14 And thou shalt put the staves into the rings on the sides of the ark, to bear the ark with them. 15 The staves shall remain fixed in the rings of the ark. 16 And thou shalt put into the ark the testimonies which I shall give thee. 17 And thou shalt make a propitiatory, a lid of pure gold; the length of two cubits and a half, and the breadth of a cubit and a half. 18 And thou shalt make two cherubs graven in gold, and thou shalt put them on both sides of the propitiatory. 19 They shall be made, one cherub on this side, and another cherub on the other side of the propitiatory; and thou shalt make the two cherubs on the two sides. 20 The cherubs shall stretch forth their wings above, overshadowing the propitiatory with their wings; and their faces shall be toward each other, the faces of the cherubs shall be toward the propitiatory. 21 And thou shalt set the propitiatory on the ark above, and thou shalt put into the ark the testimonies which I shall give thee. 22 And I will make myself known to thee from thence, and I will speak to thee above the propitiatory between the two cherubs, which are upon the ark of testimony, even in all things which I shall charge thee concerning the children of Israel. 23 And thou shalt make a golden table of pure gold, in length two cubits, and in breadth a cubit, and in height a cubit and a half. 24 And thou shalt make for it golden wreaths twisted round about, and thou shalt make for it a crown of an hand-breadth round about. 25 And thou shalt make a twisted wreath for the crown round about. 26 And thou shalt make four golden rings; and thou shalt put the four rings upon the four parts of its feet under the crown. 27 And the rings shall be for bearings for the staves, that they may bear the table with them. 28 And thou shalt make the staves of incorruptible wood, and thou shalt gild them with pure gold; and the table shall be borne with them. 29 And thou shalt make its dishes and its censers, and its bowls, and its cups, with which thou shalt offer drink-offerings: of pure gold shalt thou make them. 30 And thou shalt set upon the table shewbread before me continually. 31 And thou shalt make a candlestick of pure gold; thou shalt make the candlestick of graven work: its stem and its branches, and its bowls and its knops and its lilies shall be of one piece. 32 And six branches proceeding sideways, three branches of the candlestick from one side of it, and three branches of the candlestick from the other side. 33 And three bowls fashioned like almonds, on each branch a knop and a lily; so to the six branches proceeding from the candlestick, 34 and in the candlestick four bowls fashioned like almonds, in each branch knops and the flowers of the same. 35 A knop under two branches out of it, and a knop under four branches out of it; so to the six branches proceeding from the candlestick; and in the candlestick four bowls fashioned like almonds. 36 Let the knops and the branches be of one piece, altogether graven of one piece of pure gold. 37 And thou shalt make its seven lamps: and thou shalt set on *it* the lamps, and they shall shine from one front. 38 And thou shalt make its funnel and its snuff-dishes of pure gold. 39 All these articles *shall be* a talent of pure gold. 40 See, thou shalt make them according to the pattern shewed thee in the mount.

Ex.26 1 And thou shalt make the tabernacle, ten curtains of fine linen spun, and blue and purple, and scarlet spun *with* cherubs; thou shalt make them with work of a weaver. 2

The length of one curtain shall be eight and twenty cubits, and one curtain shall be the breadth of four cubits: there shall be the same measure to all the curtains. 3 And the five curtains shall be joined one to another, and *the other* five curtains shall be closely connected the one with the other. 4 And thou shalt make for them loops of blue on the edge of one curtain, on one side for the coupling, and so shalt thou make on the edge of the outer curtain for the second coupling. 5 Fifty loops shalt thou make for one curtain, and fifty loops shalt thou make on the part of the curtain answering to the coupling of the second, opposite *each other*, corresponding to each other at each point. 6 And thou shalt make fifty golden rings; and thou shalt join the curtains to each other with the rings, and it shall be one tabernacle. 7 And thou shalt make for a covering of the tabernacle skins with the hair on, thou shalt make them eleven skins. 8 The length of one skin thirty cubits, and the breadth of one skin four cubits: there shall be the same measure to the eleven skins. 9 And thou shalt join the five skins together, and the six skins together; and thou shalt double the sixth skin in front of the tabernacle. 10 And thou shalt make fifty loops on the border of one skin, which is in the midst for the joinings; and thou shalt make fifty loops on the edge of the second skin that joins it. 11 And thou shalt make fifty brazen rings; and thou shalt join the rings by the loops, and thou shalt join the skins, and they shall be one. 12 And thou shalt fix at the end that which is over in the skins of the tabernacle; the half of the skin that is left shalt thou fold over, according to the overplus of the skins of the tabernacle; thou shalt fold it over behind the tabernacle. 13 A cubit an this side, and a cubit on that side of that which remains of the skins, of the length of the skins of the tabernacle: it shall be folding over the sides of the tabernacle on this side and that side, that it may cover it. 14 And thou shalt make for a covering of the tabernacle rams' skins dyed red, and blue skins as coverings above. 15 And thou shalt make the posts of the tabernacle of incorruptible wood. 16 Of ten cubits shalt thou make one post, and the breadth of one post of a cubit and a half. 17 Two joints shalt thou make in one post, answering the one to the other: so shalt thou do to all the posts of the tabernacle. 18 And thou shalt make posts to the tabernacle, twenty posts on the north side. 19 And thou shalt make to the twenty posts forty silver sockets; two sockets to one post on both its sides, and two sockets to the other post on both its sides. 20 And for the next side, toward the south, twenty posts, 21 and their forty silver sockets: two sockets to one post on both its sides, and two sockets to the other post on both its sides. 22 And on the back of the tabernacle at the part which is toward the *west* thou shalt make six posts. 23 And thou shalt make two posts on the corners of the tabernacle behind. 24 And it shall be equal below, they shall be equal toward the same part from the heads to one joining; so shalt thou make to both the two corners, let them be equal. 25 And there shall be eight posts, and their sixteen silver sockets; two sockets to one post on both its sides, and two sockets to the other post. 26 And thou shalt make bars of incorruptible wood; five to one post on one side of the tabernacle, 27 and five bars to one post on the second side of the tabernacle,

and five bars to the hinder posts, on the side of the tabernacle toward the sea. 28 And let the bar in the middle between the posts go through from the one side to the other side. 29 And thou shalt gild the posts with gold; and thou shalt make golden rings, into which thou shalt introduce the bars, and thou shalt gild the bars with gold. 30 And thou shalt set up the tabernacle according to the pattern shewed thee in the mount. 31 And thou shalt make a veil of blue and purple and scarlet woven, and fine linen spun: thou shalt make it cherubs *in* woven work. 32 And thou shalt set it upon four posts of incorruptible wood overlaid with gold; and their tops *shall be* gold, and their four sockets *shall be* of silver. 33 And thou shalt put the veil on the posts, and thou shalt carry in thither within the veil the ark of the testimony; and the veil shall make a separation for you between the holy and the holy of holies. 34 And thou shalt screen with the veil the ark of the testimony in the holy of holies. 35 And thou shalt set the table outside the veil, and the candlestick opposite the table on the south side of the tabernacle; and thou shalt put the table on the north side of the tabernacle. 36 And thou shalt make a screen for the door of the tabernacle of blue, and purple, and spun scarlet and fine linen spun, the work of the embroiderer. 37 And thou shalt make for the veil five posts, and thou shalt gild them with gold; and their chapiters shall be gold; and thou shalt cast for them five brazen sockets.

Ex.27 1 And thou shalt make an altar of incorruptible wood, of five cubits in the length, and five cubits in the breadth; the altar shall be square, and the height of it shall be of three cubits. 2 And thou shalt make the horns on the four corners; the horns shall be of the same piece, and thou shalt overlay them with brass. 3 And thou shalt make a rim for the altar; and its covering and its cups, and its flesh-hooks, and its fire-pan, and all its vessels shalt thou make of brass. 4 And thou shalt make for it a brazen grate with net-work; and thou shalt make for the grate four brazen rings under the four sides. 5 And thou shalt put them below under the grate of the altar, and the grate shall extend to the middle of the altar. 6 And thou shalt make for the altar staves of incorruptible wood, and thou shalt overlay them with brass. 7 And thou shalt put the staves into the rings; and let the staves be on the sides of the altar to carry it. 8 Thou shalt make it hollow with boards: according to what was shewed thee in the mount, so thou shalt make it. 9 And thou shalt make a court for the tabernacle, curtains of the court of fine linen spun on the south side, the length of a hundred cubits for one side. 10 And their pillars twenty, and twenty brazen sockets for them, and their rings and their clasps of silver. 11 Thus *shall there be* to the side toward the north curtains of a hundred cubits in length; and their pillars twenty, and their sockets twenty of brass, and the rings and the clasps of the pillars, and their sockets overlaid with silver. 12 And in the breadth of the tabernacle toward the west curtains of fifty cubits, their pillars ten and their sockets ten. 13 And in the breadth of the tabernacle toward the south, curtains of fifty cubits; their pillars ten, and their sockets ten. 14 And the height of the curtains *shall be* of fifty cubits for the one side *of the gate*; their pillars three, and their sockets three. 15 And *for* the second side the height of the curtains *shall be* of fifteen cubits; their pillars three, and their sockets three. 16 And a veil for the door of the court, the height *of it* of twenty cubits of blue linen, and of purple, and spun scarlet, and of fine linen spun with the art of the embroiderer; their pillars four, and their sockets four. 17 All the pillars of the court round about overlaid with silver, and their chapiters silver and their brass sockets. 18 And the length of the court *shall be* a hundred *cubits* on each side, and the breadth fifty on each side, and the height five cubits of fine linen spun, and their sockets of brass. 19 And all the furniture and all the instruments and the pins of the court *shall be* of brass. 20 And do thou charge the children of Israel, and let them take for thee refined pure olive-oil beaten to burn for light, that a lamp may burn continually 21 in the tabernacle of the testimony, without the veil that is before the *ark of the* covenant, shall Aaron and his sons burn it from evening until morning, before the Lord: it is a perpetual ordinance throughout your generations of the children of Israel.

Ex.28 1 And do thou take to thyself both Aaron thy brother, and his sons, even *them* of the children of Israel; so that Aaron, and Nadab and Abiud, and Eleazar and Ithamar, sons of Aaron, may minister to me. 2 And thou shalt make holy apparel for Aaron thy brother, for honour and glory. 3 And speak thou to all those who are wise in understanding, whom I have filled with the spirit of wisdom and perception; and they shall make the holy apparel of Aaron for the sanctuary, in which *apparel* he shall minister to me as priest. 4 And these are the garments which they shall make: the breast-plate, and the shoulder-piece, and the full-length robe, and the tunic with a fringe, and the tire, and the girdle; and they shall make holy garments for Aaron and his sons to minister to me as priests. 5 And they shall take the gold, and the blue, and the purple, and the scarlet, and the fine linen. 6 And they shall make the shoulder-piece of fine linen spun, the woven work of the embroiderer. 7 It shall have two shoulder-pieces joined together, fastened on the two sides. 8 And the woven work of the shoulder-pieces which is upon it, shall be of one piece according to the work, of pure gold and blue and purple, and spun scarlet and fine twined linen. 9 And thou shalt take the two stones, the stones of emerald, and thou shalt grave on them the names of the children of Israel. 10 Six names on the first stone, and the other six names on the second stone, according to their births. 11 *It shall be* the work of the stone-engraver's art; as the graving of a seal thou shalt engrave the two stones with the names of the children of Israel. 12 And thou shalt put the two stones on the shoulders of the shoulder-piece: they are memorial-stones for the children of Israel: and Aaron shall bear the names of the children of Israel before the Lord on his two shoulders, a memorial for them. 13 And thou shalt make circlets of pure gold; 14 and thou shalt make two fringes of pure gold, variegated with flowers wreathen work; and thou shalt put the wreathen fringes on the circlets, fastening them on their shoulder-pieces in front. 15 And thou shalt make the oracle of judgment, the work of the embroiderer:

in keeping with the ephod, thou shalt make it of gold, and blue and purple, and spun scarlet, and fine linen spun. 16 Thou shalt make it square: it shall be double; of a span the length of it, and of a span the breadth. 17 And thou shalt interweave with it a texture of four rows of stone; there shall be a row of stones, a sardius, a topaz, and emerald, the first row. 18 And the second row, a carbuncle, a sapphire, and a jasper. 19 And the third row, a ligure, an agate, an amethyst: 20 and the fourth row, a chrysolite, and a beryl, and an onyx stone, set round with gold, bound together with gold: let them be according to their row. 21 And let the stones of the names of the children of Israel be twelve according to their names, engravings as of seals: let them be for the twelve tribes each according to the name. 22 And thou shalt make on the oracle woven fringes, a chain-work of pure gold. 23 And Aaron shall take the names of the children of Israel, on the oracle of judgment on his breast; a memorial before God for him as he goes into the sanctuary. 24 And thou shalt put the fringes on the oracle of judgment; thou shalt put the wreaths on both sides of the oracle, 25 and thou shalt put the two circlets on both the shoulders of the ephod in front. 26 And thou shalt put the Manifestation and the Truth on the oracle of judgment; and it shall be on the breast of Aaron, when he goes into the holy place before the Lord; and Aaron shall bear the judgments of the children of Israel on his breast before the Lord continually. 27 And thou shalt make the full-length tunic all of blue. 28 And the opening of it shall be in the middle having a fringe round about the opening, the work of the weaver, woven together in the joining of the same piece that it might not be rent. 29 And under the fringe of the robe below thou shalt make as it were pomegranates of a flowering pomegranate tree, of blue, and purple, and spun scarlet, and fine linen spun, under the fringe of the robe round about: golden pomegranates of the same shape, and bells round about between these. 30 A bell by the side of a golden pomegranate, and flower-work on the fringe of the robe round about. 31 And the sound of Aaron shall be audible when he ministers, as he goes into the sanctuary before the Lord, and has he goes out, that he die not. 32 And thou shalt make a plate *of* pure gold, and thou shalt grave on it *as* the graving of a signet, Holiness of the Lord. 33 And thou shalt put it on the spun blue cloth, and it shall be on the mitre: it shall be in the front of the mitre. 34 And it shall be on the forehead of Aaron; and Aaron shall bear away the sins of their holy things, all that the children of Israel shall sanctify of every gift of their holy things, and it shall be on the forehead of Aaron continually acceptable for them before the Lord. 35 And the fringes of the garments *shall be* of fine linen; and thou shalt make a tire of fine linen, and thou shalt make a girdle, the work of the embroiderer. 36 And for the sons of Aaron thou shalt make tunics and girdles, and thou shalt make for them tires for honour and glory. 37 And thou shalt put them on Aaron thy brother, and his sons with him, and thou shalt anoint them and fill their hands: and thou shalt sanctify them, that they may minister to me in the priest's office. 38 And thou shalt make for them linen drawers to cover the nakedness of their flesh; they shall reach from the loins to the thighs. 39

And Aaron shall have them, and his sons, whenever they enter into the tabernacle of witness, or when they shall advance to the altar of the sanctuary to minister, so they shall not bring sin upon themselves, lest they die: *it is* a perpetual statute for him, and for his seed after him.

Ex.29 1 And these are the things which thou shalt do to them: thou shalt sanctify them, so that they shall serve me in the priesthood; and thou shalt take one young calf from the herd, and two unblemished rams; 2 and unleavened loaves kneaded with oil, and unleavened cakes anointed with oil: thou shalt make them *of* fine flour of wheat. 3 And thou shalt put them on one basket, and thou shalt offer them on the basket, and the young calf and the two rams. 4 And thou shalt bring Aaron and his sons to the doors of the tabernacle of testimony, and thou shalt wash them with water. 5 And having taken the garments, thou shalt put on Aaron thy brother both the full- length robe and the ephod and the oracle; and thou shalt join for him the oracle to the ephod. 6 And thou shalt put the mitre on his head; and thou shalt put the plate, *even* the Holiness, on the mitre. 7 And thou shalt take of the anointing oil, and thou shalt pour it on his head, and shalt anoint him, 8 and thou shalt bring his sons, and put garments on them. 9 And thou shalt gird them with the girdles, and put the tires upon them, and they shall have a priestly office to me for ever; and thou shalt fill the hands of Aaron and the hands of his sons. 10 And thou shalt bring the calf to the door of the tabernacle of witness; and Aaron and his sons shall lay their hands on the head of the calf, before the Lord, by the doors of the tabernacle of witness. 11 And thou shalt slay the calf before the Lord, by the doors of the tabernacle of witness. 12 And thou shalt take of the blood of the calf, and put it on the horns of the altar with thy finger, but all the rest of the blood thou shalt pour out at the foot of the altar. 13 And thou shalt take all the fat that is on the belly, and the lobe of the liver, and the two kidneys, and the fat that is upon them, and shalt put them upon the altar. 14 But the flesh of the calf, and his skin, and his dung, shalt thou burn with fire without the camp; for it is an *offering on account* of sin. 15 And thou shalt take one ram, and Aaron and his sons shall lay their hands on the head of the ram. 16 And thou shalt kill it, and take the blood and pour it on the altar round about. 17 And thou shalt divide the ram by his several limbs, and thou shalt wash the inward parts and the feet with water, and thou shalt put them on the divided parts with the head. 18 And thou shalt offer the whole ram on the altar, a whole burnt-offering to the Lord for a sweet-smelling savour: it is an offering of incense to the Lord. 19 And thou shalt take the second ram, and Aaron and his sons shall lay their hands on the head of the ram. 20 And thou shalt kill it, and take of the blood of it, and put it on the tip of Aaron's right ear, and on the thumb of his right hand, and on the great toe of his right foot, and on the tips of the right ears of his sons, and on the thumbs of their right hands, and on the great toes of their right feet. 21 And thou shalt take of the blood from the altar, and of the anointing oil; and thou shalt sprinkle it upon Aaron and on his garments, and on his sons and on his sons' garments with him; and he shall be sanctified and his apparel, and his sons and his sons' apparel with him: but the blood of the ram thou shalt pour round about upon the altar. 22 And thou shalt take from the ram its fat, both the fat that covers the belly, and the lobe of the liver, and the two kidneys, and the fat that is upon them, and the right shoulder, for this is a consecration. 23 And one cake *made* with oil, and one cake from the basket of unleavened bread set forth before the Lord. 24 And thou shalt put them all on the hands of Aaron, and on the hands of his sons, and thou shalt separate them as a separate offering before the Lord. 25 And thou shalt take them from their hands, and shalt offer them up on the altar of whole burnt-offering for a sweet-smelling savour before the Lord: it is an offering to the Lord. 26 And thou shalt take the breast from the ram of consecration which is Aaron's, and thou shalt separate it as a separate offering before the Lord, and it shall be to thee for a portion. 27 And thou shalt sanctify the separated breast and the shoulder of removal which has been separated, and which has been removed from the ram of consecration, of the portion of Aaron and of *that of* his sons. 28 And it shall be a perpetual statute of the children of Israel to Aaron and his sons, for this is a separate offering; and it shall be a special offering from the children of Israel, from the peace-offerings of the children of Israel, a special offering to the Lord. 29 And the apparel of the sanctuary which is Aaron's shall be his son's after him, for them to be anointed in them, and to fill their hands. 30 The priest his successor from among his sons who shall go into the tabernacle of witness to minister in the holies, shall put them on seven days. 31 And thou shalt take the ram of consecration, and thou shalt boil the flesh in the holy place. 32 And Aaron and his sons shall eat the flesh of the ram, and the loaves in the basket, by the doors of the tabernacle of witness. 33 They shall eat the offerings with which they were sanctified to fill their hands, to sanctify them; and a stranger shall not eat of them, for they are holy. 34 And if *aught* be left of the flesh of the sacrifice of consecration and of the loaves until the morning, thou shalt burn the remainder with fire: it shall not be eaten, for it is a holy thing. 35 And thus shalt thou do for Aaron and for his sons according to all things that I have commanded thee; seven days shalt thou fill their hands. 36 And thou shalt sacrifice the calf of the sin-offering on the day of purification, and thou shalt purify the altar when thou dost perform consecration upon it, and thou shalt anoint it so as to sanctify it. 37 Seven days shalt thou purify the altar and sanctify it; and the altar shall be most holy, every one that touches the altar shall be hallowed. 38 And these are the offerings which thou shalt offer upon the altar; two unblemished lambs of a year old daily on the altar continually, a constant offering. 39 One lamb thou shalt offer in the morning, and the second lamb thou shalt offer in the evening. 40 And a tenth measure of fine flour mingled with the fourth part of an hin of beaten oil, and a drink-offering the fourth part of a hin of wine for one lamb. 41 And thou shalt offer the second lamb in the evening, after the manner of the morning-offering, and according to the drink-offering of the morning lamb; thou shalt offer it an offering to the Lord for a sweet- smelling savour, 42 a perpetual sacrifice throughout your generations, at the door of the tabernacle of witness before the Lord; wherein I will be known to thee from thence, so as to speak to thee. 43 And I will there give orders to the children of Israel, and I will be sanctified in my glory. 44 And I will sanctify the tabernacle of testimony and the altar, and I will sanctify Aaron and his sons, to minister as priests to me. 45 And I will be called upon among the children of Israel, and will be their God. 46 And they shall know that I am the Lord their God, who brought them forth out of the land of Egypt, to be called upon by them, and to be their God.

Ex.30 1 And thou shalt make the altar of incense of incorruptible wood. 2 And thou shalt make it a cubit in length, and a cubit in breadth: it shall be square; and the height of it shall be of two cubits, its horns shall be of the same piece. 3 And thou shalt gild its grate with pure gold, and its sides round about, and its horns; and thou shalt make for it a wreathen border of gold round- about. 4 And thou shalt make under its wreathen border two rings of pure gold; thou shalt make it to the two corners on the two sides, and they shall be bearings for the staves, so as to bear it with them. 5 And thou shalt make the staves of incorruptible wood, and shalt gild them with gold. 6 And thou shalt set it before the veil that is over the ark of the testimonies, wherein I will make myself known to thee from thence. 7 And Aaron shall burn upon it fine compound incense every morning; whensoever he trims the lamps he shall burn incense upon it. 8 And when Aaron lights the lamps in the evening, he shall burn incense upon it; a constant incense- offering always before the Lord for their generations. 9 And thou shalt not offer strange incense upon it, *nor* and offering made by fire, *nor* a sacrifice; and thou shalt not pour a drink-offering upon it. 10 And once in the year Aaron shall make atonement on its horns, he shall purge it with the blood of purification for their generations: it is most holy to the Lord. 11 And the Lord spoke to Moses, saying, 12 If thou take account of the children of Israel in the surveying of them, and they shall give every one a ransom for his soul to the Lord, then there shall not be among them a destruction in the visiting of them. 13 And this is what they shall give, as many as pass the survey, half a didrachm which is according to the didrachm of the sanctuary: twenty oboli *go to* the didrachm, but the half of the didrachm is the offering to the Lord. 14 Every one that passes the survey from twenty years old and upwards shall give the offering to the Lord. 15 The rich shall not give more, and the poor shall not give less than the half didrachm in giving the offering to the Lord, to make atonement for your souls. 16 And thou shalt take the money of the offering from the children of Israel, and shalt give it for the service of the tabernacle of testimony; and it shall be to the children of Israel a memorial before the Lord, to make atonement for your souls. 17 And the Lord spoke to Moses, saying, 18 Make a brazen laver, and a brazen base for it, for washing; and thou shalt put it between the tabernacle of witness and the altar, and thou shalt pour forth water into it. 19 And Aaron and his sons shall wash their hands and their feet with water from it. 20 Whensoever they shall go into the tabernacle of witness, they shall wash

themselves with water, so they shall not die, whensoever they advance to the altar to do service and to offer the whole burnt-offerings to the Lord. 21 They shall wash their hands and feet with water, whensoever they shall go into the tabernacle of witness; they shall wash themselves with water, that they die not; and it shall be for them a perpetual statute, for him and his posterity after him. 22 And the Lord spoke to Moses, saying, 23 Do thou also take sweet herbs, the flower of choice myrrh five hundred shekels, and the half of this two hundred and fifty shekels of sweet-smelling cinnamon, and two hundred and fifty shekels of sweet-smelling calamus, 24 and of cassia five hundred shekels of the sanctuary, and a hin of olive oil. 25 And thou shalt make it a holy anointing oil, a perfumed ointment *tempered* by the art of the perfumer: it shall be a holy anointing oil. 26 And thou shalt anoint with it the tabernacle of witness, and the ark of the tabernacle of witness, 27 and all its furniture, and the candlestick and all its furniture, and the altar of incense, 28 and the altar of whole burnt offerings and all its furniture, and the table and all its furniture, and the laver. 29 And thou shalt sanctify them, and they shall be most holy: every one that touches them shall be hallowed. 30 And thou shalt anoint Aaron and his sons, and sanctify them that they may minister to me as priests. 31 And thou shalt speak to the children of Israel, saying, This shall be to you a holy anointing oil throughout your generations. 32 On man's flesh it shall not be poured, and ye shall not make *any* for yourselves according to this composition: it is holy, and shall be holiness to you. 33 Whosoever shall make it in like manner, and whosoever shall give of it to a stranger, shall be destroyed from among his people. 34 And the Lord said to Moses, Take for thyself sweet herbs, stacte, onycha, sweet galbanum, and transparent frankincense; there shall be and equal weight of each. 35 And they shall make with it perfumed incense, tempered with the art of a perfumer, a pure holy work. 36 And of these thou shalt beat some small, and thou shalt put it before the testimonies in the tabernacle of testimony, whence I will make myself known to thee: it shall be to you a most holy incense. 37 Ye shall not make any for yourselves according to this composition; it shall be to you a holy thing for the Lord. 38 Whosoever shall make any in like manner, so as to smell it, shall perish from his people.

Ex.31 1 And the Lord spoke to Moses, saying, 2 Behold, I have called by name Beseleel the son of Urias the son of Or, of the tribe of Juda. 3 And I have filled him *with* a divine spirit of wisdom, and understanding, and knowledge, to invent in every work, 4 and to frame works, to labour in gold, and silver, and brass, and blue, and purple, and spun scarlet, 5 and works in stone, and for artificers' work in wood, to work at all works. 6 And I have appointed him and Eliab the *son* of Achisamach of the tribe of Dan, and to every one understanding in heart I have given understanding; and they shall make all things as many as I have appointed thee, — 7 the tabernacle of witness, and the ark of the covenant, and the propitiatory that is upon it, and the furniture of the tabernacle, 8 and the altars, and the table and all its furniture, 9 and the pure candlestick and all its furniture, and the laver and its base, 10 and Aaron's robes of ministry, and the robes of his sons to minister to me as priests, 11 and the anointing oil and the compound incense of the sanctuary; according to all that I have commanded thee shall they make them. 12 And the Lord spoke to Moses, saying, 13 Do thou also charge the children of Israel, saying, Take heed and keep my sabbaths; *for* they are a sign with me and among you throughout your generations, that ye may know that I am the Lord that sanctifies you. 14 And ye shall keep the sabbaths, because this is holy to the Lord for you; he that profanes it shall surely be put to death: every one who shall do a work on it, that soul shall be destroyed from the midst of his people. 15 Six days thou shalt do works, but the seventh day is the sabbath, a holy rest to the Lord; every one who shall do a work on the seventh day shall be put to death. 16 And the children of Israel shall keep the sabbaths, to observe them throughout their generations. 17 It is a perpetual covenant with me and the children of Israel, it is a perpetual sign with me; for in six days the Lord made the heaven and the earth, and on the seventh day he ceased, and rested. 18 And he gave to Moses when he left off speaking to him in mount Sina the two tables of testimony, tables of stone written *upon* with the finger of God.

Ex.32 1 And when the people saw that Moses delayed to come down from the mountain, the people combined against Aaron, and said to him, Arise and make us gods who shall go before us; for this Moses, the man who brought us forth out of the land of Egypt—we do not know what is become of him. 2 And Aaron says to them, Take off the golden ear-rings which are in the ears of your wives and daughters, and bring them to me. 3 And all the people took off the golden ear -rings that were in their ears, and brought them to Aaron. 4 And he received them at their hands, and formed them with a graving tool; and he made them a molten calf, and said, These *are* thy gods, O Israel, which have brought thee up out of the land of Egypt. 5 And Aaron having seen it built an altar before it, and Aaron made proclamation saying, To-morrow *is* a feast of the Lord. 6 And having risen early on the morrow, he offered whole burnt-offerings, and offered a peace-offering; and the people sat down to eat and drink, and rose up to play. 7 And the Lord spoke to Moses, saying, Go quickly, descend hence, for thy people whom thou broughtest out of the land of Egypt have transgressed; 8 they have quickly gone out of the way which thou commandedst; they have made for themselves a calf, and worshipped it, and sacrificed to it, and said, These are thy gods, O Israel, who brought thee up out of the land of Egypt. 9 10 And now let me alone, and I will be very angry with them and consume them, and I will make thee a great nation. 11 And Moses prayed before the Lord God, and said, Wherefore, O Lord, art thou very angry with thy people, whom thou broughtest out of the land of Egypt with great strength, and with thy high arm? 12 *Take heed* lest at any time the Egyptians speak, saying, With evil intent he brought them out to slay them in the mountains, and to consume them from off the earth; cease from thy wrathful anger, and be merciful to the sin of thy people, 13 remembering Abraam and Isaac and Jacob thy servants, to whom thou hast sworn by thyself, and hast spoken to them, saying, I will greatly multiply your seed as the stars of heaven for multitude, and all this land which thou spokest of to give to them, so that they shall possess it for ever. 14 And the Lord was prevailed upon to preserve his people. 15 And Moses turned and went down from the mountain, and the two tables of testimony were in his hands, tables of stone written on both their sides: they were written within and without. 16 And the tables were the work of God, and the writing the writing of God written on the tables. 17 And Joshua having heard the voice of the people crying, says to Moses, There is a noise of war in the camp. 18 And *Moses* says, It is not the voice of them that begin the battle, nor the voice of them that begin *the cry* of defeat, but the voice of them that begin *the banquet* of wine do I hear. 19 And when he drew nigh to the camp, he sees the calf and the dances; and Moses being very angry cast the two tables out of his hands, and broke them to pieces under the mountain. 20 And having taken the calf which they made, he consumed it with fire, and ground it very small, and scattered it on the water, and made the children of Israel to drink it. 21 And Moses said to Aaron, What has this people done to thee, that thou hast brought upon them a great sin? 22 And Aaron said to Moses, Be not angry, *my* lord, for thou knowest the impetuosity of this people. 23 For they say to me, Make us gods, which shall go before us; for as for this man Moses, who brought us out of Egypt, we do not know what is become of him. 24 And I said to them, If any one has golden ornaments, take them off; and they gave them me, and I cast them into the fire, and there came out this calf. 25 And when Moses saw that the people was scattered, —for Aaron *had* scattered them *so as to be* a rejoicing to their enemies, — 26 then stood Moses at the gate of the camp, and said, Who is on the Lord's side? let him come to me. Then all the sons of Levi came to him. 27 And he says to them, Thus saith the Lord God of Israel, Put every one his sword on his thigh, and go through and return from gate to gate through the camp, and slay every one his brother, and every one his neighbour, and every one him that is nearest to him. 28 And the sons of Levi did as Moses spoke to them, and there fell of the people in that day to the *number of* three thousand men. 29 And Moses said to them, Ye have filled your hands this day to the Lord each one on his son or on his brother, so that blessing should be given to you. 30 And it came to pass after the morrow *had begun*, that Moses said to the people, Ye have sinned a great sin; and now I will go up to God, that I may make atonement for your sin. 31 And Moses returned to the Lord and said, I pray, O Lord, this people has sinned a great sin, and they have made for themselves golden gods. 32 And now if thou wilt forgive their sin, forgive *it*; and if not, blot me out of thy book, which thou hast written. 33 And the Lord said to Moses, If any one has sinned against me, I will blot them out of my book. 34 And now go, descend, and lead this people into the place of which I spoke to thee: behold, my angel shall go before thy face; and in the day when I shall visit I will bring upon them their sin. 35 And the Lord smote the people for the making the calf, which Aaron made.

Ex.33 1 And the Lord said to Moses, Go forward, go up hence, thou and thy people, whom thou broughtest out of the land of Egypt, into the land which I swore to Abraam, and Isaac, and Jacob, saying, I will give it to your seed. 2 And I will send at the same time my angel before thy face, and he shall cast out the Amorite and the Chettite, and the Pherezite and Gergesite, and Evite, and Jebusite, and Chananite. 3 And I will bring thee into a land flowing with milk and honey; for I will not go up with thee, because thou art a stiff-necked people, lest I consume thee by the way. 4 And the people having heard this grievous saying, mourned in mourning apparel. 5 For the Lord said to the children of Israel, Ye are a stiff-necked people; take heed lest I bring on you another plague, and destroy you: now then put off your glorious apparel, and *your* ornaments, and I will shew thee what I will do to thee. 6 So the sons of Israel took off their ornaments and their array at the mount of Choreb. 7 And Moses took his tabernacle and pitched it without the camp, at a distance from the camp; and it was called the Tabernacle of Testimony: and it came to pass *that* every one that sought the Lord went forth to the tabernacle which was without the camp. 8 And whenever Moses went into the tabernacle without the camp, all the people stood every one watching by the doors of his tent; and when Moses departed, they took notice until he entered into the tabernacle. 9 And when Moses entered into the tabernacle, the pillar of the cloud descended, and stood at the door of the tabernacle, and *God* talked to Moses. 10 And all the people saw the pillar of the cloud standing by the door of the tabernacle, and all the people stood and worshipped every one at the door of his tent. 11 And the Lord spoke to Moses face to face, as if one should speak to his friend; and he retired into the camp: but his servant Joshua the son of Naue, a young man, departed not forth from the tabernacle. 12 And Moses said to the Lord, Lo! thou sayest to me, Lead on this people; but thou hast not shewed me whom thou wilt send with me, but thou hast said to me, I know thee above all, and thou hast favour with me. 13 If then I have found favour in thy sight, reveal thyself to me, that I may evidently see thee; that I may find favour in thy sight, and that I may know that this great nation *is* thy people. 14 And he says, I myself will go before thee, and give thee rest. 15 And he says to him, If thou go not up with us thyself, bring me not up hence. 16 And how shall it be surely known, that both I and this people have found favour with thee, except only if thou go with us? So both I and thy people shall be glorified beyond all the nations, as many as are upon the earth. 17 And the Lord said to Moses, I will also do for thee this thing, which thou hast spoken; for thou hast found grace before me, and I know thee above all. 18 And *Moses* says, Manifest thyself to me. 19 And *God* said, I will pass by before thee with my glory, and I will call by my name, the Lord, before thee; and I will have mercy on whom I will have mercy, and will have pity on whom I will have pity. 20 And *God* said, Thou shalt not be able to see my face; for no man shall see my face, and live. 21 And the Lord said, Behold, *there is* a place by me: thou shalt stand upon the rock; 22 and when my glory shall pass by, then I will put thee into a hole of the rock; and I will cover thee over with my hand, until I shall have passed by. 23 And I will remove my hand, and then shalt thou see my back parts; but my face shall not appear to thee.

Ex.34 1 And the Lord said to Moses, Hew for thyself two tables of stone, as also the first were, and come up to me to the mountain; and I will write upon the tables the words, which were on the first tables, which thou brokest. 2 And be ready by the morning, and thou shalt go up to the mount Sina, and shalt stand there for me on the top of the mountain. 3 And let no one go up with thee, nor be seen in all the mountain; and let not the sheep and oxen feed near that mountain. 4 And *Moses* hewed two tables of stone, as also the first were; and Moses having arisen early, went up to the mount Sina, as the Lord appointed him; and Moses took the two tables of stone. 5 And the Lord descended in a cloud, and stood near him there, and called by the name of the Lord. 6 And the Lord passed by before his face, and proclaimed, The Lord God, pitiful and merciful, longsuffering and very compassionate, and true, 7 and keeping justice and mercy for thousands, taking away iniquity, and unrighteousness, and sins; and he will not clear the guilty; bringing the iniquity of the fathers upon the children, and to the children's children, to the third and fourth generation. 8 And Moses hasted, and bowed to the earth and worshipped; 9 and said, If I have found grace before thee, let my Lord go with us; for the people is stiff-necked: and thou shalt take away our sins and our iniquities, and we will be thine. 10 And the Lord said to Moses, Behold, I establish a covenant for thee in the presence of all thy people; I will do glorious things, which have not been done in all the earth, or in any nation; and all the people among whom thou art shall see the works of the Lord, that they are wonderful, which I will do for thee. 11 Do thou take heed to all things whatsoever I command thee: behold, I cast out before your face the Amorite and the Chananite and the Pherezite, and the Chettite, and Evite, and Gergesite and Jebusite: 12 take heed to thyself, lest at any time thou make a covenant with the dwellers on the land, into which thou art entering, lest it be to thee a stumbling-block among you. 13 Ye shall destroy their altars, and break in pieces their pillars, and ye shall cut down their groves, and the graven images of their gods ye shall burn with fire. 14 For ye shall not worship strange gods, for the Lord God, a jealous name, is a jealous God; 15 lest at any time thou make a covenant with the dwellers on the land, and they go a whoring after their gods, and sacrifice to their gods, and they call thee, and thou shouldest eat of their feasts, 16 and thou shouldest take of their daughters to thy sons, and thou shouldest give of thy daughters to their sons; and thy daughters should go a whoring after their gods, and thy sons should go a whoring after their gods. 17 And thou shalt not make to thyself molten gods. 18 And thou shalt keep the feast of unleavened bread: seven days shalt thou eat unleavened bread, as I have charged thee, at the season in the month of new *corn*; for in the month of new *corn* thou camest out from Egypt. 19 The males *are* mine, everything that opens the womb; every first-born of oxen, and *every* first-born of sheep. 20 And the first-born of an ass thou shalt redeem with a sheep, and if thou wilt not redeem it thou shalt pay a price: every first-born of thy sons shalt thou redeem: thou shalt not appear before me empty. 21 Six days thou shalt work, but on the seventh day thou shalt rest: *there shall be* rest in seed- time and harvest. 22 And thou shalt keep to me the feast of weeks, the beginning of wheat- harvest; and the feast of ingathering in the middle of the year. 23 Three times in the year shall every male of thine appear before the Lord the God of Israel. 24 For when I shall have cast out the nations before thy face, and shall have enlarged thy coasts, no one shall desire thy land, whenever thou mayest go up to appear before the Lord thy God, three times in the year. 25 Thou shalt not offer the blood of my sacrifices with leaven, neither shall the sacrifices of the feast of the passover remain till the morning. 26 The first-fruits of thy land shalt thou put into the house of the Lord thy God: thou shalt not boil a lamb in his mother's milk. 27 And the Lord said to Moses, Write these words for thyself, for on these words I have established a covenant with thee and with Israel. 28 And Moses was there before the Lord forty days, and forty nights; he did not eat bread, and he did not drink water; and he wrote upon the tables these words of the covenant, the ten sayings. 29 And when Moses went down from the mountain, *there were* the two tables in the hands of Moses, —as then he went down from the mountain, Moses knew not that the appearance of the skin of his face was glorified, when God spoke to him. 30 And Aaron and all the elders of Israel saw Moses, and the appearance of the skin of his face was made glorious, and they feared to approach him. 31 And Moses called them, and Aaron and all the rulers of the synagogue turned towards him, and Moses spoke to them. 32 And afterwards all the children of Israel came to him, and he commanded them all things, whatsoever the Lord had commanded him in the mount of Sina. 33 And when he ceased speaking to them, he put a veil on his face. 34 And whenever Moses went in before the Lord to speak to him, he took off the veil till he went out, and he went forth and spoke to all the children of Israel whatsoever the Lord commanded him. 35 And the children of Israel saw the face of Moses, that it was glorified; and Moses put the veil over his face, till he went in to speak with him.

Ex.35 1 And Moses gathered all the congregation of the children of Israel together, and said, These are the words which the Lord has spoken for *you* to do them. 2 Six days shalt thou perform works, but on the seventh day *shall be* rest—a holy sabbath—a rest for the Lord: every one that does work on it, let him die. 3 Ye shall not burn a fire in any of your dwellings on the sabbath- day; I *am* the Lord. 4 And Moses spoke to all the congregation of the children of Israel, saying, This *is* the thing which the Lord has appointed you, saying, 5 Take of yourselves an offering for the Lord: every one that engages in his heart shall bring the first-fruits to the Lord; gold, silver, brass, 6 blue, purple, double scarlet spun, and fine linen spun, and goats' hair, 7 and rams' skins dyed red, and skins *dyed* blue, and incorruptible wood, 8 and sardine stones, and stones for engraving for the shoulder-piece and full-length robe. 9

And every man that is wise in heart among you, let him come and work all things whatsoever the Lord has commanded. 10 The tabernacle, and the cords, and the coverings, and the rings, and the bars, and the posts, 11 and the ark of the testimony, and its staves, and its propitiatory, and the veil, 12 and the curtains of the court, and its posts, 13 and the emerald stones, 14 and the incense, and the anointing oil, 15 and the table and all its furniture, 16 and the candle-stick for the light and all its furniture, 17 and the altar and all its furniture; 18 and the holy garments of Aaron the priest, and the garments in which they shall do service; 19 and the garments of priesthood for the sons of Aaron and the anointing oil, and the compound incense. 20 And all the congregation of the children of Israel went out from Moses. And they brought, they whose heart prompted them, and they to whomsoever it seemed good in their mind, each and offering: 21 and they brought an offering to the Lord for all the works of the tabernacle of witness, and all its services, and for all the robes of the sanctuary. 22 And the men, even every one to whom it seemed good in his heart, brought from the women, *even* brought seals and ear-rings, and finger-rings, and necklaces, and bracelets, every article of gold. 23 And all as many as brought ornaments of gold to the Lord, and with whomsoever fine linen was found; and they brought skins *dyed* blue, and rams' skins dyed red. 24 And every one that offered an offering brought silver and brass, the offerings to the Lord; and *they* with whom was found incorruptible wood; and they brought *offerings* for all the works of the preparation. 25 And every woman skilled in her heart to spin with her hands, brought spun *articles*, the blue, and purple, and scarlet and fine linen. 26 And all the women to whom it seemed good in their heart in their wisdom, spun the goats' hair. 27 And the rulers brought the emerald stones, and the stones for setting in the ephod, and the oracle, 28 and the compounds both for the anointing oil, and the composition of the incense. 29 And every man and woman whose mind inclined them to come in and do all the works as many as the Lord appointed them to do by Moses—*they* the children of Israel brought an offering to the Lord. 30 And Moses said to the children of Israel, Behold, God has called by name Beseleel the *son* of Urias the *son of* Or, of the tribe of Juda, 31 and has filled him with a divine spirit of wisdom and understanding, and knowledge of all things, 32 to labour skillfully in all works of cunning workmanship, to form the gold and the silver and the brass, 33 and to work in stone, and to fashion the wood, and to work in every work of wisdom. 34 And *God* gave improvement in understanding both to him, and to Eliab the *son* of Achisamach of the tribe of Dan. 35 And *God* filled them with wisdom, understanding *and* perception, to understand to work all the works of the sanctuary, and to weave the woven and embroidered work with scarlet and fine linen, to do all work of curious workmanship *and* embroidery.

Ex.36 1 And Beseleel wrought, and Eliab and every one wise in understanding, to whom was given wisdom and knowledge, to understand to do all the works according to the holy offices, according to all things which the Lord appointed. 2 And Moses called Beseleel and Eliab, and all that had wisdom, to whom God gave knowledge in *their* heart, and all who were freely willing to come forward to the works, to perform them. 3 And they received from Moses all the offerings, which the children of Israel brought for all the works of the sanctuary to do them; and they continued to receive the gifts brought, from those who brought them in the morning. 4 And there came all the wise men who wrought the works of the sanctuary, each according to his own work, which they wrought. 5 And one said to Moses, The people bring an abundance *too great* in proportion to all the works which the Lord has appointed *them* to do. 6 And Moses commanded, and proclaimed in the camp, saying, Let neither man nor woman any longer labour for the offerings of the sanctuary; and the people were restrained from bringing any more. 7 And they had materials sufficient for making the furniture, and they left some besides. 8 And every wise one among those that wrought made the robes of the holy places, which belong to Aaron the priest, as the Lord commanded Moses. 9 And he made the ephod of gold, and blue, and purple, and spun scarlet, and fine linen twined. 10 And the plates were divided, the threads of gold, so as to interweave with the blue and purple, and with the spun scarlet, and the fine linen twined, they made it a woven work; 11 shoulder-pieces joined from both sides, a work woven by mutual twisting of the parts into one another. 12 They made it of the same material according to the making of it, of gold, and blue, and purple, and spun scarlet, and fine linen twined, as the Lord commanded Moses; 13 and they made the two emerald stones clasped together and set in gold, graven and cut after the cutting of a seal with the names of the children of Israel; 14 and he put them on the shoulder-pieces of the ephod, *as* stones of memorial of the children of Israel, as the Lord appointed Moses. 15 And they made the oracle, a work woven with embroidery, according to the work of the ephod, of gold, and blue, and purple, and spun scarlet, and fine linen twined. 16 They made the oracle square *and* double, the length of a span, and the breadth of a span, — double. 17 And there was interwoven with it a woven work of four rows of stones, a series of stones, the first row, a sardius and topaz and emerald; 18 and the second row, a carbuncle and sapphire and jasper; 19 and the third row, a ligure and agate and amethyst; 20 and the fourth row a chrysolite and beryl and onyx set round about with gold, and fastened with gold. 21 And the stones were twelve according to the names of the children of Israel, graven according to their names like seals, each according to his own name for the twelve tribes. 22 And they made on the oracle turned wreaths, wreathen work, of pure gold, 23 and they made two golden circlets and two golden rings. 24 And they put the two golden rings on both the *upper* corners of the oracle; 25 and they put the golden wreaths on the rings on both sides of the oracle, and the two wreaths into the two couplings. 26 And they put them on the two circlets, and they put them on the shoulders of the ephod opposite *each other* in front. 27 And they made two golden rings, and put them on the two projections on the top of the oracle, and on the top of the hinder part of the ephod within. 28

And they made two golden rings, and put them on both the shoulders of the ephod under it, in front by the coupling above the connexion of the ephod. 29 And he fastened the oracle by the rings that were on it to the rings of the ephod, which were fastened with *a string* of blue, joined together with the woven work of the ephod; that the oracle should not be loosed from the ephod, as the Lord commanded Moses. 30 And they made the tunic under the ephod, woven work, all of blue. 31 And the opening of the tunic in the midst woven closely together, the opening having a fringe round about, that it might not be rent. 32 And they made on the border of the tunic below pomegranates as of a flowering pomegranate tree, of blue, and purple, and spun scarlet, and fine linen twined. 33 And they made golden bells, and put the bells on the border of the tunic round about between the pomegranates: 34 a golden bell and a pomegranate on the border of the tunic round about, for the ministration, as the Lord commanded Moses. 35 And they made vestments of fine linen, a woven work, for Aaron and his sons, 36 and the tires of fine linen, and the mitre of fine linen, and the drawers of fine linen twined; 37 and their girdles of fine linen, and blue, and purple, and scarlet spun, the work of an embroiderer, according as the Lord commanded Moses. 38 And they made the golden plate, a dedicated thing of the sanctuary, of pure gold; 39 and he wrote upon it graven letters *as* of a seal, Holiness to the Lord. 40 And they put it on the border of blue, so that it should be on the mitre above, as the Lord commanded Moses.

Ex.37 1 And they made ten curtains for the tabernacle; 2 of eight and twenty cubits the length of one curtain: the same *measure* was to all, and the breadth of one curtain was of four cubits. 3 And they made the veil of blue, and purple, and spun scarlet, and fine linen twined, the woven work with cherubs. 4 And they put it on four posts of incorruptible *wood* overlaid with gold; and their chapiters were gold, and their four sockets were silver. 5 And they made the veil of the door of the tabernacle of witness of blue, and purple, and spun scarlet, and fine linen twined, woven work with cherubs, 6 and their posts five, and the rings; and they gilded their chapiters and their clasps with gold, and they had five sockets of brass. 7 And they made the court toward the south; the curtains of the court of fine linen twined, a hundred *cubits* every way, 8 and their posts twenty, and their sockets twenty; 9 and on the north side a hundred every way, and on the south side a hundred every way, and their posts twenty and their sockets twenty. 10 And on the west side curtains of fifty cubits, their posts ten and their sockets ten. 11 And on the east side curtains of fifty cubits of fifteen cubits behind, 12 and their pillars three, and their sockets three. 13 And at the second back on this side and on that by the gate of the court, curtains of fifteen cubits, their pillars three and their sockets three; 14 all the curtains of the tabernacle of fine linen twined. 15 And the sockets of their pillars of brass, and their hooks of silver, and their chapiters overlaid with silver, and all the posts of the court overlaid with silver: 16 and the veil of the gate of the court, the work of an embroiderer of blue, and purple, and spun scarlet, and fine linen twined; the length of twenty cubits, and the height and the breadth of five cubits, made equal to the curtains of the court; 17 and their pillars four, and their sockets four of brass, and their hooks of silver, and their chapiters overlaid with silver. 18 And all the pins of the court round about of brass, and they *were* overlaid with silver. 19 And this was the construction of the tabernacle of witness, accordingly as it was appointed to Moses; so that the public service should belong to the Levites, through Ithamar the son of Aaron the priest. 20 And Beseleel the son of Urias of the tribe of Juda, did as the Lord commanded Moses. 21 And Eliab the son of Achisamach of the tribe of Dan *was there*, who was chief artificer in the woven works and needle-works and embroideries, in weaving with the scarlet and fine linen.

Ex.38 1 And Beseleel made the ark, 2 and overlaid it with pure gold within and without; 3 and he cast for it four golden rings, two on the one side, and two on the other, 4 wide *enough* for the staves, so that men should bear the ark with them. 5 And he made the propitiatory over the ark of pure gold, 6 and the two cherubs of gold; 7 one cherub on the one end of the propitiatory, and another cherub on the other end of the propitiatory, 8 overshadowing the propitiatory with their wings. 9 And he made the set table of pure gold, 10 and cast for it four rings: two on the one side and two on the other side, broad, so that *men* should lift it with the staves in them. 11 And he made the staves of the ark and of the table, and gilded them with gold. 12 And he made the furniture of the table, both the dishes, and the censers, and the cups, and the bowls with which he should offer drink-offerings, of gold. 13 And he made the candlestick which gives light, of gold; 14 the stem solid, and the branches from both its sides; 15 and blossoms proceeding from its branches, three on this side, and three on the other, made equal to each other. 16 And *as to* their lamps, which are on the ends, knops *proceeded* from them; and sockets proceeding from them, that the lamps might be upon them; and the seventh socket, on the top of the candlestick, on the summit above, entirely of solid gold. 17 And on the candlestick seven golden lamps, and its snuffers gold, and its funnels gold. 18 He overlaid the posts *with silver*, and cast for each post golden rings, and gilded the bars with gold; and he gilded the posts of the veil with gold, and made the hooks of gold. 19 He made also the rings of the tabernacle of gold; and the rings of the court, and the rings for drawing out the veil above of brass. 20 He cast the silver chapiters of the tabernacle, and the brazen chapiters of the door of the tabernacle, and the gate of the court; and he made silver hooks for the posts, he overlaid them with silver on the posts. 21 He made the pins of the tabernacle and the pins of the court of brass. 22 He made the brazen altar of the brazen censers, which belonged to the men engaged in sedition with the gathering of Core. 23 He made all the vessels of the altar and its grate, and its base, and its bowls, and the brazen flesh-hooks. 24 He made an appendage for the altar of network under the grate, beneath it as far as the middle of it; and he fastened to it four brazen rings on the four parts of the appendage of the altar, wide *enough* for the bars, so as to bear the altar with them. 25 He made the holy anointing oil and the composition of the incense, the pure work of the perfumer. 26 He made the brazen laver, and the brazen base of it of the mirrors of the women that fasted, who fasted by the doors of the tabernacle of witness, in the day in which he set it up. 27 And he made the laver, that at it Moses and Aaron and his sons might wash their hands and their feet: when they went into the tabernacle of witness, or whensoever they should advance to the altar to do service, they washed at it, as the Lord commanded Moses.

Ex.39 1 All the gold that was employed for the works according to all the fabrication of the holy things, was of the gold of the offerings, twenty-nine talents, and seven hundred and twenty shekels according to the holy shekel. 2 And the offering of silver from the men that were numbered of the congregation a hundred talents, and a thousand seven hundred and seventy-five shekels, one drachm apiece, even the half shekel, according to the holy shekel. 3 Every one that passed the survey from twenty years old and upwards to the *number of* six hundred thousand, and three thousand five hundred and fifty. 4 And the hundred talents of silver went to the casting of the hundred chapiters of the tabernacle, and to the chapiters of the veil; 5 a hundred chapiters to the hundred talents, a talent to a chapiter. 6 And the thousand seven hundred and seventy-five shekels he formed into hooks for the pillars, and he gilt their chapiters and adorned them. 7 And the brass of the offering *was* seventy talents, and a thousand five hundred shekels; 8 and they made of it the bases of the door of the tabernacle of witness, 9 and the bases of the court round about, and the bases of the gate of the court, and the pins of the tabernacle, and the pins of the court round about; 10 and the brazen appendage of the altar, and all the vessels of the altar, and all the instruments of the tabernacle of witness. 11 And the children of Israel did as the Lord commanded Moses, so did they. 12 And of the gold that remained of the offering they made vessels to minister with before the Lord. 13 And the blue that was left, and the purple, and the scarlet they made *into* garments of ministry for Aaron, so that he should minister with them in the sanctuary; 14 and they brought the garments to Moses, and the tabernacle, and its furniture, its bases and its bars and the posts; 15 and the ark of the covenant, and its bearers, and the altar and all its furniture. 16 And they made the anointing oil, and the incense of composition, and the pure candlestick, 17 and its lamps, lamps for burning, and oil for the light, 18 and the table of shewbread, and all its furniture, and the shewbread upon it, 19 and the garments of the sanctuary which belong to Aaron, and the garments of his sons, for the priestly ministry; 20 and the curtains of the court, and the posts, and the veil of the door of the tabernacle, and the gate of the court, 21 and all the vessels of the tabernacle and all its instruments: and the skins, even rams' skins dyed red, and the blue coverings, and the coverings of the other things, and the pins, and all the instruments for the works of the tabernacle of witness. 22 Whatsoever things the Lord appointed Moses, so did the children of Israel make all the furniture. 23 And Moses saw all the works; and they had done them all as the Lord commanded Moses, so had they made them; and Moses blessed them.

Ex.40 1 And the Lord spoke to Moses, saying, 2 On the first day of the first month, at the new moon, thou shalt set up the tabernacle of witness, 3 and thou shalt place *in it* the ark of the testimony, and shalt cover the ark with the veil, 4 and thou shalt bring in the table and shalt set forth that which is to be set forth on it; and thou shalt bring in the candlestick and place its lamps on it. 5 And thou shalt place the golden altar, to burn incense before the ark; and thou shalt put a covering of a veil on the door of the tabernacle of witness. 6 And thou shalt put the altar of burnt-offerings by the doors of the tabernacle of witness, and thou shalt set up the tabernacle round about, and thou shalt hallow all that belongs to it round about. 7 8 9 And thou shalt take the anointing oil, and shalt anoint the tabernacle, and all things in it; and shalt sanctify it, and all its furniture, and it shall be holy. 10 And thou shalt anoint the altar of burnt- offerings, and all its furniture; and thou shalt hallow the altar, and the altar shall be most holy. 11 12 And thou shalt bring Aaron and his sons to the doors of the tabernacle of witness, and thou shalt wash them with water. 13 And thou shalt put on Aaron the holy garments, and thou shalt anoint him, and thou shalt sanctify him, and he shall minister to me as priest. 14 And thou shalt bring up his sons, and shalt put garments on them. 15 And thou shalt anoint them as thou didst anoint their father, and they shall minister to me as priests; and it shall be that they shall have an everlasting anointing of priesthood, throughout their generations. 16 And Moses did all things whatsoever the Lord commanded him, so did he. 17 And it came to pass in the first month, in the second year after their going forth out of Egypt, at the new moon, that the tabernacle was set up. 18 And Moses set up the tabernacle, and put on the chapiters, and put the bars into their places, and set up the posts. 19 And he stretched out the curtains over the tabernacle, and put the veil of the tabernacle on it above as the Lord commanded Moses. 20 And he took the testimonies, and put them into the ark; and he put the staves by the sides of the ark. 21 And he brought the ark into the tabernacle, and put on *it* the covering of the veil, and covered the ark of the testimony, as the Lord commanded Moses. 22 And he put the table in the tabernacle of witness, on the north side without the veil of the tabernacle. 23 And he put on it the shewbread before the Lord, as the Lord commanded Moses. 24 And he put the candlestick into the tabernacle of witness, on the side of the tabernacle toward the south. 25 And he put on it its lamps before the Lord, as the Lord had commanded Moses. 26 And he put the golden altar in the tabernacle of witness before the veil; 27 and he burnt on it incense of composition, as the Lord commanded Moses. 28 29 And he put the altar of the burnt-offerings by the doors of the tabernacle. 31 And he set up the court round about the tabernacle and the altar; and Moses accomplished all the works. 34 And the cloud covered the tabernacle of witness, and the tabernacle was filled with the glory of the Lord. 35

And Moses was not able to enter into the tabernacle of testimony, because the cloud overshadowed it, and the tabernacle was filled with the glory of the Lord. 36 And when the cloud went up from the tabernacle, the children of Israel prepared to depart with their baggage. 37 And if the cloud went not up, they did not prepare to depart, till the day when the cloud went up. 38 For a cloud was on the tabernacle by day, and fire was on it by night before all Israel, in all their journeyings.

LEVITICUS

Lev.1 1 And the Lord called Moses again and spoke to him out of the tabernacle of witness, saying, Speak to the children of Israel, and thou shalt say to them, 2 If *any* man of you shall bring gifts to the Lord, ye shall bring your gifts of the cattle and of the oxen and of the sheep. 3 If his gift be a whole-burnt-offering, he shall bring an unblemished male of the herd to the door of the tabernacle of witness, he shall bring it as acceptable before the Lord. 4 And he shall lay his hand on the head of the burnt-offering as a thing acceptable for him, to make atonement for him. 5 And they shall slay the calf before the Lord; and the sons of Aaron the priests shall bring the blood, and they shall pour the blood round about on the altar, which *is* at the doors of the tabernacle of witness. 6 And having flayed the whole burnt-offering, they shall divide it by its limbs. 7 And the sons of Aaron the priests shall put fire on the altar, and shall pile wood on the fire. 8 And the sons of Aaron the priests shall pile up the divided parts, and the head, and the fat on the wood on the fire, *the wood* which is on the altar. 9 And the entrails and the feet they shall wash in water, and the priests shall put all on the altar: it is a burnt-offering, a sacrifice, a smell of sweet savour to the Lord. 10 And if his gift *be* of the sheep to the Lord, or of the lambs, or of the kids for whole-burnt-offerings, he shall bring it a male without blemish. 11 And he shall lay his hand on its head; and they shall kill it by the side of the altar, toward the north before the Lord, and the sons of Aaron the priests shall pour its blood on the altar round about. 12 And they shall divide it by its limbs, and its head and its fat, and the priests shall pile them up on the wood which is on the fire, on the altar. 13 And they shall wash the entrails and the feet with water, and the priest shall bring all the *parts* and put them on the altar: it is a burnt-offering, a sacrifice, a smell of sweet savour to the Lord. 14 And if he bring his gift, a burnt-offering to the Lord, of birds, then shall he bring his gift of doves or pigeons. 15 And the priest shall bring it to the altar, and shall wring off its head; and the priest shall put it on the altar, and shall wring out the blood at the bottom of the altar. 16 And he shall take away the crop with the feathers, and shall cast it forth by the altar toward the east to the place of the ashes. 17 And he shall break it off from the wings and shall not separate it, and the priest shall put it on the altar on the wood which is on the fire: it is a burnt-offering, a sacrifice, a sweet-smelling savour to the Lord.

Lev.2 1 And if a soul bring a gift, a sacrifice to the Lord, his gift shall be fine flour; and he shall pour oil upon it, and shall put frankincense on it: it is a sacrifice. 2 And he shall bring it to the priests the sons of Aaron: and having taken from it a handful of the fine flour with the oil, and all its frankincense, then the priest shall put the memorial of it on the altar: *it is* a sacrifice, an odour of sweet savour to the Lord. 3 And the remainder of the sacrifice shall be for Aaron and his sons, a most holy portion from the sacrifices of the Lord. 4 And if he bring as a gift a sacrifice baked from the oven, a gift to the Lord of fine flour, *he shall bring* unleavened bread kneaded with oil, and unleavened cakes anointed with oil. 5 And if thy gift *be* a sacrifice from a pan, it is fine flour mingled with oil, unleavened *offerings*. 6 And thou shalt break them into fragments and pour oil upon them: it is a sacrifice to the Lord. 7 And if thy gift be a sacrifice from the hearth, it shall be made of fine flour with oil. 8 And he shall offer the sacrifice which he shall make of these to the Lord, and shall bring it to the priest. 9 And the priest shall approach the altar, and shall take away from the sacrifice a memorial of it, and the priest shall place it on the altar: a burnt offering, a smell of sweet savour to the Lord. 10 And that which is left of the sacrifice *shall be* for Aaron and his sons, most holy from the burnt-offerings of the Lord. 11 Ye shall not leaven any sacrifice which ye shall bring to the Lord; for *as to* any leaven, or any honey, ye shall not bring of it to offer a gift to the Lord. 12 Ye shall bring them in the way of fruits to the Lord, but they shall not be offered on the altar for a sweet-smelling savour to the Lord. 13 And every gift of your sacrifice shall be seasoned with salt; omit not the salt of the covenant of the Lord from your sacrifices: on every gift of yours ye shall offer salt to the Lord your God. 14 And if thou wouldest offer a sacrifice of first-fruits to the Lord, *it shall be* new grains ground *and* roasted for the Lord; so shalt thou bring the sacrifice of the first-fruits. 15 And thou shalt pour oil upon it, and shalt put frankincense on it: it is a sacrifice. 16 And the priest shall offer the memorial of it *taken* from the grains with the oil, and all its frankincense: it is a burnt-offering to the Lord.

Lev.3 1 And if his gift to the Lord be a peace-offering, if he should bring it of the oxen, whether it be male or whether it be female, he shall bring it unblemished before the Lord. 2 And he shall lay his hands on the head of the gift, and shall slay it before the Lord, by the doors of the tabernacle of witness. And the priests the sons of Aaron shall pour the blood on the altar of burnt-offerings round about. 3 And they shall bring of the peace-offering a burnt-sacrifice to the Lord, the fat covering the belly, and all the fat on the belly. 4 And the two kidneys and the fat that is upon them; he shall take away that which is on the thighs, and the caul above the liver together with the kidneys. 5 And the priests the sons of Aaron shall offer them on the altar on the burnt-offering, on the wood which is on the fire upon the altar: *it is* a burnt-offering, a smell of sweet savour to the Lord. 6 And if his gift be of the sheep, a peace-offering to the Lord, male or female, he shall bring it unblemished. 7 If he bring a lamb for his gift, he shall bring it before the Lord. 8 And he shall lay his hands on the head of his offering, and shall slay it by the doors of the tabernacle of witness; and the priests the sons of Aaron shall pour out the blood on the altar round about. 9 And he shall bring of the peace-offering a burnt-sacrifice to the Lord: the fat and the hinder part unblemished he shall take away with the loins, and having taken away all the fat that covers the belly, and all the fat that is on the belly, 10 and both the kidneys and the fat that is upon them, *and* that which is on the thighs, and the caul which is on the liver with the kidneys, 11 the priest shall offer these on the altar: *it is* a sacrifice of sweet savour, a burnt-offering to the Lord. 12 And if his offering be of the goats, then shall he bring it before the Lord. 13 And he shall lay his hands on its head; and they shall slay it before the Lord by the doors of the tabernacle of witness; and the priests the sons of Aaron shall pour out the blood on the altar round about. 14 And he shall offer of it a burnt-offering to the Lord, *even* the fat that covers the belly, and all the fat that is on the belly. 15 And both the kidneys, and all the fat that is upon them, that which is upon the thighs, and the caul of the liver with the kidneys, shall he take away. 16 And the priest shall offer it upon the altar: *it is* a burnt-offering, a smell of sweet savour to the Lord. All the fat *belongs* to the Lord. 17 *It is* a perpetual statute throughout your generations, in all your habitations; ye shall eat no fat and no blood.

Lev.4 1 And the Lord spoke to Moses, saying, 2 Speak to the children of Israel, saying, If a soul shall sin unwillingly before the Lord, in any of the commandments of the Lord concerning things which he ought not to do, and shall do some of them; 3 if the anointed priest sin so as to cause the people to sin, then shall he bring for his sin, which he has sinned, an unblemished calf of the herd to the Lord for his sin. 4 And he shall bring the calf to the door of the tabernacle of witness before the Lord, and he shall put his hand on the head of the calf before the Lord, and shall slay the calf in the presence of the Lord. 5 And the anointed priest who has been consecrated having received of the blood of the calf, shall then bring it into the tabernacle of witness. 6 And the priest shall dip his finger into the blood, and sprinkle of the blood seven times before the Lord, over against the holy veil. 7 And the priest shall put of the blood of the calf on the horns of the altar of the compound incense which is before the Lord, which is in the tabernacle of witness; and all the blood of the calf shall he pour out by the foot of the altar of whole-burnt-offerings, which is by the doors of the tabernacle of witness. 8 and all the fat of the calf of the sin-offering shall he take off from it; the fat that covers the inwards, and all the fat that is on the inwards, 9 and the two kidneys, and the fat that is upon them, which is on the thighs, and the caul that is on the liver with the kidneys, them shall he take away, 10 as he takes it away from the calf of the sacrifice of peace-offering, so shall the priest offer it on the altar of burnt-offering. 11 And *they shall take* the skin of the calf, and all his flesh with the head and the extremities and the belly and the dung, 12 and they shall carry out the whole calf out of the camp into a clean place, where they pour out the ashes, and they shall consume it there on wood with fire: it shall be burnt on the ashes poured out. 13 And if the whole congregation of Israel trespass ignorantly, and a thing should escape the notice of the congregation, and they should do one thing forbidden of any of the commands of the Lord, which ought not to be done, and should transgress: 14 and the sin wherein they have sinned should become known to them, then shall the congregation bring an unblemished calf of the herd for a sin-offering, and they shall bring it to the doors of the tabernacle of witness. 15 And the elders of the congregation shall lay their hands on the head of the calf before the Lord, and they shall slay the calf before the Lord. 16 And the anointed priest shall bring in of the blood of the calf into the tabernacle of witness. 17 And the priest shall dip his finger into some of the blood of the calf, and shall sprinkle it seven times before the Lord, in front of the veil of the sanctuary. 18 And the priest shall put some of the blood on the horns of the altar of the incense of composition, which is before the Lord, which is in the tabernacle of witness; and he shall pour out all the blood at the bottom of the altar of whole-burnt-offerings, which is by the door of the tabernacle of witness. 19 And he shall take away all the fat from it, and shall offer it up on the altar. 20 And he shall do to the calf as he did to the calf of the sin-offering, so shall it be done; and the priest shall make atonement for them, and the trespass shall be forgiven them. 21 And they shall carry forth the calf whole without the camp, and they shall burn the calf as they burnt the former calf: it is the sin-offering of the congregation. 22 And if a ruler sin, and break one of all the commands of the Lord his God, *doing the thing* which ought not to be done, unwillingly, and shall sin and trespass, 23 and his trespass wherein he has sinned, be known to him, then shall he offer for his gift a kid of the goats, a male without blemish. 24 And he shall lay his hand on the head of the kid, and they shall kill it in the place where they kill the *victims for* whole-burnt-offerings before the Lord; it is a sin-offering. 25 And the priest shall put some of the blood of the sin-offering with his finger on the horns of the altar of whole-burnt-offering; and he shall pour out all its blood by the bottom of the altar of whole-burnt-offerings. 26 And he shall offer up all his fat on the altar, as the fat of the sacrifice of peace-offering; and the priest shall make atonement for him concerning his sin, and it shall be forgiven him. 27 And if a soul of the people of the land should sin unwillingly, in doing a thing *contrary to* any of the commandments of the Lord, which ought not to be done, and shall transgress, 28 and his sin should be known to him, wherein he has sinned, then shall he bring a kid of the goats, a female without blemish shall he bring for his sin, which he has sinned. 29 And he shall lay his hand on the head of his sin-offering, and they shall slay the kid of the sin-offering in the place where they slay the *victims for* whole-burnt-offerings. 30 And the priest shall take of its blood with his finger, and shall put it on the horns of the altar of whole-burnt-offerings; and all its blood he shall pour forth by the foot of the altar. 31 And he shall take away all the fat, as the fat is taken away from the sacrifice of peace-offering, and the priest shall offer it on the altar for a smell of sweet savour to the Lord; and the priest shall make atonement for him, and *his sin* shall be forgiven him. 32 And if he should offer a lamb for his sin-offering, he shall offer it a female without blemish. 33 And he shall lay his hand on the head of the sin-offerings, and they shall kill it in the place where they kill the *victims for* whole-burnt-offerings. 34 And the priest shall take of the blood of the sin-offering with his finger, and shall put it on the horns of the altar of whole-burnt- offerings, and he shall pour out all its blood by the bottom of the altar of whole-burnt-offering. 35 And he shall take away all his fat, as the fat of the lamb of the sacrifice of peace-offering is taken away, and the priest shall put it on the altar for a whole-burnt-offering to the Lord; and the priest shall make atonement for him for the sin which he sinned, and it shall be forgiven him.

Lev.5 1 And if a soul sin, and hear the voice of swearing, and he is a witness or has seen or been conscious, if he do not report it, he shall bear his iniquity. 2 That soul which shall touch any unclean thing, or carcase, or *that which is* unclean being taken of beasts, or the dead bodies of abominable *reptiles* which are unclean, or carcases of unclean cattle, 3 or should touch the uncleanness of a man, or whatever kind, which he may touch and be defiled by, and it should have escaped him, but afterwards he should know, —then he shall have transgressed. 4 That unrighteous soul, which determines with his lips to do evil or to do good according to whatsoever a man may determine with an oath, and it shall have escaped his notice, and he shall *afterwards* know *it*, and *so* he should sin in some one of these things: 5 —then shall he declare his sin in the tings wherein he has sinned by that sin. 6 And he shall bring for his transgressions against the Lord, for his sin which he has sinned, a ewe lamb of the flock, or a kid of the goats, for a sin-offering; and the priest shall make an atonement for him for his sin which he has sinned, and his sin shall be forgiven him. 7 And if he cannot afford a sheep, he shall bring for his sin which he has sinned, two turtle-doves or two young pigeons to the Lord; one for a sin-offering, and the other for a burnt-offering. 8 And he shall bring them to the priest, and the priest shall bring the sin-offering first; and the priest shall pinch off the head from the neck, and shall not divide the body. 9 And he shall sprinkle of the blood of the sin-offering on the side of the altar, but the rest of the blood he shall drop at the foot of the altar, for it is a sin- offering. 10 And he shall make the second a whole-burnt-offering, as it is fit; and the priest shall make atonement for his sin which he has sinned, and it shall be forgiven him. 11 And if he cannot afford a pair of turtle-doves, or two young pigeons, then shall he bring as his gift for his sin, the tenth part of an ephah of fine flour for a sin-offering; he shall not pour oil upon it, nor shall he put frankincense upon it, because it is a sin-offering. 12 And he shall bring it to the priest; and the priest having taken a handful of it, shall lay the memorial of it on the altar of whole-burnt-offerings to the Lord; it is a sin-offering. 13 And the priest shall make atonement for him for his sin, which he has sinned in one of these things, and it shall be forgiven him; and that which is left shall be the priest's, as an offering of fine flour. 14 And the Lord spoke to Moses, saying, 15 The soul which shall be really unconscious, and shall sin unwillingly in any of the holy things of the Lord, shall even bring to the Lord for his transgression, a ram of the flock without blemish, valued according to shekels of silver according to the shekel of the sanctuary, for his *transgression* wherein he transgressed. 16 And he shall make compensation for that wherein he has sinned in the holy things; and he shall add the fifth part to it, and give it to the priest; and the priest shall make atonement for him with the ram of transgression, and *his sin* shall be forgiven him. 17 And the soul which shall sin, and do one thing *against* any of the commandments of the Lord, which it is not right to do, and has not known it, and shall have transgressed, and shall have contracted guilt, 18 he shall even bring a ram without blemish from the flock, *valued* at a price of silver for his transgression to the priest; and the priest shall make atonement for his trespass of ignorance, wherein he ignorantly trespassed, and he knew it not; and it shall be forgiven him. 19 For he has surely been guilty of transgression before the Lord.

Lev.6 1 And the Lord spoke to Moses, saying, 2 The soul which shall have sinned, and willfully overlooked the commandments of the Lord, and shall have dealt falsely in the affairs of his neighbour in the matter of a deposit, or concerning fellowship, or concerning plunder, or has in anything wronged his neighbour, 3 or has found that which was lost, and shall have lied concerning it, and shall have sworn unjustly concerning *any* one of all the things, whatsoever a man may do, so as to sin hereby; 4 it shall come to pass, whensoever he shall have sinned, and transgressed, that he shall restore the plunder which he has seized, or *redress* the injury which he has committed, or restore the deposit which was entrusted to him, or the lost article which he has found of any kind, about which he swore unjustly, he shall even restore it in full; and he shall add to it a fifth part besides; he shall restore it to him whose it is in the day in which he happens to be convicted. 5 And he shall bring to the Lord for his trespass, a ram of the flock, without blemish, of value to the amount of the thing in which he trespassed. 6 And the priest shall make atonement for him before the Lord, and he shall be forgiven for any one of all the things which he did and trespassed in it. 7 And the Lord spoke to Moses, saying, 8 Charge Aaron and his sons, saying, 9 This *is* the law of whole-burnt-offering; this is the whole-burnt-offering in its burning on the altar all the night till the morning; and the fire of the altar shall burn on it, it shall not be put out. 10 And the priest shall put on the linen tunic, and he shall put the linen drawers on his body; and shall take away that which has been thoroughly burnt, which the fire shall have consumed, even the whole-burnt-offering from the altar, and he shall put it near the altar. 11 And he shall put off his robe, and put on another robe, and he shall take forth the offering that has been burnt without the camp into a clean place. 12 And the fire on the altar shall be kept burning on it, and shall not be extinguished; and the priest shall burn on it wood every morning, and shall heap on it the whole-burnt-offering, and shall lay on it the fat of the peace-offering. 13 And the fire shall always burn on the altar; it shall not be extinguished. 14 This is the law of the sacrifice, which the sons of Aaron shall bring near before the Lord, before the altar. 15 And he shall take from it a handful of the fine flour of the sacrifice with its oil, and with all its

frankincense, which are upon the sacrifice; and he shall offer up on the altar a burnt-offering as a sweet-smelling savour, a memorial of it to the Lord. 16 And Aaron and his sons shall eat that which is left of it: it shall be eaten without leaven in a holy place, they shall eat it in the court of the tabernacle of witness. 17 It shall not be baked with leaven. I have given it as a portion to them of the burnt- offerings of the Lord: it is most holy, as the offering for sin, and as the offering for trespass. 18 Every male of the priests shall eat it: it is a perpetual ordinance throughout your generations of the burnt-offerings of the Lord; whosoever shall touch them shall be hallowed. 19 And the Lord spoke to Moses, saying, 20 This is the gift of Aaron and of his sons, which they shall offer to the Lord in the day in which thou shalt anoint him; the tenth of an ephah of fine flour for a sacrifice continually, the half of it in the morning, and the half of it in the evening. 21 It shall be made with oil in a frying-pan; he shall offer it kneaded *and* in rolls, an offering of fragments, an offering of a sweet savour unto the Lord. 22 The anointed priest who is in his place, *one* of his sons, shall offer it: it is a perpetual statute, it shall all be consumed. 23 And every sacrifice of a priest shall be thoroughly burnt, and shall not be eaten. 24 And the Lord spoke to Moses, saying, 25 Speak to Aaron and to his sons, saying, This is the law of the sin- offering; —in the place where they slay the whole-burnt-offering, they shall slay the sin- offerings before the Lord: they are most holy. 26 The priest that offers it shall eat it: in a holy place it shall be eaten, in the court of the tabernacle of witness. 27 Every one that touches the flesh of it shall be holy, and on whosoever garment any of its blood shall have been sprinkled, whosoever shall have it sprinkled, shall be washed in the holy place. 28 And the earthen vessel, in whichsoever it shall have been sodden, shall be broken; and if it shall have been sodden in a brazen vessel, he shall scour it and wash it with water. 29 Every male among the priests shall eat it: it is most holy to the Lord. 30 And no offerings for sin, of whose blood there shall be brought any into the tabernacle of witness to make atonement in the holy place, shall be eaten: they shall be burned with fire. 31 And this *is* the law of the ram for the trespass-offering; it is most holy. 32 In the place where they slay the whole-burnt-offering, they shall slay the ram of the trespass-offering before the Lord, and he shall pour out the blood at the bottom of the altar round about. 33 And he shall offer all the fat from it; and the loins, and all the fat that covers the inwards, and all the fat that is upon the inwards, 34 and the two kidneys, and the fat that is upon them, that which is upon the thighs, and the caul upon the liver with the kidney, he shall take them away. 35 And the priest shall offer them on the altar a burnt-offering to the Lord; it is for trespass. 36 Every male of the priest shall eat them, in the holy place they shall eat them: they are most holy. 37 As the sin-offering, so also *is* the trespass-offering. There is one law of them; the priest who shall make atonement with it, his it shall be. 38 And *as for* the priest who offers a man's whole-burnt- offering, the skin of the whole-burnt-offering which he offers, shall be his. 39 And every sacrifice which shall be prepared in the oven, and every one which shall be prepared on the hearth, or on a frying-pan, it is the property of the priest that offers it; it shall be his. ⁴⁰ And every sacrifice made up with oil, or not made up *with oil*, shall belong to the sons of Aaron, an equal portion to each.

Lev.7 ¹ This *is* the law of the sacrifice of peace-offering, which they shall bring to the Lord. ² If a man should offer it for praise, then shall he bring, for the sacrifice of praise, loaves of fine flour made up with oil, and unleavened cakes anointed with oil, and fine flour kneaded with oil. ³ With leavened bread he shall offer his gifts, with the peace-offering of praise. ⁴ And he shall bring one of all his gifts, a separate offering to the Lord: it shall belong to the priest who pours forth the blood of the peace-offering. ⁵ And the flesh of the sacrifice of the peace-offering of praise shall be his, and it shall be eaten in the day in which it is offered: they shall not leave of it till the morning. ⁶ And if it be a vow, or he offer his gift of his own will, on whatsoever day he shall offer his sacrifice, it shall be eaten, and on the morrow. ⁷ And that which is left of the flesh of the sacrifice till the third day, shall be consumed with fire. ⁸ And if he do at all eat of the flesh on the third day, it shall not be accepted for him that offers: it shall not be reckoned to him, it is pollution; and whatsoever soul shall eat of it, shall bear his iniquity. ⁹ And whatsoever flesh shall have touched any unclean thing, it shall not be eaten, it shall be consumed with fire; every one that is clean shall eat the flesh. ¹⁰ And whatsoever soul shall eat of the flesh of the sacrifice of the peace-offering which is the Lord's, and his uncleanness be upon him, that soul shall perish from his people. ¹¹ And whatsoever soul shall touch any unclean thing, either of the uncleanness of a man, or of unclean quadrupeds, or any unclean abominable thing, and shall eat of the flesh of the sacrifice of the peace-offering, which is the Lord's, that soul shall perish from his people. ¹² And the Lord spoke to Moses, saying, ¹³ Speak to the children of Israel, saying, Ye shall eat no fat of oxen or sheep or goats. ¹⁴ And the fat of such animals as have died of themselves, or have been seized of beasts, may be employed for any work; but it shall not be eaten for food. ¹⁵ Every one that eats fat off the beasts, from which he will bring a burnt-offering to the Lord— that soul shall perish from his people. ¹⁶ Ye shall eat no blood in all your habitations, either of beasts or of birds. ¹⁷ Every soul that shall eat blood, that soul shall perish from his people. ¹⁸ And the Lord spoke to Moses, saying, ¹⁹ Thou shalt also speak to the children of Israel, saying, He that offers a sacrifice of peace-offering, shall bring his gift to the Lord also from the sacrifice of peace-offering. ²⁰ His hands shall bring the burnt-offerings to the Lord; the fat which is on the breast and the lobe of the liver, he shall bring them, so as to set them for a gift before the Lord. ²¹ And the priest shall offer the fat upon the altar, and the breast shall be Aaron's and his sons, ²² and ye shall give the right shoulder for a choice piece to the priest of your sacrifices of peace-offering. ²³ He that offers the blood of the peace-offering, and the fat, of the sons of Aaron, his shall be the right shoulder for a portion. ²⁴ For I have taken the wave- breast and shoulder of separation from the children of Israel from the sacrifices of your peace-offerings, and I have given them to Aaron the priest and his sons, a perpetual ordinance *due* from the children of Israel. ²⁵ This is the anointing of Aaron, and the anointing of his sons, *their portion* of the burnt-offerings of the Lord, in the day in which he brought them forward to minister as priests to the Lord; ²⁶ as the Lord commanded to give to them in the day in which he anointed them of the sons of Israel, a perpetual statute through their generations. ²⁷ This *is* the law of the whole-burnt-offerings, and of sacrifice, and of sin-offering, and of offering for transgression, and of the sacrifice of consecration, and of the sacrifice of peace-offering; ²⁸ as the Lord commanded Moses in the mount Sina, in the day in which he commanded the children of Israel to offer their gifts before the Lord in the wilderness of Sina.

Lev.8 ¹ And the Lord spoke to Moses, saying, ² Take Aaron and his sons, and his robes and the anointing oil, and the calf for the sin-offering, and the two rams, and the basket of unleavened bread, ³ and assemble the whole congregation at the door of the tabernacle of witness. ⁴ And Moses did as the Lord appointed him, and he assembled the congregation at the door of the tabernacle of witness. ⁵ And Moses said to the congregation, This is the thing which the Lord has commanded you to do. ⁶ And Moses brought nigh Aaron and his sons, and washed them with water, ⁷ and put on him the coat, and girded him with the girdle, and clothed him with the tunic, and put on him the ephod; ⁸ and girded him *with a girdle* according to the make of the ephod, and clasped him closely with it: and put upon it the oracle, and put upon the oracle the Manifestation and the Truth. ⁹ And he put the mitre on his head, and put upon the mitre in front the golden plate, the most holy thing, as the Lord commanded Moses. ¹⁰ And Moses took of the anointing oil, ¹¹ and sprinkled of it seven times on the altar; and anointed the altar, and hallowed it, and all things on it, and the laver, and its foot, and sanctified them; and anointed the tabernacle and all its furniture, and hallowed it. ¹² And Moses poured of the anointing oil on the head of Aaron; and he anointed him and sanctified him. ¹³ And Moses brought the sons of Aaron near, and put on them coast and girded them with girdles, and put on them bonnets, as the Lord commanded Moses. ¹⁴ And Moses brought near the calf for the sin-offering, and Aaron and his sons laid their hands on the head of the calf of the sin-offering. ¹⁵ And he slew it; and Moses took of the blood, and put it on the horns of the altar round about with his finger; and he purified the altar, and poured out the blood at the bottom of the altar, and sanctified it, to make atonement upon it. ¹⁶ And Moses took all the fat that was upon the inwards, and the lobe on the liver, and both the kidneys, and the fat that was upon them, and Moses offered them on the altar. ¹⁷ But the calf, and his hide, and his flesh, and his dung, he burnt with fire without the camp, as the Lord commanded Moses. ¹⁸ And Moses brought near the ram for a whole-burnt-offering, and Aaron and his sons laid their hands on the head of the ram. And Moses slew the ram: and Moses poured the blood on the altar round about. ¹⁹ And he divided the ram by its limbs, and Moses offered the head, and the limbs, and the fat; and he washed the belly and the feet with water. 20 And Moses offered up the whole ram on the altar: it is a whole-burnt-offering for a sweet-smelling savour; it is a burnt-offering to the Lord, as the Lord commanded Moses. 21 And Moses brought the second ram, the ram of consecration, and Aaron and his sons laid their hands on the head of the ram, and *he* slew him; 22 and Moses took of his blood, and put it upon the tip of Aaron's right ear, and on the thumb of his right hand, and on the great toe of his right foot. 23 And Moses brought near the sons of Aaron; and Moses put of the blood on the tips of their right ears, and on the thumbs of their right hands, and on the great toes of their right feet, and Moses poured out the blood on the altar round about. 24 And he took the fat, and the rump, and the fat on the belly, and the lobe of the liver, and the two kidneys, and the fat that is upon them, and the right shoulder. 25 And from the basket of consecration, which was before the Lord, he also took one unleavened loaf, and one loaf made with oil, and one cake; and put *them* upon the fat, and the right shoulder: 26 and put them all on the hands of Aaron, and upon the hands of his sons, and offered them up for a wave-offering before the Lord. 27 And Moses took them at their hands, and Moses offered them on the altar, on the whole-burnt-offering of consecration, which is a smell of sweet savour: it is a burnt-offering to the Lord. 28 And Moses took the breast, and separated it for a heave-offering before the Lord, from the ram of consecration; and it became Moses' portion, as the Lord commanded Moses. 29 And Moses took of the anointing oil, and of the blood that was on the altar, and sprinkled it on Aaron, and on his garments, and his sons, and the garments of his sons with him. 30 And he sanctified Aaron and his garments, and his sons, and the garments of his sons with him. 31 And Moses said to Aaron and to his sons, Boil the flesh in the tent of the tabernacle of witness in the holy place; and there ye shall eat it and the loaves in the basket of consecration, as it has been appointed me, *the Lord* saying, Aaron and his sons shall eat them. 32 And that which is left of the flesh and of the loaves burn ye with fire. 33 And ye shall not go out from the door of the tabernacle of witness for seven days, until the day be fulfilled, the day of your consecration; for in seven days shall he consecrate you, 34 as he did in this day on which the Lord commanded me to do so, to make an atonement for you. 35 And ye shall remain seven days at the door of the tabernacle of witness, day and night; ye shall observe the ordinances of the Lord, that ye die not; for so has the Lord God commanded me. 36 And Aaron and his sons performed all these commands which the Lord commanded Moses.

Lev.9 1 And it came to pass on the eighth day, that Moses called Aaron and his sons, and the elders of Israel, 2 and Moses said to Aaron, Take to thyself a young calf of the herd for a sin-offering, and a ram for a whole-burnt-offering, unblemished, and offer them before the Lord. 3 And speak to the elders of Israel, saying, Take one kid of the goats for a sin-offering, and a young calf, and a lamb of a year old for a whole-burnt-offering, spotless, 4 and a calf and a ram for a peace offering before the Lord, and fine flour mingled with oil, for to-day the Lord will appear among you. 5 And they took as Moses commanded them before the tabernacle of witness, and all the congregation drew nigh, and they stood before the Lord. 6 And Moses said, This is the thing which the Lord has spoken; do *it*, and the glory of the Lord shall appear among you. 7 And Moses said to Aaron, Draw nigh to the altar, and offer thy sin-offering, and thy whole-burnt-offering, and make atonement for thyself, and for thy house; and offer the gifts of the people, and make atonement for them, as the Lord commanded Moses. 8 And Aaron drew nigh to the altar, and slew the calf of his sin-offering. 9 And the sons of Aaron brought the blood to him, and he dipped his finger into the blood, and put it on the horns of the altar, and he poured out the blood at the bottom of the altar. 10 And he offered up on the altar the fat and the kidneys and the lobe of the liver of the sin-offering, according as the Lord commanded Moses. 11 And the flesh and the hide he burnt with fire outside of the camp. 12 And he slew the whole-burnt- offering; and the sons of Aaron brought the blood to him, and he poured it on the altar round about. 13 And they brought the whole-burnt-offering, according to its pieces; them and the head he put upon the altar. 14 And he washed the belly and the feet with water, and he put them on the whole-burnt-offering on the altar. 15 And he brought the gift of the people, and took the goat of the sin-offering of the people, and slew it, and purified it as also the first. 16 And he brought the whole-burnt-offering, and offered it in due form. 17 And he brought the sacrifice and filled his hands with it, and laid it on the altar, besides the morning whole-burnt-offering. 18 And he slew the calf, and the ram of the sacrifice of peace-offering of the people; and the sons of Aaron brought the blood to him, and he poured it out on the altar round about. 19 And *he took* the fat of the calf, and the hind quarters of the ram, and the fat covering the belly, and the two kidneys, and the fat upon them, and the caul on the liver. 20 And he put the fat on the breasts, and offered the fat on the altar. 21 And Aaron separated the breast and the right shoulder as a choice-offering before the Lord, as the Lord commanded Moses. 22 And Aaron lifted up his hands on the people and blessed them; and after he had offered the sin-offering, and the whole-burnt-offerings, and the peace- offerings, he came down. 23 And Moses and Aaron entered into the tabernacle of witness. And they came out and blessed all the people, and the glory of the Lord appeared to all the people. 24 And fire came forth from the Lord, and devoured the offerings on the altar, both the whole- burnt-offerings and the fat; and all the people saw, and were amazed, and fell upon their faces.

Lev.10:1 And the two sons of Aaron, Nadab and Abiud, took each his censer, and put fire therein, and threw incense thereon, and offered strange fire before the Lord, which the Lord did not command them, 2 and fire came forth from the Lord, and devoured them, and they died before the Lord. 3 And Moses said to Aaron, This is the thing which the Lord spoke, saying, I will be sanctified among them that draw night to me, and I will be glorified in the whole congregation; and Aaron was pricked *in his heart*. 4 And Moses called Misadae, and Elisaphan, sons of Oziel, sons of the brother of Aaron's father, and said to them, Draw near and take your brethren from before the sanctuary out of the camp. 5 And they came near and took them in their coats out of the camp, as Moses said. 6 And Moses said to Aaron, and Eleazar and Ithamar his sons that were left, Ye shall not make bare your heads, and ye shall not tear your garments; that ye die not, and *so* there should be wrath on all the congregation: but your brethren, *even* all the house of Israel, shall lament for the burning, with which they were burnt by the Lord. 7 And ye shall not go forth from the door of the tabernacle of witness, that ye die not; for the Lord's anointing oil *is* upon you: and they did according to the word of Moses. 8 And the Lord spoke to Aaron, saying, 9 Ye shall not drink wine nor strong drink, thou and thy sons with thee, whensoever ye enter into the tabernacle of witness, or when ye approach the altar, so shall ye not die; *it is* a perpetual statute for your generations, 10 to distinguish between sacred and profane, and between clean and unclean, 11 and to teach the children of Israel all the statutes, which the Lord spoke to them by Moses. 12 And Moses said to Aaron, and to Eleazar and Ithamar, the sons of Aaron who survived, Take the sacrifice that is left of the burnt- offerings of the Lord, and ye shall eat unleavened bread by the altar: it is most holy. 13 And ye shall eat it in the holy place; for this is a statute for thee and a statute for thy sons, of the burnt- offerings to the Lord; for so it has been commanded me. 14 And ye shall eat the breast of separation, and the shoulder of the choice-offering in the holy place, thou and thy sons and thy house with thee; for it has been given as an ordinance for thee and an ordinance for thy sons, of the sacrifices of peace-offering of the children of Israel. 15 They shall bring the shoulder of the choice-offering, and the breast of the separation upon the burnt-offerings of the fat, to separate for a separation before the Lord; and it shall be a perpetual ordinance for thee and thy sons and thy daughters with thee, as the Lord commanded Moses. 16 And Moses diligently sought the goat of the sin-offering, but it had been consumed by fire; and Moses was angry with Eleazar and Ithamar the sons of Aaron that were left, saying, 17 Why did ye not eat the sin-offering in the holy place? for because it is most holy he has given you this to eat, that ye might take away the sin of the congregation, and make atonement for them before the Lord. 18 For the blood of it was not brought into the holy place: ye shall eat it within, before *the Lord*, as the Lord commanded me. 19 And Aaron spoke to Moses, saying, If they have brought nigh to-day their sin-offerings, and their whole-burnt-offerings before the Lord, and these events have happened to me, and *yet* I should eat to-day of the sin-offerings, would it be pleasing to the Lord? 20 And Moses heard *it*, and it pleased him.

Lev.11 1 And the Lord spoke to Moses and Aaron, saying, 2 Speak ye to the sons of Israel, saying, These are the beasts which ye shall eat of all beasts that are upon the earth. 3 Every beast parting the hoof and making divisions of two claws, and chewing the cud among beasts, these ye shall eat.

4 But of these ye shall not eat, of those that chew the cud, and of those that part the hoofs, and divide claws; the camel, because it chews the cud, but does not divide the hoof, this is unclean to you. 5 And the rabbit, because it chews the cud, but does not divide the hoof, this is unclean to you. 6 And the hare, because it does not chew the cud, and does not divide the hoof, this is unclean to you. 7 And the swine, because this *animal* divides the hoof, and makes claws of the hoof, and it does not chew the cud, is unclean to you. 8 Ye shall not eat of their flesh, and ye shall not touch their carcases; these are unclean to you. 9 And these *are* what ye shall eat of all that are in the waters: all things that have fins and scales in the waters, and in the seas, and in the brooks, these ye shall eat. 10 And all things which have not fins or scales in the water, or in the seas, and in the brooks, of all which the waters produce, and of every soul living in the water, are an abomination; and they shall be abominations to you. 11 Ye shall not eat of their flesh, and ye shall abhor their carcases. 12 And all things that have not fins or scales of those that are in the waters, these are an abomination to you. 13 And these are the things which ye shall abhor of birds, and they shall not be eaten, they are an abomination: the eagle and the ossifrage, and the sea-eagle. 14 And the vulture, and the kite, and the like to it; 15 and the sparrow, and the owl, and the sea-mew, and the like to it: 16 and every raven, and the birds like it, and the hawk and his like, 17 and the night-raven and the cormorant and the stork, 18 and the red-bill, and the pelican, and swan, 19 and the heron, and the lapwing, and the like to it, and the hoopoe and the bat. 20 And all winged creatures that creep, which go upon four feet, are abominations to you. 21 But these ye shall eat of the creeping winged animals, which go upon four feet, which have legs above their feet, to leap with on the earth. 22 And these of them ye shall eat: the caterpillar and his like, and the attacus and his like, and the cantharus and his like, and the locust and his like. 23 Every creeping thing from among the birds, which has four feet, is an abomination to you. 24 And by these ye shall be defiled; every one that touches their carcases shall be unclean till the evening. 25 And every one that takes of their dead bodies shall wash his garments, and shall be unclean till the evening. 26 And whichever among the beasts divides the hoof and makes claws, and does not chew the cud, shall be unclean to you; every one that touches their dead bodies shall be unclean till evening. 27 And every one among all the wild beasts that moves upon its fore feet, which goes on all four, is unclean to you; every one that touches their dead bodies shall be unclean till evening. 28 And he that takes of their dead bodies shall wash his garments, and shall be unclean till evening: these are unclean to you. 29 And these *are* unclean to you of reptiles upon the earth, the weasel, and the mouse, and the lizard, 30 the ferret, and the chameleon, and the evet, and the newt, and the mole. 31 These are unclean to you of all the reptiles which are on the earth; every one who touches their carcases shall be unclean till evening. 32 And on whatsoever one of their dead bodies shall fall it shall be unclean; whatever wooden vessel, or garment, or skin, or sack it may be, every vessel in which work should be done, shall be dipped in water, and shall be

unclean till evening; and *then* it shall be clean. 33 And every earthen vessel into which one of these things shall fall, whatsoever is inside it, shall be unclean, and it shall be broken. 34 And all food that is eaten, on which water shall come *from such a vessel*, shall be unclean; and every beverage which is drunk in any *such* vessel, shall be unclean. 35 And every thing on which there shall fall of their dead bodies shall be unclean; ovens and stands for jars shall be broken down: these are unclean, and they shall be unclean to you. 36 Only *if the water be* of fountains of water, or a pool, or confluence of water, it shall be clean; but he that touches their carcases shall be unclean. 37 And if one of their carcases should fall upon any sowing seed which shall be sown, it shall be clean. 38 But if water be poured on any seed, and one of their dead bodies fall upon it, it is unclean to you. 39 And if one of the cattle die, which it is lawful for you to eat, he that touches their carcases shall be unclean till evening. 40 And he that eats of their carcases shall wash his garments, and be unclean till evening; and he that carries any of their carcases shall wash his garments, and bathe himself in water, and be unclean till evening. 41 And every reptile that creeps on the earth, this shall be an abomination to you; it shall not be eaten. 42 And every *animal* that creeps on its belly, and every one that goes on four *feet* continually, which abounds with feet among all the reptiles creeping upon the earth—ye shall not eat it, for it is an abomination to you. 43 And ye shall not defile your souls with any of the reptiles that creep upon the earth, and ye shall not be polluted with them, and ye shall not be unclean by them. 44 For I am the Lord your God; and ye shall be sanctified, and ye shall be holy, because I the Lord your God am holy; and ye shall not defile your souls with any of the reptiles creeping upon the earth. 45 For I am the Lord who brought you up out of the land of Egypt to be your God; and ye shall be holy, for I the Lord am holy. 46 This is the law concerning beasts and birds and every living creature moving in the water, and every living creature creeping on the earth; 47 to distinguish between the unclean and the clean; and between those that bring forth alive, such as should be eaten, and those that bring forth alive, such as should not be eaten.

Lev.12:1 And the Lord spoke to Moses, saying, 2 Speak to the children of Israel, and thou shalt say to them, Whatsoever woman shall have conceived and born a male child shall be unclean seven days, she shall be unclean according to the days of separation for her monthly courses. 3 And on the eighth day she shall circumcise the flesh of his foreskin. 4 And for thirty-three days she shall continue in her unclean blood; she shall touch nothing holy, and shall not enter the sanctuary, until the days of her purification be fulfilled. 5 But if she should have born a female child, then she shall be unclean twice seven days, according to the time of her monthly courses; and for sixty-six days shall she remain in her unclean blood. 6 And when the days of her purification shall have been fulfilled for a son or a daughter, she shall bring a lamb of a year old without blemish for a whole-burnt-offering, and a young pigeon or turtle-dove for a sin-offering to the door of the tabernacle of witness, to the priest. 7 And he shall present it before the Lord, and the priest shall make atonement for her, and shall purge her from the fountain of her blood; this is the law of her who bears a male or a female. 8 And if she cannot afford a lamb, then shall she take two turtle-doves or two young pigeons, one for a whole-burnt-offering, and one for a sin-offering; and the priest shall make atonement for her, and she shall be purified.

Lev.13 1 And the Lord spoke to Moses and Aaron, saying, 2 If any man should have in the skin of his flesh a bright clear spot, and there should be in the skin of his flesh a plague of leprosy, he shall be brought to Aaron the priest, or to one of his sons the priests. 3 And the priest shall view the spot in the skin of his flesh; and *if* the hair in the spot be changed *to* white, and the appearance of the spot be below the skin of the flesh, it is a plague of leprosy; and the priest shall look upon it, and pronounce him unclean. 4 But if the spot be clear and white in the skin of his flesh, yet the appearance of it be not deep below the skin, and its hair have not changed *itself for* white hair, but it is dark, then the priest shall separate *him that has* the spot seven days; 5 and the priest shall look on the spot the seventh day; and, behold, *if* the spot remains before him, *if* the spot has not spread in the skin, then the priest shall separate him the second time seven days. 6 And the priest shall look upon him the second time on the seventh day; and, behold, *if* the spot be dark, *and* the spot have not spread in the skin, then the priest shall pronounce him clean; for it is a *mere* mark, and the man shall wash his garments and be clean. 7 But if the bright spot should have changed and spread in the skin, after the priest has seen him for the purpose of purifying him, then shall he appear the second time to the priest, 8 and the priest shall look upon him; and, behold, *if* the mark have spread in the skin, then the priest shall pronounce him unclean: it is a leprosy. 9 And if a man have a plague of leprosy, then he shall come to the priest; 10 and the priest shall look, and, behold, if it is a white spot in the skin, and it has changed the hair to white, and *there be* some of the sound part of the quick flesh in the sore— 11 it is a leprosy waxing old in the skin of the flesh; and the priest shall pronounce him unclean, and shall separate him, because he is unclean. 12 And if the leprosy should have come out very evidently in the skin, and the leprosy should cover all the skin of the patient from the head to the feet, wheresoever the priest shall look; 13 then the priest shall look, and, behold, the leprosy has covered all the skin of the flesh; and the priest shall pronounce him clean of the plague, because it has changed all to white, it is clean. 14 But on whatsoever day the quick flesh shall appear on him, he shall be pronounced unclean. 15 And the priest shall look upon the sound flesh, and the sound flesh shall prove him to be unclean; for it is unclean, it is a leprosy. 16 But if the sound flesh be restored and changed *to* white, then shall he come to the priest; 17 and the priest shall see *him*, and, behold, *if* the plague is turned white, then the priest shall pronounce the patient clean: he is clean. 18 And if the flesh should have become an ulcer in his skin, and should be healed, 19 and there should be in the place of the ulcer a white sore, or *one* looking white and bright, or fiery, and it shall be seen by the priest; 20 then the priest shall look, and, behold, if the appearance be beneath the skin, and its hair has changed to white, then the priest shall pronounce him unclean; because it is a leprosy, it has broken out in the ulcer. 21 But if the priest look, and behold there is no white hair on it, and it be not below the skin of the flesh, and it be dark- coloured; then the priest shall separate him seven days. 22 But if it manifestly spread over the skin, then the priest shall pronounce him unclean: it is a plague of leprosy; it has broken out in the ulcer. 23 But if the bright spot should remain in its place and not spread, it is the scar of the ulcer; and the priest shall pronounce him clean. 24 And if the flesh be in his skin *in a state of* fiery inflammation, and there should be in his skin the part which is healed of the inflammation, bright, clear, and white, suffused with red or very white; 25 then the priest shall look upon him, and, behold, *if* the hair being white is changed to a bright colour, and its appearance is lower than the skin, it is a leprosy; it has broken out in the inflammation, and the priest shall pronounce him unclean: it is a plague of leprosy. 26 But if the priest should look, and, behold, there is not in the bright spot any white hair, and it should not be lower than the skin, and it should be dark, then the priest shall separate him seven days. 27 And the priest shall look upon him on the seventh day; and if the spot be much spread in the skin, then the priest shall pronounce him unclean: it is a plague of leprosy, it has broken out in the ulcer. 28 But if the bright spot remain stationary, and be not spread in the skin, but *the sore* should be dark, it is a scar of inflammation; and the priest shall pronounce him clean, for it is the mark of the inflammation. 29 And if a man or a woman have in them a plague of leprosy in the head or the beard; 30 then the priest shall look on the plague, and, behold, *if* the appearance of it be beneath the skin, and in it there be thin yellowish hair, then the priest shall pronounce him unclean: it is a scurf, it is a leprosy of the head or a leprosy of the beard. 31 And if the priest should see the plague of the scurf, and, behold, the appearance of it be not beneath the skin, and there is no yellowish hair in it, then the priest shall set apart *him that has* the plague of the scurf seven days. 32 And the priest shall look at the plague on the seventh day; and, behold, *if* the scurf be not spread, and there be no yellowish hair on it, and the appearance of the scurf is not hollow under the skin; 33 then the skin shall be shaven, but the scurf shall not be shaven; and the priest shall set aside the person having the scurf the second time for seven days. 34 And the priest shall see the scurf on the seventh day; and, behold, *if* the scurf is not spread in the skin after the man's being shaved, and the appearance of the scurf is not hollow beneath the skin, then the priest shall pronounce him clean; and he shall wash his garments, and be clean. 35 But if the scurf be indeed spread in the skin after he has been purified, 36 then the priest shall look, and, behold, *if* the scurf be spread in the skin, the priest shall not examine concerning the yellow hair, for he is unclean. 37 But if the scurf remain before *him* in its place, and a dark hair should have arisen in it, the scurf is healed: he is clean, and the priest shall pronounce him clean. 38 And if a man or woman should have in the skin of their flesh spots of a bright whiteness, 39 then the priest shall look; and, behold, there *being* bright spots of a bright whiteness in the skin of their flesh, it is a tetter; it burst forth in the skin of his flesh; he is clean. 40 And if any one's head should lose the hair, he is *only* bald, he is clean. 41 And if his head should lose the hair in front, he is forehead bald: he is clean. 42 And if there should be in his baldness of head, or his baldness of forehead, a white or fiery plague, it is leprosy in his baldness of head, or baldness of forehead. 43 And the priest shall look upon him, and, behold, if the appearance of the plague be white or inflamed in his baldness of head or baldness in front, as the appearance of leprosy in the skin of his flesh, 44 he is a leprous man: the priest shall surely pronounce him unclean, his plague is in his head. 45 And the leper in whom the plague is, let his garments be ungirt, and his head uncovered; and let him have a covering put upon his mouth, and he shall be called unclean. 46 All the days in which the plague shall be upon him, being unclean, he shall be *esteemed* unclean; he shall dwell apart, his place of sojourn shall be without the camp. 47 And if a garment have in it the plague of leprosy, a garment of wool, or a garment of flax, 48 either in the warp or in the woof, or in the linen, or in the woollen threads, or in a skin, or in any workmanship of skin, 49 and the plague be greenish or reddish in the skin, or in the garment, either in the warp, or in the woof, or in any utensil of skin, it is a plague of leprosy, and he shall show it to the priest. 50 And the priest shall look upon the plague, and the priest shall set apart *that which has* the plague seven days. 51 And the priest shall look upon the plague on the seventh day; and if the plague be spread in the garment, either in the warp or in the woof, or in the skin, in whatsoever things skins may be used in their workmanship, the plague is a confirmed leprosy; it is unclean. 52 He shall burn the garment, either the warp or woof in woollen garments or in flaxen, or in any utensil of skin, in which there may be the plague; because it is a confirmed leprosy; it shall be burnt with fire. 53 And if the priest should see, and the plague be not spread in the garments, either in the warp or in the woof, or in any utensil of skin, 54 then the priest shall give directions, and *one* shall wash that on which there may have been the plague, and the priest shall set it aside a second time for seven days. 55 And the priest shall look upon it after the plague has been washed; and *if* this, even the plague, has not changed its appearance, and the plague does not spread, it is unclean; it shall be burnt with fire: it is fixed in the garment, in the warp, or in the woof. 56 And if the priest should look, and the spot be dark after it has been washed, he shall tear it off from the garment, either from the warp or from the woof, or from the skin. 57 And if it should still appear in the garment, either in the warp or in the woof, or in any article of skin, it is a leprosy bursting forth: that wherein is the plague shall be burnt with fire. 58 And the garment, or the warp, or the woof, or any article of skin, which shall be washed, and the plague depart from it, shall also be washed again, and shall be clean. 59 This is the law of the plague of leprosy of a woollen or linen garment, either of the warp, or woof, or any leathern article, to pronounce it clean or unclean.

Lev.14 1 And the Lord spoke to Moses, saying, 2 This is the law of the leper: in whatsoever day he shall have been cleansed, then shall he be brought to the priest. 3 And the priest shall come forth out of the camp, and the priest shall look, and, behold, the plague of the leprosy is removed from the leper. 4 And the priest shall give directions, and they shall take for him that is cleansed two clean live birds, and cedar wood, and spun scarlet, and hyssop. 5 And the priest shall give direction, and they shall kill one bird over an earthen vessel over running water. 6 And as for the living bird he shall take it, and the cedar wood, and the spun scarlet, and the hyssop, and he shall dip them and the living bird into the blood of the bird that was slain over running water. 7 And he shall sprinkle seven times upon him that was cleansed of his leprosy, and he shall be clean; and he shall let go the living bird into the field. 8 and the man that has been cleansed shall wash his garments, and shall shave off all his hair, and shall wash himself in water, and shall be clean; and after that he shall go into the camp, and shall remain out of his house seven days. 9 And it shall come to pass on the seventh day, he shall shave off all his hair, his head and his beard, and his eye-brows, even all his hair shall he shave; and he shall wash his garments, and wash his body with water, and shall be clean. 10 And on the eighth day he shall take two lambs without spot of a year old, and one ewe lamp without spot of a year old, and three-tenths of fine flour for sacrifice kneaded with oil, and one small cup of oil. 11 And the priest that cleanses shall present the man under purification, and these *offerings* before the Lord, at the door of the tabernacle of witness. 12 And the priest shall take one lamb, and offer him for a trespass-offering, and the cup of oil, and set them apart for a special offering before the Lord. 13 and they shall kill the lamb in the place where they kill the whole-burnt-offerings, and the sin-offerings, in the holy places; for it is a sin-offering: as the trespass-offering, it belongs to the priest, it is most holy. 14 And the priest shall take of the blood of the trespass-offering, and the priest shall put it on the tip of the right ear of the person under cleansing, and on the thumb of his right hand, and on the great toe of his right foot. 15 And the priest shall take of the cup of oil, and shall pour it upon his own left hand. 16 And he shall dip with the finger of his right hand *into* some of the oil that is in his left hand, and he shall sprinkle with his finger seven times before the Lord. 17 And the remaining oil that is in his hand, the priest shall put on the tip of the right ear of him that is under cleansing, and on the thumb of his right hand, and on the great toe of his right foot, on the place of the blood of the trespass-offering. 18 And the remaining oil that is on the hand of the priest, the priest shall put on the head of the cleansed *leper*, and the priest shall make atonement for him before the Lord. 19 And the priest shall sacrifice the sin-offering, and the priest shall make atonement for the person under purification *to cleanse him* from his sin, and afterwards the priest shall slay the whole-burnt-offering. 20 And the priest shall offer the whole-burnt-offering, and the sacrifice upon the altar before the Lord; and the priest shall make atonement for him, and he shall be cleansed. 21 And if he should be poor, and cannot afford so much, he shall take one lamb for his transgression for a separate-offering, so as to make propitiation for him, and a tenth deal of fine flour mingled with oil for a sacrifice, and one cup of oil, 22 and two turtle-doves, or two young pigeons, as he can afford; and the one shall be for a sin-offering, and the other for a whole-burnt-offering. 23 And he shall bring them on the eighth day, to purify him, to the priest, to the door of the tabernacle of witness before the Lord. 24 And the priest shall take the lamb of the trespass- offering, and the cup of oil, and place them for a set-offering before the Lord. 25 And he shall slay the lamb of the trespass-offering; and the priest shall take of the blood of the trespass- offering, and put it on the tip of the right ear of him that is under purification, and on the thumb of his right hand, and on the great toe of his right foot. 26 And the priest shall pour of the oil on his own left hand. 27 And the priest shall sprinkle with the finger of his right hand some of the oil that is in his left hand seven times before the Lord. 28 And the priest shall put of the oil that is on his hand on the tip of the right ear of him that is under purification, and on the thumb of his right hand, and on the great toe of his right foot, on the place of the blood of the trespass- offering. 29 And that which is left of the oil which is on the hand of the priest he shall put on the head of him that is purged, and the priest shall make atonement for him before the Lord. 30 And he shall offer one of the turtle-doves or of the young pigeons, as he can afford it, 31 the one for a sin-offering, the other for a whole-burnt-offering with the meat-offering, and the priest shall make an atonement before the Lord for him that is under purification. 32 This is the law for him in whom is the plague of leprosy, and who cannot afford the offerings for his purification. 33 And the Lord spoke to Moses and Aaron, saying, 34 Whensoever ye shall enter into the land of the Chananites, which I give you for a possession, and I shall put the plague of leprosy in the houses of the land of your possession; 35 then the owner of the house shall come and report to the priest, saying, I have seen as it were a plague in the house. 36 And the priest shall give orders to remove the furniture of the house, before the priest comes in to see the plague, and *thus* none of the things in the house shall become unclean; and afterwards the priest shall go in to examine the house. 37 And he shall look on the plague, and, behold, *if* the plague is in the walls of the house, *he will see* greenish or reddish cavities, and the appearance of them *will be* beneath the surface of the walls. 38 And the priest shall come out of the house to the door of the house, and the priest shall separate the house seven days. 39 And the priest shall return on the seventh day and view the house; and, behold, *if* the plague is spread in the walls of the house, 40 then the priest shall give orders, and they shall take away the stones in which the plague is, and shall cast them out of the city into an unclean place. 41 And they shall scrape the house within round about, and shall pour out the dust scraped off outside the city into an unclean place. 42 And they shall take other scraped stones, and put them in the place of the *former* stones, and they shall take other plaster and plaster the house. 43 And if the plague should return again, and break out in the house after they have taken away the stones and after the house is scraped, and after it has been plastered, 44 then the priest shall go in and see if the plague is spread in the house: it is a confirmed leprosy in the house, it is unclean. 45 And they shall take down the house, and its timbers and its stones, and they shall carry out all the mortar without the city into an unclean place. 46 And he that goes into the house at any time, during its separation, shall be unclean until evening. 47 And he that sleeps in the house shall wash his garments, and be unclean until evening; and he that eats in the house shall wash his garments, and be unclean until evening. 48 and if the priest shall arrive and enter and see, and behold the plague be not at all spread in the house after the house has been plastered, then the priest shall declare the house clean, because the plague is healed. 49 And he shall take to purify the house two clean living birds, and cedar wood, and spun scarlet, and hyssop. 50 And he shall slay one bird in an earthen vessel over running water. 51 And he shall take the cedar wood, and the spun scarlet, and the hyssop, and the living bird; and shall dip it into the blood of the bird slain over running water, and with them he shall sprinkle the house seven times. 52 and he shall purify the house with the blood of the bird, and with the running water, and with the living bird, and with the cedar wood, and with the hyssop, and with the spun scarlet. 53 And he shall let the living bird go out of the city into the field, and shall make atonement for the house, and it shall be clean. 54 This *is* the law concerning every plague of leprosy and scurf, 55 and of the leprosy of a garment, and of a house, 56 and of a sore, and of a clear spot, and of a shining one, 57 and of declaring in what day it is unclean, and in what day it shall be purged: this *is* the law of the leprosy.

Lev.15 1 And the Lord spoke to Moses and Aaron, saying, 2 Speak to the children of Israel, and thou shalt say to them, Whatever man shall have an issue out of his body, his issue is unclean. 3 And this *is* the law of his uncleanness; whoever has a gonorrhoea out of his body, this is his uncleanness in him by reason of the issue, by which, his body is affected through the issue: all the days of the issue of his body, by which his body is affected through the issue, there is his uncleanness. 4 Every bed on which he that has the issue shall happen to lie, is unclean; and every seat on which he that has the issue may happen to sit, shall be unclean. 5 And the man who shall touch his bed, shall wash his garments, and bathe himself in water, and shall be unclean till evening. 6 And whosoever sits on the seat on which he that has the issue may have sat, shall wash his garments, and bathe himself in water, and shall be unclean until evening. 7 And he that touches the skin of him that has the issue, shall wash his garments and bathe himself in water, and shall be unclean till evening. 8 And if he that has the issue should spit upon one that is clean, *that person* shall wash his garments, and bathe himself in water, and be unclean until evening. 9 And every ass's saddle, on which the man with the issue shall have mounted, shall be unclean till evening. 10 And every one that touches whatsoever shall have been under him shall be unclean until evening; and he that takes them up shall wash his garments, and bathe himself in water, and shall be unclean until evening. 11 And whomsoever he that has the issue shall touch, if he have not rinsed his hands in water, he shall wash his garments, and bathe his body in water, and shall be unclean until evening. 12 And the earthen vessel which he that has the issue shall happen to touch, shall be broken; and a wooden vessel shall be washed with water, and shall be clean. 13 and if he that has the issue should be cleansed of his issue, then shall he number to himself seven days for his purification; and he shall wash his garments, and bathe his body in water, and shall be clean. 14 And on the eighth day he shall take to himself two turtle-doves or two young pigeons, and he shall bring them before the Lord to the doors of the tabernacle of witness, and shall give them to the priest. 15 And the priest shall offer them one for a sin-offering, and the other for a whole-burnt-offering; and the priest shall make atonement for him before the Lord for his issue. 16 And the man whose seed of copulation shall happen to go forth from him, shall then wash his whole body, and shall be unclean until evening. 17 And every garment, and every skin on which there shall be the seed of copulation shall both be washed with water, and be unclean until evening. 18 And a woman, if a man shall lie with her with seed of copulation—they shall both bathe themselves in water and shall be unclean until evening. 19 And the woman whosoever shall have an issue of blood, when her issue shall be in her body, shall be seven days in her separation; every one that touches her shall be unclean until evening. 20 And every thing whereon she shall lie in her separation, shall be unclean; and whatever she shall sit upon, shall be unclean. 21 And whosoever shall touch her bed shall wash his garments, and bathe his body in water, and shall be unclean until evening. 22 and every one that touches any vessel on which she shall sit, shall wash his garments and bathe himself in water, and shall be unclean until evening. 23 And whether it be while she is on her bed, or on a seat which she may happen to sit upon when he touches her, he shall be unclean till evening. 24 And if any one shall lie with her, and her uncleanness be upon him, he shall be unclean seven days; and every bed on which he shall have lain shall be unclean. 25 And if a woman have an issue of blood many days, not in the time of her separation; if the blood should also flow after her separation, all the days of the issue of her uncleanness *shall be* as the days of her separation: she shall be unclean. 26 And every bed on which she shall lie all the days of her flux shall be to her as the bed of her separation, and every seat whereon she shall sit shall be unclean according to the uncleanness of her separation. 27 Every one that touches it shall be unclean; and he shall wash his garments, and bathe his body in water, and shall be unclean till evening. 28 But if she shall be cleansed from her flux, then she shall number to herself seven days, and afterwards she shall be esteemed clean. 29 And on the eighth day she shall take two turtle-doves, or two young pigeons, and shall bring them to the priest, to the door of the tabernacle of witness. 30 And the priest shall offer one for a sin-offering, and the other for a whole-burnt-offering, and the priest shall make atonement for her before the Lord for her unclean flux. 31 And ye shall cause the children of Israel to beware of their uncleannesses; so they shall not die for their uncleanness, in polluting my tabernacle that is among them. 32 This is the law of the man who has an issue, and if one discharge seed of copulation, so that he should be polluted by it. 33 And *this is the law* for her that has the issue of blood in her separation, and as to the person who has an issue of seed, in his issue: *it is a law* for the male and the female, and for the man who shall have lain with her that is set apart.

Lev.16 1 And the Lord spoke to Moses after the two sons of Aaron died in bringing strange fire before the Lord, so they died. 2 And the Lord said to Moses, Speak to Aaron thy brother, and let him not come in at all times into the holy place within the veil before the propitiatory, which is upon the ark of the testimony, and he shall not die; for I will appear in a cloud on the propitiatory. 3 Thus shall Aaron enter into the holy place; with a calf of the herd for a sin- offering, and *having* a ram for a whole-burnt-offering. 4 And he shall put on the consecrated linen tunic, and he shall have on his flesh the linen drawers, and shall gird himself with a linen girdle, and shall put on the linen cap, they are holy garments; and he shall bathe all his body in water, and shall put them on. 5 And he shall take of the congregation of the children of Israel two kids of the goats for a sin-offering, and one lamb for a whole-burnt-offering. 6 And Aaron shall bring the calf for his own sin-offering, and shall make atonement for himself and for his house. 7 And he shall take the two goats, and place them before the Lord by the door of the tabernacle of witness. 8 and Aaron shall cast lots upon the two goats, one lot for the Lord, and the other for the scape-goat. 9 And Aaron shall bring forward the goat on which the lot for the Lord fell, and shall offer him for a sin-offering. 10 and the goat upon which the lot of the scape- goat came, he shall present alive before the Lord, to make atonement upon him, so as to send him away as a scape-goat, and he shall send him into the wilderness. 11 And Aaron shall bring the calf for his sin, and he shall make atonement for himself and for his house, and he shall kill the calf for his sin-offering. 12 And he shall take his censer full of coals of fire off the altar, which is before the Lord; and he shall fill his hands with fine compound incense, and shall bring it within the veil. 13 And he shall put the incense on the fire before the Lord, and the smoke of the incense shall cover the mercy-seat over the tables of testimony, and he shall not die. 14 And he shall take of the blood of the calf, and sprinkle with his finger on the mercy-seat eastward: before the mercy-seat shall he sprinkle seven times of the blood with his finger. 15 And he shall kill the goat for the sin-offering that is for the people, before the Lord; and he shall bring in of its blood within the veil, and shall do with its blood as he did with the blood of the calf, and shall sprinkle its blood on the mercy-seat, in front of the mercy-seat. 16 and he shall make atonement for the sanctuary on account of the uncleanness of the children of Israel, and for their trespasses in the matter of all their sins; and thus shall he do to the tabernacle of witness established among them in the midst of their uncleanness. 17 and there shall be no man in the tabernacle of witness, when he goes in to make atonement in the holy place, until he shall have come out; and he shall make atonement for himself, and for his house, and for all the congregation of the children of Israel. 18 And he shall come forth to the altar that is before the Lord, and he shall make atonement upon it; and he shall take of the blood of the calf, and of the blood of the goat, and shall put it on the horns of the altar round about. 19 And he shall sprinkle some of the blood upon it seven times with his finger, and shall purge it, and hallow it from the uncleanness of the children of Israel. 20 And he shall finish making atonement for the sanctuary and for the tabernacle of witness, and for the altar; and he shall make a cleansing for the priests, and he shall bring the living goat; 21 and Aaron shall lay his hands on the head of the live goat, and he shall declare over him all the iniquities of the children of Israel, and all their unrighteousness, and all their sins; and he shall lay them upon the head of the live goat, and shall send him by the hand of a ready man into the wilderness. 22 And the goat shall bear their unrighteousnesses upon him into a desert land; and Aaron shall send away the goat into the wilderness. 23 And Aaron shall enter into the tabernacle of witness, and shall put off the linen garment, which he had put on, as he entered into the holy place, and shall lay it by there. 24 And he shall bathe his body in water in the holy place, and shall put on his raiment, and shall go out and offer the whole-burnt-offering for himself and the whole-burnt-offering for the people: and shall make atonement for himself and for his house, and for the people, as for the priests. 25 And he shall offer the fat for the sin-offering on the altar. 26 And he that sends forth the goat that has been set apart to be let go, shall wash his garments, and bathe his body in water, and afterwards shall enter into the camp. 27 And the calf for the sin offering, and the goat for the sin-offering, whose blood was brought in to make atonement in the holy place, they shall carry forth out of the camp, and burn them with fire, even their skins and their flesh and their dung. 28 And he that burns them shall wash his garments, and bathe his body in water, and afterwards he shall enter into the camp. 29 And this shall be a perpetual statute for you; in the seventh month, on the tenth day of the month, ye shall humble your souls, and shall do no work, the native and the stranger who abides among you. 30 For in this day he shall make an atonement for you, to cleanse you from all your sins before the Lord, and ye shall be purged. 31 This shall be to you a most holy sabbath, a rest, and ye shall humble your souls; it is a perpetual ordinance. 32 The priest whomsoever they shall anoint shall make atonement, and whomsoever they shall consecrate to exercise the priestly office after his father; and he shall put on the linen robe, the holy garment. 33 And he shall make atonement for the most holy place, and the tabernacle of witness; and he shall make atonement for the altar, and for the priests; and he shall make atonement for all the congregation. 34 And this shall be to you a perpetual statute to make atonement for the children of Israel for all their sins: it shall be done once in the year, as the Lord commanded Moses.

Lev.17 1 And the Lord spoke to Moses, saying, 2 Speak to Aaron and to his sons, and to all the children of Israel, and thou shalt say to them, This is the word which the Lord has commanded, saying, 3 Every man of the children of Israel, or of the strangers abiding among you, who shall kill a calf, or a sheep, or a goat in the camp, or who shall kill it out of the camp, 4 and shall not bring it to the door of the tabernacle of witness, so as to sacrifice it for a whole-burnt-offering or peace-offering to the Lord to be acceptable for a sweet-smelling savour: and whosoever shall slay it without, and shall not bring it to the door of the tabernacle of witness, so as to offer it as a gift to the Lord before the tabernacle of the Lord; blood shall be imputed to that man, he has shed blood; that soul shall be cut off from his people. 5 That the children of Israel may offer their sacrifices, all that they shall slay in the fields, and bring them to the Lord unto the doors of the tabernacle of witness to the priest, and they shall sacrifice them as a peace-offering to the Lord. 6 And the priest shall pour the blood on the altar round about before the Lord by the doors of the tabernacle of witness, and shall offer the fat for a sweet-smelling savour to the Lord. 7 And they shall no longer offer their sacrifices to vain *gods* after which they go a whoring; it shall be a perpetual statute to you for your generations. 8 And thou shalt say to them, Whatever man of the children of Israel, or of the sons of the proselytes abiding among you, shall offer a whole-burnt-offering or a sacrifice, 9 and shall not bring it to the door of the tabernacle of witness to sacrifice it to the Lord, that man shall be destroyed from among his people. 10 And whatever man of the children of Israel, or of the strangers abiding among you, shall eat any blood, I will even set my face against that soul that eats blood, and will destroy it from its people. 11 For the life of flesh is its blood, and I have given it to you on the altar to make atonement for your souls; for its blood shall make atonement for the soul. 12 Therefore I said to the children of Israel, No soul of you shall eat blood, and the stranger that abides among you shall not eat blood. 13 And whatever man of the children of Israel, or of the strangers abiding among you shall take any animal in hunting, beast, or bird, which is eaten, then shall he pour out the blood, and cover it in the dust. 14 For the blood of all flesh is its life; and I said to the children of Israel, Ye shall not eat the blood of any flesh, for the life of all flesh is its blood: every one that eats it shall be destroyed. 15 And every soul which eats that which has died of itself, or is taken of beasts, either among the natives or among the strangers, shall wash his garments, and bathe himself in water, and shall be unclean until evening: then shall he be clean. 16 But if he do not wash his garments, and do not bathe his body in water, then shall he bear his iniquity.

Lev.18 1 And the Lord spoke to Moses, saying, 2 Speak to the children of Israel, and thou shalt say to them, I *am* the Lord your God. 3 Ye shall not do according to the devices of Egypt, in which ye dwelt: and according to the devices of the land of Chanaan, into which I bring you, ye shall not do; and ye shall not walk in their ordinances. 4 Ye shall observe my judgments, and shall keep my ordinances, and shall walk in them: I *am* the Lord your God. 5 So ye shall keep all my ordinances, and all my judgments, and do them; which if a man do, he shall live in them: I *am* the Lord your God. 6 No man shall draw nigh to any of his near kindred to uncover their nakedness; I *am* the Lord. 7 Thou shalt not uncover the nakedness of thy father, or the nakedness of thy mother, for she is thy mother; thou shalt not uncover her nakedness. 8 Thou shalt not uncover the nakedness of thy father's wife; it is thy father's nakedness. 9 The nakedness of thy sister by thy father or by thy mother, born at home or abroad, their nakedness thou shalt not uncover. 10 The nakedness of thy son's daughter, or thy daughter's daughter, their nakedness thou shalt not uncover; because it is thy nakedness. 11 Thou shalt not uncover the nakedness of the daughter of thy father's wife; she is thy sister by the same father: thou shalt not uncover her nakedness. 12 Thou shalt not uncover the nakedness of thy father's sister, for she is near akin to thy father. 13 Thou shalt not uncover the nakedness of thy mother's sister, for she is near akin to thy mother. 14 Thou shalt not uncover the nakedness of thy father's brother, and thou shalt not go in to his wife; for she is thy relation. 15 Thou shalt not uncover the nakedness of thy daughter-in-law, for she is thy son's wife, thou shalt not uncover her nakedness. 16 Thou shalt not uncover the nakedness of thy brother's wife: it is thy brother's nakedness. 17 The nakedness of a woman and her daughter shalt thou not uncover; her son's daughter, and her daughter's daughter, shalt thou not take, to uncover their nakedness, for they are thy kinswomen: it is impiety. 18 Thou shalt not take a wife in addition to her sister, as a rival, to uncover her nakedness in opposition to her, while she is yet living. 19 And thou shalt not go in to a woman under separation for her uncleanness, to uncover her nakedness. 20 And thou shalt not lie with thy neighbour's wife, to defile thyself with her. 21 And thou shalt not give of thy seed to serve a ruler; and thou shalt not profane my holy name; I *am* the Lord. 22 And thou shalt not lie with a man as with a woman, for it is an abomination. 23 Neither shalt thou lie with any quadruped for copulation, to be polluted with it: neither shall a woman present herself before any quadruped to have connexion with it; for it is an abomination. 24 Do not defile yourselves with any of these things; for in all these things the nations are defiled, which I drive out before you, 25 and the land is polluted; and I have recompensed their iniquity to them because of it, and the land is aggrieved with them that dwell upon it. 26 And ye shall keep all my statutes and all my ordinances, and ye shall do none of these abominations; neither the native, nor the stranger that joins himself with you: 27 (for all these abominations the men of the land did who were before you, and the land was defiled,) 28 and lest the land be aggrieved with you in your polluting it, as it was aggrieved with the nations before you. 29 For whosoever shall do any of these abominations, the souls that do them shall be destroyed from among their people. 30 And ye shall keep mine ordinances, that ye may not do any of the abominable practices, which have taken place before your time: and ye shall not be polluted in them; for I *am* the Lord your God.

Lev.19 ¹ And the Lord spoke to Moses, saying, ² Speak to the congregation of the children of Israel, and thou shalt say to them, Ye shall be holy; for I the Lord your God *am* holy. ³ Let every one of you reverence his father and his mother; and ye shall keep my sabbaths: I *am* the Lord your God. ⁴ Ye shall not follow idols, and ye shall not make to yourselves molten gods: I *am* the Lord your God. ⁵ And if ye will sacrifice a peace-offering to the Lord, ye shall offer it acceptable from yourselves. ⁶ In what day soever ye shall sacrifice it, it shall be eaten; and on the following day, and if any of it should be left till the third day, it shall be thoroughly burnt with fire. ⁷ And if it should be at all eaten on the third day, it is unfit for sacrifice: it shall not be accepted. ⁸ And he that eats it shall bear his iniquity, because he has profaned the holy things of the Lord; and the souls that eat it shall be destroyed from among their people. ⁹ And when ye reap the harvest of your land, ye shall not complete the reaping of your field with exactness, and thou shalt not gather that which falls from thy reaping. ¹⁰ And thou shalt not go over the gathering of thy vineyard, neither shalt thou gather the remaining grapes of thy vineyard: thou shalt leave them for the poor and the stranger: I am the Lord your God. ¹¹ Ye shall not steal, ye shall not lie, neither shall one bear false witness as an informer against his neighbour. ¹² And ye shall not swear unjustly by my name, and ye shall not profane the holy name of your God: I am the Lord your God. ¹³ Thou shalt not injure thy neighbour, neither do thou rob *him*, neither shall the wages of thy hireling remain with thee until the morning. ¹⁴ Thou shalt not revile the deaf, neither shalt thou put a stumbling-block in the way of the blind; and thou shalt fear the Lord thy God: I am the Lord your God. ¹⁵ Thou shalt not act unjustly in judgment: thou shalt not accept the person of the poor, nor admire the person of the mighty; with justice shalt thou judge thy neighbour. ¹⁶ Thou shalt not walk deceitfully among thy people; thou shalt not rise up against the blood of thy neighbour: I am the Lord your God. ¹⁷ Thou shalt not hate thy brother in thine heart: thou shalt in any wise rebuke thy neighbour, so thou shalt not bear sin on his account. ¹⁸ And thy hand shall not avenge thee; and thou shalt not be angry with the children of thy people; and thou shalt love thy neighbour as thyself; I am the Lord. ¹⁹ Ye shall observe my law: thou shalt not let thy cattle gender with one of a different kind, and thou shalt not sow thy vineyard with diverse seed; and thou shalt not put upon thyself a mingled garment woven of two *materials*. ²⁰ And if any one lie carnally with a woman, and she should be a home-servant kept for a man, and she has not been ransomed, *and* her freedom has not been given to her, they shall be visited *with punishment*; but they shall not die, because she was not set at liberty. ²¹ And he shall bring for his trespass to the Lord to the door of the tabernacle of witness, a ram for a trespass-offering. ²² And the priest shall make atonement for him with the ram of the trespass-offering, before the Lord, for the sin which he sinned; and the sin which he sinned shall be forgiven him. ²³ And whenever ye shall enter into the land which the Lord your God gives you, and shall plant any fruit-tree, then shall ye purge away its uncleanness; its fruit shall be three years uncleansed to you, it shall not be eaten. ²⁴ And in the fourth year all its fruit shall be holy, a subject of praise to the Lord. ²⁵ And in the fifth year ye shall eat the fruit, its produce is an increase to you. I am the Lord your God. ²⁶ Eat not on the mountains, nor shall ye employ auguries, nor divine by inspection of birds. ²⁷ Ye shall not make a round cutting of the hair of your head, nor disfigure your beard. ²⁸ And ye shall not make cuttings in your body for a *dead* body, and ye shall not inscribe on yourselves any marks. I am the Lord your God. ²⁹ Thou shalt not profane thy daughter to prostitute her; so the land shall not go a whoring, and the land be filled with iniquity. ³⁰ Ye shall keep my sabbaths, and reverence my sanctuaries: I am the Lord. ³¹ Ye shall not attend to those who have in them divining spirits, nor attach yourselves to enchanters, to pollute yourselves with them: I am the Lord your God. ³² Thou shalt rise up before the hoary head, and honour the face of the old man, and shalt fear thy God: I am the Lord your God. ³³ And if there should come to you a stranger in your land, ye shall not afflict him. ³⁴ The stranger that comes to you shall be among you as the native, and thou shalt love him as thyself; for ye were strangers in the land of Egypt: I am the Lord your God. ³⁵ Ye shall not act unrighteously in judgment, in measures and weights and scales. ³⁶ There shall be among you just balances and just weights and just liquid measure. I am the Lord your God, who brought you out of the land of Egypt. ³⁷ And ye shall keep all my law and all my ordinances, and ye shall do them: I am the Lord your God.

Lev.20 ¹ And the Lord spoke to Moses, saying, ² Thou shalt also say to the children of Israel, If *there shall be* any of the children of Israel, or of those who have become proselytes in Israel, who shall give of his seed to Moloch, let him be surely put to death; the nation upon the land shall stone him with stones. ³ And I will set my face against that man, and will cut him off from his people, because he has given of his seed to Moloch, to defile my sanctuary, and profane the name of them that are consecrated to me. ⁴ And if the natives of the land should in anywise overlook that man in giving of his seed to Moloch, so as not to put him to death; ⁵ then will I set my face against that man and his family, and I will destroy him, and all who have been of one mind with him, so that he should go a whoring to the princes, from their people. ⁶ And the soul that shall follow those who have in them divining spirits, or enchanters, so as to go a whoring after them; I will set my face against that soul, and will destroy it from among its people. ⁷ And ye shall be holy, for I the Lord your God *am* holy. ⁸ And ye shall observe my ordinances, and do them: I *am* the Lord that sanctifies you. ⁹ Every man who shall speak evil of his father or of his mother, let him die the death; has he spoken evil of his father or his mother? he shall be guilty. ¹⁰ Whatever man shall commit adultery with the wife of a man, or whoever shall commit adultery with the wife of his neighbour, let them die the death, the adulterer and the adulteress. ¹¹ And if any one should lie with his father's wife, he has uncovered his father's nakedness: let them both die the death, they are guilty. ¹² And if any one should lie with his daughter-in-law, let them both be put to death; for they have wrought impiety, they are guilty. 13 And whoever shall lie with a male as with a woman, they have both wrought abomination; let them die the death, they are guilty. 14 Whosoever shall take a woman and her mother, it is iniquity: they shall burn him and them with fire; so there shall not be iniquity among you. 15 And whosoever shall lie with a beast, let him die the death; and ye shall kill the beast. 16 And whatever woman shall approach any beast, so as to have connexion with it, ye shall kill the woman and the beast: let them die the death, they are guilty. 17 Whosoever shall take his sister by his father or by his mother, and shall see her nakedness, and she see his nakedness, it is a reproach: they shall be destroyed before the children of their family; he has uncovered his sister's nakedness, they shall bear their sin. 18 And whatever man shall lie with a woman that is set apart *for a flux*, and shall uncover her nakedness, he has uncovered her fountain, and she has uncovered the flux of her blood: they shall both be destroyed from among their generation. 19 And thou shalt not uncover the nakedness of thy father's sister, or of the sister of thy mother; for that man has uncovered the nakedness of one near akin: they shall bear their iniquity. 20 Whosoever shall lie with his near kinswoman, has uncovered the nakedness of one near akin to him: they shall die childless. 21 Whoever shall take his brother's wife, it is uncleanness; he has uncovered his brother's nakedness; they shall die childless. 22 And keep ye all my ordinances, and my judgments; and ye shall do them, and the land shall not be aggrieved with you, into which I bring you to dwell upon it. 23 And walk ye not in the customs of the nations which I drive out from before you; for they have done all these things, and I have abhorred them: 24 and I said to you, Ye shall inherit their land, and I will give it to you for a possession, *even* a land flowing with milk and honey: I *am* the Lord your God, who have separated you from all people. 25 And ye shall make a distinction between the clean and the unclean cattle, and between clean and unclean birds; and ye shall not defile your souls with cattle, or with birds, or with any creeping things of the earth, which I have separated for you by reason of uncleanness. 26 And ye shall be holy to me; because I the Lord your God *am* holy, who separated you from all nations, to be mine. 27 And *as for a* man or woman whosoever of them shall have in them a divining spirit, or be an enchanter, let them both die the death: ye shall stone them with stones, they are guilty.

Lev.21 1 And the Lord spoke to Moses, saying, Speak to the priests the sons of Aaron, and thou shalt tell them *that* they shall not defile themselves in their nation for the dead, 2 but *they may mourn* for a relative who is very near to them, for a father and mother, and sons and daughters, for a brother, 3 and for a virgin sister that is near to one, that is not espoused to a man; for these one shall defile himself. 4 He shall not defile himself suddenly among his people to profane himself. 5 And ye shall not shave your head for the dead with a baldness on the top; and they shall not shave their beard, neither shall they make gashes on their flesh. 6 They shall be holy to their God, and they shall not profane the name of their God; for they offer the sacrifices of the Lord as the gifts of their God, and they shall be holy. 7 They shall not take a woman who is a harlot and profaned, or a woman put away from her husband; for he is holy to the Lord his God. 8 And thou shalt hallow him; he offers the gifts of the Lord your God: he shall be holy, for I the Lord that sanctify them *am* holy. 9 And if the daughter of a priest should be profaned to go a whoring, she profanes the name of her father: she shall be burnt with fire. 10 And the priest that is chief among his brethren, the oil having been poured upon the head of the anointed one, and he having been consecrated to put on the garments, shall not take the mitre off his head, and shall not rend his garments: 11 neither shall he go in to any dead body, neither shall he defile himself for his father or his mother. 12 And he shall not go forth out of the sanctuary, and he shall not profane the sanctuary of his God, because the holy anointing oil of God *is* upon him: I *am* the Lord. 13 He shall take for a wife a virgin of his own tribe. 14 But a widow, or one that is put away, or profaned, or a harlot, these he shall not take; but he shall take for a wife a virgin of his own people. 15 And he shall not profane his seed among his people: I *am* the Lord that sanctifies him. 16 And the Lord spoke to Moses, saying, 17 Say to Aaron, A man of thy tribe throughout your generations, who shall have a blemish on him, shall not draw nigh to offer the gifts of his God. 18 No man who has a blemish on him shall draw nigh; a man blind, lame, with his nose disfigured, or his ears cut, 19 a man who has a broken hand or a broken foot, 20 or hump-backed, or blear-eyed, or that has lost his eye-lashes, or a man who has a malignant ulcer, or tetter, or one that has lost a testicle. 21 Whoever of the seed of Aaron the priest has a blemish on him, shall not draw nigh to offer sacrifices to thy God, because he has a blemish on him; he shall not draw nigh to offer the gifts of God. 22 The gifts of God *are* most holy, and he shall eat of the holy things. 23 Only he shall not approach the veil, and he shall not draw nigh to the altar, because he has a blemish; and he shall not profane the sanctuary of his God, for I am the Lord that sanctifies them. 24 And Moses spoke to Aaron and his sons, and to all the children of Israel.

Lev.22 1 And the Lord spoke to Moses, saying, 2 Speak to Aaron and to his sons, and let them take heed concerning the holy things of the children of Israel, so they shall not profane my holy name in any of the things which they consecrate to me: I *am* the Lord. 3 Say to them, Every man throughout your generations, whoever of all your seed shall approach to the holy things, whatsoever the children of Israel shall consecrate to the Lord, while his uncleanness is upon him, that soul shall be cut off from me: I *am* the Lord your God. 4 And the man of the seed of Aaron the priest, if he should have leprosy or issue of the reins, shall not eat of the holy things, until he be cleansed; and he that touches any uncleanness of a dead body, or the man whose seed of copulation shall have gone out from him, 5 or whosoever shall touch any unclean reptile, which will defile him, or *who shall touch* a man, whereby he shall defile him according to all his uncleanness: 6 whatsoever soul shall touch them shall be unclean until evening; he shall not eat of the holy things, unless he bathe his body in water, 7 and the sun go down, and then he shall be clean; and then shall he eat of all the holy things, for they are his bread. 8 He shall not eat that which dies of itself, or is taken of beasts, so that he should be polluted by them: I *am* the Lord. 9 And they shall keep my ordinances, that they do not bear iniquity because of them, and die because of them, if they shall profane them: I *am* the Lord God that sanctifies them. 10 And no stranger shall eat the holy things: one that sojourns with a priest, or a hireling, shall not eat the holy things. 11 But if a priest should have a soul purchased for money, he shall eat of his bread; and they that are born in his house, they also shall eat of his bread. 12 And if the daughter of a priest should marry a stranger, she shall not eat of the offerings of the sanctuary. 13 And if the daughter of priest should be a widow, or put away, and have no seed, she shall return to her father's house, as in her youth: she shall eat of her father's bread, but no stranger shall eat of it. 14 And the man who shall ignorantly eat holy things, shall add the fifth part to it, and give the holy thing to the priest. 15 And they shall not profane the holy things of the children of Israel, which they offer to the Lord. 16 So should they bring upon themselves the iniquity of trespass in their eating their holy things: for I *am* the Lord that sanctifies them. 17 And the Lord spoke to Moses, saying, 18 Speak to Aaron and his sons, and to all the congregation of Israel, and thou shalt say to them, Any man of the children of Israel, or of the strangers that abide among them in Israel, who shall offer his gifts according to all their confession and according to all their choice, whatsoever they may bring to the Lord for whole- burnt-offerings— 19 your free-will-offerings *shall* be males without blemish of the herds, or of the sheep, or of the goats. 20 They shall not bring to the Lord anything that has a blemish in it, for it shall not be acceptable for you. 21 And whatsoever man shall offer a peace-offering to the Lord, discharging a vow, or in the way of free-will-offering, or an offering in your feasts, of the herds or of the sheep, it shall be without blemish for acceptance: there shall be no blemish in it. 22 One that is blind, or broken, or has its tongue cut out, or is troubled with warts, or has a malignant ulcer, or tetters, they shall not offer these to the Lord; neither shall ye offer any of them for a burnt-offering on the altar of the Lord. 23 And a calf or a sheep with the ears cut off, or that has lost its tail, thou shalt slay them for thyself; but they shall not be accepted for thy vow. 24 That which has broken testicles, or is crushed or gelt or mutilated, —thou shalt not offer them to the Lord, neither shall ye sacrifice them upon your land. 25 Neither shall ye offer the gifts of your God of all these things by the hand of a stranger, because there is corruption in them, a blemish in them: these shall not be accepted for you. 26 And the Lord spoke to Moses, saying, 27 As for a calf, or a sheep, or a goat, whenever it is born, then shall it be seven days under its mother; and on the eighth day and after they shall be accepted for sacrifices, a burnt- offering to the Lord. 28 And a bullock and a ewe, it and its young, thou shalt not kill in one day. 29 And if thou shouldest offer a sacrifice, a vow of rejoicing to the Lord, ye shall offer it so as to be accepted for you. 30 In that same day it shall be eaten; ye shall not leave of the flesh till the morrow: I am the Lord. 31 And ye shall keep my commandments and do them. 32 And ye shall not profane the name of the Holy One, and I will be sanctified in the midst of the children of Israel. I *am* the Lord that sanctifies you, 33 who brought you out of the land of Egypt, to be your God: I *am* the Lord.

Lev.23 1 And the Lord spoke to Moses, saying, 2 Speak to the children of Israel, and thou shalt say unto them, The feasts of the Lord which ye shall call holy assemblies, these are my feasts. 3 Six days shalt thou do works, but on the seventh day is the sabbath; a rest, a holy convocation to the Lord: thou shalt not do any work, it is a sabbath to the Lord in all your dwellings. 4 These *are* the feasts to the Lord, holy convocations, which ye shall call in their seasons. 5 In the first month, on the fourteenth day of the month, between the evening times is the Lord's passover. 6 And on the fifteenth day of this month is the feast of unleavened bread to the Lord; seven days shall ye eat unleavened bread. 7 And the first day shall be a holy convocation to you: ye shall do no servile work. 8 And ye shall offer whole-burnt-offerings to the Lord seven days; and the seventh day shall be a holy convocation to you: ye shall do no servile work. 9 And the Lord spoke to Moses, saying, 10 Speak to the children of Israel, and thou shalt say to them, When ye shall enter into the land which I give you, and reap the harvest of it, then shall ye bring a sheaf, the first-fruits of your harvest, to the priest; 11 and he shall lift up the sheaf before the Lord, to be accepted for you. On the morrow of the first day the priest shall lift it up. 12 And ye shall offer on the day on which ye bring the sheaf, a lamb without blemish of a year old for a whole-burnt-offering to the Lord. 13 And its meat-offering two tenth portions of fine flour mingled with oil: it is a sacrifice to the Lord, a smell of sweet savour to the Lord, and its drink-offering the fourth part of a hin of wine. 14 And ye shall not eat bread, or the new parched corn, until this same day, until ye offer the sacrifices to your God: *it is* a perpetual statute throughout your generations in all your dwellings. 15 And ye shall number to yourselves from the day after the sabbath, from the day on which ye shall offer the sheaf of the heave-offering, seven full weeks: 16 until the morrow after the last week ye shall number fifty days, and shall bring a new meat-offering to the Lord. 17 Ye shall bring from your dwelling loaves, as a heave-offering, two loaves: they shall be of two tenth portions of fine flour, they shall be baked with leaven of the first-fruits to the Lord. 18 And ye shall bring with the loaves seven unblemished lambs of a year old, and one calf of the herd, and two rams without blemish, and they shall be a whole-burnt-offering to the Lord: and their meat-offerings and their drink-offerings *shall be* a sacrifice, a smell of sweet savour to the Lord. 19 And they shall sacrifice one kid of the goats for a sin-offering, and two lambs of a year old for a peace-offering, with the loaves of the first-fruits. 20 And the priest shall place them with the loaves of the first-fruits an offering before the Lord with the two lambs, they shall be holy to the Lord; they shall belong to the priest that brings them. 21 And ye shall call this day a convocation: it shall be holy to you; ye shall do no servile work on it: it is a perpetual ordinance throughout your generations in all your habitations. 22 And when ye shall reap the harvest of your land, ye shall not fully reap the remainder of the harvest of your field when thou reapest, and thou shalt not gather that which falls from thy reaping; thou shalt leave it for the poor and the stranger: I *am* the Lord your God. 23 And the Lord spoke to Moses, saying, 24 Speak to the children of Israel, saying, In the seventh month, on the first day of the month, ye shall have a rest, a memorial of trumpets: it shall be to you a holy convocation. 25 Ye shall do no servile work, and ye shall offer a whole- burnt-offering to the Lord. 26 And the Lord spoke to Moses, saying, 27 Also on the tenth day of this seventh month is a day of atonement: it shall be a holy convocation to you; and ye shall humble your souls, and offer a whole-burnt-offering to the Lord. 28 Ye shall do no work on this self-same day: for this is a day of atonement for you, to make atonement for you before the Lord your God. 29 Every soul that shall not be humbled in that day, shall be cut off from among its people. 30 And every soul which shall do work on that day, that soul shall be destroyed from among its people. 31 Ye shall do no manner of work: it is a perpetual statute throughout your generations in all your habitations. 32 It shall be a holy sabbath to you; and ye shall humble your souls, from the ninth day of the month: from evening to evening ye shall keep your sabbaths. 33 And the Lord spoke to Moses, saying, 34 Speak to the children of Israel, saying, On the fifteenth day of this seventh month, there shall be a feast of tabernacles seven days to the Lord. 35 And on the first day shall be a holy convocation; ye shall do no servile work. 36 Seven days shall ye offer whole-burnt-offerings to the Lord, and the eighth-day shall be a holy convocation to you; and ye shall offer whole-burnt-offerings to the Lord: it is a time of release, ye shall do no servile work. 37 These *are* the feasts to the Lord, which ye shall call holy convocations, to offer burnt-offerings to the Lord, whole-burnt-offerings and their meat-offerings, and their drink-offerings, that for each day on its day: 38 besides the sabbaths of the Lord, and besides your gifts, and besides all your vows, and besides your free-will-offerings, which ye shall give to the Lord. 39 And on the fifteenth day of this seventh month, when ye shall have completely gathered in the fruits of the earth, ye shall keep a feast to the Lord seven days; on the first day there shall be a rest, and on the eighth day a rest. 40 And on the first day ye shall take goodly fruit of trees, and branches of palm trees, and thick boughs of trees, and willows, and branches of osiers from the brook, to rejoice before the Lord your God seven days in the year. 41 *It is* a perpetual statute for your generations: in the seventh month ye shall keep it. 42 Seven days ye shall dwell in tabernacles: every native in Israel shall dwell in tents, 43 that your posterity may see, that I made the children of Israel to dwell in tents, when I brought them out of the land of Egypt: I *am* the Lord your God. 44 And Moses recounted the feasts of the Lord to the children of Israel.

Lev.24 1 And the Lord spoke to Moses, saying, 2 Charge the children of Israel, and let them take for thee pure olive oil beaten for the light, to burn a lamp continually, 3 outside the veil in the tabernacle of witness; and Aaron and his sons shall burn it from evening until morning before the Lord continually, a perpetual statute throughout your generations. 4 Ye shall burn the lamps on the pure lamp-stand before the Lord till the morrow. 5 And ye shall take fine flour, and make of it twelve loaves; each loaf shall be of two tenth parts. 6 And ye shall put them *in* two rows, each row *containing* six loaves, on the pure table before the Lord. 7 And ye shall put on *each* row pure frankincense and salt; and *these things* shall be for loaves for a memorial, set forth before the Lord. 8 On the sabbath-day they shall be set forth before the Lord continually before the children of Israel, for an everlasting covenant. 9 And they shall be for Aaron and his sons, and they shall eat them in the holy place: for this is their most holy portion of the offerings made to the Lord, a perpetual statute. 10 And there went forth a son of an Israelitish woman, and he was son of an Egyptian man among the sons of Israel; and they fought in the camp, the son of the Israelitish woman, and a man who was an Israelite. 11 And the son of the Israelitish woman named THE NAME and curse; and they brought him to Moses: and his mother's name was Salomith, daughter of Dabri of the tribe of Dan. 12 And they put him in ward, to judge him by the command of the Lord. 13 And the Lord spoke to Moses, saying, 14 Bring forth him that cursed outside the camp, and all who heard shall lay their hands upon his head, and all the congregation shall stone him. 15 And speak to the sons of Israel, and thou shalt say to them, Whosoever shall curse God shall bear his sin. 16 And he that names the name of the Lord, let him die the death: let all the congregation of Israel stone him with stones; whether he be a stranger or a native, let him die for naming the name of the Lord. 17 And whosoever shall smite a man and he die, let him die the death. 18 And whosoever shall smite a beast, and it shall die, let him render life for life. 19 And whosoever shall inflict a blemish on his neighbour, as he has done to him, so shall it be done to himself in return; 20 bruise for bruise, eye for eye, tooth for tooth: as any one may inflict a blemish on a man, so shall it be rendered to him. 21 Whosoever shall smite a man, and he shall die, let him die the death. 22 There shall be one judgment for the stranger and the native, for I *am* the Lord your God. 23 And Moses spoke to the children of Israel, and they brought him that had cursed out of the camp, and stoned him with stones: and the children of Israel did as the Lord commanded Moses.

Lev.25 1 And the Lord spoke to Moses in the mount Sina, saying, 2 Speak to the children of Israel, and thou shalt say to them, Whensoever ye shall have entered into the land, which I give to you, then the land shall rest which I give to you, for its sabbaths to the Lord. 3 Six years thou shalt sow thy field, and six years thou shall prune thy vine, and gather in its fruit. 4 But in the seventh year *shall be* a sabbath, it shall be a rest to the land, a sabbath to the Lord: thou shalt not sow thy field, and thou shalt not prune thy vine. 5 And thou shalt not gather the spontaneous produce of thy field, and thou shalt not gather fully the grapes of thy dedication: it shall be a year of rest to the land. 6 And the sabbaths of the land shall be food for thee, and for thy man-servant, and for thy maid-servant, and thy hireling, and the stranger that abides with thee. 7 And for thy cattle, and for the wild beats that are in thy land, shall every fruit of it be for food. 8 And thou shalt reckon to thyself seven sabbaths of years, seven times seven years; and they shall be to thee seven weeks of years, nine and forty years. 9 In the seventh month, on the tenth day of the month, ye shall make a proclamation with the sound of a trumpet in all your land; on the day of atonement ye shall make a proclamation with a trumpet in all your land. 10 And ye shall sanctify the year, the fiftieth year, and ye shall proclaim a release upon the land to all that inhabit it; it shall be given a year of release, a jubilee for you; and each one shall depart to his possession, and ye shall go each to his family. 11 This is a jubilee of release, the year shall be to you the fiftieth year: ye shall not sow, nor reap the produce that comes of itself from the land, neither shall ye gather its dedicated fruits. 12 For it is a jubilee of release; it shall be holy to you, ye shall eat its fruits off the fields. 13 In the year of the release *even* the jubilee of it, shall *each* one return to his possession. 14 And if thou shouldest sell a possession to thy neighbour, or if thou shouldest buy of thy neighbour, let not a man oppress his neighbour. 15 According to the number of years after the jubilee shalt thou buy of thy neighbour, according to the number of years of the fruits shall he sell to thee. 16 According as *there may be* a greater number of years he shall increase *the value of* his possession, and according as *there may be* a less number of years he shall lessen *the value of* his possession; for according to the number of his crops, so shall he sell to thee. 17 Let not a man oppress his neighbour, and thou shalt fear the Lord thy God: I am the Lord thy God. 18 And ye shall keep all my ordinances, and all my judgments; and do ye observe them, and ye shall keep them, and dwell securely in the land. 19 And the land shall yield her increase, and ye shall eat to fullness, and shall dwell securely in it. 20 And if ye should say, What shall we eat in this seventh year, if we do not sow nor gather in our fruits? 21 Then will I send my blessing upon you in the sixth year, and the land shall produce its fruits for three years. 22 And ye shall sow in the eighth year, and eat old fruits till the ninth year: until its fruit come, ye shall eat old fruits of the old. 23 And the land shall not be sold for a permanence; for the land is mine, because ye are strangers and sojourners before me. 24 And in every land of your possession, ye shall allow ransoms for the land. 25 And if thy brother who is with thee be poor, and should have sold *part* of his possession, and his kinsman who is nigh to him come, then he shall redeem the possession which his brother has sold. 26 And if one have no near kinsman, and he prosper with his hand, and he find sufficient money, *even* his ransom; 27 then shall he calculate the years of his sale, and he shall give what is due to the man to whom he sold it, and he shall return to his possession. 28 But if his hand have not prospered sufficiently, so as that he should restore the money to him, then he that bought the possessions shall have them till the sixth year of the release; and it shall go out in the release, and the owner shall return to his possession. 29 And if any one should sell an inhabited house in a walled city, then

there shall be the ransom of it, until *the time* is fulfilled: its time of ransom shall be a full year. 30 And if it be not ransomed until there be completed of its time a full year, the house which is in the walled city shall be surely confirmed to him that bought it, throughout his generations; and it shall not go out in the release. 31 But the houses in the villages which have not a wall round about them, shall be reckoned as the fields of the country: they shall always be redeemable, and they shall go out in the release. 32 And the cities of the Levites, the houses of the cities in their possession, shall be always redeemable to the Levites. 33 And if any one shall redeem a house of the Levites, then shall their sale of the houses of their possession go out in the release; because the houses of the cities of the Levites are their possession in the midst of the children of Israel. 34 And the lands set apart for their cities shall not be sold, because this is their perpetual possession. 35 And if thy brother who is with thee become poor, and he fail in resources with thee, thou shalt help him as a stranger and a sojourner, and thy brother shall live with thee. 36 Thou shalt not receive from him interest, nor increase: and thou shalt fear thy God: I *am* the Lord: and thy brother shall live with thee. 37 Thou shalt not lend thy money to him at interest, and thou shalt not lend thy meat to him to be returned with increase. 38 I *am* the Lord your God, who brought you out of the land of Egypt, to give you the land of Chanaan, so as to be your God. 39 And if thy brother by thee be lowered, and be sold to thee, he shall not serve thee with the servitude of a slave. 40 He shall be with thee as a hireling or a sojourner, he shall work for thee till the year of release: 41 and he shall go out in the release, and his children with him; and he shall go to his family, he shall hasten back to his patrimony. 42 Because these are my servants, whom I brought out of the land of Egypt; such an one shall not be sold as a *common* servant. 43 Thou shalt not oppress him with labour, and shalt fear the Lord thy God. 44 And whatever number of men-servants and maid-servants thou shalt have, thou shalt purchase male and female servants from the nations that are round about thee. 45 And of the sons of the sojourners that are among you, of these ye shall buy and of their relations, all that shall be in your lands; let them be to you for a possession. 46 And ye shall distribute them to your children after you, and they shall be to you permanent possessions for ever: but of your brethren the children of Israel, one shall not oppress his brother in labours. 47 And if a stranger or sojourner with thee wax rich, and thy brother in distress be sold to the stranger or the sojourner that is with thee, or to a proselyte by extraction; 48 after he is sold to him there shall be redemption for him, one of his brethren shall redeem him. 49 A brother of his father, or a son of his father's brother shall redeem him; or let one of his near kin of his tribe redeem him, and if he should be rich and redeem himself, 50 then shall he calculate with his purchaser from the year that he sold himself to him until the year of release: and the money of his purchase shall be as that of a hireling, he shall be with him from year to year. 51 And if any have a greater number of years *than enough*, according to these he shall pay his ransom out of his purchase-money. 52 And if but a little time be left of the years to the year of release, then shall he reckon to him according to his years, and shall pay his ransom 53 as a hireling; he shall be with him from year to year; thou shalt not oppress him with labour before thee. 54 And if he do not pay his ransom accordingly, he shall go out in the year of his release, he and his children with him. 55 For the children of Israel are my servants: they are my attendants, whom I brought out of the land of Egypt.

Lev.26 1 I *am* the Lord your God: ye shall not make to yourselves gods made with hands, or graven; neither shall ye rear up a pillar for yourselves, neither shall ye set up a stone *for* an object in your land to worship it: I am the Lord your God. 2 Ye shall keep my sabbaths, and reverence my sanctuaries: I am the Lord. 3 If ye will walk in my ordinances, and keep my commandments, and do them, 4 then will I give you the rain in its season, and the land shall produce its fruits, and the trees of the field shall yield their fruit. 5 And your threshing time shall overtake the vintage, and your vintage shall overtake your seed time; and ye shall eat your bread to the full; and ye shall dwell safely upon your land, and war shall not go through your land. 6 And I will give peace in your land, and ye shall sleep, and none *shall* make you afraid; and I will destroy the evil beasts out of your land, 7 and ye shall pursue your enemies, and they shall fall before you with slaughter. 8 And five of you shall chase a hundred, and a hundred of you shall chase tens of thousands; and your enemies shall fall before you by the sword. 9 And I will look upon you, and increase you, and multiply you, and establish my covenant with you. 10 And ye shall eat that which is old and very old, and bring forth the old to make way for the new. 11 And I will set my tabernacle among you, and my soul shall not abhor you; 12 and I will walk among you, and be your God, and ye shall be my people. 13 I am the Lord your God, who brought you out of the land of Egypt, where ye were slaves; and I broke the band of your yoke, and brought you forth openly. 14 But if ye will not hearken to me, nor obey these my ordinances, 15 but disobey them, and your soul should loathe my judgments, so that ye should not keep all my commands, so as to break my covenant, 16 then will I do thus to you: I will even bring upon you perplexity and the itch, and the fever that causes your eyes to waste away, and *disease* that consumes your life; and ye shall sow your seeds in vain, and your enemies shall eat them. 17 And I will set my face against you, and ye shall fall before your enemies, and they that hate you shall pursue you; and ye shall flee, no one pursuing you. 18 And if ye still refuse to hearken to me, then will I chasten you yet more even seven times for your sins. 19 And I will break down the haughtiness of your pride; and I will make your heaven iron, and your earth as it were brass. 20 And your strength shall be in vain; and your land shall not yield its seed, and the tree of your field shall not yield its fruit. 21 And if after this ye should walk perversely, and not be willing to obey me, I will further bring upon you seven plagues according to your sins. 22 And I will send upon you the wild beasts of the land, and they shall devour you, and shall consume your cattle: and I will make you few in number, and your ways shall be desolate. 23 And if hereupon ye are not corrected, but walk perversely towards me, 24 I also will walk with you with a perverse spirit, and I also will smite you seven times for your sins. 25 And I will bring upon you a sword avenging the cause of *my* covenant, and ye shall flee for refuge to your cities; and I will send out death against you, and ye shall be delivered into the hands of your enemies. 26 When I afflict you with famine of bread, then ten women shall bake your loaves in one oven, and they shall render your loaves by weight; and ye shall eat, and not be satisfied. 27 And if hereupon ye will not obey me, but walk perversely towards me, 28 then will I walk with you with a froward mind, and I will chasten you seven-fold according to your sins. 29 And ye shall eat the flesh of your sons, and the flesh of your daughters shall ye eat. 30 And I will render your pillars desolate, and will utterly destroy your wooden *images* made with hands; and I will lay your carcases on the carcases of your idols, and my soul shall loathe you. 31 And I will lay your cities waste, and I will make your sanctuaries desolate, and I will not smell the savour of your sacrifices. 32 And I will lay your land desolate, and your enemies who dwell in it shall wonder at it. 33 And I will scatter you among the nations, and the sword shall come upon you and consume you; and your land shall be desolate, and your cities shall be desolate. 34 Then the land shall enjoy its sabbaths all the days of its desolation. 35 And ye shall be in the land of your enemies; then the land shall keep its sabbaths, and the land shall enjoy its sabbaths all the days of its desolation: it shall keep sabbaths which it kept not among your sabbaths, when ye dwelt in it. 36 And to those who are left of you I will bring bondage into their heart in the land of their enemies; and the sound of a shaken leaf shall chase them, and they shall flee as fleeing from war, and shall fall when none pursues them. 37 And brother shall disregard brother as in war, when none pursues; and ye shall not be able to withstand your enemies. 38 And ye shall perish among the Gentiles, and the land of your enemies shall devour you. 39 And those who are left of you shall perish, because of their sins, and because of the sins of their fathers: in the land of their enemies shall they consume away. 40 And they shall confess their sins, and the sins of their fathers, that they have transgressed and neglected me, and that they have walked perversely before me, 41 and I walked with them with a perverse mind; and I will destroy them in the land of their enemies: then shall their uncircumcised heart be ashamed, and then shall they acquiesce in *the punishment of* their sins. 42 And I will remember the covenant of Jacob, and the covenant of Isaac, and the covenant of Abraam will I remember. 43 And I will remember the land, and the land shall be left of them; then the land shall enjoy her sabbaths, when it is deserted through them: and they shall accept *the punishment of* their iniquities, because they neglected my judgments, and in their soul loathed my ordinances. 44 And yet not even thus, while they were in the land of their enemies, did I overlook them, nor did I loathe them so as to consume them, to break my covenant made with them; for I am the Lord their God. 45 And I will remember their former covenant, when I brought them out of the land of Egypt, out of the house of bondage before the nation, to be their God; I am the Lord. 46 These are my judgments and my ordinances, and the law which the Lord gave between himself and the children of Israel, in the mount Sina, by the hand of Moses.

Lev.27 1 And the Lord spoke to Moses, saying, 2 Speak to the children of Israel, and thou shalt say to them, Whosoever shall vow a vow as the valuation of his soul for the Lord, 3 the valuation of a male from twenty years old to sixty years old shall be his valuation shall be fifty didrachms of silver by the standard of the sanctuary. 4 And the valuation of a female shall be thirty didrachms. 5 And if it be from five years old to twenty, the valuation of a male shall be twenty didrachms, and of a female ten didrachms. 6 And from a month old to five years old, the valuation of a male shall be five didrachms, and of a female, three didrachms of silver. 7 And if from sixty year *old* and upward, if it be a male, his valuation shall be fifteen didrachms of silver, and if a female, ten didrachms. 8 And if the man be too poor for the valuation, he shall stand before the priest; and the priest shall value him: according to what the man who has vowed can afford, the priest shall value him. 9 And if it be from the cattle that are offered as a gift to the Lord, whoever shall offer one of these to the Lord, it shall be holy. 10 He shall not change it, a good for a bad, or a bad for a good; and if he do at all change it, a beast for a beast, it and the substitute shall be holy. 11 And if it be any unclean beast, of which none are offered as a gift to the Lord, he shall set the beast before the priest. 12 And the priest shall make a valuation between the good and the bad, and accordingly as the priest shall value it, so shall it stand. 13 And if *the worshipper* will at all redeem it, he shall add the fifth part to its value. 14 And whatsoever man shall consecrate his house as holy to the Lord, the priest shall make a valuation of it between the good and the bad: as the priest shall value it, so shall it stand. 15 And if he that has sanctified it should redeem his house, he shall add to it the fifth part of the money of the valuation, and it shall be his. 16 And if a man should hallow to the Lord a part of the field of his possession, then the valuation shall be according to its seed, fifty didrachms of silver for a homer of barley. 17 And if he should sanctify his field from the year of release, it shall stand according to his valuation. 18 And if he should sanctify his field in the latter time after the release, the priest shall reckon to him the money for the remaining years, until the *next* year of release, and it shall be deducted as an equivalent from his full valuation. 19 And if he that sanctified the field would redeem it, he shall add to its value the fifth part of the money, and it shall be his. 20 And if he do not redeem the field, but should sell the field to another man, he shall not after redeem it. 21 But the field shall be holy to the Lord after the release, as separated land; the priest shall have possession of it. 22 And if he should consecrate to the Lord of a field which he has bought, which is not of the field of his possession, 23 the priest shall reckon to him the full valuation from the year of release, and he shall pay the valuation in that day *as* holy to the Lord. 24 And in the year of release the land shall be restored to the man of whom the other bought it, whose the

possession of the land was. 25 And every valuation shall be by holy weights: the didrachm shall be twenty oboli. 26 And every first-born which shall be produced among thy cattle shall be the Lord's, and no man shall sanctify it: whether calf or sheep, it is the Lord's. 27 But if he should redeem an unclean beast, according to its valuation, then he shall add the fifth part to it, and it shall be his; and if he redeem it not, it shall be sold according to its valuation. 28 And every dedicated thing which a man shall dedicate to the Lord of all that he has, whether man or beast, or of the field of his possession, he shall not sell it, nor redeem it: every devoted thing shall be most holy to the Lord. 29 And whatever shall be dedicated of men, shall not be ransomed, but shall be surely put to death. 30 Every tithe of the land, both of the seed of the land, and of the fruit of trees, is the Lord's, holy to the Lord. 31 And if a man should at all redeem his tithe, he shall add the fifth part to it, and it shall be his. 32 And every tithe of oxen, and of sheep, and whatsoever may come in numbering under the rod, the tenth shall be holy to the Lord. 33 Thou shalt not change a good for a bad, or a bad for a good; and if thou shouldest at all change it, its equivalent also shall be holy, it shall not be redeemed. 34 These are the commandments which the Lord commanded Moses for the sons of Israel in mount Sina.

NUMBERS

Num.1 1 And the Lord spoke to Moses in the wilderness of Sina, in the tabernacle of witness, on the first day of the second month, in the second year of their departure from the land of Egypt, saying, 2 Take the sum of all the congregation of Israel according to their kindreds, according to the houses of their fathers' families, according to their number by their names, according to their heads: every male 3 from twenty years old and upwards, every one that goes forth in the forces of Israel, take account of them with their strength; thou and Aaron take account of them. 4 And with you there shall be each one of the rulers according to the tribe of each: they shall be according to the houses of their families. 5 And these are the names of the men who shall be present with you; of the tribe of Ruben, Elisur the son of Sediur. 6 Of Symeon, Salamiel the son of Surisadai. 7 Of Juda, Naasson the son of Aminadab. 8 Of Issachar, Nathanael the son of Sogar. 9 Of Zabulon, Eliab the son of Chaelon. 10 Of the sons of Joseph, of Ephraim, Elisama the son of Emiud: of Manasses, Gamaliel the son of Phadasur. 11 Of Benjamin, Abidan the son of Gadeoni. 12 Of Dan, Achiezer the son of Amisadai. 13 Of Aser, Phagaiel the son of Echran. 14 Of Gad, Elisaph the son of Raguel. 15 Of Nephthali, Achire the son of Ænan. 16 These were famous men of the congregation, heads of the tribes according to their families: these are heads of thousands in Israel. 17 And Moses and Aaron took these men who were called by name. 18 And they assembled all the congregation on the first day of the month in the second year; and they registered them after their lineage, after their families, after the number of their names, from twenty years old and upwards, every male according to their number: 19 as the Lord commanded Moses, so they were numbered in the wilderness of Sina. 20 And the sons of

Ruben the first-born of Israel according to their kindreds, according to their divisions, according to the houses of their families, according to the number of their names, according to their heads, were—all males from twenty years old and upward, every one that went out with the host— 21 the numbering of them of the tribe of Ruben, was forty-six thousand and four hundred. 22 For the children of Symeon according to their kindreds, according to their divisions, according to the houses of their families, according to the number of their names, according to their polls, all males from twenty years old and upward, every one that goes out with the host, 23 the numbering of them of the tribe of Symeon, was fifty-nine thousand and three hundred. 24 For the sons of Juda according to their kindreds, according to their divisions, according to the houses of their families, according to the number of their names, according to their polls, all males from twenty years old and upward, every one that goes forth with the host, 25 the numbering of them of the tribe of Juda, was seventy-four thousand and six hundred. 26 For the sons of Issachar according to their kindreds, according to their divisions, according to the houses of their families, according to the number of their names, according to their polls, all males from twenty years old and upward, every one that goes forth with the host, 27 the numbering of them of the tribe of Issachar, was fifty-four thousand and four hundred. 28 For the sons of Zabulon according to their kindreds, according to their divisions, according to the houses of their families, according to the number of their names, according to their polls, all males from twenty years old and upward, every one that goes out with the host, 29 the numbering of them of the tribe of Zabulon, was fifty-seven thousand and four hundred. 30 For the sons of Joseph, the sons of Ephraim, according to their kindreds, according to their divisions, according to the houses of their families, according to the number of their names, according to their polls, all males from twenty years old and upward, every one that goes out with the host, 31 the numbering of them of the tribe of Ephraim, was forty thousand and five hundred. 32 For the sons of Manasse according to their kindreds, according to their divisions, according to the houses of their families, according to the number of their names, according to their polls, all males from twenty years old and upward, every one that goes out with the host, 33 the numbering of them of the tribe of Manasse, was thirty-two thousand and two hundred. 34 For the sons of Benjamin according to their kindreds, according to their divisions, according to the houses of their families, according to the number of their names, according to their polls, every male from twenty years old and upward, every one that goes forth with the host, 35 the numbering of them of the tribe of Benjamin, was thirty-five thousand and four hundred. 36 For the sons of Gad according to their kindreds, according to their divisions, according to the houses of their families, according to the number of their names, according to their polls, all males from twenty years old and upward, every one that goes forth with the host, 37 the numbering of them of the tribe of Gad, was forty and five thousand and six hundred and fifty. 38 For the sons of Dan according to their kindreds, according to their divisions, according to the houses of their families, according to the number of their names, according to their polls, all males from twenty years old and upward, every one that goes forth with the host, 39 the numbering of them of the tribe of Dan, was sixty and two thousand and seven hundred. 40 For the sons of Aser according to their kindreds, according to their divisions, according to the houses of their families, according to the number of their names, according to their polls, every male from twenty years old and upward, every one that goes forth with the host, 41 the numbering of them of the tribe of Aser, was forty and one thousand and five hundred. 42 For the sons of Nephthali according to their kindreds, according to their divisions, according to the houses of their families, according to the number of their names, according to their polls, every male from twenty years old and upward, every one who goes forth with the host, 43 the numbering of them of the tribe of Nephthali, was fifty-three thousand and four hundred. 44 This is the numbering which Moses and Aaron and the rulers of Israel, being twelve men, conducted: there was a man for each tribe, they were according to the tribe of the houses of their family. 45 And the whole numbering of the children of Israel with their host from twenty years old and upward, every one that goes out to set himself in battle array in Israel, came to 46 six hundred thousand and three thousand and five hundred and fifty. 47 But the Levites of the tribe of their family were not counted among the children of Israel. 48 And the Lord spoke to Moses, saying, 49 See, thou shalt not muster the tribe of Levi, and thou shalt not take their numbers, in the midst of the children of Israel. 50 And do thou set the Levites over the tabernacle of witness, and over all its furniture, and over all things that are in it; and they shall do service in it, and they shall encamp round about the tabernacle. 51 And in removing the tabernacle, the Levites shall take it down, and in pitching the tabernacle they shall set it up: and let the stranger that advances *to touch it* die. 52 And the children of Israel shall encamp, every man in his own order, and every man according to his company, with their host. 53 But let the Levites encamp round about the tabernacle of witness fronting it, and *so* there shall be no sin among the children of Israel; and the Levites themselves shall keep the guard of the tabernacle of witness. 54 And the children of Israel did according to all that the Lord commanded Moses and Aaron, so did they.

Num.2 1 And the Lord spoke to Moses and Aaron, saying, 2 Let the children of Israel encamp fronting *each other*, every man keeping his own rank, according to *their* standards, according to the houses of their families; the children of Israel shall encamp round about the tabernacle of witness. 3 And they that encamp first toward the east *shall be* the order of the camp of Juda with their host, and the prince of the sons of Juda, Naasson the son of Aminadab. 4 His forces that were numbered, were seventy-four thousand and six hundred. 5 And they that encamp next *shall be* of the tribe of Issachar, and the prince of the sons of Issachar *shall be* Nathanael the son of Sogar. 6 His forces that were numbered, were fifty-four thousand and four hundred. 7

And they that encamp next *shall be* of the tribe of Zabulon, and the prince of the sons of Zabulon *shall be* Eliab the son of Chaelon. 8 His forces that were numbered, were fifty-seven thousand and four hundred. 9 All that were numbered of the camp of Juda were a hundred and eighty thousand and six thousand and four hundred: they shall move first with their forces. 10 *This is* the order of the camp of Ruben; their forces *shall be* toward the south, and the prince of the children of Ruben *shall be* Elisur the son of Sediur. 11 His forces that were numbered, were forty-six thousand and five hundred. 12 And they that encamp next to him *shall be* of the tribe of Symeon, and the prince of the sons of Symeon *shall be* Salamiel the son of Surisadai. 13 His forces that were numbered, were fifty-nine thousand and three hundred. 14 And they that encamp next to them *shall be* the tribe of Gad; and the prince of the sons of Gad, Elisaph the son of Raguel. 15 His forces that were numbered, were forty-five thousand and six hundred and fifty. 16 All who were numbered of the camp of Ruben, were a hundred and fifty-one thousand and four hundred and fifty: they with their forces shall proceed in the second place. 17 And *then* the tabernacle of witness shall be set forward, and the camp of the Levites *shall be* between the camps; as they shall encamp, so also shall they commence their march, each one next in order to his fellow according to their companies. 18 The station of the camp of Ephraim *shall be* westward with their forces, and the head of the children of Ephraim *shall be* Elisama the son of Emiud. 19 His forces that were numbered, are forty thousand and five hundred. 20 And they that encamp next *shall be* of the tribe of Manasse, and the prince of the sons of Manasse, Gamaliel the son of Phadassur. 21 His forces that were numbered, were thirty-two thousand and two hundred. 22 And they that encamp next *shall be* of the tribe of Benjamin, and the prince of the sons of Benjamin, Abidan the son of Gadeoni. 23 His forces that were numbered, were thirty-five thousand and four hundred. 24 All that were numbered of the camp of Ephraim, were one hundred and eight thousand and one hundred: they with their forces shall set out third. 25 The order of the camp of Dan *shall be* northward with their forces; and the prince of the sons of Dan, Achiezer the son of Amisadai. 26 His forces that were numbered, were sixty-two thousand and seven hundred. 27 And they that encamp next to him *shall be* the tribe of Aser; and the prince of the sons of Aser, Phagiel the son of Echran. 28 His forces that were numbered, were forty-one thousand and five hundred. 29 And they that encamp next *shall be* of the tribe of Nephthali; and the prince of the children of Nephthali, Achire son Ænan. 30 His forces that were numbered were fifty-three thousand and four hundred. 31 All that were numbered of the camp of Dan, *were* a hundred and fifty-seven thousand and six hundred: they shall set out last according to their order. 32 This *is* the numbering of the children of Israel according to the houses of their families: all the numbering of the camps with their forces, *was* six hundred and three thousand, five hundred and fifty. 33 But the Levites were not numbered with them, as the Lord commanded Moses. 34 And the children of Israel did all things that the Lord commanded Moses; thus they encamped in their order, and thus they began their march in succession each according to their divisions, according to the houses of their families.

Num.3 1 And these *are* the generations of Aaron and Moses, in the day in which the Lord spoke to Moses in mount Sina. 2 And these *are* the names of the sons of Aaron; Nadab the first-born; and Abiud, Eleazar and Ithamar. 3 These *are* the names of the sons of Aaron, the anointed priests whom they consecrated to the priesthood. 4 And Nadab and Abiud died before the Lord, when they offered strange fire before the Lord, in the wilderness of Sina; and they had no children; and Eleazar and Ithamar ministered in the priests' office with Aaron their father. 5 And the Lord spoke to Moses, saying, 6 Take the tribe of Levi, and thou shalt set them before Aaron the priest, and they shall minister to him, 7 and shall keep his charges, and the charges of the children of Israel, before the tabernacle of witness, to do the works of the tabernacle. 8 And they shall keep all the furniture of the tabernacle of witness, and the charges of the children of Israel as to all the works of the tabernacle. 9 And thou shalt give the Levites to Aaron, and to his sons the priests; they are given for a gift to me of the children of Israel. 10 And thou shalt appoint Aaron and his sons over the tabernacle of witness; and they shall keep their charge of priesthood, and all things belonging to the altar, and within the veil; and the stranger that touches them shall die. 11 And the Lord spoke to Moses, saying, 12 Behold, I have taken the Levites from the midst of the children of Israel, instead of every male that opens the womb from among the children of Israel: they shall be their ransom, and the Levites shall be mine. 13 For every first-born *is* mine; in the day in which I smote every first-born in the land of Egypt, I sanctified to myself every first-born in Israel: both of man and beast, they shall be mine: I *am* the Lord. 14 And the Lord spoke to Moses in the wilderness of Sina, saying, 15 Take the number of the sons of Levi, according to the houses of their families, according to their divisions; number ye them every male from a month old and upwards. 16 And Moses and Aaron numbered them by the word of the Lord, as the Lord commanded them. 17 And these were the sons of Levi by their names; Gedson, Caath, and Merari. 18 And these *are* the names of the sons of Gedson according to their families; Lobeni and Semei: 19 and the sons of Caath according to their families; Amram and Issaar, Chebron and Oziel: 20 and the sons of Merari according to their families, Mooli and Musi; these are the families of the Levites according to the houses of their families. 21 To Gedson belongs the family of Lobeni, and the family of Semei: these are the families of Gedson. 22 The numbering of them according to the number of every male from a month old and upwards, their numbering *was* seven thousand and five hundred. 23 And the sons of Gedson shall encamp westward behind the tabernacle. 24 And the ruler of the household of the family of Gedson *was* Elisaph the son of Dael. 25 And the charge of the sons of Gedson in the tabernacle of witness *was* the tent and the veil, and the covering of the door of the tabernacle of witness, 26 and the curtains of the court, and the veil of the door of the court, which is by the tabernacle, and the remainder of all its works. 27 To Caath *belonged* one division, that of Amram, and another division, that of Issaar, and another division, that of Chebron, and another division, that of Oziel: these are the divisions of Caath, according to number. 28 Every male from a month old and upward, eight thousand and six hundred, keeping the charges of the holy things. 29 The families of the sons of Caath, shall encamp beside the tabernacle toward the south. 30 And the chief of the house of the families of the divisions of Caath, *was* Elisaphan the son of Oziel. 31 And their charge *was* the ark, and the table, and the candlestick, and the altars, and all the vessels of the sanctuary wherewith they do holy service, and the veil, and all their works. 32 And the chief over the chief of the Levites, *was* Eleazar the son of Aaron the priest, appointed to keep the charges of the holy things. 33 To Merari *belonged* the family of Mooli, and the family of Musi: these are the families of Merari. 34 The mustering of them according to number, every male from a month old and upwards, *was* six thousand and fifty. 35 And the head of the house of the families of the division of Merari, was Suriel the son of Abichail: they shall encamp by the side of the tabernacle northwards. 36 The oversight of the charge of the sons of Merari *included* the chapiters of the tabernacle, and its bars, and its pillars, and its sockets, and all their furniture, and their works, 37 and the pillars of the court round about, and their bases, and their pins, and their cords. 38 They that encamp before the tabernacle of witness on the east *shall be* Moses and Aaron and his sons, keeping the charges of the sanctuary according to the charges of the children of Israel; and the stranger that touches them, shall die. 39 All the numbering of the Levites, whom Moses and Aaron numbered by the word of the Lord, according to their families, every male from a month old and upwards, *were* two and twenty thousand. 40 And the Lord spoke to Moses, saying, Count every first-born male of the children of Israel from a month old and upwards, and take the number by name. 41 And thou shalt take the Levites for me—I *am* the Lord—instead of all the first-born of the sons of Israel, and the cattle of the Levites instead of all the first-born among the cattle of the children of Israel. 42 And Moses counted, as the Lord commanded him, every first-born among the children of Israel. 43 And all the male first-born in number by name, from a month old and upwards, were according to their numbering twenty-two thousand and two hundred and seventy-three. 44 And the Lord spoke to Moses, saying, 45 Take the Levites instead of all the first-born of the sons of Israel, and the cattle of the Levites instead of their cattle, and the Levites shall be mine; I *am* the Lord. 46 And for the ransoms of the two hundred and seventy-three which exceed the Levites in number of the first-born of the sons of Israel; 47 thou shalt even take five shekels a head; thou shalt take them according to the holy didrachm, twenty oboli to the shekel. 48 And thou shalt give the money to Aaron and to his sons, the ransom of those who exceed in number among them. 49 And Moses took the silver, the ransom of those that exceeded in number the redemption of the Levites. 50 He took the silver from the first-born of the sons of Israel, a thousand three hundred and sixty-five

shekels, according to the holy shekel. 51 And Moses gave the ransom of them that were over to Aaron and his sons, by the word of the Lord, as the Lord commanded Moses.

Num.4 1 And the Lord spoke to Moses and Aaron, saying, 2 Take the sum of the children of Caath from the midst of the sons of Levi, after their families, according to the houses of their fathers' households; 3 from twenty-five years old and upward until fifty years, every one that goes in to minister, to do all the works in the tabernacle of witness. 4 And these are the works of the sons of Caath in the tabernacle of witness; it is most holy. 5 And Aaron and his sons shall go in, when the camp is about to move, and shall take down the shadowing veil, and shall cover with it the ark of the testimony. 6 And they shall put on it a cover, even a blue skin, and put on it above a garment all of blue, and shall put the staves through *the rings*. 7 And they shall put on the table set forth for shew-bred a cloth all of purple, and the dishes, and the censers, and the cups, and the vessels with which one offers drink-offerings; and the continual loaves shall be upon it. 8 And they shall put upon it a scarlet cloth, and they shall cover it with a blue covering of skin, and they shall put the staves into it. 9 And they shall take a blue covering, and cover the candlestick that gives light, and its lamps, and its snuffers, and its funnels, and all the vessels of oil with which they minister. 10 And they shall put it, and all its vessels, into a blue skin cover; and they shall put it on bearers. 11 And they shall put a blue cloth for a cover on the golden altar, and shall cover it with a blue skin cover, and put in its staves. 12 And they shall take all the instruments of service, with which they minister in the sanctuary: and shall place them in a cloth of blue, and shall cover them with blue skin covering, and put them upon staves. 13 And he shall put the covering on the altar, and they shall cover it with a cloth all of purple. 14 And they shall put upon it all the vessels with which they minister upon it, and the fire-pans, and the flesh-hooks, and the cups, and the cover, and all the vessels of the altar; and they shall put on it a blue cover of skins, and shall put in its staves; and they shall take a purple cloth, and cover the laver and its foot, and they shall put it into a blue cover of skin, and put it on bars. 15 And Aaron and his sons shall finish covering the holy things, and all the holy vessels, when the camp begins to move; and afterwards the sons of Caath shall go in to take up *the furniture*; but shall not touch the holy things, lest they die: these shall the sons of Caath bear in the tabernacle of witness. 16 Eleazar the son of Aaron the priest is overseer—the oil of the light, and the incense of composition, and the daily meat-offering and the anointing oil, are his charge; even the oversight of the whole tabernacle, and all things that are in it in the holy place, in all the works. 17 And the Lord spoke to Moses and Aaron, saying, 18 Ye shall not destroy the family of Caath from the tribe out of the midst of the Levites. 19 This do ye to them, and they shall live and not die, when they approach the holy of holies: Let Aaron and his sons advance, and they shall place them each in his post for bearing. 20 And *so* they shall by no means go in to look suddenly upon the holy things, and die. 21 And the Lord spoke to Moses, saying, 22 Take the sum of the children of Gedson, and these according to the houses of their lineage, according to their families. 23 Take the number of them from five and twenty years old and upwards until the age of fifty, every one that goes in to minister, to do his business in the tabernacle of witness. 24 This *is* the public service of the family of Gedson, to minister and to bear. 25 And they shall bear the skins of the tabernacle, and the tabernacle of witness, and its veil, and the blue cover that was on it above, and the cover of the door of the tabernacle of witness. 26 And all the curtains of the court which were upon the tabernacle of witness, and the appendages, and all the vessels of service that they minister with they shall attend to. 27 According to the direction of Aaron and his sons shall be the ministry of the sons of Gedson, in all their ministries, and in all their works; and thou shalt take account of them by name in all things borne by them. 28 This is the service of the sons of Gedson in the tabernacle of witness, and their charge by the hand of Ithamar the son of Aaron the priest. 29 The sons of Merari according to their families, according to the houses of their lineage, take ye the number of them. 30 Take the number of them from five and twenty years old and upwards until fifty years old, every one that goes in to perform the services of the tabernacle of witness. 31 And these are the charges of the things borne by them according to all their works in the tabernacle of witness: they shall bear the chapiters of the tabernacle, and the bars, and its pillars, and its sockets, and the veil, and *there shall be* their sockets, and their pillars, and the curtain of the door of the tabernacle. 32 And they shall bear the pillars of the court round about, and *there shall be* their sockets, and *they shall bear* the pillars of the veil of the door of the court, and their sockets and their pins, and their cords, and all their furniture, and all their instruments of service: take ye their number by name, and all the articles of the charge of the things borne by them. 33 This is the ministration of the family of the sons of Merari in all their works in the tabernacle of witness, by the hand of Ithamar the son of Aaron the priest. 34 And Moses and Aaron and the rulers of Israel took the number of the sons of Caath according to their families, according to the houses of their lineage; 35 from five and twenty years old and upwards to the age of fifty years, every one that goes in to minister and do service in the tabernacle of witness. 36 And the numbering of them according to their families was two thousand, seven hundred and fifty. 37 This is the numbering of the family of Caath, every one that ministers in the tabernacle of witness, as Moses and Aaron numbered them by the word of the Lord, by the hand of Moses. 38 And the sons of Gedson were numbered according to their families, according to the houses of their lineage, 39 from five and twenty years old and upward till fifty years old, every one that goes in to minister and to do the services in the tabernacle of witness. 40 And the numbering of them according to their families, according to the houses of their lineage, *was* two thousand six hundred and thirty. 41 This *is* the numbering of the family of the sons of Gedson, every one who ministers in the tabernacle of witness; whom Moses and Aaron numbered by the word of the Lord, by the hand of Moses. 42 And also the family of the sons of Merari were numbered according to their divisions, according to the house of their fathers; 43 from five and twenty years old and upward till fifty years old, every one that goes in to minister in the services of the tabernacle of witness. 44 And the numbering of them according to their families, according to the houses of their lineage, *was* three thousand and two hundred. 45 This *is* the numbering of the family of the sons of Merari, whom Moses and Aaron numbered by the word of the Lord, by the hand of Moses. 46 All that were numbered, whom Moses and Aaron and the rulers of Israel numbered, *namely*, the Levites, according to their families and according to the houses of their lineage, 47 from five and twenty years old and upward till fifty years old, every one that goes in to the service of the works, and the *charge of* the things that are carried in the tabernacle of witness. 48 And they that were numbered were eight thousand five hundred and eighty. 49 He reviewed them by the word of the Lord by the hand of Moses, appointing each man severally over their *respective* work, and over their burdens; and they were numbered, as the Lord commanded Moses.

Num.5 1 And the Lord spoke to Moses, saying, 2 Charge the children of Israel, and let them send forth out of the camp every leper, and every one who has in issue of the reins, and every one who is unclean from a dead body. 3 Whether male or female, send them forth out of the camp; and they shall not defile their camps in which I dwell among them. 4 And the children of Israel did so, and sent them out of the camp: as the Lord said to Moses, so did the children of Israel. 5 And the Lord spoke to Moses, saying, 6 Speak to the children of Israel, saying, Every man or woman who shall commit any sin that is common to man, or if that soul shall in anywise have neglected the commandment and transgressed; 7 *that person* shall confess the sin which he has committed, and shall make satisfaction for his trespass: he *shall pay* the principal, and shall add to it the fifth part, and shall make restoration to him against whom he has trespassed. 8 But if a man have no near kinsman, so as to make satisfaction for his trespass to him, the trespass- offering paid to the Lord shall be for the priest, besides the ram of atonement, by which he shall make atonement with it for him. 9 And every first-fruits in all the sanctified things among the children of Israel, whatsoever they shall offer to the Lord, shall be for the priest himself. 10 And the hallowed things of every man shall be his; and whatever man shall give *any thing* to the priest, the gift shall be his. 11 And the Lord spoke to Moses, saying, 12 Speak to the children of Israel, and thou shalt say to them, Whosoever wife shall transgress against him, and slight and despise him, 13 and *supposing* any one shall lie with her carnally, and the thing shall be hid from the eyes of her husband, and she should conceal it and be herself defiled, and there be no witness with her, and she should not be taken; 14 and there should come upon him a spirit of jealousy, and he should be jealous of his wife, and she be defiled; or there should come upon him a spirit of jealousy, and he should be jealous of his wife, and she should not be defiled; 15 then shall the man bring his wife to the priest, and shall bring his gift for her, the tenth part of an ephah of barley-meal: he shall not pour oil upon it, neither shall he put frankincense upon it; for it is a sacrifice of jealousy, a sacrifice of memorial, recalling sin to remembrance. 16 And the priest shall bring her, and cause her to stand before the Lord. 17 And the priest shall take pure running water in an earthen vessel, and he shall take of the dust that is on the floor of the tabernacle of witness, and the priest having taken it shall cast it into the water. 18 And the priest shall cause the woman to stand before the Lord, and shall uncover the head of the woman, and shall put into her hands the sacrifice of memorial, the sacrifice of jealousy; and in the hand of the priest shall be the water of this conviction that brings the curse. 19 And the priest shall adjure her, and shall say to the woman, If no one has lain with thee, and if thou hast not transgressed so as to be polluted, being under the power of thy husband, be free from this water of the conviction that causes the curse. 20 But if being a married woman thou hast transgressed, or been polluted, and any one has lain with thee, beside thy husband: 21 then the priest shall adjure the woman by the oaths of this curse, and the priest shall say to the woman, The Lord bring thee into a curse and under an oath in the midst of thy people, in that the Lord should cause thy thigh to rot and thy belly to swell; 22 and this water bringing the curse shall enter into thy womb to cause thy belly to swell, and thy thigh to rot. And the woman shall say, So be it, So be it. 23 And the priest shall write these curses in a book, and shall blot them out with the water of the conviction that brings the curse. 24 And he shall cause the woman to drink the water of the conviction that brings the curse; and the water of the conviction that brings the curse shall enter into her. 25 And the priest shall take from the hand of the woman the sacrifice of jealousy, and shall present the sacrifice before the Lord, and shall bring it to the altar. 26 And the priest shall take a handful of the sacrifice as a memorial of it, and shall offer it up upon the altar; and afterwards he shall cause the woman to drink the water. 27 And it shall come to pass, if she be defiled, and have altogether escaped the notice of her husband, then the water of the conviction that brings the curse shall enter into her; and she shall swell in her belly, and her thigh shall rot, and the woman shall be for a curse in the midst of her people. 28 But if the woman have not been polluted, and be clean, then shall she be guiltless and shall conceive seed. 29 This is the law of jealousy, wherein a married woman should happen to transgress, and be defiled; 30 or in the case of a man on whomsoever the spirit of jealousy should come, and he should be jealous of his wife, and he should place his wife before the Lord, and the priest shall execute towards her all this law. 31 Then the man shall be clear from sin, and that woman shall bear her sin.

Num.6 1 And the Lord spoke to Moses, saying, 2 speak to the children of Israel, and thou shalt say to them, Whatsoever man or woman shall specially vow a vow to separate oneself with purity to the Lord, 3 he shall purely abstain from wine and strong drink; and he shall drink no vinegar of wine or vinegar of strong drink; and whatever is made of the grape he shall not drink; neither shall he eat fresh grapes or raisins, 4 all the days of his vow: he shall eat no one of all the things that come from the vine, wine from the grape-stones to the husk, 5 all the days of his separation:—a razor shall not come upon his head, until the days be fulfilled which he vowed to the Lord: he shall be holy, cherishing the long hair of the head, 6 all the days of his vow to the Lord: he shall not come nigh to any dead body, 7 to his father or his mother, or to his brother or his sister; he shall not defile himself for them, when they have died, because the vow of God is upon him on his head. 8 All the days of his vow he shall be holy to the Lord. 9 And if any one should die suddenly by him, immediately the head of his vow shall be defiled; and he shall shave his head in whatever day he shall be purified: on the seventh day he shall be shaved. 10 And on the eighth day he shall bring two turtledoves, or two young pigeons, to the priest, to the doors of the tabernacle of witness. 11 And the priest shall offer one for a sin-offering; and the other for a whole-burnt-offering; and the priest shall make atonement for him in the things wherein he sinned respecting the dead body, and he shall sanctify his head in that day, 12 in which he was consecrated to the Lord, *all* the days of his vow; and he shall bring a lamb of a year old for a trespass-offering; and the former days shall not be reckoned, because the head of his vow was polluted. 13 And this is the law of him that has vowed: in whatever day he shall have fulfilled the days of his vow, he shall himself bring his gift to the doors of the tabernacle of witness. 14 And he shall bring his gift to the Lord; one he-lamb of a year old without blemish for a whole-burnt- offering, and one ewe-lamb of a year old without blemish for a sin-offering, and one ram without blemish for a peace-offering; 15 and a basket of unleavened bread of fine flour, *even* loaves kneaded with oil, and unleavened cakes anointed with oil, and their meat offering, and their drink-offering. 16 And the priest shall bring them before the Lord, and shall offer his sin- offering, and his whole-burnt-offering. 17 And he shall offer the ram as a sacrifice of peace- offering to the Lord with the basket of unleavened bread; and the priest shall offer its meat-offering and its drink-offering. 18 And he that has vowed shall shave the head of his consecration by the doors of the tabernacle of witness, and shall put the hairs on the fire which is under the sacrifice of peace-offering. 19 And the priest shall take the sodden shoulder of the ram, and one unleavened loaf from the basket, and one unleavened cake, and shall put them on the hands of the votary after he has shaved off his holy hair. 20 And the priest shall present them as an offering before the Lord; it shall be the holy portion for the priest beside the breast of the heave-offering and beside the shoulder of the wave-offering: and afterwards the votary shall drink wine. 21 This is the law of the votary who shall have vowed to the Lord his gift to the Lord, concerning his vow, besides what he may be able to afford according to the value of his vow, which he may have vowed according to the law of separation. 22 And the Lord spoke to Moses, saying, 23 Speak to Aaron and to his sons, saying, Thus ye shall bless the children of Israel, saying to them, 24 The Lord bless thee and keep thee; 25 the Lord make his face to shine upon thee, and have mercy upon thee; 26 the Lord lift up his countenance upon thee, and give thee peace. 27 And they shall put my name upon the children of Israel, and I the Lord will bless them.

Num.7 1 And it came to pass in the day in which Moses finished the setting-up of the tabernacle, that he anointed it, and consecrated it, and all its furniture, and the altar and all its furniture, he even anointed them, and consecrated them. 2 And the princes of Israel brought *gifts*, twelve princes of their fathers' houses: these were the heads of tribes, these are they that presided over the numbering. 3 And they brought their gift before the Lord, six covered waggons, and twelve oxen; a waggon from two princes, and a calf from each: and they brought them before the tabernacle. 4 And the Lord spoke to Moses, saying, 5 Take of them, and they shall be for the works of the services of the tabernacle of witness: and thou shalt give them to the Levites, to each one according to his ministration. 6 And Moses took the waggons and the oxen, and gave them to the Levites. 7 And he gave two waggons and four oxen to the sons of Gedson, according to their ministrations. 8 And four waggons and eight oxen he gave to the sons of Merari according to their ministrations, by Ithamar the son of Aaron the priest. 9 But to the sons of Caath he gave them not, because they have the ministrations of the sacred things: they shall bear them on their shoulders. 10 And the rulers brought *gifts* for the dedication of the altar, in the day in which he anointed it, and the rulers brought their gifts before the altar. 11 And the Lord said to Moses, One chief each day, they shall offer their gifts a chief each day for the dedication of the altar. 12 And he that offered his gift on the first day, was Naasson the son of Aminadab, prince of the tribe of Juda. 13 And he brought his gift, one silver charger of a hundred and thirty shekels was its weight, one silver bowl, of seventy shekels according to the holy shekel; both full of fine flour kneaded with oil for a meat-offering. 14 One golden censer of ten shekels full of incense. 15 One calf of the herd, one ram, one he-lamb of a year old for a whole-burnt-offering; 16 and one kid of the goats for a sin-offering. 17 And for a sacrifice of peace-offering, two heifers, five rams, five he goats, five ewe-lambs of a year old: this *was* the gift of Naasson the son of Aminadab. 18 On the second day Nathanael son of Sogar, the prince of the tribe of Issachar, brought *his offering*. 19 And he brought his gift, one silver charger, its weight a hundred and thirty shekels, one silver bowl of seventy shekels according to the holy shekel; both full of fine flour kneaded with oil for a meat-offering. 20 One censer of ten golden shekels, full of incense. 21 One calf of the herd, one ram, one he-lamb of a year old for a whole-burnt-offering, 22 and one kid of the goats for a sin-offering. 23 And for a sacrifice, a peace-offering, two heifers, five rams, five he- goats, five ewe-lambs of a year old: this *was* the gift of Nathanael the son of Sogar. 24 On the third day the prince of the sons of Zabulon, Eliab the son of Chaelon. 25 *He brought* his gift, one silver charger, its weight a hundred and thirty shekels, one silver bowl of seventy shekels according to the holy shekel; both full of

fine flour kneaded with oil for a meat offering. 26 One golden censer of ten shekels, full of incense. 27 One calf of the herd, one ram, one he-lamb of a year old for a whole-burnt-offering, 28 and one kid of the goats for a sin-offering. 29 And for a sacrifice of peace-offering, two heifers, five rams, five he-goats, five ewe -lambs of a year old: this *was* the gift of Eliab the son of Chaelon. 30 On the fourth day Elisur the son of Sediur, the prince of the children of Ruben. 31 *He brought* his gift, one silver charger, its weight a hundred and thirty shekels, one silver bowl of seventy shekels according to the holy shekel; both full of fine flour kneaded with oil for a meat- offering. 32 One golden censer of ten shekels full of incense. 33 One calf of the herd, one ram, one he-lamb of a year old for a whole-burnt-offering, 34 and one kid of the goats for a sin-offering. 35 And for a sacrifice of peace-offering, two heifers, five rams, five he-goats, five ewe -lambs of a year old: this *was* the gift of Elisur the son of Sediur. 36 On the fifth day the prince of the children of Symeon, Salamiel the son of Surisadai. 37 *He brought* his gift, one silver charger, its weight one hundred and thirty shekels, one silver bowl of seventy shekels according to the holy shekel; both full of fine flour kneaded with oil for a meat-offering. 38 One golden censer of ten shekels, full of incense. 39 One calf of the herd, one ram, one he-lamb of a year old for a whole-burnt-offering, 40 and one kid of the goats for a sin-offering. 41 And for a sacrifice of peace-offering, two heifers, five rams, five he-goats, five ewe -lambs of a year old: this *was* the gift of Salamiel the son of Surisadai. 42 On the sixth day the prince of the sons of Gad, Elisaph the son of Raguel. 43 *He brought* his gift, one silver charger, its weight a hundred and thirty shekels, one silver bowl of seventy shekels according to the holy shekel; both full of fine flour kneaded with oil for a meat offering. 44 One golden censer of ten shekels, full of incense. 45 One calf of the herd, one ram, one he-lamb of a year old for a whole-burnt-offering, 46 and one kid of the goats for a sin- offering. 47 And for a sacrifice of peace-offering, two heifers, five rams, five he-goats, five ewe -lambs of a year old: this *was* the gift of Elisaph the son of Raguel. 48 On the seventh day the prince of the sons of Ephraim, Elisama the son of Emiud. 49 *He brought* his gift, one silver charger, its weight was a hundred and thirty shekels, one silver bowl of seventy shekels according to the holy shekel; both full of fine flour kneaded with oil for a meat-offering. 50 One golden censer of ten shekels, full of incense. 51 One calf of the herd, one ram, one he-lamb of a year old for a whole-burnt-offering, 52 and one kid of the goats for a sin-offering. 53 And for a sacrifice of peace-offering, two heifers, five rams, five he-goats, five ewe-lambs of a year old: this *was* the gift of Elisama the son of Emiud. 54 On the eighth day the prince of the sons of Manasse, Gamaliel the son of Phadassur. 55 *He brought* his gift, one silver charger, its weight one hundred and thirty shekels, one silver bowl of seventy shekels according to the holy shekel; both full of fine flour mingled with oil for a meat-offering. 56 One golden censer of ten shekels, full of incense. 57 One calf of the herd, one ram, one he-lamb of a year old for a whole-burnt-offering, 58 and one kid of the goats for a sin- offering. 59 And for a sacrifice of peace-offering two heifers, five rams, five he-goats, five ewe-lambs of a year old: this *was* the gift of Gamaliel the son of Phadassur. 60 On the ninth day the prince of the sons of Benjamin, Abidan the son of Gadeoni. 61 *He brought* his gift, one silver charger, its weight a hundred and thirty *shekels*, one silver bowl of seventy shekels according to the holy shekel; both full of fine flour mingled with oil for a meat - offering. 62 One golden censer of ten shekels, full of incense. 63 One calf of the herd, one ram, one he-lamb of a year old for a whole-burnt-offering, 64 and one kid of the goats for a sin- offering. 65 And for a sacrifice of peace-offering, two heifers, five rams, five he-goats, five ewe - lambs of a year old: this *was* the gift of Abidan the son of Gadeoni. 66 On the tenth day the prince of the sons of Dan, Achiezer the son of Amisadai. 67 *He brought* his gift, one silver charger, its weight a hundred and thirty *shekels*, one silver bowl of seventy shekels according to the holy shekel; both full of fine flour kneaded with oil for a meat- offering. 68 One golden censer of ten shekels, full of incense. 69 One calf of the herd, one ram, one he-lamb of a year old for a whole-burnt-offering, 70 and one kid of the goats for a sin-offering. 71 And for a sacrifice of peace-offering, two heifers, five rams, five he-goats, five ewe -lambs of a year old. This *was* the gift of Achiezer the son of Amisadai. 72 On the eleventh day the prince of the sons of Aser, Phageel the son of Echran. 73 *He brought* his gift, one silver charger, its weight a hundred and thirty *shekels*, one silver bowl of seventy shekels according to the holy shekel; both full of fine flour mingled with oil for a meat- offering. 74 One golden censer of ten shekels, full of incense. 75 One calf of the herd, one ram, one he-lamb of a year old for a whole-burnt-offering, 76 and one kid of the goats for a sin-offering. 77 And for a sacrifice of peace-offering, two heifers, five rams, five he-goats, five ewe -lambs of a year old: this *was* the gift of Phageel the son of Echran. 78 On the twelfth day the prince of the sons of Nephthali, Achire the son of Ænan. 79 *He brought* his gift, one silver charger, its weight a hundred and thirty shekels; one silver bowl of seventy shekels according to the holy shekel; both full of fine flour mingled with oil for a meat offering. 80 One golden censer of ten shekels, full of incense. 81 One calf of the herd, one ram, one he-lamb of a year old for a whole-burnt-offering, 82 and one kid of the goats for a sin-offering. 83 And for a sacrifice of peace-offering, two heifers, five rams, five he-goats, five ewe -lambs of a year old: this *was* the gift of Achire the son of Ænan. 84 This was the dedication of the altar in the day in which *Moses* anointed it, by the princes of the sons of Israel; twelve silver chargers, twelve silver bowls, twelve golden censers: 85 each charger of a hundred and thirty shekels, and each bowl of seventy shekels: all the silver of the vessels *was* two thousand four hundred shekels, the shekels according to the holy shekel. 86 Twelve golden censers full of incense: all the gold of the shekels, a hundred and twenty shekels. 87 All the cattle for whole-burnt-offerings, twelve calves, twelve rams, twelve he- lambs of a year old, and their meat-offerings, and their drink-offerings: and twelve kids of the goats for sin-offering. 88 All the cattle for a sacrifice of peace-offering, twenty-four heifers, sixty rams, sixty he-

goats of a year old, sixty ewe-lambs of a year old without blemish: this is the dedication of the altar, after that *Moses* consecrated *Aaron*, and after he anointed him. 89 When Moses went into the tabernacle of witness to speak to God, then he heard the voice of the Lord speaking to him from off the mercy-seat, which is upon the ark of the testimony, between the two cherubs; and he spoke to him.

Num.8 1 And the Lord spoke to Moses, saying, 2 Speak to Aaron, and thou shalt say to him, Whenever thou shalt set the lamps in order, the seven lamps shall give light opposite the candlestick. 3 And Aaron did so: on one side opposite the candlestick he lighted its lamps, as the Lord appointed Moses. 4 And this *is* the construction of the candlestick: *it is* solid, golden— its stem, and its lilies—all solid: according to the pattern which the Lord shewed Moses, so he made the candlestick. 5 And the Lord spoke to Moses, saying, 6 Take the Levites out of the midst of the children of Israel, and thou shalt purify them. 7 And thus shalt thou perform their purification: thou shalt sprinkle them with water of purification, and a razor shall come upon the whole of their body, and they shall wash their garments, and shall be clean. 8 And they shall take one calf of the herd, and its meat-offering, fine flour mingled with oil: and thou shalt take a calf of a year old of the herd for a sin-offering. 9 And thou shalt bring the Levites before the tabernacle of witness; and thou shalt assemble all the congregation of the sons of Israel. 10 And thou shalt bring the Levites before the Lord; and the sons of Israel shall lay their hands upon the Levites. 11 And Aaron shall separate the Levites for a gift before the Lord from the children of Israel: and they shall be prepared to perform the works of the Lord. 12 And the Levites shall lay their hands on the heads of the calves; and thou shalt offer one for a sin-offering, and the other for a whole-burnt-offering to the Lord, to make atonement for them. 13 And thou shalt set the Levites before the Lord, and before Aaron, and before his sons; and thou shalt give them as a gift before the Lord. 14 And thou shalt separate the Levites from the midst of the sons of Israel, and they shall be mine. 15 And afterwards the Levites shall go in to perform the works of the tabernacle of witness; and thou shalt purify them, and present them before the Lord. 16 For these are given to me for a present out of the midst of the children of Israel: I have taken them to myself instead of all the first-born of the sons of Israel that open every womb. 17 For every first-born among the children of Israel *is* mine, whether of man or beast: in the day in which I smote every first-born in the land of Egypt, I sanctified them to myself. 18 And I took the Levites in the place of every first-born among the children of Israel. 19 And I gave the Levites presented as a gift to Aaron and his sons out of the midst of the children of Israel, to do the service of the children of Israel in the tabernacle of witness, and to make atonement for the children of Israel: thus there shall be none among the sons of Israel to draw nigh to the holy things. 20 And Moses and Aaron, and all the congregation of the children of Israel, did to the Levites as the Lord commanded Moses concerning the Levites, so the sons of Israel did to them. 21 So the Levites purified themselves and washed their garments; and Aaron presented them as a gift before the Lord, and Aaron made atonement for them to purify them. 22 And afterwards the Levites went in to minister in their service in the tabernacle of witness before Aaron, and before his sons; as the Lord appointed Moses concerning the Levites, so they did to them. 23 And the Lord spoke to Moses, saying, 24 This is the *ordinance* for the Levites; From five and twenty years old and upward, they shall go in to minister in the tabernacle of witness. 25 And from fifty years old *the Levites* shall cease from the ministry, and shall not work any longer. 26 And his brother shall serve in the tabernacle of witness to keep charges, but he shall not do works: so shalt thou do to the Levites in their charges.

Num.9 1 And the Lord spoke to Moses in the wilderness of Sina in the second year after they had gone forth from the land of Egypt, in the first month, saying, 2 Speak, and let the children of Israel keep the passover in its season. 3 On the fourteenth day of the first month at even, thou shalt keep it in its season; thou shalt keep it according to its law, and according to its ordinance. 4 And Moses ordered the children of Israel to sacrifice the passover, 5 on the fourteenth day of the first month in the wilderness of Sina, as the Lord appointed Moses, so the children of Israel did. 6 And there came men who were unclean by reason of a dead body, and they were not able to keep the passover on that day; and they came before Moses and Aaron on that day. 7 And those men said to Moses, We are unclean by reason of the dead body of a man: shall we therefore fail to offer the gift to the Lord in its season in the midst of the children of Israel? 8 And Moses said to them, stand there, and I will hear what charge the Lord will give concerning you. 9 And the Lord spoke to Moses, saying, 10 Speak to the children of Israel, saying, Whatever man shall be unclean by reason of a dead body, or on a journey far off, among you, or among your posterity; he shall then keep the passover to the Lord, 11 in the second month, on the fourteenth day; in the evening they shall offer it, with unleavened bread and bitter herbs shall they eat it. 12 They shall not leave of it until the morrow, and they shall not break a bone of it; they shall sacrifice it according to the ordinance of the passover. 13 And whatsoever man shall be clean, and is not far off on a journey, and shall fail to keep the passover, that soul shall be cut off from his people, because he has not offered the gift to the Lord in its season: that man shall bear his iniquity. 14 And if there should come to you a stranger in your land, and should keep the passover to the Lord, he shall keep it according to the law of the passover and according to its ordinance: there shall be one law for you, both for the stranger, and for the native of the land. 15 And in the day in which the tabernacle was pitched the cloud covered the tabernacle, the place of the testimony; and in the evening there was upon the tabernacle as the appearance of fire till the morning. 16 So it was continually: the cloud covered it by day, and the appearance of fire by night. 17 And when the cloud went up from the tabernacle, then after that the children of Israel departed; and in whatever place the cloud rested, there the children of Israel encamped. 18 The children of Israel shall encamp by the command of the Lord, and by the command of the Lord they shall remove: all the days in which the cloud overshadows the tabernacle, the children of Israel shall encamp. 19 And whenever the cloud shall be drawn over the tabernacle for many days, then the children of Israel shall keep the charge of God, and they shall not remove. 20 And it shall be, whenever the cloud overshadows the tabernacle a number of days, they shall encamp by the word of the Lord, and shall remove by the command of the Lord. 21 And it shall come to pass, whenever the cloud shall remain from the evening till the morning, and in the morning the cloud shall go up, then shall they remove by day or by night. 22 When the cloud continues a full month overshadowing the tabernacle, the children of Israel shall encamp, and shall not depart. 23 For they shall depart by the command of the Lord:—they kept the charge of the Lord by the command of the Lord by the hand of Moses.

Num.10 1 And the Lord spoke to Moses, saying, 2 Make to thyself two silver trumpets: thou shalt make them of beaten work; and they shall be to thee for the purpose of calling the assembly, and of removing the camps. 3 And thou shalt sound with them, and all the congregation shall be gathered to the door of the tabernacle of witness. 4 And if they shall sound with one, all the rulers even the princes of Israel shall come to thee. 5 And ye shall sound an alarm, and the camps pitched eastward shall begin to move. 6 And ye shall sound a second alarm, and the camps pitched southward shall move; and ye shall sound a third alarm, and the camps pitched westward shall move forward; and ye shall sound a fourth alarm, and they that encamp toward the north shall move forward: they shall sound an alarm at their departure. 7 And whenever ye shall gather the assembly, ye shall sound, but not an alarm. 8 And the priests the sons of Aaron shall sound with the trumpets; and it shall be a perpetual ordinance for you throughout your generations. 9 And if ye shall go forth to war in your land against your enemies that are opposed to you, then shall ye sound with the trumpets; and ye shall be had in remembrance before the Lord, and ye shall be saved from your enemies. 10 And in the days of your gladness, and in your feasts, and in your new moons, ye shall sound with the trumpets at your whole burnt offerings, and at the sacrifices of your peace-offerings; and there shall be a memorial for you before your God: I *am* the Lord your God. 11 And it came to pass in the second year, in the second month, on the twentieth day of the month, the cloud went up from the tabernacle of witness. 12 And the children of Israel set forward with their baggage in the wilderness of Sina; and the cloud rested in the wilderness of Pharan. 13 And the first rank departed by the word of the Lord by the hand of Moses. 14 And they first set in motion the order of the camp of the children of Juda with their host; and over their host *was* Naasson, son of Aminadab. 15 And over the host of the tribe of the sons of Issachar, *was* Nathanael son of Sogar. 16 And over the host of the tribe of the sons of Zabulon, *was* Eliab the son of Chaelon. 17 And they shall take down the tabernacle, and the sons of

Gedson shall set forward, and the sons of Merari, who bear the tabernacle. 18 And the order of the camp of Ruben set forward with their host; and over their host *was* Elisur the son of Sediur. 19 And over the host of the tribe of the sons of Symeon, *was* Salamiel son of Surisadai. 20 And over the host of the tribe of the children of Gad, *was* Elisaph the son of Raguel. 21 And the sons of Caath shall set forward bearing the holy things, and *the others* shall set up the tabernacle until they arrive. 22 And the order of the camp of Ephraim shall set forward with their forces; and over their forces *was* Elisama the son of Semiud. 23 And over the forces of the tribes of the sons of Manasse, *was* Gamaliel the *son* of Phadassur. 24 And over the forces of the tribe of the children of Benjamin, *was* Abidan the *son* of Gadeoni. 25 And the order of the camp of the sons of Dan shall set forward the last of all the camps, with their forces: and over their forces *was* Achiezer the *son* of Amisadai. 26 And over the forces of the tribe of the sons of Aser, *was* Phageel the son of Echran. 27 And over the forces of the tribe of the sons of Nephthali, *was* Achire the son of Ænan. 28 These *are* the armies of the children of Israel; and they set forward with their forces. 29 And Moses said to Obab the son of Raguel the Madianite, the father-in-law of Moses, We are going forward to the place concerning which the Lord said, This will I give to you: Come with us, and we will do thee good, for the Lord has spoken good concerning Israel. 30 And he said to him, I will not go, but *I will go* to my land and to my kindred. 31 And he said, Leave us not, because thou hast been with us in the wilderness, and thou shalt be an elder among us. 32 And it shall come to pass if thou wilt go with us, it shall even come to pass that in whatsoever things the Lord shall do us good, we will also do thee good. 33 And they departed from the mount of the Lord a three days' journey; and the ark of the covenant of the Lord went before them a three days' journey to provide rest for them. 34 And the cloud overshadowed them by day, when they departed from the camp. 35 And it came to pass when the ark set forward, that Moses said, Arise, O Lord, and let thine enemies be scattered: let all that hate thee flee. 36 And in the resting he said, Turn again, O Lord, the thousands *and* tens of thousands in Israel.

Num.11 1 And the people murmured sinfully before the Lord; and the Lord heard *them* and was very angry; and fire was kindled among them from the Lord, and devoured a part of the camp. 2 And the people cried to Moses: and Moses prayed to the Lord, and the fire was quenched. 3 And the name of that place was called Burning; for a fire was kindled among them from the Lord. 4 And the mixed multitude among them lusted exceedingly; and they and the children of Israel sat down and wept and said, Who shall give us flesh to eat? 5 We remember the fish, which we ate in Egypt freely; and the cucumbers, and the melons, and the leeks, and the garlic, and the onions. 6 But now our soul is dried up; our eyes *turn* to nothing but to the manna. 7 And the manna is as coriander seed, and the appearance of it the appearance of hoar-frost. 8 And the people went through the field, and gathered, and ground it in the mill, or pounded it in a mortar, and baked it in a pan, and made cakes of it; and the sweetness of it was as the taste *of* wafer made with oil. 9 And when the dew came upon the camp by night, the manna came down upon it. 10 And Moses heard them weeping by their families, every one in his door: and the Lord was very angry; and the thing was evil in the sight of Moses. 11 And Moses said to the Lord, Why hast thou afflicted thy servant, and why have I not found grace in thy sight, that thou shouldest lay the weight of this people upon me? 12 Have I conceived all this people, or have I born them? that thou sayest to me, Take them into thy bosom, as a nurse would take her suckling, into the land which thou swarest to their fathers? 13 Whence have I flesh to give to all this people? for they weep to me, saying, Give us flesh, that we may eat. 14 I shall not be able to bear this people alone, for this thing is too heavy for me. 15 And if thou doest thus to me, slay me utterly, if I have found favour with thee, that I may not see my affliction. 16 And the Lord said to Moses, Gather me seventy men from the elders of Israel, whom thou thyself knowest that they are the elders of the people, and their scribes; and thou shalt bring them to the tabernacle of witness, and they shall stand there with thee. 17 And I will go down, and speak there with thee; and I will take of the spirit that is upon thee, and will put it upon them; and they shall bear together with thee the burden of the people, and thou shalt not bear them alone. 18 And to the people thou shalt say, Purify yourselves for the morrow, and ye shall eat flesh; for ye wept before the Lord, saying, Who shall give us flesh to eat? for it was well with us in Egypt: and the Lord shall allow you to eat flesh, and ye shall eat flesh. 19 Ye shall not eat one day, nor two, nor five days, nor ten days, nor twenty days; 20 ye shall eat for a full month, until *the flesh* come out at your nostrils; and it shall be nausea to you, because ye disobeyed the Lord, who is among you, and wept before him, saying, What had we to do to come out of Egypt? 21 And Moses said, The people among whom I am are six hundred thousand footmen; and thou saidst, I will give them flesh to eat, and they shall eat a whole month. 22 Shall sheep and oxen be slain for them, and shall it suffice them? or shall all the fish of the sea be gathered together for them, and shall it suffice them? 23 And the Lord said to Moses, Shall not the hand of the Lord be fully sufficient? now shalt thou know whether my word shall come to pass to thee or not. 24 And Moses went out, and spoke the words of the Lord to the people; and he gathered seventy men of the elders of the people, and he set them round about the tabernacle. 25 And the Lord came down in a cloud, and spoke to him, and took of the spirit that was upon him, and put it upon the seventy men that were elders; and when the spirit rested upon them, they prophesied and ceased. 26 And there were two men left in the camp, the name of the one was Eldad, and the name of the other Modad; and the spirit rested upon them, and these were of the number of them that were enrolled, but they did not come to the tabernacle; and they prophesied in the camp. 27 And a young man ran and told Moses, and spoke, saying, Eldad and Modad prophesy in the camp. 28 And Joshua the son of Naue, who attended on Moses, the chosen one, said, *My* lord Moses, forbid them. 29 And Moses said to him, Art thou jealous on my account?

and would that all the Lord's people were prophets; whenever the Lord shall put his spirit upon them. 30 And Moses departed into the camp, himself and the elders of Israel. 31 And there went forth a wind from the Lord, and brought quails over from the sea; and it brought them down upon the camp a day's journey on this side, and a day's journey on that side, round about the camp, as it were two cubits from the earth. 32 And the people rose up all the day, and all the night, and all the next day, and gathered quails; he that gathered least, gathered ten measures; and they refreshed themselves round about the camp. 33 The flesh was yet between their teeth, before it failed, when the Lord was wroth with the people, and the Lord smote the people with a very great plague. 34 And the name of that place was called the Graves of Lust; for there they buried the people that lusted. 35 The people departed from the Graves of Lust to Aseroth; and the people halted at Aseroth.

Num.12 1 And Mariam and Aaron spoke against Moses, because of the Ethiopian woman whom Moses took; for he had taken an Ethiopian woman. 2 And they said, Has the Lord spoken to Moses only? has he not also spoken to us? and the Lord heard it. 3 And the man Moses was very meek beyond all the men that were upon the earth. 4 And the Lord said immediately to Moses and Aaron and Mariam, Come forth all three of you to the tabernacle of witness. 5 And the three came forth to the tabernacle of witness; and the Lord descended in a pillar of a cloud, and stood at the door of the tabernacle of witness; and Aaron and Mariam were called; and both came forth. 6 And he said to them, Hear my words: If there should be of you a prophet to the Lord, I will be made known to him in a vision, and in sleep will I speak to him. 7 My servant Moses *is* not so; he is faithful in all my house. 8 I will speak to him mouth to mouth apparently, and not in dark speeches; and he has seen the glory of the Lord; and why were ye not afraid to speak against my servant Moses? 9 And the great anger of the Lord *was* upon them, and he departed. 10 And the cloud departed from the tabernacle; and, behold, Mariam was leprous, *white* as snow; and Aaron looked upon Mariam, and, behold, she *was* leprous. 11 And Aaron said to Moses, I beseech thee, my lord, do not lay sin upon us, for we were ignorant wherein we sinned. 12 Let her not be as it were like death, as an abortion coming out of his mother's womb, when *the disease* devours the half of the flesh. 13 And Moses cried to the Lord, saying, O God, I beseech thee, heal her. 14 And the Lord said to Moses, If her father had only spit in her face, would she not be ashamed seven days? let her be set apart seven days without the camp, and afterwards she shall come in. 15 And Mariam was separated without the camp seven days; and the people moved not forward till Mariam was cleansed.

Num.13 1 And afterwards the people set forth from Aseroth, and encamped in the wilderness of Pharan. 2 And the Lord spoke to Moses, saying, 3 Send for thee men, and let them spy the land of the Chananites, which I give to the sons of Israel for a possession; one man for a tribe, thou shalt send them away according to their families, every one

of them a prince. 4 And Moses sent them out of the wilderness of Pharan by the word of the Lord; all these *were* the princes of the sons of Israel. 5 And these *are* their names: of the tribe of Ruben, Samuel the son of Zachur. 6 Of the tribe of Symeon, Saphat the son of Suri. 7 Of the tribe of Judah, Chaleb the son of Jephonne. 8 Of the tribe of Issachar, Ilaal the son of Joseph. 9 Of the tribe of Ephraim, Ause the son of Naue. 10 Of the tribe of Benjamin, Phalti the son of Raphu. 11 Of the tribe of Zabulon, Gudiel the son of Sudi. 12 Of the tribe of Joseph of the sons of Manasse, Gaddi the son of Susi. 13 Of the tribe of Dan, Amiel the son of Gamali. 14 Of the tribe of Aser, Sathur the son of Michael. 15 Of the tribe of Nephthali, Nabi the son of Sabi. 16 Of the tribe of Gad, Gudiel the son of Macchi. 17 These *are* the names of the men whom Moses sent to spy out the land; and Moses called Ause the son of Naue, Joshua. 18 And Moses sent them to spy out the land of Chanaan, and said to them, Go up by this wilderness; and ye shall go up to the mountain, 19 and ye shall see the land, what it is, and the people that dwells on it, whether it is strong or weak, or *whether* they are few or many. 20 And what the land is on which they dwell, *whether* it is good or bad; and what the cities are wherein these dwell, whether they dwell in walled *cities* or unwalled. 21 And what the land is, whether rich or poor; whether there are trees in it or no: and ye shall persevere and take of the fruits of the land: and the days *were* the days of spring, the forerunners of the grape. 22 And they went up and surveyed the land from the wilderness of Sin to Rhoob, as men go in to Æmath. 23 And they went up by the wilderness, and departed as far as Chebron; and there *was* Achiman, and Sessi, and Thelami, the progeny of Enach. Now Chebron was built seven years before Tanin of Egypt. 24 And they came to the valley of the cluster and surveyed it; and they cut down thence a bough and one cluster of grapes upon it, and bore it on staves, and *they took* of the pomegranates and the figs. 25 And they called that place, The valley of the cluster, because of the cluster which the children of Israel cut down from thence. 26 And they returned from thence, having surveyed the land, after forty days. 27 And they proceeded and came to Moses and Aaron and all the congregation of the children of Israel, to the wilderness of Pharan Cades; and they brought word to them and to all the congregation, and they shewed the fruit of the land: 28 and they reported to him, and said, We came into the land into which thou sentest us, a land flowing with milk and honey; and this is the fruit of it. 29 Only the nation that dwells upon it is bold, and they have very great and strong walled towns, and we saw there the children of Enach. 30 And Amalec dwells in the land toward the south: and the Chettite and the Evite, and the Jebusite, and the Amorite dwells in the hill country: and the Chananite dwells by the sea, and by the river Jordan. 31 And Chaleb stayed the people from speaking before Moses, and said to him, Nay, but we will go up by all means, and will inherit it, for we shall surely prevail against them. 32 But the men that went up together with him said, We will not go up, for we shall not by any means be able to go up against the nation, for it is much stronger than we. 33 And they brought a horror of that land which they surveyed upon the children of Israel, saying, The land which we passed by to survey it, is a land that eats up its inhabitants; and all the people whom we saw in it are men of extraordinary stature. 34 And there we saw the giants; and we were before them as locusts, yea even so were we before them.

Num.14 1 And all the congregation lifted up their voice and cried; and the people wept all that night. 2 And all the children of Israel murmured against Moses and Aaron; and all the congregation said to them, 3 Would we had died in the land of Egypt! or in this wilderness, would we had died! and why does the Lord bring us into this land to fall in war? our wives and our children shall be for a prey: now then it is better to return into Egypt. 4 And they said one to another, Let us make a ruler, and return into Egypt. 5 And Moses and Aaron fell upon their face before all the congregation of the children of Israel. 6 But Joshua the *son* of Naue, and Chaleb the *son* of Jephonne, of *the number of* them that spied out the land, rent their garments, 7 and spoke to all the congregation of the children of Israel, saying, The land which we surveyed is indeed extremely good. 8 If the Lord choose us, he will bring us into this land, and give it us; a land which flows with milk and honey. 9 Only depart not from the Lord; and fear ye not the people of the land, for they are meat for us; for the season *of prosperity* is departed from them, but the Lord *is* among us: fear them not. 10 And all the congregation bade stone them with stones; and the glory of the Lord appeared in the cloud on the tabernacle of witness to all the children of Israel. 11 And the Lord said to Moses, How long does this people provoke me? and how long do they refuse to believe me for all the signs which I have wrought among them? 12 I will smite them with death, and destroy them; and I will make of thee and of thy father's house a great nation, and much greater than this. 13 And Moses said to the Lord, So Egypt shall hear, for thou hast brought up this people from them by thy might. 14 Moreover all the dwellers upon this land have heard that thou art Lord in the midst of this people, who, O Lord, art seen *by them* face to face, and thy cloud rests upon them, and thou goest before them by day in a pillar of a cloud, and by night in a pillar of fire. 15 And *if* thou shalt destroy this nation as one man; then all the nations that have heard thy name shall speak, saying, 16 Because the Lord could not bring this people into the land which he sware to them, he has overthrown them in the wilderness. 17 And now, O Lord, let thy strength be exalted, as thou spakest, saying, 18 The Lord *is* long-suffering and merciful, and true, removing transgressions and iniquities and sins, and he will by no means clear the guilty, visiting the sins of the fathers upon the children to the third and fourth generation. 19 Forgive this people their sin according to thy great mercy, as thou wast favourable to them from Egypt until now. 20 And the Lord said to Moses, I am gracious to them according to thy word. 21 But *as* I live and my name is living, so the glory of the Lord shall fill all the earth. 22 For all the men who see my glory, and the signs which I wrought in Egypt, and in the wilderness, and have tempted me this tenth time, and have not hearkened to my

voice, 23 surely they shall not see the land, which I sware to their fathers; but their children which are with me here, as many as know not good or evil, every inexperienced youth, to them will I give the land; but none who have provoked me shall see it. 24 But my servant Chaleb, because there was another spirit in him, and he followed me, I will bring him into the land into which he entered, and his seed shall inherit it. 25 But Amalec and the Chananite dwell in the valley: to-morrow turn and depart for the wilderness by the way of the Red Sea. 26 And the Lord spoke to Moses and Aaron, saying, 27 How long *shall I endure* this wicked congregation? I have heard their murmurings against me, *even* the murmuring of the children of Israel, which they have murmured concerning you. 28 Say to them, *As* I live, saith the Lord: surely as ye spoke into my ears, so will I do to you. 29 Your carcases shall fall in this wilderness; and all those of you that were reviewed, and those of you that were numbered from twenty years old and upward, all that murmured against me, 30 ye shall not enter into the land for which I stretched out my hand to establish you upon it; except only Chaleb the son of Jephonne, and Joshua the *son* of Naue. 31 And your little ones, who ye said should be a prey, them will I bring into the land; and they shall inherit the land, which ye rejected. 32 And your carcases shall fall in this wilderness. 33 And your sons shall be fed in the wilderness forty years, and they shall bear your fornication, until your carcases be consumed in the wilderness. 34 According to the number of the days during which ye spied the land, forty days, a day for a year, ye shall bear your sins forty years, and ye shall know my fierce anger. 35 I the Lord have spoken, Surely will I do thus to this evil congregation that has risen up together against me: in this wilderness they shall be utterly consumed, and there they shall die. 36 And the men whom Moses sent to spy out the land, and who came and murmured against it to the assembly so as to bring out evil words concerning the land, — 37 the men that spoke evil reports against the land, even died of the plague before the Lord. 38 And Joshua the son of Naue and Chaleb the son of Jephonne *still* lived of those men that went to spy out the land. 39 And Moses spoke these words to all the children of Israel; and the people mourned exceedingly. 40 And they rose early in the morning and went up to the top of the mountain, saying, Behold, we that are here will go up to the place of which the Lord has spoken, because we have sinned. 41 And Moses said, Why do ye transgress the word of the Lord? ye shall not prosper. 42 Go not up, for the Lord is not with you; so shall ye fall before the face of your enemies. 43 For Amalec and the Chananite *are* there before you, and ye shall fall by the sword; because ye have disobeyed the Lord and turned aside, and the Lord will not be among you. 44 And having forced their passage, they went up to the top of the mountain; but the ark of the covenant of the Lord and Moses stirred not out of the camp. 45 And Amalec and the Chananite that dwelt in that mountain came down, and routed them, and destroyed them unto Herman; and they returned to the camp.

Num.15 1 And the Lord spoke to Moses, saying, 2 Speak to the children of Israel, and thou shalt say to them, When ye are come into the land of your habitation, which I give to you, 3 and thou wilt offer whole-burnt-offerings to the Lord, a whole-burnt-offering or a meat-offering to perform a vow, or a free-will offering, or to offer in your feasts a sacrifice of sweet savour to the Lord, whether of the herd or the flock: 4 then he that offers his gift to the Lord shall bring a meat- offering of fine flour, a tenth part of an ephah mingled with oil, even with the fourth part of a hin. 5 And for a drink-offering ye shall offer the fourth part of a hin on the whole-burnt- offering, or on the meat-offering: for every lamb thou shalt offer so much, as a sacrifice, a smell of sweet savour to the Lord. 6 And for a ram, when ye offer it as a whole-burnt-offering or as a sacrifice, thou shalt prepare as a meat-offering two tenths of fine flour mingled with oil, the third part of a hin. 7 And ye shall offer for a smell of sweet savour to the Lord wine for a drink-offering, the third part of a hin. 8 And if ye sacrifice *a bullock* from the herd for a whole- burnt-offering or for a sacrifice, to perform a vow or a peace-offering to the Lord, 9 then *the worshipper* shall offer upon the calf a meat-offering, three tenth deals of fine flour mingled with oil, *even* the half of a hin. 10 And wine for a drink-offering the half of a hin, a sacrifice for a smell of sweet savour to the Lord. 11 Thus shalt thou do to one calf or to one ram, or to one lamb of the sheep or kid of the goats. 12 According to the number of what ye shall offer, so shall ye do to each one, according to their number. 13 Every native of the country shall do thus to offer such things as sacrifices for a smell of sweet savour to the Lord. 14 And if there should be a stranger among you in your land, or one who should be born to you among your generations, and he will offer a sacrifice, a smell of sweet savour to the Lord—as ye do, so the *whole* congregation shall offer to the Lord. 15 There shall be one law for you and for the strangers abiding among you, a perpetual law for your generations: as ye *are*, so shall the stranger be before the Lord. 16 There shall be one law and one ordinance for you, and for the stranger that abides among you. 17 And the Lord spoke to Moses, saying, 18 Speak to the sons of Israel, and thou shalt say to them, When ye are entering into the land, into which I bring you, 19 then it shall come to pass, when ye shall eat of the bread of the land, ye shall separate a wave-offering, a special offering to the Lord, the first-fruits of your dough. 20 Ye shall offer your bread a heave-offering: as a heave-offering from the threshing-floor, so shall ye separate it, 21 even the first-fruits of your dough, and ye shall give the Lord a heave-offering throughout your generations. 22 But whensoever ye shall transgress, and not perform all these commands, which the Lord spoke to Moses; 23 as the Lord appointed you by the hand of Moses, from the day which the Lord appointed you and forward throughout your generations, 24 then it shall come to pass, if a trespass be committed unwillingly, unknown to the congregation, then shall all the congregation offer a calf of the herd without blemish for a whole-burnt-offering of sweet savour to the Lord, and its meat-offering and its drink-offering according to the ordinance, and one kid of the goats for a sin-offering. 25 And the priest shall make atonement for all the congregation of the children of Israel, and *the trespass* shall

be forgiven them, because it is involuntary; and they have brought their gift, a burnt-offering to the Lord for their trespass before the Lord, even for their involuntary sins. 26 And it shall be forgiven as respects all the congregation of the children of Israel, and the stranger that is abiding among you, because *it is* involuntary to all the people. 27 And if one soul sin unwillingly, he shall bring one she-goat of a year old for a sin-offering. 28 And the priest shall make atonement for the soul that committed the trespass unwillingly, and that sinned unwillingly before the Lord, to make atonement for him. 29 There shall be one law for the native among the children of Israel, and for the stranger that abides among them, whosoever shall commit a trespass unwillingly. 30 And whatever soul either of the natives or of the strangers shall do any thing with a presumptuous hand, he will provoke God; that soul shall be cut off from his people, 31 for he has set at nought the word of the Lord and broken his commands: that soul shall be utterly destroyed, his sin *is* upon him. 32 And the children of Israel were in the wilderness, and they found a man gathering sticks on the sabbath-day. 33 And they who found him gathering sticks on the sabbath-day brought him to Moses and Aaron, and to all the congregation of the children of Israel. 34 And they placed him in custody, for they did not determine what they should do to him. 35 And the Lord spoke to Moses, saying, Let the man be by all means put to death: *do ye* all the congregation, stone him with stones. 36 And all the congregation brought him forth out of the camp; and all the congregation stoned him with stones outside the camp, as the Lord commanded Moses. 37 And the Lord spoke to Moses, saying, 38 Speak to the children of Israel, and thou shalt tell them; and let them make for themselves fringes upon the borders of their garments throughout their generations: and ye shall put upon the fringes of the borders a lace of blue. 39 And it shall be on your fringes, and ye shall look on them, and ye shall remember all the commands of the Lord, and do them: and ye shall not turn back after your imaginations, and after *the sight of your* eyes in the things after which ye go a whoring; 40 that ye may remember and perform all my commands, and ye shall be holy unto your God. 41 I *am* the Lord your God that brought you out of the land of Egypt, to be your God: I *am* the Lord your God.

Num.16 1 And Core the son of Isaar the son of Caath the son of Levi, and Dathan and Abiron, sons of Eliab, and Aun the son of Phaleth the son of Ruben, spoke; 2 and rose up before Moses, and two hundred and fifty men of the sons of Israel, chiefs of the assembly, chosen councillors, and men of renown. 3 They rose up against Moses and Aaron, and said, Let it be enough for you that all the congregation *are* holy, and the Lord *is* among them; and why do ye set up yourselves against the congregation of the Lord? 4 And when Moses heard it, he fell on his face. 5 And he spoke to Core and all his assembly, saying, God has visited and known those that are his and who are holy, and has brought them to himself; and whom he has chosen for himself, he has brought to himself. 6 This do ye: take to yourselves censers, Core and all his company; 7 and put fire on them, and put incense on them before the Lord to-morrow; and it shall come to pass that the man whom the Lord has chosen, he shall be holy: let it be enough for you, ye sons of Levi. 8 And Moses said to Core, Hearken to me, ye sons of Levi. 9 Is it a little thing for you, that the God of Israel has separated you from the congregation of Israel, and brought you near to himself to minister in the services of the tabernacle of the Lord, and to stand before the tabernacle to minister for them? 10 And he has brought thee near and all thy brethren the sons of Levi with thee, and do ye seek to be priests also? 11 Thus *it is with* thee and all thy congregation which is gathered together against God: and who is Aaron, that ye murmur against him? 12 And Moses sent to call Dathan and Abiron sons of Eliab; and they said, We will not go up. 13 Is it a little thing that thou hast brought us up to a land flowing with milk and honey, to kill us in the wilderness, *and* that thou altogether rulest over us? 14 Thou art a prince, and hast thou brought us into a land flowing with milk and honey, and hast thou given us an inheritance of land and vineyards? wouldest thou have put out the eyes of those men? we will not go up. 15 And Moses was exceeding indignant, and said to the Lord, Do thou take no heed to their sacrifice: I have not taken away the desire of any one of them, neither have I hurt any one of them. 16 And Moses said to Core, Sanctify thy company, and be ready before the Lord, thou and Aaron and they, to-morrow. 17 And take each man his censer, and ye shall put incense upon them, and shall bring each one his censer before the Lord, two hundred and fifty censers, and thou and Aaron shall bring each his censer. 18 And each man took his censer, and they put on them fire, and laid incense on them; and Moses and Aaron stood by the doors of the tabernacle of witness. 19 And Core raised up against them all his company by the door of the tabernacle of witness; and the glory of the Lord appeared to all the congregation. 20 And the Lord spoke to Moses and Aaron, saying, 21 Separate your selves from the midst of this congregation, and I will consume them at once. 22 And they fell on their faces, and said, O God, the God of spirits and of all flesh, if one man has sinned, *shall* the wrath of the Lord *be* upon the whole congregation? 23 And the Lord spoke to Moses, saying, 24 Speak to the congregation, saying, Depart from the company of Core round about. 25 And Moses rose up and went to Dathan and Abiron, and all the elders of Israel went with him. 26 And he spoke to the congregation, saying, Separate yourselves from the tents of these stubborn men, and touch nothing that belongs to them, lest ye be consumed with them in all their sin. 27 And they stood aloof from the tent of Core round about; and Dathan and Abiron went forth and stood by the doors of their tents, and their wives and their children and their store. 28 And Moses said, Hereby shall ye know that the Lord has sent me to perform all these works, that *I have* not *done them* of myself. 29 If these men shall die according to the death of all men, if also their visitation shall be according to the visitation of all men, then the Lord has not sent me. 30 But if the Lord shall shew by a wonder, and the earth shall open her mouth and swallow them up, and their houses, and their tents, and all that belongs to them, and they shall go down alive into

Hades, then ye shall know that these men have provoked the Lord. 31 And when he ceased speaking all these words, the ground clave asunder beneath them. 32 And the ground opened, and swallowed them up, and their houses, and all the men that were with Core, and their cattle. 33 And they went down and all that they had, alive into Hades; and the ground covered them, and they perished from the midst of the congregation. 34 And all Israel round about them fled from the sound of them, for they said, Lest the earth swallow us up *also*. 35 And fire went forth from the Lord, and devoured the two hundred and fifty men that offered incense. 36 And the Lord said to Moses, 37 and to Eleazar the son of Aaron the priest, Take up the brazen censers out of the midst of the men that have been burnt, and scatter the strange fire yonder, for they have sanctified the censers 38 of these sinners against their own souls, and do thou make them beaten plates a covering to the altar, because they were brought before the Lord and hallowed; and they became a sign to the children of Israel. 39 And Eleazar the son of Aaron the priest took the brazen censers, which the men who had been burnt brought near, and they put them as a covering on the altar: 40 a memorial to the children of Israel that no stranger might draw nigh, who is not of the seed of Aaron, to offer incense before the Lord; so he shall not be as Core and as they that conspired with him, as the Lord spoke to him by the hand of Moses. 41 And the children of Israel murmured the next day against Moses and Aaron, saying, Ye have killed the people of the Lord. 42 And it came to pass when the congregation combined against Moses and Aaron, that they ran impetuously to the tabernacle of witness; and the cloud covered it, and the glory of the Lord appeared. 43 And Moses and Aaron went in, in front of the tabernacle of witness. 44 And the Lord spoke to Moses and Aaron, saying, 45 Depart out of the midst of this congregation, and I will consume them at once: and they fell upon their faces. 46 And Moses said to Aaron, Take a censer, and put on it fire from the altar, and put incense on it, and carry it away quickly into the camp, and make atonement for them; for wrath is gone forth from the presence of the Lord, it has begun to destroy the people. 47 And Aaron took as Moses spoke to him, and ran among the congregation, for already the plague had begun among the people; and he put on incense, and made an atonement for the people. 48 And he stood between the dead and the living, and the plague ceased. 49 And they that died in the plague were fourteen thousand and seven hundred, besides those that died on account of Core. 50 And Aaron returned to Moses to the door of the tabernacle of witness, and the plague ceased.

Num.17 1 And the Lord spoke to Moses, saying, 2 Speak to the children of Israel, and take rods of them, according to the houses of their families, a rod from all their princes, according to the houses of their families, twelve rods, and write the name of each on his rod. 3 And write the name of Aaron on the rod of Levi; for it is one rod *for each*: they shall give *them* according to the tribe of the house of their families. 4 And thou shalt put them in the tabernacle of witness, before the testimony, where I will be made known to thee. 5 And it shall be, the man whom I shall choose, his rod shall blossom; and I will remove from me the murmuring of the children of Israel, which they murmur against you. 6 And Moses spoke to the children of Israel, and all their chiefs gave him a rod *each*, for one chief a rod, according to the house of their families, twelve rods; and the rod of Aaron *was* in the midst of the rods. 7 And Moses laid up the rods before the Lord in the tabernacle of witness. 8 And it came to pass on the morrow, that Moses and Aaron went into the tabernacle of witness; and, behold, the rod of Aaron for the house of Levi blossomed, and put forth a bud, and bloomed blossoms and produced almonds. 9 And Moses brought forth all the rods from before the Lord to all the sons of Israel; and they looked, and each one took his rod. 10 And the Lord said to Moses, Lay up the rod of Aaron before the testimonies to be kept as a sign for the children of the disobedient; and let their murmuring cease from me, and they shall not die. 11 And Moses and Aaron did as the Lord commanded Moses, so did they. 12 And the children of Israel spoke to Moses, saying, Behold, we are cut off, we are destroyed, we are consumed. 13 Every one that touches the tabernacle of the Lord, dies: shall we die utterly?

Num.18 1 And the Lord spoke to Aaron, saying, Thou and thy sons and thy father's house shall bear the sins of the holy things, and thou and thy sons shall bear the iniquity of your priesthood. 2 And take to thyself thy brethren the tribe of Levi, the family of thy father, and let them be joined to thee, and let them minister to thee; and thou and thy sons with thee *shall minister* before the tabernacle of witness. 3 And they shall keep thy charges, and the charges of the tabernacle; only they shall not approach the holy vessels and the altar, so both they and you shall not die. 4 And they shall be joined to thee, and shall keep the charges of the tabernacle of witness, in all the services of the tabernacle; and a stranger shall not approach to thee. 5 And ye shall keep the charges of the holy things, and the charges of the altar, and *so* there shall not be anger among the children of Israel. 6 And I have taken your brethren the Levites out of the midst of the children of Israel, a present given to the Lord, to minister in the services of the tabernacle of witness. 7 And thou and thy sons after thee shall keep up your priestly ministration, according to the whole manner of the altar, and that which is within the veil; and ye shall minister in the services as the office of your priesthood; and the stranger that comes near shall die. 8 And the Lord said to Aaron, And, behold, I have given you the charge of the first-fruits of all things consecrated to me by the children of Israel; and I have given them to thee as an honour, and to thy sons after thee for a perpetual ordinance. 9 And let this be to you from all the holy things that are consecrated *to me, even* the burnt-offerings, from all their gifts, and from all their sacrifices, and from every trespass-offering of theirs, and from all their sin-offerings, whatever things they give to me of all their holy things, they shall be thine and thy sons'. 10 In the most holy place shall ye eat them; every male shall eat them, thou and thy sons: they shall be holy to thee. 11 And this shall be to you of the first-fruits of their gifts, of all the wave-offerings of the children of Israel; to thee have I given them and to thy sons and thy daughters with thee, a perpetual ordinance; every clean person in thy house shall eat them. 12 Every first-offering of oil, and every first-offering of wine, their first-fruits of corn, whatsoever they may give to the Lord, to thee have I given them. 13 All the first-fruits that are in their land, whatsoever they shall offer to the Lord, shall be thine: every clean person in thy house shall eat them. 14 Every devoted thing among the children of Israel shall be thine. 15 And every thing that opens the womb of all flesh, whatsoever they bring to the Lord, whether man or beast, shall be thine: only the first-born of men shall be surely redeemed, and thou shalt redeem the first-born of unclean cattle. 16 And the redemption of them *shall be* from a month old; their valuation of five shekels—it is twenty oboli according to the holy shekel. 17 But thou shalt not redeem the first-born of calves and the first-born of sheep and the first-born of goats; they are holy: and thou shalt pour their blood upon the altar, and thou shalt offer the fat as a burnt-offering for a smell of sweet savour to the Lord. 18 And the flesh shall be thine, as also the breast of the wave-offering and as the right shoulder, it shall be thine. 19 Every special offering of the holy things, whatsoever the children of Israel shall specially offer to the Lord, I have given to thee and to thy sons and to thy daughters with thee, a perpetual ordinance: it is a covenant of salt for ever before the Lord, for thee and thy seed after thee. 20 And the Lord said to Aaron, Thou shalt have no inheritance in their land, neither shalt thou have any portion among them; for I *am* thy portion and thine inheritance in the midst of the children of Israel. 21 And, behold, I have given to the sons of Levi every tithe in Israel for an inheritance for their services, whereinsoever they perform ministry in the tabernacle of witness. 22 And the children of Israel shall no more draw nigh to the tabernacle of witness to incur fatal guilt. 23 And the Levite himself shall perform the service of the tabernacle of witness; and they shall bear their iniquities, it is a perpetual statute throughout their generations; and in the midst of the children of Israel they shall not receive an inheritance. 24 Because I have given as a distinct portion to the Levites for an inheritance the tithes of the children of Israel, whatsoever they shall offer to the Lord; therefore I said to them, In the midst of the children of Israel they shall have no inheritance. 25 And the Lord spoke to Moses, saying, 26 Thou shalt also speak to the Levites, and shalt say to them, If ye take the tithe from the children of Israel, which I have given you from them for an inheritance, then shall ye separate from it a heave-offering to the Lord, a tenth of the tenth. 27 And your heave-offerings shall be reckoned to you as corn from the floor, and an offering from the wine-press. 28 So shall ye also separate them from all the offerings of the Lord out of all your tithes, whatsoever ye shall receive from the children of Israel; and ye shall give of them an offering to the Lord to Aaron the priest. 29 Of all your gifts ye shall offer an offering to the Lord, and of every first-fruit the consecrated part from it. 30 And thou shalt say to them, When ye shall offer the first-fruits from it, then shall it be reckoned to the Levites as produce from the threshing-floor, and as produce from the wine-press. 31 And ye shall eat it in any place, ye and your families; for this is your reward for your services in the tabernacle of witness. 32 And ye shall not bear sin by reason of it, for ye shall have offered an offering of first-fruits from it, and ye shall not profane the holy things of the children of Israel, that ye die not.

Num.19 1 And the Lord spoke to Moses and Aaron, saying, 2 This is the constitution of the law, as the Lord has commanded, saying, Speak to the sons of Israel, and let them take for thee a red heifer without spot, which has no spot on her, and on which no yoke has been put. 3 And thou shalt give her to Eleazar the priest; and they shall bring her out of the camp into a clean place, and shall kill her before his face. 4 And Eleazar shall take of her blood, and sprinkle of her blood seven times in front of the tabernacle of witness. 5 And they shall burn her to ashes before him; and her skin and her flesh and her blood, with her dung, shall be consumed. 6 And the priest shall take cedar wood and hyssop and scarlet wool, and they shall cast them into the midst of the burning of the heifer. 7 And the priest shall wash his garments, and bathe his body in water, and afterwards he shall go into the camp, and the priest shall be unclean till evening. 8 And he that burns her shall wash his garments, and bathe his body, and shall be unclean till evening. 9 And a clean man shall gather up the ashes of the heifer, and lay them up in a clean place outside the camp; and they shall be for the congregation of the children of Israel to keep: it is the water of sprinkling, a purification. 10 And he that gathers up the ashes of the heifer shall wash his garments, and shall be unclean until evening; and it shall be a perpetual statute for the children of Israel and for the strangers joined to them. 11 He that touches the dead body of any man, shall be unclean seven days. 12 He shall be purified on the third day and the seventh day, and shall be clean; but if he be not purged on the third day and the seventh day, he shall not be clean. 13 Every one that touches the carcase of the person of a man, if he should have died, and *the other* not have been purified, has defiled the tabernacle of the Lord: that soul shall be cut off from Israel, because the water of sprinkling has not been sprinkled upon him; he is unclean; his uncleanness is yet upon him. 14 And this *is* the law; if a man die in a house, every one that goes into the house, and all things in the house, shall be unclean seven days. 15 And every open vessel which has not a covering bound upon it, shall be unclean. 16 And every one who shall touch a man slain by violence, or a corpse, or human bone, or sepulchre, shall be unclean seven days. 17 And they shall take for the unclean of the burnt ashes of purification, and they shall pour upon them running water into a vessel. 18 And a clean man shall take hyssop, and dip it into the water, and sprinkle it upon the house, and the furniture, and all the souls that are therein, and upon him that touched the human bone, or the slain man, or the corpse, or the tomb. 19 And the clean man shall sprinkle *the water* on the unclean on the third day and on the seventh day, and on the seventh day he shall purify himself; and *the other* shall wash his garments, and bathe himself in water, and shall be unclean until evening. 20 And whatever man

shall be defiled and shall not purify himself, that soul shall be cut off from the midst of the congregation, because he has defiled the holy things of the Lord, because the water of sprinkling has not been sprinkled upon him; he is unclean. 21 And it shall be to you a perpetual statute; and he that sprinkles the water of sprinkling shall wash his garments; and he that touches the water of sprinkling shall be unclean until evening. 22 And whatsoever the unclean man shall touch shall be unclean, and the soul that touches it shall be unclean till evening.

Num.20 1 And the children of Israel, *even* the whole congregation, came into the wilderness of Sin, in the first month, and the people abode in Cades; and Mariam died there, and was buried there. 2 And there was no water for the congregation: and they gathered themselves together against Moses and Aaron. 3 And the people reviled Moses, saying, Would we had died in the destruction of our brethren before the Lord! 4 And wherefore have ye brought up the congregation of the Lord into this wilderness, to kill us and our cattle? 5 And wherefore *is* this? Ye have brought us up out of Egypt, that we should come into this evil place; a place where there is no sowing, neither figs, nor vines, nor pomegranates, neither is there water to drink. 6 And Moses and Aaron went from before the assembly to the door of the tabernacle of witness, and they fell upon their faces; and the glory of the Lord appeared to them. 7 And the Lord spoke to Moses, saying, 8 Take thy rod, and call the assembly, thou and Aaron thy brother, and speak ye to the rock before them, and it shall give forth its waters; and ye shall bring forth for them water out of the rock, and give drink to the congregation and their cattle. 9 And Moses took his rod which was before the Lord, as the Lord commanded. 10 And Moses and Aaron assembled the congregation before the rock, and said to them, Hear me, ye disobedient ones; must we bring you water out of this rock? 11 And Moses lifted up his hand and struck the rock with his rod twice; and much water came forth, and the congregation drank, and their cattle. 12 And the Lord said to Moses and Aaron, Because ye have not believed me to sanctify me before the children of Israel, therefore ye shall not bring this congregation into the land which I have given them. 13 This is the water of Strife, because the children of Israel spoke insolently before the Lord, and he was sanctified in them. 14 And Moses sent messengers from Cades to the king of Edom, saying, Thus says thy brother Israel; Thou knowest all the distress that has come upon us. 15 And *how* our fathers went down into Egypt, and we sojourned in Egypt many days, and the Egyptians afflicted us and our fathers. 16 And we cried to the Lord, and the Lord heard our voice, and sent an angel and brought us out of Egypt; and now we are in the city of Cades, at the extremity of thy coasts. 17 We will pass through thy land: we will not go through the fields, nor through the vineyards, nor will we drink water out of thy cistern: we will go by the king's highway; we will not turn aside to the right hand or to the left, until we have passed thy borders. 18 And Edom said to him, Thou shalt not pass through me, and if otherwise, I will go forth to meet thee in war. 19 And the children of Israel say to him, We will pass by the mountain; and if I and my cattle drink of thy water, I will pay thee: but it is no matter of importance, we will go by the mountain. ²⁰ And he said, Thou shalt not pass through me; and Edom went forth to meet him with a great host, and a mighty hand. ²¹ So Edom refused to allow Israel to pass through his borders, and Israel turned away from him. ²² And they departed from Cades; and the children of Israel, even the whole congregation, came to Mount Or. ²³ And the Lord spoke to Moses and Aaron in mount Or, on the borders of the land of Edom, saying, ²⁴ Let Aaron be added to his people; for ye shall certainly not go into the land which I have given the children of Israel, because ye provoked me at the water of strife. ²⁵ Take Aaron, and Eleazar his son, and bring them up to the mount Or before all the congregation; ²⁶ and take Aaron's apparel from off him, and put it on Eleazar his son: and let Aaron die there and be added to *his people.* ²⁷ And Moses did as the Lord commanded him, and took him up to mount Or, before all the congregation. ²⁸ And he took Aaron's garments off him, and put them on Eleazar his son, and Aaron died on the top of the mountain; and Moses and Eleazar came down from the mountain. ²⁹ And all the congregation saw that Aaron was dead: and they wept for Aaron thirty days, *even* all the house of Israel.

Num.21 ¹ And Arad the Chananitish king who dwelt by the wilderness, heard that Israel came by the way of Atharin; and he made war on Israel, and carried off some of them captives. ² And Israel vowed a vow to the Lord, and said, If thou wilt deliver this people into my power, I will devote it and its cities *to thee.* ³ And the Lord hearkened to the voice of Israel, and delivered the Chananite into his power; and *Israel* devoted him and his cities, and they called the name of that place Anathema. ⁴ And having departed from mount Or by the way *leading* to the Red Sea, they compassed the land of Edom, and the people lost courage by the way. ⁵ And the people spoke against God and against Moses, saying, Why is this? Hast thou brought us ought of Egypt to slay us in the wilderness? for there is not bread nor water; and our soul loathes this light bread. ⁶ And the Lord sent among the people deadly serpents, and they bit the people, and much people of the children of Israel died. ⁷ And the people came to Moses and said, We have sinned, for we have spoken against the Lord, and against thee: pray therefore to the Lord, and let him take away the serpent from us. ⁸ And Moses prayed to the Lord for the people; and the Lord said to Moses, Make thee a serpent, and put it on a signal-*staff*; and it shall come to pass that whenever a serpent shall bite a man, every one *so* bitten that looks upon it shall live. ⁹ And Moses made a serpent of brass, and put it upon a signal-*staff*: and it came to pass that whenever a serpent bit a man, and he looked on the brazen serpent, he lived. ¹⁰ And the children of Israel departed, and encamped in Oboth. ¹¹ And having departed from Oboth, they encamped in Achalgai, on the farther side in the wilderness, which is opposite Moab, toward the east. ¹² And thence they departed, and encamped in the valley of Zared. ¹³ And they departed thence and encamped on the other

side of Arnon in the wilderness, *the country* which extends from the coasts of the Amorites; for Arnon is the borders of Moab, between Moab and the Amorites. ¹⁴ Therefore it is said in a book, A war of the Lord has set on fire Zoob, and the brooks of Arnon. ¹⁵ And he has appointed brooks to cause Er to dwell *there*; and it lies near to the coasts of Moab. ¹⁶ And thence *they came to* the well; this *is* the well of which the Lord said to Moses, Gather the people, and I will give them water to drink. ¹⁷ Then Israel sang this song at the well, Begin *to sing* of the well; ¹⁸ the princes digged it, the kings of the nations in their kingdom, in their lordship sank it in the rock: and *they went* from the well to Manthanain, ¹⁹ and from Manthanain to Naaliel, and from Naaliel to Bamoth, and from Bamoth to Janen, which is in the plain of Moab *as seen* from the top of the quarried *rock* that looks toward the wilderness. ²⁰ And Moses sent ambassadors to Seon king of the Amorites, with peaceable words, saying, ²¹ We will pass through thy land, we will go by the road; we will not turn aside to the field or to the vineyard. ²² We will not drink water out of thy well; we will go by the king's highway, until we have past thy boundaries. ²³ And Seon did not allow Israel to pass through his borders, and Seon gathered all his people, and went out to set the battle in array against Israel into the wilderness; and he came to Jassa, and set the battle in array against Israel. ²⁴ And Israel smote him with the slaughter of the sword, and they became possessors of his land, from Arnon to Jaboc, as far as the children of Amman, for Jazer is the borders of the children of Amman. ²⁵ And Israel took all their cities, and Israel dwelt in all the cities of the Amorites, in Esebon, and in all cities belonging to it. ²⁶ For Esebon is the city of Seon king of the Amorites; and he before fought against the king of Moab, and they took all his land, from Aroer to Arnon. ²⁷ Therefore say they who deal in dark speeches, Come to Esebon, that the city of Seon may be built and prepared. ²⁸ For a fire has gone forth from Esebon, a flame from the city of Seon, and has consumed as far as Moab, and devoured the pillars of Arnon. ²⁹ Woe to thee, Moab; thou art lost, thou people of Chamos: their sons are sold for preservation, and their daughters are captives to Seon king of the Amorites. ³⁰ And their seed shall perish *from* Esebon to Daebon; and their women have yet farther kindled a fire against Moab. ³¹ And Israel dwelt in all the cities of the Amorites. ³² And Moses sent to spy out Jazer; and they took it, and its villages, and cast out the Amorite that dwelt there. ³³ And having returned, they went up the road that leads to Basan; and Og the king of Basan went forth to meet them, and all his people to war to Edrain. ³⁴ And the Lord said to Moses, Fear him not; for I have delivered him and all his people, and all his land, into thy hands; and thou shalt do to him as thou didst to Seon king of the Amorites, who dwelt in Esebon. ³⁵ And he smote him and his sons, and all his people, until he left none of his to be taken alive; and they inherited his land.

Num.22 ¹ And the children of Israel departed, and encamped on the west of Moab by Jordan toward Jericho. ² And when Balac son of Sepphor saw all that Israel did to the Amorite, ³ then Moab feared the people exceedingly because they were many; and Moab was grieved before the face of the children of Israel. 4 And Moab said to the elders of Madiam, Now shall this assembly lick up all that are round about us, as a calf would lick up the green *herbs* of the field:—and Balac son of Sepphor was king of Moab at that time. 5 And he sent ambassadors to Balaam the son of Beor, to Phathura, which is on a river of the land of the sons of his people, to call him, saying, Behold, a people is come out of Egypt, and behold it has covered the face of the earth, and it has encamped close to me. 6 And now come, curse me this people, for it is stronger than we; if we may be able to smite some of them, and I will cast them out of the land: for I know that whomsoever thou dost bless, they are blessed, and whomsoever thou dost curse, they are cursed. 7 And the elders of Moab went, and the elders of Madiam, and their divining *instruments were* in their hands; and they came to Balaam, and spoke to him the words of Balac. 8 And he said to them, Tarry here the night, and I will answer you the things which the Lord shall say to me; and the princes of Moab stayed with Balaam. 9 And God came to Balaam, and said to him, Who are these men with thee? 10 And Balaam said to God, Balac son of Sepphor, king of Moab, sent them to me, saying, 11 Behold, a people has come forth out of Egypt, and has covered the face of the land, and it has encamped near to me; and now come, curse it for me, if indeed I shall be able to smite it, and cast it out of the land. 12 And God said to Balaam, Thou shalt not go with them, neither shalt thou curse the people; for they are blessed. 13 And Balaam rose up in the morning, and said to the princes of Balac, Depart quickly to your lord; God does not permit me to go with you. 14 And the princes of Moab rose, and came to Balac, and said, Balaam will not come with us. 15 And Balac yet again sent more princes and more honourable than they. 16 And they came to Balaam, and they say to him, Thus says Balac the son of Sepphor: I beseech thee, delay not to come to me. 17 For I will greatly honour thee, and will do for thee whatsoever thou shalt say; come then, curse me this people. 18 And Balaam answered and said to the princes of Balac, If Balac would give me his house full of silver and gold, I shall not be able to go beyond the word of the Lord God, to make it little or great in my mind. 19 And now do ye also tarry here this night, and I shall know what the Lord will yet say to me. 20 And God came to Balaam by night, and said to him, If these men are come to call thee, rise and follow them; nevertheless the word which I shall speak to thee, it shalt thou do. 21 And Balaam rose up in the morning, and saddled his ass, and went with the princes of Moab. 22 And God was very angry because he went; and the angel of the Lord rose up to withstand him. Now he had mounted his ass, and his two servants were with him. 23 And when the ass saw the angel of God standing opposite in the way, and his sword drawn in his hand, then the ass turned aside out of the way, and went into the field; and *Balaam* smote the ass with his staff to direct her in the way. 24 And the angel of the Lord stood in the avenues of the vines, a fence *being* on this side and a fence on that. 25 And when the ass saw the angel of God, she thrust herself against the wall, and crushed Balaam's foot against the wall, and he smote her

again. 26 And the angel of the Lord went farther, and came and stood in a narrow place where it was impossible to turn to the right or the left. 27 And when the ass saw the angel of God, she lay down under Balaam; and Balaam was angry, and struck the ass with his staff. 28 And God opened the mouth of the ass, and she says to Balaam, What have I done to thee, that thou hast smitten me this third time? 29 And Balaam said to the ass, Because thou hast mocked me; and if I *had* had a sword in my hand, I would now have killed thee. 30 And the ass says to Balaam, *Am* not I thine ass on which thou hast ridden since thy youth till this day? did I ever do thus to thee, utterly disregarding *thee*? and he said, No. 31 And God opened the eyes of Balaam, and he sees the angel of the Lord withstanding *him* in the way, and his sword drawn in his hand, and he stooped down and worshipped on his face. 32 And the angel of God said to him, Why hast thou smitten thine ass this third time? and, behold, I came out to withstand thee, for thy way was not seemly before me; and when the ass saw me, she turned away from me this third time. 33 And if she had not turned out of the way, surely now, I should have slain thee, and should have saved her alive. 34 And Balaam said to the angel of the Lord, I have sinned, for I did not know that thou wert standing opposite in the way to meet *me*; and now if it shall not be pleasing to thee *for me to go on*, I will return. 35 And the angel of the Lord said to Balaam, Go with the men: nevertheless the word which I shall speak to thee, that thou shalt take heed to speak. And Balaam went with the princes of Balac. 36 And when Balac heard that Balaam was come, he went out to meet him, to a city of Moab, which is on the borders of Arnon, which is on the *extreme* part of the borders. 37 And Balac said to Balaam, Did I not send to thee to call thee? why hast thou not come to me? shall I not indeed be able to honour thee? 38 And Balaam said to Balac, Behold, I am now come to thee: shall I be able to say anything? the word which God shall put into my mouth, that I shall speak. 39 And Balaam went with Balac, and they came to the cities of streets. 40 And Balac offered sheep and calves, and sent to Balaam and to his princes who were with him. 41 And it was morning; and Balac took Balaam, and brought him up to the pillar of Baal, and shewed him thence a part of the people.

Num.23 1 And Balaam said to Balac, Build me here seven altars, and prepare me here seven calves, and seven rams. 2 And Balac did as Balaam told him; and he offered up a calf and a ram on *every* altar. 3 And Balaam said to Balac, Stand by thy sacrifice, and I will go and see if God will appear to me and meet me, and the word which he shall shew me, I will report to thee. And Balac stood by his sacrifice. 4 And Balaam went to enquire of God; and he went straight forward, and God appeared to Balaam; and Balaam said to him, I have prepared the seven altars, and have offered a calf and a ram on *every* altar. 5 And God put a word into the mouth of Balaam, and said, thou shalt return to Balac, and thus shalt thou speak. 6 And he returned to him, and moreover he stood over his whole-burnt-offerings, and all the princes of Moab with him; and the Spirit of God came upon him. 7 And he took up his parable, and said, Balac king of Moab sent for me out of Mesopotamia, out of the mountains of the east, saying, Come, curse me Jacob, and Come, call for a curse for me upon Israel. 8 How can I curse whom the Lord curses not? or how can I devote whom God devotes not? 9 For from the top of the mountains I shall see him, and from the hills I shall observe him: behold, the people shall dwell alone, and shall not be reckoned among the nations. 10 Who has exactly calculated the seed of Jacob, and who shall number the families of Israel? let my soul die with the souls of the righteous, and let my seed be as their seed. 11 And Balac said to Balaam, What hast thou done to me? I called thee to curse my enemies, and behold thou hast greatly blessed *them*. 12 And Balaam said to Balac, Whatsoever the Lord shall put into my mouth, shall I not take heed to speak this? 13 And Balac said to him, Come yet with me to another place where thou shalt not see the people, but only thou shalt see a part of them, and shalt not see them all; and curse me them from thence. 14 And he took him to a high place of the field to the top of the quarried *rock*, and he built there seven altars, and offered a calf and a ram on *every* altar. 15 And Balaam said to Balac, Stand by thy sacrifice, and I will go to enquire of God. 16 And God met Balaam, and put a word into his mouth, and said, return to Balac, and thus shalt thou speak. 17 And he returned to him: and he also was standing by his whole-burnt-sacrifice, and all the princes of Moab with him; and Balac said to him, What has the Lord spoken? 18 And he took up his parable, and said, rise up, Balac, and hear; hearken as a witness, thou son of Sepphor. 19 God is not as man to waver, nor as the son of man to be threatened; shall he say and not perform? shall he speak and not keep *to his word*? 20 Behold, I have received *commandment* to bless: I will bless, and not turn back. 21 There shall not be trouble in Jacob, neither shall sorrow be seen in Israel: the Lord his God *is* with him, the glories of rulers *are* in him. 22 It was God who brought him out of Egypt; he has as it were the glory of a unicorn. 23 For there is no divination in Jacob, nor enchantment in Israel; in season it shall be told to Jacob and Israel what God shall perform. 24 Behold, the people shall rise up as a lion's whelp, and shall exalt himself as a lion; he shall not lie down till he have eaten the prey, and he shall drink the blood of the slain. 25 And Balac said to Balaam, Neither curse the people at all for me, nor bless them at all. 26 And Balaam answered and said to Balac, Spoke I not to thee, saying, Whatsoever thing God shall speak to me, that will I do? 27 And Balac said to Balaam, Come *and* I will remove thee to another place, if it shall please God, and curse me them from thence. 28 And Balac took Balaam to the top of Phogor, which extends to the wilderness. 29 And Balaam said to Balac, build me here seven altars, and prepare me here seven calves, and seven rams. 30 And Balac did as Balaam told him, and offered a calf and a ram on *every* altar.

Num.24 1 And when Balaam saw that it pleased God to bless Israel, he did not go according to his custom to meet the omens, but turned his face toward the wilderness. 2 And Balaam lifted up his eyes, and sees Israel encamped by their tribes; and the Spirit of God came upon him. 3 And he took up his parable and said, Balaam son of Beor says, the man who sees truly says, 4 he says who hears the oracle of the Mighty One, who saw a vision of God in sleep; his eyes were opened: 5 How goodly *are* thy habitations, Jacob, and thy tents, Israel! 6 as shady groves, and as gardens by a river, and as tents which God pitched, and as cedars by the waters. 7 There shall come a man out of his seed, and he shall rule over many nations; and the kingdom of Gog shall be exalted, and his kingdom shall be increased. 8 God led him out of Egypt; he has as it were the glory of a unicorn: he shall consume the nations of his enemies, and he shall drain their marrow, and with his darts he shall shoot through the enemy. 9 He lay down, he rested as a lion, and as a young lion; who shall stir him up? they that bless thee are blessed, and they that curse thee are cursed. 10 And Balac was angry with Balaam, and clapped his hands together; and Balac said to Balaam, I called thee to curse my enemy, and behold thou hast decidedly blessed *him* this third time. 11 Now therefore flee to thy place: I said, I will honour thee, but now the Lord has deprived thee of glory. 12 And Balaam said to Balac, Did I not speak to thy messengers also whom thou sentest to me, saying, 13 If Balac should give me his house full of silver and gold, I shall not be able to transgress the word of the Lord to make it good or bad by myself; whatsoever things God shall say, them will I speak. 14 And now, behold, I return to my place; come, I will advise thee of what this people shall do to thy people in the last days. 15 And he took up his parable and said, Balaam the son of Beor says, the man who sees truly says, 16 hearing the oracles of God, receiving knowledge from the Most High, and having seen a vision of God in sleep; his eyes were opened. 17 I will point to him, but not now; I bless him, but he draws not near: a star shall rise out of Jacob, a man shall spring out of Israel; and shall crush the princes of Moab, and shall spoil all the sons of Seth. 18 And Edom shall be an inheritance, and Esau his enemy shall be an inheritance *of Israel*, and Israel wrought valiantly. 19 And *one* shall arise out of Jacob, and destroy out of the city him that escapes. 20 And having seen Amalec, he took up his parable and said, Amalec *is* the first of the nations; yet his seed shall perish. 21 And having seen the Kenite, he took up his parable and said, thy dwelling-place *is* strong; yet though thou shouldest put thy nest in a rock, 22 and though Beor should have a skillfully contrived hiding-place, the Assyrians shall carry thee away captive. 23 And he looked upon Og, and took up his parable and said, Oh, oh, who shall live, when God shall do these things? 24 And one shall come forth from the hands of the Citians, and shall afflict Assur, and shall afflict the Hebrews, and they shall perish together. 25 And Balaam rose up and departed and returned to his place, and Balac went to his own home.

Num.25 1 And Israel sojourned in Sattin, and the people profaned itself by going a-whoring after the daughters of Moab. 2 And they called them to the sacrifices of their idols; and the people ate of their sacrifices, and worshipped their idols. 3 And Israel consecrated themselves to Beel- phegor; and the Lord was very angry with Israel. 4 And the Lord said to Moses, Take all the princes of the people, and make them examples *of judgment* for the Lord in the face of the sun, and the anger of the Lord shall be turned away from Israel. 5 And Moses said to the tribes of Israel, Slay ye every one his friend that is consecrated to Beel-phegor. 6 And, behold, a man of the children of Israel came and brought his brother to a Madianitish woman before Moses, and before all the congregation of the children of Israel; and they were weeping at the door of the tabernacle of witness. 7 And Phinees the son of Eleazar, the son of Aaron the priest, saw it, and rose out of the midst of the congregation, and took a javelin in his hand, 8 and went in after the Israelitish man into the chamber, and pierced them both through, both the Israelitish man, and the woman through her womb; and the plague was stayed from the children of Israel. 9 And those that died in the plague were four and twenty thousand. 10 And the Lord spoke to Moses, saying, 11 Phinees the son of Eleazar the son of Aaron the priest has caused my wrath to cease from the children of Israel, when I was exceedingly jealous among them, and I did not consume the children of Israel in my jealousy. 12 Thus do thou say *to him*, Behold, I give him a covenant of peace: 13 and he and his seed after him shall have a perpetual covenant of priesthood, because he was zealous for his God, and made atonement for the children of Israel. 14 Now the name of the smitten Israelitish man, who was smitten with the Madianitish woman, *was* Zambri son of Salmon, prince of a house of the tribe of Symeon. 15 And the name of the Madianitish woman who was smitten, *was* Chasbi, daughter of Sur, a prince of the nation of Ommoth: it is a chief house among the people of Madiam. 16 And the Lord spoke to Moses, saying, Speak to the children of Israel, saying, 17 Plague the Madianites as enemies, and smite them, 18 for they are enemies to you by the treachery wherein they ensnare you through Phogor, and through Chasbi their sister, daughter of a prince of Madiam, who was smitten in the day of the plague because of Phogor.

Num.26 1 And it came to pass after the plague, that the Lord spoke to Moses and Eleazar the priest, saying, 2 Take the sum of all the congregation of the children of Israel, from twenty years old and upward, according to the houses of their lineage, every one that goes forth to battle in Israel. 3 And Moses and Eleazar the priest spoke in Araboth of Moab at the Jordan by Jericho, saying, 4 *This is the numbering* from twenty years old and upward as the Lord commanded Moses. And the sons of Israel that came out of Egypt *are as follows*: 5 Ruben *was* the first-born of Israel: and the sons of Ruben, Enoch, and the family of Enoch; to Phallu belongs the family of the Phalluites. 6 To Asron, the family of Asroni: to Charmi, the family of Charmi. 7 These *are* the families of Ruben; and their numbering was forty-three thousand and seven hundred and thirty. 8 And the sons of Phallu *were* Eliab, — 9 and the sons of Eliab, Namuel, and Dathan, and Abiron: these *are* renowned men of the congregation; these are they that rose up against Moses and Aaron in the gathering of Core, in the rebellion against the Lord. 10 And the earth opened her mouth, and swallowed up them and Core, when their assembly perished, when the fire devoured the two hundred and fifty, and they were made a sign. 11 But the sons of Core died not. 12 And the sons of Symeon:—the family of the sons of Symeon: to Namuel, *belonged* the family of the Namuelites; to Jamin the family of the Jaminites; to Jachin the family of the Jachinites. 13 To Zara the family of the Zaraites; to Saul the family of the Saulites. 14 These *are* the families of Symeon according to their numbering, two and twenty thousand and two hundred. 15 And the sons of Juda, Er and Aunan; and Er and Aunan died in the land of Chanaan. 16 And these were the sons of Juda, according to their families: to Selom *belonged* the family of the Selonites; to Phares, the family of the Pharesites; to Zara, the family of the Zaraites. 17 And the sons of Phares were, to Asron, the family of the Asronites; to Jamun, the family of the Jamunites. 18 These *are* the families of Juda according to their numbering, seventy-six thousand and five hundred. 19 And the sons of Issachar according to their families: to Thola, the family of the Tholaites; to Phua, the family of the Phuaites. 20 To Jasub, the family of the Jasubites; to Samram, the family of the Samramites. 21 These *are* the families of Issachar according to their numbering, sixty-four thousand and four hundred. 22 The sons of Zabulon according to their families: to Sared, the family of the Saredites; to Allon, the family of the Allonites; to Allel, the family of the Allelites. 23 These *are* the families of Zabulon according to their numbering, sixty thousand and five hundred. 24 The sons of Gad according to their families: to Saphon, the family of the Saphonites; to Angi, the family of the Angites; to Suni, the family of the Sunites; 25 to Azeni, the family of the Azenites; to Addi, the family of the Addites: 26 to Aroadi, the family of the Aroadites; to Ariel, the family of the Arielites. 27 These *are* the families of the children of Gad according to their numbering, forty-four thousand and five hundred. 28 The sons of Aser according to their families; to Jamin, the family of the Jaminites; to Jesu, the family of the Jesusites; to Baria, the family of the Bariaites. 29 To Chober, the family of the Choberites; to Melchiel, the family of the Melchielites. 30 And the name of the daughter of Aser, Sara. 31 These *are* the families of Aser according to their numbering, forty-three thousand and four hundred. 32 The sons of Joseph according to their families, Manasse and Ephraim. 33 The sons of Manasse. To Machir the family of the Machirites; and Machir begot Galaad: to Galaad, the family of the Galaadites. 34 And these *are* the sons of Galaad; to Achiezer, the family of the Achiezerites; to Cheleg, the family of the Chelegites. 35 To Esriel, the family of the Esrielites; to Sychem, the family of the Sychemites. 36 To Symaer, the family of the Symaerites; and to Opher, the family of the Opherites. 37 And to Salpaad the son of Opher there were no sons, but daughters: and these *were* the names of the daughters of Salpaad; Mala, and Nua, and Egla, and Melcha, and Thersa. 38 These *are* the families of Manasse according to their numbering, fifty-two thousand and seven hundred. 39 And these *are* the children of Ephraim; to Suthala, the family of the Suthalanites; to Tanach, the family of the Tanachites. 40 These *are* the sons of Suthala; to Eden, the family of the Edenites. 41 These *are* the families of Ephraim according to their numbering, thirty-two thousand and five hundred: these *are* the families of the children of Joseph according to their families. 42 The sons of Benjamin according to their families; to Bale, the family of the Balites; to Asyber, the family of the Asyberites; to Jachiran, the family of the Jachiranites. 43 To Sophan, the family of the Sophanites. 44 And the sons of Bale were Adar and Noeman; to Adar, the family of the Adarites; and to Noeman, the family of the Noemanites. 45 These *are* the sons of Benjamin by their families according to their numbering, thirty-five thousand and five hundred. 46 And the sons of Dan according to their families; to Same, the family of the Sameites; these *are* the families of Dan according to their families. 47 All the families of Samei according to their numbering, sixty-four thousand and four hundred. 48 The sons of Nephthali according to their families; to Asiel, the family of the Asielites; to Gauni, the family of the Gaunites. 49 To Jeser, the family of the Jeserites; to Sellem, the family of the Sellemites. 50 These *are* the families of Nephthali, according to their numbering, forty thousand and three hundred. 51 This *is* the numbering of the children of Israel, six hundred and one thousand and seven hundred and thirty. 52 And the Lord spoke to Moses, saying, 53 To these the land shall be divided, so that they may inherit according to the number of the names. 54 To the greater number thou shalt give the greater inheritance, and to the less number thou shalt give the less inheritance: to each one, as they have been numbered, shall their inheritance be given. 55 The land shall be divided to the names by lot, they shall inherit according to the tribes of their families. 56 Thou shalt divide their inheritance by lot between the many and the few. 57 And the sons of Levi according to their families; to Gedson, the family of the Gedsonites; to Caath, the family of the Caathites; to Merari, the family of the Merarites. 58 These *are* the families of the sons of Levi; the family of the Lobenites, the family of the Chebronites, the family of the Coreites, and the family of the Musites; and Caath begot Amram. 59 And the name of his wife *was* Jochabed, daughter of Levi, who bore these to Levi in Egypt, and she bore to Amram, Aaron and Moses, and Mariam their sister. 60 And to Aaron were born both Nadab and Abiud, and Eleazar, and Ithamar. 61 And Nadab and Abiud died when they offered strange fire before the Lord in the wilderness of Sina. 62 And there were according to their numbering, twenty-three thousand, every male from a month old and upward; for they were not numbered among the children of Israel, because they have no inheritance in the midst of the children of Israel. 63 And this *is* the numbering of Moses and Eleazar the priest, who numbered the children of Israel in Araboth of Moab, at Jordan by Jericho. 64 And among these there was not a man numbered by Moses and Aaron, whom, *even* the children of Israel, they numbered in the wilderness of Sinai. 65 For the Lord said to them, They shall surely die in the wilderness; and there was not left even one of them, except Chaleb the son of Jephonne, and Joshua the *son* of Naue.

Num.27 1 And the daughters of Salpaad the son of Opher, the son of Galaad, the son of Machir, of the tribe of Manasse, of the sons of Joseph, came near; and these were their names, Maala, and Nua, and Egla, and Melcha, and Thersa; 2 and they stood before Moses, and before Eleazar the priest, and before the princes, and before all the congregation at the door of the tabernacle of witness, saying, 3 Our father died in the wilderness, and he was not in the midst of the congregation that rebelled against the Lord in the gathering of Core; for he died for his own sin, and he had no sons. Let not the name of our father be blotted out of the midst of his people, because he has no son: give us an inheritance in the midst of our father's brethren. 4 And Moses brought their case before the Lord. 5 And the Lord spoke to Moses, saying, 6 The daughters of Salpaad have spoken rightly: thou shalt surely give them a possession of inheritance in the midst of their father's brethren, and thou shalt assign their father's inheritance to them. 7 And thou shalt speak to the children of Israel, saying, 8 If a man die, and have no son, ye shall assign his inheritance to his daughter. 9 And if he have no daughter, ye shall give his inheritance to his brother. 10 And if he have no brethren, ye shall give his inheritance to his father's brother. 11 And if there be no brethren of his father, ye shall give the inheritance to his nearest relation of his tribe, to inherit his possessions; and this shall be to the children of Israel an ordinance of judgment, as the Lord commanded Moses. 12 And the Lord said to Moses, Go up to the mountain that is in the country beyond Jordan, this mount Nabau, and behold the land Chanaan, which I give to the sons of Israel for a possession. 13 And thou shalt see it, and thou also shalt be added to thy people, as Aaron thy brother was added *to them* in mount Or: 14 because ye transgressed my commandment in the wilderness of Sin, when the congregation resisted *and refused* to sanctify me; ye sanctified me not at the water before them. This is the water of Strife in Cades in the wilderness of Sin. 15 And Moses said to the Lord, 16 Let the Lord God of spirits and of all flesh look out for a man over this congregation, 17 who shall go out before them, and who shall come in before them, and who shall lead them out, and who shall bring them in; so the congregation of the Lord shall not be as sheep without a shepherd. 18 And the Lord spoke to Moses, saying, Take to thyself Joshua the son of Naue, a man who has the Spirit in him, and thou shalt lay thy hands upon him. 19 And thou shalt set him before Eleazar the priest, and thou shalt give him a charge before all the congregation, and thou shalt give a charge concerning him before them. 20 And thou shalt put of thy glory upon him, that the children of Israel may hearken to him. 21 And he shall stand before Eleazar the priest, and they shall ask of him before the Lord the judgment of the Urim: they shall go forth at his word, and at his word they shall come in, he and the children of Israel with one accord, and all the congregation. 22 And Moses did as the Lord commanded him; and he took Joshua, and set him before Eleazar the priest, and before all the congregation. 23 And he laid his hands on him, and appointed him as the Lord ordered Moses.

Num.28 1 And the Lord spoke to Moses, saying, 2 Charge the children of Israel, and thou shalt speak to them, saying, Ye shall observe to offer to me in my feasts my gifts, my presents, my burnt- offerings for a sweet-smelling savour.

³ And thou shalt say to them, These are the burnt- offerings, all that ye shall bring to the Lord; two lambs of a year old without blemish daily, for a whole-burnt offering perpetually. ⁴ Thou shalt offer one lamb in the morning, and thou shalt offer the second lamb towards evening. ⁵ And thou shalt offer the tenth part of an ephah of fine flour for a meat-offering, mingled with oil, with the fourth part of a hin. ⁶ *It is* a perpetual whole-burnt-offering, a sacrifice offered in the mount of Sina for a sweet-smelling savour to the Lord. ⁷ And its drink-offering, the fourth part of a hin to each lamb; in the holy place shalt thou pour strong drink as a drink-offering to the Lord. ⁸ And the second lamb thou shalt offer toward evening; thou shalt offer it according to its meat-offering and according to its drink-offering for a smell of sweet savour to the Lord. ⁹ And on the sabbath-day ye shall offer two lambs of a year old without blemish, and two tenth deals of fine flour mingled with oil for a meat-offering, and a drink-offering. ¹⁰ *It is* a whole- burnt-offering of the sabbaths on the sabbath days, besides the continued whole-burnt-offering, and its drink offering. ¹¹ And at the new moons ye shall bring a whole-burnt-offering to the Lord, two calves of the herd, and one ram, seven lambs of a year old without blemish. ¹² Three tenth deals of fine flour mingled with oil for one calf, and two tenth deals of fine flour mingled with oil for one ram. ¹³ A tenth deal of fine flour mingled with oil for each lamb, as a meat-offering, a sweet-smelling savour, a burnt-offering to the Lord. ¹⁴ Their drink-offering shall be the half of a hin for one calf; and the third of a hin for one ram; and the fourth part of a hin of wine for one lamb: this *is* the whole-burnt-offering monthly throughout the months of the year. ¹⁵ And *he shall offer* one kid of the goats for a sin-offering to the Lord; it shall be offered beside the continual whole-burnt-offering and its drink-offering. ¹⁶ And in the first month, on the fourteenth day of the month, *is* the passover to the Lord. ¹⁷ And on the fifteenth day of this month *is* a feast; seven days ye shall eat unleavened bread. ¹⁸ And the first day shall be to you a holy convocation; ye shall do no servile work. ¹⁹ And ye shall bring whole-burnt-offerings, a sacrifice to the Lord, two calves of the herd, one ram, seven lambs of a year old; they shall be to you without blemish. ²⁰ And their meat-offering shall be fine flour mingled with oil; three tenth deals for one calf, and two tenth deals for one ram. ²¹ Thou shalt offer a tenth for each lamb, for the seven lambs. ²² And *thou shalt offer* one kid of the goats for a sin-offering, to make atonement for you. ²³ Beside the perpetual whole- burnt-offering in the morning, which is a whole-burnt-sacrifice for a continuance, ²⁴ these shall ye thus offer daily for seven days, a gift, a sacrifice for a sweet-smelling savour to the Lord; beside the continual whole-burnt-offering, thou shalt offer its drink-offering. ²⁵ And the seventh day shall be to you a holy convocation; ye shall do no servile work in it. ²⁶ And on the day of the new corn, when ye shall offer a new sacrifice *at the festival* of weeks to the Lord, there shall be to you a holy convocation; ye shall do no servile work, ²⁷ and ye shall bring whole-burnt-offerings for a sweet-smelling savour to the Lord, two calves of the herd, one ram, seven lambs without blemish. ²⁸ Their meat-offering *shall be* fine flour mingled with oil; there shall be three tenth deals for one calf, and two tenth deals for one ram. ²⁹ A tenth for each lamb separately, for the seven lambs; and a kid of the goats, ³⁰ for a sin-offering, to make atonement for you; beside the perpetual whole-burnt-offering: and ³¹ ye shall offer to me their meat-offering. They shall be to you unblemished, and ye shall offer their drink-offerings.

Num.29 ¹ And in the seventh month, on the first day of the month, there shall be to you a holy convocation: ye shall do no servile work: it shall be to you a day of blowing the trumpets. ² And ye shall offer whole-burnt-offerings for a sweet savour to the Lord, one calf of the herd, one ram, seven lambs of a year old without blemish. ³ Their meat-offering shall be fine flour mingled with oil; three tenth deals for one calf, and two tenth deals for one ram: ⁴ a tenth deal for each several ram, for the seven lambs. ⁵ And one kid of the goats for a sin-offering, to make atonement for you. ⁶ Beside the whole-burnt-offerings for the new moon, and their meat- offerings, and their drink-offerings, and their perpetual whole-burnt-offering; and their meat-offerings and their drink-offerings according to their ordinance for a sweet-smelling savour to the Lord. ⁷ And on the tenth of this month there shall be to you a holy convocation; and ye shall afflict your souls, and ye shall do no work. ⁸ And ye shall bring near whole-burnt-offerings for a sweet-smelling savour to the Lord; burnt-sacrifices to the Lord, one calf of the herd, one ram, seven lambs of a year old; they shall be to you without blemish. ⁹ Their meat-offering shall be fine flour mingled with oil; three tenth deals for one calf, and two tenth deals for one ram. ¹⁰ A tenth deal for each several lamb, for the seven lambs. ¹¹ And one kid of the goats for a sin- offering, to make atonement for you; beside the sin-offering for atonement, and the continual whole-burnt-offering, its meat-offering, and its drink-offering according to its ordinance for a smell of sweet savour, a burnt-sacrifice to the Lord. ¹² And on the fifteenth day of this seventh month ye shall have a holy convocation; ye shall do no servile work; and ye shall keep it a feast to the Lord seven days. ¹³ And ye shall bring near whole-burnt-offerings, a sacrifice for a smell of sweet savour to the Lord, on the first day thirteen calves of the herd, two rams, fourteen lambs of a year old; they shall be without blemish. ¹⁴ their meat-offerings *shall be* fine flour mingled with oil; there shall be three tenth deals for one calf, for the thirteen calves; and two tenth deals for one ram, for the two rams. ¹⁵ A tenth deal for every lamb, for the fourteen lambs. ¹⁶ And one kid of the goats for a sin-offering; beside the continual whole-burnt-offering: there shall be their meat-offerings and their drink-offerings. ¹⁷ And on the second day twelve calves, two rams, fourteen lambs of a year old without blemish. ¹⁸ Their meat-offering and their drink-offering shall be for the calves and the rams and the lambs according to their number, according to their ordinance. ¹⁹ And one kid of the goats for a sin-offering; beside the perpetual whole-burnt-offering; their meat-offerings and their drink-offerings. ²⁰ On the third day eleven calves, two rams, fourteen lambs of a year old without blemish. ²¹ Their meat-offering and their drink-offering shall be to the calves and to the rams and to the lambs according to their number, according to their ordinance. 22 And one kid of the goats for a sin-offering; beside the continual whole-burnt-offering; *there shall be* their meat-offerings and their drink-offerings. 23 On the fourth day ten calves, two rams, fourteen lambs of a year old without spot. 24 There shall be their meat-offerings and their drink-offerings to the calves and the rams and the lambs according to their number, according to their ordinance. 25 And one kid of the goats for a sin- offering; beside the continual whole-burnt-offering *there shall be* their meat-offerings and their drink-offerings. 26 On the fifth day nine calves, two rams, fourteen lambs of a year old without spot. 27 Their meat-offerings and their drink-offerings *shall be* to the calves and the rams and the lambs according to their number, according to their ordinance. 28 And one kid of the goats for a sin- offering; beside the perpetual whole-burnt-offering; *there shall be* their meat-offerings and their drink-offerings. 29 On the sixth day eight calves, two rams, fourteen lambs of a year old without blemish. 30 There shall be their meat-offerings and their drink-offerings to the calves and rams and lambs according to their number, according to their ordinance. 31 And one kid of the goats for a sin- offering; beside the perpetual whole-burnt-offering; *there shall be* their meat-offerings and their drink-offerings. 32 On the seventh day seven calves, two rams, fourteen lambs of a year old without blemish. 33 Their meat-offerings and their drink-offerings shall be to the calves and the rams and the lambs according to their number, according to their ordinance. 34 And one kid of the goats for a sin- offering; beside the continual whole-burnt-offering; *there shall be* their meat-offerings and their drink-offerings. 35 And on the eighth day there shall be to you a release: ye shall do no servile work in it. 36 And ye shall offer whole-burnt-offerings *as* sacrifices to the Lord, one calf, one ram, seven lambs of a year old without spot. 37 *There shall be* their meat-offerings and their drink-offerings for the calf and the ram and the lambs according to their number, according to their ordinance. 38 And one kid of the goats for a sin-offering; beside the continual whole-burnt-offering; *there shall be* their meat-offerings and their drink-offerings. 39 These *sacrifices* shall ye offer to the Lord in your feasts, besides your vows; and *ye shall offer* your free-will-offerings and your whole-burnt-offerings, and your meat-offerings and your drink-offerings, and your peace-offerings.

Num.30 1 And Moses spoke to the children of Israel according to all that the Lord commanded Moses. 2 And Moses spoke to the heads of the tribes of the children of Israel, saying, This *is* the thing which the Lord has commanded. 3 Whatsoever man shall vow a vow to the Lord, or swear an oath, or bind himself with an obligation upon his soul, he shall not break his word; all that shall come out of his mouth he shall do. 4 And if a woman shall vow a vow to the Lord, or bind herself with an obligation in her youth in her father's house; and her father should hear her vows and her obligations, wherewith she has bound her soul, and her father should hold his peace at her,

then all her vows shall stand, 5 and all the obligations with which she has bound her soul, shall remain to her. 6 But if her father straitly forbid *her* in the day in which he shall hear all her vows and her obligations, which she has contracted upon her soul, they shall not stand; and the Lord shall hold her guiltless, because her father forbade her. 7 But if she should be indeed married, and her vows be upon her according to the utterance of her lips, in respect of *the obligations* which she has contracted upon her soul; 8 and her husband should hear, and hold his peace at her in the day in which he should hear, then thus shall all her vows be binding, and her obligations, which she has contracted upon her soul shall stand. 9 But if her husband should straitly forbid *her* in the day in which he should hear her, none of her vows or obligations which she has contracted upon her soul shall stand, because her husband has disallowed her, and the Lord shall hold her guiltless. 10 And the vow of a widow and of her that is put away, whatsoever she shall bind upon her soul, shall stand to her. 11 And if her vow *be made* in the house of her husband, or the obligation upon her soul with an oath, 12 and her husband should hear, and hold his peace at her, and not disallow her, then all her vows shall stand, and all the obligations which she contracted against her soul, shall stand against her. 13 But if her husband should utterly cancel the vow in the day in which he shall hear it, none of the things which shall proceed out of her lips in her vows, and in the obligations *contracted* upon her soul, shall stand to her; her husband has cancelled them, and the Lord shall hold her guiltless. 14 Every vow, and every binding oath to afflict her soul, her husband shall confirm it to her, or her husband shall cancel it. 15 But if he be wholly silent at her from day to day, then shall he bind upon her all her vows; and he shall confirm to her the obligations *which she has bound* upon herself, because he held his peace at her in the day in which he heard her. 16 And if her husband should in any wise cancel *them* after the day in which he heard *them*, then he shall bear his iniquity. 17 These *are* the ordinances which the Lord commanded Moses, between a man and his wife, and between a father and daughter in *her* youth in the house of *her* father.

Num.31 1 And the Lord spoke to Moses, saying, 2 Avenge the wrongs of the children of Israel on the Madianites, and afterwards thou shalt be added to thy people. 3 And Moses spoke to the people, saying, Arm some of you, and set yourselves in array before the Lord against Madian, to inflict vengeance on Madian from the Lord. 4 Send a thousand of each tribe from all the tribes of the children of Israel to set themselves in array. 5 And they numbered of the thousands of Israel a thousand of *each* tribe, twelve thousands; *these were* armed for war. 6 And Moses sent them away a thousand of every tribe with their forces, and Phinees the son of Eleazar the son of Aaron the priest: and the holy instruments, and the signal trumpets *were* in their hands. 7 And they set themselves in array against Madian, as the Lord commanded Moses; and they slew every male. 8 And they slew the kings of Madian together with their slain *subjects*, even Evi and Rocon, and Sur, and Ur, and

Roboc, five kings of Madian; and they slew with the sword Balaam the son of Beor with their *other* slain. 9 And they made a prey of the women of Madian, and their store, and their cattle, and all their possessions: and they spoiled their forces. 10 And they burnt with fire all their cities in the places of their habitation and they burnt their villages with fire. 11 And they took all their plunder, and all their spoils, both man and beast. 12 And they brought to Moses and to Eleazar the priest, and to all the children of Israel, the captives, and the spoils, and the plunder, to the camp to Araboth Moab, which is at Jordan by Jericho. 13 And Moses and Eleazar the priest and all the rulers of the synagogue went forth out of the camp to meet them. 14 And Moses was angry with the captains of the host, the heads of thousands and the heads of hundreds who came from the battle-array. 15 And Moses said to them, Why have ye saved every female alive? 16 For they were *the occasion* to the children of Israel by the word of Balaam of their revolting and despising the word of the Lord, because of Phogor; and there was a plague in the congregation of the Lord. 17 Now then slay every male in all the spoil, slay every woman, who has known the lying with man. 18 And as for all the captivity of women, who have not known the lying with man, save ye them alive. 19 And ye shall encamp outside the *great* camp seven days; every one who has slain and who touches a dead body, shall be purified on the third day, and ye and your captivity *shall purify yourselves* on the seventh day. 20 And ye shall purify every garment and every leathern utensil, and all furniture of goat skin, and every wooden vessel. 21 And Eleazar the priest said to the men of the host that came from the battle-array, This *is* the ordinance of the law which the Lord has commanded Moses. 22 Beside the gold, and the silver, and the brass, and the iron, and lead, and tin, 23 every thing that shall pass through the fire shall so be clean, nevertheless it shall be purified with the water of sanctification; and whatsoever will not pass through the fire shall pass through water. 24 And on the seventh day ye shall wash your garments, and be clean; and afterwards ye shall come into the camp. 25 And the Lord spoke to Moses, saying, 26 Take the sum of the spoils of the captivity both of man and beast, thou and Eleazar the priest, and the heads of the families of the congregation. 27 And ye shall divide the spoils between the warriors that went out to battle, and the whole congregation. 28 And ye shall take a tribute for the Lord from the warriors that went out to battle; one soul out of five hundred, from the men, and from the cattle, even from the oxen, and from the sheep, and from the asses; and ye shall take from their half. 29 And thou shalt give *them* to Eleazar the priest *as* the first-fruits of the Lord. 30 And from the half belonging to the children of Israel thou shalt take one in fifty from the men, and from the oxen, and from the sheep, and from the asses, and from all the cattle; and thou shalt give them to the Levites that keep the charges in the tabernacle of the Lord. 31 And Moses and Eleazar the priest did as the Lord commanded Moses. 32 And that which remained of the spoil which the warriors took, was—of the sheep, six hundred and seventy-five thousand: 33 and oxen, seventy-two thousand: 34 and asses, sixty-one thousand. 35 And persons of women who had not known lying with man, all the souls, thirty-two thousand. 36 And the half, *even* the portion of them that went out to war, from the number of the sheep, was three hundred and thirty-seven thousand and five hundred. 37 And the tribute to the Lord from the sheep was six hundred and seventy-five. 38 And the oxen, six and thirty thousand, and the tribute to the Lord seventy-two. 39 And asses, thirty thousand and five hundred, and the tribute to the Lord, sixty-one: 40 and the persons, sixteen thousand, and the tribute of them to the Lord, thirty-two souls. 41 And Moses gave the tribute to the Lord, the heave-offering of God, to Eleazar the priest, as the Lord commanded Moses; 42 from the half belonging to the children of Israel, whom Moses separated from the men of war. 43 And the half *taken* from the sheep, belonging to the congregation, was three hundred and thirty-seven thousand and five hundred. 44 And the oxen, thirty-six thousand; 45 asses, thirty thousand and five hundred; 46 and persons, sixteen thousand. 47 And Moses took of the half belonging to the children of Israel the fiftieth part, of men and of cattle, and he gave them to the Levites who keep the charges of the tabernacle of the Lord, as the Lord commanded Moses. 48 And all those who were appointed to be officers of thousands of the host, captains of thousands and captains of hundreds, approached Moses, and said to Moses, 49 Thy servants have taken the sum of the men of war with us, and not one is missing. 50 And we have brought our gift to the Lord, *every* man who has found an article of gold, whether an armlet, or a chain, or a ring, or a bracelet, or a clasp for hair, to make atonement for us before the Lord. 51 And Moses and Eleazar the priest took the gold from them, even every wrought article. 52 And all the wrought gold, even the offering that they offered to the Lord, was sixteen thousand and seven hundred and fifty shekels from the captains of thousands and the captains of hundreds. 53 For the men of war took plunder every one for himself. 54 And Moses and Eleazar the priest took the gold from the captains of thousands and captains of hundreds, and brought the vessels into the tabernacle of witness, a memorial of the children of Israel before the Lord.

Num.32 1 And the children of Ruben and the children of Gad had a multitude of cattle, very great; and they saw the land of Jazer, and the land of Galaad; and the place was a place for cattle: 2 and the children of Ruben and the children of Gad came, and spoke to Moses, and to Eleazar the priest, and to the princes of the congregation, saying, 3 Ataroth, and Daebon, and Jazer, and Namra, and Esebon, and Eleale, and Sebama, and Nabau, and Baean, 4 the land which the Lord has delivered up before the children of Israel, is pasture land, and thy servants have cattle. 5 And they said, If we have found grace in thy sight, let this land be given to thy servants for a possession, and do not cause us to pass over Jordan. 6 And Moses said to the sons of Gad and the sons of Ruben, Shall your brethren go to war, and shall ye sit here? 7 And why do ye pervert the minds of the children of Israel, that they should not cross over into the land, which the Lord gives them? 8 Did not your fathers thus, when I sent them from Cades Barne to spy out the land? 9 And they went up to the valley of the cluster, and spied the land, and turned aside the heart of the children of Israel, that they should not go into the land, which the Lord gave them. 10 And the Lord was very angry in that day, and sware, saying, 11 Surely these men who came up out of Egypt from twenty years old and upward, who know good and evil, shall not see the land which I sware *to give* to Abraam and Isaac and Jacob, for they have not closely followed after me: 12 save Caleb the son of Jephonne, who was set apart, and Joshua the son of Naue, for they closely followed after the Lord. 13 And the Lord was very angry with Israel; and for forty years he caused them to wander in the wilderness, until all the generation which did evil in the sight of the Lord was extinct. 14 Behold, ye are risen up in the room of your fathers, a combination of sinful men, to increase yet farther the fierce wrath of the Lord against Israel. 15 For ye will turn away from him to desert him yet once more in the wilderness, and ye will sin against this whole congregation. 16 And they came to him, and said, We will build here folds for our cattle, and cities for our possessions; 17 and we will arm ourselves and go as an advanced guard before the children of Israel, until we shall have brought them into their place; and our possessions shall remain in walled cities because of the inhabitants of the land. 18 We will not return to our houses till the children of Israel shall have been distributed, each to his own inheritance. 19 And we will not any longer inherit with them from the other side of Jordan and onwards, because we have our full inheritance on the side beyond Jordan eastward. 20 And Moses said to them, If ye will do according to these words, if ye will arm yourselves before the Lord for battle, 21 and every one of you will pass over Jordan fully armed before the Lord, until his enemy be destroyed from before his face, 22 and the land shall be subdued before the Lord, then afterwards ye shall return, and be guiltless before the Lord, and as regards Israel; and this land shall be to you for a possession before the Lord. 23 But if ye will not do so, ye will sin against the Lord; and ye shall know your sin, when afflictions shall come upon you. 24 And ye shall build for yourselves cities for your store, and folds for your cattle; and ye shall do that which proceeds out of your mouth. 25 And the sons of Ruben and the sons of Gad spoke to Moses, saying, Thy servants will do as our lord commands. 26 Our store, and our wives, and all our cattle shall be in the cities of Galaad. 27 But thy servants will go over all armed and set in order before the Lord to battle, as *our* lord says. 28 And Moses appointed to them *for judges* Eleazar the priest, and Joshua the son of Naue, and the chiefs of the families of the tribes of Israel. 29 And Moses said to them, If the sons of Ruben and the sons of Gad will pass over Jordan with you, every one armed for war before the Lord, and ye shall subdue the land before you, then ye shall give to them the land of Galaad for a possession. 30 But if they will not pass over armed with you to war before the Lord, then shall ye cause to pass over their possessions and their wives and their cattle before you into the land of Chanaan, and they shall inherit with you in the land of Chanaan. 31 And the sons of Ruben and the sons of Gad answered, saying, Whatsoever the Lord says to his servants,

that will we do. 32 We will go over armed before the Lord into the land of Chanaan, and ye shall give us our inheritance beyond Jordan. 33 And Moses gave to them, even to the sons of Gad and the sons of Ruben, and to the half tribe of Manasse of the sons of Joseph, the kingdom of Seon king of the Amorites, and the kingdom of Og king of Basan, the land and its cities with its coasts, the cities of the land round about. 34 And the sons of Gad built Daebon, and Ataroth, and Aroer, 35 and Sophar, and Jazer, and they set them up, 36 and Namram, and Baetharan, strong cities, and folds for sheep. 37 And the sons of Ruben built Esebon, and Eleale, and Kariatham, 38 and Beelmeon, surrounded *with walls*, and Sebama; and they called the names of the cities which they built, after their own names. 39 And a son of Machir the son of Manasse went to Galaad, and took it, and destroyed the Amorite who dwelt in it. 40 And Moses gave Galaad to Machir the son of Manasse, and he dwelt there. 41 And Jair the *son* of Manasse went and took their villages, and called them the villages of Jair. 42 And Nabau went and took Caath and her villages, and called them Naboth after his name.

Num.33 1 And these are the stages of the children of Israel, as they went out from the land of Egypt with their host by the hand of Moses and Aaron. 2 And Moses wrote their removals and their stages, by the word of the Lord: and these are the stages of their journeying. 3 They departed from Ramesses in the first month, on the fifteenth day of the first month; on the day after the passover the children of Israel went forth with a high hand before all the Egyptians. 4 And the Egyptians buried those that died of them, even all that the Lord smote, every first-born in the land of Egypt; also the Lord executed vengeance on their gods. 5 And the children of Israel departed from Ramesses, and encamped in Socchoth: 6 and they departed from Socchoth and encamped in Buthan, which is a part of the wilderness. 7 And they departed from Buthan and encamped at the mouth of Iroth, which is opposite Beel-sepphon, and encamped opposite Magdol. 8 And they departed from before Iroth, and crossed the middle of the sea into the wilderness; and they went a journey of three days through the wilderness, and encamped in Picriae. 9 And they departed from Picriae, and came to Ælim; and in Ælim *were* twelve fountains of water, and seventy palm-trees, and they encamped there by the water. 10 And they departed from Ælim, and encamped by the Red Sea. 11 And they departed from the Red Sea, and encamped in the wilderness of Sin. 12 And they departed from the wilderness of Sin, and encamped in Raphaca. 13 And they departed from Raphaca, and encamped in Ælus. 14 And they departed from Ælus, and encamped in Raphidin; and there was no water there for the people to drink. 15 And they departed from Raphidin, and encamped in the wilderness of Sina. 16 And they departed from the wilderness of Sina, and encamped at the Graves of Lust. 17 And they departed from the Graves of Lust, and encamped in Aseroth. 18 And they departed from Aseroth, and encamped in Rathama. 19 And they departed from Rathama, and encamped in Remmon Phares. 20 And they departed from Remmon

Phares, and encamped in Lebona. 21 And they departed from Lebona, and encamped in Ressan. 22 And they departed from Ressan, and encamped in Makellath. 23 And they departed from Makellath, and encamped in Saphar. 24 And they departed from Saphar, and encamped in Charadath. 25 And they departed from Charadath, and encamped in Makeloth. 26 And they departed from Makeloth, and encamped in Kataath. 27 And they departed from Kataath, and encamped in Tarath. 28 And they departed from Tarath, and encamped in Mathecca. 29 And they departed from Mathecca, and encamped in Selmona. 30 And they departed from Selmona, and encamped in Masuruth. 31 And they departed from Masuruth, and encamped in Banaea. 32 And they departed from Banaea, and encamped in the mountain Gadgad. 33 And they departed from the mountain Gadgad, and encamped in Etebatha. 34 And they departed from Etebatha, and encamped in Ebrona. 35 And they departed from Ebrona, and encamped in Gesion Gaber. 36 And they departed from Gesion Gaber, and encamped in the wilderness of Sin; and they departed from the wilderness of Sin, and encamped in the wilderness of Pharan; this is Cades. 37 And they departed from Cades, and encamped in mount Or near the land of Edom. 38 And Aaron the priest went up by the command of the Lord, and died there in the fortieth year of the departure of the children of Israel from the land of Egypt, in the fifth month, on the first *day* of the month. 39 And Aaron was a hundred and twenty-three years old, when he died in mount Or. 40 And Arad the Chananitish king (he too dwelt in the land of Chanaan) having heard when the children of Israel were entering *the land*— 41 then they departed from mount Or, and encamped in Selmona. 42 And they departed from Selmona, and encamped in Phino. 43 And they departed from Phino, and encamped in Oboth. 44 And they departed from Oboth, and encamped in Gai, on the other side *Jordan* on the borders of Moab. 45 And they departed from Gai, and encamped in Daebon Gad. 46 And they departed from Daebon Gad, and encamped in Gelmon Deblathaim. 47 And they departed from Gelmon Deblathaim, and encamped on the mountains of Abarim, over against Nabau. 48 And they departed from the mountains of Abarim, and encamped on the west of Moab, at Jordan by Jericho. 49 And they encamped by Jordan between Æsimoth, as far as Belsa to the west of Moab. 50 And the Lord spoke to Moses at the west of Moab by Jordan at Jericho, saying, 51 Speak to the children of Israel, and thou shalt say to them, Ye are to pass over Jordan into the land of Chanaan. 52 And ye shall destroy all that dwell in the land before your face, and ye shall abolish their high places, and all their molten images ye shall destroy, and ye shall demolish all their pillars. 53 And ye shall destroy all the inhabitants of the land, and ye shall dwell in it, for I have given their land to you for an inheritance. 54 And ye shall inherit their land according to your tribes; to the greater number ye shall give the larger possession, and to the smaller ye shall give the less possession; to whatsoever *part* a man's name shall go forth *by lot*, there shall be his *property*: ye shall inherit according to the tribes of your families. 55 But if ye will not destroy the

dwellers in the land from before you, then it shall come to pass that whomsoever of them ye shall leave shall be thorns in your eyes, and darts in your sides, and they shall be enemies to you on the land on which ye shall dwell; 56 and it shall come to pass that as I had determined to do to them, so I will do to you.

Num. 34 1 And the Lord spoke to Moses, saying, 2 Charge the children of Israel, and thou shalt say to them, Ye are entering into the land of Chanaan: it shall be to you for an inheritance, the land of Chanaan with its boundaries. 3 And your southern side shall be from the wilderness of Sin to the border of Edom, and your border southward shall extend on the side of the salt sea eastward. 4 And your border shall go round you from the south to the ascent of Acrabin, and shall proceed by Ennac, and the going forth of it shall be southward to Cades Barne, and it shall go forth to the village of Arad, and shall proceed by Asemona. 5 And the border shall compass from Asemona to the river of Egypt, and the sea shall be the termination. 6 And ye shall have your border on the west, the great sea shall be the boundary: this shall be to you the border on the west. 7 And this shall be your northern border; from the great sea ye shall measure to yourselves, by the side of the mountain. 8 And ye shall measure to yourselves the mountain from mount *Hor* at the entering in to Emath, and the termination of it shall be the coasts of Saradac. 9 And the border shall go out to Dephrona, and its termination shall be at Arsenain; this shall be your border from the north. 10 And ye shall measure to yourselves the eastern border from Arsenain to Sepphamar. 11 And the border shall go down from Sepphamar to Bela eastward to the fountains, and the border shall go down from Bela behind the sea Chenereth eastward. 12 And the border shall go down to Jordan, and the termination shall be the salt sea; this shall be your land and its borders round about. 13 And Moses charged the children of Israel, saying, This *is* the land which ye shall inherit by lot, even as the Lord commanded us to give it to the nine tribes and the half-tribe of Manasse. 14 For the tribe of the children of Ruben, and the tribe of the children of Gad have received *their inheritance* according to their families; and the half-tribe of Manasse have received their inheritances. 15 Two tribes and half a tribe have received their inheritance beyond Jordan by Jericho from the south eastwards. 16 And the Lord spoke to Moses, saying, 17 These *are* the names of the men who shall divide the land to you for an inheritance; Eleazar the priest and Joshua the *son* of Naue. 18 And ye shall take one ruler from *each* tribe to divide the land to you by lot. 19 And these *are* the names of the men; of the tribe of Juda Chaleb the son of Jephonne. 20 Of the tribe of Symeon, Salamiel the son of Semiud. 21 Of the tribe of Benjamin, Eldad the son of Chaslon. 22 Of the tribe of Dan the prince *was* Bacchir the son of Egli. 23 Of the sons of Joseph of the tribe of the sons of Manasse, the prince was Aniel the son of Suphi. 24 Of the tribe of the sons of Ephraim, the prince was Camuel the son of Sabathan. 25 Of the tribe of Zabulon, the prince was Elisaphan the son of Pharnac. 26 Of the tribe of the sons of Issachar, the prince was Phaltiel the son of Oza. 27 Of the tribe of the children of Aser, the prince was Achior the son of Selemi. 28 Of the tribe of Nephthali, the prince was Phadael the son of Jamiud. 29 These did the Lord command to distribute *the inheritances* to the children of Israel in the land of Chanaan.

Num.35 1 And the Lord spoke to Moses to the west of Moab by Jordan near Jericho, saying, 2 Give orders to the children of Israel, and they shall give to the Levites cities to dwell in from the lot of their possession, and they shall give to the Levites the suburbs of the cities round about them. 3 And the cities shall be for them to dwell in, and their enclosures shall be for their cattle and all their beasts. 4 And the suburbs of the cities which ye shall give to the Levites, shall be from the wall of the city and outwards two thousand cubits round about. 5 And thou shalt measure outside the city on the east side two thousand cubits, and on the south side two thousand cubits, and on the west side two thousand cubits, and on the north side two thousand cubits; and your city shall be in the midst of this, and the suburbs of the cities *as described.* 6 And ye shall give the cities to the Levites, the six cities of refuge which ye shall give for the slayer to flee thither, and in addition to these, forty-two cities. 7 Ye shall give to the Levites in all forty-eight cities, them and their suburbs. 8 And as for the cities which ye shall give out of the possession of the children of Israel, from those *that have* much *ye shall give* much, and from those that have less ye shall give less: they shall give of their cities to the Levites each one according to his inheritance which they shall inherit. 9 And the Lord spoke to Moses, saying, 10 Speak to the children of Israel, and thou shalt say to them, Ye are to cross over Jordan into the land of Chanaan. 11 And ye shall appoint to yourselves cities: they shall be to you cities of refuge for the slayer to flee to, every one who has killed another unintentionally. 12 And the cities shall be to you places of refuge from the avenger of blood, and the slayer shall not die until he stands before the congregation for judgment. 13 And the cities which ye shall assign, *even* the six cities, shall be places of refuge for you. 14 Ye shall assign three cities on the other side of Jordan, and ye shall assign three cities in the land of Chanaan. 15 It shall be a place of refuge for the children of Israel, and for the stranger, and for him that sojourns among you; these cities shall be for a place of refuge, for every one to flee thither who has killed a man unintentionally. 16 And if he should smite him with an iron instrument, and the man should die, he is a murderer; let the murderer by all means be put to death. 17 And if he should smite him with a stone *thrown* from his hand, whereby a man may die, and he *thus* die, he is a murderer; let the murderer by all means be put to death. 18 And if he should smite him with an instrument of wood from his hand, whereby he may die, and he *thus* die, he is a murderer; let the murderer by all means be put to death. 19 The avenger of blood himself shall slay the murderer: whensoever he shall meet him he shall slay him. 20 And if he should thrust him through enmity, or cast any thing upon him from an ambuscade, and the man should die, 21 or if he have smitten him with his hand through anger, and the man should die, let the man that smote him be put to death by all means, he is a murderer: let the murderer by all means be put to death: the avenger of blood shall slay the murderer when he meets him. 22 But if he should thrust him suddenly, not through enmity, or cast any thing upon him, not from an ambuscade, 23 or *smite him* with any stone, whereby a man may die, unawares, and it should fall upon him, and he should die, but he was not his enemy, nor sought to hurt him; 24 then the assembly shall judge between the smiter and the avenger of blood, according to these judgments. 25 And the congregation shall rescue the slayer from the avenger of blood, and the congregation shall restore him to his city of refuge, whither he fled for refuge; and he shall dwell there till the death of the high-priest, whom they anointed with the holy oil. 26 But if the slayer should in any wise go out beyond the bounds of the city whither he fled for refuge, 27 and the avenger of blood should find him without the bounds of the city of his refuge, and the avenger of blood should kill the slayer, he is not guilty. 28 For he ought to have remained in the city of refuge till the high-priest died; and after the death of the high-priest the slayer shall return to the land of his possession. 29 And these things shall be to you for an ordinance of judgment throughout your generations in all your dwellings. 30 Whoever kills a man, thou shalt slay the murderer on the testimony of witnesses; and one witness shall not testify against a soul that he should die. 31 And ye shall not accept ransoms for life from a murderer who is worthy of death, for he shall be surely put to death. 32 Ye shall not accept a ransom *to excuse* his fleeing to the city of refuge, so that he should again dwell in the land, until the death of the high-priest. 33 So shall ye not pollute with murder the land in which ye dwell; for this blood pollutes the land, and the land shall not be purged from the blood shed upon it, but by the blood of him that shed it. 34 And ye shall not defile the land whereon ye dwell, on which I dwell in the midst of you; for I am the Lord dwelling in the midst of the children of Israel.

Num.36 1 And the heads of the tribe of the sons of Galaad the son of Machir the son of Manasse, of the tribe of the sons of Joseph, drew near, and spoke before Moses, and before Eleazar the priest, and before the heads of the houses of the families of the children of Israel: 2 and they said, The Lord commanded our lord to render the land of inheritance by lot to the children of Israel; and the Lord appointed our lord to give the inheritance of Salpaad our brother to his daughters. 3 And they will become wives in one of the tribes of the children of Israel; so their inheritance shall be taken away from the possession of our fathers, and shall be added to the inheritance of the tribe into which the women shall marry, and shall be taken away from the portion of our inheritance. 4 And if there shall be a release of the children of Israel, then shall their inheritance be added to the inheritance of the tribe into which the women marry, and their inheritance, shall be taken away from the inheritance of our family's tribe. 5 And Moses charged the children of Israel by the commandment of the Lord, saying, Thus says the tribe of the children of Joseph. 6 This *is* the thing which the Lord has appointed the daughters of Salpaad, saying, Let them marry where they please, only let them marry *men* of their father's tribe. 7 So shall not the inheritance of the children of Israel go about from tribe to tribe, for the children of Israel shall steadfastly continue each in the inheritance of his family's tribe. 8 And whatever daughter is heiress to a property of the tribes of the children Israel, *such* women shall be married each to one of her father's tribe, that the sons of Israel may each inherit the property of his father's tribe. 9 And the inheritance shall not go about from one tribe to another, but the children of Israel shall steadfastly continue each in his own inheritance. 10 As the Lord commanded Moses, so did they to the daughters of Salpaad. 11 So Thersa, and Egla, and Melcha, and Nua, and Malaa, the daughters of Salpaad, married their cousins; 12 they were married *to men* of the tribe of Manasse of the sons of Joseph; and their inheritance was attached to the tribe of their father's family. 13 These *are* the commandments, and the ordinances, and the judgments, which the Lord commanded by the hand of Moses, at the west of Moab, at Jordan by Jericho.

DEUTERONOMY

Deut.1 1 These *are* the words which Moses spoke to all Israel on this side Jordan in the desert towards the west near the Red Sea, between Pharan Tophol, and Lobon, and Aulon, and the gold works. 2 *It is* a journey of eleven days from Choreb to mount Seir as far as Cades Barne. 3 And it came to pass in the fortieth year, in the eleventh month, on the first *day* of the month, Moses spoke to all the children of Israel, according to all things which the Lord commanded him for them: 4 after he had smitten Seon king of the Amorites who dwelt in Esebon, and Og the king of Basan who dwelt in Astaroth and in Edrain; 5 beyond Jordan in the land of Moab, Moses began to declare this law, saying, 6 The Lord your God spoke to us in Choreb, saying, Let it suffice you to have dwelt *so long* in this mountain. 7 Turn ye and depart and enter into the mountain of the Amorites, and *go* to all that dwell near about Araba, to the mountain and the plain and to the south, and the land of the Chananites near the sea, and Antilibanus, as far as the great river, the river Euphrates. 8 Behold, *God* has delivered the land before you; go in and inherit the land, which I sware to your fathers, Abraam, and Isaac, and Jacob, to give it to them and to their seed after them. 9 And I spoke to you at that time, saying, I shall not be able by myself to bear you. 10 The Lord your God has multiplied you, and, behold, ye are to-day as the stars of heaven for multitude. 11 The Lord God of your fathers add to you a thousand-fold more than you are, and bless you as he has spoken to you. 12 How shall I alone be able to bear your labour, and your burden, and your gainsayings? 13 Take to yourselves wise and understanding and prudent men for your tribes, and I will set your leaders over you. 14 And ye answered me and said, The thing which thou hast told us *is* good to do. 15 So I took of you wise and understanding and prudent men, and I set them to rule over you as rulers of thousands, and rulers of hundreds, and rulers of fifties, and rulers of tens, and officers to your judges. 16 And I charged your judges at that time, saying, Hear *causes* between your brethren, and judge rightly between a man and *his* brother, and the stranger that is with him. 17 Thou shalt not have respect to persons in judgment, thou shalt judge small and great equally; thou shalt not shrink from before the person of a man, for the judgment is God's; and whatsoever matter shall be too hard for you, ye shall bring it to me, and I will hear it. 18 And I charged upon you at that time all the commands which ye shall perform. 19 And we departed from Choreb, and went through all that great wilderness and terrible, which ye saw, by the way of the mountain of the Amorite, as the Lord our God charged us, and we came as far as Cades Barne. 20 And I said to you, Ye have come as far as the mountain of the Amorite, which the Lord our God gives to you: 21 behold, the Lord your God has delivered to us the land before you: go up and inherit it as the Lord God of your fathers said to you; fear not, neither be afraid. 22 And ye all came to me, and said, Let us send men before us, and let them go up to the land for us; and let them bring back to us a report of the way by which we shall go up, and of the cities into which we shall enter. 23 And the saying pleased me: and I took of you twelve men, one man of a tribe. 24 And they turned and went up to the mountain, and they came as far as the valley of the cluster, and surveyed it. 25 And they took in their hands of the fruit of the land, and brought it to you, and said, The land is good which the Lord our God gives us. 26 Yet ye would not go up, but rebelled against the words of the Lord our God. 27 And ye murmured in your tents, and said, Because the Lord hated us, he has brought us out of the land of Egypt to deliver us into the hands of the Amorites, to destroy us. 28 Whither do we go up? and your brethren drew away your heart, saying, *It is a* great nation and populous, and mightier than we; and *there are* cities great and walled up to heaven: moreover we saw there the sons of the giants. 29 And I said to you, Fear not, neither be ye afraid of them; 30 the Lord your God who goes before your face, he shall fight against them together with you effectually, according to all that he wrought for you in the land of Egypt; 31 and in this wilderness which ye saw, by the way of the mountain of the Amorite; how the Lord thy God will bear thee as a nursling, as if any man should nurse his child, through all the way which ye have gone until ye came to this place. 32 And in this matter ye believed not the Lord our God, 33 who goes before you in the way to choose you a place, guiding you in fire by night, shewing you the way by which ye go, and a cloud by day. 34 And the Lord heard the voice of your words, and being greatly provoked he sware, saying, 35 Not one of these men shall see this good land, which I sware to their fathers, 36 except Chaleb the son of Jephonne, he shall see it; and to him I will give the land on which he went up, and to his sons, because he attended to the things of the Lord. 37 And the Lord was angry with me for your sake, saying, Neither shalt thou by any means enter therein. 38 Joshua the son of Naue, who stands by thee, he shall enter in there; do thou strengthen him, for he shall cause Israel to inherit it. 39 And every young child who this day knows not good or evil, —they shall enter therein, and to them I will give it, and they shall inherit it. 40 And ye turned and marched into the wilderness, in the way by the Red Sea. 41

And ye answered and said, We have sinned before the Lord our God; we will go up and fight according to all that the Lord our God has commanded us: and having taken every one his weapons of war, and being gathered together, ye went up to the mountain. 42 And the Lord said to me, Tell them, Ye shall not go up, neither shall ye fight, for I am not with you; thus shall ye not be destroyed before your enemies. 43 And I spoke to you, and ye did not hearken to me; and ye transgressed the commandment of the Lord; and ye forced your way and went up into the mountain. 44 And the Amorite who dwelt in that mountain came out to meet you, and pursued you as bees do, and wounded you from Seir to Herma. 45 And ye sat down and wept before the Lord our God, and the Lord hearkened not to your voice, neither did he take heed to you. 46 And ye dwelt in Cades many days, as many days as ye dwelt *there*.

Deut.2 1 And we turned and departed into the wilderness, by the way of the Red Sea, as the Lord spoke to me, and we compassed mount Seir many days. 2 And the Lord said to me, 3 Ye have compassed this mount long enough; turn therefore toward the north. 4 And charge the people, saying, Ye are going through the borders of your brethren the children of Esau, who dwell in Seir; and they shall fear you, and dread you greatly. 5 Do not engage in war against them, for I will not give you of their land even enough to set your foot upon, for I have given mount Seir to the children of Esau as an inheritance. 6 Buy food of them for money and eat, and ye shall receive water of them by measure for money, and drink. 7 For the Lord our God has blessed thee in every work of thy hands. Consider how thou wentest through that great and terrible wilderness: behold, the Lord thy God *has been* with thee forty years; thou didst not lack any thing. 8 And we passed by our brethren the children of Esau, who dwelt in Seir, by the way of Araba from Ælon and from Gesion Gaber; and we turned and passed by the way of the desert of Moab. 9 And the Lord said to me, Do not ye quarrel with the Moabites, and do not engage in war with them; for I will not give you of their land for an inheritance, for I have given Aroer to the children of Lot to inherit. 10 Formerly the Ommin dwelt in it, a great and numerous nation and powerful, like the Enakim. 11 These also shall be accounted Raphain like the Enakim; and the Moabites call them Ommin. 12 And the Chorrhite dwelt in Seir before, and the sons of Esau destroyed them, and utterly consumed them from before them; and they dwelt in their place, as Israel did to the land of his inheritance, which the Lord gave to them. 13 Now then, arise ye, *said I*, and depart, and cross the valley of Zaret. 14 And the days in which we traveled from Cades Barne till we crossed the valley of Zaret, *were* thirty and eight years, until the whole generation of the men of war failed, dying out of the camp, as the Lord God sware to them. 15 And the hand of the Lord was upon them to destroy them out of the midst of the camp, until they were consumed. 16 And it came to pass when all the men of war dying out of the midst of the people had fallen, 17 that the Lord spoke to me, saying, 18 Thou shalt pass over this day the borders of Moab to Aroer; 19 and ye shall draw nigh to the children of Amman: do not quarrel with them, nor wage war with them; for I will not give thee of the land of the children of Amman for an inheritance, because I have given it to the children of Lot for an inheritance. 20 It shall be accounted a land of Raphain, for the Raphain dwelt there before, and the Ammanites call them Zochommin. 21 A great nation and populous, and mightier than you, as also the Enakim: yet the Lord destroyed them from before them, and they inherited *their land*, and they dwelt *there* instead of them until this day. 22 As they did to the children of Esau that dwell in Seir, even as they destroyed the Chorrhite from before them, and inherited their country, and dwelt *therein* instead of them until this day. 23 And the Evites who dwell in Asedoth to Gaza, and the Cappadocians who came out of Cappadocia, destroyed them, and dwelt in their room. 24 Now then arise and depart, and pass over the valley of Arnon: behold, I have delivered into thy hands Seon the king of Esebon the Amorite, and his land: begin to inherit *it*: engage in war with him this day. 25 Begin to put thy terror and thy fear on the face of all the nations under heaven, who shall be troubled when they have heard thy name, and shall be in anguish before thee. 26 And I sent ambassadors from the wilderness of Kedamoth to Seon king of Esebon with peaceable words, saying, 27 I will pass through thy land: I will go by the road, I will not turn aside to the right hand or to the left. 28 Thou shalt give me food for money, and I will eat; and thou shalt give me water for money, and I will drink; I will only go through on my feet: 29 as the sons of Esau did to me, who dwelt in Seir, and the Moabites who dwelt in Aroer, until I shall have passed Jordan into the land which the Lord our God gives us. 30 And Seon king of Esebon would not that we should pass by him, because the Lord our God hardened his spirit, and made his heart stubborn, that he might be delivered into thy hands, as on this day. 31 And the Lord said to me, Behold, I have begun to deliver before thee Seon the king of Esebon the Amorite, and his land, and do thou begin to inherit his land. 32 And Seon the king of Esebon came forth to meet us, he and all his people to war at Jassa. 33 And the Lord our God delivered him before our face, and we smote him, and his sons, and all his people. 34 And we took possession of all his cities at that time, and we utterly destroyed every city in succession, and their wives, and their children; we left no living prey. 35 Only we took the cattle captive, and took the spoil of the cities. 36 From Aroer, which is by the brink of the brook of Arnon, and the city which is in the valley, and as far as the mount of Galaad; there was not a city which escaped us: the Lord our God delivered all of them into our hands. 37 Only we did not draw near to the children of Amman, even all the parts bordering on the brook Jaboc, and the cities in the mountain country, as the Lord our God charged us.

Deut.3 1 And we turned and went by the way leading to Basan; and Og the king of Basan came out to meet us, he and all his people, to battle at Edraim. 2 And the Lord said to me, Fear him not, for I have delivered him, and all his people, and all his land, into thy hands; and thou shalt do to him as thou didst to Seon king of the Amorites who dwelt in Esebon. 3 And the Lord our God delivered him into our hands, even Og the king of Basan, and all his people; and we smote him until we left none of his seed. 4 And we mastered all his cities at that time; there was not a city which we took not from them; sixty cities, all the country round about Argob, belonging to king Og in Basan: 5 all strong cities, lofty walls, gates and bars; besides the very many cities of the Pherezites. 6 We utterly destroyed *them* as we dealt with Seon the king of Esebon, so we utterly destroyed every city in order, and the women and the children, 7 and all the cattle; and we took for a prey to ourselves the spoil of the cities. 8 And we took at that time the land out of the hands of the two kings of the Amorites, who were beyond Jordan, *extending* from the brook of Arnon even unto Aermon. 9 The Phoenicians call Aermon Sanior, but the Amorite has called it Sanir. 10 All the cities of Misor, and all Galaad, and all Basan as far as Elcha and Edraim, cities of the kingdom of Og in Basan. 11 For only Og the king of Basan was left of the Raphain: behold, his bed *was* a bed of iron; behold, *it is* in the chief city of the children of Ammon; the length of it *is* nine cubits, and the breadth of it four cubits, according to the cubit of a man. 12 And we inherited that land at that time from Aroer, which is by the border of the torrent Arnon, and half the mount of Galaad; and I gave his cities to Ruben and to Gad. 13 And the rest of Galaad, and all Basan the kingdom of Og I gave to the half-tribe of Manasse, and all the country round about Argob, all that Basan; it shall be accounted the land of Raphain. 14 And Jair the son of Manasse took all the country round about Argob as far as the borders of Gargasi and Machathi: he called them by his name Basan Thavoth Jair until this day. 15 And to Machir I gave Galaad. 16 And to Ruben and to Gad I gave *the land* under Galaad as far as the brook of Arnon, the border between the brook and as far as Jaboc; the brook *is* the border to the children Amman. 17 And Araba and Jordan *are* the boundary of Machanareth, even to the sea of Araba, the salt sea under Asedoth Phasga eastward. 18 And I charged you at that time, saying, The Lord your God has given you this land by lot; arm yourselves, every one *that is* powerful, and go before your brethren the children of Israel. 19 Only your wives and your children and your cattle (I know that ye have much cattle), let them dwell in your cities which I have given you; 20 until the Lord your God give your brethren rest, as also he has given to you, and they also shall inherit the land, which the Lord our God gives them on the other side of Jordan; then ye shall return, each one to his inheritance which I have given you. 21 And I commanded Joshua at that time, saying, Your eyes have seen all things, which the Lord our God did to these two kings: so shall the Lord our God do to all the kingdoms against which thou crossest over thither. 22 Ye shall not be afraid of them, because the Lord our God himself shall fight for you. 23 And I besought the Lord at that time, saying, 24 Lord God, thou hast begun to shew to thy servant thy strength, and thy power, and thy mighty hand, and thy high arm: for what God is there in heaven or on the earth, who will do as thou hast done, and according to thy might? 25 I will therefore go over and see this good land that is beyond Jordan, this good mountain and Antilibanus. 26 And the Lord because of you did not regard me, and hearkened not to me; and the Lord said to me, Let it suffice thee, speak not of this matter to me any more. 27 Go up to the top of the quarried rock, and look with thine eyes westward, and northward, and southward, and eastward, and behold *it* with thine eyes, for thou shalt not go over this Jordan. 28 And charge Joshua, and strengthen him, and encourage him; for he shall go before the face of this people, and he shall give them the inheritance of all the land which thou hast seen. 29 And we abode in the valley near the house of Phogor.

Deut.4 1 And now, Israel, hear the ordinances and judgments, all that I teach you this day to do: that ye may live, and be multiplied, and that ye may go in and inherit the land, which the Lord God of your fathers gives you. 2 Ye shall not add to the word which I command you, and ye shall not take from it: keep the commandments of the Lord our God, all that I command you this day. 3 Your eyes have seen all that the Lord our God did in *the case of* Beel-phegor; for every man that went after Beel-phegor, the Lord your God has utterly destroyed him from among you. 4 But ye that kept close to the Lord your God are all alive to-day. 5 Behold, I have shewn you ordinances and judgments as the Lord commanded me, that ye should do so in the land into which ye go to inherit it. 6 And ye shall keep and do them: for this is your wisdom and understanding before all nations, as many as shall hear all these ordinances; and they shall say, Behold, this great nation *is* a wise and understanding people. 7 For what manner of nation *is so* great, which has God so near to them as the Lord our God *is* in all things in whatsoever we may call upon him? 8 And what manner of nation *is so* great, which has righteous ordinances and judgments according to all this law, which I set before you this day? 9 Take heed to thyself, and keep thy heart diligently: forget not any of the things, which thine eyes have seen, and let them not depart from thine heart all the days of thy life; and thou shalt teach thy sons and thy sons' sons, 10 *even the things that happened in* the day in which ye stood before the Lord our God in Choreb in the day of the assembly; for the Lord said to me, Gather the people to me, and let them hear my words, that they may learn to fear me all the days which they live upon the earth, and they shall teach their sons. 11 And ye drew nigh and stood under the mountain; and the mountain burned with fire up to heaven: *there was* darkness, blackness, *and* tempest. 12 And the Lord spoke to you out of the midst of the fire a voice of words, which ye heard: and ye saw no likeness, only *ye heard* a voice. 13 And he announced to you his covenant, which he commanded you to keep, even the ten commandments; and he wrote them on two tables of stone. 14 And the Lord commanded me at that time, to teach you ordinances and judgments, that ye should do them on the land, into which ye go to inherit it. 15 And take good heed to your hearts, for ye saw no similitude in the day in which the Lord spoke to you in Choreb in the mountain out of the midst of the fire: 16 lest ye transgress, and make to yourselves a carved image, any kind of figure, the likeness of male or female, 17 the likeness of any beast of those that are on the earth, the likeness of any winged bird which flies under heaven, 18 the likeness of any reptile which creeps on the earth, the likeness of any fish of those which are in the waters under the earth; 19 and lest having looked up to the sky, and having seen the sun and the moon and the stars, and all the heavenly bodies, thou shouldest go astray and worship them, and serve them, which the Lord thy God has distributed to all the nations under heaven. 20 But God took you, and led you forth out of the land of Egypt, out of the iron furnace, out of Egypt, to be to him a people of inheritance, as at this day. 21 And the Lord God was angry with me for the things said by you, and sware that I should not go over this Jordan, and that I should not enter into the land, which the Lord thy God giveth thee for an inheritance. 22 For I am to die in this land, and shall not pass over this Jordan; but ye are to pass over, and shall inherit this good land. 23 Take heed to yourselves, lest ye forget the covenant of the Lord our God, which he made with you, and ye transgress, and make to yourselves a graven image of any of the things concerning which the Lord thy God commanded thee. 24 For the Lord thy God is a consuming fire, a jealous God. 25 And when thou shalt have begotten sons, and shalt have sons' sons, and ye shall have dwelt a long time on the land, and shall have transgressed, and made a graven image of any thing, and shall have done wickedly before the Lord your God to provoke him; 26 I call heaven and earth this day to witness against you, that ye shall surely perish from off the land, into which ye go across Jordan to inherit it there; ye shall not prolong your days upon it, but shall be utterly cut off. 27 And the Lord shall scatter you among all nations, and ye shall be left few in number among all the nations, among which the Lord shall bring you. 28 And ye shall there serve other gods, the works of the hands of men, wood and stones, which cannot see, nor can they hear, nor eat, nor smell. 29 And there ye shall seek the Lord your God, and ye shall find him whenever ye shall seek him with all your heart, and with all your soul in your affliction. 30 And all these things shall come upon thee in the last days, and thou shalt turn to the Lord thy God, and shalt hearken to his voice. 31 Because the Lord thy God is a God of pity: he will not forsake thee, nor destroy thee; he will not forget the covenant of thy fathers, which the Lord sware to them. 32 Ask of the former days which were before thee, from the day when God created man upon the earth, and *beginning* at the *one* end of heaven to the other end of heaven, if there has happened any thing like to this great event, if such a thing has been heard: 33 if a nation have heard the voice of the living God speaking out of the midst of the fire, as thou hast heard and hast lived; 34 if God has assayed to go and take to himself a nation out of the midst of *another* nation with trial, and with signs, and with wonders, and with war, and with a mighty hand, and with a high arm, and with great sights, according to all the things which the Lord our God did in Egypt in thy sight. 35 So that thou shouldest know that the Lord thy God he is God, and there is none beside him. 36 His voice was made audible from heaven to instruct thee, and he shewed thee upon the earth his great fire, and

thou heardest his words out of the midst of the fire. 37 Because he loved thy fathers, he also chose you their seed after them, and he brought thee himself with his great strength out of Egypt, 38 to destroy nations great and stronger than thou before thy face, to bring thee in, to give thee their land to inherit, as thou hast it this day. 39 An thou shalt know this day, and shalt consider in thine heart, that the Lord thy God he *is* God in heaven above, and on the earth beneath, and there is none else but he. 40 And keep ye his commandments, and his ordinances, all that I command you this day; that it may be well with thee, and with thy sons after thee, that ye may be long-lived upon the earth, which the Lord thy God giveth thee for ever. 41 Then Moses separated three cities beyond Jordan on the east, 42 that the slayer might flee thither, who should have slain his neighbour unintentionally, and should not have hated him in times past, and he shall flee to one of these cities and live: 43 Bosor in the wilderness, in the plain country of Ruben, and Ramoth in Galaad *belonging to* Gad, and Gaulon in Basan *belonging to* Manasse. 44 This *is* the law which Moses set before the children of Israel. 45 These *are* the testimonies, and the ordinances, and the judgments, which Moses spoke to the sons of Israel, when they came out of the land of Egypt: 46 on the other side of Jordan, in the valley near the house of Phogor, in the land of Seon king of the Amorites, who dwelt in Esebon, whom Moses and the sons of Israel smote when they came out of the land of Egypt. 47 And they inherited his land, and the land of Og king of Basan, two kings of the Amorites, who were beyond Jordan eastward. 48 From Aroer, which is on the border of the brook Arnon, even to the mount of Seon, which is Aermon. 49 All Araba beyond Jordan eastward under Asedoth hewn in the rock.

Deut.5 1 And Moses called all Israel, and said to them, Hear, Israel, the ordinances and judgments, all that I speak in your ears this day, and ye shall learn them, and observe to do them. 2 The Lord your God made a covenant with you in Choreb. 3 The Lord did not make this covenant with your fathers, but with you: ye are all here alive this day. 4 The Lord spoke to you face to face in the mountain out of the·midst of the fire. 5 And I stood between the Lord and you at that time to report to you the words of the Lord, (because ye were afraid before the fire, and ye went not up to the mountain) saying, 6 I am the Lord thy God, who brought thee out of the land of Egypt, out of the house of bondage. 7 Thou shalt have no other gods before my face. 8 Thou shalt not make to thyself an image, nor likeness of any thing, whatever things *are* in the heaven above, and whatever *are* in the earth beneath, and whatever *are* in the waters under the earth. 9 Thou shalt not bow down to them, nor shalt thou serve them; for I am the Lord thy God, a jealous God, visiting the sins of the fathers upon the children to the third and fourth generation to them that hate me, 10 and doing mercifully to thousands of them that love me, and that keep my commandments. 11 Thou shalt not take the name of the Lord thy God in vain, for the Lord thy God will certainly not acquit him that takes his name in vain. 12 Keep the sabbath day to sanctify it, as the Lord thy

God commanded thee. 13 Six days thou shalt work, and thou shalt do all thy works; 14 but on the seventh day *is* the sabbath of the Lord thy God: thou shalt do in it no work, thou, and thy son, and thy daughter, thy man-servant, and thy maid-servant, thine ox, and thine ass, and all thy cattle, and the stranger that sojourns in the midst of thee; that thy man-servant may rest, and thy maid, and thine ox, as well as thou. 15 And thou shalt remember that thou wast a slave in the land of Egypt, and the Lord thy God brought thee out thence with a mighty hand, and a high arm: therefore the Lord appointed thee to keep the sabbath day and to sanctify it. 16 Honour thy father and thy mother, as the Lord thy God commanded thee; that it may be well with thee, and that thou mayest live long upon the land, which the Lord thy God gives thee. 17 Thou shalt not commit murder. 18 Thou shalt not commit adultery. 19 Thou shalt not steal. 20 Thou shalt not bear false witness against thy neighbour. 21 Thou shalt not covet thy neighbour's wife; thou shalt not covet thy neighbour's house, nor his field, nor his man-servant, nor his maid, nor his ox, nor his ass, nor any beast of his, nor any thing that is thy neighbour's. 22 These words the Lord spoke to all the assembly of you in the mountain out of the midst of the fire—*there was* darkness, blackness, storm, a loud voice—and he added no more, and he wrote them on two tables of stone, and he gave them to me. 23 And it came to pass when ye heard the voice out of the midst of the fire, for the mountain burned with fire, that ye came to me, even all the heads of your tribes, and your elders: 24 and ye said, Behold, the Lord our God has shewn us his glory, and we have heard his voice out of the midst of the fire: this day we have seen that God shall speak to man, and he shall live. 25 And now let us not die, for this great fire will consume us, if we shall hear the voice of the Lord our God any more, and we shall die. 26 For what flesh *is there* which has heard the voice of the living God, speaking out of the midst of the fire, as we *have heard*, and shall live? 27 Do thou draw near, and hear all that the Lord our God shall say, and thou shalt speak to us all things whatsoever the Lord our God shall speak to thee, and we will hear, and do. 28 And the Lord heard the voice of your words as ye spoke to me; and the Lord said to me, I have heard the voice of the words of this people, even all things that they have said to thee. *They have* well *said* all that they have spoken. 29 O that there were such a heart in them, that they should fear me and keep my commands always, that it might be well with them and with their sons for ever. 30 Go, say to them, Return ye to your houses; 31 but stand thou here with me, and I will tell thee all the commands, and the ordinances, and the judgments, which thou shalt teach them, and let them do so in the land which I give them for an inheritance. 32 And ye shall take heed to do as the Lord thy God commanded thee; ye shall not turn aside to the right hand or to the left, 33 according to all the way which the Lord thy God commanded thee to walk in it, that he may give thee rest; and that it may be well with thee, and ye may prolong your days on the land which ye shall inherit.

Deut.6 1 And these *are* the commands, and the ordinances, and the judgments, as many as the Lord our God gave commandment to teach you to do so in the land on which ye enter to inherit it. 2 That ye may fear the Lord your God, keep ye all his ordinances, and his commandments, which I command thee to-day, thou, and thy sons, and thy sons' sons, all the days of thy life, that ye may live many days. 3 Hear, therefore, O Israel, and observe to do them, that it may be well with thee, and that ye may be greatly multiplied, as the Lord God of thy fathers said that he would give thee a land flowing with milk and honey: and these *are* the ordinances, and the judgments, which the Lord commanded the children of Israel in the wilderness, when they had gone forth from the land of Egypt. 4 Hear, O Israel, The Lord our God is one Lord. 5 And thou shalt love the Lord thy God with all thy mind, and with all thy soul, and all thy strength. 6 And these words, all that I command thee this day, shall be in thy heart and in thy soul. 7 And thou shalt teach them to thy children, and thou shalt speak of them sitting in the house, and walking by the way, and lying down, and rising up. 8 And thou shalt fasten them for a sign upon thy hand, and it shall be immoveable before thine eyes. 9 And ye shall write them on the lintels of your houses and of your gates. 10 And it shall come to pass when the Lord thy God shall have brought thee into the land which he sware to thy fathers, to Abraam, and to Isaac, and to Jacob, to give thee great and beautiful cities which thou didst not build, 11 houses full of all good things which thou didst not fill, wells dug in the rock which thou didst not dig, vineyards and oliveyards which thou didst not plant, then having eaten and been filled, 12 beware lest thou forget the Lord thy God that brought thee forth out of the land of Egypt, out of the house of bondage. 13 Thou shalt fear the Lord thy God, and him only shalt thou serve; and thou shalt cleave to him, and by his name thou shalt swear. 14 Go ye not after other gods of the gods of the nations round about you; 15 for the Lord thy God in the midst of thee *is* a jealous God, lest the Lord thy God be very angry with thee, and destroy thee from off the face of the earth. 16 Thou shalt not tempt the Lord thy God, as ye tempted him in the temptation. 17 Thou shalt by all means keep the commands of the Lord thy God, the testimonies, and the ordinances, which he commanded thee. 18 And thou shalt do that which is pleasing and good before the Lord thy God, that it may be well with thee, and that thou mayest go in and inherit the good land, which the Lord sware to your fathers, 19 to chase all thine enemies from before thy face, as the Lord said. 20 And it shall come to pass when thy son shall ask thee at a future time, saying, What are the testimonies, and the ordinances, and the judgments, which the Lord our God has commanded us? 21 Then shalt thou say to thy son, We were slaves to Pharao in the land of Egypt, and the Lord brought us forth thence with a mighty hand, and with a high arm. 22 And the Lord wrought signs and great and grievous wonders in Egypt, on Pharao and on his house before us. 23 And he brought us out thence to give us this land, which he sware to give to our fathers. 24 And the Lord charged us to observe all these ordinances; to fear the Lord our God, that it may be well with us for ever, that we may live, as even to-day. 25 And there shall be mercy to us, if we take heed to keep all these commands before the Lord our God, as he has commanded us.

Deut.7 1 And when the Lord thy God shall bring thee into the land, into which thou goest to possess it, and shall remove great nations from before thee, the Chettite, and Gergesite, and Amorite, and Chananite, and Pherezite, and Evite, and Jebusite, seven nations *more* numerous and stronger than you, 2 and the Lord thy God shall deliver them into thy hands, then thou shalt smite them: thou shalt utterly destroy them: thou shalt not make a covenant with them, neither shall ye pity them: 3 neither shall ye contract marriages with them: thou shalt not give thy daughter to his son, and thou shalt not take his daughter to thy son. 4 For he will draw away thy son from me, and he will serve other gods; and the Lord will be very angry with you, and will soon utterly destroy thee. 5 But thus shall ye do to them; ye shall destroy their altars, and shall break down their pillars, and shall cut down their groves, and shall burn with fire the graven images of their gods. 6 For thou art a holy people to the Lord thy God; and the Lord thy God chose thee to be to him a peculiar people beyond all nations that *are* upon the face of the earth. 7 It was not because ye are more numerous than all *other* nations that the Lord preferred you, and the Lord made choice of you: for ye are fewer in number than all *other* nations. 8 But because the Lord loved you, and as keeping the oath which he sware to your fathers, the Lord brought you out with a strong hand, and the Lord redeemed thee from the house of bondage, out of the hand of Pharao king of Egypt. 9 Thou shalt know therefore, that the Lord thy God, he *is* God, a faithful God, who keeps covenant and mercy for them that love him, and for those that keep his commandments to a thousand generations, 10 and who recompenses them that hate him to their face, to destroy them utterly; and will not be slack with them that hate him: he will recompense them to their face. 11 Thou shalt keep therefore the commands, and the ordinances, and these judgments, which I command thee this day to do. 12 And it shall come to pass when ye shall have heard these ordinances, and shall have kept and done them, that the Lord thy God shall keep for thee the covenant and the mercy, which he sware to your fathers. 13 And he will love thee, and bless thee, and multiply thee; and he will bless the off-spring of thy body, and the fruit of thy land, thy corn, and thy wine, and thine oil, the herds of thine oxen, and the flocks of thy sheep, on the land which the Lord sware to thy fathers to give to thee. 14 Thou shalt be blessed beyond all nations; there shall not be among you an impotent or barren one, or among thy cattle. 15 And the Lord thy God shall remove from thee all sickness; and none of the evil diseases of Egypt, which thou hast seen, and all that thou hast known, will he lay upon thee; but he will lay them upon all that hate thee. 16 And thou shalt eat all the spoils of the nations which the Lord thy God gives thee; thine eye shall not spare them, and thou shalt not serve their gods; for this is an offence to thee. 17 But if thou shouldest say in thine heart, This nation *is* greater than I, how shall I be able to destroy them utterly? 18 thou shalt not fear them; thou shalt surely remember all that the Lord thy God did to Pharao and to all the Egyptians: 19 the great temptations which thine eyes have seen, those signs and great wonders, the strong hand, and the high arm; how the Lord thy God brought thee forth: so the Lord your God will do to all the nations, whom thou fearest in their presence. 20 And the Lord thy God shall send against them the hornets, until they that are left and they that are hidden from thee be utterly destroyed. 21 Thou shalt not be wounded before them, because the Lord thy God in the midst of thee *is* a great and powerful God. 22 And the Lord thy God shall consume these nations before thee by little and little: thou shalt not be able to consume them speedily, lest the land become desert, and the wild beasts of the field be multiplied against thee. 23 And the Lord thy God shall deliver them into thy hands, and thou shalt destroy them with a great destruction, until ye shall have utterly destroyed them. 24 And he shall deliver their kings into your hands, and ye shall destroy their name from that place; none shall stand up in opposition before thee, until thou shalt have utterly destroyed them. 25 Ye shall burn with fire the graven images of their gods: thou shalt not covet *their* silver, neither shalt thou take to thyself gold from them, lest thou shouldest offend thereby, because it is an abomination to the Lord thy God. 26 And thou shalt not bring an abomination into thine house, so shouldest thou be an accursed thing like it; thou shalt utterly hate it, and altogether abominate it, because it is an accursed thing.

Deut.8 1 Ye shall observe to do all the commands which I charge you to-day, that ye may live and be multiplied, and enter in and inherit the land, which the Lord your God sware *to give* to your fathers. 2 And thou shalt remember all the way which the Lord thy God led thee in the wilderness, that he might afflict thee, and try thee, and that the things in thine heart might be made manifest, whether thou wouldest keep his commandments or no. 3 And he afflicted thee and straitened thee with hunger, and fed thee with manna, which thy fathers knew not; that he might teach thee that man shall not live by bread alone, but by every word that proceeds out of the mouth of God shall man live. 4 Thy garments grew not old from off thee, thy shoes were not worn from off thee, thy feet were not *painfully* hardened, lo! these forty years. 5 And thou shalt know in thine heart, that as if any man should chasten his son, so the Lord thy God will chasten thee. 6 And thou shalt keep the commands of the Lord thy God, to walk in his ways, and to fear him. 7 For the Lord thy God will bring thee into a good and extensive land, where there are torrents of waters, and fountains of deep places issuing through the plains and through the mountains: 8 a land of wheat and barley, *wherein are* vines, figs, pomegranates; a land of olive oil and honey; 9 a land on which thou shalt not eat thy bread with poverty, and thou shalt not want any thing upon it; a land whose stones are iron, and out of its mountains thou shalt dig brass. 10 And thou shalt eat and be filled, and shalt bless the Lord thy God on the good land, which he has given thee. 11 Take heed to thyself that thou forget not the Lord thy God, so as not to keep his commands, and his judgments, and ordinances, which I command thee this day: 12 lest when thou hast eaten and art full, and hast built goodly houses, and dwelt in them; 13 and thy oxen and thy sheep are multiplied to thee, and thy silver and thy gold are multiplied to thee, and all thy possessions are multiplied to thee, 14 thou shouldest be exalted in heart, and forget the Lord thy God, who brought thee out of the land of Egypt, out of the house of bondage: 15 who brought thee through that great and terrible wilderness, where *is* the biting serpent, and scorpion, and drought, where there was no water; who brought thee a fountain of water out of the flinty rock: 16 who fed thee with manna in the wilderness, which thou knewest not, and thy fathers knew not; that he might afflict thee, and thoroughly try thee, and do thee good in thy latter days. 17 Lest thou shouldest say in thine heart, My strength, and the power of mine hand have wrought for me this great wealth. 18 But thou shalt remember the Lord thy God, that he gives thee strength to get wealth; even that he may establish his covenant, which the Lord sware to thy fathers, as at this day. 19 And it shall come to pass if thou do at all forget the Lord thy God, and shouldest go after other gods, and serve them, and worship them, I call heaven and earth to witness against you this day, that ye shall surely perish. 20 As also the other nations which the Lord God destroys before your face, so shall ye perish, because ye hearkened not to the voice of the Lord your God.

Deut.9 1 Hear, O Israel: Thou goest this day across Jordan to inherit nations greater and stronger than yourselves, cities great and walled up to heaven; 2 a people great and many and tall, the sons of Enac, whom thou knowest, and concerning whom thou hast heard *say*, Who can stand before the children of Enac? 3 And thou shalt know to-day, that the Lord thy God he shall go before thy face: he is a consuming fire; he shall destroy them, and he shall turn them back before thee, and shall destroy them quickly, as the Lord said to thee. 4 Speak not in thine heart, when the Lord thy God has destroyed these nations before thy face, saying, For my righteousness the Lord brought me in to inherit this good land. 5 Not for thy righteousness, nor for the holiness of thy heart, dost thou go in to inherit their land, but because of the wickedness of these nations the Lord will destroy them from before thee, and that he may establish the covenant, which the Lord sware to our fathers, to Abraam, and to Isaac, and to Jacob. 6 And thou shalt know to-day, that *it is* not for thy righteousnesses the Lord thy God gives thee this good land to inherit, for thou art a stiff-necked people. 7 Remember, forget not, how much thou provokedst the Lord thy God in the wilderness: from the day that ye came forth out of Egypt, even till ye came into this place, ye continued to be disobedient toward the Lord. 8 Also in Choreb ye provoked the Lord, and the Lord was angry with you to destroy you; 9 when I went up into the mountain to receive the tables of stone, the tables of the covenant, which the Lord made with you, and I was in the mountain forty days and forty nights, I ate no bread and drank no water. 10 And the Lord gave me the two tables of stone written with the finger of God, and on them there had been written all the words which the Lord spoke to you

in the mountain in the day of the assembly. 11 And it came to pass after forty days and forty nights, the Lord gave me the two tables of stone, the tables of the covenant. 12 And the Lord said to me, Arise, go down quickly from hence, for thy people whom thou broughtest out of the land of Egypt have transgressed; they have gone aside quickly out of the way which I commanded them, and have made themselves a molten image. 13 And the Lord spoke to me, saying, I have spoken to thee once and again, saying, I have seen this people, and, behold, it is a stiff-necked people. 14 And now suffer me utterly to destroy them, and I will blot out their name from under heaven, and will make of thee a nation great and strong, and more numerous than this. 15 And I turned and went down from the mountain; and the mountain burned with fire to heaven; and the two tables of the testimonies *were* in my two hands. 16 And when I saw that ye had sinned against the Lord your God, and had made to yourselves a molten image, and had gone astray out of the way, which the Lord commanded you to keep; 17 then I took hold of the two tables, and cast them out of my two hands, and broke them before you. 18 And I made my petition before the Lord as also at the first forty days and forty nights: I ate no bread and drank no water, on account of all your sins which ye sinned in doing evil before the Lord God to provoke him. 19 And I was greatly terrified because of the wrath and anger, because the Lord was provoked with you utterly to destroy you; yet the Lord hearkened to me at this time also. 20 And he was angry with Aaron to destroy him utterly, and I prayed for Aaron also at that time. 21 And your sin which ye had made, *even* the calf, I took, and burnt it with fire, and pounded it and ground it down till it became fine; and it became like dust, and I cast the dust into the brook that descended from the mountain. 22 Also in the burning, and in the temptation, and at the graves of lust, ye provoked the Lord. 23 And when the Lord sent you forth from Cades Barne, saying, Go up and inherit the land which I give to you, then ye disobeyed the word of the Lord your God, and believed him not, and hearkened not to his voice. 24 Ye were disobedient in the things relating to the Lord from the day in which he became known to you. 25 And I prayed before the Lord forty days and forty nights, the number that I prayed *before*, for the Lord said that he would utterly destroy you. 26 And I prayed to God, and said, O Lord, King of gods, destroy not thy people and thine inheritance, whom thou didst redeem, whom thou broughtest out of the land of Egypt with thy great power, and with thy strong hand, and with thy high arm. 27 Remember Abraam, and Isaac, and Jacob thy servants, to whom thou swarest by thyself: look not upon the hardness of heart of this people, and their impieties, and their sins. 28 Lest the inhabitants of the land whence thou broughtest us out speak, saying, Because the Lord could not bring them into the land of which he spoke to them, and because he hated them, has he brought them forth to slay them in the wilderness. 29 And these *are* thy people and thy portion, whom thou broughtest out of the land of Egypt with thy great strength, and with thy mighty hand, and with thy high arm.

Deut.10 1 At that time the Lord said to me, Hew for thyself two stone tables as the first, and come up to me into the mountain, and thou shalt make for thyself an ark of wood. 2 And thou shalt write upon the tables the words which were on the first tables which thou didst break, and thou shalt put them into the ark. 3 So I made an ark of boards of incorruptible wood, and I hewed tables of stone like the first, and I went up to the mountain, and the two tables were in my hand. 4 And he wrote upon the tables according to the first writing the ten commandments, which the Lord spoke to you in the mountain out of the midst of the fire, and the Lord gave them to me. 5 And I turned and came down from the mountain, and I put the tables into the ark which I had made; and there they were, as the Lord commanded me. 6 And the children of Israel departed from Beeroth of the sons of Jakim *to* Misadai: there Aaron died, and there he was buried, and Eleazar his son was priest in his stead. 7 Thence they departed to Gadgad; and from Gadgad to Etebatha, a land *wherein are* torrents of water. 8 At that time the Lord separated the tribe of Levi, to bear the ark of the covenant of the Lord, to stand near before the Lord, to minister and bless in his name to this day. 9 Therefore the Levites have no part nor inheritance among their brethren; the Lord himself *is* their inheritance, as he said to them. 10 And I remained in the mount forty days and forty nights: and the Lord heard me at that time also, and the Lord would not destroy you. 11 And the Lord said to me, Go, set out before this people, and let them go in and inherit the land, which I sware to their fathers to give to them. 12 And now, Israel, what does the Lord thy God require of thee, but to fear the Lord thy God, and to walk in all his ways, and to love him, and to serve the Lord thy God with all thy heart, and with all thy soul; 13 to keep the commandments of the Lord thy God, and his ordinances, all that I charge thee to-day, that it may be well with thee? 14 Behold, the heaven and the heaven of heavens belong to the Lord thy God, the earth and all things that are in it. 15 Only the Lord chose your fathers to love them, and he chose out their seed after them, *even* you, beyond all nations, as at this day. 16 Therefore ye shall circumcise the hardness of your heart, and ye shall not harden your neck. 17 For the Lord your God, he *is* God of gods, and the Lord of lords, the great, and strong, and terrible God, who does not accept persons, nor will he by any means accept a bribe: 18 executing judgment for the stranger and orphan and widow, and he loves the stranger to give him food and raiment. 19 And ye shall love the stranger; for ye were strangers in the land of Egypt. 20 Thou shalt fear the Lord thy God, and serve him, and shalt cleave to him, and shalt swear by his name. 21 He *is* thy boast, and he *is* thy God, who has wrought in the midst of thee these great and glorious things, which thine eyes have seen. 22 With seventy souls your fathers went down into Egypt; but the Lord thy God has made thee as the stars of heaven in multitude.

Deut.11 1 Therefore thou shalt love the Lord thy God, and shalt observe his appointments, and his ordinances, and his commandments, and his judgments, always. 2 And ye shall know this day; for *I speak* not to your children, who know not and have not seen the discipline of the Lord thy God, and his wonderful works, and his strong hand, and his high arm, 3 and his miracles, and his wonders, which he wrought in the midst of Egypt on Pharao king of Egypt, and all his land; 4 and what he did to the host of the Egyptians, and to their chariots, and their cavalry, and their host; how he made the water of the Red Sea to overwhelm the face of them as they pursued after you, and the Lord destroyed them until this day; 5 and all the things which he did to you in the wilderness until ye came into this place; 6 and all the things that he did to Dathan and Abiron the sons of Eliab the son of Ruben, whom the earth opening her mouth swallowed up, and their houses, and their tents, and all their substance that was with them, in the midst of all Israel: 7 for your eyes have seen all the mighty works of the Lord, which he wrought among you to-day. 8 And ye shall keep all his commandments, as many as I command thee to-day, that ye may live, and be multiplied, and that ye may go in and inherit the land, into which ye go across Jordan to inherit it: 9 that ye may live long upon the land, which the Lord sware to your fathers to give to them, and to their seed after them, a land flowing with milk and honey. 10 For the land into which thou goest to inherit it, is not as the land of Egypt, whence ye came out, whensoever they sow the seed, and water it with their feet, as a garden of herbs: 11 but the land into which thou goest to inherit it, is a land of mountains and plains; it shall drink water of the rain of heaven. 12 A land which the Lord thy God surveys continually, the eyes of the Lord thy God are upon it from the beginning of the year to the end of the year. 13 Now if ye will indeed hearken to all the commands which I charge thee this day, to love the Lord thy God, and to serve him with all thy heart, and with all thy soul, 14 then he shall give to thy land the early and latter rain in its season, and thou shalt bring in thy corn, and thy wine, and thine oil. 15 And he shall give food in thy fields to thy cattle; and when thou hast eaten and art full, 16 take heed to thyself that thy heart be not puffed up, and ye transgress, and serve other gods, and worship them: 17 and the Lord be angry with you, and restrain the heaven; and there shall not be rain, and the earth shall not yield its fruit, and ye shall perish quickly from off the good land, which the Lord has given you. 18 And ye shall store these words in your heart and in your soul, and ye shall bind them as a sign on your hand, and it shall be fixed before your eyes. 19 And ye shall teach them to your children, so as to speak about them when thou sittest in the house, and when thou walkest by the way, and when thou sleepest, and when thou risest up. 20 And ye shall write them on the lintels of your houses, and on your gates; 21 that your days may be long, and the days of your children, upon the land which the Lord sware to your fathers to give to them, as the days of heaven upon the earth. 22 And it shall come to pass that if ye will indeed hearken to all these commands, which I charge thee to observe this day, to love the Lord our God, and to walk in all his ways, and to cleave close to him; 23 then the Lord shall cast out all these nations before you, and ye shall inherit great nations and stronger than yourselves. 24 Every place whereon the sole of your foot shall tread shall be your; from the wilderness and

Antilibanus, and from the great river, the river Euphrates, even as far as the west sea shall be your coasts. 25 No one shall stand before you; and the Lord your God will put the fear of you and the dread of you on the face of all the land, on which ye shall tread, as he told you. 26 Behold, I set before you this day the blessing and the curse; 27 the blessing, if ye hearken to the commands of the Lord your God, all that I command you this day; 28 and the curse, if ye do not hearken to the commands of the Lord our God, as many as I command you this day, and ye wander from the way which I have commanded you, having gone to serve other gods, which ye know not. 29 And it shall come to pass when the Lord thy God shall have brought thee into the land into which thou goest over to inherit it, then thou shalt put blessing on mount Garizin, and the curse upon mount Gaebal. 30 Lo! are not these beyond Jordan, behind, westward in the land of Chanaan, which lies westward near Golgol, by the high oak? 31 For ye are passing over Jordan, to go in and inherit the land, which the Lord our God gives you to inherit always, and ye shall dwell in it. 32 And ye shall take heed to do all his ordinances, and these judgments, as many as I set before you to-day.

Deut.12 1 And these *are* the ordinances and the judgments, which ye shall observe to do in the land, which the Lord God of your fathers gives you for an inheritance, all the days which ye live upon the land. 2 Ye shall utterly destroy all the places in which they served their gods, whose *land* ye inherit, on the high mountains and on the hills, and under the thick tree. 3 And ye shall destroy their altars, and break in pieces their pillars, and ye shall cut down their groves, and ye shall burn with fire the graven images of their gods, and ye shall abolish their name out of that place. 4 Ye shall not do so to the Lord your God. 5 But in the place which the Lord thy God shall choose in one of your cities to name his name there, and to be called upon, ye shall even seek *him* out and go thither. 6 And ye shall carry thither your whole-burnt-offerings, and your sacrifices, and your first-fruits, and your vowed-offerings, and your freewill-offerings, and your offerings of thanksgiving, the first-born of your herds, and of your flocks. 7 And ye shall eat there before the Lord your God, and ye shall rejoice in all the things on which ye shall lay your hand, ye and your houses, as the Lord your God has blessed you. 8 Ye shall not do altogether as we do here to-day, every man that which is pleasing in his own sight. 9 For hitherto ye have not arrived at the rest and the inheritance, which the Lord our God gives you. 10 And ye shall go over Jordan, and shall dwell in the land, which the Lord our God takes as an inheritance for you; and he shall give you rest from all your enemies round about, and ye shall dwell safely. 11 And there shall be a place which the Lord thy God shall choose for his name to be called there, thither shall ye bring all things that I order you to-day; your whole- burnt-offerings, and your sacrifices, and your tithes, and the first-fruits of your hands, and every choice gift of yours, whatsoever ye shall vow to the Lord your God. 12 And ye shall rejoice before the Lord your God, ye and your sons, and your daughters, and your men- servants and your maid-servants, and the Levite that

is at your gates; because he has no portion or inheritance with you. 13 Take heed to thyself that thou offer not thy whole-burnt-offerings in any place which thou shalt see; 14 save in the place which the Lord thy God shall choose, in one of thy tribes, there shall ye offer your whole-burnt-offerings, and there shalt thou do all things whatsoever I charge thee this day. 15 But thou shalt kill according to all thy desire, and shalt eat flesh according to the blessing of the Lord thy God, which he has given thee in every city; the unclean that is within thee and the clean shall eat it on equal terms, as the doe or the stag. 16 Only ye shall not eat the blood; ye shall pour it out on the ground as water. 17 Thou shalt not be able to eat in thy cities the tithe of thy corn, and of thy wine, and of thine oil, the first-born of thine herd and of thy flock, and all *your* vows as many as ye shall have vowed, and your thank-offerings, and the first-fruits of thine hands. 18 But before the Lord thy God thou shalt eat it, in the place which the Lord thy God shall choose for himself, thou, and thy son, and thy daughter, thy man-servant, and thy maid-servant, and the stranger that is within thy gates; and thou shalt rejoice before the Lord thy God, on whatsoever thou shalt lay thine hand. 19 Take heed to thyself that thou do not desert the Levite all the time that thou livest upon the earth. 20 And if the Lord thy God shall enlarge thy borders, as he said to thee, and thou shalt say, I will eat flesh; if thy soul should desire to eat flesh, thou shalt eat flesh according to all the desire of thy soul. 21 And if the place be far from thee, which the Lord thy God shall choose for himself, that his name be called upon it, then thou shalt kill of thy herd and of thy flock which God shall have given thee, even as I commanded thee, and thou shalt eat in thy cities according to the desire of thy soul. 22 As the doe and the stag are eaten, so shalt thou eat it; the unclean in thee and the clean shall eat it in like manner. 23 Take diligent heed that thou eat no blood, for blood *is* the life of it; the life shall not be eaten with the flesh. 24 Ye shall not eat *it*; ye shall pour it out on the ground as water. 25 Thou shalt not eat it, that it may be well with thee and with thy sons after thee, if thou shalt do that which is good and pleasing before the Lord thy God. 26 But thou shalt take thy holy things, if thou hast any, and thy vowed-offerings, and come to the place which the Lord thy God shall choose to have his name named upon it. 27 And thou shalt sacrifice thy whole-burnt-offerings, thou shalt offer the flesh upon the altar of the Lord thy God; but the blood of thy sacrifices thou shalt pour out at the foot of the altar of the Lord thy God, but the flesh thou shalt eat. 28 Beware and hearken, and thou shalt do all the commands which I charge thee, that it may be well with thee and with thy sons for ever, if thou shalt do that which is pleasing and good before the Lord thy God. 29 And if the Lord thy God shall utterly destroy the nations, to whom thou goest in thither to inherit their land, from before thee, and thou shalt inherit it, and dwell in their land; 30 take heed to thyself that thou seek not to follow them after they are destroyed before thee, saying, How do these nations act towards their gods? I will do likewise. 31 Thou shalt not do so to thy God; for they have sacrificed to their gods the abominations of the Lord which he hates, for they burn their sons and their daughters in fire to their gods. 32 Every word that I command you this day, it shalt thou observe to do: thou shalt not add to it, nor diminish from it.

Deut.13 1 And if there arise within thee a prophet, or one who dreams a dream, and he gives thee a sign or a wonder, 2 and the sign or the wonder come to pass which he spoke to thee, saying, Let us go and serve other gods, which ye know not; 3 ye shall not hearken to the words of that prophet, or the dreamer of that dream, because the Lord thy God tries you, to know whether ye love your God with all your heart and with all your soul. 4 Ye shall follow the Lord your God, and fear him, and ye shall hear his voice, and attach yourselves to him. 5 And that prophet or that dreamer of a dream, shall die; for he has spoken to make thee err from the Lord thy God who brought thee out of the land of Egypt, who redeemed thee from bondage, to thrust thee out of the way which the Lord thy God commanded thee to walk in: so shalt thou abolish the evil from among you. 6 And if thy brother by thy father or mother, or thy son, or daughter, or thy wife in thy bosom, or friend who is equal to thine own soul, entreat thee secretly, saying, Let us go and serve other gods, which neither thou nor thy fathers have known, 7 of the gods of the nations that are round about you, who are near thee or at a distance from thee, from one end of the earth to the other; 8 thou shalt not consent to him, neither shalt thou hearken to him; and thine eye shall not spare him, thou shalt feel no regret for him, neither shalt thou at all protect him: 9 thou shalt surely report concerning him, and thy hands shall be upon him among the first to slay him, and the hands of all the people at the last. 10 And they shall stone him with stones, and he shall die, because he sought to draw thee away from the Lord thy God who brought thee out of the land of Egypt, out of the house of bondage. 11 And all Israel shall hear, and fear, and shall not again do according to this evil thing among you. 12 And if in one of thy cities which the Lord God gives thee to dwell therein, thou shalt hear men saying, 13 Evil men have gone out from you, and have caused all the inhabitants of their land to fall away, saying, Let us go and worship other gods, whom ye knew not, 14 then thou shalt enquire and ask, and search diligently, and behold, *if* the thing is clearly true, and this abomination has taken place among you, 15 thou shalt utterly destroy all the dwellers in that land with the edge of the sword; ye shall solemnly curse it, and all things in it. 16 And all its spoils thou shalt gather into its public ways, and thou shalt burn the city with fire, and all its spoils publicly before the Lord thy God; and it shall be uninhabited for ever, it shall not be built again. 17 And there shall nothing of the cursed thing cleave to thy hand, that the Lord may turn from his fierce anger, and shew thee mercy, and pity thee, and multiply thee, as he sware to thy fathers; 18 if thou wilt hear the voice of the Lord thy God, to keep his commandments, all that I charge thee this day, to do that which is good and pleasing before the Lord thy God.

Deut.14 1 Ye are the children of the Lord your God: ye shall not make any baldness between you eyes for the dead. 2 For thou art a holy people to the Lord thy God, and the Lord thy God has chosen thee to be a peculiar people to himself of all the nations on the face of the earth. 3 Ye shall not eat any abominable thing. 4 These *are* the beasts which ye shall eat; the calf of the herd, and lamb of the sheep, and kid of the goats; 5 the stag, and doe, and pygarg, and wild goat, and camelopard. 6 Every beast that divides the hoofs, and makes claws of two divisions, and that chews the cud among beasts, these ye shall eat. 7 And these ye shall not eat of them that chew the cud, and of those that divide the hoofs, and make distinct claws; the camel, and the hare, and the rabbit; because they chew the cud, and do not divide the hoof, these are unclean to you. 8 And as for the swine, because he divides the hoof, and makes claws of the hoof, yet he chews not the cud, he is unclean to you; ye shall not eat of their flesh, ye shall not touch their dead bodies. 9 And these ye shall eat of all that are in the water, ye shall eat all that have fins and scales. 10 And all that have not fins and scales ye shall not eat; they are unclean to you. 11 Ye shall eat every clean bird. 12 And these of them ye shall not eat; the eagle, and the ossifrage, and the sea- eagle, 13 and the vulture, and the kite and the like to it, 14 15 and the sparrow, and the owl, and the seamew, 16 and the heron, and the swan, and the stork, 17 and the cormorant, and the hawk, and its like, and the hoopoe, and the raven, 18 and the pelican, and the diver and the like to it, and the red-bill and the bat. 19 All winged animals that creep are unclean to you; ye shall not eat of them. 20 Ye shall eat every clean bird. 21 Ye shall eat nothing that dies of itself; it shall be given to the sojourner in thy cities and he shall eat it, or thou shalt sell it to a stranger, because thou art a holy people to the Lord thy God. Thou shalt not boil a lamb in his mother's milk. 22 Thou shalt tithe a tenth of all the produce of thy seed, the fruit of thy field year by year. 23 And thou shalt eat it in the place which the Lord thy God shall choose to have his name called there; ye shall bring the tithe of thy corn and of thy wine, and of thine oil, the first-born of thy herd and of thy flock, that thou mayest learn to fear the Lord thy God always. 24 And if the journey be too far for thee, and thou art not able to bring them, because the place *is* far from thee which the Lord thy God shall choose to have his name called there, because the Lord thy God will bless thee; 25 then thou shalt sell them for money, and thou shalt take the money in thy hands, and thou shalt go to the place which the Lord thy God shall choose. 26 And thou shalt give the money for whatsoever thy soul shall desire, for oxen or for sheep, or for wine, or *thou shalt lay it out* on strong drink, or on whatsoever thy soul may desire, and thou shalt eat there before the Lord thy God, and thou shalt rejoice and thy house, 27 and the Levite that is in thy cities, because he has not a portion or inheritance with thee. 28 After three years thou shalt bring out all the tithes of thy fruits, in that year thou shalt lay it up in thy cities. 29 And the Levite shall come, because he has no part or lot with thee, and the stranger, and the orphan, and the widow which is in thy cities; and they shall eat and be filled, that the Lord thy God may bless thee in all the works which thou shalt do.

Deut.15 [1] Every seven years thou shalt make a release. [2] And this *is* the ordinance of the release: thou shalt remit every private debt which thy neighbour owes thee, and thou shalt not ask payment of it from thy brother; for it has been called a release to the Lord thy God. [3] Of a stranger thou shalt ask again whatsoever he has of thine, but to thy brother thou shalt remit his debt to thee. [4] For *thus* there shall not be a poor person in the midst of thee, for the Lord thy God will surely bless thee in the land which the Lord thy God gives thee by inheritance, that thou shouldest inherit it. [5] And if ye shall indeed hearken to the voice of the Lord your God, to keep and do all these commandments, as many as I charge thee this day, [6] (for the Lord thy God has blessed thee in the way of which he spoke to thee,)then thou shalt lend to many nations, but thou shalt not borrow; and thou shalt rule over many nations, but they shall not rule over thee. [7] And if there shall be in the midst of thee a poor *man* of thy brethren in one of thy cities in the land, which the Lord thy God gives thee, thou shalt not harden thine heart, neither shalt thou by any means close up thine hand from thy brother who is in want. [8] Thou shalt surely open thine hands to him, and shalt lend to him as much as he wants according to his need. [9] Take heed to thyself that there be not a secret thing in thine heart, an iniquity, saying, The seventh year, the year of release, draws nigh; and thine eye shall be evil to thy brother that is in want, and thou shalt not give to him, and he shall cry against thee to the Lord, and there shall be great sin in thee. [10] Thou shalt surely give to him, and thou shalt lend him as much as he wants, according as he is in need; and thou shalt not grudge in thine heart as thou givest to him, because on this account the Lord thy God will bless thee in all thy works, and in all things on which thou shalt lay thine hand. [11] For the poor shall not fail off thy land, therefore I charge thee to do this thing, saying, Thou shalt surely open thine hands to thy poor brother, and to him that is distressed upon thy land. [12] And if thy brother *or sister*, a Hebrew man or a Hebrew woman, be sold to thee, he shall serve thee six years, and in the seventh year thou shalt send him out free from thee. [13] And when thou shalt send him out free from thee, thou shalt not send him out empty. [14] Thou shalt give him provision for the way from thy flock, and from thy corn, and from thy wine; as the Lord thy God has blessed thee, thou shalt give to him. [15] And thou shalt remember that thou wast a servant in the land of Egypt, and the Lord thy God redeemed thee from thence; therefore I charge thee to do this thing. [16] And if he should say to thee, I will not go out from thee, because he continues to love thee and thy house, because he is well with thee; [17] then thou shalt take an awl, and bore his ear through to the door, and he shall be thy servant for ever; and in like manner shalt thou do to thy maid-servant. [18] It shall not seem hard to thee when they are sent out free from thee, because *thy servant* has served thee six years according to the annual hire of a hireling; so the Lord thy God shall bless thee in all things whatsoever thou mayest do. [19] Every first-born that shall be born among thy kine and thy sheep, thou shalt sanctify the males to the Lord thy God; thou shalt not work with thy first-born calf, and thou shalt not shear the first-born of thy sheep. [20] Thou shalt eat it before the Lord year by year in the place which the Lord thy God shall choose, thou and thy house. [21] And if there be in it a blemish, if it be lame or blind, an evil blemish, thou shalt not sacrifice it to the Lord thy God. [22] Thou shalt eat it in thy cities; the unclean in thee and the clean shall eat it in like manner, as the doe or the stag. [23] Only ye shall not eat the blood; thou shalt pour it out on the earth as water.

Deut.16 [1] Observe the month of new *corn*, and thou shalt sacrifice the passover to the Lord thy God; because in the month of new corn thou camest out of Egypt by night. [2] And thou shalt sacrifice the passover to the Lord thy God, sheep and oxen in the place which the Lord thy God shall choose to have his name called upon it. [3] Thou shalt not eat leaven with it; seven days shalt thou eat unleavened *bread* with it, bread of affliction, because ye came forth out of Egypt in haste; that ye may remember the day of your coming forth out of the land of Egypt all the days of your life. [4] Leaven shall not be seen with thee in all thy borders for seven days, and there shall not be left of the flesh which thou shalt sacrifice at even on the first day until the morning. [5] thou shalt not have power to sacrifice the passover in any of the cities, which the Lord thy God gives thee. [6] But in the place which the Lord thy God shall choose, to have his name called there, thou shalt sacrifice the passover at even at the setting of the sun, at the time when thou camest out of Egypt. [7] And thou shalt boil and roast and eat it in the place, which the Lord thy God shall choose; and thou shalt return in the morning, and go to thy house. [8] Six days shalt thou eat unleavened bread, and on the seventh day is a holiday, a feast to the Lord thy God: thou shalt not do in it any work, save what must be done by any one. [9] Seven weeks shalt thou number to thyself; when thou hast begun *to put* the sickle to the corn, thou shalt begin to number seven weeks. [10] And thou shalt keep the feast of weeks to the Lord thy God, accordingly as thy hand has power in as many things as the Lord thy God shall give thee. [11] And thou shalt rejoice before the Lord thy God, thou and thy son, and thy daughter, thy man-servant and thy maid-servant, and the Levite, and the stranger, and the orphan, and the widow which dwells among you, in whatsoever place the Lord thy God shall choose, that his name should be called there. [12] And thou shalt remember that thou wast a servant in the land of Egypt, and thou shalt observe and do these commands. [13] Thou shalt keep for thyself the feast of tabernacles seven days, when thou gatherest in *thy produce* from thy corn-floor and thy wine-press. [14] And thou shalt rejoice in thy feast, thou, and thy son, and thy daughter, thy man-servant, and thy maid-servant, and the Levite, and the stranger, and the orphan, and the widow that is in thy cities. [15] Seven days shalt thou keep a feast to the Lord thy God in the place which the Lord thy God shall choose for himself; and if the Lord thy God shall bless thee in all thy fruits, and in every work of thy hands, then thou shalt rejoice. [16] Three times in the year shall all thy males appear before the Lord thy God in the place which the Lord shall choose in the feast of unleavened bread, and in the feast of weeks, and in the feast of tabernacles: thou shalt not appear before the Lord thy God empty. 17 Each one according to his ability, according to the blessing of the Lord thy God which he has given thee. 18 Thou shalt make for thyself judges and officers in thy cities, which the Lord thy God gives thee in *thy* tribes, and they shall judge the people with righteous judgment: 19 they shall not wrest judgment, nor favour persons, nor receive a gift; for gifts blind the eyes of the wise, and pervert the words of the righteous. 20 Thou shalt justly pursue justice, that ye may live, and go in and inherit the land which the Lord thy God gives thee. 21 Thou shalt not plant for thyself a grove; thou shalt not plant for thyself any tree near the altar of thy God. 22 Thou shalt not set up for thyself a pillar, which the Lord thy God hates.

Deut.17 1 Thou shalt not sacrifice to the Lord thy God a calf or a sheep, in which there is a blemish, *or* any evil thing; for it is an abomination to the Lord thy God. 2 And if there should be found in any one of thy cities, which the Lord thy God gives thee, a man or a woman who shall do that which is evil before the Lord thy God, so as to transgress his covenant, 3 and they should go and serve other gods, and worship them, the sun, or the moon, or any of the host of heaven, which he commanded thee not to do, 4 and it be told thee, and thou shalt have enquired diligently, and, behold, the thing really took place, this abomination has been done in Israel; 5 then shalt thou bring out that man, or that woman, and ye shall stone them with stones, and they shall die. 6 He shall die on the testimony of two or three witnesses; a man who is put to death shall not be put to death for one witness. 7 And the hand of the witnesses shall be upon him among the first to put him to death, and the hand of the people at the last; so shalt thou remove the evil one from among yourselves. 8 And if a matter shall be too hard for thee in judgment, between blood and blood, and between cause and cause, and between stroke and stroke, and between contradiction and contradiction, matters of judgment in your cities; 9 then thou shalt arise and go up to the place which the Lord thy God shall choose, and thou shalt come to the priests the Levites, and to the judge who shall be in those days, and they shall search out *the matter* and report the judgment to thee. 10 And thou shalt act according to the thing which they shall report to thee out of the place which the Lord thy God shall choose, and thou shalt observe to do all whatsoever shall have been by law appointed to thee. 11 Thou shalt do according to the law and to the judgment which they shall declare to thee: thou shalt not swerve to the right hand or to the left from any sentence which they shall report to thee. 12 And the man whosoever shall act in haughtiness, so as not to hearken to the priest who stands to minister in the name of the Lord thy God, or the judge who shall preside in those days, that man shall die, and thou shalt remove the evil one out of Israel. 13 And all the people shall hear and fear, and shall no more commit impiety. 14 And when thou shalt enter into the land which the Lord thy God gives thee, and shalt inherit it and dwell in it, and shalt say, I will set a ruler over me, as also the other nations round about me; 15 thou shalt surely set over thee the ruler whom the Lord God shall choose: of thy brethren thou shalt set over thee a ruler; thou shalt not have power to set over thee a stranger, because he is not thy brother. 16 For he shall not multiply to himself horses, and he shall by no means turn the people back to Egypt, lest he should multiply to himself horses; for the Lord said, Ye shall not any more turn back by that way. 17 And he shall not multiply to himself wives, lest his heart turn away; and he shall not greatly multiply to himself silver and gold. 18 And when he shall be established in his government, then shall he write for himself this repetition of the law into a book by the hands of the priests the Levites; 19 and it shall be with him, and he shall read in it all the days of his life, that he may learn to fear the Lord thy God, and to keep all these commandments, and to observe these ordinances: 20 that his heart be not lifted up above his brethren, that he depart not from the commandments on the right hand or on the left; that he and his sons may reign long in his dominion among the children of Israel.

Deut.18 1 The priests, the Levites, even the whole tribe of Levi, shall have no part nor inheritance with Israel; the burnt-offerings of the Lord *are* their inheritance, they shall eat them. 2 And they shall have no inheritance among their brethren; the Lord himself *is* his portion, as he said to him. 3 And this *is* the due of the priests in the things coming from the people from those who offer sacrifices, whether it be a calf or a sheep; and thou shalt give the shoulder to the priest, and the cheeks, and the great intestine: 4 and the first-fruits of thy corn, and of thy wine, and of thine oil; and thou shalt give to him the first-fruits of the fleeces of thy sheep: 5 because the Lord has chosen him out of all thy tribes, to stand before the Lord thy God, to minister and bless in his name, himself and his sons among the children of Israel. 6 And if a Levite come from one of the cities of all the children of Israel, where he himself dwells, accordingly as his mind desires, to the place which he shall have chosen, 7 he shall minister to the name of the Lord his God, as all his brethren the Levites, who stand there present before the Lord thy God. 8 He shall eat an allotted portion, besides the sale of his hereditary property. 9 And when thou shalt have entered into the land which the Lord thy God gives thee, thou shalt not learn to do according to the abominations of those nations. 10 There shall not be found in thee one who purges his son or his daughter with fire, one who uses divination, who deals with omens, and augury, 11 a sorcerer employing incantation, one who has in him a divining spirit, and observer of signs, questioning the dead. 12 For every one that does these things is an abomination to the Lord thy God; for because of these abominations the Lord will destroy them from before thy face. 13 Thou shalt be perfect before the Lord thy God. 14 For all these nations whose *land* thou shalt inherit, they will listen to omens and divinations; but the Lord thy God has not permitted thee so *to do*. 15 The Lord thy God shall raise up to thee a prophet of thy brethren, like me; him shall ye hear: 16 according to all things which thou didst desire of the Lord thy God in Choreb in the day of the assembly, saying, We will not again hear the voice of the Lord thy God, and we will not any more see this great fire, and *so* we shall not die. 17 And the Lord said to me, They have spoken rightly all that they have said to thee. 18 I will raise up to them a prophet of their brethren, like thee; and I will put my words in his mouth, and he shall speak to them as I shall command him. 19 And whatever man shall not hearken to whatsoever words that prophet shall speak in my name, I will take vengeance on him. 20 But the prophet whosoever shall impiously speak in my name a word which I have not commanded him to speak, and whosoever shall speak in the name of other gods, that prophet shall die. 21 But if thou shalt say in thine heart, How shall we know the word which the Lord has not spoken? 22 Whatsoever words that prophet shall speak in the name of the Lord, and they shall not come true, and not come to pass, this *is* the thing which the Lord has not spoken; that prophet has spoken wickedly: ye shall not spare him.

Deut.19 1 And when the Lord thy God shall have destroyed the nations, which God gives thee, *even* the land, and ye shall inherit them, and dwell in their cities, and in their houses, 2 thou shalt separate for thyself three cities in the midst of thy land, which the Lord thy God gives thee. 3 Take a survey of thy way, and thou shalt divide the coasts of thy land, which the Lord thy God apportions to thee, into three parts, and there shall be there a refuge for every manslayer. 4 And this shall be the ordinance of the manslayer, who shall flee thither, and shall live, whosoever shall have smitten his neighbour ignorantly, whereas he hated him not in times past. 5 And whosoever shall enter with his neighbour into the thicket, to gather wood, if the hand of him that cuts wood with the axe should be violently shaken, and the axe head falling off from the handle should light on his neighbour, and he should die, he shall flee to one of these cities, and live. 6 Lest the avenger of blood pursue after the slayer, because his heart is hot, and overtake him, if the way be too long, and slay him, though there is to this man no sentence of death, because he hated him not in time past. 7 Therefore I charge thee, saying, Thou shalt separate for thy self three cities. 8 And if the Lord shall enlarge thy borders, as he sware to thy fathers, and the Lord shall give to thee all the land which he said he would give to thy fathers; 9 if thou shalt hearken to do all these commands, which I charge thee this day, to love the Lord thy God, to walk in all his ways continually; thou shalt add for thyself yet three cities to these three. 10 So innocent blood shall not be spilt in the land, which the Lord thy God gives thee to inherit, and there shall not be in thee one guilty of blood. 11 But if there should be in thee a man hating his neighbour, and he should lay wait for him, and rise up against him, and smite him, that he die, and he should flee to one of these cities, 12 then shall the elders of his city send, and take him thence, and they shall deliver him into the hands of the avengers of blood, and he shall die. 13 Thine eye shall not spare him; so shalt thou purge innocent blood from Israel, and it shall be well with thee. 14 Thou shalt not move the landmarks of thy neighbour, which thy fathers set in the inheritance, in which thou hast obtained a share in the land, which the Lord thy God gives thee to inherit. 15 One witness shall not stand to testify against a man for

any iniquity, or for any fault, or for any sin which he may commit; by the mouth of two witnesses, or by the mouth of three witnesses, shall every word be established. 16 And if an unjust witness rise up against a man, alleging iniquity against him; 17 then shall the two men between whom the controversy is, stand before the Lord, and before the priests, and before the judges, who may be in those days. 18 And the judges shall make diligent inquiry, and, behold, *if* and unjust witness has borne unjust testimony; *and* has stood up against his brother; 19 then shall ye do to him as he wickedly devised to do against his brother, and thou shalt remove the evil from yourselves. 20 And the rest shall hear and fear, and do no more according to this evil thing in the midst of you. 21 Thine eye shall not spare him: *thou shalt exact* life for life, eye for eye, tooth for tooth, hand for hand, foot for foot.

Deut.20 1 And if thou shouldest go forth to war against thine enemies, and shouldest see horse, and rider, and a people more numerous than thyself; thou shalt not be afraid of them, for the Lord thy God *is* with thee, who brought thee up out of the land of Egypt. 2 And it shall come to pass whenever thou shalt draw nigh to battle, that the priest shall draw nigh and speak to the people, and shall say to them, 3 Hear, O Israel; ye are going this day to battle against your enemies: let not your heart faint, fear not, neither be confounded, neither turn aside from their face. 4 For *it is* the Lord your God who advances with you, to fight with you against your enemies, *and* to save you. 5 And the scribes shall speak to the people, saying, What man *is* he that has built a new house, and has not dedicated it? let him go and return to his house, lest he die in the war, and another man dedicate it. 6 And what man *is* he that has planted a vineyard, and not been made merry with it? let him go and return to his house, lest he die in the battle, and another man be made merry with it. 7 And what man *is* he that has betrothed a wife, and has not taken her? let him go and return to his house, lest he die in the battle, and another man take her. 8 And the scribes shall speak further to the people, and say, What man *is* he that fears and is cowardly in his heart? Let him go and return to his house, lest he make the heart of his brother fail, as his own. 9 And it shall come to pass when the scribes shall have ceased speaking to the people, that they shall appoint generals of the army to be leaders of the people. 10 And if thou shalt draw nigh to a city to overcome them by war, then call them out peaceably. 11 If then they should answer peaceably to thee, and open to thee, it shall be that all the people found in it shall be tributary and subject to thee. 12 But if they will not hearken to thee, but wage war against thee, thou shalt invest it; 13 until the Lord thy God shall deliver it into thy hands, and thou shalt smite every male of it with the edge of the sword: 14 except the women and the stuff: and all the cattle, and whatsoever shall be in the city, and all the plunder thou shalt take as spoil for thyself, and shalt eat all the plunder of thine enemies whom the Lord thy God gives thee. 15 Thus shalt thou do to all the cities that are very far off from thee, not *being* of the cities of these nations which the Lord thy God gives thee to inherit their land. 16 *Of these* ye shall not take any thing alive; 17 but ye shall surely curse them, the Chettite, and the Amorite, and the Chananite, and the Pherezite, and the Evite, and the Jebusite, and the Gergesite; as the Lord thy God commanded thee: 18 that they may not teach you to do all their abominations, which they did to their gods, and *so* ye should sin before the Lord your God. 19 And if thou shouldest besiege a city many days to prevail against it by war to take it, thou shalt not destroy its trees, by applying an iron tool to them, but thou shalt eat of it, and shalt not cut it down: Is the tree that is in the field a man, to enter before thee into the work of the siege? 20 But the tree which thou knowest to be not fruit-bearing, this thou shalt destroy and cut down; and thou shalt construct a mound against the city, which makes war against thee, until it be delivered up.

Deut.21 1 And if one be found slain with the sword in the land, which the Lord thy God gives thee to inherit, having fallen in the field, and they do not know who has smitten *him*, 2 thine elders and thy judges shall come forth, and shall measure the distances of the cities round about the slain man: 3 and it shall be that the city which is nearest to the slain man the elders of that city shall take a heifer of the herd, which has not laboured, and which has not borne a yoke. 4 And the elders of that city shall bring down the heifer into a rough valley, which has not been tilled and is not sown, and they shall slay the heifer in the valley. 5 And the priests the Levites shall come, because the Lord God has chosen them to stand by him, and to bless in his name, and by their word shall every controversy and every stroke be *decided*. 6 And all the elders of that city who draw nigh to the slain man shall wash their hands over the head of the heifer which was slain in the valley; 7 and they shall answer and say, Our hands have not shed this blood, and our eyes have not seen *it*. 8 Be merciful to thy people Israel, whom thou hast redeemed, O Lord, that innocent blood may not be charged on thy people Israel: and the blood shall be atoned for to them. 9 And thou shalt take away innocent blood from among you, if thou shouldest do that which is good and pleasing before the Lord thy God. 10 And if when thou goest out to war against thine enemies, the Lord thy God should deliver them into thine hands, and thou shouldest take their spoil, 11 and shouldest see among the spoil a woman beautiful in countenance, and shouldest desire her, and take her to thyself for a wife, 12 and shouldest bring her within thine house: then shalt thou shave her head, and pare her nails; 13 and shalt take away her garments of captivity from off her, and she shall abide in thine house, and shall bewail her father and mother the days of a month; and afterwards thou shalt go in to her and dwell with her, and she shall be thy wife. 14 And it shall be if thou do not delight in her, thou shalt send her out free; and she shall not by any means be sold for money, thou shalt not treat her contemptuously, because thou hast humbled her. 15 And if a man have two wives, the one loved and the other hated, and both the loved and the hated should have born him *children*, and the son of the hated should be first-born; 16 then it shall be that whensoever he shall divide by inheritance his goods to his sons, he shall

not be able to give the right of the first-born to the son of the loved one, having overlooked the son of the hated, which is the first-born. 17 But he shall acknowledge the first-born of the hated one to give to him double of all things which shall be found by him, because he is the first of his children, and to him belongs the birthright. 18 And if any man has a disobedient and contentious son, who hearkens not to the voice of his father and the voice of his mother, and they should correct him, and he should not hearken to them; 19 then shall his father and his mother take hold of him, and bring him forth to the elders of his city, and to the gate of the place: 20 and they shall say to the men of their city, This our son is disobedient and contentious, he hearkens not to our voice, he is a reveler and a drunkard. 21 And the men of his city shall stone him with stones, and he shall die; and thou shalt remove the evil one from yourselves, and the rest shall hear and fear. 22 And if there be sin in any one, *and* the judgment of death *be upon him*, and he be put to death, and ye hang him on a tree: 23 his body shall not remain all night upon the tree, but ye shall by all means bury it in that day; for every one that is hanged on a tree is cursed of God; and ye shall by no means defile the land which the Lord thy God gives thee for an inheritance.

Deut.22 1 When thou seest the calf of thy brother or his sheep wandering in the way, thou shalt not overlook them; thou shalt by all means turn them back to thy brother, and thou shalt restore them to him. 2 And if thy brother do not come nigh thee, and thou dost not know him, thou shalt bring it into thy house within; and it shall be with thee until thy brother shall seek them, and thou shalt restore them to him. 3 Thus shalt thou do to his ass, and thus shalt thou do to his garment, and thus shalt thou do to every thing that thy brother has lost; whatsoever shall have been lost by him, and thou shalt have found, thou shalt not have power to overlook. 4 Thou shalt not see the ass of thy brother, or his calf, fallen in the way: thou shalt not overlook them, thou shalt surely help him to raise them up. 5 The apparel of a man shall not be on a woman, neither shall a man put on a woman's dress; for every one that does these things is an abomination to the Lord thy God. 6 And if thou shouldest come upon a brood of birds before thy face in the way or upon any tree, or upon the earth, young or eggs, and the mother be brooding on the young or the eggs, thou shalt not take the dam with the young ones. 7 Thou shalt by all means let the mother go, but thou shalt take the young to thyself; that it may be well with thee, and that thou mayest live long. 8 If thou shouldest build a new house, then shalt thou make a parapet to thy house; so thou shalt not bring blood-guiltiness upon thy house, if one should in any wise fall from it. 9 Thou shalt not sow thy vineyard with diverse seed, lest the fruit be devoted, and whatsoever seed thou mayest sow, with the fruit of thy vineyard. 10 Thou shalt not plough with an ox and an ass together. 11 Thou shalt not wear a mingled *garment*, woollen and linen together. 12 Thou shalt make fringes on the four borders of thy garments, with which soever thou mayest be clothed. 13 And if any one should take a wife, and dwell with her, and hate her, 14 and attach to her reproachful words, and bring against her an evil name, and say, I took this woman, and when I came to her I found not her tokens of virginity: 15 then the father and the mother of the damsel shall take and bring out the damsel's tokens of virginity to the elders of the city to the gate. 16 And the father of the damsel shall say to the elders, I gave this my daughter to this man for a wife; 17 and now he has hated her, and attaches reproachful words to her, saying, I have not found tokens of virginity with thy daughter; and these *are* the tokens of my daughter's virginity. And they shall unfold the garment before the elders of the city. 18 And the elders of that city shall take that man, and shall chastise him, 19 and shall fine him a hundred shekels, and shall give *them* to the father of the damsel, because he has brought forth an evil name against a virgin of Israel; and she shall be his wife: he shall never be able to put her away. 20 But if this report be true, and the tokens of virginity be not found for the damsel; 21 then shall they bring out the damsel to the doors of her father's house, and shall stone her with stones, and she shall die; because she has wrought folly among the children of Israel, to defile the house of her father by whoring: so thou shalt remove the evil one from among you. 22 And if a man be found lying with a woman married to a man, ye shall kill them both, the man that lay with the woman, and the woman: so shalt thou remove the wicked one out of Israel. 23 And if there be a young damsel espoused to a man, and a man should have found her in the city and have lain with her; 24 ye shall bring them both out to the gate of their city, and they shall be stoned with stones, and they shall die; the damsel, because she cried not in the city; and the man, because he humbled his neighbour's spouse: so shalt thou remove the evil one from yourselves. 25 But if a man find in the field a damsel that is betrothed, and he should force her and lie with her, ye shall slay the man that lay with her only. 26 And the damsel has not *committed* a sin worthy of death; as if a man should rise up against his neighbour, and slay him, so *is* this thing; 27 because he found her in the field; the betrothed damsel cried, and there was none to help her. 28 And if any one should find a young virgin who has not been betrothed, and should force *her* and lie with her, and be found, 29 the man who lay with her shall give to the father of the damsel fifty silver didrachms, and she shall be his wife, because he has humbled her; he shall never be able to put her away. 30 A man shall not take his father's wife, and shall not uncover his father's skirt.

Deut.23 1 He that is fractured or mutilated in his private parts shall not enter into the assembly of the Lord. 2 *One born* of a harlot shall not enter into the assembly of the Lord. 3 The Ammanite and Moabite shall not enter into the assembly of the Lord, even until the tenth generation he shall not enter into the assembly of the Lord, even for ever: 4 because they met you not with bread and water by the way, when ye went out of Egypt; and because they hired against thee Balaam the son of Beor of Mesopotamia to curse thee. 5 But the Lord thy God would not hearken to Balaam; and the Lord thy God changed the curses into blessings, because the Lord thy God loved thee. 6 Thou shalt not speak peaceably or profitably to them all thy days for ever. 7 Thou shalt not abhor an Edomite, because he is thy brother; thou shalt not abhor an Egyptian, because thou wast a stranger in his land. 8 If sons be born to them, in the third generation they shall enter into the assembly of the Lord. 9 And if thou shouldest go forth to engage with thine enemies, then thou shalt keep thee from every wicked thing. 10 If there should be in thee a man who is not clean by reason of his issue by night, then he shall go forth out of the camp, and he shall not enter into the camp. 11 And it shall come to pass toward evening he shall wash his body with water, and when the sun has gone down, he shall go into the camp. 12 And thou shalt have a place outside of the camp, and thou shalt go out thither, 13 and thou shalt have a trowel on thy girdle; and it shall come to pass when thou wouldest relieve thyself abroad, that thou shalt dig with it, and shalt bring back the earth and cover thy nuisance. 14 Because the Lord thy God walks in thy camp to deliver thee, and to give up thine enemy before thy face; and thy camp shall be holy, and there shall not appear in thee a disgraceful thing, and *so* he shall turn away from thee. 15 Thou shalt not deliver a servant to his master, who *coming* from his master attaches himself to thee. 16 He shall dwell with thee, he shall dwell among you where he shall please; thou shalt not afflict him. 17 There shall not be a harlot of the daughters of Israel, and there shall not be a fornicator of the sons of Israel; there shall not be an idolatress of the daughters of Israel, and there shall not be an initiated person of the sons of Israel. 18 Thou shalt not bring the hire of a harlot, nor the price of a dog into the house of the Lord thy God, for any vow; because even both are an abomination to the Lord thy God. 19 Thou shalt not lend to thy brother on usury of silver, or usury of meat, or usury of any thing which thou mayest lend out. 20 Thou mayest lend on usury to a stranger, but to thy brother thou shalt not lend on usury; that the Lord thy God may bless thee in all thy works upon the land, into which thou art entering to inherit it. 21 And if thou wilt vow a vow to the Lord thy God, thou shalt not delay to pay it; for the Lord thy God will surely require it of thee, and *otherwise* it shall be sin in thee. 22 But if thou shouldest be unwilling to vow, it is not sin in thee. 23 Thou shalt observe the words that proceed from between thy lips; and as thou hast vowed a gift to the Lord God, *so* shalt thou do that which thou hast spoken with thy mouth.

Deut.24 1 And if thou shouldest go into the corn field of thy neighbour, then thou mayest gather the ears with thy hands; but thou shalt not put the sickle to thy neighbour's corn. 2 And if thou shouldest go into the vineyard of thy neighbour, thou shalt eat grapes sufficient to satisfy thy desire; but thou mayest not put them into a vessel. 3 And if any one should take a wife, and should dwell with her, then it shall come to pass if she should not have found favour before him, because he has found some unbecoming thing in her, that he shall write for her a bill of divorcement, and give it into her hands, and he shall send her away out of his house. 4 And *if* she should go away and be married to another man; 5 and the last husband should hate her, and write for her a bill of divorcement; and should give it into her hands, and send her away out of his house, and the last husband should die, who took her to himself for a wife; 4 the former husband who sent her away shall not be able to return and take her to himself for a wife, after she has been defiled; because it is an abomination before the Lord thy God, and ye shall not defile the land, which the Lord thy God gives thee to inherit. 7 And if any one should have recently taken a wife, he shall not go out to war, neither shall any thing be laid upon him; he shall be free in his house; for one year he shall cheer his wife whom he has taken. 8 Thou shalt not take for a pledge the under millstone, nor the upper millstone; for he who does so takes life for a pledge. 9 And if a man should be caught stealing one of his brethren of the children of Israel, and having overcome him he should sell him, that thief shall die; so shalt thou remove that evil one from yourselves. 10 Take heed to thyself in *regard of* the plague of leprosy: thou shalt take great heed to do according to all the law, which the priests the Levites shall report to you; take heed to do, as I have charged you. 11 Remember all that the Lord thy God did to Mariam in the way, when ye were going out of Egypt. 12 If thy neighbour owe thee a debt, any debt whatsoever, thou shalt not go into his house to take his pledge: 13 thou shalt stand without, and the man who is in thy debt shall bring the pledge out to thee. 14 And if the man be poor, thou shalt not sleep with his pledge. 15 Thou shalt surely restore his pledge at sunset, and he shall sleep in his garment, and he shall bless thee; and it shall be mercy to thee before the Lord thy God. 16 Thou shalt not unjustly withhold the wages of the poor and needy of thy brethren, or of the strangers who are in thy cities. 17 Thou shalt pay him his wages the same day, the sun shall not go down upon it, because he is poor and he trusts in it; and he shall cry against thee to the Lord, and it shall be sin in thee. 18 The fathers shall not be put to death for the children, and the sons shall not be put to death for the fathers; every one shall be put to death for his own sin. 19 Thou shalt not wrest the judgment of the stranger and the fatherless, and widow; thou shalt not take the widow's garment for a pledge. 20 And thou shalt remember that thou wast a bondman in the land of Egypt, and the Lord thy God redeemed thee from thence; therefore I charge thee to do this thing. 21 And when thou shalt have reaped corn in thy field, and shalt have forgotten a sheaf in thy field, thou shalt not return to take it; it shall be for the stranger, and the orphan, and the widow, that the Lord thy God may bless thee in all the works of thy hands. 22 And if thou shouldest gather thine olives, thou shalt not return to collect the remainder; it shall be for the stranger, and the fatherless, and the widow, and thou shalt remember that thou wast a bondman in the land of Egypt; therefore I command thee to do this thing. 23 And when soever thou shalt gather the grapes of thy vineyard, thou shalt not glean what thou hast left; it shall be for the stranger, and the orphan, and the widow: 24 and thou shalt remember that thou wast a bondman in the land of Egypt; therefore I command thee to do this thing.

Deut.25 1 And if there should be a dispute between men, and they should come forward to judgment, and *the judges* judge, and justify the righteous, and condemn the wicked: 2 then it shall come to pass, if the unrighteous should be worthy of stripes, thou shalt lay him down before the judges, and they shall scourge him before them according to his iniquity. 3 And they shall scourge him with forty stripes in number, they shall not inflict more; for if thou shouldest scourge him *with* more stripes beyond these stripes, thy brother will be disgraced before thee. 4 Thou shalt not muzzle the ox that treads out the corn. 5 And if brethren should live together, and one of them should die, and should not have seed, the wife of the deceased shall not marry out *of the family* to a man not related: her husband's brother shall go in to her, and shall take her to himself for a wife, and shall dwell with her. 6 And it shall come to pass that the child which she shall bear, shall be named by the name of the deceased, and his name shall not be blotted out of Israel. 7 And if the man should not be willing to take his brother's wife, then shall the woman go up to the gate to the elders, and she shall say, My husband's brother will not raise up the name of his brother in Israel, my husband's brother has refused. 8 And the elders of his city shall call him, and speak to him; and if he stand and say, I will not take her: 9 then his brother's wife shall come forward before the elders, and shall loose one shoe from off his foot, and shall spit in his face, and shall answer and say, Thus shall they do to the man who will not build his brother's house in Israel. 10 And his name shall be called in Israel, The house of him that has had his shoe loosed. 11 And if men should strive together, a man with his brother, and the wife of one of them should advance to rescue her husband out of the hand of him that smites him, and she should stretch forth her hand, and take hold of his private parts; 12 thou shalt cut off her hand; thine eye shall not spare her. 13 Thou shalt not have in thy bag divers weights, a great and a small. 14 Thou shalt not have in thine house divers measures, a great and a small. 15 Thou shalt have a true and just weight, and a true and just measure, that thou mayest live long upon the land which the Lord thy God gives thee for an inheritance. 16 For every one that does this *is* an abomination to the Lord thy God, even every one that does injustice. 17 Remember what things Amalec did to thee by the way, when thou wentest forth out of the land of Egypt: 18 how he withstood thee in the way, and harassed thy rear, *even* those that were weary behind thee, and thou didst hunger and wast weary; and he did not fear God. 19 And it shall come to pass whenever the Lord thy God shall have given thee rest from all thine enemies round about thee, in the land which the Lord thy God gives thee to inherit, thou shalt blot out the name of Amalec from under heaven, and shalt not forget *to do it.*

Deut.26 1 And it shall be when thou shalt have entered into the land, which the Lord thy God gives thee to inherit it, and thou shalt have inherited it, and thou shalt have dwelt upon it, 2 that thou shalt take of the first of the fruits of thy land, which the Lord thy God gives thee, and thou shalt put them into a basket, and thou shalt go to the place which the

Lord thy God shall choose to have his name called there. 3 And thou shalt come to the priest who shall be in those days, and thou shalt say to him, I testify this day to the Lord my God, that I am come into the land which the Lord sware to our fathers to give to us. 4 And the priest shall take the basket out of thine hands, and shall set it before the altar of the Lord thy God: 5 and he shall answer and say before the Lord thy God, My father abandoned Syria, and went down into Egypt, and sojourned there with a small number, and became there a mighty nation and a great multitude. 6 And the Egyptians afflicted us, and humbled us, and imposed hard tasks on us: 7 and we cried to the Lord our God, and the Lord heard our voice, and saw our humiliation, and our labour, and our affliction. 8 And the Lord brought us out of Egypt himself with his great strength, and his mighty hand, and his high arm, and with great visions, and with signs, and with wonders. 9 And he brought us into this place, and gave us this land, a land flowing with milk and honey. 10 And now, behold, I have brought the first of the fruits of the land, which thou gavest me, O Lord, a land flowing with milk and honey: and thou shalt leave it before the Lord thy God, and thou shalt worship before the Lord thy God; 11 and thou shalt rejoice in all the good *things*, which the Lord thy God has given thee, *thou* and thy family, and the Levite, and the stranger that is within thee. 12 And when thou shalt have completed all the tithings of thy fruits in the third year, thou shalt give the second tenth to the Levite, and stranger, and fatherless, and widow; and they shall eat it in thy cities, and be merry. 13 And thou shalt say before the Lord thy God, I have fully collected the holy things out of my house, and I have given them to the Levite, and the stranger, and the orphan, and the widow, according to all commands which thou didst command me: I did not transgress thy command, and I did not forget it. 14 And in my distress I did not eat of them, I have not gathered of them for an unclean purpose, I have not given of them to the dead; I have hearkened to the voice of the Lord our God, I have done as thou hast commanded me. 15 Look down from thy holy house, from heaven, and bless thy people Israel, and the land which thou hast given them, as thou didst swear to our fathers, to give to us a land flowing with milk and honey. 16 On this day the Lord thy God charged thee to keep all the ordinances and judgments; and ye shall observe and do them, with all your heart, and with all your soul. 17 Thou hast chosen God this day to be thy God, and to walk in all his ways, and to observe his ordinances and judgments, and to hearken to his voice. 18 And the Lord has chosen thee this day that thou shouldest be to him a peculiar people, as he said, to keep his commands; 19 and that thou shouldest be above all nations, as he has made thee renowned, and a boast, and glorious, that thou shouldest be a holy people to the Lord thy God, as he has spoken.

Deut.27 1 And Moses and the elders of Israel commanded, saying, Keep all these commands, all that I command you this day. 2 And it shall come to pass in the day when ye shall cross over Jordan into the land which the Lord thy God gives thee, that thou shalt set up for thyself great stones, and shalt plaster them with plaster. 3 And thou shalt write on these stones all the words of this law, as soon as ye have crossed Jordan, when ye are entered into the land, which the Lord God of thy fathers gives thee, a land flowing with milk and honey, according as the Lord God of thy fathers said to thee. 4 And it shall be as soon as ye are gone over Jordan, ye shall set up these stones, which I command thee this day, on mount Gaebal, and thou shalt plaster them with plaster. 5 And thou shalt build there an altar to the Lord thy God, an altar of stones; thou shalt not lift up iron upon it. 6 Of whole stones shalt thou build an altar to the Lord thy God, and thou shalt offer upon it whole-burnt-offerings to the Lord thy God. 7 And thou shalt there offer a peace-offering; and thou shalt eat and be filled, and rejoice before the Lord thy God. 8 And thou shalt write upon the stones all this law very plainly. 9 And Moses and the priests the Levites spoke to all Israel, saying, Be silent and hear, O Israel; this day thou art become a people to the Lord thy God. 10 And thou shalt hearken to the voice of the Lord thy God, and shalt do all his commands, and his ordinances, as many as I command thee this day. 11 And Moses charged the people on that day, saying, 12 These shall stand to bless the people on mount Garizin having gone over Jordan; Symeon, Levi, Judas, Issachar, Joseph, and Benjamin. 13 And these shall stand for cursing on mount Gaebal; Ruben, Gad, and Aser, Zabulon, Dan, and Nephthali. 14 And the Levites shall answer and say to all Israel with a loud voice, 15 Cursed *is* the man whosoever shall make a graven or molten image, an abomination to the Lord, the work of the hands of craftsmen, and shall put it in a secret place: and all the people shall answer and say, So be it. 16 Cursed is the man that dishonours his father or his mother: and all the people shall say, So be it. 17 Cursed is he that removes his neighbour's landmarks: and all the people shall say, So be it. 18 Cursed is he that makes the blind to wander in the way: and all the people shall say, So be it. 19 Cursed is every one that shall pervert the judgment of the stranger, and orphan, and widow: and all the people shall say, So be it. 20 Cursed is he that lies with his father's wife, because he has uncovered his father's skirt: and all the people shall say, So be it. 21 Cursed is he that lies with any beast: and all the people shall say, So be it. 22 Cursed is he that lies with his sister by his father or his mother: and all the people shall say, So be it. 23 Cursed is he that lies with his daughter-in-law: and all the people shall say, So be it. Cursed is he that lies with his wife's sister: and all the people shall say, So be it. 24 Cursed is he that smites his neighbour secretly: and all the people shall say, So be it. 25 Cursed is he whosoever shall have taken a bribe to slay an innocent man: and all the people shall say, So be it. 26 Cursed is every man that continues not in all the words of this law to do them: and all the people shall say, So be it.

Deut.28 1 And it shall come to pass, if thou wilt indeed hear the voice of the Lord thy God, to observe and do all these commands, which I charge thee this day, that the Lord thy God shall set thee on high above all the nations of the earth; 2 and all these blessings shall come upon thee, and shall find thee. If thou wilt indeed hear the voice of the Lord thy

God, 3 blessed *shalt* thou *be* in the city, and blessed shalt thou be in the field. 4 Blessed shall be the offspring of thy body, and the fruits of thy land, and the herds of thy oxen, and the flocks of thy sheep. 5 Blessed shall be thy barns, and thy stores. 6 Blessed shalt thou be in thy coming in, and blessed shalt thou be in thy going out. 7 The Lord deliver thine enemies that withstand thee utterly broken before thy face: they shall come out against thee one way, and they shall flee seven ways from before thee. 8 The Lord send upon thee his blessing in thy barns, and on all on which thou shalt put thine hand, in the land which the Lord thy God gives thee. 9 The Lord raise thee up for himself a holy people, as he sware to thy fathers; if thou wilt hear the voice of the Lord thy God, and walk in all his ways. 10 And all the nations of the earth shall see thee, that the name of the Lord is called upon thee, and they shall stand in awe of thee. 11 And the Lord thy God shall multiply thee for good in the offspring of thy body, and in the offspring of thy cattle, and in the fruits of thy land, on thy land which the Lord sware to thy fathers to give to thee. 12 May the Lord open to thee his good treasure, the heaven, to give rain to thy land in season: may he bless all the works of thy hands: so shalt thou lend to many nations, but thou shalt not borrow; and thou shalt rule over many nations, but they shall not rule over thee. 13 The Lord thy God make thee the head, and not the tail; and thou shalt then be above and thou shalt not be below, if thou wilt hearken to the voice of the Lord thy God, in all things that I charge thee this day to observe. 14 Thou shalt not turn aside from any of the commandments, which I charge thee this day, to the right hand or to the left, to go after other gods to serve them. 15 But it shall come to pass, if thou wilt not hearken to the voice of the Lord thy God, to observe all his commandments, as many as I charge thee this day, then all these curses shall come on thee, and overtake thee. 16 Cursed *shalt* thou *be* in the city, and cursed shalt thou be in the field. 17 Cursed shall be thy barns and thy stores. 18 Cursed shall be the offspring of thy body, and the fruits of thy land, the herds of thine oxen, and the flocks of thy sheep. 19 Cursed shalt thou be in thy coming in, and cursed shalt thou be in thy going out. 20 The Lord send upon thee want, and famine, and consumption of all things on which thou shalt put thy hand, until he shall have utterly destroyed thee, and until he shall have consumed thee quickly because of thine evil devices, because thou hast forsaken me. 21 The Lord cause the pestilence to cleave to thee, until he shall have consumed thee off the land into which thou goest to inherit it. 22 The Lord smite thee with distress, and fever, and cold, and inflammation, and blighting, and paleness, and they shall pursue thee until they have destroyed thee. 23 And thou shalt have over thine head a sky of brass, and the earth under thee shall be iron. 24 The Lord thy God make the rain of thy land dust; and dust shall come down from heaven, until it shall have destroyed thee, and until it shall have quickly consumed thee. 25 The Lord give thee up for slaughter before thine enemies: thou shalt go out against them one way, and flee from their face seven ways; and thou shalt be a dispersion in all the kingdoms of the earth. 26 And your dead men shall be food to the birds of the sky, and to the beasts of the earth; and there shall be none to scare them away. 27 The Lord smite thee with the botch of Egypt in the seat, and with a malignant scab, and itch, so that thou canst not be healed. 28 The Lord smite thee with insanity, and blindness, and astonishment of mind. 29 And thou shalt grope at mid-day, as a blind man would grope in the darkness, and thou shalt not prosper in thy ways; and then thou shalt be unjustly treated, and plundered continually, and there shall be no helper. 30 thou shalt take a wife, and another man shall have her; thou shalt build a house, and thou shalt not dwell in it; thou shalt plant a vineyard, and shalt not gather the grapes of it. 31 Thy calf *shall be* slain before thee, and thou shalt not eat of it; thine ass shall be violently taken away from thee, and shall not be restored to thee: thy sheep shall be given to thine enemies, and thou shalt have no helper. 32 Thy sons and thy daughters shall be given to another nation, and thine eyes wasting away shall look for them: thine hand shall have no strength. 33 A nation which thou knowest not shall eat the produce of thy land, and all thy labours; and thou shalt be injured and crushed always. 34 And thou shalt be distracted, because of the sights of thine eyes which thou shalt see. 35 The Lord smite thee with an evil sore, on the knees and the legs, so that thou shalt not be able to be healed from the sole of thy foot to the crown of thy head. 36 The Lord carry away thee and thy princes, whom thou shalt set over thee, to a nation which neither thou nor thy fathers know; and thou shalt there serve other gods, wood and stone. 37 An thou shalt be there for a wonder, and a parable, and a tale, among all the nations, to which the Lord thy God shall carry thee away. 38 Thou shalt carry forth much seed into the field, and thou shalt bring in little, because the locust shall devour it. 39 Thou shalt plant a vineyard, and dress it, and shalt not drink the wine, neither shalt thou delight thyself with it, because the worm shall devour it. 40 Thou shalt have olive trees in all thy borders, and thou shalt not anoint thee with oil, because thine olive shall utterly cast *its fruit*. 41 Thou shalt beget sons and daughters, and they shall not be *thine*, for they shall depart into captivity. 42 All thy trees and the fruits of thy land shall the blight consume. 43 The stranger that is within thee shall get up very high, and thou shalt come down very low. 44 He shall lend to thee, and thou shalt not lend to him: he shall be the head, and thou shalt be the tail. 45 And all these curses shall come upon thee, and shall pursue thee, and shall overtake thee, until he shall have consumed thee, and until he shall have destroyed thee; because thou didst not hearken to the voice of the Lord thy God, to keep his commands, and his ordinances which he has commanded thee. 46 And *these things* shall be signs in thee, and wonders among thy seed for ever; 47 because thou didst not serve the Lord thy God with gladness and a good heart, because of the abundance of all things. 48 And thou shalt serve thine enemies, which the Lord will send forth against thee, in hunger, and in thirst, and in nakedness, and in the want of all things; and thou shalt wear upon thy neck a yoke of iron until he shall have destroyed thee. 49 The Lord shall bring upon thee a nation from the extremity of the earth, like the swift flying of an eagle, a nation whose voice thou shalt not understand;

50 a nation bold in countenance, which shall not respect the person of the aged and shall not pity the young. 51 And it shall eat up the young of thy cattle, and the fruits of thy land, so as not to leave to thee corn, wine, oil, the herds of thine oxen, and the flocks of thy sheep, until it shall have destroyed thee; 52 and have utterly crushed thee in thy cities, until the high and strong walls be destroyed, in which thou trustest, in all thy land; and it shall afflict thee in thy cities, which he has given to thee. 53 And thou shalt eat the fruit of thy body, the flesh of thy sons and of thy daughters, all that he has given thee, in thy straitness and thy affliction, with which thine enemy shall afflict thee. 54 He that is tender and very delicate within thee shall look with an evil eye upon his brother, and the wife in his bosom, and the children that are left, which may have been left to him; 55 so as *not* to give to one of them of the flesh of his children, whom he shall eat, because of his having nothing left him in thy straitness, and in thy affliction, with which thine enemies shall afflict thee in all thy cities. 56 And she that is tender and delicate among you, whose foot has not assayed to go upon the earth for delicacy and tenderness, shall look with an evil eye on her husband in her bosom, and her son and her daughter, 57 and her offspring that comes out between her feet, and the child which she shall bear; for she shall eat them because of the want of all things, secretly in thy straitness, and in thy affliction, with which thine enemy shall afflict thee in thy cities. 58 If thou wilt not hearken to do all the words of this law, which have been written in this book, to fear this glorious and wonderful name, the Lord thy God; 59 then the Lord shall magnify thy plagues, and the plagues of thy seed, great and wonderful plagues, and evil and abiding diseases. 60 And he shall bring upon thee all the evil pain of Egypt, of which thou wast afraid, and they shall cleave to thee. 61 And the Lord shall bring upon thee every sickness, and every plague that is not written, and every one that is written in the book of this law, until he shall have destroyed thee. 62 And ye shall be left few in number, whereas ye were as the stars of the sky in multitude; because thou didst not hearken to the voice of the Lord thy God. 63 And it shall come to pass that as the Lord rejoiced over you to do you good, and to multiply you, so the Lord will rejoice over you to destroy you; and ye shall be quickly removed from the land, into which ye go to inherit it. 64 And the Lord thy God shall scatter thee among all nations, from one end of the earth to the other; and thou shalt there serve other gods, wood and stone, which thou hast not known, nor thy fathers. 65 Moreover among those nations he will not give thee quiet, neither by any means shall the sole of thy foot have rest; and the Lord shall give thee there another and a misgiving heart, and failing eyes, and a wasting soul. 66 And thy life shall be in suspense before thine eyes; and thou shalt be afraid by day and by night, and thou shalt have no assurance of thy life. 67 In the morning thou shalt say, Would it were evening! and in the evening thou shalt say, Would it were morning! for the fear of thine heart with which thou shalt fear, and for the sights of thine eyes which thou shalt see. 68 And the Lord shall bring thee back to Egypt in ships, by the way of which I said, Thou shalt not see it again; and ye shall be sold there to your enemies for bondmen and bondwomen, and none shall buy you.

Deut.29 1 These *are* the words of the covenant, which the Lord commanded Moses to make with the children of Israel in the land of Moab, besides the covenant which he made with them in Choreb. 2 And Moses called all the sons of Israel and said to them, Ye have seen all things that the Lord did in the land of Egypt before you to Pharao and his servants, and all his land; 3 the great temptations which thine eyes have seen, the signs, and those great wonders. 4 Yet the Lord God has not given you a heart to know, and eyes to see, and ears to hear, until this day. 5 And he led you forty years in the wilderness; your garments did not grow old, and your sandals were not worn away off your feet. 6 Ye did not eat bread, ye did not drink wine or strong drink, that ye might know that I *am* the Lord your God. 7 And ye came as far as this place; and there came forth Seon king of Esebon, and Og king of Basan, to meet us in war. 8 And we smote them and took their land, and I gave it for an inheritance to Ruben and Gad, and to the half-tribe of Manasse. 9 And ye shall take heed to do all the words of this covenant, that ye may understand all things that ye shall do. 10 Ye all stand to-day before the Lord your God, the heads of your tribes, and your elders, and your judges, and your officers, every man of Israel, 11 your wives, and your children, and the stranger who is in the midst of your camp, from your hewer of wood even to your drawer of water, 12 that thou shouldest enter into the covenant of the Lord thy God and into his oaths, as many as the Lord thy God appoints thee this day; 13 that he may appoint thee to himself for a people, and he shall be thy God, as he said to thee, and as he sware to thy fathers, Abraam, and Isaac, and Jacob. 14 And I do not appoint to you alone this covenant and this oath; 15 but to those also who are here with you to-day before the Lord your God, and to those who are not here with you to-day. 16 For ye know how we dwelt in the land of Egypt, how we came through the midst of the nations through whom ye came. 17 And ye beheld their abominations, and their idols, wood and stone, silver and gold, which are among them. 18 Lest there be among you man, or woman, or family, or tribe, whose heart has turned aside from the Lord your God, having gone to serve the gods of these nations; lest there be in you a root springing up with gall and bitterness. 19 And it shall be if one shall hear the words of this curse, and shall flatter himself in his heart, saying, Let good happen to me, for I will walk in the error of my heart, lest the sinner destroy the guiltless with *him.* 20 God shall by no means be willing to pardon him, but then the wrath of the Lord and his jealousy shall flame out against that man; and all the curses of this covenant shall attach themselves to him, which are written in this book, and the Lord shall blot out his name from under heaven. 21 And the Lord shall separate that man for evil of all the children of Israel, according to all the curses of the covenant that are written in the book of this law. 22 And another generation shall say—even your sons who shall rise up after you, and the stranger who shall come from a land afar off, and shall see the plagues of that land and their diseases, which the Lord has sent upon it, 23 brimstone and burning salt, (the whole land shall not be sown, neither shall any green thing spring, nor rise upon it, as Sodom and Gomorrha were overthrown, Adama and Seboim, which the Lord overthrew in his wrath and anger:)— 24 and all the nations shall say, Why has the Lord done thus to this land? what *is* this great fierceness of anger? 25 And *men* shall say, Because they forsook the covenant of the Lord God of their fathers, the things which he appointed to their fathers, when he brought them out of the land of Egypt: 26 and they went and served other gods, which they knew not, neither did he assign *them* to them. 27 And the Lord was exceedingly angry with that land to bring upon it according to all the curses which are written in the book of this law. 28 And the Lord removed them from their land in anger, and wrath, and very great indignation, and cast them out into another land as at present. 29 The secret things *belong* to the Lord our God, but the things that are revealed *belong* to us and to our children for ever, to do all the words of this law.

Deut.30 1 And it shall come to pass when all these things shall have come upon thee, the blessing and the curse, which I have set before thy face, and thou shalt call *them* to mind among all the nations, wherein the Lord shall have scattered thee, 2 and shalt return to the Lord thy God, and shalt hearken to his voice, according to all things which I charge thee this day, with all thy heart, and with all thy soul; 3 then the Lord shall heal thine iniquities, and shall pity thee, and shall again gather thee out from all the nations, among which the Lord has scattered thee. 4 If thy dispersion be from one end of heaven to the other, thence will the Lord thy God gather thee, and thence will the Lord thy God take thee. 5 And the Lord thy God shall bring thee in from thence into the land which thy fathers have inherited, and thou shalt inherit it; and he will do thee good, and multiply thee above thy fathers. 6 And the Lord shall purge thy heart, and the heart of thy seed, to love the Lord thy God with all thy heart, and with all thy soul, that thou mayest live. 7 And the Lord thy God will put these curses upon thine enemies, and upon those that hate thee, who have persecuted thee. 8 And thou shalt return and hearken to the voice of the Lord thy God, and shall keep his commands, all that I charge thee this day. 9 And the Lord thy God shall bless thee in every work of thine hands, in the offspring of thy body, and in the offspring of thy cattle, and in the fruits of thy land, because the Lord thy God will again rejoice over thee for good, as he rejoiced over thy fathers: 10 if thou wilt hearken to the voice of the Lord thy God, to keep his commandments, and his ordinances, and his judgments written in the book of this law, if thou turn to the Lord thy God with all thine heart, and with all thy soul. 11 For this command which I give thee this day is not grievous, neither is it far from thee. 12 It is not in heaven above, *as if there were one* saying, Who shall go up for us into heaven, and shall take it for us, and we will hear and do it? 13 Neither is it beyond the sea, saying, Who will go over for us to the other side of the sea, and take it for us, and make it audible to us, and we will do it? 14 The word is very near thee, in thy mouth, and in thine heart, and in thine hands to do it. 15

Behold, I have set before thee this day life and death, good and evil. 16 If thou wilt hearken to the commands of the Lord thy God, which I command thee this day, to love the Lord thy God, to walk in all his ways, and to keep his ordinances, and his judgments; then ye shall live, and shall be many in number, and the Lord thy God shall bless thee in all the land into which thou goest to inherit it. 17 But if thy heart change, and thou wilt not hearken, and thou shalt go astray and worship other gods, and serve them, 18 I declare to you this day, that ye shall utterly perish, and ye shall by no means live long upon the land, into which ye go over Jordan to inherit it. 19 I call both heaven and earth to witness this day against you, I have set before you life and death, the blessing and the curse: choose thou life, that thou and thy seed may live; 20 to love the Lord thy God, to hearken to his voice, and cleave to him; for this *is* thy life, and the length of thy days, that thou shouldest dwell upon the land, which the Lord sware to thy fathers, Abraam, and Isaac, and Jacob, to give to them.

Deut.31 1 And Moses finished speaking all these words to all the children of Israel; 2 and said to them, I am this day a hundred and twenty years *old*; I shall not be able any longer to come in or go out; and the Lord said to me, Thou shalt not go over this Jordan. 3 The Lord thy God who goes before thee, he shall destroy these nations before thee, and thou shalt inherit them: and *it shall be* Joshua that goes before thy face, as the Lord has spoken. 4 And the Lord thy God shall do to them as he did to Seon and Og the two kings of the Amorites, who were beyond Jordan, and to their land, as he destroyed them. 5 And the Lord has delivered them to you; and ye shall do to them, as I charged you. 6 Be courageous and strong, fear not, neither be cowardly neither be afraid before them; for *it is* the Lord your God that advances with you in the midst of you, neither will he by any means forsake thee, nor desert thee. 7 And Moses called Joshua, and said to him before all Israel, Be courageous and strong; for thou shalt go in before this people into the land which the Lord sware to your fathers to give to them, and thou shalt give it to them for an inheritance. 8 And the Lord that goes with thee shall not forsake thee nor abandon thee; fear not, neither be afraid. 9 And Moses wrote the words of this law in a book, and gave it to the priests the sons of Levi who bear the ark of the covenant of the Lord, and to the elders of the sons of Israel. 10 And Moses charged them in that day, saying, After seven years, in the time of the year of release, in the feast of tabernacles, 11 when all Israel come together to appear before the Lord your God, in the place which the Lord shall choose, ye shall read this law before all Israel in their ears, 12 having assembled the people, the men, and the women, and the children, and the stranger that is in your cities, that they may hear, and that they may learn to fear the Lord your God; and they shall hearken to do all the words of this law. 13 And their sons who have not known shall hear, and shall learn to fear the Lord thy God all the days that they live upon the land, into which ye go over Jordan to inherit it. 14 And the Lord said to Moses, Behold, the days of thy death are at hand; call Joshua, and stand ye by the doors of the tabernacle of testimony, and I will give him a charge. And Moses and Joshua went to the tabernacle of testimony, and stood by the doors of the tabernacle of testimony. 15 And the Lord descended in a cloud, and stood by the doors of the tabernacle of testimony; and the pillar of the cloud stood by the doors of the tabernacle of testimony. 16 And the Lord said to Moses, Behold, thou shalt sleep with thy fathers, and this people will arise and go a whoring after the strange gods of the land, into which they are entering: and they will forsake me, and break my covenant, which I made with them. 17 And I will be very angry with them in that day, and I will leave them and turn my face away from them, and they shall be devoured; and many evils and afflictions shall come upon them; and they shall say in that day, Because the Lord my God is not with me, these evils have come upon me. 18 And I will surely turn away my face from them in that day, because of all their evil doings which they have done, because they turned aside after strange gods. 19 And now write the words of this song, and teach it to the children of Israel, and ye shall put it into their mouth, that this song may witness for me among the children of Israel to their face. 20 For I will bring them into the good land, which I sware to their fathers, to give to them a land flowing with milk and honey: and they shall eat and be filled and satisfy *themselves*, then will they turn aside after other gods, and serve them, and they will provoke me, and break my covenant. 21 And this song shall stand up to witness against them; for they shall not forget it out of their mouth, or out of the mouth of their seed; for I know their wickedness, what they are doing here this day, before I have brought them into the good land, which I sware to their fathers. 22 And Moses wrote this song in that day, and taught it to the children of Israel. 23 And he charged Joshua, and said, Be courageous and strong, for thou shalt bring the sons of Israel into the land, which the Lord sware to them, and he shall be with thee. 24 And when Moses finished writing all the words of this law in a book, even to the end, 25 then he charged the Levites who bear the ark of the covenant of the Lord, saying, 26 Take the book of this law, and ye shall put it in the side of the ark of the covenant of the Lord your God; and it shall be there among you for a testimony. 27 For I know thy provocation, and thy stiff neck; for yet during my life with you at this day, ye have been provoking in your conduct toward God: how shall ye not also be so after my death? 28 Gather together to me the heads of your tribes, and your elders, and your judges, and your officers, that I may speak in their ears all these words; and I call both heaven and earth to witness against them. 29 For I know that after my death ye will utterly transgress, and turn aside out of the way which I have commanded you; and evils shall come upon you in the latter days, because ye will do evil before the Lord, to provoke him to anger by the works of your hands. And Moses spoke all the words of this song even to the end, in the ears of the whole assembly.

Deut.32 1 Attend, O heaven, and I will speak; and let the earth hear the words out of my mouth. 2 Let my speech be looked for as the rain, and my words come down as dew, as the shower upon the herbage, and as snow upon the grass. 3 For I have called on the name of the Lord: assign ye greatness to our God. 4 *As for God*, his works *are* true, and all his ways *are* judgment: God *is* faithful, and there is no unrighteousness *in him*; just and holy *is* the Lord. 5 They have sinned, not *pleasing* him; spotted children, a froward and perverse generation. 6 Do ye thus recompense the Lord? *is the* people thus foolish and unwise? did not he himself thy father purchase thee, and make thee, and form thee? 7 Remember the days of old, consider the years for past ages: ask thy father, and he shall relate to thee, thine elders, and they shall tell thee. 8 When the Most High divided the nations, when he separated the sons of Adam, he set the bounds of the nations according to the number of the angels of God. 9 And his people Jacob became the portion of the Lord, Israel was the line of his inheritance. 10 He maintained him in the wilderness, in burning thirst and a dry land: he led him about and instructed him, and kept him as the apple of an eye. 11 As an eagle would watch over his brood, and yearns over his young, receives them having spread his wings, and takes them up on his back: 12 the Lord alone led them, there was no strange god with them. 13 He brought them up on the strength of the land; he fed them with the fruits of the fields; they sucked honey out of the rock, and oil out of the solid rock. 14 Butter of cows, and milk of sheep, with the fat of lambs and rams, of calves and kids, with fat of kidneys of wheat; and he drank wine, the blood of the grape. 15 So Jacob ate and was filled, and the beloved one kicked; he grew fat, he became thick and broad: then he forsook the God that made him, and departed from God his Saviour. 16 They provoked me to anger with strange gods; with their abominations they bitterly angered me. 17 They sacrificed to devils, and not to God; to gods whom they knew not: new and fresh *gods* came in, whom their fathers knew not. 18 Thou hast forsaken God that begot thee, and forgotten God who feeds thee. 19 And the Lord saw, and was jealous; and was provoked by the anger of his sons and daughters, 20 and said, I will turn away my face from them, and will show what shall happen to them in the last days; for it is a perverse generation, sons in whom is no faith. 21 They have provoked me to jealousy with *that which is* not God, they have exasperated me with their idols; and I will provoke them to jealousy with them that are no nation, I will anger them with a nation void of understanding. 22 For a fire has been kindled out of my wrath, it shall burn to hell below; it shall devour the land, and the fruits of it; it shall set on fire the foundations of the mountains. 23 I will gather evils upon them, and will fight with my weapons against them. 24 *They shall be* consumed with hunger and the devouring of birds, and there shall be irremediable destruction: I will send forth against them the teeth of wild beasts, with the rage of *serpents* creeping on the ground. 25 Without, the sword shall bereave them of children, and terror *shall issue* out of the secret chambers; the young man shall perish with the virgin, the suckling with him who has grown old. 26 I said, I will scatter them, and I will cause their memorial to cease from among men. 27 Were it not for the wrath of the enemy, lest they should live long, lest their enemies should combine against them; lest they should say, Our own high arm, and not the Lord, has done all these things. 28 It is a nation that has lost counsel, neither is there understanding in them. 29 They had not sense to understand: let them reserve these things against the time to come. 30 How should one pursue a thousand, and two rout tens of thousands, if God had not sold them, and the Lord delivered them up? 31 For their gods are not as our God, but our enemies *are* void of understanding. 32 For their vine *is* of the vine of Sodom, and their vine-branch of Gomorrha: their grape *is* a grape of gall, their cluster *is* one of bitterness. 33 Their wine *is* the rage of serpents, and the incurable rage of asps. 34 Lo! are not these things stored up by me, and sealed among my treasures? 35 In the day of vengeance I will recompense, whensoever their foot shall be tripped up; for the day of their destruction *is* near to them, and the judgments at hand are close upon you. 36 For the Lord shall judge his people, and shall be comforted over his servants; for he saw that they were utterly weakened, and failed in the hostile invasion, and were become feeble: 37 and the Lord said, Where are their gods on whom they trusted? 38 the fat of whose sacrifices ye ate, and ye drank the wine of their drink-offerings? let them arise and help you, and be your protectors. 39 Behold, behold that I am *he*, and there is no god beside me: I kill, and I will make to live: I will smite, and I will heal; and there is none who shall deliver out of my hands. 40 For I will lift up my hand to heaven, and swear by my right hand, and I will say, I live for ever. 41 For I will sharpen my sword like lightning, and my hand shall take hold of judgment; and I will render judgment to my enemies, and will recompense them that hate me. 42 I will make my weapons drunk with blood, and my sword shall devour flesh, *it shall glut itself* with the blood of the wounded, and from the captivity of the heads of *their* enemies that rule over them. 43 Rejoice, ye heavens, with him, and let all the angels of God worship him; rejoice ye Gentiles, with his people, and let all the sons of God strengthen themselves in him; for he will avenge the blood of his sons, and he will render vengeance, and recompense justice to his enemies, and will reward them that hate him; and the Lord shall purge the land of his people. 44 And Moses wrote this song in that day, and taught it to the children of Israel; and Moses went in and spoke all the words of this law in the ears of the people, he and Joshua the *son* of Naue. 45 And Moses finished speaking to all Israel. 46 And he said to them, Take heed with your heart to all these words, which I testify to you this day, which ye shall command your sons, to observe and do all the words of this law. 47 For this *is* no vain word to you; for it *is* your life, and because of this word ye shall live long upon the land, into which ye go over Jordan to inherit it. 48 And the Lord spoke to Moses in this day, saying, 49 Go up to the mount Abarim, this mountain Nabau which is in the land of Moab over against Jericho, and behold the land of Chanaan, which I give to the sons of Israel: 50 and die in the mount whither thou goest up, and be added to thy people; as Aaron thy brother died in mount Or, and was added to his people. 51 Because ye disobeyed my word among the children of Israel, at the waters of strife of Cades in the wilderness of Sin; because ye sanctified me not among the sons of Israel. 52 Thou shalt see the land before *thee*, but thou shalt not enter into it.

Deut.33 1 And this *is* the blessing with which Moses the man of God blessed the children of Israel before his death. 2 And he said, The Lord is come from Sina, and has appeared from Seir to us, and has hasted out of the mount of Pharan, with the ten thousands of Cades; on his right hand *were* his angels with him. 3 And he spared his people, and all his sanctified ones *are* under thy hands; and they are under thee; and he received of his words 4 the law which Moses charged us, an inheritance to the assemblies of Jacob. 5 And he shall be prince with the beloved one, when the princes of the people are gathered together with the tribes of Israel. 6 Let Ruben live, and not die; and let him be many in number. 7 And this *is the blessing* of Juda; Hear, Lord, the voice of Juda, and do thou visit his people: his hands shall contend for him, and thou shalt be a help from his enemies. 8 And to Levi he said, Give to Levi his manifestations, and his truth to the holy man, whom they tempted in the temptation; they reviled him at the water of strife. 9 Who says to his father and mother, I have not seen thee; and he knew not his brethren, and he refused to know his sons: he kept thine oracles, and observed thy covenant. 10 They shall declare thine ordinances to Jacob, and thy law to Israel: they shall place incense in *the time of* thy wrath continually upon thine altar. 11 Bless, Lord, his strength, and accept the works of his hands; break the loins of his enemies that have risen up against him, and let not them that hate him rise up. 12 And to Benjamin he said, The beloved of the Lord shall dwell in confidence, and God overshadows him always, and he rested between his shoulders. 13 And to Joseph he said, His land *is* of the blessing of the Lord, of the seasons of sky and dew, and of the deeps of wells below, 14 and of the fruits of the changes of the sun in season, and of the produce of the months, 15 from the top of the ancient mountains, and from the top of the everlasting hills, 16 and of the fullness of the land in season: and let the things pleasing to him that dwelt in the bush come on the head of Joseph, and on the crown *of him who was* glorified above his brethren. 17 His beauty *is as* the firstling of his bull, his horns *are* the horns of a unicorn; with them he shall thrust the nations at once, even from the end of the earth: these *are* the ten thousands of Ephraim, and these *are* the thousands of Manasse. 18 And to Zabulon he said, Rejoice, Zabulon, in thy going out, and Issachar in his tents. 19 They shall utterly destroy the nations, and ye shall call *men* there, and there offer the sacrifice of righteousness; for the wealth of the sea shall suckle thee, and so shall the marts of them that dwell by the sea-coast. 20 And to Gad he said, Blessed *be* he that enlarges Gad: as a lion he rested, having broken the arm and the ruler. 21 And he saw his first-fruits, that there the land of the princes gathered with the chiefs of the people was divided; the Lord wrought righteousness, and his judgment with Israel. 22 And to Dan he said, Dan *is* a lion's whelp, and shall leap out of Basan. 23 And to Nephthali he said, Nephthali *has* the fulness of good things; and let him be filled with blessing from the Lord: he shall inherit the west and the south. 24 And to Aser he said, Aser *is* blessed with children; and he shall be acceptable to his brethren: he shall dip his foot in oil. 25 His sandal shall be iron and brass; as thy days, so *shall be* thy strength. 26 There is not *any such* as the God of the beloved; he who rides upon the heaven *is* thy helper, and the magnificent One of the firmament. 27 And the rule of God shall protect thee, and *that* under the strength of the everlasting arms; and he shall cast forth the enemy from before thy face, saying, Perish. 28 And Israel shall dwell in confidence alone on the land of Jacob, with corn and wine; and the sky *shall be* misty with dew upon thee. 29 Blessed *art* thou, O Israel; who *is* like to thee, O people saved by the Lord? thy helper shall hold his shield over thee, and *his* sword *is* thy boast; and thine enemies shall speak falsely to thee, and thou shalt tread upon their neck.

Deut.34 1 And Moses went up from Araboth Moab to the mount of Nabau, to the top of Phasga, which is before Jericho; and the Lord shewed him all the mount of Galaad to Dan, and all the land of Nephthali, 2 and all the land of Ephraim and Manasse, and all the land of Juda to the farthest sea; 3 and the wilderness, and the country round about Jericho, the city of palm-trees, to Segor. 4 And the Lord said to Moses, This *is* the land of which I sware to Abraam, and Isaac, and Jacob, saying, To your seed will I give it: and I have shewed it to thine eyes, but thou shalt not go in thither. 5 So Moses the servant of the Lord died in the land of Moab by the word of the Lord. 6 And they buried him in Gai near the house of Phogor; and no one has seen his sepulchre to this day. 7 And Moses was a hundred and twenty years old at his death; his eyes were not dimmed, nor were his natural powers destroyed. 8 And the children of Israel wept for Moses in Araboth of Moab at Jordan near Jericho thirty days; and the days of the sad mourning for Moses were completed. 9 And Joshua the son of Naue was filled with the spirit of knowledge, for Moses had laid his hands upon him; and the children of Israel hearkened to him; and they did as the Lord commanded Moses. 10 And there rose up no more a prophet in Israel like Moses, whom the Lord knew face to face, 11 in all the signs and wonders, which the Lord sent him to work in Egypt on Pharao, and his servants, and all his land; 12 the great wonders, and the mighty hand which Moses displayed before all Israel.

JOSHUA

Josh.1 1 And it came to pass after the death of Moses, that the Lord spoke to Joshua the son of Naue, the minister of Moses, saying, 2 Moses my servant is dead; now then arise, go over Jordan, thou and all this people, into the land, which I give them. 3 Every spot on which ye shall tread I will give it to you, as I said to Moses. 4 The wilderness and Antilibanus, as far as the great river, the river Euphrates, and as far as the extremity of the sea; your costs shall be from the setting of the sun. 5 Not a man shall stand against you all the days of thy life; and as I was with Moses, so will I also be with thee, and I will not fail thee, or neglect thee. 6 Be strong and 'quit thyself like a man, for thou shalt divide the land to this people, which I sware to give to your fathers. 7 Be strong, therefore, and quit thyself like a man,

to observe and do as Moses my servant commanded thee; and thou shalt not turn therefrom to the right hand or to the left, that thou mayest be wise in whatsoever thou mayest do. 8 And the book of this law shall not depart out of thy mouth, and thou shalt meditate in it day and night, that thou mayest know how to do all the things that are written *in it*; then shalt thou prosper, and make thy ways prosperous, and then shalt thou be wise. 9 Lo! I have commanded thee; be strong and courageous, be not cowardly nor fearful, for the Lord thy God is with thee in all places whither thou goest. 10 And Joshua commanded the scribes of the people, saying, 11 Go into the midst of the camp of the people, and command the people, saying, Prepare provisions; for yet three days and ye shall go over this Jordan, entering in to take possession of the land, which the Lord God of your fathers gives to you. 12 And to Ruben, and to Gad, and to the half tribe of Manasse, Joshua said, 13 Remember the word which Moses the servant of the Lord commanded you, saying, the Lord your God has caused you to rest, and has given you this land. 14 Let your wives and your children and your cattle dwell in the land, which he has given you; and ye shall go over well armed before your brethren, every one of you who is strong; and ye shall fight on their side; 15 until the Lord your God shall have given your brethren rest, as also to you, and they also shall have inherited the land, which the Lord your God gives them; then ye shall depart each one to his inheritance, which Moses gave you beyond Jordan eastward. 16 And they answered Joshua and said, We will do all things which thou commandest us, and we will go to every place whither thou shalt send us. 17 Whereinsoever we hearkened to Moses we will hearken to thee; only let the Lord our God be with thee, as he was with Moses. 18 And whosoever shall disobey thee, and whosoever shall not hearken to thy words as thou shalt command him, let him die; but be thou strong and courageous.

Josh.2 1 And Joshua the son of Naue sent out of Sattin two young men to spy *the land*, saying, Go up and view the land and Jericho: and the two young men went and entered into Jericho; and they entered into the house of a harlot, whose name *was* Raab, and lodged there. 2 An it was reported to the king of Jericho, saying, Men of the sons of Israel have come in hither to spy the land. 3 And the king of Jericho sent and spoke to Raab, saying, Bring out the men that entered into thine house this night; for they are come to spy out the land. 4 And the woman took the two men and hid them; and she spoke to the messengers, saying, The men came in to me, 5 but when the gate was shut in the evening, the men went out; I know not whither they are gone: follow after them, if ye may overtake them. 6 But she *had* brought them up upon the house, and hid them in the flax-stalks that were spread by her on the house. 7 And the men followed after them in the way to Jordan to the fords; and the gate was shut. 8 And it came to pass when the men who pursued after them were gone forth, and before the spies had lain down to sleep, that she came up to them on the top of the house; 9 and she said to them, I know that the Lord has given you the land; for the fear of you has fallen upon us. 10 For we have heard that the Lord God dried up the Red Sea before you, when ye came out of the land of Egypt, and all that he did to the two kings of the Amorites, who were beyond Jordan, to Seon and Og, whom ye utterly destroyed. 11 And when we heard it we were amazed in our heart, and there was no longer any spirit in any of us because of you, for the Lord your god *is* God in heaven above, and on the earth beneath. 12 And now swear to me by the Lord God; since I deal mercifully with you, so do ye also deal mercifully with the house of my father: 13 and save alive the house of my father, my mother, and my brethren, and all my house, and all that they have, and ye shall rescue my soul from death. 14 And the men said to her, Our life for yours *even* to death: and she said, When the Lord shall have delivered the city to you, ye shall deal mercifully and truly with me. 15 And she let them down by the window; 16 and she said to them, Depart into the hill-country, lest the pursuers meet you, and ye shall be hidden there three days until your pursuers return from after you, and afterwards ye shall depart on your way. 17 And the men said to her, We are clear of this thy oath. 18 Behold, we shall enter into a part of the city, and thou shalt set a sign; thou shalt bind this scarlet cord in the window, by which thou hast let us down, and thou shalt bring in to thyself, into thy house, thy father, and thy mother, and thy brethren, and all the family of thy father. 19 And it shall come to pass that whosoever shall go outside the door of thy house, his guilt shall be upon him, and we shall be quit of this thine oath; and we will be responsible for all that shall be found with thee in thy house. 20 But if any one should injure us, or betray these our matters, we shall be quit of this thine oath. 21 And she said to them, Let it be according to your word; and she sent them out, and they departed. 22 And they came to the hill-country, and remained there three days; and the pursuers searched all the roads, and found them not. 23 And the two young men returned, and came down out of the mountain; and they went over to Joshua the son of Naue, and told him all things that had happened to them. 24 And they said to Joshua, The Lord has delivered all the land into our power, and all the inhabitants of that land tremble because of us.

Josh.2 1 And Joshua rose up early in the morning, and departed from Sattin; and they came as far as Jordan, and lodged there before they crossed over. 2 And it came to pass after three days, *that* the scribes went through the camp; 3 and they charged the people, saying, When ye shall see the ark of the covenant of the Lord our God, and our priests and the Levites bearing it, ye shall depart from your places, and ye shall go after it. 4 But let there be a distance between you and it; ye shall stand as much as two thousand cubits *from it.* Do not draw nigh to it, that ye may know the way which ye are to go; for ye have not gone the way before. 5 And Joshua said to the people, Sanctify yourselves against to-morrow, for to-morrow the Lord will do wonders among you. 6 And Joshua said to the priests, Take up the ark of the covenant of the Lord, and go before the people: and the priests took up the ark of the covenant of the Lord, and went before the people. 7 And the Lord said to Joshua,

This day do I begin to exalt thee before all the children of Israel, that they may know that as I was with Moses, so will I also be with thee. 8 And now charge the priests that bear the ark of the covenant, saying, As soon as ye shall enter on a part of the water of Jordan, then ye shall stand in Jordan. 9 And Joshua said to the children of Israel, Come hither, and hearken to the word of the Lord our God. 10 Hereby ye shall know that the living God *is* among you, and will utterly destroy from before our face the Chananite, and the Chettite and Pherezite, and the Evite, and the Amorite, and the Gergesite, and the Jebusite. 11 Behold, the ark of the covenant of the Lord of all the earth passes over Jordan. 12 Choose for yourselves twelve men of the sons of Israel, one of each tribe. 13 And it shall come to pass, when the feet of the priests that bear the ark of the covenant of the Lord of the whole earth rest in the water of Jordan, the water of Jordan *below* shall fail, and the water coming down from above shall stop. 14 And the people removed from their tents to cross over Jordan, and the priests bore the ark of the covenant of the Lord before the people. 15 And when the priests that bore the ark of the covenant of the Lord entered upon Jordan, and the feet of the priests that bore the ark of the covenant of the Lord were dipped in part of the water of Jordan; (now Jordan overflowed all its banks about the time of wheat harvest:) 16 then the waters that came down from above stopped; there stood one solid heap very far off, as far as the region of Kariathiarim, and the lower part came down to the sea of Araba, the salt sea, till it completely failed; and the people stood opposite Jericho. 17 And the priests that bore the ark of the covenant of the Lord stood on dry land in the midst of Jordan; and all the children of Israel went through on dry land, until all the people had completely gone over Jordan.

Josh.4 1 And when the people had completely passed over Jordan, the Lord spoke to Joshua, saying, 2 Take men from the people, one of each tribe, 3 and charge them; and ye shall take out of the midst of Jordan twelve fit stones, and having carried them across together with yourselves, place them in your camp, where ye shall encamp for the night. 4 And Joshua having called twelve men of distinction among the children of Israel, one of each tribe, 5 said to them, Advance before me in the presence of the Lord into the midst of Jordan, and each having taken up a stone from thence, let him carry it on his shoulders, according to the number of the twelve tribes of Israel: 6 that these may be to you continually for an appointed sign, that when thy son asks thee in future, saying, What are these stones to us? 7 then thou mayest explain to thy son, saying, The river Jordan was dried up from before the ark of the covenant of the Lord of the whole earth, when it passed it: and these stones shall be for a memorial for you for the children of Israel for ever. 8 And the children of Israel did so, as the Lord commanded Joshua; and they took up twelve stones out of the midst of Jordan, (as the Lord commanded Joshua, when the children of Israel had completely passed over,)and carried these stones with them into the camp, and laid them down there. 9 And Joshua set also other twelve stones in Jordan itself, in the place that was under the feet of the priests that bore the ark of the covenant of the Lord; and there they are to this day. 10 And the priests that bore the ark of the covenant stood in Jordan, until Joshua *had* finished all that the Lord commanded him to report to the people; and the people hasted and passed over. 11 And it came to pass when all the people had passed over, that the ark of the covenant of the Lord passed over, and the stones before them. 12 And the sons of Ruben, and the sons of Gad, and the half tribe of Manasse passed over armed before the children of Israel, as Moses commanded them. 13 Forty thousand armed for battle went over before the Lord to war, to the city of Jericho. 14 In that day the Lord magnified Joshua before all the people of Israel; and they feared him, as *they did* Moses, as long as he lived. 15 And the Lord spoke to Joshua, saying, 16 Charge the priests that bear the ark of the covenant of the testimony of the Lord, to go up out of Jordan. 17 And Joshua charged the priests, saying, Go up out of Jordan. 18 And it came to pass when the priests who bore the ark of the covenant of the Lord were gone up out of Jordan, and set their feet upon the land, *that* the water of Jordan returned impetuously to its place, and went as before over all its banks. 19 And the people went up out of Jordan on the tenth day of the first month; and the children of Israel encamped in Galgala in the region eastward from Jericho. 20 And Joshua set these twelve stones which he took out of Jordan, in Galgala, 21 saying, When your sons ask you, saying, What are these stones? 22 Tell your sons, that Israel went over this Jordan on dry land, 23 when the Lord our God had dried up the water of Jordan from before them, until they had passed over; as the Lord our God did to the Red Sea, which the Lord our God dried up from before us, until we passed over. 24 That all the nations of the earth might know, that the power of the Lord is mighty, and that ye might worship the Lord our God in every work.

Josh.5 1 And it came to pass when the kings of the Amorites who were beyond Jordan heard, and the kings of Phoenicia by the sea, that the Lord God had dried up the river Jordan from before the children of Israel when they passed over, that their hearts failed, and they were terror-stricken, and there was no sense in them because of the children of Israel. 2 And about this time the Lord said to Joshua, Make thee stone knives of sharp stone, and sit down and circumcise the children of Israel the second time. 3 And Joshua made sharp knives of stone, and circumcised the children of Israel at the place called the "Hill of Foreskins." 4 And *this is* the way in which Joshua purified the children of Israel; as many as were born in the way, and as many as were uncircumcised of them that came out of Egypt, 5 all these Joshua circumcised; for forty and two years Israel wondered in the wilderness of Mabdaris— 6 Wherefore most of the fighting men that came out of the land of Egypt, were uncircumcised, who disobeyed the commands of God; concerning whom also he determined that they should not see the land, which the Lord sware to give to their fathers, *even* a land flowing with milk and honey. 7 And in their place he raised up their sons, whom Joshua circumcised, because they were uncircumcised,

having been born by the way. 8 And when they had been circumcised they rested continuing there in the camp till they were healed. 9 And the Lord said to Joshua the son of Naue, On this day have I removed the reproach of Egypt from you: and he called the name of that place Galgala. 10 And the children of Israel kept the passover on the fourteenth day of the month at evening, to the westward of Jericho on the opposite side of the Jordan in the plain. 11 And they ate of the grain of the earth unleavened and new *corn*. 12 In this day the manna failed, after they had eaten of the corn of the land, and the children of Israel no longer had manna: and they took the fruits of the land of the Phoenicians in that year. 13 And it came to pass when Joshua was in Jericho, that he looked up with his eyes and saw a man standing before him, and *there was* a drawn sword in his hand; and Joshua drew near and said to him, Art thou for us or on the side of our enemies? 14 And he said to him, I am now come, the chief captain of the host of the Lord. 15 And Joshua fell on his face upon the earth, and said to him, Lord, what commandest thou thy servant? 16 And the captain of the Lord's host said to Joshua, Loose thy shoe off thy feet, for the place whereon thou now standest is holy.

Josh.6 1 Now Jericho was closely shut up and besieged, and none went out of it, and none came in. 2 And the Lord said to Joshua, Behold, I deliver Jericho into thy power, and its king in it, *and its* mighty men. 3 And do thou set the men of war round about it. 4 And it shall be *that* when ye shall sound with the trumpet, all the people shall shout together. 5 And when they have shouted, the walls of the city shall fall of themselves; and all the people shall enter, each one rushing direct into the city. 6 And Joshua the *son* of Naue went in to the priests, and spoke to them, saying, 7 And let seven priests having seven sacred trumpets proceed thus before the Lord, and let them sound loudly; and let the ark of the covenant of the Lord follow. 8 Charge the people to go round, and encompass the city; and let your men of war pass on armed before the Lord. 9 And let the men of war proceed before, and the priests bringing up the rear behind the ark of the covenant of the Lord *proceed* sounding the trumpets. 10 And Joshua commanded the people, saying, Cry not out, nor let any one hear your voice, until he himself declare to you the time to cry out, and then ye shall cry out. 11 And the ark of the covenant of God having gone round immediately returned into the camp, and lodged there. 12 And on the second day Joshua rose up in the morning, and the priests took up the ark of the covenant of the Lord. 13 And the seven priests bearing the seven trumpets went on before the Lord; and afterwards the men of war went on, and the remainder of the multitude went after the ark of the covenant of the Lord, and the priests sounded with the trumpets. 14 And all the rest of the multitude compassed the city six times from within a short distance, and went back again into the camp; this they did six days. 15 And on the seventh day they rose up early, and compassed the city on that day seven times. 16 And it came to pass at the seventh circuit the priests blew the trumpets; and Joshua said to the children of Israel, Shout, for the

Lord has given you the city. 17 And the city shall be devoted, it and all things that are in it, to the Lord of Hosts: only do ye save Raab the harlot, and all things in her house. 18 But keep yourselves strictly from the accursed thing, lest ye set your mind upon and take of the accursed thing, and ye make the camp of the children of Israel and accursed thing, and destroy us. 19 And all the silver, or gold, or brass, or iron, shall be holy to the Lord; it shall be carried into the treasury of the Lord. 20 And the priests sounded with the trumpets: and when the people heard the trumpets, all the people shouted at once with a loud and strong shout; and all the wall fell round about, and all the people went up into the city: 21 and Joshua devoted it to destruction, and all things that were in the city, man and woman, young man and old, and calf and ass, with the edge of the sword. 22 And Joshua said to the two young men who had acted a spies, Go into the house of the woman, and bring her out thence, and all that she has. 23 And the two young men who had spied out the city entered into the house of the woman, and brought out Raab the harlot, and her father, and her mother, and her brethren, and her kindred, and all that she had; and they set her without the camp of Israel. 24 And the city was burnt with fire with all things that were in it; only of the silver, and gold, and brass, and iron, they gave to be brought into the treasury of the Lord. 25 And Joshua saved alive Raab the harlot, and all the house of her father, and caused her to dwell in Israel until this day, because she hid the spies which Joshua sent to spy out Jericho. 26 And Joshua adjured *them* on that day before the Lord, saying, Cursed *be* the man who shall build that city: he shall lay the foundation of it in his first-born, and he shall set up the gates of it in his youngest son. And so did Hozan of Baethel; he laid the foundation in Abiron his first- born, and set up the gates of it in his youngest surviving son. 27 And the Lord was with Joshua, and his name was in all the land.

Josh.7 1 But the children of Israel committed a great trespass, and purloined *part* of the accursed thing; and Achar the son of Charmi, the son of Zambri, the son of Zara, of the tribe of Juda, took of the accursed thing; and the Lord was very angry with the children of Israel. 2 And Joshua sent men to Gai, which is by Baethel, saying, Spy out Gai: and the men went up and spied Gai. 3 And they returned to Joshua, and said to him, Let not all the people go up, but let about two or three thousand men go up and take the city by siege: carry not up thither the whole people, for *the enemy* are few. 4 And there went up about three thousand men, and they fled from before the men of Gai. 5 And the men of Gai slew of them to the number of thirty-six men, and they pursued them from the gate, and destroyed them from the steep hill; and the heart of the people was alarmed and became as water. 6 And Joshua tore his garments; and Joshua fell on the earth on his face before the Lord until evening, he and the elders of Israel; and they cast dust on their heads. 7 And Joshua said, I pray, Lord, wherefore has thy servant brought this people over Jordan to deliver them to the Amorite to destroy us? would we had remained and settled ourselves beyond Jordan. 8 And what

shall I say since Israel has turned his back before his enemy? 9 And when the Chananite and all the inhabitants of the land hear it, they shall compass us round and destroy us from off the land: and what wilt thou do *for* thy great name? 10 And the Lord said to Joshua, Rise up; why hast thou fallen upon thy face? 11 The people has sinned, and transgressed the covenant which I made with them; they have stolen from the cursed thing, and put it into their store. 12 And the children of Israel will not be able to stand before their enemies; they will turn their back before their enemies, for they have become an accursed thing: I will not any longer be with you, unless ye remove the cursed thing from yourselves. 13 Rise, sanctify the people and tell them to sanctify themselves for the morrow: thus says the Lord God of Israel, The accursed thing is among you; ye shall not be able to stand before your enemies, until ye shall have removed the cursed thing from among you. 14 And ye shall all be gathered together by your tribes in the morning, and it shall come to pass that the tribe which the Lord shall shew, ye shall bring by families; and the family which the Lord shall shew, ye shall bring by households; and the household which the Lord shall shew, ye shall bring man by man. 15 And the man who shall be pointed out, shall be burnt with fire, and all that he has; because he has transgressed the covenant of the Lord, and has wrought wickedness in Israel. 16 And Joshua rose up early, and brought the people by their tribes; and the tribe of Juda was pointed out. 17 And it was brought by their families, and family of the Zaraites was pointed out. 18 And it was brought man by man, and Achar the son of Zambri the son of Zara was pointed out. 19 And Joshua said to Achar, Give glory this day to the Lord God of Israel, and make confession; and tell me what thou hast done, and hide it not from me. 20 And Achar answered Joshua, and said, Indeed I have sinned against the Lord God of Israel: thus and thus have I done: 21 I saw in the spoil an embroidered mantle, and two hundred didrachms of silver, and one golden wedge of fifty didrachms, and I desired them and took them; and, behold, they are hid in my tent, and the silver is hid under them. 22 And Joshua sent messengers, and they ran to the tent into the camp; and these things were hidden in his tent, and the silver under them. 23 And they brought them out of the tent, and brought them to Joshua and the elders of Israel, and they laid them before the Lord. 24 And Joshua took Achar the son of Zara, and brought him to the valley of Achor, and his sons, and his daughters, and his calves, and his asses, and all his sheep, and his tent, and all his property, and all the people *were* with him; and he brought them to Emec Achor. 25 And Joshua said to Achar, Why hast thou destroyed us? the Lord destroy thee as at this day. And all Israel stoned him with stones. 26 And they set up over him a great heap of stones; and the Lord ceased from his fierce anger. Therefore he called the place Emecachor until this day.

Josh.8 1 And the Lord said to Joshua, Fear not, nor be timorous: take with thee all the men of war, and arise, go up to Gai; behold, I have given into thy hands the king of Gai, and his land. 2 And thou shalt do to Gai, as thou didst to Jericho and its king; and thou shalt take to thyself the spoil of its cattle; set now for thyself an ambush for the city behind. 3 And Joshua and all the men of war rose to go up to Gai; and Joshua chose out thirty thousand mighty men, and he sent them away by night. 4 And he charged them, saying, Do ye lie in ambush behind the city: do not go far from the city, and ye shall all be ready. 5 Land I and all with me will draw near to the city: and it shall come to pass when the inhabitants of Gai shall come forth to meet us, as before, that we will flee from before them. 6 And when they shall come out after us, we will draw them away from the city; and they will say, These men flee from before us, as also before. 7 And ye shall rise up out of the ambuscade, and go into the city. 8 Ye shall do according to this word, lo! I have commanded you. 9 And Joshua sent them, and they went to lie in ambush; and they lay between Baethel and Gai, westward of Gai. 10 And Joshua rose up early in the morning, and numbered the people; and he went up, he and the elders before the people to Gai. 11 And all the men of war went up with him, and they went forward and came over against the city eastward. 12 And the ambuscade *was* on the west side of the city. 13 14 And it came to pass when the king of Gai saw *it*, he hasted and went out to meet them direct to the battle, he and all the people *that were* with him: and he knew not that there was an ambuscade *formed* against him behind the city. 15 And Joshua and Israel saw, and retreated from before them. 16 And they pursued after the children of Israel, and they themselves went to a distance from the city. 17 There was no one left in Gai who did not pursue after Israel; and they left the city open, and pursued after Israel. 18 And the Lord said to Joshua, Stretch forth thy hand with the spear that is in thy hand toward the city, for I have delivered it into thy hands; and the liers in wait shall rise up quickly out of their place. 19 And Joshua stretched out his hand *and* his spear toward the city, and the ambuscade rose up quickly out of their place; and they came forth when he stretched out his hand; and they entered into the city, and took it; and they hasted and burnt the city with fire. 20 And when the inhabitants of Gai looked round behind them, then they saw the smoke going up out of the city to heaven, and they were no longer able to flee this way or that way. 21 And Joshua and all Israel saw that the ambuscade had taken the city, and that the smoke of the city went up to heaven; and they turned and smote the men of Gai. 22 And these came forth out of the city to meet them; and they were in the midst of the army, some *being* on this side, and some on that; and they smote them until there was not left of them one who survived and escaped. 23 And they took the king of Gai alive, and brought him to Joshua. 24 And when the children of Israel had ceased slaying all that were in Gai, and in the fields, and in the mountain on the descent, from whence they pursued them *even* to the end, then Joshua returned to Gai, and smote it with the edge of the sword. 25 And they that fell in that day, men and women, were twelve thousand: *they slew* all the inhabitants of Gai. 26 27 Beside the spoils that were in the city, all things which the children of Israel took as spoil for themselves according to the command of the Lord, as the Lord commanded Joshua. 28 And Joshua burnt the city with

fire: he made it an uninhabited heap for ever, *even* to this day. 29 And he hanged the king of Gai on a gallows; and he remained on the tree till evening: and when the sun went down, Joshua gave charge, and they took down his body from the tree, and cast it into a pit, and they set over him a heap of stones until this day.

Josh.9 1 And when the kings of the Amorites on the other side of Jordan, who were in the mountain country, and in the plain, and in all the coast of the great sea, and those who were near Antilibanus, and the Chettites, and the Chananites, and the Pherezites, and the Evites, and the Amorites, and the Gergesites, and the Jebusites, heard *of it*, 2 they came all together at the same time to make war against Joshua and Israel. 3 And the inhabitants of Gabaon heard of all that the Lord did to Jericho and Gai. 4 And they also wrought craftily, and they went and made provision and prepared themselves; and having taken old sacks on their shoulders, and old and rent and patched bottles of wine, 5 and the upper part of their shoes and their sandals old and clouted on their feet, and their garments old upon them—and the bread of their provision was dry and mouldy and corrupt. 6 And they came to Joshua into the camp of Israel to Galgala, and said to Joshua and Israel, We are come from a far land: now then make a covenant with us. 7 And the children of Israel said to the Chorrhaean, Peradventure thou dwellest amongst us; and how should I make a covenant with thee? 8 And they said to Joshua, We are thy servants: and Joshua said to them, Whence are ye, and whence have ye come? 9 And they said, Thy servants are come from a very far country in the name of the Lord thy God: for we have heard his name, and all that he did in Egypt, 10 and all that he did to the kings of the Amorites, who were beyond Jordan, to Seon king of the Amorites, and Og king of Basan, who dwelt in Astaroth and in Edrain. 11 And our elders and all that inhabit our land when they heard spoke to us, saying, Take to yourselves provision for the way, and go to meet them; and ye shall say to them, We are thy servants, and now make a covenant with us. 12 These *are* the loaves—we took them hot for our journey on the day on which we came out to come to you; and now they are dried and become mouldy. 13 And these *are* the skins of wine which we filled when new, and they are rent; and our garments and our shoes are worn out because of the very long journey. 14 And the chiefs took of their provision, and asked not *counsel of* the Lord. 15 And Joshua made peace with them, and they made a covenant with them to preserve them; and the princes of the congregation sware to them. 16 And it came to pass three days after they had made a covenant with them, they heard that they were near neighbours, and that they dwelt among them. 17 And the children of Israel departed and came to their cities; and their cities *were* Gabaon, and Kephira, and Berot, and the cities of Jarin. 18 Land the children of Israel fought not with them, because all the princes sware to them by the Lord God of Israel; and all the congregation murmured at the princes. 19 And the princes said to all the congregation: We have sworn to them by the Lord God of Israel, and now we shall not be able to touch them. 20 This we will do; take them alive, and we will preserve them: so there shall not be wrath against us by reason of the oath which we swore to them. 21 They shall live, and shall be hewers of wood and drawers of water to all the congregation, as the princes said to them. 22 And Joshua called them together and said to them, Why have ye deceived me, saying, We live very far from you; whereas ye are fellow-countrymen of those who dwell among us? 23 And now ye are cursed: there shall not fail of you a slave, or a hewer of wood, or a drawer of water to me and my God. 24 And they answered Joshua, saying, It was reported to us what the Lord thy God charged his servant Moses, to give you this land, and to destroy us and all that dwelt on it from before you; and we feared very much for our lives because of you, and *therefore* we did this thing. 25 And now, behold, we *are* in your power; do to us as it is pleasing to you, and as it seems *good* to you. 26 Aand they did so to them; and Joshua rescued them in that day out of the hands of the children of Israel, and they did not slay them. 27 And Joshua made them in that day hewers of wood and drawers of water to the whole congregation, and for the altar of God: therefore the inhabitants of Gabaon became hewers of wood and drawers of water for the altar of God until this day, even for the place which the Lord should choose. 30 Then Joshua built an alter to the Lord God of Israel in mount Gebal, 31 as Moses the servant of the Lord commanded the children of Israel, as it was written in the law of Moses, an alter of unhewn stones, on which iron had not been lifted up: and he offered there whole-burnt- offerings to the Lord, and a piece offering. And Joshua wrote upon the stones a copy of the law, *even* the law of Moses, before the children of Israel. 33 And all Israel, and their elders, and their judges, and their scribes, passed on one side and on the other, before the ark; and the priests and the levites took up the ark of the covenant of the Lord; and the stranger and the native *were there*, who were half of them near mount Gebal, as Moses the servant of the Lord commanded at first, to bless the people. 34 And afterwards Joshua read accordingly all the words of this law, the blessings and the curses, according to all things written in the law of Moses. 35 There was not a word of all that Moses charged Joshua, which Joshua read not in the ears of all men, and the women, and the children of Israel, and the strangers that joined themselves to Israel.

Josh.10 1 And when Adoni-bezec king of Jerusalem heard that Joshua had taken Gai, and had destroyed it, as he did to Jericho and its king, even so they did to Gai and its king, and that the inhabitants of Gabaon had gone over to Joshua and Israel; 2 then they were greatly terrified by them, for *the king* knew that Gabaon *was* a great city, as one of the chief cities, and all its men *were* mighty. 3 So Adoni-bezec king of Jerusalem sent to Elam king of Hebron, and to Phidon king of Jerimuth, and to Jephtha king of Lachis, and to Dabin king of Odollam, saying, 4 Come up hither to me, and help me, and let us take Gabaon; for the Gabaonites have gone over to Joshua and to the children of Israel. 5 And the five kings of the Jebusites went up, the king of Jerusalem, and the king of Chebron, and the king of Jerimuth, and the king of Lachis, and the king of Odollam,

they and all their people; and encamped around Gabaon, and besieged it. 6 And the inhabitants of Gabaon sent to Joshua into the camp to Galgala, saying, Slack not thy hands from thy servants: come up quickly to us, and help us, and rescue us; for all the kings of the Amorites who dwell in the hill country are gathered together against us. 7 And Joshua went up from Galgala, he and all the people of war with him, every one mighty in strength. 8 And the Lord said to Joshua, Fear them not, for I have delivered them into thy hands; there shall not one of them be left before you. 9 And when Joshua came suddenly upon them, he *had* advanced all the night out of Galgala. 10 And the Lord struck them with terror before the children of Israel; and the Lord destroyed them with a great slaughter at Gabaon; and they pursued them by the way of the going up of Oronin, and they smote them to Azeca and to Makeda. 11 And when they fled from the face of the children of Israel at the descent of Oronin, then the Lord cast upon them hailstones from heaven to Azeca; and they were more that died by the hailstones, than those whom the children of Israel slew with the sword in the battle. 12 Then Joshua spoke to the Lord, in the day in which the Lord delivered the Amorite into the power of Israel, when he destroyed them in Gabaon, and they were destroyed from before the children of Israel: and Joshua said, Let the sun stand over against Gabaon, and the moon over against the valley of Ælon. 13 And the sun and the moon stood still, until God executed vengeance on their enemies; and the sun stood still in the midst of heaven; it did not proceed to set till the end of one day. 14 And there was not such a day either before or after, so that God should hearken to a man, because the Lord fought on the side of Israel. 15,16 And these five kings fled, and hid themselves in a cave that is in Makeda. 17 And it was told Joshua, saying, The five kings have been found hid in the cave that is in Makeda. 18 And Joshua said, Roll stones to the mouth of the cave, and set men to watch over them. 19 But do not ye stand, but pursue after your enemies, and attack the rear of them, and do not suffer them to enter into their cities; for the Lord our God has delivered them into our hands. 20 And it came to pass when Joshua and all Israel ceased destroying them utterly with a very great slaughter, that they that escaped took refuge in the strong cities. 21 And all the people returned safe to Joshua to Makeda; and no one of the children of Israel murmured with his tongue. 22 And Joshua said, Open the cave, and bring out these five kings out of the cave. 23 And they brought out the five kings out of the cave, the king of Jerusalem, and the king of Chebron, and the king of Jerimuth, and the king of Lachis, and the king of Odollam. 24 And when they brought them out to Joshua, then Joshua called together all Israel, and the chiefs of the army that went with him, saying to them, Come forward and set your feet on their necks; and they came and set their feet on their necks. 25 And Joshua said to them, Do not fear them, neither be cowardly; be courageous and strong, for thus the Lord will do to all your enemies, against whom ye fight. 26 And Joshua slew them, and hanged them on five trees; and they hung upon the trees until the evening. 27 And it came to pass toward the setting of the sun, Joshua commanded, and they took them down from the trees, and cast them into the cave into which they *had* fled for refuge, and rolled stones to the cave, *which remain* till this day. 28 And they took Makeda on that day, and slew the inhabitants with the edge of the sword, and they utterly destroyed every living thing that was in it; and there was none left in it that was preserved and had escaped; and they did to the king of Makeda, as they did to the king of Jericho. 29 And Joshua and all Israel with him departed out of Makeda to Lebna, and besieged Lebna. 30 And the Lord delivered it into the hands of Israel: and they took it, and its king, and slew the inhabitants with the edge of the sword, and every thing breathing in it; and there was not left in it any that survived and escaped; and they did to its king, as they did to the king of Jericho. 31 And Joshua and all Israel with him departed from Lebna to Lachis, and he encamped about it, and besieged it. 32 And the Lord delivered Lachis into the hands of Israel; and they took it on the second day, and they put the inhabitants to death with the edge of the sword, and utterly destroyed it, as they had done to Lebna. 33 Then Elam the king of Gazer went up to help Lachis; and Joshua smote him and his people with the edge of the sword, until there was not left to him one that was preserved and escaped. 34 And Joshua and all Israel with him departed from Lachis to Odollam, and he besieged it and took it. 35 And the Lord delivered it into the hand of Israel; and he took it on that day, and slew the inhabitants with the edge of the sword, and slew every thing breathing in it, as they did to Lachis. 36 And Joshua and all Israel with him departed to Chebron, and encamped about it. 37 And he smote it with the edge of the sword, and all the living creatures that were in it; there was no one preserved: they destroyed it and all things in it, as they did to Odollam. 38 And Joshua and all Israel returned to Dabir; and they encamped about it; 39 and they took it, and its king, and its villages: and he smote it with the edge of the sword, and they destroyed it, and every thing breathing in it; and they did not leave in it any one that was preserved: as they did to Chebron and her king, so they did to Dabir and her king. 40 And Joshua smote all the land of the hill country, and Nageb and the plain country, and Asedoth, and her kings, they did not leave of them one that was saved: and they utterly destroyed every thing that had the breath of life, as the Lord God of Israel commanded, 41 from Cades Barne to Gaza, all Gosom, as far as Gabaon. 42 And Joshua smote, once for all, all their kings, and their land, because the Lord God of Israel fought on the side of Israel.

Josh.11 1 And when Jabis the king of Asor heard, he sent to Jobab king of Maron, and to the king of Symoon, and to the king of Aziph, 2 and to the kings who were by the great Sidon, to the hill country and to Araba opposite Keneroth, and to the plain, and to Phenaeddor, 3 and to the Chananites on the coast eastward, and to the Amorites on the coast, and the Chettites, and the Pherezites, and the Jebusites in the mountain, and the Evites, and those dwelling under *mount* Aermon in the land Massyma. 4 And they and their kings with them went forth, as the sand of the sea in multitude, and horses, and very many chariots. 5

And all the kings assembled in person, and came to the same place, and encamped at the waters of Maron to war with Israel. 6 And the Lord said to Joshua, Be not afraid of them, for to-morrow *at* this time I will put them to flight before Israel: thou shalt hough their horses, and burn their chariots with fire 7 And Joshua and all the men of war came upon them at the water of Maron suddenly; and they attacked them in the hill country. 8 And the Lord delivered them into the power of Israel; and they smote them and pursued them to great Sidon, and to Maseron, and to the plains of Massoch eastward; and they destroyed them till there was not one of them left that survived. 9 And Joshua did to them, as the Lord commanded him: he houghed their horses, and burned their chariots with fire. 10 And Joshua returned at that time, and took Asor and her king; now Asor in former time was the chief of these kingdoms. 11 And they slew with the sword all that breathed in it, and utterly destroyed them all, and there was no living thing left in it; and they burnt Asor with fire. 12 And Joshua took all the cities of the kingdoms, and their kings, and slew them with the edge of the sword; and utterly slew them, as Moses the servant of the Lord commanded. 13 But all the walled cities Israel burnt not; but Israel burnt Asor only. 14 And the children of Israel took all its spoils to themselves; and they slew all the men with the edge of the sword, until he destroyed them; they left not one of them breathing. 15 As the Lord commanded his servant Moses, even so Moses commanded Joshua; and so Joshua did, he transgressed no precept of all that Moses commanded him. 16 And Joshua took all the hill country, and all the land of Nageb, and all the land of Gosom, and the plain country, and that toward the west, and the mountain of Israel and the low country by the mountain; 17 from the mountain of Chelcha, and that which goes up to Seir, and as far as Balagad, and the plains of Libanus, under mount Aermon; and he took all their kings, and destroyed, and slew them. 18 And for many days Joshua waged war with these kings. 19 And there was no city which Israel took not; they took all in war. 20 For it was of the Lord to harden their hearts to go forth to war against Israel, that they might be utterly destroyed, that mercy should not be granted to them, but that they should be utterly destroyed, as the Lord said to Moses. 21 And Joshua came at that time, and utterly destroyed the Enakim out of the hill country, from Chebron and from Dabir, and from Anaboth, and from all the race of Israel, and from all the mountain of Juda with their cities; and Joshua utterly destroyed them. 22 There was not *any one* left of the Enakim by the children of Israel, only there was left of them in Gaza, and in Gath, and in Aseldo. 23 And Joshua took all the land, as the Lord commanded Moses; and Joshua gave them for an inheritance to Israel by division according to their tribes; and the land ceased from war.

Josh.12 1 And these *are* the kings of the land, whom the children of Israel slew, and inherited their land beyond Jordan from the east, from the valley of Arnon to the mount of Aermon, and all the land of Araba on the east. 2 Seon king of the Amorites, who dwelt in Esebon, ruling from Arnon, which is in the valley, on the side of the valley, and half of Galaad as far as Jaboc, the borders of the children of Ammon. 3 And Araba as far as the sea of Chenereth eastward, and as far as the sea of Araba; the salt sea eastward *by* the way to Asimoth, from Thaeman under Asedoth Phasga. 4 And Og king of Basan, who dwelt in Astaroth and in Edrain, was left of the giants 5 ruling from mount Aermon and from Secchai, and *over* all the land of Basan to the borders of Gergesi, and Machi, and the half of Galaad of the borders of Seon king of Esebon. 6 Moses the servant of the Lord and the children of Israel smote them; and Moses gave them by way of inheritance to Ruben, and Gad, and to the half tribe of Manasse. 7 And these *are* the kings of the Amorites, whom Joshua and the children of Israel slew beyond Jordan by the sea of Balagad in the plain of Libanus, and as far as the mountain of Chelcha, as men go up to Seir: and Joshua gave it to the tribes of Israel to inherit according to their portion; 8 in the mountain, and in the plain, and in Araba, and in Asedoth, and in the wilderness, and Nageb; the Chettite, and the Amorite, and the Chananite, and the Pherezite, and the Evite, and the Jebusite. 9 The king of Jericho, and the king of Gai, which is near Baethel; 10 the king of Jerusalem, the king of Chebron, 11 the king of Jerimuth, the king of Lachis; 12 the king of Ælam, the king of Gazer; 13 the king of Dabir, the king of Gader: 14 the king of Hermath, the king of Ader; 15 the king of Lebna, the king of Odollam, 16 the king of Elath, 17 the king of Taphut, the king of Opher, 18 the king of Ophec of Aroc, 19 the king of Asom, 20 the king of Symoon, the king of Mambroth, the king of Aziph, 21 the king of Cades, the king of Zachac, 22 the king of Maredoth, the king of Jecom of Chermel, 23 the king of Odollam *belonging to* Phennealdor, the king of Gei of Galilee: 24 the king of Thersa: all these *were* twenty-nine kings.

Josh.13 1 And Joshua *was* old and very advanced in years; and the Lord said to Joshua, Thou art advanced in years, and there is much land left to inherit. 2 And this *is* the land that is left: the borders of the Phylistines, the Gesirite, and the Chananite, 3 from the wilderness before Egypt, as far as the borders of Accaron on the left of the Chananites *the land* is reckoned to the five principalities of the Phylistines, to the inhabitant of Gaza, and of Azotus, and of Ascalon, and of Geth, and of Accaron, and to the Evite; 4 from Thaeman even to all the land of Chanaan before Gaza, and the Sidonians as far as Aphec, as far as the borders of the Amorites. 5 And all the land of Galiath of the Phylistines, and all Libanus eastward from Galgal, under the mountain Aermon as far as the entering in of Emath; 6 every one that inhabits the hill country from Libanus as far as Masereth Memphomaim. All the Sidonians, I will destroy them from before Israel; but do thou give them by inheritance to Israel, as I charged thee. 7 And now divide this land by lot to the nine tribes, and to the half tribe of Manasse. 8 From Jordan to the great sea westward thou shalt give it *them*: the great sea shall be the boundary. *But* to the two tribes and to the half tribe of Manasse, to Ruben and to Gad Moses gave *an inheritance* beyond Jordan: Moses the servant of the Lord gave *it* to them eastward, 9 from Aroer, which is on the bank of the brook of Arnon, and the city in the midst of the

valley, and all Misor from Maedaban. 10 All the cities of Seon king of the Amorites, who reigned from Esebon to the coasts of the children of Ammon; 11 and the region of Galaad, and the borders of the Gesirites and the Machatites, the whole mount of Aermon, and all the land of Basan to Acha. 12 All the kingdom of Og in the region of Basan, who reigned in Astaroth and in Edrain: he was left of the giants; and Moses smote him, and destroyed him. 13 But the children of Israel destroyed not the Gesirite and the Machatite and the Chananite; and the king of the Gesiri and the Machatite dwelt among the children of Israel until this day. 14 Only no inheritance was given to the tribe of Levi: the Lord God of Israel, he *is* their inheritance, as the Lord said to them; and this *is* the division which Moses made to the children of Israel in Araboth Moab, on the other side of Jordan, by Jericho. 15 And Moses gave the land to the tribe of Ruben according to their families. 16 And their borders were from Aroer, which is opposite the brook of Arnon, and *theirs is* the city that is in the valley of Arnon; and all Misor, 17 to Esebon, and all the cities in Misor, and Daebon, and Baemon-Baal, and the house of Meelboth; 18 and Basan, and Bakedmoth, and Maephaad, 19 and Kariathaim, and Sebama, and Serada, and Sion in mount Enab; 20 and Baethphogor, and Asedoth Phasga, and Baetthasinoth, 21 and all the cities of Misor, and all the kingdom of Seon king of the Amorites, whom Moses smote, even him and the princes of Madian, and Evi, and Roboc, and Sur, and Ur, and Robe prince of the spoils of Sion, and the inhabitants of Sion. 22 And Balaam the son of Baeor the prophet they slew in the battle. 23 And the borders of Ruben were—*even* Jordan *was the* boundary; this *is* the inheritance of the children of Ruben according to their families, *these were* their cities and their villages. 24 And Moses gave inheritance to the sons of Gad according to their families. 25 And their borders were Jazer, all the cities of Galaad, and half the land of the children of Ammon to Araba, which is before Arad. 26 And from Esebon to Araboth by Massepha, and Botanim, and Maan to the borders of Daebon, 27 and Enadom, and Othargai, and Baenthanabra, and Soccotha, and Saphan, and the rest of the kingdom of Sean king of Esebon: and Jordan shall be the boundary as far as part of the sea of Chenereth beyond Jordan eastward. 28 This *is* the inheritance of the children of Gad according to their families and according to their cities: according to their families they will turn their backs before their enemies, because their cities and their villages were according to their families. 29 And Moses gave to half the tribe of Manasse according to their families. 30 And their borders were from Maan, and all the kingdom of Basan, and all the kingdom of Og king of Basan, and all the villages of Jair, which are in the region of Basan, sixty cities: 31 and the half of Galaad, and in Astaroth, and in Edrain, royal cities of Og in the land of Basan, *Moses gave* to the sons of Machir the sons of Manasse, even to the half-tribe sons of Machir the sons of Manasse, according to their families. 32 These *are* they whom Moses caused to inherit beyond Jordan in Araboth Moab, beyond Jordan by Jericho eastward.

Josh.14 1 And these *are* they of the children of Israel that received their inheritance in the land of Chanaan, to whom Eleazar the priest, and Joshua the *son* of Naue, and the heads of the families of the tribes of the children of Israel, gave inheritance. 2 They inherited according to their lots, as the Lord commanded by the hand of Joshua to the nine tribes and the half tribe, on the other side of Jordan. 3 But to the Levites he gave no inheritance among them. 4 For the sons of Joseph were two tribes, Manasse and Ephraim; and there was none inheritance in the land given to the Levites, only cities to dwell in, and their suburbs separated for the cattle, and their cattle. 5 As the Lord commanded Moses, so did the children of Israel; and they divided the land. 6 And the children of Juda came to Joshua in Galgal, and Chaleb the *son* of Jephone the Kenezite said to him, Thou knowest the word that the Lord spoke to Moses the man of God concerning me and thee in Cades Barne. 7 For I was forty years old when Moses the servant of God sent me out of Cades Barne to spy out the land; and I returned him an answer according to his mind. 8 My brethren that went up with me turned away the heart of the people, but I applied my self to follow the Lord my God. 9 And Moses sware on that day, saying, The land on which thou art gone up, it shall be thy inheritance and thy children's for ever, because thou hast applied thyself to follow the Lord our God. 10 And now the Lord has kept me alive as he said: this *is* the forty-fifth year since the Lord spoke that word to Moses; and Israel journeyed in the wilderness; and now, behold, I *am* this day eighty-five years old. 11 I am still strong this day, as when the Lord sent me: just so strong am I now to go out and to come in for war. 12 And now I ask of thee this mountain, as the Lord said in that day; for thou heardest this word on that day; and now the Enakim are there, cities great and strong: if then the Lord should be with me, I will utterly destroy them, as the Lord said to me. 13 And Joshua blessed him, and gave Chebron to Chaleb the son of Jephone the son of Kenez for an inheritance. 14 Therefore Chebron became the inheritance of Chaleb the *son* of Jephone the Kenezite until this day, because he followed the commandment of the Lord God of Israel. 15 And the name of Chebron before was the city Argob, it *is* the metropolis of the Enakim: and the land rested from war.

Josh.15 1 And the borders of the tribe of Juda according to their families were from the borders of Idumea from the wilderness of sin, as far as Cades southward. 2 And their borders were from the south as far as a part of the salt sea from the high country that extends southward. 3 And they proceed before the ascent of Acrabin, and go out round Sena, and go up from the south to Cades Barne; and go out to Asoron, and proceed up to Sarada, and go out by the way that is west of Cades. 4 And they go out to Selmona, and issue at the valley of Egypt; and the termination of its boundaries shall be at the sea: these are their boundaries southward. 5 And their boundaries eastward *are* all the salt sea as far as Jordan; and their borders from the north, and from the border of the sea, and from part of Jordan— 6 the borders go up to Baethaglaam, and they go along from the north to Baetharaba, and the borders go on up to the stone of Baeon the son of Ruben. 7 And the borders continue on to the fourth part of the valley of Achor, and go down to Galgal, which is before the approach of Adammin, which is southward in the valley, and terminate at the water of the fountain of the sun; and their going forth shall be the fountain of Rogel. 8 And the borders go up to the valley of Ennom, behind Jebus southward; this is Jerusalem: and the borders terminate at the top of the mountain, which is before the valley of Ennom toward the sea, which is by the side of the land of Raphain northward. 9 And the border *going forth* from the top of the mountain terminates at the fountain of the water of Naphtho, and terminates at mount Ephron; and the border will lead to Baal; this is the city of Jarim. 10 And the border will go round from Baal to the sea, and will go on to the mount of Assar behind the city of Jarin northwards; this is Chaslon: and it will come down to the city of Sun, and will go on to the south. 11 And the border terminates behind Accaron northward, and the borders will terminate at Socchoth, and the borders will go on to the south, and will terminate at Lebna, and the issue of the borders will be at the sea; and their borders *shall be* toward the sea, the great sea shall be the boundary. 12 These *are* the borders of the children of Juda round about according to their families. 13 And to Chaleb the son of Jephone he gave a portion in the midst of the children of Juda by the command of God; and Joshua gave him the city of Arboc the metropolis of Enac; this is Chebron. 14 And Chaleb the son of Jephone destroyed thence the three sons of Enac, Susi, and Tholami, and Achima. 15 And Chaleb went up thence to the inhabitants of Dabir; and the name of Dabir before was the city of Letters. 16 And Chaleb said, Whosoever shall take and destroy the city of Letters, and master it, to him will I give my daughter Ascha to wife. 17 And Gothoniel the son of Chenez the brother of Chaleb took it; and he gave him Ascha his daughter to wife. 18 And it came to pass as she went out that she counselled him, saying, I will ask of my father a field; and she cried from off her ass; and Chaleb said to her, What is it? 19 And she said to him, Give me a blessing, for thou hast set me in the land of Nageb; give me Botthanis: and he gave her Gonaethla the upper, and Gonaethla the lower. 20 This *is* the inheritance of the tribe of the children of Juda. 21 And their cities were cities belonging to the tribe of the children of Juda on the borders of Edom by the wilderness, and Baeseleel, and Ara, and Asor, 22 and Icam, and Regma, and Aruel, 23 and Cades, and Asorionain, and Maenam, 24 and Balmaenan, and their villages, 25 and the cities of Aseron, this *is* Asor, 26 and Sen, and Salmaa, and Molada, 27 and Seri, and Baephalath, 28 and Cholaseola, and Beersabee; and their villages, and their hamlets, 29 Bala and Bacoc, and Asom, 30 and Elboudad, and Baethel, and Herma, 31 and Sekelac, and Macharim, and Sethennac, 32 and Labos, and Sale, and Eromoth; twenty-nine cities, and their villages. 33 In the plain country Astaol, and Raa, and Assa, 34 and Ramen, and Tano, and Iluthoth, and Maeani, 35 and Jermuth, and Odollam, and Membra, and Saocho, and Jazeca. 36 And Sacarim and Gadera, and its villages; fourteen cities, and their villages; 37 Senna, and Adasan, and Magadalgad, 38 and Dalad, and Maspha, and Jachareel, 39 and Basedoth, and

Ideadalea; 40 and Chabra, and Maches, and Maachos, 41 and Geddor, and Bagadiel, and Noman, and Machedan: sixteen cities, and their villages; 42 Lebna, and Ithac, and Anoch, 43 and Jana, and Nasib, 44 and Keilam, and Akiezi, and Kezib, and Bathesar, and Ælom: ten cities, and their villages; 45 Accaron and her villages, and their hamlets: 46 from Accaron, Gemna, and all the cities that are near Asedoth; and their villages. 47 Asiedoth, and her villages, and her hamlets; Gaza, and its villages and its hamlets as far as the river of Egypt, and the great sea is the boundary. 48 And in the hill country Samir, and Jether, and Socha, 49 and Renna and the city of Letters, this is Dabir; 50 and Anon, and Es, and Man, and Æsam, 51 and Gosom, and Chalu, and Channa, and Gelom: eleven cities, and their villages; 52 Ærem, and Remna, and Soma, 53 and Jemain, and Baethachu, and Phacua, 54 and Euma, and the city Arboc, this is Chebron, and Soraith: nine cities and their villages: 55 Maor, and Chermel, and Ozib, and Itan, 56 and Jariel, and Aricam, and Zacanaim, 57 and Gabaa, and Thamnatha; nine cities, and their villages; 58 Ælua, and Bethsur, and Geddon, 59 and Magaroth, and Baethanam, and Thecum; six cities, and their villages; Theco, and Ephratha, this is Baethleem, and Phagor, and Ætan, and Culon, and Tatam, and Thobes, and Carem, and Galem, and Thether, and Manocho: eleven cities, and their villages, 60 Cariathbaal, this is the city of Jarim, and Sotheba: two cities, and their villages: 61 and Baddargeis, and Tharabaam, and Ænon; 62 and Æochioza, and Naphlazon, and the cities of Sadon, and Ancades; seven cities, and their villages. 63 And the Jebusite dwelt in Jerusalem, and the children of Juda could not destroy them; and the Jebusites dwelt in Jerusalem to this day.

Josh.16 1 And the borders of the children of Joseph were from Jordan by Jericho eastward; and they will go up from Jericho to the hill country, to the wilderness, to Baethel Luza. 2 And they will go out to Baethel, and will proceed to the borders of Achatarothi. 3 And they will go across to the sea to the borders of Aptalim, as far as the borders of Baethoron the lower, and the going forth of them shall be to the sea. 4 And the sons of Joseph, Ephraim and Manasse, took their inheritance. 5 And the borders of the children of Ephraim were according to their families, and the borders of their inheritance were eastward to Ataroth, and Eroc as far as Baethoron the upper, and Gazara. 6 And the borders will proceed to the sea to Icasmon north of Therma; they will go round eastward to Thenasa, and Selles, and will pass on eastward to Janoca, 7 and to Macho, and Ataroth, and these are their villages; and they will come to Jericho, and will issue at Jordan. 8 And the borders will proceed from Tapho to the sea to Chelcana; and their termination will be at the sea; this is the inheritance of the tribe of Ephraim according to their families. 9 And the cities separated to the sons of Ephraim were in the midst of the inheritance of the sons of Manasse, all the cities and their villages. 10 And Ephraim did not destroy the Chananite who dwelt in Gazer; and the Chananite dwelt in Ephraim until this day, until Pharao the king of Egypt went up and took it, and burnt it with fire; and the Chananites, and Pherezites, and the dwellers in

Gaza they destroyed, and Pharao gave them for a dowry to his daughter.

Josh.17 1 And the borders of the tribe of the children of Manasse, (for he was the first-born of Joseph,) assigned to Machir the first-born of Manasse the father of Galaad, for he was a warrior, were in the land of Galaad and of Basan. 2 And there was land assigned to the other sons of Manasse according to their families; to the sons of Jezi, and to the sons of Kelez, and to the sons of Jeziel, and to the sons of Sychem, and to the sons of Symarim, and to the sons of Opher: these are the males according to their families. 3 And Salpaad the sons of Opher had no sons but daughters: and these are the names of the daughters of Salpaad; Maala, and Nua, and Egla, and Melcha, and Thersa. 4 And they stood before Eleazar the priest, and before Joshua, and before the rulers, saying, God gave a charge by the hand of Moses, to give us an inheritance in the midst of our brethren: so there was given to them by the command of the Lord an inheritance among the brethren of their father. 5 And their lot fell to them from Anassa, and to the plain of Labec of the land of Galaad, which is beyond Jordan. 6 For the daughters of the sons of Manasse inherited a portion in the midst of their brethren, and the land of Galaad was assigned to the remainder of the sons of Manasse. 7 And the borders of the sons of Manasse were Delanath, which is before the sons of Anath, and it proceeds to the borders even to Jamin and Jassib to the fountain of Thaphthoth. 8 It shall belong to Manasse, and Thapheth on the borders of Manasse shall belong to the sons of Ephraim. 9 And the borders shall go down to the valley of Carana southward by the valley of Jariel, (there is a turpentine tree belonging to Ephraim between that and the city of Manasse:) and the borders of Manasse are northward to the brook; and the sea shall be its termination. 10 Southward the land belongs to Ephraim, and northward to Manasse; and the sea shall be their cost; and northward they shall border upon Aseb, and eastward upon Issachar. 11 And Manasses shall have in the portion of Issachar and Aser Baethsan and their villages, and the inhabitants of Dor, and its villages, and the inhabitants of Mageddo, and its villages, and the third part of Mapheta, and its villages. 12 And the sons of Manasse were not able to destroy these cities; and the Chananite began to dwell in that land. 13 And it came to pass that when the children of Israel were strong, they made the Chananites subject, but they did not utterly destroy them. 14 And the sons of Joseph answered Joshua, saying, Wherefore hast thou caused us to inherit one inheritance, and one line? whereas I am a great people, and God has blessed me. 15 And Joshua said to them, If thou be a great people, go up to the forest, and clear the land for thyself, If mount Ephraim be too little for thee. 16 And they said, The mount of Ephraim does not please us, and the Chananite dwelling in it in Baethsan, and in its villages, and in the valley of Jezrael, has choice cavalry and iron. 17 And Joshua said to the sons of Joseph, If thou art a great people, and hast great strength, thou shalt not have only one inheritance. 18 For thou shalt have the wood, for there is a wood, and thou shalt clear it, and the land shall be thine;

even when thou shalt have utterly destroyed the Chananite, for he has chosen cavalry; yet thou art stronger than he.

Josh.18 1 And all the congregation of the children of Israel were assembled at Selo, and there they pitched the tabernacle of witness; and the land was subdued by them. 2 And the sons of Israel remained, *even* those who *had* not received their inheritance, seven tribes. 3 And Joshua said to the sons of Israel, How long will ye be slack to inherit the land, which the Lord our God has given you? 4 Appoint of yourselves three men of each tribe, and let them rise up and go through the land, and let them describe it before me, as it will be proper to divide it. 5 And they came to him: and he divided to them seven portions, *saying*, Juda shall stand to them a border southward, and the sons of Joseph shall stand to them northward. 6 And do ye divide the land into seven parts, and bring the description hither to me, and I will give you a lot before the Lord our God. 7 For the sons of Levi have no part among you; for the priesthood of the Lord *is* his portion; and Gad, and Ruben, and the half tribe of Manasse, have received their inheritance beyond Jordan eastward, which Moses the servant of the Lord gave to them. 8 And the men rose up and went; and Joshua charged the men who went to explore the land, saying, Go and explore the land, and come to me, and I will bring you forth a lot here before the Lord in Selo. 9 And they went, and explored the land: and they viewed it, and described it according to the cities, seven parts in a book, and brought *the book* to Joshua. 10 And Joshua cast the lot for them in Selo before the Lord. 11 And the lot of the tribe of Benjamin came forth first according to their families: and the borders of their lot came forth between the children of Juda and the children of Joseph. 12 And their borders were northward: the borders shall go up from Jordan behind Jericho northward, and shall go up to the mountain westward, and the issue of it shall be Baethon of Mabdara. 13 And the borders will go forth thence to Luz, behind Luz, from the south of it; this is Baethel: and the borders shall go down to Maatarob Orech, to the hill country, which is southward of Baethoron the lower. 14 And the borders shall pass through and proceed to the part that looks toward the sea, on the south, from the mountain in front of Baethoron southward, and its termination shall be at Cariath-Baal, this is Cariath-Jarin, a city of the children of Juda; this is the part toward the west. 15 And the south side on the part of Cariath-Baal; and the borders shall go across to Gasin, to the fountain of the water of Naphtho. 16 And the borders shall extend down on one side, this is in front of the forest of Sonnam, which is on the side of Emec Raphain northward, and it shall come down to Gaeenna behind Jebusai southward: it shall come down to the fountain of Rogel. 17 And *the borders* shall go across to the fountain of Baethsamys: 18 and shall proceed to Galiloth, which is in front by the going up of Æthamin; and they shall come down to the stone of Baeon of the sons of Ruben; and shall pass over behind Baetharaba northward, and shall go down to the borders behind the sea northward. 19 And the termination of the borders shall be at the creek of the salt sea northward to the side of Jordan southward: these are

their southern borders. 20 And Jordan shall be their boundary on the east: this *is* the inheritance of the children of Benjamin, these *are* their borders round about according to their families. 21 And the cities of the children of Benjamin according to their families *were* Jericho, and Bethagaeo, and the Amecasis, 22 and Baethabara, and Sara, and Besana, 23 and Æein, and Phara, and Ephratha, 24 and Carapha, and Cephira, and Moni, and Gabaa, twelve cities and their villages: 25 Gabaon, and Rama, and Beerotha; 26 and Massema, and Miron, and Amoke; 27 and Phira, and Caphan, and Nacan, and Selecan, and Thareela, 28 and Jebus (this is Jerusalem); and Gabaoth, Jarim, thirteen cities, and their villages; this *is* the inheritance of the sons of Benjamin according to their families.

Josh.19 1 And the second lot came out for the children of Symeon; and their inheritance was in the midst of the lots of the children of Juda. 2 And their lot was Beersabee, and Samaa, and Caladam, 3 and Arsola, and Bola, and Jason, 4 and Erthula, and Bula, and Herma, 5 and Sikelac, and Baethmachereb, and Sarsusin, 6 and Batharoth, and their fields, thirteen cities, and their villages. 7 Eremmon, and Thalcha, and Jether, and Asan; four cities and their villages, 8 round about their cities as far as Balec as *men* go to Bameth southward: this *is* the inheritance of the tribe of the children of Symeon according to their families. 9 The inheritance of the tribe of the children of Symeon *was a part* of the lot of Juda, for the portion of the children of Juda was greater than theirs; and the children of Symeon inherited in the midst of their lot. 10 And the third lot came out to Zabulon according to their families: the bounds of their inheritance shall be—Esedekgola shall be their border, 11 the sea and Magelda, and it shall reach to Baetharaba in the valley, which is opposite Jekman. 12 And the border returned from Sedduc in a contrary direction eastward from Baethsamys, to the borders of Chaselothaith, and shall pass on to Dabiroth, and shall proceed upward to Phangai. 13 And thence it shall come round in the opposite direction eastward to Gebere to the city of Catasem, and shall go on to Remmonaa Matharaoza. 14 And the borders shall come round northward to Amoth, and their going out shall be at Gaephael, 15 and Catanath, and Nabaal, and Symoon, and Jericho, and Baethman. 16 This *is* the inheritance of the tribe of the sons of Zabulon according to their families, *these* cities and their villages. 17 And the fourth lot came out to Issachar. 18 And their borders were Jazel, and Chasaloth, and Sunam, 19 and Agin, and Siona, and Reeroth, 20 and Anachereth, and Dabiron, and Kison, and Rebes, 21 and Remmas, and Jeon, and Tomman, and Æmarec, and Bersaphes. 22 And the boundaries shall border upon Gaethbor, and upon Salim westward, and Baethsamys; and the extremity of his bounds shall be Jordan. 23 This *is* the inheritance of the tribe of the children of Issachar according to their families, the cities and their villages. 24 And the fifth lot came out to Aser according to their families. 25 And their borders were Exeleketh, and Aleph, and Baethok, and Keaph, 26 and Elimelech, and Amiel, and Maasa, and the lot will border on Carmel westward, and on Sion, and Labanath. 27 And it will return westward from

Baethegeneth, and will join Zabulon and Ekgai, and Phthaeel northwards, and the borders will come to Saphthaebaethme, and Inael, and will go on to Chobamasomel, 28 and Elbon, and Raab, and Ememaon, and Canthan to great Sidon. 29 And the borders shall turn back to Rama, and to the fountain of Masphassat, and the Tyrians; and the borders shall return to Jasiph, and their going forth shall be the sea, and Apoleb, and Echozob, 30 and Archob, and Aphec, and Raau. 31 This *is* the inheritance of the tribe of the sons of Aser according to their families, the cities and their villages. 32 And the sixth lot came out to Nephthali. 33 And their borders were Moolam, and Mola, and Besemiin, and Arme, and Naboc, and Jephthamai, as far as Dodam; and their goings out were Jordan. 34 And the coasts will return westward by Athabor, and will go out thence to Jacana, and will border on Zabulon southward, and Aser will join *it* westward, and Jordan eastward. 35 And the walled cities of the Tyrians, Tyre, and Omathadaketh, and Kenereth, 36 and Armaith, and Areal, and Asor, 37 and Cades, and Assari, and the well of Asor; 38 and Keroe, and Megalaarim, and Baetthame, and Thessamys. 39 This *is* the inheritance of the tribe of the children of Nephthali. 40 And the seventh lot came out to Dan. 41 And their borders were Sarath, and Asa, and the cities of Sammaus, 42 and Salamin, and Ammon, and Silatha, 43 and Elon, and Thamnatha, and Accaron; 44 and Alcatha, and Begethon, and Gebeelan, 45 and Azor, and Banaebacat, and Gethremmon. 46 And westward of Hieracon the border *was* near to Joppa. 47 This *is* the inheritance of the tribe of the children of Dan, according to their families, these *are* their cities and their villages: and the children of Dan did not drive out the Amorite who afflicted them in the mountain; and the Amorite would not suffer them to come down into the valley, but they forcibly took from them the border of their portion. 48 And the sons of Dan went and fought against Lachis, and took it, and smote it with the edge of the sword; and they dwelt in it, and called the name of it Lasendan: and the Amorite continued to dwell in Edom and in Salamin: and the hand of Ephraim prevailed against them, and they became tribute to them. 49 And they proceeded to take possession of the land according to their borders, and the children of Israel gave an inheritance to Joshua the son of Naue among them, 50 by the command of God, and they gave him the city which he asked for, Thamnasarach, which is in the mount of Ephraim; and he built the city, and dwelt in it. 51 These *are* the divisions which Eleazar the priest divided by lot, and Joshua the *son* of Naue, and the heads of families among the tribes of Israel, according to the lots, in Selo before the Lord by the doors of the tabernacle of testimony, and they went to take possession of the land.

Josh.20 1 And the Lord spoke to Joshua, saying, 2 Speak to the children of Israel, saying, Assign the cities of refuge, *of* which I spoke to you by Moses. 3 *Even* a refuge to the slayer who has smitten a man unintentionally; and the cities shall be to you a refuge, and the slayer shall not be put to death by the avenger of blood, until he have stood before the congregation for judgment. 4 And Joshua separated Cades in Galilee in the mount Nephthali, and Sychem in the

mount Ephraim, and the city of Arboc; this is Chebron, in the mountain of Juda. 5 And beyond Jordan he appointed Bosor in the wilderness in the plain out of the tribe of Ruben, and Aremoth in Galaad out of the tribe of Gad, and Gaulon in the country of Basan out of the tribe of Manasse. 6 These *were* the cities selected for the sons of Israel, and for the stranger abiding among them, that every one who smites a soul unintentionally should flee thither, that he should not die by the hand of the avenger of blood, until he should stand before the congregation for judgment.

Josh.21 1 And the heads of the families of the sons of Levi drew near to Eleazar the priest, and to Joshua the *son* of Naue, and to the heads of families of the tribes of Israel. 2 And they spoke to them in Selo in the land of Chanaan, saying, The Lord gave commandment by Moses to give us cities to dwell in, and the country round about for our cattle. 3 So the children of Israel gave to the Levites in their inheritance by the command of the Lord the cities and the country round. 4 And the lot came out for the children of Caath; and the sons of Aaron, the priests the Levites, had by lot thirteen cities out of the tribe of Juda, and out of the tribe of Symeon, and out of the tribe of Benjamin. 5 And to the sons of Caath that were left were *given by* lot ten cities, out of the tribe of Ephraim, and out of the tribe of Dan, and out of the half tribe of Manasse. 6 And the sons of Gedson had thirteen cities, out of the tribe of Issachar, and out of the tribe of Aser, and out of the tribe of Nephthali, and out of the half tribe of Manasse in Basan. 7 And the sons of Merari according to their families had by lot twelve cities, out of the tribe of Ruben, and out of the tribe of Gad, and out of the tribe of Zabulon. 8 And the children of Israel gave to the Levites the cities and their suburbs, as the Lord commanded Moses, by lot. 9 And the tribe of the children of Juda, and the tribe of the children of Symeon, and *part* of the tribe of the children of Benjamin gave these cities, and they were assigned 10 to the sons of Aaron of the family of Caath of the sons of Levi, for the lot fell to these. 11 And they gave to them Cariatharboc the metropolis of the sons of Enac; this is Chebron in the mountain *country* of Juda, and the suburbs round it. 12 But the lands of the city, and its villages Joshua gave to the sons of Chaleb the son of Jephonne for a possession. 13 And to the sons of Aaron he gave the city of refuge for the slayer, Chebron, and the suburbs belonging to it; and Lemna and the suburbs belonging to it; 14 and Ælom and its suburbs; and Tema and its suburbs; 15 and Gella and its suburbs; and Dabir and its suburbs; 16 and Asa and its suburbs; and Tany and its suburbs; and Baethsamys and its suburbs: nine cities from these two tribes. 17 And from the tribe of Benjamin, Gabaon and its suburbs; and Gatheth and its suburbs; 18 and Anathoth and its suburbs; and Gamala and its suburbs; four cities. 19 All the cities of the sons of Aaron the priests, thirteen. 20 And to the families, *even* the sons of Caath the Levites, that were left of the sons of Caath, there was *given* their priests' city, 21 out of the tribe of Ephraim; and they gave them the slayer's city of refuge, Sychem, and its suburbs, and Gazara and its appendages, and its suburbs; 22 and Baethoron and its suburbs: four cities: 23 and the tribe of Dan, Helcothaim and its suburbs; and Gethedan and its suburbs: 24 and Ælon and its suburbs; and Getheremmon and its suburbs: four cities. 25 And out of the half tribe of Manasse, Tanach and its suburbs; and Jebatha and its suburbs; two cities. 26 In all *were given* ten cities, and the suburbs of each belonging to them, to the families of the sons of Caath that remained. 27 And *Joshua gave* to the sons of Gedson the Levites out of the other half tribe of Manasse cities set apart for the slayers, Gaulon in the country of Basan, and its suburbs; and Bosora and its suburbs; two cities. 28 And out of the tribe of Issachar, Kison and its suburbs; and Debba and its suburbs; 29 and Remmath and its suburbs; and the well of Letters, and its suburbs; four cities. 30 And out of the tribe of Aser, Basella and its suburbs; and Dabbon and its suburbs; 31 and Chelcat and its suburbs; and Raab and its suburbs; four cities. 32 And of the tribe of Nephthali, the city set apart for the slayer, Cades in Galilee, and its suburbs; and Nemmath, and its suburbs; and Themmon and its suburbs; three cities. 33 All the cities of Gedson according to their families *were* thirteen cities. 34 And to the family of the sons of Merari the Levites that remained, *he gave* out of the tribe of Zabulon, Maan and its suburbs; and Cades and its suburbs, 35 and Sella and its suburbs: three cities. 36 And beyond Jordan over against Jericho, out of the tribe of Ruben, the city of refuge for the slayer, Bosor in the wilderness; Miso and its suburbs; and Jazer and its suburbs; and Decmon and its suburbs; and Mapha and its suburbs; four cities. 37 And out of the tribe of Gad the city of refuge for the slayer, both Ramoth in Galaad, and its suburbs; Camin and its suburbs; and Esbon and its suburbs; and Jazer and its suburbs: the cities *were* four in all. 38 All *these* cities *were given* to the sons of Merari according to the families of them that were left out of the tribe of Levi; and their limits were the twelve cities. 39 All the cities of the Levites in the midst of the possession of the children of Israel, *were* forty -eight cities, 40 and their suburbs round about these cities: a city and the suburbs round about the city to all these cities: and Joshua ceased dividing the land by their borders: and the children of Israel gave a portion to Joshua because of the commandment of the Lord: they gave him the city which he asked: they gave him Thamnasachar in mount Ephraim; and Joshua built the city, and dwelt in it: and Joshua took the knives of stone, wherewith he circumcised the children of Israel that were born in the desert by the way, and put them in Thamnasachar. 41 So the Lord gave to Israel all the land which he sware to give to their fathers: and they inherited it, and dwelt in it. 42 And the Lord gave them rest round about, as he sware to their fathers: not one of all their enemies maintained his ground against them; the Lord delivered all their enemies into their hands. 43 There failed not one of the good things which the Lord spoke to the children of Israel; all came to pass.

Josh.22 1 Then Joshua called together the sons of Ruben, and the sons of Gad, and the half tribe of Manasse, 2 and said to them, Ye have heard all that Moses the servant of the Lord commanded you, and ye have hearkened to my voice in all that he commanded you. 3 Ye have not deserted your brethren these many days: until this day ye have kept the commandment of the Lord your God. 4 And now the Lord our God has given our brethren rest, as he told them: now then return and depart to your homes, and to the land of your possession, which Moses gave you on the other side Jordan. 5 But take great heed to do the commands and the law, which Moses the servant of the Lord commanded you to do; to love the Lord our God, to walk in all his ways, to keep his commands, and to cleave to him, and serve him with all your mind, and with all your soul. 6 And Joshua blessed them, and dismissed them; and they went to their homes. 7 And to *one* half the tribe of Manasse Moses gave a portion in the land of Basan, and to *the other* half Joshua gave a portion with his brethren on the other side of Jordan westward: and when Joshua sent them away to their homes, then he blessed them. 8 And they departed with much wealth to their houses, and they divided the spoil of their enemies with their brethren; very much cattle, and silver, and gold, and iron, and much raiment. 9 So the sons of Ruben, and the sons of Gad, and the half tribe of Manasse, departed from the children of Israel in Selo in the land of Chanaan, to go away into Galaad, into the land of their possession, which they inherited by the command of the Lord, by the hand of Moses. 10 And they came to Galaad of Jordan, which is in the land of Chanaan: and the children of Ruben, and the children of Gad, and the half tribe of Manasse built there an alter by Jordan, a great altar to look at. 11 And the children of Israel heard say, Behold, the sons of Ruben, and the sons of Gad, and the half tribe of Manasse have built an alter at the borders of the land of Chanaan at Galaad of Jordan, on the opposite side to the children of Israel. 12 And all the children of Israel gathered together to Selo, so as to go up and fight against them. 13 And the children of Israel sent to the sons of Ruben, and the sons of Gad, and to the sons of the half tribe of Manasse into the land of Galaad, both Phinees the son of Eleazar the son of Aaron the priest, 14 and ten of the chiefs with him; *there was* one chief of every household out of all the tribes of Israel; (the heads of families are the captains of thousands in Israel.) 15 And they came to the sons of Ruben, and to the sons of Gad, and to the half tribe of Manasse into the land of Galaad; and they spoke to them, saying, 16 Thus says the whole congregation of the Lord, What *is* this transgression that ye have transgressed before the God of Israel, to turn away today from the Lord, in that ye have built for yourselves an alter, so that ye should be apostates from the Lord? 17 Is the sin of Phogor too little for you, whereas we have not been cleansed from it until this day, though there was a plague among the congregation of the Lord? 18 And ye have this day revolted from the Lord; and it shall come to pass if ye revolt this day from the Lord, that to-morrow there shall be wrath upon all Israel. 19 And now if the land of your possession *be too* little, cross over to the land of the possession of the Lord, where the tabernacle of the Lord dwells, and receive ye an inheritance among us; and do not become apostates from God, neither do ye apostatize from the Lord, because of your having built an altar apart from the altar of the Lord our God. 20 Lo! did not Achar the *son* of Zara commit a trespass *taking* of the accursed thing, and there was wrath on the whole congregation of Israel? and he himself died alone in his own sin. 21 And the sons of Ruben, and the sons of Gad, and the half tribe of Manasse answered, and spoke to the captains of the thousands of Israel, saying, 22 God *even* God is the Lord, and God *even* God himself knows, and Israel he shall know; if we have transgressed before the Lord by apostasy, let him not deliver us this day. 23 And if we have built to ourselves an altar, so as to apostatize from the Lord our God, so as to offer upon it a sacrifice of whole-burnt-offerings, so as to offer upon it a sacrifice of peace-offering, —the Lord shall require it. 24 But we have done this for the sake of precaution *concerning this* thing, saying, Lest hereafter your sons should say to our sons, What have ye to do with the Lord God of Israel? 25 Whereas the Lord has set boundaries between us and you, even Jordan, and ye have no portion in the Lord: so your sons shall alienate our sons, that they should not worship the Lord. 26 And we gave orders to do thus, to build this altar, not for burnt-offerings, nor for meat-offerings; 27 but that this may be a witness between you and us, and between our posterity after us, that we may do service to the Lord before him, with our burnt-offerings and our meat-offerings and our peace-offerings: so your sons shall not say to our sons, hereafter, Ye have no portion in the Lord. 28 And we said, If ever it should come to pass that they should speak *so* to us, or to our posterity hereafter; then shall they say, Behold the likeness of the altar of the Lord, which our fathers made, not for the sake of burnt-offerings, nor for the sake of meat-offerings, but it is a witness between you and us, and between our sons. 29 Far be it from us therefore that we should turn away from the Lord this day so as to apostatize from the Lord, so as that we should build an altar for burnt-offerings, and for peace-offerings, besides the altar of the Lord which is before his tabernacle. 30 And Phinees the priest and all the chiefs of the congregation of Israel who were with him heard the words which the children of Ruben, and the children of Gad, and the half tribe of Manasse spoke; and it pleased them. 31 And Phinees the priest said to the sons of Ruben, and to the sons of Gad, and to the half of the tribe of Manasse, To-day we know that the Lord *is* with us, because ye have not trespassed grievously against the Lord, and because ye have delivered the children of Israel out of the hand of the Lord. 32 So Phinees the priest and the princes departed from the children of Ruben, and from the children of Gad, and from the half tribe of Manasse out of Galaad into the land of Chanaan to the children of Israel; and reported the words to them. 33 And it pleased the children of Israel; and they spoke to the children of Israel, and blessed the God of the children of Israel, and told them to go up no more to war against the others to destroy the land of the children of Ruben, and the children of Gad, and the half tribe of Manasse: so they dwelt upon it. 34 And Joshua gave a name to the altar of the children of Ruben, and the children of Gad, and the half tribe of Manasse; and said, It is a testimony in the midst of them, that the Lord is their God.

Josh.23 1 And it came to pass after many days after the Lord had given Israel rest from all his enemies round about, that Joshua was old and advanced in years. 2 And Joshua called together all the children of Israel, and their elders, and their chiefs, and their judges, and their officers; and said to them, I am old and advanced in years. 3 And ye have seen all that the Lord our God has done to all these nations before us; *for it* is the Lord your God who has fought for you. 4 See, that I have given to you these nations that are left to you by lots to your tribes, all the nations beginning at Jordan; and *some* I have destroyed; and the boundaries shall be at the great sea westward. 5 And the Lord our God, he shall destroy them before us, until they utterly perish; and he shall send against them the wild beasts, until he shall have utterly destroyed them and their kings from before you; and ye shall inherit their land, as the Lord our God said to you. 6 Do ye therefore strive diligently to observe and do all things written in the book of the law of Moses, that ye turn not to the right hand or to the left; 7 that ye go not in among these nations that are left; and the names of their gods shall not be named among you, neither shall ye serve them, neither shall ye bow down to them. 8 But ye shall cleave to the Lord our God, as ye have done until this day. 9 And the Lord shall destroy them before you, *even* great and strong nations; and no one has stood before us until this day. 10 One of you has chased a thousand, for the Lord our God, he fought for you, as he said to us. 11 And take ye great heed to love the Lord our God. 12 For if ye shall turn aside and attach yourselves to these nations that are left with you, and make marriages with them, and become mingled with them and they with you, 13 know that the Lord will no more destroy these nations from before you; and they will be to you snares and stumbling-blocks, and nails in your heels, and darts in your eyes, until ye be destroyed from off this good land, which the Lord your God has given you. 14 But I hasten to go the way *of death*, as all that are upon the earth also *do*: and ye know in your heart and in your soul, that not one word has fallen *to the ground* of all the words which the Lord our God has spoken respecting all that concerns us; there has not one of them failed. 15 And it shall come to pass, that as all the good things are come upon us which the Lord God will bring upon you all the evil things, until he shall have destroyed you from off this good land, which the Lord has given you, 16 when ye transgress the covenant of the Lord our God, which he has charged us, and go and serve other gods, and bow down to them.

Josh.24 1 And Joshua gathered all the tribe of Israel to Selo, and convoked their elders, and their officers, and their judges, and set them before God. 2 And Joshua said to all the people, Thus says the Lord God of Israel, Your fathers at first sojourned beyond the river, *even* Thara, the father of Abraam and the father of Nachor; and they served other gods. 3 And I took your father Abraam from the other side of the river, and I guided him through all the land, and I multiplied his seed; 4 and I gave to him Isaac, and to Isaac Jacob and Esau: and I gave to Esau mount Seir for him to inherit: and Jacob and his sons went down to Egypt, and became there a great and populous and mighty nation: and the Egyptians afflicted them. 5 And I smote Egypt with the wonders that I wrought among them. 6 And afterwards *God* brought out our fathers from Egypt, and ye entered into the Red Sea; and the Egyptians pursued after our fathers with chariots and horses into the Red Sea. 7 And we cried aloud to the Lord; and he put a cloud and darkness between us and the Egyptians, and he brought the sea upon them, and covered them; and your eyes have seen all that the Lord did in the land of Egypt; and ye were in the wilderness many days. 8 And he brought us into the land of the Amorites that dwelt beyond Jordan, and the Lord delivered them into our hands; and ye inherited their land, and utterly destroyed them from before you. 9 And Balac, king of Moab, son of Sepphor, rose up, and made war against Israel, and sent and called Balaam to curse us. 10 But the Lord thy God would not destroy thee; and he greatly blessed us, and rescued us out of their hands, and delivered them *to us*. 11 And ye crossed over Jordan, and came to Jericho; and the inhabitants of Jericho fought against us, the Amorite, and the Chananite, and the Pherezite, and the Evite, and the Jebusite, and the Chettite, and the Gergesite, and the Lord delivered them into our hands. 12 And he sent forth the hornet before you; and he drove them out from before you, *even* twelve kings of the Amorites, not with thy sword, nor with thy bow. 13 And he gave you a land on which ye did not labour, and cities which ye did not build, and ye were settled in them; and ye eat *of* vineyards and oliveyards which ye did not plant. 14 And now fear the Lord, and serve him in righteousness and justice; and remove the strange gods, which our fathers served beyond the river, and in Egypt; and serve the Lord. 15 But if it seem not good to you to serve the Lord, choose to yourselves this day whom ye will serve, whether the gods of your fathers that were on the other side of the river, or the gods of the Amorites, among whom ye dwell upon their land: but I and my house will serve the Lord, for he is holy. 16 And the people answered and said, Far be it from us to forsake the Lord, so as to serve other gods. 17 The Lord our God, he is God; he brought up us and our fathers from Egypt, and kept us in all the way wherein we walked, and among all the nations through whom we passed. 18 And the Lord cast out the Amorite, and all the nations that inhabited the land from before us: yea, we will serve the Lord, for he is our God. 19 And Joshua said to the people, Indeed ye will not be able to serve the Lord, for God is holy; and he being jealous will not forgive your sins and your transgressions. 20 Whensoever ye shall forsake the Lord and serve other gods, then he shall come upon you and afflict you, and consume you, because he has done you good. 21 And the people said to Joshua, Nay, but we will serve the Lord. 22 And Joshua said to the people, Ye *are* witnesses against yourselves, that ye have chosen the Lord to serve him. 23 And now take away the strange gods that are among you, and set your heart right toward the Lord God of Israel. 24 And the people said to Joshua, We will serve the Lord, and we will hearken to his voice. 25 So Joshua made a covenant with the people on that day, and gave them a law and an ordinance in Selo before the tabernacle of the God of Israel. 26 And he wrote these words in the book of the laws of God: and Joshua took a great stone, and set it up under the oak before the Lord. 27 And Joshua said to the people, Behold, this stone shall be among you for a witness, for it has heard all the words that have been spoken to it by the Lord; for he has spoken to you this day; and this *stone* shall be among you for a witness in the last days, whenever ye shall deal falsely with the Lord my God. 28 And Joshua dismissed the people, and they went every man to his place. 29 And it came to pass after these things that Joshua the son of Naue the servant of the Lord died, *at the age* of a hundred and ten years. 30 And they buried him by the borders of his inheritance in Thamnasarach in the mount of Ephraim, northward of the mount of Galaad: there they put with him into the tomb in which they buried him, the knives of stone with which he circumcised the children of Israel in Galgala, when he brought them out of Egypt, as the Lord appointed them; and there they are to this day. 31 And Israel served the Lord all the days of Joshua, and all the days of the elders that lived as long as Joshua, and all that knew all the works of the Lord which he wrought for Israel. 32 And the children of Israel brought up the bones of Joseph out of Egypt, and buried *them* in Sicima, in the portion of the land which Jacob bought of the Amorites who dwelt in Sicima for a hundred ewe-lambs; and he gave it to Joseph for a portion. 33 And it came to pass afterwards that Eleazar the high-priest the son of Aaron died, and was buried in Gabaar of Phinees his son, which he gave him in mount Ephraim. In that day the children of Israel took the ark of God, and carried it about among them; and Phinees exercised the priest's office in the room of Eleazar his father till he died, and he was buried in his own place Gabaar: but the children of Israel departed every one to their place, and to their own city: and the children of Israel worshipped Astarte, and Astaroth, and the gods of the nations round about them; and the Lord delivered them into the hands of Eglom king of Moab and he ruled over them eighteen years.

JUDGES

Judg.1 1 And it came to pass after the death of Joshua, that the children of Israel enquired of the Lord, saying, Who shall go up for us first against the Chananites, to fight against them? 2 And the Lord said, Judas shall go up: behold, I have delivered the land into his hand. 3 And Judas said to his brother Symeon, Come up with me into my lot, and let us array ourselves against the Chananites, and I also will go with thee into thy lot: and Symeon went with him. 4 And Judas went up; and the Lord delivered the Chananite and the Pherezite into their hands, and they smote them in Bezek to *the number of* ten thousand men. 5 And they overtook Adonibezek in Bezek, and fought against him; and they smote the Chananite and the Pherezite. 6 And Adonibezek fled, and they pursued after him, and took him, and cut off his thumbs and his great toes. 7 And Adonibezek said, Seventy kings, having their thumbs and their great toes cut off, gathered *their food* under my table: as I therefore have done, so God has recompensed me: and they brought him to Jerusalem, and he died there. 8 And the children of Judas fought against Jerusalem, and took it, and smote with the edge of the sword, and they burnt the city with fire. 9 And afterwards the children of Judas went down to fight with the Chananite dwelling in the hill country, and the south, and the plain country. 10 And Judas went to the Chananite who dwelt in Chebron; and Chebron came out against him; [[and the name of Chebron before was Cariatharbocsepher:]] and they smote Sessi, and Achiman, and Tholmi, children of Enac. 11 And they went up thence to the inhabitants of Dabir; but the name of Dabir was before Cariathsepher, the city of Letters. 12 And Chaleb said, Whosoever shall smite the city of Letters, and shall first take it, I will give to him Ascha my daughter to wife. 13 And Gothoniel the younger son of Kenez the brother of Chaleb took it; and Chaleb gave him his daughter Ascha to wife. 14 And it came to pass as she went in, that Gothoniel urged her to ask a field of her father; and she murmured and cried from off her ass, Thou hast sent me forth into a south land: and Chaleb said to her, What is thy request? 15 And Ascha said to him, Give me, I pray thee, a blessing, for thou hast sent me forth into a south land, and thou shalt give me the ransom of water: and Chaleb gave her according to her heart the ransom of the upper *springs* and the ransom of the low *springs*. 16 And the children of Jothor the Kenite the father-in-law of Moses went up from the city of palm-trees with the children of Judas, to the wilderness that is in the south of Juda, which is at the descent of Arad, and they dwelt with the people. 17 And Judas went with Symeon his brother, and smote the Chananite that inhabited Sepheth, and they utterly destroyed them; and they called the name of the city Anathema. 18 But Judas did not inherit Gaza nor her coasts, nor Ascalon nor her coasts, nor Accaron nor her coasts, *nor* Azotus nor the lands around it. 19 And the Lord was with Judas, and he inherited the mountain; for they were not able to destroy the inhabitants of the valley, for Rechab prevented them. 20 And they gave Chebron to Chaleb, as Moses said; and thence he inherited the three cities of the children of Enac. 21 But the children of Benjamin did not take the inheritance of the Jebusite who dwelt in Jerusalem; and the Jebusite dwelt with the children of Benjamin in Jerusalem until this day. 22 And the sons of Joseph, they also went up to Baethel; and the Lord was with them. 23 And they encamped and surveyed Baethel: and the name of the city before was Luza. 24 And the spies looked, and behold, a man went out of the city, and they took him; and they said to him, Shew us the way into the city, and we will deal mercifully with thee. 25 And he shewed them the way into the city; and they smote the city with the edge of the sword; but they let go the man and his family. 26 And the man went into the land of Chettin, and built there a city, and called the name of it Luza; this *is* its name until this day. 27 And Manasse did not drive out *the inhabitants of* Baethsan, which is a city of Scythians, nor her towns, nor her suburbs; nor Thanac, nor her towns; nor the inhabitants of Dor, nor her suburbs, nor her towns; nor the inhabitant of Balac, nor her suburbs, nor her towns; nor the inhabitants of Magedo, nor her suburbs, nor her towns; nor the inhabitants of Jeblaam, nor her suburbs, nor her towns; and the Chananite began

to dwell in this land. 28 And it came to pass when Israel was strong, that he made the Chananite tributary, but did not utterly drive them out. 29 And Ephraim did not drive out the Chananite that dwelt in Gazer; and the Chananite dwelt in the midst of him in Gazer, and became tributary. 30 And Zabulon did not drive out the inhabitants of Kedron, nor the inhabitants of Domana: and the Chananite dwelt in the midst of them, and became tributary to them. 31 And Aser did not drive out the inhabitants of Accho, and *that people* became tributary to him, nor the inhabitants of Dor, nor the inhabitants of Sidon, nor the inhabitants of Dalaph, nor Aschazi, nor Chebda, nor Nai, nor Ereo. 32 And Aser dwelt in the midst of the Chananite who inhabited the land, for he could not drive him out. 33 And Nephthali did not drive out the inhabitants of Baethsamys, nor the inhabitants of Baethanach; and Nephthali dwelt in the midst of the Chananite who inhabited the land: but the inhabitants of Bethsamys and of Baetheneth became tributary to them. 34 And the Amorite drove out the children of Dan into the mountains, for they did not suffer them to come down into the valley. 35 And the Amorite began to dwell in the mountain of shells, in which *are* bears, and foxes, in Myrsinon, and in Thalabin; and the hand of the house of Joseph was heavy upon the Amorite, and he became tributary to them. 36 And the border of the Amorite *was* from the going up of Acrabin, from the rock and upwards.

Judg.2 1 And an angel of the Lord went up from Galgal to the *place of* weeping, and to Baethel, and to the house of Israel, and said to them, Thus says the Lord, I brought you up out of Egypt, and I brought you into the land which I sware to your fathers; and I said, I will never break my covenant that I have made with you. 2 And ye shall make no covenant with them that dwell in this land, neither shall ye worship their gods; but ye shall destroy their graven images, ye shall pull down their altars: but ye hearkened not to my voice, for ye did these things. 3 And I said, I will not drive them out from before you, but they shall be for a distress to you, and their gods shall be to you for an offence. 4 And it came to pass when the angel of the Lord spoke these words to all the children of Israel, that the people lifted up their voice, and wept. 5 And they named the name of that place Weepings; and they sacrificed there to the Lord. 6 And Joshua dismissed the people, and they went every man to his inheritance, to inherit the land. 7 And the people served the Lord all the days of Joshua, and all the days of the elders that lived many days with Joshua, as many as knew all the great work of the Lord, what things he had wrought in Israel. 8 And Joshua the son of Naue, the servant of the Lord, died, a hundred and ten years old. 9 And they buried him in the border of his inheritance, in Thamnathares, in mount Ephraim, on the north of the mountain of Gaas. 10 And all that generation were laid to their fathers: and another generation rose up after them, who knew not the Lord, nor yet the work which he wrought in Israel. 11 And the children of Israel wrought evil before the Lord, and served Baalim. 12 And they forsook the Lord God of their fathers, who brought them out of the land of Egypt, and walked after other gods, of the gods of the nations round about them; and they worshipped them. 13 And they provoked the Lord, and forsook him, and served Baal and the Astartes. 14 And the Lord was very angry with Israel; and he gave them into the hands of the spoilers, and they spoiled them; and he sold them into the hands of their enemies round about, and they could not any longer resist their enemies, 15 among whomsoever they went; and the hand of the Lord was against them for evil, as the Lord spoke, and as the Lord sware to them; and he greatly afflicted them. 16 And the Lord raised up judges, and the Lord save them out of the hands of them that spoiled them: and yet they hearkened not to the judges, 17 for they went a whoring after other gods, and worshipped them; and they turned quickly out of the way in which their fathers walked to hearken to the words of the Lord; they did not so. 18 And because the Lord raised them up judges, so the Lord was with the judge, and saved them out of the hand of their enemies all the days of the judge; for the Lord was moved at their groaning by reason of them that besieged them and afflicted them. 19 And it came to pass when the judge died, that they went back, and again corrupted *themselves* worse than their fathers to go after other gods to serve them an to worship them: they abandoned not their devices nor their stubborn ways. 20 And the Lord was very angry with Israel, and said, Forasmuch as this nation has forsaken my covenant which I commanded their fathers, and has not hearkened to my voice, 21 therefore I will not any more cast out a man of the nations before their face, which Joshua the son of Naue left in the land. And *the Lord* left *them*, 22 to prove Israel with them, whether they would keep the way of the Lord, to walk in it, as their fathers kept it, or no. 23 So the Lord will leave these nations, so as not to cast them out suddenly; and he delivered them not into the hand of Joshua.

Judg.3 1 And these *are* the nations which the Lord left to prove Israel with them, all that had not known the wars of Chanaan. 2 Only for the sake of the generations of Israel, to teach them war, only the men before them knew them not. 3 The five lordships of the Phylistines, and every Chananite, and the Sidonian, and the Evite who dwelt in Libanus from the mount of Aermon to Laboemath. 4 And *this* was done in order to prove Israel by them, to know whether they would obey the commands of the Lord, which he charged their fathers by the hand of Moses. 5 And the children of Israel dwelt in the midst of the Chananite, and the Chettite, and the Amorite, and the Pherezite, and the Evite, and the Jebusite. 6 And they took their daughters for wives to themselves, and they gave their daughters to their sons, and served their gods. 7 And the children of Israel did evil in the sight of the Lord, and forgot the Lord their God, and served Baalim and the groves. 8 And the Lord was very angry with Israel, and sold them into the hand of Chusarsathaim king of Syria of the rivers: and the children of Israel served Chusarsathaim eight years. 9 And the children of Israel cried to the Lord; and the Lord raised up a saviour to Israel, and he saved them, Gothoniel the son of Kenez, the brother of Chaleb younger than himself. 10 And the Spirit of the Lord came upon him, and he judged

Israel; and he went out to war against Chusarsathaim: and the Lord delivered into his hand Chusarsathaim king of Syria of the rivers, and his hand prevailed against Chusarsathaim. 11 And the land was quiet forty years; and Gothoniel the son of Kenez died. 12 And the children of Israel continued to do evil before the Lord: and the Lord strengthened Eglom king of Moab against Israel, because they had done evil before the Lord. 13 And he gathered to himself all the children of Ammon and Amalec, and went and smote Israel, and took possession of the city of Palm-trees. 14 And the children of Israel served Eglom the king of Moab eighteen years. 15 And the children of Israel cried to the Lord; and he raised up to them a saviour, Aod the son of Gera a son of Jemeni, a man who used both hands alike: and the children of Israel sent gifts by his hand to Eglom king of Moab. 16 And Aod made himself a dagger of two edges, of a span long, and he girded it under his cloak upon his right thigh. 17 And he went, and brought the presents to Eglom king of Moab, and Eglom *was* a very handsome man. 18 And it came to pass when *Aod* had made an end of offering his gifts, that he dismissed those that brought the gifts. 19 And he himself returned from the quarries that are by Galgal; and Aod said, I have a secret errand to thee, O king! and Eglom said to him, Be silent: and he sent away from his presence all who waited upon him. 20 And Aod went in to him; and he sat in his own upper summer chamber quite alone; and Aod said, I have a message from God to thee, O king: and Eglom rose up from his throne near him. 21 And it came to pass as he arose, that Aod stretched forth his left hand, and took the dagger off his right thigh, and plunged it into his belly; 22 and drove in also the haft after the blade, and the fat closed in upon the blade, for he drew not out the dagger from his belly. 23 And Aod went out to the porch, and passed out by the appointed *guards*, and shut the doors of the chamber upon him, and locked *them*. 24 And he went out: and Eglom's servants came, and saw, and behold, the doors of the upper chamber *were* locked; and they said, Does he not uncover his feet in the summer-chamber? 25 And they waited till they were ashamed, and, behold, there was no one that opened the doors of the upper chamber; and they took the key, and opened them; and, behold, their lord was fallen down dead upon the earth. 26 And Aod escaped while they were in a tumult, and no one paid attention to him; and he passed the quarries, and escaped to Setirotha. 27 And it came to pass when Aod came into the land of Israel, that he blew the horn in mount Ephraim, and the children of Israel came down with him from the mountain, and he *was* before them. 28 And he said to them, Come down after me, for the Lord God has delivered our enemies, even Moab, into our hand; and they went down after him, and seized on the fords of Jordan before Moab, and he did not suffer a man to pass over. 29 And they smote Moab on that day about ten thousand men, every *lusty* person and every mighty man; and not a man escaped. 30 So Moab was humbled in that day under the hand of Israel, and the land had rest eighty years; and Aod judged them till he died. 31 And after him rose up Samegar the son of Dinach, and smote the Philistines to the number of six hundred men with a ploughshare *such as is drawn by* oxen; and he too delivered Israel.

Judg.4 1 And the children of Israel continued to do evil against the Lord; and Aod was dead. 2 And the Lord sold the children of Israel into the hand of Jabin king of Chanaan, who ruled in Asor; and the chief of his host was Sisara, and he dwelt in Arisoth of the Gentiles. 3 And the children of Israel cried to the Lord, because he had nine hundred chariots of iron; and he mightily oppressed Israel twenty years. 4 And Debbora, a prophetess, the wife of Lapidoth, —she judged Israel at that time. 5 And she sat under the palm-tree of Debbora between Rama and Baethel in mount Ephraim; and the children of Israel went up to her for judgment. 6 And Debbora sent and called Barac the son of Abineem out of Cades Nephthali, and she said to him, Has not the Lord God of Israel commanded thee? and thou shalt depart to mount Thabor, and shalt take with thyself ten thousand men of the sons of Nephthali and of the sons of Zabulon. 7 And I will bring to thee to the torrent of Kison Sisara the captain of the host of Jabin, and his chariots, and his multitude, and I will deliver them into thine hands. 8 And Barac said to her, If thou wilt go with me, I will go; and if thou wilt not go, I will not go; for I know not the day on which the Lord prospers his messenger with me. 9 And she said, I will surely go with thee; but know that thy honour shall not attend on the expedition on which thou goest, for the Lord shall sell Sisara into the hands of a women: and Debbora arose, and went with Barac out of Cades. 10 And Barac called Zabulon and Nephthali out of Cades, and there went up at his feet ten thousand men, and Debbora went up with him. 11 And Chaber the Kenite had removed from Caina, from the sons of Jobab the father-in-law of Moses, and pitched his tent by the oak of the covetous ones, which is near Kedes. 12 And it was told Sisara that Barac the son of Abineem was gone up to mount Thabor. 13 And Sisara summoned all his chariots, nine hundred chariots of iron and all the people with him, from Arisoth of the Gentiles to the brook of Kison. 14 And Debbora said to Barac, Rise up, for this *is* the day on which the Lord has delivered Sisara into thy hand, for the Lord shall go forth before thee: and Barac went down from mount Thabor, and ten thousand men after him. 15 And the Lord discomfited Sisara, and all his chariots, and all his army, with the edge of the sword before Barac: and Sisara descended from off his chariot, and fled on his feet. 16 And Barac pursued after the chariots and after the army, into Arisoth of the Gentiles; and the whole army of Sisara fell by the edge of the sword, there was not one left. 17 And Sisara fled on his feet to the tent of Jael the wife of Chaber the Kenite his friend: for there was peace between Jabin king of Asor and the house of Chaber the Kenite. 18 And Jael went, out to meet Sisara, and said to him, Turn aside, my lord, turn aside to me, fear not: and he turned aside to her into the tent; and she covered him with a mantle. 19 And Sisara said to her, Give me, I pray thee, a little water to drink, for I am thirsty: and she opened a bottle of milk, and gave him to drink, and covered him. 20 And Sisara said to her, Stand now by the door of the tent,

and it shall come to pass if any man come to thee, and ask of thee, and say, Is there *any* man here? then thou shalt say, There is not. 21 And Jael the wife of Chaber took a pin of the tent, and took a hammer in her hand, and went secretly to him, and fastened the pin in his temple, and it went through to the earth, and he fainted away, and darkness fell upon him and he died. 22 And, behold, Barac *was* pursuing Sisara: and Jael went out to meet him, and he said to him, Come, and I will shew thee the man whom thou seekest: and he went in to her; and, behold, Sisara was fallen dead, and the pin *was* in his temple. 23 So God routed Jabin king of Chanaan in that day before the children of Israel. 24 And the hand of the children of Israel prevailed more and more against Jabin king of Chanaan, until they utterly destroyed Jabin king of Chanaan.

Judg.5 1 And Debbora and Barac son of Abineem sang in that day, saying, 2 A revelation was made in Israel when the people were made willing: Praise ye the Lord. 3 Hear, ye kings, and hearken, rulers: I will sing, it is I *who will sing* to the Lord, it is I, I will sing a psalm to the Lord the god of Israel. 4 O Lord, in thy going forth on Seir, when thou wentest forth out of the land of Edom, the earth quaked and the heaven dropped dews, and the clouds dropped water. 5 The mountains were shaken before the face of the Lord Eloi, this Sina before the face of the Lord God of Israel. 6 In the days of Samegar son of Anath, in the days of Jael, they deserted the ways, and went in by-ways; they went in crooked paths. 7 The mighty men in Israel failed, they failed until Debbora arose, until she arose a mother in Israel. 8 They chose new gods; then the cities of rulers fought; there was not a shield or spear seen among forty thousand in Israel. 9 My heart *inclines* to the orders given in Israel; ye that are willing among the people, bless the Lord. 10 Ye that mount a she-ass at noon-day, ye that sit on the judgment-seat, and walk by the roads of them that sit in judgment by the way; declare 11 *ye that are delivered* from the noise of disturbers among the drawers of water; there shall they relate righteous acts: O Lord, increase righteous acts in Israel: then the people of the Lord went down to the cities. 12 Awake, awake, Debbora; awake, awake, utter a song: arise, Barac, and lead thy captivity captive, son of Abineem. 13 Then went down the remnant to the strong, the people of the Lord went down for him among the mighty ones from me. 14 Ephraim rooted them out in Amalec, behind thee was Benjamin among thy people: the inhabitants of Machir came down with me searching out the enemy, and from Zabulon came they that draw with the scribe's pen of record. 15 And princess in Issachar were with Debbora and Barac, thus she sent Barac on his feet in the valleys into the portions of Ruben; great *pangs* reached to the heart. 16 Why did they sit between the sheep-folds to hear the bleating of flocks for the divisions of Ruben? *there were* great searchings of heart. 17 Galaad *is* on the other side of Jordan where he pitched his tents; and why does Dan remain in ships? Aser sat down on the sea-coasts, and he will tabernacle at his ports. 18 The people Zabulon exposed their soul to death, and Nephthali came to the high places of their land. 19 Kings set themselves in array, then the kings of Chanaan fought in Thanaach at the water of Mageddo; they took no gift of money. 20 The stars from heaven set themselves in array, they set themselves *to fight* with Sisara out of their paths. 21 The brook of Kison swept them away, the ancient brook, the brook Kison: my mighty soul will trample him down. 22 When the hoofs of the horse were entangled, his mighty ones earnestly hasted 23 to curse Meroz: Curse ye *it*, said the angel of the Lord; cursed *is* every one that dwells in it, because they came not to the help of the Lord, to his help among the mighty. 24 Blessed among women be Jael wife of Chaber the Kenite; let her be blessed above women in tents. 25 He asked for water, she gave him milk in a dish; she brought butter of princes. 26 She stretched forth her left hand to the nail, and her right to the hand workman's hammer, and she smote Sisara with it, she nailed through his head and smote him; she nailed through his temples. 27 He rolled down between her feet; he fell and lay between her feet; he bowed and fell: where he bowed, there he fell dead. 28 The mother of Sisara looked down through the window out of the loophole, *saying*, Why was his chariot ashamed? why did the wheels of his chariots tarry? 29 Her wise ladies answered her, and she returned answers to herself, *saying*, 30 Will they not find him dividing the spoil? he will surely be gracious to every man: *there are* spoils of dyed garments for Sisara, spoils of various dyed garments, dyed embroidered garments, they *are* the spoils for his neck. 31 Thus let all thine enemies perish, O Lord: and they that love him shall be as the going forth of the sun in his strength. 32 And the land had rest forty years.

Judg.6 1 And the children of Israel did evil in the sight of the Lord, and the Lord gave them into the hand of Madiam seven years. 2 And the hand of Madiam prevailed against Israel: and the children of Israel made for themselves because of Madiam the caves in the mountains, and the dens, and the holes in the rocks. 3 And it came to pass when the children of Israel sowed, that Madiam and Amalec went up, and the children of the east went up together with them. 4 And they encamped against them, and destroyed their fruits until they came to Gaza; and they left not the support of life in the land of Israel, not even ox or ass among the herds. 5 For they and their stock came up, and their tents were with them, as the locust in multitude, and there was no number to them and their camels; and they came to the land of Israel, and laid it waste. 6 And Israel was greatly impoverished because of Madiam. 7 And the children of Israel cried to the Lord because of Madiam. 8 And the Lord sent a prophet to the children of Israel; and he said to them, Thus says the Lord God of Israel, I am he that brought you up out of the land of Egypt, and I brought you up out of the house of your bondage. 9 And I delivered you out of the hand of Egypt, and out of the hand of all that afflicted you, and I cast them out before you; and I gave you their land. 10 And I said to you, I *am* the Lord your God: ye shall not fear the gods of the Amorites, in whose land ye dwell; but ye hearkened not to my voice. 11 And an angel of the Lord came, and sat down under the fir tree, which was in Ephratha in the land of Joas father of Esdri; and Gedeon his son *was* threshing wheat in a wine-press in order to escape from the face of Madiam. 12 And the angel of the Lord appeared to him and said to him, The Lord *is* with thee, thou mighty in strength. 13 And Gedeon said to him, *Be gracious* with me, my Lord: but if the Lord is with us, why have these evils found us? and where are all his miracles, which our fathers have related to us, saying, Did not the Lord bring us up out of Egypt? and now he has cast us out, and given us into the hand of Madiam. 14 And the angel of the Lord turned to him, and said, Go in this thy strength, and thou shalt save Israel out of the hand of Madiam: behold, I have sent thee. 15 And Gedeon said to him, *Be gracious* with me, my Lord: whereby shall I save Israel? behold, my thousand is weakened in Manasse, and I am the least in my father's house. 16 And the angel of the Lord said to him, The Lord shall be with thee, and thou shalt smite Madiam as one man. 17 And Gedeon said to him, If now I have found mercy in thine eyes, and thou wilt do this day for me all that thou hast spoken of with me, 18 depart not hence until I come to thee, and I will bring forth an offering and offer it before thee: and he said, I will remain until thou return. 19 And Gedeon went in, and prepared a kid of the goats, and an ephah of fine flour unleavened; and he put the flesh in the basket, and poured the broth into the pot, and brought them forth to him under the turpentine tree, and drew nigh. 20 And the angel of God said to him, Take the flesh and the unleavened cakes, and put them on that rock, and pour out the broth close by: and he did so. 21 And the angel of the Lord stretched out the end of the rod that was in his hand, and touched the flesh and the unleavened bread; and fire came up out of the rock, and consumed the flesh and the unleavened bread, and the angel of the Lord vanished from his sight. 22 And Gedeon saw that he was an angel of the Lord; and Gedeon said, Ah, ah, Lord my God! for I have seen the angel of the Lord face to face. 23 And the Lord said to him, Peace be to thee, fear not, thou shalt not die. 24 And Gedeon built there an altar to the Lord, and called it The peace of the Lord, until this day, as it is still in Ephratha of the father of Esdri. 25 And it came to pass in that night, that the Lord said to him, Take the young bullock which thy father has, even the second bullock of seven years old, and thou shalt destroy the altar of Baal which thy father has, and the grove which is by it thou shalt destroy. 26 And thou shalt build an altar to the Lord thy God on the top of this Maozi in the ordering *it*, and thou shalt take the second bullock, and shalt offer up whole-burnt-offerings with the wood of the grove, which thou shalt destroy. 27 And Gedeon took ten men of his servants, and did as the Lord spoke to him: and it came to pass, as he feared the house of his father and the men of the city if he should do it by day, that he did it by night. 28 And the men of the city rose up early in the morning; and behold, the altar of Baal had been demolished, and the grove by it had been destroyed; and they saw the second bullock, which Gedeon offered on the altar that had been built. 29 And a man said to his neighbour, Who has done this thing? and they enquired and searched, and learnt that Gedeon the son of Joas had done this thing. 30 And the men of the city said to Joas, Bring out thy son, and let him die, because he has destroyed the altar of Baal, and because he has destroyed the grove that is by it. 31 And Gedeon the son of Joas said to all the men who rose up against him, Do ye now plead for Baal, or will ye save him? whoever will plead for him, let him be slain this morning: if he be a god let him plead for himself, *because* one has thrown down his altar. 32 And he called it in that day Jerobaal, saying, Let Baal plead thereby, because his altar has been thrown down. 33 And all Madiam, and Amalek, and the sons of the east gathered themselves together, and encamped in the valley of Jezrael. 34 And the Spirit of the Lord came upon Gedeon, and he blew with the horn, and Abiezer came to help after him. 35 And *Gedeon* sent messengers into all Manasse, and into Aser, and into Zabulon, and into Nephthali; and he went up to meet them. 36 And Gedeon said to God, If thou wilt save Israel by my hand, as thou hast said, 37 behold, I put the fleece of wool in the threshing-floor: if there be dew on the fleece only, and drought on all the ground, I shall know that thou wilt save Israel by my hand, as thou hast said. 38 And it was so: and he rose up early in the morning, and wrung the fleece, and dew dropped from the fleece, a bowl full of water. 39 And Gedeon said to God, Let not, I pray thee, thine anger be kindled with me, and I will speak yet once; I will even yet make one trial more with the fleece: let now the drought be upon the fleece only, and let there be dew on all the ground. 40 And God did so in that night; and there was drought on the fleece only, and on all the ground there was dew.

Judg.7 1 And Jerobaal rose early, the same is Gedeon, and all the people with him, and encamped at the fountain of Arad; and the camp of Madiam was to the north of him, *reaching* from Gabaathamorai, in the valley. 2 And the Lord said to Gedeon, The people with thee *are* many, so that I may not deliver Madiam into their hand, lest at any time Israel boast against me, saying, My hand has saved me. 3 And now speak in the ears of the people, saying, Who *is* afraid and fearful? let him turn and depart from mount Galaad: and there returned of the people twenty-two thousand, and ten thousand were left. 4 And the Lord said to Gedeon, The people is yet numerous; bring them down to the water, and I will purge them there for thee: and it shall come to pass that of whomsoever I shall say to thee, This one shall go with thee, *even* he shall go with thee; and of whomsoever I shall say to thee, This one shall not go with thee, *even* he shall not go with thee. 5 And he brought the people down to the water; and the Lord said to Gedeon, Whosoever shall lap of the water with his tongue as if a dog should lap, thou shalt set him apart, and *also* whosoever shall bow down upon his knees to drink. 6 And the number of those that lapped with their hand to their mouth was three hundred men; and all the rest of the people bowed upon their knees to drink water. 7 And the Lord said to Gedeon, I will save you by the three hundred men that lapped, and I will give Madiam into thy hand; and all the *rest of the* people shall go every one to his place. 8 And they took the provision of the people in their hand, and their horns; and he sent away every man of Israel each to his tent, and he strengthened the three hundred; and the army of Madiam were beneath him in the valley. 9 And it came to

pass in that night that the Lord said to him, Arise, go down into the camp, for I have delivered it into thy hand. 10 And if thou art afraid to go down, go down thou and thy servant Phara into the camp. 11 And thou shalt hear what they shall say, and afterwards thy hands shall be strong, and thou shalt go down into the camp: and he went down and Phara his servant to the extremity of the *companies of* fifty, which were in the camp. 12 And Madiam and Amalec and all the children of the east *were* scattered in the valley, as the locust for multitude; and there was no number to their camels, but they were as the sand on the seashore for multitude. 13 And Gedeon came, and behold a man *was* relating to his neighbour a dream, and he said, Behold, I have dreamed a dream, and behold, a cake of barley bread rolling into the camp of Madiam, and it came as far as a tent, and smote it, and it fell, and it turned it up, and the tent fell. 14 And his neighbour answered and said, This is none other than the sword of Gedeon, son of Joas, a man of Israel: God has delivered Madiam and all the host into his hand. 15 And it came to pass when Gedeon heard the account of the dream and the interpretation of it, that he worshipped the Lord, and returned to the camp of Israel, and said, Rise, for the Lord has delivered the camp of Madiam into our hand. 16 And he divided the three hundred men into three companies, and put horns in the hands of all, and empty pitchers, and torches in the pitchers: 17 and he said to them, Ye shall look at me, and so shall ye do; and behold, I will go into the beginning of the host, and it shall come to pass *that* as I do, so shall ye do. 18 And I will sound with the horn, and all ye with me shall sound with the horn round about the whole camp, and ye shall say, For the Lord and Gedeon. 19 And Gedeon and the hundred men that were with him came to the extremity of the army in the beginning of the middle watch; and they completely roused the guards, and sounded with the horns, and they broke the pitchers that were in their hands, 20 and the three companies sounded with the horns, and broke the pitchers, and held the torches in their left hands, and in their right hands their horns to sound with; and they cried out, A sword for the Lord and for Gedeon. 21 And *every* man stood in his place round about the host; and all the host ran, and sounded *an alarm*, and fled. 22 And they sounded with the three hundred horns; and the Lord set *every* man's sword in all the host against his neighbour. 23 And the host fled as far as Bethseed Tagaragatha Abel-meula to Tabath; and the men of Israel from Nephthali, and from Aser, and from all Manasse, came to help, and followed after Madiam. 24 And Gedeon sent messengers into all mount Ephraim, saying, Come down to meet Madiam, and take to yourselves the water as far as Baethera and Jordan: and every man of Ephraim cried out, and they took the water before hand unto Baethera and Jordan. 25 And they took the princess of Madiam, even Oreb and Zeb; and they slew Oreb in Sur Oreb, and they slew Zeb in Jakephzeph; and they pursued Madiam, and brought the heads of Oreb and Zeb to Gedeon from beyond Jordan.

Judg.8 1 And the men of Ephraim said to Gedeon, What *is* this *that* thou hast done to us, in that thou didst not call us when thou wentest to fight with Madiam? and they chode with him sharply. 2 And he said to them, What have I now done in comparison of you? *is* not the gleaning of Ephraim better than the vintage of Abiezer? 3 The Lord has delivered into your hand the princes of Madiam, Oreb and Zeb; and what could I do in comparison of you? Then was their spirit calmed toward him, when he spoke this word. 4 And Gedeon came to Jordan, and went over, himself and the three hundred with him, hungry, yet pursuing. 5 And he said to the men of Socchoth, Give, I pray you, bread to feed this people that follow me; because they are faint, and behold, I am following after Zebee and Salmana, kings of Madiam. 6 And the princes of Socchoth said, *Are* the hands of Zebee and Salmana now in thy hand, that we should give bread to thy host? 7 And Gedeon said, Therefore when the Lord gives Zebee and Salmana into my hand, then will I tear your flesh with the thorns of the wilderness, and the Barkenim. 8 And he went up thence to Phanuel, and spoke to them likewise: and the men of Phanuel answered him as the men of Socchoth *had* answered him. 9 And Gedeon said to the men of Phanuel, When I return in peace, I will break down this tower. 10 And Zebee and Salmana *were* in Carcar, and their host *was* with them, about fifteen thousand, all that were left of all the host of the aliens; and they that fell *were* a hundred and twenty thousand men that drew the sword. 11 And Gedeon went up by the way of them that dwelt in tents, eastward of Nabai and Jegebal; and he smote the host, and the host was secure. 12 And Zebee and Salmana fled; and he pursued after them, and took the two kings of Madiam, Zebee and Salmana, and discomfited all the army. 13 And Gedeon the son of Joas returned from the battle, down from the battle of Ares. 14 And he took prisoner a young lad of the men of Socchoth, and questioned him; and he wrote to him the names of the princes of Socchoth and of their elders, seventy-seven men. 15 And Gedeon came to the princes of Socchoth, and said, Behold Zebee and Salmana, about whom ye reproached me, saying, *Are* the hands of Zebee and Salmana now in thy hand, that we should give bread to thy men that are faint? 16 And he took the elders of the city with the thorns of the wilderness and the Barkenim, and with them he tore the men of the city. 17 And he overthrew the tower of Phanuel, and slew the men of the city. 18 And he said to Zebee and Salmana, Where *are* the men whom ye slew in Thabor? and they said, As thou, so *were* they, according to the likeness of the son of a king. 19 And Gedeon said, They were my brethren and the sons of my mother: *as* the Lord lives, if ye had preserved them alive, I would not have slain you. 20 And he said to Jether his first-born, Rise and slay them; but the lad drew not his sword, for he was afraid, for he was yet very young. 21 And Zebee and Salmana said, Rise thou and fall upon us, for thy power *is* as that of a man; and Gedeon arose, and slew Zebee and Salmana: and he took the round ornaments that were on the necks of their camels. 22 And the men of Israel said to Gedeon, Rule, *my* lord, over us, both thou, and thy son, and thy son's son; for thou hast saved us out of the hand of Madiam. 23 And Gedeon said to them, I will not rule, and my son shall not rule among you; the Lord shall rule over you. 24 And Gedeon said to them, I will make

a request of you, and do ye give me every man an earring out of his spoils: for they had golden earrings, for they were Ismaelites. 25 And they said, We will certainly give them: and he opened his garment, and each man cast therein an earring of his spoils. 26 And the weight of the golden earrings which he asked, was a thousand and seven hundred pieces of gold, besides the crescents, and the chains, and the garments, and the purple cloths that were on the kings of Madiam, and besides the chains that were on the necks of their camels. 27 And Gedeon made an ephod of it, an set it in his city in Ephratha; and all Israel went thither a whoring after it, and it became a stumbling-block to Gedeon and his house. 28 And Madiam, was straitened before the children of Israel, and they did not lift up their head any more; and the land had rest forty years in the days of Gedeon. 29 And Jerobaal the son of Joas went and sat in his house. 30 And Gedeon had seventy sons begotten of his body, for he had many wives. 31 And his concubine was in Sychem, and she also bore him a son, and gave him the name Abimelech. 32 And Gedeon son of Joas died in his city, and he was buried in the sepulchre of Joas his father in Ephratha of Abi-Esdri. 33 And it came to pass when Gedeon was dead, that the children of Israel turned, and went a whoring after Baalim, and made for themselves a covenant with Baal that he should be their god. 34 And the children of Israel remembered not the Lord their God who had delivered them out of the hand of all that afflicted them round about. 35 And they did not deal mercifully with the house of Jerobaal, (the same is Gedeon) according to all the good which he did to Israel.

Judg.9 1 And Abimelech son of Jerobaal went to Sychem to his mother's brethren; and he spoke to them and to all the kindred of the house of his mother's father, saying, 2 Speak, I pray you, in the ears of all the men of Sychem, saying, Which *is* better for you, that seventy men, even all the sons of Jerobaal, should reign over you, or that one man should reign over you? and remember that I am your bone and your flesh. 3 And his mother's brethren spoke concerning him in the ears of all the men of Sychem all these words; and their heart turned after Abimelech, for they said, He is our brother. 4 And they gave him seventy *pieces* of silver out of the house of Baalberith; and Abimelech hired for himself vain and cowardly men, and they went after him. 5 And he went to the house of his father to Ephratha, and slew his brethren the sons of Jerobaal, seventy men upon one stone; but Joatham the youngest son of Jerobaal was left, for he hid himself. 6 And all the men of Sicima, and all the house of Bethmaalo, were gathered together, and they went and made Abimelech king by the oak of Sedition, which was at Sicima. 7 And it was reported to Joatham, and he went and stood on the top of mount Garizin, and lifted up his voice, and wept, and said to them, Hear me, ye men of Sicima, and God shall hear you. 8 The trees went forth on a time to anoint a king over them; and they said to the olive, Reign over us. 9 But the olives said to them, Shall I leave my fatness, with which men shall glorify God, and go to be promoted over the trees? 10 And the trees said to the fig-tree, Come, reign over us. 11 But the fig-tree said to them, Shall I leave my sweetness an my good fruits, and go to be promoted over the trees? 12 And the trees said to the vine, Come, reign over us. 13 And the vine said to them, Shall I leave my wine that cheers God and men, and go to be promoted over the trees? 14 Then all the trees said to the bramble, Come thou and *reign* over us. 15 And the bramble said to the trees, If ye in truth anoint me to reign over you, come, stand under my shadow; and if not, let fire come out from me and devour the cedars of Libanus. 16 And now, if ye have done it in truth and integrity, and have made Abimelech king, and if ye have wrought well with Jerobaal, and with his house, and if ye have done to him according to the reward of his hand, 17 as my father fought for you, and put his life in jeopardy, and delivered you out of the hand of Madiam; 18 and ye are risen up this day against the house of my father, and have slain his sons, being seventy men, upon one stone, and have made Abimelech the son of his bondwoman king over the men of Sicima, because he is your brother: 19 if then ye have done truly and faithfully with Jerobaal, and with his house this day, rejoice ye in Abimelech, and let him also rejoice over you: 20 but if not, let fire come out from Abimelech, and devour the men of Sicima, and the house of Bethmaalo; and let fire come out from the men of Sicima and from the house of Bethmaalo, and devour Abimelech. 21 And Joatham fled, and ran away, and went as far as Baeer, and dwelt there out of the way of his brother Abimelech. 22 And Abimelech reigned over Israel three years. 23 And God sent an evil spirit between Abimelech and the men of Sicima; and the men of Sicima dealt treacherously with the house of Abimelech: 24 to bring the injury done to the seventy sons of Jerobaal, and to lay their blood upon their brother Abimelech, who slew them, and upon the men of Sicima, because they strengthened his hands to slay his brethren. 25 And the men of Sicima set liers in wait against him on the top of the mountains, and robbed every one who passed by them on the way; and it was reported to the king Abimelech. 26 And Gaal son of Jobel came, and his brethren, and passed by Sicima, and the men of Sicima trusted in him. 27 And they went out into the field, and gathered their grapes, and trod them, and made merry; and they brought *the grapes* into the house of their god, and ate and drank, and cursed Abimelech. 28 And Gaal the son of Jobel said, Who is Abimelech, and who is the son of Sychem, that we should serve him? *Is he* not the son of Jerobaal, and *is* not Zebul his steward, his servant with the son of Emmor the father of Sychem? and why should we serve him? 29 And would that this people were under my hand! then would I remove Abimelech, and I would say to him, Multiply thy host, and come out. 30 And Zebul the ruler of the city heard the words of Gaal the son of Jobel, and he was very angry. 31 And he sent messengers to Abimelech secretly, saying, Behold, Gaal the son of Jobel and his brethren are come to Sychem; and behold, they have besieged the city against thee. 32 And now rise up by night, thou and the people with thee, and lay wait in the field. 33 And it shall come to pass in the morning at sunrising, thou shalt rise up early and draw toward the city; and behold, he and the people with him will come forth

against thee, and thou shalt do to him according to thy power. 34 And Abimelech and all the people with him rose up by night, and formed an ambuscade against Sychem in four companies. 35 And Gaal the son of Jobel went forth, and stood by the door of the gate of the city: and Abimelech and the people with him rose up from the ambuscade. 36 And Gaal the son of Jobel saw the people, and said to Zebul, Behold, a people comes down from the top of the mountains: and Zebul said to him, Thou seest the shadow of the mountains as men. 37 And Gaal continued to speak and said, Behold, a people comes down westward from the part bordering on the middle of the land, and another company comes by the way of Helon Maonenim. 38 And Zebul said to him, And where is thy mouth as thou spokest, Who is Abimelech that we should serve him? *Is* not this the people whom thou despisedst? go forth now, and set the battle in array against him. 39 And Gaal went forth before the men of Sychem, and set the battle in array against Abimelech. 40 And Abimelech pursued him, and he fled from before him; and many fell down slain as far as the door of the gate. 41 And Abimelech entered into Arema, and Zebul cast out Gaal and his brethren, so that they should not dwell in Sychem. 42 And it came to pass on the second day that the people went out into the field, and *one* brought word to Abimelech. 43 And he took the people, and divided them into three companies, and formed an ambush in the field; and he looked, and, behold, the people went forth out of the city, and he rose up against them, and smote them. 44 And Abimelech and the chiefs of companies that were with him rushed forward, and stood by the door of the gate of the city; and the two *other* companies rushed forward upon all that were in the field, and smote them. 45 And Abimelech fought against the city all that day, and took the city, and slew the people that were in it, and destroyed the city, and sowed it with salt. 46 And all the men of the tower of Sychem heard, and came to the gathering of Baethel-berith. 47 And it was reported to Abimelech, that all the men of the tower of Sychem were gathered together. 48 And Abimelech went up to the mount of Selmon, and all the people that were with him; and Abimelech took an axe in his hand, and cut down a branch of a tree, and took it, and laid it on his shoulders; and said to the people that were with him, What ye see me doing, do quickly as I. 49 And they cut down likewise even every man a branch, and went after Abimelech, and laid them against the place of gathering, and burnt the place of gathering over them with fire; and they died, even all the men of the tower of Sicima, about a thousand men and women. 50 And Abimelech went out of Baethel-berith, and encamped against Thebes, and took it. 51 And there was a strong tower in the midst of the city; and thither all the men and the women of the city fled, and shut *the door* without them, and went up on the roof of the tower. 52 And Abimelech drew near to the tower, and they besieged it; and Abimelech drew near to the door of the tower to burn it with fire. 53 And a woman cast a piece of a millstone upon the head of Abimelech, and broke his skull. 54 And he cried out quickly to the young man his armour- bearer, and said to him, Draw thy sword, and slay me, lest at any time they should say, A woman slew him: and his young man thrust him through and he died. 55 And the men of Israel saw that Abimelech was dead; and they went each to his place. 56 So God requited the wickedness of Abimelech, which he wrought against his father, in slaying his seventy brethren. 57 And all the wickedness of the men of Sychem God requited upon their head; and the curse of Joatham the son of Jerobaal came upon them.

Judg.10 1 And after Abimelech Thola the son of Phua rose up to save Israel, *being* the son of his father's brother, a man of Issachar; and he dwelt in Samir in mount Ephraim. 2 And he judged Israel twenty-three years, and died, and was buried in Samir. 3 And after him arose Jair of Galaad, and he judged Israel twenty-two years. 4 And he had thirty -two sons riding on thirty-two colts, and they had thirty-two cities; and they called them Jair's towns until this day in the land of Galaad. 5 And Jair died, and was buried in Rhamnon. 6 And the children of Israel did evil again in the sight of the Lord, and served Baalim, and Astaroth, and the gods of Aram, and the gods of Sidon, and the gods of Moab, and the gods of the children of Ammon, and the gods of the Phylistines; and they forsook the Lord, and did not serve him. 7 And the Lord was very angry with Israel, and sold them into the hands of the Phylistines, and into the hand of the children of Ammon. 8 And they afflicted and bruised the children of Israel at that time eighteen years, all the children of Israel beyond Jordan in the land of the Amorite in Galaad. 9 And the children of Ammon went over Jordan to fight with Juda, and Benjamin, and with Ephraim; and the children of Israel were greatly afflicted. 10 And the children of Israel cried to the Lord, saying, We have sinned against thee, because we have forsaken God, and served Baalim. 11 And the Lord said to the children of Israel, Did I not *save you* from Egypt and from the Amorite, and from the children of Ammon, and from the Phylistines, 12 and from the Sidonians, and Amalec, and Madiam, who afflicted you? and ye cried to me, and I saved you out of their hand? 13 Yet ye forsook me and served other gods; therefore I will not save you any more. 14 Go, and cry to the gods whom ye have chosen to yourselves, and let them save you in the time of your affliction. 15 And the children of Israel said to the Lord, We have sinned: do thou to us according to all *that is* good in thine eyes; only deliver us this day. 16 And they put away the strange gods from the midst of them, and served the Lord only, and his soul was pained for the trouble of Israel. 17 And the children of Ammon went up, and encamped in Galaad; and the children of Israel were gathered together and encamped on the hill. 18 And the people the princes of Galaad said every man to his neighbour, Who *is* he that shall begin to fight against the children of Ammon? he shall even be head over all that dwell in Galaad.

Judg.11 1 And Jephthae the Galaadite *was* a mighty man; and he *was* the son of a harlot, who bore Jephthae to Galaad. 2 And the wife of Galaad bore him sons; and the sons of his wife grew up, and they cast out Jephthae, and said to him, Thou shalt not inherit in the house of our father, for thou art the son of a concubine. 3 And Jephthae

fled from the face of his brethren, and dwelt in the land of Tob; and vain men gathered to Jephthae, and went out with him. 4 And it came to pass when the children of Ammon prepared to fight with Israel, 5 that the elders of Galaad went to fetch Jephthae from the land of Tob. 6 And they said to Jephthae, Come, and be our head, and we will fight with the sons of Ammon. 7 And Jephthae said to the elders of Galaad, Did ye not hate me, and cast me out of my father's house, and banish me from you? and wherefore are ye come to me now when ye want me? 8 And the elders of Galaad said to Jephthae, Therefore have we now turned to thee, that thou shouldest go with us, and fight against the sons of Ammon, and be our head over all the inhabitants of Galaad. 9 And Jephthae said to the elders of Galaad, If ye turn me back to fight with the children of Ammon, and the Lord should deliver them before me, then will I be your head. 10 And the elders of Galaad said to Jephthae, The Lord be witness between us, if we shall not do according to thy word. 11 And Jephthae went with the elders of Galaad, and the people made him head and ruler over them: and Jephthae spoke all his words before the Lord in Massepha. 12 And Jephthae sent messengers to the king of the children of Ammon, saying, What have I to do with thee, that thou hast come against me to fight in my land? 13 And the king of the children of Ammon said to the messengers of Jephthae, Because Israel took my land when he went up out of Egypt, from Arnon to Jaboc, and to Jordan: now then return them peaceably and I will depart. 14 And Jephthae again sent messengers to the king of the children of Ammon, 15 and said to him, Thus says Jephthae, Israel took not the land of Moab, nor the land of the children of Ammon; 16 for in their going up out of Egypt Israel went in the wilderness as far as the sea of Siph, and came to Cades. 17 And Israel sent messengers to the king of Edom, saying, I will pass, if it please thee, by thy land: and the king of Edom complied not: and *Israel* also sent to the king of Moab, and he did not consent; and Israel sojourned in Cades. 18 And *they* journeyed in the wilderness, and compassed the land of Edom and the land of Moab: and they came by the east of the land of Moab, an encamped in the country beyond Arnon, and came not within the borders of Moab, for Arnon *is* the border of Moab. 19 And Israel sent messengers to Seon king of the Amorite, king of Esbon, and Israel said to him, Let us pass, we pray thee, by thy land to our place. 20 And Seon did not trust Israel to pass by his coast; and Seon gathered all his people, and they encamped at Jasa; and he set the battle in array against Israel. 21 And the Lord God of Israel delivered Seon and all his people into the hand of Israel, and they smote him; and Israel inherited all the land of the Amorite who dwelt in that land, 22 from Arnon and to Jaboc, and from the wilderness to Jordan. 23 And now the Lord God of Israel has removed the Amorite from before his people Israel, and shalt thou inherit his *land?* 24 Wilt thou not inherit those possessions which Chamos thy god shall cause thee to inherit; and shall not we inherit the *land of* all those whom the Lord our God has removed from before you? 25 And now art thou any better than Balac son of Sepphor, king of Moab? did he indeed fight with Israel, or indeed make war with him, 26 when *Israel* dwelt in Esebon and in its coasts, and in the land of Aroer and in its coasts, and in all the cities by Jordan, three hundred years? and wherefore didst thou not recover them in that time? 27 And now I have not sinned against thee, but thou wrongest me in preparing war against me: may the Lord the Judge judge this day between the children of Israel and the children of Ammon. 28 But the king of the children of Ammon hearkened not to the words of Jephthae, which he sent to him. 29 And the spirit of the Lord came upon Jephthae, and he passed over Galaad, and Manasse, and passed by the watch-tower of Galaad to the other side of the children of Ammon. 30 And Jephthae vowed a vow to the Lord, and said, If thou wilt indeed deliver the children of Ammon into my hand, 31 then it shall come to pass that whosoever shall first come out of the door of my house to meet me when I return in peace from the children of Ammon, he shall be the Lord's: I will offer him up for a whole-burnt-offering. 32 And Jephthae advanced to meet the sons of Ammon to fight against them; and the Lord delivered them into his hand. 33 And he smote them from Aroer till *one* comes to Arnon, in number twenty cities, and as far as Ebelcharmim, with a very great destruction: and the children of Ammon were straitened before the children of Israel. 34 And Jephthae came to Massepha to his house; and behold, his daughter came forth to meet him with timbrels and dances; and she was his only child, he had not another son or daughter. 35 And it came to pass when he saw her, that he rent his garments, and said, Ah, ah, my daughter, thou hast indeed troubled me, and thou wast the cause of my trouble; and I have opened my mouth against thee to the Lord, and I shall not be able to return from it. 36 And she said to him, Father, hast thou opened thy mouth to the Lord? Do to me accordingly as *the word* went out of thy mouth, in that the Lord has wrought vengeance for thee on thine enemies of the children of Ammon. 37 And she said to her father, Let my father now do this thing: let me alone for two months, and I will go up and down on the mountains, and I will bewail my virginity, I and my companions. 38 And he said, Go: and he sent her away for two months; and she went, and her companions, and she bewailed her virginity on the mountains. 39 And it came to pass at the end of the two months that she returned to her father; and he performed upon her his vow which he vowed; and she knew no man: 40 and it was an ordinance in Israel, *That* the daughters of Israel went from year to year to bewail the daughter of Jephthae the Galaadite for four days in a year.

Judg.12 1 And the men of Ephraim assembled *themselves*, and passed on to the north, and said to Jephthae, Wherefore didst thou go over to fight with the children of Ammon, and didst not call us to go with thee? we will burn thy house over thee with fire. 2 And Jephthae said to them, I and my people and the children of Ammon were very much engaged in war; and I called for you, and ye did not save me out of their hand. 3 And I saw that thou wert no helper, and I put my life in my hand, and passed on to the sons of Ammon; and the Lord delivered them into my hand: and wherefore are ye come up against me this day to

fight with me? 4 And Jephthae gathered all the men of Galaad, and fought with Ephraim; and the men of Galaad smote Ephraim, because they that were escaped of Ephraim said, Ye *are* of Galaad in the midst of Ephraim and in the midst of Manasse. 5 And Galaad took the fords of Jordan before Ephraim; and they that escaped of Ephraim said to them, Let us go over: and the men of Galaad said, Art thou an Ephrathite? and he said, No. 6 Then they said to him, Say now Stachys; and he did not rightly pronounce it so: and they took him, and slew him at the fords of Jordan; and there fell at that time of Ephraim two and forty thousand. 7 And Jephthae judged Israel six years; and Jephthae the Galaadite died, and was buried in his city Galaad. 8 And after him Abaissan of Bethleem judged Israel. 9 And he had thirty sons, and thirty daughters, whom he sent forth; and he brought in thirty daughters for his sons from without; and he judged Israel seven years. 10 And Abaissan died, and was buried in Bethleem. 11 And after him Ælom of Zabulon judged Israel ten years. 12 And Ælom of Zabulon died, and was buried in Ælom in the land of Zabulon. 13 And after him Abdon the son of Ellel, the Pharathonite, judged Israel. 14 And he had forty sons, and thirty grandsons, that rode upon seventy colts: and he judged Israel eight years. 15 And Abdon the son of Ellel, the Pharathonite, died, and was buried in Pharathon in the land of Ephraim in the mount of Amalec.

Judg.13 1 And the children of Israel yet again committed iniquity before the Lord; and the Lord delivered them into the hand of the Phylistines forty years. 2 And there was a man of Saraa, of the family of the kindred of Dan, and his name was Manoe, and his wife was barren, and bore not. 3 And an angel of the Lord appeared to the woman, and said to her, Behold, thou art barren and hast not born; yet thou shalt conceive a son. 4 And now be very cautious, and drink no wine nor strong drink, and eat no unclean thing; 5 for behold, thou art with child, and shalt bring forth a son; and there shall come no razor upon his head, for the child shall be a Nazarite to God from the womb; and he shall begin to save Israel from the hand of the Phylistines. 6 And the woman went in, and spoke to her husband, saying, A man of God came to me, and his appearance *was as* of an angel of God, very dreadful; and I did not ask him whence he was, and he did not tell me his name. 7 And he said to me, Behold, thou art with child, and shalt bring forth a son; and now drink no wine nor strong drink, and eat no unclean thing; for the child shall be holy to God from the womb until the day of his death. 8 And Manoe prayed to the Lord and said, I pray thee, O Lord my lord, *concerning* the man of God whom thou sentest; let him now come to us once more, and teach us what we shall do to the child about to be born. 9 And the Lord heard the voice of Manoe, and the angel of God came yet again to the woman; and she sat in the field, and Manoe her husband was not with her. 10 And the woman hasted, and ran, and brought word to her husband, and said to him, Behold the man who came in *the other* day to me has appeared to me. 11 And Manoe arose and followed his wife, and came to the man, and said to him, Art thou the man that spoke to the woman? and the angel said, I *am*. 12 And Manoe said, Now shall *thy* word come to pass: what shall be the ordering of the child, and our dealings with him? 13 And the angel of the Lord said to Manoe, Of all things concerning which I spoke to the woman, she shall beware. 14 She shall eat of nothing that comes of the vine yielding wine, and let her not drink wine or strong liquor, and let her not eat anything unclean: all things that I have charged her she shall observe. 15 And Manoe said to the angel of the Lord, Let us detain thee here, and prepare before thee a kid of the goats. 16 And the angel of the Lord said to Manoe, If thou shouldest detain me, I will not eat of thy bread; and if thou wouldest offer a whole-burnt-offering, to the Lord thou shalt offer it: for Manoe knew not that he *was* an angel of the Lord. 17 And Manoe said to the angel of the Lord, What *is* thy name, that *when* thy word shall come to pass, we may glorify thee? 18 And the angel of the Lord said to him, Why dost thou thus ask after my name; whereas it is wonderful? 19 And Manoe took a kid of the goats and its meat-offering, and offered it on the rock to the Lord; and *the angel* wrought a distinct work, and Manoe and his wife were looking on. 20 And it came to pass when the flame went up above the altar toward heaven, that the angel of the Lord went up in the flame; and Manoe and his wife were looking, and they fell upon their face to the earth. 21 And the angel appeared no more to Manoe and to his wife: then Manoe knew that this *was* an angel of the Lord. 22 And Manoe said to his wife, We shall surely die, because we have seen God. 23 But his wife said to him, If the Lord were pleased to slay us, he would not have received of our hand a whole-burnt-offering and a meat-offering; and he would not have shewn us all these things, neither would he have caused us to hear all these things as at this time. 24 And the woman brought forth a son, and she called his name Sampson; and the child grew, and the Lord blessed him. 25 And the Spirit of the Lord began to go out with him in the camp of Dan, and between Saraa and Esthaol.

Judg.14 1 And Sampson went down to Thamnatha, and saw a woman in Thamnatha of the daughters of the Philistines. 2 And he went up and told his father and his mother, and said, I have seen a woman in Thamnatha of the daughters of the Phylistines; and now take her to me for a wife. 3 And his father and his mother said to him, Are there no daughters of thy brethren, and *is there not* a woman of all my people, that thou goest to take a wife of the uncircumcised Philistines? And Sampson said to his father, Take her for me, for she *is* right in my eyes. 4 And his father and his mother knew not that it was of the Lord, that he sought to be revenged on the Philistines: and at that time the Philistines lorded it over Israel. 5 And Sampson and his father and his mother went down to Thamnatha, and he came to the vineyard of Thamnatha; and behold, a young lion roared in meeting him. 6 And the spirit of the Lord came powerfully upon him, and he crushed him as he would have crushed a kid of the goats, and there was nothing in his hands: and he told not his father and his mother what he had done. 7 And they went down and spoke to the woman, and she was pleasing in the eyes of Sampson. 8 And after some time he returned to take her, and he turned aside to see the carcase of the lion; and behold, a swarm of bees, and honey *were* in the mouth of the lion. 9 And he took it into his hands, and went on eating, and he went to his father and his mother, and gave to them, and they did eat; but he told them not that he took the honey out of the mouth of the lion. 10 And his father went down to the woman, and Sampson made there a banquet for seven days, for so the young men are used to do. 11 And it came to pass when they saw him, that they took thirty guests, and they were with him. 12 And Sampson said to them, I propound you a riddle: if ye will indeed tell it me, and discover it within the seven days of the feast, I will you give thirty sheets and thirty changes of raiment. 13 And if ye cannot tell it me, ye shall give me thirty napkins and thirty changes of apparel: and they said to him, Propound thy riddle, and we will hear it. 14 And he said to them, Meat came forth of the eater, and sweetness out of the strong: and they could not tell the riddle for three days. 15 And it came to pass on the fourth day, that they said to the wife of Sampson, Deceive now thy husband, and let him tell thee the riddle, lest we burn thee and thy father's house with fire: did ye invite us to do us violence? 16 And Sampson's wife wept before him, and said, Thou dost but hate me, and lovest me not; for the riddle which thou hast propounded to the children of my people thou hast not told me: and Sampson said to her, If I have not told it to my father and my mother, shall I tell it to thee? 17 And she wept before him the seven days, during which their banquet lasted: and it came to pass on the seventh day, that he told her, because she troubled him; and she told it to the children of her people. 18 And the men of the city said to him on the seventh day, before sunrise, What *is* sweeter than honey? and what *is* stronger than a lion? and Sampson said to them, If ye had not ploughed with my heifer, ye would not have known my riddle. 19 And the Spirit of the Lord came upon him powerfully, and he went down to Ascalon, and destroyed of the inhabitants thirty men, and took their garments, and gave the changes of raiment to them that told the riddle; and Sampson was very angry, and went up to the house of his father. 20 And the wife of Sampson was *given* to one of his friends, with whom he was on terms of friendship.

Judg.15 1 And it came to pass after a time, in the days of wheat harvest, that Sampson visited his wife with a kid, and said, I will go in to my wife even into the chamber: but her father did not suffer him to go in. 2 And her father spoke, saying, I said that thou didst surely hate her, and I gave her to one of thy friends: *is* not her younger sister better than she? let her be to thee instead of her. 3 And Sampson said to them, Even for once am I guiltless with regard to the Philistines, in that I do mischief among them. 4 And Sampson went and caught three hundred foxes, and took torches, and turned tail to tail, and put a torch between two tails, and fastened it. 5 And he set fire to the torches, and sent *the foxes* into the corn of the Philistines; and every thing was burnt from the threshing floor to the standing corn, and even to the vineyard and olives. 6 And the Philistines said, Who *has done* these things? and they said, Sampson the son-in-law of the Thamnite, because he has taken his wife, and given her to one of his friends; and the Philistines went up, and burnt her and her father's house with fire. 7 And Sampson said to them, Though ye may have dealt thus with her, verily I will be avenged of you, and afterwards I will cease. 8 And he smote them leg on thigh *with* a great overthrow; and went down and dwelt in a cave of the rock Etam. 9 And the Philistines went up, and encamped in Juda, and spread themselves abroad in Lechi. 10 And the men of Juda said, Why are ye come up against us? and the Philistines said, We are come up to bind Sampson, and to do to him as he has done to us. 11 And the three thousand men of Juda went down to the hole of the rock Etam, and they said to Sampson, Knowest thou not that the Philistines rule over us? and what *is* this *that* thou hast done to us? and Sampson said to them, As they did to me, so have I done to them. 12 And they said to him, We are come down to bind thee to deliver thee into the hand of the Philistines: and Sampson said to them, Swear to me that ye will not fall upon me yourselves. 13 And they spoke to him, saying, Nay, but we will only bind thee fast, and deliver thee into their hand, and will by no means slay thee: and they bound him with two new ropes, and brought him from that rock. 14 And they came to Lechi: and the Philistines shouted, and ran to meet him: and the Spirit of the Lord came mightily upon him, and the ropes that were upon his arms became as tow which is burnt with fire; and his bonds were consumed from off his hands. 15 And he found the jaw- bone of an ass that had been cast away, and he put forth his hand and took it, and smote with it a thousand men. 16 And Sampson said, With the jaw-bone of an ass I have utterly destroyed them, for with the jaw-bone of an ass I have smitten a thousand men. 17 And it came to pass when he ceased speaking, that he cast the jaw-bone out of his hand; and he called that place the Lifting of the jaw-bone. 18 And he was very thirsty, and wept before the Lord, and said, Thou hast been well pleased to grant this great deliverance by the hand of thy servant, and new shall I die for thirst, and fall into the hand of the uncircumcised? 19 And God broke open a hollow place in the jaw, and there came thence water, and he drank; and his spirit returned and he revived: therefore the name of the fountain was called 'The well of the invoker,' which is in Lechi, until this day. 20 And he judged Israel in the days of the Philistines twenty years.

Judg.16 1 And Sampson went to Gaza, and saw there a harlot, and went in to her. 2 And it was reported to the Gazites, saying, Sampson is come hither: and they compassed him and laid wait for him all night in the gate of the city, and they were quiet all the night, saying, Let us wait till the dawn appear, and we will slay him. 3 And Sampson slept till midnight, and rose up at midnight, and took hold of the doors of the gate of the city with the two posts, and lifted them up with the bar, and laid them on his shoulders, and he went up to the top of the mountain that is before Chebron, and laid them there. 4 And it came to pass after this that he loved a woman in Alsorech, and her name *was*

Dalida. 5 And the princess of the Philistines came up to her, and said to her, Beguile him, and see wherein his great strength *is*, and wherewith we shall prevail against him, and bind him to humble him; and we will give thee each eleven hundred *pieces* of silver. 6 And Dalida said to Sampson, Tell me, I pray thee, wherein *is* thy great strength, and wherewith thou shalt be bound that thou mayest be humbled. 7 And Sampson said to her, If they bind me with seven moist cords that have not been spoiled, then shall I be weak and be as one of ordinary men. 8 And the princess of the Philistines brought to her seven moist cords that had not been spoiled, and she bound him with them. 9 And the liers in wait remained with her in the chamber; and she said to him, the Philistines *are* upon thee, Sampson: and he broke the cords as if any one should break a thread of tow when it has touched the fire, and his strength was not known. 10 And Dalida said to Sampson, Behold, thou hast cheated me, and told me lies; now then tell me wherewith thou shalt be bound. 11 And he said to her, If they should bind me fast with new ropes with which work has not been done, then shall I be weak, and shall be as another man. 12 And Dalida took new ropes, and bound him with them, and the liers in wait came out of the chamber, and she said, The Philistines *are* upon thee, Sampson: and he broke them off his arms like a thread. 13 And Dalida said to Sampson, Behold, thou hast deceived me, and told me lies; tell me, I intreat thee, wherewith thou mayest be bound: and he said to her, If thou shouldest weave the seven locks of my head with the web, and shouldest fasten them with the pin into the wall, then shall I be weak as another man. 14 And it came to pass when he was asleep, that Dalida took the seven locks of his head, and wove them with the web, and fastened them with the pin into the wall, and she said, The Philistines *are* upon thee, Sampson: and he awoke out of his sleep, and carried away the pin of the web out of the wall. 15 And Dalida said to Sampson, How sayest thou, I love thee, when thy heart is not with me? this third time thou hast deceived me, and hast not told me wherein *is* thy great strength. 16 And it came to pass as she pressed him sore with her words continually, and straitened him, that his spirit failed almost to death. 17 Then he told her all his heart, and said to her, A razor has not come upon my head, because I have been a holy *one* of God from my mother's womb; if then I should be shaven, my strength will depart from me, and I shall be weak, and I shall be as all *other* men. 18 And Dalida saw that he told her all his heart, and she sent and called the princess of the Philistines, saying, Come up yet this once; for he has told me all his heart. And the chiefs of the Philistines went up to her, and brought the money in their hands. 19 And Dalida made Sampson sleep upon her knees; and she called a man, and he shaved the seven locks of his head, and she began to humble him, and his strength departed from him. 20 And Dalida said, The Philistines *are* upon thee, Sampson: and he awoke out of his sleep and said, I will go out as at former times, and shake myself; and he knew not that the Lord was departed from him. 21 And the Philistines took him, and put out his eyes, and brought him down to Gaza, and bound him with fetters of brass; and he ground in the prison-house. 22 And the hair of his head began to grow as before it was shaven. 23 And the chiefs of the Philistines met to offer a great sacrifice to their god Dagon, and to make merry; and they said, God has given into our hand our enemy Sampson. 24 And the people saw him, and sang praises to their god; for our god, *said they*, has delivered into our hand our enemy, who wasted our land, and who multiplied our slain. 25 And when their heart was merry, then they said, Call Sampson out of the prison-house, and let him play before us: and they called Sampson out of the prison-house, and he played before them; and they smote him with the palms of their hands, and set him between the pillars. 26 And Sampson said to the young man that held his hand, Suffer me to feel the pillars on which the house *rests*, and I will stay myself upon them. 27 And the house *was* full of men and woman, and there were all the chiefs of the Philistines, and on the roof *were* about three thousand men and woman looking at the sports of Sampson. 28 And Sampson wept before the Lord, and said, O Lord, my lord, remember me, I pray thee, and strengthen me, O God, yet this once, and I will requite one recompense to the Philistines for my two eyes. 29 And Sampson took hold of the two pillars of the house on which the house stood, and leaned on them, and laid hold of one with his right hand, and the other with his left. 30 And Sampson said, Let my wife perish with the Philistines: and he bowed himself mightily; and the house fell upon the princes, and upon all the people that were in it: and the dead whom Sampson slew in his death were more than those whom he slew in his life. 31 And his brethren and his father's house went down, and they took him; and they went up and buried him between Saraa and Esthaol in the sepulchre of his father Manoe; and he judged Israel twenty years.

Judg.17 1 And there was a man of mount Ephraim, and his name was Michaias. 2 And he said to his mother, The eleven hundred pieces of silver which thou tookest of thyself, and *about which* thou cursedst me, and spokest in my ears, behold, the silver *is* with me; I took it: and his mother said, Blessed *be* my son of the Lord. 3 And he restored the eleven hundred pieces of silver to his mother; and his mother said, I had wholly consecrated the money to the Lord out of my hand for my son, to make a graven and a molten *image*, and now I will restore it to thee. 4 But he returned the silver to his mother, and his mother took two hundred pieces of silver, and gave them to a silversmith, and he made it a graven and a molten image; and it was in the house of Michaias. 5 And the house of Michaias *was* to him the house of God, and he made an ephod and theraphin, and he consecrated one of his sons, and he became to him a priest. 6 And in those days there was no king in Israel; every man did that which was right in his own eyes. 7 And there was a young man in Bethleem of the tribe of Juda, and he *was* a Levite, and he was sojourning there. 8 And the man departed from Bethleem the city of Juda to sojourn in whatever place he might find; and he came as far as mount Ephraim, and to the house of Michaias to accomplish his journey. 9 And Michaias said to him, Whence comest thou? and he said to him, I am a Levite of Bethleem Juda, and I go to sojourn in any place I may find. 10 And Michaias said to him, Dwell with me, and be to me a father and a priest; and I will give thee ten pieces of silver by the year, and a change of raiment, and thy living. 11 And the Levite went and began to dwell with the man; and the young man was to him as one of his sons. 12 And Michaias consecrated the Levite, and he became to him a priest, and he was in the house of Michaias. 13 And Michaias said, Now I know that the Lord will do me good, because a Levite has become my priest.

Judg.18 1 In those days there was no king in Israel; and in those days the tribe of Dan sought for itself an inheritance to inhabit, because no inheritance had fallen to it until that day in the midst of the tribes of the children of Israel. 2 And the sons of Dan sent from their families five men of valour, from Saraa and from Esthaol, to spy out the land and to search it; and they said to them, Go and search out the land. And they came as far as the mount of Ephraim to the house of Michaias and they lodged there, 3 in the house of Michaias, and they recognised the voice of the young man the Levite, and turned in thither; and said to him, Who brought thee in hither? and what doest thou in this place? and what hast thou here? 4 And he said to them, Thus and thus did Michaias to me, and he hired me, and I became his priest. 5 And they said to him, Enquire now of God, and we shall know whether our way will prosper, on which we are going. 6 And the priest said to them, Go in peace; your way in which ye go, *is* before the Lord. 7 And the five men went on, and came to Laisa; and they saw the people in the midst of it dwelling securely, at ease as *is* the manner of the Sidonians, and there is no one perverting or shaming a matter in the land, no heir extorting treasures; and they are far from the Sidonians, and they have no intercourse with any one. 8 And the five men came to their brethren to Saraa and Esthaol, and said to their brethren, Why sit ye here *idle*? 9 And they said, Arise, and let us go up against them, for we have seen the land, and, behold, *it is* very good, yet ye are still: delay not to go, an to enter in to possess the land. 10 And whensoever ye shall go, ye shall come in upon a people secure, and the land *is* extensive, for God has given it into your hand; a place where there is no want of anything that the earth affords. 11 And there departed thence of the families of Dan, from Saraa and from Esthaol, six hundred men, girded with weapons of war. 12 And they went up, and encamped in Cariathiarim in Juda; therefore it was called in that place the camp of Dan, until this day: behold, *it is* behind Cariathiarim. 13 And they went on thence to the mount of Ephraim, and came to the house of Michaias. 14 And the five men who went to spy out the land of Laisa answered, and said to their brethren, Ye know that there is in this place an ephod, and theraphin, and a graven and a molten image; and now consider what ye shall do. 15 And they turned aside there, and went into the house of the young man, the Levite, *even* into the house of Michaias, and asked him how he was. 16 And the six hundred men of the sons of Dan who were girded with their weapons of war stood by the door of the gate. 17 And the five men who went to spy out the land went up, and entered into the house of Michaias, and the priest stood. 18 And they took the graven image, and the ephod, and the theraphin, and the molten image; and the priest said to them, What are ye doing? 19 And they said to him, Be silent, lay thine hand upon thy mouth, and come with us, and be to us a father and a priest: *is it* better for thee to be the priest of the house of one man, or to be the priest of a tribe and house for a family of Israel? 20 And the heart of the priest was glad, and he took the ephod, and the theraphin, and the graven image, and the molten image, and went in the midst of the people. 21 So they turned and departed, and put their children and their property and their baggage before them. 22 They went some distance from the house of Michaias, and, behold, Michaias and the men in the houses near Michaias' house, cried out, and overtook the children of Dan. 23 And the children of Dan turned their face, and said to Michaias, What is the matter with thee that thou hast cried out? 24 And Michaias said, Because ye have taken my graven image which I made, and my priest, and are gone; and what have I remaining? and what *is* this *that* ye say to me, Why criest thou? 25 And the children of Dan said to him, Let not thy voice be heard with us, lest angry men run upon thee, and take away thy life, and the lives of thy house. 26 And the children of Dan went their way; and Michaias saw that they were stronger than himself, and he returned to his house. 27 And the children of Dan took what Michaias had made, and the priest that he had, and they came to Laisa, to a people quiet and secure; and they smote them with the edge of the sword, and burnt the city with fire. 28 And there was no deliverer, because *the city* is far from the Sidonians, and they have no intercourse with men, and it *is* in the valley of the house of Raab; and they built the city, and dwelt in it. 29 And they called the name of the city Dan, after the name of Dan their father, who was born to Israel; and the name of the city was Ulamais before. 30 And the children of Dan set up the graven image for themselves; and Jonathan son of Gerson son of Manasse, he and his sons were priests to the tribe of Dan till the time of the carrying away of the nation. 31 And they set up for themselves the graven image which Michaias made, all the days that the house of God was in Selom; and it was so in those days *that* there was no king in Israel.

Judg.19 1 And there was a Levite sojourning in the sides of mount Ephraim, and he took to himself a concubine from Bethleem Juda. 2 And his concubine departed from him, and went away from him to the house of her father to Bethleem Juda, and she was there four months. 3 And her husband rose up, and went after her to speak kindly to her, to recover her to himself; and he had his young man with him, and a pair of asses; and she brought him into the house of her father; and the father of the damsel saw him, and was well pleased to meet him. 4 And his father-in-law, the father of the damsel, constrained him, and he stayed with him for three days; and they ate and drank, and lodged there. 5 And it came to pass on the fourth day that they rose early, and he stood up to depart; and the father of the damsel said to his son-in-law, Strengthen thy heart with a morsel of bread, and afterwards ye shall go. 6 So they two

sat down together and ate and drank: and the father of the damsel said to her husband, Tarry now the night, and let thy heart be merry. 7 And the man rose up to depart; but his father-in-law constrained him, and he stayed and lodged there. 8 And he rose early in the morning on the fifth day to depart; and the father of the damsel said, Strengthen now thine heart, and quit thyself as a soldier till the day decline; and the two ate. 9 And the man rose up to depart, he and his concubine, and his young man; but his father-in-law the father of the damsel said to him, Behold now, the day has declined toward evening; lodge here, an let thy heart rejoice; and ye shall rise early to-morrow for your journey, and thou shalt go to thy habitation. 10 But the man would not lodge there, but he arose and departed, and came to the part opposite Jebus, (this is Jerusalem,) and *there was* with him a pair of asses saddled, and his concubine *was* with him. 11 And they came as far as Jebus: and the day had far advanced, and the young man said to his master, Come, I pray thee, and let us turn aside to this city of the Jebusites, and let us lodge in it. 12 And his master said to him, We will not turn aside to a strange city, where there is not one of the children of Israel, but we will pass on as far as Gabaa. 13 And he said to his young man, Come, and let us draw nigh to one of the places, and we will lodge in Gabaa or in Rama. 14 And they passed by and went on, and the sun went down upon them near to Gabaa, which is in Benjamin. 15 And they turned aside thence to go in to lodge in Gabaa; and they went in, and sat down in the street of the city, and there was no one who conducted them into a house to lodge. 16 And behold, an old man came out of the field from his work in the evening; and the man was of mount Ephraim, and he sojourned in Gabaa, and the men of the place *were* sons of Benjamin. 17 And he lifted up his eyes, and saw a traveller in the street of the city; and the old man said to him, Whither goest thou, and whence comest thou? 18 And he said to him, We are passing by from Bethleem Juda to the sides of mount Ephraim: I am from thence, and I went as far as Bethleem Juda, and I am going home, and there is no man to take me into his house. 19 Yet is there straw and food for our asses, and bread and wine for me and my handmaid and the young man with thy servants; there is no want of anything. 20 And the old man said, Peace *be* to thee; only be every want of thine upon me, only do thou by no means lodge in the street. 21 And he brought him into his house, and made room for his asses; and they washed their feet, and ate and drank. 22 And they *were* comforting their heart, when, behold, the men of the city, sons of transgressors, compassed the house, knocking at the door: and they spoke to the old man the owner of the house, saying, Bring out the man who came into thy house, that we may know him. 23 And the master of the house came out to them, and said, Nay, brethren, do not ye wrong, I pray you, after this man has come into my house; do not ye this folly. 24 Behold my daughter a virgin, and the man's concubine: I will bring them out, and humble ye them, and do to them that which is good in your eyes; but to this man do not this folly. 25 But the men would not consent to hearken to him; so the man laid hold of his concubine, and brought her out to them; and they knew her, and abused her all night till the morning, and let her go when the morning dawned. 26 And the woman came toward morning, and fell down at the door of the house where her husband was, until it was light. 27 And her husband rose up in the morning, and opened the doors of the house, and went forth to go on his journey; and, behold, the woman his concubine had fallen down by the doors of the house, and her hands were on the threshold. 28 And he said to her, Rise, and let us go; and she answered not, for she was dead: and he took her upon his ass, and went to his place. 29 And he took his sword, and laid hold of his concubine, and divided her into twelve parts, and sent them to every coast of Israel. 30 And it was so, that every one who saw it said, *Such a day* as this has not happened nor has been seen from the day of the going up of the children of Israel out of the land of Egypt until this day: take ye counsel concerning it, and speak.

Judg.20 1 And all the children of Israel went out, and all the congregation was gathered as one man, from Dan even to Bersabee, and in the land of Galaad, to the Lord at Massepha. 2 And all the tribes of Israel stood before the Lord in the assembly of the people of God, four hundred thousand footmen that drew sword. 3 And the children of Benjamin heard that the children of Israel were gone up to Massepha: and the children of Israel came and said, Tell us, where did this wickedness take place? 4 And the Levite, the husband of the woman that was slain, answered and said, I and my concubine went to Gabaa of Benjamin to lodge. 5 And the men of Gabaa rose up against me, and compassed the house by night against me; they wished to slay me, and they have humbled my concubine, and she is dead. 6 And I laid hold of my concubine, and divided her in pieces, and sent *the parts* into every coast of the inheritance of the children of Israel; for they have wrought lewdness and abomination in Israel. 7 Behold, all ye *are* children of Israel; and consider and take counsel here among yourselves. 8 And all the people rose up as one man, saying, No one of us shall return to his tent, and no one of us shall return to his house. 9 And now this *is* the thing which shall be done in Gabaa; we will go up against it by lot. 10 Moreover we will take ten men for a hundred for all the tribes of Israel, and a hundred for a thousand, and a thousand for ten thousand, to take provision, to cause them to come to Gabaa of Benjamin, to do to it according to all the abomination, which they wrought in Israel. 11 And all the men of Israel were gathered to the city as one man. 12 And the tribes of Israel sent men through the whole tribe of Benjamin, saying, What *is* this wickedness that has been wrought among you? 13 Now then give up the men the sons of transgressors that are in Gabaa, and we will put them to death, and purge out wickedness from Israel: but the children of Benjamin consented not to hearken to the voice of their brethren the children of Israel. 14 And the children of Benjamin were gathered from their cities to Gabaa, to go forth to fight with the children of Israel. 15 And the children of Benjamin from their cities were numbered in that day, twenty-three thousand, *every* man drawing a sword, besides the inhabitants of Gabaa, who were numbered

seven hundred chosen men of all the people, able to use both hands alike; 16 All these could sling with stones at a hair, and not miss. 17 And the men of Israel, exclusive of Benjamin, were numbered four hundred thousand men that drew sword; all these *were* men of war. 18 And they arose and went up to Baethel, and enquired of God: and the children of Israel said, Who shall go up for us first to fight with the children of Benjamin? And the Lord said, Juda shall go up first as leader. 19 And the children of Israel rose up in the morning, and encamped against Gabaa. 20 And they went out, all the men of Israel, to fight with Benjamin, and engaged with them at Gabaa. 21 And the sons of Benjamin went forth from Gabaa, and they destroyed in Israel on that day two and twenty thousand men down to the ground. 22 And the men of Israel strengthened themselves, and again engaged in battle in the place where they had engaged on the first day. 23 And the children of Israel went up, and wept before the Lord till evening, and enquired of the Lord, saying, Shall we again draw nigh to battle with our brethren the children of Benjamin? and the Lord said, Go up against them. 24 And the children of Israel advanced against the children of Benjamin on the second day. 25 And the children of Benjamin went forth to meet them from Gabaa on the second day, and destroyed of the children of Israel yet further eighteen thousand men down to the ground: all these drew sword. 26 And the children of Israel and all the people went up, and came to Baethel; and they wept, and sat there before the Lord; and they fasted on that day until evening, and offered whole- burnt-offerings and perfect sacrifices, before the Lord, 27 for the ark of the Lord God *was* there in those days, 28 and Phinees the son of Eleazar the son of Aaron stood before it in those days; and the children of Israel enquired of the Lord, saying, Shall we yet again go forth to fight with our brethren the sons of Benjamin? and the Lord said, Go up, to-morrow I will give them into your hands. 29 And the children of Israel set an ambush against Gabaa round about *it*. 30 And the children of Israel went up against the children of Benjamin on the third day, and arrayed themselves against Gabaa as before. 31 And the children of Benjamin went out to meet the people, and were all drawn out of the city, and began to smite and slay the people as before in the roads, whereof one goes up to Baethel, and one to Gabaa in the field, about thirty men of Israel. 32 And the children of Benjamin said, They fall before us as at the first: but the children of Israel said, Let us flee, and draw them out from the city into the roads; and they did so. 33 And all the men rose up out of their places, and engaged in Baal Thamar; and the liers in wait of Israel advanced from their place from Maraagabe. 34 And there came over against Gabaa ten thousand chosen men out of all Israel; and the fight *was* severe; and they knew not that evil was coming upon them. 35 And the Lord smote Benjamin before the children of Israel; and the children of Israel destroyed of Benjamin in that day a hundred and twenty-five thousand men: all these drew sword. 36 And the children of Benjamin saw that they were smitten; and the men of Israel gave place to Benjamin, because they trusted in the ambuscade which they had prepared against Gabaa. 37 And when they retreated, then the liers in wait rose up, and they moved toward Gabaa, and the whole ambush came forth, and they smote the city with the edge of the sword. 38 And the children of Israel had a signal of battle with the liers in wait, that they should send up a signal of smoke from the city. 39 And the children of Israel saw that the liers in wait had seized Gabaa, and they stood in line of battle; and Benjamin began to smite down wounded ones among the men of Israel about thirty men; for they said, Surely they fall again before us, as in the first battle. 40 And the signal went up increasingly over the city as a pillar of smoke; and Benjamin looked behind him, and behold the destruction of the city went up to heaven. 41 And the men of Israel turned back, and the men of Benjamin hasted, because they saw that evil had come upon them. 42 And they turned to the way of the wilderness from before the children of Israel, and fled: but the battle overtook them, and they from the cities destroyed them in the midst of them. 43 And they cut down Benjamin, and pursued him from Nua closely till they came opposite Gabaa on the east. 44 And there fell of Benjamin eighteen thousand men: all these were men of might. 45 And the rest turned, and fled to the wilderness to the rock of Remmon; and the children of Israel picked off of them five thousand men; and the children of Israel went down after them as far as Gedan, and they smote of them two thousand men. 46 And all that fell of Benjamin were twenty-five thousand men that drew sword in that day: all these were men of might. 47 And the rest turned, and fled to the wilderness to the rock of Remmon, even six hundred men; and they sojourned four months in the rock of Remmon. 48 And the children of Israel returned to the children of Benjamin, and smote them with the edge of the sword from the city of Methla, even to the cattle, and every thing that was found in all the cities: and they burnt with fire the cities they found.

Judg.21 1 Now the children of Israel swore in Massephath, saying, No man of us shall give his daughter to Benjamin for a wife. 2 And the people came to Baethel, and sat there until evening before God: and they lifted up their voice and wept with a great weeping; 3 and said, Wherefore, O Lord God of Israel, has this come to pass, that to-day one tribe should be counted as missing from Israel? 4 And it came to pass on the morrow that the people rose up early, and built there an altar, and offered up whole-burnt-offerings and peace offerings. 5 And the children of Israel said, Who of all the tribes of Israel, went not up in the congregation to the Lord? for there was a great oath concerning those who went not up to the Lord to Massephath, saying, He shall surely be put to death. 6 And the children of Israel relented toward Benjamin their brother, and said, To-day one tribe is cut off from Israel. 7 What shall we do for wives for the rest that remain? whereas we have sworn by the Lord, not to give them of our daughters for wives. 8 And they said, What one man is there of the tribes of Israel, who went not up to the Lord to Massephath? and, behold, no man came to the camp from Jabis Galaad to the assembly. 9 And the people were numbered, and there was not there a man

from the inhabitants of Jabis Galaad. 10 And the congregation sent thither twelve thousand men of the strongest, and they charged them, saying, Go ye and smite the inhabitants of Jabis Galaad with the edge of the sword. 11 And this shall ye do: every male and every woman that has known the lying with man ye shall devote to destruction, but the virgins ye shall save alive: and they did so. 12 And they found among the inhabitants of Jabis Galaad four hundred young virgins, who had not known man by lying with him; and they brought them to Selom in the land of Chanaan. 13 And all the congregation sent and spoke to the children of Benjamin in the rock Remmon, and invited them to make peace. 14 And Benjamin returned to the children of Israel at that time, and the children of Israel gave them the women whom they had save alive of the daughters of Jabis Galaad; and they were content. 15 And the people relented for Benjamin, because the Lord had made a breach in the tribes of Israel. 16 And the elders of the congregation said, What shall we do for wives for them that remain? for the women have been destroyed out of Benjamin. 17 And they said, There must be an inheritance of them that are escaped of Benjamin; and so a tribe shall not be destroyed out of Israel. 18 For we shall not be able to give them wives of our daughters, because we swore among the children of Israel, saying, Cursed is he that gives a wife to Benjamin. 19 And they said, Lo! now there is a feast of the Lord from year to year in Selom, which is on the north of Baethel, eastward on the way that goes up from Baethel to Sychem, and from the south of Lebona. 20 And they charged the children of Benjamin, saying, Go and lie in wait in the vineyards; 21 and ye shall see; and lo! if there come out the daughters of the inhabitants of Selom to dance in dances, then shall ye go out of the vineyards and seize for yourselves every man a wife of the daughters of Selom, and go ye into the land of Benjamin. 22 And it shall come to pass, when their fathers or their brethren come to dispute with us, that we will say to them, Grant them freely to us, for we have not taken every man his wife in the battle: because ye did not give to them according to the occasion, ye transgressed. 23 And the children of Benjamin did so; and they took wives according to their number from the dancers whom they seized: and they went and returned to their inheritance, and built the cities, and dwelt in them. 24 And the children of Israel went thence at that time every man to his tribe and his kindred; and they went thence every man to his inheritance. 25 And in those days there was no king in Israel; every man did that which was right in his own sight.

RUTH

Ruth1 1 And it came to pass when the judges ruled, that there was a famine in the land: and a man went from Bethleem Juda to sojourn in the land of Moab, he, and his wife, and his two sons. 2 And the man's name was Elimelech, and his wife's name Noemin, and the names of his two sons Maalon and Chelaion, Ephrathites of Bethleem of Juda: and they came to the land of Moab, and remained there. 3 And Elimelech the husband of Noemin died; and she was left, and her two sons. 4 And they took to themselves wives, women of Moab; the name of the one *was* Orpha, and the name of the second Ruth; and they dwelt there about ten years. 5 And both Maalon and Chelaion died also; and the woman was left of her husband and her two sons. 6 And she rose up and her two daughters-in-law, and they returned out of the country of Moab, for she heard in the country of Moab that the Lord *had* visited his people to give them bread. 7 And she went forth out of the place where she was, and her two daughters-in-law with her: and they went by the way to return to the land of Juda. 8 And Noemin said to her daughter-in-law, Go now, return each to the house of her mother: the Lord deal mercifully with you, as ye have dealt with the dead, and with me. 9 The Lord grant you that ye may find rest each of you in the house of her husband: and she kissed them; and they lifted up their voice, and wept. 10 And they said to her, We will return with thee to thy people. 11 And Noemin said, Return now, my daughters; and why do ye go with me? have I yet sons in my womb to be your husbands? 12 Turn now, my daughters, for I am too old to be married: for I said, Suppose I were married, and should bear sons; 13 would ye wait for them till they should be grown? or would ye refrain from being married for their sakes? Not so, my daughters; for I am grieved for you, that the hand of the Lord has gone forth against me. 14 And they lifted up their voice, and wept again; and Orpha kissed her mother-in-law and returned to her people; but Ruth followed her. 15 And Noemin said to Ruth, Behold, thy sister-in-law has returned to her people and to her gods; turn now thou also after thy sister-in-law. 16 And Ruth said, Intreat me not to leave thee, or to return from following thee; for whithersoever thou goest, I will go, and wheresoever thou lodgest, I will lodge; thy people *shall be* my people, and thy God my God. 17 And wherever thou diest, I will die, and there will I be buried: the Lord do so to me, and more also, *if I leave thee*, for death *only* shall divide between me and thee. 18 And Noemin seeing that she was determined to go with her, ceased to speak to her any more. 19 And they went both of them until they came to Bethleem: and it came to pass, when they arrived at Bethleem, that all the city rang with them, and they said, Is this Noemin? 20 And she said to them, Nay, do not call me Noemin; call me 'Bitter,' for the Mighty One has dealt very bitterly with me. 21 I went out full, and the Lord has brought me back empty: and why call ye me Noemin, whereas the Lord has humbled me and the Mighty One has afflicted me? 22 So Noemin and Ruth the Moabitess, her daughter-in-law, returned from the country of Moab; and they came to Bethleem in the beginning of barley harvest.

Ruth2 1 And Noemin had *a friend* an acquaintance of her husband, and the man *was* a mighty man of the kindred of Elimelech, and his name *was* Booz. 2 And Ruth the Moabitess said to Noemin, Let me go now to the field, and I will glean among the ears behind the man with whomsoever I shall find favour: and she said to her, Go, daughter. 3 And she went; and came and gleaned in the field behind the reapers; and she happened by chance to come on a portion of the land of Booz, of the kindred of Elimelech. 4 And, behold, Booz came from Bethleem, and said to the reapers, The Lord *be* with you: and they said to him, The Lord bless thee. 5 And Booz said to his servant who was set over the reapers, Whose *is* this damsel? 6 And his servant who was set over the reapers answered and said, It is the Moabitish damsel who returned with Noemin out of the land of Moab. 7 And she said, I pray you, let me glean and gather among the sheaves after the reapers: and she came and stood from morning till evening, and rested not *even* a little in the field. 8 And Booz said to Ruth, Hast thou not heard, *my* daughter? go not to glean in another field; and depart not thence, join thyself here with my damsels. 9 *Let* thine eyes *be* on the field where *my men* shall reap, and thou shalt go after them: behold, I have charged the young men not to touch thee: and when you shalt thirst, then thou shalt go to the vessels, and drink of that which the young men shall have drawn. 10 And she fell upon her face, and did reverence to the ground, and said to him, How is it that I have found grace in thine eyes, that thou shouldest take notice of me, whereas I am a stranger? 11 And Booz answered and said to her, It has fully been told me how thou hast dealt with thy mother-in-law after the death of thy husband; and how thou didst leave thy father and thy mother, and the land of thy birth, and camest to a people whom thou knewest not before. 12 The Lord recompense thy work; may a full reward be given thee of the Lord God of Israel, to whom thou hast come to trust under his wings. 13 And she said, Let me find grace in thy sight, my lord, because thou hast comforted me, and because thou hast spoken kindly to thy handmaid, and behold, I shall be as one of thy servants. 14 And Booz said to her, Now *it is* time to eat; come hither, and thou shalt eat of the bread, and thou shalt dip thy morsel in the vinegar: and Ruth sat by the side of the reapers: and Booz handed her meal, and she ate, and was satisfied, and left. 15 And she rose up to glean; and Booz charged his young men, saying, Let her even glean among the sheaves, and reproach her not. 16 And do ye by all means carry it for her, and ye shall surely let fall for her some of that which is heaped up; and let her eat, and glean, and rebuke her not. 17 So she gleaned in the field till evening, and beat out that she had gleaned, and it was about an ephah of barely. 18 And she took *it* up, and went into the city: and her mother-in-law saw what she had gleaned, and Ruth brought forth and gave to her the food which she had left from what she had been satisfied with. 19 And her mother-in-law said to her, Where hast thou gleaned to-day, and where hast thou wrought? blessed be he that took notice of thee. And Ruth told her mother-in-law where she *had* wrought, and said, The name of the man with whom I wrought to-day *is* Booz. 20 And Noemin said to her daughter-in-law, Blessed is he of the Lord, because he has not failed in his mercy with the living and with the dead: and Noemin said to her, The man is near akin to us, he is one of our relations. 21 And Ruth said to her mother-in-law, Yea, he said also to me, Keep close to my damsels, until the men shall have finished all my reaping. 22 And Noemin said to Ruth her daughter-in-law, *It is* well, daughter, that thou wentest out with his damsels; thus they shall not meet thee in another field. 23 And Ruth joined herself to the damsels of Booz to glean until they had finished the barley-harvest and the wheat-harvest.

Ruth3 1 And she lodged with her mother-in-law: and Noemin her mother-in-law said to her, My daughter, shall I not seek rest for thee, that it may be well with thee? 2 And now *is* not Booz our kinsman, with whose damsels thou wast? behold, he winnows barley this night in the floor. 3 But do thou wash, and anoint thyself, and put thy raiment upon thee, and go up to the threshing-floor: do not discover thyself to the man until he has done eating and drinking. 4 And it shall come to pass when he lies down, that thou shalt mark the place where he lies down, and shalt come and lift up the covering of his feet, and shalt lie down; and he shall tell thee what thou shalt do. 5 And Ruth said to her, All that thou shalt say, I will do. 6 And she went down to the threshing-floor, and did according to all that her mother-in-law enjoined her. 7 And Booz ate and drank, and his heart was glad, and he came to lie down by the side of the heap of corn; and she came secretly, and lifted up the covering of his feet. 8 And it came to pass at midnight that the man was amazed, and troubled, and behold, a woman lay at his feet. 9 And he said, Who art thou? and she said, I am thine handmaid Ruth; spread therefore thy skirt over thine handmaid, for thou art a near relation. 10 And Booz said, Blessed *be* thou of the Lord God, *my* daughter, for thou hast made thy latter kindness greater than the former, in that thou followest not after young men, whether *any be* poor or rich. 11 And now fear not, my daughter, whatever thou shalt say I will do to thee; for all the tribe of my people knows that thou art a virtuous woman. 12 And now I am truly akin to thee; nevertheless there is a kinsman nearer than I. 13 Lodge *here* for the night, and it shall be in the morning, if he will do the part of a kinsman to thee, well— let him do it: but if he will not do the part of a kinsman to thee, I will do the kinsman's part to thee, *as* the Lord lives; lie down till the morning. 14 And she lay at his feet until the morning; and she rose up before a man could know his neighbour; and Booz said, Let it not be known that a woman came into the floor. 15 And he said to her, Bring the apron that is upon thee: and she held it, and he measured six measures of barley, and put them upon her, and she went into the city. 16 And Ruth went in to her mother-in-law, and she said to her, *My* daughter! and *Ruth* told her all that the man had done to her. 17 And she said to her, He gave me these six measures of barley, for he said to me, Go not empty to thy mother-in-law. 18 And she said, Sit still, *my* daughter, until thou shalt know how the matter will fall out; for the man will not rest until the matter be accomplished this day.

Ruth4 1 And Booz went up to the gate, and sat there; and behold, the relative passed by, of whom Booz spoke: and Booz said to him, Turn aside, sit down here, such a one: and he turned aside and sat down. 2 And Booz took ten men of the elders of the city, and said, Sit ye here; and they sat down. 3 And Booz said to the relative, *The matter regards* the portion of the field which was our brother Elimelech's which was given to Noemin, now returning out of the land of Moab; 4 and I said, I will inform thee, saying, Buy it

before those that sit, and before the elders of my people: if thou wilt redeem it, redeem it, but if thou wilt not redeem it, tell me, and I shall know; for there is no one beside thee to do the office of a kinsman, and I am after thee: and he said, I am *here*, I will redeem it. 5 And Booz said, In the day of thy buying the field of the hand of Noemin and of Ruth the Moabitess the wife of the deceased, thou must also buy her, so as to raise up the name of the dead upon his inheritance. 6 And the kinsman said, I shall not be able to redeem it for myself, lest I mar my own inheritance; do thou redeem my right for thyself, for I shall not be able to redeem *it*. 7 And this *was* in former time the ordinance in Israel for redemption, and for a bargain, to confirm every word: A man loosed his shoe, and gave it to his neighbour that redeemed his right; and this was a testimony in Israel. 8 And the kinsman said to Booz, Buy my right for thyself: and he took off his shoe and gave it to him. 9 And Booz said to the elders and to all the people, Ye *are* this day witnesses, that I have bought all that was Elimelech's, and all that belonged to Chelaion and Maalon, of the hand of Noemin. 10 Moreover I have bought for myself for a wife Ruth the Moabitess, the wife of Maalon, to raise up the name of the dead upon his inheritance; so the name of the dead shall not be destroyed from among his brethren, and from the tribe of his people: ye *are* this day witnesses. 11 And all the people who were in the gate said, *We are* witnesses: and the elders said, The Lord make thy wife who goes into thy house, as Rachel and as Lia, who both *together* built the house of Israel, and wrought mightily in Ephratha, and there shall be a name *to thee* in Bethleem. 12 And let thy house be as the house of Phares, whom Thamar bore to Juda, of the seed which the Lord shall give thee of this handmaid. 13 And Booz took Ruth, and she became his wife, and he went in to her; and the Lord gave her conception, and she bore a son. 14 And the woman said to Noemin, Blessed *is* the Lord, who has not suffered a redeemer to fail thee this day, even to make thy name famous in Israel. 15 And he shall be to thee a restorer of thy soul, and one to cherish thy old age; for thy daughter- in-law which has loved thee, who is better to thee than seven sons, has born him. 16 And Noemin took the child and laid it in her bosom, and became a nurse to it. 17 And the neighbours gave it a name, saying, A son has been born to Noemin; and they called his name Obed; this *is* the father of Jessae the father of David. 18 And these *are* the generations of Phares: Phares begot Esrom: 19 Esrom begot Aram; and Aram begot Aminadab. 20 And Aminadab begot Naasson; and Naasson begot Salmon. 21 And Salmon begot Booz; and Booz begot Obed. 22 And Obed begot Jessae; and Jessae begot David.

1 KINGDOMS (I SAMUEL)

1-Kgdms1 1 There was a man of Armathaim Sipha, of mount Ephraim, and his name *was* Helkana, a son of Jeremeel the son of Elias the son of Thoke, in Nasib Ephraim. 2 And he *had* two wives; the name of the one *was* Anna, and the name of the second Phennana. And Phennana had children, but Anna had no child. 3 And the man went up from year to year from his city, from

Armathaim, to worship and sacrifice to the Lord God of Sabaoth at Selom: and *there were* Heli and his two sons Ophni and Phinees, the priests of the Lord. 4 And the day came, and Helkana sacrificed, and gave portions to his wife Phennana and her children. 5 And to Anna he gave a prime portion, because she had no child, only Helkana loved Anna more than the other; but the Lord *had* closed her womb. 6 For the Lord gave her no child in her affliction, and according to the despondency of her affliction; and she was dispirited on this account, that the Lord shut up her womb so as not to give her a child. 7 So she did year by year, in going up to the house of the Lord; and she was dispirited, and wept, and did not eat. 8 And Helkana her husband said to her, Anna: and she said to him, Here *am* I, my lord: and he said to her, What ails thee that thou weepest? and why dost thou not eat? and why does thy heart smite thee? *am* I not better to thee than ten children? 9 And Anna rose up after they had eaten in Selom, and stood before the Lord: and Heli the priest *was* on a seat by the threshold of the temple of the Lord. 10 And she *was* very much grieved in spirit, and prayed to the Lord, and wept abundantly. 11 And she vowed a vow to the Lord, saying, O Lord God of Sabaoth, if thou welt indeed look upon the humiliation of thine handmaid, and remember me, and give to thine handmaid a man- child, then will I indeed dedicate him to thee till the day of his death; and he shall drink no wine nor strong drink, and no razor shall come upon his head. 12 And it came to pass, while she was long praying before the Lord, that Heli the priest marked her mouth. 13 And she was speaking in her heart, and her lips moved, but her voice was not heard: and Heli accounted her a drunken woman. 14 And the servant of Heli said to her, How long wilt thou be drunken? take away thy wine from thee, and go out from the presence of the Lord. 15 And Anna answered and said, Nay, my lord, *I live* in a hard day, and I have not drunk wine or strong drink, and I pour out my soul before the Lord. 16 Count not thy handmaid for a pestilent woman, for by reason of the abundance of my importunity I have continued *my prayer* until now. 17 And Heli answered and said to her, Go in peace: the God of Israel give thee all thy petition, which thou hast asked of him. 18 And she said, Thine handmaid has found favour in thine eyes: and the woman went her way, and entered into her lodging, and ate and drank with her husband, and her countenance was no more sad. 19 And they rise early in the morning, and worship the Lord, and they go their way: and Helkana went into his house at Armathaim, and knew his wife Anna; and the Lord remembered her, and she conceived. 20 And it came to pass when the time was come, that she brought forth a son, and called his name Samuel, and said, Because I asked him of the Lord God of Sabaoth. 21 And the man Helkana and all his house went up to offer in Selom the yearly sacrifice, and his vows, and all the tithes of his land. 22 But Anna did not go up with him, for she said to her husband, *I will not go up* until the child goes up, when I have weaned him, and he shall be presented before the Lord, and he shall abide there continually. 23 And Helkana her husband said to her, Do that which is good in thine eyes, abide still until thou shalt have weaned him; but may the Lord establish that which comes out of thy mouth: and the woman tarried, and suckled her son until she had weaned him. 24 And she went up with him to Selom with a calf of three years old, and loaves, and an ephah of fine flour, and a bottle of wine: and she entered into the house of the Lord in Selom, and the child with them. 25 And they brought him before the Lord; and his father slew his offering which he offered from year to year to the Lord; and he brought near the child, and slew the calf; and Anna the mother of the child brought him to Heli. 26 And she said, I pray thee, my lord, as thy soul liveth, I *am* the woman that stood in thy presence with thee while praying to the Lord. 27 For this child I prayed; and the Lord has given me my request that I asked of him. 28 And I lend him to the Lord all his days that he lives, a loan to the Lord: and she said,

1-Kgdms2 1 My heart is established in the Lord, my horn is exalted in my God; my mouth is enlarged over my enemies, I have rejoiced in thy salvation. 2 For there is none holy as the Lord, and there is none righteous as our God; there is none holy besides thee. 3 Boast not, and utter not high things; let not high-sounding words come out of your mouth, for the Lord *is* a God of knowledge, and God prepares his own designs. 4 The bow of the mighty has waxed feeble, and the weak have girded themselves with strength. 5 They that were full of bread are brought low; and the hungry have forsaken the land; for the barren has born seven, and she that abounded in children has waxed feeble. 6 The Lord kills and makes alive; he brings down to the grave, and brings up. 7 The Lord makes poor, and makes rich; he brings low, and lifts up. 8 He lifts up the poor from the earth, and raises the needy from the dunghill; to seat him with the princes of the people, and causing them to inherit the throne of glory: 9 granting his petition to him that prays; and he blesses the years of the righteous, for by strength cannot man prevail. 10 The Lord will weaken his adversary; the Lord *is* holy. Let not the wise man boast in his wisdom, nor let the mighty man boast in his strength, and let not the rich man boast in his wealth; but let him that boasts boast in this, to understand and know the Lord, and to execute judgment and justice in the midst of the earth. The Lord has gone up to the heavens, and has thundered: he will judge the extremities of the earth, and he gives strength to our kings, and will exalt the horn of his Christ. And she left him there before the Lord,11 and departed to Armathaim: and the child ministered in the presence of the Lord before Heli the priest. 12 And the sons of Heli the priest *were* evil sons, not knowing the Lord. 13 And the priest's claim from every one of the people that sacrificed *was this:* the servant of the priest came when the flesh was in seething, and a flesh- hook of three teeth *was* in his hand. 14 And he struck it into the great caldron, or into the brazen vessel, or into the pot, and whatever came up with the flesh-hook, the priest took for himself: so they did to all Israel that came to sacrifice to the Lord in Selom. 15 And before the fat was burnt for a sweet savour, the servant of the priest would come, and say to the man that sacrificed, Give flesh to roast for the priest, and I will by no means take of thee sodden flesh out of the caldron. 16 And *if* the man that sacrificed said, First let the fat be burned, as it is fit, and take for thyself of all things which thy soul desires: then he would say, Nay, for thou shalt give it me now; and if not I will take it by force. 17 So the sin of the young men was very great before the Lord, for they set at nought the offering of the Lord. 18 And Samuel ministered before the Lord, a child girt with a linen ephod. 19 And his mother made him a little doublet, and brought it to him from year to year, in her going up in company with her husband to offer the yearly sacrifice. 20 And Heli blessed Helcana and his wife, saying The Lord recompense to thee seed of this woman, in return for the loan which thou hast lent to the Lord: and the man returned to his place. 21 And the Lord visited Anna, and she bore yet three sons, and two daughters. And the child Samuel grew before the Lord. 22 And Heli *was* very old, and he heard what his sons did to the children of Israel. 23 And he said to them, Why do ye according to this thing, which I hear from the mouth of all the people of the Lord? 24 Nay *my* sons, for the report which I hear *is* not good; do not so, for the reports which I hear *are* not good, so that the people do not serve God. 25 If a man should at all sin against another, then shall they pray for him to the Lord; but if a man sin against the Lord, who shall intreat for him? But they hearkened not to the voice of their father, because the Lord would by all means destroy them. 26 And the child Samuel advanced, and was in favour with God and with men. 27 And a man of God came to Heli, and said, Thus says the Lord, I plainly revealed myself to the house of thy father, when they were servants in Egypt to the house of Pharao. 28 And I chose the house of thy father out of all the tribes of Israel to minister to me in the priest's office, to go up to my altar, and to burn incense, and to wear an ephod. And I gave to the house of thy father all the offerings by fire of the children of Israel for food. 29 And wherefore hast thou looked upon my incense-offering and my meat-offering with a shameless eye, and hast honoured thy sons above me, so that they should bless themselves with the first-fruits of every sacrifice of Israel before me? 30 Therefore thus says the Lord God of Israel, I said, Thy house and the house of thy father shall pass before me for ever: but now the Lord says, That be far from me; for I will only honour them that honour me, and he that sets me at nought shall be despised. 31 Behold, the days come when I will destroy thy seed and the seed of thy father's house. 32 And thou shalt not have an old man in my house for ever. 33 And *if* I do not destroy a man of thine from my altar, *it shall be* that his eyes may fail and his soul may perish; and every one that remains in thy house shall fall by the sword of men. 34 And this which shall come upon thy two sons Ophni and Phinees shall be a sign to thee; in one day they shall both die. 35 And I will raise up to myself a faithful priest, who shall do all that is in my heart and in my soul; and I will build him a sure house, and he shall walk before my Christ for ever. 36 And it shall come to pass that he that survives in thy house, shall come to do obeisance before him for a little piece of silver, saying, Put me into one of thy priest's offices to eat bread.

1-Kgdms3 1 And the child Samuel ministered to the Lord before Heli the priest: and the word of the Lord was precious in those days, there was no distinct vision. 2 And it came to pass at that time that Heli was sleeping in his place; and his eyes began to fail, and could not see. 3 And the lamp of God *was burning* before it was trimmed, and Samuel slept in the temple, where *was* the ark of God. 4 And the Lord called, Samuel, Samuel; and he said, Behold, *here am* I. 5 And he ran to Heli, and said, *Here am* I, for thou didst call me: and he said, I did not call thee; return, go to sleep; and he returned and went to sleep. 6 And the Lord called again, Samuel, Samuel: and he went to Heli the second time, and said, Behold *here am* I, for thou didst call me: and he said, I called thee not; return, go to sleep. 7 And *it was* before Samuel knew the Lord, and *before* the word of the Lord was revealed to him. 8 And the Lord called Samuel again for the third time: and he arose and went to Heli, and said, Behold, I *am here*, for thou didst call me: and Heli perceived that the Lord *had* called the child. 9 And he said, Return, child, go to sleep; and it shall come to pass if he shall call thee, that thou shalt say, Speak for thy servant hears: and Samuel went and lay down in his place. 10 And the Lord came, and stood, and called him as before: and Samuel said, Speak, for thy servant hears. 11 And the Lord said to Samuel, Behold, I execute my words in Israel; whoever hears them, both his ears shall tingle. 12 In that day I will raise up against Heli all things that I have said against his house; I will begin, and I will make an end. 13 And I have told him that I will be avenged on his house perpetually for the iniquities of his sons, because his sons spoke evil against God, and he did not admonish them. 14 And *it shall* not *go on* so; I have sworn to the house of Eli, the iniquity of the house of Eli shall not be atoned for with incense or sacrifices for ever. 15 And Samuel slept till morning, and rose early in the morning, and opened the doors of the house of the Lord; and Samuel feared to tell *Heli* the vision. 16 And Heli said to Samuel, Samuel, *my* son; and he said, Behold, *here am* I. 17 And he said, What *was* the word that was spoken to thee? I pray thee hide it not from me: may God do these things to thee, and more also, if thou hide from me any thing of all the words that were spoken to thee in thine ears. 18 And Samuel reported all the words, and hid them not from him. And Heli said, He *is* the Lord, he shall do that which is good in his sight. 19 And Samuel grew, and the Lord was with him, and there did not fall one of his words to the ground. 20 And all Israel knew from Dan even to Bersabee, that Samuel *was* faithful as a prophet to the Lord. 21 And the Lord manifested himself again in Selom, for the Lord revealed himself to Samuel; and Samuel was accredited to all Israel as a prophet to the Lord from one end of the land to the other: and Heli *was* very old, and his sons kept advancing *in wickedness*, and their way *was* evil before the Lord.

1-Kgdms4 1 And it came to pass in those days that the Philistines gathered themselves together against Israel to war; and Israel went out to meet them and encamped at Abenezer, and the Philistines encamped in Aphec. 2 And the Philistines prepare to fight with Israel, and the battle was turned against them; and the men of Israel fell before the Philistines, and there were smitten in the battle in the field four thousand men. 3 And the people came to the camp, and the elders of Israel said, Why has the Lord caused us to fall this day before the Philistines? let us take the ark of our God out of Selom, and let it proceed from the midst of us, and it shall save us from the hand of our enemies. 4 And the people sent to Selom, and they take thence the ark of the Lord who dwells between the cherubs: and both the sons of Heli, Ophni and Phinees, *were* with the ark. 5 And it came to pass when the ark of the Lord entered into the camp, that all Israel cried out with a loud voice, and the earth resounded. 6 And the Philistines heard the cry, and the Philistines said, What *is* this great cry in the camp of the Hebrews: and they understood that the ark of the Lord was come into the camp. 7 And the Philistines feared, and said, These are the Gods that are come to them into the camp. 8 Woe to us, O Lord, deliver us to-day for such a thing has not happened aforetime: woe to us, who shall deliver us out of the hand of these mighty Gods? these *are* the Gods that smote Egypt with every plague, and in the wilderness. 9 Strengthen yourselves and behave yourselves like men, O ye Philistines, that ye may not serve the Hebrews as they have served us, but be ye men and fight with them. 10 And they fought with them; and the men of Israel fall, and they fled every man to his ten; and there was a very great slaughter; and there fell of Israel thirty thousand fighting men. 11 And the ark of God was taken, and both the sons of Heli, Ophni, and Phinees, died. 12 And there ran a man of Benjamin out of the battle, and he came to Selom on that day: and his clothes *were* rent, and earth *was* upon his head. 13 And he came, an behold, Heli was upon the seat by the gate looking along the way, for his heart was greatly alarmed for the ark of God: and the man entered into the city to bring tidings; and the city cried out. 14 And Heli heard the sound of the cry, and said, What *is* the voice of this cry? and the men hasted and went in, and reported to Heli. 15 Now Heli *was* ninety years old, and his eyes were fixed, and he saw not. 16 And Heli said to them that stood round about him, What *is* the voice of this sound? And the man hasted and advanced to Heli, and said to him, I am he that is come out of the camp, and I have fled from the battle to-day: and Heli said, What *is* the even, *my* son? 17 And they young man answered and said, The men of Israel fled from the face of the Philistines, and there was a great slaughter among the people, and both thy sons are dead, and the ark of God is taken. 18 And it came to pass, when he mentioned the ark of God, that he fell from the seat backward near the gate, and his back was broken, and he died, for *he was* an old man and heavy: and he judged Israel twenty years. 19 And his daughter-in-law the wife of Phinees *was* with child, *about* to bring forth; and she heard the tidings, that the ark of God was taken, and that her father-in-law and her husband were dead; and she wept and was delivered, for her pains came upon her. 20 And in her time she was at the point of death; and the women that stood by her, said to her, Fear not, for thou hast born a son: but she answered not, and her heart did not regard it. 21 And she called the child Uaebarchaboth, because of the ark of God, and because of her father-in-law, and because of her husband. 22 And they said, The glory of Israel is departed, forasmuch as the ark of the Lord is taken.

1-Kgdms5 1 And the Philistines took the ark of God, and brought it from Abenezer to Azotus. 2 And the Philistines took the ark of the Lord, and brought it into the house of Dagon, and set it by Dagon. 3 And the people of Azotus rose early, and entered into the house of Dagon; and looked, and behold, Dagon had fallen on his face before the ark of the Lord: and they lifted up Dagon, and set him in his place. And the hand of the Lord was heavy upon the Azotians, and he plagued them, and he smote them in their secret parts, Azotus and her coasts. 4 And it came to pass when they rose early in the morning, behold, Dagon had fallen on his face before the ark of the covenant of the Lord; and the head of Dagon and both the palms of his hands *were* cut off each before the threshold, and both the wrists of his hands had fallen on the floor of the porch; only the stump of Dagon was left. 5 Therefore the priests of Dagon, and every one that enters into the house of Dagon, do not tread upon the threshold of the house of Dagon in Azotus until this day, for they step over. 6 And the hand of the Lord was heavy upon Azotus, and he brought evil upon them, and it burst out upon them into the ships, and mice sprang up in the midst of their country, and there was a great and indiscriminate mortality in the city. 7 And the men of Azotus saw that *it was* so, and they said, The ark of the God of Israel shall not abide with us, for his hand *is* heavy upon us and upon Dagon our god. 8 And they send and gather the lords of the Philistines to them, and say, What shall we do to the ark of the God of Israel? and the Gittites say, Let the ark of God come over to us; and the ark of the God of Israel came to Geth. 9 And it came to pass after it went about to Geth, that the hand of the Lord comes upon the city, a very great confusion; and he smote the men of the city small and great, and smote them in their secret parts: and the Gittites made to themselves images of emerods. 10 And they send away the ark of God to Ascalon; and it came to pass when the ark of God went into Ascalon, that the men of Ascalon cried out, saying, Why have ye brought back the ark of the God of Israel to us, to kill us and our people? 11 And they send and gather the lords of the Philistines, and they said, Send away the ark of the God of Israel, and let it lodge in its place; and let it not slay us and our people. 12 For there was a very great confusion in all the city, when the ark of the God of Israel entered there; and those, who lived and died not were smitten with emerods; and the cry of the city went up to heaven.

1-Kgdms6 1 And the ark was seven months in the country of the Philistines, and their land brought forth swarms of mice. 2 And the Philistines call their priests, and their prophets, and their enchanters, saying, What shall we do to the ark of the Lord? teach us wherewith we shall send it away to its place. 3 And they said, If ye send away the ark of the covenant of the Lord God of Israel, do not on any account send it away empty, but by all means render to it an offering for the plague; and then shall ye be healed, and an atonement shall be made for you: should not his hand be *thus* stayed from off you? 4 And they say, What *is* the offering for the plague *which* we shall return to it? and they said, 5 According to the number of the lords of the Philistines, five golden emerods, for the plague was on you, and on your rulers, and on the people; and golden mice, the likeness of the mice that destroy your land:·and ye shall give glory to the Lord, that he may lighten his hand from off you, and from off your gods, and from off your land. 6 And why do ye harden your hearts, as Egypt and Pharao hardened their hearts? *was it* not *so* when he mocked them, *that* they let the people go, and they departed? 7 And now take wood and make a new wagon, and take two cows, that have calved for the first time, without their calves; and do ye yoke the cows to the wagon, and lead away the calves from behind them home. 8 And ye shall take the ark and put it on the wagon; and ye shall restore to it the golden articles for the trespass-offering in a coffer by the side of it: and ye shall let it go, and sent it away, and ye shall depart. 9 And ye shall see, if it shall go the way of its coasts along by Baethsamys, he has brought upon us this great affliction; and if not, then shall we know that his hand has not touched us, but this *is a* chance *which* has happened to us. 10 And the Philistines did so; and they took two cows that had calved for the first time, and yoked them to the waggon, and shut up their calves at home. 11 And they set the ark of the Lord, and the coffer, and the golden mice, on the waggon. 12 And the cows went straight on the way to the way of Baethsamys, they went along one track; and laboured, and turned not aside to the right hand or to the left, and the lords of the Philistines went after it as far as the coasts of Baethsamys. 13 And the men of Baethsamys were reaping the wheat harvest in the valley; and they lifted up their eyes, and saw the ark of the Lord, and rejoiced to meet it. 14 And the waggon entered into the field of Osee, which was in Baethsamys, and they set there by it a great stone; and they split the wood of the waggon, and offered up the cows for a whole-burnt- offering to the Lord. 15 And the Levites brought up the ark of the Lord, and the coffer with it, and the golden articles upon it, and placed them on the great stone, and the men of Baethsamys offered whole-burnt-offerings and meat offerings on that day to the Lord. 16 And the five lords of the Philistines saw, and returned to Ascalon in that day. 17 And these *are* the golden emerods which the lords of the Philistines gave as a trespass-offering to the Lord; for Azotus one, for Gaza one, for Ascalon one, for Geth one, for Accaron one. 18 And the golden mice according to the number of all the cities of the Philistines, belonging to the five lords, from the fenced city to the village of the Pherezite, and to the great stone, on which they placed the ark of the covenant of the Lord, that was in the field of Osee the Baethsamysite. 19 And the sons of Jechonias were not pleased with the men of Baethsamys, because they saw the ark of the Lord; and *the Lord* smote among them seventy men, and fifty thousand men: and the people mourned, because the Lord had inflicted on the people, a very great plague. 20 And the men of Baethsamys said, Who shall be able to pass before this holy Lord God? and to whom shall the ark of the Lord go up from us? 21 And they send messengers to the inhabitants of Cariathiarim, saying, The Philistines have brought back the ark of the Lord, go down and take it home to yourselves.

1-Kgdms7 1 And the men of Cariathiarim come, and bring up the ark of the covenant of the Lord: and they bring it into the house of Aminadab in the hill; and they sanctified Eleazar his son to keep the ark of the covenant of the Lord. 2 And it came to pass from the time that the ark was in Cariathiarim, the days were multiplied, and *the time* was twenty years; and all the house of Israel looked after the Lord. 3 And Samuel spoke to all the house of Israel, saying, If ye do with all your heart return to the Lord, take away the strange gods from the midst of you, and the groves, and prepare your hearts to *serve* the Lord, and serve him only; and he shall deliver you from the hand of the Philistines. 4 And the children of Israel took away Baalim and the groves of Astaroth, and served the Lord only. 5 And Samuel said, Gather all Israel to Massephath, and I will pray for you to the Lord. 6 And they were gathered together to Massephath, and they drew water, and poured it out upon the earth before the Lord. And they fasted on that day, and said, We have sinned before the Lord. And Samuel judged the children of Israel in Massephath. 7 And the Philistines heard that all the children of Israel were gathered together to Massephath: and the lords of the Philistines went up against Israel: and the children of Israel heard, and they feared before the Philistines. 8 And the children of Israel said to Samuel, Cease not to cry to the Lord thy God for us, and he shall save us out of the hand of the Philistines. 9 And Samuel took a sucking lamb, and offered it up as a whole-burnt-offering with all the people to the Lord: and Samuel cried to the Lord for Israel, and the Lord heard him. 10 And Samuel was offering the whole-burnt-offering; and the Philistines drew near to war against Israel; and the Lord thundered with a mighty sound in that day upon the Philistines, and they were confounded and overthrown before Israel. 11 And the men of Israel went forth out of Massephath, and pursued the Philistines, and smote them to the parts under Baethchor. 12 And Samuel took a stone, and set it up between Massephath and the old *city*; and he called the name of it Abenezer, stone of the helper; and he said, Hitherto has the Lord helped us. 13 So the Lord humbled the Philistines, and they did not anymore come into the border of Israel; and the hand of the Lord was against the Philistines all the days of Samuel. 14 And the cities which the Philistines took from the children of Israel were restored; and they restored them to Israel from Ascalon to Azob: and they took the coast of Israel out of the hand of the Philistines; and there was peace between Israel and the Amorite. 15 And Samuel judged Israel all the days of his life. 16 And he went year by year, and went round Baethel, and Galgala, and Massephath; and he judged Israel in all these consecrated places. 17 And his return was to Armathaim, because there was his house; and there he judged Israel, and built there an altar to the Lord.

1-Kgdms8 1 And it came to pass when Samuel was old, that he made his sons judges over Israel. 2 And these *are* the names of his sons; Joel the first-born, and the name of the second Abia, judges in Bersabee. 3 And his sons did not walk in his way; and they turned aside after gain, and took gifts, and perverted judgments. 4 And the men of Israel gather themselves together, and come to Armathaim to Samuel, 5 and they said to him, Behold, thou art grown old, and thy sons walk not in thy way; and now set over us a king to judge us, as also the other nations *have*. 6 And the thing *was* evil in the eyes of Samuel, when they said, Give us a king to judge us: and Samuel prayed to the Lord. 7 And the Lord said to Samuel, Hear the voice of the people, in whatever they shall say to thee; for they have not rejected thee, but they have rejected me from reigning over them. 8 According to all their doings which they have done to me, from the day that I brought them out of Egypt until this day, even *as* they have deserted me, and served other gods, so they do also to thee. 9 And now hearken to their voice; only thou shalt solemnly testify to them, and thou shalt describe to them the manner of the king who shall reign over them. 10 And Samuel spoke every word of the Lord to the people who asked of him a king. 11 And he said, This shall be the manner of the king that shall rule over you: he shall take your sons, and put them in his chariots, and among his horsemen, and running before his chariots, 12 and *his manner shall be* to make them to himself captains of hundreds and captains of thousands; and to reap his harvest, and gather his vintage, and prepare his instruments of war, and the implements of his chariots. 13 And he will take your daughters to be perfumers, and cooks, and bakers. 14 And he will take your fields, and your vineyards, and your good oliveyards, and give them to his servants. 15 And he will take the tithe of your seeds and your vineyards, and give *it* to his eunuchs, and to his servants. 16 And he will take your servants, and your handmaids, and your good herds and your asses, and will take the tenth of them for his works. 17 And he will tithe your flocks; and ye shall be his servants. 18 And ye shall cry out in that day because of your king whom ye have chosen to yourselves, and the Lord shall not hear you in those days, because ye have chosen to yourselves a king. 19 But the people would not hearken to Samuel; and they said to him, Nay, but there shall be a king over us. 20 An we also will be like all the nations; and our king shall judge us, and shall go out before us, and fight our battles. 21 And Samuel heard all the words of the people, and spoke them in the ears of the Lord. 22 And the Lord said to Samuel, Hearken to their voice, and appoint them a king. And Samuel said to the men of Israel, Let each man depart to his city.

1-Kgdms9 1 And *there was* a man of the sons of Benjamin, and his name *was* Kis, the son of Abiel, the son of Jared, the son of Bachir, the son of Aphec, the son of a Benjamite, a man of might. 2 And this man *had* a son, and his name was Saul, of great stature, a goodly man; and there was not among the sons of Israel a goodlier than he, high above all the people from his shoulders and upward. 3 And the asses of Kis the father of Saul were lost; and Kis said to Saul his son, Take with thee one of the young men, and arise ye, and go seek the asses. 4 And they went through mount Ephraim, and they went through the land of Selcha, and found them not: and they passed through the land of Segalim, and they were not there: and they passed through the land of Jamin, and found them not. 5 And when they came to Siph, then Saul said to his young man that was with him, Come and let us return, lest my father leave the asses, and take care for us. 6 And the young man said to him, Behold now, *there is* a man of God in this city, and the man *is* of high repute; all that he shall speak will surely come to pass: now then let us go, that he may tell us our way on which we have set out. 7 And Saul said to his young man that was with him, Lo, then, we will go; but what shall we bring the man of God? for the loaves are spent out of our vessels, and we have nothing more with us that belongs to us to bring to the man of God. 8 And the young man answered Saul again, and said, Behold, there is found in my hand a fourth part of a shekel of silver; and thou shalt give it to the man of God, and he shall tell us our way. 9 Now before time in Israel every one in going to enquire of God said, Come and let us go to the seer; for the people beforetime called the prophet, the seer. 10 And Saul said to his servant, Well said, come and let us go: and they went to the city where the man of God was. 11 As they went up the ascent to the city, they find damsels come out to draw water, and they say to them, Is the seer here? 12 And the virgins answered them, and they say to them, He is: behold, *he is* before you: now he is coming to the city, because of the day, for to-day *there is* a sacrifice for the people in Bama. 13 As soon as ye shall enter into the city, so shall ye find him in the city, before he goes up to Bama to eat; for the people will not eat until he comes in, for he blesses the sacrifice, and afterwards the guests eat; now then go up, for ye shall find him because of the holiday. 14 And they go up to the city; and as they were entering into the midst of the city, behold, Samuel came out to meet them, to go up to Bama. 15 And the Lord uncovered the ear of Samuel one day before Saul came to him, saying, 16 At this time to-morrow I will send to thee a man out of the land of Benjamin, and thou shalt anoint him to be ruler over my people Israel, and he shall save my people out of the hand of the Philistines; for I have looked upon the humiliation of my people, for their cry is come unto me. 17 And Samuel looked upon Saul, and the Lord answered him, Behold the man of whom I spoke to thee, this one shall rule over my people. 18 And Saul drew near to Samuel into the midst of the city, and said, Tell me now which *is* the house of the seer? 19 And Samuel answered Saul, and said, I am he: go up before me to Bama, and eat with me to-day, and I will send thee away in the morning, and I will tell thee all that is in thine heart. 20 And concerning thine asses that have been lost now these three days, care not for them, for they are found. And to whom does the excellency of Israel belong? does it not to thee and to thy father's house? 21 And Saul answered and said, Am not I the son of a Benjamite, the least tribe of the people of Israel? and of the least family of the whole tribe of Benjamin? and why hast thou spoken to me according to this word? 22 And Samuel took Saul and his servant, and brought them to the inn, and set them there a place among the chief of those that were called, about seventy men. 23 And Samuel said to the cook, Give me the portion which I gave thee, which I told thee to set by thee. 24 Now the cook *had* boiled the shoulder, and he set it before Saul; and Samuel said to Saul, Behold that which is left: set before thee, an eat; for it is set thee for a testimony in preference to the others; take *of it*: and Saul ate with Samuel on that day. 25 And he went down from Bama into the city; and they prepared a lodging for Saul on the roof, and he lay down. 26 An it came to pass when the morning dawned, that Samuel called Saul on the roof, saying, Rise up, and I will dismiss thee. And Saul arose, and he and Samuel went out. 27 As they went down to a part of the city, Samuel said to Saul, Speak to the young man, and let him pass on before us; and do thou stand as to-day, and hearken to the word of God.

1-Kgdms10 1 And Samuel took a vial of oil, and poured *it* on his head, and kissed him, and said to him, Has not the Lord anointed thee for a ruler over his people, over Israel? and thou shalt rule among the people of the Lord, and thou shalt save them out of the hand of their enemies; and this *shall be* the sign to thee that the Lord has anointed thee for a ruler over his inheritance. 2 *As soon* as thou shalt have departed this day from me, thou shalt find two men by the burial-place of Rachel on the mount of Benjamin, exulting greatly; and they shall say to thee, The asses are found which ye went to seek; and, behold, thy father has given up the matter of the asses, and he is anxious for you, saying, What shall I do for my son? 3 And thou shalt depart thence, and shalt go beyond that as far as the oak of Thabor, and thou shalt find there three men going up to God to Baethel, one bearing three kids, and another bearing three vessels of bread, and another bearing a bottle of wine. 4 And they shall ask thee how thou doest, and shall give thee two presents of bread, and thou shall receive them of their hand. 5 And afterward thou shalt go to the hill of God, where is the encampment of the Philistines; there *is* Nasib the Philistine: an it shall come to pass when ye shall have entered into the city, that thou shalt meet a band of prophets coming down from the Bama; and before them will be lutes, and a drum, and a pipe, and a harp, and they shall prophesy. 6 And the Spirit of the Lord shall come upon thee, and thou shalt prophesy with them, and shalt be turned into another man. 7 And it shall come to pass when these signs shall come upon thee, —*then* do thou whatsoever thy hand shall find, because God *is* with thee. 8 And thou shalt go down in front of Galgal, and behold, I come down to thee to offer a whole-burnt-offering and peace-offerings: seven days shalt thou wait until I shall come to thee, and I will make known to thee what thou shalt do. 9 And it came to pass when he turned his back to depart from Samuel, God gave him another heart; and all these signs came to pass in that day. 10 And he comes thence to the hill, and behold a band of prophets opposite to him; and the Spirit of God came upon him, and he prophesied in the midst of them. 11 And all that had known him before came, and saw, and behold, he *was* in the midst of the prophets: and the people said every one to his neighbour, What *is* this that has happened to the son of Kis? *is* Saul also among the prophets? 12 And one of them answered and said, And who *is* his father? and

therefore it became a proverb, *Is* Saul also among the prophets? 13 And he ceased prophesying, and comes to the hill. 14 And his kinsman said to him and to his servant, Whither went ye? and they said, To seek the asses; and we saw that they were lost, and we went in to Samuel. 15 And his kinsman said to Saul, Tell me, I pray thee, What did Samuel say to thee? 16 And Saul said to his kinsman, he verily told me that the asses were found. But the matter of the kingdom he told him not. 17 And Samuel summoned all the people before the Lord to Massephath. 18 And he said to the children of Israel, Thus has the Lord God of Israel spoken, saying, I brought up the children of Israel out of Egypt, and I rescued you out of the hand of Pharao king of Egypt, and out of all the kingdoms that afflicted you. 19 And ye have this day rejected God, who is himself your Deliverer out of all your evils and afflictions; and ye said, Nay, but thou shalt set a king over us: and now stand before the Lord according to your tribes, and according to your families. 20 And Samuel brought nigh all the tribes of Israel, and the tribe of Benjamin is taken by lot. 21 And he brings near the tribe of Benjamin by families, and the family of Mattari is taken by lot: and they bring near the family of Mattari, man by man, and Saul the son of Kis is taken; and he sought him, but he was not found. 22 And Samuel asked yet again of the Lord, Will the man come hither? and the Lord said, Behold, he is hid among the stuff. 23 And he ran and took him thence, and he set him in the midst of the people; and he was higher than all the people by his shoulders and upwards. 24 And Samuel said to all the people, Have ye seen whom the Lord has chosen to himself, that there is none like to him among you all? And all the people took notice, and said, Let the king live! 25 And Samuel told the people the manner of the king, and wrote it in a book, and set it before the Lord: and Samuel sent away all the people, and each went to his place. 26 And Saul departed to his house to Gabaa; and there went with Saul mighty men whose hearts God had touched. 27 But evil men said, Who *is* this man *that* shall save us? and they despised him, and brought him no gifts.

1-Kgdms11 1 And it came to pass about a month after this, that Naas the Ammanite went up, and encamped against Jabis Galaad: and all the men of Jabis said to Naas the Ammanite, Make a covenant with us, and we will serve thee. 2 Naas the Ammanite said to them, On these terms will I make a covenant with you, that I should put out all your right eyes, and I will lay a reproach upon Israel. 3 And the men of Jabis say to him, Allow us seven days, and we will send messengers into all the coasts of Israel: if there should be no one to deliver us, we will come out to you. 4 And the messengers came to Gabaa to Saul, and they speak the words into the ears of the people; and all the people lifted up their voice, and wept. 5 And, behold, Saul came after the early morning out of the field: and Saul said, Why does the people week? and they tell him the words of the men of Jabis. 6 And the Spirit of the Lord came upon Saul when he heard these words, and his anger was greatly kindled against them. 7 And he took two cows, and cut them in pieces, and sent them into all the coasts of Israel by the hand of messengers, saying, Whoso comes not forth after Saul and after Samuel, so shall they do to his oxen: and a transport from the Lord came upon the people of Israel, and they came out to battle as one man. 8 And he reviews them at Bezec in Bama, every man of Israel six hundred thousand, and the men of Juda seventy thousand. 9 And he said to the messengers that came, Thus shall ye say to the men of Jabis, To-morrow ye shall have deliverance when the sun is hot; and the messengers came to the city, and told the men of Jabis, and they rejoiced. 10 And the men of Jabis said to Naas the Ammanite, To-morrow we will come forth to you, and ye shall do to us what seems good in your sight. 11 And it came to pass on the morrow, that Saul divided the people into three companies, and they go into the midst of the camp in the morning watch, and they smote the children of Ammon until the day was hot; at it came to pass that those who were left were scattered, and there were not left among them two together. 12 And the people said to Samuel, Who has said that Saul shall not reign over us? Give up the men, and we will put them to death. 13 And Saul said, No man shall die this day, for to-day the Lord has wrought deliverance in Israel. 14 And Samuel spoke to the people, saying, Let us go to Galgala, and there renew the kingdom. 15 And all the people went to Galgala, and Samuel anointed Saul there to be king before the Lord in Galgala, and there he offered meat-offerings and peace-offerings before the Lord: and Samuel and all Israel rejoiced exceedingly.

1-Kgdms12 1 And Samuel said to all Israel, Behold, I have hearkened to your voice in all things that ye have said to me, and I have set a king over you. 2 And now, behold, the king goes before you; and I am grown old and shall rest; and, behold, my sons *are* among you; and, behold, I have gone about before you from my youth to this day. 3 Behold, *here am* I, answer against me before the Lord and before his anointed: whose calf have I taken? or whose ass have I taken? or whom of you have I oppressed? or from whose hand have I taken a bribe, even *to* a sandal? bear witness against me, and I will make restitution to you. 4 And they said to Samuel, Thou hast not injured us, and thou hast not oppressed us; and thou hast not afflicted us, and thou hast not taken anything from any one's hand. 5 And Samuel said to the people, The Lord *is* witness among you, and his anointed *is* witness this day, that ye have not found anything in my hand: and they said, *He is* witness. 6 And Samuel spoke to the people, saying, The Lord who appointed Moses and Aaron *is* witness, who brought our fathers up out of Egypt. 7 And now stand still, and I will judge you before the Lord; and I will relate to you all the righteousness of the Lord, the things which he has wrought among you and your fathers. 8 When Jacob and his sons went into Egypt, and Egypt humbled them, then our fathers cried to the Lord, and the Lord sent Moses and Aaron; and they brought our fathers out of Egypt, and he made them to dwell in this place. 9 And they forgot the Lord their God, and he sold them into the hands of Sisara captain of the host of Jabis king of Asor, and into the hands of the Philistines, and into the hands of the king of Moab;

and he fought with them. 10 And they cried to the Lord, and said, We have sinned, for we have forsaken the Lord, and have served Baalim and the groves: and now deliver us out of the hand of our enemies, and we will serve thee. 11 And he sent Jerobaal, and Barac, and Jephthae, and Samuel, and rescued us out of the hand of our enemies round about, and ye dwelt in security. 12 And ye saw that Naas king of the children of Ammon came against you, and ye said, Nay, none but a king shall reign over us; whereas the Lord our God *is* our king. 13 And now behold the king whom ye have chosen; and behold, the Lord has set a king over you. 14 If ye should fear the Lord, and serve him, and hearken to his voice, and not resist the mouth of the Lord, and ye and your king that reigns over you should follow the Lord, *well.* 15 But if ye should not hearken to the voice of the Lord, and ye should resist the mouth of the Lord, then shall the hand of the Lord be upon you and upon your king. 16 And now stand still, and see this great thing, which the Lord will do before your eyes. 17 *Is it* not wheat-harvest to-day? I will call upon the Lord, and he shall send thunder and rain; and know ye and see, that your wickedness *is* great which ye have wrought before the Lord, having asked for yourselves a king. 18 And Samuel called upon the Lord, and the Lord sent thunders and rain in that day; and all the people feared greatly the Lord and Samuel. 19 And all the people said to Samuel, Pray for thy servants to the Lord thy God, and let us not die; for we have added to all our sins this iniquity, in asking for us a king. 20 And Samuel said to the people, Fear not: ye have *indeed* wrought all this iniquity; only turn not from following the Lord, and serve the Lord with all your heart. 21 And turn not aside after the *gods* that are nothing, who will do nothing, and will not deliver *you*, because they are nothing. 22 For the Lord will not cast off his people for his great name's sake, because the Lord graciously took you to himself for a people. 23 And far be it from me to sin against the Lord in ceasing to pray for you: but I will serve the Lord, and shew you the good and the right way. 24 Only fear the Lord, and serve him in truth and with all your heart, for ye see what great things he has wrought with you. 25 But if ye continue to do evil, then shall ye and your king be consumed.

1-Kgdms13 1,2 And Saul chooses for himself three thousand men of the men of Israel: and there were with Saul two thousand who were in Machmas, and in mount Baethel, and a thousand were with Jonathan in Gabaa of Benjamin: and he sent the rest of the people every man to his tent. 3 And Jonathan smote Nasib the Philistine that dwelt in the hill; and the Philistines hear of it, and Saul sounds the trumpet through all the land, saying, The servants have despised *us.* 4 And all Israel heard say, Saul has smitten Nasib the Philistine; now Israel had been put to shame before the Philistines; and the children of Israel went up after Saul in Galgala. 5 And the Philistines gather together to war with Israel; and then come up against Israel thirty thousand chariots, and six thousand horsemen, and people as the sand by the seashore for multitude: and they come up, and encamp in Machmas, opposite Baethoron southward. 6 And the men of Israel saw that they were in a strait so that they could not draw nigh, and the people hid themselves in caves, and sheepfolds, and rocks, and ditches, and pits. 7 And they that went over went over Jordan to the land of Gad and Galaad: and Saul was yet in Galgala, and all the people followed after him in amazement. 8 And he continued seven days for the appointed testimony, as Samuel told him, and Samuel came not to Galgala, and his people were dispersed from him. 9 And Saul said, Bring hither *victims*, that I may offer whole-burnt- offerings and peace-offerings: and he offered the whole-burnt-offering. 10 And it came to pass when he had finished offering the whole-burnt-offering, that Samuel arrived, and Saul went out to meet him, *and* to bless him. 11 And Samuel said, What hast thou done? and Saul said, Because I saw how the people were scattered from me, and thou was not present as thou purposedst according to the set time of the days, and the Philistines were gathered to Machmas. 12 Then I said, Now will the Philistines come down to me to Galgala, and I have not sought the face of the Lord: so I forced myself and offered the whole-burnt-offering. 13 And Samuel said to Saul, Thou hast done foolishly; for thou hast not kept my command, which the Lord commanded thee, as now the Lord would have confirmed thy kingdom over Israel for ever. 14 But now thy kingdom shall not stand to thee, and the Lord shall seek for himself a man after his own heart; and the Lord shall appoint him to be a ruler over his people, because thou hast not kept all that the Lord commanded thee. 15 And Samuel arose, and departed from Galgala, and the remnant of the people went after Saul to meet *him* after the men of war, when they had come out of Galgala to Gabaa of Benjamin. And Saul numbered the people that were found with him, about six hundred men. 16 And Saul and Jonathan his son, and the people that were found with them, halted in Gabaa, of Benjamin; and they wept: and the Philistines had encamped in Machmas. 17 And men came forth to destroy out of the land of the Philistines in three companies; one company turning by the way of Gophera toward the land of Sogal, 18 and another company turning the way of Baethoron, and another company turning by the way of Gabae that turns aside to Gai of Sabim. 19 And there was not found a smith in all the land of Israel, for the Philistines said, Lest the Hebrews make themselves sword or spear. 20 And all Israel went down to the Land of the Philistines to forge every one his reaping-hook and his tool, and every one his axe and his sickle. 21 And it was near the time of vintage: and their tools were *valued at* three shekels for a plough-share, and there was the same rate for the axe and the sickle. 22 And it came to pass in the days of the war of Machmas, that there was not a sword or spear found in the hand of all the people, that were with Saul and Jonathan; but with Saul and Jonathan his son was there found. 23 And there went out some from the camp of the Philistines to the place beyond Machmas.

1-Kgdms14 1 And when a certain day arrived, Jonathan the son of Saul said to the young man that bore his armour, Come, and let us go over to Messab of the Philistines that is on the other side yonder; but he told not his father. 2 And Saul sat on the top of the hill under the pomegranate tree that is in Magdon, and there were with him about six hundred men. 3 And Achia son of Achitob, the brother of Jochabed the son of Phinees, the son of Heli, *was* the priest of God in Selom wearing an ephod: and the people knew not that Jonathan was gone. 4 And in the midst of the passage whereby Jonathan sought to pass over to the encampment of the Philistines, there was both a sharp rock on this side, and a sharp rock on the other side: the name of the one *was* Bases, and the name of the other Senna. 5 The one way *was* northward to one coming to Machmas, and the other way *was* southward to one coming to Gabae. 6 And Jonathan said to the young man that bore his armour, Come, let us go over to Messab of these uncircumcised, if *peradventure* the Lord may do something for us; for the Lord is not straitened to save by many or by few. 7 And his armour-bearer said to him, Do all that thine heart inclines toward: behold, I *am* with thee, my heart *is* as thy heart. 8 And Jonathan said, Behold, we will go over to the men, and will come down suddenly upon them. 9 If they should say thus to us, Stand aloof there until we shall send you word; then we will stand still by ourselves, and will not go up against them. 10 *But* if they should say thus to us, Come up to us; then will we go up, for the Lord has delivered them into our hands; this *shall be* a sign to us. 11 And they both went in to Messab of the Philistines; and the Philistines said, Behold, the Hebrews come forth out of their Caves, where they had hidden themselves. 12 And the men of Messab answered Jonathan and his armour-bearer, and said, Come up to us, and we will shew you a thing: and Jonathan said to his armour-bearer, Come up after me, for the Lord has delivered them into the hands of Israel. 13 And Jonathan went up on his hands and feet, and his armour-bearer with him; and they looked on the face of Jonathan, and he smote them, and his armour-bearer did smite *them* after him. 14 And the first slaughter which Jonathan and his armour-bearer effected was twenty men, with darts and slings, and pebbles of the field. 15 And there was dismay in the camp, and in the field; and all the people in Messab, and the spoilers were amazed; and they would not act, and the land was terror-struck, and there was dismay from the lord. 16 And the watchmen of Saul beheld in Gabaa of Benjamin, and, behold, the army was thrown into confusion on every side. 17 And Saul said to the people with him, Number yourselves now, and see who has gone out from you: and they numbered themselves, and behold, Jonathan and his armour-bearer were not found. 18 And Saul said to Achia, Bring the ephod; for he wore the ephod in that day before Israel. 19 And it came to pass while Saul was speaking to the priest, that the sound in the camp of the Philistines continued to increase greatly; and Saul said to the priest, Withdraw thy hands. 20 And Saul went up and all the people that were with him, and they come to the battle: and, behold, *every* man's sword was against his neighbour, a very great confusion. 21 And the servants who had been before with the Philistines, who had gone up to the army, turned themselves also to be with the Israelites who were with Saul and Jonathan. 22 And all the Israelites who were hidden in mount Ephraim heard also that the Philistines fled; and they also gather themselves after them to battle: and the Lord saved Israel in that day; and the war passed through Bamoth; and all the people with Saul were about ten thousand men. 23 And the battle extended itself to every city in the mount Ephraim. 24 And Saul committed a great trespass of ignorance in that day, and he lays a curse on the people, saying, Cursed *is* the man who shall eat bread before the evening; so I will avenge myself on my enemy: and none of the people tasted bread, though all the land was dining. 25 And Jaal was a wood abounding in swarms of bees on the face of the ground. 26 And the people went into the place of the bees, and, behold, they continued speaking; and, behold, there was none that put his hand to his mouth, for the people feared the oath of the Lord. 27 And Jonathan had not heard when his father adjured the people; and he reached forth the end of the staff that was in his hand, an dipped it into the honeycomb, and returned his hand to his mouth, and his eyes recovered their sight. 28 And one of the people answered and said, Thy father solemnly adjured the people, saying, Cursed *is* the man who shall eat bread to-day. And the people were very faint, 29 and Jonathan knew it, and said, My father has destroyed the land: see how my eyes have received sight *now* that I have tasted a little of this honey. 30 Surely if the people had this day eaten freely of the spoils of their enemies which they found, the slaughter among the Philistines would have been greater. 31 And on that day he smote some of the Philistines in Machmas; and the people were very weary. 32 And the people turned to the spoil; and the people took flocks, and herds, and calves, and slew them on the ground, and the people ate with the blood. 33 And it was reported to Saul, saying, The people have sinned against the Lord, eating with the blood: and Saul said, Out of Getthaim roll a great stone to me hither. 34 And Saul said, Disperse yourselves among the people, and tell them to bring hither every one his calf, and every one his sheep: and let them slay it on this *stone* and sin not against the Lord in eating with the blood: and the people brought each one that which was in his hand, and they slew *them* there. 35 And Saul built an altar there to the Lord: this was the first altar that Saul built to the Lord. 36 And Saul said, Let us go down after the Philistines this night, and let us plunder among them till the day break, and let us not leave a man among them. And they said, Do all that is good in thy sight: and the priest said, let us draw nigh hither to God. 37 And Saul enquired of God, If I go down after the Philistines, wilt thou deliver them into the hands of Israel? And he answered him not in that day. 38 And Saul said, Bring hither all the chiefs of Israel, and know and see by whom this sin has been committed this day. 39 For as the Lord lives who has saved Israel, if answer should be against my son Jonathan, he shall surely die. And there was no one that answered out of all the people. 40 And he said to all the men of Israel, Ye shall be under subjection, and I an Jonathan my son will be under subjection: and the people said to Saul, Do that which is good in thy sight. 41 And Saul said, O Lord God of Israel, why hast thou not answered thy servant this day? *is* the iniquity in me, or in Jonathan my son? Lord God of Israel, give clear *manifestations*, and if *the* lot should declare

this, give, I pray thee, to thy people of Israel, give, I pray, holiness. And Jonathan and Saul are taken, and the people escaped. 42 And Saul said, Cast *lots* between me and my son Jonathan: whomsoever the Lord shall cause to be taken by lot, let him die: and the people said to Saul, This thing is not *to be done*: and Saul prevailed against the people, and they cast *lots* between him and Jonathan his son, and Jonathan is taken by lot. 43 And Saul said to Jonathan, Tell me what thou hast done: and Jonathan told him, and said, I did indeed taste a little honey, with the end of my staff that was in my hand, and, lo! I *am to* die. 44 And Saul said to him, God do so to me, and more also, thou shalt surely die to-day. 45 And the people said to Saul, Shall he that has wrought this great salvation in Israel be put to death this day? *As* the Lord lives, there shall not fall to the ground one of the hairs of his head; for the people of God have wrought successfully this day. And the people prayed for Jonathan in that day, and he died not. 46 And Saul went up from following the Philistines; and the Philistines departed to their place. 47 And Saul received the kingdom, by lot he inherits the office *of ruling* over Israel: and he fought against all his enemies round about, against Moab, and against the children of Ammon, and against the children of Edom, and against Baethaeor, and against the king of Suba, and against the Philistines: whithersoever he turned, he was victorious. 48 And he wrought valiantly, and smote Amalec, and rescued Israel out of the hand of them that trampled on him. 49 And the sons of Saul were Jonathan, and Jessiu, and Melchisa: and *these were* the names of his two daughters, the name of the first-born Merob, and the name of the second Melchol. 50 And the name of his wife was Achinoom, the daughter of Achimaa: and the name of his captain of the host was Abenner, the son of Ner, son of a kinsman of Saul. 51 And Kis *was* the father of Saul, and Ner, the father of Abenezer, *was* son of Jamin, son of Abiel. 52 And the war was vehement against the Philistines all the days of Saul; and when Saul saw any mighty man, and any valiant man, then he took them to himself.

1-Kgdms15 1 And Samuel said to Saul, The Lord sent me to anoint thee king over Israel: and now hear the voice of the Lord. 2 Thus said the Lord of hosts, Now will I take vengeance for what Amalec did to Israel, when he met him in the way as he came up out of Egypt. 3 And now go, and thou shalt smite Amalec and Hierim and all that belongs to him, and thou shalt not save anything of him alive, but thou shalt utterly destroy him: and thou shalt devote him and all his to *destruction*, and thou shalt spare nothing belonging to him; and thou shalt slay both man and woman, and infant and suckling, and calf and sheep, and camel and ass. 4 And Saul summoned the people, and he numbered them in Galgala, four hundred thousand regular troops, and Juda thirty thousand regular troops. 5 And Saul came to the cities of Amalec, and laid wait in the valley. 6 And Saul said to the Kinite, Go, and depart out of the midst of the Amalekites, lest I put thee with them; for thou dealedst mercifully with the children of Israel when they went up out of Egypt. So the Kinite departed from the midst of Amalec. 7 And Saul smote Amalec from Evilat to Sur fronting Egypt. 8 And he took Agag the king of Amalec alive, and he slew all the people and Hierim with the edge of the sword. 9 And Saul and all the people saved Agag alive, and the best of the flocks, and of the herds, and of the fruits, of the vineyards, and of all the good things; and they would not destroy them: but every worthless and refuse thing they destroyed. 10 And the word of the Lord came to Samuel, saying, 11 I have repented that I have made Saul to be king: for he has turned back from following me, and has not kept my word. And Samuel was grieved, and cried to the Lord all night. 12 And Samuel rose early and went to meet Israel in the morning, and it was told Saul, saying, Samuel has come to Carmel, and he has raised up help for himself: and he turned his chariot, and came down to Galgala to Saul; and, behold, he was offering up a whole-burnt-offering to the Lord, the chief of the spoils which he brought out of Amalec. 13 And Samuel came to Saul: and Saul said to him, Blessed *art* thou of the Lord: I have performed all that the Lord said. 14 And Samuel said, What then *is* the bleating of this flock in my ears, and the sound of the oxen which I hear? 15 And Saul said, I have brought them out of Amalec, that which the people preserved, even the best of the sheep, and of the cattle, that it might be sacrificed to the Lord thy God, and the rest have I utterly destroyed. 16 And Samuel said to Saul, Stay, and I will tell thee what the Lord has said to me this night: and he said to him, Say on. 17 And Samuel said to Saul, Art thou not little in his eyes, *though* a leader of one of the tribes of Israel? and *yet* the Lord anointed thee to be king over Israel. 18 And the Lord sent thee on a journey, and said to thee, Go, and utterly destroy: thou shalt slay the sinners against me, *even* the Amalekites; and thou shalt war against them until thou have consumed them. 19 And why didst not thou hearken to the voice of the Lord, but didst haste to fasten upon the spoils, and didst that which was evil in the sight of the Lord? 20 And Saul said to Samuel, Because I listened to the voice of the people: yet I went the way by which the Lord sent me, and I brought Agag the king of Amalec, and I destroyed Amalec. 21 But the people took of the spoils the best flocks and herds *out* of that which was destroyed, to sacrifice before the Lord our God in Galgal. 22 And Samuel said, Does the Lord take pleasure in whole-burnt-offerings and sacrifices, as in hearing the words of the Lord? behold, obedience *is* better than a good sacrifice, and hearkening than the fat of rams. 23 For sin is *as* divination; idols bring on pain and grief. Because thou hast rejected the word of the Lord, the Lord also shall reject thee from being king over Israel. 24 And Saul said to Samuel, I have sinned, in that I have transgressed the word of the Lord and thy direction; for I feared the people, and I hearkened to their voice. 25 And now remove, I pray thee, my sin, and turn back with me, and I will worship the Lord thy God. 26 And Samuel said to Saul, I will not turn back with thee, for thou hast rejected the word of the Lord, and the Lord will reject thee from being king over Israel. 27 And Samuel turned his face to depart, and Saul caught hold of the skirt of his garment, and tore it. 28 And Samuel said to him, The Lord has rent thy kingdom from Israel out of thy hand this day, and will give it to thy neighbour who is better than thou. 29 And Israel shall be divided to two: and *God* will not turn nor repent, for he is not as a man to repent. 30 And Saul said, I have sinned; yet honour me, I pray thee, before the elders of Israel, and before my people; and turn back with me, and I will worship the Lord thy God. 31 So Samuel turned back after Saul, and he worshipped the Lord. 32 And Samuel said, Bring me Agag the king of Amalec: and Agag came to him trembling; and Agag said Is death thus bitter? 33 And Samuel said to Agag, As thy sword has bereaved women of their children, so shall thy mother be made childless among women: and Samuel slew Agag before the Lord in Galgal. 34 And Samuel departed to Armathaim, and Saul went up to his house at Gabaa. 35 And Samuel did not see Saul again till the day of his death, for Samuel mourned after Saul, and the Lord repented that he had made Saul king over Israel.

1-Kgdms16 1 And the Lord said to Samuel, How long dost thou mourn for Saul, whereas I have rejected him from reigning over Israel? Fill thy horn with oil, and come, I will send thee to Jessae, to Bethleem; for I have seen among his sons a king for me. 2 And Samuel said, How can I go? whereas Saul will hear of it, and slay me: and the Lord said, Take a heifer in thine hand and thou shall say, I am come to sacrifice to the Lord. 3 And thou shalt call Jessae to the sacrifice, and I will make known to thee what thou shalt do; and thou shalt anoint him whom I shall mention to thee. 4 And Samuel did all that the Lord told him; and he came to Bethleem: and the elders of the city were amazed at meeting him, and said, Dost thou come peaceably, thou Seer? 5 And he said, Peaceably: I am come to sacrifice to the Lord. Sanctify yourselves, and rejoice with me this day: and he sanctified Jessae and his sons, and he called them to the sacrifice. 6 And it came to pass when they came in, that he saw Eliab, and said, Surely the Lord's anointed *is* before him. 7 But the Lord said to Samuel, Look not on his appearance, nor on his stature, for I have rejected him; for God sees not as man looks; for man looks at the outward appearance, but God looks at the heart. 8 And Jessae called Aminadab, and he passed before Samuel: and he said, Neither has God chosen this one. 9 And Jessae caused Sama to pass by: and he said, Neither has God chosen this one. 10 And Jessae caused his seven sons to pass before Samuel: and Samuel said, the Lord has not chosen these. 11 And Samuel said to Jessae, Hast thou no more sons? And Jessae said, *There is* yet a little one; behold, he tends the flock. And Samuel said to Jessae, Send and fetch him for we may not sit down till he comes. 12 And he sent and fetched him: and he was ruddy, with beauty of eyes, and very goodly to behold. And the Lord said to Samuel, Arise, and anoint David, for he is good. 13 And Samuel took the horn of oil, and anointed him in the midst of his brethren: and the Spirit of the Lord came upon David from that day forward: and Samuel arose, and departed to Armathaim. 14 And the Spirit of the Lord departed from Saul, and an evil spirit from the Lord tormented him. 15 And Saul's servants said to him, Behold now, and evil spirit from the Lord torments thee. 16 Let now thy servants speak before thee, and let them seek for our lord a man skilled to play on the harp; and it shall come to pass when an evil spirit comes upon thee and he shall play on his harp, that thou shalt be well, and he shall refresh thee. 17 And Saul said to his servants, Look now out for me a skillful player, and bring him to me. 18 And one of his servants answered and said, Behold, I have seen a son of Jessae the Bethleemite, and he understands playing *on the harp*, and the man *is* prudent, and a warrior, and wise in speech, and the man *is* handsome, and the Lord *is* with him. 19 And Saul sent messengers to Jessae, saying, Send to me thy son David who is with thy flock. 20 And Jessae took a homer of bread, and a bottle of wine, and one kid of the goats, and sent them by the hand of his son David to Saul. 21 And David went in to Saul, and stood before him; and he loved him greatly; and he became his armour-bearer. 22 And Saul sent to Jessae, saying, Let David, I pray thee, stand before me, for he has found grace in my eyes. 23 And it came to pass when the evil spirit was upon Saul, that David took his harp, and played with his hand: and Saul was refreshed, and *it was* well with him, and the evil spirit departed from him.

1-Kgdms17 1 And the Philistines gather their armies to battle, and gather themselves to Socchoth of Judaea, and encamp between Socchoth and Azeca Ephermen. 2 And Saul and the men of Israel gather together, and they encamp in the valley, and set the battle in array against the Philistines. 3 And the Philistines stand on the mountain on one side, and Israel stands on the mountain on the other side, and the valley was between them. 4 And there went forth a mighty man out of the army of the Philistines, Goliath, by name, out of Geth, his height *was* four cubits and a span. 5 And *he had* a helmet upon his head, and he wore a breastplate of chain armour; and the weight of his breastplate *was* five thousand shekels of brass and iron. 6 And greaves of grass *were* upon his legs, and a brazen target *was* between his shoulders. 7 And the staff of his spear *was* like a weaver's beam, and the spear's head *was formed* of six hundred shekels of iron; and his armour-bearer went before him. 8 And he stood and cried to the army of Israel, and said to them, Why are ye come forth to set yourselves in battle array against us? Am not I a Philistine, and ye He brews of Saul? Choose for yourselves a man, and let him come down to me. 9 And if he shall be able to fight against me, and shall smite me, then will we be your servants: but if I should prevail and smite him, ye shall be our servants, and serve us. 10 And the Philistine said, Behold, I have defied the armies of Israel this very day: give me a man, and we will both of us fight in single combat. 11 And Saul and all Israel heard these words of the Philistine, and they were dismayed, and greatly terrified. 32 And David said to Saul, Let not, I pray thee, the heart of my lord be dejected within him: thy servant will go, and fight with this Philistine. 33 And Saul said to David, Thou wilt not in anywise be able to go against this Philistine to fight with him, for thou art a mere youth, and he a man of war from his youth. 34 And David said to Saul, Thy servant was tending the flock for his father; and when a lion came and a she-bear, and took a sheep out of the flock, 35 then I went forth after him, and smote him, and drew *the spoil* out of his mouth: and as he rose up against me, then I caught hold of his throat, and

smote him, and slew him. 36 Thy servant smote both the lion and the bear, and the uncircumcised Philistine shall be as one of them: shall I not go and smite him, and remove this day a reproach from Israel? For who *is* this uncircumcised one, who has defied the army of the living God? 37 The Lord who delivered me out of the paw of the lion and out of the paw of the bear, he will deliver me out of the hand of this uncircumcised Philistine. And Saul said to David, Go, and the Lord shall be with thee. 38 And Saul clothed David with a military coat, and *put* his brazen helmet on his head. 39 And he girt David with his sword over his coat: and he made trial walking *with them* once and again: and David said to Saul, I shall not be able to go with these, for I have not proved *them*: so they remove them from him. 40 And he took his staff in his hand, and he chose for himself five smooth stones out of the brook, and put them in the shepherd's scrip which he had for his store, and his sling was in his hand; and he approached the Philistine. 41 42 And Goliath saw David, and despised him; for he was a lad, and ruddy, with a fair countenance. 43 And the Philistine said to David, Am I as a dog, that thou comest against me with a staff and stones? [and David said, Nay, but worse than a dog.] And the Philistine cursed David by his gods. 44 And the Philistine said to David, Come to me, and I will give thy flesh to the birds of the air, and to the beasts of the earth. 45 And David said to the Philistine, Thou comest to me with sword, and with spear, and with shield; but I come to thee in the name of the Lord God of hosts of the army of Israel, which thou hast defied 46 this day. And the Lord shall deliver thee this day into my hand; and I will slay thee, and take away thy head from off thee, and will give thy limbs and the limbs of the army of the Philistines this day to the birds of the sky, and to the wild beasts of the earth; and all the earth shall know that there is a God in Israel. 47 And all this assembly shall know that the Lord delivers not by sword or spear, for the battle *is* the Lord's, and the Lord will deliver you into our hands. 48 And the Philistine arose and went to meet David. 49 And David stretched out his hand to his scrip, and took thence a stone, and slang it, and smote the Philistine on his forehead, and the stone penetrated through the helmet into his forehead, and he fell upon his face to the ground. 50 51 And David ran, and stood upon him, and took his sword, and slew him, and cut off his head: and the Philistines saw that their champion was dead, and they fled. 52 And the men of Israel and Juda arose, and shouted and pursued them as far as the entrance to Geth, and as far as the gate of Ascalon: and the slain men of the Philistines fell in the way of the gates, both to Geth, and to Accaron. 53 And the men of Israel returned from pursuing after the Philistines, and they destroyed their camp. 54 And David took the head of the Philistine, and brought it to Jerusalem; but he put his armour in his tent.

1-Kgdms18 1 And there came out women in dances to meet David out of all the cities of Israel, with timbrels, and with rejoicing, and with cymbals. 7 And the women began *the strain*, and said, Saul has smitten his thousands, and David his ten thousands. 8 And it seemed evil in the eyes of Saul concerning this matter, and he said, To David they have given ten thousands, and to me they have given thousands. 9,10,11,12 And Saul was alarmed on account of David. 13 And he removed him from him, and made him a captain of a thousand for himself; and he went out and came in before the people. 14 And David was prudent in all his ways, and the Lord was with him. 15 And Saul saw that he was very wise, and he was afraid of him. 16 And all Israel and Juda loved David, because he came in and went out before the people. 17,18,19,20 And Melchol the daughter of Saul loved David; and it was told Saul, and the thing was pleasing in his eyes. 21 And Saul said, I will give her to him, and she shall be a stumbling-block to him. Now the hand of the Philistines was against Saul. 22 And Saul charged his servants, saying, Speak ye privately to David, saying, Behold, the king delights in thee, and all his servants love thee, and do thou becomes the king's son-in-law. 23 And the servants of Saul spoke these words in the ears of David; and David said, *Is it* a light thing in your eyes to become son-in-law to the king? Whereas I *am* an humble man, an not honourable? 24 And the servants of Saul reported to him according to these words, which David spoke. 25 And Saul said, Thus shall ye speak to David, The king wants no gift but a hundred foreskins of the Philistines, to avenge himself on the kings enemies. Now Saul thought to cast him into the hands of the Philistines. 26 And the servants of Saul report these words to David, and David was well pleased to become the son-in-law to the king. 27 And David arose, and went, he and his men, and smote among the Philistines a hundred men: and he brought their foreskins, and he becomes the king's son-in-law, and *Saul* gives him Melchol his daughter to wife. 28 And Saul saw that the Lord *was* with David, and *that* all Israel loved him. 29 And he was yet more afraid of David.

1-Kgdms19 1 And Saul spoke to Jonathan his son, and to all his servants, to slay David. 2 And Jonathan, Saul's son, loved David much: and Jonathan told David, saying, Saul seeks to kill thee: take heed to thyself therefore to-morrow morning, and hide thyself, and dwell in secret. 3 And I will go forth, and stand near my father in the field where thou shalt be, and I will speak concerning thee to my father; and I will see what his answer may be, and I will tell thee. 4 And Jonathan spoke favorably concerning David to Saul his father, and said to him, Let not the king sin against thy servant David, for he has not sinned against thee, and his deeds *are* very good. 5 And he put his life in his hand, and smote the Philistine, and the Lord wrought a great deliverance; and all Israel saw, and rejoiced: why then dost thou sin against innocent blood, to slay David without a cause? 6 And Saul hearkened to the voice of Jonathan; and Saul swore, saying, *As* the Lord lives, he shall not die. 7 And Jonathan called David, and told him all these words; and Jonathan brought David in to Saul, and he was before him as in former times. 8 And there was again war against Saul; and David did valiantly, and fought against the Philistines, and smote them with a very great slaughter, and they fled from before him. 9 And an evil spirit from God was upon Saul, and he was resting in his house, and a spear *was* in his hand, and David was playing on the harp with his hands. 10

And Saul sought to smite David with the spear; and David withdrew *suddenly* from the presence of Saul; and he drove the spear into the wall; and David retreated and escaped. 11 And it came to pass in that night, that Saul sent messengers to the house of David to watch him, in order to slay him in the morning; and Melchol David's wife told him, saying, Unless thou save thy life this night, to- morrow thou shalt be slain. 12 So Melchol lets David down by the window, and he departed, and fled, and escaped. 13 And Melchol took images, and laid them on the bed, and she put the liver of a goat by his head, and covered them with clothes. 14 And Saul sent messengers to take David; and they say that he is sick. 15 And he sends to David, saying, Bring him to me on the bed, that I may slay him. 16 And the messengers come, and, behold, the images *were* on the bed, and the goat's liver at his head. 17 And Saul said to Melchol, Why hast thou thus deceived me, and suffered my enemy to depart, and he has escaped? and Melchol said to Saul, He said, let me go, and if not, I will slay thee. 18 So David fled, and escaped, and comes to Samuel to Armathaim, and tells him all that Saul had done to him: and Samuel and David went, and dwelt in Navath in Rama. 19 And it was told Saul, saying, Behold, David *is* in Navath in Rama. 20 And Saul sent messengers to take David, and they saw the assembly of the prophets, and Samuel stood *as* appointed over them; and the Spirit of God came upon the messengers of Saul, and they prophesy. 21 And it was told Saul, and he sent other messengers, and they also prophesied: and Saul sent again a third set of messengers, and they also prophesied. 22 And Saul was very angry, and went himself also to Armathaim, and he comes as far as the well of the threshing floor that is in Sephi; and he asked and said, Where *are* Samuel and David? And they said, Behold, in Navath in Rama. 23 And he went thence to Navath in Rama: and there came the Spirit of God upon him also, and he went on prophesying till he came to Navath in Rama. 24 And he took off his clothes, and prophesied before them; and lay down naked all that day and all that night: therefore they said, *Is* Saul also among the prophets?

1-Kgdms20 1 And David fled from Navath in Rama, and comes into the presence of Jonathan; and he said, What have I done, and what *is* my fault, and wherein have I sinned before thy father, that he seeks my life? 2 And Jonathan said to him, Far be it from thee: thou shalt not die: behold, my father will not do any thing great or small without discovering it to me; and why should my father hide this matter from me? This thing is not *so*. 3 And David answered Jonathan, and said, Thy father knows surely that I have found grace in thy sight, and he said, Let not Jonathan know this, lest he refuse his consent: but *as* the Lord lives and thy soul lives, as I said, *the space* is filled up between me and death. 4 And Jonathan said to David, What does thy soul desire, and what shall I do for thee. 5 And David said to Jonathan, Behold, to-morrow *is* the new moon, and I shall not on any account sit down to eat, but thou shalt let me go, and I will hide in the plain till the evening. 6 And if thy father do in anywise enquire for me, then shalt thou say, David earnestly asked leave of me to run to Bethleem his city, for *there is* there, a yearly sacrifice for all the family. 7 If he shall say thus, Well, —*all is* safe for thy servant: but if he shall answer harshly to thee, know that evil is determined by him. 8 And thou shalt deal mercifully with thy servant; for thou hast brought thy servant into a covenant of the Lord with thyself: and if there is iniquity in thy servant, slay me thyself; but why dost thou thus bring me to thy father? 9 And Jonathan said, That be far from thee: for if I surely know that evil is determined by my father to come upon thee, although it should not be against thy cities, I will tell thee. 10 And David said to Jonathan, Who can tell me if thy father should answer roughly? 11 And Jonathan said to David, Go, and abide in the field. And they went out both into the field. 12 And Jonathan said to David, the Lord God of Israel knows that I will sound my father as I have an opportunity, three several times, and, behold, *if good* should be determined concerning David, and I do not send to thee to the field, 13 God do so to Jonathan and more also: as I shall *also* report the evil to thee, and make it known to thee, and I will let thee go; and thou shalt depart in peace, and the Lord shall be with thee, as he was with my father. 14 And if indeed I continue to live, then shalt thou deal mercifully with me; and if I indeed die, 15 16 thou shalt not withdraw thy mercy from my house for ever: and if thou doest not, when the Lord cuts off the enemies of David each from the face of the earth, *should it happen* that the name of Jonathan be discovered by the house of David, then let the Lord seek out the enemies of David. 17 And Jonathan swore yet again to David, because he loved the soul of him that loved him. 18 And Jonathan said, To-morrow *is* the new moon, and thou wilt be enquired for, because thy seat will be observed as vacant. 19 And thou shalt stay three days, and watch an opportunity, and shalt come to thy place where thou mayest hide thyself in the day of thy business, and thou shalt wait by that ergab. 20 And I will shoot three arrows, aiming them at a mark. 21 And behold, I *will* send a lad, saying, Go find me the arrow. 22 If I should expressly say to the lad, The arrow *is* here, and on this side of thee, take it; *then* come, for it is well with thee, and there is no reason *for fear, as* the Lord lives: *but if I* should say thus to the young man, The arrow *is* on that side of thee, and beyond; go, for the Lord hath sent thee away. 23 And as for the word which thou and I have spoken, behold, the Lord *is* witness between me and thee for ever. 24 So David hides himself in the field, and the *new* month arrives, and the king comes to the table to eat. 25 And he sat upon his seat as in former times, even on his seat by the wall, and he went before Jonathan; and Abenner sat on one side of Saul, and the place of David was empty. 26 And Saul said nothing on that day, for he said, It seems to have fallen out that he is not clean, because he has not purified himself. 27 And it came to pass on the morrow, on the second day of the month, that the place of David was empty; and Saul said to Jonathan his son, Why has not the son of Jessae attended both yesterday and today at the table? 28 And Jonathan answered Saul, and said to him, David asked leave of me to go as far as Bethleem his city; 29 and he said, Let me go, I pray thee, for we have a family sacrifice in the city, and my brethren have sent for me; and now, if I have found grace in thine eyes, I will even go over and see my brethren: therefore he is not present at the table of the king. 30 And Saul was exceedingly angry with Jonathan, and said to him, Thou son of traitorous damsels! for do I not know that thou art an accomplice with the son of Jessae to thy same, and to the shame of thy mother's nakedness? 31 For so long as the son of Jessae lives upon the earth, thy kingdom shall not be established: now then send and take the young man, for he shall surely die. 32 And Jonathan answered Saul, Why is he to die? What has he done? 33 And Saul lifted up his spear against Jonathan to slay him: so Jonathan knew that this evil was determined on by his father to slay David. 34 And Jonathan sprang up from the table in great anger, and did not eat bread on the second *day* of the month, for he grieved bitterly for David, because his father determined *on mischief* against him. 35 And morning came, and Jonathan went out to the field, as he appointed *to do* for a signal to David, and a little boy *was* with him. 36 And he said to the boy, Run, find me the arrows which I shoot: and the boy ran, and *Jonathan* shot an arrow, and sent it beyond *him.* 37 And the boy came to the place where the arrow was which Jonathan shot; and Jonathan cried out after the lad, and said, The arrow *is* on that side of thee and beyond thee. 38 And Jonathan cried out after his boy, saying, Make all speed, and stay not. And Jonathan's boy gathered up the arrows, and brought the arrows to his master. 39 And the boy knew nothing, only Jonathan and David *knew.* 40 And Jonathan gave his weapons to his boy, and said to his boy, Go, enter into the city. 41 And when the lad went in, then David arose from the argab, and fell upon his face, and did obeisance to him three times, and they kissed each other, and wept for each other, for a great while. 42 And Jonathan said to David, Go in peace, and as we have both sworn in the name of the Lord, saying, The Lord shall be witness between me and thee, and between my seed and thy seed for ever—*even so let it be.* And David arose and departed, and Jonathan went into the city.

1-Kgdms21 1 And David comes to Nomba to Abimelech the priest: and Abimelech was amazed at meeting him, and said to him, Why *art* thou alone, and nobody with thee? 2 And David said to the priest, The king gave me a command to-day, and said to me, Let no one know the matter on which I send thee, an concerning which I have charged thee: and I have charged my servants *to be* in the place that is called, The faithfulness of God, phellani maemoni. 3 And now if there are under thy hand five loaves, give into my hand what is ready. 4 And the priest answered David, and said, There are no common loaves under my hand, for I have none but holy loaves: if the young men have been kept at least from women, then they shall eat *them.* 5 And David answered the priest, and said to him, Yea, we have been kept from women for three days: when I came forth for the journey all the young men were purified; but this expedition is unclean, wherefore it shall be sanctified this day because of my weapons. 6 So Abimelech the priest gave him the shewbread; for there were no loaves there, but only the presence loaves which had been removed from the presence of the Lord, in order that hot bread should be set on, on the day on which he took them. 7 And there was there on that day one of Saul's servants detained before the Lord, and his name *was* Doec the Syrian, tending the mules of Saul. 8 And David said to Abimelech, See if there is here under thy hand spear or sword, for I have not brought in my hand my sword or my weapons, for the word of the king was urgent. 9 And the priest said, Behold the sword of Goliath the Philistine, whom thou smotest in the valley of Ela; and it is wrapt in a cloth: if thou wilt take it, take it for thyself, for there is no other except it here. And David said, Behold, there is none like it; give it me. 10 And he gave it him; and David arose, and fled in that day from he presence of Saul: and David came to Anchus king of Geth. 11 And the servants of Anchus said to him, *Is* not this David the king of the land? Did not the dancing women begin the son to him, saying, Saul has smitten his thousand, and David his ten thousands? 12 And David laid up the words in his heart, and was greatly afraid of Anchus king of Geth. 13 And he changed his appearance before him, and feigned himself a false character in that day; and drummed upon the doors of the city, and used extravagant gestures with his hands, and fell against the doors of the gate, and his spittle ran down upon his beard. 14 And Anchus said to his servants, Lo! ye see the man *is* mad: why have ye brought him in to me? 15 *Am* I in want of madmen, that ye have brought him in to me to play the madman? He shall not come into the house.

1-Kgdms22 1 And David departed thence, and escaped; and he comes to the cave of Odollam, and his brethren hear, and the house of his father, and they go down to him there. 2 And there gathered to him every one that was in distress, and every one that was in debt, and every one that was troubled in mind; and he was a leader over them, and there were with him about four hundred men. 3 And David departed thence to Massephath of Moab, and said to the king of Moab, Let, I pray thee, my father and my mother be with thee, until I know what God will do to me. 4 And he persuaded the King of Moab, and they dwell with him continually, while David was in the hold. 5 And Gad the prophet said to David, Dwell not in the hold: go, and thou shalt enter the land of Juda. So David went, and came and dwelt in the city of Saric. 6 And Saul heard that David was discovered, and his men with him: now Saul dwelt in the hill below the field that is in Rama, and his spear *was* in his hand, and all his servants stood near him. 7 And Saul said to his servants that stood by him, Hear now, ye sons of Benjamin, will the son of Jessae indeed give all of you fields and vineyards, and will he make you all captains of hundreds and captains of thousands? 8 That ye are conspiring against me, and there is no one that informs me, whereas my son has made a covenant with the son of Jessae, and there is no one of you that is sorry for me, or informs me, that my son has stirred up my servant against me for an enemy, as *it is* this day? 9 And Doec the Syrian who was over the mules of Saul answered and said, I saw the son of Jessae as he came to Nomba to Abimelech son of Achitob the priest. 10 And *the priest* enquired of God for him, and gave him provision, and gave him the sword of

Goliath the Philistine. 11 And the king sent to call Abimelech son of Achitob and all his father's sons, the priests that were in Nomba; and they all came to the king. 12 And Saul said, Hear now, thou son of Achitob. And he said, Lo! I *am here*, speak, *my* lord. 13 And Saul said to him, Why have thou and the son of Jessae conspired against me, that thou shouldest give him bread and a sword, and shouldest enquire of God for him, to raise him up against me as an enemy, as *he is* this day? 14 And he answered the king, and said, And who *is* there among all thy servants faithful as David, and *he is* a son-in-law of the king, and *he is* executor of all thy commands, and *is* honourable in thy house? 15 Have I begun to-day to enquire of God for him? By no means: let not the king bring a charge against his servant, and against thee whole of my father's house; for thy servant knew not in all these matters anything great or small. 16 And king Saul said, Thou shalt surely die, Abimelech, thou, and all thy father's house. 17 And the king said to the footmen that attended on him, Draw nigh and slay the priests of the Lord, because their hand *is* with David, and because they knew that he fled, and they did not inform me. But the servants of the king would not lift their hands to fall upon the priest of the Lord. 18 And the king said to Doec, Turn thou, and fall upon the priests: and Doec the Syrian turned, and slew the priests of the Lord in that day, three hundred and five men, all wearing an ephod. 19 And he smote Nomba the city of the priest with the edge of the sword, both man, and woman, infant and suckling, and calf, and ox, and sheep. 20 And one son of Abimelech son of Achitob escapes, and his name *was* Abiathar, and he fled after David. 21 And Abiathar told David that Saul had slain all the priests of the Lord. 22 And David said to Abiathar, I knew it in that day, that Doec the Syrian would surely tell Saul: I am guilty of the death of the house of thy father. 23 Dwell with me; fear not, for wherever I shall seek a place *of safety* for my life, I will also seek a place for thy life, for thou art safely guarded *while* with me.

1-Kgdms23 1 And it was told David, saying, behold, the Philistines war in Keila, and they rob, they trample on the threshing-floors. 2 And David enquired of the Lord, saying, Shall I go and smite these Philistines? And the Lord said, Go, and thou shalt smite these Philistines, and shalt save Keila. 3 And the men of David said to him, Behold, we are afraid here in Judea; and how shall it be if we go to Keila? Shall we go after the spoils of the Philistines? 4 And David enquired yet again of the Lord; and the Lord answered him, and said to him, Arise and go down to Keila, for I will deliver the Philistines into thy hands. 5 So David and his men with him went to Keila, and fought with the Philistines; and they fled from before him, and he carried off their cattle, and smote them with a great slaughter, and David rescued the inhabitants of Keila. 6 And it came to pass when Abiathar the son of Achimelech fled to David, that he went down with David to Keila, having and ephod in his hand. 7 And it was told Saul that David was come to Keila: and Saul said, God has sold him into my hands, for he is shut up, having entered into a city that has gates and bars. 8 And Saul charged all the people to go down to war to Keila, to besiege David and his men. 9 And David knew that Saul spoke openly of mischief against him: and David said to Abiathar the priest, Bring the ephod of the Lord. 10 And David said, Lord God of Israel, thy servant has indeed heard, that Saul seeks to come against Keila to destroy the city on my account. 11 Will *the place* be shut up? And now will Saul come down, as thy servant has heard? Lord God of Israel, tell thy servant. And the Lord said, It will be shut up. 12,13 And David arose, and the men with him, in number about four hundred, and they went forth from Keila, and went whithersoever they could go: and it was told Saul that David had escaped from Keila, and he forbore to come. 14 And he dwelt in Maserem in the wilderness, in the narrow *passes*, and dwelt in the wilderness in mount Ziph, in the dry country. And Saul sought him continually, but the Lord delivered him not into his hands. 15 And David perceived that Saul went forth to seek David; and David was in the dry mountain in the New Ziph. 16 And Jonathan son of Saul rose, and went to David to Caene, and strengthened his hands in the Lord. 17 And he said to him, Fear not, for the hand of Saul my father shall not find thee; and thou shalt be king over Israel, and I shall be second to thee; and Saul my father knows it. 18 So they both made a covenant before the Lord; and David dwelt in Caene, and Jonathan went to his home. 19 And the Ziphites came up out of the dry country to Saul to the hill, saying, Behold, is not David hidden with us in Messara, in the narrows in Caene in the hill of Echela, which is on the right of Jessaemon? 20 And now *according to* all the king's desire to come down, let him come down to us; they have shut him up into the hands of the king. 21 And Saul said to them, Blessed *be* ye of the Lord, for ye have been grieved on my account. 22 Go, I pray you, and make preparations yet, and notice his place where his foot shall be, quickly, in that place which ye spoke of, lest by any means he should deal craftily. 23 Take notice, then, and learn, and I will go with you; and it shall come to pass that if he is in the land, I will search him out among all the thousands of Juda. 24 And the Ziphites arose, and went before Saul: and David and his men *were* in the wilderness of Maon, westward, to the right of Jessaemon. 25 And Saul and his men went to seek him: and they brought word to David, and he went down to the rock that was in the wilderness of Maon: and Saul heard, and followed after David to the wilderness of Maon. 26 And Saul and his men go on one side of the mountain, and David and his men are on the other side of the mountain: and David was hiding himself to escape from Saul: and Saul and his men encamped against David and his men, in order to take them. 27 And there came a messenger to Saul, saying, Haste thee, and come hither, for the Philistines have invaded the land. 28 So Saul returned from following after David, and went to meet the Philistines: therefore that place was called The divided Rock.

1-Kgdms24 1 And David rose up from thence, and dwelt in the narrow passes of Engaddi. 2 And it came to pass when Saul returned from pursuing after the Philistines, that it was reported to him, saying, David *is* in the wilderness of Engaddi. 3 And he took with him three thousand men, chosen out of all Israel, and went to seek David and his men in front of Saddaeem. 4 And he came to the flocks of sheep that were by the way, and there was a cave there; and Saul went in to make preparation, and David and his men were sitting in the inner part of the cave. 5 And the men of David said to him, Behold, this *is* the day of which the Lord spoke to thee, that he would deliver thine enemy into thy hands; and thou shalt do to him as *it is* good in thy sight. So David arose and cut off the skirt of Saul's garment secretly. 6 And it came to pass after this that David's heart smote him, because he had cut off the skirt of his garment. 7 And David said to his men, The Lord forbid it me, that I should do this ting to my lord the anointed of the Lord, to lift my hand against him; for he is the anointed of the Lord. 8 So David persuaded his men by *his* words, and did not suffer them to arise and slay Saul: and Saul arose and went his way. 9 And David rose up *and went* after him out of the cave: and David cried after Saul, saying, *My* lord, O king! and Saul looked behind him, and David bowed with his face to the ground, and did obeisance to him. 10 And David said to Saul, Why dost thou hearken to the words of the people, saying, Behold, David seeks thy life? 11 Behold, thine eyes have seen this day how that the Lord has delivered thee this day into my hands in the cave; and I would not slay thee, but spared thee, and said, I will not lift up my hand against my lord, for he is the Lord's anointed. 12 And behold, the skirt of thy mantle *is* in my hand, I cut off the skirt, and did not slay thee: know then and see to-day, there is no evil in my hand, nor impiety, nor rebellion; and I have not sinned against thee, yet thou layest snares for my soul to take it. 13 The Lord judge between me and thee, and the Lord requite thee on thyself: but my hand shall not be upon thee. 14 As the old proverb says, Transgression will proceed from the wicked ones: but my hand shall not be upon thee. 15 And now after whom dost thou come forth, O king of Israel? After whom dost thou pursue? After a dead dog, and after a flea? 16 The Lord be judge and umpire between me and thee, the Lord look upon and judge my cause, and rescue me out of thy hand. 17 And it came to pass when David had finished speaking these words to Saul, that Saul said, *Is* this thy voice, Son David? And Saul lifted up his voice, and wept. 18 And Saul said to David, Thou *art* more righteous that I, for thou hast recompensed me good, but I have recompensed thee evil. 19 And thou hast told me to-day what good thou hast done me, how the Lord shut me up into thy hands to-day, and thou didst not slay me. 20 And if any one should find his enemy in distress, and should send him forth in a good way, then the Lord will reward him good, as thou has done this day. 21 And now, behold, I know that thou shalt surely reign, and the kingdom of Israel shall be established in thy hand. 22 Now then swear to me by the Lord, that thou wilt not destroy my seed after me, that thou wilt not blot out my name from the house of my father. 23 So David swore to Saul: and Saul departed to his place, and David and his men went up to the strong-hold of Messera.

1-Kgdms25 1 And Samuel died, and all Israel assembled, and bewailed him, and they bury him in his house in

Armathaim: and David arose, and went down to the wilderness of Maon. 2 And there was a man in Maon, and his flocks were in Carmel, and *he was* a very great man; and he had three thousand sheep, and a thousand she-goats: and he happened to be shearing his flock in Carmel. 3 And the man's name *was* Nabal, and his wife's name *was* Abigaia: and his wife *was* of good understanding and very beautiful in person: but the man *was* harsh, and evil in his doings, and the man *was* churlish. 4 And David heard in the wilderness, that Nabal the Carmelite was shearing his sheep. 5 And David sent ten young men, and he said to the young men, Go up to Carmel, and go to Nabal, and ask him in my name how he is. 6 And thus shall ye say, May thou and thy house seasonably prosper, and all thine be in prosperity. 7 And now, behold, I have heard that thy shepherds who were with is in the wilderness are shearing thy sheep, and we hindered them not, neither did we demand any thing from them all the time they were in Carmel. 8 Ask thy servants, and they will tell thee. Let then thy servants find grace in thine eyes, for we are come on a good day; give we pray thee, whatsoever thy hand may find, to thy son David. 9 So the servants come and speak these words to Nabal, according to all these words in the name of David. 10 And Nabal sprang up, and answered the servants of David, and said, Who *is* David? and who *is* the son of Jessae? Now-a-days there is abundance of servants who depart every one from his master. 11 And shall I take my bread, and my wine, and my beasts that I have slain for my shearers, and shall I give them to men of whom I know not whence they are? 12 So the servants of David turned back, and returned, and came and reported to David according to these words. 13 And David said to his men, Gird on every man his sword. And they went up after David, about four hundred men: and two hundred abode with the stuff. 14 And one of the servants reported to Abigaia the wife of Nabal, saying, Behold, David sent messengers out of the wilderness to salute our lord; but he turned away from them. 15 And the men were very good to us; they did not hinder us, neither did they demand from us any thing all the days that we were with them. 16 And when we were in the field, they were as a wall round about us, both by night and by day, all the days that we were with them feeding the flock. 17 And now do thou consider, and see what thou wilt do; for mischief is determined against our lord and against his house; and he *is* a vile character, and one cannot speak to him. 18 And Abigaia hasted, and took two hundred loaves, and two vessels of wine, and five sheep ready dressed, and five ephahs of fine flour, and one homer of dried grapes, and two hundred cakes of figs, and put them upon asses. 19 And she said to her servants, Go on before me, and behold I come after you: but she told not her husband. 20 And it came to pass when she had mounted her ass and was going down by the covert of the mountain, behold, David and his men came down to meet her, and she met them. 21 And David said, Perhaps I have kept all his possessions in the wilderness that he should wrong me, and we did not order the taking anything of all his goods; yet he has rewarded me evil for good. 22 So God do to David and more also, if I leave one male of all that belong to Nabal until the morning. 23 And Abigaia saw David, and she hasted and alighted from her ass; and she felt before David on her face, and did obeisance to him, *bowing* to the ground 24 *even* to his feet, and said, On me, my lord, be my wrong: let, I pray thee, thy servant speak in thine ears, and hear thou the words of thy servant. 25 Let not my lord, I pray thee, take to heart this pestilent man, for according to his name, so is he; Nabal *is* his name, and folly *is* with him: but I thy handmaid saw not the servants of my lord whom thou didst send. 26 And now, my lord, *as* the Lord lives, and thy soul lives, as the Lord has kept thee from coming against innocent blood, and from executing vengeance for thyself, now therefore let thine enemies, and those that seek evil against my lord, become as Nabal. 27 And now accept this token of goodwill, which thy servant has brought to my lord, and thou shalt give it to the servants that wait on my lord. 28 Remove, I pray thee, the trespass of thy servant; for the Lord will surely make for my lord a sure house, for the Lord fights the battles of my lord, and there shall no evil be ever found in thee. 29 And *if* a man shall rise up persecuting thee and seeking thy life, yet shall the life of my lord be bound up in the bundle of life with the Lord God, and thou shalt whirl the life of thine enemies *as* in the midst of a sling. 30 And it shall be when the Lord shall have wrought for my lord all the good things he has spoken concerning thee, and shall appoint thee to be ruler over Israel; 31 then this shall not be an abomination and offence to my lord, to have shed innocent blood without cause, and for my lord to have avenged himself: and so may the Lord do good to my lord, and thou shalt remember thine handmaid to do her good. 32 And David said to Abigaia, Blessed *be* the Lord God of Israel, who sent thee this very day to meet me: 33 and blessed *be* thy conduct, and blessed *be* thou, who hast hindered me this very day from coming to shed blood, and from avenging myself. 34 But surely as the Lord God of Israel lives, who hindered me this day from doing thee harm, if thou hadst not hasted and come to meet me, then I said, There shall *surely* not be left to Nabal till the morning one male. 35 And David took of her hand all that she brought to him, and said to her, Go in peace to thy house: see, I have hearkened to thy voice, and accepted thy petition. 36 And Abigaia came to Nabal: and, behold, he had a banquet in this house, as the banquet of a king, and the heart of Nabal *was* merry within him, and he *was* very drunken: and she told him nothing great or small till the morning light. 37 And it came to pass in the morning, when Nabal recovered from his wine, his wife told him these words; and his heart died within him, and he became as a stone. 38 And it came to pass after about ten days, that the Lord smote Nabal, and he died. 39 And David heard it and said, Blessed *be* the Lord, who has judged the cause of my reproach at the hand of Nabal, and has delivered his servant from the power of evil; and the Lord has returned the mischief of Nabal upon his own head. And David sent and spoke concerning Abigaia, to take her to himself for a wife. 40 So the servants of David came to Abigaia to Carmel, and spoke to her, saying, David has sent us to thee, to take thee to himself for a wife. 41 And she arose, and did reverence with her face to the earth, and said, Behold, thy servant *is* for an handmaid to wash the feet of thy servants. 42 And Abigaia arose, and mounted her ass, and five damsels followed her: and she went after the servants of David, and became his wife. 43 And David took Achinaam out of Jezrael, and they were both his wives. 44 And Saul gave Melchol his daughter, David's wife, to Phalti the son of Amis who was of Romma.

1-Kgdms26 1 And the Ziphites come out of the dry country to Saul to the hill, saying, Behold, David hides himself with us in the hill Echela, opposite Jessemon. 2 And Saul arose, and went down to the wilderness of Ziph, and with him *went* three thousand men chosen out of Israel, to seek David in the wilderness of Ziph. 3 And Saul encamped in the hill of Echela in front of Jessemon, by the way, and David dwelt in the wilderness: and David saw that Saul came after him into the wilderness. 4 And David sent spies, and ascertained that Saul was come prepared out of Keila. 5 And David arose secretly, and goes into the place where Saul was sleeping, and there *was* Abenner the son of Ner, the captain of his host: and Saul was sleeping in a chariot, and the people had encamped along round about him. 6 And David answered and spoke to Abimelech the Chettite, and to Abessa the son Saruia the brother of Joab, saying, Who will go in with me to Saul into the camp? And Abessa said, I will go in with thee. 7 So David and Abessa go in among the people by night: and behold, Saul was fast asleep in the chariot, and his spear was stuck in the ground near his head, and Abenner and his people slept round about him. 8 And Abessa said to David, The Lord has this day shut up thine enemy into thine hands, and now I will smite him to the earth with the spear to the ground once *for all*, and I will not smite him again. 9 And David said to Abessa, Do not lay him low, for who shall lift up his hand against the anointed of the Lord, and be guiltless? 10 And David said, *As* the Lord lives, if the Lord smite him not, or his day come and he die, or he go down to battle and be added *to his fathers, do not so.* 11 The Lord forbid it me that I should lift up my hand against the anointed of the Lord: and now take, I pray thee, the spear from his bolster, and the pitcher of water, and let us return home. 12 So David took the spear, and the pitcher of water from his bolster, and they went home: and there was no one that saw, and no one that knew, and there was no one that awoke, all being asleep, for a stupor from the Lord had fallen upon them. 13 So David went over to the other side, and stood on the top of a hill afar off, and *there was* a good distance between them. 14 And David called to the people, and spoke to Abenner, saying, Wilt thou not answer, Abenner? and Abenner answered and said, Who art thou that callest? 15 And David said to Abenner, *Art* not thou a man? and who *is* like thee in Israel? Why then dost thou not guard thy lord the king? for one out of the people went in to destroy thy lord the king. 16 And this thing *is* not good which thou hast done. *As* the Lord lives, ye are worthy of death, ye who guard your lord the king, the anointed of the Lord: and now behold, I pray you, the spear of the king, and the cruse of water: where are the articles that should be at his head? 17 And Saul recognized the voice of David, and said, *Is* this

thy voice, son David? and David said, I *am* thy servant, *my* lord, O king. 18 And he said, Why does my lord thus pursue after his servant? for in what have I sinned? and what unrighteousness has been found in me? 19 And now let my lord the king hear the word of his servant. If God stirs thee up against me, let thine offering be acceptable: but if the sons of men, they *are* cursed before the Lord, for they have cast me out this day so that I should not be established in the inheritance of the Lord, saying, Go, serve other Gods. 20 And now let not my blood fall to the ground before the Lord, for the king of Israel has come forth to seek thy life, as the night hawk pursues *its prey* in the mountains. 21 And Saul said, I have sinned: turn, son David, for I will not hurt thee, because my life was precious in thine eyes; and to-day I have been foolish and have erred exceedingly. 22 And David answered and said, Behold, the spear of the king: let one of the servants come over and take it. 23 And the Lord shall recompense each according to his righteousness and his truth, since the Lord delivered thee this day into my hands, and I would not lift my hand against the Lord's anointed. 24 And, behold, as thy life has been precious this very day in my eyes, so let my life be precious before the Lord, and may he protect me, and deliver me out of all affliction. 25 And Saul said to David, Blessed *be* thou, *my* son; and thou shalt surely do valiantly, and surely prevail. And David went on his way, and Saul returned to his place.

1-Kgdms27 1 And David said in his heart, Now shall I be one day delivered *for death* into the hands of Saul; and there is no good thing for me unless I should escape into the land of the Philistines, and Saul should cease from seeking me through every coast of Israel: so I shall escape out of his hand. 2 So David arose, and the six hundred men that were with him, and he went to Anchus, son Ammach, king of Geth. 3 And David dwelt with Anchus, he and his men, each with his family; and David and both his wives, Achinaam, the Jezraelitess, and Abigaia the wife of Nabal the Carmelite. 4 And it was told Saul that David had fled to Geth; and he no longer sought after him. 5 And David said to Anchus, If now thy servant has found grace in thine eyes, let them give me, I pray thee, a place in one of the cities in the country, and I will dwell there: for why does thy servant dwell with thee in a royal city? 6 And he gave him Sekelac in that day: therefore Sekelac came into possession of the king of Judea to this day. 7 And the number of the days that David dwelt in the country of the Philistines was four months. 8 And David and his men went up, and made an attack on all the Gesirites and on the Amalekites: and behold, the land was inhabited, (even the land from Gelampsur) by those who come from the fortified *cities* even to the land of Egypt. 9 And he smote the land, and saved neither man nor woman alive; and they took flocks, and herds, and asses, and camels, and raiment; and they returned and came to Anchus. 10 And Anchus said to David, On whom have ye made an attack to-day? And David said to Anchus, On the south of Judea, and on the south of Jesmega, and on the south of the Kenezite. 11 And I have not saved man or woman alive to bring them to Geth, saying, Lest they carry a report to Geth against us, saying, These things David does. And this was his manner all the days that David dwelt in the country of the Philistines. 12 So David had the full confidence of Anchus, who said, He is thoroughly disgraced among his people in Israel and he shall be my servant for ever.

1-Kgdms28 1 And it came to pass in those days that the Philistines gathered themselves together with their armies to go out to fight with Israel; and Anchus said to David, Know surely, that thou shalt go forth to battle with me, *thou*, and thy men. 2 And David said to Anchus, Thus now thou shalt know what thy servant will do. And Anchus said to David, So will I make thee captain of my body-guard continually. 3 And Samuel died, and all Israel lamented for him, and they bury him in his city, in Armathaim. And Saul had removed those who had in them divining spirits, and the wizards, out of the land. 4 And the Philistines assemble themselves, and come and encamp in Sonam: and Saul gathers all the men of Israel, and they encamp in Gelbue. 5 And Saul saw the camp of the Philistines, and he was alarmed, and his heart was greatly dismayed. 6 And Saul enquired of the Lord; and the Lord answered him not by dreams, nor by manifestations, nor by prophets. 7 Then Saul said to his servants, Seek for me a woman who has in her a divining spirit, and I will go to her, and enquire of her: and his servants said to him, Behold, *there is* a woman who has in her a divining spirit at Aendor. 8 And Saul disguised himself, and put on other raiment, and he goes, and two men with him, and they come to the woman by night; and he said to her, Divine to me, I pray thee, by the divining spirit within thee, and bring up to me him whom I shall name to thee. 9 And the woman said to him, Behold now, thou knowest what Saul has done, how he has cut off those who had in them divining spirits, and the wizards from the land, and why dost thou spread a snare for my life to destroy it? 10 And Saul swore to her, and said, *As* the Lord lives, no injury shall come upon thee on this account. 11 And the woman said, Whom shall I bring up to thee? and he said, Bring up to me Samuel. 12 And the woman saw Samuel, and cried out with a loud voice: and the woman said to Saul, Why hast thou deceived me? for thou art Saul. 13 And the king said to her, Fear not; tell me whom thou has seen. And the woman said to him, I saw gods ascending out of the earth. 14 And he said to her, What didst thou perceive? and she said to him, An upright man ascending out of the earth, and he *was* clothed with a mantle. And Saul knew that this was Samuel, and he stooped with his face to the earth, and did obeisance to him. 15 And Samuel said, Why hast thou troubled me, that I should come up? And Saul said, I am greatly distressed, and the Philistines war against me, and God has departed from me, and no longer hearkens to me either by the hand of the prophets or by dreams: and now I have called thee to tell me what I shall do. 16 And Samuel said, Why askest thou me, whereas the Lord has departed from thee, and taken part with thy neighbour? 17 And the Lord has done to thee, as the Lord spoke by me; and the Lord will rend thy kingdom out of thy hand, and will give it to thy neighbour David. 18 because thou didst not hearken to the voice of the Lord, and didst not execute his fierce anger upon Amalec, therefore the Lord has done this thing to thee this day. 19 And the Lord shall deliver Israel with thee into the hands of the Philistines, and to-morrow thou and thy sons with thee shall fall, and the Lord shall deliver the army of Israel into the hands of the Philistines. 20 And Saul instantly fell at his full length upon the earth, and was greatly afraid because of the words of Samuel; and there was no longer any strength in him, for he had eaten no bread all that day, and all that night. 21 And the woman went in to Saul, and saw that he was greatly disquieted, and said to him, Behold now, thine handmaid has hearkened to thy voice, and I have put my life in my hand, and have heard the words which thou has spoken to me. 22 And now hearken, I pray thee, to the voice of thine handmaid, and I will set before thee a morsel of bread, and eat, and thou shalt be strengthened, for thou wilt be going on thy way. 23 But he would not eat; so his servants and the woman constrained him, and he hearkened to their voice, and rose up from the earth, and sat upon a bench. 24 And the woman had a fat heifer in the house; and she hasted and slew it; and she took meal and kneaded it, and baked unleavened cakes. 25 And she brought *the meat* before Saul, and before his servants; and they ate, and rose up, and departed that night.

1-Kgdms29 1 And the Philistines gather all their armies to Aphec, and Israel encamped in Aendor, which is in Jezrael. 2 And the lords of the Philistines went on by hundreds and thousands, and David and his men went on in the rear with Anchus. 3 And the lords of the Philistines said, Who *are* these that pass by? And Anchus said to the captains of the Philistines, *Is* not this David the servant of Saul king of Israel? He has been with us some time, even this second year, and I have not found any fault in him from the day that he attached himself to me even until this day. 4 And the captains of the Philistines were displeased at him, and they say to him, Send the man away, and let him return to his place, where thou didst set him; and let him not come with us to the war, and let him not be a traitor in the camp: and wherewith will he be reconciled to his master? Will it not be with the heads of those men? 5 *Is* not this David whom they celebrated in dances, saying, Saul has smitten his thousands, and David his ten thousands? 6 And Anchus called David, and said to him, *As* the Lord lives, thou *art* right and approved in my eyes, and *so is* thy going out and thy coming in with me in the army, and I have not found *any* evil to charge against thee from the day that thou camest to me until this day: but thou art not approved in the eyes of the lords. 7 Now then return and go in peace, thus thou shalt not do evil in the sight of the lords of the Philistines. 8 And David said to Anchus, What have I done to thee? and what hast thou found in thy servant from the *first* day that I was before thee even until this day, that I should not come and war against the enemies of the lord my king? 9 And Anchus answered David, I know that thou *art* good in my eyes, but the lords of the Philistines say, He shall not come with us to the war. 10 Now then rise up early in the morning, thou and the servants of thy lord that are come with thee, and go to the place where I appointed you, and entertain no evil thought in thy heart, for thou *art* good in my sight: and rise early for your journey when it is light, and depart. 11 So David arose early, he and his men, to depart and guard the land of the Philistines: and the Philistines went up to Jezrael to battle.

1-Kgdms30 1 And it came to pass when David and his men had entered Sekelac on the third day, that Amalec had made an incursion upon the south, and upon Sekelac, and smitten Sekelac, and burnt it with fire. 2 And as to the women and all things that were in it, great and small, they slew neither man nor woman, but carried them captives, and went on their way. 3 And David and his men came into the city, and, behold, it was burnt with fire; and their wives, and their sons, and their daughters were carried captive. 4 And David and his men lifted up their voice, and wept till there was no longer any power within them to weep. 5 And both the wives of David were carried captive, Achinaam, the Jezraelitess, and Abigaia the wife of Nabal the Carmelite. 6 And David was greatly distressed, because the people spoke of stoning him, because the soul of all the people was grieved, each for his sons and his daughters: but David strengthened himself in the Lord his God. 7 And David said to Abiathar the priest the son of Achimelech, Bring near the ephod. 8 And David enquired of the Lord, saying, Shall I pursue after this troop? shall I overtake them? and he said to him, Pursue, for thou shalt surely overtake them, and thou shalt surely rescue *the captives*. 9 So David went, he an the six hundred men with him, an they come as far as the brook Bosor, and the superfluous ones stopped. 10 And he pursued them with four hundred men; and there remained behind two hundred men, who tarried on the other side of the brook Bosor. 11 And they find an Egyptian in the field, and they take him, and bring him to David; and they gave him bread and he ate, and they caused him to drink water. 12 And they gave him a piece of a cake of figs, and he ate, and his spirit was restored in him; for he had not eaten bread, and had not drunk water three days and three nights. 13 And David said to him, Whose art thou? and whence art thou? and the young man the Egyptian said, I am the servant of an Amalekite; and my master left me, because I was taken ill three days ago. 14 And we made an incursion on the south of the Chelethite, and on the parts of Judea, and on the south of Chelub, and we burnt Sekelac with fire. 15 And David said to him, Wilt thou bring me down to this troop? And he said, Swear now to me by God, that thou wilt not kill me, and that thou wilt not deliver me into the hands of my master, and I will bring thee down upon this troop. 16 So be brought him down thither, and behold, they *were* scattered abroad upon the surface of the whole land, eating and drinking, and feasting by *reason of* all the great spoils which they had taken out of the land of the Philistines, and out of the land of Juda. 17 And David came upon them, and smote them from the morning till the evening, and on the next day; and not one of them escaped, except four hundred young men, who were mounted on camels, and fled. 18 And David recovered all that the Amalekites had taken, and he rescued both his wives. 19 And nothing was wanting to them of great or small, either of the spoils, or the sons and daughters, or anything that they had taken of theirs; and David recovered all. 20 And he took all the flocks, and the herds, and led them away before the spoils: and it was said of these spoils, These *are* the spoils of David. 21 And David comes to the two hundred men who were left behind that they should not follow after David, and he had caused them to remain by the brook of Bosor; and they came forth to meet David, and to meet his people with him: and David drew near to the people, and they asked him how he did. 22 Then every ill-disposed and bad man of the soldiers who had gone with David, answered and said, Because they did not pursue together with us, we will not give them of the spoils which we have recovered, only let each one lead away with him his wife and his children, and let them return. 23 And David said, Ye shall not do so, after the Lord has delivered *the enemy* to us, and guarded us, and the Lord has delivered into our hands the troop that came against u. 24 And who will hearken to these your words? for they are not inferior to us; for according to the portion of him that went down to the battle, so shall be the portion of him that abides with the baggage; they shall share alike. 25 And it came to pass from that day forward, that it became an ordinance and a custom in Israel until this day. 26 And David came to Sekelac, and sent of the spoils to the elders of Juda, and to his friends, saying, Behold *some* of the spoils of the enemies of the Lord; 27 to those in Baethsur, and to those in Rama of the south, and to those in Gethor. 28 And to those in Aroer, and to those in Ammadi, and to those in Saphi, and to those in Esthie, 29 and to those in Geth, and to those in Cimath, and to those in Saphec, and to those in Themath, and to those in Carmel, and to those in the cities of Jeremeel, and to those in the cities of the Kenezite; 30 and to those in Jerimuth, and to those in Bersabee, and to those in Nombe, 31 and to those in Chebron, and to all the places which David and his men had passed through.

1-Kgdms31 1 And the Philistines fought with Israel: and the men of Israel fled from before the Philistines, and they fall down wounded in the mountain in Gelbue. 2 And the Philistines press closely on Saul and his sons, and the Philistines smite Jonathan, and Aminadab, and Melchisa son of Saul. 3 And the battle prevails against Saul, and the shooters with arrows, even the archers find him, and he was wounded under the ribs. 4 And Saul said to his armour-bearer, Draw thy sword and pierce me through with it; lest these uncircumcised come and pierce me through, and mock me. But his armour-bearer would not, for he feared greatly: so Saul took his sword and fell upon it. 5 And his armour-bearer saw that Saul was dead, and he fell also himself upon his sword, and died with him. 6 So Saul died, and his three sons, and his armour- bearer, in that day together. 7 And the men of Israel who were on the other side of the valley, and those beyond Jordan, saw that the men of Israel fled, and that Saul and his sons were dead; and they leave their cities and flee: and the Philistines come and dwell in them. 8 And it came to pass on the morrow that the Philistines come to strip the dead, and they find Saul and his three sons fallen on the mountains of Gelbue.

9 And they turned him, and stripped off his armour, and sent it into the land of the Philistines, sending round glad tidings to their idols and to the people. 10 And they set up his armour at the temple of Astarte, and they fastened his body on the wall of Baethsam. 11 And the inhabitants of Jabis Galaad hear what the Philistines did to Saul. 12 And they rose up, *even* every man of might, and marched all night, and took the body of Saul and the body of Jonathan his son from the wall of Baethsam; and they bring them to Jabis, and burn them there. 13 And they take their bones, and bury them in the field that is in Jabis, and fast seven days.

2 KINGDOMS (II SAMUEL)

2-Kgdms1 1 And it came to pass after Saul was dead, that David returned from smiting Amalec, and David abode two days in Sekelac. 2 And it came to pass on the third day, that, behold, a man came from the camp, from the people of Saul, and his garments were rent, and earth *was* upon his head: and it came to pass when he went in to David, that he fell upon the earth, and did obeisance to him. 3 And David said to him, Whence comest thou? and he said to him, I have escaped out of the camp of Israel. 4 And David said to him, What *is* the matter? tell me. And he said, The people fled out of the battle, and many of the people have fallen and are dead, and Saul and Jonathan his son are dead. 5 And David said to the young man who brought him the tidings, How knowest thou that Saul and Jonathan his son are dead? 6 And the young man that brought the tidings, said to him, I happened accidentally to be upon mount Gelbue; and, behold, Saul was leaning upon his spear, and, behold, the chariots and captains of horse pressed hard upon him. 7 And he looked behind him, and saw me, and called me; and I said, Behold, *here am* I. 8 And he said to me, Who art thou? and I said, I am an Amalekite. 9 And he said to me, Stand, I pray thee, over me, and slay me, for a dreadful darkness has come upon me, for all my life *is* in me. 10 So I stood over him and slew him, because I knew he would not live after he was fallen; and I took the crown that was upon his head, and the bracelet that was upon his arm, and I have brought them hither to my lord. 11 And David laid hold of his garments, and rent them; and all the men who were with him rent their garments. 12 And they lamented, and wept, and fasted till evening, for Saul and for Jonathan his son, and for the people of Juda, and for the house of Israel, because they were smitten with the sword. 13 And David said to the young man who brought the tidings to him, Whence art thou? and he said, I am the son of an Amalekite sojourner. 14 And David said to him, How was it thou wast not afraid to lift thy hand to destroy the anointed of the Lord? 15 And David called one of his young men, and said, Go and fall upon him: and he smote him, and he died. 16 And David said to him, Thy blood *be* upon thine own head; for thy mouth has testified against thee, saying, I have slain the anointed of the Lord. 17 And David lamented with this lamentation over Saul and over Jonathan his son. 18 And he gave orders to teach it the sons of Juda: behold, it is written in the book of Right. 19 Set up a pillar, O Israel, for the slain that died upon thy high places: how are the mighty fallen! 20 Tell it not in Geth, and tell it not as glad tidings in the streets of Ascalon, lest the daughters of the Philistines rejoice, lest the daughters of the uncircumcised triumph. 21 Ye mountains of Gelbue, let not dew no rain descend upon you, nor fields of first-fruits *be upon you*, for there the shield of the mighty ones has been grievously assailed; the shield of Saul was not anointed with oil. 22 From the blood of the slain, and from the fat of the mighty, the bow of Jonathan returned not empty; and the sword of Saul turned not back empty. 23 Saul and Jonathan, the beloved and the beautiful, were not divided: comely *were they* in their life, and in their death they were not divided: *they were* swifter than eagles, and they were stronger than lions. 24 Daughters of Israel, weep for Saul, who clothed you with scarlet together with your adorning, who added golden ornaments to your apparel. 25 How are the mighty fallen in the midst of the battle! O Jonathan, even the slain ones upon thy high places! 26 I am grieved for thee, my brother Jonathan; thou wast very lovely to me; thy love to me was wonderful beyond the love of women. 27 How are the mighty fallen, and the weapons of war perished!

2-Kgdms2 1 And it came to pass after this that David enquired of the Lord, saying, Shall I go up into one of the cities of Juda? and the Lord said to him, Go up. And David said, Whither shall I go up? and he said, To Chebron. 2 And David went up thither to Chebron, *he* and both his wives, Achinaam the Jezraelitess, and Abigaia the wife of Nabal the Carmelite, 3 and the men that were with him, every one and his family; and they dwelt in the cities of Chebron. 4 And the men of Judea come, and anoint David there to reign over the house of Juda; and they reported to David, saying, The men of Jabis of the country of Galaad have buried Saul. 5 And David sent messengers to the rulers of Jabis of the country of Galaad, and David said to them, Blessed be ye of the Lord, because ye have wrought this mercy toward your lord, even toward Saul the anointed of the Lord, and ye have buried him and Jonathan his son. 6 And now may the Lord deal in mercy and truth towards you: and I also will requite towards you this good deed, because ye have done this. 7 And now let your hands be made strong, and be valiant; for your master Saul is dead, and moreover the house of Juda have anointed me to be king over them. 8 But Abenner, the son of Ner, the commander-in-chief of Saul's army, took Jebosthe son of Saul, and brought him up from the camp to Manaem 9 and made him king over the land of Galaad, and over Thasiri, and over Jezrael, and over Ephraim, and over Benjamin, and over all Israel. 10 Jebosthe, Saul's son *was* forty years old, when he reigned over Israel; and he reigned two years, but not over the house of Juda, who followed David. 11 And the days which David reigned in Chebron over the house of Juda were seven years and six months. 12 And Abenner the son of Ner went forth, and the servants of Jebosthe the son of Saul, from Manaem to Gabaon. 13 And Joab the son of Saruia, and the servants of David, went forth from Chebron, and met them at the fountain of Gabaon, at the same place: and these sat down by the fountain on this side, and those by the fountain on that

179

side. 14 And Abenner said to Joab, Let now the young men arise, and play before us. And Joab said, Let them arise. 15 And there arose and passed over by number twelve of the children of Benjamin, belonging to Jebosthe the son of Saul, and twelve of the servants of David. 16 And they seized every one the head of his neighbour with his hand, and his sword *was thrust* into the side of his neighbour, and they fall down together: and the name of that place was called The portion of the treacherous ones, which is in Gabaon. 17 And the battle was very severe on that day; and Abenner and the men of Israel were worsted before the servants of David. 18 And there were there the three sons of Saruia, Joab, and Abessa, and Asael: and Asael was swift in his feet as a roe in the field. 19 And Asael followed after Abenner, and turned not to go to the right hand or to the left from following Abenner. 20 And Abenner looked behind him, and said, Art thou Asael himself? and he said, I am. 21 And Abenner said to him, Turn thou to the right hand or to the left, and lay hold for thyself on one of the young men, and take to thyself his armour: but Asel would not turn back from following him. 22 And Abenner said yet again to Asael, Stand aloof from me, lest I smite thee to the ground? and how should I lift up my face to Joab? 23 And what does this mean? return to Joab thy brother? But he would not stand aloof; and Abenner smites him with the hinder end of the spear on the loins, and the spear went out behind him, and he falls there and dies on the spot: and it came to pass that every one that came to the place where Asael fell and died, stood still. 24 And Joab and Abessa pursued after Abenner, and the sun went down: and they went as far as the hill of Amman, which is in the front of Gai, by the desert way of Gabaon. 25 And the children of Benjamin who followed Abenner gather themselves together, and they formed themselves into one body, and stood on the top of a hill. 26 And Abenner called Joab, and said, Shall the sword devour perpetually? knowest thou not that it will be bitter at last? How long then wilt thou refuse to tell the people to turn from following our brethren? 27 And Joab said, As the Lord lives, if thou hadst not spoken, even from the morning the people had gone up every one from following his brother. 28 And Joab sounded the trumpet, and all the people departed, and did not pursue after Israel, and did not fight any longer. 29 And Abenner and his men departed at evening, *and went* all that night, and crossed over Jordan, and went along the whole adjacent *country*, and they come to the camp. 30 And Joab returned from following Abenner, and he assembled all the people, and there were missing of the people of David, nineteen men, and Asael. 31 And the servants of David smote of the children of Benjamin, of the men of Abenner, three hundred and sixty men belonging to him. 32 And they take up Asael, and bury him in the tomb of his father in Bethleem. And Joab and the men with him went all the night, and the morning rose upon them in Chebron.

2-Kgdms3 1 And there was war for a long time between the house of Saul and the house of David; and the house of David grew continually stronger; but the house of Saul grew continually weaker. 2 And sons were born to David in Chebron: and his first-born was Ammon the son of Achinoom the Jezraelitess. 3 And his second son *was* Daluia, the son of Abigaia the Carmelitess; and the third, Abessalom the son of Maacha the daughter of Tholmi the king of Gessir. 4 And the fourth *was* Ornia, the son of Aggith, and the fifth *was* Saphatia, the son of Abital. 5 And the sixth *was* Jetheraam, the son of Ægal the wife of David. These were born to David in Chebron. 6 And it came to pass while there was war between the house of Saul and the house of David, that Abenner was governing the house of Saul. 7 And Saul had a concubine, Respha, the daughter of Jol; and Jebosthe the son of Saul said to Abenner, Why hast thou gone in to my father's concubine? 8 And Abenner was very angry with Jebosthe for this saying; and Abenner said to him, Am I a dog's head? I have this day wrought kindness with the house of Saul thy father, and with his brethren and friends, and have not gone over to the house of David, and dost thou this day seek a charge against me concerning injury to a woman? 9 God do thus and more also to Abenner, if as the Lord swore to David, so do I not to him this day; 10 to take away the kingdom from the house of Saul, and to raise up the throne of David over Israel and over Juda from Dan to Bersabee. 11 And Jebosthe could not any longer answer Abenner a word, because he feared him. 12 And Abenner sent messengers to David to Thaelam where he was, immediately, saying, Make thy covenant with me, and, behold, my hand *is* with thee to bring back to thee all the house of Israel. 13 And David said, With a good will I will make with thee a covenant: only I demand one condition of thee, saying, Thou shalt not see my face, unless thou bring Melchol the daughter of Saul, when thou comest to see my face. 14 And David sent messengers to Jebosthe the son of Saul, saying, Restore me my wife Melchol, whom I took for a hundred foreskins of the Philistines. 15 And Jebosthe sent, and took her from her husband, *even* from Phaltiel the son of Selle. 16 And her husband went with her weeping behind her as far as Barakim. And Abenner said to him, Go, return; and he returned. 17 And Abenner spoke to the elders of Israel, saying, In former days ye sought David to reign over you; 18 and now perform *it*: for the Lord has spoken concerning David, saying, By the hand of my servant David I will save Israel out of the hand of all their enemies. 19 And Abenner spoke in the ears of Benjamin: and Abenner went to speak in the ears of David at Chebron, all that seemed good in the eyes of Israel and in the eyes of the house of Benjamin. 20 And Abenner came to David to Chebron, and with him twenty men: and David made for Abenner and his men with him a banquet of wine. 21 And Abenner said to David, I will arise now, and go, and gather to my lord the king all Israel; and I will make with him a covenant, and thou shalt reign over all whom thy soul desires. And David sent away Abenner, and he departed in peace. 22 And, behold, the servants of David and Joab arrived from their expedition, and they brought much spoil with them: and Abenner was not with David in Chebron, because he had sent him away, and he had departed in peace. 23 And Joab and all his army came, and it was reported to Joab, saying, Abenner the son of Ner is come to David, and David has let him go, and he has departed in peace. 24 And Joab went in to the king, and said, What *is* this *that* thou hast done? behold, Abenner came to thee; and why hast thou let him go, and he has departed in peace? 25 Knowest thou not the mischief of Abenner the son of Ner, that he came to deceive thee, and to know thy going out and thy coming in, and to know all things that thou doest? 26 And Joab returned from David, and sent messengers to Abenner after *him*; and they bring him back from the well of Seiram: but David knew *it* not. 27 And he brought back Abenner to Chebron, and Joab caused him to turn aside from the gate to speak to him, laying wait for him: and he smote him there in the loins, and he died for the blood of Asael the brother of Joab. 28 And David heard *of it* afterwards, and said, I and my kingdom are guiltless before the Lord even for ever of the blood of Abenner the son of Ner. 29 Let it fall upon the head of Joab, and upon all the house of his father; and let there not be wanting of the house of Joab one that has an issue, or a leper, or that leans on a staff, or that falls by the sword, or that wants bread. 30 For Joab and Abessa his brother laid wait continually for Abenner, because he slew Asael their brother at Gabaon in the battle. 31 And David said to Joab and to all the people with him, Rend your garments, and gird yourselves with sackcloth, and lament before Abenner. And king David followed the bier. 32 And they bury Abenner in Chebron: and the king lifted up his voice, and wept at his tomb, and all the people wept for Abenner. 33 And the king mourned over Abenner, and said, Shall Abenner die according to the death of Nabal? 34 Thy hands were not bound, and thy feet *were* not *put* in fetters: *one* brought *thee* not near as Nabal; thou didst fall before children of iniquity. 35 And all the people assembled to weep for him. And all the people came to cause David to eat bread while it was yet day: and David swore, saying, God do so to me, and more also, if I eat bread or any thing else before the sun goes down. 36 And all the people took notice, and all things that the king did before the people were pleasing in their sight. 37 So all the people and all Israel perceived in that day, that it was not of the king to slay Abenner the son of Ner. 38 And the king said to his servants, Know ye not that a great prince is this day fallen in Israel? 39 And that I am this day a *mere* kinsman *of his*, and *as it were* a subject; but these men the sons of Saruia are too hard for me: the Lord reward the evil-doer according to his wickedness.

2-Kgdms4 1 And Jebosthe the son of Saul heard that Abenner the son of Ner had died in Chebron; and his hands were paralyzed, and all the men of Israel grew faint. 2 And Jebosthe the son of Saul had two men that were captains of bands: the name of the one *was* Baana, and the name of the other Rechab, sons of Remmon the Berothite of the children of Benjamin; for Beroth was reckoned to the children of Benjamin. 3 And the Berothites ran away to Gethaim, and were sojourners there until this day. 4 And Jonathan Saul's son *had* a son lame of his feet, five years old, and he was *in the way* when the news of Saul and Jonathan his son came from Jezrael, and his nurse took him up, and fled; and it came to pass as he hasted and retreated, that he fell, and was lamed. And his name *was* Memphibosthe. 5 And Rechab and Baana the sons of Remmon the Berothite went, and they came in the heat of the day into the house of Jebosthe; and he was sleeping on a bed at noon. 6 And, behold, the porter of the house winnowed wheat, and he slumbered and slept: and the brothers Rechab and Baana went privily into the house: 7 And Jebosthe was sleeping on his bed in his chamber: and they smite him, and slay him, and take off his head: and they took his head, and went all the night by the western road. 8 And they brought the head of Jebosthe to David to Chebron, and they said to the king, Behold the head of Jebosthe the son of Saul thy enemy, who sought thy life; and the Lord has executed for my lord the king vengeance on his enemies, as *it is* this day: even on Saul thy enemy, and on his seed. 9 And David answered and Rechab and Baana his brother, the sons of Remmon the Berothite, and said to them, *As* the Lord lives, who has redeemed my soul out of all affliction; 10 he that reported to me that Saul was dead, even he was as one bringing glad tidings before me: but I seized him and slew him in Sekelac, to whom I ought, *as he thought*, to have given a reward for his tidings. 11 And now evil men have slain a righteous men in his house on his bed: now then I will require his blood of your hand, and I will destroy you from off the earth. 12 And David commanded his young men, and they slay them, and cut off their hands and their feet; and they hung them up at the fountain in Chebron: and they buried the head of Jebosthe in the tomb of Abenezer the son of Ner.

2-Kgdms5 1 And all the tribes of Israel come to David to Chebron, and they said to him, Behold, we *are* thy bone and thy flesh. 2 And heretofore Saul being king over us, thou was he that didst lead out and bring in Israel: and the Lord said to thee, Thou shalt feed my people Israel, and thou shalt be for a leader to my people Israel. 3 And all the elders of Israel come to the king to Chebron; and king David made a covenant with them in Chebron before the Lord; and they anoint David king over all Israel. 4 David *was* thirty years old when he began to reign, and he reigned forty years. 5 Seven years and six months he reigned in Chebron over Juda, and thirty- three years he reigned over all Israel and Juda in Jerusalem. 6 And David and his men, departed to Jerusalem, to the Jebusite that inhabited the land: and it was said to David, Thou shalt not come in hither: for the blind and the lame withstood him, saying, David shall not come in hither. 7 And David took first the hold of Sion: this *is* the city of David. 8 And David said on that day, Every one that smites the Jebusite, let him attack with the dagger both the lame and the blind, and those that hate the soul of David. Therefore they say, The lame and the blind shall not enter into the house of the Lord. 9 And David dwelt in the hold, and it was called the city of David, and he built the city itself round about from the citadel, and *he built* his own house. 10 And David advanced and became great, and the Lord Almighty *was* with him. 11 And Chiram king of Tyre sent messengers to David, and cedar wood, and carpenters, and stone-masons: and they built a house for David. 12 And David knew that the Lord had prepared him to be king over

Israel, and that his kingdom was exalted for the sake of his people Israel. 13 And David took again wives and concubines out of Jerusalem, after he came from Chebron: and David had still more sons and daughters born to him. 14 And these *are* the names of those that were born to him in Jerusalem; Sammus, and Sobab, and Nathan, and Solomon. 15 And Ebear, and Elisue, and Naphec, and Jephies. 16 And Elisama, and Elidae, and Eliphalath, (5:16A) Samae, Jessibath, Nathan, Galamaan, Jebaar, Theesus, Eliphalat, Naged, Naphec, Janathan, Leasamys, Baalimath, Eliphaath. 17 And the Philistines heard that David was anointed king over Israel; and all the Philistines went up to seek David; and David heard of it, and went down to the strong hold. 18 And the Philistines came, and assembled in the valley of the giants. 19 And David enquired of the Lord, saying, Shall I go up against the Philistines? and wilt thou deliver them into my hands? and the Lord said to David, Go up, for I will surely deliver the Philistines into thine hands. 20 And David came from Upper Breaches, and smote the Philistines there: and David said, The Lord has destroyed the hostile Philistines before me, as water is dispersed; therefore the name of that place was called Over Breaches. 21 And they leave there their gods, and David and his men with him took them. 22 And the Philistines came up yet again, and assembled in the valley of Giants. 23 And David enquired of the Lord: and the Lord said, Thou shalt not go up to meet them: turn from them, and thou shalt meet them near the place of weeping. 24 And it shall come to pass when thou hearest the sound of a clashing together from the grove of weeping, then thou shalt go down to them, for then the Lord shall go forth before thee to make havoc in the battle with the Philistines. 25 And David did as the Lord commanded him, and smote the Philistines from Gabaon as far as the land of Gazera.

2-Kgdms6 1 And David again gathered all the young men of Israel, about seventy thousand. 2 And David arose, and went, he and all the people that were with him, and some of the rulers of Juda, on an expedition *to a distant place*, to bring back thence the ark of God, on which the name of the Lord of Host who dwells between the cherubs upon it is called. 3 And they put the ark of the Lord on a new waggon, and took it out of the house of Aminadab who lived on the hill, and Oza and his brethren the sons of Aminadab drove the waggon with the ark. 4 And his brethren went before the ark. 5 And David and the children of Israel *were* playing before the Lord on well-tuned instruments mightily, and with songs, and with harps, and with lutes, and with drums, and with cymbals, and with pipes. 6 And they come as far as the threshing floor of Nachor: and Oza reached forth his hand to the ark of God to keep it steady, and took hold of it; for the ox shook it out of its place. 7 And the Lord was very angry with Oza; and God smote him there: and he died there by the ark of the Lord before God. 8 And David was dispirited because the Lord made a breach upon Oza; and that place was called the breach of Oza until this day. 9 And David feared the Lord in that day, saying, How shall the ark of the Lord come in to me? 10 And David would not bring in the ark of

the covenant of the Lord to himself into the city of David: and David turned it aside into the house of Abeddara the Gethite. 11 And the ark of the Lord lodged in the house of Abeddara the Gethite three months, and the Lord blessed all the house of Abeddara, and all his possessions. 12 And it was reported to king David, saying, The Lord has blessed the house of Abeddara, and all that he has, because of the ark of the Lord. And David went, and brought up the Ark of the Lord from the house of Abeddara to the city of David with gladness. 13 And there were with him bearing the ark seven bands, and for a sacrifice a calf and lambs. 14 And David sounded with well-tuned instruments before the Lord, and David *was* clothed with a fine long robe. 15 And David and all the house of Israel brought up the ark of the Lord with shouting, and with the sound of a trumpet. 16 And it came to pass as the ark arrived at the city of David, that Melchol the daughter of Saul looked through the window, and saw king David dancing and playing before the Lord; and she despised him in her heart. 17 And they bring the ark of the Lord, and set it in its place in the midst of the tabernacle which David pitched for it: and David offered whole-burnt-offerings before the Lord, *and* peace-offerings. 18 And David made an end of offering the whole-burnt-offerings and peace-offerings, and blessed the people in the name of the Lord of Hosts. 19 And he distributed to all the people, even to all the host of Israel from Dan to Bersabee, both men and women, to every one a cake of bread, and a joint of meat, and a cake from the frying-pan: and all the people departed every one to his home. 20 And David returned to bless his house. And Melchol the daughter of Saul came out to meet David and saluted him, and said, How was the king of Israel glorified to-day, who was to-day uncovered in the eyes of the handmaids of his servants, as one of the dancers wantonly uncovers himself! 21 And David said to Melchol, I will dance before the Lord. Blessed *be* the Lord who chose me before thy father, and before all his house, to make me head over his people, even over Israel: therefore I will play, and dance before the Lord. 22 And I will again uncover myself thus, and I will be vile in thine eyes, and with the maid-servants by whom thou saidst that I was not had in honour. 23 And Melchol the daughter of Saul had no child till the day of her death.

2-Kgdms7 1 And it came to pass when the king sat in his house, and the Lord had given him an inheritance on every side *free* from all his enemies round about him; 2 that the king said to Nathan the prophet, Behold now, I live in a house of cedar, and the ark of the Lord dwells in the midst of a tent. 3 And Nathan said to the king, Go and do all that *is* in thine heart, for the Lord *is* with thee. 4 And it came to pass in that night, that the word of the Lord came to Nathan, saying, 5 Go, and say to my servant David, Thus says the Lord, Thou shalt not build me a house for me to dwell in. 6 For I have not dwelt in a house from the day that I brought up the children of Israel out of Egypt to this day, but I have been walking in a lodge and in a tent, 7 wheresoever I went with all Israel. Have I ever spoken to any of the tribes of Israel, which I commanded to tend my people Israel, saying, Why have ye not built me a house of

Cedar? 8 And now thus shalt thou say to my servant David, Thus says the Lord Almighty, I took thee from the sheep-cote, that thou shouldest be a prince over my people, over Israel. 9 And I was with thee wheresoever thou wentest, and I destroyed all thine enemies before thee, and I made thee renowned according to the renown of the great ones on the earth. 10 And I will appoint a place for my people Israel, and will plant them, and they shall dwell by themselves, and shall be no more distressed; and the son of iniquity shall no more afflict them, as he *has done* from the beginning, 11 from the days when I appointed judges over my people Israel: and I will give thee rest from all thine enemies, and the Lord will tell thee that thou shalt build a house to him. 12 And it shall come to pass when thy days shall have been fulfilled, and thou shalt sleep with thy fathers, that I will raise up thy seed after thee, even thine own issue, and I will establish his kingdom. 13 He shall build for me a house to my name, and I will set up his throne even for ever. 14 I will be to him a father, and he shall be to me a son. And when he happens to transgress, then will I chasten him with the rod of men, and with the stripes of the sons of men. 15 But my mercy I will not take from him, as I took it from those whom I removed from my presence. 16 And his house shall be made sure, and his kingdom for ever before me, and his throne shall be set up for ever. 17 According to all these words, and according to all this vision, so Nathan spoke to David. 18 And king David came in, and sat before the Lord, and said, Who am I, O Lord, my Lord, and what *is* my house, that thou hast loved me hitherto? 19 Whereas I was very little before thee, O Lord, my Lord, yet thou spokest concerning the house of thy servant for a long time to *to come*. And *is* this the law of man, O Lord, my Lord? 20 And what shall David yet say to thee? and now thou knowest thy servant, O Lord, my Lord. 21 And thou hast wrought for thy servant's sake, and according to thy heart thou hast wrought all this greatness, to make it known to thy servant, 22 that he may magnify thee, O my Lord; for there is no one like thee, and there is no God, but thou among all of whom we have heard with our ears. 23 And what other nation in the earth *is* as thy people Israel? whereas God was his guide, to redeem for himself a people to make thee a name, to do mightily and nobly, so that thou shouldest cast out nations an *their* tabernacles from the presence of thy people, whom thou didst redeem for thyself out of Egypt? 24 And thou has prepared for thyself thy people Israel to be a people for ever, and thou, Lord, art become their God. 25 And now, O my Lord, the Almighty Lord God of Israel, confirm the word for ever which thou hast spoken concerning thy servant and his house: and now as thou hast said, 26 Let thy name be magnified for ever. 27 Almighty Lord God of Israel, thou hast uncovered the ear of thy servant, saying, I will build thee a house: therefore thy servant has found *in* his heart to pray this prayer to thee. 28 And now, O Lord my Lord, thou art God; and thy words will be true, and thou hast spoken these good things concerning thy servant. 29 And now begin and bless the house of thy servant, that it may continue for ever before thee; for thou, O Lord, my Lord, hast spoken, and the house of thy servant shall be blessed with thy blessing so as to continue for ever.

2-Kgdms8 1 And it came to pass after this, that David smote the Philistines, and put them to flight, and David took the tribute from out of the hand of the Philistines. 2 And David smote Moab, and measured them out with lines, having laid them down on the ground: and there were two lines for slaying, and two lines he kept alive: and Moab became servants to David, yielding tribute. 3 And David smote Adraazar the son of Raab king of Suba, as he went to extend his power to the river Euphrates. 4 And David took a thousand of his chariots, and seven thousand horsemen, and twenty thousand footmen: and David houghed all his chariot *horses*, and he reserved to himself a hundred chariots. 5 And Syria of Damascus comes to help Adraazar king of Suba, and David smote twenty-two thousand men belonging to the Syrian. 6 And David placed a garrison in Syria near Damascus, and the Syrians became servants and tributaries to David: and the Lord preserved David whithersoever he went. 7 And David took the golden bracelets which were on the servants of Adraazar king of Suba, and brought them to Jerusalem. And Susakim king of Egypt took them, when he went up to Jerusalem in the days of Roboam son of Solomon. 8 And king David took from Metebac, and from the choice cities of Adraazar, very much brass: with that Solomon made the brazen sea, and the pillars, and the lavers, and all the furniture. 9 And Thou the king of Hemath heard that David had smitten all the host of Adraazar. 10 And Thou sent Jedduram his son to king David, to ask him of his welfare, and to congratulate him on his fighting against Adraazar and smiting him, for he was an enemy to Adraazar: and in his hands were vessels of silver, and vessels of gold, and vessels of brass. 11 And these king David consecrated to the Lord, with the silver and with the gold which he consecrated out of all the cities which he conquered, 12 out of Idumea, and out of Moab, and from the children of Ammon, and from the Philistines, and from Amalec, and from the spoils of Adraazar son of Raab king of Suba. 13 And David made *himself* a name: and when he returned he smote Idumea in Gebelem to *the number of* eighteen thousand. 14 And he set garrisons in Idumea, even in all Idumea: and all the Idumeans were servants to the king. And the Lord preserved David wherever he went. 15 And David reigned over all Israel: and David wrought judgment and justice over all his people. 16 And Joab the son of Saruia *was* over the host; and Josaphat the son of Achilud *was keeper* of the records. 17 And Sadoc the son of Achitob, and Achimelech son of Abiathar, *were* priests; and Sasa *was* the scribe, 18 and Banaeas son of Jodae *was* councillor, and the Chelethite and the Phelethite, and the sons of David, were princes of the court.

2-Kgdms9 1 And David said, Is there yet any one left in the house of Saul, that I may deal kindly with him for Jonathan's sake? 2 And there was a servant of the house of Saul, and his name was Siba: and they call him to David; and the king said to him, Art thou Siba? and he said, I *am* thy servant. 3 And the king said, Is there yet a man left of the house of Saul, that I may act towards him with the mercy of God? and Siba said to the king, There is yet a son of Jonathan, lame *of* his feet. 4 And the king said, Where *is* he? and Siba said to the king, Behold, *he is* in the house of Machir the son of Amiel of Lodabar. 5 And king David went, and took him out of the house of Machir the son Amiel of Lodabar. 6 And Memphibosthe the son of Jonathan the son of Saul comes to the king David, and he fell upon his face and did obeisance to him: and David said to him, Memphibosthe: and he said, Behold thy servant. 7 And David said to him, Fear not, for I will surely deal mercifully with thee for the sake of Jonathan thy father, and I will restore to thee all the land of Saul the father of thy father; and thou shalt eat bread at my table continually. 8 And Memphibosthe did obeisance, and said, Who am I thy servant, that thou hast looked upon a dead dog like me? 9 And the king called Siba the servant of Saul, and said to him, All that belonged to Saul and to all his house have I given to the son of thy lord. 10 And thou, and thy sons, and thy servants, shall till the land for him; and thou shalt bring in bread to the son of thy lord, and he shall eat bread: and Memphibosthe the son of thy lord shall eat bread continually at my table. Now Siba had fifteen sons and twenty servants. 11 And Siba said to the king, According to all that my lord the king has commanded his servant, so will thy servant do. And Memphibosthe did eat at the table of David, as one of the sons of the king. 12 And Memphibosthe had a little son, and his name *was* Micha: and all the household of Siba *were* servants to Memphibosthe. 13 And Memphibosthe dwelt in Jerusalem, for he continually ate at the table of the king; and he was lame in both his feet.

2-Kgdms10 1 And it came to pass after this that the king of the children of Ammon died, and Annon his son reigned in his stead. 2 And David said, I will shew mercy to Annon the son of Naas, as his father dealt mercifully with me. And David sent to comfort him concerning his father by the hand of his servants; and the servants of David came into the land of the children of Ammon. 3 And the princes of the children of Ammon said to Annon their lord, *Is it* to honour thy father before thee that David has sent comforters to thee? Has not David rather sent his servants to thee that they should search the city, and spy it out and examine it? 4 And Annon took the servants of David, and shaved their beards, and cut off their garments in the midst as far as their haunches, and sent them away. 5 And they brought David word concerning the men; and he sent to meet them, for the men were greatly dishonoured: and the king said, Remain in Jericho till your beards have grown, and *then* ye shall return. 6 And the children of Ammon saw that the people of David were ashamed; and the children of Ammon sent, and hired the Syrians of Baethraam, and the Syrians of Suba, and Roob, twenty thousand footmen, and the king of Amalec with a thousand men, and Istob with twelve thousand men. 7 And David heard, and sent Joab and all his host, *even* the mighty men. 8 And the children of Ammon went forth, and set the battle in array by the door of the gate: *those* of Syria, Suba, and Roob, and Istob, and Amalec, being by themselves in the field. 9 And Joab saw that the front of the battle was against him from that which was opposed in front and from behind, and he

chose out *some* of all the young men of Israel, and they set themselves in array against Syria. 10 And the rest of the people he gave into the hand of Abessa his brother, and they set the battle in array opposite to the children of Ammon. 11 And he said, If Syria be too strong for me, then shall ye help me: and if the children of Ammon be too strong for thee, then will we be ready to help thee. 12 Be thou courageous, and let us be strong for our people, and for the sake of the cities of our God, and the Lord shall do that which is good in his eyes. 13 And Joab and his people with him advanced to battle against Syria, and they fled from before him. 14 And the children of Ammon saw that the Syrians were fled, and they fled from before Abessa, and entered into the city: and Joab returned from the children of Ammon, and came to Jerusalem. 15 And the Syrians saw that they were worsted before Israel, and they gathered themselves together. 16 And Adraazar sent and gathered the Syrians from the other side of the river Chalamak, and they came to Ælam; and Sobac the captain of the host of Adraazar *was* at their head. 17 And it was reported to David, and he gathered all Israel, and went over Jordan, and came to Ælam: and the Syrians set the battle in array against David, and fought with him. 18 And Syria fled from before Israel, and David destroyed of Syria seven hundred chariots, and forty thousand horsemen, and he smote Sobac the captain of his host, and he died there. 19 And all the kings the servants of Adraazar saw that they were put to the worse before Israel, and they went over to Israel, and served them: and Syria was afraid to help the children of Ammon any more.

2-Kgdms11 1 And it came to pass when the time o the year for kings going out *to battle* had come round, that David sent Joab, and his servants with him, and all Israel; and they destroyed the children of Ammon, and besieged Rabbath: but David remained at Jerusalem. 2 And it came to pass toward evening, that David arose off his couch, and walked on the roof of the king's house, and saw from the roof a woman bathing; and the woman was very beautiful to look upon. 3 And David sent and enquired about the woman: and *one* said, *Is* not this Bersabee the daughter of Eliab, the wife of Urias the Chettite? 4 And David sent messengers, and took her, and went in to her, and he lay with her: and she was purified from her uncleanness, and returned to her house. 5 And the woman conceived; and she sent and told David, and said, I am with child. 6 And David sent to Joab, saying, Send me Urias the Chettite; and Joab sent Urias to David. 7 And Urias arrived and went in to him, and David asked him how Joab was, and how the people were, and how the war went on. 8 And David said to Urias, Go to thy house, and wash thy feet: and Urias departed from the house of the king, and a portion *of meat* from the king followed him. 9 And Urias slept at the door of the king with the servants of his lord, and went not down to his house. 10 And they brought David word, saying, Urias has not gone down to his house. And David said to Urias, Art thou not come from a journey? why hast thou not gone down to thy house? 11 And Urias said to David, The ark, and Israel, and Juda dwell in tents; and my lord Joab, and the servants of my lord, are encamped in the open fields; and shall I go into my house to eat and drink, and lie with my wife? how *should I do this? as* thy soul lives, I will not do this thing. 12 And David said to Urias, Remain here to-day also, and to-morrow I will let thee go. So Urias remained in Jerusalem that day and the day following. 13 And David called him, and he ate before him and drank, and he made him drunk: and he went out in the evening to lie upon his bed with the servants of his lord, and went not down to his house. 14 And the morning came, and David wrote a letter to Joab, and sent it by the hand of Urias. 15 And he wrote in the letter, saying, Station Urias in front of the severe *part* of the fight, and retreat from behind him, so shall he be wounded and die. 16 And it came to pass while Joab was watching against the city, that he set Urias in a place where he knew that valiant men were. 17 And the men of the city went out, and fought with Joab: and some of the people of the servants of David fell, and Urias the Chettite died also. 18 And Joab sent, and reported to David all the events of the war, so as to tell them to the king. 19 And he charged the messenger, saying, When thou hast finished reporting all the events of the war to the king, 20 then it shall come to pass if the anger of the king shall arise, and he shall say to thee, Why did ye draw nigh to the city to fight? knew ye not that they would shoot from off the wall? 21 Who smote Abimelech the son of Jerobaal son of Ner? did not a woman cast a piece of a millstone upon him from above the wall, and he died in Thamasi? why did ye draw near to the wall? then thou shalt say, Thy servant Urias the Chettite is also dead. 22 And the messenger of Joab went to the king to Jerusalem, and he came and reported to David all that Joab told him, all the affairs of the war. And David was very angry with Joab, and said to the messenger, Why did ye draw nigh to the wall to fight? knew ye not that ye would be wounded from off the wall? Who smote Abimelech the son of Jerobaal? did not a woman cast upon him a piece of millstone from the wall, and he died in Thamasi? why did ye draw near to the wall? 23 And the messenger said to David, The men prevailed against us, and they came out against us into the field, and we came upon them even to the door of the gate. 24 And the archers shot at thy servants from off the wall, and some of the king's servants died, and thy servant Urias the Chettite is dead also. 25 And David said to the messenger, Thus shalt thou say to Joab, Let not the matter be grievous in thine eyes, for the sword devours one way at one time and another way at another: strengthen thine array against the city, and destroy it, and strengthen him. 26 And the wife of Urias heard that Urias her husband was dead, and she mourned for her husband. 27 And the time of mourning expired, and David sent and took her into his house, and she became his wife, and bore him a son: but the thing which David did was evil in the eyes of the Lord.

2-Kgdms12 1 And the Lord sent Nathan the prophet to David; and he went in to him, and said to him, There were two men in one city, one rich and the other poor. 2 And the rich *man* had very many flocks and herds. 3 But the poor *man had* only one little ewe lamb, which he had purchased, and preserved, and reared; an it grew up with himself and his children in common; it ate of his bread and drank of his cup, and slept in his bosom, and was to him as a daughter. 4 And a traveller came to the rich man, and he spared to take of his flocks and of his herds, to dress for the traveller that came to him; and he took the poor man's lamb, and dressed it for the man that came to him. 5 And David was greatly moved with anger against the man; and David said to Nathan, *As* the Lord lives, the man that did this thing shall surely die. 6 And he shall restore the lamb seven-fold, because he has not spared. 7 And Nathan said to David, Thou art the man that has done this. Thus says the Lord God of Israel, I anointed thee to be king over Israel, and I rescued thee out the hand of Saul; 8 and I gave thee the house of thy lord, and the wives of thy lord into thy bosom, and I gave to thee the house of Israel and Juda; and if that had been little, I would have given thee yet more. 9 Why hast thou set at nought the word of the Lord, to do that which is evil in his eyes? thou hast slain Urias the Chettite with the sword, and thou hast taken his wife to be thy wife, and thou hast slain him with the sword of the children of Ammon. 10 Now therefore the sword shall not depart from thy house for ever, because thou has set me at nought, and thou hast taken the wife of Urias the Chettite, to be thy wife. 11 Thus says the Lord, Behold, I will raise up against thee evil out of thy house, and I will take thy wives before thine eyes, and will give them to thy neighbour, and he shall lie with thy wives in the sight of this sun. 12 For thou didst it secretly, but I will do this thing in the sight of all Israel, and before the sun. 13 And David said to Nathan, I have sinned against the Lord. And Nathan said to David, And the Lord has put away thy sin; thou shalt not die. 14 Only because thou hast given great occasion of provocation to the enemies of the Lord by this thing, thy son also that is born to thee shall surely die. 15 And Nathan departed to his house. And the Lord smote the child, which the wife of Urias the Chettite bore to David, and it was ill. 16 And David enquired of God concerning the child, and David fasted, and went in and lay all night upon the ground. 17 And the elders of his house arose *and went* to him to raise him up from the ground, but he would not *rise*, nor did he eat bread with them. 18 And it came to pass on the seventh day that the child died: and the servants of David were afraid to tell him that the child was dead; for they said, Behold, while the child was yet alive we spoke to him, and he hearkened not to our voice; and thou should we tell him that the child is dead?—so would he do *himself* harm. 19 And David understood that his servants were whispering, and David perceived that the child was dead: and David said to his servants, Is the child dead? and they said, He is dead. 20 Then David rose up from the earth, and washed, and anointed himself, and changed his raiment, and went into the house of God, and worshipped him; and went into his own house, and called for bread to eat, and they set bread before him and he ate. 21 And his servants said to him, What *is* this thing that thou hast done concerning the child? while it was yet living thou didst fast, and weep, and watch: and when the child was dead thou didst rise up, and didst eat bread, and drink. 22 And David said, While the child yet lived, I fasted and wept; for I said, Who knows if the Lord will pity me, and the child live? 23 But now it is dead, why should I fast thus? shall I be able to bring him back again? I shall go to him, but he shall not return to me. 24 And David comforted Bersabee his wife, and he went in to her, and lay with her; and she conceived and bore a son, and he called his named Solomon, and the Lord loved him. 25 And he sent by the hand of Nathan the prophet, and called his name Jeddedi, for the Lord's sake. 26 And Joab fought against Rabbath of the children of Ammon, and took the royal city. 27 And Joab sent messengers to David, and said, I have fought against Rabbath, and taken the city of waters. 28 And now gather the rest of the people, and encamp against the city, an take it beforehand; lest I take the city first, and my name be called upon it. 29 And David gathered all the people, and went to Rabbath, and fought against it, and took it. 30 And he took the crown of Molchom their king from off his head, and the weight of it was a talent of gold, with precious stones, and it was upon the head of David; and he carried forth very much spoil of the city. 31 And he brought forth the people that were in it, and put them under the saw, and under iron harrows, and axes of iron, and made them pass through the brick -kiln: and thus he did to all the cities of the children of Ammon. And David and all the people returned to Jerusalem.

2-Kgdms13 1 And it happened after this that Abessalom the son of David had a very beautiful sister, and her name *was* Themar; and Amnon the son of David loved her. 2 And Amnon was distressed even to sickness, because of Themar his sister; for she was a virgin, and it seemed very difficult for Amnon to do anything to her. 3 And Amnon had a friend, and his name *was* Jonadab, the son of Samaa the brother of David: and Jonadab *was* a very cunning man. 4 And he said to him, What ails thee that thou art thus weak? O son of the king, morning by morning? wilt thou not tell me? and Ammon said, I love Themar the sister of my brother Abessalom. 5 And Jonadab said to him, Lie upon thy bed, and make thyself sick, and thy father shall come in to see thee; and thou shalt say to him, Let, I pray thee, Themar my sister come, and feed me with morsels, and let her prepare food before my eyes, that I may see and eat at her hands. 6 So Ammon lay down, and made himself sick; and the king came in to see him: and Amnon said to the king, Let, I pray thee, my sister Themar come to me, and make a couple of cakes in my sight, and I will eat them at her hand. 7 And David sent to Themar to the house, saying, Go now to thy brother's house, and dress him food. 8 And Themar went to the house of her brother Amnon, and he *was* lying down: and she took the dough and kneaded it, and made cakes in his sight, and baked the cakes. 9 And she took the frying pan and poured them out before him, but he would not eat. And Amnon said, Send out every man from about me. And they removed every man from about him. 10 And Amnon said to Themar, Bring in the food into the closet, and I will eat of thy hand. And Themar took the cakes which she had made, and brought them to her brother Amnon into the chamber. 11 And she brought *them* to him to eat, and he caught hold of her, and said to her,

Come, lie with me, my sister. 12 And she said to him, Nay, my brother, do not humble me, for it ought not to be so done in Israel; do not this folly. 13 And I, whither shall I remove my reproach? and thou shalt be as one of the fools in Israel. And now, speak, I pray thee, to the king, for surely he will not keep me from thee. 14 But Amnon would not hearken to her voice; and he prevailed against her, and humbled her, and lay with her. 15 Then Amnon hated her with very great hatred; for the hatred with which he hated her was greater than the love with which he had loved her, for the last wickedness was greater than the first: and Amnon said to her, Rise, and be gone. 16 And Themar spoke to him concerning this great mischief, greater, *said she*, than the other that thou didst me, to send me away: but Amnon would not hearken to her voice. 17 And he called his servant who had charge of the house, and said to him, Put now this *woman* out from me, and shut the door after her. 18 And she had on her a variegated robe, for so were the king's daughters that were virgins attired in their apparel: and his servant led her forth, and shut the door after her. 19 And Themar took ashes, and put them on her head; and she rent the variegated garment that was upon her: and she laid her hands on her head, and went crying continually. 20 And Abessalom her brother said to her, Has thy brother Amnon been with thee? now then, my sister, be silent, for he is thy brother: be not careful to mention this matter. So Themar dwelt as a widow in the house of her brother Abessalom. 21 And king David heard of all these things, and was very angry; but he did not grieve the spirit of his son Amnon, because be loved him, for he was his first-born. 22 And Abessalom spoke not to Amnon, good or bad, because Abessalom hated Amnon, on account of his humbling his sister Themar. 23 And it came to pass at the end of two whole years, that they were shearing *sheep* for Abessalom in Belasor near Ephraim: and Abessalom invited all the king's sons. 24 And Abessalom came to the king, and said, Behold, thy servant has a sheep-shearing; let now the king and his servants go with thy servant. 25 And the king said to Abessalom, Nay, my son, let us not all go, and let us not be burdensome to thee. And he pressed him; but he would not go, but blessed him. 26 And Abessalom said to him, And if not, let I pray thee, my brother Amnon go with us. And the king said to him, Why should he go with thee? 27 And Abessalom pressed him, and he sent with him Amnon and all the king's sons; and Abessalom made a banquet like the banquet of the king. 28 And Abessalom charged his servants, saying, Mark when the heart of Amnon shall be merry with wine, and I shall say to you, Smite Amnon, and slay him: fear not; for is it not I that command you? Be courageous, and be valiant. 29 And the servants of Abessalom did to Amnon as Abessalom commanded them: and all the sons of the king rose up, and they mounted every man his mule, and fled. 30 And it came to pass, when they were in the way, that a report came to David, saying, Abessalom has slain all the king's sons, and there is not one of them left. 31 Then the king arose, and rent his garments, and lay upon the ground: and all his servants that were standing round him rent their garments. 32 And Jonadab the son of Samaa brother of

David, answered and said, Let not my Lord the king say that he has slain all the young men the sons of the king, for Amnon only of them all is dead; for he was appointed *to death* by the mouth of Abessalom from the day that he humbled his sister Themar. 33 And now let not my lord the king take the matter to heart, saying, All the king's sons are dead: for Amnon only of them is dead. 34 And Abessalom escaped: and the young man the watchman, lifted up his eyes, and looked; and, behold, much people went in the way behind him from the side of the mountain in the descent: and the watchman came and told the king, and said, I have seen men by the way of Oronen, by the side of the mountain. 35 And Jonadab said to the king, Behold, the king's sons are present: according to the word of thy servant, so has it happened. 36 And it came to pass when he had finished speaking, that, behold, the king's sons came, and lifted up their voices and wept: and the king also and all his servants wept with a very great weeping. 37 But Abessalom fled, and went to Tholmi son of Emiud the king of Gedsur to the land of Chamaachad: and king David mourned for his son continually. 38 So Abessalom fled, and departed to Gedsur, and was there three years. 39 And king David ceased to go out after Abessalom, for he was comforted concerning Amnon, touching his death.

2-Kgdms14 1 And Joab the son of Saruia knew that the heart of the king was toward Abessalom. 2 And Joab sent to Thecoe, and took thence a cunning woman, and said to her, Mourn, I pray thee, and put on mourning apparel, and anoint thee not with oil, and thou shalt be as a woman mourning for one that is dead thus for many days. 3 And thou shalt go to the king, and speak to him according to this word. And Joab put the words in her mouth. 4 So the woman of Thecoe went in to the king and fell upon her face to the earth, and did him obeisance, and said, Help, O king, help. 5 And the king said to her, What is the matter with thee? And she said, I am indeed a widow woman, and my husband is dead. 6 And moreover thy handmaid had two sons, and they fought together in the field, and there was no one to part them; and the one smote the other his brother, and slew him. 7 And behold the whole family rose up against thine handmaid, and they said, Give up the one that smote his brother, and we will put him to death for the life of his brother, whom he slew, and we will take away even your heir: so they will quench my coal that is left, so as not to leave my husband remnant or name on the face of the earth. 8 And the king said to the woman, Go in peace to thy house, and I will give commandment concerning thee. 9 And the woman of Thecoe said to the king, On me, my lord, O king, and on my father's house *be* the iniquity, and the king and his throne *be* guiltless. 10 And the king said, Who was it that spoke to thee? thou shalt even bring him to me, and *one* shall not touch him any more. 11 And she said, Let now the king remember concerning his Lord God in that the avenger of blood is multiplied to destroy, and let them not take away my son. And he said, *As* the lord lives, not a hair of thy son shall fall to the ground. 12 And the woman said, Let now thy servant speak a word to my lord the king. And he said, Say on. 13 And the woman said, Why

hast thou devised this thing against the people of God? or *is* this word out of the king's mouth as a transgression, so that the king should not bring back his banished? 14 For we shall surely die, and be as water poured upon the earth, which shall not be gathered up, and God shall take the life, even as he devises to thrust forth from him his outcast. 15 And now whereas I came to speak this word to my lord the king, *the reason is* that the people will see me, and thy handmaid will say, Let one now speak to my lord the king, if peradventure the king will perform the request of his handmaid; 16 for the king will hear. Let him rescue his handmaid out of the hand of the man that seeks to cast out me and my son from the inheritance of God. 17 And the woman said, If now the word of my lord the king be gracious, —*well*: for as an angel of God, so *is* my lord the king, to hear good and evil: and the Lord thy God shall be with thee. 18 And the king answered, and said to the woman, Hide not from me, I pray thee, the matter which I ask thee. And the woman said, Let my lord the king by all means speak. 19 And the king said, *Is* not the hand of Joab in all this matter with thee? and the woman said to the king, *As* thy soul lives, my lord, O king, there is no turning to the right hand or to the left from all that my lord the king has spoken; for thy servant Joab himself charged me, and he put all these words in the mouth of thine handmaid. 20 In order that this form of speech might come about *it was* that thy servant Joab has framed this matter: and my lord is wise as *is* the wisdom of an angel of God, to know all things that are in the earth. 21 And the king said to Joab, Behold now, I have done to thee according to this thy word: go, bring back the young man Abessalom. 22 And Joab fell on his face to the ground, and did obeisance, and blessed the king: and Joab said, To-day thy servant knows that I have found grace in thy sight, my lord, O king, for my lord the king has performed the request of his servant. 23 And Joab arose, and went to Gedsur, and brought Abessalom to Jerusalem. 24 And the king said, Let him return to his house, and not see my face. And Abessalom returned to his house, and saw not the king's face. 25 And there was not a man in Israel so very comely as Abessalom: from the sole of his foot even to the crown of his head there was no blemish in him. 26 And when he polled his head, (and it was at the beginning of every year that he polled it, because it grew, heavy upon him,) even when he polled it, he weighed the hair of his head, two hundred shekels according to the royal shekel. 27 And there were born to Abessalom three sons and one daughter, and her name was Themar: she was a very beautiful woman, and she becomes the wife of Roboam son of Solomon, and she bears to him Abia. 28 And Abessalom remained in Jerusalem two full years, and he saw not the king's face. 29 And Abessalom sent to Joab to bring him in to the king, and he would not come to him: and he sent to him the second time, and he would not come. 30 And Abessalom said to his servants, Behold, Joab's portion in the field *is* next to mine, and he has in it barley; go and set it on fire. And the servants of Abessalom set the field on fire: and the servants of Joab come to him with their clothes rent, and they said to him, The servants of Abessalom have set the field on fire. 31 And Joab arose, and came to Abessalom into the house, and said to him, Why have thy servants set my field on fire? 32 And Abessalom said to Joab, Behold, I sent to thee, saying, Come hither, and I will send thee to the king, saying, Why did I come out of Gedsur? it would have been better for me to have remained there: and now, behold, I have not seen the face of the king; but if there is iniquity in me, then put me to death. 33 And Joab went in to the king, and brought him word: and he called Abessalom, and he went in to the king, and did him obeisance, and fell upon his face to the ground, even in the presence of the king; and the king kissed Abessalom.

2-Kgdms15 1 And it came to pass after this that Abessalom prepared for himself chariots and horses, and fifty men to run before him. 2 And Abessalom rose early, and stood by the side of the way of the gate: and it came to pass that every man who had a cause, came to the king for judgment, and Abessalom cried to him, and said to him, Of what city art thou? And he said, Thy servant *is* of one of the tribes of Israel. 3 And Abessalom said to him, See, thy affairs *are* right and clear, yet thou hast no one *appointed* of the king to hear thee. 4 And Abessalom said, O that one would make me a judge in the land; then every man who had a dispute or a cause would come to me, and I would judge him! 5 And it came to pass when a man came near to do him obeisance, that he stretched out his hand, and took hold of him, and kissed him. 6 And Abessalom did after this manner to all Israel that came to the king for judgment; and Abessalom gained the hearts of the men of Israel. 7 And it came to pass after forty years, that Abessalom said to his father, I will go now, and pay my vows, which I vowed to the Lord in Chebron. 8 For thy servant vowed a vow when I dwelt at Gedsur in Syria, saying, If the Lord should indeed restore me to Jerusalem, then will I serve the Lord. 9 And the king said to him, Go in peace. And he arose and went to Chebron. 10 And Abessalom sent spies throughout all the tribes of Israel, saying, When ye hear the sound of the trumpet, then shall ye say, Abessalom is become king in Chebron. 11 And there went with Abessalom two hundred chosen men from Jerusalem; and they went in their simplicity, and knew not anything. 12 And Abessalom sent to Achitophel the Theconite, the counsellor of David, from his city, from Gola, where he was sacrificing: and there was a strong conspiracy; and the people with Abessalom were increasingly numerous. 13 And there came a messenger to David, saying, the heart of the men of Israel is gone after Abessalom. 14 And David said to all his servants who were with him in Jerusalem, Rise, and let us flee, for we have no refuge from Abessalom: make haste and go, lest he overtake us speedily, and bring evil upon us, and smite the city with the edge of the sword. 15 And the king's servants said to the king, In all things which our lord the king chooses, behold *we are* thy servants. 16 And the king and all his house went out on foot: and the king left ten women of his concubines to keep the house. 17 And the king and all his servants went out on foot; and abode in a distant house. 18 And all his servants passed on by his side, and every Chelethite, and every Phelethite, and they stood by the olive

tree in the wilderness: and all the people marched near him, and all his court, and all the men of might, and all the men of war, six hundred: and they were present at his side: and every Chelethite, and every Phelethite, and all the six hundred Gittites that came on foot out of Geth, and they went on before the king. 19 And the king said to Ethi, the Gittite, Why dost thou also go with us? return, and dwell with the king, for thou art a stranger, and thou has come forth as a sojourner out of thy place. 20 Whereas thou camest yesterday, shall I to-day cause thee to travel with us, and shalt thou *thus* change thy place? thou didst come forth yesterday, and to-day shall I set thee in motion to go along with us? I indeed will go whithersoever I may go: return then, and cause thy brethren to return with thee, and may the Lord deal mercifully and truly with thee. 21 And Ethi answered the king and said, *As* the Lord lives and as my lord the king lives, in the place wheresoever my lord shall be, whether it be for death or life, there shall thy servant be. 22 And the king said to Ethi, Come and pass over with me. So Ethi the Gittite and the king passed over, and all his servants, and all the multitude with him. 23 And all the country wept with a loud voice. And all the people passed by over the brook of Kedron; and the king crossed the brook Kedron: and all the people and the king passed on toward the way of the wilderness. 24 And behold also Sadoc, and all the Levites were with him, bearing the ark of the covenant of the Lord from Baethar: and they set down the ark of God; and Abiathar went up, until all the people had passed out of the city. 25 And the king said to Sadoc, Carry back the ark of God into the city: if I should find favour in the eyes of the Lord, then will he bring me back, and he will shew me it and its beauty. 26 But if he should say thus, I have no pleasure in thee; behold, *here* I am, let him do to me according to that which is good in his eyes. 27 And the king said to Sadoc the priest, Behold, thou shalt return to the city in peace, and Achimaas thy son, and Jonathan the son of Abiathar, your two sons with you. 28 Behold, I continue in arms in Araboth of the desert, until there come tidings from you to report to me. 29 So Sadoc and Abiathar brought back the ark of the Lord to Jerusalem, and it continued there. 30 And David went up by the ascent of *the mount of* Olives, ascending and weeping, and had his head covered, and went barefooted: and all the people that were with him covered *every* man his head; and they went up, ascending and weeping. 31 And it was reported to David, saying, Achitophel also *is* among the conspirators with Abessalom. And David said, O Lord my God, disconcert, I pray thee, the counsel of Achitophel. 32 And David came as far as Ros, where he worshipped God: and behold, Chusi the chief friend of David came out to meet him, having rent his garment, and earth *was* upon his head. 33 And David said to him, If thou shouldest go over with me, then wilt thou be a burden to me; 34 but if thou shall return to the city, and shalt say to Abessalom, Thy brethren are passed over, and the king thy father is passed over after me: and now I am thy servant, O king, suffer me to live: at one time even of late I was the servant of thy father, and now I *am* thy humble servant—so shalt thou disconcert for me, the counsel of Achitophel. 35 And, behold, *there are* there with thee Sadoc and Abiathar the priests; and it shall be that every word that thou shalt hear of the house of the king, thou shalt report it to Sadoc and Abiathar the priests. 36 Behold, *there are* there with them their two sons, Achimaas the son of Sadoc, and Jonathan the son of Abiathar; and by them ye shall report to me every word which ye shall hear. 37 So Chusi the friend of David went into the city, and Abessalom was lately gone into Jerusalem.

2-Kgdms16 1 And David passed on a little way from Ros; and, behold, Siba the servant of Memphibosthe *came* to meet him; and he had a couple of asses laden, and upon them two hundred loaves, and a hundred *bunches of* raisins, and a hundred *cakes of* dates, and bottle of wine. 2 And the king said to Siba, What meanest thou by these? and Siba, said, The asses *are* for the household of the king to sit upon, and the loaves and the dates *are* for the young men to eat, and the wine *is* for them that are faint in the wilderness to drink. 3 And the king said, And where *is* the son of thy master? and Siba said to the king, Behold, he remains in Jerusalem; for he said, To-day shall the house of Israel restore to me the kingdom of my father. 4 And the king said to Siba, Behold, all Memphibosthe's property *is* thine. And Siba did obeisance and said, My lord, O king, let me find grace in thine eyes. 5 And king David came to Baurim; and, behold, there came out from thence a man of the family of the house of Saul, and his name *was* Semei the son of Gera. He came forth and cursed as he went, 6 and cast stones at David, and at all the servants of king David: and all the people and all the mighty men were on the right and left hand of the king. 7 And thus Semei said when he cursed him, Go out, go out, thou bloody man, and man of sin. 8 The Lord has returned upon thee all the blood of the house of Saul, because thou hast reigned in his stead; and the Lord has given the kingdom into the hand of Abessalom thy son: and, behold, thou *art taken* in thy mischief, because thou *art* a bloody man. 9 And Abessa the son of Saruia said to the king, Why does this dead dog curse my lord the king? let me go over now and take off his head. 10 And the king said, What have I to do with you, ye sons of Saruia? even let him alone, and so let him curse, for the Lord has told him to curse David: and who shall say, Why hast thou done thus? 11 And David said to Abessa and to all his servants, Behold, my son who came forth out of my bowels seeks my life; still more now may the son of Benjamin: let him curse, because the Lord has told him. 12 If by any means the Lord may look on my affliction, thus shall he return me good for his cursing this day. 13 And David and all the men with him went on the way: and Semei went by the side of the hill next to him, cursing as he went, and casting stones at him, and sprinkling him with dirt. 14 And the king, and all the people with him, came away and refreshed themselves there. 15 And Abessalom and all the men of Israel went into Jerusalem, and Achitophel with him. 16 And it came to pass when Chusi the chief friend of David came to Abessalom, that Chusi said to Abessalom, Let the king live. 17 And Abessalom said to Chusi, *Is* this thy kindness to thy friend? why wentest thou not forth with thy friend? 18 And Chusi said to Abessalom, Nay, but following whom the Lord, and this people, and all Israel have chosen, —his will I be, and with him I will dwell. 19 And again, whom shall I serve? should I not in the presence of his son? As I served in the sight of thy father, so will I be in thy presence. 20 And Abessalom said to Achitophel, Deliberate among yourselves concerning what we should do. 21 And Achitophel said to Abessalom, Go in to thy father's concubines, whom he left to keep his house; and all Israel shall hear that thou hast dishonoured thy father; and the hands of all that are with thee shall be strengthened. 22 And they pitched a tent for Abessalom on the roof, and Abessalom went in to his father's concubines in the sight of all Israel. 23 And the counsel of Achitophel, which he counselled in former days, *was* as if one should enquire of the word of God: so *was* all the counsel of Achitophel both to David and also to Abessalom.

2-Kgdms17 1 And Achitophel said to Abessalom, Let me now choose out for myself twelve thousand men, and I will arise and follow after David this night: 2 and I will come upon him when he *is* weary and weak-handed, and I will strike him with terror; and all the people with him shall flee, and I will smite the king only of all. 3 And I will bring back all the people to thee, as a bride returns to her husband: only thou seekest the life of one man, and all the people shall have peace. 4 And the saying *was* right in the eyes of Abessalom, and in the eyes of all the elders of Israel. 5 And Abessalom said, Call now also Chusi the Arachite, and let us hear what *is* in his mouth, even in his also. 6 And Chusi went in to Abessalom, and Abessalom spoke to him, saying, After this manner spoke Achitophel: shall we do according to his word? but if not, do thou speak. 7 And Chusi said to Abessalom, This counsel which Achitophel has counselled this one time *is* not good. 8 And Chusi said, Thou knowest thy father and his men, that they are very mighty, and bitter in their spirit, as a bereaved bear in the field, [[and as a wild boar in the plain]]: and thy father *is* a man of war, and will not give the people rest. 9 For, behold, he is now hidden in one of the hills or in some *other* place: and it shall come to pass when he falls upon them at the beginning, that *some one* will certainly hear, and say, There has been a slaughter among the people that follow after Abessalom. 10 Then even he *that is* strong, whose heart is as the heart of a lion, —it shall utterly melt: for all Israel knows that thy father *is* mighty, and they that are with him *are* mighty men. 11 For thus I have surely given counsel, that all Israel be generally gathered to thee from Dan even to Bersabee, as the sand that is upon the sea-shore for multitude: and that thy presence go in the midst of them. 12 And we will come upon him in one of the places where we shall find him, and we will encamp against him, as the dew falls upon the earth; and we will not leave of him and of his men so much as one. 13 And if he shall have taken refuge with his army in a city, then shall all Israel take ropes to that city, and we will draw it even into the river, that there may not be left there even a stone. 14 And Abessalom, and all the men of Israel said, The counsel of Chusi the Arachite *is* better than the counsel of Achitophel. For the Lord ordained to disconcert the good counsel of Achitophel, that the Lord might bring all evil upon Abessalom. 15 And Chusi the Arachite said to Sadoc and Abiathar the priests, Thus and thus Achitophel counselled Abessalom and the elders of Israel; and thus and thus have I counselled. 16 And now send quickly and report to David, saying, Lodge not this night in Araboth of the wilderness: even go and make haste, lest *one* swallow up the king, and all the people with him. 17 And Jonathan and Achimaas stood by the well of Rogel, and a maid-servant went and reported to them, and they go and tell king David; for they might not be seen to enter into the city. 18 But a young man saw them and told Abessalom: and the two went quickly, and entered into the house of a man in Baurim; and he had a well in his court, and they went down into it. 19 And a woman took a covering, and spread it over the mouth of the well, and spread out ground corn upon it to dry, and the thing was not known. 20 And the servants of Abessalom came to the woman into the house, and said, Where *are* Achimaas and Jonathan? and the woman said to them, They are gone a little way beyond the water. And they sought and found them not, and returned to Jerusalem. 21 And it came to pass after they were gone, that they came up out of the pit, and went on their way; and reported to king David, and said to David, Arise ye and go quickly over the water, for thus has Achitophel counselled concerning you. 22 And David rose up and all the people with him, and they passed over Jordan till the morning light; there was not one missing who did not pass over Jordan. 23 And Achitophel saw that his counsel was not followed, and he saddled his ass, and rose and departed to his house into his city; and he gave orders to his household, and hanged himself, and died, and was buried in the sepulchre of his father. 24 And David passed over to Manaim: and Abessalom crossed over Jordan, he and all the men of Israel with him. 25 And Abessalom appointed Amessai in the room of Joab over the host. And Amessai was the son of a man whose name was Jether of Jezrael: he went in to Abigaia the daughter of Naas, the sister of Saruia the mother of Joab. 26 And all Israel and Abessalom encamped in the land of Galaad. 27 And it came to pass when David came to Manaim, that Uesbi the son of Naas of Rabbath of the sons of Ammon, and Machir son of Amiel of Lodabar, and Berzelli the Galaadite of Rogellim, 28 brought ten embroidered beds, (with double coverings,)and ten caldrons, and earthenware, and wheat, and barley, and flour, and meal, and beans, and pulse, 29 and honey, and butter, and sheep, and cheeses of kine: and they brought them to David and to his people with him to eat; for *one* said, The people *is* faint and hungry and thirsty in the wilderness.

2-Kgdms18 1 And David numbered the people with him, and set over them captains of thousands and captains of hundreds. 2 And David sent away the people, the third part under the hand of Joab, and the third part under the hand of Abessa the son of Saruia, the brother of Joab, and the third part under the hand of Ethi the Gittite. And David said to the people, I also will surely go out with you. 3 And they said, Thou shalt not go out: for if we should indeed flee, they will not care for us; and if half of us should die,

they will not mind us; for thou *art* as ten thousand of us: and now *it is* well that thou shalt be to us an aid to help us in the city. 4 And the king said to them, Whatsoever shall seem good in your eyes I will do. And the king stood by the side of the gate, and all the people went out by hundreds and by thousands. 5 And the king commanded Joab and Abessa and Ethi, saying, Spare for my sake the young man Abessalom. And all the people heard the king charging all the commanders concerning Abessalom. 6 And all the people went out into the wood against Israel; and the battle was in the wood of Ephraim. 7 And the people of Israel fell down there before the servants of David, and there was a great slaughter in that day, *even* twenty thousand men. 8 And the battle there was scattered over the face of all the land: and the wood consumed more of the people than the sword consumed among the people in that day. 9 And Abessalom went to meet the servants of David: and Abessalom was mounted on his mule, and the mule came under the thick boughs of a great oak; and his head was entangled in the oak, and he was suspended between heaven and earth; and the mule passed on from under him. 10 And a man saw it, and reported to Joab, and said, Behold, I saw Abessalom hanging in an oak. 11 And Joab said to the man who reported it to him, And, behold, thou didst see him: why didst thou not smite him there to the ground? and I would have given thee ten *pieces* of silver, and a girdle. 12 And the man said to Joab, Were I even to receive a thousand shekels of silver, I would not lift my hand against the king's son; for in our ears the king charged thee and Abessa and Ethi, saying, Take care of the young man Abessalom for me, 13 so as to do no harm to his life: and nothing of the matter will be concealed from the king, and thou wilt set thyself against me. 14 And Joab said, I will begin this; I will not thus remain with thee. And Joab took three darts in his hand, and thrust them into the heart of Abessalom, while he was yet alive in the heart of the oak. 15 And ten young men that bore Joab's armour compassed Abessalom, and smote him and slew him. 16 And Joab blew the trumpet, and the people returned from pursuing Israel, for Joab spared the people. 17 And he took Abessalom, and cast him into a great cavern in the wood, into a deep pit, and set up over him a very great heap of stones: and all Israel fled every man to his tent. 18 Now Abessalom while yet alive had taken and set up for himself the pillar near which he was taken, and set it up so as to have the pillar in the king's dale; for he said he had no son to keep his name in remembrance: and he called the pillar, Abessalom's hand, until this day. 19 And Achimaas the son of Sadoc said, Let me run now and carry glad tidings to the king, for the Lord has delivered him from the hand of his enemies. 20 And Joab said to him, Thou *shalt* not *be* a messenger of glad tidings this day; thou shalt bear them another day; but on this day thou shalt bear no tidings, because the king's son is dead. 21 And Joab said to Chusi, Go, report to the king all that thou hast seen. And Chusi did obeisance to Joab, and went out. 22 And Achimaas the son of Sadoc said again to Joab, Nay, let me also run after Chusi. And Joab said, Why wouldest thou thus run, my son? attend, thou hast no tidings for profit if thou go. 23 And he said, Why should I not run? and Joab said to him, Run. And Achimaas ran along the way of Kechar, and outran Chusi. 24 And David was sitting between the two gates: and the watchman went up on the top of the gate of the wall, and lifted up his eyes, and looked, and behold a man running alone before him. 25 And the watchman cried out, and reported to the king. And the king said, If he be alone, *there are* good tidings in his mouth. And the man came and drew near. 26 And the watchman saw another man running: and the watchman cried at the gate, and said, And look, another man running alone. And the king said, He also brings glad tidings. 27 And the watchman said, I see the running of the first as the running of Achimaas the son of Sadoc. And the king said, He *is* a good man, and will come to *report* glad tidings. 28 And Achimaas cried out and said to the king, Peace. And he did obeisance to the king with his face to the ground, and said, Blessed *be* the Lord thy God, who has delivered up the men that lifted up their hands against my lord the king. 29 And the king said, *Is* the young man Abessalom safe? and Achimaas said, I saw a great multitude *at the time* of Joab's sending the king's servant and thy servant, and I knew not what was there. 30 And the king said, Turn aside, stand still here. And he turned aside, and stood. 31 And, behold, Chusi came up, and said to the king, Let my lord the king hear glad tidings, for the Lord has avenged thee this day upon all them that rose up against thee. 32 And the king said to Chusi, Is it well with the young man Abessalom? and Chusi said, Let the enemies of my lord the king, and all whosoever have risen up against him for evil, be as that young man. 33 And the king was troubled, and went to the chamber over the gate, and wept: and thus he said as he went, My son Abessalom, my son, my son Abessalom; would God I had died for thee, *even* I *had died* for thee, Abessalom, my son, my son!

2-Kgdms19 1 And they brought Joab word, saying, Behold, the king weeps and mourns for Abessalom. 2 And the victory was turned that day into mourning to all the people, for the people heard say that day, The king grieves after his son. 3 And the people stole away that day to go into the city, as people steal away when they are ashamed as they flee in the battle. 4 And the king hid his face: and the king cried with a loud voice, My son Abessalom! Abessalom my son! 5 And Joab went in to the king, into the house, and said, Thou hast this day shamed the faces of all thy servants that have delivered thee this day, and *have saved* the lives of thy sons and of thy daughters, and the lives of thy wives, and of thy concubines, 6 forasmuch as thou lovest them that hate thee, and hatest them that love thee; and thou hast this day declared, that thy princes and thy servants are nothing *in thy sight*: for I know this day, that if Abessalom were alive, *and* all of us dead to-day, then it would have been right in thy sight. 7 And now arise, and go forth, and speak comfortably to thy servants; for I have sworn by the Lord, that unless thou wilt go forth to-day, there shall not a man remain with thee this night: and know for thyself, this thing *will* indeed *be* evil to thee beyond all the evil that has come upon thee from thy youth until now. 8 Then the king arose, and sat in the gate: and all the people reported, saying,

Behold, the king sits in the gate. And all the people went in before the king to the gate; for Israel had fled every man to his tent. 9 And all the people disputed among all the tribes of Israel, saying, King David delivered us from all our enemies, and he rescued us from the hand of the Philistines: and now he has fled from the land, and from his kingdom, and from Abessalom. 10 And Abessalom, whom we anointed over us, is dead in battle: and now why are ye silent about bringing back the king? And the word of all Israel came to the king. 11 And king David sent to Sadoc and Abiathar the priests, saying, Speak to the elders of Israel, saying, Why are ye the last to bring back the king to his house? whereas the word of all Israel is come to the king to his house. 12 Ye *are* my brethren, ye *are* my bones and my flesh: why are ye the last to bring back the king to his house? 13 And ye shall say to Amessai, *Art* thou not my bone and my flesh? and now God do so to me, and more also, if thou shalt not be commander of the host before me continually in the room of Joab. 14 And he bowed the heart of all the men of Juda as that of one man; and they sent to the king, saying, Return thou, and all thy servants. 15 And the king returned, and came as far s Jordan. And the men of Juda came to Galgala on their way to meet the king, to cause the king to pass over Jordan. 16 And Semei the son of Gera, the Benjamite, of Baurim, hasted and went down with the men of Juda to meet king David. 17 And a thousand men of Benjamin *were* with him, and Siba the servant of the house of Saul, and his fifteen sons with him, and his twenty servants with him: and they went directly down to Jordan before the king, 18 and they performed the service of bringing the king over; and there went over a ferry-boat to remove the household of the king, and to do that which was right in his eyes. And Semei the son of Gera fell on his face before the king, as he went over Jordan; 19 and said to the king, Let not my lord now impute iniquity, and remember not all the iniquity of thy servant in the day in which my lord went out from Jerusalem, so that the king should mind it. 20 For thy servant knows that I have sinned: and, behold, I am come to-day before all Israel and the house of Joseph, to go down and meet my lord the king. 21 And Abessai the son of Saruia answered and said, Shall not Semei therefore be put to death, because he cursed the Lord's anointed? 22 And David said, What have I to do with you, ye sons of Saruia, that ye as it were lie in wait against me this day? to-day no man in Israel shall be put to death, for I know not if I this day reign over Israel. 23 And the king said to Semei, Thou shalt not die: and the king swore to him. 24 And Memphibosthe the son of Saul's son went down to meet the king, and had not dressed his feet, nor pared his nails, nor shaved himself, neither had he washed his garments, from the day that the king departed, until the day when he arrived in peace. 25 And it came to pass when he went into Jerusalem to meet the king, that the king said to him, Why didst thou not go with me, Memphibosthe? 26 And Memphibosthe said to him, My lord, O king, my servant deceived me; for thy servant said to him, Saddle me the ass, and I will ride upon it, and go with the king; for thy servant *is* lame. 27 And he has dealt deceitfully with thy servant to my lord the king: but my lord the king *is* as an angel of God, and do thou that which is good in thine eyes. 28 For all the house of my father were but as dead men before my lord the king; yet thou hast set thy servant among them that eat at thy table: and what right have I any longer even to cry to the king? 29 And the king said to him, Why speakest thou any longer of thy matters? I have said, Thou and Siba shall divide the land. 30 And Memphibosthe said to the king, Yea, let him take all, since my lord the king has come in peace to his house. 31 And Berzelli the Galaadite came down from Rogellim, and crossed over Jordan with the king, that he might conduct the king over Jordan. 32 And Berzelli was a very old man, eighty years old; and he had maintained the king when he dwelt in Manaim; for he was a very great man. 33 And the king said to Berzelli, Thou shalt go over with me, and I will nourish thine old age with me in Jerusalem. 34 And Berzelli said to the king, How many *are* the days of the years of my life, that I should go up with the king to Jerusalem? 35 I am this day eighty years old: can I then distinguish between good and evil? Can thy servant taste any longer what I eat or drink? can I any longer hear the voice of singing men or singing women? and wherefore shall thy servant any longer be a burden to my lord the king? 36 Thy servant will go a little way over Jordan with the king: and why does the king return me this recompense? 37 Let, I pray thee, thy servant remain, and I will die in my city, by the tomb of my father and of my mother. And, behold, thy servant Chamaam shall go over with my lord the king; and do thou to him as it seems good in thine eyes. 38 And the king said, Let Chamaam go over with me, and I will do to him what is good in my sight; and whatsoever thou shalt choose at my hand, I will do for thee. 39 And all the people went over Jordan, and the king went over; and the king kissed Berzelli, and blessed him; and he returned to his place. 40 And the king went over to Galgala, and Chamaam went over with him: and all the men of Juda went over with the king, and also half the people of Israel. 41 And behold, all the men of Israel came to the king, and said to the king, Why have our brethren the men of Juda stolen thee away, and caused the king and all his house to pass over Jordan, and all the men of David with him? 42 And all the men of Juda answered the men of Israel, and said, Because the king is near of kin to us: and why were you thus angry concerning this matter? have we indeed eaten of the king's food? or has he given us a gift, or has he sent us a portion? 43 And the men of Israel answered the men of Juda, and said, We have ten parts in the king, and we are older than you, we have also an interest in David above you: and why have ye thus insulted us, and why was not our advice taken before that of Juda, to bring back our king? And the speech of the men of Juda was sharper than the speech of the men of Israel.

2-Kgdms20 1 And there was a transgressor *so* called there, and his name was Sabee, a Benjamite, the son of Bochori: and he blew the trumpet, and said, We have no portion in David, neither have we *any* inheritance in the son of Jessae: to thy tents, O Israel, every one. 2 And all the men of Israel went up from following David after Sabee the son of Bochori: but the men of Juda adhered to their king, from

Jordan even to Jerusalem. 3 And David went into his house at Jerusalem: and the king took the ten women his concubines, whom he had left to keep the house, and he put them in a place of custody, and maintained them, and went not in to them; and they were kept living as widows, till the day of their death. 4 And the king said to Amessai, Call to me the men of Juda for three days, and do thou be present here. 5 And Amessai went to call Juda, and delayed beyond the time which David appointed him. 6 And David said to Amessai, Now shall Sabee the son of Bochori do us more harm than Abessalom: now then take thou with thee the servants of thy lord, and follow after him, lest he find for himself strong cities, so will he blind our eyes. 7 And there went out after him Amessai and the men of Joab, and the Cherethites, and the Phelethites, and all the mighty men: and they went out from Jerusalem to pursue after Sabee the son of Bochori. 8 And they *were* by the great stone that is in Gabaon: and Amessai went in before them: and Joab had upon him a military cloak over his apparel, and over it he was girded with a dagger fastened upon his loins in its scabbard: and the dagger came out, it even came out and fell. 9 And Joab said to Amessai, Art thou in health, *my* brother? and the right hand of Joab took hold of the beard of Amessai to kiss him. 10 And Amessai observed not the dagger that was in the hand of Joab: and Joab smote him with it on the loins, and his bowels were shed out upon the ground, and he did not repeat the blow, and he died: and Joab and Abessai his brother pursued after Sabee the son of Bochori. 11 And there stood over him one of the servants of Joab, and said, Who *is* he that is for Joab, and who *is* on the side of David following Joab? 12 And Amessai *was* weltering in blood in the midst of the way. And a man saw that all the people stood still; and he removed Amessai out of the path into a field, and he cast a garment upon him, because he saw every one that came to him standing still. 13 And when he was quickly removed from the road, every man of Israel passed after Joab to pursue after Sabee the son of Bochori. 14 And he went through all the tribes of Israel to Abel, and to Bethmacha; and all in Charri too were assembled, and followed after him. 15 And they came and besieged him in Abel and Phermacha: and they raised a mound against the city and it stood close to the wall; and all the people with Joab proposed to throw down the wall. 16 And a wise woman cried from the wall, and said, Hear, hear; say, I pray ye, to Joab, Draw near hither, and I will speak to him. 17 And he drew nigh to her, and the woman said to him, Art thou Joab? and he said, I *am*. And she said to him, Hear the words of thy handmaid; and Joab said, I do hear. 18 And she spoke, saying, Of old time they said thus, Surely one was asked in Abel, and Dan, whether the faithful in Israel failed in what they purposed; they will surely ask in Abel, even in like manner, whether they have failed. 19 I am a peaceable one of the strong ones in Israel; but thou seekest to destroy a city and a mother city in Israel: why dost thou seek to ruin the inheritance of the Lord? 20 And Joab answered and said, Far be it, far be it from me, that I should ruin or destroy. 21 Is not the case thus, that a man of mount Ephraim, Sabee, son of Bochori by name, has even lifted up his hand against king David? Give him only to me, and I will depart from the city. And the woman said to Joab, Behold, his head shall be thrown to thee over the wall. 22 And the woman went in to all the people, and she spoke to all the city in her wisdom; and they took off the head of Sabee the son of Bochori; and took it away and threw it to Joab: and he blew the trumpet, and the people separated from the city away from him, every man to his tent: and Joab returned to Jerusalem to the king. 23 And Joab *was* over all the forces of Israel: and Banaias the son of Jodae *was* over the Cherethites and over the Phelethites. 24 And Adoniram *was* over the tribute: and Josaphath the son of Achiluth *was* recorder. 25 And Susa *was* scribe: and Sadoc and Abiathar *were* priests. 26 Moreover Iras the *son of* Iarin was priest to David.

2-Kgdms21 1 And there was a famine in the days of David three years, year after year; and David sought the face of the Lord. And the Lord said, *There is* guilt upon Saul and his house because of his bloody murder, whereby he slew the Gabaonites. 2 And King David called the Gabaonites, and said to them; —(now the Gabaonites are not the children of Israel, but *are* of the remnant of the Amorite, and the children of Israel had sworn to them: but Saul sought to smite them in his zeal for the children of Israel and Juda.) 3 And David said to the Gabaonites, What shall I do to you? and wherewithal shall I make atonement, that ye may bless the inheritance of the Lord? 4 And the Gabaonites said to him, We have no *question about* silver or gold with Saul and with his house; and there is no man for us to put to death in Israel. 5 And he said, What say ye? speak, and I will do it for you. And they said to the king, The man who would have made an end of us, and persecuted us, who plotted against us to destroy us, let us utterly destroy him, so that he shall have no standing in all the coasts of Israel. 6 Let one give us seven men of his sons, and let us hang them up in the sun to the Lord in Gabaon of Saul, as chosen out for the Lord. And the king said, I will give *them*. 7 But the king spared Memphibosthe son of Jonathan the son of Saul, because of the oath of the Lord that was between them, even between David and Jonathan the son of Saul. 8 And the king took the two sons of Respha the daughter of Aia, whom she bore to Saul, Hermonoi and Memphibosthe, and the five sons of Michol daughter of Saul, whom she bore to Esdriel son of Berzelli the Moulathite. 9 And he gave them into the hand of the Gabaonites, and they hanged them up to the sun in the mountain before the lord: and they fell, even the seven together: moreover they were put to death in the days of harvest at the commencement, in the beginning of barley-harvest. 10 And Respha the daughter of Aia took sackcloth, and fixed it for herself on the rock in the beginning of barley harvest, until water dropped upon them out of heaven: and she did not suffer the birds of the air to rest upon them by day, nor the beasts of the field by night. 11 And it was told David what Respha the daughter of Aia the concubine of Saul had done, [and they were faint, and Dan, the son of Joa of the offspring of the giants overtook them.] 12 And David went and took the bones of Saul, and the bones of Jonathan his son, from the men of the sons of Jabis Galaad, who stole them from the street of Baethsan; for the Philistines set them there in the day in which the Philistines smote Saul in Gelbue. 13 And he carried up thence the bones of Saul and the bones of Jonathan his son, and gathered the bones of them that had been hanged. 14 And they buried the bones of Saul and the bones of Jonathan his son, and the bones of them that had been hanged, in the land of Benjamin in the hill, in the sepulchre of Cis his father; and they did all things that the king commanded: and after this God hearkened to *the prayers of the land*. 15 And there was yet war between the Philistines and Israel: and David went down and his servants with him, and they fought with the Philistines, and David went. 16 And Jesbi, who was of the progeny of Rapha, and the head of whose spear *was* three hundred shekels of brass in weight, who also was girt with a club, even he thought to smite David. 17 And Abessa the son of Saruia helped him and smote the Philistine, and slew him. Then the men of David swore, saying, Thou shalt not any longer go out with us to battle, and thou shalt not quench the lamp of Israel. 18 And after this there was a battle again with the Philistines in Geth: then Sebocha the Astatothite slew Seph of the progeny of Rapha. 19 And there was a battle in Rom with the Philistines; and Eleanan son of Ariorgim the Bethleemite slew Goliath the Gittite; and the staff of his spear *was* as a weaver's beam. 20 And there was yet a battle in Geth: and there was a man of stature, and the fingers of his hands and the toes of his feet *were* six on each, four and twenty in number: and he also was born to Rapha. 21 And he defied Israel, and Jonathan son of Semei brother of David, smote him. 22 These four were born descendants of the giants in Geth, the family of Rapha; and they fell by the hand of David, and by the hand of his servants.

2-Kgdms22 1 And David spoke to the Lord the words of this song, in the day in which the Lord rescued him out of the hand of all his enemies, and out of the hand of Saul. 2 And the song was thus: O Lord, my rock, and my fortress, and my deliverer, 3 my God; he shall be to me my guard, I will trust in him: *he is* my protector, and the horn of my salvation, my helper, and my sure refuge; thou shalt save me from the unjust man. 4 I will call upon the Lord who is worthy to be praised, and I shall be saved from my enemies. 5 For the troubles of death compassed me, the floods of iniquity amazed me: 6 the pangs of death surrounded me, the agonies of death prevented me. 7 When I am afflicted I will call upon the Lord, and will cry to my God, and he shall hear my voice out of his temple, and my cry shalt come into his ears. 8 And the earth was troubled and quaked, and the foundations of heaven were confounded and torn asunder, because the Lord was wroth with them. 9 There went up a smoke in his wrath, and fire out of his mouth devours: coals were kindled at it. 10 And he bowed the heavens, and came down, and *there was* darkness under his feet. 11 And he rode upon the cherubs and did fly, and was seen upon the wings of the wind. 12 And he made darkness his hiding-place; his tabernacle round about him was the darkness of waters, he condensed it with the clouds of the air. 13 At the brightness before him coals of fire were kindled. 14 The Lord thundered out of heaven, and the Most High uttered his voice. 15 And he sent forth arrows, and scattered them, and he flashed lightning, and dismayed them. 16 And the channels of the sea were seen, and the foundations of the world were discovered, at the rebuke of the Lord, at the blast of the breath of his anger. 17 He sent from above and took me; he drew me out of many waters. 18 He delivered me from my strong enemies, from them that hated me, for they were stronger than I. 19 The days of my affliction prevented me; but the Lord was my stay. 20 And he brought me into a wide place, and rescued me, because he delighted in me. 21 And the Lord recompensed me according to my righteousness; even according to the purity of my hands did he recompense me. 22 Because, I kept the ways of the Lord, and did not wickedly depart from my God. 23 For all his judgments and his ordinances *were* before me: I departed not from them. 24 And I shall be blameless before him, and will keep myself from my iniquity. 25 And the Lord will recompense me according to my righteousness, and according to the purity of my hands in his eye-sight. 26 With the holy thou wilt be holy, and with the perfect man thou will be perfect, 27 and with the excellent thou wilt be excellent, and with the froward thou will be froward. 28 And thou wilt save the poor people, and wilt bring down the eyes of the haughty. 29 For thou, Lord, *art* my lamp, and the Lord shall shine forth to me in my darkness. 30 For by thee shall I run *as* a girded man, and by my God shall I leap over a wall. 31 As for the Mighty One, his way *is* blameless: the word of the Lord *is* strong *and* tried in the fire: he is a protector to all that put their trust in him. 32 Who *is* strong, but the Lord? and who will be a Creator except our God? 33 *It is* the Mighty One who strengthens me with might, and has prepared my way without fault. 34 He makes my feet like hart's feet, and sets me upon the high places. 35 He teaches my hands to war, and has broken a brazen bow by my arm. 36 And thou hast given me the shield of my salvation, and thy propitious dealing has increased me, 37 so as to make room under me for my going, and my legs did not totter. 38 I will pursue my enemies, and will utterly destroy them; and I will not turn again till I have consumed them. 39 And I will crush them, and they shall not rise; and they shall fall under my feet. 40 And thou shalt strengthen me with power for the war; thou shalt cause them that rise up against me to bow down under me. 41 And thou hast caused mine enemies to flee before me, even them that hated me, and thou hast slain them. 42 They shall cry, and there shall be no helper; to the Lord, but he hearkens not to them. 43 And I ground them as the dust of the earth, I beat them small as the mire of the streets. 44 And thou shalt deliver me from the striving of the peoples, thou shalt keep me *to be* the head of the Gentiles: a people which I knew not served me. 45 The strange children feigned *obedience* to me; they hearkened to me as soon as they heard. 46 The strange children shall be cast away, and shall be overthrown out of their hiding places. 47 The Lord lives, and blessed *be* my guardian, and my God, my strong keeper, shall be exalted. 48 The Lord who avenges me *is* strong, chastening the nations under me, 49 and bringing me out from my enemies: and thou shalt set me on high from among those that rise up against me: thou shalt deliver me from the violent man. 50 Therefore will I confess to thee, O Lord, among the Gentiles, and sing to thy name. 51 He magnifies the salvation of his king, and works mercy for his anointed, even for David and for his seed for ever.

2-Kgdms23 1 And these *are* the last words of David. Faithful *is* David the son of Jessae, and faithful the man whom the Lord raised up to be the anointed of the God of Jacob, and beautiful *are* the psalms of Israel. 2 The Spirit of the Lord spoke by me, and his word *was* upon my tongue. 3 The God of Israel says, A watchman out of Israel spoke to me a parable: I said among men, How will ye strengthen the fear of the anointed? 4 And in the morning light of God, let the sun arise in the morning, from the light of which the Lord passed on, and as it were from the rain of the tender grass upon the earth. 5 For my house *is* not so with the Mighty One: for he has made an everlasting covenant with me, ready, guarded at every time; for all my salvation and all my desire *is*, that the wicked should not flourish. 6 All these *are* as a thorn thrust forth, for they shall not be taken with the hand, 7 and a man shall not labour among them; and *one shall have* that which is fully armed with iron, and the staff of a spear, an he shall burn them with fire, and they shall be burnt in their shame. 8 These *are* the names of the mighty men of David: Jebosthe the Chananite is a captain of the third *part*: Adinon the Asonite, he drew his sword against eight hundred soldiers at once. 9 And after him Eleanan the son of his uncle, son of Dudi who was among the three mighty men with David; and when he defied the Philistines they were gathered there to war, and the men of Israel went up. 10 He arose an smote the Philistines, until his hand was weary, and his hand clave to the sword: and the Lord wrought a great salvation in that day, and the people rested behind him only to strip *the slain*. 11 And after him Samaia the son of Asa the Arachite: and the Philistines were gathered to Theria; and there was there a portion of ground full of lentiles; and the people fled before the Philistines. 12 And he stood firm in the midst of the portion, and rescued it, and smote the Philistines; and the Lord wrought a great deliverance. 13 And three out of the thirty went down, and came to Cason to David, to the cave of Odollam; and *there was* an army of the Philistines, and they encamped in the valley of Raphain. 14 And David *was* then in the strong hold, and the garrison of the Philistines *was* then in Bethleem. 15 And David longed, and said, Who will give me water to drink out of the well that is in Bethleem by the gate? now the band of the Philistines *was* then in Bethleem. 16 And the three mighty men broke through the host of the Philistines, and drew water out of the well that was in Bethleem in the gate: and they took it, and brought it to David, and he would not drink it, but poured it out before the Lord. 17 And he said, O Lord, forbid that I should do this, that I should drink of the blood of the men who went at *the risk of* their lives: and he would not drink it. These things did these three mighty men. 18 And Abessa the brother of Joab the son of Saruia, he *was* chief among the three, and he lifted up his spear against three hundred whom he slew; and he had a name among three. 19 Of those three *he was* most honourable, and he became a chief over them, but he reached not to the *first* three. 20 And Banaeas the son of Jodae, he was abundant in *mighty* deeds, from Cabeseel, and he smote the two sons of Ariel of Moab: and he went down and smote a lion in the midst of a pit on a snowy day. 21 He smote an Egyptian, a wonderful man, and in the hand of the Egyptian *was* a spear as the side of a ladder; and he went down to him with a staff, and snatched the spear from the Egyptian's hand, and slew him with his own spear. 22 These things did Banaeas the son of Jodae, and he had a name among the three mighty men. 23 He was honourable among the *second* three, but he reached not to the *first* three: and David made him his reporter. And these *are* the names of King David's mighty men. 24 Asael Joab's brother; he *was* among the thirty. Eleanan son of Dudi his uncle in Bethleem. 25 Saema the Rudaean. 26 Selles the Kelothite: Iras the son of Isca the Thecoite. 27 Abiezer the Anothite, of the sons of the Anothite. 28 Ellon the Aoite; Noere the Netophatite. 29 Esthai the son of Riba of Gabaeth, son of Benjamin the Ephrathite; Asmoth the Bardiamite; Emasu the Salabonite: 30 Adroi of the brooks. 31 Gadabiel son of the Arabothaeite. 32 the sons of Asan, Jonathan; 33 Samnan the Arodite; Amnan the son of Arai the Saraurite. 34 Aliphaleth the son of Asbites, the son of the Machachachite; Eliab the son of Achitophel the Gelonite. 35 Asarai the Carmelite the son of Uraeoerchi. 36 Gaal the son of Nathana. The son of much valour, *the son* of Galaaddi. Elie the Ammanite. 37 Gelore the Bethorite, armour-bearer to Joab, son of Saruia. 38 Iras the Ethirite. Gerab the Ethenite. 39 Urias the Chettite: thirty-seven in all.

2-Kgdms 24 1 And the Lord caused his anger to burn forth again in Israel, and *Satan* stirred up David against them, saying, Go, number Israel and Juda. 2 And the king said to Joab commander of the host, who was with him, Go now through all the tribes of Israel and Juda, from Dan even to Bersabee, and number the people, and I will know the number of the people. 3 And Joab said to the king, Now may the Lord add to the people a hundred-fold as many as they are, and *may* the eyes of my lord the king see it: but why does my lord the king desire this thing? 4 Nevertheless the word of the king prevailed against Joab an the captains of the host: And Joab and the captains of the host went out before the king to number the people of Israel. 5 And they went over Jordan, and encamped in Aroer, on the right of the city which is in the midst of the valley of Gad and Eliezer. 6 And they came to Galaad, and into the land of Thabason, which is Adasai, and they came to Danidan and Udan, and compassed Sidon. 7 And they came to Mapsar of Tyre, and to all the cities of the Evite and the Chananite: and they came by the South of Juda to Bersabee. 8 And they compassed the whole land; and they arrived at Jerusalem at the end of nine months and twenty days. 9 And Joab gave in the number of the census of the people to the king: and Israel consisted of eight hundred thousand men of might that drew sword; and the men of Juda, five hundred thousand fighting men. 10 And the heart of David smote him after he had numbered the people; and David said to the Lord, I have sinned grievously, O Lord, *in* what I have

now done: remove, I pray thee, the iniquity of thy servant, for I have been exceedingly foolish. 11 And David rose early in the morning, and the word of the Lord came to the prophet Gad, the seer, saying, Go, and speak to David, saying, 12 Thus saith the Lord, I bring *one of* three things upon thee: now choose thee one of them, and I will do *it* to thee. 13 And Gad went in to David, and told him, and said to him, Choose *one of these things* to befall thee, whether there shall come upon thee *for* three years famine in thy land; or that thou shouldest flee three months before thine enemies, and they should pursue thee; or that there should be *for* three days mortality in thy land. Now then decide, and see what answer I shall return to him that sent me. 14 And David said to Gad, On every side I am much straitened: let me fall now into the hands of the Lord, for his compassions *are* very many; and let me not fall into the hands of man. 15 So David chose for himself the mortality: and *they were* the days of wheat-harvest; and the Lord sent a pestilence upon Israel from morning till noon, and the plague began among the people; and there died of the people from Dan even to Bersabee seventy thousand men. 16 And the angel of the Lord stretched out his hand against Jerusalem to destroy it, and the Lord repented of the evil, and said to the angel that destroyed the people, *It is* enough now, withhold thine hand. And the angel of the Lord was by the threshing-floor of Orna the Jebusite. 17 And David spoke to the Lord when he saw the angel smiting the people, and he said, Behold, it is I that have done wrong, but these sheep what have they done? Let thy hand, I pray thee, be upon me, and upon my father's house. 18 And Gad came to David in that day, and said to him, Go up, and set up to the Lord and altar in the threshing-floor of Orna the Jebusite. 19 And David went up according to the word of Gad, as the Lord commanded him. 20 And Orna looked out, and saw the king and his servants coming on before him: and Orna went forth, and did obeisance to the king with his face to the earth. 21 And Orna said, Why has my lord the king come to his servant? and David said, To buy of thee the threshing-floor, in order to build an altar to the Lord that the plague may be restrained from off the people. 22 And Orna said to David, Let my lord the king take and offer to the Lord that which is good in his eyes: behold, *here are* oxen for a whole-burnt-offering, and the wheels and furniture of the oxen for wood. 23 Orna gave all to the king: and Orna said to the king, The Lord thy God bless thee. 24 And the king said to Orna, Nay, but I will surely buy it of thee at a fair price, and I will not offer to the Lord my God a whole-burnt-offering for nothing. So David purchased the threshing-floor and the oxen for fifty shekels of silver. 25 And David built there an altar to the Lord, and offered up whole-burnt-offerings and peace- offerings: and Solomon made an addition to the altar afterwards, for it was little at first. And the Lord hearkened to the land, and the plague was stayed from Israel.

3 KINGDOMS (I KINGS)

3-Kgdms 1 1 And king David *was* old and advanced in days, and they covered him with clothes, and he was not warmed. 2 And his servants said, Let them seek for the king a young virgin, and she shall wait on the king, and cherish him, and lie with him, and my lord the king shall be warmed. 3 So they sought for a fair damsel out of all the coasts of Israel; and they found Abisag the Somanite, and they brought her to the king. 4 And the damsel was extremely beautiful, and she cherished the king, and ministered to him, but the king knew her not. 5 And Adonias the son of Aggith exalted himself, saying, I will be king; and he prepared for himself chariots and horses, and fifty men to run before him. 6 And his father never at any time checked him, saying, Why hast thou done *thus*? and he was also very handsome in appearance, and his mother bore him after Abessalom. 7 And he conferred with Joab the son of Saruia, and with Abiathar the priest, and they followed after Adonias. 8 But Sadoc the priest, and Banaeas the son of Jodae, and Nathan the prophet, and Semei, and Resi, and the mighty men of David, did not follow Adonias. 9 And Adonias sacrificed sheep and calves and lambs by the stone of Zoelethi, which was near Rogel: and he called all his brethren, and all the adult *men* of Juda, servants of the king. 10 But Nathan the prophet, and Banaeas, and the mighty *men*, and Solomon his brother, he did not call. 11 And Nathan spoke to Bersabee the mother of Solomon, saying, Hast thou not heard that Adonias the son of Aggith reigns, and our lord David knows it not? 12 And now come, let me, I pray, give thee counsel, and thou shalt rescue thy life, and the life of thy son Solomon. 13 Haste, and go in to king David, and thou shalt speak to him, saying, Hast not thou, my lord, O king, sworn to thine handmaid, saying, Thy son Solomon shall reign after me, and he shall sit upon my throne? why then does Adonias reign? 14 And behold, while thou art still speaking there with the king, I also will come in after thee, and will confirm thy words. 15 So Bersabee went in to the king into the chamber: and the king was very old, and Abisag the Somanite was ministering to the king. 16 And Bersabee bowed, and did obeisance to the king; and the king said, What is thy request? 17 And she said, My lord, thou didst swear by the Lord thy God to thine handmaid, saying, Thy son Solomon shall reign after me, and shall sit upon my throne. 18 And now, behold, Adonias reigns, and thou, my lord, O king, knowest *it* not. 19 And he has sacrificed calves and lambs and sheep in abundance, and has called all the king's sons, and Abiathar the priest and Joab the commander-in-chief of the host; but Solomon thy servant he has not called. 20 And thou, my lord, O king, — the eyes of all Israel *are* upon thee, to tell them who shall sit upon the throne of my lord the king after him. 21 And it shall come to pass, when my lord the king shall sleep with his fathers, that I and Solomon my son shall be offenders. 22 And behold, while she was yet talking with the king, Nathan the prophet came. And it was reported to the king, 23 Behold, Nathan the prophet *is here*: and he came in to the king's presence, and did obeisance to the king with his face to the ground. 24 And Nathan said, My lord, O king, didst thou say, Adonias shall reign after me, and he shall sit upon my throne? 25 For he has gone down to-day, and has sacrificed calves and lambs and sheep in abundance, and has called all the king's sons, and the chiefs of the army, and Abiathar the priest; and, behold, they are eating and drinking before him, and they said, *Long* live king Adonias. 26 But he has not invited me thy servant, and Sadoc the priest, and Banaeas the son of Jodae, and Solomon thy servant. 27 Has this matter happened by the authority of my lord the king, and hast thou not made known to thy servant who shall sit upon the throne of my lord the king after him? 28 And king David answered and said, Call me Bersabee: and she came in before the king, and stood before him. 29 And the king swore, and said, *As* the Lord lives who redeemed my soul out of all affliction, 30 as I swore to thee by the Lord God of Israel, saying, Solomon thy son shall reign after me, and he shall sit upon my throne in my stead, so will I do this day. 31 And Bersabee bowed with her face to the ground, and did obeisance to the king, and said, Let my lord king David live for ever. 32 And king David said, Call me Sadoc the priest, and Nathan the prophet, and Banaeas the son of Jodae: and they came in before the king. 33 And the king said to them, Take the servants of your lord with you, and mount my son Solomon upon my own mule, and bring him down to Gion. 34 And there let Sadoc the priest and Nathan the prophet anoint him to be king over Israel, and do ye sound the trumpet, and ye shall say, Let king Solomon live. 35 And he shall sit upon my throne, and reign in my stead: and I have given charge that he should be for a prince over Israel and Juda. 36 And Banaeas the son of Jodae answered the king and said, So let it be: may the Lord God of my lord the king confirm *it*. 37 As the Lord was with my lord the king, so let him be with Solomon, and let him exalt his throne beyond the throne of my lord king David. 38 And Sadoc the priest went down, and Nathan the prophet, and Banaeas son of Jodae, and the Cherethite, and the Phelethite, and they mounted Solomon upon the mule of king David, and led him away to Gion. 39 And Sadoc the priest took the horn of oil out of the tabernacle, and anointed Solomon, and blew the trumpet; and all the people said, Let king Solomon live. 40 And all the people went up after him, and they danced in choirs, and rejoiced with great joy, and the earth quaked with their voice. 41 And Adonias and all his guests heard, and they had *just* left off eating: and Joab heard the sound of the trumpet, and said, What *means* the voice of the city in tumult? 42 While he was yet speaking, behold, Jonathan the son of Abiathar the priest came in: and Adonias said, Come in, for thou art a mighty man, and *thou comest* to bring glad tidings. 43 And Jonathan answered and said, Verily our lord king David has made Solomon king: 44 and the king has sent with him Sadoc the priest, and Nathan the prophet, and Banaeas the son of Jodae, and the Cherethite, and the Phelethite, and they have mounted him on the king's mule; 45 and Sadoc the priest and Nathan the prophet have anointed him in Gion, and have gone up thence rejoicing, and the city resounded: this *is* the sound which ye have heard. 46 And Solomon is seated upon the throne of the kingdom. 47 And the servants of the king have gone in to bless our lord king David, saying, God make the name of Solomon better than thy name, and make his throne greater than thy throne; and the king worshipped upon his bed. 48 Moreover thus said the king, Blessed *be* the Lord God of Israel, who has this day appointed one of my seed sitting on my throne, and my eyes see it. 49 And all the guests of Adonias were dismayed, and every man went his way. 50 And Adonias feared because of Solomon, and arose, and departed, and laid hold on the horns of the altar. 51 And it was reported to Solomon, saying, Behold, Adonias fears king Solomon, and holds the horns of the altar, saying, Let Solomon swear to me this day, that he will not slay his servant with the sword. 52 And Solomon said, If he should be a valiant man, there shall not a hair of his fall to the ground; but if evil be found in him, he shall die. 53 And king Solomon sent, and they brought him away from the altar; and he went in and did obeisance to king Solomon: and Solomon said to him, Go to thy house.

3-Kgdms2 1 And the days of David drew near that he should die: and he addressed his son Solomon, saying, I go the way of all the earth: 2 but be thou strong, and shew thyself a man; 3 and keep the charge of the Lord thy God, to walk in his ways, to keep the commandments and the ordinances and the judgments which are written in the law of Moses; that thou mayest understand what thou shalt do in all things that I command thee: 4 that the Lord may confirm his word which he spoke, saying, If thy children shall take heed to their way to walk before me in truth with all their heart, *I promise thee*, saying, there shall not fail thee a man on the throne of Israel. 5 Moreover thou knowest all that Joab the son of Saruia did to me, what he did to the two captains of the forces of Israel, to Abenner the son of Ner, and to Amessai the son of Jether, that he slew them, and shed the blood of war in peace, and put innocent blood on his girdle that was about his loins, and on his sandal that was on his foot. 6 Therefore thou shalt deal *with him* according to thy wisdom, and thou shalt not bring down his grey hairs in peace to the grave. 7 But thou shalt deal kindly with the sons of Berzelli the Galaadite, and they shall be among those that eat at thy table; for thus they drew nigh to me when I fled from the face of thy brother Abessalom. 8 And, behold, *there is* with thee Semei the son of Gera, a Benjamite of Baurim: and he cursed me with a grievous curse in the day when I went into the camp; and he came down to Jordan to meet me, and I swore to him by the Lord, saying, I will not put thee to death with the sword. 9 But thou shalt by no means hold him guiltless, for thou art a wise man, and wilt know what thou shalt do to him, and shalt bring down his grey hairs with blood to the grave. 10 And David slept with his fathers, and was buried in the city of David. 11 And the days which David reigned over Israel *were* forty years; he reigned seven years in Chebron, and thirty-three years in Jerusalem. 12 And Solomon sat on the throne of his father David, and his kingdom was established greatly. 13 And Adonias the son of Aggith came in to Bersabee the mother of Solomon, and did obeisance to her: and she said, Dost thou enter peaceably? and he said, Peaceably: 14 I have business with thee. And she said to him, Say on. 15 And he said to her, Thou knowest that the kingdom was mine, and all Israel turned their face toward me for a king; but the kingdom was turned *from me* and became my brother's: for it was *appointed* to him from the Lord. 16 And now I make one

request of thee, do not turn away thy face. And Bersabee said to him, Speak *on*. 17 And he said to her, Speak, I pray thee, to king Solomon, for he will not turn away his face from thee, and let him give me Abisag the Somanite for a wife. 18 And Bersabee said, Well; I will speak for thee to the king. 19 And Bersabee went in to king Solomon to speak to him concerning Adonias; and the king rose up to meet her, and kissed her, and sat on the throne, and a throne was set for the mother of the king, and she sat on his right hand. 20 And she said to him, I ask of thee one little request; turn not away my face from thee. And the king said to her, Ask, my mother, and I will not reject thee. 21 And she said, Let, I pray thee, Abisag the Somanite be given to Adonias thy brother to wife. 22 And king Solomon answered and said to his mother, And why hast thou asked Abisag for Adonias? ask for him the kingdom also; for he *is* my elder brother, and he has for his companion Abiathar the priest, and Joab the son of Saruia the commander-in-chief. 23 And king Solomon swore by the Lord, saying, God do so to me, and more also, *if it be not* that Adonias has spoken this word against his own life. 24 And now *as* the Lord lives who has established me, and set me on the throne of my father David, and he has made me a house, as the Lord spoke, this day shall Adonias be put to death. 25 So king Solomon sent by the hand of Banaeas the son of Jodae, and he slew him, and Adonias died in that day. 26 And the king said to Abiathar the priest, Depart thou quickly to Anathoth to thy farm, for thou art worthy of death this day; but I will not slay thee, because thou hast borne the ark of the covenant of the Lord before my father, and because thou was afflicted in all things wherein my father was afflicted. 27 And Solomon removed Abiathar from being a priest of the Lord, that the word of the Lord might be fulfilled, which he spoke concerning the house of Heli in Selom. 28 And the report came to Joab son of Saruia; for Joab had turned after Adonias, and he went not after Solomon: and Joab fled to the tabernacle of the Lord, and caught hold of the horns of the altar. 29 And it was told Solomon, saying, Joab has fled to the tabernacle of the Lord, and lo! he has hold of the horns of the altar. And king Solomon sent to Joab, saying, What ails thee, that thou hast fled to the altar? and Joab said, Because I was afraid of thee, and fled for refuge to the Lord. And Solomon sent Banaeas son of Jodae, saying, Go and slay him, and bury him. 30 And Banaeas son of Jodae came to Joab to the tabernacle of the Lord, and said to him, Thus says the king, Come forth. And Joab said, I will not come forth, for I will die here. And Banaeas son of Jodae returned and spoke to the king, saying, Thus has Joab spoken, and thus has he answered me. 31 And the king said to him, Go, and do to him as he has spoken, and kill him: and thou shalt bury him, and thou shalt remove this day the blood which he shed without cause, from me and from the house of my father. 32 And the Lord has returned upon his own head the blood of his unrighteousness, inasmuch as he attacked two men more righteous and better than himself, and slew them with the sword, and my father David knew not of their blood, *even* Abenner the son of Ner the commander-in-chief of Israel, and Amessa the son of Jether the commander-in-chief of Juda. 33 And their blood is returned upon his head, and upon the head of his seed for ever: but to David, and his seed, and his house, and his throne, may there be peace for ever from the Lord. [34] So Banaeas son of Jodae went up, and attacked him, and slew him, and buried him in his house in the wilderness. [35] And the king appointed Banaeas son of Jodae in his place over the host; and the kingdom was established in Jerusalem; and as for Sadoc the priest, the king appointed him to be high priest in the room of Abiathar. And Solomon son of David reigned over Israel and Juda in Jerusalem: and the Lord gave understanding to Solomon, and very much wisdom, and largeness of heart, as the sand by the sea-shore. And the wisdom of Solomon abounded exceedingly beyond the wisdom of all the ancients, and beyond all the wise men of Egypt: and he took the daughter of Pharao, and brought her into the city of David, until he had finished building his own house, and the house of the Lord first, and the wall of Jerusalem round about. In seven years he made and finished them. And Solomon had seventy thousand bearers of burdens, and eight thousand hewers of stone in the mountain: and Solomon made the sea, and the bases, and the great lavers, and the pillars, and the fountain of the court, and the brazen sea-and he built the citadel as a defence above it, he made a breach in the wall of the city of David: thus the daughter of Pharao went up out of the city of David to her house which he built for her. Then he built the citadel: and Solomon offered up three whole-burnt-offerings in the year, and peace-offerings on the altar which he built to the Lord, and he burnt incense before the Lord, and finished the house. And these are the chief persons who presided over the works of Solomon; three thousand and six hundred masters of the people that wrought the works. And he burit Assur, and Magdo, and Gazer, and upper Baethoron, and Ballath: only after he had built the house of the Lord, and the wall of Jerusalem round about, afterwards he built these cities. And when David was yet living, he charged Solomon, saying, Behold, there is with thee Semei the son of Gera, of the seed of Benjamin out of Chebron: he cursed me with a grievous curse in the day when I went into the camp; and he came down to meet me at Jordan, and I swore to him by the Lord, saying, He shall not be slain with the sword. But now do not thou hold him guiltless, for thou art a man of understanding, and thou wilt know what thou shalt do to him, and thou shalt bring down his grey hairs with blood to the grave. [36] And the king called Semei, and said to him, Build thee a house in Jerusalem, and dwell there, and thou shalt not go out thence any whither. [37] And it shall come to pass in the day that thou shalt go forth and cross over the brook Kedron, know assuredly that thou shalt certainly die: thy blood shall be upon thine head. And the king caused him to swear in that day. [38] And Semei said to the king, Good is the word that thou hast spoken, my lord O king: thus will thy servant do. And Semei dwelt in Jerusalem three years. [39] And it came to pass after the three years, that two servants of Semei ran away to Anchus son of Maacha king of Geth: and it was told Semei, saying, Behold, thy servants are in Geth. [40] And Semei rose up, and saddled his ass, and went to Geth to Anchus to seek out his servants: and Semei

went, and brought his servants out of Geth. [41] And it was told Solomon, saying, Semei is gone out of Jerusalem to Geth, and has brought back his servants. [42] And the king sent and called Semei, and said to him, Did I not adjure thee by the Lord, and testify to thee, saying, In whatsoever day thou shalt go out of Jerusalem, and go to the right or left, know certainly that thou shalt assuredly die? [43] And why hast thou not kept the oath of the Lord, and the commandment which I commanded thee? [44] And the king said to Semei, Thou knowest all thy mischief which thy heart knows, which thou didst to David my father: and the Lord has recompensed thy mischief on thine own head. [45] And king Solomon is blessed, and the throne of David shall be established before the Lord for ever. [46] And Solomon commanded Banaeas the son of Jodae, and he went forth and slew him. And king Solomon was very prudent and wise: and Juda and Israel were very many, as the sand which is by the sea for multitude, eating, and drinking, and rejoicing: and Solomon was chief in all the kingdoms, and they brought gifts, and served Solomon all the days of his life. And Solomon began to open the domains of Libanus, and he built Thermae in the wilderness. And this was the daily provision of Solomon, thirty measures of fine flour, and sixty measures of ground meal, ten choice calves, and twenty oxen from the pastures, and a hundred sheep, besides stags, and does, and choice fed birds. For he ruled in all the country on this side the river, from Raphi unto Gaza, over all the kings on this side the river: and he was at peace on all sides round about; and Juda and Israel dwelt safely, every one under his vine and under his fig tree, eating and drinand feasting, from Dan even to Bersabee, all the days of Solomon. And these were the princes of Solomon; Azariu son of Sadoc the priest, and Orniu son of Nathan chief of the officers, and he went to his house; and Suba the scribe, and Basa son of Achithalam recorder, and Abi son of Joab commander-in-chief, and Achire son of Edrai was over the levies, and Banaeas son of Jodae over the household and over the brickwork, and Cachur the son of Nathan was counsellor. And Solomon had forty thousand brood mares for his chariots, and twelve thousand horses. And he reigned over all the kings from the river and to the land of the Philistines, and to the borders of Egypt: so Solomon the son of David reigned over Israel and Juda in Jerusalem.

3-Kgdms1 [1,2] Nevertheless the people burnt incense on the high places, because a house had not yet been built to the Lord. [3] And Solomon loved the Lord, so as to walk in the ordinances of David his father; only he sacrificed and burnt incense on the high places. [4] And he arose and went to Gabaon to sacrifice there, for that was the highest place, and great: Solomon offered a whole- burnt-offering of a thousand victims on the altar in Gabaon. [5] And the Lord appeared to Solomon in a dream by night, and the Lord said to Solomon, Ask some petition for thyself. [6] And Solomon said, Thou hast dealt very mercifully with thy servant David my father according as he walked before thee in truth, and in righteousness, and in uprightness of heart with thee, and thou hast kept for him this great mercy, to set his son upon his throne, as *it is* this day. 7 And now, O Lord my God, thou hast appointed thy servant in the room of David my father; and I am a little child, and know not my going out an my coming in. 8 But thy servant *is* in the midst of thy people, whom thou hast chosen, a great people, which cannot be numbered. 9 Thou shalt give therefore to thy servant a heart to hear and to judge thy people justly, and to discern between good and evil: for who will be able to judge this thy great people? 10 And it was pleasing before the Lord, that Solomon asked this thing. 11 And the Lord said to him, Because thou hast asked this thing of me, and hast not asked for thyself long life, and hast not asked wealth, nor hast asked the lives of thine enemies, but hast asked for thyself understanding to hear judgment; 12 behold, I have done according to thy word: behold, I have given thee an understanding and wise heart: there has not been *any one* like thee before thee, and after thee there shall not arise one like thee. 13 And I have given thee what thou hast not asked, wealth and glory, so that there has not been any one like thee among kings. 14 And if thou wilt walk in my way, to keep my commandments and my ordinances, as David thy father walked, then will I multiply thy days. 15 And Solomon awoke, and, behold, *it was* a dream: and he arose and came to Jerusalem, and stood before the altar that was in front of the ark of the covenant of the Lord in Sion: and he offered whole-burnt-offerings, and sacrificed peace- offerings, and made a great banquet for himself and all his servants. 16 Then there appeared two harlots before the king, and they stood before him. 17 And the one woman said, Hear me, *my* lord; I and this woman dwelt in one house, and we were delivered in the house. 18 And it came to pass on the third day after I was delivered, this woman also was delivered: and we *were* together; and there was no one with us besides our two selves in the house. 19 And this woman's child died in the night; because she overlaid it. 20 and she arose in the middle of the night, and took my son from my arms, and laid him in her bosom, and laid her dead son in my bosom. 21 and I arose in the morning to suckle my son, and he was dead: and, behold, I considered him in the morning, and, behold, it was not my son whom I bore. 22 And the other woman said, No, but the living *is* my son, and the dead *is* thy son. So they spoke before the king. 23 and the king said to them, Thou sayest, This *is* my son, *even* the living *one*, and this woman's son *is* the dead one: and thou sayest, No, but the living *is* my son, and the dead *is* thy son. 24 And the king said, Fetch a sword. And they brought a sword before the king. 25 And the king said, Divide the live child, the suckling, in two; and give half of it to one, and half of it to the other. 26 And the woman whose the living child was, answered and said to the king, (for her bowels yearned over her son) and she said, I pray thee, *my* lord, give her the child, and in nowise slay it. But the other said, Let it be neither mine nor hers; divide *it*. 27 Then the king answered and said, Give the child to her that said, 'Give it to her, and by no means slay it:' she *is* its mother. 28 and all Israel heard this judgment which the king judged, and they feared before the king; because they saw that the wisdom of God *was* in him, to execute judgment.

3-Kgdms4 1 And king Solomon reigned over Israel. 2 And these *are* the princes which he had; Azarias son of Sadoc. 3 Eliaph, and Achia son of Seba, scribes; and Josaphat son of Achilud, recorder. 4 And Banaeas son of Jodae over the host; and Sadoc and Abiathar *were* priests. 5 And Ornia the son of Nathan *was* over the officers; and Zabuth son of Nathan *was* the king's friend. 6 And Achisar was steward, and Eliac the *chief* steward; and Eliab the son of Saph *was* over the family: and Adoniram the son of Audon over the tribute. 7 And Solomon had twelve officers over all Israel, to provide for the king and his household; each one's turn came to supply for a month in the year. 8 And these *were* their names: Been the son of Or in the mount of Ephraim, one. 9 The son of Dacar, in Makes, and in Salabin, and Baethsamys, and Elon as far as Bethanan, one. 10 The son of Esdi in Araboth; his *was* Socho, and all the land of Opher. 11 All Nephthador *belonged to* the son of Aminadab, Tephath daughter of Solomon was his wife, one. 12 Bana son of Achiluth *had* Ithaanach, and Mageddo, and *his was* the whole house of San which was by Sesathan below Esrae, and from Bethsan as far as Sabelmaula, as far as Maeber Lucam, one. 13 The son of Naber in Raboth Galaad, to him *fell* the lot of Ergab in Basan, sixty great cities with walls, and brazen bars, one. 14 Achinadab son of Saddo, *had* Maanaim. 15 Achimaas *was* in Nephthalim, and he took Basemmath daughter of Solomon to wife, one. 16 Baana son of Chusi, in Aser and in Baaloth, one, 17 Josaphat son of Phuasud *was* in Issachar. 18 Semei son of Ela, in Benjamin. 19 Gaber son of Adai in the land of Gad, *the land* of Seon king of Esebon, and of Og king of Basan, and one officer in the land of Juda. 20 21 22 And these *were* the requisite supplies for Solomon: in one day thirty measures of fine flour, and sixty measures of fine pounded meal, 23 and ten choice calves, and twenty pastured oxen, and a hundred sheep, besides stags, and choice fatted does. 24 For he had dominion on this side the river, and he was at peace on all sides round about. 25,26,27 And thus the officers provided king Solomon: and *they execute* every one in his month all the orders for the table of the king, they omit nothing. 28 And they carried the barley and the straw for the horses and the chariots to the place where the king might be, each according to his charge. 29 And the Lord gave understanding to Solomon, and very much wisdom, and enlargement of heart, as the sand on the seashore. 30 And Solomon abounded greatly beyond the wisdom of all the ancients, and beyond all the wise men of Egypt. 31 And he was wiser than all *other* men: and he was wiser than Gaethan the Zarite, and *than* Ænan, and *than* Chalcad and Darala the son of Mal. 32 And Solomon spoke three thousand proverbs, and his songs were five thousand. 33 And he spoke of trees, from the cedar in Libanus even to the hyssop which comes out through the wall: he spoke also of cattle, and of birds, and of reptiles, and of fishes. 34 And all the nations came to hear the wisdom of Solomon, and *ambassadors* from all the kings of the earth, as many as heard of his wisdom. And Solomon took to himself the daughter of Pharao to wife, and brought her into the city of David until he had finished the house of the Lord, and his own house, and the wall of Jerusalem. Then went up Pharao the king of Egypt, and took Gazer, and burnt it and the Chananite dwelling in Mergab; and Pharao gave them as a dowry to his daughter the wife of Solomon: and Solomon rebuilt Gazer.

3-Kgdms5 1 And Chiram king of Tyre sent his servants to anoint Solomon in the room of David his father, because Chiram always loved David. 2 And Solomon sent to Chiram, saying, 3 Thou knewest my father David, that he could not build a house to the name of the Lord my God because of the wars that compassed him about, until the Lord put them under the soles of his feet. 4 And now the Lord my God has given me rest round about; there is no one plotting against *me*, and there is no evil trespass *against me*. 5 And, behold, I intend to build a house to the name of the Lord my God, as the Lord God spoke to my father David, saying, Thy son whom I will set on thy throne in thy place, he shall build a house to my name. 6 And now command, and let *men* cut wood for me out of Libanus: and, behold, my servants *shall be* with thy servants, and I will give thee the wages of thy service, according to all that thou shalt say, because thou knowest that we have no one skilled in cutting timber like the Sidonians. 7 And it came to pass, as soon as Chiram heard the words of Solomon, that he rejoiced greatly, and said, Blessed *be* God to-day, who has given to David a wise son over this numerous people. 8 And he sent to Solomon, saying, I have listened concerning all that thou hast sent to me for: I will do all thy will: *as for* timber of cedar and fir, 9 my servants shall bring them down from Libanus to the sea: I will form them *into* rafts, *and bring them* to the place which thou shalt send to me *about*; and I will land them there, and thou shalt take *them* up: and thou shalt do my will, in giving bread to my household. 10 So Chiram gave to Solomon cedars, and fir trees, and all his desire. 11 And Solomon gave to Chiram twenty thousand measures of wheat as food for his house, and twenty thousand baths of beaten oil thus Solomon gave to Chiram yearly. 12 And the Lord gave wisdom to Solomon as he promised him; and there was peace between Chiram and Solomon, and they made a covenant between them. 13 And the king raised a levy out of all Israel, and the levy was thirty thousand men. 14 And he sent them to Libanus, ten thousand taking turn every month: they were a month in Libanus and two months at home: and Adoniram *was* over the levy. 15 And Solomon had seventy thousand bearers of burdens, and eighty thousand hewers of stone in the mountain; 16 besides the rulers that were appointed over the works of Solomon, *there were* three thousand six hundred masters who wrought in the works. 17 18 And they prepared the stones and the timber *during* three years.

3-Kgdms6 0 And it came to pass in the four hundred and fortieth year after the departure of the children of Israel out of Egypt, in the fourth year and second month of the reign of king Solomon over Israel, 17 that the king commanded that they should take great *and* costly stones for the foundation of the house, and hewn stones. 18 And the men of Solomon, and the men of Chiram hewed *the stones*, and laid them *for a foundation*. 1 In the fourth year he laid the foundation of the house of the Lord, in the month Ziu, even in the second month. 38 In the eleventh year, in the month Baal, this *is* the eighth month, the house was completed according to all its plan, and according to all its arrangement. 2 And the house which the king built to the Lord *was* forty cubits in length, and twenty cubits in breadth, and its height five and twenty cubits. 3 And the porch in front of the temple—twenty cubits *was* its length according to the breadth of the house in front of the house: and he built the house, and finished it. 4 And he made to the house secret windows inclining inward. 5 And against the wall of the house he set chambers round about the temple and the ark. 6 The under side *was* five cubits broad, and the middle *part* six, and the third *was* seven cubits broad; for he formed an interval to the house round about without the house, that they might not touch the walls of the house. 7 And the house was built in the construction of it with rough hewn stones: and there was not heard in the house in the building of it hammer or axe, or any iron tool. 8 And the porch of the under side *was* below the right wing of the house, and *there was* a winding ascent into the middle *chamber*, and from the middle to the third story. 9 So he built the house and finished it; and he made the ceiling of the house with cedars. 10 And he made the partitions through all the house, each five cubits high, and enclosed each partition with cedar boards. 11 12 13 14 15 And he framed the walls of the house within with cedar boards, from the floor of the house and on to the inner walls and to the beams: he lined the parts enclosed with boards within, and compassed the inward parts of the house with planks of fir. 16 And he built the twenty cubits from the top of the wall, one side from the floor to the beams, and he made it from the oracle to the most holy place. 17 And the temple was forty cubits *in extent*, 18 19 in front of the oracle in the midst of the house within, *in order* to put there the ark of the covenant of the Lord. 20 The length *was* twenty cubits, and the breadth *was* twenty cubits, and the height of it was twenty cubits. And he covered it with perfect gold, and he made an altar in front of the oracle, and covered it with gold. 21 22 And he covered the whole house with gold, till he had finished *gilding* the whole house. 23 And he made in the oracle two cherubs of ten cubits measured size. 24 And the wing of one cherub was five cubits, and his other wing was five cubits; ten cubits from the tip of one wing to the tip of the other wing. 25 Thus it was with the other cherub, both were alike finished with one measure. 26 And the height of the one cherub *was* ten cubits, and so *was it* with the second cherub. 27 And both the cherubs *were* in the midst of the innermost part of the house; and they spread out their wings, and one wing touched the wall, and the wing of the other cherub touched the other wall; and their wings in the midst of the house touched each other. 28 And he covered the cherubs with gold. 29 He graved all the walls of the house round about with the graving of cherubs, and *he sculptured* palm trees within and without *the house*. 30 And he covered the floor of the house within and without with gold. 31 And for the door-way of the oracle he made doors of juniper wood, *there were* porches in a four-fold way. 32 33 34 In both the doors *were* planks of fir; the one door had two leaves and their hinges, and the other door had two leaves and turned *on hinges*, 35 being carved with cherubs, and *there were* palm-trees and open flower-leaves, and it *was* overlaid with gold gilt upon the engraving. 36 And he built the inner court, three rows of hewn stones, and a row of wrought cedar round about, and he made the curtain of the court of the porch of the house that was in front of the temple. 37 38 13 And king Solomon sent, and took Chiram out of Tyre, 14 the son of a widow woman; and he *was* of the tribe of Nephthalim, and his father *was* a Tyrian; a worker in brass, andaccomplished in art and skill and knowledge to work every work in brass: and he was brought in to king Solomon, and he wrought all the works. 15 And he cast the two pillars for the porch of the house: eighteen cubits *was* the height of *each* pillar, and a circumference of fourteen cubits encompassed it, even the thickness of the pillar: the flutings *were* four fingers *wide*, and thus *was* the other pillar *formed*. 16 And he made two molten chapiters to put on the heads of the pillars: five cubits *was* the height of one chapiter, and five cubits *was* the height of the other chapiter. 17 And he made two ornaments of net-work to cover the chapiters of the pillars; even a net for one chapiter, and a net for the other chapiter. 18 And hanging work, two rows of brazen pomegranates, formed with net-work, hanging work, row upon row: and thus he framed *the ornaments* for the second chapiter. 19 And on the heads of the pillars he made lily-work against the porch, of four cubits, 20 and a chamber over both the pillars, and above the sides an addition *equal to* the chamber in width. 21 And he set up the pillars of the porch of the temple: and he set up the one pillar, and called its name Jachum: and he set up the second pillar, and called its name Boloz. 22 23 And he made the sea, ten cubits from one rim to the other, the same was completely circular round about: its height *was* five cubits, and its circumference thirty-three cubits. 24 And stays underneath its rim round about compassed it ten cubits round; 25 And *there were* twelve oxen under the sea: three looking to the north, and three looking to the west, and three looking to the south, and three looking to the east: and all their hinder parts *were* inward, and the sea *was* above upon them. 26 and its rim *was* as the work of the rim of a cup, a lily-flower, and the thickness of it *was* a span. 27 And he made ten brazen bases: five cubits *was* the length of one base, and four cubits the breadth of it, and its height *was* six cubits. 28 And this work of the bases *was* formed with a border the them, and *there was* a border between the ledges. 29 And upon their borders between the projection *were* lions, and oxen, and cherubs: and on the projections, even so above, and also below *were* the places of lions and oxen, hanging work. 30 And *there were* four brazen wheels to one base; and *there were* brazen bases, and their four sides *answering to them*, side pieces under the bases. 31 And *there were* axles in the wheels under the base. 32 And the height of one wheel *was* a cubit and a half. 33 And the work of the wheels *was* as the work of chariot wheels: their axles, and their felloes, and *the rest of* their work, *were* all molten. 34 The four side pieces were at the four corners of each base; its shoulders *were formed* of the base. 35 And on the top of the base half a cubit *was* the size of it, *there was* a circle on the top of the base, and *there was* the top of its spaces and its borders: and it was open at the top of its spaces. 36 And its borders *were* cherubs, and lions, and palm-trees, upright, each *was* joined in front *and* within and round about. 37 According to the same form he made all the ten bases, *even* one order and one measure to all. 38 And he made ten brazen lavers, each laver containing forty baths, *and* measuring four cubits, each laver *placed* on a several base throughout the ten bases. 39 And he put five bases on the right side of the house, and five on the left side of the house: and the sea was placed on the right side of the house eastward in the direction of the south. 40 And Chiram made the caldrons, and the pans, and the bowls; and Chiram finished making all the works that he wrought for king Solomon in the house of the Lord: 41 two pillars and the wreathen works of the pillars on the heads of the two pillars; and the two net-works to cover both the wreathen works of the flutings that were upon the pillars. 42 The four hundred pomegranates for both the net-works, two rows of pomegranates for one net-work, to cover both the wreathen works of the bases belonging to both pillars. 43 And the ten bases, and the ten lavers upon the bases. 44 And one sea, and the twelve oxen under the sea. 45 And the caldrons, and pans, and bowls, and all the furniture, which Chiram made for king Solomon for the house of the Lord: and *there were* eight and forty pillars of the house of the king and of the house of the Lord: all the works of the king which Chiram made were entirely of brass. 46 In the country round about Jordan did he cast them, in the clay land between Socchoth and Sira. 47 There was no reckoning of the brass of which he made all these works, from the very great abundance, there was no end of the weight of the brass. 48 And king Solomon took the furniture which *Chiram* made for the house of the Lord, the golden altar, and the golden table of shewbread. 49 And *he put* the five candlesticks on the left, and five on the right in front of the oracle, *being* of pure gold, and the lamp-stands, and the lamps, and the snuffers of gold. 50 And *there were made* the porches, and the nails, and the bowls, and the spoons, and the golden censers, of pure gold: and the panels of the doors of the innermost part of the house, *even* the holy of holies, and the golden doors of the temple. 51 So the work of the house of the Lord which Solomon wrought was finished; and Solomon brought in the holy things of David his father, and all the holy things of Solomon; he put the silver, and the gold, and the furniture, into the treasures of the house of the Lord.

3-Kgdms7 1 And Solomon built a house for himself in thirteen years. 2 And he built the house with the wood of Libanus; its length *was* a hundred cubits, and its breadth *was* fifty cubits, and its height *was* of thirty cubits, and *it was made* with three rows of cedar pillars, and the pillars had side-pieces of cedar. 3 And he formed the house with chambers above on the sides of the pillars, and the number of the pillars *was each* row forty and five, 4 and *there were* three chambers, and space against space in three rows. 5 And all the doors and spaces formed like chambers *were* square, and from door to door *was a correspondence* in three rows. 6 And *he made* the porch of the pillars, *they were* fifty *cubits* long and fifty broad, the porch joining them in front; and the *other* pillars and the thick beam *were* in front of the house by the porches. 7 And *there was* the Porch of seats where he would judge, the porch of judgment. 8 And their house where he would dwell, *had* one court communicating with these according to this work; and *he built* the house for the daughter of Pharao whom Solomon had taken, according to this porch. 9 All these *were* of costly stones, sculptured at intervals within even from the foundation even to the top, and outward to the great court, 10 founded with large costly stones, stones of ten cubits and eight cubits *long.* 11 And above with costly stones, according to the measure of hewn stones, and with cedars. 12 *There were* three rows of hewn *stones* round about the great hall, and a row of sculptured cedar: and Solomon finished all his house.

3-Kgdms8 1 And it came to pass when Solomon had finished building the house of the Lord and his own house after twenty years, then king Solomon assembled all the elders of Israel in Sion, to bring the ark of the covenant of the Lord out of the city of David, this is Sion, 2 in the month of Athanin. 3 And the priests took up the ark, 4 and the tabernacle of testimony, and the holy furniture that was in the tabernacle of testimony. 5 And the king and all Israel *were occupied* before the ark, sacrificing sheep *and* oxen, without number. 6 And the priests bring in the ark into its place, into the oracle of the house, even into the holy of holies, under the wings of the cherubs. 7 For the cherubs spread out their wings over the place of the ark, and the cherubs covered the ark and its holy things above. 8 And the holy staves projected, and the ends of the holy staves appeared out of the holy places in front of the oracle, and were not seen without. 9 There was nothing in the ark except the two tables of stone, the tables of the covenant which Moses put *there* in Choreb, which *tables* the Lord made *as a covenant* with the children of Israel in their going forth from the land of Egypt. 10 And it came to pass when the priests departed out of the holy place, that the cloud filled the house. 11 And the priests could not stand to minister because of the cloud, because the glory of the Lord filled the house. 12 13 14 And the king turned his face, and the king blessed all Israel, (and the whole assembly of Israel stood:) 15 and he said, Blessed *be* the Lord God of Israel to-day, who spoke by his mouth concerning David my father, and has fulfilled it with his hands, saying, 16 From the day that I brought out my people Israel out of Egypt, I have not chosen a city in *any* one tribe of Israel to build a house, so that my name should be there: but I chose Jerusalem that my name should be there, and I chose David to be over my people Israel. 17 And it was in the heart of my father to build a house to the name of the Lord God of Israel. 18 And the Lord said to David my father, Forasmuch as it came into thine heart to build a house to my name, thou didst well that it came upon thine heart. 19 Nevertheless thou shalt not build the house, but thy son that has proceeded out of thy bowels, he shall build the house to my name. 20 And the Lord has confirmed the word that he spoke, and I am risen up in the place of my father David, and I have sat down on the throne of Israel, as the Lord spoke, and I have built the house to the name of the Lord God of Israel. 21 And I have set there a place for the ark, in which is the covenant of the Lord, which the Lord made with our fathers, when he brought them out of the land of Egypt. 22 And Solomon stood up in front of the altar before all the congregation of Israel; and he spread out his hands toward heaven: 23 and he said, Lord God of Israel, there is no God like thee in heaven above and on the earth beneath, keeping covenant and mercy with thy servant who walks before thee with all his heart; 24 which thou hast kept toward thy servant David my father: for thou hast spoken by thy mouth and thou hast fulfilled it with thine hands, as *at* this day. 25 And now, O Lord God of Israel, keep for thy servant David my father, *the promises* which thou hast spoken to him, saying, There shall not be taken from thee a man sitting before me on the throne of Israel, provided only thy children shall take heed to their ways, to walk before me as thou hast walked before me. 26 And now, O Lord God of Israel, let, I pray thee, thy word to David my father be confirmed. 27 But will God indeed dwell with men upon the earth? if the heaven and heaven of heavens will not suffice thee, how much less even this house which I have built to thy name? 28 Yet, O Lord God of Israel, thou shalt look upon my petition, to hear the prayer which thy servant prays to thee in thy presence this day, 29 that thine eyes may be open toward this house day and night, even toward the place which thou saidst, My name shall be there, to hear the prayer which thy servant prays at this place day and night. 30 And thou shalt hearken to the prayer of thy servant, and of thy people Israel, which they shall pray toward this place; and thou shalt hear in thy dwelling-place in heaven, and thou shalt do and be gracious. 31 Whatsoever trespasses any *one* shall commit against his neighbor,—and if he shall take upon him an oath so that he should swear, and he shall come and make confession before thine altar in this house, 32 then shalt thou hear from heaven, and do, and thou shalt judge thy people Israel, that the wicked should be condemned, to recompense his way upon his head; and to justify the righteous, to give to him according to his righteousness. 33 When thy people Israel falls before enemies, because they shall sin against thee, and they shall return and confess to thy name, and they shall pray and supplicate in this house, 34 then shalt thou hear from heaven, and be gracious to the sins of thy people Israel, and thou shalt restore them to the land which thou gavest to their fathers. 35 When the heaven is restrained, and there is no rain, because they shall sin against thee, and the shall pray toward this place, and they shall make confession to thy name, and shall turn from their sins when thou shalt have humbled them, 36 then thou shalt hear from heaven, and be merciful to the sins of thy servant and of thy people Israel; for thou shalt shew them the good way to walk in it, and thou shalt give rain upon the earth which thou hast given to thy people for an inheritance. 37 If there should be famine, if there should be death, because there should be blasting, locust, or if there be mildew, and if their enemy oppress them in *any* one of their cities, *with regard to* every calamity, every trouble, 38 every prayer, every supplication whatever shall be made by any man, as they shall know each the plague of his heart, and shall spread abroad his hands to this house, 39 then shalt thou hearken from heaven, out of thine established dwelling-place, and shalt be merciful, and shalt do, and recompense to *every* man according to his ways, as thou shalt know his heart, for thou alone knowest the heart of all the children of men: 40 that they may fear thee all the days that they live upon the land, which thou hast given to our fathers. 41 And for the stranger who is not of thy people, 42 when they shall come and pray toward this place, 43 then shalt thou hear *them* from heaven, out of thine established dwelling-place, and thou shalt do according to all that the stranger shall call upon thee for, that all the nations may know thy name, and fear thee, as *do* thy people Israel, and may know that thy name has been called on this house which I have builded. 44 *If it be* that thy people shall go forth to war against their enemies in the way by which thou shalt turn them, and pray in the name of the Lord toward the city which thou hast chosen, and the house which I have built to thy name, 45 then shalt thou hear from heaven their supplication and their prayer, and shalt execute judgment for them. 46 *If it be* that they shall sin against thee, (for there is not a man who will not sin,) and thou shalt bring them and deliver them up before their enemies, and they that take *them* captive shall carry *them* to a land far or near, 47 and they shall turn their hearts in the land whither they have been carried captives, and turn in the land of their sojourning, and supplicate thee, saying, We have sinned, we have done unjustly, we have transgressed, 48 and they shall turn to thee with all their heart, and with all their soul, in the land of their enemies whither thou hast carried them captives, and shall pray to thee toward their land which thou hast given to their fathers, and the city which thou hast chosen, and the house which I have built to thy name: 49 then shalt thou hear from heaven thine established dwelling-place, 50 and thou shalt be merciful to their unrighteousness wherein they have trespassed against thee, and according to all their transgressions wherewith they have transgressed against thee, and thou shalt cause them to be pitied before them that carried them captives, and they shall have compassion on them: 51 for *they are* thy people and thine inheritance, whom thou broughtest out of the land of Egypt, out of the midst of the furnace of iron. 52 And let thine eyes and thine ears be opened to the supplication of thy servant, and to the supplication of thy people Israel, to hearken to them in all things for which they shall call upon thee. 53 Because thou hast set them apart for an inheritance to thyself out of all the nations of the earth, as thou spokest by the hand of thy servant Moses, when thou broughtest our fathers out of the land of Egypt, O Lord God.—Then spoke Solomon concerning the house, when he had finished building it—He manifested the sun in the heaven: the Lord said he would dwell in darkness: build thou my house, a beautiful house for thyself to dwell in anew. Behold, is not this written in the book of the song? 54 And it came to pass when Solomon had finished praying to the Lord all this prayer and supplication, that he rose up from before the altar of the Lord, *after* having knelt upon his knees, and his hands *were* spread out

towards heaven. 55 And he stood, and blessed all the congregation of Israel with a loud voice, saying, 56 Blessed *be* the Lord this day, who has given rest to his people Israel, according to all that he said: there has not failed one word among all his good words which he spoke by the hand of his servant Moses. 57 May the Lord our God be with us, as he was with our fathers; let him not desert us nor turn from us, 58 that he may turn our hearts toward him to walk in all his ways, and to keep all his commandments, and his ordinances which he commanded our fathers. 59 And let these words, which I have prayed before the Lord our God, *be* near to the Lord our God day and night, to maintain the cause of thy servant, and the cause of thy people Israel for ever. 60 that all the nations of the earth may know that the Lord God, he *is* God, and there is none beside. 61 And let our hearts be perfect toward the Lord our God, to walk also holily in his ordinances, and to keep his commandments, as at this day. 62 And the king and all the children of Israel offered sacrifice before the Lord. 63 And king Solomon offered for the sacrifices of peace-offering which he sacrificed to the Lord, two and twenty thousand oxen, and hundred and twenty thousand sheep: and the king and all the children of Israel dedicated the house of the Lord. 64 In that day the king consecrated the middle of the court in the front of the house of the Lord; for there he offered the whole-burnt- offering, and the sacrifices, and the fat of the peace-offerings, because the brazen altar which was before the Lord *was too* little to bear the whole-burnt-offering and the sacrifices of peace- offerings. 65 And Solomon kept the feast in that day, and all Israel with him, even a great assembly from the entering in of Hemath to the river of Egypt, before the Lord our God in the house which he built, eating and drinking, and rejoicing before the Lord our God seven days. 66 And on the eighth day he sent away the people: and they blessed the king, and each departed to his tabernacle rejoicing, and *their* heart *was* glad because of the good things which the Lord had done to his servant David, and to Israel his people.

3-Kgdms9 1 And it came to pass when Solomon had finished building the house of the Lord, and the king's house, and all the work of Solomon, whatever he wished to perform, 2 that the Lord appeared to Solomon a second time, as he appeared in Gabaon. 3 And the Lord said to him, I have heard the voice of thy prayer, and thy supplication which thou madest before me: I have done for thee according to all thy prayer: I have hallowed this house which thou hast built to put my name there for ever, and mine eyes and my heart shall be there always. 4 And if thou wilt walk before me as David thy father walked, in holiness of heart and uprightness, and so as to do according to all that I commanded him, and shalt keep my ordinances and my commandments: 5 then will I establish the throne of thy kingdom in Israel for ever, as I spoke to David thy father, saying, There shall not fail thee a man to rule in Israel. 6 But if ye or your children do in any wise revolt from me, and do not keep my commandments and my ordinances, which Moses set before you, and ye go and serve other gods, and worship them: 7 then will I cut off Israel from the land which I have given them, and this house which I have consecrated to my name I will cast out of my sight; and Israel shall be a desolation and a by-word to all nations. 8 And this house, which is high, shall be *so that* every one that passes by it shall be amazed, and shall hiss; and they shall say, Wherefore has the Lord done thus to this land, and to this house? 9 And *men* shall say, Because they forsook the Lord their God, who brought out their fathers from Egypt, out of the house of bondage, and they attached themselves to strange gods, and worshipped them, and served them: therefore the Lord has brought this evil upon them. Then Solomon brought up the daughter of Pharao out of the city of David into his house which he built for himself in those days. 10 *During* twenty years in which Solomon was building the two houses, the house of the Lord, and the house of the king, 11 Chiram king of Tyre helped Solomon with cedar wood, and fir wood, and with gold, and all that he wished for: then the king gave Chiram twenty cities in the land of Galilee. 12 So Chiram departed from Tyre, and went into Galilee to see the cities which Solomon gave to him; and they pleased him not. And he said, 13 What *are* these cities which thou hast given me, brother? And he called them Boundary until this day. 14 And Chiram brought to Solomon a hundred and twenty talents of gold, 25 26 even that for which king Solomon built a ship in Gasion Gaber near Ælath on the shore of the extremity of the sea in the land of Edom. 27 And Chiram sent in the ship together with the servants of Solomon servants of his own, mariners to row, men acquainted with the sea. 28 And they came to Sophira, and took thence a hundred and twenty talents of gold, and brought them to king Solomon.

3-Kgdms10 1 And the queen of Saba heard of the name of Solomon, and the name of the Lord, and she came to try him with riddles. 2 And she came to Jerusalem with a very great train; and *there came* camels bearing spices, and very much gold, and precious stones: and she came in to Solomon, and told him all that was in her heart. 3 And Solomon answered all her questions: and there was not a question overlooked by the king which he did not answer her. 4 And the queen of Saba saw all the wisdom of Solomon, and the house which he built, 5 and the provision of Solomon and the sitting of his attendants, and the standing of his servants, and his raiment, and his cup-bearers, and his whole-burnt-offering which he offered in the house of the Lord, and she was utterly amazed. 6 And she said to king Solomon, *It was* a true report which I heard in my land of thy words and thy wisdom. 7 But I believed not them that told me, until I came and my eyes saw: and, behold, the words as they reported to me are not the half: thou hast exceeded in goodness all the report which I heard in my land. 8 Blessed *are* thy wives, blessed *are* these thy servants who stand before thee continually, who hear all thy wisdom. 9 Blessed be the Lord thy God, who has taken pleasure in thee, to set thee upon the throne of Israel, because the Lord loved Israel to establish *him* for ever; and he has made thee king over them, to execute judgment with justice, and in their causes. 10 And she *gave* to Solomon a hundred and twenty talents of gold, and very many spices, and precious stones: there had not come any other spices so abundant as those which the queen of Saba gave to king Solomon. 11 And the ship of Chiram which brought the gold from Suphir, brought very much hewn timber and precious stones. 12 And the king made the hewn timber *into* buttresses of the house of the Lord and the king's house, and lyres and harps for singers: such hewn timber had not come upon the earth, nor have been seen anywhere until this day. 13 And king Solomon gave to the queen of Saba all that she desired, whatsoever she asked, besides all that he had given her by the hand of king Solomon: and she returned, and came into her own land, she and her servants. 14 And the weight of gold that came to Solomon in one year was six hundred and sixty-six talents of gold. 15 Besides the tributes of them that were subjects, both merchants and all the kings of the *country* beyond *the river*, and of the princess of the land. 16 And Solomon made three hundred spears of beaten gold: three hundred shekels of gold were upon one spear. 17 And three hundred shields of beaten gold: and three pounds of gold were in one shield: and the king put them in the house of the forest of Lebanon. 18 And the king made a great ivory throne, and gilded it with pure gold. 19 The throne *had* six steps, and calves in bold relief to the throne behind it, and side-pieces on either hand of the place of the seat, and two lions standing by the side-pieces, 20 and twelve lions standing there on the six steps on either side: it was not so done in any *other* kingdom. 21 And all the vessels made by Solomon *were* of gold, and the lavers *were* golden, and all the vessels of the house of the forest of Lebanon were of pure gold; there was no silver, for it was not accounted of in the days of Solomon. 22 For Solomon had a ship of Tharsis in the sea with the ships of Chiram: one ship came to the king every three years out of Tharsis, *laden with* gold and silver, and wrought stones, and hewn stones. This was the arrangement of the provision which king Solomon fetched to build the house of the Lord, and the house of the king, and the wall of Jerusalem, and the citadel; to fortify the city of David, and Assur, and Magdal, and Gazer, and Baethoron the upper, and Jethermath, and all the cities of the chariots, and all the cities of the horsemen, and the fortification of Solomon which he purposed to build in Jerusalem and in all the land, so that none of the people should rule over him that was left of the Chettite and the Amorite, and the Pherezite, and the Chananite, and the Evite, and the Jebusite, and the Gergesite, who were not of the children of Israel, their descendants who had been left with him in the land, whom the children of Israel could not utterly destroy; and Solomon made them tributaries until this day. But of the children of Israel Solomon made nothing; for they were warriors, and his servants and rulers, and captains of the third order, and the captains of his chariots, and his horsemen. 23 And Solomon increased beyond all the kings of the earth in wealth and wisdom. 24 And all the kings of the earth sought the presence of Solomon, to hear his wisdom which the Lord *had* put into his heart. 25 And they brought every one their gifts, vessels of gold, and raiment, and stacte, and spices, and horses, and mules, a rate year by year. 26 And Solomon had four thousand mares for his chariots, and twelve thousand horsemen: and he put them in the cities of his chariots, and with the king in Jerusalem: and he ruled over all the kings from the river to the land of the Philistines, and to the borders of Egypt. 27 And the king made gold and silver in Jerusalem as stones, and he made cedars as the sycamores in the plain for multitude. 28 And the goings forth of Solomon's horsemen *was* also out of Egypt, and the king's merchants *were* of Thecue; and they received them out of Thecue at a price. 29 And that which proceeded out of Egypt went up *thus, even* a chariot for a hundred *shekels* of silver, and a horse for fifty *shekels* of silver: and thus for all the kings of the Chettians, and the kings of Syria, they came out by sea.

3-Kgdms11 0 And king Solomon was a lover of women. 3 And he had seven hundred wives, princesses, and three hundred concubines. 1 And he took strange women, as well as the daughter of Pharao, Moabitish, Ammanitish women, Syrians and Idumeans, Chettites, and Amorites; 2 of the nations concerning whom the Lord forbade the children of Israel, *saying,* Ye shall not go in to them, and they shall not come in to you, lest they turn away your hearts after their idols: Solomon clave to these in love. 4 And it came to pass in the time of the old age of Solomon, that his heart was not perfect with the Lord his God, as *was* the heart of David his father. 5 and to Astarte the abomination of the Sidonians. 7 Then Solomon built a high place to Chamos the idol of Moab, and to their king the idol of the children of Ammon, 8 And thus he acted towards all his strange wives, who burnt incense and sacrificed to their idols. 6 And Solomon did that which was evil in the sight of the Lord: he went not after the Lord, as David his father. And the strange women turned away his heart after their gods. 9 And the Lord was angry with Solomon, because he turned away his heart from the Lord God of Israel, who had appeared twice to him, 10 and charged him concerning this matter, by no means to go after other gods, but to take heed to do what the Lord God commanded him; neither was his heart perfect with the Lord, according to the heart of David his father. 11 And the Lord said to Solomon, Because it has been thus with thee, and thou hast not kept my commandments and my ordinances which I commanded thee, I will surely rend thy kingdom out of thy hand, and give it to thy servant. 12 Only in thy days I will not do it for David thy father's sake: *but* I will take it out of the hand of thy son. 13 Only I will not take away the whole kingdom: I will give one tribe to thy son for David my servant's sake, and for the sake of Jerusalem, the city which I have chosen. 14 And the Lord raised up and enemy to Solomon, Ader the Idumaean, and Esrom son of Eliadae who *dwelt* in Raama, *and* Adadezer king of Suba his master; (and men gathered to him, and he was head of the conspiracy, and he seized on Damasec,)and they were adversaries to Israel all the days of Solomon: and Ader the Idumaean *was* of the seed royal in Idumaea. 15 And it happened, that while David was utterly destroying Edom, while Joab captain of the host was going to bury the dead, when they slew every male in Idumaea; 16 (for Joab and all Israel abode there six months in Idumaea, until he utterly destroyed every male in Idumaea;) 17 that Ader ran away, he and all the Idumaeans of the servants of his father with him; and they went into Egypt; and Ader *was then* a little child. 18 And there rise up men out of the city of Madiam, and they come to Pharan, and take men with them, and come to Pharao king of Egypt: and Ader went in to Pharao, and he gave him a house, and appointed him provision. 19 And Ader found great favour in the sight of Pharao, and he gave him his wife's sister in marriage, the elder sister of Thekemina. 20 And the sister of Thekemina bore to him, *even* to Ader, Ganebath her son; and Thekemina brought him up in the midst of the sons of Pharao, and Ganebath was in the midst of the sons of Pharao. 21 And Ader heard in Egypt that David slept with his fathers, and that Joab the captain of the host was dead; and Ader said to Pharao, Let me go, and I will return to my country. 22 And Pharao said to Ader, What lackest thou with me? that lo! thou seekest to depart to thy country? and Ader said to him, By all means let me go. 23 So Ader returned to his country; this *is* the mischief which Ader did, and he was a bitter enemy of Israel, and he reigned in the land of Edom. 26 And Jeroboam the son of Nabat, the Ephrathite of Sarira, the son of a widow, *was* servant of Solomon. 27 And this *was* the occasion of his lifting up *his* hands against king Solomon: now king Solomon built the citadel, he completed the fortification of the city of David his father. 28 And the man Jeroboam was very strong; and Solomon saw the young man that he was active, and he set him over the levies of the house of Joseph. 29 And it came to pass at that time, that Jeroboam went forth from Jerusalem, and Achia the Selonite the prophet found him in the way, and caused him to turn aside out of the way: and Achia was clad with a new garment, and they two *were* alone in the field. 30 And Achia laid hold of his new garment that was upon him, and tore it *into* twelve pieces: 31 and he said to Jeroboam, Take to thyself ten pieces, for thus saith the Lord God of Israel, Behold, I rend the kingdom out of the hand of Solomon, and will give thee ten tribes. 32 Yet he shall have two tribes, for my servant David's sake, and for the sake of Jerusalem, the city which I have chosen out of all the tribes of Israel. 33 Because he forsook me, and sacrificed to Astarte the abomination of the Sidonians, and to Chamos, and to the idols of Moab, and to their king the abomination of the children of Ammon, and he walked not in my ways, to do that which was right before me, as David his father *did.* 34 Howbeit I will not take the whole kingdom out of his hand, (for I will certainly resist him all the days of his life,) for David my servant's sake, whom I have chosen. 35 But I will take the kingdom out of the hand of his son, and give thee ten tribes. 36 But to his son I will give the two *remaining* tribes, that my servant David may have an establishment continually before me in Jerusalem, the city which I have chosen for myself to put my name there. 37 And I will take thee, and thou shalt reign as thy soul desires, and thou shalt be king over Israel. 38 And it shall come to pass, if thou wilt keep all the commandments that I shall give thee, and wilt walk in my ways, and do that which is right before me, to keep my ordinances and my commandments, as David my servant did, that I will be with thee, and will build thee a sure house, as I built to David. 39 40 And Solomon sought to slay Jeroboam: but he arose and fled into Egypt, to Susakim king of Egypt, and he was in Egypt until Solomon died. 41 And the rest of the history of Solomon, and all that he did, and all his wisdom, behold are not these things written in the book of the life of Solomon? 42 And the days *during* which Solomon reigned in Jerusalem over all Israel *were* forty years. 43 And Solomon slept with his fathers, and they buried him in the city of David his father. And it came to pass when Jeroboam son of Nabat heard *of it*, even while he was yet in Egypt as he fled from the face of Solomon and dwelt in Egypt, he straightway comes into his own city, into the land of Sarira in the mount of Ephraim. And king Solomon slept with his fathers, and Roboam his son reigned in his stead.

3-Kgdms12 1 And king Roboam goes to Sikima; for all Israel were coming to Sikima to make him king. 2,3 And the people spoke to king Roboam, saying, Thy father made our yoke heavy; 4 but do thou now lighten somewhat of the hard service of thy father, and of his heavy yoke which he put upon us, and we will serve thee. 5 And he said to them, Depart for three days, and return to me. And they departed. 6 And the king referred *the matter* to the elders, who stood before Solomon his father while he was yet living, saying, How do ye advise that I should answer this people? 7 And they spoke to him, saying, If thou wilt this day be a servant to this people, and wilt serve them, and wilt speak to them good words, then will they be thy servants continually. 8 But he forsook the counsel of the old men which they gave him, and consulted with the young men who were brought up with him, who stood in his presence. 9 And he said to them, What counsel do ye give? And what shall I answer to this people who speak to me, saying, Lighten somewhat of the yoke which thy father has put upon us? 10 And the young men who had been brought up with him, who stood before his face, spoke to him, saying, Thus shalt thou say to this people who have spoken to thee, saying, Thy father made our yoke heavy, and do thou now lighten it from off us: thus shalt say to them, My little *finger shall be* thicker than my father's loins. 11 And whereas my father did lade you with a heavy yoke, I also will add to your yoke: my father chastised you with whips, but I will chastise you with scorpions. 12 And all Israel came to king Roboam on the third day, as the king spoke to them, saying, Return to me on the third day. 13 And the king answered the people harshly; and Roboam forsook the counsel of the old men which they counselled him. 14 And he spoke to them according to the counsel of the young men, saying, My father made your yoke heavy, and I will add to your yoke: my father chastised you with whips, but I will chastise you with scorpions. 15 And the king hearkened not to the people, because the change was from the Lord, that he might establish his word which he spoke by Achia the Selonite concerning Jeroboam the son of Nabat. 16 And all Israel saw that the king did not hearken to them: and the people answered the king, saying, What portion have we in David? neither have we any inheritance in the son of Jessae. Depart, O Israel, to thy tents: now feed thine own house,

David. So Israel departed to his tents. 17 18 And the king sent Adoniram who was over the tribute; and they stoned him with stones, and he died: and king Roboam made haste to rise to flee to Jerusalem. 19 So Israel rebelled against the house of David until this day. 20 And it came to pass when all Israel heard that Jeroboam had returned out of Egypt, that they sent and called him to the assembly, and they made him king over Israel: and none followed the house of David except the tribe of Juda and Benjamin only. 21 And Roboam went into Jerusalem, and he assembled the congregation of Juda, and the tribe of Benjamin, a hundred and twenty thousand young men, warriors, to fight against the house of Israel, to recover the kingdom to Roboam the son of Solomon. 22 And the word of the Lord came to Samaia the man of God, saying, 23 Speak to Roboam the son of Solomon, king of Juda, and to all the house of Juda and Benjamin, and to the remnant of the people, saying, 24 Thus saith the Lord, Ye shall not go up, neither shall ye fight with your brethren the sons of Israel: return each man to his own home; for this thing is from me; and they hearkened to the word of the Lord, and they ceased from going up, according to the word of the Lord. So king Solomon sleeps with his fathers, and is buried with his fathers in the city of David; and Roboam his son reigned in his stead in Jerusalem, being sixteen years old when he began to reign, and he reigned twelve years I Jerusalem: and his mother's name *was* Naanan, daughter of Ana son of Naas king of the children of Ammon. And he did that which was evil in the sight of the Lord, and walked not in the way of David his father. And there was a man of mount Ephraim, a servant to Solomon, and his name was Jeroboam: and the name of his mother was Sarira, a harlot: and Solomon made him head of the levies of the house of Joseph: and he built for Solomon Sarira in mount Ephraim; and he had three hundred chariots of horses: he built the citadel with the levies of the house of Ephraim; he fortified the city of David, and aspired to the kingdom, And Solomon sought to kill him; and he was afraid, and escaped to Susakim king of Egypt, and was with him until Solomon died. And Jeroboam heard in Egypt that Solomon was dead: and he spoke in the ears of Susakim king of Egypt, saying, Let me go, and I will depart into my land: and Susakim said to him, Ask and request, and I will grant it thee. And Susakim gave to Jeroboam Ano the eldest sister of Thekemina his wife: she was great among the daughters of the king, and she bore to Jeroboam Abia his son: and Jeroboam said to Susakim, Let me indeed go, and I will depart. And Jeroboam departed out of Egypt, and came into the land of Saria that was in mount Ephraim, and thither the whole in mount Ephraim, and thither the whole tribe of Ephraim assembles, and Jeroboam built a fortress there. And his young child was sick with a very severe sickness; and Jeroboam went to enquire concerning the child: and he said to Ano his wife, Arise, go, enquire of God concerning the child, whether he shall recover from his sickness. Now there was a man in Selom, an his name *was* Achia: and he was sixty years old, and the word of the Lord was with him. And Jeroboam said to his wife, Arise, and take in thine hand loaves for the man of God, and cakes for his children, and grapes, and a pot of honey. And the woman arose, and took in her hand bread, and two cakes, and grapes, and a pot of honey, for Achia: and the man *was* old, and his eyes were dim, so that he could not see. And she arose, up from Sarira and went; and it came to pass when she had come into the city to Achia the Selonite, that Achia said to his servant, Go out now to meet Ano the wife of Jeroboam, and thou shalt say to her, Come in, and stand not *still*: for thus saith the Lord, I send grievous tidings to thee. And Ano went in to the man of God; and Achia said to her, Why hast thou brought me bread and grapes, and cakes, and a pot of honey? Thus saith the Lord, Behold, thou shalt depart from me, and it shall come to pass when thou hast entered into the city, *even* into Sarira, that thy maidens shall come out to meet thee, and shall say to thee, The child is dead: for thus saith the Lord, Behold, I will destroy every male of Jeroboam, and there shall be the dead of Jeroboam in the city, *them* the dogs shall eat, and him that eat, and he shall lament for the child, saying, *Woe is me,* Lord! For there has been found in him some good thing touching the Lord. And the woman departed, when she heard this: and it came to pass as she entered into Sarira, that the child died; and there came forth a wailing to meet *her.* And Jeroboam went to Sikima in mount Ephraim, and assembled there the tribes of Israel; and Roboam the son of Solomon went up thither. And the word of the Lord came to Samaias son of Enlami, saying, Take to thyself a new garment which has not gone into the water, and rend it into twelve piees; and thou shalt five some to Jeroboam, and shalt say to him, thus saith the Lord, Take to thyself ten pieces to cover thee: and Jeroboam took *them*: and Samaias said, Thus saith the Lord concerning the ten tribes of Israel. And the people said to Roboam the son of Solomon, Thy father make his yoke heavy upon us, and made the meat of his table heavy; and now thou shalt lighten them upon us, and we will serve thee. And Roboam said to the people, Wait three days, and I will return you an answer: and Roboam said, Bring in to me the elders, and I will take counsel with them what I shall answer to the people on the third day, So Roboam spoke in their ears, as the people sent to him to *say*: and the elders of the people said, Thus the people have spoken to thee. And Roboam rejected their counsel, and it pleased him not: and he sent and brought in thouse who had been brought up with him; and he said to them, Thus and thus has the people sent to me to say: and they that had been brought up with him said, Thus shalt thou speak to the people saying, My little *finger* shall be thicker than my father's loins; my father scourged you with whips, but I will rule you with scorpions. And the saying pleased Roboam, and he answered the people as the young men, they that were brought up with him, counselled him: and all the people spoke as one man, every one to his neighbor, and they cried out all together, saying, We have no part in David, nor inheritance in the son of Jessae: to they tents, O Israel, every one; for this man is not for a prince or a ruler over us. And all the people was dispersed from Sikima, and they departed every one to his tent: and Roboam strengthened him self and departed, and mounted his chariot, and entered into Jerusalem: and there follow

him the whole tribe of Juda, and the whole tribe of Benjamin. And it came to pass at the beginning of the year, that Roboam gathered all the men of Juda and Benjamin, and went up to fight with Jeroboam at Sikima. And the word of the Lord came to Sameas the man of God, saying, Speak to Roboam king of Juda, and to all the house of Juda and Benjamin, and to the remnant of the people, saying, Thus saith the Lord, Ye shall not go up, neither shall ye fight with your brethren the sons of Israel: return every man to his house, for this thing is from me. And they hearkened to the word of the Lord, and forbore to go up, according to the word of the Lord. 25 And Jeroboam built Sikima in mount Ephraim and dwelt in it, and went forth thence and built Phanuel. 26 And Jeroboam said in his heart, Behold, now the kingdom will return to the house of David. 27 If this people shall go up to offer sacrifice in the house of the Lord at Jerusalem, then the heart of the people will return to the Lord, and to their master, to Roboam king of Juda, and they will slay me. 28 And the king took counsel, and went, and made two golden heifers, and said to the people, Let it suffice you to have gone *hitherto* to Jerusalem: behold thy gods, O Israel, who brought thee up out of the land of Egypt. 29 And he put one in Bethel, and he put the other in Dan. 30 And this thing became a sin; and the people went before one as far as Dan, and left the house of the Lord. 31 And he made houses on the high places, and made priests of any part of the people, who were not of the sons of Levi. 32 And Jeroboam appointed a feast in the eighth month, on the fifteenth day of the month, according to the feast in the land of Juda; 33 and went up to the altar which he made in Baethel to sacrifice to the heifers which he made, and he placed in Baethel the priests of the high places which he had made. And he went up to the altar which he had made, on the fifteenth day in the eighth month, at the feast which he devised out of his own heart; and he made a feast to the children of Israel, and went up to the altar to sacrifice.

3-Kgdms13 1 And behold, there came a man of God out of Juda by the word of the Lord to Baethel, and Jeroboam stood at the altar to sacrifice. 2 And he cried against the altar by the word of the Lord, and said, O altar, altar, thus saith the Lord, Behold, a son is *to be* born to the house of David, Josias by name; and he shall offer upon thee the priests of the high places, *even* of them that sacrifice upon thee, and *he* shall burn men's bones upon thee. 3 And in that day one shall give a sign, saying, This *is* the word which the Lord has spoken, saying, Behold, the altar is rent, and the fatness upon it shall be poured out. 4 And it came to pass when king Jeroboam heard the words of the man of God who called on the altar that was in Baethel, that the king stretched forth his hand from the altar, saying, Take hold of him. And, behold, his hand, which he stretched forth against him, withered, and he could not draw it back to himself. 5 And the altar was rent, and the fatness was poured out from the altar, according to the sign which the man of God gave by the word of the Lord. 6 And king Jeroboam said to the man of God, Intreat the Lord thy God, and let my hand be restored to me. And the man of

God intreated the Lord, and he restored the king's hand to him, and it became as before. 7 And the king said to the man of God, Enter with me into the house, and dine, and I will give thee a gift. 8 And the man of God said to the king, If thou shouldest give me the half of thine house, I would not go in with thee, neither will I eat bread, neither will I drink water in this place; for thus the Lord charged me by *his* word, saying, 9 Eat no bread, and drink no water, and return not by the way by which thou camest. 10 So he departed by another way, and returned not by the way by which he came to Baethel. 11 And there dwelt an old prophet in Baethel; and his sons came and told him all the works that the man of God did on that day in Baethel, and the words which he spoke to the king: and they turned the face of their father. 12 And their father spoke to them, saying, Which way went he? and his sons shew him the way by which the man of God who came out of Juda went up. 13 And he said to his sons, Saddle me the ass: and they saddled him the ass, and he mounted it, 14 and went after the man of God, and found him sitting under an oak: and he said to him, Art thou the man of God that came out of Juda? And he said to him, I *am*. 15 And he said to him, Come with me, and eat bread. 16 And he said, I shall not by any means be able to return with thee, neither will I eat bread, neither will I drink water in this place. 17 For thus the Lord commanded me by word, saying, Eat not bread there, and drink not water, and return not thither by the way by which thou camest. 18 And he said to him, I also am a prophet as thou *art*; and an angel spoke to me by the word of the Lord, saying, Bring him back to thee into thy house, and let him eat bread and drink water: but he lied to him. 19 And he brought him back, and he ate bread and drank water in his house. 20 And it came to pass while they were sitting at the table, that the word of the Lord came to the prophet that brought him back; 21 and he spoke to the man of God that came out of Juda, saying, Thus saith the Lord, Because thou hast resisted the word of the Lord, and hast not kept the commandment which the Lord thy God commanded thee, 22 but hast returned, and eaten bread and drunk water in the place of which he spoke to thee, saying, Thou shalt not eat bread, and shalt not drink water; *therefore* thy body shall in nowise enter into the sepulchre of thy fathers. 23 And it came to pass after he had eaten bread and drunk water, that he saddled the ass for him, and he turned and departed. 24 And a lion found him in the way, and slew him; and his body was cast out in the way, and the ass was standing by it, and the lion *also* was standing by the body. 25 And, behold, men *were* passing by, and saw the carcase cast in the way, and the lion was standing near the carcase: and they went in and spoke *of it* in the city where the old prophet dwelt. 26 And *the prophet* that turned him back out of the way heard, and said, This is the man of God who rebelled against the word of the Lord. 27 28 And he went and found the body cast in the way, and the ass and the lion were standing by the body: and the lion had not devoured the body of the man of God, and had not torn the ass. 29 And the prophet took up the body of the man of God, and laid it on his ass; and the prophet brought him back to his city, to bury him in his own tomb, 30 and they bewailed him, *saying*, Alas, brother. 31 And it came to pass after he had lamented him, that he spoke to his sons, saying, Whenever I die, bury me in this tomb wherein the man of God is buried; lay me by his bones, that my bones may be preserved with his bones. 32 For the word will surely come to pass which he spoke by the word of the Lord against the altar in Baethel, and against the high houses in Samaria. 33 And after this Jeroboam turned not from his sin, but he turned and made of part of the people priests of the *high places*: whoever would, he consecrated him, and he became a priest for the high places. 34 And this thing became sin to the house of Jeroboam, even to its destruction and its removal from the face of the earth.

3-Kgdms14 1 And Roboam son of Solomon ruled over Juda. Roboam was forty and one years old when he began to reign, and he reigned seventeen years in the city Jerusalem, which the Lord chose to put his name there out of all the tribes of Israel: and his mother's name *was* Naama the Ammonitess. 22 And Roboam did evil in the sight of the Lord; and he provoked him in all the things which their fathers did in their sins which they sinned. 23 And they built for themselves high places, and pillars, and *planted* groves on every high hill, and under every shady tree. 24 And there was a conspiracy in the land, and they did according to all the abominations of the nations which the Lord removed from before the children of Israel. 25 And it came to pass in the fifth year of the reign of Roboam, Susakim king of Egypt came up against Jerusalem; 26 and took all the treasures of the house of the Lord, and the treasures of the king's house, and the golden spears which David took out of the hand of the sons of Adrazaar king of Suba, and brought them into Jerusalem, even all that he took, *and* the golden shields which Solomon had made, [and carried them away into Egypt.] 27 And king Roboam made brazen shields instead of them; and the chiefs of the body guard, who kept the gate of the house of the king, were placed in charge over them. 28 And it came to pass when the king went into the house of the Lord, that the body guard took them up, and fixed them in the chamber of the body guard. 29 And the rest of the history of Roboam, and all that he did, behold, are they not written in the book of the chronicles of the kings of Juda? 30 And there was war between Roboam and Jeroboam continually. 31 And Roboam slept with his fathers, and was buried with his fathers in the city of David: and Abiu his son reigned in his stead.

3-Kgdms15 1 And in the eighteenth year of the reign of Jeroboam son of Nabat, Abiu son of Roboam reigns over Juda. 2 And he reigned three years over Jerusalem: and his mother's name *was* Maacha, daughter of Abessalom. 3 And he walked in the sins of his father which he wrought in his presence, and his heart was not perfect with the Lord his God, as *was* the heart of his father *David*. 4 Howbeit for David's sake the Lord gave him a remnant, that he might establish his children after him, and might establish Jerusalem. 5 Forasmuch as David did that which was right in the sight of the Lord: he turned not from any thing that he commanded him all the days of his life. 6 7 And the rest of the history of Abiu, and all that he did, behold, are not these written in the book of the chronicles of the kings of Juda? And there was war between Abiu and Jeroboam. 8 And Abiu slept with his fathers in the twenty-fourth year of Jeroboam; and he is buried with his fathers in the city of David: And Asa his son reigns in his stead. 9 In the four and twentieth year of Jeroboam king of Israel, Asa begins to reign over Juda. 10 And he reigned forty-one years in Jerusalem: and his mother's name *was* Ana, daughter of Abessalom. 11 And Asa did that which was right in the sight of the Lord, as David his father. 12 And he removed the sodomites out of the land, and abolished all the practices which his fathers had kept up. 13 And he removed Ana his mother from being queen, forasmuch as she gathered a meeting in her grove: and Asa cut down her retreats, and burnt them with fire in the brook of Kedron. 14 But he removed not the high places; nevertheless the heart of Asa was perfect with the Lord all his days. 15 And he brought in the pillars of his father, he even brought in his gold and silver pillars into the house of the Lord, and *his* vessels. 16 And there was war between Asa and Baasa king of Israel all their days. 17 And Baasa king of Israel went up against Juda, and built Rama, so that no one should go out or come in for Asa king of Juda. 18 And Asa took all the silver and the gold that was found in the treasures of the house of the Lord, and in the treasures of the king's house, and gave them into the hands of his servants; and king Asa sent them out to the son of Ader, the son of Taberema son of Azin king of Syria, who dwelt in Damascus, saying, 19 Make a covenant between me and thee, and between my father and thy father: lo! I have sent forth to thee gold and silver *for* gifts: come, break thy league with Baasa king of Israel, that he may go up from me. 20 And the son of Ader hearkened to king Asa, and sent the chiefs of his forces to the cities of Israel; and they smote Ain, Dan, and Abel of the house of Maacha, and all Chennereth, as far as the whole land of Nephthali. 21 And it came to pass when Baasa heard it, that he left off building Rama, and returned to Thersa. 22 And king Asa charged all Juda without exception: and they take up the stones of Rama and its timbers *with* which Baasa was building; and king Asa built with them upon the whole hill of Benjamin, and the watch-tower. 23 And the rest of the history of Asa, and all his mighty deeds which he wrought, and the cities which he built, behold, are not these written in the book of the chronicles of the kings of Juda? Nevertheless in the time of his old age he was diseased in his feet. 24 And Asa slept with his fathers, and was buried with his fathers in the city of David his father: and Josaphat his son reigns in his stead. 25 And Nabat son of Jeroboam reigns over Israel in the second year of Asa king of Juda, and he reigned two years in Israel. 26 And he did that which was evil in the sight of the Lord, and walked in the way of his father, and in his sins wherein he caused Israel to sin. 27 And Baasa son of Achia, *who was* over the house of Belaan son of Achia, conspired against him, and smote him in Gabathon of the Philistines; for Nabat and all Israel were besieging Gabathon. 28 And Baasa slew him in the third year of Asa son of Asa king of Juda; and reigned in his stead. 29 And it came to pass when he reigned, that he smote the whole house of Jeroboam, and left none that breathed of Jeroboam, until he has destroyed him utterly, according to the word of the Lord which he spoke by his servant Achia the Selonite, 30 for the sins of Jeroboam, who led Israel into sin, even by his provocation wherewith he provoked the Lord God of Israel. 31 And the rest of the history of Nabat, and all that he did, behold, are not these written in the book of the chronicles of the kings of Israel? 32,33 And in the third year of Asa king of Juda, Baasa the son of Achia begins to reign over Israel in Thersa, twenty and four years. 34 And he did that which was evil in the sight of the Lord, and walked in the way of Jeroboam the son of Nabat, and in his sins, as he caused Israel to sin.

3-Kgdms16 1 And the word of the Lord came by the hand of Ju son of Anani to Baasa, *saying*, 2 Forasmuch as I lifted thee up from the earth, and made thee ruler over my people Israel; and thou hast walked in the way of Jeroboam, and hast caused my people Israel to sin, to provoke me with their vanities; 3 Behold, I raise up *enemies* after Baasa, and after his house; and I will make thy house as the house of Jeroboam son of Nabat. 4 Him the dies of Baasa in the city the dogs shall devour, and him that dies of his in the field the birds of the sky shall devour. 5 Now the rest of the history of Baasa, and all that he did, and his mighty acts, behold, are not these written in the book of the chronicles of the kings of Israel? 6 And Baasa slept with his fathers, and they bury him in Thersa; and Ela his son reigns in his stead. 7 And the Lord spoke by Ju the son of Anani against Baasa, and against his house, *even* all the evil which he wrought before the Lord to provoke him to anger by the works of his hands, in being like the house of Jeroboam; and because he smote him. 8 And Ela son of Baasa reigned over Israel two years in Thersa. 9 And Zambri, captain of half his cavalry, conspired against him, while he was in Thersa, drinking himself drunk in the house of Osa the steward at Thersa. 10 And Zambri went in and smote him and slew him, and reigned in his stead. 11 And it came to pass when he reigned, when he sat upon his throne, 12 that he smote all the house of Baasa, according to the word which the Lord spoke against the house of Baasa, and to Ju the prophet, 13 for all the sins of Baasa and Ela his son, as he led Israel astray to sin, to provoke the Lord God of Israel with their vanities. 14 And the rest of the deeds of Ela which he did, behold, are not these written in the book of the chronicles of the kings of Israel? 15 And Zambri reigned in Thersa seven days: and the army of Israel *was* encamped against Gabathon of the Philistines. 16 And the people heard in the army, saying, Zambri has conspired and smitten the king: and the people of Israel made Ambri the captain of the host king in that day in the camp over Israel. 17 And Ambri went up, and all Israel with him, out of Gabathon; and they besieged Thersa. 18 And it came to pass when Zambri saw that his city was taken, that he goes into the inner chamber of the house of the king, and burnt the king's house over him, and died. 19 Because of his sins which he committed, doing that which was evil in the sight of the Lord, so as to walk in the way of Jeroboam the son of Nabat, and in his sins wherein he caused Israel to sin. 20

And the rest of the history of Zambri, and his conspiracies wherein he conspired, behold, are not these written in the book of the chronicles of the kings of Israel? 21 Then the people of Israel divides; half the people goes after Thamni the son of Gonath to make him king; and half the people goes after Ambri. 22 The people that followed Ambri overpowered the people that followed Thamni son of Gonath; and Thamni died and Joram his brother at that time, and Ambri reigned after Thamni. 23 In the thirty-first year of king Asa, Ambri begins to reign over Israel twelve years: he reigns six years in Thersa. 24 And Ambri bought the mount Semeron of Semer the lord of the mountain for two talents of silver; and he built *upon* the mountain, and they called the name of the mountain *on* which he built, after the name of Semer the lord of the mount, Semeron. 25 And Ambri did that which was evil in the sight of the Lord, and wrought wickedly beyond all that were before him. 26 And he walked in all the way of Jeroboam the son of Nabat, and in his sins wherewith he caused Israel to sin, to provoke the Lord God of Israel by their vanities. 27 And the rest of the acts of Ambri, and all that he did, and all his might, behold, *are* not these things written in the book of the chronicles of the kings of Israel? 28 And Ambri slept with his fathers, and is buried in Samaria; and Achaab his son reigns in his stead. And in the eleventh year of Ambri Josaphat the son of Asa reigns, *being* thirty-five years old in the beginning of his reign, and he reigned twenty-five years in Jerusalem: and his mother's name *was* Gazuba, daughter of Seli. And he walked in the way of Asa his father, and turned not from it, *even* from doing right in the eyes of the Lord: only they removed not *any* of the high places; they sacrificed and burnt incense on the high places. Now the engagements which Josaphat made with the king of Israel, and all his mighty deeds which he performed, and the enemies whom he fought against, behold, *are* not these written in the book of the chronicles of the kings of Juda? and the remains of the prostitution which they practiced in the days of Asa his father, he removed out of the land: and there was no king in Syria, *but* a deputy. And king Josaphat made a ship at Tharsis to go to Sophir for gold: but it went not, for the ship was broken at Gasion Gaber. Then the king of Israel said to Josaphat, I will send forth thy servants and my servants in the ship: but Josaphat would not. And Josaphat slept with his fathers, and is buried with his fathers in the city of David: and Joram his son reigned in his stead. 29 In the second year of Josaphat king of Juda, Achaab son of Ambri reigned over Israel in Samaria twenty-two years. 30 And Achaab did that which was evil in the sight of the Lord, and did more wickedly than all that were before him. 31 And it was not enough for him to walk in the sins of Jeroboam the son of Nabat, but he took to wife, Jezabel the daughter of Jethebaal king of the Sidonians; and he went and served Baal, and worshiped him. 32 And he set up an alter to Baal, in the house of his abominations, which he built in Samaria. 33 And Achaab made a grove; and Achaab did yet more abominably, to provoke the Lord God of Israel, and *to sin against* his own life so that he should be destroyed: he did evil above all the kings of Israel that were before him. 34 And in his days Achiel the Baethelite built

Jericho: he laid the foundation of it in Abiron his first-born, and he set up the doors of it in Segub his younger son, according to the word of the Lord which he spoke by Joshua the son of Naue.

3-Kgdms17 1 And Eliu the prophet, the Thesbite of Thesbae of Galaad, said to Achaab, As the Lord God of hosts, the God of Israel, lives, before whom I stand, there shall not be these years dew nor rain, except by the word of my mouth. 2 And the word of the Lord came to Eliu, *saying,* 3 Depart hence eastward, and hide thee by the brook of Chorrath, that is before Jordan. 4 And it shall be *that* thou shalt drink water of the brook, and I will charge the ravens to feed thee there. 5 And Eliu did according to the word of the Lord, and he sat by the brook of Chorrath before Jordan. 6 And the ravens brought him loaves in the morning, and flesh in the evening and he drank water of the brook. 7 And it came to pass after some time, that the brook was dried up, because there had been no rain upon the earth. 8 And the word of the Lord came to Eliu, *saying,* 9 Arise, and go to Sarepta of the Sidonian *land*: behold, I have there commanded a widow-woman to maintain thee. 10 And he arose and went to Sarepta, and came to the gate of the city: and, behold, a widow-woman was there gathering sticks; and Eliu cried after her, and said to her, Fetch me, I pray thee, a little water in a vessel, that I may drink. 11 And she went to fetch it; and Eliu cried after her, and said, Bring me, I pray thee, a morsel of the bread that is in thy hand. 12 And the woman said, *As* the Lord thy God lives, I have not a cake, but only a handful of meal in the pitcher, and a little oil in a cruse, and, behold, I am going to gather two sticks, and I shall go in and dress it for myself and my children, and we shall eat it and die. 13 And Eliu said to her, Be of good courage, go in and do according to thy word: but make me thereof a little cake, and thou shalt bring *it* out to me first, and thou shalt make *some* for thyself and thy children last. 14 For thus saith the Lord, The pitcher of meal shall not fail, and the cruse of oil shall not diminish, until the day that the Lord gives rain upon the earth. 15 And the woman went and did *so,* and did eat, she, and he, and her children. 16 And the pitcher of meal failed not, and the cruse of oil was not diminished, according to the word of the Lord which he spoke by the hand of Eliu. 17 And it came to pass afterward, that the son of the woman the mistress of the house was sick; and his sickness was very severe, until there was no breath left in him. 18 And she said to Eliu, What have I to do with thee, O man of God? hast thou come in to me to bring my sins to remembrance, and to slay my son? 19 And Eliu said to the woman, Give me thy son. And he took him out of her bosom, and took him up to the chamber in which he himself lodged, and laid him on the bed. 20 And Eliu cried aloud, and said, Alas, O Lord, the witness of the widow with whom I sojourn, thou hast wrought evil *for her* in slaying her son. 21 And he breathed on the child thrice, and called on the Lord, and said, O Lord my God, let, I pray thee, the soul of this child return to him. 22 And it was so, and the child cried out, 23 and he brought him down from the upper chamber into the house, and gave him to his mother; and Eliu said, See, thy son lives. 24

And the woman said to Eliu, Behold, I know that thou *art* a man of God, and the word of the Lord in thy mouth *is* true.

3-Kgdms18 1 And it came to pass after many days, that the word of the Lord came to Eliu in the third year, saying, Go, and appear before Achaab, and I will bring rain upon the face of the earth. 2 And Eliu went to appear before Achaab: and the famine *was* severe in Samaria. 3 And Achaab called Abdiu the steward. Now Abdiu feared the Lord greatly. 4 And it came to pass when Jezabel smote the prophets of the Lord, that Abdiu took a hundred prophets, and hid them by fifty in a cave, and fed them with bread and water. 5 And Achaab said to Abdiu, Come, and let us go through the land, and to the fountains of water, and to the brooks, if by any means we may find grass, and may save the horses and mules, and so they will not perish from the tents. 6 And they made a division of the way between them to pass through it: Achaab went one way, and Abdiu went by another way alone. 7 And Abdiu was alone in the way; and Eliu came alone to meet him: and Abdiu hasted, and fell upon his face, and said, My lord Eliu, art thou *indeed* he? 8 And Eliu said to him, I *am*: go say to thy master, Behold, Eliu *is here*. 9 And Abdiu said, What sin have I committed, that thou givest thy servant into the hand of Achaab to slay me? 10 *As* the Lord thy God lives, there is not a nation or kingdom, whither my lord has not sent to seek thee; and if they said, He is not *here*, then has he set fire to the kingdom and its territories, because he has not found thee. 11 And now thou sayest, Go, tell thy lord, Behold, Eliu *is here*. 12 And it shall come to pass when I shall have departed from thee, that the Spirit of the Lord shall carry thee to a land which I know not, and I shall go in to tell the matter to Achaab, and he will not find thee and will slay me: yet thy servant fears the Lord from his youth. 13 Has it not been told to thee my lord, what I did when Jezabel slew the prophets of the Lord, that I hid a hundred men of the prophets of the Lord, by fifty in a cave, and fed them with bread and water? 14 And now thou sayest to me, Go, say to thy master, Behold, Eliu *is here*: and he shall slay me. 15 And Eliu said, *As* the Lord of Hosts before whom I stand lives, to -day I will appear before him. 16 And Abdiu went to meet Achaab, and told him: and Achaab hasted forth, and went to meet Eliu. 17 And it came to pass when Achaab saw Eliu, that Achaab said to Eliu, Art thou he that perverts Israel? 18 And Eliu said, I do not pervert Israel; but it is thou and thy father's house, in that ye forsake the Lord your God, and thou hast gone after Baalim. 19 And now send, gather to me all Israel to mount Carmel, and the prophets of shame four hundred and fifty, and the prophets of the groves four hundred, that eat *at* Jezabel's table. 20 And Achaab sent to all Israel, and gathered all the prophets to mount Carmel. 21 And Eliu drew near to them all: and Eliu said to them, How long wilt ye halt on both feet? if the Lord be God, follow him; but if Baal, follow him. And the people answered not a word. 22 And Eliu said to the people, I am left, the only one prophet of the Lord; and the prophets of Baal *are* four hundred and fifty men, and the prophets of the groves four hundred. 23 Let them give us

two oxen, and let them choose one for themselves, and cut it in pieces, and lay it on the wood, and put no fire *on* the wood: and I will dress the other bullock, and put on no fire. 24 And do ye call loudly on the name of your gods, and I will call on the name of the Lord my God, and it shall come to pass that the God who shall answer by fire, he *is* God. And all the people answered and said, The word which thou hast spoken *is* good. 25 And Eliu said to the prophets of shame, Choose to yourselves one calf, and dress it first, for ye *are* many; and call ye on the name of your god; but apply no fire. 26 And they took the calf and drest it, and called on the name of Baal from morning till noon, and said, hear us, O Baal, hear us. And there was no voice, neither was there hearing, and they ran up and down on the alter which they *had* made. 27 And it was noon, and Eliu the Thesbite mocked them, and said, Call with a loud voice, for he is a god; for he is meditating, or else perhaps he is engaged in business, or perhaps he is asleep, and is to be awaked. 28 And they cried with a loud voice, and cut themselves according to their custom with knives and lancets until the blood gushed out upon them. 29 And they prophesied until the evening came; and it came to pass as it was the time of the offering of the sacrifice, that Eliu the Thesbite spoke to the prophets of the abominations, saying, Stand by for the present, and I will offer my sacrifice. And they stood aside and departed. 30 And Eliu said to the people, Come near to me. And all the people came near to him. 31 And Eliu took twelve stones, according to the number of the tribes of Israel, as the Lord spoke to him, saying, Israel shall be thy name. 32 And he built up the stones in the name of the Lord, and repaired the altar that had been broken down; and he made a trench that would hold two measures of seed round about the altar. 33 And he piled the cleft wood on the altar which he *had* made, and divided the whole-burnt-offering, and laid *it* on the wood, and laid *it* in order on the altar, and said, Fetch me four pitchers of water, and pour *it* on the whole-burnt-offering, and on the wood. And they did so. 34 And he said, Do it the second time. And they did it the second time. And he said, Do it the third time. And they did it the third time. 35 And the water ran round about the altar, and they filled the trench with water. 36 And Eliu cried aloud to the heaven, and said, Lord God of Abraam, and Isaac, and Israel, answer me, O Lord, answer me this day by fire, and let all this people know that thou art the Lord, the God of Israel, and I *am* thy servant, and for thy sake I have wrought these works. 37 Hear me, O Lord, hear me, and let this people know that thou art the Lord God, and thou hast turned back the heart of this people. 38 Then fire fell from the Lord out of heaven, and devoured the whole-burnt-offerings, and the wood and the water that was in the trench, and the fire licked up the stones and the earth. 39 And all the people fell upon their faces, and said, Truly the Lord *is* God; he *is* God. 40 And Eliu said to the people, Take the prophets of Baal; let not one of them escape. And they took them; and Eliu brings them down to the brook Kisson, and he slew them there. 41 And Eliu said to Achaab, Go up, and eat and drink, for *there is* a sound of the coming of rain. 42 And Achaab went up to eat and to drink; and Eliu went up to Carmel, and stooped to the ground, and put his face between his knees, 43 and said to his servant, Go up, and look toward the sea. And the servant looked, and said, There is nothing: and Eliu said, Do thou then go again seven times. 44 And the servant went again seven times: and it came to pass at the seventh time, that, behold, a little cloud like the sole of a man's foot brought water; and he said, Go up, and say to Achaab, make ready thy chariot, and go down, lest the rain overtake thee. 45 And it came to pass in the meanwhile, that the heaven grew black with clouds and wind, and there was a great rain. And Achaab wept, and went to Jezrael. 46 And the hand of the Lord *was* upon Eliu, and he girt up his loins, and ran before Achaab to Jezrael.

3-Kgdms19 1 And Achaab told Jezabel his wife all that Eliu *had* done, and how he *had* slain the prophets with the sword. 2 And Jezabel sent to Eliu, and said, If thou art Eliu and I am Jezabel, God do so to me, and more also, if I do not make thy life by this time to-morrow as the life of one of them. 3 And Eliu feared, and rose, and departed for his life: and he comes to Bersabee *to* the land of Juda, and he left his servant there. 4 And he himself went a day's journey in the wilderness, and came and sat under a juniper tree; and asked concerning his life that he might die, and said, Let it be enough now, O Lord, take, I pray thee, my life from me; for I am no better than my fathers. 5 And he lay down and slept there under a tree; and behold, some one touched him, and said to him, Arise and eat. 6 And Eliu looked, and, behold, at his head there was a cake of meal and a cruse of water; and he arose, and ate and drank, and returned and lay down. 7 And the angel of the Lord returned again, and touched him, and said to him, Arise, and eat, for the journey *is* far from thee. 8 And he arose, and ate and drank, and went in the strength of that meat forty days and forty nights to mount Choreb. 9 And he entered there into a cave, and rested there; and, behold, the word of the Lord *came* to him, and he said, What *doest* thou here, Eliu? 10 And Eliu said, I have been very jealous for the Lord Almighty, because the children of Israel have forsaken thee: they have digged down thine altars, and have slain thy prophets with the sword; and I only am left alone, and they seek my life to take it. 11 And he said, Thou shalt go forth to-morrow, and shalt stand before the Lord in the mount; behold, the Lord will pass by. And, behold, a great *and* strong wind rending the mountains, and crushing the rocks before the Lord; *but* the Lord *was* not in the wind; and after the wind an earthquake; *but* the Lord *was* not in the earthquake: 12 and after the earthquake a fire; *but* the Lord *was* not in the fire: and after the fire the voice of a gentle breeze. 13 And it came to pass when Eliu heard, that he wrapt his face in his mantle, and went forth and stood in the cave: and, behold, a voice *came* to him and said, What *doest* thou here, Eliu? 14 And Eliu said, I have been very jealous for the Lord Almighty; for the children of Israel have forsaken thy covenant, and they have overthrown thine altars, and have slain thy prophets with the sword! and I am left entirely alone, and they seek my life to take it. 15 And the Lord said to him, Go, return, and thou shalt come into the way of the wilderness of Damascus: and thou shalt go and anoint Azael to be king over Syria. 16 And Ju the son of Namessi shalt thou anoint to be king over Israel; and Elisaie the son of Saphat shalt thou anoint to be prophet in thy room. 17 And it shall come to pass, that him that escapes from the sword of Azael, Ju shall slay; and him that escapes from the sword of Ju, Elisaie shall slay. 18 And thou shalt leave in Israel seven thousand men, all the knees which had not bowed themselves to Baal, and every mouth which had not worshipped him. 19 And he departed thence, and finds Elisaie the son of Saphat, and he was ploughing with oxen; *there were* twelve yoke before him, and he with the twelve, and he passed by to him, and cast his mantle upon him. 20 And Elisaie left the cattle, and ran after Eliu and said, I will kiss my father, and follow after thee. And Eliu said, Return, for I have done *a work* for thee. 21 And he returned from following him, and took a yoke of oxen, and slew them, and boiled them with the instruments of the oxen, and gave to the people, and they ate: and he arose, and went after Eliu, and ministered to him.

3-Kgdms20 1 And Nabuthai the Jezraelite had a vineyard, near the threshingfloor of Achaab king of Samaria. 2 And Achaab spoke to Nabuthai, saying, Give me thy vineyard, and I will have it for a garden of herbs, for it *is* near my house: and I will give thee another vineyard better than it; or if it please thee, I will give thee money, the price of this thy vineyard, and I will have it for a garden of herbs. 3 And Nabuthai said to Achaab, My God forbid me that I should give thee the inheritance of my fathers. 4 And the spirit of Achaab was troubled, and he lay down upon his bed, and covered his face, and ate no bread. 5 And Jezabel his wife went in to him, and spoke to him, *saying*, Why *is* thy spirit troubled, and *why* dost thou eat no bread? 6 And he said to her, Because I spoke to Nabuthai the Jezraelite, saying, Give me thy vineyard for money; or if thou wilt, I will give thee another vineyard for it: and he said, I will not give thee the inheritance of my fathers. 7 And Jezabel his wife said to him, Dost thou now thus act the king over Israel? arise, and eat bread, and be thine own *master*, and I will give thee the vineyard of Nabuthai the Jezraelite. 8 And she wrote a letter in the name of Achaab, and sealed it with his seal, and sent the letter to the elders, and to the freemen who dwelt with Nabuthai. 9 And it was written in the letters, saying, Keep a fast, and set Naboth in a chief place among the people. 10 And set two men, sons of transgressors, before him, and let them testify against him, saying, He blessed God and the king: and let them lead him forth, and stone him, and let them die. 11 And the men of his city, the elders, and the nobles who dwelt in his city, did as Jezabel sent to them, and as it had been written in the letters which she sent to them. 12 And they proclaimed a fast, and set Nebuthai in a chief place among the people. 13 And two men, sons of transgressors, came in, and sat opposite him, and bore witness against him, saying, Thou hast blessed God and the king. And they led him forth out of the city, and stoned him with stones, and he died. 14 And they sent to Jezabel, saying, Nabuthai is stoned, and is dead. 15 And it came to pass, when Jezabel heard *it*, that she said to Achaab, Arise, take possession of the vineyard of Nabuthai the Jezraelite, who would not sell it to thee: for Nebuthai is not alive, for he is dead. 16 And it came to pass, when Achaab heard that Nabuthai the Jezraelite was dead, that he rent his garments, and put on sackcloth. And it came to pass afterward, that Achaab arose and went down to the vineyard of Nabuthai the Jezraelite, to take possession of it. 17 And the Lord spoke to Eliu the Thesbite, saying, 18 Arise, and go down to meet Achaab king of Israel, who is in Samaria, for he *is* in the vineyard of Nabuthai, for he has gone down thither to take possession of it. 19 And thou shalt speak to him, saying, Thus saith the Lord, Forasmuch as thou hast slain and taken possession, therefore thus saith the Lord, In every place where the swine and the dogs have licked the blood of Nabuthai, there shall the dogs lick thy blood; and the harlots shall wash themselves in thy blood. 20 And Achaab said to Eliu, Hast thou found me, mine enemy? and he said, I have found *thee*: because thou hast wickedly sold thyself to work evil in the sight of the Lord, to provoke him to anger; 21 behold, I bring evil upon thee: and I will kindle a fire after thee, and I will utterly destroy every male of Achaab, and him that is shut up and him that is left in Israel. 22 And I will make thy house as the house of Jeroboam the son of Nabat, and as the house of Baasa son of Achia, because of the provocations wherewith thou hast provoked *me*, and caused Israel to sin. 23 And the Lord spoke of Jezabel, saying, The dogs shall devour her within the fortification of Jezrael. 24 Him that is dead of Achaab in the city shall the dogs eat, and him that is dead of him in the field shall the birds of the sky eat. 25 But Achaab *did* wickedly, in that he sold himself to do that which was evil in the sight of the Lord, as his wife Jezabel led him astray. 26 And he did very abominably in following after the abominations, according to all that the Amorite did, whom the Lord utterly destroyed from before the children of Israel. 27 And because of the word, Achaab was pierced with sorrow before the Lord, and he both went weeping, and rent his garment, and girt sackcloth upon his body, and fasted; he put on sackcloth also in the day that he smote Nabuthai the Jezraelite, and went his way. 28 And the word of the Lord came by the hand of his servant Eliu concerning Achaab, and the Lord said, 29 Hast thou seen how Achaab has been pricked *to the heart* before me? I will not bring on the evil in his days, but in his son's days will I bring on the evil.

3-Kgdms21 1 And the son of Ader gathered all his forces, and went up and besieged Samaria, *he* and thirty-two kings with him, and all *his* horse and chariots: and they went up and besieged Samaria, and fought against it. 2 And he sent into the city to Achaab king of Israel, and said to him, Thus says the son of Ader, 3 Thy silver and thy gold are mine, and thy wives and thy children are mine. 4 And the king of Israel answered and said, As thou hast said, my lord, O king, I am thine, and all mine *also*. 5 And the messengers came again, and said, Thus says the son of Ader, I sent to thee, saying, Thou shalt give me thy silver and thy gold, and thy wives and thy children. 6 For at this time to- morrow I will send my servants to thee, and they shall search thy house, and the houses of thy servants, and it shall be that all the desirable objects of their eyes on which they shall lay their hands, they shall even take *them*. 7 And the king of Israel called all the elders of the land, and said, Take notice now and consider, that this man seeks mischief: for he has sent to me concerning my wives, and concerning my sons, an concerning my daughters: I have not kept back from him my silver and my gold. 8 And the elders and all the people said to him, Hearken not, and consent not. 9 And he said to the messengers of the son of Ader, Say to your master, All things that thou hast sent to thy servant about at first I will do; but this thing I shall not be able to do. And the men departed, and carried back the answer to him. 10 And the son of Ader sent to him, saying, So do God to me, and more also, if the dust of Samaria shall suffice for foxes to all the people, even my infantry. 11 And the king of Israel answered and said, Let it be sufficient; let not the humpbacked boast as he that is upright. 12 And it came to pass when he returned him this answer, he and all the kings with him were drinking in tents: and he said to his servants, Form a trench. And they made a trench against the city. 13 And, behold, a prophet came to Achaab king of Israel, and said, Thus saith the Lord, Hast thou seen this great multitude? behold, I give it this day into thine hands; and thou shalt know that I *am* the Lord. 14 And Achaab said, Whereby? And he said, Thus saith the Lord, by the young men of the heads of the districts. And Achaab said, Who shall begin the battle? and he said, Thou. 15 And Achaab numbered the young men the heads of the districts, and they were two hundred and thirty: and afterwards he numbered the people, *even* every man fit for war, seven thousand. 16 And he went forth at noon, an the son of Ader was drinking *and* getting drunk in Socchoth, he and the kings, *even* thirty and two kings, his allies. 17 And the young men the heads of the districts went forth first; and they send and report to the king of Syria, saying, There are men come forth out of Samaria. 18 And he said to them, If they come forth peaceably, take them alive; and if they come forth to war, take them alive: 19 and let not the young men the heads of the districts go forth of the city. And the force that was behind them 20 smote each one the man next to him; and each one a second time smote the man next to him: and Syria fled, and Israel pursued them; and the son of Ader, *even* the king of Syria, escapes on the horse of a horseman. 21 And the king of Israel went forth, and took all the horses and the chariots, and smote *the enemy* with a great slaughter in Syria. 22 And the prophet came to the king of Israel, and said, Strengthen thyself, and observe, and see what thou shalt do; for at the return of the year the son of Ader king of Syria comes up against thee. 23 And the servants of the king of Syria, even they said, The God of Israel *is* a God of mountains, and not a God of valleys; therefore has he prevailed against us: but if we should fight against them in the plain, verily we shall prevail against them. 24 And do thou this thing: Send away the kings, each one to his place, and set princes in their stead. 25 And we will give thee *another* army according to the army that was destroyed, and cavalry according to the cavalry, and chariots according to the chariots, and we will fight against them in the plain, and we shall prevail against them. And he hearkened to their voice, and did so. 26 And it came to pass at the return of the year, that the son of Ader reviewed Syria, and went up to Apheca to war against Israel. 27 And the children of Israel were numbered, and came to meet them: and Israel encamped before them as two little flocks of goats, but Syria filled the land. 28 And there came the man of God, and said to the king of Israel, Thus saith the Lord, Because Syria has said, The Lord God of Israel is a God of the hills, and he is not a God of the valleys, therefore will I give this great army into thy hand, and thou shalt know that I am the Lord. 29 And they encamp one over against the other before them seven days. And it came to pass on the seventh day that the battle drew on, and Israel smote Syria, even a hundred thousand footmen in one day. 30 And the rest fled to Apheca, into the city; and the wall fell upon twenty- seven thousand men that were left: and the son of Ader fled, and entered into an inner chamber, into a closet. 31 And he said to his servants, I know that the kings of Israel are merciful kings: let us now put sackcloth upon our loins, and ropes upon our heads, and let us go forth to the king of Israel, if by any means he will save our souls alive. 32 So they girt sackcloth upon their loins, and put ropes upon their heads, and said to the king of Israel, Thy servant the son of Ader says, Let our souls live, I pray thee. And he said, Does he yet live? He is my brother. 33 And the men divined, and offered drink-offerings; and they caught the word out of his mouth, and said, Thy brother the son of Ader. And he said, Go ye in and fetch him. And the son of Ader went out to him, and they cause him to go up to him into the chariot. 34 And he said to him, The cities which my father took from thy father I will restore to thee; and thou shalt make streets for thyself in Damascus, as my father made streets in Samaria; and I will let thee go with a covenant. And he made a covenant with him, and let him go. 35 And a certain man of the sons of the prophets said to his neighbour by the word of the Lord, Smite me, I pray, And the man would not smite him. 36 And he said to him, Because thou hast not hearkened to the voice of the Lord, therefore, behold, as thou departest from me, a lion shall smite thee: and he departed from him, and a lion found him, and smote him. 37 And he finds another man, and says, Smite me, I pray thee. And the man smote him, and in smiting wounded him. 38 And the prophet went and stood before the king of Israel by the way, and bound his eyes with a bandage. 39 And it came to pass as the king passed by, that he cried aloud to the king, and said, Thy servant went out to war, and, behold, a man brought another man to me, and said to me, Keep his man; and if he should by any means escape, then thy life shall go for his life, or thou shalt pay a talent of silver. 40 And it came to pass, that thy servant looked round this way and that way, and the man was gone. And the king of Israel said to him, Behold, thou hast also destroyed snares set for me. 41 And he hasted, and took away the bandage from his eyes; and the king of Israel recognized him, that he was one of the prophets. 42 And he said to him, Thus saith the Lord, Because thou hast suffered to escape out of thine hand a man appointed to destruction, therefore thy life shall go for his life, and thy

people for his people. 43 And the king of Israel departed confounded and discouraged, and came to Samaria.

3-Kgdms22 1 And he rested three years, and there was no war between Syria and Israel. 2 And it came to pass in the third year, that Josaphat king of Juda went down to the king of Israel. 3 And the king of Israel said to his servants, Know ye that Remmath Galaad is ours, and we are slow to take it out of the hand of the king of Syria? 4 And the king of Israel said to Josaphat, Wilt thou go up with us to Remmath Galaad to battle? 5 And Josaphat said, As I am, so art thou also; as my people, so is thy people; as my horses, so are thy horses. And Josaphat king of Juda said to the king of Israel, Enquire, I pray thee, of the Lord to-day. 6 And the king of Israel gathered all the prophets together, about four hundred men; and the king said to them, Shall I go up to Remmath Galaad to battle, or shall I forbear? and they said, Go up, and the Lord will surely give it into the hands of the king. 7 And Josaphat said to the king of Israel, Is there not here a prophet of the Lord, that we may enquire of the Lord by him? 8 And the king of Israel said to Josaphat, There is one man here for us to enquire of the Lord by; but I hate him, for he does not speak good of me, but only evil; Michaias son of Jemblaa. And Josaphat king of Juda said, Let not the king say so. 9 And the king of Israel called a eunuch and said, Bring hither quickly Michaias son of Jemblaa. 10 And the king of Israel and Josaphat king of Juda sat, each on his throne, armed in the gates of Samaria; and all the prophets prophesied before them. 11 And Sedekias son of Chanaan made for himself iron horns, and said, Thus saith the Lord, With these thou shalt push Syria, until it be consumed. 12 And all the prophets prophesied in like manner, saying, Go up to Remmath Galaad, and the thing shall prosper, and the Lord shall deliver it and the king of Syria into thine hands. 13 And the messenger that went to call Michaias spoke to him, saying, Behold now, all the prophets speak with one mouth good concerning the king, let now thy words be like the words of one of them, and speak good things. 14 And Michaias said, As the Lord lives, whatsoever the Lord shall say to me, that will I speak. 15 And he came to the king: and the king said to him, Michaias, shall I go up to Remmath Galaad to battle, or shall I forbear? and he said, Go up, and the Lord shall deliver it into the hand of the king. 16 And the king said to him, How often shall I adjure thee, that thou speak to me truth in the name of the Lord? 17 And he said, Not so. I saw all Israel scattered on the mountains as a flock without a shepherd: and the Lord said, Is not God lord of these? let each one return to his home in peace. 18 And the king of Israel said to Josaphat king of Juda, Did I not say to thee that this man does not prophesy good to me, for he speaks nothing but evil? 19 And Michaias said, Not so, it is not I: hear the word of the Lord; it is not so. I saw the God of Israel sitting on his throne, and all the host of heaven stood about him on his right hand and on his left. 20 And the Lord said, Who will deceive Achaab king of Israel, that he may go up and fall in Remmath Galaad? and one spoke one way, and another another way. 21 And there came forth a spirit and stood before the Lord, and said, I will deceive him. 22

And the Lord said to him, Whereby? And he said, I will go forth, and will be a false spirit in the mouth of all his prophets. And he said, Thou shalt deceive him, yea, and shalt prevail: go forth, and do so. 23 And now, behold, the Lord has put a false spirit in the mouth of all these thy prophets, and the Lord has spoken evil against thee. 24 And Sedekias the son of Chanaan came near and smote Michaias on the cheek, and said, What sort of a spirit of the Lord *has* spoken in thee? 25 And Michaias said, Behold, thou shalt see in that day, when thou shalt go into an innermost chamber to hide thyself there. 26 And the king of Israel said, Take Michaias, and convey him away to Semer the keeper of the city; 27 and tell Joas the king's son to put this *fellow* in prison, and to feed him with bread of affliction and water of affliction until I return in peace. 28 And Michaias said, If thou return at all in peace, the Lord has not spoken by me. 29 So the king of Israel went up, and Josaphat king of Juda with him to Remmath Galaad. 30 And the king of Israel said to Josaphat king of Juda, I will disguise myself, and enter into the battle, and do thou put on my raiment. So the king of Israel disguised himself, and went into the battle. 31 And the king of Syria had charged the thirty-two captains of his chariots, saying, Fight not *against* small or great, but against the king of Israel only. 32 And it came to pass, when the captains of the chariots saw Josaphat king of Juda, that they said, this seems *to be* the king of Israel. And they compassed him about to fight *against* him; and Josaphat cried out. 33 And it came to pass, when the captains of the chariots saw that this was not the king of Israel, that they returned from him. 34 And one drew a bow with a good aim, and smote the king of Israel between the lungs and the breast-plate: and he said to his charioteer, Turn thine hands, and carry me away out of the battle, for I am wounded. 35 And the war was turned in that day, and the king was standing on the chariot, against Syria from morning till evening; and he shed the blood out of his wound, into the bottom of the chariot, and died at even, and the blood ran out of the wound into the bottom of the chariot. 36 And the herald of the army stood at sunset, saying, Let every man go to his own city and his own land, 37 for the king is dead. And they came to Samaria, and buried the king in Samaria. 38 And they washed the chariot at the fountain of Samaria; and the swine and the dogs licked up the blood, and the harlots washed themselves in the blood, according to the word of the Lord which he spoke. 39 And the rest of the acts of Achaab, and all that he did, and the ivory house which he built, and all the cities which he built, behold, *are* not these things written in the book of the chronicles of the kings of Israel? 40 And Achaab slept with his fathers, and Ochozias his son reigned in his stead. 41 And Josaphat the son of Asa reigned over Juda: in the fourth year of Achaab king of Israel began Josaphat to reign. 42 Thirty and five years old *was he* when he began to reign, and he reigned twenty and five years in Jerusalem; and his mother's name *was* Azuba daughter of Salai. 43 And he walked in all the way of Asa his father: he turned not from it, even from doing that which was right in the eyes of the Lord. 44 Only he took not away *any* of the high places: the people still sacrificed and burnt incense on the high places. 45 And Josaphat was at peace with the king of Israel. 46 And the rest of the acts of Josaphat, and his mighty deeds, whatever he did, behold, *are* not these things written in the book of the chronicles of the kings of Juda? 46 47 48 49 50 51 And Josaphat slept with his fathers, and was buried by his fathers in the city of David his father, and Joram his son reigned in his stead. 52 And Ochozias son of Achaab reigned over Israel in Samaria: in the seventeenth year of Josaphat king of Juda, Ochozias son of Achaab reigned over Israel in Samaria two years. 53 And he did that which was evil in the sight of the Lord, and walked in the way of Achaab his father, and in the way of Jezabel his mother, and in the sins of the house of Jeroboam the son of Nabat, who caused Israel to sin. 54 And he served Baalim, and worshipped them, and provoked the Lord God of Israel, according to all that had been done before him.

4 KINGDOMS (II KINGS)

4-Kgdms1 1 And Moab repelled against Israel after the death of Achaab. 2 And Ochozias fell through the lattice that was in his upper chamber in Samaria and was sick; and he sent messengers, and said to them, Go and enquire of Baal fly, the god of Accaron, whether I shall recover of this my sickness. And they went to enquire of him. 3 And an angel of the Lord called Eliu the Thesbite, saying, Arise, and go to meet the messengers of Ochozias king of Samaria, and thou shalt say to them, *Is it* because there is no God in Israel, *that* ye go to enquire of Baal fly, the God of Accaron? but *it shall* not *be* so. 4 For thus saith the Lord, The bed on which thou art gone up, thou shalt not come down from it, for thou shalt surely die. And Eliu went, and said *so* to them. 5 And the messengers returned to him, and he said to them, Why have ye returned? 6 And they said to him, A man came up to meet us, and said to us, Go, return to the king that sent you, and say to him, Thus saith the Lord, *Is it* because there is no God in Israel, *that* thou goest to enquire of Baal fly, the God of Accaron? *it shall* not *be* so: the bed on which thou art gone up, thou shalt not come down from it, for thou shalt surely die. 7 So they returned and reported to the king as Eliu said: and he said to them, What *was* the manner of the man who went up to mid you, and spoke to you these·words? 8 And they said to him, *He was* a hairy man, and girt with a leathern girdle about his loins. And he said, This is Eliu the Thesbite. 9 And he sent to him a captain of fifty and his fifty; and he went up to him: and, behold, Eliu sat on the top of a mountain. And the captain of fifty spoke to him, and said, O man of God, the king has called thee, come down. 10 And Eliu answered and said to the captain of fifty, And if I *am* a man of God, fire shall come down out of heaven, and devour thee and thy fifty. And fire came down out of heaven, and devoured him and his fifty. 11 And the king sent a second time to him another captain of fifty, and his fifty. And the captain of fifty spoke to him, and said, O man of God, thus says the king, Come down quickly. 12 And Eliu answered and spoke to him, and said, If I *am* a man of God, fire shall come down out of heaven, and devour thee and thy fifty. And fire came down out of heaven, and devoured him and his fifty. 13 And the king sent yet again a captain and his fifty.

And the third captain of fifty came, and knelt on his knees before Eliu, and entreated him, and spoke to him and said, O man of God, let my life, and the life of these fifty thy servants, be precious in thine eyes. 14 Behold, fire came down from heaven, and devoured the two first captains of fifty: and now, I pray, let my life be precious in thine eyes. 15 And the angel of the Lord spoke to Eliu, and said, Go down with him, be not afraid of them. And Eliu rose up, and went down with him to the king. 16 And Eliu spoke to him, and said, Thus saith the Lord, Why hast thou sent messengers to enquire of Baal fly, the god of Accaron? *it shall* not *be* so: the bed on which thou art gone up, thou shalt not come down from it, for thou shalt surely die. 17 So he died according to the word of the Lord which Eliu has spoken. 18 And the rest of the acts of Ochozias which he did, behold, *are* they not written in the book of the chronicles of the kings of Israel? and Joram son of Achaab reigns over Israel in Samaria twelve years *beginning* in the eighteenth year of Josaphat king of Juda: and he did that which was evil in the sight of the Lord, only not as his brethren, nor as his mother: and he removed the pillars of Baal which his father made, and broke them in pieces: only he was joined to the sins of the house of Jeroboam, who led Israel to sin; he departed not from them. And the Lord was very angry with the house of Achaab.

4-Kgdms2 1 And it came to pass, when the Lord was going to take Eliu with a whirlwind as it were into heaven, that Eliu and Elisaie went out of Galgala. 2 And Eliu said to Elisaie, Stay here, I pray thee; for God has sent me to Baethel. And Elisaie said, *As* the Lord lives and thy soul lives, I will not leave thee; so they came to Baethel. 3 And the sons of the prophets who were in Baethel came to Elisaie, and said to him, Dost thou know, that the Lord this day is going to take thy lord away from thy head? And he said, Yea, I know *it*; be silent. 4 And Eliu said to Elisaie, Stay here, I pray thee; for the Lord has sent me to Jericho. And he said, *As* the Lord lives and thy soul lives, I will not leave thee. And they came to Jericho. 5 And the sons of the prophets who were in Jericho drew near to Elisaie, and said to him, Dost thou know that the Lord is about to take away thy master to-day from thy head? And he said, Yea, I know *it*; hold your peace. 6 And Eliu said to him, Stay here, I pray thee, for the Lord has sent me to Jordan. And Elisaie said, *As* the Lord lives and thy soul lives, I will not leave thee: and they both went on. 7 And fifty men of the sons of the prophets *went also*, and they stood opposite afar off: and both stood on *the bank* of Jordan. 8 And Eliu took his mantle, and wrapped it together, and smote the water: and the water was divided on this side and on that side, and they both went over on dry ground. 9 And it came to pass while they were crossing over, that Eliu said to Elisaie, Ask what I shall do for thee before I am taken up from thee. And Elisaie said, Let there be, I pray thee, a double *portion* of thy spirit upon me. 10 And Eliu said, Thou hast asked a hard thing: if thou shalt see me when I am taken up from thee, then shall it be so to thee; and if not, it shall not be *so*. 11 And it came to pass as they were going, they went on talking; and, behold, a chariot of fire, and horses of fire, and

it separated between them both; and Eliu was taken up in a whirlwind as it were into heaven. 12 And Elisaie saw, and cried, Father, father, the chariot of Israel, and the horseman thereof! And he saw him no more: and he took hold of his garments, and rent them into two pieces. 13 And Elisaie took up the mantle of Eliu, which fell from off him upon Elisaie; and Elisaie returned, and stood upon the brink of Jordan; 14 and he took the mantle of Eliu, which fell from off him, and smote the water, and said, Where is the Lord God of Eliu? and he smote the waters, and they were divided hither and thither; and Elisaie went over. 15 And the sons of the prophets who were in Jericho on the opposite side saw him, and said, The spirit of Eliu has rested upon Elisaie. And they came to meet him, and did obeisance to him to the ground. 16 And they said to him, Behold now, *there are* with thy servants fifty men of strength: let them go now, and seek thy lord: peradventure the Spirit of the Lord has taken him up, and cast him into Jordan, or on one of the mountains, or on one of the hills. And Elisaie said, Ye shall not send. 17 And they pressed him until he was ashamed; and he said, Send. And they sent fifty men, and sought three days, and found him not. 18 And they returned to him, for he dwelt in Jericho: and Elisaie said, Did I not say to you, Go not? 19 And the men of the city said to Elisaie, Behold, the situation of the city *is* good, as *our* lord sees; but the waters *are* bad, and the ground barren. 20 And Elisaie said, Bring me a new pitcher, and put salt in it. And they took *one*, and brought *it* to him. 21 And Elisaie went out to the spring of the waters, and cast salt therein, and says, Thus saith the Lord, I have healed these waters; there shall not be any longer death thence or barren *land*. 22 And the waters were healed until this day, according to the word of Elisaie which he spoke. 23 And he went up thence to Baethel: and as he was going up by the way there came up also little children from the city, and mocked him, and said to him, Go up, bald-head, go up. 24 And he turned after them, and saw them, and cursed them in the name of the Lord. And, behold, there came out two bears out of the wood, and they tore forty and two children of them. 25 And he went thence to mount Carmel, and returned thence to Samaria.

4-Kgdms3 1 And Joram the son of Achaab began to reign in Israel in the eighteenth year of Josaphat king of Juda, and he reigned twelve years. 2 And he did that which was evil in the sight of the Lord, only not as his father, nor as his mother: and he removed the pillars of Baal which his father had made. 3 Only he adhered to the sin of Jeroboam the son of Nabat, who made Israel to sin; he departed not from it. 4 And Mosa king of Moab was a sheep-master, and he rendered to the king of Israel in the beginning *of the year*, a hundred thousand lambs, and a hundred thousand rams, with the wool. 5 And it came to pass, after the death of Achaab, that the king of Moab rebelled against the king of Israel. 6 And king Joram went forth in that day out of Samaria, and numbered Israel. 7 And he went and sent to Josaphat king of Juda, saying, The king of Moab has rebelled against me: wilt thou go with me against Moab to war? And he said, I will go up: thou art as I, I am as thou;

as my people, so *is* thy people, as my horses, so *are* thy horses. 8 And he said, What way shall I go up? and he said, The way of the wilderness of Edom. 9 And the king of Israel went, and the king of Juda, and the king of Edom: and they fetched a compass of seven days' journey; and there was no water for the army, and for the cattle that went with them. 10 And the king of Israel said, Alas! that the Lord should have called the three kings on their way, to give them into the hand of Moab. 11 And Josaphat said, Is there not here a prophet of the Lord, that we may enquire of the Lord by him? And one of the servants of the king of Israel answered and said, *There is* here Elisaie son of Saphat, who poured water on the hands of Eliu. 12 And Josaphat said, He has the word of the Lord. And the king of Israel, and Josaphat king of Juda, and the king of Edom, went down to him. 13 And Elisaie said to the king of Israel, What have I to do with thee? go to the prophets of thy father, and the prophets of thy mother. And the king of Israel said to him, Has the Lord called the three kings to deliver them into the hands of Moab? 14 And Elisaie said, *As* the Lord of hosts before whom I stand lives, unless I regarded the presence of Josaphat the king of Juda, I would not have looked on thee, nor seen thee. 15 And now fetch me a harper. And it came to pass, as the harper harped, that the hand of the Lord came upon him. 16 And he said, Thus saith the Lord, Make this valley full of trenches. 17 For thus saith the Lord, Ye shall not see wind, neither shall ye see rain, yet this valley shall be filled with water, and ye, and your flocks, and your cattle shall drink. 18 And this *is* a light *thing* in the eyes of the Lord: I will also deliver Moab into your hand. 19 And ye shall smite every strong city, and ye shall cut down every good tree, and ye shall stop all wells of water, and spoil every good piece *of land* with stones. 20 And it came to pass in the morning, when the sacrifice was offered, that, behold! waters came from the way of Edom, and the land was filled with water. 21 And all Moab heard that the three kings were come up to fight against them; and they cried out on every *side, even* all that were girt with a girdle, and they said, Ho! and stood upon the border. 22 And they rose early in the morning, and the sun rose upon the waters, and Moab saw the waters on the opposite side red as blood. 23 And they said, This *is* the blood of the sword; and the kings have fought, and each man has smitten his neighbour; now then to the spoils, Moab. 24 And they entered into the camp of Israel; and Israel arose and smote Moab, and they fled from before them; and they went on and smote Moab as they went. 25 And they razed the cities, and cast every man his stone on every good piece *of land* and filled it; and they stopped every well, and cut down every good tree, until they left *only* the stones of the wall cast down; and the slingers compassed *the land*, and smote it. 26 And the king of Moab saw that the battle prevailed against him; and he took with him seven hundred men that drew sword, to cut through to the king of Edom: and they could not. 27 And he took his eldest son whom he had designed to reign in his stead, and offered him up for a whole-burnt-offering on the walls. And there was a great indignation against Israel; and they departed from him, and returned to their land.

4-Kgdms4 1 And one of the wives of the sons of the prophets cried to Elisaie, saying, Thy servant my husband is dead; and thou knowest that thy servant feared the Lord: and the creditor is come to take my two sons to be his servants. 2 And Elisaie said, What shall I do for thee? tell me what thou hast in the house. And she said, Thy servant has nothing in the house, except oil wherewith I anoint myself. 3 And he said to her, Go, borrow for thyself vessels without of all thy neighbours, *even* empty vessels; borrow not a few. 4 And thou shalt go in and shut the door upon thee and upon thy sons, and thou shalt pour forth into these vessels, and remove that which is filled. 5 And she departed from him, and shut the door upon herself and upon her sons: they brought the vessels near to her, and she poured in until the vessels were filled. 6 And she said to her sons, Bring me yet a vessel. And they said to her, There is not a vessel more. And the oil stayed. 7 And she came and told the man of God: and Elisaie said, Go, and sell the oil, and thou shalt pay thy debts, and thou and thy sons shall live of the remaining oil. 8 And a day came, when Elisaie passed over to Soman, and *there was* a great lady there, and she constrained him to eat bread: and it came to pass as often as he went into *the city, that* he turned aside to eat there. 9 And the woman said to her husband, See now, I know that this *is* a holy man of God who comes over continually to us. 10 Let us now make for him an upper chamber, a small place; and let us put there for him a bed, and a table, and a stool, and a candlestick: and it shall come to pass that when he comes in to us, he shall turn in thither. 11 And a day came, and he went in thither, and turned aside into the upper chamber, and lay there. 12 And he said to Giezi his servant, Call me this Somanite. and he called her, and she stood before him. 13 And he said to him, Say now to her, Behold, thou hast taken all this trouble for us; what should I do for thee? Hast thou any request *to make* to the king, or to the captain of the host? And she said, I dwell in the midst of my people. 14 And he said to Giezi, What must we do for her? and Giezi his servant said, Indeed she has no son, and her husband *is* old. 15 And he called her, and she stood by the door. 16 And Elisaie said to her, At this time *next year*, as the season *is*, thou *shalt be* alive, and embrace a son. And she said, Nay, my lord, do not lie to thy servant. 17 And the woman conceived, and bore a son at the very time, as the season was, being alive, as Elisaie said to her. 18 And the child grew: and it came to pass when he went out to his father to the reapers, 19 that he said to his father, My head, my head. and *his father* said to a servant, carry him to his mother. 20 And he˙ carried him to his mother, and he lay upon her knees till noon, and died. 21 And she carried him up and laid him on the bed of the man of god; and she shut the door upon him, and went out. 22 And she called her husband, and said, Send now for me one of the young men, and one of the asses, and I will ride quickly to the man of God, and return. 23 And he said, Why art thou going to him to-day? It is neither new moon, nor the Sabbath. And she said, *It is* well. 24 And she saddled the ass, and said to her servant, Be quick, proceed: spare not on my account to ride, unless I shall tell thee. Go, and thou shalt proceed, and come to the man of God to mount

Carmel. 25 And she rode and came to the man of God to the mountain: and it came to pass when Elisaie saw her coming, that he said to Giezi his servant, See now, that Somanite comes. 26 Now run to meet her, and thou shalt say, Is it well with thee? is it well with thy husband? is it well with the child? and she said, It is well. 27 And she came to Elisaie to the mountain, and laid hold of his feet; and Giezi drew near to thrust her away. And Elisaie said, Let her alone, for her soul is much grieved in her, and the Lord has hidden it from me, and has not told it me. 28 And she said, Did I ask a son of my lord? For did I not say, Do not deal deceitfully with me? 29 And Elisaie said to Giezi, Gird up thy loins, and take my staff in thy hand, and go: if thou meet any man, thou shalt not salute him, and if a man salute thee thou shalt not answer him: and thou shalt lay my staff on the child's face. 30 And the mother of the child said, As the Lord lives and as thy soul lives, I will not leave thee. And Elisaie arose, and went after her. 31 And Giezi went on before her, and laid his staff on the child's face: but there was neither voice nor any hearing. So he returned to meet him, and told him, saying, The child is not awaked. 32 And Elisaie went into the house, and, behold, the dead child was laid upon his bed. 33 And Elisaie went into the house, and shut the door upon themselves, the two, and prayed to the Lord. 34 And he went up, and lay upon the child, and put his mouth upon his mouth, and his eyes upon his eyes, and his hands upon his hands; and bowed himself upon him, and the flesh of the child grew warm. 35 And he returned, and walked up and down in the house: and he went up, and bowed himself on the child seven times; and the child opened his eyes. 36 And Elisaie cried out to Giezi, and said, Call this Somanite. So he called her, and she came in to him: and Elisaie said, Take thy son. 37 And the woman went in, and fell at his feet, and did obeisance bowing to the ground; and she took her son, and went out. 38 And Elisaie returned to Galgala: and a famine was in the land; and the sons of the prophets sat before him: and Elisaie said to his servant, Set on the great pot, and boil pottage for the sons of the prophets. 39 And he went out into the field to gather herbs, and found a vine in the field, and gathered of it wild gourds, his garment full; and he cast it into the caldron of pottage, for they knew them not. 40 And he poured it out for the men to eat: and it came to pass, when they were eating of the pottage, that lo! they cried out, and said, There is death in the pot, O man of God. And they could not eat. 41 And he said, Take meal, and cast it into the pot. And Elisaie said to his servant Giezi, Pour out for the people, and let them eat. And there was no longer there any hurtful thing in the pot. 42 And there came a man over from Baetharisa, and brought to the man of God twenty barley loaves and cakes of figs, of the first-fruits. And he said, Give to the people, and let them eat. 43 And his servant said, Why should I set this before a hundred men? and he said, Give to the people, and let them eat; for thus saith the Lord, They shall eat and leave. 44 And they ate and left, according to the word of the Lord.

4-Kgdms5 1 Now Naiman, the captain of the host of Syria, was a great man before his master, and highly respected, because by him the Lord had given deliverance to Syria, and the man was mighty in strength, but a leper. 2 And the Syrians went forth in small bands, and took captive out of the land of Israel a little maid: and she waited on Naiman's wife. 3 And she said to her mistress, O that my lord were before the prophet of God in Samaria; then he would recover him from his leprosy. 4 And she went in and told her lord, and said, Thus and thus spoke the maid from the land of Israel. 5 And the king of Syria said to Naiman, Go to, go, and I will send a letter to the king of Israel. And he went, and took in his hand ten talents of silver, and six thousand pieces of gold, and ten changes of raiment. 6 And he brought the letter to the king of Israel, saying, Now then, as soon as this letter shall reach thee, behold, I have sent to thee my servant Naiman, and thou shalt recover him from his leprosy. 7 And it came to pass, when the king of Israel read the letter, that he rent his garments, and said, Am I God, to kill and to make alive, that this man sends to me to recover a man of his leprosy? consider, however, I pray you, and see that this man seeks an occasion against me. 8 And it came to pass, when Elisaie heard that the king of Israel had rent his garments, that he sent to the king of Israel, saying, Wherefore hast thou rent thy garments? Let Naiman, I pray thee, come to me, and let him know that there is a prophet in Israel. 9 So Naiman came with horse and chariot, and stood at the door of the house of Elisaie. 10 And Elisaie sent a messenger to him, saying, Go and wash seven times in Jordan, and thy flesh shall return to thee, and thou shalt be cleansed. 11 And Naiman was angry, and departed, and said, Behold, I said, He will by all means come out to me, and stand, and call on the name of his God, and lay his hand upon the place, and recover the leper. 12 Are not the Abana and Pharphar, rivers of Damascus, better than all the waters of Israel? may I not go and wash in them, and be cleansed? and he turned and went away in a rage. 13 And his servants came near and said to him, Suppose the prophet had spoken a great thing to thee, wouldest thou not perform it? yet he has but said to thee, Wash, and be cleansed. 14 So Naiman went down, and dipped himself seven times in Jordan, according to the word of Elisaie: and his flesh returned to him as the flesh of a little child, and he was cleansed. 15 And he and all his company returned to Elisaie, and he came and stood before him, and said, Behold, I know that there is no God in all the earth, save only in Israel: and now receive a blessing of thy servant. 16 And Elisaie said, As the Lord lives, before whom I stand, I will not take one. And he pressed him to take one: but he would not. 17 And Naiman said, Well then, if not, let there be given to thy servant, I pray thee, the load of a yoke of mules; and thou shalt give me of the red earth: for henceforth thy servant will not offer whole-burnt-offering or sacrifice to other gods, but only to the Lord by reason of this thing. 18 And l let the Lord be propitious to thy servant when my master goes into the house of Remman to worship there, and he shall lean on my hand, and I shall bow down in the house of Remman when he bows down in the house of Remman; even let the Lord, I pray, be merciful to thy servant in this matter. 19 And Elisaie said to Naiman, Go in peace. And he departed from him a little way. 20 And Giezi the servant of Elisaie said, Behold, my Lord has spared this Syrian Naiman, so as not to take of his hand what he has brought: as the Lord lives, I will surely run after him, and take somewhat of him. 21 So Giezi followed after Naiman: and Naiman saw him running after him, and turned back from his chariot to meet him. 22 And *Giezi* said, All is well: my master has sent me, saying, Behold, now are there come to me two young men of the sons of the prophets from mount Ephraim; give them, I pray thee, a talent of silver, and two changes of raiment. 23 And *Naiman* said, Take two talents of silver. And he took two talents of silver in two bags, and two changes of raiment, and put them upon two of his servants, and they bore them before him. 24 And he came to a secret place, and took them from their hands, and laid them up in the house, and dismissed the men. 25 And he went in himself and stood before his master; and Elisaie said to him, 26 Whence *comest thou*, Giezi? and Giezi said, Thy servant has not been hither or thither. And Elisaie said to him, Went not my heart with thee, when the man returned from his chariot to meet thee? and now thou hast received silver, and now thou hast received raiment, and olive yards, and vineyards, and sheep, and oxen, and menservants, and maidservants. 27 The leprosy also of Naiman shall cleave to thee, and to thy seed for ever. And he went out from his presence leprous, like snow.

4-Kgdms6 1 And the sons of the prophets said to Elisaie, Behold now, the place wherein we dwell before thee is too narrow for us. 2 Let us go, we pray thee, unto Jordan, and take thence every man a beam, and make for ourselves a habitation there. 3 And he said, Go. And one of them said gently, Come with thy servants. And he said, I will go. 4 And he went with them, and they came to Jordan, and began to cut down wood. 5 And behold, one was cutting down a beam, and the axe head fell into the water: and he cried out, Alas! master: and it was hidden. 6 And the man of God said, Where did it fall? and he shewed him the place: and he broke off a stick, and threw it in there, and the iron came to the surface. 7 And he said, Take it up to thyself. And he stretched out his hand, and took it. 8 And the king of Syria was at war with Israel: and he consulted with his servants, saying, I will encamp in such a place. 9 And Elisaie sent to the king of Israel, saying, Take heed that thou pass not by that place, for the Syrians are hidden there. 10 And the king of Israel sent to the place which Elisaie mentioned to him, and saved himself thence not once or twice. 11 And the mind of the king of Syria was very much disturbed concerning this thing; and he called his servants, and said to them, Will ye not tell me who betrays me to the king of Israel? 12 And one of his servants said, Nay, my Lord, O king, for Elisaie the prophet that is in Israel reports to the king of Israel all the words whatsoever thou mayest say in thy bedchamber. 13 And he said, Go, see where this man *is*, and I will send and take him. And they sent word to him, saying, Behold, *he is* in Dothaim. 14 And he sent thither horses, and chariots, and a mighty host: and they came by night, and compassed about the city. 15 And the servant of Elisaie rose up early and went out; and, behold, a host compassed the city, and horses and chariots: and the servant said to him, O master, what shall we do? 16 And Elisaie said, Fear not, for they who are with us *are* more than they that are with them. 17 And Elisaie prayed, and said, Lord, open, I pray thee, the eyes of the servant, and let him see. And the Lord opened his eyes, and he saw: and, behold, the mountain *was* full of horses, and there were chariots of fire round about Elisaie. 18 And they came down to him; and he prayed to the Lord, and said, Smite, I pray thee, this people with blindness. And he smote them with blindness, according to the word of Elisaie. 19 And Elisaie said to them, This *is* not the city, and this *is* not the way: follow me, and I will bring you to the man whom ye seek. And he led them away to Samaria. 20 And it came to pass when they entered into Samaria, that Elisaie said, Open, I pray thee, O Lord, their eyes, and let them see. And the Lord opened their eyes, and they saw; and, behold, they were in the midst of Samaria. 21 And the king of Israel said to Elisaie, when he saw them, Shall I *not* verily smite them, *my* father? 22 And he said, Thou shalt not smite them, unless thou wouldest smite those whom thou hast taken captive with thy sword and with thy bow: set bread and water before them, and let them eat and drink, and depart to their master. 23 And he set before them a great feast, and they ate and drank: and he dismissed them and they departed to their master. And the bands of Syria came no longer into the land of Israel. 24 And it came to pass after this, that the son of Ader king of Syria gathered all his army, and went up, and besieged Samaria. 25 And there was a great famine in Samaria: and, behold, they besieged it, until an ass's head was *valued* at fifty pieces of silver, and the fourth part of a cab of dove's dung at five pieces of silver. 26 And the king of Israel was passing by on the wall, and a woman cried to him, saying, Help, my lord, O king. 27 And he said to her, Unless the Lord help thee, whence shall I help thee? from the corn-floor, or from the wine-press? 28 And the king said to her, What is *the matter* with thee? And the woman said to him, This *woman* said to me, Give thy son, and we will eat him to-day, and we will eat my son to-morrow. 29 So we boiled my son, and ate him; and I said to her on the second day, Give thy son, and let us eat him: and she has hidden her son. 30 And it came to pass, when the king of Israel heard the words of the woman, *that* he rent his garments; and he passed by on the wall, and the people saw sackcloth within upon his flesh. 31 And he said, God do so to me and more also, if the head of Elisaie shall stand upon him this day. 32 And Elisaie was sitting in his house, and the elders were sitting with him; and *the king* sent a man before him: before the messenger came to him, he also said to the elders, Do ye see that this son of a murderer has sent to take away my head? See, as soon as the messenger shall have come, shut the door, and forcibly detain him at the door: *is* not the sound of his master's feet behind him? 33 While he was yet speaking with them, behold, a messenger came to him: and he said, Behold, this evil *is* of the Lord; why should I wait for the Lord any longer?

4-Kgdms7 1 And Elisaie said, Hear thou the word of the Lord; Thus saith the Lord, As at this time, to- morrow a measure of fine flour *shall be sold* for a shekel, and two measures of barley for a shekel, in the gates of Samaria. 2 And the officer on whose hand the king rested, answered Elisaie, and said, Behold, *if* the Lord shall make flood-gates in heaven, might this thing be? and Elisaie said, Behold, thou shalt see with thine eyes, but shalt not eat thereof. 3 And there were four leprous men by the gate of the city: and one said to his neighbour, Why sit we here until we die? 4 If we should say, Let us go into the city, then *there is* famine in the city, and we shall die there: and if we sit here, then we shall die. Now then come, and let us fall upon the camp of the Syrians: if they should take us alive, then we shall live; and if they should put us to death, then we shall *only* die. 5 And they rose up while it was yet night, to go into the camp of Syria; and they came into a part of the camp of Syria, and behold, there *was* no man there. 6 For the Lord had made the army of Syria to hear a sound of chariots, and a sound of horses, *even* the sound of a great host: and *each* man said to his fellow, Now has the king of Israel hired against us the kings of the Chettites, and the kings of Egypt, to come against us. 7 And they arose and fled while it was yet dark, and left their tents, and their horses, and their asses in the camp, as they were, and fled for their lives. 8 And these lepers entered a little way into the camp, and went into one tent, and ate and drank, and took thence silver, and gold, and raiment; and they went and returned thence, and entered into another tent, and took thence, and went and hid *the spoil*. 9 And *one* man said to his neighbour, We are not doing *well* thus: this day is a day of glad tidings, and we hold our peace, and are waiting till the morning light, and shall find mischief: now them come, and let us go into *the city*, and report to the house of the king. 10 So they went and cried toward the gate of the city, and reported to them, saying, We went into the camp of Syria, and, behold, there is not there a man, nor voice of man, only horses tied and asses, and their tents as they were. 11 And the porters cried aloud, and reported to the house of the king within. 12 And the king rose up by night, and said to his servants, I will now tell you what the Syrians have done to us. They knew that we are hungry; and they have gone forth from the camp and hidden themselves in the field, saying, They will come out of the city, and we shall catch them alive, and go into the city. 13 And one of his servants answered and said, Let them now take five of the horses that were left, which were left here; behold, they are the number left to all the multitude of Israel; and we will send thither and see. 14 So they took two horsemen; and the king of Israel sent after the king of Syria, saying, Go, and see. 15 And they went after them even to Jordan: and, behold, all the way was full of garments and vessels, which the Syrians had cast away in their panic. and the messengers returned, and brought word to the king. 16 And the people went out, and plundered the camp of Syria: and a measure of fine flour was sold for a shekel, according to the word of the Lord, and two measures of barley for a shekel. 17 And the king appointed the officer on whose hand the king leaned *to have charge* over the gate: and the people trampled on him in the gate, and he died, as the man of God *had* said, who spoke when the messenger came down to him. 18 So it came to pass as Elisaie had spoken to the king, saying, Two measures of barley *shall be sold* for a shekel, and a measure of fine flour for a shekel; and it shall be as at this time to-morrow in the gate of Samaria. 19 And the officer answered Elisaie, and said, Behold, *if* the Lord makes flood-gates in heaven, shall this thing be? and Elisaie said, Behold, thou shalt see *it* with thine eyes, but thou shalt not eat thereof. 20 And it was so: for the people trampled on him in the gate, and he died.

4-Kgdms8 1 And Elisaie spoke to the woman, whose son he *had* restored to life, saying, Arise, and go thou and thy house, and sojourn wherever thou mayest sojourn: for the Lord has called for a famine upon the land; indeed it is come upon the land *for* seven years. 2 And the woman arose, and did according to the word of Elisaie, both she and her house; and they sojourned in the land of the Philistines seven years. 3 And it came to pass after the expiration of the seven years, that the woman returned out of the land of the Philistines to the city; and came to cry to the king for her house and for her lands. 4 And the king spoke to Giezi the servant of Elisaie the man of God, saying, Tell me, I pray thee, all the great things which Elisaie has done. 5 And it came to pass, as he was telling the king how he had restored to life the dead son, behold, the woman whose son Elisaie restored to life *came* crying to the king for her house and for her lands. And Giezi said, My lord, O king, this *is* the woman, and this *is* her son, whom Elisaie restored to life. 6 And the king asked the woman, and she told him: and the king appointed her a eunuch, saying, Restore all that was hers, and all the fruits of the field from the day that she left the land until now. 7 And Elisaie came to Damascus; and the king of Syria the son of Ader was ill, and they brought him word, saying, The man of God is come hither. 8 And the king said to Azael, Take in thine hand a present, and go to meet the man of God, and enquire of the Lord by him, saying, Shall I recover of this my disease? 9 And Azael went to meet him, and he took a present in his hand, and all the good things of Damascus, forty camels' load, and came and stood before him, and said to Elisaie, Thy son the son of Ader, the king of Syria, has sent me to thee to enquire, saying, Shall I recover of this my disease? 10 And Elisaie said, Go, say, Thou shalt certainly live; yet the Lord has shewed me that thou shalt surely die. 11 And he stood before him, and fixed *his countenance* till he was ashamed: and the man of God wept. 12 And Azael said, Why does my lord weep? And he said, Because I know all the evil that thou wilt do to the children of Israel: thou wilt utterly destroy their strong holds with fire, and thou wilt slay their choice men with the sword, and thou wilt dash their infants *against the ground*, and their women with child thou wilt rip up. 13 And Azael said, Who is thy servant? a dead dog, that he should do this thing? And Elisaie said, The Lord has shewn me thee ruling over Syria. 14 And he departed from Elisaie, and went in to his lord; and he said to him, What said Elisaie to thee? and he said, He said to me, Thou shalt surely live. 15 And it came to pass on the next day that he took a thick cloth, and dipped it in water, and put it on his face, and he died: and Azael reigned in his stead. 16 In the fifth year of Joram son of Achaab king of Israel, and while Josaphat was king of Juda, Joram the son of Josaphat king of Juda began to reign. 17 Thirty and two years old was he when he began to reign, and he reigned eight years in Jerusalem. 18 And he walked in the way of the kings of Israel, as did the house of Achaab; for the daughter of Achaab was his wife: and he did that which was evil in the sight of the Lord. 19 But the Lord would not destroy Juda for David his servant's sake, as he said he would give a light to him and to his sons continually. 20 In his days Edom revolted from under the hand of Juda, and they made a king over themselves. 21 And Joram went up to Sior, and all the chariots that were with him: and it came to pass after he had arisen, that he smote Edom who compassed him about, and the captains of the chariots; and the people fled to their tents. 22 Yet Edom revolted from under the hand of Juda till this day. Then Lobna revolted at that time. 23 And the rest of the acts of Joram, and all that he did, behold, are not these written in the book of the chronicles of the kings of Juda? 24 So Joram slept with his fathers, and was buried with his fathers in the city of his father David: and Ochozias his son reigned in his stead. 25 In the twelfth year of Joram son of Achaab king of Israel, Ochozias son of Joram began to reign. 26 Twenty and two years old was Ochozias when he began to reign, and he reigned one year in Jerusalem: and the name of his mother was Gotholia, daughter of Ambri king of Israel. 27 And he walked in the way of the house of Achaab, and did that which was evil in the sight of the Lord, as did the house of Achaab. 28 And he went with Joram the son of Achaab to war against Azael king of the Syrians in Remmoth Galaad; and the Syrians wounded Joram. 29 And king Joram returned to be healed in Jezrael of the wounds with which they wounded him in Remmoth, when he fought with Azael king of Syria. And Ochozias son of Joram went down to see Joram the son of Achaab in Jezrael, because he was sick.

4-Kgdms9 1 And Elisaie the prophet called one of the sons of the prophets, and said to him, Gird up thy loins, and take this cruse of oil in thy hand, and go to Remmoth Galaad. 2 And thou shalt enter there, and shalt see there Ju the son of Josaphat son of Namessi, and shalt go in and make him rise up from among his brethren, and shalt bring him into a secret chamber. 3 And thou shalt take the cruse of oil, and pour it on his head, and say thou, Thus saith the Lord, I have anointed thee king over Israel: and thou shalt open the door, and flee, and not tarry. 4 And the young man the prophet went to Remmoth Galaad. 5 And he went in, and, behold, the captains of the host were sitting; and he said, I have a message to thee, O captain. And Ju said, To which of all us? And he said, To thee, O captain. 6 And he arose, and went into the house: and he poured the oil upon his head, and said to him, Thus saith the Lord God of Israel, I have anointed thee to be king over the people of the Lord, even over Israel. 7 And thou shalt utterly destroy the house of Achaab thy master from before me, and shalt avenge the blood of my servants the prophets, and the blood of all the servants of the Lord, at the hand of Jezabel, 8 and at the hand of the whole house of Achaab: and thou shalt utterly cut off from the house of Achaab every male, and him that is shut up and left in Israel. 9 And I will make the house of Achaab like the house of Jeroboam the son of Nabat, and as the house of Baasa the son of Achia. 10 And the dogs shall eat Jezabel in the portion of Jezreel, and there shall be none to bury her. And he opened the door, and fled. 11 And Ju went forth to the servants of his lord, and they said to him, Is all well? Why came this mad fellow in to thee? And he said to them, Ye know the man, and his communication. 12 And they said, It is wrong: tell us now. And Ju said to them, Thus and thus spoke he to me, saying, —and he said, Thus saith the Lord, I have anointed thee to be king over Israel. 13 And when they heard it, they hasted, and took every man his garment, and put it under him on the top of the stairs, and blew with the trumpet, and said, Ju is king. 14 So Ju the son of Josaphat the son of Namessi conspired against Joram, and Joram was defending Remmoth Galaad, he and all Israel, because of Azael king of Syria. 15 And king Joram had returned to be healed in Jezrael of the wounds which the Syrians had given him, in his war with Azael king of Syria. And Ju said, If your heart is with me, let there not go forth out of the city one fugitive to go and report to Jezrael. 16 And Ju rode and advanced, and came down to Jezrael; for Joram king of Israel was getting healed in Jezrael of the arrow-wounds wherewith the Syrians had wounded him in Rammath in the war with Azael king of Syria; for he was strong and a mighty man: and Ochozias king of Juda was come down to see Joram. 17 And there went up a watchman upon the tower of Jezrael, and saw the dust made by Ju as he approached; and he said, I see dust. And Joram said, Take a horseman, and send to meet them, and let him say, Peace. 18 And there went a horseman to meet them, and said, Thus says the king, Peace. And Ju said, What hast thou to do with peace? turn behind me. And the watchman reported, saying, The messenger came up to them, and has not returned. 19 And he sent another horseman, and he came to him, and said, Thus says the king, Peace. And Ju said, What hast thou to do with peace? turn behind me. 20 And the watchman reported, saying, He came up to them, and has not returned: and the driver drives Ju the son of Namessi, for it is with furious haste. 21 And Joram said, Make ready. And one made ready the chariot: and Joram the king of Israel went forth, and Ochozias king of Juda, each in his chariot, and they went to meet Ju, and found him in the portion of Nabuthai the Jezraelite. 22 And it came to pass when Joram saw Ju, that he said, Is it peace, Ju? And Ju said, How can it be peace? as yet there are the whoredoms of thy mother Jezabel, and her abundant witchcrafts. 23 And Joram turned his hands, and fled, and said to Ochozias, Treachery, Ochozias. 24 And Ju bent his bow with his full strength, and smote Joram between his arms, and his arrow went out at his heart, and he bowed upon his knees. 25 And Ju said to Badecar his chief officer, Cast him into the portion of ground of Nabuthai the Jezraelite, for I and thou remember, riding as we were on chariots after Achaab his father, that the Lord took up this burden against him, saying, 26 Surely, I have seen yesterday the blood of Nabuthai, and the blood of his sons, saith the Lord; and I will recompense him in this portion, saith the Lord. Now then, I pray thee, take him up and cast him into the portion, according to the word of the Lord. 27 And Ochozias king of Juda saw *it*, and fled by the way of Baethgan. And Ju pursued after him, and said, *Slay* him also. And one smote him in the chariot at the going up of Gai, which is Jeblaam: and he fled to Mageddo, and died there. 28 And his servants put him on a chariot, and brought him to Jerusalem, and they buried him in his sepulchre in the city of David. 29 And in the eleventh year of Joram king of Israel, Ochozias began to reign over Juda. 30 And Ju came to Jezrael; and Jezabel heard *of it*, and coloured her eyes, and adorned her head, and looked through the window. 31 And Ju entered into the city; and she said, Had Zambri, the murderer of his master, peace? 32 And he lifted up his face toward the window, and saw her, and said, Who art thou? Come down with me. And two eunuchs looked down towards him. 33 And he said, Throw her *down*. And they threw her *down*; and some of her blood was sprinkled on the wall, and on the horses: and they trampled on her. 34 And *Ju* went in and ate and drank, and said, Look now, after this cursed woman, and bury her, for she is a king's daughter. 35 And they went to bury her; but they found nothing of her but the skull, and the feet, and the palms of her hands. 36 And they returned and told him. And he said, *It is* the word of the Lord, which he spoke by the hand of Eliu the Thesbite, saying, In the portion of Jezrael shall the dogs eat the flesh of Jezabel. 37 And the carcass of Jezabel shall be as dung on the face of the field in the portion of Jezrael, so that they shall not say, *This is* Jezabel.

4-Kgdms10 1 And Achaab *had* seventy sons in Samaria. And Ju wrote a letter, and sent it into Samaria to the rulers of Samaria, and to the elders, and to the guardians of *the children of* Achaab, saying. 2 Now then, as soon as this letter shall have reached you, whereas *there are* with you the sons of your master, and with you chariots and horses, and strong cities, and arms, 3 do ye accordingly look out the best and fittest among your master's sons, and set him on the throne of his father, and fight for the house of your master. 4 And they feared greatly, and said, Behold, two kings stood not before him: and how shall we stand? 5 So they that were over the house, and they that were over the city, and the elders and the guardians, sent to Ju, saying, We also *are* thy servants, and whatsoever thou shalt say to us we will do; we will not make *any* man king: we will do that which is right in thine eyes. 6 And Ju wrote them a second letter, saying, If ye *are* for me, and hearken to my voice, take the heads of the men your master's sons, and bring *them* to me at this time to-morrow in Jezrael. Now the sons of the king were seventy men; these great men of the city brought them up. 7 And it came to pass, when the letter came to them, that they took the king's sons, and slew them, *even* seventy men, and put their heads in baskets, and sent them to him at Jezrael. 8 And a messenger came and told *him*, saying, They have brought the heads of the king's sons. And he said, Lay them *in* two heaps by the door of the gate until the morning. 9 And the morning came, and he went forth, and stood, and said to all the people, Ye are righteous: behold, I conspired against my master, and slew him: but who slew all these? 10 See now that there shall not fall to the ground anything of the word of the Lord which the Lord spoke against the house of Achaab: for the Lord has performed all that he spoke of by the hand of his servant Eliu. 11 And Ju smote all that were left of the house of Achaab in Jezrael, and all his great men, and his acquaintance, and his priests, so as not to leave him *any* remnant. 12 And he arose and went to Samaria, *and* he *was* in the house of sheep-shearing in the way. 13 And Ju found the brethren of Ochozias king of Juda, and said, Who *are* ye? And they said, We *are* the brethren of Ochozias, and we have come down to salute the sons of the king, and the sons of the queen. 14 And he said, Take them alive. And they slew them at the shearing-house, forty and two men: he left not a man of them. 15 And he went thence and found Jonadab the son of Rechab *coming* to meet him; and he saluted him, and Ju said to him, Is thy heart right with my heart, as my heart *is* with thy heart? And Jonadab said, It is. And Ju said, If it is then, give me thy hand. And he gave him his hand, and he took him up to him into the chariot. 16 And he said to him, Come with me, and see me zealous for the Lord. And he caused him to sit in his chariot. 17 And he entered into Samaria, and smote all that were left of Achaab in Samaria, until he had utterly destroyed him, according to the word of the Lord, which he spoke to Eliu. 18 And Ju gathered all the people, and said to them, Achaab served Baal a little; Ju shall serve him much. 19 Now then do all *ye* the prophets of Baal call all his servants and his priests to me; let not a man be wanting: for I have a great sacrifice *to offer* to Baal; every one who shall be missing shall die. But Ju did it in subtilty, that he might destroy the servants of Baal. 20 And Ju said, Sanctify a solemn festival to Baal, and they made a proclamation. 21 And Ju sent throughout all Israel, saying, Now then let all *Baal's* servants, and all his priests, and all his prophets *come*, let none be lacking: for I am going to offer a great sacrifice; whosoever shall be missing, shall not live. So all the servants of Baal came, and all his priests, and all his prophets: there was not one left who came not. And they entered into the house of Baal; and the house of Baal was filled from one end to the other. 22 And he said to the man who was over the house of the wardrobe, Bring forth a robe for all the servants of Baal. And the keeper of the robes brought forth to them. 23 And Ju and Jonadab the son of Rechab entered into the house of Baal, and said to the servants of Baal, Search, and see whether there is among you any of the servants of the Lord, or only the servants of Baal, by themselves. 24 And he went in to offer sacrifices and whole-burnt-offerings; and Ju set for himself eighty men without, and said, Every man who shall escape of the men whom I bring into your hand, the life of him *that spares him* shall go for his life. 25 And it came to pass, when he had finished offering the whole-burnt-offering, that Ju said to the footmen and to the officers, Go ye in and slay them; let not a man of them escape. So they smote them with the edge of the sword, and the footmen and the officers cast *the bodies* forth, and went to the city of the house of Baal. 26 And they brought out the pillar of Baal, and burnt it. 27 And they tore down the pillars of Baal, and made his house a draught-house until this day. 28 So Ju abolished Baal out of Israel. 29 Nevertheless Ju departed not from following the sins of Jeroboam the son of Nabat, who led Israel to sin: *these were* the golden heifers in Baethel and in Dan. 30 And the Lord said to Ju, Because of all thy deeds wherein thou hast acted well in doing that which was right in my eyes, according to all things which thou hast done to the house of Achaab *as they were* in my heart, thy sons to the fourth generation shall sit upon the throne of Israel. 31 But Ju took no heed to walk in the law of the Lord God of Israel with all his heart: he departed not from following the sins of Jeroboam, who made Israel to sin. 32 In those days the Lord began to cut Israel short; and Azael smote them in every coast of Israel; 33 from Jordan eastward all the land of Galaad belonging to the Gadites, of Gaddi and that of Ruben, and of Manasses, from Aroer, which is on the brink of the brook of Arnon, and Galaad and Basan. 34 And the rest of the acts of Ju, and all that he did, and all his might, and the wars wherein he engaged, *are* not these things written in the book of the chronicles of the kings of Israel? 35 And Ju slept with his fathers; and they buried him in Samaria: and Joachaz his son reigned in his stead. 36 And the days which Ju reigned over Israel *were* twenty-eight years in Samaria.

4-Kgdms11 1 And Gotholia the mother of Ochozias saw that her son was dead, and she destroyed all the seed royal. 2 And Josabee daughter of king Joram, sister of Ochozias, took Joas the son of her brother, and stole him from among the king's sons that were put to death, *secreting* him and his nurse in the bedchamber, and hid him from the face of Gotholia, and he was not slain. 3 And he remained with her hid in the house of the Lord six years: and Gotholia reigned over the land. 4 And in the seventh year Jodae sent and took the captains of hundreds of the Chorri and of the Rhasim, and brought them to him into the house of the Lord, and made a covenant of the Lord with them, and adjured them, and Jodae shewed them the king's son. 5 And charged them, saying, This *is* the thing which ye shall do. 6 Let a third part of you go in *on* the sabbath-day, and keep ye the watch of the king's house in the porch; and another third in the gate of the high way, and a third at the gate behind the footmen; and keep ye the guard of the house. 7 And there *shall be* two parties among you, even every one that goes out on the Sabbath, and they shall keep the guard of the Lord's house before the king. 8 And do ye compass the king about every man with his weapon in his hand, and he that goes into the ranges shall die: and they shall be with the king in his going out and in his coming in. 9 And the captains of hundreds did all things that the wise Jodae commanded; and they took each his men, both those that went in on the sabbath-day, and those that went out on the sabbath-day, and went in to Jodae the priest. 10 And the priest gave to the captains of hundreds the swords and spears of king David that were in the house of the Lord. 11 And the footmen stood each with his weapon in his hand from the right corner of the house to the left corner of the house, *by* the altar and the house round about the king. 12 And he brought forth the king's son, and put upon him the crown and *gave him* the

testimony; and he made him king, and anointed him: and they clapped *their* hands, and said, Long live the king. 13 And Gotholia heard the sound of the people running, and she went in to the people to the house of the Lord. 14 And she looked, and, behold, the king stood near a pillar according to the manner; and the singers and the trumpeters were before the king and all the people of the land *even* rejoicing and sounding with trumpets: and Gotholia rent her garments, and cried, A conspiracy, a conspiracy. 15 And Jodae the priest commanded the captains of hundreds who were over the host, and said to them, Bring her forth without the ranges, *and* he that goes in after her shall certainly die by the sword. For the priest said, Let her not however be slain in the house of the Lord. 16 And they laid hands upon her, and went in by the way of the horses' entrance into the house of the Lord, and she was slain there. 17 And Jodae made a covenant between the Lord and the king and the people, that they should be the Lord's people; also between the king and the people. 18 And all the people of the land went into the house of Baal, and tore it down, and completely broke in pieces his altars and his images, and they slew Mathan the priest of Baal before the altars. And the priest appointed overseers over the house of the Lord. 19 And he took the captains of the hundreds, and the Chorri, and the Rhasim, and all the people of the land, and brought down the king out of the house of the Lord; and they went in by the way of the gate of the footmen of the king's house, and seated him there on the throne of the kings. 20 And all the people of the land rejoiced, and the city was at rest: and they slew Gotholia with the sword in the house of the king. 21 Joas *was* seven years old when he began to reign.

4-Kgdms12 1 Joas began to reign in the seventh year of Ju, and he reigned forty years in Jerusalem: and his mother's name *was* Sabia of Bersabee. 2 And Joas did that which was right in the sight of the Lord all the days that Jodae the priest instructed him. 3 Only there were not *any* of the high places removed, and the people still sacrificed there, and burned incense on the high places. 4 And Joas said to the priests, *As for* all the money of the holy things that is brought into the house of the Lord, the money of valuation, *as* each man brings the money of valuation, all the money which any man may feel disposed to bring into the house of the Lord, 5 let the priests take it to themselves, every man from *the proceeds of* his sale: and they shall repair the breaches of the house in all *places* wheresoever a breach shall be found. 6 And it came to pass in the twenty-third year of king Joas the priests *had* not repaired the breaches of the house. 7 And king Joas called Jodae the priest, and the *other* priests, and said to them, Why have ye not repaired the breaches of the house? now then receive no *more* money from your sales, for ye shall give it to *repair the* breaches of the house. 8 And the priests consented to receive no more money of the people, and not to repair the breaches of the house. 9 And Jodae the priest took a chest, and bored a hole in the lid of it, and set it by the altar in the house of a man *belonging to* the house of the Lord, and the priests that kept the door put *therein* all the money that was found in the house of the Lord. 10 And it came to pass, when they saw that *there was* much money in the chest, that the king's scribe and the high priest went up, and they tied up and counted the money that was found in the house of the Lord. 11 And they gave the money that had been collected into the hands of them that wrought the works, the overseers of the house of the Lord; and they gave it out to the carpenters and to the builders that wrought in the house of the Lord. 12 And to the masons, and to the hewers of stone, to purchase timber and hewn stone to repair the breaches of the house of the Lord, for all that was spent on the house of the Lord to repair *it*. 13 Only there were not to be made for the house of the Lord silver plates, studs, bowls, or trumpets, any vessel of gold or vessel of silver, of the money that was brought into the house of the Lord: 14 for they were to give it to the workmen, and they repaired therewith the house of the Lord. 15 Also they took no account of the men into whose hands they gave the money to give to the workmen, for they acted faithfully. 16 Money for a sin-offering, and money for a trespass-offering, whatever happened to be brought into the house of the Lord, went to the priests. 17 Then went up Azael king of Syria, and fought against Geth, and took it: and Azael set his face to go against Jerusalem. 18 And Joas king of Juda took all the holy things which Josaphat, and Joram, Ochozias, his fathers, and kings of Juda *had* consecrated, and what he had himself dedicated, and all the gold that was found in the treasures of the Lord's house and the king's house, and he sent *them* to Azael king of Syria; and he went up from Jerusalem. 19 And the rest of the acts of Joas, and all that he did, behold, *are* not these things written in the book of the chronicles of the kings of Juda? 20 And his servants rose up and made a conspiracy, and smote Joas in the house of Mallo that is in Sela. 21 And Jezirchar the son of Jemuath, and Jezabuth Somer's son, his servants, smote him, and he died; and they buried him with his fathers in the city of David: and Amessias his son reigned in his stead.

4-Kgdms13 1 In the twenty-third year of Joas son of Ochozias king of Juda began Joachaz the son of Ju to reign in Samaria, *and he reigned* seventeen years. 2 And he did that which was evil in the sight of the Lord, and walked after the sins of Jeroboam the son of Nabat, who led Israel to sin; he departed not from them. 3 And the Lord was very angry with Israel, and delivered them into the hand of Azael king of Syria, and into the hand of the son of Ader son of Azael, all their days. 4 And Joachaz besought the Lord, and the Lord hearkened to him, for he saw the affliction of Israel, because the king of Syria afflicted them. 5 And the Lord gave deliverance to Israel, and they escaped from under the hand of Syria: and the children of Israel dwelt in their tents as heretofore. 6 Only they departed not from the sins of the house of Jeroboam, who led Israel to sin: they walked in them—moreover the grove also remained in Samaria. 7 Whereas there was not left any army to Joachaz, except fifty horsemen, and ten chariots, and ten thousand infantry: for the king of Syria had destroyed them, and they made them as dust for trampling. 8 And the rest of the acts of Joachaz, and all that he did, and his mighty acts *are* not

these things written in the book of the chronicles of the kings of Israel? 9 And Joachaz slept with his fathers, and they buried him in Samaria: and Joas his son reigned in his stead. 10 In the thirty-seventh year of Joas king of Juda, Joas the son of Joachaz began to reign over Israel in Samaria sixteen years. 11 And he did that which was evil in the sight of the Lord; he departed not from all the sin of Jeroboam the son of Nabat, who led Israel to sin: he walked in it. 12 And the rest of the acts of Joas, and all that he did, and his mighty acts which he performed together with Amessias king of Juda, *are* not these written in the book of the chronicles of the kings of Israel? 13 And Joas slept with his fathers, and Jeroboam sat upon his throne, and he was buried in Samaria with the kings of Israel. 14 Now Elisaie was sick of his sickness, whereof he died: and Joas king of Israel went down to him, and wept over his face, and said, *My* father, *my* father, the chariot of Israel, and the horseman thereof! 15 And Elisaie said to him, Take bow and arrows. And he took to himself a bow and arrows. 16 And he said to the king, Put thy hand on the bow. And Joas put his hand upon *it*: and Elisaie put his hands upon the king's hands. 17 And he said, Open the window eastward. And he opened it. And Elisaie said, Shoot. And he shot. And *Elisaie* said, The arrow of the Lord's deliverance, and the arrow of deliverance from Syria; and thou shalt smite the Syrians in Aphec until thou have consumed them. 18 And Elisaie said to him, Take bow and arrows. And he took them. And *he* said to the king of Israel, Smite upon the ground. And the king smote three times, and stayed. 19 And the man of God was grieved at him, and said, If thou hadst smitten five or six times, then thou shouldest have smitten Syria till thou hadst consumed them; but now thou shalt smite Syria *only* thrice. 20 And Elisaie died, and they buried him. And the bands of the Moabites came into the land, at the beginning of the year. 21 And it came to pass as they were burying a man, that behold, they saw a band *of men*, and they cast the man into the grave of Elisaie: and as soon as he touched the bones of Elisaie, he revived and stood up on his feet. 22 And Azael greatly afflicted Israel all the days of Joachaz. 23 And the Lord had mercy and compassion upon them, and had respect to them because of his covenant with Abraam, and Isaac, and Jacob; and the Lord would not destroy them, and did not cast them out from his presence. 24 And Azael king of Syria died, and the son of Ader his son reigned in his stead. 25 And Joas the son of Joachaz returned, and took the cities out of the hand of the son of Ader the son of Azael, which he had taken out of the hand of Joachaz his father in the war: thrice did Joas smite him, and he recovered the cities of Israel.

4-Kgdms14 1 In the second year of Joas the son of Joachaz king of Israel, did Amessias also the son of Joas the king of Juda begin to reign. 2 Twenty and five years old was he when he began to reign, and he reigned twenty and nine years in Jerusalem: and his mother's name *was* Joadim of Jerusalem. 3 And he did that which was right in the sight of the Lord, but not as David his father: he did according to all things that his father Joas did. 4 Only he removed not the high places: as yet the people sacrificed and burnt incense on the high places. 5 And it came to pass when the kingdom was established in his hand, that he slew his servants that had slain the king his father. 6 But he slew not the sons of those that had slain him; according as it is written in the book of the laws of Moses, as the Lord gave commandment, saying, The fathers shall not be put to death for the children, and the children shall not be put to death for the fathers; but every one shall die for his own sins. 7 He smote of Edom ten thousand in the valley of salt, and took the Rock in the war, and called its name Jethoel until this day. 8 Then Amessias sent messengers to Joas son of Joachaz son of Ju king of Israel, saying, Come, let us look one another in the face. 9 And Joas the king of Israel sent to Amessias king of Juda, saying, The thistle that was in Libanus sent to the cedar that was in Libanus, saying, Give my daughter to thy son to wife: and the wild beasts of the field that were in Libanus passed by and trod down the thistle. 10 Thou hast smitten and wounded Edom, and thy heart has lifted thee up: stay at home and glorify thyself; for wherefore art thou quarrelsome to thy hurt? So *both* thou wilt fall and Juda with thee. 11 Nevertheless Amessias hearkened not: so Joas king of Israel went up, and he and Amessias king of Juda looked one another in the face in Baethsamys of Juda. 12 And Juda was overthrown before Israel, and *every* man fled to his tent. 13 And Joas king of Israel took Amessias the son of Joas the son of Ochozias, in Baethsamys; and he came to Jerusalem, and broke down the wall of Jerusalem, *beginning* at the gate of Ephraim as far as the gate of the corner, four hundred cubits. 14 And he took the gold, and the silver, and all the vessels that were found in the house of the Lord, and in the treasures of the king's house, and the hostages, and returned to Samaria. 15 And the rest of the acts of Joas, *even* all that he did in his might, how he warred with Amessias king of Juda, are not these things written in the book of the chronicles of the kings of Israel? 16 And Joas slept with his fathers, and was buried in Samaria with the kings of Israel; and Jeroboam his son reigned in his stead. 17 And Amessias the son of Joas king of Juda lived after the death of Joas son of Joachaz king of Israel fifteen years. 18 And the rest of the acts of Amessias, and all that he did, *are* not these written in the book of the chronicles of the kings of Juda? 19 And they formed a conspiracy against him in Jerusalem, and he fled to Lachis: and they sent after him to Lachis, and slew him there. 20 And they brought him upon horses; and he was buried in Jerusalem with his fathers in the city of David. 21 And all the people of Juda took Azarias, and he was sixteen years old, and made him king in the room of his father Amessias. 22 He built Æloth, and restored it to Juda, after the king slept with his fathers. 23 In the fifteenth year of Amessias son of Joas king of Juda began Jeroboam son of Joas to reign over Israel in Samaria forty and one years. 24 And he did that which was evil in the sight of the Lord: he departed not from all the sins of Jeroboam the son of Nabat, who led Israel to sin. 25 He recovered the coast of Israel from the entering in of Æmath to the sea of Araba, according to the word of the Lord God of Israel, which he spoke by his servant Jonas the son of Amathi, the prophet of Gethchopher. 26 For the Lord saw *that* the affliction of Israel *was* very bitter, and that they were few in number, straitened and in want, and destitute, and Israel had no helper. 27 And the Lord said that he would not blot out the seed of Israel from under heaven; so he delivered them by the hand of Jeroboam the son of Joas. 28 And the rest of the acts of Jeroboam and all that he did, and his mighty deeds, which he achieved in war, and how he recovered Damascus and Æmath to Juda in Israel, *are* not these things written in the book of the chronicles of the kings of Israel? 29 And Jeroboam slept with his fathers, even with the kings of Israel; and Zacharias his son reigned in his stead.

4-Kgdms15 1 In the twenty-seventh year of Jeroboam king of Israel Azarias the son of Amessias king of Juda began to reign. 2 Sixteen years old was he when he began to reign, and he reigned fifty- two years in Jerusalem: and his mother's name was Jechelia of Jerusalem. 3 And he did that which was right in the eyes of the Lord, according to all things that Amessias his father did. 4 Only he took not away *any* of the high places: as yet the people sacrificed and burnt incense on the high places. 5 And the Lord plagued the king, and he was leprous till the day of his death; and he reigned in a separate house. And Joatham the king's son *was* over the household, judging the people of the land. 6 And the rest of the acts of Azarias, and all that he did, *are* not these written in the book of the chronicles of the kings of Juda? 7 And Azarias slept with his fathers, and they buried him with his fathers in the city of David: and Joatham his son reigned in his stead. 8 In the thirty and eighth year of Azarias king of Juda Zacharias the son of Jeroboam began to reign over Israel in Samaria six months. 9 And he did that which was evil in the eyes of the Lord, as his fathers had done: he departed not from all the sins of Jeroboam the son of Nabat, who made Israel to sin. 10 And Sellum the son of Jabis *and others* conspired against him, and they smote him *in* Keblaam, and slew him, and he reigned in his stead. 11 And the rest of the acts of Zacharias, behold, they are written in the book of the chronicles of the kings of Israel. 12 *This was* the word of the Lord which he spoke to Ju, saying, Thy sons of the fourth generation shall sit upon the throne of Israel: and it was so. 13 And Sellum the son of Jabis reigned: and in the thirty and ninth year of Azarias king of Juda began Sellum to reign a full month in Samaria. 14 And Manaem the son of Gaddi went up out of Tharsila, and came to Samaria, and smote Sellum the son of Jabis in Samaria, and slew him. 15 And the rest of the acts of Sellum, and his conspiracy wherein he was engaged, behold, they are written in the book of the chronicles of the kings of Israel. 16 Then Manaem smote both Thersa and all that was in it, and its borders extending beyond Thersa, because they opened not to him: and he smote it, and ripped up the women with child. 17 In the thirty and ninth year of Azarias king of Juda began Manaem the son of Gaddi to reign over Israel in Samaria ten years. 18 And he did that which was evil in the sight of the Lord: he departed not from all the sins of Jeroboam the son of Nabat, who led Israel to sin. 19 In his days went up Phua king of the Assyrians against the land: and Manaem gave to Phua a thousand talents of silver to aid him with his power. 20 And Manaem raised the silver *by a tax* upon Israel, even on every mighty man in wealth, to give to the king of the Assyrians, fifty shekels *levied* on each man; and the king of the Assyrians departed, and remained not there in the land. 21 And the rest of the acts of Manaem, and all that he did, behold, are not these written in the book of the chronicles of the kings of Israel? 22 And Manaem slept with his fathers; and Phakesias his son reigned in his stead. 23 In the fiftieth year of Azarias king of Juda, began Phakesias the son of Manaem to reign over Israel in Samaria two years. 24 And he did that which was evil in the sight of the Lord: he departed not from the sins of Jeroboam the son of Nabat, who made Israel to sin. 25 And Phakee the son of Romelias, his officer, conspired against him, and smote him in Samaria in the front of the king's house, with Argob and Aria, and with him *there were* fifty men of the four hundred: and he slew him, and reigned in his stead. 26 And the rest of the acts of Phakesias, and all that he did, behold, they are written in the book of the chronicles of the kings of Israel. 27 In the fifty-second year of Azarias king of Juda began Phakee the son of Romelias to reign over Israel in Samaria twenty years. 28 And he did that which was evil in the eyes of the Lord: he departed not from all the sins of Jeroboam the son of Nabat, who led Israel to sin. 29 In the days of Phakee king of Israel came Thalgath-phellasar king of the Assyrians, and took Ain, and Abel, and Thamaacha, and Anioch, and Kenez, and Asor, and Galaa, and Galilee, *even* all the land of Nephthali, and carried them away to the Assyrians. 30 And Osee son of Ela formed a conspiracy against Phakee the son of Romelias, and smote him, and slew him, and reigned in his stead, in the twentieth year of Joatham the son of Azarias. 31 And the rest of the acts of Phakee, and all that he did, behold, these *are* written in the book of the chronicles of the kings of Israel. 32 In the second year of Phakee son of Romelias king of Israel began Joatham the son of Azarias king of Juda to reign. 33 Twenty and five years old was he when he began to reign, and he reigned sixteen years in Jerusalem: and his mother's name *was* Jerusa daughter of Sadoc. 34 And he did that which was right in the sight of the Lord, according to all things that his father Azarias did. 35 Nevertheless he took not away the high places: as yet the people sacrificed and burnt incense on the high places. He built the upper gate of the Lord's house. 36 And the rest of the acts of Joatham, and all that he did, *are* not these written in the book of the chronicles of the kings of Juda? 37 In those days the Lord began to send forth against Juda Raasson king of Syria, and Phakee son of Romelias. 38 And Joatham slept with his fathers, and was buried with his fathers in the city of David his father: and Achaz his son reigned in his stead.

4-Kgdms16 1 In the seventeenth year of Phakee son of Romelias began Achaz the son of Joatham king of Juda to reign. 2 Twenty years old was Achaz when he began to reign, and he reigned sixteen years in Jerusalem; and he did not that which was right in the eyes of the Lord his God faithfully, as David his father *had done*. 3 And he walked in the way of the kings of Israel, yea, he made his son to pass through the fire, according to the abominations of the heathen whom the Lord cast out from before the children of Israel. 4 And he sacrificed and burnt incense on the high places, and upon the hills, and under every shady tree. 5 Then went up Raasson king of Syria and Phakee son of Romelias king of Israel against Jerusalem to war, and besieged Achaz, but could not prevail *against him*. 6 At that time Raasson king of Syria recovered Ælath to Syria, and drove out the Jews from Ælath, and the Idumeans came to Ælath, and dwelt there until this day. 7 And Achaz sent messengers to Thalgath-phellasar king of the Assyrians, saying, I am thy servant and thy son: come up, deliver me out of the hand of the king of Syria, and out of the hand of the king of Israel, who are rising up against me. 8 And Achaz took the silver and the gold that was found in the treasures of the house of the Lord, and of the king's house, and sent gifts to the king. 9 And the king of the Assyrians hearkened to him: and the king of the Assyrians went up to Damascus and took it, and removed the inhabitants, and slew king Raasson. 10 And king Achaz went to Damascus to meet Thalgath-phellasar king of the Assyrians at Damascus; and he saw an altar at Damascus. And king Achaz sent to Urias the priest the pattern of the altar, and its proportions, and all its workmanship. 11 And Urias the priest built the altar, according to all *the directions* which king Achaz sent from Damascus. 12 And the king saw the altar, and went up to it, 13 and offered his whole-burnt-offering, and his meat-offering, and his drink-offering, and poured out the blood of his peace-offerings on the brazen altar that was before the Lord. 14 And he brought forward *the one* before the house of the Lord from between the altar and the house of the Lord, and he set it openly by the side of the altar northwards. 15 And king Achaz charged Urias the priest, saying, Offer upon the great altar the whole-burnt-offering in the morning and the meat-offering in the evening, and the whole-burnt-offering of the king, and his meat-offering, and the whole-burnt-offering of all the people, and their meat-offering, and their drink-offering; and thou shalt pour all the blood of the whole-burnt-offering, and all the blood of *any other* sacrifice upon it: and the brazen altar shall be for me in the morning. 16 And Urias the priest did according to all that king Achaz commanded him. 17 And king Achaz cut off the borders of the bases, and removed the laver from off them, and took down the sea from the brazen oxen that were under it, and set it upon a base of stone. 18 And he made a base for the throne in the house of the Lord, and he turned the king's entrance without in the house of the Lord because of the king of the Assyrians. 19 And the rest of the acts of Achaz, even all that he did, *are* not these written in the book of the chronicles of the kings of Juda? 20 And Achaz slept with his fathers, and was buried in the city of David: and Ezekias his son reigned in his stead.

4-Kgdms17 1 In the twelfth year of Achaz king of Juda began Osee the son of Ela to reign in Samaria over Israel nine years. 2 And he did evil in the eyes of the Lord, only not as the kings of Israel that were before him. 3 Against him came up Salamanassar king of the Assyrians; and Osee became his servant, and rendered him tribute. 4 And the king of the Assyrians found iniquity in Osee, in that he sent messengers to Segor king of Egypt, and brought not a tribute to the king of the Assyrians in that year: and the king of the Assyrians besieged him, and bound him in the prison-house. 5 And the king of the Assyrians went up against all the land, and went up to Samaria, and besieged it *for* three years. 6 In the ninth year of Osee the king of the Assyrians took Samaria, and carried Israel away to the Assyrians, and settled them in Alae, and in Abor, *near the* rivers of Gozan, and *in* the mountains of the Medes. 7 For it came to pass that the children of Israel *had* transgressed against the Lord their God, who had brought them up out of the land of Egypt, from under the hand of Pharao king of Egypt, and they feared other gods, 8 and walked in the statutes of the nations which the Lord cast out before the face of the children of Israel, and of the kings of Israel as many as did *such things*, 9 and *in those* of the children of Israel as many as secretly practised customs, not as *they should have done*, against the Lord their God: 10 and they built for themselves high places in all their cities, from the tower of the watchmen to the fortified city. And they made for themselves pillars and groves on every high hill, and under every shady tree. 11 And burned incense there on all high places, as the nations *did* whom the Lord removed from before them, and dealt with familiar spirits, and they carved *images* to provoke the Lord to anger. 12 And they served the idols, of which the Lord said to them, Ye shall not do this thing *against* the Lord. 13 And the Lord testified against Israel and against Juda, even by the hand of all his prophets, *and* of every seer, saying, Turn ye from your evil ways, and keep my commandments and my ordinances, and all the law which I commanded your fathers, *and* all that I sent to them by the hand of my servants the prophets. 14 But they hearkened not, and made their neck harder than the neck of their fathers. 15 And they kept not any of his testimonies which he charged them; and they walked after vanities, and became vain, and after the nations round about them, concerning which the Lord had charged them not to do accordingly. 16 They forsook the commandments of the Lord their God, and made themselves graven images, *even* two heifers, and they made groves, and worshipped all the host of heaven, and served Baal. 17 And they caused their sons and their daughters to pass through the fire, and used divinations and auspices, and sold themselves to work wickedness in the sight of the Lord, to provoke him. 18 And the Lord was very angry with Israel, and removed them out of his sight; and there was only left the tribe of Juda quite alone. 19 Nay even Juda kept not the commandments of the Lord their God, but they walked according to the customs of Israel which they practised, and rejected the Lord. 20 And the Lord was angry with the whole seed of Israel, and troubled them, and gave them into the hand of them that spoiled them, until he cast them out of his presence. 21 Forasmuch as Israel revolted from the house of David, and they made Jeroboam the son of Nabat king: and Jeroboam drew off Israel from following the Lord, and led them to sin a great sin. 22 And the children of Israel walked in all the sin of Jeroboam which he committed; they departed not from it, 23 until the Lord removed Israel from his presence, as the Lord spoke by all his servants the prophets; and Israel was removed from off their land to the Assyrians until this day. 24 And the king of Assyria brought from Babylon the men of Chutha, *and men* from Aia, and from Æmath, and Seppharvaim, and they were settled in the cities of Samaria in the place of the children of Israel: and they inherited Samaria, and were settled in its cities. 25 And it was so at the beginning of their establishment there *that* they feared not the Lord, and the Lord sent lions among them, and they slew some of them. 26 And they spoke to the king of the Assyrians, saying, The nations whom thou hast removed and substituted in the cities of Samaria *for the Israelites*, know not the manner of the God of the land: and he has sent the lions against them, and, behold, they are slaying them, because they know not the manner of the God of the land. 27 And the king of the Assyrians commanded, saying, Bring some *Israelites* thence, and let them go and dwell there, and they shall teach them the manner of the God of the land. 28 And they brought one of the priests whom they had removed from Samaria, and he settled in Baethel, and taught them how they should fear the Lord. 29 But the nations made each their own gods, and put them in the house of the high places which the Samaritans *had* made, each nation in the cities in which they dwelt. 30 And the men of Babylon made Socchoth Benith, and the men of Chuth made Ergel, and the men of Haemath made Asimath. 31 And the Evites made Eblazer and Tharthac, and the *inhabitant* of Seppharvaim *did evil* when they burnt their sons in the fire to Adramelech and Anemelech, the gods of Seppharvaim. 32 And they feared the Lord, yet they established their abominations in the houses of the high places which they made in Samaria, each nation in the city in which they dwelt: and they feared the Lord, and they made for themselves priests of the high places, and sacrificed for themselves in the house of the high places. 33 And they feared the Lord, and served their gods according to the manner of the nations, whence *their lords* brought them. 34 Until this day they did according to their manner: they fear *the Lord*, and they do according to their customs, and according to their manner, and according to the law, and according to the commandment which the Lord commanded the sons of Jacob, whose name he made Israel. 35 And the Lord made a covenant with them, and charged them, saying, Ye shall not fear other gods, neither shall ye worship them, nor serve them, nor sacrifice to them: 36 but only to the Lord, who brought you up out of the land of Egypt with great strength and with a high arm: him shall ye fear, and him shall ye worship; to him shall ye sacrifice. 37 Ye shall observe continually the ordinances, and the judgments, and the law, and the commandments which he wrote for you to do; and ye shall not fear other gods. 38 Neither shall ye forget the covenant which he made with you: and ye shall not fear other gods. 39 But ye shall fear the Lord your God, and he shall deliver you from all your enemies. 40 Neither shall ye comply with their practice, which they follow. 41 So these nations feared the Lord, and served their graven images: yea, their sons and their son's sons do until this day even as their fathers did.

4-Kgdms18 [1] And it came to pass in the third year of Osee son of Ela king of Israel *that* Ezekias son of Achaz king of Juda began to reign. [2] Five and twenty years old was he when he began to reign, and he reigned twenty and nine years in Jerusalem: and his mother's name *was* Abu, daughter of Zacharias. [3] And he did that which was right in the sight of the Lord, according to all that his father David did. [4] He removed the high places, and broke in pieces the pillars, and utterly destroyed the groves, and the brazen serpent which Moses made: because until those days the children of Israel burnt incense to it: and he called it Neesthan. [5] He trusted in the Lord God of Israel; and after him there was not any like him among the kings of Juda, nor among those that were before him. [6] And he clave to the Lord, he departed not from following him; and he kept his commandments, as many as he commanded Moses. [7] And the Lord was with him; and he was wise in all that he undertook: and he revolted from the king of the Assyrians, and served him not. [8] He smote the Philistines *even* to Gaza, and to the border of it, from the tower of the watchmen even to the strong city. [9] And it came to pass in the fourth year of King Ezekias (this is the seventh year of Osee son of Ela king of Israel,)*that* Salamanassar king of the Assyrians came up against Samaria, and besieged it. [10] And he took it at the end of three years, in the sixth year of Ezekias, (this *is* the ninth year of Osee king of Israel, when Samaria was taken.) [11] And the king of the Assyrians carried away the Samaritans to Assyria, and put them in Alae and in Abor, *by* the river Gozan, and *in* the mountains of the Medes; [12] because they hearkened not to the voice of the Lord their God, and transgressed his covenant, *even* in all things that Moses the servant of the Lord commanded, and hearkened not *to them*, nor did *them*. [13] And in the fourteenth year of king Ezekias came up Sennacherim king of the Assyrians against the strong cities of Juda, and took them. [14] And Ezekias king of Juda sent messengers to the king of the Assyrians to Lachis, saying, I have offended; depart from me: whatsoever thou shalt lay upon me, I will bear. And the king of Assyria laid upon Ezekias king of Juda *a tribute of* three hundred talents of silver, and thirty talents of gold. [15] And Ezekias gave all the silver that was found in the house of the Lord, and in the treasures of the king's house. [16] At that time Ezekias cut off *the gold from* the doors of the temple, and *from* the pillars which Ezekias king of Juda *had* overlaid with gold, and gave it to the king of the Assyrians. [17] And the king of the Assyrians sent Tharthan and Raphis and Rapsakes from Lachis to king Ezekias with a strong force against Jerusalem. And they went up and came to Jerusalem, and stood by the aqueduct of the upper pool, which is by the way of the fuller's field. [18] And they cried to Ezekias: and there came to him Heliakim the son of Chelcias the steward, and Somnas the scribe, and Joas the son of Saphat the recorder. [19] And Rapsakes said to them, Say now to Ezekias, Thus says the king, the great king of the Assyrians, What *is* this confidence wherein thou trustest? [20] Thou hast said, (but *they are* mere words,)*I have* counsel and strength for war. Now then in whom dost thou trust, that thou hast revolted from me? [21] See now, art thou trusting for thyself on this broken staff of reed, *even* upon Egypt? whosoever shall stay himself upon it, it shall even go into his hand, and pierce it: so *is* Pharao king of Egypt to all that trust on him. [22] And whereas thou hast said to me, We trust on the Lord God: *is* not this he, whose high places and altars Ezekias has removed, and has said to Juda and Jerusalem, Ye shall worship before this altar in Jerusalem? [23] And now, I pray you, make and agreement with my lord the king of the Assyrians, and I will give thee two thousand horses, if thou shalt be able on thy part to set riders upon them. [24] How then wilt thou turn away the face of one petty governor, from among the least of my lord's servants? whereas thou trustest for thyself on Egypt for chariots and horsemen. [25] And now have we come up without the Lord against this place to destroy it? The Lord said to me, Go up against this land, and destroy it. [26] And Heliakim the son of Chelkias, and Somnas, and Joas, said to Rapsakes, Speak now to thy servants in the Syrian language, for we understand it; and speak not with us in the Jewish language: and why dost thou speak in the ears of the people that are on the wall? [27] And Rapsakes said to them, Has my master sent me to thy master, and to thee, to speak these words? *has he* not *sent me* to the men who sit on the wall, that they may eat their own dung, and drink their own water together with you. [28] And Rapsakes stood, and cried with a loud voice in the Jewish language, and spoke, and said, Hear the words of the great king of the Assyrians: [29] thus says the king, Let not Ezekias encourage you with words: for he shall not be able to deliver you out of his hand. [30] And let not Ezekias cause you to trust on the Lord, saying, The Lord will certainly deliver us; this city shall not be delivered into the hand of the king of the Assyrians: hearken not to Ezekias: [31] for thus says the king of the Assyrians, Gain my favour, and come forth to me, and every man shall drink *of the wine* of his own vine, and every man shall eat of his own fig-tree, and shall drink water out of his own cistern; [32] until I come and remove you to a land like your own land, a land of corn and wine, and bread and vineyards, a land of olive oil, and honey, and ye shall live and not die: and do not ye hearken to Ezekias, for he deceives you, saying, The Lord shall deliver you. [33] Have the Gods of the nations at all delivered each their own land out of the hand of the king of the Assyrians? [34] Where is the god of Haemath, and of Arphad? where is the god of Seppharvaim, Ana, and Aba? for have they delivered Samaria out of my hand? [35] Who *is there* among all the gods of the countries, who have delivered their countries out of my hand, that the Lord should deliver Jerusalem out of my hand? [36] But *the men* were silent, and answered him not a word: for *there was* a commandment of the king, saying, Ye shall not answer him. [37] And Heliakim the son of Chelcias, the steward, and Somnas the scribe, and Joas the son of Saphat the recorder came in to Ezekias, having rent their garments; and they reported to him the words of Rapsakes.

4-Kgdms19 [1] And it came to pass when king Ezekias heard it, that he rent his clothes, and put on sackcloth, an went into the house of the Lord. [2] And he sent Heliakim the steward, and Somnas the scribe, and the elders of the priests, clothed with sackcloth, to Esaias the prophet the son of Amos. 3 And they said to him, Thus says Ezekias, This day *is* a day of tribulation, and rebuke, and provocation: for the children are come to the travail-*pangs*, but the mother has no strength. 4 Peradventure the Lord thy God will hear all the words of Rapsakes, whom the king of Assyria his master has sent to reproach the living God and to revile him with the words which the Lord thy God has heard: and thou shalt offer *thy* prayer for the remnant that is found. 5 So the servants of king Ezekias came to Esaias. 6 And Esaias said to them, Thus shall ye say to your master, Thus saith the Lord, Be not afraid of the words which thou hast heard, wherewith the servants of the king of the Assyrians have blasphemed. 7 Behold, I send a blast upon him, and he shall hear a report, and shall return to his own land; and I will overthrow him with the sword in his own land. 8 So Rapsakes returned, and found the king of Assyria warring against Lobna: for he heard that he *had* departed from Lachis. 9 And he heard concerning Tharaca king of the Ethiopians, saying, Behold, he is come forth to fight with thee: and he returned, and sent messengers to Ezekias, saying, 10 Let not thy God on whom thou trustest encourage thee, saying, Jerusalem shall not be delivered into the hands of the king of the Assyrians. 11 Behold, thou hast heard all that the kings of the Assyrians have done in all the lands, to waste them utterly: and shalt thou be delivered? 12 Have the gods of the nations at all delivered them, whom my fathers destroyed; both Gozan, and Charran, and Raphis, and the sons of Edem who were in Thaesthen? 13 Where is the king of Haemath, and the king of Arphad? and where is the king of the city of Seppharvaim, of Ana, and Aba? 14 And Ezekias took the letter from the hand of the messengers, and read it: and he went up to the house of the Lord, an Ezekias spread it before the Lord, 15 and said, O Lord God of Israel that dwellest over the cherubs, thou art the only god in all the kingdoms of the earth; thou hast made heaven and earth. 16 Incline thine ear, O Lord, and hear: open, Lord, thine eyes, and see: and hear the words of Sennacherim, which he has sent to reproach the living God. 17 For truly, Lord, the kings of Assyria have wasted the nations, 18 and have cast their gods into the fire: because they are no gods, but the works of men's hands, wood and stone; and they have destroyed them. 19 And now, O Lord our God, deliver us out of his hand, and all the kingdoms of the earth shall know that thou alone *art* the Lord God. 20 And Esaias the son of Amos sent to Ezekias, saying, Thus saith the Lord God of hosts, the God of Israel, I have heard thy prayer to me concerning Sennacherim king of the Assyrians. 21 This *is* the word which the Lord has spoken against him; The virgin daughter of Sion has made light of thee, and mocked thee; the daughter of Jerusalem has shaken her head at thee. 22 Whom hast thou reproached, and whom hast thou reviled? and against whom hast thou lifted up thy voice, and raised thine eyes on high? *Is it* against the Holy One of Israel? 23 By thy messengers thou has reproached the Lord, and hast said, I will go up with the multitude of my chariots, to the height of the mountains, to the sides of Libanus, and I have cut down the height of his cedar, *and* his choice cypresses; and I have come into the midst of the forest and

of Carmel. 24 I have refreshed *myself*, and have drunk strange waters, and I have dried up with the sole of my foot all the rivers of fortified places. 25 I have brought about *the matter*, I have brought it to a conclusion; and it is come to the destruction of the bands of warlike prisoners, *even of* strong cities. 26 And they that dwelt in them were weak in hand, they quaked and were confounded, they became *as* grass of the field, or *as* the green herb, the grass *growing on* houses, and that which is trodden down by him that stands *upon it.* 27 But I know thy down-sitting, and thy going forth, and thy rage against me. 28 Because thou was angry against me, and thy fierceness is come up into my ears, therefore will I put my hooks in thy nostrils, and my bridle in thy lips, and I will turn thee back by the way by which thou camest. 29 And this shall be a sign to thee; eat this year the things that grow of themselves, and in the second year the things which spring up: and in the third year *let there be* sowing, and reaping, and planting of vineyards, and eat ye the fruit of them. 30 And he shall increase him that has escaped of the house of Juda: and the remnant *shall strike* root beneath, and it shall produce fruit above. 31 For from Jerusalem shall go forth a remnant, and he that escapes from the mountain of Sion: the zeal of the Lord of host shall do this. 32 *Is it* not so? Thus saith the Lord concerning the king of the Assyrians, He shall not enter into this city, and he shall not shoot an arrow there, neither shall a shield come against it, neither shall he heap a mound against it. 33 By the way by which he comes, by it shall he return, and he shall not enter into this city, saith the Lord. 34 And I will defend this city as with a shield, for my own sake, and for my servant David's sake. 35 And it came to pass at night that the angel of the Lord went forth, an smote in the camp of the Assyrians a hundred and eighty-five thousand: and they rose early in the morning, and, behold, *these were* all dead corpses. 36 And Sennacherim king of the Assyrians departed, and went and returned, and dwelt in Nineve. 37 And it came to pass, while he was worshipping in the house of Meserach his god, that Adramelech and Sarasar his sons smote him with the sword: and they escaped into the land of Ararath; and Asordan his son reigned in his stead.

4-Kgdms21 1 In those days was Ezekias sick *even* to death. And the prophet Esaias the son of Amos came in to him, and said to him, Thus saith the Lord, Give charge to thy household; *for* thou shalt die, and not live. 2 And Ezekias turned to the wall, and prayed to the Lord, saying, 3 Lord, remember, I pray thee, how I have walked before thee in truth and with a perfect heart, and have done that which is good in thine eyes. And Ezekias wept with a great weeping. 4 And Esaias was in the middle court, and the word of the Lord came to him, saying, 5 Turn back, and thou shalt say to Ezekias the ruler of my people, Thus saith the Lord God of thy father David, I have heard thy prayer, I have seen thy tears: behold, I will heal thee: on the third day thou shalt go up to the house of the Lord. 6 And I will add to thy days fifteen years; and I will deliver thee and this city out of the hand of the king of the Assyrians, and I will defend this city for my own sake, and for my servant's David sake. 7 And he said, Let them take a cake of figs, and lay it upon the ulcer, and he shall be well. 8 And Ezekias said to Esaias, What *is* the sign that the Lord will heal me, and I shall go up to the house of the Lord on the third day? 9 And Esaias said, This *is* the sign from the Lord, that the Lord will perform the word which he has spoken, the shadow *of the dial* shall advance ten degrees: *or* if it should go back ten degrees *this would also be the sign*. 10 And Ezekias said, *It is* a light thing for the shadow to go down ten degrees: nay, but let the shadow return ten degrees backward on the dial. 11 And Esaias the prophet cried to the Lord: and the shadow returned back ten degrees on the dial. 12 At that time Marodach Baladan, son of Baladan king of Babylon, sent letters and a present to Ezekias, because he had heard that Ezekias was sick. 13 And Ezekias rejoiced at them, and shewed all the house of his spices, the silver and the gold, the spices, and the fine oil, and the armory, and all that was found in his treasures: there was nothing which Ezekias did not shew them in his house, and in all his dominion. 14 And Esaias the prophet went in to king Ezekias, and said to him, What said these men? and whence came they to thee? And Ezekias said, they came to me from a distant land, *even* from Babylon. 15 And he said, What saw they in thy house? And he said, They saw all things that *are* in my house: there was nothing in my house which I shewed not to them; yea, all that was in my treasures also. 16 And Esaias said to Ezekias, Hear the word of the Lord: 17 Behold, the days come, that all things that are in thy house shall be taken, and all that thy fathers have treasured up until this day, to Babylon; and there shall not fail a word, which the Lord has spoken. 18 And as for thy sons which shall come forth of thee, which thou shalt beget, *the enemy* shall take them, and they shall be eunuchs in the house of the king of Babylon. 19 And Ezekias said to Esaias, Good *is* the word of the Lord which he has spoken: *only* let there be peace in my days. 20 And the rest of the acts of Ezekias, and all his might, and all that he made, the fountain and the aqueduct, and *how* he brought water into the city, *are* not these things written in the book of the chronicles of the kings of Juda? 21 And Ezekias slept with his fathers: and Manasses his son reigned in his stead.

4-Kgdms21 1 Manasses *was* twelve years old when he began to reign, and he reigned fifty-five years in Jerusalem: and his mother's name *was* Apsiba. 2 And he did that which was evil in the eyes of the Lord, according to the abominations of the nations which the Lord cast out from before the children of Israel. 3 And he built again the high places, which Ezekias his father *had* demolished; and set up an altar to Baal, and made groves as Achaab king of Israel *made them*, and worshipped all the host of heaven, and served them. 4 And he built an altar in the house of the Lord, whereas he had said, In Jerusalem I will place my name. 5 And he built an altar to all the host of heaven in the two courts of the house of the Lord. 6 And he caused his sons to pass through the fire, and used divination and auspices, and made groves, and multiplied wizards, so as to do that which was evil in the sight of the Lord, to provoke him to anger. 7 And he set up the graven image of the grove in the house of which the Lord said to David, and to Solomon his son, In this house, and in Jerusalem which I have chosen out of all the tribes

of Israel, will I even place my name for ever. 8 And I will not again remove the foot of Israel from the land which I gave to their fathers, *even of those* who shall keep all that I commanded, according to all the commandments which my servant Moses commanded them. 9 But they hearkened not; and Manasses led them astray to do evil in the sight of the Lord, beyond the nations whom the Lord utterly destroyed from before the children of Israel. 10 And the Lord spoke by his servants the prophets, saying, 11 Forasmuch as Manasses the king of Juda has wrought all these evil abominations, beyond all that the Amorite did, who lived before *him*, and has led Juda also into sin by their idols, 12 *it shall* not *be* so. Thus saith the Lord God of Israel, Behold, I bring calamities upon Jerusalem and Juda, so that both the ears of every one that hears shall tingle. 13 And I will stretch out over Jerusalem the measure of Samaria, and the plummet of the house of Achaab: and I will wipe Jerusalem as a jar is wiped, and turned upside down in the wiping. 14 And I will reject the remnant of my inheritance, and will deliver them into the hands of their enemies; and they shall be for a plunder and for a spoil to all their enemies: 15 forasmuch as they have done wickedly in my sight, and have provoked me from the day that I brought out their fathers out of Egypt, even until this day. 16 Moreover Manasses shed very much innocent blood, until he filled Jerusalem *with it* from one end to the other, beside his sins with which he caused Juda to sin, in doing evil in the eyes of the Lord. 17 And the rest of the acts of Manasses, and all that he did, and his sin which he sinned, *are* not these things written in the book of the chronicles of the kings of Juda? 18 And Manasses slept with his fathers, and was buried in the garden of his house, *even* in the garden of Oza: and Amos his son reigned in his stead. 19 Twenty and two years old *was* Amos when he began to reign, and he reigned two years in Jerusalem: and his mother's name *was* Mesollam, daughter of Arus of Jeteba. 20 And he did that which was evil in the sight of the Lord, as Manasses his father did. 21 And he walked in all the way in which his father walked, and served the idols which his father served, and worshipped them. 22 And he forsook the Lord God of his fathers, and walked not in the way of the Lord. 23 And the servants of Amos conspired against him, and slew the king in his house. 24 And the people of the land slew all that had conspired against king Amos; and the people of the land made Josias king in his room. 25 And the rest of the acts of Amos, *even* all that he did, behold, *are* not these written in the book of the chronicles of the kings of Juda? 26 And they buried him in his tomb in the garden of Oza: and Josias his son reigned in his stead.

4-Kgdms22 1 Josias *was* eight years old when he began to reign, and he reigned thirty and one years in Jerusalem: and his mother's name *was* Jedia, daughter of Edeia of Basuroth. 2 And he did that which was right in the sight of the Lord, and walked in all the way of David his father; he turned not aside to the right hand or to the left. 3 And it came to pass in the eighteenth year of king Josias, in the eighth month, the king sent Sapphan the son of Ezelias the son of Mesollam, the scribe of the house of the Lord, saying, 4 Go up to Chelcias the high priest, and take account of the money that is brought into the house of the Lord, which they that keep the door have collected of the people. 5 And let them give it into the hand of the workmen that are appointed in the house of the Lord. And he gave it to the workmen in the house of the Lord, to repair the breaches of the house, 6 *even* to the carpenters, and builders, and masons, *and* also to purchase timber and hewn stones, to repair the breaches of the house. 7 Only they did not call them to account for the money that was given to them, because they dealt faithfully. 8 And Chelcias the high priest said to Saphan the scribe, I have found the book of the law in the house of the Lord. And Chelcias gave the book to Sapphan, and he read it. 9 And he went into the house of the Lord to the king, and reported the matter to the king, and said, Thy servants have collected the money that was found in the house of the Lord, and have given it into the hand of the workmen that are appointed in the house of the Lord. 10 And Sapphan the scribe spoke to the king, saying, Chelcias the priest has given me a book. And Sapphan read it before the king. 11 And it came to pass, when the king heard the words of the book of the law, that he rent his garments. 12 And the king commanded Chelcias the priest, and Achikam the son of Sapphan, and Achobor the son of Michaias, and Sapphan the scribe, and Asaias the king's servant, saying, 13 Go, enquire of the Lord for me, and for all the people, and for all Juda, and concerning the words of this book that has been found: for the wrath of the Lord that has been kindled against us *is* great, because our fathers hearkened not to the words of this book, to do according to all the things written concerning us. 14 So Chelcias the priest went, and Achicam, and Achobor, and Sapphan, and Asaias, to Olda the prophetess, the mother of Sellem the son of Thecuan son of Aras, keeper of the robes; and she dwelt in Jerusalem in Masena; and they spoke to her. 15 And she said to them, Thus saith the Lord God of Israel, Say to the man that sent you to me, 16 Thus saith the Lord, Behold, I bring evil upon this place, and upon them that dwell in it, *even* all the words of the book which the king of Juda has read: 17 because they have forsaken me, and burnt incense to other gods, that they might provoke me with the works of their hands: therefore my wrath shall burn forth against this place, and shall not be quenched. 18 And to the king of Juda that sent you to enquire of the Lord, —thus shall ye say to him, Thus saith the Lord God of Israel, *As for* the words which thou hast heard; 19 because thy heart was softened, and thou was humbled before *me*, when thou heardest all that I spoke against this place, and against the inhabitants of it, that it should be utterly destroyed and accursed, and thou didst rend thy garments, and weep before me; I also have heard, saith the Lord. 20 It shall not be so *therefore*: behold, I *will* add thee to thy fathers, and thou shalt be gathered to thy tomb in peace, and thine eyes shall not see *any* among all the evils which I bring upon this place.

4-Kgdms23 1 So they reported the word to the king: and the king sent and gathered all the elders of Juda and Jerusalem to himself. 2 And the king went up to the house of the Lord, and every man of Juda and all who dwelt in Jerusalem with him, and the priests, and the prophets, and all the people small and great; and he read in their ears all the words of the book of the covenant that was found in the house of the Lord. 3 And the king stood by a pillar, and made a covenant before the Lord, to walk after the Lord, to keep his commandments and his testimonies and his ordinances with all the heart and with all the soul, to confirm the words of this covenant; *even* the things written in this book. And all the people stood to the covenant. 4 And the king commanded Chelcias the high priest, and the priests of the second order, and them that kept the door, to bring out of the temple of the Lord all the vessels that were made for Baal, and for the grove, and all the host of heaven, and he burned them without Jerusalem in the fields of Kedron, and took the ashes of them to Baethel. 5 And he burned the idolatrous priests, whom the kings of Juda *had* appointed, (and they burned incense in the high places and in the cities of Juda, and the places around about Jerusalem); and them that burned incense to Baal, and to the sun, and to the moon, and to Mazuroth, and to all the host of heaven. 6 And he carried out the grove from the house of the Lord to the brook Kedron, and burned it at the brook Kedron, and reduced it to powder, and cast its powder on the sepulchres of the sons of the people. 7 And he pulled down the house of the sodomites that were by the house of the Lord, where the women wove tents for the grove. 8 And he brought up all the priest from the cities of Juda, and defiled the high places where the priests burned incense, from Gaebal even to Bersabee; and he pulled down the house of the gates that was by the door of the gate of Joshua the ruler of the city, on a man's left hand at the gate of the city. 9 Only the priests of the high places went not up to the altar of the Lord in Jerusalem, for they only ate leavened bread in the midst of their brethren. 10 And he defiled Tapheth which is in the valley of the son of Ennom, *constructed* for a man to cause his son or his daughter to pass through fire to Moloch. 11 And he burned the horses which the king of Juda had given to the sun in the entrance of the house of the Lord, by the treasury of Nathan the king's eunuch, in the suburbs; and he burned the chariot of the sun with fire. 12 And the altars that were on the roof of the upper chamber of Achaz, which the kings of Juda had made, and the altars which Manasses had made in the two courts of the house of the Lord, did the king pull down and forcibly remove from thence, and cast their dust into the brook of Kedron. 13 And the king defiled the house that was before Jerusalem, on the right hand of the mount of Mosthath, which Solomon king of Israel built to Astarte the abomination of the Sidonians, and to Chamos the abomination of Moab, and to Moloch the abomination of the children of Ammon. 14 And he broke in pieces the pillars, and utterly destroyed the groves, and filled their places with the bones of men. 15 Also the high altar in Baethel, which Jeroboam the son of Nabat, who made Israel to sin, had made, even that high altar he tore down, and broke in pieces the stones of it, and reduced it to powder, and burnt the grove. 16 And Josias turned aside, and saw the tombs that were there in the city, and sent, and took the bones out of the tombs, and burnt them on the altar, and defiled it, according to the word of the Lord which the man of God spoke, when Jeroboam stood by the altar at the feast: and he turned and raised his eyes to the tomb of the man of God that spoke these words. 17 And he said, What *is* that mound which I see? And the men of the city said to him, *It is the grave of* the man of God that came out of Juda, and uttered these imprecations which he imprecated upon the altar of Baethel. 18 And he said, Let him alone; let no one disturb his bones. So his bones were spared, together with the bones of the prophet that came out of Samaria. 19 Moreover Josias removed all the houses of the high places that were in the cities of Samaria, which the kings of Israel made to provoke the Lord, and did to them all that he did in Baethel. 20 And he sacrificed all the priests of the high places that were there on the altars, and burnt the bones of men upon them, and returned to Jerusalem. 21 And the king commanded all the people, saying, Keep the passover to the Lord your God, as it is written in the book of this covenant. 22 For a passover *such as* this had not been kept from the days of the judges who judged Israel, even all the days of the kings of Israel, and of the kings of Juda. 23 But in the eighteenth year of king Josias, was the passover kept to the Lord in Jerusalem. 24 Moreover Josias removed the sorcerers, and the wizards, and the theraphin, and the idols, and all the abominations that had been set up in the land of Juda and in Jerusalem, that he might keep the words of the law that were written in the book, which Chelcias the priest found in the house of the Lord. 25 There was no king like him before him, who turned to the Lord with all his heart, and with all his soul, and with all his strength, according to all the law of Moses; and after him there rose not one like him. 26 Nevertheless the Lord turned not from the fierceness of his great anger, wherewith he was wroth in his anger against Juda, because of the provocations, wherewith Manasses provoked him. 27 And the Lord said, I will also remove Juda from my presence, as I removed Israel, and will reject this city which I have chosen *even* Jerusalem, and the house *of* which I said, My name shall be there. 28 And the rest of the acts of Josias, and all that he did, *are* not these things written in the book of the chronicles of the kings of Juda? 29 And in his days went up Pharao Nechao king of Egypt against the king of the Assyrians to the river Euphrates: and Josias went out to meet him: and Nechao slew him in Mageddo when he saw him. 30 And his servants carried him dead from Mageddo, and brought him to Jerusalem, and buried him in his sepulchre: and the people of the land took Joachaz the son of Josias, and anointed him, and made him king in the room of his father. 31 Twenty and three years old was Joachaz when he began to reign, and he reigned three months in Jerusalem: and his mother's name *was* Amital, daughter of Jeremias of Lobna. 32 And he did that which was evil in the sight of the Lord, according to all that his fathers did. 33 And Pharao Necchao removed him to Rablaam in the land of Emath, so that he should not reign in Jerusalem; and imposed a tribute on the land, a hundred talents of silver, and a hundred talents of gold. 34 And Pharao Nechao made Eliakim son of Josias king of Juda king over them in the place of his father Josias, and he changed his name *to* Joakim, and he took Joachaz and brought him to Egypt, and he died there. 35 And Joakim gave the silver and the gold to Pharao; but he assessed the land to give the money at the command of Pharao: they gave the silver and the gold *each* man according to his assessment together with the people of the land to give to Pharao Nechao. 36 Twenty-five years old *was* Joakim when he began to reign, and he reigned eleven years in Jerusalem: and his mother's name *was* Jeldaph, daughter of Phadail of Ruma. 37 And he did that which was evil in the eyes of the lord, according to all that his fathers had done.

4-Kgdms24 1 In his days went up Nabuchodonosor king of Babylon, and Joakim became his servant three years; and *then* he turned and revolted from him. 2 And the lord sent against him the bands of the Chaldeans, and the bands of Syria, and the bans of Moab, and the bands of the children of Ammon, and sent them into the land of Juda to prevail *against it*, according to the word of the Lord, which he spoke by his servants the prophets. 3 Moreover it was the purpose of the Lord concerning Juda, to remove them from his presence, because of the sins of Manasses, according to all that he did. 4 Moreover he shed innocent blood, and filled Jerusalem with innocent blood, and the Lord would not pardon *it*. 5 And the rest of the acts of Joakim, and all that he did, behold, *are* not these written in the book of the chronicles of the kings of Juda? 6 And Joakim slept with his fathers: and Joachim his son reigned in his stead. 7 And the king of Egypt came no more out of his land: for the king of Babylon took away all that belonged to the king of Egypt from the river of Egypt as far as the river Euphrates. 8 Eighteen years old *was* Joachim when he began to reign, an he reigned three months in Jerusalem: and his mother's name *was* Nestha, daughter of Ellanastham, of Jerusalem. 9 And he did that which was evil in the sight of the Lord, according to all that his father did. 10 At that time went up Nabuchodonosor king of Babylon to Jerusalem, and the city was besieged. 11 And Nabuchodonosor king of Babylon came against the city, and his servants besieged it. 12 And Joachim king of Juda came forth to the king of Babylon, he and his servants, and his mother, and his princes, and his eunuchs; and the king of Babylon took him in the eighth year of his reign. 13 And he brought forth thence all the treasures of the house of the Lord, and the treasures of the king's house, and he cut up all the golden vessels which Solomon the king of Israel *had* made in the temple of the Lord, according to the word of the Lord. 14 And he carried away *the inhabitants of* Jerusalem, and all the captains, and the mighty men, taking captive ten thousand prisoners, and every artificer and smith: and only the poor of the land were left. 15 And he carried Joachim away to Babylon, and the king's mother, and the king's wives, and his eunuchs: and he carried away the mighty men of the land into captivity from Jerusalem to Babylon. 16 And all the men of might, even seven thousand, and one thousand artificers and smiths: all *were* mighty *men* fit for war; and the king of Babylon carried them captive to Babylon. 17 And the king of Babylon made Batthanias his son king in his stead, and called his name Sedekias. 18 Twenty and one years old *was* Sedekias when he began to reign, and he reigned eleven years in Jerusalem: and his mother's name *was* Amital daughter of Jeremias. 19 And he did that which was evil in the sight of the Lord, according to all that Joachim did. 20 For it was according to the Lord's anger against Jerusalem and on Juda, until he cast them out of his presence, that Sedekias revolted against the king of Babylon.

4-Kgdms25 1 And it came to pass in the ninth year of his reign, in the tenth month, *that* Nabuchodonosor king of Babylon came, and all his host, against Jerusalem; and he encamped against it, and built a mound against it. 2 And the city was besieged until the eleventh year of king Sedekias on the ninth day of the month. 3 And the famine prevailed in the city, and there was no bread for the people of the land. 4 And the city was broken up, and all the men of war went forth by night, by the way of the gate between the walls, this is *the gate* of the king's garden: and the Chaldeans *were set* against the city round about: and *the king* went by the way of the plain. 5 And the force of the Chaldeans pursued the king, and overtook him in the plains of Jericho: and all his army was dispersed from about him. 6 And they took the king, and brought him to the king of Babylon to Reblatha; and he gave judgment upon him. 7 And he slew the sons of Sedekias before his eyes, and put out the eyes of Sedekias, and bound him in fetters, and brought him to Babylon. 8 And in the fifth month, on the seventh day of the month (this *is* the nineteenth year of Nabuchodonosor king of Babylon), came Nabuzardan, captain of the guard, who stood before the king of Babylon, to Jerusalem. 9 And he burnt the house of the Lord, and the king's house, and all the houses of Jerusalem, even every house did the captain of the guard burn. 10 And the force of the Chaldeans pulled down the wall of Jerusalem round about. 11 And Nabuzardan the captain of the guard removed the rest of the people that were left in the city, and the men who had deserted to the king of Babylon, and the rest of the multitude. 12 But the captain of the guard left of the poor of the land to be vine-dressers and husbandmen. 13 And the Chaldeans broke to pieces the brazen pillars that were in the house of the Lord, and the bases, and the brazen sea that was in the house of the Lord, and carried their brass to Babylon. 14 And the caldrons, and the shovels, and the bowls, and the censers, and all the brazen vessels with which they minister, he took. 15 And the captain of the guard took the fire- pans, and the gold and silver bowls. 16 Two pillars, and one sea, and the bases which Solomon made for the house of the Lord: there was no weight of the brass of all the vessels. 17 The height of one pillar *was* eighteen cubits, and the chapiter upon it was of brass: and the height of the chapiter was three cubits: the border, and the pomegranates on the chapiter round about were all of brass: and so it was with the second pillar with its border. 18 And the captain of the guard took Saraias the high-priest, and Sophonias the second in order, and the three doorkeepers. 19 And they took out of the city one eunuch who was commander of the men of war, and five men that saw the face of the king, that were found in the city, and the secretary of the commander-in-chief, who took account of the people of the land, and sixty men of the people of the land that were found in the city. 20 And Nabuzardan the captain of the guard took them, and brought them to the king of Babylon to Reblatha. 21 And the king of Babylon smote them and slew them at Reblatha in the land of Æmath. So Juda was carried away from his land. 22 And *as for* the people that were left in the land of Juda, whom Nabuchodonosor king of Babylon left, even over them he set Godolias son of Achicam son of Saphan. 23 And all the captains of the host, they and their men, heard that the king of Babylon had *thus* appointed Godolias, and they came to Godolias to Massephath, both Ismael the son of Nathanias, and Jona son of Careth, and Saraias, son of Thanamath the Netophathite, and Jezonias son of a Machathite, they and their men. 24 And Godolias swore to them and their men, and said to them, Fear not the incursion of the Chaldeans; dwell in the land, and serve the king of Babylon, and it shall be well with you. 25 And it came to pass in the seventh month *that* Ismael son of Nathanias son of Helisama, of the seed royal, came, and ten men with him, and he smote Godolias, that he died, *him* and the Jews and the Chaldeans that were with him in Massepha. 26 And all the people, great and small rose up, *they* and the captains of the forces, and went into Egypt; because they were afraid of the Chaldeans. 27 And it came to pass in the thirty-seventh year of the carrying away of Joachim king of Juda, in the twelfth month, on the twenty-seventh day of the month, *that* Evialmarodec king of Babylon in the *first* year of his reign lifted up the head of Joachim king of Juda, and brought him out of his prison-house. 28 And he spoke kindly to him, and set his throne above the thrones of the kings that were with him in Babylon; 29 And changed his prison garments: and he ate bread continually before him all the days of his life. 30 And his portion, a continual portion, was given him out of the house of the king, a daily rate for every day all the days of his life.

1 CHRONICLES

1-Chron.1 1 Adam, Seth, Enos, 2 and Cainan, Maleleel, Jared, 3 Enoch, Mathusala, Lamech, 4 Noe: the sons of Noe, Sem, Cham, Japheth. 5 The sons of Japheth, Gamer, Magog, Madaim, Jovan, Helisa, Thobel, Mosoch, and Thiras. 6 And the sons of Gamer, Aschanaz, and Riphath, and Thorgama. 7 And the sons of Jovan, Helisa, and Tharsis, the Citians, and Rhodians. 8 And the sons of Cham, Chus, and Mesraim, Phud and Chanaan. 9 And the sons of Chus, Saba, and Evila, and Sabatha, and Regma, and Sebethaca: and the sons of Regma, Saba, and Dadan. 10 And Chus begot Nebrod: he began to be a mighty hunter on the earth. 17 The sons of Sem, Ælam, and Assur, 18 and Arphaxad, Sala, 25 Eber, Pheleg, Ragan, 26 Seruch, Nachor, Tharrha, 27 Abraam. 28 And the sons of Abraam, Isaac, and Ismael. 29 And these *are* their generations: the first-born of Ismael, Nabaeoth, and Kedar, Nabdeel, Massam, 30 Masma, Iduma, Masse, Chondan, Thaeman, 31 Jettur, Naphes, Kedma: these *are* the sons of Ismael. 32 And the sons of Chettura Abraam's concubine:—and she bore him

Zembram, Jexan, Madiam, Madam, Sobac, Soe: and the sons of Jexan; Daedan, and Sabai; 33 and the sons of Madiam; Gephar, and Opher, and Enoch, and Abida, and Eldada; all these *were* the sons of Chettura. 34 And Abraam begot Isaac: and the sons of Isaac *were* Jacob, and Esau. 35 The sons of Esau, Eliphaz, and Raguel, and Jeul, and Jeglom, and Core. 36 The sons of Eliphaz: Thaeman, and Omar, Sophar, and Gootham, and Kenez, and Thamna, and Amalec. 37 And the sons of Raguel, Naches, Zare, Some, and Moze. 38 The sons of Seir, Lotan, Sobal, Sebegon, Ana, Deson, Osar, and Disan. 39 And the sons of Lotan, Chorri, and Æman; and the sister of Lotan *was* Thamna. 40 The sons of Sobal; Alon, Machanath, Taebel, Sophi, and Onan: and the sons of Sebegon; Æth, and Sonan. 41 The sons of Sonan, Daeson: and the sons of Daeson; Emeron, and Asebon, and Jethram, and Charran. 42 And the sons of Hosar, Balaam, and Zucam, and Acan: the sons of Disan, Os, and Aran. 43 And these *are* their kings, Balac the son of Beor; and the name of his city *was* Dennaba. 44 And Balac died, and Jobab the son of Zara of Bosorrha reigned in his stead. 45 And Jobab died, and Asom of the land of the Thaemanites reigned in his stead. 46 And Asom died, and Adad the son of Barad reigned in his stead, who smote Madiam in the plain of Moab: and the name of his city *was* Gethaim. 47 And Adad died, and Sebla of Masecca reigned in his stead. 48 And Sebla died, and Saul of Rhoboth by the river reigned in his stead. 49 And Saul died, and Balaennor son of Achobor reigned in his stead. 50 And Balaennor died, and Adad son of Barad reigned in his stead; and the name of his city *was* Phogor. 51 The princes of Edom: prince Thamna, prince Golada, prince Jether, 52 prince Elibamas, prince Elas, prince Phinon, 53 prince Kenez, prince Thaeman, prince Babsar, prince Magediel, 54 prince Zaphoin. These *are* the princes of Edom.

1-Chron.2 1 These *are* the names of the sons of Israel; 2 Ruben, Symeon, Levi, Juda, Issachar, Zabulon, Dan, Joseph, Benjamin, Nephthali, Gad, Aser. 3 The sons of Juda; Er, Aunan, Selom. *These* three were born to him of the daughter of Sava the Chananitish woman: and Er, the first-born of Juda, *was* wicked before the Lord, and he slew him. 4 And Thamar his daughter-in-law bore to him Phares, and Zara: all the sons of Juda *were* five. 5 The sons of Phares, Esrom, and Jemuel. 6 And the sons of Zara, Zambri, and Ætham, and Æmuan, and Calchal, and Darad, *in* all five. 7 And the sons of Charmi; Achar the troubler of Israel, who was disobedient in the accursed thing. 8 And the sons of Ætham; Azarias, 9 and the sons of Esrom who were born to him; Jerameel, and Aram, and Chaleb. 10 And Aram begot Aminadab, and Aminadab begot Naasson, chief of the house of Juda. 11 And Naasson begot Salmon, and Salmon begot Booz, 12 and Booz begot Obed, and Obed begot Jessae. 13 And Jessae begot his first-born Eliab, Aminadab *was* the second, Samaa the third, 14 Nathanael the fourth, Zabdai the fifth, 15 Asam the sixth, David the seventh. 16 And their sister *was* Saruia, and *another* Abigaia: and the sons of Saruia *were* Abisa, and Joab, and Asael, three. 17 And Abigaia bore Amessab: and the father of Amessab *was* Jothor the Ismaelite. 18 And Chaleb the son of Esrom took Gazuba to wife, and Jerioth: and these *were* her sons; Jasar, and Subab, and Ardon. 19 And Gazuba died; and Chaleb took to himself Ephrath, and she bore to him Or. 20 And Or begot Uri, and Uri begot Beseleel. 21 And after this Esron went in to the daughter of Machir the father of Galaad, and he took her when he was sixty-five years old; and she bore him Seruch. 22 And Seruch begot Jair, and he had twenty-three cities in Galaad. 23 And he took Gedsur and Aram, the towns of Jair from them; *with* Canath and its towns, sixty cities. All these *belonged to* the sons of Machir the father of Galaad. 24 And after the death of Esron, Chaleb came to Ephratha; and the wife of Esron *was* Abia; and she bore him Ascho the father of Thecoe. 25 And the sons of Jerameel the first-born of Esron *were*, the first-born Ram, and Banaa, and Aram, and Asan his brother. 26 And Jerameel had another wife, and her name *was* Atara: she is the mother of Ozom. 27 And the sons of Ram the first-born of Jerameel were Maas, and Jamin, and Acor. 28 And the sons of Ozom were, Samai, and Jadae: and the sons of Samai; Nadab, and Abisur. 29 And the name of the wife of Abisur *was* Abichaia, and she bore him Achabar, and Moel. 30 And the sons of Nadab; Salad and Apphain; and Salad died without children. 31 And the sons of Apphain, Isemiel; and the sons of Isemiel, Sosan; and the sons of Sosan, Dadai. 32 And the sons of Dadai, Achisamas, Jether, Jonathan: and Jether died childless. 33 And the sons of Jonathan; Phaleth, and Hozam. These were the sons of Jerameel. 34 And Sosan had no sons, but daughters. And Sosan had an Egyptian servant, and his name *was* Jochel. 35 And Sosan gave his daughter to Jochel his servant to wife; and she bore him Ethi. 36 And Ethi begot Nathan, and Nathan begot Zabed, 37 and Zabed begot Aphamel, and Aphamel begot Obed. 38 And Obed begot Jeu, and Jeu begot Azarias. 39 And Azarias begot Chelles, and Chelles begot Eleasa, 40 and Eleasa begot Sosomai, and Sosomai begot Salum, 41 and Salum begot Jechemias, and Jechemias begot Elisama, and Elisama begot Ismael. 42 And the sons of Chaleb the brother of Jerameel *were*, Marisa his first-born, he *is* the father of Ziph:—and the sons of Marisa the father of Chebron. 43 And the sons of Chebron; Core, and Thapphus, and Recom, and Samaa. 44 And Samaa begot Raem the father of Jeclan: and Jeclan begot Samai. 45 And his son *was* Maon: and Maon *is* the father of Baethsur. 46 And Gaepha the concubine of Chaleb bore Aram, and Mosa, and Gezue. 47 And the sons of Addai *were* Ragem, and Joatham, and Sogar, and Phalec, and Gaepha, and Sagae. 48 And Chaleb's concubine Mocha bore Saber, and Tharam. 49 She bore also Sagae the father of Madmena, and Sau the father of Machabena, and the father of Gaebal: and the daughter of Chaleb *was* Ascha. 50 These were the sons of Chaleb: the sons of Or the first-born of Ephratha; Sobal the father of Cariathiarim, 51 Salomon the father of Baetha, Lammon the father of Baethlaem, and Arim the father of Bethgedor. 52 And the sons of Sobal the father of Cariathiarim were Araa, and Æsi, and Ammanith, 53 and Umasphae, cities of Jair; Æthalim, and Miphithim, and Hesamathim, and Hemasaraim; from these went forth the Sarathaeans, and the sons of Esthaam. 54 The sons of Salomon; Baethlaem, the Netophathite, Ataroth of the house of Joab, and half of the family of Malathi, Esari. 55 The families of the scribes dwelling in Jabis; Thargathiim, and Samathiim, and Sochathim, these *are* the Kinaeans that came of Hemath, the father of the house of Rechab.

1-Chron.3 1 Now these were the sons of David that were born to him in Chebron; the first-born Amnon, *born* of Achinaam the Jezraelitess; the second Damniel, of Abigaia the Carmelitess. 2 The third, Abessalom, the son of Mocha the daughter of Tholmai king of Gedsur; the fourth, Adonia the son of Aggith. 3 The fifth, Saphatia, *the son of* Abital; the sixth, Jethraam, *born* of Agla his wife. 4 Six were born to him in Chebron; and he reigned there seven years and six months: and he reigned thirty-three years in Jerusalem. 5 And these were born to him in Jerusalem; Samaa, Sobab, Nathan, and Solomon; four *of* Bersabee the daughter of Amiel: 6 and Ebaar, and Elisa, and Eliphaleth, 7 and Nagai, and Naphec, and Japhie, 8 and Helisama, and Eliada, and Eliphala, nine. 9 All *these were* the sons of David, besides the sons of the concubines, and *there was also* Themar their sister. 10 The sons of Solomon; Roboam, Abia his son, Asa his son, Josaphat his son, 11 Joram his son, Ochozias his son, Joas his son, 12 Amasias his son, Azarias his son, Joathan his son, 13 Achaz his son, Ezekias his son, Manasses his son, 14 Amon his son, Josia his son. 15 And the sons of Josia; the first-born Joanan, the second Joakim, the third Sedekias, the fourth Salum. 16 And the sons of Joakim; Jechonias his son, Sedekias his son. 17 And the sons of Jechonias; Asir, Salathiel his son, 18 Melchiram, and Phadaias, and Sanesar, and Jekimia, and Hosamath, and Nabadias. 19 And the sons of Phadaias; Zorobabel, and Semei: and the sons of Zorobabel; Mosollam, and Anania, and Salomethi *was* their sister. 20 And Asube, and Ool, and Barachia, and Asadia, and Asobed, five. 21 And the sons of Anania, Phalettia, and Jesias his son, Raphal his son, Orna his son, Abdia his son, Sechenias his son. 22 And the son of Sechenias; Samaia: and the sons of Samaia; Chattus, and Joel, and Berri and Noadia, and Saphath, six. 23 And the sons of Noadia: Elithenan, and Ezekia, and Ezricam, three. 24 And the sons of Elithenan; Odolia, and Heliasebon, and Phadaia, and Akub, and Joanan, and Dalaaia, and Anan, seven.

1-Chron.4 1 And the sons of Juda; Phares, Esrom, and Charmi, and Or, Subal, 2 and Rada his son; and Subal begot Jeth; and Jeth begot Achimai, and Laad: these *are* the generations of the Arathites. 3 And these *are* the sons of Ætam; Jezrael and Jesman, and Jebdas: and their sister's name *was* Eselebbon. 4 And Phanuel the father of Gedor, and Jazer the father of Osan: these *are* the sons of Or, the first-born of Ephratha, the father of Baethalaen. 5 And Asur the father of Thecoe had two wives, Aoda and Thoada. 6 And Aoda bore to him Ochaia, and Ephal, and Thaeman, and Aasther: all these *were* the sons of Aoda. 7 And the sons of Thoada; Sereth, and Saar, and Esthanam. 8 And Coe begot Enob, and Sabatha, and the progeny of the brother of Rechab, the son of Jarin. 9 And Igabes was more famous than his brethren; and his mother called his name Igabes, saying, I have born as a sorrowful one. 10 And Igabes called on the God of Israel, saying, O that thou wouldest indeed bless me, and enlarge my coasts, and that thy hand might be with me, and that thou wouldest make me know that thou wilt not grieve me! And God granted him all that he asked. 11 And Chaleb the father of Ascha begot Machir; he *was* the father of Assathon. 12 He begot Bathraias, and Bessee, and Thaeman the founder of the city of Naas the brother of Eselom the Kenezite: these *were* the men of Rechab. 13 And the sons of Kenez; Gothoniel, and Saraia: and the sons of Gothoniel; Athath. 14 And Manathi begot Gophera: and Saraia begot Jobab, the father of Ageaddair, for they were artificers. 15 And the sons of Chaleb the son of Jephonne; Er, Ada, and Noom: and the sons of Ada, Kenez. 16 And the sons of Aleel, Zib, and Zepha, and Thiria, and Eserel. 17 And the sons of Esri; Jether, Morad, and Apher, and Jamon: and Jether begot Maron, and Semei, and Jesba the father of Esthaemon. 18 And his wife, that *is* Adia, bore Jared the father of Gedor, and Aber the father of Sochon, and Chetiel the father of Zamon: and these *are* the sons of Betthia the daughter of Pharao, whom Mored took. 19 And the sons of the wife of Iduia the sister of Nachaim the father of Keila; Garmi, and Esthaemon the Nochathite. 20 And the sons of Semon; Amnon, and Ana the son of Phana, and Inon: and the sons of Sei, Zoan, and the sons of Zoab. 21 The sons of Selom the son of Juda; Er the father of Lechab, and Laada the father of Marisa, and the offspring of the family of Ephrathabac *belonging to* the house of Esoba. 22 And Joakim, and the men of Chozeba, and Joas, and Saraph, who dwelt in Moab, and he changed their names to Abederin and Athukiim. 23 These *are* the potters who dwelt in Ataim and Gadira with the king: they grew strong in his kingdom, and dwelt there. 24 The sons of Semeon; Namuel, and Jamin, Jarib, Zares, Saul: 25 Salem his son, Mabasam his son, Masma his son: 26 Amuel his son, Sabud his son, Zacchur his son, Semei his son. 27 Semei *had* sixteen sons, and six daughters; and his brethren had not many sons, neither did all their families multiply as the sons of Juda. 28 And they dwelt in Bersabee, and Molada, and in Esersual, 29 and in Balaa, and in Æsem, and in Tholad, 30 and in Bathuel, and in Herma, and in Sikelag, 31 and in Baethmarimoth, and Hemisuseosin, and the house of Baruseorim: these *were* their cities until *the time of* king David. 32 And their villages *were* Ætan, and En, Remnon, and Thocca, and Æsar, five cities. 33 And all their villages *were* round about these cities, as far as Baal: this *was* their possession, and their distribution. 34 And Mosobab, and Jemoloch, and Josia the son of Amasia; 35 and Joel, and Jeu the son of Asabia, the son of Sarau, the son of Asiel; 36 and Elionai, and Jocaba, and Jasuia, and Asaia, and Jediel, and Ismael, and Banaias; 37 and Zuza the son of Saphai, the son of Alon, the son of Jedia, the son of Semri, the son of Samaias. 38 These went by the names of princes in their families, and they increased abundantly in their fathers' households. 39 And they went till they came to Gerara, to the east of Gai, to seek pasture for their cattle. 40 And they found abundant and good pastures, and the land before them *was* wide, and *there was* peace and quietness; for *there were* some of the children of Cham who dwelt there before. 41 And these who are written by name came in the days of Ezekias king of Juda, and they smote the people's houses, and the Minaeans whom they found there, and utterly destroyed them until this day: and they dwelt in their place, because *there was* pasture there for their cattle. 42 And some of them, *even* of the sons of Symeon, went to mount Seir, *even* five hundred men; and Phalaettia, and Noadia, and Raphaia, and Oziel, sons of Jesi, *were* their rulers. 43 And they smote the remnant that were left of Amalec, until this day.

1-Chron.5 1 And the sons of Ruben the first-born of Israel (for he *was* the first-born; but because of his going up to his father's couch, *his father* gave his blessing to his son Joseph, *even* the son of Israel; and he was not reckoned as first-born; 2 for Judas *was* very mighty even among his brethren, and one was to be a ruler out of him: but the blessing *was* Joseph's). 3 The sons of Ruben the first-born of Israel; Enoch, and Phallus, Asrom, and Charmi. 4 The sons of Joel; Semei, and Banaia his son: and the sons of Gug the son of Semei. 5 His son *was* Micha, his son Recha, his son Joel, 6 his son Beel, whom Thagla-phallasar king of Assyria carried away captive: he *is* the chief of the Rubenites. 7 And his brethren in his family, in their distribution according to their generations; the chief, Joel, and Zacharia. 8 And Balec the son of Azuz, the son of Sama, the son of Joel: he dwelt in Aroer, and even to Naban, and Beelmasson. 9 And he dwelt eastward to the borders of the wilderness, from the river Euphrates: for they had much cattle in the land of Galaad. 10 And in the days of Saul they made war upon the sojourners *in the land*; and they fell into their hands, all of them dwelling in their tents eastward of Galaad. 11 The sons of Gad dwelt over against them in the land of Basan even to Sela. 12 Joel the first- born, and Sapham the second, and Janin the scribe in Basan. 13 And their brethren according to the houses of their fathers; Michael, Mosollam, and Sebee, and Joree, and Joachan, and Zue, and Obed, seven. 14 These *are* the sons of Abichaia the son of Uri, the son of Idai, the son of Galaad, the son of Michael, the son of Jesai, the son of Jeddai, the son of Buz, 15 *who was* the brother of the son of Abdiel, the son of Guni, *he was* chief of the house of their families. 16 They dwelt in Galaad, in Basan, and in their villages, and *in* all the country round about Saron to the border. 17 The enumeration of *them* all took place in the days of Joatham king of Juda, and in the days of Jeroboam king of Israel. 18 The sons of Ruben and Gad, and the half-tribe of Manasse, of mighty men, bearing shields and sword, and bending the bow, and skilled in war, *were* forty and four thousand and seven hundred and sixty, going forth to battle. 19 And they made war with the Agarenes, and Itureans, and Naphiseans, and Nadabeans, 20 and they prevailed against them: and the Agaraeans were given into their hands, *they* and all their tents: for they cried to God in the battle, and he hearkened to them, because they trusted on him. 21 And they took captive their store; five thousand camels, and two hundred and fifty thousand sheep, two thousand asses, and a hundred thousand men. 22 For many fell slain, because the war *was* of God. And they dwelt in their place until the captivity. 23 And the half-tribe of Manasse dwelt from Basan to Baal, Ermon, and Sanir, and *to* the mount Aermon: and they increased in Libanus. 24

And these were the heads of the houses of their families; Opher, and Sei, and Eliel, and Jeremia, and Oduia, and Jediel, mighty men of valour, men of renown, heads of the houses of their families. 25 But they rebelled against the God of their fathers, and went a-whoring after the gods of the nations of the land, whom God cast out from before them. 26 And the God of Israel stirred up the spirit of Phaloch king of Assyria, and the spirit of Thagla-phallasar king of Assyria, and carried away Ruben and Gaddi, and the half-tribe of Manasse, and brought them to Chaach, and Chabor, and to the river Gozan, until this day.

1-Chron.6 1 The sons of Levi: Gedson, Caath, and Merari. 2 And the sons of Caath; Ambram, and Issaar, Chebron, and Oziel. 3 And the sons of Ambram; Aaron, and Moses, and Mariam: and the sons of Aaron; Nadab, and Abiud, Eleazar, and Ithamar. 4 Eleazar begot Phinees, Phinees begot Abisu; 5 Abisu begot Bokki, and Bokki begot Ozi; 6 Ozi begot Zaraia, Zaraia begot Mariel; 7 and Mariel begot Amaria, and Amaria begot Achitob; 8 and Achitob begot Sadoc, and Sadoc begot Achimaas; 9 and Achimaas begot Azarias, and Azarias begot Joanan; 10 and Joanan begot Azarias: he ministered as priest in the house which Solomon built in Jerusalem. 11 And Azarias begot Amaria, and Amaria begot Achitob; 12 and Achitob begot Sadoc, and Sadoc begot Salom; 13 and Salom begot Chelcias, and Chelcias begot Azarias; 14 and Azarias begot Saraia, and Saraias begot Josadac. 15 And Josadac went into captivity with Juda and Jerusalem under Nabuchodonosor. 16 The sons of Levi: Gedson, Caath, and Merari. 17 And these *are* the names of the sons of Gedson; Lobeni, and Semei. 18 The sons of Caath; Ambram, and Issaar, Chebron, and Oziel. 19 The sons of Merari; Mooli and Musi: and these *are* the families of Levi, according to their families. 20 To Gedson—to Lobeni his son—*were born* Jeth his son, Zammath his son, 21 Joab his son, Addi his son, Zara his son, Jethri his son. 22 The sons of Caath; Aminadab his son, Core his son, Aser his son; 23 Helcana his son, Abisaph his son, Aser his son: 24 Thaath his son, Uriel his son, Ozia his son, Saul his son. 25 And the sons of Helcana; Amessi, and Achimoth. 26 Helcana his son, Suphi his son, Cainaath his son; 27 Eliab his son, Jeroboam his son, Helcana his son. 28 The sons of Samuel; the first-born Sani, and Abia. 29 The sons of Merari; Mooli, Lobeni his son, Semei his son, Oza his son; 30 Samaa his son, Angia his son, Asaias his son. 31 And these *were the men* whom David set over the service of the singers in the house of the Lord when the ark was at rest. 32 And they ministered in front of the tabernacle of witness *playing* on instruments, until Solomon built the house of the Lord in Jerusalem; and they stood according to their order for their services. 33 And these *were the men* that stood, and their sons, of the sons of Caath: Æman the psalm singer, son of Joel, the son of Samuel, 34 the son of Helcana, the son of Jeroboam, the son of Eliel, the son of Thoas, 35 the son of Suph, the son of Helcana, the son of Maath, the son of Amathi, 36 the son of Helcana, the son of Joel, the son of Azarias, the son of Japhanias, 37 the son of Thaath, the son of Aser, the son of Abiasaph, the son of Core, 38 the son of Isaar, the son of Caath, the son of Levi, the son of Israel. 39 And his brother Asaph, who stood at his right hand; Asaph the son of Barachias, the son of Samaa, 40 the son of Michael, the son of Baasia, the son of Melchia, 41 the son of Athani, the son of Zaarai, 42 the son of Adai, the son of Ætham, the son of Zammam, the son of Semei, 43 the son of Jeeth, the son of Gedson, the son of Levi. 44 And the sons of Merari their brethren on the left hand: Ætham the son of Kisa, the son of Abai, the son of Maloch, 45 the son of Asebi, 46 the son of Amessias, the son of Bani, the son of Semer, 47 the son of Mooli, the son of Musi, the son of Merari, the son of Levi. 48 And their brethren according to the houses of their fathers, *were* the Levites who were appointed to all the work of ministration of the tabernacle of the house of God. 49 And Aaron and his sons *were* to burn incense on the altar of whole-burnt-offerings, and on the altar of incense, for all the ministry *in* the holy of holies, and to make atonement for Israel, according to all things that Moses the servant of the Lord commanded. 50 And these *are* the sons of Aaron; Eleazar his son, Phinees his son, Abisu his son, 51 Bokki his son, Ozi his son, Saraia his son, 52 Mariel his son, Amaria his son, Achitob his son, 53 Sadoc his son, Achimaas his son. 54 And these *are* their residences in their villages, in their coasts, to the sons of Aaron, to their family the Caathites: for they had the lot. 55 And they gave them Chebron in the land of Juda, and its suburbs round about it. 56 But the fields of the city, and its villages, they gave to Chaleb the son of Jephonne. 57 And to the sons of Aaron they gave the cities of refuge, *even* Chebron, and Lobna and her suburbs round about, and Selna and her suburbs, and Esthamo and her suburbs, 58 and Jethar and her suburbs, and Dabir and her suburbs, 59 and Asan and her suburbs, and Baethsamys and her suburbs: 60 and of the tribe of Benjamin Gabai and her suburbs, and Galemath and her suburbs, and Anathoth and her suburbs: all their cities *were* thirteen cities according to their families. 61 And to the sons of Caath that were left of their families, *there were given* out of the tribe, *namely*, out of the half-tribe of Manasse, by lot, ten cities. 62 And to the sons of Gedson according to their families *there were given* thirteen cities of the tribe of Issachar, of the tribe of Aser, of the tribe of Nephthali, of the tribe of Manasse in Basan. 63 And to the sons of Merari according to their families *there were given*, by lot, twelve cities of the tribe of Ruben, of the tribe of Gad, *and* of the tribe of Zabulon. 64 So the children of Israel gave to the Levites the cities and their suburbs. 65 And they gave by lot out of the tribe of the children of Juda, and out of the tribe of the children of Symeon, and out of the tribe of the children of Benjamin, these cities which they call by name. 66 And *to the members* of the families of the sons of Caath there were also given the cities of their borders out of the tribe of Ephraim. 67 And they gave them the cities of refuge, Sychem and her suburbs in mount Ephraim, and Gazer and her suburbs, 68 and Jecmaan and her suburbs, and Baethoron and her suburbs, 69 and Ælon and her suburbs, and Gethremmon and her suburbs: 70 and of the half-tribe of Manasse Anar and her suburbs, and Jemblaan and her suburbs, to the sons of Caath that were left, according to *each several* family. 71 To the sons of Gedson from the families of the half-tribe of Manasse *they*

gave Golan of Basan and her suburbs, and Aseroth and her suburbs. 72 And out of the tribe of Issachar, Kedes and her suburbs, and Deberi and her suburbs, and Dabor and her suburbs, 73 and Ramoth, and Ænan and her suburbs. 74 And of the tribe of Aser; Maasal and her suburbs, and Abdon and her suburbs, 75 and Acac and her suburbs, and Roob and her suburbs. 76 And of the tribe of Nephthali; Kedes in Galilee and her suburbs, and Chamoth and her suburbs, and Kariathaim and her suburbs. 77 To the sons of Merari that were left, *they gave* out of the tribe of Zabulon Remmon and her suburbs, and Thabor and her suburbs: 78 out of *the country* beyond Jordan; Jericho westward of Jordan: out of the tribe of Ruben; Bosor in the wilderness and her suburbs, and Jasa and her suburbs, 79 and Kadmoth and her suburbs, and Maephla and her suburbs. 80 Out of the tribe of Gad; Rammoth Galaad and her suburbs, and Maanaim and her suburbs, 81 and Esebon and her suburbs, and Jazer and her suburbs.

1-Chron.7 1 And *as* to the sons of Issachar, *they were* Thola, and Phua, and Jasub, and Semeron, four. 2 And the sons of Thola; Ozi, Raphaia, and Jeriel, and Jamai, and Jemasan, and Samuel, chiefs of their fathers' houses *belonging to* Thola, men of might according to their generations; their number in the days of David *was* twenty and two thousand and six hundred. 3 And the sons of Ozi; Jezraia: and the sons of Jezraia; Michael, Abdiu, and Joel, and Jesia, five, all rulers. 4 And with them, according to their generations, according to the houses of their families, *were men* mighty to set *armies* in array for war, thirty and six thousand, for they had multiplied *their* wives and children. 5 And their brethren among all the families of Issachar, also mighty men, *were* eighty-seven thousand—*this was* the number of them all. 6 The sons of Benjamin; Bale, and Bachir, and Jediel, three. 7 And the sons of Bale; Esebon, and Ozi, and Oziel, and Jerimuth, and Uri, five; heads of houses of families, mighty men; and their number *was* twenty and two thousand and thirty-four. 8 And the sons of Bachir; Zemira, and Joas, and Eliezer, and Elithenan, and Amaria, and Jerimuth, and Abiud, and Anathoth, and Eleemeth: all these *were* the sons of Bachir. 9 And their number according to their generations, (*they were* chiefs of their fathers' houses, men of might), *was* twenty thousand and two hundred. 10 And the sons of Jediel; Balaan: and the sons of Balaan; Jaus, and Benjamin, and Aoth, and Chanana, and Zaethan, and Tharsi, and Achisaar. 11 All these *were* the sons of Jediel, chiefs of their families, men of might, seventeen thousand and two hundred, going forth to war with might. 12 And Sapphin, and Apphin, and the sons of Or, Asom, whose son *was* Aor. 13 The sons of Nephthali; Jasiel, Goni, and Aser, and Sellum, his sons, Balam his son. 14 The sons of Manasse; Esriel, whom his Syrian concubine bore; and she bore to him also Machir the father of Galaad. 15 And Machir took a wife for Apphin and Sapphin, and his sister's name was Moocha; and the name of the second *son* was Sapphaad; and to Sapphaad were born daughters. 16 And Moocha the wife of Machir bore a son, and called his name Phares; and his brother's name *was* Surus; his sons *were* Ulam, and Rocom. 17 And the sons of Ulam; Badam. These *were* the sons of Galaad, the son of Machir, the son of Manasse. 18 And his sister Malecheth bore Isud, and Abiezer, and Maela. 19 And the sons of Semira were, Aim, and Sychem, and Lakim, and Anian. 20 And the sons of Ephraim; Sothalath, and Barad his son, and Thaath his son, Elada his son, Saath his son, 21 and Zabad his son, Sothele his son, and Azer, and Elead: and the men of Geth who were born in the land slew them, because they went down to take their cattle. 22 And their father Ephraim mourned many days, and his brethren came to comfort him. 23 And he went in to his wife, and she conceived, and bore a son, and he called his name Beria, because, *said he*, he was afflicted in my house. 24 And his daughter *was* Saraa, and he was among them that were left, and he built Baethoron the upper and the lower. And the descendants of Ozan *were* Seera, 25 and Raphe his son, Saraph and Thalees his sons, Thaen his son. 26 To Laadan his son *was born his* son Amiud, his son Helisamai, *his* son 27 Nun, *his* son Jesue, *these were* his sons. 28 And their possession and their dwelling *were* Baethel and her towns, to the east Noaran, westward Gazer and her towns, and Sychem and her towns, as far as Gaza and her towns. 29 And as far as the borders of the sons of Manasse, Baethsaan and her towns, Thanach and her towns, Mageddo and her towns, Dor and her towns. In this the children of Joseph the son of Israel dwelt. 30 The sons of Aser; Jemna, and Suia, and Isui, and Beria, and Sore their sister. 31 And the sons of Beria; Chaber, and Melchiel; he *was* the father of Berthaith. 32 And Chaber begot Japhlet, and Samer, and Chothan, and Sola their sister. 33 And the sons of Japhlet; Phasec, and Bamael, and Asith: these *are* the sons of Japhlet. 34 And the sons of Semmer; Achir, and Rooga, and Jaba, and Aram. 35 And the sons of Elam his brother; Sopha, and Imana, and Selles, and Amal. 36 The sons of Sopha; Sue, and Arnaphar, and Suda, and Barin, and Imran, 37 and Basan, and Oa, and Sama, and Salisa, and Jethra, and Beera. 38 And the sons of Jether, Jephina, and Phaspha, and Ara. 39 And the sons of Ola; Orech, Aniel, and Rasia. 40 All these *were* the sons of Aser, all heads of families, choice, mighty men, chief leaders: their number for battle array—their number *was* twenty-six thousand men.

1-Chron.8 1 Now Benjamin begot Bale his first-born, and Asbel his second *son*, Aara the third, Noa the fourth, 2 and Rapha the fifth. 3 And the sons of Bale were, Adir, and Gera, and Abiud, 4 and Abessue, and Noama, and Achia, 5 and Gera, and Sephupham, and Uram. 6 These *were* the sons of Aod: these are the heads of families to them that dwell in Gabee, and they removed them to Machanathi: 7 and Nooma, and Achia and Gera, he removed them, and he begot Aza, and Jachicho. 8 And Saarin begot *children* in the plain of Moab, after that he had sent away Osin and Baada his wives. 9 And he begot of his wife Ada, Jolab, and Sebia, and Misa, and Melchas, 10 and Jebus, and Zabia, and Marma: these *were* heads of families. 11 And of Osin he begot Abitol, and Alphaal. 12 And the sons of Alphaal; Obed, Misaal, Semmer: he built Ona, and Lod, and its towns: 13 and Beria, and Sama; these *were* heads of families among the dwellers in Elam, and they drove out the inhabitants of Geth. 14 And his brethren *were* Sosec, and Arimoth, 15 and Zabadia, and Ored, and Eder, 16 and Michael, and Jespha, and Joda, the sons of Beria: 17 and Zabadia, and Mosollam, and Azaki, and Abar, 18 and Isamari, and Jexlias, and Jobab, the sons of Elphaal: 19 and Jakim, and Zachri, and Zabdi, 20 and Elionai, and Salathi, 21 and Elieli, and Adaia, and Baraia, and Samarath, sons of Samaith: 22 and Jesphan, and Obed, and Eliel, 23 and Abdon, and Zechri, and Anan, 24 and Anania, and Ambri, and Ælam, *and* Anathoth, 25 and Jathin, and Jephadias, and Phanuel, the sons of Sosec: 26 and Samsari, and Saarias, and Gotholia, 27 and Jarasia, and Eria, and Zechri, son of Iroam. 28 These *were* heads of families, chiefs according to their generations: these dwelt in Jerusalem. 29 And the father of Gabaon dwelt in Gabaon; and his wife's name was Moacha. 30 And her first-born son was Abdon, and Sur, and Kis, and Baal, and Nadab, and Ner, 31 and Gedur and his brother, and Zacchur, and Makeloth. 32 And Makeloth begot Samaa: for these dwelt in Jerusalem in the presence of their brethren with their brethren. 33 And Ner begot Kis, and Kis begot Saul, and Saul begot Jonathan, and Melchisue, and Aminadab, and Asabal. 34 And the son of Jonathan *was* Meribaal; and Meribaal begot Micha. 35 And the sons of Micha; Phithon, and Melach, and Tharach, and Achaz. 36 And Achaz begot Jada, and Jada begot Salaemath, and Asmoth, and Zambri; and Zambri begot Maesa; 37 and Maesa begot Baana: Rhaphaea *was* his son, Elasa his son, Esel his son. 38 And Esel *had* six sons, and these *were* their name; Ezricam his first-born, and Ismael, and Saraia, and Abdia, and Anan, and Asa: all these *were* the sons of Esel. 39 And the sons of Asel his brother; Ælam his first-born, and Jas the second, and Eliphalet the third. 40 And the sons of Ælam were mighty men, bending the bow, and multiplying sons and grandsons, a hundred *and* fifty. All these *were* of the sons of Benjamin.

1-Chron.9 1 And *this is* all Israel, *even* their enrolment: and these *are* written down in the book of the kings of Israel and Juda, with the *names of them* that were carried away to Babylon for their transgressions. 2 And they that dwelt before in their possessions in the cities of Israel, the priests, the Levites, and the appointed ones. 3 And there dwelt in Jerusalem some of the children of Juda, and of the children of Benjamin, and of the children of Ephraim, and Manasse. 4 And Gnothi, and the son of Samiud, the son of Amri, the son of Ambraim, the son of Buni, son of the sons of Phares, the son of Juda. 5 And of the Selonites; Asaia his first-born, and his sons. 6 Of the sons of Zara; Jeel, and their brethren, six hundred and ninety. 7 And of the sons of Benjamin; Salom, son of Mosollam, son of Odouia, son of Asinu. 8 And Jemnaa son of Jeroboam, and Elo: these *are* the sons of Ozi the son of Machir: and Mosollam, son of Saphatia, son of Raguel, son of Jemnai; 9 and their brethren according to their generations, nine hundred and fifty-six, all the men *were* heads of families according to the houses of their fathers. 10 And of the priests; Jodae, and Joarim, and Jachin, 11 and Azaria the son of Chelcias, the son of Mosollam, the son of Sadoc, the son of Maraioth, the son of Achitob, the ruler of the house of God; 12 and Adaia son of Iraam, son of Phascor, son of Melchia, and Maasaia son of Adiel, son of Ezira, son of Mosollam, son of Maselmoth, son of Emmer; 13 and their brethren, chiefs of their families, a thousand seven hundred and sixty, mighty *men* for the work of the ministration of the house of God. 14 And of the Levites; Samaia son of Asob, son of Ezricam, son of Asabia, of the sons of Merari. 15 And Bacbacar, and Ares, and Galaal, and Matthanias son of Micha, son of Zechri, son of Asaph; 16 and Abdia, son of Samia, son of Galaal, son of Idithun, and Barachia son of Ossa, son of Helcana—who dwelt in the villages of the Notephatites. 17 The door-keepers; Salom, Acum, Telmon, and Diman, and their brethren; Salom *was* the chief; 18 and *he waited* hitherto in the king's gate eastward: these *are* the gates of the companies of the sons of Levi. 19 And Sellum the son of Core, the son of Abiasaph, the son of Core, and his brethren belonging to the house of his father, the Corites *were* over the works of the service, keeping the watches of the tabernacle, and their fathers over the camp of the Lord, keeping the entrance. 20 And Phinees son of Eleazar was head over them before the Lord, and these *were* with him. 21 Zacharias the son of Mosollami *was* keeper of the door of the tabernacle of witness. 22 All the chosen porters in the gates *were* two hundred and twelve, these *were* in their courts, *this was* their distribution: these David and Samuel the seer established in their charge. 23 And these and their sons *were* over the gates in the house of the Lord, and in the house of the tabernacle, to keep watch. 24 The gates were toward the four winds, eastward, westward, northward, southward. 25 And their brethren *were* in their courts, to enter in weekly from time to time with these. 26 For four strong *men* have the charge of the gates; and the Levites were over the chambers, and they keep watch over the treasures of the house of God. 27 For the charge *was* upon them, and these *were* charged with the keys to open the doors of the temple every morning. 28 And *some* of them *were appointed* over the vessels of service, that they should carry them in by number, and carry them out by number. 29 And *some* of them *were* appointed over the furniture, and over all the holy vessels, and over the fine flour, the wine, the oil, the frankincense, and the spices. 30 And some of the priests were makers of the ointment, and *appointed to prepare* the spices. 31 And Matthathias of the Levites, (he *was* the first-born of Salom the Corite,)*was set* in charge over the sacrifices of meat-offering of the pan belonging to the high priest. 32 And Banaias the Caathite, from among their brethren, *was set* over the shewbread, to prepare it every sabbath. 33 And these *were* the singers, heads of families of the Levites, *to whom were* established daily courses, for they were employed in the services day and night. 34 These *were* the heads of the families of the Levites according to their generations; these chiefs dwelt in Jerusalem. 35 And Jeel the father of Gabaon dwelt in Gabaon; and his wife's name *was* Moocha. 36 And his first-born son *was* Abdon, and *he had* Sur, and Kis, and Baal, and Ner, and Nadab, 37 and Gedur and *his* brother, and Zacchur, and Makeloth. 38 And Makeloth begot Samaa: and these dwelt in the midst of their brethren in Jerusalem, *even* in the midst of their brethren. 39 And Ner begot Kis, and Kis begot Saul, and

Saul begot Jonathan, and Melchisue, and Aminadab, and Asabal. 40 And the son of Jonathan *was* Meribaal: and Meribaal begot Micha. 41 And the sons of Micha *were* Phithon and Malach, and Tharach. 42 And Achaz begot Jada: and Jada begot Galemeth, and Gazmoth, and Zambri; and Zambri begot Massa. 43 And Massa begot Baana, and Rhaphaia *was* his son, Elasa his son, Esel his son. 44 And Esel had six sons, and these *were* their names; Esricam his first-born, and Ismael, and Saraia, and Abdia, and Anan, and Asa: these *were* the sons of Esel.

1-Chron.10 1 Now the Philistines warred against Israel; and they fled from before the Philistines, and fell down slain in mount Gelbue. 2 And the Philistines pursued after Saul, and after his sons; and the Philistines smote Jonathan, and Aminadab, and Melchisue, sons of Saul. 3 And the battle prevailed against Saul, and the archers hit him with bows and arrows, and they were wounded of the bows. 4 And Saul said to his armour-bearer, Draw thy sword, and pierce me through with it, lest these uncircumcised come and mock me. But his armour-bearer would not, for he was greatly afraid: so Saul took a sword, and fell upon it. 5 And his armour-bearer saw that Saul was dead, and he also fell upon his sword. 6 So Saul died, and his three sons on that day, and all his family died at the same time. 7 And all the men of Israel that were in the valley saw that Israel fled, and that Saul and his sons were dead, and they left their cities, and fled: and the Philistines came and dwelt in them. 8 And it came to pass on the next *day* that the Philistines came to strip the slain, and they found Saul and his sons fallen on mount Gelbue. 9 And they stripped him, and took his head, and his armour, and sent them into the land of the Philistines round about, to proclaim the glad tidings to their idols, and to the people. 10 And they put their armour in the house of their god, and they put his head in the house of Dagon. 11 And all the dwellers in Galaad heard of all that the Philistines had done to Saul and to Israel. 12 And all the mighty men rose up from Galaad, and they took the body of Saul, and the bodies of his sons, and brought them to Jabis, and buried their bones under the oak in Jabis, and fasted seven days. 13 So Saul died for his transgressions, wherein he transgressed against God, against the word of the Lord, forasmuch as he kept *it* not, because Saul enquired of a wizard to seek *counsel*, and Samuel the prophet answered him: 14 and he sought not the Lord: so he slew him, and turned the kingdom to David the son of Jesse.

1-Chron.11 1 And all Israel came to David in Chebron, saying, Behold, we *are* thy bones and thy flesh. 2 And heretofore when Saul was king, thou wast he that led Israel in and out, and the Lord of Israel said to thee, Thou shalt feed my people Israel, and thou shalt be for a ruler over Israel. 3 And all the elders of Israel came to the king to Chebron; and king David made a covenant with them in Chebron before the Lord: and they anointed David to be king over Israel, according to the word of the Lord by Samuel. 4 And the king and his men went to Jerusalem, this *is* Jebus; and there the Jebusites the inhabitants of the land said to David, 5 Thou shalt not enter in hither. But he took the strong hold of Sion: this *is* the city of David. 6 And

David said, Whoever first smites the Jebusite, even he shall be chief and captain. And Joab the son of Saruia went up first, and became chief. 7 And David dwelt in the strong hold; therefore he called it the city of David. 8 And he fortified the city round about. 9 And David continued to increase, and the Lord Almighty *was* with him. 10 And these *are* the chiefs of the mighty men, whom David had, who strengthened *themselves* with him in his kingdom, with all Israel, to make him king, according to the word of the Lord concerning Israel. 11 And this *is* the list of the mighty *men* of David; Jesebada, son of Achaman, first of the thirty: he drew his sword once against three hundred whom he slew at one time. 12 And after him Eleazar son of Dodai, the Achochite: he was among the three mighty men. 13 He was with David in Phasodamin, and the Philistines were gathered there to battle, and *there was* a portion of the field full of barley; and the people fled before the Philistines. 14 And he stood in the midst of the portion, and rescued it, and smote the Philistines; and the Lord wrought a great deliverance. 15 And three of the thirty chiefs went down to the rock to David, to the cave of Odollam, and the camp of the Philistines *was* in the giants' valley. 16 And David *was* then in the hold, and the garrison of the Philistines *was* then in Bethleem. 17 And David longed, and said, Who will give me water to drink of the well of Bethleem, that is in the gate? 18 And the three broke through the camp of the Philistines, and they drew water out of the well that was in Bethleem, which was in the gate, and they took it, and came to David: but David would not drink it, and poured it out to the Lord, and said, 19 God forbid that I should do this thing: shall I drink the blood of these men with their lives? for with *the peril of* their lives they brought it. So he would not drink it. These things did the three mighty *men*. 20 And Abisa the brother of Joab, he was chief of three: he drew his sword against three hundred slain at one time, and he had a name among the *second* three. 21 He was more famous than the two *others* of the three, and he was chief *over* them; yet he reached not to the *first* three. 22 And Banaia the son of Jodae was the son of a mighty man: many *were* his acts for Cabasael: he smote two lion-like men of Moab, and he went down and smote a lion in a pit on a snowy day. 23 And he smote an Egyptian, a wonderful man five cubits *high*; and in the hand of the Egyptian *there was* a spear like a weavers' beam; and Banaia went down to him with a staff, and took the spear out of the Egyptian's hand, and slew him with his own spear. 24 These things did Banaia son of Jodae, and his name *was* among the three mighties. 25 He was distinguished beyond the thirty, yet he reached not to the *first* three: and David set him over his family. 26 And the mighty *men* of the forces *were*, Asael the brother of Joab, Eleanan the son of Dodoe of Bethleem, 27 Samaoth the Arorite, Chelles the Phelonite, 28 Ora the son of Ekkis the Thecoite, Abiezer the Anathothite, 29 Sobochai the Usathite, Eli the Achonite, 30 Marai the Netophathite, Chthaod the son of Nooza the Netophathite, 31 Airi the son of Rebie of the hill of Benjamin, Banaias the Pharathonite, 32 Uri of Nachali Gaas, Abiel the Garabaethite, 33 Azbon the Baromite, Eliaba the Salabonite, 34 the son of Asam the Gizonite, Jonathan the son of Sola the Ararite, 35 Achim the son of Achar the Ararite, Elphat the son of Thyrophar 36 the Mechorathrite, Achia the Phellonite, 37 Esere the Charmadaite, Naarai the son of Azobai, 38 Joel the son of Nathan, Mebaal son of Agari, 39 Sele the son of Ammoni, Nachor the Berothite, armour-bearer to the son of Saruia, 40 Ira the Jethrite, Gaber the Jethrite, 41 Uria the Chettite, Zabet son of Achaia, 42 Adina son of Saeza, a chief of Ruben, and thirty with him, 43 Anan the son of Moocha, and Josaphat the Matthanite, 44 Ozia the Astarothite, Samatha and Jeiel sons of Chotham the Ararite, 45 Jediel the son of Sameri, and Jozae his brother the Thosaite, 46 Eliel the Maoite, and Jaribi, and Josia his son, Ellaam, and Jethama the Moabite, 47 Daliel, and Obeth, and Jessiel of Mesobia.

1-Chron.12 1 And these *are* they that came to Sikelag, when he yet kept himself close because of Saul the son of Kis; and these *were* among the mighty, aiding *him* in war, 2 and *using* the bow with the right hand and with the left, and slingers with stones, and *shooters* with bows. Of the brethren of Saul of Benjamin, 3 the chief *was* Achiezer, and Joas son of Asma the Gabathite, and Joel and Jophalet, sons of Asmoth, and Berchia, and Jeul of Anathoth, 4 and Samaias the Gabaonite a mighty man among the thirty, and over the thirty; *and* Jeremia, and Jeziel, and Joanan, and Jozabath of Gadarathiim, 5 Azai and Arimuth, and Baalia, and Samaraia, and Saphatias of Charaephiel, 6 Helcana, and Jesuni, and Ozriel, and Jozara, and Sobocam, and the Corites, 7 and Jelia and Zabadia, sons of Iroam, and the *men* of Gedor. 8 And from Gad these separated themselves to David from the wilderness, strong mighty men of war, bearing shields and spears, and their faces *were as* the face of a lion, and they were nimble as roes upon the mountains in speed. 9 Aza the chief, Abdia the second, Eliab the third, 10 Masmana the fourth, Jeremias the fifth, 11 Jethi the sixth, Eliab the seventh, 12 Joanan the eighth, Eleazer the ninth, 13 Jeremia the tenth, Melchabanai the eleventh. 14 These *were* chiefs of the army of the sons of Gad, the least one commander of a hundred, and the greatest one of a thousand. 15 These *are* the *men* that crossed over Jordan in the first month, and it had overflowed all its banks; and they drove out all the inhabitants of the valleys, from the east to the west. 16 And there came *some* of the sons of Benjamin and Juda to the assistance of David. 17 And David went out to meet them, and said to them, If ye are come peaceably to me, let my heart be at peace with you: but if *ye are come* to betray me to my enemies unfaithfully, the God of your fathers look upon it, and reprove it. 18 And the Spirit came upon Amasai, a captain of the thirty, and he said, Go, David, son of Jesse, thou and thy people, peace, peace be to thee, and peace to thy helpers, for thy God has helped thee. And David received them, and made them captains of the forces. 19 And *some* came to David from Manasse, when the Philistines came against Saul to war: and he helped them not, because the captains of the Philistines took counsel, saying, With the heads of those men will he return to his master Saul. 20 When David was going to Sikelag, there came to him of Manasse, Edna and Jozabath, and Rodiel, and Michael, and Josabaith, and Elimuth, and Semathi: *these* are the captains of thousands of Manasse. 21 And they fought on the side of David against a troop, for they *were* all men of might; and they were commanders in the army, *because* of *their* might. 22 For daily men came to David, *till they amounted* to a great force, as the force of God. 23 And these *are* the names of the commanders of the army, who came to David to Chebron, to turn the kingdom of Saul to him according to the word of the Lord. 24 The sons of Juda, bearing shields and spears, six thousand and eight hundred mighty in war. 25 Of the sons of Symeon mighty for battle, seven thousand and a hundred. 26 Of the sons of Levi, four thousand and six hundred. 27 And Joadas the chief *of the family* of Aaron, and with him three thousand and seven hundred. 28 And Sadoc, a young *man* mighty in strength, and *there were* twenty-two leaders of his father's house. 29 And of the sons of Benjamin, the brethren of Saul, three thousand: and still the greater part of them kept the guard of the house of Saul. 30 And of the sons of Ephraim, twenty thousand and eight hundred mighty men, famous in the houses of their fathers. 31 And of the half-tribe of Manasse, eighteen thousand, even *those* who were named by name, to make David king. 32 And of the sons of Issachar having wisdom with regard to the times, knowing what Israel should do, two hundred; and all their brethren with them. 33 And of Zabulon they that went out to battle, with all weapons of war, *were* fifty thousand to help David, not weak-handed. 34 And of Nephthali a thousand captains, and with them *men* with shields and spears, thirty-seven thousand. 35 And of the Danites *men* ready for war twenty-eight thousand and eight hundred. 36 And of Aser, they that went out to give aid in war, forty thousand. 37 And from the country beyond Jordan, from Ruben, and the Gadites, and from the half-tribe of Manasse, a hundred and twenty thousand, with all weapons of war. 38 All these *were* men of war, setting *the army* in battle array, with a peaceful mind *towards him*, and they came to Chebron to make David king over all Israel: and the rest of Israel *were of* one mind to make David king. 39 And they were there three days eating and drinking, for their brethren *had* made preparations. 40 And their neighbours, as far as Issachar and Zabulon and Nephthali, brought to them upon camels, and asses, and mules, and upon calves, victuals, meal, cakes of figs, raisins, wine, and oil, calves and sheep abundantly: for *there was* joy in Israel.

1-Chron.13 1 And David took counsel with the captains of thousands and captains of hundreds, *even with* every commander. 2 And David said to the whole congregation of Israel, If it *seem* good to you, and it should be prospered by the Lord our God, let us send to our brethren that are left in all the land of Israel, and let the priests the Levites who are with them in the cities of their possession *come*, and let them be gathered to us. 3 And let us bring over to us the ark of our God; for men have not enquired *at* it since the days of Saul. 4 And all the congregation said that they would do thus; for the saying was right in the eyes of all the people. 5 So David assembled all Israel, from the borders of Egypt even to the entering in of Hemath, to bring in the ark of God from the city of Jarim. 6 And David brought it up: and all Israel went up to the city of David, which belonged to Juda, to bring up thence the ark of the Lord God who sits between the cherubim, whose name is called *on it*. 7 And they set the ark of God on a new waggon *brought* out of the house of Aminadab: and Oza and his brethren drove the waggon. 8 And David and all Israel *were* playing before the Lord with all their might, and *that* together with singers, and with harps, and with lutes, with timbrels, and with cymbals, and with trumpets. 9 And they came as far as the threshing-floor: and Oza put forth his hand to hold the ark, because the bullock moved it from *its place*. 10 And the Lord was very angry with Oza, and smote him there, because of his stretching forth his hand upon the ark: and he died there before God. 11 And David was dispirited, because the Lord *had* made a breach on Oza: and he called that place the Breach of Oza until this day. 12 And David feared God that day, saying, How shall I bring the ark of God in to myself? 13 So David brought not the ark home to himself into the city of David, but he turned it aside into the house of Abeddara the Gethite. 14 And the ark of God abode in the house of Abeddara three months: and God blessed Abeddara and all that he had.

1-Chron.14 1 And Chiram king of Tyre sent messengers to David, and cedar timbers, and masons, and carpenters, to build a house for him. 2 And David knew that the Lord *had* designed him to be king over Israel; because his kingdom was highly exalted, on account of his people Israel. 3 And David took more wives in Jerusalem: and there were born to David more sons and daughters. 4 And these *are* the names of those that were born, who were *born* to him in Jerusalem; Samaa, Sobab, Nathan, and Solomon, 5 and Baar, and Elisa, and Eliphaleth, 6 and Nageth, and Naphath, and Japhie, 7 and Elisamae, and Eliade, and Eliphala. 8 And the Philistines heard that David was anointed king over all Israel: and all the Philistines went up to seek David; and David heard *it*, and went out to meet them. 9 And the Philistines came and assembled together in the giants' valley. 10 And David enquired of God, saying, Shall I go up against the Philistines? and wilt thou deliver them into my hand? And the Lord said to him, Go up, and I will deliver them into thy hands. 11 And he went up to Baal Pharasin, and David smote them there; and David said, God has broken through enemies by my hand like a breach of water: therefore he called the name of that place, the Breach of Pharasin. 12 And the Philistines left their gods there; and David gave orders to burn them with fire. 13 And the Philistines once more assembled themselves in the giants' valley. 14 And David enquired of God again; and God said to him, Thou shalt not go after them; turn away from them, and thou shalt come upon them near the pear trees. 15 And it shall be, when thou shalt hear the sound of their tumult in the tops of the pear trees, then thou shalt go into the battle: for God has gone out before thee to smite the army of the Philistines. 16 And he did as God commanded him: and he smote the army of the Philistines from Gabaon to Gazera. 17 And the name of David was *famous* in all the land; and the Lord put the terror of him on all the nations.

1-Chron.15 1 And *David* made for himself houses in the city of David, and he prepared a place for the ark of God, and made a tent for it. 2 Then said David, It is not *lawful for any* to bear the ark of God, but the Levites; for the Lord has chosen them to bear the ark of the Lord, and to minister to him for ever. 3 And David assembled all Israel at Jerusalem, to bring up the ark of the Lord to the place which he *had* prepared for it. 4 And David gathered together the sons of Aaron the Levites. 5 Of the sons of Caath; *there was* Uriel the chief, and his brethren, a hundred and twenty. 6 Of the sons of Merari; Asaia the chief, and his brethren, two hundred and twenty. 7 Of the sons of Gedson; Joel the chief, and his brethren, a hundred and thirty. 8 Of the sons of Elisaphat; Semei the chief, and his brethren, two hundred. 9 Of the sons of Chebrom; Eliel the chief, and his brethren eighty. 10 Of the sons of Oziel; Aminadab the chief, and his brethren a hundred and twelve. 11 And David called Sadoc and Abiathar the priests, and the Levites, Uriel, Asaia, and Joel, and Semaia, and Eliel, and Aminadab, 12 and said to them, Ye *are* the heads of the families of the Levites: sanctify yourselves, you and your brethren, and ye shall carry up the ark of the God of Israel, *to the place* which I have prepared for it. 13 For because ye were not *ready* at the first, our God made a breach upon us, because we sought him not according to the ordinance. 14 So the priests and the Levites sanctified themselves, to bring up the ark of the God of Israel. 15 And the sons of the Levites took the ark of God, (as Moses commanded by the word of God according to the scripture) upon their shoulders with staves. 16 And David said to the chiefs of the Levites, Set your brethren the singers with musical instruments, lutes, harps, and cymbals, to sound aloud with a voice of joy. 17 So the Levites appointed Æman the son of Joel; Asaph the son of Barachias *was one* of his brethren; and Æthan the son of Kisaeus was of the sons of Merari their brethren; 18 and with them their brethren of the second rank, Zacharias, and Oziel, and Semiramoth, and Jeiel, and Elioel, and Eliab, and Banaia, and Maasaia, and Matthathia, and Eliphena, and Makellia, and Abdedom, and Jeiel, and Ozias, the porters. 19 And the singers, Æman, Asaph, and Æthan, with brazen cymbals to make *a sound* to be heard. 20 Zacharias, and Oziel, Semiramoth, Jeiel, Oni, Eliab, Maasaeas, Banaeas, with lutes, on alaemoth. 21 And Mattathias, and Eliphalu, and Makenia, and Abdedom, and Jeiel, and Ozias, with harps of Amasenith, to make a loud noise. 22 And Chonenia chief of the Levites *was* master of the bands, because he was skilful. 23 And Barachia and Elcana *were* door-keepers of the ark. 24 And Somnia, and Josaphat, and Nathanael, and Amasai, and Zacharia, and Banaea, and Eliezer, the priests, were sounding with trumpets before the ark of God: and Abdedom and Jeia *were* door-keepers of the ark of God. 25 So David, and the elders of Israel, and the captains of thousands, went to bring up the ark of the covenant from the house of Abdedom with gladness. 26 And it came to pass when God strengthened the Levites bearing the ark of the covenant of the Lord, that they sacrificed seven calves and seven rams. 27 And David *was* girt with a fine linen robe, and all the Levites *who were* bearing the ark of the covenant of the Lord, and the singers, and Chonenias the master of the band of singers; also upon David *there was* a robe of fine linen. 28 And all Israel brought up the ark of the covenant of the Lord with shouting, and with the sound of a horn, and with trumpets, and with cymbals, playing loudly on lutes and harps. 29 And the ark of the covenant of the Lord arrived, and came to the city of David; and Melchol the daughter of Saul looked down through the window, and saw king David dancing and playing: and she despised him in her heart.

1-Chron.16 1 So they brought in the ark of God, and set it in the midst of the tabernacle which David pitched for it; and they offered whole-burnt-offerings and peace-offerings before God. 2 And David finished offering up whole-burnt-offerings and peace-offerings, and blessed the people in the name of the Lord. 3 And he divided to every man of Israel (both men and women), to *every* man one baker's loaf, and a cake. 4 And he appointed before the ark of the covenant of the Lord, Levites to minister *and* lift up the voice, and to give thanks and praise the Lord God of Israel: 5 Asaph *was* the chief, and next to him Zacharias, Jeiel, Semiramoth, and Jeiel, Mattathias, Eliab, and Banaeas, and Abdedom: and Jeiel sounding with musical instruments, lutes *and* harps, and Asaph with cymbals: 6 and Banaeas and Oziel the priests *sounding* continually with trumpets before the ark of the covenant of God in that day. 7 Then David first gave orders to praise the Lord by the hand of Asaph and his brethren. 8 Song. Give thanks to the Lord, call upon him by his name, make known his designs among the people. 9 Sing *songs* to him, and sing hymns to him, relate to all *people* his wonderful deeds, which the Lord has wrought. 10 Praise his holy name, the heart that seeks his pleasure shall rejoice. 11 Seek the Lord and be strong, seek his face continually. 12 Remember his wonderful works which he has wrought, his wonders, and the judgments of his mouth; 13 *ye* seed of Israel his servants, *ye* seed of Jacob his chosen ones. 14 He *is* the Lord our God; his judgments *are* in all the earth. 15 Let us remember his covenant for ever, his word which he commanded to a thousand generations, 16 which he covenanted with Abraham, and his oath *sworn* to Isaac. 17 He confirmed it to Jacob for an ordinance, to Israel *as* an everlasting covenant, 18 saying, To thee will I give the land of Chanaan, the line of your inheritance: 19 when they were few in number, when they were but little, and dwelt as strangers in it; 20 and went from nation to nation, and from one kingdom to another people. 21 He suffered not a man to oppress them, and he reproved kings for their sakes, 22 saying, Touch not my anointed ones, and deal not wrongfully with my prophets. 23 Sing ye to the Lord, all the earth; proclaim his salvation from day to day. 24 Declare among the nations his glory, his wondrous deeds among all peoples. 25 For the Lord *is* great, and greatly to be praised: he *is* to be feared above all gods. 26 For all the gods of the nations *are* idols; but our God made the heavens. 27 Glory and praise *are* in his presence; strength and rejoicing *are* in his place. 28 Give to the Lord, ye families of the nations, give to the Lord glory and strength. 29 Give to the Lord the glory *belonging* to his name: take gifts and offer *them* before him; and worship the Lord in his holy courts. 30 Let the whole earth fear before him; let the earth be established, and not be moved. 31 Let the heavens rejoice, and let the earth exult; and let them say among the nations, The Lord reigns. 32 The sea with its fullness shall resound and the tree of the field, and all things in it. 33 Then shall the trees of the wood rejoice before the Lord, for he is come to judge the earth. 34 Give thanks to the Lord, for *it is* good, for his mercy *is* for ever. 35 And say ye, Save us, O God of our salvation, and gather us, and rescue us from among the heathen, that we may praise thy holy name, and glory in thy praises. 36 Blessed *be* the Lord God of Israel from everlasting and to everlasting: And all the people shall say, Amen. So they praised the Lord. 37 And they left there Asaph and his brethren before the ark of the covenant of the Lord, to minister before the ark continually, according to the service of each day: from day to day. 38 And Abdedom and his brethren *were* sixty and eight; and Abdedom the son of Idithun, and Osa, *were* to be door-keepers. 39 And *they appointed* Sadoc the priest, and his brethren the priests, before the tabernacle of the Lord in the high place in Gabaon, 40 to offer up whole-burnt - offerings continually morning and evening, and according to all things written in the law of the Lord, which he commanded the children of Israel by Moses the servant of God. 41 And with him *were* Æman and Idithun, and the rest chosen out by name to praise the Lord, for his mercy *endures* for ever. 42 And with them *there were* trumpets and cymbals to sound aloud, and musical instruments for the songs of God: and the sons of Idithun *were* at the gate. 43 And all the people went every one to his home: and David returned to bless his house.

1-Chron.17 1 And it came to pass as David dwelt in his house, that David said to Nathan the prophet, Behold, I dwell in a house of cedar, but the ark of the covenant of the Lord *is* under *curtains* of skins. 2 And Nathan said to David, Do all that is in thy heart; for God *is* with thee. 3 And it came to pass in that night, that the word of the Lord came to Nathan, *saying*, 4 Go and say to David my servant, Thus said the Lord, Thou shalt not build me a house for me to dwell in it. 5 For I have not dwelt in a house from the day that I brought up Israel until this day, but I have been in a tabernacle and a tent, 6 in all places through which I have gone with all Israel: did I ever speak to *any* one tribe of Israel whom I commanded to feed my people, saying, *Why is it* that ye have not built me a house of cedar? 7 And now thus shalt thou say to my servant David, Thus saith the Lord Almighty, I took thee from the sheepfold, from following the flocks, to be a ruler over my people Israel: 8 and I was with thee in all places whither thou wentest, and I destroyed all thine enemies from before thee, and I made for thee a name according to the name of the great ones that are upon the earth. 9 And I will appoint a place for my people Israel, and I will plant him, and he shall dwell by himself, and shall no longer be anxious; and the son of iniquity shall no longer afflict him, as at the beginning, 10 and from the days when I appointed judges over my people Israel. Also I have humbled all thine enemies, and I will increase thee, and the Lord will build thee a house. 11 And

it shall come to pass when thy days shall be fulfilled, and thou shalt sleep with thy fathers, that I will raise up thy seed after thee, which shall be of thy bowels, and I will establish his kingdom. 12 He shall build me a house, and I will set up his throne for ever. 13 I will be to him a father, and he shall be to me a son: and my mercy will I not withdraw from him, as I withdrew *it* from them that were before thee. 14 And I will establish him in my house and in my kingdom for ever; and his throne shall be set up for ever. 15 According to all these words, and according to all this vision, so spoke Nathan to David. 16 And king David came and sat before the Lord, and said, Who am I, O Lord God? and what *is* my house, that thou hast loved me for ever? 17 And these things were little in thy sight, O God: thou hast also spoken concerning the house of thy servant for a long time to come, and thou hast looked upon me as a man looks upon his fellow, and hast exalted me, O Lord God. 18 What shall David do more toward thee to glorify *thee*? and thou knowest thy servant. 19 And thou hast wrought all this greatness according to thine heart. 20 O Lord, there is none like thee, and there is no God beside thee, according to all things which we have heard with our ears. 21 Neither is there another nation upon the earth *such* as thy people Israel, whereas God led him in the way, to redeem a people for himself, to make for himself a great and glorious name, to cast out nations from before thy people, whom thou redeemedst out of Egypt. 22 And thou hast appointed thy people Israel as a people to thyself for ever; and thou, Lord, didst become a God to them. 23 And now, Lord, let the word which thou spokest to thy servant, and concerning his house, be confirmed for ever, and do thou as thou hast spoken. 24 And let thy name *be* established and magnified for ever, *men* saying, Lord, Lord, Almighty God of Israel: and *let* the house of thy servant David *be* established before thee. 25 For thou, O Lord my God, hast revealed to the ear of thy servant that thou wilt build him a house; therefore thy servant has found a willingness to pray before thee. 26 And now, Lord, thou thyself art God, and thou hast spoken these good things concerning thy servant. 27 And now thou hast begun to bless the house of thy servant, so that it should continue for ever before thee: for thou, Lord, hast blessed *it*, and do thou bless *it* for ever.

1-Chron.18 1 And it came to pass afterwards, that David smote the Philistines, and routed them, and took Geth and its villages out of the hand of the Philistines. 2 And he smote Moab; and the Moabites became servants to David, *and* tributaries. 3 And David smote Adraazar king of Suba of Emath, as he was going to establish power toward the river Euphrates. 4 And David took of them a thousand chariots, and seven thousand horsemen, and twenty thousand infantry: and David houghed all the chariot *horses*, but there were reserved of them a hundred chariots. 5 And the Syrian came from Damascus to help Adraazar king of Suba; and David smote of the Syrian *army* twenty and two thousand men. 6 And David put a garrison in Syria near Damascus; and they became tributary servants to David: and the Lord delivered David wherever he went. 7 And David took the golden collars that were on the servants of Adraazar, and brought them to Jerusalem. 8 And David took out of Matabeth, and out of the chief cities of Adraazar very much brass: of this Solomon made the brazen sea, and the pillars, and the brazen vessels. 9 And Thoa king of Emath heard that David had smitten the whole force of Adraazar king of Suba. 10 And he sent Aduram his son to king David to ask how he was, and to congratulate him because he had fought against Adraazar, and smitten him; for Thoa was the enemy of Adraazar. 11 And all the golden and silver and brazen vessels, even these king David consecrated to the Lord, with the silver and the gold which he took from all the nations; from Idumaea, and Moab, and from the children of Ammon, and from the Philistines, and from Amalec. 12 And Abesa son of Saruia smote the Idumeans in the valley of Salt, eighteen thousand. 13 And he put garrisons in the valley; and all the Idumaeans became David's servants: and the Lord delivered David wherever he went. 14 So David reigned over all Israel; and he executed judgment and justice to all his people. 15 And Joab the son of Saruia *was* over the army, and Josaphat the son of Achilud *was* recorder. 16 And Sadoc son of Achitob, and Achimelech son of Abiathar, *were* the priests; and Susa *was* the scribe; 17 and Banaeas the son of Jodae *was* over the Cherethite and the Phelethite, and the sons of David were the chief deputies of the king.

1-Chron.19 1 And it came to pass after this, *that* Naas the king of the children of Ammon died, and Anan his son reigned in his stead. 2 And David said, I will act kindly toward Anan the son of Naas, as his father acted kindly towards me. And David sent messengers to condole with him on the death of his father. So the servants of David came into the land of the children of Ammon to Anan, to comfort him. 3 And the chiefs of the children of Ammon said to Anan, Is it to honour thy father before thee, that David has sent comforters to thee? Have not his servants come to thee that they might search the city, and to spy out the land? 4 And Anan took the servants of David, and shaved them, and cut off the half of their garments as far as their tunic, and sent them away. 5 And there came men to report to David concerning the men: and he sent to meet them, for they were greatly disgraced: and the king said, Dwell in Jericho until your beards have grown, and return. 6 And the children of Ammon saw that the people of David were ashamed, and Anan and the children of Ammon sent a thousand talents of silver to hire for themselves chariots and horsemen out of Syria of Mesopotamia, and out of Syria Maacha, and from Sobal. 7 And they hired for themselves two and thirty thousand chariots, and the king of Maacha and his people; and they came and encamped before Medaba: and the children of Ammon assembled out of their cities, and came to fight. 8 And David heard, and sent Joab and all the host of mighty men. 9 And the children of Ammon came forth, and set themselves in array for battle by the gate of the city: and the kings that were come forth encamped by themselves in the plain. 10 And Joab saw that they were fronting *him* to fight against him before and behind, and he chose *some* out of all the young men of Israel, and they set themselves in array against the Syrian. 11

And the rest of the people he gave into the hand of his brother Abesai, and they set themselves in array against the children of Ammon. 12 And he said, If the Syrian should prevail against me, then shalt thou deliver me: and if the children of Ammon should prevail against thee, then will I deliver thee. 13 Be of good courage, and let us be strong, for our people, and for the cities of our God: and the Lord shall do what *is* good in his eyes. 14 So Joab and the people that were with him set themselves in battle array against the Syrians, and they fled from them. 15 And the children of Ammon saw that the Syrians fled, and they also fled from before Abesai, and from before Joab his brother, and they came to the city: and Joab came to Jerusalem. 16 And the Syrian saw that Israel had defeated him, and he sent messengers, and they brought out the Syrians from beyond the river; and Sophath the commander-in-chief of the forces of Adraazar *was* before them. 17 And it was told David; and he gathered all Israel, and crossed over Jordan, and came upon them, and set the battle in array against them. So David set *his army* in array to fight against the Syrians, and they fought against him. 18 And the Syrians fled from before Israel; and David slew of the Syrians seven thousand *riders in* chariots, and forty thousand infantry, and he slew Sophath the commander-in-chief of the forces. 19 And the servants of Adraazar saw that they were defeated before Israel, and they made peace with David and served him: and the Syrians would not any more help the children of Ammon.

1-Chron.20 1 And it came to pass at the return of the year, at the *time of the* going forth of kings *to war*, that Joab gathered the whole force of the army, and they ravaged the land of the children of Ammon; and he came and besieged Rabba. But David abode in Jerusalem. And Joab smote Rabba and destroyed it. 2 And David took the crown of Molchom their king off his head, and the weight of it was found *to be* a talent of gold, and on it were precious stones; and it was *placed* on the head of David: and he brought out the spoils of the city *which were* very great. 3 And he brought out the people that were in it, and sawed them asunder with saws, and *cut them* with iron axes, and with harrows: and thus David did to all the children of Ammon. And David and all his people returned to Jerusalem. 4 And it came to pass afterward that there was again war with the Philistines in Gazer: then Sobochai the Sosathite smote Saphut of the sons of the giants, and laid him low. 5 And there *was* war again with the Philistines; and Eleanan the son of Jair smote Lachmi the brother of Goliath the Gittite, and the wood of his spear *was* as a weavers' beam. 6 And there was again war in Geth, and there was a man of extraordinary size, and his fingers *and toes were* six on each hand and foot, four and twenty; and he was descended from the giants. 7 And he defied Israel, and Jonathan the son of Samaa the brother of David slew him. 8 These were born to Rapha in Geth; all four were giants, and they fell by the hand of David, and by the hand of his servants.

1-Chron.21 1 And the devil stood up against Israel, and moved David to number Israel. 2 And king David said to Joab and to the captains of the forces, Go, number Israel from Bersabee even to Dan, and bring me *the account*, and I shall know their number. 3 And Joab said, May the Lord add to his people, a hundred-fold as many as they *are*, and *let* the eyes of my lord the king see *it*: all *are* the servants of my lord. Why does my lord seek this thing? *do it not*, lest it become a sin to Israel. 4 Nevertheless the king's word prevailed against Joab; and Joab went out and passed through all Israel, and came to Jerusalem. 5 And Joab gave the number of the mustering of the people to David: and all Israel was a million and a hundred thousand men that drew sword: and the sons of Juda *were* four hundred and seventy thousand men that drew sword. 6 But he numbered not Levi and Benjamin among them; for the word of the king was painful to Joab. 7 And *there was* evil in the sight of the Lord respecting this thing; and he smote Israel. 8 And David said to God, I have sinned exceedingly, in that I have done this thing: and now, I pray thee, remove the sin of thy servant; for I have been exceedingly foolish. 9 And the Lord spoke to Gad the seer, saying, 10 Go and speak to David, saying, Thus saith the Lord, I bring three things upon thee: choose one of them for thyself, and I will do it to thee. 11 And Gad came to David, and said to him, Thus saith the Lord, Choose for thyself, 12 either three years of famine, or that thou shouldest flee three months from the face of thine enemies, and the sword of thine enemies *shall be employed* to destroy thee, or that the sword of the Lord and pestilence *should be* three days in the land, and the angel of the Lord *shall be* destroying in all the inheritance of Israel. And now consider what I shall answer to him that sent the message. 13 And David said to Gad, They are very hard for me, even *all* the three: let me fall now into the hands of the Lord, for his mercies *are* very abundant, and let me not fall by any means into the hands of man. 14 So the Lord brought pestilence upon Israel: and there fell of Israel seventy thousand men. 15 And God sent an angel to Jerusalem to destroy it: and as he was destroying, the Lord saw, and repented for the evil, and said to the angel that was destroying, Let it suffice thee; withhold thine hand. And the angel of the Lord stood by the threshing-floor of Orna the Jebusite. 16 And David lifted up his eyes, and saw the angel of the Lord, standing between the earth and the heaven, and his sword drawn in his hand, stretched out over Jerusalem: and David and the elders clothed in sackcloth, fell upon their faces. 17 And David said to God, *Was it* not I *that* gave orders to number the people? and I am the guilty one; I have greatly sinned: but these sheep, what have they done? O Lord God, let thy hand be upon me, and upon my father's house, and not on thy people for destruction, O Lord! 18 And the angel of the Lord told Gad to tell David, that he should go up to erect and altar to the Lord, in the threshing-floor of Orna the Jebusite. 19 And David went up according to the word of Gad, which he spoke in the name of the Lord. 20 And Orna turned and saw the king; and he hid himself and his four sons with him. Now Orna was threshing wheat. 21 And David came to Orna; and Orna came forth from the threshing-floor, and did obeisance to David with his face to the ground. 22 And David said to Orna, Give me thy place of the threshing-floor, and I will build upon it an altar to the Lord: give it me for its worth in money, and the plague shall cease from *among* the people. 23 And Orna said to David, Take it to thyself, and let my lord the king do what is right in his eyes: see, I have given the calves for a whole-burnt-offering, and the plough for wood, and the corn for a meat-offering; I have given all. 24 And king David said to Orna, Nay; for I will surely buy it for its worth in money: for I will not take thy property for the Lord, to offer a whole-burnt-offering to the Lord without cost *to myself*. 25 And David gave to Orna for his place six hundred shekels of gold *by* weight. 26 And David built there an altar to the Lord, and offered up whole-burnt-offerings and peace- offerings: and he cried to the Lord, and he answered him by fire out of heaven on the altar of whole-burnt-offerings, and *it* consumed the whole-burnt-offering. 27 And the Lord spoke to the angel; and he put up the sword into its sheath. 28 At that time when David saw that the Lord answered him in the threshing-floor of Orna the Jebusite, he also sacrificed there. 29 And the tabernacle of the Lord which Moses made in the wilderness, and the altar of whole-burnt-offerings, *were* at that time in the high place at Gabaon. 30 And David could not go before it to enquire of God; for he hasted not because of the sword of the angel of the Lord.

1-Chron.22 1 And David said, This is the house of the Lord God, and this *is* the altar for whole-burnt- offering for Israel. 2 And David gave orders to gather all the strangers that were in the land of Israel; and he appointed stone-hewers to hew polished stones to build the house to God. 3 And David prepared much iron for the nails of the doors and the gate; the hinges also and brass in abundance, there was no weighing *of it*. 4 And cedar threes without number: for the Sidonians and the Tyrians brought cedar trees in abundance to David. 5 And David said, My son Solomon *is* a tender child, and the house *for me* to build to the Lord *is* for superior magnificence for a name and for a glory through all the earth: I will make preparation for it. And David prepared abundantly before his death. 6 And he called Solomon his son, and commanded him to build the house for the Lord God of Israel. 7 And David said to Solomon, *My* child, it was in my heart to build a house to the name of the Lord God. 8 But the word of the Lord came to me, saying, Thou hast shed blood abundantly, and hast carried on great wars: thou shalt not build a house to my name, because thou hast shed much blood upon the earth before me. 9 Behold, a son shall be born to thee, he shall be a man of rest; and I will give him rest from all his enemies round about: for his name *shall be* Solomon, and I will give peace and quietness to Israel in his days. 10 He shall build a house to my name; and he shall be a son to me, and I will be a father to him; and I will establish the throne of his kingdom in Israel for ever. 11 And now, my son, the Lord shall be with thee, and prosper *thee*; and thou shalt build a house to the Lord thy God, as he spoke concerning thee. 12 Only may the Lord give thee wisdom and prudence, and strengthen thee over Israel, both to keep and to do the law of the Lord thy God. 13 Then will he prosper *thee*, if thou take heed to do the commandments and judgments which the Lord commanded Moses for Israel: be courageous and strong; fear not, nor be terrified. 14 And, behold, I according to my poverty have prepared for the house of the Lord a hundred thousand talents of gold, and a million talents of silver, and brass and iron without measure; for it is abundant; and I have prepared timber and stones; and do thou add to these. 15 And *of them that are* with thee do thou add to the multitude of workmen; *let there be* artificers and masons, and carpenters, and every skilful *workman* in every work; 16 in gold and silver, brass and iron, *of which* there is no number. Arise and do, and the Lord *be* with thee. 17 And David charged all the chief men of Israel to help Solomon his son, *saying*, 18 *Is* not the Lord with you? and he has given you rest round about, for he has given into your hands the inhabitants of the land; and the land is subdued before the Lord, and before his people. 19 Now set your hearts and souls to seek after the Lord your God: and rise, and build a sanctuary to your God to carry in the ark of the covenant of the Lord, and the holy vessels of God, into the house that is to be built to the name of the Lord.

1-Chron.23 1 And David was old and full of days; and he made Solomon his son king over Israel in his stead. 2 And he assembled all the chief men of Israel, and the priests, and the Levites. 3 And the Levites numbered *themselves* from thirty years old and upward; and their number by their polls amounted to thirty and eight thousand men. 4 Of the overseers over the works of the house of the Lord *there were* twenty-four thousand, and *there were* six thousand scribes and judges; 5 and four thousand door-keepers, and four thousand to praise the Lord with instruments which he made to praise the Lord. 6 And David divided them *into* daily courses, for the sons of Levi, for Gedson, Caath, and Merari. 7 And for *the family of* Gedson, Edan, and Semei. 8 The sons of Edan *were* Jeiel, the chief, and Zethan, and Joel, three. 9 The sons of Semei; Salomith, Jeiel, and Dan, three: these *were* the chiefs of the families of Edan. 10 And to the sons of Semei, Jeth, and Ziza, and Joas, and Beria: these *were* the four sons of Semei. 11 And Jeth was the chief, and Ziza the second: and Joas and Beria did not multiply sons, and they became *only* one reckoning according to the house of their father. 12 The sons of Caath; Ambram, Isaar, Chebron, Oziel, four. 13 The sons of Ambram; Aaron and Moses: and Aaron was appointed for the consecration of the most holy things, he and his sons for ever, to burn incense before the Lord, to minister and bless in his name for ever. 14 And *as for* Moses the man of God, his sons were reckoned to the tribe of Levi. 15 The sons of Moses; Gersam, and Eliezer. 16 The sons of Gersam; Subael the chief. 17 And the sons of Eliezer were, Rabia the chief: and Eliezer had no other sons; but the sons of Rabia were very greatly multiplied. 18 The sons of Isaar; Salomoth the chief. 19 The sons of Chebron; Jeria the chief, Amaria the second, Jeziel the third, Jekemias the fourth. 20 The sons of Oziel; Micha the chief, and Isia the second. 21 The sons of Merari; Mooli, and Musi: the sons of Mooli; Eleazar, and Kis. 22 And Eleazar died, and he had no sons, but daughters: and the sons of Kis, their brethren, took them. 23 The sons of Musi; Mooli, and Eder, and Jarimoth, three. 24 These *are* the sons of Levi according to the houses of their fathers; chiefs

of their families according to their numbering, according to the number of their names, according to their polls, doing the works of service of the house of the Lord, from twenty years old and upward. 25 For David said, The Lord God of Israel has given rest to his people, and has taken up his abode in Jerusalem for ever. 26 And the Levites bore not the tabernacle, and all the vessels of it for its service. 27 For by the last words of David was the number of the Levites *taken* from twenty years old and upward. 28 For he appointed them to wait on Aaron, to minister in the house of the Lord, over the courts, and over the chambers, and over the purification of all the holy things, and over the works of the service of the house of God; 29 and for the shew-bread, and for the fine flour of the meat-offering, and for the unleavened cakes, and for the fried cake, and for the dough, and for every measure; 30 and to stand in the morning to praise and give thanks to the Lord, and so in the evening; 31 and *to be* over all the whole-burnt-offerings that were offered up to the Lord on the sabbaths, and at the new moons, and at the feasts, by number, according to the order *given* to them, continually before the Lord. 32 And they are to keep the charge of the tabernacle of witness, and the charge of the holy place, and the charges of the sons of Aaron their brethren, to minister in the house of the Lord.

1-Chron.24 1 And *they number* the sons of Aaron in *their* division, Nadab, and Abiud, and Eleazar, and Ithamar. 2 And Nadab and Abiud died before their father, and they had no sons: so Eleazar and Ithamar the sons of Aaron ministered as priests. 3 And David distributed them, even Sadoc of the sons of Eleazar, and Achimelech of the sons of Ithamar, according to their numbering, according to their service, according to the houses of their fathers. 4 And there were found *among* the sons of Eleazar more chiefs of the mighty ones, than of the sons of Ithamar: and he divided them, sixteen heads of families to the sons of Eleazar, eight according to *their* families to the sons of Ithamar. 5 And he divided them according to their lots, one with the other; for there were those who had charge of the holy things, and those who had charge of the *house* of the Lord among the sons of Eleazar, and among the sons of Ithamar. 6 And Samaias the son of Nathanael, the scribe, *of the family* of Levi, wrote them down before the king, and the princes, and Sadoc the priest, and Achimelech the son of Abiathar *were present*; and the heads of the families of the priests and the Levites, each of a household *were assigned* one to Eleazar, and one to Ithamar. 7 And the first lot came out to Joarim, the second to Jedia, 8 the third to Charib, the fourth to Seorim, 9 the fifth to Melchias, the sixth to Meiamin, 10 the seventh to Cos, the eighth to Abia, 11 the ninth to Jesus, the tenth to Sechenias, 12 the eleventh to Eliabi, the twelfth to Jacim, 13 the thirteenth to Oppha, the fourteenth to Jesbaal, 14 the fifteenth to Belga, the sixteenth to Emmer, 15 the seventeenth to Chezin, the eighteenth to Aphese, 16 the nineteenth to Phetaea, the twentieth to Ezekel, 17 the twenty-first to Achim, the twenty-second to Gamul, 18 the twenty- third to Adallai, the twenty-fourth to Maasai. 19 This *is* their numbering according to their service to go into the house of the Lord, according to their appointment by the hand of Aaron their father, as the Lord God of Israel commanded. 20 And for the sons of Levi that were left, *even* for the sons of Ambram, Sobael: for the sons of Sobael, Jedia. 21 For Raabia, the chief *was Isaari*, 22 and for Isaari, Salomoth: for the sons of Salomoth, Jath. 23 The sons of Ecdiu; Amadia the second, Jaziel the third, Jecmoam the fourth. 24 For the sons of Oziel, Micha: the sons of Micha; Samer. 25 The brother of Micha; Isia, the son of Isia; Zacharia. 26 The sons of Merari, Mooli, and Musi: the sons of Ozia, 27 *That is, the sons* of Merari by Ozia, —his sons *were* Isoam, and Sacchur, and Abai. 28 To Mooli *were born* Eleazar, and Ithamar; and Eleazar died, and had no sons. 29 For Kis; the sons of Kis; Jerameel. 30 And the sons of Musi; Mooli, and Eder, and Jerimoth. These *were* the sons of the Levites according to the houses of their families. 31 And they also received lots as their brethren the sons of Aaron before the king; Sadoc also, and Achimelech, and the chiefs of the families of the priests and of the Levites, principal heads of families, even as their younger brethren.

1-Chron.25 1 And king David and the captains of the host appointed to their services the sons of Asaph, and of Æman, and of Idithun, prophesiers with harps, and lutes, and cymbals: and their number was according to their polls serving in their ministrations. 2 The sons of Asaph; Sacchur, Joseph, and Nathanias, and Erael: the sons of Asaph *were* next the king. 3 To Idithun *were reckoned* the sons of Idithun, Godolias, and Suri, and Iseas, and Asabias, and Matthathias, six after their father Idithun, sounding loudly on the harp thanksgiving and praise to the Lord. 4 To Æman *were reckoned* the sons of Æman, Bukias, and Matthanias, and Oziel, and Subael, and Jerimoth, and Ananias, and Anan, and Heliatha, and Godollathi, and Rometthiezer, and Jesbasaca, and Mallithi, and Otheri, and Meazoth. 5 All these *were* the sons of Æman the king's chief player in the praises of God, to lift up the horn. And God gave to Æman fourteen sons, and three daughters. 6 All these sang hymns with their father in the house of God, with cymbals, and lutes, and harps, for the service of the house of God, near the king, and Asaph, and Idithun, and Æman. 7 And the number of them after their brethren, those instructed to sing to God, every one that understood *singing* was two hundred and eighty-eight. 8 And they also cast lots for the daily courses, for the great and the small *of them*, of the perfect ones and the learners. 9 And the first lot of his sons and of his brethren came forth to Asaph the son of Joseph, *namely*, Godolias: the second Heneia, his sons and his brethren *being* twelve. 10 The third Zacchur, his sons and his brethren *were* twelve: 11 the fourth Jesri, his sons and his brethren *were* twelve: 12 the fifth Nathan, his sons and his brethren, twelve: 13 the sixth Bukias, his sons and his brethren, twelve: 14 the seventh Iseriel, his sons and his brethren, twelve: 15 the eighth Josia, his sons and his brethren, twelve: 16 the ninth Matthanias, his sons and his brethren, twelve: 17 the tenth Semeia, his sons and his brethren, twelve: 18 the eleventh Asriel, his sons and his brethren, twelve: 19 the twelfth Asabia, his sons and his brethren, twelve: 20 the thirteenth Subael, his sons and his brethren, twelve: 21 the fourteenth Matthathias, his sons and his brethren, twelve: 22 the fifteenth Jerimoth, his sons and his brethren, twelve: 23 the sixteenth Anania, his sons and his brethren, twelve: 24 the seventeenth Jesbasaca, his sons and his brethren, twelve: 25 the eighteenth Ananias, his sons and his brethren, twelve: 26 the nineteenth Mallithi, his sons and his brethren, twelve: 27 the twentieth Heliatha, his sons and his brethren, twelve: 28 the twenty-first Otheri, his sons and his brethren, twelve: 29 the twenty-second Godollathi, his sons and his brethren, twelve: 30 the twenty-third Meazoth, his sons and his brethren, twelve: 31 the twenty-fourth Rometthiezer, his sons and his brethren, twelve:

1-Chron.26 1 And for the divisions of the gates: the sons of the Corites *were* Mosellemia, of the sons of Asaph. 2 And Mosellemia's first-born son *was* Zacharias, the second Jadiel, the third Zabadia, the fourth Jenuel, 3 the fifth Jolam, the sixth Jonathan, the seventh Elionai, the eighth Abdedom. 4 And to Abdedom *there were born* sons, Samaias the first-born, Jozabath the second, Joath the third, Sachar the fourth, Nathanael the fifth, 5 Amiel the sixth, Issachar the seventh, Phelathi the eighth: for God blessed him. 6 And to Samaias his son were born the sons of his first-born, chiefs over the house of their father, for they were mighty. 7 The sons of Samai; Othni, and Raphael, and Obed, and Elzabath, and Achiud, mighty men, Heliu, and Sabachia, and Isbacom. 8 All *these were* of the sons of Abdedom, they and their sons and their brethren, doing mightily in service: in all sixty-two *born* to Abdedom. 9 And Mosellemia *had* eighteen sons and brethren, mighty men. 10 And to Osa of the sons of Merari *there were born* sons, keeping the dominion; though he was not the first-born, yet his father made him chief of the second division. 11 Chelcias the second, Tablai the third, Zacharias the fourth: all these *were* the sons and brethren of Osa, thirteen. 12 To these *were assigned* the divisions of the gates, to the chiefs of the mighty men the daily courses, even their brethren, to minister in the house of the Lord. 13 And they cast lots for the small as well as for the great, for the several gates, according to their families. 14 And the lot of the east gates fell to Selemias, and Zacharias: the sons of Soaz cast lots for Melchias, and the lot came out northward. 15 To Abdedom *they gave by lot* the south, opposite the house of Esephim. 16 *They gave the lot* for the second to Osa westward, after the gate of the chamber by the ascent, watch against watch. 17 Eastward *were* six *watchmen* in the day; northward four by the day; southward four by the day; and two at the Esephim, 18 to relieve guard, also for Osa westward after the chamber-gate, three. *There was* a ward over against the ward of the ascent eastward, six *men* in a day, and four for the north, and four for the south, and at the Esephim two to relieve guard, and four by the west, and two to relieve guard at the pathway. 19 These *are* the divisions of the porters for the sons of Core, and to the sons of Merari. 20 And the Levites their brethren *were* over the treasures of the house of the Lord, and over the treasures of the hallowed things. 21 These *were* the sons of Ladan, the sons of the Gersonite: to Ladan *belonged* the heads of the families: *the* son of Ladan the Gersonite *was* Jeiel. 22 The sons of Jeiel *were* Zethom, and Joel; brethren *who were* over the treasures of the house of the Lord. 23 To Ambram and Issaar belonged Chebron, and Oziel. 24 And Subael the *son* of Gersam, the *son* of Moses, *was* over the treasures. 25 And Rabias *was* son to his brother Eliezer, and *so was* Josias, and Joram, and Zechri, and Salomoth. 26 This Salomoth and his brethren *were* over all the sacred treasures, which David the king and the heads of families consecrated, *and* the captains of thousands and captains of hundreds, and princes of the host, 27 things which he took out of cities and from the spoils, and consecrated some of them, so that the building of the house of God should not want *supplies;* 28 and over all the holy things of God dedicated by Samuel the prophet, and Saul the son of Kis, and Abenner the son of Ner, and Joab the son of Saruia, whatsoever they sanctified *was* by the hand of Salomoth and his brethren. 29 For the Issaarites, Chonenia, and *his* sons *were over* the outward ministration over Israel, to record and to judge. 30 For the Chebronites, Asabias and his brethren, a thousand and seven hundred mighty men, *were* over the charge of Israel beyond Jordan westward, for all the service of the Lord and work of the king. 31 Of the *family* of Chebron Urias *was* chief, even of the Chebronites according to their generations, according to their families. In the fortieth year of his reign they were numbered, and there were found mighty men among them in Jazer of Galaad. 32 And his brethren *were* two thousand seven hundred mighty men, chiefs of their families, and king David set them over the Rubenites, and the Gaddites, and the half-tribe of Manasse, for every ordinance of the Lord, and business of the king.

1-Chron.27 1 Now the sons of Israel according to their number, heads of families, captains of thousands and captains of hundreds, and scribes ministering to the king, and for every affair of the king according to *their* divisions, *for* every ordinance of coming in and going out monthly, for all the months of the year, one division of them *was* twenty-four thousand. 2 And over the first division of the first month *was* Isboaz the son of Zabdiel: in his division *were* twenty-four thousand. 3 Of the sons of Tharez *one* was chief of all the captains of the host for the first month. 4 And over the division of the second month *was* Dodia the son of Ecchoc, and over his division *was* Makelloth also chief: and in his division *were* twenty and four thousand, chief men of the host. 5 The third for the third month *was* Banaias the son of Jodae the chief priest: and in his division *were* twenty and four thousand. 6 This Banaeas *was* more mighty than the thirty, and over the thirty: and Zabad his son *was* over his division. 7 The fourth for the fourth month *was* Asael the brother of Joab, and Zabadias his son, and his brethren: and in his division *were* twenty and four thousand. 8 The fifth chief for the fifth month *was* Samaoth the Jezraite: and in his division *were* twenty and four thousand. 9 The sixth for the sixth month *was* Hoduias the son of Ekkes the Thecoite: and in his division *were* twenty and four thousand. 10 The seventh for the seventh month *was* Chelles of Phallus of the children of Ephraim: and in his division *were* twenty and four thousand. 11 The eighth

for the eighth month *was* Sobochai the Usathite, *belonging* to Zarai: and in his division *were* twenty and four thousand. 12 The ninth for the ninth month *was* Abiezer of Anathoth, of the land of Benjamin: and in his division *were* twenty and four thousand. 13 The tenth for the tenth month *was* Meera the Netophathite, *belonging* to Zarai: and in his division *were* twenty and four thousand. 14 The eleventh for the eleventh month *was* Banaias of Pharathon, of the sons of Ephraim: and in his division *were* twenty and four thousand. 15 The twelfth for the twelfth month *was* Choldia the Netophathite, *belonging* to Gothoniel: and in his division *were* twenty and four thousand. 16 And over the tribes of Israel, the chief for Ruben *was* Eliezer the son of Zechri: for Symeon, Saphatias the son of Maacha: 17 for Levi, Asabias the son of Camuel: for Aaron, Sadoc: 18 for Juda, Eliab of the brethren of David: for Issachar, Ambri the son of Michael: 19 for Zabulon, Samaeas the son of Abdiu: for Nephthali, Jerimoth the son of Oziel: 20 for Ephraim, Ose the son of Ozia: for the half-tribe of Manasse, Joel the son of Phadaea: 21 for the half-tribe of Manasse in the land of Galaad, Jadai the son of Zadaeas, for the sons of Benjamin, Jasiel the son of Abenner: 22 for Dan, Azariel the son of Iroab: these *are* the chiefs of the tribes of Israel. 23 But David took not their number from twenty years old and under: because the Lord said that he would multiply Israel as the stars of the heaven. 24 And Joab the son of Saruia began to number the people, and did not finish the work, for there was hereupon wrath on Israel; and the number was not recorded in the book of the chronicles of king David. 25 And over the king's treasures *was* Asmoth the son of Odiel; and over the treasures in the country, and in the towns, and in the villages, and in the towers, *was* Jonathan the son of Ozia. 26 And over the husbandmen who tilled the ground *was* Esdri the son of Chelub. 27 And over the fields *was* Semei of Rael; and over the treasures of wine in the fields *was* Zabdi the son of Sephni. 28 And over the oliveyards, and over the sycamores in the plain country *was* Ballanan the Gedorite; and over the stores of oil *was* Joas. 29 And over the oxen pasturing in Saron *was* Satrai the Saronite; and over the oxen in the valleys *was* Sophat the son of Adli. 30 And over the camels *was* Abias the Ismaelite; and over the asses *was* Jadias of Merathon. 31 And over the sheep *was* Jaziz the Agarite. All these *were* superintendents of the substance of king David. 32 And Jonathan, David's uncle by the father's side, *was* a counsellor, a wise man: and Jeel the son of Achami *was* with the king's sons. 33 Achitophel *was* the king's counsellor: and Chusi the chief friend of the king. 34 And after this Achitophel Jodae the son of Banaeas *came* next, and Abiathar: and Joab *was* the king's commander-in-chief.

1-Chron.28 1 And David assembled all the chief *men* of Israel, the chief of the judges, and all the chief *men* of the courses *of attendance* on the person of the king, and the captains of thousands and hundreds, and the treasurers, and the lords of his substance, and of all the king's property, and of his sons, together with the eunuchs, and the mighty men, and the warriors of the army, at Jerusalem. 2 And David stood in the midst of the assembly, and said,

Hear me, my brethren, and my people: it was in my heart to build a house of rest for the ark of the covenant of the Lord, and a place for the feet of our Lord, and I prepared *materials* suitable for the building: 3 but God said, Thou shalt not build me a house to call my name upon it, for thou art a man of war, and hast shed blood. 4 Yet the Lord God of Israel chose me out of the whole house of my father to be king over Israel for ever; and he chose Juda as the kingly *house*, and out of the house of Juda *he chose* the house of my father; and among the sons of my father he preferred me, that I should be king over all Israel. 5 And of all my sons, (for the Lord has given me many sons,)he has chosen Solomon my son, to set him on the throne of the kingdom of the Lord over Israel. 6 And God said to me, Solomon thy son shall build my house and my court: for I have chosen him to be my son, and I will be to him a father. 7 And I will establish his kingdom for ever, if he continue to keep my commandments, and my judgments, as *at* this day. 8 And now *I charge you* before the whole assembly of the Lord, and in the audience of our God, keep and seek all the commandments of the Lord our God, that ye may inherit the good land, and leave it for your sons to inherit after you for ever. 9 And now, *my* son Solomon, know the God of thy fathers, and serve him with a perfect heart and willing soul: for the Lord searches all hearts, and knows every thought: if thou seek him, he will be found of thee; but if thou shouldest forsake him, he will forsake thee for ever. 10 See now, for the Lord has chosen thee to build him a house for a sanctuary, be strong and do *it*. 11 And David gave Solomon his son the plan of the temple, and its buildings, and its treasuries, and its upper chambers, and the inner store-rooms, and the place of the atonement, 12 and the plan which he had in his mind of the courts of the house of the Lord, and of all the chambers round about, *designed* for the treasuries of the house of God, and of the treasuries of the holy things, and of the chambers for resting: 13 and *the plan* of the courses of the priests and Levites, for all the work of the service of the house of the Lord, and of the stores of vessels for ministration of the service of the house of the Lord. 14 And *he gave him* the account of their weight, both of gold and silver *vessels*. 15 He gave him the weight of the candlesticks, and of the lamps. 16 He gave him likewise the weight of the tables of shewbread, of each table of gold, and likewise of the *tables of* silver: 17 also of the flesh-hooks, and vessels for drink-offering, and golden bowls: and the weight of the gold and silver *articles*, and censers, *and* bowls, according to the weight of each. 18 And he shewed him the weight *of the utensils* of the altar of incense, *which was* of pure gold, and the plan of the chariot of the cherubs that spread out their wings, and overshadowed the ark of the covenant of the Lord. 19 David gave all to Solomon in the Lord's handwriting, according to the knowledge given him of the work of the pattern. 20 And David said to Solomon his son, Be strong, and play the man, and do: fear not, neither be terrified; for the Lord my God *is* with thee; he will not forsake thee, and will not fail thee, until thou hast finished all the work of the service of the house of the Lord. And behold the pattern of the temple, even his house, and its treasury, and the upper chambers, and the inner store-

rooms, and the place of propitiation, and the plan of the house of the Lord. 21 And see, *here are* the courses of the priests and Levites for all the service of the house of the Lord, and *there shall be* with thee *men* for every workmanship, and every one of ready skill in every art: also the chief men and all the people, *ready* for all thy commands.

1-Chron.29 1 And David the king said to all the congregation, Solomon my son, whom the Lord has chosen, *is* young and tender, and the work *is* great; for *it is* not for man, but for the Lord God. 2 I have prepared according to all *my* might for the house of my God gold, silver, brass, iron, wood, onyx stones, and costly and variegated stones for setting, and every precious stone, and much Parian *marble*. 3 And still farther, because I took pleasure in the house of my God, I have gold and silver which I have procured for myself, and, behold, I have given them to the house of my God over and above, beyond what I have prepared for the holy house. 4 Three thousand talents of gold of Suphir, and seven thousand talents of fine silver, for the overlaying of the walls of the sanctuary: 5 *for thee to use* the gold for *things of* gold, and the silver for things of silver, and for every work by the hand of the artificers. And who is willing to dedicate himself in work this day for the Lord? 6 Then the heads of families, and the princes of the children of Israel, and the captains of thousands and captains of hundreds, and the overseers of the works, and the king's builders, offered willingly. 7 And they gave for the works of the house of the Lord five thousand talents of gold, and ten thousand gold *pieces*, and ten thousand talents of silver, and eighteen thousand talents of brass, and a hundred thousand talents of iron. 8 And they who had *precious* stone, gave it into the treasuries of the house of the Lord by the hand of Jeiel the Gedsonite. 9 And the people rejoiced because of the willingness, for they offered willingly to the Lord with a full heart: and king David rejoiced greatly. 10 And king David blessed the Lord before the congregation, saying, Blessed art thou, O Lord God of Israel, our Father, from everlasting and to everlasting. 11 Thine, O Lord, *is* the greatness, and the power, and the glory, and the victory, and the might: for thou art Lord of all things that are in heaven and upon the earth: before thy face every king and nation is troubled. 12 From thee *come* wealth and glory: thou, O Lord, rulest over all, the Lord of all dominion, and in thy hand *is* strength and rule; and *thou art* almighty with thy hand to increase and establish all things. 13 And now, Lord, we give thanks to thee, and praise thy glorious name. 14 But who am I, and what *is* my people, that we have been able to be thus forward *in offering* to thee? for all things *are* thine, and of thine own have we given thee, 15 for we are strangers before thee, and sojourners, as all our fathers *were*: our days upon the earth *are* as a shadow, and there is no remaining. 16 O Lord our God, as for all this abundance which I have prepared that a house should be built to thy holy name, it is of thy hand, and all *is* thine. 17 And I know, Lord, that thou art he that searches the hearts, and thou lovest righteousness. I have willingly offered all these things in simplicity of heart; and now I have seen with joy thy people here present, willingly offering to thee. 18 O

Lord God of Abraham, and Isaac, and Israel, our fathers, preserve these things in the thought of the heart of thy people for ever, and direct their hearts to thee. 19 And to Solomon my son give a good heart, to perform thy commandments, and *to observe* thy testimonies, and thine ordinances, and to accomplish the building of thy house. 20 And David said to the whole congregation, Bless ye the Lord our God. And all the congregation blessed the Lord God of their fathers, and they bowed the knee and worshipped the Lord, and *did obeisance* to the king. 21 And David sacrificed to the Lord, and offered up whole-burnt-offerings to the Lord on the morrow after the first day, a thousand calves, a thousand rams, a thousand lambs, and their drink-offerings, and sacrifices in abundance for all Israel. 22 And they ate and drank joyfully that day before the Lord: and they made Solomon the son of David king a second time, and anointed him king before the Lord, and Sadoc to the priesthood. 23 And Solomon sat upon the throne of his father David, and was highly honoured; and all Israel obeyed him. 24 The princes, and the mighty men, and all the sons of king David his father, were subject to him. 25 And the Lord magnified Solomon over all Israel, and gave him royal glory, such as was not upon any king before him. 26 And David the son of Jessae reigned over Israel forty years; 27 seven years in Chebron, and thirty-three years in Jerusalem. 28 And he died in a good old age, full of days, in wealth, and glory: and Solomon his son reigned in his stead. 29 And the rest of the acts of David, the former and the latter, are written in the history of Samuel the seer, and in the history of Nathan the prophet, and in the history of Gad the seer, 30 concerning all his reign, and his power, and the times which went over him, and over Israel, and over all the kingdoms of the earth.

2 CHRONICLES

2-Chron.1 1 And Solomon the son of David was established over his kingdom, and the Lord his God was with him, and increased him exceedingly. 2 And Solomon spoke to all Israel, to the captains of thousands, and to the captains of hundreds, and to the judges, and to all the rulers over Israel, even the heads of the families; 3 and Solomon and all the congregation went to the high place that was in Gabaon, where was God's tabernacle of witness, which Moses the servant of the Lord made in the wilderness. 4 But David had brought up the ark of God out of the city of Cariathiarim; for David had prepared a place for it, for he had pitched a tabernacle for it in Jerusalem. 5 And the brazen altar which Beseleel the son of Urias, the son of Or, had made, was there before the tabernacle of the Lord: and Solomon and the congregation enquired at it. 6 And Solomon brought *victims* thither to the brazen altar that was before the Lord in the tabernacle, and offered upon it a thousand whole-burnt-offerings. 7 In that night God appeared to Solomon, and said to him, Ask what I shall give thee. 8 And Solomon said to God, Thou hast dealt very mercifully with my father David, and hast made me king in his stead. 9 And now, O Lord God, let, I pray thee, thy name be established upon David my father; for thou hast made me king over a people numerous as the dust of the

earth. 10 Now give me wisdom and understanding, that I may go out and come in before this people: for who shall judge this thy great people? 11 And God said to Solomon, Because this was in thy heart, and thou hast not asked great wealth, nor glory, nor the life of thine enemies, and thou hast not asked long life; but hast asked for thyself wisdom and understanding, that thou mightest judge my people, over whom I have made thee king: 12 I give thee this wisdom and understanding; and I will give thee wealth, and riches, and glory, so that there shall not have been *any* like thee among the kings before thee, neither shall there be such after thee. 13 And Solomon came from the high place that was in Gabaon to Jerusalem, *from* before the tabernacle of witness, and reigned over Israel. 14 And Solomon collected chariots and horsemen: and he had fourteen hundred chariots, and twelve thousand horsemen: and he set them in the cities of chariots, and the people *were* with the king in Jerusalem. 15 And the king made silver and gold in Jerusalem *to be* as stones, and cedars in Judea as sycamores in the plain for multitude. 16 And Solomon imported horses from Egypt, and the charge of the king's merchants for going *was as follows*, and they traded, 17 and went and brought out of Egypt a chariot for six hundred *pieces* of silver, and a horse for a hundred and fifty *pieces* of silver: and so they brought for all the kings of the Chettites, and for the kings of Syria by their means.

2-Chron.2 1 And Solomon said that he would build a house to the name of the Lord, and a house for his kingdom. 2 And Solomon gathered seventy thousand men that bore burdens, and eighty thousand hewers of stone in the mountain, and *there were* three thousand six hundred superintendents over them. 3 And Solomon sent to Chiram king of Tyre, saying, Whereas thou didst deal *favourably* with David my father, and didst send him cedars to build for himself a house to dwell in, 4 behold, I also his son am building a house to the name of the Lord my God, to consecrate it to him, to burn incense before him, and *to offer* shewbread continually, and to offer up whole-burnt-offerings continually morning and evening, and on the sabbaths, and at the new moons, and at the feasts of the Lord our God: this *is* a perpetual *statute* for Israel. 5 And the house which I am building *is to be* great: for the Lord our God *is* great beyond all gods. 6 And who will be able to build him a house? for the heaven and heaven of heavens do not bear his glory: and who am I, that I should build him a house, save only to burn incense before him? 7 And now send me a man wise and skilled to work in gold, and in silver, and in brass, and in iron, and in purple, and in scarlet, and in blue, and one that knows how to grave together with the craftsmen who are with me in Juda and in Jerusalem, which materials my father David prepared. 8 And send me from Libanus cedar wood, and wood of juniper, and pine; for I know that thy servants are skilled in cutting timber in Libanus: and, behold, thy servants shall go with my servants, 9 to prepare timber for me in abundance: for the house which I am building *must be* great and glorious. 10 And, behold, I have given freely to thy servants that work and cut the wood, corn for food, *even* twenty thousand measures of wheat, and twenty thousand measures of barley, and twenty thousand measures of wine, and twenty thousand measures of oil. 11 And Chiram king of Tyre answered in writing, and sent to Solomon, saying, Because the Lord loved his people, he made thee king over them. 12 And Chiram said, Blessed *be* the Lord God of Israel, who made heaven and earth, who has given to king David a wise son, and one endowed with knowledge and understanding, who shall build a house for the Lord, and a house for his kingdom. 13 And now I have sent thee a wise and understanding man *who belonged* to Chiram my father 14 (his mother *was* of the daughters of Dan, and his father *was* a Tyrian), skilled to work in gold, and in silver, and in brass, and in iron, and in stones and wood; and to weave with purple, and blue, and fine linen, and scarlet; and to engrave, and to understand every device, whatsoever thou shalt give him *to do* with thy craftsmen, and the craftsmen of my lord David thy father. 15 And now, the wheat, and the barley, and the oil, and the wine which my lord mentioned, let him send to his servants. 16 And we will cut timber out of Libanus according to all thy need, and we will bring it on rafts to the sea of Joppa, and thou shalt bring it to Jerusalem. 17 And Solomon gathered all the foreigners that were in the land of Israel, after the numbering with which David his father numbered them; and there were found a hundred and fifty-three thousand six hundred. 18 And he made of them seventy thousand burden-bearers, and eighty thousand hewers of stone, and three thousand six hundred taskmasters over the people.

2-Chron.3 1 And Solomon began to build the house of the Lord in Jerusalem in the mount of Amoria, where the Lord appeared to his father David, in the place which David had prepared in the threshing-floor of Orna the Jebusite. 2 And he began to build in the second month, in the fourth year of his reign. 3 And thus Solomon began to build the house of God: the length in cubits—even the first measurement from end to end, was sixty cubits, and the breadth twenty cubits. 4 And the portico in front of the house, its length in front of the breadth of the house *was* twenty cubits, and its height a hundred and twenty cubits: and he gilded it within with pure gold. 5 And he lined the great house with cedar wood, and gilded it with pure gold, and carved upon it palm- trees and chains. 6 And he garnished the house with precious stones for beauty; and he gilded it with gold of the gold from Pharuim. 7 And he gilded the house, and its *inner* walls, and the door-posts, and the roofs, and the doors with gold; and he carved cherubs on the walls. 8 And he built the holy of holies, its length was according to the front *of the other house*, the breadth of the house *was* twenty cubits, and the length twenty cubits: and he gilded *it* with pure gold for cherubs, to *the amount of* six hundred talents. 9 And the weight of the nails, *even* the weight of each was fifty shekels of gold: and he gilded the upper chamber with gold. 10 And he made two cherubs in the most holy house, wood-work, and he gilded them with gold. 11 And the wings of the cherubs were twenty cubits in length: and one wing of five cubits touched the wall of the house: and the other wing of five cubits touched the wing of the other cherub. 12 13 And

the wings of these cherubs expanded were of the length of twenty cubits: and they stood upon their feet, and their faces were toward the house. 14 And he made the vail of blue, and purple, and scarlet, and fine linen, and wove cherubs in it. 15 Also he made in front of the house two pillars, in height thirty-five cubits, and their chapters of five cubits. 16 And he made chains, *as* in the oracle, and put *them* on the heads of the pillars; and he made a hundred pomegranates, and put them on the chains. 17 And he set up the pillars in front of the temple, one on the right hand and the other on the left: and he called the name of the one on the right hand 'Stability,' and the name of the one on the left 'Strength.'

2-Chron.4 1 And he made a brazen altar, the length of it twenty cubits, and the breadth twenty cubits, and the height ten cubits. 2 And he made the molten sea, in diameter ten cubits, entirely round, and the height of it five cubits, and the circumference thirty cubits. 3 And beneath it the likeness of calves, they compass it round about: ten cubits compass the laver round about, they cast the calves two rows in their casting, 4 wherein they made them twelve calves, —three looking northwards, and three westwards, and three southwards, and three eastwards: and the sea was upon them above, *and* their hinder parts were inward. 5 And its thickness was a hand-breadth, and its brim as the brim of a cup, graven with flowers of lilies, holding three thousand measures: and he finished *it*. 6 And he made ten lavers, and set five on the right hand, and five on the left, to wash in them the instruments of the whole-burnt-offerings, and to rinse *the vessels* in them; and the sea *was* for the priests to wash in. 7 And he made the ten golden candlesticks according to their pattern, and he put them in the temple, five on the right hand, and five on the left. 8 And he made ten tables, and put them in the temple, five on the right hand, and five on the left: and he made a hundred golden bowls. 9 Also he made the priests' court, and the great court, and doors to the court, and their panels *were* overlaid with brass. 10 And he set the sea at the corner of the house on the right, as it were fronting the east. 11 And Chiram made the fleshhooks, and the fire-pans, and the grate of the altar, and all its instruments: and Chiram finished doing all the work which he wrought for king Solomon in the house of God: 12 two pillars, and upon them an embossed work for the chapiters on the heads of the two pillars, and two nets to cover the heads of the chapiters which are on the heads of the pillars; 13 and four hundred golden bells for the two nets, and two rows of pomegranates in each net, to cover the two embossed rims of the chapiters which are upon the pillars. 14 And he made the ten bases, and he made the lavers upon the bases; 15 and the one sea, and the twelve calves under it; 16 and the foot-baths, and the buckets, and the caldrons, and the flesh-hooks, and all their furniture (which Chiram made, and brought to king Solomon in the house of the Lord) of pure brass. 17 In the country round about Jordan the king cast them, in the clay ground in the house of Socchoth, and between *that and* Saredatha. 18 So Solomon made all these vessels in great abundance, for the quantity of brass failed not. 19 And Solomon made all the vessels of the house of the Lord, and the golden altar, and the tables, and upon them *were to be* the loaves of shewbread; 20 also the candlesticks, and the lamps to give light according to the pattern, and in front of the oracle, of pure gold. 21 And their snuffers, and their lamps *were made*, and *he made* the bowls, and the censers, and the fire-pans, of pure gold. 22 And *there was* the inner door of the house *opening* into the holy of holies, and *he made* the inner doors of the temple of gold. So all the work which Solomon wrought for the house of the Lord was finished.

2-Chron.5 1 And Solomon brought in the holy things of his father David, the silver, and the gold, and the *other* vessels, and put them in the treasury of the house of the Lord. 2 Then Solomon assembled all the elders of Israel, and all the heads of the tribes, *even* the leaders of the families of the children of Israel, to Jerusalem, to bring up the ark of the covenant of the Lord out of the city of David, —this *is* Sion. 3 And all Israel were assembled *unto* the king in the feast, this *is* the seventh month. 4 And all the elders of Israel came; and all the Levites took up the ark, 5 and the tabernacle of witness, and all the holy vessels that were in the tabernacle; and the priests and the Levites brought it up. 6 And king Solomon, and all the elders of Israel, and the religious of them, and they of them that were gathered before the ark, *were* sacrificing calves and sheep, which could not be numbered or reckoned for multitude. 7 And the priests brought in the ark of the covenant of the Lord into its place, into the oracle of the house, *even* into the holy of holies, under the wings of the cherubs. 8 And the cherubs stretched out their wings over the place of the ark, and the cherubs covered the ark, and its staves above. 9 And the staves projected, and the heads of the staves were seen from the holy place in front of the oracle, they were not seen without: and there they were to this day. 10 There was nothing in the ark except the two tables which Moses placed *there* in Choreb, which God gave in covenant with the children of Israel, when they went out of the land of Egypt. 11 And it came to pass, when the priests when out of the holy place, (for all the priests that were found were sanctified, they were not *then* arranged according to their daily course,) 12 that all the singing Levites *assigned* to the sons of Asaph, to Æman, to Idithun, and to his sons, and to his brethren, of them that were clothed in linen garments, with cymbals and lutes and harps, *were* standing before the altar, and with them a hundred and twenty priests, blowing trumpets. 13 And there was one voice in the trumpeting and in the psalm-singing, and in the loud utterance with one voice to give thanks and praise the Lord; and when they raised their voice together with trumpets and cymbals, and instruments of music, and said, Give thanks to the Lord, for *it is* good, for his mercy *endures* for ever:—then the house was filled with the cloud of the glory of the Lord. 14 And the priests could not stand to minister because of the cloud: for the glory of the Lord filled the house of God.

2-Chron.6 1 Then said Solomon, The Lord said that he would dwell in thick darkness. 2 But I have built a house to thy name, holy to thee, and prepared *for thee* to dwell in for ever. 3 And the king turned his face, and blessed all the congregation of Israel: and all the congregation of Israel stood by. 4 And he said, Blessed *be* the Lord God of Israel: he has even fulfilled with his hands as he spoke with his mouth to my father David, saying, 5 From the day when I brought up my people out of the land of Egypt, I chose no city of all the tribes of Israel, to build a house that my name should be there; neither did I choose a man to be a leader over my people Israel. 6 But I chose Jerusalem that my name should be there; and I chose David to be over my people Israel. 7 And it came into the heart of David my father, to build a house for the name of the Lord God of Israel. 8 But the Lord said to my father David, Whereas it came into thy heart to build a house for my name, thou didst well that it came into thy heart. 9 Nevertheless thou shalt not build the house; for thy son who shall come forth out of thy loins, he shall build the house for my name. 10 And the Lord has confirmed this word, which he spoke; and I am raised up in the room of my father David, and I sit upon the throne of Israel as the Lord said, and I have built the house for the name of the Lord God of Israel: 11 and I have set there the ark in which *is* the covenant of the Lord, which he made with Israel. 12 And he stood before the altar of the Lord in the presence of all the congregation of Israel, and spread out his hands. 13 For Solomon *had* made a brazen scaffold, and set it in the midst of the court of the sanctuary; the length of it *was* five cubits, and the breadth of it five cubits, and the height of it three cubits: and he stood upon it, and fell upon his knees before the whole congregation of Israel, and spread abroad his hands to heaven, 14 and said, Lord God of Israel, there is no God like thee in heaven, or on the earth; keeping covenant and mercy with thy servants that walk before thee with *their* whole heart. 15 Even as thou hast kept *them* with thy servant David my father, as thou hast spoken to him in words:— thou hast both spoken with thy mouth, and hast fulfilled *it* with thy hands, as it is this day. 16 and now, Lord God of Israel, keep with thy servant David my father the things which thou spokest to him, saying, There shall not fail thee a man before me sitting on the throne of Israel, if only thy sons will take heed to their way to walk in my law, as thou didst walk before me. 17 And now, Lord God of Israel, let, I pray thee, thy word be confirmed, which thou hast spoken to thy servant David. 18 For will God indeed dwell with men upon the earth? if the heaven and the heaven of heavens will not suffice thee, what then is this house which I have built? 19 Yet thou shalt have respect to the prayer of thy servant, and to my petition, O Lord God, so as to hearken to the petition and the prayer which thy servant prays before thee this day: 20 so that thine eyes should be open over this house by day and by night, towards this place, whereon thou saidst thy name should be called, so as to hear the prayer which thy servant prays towards this house. 21 And thou shalt hear the supplication of thy servant, and of thy people Israel, whatsoever prayers they shall make towards this place: and thou shalt hearken in thy dwelling-place out of heaven, yea thou shalt hear, and be merciful. 22 If a man sin against his neighbour, and he bring an oath upon him so as to make him swear, and he come and swear before the altar in this house; 23 then shalt thou hearken out of heaven, and do, and judge thy servants, to recompense the transgressor, and to return his ways upon his head: and to justify the righteous, to recompense him according to his righteousness. 24 And if thy people Israel should be put to the worse before the enemy, if they should sin against thee, and *then* turn and confess to thy name, and pray and make supplication before thee in this house; 25 then shalt thou hearken out of heaven and shalt be merciful to the sins of thy people Israel, and thou shalt restore them to the land which thou gavest to them and to their fathers. 26 When heaven is restrained, and there is no rain, because they shall have sinned against thee, and *when* they shall pray towards this place, and praise thy name, and shall turn from their sins, because thou shalt afflict them; 27 then shalt thou hearken from heaven, and thou shalt be merciful to the sins of thy servants, and of thy people Israel; for thou shalt shew them the good way in which they shall walk; and thou shalt send rain upon thy land, which thou gavest to thy people for an inheritance. 28 If there should be famine upon the land, if there should be death, a pestilent wind an blight; if there should be locust and caterpiller, and if the enemy should harass them before their cities: in whatever plague and whatever distress *they may be*; 29 Then whatever prayer and whatever supplication shall be made by any man and all thy people Israel, if a man should know his own plague and his own sickness, and should spread forth his hands toward this house; 30 then shalt thou hear from heaven, out of thy prepared dwelling-place, and shalt be merciful, and shalt recompense to the man according to his ways, as thou shalt know his heart *to be*; for thou alone knowest the heart of the children of men: 31 that they may reverence all thy ways all the days which they live upon the face of the land, which thou gavest to our fathers. 32 And every stranger who is not himself of thy people Israel, and who shall have come from a distant land because of thy great name, and thy mighty hand, and thy high arm; when they shall come and worship toward this place; — 33 then shalt thou hearken out of heaven, out of thy prepared dwelling-place, and shalt do according to all that the stranger shall call upon thee for; that all the nations of the earth may know thy name, and that they may fear thee, as thy people Israel *do*, and that they may know that thy name is called upon this house which I have built. 34 And if thy people shall go forth to war against their enemies by the way by which thou shalt send them, and shall pray to thee toward this city which thou hast chosen, and *toward* the house which I have built to thy name; 35 then shalt thou hear out of heaven their prayer and their supplication, and maintain their cause. 36 Whereas if they shall sin against thee, (for there is no man who will not sin,) and thou shalt smite them, and deliver them up before their enemies, and they that take them captive shall carry them away into a land of enemies, to a land far off or near; 37 and *if* they shall repent in their land whither they were carried captive, and shall also turn and make supplication to thee in their captivity, saying, We have sinned, we have transgressed, we have wrought unrighteously; 38 and *if* they shall turn to thee with all their heart and all their soul in the land of them that carried them captives, whither they carried them captives, and shall pray toward their land which thou gavest to their fathers, and the city which thou didst choose, and the house which I built to thy name:— 39 then shalt thou hear out of heaven, out of thy prepared dwelling- place, their prayer and their supplication, and thou shalt execute justice, and shalt be merciful to thy people that sin against thee. 40 And now, Lord, let, I pray thee, thine eyes be opened, and thine ears be attentive to the petition *made in* this place. 41 And now, O Lord God, arise into thy resting-place, thou, and the ark of thy strength: let thy priests, O Lord God, clothe themselves with salvation, and thy sons rejoice in prosperity. 42 O Lord God, turn not away the face of thine anointed: remember the mercies of thy servant David.

2-Chron.7 1 And when Solomon had finished praying, then the fire came down from heaven, and devoured the whole-burnt-offerings and the sacrifices; and the glory of the Lord filled the house. 2 And the priests could not enter into the house of the Lord at that time, for the glory of the Lord filled the house. 3 And all the children of Israel saw the fire descending, and the glory of the Lord was upon the house: and they fell upon their face to the ground on the pavement, and worshipped, and praised the Lord; for *it is* good *to do so*, because his mercy *endures* for ever. 4 And the king and all the people *were* offering sacrifices before the Lord. 5 And king Solomon offered a sacrifice of calves twenty and two thousand, of sheep a hundred and twenty thousand: so the king and all the people dedicated the house of God. 6 And the priests were standing at their watches, and the Levites with instruments of music of the Lord, belonging to king David, to give thanks before the Lord, for his mercy *endures* for ever, with the hymns of David, by their ministry: and the priests were blowing the trumpets before them, and all Israel standing. 7 And Solomon consecrated the middle of the court that was in the house of the Lord: for he offered there the whole-burnt-offerings and the fat of the peace-offerings, for the brazen altar which Solomon had made was not sufficient to receive the whole-burnt-offerings, and the meat - offerings, and the fat. 8 And Solomon kept the feast at that time seven days, and all Israel with him, a very great assembly, from the entering in of Æmath, and as far as the river of Egypt. 9 And on the eighth day he kept a solemn assembly: for he kept a feast of seven days as the dedication of the altar. 10 And on the twenty-third day of the seventh month he dismissed the people to their tents, rejoicing, and with a glad heart because of the good deeds which the Lord had done to David, and to Solomon, and to Israel his people. 11 So Solomon finished the house of the Lord, and the king's house: and in whatever Solomon wished in his heart to do in the house of the Lord and in his own house, he prospered. 12 And the Lord appeared to Solomon by night, and said to him, I have heard thy prayer, and I have chosen this place to myself for a house of sacrifice. 13 If I should restrain the heaven and there should be no rain, and if I should command the locust to devour the trees, and if I should send pestilence upon my people; 14 then if my people, on whom my name is called, should repent, and pray, and seek my face, and turn from their evil ways, I also will hear from heaven, and I will be merciful to their sins, and I will heal their land. 15 And now my eyes shall be open, and my ears attentive to the prayer of this place. 16 And now I have chosen and sanctified this house, that my name should be there for ever: and my eyes and my heart shall be there always. 17 And if thou wilt walk before me as David thy father *did*, and wilt do according to all that I have commanded thee, and wilt keep my ordinances and my judgments; 18 then will I establish the throne of thy kingdom, as I covenanted with David thy father, saying, There shall not fail thee a man ruling in Israel. 19 But if ye should turn away, and forsake my ordinances and my commandments, which I have set before you, and go and serve other gods, and worship them; 20 then will I remove you from the land which I gave them; and this house which I have consecrated to my name I will remove out of my sight, and I will make it a proverb and a by-word among all nations. 21 And *as for* this lofty house, every one that passes by it shall be amazed, and shall say, Wherefore has the Lord done *thus* to this land, and to this house? 22 And *men* shall say, Because they forsook the Lord God of their fathers, who brought them out of the land of Egypt, and they attached themselves to other gods, and worshipped them, and served them: and therefore he has brought upon them all this evil.

2-Chron.8 1 And it came to pass after twenty years, in which Solomon built the house of the Lord, and his own house, 2 that Solomon rebuilt the cities which Chiram had given to Solomon, and caused the children of Israel to dwell in them. 3 And Solomon came to Baesoba, and fortified it. 4 And he built Thoedmor in the wilderness, and all the strong cities which he built in Emath. 5 And he built Baethoron the upper, and Baethoron the lower, strong cities, —they had walls, gates, and bars; 6 and Balaath, and all the strong cities which Solomon had, and all his chariot cities, and cities of horsemen, and all things that Solomon desired according to his desire of building, in Jerusalem, and in Libanus, and in all his kingdom. 7 *As for* all the people that was left of the Chettites, and the Amorites, and the Pherezites, and the Evites, and the Jebusites, who are not of Israel, 8 but were of the children of them whom the children Israel destroyed not, that were left after them in the land, even them did Solomon make tributaries to this day. 9 But Solomon did not make any of the children of Israel servants in his kingdom; for, behold, *they were* warriors and rulers, and mighty *men*, and captains of chariots and horsemen. 10 And these are the chiefs of the officers of king Solomon, two hundred and fifty overseeing the work among the people. 11 And Solomon brought up the daughter of Pharao from the city of David to the house which he had built for her: for he said, My wife shall not dwell in the city of David, the king of Israel, for *the place* is holy into which the ark of the Lord has entered. 12 Then Solomon offered up to the Lord whole-burnt-offerings on the altar which he had built to the Lord before the temple, 13 according to the daily rate, to offer up *sacrifices* according

to the commandments of Moses, on the sabbaths, and at the new moons, and at the feasts, three times in the year, at the feast of unleavened bread, and at the feast of weeks, and at the feast of tabernacles. 14 And he established, according to the order of his father David, the courses of the priests, and *that* according to their public ministrations: and the Levites *were appointed* over their charges, to praise and minister before the priests according to the daily order: and the porters were appointed according to their courses to the different gates: for thus *were* the commandments of David the man of God. 15 They transgressed not the commandments of the king concerning the priests and the Levites with regard to everything else, and with regard to the treasures. 16 Now all the work had been prepared from the day when the foundation was laid, until Solomon finished the house of the Lord. 17 Then Solomon went to Gasion Gaber, and to Ælath near the sea in the land of Idumea. 18 And Chiram sent by the hand of his servants ships, and servants skilled in naval affairs; and they went with the servants of Solomon to Sophira, and brought thence four hundred and fifty talents of gold, and they came to king Solomon.

2-Chron.9 1 And the queen of Saba heard *of* the name of Solomon, and she came to Jerusalem with a very large force, to prove Solomon with hard questions, and *she had* camels bearing spices in abundance, and gold, and precious stones: and she came to Solomon, and told him all that was in her mind. 2 And Solomon told her all her words; and there passed not a word from Solomon which he told her not. 3 And the queen of Saba saw the wisdom of Solomon, and the house which he had built, 4 and the meat of the tables, and the sitting of his servants, and the standing of his ministers, and their raiment; and his cupbearers, and their apparel; and the whole-burnt-offerings which he offered up in the house of the Lord; then she was in ecstasy. 5 And she said to the king, *It was* a true report which I heard in my land concerning thy words, and concerning thy wisdom. 6 Yet I believed not the reports until I came, and my eyes saw: and, behold, the half of the abundance of thy wisdom was not told me: thou hast exceeded the report which I heard. 7 Blessed *are* thy men, blessed *are* these thy servants, who stand before thee continually, and hear thy wisdom. 8 Blessed be the Lord thy God, who took pleasure in thee, to set thee upon his throne for a king, to the Lord thy God: forasmuch as the Lord thy God loved Israel to establish them for ever, therefore he has set thee over them for a king to execute judgment and justice. 9 And she gave the king a hundred and twenty talents of gold, and spices in very great abundance, and precious stones: and there were not *any where else* such spices as those which the queen of Saba gave king Solomon. 10 And the servants of Solomon and the servants of Chiram brought gold to Solomon out of Suphir, and pine timber, and precious stones. 11 And the king made of the pine timber steps to the house of the Lord, and to the king's house, and harps and lutes for the singers: and such were not seen before in the land of Juda. 12 And king Solomon gave to the queen of Saba all that she requested, besides all that she brought to king Solomon: and she returned to her *own* land. 13 And the weight of the gold that was brought to Solomon in one year was six hundred and sixty-six talents of gold, 14 besides what the men who were regularly appointed and the merchants brought, and all the kings of Arabia and princes of the land: all brought gold and silver to king Solomon. 15 And king Solomon made two hundred shields of beaten gold: there were six hundred *shekels* of pure gold to one shield. 16 And three hundred buckles of beaten gold: *the weight* of three hundred gold shekels went to one buckler: and the king placed them in the house of the forest of Lebanon. 17 And the king made a great throne of ivory, and he gilded it with pure gold. 18 And *there were* six steps to the throne, riveted with gold, and elbows on either side of the seat of the throne, and two lions standing by the elbows: 19 and twelve lions standing there on the six steps on each side. There was not the like in any *other* kingdom. 20 And all king Solomon's vessels were of gold, and all the vessels of the house of the forest of Lebanon were covered with gold: silver was not thought anything of in the days of Solomon. 21 For a ship went for the king to Tharsis with the servants of Chiram: once every three years came vessels from Tharsis to the king, laden with gold, and silver, and ivory, and apes. 22 And Solomon exceeded all *other* kings both in riches and wisdom. 23 And all the kings of the earth sought the presence of Solomon, to hear his wisdom, which God had put in his heart. 24 And they brought every one his gifts, silver vessels and golden vessels, and raiment, myrrh and spices, horses and mules, a rate every year. 25 And Solomon had four thousand mares for chariots, and twelve thousand horsemen; and he put them in the chariot cities, and with the king in Jerusalem. 26 And he rules over all the kings from the river even to the land of the Philistines, and to the borders of Egypt. 27 And the king made gold and silver in Jerusalem as stones, and cedars as the sycamore trees in the plain for abundance. 28 And Solomon imported horses from Egypt, and from every *other* country. 29 And the rest of the acts of Solomon, the first and the last, behold, these are written in the words of Nathan the prophet, and in the words of Achia the Selonite, and in the visions of Joel the seer concerning Jeroboam the son of Nabat. 30 And Solomon reigned over all Israel forty years. 31 And Solomon fell asleep, and they buried him in the city of David his father: and Roboam his son reigned in his stead.

2-Chron.10 1 And Roboam came to Sychem: for all Israel came to Sychem to make him king. 2 And it came to pass when Jeroboam the son of Nabat heard *it*, (now he was in Egypt, forasmuch as he had fled thither from the face of king Solomon, and Jeroboam dwelt in Egypt,) that Jeroboam returned out of Egypt. 3 And they sent and called him: and Jeroboam and all the congregation came to Roboam, saying, 4 Thy father made our yoke grievous: now then abate *somewhat* of thy father's grievous rule, and of his heavy yoke which he put upon us, and we will serve thee. 5 And he said to them, Go away for three days, and *then* come to me. So the people departed. 6 And king Roboam assembled the elders that stood before his father Solomon in his life-time, saying, How do ye counsel *me* to return an

answer to this people? 7 And they spoke to him, saying, If thou wouldest this day befriend this people, and be kind to them, and speak to them good words, then will they be thy servants for ever. 8 But he forsook the advice of the old men, who took counsel with him, and he took counsel with the young men who had been brought up with him, who stood before him. 9 And he said to them, What do ye advise that I should answer this people, who spoke to me, saying, Ease *somewhat* of the yoke which thy father laid upon us? 10 And the young men that had been brought up with him spoke to him, saying, Thus shalt thou speak to the people that spoke to thee, saying, Thy father made our yoke heavy, and do thou lighten *somewhat of it* from us; thus shalt thou say, My little finger *shall be* thicker than my father's loins. 11 And whereas my father chastised you with a heavy yoke, I will also add to your yoke: my father chastised you with whips, and I will chastise you with scorpions. 12 And Jeroboam and all the people came to Roboam on the third day, as the king had spoken, saying, Return to me on the third day. 13 And the king answered harshly; and king Roboam forsook the counsel of the old men, 14 and spoke to them according to the counsel of the young men, saying, My father made your yoke heavy, but I will add to it: my father chastised you with whips, but I will chastise you with scorpions. 15 And the king hearkened not to the people, for there was a change *of their minds* from God, saying, The Lord has confirmed his word, which he spoke by the hand of Achia the Selonite concerning Jeroboam the son of Nabat, and *concerning* all Israel; 16 for the king did not hearken to them. And the people answered the king, saying, What portion have we in David, or inheritance in the son of Jessae? to thy tents, O Israel: now see to thine own house, David. So all Israel went to their tents. 17 But the men of Israel, even those who dwelt in the cities of Juda, *remained* and made Roboam king over them. 18 And king Roboam sent to them Adoniram that was over the tribute; and the children of Israel stoned him with stones, and he died. And king Roboam hasted to mount *his* chariot, to flee to Jerusalem. 19 So Israel rebelled against the house of David until this day.

2-Chron.11 1 And Roboam came to Jerusalem; and he assembled Juda and Benjamin, a hundred and eighty thousand young men fit for war, and he waged war with Israel to recover the kingdom to Roboam. 2 And the Word of the Lord came to Samaias the man of God, saying, 3 Speak to Roboam the *son* of Solomon, and to all Juda and Benjamin, saying, 4 Thus saith the Lord, Ye shall not go up, and ye shall not war against your brethren: return every one to his home; for this thing is of me. And they hearkened to the word of the Lord, and returned from going against Jeroboam. 5 And Roboam dwelt in Jerusalem, and he built walled cities in Judea. 6 And he built Bethleem, and Ætan and Thecoe, 7 and Baethsura, and Sochoth, and Odollam, 8 and Geth, and Marisa, and Ziph, 9 and Adorai, and Lachis, and Azeca, 10 and Saraa, and Ælom, and Chebron, which belong to Juda and Benjamin, walled cities. 11 And he fortified them with walls, and placed in them captains, and stores of provisions, oil and wine, 12 shields and spears in every several city, and he fortified them very strongly, and he had on his side Juda and Benjamin. 13 And the priests and the Levites who were in all Israel were gathered to him out of all the coasts. 14 For the Levites left the tents of their possession, and went to Juda to Jerusalem, because Jeroboam and his sons had ejected them so that they should not minister to the Lord. 15 And he made for himself priests of the high places, and for the idols, and for the vanities, and for the calves which Jeroboam made. 16 And he cast out from the tribes of Israel those who set their heart to seek the Lord God of Israel: and they came to Jerusalem, to sacrifice to the Lord God of their fathers. 17 And they strengthened the kingdom of Juda; and *Juda* strengthened Roboam the *son* of Solomon for three years, for he walked three years in the ways of David and Solomon. 18 And Roboam took to himself for a wife, Moolath daughter of Jerimuth the son of David, and Abigaia daughter of Heliab the son of Jessae. 19 And she bore him sons; Jeus, and Samoria, and Zaam. 20 And afterwards he took to himself Maacha the daughter of Abessalom; and she bore him Abia, and Jetthi, and Zeza, and Salemoth. 21 And Roboam loved Maacha the daughter of Abessalom more than all his wives and all his concubines: for he had eighteen wives and sixty concubines; and he begot twenty-eight sons, and sixty daughters. 22 And he made Abia the son of Maacha chief, *even* a leader among his brethren, for he intended to make him king. 23 And he was exalted beyond all his *other* sons in all the coasts of Juda and Benjamin, and in the strong cities; and he gave them provisions in great abundance: and he desired many wives.

2-Chron.12 1 And it came to pass when the kingdom of Roboam was established, and when he had grown strong, *that* he forsook the commandments of the Lord, and all Israel with him. 2 And it came to pass in the fifth year of the reign of Roboam, Susakim king of Egypt came up against Jerusalem, because they had sinned against the Lord, 3 with twelve hundred chariots, and sixty thousand horses: and there was no number of the multitude that came with him from Egypt; Libyans, Trogodytes, and Ethiopians. 4 And they obtained possession of the strong cities, which were in Juda, and came to Jerusalem. 5 And Samaias the prophet came to Roboam, and to the princes of Juda that were gathered to Jerusalem for fear of Susakim, and said to them, Thus said the Lord, Ye have left me, and I will leave you in the hand of Susakim. 6 And the elders of Israel and the king were ashamed, and said, The Lord *is* righteous. 7 And when the Lord saw that they repented, then came the word of the Lord to Samaias, saying, They have repented; I will not destroy them, but I will set them in safety for a little while, and my wrath shall not be poured out on Jerusalem. 8 Nevertheless they shall be servants, and know my service, and the service of the kings of the earth. 9 So Susakim king of Egypt went up against Jerusalem, and took the treasures that were in the house of the Lord, and the treasures that were in the king's house: he took all; and he took the golden shields which Solomon had made. 10 And king Roboam made brazen shields instead of them.

And Susakim set over him captains of footmen, as keepers of the gate of the king. 11 And it came to pass, when the king went into the house of the Lord, the guards and the footmen went in, and they that returned to meet the footmen. 12 And when he repented, the anger of the Lord turned from him, and did not destroy him utterly; for there were good things in Juda. 13 So king Roboam strengthened *himself* in Jerusalem, and reigned: and Roboam was forty and one years old when he began to reign, and he reigned seventeen years in Jerusalem, in the city which the Lord chose out of all the tribes of the children of Israel to call his name there: and his mother's name was Noomma the Ammanitess. 14 And he did evil, for he directed not his heart to seek the Lord. 15 And the acts of Roboam, the first and the last, behold, are they not written in the book of Samaia the prophet, and Addo the seer, with his achievements. 16 And Roboam made war with Jeroboam all *his* days. And Roboam died with his fathers, and was buried in the city of David: and Abia his son reigned in his stead.

2-Chron.13 1 In the eighteenth year of the reign of Jeroboam Abia began to reign over Juda. 2 He reigned three years in Jerusalem. And his mother's name *was* Maacha, daughter of Uriel of Gabaon. And there was war between Abia and Jeroboam. 3 And Abia set the battle in array with an army, with mighty men of war, *even* four hundred thousand mighty men: and Jeroboam set the battle in array against him with eight hundred thousand, *they were* mighty warriors of the host. 4 And Abia rose up from the mount Somoron, which is in mount Ephraim, and said, Hear ye, Jeroboam, and all Israel: 5 *Is it* not for you to know that the Lord God of Israel has given a king over Israel for ever to David, and to his sons, by a covenant of salt? 6 But Jeroboam the *son* of Nabat, the servant of Solomon *the son* of David, is risen up, and has revolted from his master: 7 and there are gathered to him pestilent men, transgressors, and he has risen up against Roboam the *son* of Solomon, while Roboam was young and fearful in heart, and he withstood him not. 8 And now ye profess to resist the kingdom of the Lord in the hand of the sons of David; and ye *are* a great multitude, and with you are golden calves, which Jeroboam made you for gods. 9 Did ye not cast out the priests of the Lord, the sons of Aaron, and the Levites, and make to yourselves priests of the people of any *other* land? whoever came to consecrate himself with a calf of the heard and seven rams, he forthwith became a priest to that which is no god. 10 But we have not forsaken the Lord our God, and his priests, the sons of Aaron, and the Levites, minister to the Lord; and in their daily courses 11 they sacrifice to the Lord whole-burnt- offering, morning and evening, and compound incense, and *set* the shewbread on the pure table; and *there is* the golden candlestick, and the lamps for burning, to light in the evening: for we keep the charge of the Lord God of our fathers; but ye have forsaken him. 12 And, behold, the Lord and his priests are with us at our head, and the signal trumpets to sound an alarm over us. Children of Israel, fight not against the Lord God of our fathers; for ye shall not prosper. 13 Now Jeroboam had caused an ambush to come round upon him from behind: and he *himself* was before Juda, and the ambush behind. 14 And Juda looked back, and, behold, the battle *was* against them before and behind: and they cried to the Lord, and the priests sounded with the trumpets. 15 And the men of Juda shouted: and it came to pass, when the men of Juda shouted, that the Lord smote Jeroboam and Israel before Abia and Juda. 16 And the children of Israel fled from before Juda; and the Lord delivered them into their hands. 17 And Abia and his people smote them with a great slaughter: and there fell slain of Israel five hundred thousand mighty men. 18 So the children of Israel were brought low in that day, and the children of Juda prevailed, because they trusted on the Lord God of their fathers. 19 And Abia pursued after Jeroboam, and he took from him the cities, Baethel and her towns, and Jesyna and her towns, and Ephron and her towns. 20 And Jeroboam did not recover strength again all the days of Abia: and the Lord smote him, and he died. 21 But Abia strengthened himself, and took to himself fourteen wives, and he begot twenty-two sons, and sixteen daughters. 22 And the rest of the acts of Abia, and his deeds, and his sayings, are written in the book of the prophet Addo.

2-Chron.14 1 And Abia died with his fathers, and they buried him in the city of David; and Asa his son reigned in his stead. In the days of Asa the land of Juda had rest ten years. 2 And he did that which was good and right in the sight of the Lord his God. 3 And he removed the altars of the strange *gods*, and the high places, and broke the pillars in pieces, and cut down the groves: 4 and he told Juda to seek earnestly the Lord God of their fathers, and to perform the law and commandments. 5 And he removed from all the cities of Juda the altars and the idols, and established in quietness 6 fortified cities in the land of Juda; for the land was quiet, and he had no war in these years; for the Lord gave him rest. 7 And he said to Juda, Let us fortify these cities, and make walls, and towers, and gates, and bars: we shall prevail over the land, for as we have sought out the Lord our God, he has sought out us, and has given us rest round about, and prospered us. 8 And Asa had a force of armed men bearing shields and spears in the land of Juda, *even* three hundred thousand, and in the land of Benjamin two hundred and eighty thousand targeteers and archers: all these were mighty warriors. 9 And Zare the Ethiopian went out against them, with a force of a million, and three hundred chariots; and came to Maresa. 10 And Asa went out to meet him, and set the battle in array in the valley north of Maresa. 11 And Asa cried to the Lord his God, and said, O Lord, it is not impossible with thee to save by many or by few: strengthen us, O Lord our God; for we trust in thee, and in thy name have we come against this great multitude. O Lord our God, let not man prevail against thee. 12 And the Lord smote the Ethiopians before Juda; and the Ethiopians fled. 13 And Asa and his people pursued them to Gedor; and the Ethiopians fell, so that they could not recover themselves; for they were crushed before the Lord, and before his host; and they took many spoils. 14 And they destroyed their towns roundabout Gedor; for a terror of the Lord was upon them: and they spoiled all their cities, for they had much spoil. 15 Also they destroyed the tents of cattle, and the Alimazons, and took many sheep and camels, and returned to Jerusalem.

2-Chron.15 1 And Azarias the son of Oded—upon him came the Spirit of the Lord, 2 and he went out to meet Asa, and all Juda and Benjamin, and said, Hear me, Asa, and all Juda and Benjamin. The Lord *is* with you, while ye are with him; and if ye seek him out, he will be found of you; but if ye forsake him, he will forsake you. 3 And Israel *has been* a long time without the true God, and without a priest to expound *the truth*, and without the law. 4 But he shall turn them to the Lord God of Israel, and he will be found of them. 5 And in that time there is no peace to one going out, or to one coming in, for the terror of the Lord is upon all that inhabit the lands. 6 And nation shall fight against nation, and city against city; for God has confounded them with every *kind of* affliction. 7 But be ye strong, and let not your hands be weakened: for there is a reward for your work. 8 And when *Asa* heard these words, and the prophesy of Adad the prophet, then he strengthened himself, and cast out the abominations from all the land of Juda and Benjamin, and from the cities which Jeroboam possessed, in mount Ephraim, and he renewed the altar of the Lord, which was before the temple of the Lord. 9 And he assembled Juda and Benjamin, and the strangers that dwelt with him, of Ephraim, and of Manasse, and of Symeon: for many of Israel were joined to him, when they saw that the Lord his God was with him. 10 And they assembled at Jerusalem in the third month, in the fifteenth year of the reign of Asa. 11 And he sacrificed to the Lord in that day of the spoils which they brought, seven hundred calves and seven thousand sheep. 12 And he entered into a covenant that they should seek the Lord God of their fathers with all their heart and with all their soul. 13 And that whoever should not seek the Lord God of Israel, should die, whether young or old, whether man or woman. 14 And they swore to the Lord with a loud voice, and with trumpets, and with cornets. 15 And all Juda rejoiced concerning the oath: for they swore with all their heart, and they sought him with all their desires; and he was found of them: and the Lord gave them rest round about. 16 And he removed Maacha his mother from being priestess to Astarte; and he cut down the idol, and burnt it in the brook of Kedron. 17 Nevertheless they removed not the high places: they still existed in Israel: nevertheless the heart of Asa was perfect all his days. 18 And he brought in the holy things of David his father, and the holy things of the house of God, silver, and gold, and vessels. 19 And there was no war *waged* with him until the thirty-fifth year of the reign of Asa.

2-Chron.16 1 And in the thirty-eighth year of the reign of Asa, the king of Israel went up against Juda, and built Rama, so as not to allow egress or ingress to Asa king of Juda. 2 And Asa took silver and gold out of the treasures of the house of the Lord, and of the king's house, and sent *them* to the son of Ader king of Syria, which dwelt in Damascus, saying, 3 Make a covenant between me and thee, and between my father and thy father: behold, I have sent thee gold and silver: come, and turn away from me Baasa king of Israel, and let him depart from me. 4 And the son of Ader hearkened to king Asa, and sent the captains of his host against the cities of Israel; and smote Æon, and Dan, and Abelmain, and all the country round Nephthali. 5 And it came to pass when Baasa heard *it* he left off building Rama, and put a stop to his work: 6 then king Asa took all Juda, and took the stones of Rama, and its timber, *with* which Baasa *had* built; and he built with them Gabae and Maspha. 7 And at that time came Anani the prophet to Asa king of Juda, and said to him, Because thou didst trust on the king of Syria, and didst not trust on the Lord thy God, therefore the army of Syria is escaped out of thy hand. 8 Were not the Ethiopians and Libyans a great force, in courage, in horsemen, in great numbers? and did not He deliver them into thy hands, because thou trustedst in the Lord? 9 For the eyes of the Lord look upon all the earth, to strengthen every heart that is perfect toward him. In this thou hast done foolishly; henceforth there shall be war with thee. 10 And Asa was angry with the prophet, and put him in prison, for he was angry at this: and Asa vexed some of the people at that time. 11 And, behold, the acts of Asa, the first and the last, *are* written in the book of the kings of Juda and Israel. 12 And Asa was diseased *in* his feet in the thirty-ninth year of his reign, until he was very ill: but in his disease he sought not to the Lord, but to the physicians. 13 And Asa slept with his fathers, and died in the fortieth year of his reign. 14 And they buried him in the sepulchre which he had dug for himself in the city of David, and they laid him on a bed, and filled *it* with spices and *all* kinds of perfumes of the apothecaries; and they made for him a very great funeral.

2-Chron.17 1 And Josaphat his son reigned in his stead, Josaphat strengthened himself against Israel. 2 And he put garrisons in all the strong cities of Juda, and appointed captains in all the cities of Juda, and in the cities of Ephraim, which Asa his father had taken. 3 And the Lord was with Josaphat, for he walked in the first ways of his father, and did not seek to idols; 4 but he sought to the Lord God of his father, and walked in the commandments of his father, and not according to the works of Israel. 5 And the Lord prospered the kingdom in his hand; and all Juda gave gifts to Josaphat; and he had great wealth and glory. 6 And his heart was exalted in the way of the Lord; and he removed the high places and the groves from the land of Juda. 7 And in the third year of his reign, he sent his chief men, and his mighty men, Abdias and Zacharias, and Nathanael, and Michaias, to teach in the cities of Juda. 8 And with them *were* the Levites, Samaias, and Nathanias, and Zabdias, and Asiel, and Semiramoth, and Jonathan, and Adonias, and Tobias, and Tobadonias, Levites, and with them Elisama and Joram, the priests. 9 And they taught in Juda, and *there was* with them the book of the law of the Lord, and they passed through the cities of Juda, and taught the people. 10 And a terror of the Lord was upon all the kingdoms of the land round about Juda, and they made no war against Josaphat. 11 And *some* of the Philistines brought to Josaphat gifts, and silver, and presents; and the Arabians brought him seven thousand seven hundred rams. 12 And

Josaphat increased in greatness exceedingly, and built in Judea places of abode, and strong cities. 13 And he had many works in Judea: and the mighty men of war, *the men* of strength, *were* in Jerusalem. 14 And this *is* their number according to the houses of their fathers; even the captains of thousands in Juda *were*, Ednas the chief, and with him mighty men of strength three hundred thousand. 15 And after him, Joanan the captain, and with him two hundred eighty thousand. 16 And after him Amasias the *son* of Zari, who was zealous for the Lord; and with him two hundred thousand mighty men of strength. 17 And out of Benjamin *there was* a mighty man of strength, even Eliada, and with him two hundred thousand archers and targeteers. 18 And after him Jozabad, and with him a hundred and eighty thousand mighty men of war. 19 These were the king's servants besides those whom the king put in the strong cities in all Judea.

2-Chron.18 1 And Josaphat had yet great wealth and glory, and he connected himself by marriage with the house of Achaab. 2 And he went down after a term of years to Achaab to Samaria: and Achaab slew for him sheep and calves, in abundance, and for the people with him, and he much desired him to go up with him to Ramoth of the country of Galaad. 3 And Achaab king of Israel said to Josaphat king of Juda, Wilt thou go with me to Ramoth of the country of Galaad? And he said to him, As I *am*, so also *art* thou, as thy people, *so also is* my people with thee for the war. 4 And Josaphat said to the king of Israel, Seek, I pray thee, the Lord to-day. 5 And the king of Israel gathered the prophets, four hundred men, and said to them, Shall I go to Ramoth Galaad to battle, or shall I forbear? And they said, Go up, and God shall deliver *it* into the hands of the king. 6 And Josaphat said, Is there not here a prophet of the Lord besides, that we may enquire of him? 7 And the king of Israel said to Josaphat, There is yet one man by whom to enquire of the Lord; but I hate him, for he does not prophesy concerning me for good, for all his days *are* for evil: this *is* Michaias the son of Jembla. And Josaphat said, Let not the king say so. 8 And the king called an eunuch, and said, *Fetch* quickly Michaias the son of Jembla. 9 And the king of Israel and Josaphat king of Juda were sitting each on his throne, and clothed in their robes, sitting in the open space at the entrance of the gate of Samaria: and all the prophets were prophesying before them. 10 And Sedekias son of Chanaan made for himself iron horns, and said, Thus saith the Lord, With these thou shalt thrust Syria until it be consumed. 11 And all the prophets prophesied so, saying, Go up to Ramoth Galaad, and thou shalt prosper; and the Lord shall deliver it into the hands of the king. 12 And the messenger that went to call Michaias spoke to him, saying, Behold, the prophets have spoken favourably concerning the king with one mouth; let now, I pray thee, thy words be as *the words* of one of them, and do thou speak good things. 13 And Michaias said, *As* the Lord lives, whatever God shall say to me, that will I speak. 14 And he came to the king, and the king said to him, Michaias, shall I go up to Ramoth Galaad to battle, or shall I forbear? And he said, Go up, and thou shalt prosper, and they shall be given into your hands. 15 And the king said to him, How often shall I solemnly charge thee that thou speak to me nothing but truth in the name of the Lord? 16 And he said, I saw Israel scattered on the mountains, as sheep without a shepherd: and the Lord said, These have no commander; let each return to his home in peace. 17 And the king of Israel said to Josaphat, Said I not to thee, that he would not prophesy concerning me good, but evil? 18 But he said, Not so. Hear ye the word of the Lord: I saw the Lord sitting on his throne, and all the host of heaven stood by on his right hand and on his left. 19 And the Lord said, Who will deceive Achaab king of Israel, that he may go up, and fall in Ramoth Galaad? And one spoke this way, and another spoke that way. 20 And there came forth a spirit, and stood before the Lord, and said, I will deceive him. And the Lord said, Whereby? 21 And he said, I will go forth, and will be a lying spirit in the mouth of all his prophets. And *the Lord* said, Thou shalt deceive *him*, and shalt prevail: go forth, and do so. 22 And now, behold, the Lord has put a false spirit in the mouth of these thy prophets, and the Lord has spoken evil against thee. 23 Then Sedekias the son of Chanaan drew near, and smote Michaias on the cheek, and said to him, By what way passed the Spirit of the Lord from me to speak to thee? 24 And Michaias said, Behold, thou shalt see in that day, when thou shalt go from chamber to chamber to hide thyself. 25 And the king of Israel said, Take Michaias, and carry him back to Emer the governor of the city, and to Joas the captain, the king's son; 26 and ye shall say, Thus said the king, Put this fellow into the prison house, and let him eat the bread of affliction, and *drink* the water of affliction, until I return in peace. 27 And Michaias said, If thou do at all return in peace, the Lord has not spoken by me. And he said, Hear, all ye people. 28 So the king of Israel, and Josaphat king of Juda, went up to Ramoth Galaad. 29 And the king of Israel said to Josaphat, Disguise me, and I will enter into the battle: and do thou put on my raiment. so the king of Israel disguised himself, and entered into the battle. 30 Now the king of Syria had commanded the captains of the chariots that were with him, saying, Fight neither against small nor great, but only against the king of Israel. 31 And it came to pass, when the captains of the chariots saw Josaphat, that they said, It is the king of Israel: and they compassed him about to fight against him: and Josaphat cried out, and the Lord delivered him; and God turned them away from him. 32 And it came to pass, when the captains of the chariots saw that it was not the king of Israel, that they turned away from him. 33 And a man drew a bow with a good aim, and smote the king of Israel between the lungs and the breast-plate: and he said to the charioteer, Turn thine hand, drive me out of the battle, for I am wounded. 34 And the battle turned in that day; and the king of Israel remained on the chariot against Syria until evening, and died at sunset.

2-Chron.19 1 And Josaphat king of Juda returned to his house at Jerusalem. 2 And there went out to meet him Jeu the prophet the son of Anani, and said to him, King Josaphat, doest thou help a sinner, or act friendly towards one hated of the Lord? Therefore has wrath come upon thee from the Lord. 3 Nevertheless *some* good things have been found in thee, forasmuch as thou didst remove the groves from the land of Juda, and didst direct thine heart to seek after the Lord. 4 And Josaphat dwelt in Jerusalem: and he again went out among the people from Bersabee to the mount of Ephraim, and turned them back to the Lord God of their fathers. 5 And he appointed judges in all the strong cities of Juda, city by city. 6 And he said to the judges, Take good heed what ye do: for ye judge not for man, but for the Lord, and with you are matters of judgment. 7 And now let the fear of the Lord be upon you, and be wary, and do *your duty*: for there is no unrighteousness with the Lord our God, neither *is it for him* to respect persons, nor take bribes. 8 Moreover Josaphat appointed in Jerusalem some of the priests, and Levites, and heads of houses of Israel, for the judgment of the Lord, and to judge the dwellers in Jerusalem. 9 And he charged them, saying, Thus shall ye do in the fear of the Lord, in truth and with a perfect heart. 10 Whatsoever man of your brethren that dwell in their cities *shall bring* the cause that comes before you, between blood *and* blood, and between precept and commandment, and ordinances and judgments, ye shall even decide for them; so they shall not sin against the Lord, and there shall not be wrath upon you, and upon your brethren: thus ye shall do, and ye shall not sin. 11 And, behold, Amarias the priest is head over you in every matter of the Lord; and Zabdias the son of Ismael is head over the house of Juda in every matter of the king; and the scribes and Levites are before you: be strong and active, and the Lord shall be with the good.

2-Chron.20 1 And after this came the children of Moab, and the children of Ammon, and with them *some* of the Minaeans, against Josaphat to battle. 2 And they came and told Josaphat, saying, There is come against thee a great multitude from Syria, from beyond the sea; and, behold, they are in Asasan Thamar, this is Engadi. 3 And Josaphat was alarmed, and set his face to seek the Lord earnestly, and he proclaimed a fast in all Juda. 4 And Juda gathered themselves together to seek after the Lord: even from all the cities of Juda they came to seek the Lord. 5 And Josaphat stood up in the assembly of Juda in Jerusalem, in the house of the Lord, in front of the new court. 6 And he said, O Lord God of my fathers, art not thou God in heaven above, and art not thou Lord of all the kingdoms of the nations? and *is there* not in thy hand the might of dominion, and there is no one who can resist thee? 7 Art not thou the Lord that didst destroy the inhabitants of this land before the face of thy people Israel, and didst give it to thy beloved seed of Abraham for ever? 8 And they dwelt in it, and built in it a sanctuary to thy name, saying, 9 If there should come upon us evils, sword, judgment, pestilence, famine, we will stand before this house, and before thee, (for thy name *is* upon this house,)and we will cry to thee because of the affliction, and thou shalt hear, and deliver. 10 And now, behold, the children of Ammon, and Moab, and mount Seir, with regard to whom thou didst not permit Israel to pass through their border, when they had come out of the land of Egypt, (for they turned away from them, and did not destroy them;)— 11 yet now, behold, they make attempts against us, to come forth to cast us out from our inheritance which thou gavest us. 12 O Lord our God, wilt thou not judge them? for we have no strength to resist this great multitude that is come against us; and we know not what we shall do to them: but our eyes are toward thee. 13 And all Juda was standing before the Lord, and their children, and their wives. 14 And Oziel the *son* of Zacharias, of the children of Banaias, of the sons of Eleiel, the sons of Matthanias the Levite, of the sons of Asaph, —upon him came the Spirit of the Lord in the assembly: 15 and he said, Hear ye, all Juda, and the dwellers in Jerusalem, and king Josaphat: Thus saith the Lord to you, even you, Fear not, neither be alarmed, before all this great multitude; for the battle is not years, but God's. 16 To-morrow go ye down against them: behold, they come up by the ascent of Assis, and ye shall find them at the extremity of the river of the wilderness of Jeriel. 17 It is not for you to fight: understand these things, and see the deliverance of the Lord with you, Juda and Jerusalem: fear not, neither be afraid to go forth to-morrow to meet them; and the Lord shall be with you. 18 And Josaphat bowed with his face *to the ground* with all Juda and the dwellers in Jerusalem, *and* they fell before the Lord to worship the Lord. 19 And the Levites of the children of Caath, and *they* of the sons of Core, rose up to praise the Lord God of Israel with a loud voice on high. 20 And they rose early in the morning and went out to the wilderness of Thecoe: and as they went out, Josaphat stood and cried, and said, Hear me, Juda, and the dwellers in Jerusalem; put your trust in the Lord God, and your trust shall be honored; trust in his prophet, and ye shall prosper. 21 And he took counsel with the people, and set appointed men to sing psalms and praises, to give thanks, and sing the holy songs of praise in going forth before the host: and they said, Give thanks to the Lord, for his mercy *endures* for ever. 22 And when they began the praise and thanksgiving, the Lord caused the children of Ammon to fight against Moab, and *the inhabitants of* mount Seir that came out against Juda; and they were routed. 23 Then the children of Ammon and Moab rose up against the dwellers in mount Seir, to destroy and consume them; and when they had made an end of *destroying* the inhabitants of Seir, they rose up against one another so that they were utterly destroyed. 24 And Juda came to the watch-tower of the wilderness, and looked, and saw the multitude, and, behold, *they were* all fallen dead upon the earth, not one escaped. 25 And Josaphat and his people went out to spoil them, and they found much cattle, and furniture, and spoils, and precious things: and they spoiled them, and they were three days gathering the spoil, for it was abundant. 26 And it came to pass on the fourth day they were gathered to the Valley of Blessing; for there they blessed the Lord: therefore they called the name of the place the Valley of Blessing, until this day. 27 And all the men of Juda returned to Jerusalem, and Josaphat led them with great joy; for the Lord gave them joy over their enemies. 28 And they entered into Jerusalem with lutes and harps and trumpets, *going* into the house of the lord. 29 And there was a terror of the Lord upon all the kingdoms of the land, when they heard that the Lord fought against the enemies of Israel. 30 And the kingdom of Josaphat was at peace; and his God gave him rest round about. 31 And Josaphat reigned over Juda, being thirty-five years *old* when he began to reign, and he reigned twenty-five years in Jerusalem: and his mother's name was Azuba, daughter of Sali. 32 And he walked in the ways of his father Asa, and turned not aside from doing that which was right in the sight of the Lord. 33 nevertheless the high places yet remained; and as yet the people did not direct their heart to the Lord God of their fathers. 34 And the rest of the acts of Josaphat, the first and the last, behold, they are written in the history of Jeu *the son* of Anani, who wrote the book of the kings of Israel. 35 And afterwards Josaphat king of Juda entered into an alliance with Ochozias king of Israel, (now this was an unrighteous man,) 36 by acting *with* and going to him, to build ships to go to Tharsis: and he built ships in Gasion Gaber. 37 And Eliezer thee *son* of Dodia of Marisa prophesied against Josaphat, saying, Forasmuch as thou hast allied thyself with Ochozias, the Lord has broken thy work, and thy vessels have been wrecked. And they could not go to Tharsis.

2-Chron.21 1 And Josaphat slept with his fathers, and was buried in the city of David: and Joran his son reigned in his stead. 2 And he had brothers, the six sons of Josaphat, Azarias, and Jeiel, and Zacharias, and Azarias, and Michael, and Zaphatias: all these *were* the sons of Josaphat king of Juda. 3 And their father gave them many gifts, silver, and gold, and arms, together with fortified cities in Juda: but he gave the kingdom to Joram, for he *was* the first-born. 4 And Joram entered upon his kingdom, and strengthened himself, and slew all his brothers with the sword, and *some* of the princes of Israel. 5 When he was thirty and two years old, Joram succeeded to his kingdom, and he reigned eight years in Jerusalem. 6 And he walked in the way of the kings of Israel, as did the house of Achaab; for a daughter of Achaab was his wife: and he did that which was evil in the sight of the Lord: 7 nevertheless the Lord would not utterly destroy the house of David, because of the covenant which he made with David, and as he said to him that he would give a light to him and his sons for ever. 8 In those days Edom revolted from Juda, and they made a king over themselves. 9 And Joram went with the princes, and all the cavalry with him: and it came to pass that he arose by night, and smote Edom that compassed him about, and the captains of the chariots, and the people fled to their tents. 10 And Edom revolted from Juda until this day. Then Lomna at that time revolted from *under* his hand, because he forsook the Lord God of his fathers. 11 For he built high places in the cities of Juda, and caused the dwellers in Jerusalem to go a-whoring, and led Juda astray. 12 And there came to him *a message* in writing from Eliu the prophet, saying, Thus saith the Lord God of thy father David, Because thou hast not walked in the way of thy father Josaphat, nor in the ways of Asa king of Juda, 13 but hast walked in the ways of the kings of Israel, and hast caused Juda and the dwellers in Jerusalem to go a-whoring, as the house of Achaab caused *Israel* to go a-whoring, and thou hast slain thy brethren, the sons of thy father, who were better than thyself; 14 behold, the Lord shall smite thee with a great plague among thy people, and thy sons, and thy wives, and all thy store: 15 and thou *shalt be afflicted* with a grievous disease, with a disease of the bowels, until thy bowels shall fall out day by day with the sickness. 16 So the Lord stirred up the Philistines against Joram, and the Arabians, and those who bordered on the Æthiopians: 17 and they went up against Juda, and prevailed against them, and took away all the store which they found in the house of the king, and his sons, and his daughters; and there was no son left to him but Ochozias the youngest of his sons. 18 And after all these things the Lord smote him in the bowels with an incurable disease. 19 And it continued from day to day: and when the time of the days came *to* two years, his bowels fell out with the disease, and he died by a grievous distemper: and his people performed no funeral, like the funeral of his fathers. 20 He was thirty and two years old when he began to reign, and he reigned eight years in Jerusalem. And he departed without honour, and was buried in the city of David, but not in the tombs of the kings.

2-Chron.22 1 And the inhabitants of Jerusalem made Ochozias his youngest son king in his stead: for the band of robbers that came against them, even the Arabians and the Alimazonians, had slain all the elder ones. So Ochozias son of Joram king of Juda reigned. 2 Ochozias began to reign when he was twenty years old, and he reigned one year in Jerusalem: and his mother's name was Gotholia, the daughter of Ambri. 3 And he walked in the way of the house of Achaab; for his mother was his counsellor to do evil. 4 And he did that which was evil in the sight of the Lord as the house of Achaab *had done*: for they were his counselors after the death of his father to his destruction. 5 And he walked in their counsels, and he went with Joram son of Achaab king of Israel to war against Azael king of Syria to Ramoth Galaad: and the archers smote Joram. 6 And Joram returned to Jezrael to be healed of the wounds wherewith the Syrians smote him in Ramoth, when he fought against Azael king of Syria. And Ochozias son of Joram, king of Juda, went down to see Joram the son of Achaab at Jezrael because he was sick. 7 And destruction from God came upon Ochozias in *his* coming to Joram; for when he had come, Joram went out with him against Jeu the son of Namessei, the anointed of the Lord against the house of Achaab. 8 And it came to pass, when Jeu was taking vengeance on the house of Achaab, that he found the princes of Juda and the brethren of Ochozias ministering to Ochozias, and he slew them. 9 And he gave orders to seek Ochozias: and they took him while he was healing his wounds in Samaria, and they brought him to Jeu, and he slew him; and they buried him, for they said, He is the son of Josaphat, who sought the Lord with all his heart. So there was none in the house of Ochozias to secure their power in the kingdom. 10 And Gotholia the mother of Ochozias saw that her son was dead, and she arose and destroyed all the seed royal in the house of Juda. 11 But Josabeeth, the daughter of the king, took Joas the son of Ochozias and rescued him secretly out of the midst of the sons of the king that were put to death, and she placed him

and his nurse in a bedchamber. So Josabeeth daughter of king Joram, sister of Ochozias, wife of Jodae the priest, hid him, and she *even* hid him from Gotholia, and she did not slay him. 12 And he was with him hid in the house of God six years; and Gotholia reigned over the land.

2-Chron.23 1 And in the eighth year Jodae strengthened *himself*, and took the captains of hundreds, Azarias the son of Joram, and Ismael the son of Joanan, and Azarias the son of Obed, and Maasaeas the son of Adia, and Elisaphan the son of Zacharias, with him unto the house of the Lord. 2 And they went round about Juda, and gathered the Levites out of all the cities of Juda, and heads of the families of Israel, and they came to Jerusalem. 3 and all the congregation of Juda made a covenant with the king in the house of God. And he shewed them the king's son, and said to them, Lo, let the king's son reign, as the Lord said concerning the house of David. 4 Now this *is* the thing which ye shall do. Let a third part of you, *even* of the priests and of the Levites, enter in on the sabbath, even into the gates of the entrances; 5 and let a third part be in the house of the king; and another third at the middle gate: and all the people in the courts of the Lord's house. 6 And let not *any one* enter into the house of the Lord, except the priests and the Levites, and the servants of the Levites; they shall enter in, because they are holy: and let all the people keep the watch of the Lord. 7 And the Levites shall compass the king round about, every man's weapon in his hand; and whoever *else* goes into the house shall die: but they shall be with the king when he goes out, and when he comes in. 8 And the Levites and all Juda did according to all that the priest Jodae commanded them, and they took each his men from the beginning of the sabbath to the end of the sabbath, for Jodae the priest did not dismiss the courses. 9 And Jodae gave to the men the swords, and the shields, and the arms, which *had* belonged to King David, in the house of God. 10 And he set the whole people, every man with his arms, from the right side of the house to the left side of the altar and the house, over against the king round about. 11 And he brought out the king's son, and put on him the crown and the testimony, and Jodae the priest and his sons proclaimed him king, and anointed him, and said, Long live the king! 12 And Gotholia heard the sound of the people running, and acknowledging and praising the king: and she went in to the king into the house of the Lord. 13 And she looked, and, behold, the king *stood* in his place, and the princes and trumpets were at the entrance, and the princes were round the king: and all the people of the land rejoiced, and sounded the trumpets, and there were the singers singing with instruments, and singing hymns of praise. and Gotholia rent her robe, and cried, ye surely are plotting against *me*. 14 And Jodae the priest went forth, and Jodae the priest charged the captains of hundreds, even the captains of the host, and said to them, Thrust her forth outside the house, and follow her, and let her be slain with the sword. For the priest said, Let her not be slain in the house of the Lord. 15 So they let her go *out*; and she went through the horsemen's gate of the house of the king, and they slew her there. 16 And Jodae made a covenant between himself, and the people, and the king, that the people should be the Lord's. 17 And all the people of the land went into the house of Baal, and tore down it and its altars, and they ground his images to powder, and they slew Matthan the priest of Baal before his altars. 18 And Jodae the priest committed the works of the house of the Lord into the and of the priests and Levites, and he re-established the courses of the priests and Levites which David appointed over the house of the Lord, and *he appointed them* to offer whole-burnt-offerings to the Lord, as it is written in the law of Moses, with gladness, and with songs by the hand of David. 19 And the porters stood at the gates of the house of the Lord, that no one unclean in any respect should enter in. 20 And he took the heads of families, and the mighty men, and the chiefs of the people, and all the people of the land, and they conducted the king into the house of the Lord; and he went through the inner gate into the king's house, and they seated the king on the throne of the kingdom. 21 And all the people of the land rejoiced; and the city was quiet: and they slew Gotholia.

2-Chron.24 1 Joas was seven years old when he began to reign, and he reigned forty years in Jerusalem: and his mother's name was Sabia of Bersabee. 2 And Joas did that which right in the sight of the Lord all the days of Jodae the priest. 3 And Jodae took to himself two wives, and they bore sons and daughters. 4 And it came to pass afterward that it came into the heart of Joas to repair the house of the Lord. 5 And he gathered the priests and the Levites, and said to them, Go out into the cities of Juda, and collect money of all Israel to repair the house of the Lord from year to year, and make haste to speak *of it*. But the Levites hasted not. 6 And king Joas called Jodae the chief, and said to him, Why hast thou not looked after the Levites, so that they should bring from Juda and Jerusalem that which was prescribed by Moses the man of God, when he assembled Israel at the tabernacle of witness? 7 For Gotholia was a transgressor, and her sons tore down the house of God; for they offered the holy things of the house of the Lord to Baalim. 8 And the king said, Let a box be made, and let it be put at the gate of the house of the Lord without. 9 And let *men* proclaim in Juda an in Jerusalem, that *the people* should bring to the Lord, as Moses the servant of God spoke concerning Israel in the wilderness. 10 And all the princes and all the people gave, and brought in, and cast into the box until it was filled. 11 And it came to pass, when they brought in the box to the officers of the king by the hand of the Levites, and when they saw that the money was more than sufficient, then came the king's scribe, and the officer of the high priest, and emptied the box, and restored it to its place. Thus they did day by day, and collected much money. 12 And the king and Jodae the priest gave it to the workmen employed in the service of the house of the Lord, and they hired masons and carpenters to repair the house of the Lord, also smiths and braziers to repair the house of the Lord. 13 And the workmen wrought, and the works prospered in their hands, and they established the house of the Lord on its foundation, and strengthened *it*. 14 And when they had finished *it*, they brought to the king and to

Jodae the remainder of the money, and they made vessels for the house of the Lord, vessels of service for whole-burnt-offerings, and gold and silver *censers*: and they offered up whole-burnt-offerings in the house of the Lord continually all the days of Jodae. 15 And Jodae grew old, being full of days, and he died, being a hundred and thirty years old at his death. 16 And they buried him with the kings in the city of David, because he had dealt well with Israel, and with God and his house. 17 And it came to pass after the death of Jodae, *that* the princes of Juda went in, and did obeisance to the king. Then the king hearkened to them. 18 And they forsook the house of the Lord God of their fathers, and served the Astartes and idols: and there was wrath upon Juda and Jerusalem in that day. 19 yet he sent prophets to them, to turn them to the Lord; but they hearkened not: and he testified to them, but they obeyed not. 20 And the Spirit of God came upon Azarias the son of Jodae the priest, and he stood up above the people, and said, Thus saith the Lord, Why do ye transgress the commandments of the Lord? so shall ye not prosper; for ye have forsaken the Lord, and he will forsake you. 21 And they conspired against him, and stone him by command of king Joas in the court of the Lord's house. 22 So Joas remembered not the kindness which his father Jodae had exercised towards him, but slew his son. And as he died, he said, The Lord look upon *it*, and judge. 23 And it came to pass after the end of the year, *that* the host of Syria went up against him, and came against Juda and Jerusalem: and they slew all the chiefs of the people among the people, and all their spoils they sent to the king of Damascus. 24 For the army of Syria came with few men, yet God gave into their hands a very large army, because they had forsaken the God of their fathers; and he brought judgments on Joas. 25 And after they had departed from him, when they had left him in sore diseases, then his servants conspired against him because of the blood of the son of Jodae the priest, and slew him on his bed, and he died, and they buried him in the city of David, but they buried him not in the sepulchre of the kings. 26 And they that conspired against him were Zabed the son of Samaath the Ammanite, and Jozabed the son of Samareth the Moabite. 27 And all his sons, and the five came to him: and the other *matters*, behold, they are written in the book of the kings. And Amasias his son reigned in his stead.

2-Chron.25 1 Amasias began to reign when he was twenty and five years old, and he reigned twenty-nine years in Jerusalem; and his mother's name *was* Joadaen of Jerusalem. 2 And he did that which was right in the sight of the Lord, but not with a perfect heart. 3 And it came to pass, when the kingdom was established in his hand, that he slew his servants who had slain the king his father. 4 But he slew not their sons, according to the covenant of the law of the Lord, as it is written, *and* as the Lord commanded, saying, The fathers shall not die for the children, and the sons shall not die for the fathers, but they shall die each for his own sin. 5 And Amasias assembled the house of Juda, and appointed them according to the houses of their families for captains of thousands and captains of hundreds in all

Juda and Jerusalem: and he numbered them from twenty years old and upwards, and found them three hundred thousand able to go out to war, holding spear and shield. 6 Also he hired of Israel a hundred thousand mighty *men for* a hundred talents of silver. 7 And there came a man of God to him, saying, O king, let not the host of Israel go with thee; for the Lord is not with Israel, *even* all the sons of Ephraim. 8 For if thou shalt undertake to strengthen *thyself* with these, then the lord shall put thee to flight before the enemies: for it is of the Lord both to strengthen and to put to flight. 9 And Amasias said to the man of God, But what shall I do *for* the hundred talents which I have given to the army of Israel? And the man of God said, The Lord can give thee much more than these. 10 And Amasias separated from the army that came to him from Ephraim, that they might go away to their place; and they were very angry with Juda, and they returned to their place with great wrath. 11 And Amasias strengthened *himself*, and took his people, and went to the valley of salt, and smote there the children of Seir ten thousand. 12 And the children of Juda took ten thousand prisoners, and they carried them to the top of the precipice, and cast them headlong from the top of the precipice, and they were all dashed to pieces. 13 And the men of the host whom Amasias sent back so that they should not go with him to battle, *went* and attacked the cities of Juda, from Samaria to Baethoron; and they smote three thousand among them, and took much spoil. 14 And it came to pass, after Amasias had returned from smiting Idumea, that he brought home the gods of the children of Seir, and set them up for himself as gods, and bowed down before them, and he sacrificed to them. 15 And the anger of the Lord came upon Amasias, and he sent him a prophet, and he said to him, Why hast thou sought the gods of the people, which have not rescued their own people out of thine hand? 16 And it came to pass when the prophet was speaking to him, that he said to him, have I made thee king's counsellor? take heed lest thou be scourged: and the prophet forebore, and said, I know that *God* is disposed against thee to destroy thee, because thou hast done this thing, and hast not hearkened to my counsel. 17 And Amasias king of Juda took counsel, and sent to Joas, son of Joachaz, son of Jeu, king of Israel, saying, Come, and let us look one another in the face. 18 And Joas king of Israel sent to Amasias king of Juda, saying, The thistle that was in Libanus sent to the cedar that was in Libanus, saying, Give thy daughter to my son to wife; but, behold, thy wild beasts of the field that are in Libanus shall come: and the wild beasts did come, and trod down the thistle. 19 Thou hast said, Behold, I have smitten Idumea, and thy stout heart exalts thee: now stay at home; for why dost thou implicate thyself in mischief, that thou shouldest fall, and Juda with thee. 20 Nevertheless Amasias hearkened not, for it was of the Lord to deliver him into *the enemy's* hands, because he sought after the gods of the Idumeans. 21 So Joas king of Israel went up; and they saw one another, he and Amasias king of Juda, in Baethsamys, which is of Juda. 22 And Juda was put to flight before Israel, and they fled every man to his tent. 23 And Joas king of Israel took prisoner Amasias king of Juda, *son* of Joas, son of Joachaz, in Baethsamys,

and brought him to Jerusalem; and he pulled down *part* of the wall of Jerusalem from the gate of Ephraim to the corner gate, four hundred cubits. 24 And *he took* all the gold and the silver, and all the vessels that were found in the house of the Lord and with Abdedom, and the treasures of the king's house, and the hostages, and he returned to Samaria. 25 And Amasias the *son* of Joas king of Juda lived after the death of Joas the *son* of Joachaz king of Israel fifteen years. 26 And the rest of the acts of Amasias, the first and the last, Lo! are they not written in the book of the kings of Juda and Israel? 27 And at the time when Amasias departed from the Lord, then they formed a conspiracy against him; and he fled from Jerusalem to Lachis: and they sent after him to Lachis, and slew him there. 28 And they took him up on horses, and buried him with his fathers in the city of David.

2-Chron.26 1 Then all the people of the land took Ozias, and he was sixteen years old, and they made him king in the room of his father Amasias. 2 He built Ælath, he recovered it to Juda, after the king slept with his fathers. 3 Ozias began to reign at the age of sixteen years, and he reigned fifty-two years in Jerusalem: and his mother's name was Jechelia of Jerusalem. 4 And he did that which was right in the sight of the Lord, according to all that Amasias his father did. 5 And he sought the Lord in the days of Zacharias, who understood the fear of the Lord; and in his days he sought the Lord, and the Lord prospered him. 6 And he went out and fought against the Philistines, and pulled down the walls of Geth, and the walls of Jabner, and the walls of Azotus, and he built cities *near* Azotus, and among the Philistines. 7 And the Lord strengthened him against the Philistines, and against the Arabians that dwelt on the rock, and against the Minaeans. 8 And the Minaeans gave gifts to Ozias; and his fame spread as far as the entering in of Egypt, for he strengthened *himself* exceedingly. 9 And Ozias built towers in Jerusalem, both at the gate of the corners, and at the valley gate, and at the corners and he fortified them. 10 And he built towers in the wilderness, and dug many wells, for he had many cattle in the low country and in the plain; and vinedressers in the mountain country and in Carmel: for he was a husbandman. 11 And Ozias had a host of warriors, and that went out orderly to war, and returned orderly in number; and their number was *made* by the hand of Jeiel the scribe, and Maasias the judge, by the hand of Ananias the king's deputy. 12 The whole number of the chiefs of families of the mighty men of war *was* two thousand six hundred; 13 and with them was a warrior force, three hundred thousand and seven thousand and five hundred: these waged war mightily to help the king against *his* enemies. 14 And Ozias prepared for them, *even* for all the host, shields, and spears, and helmets, and breastplates, and bows, and slings for stones. 15 And he made in Jerusalem machines invented by a wise contriver, to be upon the towers and upon the corners, to cast darts and great stones: and *the fame* of their preparation was heard at a distance; for he was wonderfully helped, till he was strong. 16 And when he was strong, his heart was lifted up to his destruction; and he transgressed against the Lord his God, and went into the temple of the Lord to turn incense on the altar of incense. 17 And there went in after him Azarias the priest, and with him eighty priests of the Lord, mighty men. 18 And they withstood Ozias the king, and said to him, *It is* not for thee, Ozias, to burn incense to the Lord, but only for the priests the sons of Aaron, who are consecrated to sacrifice: go forth of the sanctuary, for thou hast departed from the Lord; and this shall not be for glory to thee from the Lord god. 19 And Ozias was angry, and in his hand *was* the censer to burn incense in the temple: and when he was angry with the priests, then the leprosy rose up in his forehead before the priests in the house of the Lord, over the altar of incense. 20 And Azarias the chief priest, and the *other* priests, turned *to look* at him, and, behold, he *was* leprous in his forehead; and they got him hastily out thence, for he also hasted to go out, because the Lord had rebuked him. 21 And Ozias the king was a leper to the day of his death, and he dwelt *as* a leper in a separate house; for he was cut off from the house of the Lord: and Joathan his son *was set* over his kingdom, judging the people of the land. 22 And the rest of the acts of Ozias, the first and the last, *are* written by Jessias the prophet. 23 And Ozias slept with his fathers, and they buried him with his fathers in the field of the burial *place* of the kings, for they said, He is a leper; and Joatham his son reigned in his stead.

2-Chron.27 1 Joatham *was* twenty and five years old when he began to reign, and he reigned sixteen years in Jerusalem: and his mother's name *was* Jerusa, daughter of Sadoc. 2 And he did that which was right in the sight of the Lord, according to all that his father Ozias did: but he went not into the temple of the Lord. And still the people corrupted themselves. 3 He built the high gate of the house of the Lord, and he built much in the wall of Opel. 4 In the mountain of Juda, and in the woods, *he built* both dwelling-places and towers. 5 He fought against the king of the children of Ammon, and prevailed against him: and the children of Ammon gave him even annually a hundred talents of silver, and ten thousand measures of wheat, and ten thousand of barley. These the king of the children of Ammon brought to him annually in the first and second and third years. 6 Joatham grew strong, because he prepared his ways before the Lord his God. 7 And the rest of the acts of Joatham, and his war, and his deeds, behold, *they are* written in the book of the kings of Juda and Israel. 8 9 And Joatham slept with his fathers, and was buried in the city of David: and Achaz his son reigned in his stead.

2-Chron.28 1 Achaz was five and twenty years old when he began to reign, and he reigned sixteen years in Jerusalem: and he did not that which was right in the sight of the Lord, as David his father. 2 But he walked in the ways of the kings of Israel, for he made graven images. 3 And *he sacrificed* to their idols in the valley of Benennom, and passed his children through the fire, according to the abominations of the heathen, whom the Lord cast out from before the children of Israel. 4 And he burnt incense upon the high places, and upon the roofs, and under every shady tree. 5 And the Lord his God delivered him into the hand of the king of Syria; and he smote him, and took captive of them a great band of prisoners, and carried him to Damascus. Also *God* delivered him into the hands of the king of Israel, who smote him with a great slaughter. 6 And Phakee the son of Romelias king of Israel, slew in Juda in one day a hundred and twenty thousand mighty men; because they had forsaken the Lord God of their fathers. 7 And Zechri, a mighty man of Ephraim, slew Maasias the king's son, and Ezrican the chief of his house, and Elcana the king's deputy. 8 And the children of Israel took captive of their brethren three hundred thousand, women, and sons, and daughters, and they spoiled them of much property, and brought the spoils to Samaria. 9 And there was there a prophet of the Lord, his name *was* Oded: and he went out to meet the host that were coming to Samaria, and said to them, Behold, the wrath of the Lord God of your fathers *is* upon Juda, and he has delivered them into your hands, and ye have slain them in wrath, and it has reached even to heaven. 10 And now ye talk of keeping the children of Juda and Jerusalem for servants and handmaidens. Lo, am I not with you to testify for the Lord your God? 11 And now hearken to me, and restore the prisoners of your brethren whom ye have taken: for the fierce anger of the Lord *is* upon you. 12 And the chiefs of the sons of Ephraim rose up, Udias the son of Joanas, and Barachias the son of Mosolamoth, and Ezekias the son of Sellem, and Amasias the son of Eldai, against those that came from the war, 13 and said to them, Ye shall not bring in hither the prisoners to us, for whereas sin against the Lord *is* upon us, ye mean to add to our sins, and to our trespass: for our sin *is* great, and the fierce anger of the Lord *is* upon Israel. 14 So the warriors left the prisoners and the spoils before the princes and all the congregation. 15 And the men who were called by name rose up, and took hold of the prisoners, and clothed all the naked from the spoils, and gave them garments and shoes, and gave them *food* to eat, and *oil* to anoint themselves *with*, and they helped also every one that was weak with asses, and placed them in Jericho, the city of palm-trees, with their brethren; and they returned to Samaria. 16 At that time king Achaz sent to the king of Assyria to help him, and on this occasion, 17 because the Idumeans had attacked *him*, and smitten Juda, and taken a number of prisoners. 18 Also the Philistines had made an attack on the cities of the plain country, and the cities of the south of Juda, and taken Baethsamys, and [[the things in the house of the Lord, and the things in the house of the king, and of the princes: and they gave to the king]] Ælon, and Galero, and Socho and her villages, and Thamna and her villages, and Gamzo and her villages: and they dwelt there. 19 For the Lord humbled Juda because of Achaz king of Juda, because he grievously departed from the Lord. 20 And there came against him Thalgaphellasar king of Assyria, and he afflicted him. 21 And Achaz took the things *that were* in the house of the Lord, and the things in the house of the king, and of the princes, and gave them to the king of Assyria: but he was no help to him, 22 but only *troubled him* in his affliction: and he departed yet more from the Lord, and king Achaz said, 23 I will seek after the gods of Damascus that smite me. And he said, Forasmuch as the gods of the king of Syria themselves strengthen them, therefore will I sacrifice to them, and they will help me. But they became a stumbling-block to him, and to all Israel. 24 And Achaz removed the vessels of the house of the Lord, and cut them in pieces, and shut the doors of the house of the Lord, and made to himself altars in every corner in Jerusalem: 25 and in each several city in Juda he made high places to burn incense to strange gods: and they provoked the Lord God of their fathers. 26 And the rest of his acts, and his deeds, the first and the last, behold, *they are* written in the book of the kings of Juda and Israel. 27 And Achaz slept with his fathers, and was buried in the city of David; for they did not bring him into the sepulchres of the kings of Israel: and Ezekias his son reigned in his stead.

2-Chron.29 1 And Ezekias began to reign at the age of twenty-five years, and he reigned twenty-nine years in Jerusalem: and his mother's name was Abia, daughter of Zacharias. 2 And he did that which was right in the sight of the Lord, according to all that his father David had done. 3 And it came to pass, when he was established over his kingdom, in the first month, he opened the doors of the house of the Lord, and repaired them. 4 And he brought in the priests and the Levites, and put them on the east side, 5 and said to them, Hear, ye Levites: now sanctify yourselves, and sanctify the house of the Lord God of your fathers, and cast out the impurity from the holy places. 6 For our fathers have revolted, and done that which was evil before the Lord our God, and have forsaken him, and have turned away their face from the tabernacle of the Lord, and have turned *their* back. 7 And they have shut up the doors of the temple, and put out the lamps, and have not burnt incense, and have not offered whole-burnt-offerings in the holy *place* to the God of Israel. 8 And the Lord was very angry with Juda and Jerusalem, and made them an astonishment, and a desolation, and a hissing, as ye see with your eyes. 9 And, behold, your fathers have been smitten with the sword, and your sons and your daughters and your wives are in captivity in a land not their own, as it is even now. 10 Therefore it is now in my heart to make a covenant, a covenant with the Lord God of Israel, that he may turn away his fierce wrath from us. 11 And now be not wanting *to your duty*, for the Lord has chosen you to stand before him to minister, and to be ministers and burners of incense to him. 12 Then the Levites rose up, Maath the son of Amasi, and Joel the son of Azarias, of the sons of Caath: and of the sons of Merari, Kis the son of Abdi, and Azarias the son of Haelel: and of the sons of Gedsoni, Jodaad the son of Zemmath, and Joadam: these *were* the sons of Joacha. 13 And of the sons of Elisaphan; Zambri, and Jeiel: and of the sons of Asaph; Zacharias, and Matthanias: 14 and of the sons of Æman; Jeiel, and Semei: and of the sons of Idithun; Samaisa, and Oziel. 15 And they gathered their brethren, and they purified themselves according to the king's command by the order of the Lord, to purify the house of the Lord. 16 And the priests entered into the house of the Lord, to purify *it*, and they cast out all the uncleanness that was found in the house of the Lord, even into the court of the house of the Lord: and the Levites received *it* to cast into the brook of Kedron without. 17 And

Ezekias began on the first day, *even* on the new moon of the first month, to purify, and on the eighth day of the month they entered into the temple of the Lord: and they purified the house of the Lord in eight days; and on the thirteenth day of the first month they finished *the work.* 18 And they went in to king Ezekias, and said, We have purified all the things in the house of the Lord, the altar of whole-burnt-offering, and its vessels, and the table of shew-bread, and its vessels; 19 and all the vessels which king Achaz polluted in his reign, in his apostasy, we have prepared and purified: behold, they are before the altar of the Lord. 20 And king Ezekias rose early in the morning, and gathered the chief men of the city, and went up to the house of the Lord. 21 And he brought seven calves, seven rams, seven lambs, seven kids of goats for a sin-offering, for the kingdom, and for the holy things, and for Israel: and he told the priests the sons of Aaron to go up to the altar of the Lord. 22 And they slew the calves, and the priests received the blood, and poured it on the altar: and they slew the rams, and poured the blood upon the altar: also they slew the lambs, and poured the blood round the altar. 23 And they brought the goats for a sin-offering before the king and the congregation; and laid their hands upon them. 24 And the priests slew them, and offered their blood as a propitiation on the altar; and they made atonement for all Israel: for the king said, The whole-burnt- offering, and the sin-offering *are* for all Israel. 25 And he stationed the Levites in the house of the Lord with cymbals, and lutes, and harps, according to the commandment of king David, and of Gad the king's seer, and Nathan the prophet: for by the commandment of the Lord the order *was* in the hand of the prophets. 26 And the Levites stood with the instruments of David, and the priests with the trumpets. 27 And Ezekias told *them* to offer up the whole-burnt-offering on the altar: and when they began to offer the whole-burnt-offering, they began to sing to the Lord, and the trumpets *accompanied* the instruments of David king of Israel. 28 And all the congregation worshipped, and the psalm- singers *were* singing, and the trumpets sounding, until the whole-burnt-sacrifice had been completely offered. 29 And when they had done offering *it*, the king and all that were present bowed, and worshipped. 30 And king Ezekias and the princes told the Levites to sing hymns to the Lord in the words of David, and of Asaph the prophet: and they sang hymns with gladness, and fell down and worshipped. 31 Then Ezekias answered and said, Now ye have consecrated yourselves to the Lord, bring near and offer sacrifices of praise in the house of the Lord. And the congregation brought sacrifices and thank-offerings into the house of the Lord; and every one who was ready in his heart *brought* whole-burnt-offerings. 32 And the number of the whole-burnt-offerings which the congregation brought, was seventy calves, a hundred rams, two hundred lambs: all these *were* for a whole-burnt-offering to the Lord. 33 And the consecrated calves were six hundred, *and* the sheep three thousand. 34 But the priests were few, and could not flay the whole-burnt-offering, so their brethren the Levites helped them, until the work was finished, and until the priests had purified themselves: for the Levites *more* zealously purified *themselves* than the priests. 35 And the whole-burnt-offering *was* abundant, with the fat of the complete peace-offering, and the drink-offerings of the whole-burnt-sacrifice. So the service was established in the house of the Lord. 36 And Ezekias and all the people rejoiced, because God has prepared the people: for the thing was done suddenly.

2-Chron.30 1 And Ezekias sent to all Israel and Juda, and wrote letters to Ephraim and Manasse, that they should come into the house of the Lord to Jerusalem, to keep the passover to the Lord God of Israel. 2 For the king, and the princes, and all the congregation in Jerusalem, designed to keep the passover in the second month. 3 For they could not keep it at that time, because a sufficient number of priest had not purified themselves, and the people was not gathered to Jerusalem. 4 And the proposal pleased the king and the congregation. 5 And they established a decree that a proclamation should go through all Israel, from Bersabee to Dan, that they should come and keep the passover to the Lord God of Israel at Jerusalem: for the multitude had not done it lately according to the scripture. 6 And the posts went with the letters from the king and the princes to all Israel and Juda, according to the command of the king, saying, Children of Israel, return to the Lord God of Abraam, and Isaac, and Israel, and bring back them that have escaped *even* those that were left of the hand of the king of Assyria. 7 And be not as your fathers, and your brethren, who revolted from the Lord God of their fathers, and he gave them up to desolation, as ye see. 8 And now harden not your hearts, as your fathers *did*: give glory to the Lord God, and enter into his sanctuary, which he has sanctified for ever: and serve the Lord your God, and he shall turn away *his* fierce anger from you. 9 For when ye turn to the Lord, your brethren and your children shall be pitied before all that have carried them captives, and he will restore *you* to this land: for the Lord our God is merciful and pitiful, and will not turn away his face from you, if we return to him. 10 So the posts went through from city to city in mount Ephraim, and Manasse, and as far as Zabulon: and they as it were laughed them to scorn, and mocked them. 11 But the men of Aser, and *some* of Manasses and of Zabulon, were ashamed, and came to Jerusalem and Juda. 12 And the hand of the Lord was *present* to give them one heart to come, to do according to the commands of the king and of the princes, by the word of the Lord. 13 And a great multitude were gathered to Jerusalem to keep the feast of unleavened bread in the second month, a very great congregation. 14 And they arose, and took away the altars that were in Jerusalem, and all on which they burnt incense to false *gods* they tore down and cast into the brook Kedron. 15 Then they killed the passover on the fourteenth day of the second month: and the priests and the Levites repented, and purified *themselves*, and brought whole- burnt-offerings into the house of the Lord. 16 And they stood at their post, according to their ordinance, according to the commandment of Moses the man of God: and the priests received the blood from the hand of the Levites. 17 For a great part of the congregation was not sanctified; and the Levites were *ready* to kill the passover for every one who

could not sanctify himself to the Lord. 18 For the greatest part of the people of Ephraim, and Manasse, and Issachar, and Zabulon, had not purified *themselves*, but ate the passover contrary to the scripture. On this account also Ezekias prayed concerning them, saying, 19 The good Lord be merciful with regard to every heart that sincerely seeks the Lord God of their fathers, and *is* not *purified* according to the purification of the sanctuary. 20 And the Lord hearkened to Ezekias, and healed the people. 21 And the children of Israel who were present in Jerusalem kept the feast of unleavened bread seven days with great joy; and they continued to sing hymns to the Lord daily, and the priests and the Levites *played* on instruments to the Lord. 22 And Ezekias encouraged all the Levites, and those that had good understanding of the Lord: and they completely kept the feast of unleavened bread seven days, offering peace-offerings, and confessing to the Lord God of their fathers. 23 And the congregation purposed together to keep other seven days: and they kept seven days with gladness. 24 For Ezekias set apart for Juda, *even* for the congregation, a thousand calves and seven thousand sheep; and the princes set apart for the people a thousand calves and ten thousand sheep: and the holy things of the priests abundantly. 25 And all the congregation, the priests and the Levites, rejoiced, and all the congregation of Juda, and they that were present of Jerusalem, and the strangers that came from the land of Israel, and the dwellers in Juda. 26 And there was great joy in Jerusalem: from the days of Solomon the son of David king of Israel there was not such a feast in Jerusalem. 27 Then the priests the Levites rose up and blessed the people: and their voice was heard, and their prayer came into his holy dwelling-place, *even* into heaven.

2-Chron.31 1 And when all these things were finished, all Israel that were found in the cities of Juda went out, and broke in pieces the pillars, and cut down the groves, and tore down the high places and the altars out of all Judea and Benjamin, also of Ephraim and Manasse, till they made an end: and all Israel returned, every one to his inheritance, and to their cities. 2 And Ezekias appointed the courses of the priests and the Levites, and the courses of each one according to his ministry, to the priests and to the Levites, for the whole-burnt-offering, and for the peace-offering, and to praise, and to give thanks, and to minister in the gates, *and* in the courts of the house of the Lord. 3 And the king's proportion out of his substance *was appointed* for the whole-burnt-offerings, the morning and the evening one, and the whole-burnt-offerings for the sabbaths, and for the new moons, and for the feasts that were ordered in the law of the Lord. 4 And they told the people who dwelt in Jerusalem, to give the portion of the priests and the Levites, that they might be strong in the ministry of the house of the Lord. 5 And as he gave the command, Israel brought abundantly first-fruits of corn, and wine, and oil, and honey, and every fruit of the field: and the children of Israel and Juda brought tithes of everything abundantly. 6 And they that dwelt in the cities of Juda themselves also brought tithes of calves and sheep, and tithes of goats, and consecrated them to the Lord their God, and they brought them and laid them in heaps. 7 In the third month the heaps began to be piled, and in the seventh month they were finished. 8 And Ezekias and the princes came and saw the heaps, and blessed the Lord, and his people Israel. 9 Then Ezekias enquired of the priests and the Levites concerning the heaps. 10 And Azarias the priest, the chief over the house of Sadoc, spoke to him, and said, From the time that the first-fruits began to be brought into the house of the Lord, we have eaten and drunk, and left even abundantly; for the Lord has blessed his people, and we have left to this amount. 11 And Ezekias told them yet farther to prepare chambers for the house of the Lord; and they prepared *them*, 12 and they brought thither the first-fruits and the tithes faithfully: and Chonenias the Levite was superintendent over them, and Semei his brother was next. 13 and Jeiel, and Ozias, and Naeth, and Asael, and Jerimoth, and Jozabad, and Eliel, and Samachia, and Maath, and Banaias, and his sons, were appointed by Chonenias and Semei his brother, as Ezekias the king, and Azarias who was over the house of the Lord commanded. 14 And Core, the *son* of Jemna the Levite, the porter eastward, *was* over the gifts, to distribute the first-fruits of the Lord, and the most holy things, 15 by the hand of Odom, and Benjamin, and Jesus, and Semei, and Amarias, and Sechonias, by the hand of the priests faithfully, to give to their brethren according to the courses, as well to great as small; 16 besides the increase of males from three years old and upward, to every one entering into the house of the Lord, *a portion* according to a daily rate, for service in the daily courses of their order. 17 This *is* the distribution of the priests according to the houses of their families; and the Levites in their daily courses from twenty years old and upward *were* in *their* order, 18 to assign stations for all the increase of their sons and their daughters, for the whole number: for they faithfully sanctified the holy place. 19 As for the sons of Aaron that executed the priests' office, —even those from their cities the men in each several city who were named expressly, —*were appointed* to give a portion to every male among the priests, and to every one reckoned among the Levites. 20 And Ezekias did so through all Juda, and did that which was good and right before the Lord his God. 21 And in every work which he began in service in the house of the Lord, and in the law, and in the ordinances, he sought his God with all his soul, and wrought, and prospered.

2-Chron.32 1 And after these things and this faithful dealing, came Sennacherim king of the Assyrians, and he came to Juda, and encamped against the fortified cities, and intended to take them for himself. 2 And Ezekias saw that Sennacherim was come, and *that* his face *was set* to fight against Jerusalem. 3 And he took counsel with his elders and his mighty *men* to stop the wells of water which were without the city: and they helped him. 4 And he collected many people, and stopped the wells of water, and the river that flowed through the city, saying, Lest the king of Assyria come, and find much water, and strengthen *himself*. 5 And Ezekias strengthened *himself*, and built all the wall that had been pulled down, and the towers, and another wall in front without, and fortified the strong place of the city of David,

and prepared arms in abundance. 6 And he appointed captains of war over the people, and they were gathered to *meet* him to the open place of the gate of the valley, and he encouraged them, saying, 7 Be strong and courageous, and fear not, neither be dismayed before the King of Assyria, and before all the nation that *is* with him: for *there are* more with us than with him. 8 With him *are* arms of flesh; but with us *is* the Lord our God to save *us*, and to fight our battle. And the people were encouraged at the words of Ezekias king of Juda. 9 And afterward Sennacherim king of the Assyrians sent his servants to Jerusalem; and *he went* himself against Lachis, and all his army with him, and sent to Ezekias king of Juda, and to all Juda that *was* in Jerusalem, saying, 10 Thus says Sennacherim king of the Assyrians, On what do ye trust, that ye will remain in the siege in Jerusalem? 11 Does not Ezekias deceive you, to deliver you to death and famine and thirst, saying, The Lord our God will deliver us out of the hand of the king of Assyria? 12 Is not this Ezekias who has taken down his altars and his high places and has spoken to Juda and the dwellers in Jerusalem, saying, Ye shall worship before this altar and burn incense upon it? 13 Know ye not what I and my fathers have done to all the nations of the countries? Could the gods of the nations of all the earth at all rescue their people out of my hand? 14 Who is there among all the gods of those nations whom my fathers utterly destroyed, *worthy of trust*? Could they deliver their people out of my hand, that your God should deliver you out of my hand? 15 Now then, let not Ezekias deceive you, and let him not make you thus confident, and believe him not: for no god of any kingdom or nation is at all able to deliver his people out of my hand, or the hand of my fathers: therefore your God shall not deliver you out of my hand. 16 And his servants continued to speak against the Lord God, and against his servant Ezekias. 17 And he wrote a letter to reproach the Lord God of Israel, and spoke concerning him, saying, As the gods of the nations of the earth have not delivered their people out of my hand, so the God of Ezekias shall by no means deliver his people out of my hand. 18 And he cried with a loud voice in the Jews' language to the people of Jerusalem on the wall, *calling them* to assist them, and pull down *the walls*, that they might take the city. 19 And he spoke against the God of Jerusalem, even as against the gods of the nations of the earth, the works of the hands of men. 20 And king Ezekias and Esaias the prophet the son of Amos prayed concerning these things, and they cried to heaven. 21 And the Lord sent an angel, and he destroyed every mighty man and warrior, and leader and captain in the camp of the king of Assyria: and he returned with shame of face to his own land and came into the house of his god: and *some* of them that came out of his bowels slew him with the sword. 22 So the Lord delivered Ezekias and the dwellers in Jerusalem out of the hand of Sennacherim King of Assyria, and out of the hand of all *his enemies*, and gave them rest round about. 23 And many brought gifts to the Lord to Jerusalem, and presents to Ezekias king of Juda; and he was exalted in the eyes of all the nations after these things. 24 In those days Ezekias was sick even to death, and prayed to the Lord: and he hearkened to him, and gave him a sign. 25 But Ezekias did not recompense the Lord according to the return which he made him, but his heart was lifted up: and wrath came upon him, and upon Juda and Jerusalem. 26 And Ezekias humbled himself after the exaltation of his heart, he and the dwellers in Jerusalem; and the wrath of the Lord did not come upon them in the days of Ezekias. 27 And Ezekias had wealth and very great glory: and he made for himself treasuries of gold, and silver, and precious stones, also for spices, and stores for arms, and for precious vessels; 28 and cities for the produce of corn, and wine, and oil; and stalls and mangers for every *kind of* cattle, and folds for flocks; 29 and cities which he built for himself, and store of sheep and oxen in abundance, for the Lord gave him a very great store. 30 The same Ezekias stopped up the course of the water of Gion above, and brought the water down straight south of the city of David. And Ezekias prospered in all his works. 31 Notwithstanding, in regard to the ambassadors of the princes of Babylon, who were sent to him to enquire of him *concerning* the prodigy which came upon the land, the Lord left him, to try him, to know what was in his heart. 32 And the rest of the acts of Ezekias, and his kindness, behold, they are written in the prophecy of Esaias the son of Amos the prophet, and in the book of the kings of Juda and Israel. 33 And Ezekias slept with his fathers, and they buried him in a high place among the sepulchres of the sons of David: and all Juda and the dwellers in Jerusalem gave him glory and honour at his death. And Manasses his son reigned in his stead.

2-Chron.33 1 Manasses was twelve years old when he began to reign, and he reigned fifty-five years in Jerusalem. 2 And he did that which was evil in the sight of the Lord, according to all the abominations of the heathen, whom the Lord destroyed from before the face of the children of Israel. 3 And he returned and built the high places, which his father Ezekias had pulled down, and set up images to Baalim, and made groves, and worshipped all the host of heaven, and served them. 4 And he built altars in the house of the Lord, concerning which the Lord said, In Jerusalem shall be my name for ever. 5 And he built altars to all the host of heaven in the two courts of the house of the Lord. 6 He also passed his children through the fire in the valley of Benennom; and he divined, and used auspices, and sorceries, and appointed those who had divining spirits, and enchanters, and wrought abundant wickedness before the Lord, to provoke him. 7 And he set the graven *image*, the molten *statue*, the idol which he made, in the house of God, of which God had said to David and to Solomon his son, In this house, and Jerusalem, which I have chosen out of all the tribes of Israel, I will put my name for ever; 8 and I will not again remove the foot of Israel from the land which I gave to their fathers, if only they will take heed to do all things which I have commanded them, according to all the law and the ordinances and the judgments *given* by the hand of Moses. 9 So Manasses led astray Juda and the inhabitants of Jerusalem, to do evil beyond all the nations which the Lord cast out from before the children of Israel. 10 And the Lord spoke to Manasses, and to his people: but they hearkened not. 11 And the Lord brought upon them the captains of the host of the king of Assyria, and they took Manasses in bonds, and bound him in fetters, and brought him to Babylon. 12 And when he was afflicted, he sought the face of the Lord his God, and was greatly humbled before the face of the God of his fathers; 13 and he prayed to him: and he hearkened to him, and listened to his cry, and brought him back to Jerusalem to his kingdom: and Manasses knew that the Lord he is God. 14 And afterward he built a wall without the city of David, from the southwest southward in the valleys and at the entrance through the fish-gate, as men go out by the gate round about, even as far as Opel: and he raised it much, and set captains of the host in all the fortified cities in Juda. 15 And he removed the strange gods, and the graven *image* out of the house of the Lord, and all the altars which he had built in the mount of the house of the Lord, and in Jerusalem, and without the city. 16 And he repaired the altar of the Lord, and offered upon it a sacrifice of peace-offering and thank-offering, and he told Juda to serve the Lord God of Israel. 17 Nevertheless the people still sacrificed on the high places, only to the Lord their God. 18 And the rest of the acts of Manasses, and his prayer to God, and the words of the seers that spoke to him in the name of the God of Israel, 19 behold, *they are* in the account of his prayer; and *God* hearkened to him. And all his sins, and his backslidings, and the spots on which he built the high places, and set there groves and graven images, before he repented, behold, they are written in the books of the seers. 20 And Manasses slept with his fathers, and they buried him in the garden of his house: and Amon his son reigned in his stead. 21 Amon was twenty and two years old when he began to reign, and he reigned two years in Jerusalem. 22 And he did that which was evil in the sight of the Lord, as his father Manasses did: and Amon sacrificed to all the idols which his father Manasses had made, and served them. 23 And he was not humbled before the Lord as his father Manasses was humbled; for his son Amon abounded in transgression. 24 And his servants conspired against him, and slew him in his house. 25 And the people of the land slew the men who had conspired against king Amon; and the people of the land made Josias his son king in his stead.

2-Chron.34 1 Josias was eight years old when he began to reign, and he reigned thirty-one years in Jerusalem. 2 And he did that which was right in the sight of the Lord, and walked in the ways of his father David, and turned not aside to the right hand or to the left. 3 And in the eighth year of his reign, and he *being* yet a youth, he began to seek the Lord God of his father David: and in the twelfth year of his reign he began to purge Juda and Jerusalem from the high places, and the groves, and the ornaments for the altars, and the molten images. 4 And he pulled down the altars of Baalim that were before his face, and the high places that were above them; and he cut down the groves, and the graven images, and broke in pieces the molten images, and reduced them to powder, and cast *it* upon the surface of the tombs of those who *had* sacrificed to them. 5 And he burnt the bones of the priests upon the altars, and purged Juda and

Jerusalem. 6 And *he did so* in the cities of Manasse, and Ephraim, and Symeon, and Nephthali, and the places round about them. 7 And he pulled down the altars and the groves, and he cut the idols in small pieces, and cut off all the high places from all the land of Israel, and returned to Jerusalem. 8 And in the eighteenth year of his reign, after having cleansed the land, and the house, he sent Saphan the son of Ezelias, and Maasa prefect of the city, and Juach son of Joachaz his recorder, to repair the house of the Lord his God. 9 And they came to Chelcias the high priest, and gave the money that was brought into the house of God, which the Levites who kept the gate collected of the hand of Manasse and Ephraim, and of the princes, and of every one that was left in Israel, and of the children of Juda and Benjamin, and of the dwellers in Jerusalem. 10 And they gave it into the hand of the workmen, who were appointed in the house of the Lord, and they gave it to the workmen who wrought in the house of the Lord, to repair and strengthen the house. 11 They gave *it* also to the carpenters and builders, to buy squared stones, and timber for beams to cover the houses which the kings of Juda had destroyed. 12 And the men *were* faithfully *engaged* in the works: and over them were superintendents, Jeth and Abdias, Levites of the sons of Merari, and Zacharias and Mosollam, of the sons of Caath, *appointed* to oversee; and every Levite, and every one that understood *how* to play on musical instruments. 13 And *overseers were* over the burden-bearers, and over all the workmen in the respective works; and of the Levites *were appointed* scribes, and judges, and porters. 14 And when they brought forth the money that had been brought into the house of the Lord, Chelcias the priest found a book of the law of the Lord *given* by the hand of Moses. 15 And Chelcias answered and said to Saphan the scribe, I have found a book of the law in the house of the Lord. And Chelcias gave the book to Saphan. 16 And Saphan brought in the book to the king, and moreover gave an account to the king, *saying, This is* all the money given into the hand of thy servants that work. 17 And they have collected the money that was found in the house of the Lord, and given it into the hand of the overseers, and into the hand of them that do the work. 18 And Saphan the scribe brought word to the king, saying, Chelcias the priest has given me a book. And Saphan read it before the king. 19 And it came to pass, when the king heard the words of the law, that he rent his garments. 20 And the king commanded Chelcias, and Achicam the son of Saphan, and Abdom the son of Michaias, and Saphan the scribe, and Asia the servant of the king, saying, 21 Go, enquire of the Lord for me, and for every one that is left in Israel and Juda, concerning the words of the book that is found: for great is the wrath of the Lord *which* has been kindled amongst us, because our fathers have not hearkened to the words of the Lord, to do according to all the things written in this book. 22 And Chelcias went, and *the others* whom the king told, to Olda the prophetess, the wife of Sellem son of Thecoe, son of Aras, who kept the commandments; and she dwelt in Jerusalem in the second *quarter*: and they spoke to her accordingly. 23 And she said to them, Thus has the Lord God of Israel said, Tell the man who sent you to me, 24

Thus saith the Lord, Behold, I bring evil upon this place, *even* all the words that are written in the book that was read before the king of Juda: 25 because they have forsaken me, and burnt incense to strange gods, that they might provoke me by all the works of their hands; and my wrath is kindled against this place, and it shall not be quenched. 26 And concerning the king of Juda, who sent you to seek the Lord, —thus shall ye say to him, Thus saith the Lord God of Israel, *As for* the words which thou has heard, 27 forasmuch as thy heart was ashamed, and thou was humbled before me when thou heardest my words against this place, and against the inhabitants of it, and thou wast humbled before me, and didst rend thy garments, and didst weep before me; I also have heard, saith the Lord. 28 Behold, I *will* gather thee to thy fathers, and thou shalt be gathered to thy grave in peace, and thine eyes shall not look upon all the evils which I am bringing upon this place, and upon the inhabitants of it. And they brought back word to the king. 29 And the king sent and gathered the elders of Juda and Jerusalem. 30 And the king went up to the house of the Lord, *he* and all Juda, and the inhabitants of Jerusalem, and the priests, and the Levites, and all the people great and small: and he read in their ears all the words of the book of the covenant that were found in the house of the Lord. 31 And the king stood at a pillar, and made a covenant before the Lord, to walk before the Lord, to keep his commandments and testimonies, and his ordinances, with all *his* heart and with all *his* soul, so as to perform the words of the covenant that were written in this book. 32 And he caused all that were found in Jerusalem and Benjamin to stand; and the inhabitants of Jerusalem made a covenant in the house of the Lord God of their fathers. 33 And Josias removed all the abominations out of the whole land which belonged to the children of Israel, and caused all that were found in Jerusalem and in Israel, to serve the Lord their God all his days: he departed not from following the Lord God of his fathers.

2-Chron.35 1 And Josias kept a passover to the Lord his God; and sacrificed the passover on the fourteenth day of the first month. 2 And he appointed the priests at their charges, and encouraged them for the services of the house of the Lord. 3 And he told the Levites that were able *to act* in all Israel, that they should consecrate themselves to the Lord: and they put the holy ark in the house which Solomon the son of David king of Israel built: and the king said, Ye must not carry anything on your shoulders: now then minister to the Lord your God, and to his people Israel. 4 And prepare yourselves according to the houses of your families, and according to your daily courses, according to the writing of David king of Israel, and *the order* by the hand of his son Solomon. 5 And stand ye in the house according to the divisions of the houses of your families for your brethren the sons of the people; *so* also let there be for the Levites a division of the house of their family. 6 And kill ye the passover, and prepare *it* for your brethren, to do according to the word of the Lord, by the hand of Moses. 7 And Josias gave as an offering to the children of the people, sheep, and lambs, and kids of the young of the goats, all for the passover, *even for* all that were found, in number *amounting to* thirty thousand, and three thousand calves, these *were* of the substance of the king. 8 And his princes gave an offering to the people, and to the priests, and to the Levites: and Chelcias and Zacharias and Jeiel the chief men gave to the priests of the house of God, they even gave for the passover sheep, and lambs, and kids, two thousand six hundred, and three hundred calves. 9 And Chonenias, and Banaeas, and Samaeas, and Nathanael his brother, and Asabias, and Jeiel, and Jozabad, heads of the Levites, gave an offering to the Levites for the passover, of five thousand sheep and five hundred calves. 10 And the service was duly ordered, and the priests stood in their place, and the Levites in their divisions, according to the command of the king. 11 And they slew the passover, and the priests sprinkled the blood from their hand, and the Levites flayed *the victims*. 12 And they prepared the whole-burnt-offering to give to them, according to the division by the houses of families, *even* to the sons of the people, to offer to the Lord, as it is written in the book of Moses. 13 And thus *they did* till the morning. And they roasted the passover with fire according to the ordinance; and boiled the holy *pieces* in copper vessels and caldrons, and *the feast* went on well, and they quickly served all the children of the people. 14 And after they had prepared for themselves and for the priests, for the priests *were engaged* in offering the whole-burnt-offerings and the fat until night, then the Levites prepared for themselves, and for their brethren the sons of Aaron. 15 And the sons of Asaph the psalm- singers *were* at their post according to the commands of David, and Asaph, and Æman, and Idithom, the prophets of the king: also, the chiefs and the porters of the several gates; —it was not for them to stir from the service of the holy things, for their brethren the Levites prepared for them. 16 So all the service of the Lord was duly ordered and prepared in that day, for keeping the passover, and offering the whole-burnt-sacrifices on the altar of the Lord, according to the command of king Josias. 17 And the children of Israel that were present kept the passover at that time, and the feast of unleavened bread seven days. 18 And there was no passover like it in Israel from the days of Samuel the prophet, or any king of Israel: they kept not such a passover as Josias, and the priests, and the Levites, and all Juda and Israel that were present, and the dwellers in Jerusalem, kept to the Lord. 19 In the eighteenth year of the reign of Josias this passover was kept, after all these things that Josias did in the house. And king Josias burnt those who had in them a divining spirit, and the wizards, and the images, and the idols, and the sodomites which were in the land of Juda and in Jerusalem, that he might confirm the words of the law that were written in the book which Chelcias the priest found in the house of the Lord. There was no *king* like him before him, who turned to the Lord with all his heart, and all his soul, and all his strength, according to all the law of Moses, and after him there rose up none like him. Nevertheless the Lord turned not from the anger of his fierce wrath, wherewith the Lord was greatly angry against Juda, for all the provocations wherewith Manasses provoked him: and the Lord said, I will even remove Juda

also from my presence, as I have removed Israel, and I have rejected the city which I chose, *even* Jerusalem, and thehouse of which I said, My name shall be there. 20 And Pharao Nechao king of Egypt went up against the king of the Assyrians to the river Euphrates, and king Josias went to meet him. 21 And he sent messengers to him, saying, What have I to do with thee, O king of Juda? I am not come to-day to war against thee; and God has told me to hasten: beware of the God that is with me, lest he destroy thee. 22 However, Josias turned not his face from him, but strengthened himself to fight against him, and hearkened not to the words of Nechao by the mouth of God, and he came to fight in the plain of Mageddo. 23 And the archers shot at king Josias; and the king said to his servants, Take me away, for I am severely wounded. 24 And his servants lifted him out of the chariot, and put him in the second chariot which he had, and brought him to Jerusalem; and he died, and was buried with his fathers: and all Juda and Jerusalem lamented over Josias. 25 And Jeremias mourned over Josias, and all the chief men and chief women uttered a lamentation over Josias until this day: and they made it an ordinance for Israel, and, behold, it is written in the lamentations. 26 And the rest of the acts of Josias, and his hope, are written in the law of the Lord. 27 And his acts, the first and the last, behold, *they are* written in the book of the kings of Israel and Judah.

2-Chron.36 1 And the people of the land took Joachaz the son of Josias, and anointed him, and made him king over Jerusalem in the room of his father. 2 Joachaz *was* twenty-three years old when he began to reign, and he reigned three months in Jerusalem: and his mother's name was Amital, daughter of Jeremias of Lobna. And he did that which was evil in the sight of the Lord, according to all that his fathers had done. And Pharao Nechao bound him in Deblatha in the land of Æmath, that he might not reign in Jerusalem. 3 And the king brought him over to Egypt; and imposed a tribute on the land, a hundred talents of silver and a talent of gold. 4 And Pharao Nechao made Eliakim the son of Josias king over Juda in the room of his father Josias, and changed his name *to* Joakim. And Pharao Nechao took his brother Joachaz and brought him into Egypt, and he died there: but *he* had given the silver and gold to Pharao. At that time the land began to be taxed to give the money at the command of Pharao; and every one as he could borrowed the silver and the gold of the people of the land, to give to Pharao Nechao. 5 Joachim was twenty-five years old when he began to reign, and he reigned eleven years in Jerusalem: and his mother's name *was* Zechora, daughter of Nerias of Rama. And he did that which was evil in the sight of the Lord, according to all that his fathers did. In his days came Nabuchodonosor king of Babylon into the land, and he served him three years, and *then* revolted from him. And the Lord sent against them the Chaldeans, and plundering parties of Syrians, and plundering parties of the Moabites, and of the children of Ammon, and of Samaria; but after this they departed, according to the word of the Lord by the hand of his servants the prophets. Nevertheless the wrath of the Lord was upon Juda, so that they should be removed from his presence, because of the sins of Manasses in all that he did, and for the innocent blood which Joakim shed, for he had filled Jerusalem with innocent blood; yet the Lord would not utterly destroy them. 6 And Nabuchodonosor king of Babylon came up against him, and bound him with brazen fetters, and carried him away to Babylon. 7 And he carried away a part of the vessels of the house of the Lord to Babylon, and put them in his temple in Babylon. 8 And the rest of the acts of Joakim, and all that he did, behold, *are* not these things written in the book of the chronicles of the kings of Juda? And Joakim slept with his fathers, and was buried with his fathers in Ganozae: and Jechonias his son reigned in his stead. 9 Jechonias *was* eight years old when he began to reign, and he reigned three months and ten days in Jerusalem, and did that which was evil in the sight of the Lord. 10 And at the turn of the year, king Nabuchodonosor sent, and brought him to Babylon, with the precious vessels of the house of the Lord, and made Sedekias his father's brother king over Juda and Jerusalem. 11 Sedekias *was* twenty-one years old when he began to reign, and be reigned eleven years in Jerusalem. 12 And he did that which was evil in the sight of the Lord his God: he was not ashamed before the prophet Jeremias, nor because of the word of the Lord; 13 in that he rebelled against king Nabuchodonosor, which he adjured him by God *not to do*: but he stiffened his neck, and hardened his heart, so as not to return to the Lord God of Israel. 14 And all the great men of Juda, and the priests, and the people of the land transgressed abundantly in the abominations of the heathen, and polluted the house of the Lord which *was* in Jerusalem. 15 And the Lord God of their fathers sent by the hand of his prophets; rising early and sending his messengers, for he spared his people, and his sanctuary. 16 Nevertheless they sneered at his messengers, and set at nought his words, and mocked his prophets, until the wrath of the Lord rose up against his people, till there was no remedy. 17 And he brought against them the king of the Chaldeans, and slew their young men with the sword in the house of his sanctuary, and did not spare Sedekias, and had no mercy upon their virgins, and they led away their old men: he delivered all things into their hands. 18 And all the vessels of the house of God, the great and the small, and the treasures of the house of the Lord, and all the treasures of the king and the great men; he brought all to Babylon. 19 And he burnt the house of the Lord, and broke down the wall of Jerusalem, and burnt its palaces with fire, and *utterly destroyed* every beautiful vessel. 20 And he carried away the remnant to Babylon; and they were servants to him and to his sons until *the establishment of* the kingdom of the Medes. 21 That the word of the Lord by the mouth of Jeremias might be fulfilled, until the land should enjoy its sabbaths in resting *and* sabbath keeping all the days of its desolation, till the accomplishment of seventy years. 22 In the first year of Cyrus king of the Persians, after the fulfillment of the word of the Lord by the mouth of Jeremias, the Lord stirred up the spirit of Cyrus king of the Persians, and told him to make proclamation in writing throughout all his kingdom, saying, 23 Thus says Cyrus king of the Persians to all the kingdoms of the earth, The Lord God of heaven has given me *power*, and he has commanded me to build a house to him in Jerusalem, in Judea. Who *is there* of you of all his people? His God shall be with him, and let him go up.

EZRA

Ezra1 1 Now in the first year of Cyrus king of the Persians, that the word of the Lord by the mouth of Jeremias might be fulfilled, the Lord stirred up the spirit of Cyrus king of the Persians, and he issued a proclamation through all his kingdom, and that in writing, saying, 2 Thus said Cyrus king of the Persians, The Lord God of heaven has given me all the kingdoms of the earth, and he has given me a charge to build him a house in Jerusalem that is in Judea. 3 Who *is* there among you of all his people? for his God shall be with him, and he shall go up to Jerusalem that is in Judea, and let him build the house of the God of Israel: he *is* the God that is in Jerusalem. 4 And *let* every *Jew* that is left *go* from every place where he sojourns, and the men of his place shall help him with silver, and gold, and goods, and cattle, together with the voluntary offering for the house of God that is in Jerusalem. 5 Then the chiefs of the families of Juda and Benjamin arose, and the priests, and the Levites, all whose spirit the Lord stirred up to go up to build the house of the Lord that *is* in Jerusalem. 6 And all that were round about strengthened their hands with vessels of silver, with gold, with goods, and with cattle, and with presents, besides the voluntary offerings. 7 And king Cyrus brought out the vessels of the house of the Lord, which Nabuchodonosor had brought from Jerusalem, and put in the house of his god. 8 And Cyrus king of the Persians brought them out by the hand of Mithradates the treasurer, and he numbered them to Sasabasar, the chief man of Juda. 9 And this *is* their number: thirty gold basons, and a thousand silver basons, nine and twenty changes, thirty golden goblets, 10 and four hundred *and* ten double silver *vessels*, and a thousand other vessels. 11 All the gold and silver vessels were five thousand four hundred, *even* all that went up with Sasabasar from the *place of* transportation, from Babylon to Jerusalem.

Ezra2 1 And these *are* the people of the land that went up, of the number of prisoners who were removed, whom Nabuchodonosor king of Babylon carried away to Babylon, and they returned to Juda and Jerusalem, every man to his city; 2 who came with Zorobabel: Jesus, Neemias, Saraias, Reelias, Mardochaeus, Balasan, Masphar, Baguai, Reum, Baana. The number of the people of Israel: 3 the children of Phares, two thousand one hundred and seventy-two. 4 The children of Saphatia, three hundred and seventy-two. 5 The children of Ares, seven hundred and seventy-five. 6 The children of Phaath Moab, belonging to the sons of Jesue *and* Joab, two thousand eight hundred and twelve. 7 The children of Ælam, a thousand two hundred and fifty-four. 8 The children of Zatthua, nine hundred and forty-five.

9 The children of Zacchu, seven hundred and sixty. 10 The children of Banui, six hundred and forty-two. 11 The children of Babai, six hundred and twenty-three. 12 The children of Asgad, a thousand two hundred and twenty-two. 13 The children of Adonicam, six hundred and sixty-

six. 14 The children of Bague, two thousand and fifty-six. 15 The children of Addin, four hundred and fifty-four. 16 The children of Ater *the son* of Ezekias, ninety eight. 17 The children of Bassu, three hundred and twenty-three. 18 The children of Jora, a hundred and twelve. 19 The children of Asum, two hundred and twenty-three. 20 The children of Gaber, ninety-five. 21 The children of Bethlaem, a hundred and twenty-three. 22 The children of Netopha, fifty-six. 23 The children of Anathoth, a hundred and twenty-eight. 24 The children of Azmoth, forty-three. 25 The children of Cariathiarim, Chaphira, and Beroth, seven hundred and forty-three. 26 The children of Rama and Gabaa, six hundred and twenty-one. 27 The men of Machmas, a hundred and twenty-two. 28 The men of Baethel and Aia, four hundred and twenty-three. 29 The children of Nabu, fifty-two. 30 The children of Magebis, a hundred and fifty-six. 31 The children of Elamar, a thousand two hundred and fifty-four. 32 The children of Elam, three hundred and twenty. 33 The children of Lodadi and Ono, seven hundred and twenty-five. 34 The children of Jericho, three hundred and forty-five. 35 The children of Senaa, three thousand six hundred and thirty. 36 And the priests, the sons of Jedua, *belonging to* the house of Jesus, *were* nine hundred and seventy-three. 37 The children of Emmer, a thousand *and* fifty-two. 38 The children of Phassur, a thousand two hundred *and* forty-seven. 39 The children of Erem, a thousand *and* seven. 40 And the Levites, the sons of Jesus and Cadmiel, belonging to the sons of Oduia, seventy-four. 41 The sons of Asaph, singers, a hundred *and* twenty-eight. 42 The children of the porters, the children of Sellum, the children of Ater, the children of Telmon, the children of Acub, the children of Atita, the children of Sobai, *in* all a hundred *and* thirty-nine. 43 The Nathinim: the children of Suthia, the children of Asupha, the children of Tabaoth, 44 the sons of Cades, the children of Siaa, the children of Phadon, 45 the children of Labano, the children of Agaba, the sons of Acub, 46 the children of Agab, the children of Selami, the children of Anan, 47 the children of Geddel, the children of Gaar, the children of Raia, 48 the children of Rason, the children of Necoda, the children of Gazem, 49 the children of Azo, the children of Phase, the children of Basi, 50 the children of Asena, the children of Mounim, the children of Nephusim, 51 the children of Bacbuc, the children of Acupha, the children of Arur, 52 the children of Basaloth, the children of Mauda, the children of Arsa, 53 the children of Barcos, the children of Sisara, the children of Thema, 54 the children of Nasthie, the children of Atupha. 55 The children of the servants of Solomon: the children of Sotai, the children of Sephera, the children of Phadura, 56 the children of Jeela, the children of Darcon, the children of Gedel, 57 the children of Saphatia, the children of Atil, the children of Phacherath, the children of Aseboim, the children of Emei. 58 All the Nathanim, and the sons of Abdeselma *were* three hundred and ninety-two. 59 And these *are* they that went up from Thelmelech, Thelaresa, Cherub, Hedan, Emmer: and they were not able to tell the house of their fathers, and their seed, whether they were of Israel: 60 the children of Dalaea, the children of Bua, the children of Tobias, the children of Necoda, six hundred *and* fifty-two.

61 And of the children of the priests, the children of Labeia, the children of Akkus, the children of Berzellai, who took a wife of the daughter of Berzellai the Galaadite, and was called by their name. 62 These sought their genealogy *as though* they had been reckoned, but they were not found; and they were removed, *as polluted*, from the priesthood. 63 And the Athersastha told them that they should not eat of the most holy things, until a priest should arise with Lights and Perfections. 64 And all the congregation together *were* about forty-two thousand three hundred and sixty; 65 besides their men-servants and maid-servants, *and* these were seven thousand three hundred *and* thirty-seven: and *among* these were two hundred singing men and singing women. 66 Their horses *were* seven hundred *and* thirty-six, their mules, two hundred *and* forty-five. 67 Their camels, four hundred *and* thirty-five; their asses, six thousand seven hundred *and* twenty. 68 And *some* of the chiefs of families, when they went into the house of the Lord that was in Jerusalem, offered willingly for the house of God, to establish it on its prepared place. 69 According to their power they gave into the treasury of the work pure gold sixty-one thousand pieces, and five thousand pounds of silver, and one hundred priests' garments. 70 So the priests, and the Levites, and some of the people, and the singers, and the porters, and the Nathinim, dwelt in their cities, and all Israel in their cities.

Ezra3 1 And the seventh month came on, and the children of Israel *were* in their cities, and the people assembled as one man at Jerusalem. 2 Then stood up Jesus the *son* of Josedec, and his brethren the priests, and Zorobabel the *son* of Salathiel, and his brethren, and they built the altar of the God of Israel, to offer upon it whole-burnt-offerings, according to the things that were written in the law of Moses the man of God. 3 And they set up the altar on its place, for there was a terror upon them because of the people of the lands: and the whole-burnt-offerings was offered up upon it to the Lord morning and evening. 4 And they kept the feast of tabernacles, according to that which was written, and *offered* whole-burnt-offerings daily in number according to the ordinance, the exact daily rate. 5 And after this the perpetual whole-burnt-offering, and *offering* for the season of new moon, and for all the hallowed feasts to the Lord, and for every one that offered a free-will-offering to the Lord. 6 On the first day of the seventh month they began to offer whole-burnt-offerings to the Lord: but the foundation of the house of the Lord was not laid. 7 And they gave money to the stone-hewers and carpenters, and meat and drink, and oil, to the Sidonians, and Tyrians, to bring cedar trees from Libanus to the sea of Joppa, according to the grant of Cyrus king of the Persians to them. 8 And in the second year of their coming to the house of God in Jerusalem, in the second month, began Zorobabel the *son* of Salathiel, and Jesus the *son* of Josedec, and the rest of their brethren the priests and the Levites, and all who came from the captivity to Jerusalem, and they appointed the Levites, from twenty years old and upward, over the workmen in the house of the Lord. 9 And Jesus and his sons and his brethren stood, Cadmiel and his sons the sons of Juda, over them that wrought the works in the house of God: the sons of Enadad, their sons and their brethren the Levites. 10 And they laid a foundation for building the house of the Lord: and the priests in their robes stood with trumpets and the Levites the sons of Asaph with cymbals, to praise the Lord, according to the order of David king of Israel. 11 And they answered *each other* with praise and thanksgiving to the Lord, *saying*, For *it is* good, for his mercy to Israel *endures* for ever. And all the people shouted with a loud voice to praise the Lord at the laying the foundation of the house of the Lord. 12 But many of the priests and the Levites, and the elder men, heads of families, who had seen the former house on its foundation, and *who saw* this house with their eyes, wept with a loud voice: but the multitude shouted with joy to raise a song. 13 And the people did not distinguish the voice of the glad shout from the voice of the weeping of the people: for the people shouted with a loud voice, and the voice was heard even from afar off.

Ezra4 1 And they that afflicted Juda and Benjamin heard, that the children of the captivity were building a house to the Lord God of Israel. 2 And they drew near to Zorobabel, and to the heads of families, and said to them, We will build with you; for as ye *do*, we seek *to serve* our God, and we do sacrifice to him from the days of Asaradan king of Assur, who brought us hither. 3 then Zorobabel, and Jesus and the rest of the heads of the families of Israel said to them, *It is* not for us and you to build a house to our God, for we ourselves will build together to the Lord our God, as Cyrus the king of the Persians commanded us. 4 And the people of the land weakened the hands of the people of Juda, and hindered them in building, 5 and *continued* hiring *persons* against them, plotting to frustrate their counsel, all the days of Cyrus king of the Persians, and until the reign of Darius king of the Persians. 6 And in the reign of Assuerus, even in the beginning of his reign, they wrote a letter against the inhabitants of Juda and Jerusalem. 7 And in the days of Arthasastha, Tabeel wrote peaceably to Mithradates and to the rest of his fellow-servants: the tribute-gatherer wrote to Arthasastha king of the Persians a writing in the Syrian tongue, and *the same* interpreted. 8 Reum the chancellor, and Sampsa the scribe wrote an epistle against Jerusalem to King Arthasastha, *saying,* 9 Thus has judged Reum the chancellor, and Sampsa the scribe, and the rest of our fellow-servants, the Dinaeans, the Apharsathachaeans, the Tarphalaeans, the Apharsaeans, the Archyaeans, the Babylonians, the Susanachaeans, Davaeans, 10 and the rest of the nations whom the great and noble Assenaphar removed, and settled them in the cities of Somoron, and the rest *of them* beyond the river. 11 This *is* the purport of the letter, which they sent to him: Thy servants the men beyond the river to king Arthasastha. 12 Be it known to the king, that the Jews who came up from thee to us have come to Jerusalem the rebellious and wicked city, which they are building, and its walls are set in order, and they have established the foundations of it. 13 Now then be it known to the king, that if that city be built up, and its walls completed, thou shalt have no tribute, neither will they pay

anything, and this injures kings. 14 And it is not lawful for us to see the dishonour of the king: therefore have we sent and made known *the matter* to the king; 15 That examination may be made in thy fathers' book of record; and thou shalt find, and thou shalt know that city *is* rebellious, and does harm to kings and countries, and there are in the midst of it from very old time refuges for *runaway* slaves: therefore this city has been made desolate. 16 We therefore declare to the king, that, if that city be built, and its walls be set up, thou shalt not have peace. 17 Then the king sent to Reum the chancellor, and Sampsa the scribe, and the rest of their fellow-servants who dwelt in Samaria, and the rest beyond the river, *saying,*Peace; and he says, 18 The tribute-gatherer whom ye sent to us, has been called before me. 19 And a decree has been made by me, and we have examined, and found that city of old time exalts itself against kings, and that rebellions and desertions take place within it. 20 And there were powerful kings in Jerusalem, and they ruled over all the *country* beyond the river, and abundant revenues and tribute were given to them. 21 Now therefore make a decree to stop the work of those men, and that city shall no more be built. 22 *See* that ye be careful of the decree, *not* to be remiss concerning this matter, lest at any time destruction should abound to the harm of kings. 23 Then the tribute-gatherer of king Arthasastha read *the letter* before Reum the chancellor, and Sampsa the scribe, and his fellow-servants: and they went in haste to Jerusalem and through Juda, and caused them to cease with horses and an *armed* force. 24 Then ceased the work of the house of God in Jerusalem, and it was at a stand until the second year of the reign of Darius king of the Persians.

Ezra5 1 And Aggaeus the prophet, and Zacharias the *son* of Addo, prophesied a prophesy to the Jews in Juda and Jerusalem in the name of the God of Israel, *even* to them. 2 Then rose up Zorobabel the *son* of Salathiel, and Jesus the son of Josedec, and began to build the house of God that was in Jerusalem: and with them *were* the prophets of God assisting them. 3 At the same time came there upon them Thanthanai, the governor on this side the river, and Satharbuzanai, and their fellow-servants, and spoke thus to them, Who has ordained a decree for you to build this house, and to *provide* this preparation? 4 Then they spoke thus to them, What are the names of the men that build this city? 5 But the eyes of God were upon the captivity of Juda, and they did not cause them to cease till the decree was brought to Darius; and then was sent by the tribute-gatherer concerning this 6 the copy of a letter, which Thanthanai, the governor of the part on this side the river, and Satharbuzanai, and their fellow- servants the Apharsachaeans who were on this side of the river, sent to king Darius. 7 They sent an account to him, and thus it was written in it: All peace to king Darius. 8 Be it known to the king, that we went into the land of Judea, to the house of the great God; and it is building with choice stones, and they are laying timbers in the walls, and that work is prospering, and goes on favorably in their hands. 9 Then we asked those elders, and thus we said to them, Who gave you the order to build this house, and to *provide* this preparation?

10 And we asked them their names, *in order* to declare *them* to thee, so as to write to thee the names of their leading men. 11 And they answered us thus, saying, We *are* the servants of the God of heaven and earth, and we *are* building the house which had been built many years before this, and a great king of Israel built it, and established it for them. 12 But after that our fathers provoked the God of heaven, he gave them into the hands of Nabuchodonosor the Chaldean, king of Babylon, and he destroyed this house, and carried the people captive to Babylon. 13 And in the first year of king Cyrus, Cyrus the king made a decree that this house of God should be built. 14 And the gold and silver vessels of the house of God, which Nabuchodonosor brought out from the house that was in Jerusalem, and carried them into the temple of the king, them did king Cyrus bring out from the temple of the king, and gave them to Sabanasar the treasurer, who was over the treasurer; 15 and said to him, Take all the vessels, and go, put them in the house that is in Jerusalem in their place. 16 Then that Sabanazar came, and laid the foundations of the house of God in Jerusalem: and from that time even until now it has been building, and has not been finished. 17 And now, if it *seem* good to the king, lest search be made in the treasure-house of the king at Babylon, that thou mayest know *if it be* that a decree was made by king Cyrus to build that house of God that was in Jerusalem, and let the king send to us when he has learnt concerning this *matter.*

Ezra6 1 Then Darius the king made a decree, and caused a search to be made in the record-offices, where the treasure is stored in Babylon. 2 And there was found in the city, in the palace, a volume, and this was the record written in it. 3 In the first year of king Cyrus, Cyrus the king made a decree concerning the holy house of God that was in Jerusalem, *saying,*Let the house be built, and the place where they sacrifice the sacrifices. (Also he appointed its elevation, in height sixty cubits; its breadth *was* of sixty cubits.) 4 And *let there be* three strong layers of stone, and one layer of timber; and the expense shall be paid out of the house of the king. 5 And the silver and the gold vessels of the house of God, which Nabuchodonosor carried off from the house that was in Jerusalem, and carried to Babylon, let them even be given, and be carried to the temple that is in Jerusalem, and put in the place where they were set in the house of God. 6 Now, ye rulers beyond the river, Satharbuzanai, and their fellow-servants the Apharsachaeans, who *are* on the other side of the river, give *these things*, keeping far from that place. 7 Now let alone the work of the house of God: let the rulers of the Jews and the elders of the Jews build that house of God on its place. 8 Also a decree has been made by me, if haply ye may do somewhat in concert with the elders of the Jews for the building of that house of God: to wit, out of the king's property, *even* the tributes beyond the river, let there be money to defray the expenses carefully granted to those men, so that they be not hindered. 9 And whatever need *there may be*, ye shall give both the young of bulls and rams, and lambs for whole-burnt-offerings to the God of heaven, wheat, salt, wine, oil:—let it be given them according to the word of the priests that are in Jerusalem,

day by day whatsoever they shall ask; 10 that they may offer sweet savours to the God of heaven, and that they may pray for the life of the king and his sons. 11 And a decree has been made by me, that every man who shall alter this word, timber shall be pulled down from his house, and let him be lifted up and slain upon it, and his house shall be confiscated. 12 And may the God whose name dwells there, overthrow every king and people who shall stretch out his hand to alter or destroy the house of God which is in Jerusalem. I Darius have made a decree; let it be diligently *attended to.* 13 Then Thanthanai the governor on this side beyond the river, Satharbuzanai, and his fellow- servants, according to that which king Darius sent, so they did diligently. 14 And the elders of the Jews and the Levites built, at the prophecy of Aggaeus the prophet, and Zacharias the son of Addo: and they built up, and finished *it*, by the decree of the God of Israel, and by the decree of Cyrus, and Darius, and Arthasastha, kings of the Persians. 15 And they finished this house by the third day of the month Adar, which is the sixth year of the reign of Darius the king. 16 And the children of Israel, the priests, and the Levites, and the rest of the children of the captivity, kept the dedication of the house of God with gladness. 17 And they offered for the dedication of the house of God a hundred calves, two hundred rams, four hundred lambs, twelve kids of the goats for a sin-offering for all Israel, according to the number of the tribes of Israel. 18 And they set the priests in their divisions, and the Levites in their separate orders, for the services of God in Jerusalem, according to the writing of the book of Moses. 19 And the children of the captivity kept the passover on the fourteenth day of the first month. 20 For the priests and Levites were purified, all were clean to a man, and they slew the passover for all the children of the captivity, and for their brethren the priests, and for themselves. 21 And the children of Israel ate the passover, *even* they that were of the captivity, and every one who separated himself to them from the uncleanness of the nations of the land, to seek the Lord God of Israel. 22 and they kept the feast of unleavened bread seven days with gladness, because the Lord made them glad, and he turned the heart of the king of Assyria to them, to strengthen their hands in the works of the house of the God of Israel.

Ezra7 1 Now after these things, in the reign of Arthasastha king of the Persians, came up Esdras the son of Saraias, the son of Azarias, the son of Chelcias, 2 the son of Selum, the son of Sadduc, the son of Achitob, 3 the son of Samarias, the son of Esria, the son of Mareoth, 4 the son of Zaraia, the son of Ozias, the son of Bokki, 5 the son of Abisue, the son of Phinees, the son of Eleazar, the son of Aaron the first priest. 6 This Esdras went up out of Babylon; and he was a ready scribe in the law of Moses, which the Lord God of Israel gave: and the king gave him *leave*, for the hand of the Lord his God was upon him in all things which he sought. 7 And *some* of the children of Israel went up, and *some* of the priests, and of the Levites, and the singers, and the door-keepers, and the Nathinim, to Jerusalem, in the seventh year of Arthasastha the king. 8 And they came to

Jerusalem in the fifth month, this *was* the seventh year of the king. 9 For in the first *day* of the first month he began the going up from Babylon, and in the first day of the fifth month, they came to Jerusalem, for the good hand of his God was upon him. 10 For Esdras had determined in his heart to seek the law, and to do and teach the ordinances and judgments in Israel. 11 And this *is* the copy of the order which Arthasastha gave to Esdras the priest, the scribe of the book of the words of the commandments of the Lord, and of his ordinances to Israel. 12 Arthasastha, king of kings, to Esdras, the scribe of the law of the Lord God of heaven, Let the order and the answer be accomplished. 13 A decree is made by me, that every one who is willing in my kingdom of the people of Israel, and of the priests and Levites, to go to Jerusalem, *be permitted* to go with thee. 14 *One* has been sent from the king and the seven councillors, to visit Judea and Jerusalem, according to the law of their God that is in thine hand. 15 And for the house of the Lord *there have been sent* silver and gold, which the king and the councillors have freely given to the God of Israel, who dwells in Jerusalem. 16 And all the silver and gold, whatsoever thou shalt find in all the land of Babylon, with the freewill-offering of the people, and the priests that offer freely for the house of God which is in Jerusalem. 17 And as for every one that arrives *there*, speedily order him by this letter *to bring* calves, rams, lambs, and their meat-offerings, and their drink-offerings; and thou shalt offer them on the altar of the house of your God which is in Jerusalem. 18 And whatever it shall seem good to thee and to thy brethren to do with the rest of the silver and the gold, do as it is pleasing to your God. 19 And deliver the vessels that are given thee for the service of the house of God, before God in Jerusalem. 20 And as to the rest of the need of the house of thy God, thou shalt give from the king's treasure-houses, 21 and from me, whatever it shall seem *good* to thee to give. I king Arthasastha have made a decree for all the treasuries that are in the *country* beyond the river, that whatever Esdras the priest and scribe of the God of heaven may ask you, it shall be done speedily, 22 to *the amount of* a hundred talents of silver, and a hundred measures of wheat, and a hundred baths of wine, and a hundred baths of oil, and salt without reckoning. 23 Let whatever is in the decree of the God of heaven, be done: take heed lest any one make an attack on the house of the God of heaven, lest at any time there shall be wrath against the realm of the king and his sons. 24 Also this has been declared to you, with respect to all the priests, and Levites, the singers, porters, Nathinim and ministers of the house of God, let no tribute be *paid* to thee; thou shalt not have power to oppress them. 25 And thou, Esdras, as the wisdom of God *is* in thy hand, appoint scribes and judges, that they may judge for all the people beyond the river, all that know the law of the Lord thy God; and ye shall make it known to him that knows not. 26 And whosoever shall not do the law of God, and the law of the king readily, judgment shall be taken upon him, whether for death or for chastisement, or for a fine of his property, or casting into prison. 27 Blessed *be* the Lord God of our fathers, who has put it thus into the heart of the king, to glorify the house of the Lord which is in Jerusalem; 28 and

has given me favour in the eyes of the king, and of his councillors, and all the rulers of the king, the exalted ones. And I was strengthened according to the good hand of God upon me, and I gathered chief men of Israel to go up with me.

Ezra8 1 And these *are* the heads of their families, the leaders that went up with me in the reign of Arthasastha the king of Babylon. 2 Of the sons of Phinees; Gerson: of the sons of Ithamar; Daniel: of the sons of David; Attus. 3 Of the sons of Sachania, and the sons of Phoros; Zacharias: and with him a company *of* a hundred and fifty. 4 Of the sons of Phaath-Moab; Eliana the son of Saraia, and with him two hundred that were males. 5 And of the sons of Zathoes; Sechenias the son of Aziel, and with him three hundred males. 6 And of the sons of Adin; Obeth the son of Jonathan, and with him fifty males. 7 And of the sons of Elam; Isaeas the son of Athelia, and with him seventy males. 8 And of the sons of Saphatia; Zabadias the son of Michael, and with him eighty males. 9 And of the sons of Joab; Abadia the son of Jeiel, and with him two hundred and eighteen males. 10 And of the sons of Baani; Selimuth the son of Josephia, and with him a hundred and sixty males. 11 And of the sons of Babi; Zacharias the son of Babi, and with him twenty-eight males. 12 And of the sons of Asgad; Joanan the son of Accatan, and with him a hundred and ten males. 13 And of the sons of Adonicam *were the* last, and these *were* their names, Eliphalat, Jeel, and Samaea, and with them sixty males. 14 And of the sons of Baguae, Uthai, and Zabud, and with him seventy males. 15 And I gathered them to the river that comes to Evi, and we encamped there three days: and I reviewed the people and the priests, and found none of the sons of Levi there. 16 And I sent men of understanding to Eleazar, to Ariel, to Semeias, and to Alonam, and to Jarib, and to Elnatham, and to Nathan, and to Zacharias, and to Mesollam, and to Joarim, and to Elnathan. 17 And I forwarded them to the rulers with the money of the place, and I put words in their mouth to speak to their brethren the Athinim with the money of the place, that they should bring us singers for the house of our God. 18 And they came to us, as the good hand of our God was upon us, even a man of understanding of the sons of Mooli, the son of Levi, the son of Israel, and at the commencement came his sons and his brethren, eighteen. 19 And Asebia, and Isaia of the sons of Merari, his brethren and his sons, twenty. 20 And of the Nathinim; whom David and the princes had appointed for the service of the Levites *there were* two hundred and twenty Nathinim; all were gathered by *their* names. 21 And I proclaimed there a fast, at the river Aue, that *we* should humble ourselves before our God, to seek of him a straight way for us, and for our children, and for all our property. 22 For I was ashamed to ask of the king a guard and horsemen to save us from the enemy in the way: for we had spoken to the king, saying, The hand of our God *is* upon all that seek him, for good; but his power and his wrath *are* upon all that forsake him. 23 So we fasted, and asked of our God concerning this; and he hearkened to us. 24 And I gave charge to twelve of the chiefs of the priests, to Saraia, to

Asabia, and ten of their brethren with them. 25 And I weighed to them the silver, and the gold, and the vessels of the first-fruits of the house of our God, which the king, and his councillors, and his princes, and all Israel that were found, had dedicated. 26 I even weighed into their hands six hundred and fifty talents of silver, and a hundred silver vessels, and a hundred talents of gold; 27 and twenty golden bowls, *weighing* about a thousand drachms, and superior vessels of fine shining brass, *precious* as gold. 28 And I said to them, Ye *are* holy to the Lord; and the vessels *are* holy; and the silver and the gold are freewill-offerings to the Lord God of our fathers. 29 Be watchful and keep them, until ye weigh *them* before the chief priests and the Levites, and the chiefs of families in Jerusalem, at the chambers of the house of the Lord. 30 So the priests and the Levites took the weight of the silver, and the gold, and the vessels, to bring to Jerusalem into the house of our God. 31 And we departed from the river of Aue on the twelfth day of the first month, to come to Jerusalem: and the hand of our God was upon us, and delivered us from the hand of the enemy and adversary in the way. 32 And we came to Jerusalem, and abode there three days. 33 And it came to pass on the fourth day that we weighed the silver, and the gold, and the vessels, in the house of our God, into the hand of Merimoth the son of Uria the priest; and with him *was* Eleazar the son of Phinees, and with them Jozabad the son of Jesus, and Noadia the son of Banaia, the Levites. 34 All things *were reckoned* by number and weight, and the whole weight was written *down*. 35 At that time the children of the banishment that came from the captivity offered whole-burnt- offerings to the God of Israel, twelve calves for all Israel, ninety-six rams, seventy-seven lambs, twelve goats for a sin-offering; all whole-burnt-offerings to the Lord. 36 And they gave the king's mandate to the king's lieutenants, and the governors beyond the river: and they honoured the people and the house of God.

Ezra9 1 And when these things were finished, the princes drew near to me, saying, The people of Israel, and the priests, and the Levites, have not separated themselves from the people of the lands in their abominations, *even* the Chananite, the Ethite, the Pherezite, the Jebusite, the Ammonite, the Moabite, and the Moserite and the Amorite. 2 For they have taken of their daughters for themselves and their sons; and the holy seed has passed among the nations of the lands, and the hand of the rulers *has been* first in this transgression. 3 And when I heard this thing, I rent my garments, and trembled, and plucked *some* of the hairs of my head and of my beard, and sat down mourning. 4 Then there assembled to me all that followed the word of the God of Israel, on account of the transgression of the captivity; and I remained mourning until the evening sacrifice. 5 And at the evening sacrifice I rose up from my humiliation; and when I had rent my garments, then I trembled, and I bow myself on my knees, and spread out my hands to the Lord God, 6 and I said, O Lord, I am ashamed and confounded, O my God, to lift up my face to thee: for our transgressions have abounded over our head, and our trespasses have increased even to heaven.

7 From the days of our fathers we have been in a great trespass until this day: and because of our iniquities we, and our kings, and our children, have been delivered into the hand of the kings of the Gentiles by the sword, and by captivity, and by spoil, and with shame of our face, as at this day. 8 And now our God has dealt mercifully with us, so as to leave us to escape, and to give us an establishment in the place of his sanctuary, to enlighten our eyes, and to give a little quickening in our servitude. 9 For we are slaves, yet in our servitude the Lord our God has not deserted us; and he has extended favour to us in the sight of the kings of the Persians, to give us a quickening, that they should raise up the house of our God, and restore the desolate places of it, and to give us a fence in Juda and Jerusalem. 10 What shall we say, our God, after this? for we have forsaken thy commandments, 11 which thou hast given us by the hand of thy servants the prophets, saying, The land, into which ye go to inherit it, is a land subject to disturbance by the removal of the people of the nations for their abominations, wherewith they have filled it from one end to the other by their uncleanness. 12 And now give not your daughters to their sons, and take not of their daughters for your sons, neither shall ye seek their peace or their good for ever: that ye may be strong, and eat the good of the land, and transmit it as an inheritance to your children for ever. 13 And after all that is come upon us because of our evil deeds, and our great trespass, *it is clear* that there is none such as our God, for thou has lightly visited our iniquities, and given us deliverance; 14 whereas we have repeatedly broken thy commandments, and intermarried with the people of the lands: be not very angry with us to *our* utter destruction, so that there should be no remnant or escaping one. 15 O Lord God of Israel, thou *art* righteous; for we remain *yet* escaped, as at this day: behold, we *are* before thee in our trespasses: for we cannot stand before thee on this account.

Ezra10 1 So when Esdras *had* prayed, and when he *had* confessed, weeping and praying before the house of God, a very great assembly of Israel came together to him, men and women and youths; for the people wept, and wept aloud. 2 And Sechenias the son of Jeel, of the sons of Elam, answered and said to Esdras, We have broken covenant with our God, and have taken strange wives of the nations of the land: yet now there is patience *of hope* to Israel concerning this thing. 3 Now then let us make a covenant with our God, to put away all the wives, and their offspring, as thou shalt advise: 4 arise, and alarm them with the commands of our God; and let *it* be done according to the law. Rise up, for the matter *is* upon thee; and we *are* with thee: be strong and do. 5 Then Esdras arose, and caused the rulers, the priests, and Levites, and all Israel, to swear that they would do according to this word: and they swore. 6 And Esdras rose up from before the house of God, and went to the treasury of Joanan the son of Elisub; he even went thither: he ate no bread, and drank no water; for he mourned over the unfaithfulness *of them* of the captivity. 7 And they made proclamation throughout Juda and Jerusalem to all the children of the captivity, that they should assemble at Jerusalem, *saying*, 8 Every one who shall not arrive within three days, as *is* the counsel of the rulers and the elders, all his substance shall be forfeited, and he shall be separated from the congregation of the captivity. 9 So all the men of Juda and Benjamin assembled at Jerusalem within the three days. This *was* the ninth month: on the twentieth day·of the month all the people sat down in the street of the house of the Lord, because of their alarm concerning the word, and because of the storm. 10 And Esdras the priest arose, and said to them, Ye have broken covenant, and have taken strange wives, to add to the trespass of Israel. 11 Now therefore give praise to the Lord God of our fathers, and do that which is pleasing in his sight: and separate yourselves from the peoples of the land, and from the strange wives. 12 Then all the congregation answered and said, This thy word *is* powerful upon us to do it. 13 But the people *is* numerous, and the season *is* stormy, and there is no power to stand without, and the work is more than enough for one day or for two; for we have greatly sinned in this matter. 14 Let now our rulers stand, and for all those in our cities who have taken strange wives, let them come at appointed times, and with them elders from every several city, and judges, to turn away the fierce wrath of our God from us concerning this matter. 15 Only Jonathan the son of Asael, and Jazias the son of Thecoe *were* with me concerning this; and Mesollam, and Sabbathai the Levite helped them. 16 And the children of the captivity did thus: and Esdras the priest, and heads of families according to *their* house were separated, and all by their names, for they returned in the first day of the tenth month to search out the matter. 17 And they made an end with all the men who had taken strange wives by the first day of the first month. 18 And there were found *some* of the sons of the priests who had taken strange wives: of the sons of Jesus the son of Josedec, and his brethren; Maasia, and Eliezer, and Jarib, and Gadalia. 19 And they pledged themselves to put away their wives, and *offered* a ram of the flock for a trespass-offering because of their trespass. 20 And of the sons of Emmer; Anani, and Zabdia. 21 And of the sons of Eram; Masael, and Elia, and Samaia, and Jeel, and Ozia. 22 And of the sons of Phasur; Elionai, Maasia, and Ismael, and Nathanael, and Jozabad, and Elasa. 23 And of the Levites; Jozabad, and Samu, and Colia (he *is* Colitas,)and Phetheia, and Judas, and Eliezer. 24 And of the singers; Elisab: and of the porters; Solmen, and Telmen, and Oduth. 25 Also of Israel: of the sons of Phoros; Ramia, and Azia, and Melchia, and Meamin, and Eleazar, and Asabia, and Banaia. 26 And of the sons of Helam; Matthania, and Zacharia, and Jaiel, and Abdia, and Jarimoth, and Elia. 27 And of the sons of Zathua; Elionai, Elisub, Matthanai, and Armoth, and Zabad, and Oziza. 28 And of the sons of Babei; Joanan, Anania, and Zabu, and Thali. 29 And of the sons of Banui; Mosollam, Maluch, Adaias, Jasub, and Saluia, and Remoth. 30 And of the sons of Phaath Moab; Edne, and Chalel, and Banaia, Maasia, Matthania, Beseleel, and Banui, and Manasse. 31 And of the sons of Eram; Eliezer, Jesia, Melchia, Samaias, Semeon, 32 Benjamin, Baluch, Samaria. 33 And of the sons of Asem; Metthania, Matthatha, Zadab, Eliphalet, Jerami, Manasse,

Semei. 34 And of the sons of Bani; Moodia, Amram, Uel, 35 Banaia, Badaia, Chelkia, 36 Uvania, Marimoth, Eliasiph, 37 Matthania, Matthanai: 38 and *so* did the children of Banui, and the children of Semei, 39 and Selemia, and Nathan, and Adaia, 40 Machadnabu, Sesei, Sariu, 41 Ezriel, and Selemia, and Samaria, 42 and Sellum, Amaria, Joseph. 43 Of the sons of Nabu; Jael, Matthanias, Zabad, Zebennas, Jadai, and Joel, and Banaia. 44 All these had taken strange wives, and had begotten sons of them.

1 ESDRAS

1-Esdras1 1 And Josias held the feast of the passover in Jerusalem unto his Lord, and offered the passover the fourteenth day of the first month; 2 Having set the priests according to their daily courses, being arrayed in long garments, in the temple of the Lord. 3 And he spake unto the Levites, the holy ministers of Israel, that they should hallow themselves unto the Lord, to set the holy ark of the Lord in the house that king Solomon the son of David had built: 4 And said, Ye shall no more bear the ark upon your shoulders: now therefore serve the Lord your God, and minister unto his people Israel, and prepare you after your families and kindreds, 5 According as David the king of Israel prescribed, and according to the magnificence of Solomon his son: and standing in the temple according to the several dignity of the families of you the Levites, who minister in the presence of your brethren the children of Israel, 6 Offer the passover in order, and make ready the sacrifices for your brethren, and keep the passover according to the commandment of the Lord, which was given unto Moses. 7 And unto the people that was found there Josias gave thirty thousand lambs and kids, and three thousand calves: these things were given of the king's allowance, according as he promised, to the people, to the priests, and to the Levites. 8 And Helkias, Zacharias, and Syelus, the governors of the temple, gave to the priests for the passover two thousand and six hundred sheep, and three hundred calves. 9 And Jeconias, and Samaias, and Nathanael his brother, and Assabias, and Ochiel, and Joram, captains over thousands, gave to the Levites for the passover five thousand sheep, and seven hundred calves. 10 And when these things were done, the priests and Levites, having the unleavened bread, stood in very comely order according to the kindreds, 11 And according to the several dignities of the fathers, before the people, to offer to the Lord, as it is written in the book of Moses: and thus did they in the morning. 12 And they roasted the passover with fire, as appertaineth: as for the sacrifices, they sod them in brass pots and pans with a good savour, 13 And set them before all the people: and afterward they prepared for themselves, and for the priests their brethren, the sons of Aaron. 14 For the priests offered the fat until night: and the Levites prepared for themselves, and the priests their brethren, the sons of Aaron. 15 The holy singers also, the sons of Asaph, were in their order, according to the appointment of David, to wit, Asaph, Zacharias, and Jeduthun, who was of the king's retinue. 16 Moreover the porters were at every gate; it was not lawful for any to go from his ordinary service: for their brethren the Levites prepared for them. 17 Thus were the things that belonged to the sacrifices of the Lord accomplished in that day, that they might hold the passover, 18 And offer sacrifices upon the altar of the Lord, according to the commandment of king Josias. 19 So the children of Israel which were present held the passover at that time, and the feast of sweet bread seven days. 20 And such a passover was not kept in Israel since the time of the prophet Samuel. 21 Yea, all the kings of Israel held not such a passover as Josias, and the priests, and the Levites, and the Jews, held with all Israel that were found dwelling at Jerusalem. 22 In the eighteenth year of the reign of Josias was this passover kept. 23 And the works or Josias were upright before his Lord with an heart full of godliness. 24 As for the things that came to pass in his time, they were written in former times, concerning those that sinned, and did wickedly against the Lord above all people and kingdoms, and how they grieved him exceedingly, so that the words of the Lord rose up against Israel. 25 Now after all these acts of Josias it came to pass, that Pharaoh the king of Egypt came to raise war at Carchamis upon Euphrates: and Josias went out against him. 26 But the king of Egypt sent to him, saying, What have I to do with thee, O king of Judea? 27 I am not sent out from the Lord God against thee; for my war is upon Euphrates: and now the Lord is with me, yea, the Lord is with me hasting me forward: depart from me, and be not against the Lord. 28 Howbeit Josias did not turn back his chariot from him, but undertook to fight with him, not regarding the words of the prophet Jeremy spoken by the mouth of the Lord: 29 But joined battle with him in the plain of Magiddo, and the princes came against king Josias. 30 Then said the king unto his servants, Carry me away out of the battle; for I am very weak. And immediately his servants took him away out of the battle. 31 Then gat he up upon his second chariot; and being brought back to Jerusalem died, and was buried in his father's sepulchre. 32 And in all Jewry they mourned for Josias, yea, Jeremy the prophet lamented for Josias, and the chief men with the women made lamentation for him unto this day: and this was given out for an ordinance to be done continually in all the nation of Israel. 33 These things are written in the book of the stories of the kings of Judah, and every one of the acts that Josias did, and his glory, and his understanding in the law of the Lord, and the things that he had done before, and the things now recited, are reported in the book of the kings of Israel and Judea. 34 And the people took Joachaz the son of Josias, and made him king instead of Josias his father, when he was twenty and three years old. 35 And he reigned in Judea and in Jerusalem three months: and then the king of Egypt deposed him from reigning in Jerusalem. 36 And he set a tax upon the land of an hundred talents of silver and one talent of gold. 37 The king of Egypt also made king Joacim his brother king of Judea and Jerusalem. 38 And he bound Joacim and the nobles: but Zaraces his brother he apprehended, and brought him out of Egypt. 39 Five and twenty years old was Joacim when he was made king in the land of Judea and Jerusalem; and he did evil before the Lord. 40 Wherefore against him Nabuchodonosor the king of Babylon came up, and bound him with a chain of brass,

and carried him into Babylon. 41 Nabuchodonosor also took of the holy vessels of the Lord, and carried them away, and set them in his own temple at Babylon. 42 But those things that are recorded of him, and of his uncleanness and impiety, are written in the chronicles of the kings. 43 And Joacim his son reigned in his stead: he was made king being eighteen years old; 44 And reigned but three months and ten days in Jerusalem; and did evil before the Lord. 45 So after a year Nabuchodonosor sent and caused him to be brought into Babylon with the holy vessels of the Lord; 46 And made Zedechias king of Judea and Jerusalem, when he was one and twenty years old; and he reigned eleven years: 47 And he did evil also in the sight of the Lord, and cared not for the words that were spoken unto him by the prophet Jeremy from the mouth of the Lord. 48 And after that king Nabuchodonosor had made him to swear by the name of the Lord, he forswore himself, and rebelled; and hardening his neck, his heart, he transgressed the laws of the Lord God of Israel. 49 The governors also of the people and of the priests did many things against the laws, and passed all the pollutions of all nations, and defiled the temple of the Lord, which was sanctified in Jerusalem. 50 Nevertheless the God of their fathers sent by his messenger to call them back, because he spared them and his tabernacle also. 51 But they had his messengers in derision; and, look, when the Lord spake unto them, they made a sport of his prophets: 52 So far forth, that he, being wroth with his people for their great ungodliness, commanded the kings of the Chaldees to come up against them; 53 Who slew their young men with the sword, yea, even within the compass of their holy temple, and spared neither young man nor maid, old man nor child, among them; for he delivered all into their hands. 54 And they took all the holy vessels of the Lord, both great and small, with the vessels of the ark of God, and the king's treasures, and carried them away into Babylon. 55 As for the house of the Lord, they burnt it, and brake down the walls of Jerusalem, and set fire upon her towers: 56 And as for her glorious things, they never ceased till they had consumed and brought them all to nought: and the people that were not slain with the sword he carried unto Babylon: 57 Who became servants to him and his children, till the Persians reigned, to fulfil the word of the Lord spoken by the mouth of Jeremy: 58 Until the land had enjoyed her sabbaths, the whole time of her desolation shall she rest, until the full term of seventy years.

1-Esdras2 1 In the first year of Cyrus king of the Persians, that the word of the Lord might be accomplished, that he had promised by the mouth of Jeremy; 2 The Lord raised up the spirit of Cyrus the king of the Persians, and he made proclamation through all his kingdom, and also by writing, 3 Saying, Thus saith Cyrus king of the Persians; The Lord of Israel, the most high Lord, hath made me king of the whole world, 4 And commanded me to build him an house at Jerusalem in Jewry. 5 If therefore there be any of you that are of his people, let the Lord, even his Lord, be with him, and let him go up to Jerusalem that is in Judea, and build the house of the Lord of Israel: for he is the Lord that dwelleth in Jerusalem. 6 Whosoever then dwell in the places about, let them help him, those, I say, that are his neighbours, with gold, and with silver, 7 With gifts, with horses, and with cattle, and other things, which have been set forth by vow, for the temple of the Lord at Jerusalem. 8 Then the chief of the families of Judea and of the tribe of Benjamin stood up; the priests also, and the Levites, and all they whose mind the Lord had moved to go up, and to build an house for the Lord at Jerusalem, 9 And they that dwelt round about them, and helped them in all things with silver and gold, with horses and cattle, and with very many free gifts of a great number whose minds were stirred up thereto. 10 King Cyrus also brought forth the holy vessels, which Nabuchodonosor had carried away from Jerusalem, and had set up in his temple of idols. 11 Now when Cyrus king of the Persians had brought them forth, he delivered them to Mithridates his treasurer: 12 And by him they were delivered to Sanabassar the governor of Judea. 13 And this was the number of them; A thousand golden cups, and a thousand of silver, censers of silver twenty nine, vials of gold thirty, and of silver two thousand four hundred and ten, and a thousand other vessels. 14 So all the vessels of gold and of silver, which were carried away, were five thousand four hundred threescore and nine. 15 These were brought back by Sanabassar, together with them of the captivity, from Babylon to Jerusalem. 16 But in the time of Artaxerxes king of the Persians Belemus, and Mithridates, and Tabellius, and Rathumus, and Beeltethmus, and Semellius the secretary, with others that were in commission with them, dwelling in Samaria and other places, wrote unto him against them that dwelt in Judea and Jerusalem these letters following; 17 To king Artaxerxes our lord, Thy servants, Rathumus the storywriter, and Semellius the scribe, and the rest of their council, and the judges that are in Celosyria and Phenice. 18 Be it now known to the lord king, that the Jews that are up from you to us, being come into Jerusalem, that rebellious and wicked city, do build the marketplaces, and repair the walls of it and do lay the foundation of the temple. 19 Now if this city and the walls thereof be made up again, they will not only refuse to give tribute, but also rebel against kings. 20 And forasmuch as the things pertaining to the temple are now in hand, we think it meet not to neglect such a matter, 21 But to speak unto our lord the king, to the intent that, if it be thy pleasure it may be sought out in the books of thy fathers: 22 And thou shalt find in the chronicles what is written concerning these things, and shalt understand that that city was rebellious, troubling both kings and cities: 23 And that the Jews were rebellious, and raised always wars therein; for the which cause even this city was made desolate. 24 Wherefore now we do declare unto thee, O lord the king, that if this city be built again, and the walls thereof set up anew, thou shalt from henceforth have no passage into Celosyria and Phenice. 25 Then the king wrote back again to Rathumus the storywriter, to Beeltethmus, to Semellius the scribe, and to the rest that were in commission, and dwellers in Samaria and Syria and Phenice, after this manner; 26 I have read the epistle which ye have sent unto me: therefore I commanded to make diligent search, and it hath been found that that city was

from the beginning practising against kings; 27 And the men therein were given to rebellion and war: and that mighty kings and fierce were in Jerusalem, who reigned and exacted tributes in Celosyria and Phenice. 28 Now therefore I have commanded to hinder those men from building the city, and heed to be taken that there be no more done in it; 29 And that those wicked workers proceed no further to the annoyance of kings, 30 Then king Artaxerxes his letters being read, Rathumus, and Semellius the scribe, and the rest that were in commission with them, removing in haste toward Jerusalem with a troop of horsemen and a multitude of people in battle array, began to hinder the builders; and the building of the temple in Jerusalem ceased until the second year of the reign of Darius king of the Persians.

1-Esdras3 1 Now when Darius reigned, he made a great feast unto all his subjects, and unto all his household, and unto all the princes of Media and Persia, 2 And to all the governors and captains and lieutenants that were under him, from India unto Ethiopia, of an hundred twenty and seven provinces. 3 And when they had eaten and drunken, and being satisfied were gone home, then Darius the king went into his bedchamber, and slept, and soon after awaked. 4 Then three young men, that were of the guard that kept the king's body, spake one to another; 5 Let every one of us speak a sentence: he that shall overcome, and whose sentence shall seem wiser than the others, unto him shall the king Darius give great gifts, and great things in token of victory: 6 As, to be clothed in purple, to drink in gold, and to sleep upon gold, and a chariot with bridles of gold, and an headtire of fine linen, and a chain about his neck: 7 And he shall sit next to Darius because of his wisdom, and shall be called Darius his cousin. 8 And then every one wrote his sentence, sealed it, and laid it under king Darius his pillow; 9 And said that, when the king is risen, some will give him the writings; and of whose side the king and the three princes of Persia shall judge that his sentence is the wisest, to him shall the victory be given, as was appointed. 10 The first wrote, Wine is the strongest. 11 The second wrote, The king is strongest. 12 The third wrote, Women are strongest: but above all things Truth beareth away the victory. 13 Now when the king was risen up, they took their writings, and delivered them unto him, and so he read them: 14 And sending forth he called all the princes of Persia and Media, and the governors, and the captains, and the lieutenants, and the chief officers; 15 And sat him down in the royal seat of judgment; and the writings were read before them. 16 And he said, Call the young men, and they shall declare their own sentences. So they were called, and came in. 17 And he said unto them, Declare unto us your mind concerning the writings. Then began the first, who had spoken of the strength of wine; 18 And he said thus, O ye men, how exceeding strong is wine! it causeth all men to err that drink it: 19 It maketh the mind of the king and of the fatherless child to be all one; of the bondman and of the freeman, of the poor man and of the rich: 20 It turneth also every thought into jollity and mirth, so that a man remembereth neither sorrow nor debt: 21 And it maketh every heart rich, so that a man remembereth neither king nor governor; and it maketh to speak all things by talents: 22 And when they are in their cups, they forget their love both to friends and brethren, and a little after draw out swords: 23 But when they are from the wine, they remember not what they have done. 24 O ye men, is not wine the strongest, that enforceth to do thus? And when he had so spoken, he held his peace.

1-Esdras4 1 Then the second, that had spoken of the strength of the king, began to say, 2 O ye men, do not men excel in strength that bear rule over sea and land and all things in them? 3 But yet the king is more mighty: for he is lord of all these things, and hath dominion over them; and whatsoever he commandeth them they do. 4 If he bid them make war the one against the other, they do it: if he send them out against the enemies, they go, and break down mountains walls and towers. 5 They slay and are slain, and transgress not the kings commandment: if they get the victory, they bring all to the king, as well the spoil, as all things else. 6 Likewise for those that are no soldiers, and have not to do with wars, but use husbandry, when they have reaped again that which they had sown, they bring it to the king, and compel one another to pay tribute unto the king. 7 And yet he is but one man: if he command to kill, they kill; if he command to spare, they spare; 8 If he command to smite, they smite; if he command to make desolate, they make desolate; if he command to build, they build; 9 If he command to cut down, they cut down; if he command to plant, they plant. 10 So all his people and his armies obey him: furthermore he lieth down, he eateth and drinketh, and taketh his rest: 11 And these keep watch round about him, neither may any one depart, and do his own business, neither disobey they him in any thing. 12 O ye men, how should not the king be mightiest, when in such sort he is obeyed? And he held his tongue. 13 Then the third, who had spoken of women, and of the truth, (this was Zorobabel) began to speak. 14 O ye men, it is not the great king, nor the multitude of men, neither is it wine, that excelleth; who is it then that ruleth them, or hath the lordship over them? are they not women? 15 Women have borne the king and all the people that bear rule by sea and land. 16 Even of them came they: and they nourished them up that planted the vineyards, from whence the wine cometh. 17 These also make garments for men; these bring glory unto men; and without women cannot men be. 18 Yea, and if men have gathered together gold and silver, or any other goodly thing, do they not love a woman which is comely in favour and beauty? 19 And letting all those things go, do they not gape, and even with open mouth fix their eyes fast on her; and have not all men more desire unto her than unto silver or gold, or any goodly thing whatsoever? 20 A man leaveth his own father that brought him up, and his own country, and cleaveth unto his wife. 21 He sticketh not to spend his life with his wife. and remembereth neither father, nor mother, nor country. 22 By this also ye must know that women have dominion over you: do ye not labour and toil, and give and bring all to the woman? 23 Yea, a man taketh his sword, and goeth his way to rob and to steal, to sail upon the sea and upon rivers; 24 And looketh upon a lion, and goeth in the darkness; and when he hath stolen, spoiled, and robbed, he bringeth it to his love. 25 Wherefore a man loveth his wife better than father or mother. 26 Yea, many there be that have run out of their wits for women, and become servants for their sakes. 27 Many also have perished, have erred, and sinned, for women. 28 And now do ye not believe me? is not the king great in his power? do not all regions fear to touch him? 29 Yet did I see him and Apame the king's concubine, the daughter of the admirable Bartacus, sitting at the right hand of the king, 30 And taking the crown from the king's head, and setting it upon her own head; she also struck the king with her left hand. 31 And yet for all this the king gaped and gazed upon her with open mouth: if she laughed upon him, he laughed also: but if she took any displeasure at him, the king was fain to flatter, that she might be reconciled to him again. 32 O ye men, how can it be but women should be strong, seeing they do thus? 33 Then the king and the princes looked one upon another: so he began to speak of the truth. 34 O ye men, are not women strong? great is the earth, high is the heaven, swift is the sun in his course, for he compasseth the heavens round about, and fetcheth his course again to his own place in one day. 35 Is he not great that maketh these things? therefore great is the truth, and stronger than all things. 36 All the earth crieth upon the truth, and the heaven blesseth it: all works shake and tremble at it, and with it is no unrighteous thing. 37 Wine is wicked, the king is wicked, women are wicked, all the children of men are wicked, and such are all their wicked works; and there is no truth in them; in their unrighteousness also they shall perish. 38 As for the truth, it endureth, and is Always strong; it liveth and conquereth for evermore. 39 With her there is no accepting of persons or rewards; but she doeth the things that are just, and refraineth from all unjust and wicked things; and all men do well like of her works. 40 Neither in her judgment is any unrighteousness; and she is the strength, kingdom, power, and majesty, of all ages. Blessed be the God of truth. 41 And with that he held his peace. And all the people then shouted, and said, Great is Truth, and mighty above all things. 42 Then said the king unto him, Ask what thou wilt more than is appointed in the writing, and we will give it thee, because thou art found wisest; and thou shalt sit next me, and shalt be called my cousin. 43 Then said he unto the king, Remember thy vow, which thou hast vowed to build Jerusalem, in the day when thou camest to thy kingdom, 44 And to send away all the vessels that were taken away out of Jerusalem, which Cyrus set apart, when he vowed to destroy Babylon, and to send them again thither. 45 Thou also hast vowed to build up the temple, which the Edomites burned when Judea was made desolate by the Chaldees. 46 And now, O lord the king, this is that which I require, and which I desire of thee, and this is the princely liberality proceeding from thyself: I desire therefore that thou make good the vow, the performance whereof with thine own mouth thou hast vowed to the King of heaven. 47 Then Darius the king stood up, and kissed him, and wrote letters for him unto all the treasurers and lieutenants and captains and governors, that they should safely convey on their way both him, and all those that go up with him to build Jerusalem. 48 He wrote letters also unto the lieutenants that were in Celosyria and Phenice, and unto them in Libanus, that they should bring cedar wood from Libanus unto Jerusalem, and that they should build the city with him. 49 Moreover he wrote for all the Jews that went out of his realm up into Jewry, concerning their freedom, that no officer, no ruler, no lieutenant, nor treasurer, should forcibly enter into their doors; 50 And that all the country which they hold should be free without tribute; and that the Edomites should give over the villages of the Jews which then they held: 51 Yea, that there should be yearly given twenty talents to the building of the temple, until the time that it were built; 52 And other ten talents yearly, to maintain the burnt offerings upon the altar every day, as they had a commandment to offer seventeen: 53 And that all they that went from Babylon to build the city should have free liberty, as well they as their posterity, and all the priests that went away. 54 He wrote also concerning. the charges, and the priests' vestments wherein they minister; 55 And likewise for the charges of the Levites, to be given them until the day that the house were finished, and Jerusalem builded up. 56 And he commanded to give to all that kept the city pensions and wages. 57 He sent away also all the vessels from Babylon, that Cyrus had set apart; and all that Cyrus had given in commandment, the same charged he also to be done, and sent unto Jerusalem. 58 Now when this young man was gone forth, he lifted up his face to heaven toward Jerusalem, and praised the King of heaven, 59 And said, From thee cometh victory, from thee cometh wisdom, and thine is the glory, and I am thy servant. 60 Blessed art thou, who hast given me wisdom: for to thee I give thanks, O Lord of our fathers. 61 And so he took the letters, and went out, and came unto Babylon, and told it all his brethren. 62 And they praised the God of their fathers, because he had given them freedom and liberty 63 To go up, and to build Jerusalem, and the temple which is called by his name: and they feasted with instruments of musick and gladness seven days.

1-Esdras5 1 After this were the principal men of the families chosen according to their tribes, to go up with their wives and sons and daughters, with their menservants and maidservants, and their cattle. 2 And Darius sent with them a thousand horsemen, till they had brought them back to Jerusalem safely, and with musical *instruments* tabrets and flutes. 3 And all their brethren played, and he made them go up together with them. 4 And these are the names of the men which went up, according to their families among their tribes, after their several heads. 5 The priests, the sons of Phinees the son of Aaron: Jesus the son of Josedec, the son of Saraias, and Joacim the son of Zorobabel, the son of Salathiel, of the house of David, out of the kindred of Phares, of the tribe of Judah; 6 Who spake wise sentences before Darius the king of Persia in the second year of his reign, in the month Nisan, which is the first month. 7 And these are they of Jewry that came up from the captivity, where they dwelt as strangers, whom Nabuchodonosor the king of Babylon had carried away unto Babylon. 8 And they returned unto Jerusalem, and to the other parts of Jewry, every man to his own city, who came with Zorobabel, with Jesus, Nehemias, and Zacharias, and Reesaias, Enenius, Mardocheus, Beelsarus, Aspharasus, Reelius, Roimus, and Baana, their guides. 9 The number of them of the nation, and their governors, sons of Phoros, two thousand an hundred seventy and two; the sons of Saphat, four hundred seventy and two: 10 The sons of Ares, seven hundred fifty and six: 11 The sons of Phaath Moab, two thousand eight hundred and twelve: 12 The sons of Elam, a thousand two hundred fifty and four: the sons of Zathui, nine hundred forty and five: the sons of Corbe, seven hundred and five: the sons of Bani, six hundred forty and eight: 13 The sons of Bebai, six hundred twenty and three: the sons of Sadas, three thousand two hundred twenty and two: 14 The sons of Adonikam, six hundred sixty and seven: the sons of Bagoi, two thousand sixty and six: the sons of Adin, four hundred fifty and four: 15 The sons of Aterezias, ninety and two: the sons of Ceilan and Azetas threescore and seven: the sons of Azuran, four hundred thirty and two: 16 The sons of Ananias, an hundred and one: the sons of Arom, thirty two: and the sons of Bassa, three hundred twenty and three: the sons of Azephurith, an hundred and two: 17 The sons of Meterus, three thousand and five: the sons of Bethlomon, an hundred twenty and three: 18 They of Netophah, fifty and five: they of Anathoth, an hundred fifty and eight: they of Bethsamos, forty and two: 19 They of Kiriathiarius, twenty and five: they of Caphira and Beroth, seven hundred forty and three: they of Pira, seven hundred: 20 They of Chadias and Ammidoi, four hundred twenty and two: they of Cirama and Gabdes, six hundred twenty and one: 21 They of Macalon, an hundred twenty and two: they of Betolius, fifty and two: the sons of Nephis, an hundred fifty and six: 22 The sons of Calamolalus and Onus, seven hundred twenty and five: the sons of Jerechus, two hundred forty and five: 23 The sons of Annas, three thousand three hundred and thirty. 24 The priests: the sons of Jeddu, the son of Jesus among the sons of Sanasib, nine hundred seventy and two: the sons of Meruth, a thousand fifty and two: 25 The sons of Phassaron, a thousand forty and seven: the sons of Carme, a thousand and seventeen. 26 The Levites: the sons of Jessue, and Cadmiel, and Banuas, and Sudias, seventy and four. 27 The holy singers: the sons of Asaph, an hundred twenty and eight. 28 The porters: the sons of Salum, the sons of Jatal, the sons of Talmon, the sons of Dacobi, the sons of Teta, the sons of Sami, in all an hundred thirty and nine. 29 The servants of the temple: the sons of Esau, the sons of Asipha, the sons of Tabaoth, the sons of Ceras, the sons of Sud, the sons of Phaleas, the sons of Labana, the sons of Graba, 30 The sons of Acua, the sons of Uta, the sons of Cetab, the sons of Agaba, the sons of Subai, the sons of Anan, the sons of Cathua, the sons of Geddur, 31 The sons of Airus, the sons of Daisan, the sons of Noeba, the sons of Chaseba, the sons of Gazera, the sons of Azia, the sons of Phinees, the sons of Azara, the sons of Bastai, the sons of Asana, the sons of Meani, the sons of Naphisi, the sons of Acub, the sons of Acipha, the sons of Assur, the sons of

Pharacim, the sons of Basaloth, 32 The sons of Meeda, the sons of Coutha, the sons of Charea, the sons of Charcus, the sons of Aserer, the sons of Thomoi, the sons of Nasith, the sons of Atipha. 33 The sons of the servants of Solomon: the sons of Azaphion, the sons of Pharira, the sons of Jeeli, the sons of Lozon, the sons of Israel, the sons of Sapheth, 34 The sons of Hagia, the sons of Pharacareth, the sons of Sabi, the sons of Sarothie, the sons of Masias, the sons of Gar, the sons of Addus, the sons of Suba, the sons of Apherra, the sons of Barodis, the sons of Sabat, the sons of Allom. 35 All the ministers of the temple, and the sons of the servants of Solomon, were three hundred seventy and two. 36 These came up from Thermeleth and Thelersas, Charaathalar leading them, and Aalar; 37 Neither could they shew their families, nor their stock, how they were of Israel: the sons of Ladan, the son of Ban, the sons of Necodan, six hundred fifty and two. 38 And of the priests that usurped the office of the priesthood, and were not found: the sons of Obdia, the sons of Accoz, the sons of Addus, who married Augia one of the daughters of Barzelus, and was named after his name. 39 And when the description of the kindred of these men was sought in the register, and was not found, they were removed from executing the office of the priesthood: 40 For unto them said Nehemias and Atharias, that they should not be partakers of the holy things, till there arose up an high priest clothed with doctrine and truth. 41 So of Israel, from them of twelve years old and upward, they were all in number forty thousand, beside menservants and womenservants two thousand three hundred and sixty. 42 Their menservants and handmaids were seven thousand three hundred forty and seven: the singing men and singing women, two hundred forty and five: 43 Four hundred thirty and five camels, seven thousand thirty and six horses, two hundred forty and five mules, five thousand five hundred twenty and five beasts used to the yoke. 44 And certain of the chief of their families, when they came to the temple of God that is in Jerusalem, vowed to set up the house again in his own place according to their ability, 45 And to give into the holy treasury of the works a thousand pounds of gold, five thousand of silver, and an hundred priestly vestments. 46 And so dwelt the priests and the Levites and the people in Jerusalem, and in the country, the singers also and the porters; and all Israel in their villages. 47 But when the seventh month was at hand, and when the children of Israel were every man in his own place, they came all together with one consent into the open place of the first gate which is toward the east. 48 Then stood up Jesus the son of Josedec, and his brethren the priests and Zorobabel the son of Salathiel, and his brethren, and made ready the altar of the God of Israel, 49 To offer burnt sacrifices upon it, according as it is expressly commanded in the book of Moses the man of God. 50 And there were gathered unto them out of the other nations of the land, and they erected the altar upon his own place, because all the nations of the land were at enmity with them, and oppressed them; and they offered sacrifices according to the time, and burnt offerings to the Lord both morning and evening. 51 Also they held the feast of tabernacles, as it is commanded in the law, and offered sacrifices daily, as was meet: 52 And after that, the continual oblations, and the sacrifice of the sabbaths, and of the new moons, and of all holy feasts. 53 And all they that had made any vow to God began to offer sacrifices to God from the first day of the seventh month, although the temple of the Lord was not yet built. 54 And they gave unto the masons and carpenters money, meat, and drink, with cheerfulness. 55 Unto them of Zidon also and Tyre they gave carrs, that they should bring cedar trees from Libanus, which should be brought by floats to the haven of Joppa, according as it was commanded them by Cyrus king of the Persians. 56 And in the second year and second month after his coming to the temple of God at Jerusalem began Zorobabel the son of Salathiel, and Jesus the son of Josedec, and their brethren, and the priests, and the Levites, and all they that were come unto Jerusalem out of the captivity: 57 And they laid the foundation of the house of God in the first day of the second month, in the second year after they were come to Jewry and Jerusalem. 58 And they appointed the Levites from twenty years old over the works of the Lord. Then stood up Jesus, and his sons and brethren, and Cadmiel his brother, and the sons of Madiabun, with the sons of Joda the son of Eliadun, with their sons and brethren, all Levites, with one accord setters forward of the business, labouring to advance the works in the house of God. So the workmen built the temple of the Lord. 59 And the priests stood arrayed in their vestments with musical instruments and trumpets; and the Levites the sons of Asaph had cymbals, 60 Singing songs of thanksgiving, and praising the Lord, according as David the king of Israel had ordained. 61 And they sung with loud voices songs to the praise of the Lord, because his mercy and glory is for ever in all Israel. 62 And all the people sounded trumpets, and shouted with a loud voice, singing songs of thanksgiving unto the Lord for the rearing up of the house of the Lord. 63 Also of the priests and Levites, and of the chief of their families, the ancients who had seen the former house came to the building of this with weeping and great crying. 64 But many with trumpets and joy shouted with loud voice, 65 Insomuch that the trumpets might not be heard for the weeping of the people: yet the multitude sounded marvellously, so that it was heard afar off. 66 Wherefore when the enemies of the tribe of Judah and Benjamin heard it, they came to know what that noise of trumpets should mean. 67 And they perceived that they that were of the captivity did build the temple unto the Lord God of Israel. 68 So they went to Zorobabel and Jesus, and to the chief of the families, and said unto them, We will build together with you. 69 For we likewise, as ye, do obey your Lord, and do sacrifice unto him from the days of Azbazareth the king of the Assyrians, who brought us hither. 70 Then Zorobabel and Jesus and the chief of the families of Israel said unto them, It is not for us and you to build together an house unto the Lord our God. 71 We ourselves alone will build unto the Lord of Israel, according as Cyrus the king of the Persians hath commanded us. 72 But the heathen of the land lying heavy upon the inhabitants of Judea, and holding them strait, hindered their building; 73 And by their secret plots, and popular persuasions and commotions, they hindered the finishing of the building all the time that king Cyrus lived: so they were hindered from building for the space of two years, until the reign of Darius.

1-Esdras6 1 Now in the second year of the reign of Darius Aggeus and Zacharias the son of Addo, the prophets, prophesied unto the Jews in Jewry and Jerusalem in the name of the Lord God of Israel, which was upon them. 2 Then stood up Zorobabel the son of Salatiel, and Jesus the son of Josedec, and began to build the house of the Lord at Jerusalem, the prophets of the Lord being with them, and helping them. 3 At the same time came unto them Sisinnes the governor of Syria and Phenice, with Sathrabuzanes and his companions, and said unto them, 4 By whose appointment do ye build this house and this roof, and perform all the other things? and who are the workmen that perform these things? 5 Nevertheless the elders of the Jews obtained favour, because the Lord had visited the captivity; 6 And they were not hindered from building, until such time as signification was given unto Darius concerning them, and an answer received. 7 The copy of the letters which Sisinnes, governor of Syria and Phenice, and Sathrabuzanes, with their companions, rulers in Syria and Phenice, wrote and sent unto Darius; To king Darius, greeting: 8 Let all things be known unto our lord the king, that being come into the country of Judea, and entered into the city of Jerusalem we found in the city of Jerusalem the ancients of the Jews that were of the captivity 9 Building an house unto the Lord, great and new, of hewn and costly stones, and the timber already laid upon the walls. 10 And those works are done with great speed, and the work goeth on prosperously in their hands, and with all glory and diligence is it made. 11 Then asked we these elders, saying, By whose commandment build ye this house, and lay the foundations of these works? 12 Therefore to the intent that we might give knowledge unto thee by writing, we demanded of them who were the chief doers, and we required of them the names in writing of their principal men. 13 So they gave us this answer, We are the servants of the Lord which made heaven and earth. 14 And as for this house, it was builded many years ago by a king of Israel great and strong, and was finished. 15 But when our fathers provoked God unto wrath, and sinned against the Lord of Israel which is in heaven, he gave them over into the power of Nabuchodonosor king of Babylon, of the Chaldees; 16 Who pulled down the house, and burned it, and carried away the people captives unto Babylon. 17 But in the first year that king Cyrus reigned over the country of Babylon Cyrus the king wrote to build up this house. 18 And the holy vessels of gold and of silver, that Nabuchodonosor had carried away out of the house at Jerusalem, and had set them in his own temple those Cyrus the king brought forth again out of the temple at Babylon, and they were delivered to Zorobabel and to Sanabassarus the ruler, 19 With commandment that he should carry away the same vessels, and put them in the temple at Jerusalem; and that the temple of the Lord should be built in his place. 20 Then the same Sanabassarus, being come hither, laid the foundations

of the house of the Lord at Jerusalem; and from that time to this being still a building, it is not yet fully ended. 21 Now therefore, if it seem good unto the king, let search be made among the records of king Cyrus: 22 And if it be found that the building of the house of the Lord at Jerusalem hath been done with the consent of king Cyrus, and if our lord the king be so minded, let him signify unto us thereof. 23 Then commanded king Darius to seek among the records at Babylon: and so at Ecbatana the palace, which is in the country of Media, there was found a roll wherein these things were recorded. 24 In the first year of the reign of Cyrus king Cyrus commanded that the house of the Lord at Jerusalem should be built again, where they do sacrifice with continual fire: 25 Whose height shall be sixty cubits and the breadth sixty cubits, with three rows of hewn stones, and one row of new wood of that country; and the expenses thereof to be given out of the house of king Cyrus: 26 And that the holy vessels of the house of the Lord, both of gold and silver, that Nabuchodonosor took out of the house at Jerusalem, and brought to Babylon, should be restored to the house at Jerusalem, and be set in the place where they were before. 27 And also he commanded that Sisinnes the governor of Syria and Phenice, and Sathrabuzanes, and their companions, and those which were appointed rulers in Syria and Phenice, should be careful not to meddle with the place, but suffer Zorobabel, the servant of the Lord, and governor of Judea, and the elders of the Jews, to build the house of the Lord in that place. 28 I have commanded also to have it built up whole again; and that they look diligently to help those that be of the captivity of the Jews, till the house of the Lord be finished: 29 And out of the tribute of Celosyria and Phenice a portion carefully to be given these men for the sacrifices of the Lord, that is, to Zorobabel the governor, for bullocks, and rams, and lambs; 30 And also corn, salt, wine, and oil, and that continually every year without further question, according as the priests that be in Jerusalem shall signify to be daily spent: 31 That offerings may be made to the most high God for the king and for his children, and that they may pray for their lives. 32 And he commanded that whosoever should transgress, yea, or make light of any thing afore spoken or written, out of his own house should a tree be taken, and he thereon be hanged, and all his goods seized for the king. 33 The Lord therefore, whose name is there called upon, utterly destroy every king and nation, that stretcheth out his hand to hinder or endamage that house of the Lord in Jerusalem. 34 I Darius the king have ordained that according unto these things it be done with diligence.

1-Esdras7 1 Then Sisinnes the governor of Celosyria and Phenice, and Sathrabuzanes, with their companions following the commandments of king Darius, 2 Did very carefully oversee the holy works, assisting the ancients of the Jews and governors of the temple. 3 And so the holy works prospered, when Aggeus and Zacharias the prophets prophesied. 4 And they finished these things by the commandment of the Lord God of Israel, and with the consent of Cyrus, Darius, and Artaxerxes, kings of Persia.

5 And thus was the holy house finished in the three and twentieth day of the month Adar, in the sixth year of Darius king of the Persians 6 And the children of Israel, the priests, and the Levites, and others that were of the captivity, that were added unto them, did according to the things written in the book of Moses. 7 And to the dedication of the temple of the Lord they offered an hundred bullocks two hundred rams, four hundred lambs; 8 And twelve goats for the sin of all Israel, according to the number of the chief of the tribes of Israel. 9. The priests also and the Levites stood arrayed in their vestments, according to their kindreds, in the service of the Lord God of Israel, according to the book of Moses: and the porters at every gate. 10 And the children of Israel that were of the captivity held the passover the fourteenth day of the first month, after that the priests and the Levites were sanctified. 11 They that were of the captivity were not all sanctified together: but the Levites were all sanctified together. 12 And so they offered the passover for all them of the captivity, and for their brethren the priests, and for themselves. 13 And the children of Israel that came out of the captivity did eat, even all they that had separated themselves from the abominations of the people of the land, and sought the Lord. 14 And they kept the feast of unleavened bread seven days, making merry before the Lord, 15 For that he had turned the counsel of the king of Assyria toward them, to strengthen their hands in the works of the Lord God of Israel.

1-Esdras8

1 And after these things, when Artaxerxes the king of the Persians reigned came Esdras the son of Saraias, the son of Ezerias, the son of Helchiah, the son of Salum, 2 The son of Sadduc, the son of Achitob, the son of Amarias, the son of Ezias, the son of Meremoth, the son of Zaraias, the son of Savias, the son of Boccas, the son of Abisum, the son of Phinees, the son of Eleazar, the son of Aaron the chief priest. 3 This Esdras went up from Babylon, as a scribe, being very ready in the law of Moses, that was given by the God of Israel. 4 And the king did him honour: for he found grace in his sight in all his requests. 5 There went up with him also certain of the children of Israel, of the priest of the Levites, of the holy singers, porters, and ministers of the temple, unto Jerusalem, 6 In the seventh year of the reign of Artaxerxes, in the fifth month, this was the king's seventh year; for they went from Babylon in the first day of the first month, and came to Jerusalem, according to the prosperous journey which the Lord gave them. 7 For Esdras had very great skill, so that he omitted nothing of the law and commandments of the Lord, but taught all Israel the ordinances and judgments. 8 Now the copy of the commission, which was written from Artaxerxes the king, and came to Esdras the priest and reader of the law of the Lord, is this that followeth; 9 King Artaxerxes unto Esdras the priest and reader of the law of the Lord sendeth greeting: 10 Having determined to deal graciously, I have given order, that such of the nation of the Jews, and of the priests and Levites being within our realm, as are willing and desirous should go with thee unto Jerusalem. 11 As many therefore as have a mind thereunto, let them depart with thee, as it hath seemed good both to me and my seven friends the counsellors; 12 That they may look unto the affairs of Judea and Jerusalem, agreeably to that which is in the law of the Lord; 13 And carry the gifts unto the Lord of Israel to Jerusalem, which I and my friends have vowed, and all the gold and silver that in the country of Babylon can be found, to the Lord in Jerusalem, 14 With that also which is given of the people for the temple of the Lord their God at Jerusalem: and that silver and gold may be collected for bullocks, rams, and lambs, and things thereunto appertaining; 15 To the end that they may offer sacrifices unto the Lord upon the altar of the Lord their God, which is in Jerusalem. 16 And whatsoever thou and thy brethren will do with the silver and gold, that do, according to the will of thy God. 17 And the holy vessels of the Lord, which are given thee for the use of the temple of thy God, which is in Jerusalem, thou shalt set before thy God in Jerusalem. 18 And whatsoever thing else thou shalt remember for the use of the temple of thy God, thou shalt give it out of the king's treasury. 19 And I king Artaxerxes have also commanded the keepers of the treasures in Syria and Phenice, that whatsoever Esdras the priest and the reader of the law of the most high God shall send for, they should give it him with speed, 20 To the sum of an hundred talents of silver, likewise also of wheat even to an hundred cors, and an hundred pieces of wine, and other things in abundance. 21 Let all things be performed after the law of God diligently unto the most high God, that wrath come not upon the kingdom of the king and his sons. 22 I command you also, that ye require no tax, nor any other imposition, of any of the priests, or Levites, or holy singers, or porters, or ministers of the temple, or of any that have doings in this temple, and that no man have authority to impose any thing upon them. 23 And thou, Esdras, according to the wisdom of God ordain judges and justices, that they may judge in all Syria and Phenice all those that know the law of thy God; and those that know it not thou shalt teach. 24 And whosoever shall transgress the law of thy God, and of the king, shall be punished diligently, whether it be by death, or other punishment, by penalty of money, or by imprisonment. 25 Then said Esdras the scribe, Blessed be the only Lord God of my fathers, who hath put these things into the heart of the king, to glorify his house that is in Jerusalem: 26 And hath honoured me in the sight of the king, and his counsellors, and all his friends and nobles. 27 Therefore was I encouraged by the help of the Lord my God, and gathered together men of Israel to go up with me. 28 And these are the chief according to their families and several dignities, that went up with me from Babylon in the reign of king Artaxerxes: 29 Of the sons of Phinees, Gerson: of the sons of Ithamar, Gamael: of the sons of David, Lettus the son of Sechenias: 30 Of the sons of Pharez, Zacharias; and with him were counted an hundred and fifty men: 31 Of the sons of Pahath Moab, Eliaonias, the son of Zaraias, and with him two hundred men: 32 Of the sons of Zathoe, Sechenias the son of Jezelus, and with him three hundred men: of the sons of Adin, Obeth the son of Jonathan, and with him two hundred and fifty men: 33 Of the sons of Elam, Josias son of Gotholias, and with him seventy men: 34 Of the sons of Saphatias, Zaraias son of

Michael, and with him threescore and ten men: 35 Of the sons of Joab, Abadias son of Jezelus, and with him two hundred and twelve men: 36 Of the sons of Banid, Assalimoth son of Josaphias, and with him an hundred and threescore men: 37 Of the sons of Babi, Zacharias son of Bebai, and with him twenty and eight men: 38 Of the sons of Astath, Johannes son of Acatan, and with him an hundred and ten men: 39 Of the sons of Adonikam the last, and these are the names of them, Eliphalet, Jewel, and Samaias, and with them seventy men: 40 Of the sons of Bago, Uthi the son of Istalcurus, and with him seventy men. 41 And these I gathered together to the river called Theras, where we pitched our tents three days: and then I surveyed them. 42 But when I had found there none of the priests and Levites, 43 Then sent I unto Eleazar, and Iduel, and Masman, 44 And Alnathan, and Mamaias, and Joribas, and Nathan, Eunatan, Zacharias, and Mosollamon, principal men and learned. 45 And I bade them that they should go unto Saddeus the captain, who was in the place of the treasury: 46 And commanded them that they should speak unto Daddeus, and to his brethren, and to the treasurers in that place, to send us such men as might execute the priests' office in the house of the Lord. 47 And by the mighty hand of our Lord they brought unto us skilful men of the sons of Moli the son of Levi, the son of Israel, Asebebia, and his sons, and his brethren, who were eighteen. 48 And Asebia, and Annuus, and Osaias his brother, of the sons of Channuneus, and their sons, were twenty men. 49 And of the servants of the temple whom David had ordained, and the principal men for the service of the Levites to wit, the servants of the temple two hundred and twenty, the catalogue of whose names were shewed. 50 And there I vowed a fast unto the young men before our Lord, to desire of him a prosperous journey both for us and them that were with us, for our children, and for the cattle: 51 For I was ashamed to ask the king footmen, and horsemen, and conduct for safeguard against our adversaries. 52 For we had said unto the king, that the power of the Lord our God should be with them that seek him, to support them in all ways. 53 And again we besought our Lord as touching these things, and found him favourable unto us. 54 Then I separated twelve of the chief of the priests, Esebrias, and Assanias, and ten men of their brethren with them: 55 And I weighed them the gold, and the silver, and the holy vessels of the house of our Lord, which the king, and his council, and the princes, and all Israel, had given. 56 And when I had weighed it, I delivered unto them six hundred and fifty talents of silver, and silver vessels of an hundred talents, and an hundred talents of gold, 57 And twenty golden vessels, and twelve vessels of brass, even of fine brass, glittering like gold. 58 And I said unto them, Both ye are holy unto the Lord, and the vessels are holy, and the gold and the silver is a vow unto the Lord, the Lord of our fathers. 59 Watch ye, and keep them till ye deliver them to the chief of the priests and Levites, and to the principal men of the families of Israel, in Jerusalem, into the chambers of the house of our God. 60 So the priests and the Levites, who had received the silver and the gold and the vessels, brought them unto Jerusalem, into the temple of the Lord. 61 And from the river Theras we departed the twelfth day of the first month, and came to Jerusalem by the mighty hand of our Lord, which was with us: and from the beginning of our journey the Lord delivered us from every enemy, and so we came to Jerusalem. 62 And when we had been there three days, the gold and silver that was weighed was delivered in the house of our Lord on the fourth day unto Marmoth the priest the son of Iri. 63 And with him was Eleazar the son of Phinees, and with them were Josabad the son of Jesu and Moeth the son of Sabban, Levites: all was delivered them by number and weight. 64 And all the weight of them was written up the same hour. 65 Moreover they that were come out of the captivity offered sacrifice unto the Lord God of Israel, even twelve bullocks for all Israel, fourscore and sixteen rams, 66 Threescore and twelve lambs, goats for a peace offering, twelve; all of them a sacrifice to the Lord. 67 And they delivered the king's commandments unto the king's stewards' and to the governors of Celosyria and Phenice; and they honoured the people and the temple of God. 68 Now when these things were done, the rulers came unto me, and said, 69 The nation of Israel, the princes, the priests and Levites, have not put away from them the strange people of the land, nor the pollutions of the Gentiles to wit, of the Canaanites, Hittites, Pheresites, Jebusites, and the Moabites, Egyptians, and Edomites. 70 For both they and their sons have married with their daughters, and the holy seed is mixed with the strange people of the land; and from the beginning of this matter the rulers and the great men have been partakers of this iniquity. 71 And as soon as I had heard these things, I rent my clothes, and the holy garment, and pulled off the hair from off my head and beard, and sat me down sad and very heavy. 72 So all they that were then moved at the word of the Lord God of Israel assembled unto me, whilst I mourned for the iniquity: but I sat still full of heaviness until the evening sacrifice. 73 Then rising up from the fast with my clothes and the holy garment rent, and bowing my knees, and stretching forth my hands unto the Lord, 74 I said, O Lord, I am confounded and ashamed before thy face; 75 For our sins are multiplied above our heads, and our ignorances have reached up unto heaven. 76 For ever since the time of our fathers we have been and are in great sin, even unto this day. 77 And for our sins and our fathers' we with our brethren and our kings and our priests were given up unto the kings of the earth, to the sword, and to captivity, and for a prey with shame, unto this day. 78 And now in some measure hath mercy been shewed unto us from thee, O Lord, that there should be left us a root and a name in the place of thy sanctuary; 79 And to discover unto us a light in the house of the Lord our God, and to give us food in the time of our servitude. 80 Yea, when we were in bondage, we were not forsaken of our Lord; but he made us gracious before the kings of Persia, so that they gave us food; 81 Yea, and honoured the temple of our Lord, and raised up the desolate Sion, that they have given us a sure abiding in Jewry and Jerusalem. 82 And now, O Lord, what shall we say, having these things? for we have transgressed thy commandments, which thou gavest by the hand of thy servants the prophets, saying, 83 That the land, which ye enter into to possess as an heritage, is a land polluted with the pollutions of the strangers of the land, and they have filled it with their uncleanness. 84 Therefore now shall ye not join your daughters unto their sons, neither shall ye take their daughters unto your sons. 85 Moreover ye shall never seek to have peace with them, that ye may be strong, and eat the good things of the land, and that ye may leave the inheritance of the land unto your children for evermore. 86 And all that is befallen is done unto us for our wicked works and great sins; for thou, O Lord, didst make our sins light, 87 And didst give unto us such a root: but we have turned back again to transgress thy law, and to mingle ourselves with the uncleanness of the nations of the land. 88 Mightest not thou be angry with us to destroy us, till thou hadst left us neither root, seed, nor name? 89 O Lord of Israel, thou art true: for we are left a root this day. 90 Behold, now are we before thee in our iniquities, for we cannot stand any longer by reason of these things before thee. 91 And as Esdras in his prayer made his confession, weeping, and lying flat upon the ground before the temple, there gathered unto him from Jerusalem a very great multitude of men and women and children: for there was great weeping among the multitude. 92 Then Jechonias the son of Jeelus, one of the sons of Israel, called out, and said, O Esdras, we have sinned against the Lord God, we have married strange women of the nations of the land, and now is all Israel aloft. 93 Let us make an oath to the Lord, that we will put away all our wives, which we have taken of the heathen, with their children, 94 Like as thou hast decreed, and as many as do obey the law of the Lord. 95 Arise and put in execution: for to thee doth this matter appertain, and we will be with thee: do valiantly. 96 So Esdras arose, and took an oath of the chief of the priests and Levites of all Israel to do after these things; and so they sware.

1-Esdras9 1 Then Esdras rising from the court of the temple went to the chamber of Joanan the son of Eliasib, 2 And remained there, and did eat no meat nor drink water, mourning for the great iniquities of the multitude. 3 And there was a proclamation in all Jewry and Jerusalem to all them that were of the captivity, that they should be gathered together at Jerusalem: 4 And that whosoever met not there within two or three days according as the elders that bare rule appointed, their cattle should be seized to the use of the temple, and himself cast out from them that were of the captivity. 5 And in three days were all they of the tribe of Judah and Benjamin gathered together at Jerusalem the twentieth day of the ninth month. 6 And all the multitude sat trembling in the broad court of the temple because of the present foul weather. 7 So Esdras arose up, and said unto them, Ye have transgressed the law in marrying strange wives, thereby to increase the sins of Israel. 8 And now by confessing give glory unto the Lord God of our fathers, 9 And do his will, and separate yourselves from the heathen of the land, and from the strange women. 10 Then cried the whole multitude, and said with a loud voice, Like as thou hast spoken, so will we do. 11 But forasmuch as the people are many, and it is foul weather, so that we cannot

stand without, and this is not a work of a day or two, seeing our sin in these things is spread far: 12 Therefore let the rulers of the multitude stay, and let all them of our habitations that have strange wives come at the time appointed, 13 And with them the rulers and judges of every place, till we turn away the wrath of the Lord from us for this matter. 14 Then Jonathan the son of Azael and Ezechias the son of Theocanus accordingly took this matter upon them: and Mosollam and Levis and Sabbatheus helped them. 15 And they that were of the captivity did according to all these things. 16 And Esdras the priest chose unto him the principal men of their families, all by name: and in the first day of the tenth month they sat together to examine the matter. 17 So their cause that held strange wives was brought to an end in the first day of the first month. 18 And of the priests that were come together, and had strange wives, there were found: 19 Of the sons of Jesus the son of Josedec, and his brethren; Matthelas and Eleazar, and Joribus and Joadanus. 20 And they gave their hands to put away their wives and to offer rams to make reconcilement for their errors. 21 And of the sons of Emmer; Ananias, and Zabdeus, and Eanes, and Sameius, and Hiereel, and Azarias. 22 And of the sons of Phaisur; Elionas, Massias Israel, and Nathanael, and Ocidelus and Talsas. 23 And of the Levites; Jozabad, and Semis, and Colius, who was called Calitas, and Patheus, and Judas, and Jonas. 24 Of the holy singers; Eleazurus, Bacchurus. 25 Of the porters; Sallumus, and Tolbanes. 26 Of them of Israel, of the sons of Phoros; Hiermas, and Eddias, and Melchias, and Maelus, and Eleazar, and Asibias, and Baanias. 27 Of the sons of Ela; Matthanias, Zacharias, and Hierielus, and Hieremoth, and Aedias. 28 And of the sons of Zamoth; Eliadas, Elisimus, Othonias, Jarimoth, and Sabatus, and Sardeus. 29 Of the sons of Babai; Johannes, and Ananias and Josabad, and Amatheis. 30 Of the sons of Mani; Olamus, Mamuchus, Jedeus, Jasubus, Jasael, and Hieremoth. 31 And of the sons of Addi; Naathus, and Moosias, Lacunus, and Naidus, and Mathanias, and Sesthel, Balnuus, and Manasseas. 32 And of the sons of Annas; Elionas and Aseas, and Melchias, and Sabbeus, and Simon Chosameus. 33 And of the sons of Asom; Altaneus, and Matthias, and Baanaia, Eliphalet, and Manasses, and Semei. 34 And of the sons of Maani; Jeremias, Momdis, Omaerus, Juel, Mabdai, and Pelias, and Anos, Carabasion, and Enasibus, and Mamnitanaimus, Eliasis, Bannus, Eliali, Samis, Selemias, Nathanias: and of the sons of Ozora; Sesis, Esril, Azaelus, Samatus, Zambis, Josephus. 35 And of the sons of Ethma; Mazitias, Zabadaias, Edes, Juel, Banaias. 36 All these had taken strange wives, and they put them away with their children. 37 And the priests and Levites, and they that were of Israel, dwelt in Jerusalem, and in the country, in the first day of the seventh month: so the children of Israel were in their habitations. 38 And the whole multitude came together with one accord into the broad place of the holy porch toward the east: 39 And they spake unto Esdras the priest and reader, that he would bring the law of Moses, that was given of the Lord God of Israel. 40 So Esdras the chief priest brought the law unto the whole multitude from man to woman, and to all the priests, to hear law in the first day of the seventh month. 41 And he read in the broad court before the holy porch from morning unto midday, before both men and women; and the multitude gave heed unto the law. 42 And Esdras the priest and reader of the law stood up upon a pulpit of wood, which was made for that purpose. 43 And there stood up by him Mattathias, Sammus, Ananias, Azarias, Urias, Ezecias, Balasamus, upon the right hand: 44 And upon his left hand stood Phaldaius, Misael, Melchias, Lothasubus, and Nabarias. 45 Then took Esdras the book of the law before the multitude: for he sat honourably in the first place in the sight of them all. 46 And when he opened the law, they stood all straight up. So Esdras blessed the Lord God most High, the God of hosts, Almighty. 47 And all the people answered, Amen; and lifting up their hands they fell to the ground, and worshipped the Lord. 48 Also Jesus, Anus, Sarabias, Adinus, Jacubus, Sabateas, Auteas, Maianeas, and Calitas, Azarias, and Joazabdus, and Ananias, Biatas, the Levites, taught the law of the Lord, making them withal to understand it. 49 Then spake Attharates unto Esdras the chief priest. and reader, and to the Levites that taught the multitude, even to all, saying, 50 This day is holy unto the Lord; (for they all wept when they heard the law:) 51 Go then, and eat the fat, and drink the sweet, and send part to them that have nothing; 52 For this day is holy unto the Lord: and be not sorrowful; for the Lord will bring you to honour. 53 So the Levites published all things to the people, saying, This day is holy to the Lord; be not sorrowful. 54 Then went they their way, every one to eat and drink, and make merry, and to give part to them that had nothing, and to make great cheer; 55 Because they understood the words wherein they were instructed, and for the which they had been assembled.

NEHEMIAH

Neh.1 1 The words of Neemias the son of Chelcia. And it came to pass in the month Chaseleu, of the twentieth year, that I was in Susan the palace. 2 And Anani, one of my brethren, came, he and *some* men of Juda; and I asked them concerning those that had escaped, who had been left of the captivity, and concerning Jerusalem. 3 And they said to me, The remnant, *even* those that are left of the captivity, *are* there in the land, in great distress and reproach: and the walls of Jerusalem *are* thrown down, and its gates are burnt with fire. 4 And it came to pass, when I heard these words, *that* I sat down and wept, and mourned for *several* days, and continued fasting and praying before the God of heaven. 5 And I said, Nay, I pray thee, O Lord God of heaven, the mighty, the great and terrible, keeping thy covenant and mercy to them that love him, and to those that keep his commandments: 6 let now thine ear be attentive, and thine eyes open, that thou mayest hear the prayer of thy servant, which I pray before thee at this time, this day *both* day and night, for the children of Israel thy servants, and make confession for the sins of the children of Israel, which we have sinned against thee: both I and the house of my father have sinned. 7 We have altogether broken *covenant* with thee, and we have not kept the commandments, and the ordinances, and the judgments, which thou didst command

thy servant Moses. 8 Remember, I pray thee, the word wherewith thou didst charge thy servant Moses, saying, If ye break covenant *with me*, I will disperse you among the nations. 9 But if ye turn again to me, and keep my commandments, and do them; if ye should be scattered under the utmost *bound* of heaven, thence will I gather them, and I will bring them into the place which I have chosen to cause my name to dwell there. 10 Now they *are* thy servants and thy people, whom thou hast redeemed with thy great power, and with thy strong hand. 11 *Turn* not *away*, I pray thee, O Lord, but let thine ear be attentive to the prayer of thy servant, and to the prayer of thy servants, who desire to fear thy name: and prosper, I pray thee, thy servant this day, and cause him to find mercy in the sight of this man. Now I was the king's cup-bearer.

Neh.2 1 And it came to pass in the month Nisan of the twentieth year of king Arthasastha, that the wine was before me: and I took the wine, and gave *it* to the king: and there was not another before him. 2 And the king said to me, Why is thy countenance sad, and dost thou not control thyself? and now this is nothing but sorrow of heart. Then I was very much alarmed, 3 and I said to the king, Let the king live for ever: why should not my countenance be said, forasmuch as the city, even the home of the sepulchres of my fathers, has been laid waste, and her gates have been devoured with fire? 4 And the king said to me, For what dost thou ask thus? So I prayed to the God of heaven. 5 And I said to the king, If *it seem* good to the king, and if thy servant shall have found favour in thy sight, *I ask* that *thou* wouldest send him into Juda, to the city of the sepulchres of my fathers; then will I rebuild it. 6 And the king, and his concubine that sat next to him, said to me, For how long will thy journey be, and when wilt thou return? and *the proposal* was pleasing before the king, and he sent me away, and I appointed him a time. 7 And I said to the king, If *it seem* good to the king, let him give me letters to the governors beyond the river, so as to forward me till I come to Juda; 8 and a letter to Asaph the keeper of the garden which belongs to the king, that he may give me timber to cover the gates, and for the wall of the city, and for the house into which I shall enter. And the king gave to me, according as the good hand of God *was upon me.* 9 And I came to the governors beyond the river, and I gave them the king's letters. (Now the king had sent with me captains of the army and horsemen.) 10 And Sanaballat the Aronite heard *it*, and Tobia the servant, the Ammonite, and it was grievous to them that a man was come to seek good for the children of Israel. 11 So I came to Jerusalem, and was there three days. 12 And I rose up by night, I and a few men with me; and I told no man what God put into my heart to do with Israel; and there was no beast with me, except the beast which I rode upon. 13 And I went forth by the gate of the valley by night, and to the mouth of the well of fig trees, and to the dung-gate: and I mourned over the wall of Jerusalem which they were destroying, and her gates were devoured with fire. 14 And I passed on to the fountain gate, and to the king's pool; and there was no room for the beast to pass under me. 15 And I went up by the wall of the brook by night, and mourned over the wall, and passed through the gate of the valley, and returned. 16 And the sentinels knew not why I went, nor what I was doing; and until that time I told *it* not to the Jews, or to the priests, or to the nobles, or to the captains, or to the rest *of the men* who wrought the works. 17 Then I said to them, Ye see this evil, in which we are, how Jerusalem is desolate, and her gates have been set on fire: come, and let us build throughout the wall of Jerusalem, and we shall be no longer a reproach. 18 And I told them of the hand of God which was good upon me, also about the words of the king which he spoke to me: and I said, Let us arise and build. And their hands were strengthened for the good *work*. 19 And Sanaballat the Aronite, and Tobia the servant, the Ammonite, and Gesam the Arabian, heard *it*, and they laughed us to scorn, and came to us, and said, What *is* this thing that ye are doing? are ye revolting against the king? 20 And I answered them, and said to them, The God of heaven, he shall prosper us, and we his servants are pure, and we will build: but ye have no part, nor right, nor memorial, in Jerusalem.

Neh.3 1 Then Eliasub the high priest, and his brethren the priests, rose up, and built the sheep-gate; they sanctified it, and set up the doors of it; even to the tower of the hundred they sanctified *it*, to the tower of Anameel. 2 And *they builded* by the side of the men of Jericho, and by the side of the sons of Zacchur, the son of Amari. 3 And the sons of Asana built the fish-gate; they roofed it, and covered in its doors, and bolts, and bars. 4 And next to them *the order* reached to Ramoth the son of Uria, the son of Accos, and next to them Mosollam son of Barachias the son of Mazebel took *his* place: and next to them Sadoc the son of Baana took *his* place. 5 And next to them the Thecoim took *their* place; but the Adorim applied not their neck to their service. 6 And Joida the son of Phasec, and Mesulam son of Basodia, repaired the old gate; they covered it in, and set up its doors, and its bolts, and its bars. 7 And next to them repaired Maltias the Gabaonite, and Evaron the Meronothite, the men of Gabaon and Maspha, to the throne of the governor on this side the river. 8 And next to him Oziel the son of Arachias of the smiths, carried on the repairs: and next to them Ananias the son of one of the apothecaries repaired, and they finished Jerusalem to the broad wall. 9 And next to them repaired Raphaea the son of Sur, the ruler of half the district round about Jerusalem. 10 And next to them repaired Jedaia the son of Eromaph, and *that* in front of his house: and next to him repaired Attuth son of Asabania. 11 And next *to him* repaired Melchias son of Heram, and Asub son of Phaat Moab, even to the tower of the furnaces. 12 And next to him repaired Sallum the son of Alloes, the ruler of half the district round about Jerusalem, he and his daughters. 13 Anun and the inhabitants of Zano repaired the gate of the valley: they built it, and set up its doors, and its bolts, and its bars, and a thousand cubits of the wall as far as the dung-gate. 14 And Melchia the son of Rechab, the ruler of the district round about Beth-accharim, repaired the dung-gate, he and his sons; and they covered it, and set up its doors, and its bolts, and its bars. 15 But Solomon the son of Choleze repaired the gate of the fountain, the ruler

of part of Maspha; he built it, and covered it, and set up its doors and its bars, and the wall of the pool of the skins by the meadow of the king, and as far as the steps that lead down from the city of David. 16 After him repaired Neemias son of Azabuch, ruler of half the district round about Bethsur, as far as the garden of David's sepulchre, and as far as the artificial pool, and as far as the house of the mighty men. 17 After him repaired the Levites, *even* Raum the son of Bani: next to him repaired Asabia, ruler of half the district round about Keila, in his district. 18 And after him repaired his brethren, Benei son of Enadad, ruler of half the district round about Keila. 19 And next to him repaired Azur the son of Joshua, ruler of Masphai, another portion of the tower of ascent, where it meets the corner. 20 After him repaired Baruch the son of Zabu, a second portion, from the corner as far as the door of the house of Eliasub the high priest. 21 After him repaired Meramoth the son of Uria the son of Accos, a second part from the door of the house of Eliasub, to the end of the house of Eliasub. 22 And after him repaired the priests, the men of Ecchechar. 23 And after him repaired Benjamin and Asub over against their house: and after him repaired Azarias son of Maasias the son of Ananias, *the parts* near to his house. 24 After him repaired Bani the son of Adad, another portion from the house of Azaria as far as the corner and to the turning, 25 of Phalach the son of Uzai, opposite the corner, and *where is* also the tower that projects from the king's house, even the upper one of the prison-house: and after him *repaired* Phadaea the son of Phoros. 26 And the Nathinim dwelt in Ophal, as far as the garden of the water-gate eastward, and *there is* the projecting tower. 27 And after them the Thecoim repaired, another portion opposite the great projecting tower, even as far as the wall of Ophla. 28 The priests repaired above the horse-gate, *every* man over against his own house. 29 And after him Sadduc the son of Emmer repaired opposite his own house: and after him repaired Samaea son of Sechenia, guard of the east-gate. 30 After him repaired Anania son of Selemia, and Anom, the sixth son of Seleph, another portion: after him Mesulam the son of Barachia repaired over against his treasury. 31 After him repaired Melchia the son of Sarephi as far as the house of the Nathinim, and the chapmen over against the gate of Maphecad, and as far as the steps of the corner. 32 And between *that and* the sheep-gate the smiths and chapmen repaired.

Neh.4 1 Now it came to pass, when Sanaballat heard that we were building the wall, that it was grievous to him, and he was very angry, and railed against the Jews. 2 And he said before his brethren (that *is* the army of the Samaritans) *Is it true* that these Jews are building their city? do they indeed offer sacrifices? will they prevail? and will they this day restore the stones, after they have been burnt and made a heap of rubbish? 3 And Tobias the Ammanite came near to him, and said to them, Do they sacrifice or eat in their place? shall not a fox go up and pull down their wall of stones? 4 Hear, O our God, for we have become a scorn; and return thou their reproach upon their head, and make them a scorn in a land of captivity, 5 and do not cover *their* iniquity. 6 7 But it came to pass, when Sanaballat and Tobia, and the Arabians, and the Ammanites, heard that the building of the walls of Jerusalem was advancing, *and* that the breaches began to be stopped, that it appeared very grievous to them. 8 And all of them assembled together, to come to fight against Jerusalem, and to destroy it utterly. 9 So we prayed to our God and set watchmen against them day and night, because of them. 10 And Juda said, The strength of the enemies is broken, yet *there is* much rubbish, and we shall not be able to build the wall. 11 And they that afflicted us said, They shall not know, and they shall not see, until we come into the midst of them, and slay them, and cause the work to cease. 12 And it came to pass, when the Jews who lived near them came, that they said to us, They are coming up against us from every quarter. 13 So I set *men* in the lowest part of the place behind the wall in the lurking-places, I even set the people according to their families, with their swords, their spears, and their bows. 14 And I looked, and arose, and said to the nobles, and to the captains, and to the rest of the people, Be not afraid of them: remember our great and terrible God, and fight for your brethren, your sons, your daughters, your wives, and your houses. 15 And it came to pass, when our enemies heard that it was made known to us, and God had frustrated their counsel, that we all returned to the wall, *every* man to his work. 16 And it came to pass from that day *that* half of them that had been driven forth, wrought the work, and half of them kept guard; and *there were* spears, and shields, and bows, and breast-plates, and rulers behind the whole house of Juda, 17 even of them that were building the wall:—and those who carried the burdens *were* under arms: *each* with one hand wrought his work, and with the other held his dart. 18 And the builders *wrought* each man having his sword girt upon his loins, and so they built: and the trumpeter with his trumpet next to him. 19 And I said to the nobles, and to the rulers, and to the rest of the people, The work *is* great and abundant, and we are dispersed upon the wall, each at a great distance from his brother. 20 In whatsoever place ye shall hear the sound of the cornet, thither gather yourselves together to us; and our God shall fight for us. 21 So we *continued* labouring at the work: and half of them held the spears from the rising of the morning until the stars appeared. 22 And at that time I said to the people, Lodge ye every man with his servant in the midst of Jerusalem, and let the night be a watch-time to you, and the day a work-time. 23 And I was *there*, and the watchmen behind me, and there was not a man of us that put off his garments.

Neh.5 1 And the cry of the people and their wives *was* great against their brethren the Jews. 2 And some said, We *are* numerous with our sons and our daughters; so we will take corn, and eat, and live. 3 And some said, *As to* our fields and vineyards and houses, let us pledge *them*, and we will take corn, and eat. 4 And some said, We have borrowed money for the king's tributes: —our fields, and our vineyards, and houses *are pledged*. 5 And now our flesh *is* as the flesh of our brethren, our children *are* as their children: yet, behold, we are reducing our sons and our daughters to slavery, and

some of our daughters are enslaved: and there is no power of our hands, for our fields and our vineyards *belong* to the nobles. 6 And I was much grieved as I heard their cry and these words. 7 And my heart took counsel within me, and I contended against the nobles, and the princes, and I said to them, Should every man demand of his brother what ye demand? And I appointed against them a great assembly, 8 and I said to them, We of our free-will have redeemed our brethren the Jews that were sold to the Gentiles; and do ye sell your brethren? and shall they be delivered to us? And they were silent, and found no answer. 9 And I said, The thing which ye do *is* not good; ye will not so walk in the fear of our God because of the reproach of the Gentiles our enemies. 10 Both my brethren, and my acquaintances, and I, have lent them money and corn: let us now leave off this exaction. 11 Restore to them, I pray, as at this day, their fields, and their vineyards, and their olive-yards, and their houses, and bring forth to them corn and wine and oil of the money. 12 And they said, We will restore, and we will not exact of them; we will do thus as thou sayest. Then I called the priests, and bound them by oath to do according to this word. 13 And I shook out my garment, and said, So may God shake out every man who shall not keep to this word, from his house, and from his labours, he shall be even thus shaken out, as an outcast and empty. And all the congregation said, Amen, and they praised the Lord: and the people did this thing. 14 From the day that he charged me to be their ruler in the land of Juda, from the twentieth year even to the thirty-second year of Arthasastha, twelve years, I and my brethren ate not *provision* extorted from them. 15 But as for the former acts of extortion wherein *those who were* before me oppressed them, they even took of them their last money, forty didrachms for bread and wine; and the *very* outcasts of them exercised authority over the people: but I did not so, because of the fear of God. 16 Also in the work of the wall I treated them not with rigor, I bought not land: and all that were gathered together *came* thither to the work. 17 And the Jews, to *the number of* a hundred and fifty men, besides those coming to us from the nations round about, *were* at my table. 18 And there came *to me* for one day one calf, and I had six choice sheep and a goat; and every ten days wine in abundance of all sorts: yet with these I required not the bread of extortion, because the bondage was heavy upon this people. 19 Remember me, O God, for good, *in* all that I have done to this people.

Neh.6 1 Now it came to pass, when Sanaballat, and Tobias, and Gesam the Arabian, and the rest of our enemies, heard that I had built the wall, and *that* there was no opening left therein; (*but* hitherto I had not set up the doors on the gates;) 2 that Sanaballat and Gesam sent to me, saying, Come and let us meet together in the villages in the plain of Ono. But they *were* plotting to do me mischief. 3 So I sent messengers to them, saying, I am doing a great work, and I shall not be able to come down, lest the work should cease: as soon as I shall have finished it, I will come down to you. 4 And they sent to me *again* to this effect; and I sent them *word* accordingly. 5 Then Sanaballat sent his servant to me with an open letter in his hand. 6 And in it was written, It has been reported among the Gentiles that thou and the Jews are planning to revolt: therefore thou art building the wall, and thou wilt be a king to them. 7 And moreover thou has appointed prophets to thyself, that thou mightest dwell in Jerusalem as a king over Juda: and now these words will be reported to the king. Now then, come, let us take counsel together. 8 And I sent to him, saying, It has not happened according to these words, *even* as thou sayest, for thou framest them falsely out of thy heart. 9 For all were trying to alarm us, saying, Their hands shall be weakened from this work, and it shall not be done. Now therefore I have strengthened my hands. 10 And I came into the house of Semei the son of Dalaia the Son of Metabeel, and he was shut up; and he said, Let us assemble together in the house of God, in the midst of it, and let us shut the doors of it; for they are coming by night to slay thee. 11 And I said, Who is the man that shall enter into the house, that he may live? 12 And I observed, and, behold, God had not sent him, for the prophecy was a fable *devised* against me: 13 and Tobias and Sanaballat had hired against me a multitude, that I might be frightened, and do this, and sin, and become to them an ill name, that they might reproach me. 14 Remember, O God, Tobias and Sanaballat, according to these their deeds, and the prophetess Noadia, and the rest of the prophets who tried to alarm me. 15 So the wall was finished on the twenty-fifth day of the *month* Elul, in fifty-two days. 16 And it came to pass, when all our enemies heard *of it*, that all the nations round about us feared, and great alarm fell upon them, and they knew that it was of our God that this work should be finished. 17 And in those days letters came to Tobias from many nobles of Juda, and those of Tobias came to them. 18 For many in Juda were bound to him by oath, because he was son-in-law of Sechenias the son of Herae; and Jonan his son had taken the daughter of Mesulam the son of Barachia to wife. 19 And they reported his words to me, and carried out my words to him: and Tobias sent letters to terrify me.

Neh.7 1 And it came to pass, when the wall was built, and I had set up the doors, and the porters and the singers and the Levites were appointed, 2 that I gave charge to Ananias my brother, and Ananias the ruler of the palace, over Jerusalem: for he was a true man, and one that feared God beyond many. 3 And I said to them, The gates of Jerusalem shall not be opened till sunrise; and while they are still watching, let the doors be shut, and bolted; and set watches of them that dwell in Jerusalem, *every* man at his post, and *every* man over against his house. 4 Now the city *was* wide and large; and the people *were* few in it, and the houses were not built. 5 And God put *it* into my heart, and I gathered the nobles, and the rulers, and the people, into companies: and I found a register of the company that came up first, and I found written in it as follows: 6 Now these *are* the children of the country, that came up from captivity, of the number which Nabuchodonosor king of Babylon carried away, and they returned to Jerusalem and to Juda, *every* man to his city; 7 with Zorobabel, and Jesus, and Neemia, Azaria, and Reelma, Naemani, Mardochaeus, Balsan, Maspharath, Esdra, Boguia, Inaum, Baana, Masphar, men of the people of Israel. 8 The children of Phoros, two thousand one hundred and seventy-two. 9 The children of Saphatia, three hundred and seventy-two. 10 The children of Era, six hundred and fifty-two. 11 The children of Phaath Moab, with the children of Jesus and Joab, two thousand six hundred and eighteen. 12 The children of Ælam, a thousand two hundred and fifty-four. 13 The children of Zathuia, eight hundred and forty-five. 14 The children of Zacchu, seven hundred and sixty. 15 The children of Banui, six hundred and forty-eight. 16 The children of Bebi, six hundred and twenty-eight. 17 The children of Asgad, two thousand three hundred and twenty-two. 18 The children of Adonicam, six hundred and sixty-seven. 19 The children of Bagoi, two thousand and sixty-seven. 20 The children of Edin, six hundred and fifty-five. 21 The children of Ater, *the son* of Ezekias, ninety-eight. 22 The children of Esam, three hundred and twenty-eight. 23 The children of Besei, three hundred and twenty-four. 24 The children of Ariph, a hundred and twelve: the children of Asen, two hundred and twenty- three. 25 The children of Gabaon, ninety-five. 26 The children of Baethalem, a hundred and twenty-three: the children of Atopha, fifty-six. 27 The children of Anathoth, a hundred and twenty-eight. 28 The men of Bethasmoth, forty-two. 29 The men of Cariatharim, Caphira, and Beroth, seven hundred and forty-three. 30 The men of Arama and Gabaa, six hundred and twenty. 31 The men of Machemas, a hundred and twenty-two. 32 The men of Baethel and Ai, a hundred and twenty-three. 33 The men of Nabia, a hundred an fifty-two. 34 The men of Elamaar, one thousand two hundred and fifty-two. 35 The children of Eram, three hundred and twenty. 36 The children of Jericho, three hundred and forty-five. 37 The children of Lodadid and Ono, seven hundred and twenty-one. 38 The children of Sanana, three thousand nine hundred and thirty. 39 The priests; the sons of Jodae, *pertaining* to the house of Jesus, nine hundred and seventy-three. 40 The children of Emmer, one thousand and fifty-two. 41 The children of Phaseur, one thousand two hundred and forty-seven. 42 The children of Eram, a thousand and seventeen. 43 The Levites; the children of Jesus the son of Cadmiel, with the children of Uduia, seventy- four. 44 The singers; the children of Asaph, a hundred and forty-eight. 45 The porters; the children of Salum, the children of Ater, the children of Telmon, the children of Acub, the children of Atita, the children of Sabi, a hundred and thirty-eight. 46 The Nathinim; the children of Sea, the children of Aspha, the children of Tabaoth, 47 the children of Kiras, the children of Asuia, the children of Phadon, 48 the children of Labana, the children of Agaba, the children of Selmei, 49 the children of Anan, the children of Gadel, the children of Gaar, 50 the children of Raaia, the children of Rasson, the children of Necoda, 51 the children of Gezam, the children of Ozi, the children of Phese, 52 the children of Besi, the children of Meinon, the children of Nephosasi, 53 the children of Bacbuc, the children of Achipha, the children of Arur, 54 the children of Basaloth, the children of Mida, the children of Adasan, 55 the children of Barcue, the children of Sisarath, the children of Thema, 56 the children of Nisia, the children of Atipha. 57 The children of the servants of Solomon; the children of Sutei, the children of Sapharat, the children of Pherida, 58 the children of Jelel, the children of Dorcon, the children of Gadael, 59 the children of Saphatia, the children of Ettel, the children of Phacarath, the children of Sabaim, the children of Emim. 60 All the Nathinim, and children of the servants of Solomon, *were* three hundred and ninety-two. 61 And these went up from Thelmeleth, Thelaresa, Charub, Eron, Jemer: but they could not declare the houses of their families, or their seed, whether they were of Israel. 62 The children of Dalaia, the children of Tobia, the children of Necoda, six hundred and forty-two. 63 And of the priests; the children of Ebia, the children of Acos, the children of Berzelli, for they took wives of the daughters of Berzelli the Galaadite, and they were called by their name. 64 These sought the pedigree of their company, and it was not found, and they were removed *as polluted* from the priesthood. 65 And the Athersastha said, that they should not eat of the most holy things, until a priest should stand up to give light. 66 And all the congregation was about forty-two thousand three hundred and sixty, 67 besides their men-servants and their maid-servants: these were seven thousand three hundred and thirty seven: and the singing-men and singing-women, two hundred and forty-five. 68 69 Two thousand seven hundred asses. 70 And part of the heads of families gave into the treasury to Neemias for the work a thousand pieces of gold, fifty bowls, and thirty priests' *garments*. 71 And *some* of the heads of families gave into the treasuries of the work, twenty thousand pieces of gold, and two thousand three hundred pounds of silver. 72 And the rest of the people gave twenty thousand pieces of gold, and two thousand two hundred pounds of silver, and sixty-seven priests' *garments*. 73 And the priests, and Levites, and porters, and singers, and *some* of the people, and the Nathinim, and all Israel, dwelt in their cities.

Neh.8 1 And the seventh month arrived, and the children of Israel *were settled* in their cities; and all the people were gathered as one man to the broad place before the water-gate, and they told Esdras the scribe to bring the book of the law of Moses, which the Lord commanded Israel. 2 So Esdras the priest brought the law before the congregation both of men and women, and every one who had understanding *was present* to hearken, on the first day of the seventh month. 3 And he read in it from the time of sun-rise to the middle of the day, before the men and the women; and they understood *it*, and the ears of all the people *were attentive* to the book of the law. 4 And Esdras the scribe stood on a wooden stage, and there stood next to him Mattathias, and Samaeas, and Ananias, and Urias, and Chelcia, and Massia, on his right hand; and on his left Phadaeas, and Misael, and Melchias, and Asom, and Asabadma, and Zacharias, and Mesollam. 5 And Esdras opened the book before all the people, for he was above the people; and it came to pass when he had opened it, *that* all the people stood. 6 And Esdras blessed the Lord, the great God: and all the people answered, and said, Amen, lifting up their hands: and they bowed down and worshipped the Lord with their face to the ground. 7 And Jesus and Banaias and Sarabias instructed the people in the law, and the people *stood* in their place. 8 And they read in the book of the law of God, and Esdras taught, and instructed them distinctly in the knowledge of the Lord, and the people understood *the law* in the reading. 9 And Neemias, and Esdras the priest and scribe, and the Levites, and they that instructed the people, spoke and said to all the people, It is a holy day to the Lord our God; do not mourn, nor weep. For all the people wept when they heard the words of the law. 10 And *the governor* said to them, Go, eat the fat, and drink the sweet, and send portions to them that have nothing; for the day is holy to our Lord: and faint not, for the Lord is our strength. 11 And the Levites caused all the people to be silent, saying, Be silent, for *it is* a holy day, and despond not. 12 So all the people departed to eat, and to drink, and to send portions, and to make great mirth, for they understood the words which he made known to them. 13 And on the second day the heads of families assembled with all the people, *also* the priests and Levites, to Esdras the scribe, to attend to all the words of the law. 14 And they found written in the law which the Lord commanded Moses, that the children of Israel should dwell in booths, in the feast in the seventh month: 15 and that they should sound with trumpets in all their cities, and in Jerusalem. And Esdras said, Go forth to the mountain, and bring branches of olive, and branches of cypress trees, and branches of myrtle, and branches of palm trees, and branches of *every* thick tree, to make booths, according to that which was written. 16 And the people went forth, and brought *them*, and made booths for themselves, each one upon his roof, and in their courts, and in the courts of the house of God, and in the streets of the city, and as far as the gate of Ephraim. 17 And all the congregation who had returned from the captivity, made booths, and dwelt in booths: for the children of Israel *had* not done so from the days of Jesus the son of Naue until that day: and there was great joy. 18 And *Esdras* read in the book of the law of God daily, from the first day even to the last day: and they kept the feast seven days; and on the eighth day a solemn assembly, according to the ordinance.

Neh.9 1 Now on the twenty-fourth day of this month the children of Israel assembled with fasting, and in sackcloths, and with ashes on their head. 2 And the children of Israel separated themselves from every stranger, and stood and confessed their sins, and the iniquities of their fathers. 3 And they stood in their place, and read in the book of the law of the Lord their god: and they confessed *their sins* to the Lord, and worshipped the Lord their God. 4 *And* there stood upon the stairs, of the Levites, Jesus, and the sons of Cadmiel, Sechenia the son of Sarabia, sons of Choneni; and they cried with a loud voice to the Lord their God. 5 And the Levites, Jesus and Cadmiel, said, Rise up, bless the Lord our God forever and ever: and let them bless thy glorious name, and exalt it with all blessing and praise. 6 And Esdras said, Thou art the only true Lord; thou madest the heaven, and the heaven of heavens, and all their array, the earth, and all things that are in it, the seas, and all things in them; and thou quickenest all things, and the hosts of heaven worship thee. 7 Thou art the Lord God, thou didst choose Abram, and broughtest him out of the land of the Chaldeans, and gavest him the name of Abraam: 8 and thou foundest his heart faithful before thee, and didst make a covenant with him to give to him and to his seed the land of the Chananites, and the Chettites, and Amorites, and Pherezites, and Jebusites, and Gergesites; and thou hast confirmed thy words, for thou *art* righteous. 9 And thou sawest the affliction of our fathers in Egypt, and thou heardest their cry at the Red Sea. 10 And thou shewedst signs and wonders in Egypt, on Pharao and all his servants, and on all the people of his land: for thou knowest that they behaved insolently against them: and thou madest thyself a name, as at this day. 11 And thou didst cleave the sea before them, and they passed through the midst of the sea on dry land; and thou didst cast into the deep them that were about to pursue them, as a stone in the mighty water. 12 And thou guidedst them by day by a pillar of cloud, and by night by a pillar of fire, to enlighten for them the way wherein they should walk. 13 Also thou camest down upon mount Sina, and thou spakest to them out of heaven, and gavest them right judgments, and laws of truth, ordinances, and good commandments. 14 And thou didst make known to them thy holy sabbath; thou didst enjoin upon them commandments, and ordinances, and a law, by the hand of thy servant Moses. 15 And thou gavest them bread from heaven for their food, and thou broughtest them forth water from a rock for their thirst; and thou badest them go in to inherit the land over which thou stretchedst out thy hand to give *it* them. 16 But they and our fathers behaved proudly, and hardened their neck, and did not hearken to thy commandments, 17 and refused to listen, and remembered not thy wonders which thou wroughtest with them; and they hardened their neck, and appointed a leader to return to their slavery in Egypt: but thou, O God, *art* merciful and compassionate, long-suffering, and abundant in mercy, and thou didst not forsake them. 18 And still farther they even made to themselves a molten calf, and said, These *are* the gods that brought us up out of Egypt: and they wrought great provocations. 19 Yet thou in thy great compassions didst not forsake them in the wilderness: thou didst not turn away from them the pillar of the cloud by day, to guide them in the way, nor the pillar of fire by night, to enlighten for them the way wherein they should walk. 20 And thou gavest thy good Spirit to instruct them, and thou didst not withhold thy manna from their mouth, and gavest them water in their thirst. 21 And thou didst sustain them forty years in the wilderness; thou didst not allow anything to fail them: their garments did not wax old, and their feet were not bruised. 22 Moreover, thou gavest them kingdoms, and didst divide nations to them: and they inherited the land of Seon king of Esebon, and the land of Og king of Basan. 23 And thou didst multiply their children as the stars of heaven, and broughtest them into the land of which thou spokest to their fathers; 24 And they inherited it: and thou didst destroy from before them the dwellers in the land of the Chananites, and thou gavest into their hands them and their kings, and the nations of the land, to do unto them as it pleased them. 25 And they took lofty cities,

and inherited houses full of all good things, wells dug, vineyards, and oliveyards, and every fruit tree in abundance: so they ate, and were filled, and grew fat, and rioted in thy great goodness. 26 But they turned, and revolted from thee, and cast thy law behind their backs; and they slew thy prophets, who testified against them to turn them back to thee, and they wrought great provocations. 27 Then thou gavest them into the hand of them that afflicted them, and they did afflict them: and they cried to thee in the time of their affliction, and thou didst hear them from thy heaven, and in thy great compassions gavest them deliverers, and didst save them from the hand of them that afflicted them. 28 But when they rested, they did evil again before thee: so thou leftest them in the hands of their enemies, and they ruled over them: and they cried again to thee, and thou heardest *them* from heaven, and didst deliver them in thy great compassions. 29 And thou didst testify against them, to bring them back to thy law: but they hearkened not, but sinned against thy commandments and thy judgments, which if a man do, he shall live in them; and they turned their back, and hardened their neck, and heard not. 30 Yet thou didst bear long with them many years, and didst testify to them by thy Spirit by the hand of thy prophets: but they hearkened not; so thou gavest them into the hand of the nations of the land. 31 But thou in thy many mercies didst not appoint them to destruction, and didst not forsake them; for thou art strong, and merciful, and pitiful. 32 And now, O our God, the powerful, the great, the mighty, and the terrible, keeping thy covenant and thy mercy, let not all the trouble seem little in thy sight which has come upon us, and our kings, and our princes, and our priests, and our prophets, and our fathers, and upon all thy people, from the days of the kings of Assur even to this day. 33 But thou *art* righteous in all the things that come upon us; for thou hast wrought faithfully, but we have greatly sinned. 34 And our kings, and our princes, and our priests, and our fathers, have not performed thy law, and have not given heed to thy commandments, and *have not kept* thy testimonies which thou didst testify to them. 35 And they did not serve thee in thy kingdom, and in thy great goodness which thou gavest to them, and in the large and fat land which thou didst furnish before them, and they turned not from their evil devices. 36 Behold, we are servants this day, and *as for* the land which thou gavest to our fathers to eat the fruit of it and the good things of it, behold, we are servants upon it: 37 and its produce *is* abundant for the kings whom thou didst appoint over us because of our sins; and they have dominion over our bodies, and over our cattle, as it pleases them, and we are in great affliction. 38 And in regard to all these circumstances we make a covenant, and write *it*, and our princes, our Levites, *and* our priests, set their seal to *it*.

Neh.10 1 And over them that sealed were Neemias the Artasastha, son of Achalia, and Zedekias, 2 the son of Araea, and Azaria, and Jeremia, 3 Phasur, Amaria, Melchia, 4 Attus, Sebani, Maluch, 5 Iram, Meramoth, Abdia, 6 Daniel, Gannathon, Baruch, 7 Mesulam, Abia, Miamin, 8 Maazia, Belgai, Samaia; these *were* priests. 9 And the Levites; Jesus the son of Azania, Banaiu of the sons of Enadad, Cadmiel

10 and his brethren, Sabania, Oduia, Calitan, Phelia, Anan, 11 Micha, Roob, Asebias, 12 Zacchor, Sarabia, Sebania, 13 Odum, the sons of Banuae. 14 The heads of the people; Phoros, Phaath Moab, Elam, Zathuia, 15 the sons of Bani, Asgad, Bebai, 16 Adania, Bagoi, Hedin 17 Ater, Ezekia, Azur, 18 Oduia, Esam, Besi, 19 Ariph, Anathoth, Nobai, 20 Megaphes, Mesullam, Ezir, 21 Mesozebel, Saduc, Jeddua, 22 Phaltia, Anan, Anaea, 23 Osee, Anania, Asub, 24 Aloes, Phalai, Sobec, 25 Reum, Essabana, Maasia, 26 and Aia, Ænan, Enam, 27 Maluch, Eram, Baana. 28 And the rest of the people, the priests, the Levites, the porters, the singers, the Nathinim, and every one who drew off from the nations of the land to the law of God, their wives, their sons, their daughters, every one who had knowledge and understanding, 29 were urgent with their brethren, and bound them under a curse, and entered into a curse, and into an oath, to walk in the law of God, which was given by the hand of Moses, the servant of God; to keep and to do all the commandments of the Lord, and his judgments, and his ordinances; 30 and that we will not, *they said,*give our daughters to the people of the land, nor will we take their daughters to our sons. 31 And *as for* the people of the land who bring wares and all *manner of* merchandise to sell on the sabbath-day, we *will* not buy of them on the sabbath or on the holy day: and we will leave the seventh year, and the exaction of every debt. 32 And we will impose ordinances upon ourselves, to levy on ourselves the third part of a didrachm yearly for the service of the house of our God; 33 the shewbread, and the continual meat-offering, and for the continual whole-burnt-offering, of the sabbaths, of the new moon, for the feast, and for the holy things, and the sin-offerings, to make atonement for Israel, and for the works of the house of our God. 34 And we cast lots for the office of wood-bearing, *we* the priests, and the Levites, and the people, to bring *wood* into the house of our God, according to the house of our families, at certain set times, year by year, to burn on the altar of the Lord our God, as it is written in the law: 35 and to bring the first-fruits of our land, and the first-fruits of the fruit of every tree, year by year, into the house of the Lord: 36 the first-born of our sons, and of our cattle, as it is written in the law, and the first-born of our herds and of our flocks, to bring to the house of our God, for the priests that minister in the house of our God. 37 And the first-fruits of our corn, and the fruit of every tree, of wine, and of oil, will we bring to the priests to the treasury of the house of God; and a tithe of our land to the Levites: for the Levites themselves shall receive tithes in all the cities of the land we cultivate. 38 And the priest the son of Aaron shall be with the Levites in the tithe of the Levite: and the Levites shall bring up the tenth part of *their* tithe to the house of our God, into the treasuries of the house of God. 39 For the children of Israel and the children of Levi shall bring into the treasuries the first-fruits of the corn, and wine, and oil; and there *are* the holy vessels, and the priests, and the ministers, and the porters, and the singers: and we will not forsake the house of our God.

Neh.11 1 And the chiefs of the people dwelt in Jerusalem: and the rest of the people cast lots, to bring one of *every* ten to dwell in Jerusalem the holy city, and nine parts in the *other* cities. 2 And the people blessed all the men that volunteered to dwell in Jerusalem. 3 Now these *are* the chiefs of the province who dwelt in Jerusalem, and in the cities of Juda; *every* man dwelt in his possession in their cities: Israel, the priests, and the Levites, and the Nathinim, and the children of the servants of Solomon. 4 And there dwelt in Jerusalem *some* of the children of Juda, and of the children of Benjamin. Of the children of Juda; Athaia son of Azia, the son of Zacharia, the son of Samaria, the son of Saphatia, the son of Maleleel, and *some* of the sons of Phares; 5 and Maasia son of Baruch, son of Chalaza, son of Ozia, son of Adaia, son of Joarib, son of Zacharias, son of Seloni. 6 All the sons of Phares who dwelt in Jerusalem *were* four hundred and sixty-eight men of might. 7 And these *were* the children of Benjamin; Selo son of Mesulam, son of Joad, son of Phadaia, son of Coleia, son of Maasias, son of Ethiel, son of Jesia. 8 And after him Gebe, Seli, nine hundred and twenty-eight. 9 And Joel son of Zechri *was* overseer over them: and Juda son of Asana was second in the city. 10 Of the priests: both Jadia son of Joarib, and Jachin. 11 Saraia, son of Elchia, son of Mesulam, son of Sadduc, son of Marioth, son of Ætoth, was over the house of God. 12 And their brethren doing the work of the house were eight hundred and twenty-two: and Adaia son of Jeroam, son of Phalalia, son of Amasi, son of Zacharia, son of Phassur, son of Melchia, 13 and his brethren, chiefs of families, two hundred and forty-two: and Amasia son of Esdriel, son of Mesarimith, son of Emmer, 14 and his brethren, mighty men of war, a hundred and twenty-eight: and *their* overseer *was* Badiel son of *one of the* great men. 15 And of the Levites; Samaia, son of Esricam, 16 17 Matthanias son of Micha, and Jobeb son of Samui, 18 two hundred and eighty-four. 19 And the porters; Acub, Telamin, and their brethren, a hundred and seventy-two. 20 21 22 And the overseer of the Levites *was* the son of Bani, son of Ozi, son of Asabia, the son of Micha. Of the sons of Asaph the singers *some were* over the house of God, 23 For so was the king's commandment concerning them. 24 And Phathaia son of Baseza was in attendance on the king in every matter for the people, 25 and with regard to villages in their country district: and *some* of the children of Juda dwelt in Cariatharboc, 26 and in Jesu, 27 and in Bersabee: 28 29 30 And their villages *were* Lachis and her hands: and they pitched their tents in Bersabee. 31 And the children of Benjamin *dwelt* from Gabaa *to* Machmas. 32 33 34 35 36 And of the Levites there were divisions to Juda *and* to Benjamin.

Neh.12 1 Now these *are* the priests and the Levites that went up with Zorobabel the son of Salathiel and Jesus: Saraia, Jeremia, Esdra, 2 Amaria, Maluch, 3 Sechenia. 4 5 6 7 These *were* the chiefs of the priests, and their brethren in the days of Jesus. 8 And the Levites *were*, Jesus, Banui, Cadmiel, Sarabia, Jodae, Matthania: he *was* over the bands, 9 and his brethren *were appointed* to the daily courses. 10 And Jesus begot Joakim, and Joakim begot Eliasib, and Eliasib *begot* Jodae, 11 and Jodae begot Jonathan, and Jonathan begot Jadu. 12 And in the days of Joakim, his brethren the priests and the heads of families *were, belonging* to Saraia,

Amaria; to Jeremia, Anania; 13 to Esdra, Mesulam; to Amaria, Joanan; 14 to Amaluch, Jonathan; to Sechenia, Joseph; 15 to Are, Mannas; to Marioth, Elcai; 16 to Adadai, Zacharia; to Ganathoth, Mesolam; 17 to Abia, Zechri; to Miamin, Maadai; to Pheleti, *one*; 18 to Balgas, Samue; to Semia, Jonathan; 19 to Joarib, Matthanai; to Edio, Ozi; 20 to Salai, Callai; to Amec, Abed; 21 to Elkia, Asabias; to Jedeiu, Nathanael. 22 The Levites in the days of Eliasib, Joada, and Joa, and Joanan, and Idua, *were* recorded heads of families: also the priests, in the reign of Darius the Persian. 23 And the sons of Levi, heads of families, *were* written in the book of the chronicles, even to the days of Joanan son of Elisue. 24 And the heads of the Levites *were* Asabia, and Sarabia, and Jesu: and the sons of Cadmiel, and their brethren over against them, were to sing hymns of praise, according to the commandment of David the man of God, course by course. 25 When I gathered the porters, 26 *it was* in the days of Joakim son of Jesus, son of Josedec, and in the days of Neemia: and Esdras the priest *was* scribe. 27 And at the dedication of the wall of Jerusalem they sought the Levites in their places, to bring them to Jerusalem, to keep a feast of dedication and gladness with thanksgiving, and they sounded cymbals with songs, and *had* psalteries and harps. 28 And the sons of the singers were assembled both from the neighbourhood round about to Jerusalem, and from the villages, 29 and from the country: for the singers built themselves villages by Jerusalem. 30 And the priests and the Levites purified themselves, and they purified the people, and the porters, and the wall. 31 And they brought up the princes of Juda on the wall, and they appointed two great *companies* for thanksgiving, and they passed on the right hand on the wall of the dung-gate. 32 And after them went Osaia, and half the princes of Juda, 33 and Azarias, and Esdras, and Mesollam, 34 and Juda, and Benjamin, and Samaias and Jeremia. 35 And *some* of the sons of the priest with trumpets, Zacharias son of Jonathan, son of Samaias, son of Matthania, son of Michaia, son of Zacchur, son of Asaph: 36 and his brethren, Samaia, and Oziel, Gelol, Jama, Aia, Nathanael, and Juda, Anani, to praise with the hymns of David the man of God; and Esdras the scribe *was* before them, 37 at the gate, to praise before them, and they went up by the steps of the city of David, in the ascent of the wall, above the house of David, even to the water -gate 38 39 of Ephraim, and to the fish-gate, and by the tower of Anameel, and as far as the sheep-gate. 40 41 42 And the singers were heard, and were numbered. 43 And in that day they offered great sacrifices, and rejoiced; for God had made them very joyful: and their wives and their children rejoiced: and the joy in Jerusalem was heard from afar off. 44 And in that day they appointed men over the treasuries, for the treasures, the first-fruits, and the tithes, and *for* the chiefs of the cities who were assembled among them, *to furnish* portions for the priests and Levites: for *there was* joy in Juda over the priests and over the Levites that waited. 45 And they kept the charges of their God, and the charges of the purification, and *ordered* the singers and the porters, according to the commandments of David and his son Solomon. 46 For in the days of David Asaph was originally first of the singers, and *they sang* hymns and praise to God.

47 And all Israel in the days of Zorobabel, and in the days of Neemias, gave the portions of the singers and the porters, a daily rate: and consecrated them to the Levites: and the Levites consecrated them to the sons of Aaron.

Neh.13 1 In that day they read in the book of Moses in the ears of the people; and it was found written in it, that the Ammonites and Moabites should not enter into the congregation of God for ever; 2 because they met not the children of Israel with bread and water, but hired Balaam against them to curse them: but our God turned the curse into a blessing. 3 And it came to pass, when they heard the law, that they were separated, *even* every alien in Israel. 4 And before this time Eliasib the priest dwelt in the treasury of the house of our God, connected with Tobias; 5 and he made himself a great treasury, and there they were formerly in the habit of bestowing the offerings, and the frankincense, and the vessels, and the tithe of the corn, and the wine, and the oil, the ordered portion of the Levites, and singers, and porters; and the first-fruits of the priests. 6 But in all this *time* I was not in Jerusalem; for in the thirty-second year of Arthasastha king of Babylon I came to the king, and after a certain time I made my request of the king; 7 and I came to Jerusalem, and I understood the mischief which Eliasib had done in the case of Tobias, in making for him a treasury in the court of the house of God. 8 And it appeared very evil to me: so I cast forth all the furniture of the house of Tobias from the treasury. 9 And I gave orders, and they purified the treasuries: and I restored thither the vessels of the house of God, *and* the offerings, and the frankincense. 10 And I understood that the portion of the Levites had not been given: and they had fled every one to his field, the Levites and the singers doing the work. 11 And I strove with the commanders, and said, Wherefore has the house of God been abandoned? and I assembled them, and set them in their place. 12 And all Juda brought a tithe of the wheat and the wine and the oil into the treasuries, 13 to the charge of Selemia the priest, and Sadoc the scribe, and Phadaea of the Levites: and next to them *was* Anan the son of Zacchur, son of Matthanias; for they were accounted faithful: *it was* their office to distribute to their brethren. 14 Remember me, O God, in this, and let not my kindness be forgotten which I have wrought in *regard to* the house of the Lord God. 15 In those days I saw in Juda *men* treading wine-presses on the sabbath, and carrying sheaves, and loading asses with both wine, and grapes, and figs, and every *kind of* burden, and bringing them into Jerusalem on the sabbath-day: 16 and I testified in the day of their sale. Also their dwelt in it *men* bringing fish, and selling every *kind of* merchandise to the children of Juda and in Jerusalem on the sabbath. 17 And I strove with the free children of Juda, and said to them, What *is* this evil thing which ye do, and profane the sabbath-day? 18 Did not your fathers thus, and our God brought upon them and upon us and upon this city all these evils? and do ye bring additional wrath upon Israel by profaning the sabbath? 19 And it came to pass, when the gates were set up in Jerusalem, before the sabbath, that I spoke, and they shut the gates; and I gave orders that they should not be opened till after the sabbath:

and I set *some* of my servants at the gates, that none should bring *in* burdens on the sabbath-day. 20 So all *the merchants* lodged, and carried on traffic without Jerusalem once or twice. 21 Then I testified against them, and said to them, Why do ye lodge in front of the wall? if ye do so again, I will stretch out my hand upon you. From that time they came not on the sabbath. 22 and I told the Levites who were purifying themselves, and came and kept the gates, that they should sanctify the sabbath-day. Remember me, O God, for these things, and spare me according to the abundance of thy mercy. 23 And in those days I saw the Jews who had married women of Ashdod, of Ammon, *and* of Moab: 24 and their children spoke half in the language of Ashdod, and did not know how to speak in the Jewish language. 25 And I strove with them and cursed them; and I smote some of them, and plucked off their hair, and made them swear by God, *saying,* Ye shall not give your daughters to their sons, and ye shall not take of their daughters to your sons. 26 Did not Solomon king of Israel sin thus? though there was no king like him among many nations, and he was beloved of God, and God made him king over all Israel; yet strange women turned him aside. 27 So we will not hearken to you to do all this evil, to break covenant with our God, —to marry strange wives. 28 and Elisub the high priest, *one* of the sons of Joada, *being* son-in-law of Sanaballat the Uranite, I chased him away from me. 29 Remember them, O God, for their *false* connection with the priesthood, and *the breaking* the covenant of the priesthood, and *for defiling* the Levites. 30 So I purged them from all foreign connection, and established courses for the priests and the Levites, *every* man according to his work. 31 And the offering of the wood-bearers *was* at certain set times, and in the *times of the* first-fruits. Remember me, O our God, for good.

TOBIT

Tob.1 1 The book of the words of Tobit, son of Tobiel, the son of Ananiel, the son of Aduel, the son of Gabael, of the seed of Asael, of the tribe of Nephthali; 2 Who in the time of Enemessar king of the Assyrians was led captive out of Thisbe, which is at the right hand of that city, which is called properly Nephthali in Galilee above Aser. 3 I Tobit have walked all the days of my life in the ways of truth and justice, and I did many almsdeeds to my brethren, and my nation, who came with me to Nineve, into the land of the Assyrians. 4 And when I was in mine own country, in the land of Israel being but young, all the tribe of Nephthali my father fell from the house of Jerusalem, which was chosen out of all the tribes of Israel, that all the tribes should sacrifice there, where the temple of the habitation of the most High was consecrated and built for all ages. 5 Now all the tribes which together revolted, and the house of my father Nephthali, sacrificed unto the heifer Baal. 6 But I alone went often to Jerusalem at the feasts, as it was ordained unto all the people of Israel by an everlasting decree, having the firstfruits and tenths of increase, with that which was first shorn; and them gave I at the altar to the priests the children of Aaron. 7 The first tenth part of all increase I gave to the sons of Aaron, who ministered at Jerusalem: another tenth part I sold away, and went, and spent it every year at Jerusalem: 8 And the third I gave unto them to whom it was meet, as Debora my father's mother had commanded me, because I was left an orphan by my father. 9 Furthermore, when I was come to the age of a man, I married Anna of mine own kindred, and of her I begat Tobias. 10 And when we were carried away captives to Nineve, all my brethren and those that were of my kindred did eat of the bread of the Gentiles. 11 But I kept myself from eating; 12 Because I remembered God with all my heart. 13 And the most High gave me grace and favour before Enemessar, so that I was his purveyor. 14 And I went into Media, and left in trust with Gabael, the brother of Gabrias, at Rages a city of Media ten talents of silver. 15 Now when Enemessar was dead, Sennacherib his son reigned in his stead; whose estate was troubled, that I could not go into Media. 16 And in the time of Enemessar I gave many alms to my brethren, and gave my bread to the hungry, 17 And my clothes to the naked: and if I saw any of my nation dead, or cast about the walls of Nineve, I buried him. 18 And if the king Sennacherib had slain any, when he was come, and fled from Judea, I buried them privily; for in his wrath he killed many; but the bodies were not found, when they were sought for of the king. 19 And when one of the Ninevites went and complained of me to the king, that I buried them, and hid myself; understanding that I was sought for to be put to death, I withdrew myself for fear. 20 Then all my goods were forcibly taken away, neither was there any thing left me, beside my wife Anna and my son Tobias. 21 And there passed not five and fifty days, before two of his sons killed him, and they fled into the mountains of Ararath; and Sarchedonus his son reigned in his stead; who appointed over his father's accounts, and over all his affairs, Achiacharus my brother Anael's son. 22 And Achiacharus intreating for me, I returned to Nineve. Now Achiacharus was cupbearer, and keeper of the signet, and steward, and overseer of the accounts: and Sarchedonus appointed him next unto him: and he was my brother's son.

Tob.2 1 Now when I was come home again, and my wife Anna was restored unto me, with my son Tobias, in the feast of Pentecost, which is the holy feast of the seven weeks, there was a good dinner prepared me, in the which I sat down to eat. 2 And when I saw abundance of meat, I said to my son, Go and bring what poor man soever thou shalt find out of our brethren, who is mindful of the Lord; and, lo, I tarry for thee. 3 But he came again, and said, Father, one of our nation is strangled, and is cast out in the marketplace. 4 Then before I had tasted of any meat, I started up, and took him up into a room until the going down of the sun. 5 Then I returned, and washed myself, and ate my meat in heaviness, 6 Remembering that prophecy of Amos, as he said, Your feasts shall be turned into mourning, and all your mirth into lamentation. 7 Therefore I wept: and after the going down of the sun I went and made a grave, and buried him. 8 But my neighbours mocked me, and said, This man is not yet afraid to be put to death for this matter: who fled away; and yet, lo, he burieth the dead again. 9 The same night also I returned from the burial, and slept by the wall of my courtyard, being polluted and my face was uncovered: 10 And I knew not that there were sparrows in the wall, and mine eyes being open, the sparrows muted warm dung into mine eyes, and a whiteness came in mine eyes: and I went to the physicians, but they helped me not: moreover Achiacharus did nourish me, until I went into Elymais. 11 And my wife Anna did take women's works to do. 12 And when she had sent them home to the owners, they paid her wages, and gave her also besides a kid. 13 And when it was in my house, and began to cry, I said unto her, From whence is this kid? is it not stolen? render it to the owners; for it is not lawful to eat any thing that is stolen. 14 But she replied upon me, It was given for a gift more than the wages. Howbeit I did not believe her, but bade her render it to the owners: and I was abashed at her. But she replied upon me, Where are thine alms and thy righteous deeds? behold, thou and all thy works are known.

Tob.3 1 Then I being grieved did weep, and in my sorrow prayed, saying, 2 O Lord, thou art just, and all thy works and all thy ways are mercy and truth, and thou judgest truly and justly for ever. 3 Remember me, and look on me, punish me not for my sins and ignorances, and the sins of my fathers, who have sinned before thee: 4 For they obeyed not thy commandments: wherefore thou hast delivered us for a spoil, and unto captivity, and unto death, and for a proverb of reproach to all the nations among whom we are dispersed. 5 And now thy judgments are many and true: deal with me according to my sins and my fathers': because we have not kept thy commandments, neither have walked in truth before thee. 6 Now therefore deal with me as seemeth best unto thee, and command my spirit to be taken from me, that I may be dissolved, and become earth: for it is profitable for me to die rather than to live, because I have heard false reproaches, and have much sorrow: command therefore that I may now be delivered out of this distress, and go into the everlasting place: turn not thy face away from me. 7 It came to pass the same day, that in Ecbatane a city of Media Sara the daughter of Raguel was also reproached by her father's maids; 8 Because that she had been married to seven husbands, whom Asmodeus the evil spirit had killed, before they had lain with her. Dost thou not know, said they, that thou hast strangled thine husbands? thou hast had already seven husbands, neither wast thou named after any of them. 9 Wherefore dost thou beat us for them? if they be dead, go thy ways after them, let us never see of thee either son or daughter. 10 When she heard these things, she was very sorrowful, so that she thought to have strangled herself; and she said, I am the only daughter of my father, and if I do this, it shall be a reproach unto him, and I shall bring his old age with sorrow unto the grave. 11 Then she prayed toward the window, and said, Blessed art thou, O Lord my God, and thine holy and glorious name is blessed and honourable for ever: let all thy works praise thee for ever. 12 And now, O Lord, I set I mine eyes and my face toward thee, 13 And say, Take me out of the earth, that I may hear no more the reproach. 14 Thou knowest, Lord, that I am pure from all sin with man, 15 And

that I never polluted my name, nor the name of my father, in the land of my captivity: I am the only daughter of my father, neither hath he any child to be his heir, neither any near kinsman, nor any son of his alive, to whom I may keep myself for a wife: my seven husbands are already dead; and why should I live? but if it please not thee that I should die, command some regard to be had of me, and pity taken of me, that I hear no more reproach. 16 So the prayers of them both were heard before the majesty of the great God. 17 And Raphael was sent to heal them both, that is, to scale away the whiteness of Tobit's eyes, and to give Sara the daughter of Raguel for a wife to Tobias the son of Tobit; and to bind Asmodeus the evil spirit; because she belonged to Tobias by right of inheritance. The selfsame time came Tobit home, and entered into his house, and Sara the daughter of Raguel came down from her upper chamber.

Tob.4 1 In that day Tobit remembered the money which he had committed to Gabael in Rages of Media, 2 And said with himself, I have wished for death; wherefore do I not call for my son Tobias that I may signify to him of the money before I die? 3 And when he had called him, he said, My son, when I am dead, bury me; and despise not thy mother, but honour her all the days of thy life, and do that which shall please her, and grieve her not. 4 Remember, my son, that she saw many dangers for thee, when thou wast in her womb: and when she is dead, bury her by me in one grave. 5 My son, be mindful of the Lord our God all thy days, and let not thy will be set to sin, or to transgress his commandments: do uprightly all thy life long, and follow not the ways of unrighteousness. 6 For if thou deal truly, thy doings shall prosperously succeed to thee, and to all them that live justly. 7 Give alms of thy substance; and when thou givest alms, let not thine eye be envious, neither turn thy face from any poor, and the face of God shall not be turned away from thee. 8 If thou hast abundance give alms accordingly: if thou have but a little, be not afraid to give according to that little: 9 For thou layest up a good treasure for thyself against the day of necessity. 10 Because that alms do deliver from death, and suffereth not to come into darkness. 11 For alms is a good gift unto all that give it in the sight of the most High. 12 Beware of all whoredom, my son, and chiefly take a wife of the seed of thy fathers, and take not a strange woman to wife, which is not of thy father's tribe: for we are the children of the prophets, Noe, Abraham, Isaac, and Jacob: remember, my son, that our fathers from the beginning, even that they all married wives of their own kindred, and were blessed in their children, and their seed shall inherit the land. 13 Now therefore, my son, love thy brethren, and despise not in thy heart thy brethren, the sons and daughters of thy people, in not taking a wife of them: for in pride is destruction and much trouble, and in lewdness is decay and great want: for lewdness is the mother of famine. 14 Let not the wages of any man, which hath wrought for thee, tarry with thee, but give him it out of hand: for if thou serve God, he will also repay thee: be circumspect my son, in all things thou doest, and be wise in all thy conversation. 15 Do that to no man which thou hatest: drink not wine to make thee drunken:

neither let drunkenness go with thee in thy journey. 16 Give of thy bread to the hungry, and of thy garments to them that are naked; and according to thine abundance give alms: and let not thine eye be envious, when thou givest alms. 17 Pour out thy bread on the burial of the just, but give nothing to the wicked. 18 Ask counsel of all that are wise, and despise not any counsel that is profitable. 19 Bless the Lord thy God alway, and desire of him that thy ways may be directed, and that all thy paths and counsels may prosper: for every nation hath not counsel; but the Lord himself giveth all good things, and he humbleth whom he will, as he will; now therefore, my son, remember my commandments, neither let them be put out of thy mind. 20 And now I signify this to they that I committed ten talents to Gabael the son of Gabrias at Rages in Media. 21 And fear not, my son, that we are made poor: for thou hast much wealth, if thou fear God, and depart from all sin, and do that which is pleasing in his sight.

Tob.5 1 Tobias then answered and said, Father, I will do all things which thou hast commanded me: 2 But how can I receive the money, seeing I know him not? 3 Then he gave him the handwriting, and said unto him, Seek thee a man which may go with thee, whiles I yet live, and I will give him wages: and go and receive the money. 4 Therefore when he went to seek a man, he found Raphael that was an angel. 5 But he knew not; and he said unto him, Canst thou go with me to Rages? and knowest thou those places well? 6 To whom the angel said, I will go with thee, and I know the way well: for I have lodged with our brother Gabael. 7 Then Tobias said unto him, Tarry for me, till I tell my father. 8 Then he said unto him, Go and tarry not. So he went in and said to his father, Behold, I have found one which will go with me. Then he said, Call him unto me, that I may know of what tribe he is, and whether he be a trusty man to go with thee. 9 So he called him, and he came in, and they saluted one another. 10 Then Tobit said unto him, Brother, shew me of what tribe and family thou art. 11 To whom he said, Dost thou seek for a tribe or family, or an hired man to go with thy son? Then Tobit said unto him, I would know, brother, thy kindred and name. 12 Then he said, I am Azarias, the son of Ananias the great, and of thy brethren. 13 Then Tobit said, Thou art welcome, brother; be not now angry with me, because I have enquired to know thy tribe and thy family; for thou art my brother, of an honest and good stock: for I know Ananias and Jonathas, sons of that great Samaias, as we went together to Jerusalem to worship, and offered the firstborn, and the tenths of the fruits; and they were not seduced with the error of our brethren: my brother, thou art of a good stock. 14 But tell me, what wages shall I give thee? wilt thou a drachm a day, and things necessary, as to mine own son? 15 Yea, moreover, if ye return safe, I will add something to thy wages. 16 So they were well pleased. Then said he to Tobias, Prepare thyself for the journey, and God send you a good journey. And when his son had prepared all things far the journey, his father said, Go thou with this man, and God, which dwelleth in heaven, prosper your journey, and the angel of God keep you company. So they went forth both,

and the young man's dog with them. 17 But Anna his mother wept, and said to Tobit, Why hast thou sent away our son? is he not the staff of our hand, in going in and out before us? 18 Be not greedy to add money to money: but let it be as refuse in respect of our child. 19 For that which the Lord hath given us to live with doth suffice us. 20 Then said Tobit to her, Take no care, my sister; he shall return in safety, and thine eyes shall see him. 21 For the good angel will keep him company, and his journey shall be prosperous, and he shall return safe. 22 Then she made an end of weeping.

Tob.6 1 And as they went on their journey, they came in the evening to the river Tigris, and they lodged there. 2 And when the young man went down to wash himself, a fish leaped out of the river, and would have devoured him. 3 Then the angel said unto him, Take the fish. And the young man laid hold of the fish, and drew it to land. 4 To whom the angel said, Open the fish, and take the heart and the liver and the gall, and put them up safely. 5 So the young man did as the angel commanded him; and when they had roasted the fish, they did eat it: then they both went on their way, till they drew near to Ecbatane. 6 Then the young man said to the angel, Brother Azarias, to what use is the heart and the liver and the gal of the fish? 7 And he said unto him, Touching the heart and the liver, if a devil or an evil spirit trouble any, we must make a smoke thereof before the man or the woman, and the party shall be no more vexed. 8 As for the gall, it is good to anoint a man that hath whiteness in his eyes, and he shall be healed. 9 And when they were come near to Rages, 10 The angel said to the young man, Brother, to day we shall lodge with Raguel, who is thy cousin; he also hath one only daughter, named Sara; I will speak for her, that she may be given thee for a wife. 11 For to thee doth the right of her appertain, seeing thou only art of her kindred. 12 And the maid is fair and wise: now therefore hear me, and I will speak to her father; and when we return from Rages we will celebrate the marriage: for I know that Raguel cannot marry her to another according to the law of Moses, but he shall be guilty of death, because the right of inheritance doth rather appertain to thee than to any other. 13 Then the young man answered the angel, I have heard, brother Azarias that this maid hath been given to seven men, who all died in the marriage chamber. 14 And now I am the only son of my father, and I am afraid, lest if I go in unto her, I die, as the other before: for a wicked spirit loveth her, which hurteth no body, but those which come unto her; wherefore I also fear lest I die, and bring my father's and my mother's life because of me to the grave with sorrow: for they have no other son to bury them. 15 Then the angel said unto him, Dost thou not remember the precepts which thy father gave thee, that thou shouldest marry a wife of thine own kindred? wherefore hear me, O my brother; for she shall be given thee to wife; and make thou no reckoning of the evil spirit; for this same night shall she be given thee in marriage. 16 And when thou shalt come into the marriage chamber, thou shalt take the ashes of perfume, and shalt lay upon them some of the heart and liver of the fish, and shalt make a smoke with it: 17 And the devil shall smell it, and flee away, and never come again any more: but when thou shalt come to her, rise up both of you, and pray to God which is merciful, who will have pity on you, and save you: fear not, for she is appointed unto thee from the beginning; and thou shalt preserve her, and she shall go with thee. Moreover I suppose that she shall bear thee children. Now when Tobias had heard these things, he loved her, and his heart was effectually joined to her.

Tob.7 1 And when they were come to Ecbatane, they came to the house of Raguel, and Sara met them: and after they had saluted one another, she brought them into the house. 2 Then said Raguel to Edna his wife, How like is this young man to Tobit my cousin! 3 And Raguel asked them, From whence are ye, brethren? To whom they said, We are of the sons of Nephthalim, which are captives in Nineve. 4 Then he said to them, Do ye know Tobit our kinsman? And they said, We know him. Then said he, Is he in good health? 5 And they said, He is both alive, and in good health: and Tobias said, He is my father. 6 Then Raguel leaped up, and kissed him, and wept, 7 And blessed him, and said unto him, Thou art the son of an honest and good man. But when he had heard that Tobit was blind, he was sorrowful, and wept. 8 And likewise Edna his wife and Sara his daughter wept. Moreover they entertained them cheerfully; and after that they had killed a ram of the flock, they set store of meat on the table. Then said Tobias to Raphael, Brother Azarias, speak of those things of which thou didst talk in the way, and let this business be dispatched. 9 So he communicated the matter with Raguel: and Raguel said to Tobias, Eat and drink, and make merry: 10 For it is meet that thou shouldest marry my daughter: nevertheless I will declare unto thee the truth. 11 I have given my daughter in marriage to seven men, who died that night they came in unto her: nevertheless for the present be merry. But Tobias said, I will eat nothing here, till we agree and swear one to another. 12 Raguel said, Then take her from henceforth according to the manner, for thou art her cousin, and she is thine, and the merciful God give you good success in all things. 13 Then he called his daughter Sara, and she came to her father, and he took her by the hand, and gave her to be wife to Tobias, saying, Behold, take her after the law of Moses, and lead her away to thy father. And he blessed them; 14 And called Edna his wife, and took paper, and did write an instrument of covenants, and sealed it. 15 Then they began to eat. 16 After Raguel called his wife Edna, and said unto her, Sister, prepare another chamber, and bring her in thither. 17 Which when she had done as he had bidden her, she brought her thither: and she wept, and she received the tears of her daughter, and said unto her, 18 Be of good comfort, my daughter; the Lord of heaven and earth give thee joy for this thy sorrow: be of good comfort, my daughter.

Tob.8 1 And when they had supped, they brought Tobias in unto her. 2 And as he went, he remembered the words of Raphael, and took the ashes of the perfumes, and put the heart and the liver of the fish thereupon, and made a smoke therewith. 3 The which smell when the evil spirit had smelled, he fled into the utmost parts of Egypt, and the angel bound him. 4 And after that they were both shut in

together, Tobias rose out of the bed, and said, Sister, arise, and let us pray that God would have pity on us. 5 Then began Tobias to say, Blessed art thou, O God of our fathers, and blessed is thy holy and glorious name for ever; let the heavens bless thee, and all thy creatures. 6 Thou madest Adam, and gavest him Eve his wife for an helper and stay: of them came mankind: thou hast said, It is not good that man should be alone; let us make unto him an aid like unto himself. 7 And now, O Lord, I take not this my sister for lush but uprightly: therefore mercifully ordain that we may become aged together. 8 And she said with him, Amen. 9 So they slept both that night. And Raguel arose, and went and made a grave, 10 Saying, I fear lest he also be dead. 11 But when Raguel was come into his house, 12 He said unto his wife Edna. Send one of the maids, and let her see whether he be alive: if he be not, that we may bury him, and no man know it. 13 So the maid opened the door, and went in, and found them both asleep, 14 And came forth, and told them that he was alive. 15 Then Raguel praised God, and said, O God, thou art worthy to be praised with all pure and holy praise; therefore let thy saints praise thee with all thy creatures; and let all thine angels and thine elect praise thee for ever. 16 Thou art to be praised, for thou hast made me joyful; and that is not come to me which I suspected; but thou hast dealt with us according to thy great mercy. 17 Thou art to be praised because thou hast had mercy of two that were the only begotten children of their fathers: grant them mercy, O Lord, and finish their life in health with joy and mercy. 18 Then Raguel bade his servants to fill the grave. 19 And he kept the wedding feast fourteen days. 20 For before the days of the marriage were finished, Raguel had said unto him by an oath, that he should not depart till the fourteen days of the marriage were expired; 21 And then he should take the half of his goods, and go in safety to his father; and should have the rest when I and my wife be dead.

Tob.9 1 Then Tobias called Raphael, and said unto him, 2 Brother Azarias, take with thee a servant, and two camels, and go to Rages of Media to Gabael, and bring me the money, and bring him to the wedding. 3 For Raguel hath sworn that I shall not depart. 4 But my father counteth the days; and if I tarry long, he will be very sorry. 5 So Raphael went out, and lodged with Gabael, and gave him the handwriting: who brought forth bags which were sealed up, and gave them to him. 6 And early in the morning they went forth both together, and came to the wedding: and Tobias blessed his wife.

Tob.10 1 Now Tobit his father counted every day: and when the days of the journey were expired, and they came not, 2 Then Tobit said, Are they detained? or is Gabael dead, and there is no man to give him the money? 3 Therefore he was very sorry. 4 Then his wife said unto him, My son is dead, seeing he stayeth long; and she began to wail him, and said, 5 Now I care for nothing, my son, since I have let thee go, the light of mine eyes. 6 To whom Tobit said, Hold thy peace, take no care, for he is safe. 7 But she said, Hold thy peace, and deceive me not; my son is dead. And she went out every day into the way which they went, and did eat no meat on the daytime, and ceased not whole nights to bewail her son Tobias, until the fourteen days of the wedding were expired, which Raguel had sworn that he should spend there. Then Tobias said to Raguel, 8 Let me go, for my father and my mother look no more to see me. 9 But his father in law said unto him, Tarry with me, and I will send to thy father, and they shall declare unto him how things go with thee. 10 But Tobias said, No; but let me go to my father. 11 Then Raguel arose, and gave him Sara his wife, and half his goods, servants, and cattle, and money: 12 And he blessed them, and sent them away, saying, The God of heaven give you a prosperous journey, my children. 13 And he said to his daughter, Honour thy father and thy mother in law, which are now thy parents, that I may hear good report of thee. And he kissed her. Edna also said to Tobias, The Lord of heaven restore thee, my dear brother, and grant that I may see thy children of my daughter Sara before I die, that I may rejoice before the Lord: behold, I commit my daughter unto thee of special trust; where are do not entreat her evil.

Tob.11 1 After these things Tobias went his way, praising God that he had given him a prosperous journey, and blessed Raguel and Edna his wife, and went on his way till they drew near unto Nineve. 2 Then Raphael said to Tobias, Thou knowest, brother, how thou didst leave thy father: 3 Let us haste before thy wife, and prepare the house. 4 And take in thine hand the gall of the fish. So they went their way, and the dog went after them. 5 Now Anna sat looking about toward the way for her son. 6 And when she espied him coming, she said to his father, Behold, thy son cometh, and the man that went with him. 7 Then said Raphael, I know, Tobias, that thy father will open his eyes. 8 Therefore anoint thou his eyes with the gall, and being pricked therewith, he shall rub, and the whiteness shall fall away, and he shall see thee. 9 Then Anna ran forth, and fell upon the neck of her son, and said unto him, Seeing I have seen thee, my son, from henceforth I am content to die. And they wept both. 10 Tobit also went forth toward the door, and stumbled: but his son ran unto him, 11 And took hold of his father: and he strake of the gall on his fathers' eyes, saying, Be of good hope, my father. 12 And when his eyes began to smart, he rubbed them; 13 And the whiteness pilled away from the corners of his eyes: and when he saw his son, he fell upon his neck. 14 And he wept, and said, Blessed art thou, O God, and blessed is thy name for ever; and blessed are all thine holy angels: 15 For thou hast scourged, and hast taken pity on me: for, behold, I see my son Tobias. And his son went in rejoicing, and told his father the great things that had happened to him in Media. 16 Then Tobit went out to meet his daughter in law at the gate of Nineve, rejoicing and praising God: and they which saw him go marvelled, because he had received his sight. 17 But Tobias gave thanks before them, because God had mercy on him. And when he came near to Sara his daughter in law, he blessed her, saying, Thou art welcome, daughter: God be blessed, which hath brought thee unto us, and blessed be thy father and thy mother. And there was joy among all his brethren which were at Nineve. 18 And

Achiacharus, and Nasbas his brother's son, came: 19 And Tobias' wedding was kept seven days with great joy.

Tob.12 1 Then Tobit called his son Tobias, and said unto him, My son, see that the man have his wages, which went with thee, and thou must give him more. 2 And Tobias said unto him, O father, it is no harm to me to give him half of those things which I have brought: 3 For he hath brought me again to thee in safety, and made whole my wife, and brought me the money, and likewise healed thee. 4 Then the old man said, It is due unto him. 5 So he called the angel, and he said unto him, Take half of all that ye have brought and go away in safety. 6 Then he took them both apart, and said unto them, Bless God, praise him, and magnify him, and praise him for the things which he hath done unto you in the sight of all that live. It is good to praise God, and exalt his name, and honourably to shew forth the works of God; therefore be not slack to praise him. 7 It is good to keep close the secret of a king, but it is honourable to reveal the works of God. Do that which is good, and no evil shall touch you. 8 Prayer is good with fasting and alms and righteousness. A little with righteousness is better than much with unrighteousness. It is better to give alms than to lay up gold: 9 For alms doth deliver from death, and shall purge away all sin. Those that exercise alms and righteousness shall be filled with life: 10 But they that sin are enemies to their own life. 11 Surely I will keep close nothing from you. For I said, It was good to keep close the secret of a king, but that it was honourable to reveal the works of God. 12 Now therefore, when thou didst pray, and Sara thy daughter in law, I did bring the remembrance of your prayers before the Holy One: and when thou didst bury the dead, I was with thee likewise. 13 And when thou didst not delay to rise up, and leave thy dinner, to go and cover the dead, thy good deed was not hid from me: but I was with thee. 14 And now God hath sent me to heal thee and Sara thy daughter in law. 15 I am Raphael, one of the seven holy angels, which present the prayers of the saints, and which go in and out before the glory of the Holy One. 16 Then they were both troubled, and fell upon their faces: for they feared. 17 But he said unto them, Fear not, for it shall go well with you; praise God therefore. 18 For not of any favour of mine, but by the will of our God I came; wherefore praise him for ever. 19 All these days I did appear unto you; but I did neither eat nor drink, but ye did see a vision. 20 Now therefore give God thanks: for I go up to him that sent me; but write all things which are done in a book. 21 And when they arose, they saw him no more. 22 Then they confessed the great and wonderful works of God, and how the angel of the Lord had appeared unto them.

Tob.13 1 Then Tobit wrote a prayer of rejoicing, and said, Blessed be God that liveth for ever, and blessed be his kingdom. 2 For he doth scourge, and hath mercy: he leadeth down to hell, and bringeth up again: neither is there any that can avoid his hand. 3 Confess him before the Gentiles, ye children of Israel: for he hath scattered us among them. 4 There declare his greatness, and extol him before all the living: for he is our Lord, and he is the God our Father for ever. 5 And he will scourge us for our iniquities, and will have mercy again, and will gather us out of all nations, among whom he hath scattered us. 6 If ye turn to him with your whole heart, and with your whole mind, and deal uprightly before him, then will he turn unto you, and will not hide his face from you. Therefore see what he will do with you, and confess him with your whole mouth, and praise the Lord of might, and extol the everlasting King. In the land of my captivity do I praise him, and declare his might and majesty to a sinful nation. O ye sinners, turn and do justice before him: who can tell if he will accept you, and have mercy on you? 7 I will extol my God, and my soul shall praise the King of heaven, and shall rejoice in his greatness. 8 Let all men speak, and let all praise him for his righteousness. 9 O Jerusalem, the holy city, he will scourge thee for thy children's works, and will have mercy again on the sons of the righteous. 10 Give praise to the Lord, for he is good: and praise the everlasting King, that his tabernacle may be builded in thee again with joy, and let him make joyful there in thee those that are captives, and love in thee for ever those that are miserable. 11 Many nations shall come from far to the name of the Lord God with gifts in their hands, even gifts to the King of heaven; all generations shall praise thee with great joy. 12 Cursed are all they which hate thee, and blessed shall all be which love thee for ever. 13 Rejoice and be glad for the children of the just: for they shall be gathered together, and shall bless the Lord of the just. 14 O blessed are they which love thee, for they shall rejoice in thy peace: blessed are they which have been sorrowful for all thy scourges; for they shall rejoice for thee, when they have seen all thy glory, and shall be glad for ever. 15 Let my soul bless God the great King. 16 For Jerusalem shall be built up with sapphires and emeralds, and precious stone: thy walls and towers and battlements with pure gold. 17 And the streets of Jerusalem shall be paved with beryl and carbuncle and stones of Ophir. 18 And all her streets shall say, Alleluia; and they shall praise him, saying, Blessed be God, which hath extolled it for ever.

Tob.14 1 So Tobit made an end of praising God. 2 And he was eight and fifty years old when he lost his sight, which was restored to him after eight years: and he gave alms, and he increased in the fear of the Lord God, and praised him. 3 And when he was very aged he called his son, and the sons of his son, and said to him, My son, take thy children; for, behold, I am aged, and am ready to depart out of this life. 4 Go into Media my son, for I surely believe those things which Jonas the prophet spake of Nineve, that it shall be overthrown; and that for a time peace shall rather be in Media; and that our brethren shall lie scattered in the earth from that good land: and Jerusalem shall be desolate, and the house of God in it shall be burned, and shall be desolate for a time; 5 And that again God will have mercy on them, and bring them again into the land, where they shall build a temple, but not like to the first, until the time of that age be fulfilled; and afterward they shall return from all places of their captivity, and build up Jerusalem gloriously, and the house of God shall be built in it for ever with a glorious building, as the prophets have spoken thereof. 6 And all

nations shall turn, and fear the Lord God truly, and shall bury their idols. 7 So shall all nations praise the Lord, and his people shall confess God, and the Lord shall exalt his people; and all those which love the Lord God in truth and justice shall rejoice, shewing mercy to our brethren. 8 And now, my son, depart out of Nineve, because that those things which the prophet Jonas spake shall surely come to pass. 9 But keep thou the law and the commandments, and shew thyself merciful and just, that it may go well with thee. 10 And bury me decently, and thy mother with me; but tarry no longer at Nineve. Remember, my son, how Aman handled Achiacharus that brought him up, how out of light he brought him into darkness, and how he rewarded him again: yet Achiacharus was saved, but the other had his reward: for he went down into darkness. Manasses gave alms, and escaped the snares of death which they had set for him: but Aman fell into the snare, and perished. 11 Wherefore now, my son, consider what alms doeth, and how righteousness doth deliver. When he had said these things, he gave up the ghost in the bed, being an hundred and eight and fifty years old; and he buried him honourably. 12 And when Anna his mother was dead, he buried her with his father. But Tobias departed with his wife and children to Ecbatane to Raguel his father in law, 13 Where he became old with honour, and he buried his father and mother in law honourably, and he inherited their substance, and his father Tobit's. 14 And he died at Ecbatane in Media, being an hundred and seven and twenty years old. 15 But before he died he heard of the destruction of Nineve, which was taken by Nabuchodonosor and Assuerus: and before his death he rejoiced over Nineve.

JUDITH

Jth.1 1 In the twelfth year of the reign of Nabuchodonosor, who reigned in Nineve, the great city; in the days of Arphaxad, which reigned over the Medes in Ecbatane, 2 And built in Ecbatane walls round about of stones hewn three cubits broad and six cubits long, and made the height of the wall seventy cubits, and the breadth thereof fifty cubits: 3 And set the towers thereof upon the gates of it an hundred cubits high, and the breadth thereof in the foundation threescore cubits: 4 And he made the gates thereof, even gates that were raised to the height of seventy cubits, and the breadth of them was forty cubits, for the going forth of his mighty armies, and for the setting in array of his footmen: 5 Even in those days king Nabuchodonosor made war with king Arphaxad in the great plain, which is the plain in the borders of Ragau. 6 And there came unto him all they that dwelt in the hill country, and all that dwelt by Euphrates, and Tigris and Hydaspes, and the plain of Arioch the king of the Elymeans, and very many nations of the sons of Chelod, assembled themselves to the battle. 7 Then Nabuchodonosor king of the Assyrians sent unto all that dwelt in Persia, and to all that dwelt westward, and to those that dwelt in Cilicia, and Damascus, and Libanus, and Antilibanus, and to all that dwelt upon the sea coast, 8 And to those among the nations that were of Carmel, and Galaad, and the higher Galilee, and the great plain of Esdrelom, 9 And to all that were in Samaria and the cities thereof, and beyond Jordan unto Jerusalem, and Betane, and Chelus, and Kades, and the river of Egypt, and Taphnes, and Ramesse, and all the land of Gesem, 10 Until ye come beyond Tanis and Memphis, and to all the inhabitants of Egypt, until ye come to the borders of Ethiopia. 11 But all the inhabitants of the land made light of the commandment of Nabuchodonosor king of the Assyrians, neither went they with him to the battle; for they were not afraid of him: yea, he was before them as one man, and they sent away his ambassadors from them without effect, and with disgrace. 12 Therefore Nabuchodonosor was very angry with all this country, and sware by his throne and kingdom, that he would surely be avenged upon all those coasts of Cilicia, and Damascus, and Syria, and that he would slay with the sword all the inhabitants of the land of Moab, and the children of Ammon, and all Judea, and all that were in Egypt, till ye come to the borders of the two seas. 13 Then he marched in battle array with his power against king Arphaxad in the seventeenth year, and he prevailed in his battle: for he overthrew all the power of Arphaxad, and all his horsemen, and all his chariots, 14 And became lord of his cities, and came unto Ecbatane, and took the towers, and spoiled the streets thereof, and turned the beauty thereof into shame. 15 He took also Arphaxad in the mountains of Ragau, and smote him through with his darts, and destroyed him utterly that day. 16 So he returned afterward to Nineve, both he and all his company of sundry nations being a very great multitude of men of war, and there he took his ease, and banqueted, both he and his army, an hundred and twenty days.

Jth.2 1 And in the eighteenth year, the two and twentieth day of the first month, there was talk in the house of Nabuchodonosor king of the Assyrians that he should, as he said, avenge himself on all the earth. 2 So he called unto him all his officers, and all his nobles, and communicated with them his secret counsel, and concluded the afflicting of the whole earth out of his own mouth. 3 Then they decreed to destroy all flesh, that did not obey the commandment of his mouth. 4 And when he had ended his counsel, Nabuchodonosor king of the Assyrians called Holofernes the chief captain of his army, which was next unto him, and said unto him. 5 Thus saith the great king, the lord of the whole earth, Behold, thou shalt go forth from my presence, and take with thee men that trust in their own strength, of footmen an hundred and twenty thousand; and the number of horses with their riders twelve thousand. 6 And thou shalt go against all the west country, because they disobeyed my commandment. 7 And thou shalt declare unto that they prepare for me earth and water: for I will go forth in my wrath against them and will cover the whole face of the earth with the feet of mine army, and I will give them for a spoil unto them: 8 So that their slain shall fill their valleys and brooks and the river shall be filled with their dead, till it overflow: 9 And I will lead them captives to the utmost parts of all the earth. 10 Thou therefore shalt go forth. and take beforehand for me all their coasts: and if they will yield themselves unto thee, thou shalt reserve them for me till the day of their

punishment. 11 But concerning them that rebel, let not thine eye spare them; but put them to the slaughter, and spoil them wheresoever thou goest. 12 For as I live, and by the power of my kingdom, whatsoever I have spoken, that will I do by mine hand. 13 And take thou heed that thou transgress none of the commandments of thy lord, but accomplish them fully, as I have commanded thee, and defer not to do them. 14 Then Holofernes went forth from the presence of his lord, and called all the governors and captains, and the officers of the army of Assur; 15 And he mustered the chosen men for the battle, as his lord had commanded him, unto an hundred and twenty thousand, and twelve thousand archers on horseback; 16 And he ranged them, as a great army is ordered for the war. 17 And he took camels and asses for their carriages, a very great number; and sheep and oxen and goats without number for their provision: 18 And plenty of victual for every man of the army, and very much gold and silver out of the king's house. 19 Then he went forth and all his power to go before king Nabuchodonosor in the voyage, and to cover all the face of the earth westward with their chariots, and horsemen, and their chosen footmen. 20 A great number also sundry countries came with them like locusts, and like the sand of the earth: for the multitude was without number. 21 And they went forth of Nineve three days' journey toward the plain of Bectileth, and pitched from Bectileth near the mountain which is at the left hand of the upper Cilicia. 22 Then he took all his army, his footmen, and horsemen and chariots, and went from thence into the hill country; 23 And destroyed Phud and Lud, and spoiled all the children of Rasses, and the children of Israel, which were toward the wilderness at the south of the land of the Chellians. 24 Then he went over Euphrates, and went through Mesopotamia, and destroyed all the high cities that were upon the river Arbonai, till ye come to the sea. 25 And he took the borders of Cilicia, and killed all that resisted him, and came to the borders of Japheth, which were toward the south, over against Arabia. 26 He compassed also all the children of Madian, and burned up their tabernacles, and spoiled their sheepcotes. 27 Then he went down into the plain of Damascus in the time of wheat harvest, and burnt up all their fields, and destroyed their flocks and herds, also he spoiled their cities, and utterly wasted their countries, and smote all their young men with the edge of the sword. 28 Therefore the fear and dread of him fell upon all the inhabitants of the sea coasts, which were in Sidon and Tyrus, and them that dwelt in Sur and Ocina, and all that dwelt in Jemnaan; and they that dwelt in Azotus and Ascalon feared him greatly.

Jth.3 1 So they sent ambassadors unto him to treat of peace, saying, 2 Behold, we the servants of Nabuchodonosor the great king lie before thee; use us as shall be good in thy sight. 3 Behold, our houses, and all our places, and all our fields of wheat, and flocks, and herds, and all the lodges of our tents lie before thy face; use them as it pleaseth thee. 4 Behold, even our cities and the inhabitants thereof are thy servants; come and deal with them as seemeth good unto thee. 5 So the men came to Holofernes, and declared unto him after this manner. 6 Then came he down toward the sea coast, both he and his army, and set garrisons in the high cities, and took out of them chosen men for aid. 7 So they and all the country round about received them with garlands, with dances, and with timbrels. 8 Yet he did cast down their frontiers, and cut down their groves: for he had decreed to destroy all the gods of the land, that all nations should worship Nabuchodonosor only, and that all tongues and tribes should call upon him as god. 9 Also he came over against Esdraelon near unto Judea, over against the great strait of Judea. 10 And he pitched between Geba and Scythopolis, and there he tarried a whole month, that he might gather together all the carriages of his army.

Jth.4 1 Now the children of Israel, that dwelt in Judea, heard all that Holofernes the chief captain of Nabuchodonosor king of the Assyrians had done to the nations, and after what manner he had spoiled all their temples, and brought them to nought. 2 Therefore they were exceedingly afraid of him, and were troubled for Jerusalem, and for the temple of the Lord their God: 3 For they were newly returned from the captivity, and all the people of Judea were lately gathered together: and the vessels, and the altar, and the house, were sanctified after the profanation. 4 Therefore they sent into all the coasts of Samaria, and the villages and to Bethoron, and Belmen, and Jericho, and to Choba, and Esora, and to the valley of Salem: 5 And possessed themselves beforehand of all the tops of the high mountains, and fortified the villages that were in them, and laid up victuals for the provision of war: for their fields were of late reaped. 6 Also Joacim the high priest, which was in those days in Jerusalem, wrote to them that dwelt in Bethulia, and Betomestham, which is over against Esdraelon toward the open country, near to Dothaim, 7 Charging them to keep the passages of the hill country: for by them there was an entrance into Judea, and it was easy to stop them that would come up, because the passage was straight, for two men at the most. 8 And the children of Israel did as Joacim the high priest had commanded them, with the ancients of all the people of Israel, which dwelt at Jerusalem. 9 Then every man of Israel cried to God with great fervency, and with great vehemency did they humble their souls: 10 Both they, and their wives and their children, and their cattle, and every stranger and hireling, and their servants bought with money, put sackcloth upon their loins. 11 Thus every man and women, and the little children, and the inhabitants of Jerusalem, fell before the temple, and cast ashes upon their heads, and spread out their sackcloth before the face of the Lord: also they put sackcloth about the altar, 12 And cried to the God of Israel all with one consent earnestly, that he would not give their children for a prey, and their wives for a spoil, and the cities of their inheritance to destruction, and the sanctuary to profanation and reproach, and for the nations to rejoice at. 13 So God heard their prayers, and looked upon their afflictions: for the people fasted many days in all Judea and Jerusalem before the sanctuary of the Lord Almighty. 14 And Joacim the high priest, and all the priests that stood before the Lord, and they which ministered unto the Lord, had their loins girt with sackcloth, and offered the daily burnt offerings, with the vows and free gifts of the people, 15 And had ashes on their mitres, and cried unto the Lord with all their power, that he would look upon all the house of Israel graciously.

Jth.5 1 Then was it declared to Holofernes, the chief captain of the army of Assur, that the children of Israel had prepared for war, and had shut up the passages of the hill country, and had fortified all the tops of the high hills and had laid impediments in the champaign countries: 2 Wherewith he was very angry, and called all the princes of Moab, and the captains of Ammon, and all the governors of the sea coast, 3 And he said unto them, Tell me now, ye sons of Chanaan, who this people is, that dwelleth in the hill country, and what are the cities that they inhabit, and what is the multitude of their army, and wherein is their power and strength, and what king is set over them, or captain of their army; 4 And why have they determined not to come and meet me, more than all the inhabitants of the west. 5 Then said Achior, the captain of all the sons of Ammon, Let my lord now hear a word from the mouth of thy servant, and I will declare unto thee the truth concerning this people, which dwelleth near thee, and inhabiteth the hill countries: and there shall no lie come out of the mouth of thy servant. 6 This people are descended of the Chaldeans: 7 And they sojourned heretofore in Mesopotamia, because they would not follow the gods of their fathers, which were in the land of Chaldea. 8 For they left the way of their ancestors, and worshipped the God of heaven, the God whom they knew: so they cast them out from the face of their gods, and they fled into Mesopotamia, and sojourned there many days. 9 Then their God commanded them to depart from the place where they sojourned, and to go into the land of Chanaan: where they dwelt, and were increased with gold and silver, and with very much cattle. 10 But when a famine covered all the land of Chanaan, they went down into Egypt, and sojourned there, while they were nourished, and became there a great multitude, so that one could not number their nation. 11 Therefore the king of Egypt rose up against them, and dealt subtilly with them, and brought them low with labouring in brick, and made them slaves. 12 Then they cried unto their God, and he smote all the land of Egypt with incurable plagues: so the Egyptians cast them out of their sight. 13 And God dried the Red sea before them, 14 And brought them to mount Sina, and Cades-Barne, and cast forth all that dwelt in the wilderness. 15 So they dwelt in the land of the Amorites, and they destroyed by their strength all them of Esebon, and passing over Jordan they possessed all the hill country. 16 And they cast forth before them the Chanaanite, the Pherezite, the Jebusite, and the Sychemite, and all the Gergesites, and they dwelt in that country many days. 17 And whilst they sinned not before their God, they prospered, because the God that hateth iniquity was with them. 18 But when they departed from the way which he appointed them, they were destroyed in many battles very sore, and were led captives into a land that was not their's, and the temple of their God was cast to the ground, and their cities were taken by the enemies. 19 But now are they returned to their God, and are come up from the places where they were scattered, and have possessed Jerusalem, where their sanctuary is, and are seated in the hill country; for it was desolate. 20 Now therefore, my lord and governor, if there be any error against this people, and they sin against their God, let us consider that this shall be their ruin, and let us go up, and we shall overcome them. 21 But if there be no iniquity in their nation, let my lord now pass by, lest their Lord defend them, and their God be for them, and we become a reproach before all the world. 22 And when Achior had finished these sayings, all the people standing round about the tent murmured, and the chief men of Holofernes, and all that dwelt by the sea side, and in Moab, spake that he should kill him. 23 For, say they, we will not be afraid of the face of the children of Israel: for, lo, it is a people that have no strength nor power for a strong battle 24 Now therefore, lord Holofernes, we will go up, and they shall be a prey to be devoured of all thine army.

Jth.6 1 And when the tumult of men that were about the council was ceased, Holofernes the chief captain of the army of Assur said unto Achior and all the Moabites before all the company of other nations, 2 And who art thou, Achior, and the hirelings of Ephraim, that thou hast prophesied against us as to day, and hast said, that we should not make war with the people of Israel, because their God will defend them? and who is God but Nabuchodonosor? 3 He will send his power, and will destroy them from the face of the earth, and their God shall not deliver them: but we his servants will destroy them as one man; for they are not able to sustain the power of our horses. 4 For with them we will tread them under foot, and their mountains shall be drunken with their blood, and their fields shall be filled with their dead bodies, and their footsteps shall not be able to stand before us, for they shall utterly perish, saith king Nabuchodonosor, lord of all the earth: for he said, None of my words shall be in vain. 5 And thou, Achior, an hireling of Ammon, which hast spoken these words in the day of thine iniquity, shalt see my face no more from this day, until I take vengeance of this nation that came out of Egypt. 6 And then shall the sword of mine army, and the multitude of them that serve me, pass through thy sides, and thou shalt fall among their slain, when I return. 7 Now therefore my servants shall bring thee back into the hill country, and shall set thee in one of the cities of the passages: 8 And thou shalt not perish, till thou be destroyed with them. 9 And if thou persuade thyself in thy mind that they shall be taken, let not thy countenance fall: I have spoken it, and none of my words shall be in vain. 10 Then Holofernes commanded his servants, that waited in his tent, to take Achior, and bring him to Bethulia, and deliver him into the hands of the children of Israel. 11 So his servants took him, and brought him out of the camp into the plain, and they went from the midst of the plain into the hill country, and came unto the fountains that were under Bethulia. 12 And when the men of the city saw them, they took up their weapons, and went out of the city to the top of the hill: and every man that used a sling kept them

from coming up by casting of stones against them. 13 Nevertheless having gotten privily under the hill, they bound Achior, and cast him down, and left him at the foot of the hill, and returned to their lord. 14 But the Israelites descended from their city, and came unto him, and loosed him, and brought him to Bethulia, and presented him to the governors of the city: 15 Which were in those days Ozias the son of Micha, of the tribe of Simeon, and Chabris the son of Gothoniel, and Charmis the son of Melchiel. 16 And they called together all the ancients of the city, and all their youth ran together, and their women, to the assembly, and they set Achior in the midst of all their people. Then Ozias asked him of that which was done. 17 And he answered and declared unto them the words of the council of Holofernes, and all the words that he had spoken in the midst of the princes of Assur, and whatsoever Holofernes had spoken proudly against the house of Israel. 18 Then the people fell down and worshipped God, and cried unto God. saying, 19 O Lord God of heaven, behold their pride, and pity the low estate of our nation, and look upon the face of those that are sanctified unto thee this day. 20 Then they comforted Achior, and praised him greatly. 21 And Ozias took him out of the assembly unto his house, and made a feast to the elders; and they called on the God of Israel all that night for help.

Jth.7 1 The next day Holofernes commanded all his army, and all his people which were come to take his part, that they should remove their camp against Bethulia, to take aforehand the ascents of the hill country, and to make war against the children of Israel. 2 Then their strong men removed their camps in that day, and the army of the men of war was an hundred and seventy thousand footmen, and twelve thousand horsemen, beside the baggage, and other men that were afoot among them, a very great multitude. 3 And they camped in the valley near unto Bethulia, by the fountain, and they spread themselves in breadth over Dothaim even to Belmaim, and in length from Bethulia unto Cynamon, which is over against Esdraelon. 4 Now the children of Israel, when they saw the multitude of them, were greatly troubled, and said every one to his neighbour, Now will these men lick up the face of the earth; for neither the high mountains, nor the valleys, nor the hills, are able to bear their weight. 5 Then every man took up his weapons of war, and when they had kindled fires upon their towers, they remained and watched all that night. 6 But in the second day Holofernes brought forth all his horsemen in the sight of the children of Israel which were in Bethulia, 7 And viewed the passages up to the city, and came to the fountains of their waters, and took them, and set garrisons of men of war over them, and he himself removed toward his people. 8 Then came unto him all the chief of the children of Esau, and all the governors of the people of Moab, and the captains of the sea coast, and said, 9 Let our lord now hear a word, that there be not an overthrow in thine army. 10 For this people of the children of Israel do not trust in their spears, but in the height of the mountains wherein they dwell, because it is not easy to come up to the tops of their mountains. 11 Now therefore, my lord, fight not against them in battle array, and there shall not so much as one man of thy people perish. 12 Remain in thy camp, and keep all the men of thine army, and let thy servants get into their hands the fountain of water, which issueth forth of the foot of the mountain: 13 For all the inhabitants of Bethulia have their water thence; so shall thirst kill them, and they shall give up their city, and we and our people shall go up to the tops of the mountains that are near, and will camp upon them, to watch that none go out of the city. 14 So they and their wives and their children shall be consumed with fire, and before the sword come against them, they shall be overthrown in the streets where they dwell. 15 Thus shalt thou render them an evil reward; because they rebelled, and met not thy person peaceably. 16 And these words pleased Holofernes and all his servants, and he appointed to do as they had spoken. 17 So the camp of the children of Ammon departed, and with them five thousand of the Assyrians, and they pitched in the valley, and took the waters, and the fountains of the waters of the children of Israel. 18 Then the children of Esau went up with the children of Ammon, and camped in the hill country over against Dothaim: and they sent some of them toward the south, and toward the east over against Ekrebel, which is near unto Chusi, that is upon the brook Mochmur; and the rest of the army of the Assyrians camped in the plain, and covered the face of the whole land; and their tents and carriages were pitched to a very great multitude. 19 Then the children of Israel cried unto the Lord their God, because their heart failed, for all their enemies had compassed them round about, and there was no way to escape out from among them. 20 Thus all the company of Assur remained about them, both their footmen, chariots, and horsemen, four and thirty days, so that all their vessels of water failed all the inhabitants of Bethulia. 21 And the cisterns were emptied, and they had not water to drink their fill for one day; for they gave them drink by measure. 22 Therefore their young children were out of heart, and their women and young men fainted for thirst, and fell down in the streets of the city, and by the passages of the gates, and there was no longer any strength in them. 23 Then all the people assembled to Ozias, and to the chief of the city, both young men, and women, and children, and cried with a loud voice, and said before all the elders, 24 God be judge between us and you: for ye have done us great injury, in that ye have not required peace of the children of Assur. 25 For now we have no helper: but God hath sold us into their hands, that we should be thrown down before them with thirst and great destruction. 26 Now therefore call them unto you, and deliver the whole city for a spoil to the people of Holofernes, and to all his army. 27 For it is better for us to be made a spoil unto them, than to die for thirst: for we will be his servants, that our souls may live, and not see the death of our infants before our eyes, nor our wives nor our children to die. 28 We take to witness against you the heaven and the earth, and our God and Lord of our fathers, which punisheth us according to our sins and the sins of our fathers, that he do not according as we have said this day. 29 Then there was great weeping with one consent in the midst of the assembly; and they cried unto the Lord God

with a loud voice. 30 Then said Ozias to them, Brethren, be of good courage, let us yet endure five days, in the which space the Lord our God may turn his mercy toward us; for he will not forsake us utterly. 31 And if these days pass, and there come no help unto us, I will do according to your word. 32 And he dispersed the people, every one to their own charge; and they went unto the walls and towers of their city, and sent the women and children into their houses: and they were very low brought in the city.

Jth.8 1 Now at that time Judith heard thereof, which was the daughter of Merari, the son of Ox, the son of Joseph, the son of Ozel, the son of Elcia, the son of Ananias, the son of Gedeon, the son of Raphaim, the son of Acitho, the son of Eliu, the son of Eliab, the son of Nathanael, the son of Samael, the son of Salasadal, the son of Israel. 2 And Manasses was her husband, of her tribe and kindred, who died in the barley harvest. 3 For as he stood overseeing them that bound sheaves in the field, the heat came upon his head, and he fell on his bed, and died in the city of Bethulia: and they buried him with his fathers in the field between Dothaim and Balamo. 4 So Judith was a widow in her house three years and four months. 5 And she made her a tent upon the top of her house, and put on sackcloth upon her loins and ware her widow's apparel. 6 And she fasted all the days of her widowhood, save the eves of the sabbaths, and the sabbaths, and the eves of the new moons, and the new moons and the feasts and solemn days of the house of Israel. 7 She was also of a goodly countenance, and very beautiful to behold: and her husband Manasses had left her gold, and silver, and menservants and maidservants, and cattle, and lands; and she remained upon them. 8 And there was none that gave her an ill word; ar she feared God greatly. 9 Now when she heard the evil words of the people against the governor, that they fainted for lack of water; for Judith had heard all the words that Ozias had spoken unto them, and that he had sworn to deliver the city unto the Assyrians after five days; 10 Then she sent her waitingwoman, that had the government of all things that she had, to call Ozias and Chabris and Charmis, the ancients of the city. 11 And they came unto her, and she said unto them, Hear me now, O ye governors of the inhabitants of Bethulia: for your words that ye have spoken before the people this day are not right, touching this oath which ye made and pronounced between God and you, and have promised to deliver the city to our enemies, unless within these days the Lord turn to help you. 12 And now who are ye that have tempted God this day, and stand instead of God among the children of men? 13 And now try the Lord Almighty, but ye shall never know any thing. 14 For ye cannot find the depth of the heart of man, neither can ye perceive the things that he thinketh: then how can ye search out God, that hath made all these things, and know his mind, or comprehend his purpose? Nay, my brethren, provoke not the Lord our God to anger. 15 For if he will not help us within these five days, he hath power to defend us when he will, even every day, or to destroy us before our enemies. 16 Do not bind the counsels of the Lord our God: for God is not as man, that he may be threatened; neither is he as the son of man, that he should be wavering. 17 Therefore let us wait for salvation of him, and call upon him to help us, and he will hear our voice, if it please him. 18 For there arose none in our age, neither is there any now in these days neither tribe, nor family, nor people, nor city among us, which worship gods made with hands, as hath been aforetime. 19 For the which cause our fathers were given to the sword, and for a spoil, and had a great fall before our enemies. 20 But we know none other god, therefore we trust that he will not dispise us, nor any of our nation. 21 For if we be taken so, all Judea shall lie waste, and our sanctuary shall be spoiled; and he will require the profanation thereof at our mouth. 22 And the slaughter of our brethren, and the captivity of the country, and the desolation of our inheritance, will he turn upon our heads among the Gentiles, wheresoever we shall be in bondage; and we shall be an offence and a reproach to all them that possess us. 23 For our servitude shall not be directed to favour: but the Lord our God shall turn it to dishonour. 24 Now therefore, O brethren, let us shew an example to our brethren, because their hearts depend upon us, and the sanctuary, and the house, and the altar, rest upon us. 25 Moreover let us give thanks to the Lord our God, which trieth us, even as he did our fathers. 26 Remember what things he did to Abraham, and how he tried Isaac, and what happened to Jacob in Mesopotamia of Syria, when he kept the sheep of Laban his mother's brother. 27 For he hath not tried us in the fire, as he did them, for the examination of their hearts, neither hath he taken vengeance on us: but the Lord doth scourge them that come near unto him, to admonish them. 28 Then said Ozias to her, All that thou hast spoken hast thou spoken with a good heart, and there is none that may gainsay thy words. 29 For this is not the first day wherein thy wisdom is manifested; but from the beginning of thy days all the people have known thy understanding, because the disposition of thine heart is good. 30 But the people were very thirsty, and compelled us to do unto them as we have spoken, and to bring an oath upon ourselves, which we will not break. 31 Therefore now pray thou for us, because thou art a godly woman, and the Lord will send us rain to fill our cisterns, and we shall faint no more. 32 Then said Judith unto them, Hear me, and I will do a thing, which shall go throughout all generations to the children of our nation. 33 Ye shall stand this night in the gate, and I will go forth with my waitingwoman: and within the days that ye have promised to deliver the city to our enemies the Lord will visit Israel by mine hand. 34 But enquire not ye of mine act: for I will not declare it unto you, till the things be finished that I do. 35 Then said Ozias and the princes unto her, Go in peace, and the Lord God be before thee, to take vengeance on our enemies. 36 So they returned from the tent, and went to their wards.

Jth.9 1 Judith fell upon her face, and put ashes upon her head, and uncovered the sackcloth wherewith she was clothed; and about the time that the incense of that evening was offered in Jerusalem in the house of the Lord Judith cried with a loud voice, and said, 2 O Lord God of my father

Simeon, to whom thou gavest a sword to take vengeance of the strangers, who loosened the girdle of a maid to defile her, and discovered the thigh to her shame, and polluted her virginity to her reproach; for thou saidst, It shall not be so; and yet they did so: 3 Wherefore thou gavest their rulers to be slain, so that they dyed their bed in blood, being deceived, and smotest the servants with their lords, and the lords upon their thrones; 4 And hast given their wives for a prey, and their daughters to be captives, and all their spoils to be divided among thy dear children; which were moved with thy zeal, and abhorred the pollution of their blood, and called upon thee for aid: O God, O my God, hear me also a widow. 5 For thou hast wrought not only those things, but also the things which fell out before, and which ensued after; thou hast thought upon the things which are now, and which are to come. 6 Yea, what things thou didst determine were ready at hand, and said, Lo, we are here: for all thy ways are prepared, and thy judgments are in thy foreknowledge. 7 For, behold, the Assyrians are multiplied in their power; they are exalted with horse and man; they glory in the strength of their footmen; they trust in shield, and spear, and bow, and sling; and know not that thou art the Lord that breakest the battles: the Lord is thy name. 8 Throw down their strength in thy power, and bring down their force in thy wrath: for they have purposed to defile thy sanctuary, and to pollute the tabernacle where thy glorious name resteth and to cast down with sword the horn of thy altar. 9 Behold their pride, and send thy wrath upon their heads: give into mine hand, which am a widow, the power that I have conceived. 10 Smite by the deceit of my lips the servant with the prince, and the prince with the servant: break down their stateliness by the hand of a woman. 11 For thy power standeth not in multitude nor thy might in strong men: for thou art a God of the afflicted, an helper of the oppressed, an upholder of the weak, a protector of the forlorn, a saviour of them that are without hope. 12 I pray thee, I pray thee, O God of my father, and God of the inheritance of Israel, Lord of the heavens and earth, Creator of the waters, king of every creature, hear thou my prayer: 13 And make my speech and deceit to be their wound and stripe, who have purposed cruel things against thy covenant, and thy hallowed house, and against the top of Sion, and against the house of the possession of thy children. 14 And make every nation and tribe to acknowledge that thou art the God of all power and might, and that there is none other that protecteth the people of Israel but thou.

Jth.10 1 Now after that she had ceased to cry unto the God of Israel, and had made an end of all these words. 2 She rose where she had fallen down, and called her maid, and went down into the house in the which she abode in the sabbath days, and in her feast days, 3 And pulled off the sackcloth which she had on, and put off the garments of her widowhood, and washed her body all over with water, and anointed herself with precious ointment, and braided the hair of her head, and put on a tire upon it, and put on her garments of gladness, wherewith she was clad during the life of Manasses her husband. 4 And she took sandals upon her feet, and put about her her bracelets, and her chains, and her rings, and her earrings, and all her ornaments, and decked herself bravely, to allure the eyes of all men that should see her. 5 Then she gave her maid a bottle of wine, and a cruse of oil, and filled a bag with parched corn, and lumps of figs, and with fine bread; so she folded all these things together, and laid them upon her. 6 Thus they went forth to the gate of the city of Bethulia, and found standing there Ozias and the ancients of the city, Chabris and Charmis. 7 And when they saw her, that her countenance was altered, and her apparel was changed, they wondered at her beauty very greatly, and said unto her. 8 The God, the God of our fathers give thee favour, and accomplish thine enterprizes to the glory of the children of Israel, and to the exaltation of Jerusalem. Then they worshipped God. 9 And she said unto them, Command the gates of the city to be opened unto me, that I may go forth to accomplish the things whereof ye have spoken with me. So they commanded the young men to open unto her, as she had spoken. 10 And when they had done so, Judith went out, she, and her maid with her; and the men of the city looked after her, until she was gone down the mountain, and till she had passed the valley, and could see her no more. 11 Thus they went straight forth in the valley: and the first watch of the Assyrians met her, 12 And took her, and asked her, Of what people art thou? and whence comest thou? and whither goest thou? And she said, I am a woman of the Hebrews, and am fled from them: for they shall be given you to be consumed: 13 And I am coming before Holofernes the chief captain of your army, to declare words of truth; and I will shew him a way, whereby he shall go, and win all the hill country, without losing the body or life of any one of his men. 14 Now when the men heard her words, and beheld her countenance, they wondered greatly at her beauty, and said unto her, 15 Thou hast saved thy life, in that thou hast hasted to come down to the presence of our lord: now therefore come to his tent, and some of us shall conduct thee, until they have delivered thee to his hands. 16 And when thou standest before him, be not afraid in thine heart, but shew unto him according to thy word; and he will entreat thee well. 17 Then they chose out of them an hundred men to accompany her and her maid; and they brought her to the tent of Holofernes. 18 Then was there a concourse throughout all the camp: for her coming was noised among the tents, and they came about her, as she stood without the tent of Holofernes, till they told him of her. 19 And they wondered at her beauty, and admired the children of Israel because of her, and every one said to his neighbour, Who would despise this people, that have among them such women? surely it is not good that one man of them be left who being let go might deceive the whole earth. 20 And they that lay near Holofernes went out, and all his servants and they brought her into the tent. 21 Now Holofernes rested upon his bed under a canopy, which was woven with purple, and gold, and emeralds, and precious stones. 22 So they shewed him of her; and he came out before his tent with silver lamps going before him. 23 And when Judith was come before him and his servants they all marvelled at the beauty of her countenance; and she fell down upon her face, and did reverence unto him: and his servants took her up.

Jth.11 1 Then said Holofernes unto her, Woman, be of good comfort, fear not in thine heart: for I never hurt any that was willing to serve Nabuchodonosor, the king of all the earth. 2 Now therefore, if thy people that dwelleth in the mountains had not set light by me, I would not have lifted up my spear against them: but they have done these things to themselves. 3 But now tell me wherefore thou art fled from them, and art come unto us: for thou art come for safeguard; be of good comfort, thou shalt live this night, and hereafter: 4 For none shall hurt thee, but entreat thee well, as they do the servants of king Nabuchodonosor my lord. 5 Then Judith said unto him, Receive the words of thy servant, and suffer thine handmaid to speak in thy presence, and I will declare no lie to my lord this night. 6 And if thou wilt follow the words of thine handmaid, God will bring the thing perfectly to pass by thee; and my lord shall not fail of his purposes. 7 As Nabuchodonosor king of all the earth liveth, and as his power liveth, who hath sent thee for the upholding of every living thing: for not only men shall serve him by thee, but also the beasts of the field, and the cattle, and the fowls of the air, shall live by thy power under Nabuchodonosor and all his house. 8 For we have heard of thy wisdom and thy policies, and it is reported in all the earth, that thou only art excellent in all the kingdom, and mighty in knowledge, and wonderful in feats of war. 9 Now as concerning the matter, which Achior did speak in thy council, we have heard his words; for the men of Bethulia saved him, and he declared unto them all that he had spoken unto thee. 10 Therefore, O lord and governor, reject not his word; but lay it up in thine heart, for it is true: for our nation shall not be punished, neither can sword prevail against them, except they sin against their God. 11 And now, that my lord be not defeated and frustrate of his purpose, even death is now fallen upon them, and their sin hath overtaken them, wherewith they will provoke their God to anger whensoever they shall do that which is not fit to be done: 12 For their victuals fail them, and all their water is scant, and they have determined to lay hands upon their cattle, and purposed to consume all those things, that God hath forbidden them to eat by his laws: 13 And are resolved to spend the firstfruits of the the tenths of wine and oil, which they had sanctified, and reserved for the priests that serve in Jerusalem before the face of our God; the which things it is not lawful for any of the people so much as to touch with their hands. 14 For they have sent some to Jerusalem, because they also that dwell there have done the like, to bring them a licence from the senate. 15 Now when they shall bring them word, they will forthwith do it, and they shall be given to thee to be destroyed the same day. 16 Wherefore I thine handmaid, knowing all this, am fled from their presence; and God hath sent me to work things with thee, whereat all the earth shall be astonished, and whosoever shall hear it. 17 For thy servant is religious, and serveth the God of heaven day and night: now therefore, my lord, I will remain with thee, and thy servant will go out by night into the valley, and I will pray unto God, and he will tell me when they have committed their sins: 18 And I will come and shew it unto thee: then thou shalt go forth with all thine army, and there shall be none of them that shall resist thee. 19 And I will lead thee through the midst of Judea, until thou come before Jerusalem; and I will set thy throne in the midst thereof; and thou shalt drive them as sheep that have no shepherd, and a dog shall not so much as open his mouth at thee: for these things were told me according to my foreknowledge, and they were declared unto me, and I am sent to tell thee. 20 Then her words pleased Holofernes and all his servants; and they marvelled at her wisdom, and said, 21 There is not such a woman from one end of the earth to the other, both for beauty of face, and wisdom of words. 22 Likewise Holofernes said unto her. God hath done well to send thee before the people, that strength might be in our hands and destruction upon them that lightly regard my lord. 23 And now thou art both beautiful in thy countenance, and witty in thy words: surely if thou do as thou hast spoken thy God shall be my God, and thou shalt dwell in the house of king Nabuchodonosor, and shalt be renowned through the whole earth.

Jth.12 1 Then he commanded to bring her in where his plate was set; and bade that they should prepare for her of his own meats, and that she should drink of his own wine. 2 And Judith said, I will not eat thereof, lest there be an offence: but provision shall be made for me of the things that I have brought. 3 Then Holofernes said unto her, If thy provision should fail, how should we give thee the like? for there be none with us of thy nation. 4 Then said Judith unto him As thy soul liveth, my lord, thine handmaid shall not spend those things that I have, before the Lord work by mine hand the things that he hath determined. 5 Then the servants of Holofernes brought her into the tent, and she slept till midnight, and she arose when it was toward the morning watch, 6 And sent to Holofernes, saying, Let my lord now command that thine handmaid may go forth unto prayer. 7 Then Holofernes commanded his guard that they should not stay her: thus she abode in the camp three days, and went out in the night into the valley of Bethulia, and washed herself in a fountain of water by the camp. 8 And when she came out, she besought the Lord God of Israel to direct her way to the raising up of the children of her people. 9 So she came in clean, and remained in the tent, until she did eat her meat at evening. 10 And in the fourth day Holofernes made a feast to his own servants only, and called none of the officers to the banquet. 11 Then said he to Bagoas the eunuch, who had charge over all that he had, Go now, and persuade this Hebrew woman which is with thee, that she come unto us, and eat and drink with us. 12 For, lo, it will be a shame for our person, if we shall let such a woman go, not having had her company; for if we draw her not unto us, she will laugh us to scorn. 13 Then went Bagoas from the presence of Holofernes, and came to her, and he said, Let not this fair damsel fear to come to my lord, and to be honoured in his presence, and drink wine, and be merry with us and be made this day as one of the daughters of the Assyrians, which serve in the house of Nabuchodonosor. 14 Then said Judith unto him, Who am I now, that I should gainsay my lord? surely whatsoever pleaseth him I will do speedily, and it shall be my joy unto the day of my death. 15 So she arose, and decked herself with her apparel and all her woman's attire, and her maid went and laid soft skins on the ground for her over against Holofernes, which she had received of Bagoas for her daily use, that she might sit and eat upon them. 16 Now when Judith came in and sat down, Holofernes his heart was ravished with her, and his mind was moved, and he desired greatly her company; for he waited a time to deceive her, from the day that he had seen her. 17 Then said Holofernes unto her, Drink now, and be merry with us. 18 So Judith said, I will drink now, my lord, because my life is magnified in me this day more than all the days since I was born. 19 Then she took and ate and drank before him what her maid had prepared. 20 And Holofernes took great delight in her, and drank more wine than he had drunk at any time in one day since he was born.

Jth.13 1 Now when the evening was come, his servants made haste to depart, and Bagoas shut his tent without, and dismissed the waiters from the presence of his lord; and they went to their beds: for they were all weary, because the feast had been long. 2 And Judith was left along in the tent, and Holofernes lying along upon his bed: for he was filled with wine. 3 Now Judith had commanded her maid to stand without her bedchamber, and to wait for her. coming forth, as she did daily: for she said she would go forth to her prayers, and she spake to Bagoas according to the same purpose. 4 So all went forth and none was left in the bedchamber, neither little nor great. Then Judith, standing by his bed, said in her heart, O Lord God of all power, look at this present upon the works of mine hands for the exaltation of Jerusalem. 5 For now is the time to help thine inheritance, and to execute thine enterprizes to the destruction of the enemies which are risen against us. 6 Then she came to the pillar of the bed, which was at Holofernes' head, and took down his fauchion from thence, 7 And approached to his bed, and took hold of the hair of his head, and said, Strengthen me, O Lord God of Israel, this day. 8 And she smote twice upon his neck with all her might, and she took away his head from him. 9 And tumbled his body down from the bed, and pulled down the canopy from the pillars; and anon after she went forth, and gave Holofernes his head to her maid; 10 And she put it in her bag of meat: so they twain went together according to their custom unto prayer: and when they passed the camp, they compassed the valley, and went up the mountain of Bethulia, and came to the gates thereof. 11 Then said Judith afar off, to the watchmen at the gate, Open, open now the gate: God, even our God, is with us, to shew his power yet in Jerusalem, and his forces against the enemy, as he hath even done this day. 12 Now when the men of her city heard her voice, they made haste to go down to the gate of their city, and they called the elders of the city. 13 And then they ran all together, both small and great, for it was strange unto them that she was come: so they opened the gate, and received them, and made a fire for a light, and stood round about them. 14 Then she said to them with a loud voice, Praise, praise God, praise God, I say, for he hath not taken away his mercy from the house of Israel, but hath destroyed our enemies by mine hands this night. 15 So she took the head out of the bag, and shewed it, and said unto them, behold the head of Holofernes, the chief captain of the army of Assur, and behold the canopy, wherein he did lie in his drunkenness; and the Lord hath smitten him by the hand of a woman. 16 As the Lord liveth, who hath kept me in my way that I went, my countenance hath deceived him to his destruction, and yet hath he not committed sin with me, to defile and shame me. 17 Then all the people were wonderfully astonished, and bowed themselves and worshipped God, and said with one accord, Blessed be thou, O our God, which hast this day brought to nought the enemies of thy people. 18 Then said Ozias unto her, O daughter, blessed art thou of the most high God above all the women upon the earth; and blessed be the Lord God, which hath created the heavens and the earth, which hath directed thee to the cutting off of the head of the chief of our enemies. 19 For this thy confidence shall not depart from the heart of men, which remember the power of God for ever. 20 And God turn these things to thee for a perpetual praise, to visit thee in good things because thou hast not spared thy life for the affliction of our nation, but hast revenged our ruin, walking a straight way before our God. And all the people said; So be it, so be it.

Jth.14 1 Then said Judith unto them, Hear me now, my brethren, and take this head, and hang it upon the highest place of your walls. 2 And so soon as the morning shall appear, and the sun shall come forth upon the earth, take ye every one his weapons, and go forth every valiant man out of the city, and set ye a captain over them, as though ye would go down into the field toward the watch of the Assyrians; but go not down. 3 Then they shall take their armour, and shall go into their camp, and raise up the captains of the army of Assur, and shall run to the tent of Holofernes, but shall not find him: then fear shall fall upon them, and they shall flee before your face. 4 So ye, and all that inhabit the coast of Israel, shall pursue them, and overthrow them as they go. 5 But before ye do these things, call me Achior the Ammonite, that he may see and know him that despised the house of Israel, and that sent him to us as it were to his death. 6 Then they called Achior out of the house of Ozias; and when he was come, and saw the head of Holofernes in a man's hand in the assembly of the people, he fell down on his face, and his spirit failed. 7 But when they had recovered him, he fell at Judith's feet, and reverenced her, and said, Blessed art thou in all the tabernacles of Juda, and in all nations, which hearing thy name shall be astonished. 8 Now therefore tell me all the things that thou hast done in these days. Then Judith declared unto him in the midst of the people all that she had done, from the day that she went forth until that hour she spake unto them. 9 And when she had left off speaking, the people shouted with a loud voice, and made a joyful noise in their city. 10 And when Achior had seen all that the God of Israel had done, he believed in God greatly, and

circumcised the flesh of his foreskin, and was joined unto the house of Israel unto this day. 11 And as soon as the morning arose, they hanged the head of Holofernes upon the wall, and every man took his weapons, and they went forth by bands unto the straits of the mountain. 12 But when the Assyrians saw them, they sent to their leaders, which came to their captains and tribunes, and to every one of their rulers. 13 So they came to Holofernes' tent, and said to him that had the charge of all his things, Waken now our lord: for the slaves have been bold to come down against us to battle, that they may be utterly destroyed. 14 Then went in Bagoas, and knocked at the door of the tent; for he thought that he had slept with Judith. 15 But because none answered, he opened it, and went into the bedchamber, and found him cast upon the floor dead, and his head was taken from him. 16 Therefore he cried with a loud voice, with weeping, and sighing, and a mighty cry, and rent his garments. 17 After he went into the tent where Judith lodged: and when he found her not, he leaped out to the people, and cried, 18 These slaves have dealt treacherously; one woman of the Hebrews hath brought shame upon the house of king Nabuchodonosor: for, behold, Holofernes lieth upon the ground without a head. 19 When the captains of the Assyrians army heard these words, they rent their coats and their minds were wonderfully troubled, and there was a cry and a very great noise throughout the camp.

Jth.15 1 And when they that were in the tents heard, they were astonished at the thing that was done. 2 And fear and trembling fell upon them, so that there was no man that durst abide in the sight of his neighbour, but rushing out all together, they fled into every way of the plain, and of the hill country. 3 They also that had camped in the mountains round about Bethulia fled away. Then the children of Israel, every one that was a warrior among them, rushed out upon them. 4 Then sent Ozias to Betomasthem, and to Bebai, and Chobai, and Cola and to all the coasts of Israel, such as should tell the things that were done, and that all should rush forth upon their enemies to destroy them. 5 Now when the children of Israel heard it, they all fell upon them with one consent, and slew them unto Chobai: likewise also they that came from Jerusalem, and from all the hill country, (for men had told them what things were done in the camp of their enemies) and they that were in Galaad, and in Galilee, chased them with a great slaughter, until they were past Damascus and the borders thereof. 6 And the residue that dwelt at Bethulia, fell upon the camp of Assur, and spoiled them, and were greatly enriched. 7 And the children of Israel that returned from the slaughter had that which remained; and the villages and the cities, that were in the mountains and in the plain, gat many spoils: for the multitude was very great. 8 Then Joacim the high priest, and the ancients of the children of Israel that dwelt in Jerusalem, came to behold the good things that God had shewed to Israel, and to see Judith, and to salute her. 9 And when they came unto her, they blessed her with one accord, and said unto her, Thou art the exaltation of Jerusalem, thou art the great glory of Israel, thou art the great rejoicing of our nation: 10 Thou hast done all these things by thine hand: thou hast done much good to Israel, and God is pleased therewith: blessed be thou of the Almighty Lord for evermore. And all the people said, So be it. 11 And the people spoiled the camp the space of thirty days: and they gave unto Judith Holofernes his tent, and all his plate, and beds, and vessels, and all his stuff: and she took it and laid it on her mule; and made ready her carts, and laid them thereon. 12 Then all the women of Israel ran together to see her, and blessed her, and made a dance among them for her: and she took branches in her hand, and gave also to the women that were with her. 13 And they put a garland of olive upon her and her maid that was with her, and she went before all the people in the dance, leading all the women: and all the men of Israel followed in their armour with garlands, and with songs in their mouths.

Jth.16 1 Then Judith began to sing this thanksgiving in all Israel, and all the people sang after her this song of praise. 2 And Judith said, Begin unto my God with timbrels, sing unto my Lord with cymbals: tune unto him a new psalm: exalt him, and call upon his name. 3 For God breaketh the battles: for among the camps in the midst of the people he hath delivered me out of the hands of them that persecuted me. 4 Assur came out of the mountains from the north, he came with ten thousands of his army, the multitude whereof stopped the torrents, and their horsemen have covered the hills. 5 He bragged that he would burn up my borders, and kill my young men with the sword, and dash the sucking children against the ground, and make mine infants as a prey, and my virgins as a spoil. 6 But the Almighty Lord hath disappointed them by the hand of a woman. 7 For the mighty one did not fall by the young men, neither did the sons of the Titans smite him, nor high giants set upon him: but Judith the daughter of Merari weakened him with the beauty of her countenance. 8 For she put off the garment of her widowhood for the exaltation of those that were oppressed in Israel, and anointed her face with ointment, and bound her hair in a tire, and took a linen garment to deceive him. 9 Her sandals ravished his eyes, her beauty took his mind prisoner, and the fauchion passed through his neck. 10 The Persians quaked at her boldness, and the Medes were daunted at her hardiness. 11 Then my afflicted shouted for joy, and my weak ones cried aloud; but they were astonished: these lifted up their voices, but they were overthrown. 12 The sons of the damsels have pierced them through, and wounded them as fugatives' children: they perished by the battle of the Lord. 13 I will sing unto the Lord a new song: O Lord, thou art great and glorious, wonderful in strength, and invincible. 14 Let all creatures serve thee: for thou spakest, and they were made, thou didst send forth thy spirit, and it created them, and there is none that can resist thy voice. 15 For the mountains shall be moved from their foundations with the waters, the rocks shall melt as wax at thy presence: yet thou art merciful to them that fear thee. 16 For all sacrifice is too little for a sweet savour unto thee, and all the fat is not sufficient for thy burnt offering: but he that feareth the Lord is great at all times. 17 Woe to the nations that rise up against my kindred! the Lord Almighty will take vengeance of them in the day of judgment, in putting fire and worms in their flesh; and they shall feel them, and weep for ever. 18 Now as soon as they entered into Jerusalem, they worshipped the Lord; and as soon as the people were purified, they offered their burnt offerings, and their free offerings, and their gifts. 19 Judith also dedicated all the stuff of Holofernes, which the people had given her, and gave the canopy, which she had taken out of his bedchamber, for a gift unto the Lord. 20 So the people continued feasting in Jerusalem before the sanctuary for the space of three months and Judith remained with them. 21 After this time every one returned to his own inheritance, and Judith went to Bethulia, and remained in her own possession, and was in her time honourable in all the country. 22 And many desired her, but none knew her all the days of her life, after that Manasses her husband was dead, and was gathered to his people. 23 But she increased more and more in honour, and waxed old in her husband's house, being an hundred and five years old, and made her maid free; so she died in Bethulia: and they buried her in the cave of her husband Manasses. 24 And the house of Israel lamented her seven days: and before she died, she did distribute her goods to all them that were nearest of kindred to Manasses her husband, and to them that were the nearest of her kindred. 25 And there was none that made the children of Israel any more afraid in the days of Judith, nor a long time after her death.

ESTHER

In the second year of the reign of Artaxerxes the great king, on the first *day* of Nisan, Mardochaeus the *son* of Jarius, the *son* of Semeias, the *son* of Cisaus, of the tribe of Benjamine, a Jew dwelling in the city Susa, a great man, serving in the king's palace, saw a vision. Now he was of the captivity which Nabuchodonosor king of Babylon had carried captive from Jerusalem, with Jachonias the king of Judea. And this was his dream: Behold, voices and a noise, thunders and earthquake, tumult upon the earth. And, behold, two great serpents came forth, both ready for conflict, and there came from them a great voice, and by their voice every nation was prepared for battle, even to fight against the nation of the just. And, behold, a day of darkness and blackness, tribulation and anguish, affection and tumult upon the earth. And all the righteous nation was troubled, fearing their own afflictions; and they prepared to die, and cried to God: and from their cry there came as it were a great river from a little fountain , *even* much water. And light and the sun arose, and the lowly were exalted, and devoured the honorable. And Mardochaeus who had seen this vision and what God desired to do, having awoke, kept it in his heart, and desired by all means to interpret it, even till night. And Mardochaeus rested quiet in the palace with Gabatha and Tharrha the king's two chamberlains, eunuchs who guarded the palace. And he heard their reasoning and searched out their plans, and learnt that they were preparing to lay hands on king Artaxerxes: and he informed the king concerning them. And the king examined the two chamberlains, and they confessed, and were executed. And the king wrote these things for a memorial: also Mardochaeus wrote concerning these matters. And the king commanded Mardochaeus to attend in the palace, and gave gifts for this service. And Aman the son of Amadathes the Bugean was honourable in the sight of the king, and he endeavored to hurt Mardochaeus and his people, because of the two chamberlains of the king.

Est.1 1 And it came to pass after these things in the days of Artaxerxes, —(this Artaxerxes ruled over a hundred and twenty-seven provinces from India)— 2 in those days, when king Artaxerxes was on the throne in the city of Susa, 3 in the third year of his reign, he made a feast to his friends, and the other nations, and to the nobles of the Persians and Medes, and the chief of the satraps. 4 And after this, after he had shewn to them the wealth of his kingdom, and the abundant glory of his wealth during a hundred and eighty days, 5 when, *I say*, the days of the marriage feast were completed, the king made a banquet to the nations who were present in the city six days, in the court of the king's house, 6 *which was* adorned with *hangings* of fine linen and flax on cords of fine linen and purple, fastened to golden and silver studs, on pillars of Parian marble and stone: *there were* golden and silver couches on a pavement of emerald stone, and of pearl, and of Parian stone, and open-worked coverings variously flowered, *having* roses worked round about; 7 gold and silver cups, and a small cup of carbuncle set out of the value of thirty thousand talents, abundant and sweet wine, which the king himself drank. 8 And this banquet was not according to the appointed law; but so the king would have it: and he charged the stewards to perform his will and that of the company. 9 Also Astin the queen made a banquet for the women in the palace where king Artaxerxes *dwelt.* 10 Now on the seventh day the king, being merry, told Aman, and Bazan, and Tharrha, and Barazi, and Zatholtha, and Abataza, and Tharaba, the seven chamberlains, servants of king Artaxerxes, 11 to bring in the queen to him, to enthrone her, and crown her with the diadem, and to shew her to the princes, and her beauty to the nations: for she was beautiful. 12 But queen Astin hearkened not to him to come with the chamberlains: so the king was grieved and angered. 13 And he said to his friends, Thus hast Astin spoken: pronounce therefore upon this *case* law and judgment. 14 So Arkesaeus, and Sarsathaeus, and Malisear, the princes of the Persians and Medes, who were near the king, who sat chief *in rank* by the king, drew near to him, 15 and reported to him according to the laws how it was proper to do to queen Astin, because she had not done the things commanded of the king by the chamberlains. 16 And Muchaeus said to the king and to the princes, Queen Astin has not wronged the king only, but also all the king's rulers and princes: 17 for he has told them the words of the queen, and how she disobeyed the king. As then, *said he*, she refused *to obey* king Artaxerxes, 18 so this day shall the other ladies of the chiefs of the Persians and Medes, having heard what she said to the king, dare in the same way to dishonour their husbands. 19 If then it seem good to the king, let him make a royal decree, and let it be written according to the laws of the Medes and Persians, and let him not alter *it*: and let not the queen come in to him any more; and let the king give her royalty to a woman

better than she. 20 And let the law of the king which he shall have made, be widely proclaimed, in his kingdom: and so shall all the women give honour to their husbands, from the poor even to the rich. 21 And the saying pleased the king and the princes; and the king did as Muchaeus had said, 22 and sent into all his kingdom through the several provinces, according to their language, in order that men might be feared in their own houses.

Est.2 1 And after this the king's anger was pacified, and he no more mentioned Astin, bearing in mind what she had said, and how he had condemned her. 2 Then the servants of the king said, Let there be sought for the king chaste *and* beautiful young virgins. 3 And let the king appoint local governors in all the provinces of his kingdom, and let them select fair *and* chaste young damsels *and bring them* to the city Susa, into the women's apartment, and let them be consigned to the king's chamberlain, the keeper of the women; and let things for purification and other attendance be given *to them.* 4 And let the woman who shall please the king be queen instead of Astin. And the thing pleased the king; and he did so. 5 Now there was a Jew in the city Susa, and his name was Mardochaeus, the *son* of Jairus, *the son* of Semeias, *the son* of Cisaeus, of the tribe of Benjamin; 6 who had been brought a prisoner from Jerusalem, which Nabuchodonosor king of Babylon had carried into captivity. 7 And he had a foster child, daughter of Aminadab his father's brother, and her name *was* Esther; and when her parents were dead, he brought her up for a wife for himself: and the damsel was beautiful. 8 And because the king's ordinance was published, many damsels were gathered to the city Susa under the hand of Gai; and Esther was brought to Gai the keeper of the women. 9 And the damsel pleased him, and she found favour in his sight; and he hasted to give her the things for purification, and her portion, and the seven maidens appointed her out of the palace: and he treated her and her maidens well in the women's apartment. 10 But Esther discovered not her family nor her kindred: for Mardochaeus had charged her not to tell. 11 But Mardochaeus used to walk every day by the women's court, to see what would become of Esther. 12 Now this was the time for a virgin to go into the king, when she should have fulfilled twelve months; for so are the days of purification fulfilled, six months while they are anointing themselves with oil of myrrh, and six months with spices and women's purifications. 13 And then *the damsel* goes in to the king; and *the officer* to whomsoever he shall give the command, will bring her to come in with him from the women's apartment to the king's chamber. 14 She enters in the evening, and in the morning she departs to the second women's apartment, where Gai the king's chamberlain *is* keeper of the women: and she goes not in to the king again, unless she should be called by name. 15 And when the time was fulfilled for Esther the daughter of Aminadab the brother of Mardochaeus' father to go in to the king, she neglected nothing which the chamberlain, the women's keeper, commanded; for Esther found grace in the sight of all that looked upon her. 16 So Esther went in to king Artaxerxes in the twelfth month, which is Adar, in the seventh year of his reign. 17 And the king loved Esther, and she found favour beyond all the *other* virgins: and he put on her the queen's crown. 18 And the king made a banquet for all his friends and great men for seven days, and he highly celebrated the marriage of Esther; and he made a release to those who were under his dominion. 19 But Mardochaeus served in the palace. 20 Now Esther had not discovered her kindred; for so Mardochaeus commanded her, to fear God, and perform his commandments, as when she was with him: and Esther changed not her manner of life. 21 And two chamberlains of the king, the chiefs of the body-guard, were grieved, because Mardochaeus was promoted; and they sought to kill king Artaxerxes. 22 And the matter was discovered to Mardochaeus, and he made it known to Esther, and she declared to the king the matter of the conspiracy. 23 And the king examined the two chamberlains, and hanged them: and the king gave orders to make a note for a memorial in the royal records of the good offices of Mardochaeus, as a commendation.

Est.3 1 And after this king Artaxerxes highly honoured Aman *son* of Amadathes, the Bugaean, and exalted him, and set his seat above all his friends. 2 And all in the palace did him obeisance, for so the king had given orders to do: but Mardochaeus did not do him obeisance. 3 And they in the king's palace said to Mardochaeus, Mardochaeus, why dost thou transgress the commands of the king? 4 *Thus* they spoke daily to him, but he hearkened not unto them; so they represented to Aman that Mardochaeus resisted the commands of the king: and Mardochaeus had shewn to them that he was a Jew. 5 And when Aman understood that Mardochaeus did not obeisance to him, he was greatly enraged, 6 and took counsel to destroy utterly all the Jews who were under the rule of Artaxerxes. 7 And he made a decree in the twelfth year of the reign of Artaxerxes, and cast lots daily and monthly, to slay in one day the race of Mardochaeus: and the lot fell on the fourteenth *day* of the month which is Adar. 8 And he spoke to king Artaxerxes, saying, There is a nation scattered among the nations in all thy kingdom, and their laws differ from *those of* all the *other* nations; and they disobey the laws of the king; and it is not expedient for the king to let them alone. 9 If it seem good to the king, let him make a decree to destroy them: and I will remit into the king's treasury ten thousand talents of silver. 10 And the king took off his ring, and gave it into the hands of Aman, to seal the decrees against the Jews. 11 And the king said to Aman, Keep the silver, and treat the nation as thou wilt. 12 So the king's recorders were called in the first month, on the thirteenth *day*, and they wrote as Aman commanded to the captains and governors in every province, from India even to Ethiopia, to a hundred and twenty-seven provinces; and to the rulers of the nations according to their *several* languages, in the name of king Artaxerxes. 13 And *the message* was sent by posts throughout the kingdom of Artaxerxes, to destroy utterly the race of the Jews on the first day of the twelfth month, which is Adar, and to plunder their goods. And the following is the copy of the letter; The great king Artaxerxes writes thus to

the rulers and inferior governors of a hundred and twenty-seven provinces, from India even to Ethiopia, who hold authority under *him*. Ruling over many nations and having obtained dominion over the whole world, I was minded (not elated by the confidence of power, but ever conducting *myself* with great moderation and gentleness) to make the lives of *my* subjects continually tranquil, desiring both to maintain the kingdom quiet and orderly to *its* utmost limits, and to restore the peace desired by all men. But when I had enquired of my counsellors how this should be brought to pass. Aman, who excels in soundness of judgment among us, and has been manifestly well inclined without wavering and with unshaken fidelity, and had obtained the second post in the kingdom, informed us that a certain ill-disposed people is mixed up with all the tribes throughout the world, opposed in their law to every *other* nation, and continually neglecting the commands of the king, so that the united government blamelessly administered by us is not quietly established. Having then conceived that this nation *alone of all others* is continually set in opposition to every man, introducing as a change a foreign code of laws, and injuriously plotting to accomplish the worst of evils against our interests, and against the happy establishment of the monarchy; we signified to you in the letter written by Aman, who is set over *the public* affairs and is our second governor, to destroy them all utterly with their wives and children by the swords of the enemies, without pitying or sparing any, on the fourteenth day of the twelfth month Adar, of the present year; that the people aforetime and now ill- disposed *to us* having been violently consigned to death in one day, may hereafter secure to us continually a well constituted and quiet *state of affairs*. 14 And the copies of the letters were published in every province; and an order was given to all the nations to be ready against that day. 15 And the business was hastened, and *that* at Susa: and the king and Aman began to drink; but the city was troubled.

Est.4 1 But Mardochaeus having perceived what was done, rent his garments, and put on sackcloth, and sprinkled dust upon himself; and having rushed forth through the open street of the city, he cried with a loud voice, A nation that has done no wrong is going to be destroyed. 2 And he came to the king's gate, and stood; for it was not lawful for him to enter into the palace, wearing sackcloth and ashes. 3 And in every province where the letters were published, *there was* crying and lamentation and great mourning on the part of the Jews: they spread for themselves sackcloth and ashes. 4 And the queen's maids and chamberlains went in and told her: and when she had heard what was done, she was disturbed; and she sent to clothe Mardochaeus, and take away his sackcloth; but he consented not. 5 So Esther called for her chamberlain Achrathaeus, who waited upon her; and she sent to learn the truth from Mardochaeus. 6 7 And Mardochaeus shewed him what was done, and the promise which Aman had made the king of ten thousand talents *to be paid* into the treasury, that he might destroy the Jews. 8 And he gave him the copy *of the writing* that was published in Susa concerning their destruction, to shew to Esther; and told him to charge her to go in and intreat the king, and to beg him for the people, remembering, *said he*, the days of thy low estate, how thou wert nursed by my hand: because Aman who holds the next place to the king has spoken against us for death. Do thou call upon the Lord, and speak to the king concerning us, to deliver us from death. 9 So Achrathaeus went in and told her all these words. 10 And Esther said to Achrathaeus, Go to Mardochaeus, and say, 11 All the nations of the empire know, that whoever, man or woman, shall go in to the king into the inner court uncalled, that person cannot live: only to whomsoever the king shall stretch out *his* golden sceptre, he shall live: and I have not been called to go into the king, for these thirty days. 12 And Achrathaeus reported to Mardochaeus all the words of Esther. 13 Then Mardochaeus said to Achrathaeus, Go, and say to her, Esther, say not to thyself that thou alone wilt escape in the kingdom, more than all the *other* Jews. 14 For if thou shalt refuse to hearken on this occasion, help and protection will be to the Jews from another quarter; but thou and thy father's house will perish: and who knows, if thou hast been made queen for this *very* occasion? 15 And Esther sent the *man* that came to her to Mardochaeus, saying, 16 Go and assemble the Jews that are in Susa, and fast ye for me, and eat not and drink not for three days, night and day: and I also and my maidens will fast; and then I will go in to the king contrary to the law, even if I must die. 17 So Mardochaeus went and did all that Esther commanded him. [And he besought the Lord, making mention of all the works of the Lord; and he said, Lord God, king ruling over all, for all things are in thy power, and there is no one that shall oppose thee, in thy purpose to save Israel. - For thou hast made the heaven and the earth and every wonderful thing in the *world* under heaven. And thou art Lord of all, and there is no one who shall resist thee Lord. Thou knowest all things: thou knowest, Lord, that it is not in insolence, nor haughtiness, nor love of glory, that I have done this, to refuse obeisance to the haughty Aman. For I would gladly have kissed the soles of his feet for the safety of Israel. But I have done this, that I might not set the glory of man above the glory of God: and I will not worship any one except thee, my Lord, and I will not do these things in haughtiness. And now, O Lord God, the King, the God of Abraam, spare thy people, for *our enemies* are looking upon us to *our* destruction, and they have desired to destroy thine ancient inheritance. Do not overlook thy peculiar people, whom thou hast redeemed for thyself out of the land of Egypt. Hearken to my prayer, and be propitious to thine inheritance, and turn our mourning into gladness, that we may live and sing praise to thy name, O Lord; and do not utterly destroy the mouth of them that praise thee, O Lord. And all Israel cried with *all* their might, for death *was* before their eyes. And queen Esther betook herself for refuge to the Lord, being taken *as it were* in the agony of death. And having taken off her glorious apparel, she put on garments of distress and mourning; and instead of grand perfumes she filled her head with ashes and dung, and she greatly brought down her body, and she filled every place of her glad adorning with the *torn* curls of her hair. And she

besought the Lord God of Israel, and said, O my Lord, thou alone art our king: help me *who am* destitute, and have no helper but thee, for my danger *is* near at hand. I have heard from my birth, in the tribe of my kindred that thou, Lord, tookest Israel out of all the nations, and our fathers out of all their kindred for a perpetual inheritance, and hast wrought for them all that thou hast said. And now we have sinned before thee, and thou hast delivered us into the hands of our enemies, because we honoured their gods: thou art righteous, O Lord. But now they have not been contented with the bitterness of our slavery, but have laid their hands on the hands of their idols, *in order* to abolish the decree of thy mouth, and utterly to destroy thine inheritances, and to stop the mouth of them that praise thee, and to extinguish the glory of thine house and thine alter, and to open the mouth of the Gentiles to *speak* the praises of vanities, and *in order* that a mortal king should be admired for ever. O Lord, do not resign thy scepter to them that are not, and let them not laugh at our fall, but turn their counsel, against themselves, and make an example of him who has begun *to injure* us. Remember *us*, O Lord, manifest thyself in the time of our affliction, and encourage me, O King of gods, and ruler of all dominion. Put harmonious speech into my mouth before the lion, and turn his heart to hate him that fights against us, to the utter destruction of him that consent with him. But deliver us by thine hand, and help me *who am* destitute, and have none but the, O Lord. Thou knowest all things, and knowest that I hate the glory of transgressors, and that I abhor the couch of the uncircumcised, and of every stranger. Thou knowest my necessity, for I abhor the symbol of my proud station, which is upon my head in the days of my splendour: I abhor it as a menstruous cloth, and I wear it not in the days of my tranquility. And thy handmaid has not eaten *at* the table of Aman, and I have not honoured the banquet of the king, neither have I drunk wine of libations. Neither has thy handmaid rejoiced since the day of my promotion until now, except in thee, O Lord God of Abraam. O god, who has power over all, hearken to the voice of the desperate, and deliver us from the hand of them that devise mischief; and deliver me from my fear.

Est.5 1 And it came to pass on the third day, when she had ceased praying, that she put off her mean dress, and put on her glorious apparel. And being splendidly arrayed, *and* having called upon God the Overseer and Preserver of all things, she took her two maids, and she leaned upon one, as a delicate female, and the other followed bearing her train. And she *was* blooming in the perfection of her beauty; and her face *was* cheerful, and *it were* benevolent, but her heart *was* straitened for fear. And having passed through all the doors, she stood before the king: and he was sitting upon his royal throne, and he had put on all his glorious apparel, *covered* all over with gold and precious stones, and was very terrible. And having raised his face resplendent with glory, he looked with intense anger: and the queen fell, and changed her colour as she fainted; and she bowed herself upon the head of the maid that went before *her*. But God changed the spirit of the king gentleness, and in intense feeling he sprang from off his throne, and took her into his arms, until she recovered: and he comforted her with peaceable words, and said to her, What is *the matter*, Esther? I *am* thy brother; be of good cheer, thou shalt not die, for our command is openly declared *to thee*, Draw nigh. 2 And having raised the golden sceptre he laid it upon her neck, and embraced her, and said, Speak to me. And she said to him, I saw thee, *my* lord, as an angel of God, and my heart was troubled for fear of thy glory; for thou, *my* lord, art to be wondered at, and thy face *is* full of grace. And while she was speaking, she fainted and fell. Then the king was troubled, and all his servants comforted her. 3 And the king said, What wilt thou, Esther? and what is thy request? *ask* even to the half of my kingdom, and it shall be thine. 4 And Esther said, To-day is my great day: if then it seem good to the king, let both him and Aman come to the feast which I will prepare this day. 5 And the king said, Hasten Aman hither, that we may perform the word of Esther. So they both come to the feast of which Esther had spoken. 6 And at the banquet the king said to Esther, What is *thy request*, queen Esther? *speak*, and thou shalt have all that thou requirest. 7 And she said, My request and my petition *are*: 8 if I have found favour in the sight of the king, let the king and Aman come again to-morrow to the feast which I shall prepare for them, and to-morrow I will do the same. 9 So Aman went out from the king very glad *and* merry: but when Aman saw Mardochaeus the Jew in the court, he was greatly enraged. 10 And having gone into his own house, he called his friends, and his wife Zosara. 11 And he shewed them his wealth, and the glory with which the king had invested him, and how he had caused him to take precedence and bear chief rule in the kingdom. 12 And Aman said, The queen has called no one to the feast with the king but me, and I am invited to-morrow. 13 But these things please me not, while I see Mardochaeus the Jew in the court. 14 And Zosara his wife and his friends said to him, Let there be a gallows made for thee of fifty cubits, and in the morning do thou speak to the king, and let Mardochaeus be hanged on the gallows: but do thou go in to the feast with the king, and be merry. And the saying pleased Aman, and the gallows was prepared.

Est.6 1 But the Lord removed sleep from the king that night: and he told his servant to bring in the books, the registers of daily events, to read to him. 2 And he found the records written concerning Mardochaeus, how he had told the king concerning the two chamberlains of the king, when they were keeping guard, and sought to lay hands on Artaxerxes. 3 And the king said, What honour or favour have we done to Mardochaeus? And the king's servants said, Thou hast not done anything to him. 4 And while the king was enquiring about the kindness of Mardochaeus, behold, Aman *was* in the court. And the king said, Who *is* in the court? Now Aman was come in to speak to the king, that he should hang Mardochaeus on the gallows, which he had prepared. 5 And the king's servants said, Behold, Aman stands in the court. And the king said, Call him. 6 And the king said to Aman, What shall I do to the man whom I wish to honour? And Aman said within himself, Whom would

the king honour but myself? 7 and he said to the king, As for the man whom the king wishes to honour, 8 let the king's servants bring the robe of fine linen which the king puts on, and the horse on which the king rides, 9 and let him give *it* to one of the king's noble friends, and let him array the man whom the king loves; and let him mount him on the horse, and proclaim through the street of the city, saying, Thus shall it be *done* to every man whom the king honours. 10 Then the king said to Aman, Thou hast well said: so do to Mardochaeus the Jew, who waits in the palace, and let not a word of what thou hast spoken be neglected. 11 So Aman took the robe and the horse, and arrayed Mardochaeus, and mounted him on the horse, and went through the street of the city, and proclaimed, saying, Thus shall it be to every man whom the king wishes to honour. 12 And Mardochaeus returned to the palace: but Aman went home mourning, and having his head covered. 13 And Aman related the events that had befallen him to Zosara his wife, and to *his* friends: and his friends and his wife said to him, If Mardochaeus *be* of the race of the Jews, *and* thou hast begun to be humbled before him, thou wilt assuredly fall, and thou wilt not be able to withstand him, for the living God *is* with him. 14 While they were yet speaking, the chamberlains arrived, to hasten Aman to the banquet which Esther had prepared.

Est.7 1 So the king and Aman went in to drink with the queen. 2 And the king said to Esther at the banquet on the second day, What is it, queen Esther? and what *is* thy request, and what *is* thy petition? and it shall be *done* for thee, to the half of my kingdom. 3 And she answered and said, If I have found favour in the sight of the king, let *my* life be granted to my petition, and my people to my request. 4 For both I and my people are sold for destruction, and pillage, and slavery; *both* we and our children for bondmen and bondwomen: and I consented not to it, for the slanderer *is* not worthy of the king's palace. 5 And the king said, Who *is* this that has dared to do this thing? 6 And Esther said, the adversary *is* Aman, this wicked man. Then Aman was troubled before the king and the queen. 7 And the king rose up from the banquet to go into the garden: and Aman began to intreat the queen; for he saw that he was in an evil case. 8 And the king returned from the garden; and Aman had fallen upon the bed, intreating the queen. And the king said, Wilt thou even force *my* wife in my house? And when Aman heard it, he changed countenance. 9 And Bugathan, one of the chamberlains, said to the king, Behold, Aman has also prepared a gallows for Mardochaeus, who spoke concerning the king, and a gallows of fifty cubits high has been set up in the premises of Aman. And the king said, Let him be hanged thereon. 10 So Aman was hanged on the gallows that had been prepared for Mardochaeus: and then the king's wrath was appeased.

Est.8 1 And in that day king Artaxerxes gave to Esther all that belonged to Aman the slanderer: and Mardochaeus was called by the king; for Esther had shewn that he was related to her. 2 And the king took the ring which he had taken away from Aman, and gave it to Mardochaeus: and

Esther appointed Mardochaeus over all that had been Aman's. 3 And she spoke yet again to the king, and fell at his feet, and besought *him* to do away the mischief of Aman, and all that he had done against the Jews. 4 Then the king stretched out to Esther the golden sceptre: and Esther arose to stand near the king. 5 And Esther said, If it seem good to thee, and I have found favour *in thy sight*, let an order be sent that the letters sent by Aman may be reversed, that were written for the destruction of the Jews, who are in thy kingdom. 6 For how shall I be able to look upon the affliction of my people, and how shall I be able to survive the destruction of my kindred? 7 And the king said to Esther, If I have given and freely granted thee all that was Aman's, and hanged him on a gallows, because he laid his hands upon the Jews, what dost thou yet further seek? 8 Write ye also in my name, as it seems good to you, and seal *it* with my ring: for whatever *orders* are written at the command of the king, and sealed with my ring, it is not lawful to gainsay them. 9 So the scribes were called in the first-month, which is Nisan, on the three and twentieth day of the same year; and *orders* were written to the Jews, whatever *the king had* commanded to the local governors and chiefs of the satraps, from India even to Ethiopia, a hundred and twenty-seven satraps, according to the several provinces, according to their dialects. 10 And they were written by order of the king, and sealed with his ring, and they sent the letters by the posts: 11 wherein he charged them to use their *own* laws in every city, and to help each other, and to treat their adversaries, and those who attacked them, as they pleased, 12 on one day in all the kingdom of Artaxerxes, on the thirteenth *day* of the twelfth month, which is Adar. 13 And let the copies be posted in conspicuous places throughout the kingdom, and let all the Jews be ready against this day, to fight against their enemies. And the following is the copy of the letter of the orders. The great king Artaxerxes sends greetings to the rulers of provinces *in* a hundred and twenty- seven satrapies, from India to Ethiopia, even to those who are faithful to our interests. Many who have been frequently honored by the most abundant kindness of their benefactors have conceived ambitious designs, and not only endeavour to hurt our subjects, but moreover, not being able to bear prosperity, they also endeavour to plot against their own benefactors. And they not only would utterly abolish gratitude from among men, but also, elated by the boastings of men who are strangers to all that is good, they supposed that they shall escape the sin-hating vengeance of the ever-seeing God. And oftentimes *evil* exhortation has made partakers of the guilt of shedding innocent blood, and has involved in irremediable calamities, many of those who had been appointed to offices of authority, who had been entrusted with the management of their friends' affairs; while *men*, by the false sophistry of an evil disposition, have deceived the simple candour of the ruling powers. And it is possible to see *this*, not so much from more ancient traditionary accounts, as it is immediately in your power *to see it* by examining what things have been wickedly perpetrated by the baseness of men unworthily holding power. And *it is right* to take heed with regard to

the future, that we may maintain the government in undistributed peace for all men, adopting *needful* changes, and ever judging those cases which come under our notices, with truly equitable decision. For whereas Aman, a Macedonian, the son of Amadathes, in reality an alien from the blood of the Persians, and differing widely from our mild course of government, having been hospitable entertained by us, obtained so large a share of our universal kindness, as to be called our father, and to continue the person next to the royal throne, reverenced of all; *he however*, overcome by the pride *of his station*, endeavored to deprive us of our dominion, and our life: having by various and subtle artifices demanded for destruction both Mardochaeus our deliverer and perpetual benefactor, and Esther the blameless consort of *our* kingdom, with their whole nation. For by these methods he thought, having surprised us in a defenceless state, to transfer the dominion of the Persians to the Macedonians. But we find that the Jews, who have been consigned to destruction by the most abominable of men, are not malefactors, but living according to the justest laws, and being the sons of the living God, the most high and mighty, who maintains the kingdom. to us as well as to our forefathers, in the most excellent order. Ye will therefore do well in refusing to obey the letter sent by Aman the son of Amadathes, because he that has done these things, has been hanged with his whole family at the gates of Susa, Almighty God having swiftly returned to him a worthy recompence, *We enjoin you* then, having openly published a copy of this letter in every place, to give the Jews permission to use their own lawful customs, and to strengthen them, that on the thirteenth of the twelfth month Adar, on the self-same day, they may defend themselves against those who attack them in a time of affliction. For in the place of the destruction of the chosen race, Almighty God has granted them this *time of* gladness. Do ye therefore also, among your *notable* feasts, keep a distinct day with all festivity, that both now and hereafter it may be a day of deliverance to us and who are well disposed toward the Persians, but to those that plotted against us a memorial of destruction. And every city and province collectively, which shall not do accordingly, shall be consumed with vengeance by spear and fire: it shall be made not only inaccessible to men, but most hateful to wild beasts and birds for ever.] And let the copies be posted in conspicuous places throughout the kingdom and let all the Jews be ready against this day, to fight against their enemies. 14 So the horsemen went forth with haste to perform the king's commands; and the ordinance was also published in Susa. 15 And Mardochaeus went forth robed in the royal apparel, and wearing a golden crown, and a diadem of fine purple linen: and the people in Susa saw *it* and rejoiced. 16 And the Jews had light and gladness, 17 in every city and province wherever the ordinance was published: wherever the proclamation took place, the Jews had joy and gladness, feasting and mirth: and many of the Gentiles were circumcised, and became Jews, for fear of the Jews.

Est.9 1 For in the twelfth month, on the thirteenth day of the month which is Adar, the letters written by the king arrived. 2 In that day the adversaries of the Jews perished: for no one resisted, through fear of them. 3 For the chiefs of the satraps, and the princes and the royal scribes, honoured the Jews; for the fear of Mardochaeus lay upon them. 4 For the order of the king was in force, that he should be celebrated in all the kingdom. 5 6 And in the city Susa the Jews slew five hundred men: 7 both Pharsannes, and Delphon and Phasga, 8 and Pharadatha, and Barea, and Sarbaca, 9 and Marmasima, and Ruphaeus, and Arsaeus, and Zabuthaeus, 10 the ten sons of Aman the son of Amadathes the Bugaean, the enemy of the Jews, and they plundered *their property* on the same day: 11 and the number of them that perished in Susa was rendered to the king. 12 And the king said to Esther, The Jews have slain five hundred men in the city Susa; and how, thinkest thou, have they used them in the rest of the country? What then dost thou yet ask, that it may be *done* for thee? 13 And Esther said to the king, let it be granted to the Jews so to treat them tomorrow as to hand the ten sons of Aman. 14 And he permitted it to be so done; and he gave up to the Jews of the city the bodies of the sons of Aman to hang. 15 And the Jews assembled in Susa on the fourteenth *day* of Adar, and slew three hundred men, but plundered no property. 16 And the rest of the Jews who were in the kingdom assembled, and helped one another, and obtained rest from their enemies: for they destroyed fifteen thousand of them on the thirteenth *day* of Adar, but took no spoil. 17 And they rested on the fourteenth of the same month, and kept it as a day of rest with joy and gladness. 18 And the Jews in the city Susa assembled also on the fourteenth *day* and rested; and they kept also the fifteenth with joy and gladness. 19 On this account then *it is that* the Jews dispersed in every foreign land keep the fourteenth of Adar *as* a holy day with joy, sending portions each to his neighbour. 20 And Mardochaeus wrote these things in a book, and sent them to the Jews, as many as were in the kingdom of Artaxerxes, both them that were near and them that were afar off, 21 to establish these *as* joyful days, and to keep the fourteenth and fifteenth of Adar; 22 for on these days the Jews obtained rest from their enemies; and *as to* the month, which was Adar, in which a change was made for them, from mourning to joy, and from sorrow to a good day, to spend the whole of it *in* good days of feasting and gladness, sending portions to their friends, and to the poor. 23 And the Jews consented *to this* accordingly as Mardochaeus wrote to them, 24 *shewing* how Aman the son of Amadathes the Macedonian fought against them, how he made a decree and cast lots to destroy them utterly; 25 also how he went in to the king, telling *him* to hang Mardochaeus: but all the calamities he tried to bring upon the Jews came upon himself, and he was hanged, and his children. 26 Therefore these days were called Phrurae, because of the lots; (for in their language they are called Phrurae;)because of the words of this letter, and *because of* all they suffered on this account, and all that happened to them. 27 And *Mardochaeus* established it, and the Jews took upon themselves, and upon their seed, and upon those that were joined to them *to observe it*, neither would they on any account behave differently: but these days *were to be* a memorial kept in every

generation, and city, and family, and province. 28 And these days of the Phrurae, *said they,*shall be kept for ever, and their memorial shall not fail in any generation. 29 And queen Esther, the daughter of Aminadab, and Mardochaeus the Jew, wrote all that they had done, and the confirmation of the letter of Phrurae. 30 31 And Mardochaeus and Esther the queen appointed *a fast* for themselves privately, even at that time also having formed their plan against their own health. 32 And Esther established it by a command for ever, and it was written for a memorial.

Est.10 1 And the king levied *a tax* upon *his* kingdom both by land and sea. 2 And *as for* his strength and valour, and the wealth and glory of his kingdom, behold, they are written in the book of the Persians and Medes, for a memorial. 3 And Mardochaeus was viceroy to king Artaxerxes, and was a great man in the kingdom, and honoured by the Jews, and passed his life beloved of all his nation. And Mardocheus said, These things have been done of God. For I remember the dream which I had concerning these matters: for not one particular of them has failed. *There was* the little fountain which became a river, and there was light, and the sun and much water. The river is Esther, whom the king married, and made queen. And the two serpents are I and Aman. And the nations are those *nations* that combined to destroy the name of the Jews. But *as for* my nation, this is Israel, *even* they that cried to God and were delivered: for the Lord delivered his people. And the Lord rescued us out of all these calamities; and God wrought such signs and great wonders as have not been done among the nations. Therefore did he ordain two lots. One for the people of God, and one for all the other *nations*. And these two lots came for an appointed season, and for a day of judgment, before God, and for all the nations. And God remembered his people, and vindicated his inheritance. And they shall observe these days in the month Adar, on the fourteenth and on the fifteenth *day* of the month, with an assembly, and joy and gladness before God, throughout the generations for ever among his people Israel. In the fourth year of the reign of Ptolemeus and Cleopatra, Dositheus, who said he was a priest and Levite, and Ptolemeus his son, brought this epistle of Phurim, which they said was the same, and that Lysimachus the son of Ptolemeus, that was in Jerusalem, had interpreted it.

1 MACCABEES

1-Macc.1 1 And it happened, after that Alexander son of Philip, the Macedonian, who came out of the land of Chettiim, had smitten Darius king of the Persians and Medes, that he reigned in his stead, the first over Greece, 2 And made many wars, and won many strong holds, and slew the kings of the earth, 3 And went through to the ends of the earth, and took spoils of many nations, insomuch that the earth was quiet before him; whereupon he was exalted and his heart was lifted up. 4 And he gathered a mighty strong host and ruled over countries, and nations, and kings, who became tributaries unto him. 5 And after these things he fell sick, and perceived that he should die. 6 Wherefore he called his servants, such as were honourable, and had been brought up with him from his youth, and parted his kingdom among them, while he was yet alive. 7 So Alexander reigned twelve years, and then died. 8 And his servants bare rule every one in his place. 9 And after his death they all put crowns upon themselves; so did their sons after them many years: and evils were multiplied in the earth. 10 And there came out of them a wicked root Antiochus *surnamed* Epiphanes, son of Antiochus the king, who had been an hostage at Rome, and he reigned in the hundred and thirty and seventh year of the kingdom of the Greeks. 11 In those days went there out of Israel wicked men, who persuaded many, saying, Let us go and make a covenant with the heathen that are round about us: for since we departed from them we have had much sorrow. 12 So this device pleased them well. 13 Then certain of the people were so forward herein, that they went to the king, who gave them licence to do after the ordinances of the heathen: 14 Whereupon they built a place of exercise at Jerusalem according to the customs of the heathen: 15 And made themselves uncircumcised, and forsook the holy covenant, and joined themselves to the heathen, and were sold to do mischief. 16 Now when the kingdom was established before Antiochus, he thought to reign over Egypt that he might have the dominion of two realms. 17 Wherefore he entered into Egypt with a great multitude, with chariots, and elephants, and horsemen, and a great navy, 18 And made war against Ptolemee king of Egypt: but Ptolemee was afraid of him, and fled; and many were wounded to death. 19 Thus they got the strong cities in the land of Egypt and he took the spoils thereof. 20 And after that Antiochus had smitten Egypt, he returned again in the hundred forty and third year, and went up against Israel and Jerusalem with a great multitude, 21 And entered proudly into the sanctuary, and took away the golden altar, and the candlestick of light, and all the vessels thereof, 22 And the table of the shewbread, and the pouring vessels, and the vials. and the censers of gold, and the veil, and the crown, and the golden ornaments that were before the temple, all which he pulled off. 23 He took also the silver and the gold, and the precious vessels: also he took the hidden treasures which he found. 24 And when he had taken all away, he went into his own land, having made a great massacre, and spoken very proudly. 25 Therefore there was a great mourning in Israel, in every place where they were; 26 So that the princes and elders mourned, the virgins and young men were made feeble, and the beauty of women was changed. 27 Every bridegroom took up lamentation, and she that sat in the marriage chamber was in heaviness, 28 The land also was moved for the inhabitants thereof, and all the house of Jacob was covered with confusion. 29 And after two years fully expired the king sent his chief collector of tribute unto the cities of Juda, who came unto Jerusalem with a great multitude, 30 And spake peaceable words unto them, but all was deceit: for when they had given him credence, he fell suddenly upon the city, and smote it very sore, and destroyed much people of Israel. 31 And when he had taken the spoils of the city, he set it on fire, and pulled down the houses and walls thereof on every side. 32 But the women and children took they captive, and possessed the cattle. 33 Then builded they the city of David with a great

and strong wall, and with mighty towers, and made it a strong hold for them. 34 And they put therein a sinful nation, wicked men, and fortified themselves therein. 35 They stored it also with armour and victuals, and when they had gathered together the spoils of Jerusalem, they laid them up there, and so they became a sore snare: 36 For it was a place to lie in wait against the sanctuary, and an evil adversary to Israel. 37 Thus they shed innocent blood on every side of the sanctuary, and defiled it: 38 Insomuch that the inhabitants of Jerusalem fled because of them: whereupon the city was made an habitation of strangers, and became strange to those that were born in her; and her own children left her. 39 Her sanctuary was laid waste like a wilderness, her feasts were turned into mourning, her sabbaths into reproach her honour into contempt. 40 As had been her glory, so was her dishonour increased, and her excellency was turned into mourning. 41 Moreover king Antiochus wrote to his whole kingdom, that all should be one people, 42 And every one should leave his laws: so all the heathen agreed according to the commandment of the king. 43 Yea, many also of the Israelites consented to his religion, and sacrificed unto idols, and profaned the sabbath. 44 For the king had sent letters by messengers unto Jerusalem and the cities of Juda that they should follow the strange laws of the land, 45 And forbid burnt offerings, and sacrifice, and drink offerings, in the temple; and that they should profane the sabbaths and festival days: 46 And pollute the sanctuary and holy people: 47 Set up altars, and groves, and chapels of idols, and sacrifice swine's flesh, and unclean beasts: 48 That they should also leave their children uncircumcised, and make their souls abominable with all manner of uncleanness and profanation: 49 To the end they might forget the law, and change all the ordinances. 50 And whosoever would not do according to the commandment of the king, he said, he should die. 51 In the selfsame manner wrote he to his whole kingdom, and appointed overseers over all the people, commanding the cities of Juda to sacrifice, city by city. 52 Then many of the people were gathered unto them, to wit every one that forsook the law; and so they committed evils in the land; 53 And drove the Israelites into secret places, even wheresoever they could flee for succour. 54 Now the fifteenth day of the month Casleu, in the hundred forty and fifth year, they set up the abomination of desolation upon the altar, and builded idol altars throughout the cities of Juda on every side; 55 And burnt incense at the doors of their houses, and in the streets. 56 And when they had rent in pieces the books of the law which they found, they burnt them with fire. 57 And whosoever was found with any the book of the testament, or if any committed to the law, the king's commandment was, that they should put him to death. 58 Thus did they by their authority unto the Israelites every month, to as many as were found in the cities. 59 Now the five and twentieth day of the month they did sacrifice upon the idol altar, which was upon the altar of God. 60 At which time according to the commandment they put to death certain women, that had caused their children to be circumcised. 61 And they hanged the infants about their necks, and rifled their houses, and slew them that had circumcised them. 62

Howbeit many in Israel were fully resolved and confirmed in themselves not to eat any unclean thing. 63 Wherefore the rather to die, that they might not be defiled with meats, and that they might not profane the holy covenant: so then they died. 64 And there was very great wrath upon Israel.

1-Macc.2 1 In those days arose Mattathias the son of John, the son of Simeon, a priest of the sons of Joarib, from Jerusalem, and dwelt in Modin. 2 And he had five sons, Joannan, called Caddis: 3 Simon; called Thassi: 4 Judas, who was called Maccabeus: 5 Eleazar, called Avaran: and Jonathan, whose surname was Apphus. 6 And when he saw the blasphemies that were committed in Juda and Jerusalem, 7 He said, Woe is me! wherefore was I born to see this misery of my people, and of the holy city, and to dwell there, when it was delivered into the hand of the enemy, and the sanctuary into the hand of strangers? 8 Her temple is become as a man without glory. 9 Her glorious vessels are carried away into captivity, her infants are slain in the streets, her young men with the sword of the enemy. 10 What nation hath not had a part in her kingdom and gotten of her spoils? 11 All her ornaments are taken away; of a free woman she is become a bondslave. 12 And, behold, our sanctuary, even our beauty and our glory, is laid waste, and the Gentiles have profaned it. 13 To what end therefore shall we live any longer? 14 Then Mattathias and his sons rent their clothes, and put on sackcloth, and mourned very sore. 15 In the mean while the king's officers, such as compelled the people to revolt, came into the city Modin, to make them sacrifice. 16 And when many of Israel came unto them, Mattathias also and his sons came together. 17 Then answered the king's officers, and said to Mattathias on this wise, Thou art a ruler, and an honourable and great man in this city, and strengthened with sons and brethren: 18 Now therefore come thou first, and fulfil the king's commandment, like as all the heathen have done, yea, and the men of Juda also, and such as remain at Jerusalem: so shalt thou and thy house be in the number of the king's friends, and thou and thy children shall be honoured with silver and gold, and many rewards. 19 Then Mattathias answered and spake with a loud voice, Though all the nations that are under the king's dominion obey him, and fall away every one from the religion of their fathers, and give consent to his commandments: 20 Yet will I and my sons and my brethren walk in the covenant of our fathers. 21 God forbid that we should forsake the law and the ordinances. 22 We will not hearken to the king's words, to go from our religion, either on the right hand, or the left. 23 Now when he had left speaking these words, there came one of the Jews in the sight of all to sacrifice on the altar which was at Modin, according to the king's commandment. 24 Which thing when Mattathias saw, he was inflamed with zeal, and his reins trembled, neither could he forbear to shew his anger according to judgment: wherefore he ran, and slew him upon the altar. 25 Also the king's commissioner, who compelled men to sacrifice, he killed at that time, and the altar he pulled down. 26 Thus dealt he zealously for the law of God like as Phinees did unto Zambri the son of Salom. 27 And Mattathias cried throughout the city with a loud voice, saying, Whosoever is zealous of the law, and maintaineth the covenant, let him follow me. 28 So he and his sons fled into the mountains, and left all that ever they had in the city. 29 Then many that sought after justice and judgment went down into the wilderness, to dwell there: 30 Both they, and their children, and their wives; and their cattle; because afflictions increased sore upon them. 31 Now when it was told the king's servants, and the host that was at Jerusalem, in the city of David, that certain men, who had broken the king's commandment, were gone down into the secret places in the wilderness, 32 They pursued after them a great number, and having overtaken them, they camped against them, and made war against them on the sabbath day. 33 And they said unto them, Let that which ye have done hitherto suffice; come forth, and do according to the commandment of the king, and ye shall live. 34 But they said, We will not come forth, neither will we do the king's commandment, to profane the sabbath day. 35 So then they gave them the battle with all speed. 36 Howbeit they answered them not, neither cast they a stone at them, nor stopped the places where they lay hid; 37 But said, Let us die all in our innocency: heaven and earth will testify for us, that ye put us to death wrongfully. 38 So they rose up against them in battle on the sabbath, and they slew them, with their wives and children and their cattle, to the number of a thousand people. 39 Now when Mattathias and his friends understood hereof, they mourned for them right sore. 40 And one of them said to another, If we all do as our brethren have done, and fight not for our lives and laws against the heathen, they will now quickly root us out of the earth. 41 At that time therefore they decreed, saying, Whosoever shall come to make battle with us on the sabbath day, we will fight against him; neither will we die all, as our brethren that were murdered in the secret places. 42 Then came there unto him a company of Assideans who were mighty men of Israel, even all such as were voluntarily devoted unto the law. 43 Also all they that fled for persecution joined themselves unto them, and were a stay unto them. 44 So they joined their forces, and smote sinful men in their anger, and wicked men in their wrath: but the rest fled to the heathen for succour. 45 Then Mattathias and his friends went round about, and pulled down the altars: 46 And what children soever they found within the coast of Israel uncircumcised, those they circumcised valiantly. 47 They pursued also after the proud men, and the work prospered in their hand. 48 So they recovered the law out of the hand of the Gentiles, and out of the hand of kings, neither suffered they the sinner to triumph. 49 Now when the time drew near that Mattathias should die, he said unto his sons, Now hath pride and rebuke gotten strength, and the time of destruction, and the wrath of indignation: 50 Now therefore, my sons, be ye zealous for the law, and give your lives for the covenant of your fathers. 51 Call to remembrance what acts our fathers did in their time; so shall ye receive great honour and an everlasting name. 52 Was not Abraham found faithful in temptation, and it was imputed unto him for righteousness? 53 Joseph in the time of his distress kept the commandment and was made lord of Egypt. 54 Phinees our father in being zealous and fervent obtained the covenant of an everlasting priesthood. 55 Jesus for fulfilling the word was made a judge in Israel. 56 Caleb for bearing witness before the congregation received the heritage of the land. 57 David for being merciful possessed the throne of an everlasting kingdom. 58 Elias for being zealous and fervent for the law was taken up into heaven. 59 Ananias, Azarias, and Misael, by believing were saved out of the flame. 60 Daniel for his innocency was delivered from the mouth of lions. 61 And thus consider ye throughout all ages, that none that put their trust in him shall be overcome. 62 Fear not then the words of a sinful man: for his glory shall be dung and worms. 63 To day he shall be lifted up and to morrow he shall not be found, because he is returned into his dust, and his thought is come to nothing. 64 Wherefore, ye my sons, be valiant and shew yourselves men in the behalf of the law; for by it shall ye obtain glory. 65 And behold, I know that your brother Simon is a man of counsel, give ear unto him alway: he shall be a father unto you. 66 As for Judas Maccabeus, he hath been mighty and strong, even from his youth up: let him be your captain, and fight the battle of the people. 67 Take also unto you all those that observe the law, and avenge ye the wrong of your people. 68 Recompense fully the heathen, and take heed to the commandments of the law. 69 So he blessed them, and was gathered to his fathers. 70 And he died in the hundred forty and sixth year, and his sons buried him in the sepulchres of his fathers at Modin, and all Israel made great lamentation for him.

1-Macc.3 1 Then his son Judas, called Maccabeus, rose up in his stead. 2 And all his brethren helped him, and so did all they that held with his father, and they fought with cheerfulness the battle of Israel. 3 So he gat his people great honour, and put on a breastplate as a giant, and girt his warlike harness about him, and he made battles, protecting the host with his sword. 4 In his acts he was like a lion, and like a lion's whelp roaring for his prey. 5 For He pursued the wicked, and sought them out, and burnt up those that vexed his people. 6 Wherefore the wicked shrunk for fear of him, and all the workers of iniquity were troubled, because salvation prospered in his hand. 7 He grieved also many kings, and made Jacob glad with his acts, and his memorial is blessed for ever. 8 Moreover he went through the cities of Juda, destroying the ungodly out of them, and turning away wrath from Israel: 9 So that he was renowned unto the utmost part of the earth, and he received unto him such as were ready to perish. 10 Then Apollonius gathered the Gentiles together, and a great host out of Samaria, to fight against Israel. 11 Which thing when Judas perceived, he went forth to meet him, and so he smote him, and slew him: many also fell down slain, but the rest fled. 12 Wherefore Judas took their spoils, and Apollonius' sword also, and therewith he fought all his life long. 13 Now when Seron, a prince of the army of Syria, heard say that Judas had gathered unto him a multitude and company of the faithful to go out with him to war; 14 He said, I will get me a name and honour in the kingdom; for I will go fight with Judas and them that are with him, who despise the king's commandment. 15 So he made him ready to go up, and there went with him a mighty host of the ungodly to help him, and to be avenged of the children of Israel. 16 And when he came near to the going up of Bethhoron, Judas went forth to meet him with a small company: 17 Who, when they saw the host coming to meet them, said unto Judas, How shall we be able, being so few, to fight against so great a multitude and so strong, seeing we are ready to faint with fasting all this day? 18 Unto whom Judas answered, It is no hard matter for many to be shut up in the hands of a few; and with the God of heaven it is all one, to deliver with a great multitude, or a small company: 19 For the victory of battle standeth not in the multitude of an host; but strength cometh from heaven. 20 They come against us in much pride and iniquity to destroy us, and our wives and children, and to spoil us: 21 But we fight for our lives and our laws. 22 Wherefore the Lord himself will overthrow them before our face: and as for you, be ye not afraid of them. 23 Now as soon as he had left off speaking, he leapt suddenly upon them, and so Seron and his host was overthrown before him. 24 And they pursued them from the going down of Bethhoron unto the plain, where were slain about eight hundred men of them; and the residue fled into the land of the Philistines. 25 Then began the fear of Judas and his brethren, and an exceeding great dread, to fall upon the nations round about them: 26 Insomuch as his fame came unto the king, and all nations talked of the battles of Judas. 27 Now when king Antiochus heard these things, he was full of indignation: wherefore he sent and gathered together all the forces of his realm, even a very strong army. 28 He opened also his treasure, and gave his soldiers pay for a year, commanding them to be ready whensoever he should need them. 29 Nevertheless, when he saw that the money of his treasures failed and that the tributes in the country were small, because of the dissension and plague, which he had brought upon the land in taking away the laws which had been of old time; 30 He feared that he should not be able to bear the charges any longer, nor to have such gifts to give so liberally as he did before: for he had abounded above the kings that were before him. 31 Wherefore, being greatly perplexed in his mind, he determined to go into Persia, there to take the tributes of the countries, and to gather much money. 32 So he left Lysias, a nobleman, and one of the blood royal, to oversee the affairs of the king from the river Euphrates unto the borders of Egypt: 33 And to bring up his son Antiochus, until he came again. 34 Moreover he delivered unto him the half of his forces, and the elephants, and gave him charge of all things that he would have done, as also concerning them that dwelt in Juda and Jerusalem: 35 To wit, that he should send an army against them, to destroy and root out the strength of Israel, and the remnant of Jerusalem, and to take away their memorial from that place; 36 And that he should place strangers in all their quarters, and divide their land by lot. 37 So the king took the half of the forces that remained, and departed from Antioch, his royal city, the hundred forty and seventh year; and having passed the river Euphrates, he went through the high countries. 38 Then Lysias chose Ptolemee the son of

Dorymenes, Nicanor, and Gorgias, mighty men of the king's friends: 39 And with them he sent forty thousand footmen, and seven thousand horsemen, to go into the land of Juda, and to destroy it, as the king commanded. 40 So they went forth with all their power, and came and pitched by Emmaus in the plain country. 41 And the merchants of the country, hearing the fame of them, took silver and gold very much, with servants, and came into the camp to buy the children of Israel for slaves: a power also of Syria and of the land of the Philistines joined themselves unto them. 42 Now when Judas and his brethren saw that miseries were multiplied, and that the forces did encamp themselves in their borders: for they knew how the king had given commandment to destroy the people, and utterly abolish them; 43 They said one to another, Let us restore the decayed fortune of our people, and let us fight for our people and the sanctuary. 44 Then was the congregation gathered together, that they might be ready for battle, and that they might pray, and ask mercy and compassion. 45 Now Jerusalem lay void as a wilderness, there was none of her children that went in or out: the sanctuary also was trodden down, and aliens kept the strong hold; the heathen had their habitation in that place; and joy was taken from Jacob, and the pipe with the harp ceased. 46 Wherefore the Israelites assembled themselves together, and came to Maspha, over against Jerusalem; for in Maspha was the place where they prayed aforetime in Israel. 47 Then they fasted that day, and put on sackcloth, and cast ashes upon their heads, and rent their clothes, 48 And laid open the book of the law, wherein the heathen had sought to paint the likeness of their images. 49 They brought also the priests' garments, and the firstfruits, and the tithes: and the Nazarites they stirred up, who had accomplished their days. 50 Then cried they with a loud voice toward heaven, saying, What shall we do with these, and whither shall we carry them away? 51 For thy sanctuary is trodden down and profaned, and thy priests are in heaviness, and brought low. 52 And lo, the heathen are assembled together against us to destroy us: what things they imagine against us, thou knowest. 53 How shall we be able to stand against them, except thou, O God, be our help? 54 Then sounded they with trumpets, and cried with a loud voice. 55 And after this Judas ordained captains over the people, even captains over thousands, and over hundreds, and over fifties, and over tens. 56 But as for such as were building houses, or had betrothed wives, or were planting vineyards, or were fearful, those he commanded that they should return, every man to his own house, according to the law. 57 So the camp removed, and pitched upon the south side of Emmaus. 58 And Judas said, arm yourselves, and be valiant men, and see that ye be in readiness against the morning, that ye may fight with these nations, that are assembled together against us to destroy us and our sanctuary: 59 For it is better for us to die in battle, than to behold the calamities of our people and our sanctuary. 60 Nevertheless, as the will of God is in heaven, so let him do.

1-Macc.4 1 Then took Gorgias five thousand footmen, and a thousand of the best horsemen, and removed out of the camp by night; 2 To the end he might rush in upon the camp of the Jews, and smite them suddenly. And the men of the fortress were his guides. 3 Now when Judas heard thereof he himself removed, and the valiant men with him, that he might smite the king's army which was at Emmaus, 4 While as yet the forces were dispersed from the camp. 5 In the mean season came Gorgias by night into the camp of Judas: and when he found no man there, he sought them in the mountains: for said he, These fellows flee from us 6 But as soon as it was day, Judas shewed himself in the plain with three thousand men, who nevertheless had neither armour nor swords to their minds. 7 And they saw the camp of the heathen, that it was strong and well harnessed, and compassed round about with horsemen; and these were expert of war. 8 Then said Judas to the men that were with him, Fear ye not their multitude, neither be ye afraid of their assault. 9 Remember how our fathers were delivered in the Red sea, when Pharaoh pursued them with an army. 10 Now therefore let us cry unto heaven, if peradventure the Lord will have mercy upon us, and remember the covenant of our fathers, and destroy this host before our face this day: 11 That so all the heathen may know that there is one who delivereth and saveth Israel. 12 Then the strangers lifted up their eyes, and saw them coming over against them. 13 Wherefore they went out of the camp to battle; but they that were with Judas sounded their trumpets. 14 So they joined battle, and the heathen being discomfited fled into the plain. 15 Howbeit all the hindmost of them were slain with the sword: for they pursued them unto Gazera, and unto the plains of Idumea, and Azotus, and Jamnia, so that there were slain of them upon a three thousand men. 16 This done, Judas returned again with his host from pursuing them, 17 And said to the people, Be not greedy of the spoil inasmuch as there is a battle before us, 18 And Gorgias and his host are here by us in the mountain: but stand ye now against our enemies, and overcome them, and after this ye may boldly take the spoils. 19 As Judas was yet speaking these words, there appeared a part of them looking out of the mountain: 20 Who when they perceived that the Jews had put their host to flight and were burning the tents; for the smoke that was seen declared what was done: 21 When therefore they perceived these things, they were sore afraid, and seeing also the host of Judas in the plain ready to fight, 22 They fled every one into the land of strangers. 23 Then Judas returned to spoil the tents, where they got much gold, and silver, and blue silk, and purple of the sea, and great riches. 24 After this they went home, and sung a song of thanksgiving, and praised the Lord in heaven: because it is good, because his mercy endureth forever. 25 Thus Israel had a great deliverance that day. 26 Now all the strangers that had escaped came and told Lysias what had happened: 27 Who, when he heard thereof, was confounded and discouraged, because neither such things as he would were done unto Israel, nor such things as the king commanded him were come to pass. 28 The next year therefore following Lysias gathered together threescore thousand choice men of foot, and five thousand horsemen, that he might subdue them. 29 So they came into Idumea, and pitched their tents at Bethsura, and Judas met them with ten thousand men. 30 And when he saw that mighty army, he prayed and said, Blessed art thou, O Saviour of Israel, who didst quell the violence of the mighty man by the hand of thy servant David, and gavest the host of strangers into the hands of Jonathan the son of Saul, and his armourbearer; 31 Shut up this army in the hand of thy people Israel, and let them be confounded in their power and horsemen: 32 Make them to be of no courage, and cause the boldness of their strength to fall away, and let them quake at their destruction: 33 Cast them down with the sword of them that love thee, and let all those that know thy name praise thee with thanksgiving. 34 So they joined battle; and there were slain of the host of Lysias about five thousand men, even before them were they slain. 35 Now when Lysias saw his army put to flight, and the manliness of Judas' soldiers, and how they were ready either to live or die valiantly, he went into Antiochia, and gathered together a company of strangers, and having made his army greater than it was, he purposed to come again into Judea. 36 Then said Judas and his brethren, Behold, our enemies are discomfited: let us go up to cleanse and dedicate the sanctuary. 37 Upon this all the host assembled themselves together, and went up into mount Sion. 38 And when they saw the sanctuary desolate, and the altar profaned, and the gates burned up, and shrubs growing in the courts as in a forest, or in one of the mountains, yea, and the priests' chambers pulled down; 39 They rent their clothes, and made great lamentation, and cast ashes upon their heads, 40 And fell down flat to the ground upon their faces, and blew an alarm with the trumpets, and cried toward heaven. 41 Then Judas appointed certain men to fight against those that were in the fortress, until he had cleansed the sanctuary. 42 So he chose priests of blameless conversation, such as had pleasure in the law: 43 Who cleansed the sanctuary, and bare out the defiled stones into an unclean place. 44 And when as they consulted what to do with the altar of burnt offerings, which was profaned; 45 They thought it best to pull it down, lest it should be a reproach to them, because the heathen had defiled it: wherefore they pulled it down, 46 And laid up the stones in the mountain of the temple in a convenient place, until there should come a prophet to shew what should be done with them. 47 Then they took whole stones according to the law, and built a new altar according to the former; 48 And made up the sanctuary, and the things that were within the temple, and hallowed the courts. 49 They made also new holy vessels, and into the temple they brought the candlestick, and the altar of burnt offerings, and of incense, and the table. 50 And upon the altar they burned incense, and the lamps that were upon the candlestick they lighted, that they might give light in the temple. 51 Furthermore they set the loaves upon the table, and spread out the veils, and finished all the works which they had begun to make. 52 Now on the five and twentieth day of the ninth month, which is called the month Casleu, in the hundred forty and eighth year, they rose up betimes in the morning, 53 And offered sacrifice according to the law upon the new altar of burnt offerings, which they had made. 54 Look, at what time and what day the heathen had profaned it, even in that was it dedicated with songs, and cithems, and harps, and cymbals. 55 Then all the people fell upon their faces, worshipping and praising the God of heaven, who had given them good success. 56 And so they kept the dedication of the altar eight days and offered burnt offerings with gladness, and sacrificed the sacrifice of deliverance and praise. 57 They decked also the forefront of the temple with crowns of gold, and with shields; and the gates and the chambers they renewed, and hanged doors upon them. 58 Thus was there very great gladness among the people, for that the reproach of the heathen was put away. 59 Moreover Judas and his brethren with the whole congregation of Israel ordained, that the days of the dedication of the altar should be kept in their season from year to year by the space of eight days, from the five and twentieth day of the month Casleu, with mirth and gladness. 60 At that time also they builded up the mount Sion with high walls and strong towers round about, lest the Gentiles should come and tread it down as they had done before. 61 And they set there a garrison to keep it, and fortified Bethsura to preserve it; that the people might have a defence against Idumea.

1-Macc.5 1 Now when the nations round about heard that the altar was built and the sanctuary renewed as before, it displeased them very much. 2 Wherefore they thought to destroy the generation of Jacob that was among them, and thereupon they began to slay and destroy the people. 3 Then Judas fought against the children of Esau in Idumea at Arabattine, because they besieged Gael: and he gave them a great overthrow, and abated their courage, and took their spoils. 4 Also he remembered the injury of the children of Bean, who had been a snare and an offence unto the people, in that they lay in wait for them in the ways. 5 He shut them up therefore in the towers, and encamped against them, and destroyed them utterly, and burned the towers of that place with fire, and all that were therein. 6 Afterward he passed over to the children of Ammon, where he found a mighty power, and much people, with Timotheus their captain. 7 So he fought many battles with them, till at length they were discomfited before him; and he smote them. 8 And when he had taken Jazar, with the towns belonging thereto, he returned into Judea. 9 Then the heathen that were at Galaad assembled themselves together against the Israelites that were in their quarters, to destroy them; but they fled to the fortress of Dathema. 10 And sent letters unto Judas and his brethren, The heathen that are round about us are assembled together against us to destroy us: 11 And they are preparing to come and take the fortress whereunto we are fled, Timotheus being captain of their host. 12 Come now therefore, and deliver us from their hands, for many of us are slain: 13 Yea, all our brethren that were in the places of Tobie are put to death: their wives and their children also they have carried away captives, and borne away their stuff; and they have destroyed there about a thousand men. 14 While these letters were yet reading, behold, there came other messengers from Galilee with their clothes rent, who reported on this wise, 15 And said, They of Ptolemais, and of Tyrus, and Sidon, and all Galilee of the Gentiles, are assembled together against us to consume us. 16 Now when Judas and the people heard these words, there assembled a great congregation together, to consult what they should do for their brethren, that were in trouble, and assaulted of them. 17 Then said Judas unto Simon his brother, Choose thee out men, and go and deliver thy brethren that are in Galilee, for I and Jonathan my brother will go into the country of Galaad. 18 So he left Joseph the son of Zacharias, and Azarias, captains of the people, with the remnant of the host in Judea to keep it. 19 Unto whom he gave commandment, saying, Take ye the charge of this people, and see that ye make not war against the heathen until the time that we come again. 20 Now unto Simon were given three thousand men to go into Galilee, and unto Judas eight thousand men for the country of Galaad. 21 Then went Simon into Galilee, where he fought many battles with the heathen, so that the heathen were discomfited by him. 22 And he pursued them unto the gate of Ptolemais; and there were slain of the heathen about three thousand men, whose spoils he took. 23 And those that were in Galilee, and in Arbattis, with their wives and their children, and all that they had, took he away with him, and brought them into Judea with great joy. 24 Judas Maccabeus also and his brother Jonathan went over Jordan, and travelled three days' journey in the wilderness, 25 Where they met with the Nabathites, who came unto them in a peaceable manner, and told them every thing that had happened to their brethren in the land of Galaad: 26 And how that many of them were shut up in Bosora, and Bosor, and Alema, Casphor, Maked, and Carnaim; all these cities are strong and great: 27 And that they were shut up in the rest of the cities of the country of Galaad, and that against to morrow they had appointed to bring their host against the forts, and to take them, and to destroy them all in one day. 28 Hereupon Judas and his host turned suddenly by the way of the wilderness unto Bosora; and when he had won the city, he slew all the males with the edge of the sword, and took all their spoils, and burned the city with fire, 29 From whence he removed by night, and went till he came to the fortress. 30 And betimes in the morning they looked up, and, behold, there was an innumerable people bearing ladders and other engines of war, to take the fortress: for they assaulted them. 31 When Judas therefore saw that the battle was begun, and that the cry of the city went up to heaven, with trumpets, and a great sound, 32 He said unto his host, Fight this day for your brethren. 33 So he went forth behind them in three companies, who sounded their trumpets, and cried with prayer. 34 Then the host of Timotheus, knowing that it was Maccabeus, fled from him: wherefore he smote them with a great slaughter; so that there were killed of them that day about eight thousand men. 35 This done, Judas turned aside to Maspha; and after he had assaulted it he took and slew all the males therein, and received the spoils thereof and burnt it with fire. 36 From thence went he, and took Casphon, Maged, Bosor, and the other cities of the country of Galaad. 37 After these things gathered Timotheus another host and encamped against Raphon beyond the brook. 38 So Judas sent men to espy the host, who brought him word, saying, All the heathen that be round about us are assembled unto them,

even a very great host. 39 He hath also hired the Arabians to help them and they have pitched their tents beyond the brook, ready to come and fight against thee. Upon this Judas went to meet them. 40 Then Timotheus said unto the captains of his host, When Judas and his host come near the brook, if he pass over first unto us, we shall not be able to withstand him; for he will mightily prevail against us: 41 But if he be afraid, and camp beyond the river, we shall go over unto him, and prevail against him. 42 Now when Judas came near the brook, he caused the scribes of the people to remain by the brook: unto whom he gave commandment, saying, Suffer no man to remain in the camp, but let all come to the battle. 43 So he went first over unto them, and all the people after him: then all the heathen, being discomfited before him, cast away their weapons, and fled unto the temple that was at Carnaim. 44 But they took the city, and burned the temple with all that were therein. Thus was Carnaim subdued, neither could they stand any longer before Judas. 45 Then Judas gathered together all the Israelites that were in the country of Galaad, from the least unto the greatest, even their wives, and their children, and their stuff, a very great host, to the end they might come into the land of Judea. 46 Now when they came unto Ephron, (this was a great city in the way as they should go, very well fortified) they could not turn from it, either on the right hand or the left, but must needs pass through the midst of it. 47 Then they of the city shut them out, and stopped up the gates with stones. 48 Whereupon Judas sent unto them in peaceable manner, saying, Let us pass through your land to go into our own country, and none shall do you any hurt; we will only pass through on foot: howbeit they would not open unto him. 49 Wherefore Judas commanded a proclamation to be made throughout the host, that every man should pitch his tent in the place where he was. 50 So the soldiers pitched, and assaulted the city all that day and all that night, till at the length the city was delivered into his hands: 51 Who then slew all the males with the edge of the sword, and rased the city, and took the spoils thereof, and passed through the city over them that were slain. 52 After this went they over Jordan into the great plain before Bethsan. 53 And Judas gathered together those that came behind, and exhorted the people all the way through, till they came into the land of Judea. 54 So they went up to mount Sion with joy and gladness, where they offered burnt offerings, because not one of them were slain until they had returned in peace. 55 Now what time as Judas and Jonathan were in the land of Galaad, and Simon his brother in Galilee before Ptolemais, 56 Joseph the son of Zacharias, and Azarias, captains of the garrisons, heard of the valiant acts and warlike deeds which they had done. 57 Wherefore they said, Let us also get us a name, and go fight against the heathen that are round about us. 58 So when they had given charge unto the garrison that was with them, they went toward Jamnia. 59 Then came Gorgias and his men out of the city to fight against them. 60 And so it was, that Joseph and Azarias were put to flight, and pursued unto the borders of Judea: and there were slain that day of the people of Israel about two thousand men. 61 Thus was there a great overthrow among the children of Israel, because they were not obedient unto Judas and his brethren, but thought to do some valiant act. 62 Moreover these men came not of the seed of those, by whose hand deliverance was given unto Israel. 63 Howbeit the man Judas and his brethren were greatly renowned in the sight of all Israel, and of all the heathen, wheresoever their name was heard of; 64 Insomuch as the people assembled unto them with joyful acclamations. 65 Afterward went Judas forth with his brethren, and fought against the children of Esau in the land toward the south, where he smote Hebron, and the towns thereof, and pulled down the fortress of it, and burned the towers thereof round about. 66 From thence he removed to go into the land of the Philistines, and passed through Samaria. 67 At that time certain priests, desirous to shew their valour, were slain in battle, for that they went out to fight unadvisedly. 68 So Judas turned to Azotus in the land of the Philistines, and when he had pulled down their altars, and burned their carved images with fire, and spoiled their cities, he returned into the land of Judea.

1-Macc.6 1 About that time king Antiochus travelling through the high countries heard say, that Elymais in the country of Persia was a city greatly renowned for riches, silver, and gold; 2 And that there was in it a very rich temple, wherein were coverings of gold, and breastplates, and shields, which Alexander, son of Philip, the Macedonian king, who reigned first among the Grecians, had left there. 3 Wherefore he came and sought to take the city, and to spoil it; but he was not able, because they of the city, having had warning thereof, 4 Rose up against him in battle: so he fled, and departed thence with great heaviness, and returned to Babylon. 5 Moreover there came one who brought him tidings into Persia, that the armies, which went against the land of Judea, were put to flight: 6 And that Lysias, who went forth first with a great power was driven away of the Jews; and that they were made strong by the armour, and power, and store of spoils, which they had gotten of the armies, whom they had destroyed: 7 Also that they had pulled down the abomination, which he had set up upon the altar in Jerusalem, and that they had compassed about the sanctuary with high walls, as before, and his city Bethsura. 8 Now when the king heard these words, he was astonished and sore moved: whereupon he laid him down upon his bed, and fell sick for grief, because it had not befallen him as he looked for. 9 And there he continued many days: for his grief was ever more and more, and he made account that he should die. 10 Wherefore he called for all his friends, and said unto them, The sleep is gone from mine eyes, and my heart faileth for very care. 11 And I thought with myself, Into what tribulation am I come, and how great a flood of misery is it, wherein now I am! for I was bountiful and beloved in my power. 12 But now I remember the evils that I did at Jerusalem, and that I took all the vessels of gold and silver that were therein, and sent to destroy the inhabitants of Judea without a cause. 13 I perceive therefore that for this cause these troubles are come upon me, and, behold, I perish through great grief in a strange land. 14 Then called he for Philip, one of his friends, who he made ruler over all his realm, 15 And gave him the crown, and his robe, and his signet, to the end he should bring up his son Antiochus, and nourish him up for the kingdom. 16 So king Antiochus died there in the hundred forty and ninth year. 17 Now when Lysias knew that the king was dead, he set up Antiochus his son, whom he had brought up being young, to reign in his stead, and his name he called Eupator. 18 About this time they that were in the tower shut up the Israelites round about the sanctuary, and sought always their hurt, and the strengthening of the heathen. 19 Wherefore Judas, purposing to destroy them, called all the people together to besiege them. 20 So they came together, and besieged them in the hundred and fiftieth year, and he made mounts for shot against them, and other engines. 21 Howbeit certain of them that were besieged got forth, unto whom some ungodly men of Israel joined themselves: 22 And they went unto the king, and said, How long will it be ere thou execute judgment, and avenge our brethren? 23 We have been willing to serve thy father, and to do as he would have us, and to obey his commandments; 24 For which cause they of our nation besiege the tower, and are alienated from us: moreover as many of us as they could light on they slew, and spoiled our inheritance. 25 Neither have they stretched out their hand against us only, but also against their borders. 26 And, behold, this day are they besieging the tower at Jerusalem, to take it: the sanctuary also and Bethsura have they fortified. 27 Wherefore if thou dost not prevent them quickly, they will do the greater things than these, neither shalt thou be able to rule them. 28 Now when the king heard this, he was angry, and gathered together all his friends, and the captains of his army, and those that had charge of the horse. 29 There came also unto him from other kingdoms, and from isles of the sea, bands of hired soldiers. 30 So that the number of his army was an hundred thousand footmen, and twenty thousand horsemen, and two and thirty elephants exercised in battle. 31 These went through Idumea, and pitched against Bethsura, which they assaulted many days, making engines of war; but they of Bethsura came out, and burned them with fire, and fought valiantly. 32 Upon this Judas removed from the tower, and pitched in Bathzacharias, over against the king's camp. 33 Then the king rising very early marched fiercely with his host toward Bathzacharias, where his armies made them ready to battle, and sounded the trumpets. 34 And to the end they might provoke the elephants to fight, they shewed them the blood of grapes and mulberries. 35 Moreover they divided the beasts among the armies, and for every elephant they appointed a thousand men, armed with coats of mail, and with helmets of brass on their heads; and beside this, for every beast were ordained five hundred horsemen of the best. 36 These were ready at every occasion: wheresoever the beast was, and whithersoever the beast went, they went also, neither departed they from him. 37 And upon the beasts were there strong towers of wood, which covered every one of them, and were girt fast unto them with devices: there were also upon every one two and thirty strong men, that fought upon them, beside the Indian that ruled him. 38 As for the remnant of the horsemen, they set them on this side and that side at the two parts of the host giving them signs what to do, and being harnessed all over amidst the ranks. 39 Now when the sun shone upon the shields of gold and brass, the mountains glistered therewith, and shined like lamps of fire. 40 So part of the king's army being spread upon the high mountains, and part on the valleys below, they marched on safely and in order. 41 Wherefore all that heard the noise of their multitude, and the marching of the company, and the rattling of the harness, were moved: for the army was very great and mighty. 42 Then Judas and his host drew near, and entered into battle, and there were slain of the king's army six hundred men. 43 Eleazar also, surnamed Savaran, perceiving that one of the beasts, armed with royal harness, was higher than all the rest, and supposing that the king was upon him, 44 Put himself in jeopardy, to the end he might deliver his people, and get him a perpetual name: 45 Wherefore he ran upon him courageously through the midst of the battle, slaying on the right hand and on the left, so that they were divided from him on both sides. 46 Which done, he crept under the elephant, and thrust him under, and slew him: whereupon the elephant fell down upon him, and there he died. 47 Howbeit the rest of the Jews seeing the strength of the king, and the violence of his forces, turned away from them. 48 Then the king's army went up to Jerusalem to meet them, and the king pitched his tents against Judea, and against mount Sion. 49 But with them that were in Bethsura he made peace: for they came out of the city, because they had no victuals there to endure the siege, it being a year of rest to the land. 50 So the king took Bethsura, and set a garrison there to keep it. 51 As for the sanctuary, he besieged it many days: and set there artillery with engines and instruments to cast fire and stones, and pieces to cast darts and slings. 52 Whereupon they also made engines against their engines, and held them battle a long season. 53 Yet at the last, their vessels being without victuals, (for that it was the seventh year, and they in Judea that were delivered from the Gentiles, had eaten up the residue of the store;) 54 There were but a few left in the sanctuary, because the famine did so prevail against them, that they were fain to disperse themselves, every man to his own place. 55 At that time Lysias heard say, that Philip, whom Antiochus the king, whiles he lived, had appointed to bring up his son Antiochus, that he might be king, 56 Was returned out of Persia and Media, and the king's host also that went with him, and that he sought to take unto him the ruling of the affairs. 57 Wherefore he went in all haste, and said to the king and the captains of the host and the company, We decay daily, and our victuals are but small, and the place we lay siege unto is strong, and the affairs of the kingdom lie upon us: 58 Now therefore let us be friends with these men, and make peace with them, and with all their nation; 59 And covenant with them, that they shall live after their laws, as they did before: for they are therefore displeased, and have done all these things, because we abolished their laws. 60 So the king and the princes were content: wherefore he sent unto them to make peace; and they accepted thereof. 61 Also the king and the princes made an oath unto them: whereupon they went out of the strong hold. 62 Then the king entered into mount Sion; but when he saw the strength of the place, he broke his oath that he had made, and gave commandment to pull down the wall round about. 63 Afterward departed he in all haste, and returned unto Antiochia, where he found Philip to be master of the city: so he fought against him, and took the city by force.

1-Macc.7 1 In the hundred and one and fiftieth year Demetrius the son of Seleucus departed from Rome, and came up with a few men unto a city of the sea coast, and reigned there. 2 And as he entered into the palace of his ancestors, so it was, that his forces had taken Antiochus and Lysias, to bring them unto him. 3 Wherefore, when he knew it, he said, Let me not see their faces. 4 So his host slew them. Now when Demetrius was set upon the throne of his kingdom, 5 There came unto him all the wicked and ungodly men of Israel, having Alcimus, who was desirous to be high priest, for their captain: 6 And they accused the people to the king, saying, Judas and his brethren have slain all thy friends, and driven us out of our own land. 7 Now therefore send some man whom thou trustest, and let him go and see what havock he hath made among us, and in the king's land, and let him punish them with all them that aid them. 8 Then the king chose Bacchides, a friend of the king, who ruled beyond the flood, and was a great man in the kingdom, and faithful to the king, 9 And him he sent with that wicked Alcimus, whom he made high priest, and commanded that he should take vengeance of the children of Israel. 10 So they departed, and came with a great power into the land of Judea, where they sent messengers to Judas and his brethren with peaceable words deceitfully. 11 But they gave no heed to their words; for they saw that they were come with a great power. 12 Then did there assemble unto Alcimus and Bacchides a company of scribes, to require justice. 13 Now the Assideans were the first among the children of Israel that sought peace of them: 14 For said they, One that is a priest of the seed of Aaron is come with this army, and he will do us no wrong. 15 So he spake unto them, peaceably, and sware unto them, saying, we will procure the harm neither of you nor your friends. 16 Whereupon they believed him: howbeit he took of them threescore men, and slew them in one day, according to the words which he wrote, 17 The flesh of thy saints have they cast out, and their blood have they shed round about Jerusalem, and there was none to bury them. 18 Wherefore the fear and dread of them fell upon all the people, who said, There is neither truth nor righteousness in them; for they have broken the covenant and oath that they made. 19 After this, removed Bacchides from Jerusalem, and pitched his tents in Bezeth, where he sent and took many of the men that had forsaken him, and certain of the people also, and when he had slain them, he cast them into the great pit. 20 Then committed he the country to Alcimus, and left with him a power to aid him: so Bacchides went to the king. 21 But Alcimus contended for the high priesthood. 22 And unto him resorted all such as troubled the people, who, after they had gotten the land of Juda into their power, did much hurt in Israel. 23 Now when Judas saw all the mischief that Alcimus and his company had done among the

Israelites, even above the heathen, 24 He went out into all the coasts of Judea round about, and took vengeance of them that had revolted from him, so that they durst no more go forth into the country. 25 On the other side, when Alcimus saw that Judas and his company had gotten the upper hand, and knew that he was not able to abide their force, he went again to the king, and said all the worst of them that he could. 26 Then the king sent Nicanor, one of his honourable princes, a man that bare deadly hate unto Israel, with commandment to destroy the people. 27 So Nicanor came to Jerusalem with a great force; and sent unto Judas and his brethren deceitfully with friendly words, saying, 28 Let there be no battle between me and you; I will come with a few men, that I may see you in peace. 29 He came therefore to Judas, and they saluted one another peaceably. Howbeit the enemies were prepared to take away Judas by violence. 30 Which thing after it was known to Judas, to wit, that he came unto him with deceit, he was sore afraid of him, and would see his face no more. 31 Nicanor also, when he saw that his counsel was discovered, went out to fight against Judas beside Capharsalama: 32 Where there were slain of Nicanor's side about five thousand men, and the rest fled into the city of David. 33 After this went Nicanor up to mount Sion, and there came out of the sanctuary certain of the priests and certain of the elders of the people, to salute him peaceably, and to shew him the burnt sacrifice that was offered for the king. 34 But he mocked them, and laughed at them, and abused them shamefully, and spake proudly, 35 And sware in his wrath, saying, Unless Judas and his host be now delivered into my hands, if ever I come again in safety, I will burn up this house: and with that he went out in a great rage. 36 Then the priests entered in, and stood before the altar and the temple, weeping, and saying, 37 Thou, O Lord, didst choose this house to be called by thy name, and to be a house of prayer and petition for thy people: 38 Be avenged of this man and his host, and let them fall by the sword: remember their blasphemies, and suffer them not to continue any longer. 39 So Nicanor went out of Jerusalem, and pitched his tents in Bethhoron, where an host out of Syria met him. 40 But Judas pitched in Adasa with three thousand men, and there he prayed, saying, 41 O Lord, when they that were sent from the king of the Assyrians blasphemed, thine angel went out, and smote an hundred fourscore and five thousand of them. 42 Even so destroy thou this host before us this day, that the rest may know that he hath spoken blasphemously against thy sanctuary, and judge thou him according to his wickedness. 43 So the thirteenth day of the month Adar the hosts joined battle: but Nicanor's host was discomfited, and he himself was first slain in the battle. 44 Now when Nicanor's host saw that he was slain, they cast away their weapons, and fled. 45 Then they pursued after them a day's journey, from Adasa unto Gazera, sounding an alarm after them with their trumpets. 46 Whereupon they came forth out of all the towns of Judea round about, and closed them in; so that they, turning back upon them that pursued them, were all slain with the sword, and not one of them was left. 47 Afterwards they took the spoils, and the prey, and smote off Nicanor's head, and his right hand,

which he stretched out so proudly, and brought them away, and hanged them up toward Jerusalem. 48 For this cause the people rejoiced greatly, and they kept that day a day of great gladness. 49 Moreover they ordained to keep yearly this day, being the thirteenth of Adar. 50 Thus the land of Juda was in rest a little while.

1-Macc.8 1 Now Judas had heard of the fame of the Romans, that they were mighty and valiant men, and such as would lovingly accept all that joined themselves unto them, and make a league of amity with all that came unto them; 2 And that they were men of great valour. It was told him also of their wars and noble acts which they had done among the Galatians, and how they had conquered them, and brought them under tribute; 3 And what they had done in the country of Spain, for the winning of the mines of the silver and gold which is there; 4 And that by their policy and patience they had conquered all the place, though it were very far from them; and the kings also that came against them from the uttermost part of the earth, till they had discomfited them, and given them a great overthrow, so that the rest did give them tribute every year: 5 Beside this, how they had discomfited in battle Philip, and Perseus, king of the Citims, with others that lifted up themselves against them, and had overcome them: 6 How also Antiochus the great king of Asia, that came against them in battle, having an hundred and twenty elephants, with horsemen, and chariots, and a very great army, was discomfited by them; 7 And how they took him alive, and covenanted that he and such as reigned after him should pay a great tribute, and give hostages, and that which was agreed upon, 8 And the country of India, and Media and Lydia and of the goodliest countries, which they took of him, and gave to king Eumenes: 9 Moreover how the Grecians had determined to come and destroy them; 10 And that they, having knowledge thereof sent against them a certain captain, and fighting with them slew many of them, and carried away captives their wives and their children, and spoiled them, and took possession of their lands, and pulled down their strong holds, and brought them to be their servants unto this day: 11 It was told him besides, how they destroyed and brought under their dominion all other kingdoms and isles that at any time resisted them; 12 But with their friends and such as relied upon them they kept amity: and that they had conquered kingdoms both far and nigh, insomuch as all that heard of their name were afraid of them: 13 Also that, whom they would help to a kingdom, those reign; and whom again they would, they displace: finally, that they were greatly exalted: 14 Yet for all this none of them wore a crown or was clothed in purple, to be magnified thereby: 15 Moreover how they had made for themselves a senate house, wherein three hundred and twenty men sat in council daily, consulting alway for the people, to the end they might be well ordered: 16 And that they committed their government to one man every year, who ruled over all their country, and that all were obedient to that one, and that there was neither envy nor emulation among them. 17 In consideration of these things, Judas chose Eupolemus the son of John, the son of Accos, and Jason the son of

Eleazar, and sent them to Rome, to make a league of amity and confederacy with them, 18 And to intreat them that they would take the yoke from them; for they saw that the kingdom of the Grecians did oppress Israel with servitude. 19 They went therefore to Rome, which was a very great journey, and came into the senate, where they spake and said. 20 Judas Maccabeus with his brethren, and the people of the Jews, have sent us unto you, to make a confederacy and peace with you, and that we might be registered your confederates and friends. 21 So that matter pleased the Romans well. 22 And this is the copy of the epistle which the senate wrote back again in tables of brass, and sent to Jerusalem, that there they might have by them a memorial of peace and confederacy: 23 Good success be to the Romans, and to the people of the Jews, by sea and by land for ever: the sword also and enemy be far from them, 24 If there come first any war upon the Romans or any of their confederates throughout all their dominion, 25 The people of the Jews shall help them, as the time shall be appointed, with all their heart: 26 Neither shall they give any thing unto them that make war upon them, or aid them with victuals, weapons, money, or ships, as it hath seemed good unto the Romans; but they shall keep their covenants without taking any thing therefore. 27 In the same manner also, if war come first upon the nation of the Jews, the Romans shall help them with all their heart, according as the time shall be appointed them: 28 Neither shall victuals be given to them that take part against them, or weapons, or money, or ships, as it hath seemed good to the Romans; but they shall keep their covenants, and that without deceit. 29 According to these articles did the Romans make a covenant with the people of the Jews. 30 Howbeit if hereafter the one party or the other shall think to meet to add or diminish any thing, they may do it at their pleasures, and whatsoever they shall add or take away shall be ratified. 31 And as touching the evils that Demetrius doeth to the Jews, we have written unto him, saying, Wherefore thou made thy yoke heavy upon our friends and confederates the Jews? 32 If therefore they complain any more against thee, we will do them justice, and fight with thee by sea and by land.

1-Macc.9 1 Furthermore, when Demetrius heard the Nicanor and his host were slain in battle, he sent Bacchides and Alcimus into the land of Judea the second time, and with them the chief strength of his host: 2 Who went forth by the way that leadeth to Galgala, and pitched their tents before Masaloth, which is in Arbela, and after they had won it, they slew much people. 3 Also the first month of the hundred fifty and second year they encamped before Jerusalem: 4 From whence they removed, and went to Berea, with twenty thousand footmen and two thousand horsemen. 5 Now Judas had pitched his tents at Eleasa, and three thousand chosen men with him: 6 Who seeing the multitude of the other army to be so great were sore afraid; whereupon many conveyed themselves out of the host, insomuch as abode of them no more but eight hundred men. 7 When Judas therefore saw that his host slipt away, and that the battle pressed upon him, he was sore troubled in mind, and much distressed, for that he had no time to gather them together. 8 Nevertheless unto them that remained he said, Let us arise and go up against our enemies, if peradventure we may be able to fight with them. 9 But they dehorted him, saying, We shall never be able: let us now rather save our lives, and hereafter we will return with our brethren, and fight against them: for we are but few. 10 Then Judas said, God forbid that I should do this thing, and flee away from them: if our time be come, let us die manfully for our brethren, and let us not stain our honour. 11 With that the host of Bacchides removed out of their tents, and stood over against them, their horsemen being divided into two troops, and their slingers and archers going before the host and they that marched in the foreward were all mighty men. 12 As for Bacchides, he was in the right wing: so the host drew near on the two parts, and sounded their trumpets. 13 They also of Judas' side, even they sounded their trumpets also, so that the earth shook at the noise of the armies, and the battle continued from morning till night. 14 Now when Judas perceived that Bacchides and the strength of his army were on the right side, he took with him all the hardy men, 15 Who discomfited the right wing, and pursued them unto the mount Azotus. 16 But when they of the left wing saw that they of the right wing were discomfited, they followed upon Judas and those that were with him hard at the heels from behind: 17 Whereupon there was a sore battle, insomuch as many were slain on both parts. 18 Judas also was killed, and the remnant fled. 19 Then Jonathan and Simon took Judas their brother, and buried him in the sepulchre of his fathers in Modin. 20 Moreover they bewailed him, and all Israel made great lamentation for him, and mourned many days, saying, 21 How is the valiant man fallen, that delivered Israel! 22 As for the other things concerning Judas and his wars, and the noble acts which he did, and his greatness, they are not written: for they were very many. 2 3 Now after the death of Judas the wicked began to put forth their heads in all the coasts of Israel, and there arose up all such as wrought iniquity. 24 In those days also was there a very great famine, by reason whereof the country revolted, and went with them. 25 Then Bacchides chose the wicked men, and made them lords of the country. 26 And they made enquiry and search for Judas' friends, and brought them unto Bacchides, who took vengeance of them, and used them despitefully. 27 So was there a great affliction in Israel, the like whereof was not since the time that a prophet was not seen among them. 28 For this cause all Judas' friends came together, and said unto Jonathan, 29 Since thy brother Judas died, we have no man like him to go forth against our enemies, and Bacchides, and against them of our nation that are adversaries to us. 30 Now therefore we have chosen thee this day to be our prince and captain in his stead, that thou mayest fight our battles. 31 Upon this Jonathan took the governance upon him at that time, and rose up instead of his brother Judas. 32 But when Bacchides gat knowledge thereof, he sought for to slay him 33 Then Jonathan, and Simon his brother, and all that were with him, perceiving that, fled into the wilderness of Thecoe, and pitched their tents by the water of the pool Asphar. 34 Which when Bacchides understood, he came near to Jordan with all his host upon the sabbath day. 35 Now Jonathan had sent his brother John, a captain of the people, to pray his friends the Nabathites, that they might leave with them their carriage, which was much. 36 But the children of Jambri came out of Medaba, and took John, and all that he had, and went their way with it. 37 After this came word to Jonathan and Simon his brother, that the children of Jambri made a great marriage, and were bringing the bride from Nadabatha with a great train, as being the daughter of one of the great princes of Chanaan. 38 Therefore they remembered John their brother, and went up, and hid themselves under the covert of the mountain: 39 Where they lifted up their eyes, and looked, and, behold, there was much ado and great carriage: and the bridegroom came forth, and his friends and brethren, to meet them with drums, and instruments of musick, and many weapons. 40 Then Jonathan and they that were with him rose up against them from the place where they lay in ambush, and made a slaughter of them in such sort, as many fell down dead, and the remnant fled into the mountain, and they took all their spoils. 41 Thus was the marriage turned into mourning, and the noise of their melody into lamentation. 42 So when they had avenged fully the blood of their brother, they turned again to the marsh of Jordan. 43 Now when Bacchides heard hereof, he came on the sabbath day unto the banks of Jordan with a great power. 44 Then Jonathan said to his company, Let us go up now and fight for our lives, for it standeth not with us to day, as in time past: 45 For, behold, the battle is before us and behind us, and the water of Jordan on this side and that side, the marsh likewise and wood, neither is there place for us to turn aside. 46 Wherefore cry ye now unto heaven, that ye may be delivered from the hand of your enemies. 47 With that they joined battle, and Jonathan stretched forth his hand to smite Bacchides, but he turned back from him. 48 Then Jonathan and they that were with him leapt into Jordan, and swam over unto the other bank: howbeit the other passed not over Jordan unto them. 49 So there were slain of Bacchides' side that day about a thousand men. 50 Afterward returned Bacchides to Jerusalem and repaired the strong cites in Judea; the fort in Jericho, and Emmaus, and Bethhoron, and Bethel, and Thamnatha, Pharathoni, and Taphon, these did he strengthen with high walls, with gates and with bars. 51 And in them he set a garrison, that they might work malice upon Israel. 52 He fortified also the city Bethsura, and Gazera, and the tower, and put forces in them, and provision of victuals. 53 Besides, he took the chief men's sons in the country for hostages, and put them into the tower at Jerusalem to be kept. 54 Moreover in the hundred fifty and third year, in the second month, Alcimus commanded that the wall of the inner court of the sanctuary should be pulled down; he pulled down also the works of the prophets 55 And as he began to pull down, even at that time was Alcimus plagued, and his enterprises hindered: for his mouth was stopped, and he was taken with a palsy, so that he could no more speak any thing, nor give order concerning his house. 56 So Alcimus died at that time with great torment. 57 Now when Bacchides saw that Alcimus was dead, he returned to the king: whereupon the

land of Judea was in rest two years. 58 Then all the ungodly men held a council, saying, Behold, Jonathan and his company are at ease, and dwell without care: now therefore we will bring Bacchides hither, who shall take them all in one night. 59 So they went and consulted with him. 60 Then removed he, and came with a great host, and sent letters privily to his adherents in Judea, that they should take Jonathan and those that were with him: howbeit they could not, because their counsel was known unto them. 61 Wherefore they took of the men of the country, that were authors of that mischief, about fifty persons, and slew them. 62 Afterward Jonathan, and Simon, and they that were with him, got them away to Bethbasi, which is in the wilderness, and they repaired the decays thereof, and made it strong. 63 Which thing when Bacchides knew, he gathered together all his host, and sent word to them that were of Judea. 64 Then went he and laid siege against Bethbasi; and they fought against it a long season and made engines of war. 65 But Jonathan left his brother Simon in the city, and went forth himself into the country, and with a certain number went he forth. 66 And he smote Odonarkes and his brethren, and the children of Phasiron in their tent. 67 And when he began to smite them, and came up with his forces, Simon and his company went out of the city, and burned up the engines of war, 68 And fought against Bacchides, who was discomfited by them, and they afflicted him sore: for his counsel and travail was in vain. 69 Wherefore he was very wroth at the wicked men that gave him counsel to come into the country, inasmuch as he slew many of them, and purposed to return into his own country. 70 Whereof when Jonathan had knowledge, he sent ambassadors unto him, to the end he should make peace with him, and deliver them the prisoners. 71 Which thing he accepted, and did according to his demands, and sware unto him that he would never do him harm all the days of his life. 72 When therefore he had restored unto him the prisoners that he had taken aforetime out of the land of Judea, he returned and went his way into his own land, neither came he any more into their borders. 73 Thus the sword ceased from Israel: but Jonathan dwelt at Machmas, and began to govern the people; and he destroyed the ungodly men out of Israel.

1-Macc.10 1 In the hundred and sixtieth year Alexander, the son of Antiochus surnamed Epiphanes, went up and took Ptolemais: for the people had received him, by means whereof he reigned there, 2 Now when king Demetrius heard thereof, he gathered together an exceeding great host, and went forth against him to fight. 3 Moreover Demetrius sent letters unto Jonathan with loving words, so as he magnified him. 4 For said he, Let us first make peace with him, before he join with Alexander against us: 5 Else he will remember all the evils that we have done against him, and against his brethren and his people. 6 Wherefore he gave him authority to gather together an host, and to provide weapons, that he might aid him in battle: he commanded also that the hostages that were in the tower should be delivered him. 7 Then came Jonathan to Jerusalem, and read the letters in the audience of all the people, and of them that were in the tower: 8 Who were sore afraid, when they heard that the king had given him authority to gather together an host. 9 Whereupon they of the tower delivered their hostages unto Jonathan, and he delivered them unto their parents. 10 This done, Jonathan settled himself in Jerusalem, and began to build and repair the city. 11 And he commanded the workmen to build the walls and the mount Sion and about with square stones for fortification; and they did so. 12 Then the strangers, that were in the fortresses which Bacchides had built, fled away; 13 Insomuch as every man left his place, and went into his own country. 14 Only at Bethsura certain of those that had forsaken the law and the commandments remained still: for it was their place of refuge. 15 Now when king Alexander had heard what promises Demetrius had sent unto Jonathan: when also it was told him of the battles and noble acts which he and his brethren had done, and of the pains that they had endured, 16 He said, Shall we find such another man? now therefore we will make him our friend and confederate. 17 Upon this he wrote a letter, and sent it unto him, according to these words, saying, 18 King Alexander to his brother Jonathan sendeth greeting: 19 We have heard of thee, that thou art a man of great power, and meet to be our friend. 20 Wherefore now this day we ordain thee to be the high priest of thy nation, and to be called the king's friend; (and therewithal he sent him a purple robe and a crown of gold:) and require thee to take our part, and keep friendship with us. 21 So in the seventh month of the hundred and sixtieth year, at the feast of the tabernacles, Jonathan put on the holy robe, and gathered together forces, and provided much armour. 22 Whereof when Demetrius heard, he was very sorry, and said, 23 What have we done, that Alexander hath prevented us in making amity with the Jews to strengthen himself? 24 I also will write unto them words of encouragement, and promise them dignities and gifts, that I may have their aid. 25 He sent unto them therefore to this effect: King Demetrius unto the people of the Jews sendeth greeting: 26 Whereas ye have kept covenants with us, and continued in our friendship, not joining yourselves with our enemies, we have heard hereof, and are glad. 27 Wherefore now continue ye still to be faithful unto us, and we will well recompense you for the things ye do in our behalf, 28 And will grant you many immunities, and give you rewards. 29 And now do I free you, and for your sake I release all the Jews, from tributes, and from the customs of salt, and from crown taxes, 30 And from that which appertaineth unto me to receive for the third part or the seed, and the half of the fruit of the trees, I release it from this day forth, so that they shall not be taken of the land of Judea, nor of the three governments which are added thereunto out of the country of Samaria and Galilee, from this day forth for evermore. 31 Let Jerusalem also be holy and free, with the borders thereof, both from tenths and tributes. 32 And as for the tower which is at Jerusalem, I yield up authority over it, and give the high priest, that he may set in it such men as he shall choose to keep it. 33 Moreover I freely set at liberty every one of the Jews, that were carried captives out of the land of Judea into any part of my kingdom, and I will that all my officers remit the tributes even of their cattle. 34 Furthermore I will that all the feasts, and sabbaths, and new moons, and solemn days, and the three days before the feast, and the three days after the feast shall be all of immunity and freedom for all the Jews in my realm. 35 Also no man shall have authority to meddle with or to molest any of them in any matter. 36 I will further, that there be enrolled among the king's forces about thirty thousand men of the Jews, unto whom pay shall be given, as belongeth to all king's forces. 37 And of them some shall be placed in the king's strong holds, of whom also some shall be set over the affairs of the kingdom, which are of trust: and I will that their overseers and governors be of themselves, and that they live after their own laws, even as the king hath commanded in the land of Judea. 38 And concerning the three governments that are added to Judea from the country of Samaria, let them be joined with Judea, that they may be reckoned to be under one, nor bound to obey other authority than the high priest's. 39 As for Ptolemais, and the land pertaining thereto, I give it as a free gift to the sanctuary at Jerusalem for the necessary expenses of the sanctuary. 40 Moreover I give every year fifteen thousand shekels of silver out of the king's accounts from the places appertaining. 41 And all the overplus, which the officers payed not in as in former time, from henceforth shall be given toward the works of the temple. 42 And beside this, the five thousand shekels of silver, which they took from the uses of the temple out of the accounts year by year, even those things shall be released, because they appertain to the priests that minister. 43 And whosoever they be that flee unto the temple at Jerusalem, or be within the liberties hereof, being indebted unto the king, or for any other matter, let them be at liberty, and all that they have in my realm. 44 For the building also and repairing of the works of the sanctuary expenses shall be given of the king's accounts. 45 Yea, and for the building of the walls of Jerusalem, and the fortifying thereof round about, expenses shall be given out of the king's accounts, as also for the building of the walls in Judea. 46 Now when Jonathan and the people heard these words, they gave no credit unto them, nor received them, because they remembered the great evil that he had done in Israel; for he had afflicted them very sore. 47 But with Alexander they were well pleased, because he was the first that entreated of true peace with them, and they were confederate with him always. 48 Then gathered king Alexander great forces, and camped over against Demetrius. 49 And after the two kings had joined battle, Demetrius' host fled: but Alexander followed after him, and prevailed against them. 50 And he continued the battle very sore until the sun went down: and that day was Demetrius slain. 51 Afterward Alexander sent ambassadors to Ptolemee king of Egypt with a message to this effect: 52 Forasmuch as I am come again to my realm, and am set in the throne of my progenitors, and have gotten the dominion, and overthrown Demetrius, and recovered our country; 53 For after I had joined battle with him, both he and his host was discomfited by us, so that we sit in the throne of his kingdom: 54 Now therefore let us make a league of amity together, and give me now thy daughter to wife: and I will be thy son in law, and will give both thee and her as according to thy dignity. 55 Then Ptolemee the king gave answer, saying, Happy be the day wherein thou didst return into the land of thy fathers, and satest in the throne of their kingdom. 56 And now will I do to thee, as thou hast written: meet me therefore at Ptolemais, that we may see one another; for I will marry my daughter to thee according to thy desire. 57 So Ptolemee went out of Egypt with his daughter Cleopatra, and they came unto Ptolemais in the hundred threescore and second year: 58 Where king Alexander meeting him, he gave unto him his daughter Cleopatra, and celebrated her marriage at Ptolemais with great glory, as the manner of kings is. 59 Now king Alexander had written unto Jonathan, that he should come and meet him. 60 Who thereupon went honourably to Ptolemais, where he met the two kings, and gave them and their friends silver and gold, and many presents, and found favour in their sight. 61 At that time certain pestilent fellows of Israel, men of a wicked life, assembled themselves against him, to accuse him: but the king would not hear them. 62 Yea more than that, the king commanded to take off his garments, and clothe him in purple: and they did so. 63 And he made him sit by himself, and said into his princes, Go with him into the midst of the city, and make proclamation, that no man complain against him of any matter, and that no man trouble him for any manner of cause. 64 Now when his accusers saw that he was honoured according to the proclamation, and clothed in purple, they fled all away. 65 So the king honoured him, and wrote him among his chief friends, and made him a duke, and partaker of his dominion. 66 Afterward Jonathan returned to Jerusalem with peace and gladness. 67 Furthermore in the; hundred threescore and fifth year came Demetrius son of Demetrius out of Crete into the land of his fathers: 68 Whereof when king Alexander heard tell, he was right sorry, and returned into Antioch. 69 Then Demetrius made Apollonius the governor of Celosyria his general, who gathered together a great host, and camped in Jamnia, and sent unto Jonathan the high priest, saying, 70 Thou alone liftest up thyself against us, and I am laughed to scorn for thy sake, and reproached: and why dost thou vaunt thy power against us in the mountains? 71 Now therefore, if thou trustest in thine own strength, come down to us into the plain field, and there let us try the matter together: for with me is the power of the cities. 72 Ask and learn who I am, and the rest that take our part, and they shall tell thee that thy foot is not able to stand before our face; for thy fathers have twice been put to flight in their own land. 73 Wherefore now thou shalt not be able to abide the horsemen and so great a power in the plain, where is neither stone nor flint, nor place to flee unto. 74 So when Jonathan heard these words of Apollonius, he was moved in his mind, and choosing ten thousand men he went out of Jerusalem, where Simon his brother met him for to help him. 75 And he pitched his tents against Joppa: but; they of Joppa shut him out of the city, because Apollonius had a garrison there. 76 Then Jonathan laid siege unto it: whereupon they of the city let him in for fear: and so Jonathan won Joppa. 77 Whereof when Apollonius heard,

he took three thousand horsemen, with a great host of footmen, and went to Azotus as one that journeyed, and therewithal drew him forth into the plain. because he had a great number of horsemen, in whom he put his trust. 78 Then Jonathan followed after him to Azotus, where the armies joined battle. 79 Now Apollonius had left a thousand horsemen in ambush. 80 And Jonathan knew that there was an ambushment behind him; for they had compassed in his host, and cast darts at the people, from morning till evening. 81 But the people stood still, as Jonathan had commanded them: and so the enemies' horses were tired. 82 Then brought Simon forth his host, and set them against the footmen, (for the horsemen were spent) who were discomfited by him, and fled. 83 The horsemen also, being scattered in the field, fled to Azotus, and went into Bethdagon, their idol's temple, for safety. 84 But Jonathan set fire on Azotus, and the cities round about it, and took their spoils; and the temple of Dagon, with them that were fled into it, he burned with fire. 85 Thus there were burned and slain with the sword well nigh eight thousand men. 86 And from thence Jonathan removed his host, and camped against Ascalon, where the men of the city came forth, and met him with great pomp. 87 After this returned Jonathan and his host unto Jerusalem, having any spoils. 88 Now when king Alexander heard these things, he honoured Jonathan yet more. 89 And sent him a buckle of gold, as the use is to be given to such as are of the king's blood: he gave him also Accaron with the borders thereof in possession.

1-Macc.11 1 And the king of Egypt gathered together a great host, like the sand that lieth upon the sea shore, and many ships, and went about through deceit to get Alexander's kingdom, and join it to his own. 2 Whereupon he took his journey into Syria in peaceable manner, so as they of the cities opened unto him, and met him: for king Alexander had commanded them so to do, because he was his brother in law. 3 Now as Ptolemee entered into the cities, he set in every one of them a garrison of soldiers to keep it. 4 And when he came near to Azotus, they shewed him the temple of Dagon that was burnt, and Azotus and the suburbs thereof that were destroyed, and the bodies that were cast abroad and them that he had burnt in the battle; for they had made heaps of them by the way where he should pass. 5 Also they told the king whatsoever Jonathan had done, to the intent he might blame him: but the king held his peace. 6 Then Jonathan met the king with great pomp at Joppa, where they saluted one another, and lodged. 7 Afterward Jonathan, when he had gone with the king to the river called Eleutherus, returned again to Jerusalem. 8 King Ptolemee therefore, having gotten the dominion of the cities by the sea unto Seleucia upon the sea coast, imagined wicked counsels against Alexander. 9 Whereupon he sent ambassadors unto king Demetrius, saying, Come, let us make a league betwixt us, and I will give thee my daughter whom Alexander hath, and thou shalt reign in thy father's kingdom: 10 For I repent that I gave my daughter unto him, for he sought to slay me. 11 Thus did he slander him, because he was desirous of his kingdom. 12 Wherefore he took his daughter from him, and gave her to Demetrius, and forsook Alexander, so that their hatred was openly known. 13 Then Ptolemee entered into Antioch, where he set two crowns upon his head, the crown of Asia, and of Egypt. 14 In the mean season was king Alexander in Cilicia, because those that dwelt in those parts had revolted from him. 15 But when Alexander heard of this, he came to war against him: whereupon king Ptolemee brought forth his host, and met him with a mighty power, and put him to flight. 16 So Alexander fled into Arabia there to be defended; but king Ptolemee was exalted: 17 For Zabdiel the Arabian took off Alexander's head, and sent it unto Ptolemee. 18 King Ptolemee also died the third day after, and they that were in the strong holds were slain one of another. 19 By this means Demetrius reigned in the hundred threescore and seventh year. 20 At the same time Jonathan gathered together them that were in Judea to take the tower that was in Jerusalem: and he made many engines of war against it. 21 Then came ungodly persons, who hated their own people, went unto the king, and told him that Jonathan besieged the tower, 22 Whereof when he heard, he was angry, and immediately removing, he came to Ptolemais, and wrote unto Jonathan, that he should not lay siege to the tower, but come and speak with him at Ptolemais in great haste. 23 Nevertheless Jonathan, when he heard this, commanded to besiege it still: and he chose certain of the elders of Israel and the priests, and put himself in peril; 24 And took silver and gold, and raiment, and divers presents besides, and went to Ptolemais unto the king, where he found favour in his sight. 25 And though certain ungodly men of the people had made complaints against him, 26 Yet the king entreated him as his predecessors had done before, and promoted him in the sight of all his friends, 27 And confirmed him in the high priesthood, and in all the honours that he had before, and gave him preeminence among his chief friends. 28 Then Jonathan desired the king, that he would make Judea free from tribute, as also the three governments, with the country of Samaria; and he promised him three hundred talents. 29 So the king consented, and wrote letters unto Jonathan of all these things after this manner: 30 King Demetrius unto his brother Jonathan, and unto the nation of the Jews, sendeth greeting: 31 We send you here a copy of the letter which we did write unto our cousin Lasthenes concerning you, that ye might see it. 32 King Demetrius unto his father Lasthenes sendeth greeting: 33 We are determined to do good to the people of the Jews, who are our friends, and keep covenants with us, because of their good will toward us. 34 Wherefore we have ratified unto them the borders of Judea, with the three governments of Apherema and Lydda and Ramathem, that are added unto Judea from the country of Samaria, and all things appertaining unto them, for all such as do sacrifice in Jerusalem, instead of the payments which the king received of them yearly aforetime out of the fruits of the earth and of trees. 35 And as for other things that belong unto us, of the tithes and customs pertaining unto us, as also the saltpits, and the crown taxes, which are due unto us, we discharge them of them all for their relief. 36 And nothing hereof shall be revoked from this time forth for ever. 37

Now therefore see that thou make a copy of these things, and let it be delivered unto Jonathan, and set upon the holy mount in a conspicuous place. 38 After this, when king Demetrius saw that the land was quiet before him, and that no resistance was made against him, he sent away all his forces, every one to his own place, except certain bands of strangers, whom he had gathered from the isles of the heathen: wherefore all the forces of his fathers hated him. 39 Moreover there was one Tryphon, that had been of Alexander's part afore, who, seeing that all the host murmured against Demetrius, went to Simalcue the Arabian that brought up Antiochus the young son of Alexander, 40 And lay sore upon him to deliver him this young Antiochus, that he might reign in his father's stead: he told him therefore all that Demetrius had done, and how his men of war were at enmity with him, and there he remained a long season. 41 In the mean time Jonathan sent unto king Demetrius, that he would cast those of the tower out of Jerusalem, and those also in the fortresses: for they fought against Israel. 42 So Demetrius sent unto Jonathan, saying, I will not only do this for thee and thy people, but I will greatly honour thee and thy nation, if opportunity serve. 43 Now therefore thou shalt do well, if thou send me men to help me; for all my forces are gone from me. 44 Upon this Jonathan sent him three thousand strong men unto Antioch: and when they came to the king, the king was very glad of their coming. 45 Howbeit they that were of the city gathered themselves together into the midst of the city, to the number of an hundred and twenty thousand men, and would have slain the king. 46 Wherefore the king fled into the court, but they of the city kept the passages of the city, and began to fight. 47 Then the king called to the Jews for help, who came unto him all at once, and dispersing themselves through the city slew that day in the city to the number of an hundred thousand. 48 Also they set fire on the city, and gat many spoils that day, and delivered the king. 49 So when they of the city saw that the Jews had got the city as they would, their courage was abated: wherefore they made supplication to the king, and cried, saying, 50 Grant us peace, and let the Jews cease from assaulting us and the city. 51 With that they cast away their weapons, and made peace; and the Jews were honoured in the sight of the king, and in the sight of all that were in his realm; and they returned to Jerusalem, having great spoils. 52 So king Demetrius sat on the throne of his kingdom, and the land was quiet before him. 53 Nevertheless he dissembled in all that ever he spake, and estranged himself from Jonathan, neither rewarded he him according to the benefits which he had received of him, but troubled him very sore. 54 After this returned Tryphon, and with him the young child Antiochus, who reigned, and was crowned. 55 Then there gathered unto him all the men of war, whom Demetrius had put away, and they fought against Demetrius, who turned his back and fled. 56 Moreover Tryphon took the elephants, and won Antioch. 57 At that time young Antiochus wrote unto Jonathan, saying, I confirm thee in the high priesthood, and appoint thee ruler over the four governments, and to be one of the king's friends. 58 Upon this he sent him golden vessels to be served in, and gave him leave to drink in gold, and to be clothed in purple, and to wear a golden buckle. 59 His brother Simon also he made captain from the place called The ladder of Tyrus unto the borders of Egypt. 60 Then Jonathan went forth, and passed through the cities beyond the water, and all the forces of Syria gathered themselves unto him for to help him: and when he came to Ascalon, they of the city met him honourably. 61 From whence he went to Gaza, but they of Gaza shut him out; wherefore he laid siege unto it, and burned the suburbs thereof with fire, and spoiled them. 62 Afterward, when they of Gaza made supplication unto Jonathan, he made peace with them, and took the sons of their chief men for hostages, and sent them to Jerusalem, and passed through the country unto Damascus. 63 Now when Jonathan heard that Demetrius' princes were come to Cades, which is in Galilee, with a great power, purposing to remove him out of the country, 64 He went to meet them, and left Simon his brother in the country. 65 Then Simon encamped against Bethsura and fought against it a long season, and shut it up: 66 But they desired to have peace with him, which he granted them, and then put them out from thence, and took the city, and set a garrison in it. 67 As for Jonathan and his host, they pitched at the water of Gennesar, from whence betimes in the morning they gat them to the plain of Nasor. 68 And, behold, the host of strangers met them in the plain, who, having laid men in ambush for him in the mountains, came themselves over against him. 69 So when they that lay in ambush rose out of their places and joined battle, all that were of Jonathan's side fled; 70 Insomuch as there was not one of them left, except Mattathias the son of Absalom, and Judas the son of Calphi, the captains of the host. 71 Then Jonathan rent his clothes, and cast earth upon his head, and prayed. 72 Afterwards turning again to battle, he put them to flight, and so they ran away. 73 Now when his own men that were fled saw this, they turned again unto him, and with him pursued them to Cades, even unto their own tents, and there they camped. 74 So there were slain of the heathen that day about three thousand men: but Jonathan returned to Jerusalem.

1-Macc.12 1 Now when Jonathan saw that time served him, he chose certain men, and sent them to Rome, for to confirm and renew the friendship that they had with them. 2 He sent letters also to the Lacedemonians, and to other places, for the same purpose. 3 So they went unto Rome, and entered into the senate, and said, Jonathan the high priest, and the people of the Jews, sent us unto you, to the end ye should renew the friendship, which ye had with them, and league, as in former time. 4 Upon this the Romans gave them letters unto the governors of every place that they should bring them into the land of Judea peaceably. 5 And this is the copy of the letters which Jonathan wrote to the Lacedemonians: 6 Jonathan the high priest, and the elders of the nation, and the priests, and the other of the Jews, unto the Lacedemonians their brethren send greeting: 7 There were letters sent in times past unto Onias the high priest from Darius, who reigned then among you, to signify that ye are our brethren, as the copy here underwritten doth specify. 8 At which time Onias entreated the ambassador that was sent honourably, and received the letters, wherein declaration was made of the league and friendship. 9 Therefore we also, albeit we need none of these things, that we have the holy books of scripture in our hands to comfort us, 10 Have nevertheless attempted to send unto you for the renewing of brotherhood and friendship, lest we should become strangers unto you altogether: for there is a long time passed since ye sent unto us. 11 We therefore at all times without ceasing, both in our feasts, and other convenient days, do remember you in the sacrifices which we offer, and in our prayers, as reason is, and as it becometh us to think upon our brethren: 12 And we are right glad of your honour. 13 As for ourselves, we have had great troubles and wars on every side, forsomuch as the kings that are round about us have fought against us. 14 Howbeit we would not be troublesome unto you, nor to others of our confederates and friends, in these wars: 15 For we have help from heaven that succoureth us, so as we are delivered from our enemies, and our enemies are brought under foot. 16 For this cause we chose Numenius the son of Antiochus, and Antipater he son of Jason, and sent them unto the Romans, to renew the amity that we had with them, and the former league. 17 We commanded them also to go unto you, and to salute and to deliver you our letters concerning the renewing of our brotherhood. 18 Wherefore now ye shall do well to give us an answer thereto. 19 And this is the copy of the letters which Oniares sent. 20 Areus king of the Lacedemonians to Onias the high priest, greeting: 21 It is found in writing, that the Lacedemonians and Jews are brethren, and that they are of the stock of Abraham: 22 Now therefore, since this is come to our knowledge, ye shall do well to write unto us of your prosperity. 23 We do write back again to you, that your cattle and goods are our's, and our's are your's We do command therefore our ambassadors to make report unto you on this wise. 24 Now when Jonathan heard that Demetrius' princes were come to fight against him with a greater host than afore, 25 He removed from Jerusalem, and met them in the land of Amathis: for he gave them no respite to enter his country. 26 He sent spies also unto their tents, who came again, and told him that they were appointed to come upon them in the night season. 27 Wherefore so soon as the sun was down, Jonathan commanded his men to watch, and to be in arms, that all the night long they might be ready to fight: also he sent forth sentinels round about the host. 28 But when the adversaries heard that Jonathan and his men were ready for battle, they feared, and trembled in their hearts, and they kindled fires in their camp. 29 Howbeit Jonathan and his company knew it not till the morning: for they saw the lights burning. 30 Then Jonathan pursued after them, but overtook them not: for they were gone over the river Eleutherus. 31 Wherefore Jonathan turned to the Arabians, who were called Zabadeans, and smote them, and took their spoils. 32 And removing thence, he came to Damascus, and so passed through all the country, 33 Simon also went forth, and passed through the country unto Ascalon, and the holds there adjoining, from whence he turned aside to

Joppa, and won it. 34 For he had heard that they would deliver the hold unto them that took Demetrius' part; wherefore he set a garrison there to keep it. 35 After this came Jonathan home again, and calling the elders of the people together, he consulted with them about building strong holds in Judea, 36 And making the walls of Jerusalem higher, and raising a great mount between the tower and the city, for to separate it from the city, that so it might be alone, that men might neither sell nor buy in it. 37 Upon this they came together to build up the city, forasmuch as part of the wall toward the brook on the east side was fallen down, and they repaired that which was called Caphenatha. 38 Simon also set up Adida in Sephela, and made it strong with gates and bars. 39 Now Tryphon went about to get the kingdom of Asia, and to kill Antiochus the king, that he might set the crown upon his own head. 40 Howbeit he was afraid that Jonathan would not suffer him, and that he would fight against him; wherefore he sought a way how to take Jonathan, that he might kill him. So he removed, and came to Bethsan. 41 Then Jonathan went out to meet him with forty thousand men chosen for the battle, and came to Bethsan. 42 Now when Tryphon saw Jonathan came with so great a force, he durst not stretch his hand against him; 43 But received him honourably, and commended him unto all his friends, and gave him gifts, and commanded his men of war to be as obedient unto him, as to himself. 44 Unto Jonathan also he said, Why hast thou brought all this people to so great trouble, seeing there is no war betwixt us? 45 Therefore send them now home again, and choose a few men to wait on thee, and come thou with me to Ptolemais, for I will give it thee, and the rest of the strong holds and forces, and all that have any charge: as for me, I will return and depart: for this is the cause of my coming. 46 So Jonathan believing him did as he bade him, and sent away his host, who went into the land of Judea. 47 And with himself he retained but three thousand men, of whom he sent two thousand into Galilee, and one thousand went with him. 48 Now as soon as Jonathan entered into Ptolemais, they of Ptolemais shut the gates and took him, and all them that came with him they slew with the sword. 49 Then sent Tryphon an host of footmen and horsemen into Galilee, and into the great plain, to destroy all Jonathan's company. 50 But when they knew that Jonathan and they that were with him were taken and slain, they encouraged one another; and went close together, prepared to fight. 51 They therefore that followed upon them, perceiving that they were ready to fight for their lives, turned back again. 52 Whereupon they all came into the land of Judea peaceably, and there they bewailed Jonathan, and them that were with him, and they were sore afraid; wherefore all Israel made great lamentation. 53 Then all the heathen that were round about then sought to destroy them: for said they, They have no captain, nor any to help them: now therefore let us make war upon them, and take away their memorial from among men.

1-Macc.13 1 Now when Simon heard that Tryphon had gathered together a great host to invade the land of Judea, and destroy it, 2 And saw that the people was in great trembling and fear, he went up to Jerusalem, and gathered the people together, 3 And gave them exhortation, saying, Ye yourselves know what great things I, and my brethren, and my father's house, have done for the laws and the sanctuary, the battles also and troubles which we have seen. 4 By reason whereof all my brethren are slain for Israel's sake, and I am left alone. 5 Now therefore be it far from me, that I should spare mine own life in any time of trouble: for I am no better than my brethren. 6 Doubtless I will avenge my nation, and the sanctuary, and our wives, and our children: for all the heathen are gathered to destroy us of very malice. 7 Now as soon as the people heard these words, their spirit revived. 8 And they answered with a loud voice, saying, Thou shalt be our leader instead of Judas and Jonathan thy brother. 9 Fight thou our battles, and whatsoever, thou commandest us, that will we do. 10 So then he gathered together all the men of war, and made haste to finish the walls of Jerusalem, and he fortified it round about. 11 Also he sent Jonathan the son of Absalom, and with him a great power, to Joppa: who casting out them that were therein remained there in it. 12 So Tryphon removed from Ptolemais with a great power to invade the land of Judea, and Jonathan was with him in ward. 13 But Simon pitched his tents at Adida, over against the plain. 14 Now when Tryphon knew that Simon was risen up instead of his brother Jonathan, and meant to join battle with him, he sent messengers unto him, saying, 15 Whereas we have Jonathan thy brother in hold, it is for money that he is owing unto the kings treasure, concerning the business that was committed unto him. 16 Wherefore now send an hundred talents of silver, and two of his sons for hostages, that when he is at liberty he may not revolt from us, and we will let him go. 17 Hereupon Simon, albeit he perceived that they spake deceitfully unto him yet sent he the money and the children, lest peradventure he should procure to himself great hatred of the people: 18 Who might have said, Because I sent him not the money and the children, therefore is Jonathan dead. 19 So he sent them the children and the hundred talents: howbeit Tryphon dissembled neither would he let Jonathan go. 20 And after this came Tryphon to invade the land, and destroy it, going round about by the way that leadeth unto Adora: but Simon and his host marched against him in every place, wheresoever he went. 21 Now they that were in the tower sent messengers unto Tryphon, to the end that he should hasten his coming unto them by the wilderness, and send them victuals. 22 Wherefore Tryphon made ready all his horsemen to come that night: but there fell a very great snow, by reason whereof he came not. So he departed, and came into the country of Galaad. 23 And when he came near to Bascama he slew Jonathan, who was buried there. 24 Afterward Tryphon returned and went into his own land. 25 Then sent Simon, and took the bones of Jonathan his brother, and buried them in Modin, the city of his fathers. 26 And all Israel made great lamentation for him, and bewailed him many days. 27 Simon also built a monument upon the sepulchre of his father and his brethren, and raised it aloft to the sight, with hewn stone behind and before. 28 Moreover he set up seven pyramids, one against another, for his father, and his mother, and his four brethren. 29 And in these he made cunning devices, about the which he set great pillars, and upon the pillars he made all their armour for a perpetual memory, and by the armour ships carved, that they might be seen of all that sail on the sea. 30 This is the sepulchre which he made at Modin, and it standeth yet unto this day. 31 Now Tryphon dealt deceitfully with the young king Antiochus, and slew him. 32 And he reigned in his stead, and crowned himself king of Asia, and brought a great calamity upon the land. 33 Then Simon built up the strong holds in Judea, and fenced them about with high towers, and great walls, and gates, and bars, and laid up victuals therein. 34 Moreover Simon chose men, and sent to king Demetrius, to the end he should give the land an immunity, because all that Tryphon did was to spoil. 35 Unto whom king Demetrius answered and wrote after this manner: 36 King Demetrius unto Simon the high priest, and friend of kings, as also unto the elders and nation of the Jews, sendeth greeting: 37 The golden crown, and the scarlet robe, which ye sent unto us, we have received: and we are ready to make a stedfast peace with you, yea, and to write unto our officers, to confirm the immunities which we have granted. 38 And whatsoever covenants we have made with you shall stand; and the strong holds, which ye have builded, shall be your own. 39 As for any oversight or fault committed unto this day, we forgive it, and the crown tax also, which ye owe us: and if there were any other tribute paid in Jerusalem, it shall no more be paid. 40 And look who are meet among you to be in our court, let then be enrolled, and let there be peace betwixt us. 41 Thus the yoke of the heathen was taken away from Israel in the hundred and seventieth year. 42 Then the people of Israel began to write in their instruments and contracts, In the first year of Simon the high priest, the governor and leader of the Jews. 43 In those days Simon camped against Gaza and besieged it round about; he made also an engine of war, and set it by the city, and battered a certain tower, and took it. 44 And they that were in the engine leaped into the city; whereupon there was a great uproar in the city: 45 Insomuch as the people of the city rent their clothes, and climbed upon the walls with their wives and children, and cried with a loud voice, beseeching Simon to grant them peace. 46 And they said, Deal not with us according to our wickedness, but according to thy mercy. 47 So Simon was appeased toward them, and fought no more against them, but put them out of the city, and cleansed the houses wherein the idols were, and so entered into it with songs and thanksgiving. 48 Yea, he put all uncleanness out of it, and placed such men there as would keep the law, and made it stronger than it was before, and built therein a dwellingplace for himself. 49 They also of the tower in Jerusalem were kept so strait, that they could neither come forth, nor go into the country, nor buy, nor sell: wherefore they were in great distress for want of victuals, and a great number of them perished through famine. 50 Then cried they to Simon, beseeching him to be at one with them: which thing he granted them; and when he had put them out from thence, he cleansed the tower from pollutions: 51 And entered into it the three and twentieth day of the second month in the hundred seventy and first year, with thanksgiving, and branches of palm trees, and with harps, and cymbals, and with viols, and hymns, and songs: because there was destroyed a great enemy out of Israel. 52 He ordained also that that day should be kept every year with gladness. Moreover the hill of the temple that was by the tower he made stronger than it was, and there he dwelt himself with his company. 53 And when Simon saw that John his son was a valiant man, he made him captain of all the hosts; and he dwelt in Gazera.

1-Macc.14 1 Now in the hundred threescore and twelfth year king Demetrius gathered his forces together, and went into Media to get him help to fight against Tryphon. 2 But when Arsaces, the king of Persia and Media, heard that Demetrius was entered within his borders, he sent one of his princes to take him alive: 3 Who went and smote the host of Demetrius, and took him, and brought him to Arsaces, by whom he was put in ward. 4 As for the land of Judea, that was quiet all the days of Simon; for he sought the good of his nation in such wise, as that evermore his authority and honour pleased them well. 5 And as he was honourable in all his acts, so in this, that he took Joppa for an haven, and made an entrance to the isles of the sea, 6 And enlarged the bounds of his nation, and recovered the country, 7 And gathered together a great number of captives, and had the dominion of Gazera, and Bethsura, and the tower, out of the which he took all uncleanness, neither was there any that resisted him. 8 Then did they till their ground in peace, and the earth gave her increase, and the trees of the field their fruit. 9 The ancient men sat all in the streets, communing together of good things, and the young men put on glorious and warlike apparel. 10 He provided victuals for the cities, and set in them all manner of munition, so that his honourable name was renowned unto the end of the world. 11 He made peace in the land, and Israel rejoiced with great joy: 12 For every man sat under his vine and his fig tree, and there was none to fray them: 13 Neither was there any left in the land to fight against them: yea, the kings themselves were overthrown in those days. 14 Moreover he strengthened all those of his people that were brought low: the law he searched out; and every contemner of the law and wicked person he took away. 15 He beautified the sanctuary, and multiplied vessels of the temple. 16 Now when it was heard at Rome, and as far as Sparta, that Jonathan was dead, they were very sorry. 17 But as soon as they heard that his brother Simon was made high priest in his stead, and ruled the country, and the cities therein: 18 They wrote unto him in tables of brass, to renew the friendship and league which they had made with Judas and Jonathan his brethren: 19 Which writings were read before the congregation at Jerusalem. 20 And this is the copy of the letters that the Lacedemonians sent; The rulers of the Lacedemonians, with the city, unto Simon the high priest, and the elders, and priests, and residue of the people of the Jews, our brethren, send greeting: 21 The ambassadors that were sent unto our people certified us of your glory and honour: wherefore we were glad of their coming, 22 And did register the things that they spake in the council of the people in this manner; Numenius son of Antiochus, and Antipater son of Jason, the Jews' ambassadors, came unto us to renew the friendship they had with us. 23 And it pleased the people to entertain the men honourably, and to put the copy of their ambassage in publick records, to the end the people of the Lacedemonians might have a memorial thereof: furthermore we have written a copy thereof unto Simon the high priest. 24 After this Simon sent Numenius to Rome with a great shield of gold of a thousand pound weight to confirm the league with them. 25 Whereof when the people heard, they said, What thanks shall we give to Simon and his sons? 26 For he and his brethren and the house of his father have established Israel, and chased away in fight their enemies from them, and confirmed their liberty. 27 So then they wrote it in tables of brass, which they set upon pillars in mount Sion: and this is the copy of the writing; The eighteenth day of the month Elul, in the hundred threescore and twelfth year, being the third year of Simon the high priest, 28 At Saramel in the great congregation of the priests, and people, and rulers of the nation, and elders of the country, were these things notified unto us. 29 Forasmuch as oftentimes there have been wars in the country, wherein for the maintenance of their sanctuary, and the law, Simon the son of Mattathias, of the posterity of Jarib, together with his brethren, put themselves in jeopardy, and resisting the enemies of their nation did their nation great honour: 30 (For after that Jonathan, having gathered his nation together, and been their high priest, was added to his people, 31 Their enemies prepared to invade their country, that they might destroy it, and lay hands on the sanctuary: 32 At which time Simon rose up, and fought for his nation, and spent much of his own substance, and armed the valiant men of his nation and gave them wages, 33 And fortified the cities of Judea, together with Bethsura, that lieth upon the borders of Judea, where the armour of the enemies had been before; but he set a garrison of Jews there: 34 Moreover he fortified Joppa, which lieth upon the sea, and Gazera, that bordereth upon Azotus, where the enemies had dwelt before: but he placed Jews there, and furnished them with all things convenient for the reparation thereof.) 35 The people therefore sang the acts of Simon, and unto what glory he thought to bring his nation, made him their governor and chief priest, because he had done all these things, and for the justice and faith which he kept to his nation, and for that he sought by all means to exalt his people. 36 For in his time things prospered in his hands, so that the heathen were taken out of their country, and they also that were in the city of David in Jerusalem, who had made themselves a tower, out of which they issued, and polluted all about the sanctuary, and did much hurt in the holy place: 37 But he placed Jews therein. and fortified it for the safety of the country and the city, and raised up the walls of Jerusalem. 38 King Demetrius also confirmed him in the high priesthood according to those things, 39 And made him one of his friends, and honoured him with great honour. 40 For he had heard say, that the Romans had called the Jews their friends and confederates and brethren; and that they had entertained the

ambassadors of Simon honourably; 41 Also that the Jews and priests were well pleased that Simon should be their governor and high priest for ever, until there should arise a faithful prophet; 42 Moreover that he should be their captain, and should take charge of the sanctuary, to set them over their works, and over the country, and over the armour, and over the fortresses, that, I say, he should take charge of the sanctuary; 43 Beside this, that he should be obeyed of every man, and that all the writings in the country should be made in his name, and that he should be clothed in purple, and wear gold: 44 Also that it should be lawful for none of the people or priests to break any of these things, or to gainsay his words, or to gather an assembly in the country without him, or to be clothed in purple, or wear a buckle of gold; 45 And whosoever should do otherwise, or break any of these things, he should be punished. 46 Thus it liked all the people to deal with Simon, and to do as hath been said. 47 Then Simon accepted hereof, and was well pleased to be high priest, and captain and governor of the Jews and priests, and to defend them all. 48 So they commanded that this writing should be put in tables of brass, and that they should be set up within the compass of the sanctuary in a conspicuous place; 49 Also that the copies thereof should be laid up in the treasury, to the end that Simon and his sons might have them.

1-Macc.15 1 Moreover Antiochus son of Demetrius the king sent letters from the isles of the sea unto Simon the priest and prince of the Jews, and to all the people; 2 The contents whereof were these: King Antiochus to Simon the high priest and prince of his nation, and to the people of the Jews, greeting: 3 Forasmuch as certain pestilent men have usurped the kingdom of our fathers, and my purpose is to challenge it again, that I may restore it to the old estate, and to that end have gathered a multitude of foreign soldiers together, and prepared ships of war; 4 My meaning also being to go through the country, that I may be avenged of them that have destroyed it, and made many cities in the kingdom desolate: 5 Now therefore I confirm unto thee all the oblations which the kings before me granted thee, and whatsoever gifts besides they granted. 6 I give thee leave also to coin money for thy country with thine own stamp. 7 And as concerning Jerusalem and the sanctuary, let them be free; and all the armour that thou hast made, and fortresses that thou hast built, and keepest in thine hands, let them remain unto thee. 8 And if anything be, or shall be, owing to the king, let it be forgiven thee from this time forth for evermore. 9 Furthermore, when we have obtained our kingdom, we will honour thee, and thy nation, and thy temple, with great honour, so that your honour shall be known throughout the world. 10 In the hundred threescore and fourteenth year went Antiochus into the land of his fathers: at which time all the forces came together unto him, so that few were left with Tryphon. 11 Wherefore being pursued by king Antiochus, he fled unto Dora, which lieth by the sea side: 12 For he saw that troubles came upon him all at once, and that his forces had forsaken him. 13 Then camped Antiochus against Dora, having with him an hundred and twenty thousand men of war, and eight thousand horsemen. 14 And when he had compassed the city round about, and joined ships close to the town on the sea side, he vexed the city by land and by sea, neither suffered he any to go out or in. 15 In the mean season came Numenius and his company from Rome, having letters to the kings and countries; wherein were written these things: 16 Lucius, consul of the Romans unto king Ptolemee, greeting: 17 The Jews' ambassadors, our friends and confederates, came unto us to renew the old friendship and league, being sent from Simon the high priest, and from the people of the Jews: 18 And they brought a shield of gold of a thousand pound. 19 We thought it good therefore to write unto the kings and countries, that they should do them no harm, nor fight against them, their cities, or countries, nor yet aid their enemies against them. 20 It seemed also good to us to receive the shield of them. 21 If therefore there be any pestilent fellows, that have fled from their country unto you, deliver them unto Simon the high priest, that he may punish them according to their own law. 22 The same things wrote he likewise unto Demetrius the king, and Attalus, to Ariarathes, and Arsaces, 23 And to all the countries and to Sampsames, and the Lacedemonians, and to Delus, and Myndus, and Sicyon, and Caria, and Samos, and Pamphylia, and Lycia, and Halicarnassus, and Rhodus, and Aradus, and Cos, and Side, and Aradus, and Gortyna, and Cnidus, and Cyprus, and Cyrene. 24 And the copy hereof they wrote to Simon the high priest. 25 So Antiochus the king camped against Dora the second day, assaulting it continually, and making engines, by which means he shut up Tryphon, that he could neither go out nor in. 26 At that time Simon sent him two thousand chosen men to aid him; silver also, and gold, and much armour. 27 Nevertheless he would not receive them, but brake all the covenants which he had made with him afore, and became strange unto him. 28 Furthermore he sent unto him Athenobius, one of his friends, to commune with him, and say, Ye withhold Joppa and Gazera; with the tower that is in Jerusalem, which are cities of my realm. 29 The borders thereof ye have wasted, and done great hurt in the land, and got the dominion of many places within my kingdom. 30 Now therefore deliver the cities which ye have taken, and the tributes of the places, whereof ye have gotten dominion without the borders of Judea: 31 Or else give me for them five hundred talents of silver; and for the harm that ye have done, and the tributes of the cities, other five hundred talents: if not, we will come and fight against you 32 So Athenobius the king's friend came to Jerusalem: and when he saw the glory of Simon, and the cupboard of gold and silver plate, and his great attendance, he was astonished, and told him the king's message. 33 Then answered Simon, and said unto him, We have neither taken other men's land, nor holden that which appertaineth to others, but the inheritance of our fathers, which our enemies had wrongfully in possession a certain time. 34 Wherefore we, having opportunity, hold the inheritance of our fathers. 35 And whereas thou demandest Joppa and Gazera, albeit they did great harm unto the people in our country, yet will we give thee an hundred talents for them. Hereunto Athenobius answered him not a word; 36 But returned in a rage to the king, and made report unto him of these speeches, and of the glory of Simon, and of all that he had seen: whereupon the king was exceeding wroth. 37 In the mean time fled Tryphon by ship unto Orthosias. 38 Then the king made Cendebeus captain of the sea coast, and gave him an host of footmen and horsemen, 39 And commanded him to remove his host toward Judea; also he commanded him to build up Cedron, and to fortify the gates, and to war against the people; but as for the king himself, he pursued Tryphon. 40 So Cendebeus came to Jamnia and began to provoke the people and to invade Judea, and to take the people prisoners, and slay them. 41 And when he had built up Cedron, he set horsemen there, and an host of footmen, to the end that issuing out they might make outroads upon the ways of Judea, as the king had commanded him.

1-Macc.16 1 Then came up John from Gazera, and told Simon his father what Cendebeus had done. 2 Wherefore Simon called his two eldest sons, Judas and John, and said unto them, I, and my brethren, and my father's house, have ever from my youth unto this day fought against the enemies of Israel; and things have prospered so well in our hands, that we have delivered Israel oftentimes. 3 But now I am old, and ye, by God's mercy, are of a sufficient age: be ye instead of me and my brother, and go and fight for our nation, and the help from heaven be with you. 4 So he chose out of the country twenty thousand men of war with horsemen, who went out against Cendebeus, and rested that night at Modin. 5 And when as they rose in the morning, and went into the plain, behold, a mighty great host both of footmen and horsemen came against them: howbeit there was a water brook betwixt them. 6 So he and his people pitched over against them: and when he saw that the people were afraid to go over the water brook, he went first over himself, and then the men seeing him passed through after him. 7 That done, he divided his men, and set the horsemen in the midst of the footmen: for the enemies' horsemen were very many. 8 Then sounded they with the holy trumpets: whereupon Cendebeus and his host were put to flight, so that many of them were slain, and the remnant gat them to the strong hold. 9 At that time was Judas John's brother wounded; but John still followed after them, until he came to Cedron, which Cendebeus had built. 10 So they fled even unto the towers in the fields of Azotus; wherefore he burned it with fire: so that there were slain of them about two thousand men. Afterward he returned into the land of Judea in peace. 11 Moreover in the plain of Jericho was Ptolemeus the son of Abubus made captain, and he had abundance of silver and gold: 12 For he was the high priest's son in law. 13 Wherefore his heart being lifted up, he thought to get the country to himself, and thereupon consulted deceitfully against Simon and his sons to destroy them. 14 Now Simon was visiting the cities that were in the country, and taking care for the good ordering of them; at which time he came down himself to Jericho with his sons, Mattathias and Judas, in the hundred threescore and seventeenth year, in the eleventh month, called Sabat: 15 Where the son of Abubus receiving them deceitfully into a little hold, called Docus, which he had built, made them a great banquet: howbeit he had hid men there. ¹⁶ So when Simon and his sons had drunk largely, Ptolemee and his men rose up, and took their weapons, and came upon Simon into the banqueting place, and slew him, and his two sons, and certain of his servants. ¹⁷ In which doing he committed a great treachery, and recompensed evil for good. ¹⁸ Then Ptolemee wrote these things, and sent to the king, that he should send him an host to aid him, and he would deliver him the country and cities. ¹⁹ He sent others also to Gazera to kill John: and unto the tribunes he sent letters to come unto him, that he might give them silver, and gold, and rewards. ²⁰ And others he sent to take Jerusalem, and the mountain of the temple. ²¹ Now one had run afore to Gazera and told John that his father and brethren were slain, and, quoth he, Ptolemee hath sent to slay thee also. ²² Hereof when he heard, he was sore astonished: so he laid hands on them that were come to destroy him, and slew them; for he knew that they sought to make him away. ²³ As concerning the rest of the acts of John, and his wars, and worthy deeds which he did, and the building of the walls which he made, and his doings, ²⁴ Behold, these are written in the chronicles of his priesthood, from the time he was made high priest after his father.

2 MACCABEES

2-Macc.1 ¹ The brethren, the Jews that be at Jerusalem and in the land of Judea, wish unto the brethren, the Jews that are throughout Egypt health and peace: ² God be gracious unto you, and remember his covenant that he made with Abraham, Isaac, and Jacob, his faithful servants; ³ And give you all an heart to serve him, and to do his will, with a good courage and a willing mind; ⁴ And open your hearts in his law and commandments, and send you peace, ⁵ And hear your prayers, and be at one with you, and never forsake you in time of trouble. ⁶ And now we be here praying for you. ⁷ What time as Demetrius reigned, in the hundred threescore and ninth year, we the Jews wrote unto you in the extremity of trouble that came upon us in those years, from the time that Jason and his company revolted from the holy land and kingdom, ⁸ And burned the porch, and shed innocent blood: then we prayed unto the Lord, and were heard; we offered also sacrifices and fine flour, and lighted the lamps, and set forth the loaves. ⁹ And now see that ye keep the feast of tabernacles in the month Casleu. ¹⁰ In the hundred fourscore and eighth year, the people that were at Jerusalem and in Judea, and the council, and Judas, sent greeting and health unto Aristobulus, king Ptolemeus' master, who was of the stock of the anointed priests, and to the Jews that were in Egypt: ¹¹Insomuch as God hath delivered us from great perils, we thank him highly, as having been in battle against a king. ¹² For he cast them out that fought within the holy city. ¹³ For when the leader was come into Persia, and the army with him that seemed invincible, they were slain in the temple of Nanea by the deceit of Nanea's priests. ¹⁴ For Antiochus, as though he would marry her, came into the place, and his friends that were with him, to receive money in name of a dowry. ¹⁵ Which when the priests of Nanea had set forth, and he was entered with a small company into the compass of the temple, they shut the temple as soon as Antiochus was come in: ¹⁶ And opening a privy door of the roof, they threw stones like thunderbolts, and struck down the captain, hewed them in pieces, smote off their heads and cast them to those that were without. ¹⁷ Blessed be our God in all things, who hath delivered up the ungodly. ¹⁸ Therefore whereas we are now purposed to keep the purification of the temple upon the five and twentieth day of the month Casleu, we thought it necessary to certify you thereof, that ye also might keep it, as the feast of the tabernacles, and of the fire, which was given us when Neemias offered sacrifice, after that he had builded the temple and the altar. ¹⁹ For when our fathers were led into Persia, the priests that were then devout took the fire of the altar privily, and hid it in an hollow place of a pit without water, where they kept it sure, so that the place was unknown to all men. ²⁰ Now after many years, when it pleased God, Neemias, being sent from the king of Persia, did send of the posterity of those priests that had hid it to the fire: but when they told us they found no fire, but thick water; ²¹ Then commanded he them to draw it up, and to bring it; and when the sacrifices were laid on, Neemias commanded the priests to sprinkle the wood and the things laid thereupon with the water. ²² When this was done, and the time came that the sun shone, which afore was hid in the cloud, there was a great fire kindled, so that every man marvelled. ²³ And the priests made a prayer whilst the sacrifice was consuming, I say, both the priests, and all the rest, Jonathan beginning, and the rest answering thereunto, as Neemias did. ²⁴ And the prayer was after this manner; O Lord, Lord God, Creator of all things, who art fearful and strong, and righteous, and merciful, and the only and gracious King, ²⁵ The only giver of all things, the only just, almighty, and everlasting, thou that deliverest Israel from all trouble, and didst choose the fathers, and sanctify them: ²⁶ Receive the sacrifice for thy whole people Israel, and preserve thine own portion, and sanctify it. ²⁷ Gather those together that are scattered from us, deliver them that serve among the heathen, look upon them that are despised and abhorred, and let the heathen know that thou art our God. ²⁸ Punish them that oppress us, and with pride do us wrong. ²⁹ Plant thy people again in thy holy place, as Moses hath spoken. ³⁰ And the priests sung psalms of thanksgiving. ³¹ Now when the sacrifice was consumed, Neemias commanded the water that was left to be poured on the great stones. ³² When this was done, there was kindled a flame: but it was consumed by the light that shined from the altar. ³³ So when this matter was known, it was told the king of Persia, that in the place, where the priests that were led away had hid the fire, there appeared water, and that Neemias had purified the sacrifices therewith. ³⁴ Then the king, inclosing the place, made it holy, after he had tried the matter. ³⁵ And the king took many gifts, and bestowed thereof on those whom he would gratify. ³⁶ And Neemias called this thing Naphthar, which is as much as to say, a cleansing: but many men call it Nephi.

2-Macc.2 ¹ It is also found in the records, that Jeremy the prophet commanded them that were carried away to take of the fire, as it hath been signified: 2 And how that the prophet, having given them the law, charged them not to forget the commandments of the Lord, and that they should not err in their minds, when they see images of silver and gold, with their ornaments. 3 And with other such speeches exhorted he them, that the law should not depart from their hearts. 4 It was also contained in the same writing, that the prophet, being warned of God, commanded the tabernacle and the ark to go with him, as he went forth into the mountain, where Moses climbed up, and saw the heritage of God. 5 And when Jeremy came thither, he found an hollow cave, wherein he laid the tabernacle, and the ark, and the altar of incense, and so stopped the door. 6 And some of those that followed him came to mark the way, but they could not find it. 7 Which when Jeremy perceived, he blamed them, saying, As for that place, it shall be unknown until the time that God gather his people again together, and receive them unto mercy. 8 Then shall the Lord shew them these things, and the glory of the Lord shall appear, and the cloud also, as it was shewed under Moses, and as when Solomon desired that the place might be honourably sanctified. 9 It was also declared, that he being wise offered the sacrifice of dedication, and of the finishing of the temple. 10 And as when Moses prayed unto the Lord, the fire came down from heaven, and consumed the sacrifices: even so prayed Solomon also, and the fire came down from heaven, and consumed the burnt offerings. 11 And Moses said, Because the sin offering was not to be eaten, it was consumed. 12 So Solomon kept those eight days. 13 The same things also were reported in the writings and commentaries of Neemias; and how he founding a library gathered together the acts of the kings, and the prophets, and of David, and the epistles of the kings concerning the holy gifts. 14 In like manner also Judas gathered together all those things that were lost by reason of the war we had, and they remain with us, 15 Wherefore if ye have need thereof, send some to fetch them unto you. 16 Whereas we then are about to celebrate the purification, we have written unto you, and ye shall do well, if ye keep the same days. 17 We hope also, that the God, that delivered all his people, and gave them all an heritage, and the kingdom, and the priesthood, and the sanctuary, 18 As he promised in the law, will shortly have mercy upon us, and gather us together out of every land under heaven into the holy place: for he hath delivered us out of great troubles, and hath purified the place. 19 Now as concerning Judas Maccabeus, and his brethren, and the purification of the great temple, and the dedication of the altar, 20 And the wars against Antiochus Epiphanes, and Eupator his son, 21 And the manifest signs that came from heaven unto those that behaved themselves manfully to their honour for Judaism: so that, being but a few, they overcame the whole country, and chased barbarous multitudes, 22 And recovered again the temple renowned all the world over, and freed the city, and upheld the laws which were going down, the Lord being gracious unto them with all favour: 23 All these things, I say, being declared by Jason of Cyrene in five books, we will assay to abridge in one volume. 24 For considering the infinite number, and the difficulty which they find that desire to look into the narrations of the story, for the variety of the matter, 25 We have been careful, that they that will read may have delight, and that they that are desirous to commit to memory might have ease, and that all into whose hands it comes might have profit. 26 Therefore to us, that have taken upon us this painful labour of abridging, it was not easy, but a matter of sweat and watching; 27 Even as it is no ease unto him that prepareth a banquet, and seeketh the benefit of others: yet for the pleasuring of many we will undertake gladly this great pains; 28 Leaving to the author the exact handling of every particular, and labouring to follow the rules of an abridgement. 29 For as the master builder of a new house must care for the whole building; but he that undertaketh to set it out, and paint it, must seek out fit things for the adorning thereof: even so I think it is with us. 30 To stand upon every point, and go over things at large, and to be curious in particulars, belongeth to the first author of the story: 31 But to use brevity, and avoid much labouring of the work, is to be granted to him that will make an abridgment. 32 Here then will we begin the story: only adding thus much to that which hath been said, that it is a foolish thing to make a long prologue, and to be short in the story itself.

2-Macc.3 1 Now when the holy city was inhabited with all peace, and the laws were kept very well, because of the godliness of Onias the high priest, and his hatred of wickedness, 2 It came to pass that even the kings themselves did honour the place, and magnify the temple with their best gifts; 3 Insomuch that Seleucus of Asia of his own revenues bare all the costs belonging to the service of the sacrifices. 4 But one Simon of the tribe of Benjamin, who was made governor of the temple, fell out with the high priest about disorder in the city. 5 And when he could not overcome Onias, he gat him to Apollonius the son of Thraseas, who then was governor of Celosyria and Phenice, 6 And told him that the treasury in Jerusalem was full of infinite sums of money, so that the multitude of their riches, which did not pertain to the account of the sacrifices, was innumerable, and that it was possible to bring all into the king's hand. 7 Now when Apollonius came to the king, and had shewed him of the money whereof he was told, the king chose out Heliodorus his treasurer, and sent him with a commandment to bring him the foresaid money. 8 So forthwith Heliodorus took his journey; under a colour of visiting the cities of Celosyria and Phenice, but indeed to fulfil the king's purpose. 9 And when he was come to Jerusalem, and had been courteously received of the high priest of the city, he told him what intelligence was given of the money, and declared wherefore he came, and asked if these things were so indeed. 10 Then the high priest told him that there was such money laid up for the relief of widows and fatherless children: 11 And that some of it belonged to Hircanus son of Tobias, a man of great dignity, and not as that wicked Simon had misinformed: the sum whereof in all was four hundred talents of silver, and two hundred of gold: 12 And that it was altogether impossible that such wrongs should be done unto them, that had committed it to the holiness of the place, and to the majesty and inviolable sanctity of the temple, honoured over all the world. 13 But Heliodorus, because of the king's commandment given him, said, That in any wise it must be brought into the king's treasury. 14 So at the day which he appointed he entered in to order this matter: wherefore there was no small agony throughout the whole city. 15 But the priests, prostrating themselves before the altar in their priests' vestments, called unto heaven upon him that made a law concerning things given to he kept, that they should safely be preserved for such as had committed them to be kept. 16 Then whoso had looked the high priest in the face, it would have wounded his heart: for his countenance and the changing of his colour declared the inward agony of his mind. 17 For the man was so compassed with fear and horror of the body, that it was manifest to them that looked upon him, what sorrow he had now in his heart. 18 Others ran flocking out of their houses to the general supplication, because the place was like to come into contempt. 19 And the women, girt with sackcloth under their breasts, abounded in the streets, and the virgins that were kept in ran, some to the gates, and some to the walls, and others looked out of the windows. 20 And all, holding their hands toward heaven, made supplication. 21 Then it would have pitied a man to see the falling down of the multitude of all sorts, and the fear of the high priest being in such an agony. 22 They then called upon the Almighty Lord to keep the things committed of trust safe and sure for those that had committed them. 23 Nevertheless Heliodorus executed that which was decreed. 24 Now as he was there present himself with his guard about the treasury, the Lord of spirits, and the Prince of all power, caused a great apparition, so that all that presumed to come in with him were astonished at the power of God, and fainted, and were sore afraid. 25 For there appeared unto them an horse with a terrible rider upon him, and adorned with a very fair covering, and he ran fiercely, and smote at Heliodorus with his forefeet, and it seemed that he that sat upon the horse had complete harness of gold. 26 Moreover two other young men appeared before him, notable in strength, excellent in beauty, and comely in apparel, who stood by him on either side; and scourged him continually, and gave him many sore stripes. 27 And Heliodorus fell suddenly unto the ground, and was compassed with great darkness: but they that were with him took him up, and put him into a litter. 28 Thus him, that lately came with a great train and with all his guard into the said treasury, they carried out, being unable to help himself with his weapons: and manifestly they acknowledged the power of God. 29 For he by the hand of God was cast down, and lay speechless without all hope of life. 30 But they praised the Lord, that had miraculously honoured his own place: for the temple; which a little afore was full of fear and trouble, when the Almighty Lord appeared, was filled with joy and gladness. 31 Then straightways certain of Heliodorus' friends prayed Onias, that he would call upon the most High to grant him his life, who lay ready to give up the ghost. 32 So the high priest, suspecting lest the king should misconceive that some treachery had been done to Heliodorus by the Jews, offered a sacrifice for the health of the man. 33 Now as the high priest was making an atonement, the same young men in the same clothing appeared and stood beside Heliodorus, saying, Give Onias the high priest great thanks, insomuch as for his sake the Lord hath granted thee life: 34 And seeing that thou hast been scourged from heaven, declare unto all men the mighty power of God. And when they had spoken these words, they appeared no more. 35 So Heliodorus, after he had offered sacrifice unto the Lord, and made great vows unto him that had saved his life, and saluted Onias, returned with his host to the king. 36 Then testified he to all men the works of the great God, which he had seen with his eyes. 37 And when the king Heliodorus, who might be a fit man to be sent yet once again to Jerusalem, he said, 38 If thou hast any enemy or traitor, send him thither, and thou shalt receive him well scourged, if he escape with his life: for in that place, no doubt; there is an especial power of God. 39 For he that dwelleth in heaven hath his eye on that place, and defendeth it; and he beateth and destroyeth them that come to hurt it. 40 And the things concerning Heliodorus, and the keeping of the treasury, fell out on this sort.

2-Macc.4 1 This Simon now, of whom we spake afore, having been a betrayer of the money, and of his country, slandered Onias, as if he ha terrified Heliodorus, and been the worker of these evils. 2 Thus was he bold to call him a traitor, that had deserved well of the city, and tendered his own nation, and was so zealous of the laws. 3 But when their hatred went so far, that by one of Simon's faction murders were committed, 4 Onias seeing the danger of this contention, and that Apollonius, as being the governor of Celosyria and Phenice, did rage, and increase Simon's malice, 5 He went to the king, not to be an accuser of his countrymen, but seeking the good of all, both publick and private: 6 For he saw that it was impossible that the state should continue quiet, and Simon leave his folly, unless the king did look thereunto. 7 But after the death of Seleucus, when Antiochus, called Epiphanes, took the kingdom, Jason the brother of Onias laboured underhand to be high priest, 8 Promising unto the king by intercession three hundred and threescore talents of silver, and of another revenue eighty talents: 9 Beside this, he promised to assign an hundred and fifty more, if he might have licence to set him up a place for exercise, and for the training up of youth in the fashions of the heathen, and to write them of Jerusalem by the name of Antiochians. 10 Which when the king had granted, and he had gotten into his hand the rule he forthwith brought his own nation to Greekish fashion. 11 And the royal privileges granted of special favour to the Jews by the means of John the father of Eupolemus, who went ambassador to Rome for amity and aid, he took away; and putting down the governments which were according to the law, he brought up new customs against the law: 12 For he built gladly a place of exercise under the tower itself, and brought the chief young men under his subjection, and made them wear a hat. 13 Now such was the height of Greek fashions, and increase of heathenish manners, through the exceeding profaneness of Jason, that ungodly wretch, and no high priest; 14 That the priests had no courage to serve any more at the altar, but despising the temple, and neglecting the sacrifices, hastened to be partakers of the unlawful allowance in the place of exercise, after the game of Discus called them forth; 15 Not setting by the honours of their fathers, but liking the glory of the Grecians best of all. 16 By reason whereof sore calamity came upon them: for they had them to be their enemies and avengers, whose custom they followed so earnestly, and unto whom they desired to be like in all things. 17 For it is not a light thing to do wickedly against the laws of God: but the time following shall declare these things. 18 Now when the game that was used every faith year was kept at Tyrus, the king being present, 19 This ungracious Jason sent special messengers from Jerusalem, who were Antiochians, to carry three hundred drachms of silver to the sacrifice of Hercules, which even the bearers thereof thought fit not to bestow upon the sacrifice, because it was not convenient, but to be reserved for other charges. 20 This money then, in regard of the sender, was appointed to Hercules' sacrifice; but because of the bearers thereof, it was employed to the making of gallies. 21 Now when Apollonius the son of Menestheus was sent into Egypt for the coronation of king Ptolemeus Philometor, Antiochus, understanding him not to be well affected to his affairs, provided for his own safety: whereupon he came to Joppa, and from thence to Jerusalem: 22 Where he was honourably received of Jason, and of the city, and was brought in with torch alight, and with great shoutings: and so afterward went with his host unto Phenice. 23 Three years afterward Jason sent Menelaus, the aforesaid Simon's brother, to bear the money unto the king, and to put him in mind of certain necessary matters. 24 But he being brought to the presence of the king, when he had magnified him for the glorious appearance of his power, got the priesthood to himself, offering more than Jason by three hundred talents of silver. 25 So he came with the king's mandate, bringing nothing worthy the high priesthood, but having the fury of a cruel tyrant, and the rage of a savage beast. 26 Then Jason, who had undermined his own brother, being undermined by another, was compelled to flee into the country of the Ammonites. 27 So Menelaus got the principality: but as for the money that he had promised unto the king, he took no good order for it, albeit Sostratis the ruler of the castle required it: 28 For unto him appertained the gathering of the customs. Wherefore they were both called before the king. 29 Now Menelaus left his brother Lysimachus in his stead in the priesthood; and Sostratus left Crates, who was governor of the Cyprians. 30 While those things were in doing, they of Tarsus and Mallos made insurrection, because they were given to the king's concubine, called Antiochus. 31 Then came the king in all haste to appease matters, leaving Andronicus, a man in authority, for his deputy. 32 Now Menelaus, supposing that he had gotten a convenient time, stole certain vessels of gold out of the temple, and gave some of them to Andronicus, and some he sold into Tyrus and the cities round about. 33 Which when Onias knew of a surety, he reproved him, and withdrew himself into a sanctuary at Daphne, that lieth by Antiochia. 34 Wherefore Menelaus,

taking Andronicus apart, prayed, him to get Onias into his hands; who being persuaded thereunto, and coming to Onias in deceit, gave him his right hand with oaths; and though he were suspected by him, yet persuaded he him to come forth of the sanctuary: whom forthwith he shut up without regard of justice. 35 For the which cause not only the Jews, but many also of other nations, took great indignation, and were much grieved for the unjust murder of the man. 36 And when the king was come again from the places about Cilicia, the Jews that were in the city, and certain of the Greeks that abhorred the fact also, complained because Onias was slain without cause. 37 Therefore Antiochus was heartily sorry, and moved to pity, and wept, because of the sober and modest behaviour of him that was dead. 38 And being kindled with anger, forthwith he took away Andronicus his purple, and rent off his clothes, and leading him through the whole city unto that very place, where he had committed impiety against Onias, there slew he the cursed murderer. Thus the Lord rewarded him his punishment, as he had deserved. 39 Now when many sacrileges had been committed in the city by Lysimachus with the consent of Menelaus, and the fruit thereof was spread abroad, the multitude gathered themselves together against Lysimachus, many vessels of gold being already carried away. 40 Whereupon the common people rising, and being filled with rage, Lysimachus armed about three thousand men, and began first to offer violence; one Auranus being the leader, a man far gone in years, and no less in folly. 41 They then seeing the attempt of Lysimachus, some of them caught stones, some clubs, others taking handfuls of dust, that was next at hand, cast them all together upon Lysimachus, and those that set upon them. 42 Thus many of them they wounded, and some they struck to the ground, and all of them they forced to flee: but as for the churchrobber himself, him they killed beside the treasury. 43 Of these matters therefore there was an accusation laid against Menelaus. 44 Now when the king came to Tyrus, three men that were sent from the senate pleaded the cause before him: 45 But Menelaus, being now convicted, promised Ptolemee the son of Dorymenes to give him much money, if he would pacify the king toward him. 46 Whereupon Ptolemee taking the king aside into a certain gallery, as it were to take the air, brought him to be of another mind: 47 Insomuch that he discharged Menelaus from the accusations, who notwithstanding was cause of all the mischief: and those poor men, who, if they had told their cause, yea, before the Scythians, should have been judged innocent, them he condemned to death. 48 Thus they that followed the matter for the city, and for the people, and for the holy vessels, did soon suffer unjust punishment. 49 Wherefore even they of Tyrus, moved with hatred of that wicked deed, caused them to be honourably buried. 50 And so through the covetousness of them that were of power Menelaus remained still in authority, increasing in malice, and being a great traitor to the citizens.

2-Macc.5 1 About the same time Antiochus prepared his second voyage into Egypt: 2 And then it happened, that through all the city, for the space almost of forty days, there were seen horsemen running in the air, in cloth of gold, and armed with lances, like a band of soldiers, 3 And troops of horsemen in array, encountering and running one against another, with shaking of shields, and multitude of pikes, and drawing of swords, and casting of darts, and glittering of golden ornaments, and harness of all sorts. 4 Wherefore every man prayed that that apparition might turn to good. 5 Now when there was gone forth a false rumour, as though Antiochus had been dead, Jason took at the least a thousand men, and suddenly made an assault upon the city; and they that were upon the walls being put back, and the city at length taken, Menelaus fled into the castle: 6 But Jason slew his own citizens without mercy, not considering that to get the day of them of his own nation would be a most unhappy day for him; but thinking they had been his enemies, and not his countrymen, whom he conquered. 7 Howbeit for all this he obtained not the principality, but at the last received shame for the reward of his treason, and fled again into the country of the Ammonites. 8 In the end therefore he had an unhappy return, being accused before Aretas the king of the Arabians, fleeing from city to city, pursued of all men, hated as a forsaker of the laws, and being had in abomination as an open enemy of his country and countrymen, he was cast out into Egypt. 9 Thus he that had driven many out of their country perished in a strange land, retiring to the Lacedemonians, and thinking there to find succour by reason of his kindred: 10 And he that had cast out many unburied had none to mourn for him, nor any solemn funerals at all, nor sepulchre with his fathers. 11 Now when this that was done came to the king's ear, he thought that Judea had revolted: whereupon removing out of Egypt in a furious mind, he took the city by force of arms, 12 And commanded his men of war not to spare such as they met, and to slay such as went up upon the houses. 13 Thus there was killing of young and old, making away of men, women, and children, slaying of virgins and infants. 14 And there were destroyed within the space of three whole days fourscore thousand, whereof forty thousand were slain in the conflict; and no fewer sold than slain. 15 Yet was he not content with this, but presumed to go into the most holy temple of all the world; Menelaus, that traitor to the laws, and to his own country, being his guide: 16 And taking the holy vessels with polluted hands, and with profane hands pulling down the things that were dedicated by other kings to the augmentation and glory and honour of the place, he gave them away. 17 And so haughty was Antiochus in mind, that he considered not that the Lord was angry for a while for the sins of them that dwelt in the city, and therefore his eye was not upon the place. 18 For had they not been formerly wrapped in many sins, this man, as soon as he had come, had forthwith been scourged, and put back from his presumption, as Heliodorus was, whom Seleucus the king sent to view the treasury. 19 Nevertheless God did not choose the people for the place's sake, but the place for the people's sake. 20 And therefore the place itself, that was partaker with them of the adversity that happened to the nation, did afterward communicate in the benefits sent from the Lord: and as it was forsaken in the wrath of the Almighty, so again, the great Lord being reconciled, it was set up with all glory. 21 So when Antiochus had carried out of the temple a thousand and eight hundred talents, he departed in all haste unto Antiochia, weening in his pride to make the land navigable, and the sea passable by foot: such was the haughtiness of his mind. 22 And he left governors to vex the nation: at Jerusalem, Philip, for his country a Phrygian, and for manners more barbarous than he that set him there; 23 And at Garizim, Andronicus; and besides, Menelaus, who worse than all the rest bare an heavy hand over the citizens, having a malicious mind against his countrymen the Jews. 24 He sent also that detestable ringleader Apollonius with an army of two and twenty thousand, commanding him to slay all those that were in their best age, and to sell the women and the younger sort: 25 Who coming to Jerusalem, and pretending peace, did forbear till the holy day of the sabbath, when taking the Jews keeping holy day, he commanded his men to arm themselves. 26 And so he slew all them that were gone to the celebrating of the sabbath, and running through the city with weapons slew great multitudes. 27 But Judas Maccabeus with nine others, or thereabout, withdrew himself into the wilderness, and lived in the mountains after the manner of beasts, with his company, who fed on herbs continually, lest they should be partakers of the pollution.

2-Macc.6 1 Not long after this the king sent an old man of Athens to compel the Jews to depart from the laws of their fathers, and not to live after the laws of God: 2 And to pollute also the temple in Jerusalem, and to call it the temple of Jupiter Olympius; and that in Garizim, of Jupiter the Defender of strangers, as they did desire that dwelt in the place. 3 The coming in of this mischief was sore and grievous to the people: 4 For the temple was filled with riot and revelling by the Gentiles, who dallied with harlots, and had to do with women within the circuit of the holy places, and besides that brought in things that were not lawful. 5 The altar also was filled with profane things, which the law forbiddeth. 6 Neither was it lawful for a man to keep sabbath days or ancient fasts, or to profess himself at all to be a Jew. 7 And in the day of the king's birth every month they were brought by bitter constraint to eat of the sacrifices; and when the fast of Bacchus was kept, the Jews were compelled to go in procession to Bacchus, carrying ivy. 8 Moreover there went out a decree to the neighbour cities of the heathen, by the suggestion of Ptolemee, against the Jews, that they should observe the same fashions, and be partakers of their sacrifices: 9 And whoso would not conform themselves to the manners of the Gentiles should be put to death. Then might a man have seen the present misery. 10 For there were two women brought, who had circumcised their children; whom when they had openly led round about the city, the babes handing at their breasts, they cast them down headlong from the wall. 11 And others, that had run together into caves near by, to keep the sabbath day secretly, being discovered by Philip, were all burnt together, because they made a conscience to help themselves for the honour of the most sacred day. 12 Now I beseech those that read this book, that they be not discouraged for these calamities, but that they judge those punishments not to be for destruction, but for a chastening of our nation. 13 For it is a token of his great goodness, when wicked doers are not suffered any long time, but forthwith punished. 14 For not as with other nations, whom the Lord patiently forbeareth to punish, till they be come to the fulness of their sins, so dealeth he with us, 15 Lest that, being come to the height of sin, afterwards he should take vengeance of us. 16 And therefore he never withdraweth his mercy from us: and though he punish with adversity, yet doth he never forsake his people. 17 But let this that we at spoken be for a warning unto us. And now will we come to the declaring of the matter in a few words. 18 Eleazar, one of the principal scribes, an aged man, and of a well favoured countenance, was constrained to open his mouth, and to eat swine's flesh. 19 But he, choosing rather to die gloriously, than to live stained with such an abomination, spit it forth, and came of his own accord to the torment, 20 As it behoved them to come, that are resolute to stand out against such things, as are not lawful for love of life to be tasted. 21 But they that had the charge of that wicked feast, for the old acquaintance they had with the man, taking him aside, besought him to bring flesh of his own provision, such as was lawful for him to use, and make as if he did eat of the flesh taken from the sacrifice commanded by the king; 22 That in so doing he might be delivered from death, and for the old friendship with them find favour. 23 But he began to consider discreetly, and as became his age, and the excellency of his ancient years, and the honour of his gray head, whereon was come, and his most honest education from a child, or rather the holy law made and given by God: therefore he answered accordingly, and willed them straightways to send him to the grave. 24 For it becometh not our age, said he, in any wise to dissemble, whereby many young persons might think that Eleazar, being fourscore years old and ten, were now gone to a strange religion; 25 And so they through mine hypocrisy, and desire to live a little time and a moment longer, should be deceived by me, and I get a stain to mine old age, and make it abominable. 26 For though for the present time I should be delivered from the punishment of men: yet should I not escape the hand of the Almighty, neither alive, nor dead. 27 Wherefore now, manfully changing this life, I will shew myself such an one as mine age requireth, 28 And leave a notable example to such as be young to die willingly and courageously for the honourable and holy laws. And when he had said these words, immediately he went to the torment: 29 They that led him changing the good will they bare him a little before into hatred, because the foresaid speeches proceeded, as they thought, from a desperate mind. 30 But when he was ready to die with stripes, he groaned, and said, It is manifest unto the Lord, that hath the holy knowledge, that whereas I might have been delivered from death, I now endure sore pains in body by being beaten: but in soul am well content to suffer these things, because I fear him. 31 And thus this man died, leaving his death for an example of a noble courage, and a memorial of virtue, not only unto young men, but unto all his nation.

2-Macc.7 1 It came to pass also, that seven brethren with their mother were taken, and compelled by the king against the law to taste swine's flesh, and were tormented with scourges and whips. 2 But one of them that spake first said thus, What wouldest thou ask or learn of us? we are ready to die, rather than to transgress the laws of our fathers. 3 Then the king, being in a rage, commanded pans and caldrons to be made hot: 4 Which forthwith being heated, he commanded to cut out the tongue of him that spake first, and to cut off the utmost parts of his body, the rest of his brethren and his mother looking on. 5 Now when he was thus maimed in all his members, he commanded him being yet alive to be brought to the fire, and to be fried in the pan: and as the vapour of the pan was for a good space dispersed, they exhorted one another with the mother to die manfully, saying thus, 6 The Lord God looketh upon us, and in truth hath comfort in us, as Moses in his song, which witnessed to their faces, declared, saying, And he shall be comforted in his servants. 7 So when the first was dead after this number, they brought the second to make him a mocking stock: and when they had pulled off the skin of his head with the hair, they asked him, Wilt thou eat, before thou be punished throughout every member of thy body? 8 But he answered in his own language, and said, No. Wherefore he also received the next torment in order, as the former did. 9 And when he was at the last gasp, he said, Thou like a fury takest us out of this present life, but the King of the world shall raise us up, who have died for his laws, unto everlasting life. 10 After him was the third made a mocking stock: and when he was required, he put out his tongue, and that right soon, holding forth his hands manfully. 11 And said courageously, These I had from heaven; and for his laws I despise them; and from him I hope to receive them again. 12 Insomuch that the king, and they that were with him, marvelled at the young man's courage, for that he nothing regarded the pains. 13 Now when this man was dead also, they tormented and mangled the fourth in like manner. 14 So when he was ready to die he said thus, It is good, being put to death by men, to look for hope from God to be raised up again by him: as for thee, thou shalt have no resurrection to life. 15 Afterward they brought the fifth also, and mangled him. 16 Then looked he unto the king, and said, Thou hast power over men, thou art corruptible, thou doest what thou wilt; yet think not that our nation is forsaken of God; 17 But abide a while, and behold his great power, how he will torment thee and thy seed. 18 After him also they brought the sixth, who being ready to die said, Be not deceived without cause: for we suffer these things for ourselves, having sinned against our God: therefore marvellous things are done unto us. 19 But think not thou, that takest in hand to strive against God, that thou shalt escape unpunished. 20 But the mother was marvellous above all, and worthy of honourable memory: for when she saw her seven sons slain within the space of one day, she bare it with a good courage, because of the hope that she had in the Lord. 21 Yea, she exhorted every one of them in her own language, filled with courageous spirits; and stirring up her womanish thoughts with a manly stomach, she said unto them, 22 I cannot tell how ye came into my womb: for I neither gave you breath nor life, neither was it I that formed the members of every one of you; 23 But doubtless the Creator of the world, who formed the generation of man, and found out the beginning of all things, will also of his own mercy give you breath and life again, as ye now regard not your own selves for his laws' sake. 24 Now Antiochus, thinking himself despised, and suspecting it to be a reproachful speech, whilst the youngest was yet alive, did not only exhort him by words, but also assured him with oaths, that he would make him both a rich and a happy man, if he would turn from the laws of his fathers; and that also he would take him for his friend, and trust him with affairs. 25 But when the young man would in no case hearken unto him, the king called his mother, and exhorted her that she would counsel the young man to save his life. 26 And when he had exhorted her with many words, she promised him that she would counsel her son. 27 But she bowing herself toward him, laughing the cruel tyrant to scorn, spake in her country language on this manner; O my son, have pity upon me that bare thee nine months in my womb, and gave thee such three years, and nourished thee, and brought thee up unto this age, and endured the troubles of education. 28 I beseech thee, my son, look upon the heaven and the earth, and all that is therein, and consider that God made them of things that were not; and so was mankind made likewise. 29 Fear not this tormentor, but, being worthy of thy brethren, take thy death that I may receive thee again in mercy with thy brethren. 30 Whiles she was yet speaking these words, the young man said, Whom wait ye for? I will not obey the king's commandment: but I will obey the commandment of the law that was given unto our fathers by Moses. 31 And thou, that hast been the author of all mischief against the Hebrews, shalt not escape the hands of God. 32 For we suffer because of our sins. 33 And though the living Lord be angry with us a little while for our chastening and correction, yet shall he be at one again with his servants. 34 But thou, O godless man, and of all other most wicked, be not lifted up without a cause, nor puffed up with uncertain hopes, lifting up thy hand against the servants of God: 35 For thou hast not yet escaped the judgment of Almighty God, who seeth all things. 36 For our brethren, who now have suffered a short pain, are dead under God's covenant of everlasting life: but thou, through the judgment of God, shalt receive just punishment for thy pride. 37 But I, as my brethren, offer up my body and life for the laws of our fathers, beseeching God that he would speedily be merciful unto our nation; and that thou by torments and plagues mayest confess, that he alone is God; 38 And that in me and my brethren the wrath of the Almighty, which is justly brought upon our nation, may cease. 39 Than the king' being in a rage, handed him worse than all the rest, and took it grievously that he was mocked. 40 So this man died undefiled, and put his whole trust in the Lord. 41 Last of all after the sons the mother died. 42 Let this be enough now to have spoken concerning the idolatrous feasts, and the extreme tortures.

2-Macc.8 1 Then Judas Maccabeus, and they that were with him, went privily into the towns, and called their kinsfolks together, and took unto them all such as continued in the Jews' religion, and assembled about six thousand men. 2 And they called upon the Lord, that he would look upon the people that was trodden down of all; and also pity the temple profaned of ungodly men; 3 And that he would have compassion upon the city, sore defaced, and ready to be made even with the ground; and hear the blood that cried unto him, 4 And remember the wicked slaughter of harmless infants, and the blasphemies committed against his name; and that he would shew his hatred against the wicked. 5 Now when Maccabeus had his company about him, he could not be withstood by the heathen: for the wrath of the Lord was turned into mercy. 6 Therefore he came at unawares, and burnt up towns and cities, and got into his hands the most commodious places, and overcame and put to flight no small number of his enemies. 7 But specially took he advantage of the night for such privy attempts, insomuch that the fruit of his holiness was spread every where. 8 So when Philip saw that this man increased by little and little, and that things prospered with him still more and more, he wrote unto Ptolemeus, the governor of Celosyria and Phenice, to yield more aid to the king's affairs. 9 Then forthwith choosing Nicanor the son of Patroclus, one of his special friends, he sent him with no fewer than twenty thousand of all nations under him, to root out the whole generation of the Jews; and with him he joined also Gorgias a captain, who in matters of war had great experience. 10 So Nicanor undertook to make so much money of the captive Jews, as should defray the tribute of two thousand talents, which the king was to pay to the Romans. 11 Wherefore immediately he sent to the cities upon the sea coast, proclaiming a sale of the captive Jews, and promising that they should have fourscore and ten bodies for one talent, not expecting the vengeance that was to follow upon him from the Almighty God. 12 Now when word was brought unto Judas of Nicanor's coming, and he had imparted unto those that were with him that the army was at hand, 13 They that were fearful, and distrusted the justice of God, fled, and conveyed themselves away. 14 Others sold all that they had left, and withal besought the Lord to deliver them, sold by the wicked Nicanor before they met together: 15 And if not for their own sakes, yet for the covenants he had made with their fathers, and for his holy and glorious name's sake, by which they were called. 16 So Maccabeus called his men together unto the number of six thousand, and exhorted them not to be stricken with terror of the enemy, nor to fear the great multitude of the heathen, who came wrongly against them; but to fight manfully, 17 And to set before their eyes the injury that they had unjustly done to the holy place, and the cruel handling of the city, whereof they made a mockery, and also the taking away of the government of their forefathers: 18 For they, said he, trust in their weapons and boldness; but our confidence is in the Almighty who at a beck can cast down both them that come against us, and also all the world. 19 Moreover, he recounted unto them what helps their forefathers had found, and how they were delivered, when under Sennacherib an hundred fourscore and five thousand perished. 20 And he told them of the battle that they had in Babylon with the Galatians, how they came but eight thousand in all to the business, with four thousand Macedonians, and that the Macedonians being perplexed, the eight thousand destroyed an hundred and twenty thousand because of the help that they had from heaven, and so received a great booty. 21 Thus when he had made them bold with these words, and ready to die for the law and the country, he divided his army into four parts; 22 And joined with himself his own brethren, leaders of each band, to wit Simon, and Joseph, and Jonathan, giving each one fifteen hundred men. 23 Also he appointed Eleazar to read the holy book: and when he had given them this watchword, The help of God; himself leading the first band, 24 And by the help of the Almighty they slew above nine thousand of their enemies, and wounded and maimed the most part of Nicanor's host, and so put all to flight; 25 And took their money that came to buy them, and pursued them far: but lacking time they returned: 26 For it was the day before the sabbath, and therefore they would no longer pursue them. 27 So when they had gathered their armour together, and spoiled their enemies, they occupied themselves about the sabbath, yielding exceeding praise and thanks to the Lord, who had preserved them unto that day, which was the beginning of mercy distilling upon them. 28 And after the sabbath, when they had given part of the spoils to the maimed, and the widows, and orphans, the residue they divided among themselves and their servants. 29 When this was done, and they had made a common supplication, they besought the merciful Lord to be reconciled with his servants for ever. 30 Moreover of those that were with Timotheus and Bacchides, who fought against them, they slew above twenty thousand, and very easily got high and strong holds, and divided among themselves many spoils more, and made the maimed, orphans, widows, yea, and the aged also, equal in spoils with themselves. 31 And when they had gathered their armour together, they laid them up all carefully in convenient places, and the remnant of the spoils they brought to Jerusalem. 32 They slew also Philarches, that wicked person, who was with Timotheus, and had annoyed the Jews many ways. 33 Furthermore at such time as they kept the feast for the victory in their country they burnt Callisthenes, that had set fire upon the holy gates, who had fled into a little house; and so he received a reward meet for his wickedness. 34 As for that most ungracious Nicanor, who had brought a thousand merchants to buy the Jews, 35 He was through the help of the Lord brought down by them, of whom he made least account; and putting off his glorious apparel, and discharging his company, he came like a fugitive servant through the midland unto Antioch having very great dishonour, for that his host was destroyed. 36 Thus he, that took upon him to make good to the Romans their tribute by means of captives in Jerusalem, told abroad, that the Jews had God to fight for them, and therefore they could not be hurt, because they followed the laws that he gave them.

2-Macc.9 1 About that time came Antiochus with dishonour out of the country of Persia 2 For he had entered the city called Persepolis, and went about to rob the temple, and to hold the city; whereupon the multitude running to defend themselves with their weapons put them to flight; and so it happened, that Antiochus being put to flight of the inhabitants returned with shame. 3 Now when he came to Ecbatane, news was brought him what had happened unto Nicanor and Timotheus. 4 Then swelling with anger. he thought to avenge upon the Jews the disgrace done unto him by those that made him flee. Therefore commanded he his chariotman to drive without ceasing, and to dispatch the journey, the judgment of God now following him. For he had spoken proudly in this sort, That he would come to Jerusalem and make it a common burying place of the Jews. 5 But the Lord Almighty, the God of Israel, smote him with an incurable and invisible plague: or as soon as he had spoken these words, a pain of the bowels that was remediless came upon him, and sore torments of the inner parts; 6 And that most justly: for he had tormented other men's bowels with many and strange torments. 7 Howbeit he nothing at all ceased from his bragging, but still was filled with pride, breathing out fire in his rage against the Jews, and commanding to haste the journey: but it came to pass that he fell down from his chariot, carried violently; so that having a sore fall, all the members of his body were much pained. 8 And thus he that a little afore thought he might command the waves of the sea, (so proud was he beyond the condition of man) and weigh the high mountains in a balance, was now cast on the ground, and carried in an horselitter, shewing forth unto all the manifest power of God. 9 So that the worms rose up out of the body of this wicked man, and whiles he lived in sorrow and pain, his flesh fell away, and the filthiness of his smell was noisome to all his army. 10 And the man, that thought a little afore he could reach to the stars of heaven, no man could endure to carry for his intolerable stink. 11 Here therefore, being plagued, he began to leave off his great pride, and to come to the knowledge of himself by the scourge of God, his pain increasing every moment. 12 And when he himself could not abide his own smell, he said these words, It is meet to be subject unto God, and that a man that is mortal should not proudly think of himself if he were God. 13 This wicked person vowed also unto the Lord, who now no more would have mercy upon him, saying thus, 14 That the holy city (to the which he was going in haste to lay it even with the ground, and to make it a common buryingplace,) he would set at liberty: 15 And as touching the Jews, whom he had judged not worthy so much as to be buried, but to be cast out with their children to be devoured of the fowls and wild beasts, he would make them all equals to the citizens of Athens: 16 And the holy temple, which before he had spoiled, he would garnish with goodly gifts, and restore all the holy vessels with many more, and out of his own revenue defray the charges belonging to the sacrifices: 17 Yea, and that also he would become a Jew himself, and go through all the world that was inhabited, and declare the power of God. 18 But for all this his pains would not cease: for the just judgment of God was come upon him:

therefore despairing of his health, he wrote unto the Jews the letter underwritten, containing the form of a supplication, after this manner: 19 Antiochus, king and governor, to the good Jews his citizens wisheth much joy, health, and prosperity: 20 If ye and your children fare well, and your affairs be to your contentment, I give very great thanks to God, having my hope in heaven. 21 As for me, I was weak, or else I would have remembered kindly your honour and good will returning out of Persia, and being taken with a grievous disease, I thought it necessary to care for the common safety of all: 22 Not distrusting mine health, but having great hope to escape this sickness. 23 But considering that even my father, at what time he led an army into the high countries. appointed a successor, 24 To the end that, if any thing fell out contrary to expectation, or if any tidings were brought that were grievous, they of the land, knowing to whom the state was left, might not be troubled: 25 Again, considering how that the princes that are borderers and neighbours unto my kingdom wait for opportunities, and expect what shall be the event. I have appointed my son Antiochus king, whom I often committed and commended unto many of you, when I went up into the high provinces; to whom I have written as followeth: 26 Therefore I pray and request you to remember the benefits that I have done unto you generally, and in special, and that every man will be still faithful to me and my son. 27 For I am persuaded that he understanding my mind will favourably and graciously yield to your desires. 28 Thus the murderer and blasphemer having suffered most grievously, as he entreated other men, so died he a miserable death in a strange country in the mountains. 29 And Philip, that was brought up with him, carried away his body, who also fearing the son of Antiochus went into Egypt to Ptolemeus Philometor.

2-Macc.10 1 Now Maccabeus and his company, the Lord guiding them, recovered the temple and the city: 2 But the altars which the heathen had built in the open street, and also the chapels, they pulled down. 3 And having cleansed the temple they made another altar, and striking stones they took fire out of them, and offered a sacrifice after two years, and set forth incense, and lights, and shewbread. 4 When that was done, they fell flat down, and besought the Lord that they might come no more into such troubles; but if they sinned any more against him, that he himself would chasten them with mercy, and that they might not be delivered unto the blasphemous and barbarous nations. 5 Now upon the same day that the strangers profaned the temple, on the very same day it was cleansed again, even the five and twentieth day of the same month, which is Casleu. 6 And they kept the eight days with gladness, as in the feast of the tabernacles, remembering that not long afore they had held the feast of the tabernacles, when as they wandered in the mountains and dens like beasts. 7 Therefore they bare branches, and fair boughs, and palms also, and sang psalms unto him that had given them good success in cleansing his place. 8 They ordained also by a common statute and decree, That every year those days should be kept of the whole nation of the Jews. 9 And this

was the end of Antiochus, called Epiphanes. 10 Now will we declare the acts of Antiochus Eupator, who was the son of this wicked man, gathering briefly the calamities of the wars. 11 So when he was come to the crown, he set one Lysias over the affairs of his realm, and appointed him his chief governor of Celosyria and Phenice. 12 For Ptolemeus, that was called Macron, choosing rather to do justice unto the Jews for the wrong that had been done unto them, endeavoured to continue peace with them. 13 Whereupon being accused of the king's friends before Eupator, and called traitor at every word because he had left Cyprus, that Philometor had committed unto him, and departed to Antiochus Epiphanes, and seeing that he was in no honourable place, he was so discouraged, that he poisoned himself and died. 14 But when Gorgias was governor of the holds, he hired soldiers, and nourished war continually with the Jews: 15 And therewithal the Idumeans, having gotten into their hands the most commodious holds, kept the Jews occupied, and receiving those that were banished from Jerusalem, they went about to nourish war. 16 Then they that were with Maccabeus made supplication, and besought God that he would be their helper; and so they ran with violence upon the strong holds of the Idumeans, 17 And assaulting them strongly, they won the holds, and kept off all that fought upon the wall, and slew all that fell into their hands, and killed no fewer than twenty thousand. 18 And because certain, who were no less than nine thousand, were fled together into two very strong castles, having all manner of things convenient to sustain the siege, 19 Maccabeus left Simon and Joseph, and Zaccheus also, and them that were with him, who were enough to besiege them, and departed himself unto those places which more needed his help. 20 Now they that were with Simon, being led with covetousness, were persuaded for money through certain of those that were in the castle, and took seventy thousand drachms, and let some of them escape. 21 But when it was told Maccabeus what was done, he called the governors of the people together, and accused those men, that they had sold their brethren for money, and set their enemies free to fight against them. 22 So he slew those that were found traitors, and immediately took the two castles. 23 And having good success with his weapons in all things he took in hand, he slew in the two holds more than twenty thousand. 24 Now Timotheus, whom the Jews had overcome before, when he had gathered a great multitude of foreign forces, and horses out of Asia not a few, came as though he would take Jewry by force of arms. 25 But when he drew near, they that were with Maccabeus turned themselves to pray unto God, and sprinkled earth upon their heads, and girded their loins with sackcloth, 26 And fell down at the foot of the altar, and besought him to be merciful to them, and to be an enemy to their enemies, and an adversary to their adversaries, as the law declareth. 27 So after the prayer they took their weapons, and went on further from the city: and when they drew near to their enemies, they kept by themselves. 28 Now the sun being newly risen, they joined both together; the one part having together with their virtue their refuge also unto the Lord for a pledge of their success and victory: the other side making their rage leader of their battle 29 But when the battle waxed strong, there appeared unto the enemies from heaven five comely men upon horses, with bridles of gold, and two of them led the Jews, 30 And took Maccabeus betwixt them, and covered him on every side weapons, and kept him safe, but shot arrows and lightnings against the enemies: so that being confounded with blindness, and full of trouble, they were killed. 31 And there were slain of footmen twenty thousand and five hundred, and six hundred horsemen. 32 As for Timotheus himself, he fled into a very strong hold, called Gazara, where Chereas was governor. 33 But they that were with Maccabeus laid siege against the fortress courageously four days. 34 And they that were within, trusting to the strength of the place, blasphemed exceedingly, and uttered wicked words. 35 Nevertheless upon the fifth day early twenty young men of Maccabeus' company, inflamed with anger because of the blasphemies, assaulted the wall manly, and with a fierce courage killed all that they met withal. 36 Others likewise ascending after them, whiles they were busied with them that were within, burnt the towers, and kindling fires burnt the blasphemers alive; and others broke open the gates, and, having received in the rest of the army, took the city, 37 And killed Timotheus, that was hid in a certain pit, and Chereas his brother, with Apollophanes. 38 When this was done, they praised the Lord with psalms and thanksgiving, who had done so great things for Israel, and given them the victory.

2-Macc.11 1 Not long after the, Lysias the king's protector and cousin, who also managed the affairs, took sore displeasure for the things that were done. 2 And when he had gathered about fourscore thousand with all the horsemen, he came against the Jews, thinking to make the city an habitation of the Gentiles, 3 And to make a gain of the temple, as of the other chapels of the heathen, and to set the high priesthood to sale every year: 4 Not at all considering the power of God but puffed up with his ten thousands of footmen, and his thousands of horsemen, and his fourscore elephants. 5 So he came to Judea, and drew near to Bethsura, which was a strong town, but distant from Jerusalem about five furlongs, and he laid sore siege unto it. 6 Now when they that were with Maccabeus heard that he besieged the holds, they and all the people with lamentation and tears besought the Lord that he would send a good angel to deliver Israel. 7 Then Maccabeus himself first of all took weapons, exhorting the other that they would jeopard themselves together with him to help their brethren: so they went forth together with a willing mind. 8 And as they were at Jerusalem, there appeared before them on horseback one in white clothing, shaking his armour of gold. 9 Then they praised the merciful God all together, and took heart, insomuch that they were ready not only to fight with men, but with most cruel beasts, and to pierce through walls of iron. 10 Thus they marched forward in their armour, having an helper from heaven: for the Lord was merciful unto them 11 And giving a charge upon their enemies like lions, they slew eleven thousand footmen, and sixteen hundred horsemen, and put all the other to flight. 12 Many of them also being wounded escaped naked; and Lysias himself fled away shamefully, and so escaped. 13 Who, as he was a man of understanding, casting with himself what loss he had had, and considering that the Hebrews could not be overcome, because the Almighty God helped them, he sent unto them, 14 And persuaded them to agree to all reasonable conditions, and promised that he would persuade the king that he must needs be a friend unto them. 15 Then Maccabeus consented to all that Lysias desired, being careful of the common good; and whatsoever Maccabeus wrote unto Lysias concerning the Jews, the king granted it. 16 For there were letters written unto the Jews from Lysias to this effect: Lysias unto the people of the Jews sendeth greeting: 17 John and Absalon, who were sent from you, delivered me the petition subscribed, and made request for the performance of the contents thereof. 18 Therefore what things soever were meet to be reported to the king, I have declared them, and he hath granted as much as might be. 19 And if then ye will keep yourselves loyal to the state, hereafter also will I endeavour to be a means of your good. 20 But of the particulars I have given order both to these and the other that came from me, to commune with you. 21 Fare ye well. The hundred and eight and fortieth year, the four and twentieth day of the month Dioscorinthius. 22 Now the king's letter contained these words: King Antiochus unto his brother Lysias sendeth greeting: 23 Since our father is translated unto the gods, our will is, that they that are in our realm live quietly, that every one may attend upon his own affairs. 24 We understand also that the Jews would not consent to our father, for to be brought unto the custom of the Gentiles, but had rather keep their own manner of living: for the which cause they require of us, that we should suffer them to live after their own laws. 25 Wherefore our mind is, that this nation shall be in rest, and we have determined to restore them their temple, that they may live according to the customs of their forefathers. 26 Thou shalt do well therefore to send unto them, and grant them peace, that when they are certified of our mind, they may be of good comfort, and ever go cheerfully about their own affairs. 27 And the letter of the king unto the nation of the Jews was after this manner: King Antiochus sendeth greeting unto the council, and the rest of the Jews: 28 If ye fare well, we have our desire; we are also in good health. 29 Menelaus declared unto us, that your desire was to return home, and to follow your own business: 30 Wherefore they that will depart shall have safe conduct till the thirtieth day of Xanthicus with security. 31 And the Jews shall use their own kind of meats and laws, as before; and none of them any manner of ways shall be molested for things ignorantly done. 32 I have sent also Menelaus, that he may comfort you. 33 Fare ye well. In the hundred forty and eighth year, and the fifteenth day of the month Xanthicus. 34 The Romans also sent unto them a letter containing these words: Quintus Memmius and Titus Manlius, ambassadors of the Romans, send greeting unto the people of the Jews. 35 Whatsoever Lysias the king's cousin hath granted, therewith we also are well pleased. 36 But touching such things as he judged to be referred to the king, after ye have advised thereof, send one forthwith, that we may declare as it is convenient for you: for we are now going to Antioch. 37 Therefore send some with speed, that we may know what is your mind. 38 Farewell. This hundred and eight and fortieth year, the fifteenth day of the month Xanthicus.

2-Macc.12 1 When these covenants were made, Lysias went unto the king, and the Jews were about their husbandry. 2 But of the governors of several places, Timotheus, and Apollonius the son of Genneus, also Hieronymus, and Demophon, and beside them Nicanor the governor of Cyprus, would not suffer them to be quiet and live in peace. 3 The men of Joppa also did such an ungodly deed: they prayed the Jews that dwelt among them to go with their wives and children into the boats which they had prepared, as though they had meant them no hurt. 4 Who accepted of it according to the common decree of the city, as being desirous to live in peace, and suspecting nothing: but when they were gone forth into the deep, they drowned no less than two hundred of them. 5 When Judas heard of this cruelty done unto his countrymen, he commanded those that were with him to make them ready. 6 And calling upon God the righteous Judge, he came against those murderers of his brethren, and burnt the haven by night, and set the boats on fire, and those that fled thither he slew. 7 And when the town was shut up, he went backward, as if he would return to root out all them of the city of Joppa. 8 But when he heard that the Jamnites were minded to do in like manner unto the Jews that dwelt among them, 9 He came upon the Jamnites also by night, and set fire on the haven and the navy, so that the light of the fire was seen at Jerusalem two hundred and forty furlongs off. 10 Now when they were gone from thence nine furlongs in their journey toward Timotheus, no fewer than five thousand men on foot and five hundred horsemen of the Arabians set upon him. 11 Whereupon there was a very sore battle; but Judas' side by the help of God got the victory; so that the Nomades of Arabia, being overcome, besought Judas for peace, promising both to give him cattle, and to pleasure him otherwise. 12 Then Judas, thinking indeed that they would be profitable in many things, granted them peace: whereupon they shook hands, and so they departed to their tents. 13 He went also about to make a bridge to a certain strong city, which was fenced about with walls, and inhabited by people of divers countries; and the name of it was Caspis. 14 But they that were within it put such trust in the strength of the walls and provision of victuals, that they behaved themselves rudely toward them that were with Judas, railing and blaspheming, and uttering such words as were not to be spoken. 15 Wherefore Judas with his company, calling upon the great Lord of the world, who without rams or engines of war did cast down Jericho in the time of Joshua, gave a fierce assault against the walls, 16 And took the city by the will of God, and made unspeakable slaughters, insomuch that a lake two furlongs broad near adjoining thereunto, being filled full, was seen running with blood. 17 Then departed they from thence seven hundred and fifty furlongs, and came to Characa unto the Jews that are called Tubieni. 18 But as for Timotheus, they found him not in the places: for before he had dispatched any thing, he departed from thence, having left a very strong garrison in a certain hold. 19 Howbeit Dositheus and Sosipater, who were of Maccabeus' captains, went forth, and slew those that Timotheus had left in the fortress, above ten thousand men. 20 And Maccabeus ranged his army by bands, and set them over the bands, and went against Timotheus, who had about him an hundred and twenty thousand men of foot, and two thousand and five hundred horsemen. 21 Now when Timotheus had knowledge of Judas' coming, he sent the women and children and the other baggage unto a fortress called Carnion: for the town was hard to besiege, and uneasy to come unto, by reason of the straitness of all the places. 22 But when Judas his first band came in sight, the enemies, being smitten with fear and terror through the appearing of him who seeth all things, fled amain, one running into this way, another that way, so as that they were often hurt of their own men, and wounded with the points of their own swords. 23 Judas also was very earnest in pursuing them, killing those wicked wretches, of whom he slew about thirty thousand men. 24 Moreover Timotheus himself fell into the hands of Dositheus and Sosipater, whom he besought with much craft to let him go with his life, because he had many of the Jews' parents, and the brethren of some of them, who, if they put him to death, should not be regarded. 25 So when he had assured them with many words that he would restore them without hurt, according to the agreement, they let him go for the saving of their brethren. 26 Then Maccabeus marched forth to Carnion, and to the temple of Atargatis, and there he slew five and twenty thousand persons. 27 And after he had put to flight and destroyed them, Judas removed the host toward Ephron, a strong city, wherein Lysias abode, and a great multitude of divers nations, and the strong young men kept the walls, and defended them mightily: wherein also was great provision of engines and darts. 28 But when Judas and his company had called upon Almighty God, who with his power breaketh the strength of his enemies, they won the city, and slew twenty and five thousand of them that were within, 29 From thence they departed to Scythopolis, which lieth six hundred furlongs from Jerusalem, 30 But when the Jews that dwelt there had testified that the Scythopolitans dealt lovingly with them, and entreated them kindly in the time of their adversity; 31 They gave them thanks, desiring them to be friendly still unto them: and so they came to Jerusalem, the feast of the weeks approaching. 32 And after the feast, called Pentecost, they went forth against Gorgias the governor of Idumea, 33 Who came out with three thousand men of foot and four hundred horsemen. 34 And it happened that in their fighting together a few of the Jews were slain. 35 At which time Dositheus, one of Bacenor's company, who was on horseback, and a strong man, was still upon Gorgias, and taking hold of his coat drew him by force; and when he would have taken that cursed man alive, a horseman of Thracia coming upon him smote off his shoulder, so that Gorgias fled unto Marisa. 36 Now when they that were with Gorgias had fought long, and were weary, Judas called upon the Lord, that he would shew himself to be their helper and leader of the battle. 37 And with that he began in his own language, and sung psalms with a loud voice, and rushing unawares upon Gorgias' men, he put them to flight. 38 So Judas gathered his host, and came into the city of Odollam, And when the seventh day came, they purified themselves, as the custom was, and kept the sabbath in the same place. 39 And upon the day following, as the use had been, Judas and his company came to take up the bodies of them that were slain, and to bury them with their kinsmen in their fathers' graves. 40 Now under the coats of every one that was slain they found things consecrated to the idols of the Jamnites, which is forbidden the Jews by the law. Then every man saw that this was the cause wherefore they were slain. 41 All men therefore praising the Lord, the righteous Judge, who had opened the things that were hid, 42 Betook themselves unto prayer, and besought him that the sin committed might wholly be put out of remembrance. Besides, that noble Judas exhorted the people to keep themselves from sin, forsomuch as they saw before their eyes the things that came to pass for the sins of those that were slain. 43 And when he had made a gathering throughout the company to the sum of two thousand drachms of silver, he sent it to Jerusalem to offer a sin offering, doing therein very well and honestly, in that he was mindful of the resurrection: 44 For if he had not hoped that they that were slain should have risen again, it had been superfluous and vain to pray for the dead. 45 And also in that he perceived that there was great favour laid up for those that died godly, it was an holy and good thought. Whereupon he made a reconciliation for the dead, that they might be delivered from sin.

2-Macc.13 1 In the hundred forty and ninth year it was told Judas, that Antiochus Eupator was coming with a great power into Judea, 2 And with him Lysias his protector, and ruler of his affairs, having either of them a Grecian power of footmen, an hundred and ten thousand, and horsemen five thousand and three hundred, and elephants two and twenty, and three hundred chariots armed with hooks. 3 Menelaus also joined himself with them, and with great dissimulation encouraged Antiochus, not for the safeguard of the country, but because he thought to have been made governor. 4 But the King of kings moved Antiochus' mind against this wicked wretch, and Lysias informed the king that this man was the cause of all mischief, so that the king commanded to bring him unto Berea, and to put him to death, as the manner is in that place. 5 Now there was in that place a tower of fifty cubits high, full of ashes, and it had a round instrument which on every side hanged down into the ashes. 6 And whosoever was condemned of sacrilege, or had committed any other grievous crime, there did all men thrust him unto death. 7 Such a death it happened that wicked man to die, not having so much as burial in the earth; and that most justly: 8 For inasmuch as he had committed many sins about the altar, whose fire and ashes were holy, he received his death in ashes. 9 Now the king came with a barbarous and haughty mind to do far worse to the Jews, than had been done in his father's time.

10 Which things when Judas perceived, he commanded the multitude to call upon the Lord night and day, that if ever at any other time, he would now also help them, being at the point to be put from their law, from their country, and from the holy temple: 11 And that he would not suffer the people, that had even now been but a little refreshed, to be in subjection to the blasphemous nations. 12 So when they had all done this together, and besought the merciful Lord with weeping and fasting, and lying flat upon the ground three days long, Judas, having exhorted them, commanded they should be in a readiness. 13 And Judas, being apart with the elders, determined, before the king's host should enter into Judea, and get the city, to go forth and try the matter in fight by the help of the Lord. 14 So when he had committed all to the Creator of the world, and exhorted his soldiers to fight manfully, even unto death, for the laws, the temple, the city, the country, and the commonwealth, he camped by Modin: 15 And having given the watchword to them that were about him, Victory is of God; with the most valiant and choice young men he went in into the king's tent by night, and slew in the camp about four thousand men, and the chiefest of the elephants, with all that were upon him. 16 And at last they filled the camp with fear and tumult, and departed with good success. 17 This was done in the break of the day, because the protection of the Lord did help him. 18 Now when the king had taken a taste of the manliness of the Jews, he went about to take the holds by policy, 19 And marched toward Bethsura, which was a strong hold of the Jews: but he was put to flight, failed, and lost of his men: 20 For Judas had conveyed unto them that were in it such things as were necessary. 21 But Rhodocus, who was in the Jews' host, disclosed the secrets to the enemies; therefore he was sought out, and when they had gotten him, they put him in prison. 22 The king treated with them in Bethsura the second time, gave his hand, took their's, departed, fought with Judas, was overcome; 23 Heard that Philip, who was left over the affairs in Antioch, was desperately bent, confounded, intreated the Jews, submitted himself, and sware to all equal conditions, agreed with them, and offered sacrifice, honoured the temple, and dealt kindly with the place, 24 And accepted well of Maccabeus, made him principal governor from Ptolemais unto the Gerrhenians; 25 Came to Ptolemais: the people there were grieved for the covenants; for they stormed, because they would make their covenants void: 26 Lysias went up to the judgment seat, said as much as could be in defence of the cause, persuaded, pacified, made them well affected, returned to Antioch. Thus it went touching the king's coming and departing.

2-Macc.14 1 After three years was Judas informed, that Demetrius the son of Seleucus, having entered by the haven of Tripolis with a great power and navy, 2 Had taken the country, and killed Antiochus, and Lysias his protector. 3 Now one Alcimus, who had been high priest, and had defiled himself wilfully in the times of their mingling with the Gentiles, seeing that by no means he could save himself, nor have any more access to the holy altar, 4 Came to king Demetrius in the hundred and one and fiftieth year, presenting unto him a crown of gold, and a palm, and also of the boughs which were used solemnly in the temple: and so that day he held his peace. 5 Howbeit having gotten opportunity to further his foolish enterprise, and being called into counsel by Demetrius, and asked how the Jews stood affected, and what they intended, he answered thereunto: 6 Those of the Jews that he called Assideans, whose captain is Judas Maccabeus, nourish war and are seditious, and will not let the rest be in peace. 7 Therefore I, being deprived of mine ancestors' honour, I mean the high priesthood, am now come hither: 8 First, verily for the unfeigned care I have of things pertaining to the king; and secondly, even for that I intend the good of mine own countrymen: for all our nation is in no small misery through the unadvised dealing of them aforesaid. 9 Wherefore, O king, seeing knowest all these things, be careful for the country, and our nation, which is pressed on every side, according to the clemency that thou readily shewest unto all. 10 For as long as Judas liveth, it is not possible that the state should be quiet. 11 This was no sooner spoken of him, but others of the king's friends, being maliciously set against Judas, did more incense Demetrius. 12 And forthwith calling Nicanor, who had been master of the elephants, and making him governor over Judea, he sent him forth, 13 Commanding him to slay Judas, and to scatter them that were with him, and to make Alcimus high priest of the great temple. 14 Then the heathen, that had fled out of Judea from Judas, came to Nicanor by flocks, thinking the harm and calamities of the Jews to be their welfare. 15 Now when the Jews heard of Nicanor's coming, and that the heathen were up against them, they cast earth upon their heads, and made supplication to him that had established his people for ever, and who always helpeth his portion with manifestation of his presence. 16 So at the commandment of the captain they removed straightways from thence, and came near unto them at the town of Dessau. 17 Now Simon, Judas' brother, had joined battle with Nicanor, but was somewhat discomfited through the sudden silence of his enemies. 18 Nevertheless Nicanor, hearing of the manliness of them that were with Judas, and the courageousness that they had to fight for their country, durst not try the matter by the sword. 19 Wherefore he sent Posidonius, and Theodotus, and Mattathias, to make peace. 20 So when they had taken long advisement thereupon, and the captain had made the multitude acquainted therewith, and it appeared that they were all of one mind, they consented to the covenants, 21 And appointed a day to meet in together by themselves: and when the day came, and stools were set for either of them, 22 Judas placed armed men ready in convenient places, lest some treachery should be suddenly practised by the enemies: so they made a peaceable conference. 23 Now Nicanor abode in Jerusalem, and did no hurt, but sent away the people that came flocking unto him. 24 And he would not willingly have Judas out of his sight: for he love the man from his heart 25 He prayed him also to take a wife, and to beget children: so he married, was quiet, and took part of this life. 26 But Alcimus, perceiving the love that was betwixt them, and considering the covenants that were made, came to Demetrius, and told

him that Nicanor was not well affected toward the state; for that he had ordained Judas, a traitor to his realm, to be the king's successor. 27 Then the king being in a rage, and provoked with the accusations of the most wicked man, wrote to Nicanor, signifying that he was much displeased with the covenants, and commanding him that he should send Maccabeus prisoner in all haste unto Antioch. 28 When this came to Nicanor's hearing, he was much confounded in himself, and took it grievously that he should make void the articles which were agreed upon, the man being in no fault. 29 But because there was no dealing against the king, he watched his time to accomplish this thing by policy. 30 Notwithstanding, when Maccabeus saw that Nicanor began to be churlish unto him, and that he entreated him more roughly than he was wont, perceiving that such sour behaviour came not of good, he gathered together not a few of his men, and withdrew himself from Nicanor. 31 But the other, knowing that he was notably prevented by Judas' policy, came into the great and holy temple, and commanded the priests, that were offering their usual sacrifices, to deliver him the man. 32 And when they sware that they could not tell where the man was whom he sought, 33 He stretched out his right hand toward the temple, and made an oath in this manner: If ye will not deliver me Judas as a prisoner, I will lay this temple of God even with the ground, and I will break down the altar, and erect a notable temple unto Bacchus. 34 After these words he departed. Then the priests lifted up their hands toward heaven, and besought him that was ever a defender of their nation, saying in this manner; 35 Thou, O Lord of all things, who hast need of nothing, wast pleased that the temple of thine habitation should be among us: 36 Therefore now, O holy Lord of all holiness, keep this house ever undefiled, which lately was cleansed, and stop every unrighteous mouth. 37 Now was there accused unto Nicanor one Razis, one of the elders of Jerusalem, a lover of his countrymen, and a man of very good report, who for his kindness was called a father of the Jews. 38 For in the former times, when they mingled not themselves with the Gentiles, he had been accused of Judaism, and did boldly jeopard his body and life with all vehemency for the religion of the Jews. 39 So Nicanor, willing to declare the hate that he bare unto the Jews, sent above five hundred men of war to take him: 40 For he thought by taking him to do the Jews much hurt. 41 Now when the multitude would have taken the tower, and violently broken into the outer door, and bade that fire should be brought to burn it, he being ready to be taken on every side fell upon his sword; 42 Choosing rather to die manfully, than to come into the hands of the wicked, to be abused otherwise than beseemed his noble birth: 43 But missing his stroke through haste, the multitude also rushing within the doors, he ran boldly up to the wall, and cast himself down manfully among the thickest of them. 44 But they quickly giving back, and a space being made, he fell down into the midst of the void place. 45 Nevertheless, while there was yet breath within him, being inflamed with anger, he rose up; and though his blood gushed out like spouts of water, and his wounds were grievous, yet he ran through the midst of the throng; and standing upon a steep rock, 46 When as his blood was now quite gone, he plucked out his bowels, and taking them in both his hands, he cast them upon the throng, and calling upon the Lord of life and spirit to restore him those again, he thus died.

2-Macc.15 1 But Nicanor, hearing that Judas and his company were in the strong places about Samaria, resolved without any danger to set upon them on the sabbath day. 2 Nevertheless the Jews that were compelled to go with him said, O destroy not so cruelly and barbarously, but give honour to that day, which he, that seeth all things, hath honoured with holiness above all other days. 3 Then the most ungracious wretch demanded, if there were a Mighty one in heaven, that had commanded the sabbath day to be kept. 4 And when they said, There is in heaven a living Lord, and mighty, who commanded the seventh day to be kept: 5 Then said the other, And I also am mighty upon earth, and I command to take arms, and to do the king's business. Yet he obtained not to have his wicked will done. 6 So Nicanor in exceeding pride and haughtiness determined to set up a publick monument of his victory over Judas and them that were with him. 7 But Maccabeus had ever sure confidence that the Lord would help him: 8 Wherefore he exhorted his people not to fear the coming of the heathen against them, but to remember the help which in former times they had received from heaven, and now to expect the victory and aid, which should come unto them from the Almighty. 9 And so comforting them out of the law and the prophets, and withal putting them in mind of the battles that they won afore, he made them more cheerful. 10 And when he had stirred up their minds, he gave them their charge, shewing them therewithal the falsehood of the heathen, and the breach of oaths. 11 Thus he armed every one of them, not so much with defence of shields and spears, as with comfortable and good words: and beside that, he told them a dream worthy to be believed, as if it had been so indeed, which did not a little rejoice them. 12 And this was his vision: That Onias, who had been high priest, a virtuous and a good man, reverend in conversation, gentle in condition, well spoken also, and exercised from a child in all points of virtue, holding up his hands prayed for the whole body of the Jews. 13 This done, in like manner there appeared a man with gray hairs, and exceeding glorious, who was of a wonderful and excellent majesty. 14 Then Onias answered, saying, This is a lover of the brethren, who prayeth much for the people, and for the holy city, to wit, Jeremias the prophet of God. 15 Whereupon Jeremias holding forth his right hand gave to Judas a sword of gold, and in giving it spake thus, 16 Take this holy sword, a gift from God, with the which thou shalt wound the adversaries. 17 Thus being well comforted by the words of Judas, which were very good, and able to stir them up to valour, and to encourage the hearts of the young men, they determined not to pitch camp, but courageously to set upon them, and manfully to try the matter by conflict, because the city and the sanctuary and the temple were in danger. 18 For the care that they took for their wives, and their children, their brethren, and folks, was in least account with them: but the greatest and principal fear was for the holy temple. 19 Also they that were in the city took not the least care, being troubled for the conflict abroad. 20 And now, when as all looked what should be the trial, and the enemies were already come near, and the army was set in array, and the beasts conveniently placed, and the horsemen set in wings, 21 Maccabeus seeing the coming of the multitude, and the divers preparations of armour, and the fierceness of the beasts, stretched out his hands toward heaven, and called upon the Lord that worketh wonders, knowing that victory cometh not by arms, but even as it seemeth good to him, he giveth it to such as are worthy: 22 Therefore in his prayer he said after this manner; O Lord, thou didst send thine angel in the time of Ezekias king of Judea, and didst slay in the host of Sennacherib an hundred fourscore and five thousand: 23 Wherefore now also, O Lord of heaven, send a good angel before us for a fear and dread unto them; 24 And through the might of thine arm let those be stricken with terror, that come against thy holy people to blaspheme. And he ended thus. 25 Then Nicanor and they that were with him came forward with trumpets and songs. 26 But Judas and his company encountered the enemies with invocation and prayer. 27 So that fighting with their hands, and praying unto God with their hearts, they slew no less than thirty and five thousand men: for through the appearance of God they were greatly cheered. 28 Now when the battle was done, returning again with joy, they knew that Nicanor lay dead in his harness. 29 Then they made a great shout and a noise, praising the Almighty in their own language. 30 And Judas, who was ever the chief defender of the citizens both in body and mind, and who continued his love toward his countrymen all his life, commanded to strike off Nicanor's head, and his hand with his shoulder, and bring them to Jerusalem. 31 So when he was there, and called them of his nation together, and set the priests before the altar, he sent for them that were of the tower, 32 And shewed them vile Nicanor's head, and the hand of that blasphemer, which with proud brags he had stretched out against the holy temple of the Almighty. 33 And when he had cut out the tongue of that ungodly Nicanor, he commanded that they should give it by pieces unto the fowls, and hang up the reward of his madness before the temple. 34 So every man praised toward the heaven the glorious Lord, saying, Blessed be he that hath kept his own place undefiled. 35 He hanged also Nicanor's head upon the tower, an evident and manifest sign unto all of the help of the Lord. 36 And they ordained all with a common decree in no case to let that day pass without solemnity, but to celebrate the thirtieth day of the twelfth month, which in the Syrian tongue is called Adar, the day before Mardocheus' day. 37 Thus went it with Nicanor: and from that time forth the Hebrews had the city in their power. And here will I make an end. 38 And if I have done well, and as is fitting the story, it is that which I desired: but if slenderly and meanly, it is that which I could attain unto. 39 For as it is hurtful to drink wine or water alone; and as wine mingled with water is pleasant, and delighteth the taste: even so speech finely framed delighteth the ears of them that read the story. And here shall be an end.

3 MACCABEES

3-Macc.1 [1] Now Philopater, on learning from those who came back that Antiochus had made himself master of the places which belonged to himself, sent orders to all his footmen and horsemen, took with him his sister Arsinoe, and marched out as far as the parts of Raphia, where Antiochus and his forces encamped. [2] And one Theodotus, intending to carry out his design, took with him the bravest of the armed men who had been before committed to his trust by Ptolemy, and got through at night to the tent of Ptolemy, to kill him on his own responsibility, and so to end the war. [3] But Dositheus, called the son of Drimulus, by birth a Jew, afterward a renegade from the laws and observances of his country, conveyed Ptolemy away, and made an obscure person lie down in his stead in the tent. It befell this man to receive the fate which was meant for the other. [4] A fierce battle then took place; and the men of Antiochus prevailing, Arsinoe continually went up and down the ranks, and with dishevelled hair, with tears and entreaties, begged the soldiers to fight manfully for themselves, their children, and wives; and promised that if they proved conquerors, she would give them two minae of gold apiece. [5] It thus fell out that their enemies were defeated in hand-to-hand encounter, and that many of them were taken prisoners. [6] Having vanquished this attempt, the king then decided to proceed to the neighbouring cities, and encourage them. [7] By doing this, and by making donations to their temples, he inspired his subjects with confidence. [8] The Jews sent some of their council and of their elders to him. The greetings, guest-gifts, and congratulations of the past, bestowed by them, filled him with the greater eagerness to visit their city. [9] Having arrived at Jerusalem, sacrificed, and offered thank-offerings to the Greatest God, and done whatever else was suitable to the sanctity of the place, and entered the inner court, [10] he was so struck with the magnificence of the place, and so wondered at the orderly arrangements of the temple, that he considered entering the sanctuary itself. [11] And when they told him that this was not permissible, none of the nation, no, nor even the priests in general, but only the supreme high priest of all, and he only once in a year, being allowed to go in, he would by no means give way. [12] Then they read the law to him; but he persisted in obtruding himself, exclaiming, that he ought to be allowed: and saying Be it that they were deprived of this honour, I ought not to be. [13] And he put the question, Why, when he entered all the temples, none of the priests who were present forbad him? [14] He was thoroughly answered by some one, That he did wrong to boast of this. [15] Well; since I have done this, said he, be the cause what it may, shall I not enter with or without your consent? [16] And when the priests fell down in their sacred vestments imploring the Greatest God to come and help in time of need, and to avert the violence of the fierce aggressor, and when they filled the temple with lamentations and tears, [17] then those who had been left behind in the city were scared, and rushed forth, uncertain of the event. [18] Virgins, who had been shut up within their chambers, came out with their mothers, scattering dust and ashes on their heads, and filling the streets with outcries. [19] Women, but recently separated off, left their bridal chambers, left the reserve that befitted them, and ran about the city in a disorderly manner. [20] New-born babes were deserted by the mothers or nurses who waited upon them; some here, some there, in houses, or in fields; these now, with an ardour which could not be checked, swarmed into the Most High temple. [21] Various were the prayers offered up by those who assembled in this place, on account of the unholy attempt of the king. [22] Along with these there were some of the citizens who took courage, and would not submit to his obstinacy, and his intention of carrying out his purpose. [23] Calling out to arms, and to die bravely in defence of the law of their fathers, they created a great uproar in the place, and were with difficulty brought back by the aged and the elders to the station of prayer which they had occupied before. [24] During this time the multitude kept on praying. [25] The elders who surrounded the king strove in many ways to divert his haughty mind from the design which he had formed. [26] He, in his hardened mood, insensible to all persuasion, was going onwards with the view of carrying out this design. [27] Yet even his own officers, when they saw this, joined the Jews in an appeal to Him who has all power, to aid in the present crisis, and not wink at such overweening lawlessness. [28] Such was the frequency and the vehemence of the cry of the assembled crowd, that an indescribable noise ensued. [29] Not the men only, but the very walls and floor seemed to sound forth; all things preferring dissolution rather than to see the place defiled.

3-Macc.2 [1] Now was it that the high priest Simon bowed his knees over against the holy place, and spread out his hands in reverent form, and uttered the following supplication: [2] O Lord, Lord, King of the heavens, and Ruler of the whole creation, Holy among the holy, sole Governor, Almighty, give ear to us who are oppressed by a wicked and profane one, who exulteth in his confidence and strength. [3] It is thou, the Creator of all, the Lord of the universe, who art a righteous Governor, and judgest all who act with pride and insolence. [4] It was thou who didst destroy the former workers of unrighteousness, among whom were the giants, who trusted in their strength and hardihood, by covering them with a measureless flood. [5] It was thou who didst make the Sodomites, those workers of exceeding iniquity, men notorious for their vices, an example to after generations, when thou didst cover them with fire and brimstone. [6] Thou didst make known thy power when thou causedst the bold Pharaoh, the enslaver of thy people, to pass through the ordeal of many and diverse inflictions. [7] And thou rolledst the depths of the sea over him, when he made pursuit with chariots, and with a multitude of followers, and gavest a safe passage to those who put their trust in thee, the Lord of the whole creation. [8] These saw and felt the works of thine hands, and praised thee the Almighty. [9] Thou, O King, when thou createdst the illimitable and measureless earth, didst choose out this city: thou didst make this place sacred to thy name, albeit thou needest nothing: thou didst glorify it with thine illustrious presence, after constructing it to the glory of thy great and honourable name. ¹⁰ And thou didst promise, out of love to the people of Israel, that should we fall away from thee, and become afflicted, and then come to this house and pray, thou wouldest hear our prayer. ¹¹ Verily thou art faithful and true. ¹² And when thou didst often aid our fathers when hard pressed, and in low estate, and deliveredst them out of gret dangers, ¹³ see now, holy King, how through our many and great sins we are borne down, and made subject to our enemies, and are become weak and powerless. ¹⁴ We being in this low condition, this bold and profane man seeks to dishonour this thine holy place, consecrated out of the earth to the name of thy Majesty. ¹⁵ Thy dwelling place, the heaven of heavens, is indeed unapproachable to men. ¹⁶ But since it seemed good to thee to exhibit thy glory among thy people Israel, thou didst sanctify this place. ¹⁷ Punish us not by means of the uncleanness of their men, nor chastise us by means of their profanity; lest the lawless ones should boast in their rage, and exult in exuberant pride of speech, and say, ¹⁸ We have trampled upon the holy house, as idolatrous houses are trampled upon. ¹⁹ Blot out our iniquities, and do away with our errors, and shew forth thy compassion in this hour. ²⁰ Let thy mercies quickly go before us. Grant us peace, that the cast down and broken hearted may praise thee with their mouth. ²¹ At that time God, who seeth all things, who is beyond all Holy among the holy, heard that prayer, so suitable; and scourged the man greatly uplifted with scorn and insolence. ²² Shaking him to and fro as a reed is shaken with the wind, he cast him upon the pavement, powerless, with limbs paralyzed; by a righteous judgment deprived of the faculty of speech. ²³ His friends and bodyguards, beholding the swift recompense which had suddenly overtaken him, struck with exceeding terror, and fearing that he would die, speedily removed him. ²⁴ When in course of time he had come to himself, this severe check caused no repentance within him, but he departed with bitter threatenings. ²⁵ He proceeded to Egypt, grew worse in wickedness through his beforementioned companions in wine, who were lost to all goodness; ²⁶ and not satisfied with countless acts of impiety, his audacity so increased that he raised evil reports there, and many of his friends, watching his purpose attentively, joined in furthering his will. ²⁷ His purpose was to indict a public stigma upon our race; wherefore he erected a pillar at the tower-porch, and caused the following inscription to be engraved upon it: ²⁸ That entrance to their own temple was to be refused to all those who would not sacrifice; that all the Jews were to be registered among the common people; that those who resisted were to be forcibly seized and put to death; ²⁹ that those who were thus registered, were to be marked on their persons by the ivy-leaf symbol of Dionysus, and to be set apart with these limited rights. ³⁰ To do away with the appearance of hating them all, he had it written underneath, that if any of them should elect to enter the community of those initiated in the rites, these should have equal rights with the Alexandrians. ³¹ Some of those who were over the city, therefore, abhorring any approach to the city of piety, unhesitatingly gave in to the king, and expected to derive some great honour from a future connection with him. ³²

A nobler spirit, however, prompted the majority to cling to their religious observances, and by paying money that they might live unmolested, these sought to escape the registration: ³³ cheerfully looking forward to future aid, they abhorred their own apostates, considering them to be national foes, and debarring them from the common usages of social intercourse.

3-Macc.3 ¹ On discovering this, so incensed was the wicked king, that he no longer confined his rage to the Jews in Alexandria. Laying his hand more heavily upon those who lived in the country, he gave orders that they should be quickly collected into one place, and most cruelly deprived of their lives. ² While this was going on, an invidious rumour was uttered abroad by men who had banded together to injure the Jewish race. The purport of their charge was, that the Jews kept them away from the ordinances of the law. ³ Now, while the Jews always maintained a feeling of un- swerving loyalty towards the kings, yet, as they worshipped God, and observed his law, they made certain distinctions, and avoided certain things. Hence some persons held them in odium; although, as they adorned their conversation with works of righteousness, they had established themselves in the good opinion of the world. ⁶ What all the rest of mankind said, was, however, made of no account by the foreigners; ⁷ who said much of the exclusiveness of the Jews with regard to their worship and meats; they alleged that they were men unsociable, hostile to the king's interests, refusing to associate with him or his troops. By this way of speaking, they brought much odium upon them. ⁸ Nor was this unexpected uproar and sudden conflux of people unobserved by the Greeks who lived in the city, concerning men who had never harmed them: yet to aid them was not in their power, since all was oppression around; but they encouraged them in their troubles, and expected a favourable turn of affairs: ⁹ He who knoweth all things, will not, [said they,] disregard so great a people. ¹⁰ Some of the neighbors, friends, and fellow dealers of the Jews, even called them secretly to an interview, pledged them their assistance, and promised to do their very utmost for them. ¹¹ Now the king, elated with his prosperous fortune, and not regarding the superior power of God, but thinking to persevere in his present purpose, wrote the following letter to the prejudice of the Jews. ¹² King Ptolemy Philopater, to the commanders and soldiers in Egypt, and in all places, health and happiness! ¹³ I am right well; and so, too, are my affairs. ¹⁴ Since our Asiatic campaign, the particulars of which ye know, and which by the aid of the gods, not lightly given, and by our own vigour, has been brought to a successful issue according to our expectation, ¹⁵ we resolved, not with strength of spear, but with gentleness and much humanity, as it were to nurse the inhabitants of Coele-Syria and Phoenicia, and to be their willing benefactors. ¹⁶ So, having bestowed considerable sums of money upon the temples of the several cities, we proceeded even as far as Jerusalem; and went up to honour the temple of these wretched beings who never cease from their folly. ¹⁷ To outward appearance they received us willingly; but belied that appearance by their deeds. When we were eager to enter their temple, and to honour it with the most beautiful and exquisite gifts, 18 they were so carried away by their old arrogance, as to forbid us the entrance; while we, out of our forbearance toward all men, refrained from exercising our power upon them. 19 And thus, exhibiting their enmity against us, they alone among the nations lift up their heads against kings and benefactors, as men unwilling to submit to any thing reasonable. 20 We then, having endeavoured to make allowance for the madness of these persons, and on our victorious return treating all people in Egypt courteously, acted in a manner which was befitting. 21 Accordingly, bearing no ill-will against their kinsmen [at Jerusalem,] but rather remembering our connection with them, and the numerous matters with sincere heart from a remote period entrusted to them, we wished to venture a total alteration of their state, by bestowing upon them the rights of citizens of Alexandria, and to admit them to the everlasting rites of our solemnities. 22 All this, however, they have taken in a very different spirit. With their innate malignity, they have spurned the fair offer; and constantly inclining to evil, 23 have rejected the inestimable rights. Not only so, but by using speech, and by refraining from speech, they abhor the few among them who are heartily disposed towards us; ever deeming that their ignoble course of procedure will force us to do away with our reform. 24 Having then, received certain proofs that these [Jews] bear us every sort of ill-will, we must look forward to the possibility of some sudden tumult among ourselves, when these impious men may turn traitors and barbarous enemies. 25 As soon, therefore, as the contents of this letter become known to you, in that same hour we order those [Jews] who dwell among you, with wives and children, to be sent to us, vilified and abused, in chains of iron, to undergo a death, cruel and ignominious, suitable to men disaffected. 26 For by the punishment of them in one body we perceive that we have found the only means of establishing our affairs for the future on a firm and satisfactory basis. 27 Whosoever shall shield a Jew, whether it be old man, child, or suckling, shall with his whole house be tortured to death. 28 Whoever shall inform against the [Jews,] besides receiving the property of the person charged, shall be presented with two thousand drachmae from the royal treasury, shall be made free, and shall be crowned. 29 Whatever place shall shelter a Jew, shall, when he is hunted forth, be put under the ban of fire, and be for ever rendered useless to every living being for all time to come. 30 Such was the purport of the king's letter.

3-Macc.4 1 Wherever this decree was received, the people kept up a revelry of joy and shouting; as if their long-pent-up, hardened hatred, were now to shew itself openly. 2 The Jews suffered great throes of sorrow, and wept much; while their hearts, all things around being lamentable, were set on fire as they bewailed the sudden destruction which was decreed against them. 3 What home, or city, or place at all inhabited, or what streets were there, which their condition did not fill with wailing and lamentation? 4 They were sent out unanimously by the generals in the several cities, with such stern and pitiless feeling, that the exceptional nature

of the infliction moved even some of their enemies. These, influenced by sentiments of common humanity, and reflecting upon the uncertain issue of life, shed tears at this their miserable expulsion. 5 A multitude of aged hoary-haired old men, were driven along with halting bending feet, urged onward by the impulse of a violent, shameless force to quick speed. 6 Girls who had entered the bridal chamber quite lately, to enjoy the partnership of marriage, exchanged pleasure for misery; and with dust scattered upon their myrrh-anointed heads, were hurried along unveiled; and, in the midst of outlandish insults, set up with one accord a lamentable cry in lieu of the marriage hymn. 7 Bound, and exposed to public gaze, they were hurried violently on board ship. 8 The husbands of these, in the prime of their youthful vigour, instead of crowns wore halters round their necks; instead of feasting and youthful jollity, spent the rest of their nuptial days in wailings, and saw only the grave at hand. 9 They were dragged along by unyielding chains, like wild beasts: of these, some had their necks thrust into the benches of the rowers; while the feet of others were enclosed in hard fetters. 10 The planks of the deck above them barred out the light, and shut out the day on every side, so that they might be treated like traitors during the whole voyage. 11 They were conveyed accordingly in this vessel, and at the end of it arrived at Schedia. The king had ordered them to be cast into the vast hippodrome, which was built in front of the city. This place was well adapted by its situation to expose them to the gaze of all comers into the city, and of those who went from the city into the country. Thus they could hold no communication with his forces; nay, were deemed unworthy of any civilized accommodation. 12 When this was done, the king, hearing that their brethren in the city often went out and lamented the melancholy distress of these victims, 13 was full of rage, and commanded that they should be carefully subjected to the same (and not one whit milder) treatment. 14 The whole nation was now to be registered. Every individual was to be specified by name; not for that hard servitude of labour which we have a little before mentioned, but that he might expose them to the before-mentioned tortures; and finally, in the short space of a day, might extirpate them by his cruelties 15 The registering of these men was carried on cruelly, zealously, assiduously, from the rising of the sun to its going down, and was not brought to an end in forty days. 16 The king was filled with great and constant joy, and celebrated banquets before the temple idols. His erring heart, far from the truth, and his profane mouth, gave glory to idols, deaf and incapable of speaking or aiding, and uttered unworthy speech against the Greatest God. 17 At the end of the above-mentioned interval of time, the registrars brought word to the king that the multitude of the Jews was too great for registration, 18 inasmuch as there were many still left in the land, of whom some were in inhabited houses, and others were scattered about in various places; so that all the commanders in Egypt were insufficient for the work. 19 The king threatened them, and charged them with taking bribes, in order to contrive the escape of the Jews: but was clearly convinced of the truth of what had been said. 20

They said, and proved, that paper and pens had failed them for the carrying out of their purpose. 21 Now this was an active interference of the unconquerable Providence which assisted the Jews from heaven.

3-Macc.5 1 Then he called Hermon, who had charge of the elephants. Full of rage, altogether fixed in his furious design, 2 he commanded him, with a quantity of unmixed wine and handfuls of incense [infused] to drug the elephants early on the following day. These five hundred elephants were, when infuriated by the copious draughts of frankincense, to be led up to the execution of death upon the Jews. 3 The king, after issuing these orders, went to his feasting, and gathered together all those of his friends and of the army who hated the Jews the most. 4 The master of the elephants, Hermon, fulfilled his commission punctually. 5 The underlings appointed for the purpose went out about eventide and bound the hands of the miserable victims, and took other precautions for their security at night, thinking that the whole race would perish together. 6 The heathen believed the Jews to be destitute of all protection; for chains fettered them about. 7 they invoked the Almighty Lord, and ceaselessly besought with tears their merciful God and Father, Ruler of all, Lord of every power, 8 to overthrow the evil purpose which was gone out against them, and to deliver them by extraordinary manifestation from that death which was in store for them. 9 Their litany so earnest went up to heaven. 10 Then Hermon, who had filled his merciless elephants with copious draughts of mingled wine and frankincense, came early to the palace to certify the kind thereof. 11 He, however, who has sent his good creature sleep from all time by night or by day thus gratifying whom he wills, diffused a portion thereof now upon the king. 12 By this sweet and profound influence of the Lord he was held fast, and thus his unjust purpose was quite frustrated, and his unflinching resolve greatly falsified. 13 But the Jews, having escaped the hour which had been fixed, praised their holy God, and again prayed him who is easily reconciled to display the power of his powerful hand to the overweening Gentiles. 14 The middle of the tenth hour had well nigh arrived, when the master- bidder, seeing the guests who were bidden collected, came and shook the king. 15 He gained his attention with difficulty, and hinting that the mealtime was getting past, talked the matter over with him. 16 The kind listened to this, and then turning aside to his potations, commanded the guests to sit down before him. 17 This done, he asked them to enjoy themselves, and to indulge in mirth at this somewhat late hour of the banquet. 18 Conversation grew on, and the king sent for Hermon, and enquired of him, with fierce denunciations, why the Jews had been allowed to outlive that day. 19 Hermon explained that he had done his bidding over night; and in this he was confirmed by his friends. 20 The king, then, with a barbarity exceeding that of Phalaris, said, That they might thank his sleep of that day. Lose no time, and get ready the elephants against tomorrow, as you did before, for the destruction of these accursed Jews. 21 When the king said this, the company present were glad, and approved; and then each man went to his own home. 22 Nor did they employ the night in sleep, so much as in contriving cruel mockeries for those deemed miserable. 23 The morning cock had just crowed, and Hermon, having harnessed the brutes, was stimulating them in the great colonnade. 24 The city crowds were collected together to see the hideous spectacle, and waited impatiently for the dawn. 25 The Jews, breathless with momentary suspense, stretched forth their hands, and prayed the Greatest God, in mournful strains, again to help them speedily. 26 The sun's rays were not yet shed abroad, and the king was waiting for his friends, when Hermon came to him, calling him out, and saying, That his desires could now be realized. 27 The king, receiving him, was astonished at his unwonted exit; and, overwhelmed with a spirit of oblivion about everything, enquired the object of this earnest preparation. 28 But this was the wroking of that Almighty God who had made him forget all his purpose. 29 Hermon, and all his friends, pointed out the preparation of the animals. they are ready, O king, according to your own strict injunction. 30 The king was filled with fierce anger at these words; for, by the Providence of God regarding these things, his mind had become entirely confused. He looked hard at Hermon, and threatened him as follows: 31 Your parents, or your children, were they here, to these wild beasts a large repast they should have furnished; not these innocent Jews, who me and my forefathers loyally have served. 32 Had it not been for familar friendship, and the claims of your office, your life should have gone for theirs. 33 Hermon, being threatened in this unexpected and alarming manner, was troubled in visage, and depressed in countenance. 34 The friends, too, stole out one by one, and dismissed the assembled multitudes to their respective occupations. 35 The Jews, having heard of these events, praised the glorious God and King of kings, because they had obtained this help, too, from him. 36 Now the king arranged another banquet after the same manner, and proclaimed an invitation to mirth. 27 And he summoned Hermon to his presence, and said, with threats, How often, O wretch, must I repeat my orders to thee about these same persons? 28 Once more, arm the elephants against the morrow for the extermination of the Jews. 39 His kinsmen, who were reclining with him, wondered at his instability, and thus expressed themselves: 40 O king, how long dost thou make trial of us, as of men bereft of reason? This is the third time that thou hast ordered their destruction. When the thing is to be done, thou changest thy mind, and recallest thy instructions. 41 For this cause the feeling of expectation causes tumult in the city: it swarms with factions; and is continually on the point of being plundered. 42 The king, just like another Phalaris, a prey to thoughtlessness, made no account of the changes which his own mind had undergone, issuing in the deliverance of the Jews. He swore a fruitless oath, and determined forthwith to send them to hades, crushed by the knees and feet of the elephants. 43 He would also invade Judea, and level its towns with fire and the sword; and destroy that temple which the heathen might not enter, and prevent sacrifices ever after being offered up there. 44 Joyfully his friends broke up, together with his kinsmen; and, trusting in his determination, arranged their forces in guard at the most convenient places of the city. 45 And the master of the elephants urged the beasts into an almost maniacal state, drenched them with incense and wine, and decked them with frightful instruments. 46 About early morning, when the city was now filled with an immense number of people at the hippodrome, he entered the palace, and called the king to the business in hand. 47 The king's heart teemed with impious rage; and he rushed forth with the mass, along with the elephants. With feelings unsoftened, and eyes pitiless, he longed to gaze at the hard and wretched doom of the abovementioned [Jews]. 48 But the [Jews,] when the elephants went out at the gate, followed by the armed force; and when they saw the dust raised by the throng, and heard the loud cries of the crowd, 49 thought that they had come to the last moment of their lives, to the end of what they had tremblingly expected. They gave way, therefore, to lamentations and moans: they kissed each other: those nearest of kin to each other hung about one another's necks: fathers about their sons, mother their daughters: other women held their infants to their breasts, which drew what seemed their last milk. 50 Nevertheless, when they reflected upon the succour before granted them from heaven, they prostrated themselves with one accord; removed even the sucking children from the breasts, and 51 sent up an exceeding great cry entreating the Lord of all power to reveal himself, and have mercy upon those who now lay at the gates of hades.

3-Macc.6 1 And Eleazar, an illustrious priest of the country, who had attained to length of day, and whose life had been adorned with virtue, caused the presbyters who were about him to cease to cry out to the holy God, and prayed thus: 2 O king, mighty in power, most high, Almighty God, who regulates the whole creation with thy tender mercy, 3 look upon the seed of Abraham, upon the children of the sanctified Jacob, thy sanctified inheritance, O Father, now being wrongfully destroyed as strangers in a strange land. 4 Thou destroyedst Pharaoh, with his hosts of chariots, when that lord of this same Egypt was uplifted with lawless hardihood and loud-sounding tongue. Shedding the beams of thy mercy upon the race of Israel, thou didst overwhelm him with his proud army. 5 When Sennacherim, the grievous king of the Assyrians, glorying in his countless hosts, had subdued the whole land with his spear, and was lifting himself against thine holy city, with boastings grievous to be endured, thou, O Lord, didst demolish him and didst shew forth thy might to many nations. 6 When the three friends in the land of Babylon of their own will exposed their lives to the fire rather than serve vain things, thou didst send a dewy coolness through the fiery furnace, and bring the fire upon all their adversaries. 7 It was thou who, when Daniel was hurled, through slander and envy, as a prey to lions down below, didst bring him back against unhurt to light. 8 When Jonah was pining away in the belly of the sea-bred monster, thou didst look upon him, O Father, and recover him to the sight of his own. 9 And now, thou who hatest insolence; thou who dost abound in mercy; thou who art the protector of all things; appear quickly to those of the race of Israel, who are insulted by abhorred, lawless gentiles. 10 If our life has during our exile been stained with iniquity, deliver us from the hand of the enemy, and destroy us, O Lord, by the death which thou preferrest. 11 Let not the vain-minded congratulate vain idols at the destruction of thy beloved, saying, Neither did their god deliver them. 12 Thou, who art All-powerful and Almighty, O Eternal One, behold! have mercy upon us who are being withdrawn from life, like traitors, by the unreasoning insolence of lawless men. 13 Let the heathen cower before thine invincible might today, O glorious One, who hast all power to save the race of Jacob. 14 The whole band of infants and their parents with tears beseech thee. 15 Let it be shewn to all the nations that thou art with us, O Lord, and hast not turned thy face away from us; but as thou saidst that thou wouldst not forget them even in the land of their enemies, so do thou fulfil this saying, O Lord. 16 Now, at the time that Eleazar had ended his prayer, the king came along to the hippodrome, with the wild beasts, and with his tumultuous power. 17 When the Jews saw this, they uttered a loud cry to heaven, so that the adjacent valleys resounded, and caused an irrepressible lamentation throughout the army. 18 Then the all-glorious, all-powerful, and true God, displayed his holy countenance, and opened the gates of heaven, from which two angels, dreadful of form, came down and were visible to all but the Jews. 19 And they stood opposite, and filled the enemies' host with confusion and cowardice; and bound them with immoveable fetters. 20 And a cold shudder came over the person of the king, and oblivion paralysed the vehemence of his spirit. 21 They turned back the animals upon the armed forces which followed them; and the animals trod them down, and destroyed them. 22 The king's wrath was converted into compassion; and he wept at his own machinations. 23 For when he heard the cry, and saw them all on the verge of destruction, with tears he angrily threatened his friends, saying, 24 Ye have governed badly; and have exceeded tyrants in cruelty; and me your benefactor ye have laboured to deprive at once of my dominion and my life, by secretly devising measures injurious to the kingdom. 25 Who has gathered here, unreasonably removing each from his home, those who, in fidelity to us, had held the fortresses of the country? 26 Who has thus consigned to unmerited punishments those who in good will towards us from the beginning have in all things surpassed all nations, and who often have engaged in the most dangerous undertakings? 27 Loose, loose the unjust bonds; send them to their homes in peace, and deprecate what has been done. 28 Release the sons of the almighty living God of heaven, who from our ancestors' times until now has granted a glorious and uninterrupted prosperity to our affairs. 29 These things he said; and they, released the same moment, having now escaped death, praised God their holy Saviour. 30 The king then departed to the city, and called his financier to him, and bade him provide a seven days' quantity of wine and other materials for feasting for the Jews. He decided that they should keep a gladsome festival of deliverance in the very place in which they expected to meet with their destruction. 31 Then they who were before despised and nigh unto hades, yea, rather advanced into it, partook of the cup of salvation, instead of a grievous and lamentable death. Full of exultation, they parted out the place intended for their fall and burial into banqueting booths. 32 Ceasing their miserable strain of woe, they took up the subject of their fatherland, hymning in praise God their wonder-working Saviour. All groans, all wailing, were laid aside: they formed dances in token of serene joy. 33 So, also, the king collected a number of guests for the occasion, and returned unceasing thanks with much magnificence for the unexpected deliverance afforded him. 34 Those who had marked them out as for death and for carrion, and had registered them with joy, howled aloud, and were clothed with shame, and had the fire of their rage ingloriously put out. 35 But the Jews, as we just said, instituted a dance, and then gave themselves up to feasting, glad thanksgivings, and psalms. 36 They made a public ordinance to commemorate these things for generations to come, as long as they should be sojourners. They thus established these days as days of mirth, not for the purpose of drinking or luxury, but because God had saved them. 37 They requested the king to send them back to their homes. 38 They were being enrolled from the twenty-fifth of Pachon to the fourth of Epiphi, a period of forty days: the measures taken for their destruction lasted from the fifth of Epiphi till the seventh, that is, three days. 39 The Ruler over all did during this time manifest forth his mercy gloriously, and did deliver them all together unharmed. 40 They feasted upon the king's provision up to the fourteenth day, and then asked to be sent away. 41 The king commended them, and wrote the subjoined letter, of magnanimous import for them, to the commanders of every city.

3-Macc.7 1 King Ptolemy Philopator to the commanders throughout Egypt, and to all who are set over affairs, joy and strength. 2 We, too, and our children are well; and God has directed our affairs as we wish. 3 Certain of our friends did of malice vehemently urge us to punish the Jews of our realm in a body, with the infliction of a monstrous punishment. 4 They pretended that our affairs would never be in a good state till this took place. Such, they said, was the hatred borne by the Jews to all other people. 5 They brought them fettered in grievous chains as slaves, nay, as traitors. Without enquiry or examination they endeavoured to annihilate them. They buckled themselves with a savage cruelty, worse than Scythian custom. 6 For this cause we severely threatened them; yet, with the clemency which we are wont to extend to all men, we at length permitted them to live. Finding that the God of heaven cast a shield of protection over the Jews so as to preserve them, and that he fought for them as a father always fights for his sons; 7 and taking into consideration their constancy and fidelity towards us and towards our ancestors, we have, as we ought, acquitted them of every sort of charge. 8 And we have dismissed them to their several homes; bidding all men everywhere to do them no wrong, or unrighteously revile them about the past. 9 For know ye, that should we conceive any evil design, or in any way aggrieve them, we

shall ever have as our opposite, not man, but the highest God, the ruler of all might. From Him there will be no escape, as the avenger of such deeds. Fare ye well. 10 When they had received this letter, they were not forward to depart immediately. They petitioned the king to be allowed to inflict fitting punishment upon those of their race who had willingly transgressed the holy god, and the law of God. 11 They alleged that men who had for their bellies' sake transgressed the ordinances of God, would never be faithful to the interests of the king. 12 The king admitted the truth of this reasoning, and commended them. Full power was given them, without warrant or special commission, to destroy those who had transgressed the law of God boldly in every part of the king's dominions. 13 Their priests, then, as it was meet, saluted him with good wishes, and all the people echoed with the Hallelujah. They then joyfully departed. 14 Then they punished and destryed with ignominy every polluted Jew that fell in their way; 15 slaying thus, in that day, above three hundred men, and esteeming this destruction of the wicked a season of joy. 16 They themselves having held fast their God unto death, and having enjoyed a full deliverance, departed from the city garlanded with sweet-flowered wreaths of every kind. Uttering exclamations of joy, with songs of praise, and melodious hymns they thanked the God of their fathers, the eternal Saviour of Israel. 17 Having arrived at Ptolemais, called from the specialty of that district Rose-bearing, where the fleet, in accordance with the general wish, waited for them seven days, 18 they partook of a banquet of deliverance, for the king generously granted them severally the means of securing a return home. 19 They were accordingly brought back in peace, while they gave utterance to becoming thanks; and they determined to keep these days during their sojourn as days of joyfulness. 20 These they registered as sacred upon a pillar, when they had dedicated the place of their festivity to be one of prayer. They departed unharmed, free, abundant in joy, preserved by the king's command, by land, by sea, and by river, each to his own home. 21 They had more weight than before among their enemies; and were honoured and feared, and no one in any way robbed them of their goods. 22 Every man received back his own, according to inventory; those who had obtained their goods, giving them up with the greatest terror. For the greatest God wrought with perfectness wonders for their salvation. 23 Blessed be the Redeemer of Israel unto everlasting. Amen.

4 MACCABEES

4-Macc.1 1 As I am going to demonstrate a most philosophical proposition, namely, that religious reasoning is absolute master of the passions, I would willingly advise you to give the utmost heed to philosophy. 2 For reason is necessary to every one as a step to science: and more especially does it embrace the praise of prudence, the highest virtue. 3 If, then, reasoning appears to hold the mastery over the passions which stand in the way of temperance, such as gluttony and lust, 4 it surely also and manifestly has the rule over the affections which are contrary to justice, such as malice; and of those which are hindrances to manliness, as wrath, and pain, and fear. 5 How, then, is it, perhaps some may say, that reasoning, if it rule the affections, is not also master of forgetfulness and ignorance? They attempt a ridiculous argument. 6 For reasoning does not rule over its own affections, but over such as are contrary to justice, and manliness and temperance, and prudence; and yet over these, so as to withstand, without destroying them. 7 I might prove to you, from may other considerations, that religious reasoning is sole master of the passions; 8 but I shall prove it with the greatest force from the fortitude of Eleazar, and seven brethren, and their mother, who suffered death in defence of virtue. 9 For all these, contemning pains even unto death, by this contempt, demonstrated that reasoning has command over the passions. 10 For their virtues, then, it is right that I should commend those men who died with their mother at this time in behalf of rectitude; and for their honours, I may count them happy. 11 For they, winning admiration not only from men in general, but even from the persecutors, for their manliness and endurance, became the means of the destruction of the tyranny against their nation, having conquered the tyrant by their endurance, so that by them their country was purified. 12 But we may now at once enter upon the question, having commenced, as is our wont, with laying down the doctrine, and so proceed to the account of these persons, giving glory to the all wise God. 13 The question, therefore, is, whether reasoning be absolute master of the passions. 14 Let us determine, then, What is reasoning? and what passion? and how many forms of the passions? and whether reasoning bears sway over all of these? 15 Reasoning is, then, intellect accompanied by a life of rectitude, putting foremost the consideration of wisdom. 16 And wisdom is a knowledge of divine and human things, and of their causes. 17 And this is contained in the education of the law; by means of which we learn divine things reverently, and human things profitably. 18 And the forms of wisdom are prudence, and justice, and manliness, and temperance. 19 The leading one of these is prudence; by whose means, indeed, it is that reasoning bears rule over the passions. 20 Of the passions, pleasure and pain are the two most comprehensive; and they also by nature refer to the soul. 21 And there are many attendant affections surrounding pleasure and pain. 22 Before pleasure is lust; and after pleasure, joy. 23 And before pain is fear; and after pain is sorrow. 24 Wrath is an affection, common to pleasure and to pain, if any one will pay attention when it comes upon him. 25 And there exists in pleasure a malicious disposition, which is the most multiform of all the affections. 26 In the soul it is arrogance, and love of money, and vaingloriousness, and contention, and faithlessness, and the evil eye. 27 In the body it is greediness and gormandizing, and solitary gluttony. 28 As pleasure and pain are, therefore, two growth of the body and the soul, so there are many offshoots of these passions. 29 And reasoning, the universal husbandman, purging, and pruning these severally, and binding round, and watering, and transplanting, in every way improves the materials of the morals and affections. 30 For reasoning is the leader of the virtues, but it is the sole ruler of the passions. Observe then first, through the very things which stand in the way of temperance, that reasoning is absolute ruler of the passions. 31 Now temperance consists of a command over the lusts. 32 But of the lusts, some belong to the soul, others to the body: and over each of these classes the reasoning appears to bear sway. 33 For whence is it, otherwise, that when urged on to forbidden meats, we reject the gratification which would ensue from them? Is it not because reasoning is able to command the appetites? I believe so. 34 Hence it is, then, that when lusting after water-animals and birds, and fourfooted beasts, and all kinds of food which are forbidden us by the law, we withhold ourselves through the mastery of reasoning. 35 For the affections of our appetites are resisted by the temperate understanding, and bent back again, and all the impulses of the body are reined in by reasoning.

4-Macc.2 1 And what wonder? if the lusts of the soul, after participation with what is beautiful, are frustrated, 2 on this ground, therefore, the temperate Joseph is praised in that by reasoning, he subdued, on reflection, the indulgence of sense. 3 For, although young, and ripe for sexual intercourse, he abrogated by reasoning the stimulus of his passions. 4 And it is not merely the stimulus of sensual indulgence, but that of every desire, that reasoning is able to master. 5 For instance, the law says, Thou shalt not covet thy neighbour's wife, nor anything that belongs to thy neighbour. 6 Now, then, since it is the law which has forbidden us to desire, I shall much the more easily persuade you, that reasoning is able to govern our lusts, just as it does the affections which are impediments to justice. 7 Since in what way is a solitary eater, and a glutton, and a drunkard reclaimed, unless it be clear that reasoning is lord of the passions? 8 A man, therefore, who regulates his course by the law, even if he be a lover of money, straightway puts force upon his own disposition; lending to the needy without interest, and cancelling the debt of the incoming sabbath. 9 And should a man be parsimonious, he is ruled by the law acting through reasoning; so that he does not glean his harvest crops, nor vintage: and in reference to other points we may perceive that it is reasoning that conquers his passions. 10 For the law conquers even affection toward parents, not surrendering virtue on their account. 11 And it prevails over marriage love, condemning it when transgressing law. 12 And it lords it over the love of parents toward their children, for they punish them for vice; and it domineers over the intimacy of friends, reproving them when wicked. 13 And think it not a strange assertion that reasoning can in behalf of the law conquer even enmity. 14 It alloweth not to cut down the cultivated herbage of an enemy, but preserveth it from the destroyers, and collecteth their fallen ruins. 15 And reason appears to be master of the more violent passions, as love of empire and empty boasting, and slander. 16 For the temperate understanding repels all these malignant passions, as it does wrath: for it masters even this. 17 Thus Moses, when angered against Dathan and Abiram, did nothing to them in wrath, but regulated his anger by reasoning. 18 For the temperate mind is able, as I said, to be superior to the passions, and to transfer some, and destroy others. 19 For why, else, does our most wise father Jacob blame Simeon and Levi for having irrationally slain the whole race of the Shechemites, saying, Cursed be their anger. 20 For if reasoning did not possess the power of subduing angry affections, he would not have spoken thus. 21 For at the time when God created man, He implanted within him his passions and moral nature. 22 And at that time He enthroned above all the holy leader mind, through the medium of the senses. 23 And He gave a law to this mind, by living according to which it will maintain a temperate, and just, and good, and manly reign. 24 How, then, a man may say, if reasoning be master of the passions, has it no control over forgetfulness and ignorance?

4-Macc.3 1 The argument is exceedingly ridiculous: for reasoning does not appear to bear sway over its own affections, but over those of the body, 2 in such a way as that any one of you may not be able to root out desire, but reasoning will enable you to avoid being enslaved to it. 3 One may not be able to root out anger from the soul, but it is possible to withstand anger. 4 Any one of you may not be able to eradicate malice, but reasoning has force to work with you to prevent you yielding to malice. 5 For reasoning is not an eradicator, but an antagonist of the passions. 6 And this may be more clearly comprehended from the thirst of king David. 7 For after David had been attacking the Philistines the whole day, he with the soldiers of his nation slew many of them; 8 then when evening came, sweating and very weary, he came to the royal tent, about which the entire host of our ancestors was encamped. 9 Now all the rest of them were at supper; 10 but the king, being very much athirst, although he had numerous springs, could not by their means quench his thirst; 11 but a certain irrational longing for the water in the enemy's camp grew stronger and fiercer upon him, and consumed him with languish. 12 Wherefore his body-guards being troubled at this longing of the king, two valiant young soldiers, reverencing the desire of the king, put on their panoplies, and taking a pitcher, got over the ramparts of the enemies: 13 and unperceived by the guardians of the gate, they went throughout the whole camp of the enemy in quest. 14 And having boldly discovered the fountain, they filled out of it the draught for the king. 15 But he, though parched with thirst, reasoned that a draught reputed of equal value to blood, would be terribly dangerous to his soul. 16 Wherefore, setting up reasoning in opposition to his desire, he poured out the draught to God. 17 For the temperate mind has power to conquer the pressure of the passions, and to quench the fires of excitement, 18 and to wrestle down the pains of the body, however excessive; and, through the excellency of reasoning, to abominate all the assaults of the passions. 19 But the occasion now invites us to give an illustration of temperate reasoning from history. 20 For at a time when our fathers were in possession of undisturbed peace through obedience to the law, and were prosperous, so that Seleucus Nicanor, the king of Asia, both assigned them money for divine service, and accepted their form of government, 21 then certain persons, bringing in new things contrary to the general unanimity, in various ways fell into calamities.

4-Macc.4 1 For a certain man named Simon, who was in opposition to Onias, who once held the high priesthood for life, and was an honourable and good man, after that by slandering him in every way, he could not injure him with the people, went away as an exile, with the intention of betraying his country. 2 Whence coming to Apollonius, the military governor of Syria, and Phoenicia, and Cilicia, he said, 3 Having good will to the king's affairs, I am come to inform thee that infinite private wealth is laid up in the treasuries of Jerusalem which do not belong to the temple, but pertain to king Seleucus. 4 Apollonius, acquainting himself with the particulars of this, praised Simon for his care of the king's interests, and going up to Seleucus informed him of the treasure; 5 and getting authority about it, and quickly advancing into our country with the accursed Simon and a very heavy force, 6 he said that he came with the commands of the king that he should take the private money of the treasure. 7 And the nation, indignant at this proclamation, and replying to the effect that it was extremely unfair that those who had committed deposits to the sacred treasury should be deprived of them, resisted as well as they could. 8 But Appolonius went away with threats into the temple. 9 And the priests, with the women and children, having supplicated God to throw his shield over the holy, despised place, 10 and Appolonius going up with his armed force to the seizure of the treasure,--there appeared from heaven angels riding on horseback, all radiant in armour, filling them with much fear and trembling. 11 And Apollonius fell half dead upon the court which is open to all nations, and extended his hands to heaven, and implored the Hebrews, with tears, to pray for him, and propitiate the heavenly host. 12 For he said that he had sinned, so as to be consequently worthy of death; and that if he were saved, he would celebrate to all men the blessedness of the holy place. 13 Onias the high priest, induced by these words, although for other reasons anxious that king Seleucus should not suppose that Apollonius was slain by human device and not by Divine punishment, prayed for him; 14 and he being thus unexpectedly saved, departed to manifest to the king what had happened to him. 15 But on the death of Seleucus the king, his son Antiochus Epiphanes succeeds to the kingdom: a man of haughty pride and terrible. 16 Who having deposed Onias from the high priesthood, appointed his brother Jason to be high priest: 17 who had made a covenant, if he would give him this authority, to pay yearly three thousand six hundred and sixty talents. 18 And he committed to him the high priesthood and rulership over the nation. 19 And he both changed the manner of living of the people, and perverted their civil customs into all lawlessness. 20 So that he not only erected a gymnasium on the very citadel of our country, [but neglected] the guardianship of the temple. 21 At which Divine vengeance being grieved, instigated Antiochus himself against them. 22 For being at war with Ptolemy in Egypt, he heard that on a report of his death being spread abroad, the inhabitants of Jerusalem had exceedingly rejoiced, and he quickly marched against them. 23 And having subdued them, he established a decree that if any of them lived according to the laws of his country he should die. 24 And when he could by no means destroy by his decrees the obedience to the law of the nation, but saw all his threats and punishments without effect, 25 for even women, because they continued to circumcise their children, were flung down a precipice along with them, knowing beforehand of the punishment. 26 When, therefore, his decrees were disregarded by the people, he himself compelled by means of tortures every one of this race, by tasting forbidden meats, to abjure the Jewish religion.

4-Macc.5 1 The tyrant Antiochus, therefore, sitting in public state with his assessors upon a certain lofty place, with his armed troops standing in a circle around him, commanded his spearbearers to seize every one of the Hebrews, and to compel them to taste swine's flesh, and things offered to idols. 2, 3 And should any of them be unwilling to eat the accursed food, they were to be tortured on the wheel, and so killed. 4 And when many had been seized, a foremost man of the assembly, a Hebrew, by name Eleazar, a priest by family, by profession a lawyer, and advanced in years, and for this reason known to many of the king's followers, was brought near to him. 5 And Antiochus seeing him, said, 6 I would counsel thee, old man, before thy tortures begin, to tasted the swine's flesh, and save your life; for I feel respect for your age and hoary head, which since you have had so long, you appear to me to be no philosopher in retaining the superstition of the Jews. 7 For wherefore, since nature has conferred upon you the most excellent flesh of this animal, do you loathe it? 8 It seems senseless not to enjoy what is pleasant, yet not disgraceful; and from notions of sinfulness, to reject the boons of nature. 9 And you will be acting, I think, still more senselessly, if you follow vain conceits about the truth. 10 And you will, moreover, be despising me to your own punishment. 11 Will you not awake from your trifling philosophy? and give up the folly of your notions; and, regaining understanding worthy of your age, search into the truth of an expedient course? 12 and, reverencing my kindly admonition, have pity upon your own years? 13 For, bear in mind, that if there be any power which watches over this religion of yours, it will pardon you for all transgressions of the law which you commit through compulsion. 14 While the tyrant incited him in this manner to the unlawful eating of flesh, Eleazar begged permission to speak. 15 And having received power to speak, he began thus to deliver himself: 16 We, O Antiochus, who are persuaded that we live under a divine law, consider no compulsion to be so forcible as obedience to that law; 17 wherefore we consider that we ought not in any point to transgress the law. 18 And indeed, were our law (as you suppose) not truly divine, and if we wrongly think it divine, we should have no right even in that case to destroy our sense of religion. 19 think not eating the unclean, then, a trifling offense. 20 For transgression of the law, whether in small or great matters, is of equal moment; 21 for in either case the law is equally slighted. 22

But thou deridest our philosophy, as though we lived irrationally in it. 23 Yet it instructs us in temperance, so that we are superior to all pleasures and lusts; and it exercises us in manliness, so that we cheerfully undergo every grievance. 24 And it instructs us in justice, so that in all our dealoings we render what is due; and it teaches us piety, so that we worship the one only God becomingly. 25 Wherefore it is that we eat not the unclean; for believing that the law was established by God, we are convinced that the Creator of the world, in giving his laws, sympathises with our nature. 26 Those things which are convenient to our souls, he has directed us to eat; but those which are repugnant to them, he has interdicted. 27 But, tyrant-like, thou not only forcest us to break the law, but also to eat, that thou mayest ridicule us as we thus profanely eat: 28 but thou shalt not have this cause of laughter against me; 29 nor will I transgress the sacred oaths of my forefathers to keep the law. 30 No, not if you pluck out my eyes, and consume my entrails. 31 I am not so old, and void of manliness, but that my rational powers are youthful in defence of my religion. 32 Now then; prepare your wheels, and kindle a fiercer flame. 33 I will not so compassionate my old age, as on my account to break the law of my country. 34 I will not belie thee, O law, my instructor! or forsake thee, O beloved self-control! 35 I will not put thee to shame, O philosopher Reason; or deny thee, O honoured priesthood, and science of the law. 36 Mouth! thou shalt not pollute my old age, nor the full stature of a perfect life. 37 My fathers shall receive me pure, not having quailed before your compulsion, though unto death. 38 For over the ungodly thou shalt tyrannize; but thou shalt not lord it over my thoughts about religion, either by thine arguments, or through deeds.

4-Macc.6 1 When Eleazar had in this manner answered the exhortations of the tyrant, the spearbearers came up, and rudely haled Eleazar to the instruments of torture. 2 And first, they stripped the old man, adorned as he was with the comeliness of piety. 3 Then tying back his arms and hands, they disdainfully used him with stripes; 4 a herald opposite crying out, Obey the commands of the king. 5 But Eleazar, the high-minded and truly noble, as one tortured in a dream, regarded it not all. 6 But raising his eyes on high to heaven, the old man's flesh was stripped off by the scourges, and his blood streamed down, and his sides were pierced through. 7 And falling upon the ground, from his body having no power to support the pains, he yet kept his reasoning upright and unbending. 8 then one of the harsh spearbearers leaped upon his belly as he was falling, to force him upright. 9 But he endured the pains, and despised the cruelty, and persevered through the indignities; 10 and like a noble athlete, the old man, when struck, vanquished his torturers. 11 His countenance sweating, and he panting for breath, he was admired by the very torturers for his courage. 12 Wherefore, partly in pity for his old age, 13 partly from the sympathy of acquaintance, and partly in admiration of his endurance, some of the attendants of the king said, Why do you unreasonably destroy yourself, O Eleazar, with these miseries? 14 We will bring you some meat cooked by yourself, and do you save yourself by pretending that you have eaten swine's flesh. 16 And Eleazar, as though the advice more painfully tortured him, cried out, 17 Let not us who are children of Abraham be so evil advised as by giving way to make use of an unbecoming pretence; 18 for it were irrational, if having lived up to old age in all truth, and having scrupulously guarded our character for it, we should now turn back, 19 and ourselves should become a pattern of impiety to the young, as being an example of pollution eating. 20 It would be disgraceful if we should live on some short time, and that scorned by all men for cowardice, 21 and be condemned by the tyrant for unmanliness, by not contending to the death for our divine law. 22 Wherefore do you, O children of Abraham, die nobly for your religion. 23 Ye spearbearers of the tyrant, why do ye linger? 24 Beholding him so high-minded against misery, and not changing at their pity, they led him to the fire: 25 then with their wickedly-contrived instruments they burnt him on the fire, and poured stinking fluids down into his nostrils. 26 And he being at length burnt down to the bones, and about to expire, raised his eyes Godward, and said, 27 Thou knowest, O God, that when I might have been saved, I am slain for the sake of the law by tortures of fire. 28 Be merciful to thy people, and be satisfied with the punishment of me on their account. 29 Let my blood be a purification for them, and take my life in recompense for theirs. 30 Thus speaking, the holy man departed, noble in his torments, and even to the agonies of death resisted in his reasoning for the sake of the law. 31 Confessedly, therefore, religious reasoning is master of the passions. 32 For had the passions been superior to reasoning, I would have given them the witness of this mastery. 33 But now, since reasoning conquered the passions, we befittingly awared it the authority of first place. 34 And it is but fair that we should allow, that the power belongs to reasoning, since it masters external miseries. 35 Ridiculous would it be were it not so; and I prove that reasoning has not only mastered pains, but that it is also superior to the pleasures, and withstands them.

4-Macc.7 1 The reasoning of our father Eleazar, like a first-rate pilot, steering the vessel of piety in the sea of passions, 2 and flouted by the threats of the tyrant, and overwhelmed with the breakers of torture, 3 in no way shifted the rudder of piety till it sailed into the harbour of victory over death. 4 Not so has ever a city, when besieged, held out against many and various machines, as did that holy man, when his pious soul was tried with the fiery trial of tortures and rackings, move his besiegers through the religious reasoning that shielded him. 5 For father Eleazar, projecting his disposition, broke the raging wabves of the passions as with a jutting promontory. 6 O priest worthy of the priesthood! thou didst not pollute thy sacred teeth; nor make thine appetite, which had always embraced the clean and lawful, a partaker of profanity. 7 O harmonizer with the law, and sage devoted to a divine life! 8 Of such a character ought those to be who perform the duties of the law at the risk of their own blood, and defend it with generous sweat by sufferings even unto death. 9 Thou, father, hast gloriously established our right government by thy endurance; and making of much account our service past, prevented its destruction, and, by thy deeds, hast made credible the words of philosophy. 10 O aged man of more power than tortures, elder more vigorous than fire, greatest king over the passions, Eleazar! 11 For as father Aaron, armed with a censer, hastening through the consuming fire, vanquished the flame-bearing angel, 12 so, Eleazar, the descendant of Aaron, wasted away by the fire, did not give up his reasoning. 13 And, what is most wonderful, though an old man, though the labours of his body were now spent, and his fibres were relaxed, and his sinews worn out, he recovered youth. 14 By the spirit of reasoning, and the reasoning of Isaac, he rendered powerless the many-headed instrument. 15 O blessed old age, and reverend hoar head, and life obedient to the law, which the faithful seal of death perfected. 16 O If, then, an old man, through religion, despised tortures even unto death, confessedly religious reasoning is ruler of the passions. 17 But perhaps some might say, It is not all who conquer passions, as all do not possess wise reasoning. 18 But they who have meditated upon religion with their whole heart, these alone can master the passions of the flesh; 19 they who believe that to God they die not; for, as our forefathers, Abraham, Isaac, Jacob, they live to God. 20 This circumstance, then, is by no means an objection, that some who have weak reasoning, are governed by their passions: 21 since what person, walking religiously by the whole rule of philosophy, and believing in God, 22 and knowing that it is a blessed thing to endure all kinds of hardships for virture, would not, for the sake of religion, master his passion? 23 For the wise and brave man only is lord over his passions. 24 Whence it is, that even boys, imbued with the philosophy of religious reasoning, have conquered still more bitter tortures: 25 for when the tyrant was manifestly vanquished in his first attempt, in being unable to force the old man to eat the unclean thing,-

4-Macc.8 1 Then, indeed, vehemently swayed with passion, he commanded to bring others of the adult Hebrews, and if they would eat of the unclean thing, to let them go when they had eaten; but if they objected, to torment them more grievously. 2 The tyrant having given this charge, seven brethren were brought into his presence, along with their aged mother, handsome, and modest, and well-born, and altogether comely. 3 Whom, when the tyrant beheld, encircling their mother as in a dance, he was pleased at them; and being struck with their becoming and ingenuous mien, smiled upon them, and calling them near, said: 4 O youths, with favourable feelings, I admire the beauty of each of you; and greatly honouring so numerous a band of brethren, I not only counsel you not to share the madness of the old man who has been tortured before, 5 but I do beg you to yield, and to enjoy my friendship; for I possess the power, not only of punishing those who disobey my commands, but of doing good to those who obey them. 6 Put confidence in me, then, and you shall receive places of authority in my government, if you forsake your national ordinance, 7 and, conforming to the Greek mode of life, alter your rule, and revel in youth's delights. 8 For if you provoke me by your disobedience, you will compel me to destroy you, every one, with terrible punishments by tortures. 9 Have mercy, then, upon your own selves, whom I, although an enemy, compassionate for your age and comeliness. 10 Will you not reason upon this--that if you disobey, there will be nothing left for you but to die in tortures? 11 Thus speaking, he ordered the instruments of torture to be brought forward, that very fear might prevail upon them to eat unclean meat. 12 And when the spearman brought forward the wheels, and the racks, and the hooks, and catapeltae, and caldrons, pans, and finger-racks, and iron hands and wedges, and bellows, the tyrant continue: 13 Fear, young men, and the righteousness which ye worship will be merciful to you if you err from compulsion. 14 Now they having listened to these words of persuasion, and seeing the fearful instruments, not only were not afraid, but even answered the arguments of the tyrant, and through their good reasoning destroyed his power. 15 Now let us consider the matter: had any of them been weak-spirited and cowardly among them, what reasonings would they have employed but these? 16 O wretched that we are, and exceeding senseless! when the king exhorts us, and calls us to his bounty, should we not obey him? 17 Why do we cheer ourselves with vain counsels, and venture upon a disobedience bringing death? 18 Shall we not fear, O brethren, the instruments of torture and weigh the threatenings of torment and shun this vain-glory and destructive pride? 19 Let us have compassion upon our age and relent over the years of our mother. 20 And let us bear in mind that we shall be dying as rebels. 21 And Divine Justice will pardon us if we fear the king through necessity. 22 Why withdraw ourselves from a most sweet life, and deprive ourselves of this pleasant world? 23 Let us not oppose necessity, nor seek vain-glory by our own excruciation. 24 The law itself is not forward to put us to death, if we dread torture. 25 Whence has such angry zeal taken root in us, and such fatal obstinacy approved itself to us, when we might live unmolested by the king? 26 But nothing of this kind did the young men say or think when about to be tortured. 27 For they were well aware of the sufferings, and masters of the pains. So that as soon as the tyrant had ceased counseling them to eat the unclean, they altogether with one voice, as from the same heart said:

4-Macc.9 1 Why delayest thou, O tyrant? for we are readier to die than to transgress the injunctions of our fathers. 2 And we should be disgracing our fathers if we did not obey the law, and take knowledge for our guide. 3 O tyrant, counsellor of law-breaking, do not, hating us as thou dost, pity us more than we pity ourselves. 4 For we account escape to be worse than death. 5 And you think to scare us, by threatening us with death by tortures, as though thou hadst learned nothing by the death of Eleazar. 6 But if aged men of the Hebrews have died in the cause of religion after enduring torture, more rightly should we younger men die, scorning your cruel tortures, which our aged instructor overcame. 7 Make the attempt, then, O tyrant; and if thou puttest us to death for our religion, think not that thou harmest us by torturing us. 8 For we through this ill-treatment and endurance shall bear off the rewards of

virtue. 9 But thou, for the wicked and despotic slaughter of us, shalt, from the Divine vengeance, endure eternal torture by fire. 10 When they had thus spoken, the tyrant was not only exasperated against them as being refractory, but enraged with them as being ungrateful. 11 So that, at his bidding, the torturers brought forth the eldest of them, and tearing through his tunic, bound his hands and arms on each side with thongs. 12 And when they had laboured hard without effect in scourging him, they hurled him upon the wheel. 13 And the noble youth, extended upon this, became dislocated. 14 And with every member disjointed, he exclaimed in expostulation, 15 O most accursed tyrant, and enemy of heavenly justice, and cruel-hearted, I am no murderer, nor sacrilegious man, whom thou thus ill-usest; but a defender of the Divine law. 16 And when the spearmen said, Consent to eat, that you may be released from your tortures,-- 17 he answered, Not so powerful, O accursed ministers, is your wheel, as to stifle my reasoning; cut my limbs, and burn my flesh, and twist my joints. 18 For through all my torments I will convince you that the children of the Hebrews are alone unconquered in behalf of virtue. 19 While he was saying this, they heaped up fuel, and setting fire to it, strained him upon the wheel still more. 20 And the wheel was defiled all over with blood, and the hot ashes were quenched by the droppings of gore, and pieces of flesh were scattered about the axles of the machine. 21 And although the framework of his bones was now destroyed the high-minded and Abrahamic youth did not groan. 22 But, as though transformed by fire into immortality, he nobly endured the rackings, saying 23 Imitate me, O brethren, nor ever desert your station, nor abjure my brotherhood in courage: fight the holy and honourable fight of religion; 24 by which means our just and paternal Providence, becoming merciful to the nation, will punish the pestilent tyrant. 25 And saying this, the revered youth abruptly closed his life. 26 And when all admired his courageous soul, the spearmen brought forward him who was second in point of age, and having put on iron hands, bound him with pointed hooks to the catapelt. 27 And when, on enquiring whether he would eat before he was tortured, they heard his noble sentiment, 28 after they with the iron hands had violently dragged all the flesh from the neck to the chin, the panther-like beasts tore off the very skin of his head: but he, bearing with firmness this misery, said, 29 How sweet is every form of death for the religion of our fathers! and he said to the tyrant, 30 Thinkest thou not, most cruel of all tyrants, that thou art now tortured more than I, finding thine overweening conception of tyranny conquered by our patience in behalf of our religion? 31 For I lighten my suffering by the pleasures which are connected with virtue. 32 But thou art tortured with threatenings for impiety; and thou shalt not escape, most corrupt tyrant, the vengeance of Divine wrath.

4-Macc.10 1 Now this one, having endured this praiseworthy death, the third was brought along, and exhorted by many to taste and save his life. 2 But he cried out and said, Know ye not, that the father of those who are dead, begat me also; and that the same mother bare me; and that I was brought up in the same tenets? 3 I abjure not the noble relationship of my brethren. 4 Now then, whatever instrument of vengeance ye have, apply it to my body, for ye are not able to touch, even if ye wish it, my soul. 5 But they, highly incensed at his boldness of speech, dislocated his hands and feet with racking engines, and wrenching them from their sockets, dismembered him. 6 And they dragged round his fingers, and his arms, and his legs, and his ankles. 7 And not being able by any means to strangle him, they tore off his skin, together with the extreme tips of his fingers, flayed him, and then haled him to the wheel; 8 around which his vertebral joints were loosened, and he saw his own flesh torn to shreds, and streams of blood flowing from his entrails. 9 And when about to die, he said, 10 We, O accursed tyrant, suffer this for the sake of Divine education and virtue. 11 But thou, for thine impiety and blood-shedding, shalt endure indissoluble torments. 12 And thus having died worthily of his brethren, they dragged forward the fourth, saying, 13 Do not thou share the madness of thy brethren: but give regard to the king, and save thyself. 14 But he said to them, You have not a fire so scorching as to make me play the coward. 15 By the blessed death of my brethren, and the eternal punishment of the tyrant, and the glorious life of the pious, I will not repudiate the noble brotherhood. 16 Invent, O tyrant, tortures; that you may learn, even through them, that I am the brother of those tormented before. 17 When he had said this, the blood-thirsty, and murderous, and unhallowed Antiochus ordered his tongue to be cut out. 18 But he said, Even if you take away the organ of speech, yet God hears the silent. 19 Behold, my tongue is extended, cut it off; for not for that halt thou extirpate our reasoning. 20 Gladly do we lose our limbs in behalf of God. 21 But God shall speedily find you, since you cut off the tongue, the instrument of divine melody.

4-Macc.11 1 And when he had died, disfigured in his torments, the fifth leaped forward, and said, 2 I intend not, O tyrant, to get excused from the torment which is in behalf of virtue. 3 But I have come of mine own accord, that by the death of me, you may owe heavenly vengeance a punishment for more crimes. 4 O thou hater of virtue and of men, what have we done that thou thus revellest in our blood? 5 Does it seem evil to thee that we worship the Founder of all things, and live according to his surpassing law? 6 But this is worthy of honours, not torments; 7 hadst thou been capable of the higher feelings of men, and possessed the hope of salvation from God. 8 Behold now, being alien from God, thou makest war against those who are religious toward God. 9 As he said this, the spearbearers bound him, and drew him to the catapelt: 10 to which binding him at his knees, and fastening them with iron fetters, they bent down his loins upon the wedge of the wheel; and his body was then dismembered, scorpion-fashion. 11 With his breath thus confined, and his body strangled, he said, 12 A great favour thou bestowest upon us, O tyrant, by enabling us to manifest our adherence to the law by means of nobler sufferings. 13 He also being dead, the sixth, quite a youth, was brought out; and on the tyrant asking him whether he would eat and be delivered, he said, 14 I am indeed younger than my brothers, but in understanding I am am as old; 15 for having been born and reared unto the same end, we are bound to die also in behalf of the same cause. 16 So that if ye think proper to torment us for not eating the unclean;--torment! 17 As he said this, they brought him to the wheel. 18 Extended upon which, with limbs racked and dislocated, he was gradually roasted from beneath. 19 And having heated sharp spits, they approached them to his back; and having transfixed his sides, they burned away his entrails. 20 And he, while tormented, said, O period good and holy, in which, for the sake of religion, we brethren have been called to the contest of pain, and have not been conquered. 21 For religious understanding, O tyrant, is unconquered. 22 Armed with upright virtue, I also shall depart with my brethren. 23 I, too, bearing with me a great avenger, O deviser of tortures, and enemy of the truly pious. 24 We six youths have destroyed thy tyranny. 25 For is not your inability to overrule our reasoning, and to compel us to eat the unclean, thy destruction? 26 Your fire is cold to us, your catapelts are painless, and your violence harmless. 27 For the guards not of a tyrant but of a divine law are our defenders: through this we keep our reasoning unconquered.

4-Macc.12 1 When he, too, had undergone blessed martyrdom, and died in the caldron into which he had been thrown, the seventh, the youngest of all, came forward: 2 whom the tyrant pitying, though he had been dreadfully reproached by his brethren, 3 seeing him already encompassed with chains, had him brought nearer, and endeavoured to counsel him, saying, 4 Thou seest the end of the madness of thy brethren: for they have died to torture through disobedience; and you, if disobedient, having been miserably tormented, will yourself perish prematurely. 5 But if you obey, you shall be my friend, and have a charge over the affairs of the kingdom. 6 And having thus exhorted him, he sent for the mother of the boy; that, by condoling with her for the loss of so many sons, he might incline her, through the hope of safety, to render the survivor obedient. 7 And he, after his mother had urged him on in the Hebrew tongue, (as we shall soon relate) saith, 8 Release me that I may speak to the king and all his friends. 9 And they, rejoicing exceedingly at the promise of the youth, quickly let him go. 10 And he, running up to the pans, said, 11 Impious tyrant, and most blasphemous man, wert thou not ashamed, having received prosperity and a kingdom from God, to slay His servants, and to rack the doers of godliness? 12 Wherefore the divine vengeance is reserving thee for eternal fire and torments, which shall cling to thee for all time. 13 Wert thou not ashamed, man as thou art, yet most savage, to cut out the tongues of men of like feeling and origin, and having thus abused to torture them? 14 But they, bravely dying, fulfilled their religion towards God. 15 But thou shalt groan according to thy deserts for having slain without cause the champions of virtue. 16 Wherefore, he continued, I myself, being about to die, 17 will not forsake my brethren. 18 And I call upon the God of my fathers to be merciful to my race. 19 But thee, both living and dead, he will punish. 20 Thus having prayed, he hurled himself into the pans; and so expired.

4-Macc.13 1 If then, the seven brethren despised troubles even unto death, it is confessed on all sides that righteous reasoning is absolute master over the passions. 2 For just as if, had they as slaves to the passions, eaten of the unholy, we should have said that they had been conquered by the; 3 now it is not so: but by means of the reasoning which is praised by God, they mastered their passions. 4 And it is impossible to overlook the leadership of reflection: for it gained the victory over both passions and troubles. 5 How, then, can we avoid according to these men mastery of passion through right reasoning, since they drew not back from the pains of fire? 6 For just as by means of towers projecting in front of harbours men break the threatening waves, and thus assure a still course to vessels entering port, 7 so that seven-towered right-reasoning of the young men, securing the harbour of religion, conquered the intemperance of passions. 8 For having arranged a holy choir of piety, they encouraged one another, saying, 9 Brothers, may we die brotherly for the law. Let us imitate the three young men in Assyria who despised the equally afflicting furnace. 10 Let us not be cowards in the manifestation of piety. 11 And one said, Courage, brother; and another, Nobly endure. 12 And another, Remember of what stock ye are; and by the hand of our father Isaac endured to be slain for the sake of piety. 13 And one and all, looking on each other serene and confident, said, Let us sacrifice with all our heart our souls to God who gave them, and employ our bodies for the keeping of the law. 14 Let us not fear him who thinketh he killeth; 15 for great is the trial of soul and danger of eternal torment laid up for those who transgress the commandment of God. 16 Let us arm ourselves, therefore, in the abnegation of the divine reasoning. 17 If we suffer thus, Abraham, and Isaac, and Jacob will receive us, and all the fathers will commend us. 18 And as each one of the brethren was haled away, the rest exclaimed, Disgrace us not, O brother, nor falsify those who died before you. 19 Now you are not ignorant of the charm of brotherhood, which the Divine and all wise Providence hath imparted through fathers to children, and hath engendered through the mother's womb. 20 In which these brothers having remained an equal time, and having been formed for the same period, and been increased by the same blood, and having been perfected through the same principle of life, 21 and having been brought forth at equal intervals, and having sucked milk from the same fountains, hence their brotherly souls are reared up lovingly together; 22 and increase the more powerfully by reason of this simultaneous rearing, and by daily intercourse, and by other education, and exercise in the law of God. 23 Brotherly love being thus sympathetically constituted, the seven brethren had a more sympathetic mutual harmony. 24 For being educated in the same law, and practising the same virtues, and reared up in a just course of life, they increased this harmony with each other. 25 For a like ardour for what is right and honourable increased their fellow-feeling towards each other. 26 For it acting along with religion, made their brotherly feeling more desirable to them. 27 And yet, although nature and intercourse and virtuous morals increased their brotherly love those who were left endured to behold their brethren, who were illused for their religion, tortured even unto death.

4-Macc.14 1 And more that this, they even urged them on to this ill-treatment; so that they not only despised pains themselves, but they even got the better of their affections of brotherly love. 2 O reasonings more royal than a king, and freer than freemen! 3 Sacred and harmonius concert of the seven brethern as concerning piety! 4 None of the seven youths turned cowardly, or shrank back from death. 5 But all of them, as though running the road to immortality, hastened on to death through tortures. 6 For just as hands and feet are moved sympathetically with the directions of the soul, so those holy youths agreed unto death for religion's sake, as through the immortal soul of religion. 7 O holy seven of harmonious brethren! for as the seven days of creation, about religion, 8 so the youths, circling around the number seven, annulled the fear of torments. 9 We now shudder at the recital of the affliction of those young men; but they not only beheld, and not only heard the immediate execution of the threat, but undergoing it, persevered; and that through the pains of fire. 10 And what could be more painful? for the power of fire, being sharp and quick, speedily dissolved their bodies. 11 And think it not wonderful that reasoning bore rule over those men in their torments, when even a woman's mind despised more manifold pains. 12 For the mother of those seven youths endured the rackings of each of her children. 13 And consider how comprehensive is the love of offspring, which draws every one to sympathy of affection, 14 where irrational animals possess a similar sympathy and love for their offspring with men. 15 The tame birds frequenting the roofs of our houses, defend their fledglings. 16 Others build their nests, and hatch their young, in the tops of mountains and in the precipices of valleys, and the holes and tops of trees, and keep off the intruder. 17 And if not able to do this, they fly circling round them in agony of affection, calling out in their own note, and save their offspring in whatever manner they are able. 18 But why should we point attention to the sympathy toward children shewn by irrational animals? 19 The very bees, at the season of honey-making, attack all who approach; and pierce with their sting, as with a sword, those who draw near their hive, and repel them even unto death. 20 But sympathy with her children did not turn aside the mother of the young men, who had a spirit kindred with that of Abraham.

4-Macc.15 1 O reasoning of the sons, lord over the passions, and religion more desirable to a mother than progeny! 2 The mother, when two things were set before here, religion and the safety of her seven sons for a time, on the conditional promise of a tyrant, 3 rather elected the religion which according to God preserves to eternal life. 4 O in what way can I describe ethically the affections of parents toward their children, the resemblance of soul and of form engrafted into the small type of a child in a wonderful manner, especially through the greater sympathy of mothers with the feelings of those born of them! 5 for by how much mothers are by nature weak in disposition and prolific in offspring, by so much the fonder they are of children. 6 And of all mothers the mother of the seven was the fondest of children, who in seven childbirths had deeply engendered love toward them; 7 and through her many pains undergone in connection with each one, was compelled to feel sympathy with them; 8 yet, through fear of God, who neglected the temporary salvation of her children. 9 Not but that, on account of the excellent disposition to the law, her maternal affection toward them was increased. 10 For they were both just and temperate, and manly, and high-minded, and fond of their brethren, and so fond of their mother that even unto death they obeyed her by observing the law. 11 And yet, though there were so many circumstances connected with love of children to draw on a mother to sympathy, in the case of none of them were the various tortures able to pervert her principle. 12 But she inclined each one separately and all together to death for religion. 13 O holy nature and parental feeling, and reward of bringing up children, and unconquerable maternal affection! 14 At the racking and roasting of each one of them, the observant mother was prevented by religion from changing. 15 She beheld her children's flesh dissolving around the fire; and their extremities quivering on the ground, and the flesh of their heads dropped forwards down to their beards, like masks. 16 O thou mother, who wast tried at this time with bitterer pangs than those of parturition! 17 O thou only woman who hast brought forth perfect holiness! 18 Thy first-born, expiring, turned thee not; nor the second, looking miserable in his torments; nor the third, breathing out his soul. 19 Nor when thou didst behold the eyes of each of them looking sternly upon their tortures, and their nostrils foreboding death, didst thou weep! 20 When thou didst see children's flesh heaped upon children's flesh that had been torn off, heads decapitated upon heads, dead falling upon the dead, and a choir of children turned through torture into a burying ground, thou lamentedst not. 21 Not so do siren melodies, or songs of swans, attract the hearers to listening, O voices of children calling upon your mother in the midst of torments! 22 With what and what manner of torments was the mother herself tortured, as her sons were undergoing the wheel and the fires! 23 But religious reasoning, having strengthened her courage in the midst of sufferings, enabled her to forego, for the time, parental love. 24 Although beholding the destruction of seven children, the noble mother, after one embrace, stripped off [her feelings] through faith in God. 25 For just as in a council-room, beholding in her own soul vehement counsellors, nature and parentage and love of her children, and the racking of her children, 26 she holding two votes, one for the death, the other for the preservation of her children, 27 did not lean to that which would have saved her children for the safety of a brief space. 28 But this daughter of Abraham remembered his holy fortitude. 29 O holy mother of a nation avenger of the law, and defender of religion, and prime bearer in the battle of the affections! 30 O thou nobler in endurance than males, and more manly

than men in patience! 31 For as the ark of Noah, bearing the world in the world-filling flood, bore up against the waves, 32 so thou, the guardian of the law, when surrounded on every side by the flood of passions, and straitened by violent storms which were the torments of they children, didst bear up nobly against the storms against religion.

4-Macc.16 1 If, then, even a woman, and that an aged one, and the mother of seven children, endured to see her children's torments even unto death, confessedly religious reasoning is master even of the passions. 2 I have proved, then, that not only men have obtained the mastery of their passions, but also that a woman despised the greatest torments. 3 And not so fierce were the lions round Daniel, nor the furnace of Misael burning with most vehement fires as that natural love of children burned within her, when she beheld her seven sons tortured. 4 But with the reasoning of religion the mother quenched passions so great and powerful. 5 For we must consider also this: that, had the woman been faint hearted, as being their other, she would have lamented over them; and perhaps might have spoken thus: 6 Ah! wretched I, and many times miserable; who having born seven sons, have become the mother of none. 7 O seven useless childbirths, and seven profitless periods of labour, and fruitless givings of suck, and miserable nursings at the breast. 8 Vainly, for your sakes, O sons, have I endured many pangs, and the more difficult anxieties of rearing. 9 Alas, of my children, some of you unmarried, and some who have married to no profit, I shall not see your children, nor be felicitated as a grandmother. 10 Ah, that I who had many and fair children, should be a lone widow full of sorrows! 11 Nor, should I die, shall I have a son to bury me. But with such a lament is this the holy and God-fearing mother bewailed none of them. 12 Nor did she divert any of them from death, nor grieve for them as for the dead. 13 But as one possessed with an adamantine mind, and as one bringing forth again her full number of sons to immortality, she rather with supplication exhorted them to death in behalf of religion. 14 O woman, soldier of God for religion, thou, aged and a female, hast conquered through endurance even a tyrant; and though but weak, hast been found more powerful in deeds and words. 15 For when thou wast seized along with thy children, thou stoodest looking upon Eleazar in torments, and saidst to thy sons in the Hebrew tongue, 16 O sons, noble is the contest; to which you being called as a witness for the nation, strive zealously for the laws of your country. 17 For it were disgraceful that this old man should endure pains for the sake of righteousness, and that you who are younger should be afraid of the tortures. 18 Remember that through God ye obtained existence, and have enjoyed it. 19 And on this second account ye ought to bear every affliction because of God. 20 For whom also our father Abraham was forward to sacrifice Isaac our progenitor, and shuddered not at the sight of his own paternal hand descending down with the sword upon him. 21 And the righteous Daniel was cast unto the lions; and Ananias, and Azarias, and Misael, were slung out into a furnace of fire; yet they endured through God. 22 You, then, having the same faith towards God, be not troubled. 23 For it is unreasonable that they who know religion should not stand up against troubles. 24 With these arguments, the mother of seven, exhorting each of her sons, over-persuaded them from transgressing the commandment of God. 25 And they saw this, too, that they who die for God, live to God; as Abraham, and Isaac, and Jacob, and all the patriarchs.

4-Macc.17 1 And some of the spearbearers said, that when she herself was about to be seized for the purpose of being put to death, she threw herself upon the pile, rather than they should touch her person. 2 O thou mother, who together with seven children didst destroy the violence of the tyrant, and render void his wicked intentions, and exhibit the nobleness of faith! 3 For thou, as an house bravely built upon the pillar of thy children, didst bear without swaying, the shock of tortures. 4 Be of good cheer, therefore, O holy-minded mother! holding the firm [substance of the] hope of your steadfastness with God. 5 Not so gracious does the moon appear with the stars in heaven, as thou art established honourable before God, and fixed in the firmament with thy sons who thou didst illuminate with religion to the stars. 6 For thy bearing of children was after the fashion of a child of Abraham. 7 And, were it lawful for us to paint as on a tablet the religion of thy story, the spectators would not shudder at beholding the mother of seven children enduring for the sake of religion various tortures even unto death. 8 And it had been a worth thing to have inscribed upon the tomb itself these words as a memorial to those of the nation, 9 Here an aged priest, and an aged woman, and seven sons, are buried through the violence of a tyrant, who wished to destroy the polity of the Hebrews. 10 These also avenged their nation, looking unto God, and enduring torments unto death. 11 For it was truly a divine contest which was carried through by them. 12 For at that time virtue presided over the contest, approving the victory through endurance, namely, immortality, eternal life. 13 Eleazar was the first to contend: and the mother of the seven children entered the contest; and the brethren contended. 14 The tyrant was the opposite; and the world and living men were the spectators. 15 And reverence for God conquered, and crowned her own athletes. 16 Who did not admire those champions of true legislation? who were not astonied? 17 The tyrant himself, and all their council, admired their endurance; 18 through which, also, they now stand beside the divine throne, and live a blessed life. 19 For Moses saith, And all the saints are under thine hands. 20 These, therefore, having been sanctified through God, have been honoured not only with this honour, but that also by their means the enemy did not overcome our nation; 21 and that the tyrant was punished, and their country purified. 22 For they became the atnipoised to the sin of the nation; and the Divine Providence saved Israel, aforetime afflicted, by the blood of those pious ones, and the propitiatory death. 23 For the tyrant Antiochus, looking to their manly virtue, and to their endurance in torture, proclaimed that endurance as an example to his soldiers. 24 And they proved to be to him noble and brave for land battles and for sieges; and he conquered and stormed the towns of all his enemies.

4-Macc.18 1 O Israelitish children, descendants of the seed of Abraham, obey this law, and in every way be religious. 2 Knowing that religious reasoning is lord of the passions, and those not only inward but outward. 3 When those persons giving up their bodies to pains for the sake of religion, were not only admired by men, but were deemed worthy of a divine portion. 4 And the nation through them obtained peace, and having renewed the observance of the law in their country, drove the enemy out of the land. 5 And the tyrant Antiochus was both punished upon earth, and is punished now he is dead; for when he was quite unable to compel the Israelites to adopt foreign customs, and to desert the manner of life of their fathers, 6 then, departing from Jerusalem, he made war against the Persians. 7 And the righteous mother of the seven children spake also as follows to her offspring: I was a pure virgin, and went not beyond my father's house; but I took care of the built-up rib. 8 No destroyer of the desert, *or* ravisher of the plain, injured me; nor did the destructive, deceitful snake, make spoil of my chaste virginity; and I remained with my husband during the period of my prime. 9 And these my children, having arrive at maturity, their father died: blessed was he! for having sought out a life of fertility in children, he was not grieved with a period of loss of children. 10 And he used to teach you, when yet with you, the law and the prophets. 11 He used to read to you the slaying of Abel by Cain, and the offering up of Isaac, and the imprisonment of Joseph. 12 And he used to tell you of the zealous Phinehas; and informed you of Ananias and Azarias, and Misael in the fire. 13 And he used to glorify Daniel, who was in the den of lions, and pronounce him blessed. 14 And he used to put you in mind of the scripture of Esaias, which saith, Even if thou pass through the fire, it shall not burn thee. 15 He chanted to you David, the hymn-writer, who saith, Many are the afflictions of the just. 16 He declared the proverbs of Solomon, who saith, He is a tree of life to all those who do His will. 17 He used to verify Ezekiel, who said, Shall these dry bones live? 18 For he did not forget the song which Moses taught, proclaiming, I will kill, and I will make to live. 19 This is our life, and the length of our days. 20 O that bitter, and yet not bitter, day when the bitter tyrant of the Greeks, quenching fire with fire in his cruel caldrons, brought with boiling rage the seven sons of the daughter of Abraham to the catapelt, and to all his torments! 21 He pierced the balls of their eyes, and cut out their tongues, and put them to death with varied tortures. 22 Wherefore divine retribution pursued and will pursue the pestilent wretch. 23 But the children of Abraham, with their victorious mother, are assembled together to the choir of their fathers; having received pure and immortal souls from God. 24 To whom be glory for ever and ever. Amen.

JOB

Job.1 1 There was a certain man in the land of Ausis, whose name *was* Job; and than man was true, blameless, righteous, *and* godly, abstaining from everything evil. 2 And he had seven sons and three daughters. 3 And his cattle consisted of seven thousand sheep, three thousand camels, five hundred yoke of oxen, five hundred she-asses in the pastures, and a very great household, and he had a great husbandry on the earth; and that man was *most* noble of the *men* of the east. 4 And his sons visiting one another prepared a banquet every day, taking with them also their three sisters to eat and drink with them. 5 And when the days of the banquet were completed, Job sent and purified them, having risen up in the morning, and offered sacrifices for them, according to their number, and one calf for a sin-offering for their souls: for Job said, Lest peradventure my sons have thought evil in their minds against God. Thus, then Job did continually. 6 And it came to pass on a day, that behold, the angels of God came to stand before the Lord, and the devil came with them. 7 And the Lord said to the devil, Whence art thou come? And the devil answered the Lord, and said, I am come from compassing the earth, and walking up and down in the world. 8 And the Lord said to him, Hast thou diligently considered my servant Job, that there is none like him on the earth, a man blameless, true, godly, abstaining from everything evil? 9 Then the devil answered, and said before the Lord, Does Job worship the Lord for nothing? 10 Hast thou not made a hedge about him, and about his household, and all his possessions round about? and hast thou not blessed the works of his hands, and multiplied his cattle upon the land? 11 But put forth thine hand, and touch all that he has: verily he will bless thee to *thy* face. 12 Then the Lord said to the devil, Behold, I give into thine hand all that he has, but touch not himself. So the devil went out from the presence of the Lord. 13 And it came to pass on a certain day, that Job's sons and his daughters were drinking wine in the house of their elder brother. 14 And, behold, there came a messenger to Job, and said to him, The yokes of oxen were ploughing, and the she-asses were feeding near them; 15 and the spoilers came and took them for a prey, and slew the servants with the sword; and I having escaped alone am come to tell thee. 16 While he was yet speaking, there came another messenger, and said to Job, Fire has fallen from heaven, and burnt up the sheep, and devoured the shepherds like wise; and I having escaped alone am come to tell thee. 17 While he was yet speaking, there came another messenger, and said to Job, The horsemen formed three companies against us, and surrounded the camels, and took them for a prey, and slew the servants with the sword; and I only escaped, and am come to tell thee. 18 While he is yet speaking, another messenger comes, saying to Job, While thy sons and thy daughters were eating and drinking with their elder brother, 19 suddenly a great wind came on from the desert, and caught the four corners of the house, and the house fell upon thy children, and they are dead; and I have escaped alone, and am come to tell thee. 20 So Job arose, and rent his garments, and shaved the hair of his head, and fell on the earth, and worshipped, 21 and said, I myself came forth naked from my mother's womb, and naked shall I return thither; the Lord gave, the Lord has taken away: as it seemed good to the Lord, so has it come to pass; blessed be the name of the Lord. 22 In all

these events that befell him Job sinned not at all before the Lord, and did not impute folly to God.

Job.2 1 And it came to pass on a certain day, that the angels of God came to stand before the Lord, and the devil came among them to stand before the Lord. 2 And the Lord, said to the devil, Whence comest thou? Then the devil said before the Lord, I am come from going through the world, and walking about the whole earth. 3 And the Lord said to the devil, Hast thou then observed my servant Job, that there is none of *men* upon the earth like him, a harmless, true, blameless, godly man, abstaining from all evil? and he yet cleaves to innocence, whereas thou has told *me* to destroy his substance without cause? 4 And the devil answered and said to the Lord, Skin for skin, all that a man has will he give as a ransom for his life. 5 Nay, but put forth thine hand, and touch his bones and his flesh: verily he will bless thee to *thy* face. 6 And the Lord said to the devil, Behold, I deliver him up to thee; only save his life. 7 So the devil went out from the Lord, and smote Job with sore boils from *his* feet to *his* head. 8 And he took a potsherd to scrape away the discharge, and sat upon a dung-heap outside the city. 9 And when much time had passed, his wife said to him, How long wilt thou hold out, saying, Behold, I wait yet a little while, expecting the hope of my deliverance? for, behold, thy memorial is abolished from the earth, *even thy* sons and daughters, the pangs and pains of my womb which I bore in vain with sorrows; and thou thyself sittest down to spend the nights in the open air among the corruption of worms, and I am a wanderer and a servant from place to place and house to house, waiting for the setting of the sun, that I may rest from my labours and my pangs which now beset me: but say some word against the Lord, and die. 10 But he looked on her, and said to her, Thou hast spoken like one of the foolish women. If we have received good things of the hand of the Lord, shall we not endure evil things? In all these things that happened to him, Job sinned not at all with his lips before God. 11 Now his three friends having heard of all the evil that was come upon him, came to him each from his own country: Eliphaz the king of the Thaemans, Baldad sovereign of the Saucheans, Sophar king of he Minaeans: and they came to him with one accord, to comfort and to visit him. 12 And when they saw him from a distance they did not know him; and they cried with a loud voice, and wept, and rent every one his garment, and sprinkled dust upon *their heads*, 13 and they sat down beside him seven days and seven nights, and no one of them spoke; for they saw that his affliction was dreadful and very great.

Job.3 1 After this Job opened his mouth, and cursed his day, 2 saying, 3 Let the day perish in which I was born, and that night in which they said, Behold a man-child! 4 Let that night be darkness, and let not the Lord regard it from above, neither let light come upon it. 5 But let darkness and the shadow of death seize it; let blackness come upon it; 6 let that day and night be cursed, let darkness carry them away; let it not come into the days of the year, neither let it be numbered with the days of the months. 7 But let that night be pain, and let not mirth come upon it, nor joy. 8 But let him that curses that day curse it, *even* he that is ready to attack the great whale. 9 Let the stars of that night be darkened; let it remain *dark*, and not come into light; and let it not see the morning star arise: 10 because it shut not up the gates of my mother's womb, for *so* it would have removed sorrow from my eyes. 11 For why died I not in the belly? and *why* did I not come forth from the womb and die immediately? 12 and why did the knees support me? and why did I suck the breasts? 13 Now I should have lain down and been quiet, I should have slept and been at rest, 14 with kings *and* councillors of the earth, who gloried in *their* swords; 15 or with rulers, whose gold was abundant, who filled their houses with silver: 16 or *I should have been* as an untimely birth proceeding from his mother's womb, or as infants who never saw light. 17 There the ungodly have burnt out the fury of rage; there the wearied in body rest. 18 And the men of old time have together ceased to hear the exactor's voice. 19 The small and great are there, and the servant that feared his lord. 20 For why is light given to those who are in bitterness, and life to those souls which are in griefs? 21 who desire death, and obtain it not, digging *for it* as *for* treasures; 22 and would be very joyful if they should gain it? 23 Death *is* rest to *such* a man, for God has hedged him in. 24 For my groaning comes before my food, and I weep being beset with terror. 25 For the terror of which I meditated has come upon me, and that which I had feared has befallen me. 26 I was not at peace, nor quiet, nor had I rest; yet wrath came upon me.

Job.4 1 Then Eliphaz the Thaemanite answered and said, 2 Hast thou been often spoken to in distress? but who shall endure the force of thy words? 3 For whereas thou hast instructed many, and hast strengthened the hands of the weak one, 4 and hast supported the failing with words, and hast imparted courage to feeble knees. 5 Yet now *that* pain has come upon thee, and touched thee, thou art troubled. 6 Is not thy fear *founded* in folly, thy hope also, and the mischief of thy way? 7 Remember then who has perished, being pure? or when were the true-hearted utterly destroyed? 8 Accordingly as I have seen men ploughing barren places, and they that sow them will reap sorrows for themselves. 9 They shall perish by the command of the Lord, and shall be utterly consumed by the breath of his wrath. 10 The strength of the lion, and the voice of the lioness, and the exulting cry of serpents are quenched. 11 The old lion has perished for want of food, and the lions' whelps have forsaken one another. 12 But if there had been any truth in thy words, none of these evils would have befallen thee. Shall not mine ear receive excellent *revelations* from him? 13 But *as when* terror falls upon men, with dread and a sound in the night, 14 horror and trembling seized me, and caused all my bones greatly to shake. 15 And a spirit came before my face; and my hair and flesh quivered. 16 I arose and perceived it not: I looked, and there, was no form before my eyes: but I only heard a breath and a voice, *saying,* 17 What, shall a mortal be pure before the Lord? or a man be blameless in regard to his works? 18 Whereas he trust not in his servants, and perceives perverseness in his angels. 19 But *as for* them that dwell in houses of clay, of whom we

also are formed of the same clay, he smites them like a moth. 20 And from the morning to evening they no longer exist: they have perished, because they cannot help themselves. 21 For he blows upon them, and they are withered: they have perished for lack of wisdom.

Job.5 1 But call, if any one will hearken to thee, or if thou shalt see any of the holy angels. 2 For wrath destroys the foolish one, and envy slays him that has gone astray. 3 And I have seen foolish ones taking root: but suddenly their habitation was devoured. 4 Let their children be far from safety, and let them be crushed at the doors of vile men, and let there be no deliverer. 5 For what they have collected, the just shall eat; but they shall not be delivered out of calamities: let their strength be utterly exhausted. 6 For labour cannot by any means come out of the earth, nor shall trouble spring out of the mountains: 7 yet man is born to labour, and *even so* the vulture's young seek the high places. 8 Nevertheless I will beseech the Lord, and will call upon the Lord, the sovereign of all; 9 who does great things and untraceable, glorious things also, and marvellous, of which there is no number: 10 who gives rain upon the earth, sending water on the earth: 11 who exalts the lowly, and raises up them that are lost: 12 frustrating the counsels of the crafty, and their hands shall not perform the truth: 13 who takes the wise in their wisdom, and subverts the counsel of the crafty 14 In the day darkness shall come upon them, and let them grope in the noon-day even as in the night: 15 and let them perish in war, and let the weak escape from the hand of the mighty. 16 And let the weak have hope, but the mouth of the unjust be stopped. 17 But blessed *is* the man whom the Lord has reproved; and reject not thou the chastening of the Almighty. 18 for he causes *a man* to be in pain, and restores *him* again: he smites, and his hands heal. 19 Six time he shall deliver thee out of distresses: and in the seventh harm shall not touch thee. 20 In famine he shall deliver thee from death: and in war he shall free thee from the power of the sword. 21 He shall hide thee from the scourge of the tongue: and thou shalt not be afraid of coming evils. 22 Thou shalt laugh at the unrighteous and the lawless: and thou shalt not be afraid of wild beasts. 23 For the wild beasts of the field shall be at peace with thee. 24 Then shalt thou know that thy house shall be at peace, and the provision for thy tabernacle shall not fail. 25 And thou shalt know that thy seed *shall be* abundant; and thy children shall be like the herbage of the field. 26 And thou shalt come to the grave like ripe corn reaped in its season, or as a heap of the corn-flour collected in proper time. 27 Behold, we have thus sought out these matters; these are what we have heard: but do thou reflect with thyself, if thou hast done anything *wrong.*

Job.6 1 But Job answered and said, 2 Oh that one would indeed weigh the wrath that is upon me, and take up my griefs in a balance together! 3 And verily they would be heavier than the sand by the seashore: but, as it seems, my words are vain. 4 For the arrows of the Lord are in my body, whose violence drinks up my blood: whenever I am going to speak, they pierce me. 5 What then? will the wild ass bray for nothing, if he is not seeking food? or again, will the ox low at the manger, when he has a fodder? 6 Shall bread be eaten without salt? or again, is there taste in empty words? 7 For my wrath cannot cease; for I perceive my food as the smell of a lion *to be* loathsome. 8 For oh that he would grant *my desire*, and my petition might come, and the Lord would grant my hope! 9 Let the Lord begin and wound me, but let him not utterly destroy me. 10 Let the grave be my city, upon the walls of which I have leaped: I will not shrink from it; for I have not denied the holy words of my God. 11 For what is my strength, that I continue? what is my time, that my soul endures? 12 Is my strength the strength of stones? or is my flesh of brass? 13 Or have I not trusted in him? but help is *far* from me. 14 Mercy has rejected me; and the visitation of the Lord has disregarded me. 15 My nearest relations have not regarded me; they have passed me by like a failing brook, or like a wave. 16 They who used to reverence me, now have come against me like snow or congealed ice. 17 When it has melted at the approach of heat, it is not known what it was. 18 Thus I also have been deserted of all; and I am ruined, and become an outcast. 19 Behold the ways of the Thaemanites, ye that mark the paths of the Sabaeans. 20 They too that trust in cities and riches shall come to shame. 21 But ye also have come to me without pity; so that beholding my wound ye are afraid. 22 What? have I made any demand of you? or do I ask for strength from you, 23 to deliver me from enemies, or to rescue me from the hand of the mighty ones? 24 Teach ye me, and I will be silent: if in anything I have erred, tell me. 25 But as it seems, the words of a true man are vain, because I do not ask strength of you. 26 Neither will your reproof cause me to cease my words, for neither will I endure the sound of your speech. 27 Even because ye attack the fatherless, and insult your friend. 28 But now, having looked upon your countenances, I will not lie. 29 Sit down now, and let there not be unrighteousness; and unite again with the just. 30 For there is no injustice in my tongue; and does not my throat meditate understanding?

Job.7 1 Is not the life of man upon earth a state of trial? and his existence as that of a hireling by the day? 2 Or as a servant that fears his master, and one who has grasped a shadow? or as a hireling waiting for his pay? 3 So have I also endured months of vanity, and nights of pain have been appointed me. 4 Whenever I lie down, I say, When *will it be* day? and whenever I rise up, again *I say* when *will it be* evening? and I am full of pains from evening to morning. 5 And my body is covered with loathsome worms; and I waste away, scraping off clods of dust from my eruption. 6 And my life is lighter than a word, and has perished in vain hope. 7 Remember then that my life is breath, and mine eye shalt not yet again see good. 8 The eye of him that sees me shall not see me *again*: thine eyes are upon me, and I am no more. 9 *I am* as a cloud that is cleared away from the sky: for if a man go down to the grave, he shall not come up again: 10 and he shall surely not return to his own house, neither shall his place know him any more. 11 Then neither will I refrain my mouth: I will speak being in distress; being in anguish I will disclose the bitterness of my soul. 12 Am I a sea, or a serpent, that thou hast set a watch over me? 13 I

said that my bed should comfort me, and I would privately counsel with myself on my couch. 14 Thou scarest me with dreams, and dost terrify me with visions. 15 Thou wilt separate life from my spirit; and yet *keep* my bones from death. 16 For I shall not live for ever, that I should patiently endure: depart from me, for my life *is* vain. 17 For what is man, that thou hast magnified him? or that thou givest heed to him? 18 Wilt thou visit him till the morning, and judge him till *the time of* rest? 19 How long dost thou not let me alone, nor let me go, until I shall swallow down my spittle? 20 If I have sinned, what shall I be able to do, O thou that understandest the mind of men? why hast thou made me as thine accuser, and *why* am I a burden to thee? 21 Why hast thou not forgotten my iniquity, and purged my sin? but now I shall depart to the earth; and in the morning I am no more.

Job.8 1 Then Baldad the Sauchite answered, and said, 2 How long wilt thou speak these things, *how long shall* the breath of thy mouth *be* abundant in words? 3 Will the Lord be unjust when he judges; or will he that has made all things pervert justice? 4 If thy sons have sinned before him, he has cast them away because of their transgression. 5 But be thou early in prayer to the Lord Almighty. 6 If thou art pure and true, he will hearken to thy supplication, and will restore to thee the habitation of righteousness. 7 Though then thy beginning should be small, yet thy end should be unspeakably great. 8 For ask of the former generation, and search diligently among the race of *our* fathers: 9 (for we are of yesterday, and know nothing; for our life upon the earth is a shadow:) 10 shall not these teach thee, and report *to thee*, and bring out words from *their* heart? 11 Does the rush flourish without water, or shall the flag grow up without moisture? 12 When it is yet on the root, and *though* it has not been cut down, does not any herb wither before it has received moisture? 13 Thus then shall be the end of all that forget the Lord: for the hope of the ungodly shall perish. 14 For his house shall be without inhabitants, and his tent shall prove a spider's web. 15 If he should prop up his house, it shall not stand: and when he has taken hold of it, it shall not remain. 16 For it is moist under the sun, and his branch shall come forth out of his dung-heap. 17 He lies down upon a gathering of stones, and shall live in the mist of flints. 18 If *God* should destroy *him*, his place shall deny him. Hast thou not seen such things, 19 that such is the overthrow of the ungodly? and out of the earth another shall grow. 20 For the Lord will by no means reject the harmless man; but he will not receive any gift of the ungodly. 21 But he will fill with laughter the mouth of the sincere, and their lips with thanksgiving. 22 But their adversaries shall clothe themselves with shame; and the habitation of the ungodly shall perish.

Job.9 1 Then Job answered and said, 2 I know of a truth that it is so: for how shall a mortal man be just before the Lord? 3 For if he would enter into judgment with him, *God* would not hearken to him, so that he should answer to one of his charges of a thousand. 4 For he is wise in mind, and mighty, and great: who has hardened himself against him and endured? 5 Who wears out the mountains, and *men* know it not: who overturns them in anger. 6 Who shakes the *earth* under heaven from its foundations, and its pillars totter. 7 Who commands the sun, and it rises not; and he seals up the stars. 8 Who alone has stretched out the heavens, and walks on the sea as on firm ground. 9 Who makes Pleias, and Hesperus, and Arcturus, and the chambers of the south. 10 Who does great and unsearchable things; glorious also and excellent things, innumerable. 11 If ever he should go beyond me, I shall not see him: if he should pass by me, neither thus have I known *it*. 12 If he would take away, who shall turn him back? or who shall say to him, What hast thou done? 13 For *if* he has turned away *his* anger, the whales under heaven have stooped under him. 14 Oh then that he would hearken to me, or judge my cause. 15 For though I be righteous, he will not hearken to me: I will intreat his judgment. 16 And if I should call and he should not hearken, I cannot believe that he has listened to my voice. 17 Let him not crush me with a dark storm: but he has made by bruises many without cause. 18 For he suffers me not to take breath, but he has filled me with bitterness. 19 For indeed he is strong in power: who then shall resist his judgment? 20 For though I should seem righteous, my mouth will be profane: and though I should seem blameless, I shall be proved perverse. 21 For even if I have sinned, I know it not *in* my soul: but my life is taken away. 22 Wherefore I said, Wrath slays the great and mighty man. 23 For the worthless die, but the righteous are laughed to scorn. 24 For they are delivered into the hands of the unrighteous *man*: he covers the faces of the judges *of the earth*: but if it be not he, who is it? 25 But my life is swifter than a post: *my days* have fled away, and they knew it not. 26 Or again, is there a trace of *their* path *left* by ships? or is there one of the flying eagle as it seeks *its* prey? 27 And if I should say, I will forget to speak, I will bow down my face and groan; 28 I quake in all my limbs, for I know that thou wilt not leave me alone *as* innocent. 29 But since I am ungodly, why have I not died? 30 For if I should wash myself with snow, and purge myself with pure hands, 31 thou hadst thoroughly plunged me in filth, and my garment had abhorred me. 32 For thou art not man like me, with whom I could contend, that we might come together to judgment. 33 Would that *he* our mediator were *present*, and a reprover, and one who should hear *the cause* between both. 34 Let him remove *his* rod from me, and let not his fear terrify me: 35 so shall I not be afraid, but I will speak: for I am not thus conscious *of guilt*.

Job.10 1 Weary in my soul, I will pour my words with groans upon him: I will speak being straitened in the bitterness of my soul. 2 And I will say to the Lord, Do not teach me to be impious; and wherefore hast thou thus judged me? 3 Is it good before thee if I be unrighteous? for thou hast disowned the work of thy hands, and attended to the counsel of the ungodly. 4 Or dost thou see as a mortal sees? or wilt thou look as a man sees? 5 Or is thy life human, or thy years *the years* of a man, 6 that thou hast enquired into mine iniquity, and searched out my sins? 7 For thou knowest that I have not committed iniquity: but who is he that can deliver out of thy hands? 8 Thy hands have formed me and made me; afterwards thou didst change *thy mind*,

and smite me. 9 Remember that thou hast made me *as* clay, and thou dost turn me again to earth. 10 Hast thou not poured me out like milk, and curdled me like cheese? 11 And thou didst clothe me with skin and flesh, and frame me with bones and sinews. 12 And thou didst bestow upon me life and mercy, and thy oversight has preserved my spirit. 13 Having these things in thyself, I know that thou canst do all things; for nothing is impossible with thee. 14 And if I should sin, thou watchest me; and thou hast not cleared me from iniquity. 15 Or if I should be ungodly, woe is me: and if I should be righteous, I cannot lift myself up, for I am full of dishonour. 16 For I am hunted like a lion for slaughter; for again thou hast changed and art terribly destroying me; 17 renewing against me my torture: and thou hast dealt with me in great anger, and thou hast brought trials upon me. 18 Why then didst thou bring me out of the womb? and why did I not die, and no eye see me, 19 and I become as if I had not been? for why was I not carried from the womb to the grave? 20 Is not the time of my life short? suffer me to rest a little, 21 before I go whence I shall not return, to a land of darkness and gloominess; 22 to a land of perpetual darkness, where there is no light, neither *can any one* see the life of mortals.

Job.11 1 Then Sophar the Minaean answered and said, 2 He that speaks much, should also hear on the other side: or does the fluent speaker think himself to be righteous? blessed *is* the short lived offspring of woman. 3 Be not a speaker of many words; for is there none to answer thee? 4 For say not, I am pure in my works, and blameless before him. 5 But oh that the Lord would speak to thee, and open his lips to thee! 6 Then shall he declare to thee the power of wisdom; for it shall be double of that which is with thee: and then shalt thou know, that a just recompence of thy sins has come to thee from the Lord. 7 Wilt thou find out the traces of the Lord? or hast thou come to the end *of that* which the Almighty has made? 8 Heaven *is* high; and what wilt thou do? and there are deeper things than those in hell; what dost thou know? 9 Or longer than the measure of the earth, or the breadth of the sea. 10 And if he should overthrow all things, who will say to him, What hast thou done? 11 For he knows the works of transgressors; and when he sees wickedness, he will not overlook *it*. 12 But man vainly buoys himself up with words; and a mortal born of woman *is* like an ass in the desert. 13 For if thou hast made thine heart pure, and liftest up *thine* hands towards him; 14 if there is any iniquity in thy hands, put if far from thee, and let not unrighteousness lodge in thy habitation. 15 For thus shall thy countenance shine again, as pure water; and thou shalt divest thyself of uncleanness, and shalt not fear. 16 And thou shalt forget trouble, as a wave that has passed by; and thou shalt not be scared. 17 And thy prayer *shall be* as the morning star, and life shall arise to thee *as* from the noonday. 18 And thou shalt be confident, because thou hast hope; and peace shall dawn to thee from out of anxiety and care. 19 For thou shalt be at ease, and there shall be no one to fight against thee; and many shall charge, and make supplication to thee. 20 But safety shall fail them; for their hope is destruction, and the eyes of the ungodly shall waste away.

Job.12 1 And Job answered and said, 2 So then ye *alone* are men, and wisdom shall die with you? 3 *But* I also have a heart as well as you. 4 For a righteous and blameless man has become a subject for mockery. 5 For it had been ordained that he should fall under others at the appointed time, and that his houses should be spoiled by transgressors: let not however any one trust that, being evil, he shall be *held* guiltless, 6 even as many as provoke the Lord, as if there were indeed to be no inquisition *made* of them. 7 But ask now the beasts, if they may speak to thee; and the birds of the air, if they may declare to thee. 8 Tell the earth, if it may speak to thee: and the fishes of the sea shall explain to thee. 9 Who then has not known in all these things, that the hand of the Lord has made them? 10 Whereas the life of all living things is in his hand, and the breath of every man. 11 For the ear tries words, and the palate tastes meats. 12 In length of time is wisdom, and in long life knowledge. 13 With him are wisdom and power, with him counsel and understanding. 14 If he should cast down, who will build up? if he should shut up against man, who shall open? 15 If he should withhold the water, he will dry the earth: and if he should let it loose, he overthrows and destroys it. 16 With him are strength and power: he has knowledge and understanding. 17 He leads counsellors away captive, and maddens the judges of the earth. 18 He seats kings upon thrones, and girds their loins with a girdle. 19 He sends away priests into captivity, and overthrows the mighty ones of the earth. 20 He changes the lips of the trusty, and he knows the understanding of the elders. 21 He pours dishonour upon princes, and heals the lowly. 22 Revealing deep things out of darkness: and he has brought into light the shadow of death. 23 Causing the nations to wander, and destroying them: overthrowing the nations, and leading them *away.* 24 Perplexing the minds of the princes of the earth: and he causes them to wander in a way, they have not known, *saying,* 25 Let them grope *in* darkness, and *let there be* no light, and let them wander as a drunken man.

Job.13 1 Behold, mine eye has seen these things, and mine ear has heard *them.* 2 And I know all that ye too know; and I have not less understanding than you. 3 Nevertheless I will speak to the Lord, and I will reason before him, if he will. 4 But ye are all bad physicians, and healers of diseases. 5 But would that ye were silent, and it would be wisdom to you in the end. 6 But hear ye the reasoning of my mouth, and attend to the judgment of my lips. 7 Do ye not speak before the Lord, and utter deceit before him? 8 Or will ye draw back? nay do, ye yourselves be judges. 9 For *it were* well if he would thoroughly search you: for though doing all things *in your power* ye should attach yourselves to him, 10 he will not reprove you at all the less: but if moreover ye should secretly respect persons, 11 shall not his whirlpool sweep you round, and terror from him fall upon you? 12 And your glorying shall prove in the end to you like ashes, and your body *like a body* of clay. 13 Be silent, that I may speak, and cease from *mine* anger, 14 while I may take my flesh in my teeth, and put my life in my hand. 15 Though the Mighty One should lay hand upon me, forasmuch as he has begun, verily I will speak, and plead before him. 16 And this shall turn to me for salvation; for fraud shall have no entrance before him. 17 Hear, hear ye my words, for I will declare in your hearing. 18 Behold, I am near my judgment: I know that I shall appear evidently just. 19 For who is he that shall plead with me, that I should now be silent, and expire? 20 But grant me two things: then I will not hide myself from thy face. 21 Withhold *thine* hand from me: and let not thy fear terrify me. 22 Then shalt thou call, and I will hearken to thee: or thou shalt speak, and I will give thee an answer. 23 How many are my sins and my transgressions? teach me what they are. 24 Wherefore hidest thou thyself from me, and deemest me thine enemy? 25 Wilt thou be startled *at me,* as *at* a leaf shaken by the wind? or wilt thou set thyself against me as against grass borne upon the breeze? 26 for thou hast written evil things against me, and thou hast compassed me with the sins of my youth. 27 And thou hast placed my foot in the stocks; and thou hast watched all my works, and hast penetrated my heels. 28 *I am as* that which waxes old like a bottle, or like a moth-eaten garment.

Job.14 1 For a mortal born of a woman *is* short lived, and full of wrath. 2 Or he falls like a flower that has bloomed; and he departs like a shadow, and cannot continue. 3 Hast thou not taken account even of him, and caused him to enter into judgment before thee? 4 For who shall be pure from uncleanness? not even one; 5 if even his life should be *but* one day upon the earth: and his months are numbered by him: thou hast appointed *him* for a time, and he shall by no means exceed *it.* 6 Depart from him, that he may be quiet, and take pleasure in his life, *though* as a hireling. 7 For there is hope for a tree, even if it should be cut down, *that* it shall blossom again, and its branch shall not fail. 8 For though its root should grow old in the earth, and its stem die in the rock; 9 it will blossom from the scent of water, and will produce a crop, as one newly planted. 10 But a man that has died is utterly gone; and when a mortal has fallen, he is no more. 11 For the sea wastes in *length of* time, and a river fails and is dried up. 12 And man that has lain down *in death* shall certainly not rise again till the heaven be dissolved, and they shall not awake from their sleep. 13 For oh that thou hadst kept me in the grave, and hadst hidden me until thy wrath should cease, and thou shouldest set me a time in which thou wouldest remember me! 14 For if a man should die, shall he live *again*, having accomplished the days of his life? I will wait till I exist again? 15 Then shalt thou call, and I will hearken to thee: but do not thou reject the work of thine hands. 16 But thou hast numbered my devices: and not one of my sins shall escape thee? 17 An thou hast sealed up my transgressions in a bag, and marked if I have been guilty of any transgression unawares. 18 And verily a mountain falling will utterly be destroyed, and a rock shall be worn out of its place. 19 The waters wear the stones, and waters falling headlong *overflow* a heap of the earth: and thou destroyest the hope of man. 20 Thou drivest him to an end, and he is gone: thou settest thy face against him, and sendest him away; 21 and though his children be multiplied, he knows *it* not; and if they be few, he is not aware. 22 But his flesh is in pain, and his soul mourns.

Job.15 1 Then Eliphaz the Thaemanite answered and said, 2 Will a wise man give for answer a *mere* breath of wisdom? and does he fill up the pain of his belly, 3 reasoning with improper sayings, and with words wherein is no profit? 4 Hast not thou moreover cast off fear, and accomplished such words before the Lord? 5 Thou art guilty by the words of thy mouth, neither hast thou discerned the words of the mighty. 6 Let thine own mouth, and not me, reprove thee: and thy lips shall testify against thee. 7 What! art thou the first man that was born? or wert thou established before the hills? 8 Or hast thou heard the ordinance of the Lord? or has God used thee as *his* counsellor? and has wisdom come *only* to thee? 9 For what knowest thou, that, we know not? or what understandest thou, which we do not also? 10 Truly among us *are* both the old and very aged man, more advanced in days than thy father. 11 Thou hast been scourged for *but* few of thy sins: thou hast spoken haughtily *and* extravagantly. 12 What has thine heart dared? or what have thine eyes *aimed at*, 13 that thou hast vented *thy* rage before the Lord, and delivered such words from *thy* mouth? 14 For who, being a mortal, *is such* that he shall be blameless? or, *who that is* born of a woman, that he should be just? 15 Forasmuch as he trusts not his saints; and the heaven is not pure before him. 16 Alas then, abominable and unclean is man, drinking unrighteousness as a draught. 17 But I will tell thee, hearken to me; I will tell thee now what I have seen; 18 things wise men say, and their fathers have not hidden. 19 To them alone the earth was given, and no stranger came upon them. 20 All the life of the ungodly *is spent* in care, and the years granted to the oppressor are numbered. 21 And his terror is in his ears: just when he seems to be at peace, his overthrow will come. 22 Let him not trust that he shall return from darkness, for he has been already made over to the power of the sword. 23 And he has been appointed to be food for vultures; and he knows within himself that he is doomed to be a carcass: and a dark day shall carry him away as with a whirlwind. 24 Distress also and anguish shall come upon him: he shall fall as a captain in the first rank. 25 For he has lifted his hands against the Lord, and he has hardened his neck against the Almighty Lord. 26 And he has run against him with insolence, on the thickness of the back of his shield. 27 For he has covered his face with his fat, and made layers of fat upon his thighs. 28 And let him lodge in desolate cities, and enter into houses without inhabitant: and what they have prepared, others shall carry away. 29 Neither shall he at all grow rich, nor shall his substance remain: he shall not cast a shadow upon the earth. 30 Neither shall he in any wise escape the darkness: let the wind blast his blossom, and let his flower fall off. 31 Let him not think that he shall endure; for his end shall be vanity. 32 His harvest shall perish before the time, and his branch shall not flourish. 33 And let him be gathered as the unripe grape before the time, and let him fall as the blossom of the olive. 34 For death is the witness of an ungodly man, and fire shall burn the houses of them that receive gifts. 35 And

he shall conceive sorrows, and his end shall be vanity, and his belly shall bear deceit.

Job.16 1 But Job answered and said, 2 I have heard many such things: poor comforters are ye all. 3 What! is there any reason in vain words? or what will hinder thee from answering? 4 I also will speak as ye *do*: if indeed your soul were in my *soul's* stead, 5 then would I insult you with words, and I would shake my head at you. 6 And would there were strength in my mouth, and I would not spare the movement of my lips. 7 For if I should speak, I shall not feel the pain of my wound: and if I should be silent, how shall I be wounded the less? 8 But now he has made me weary, and a worn-out fool; and thou hast laid hold of me. 9 My falsehood has become a testimony, and has risen up against me: it has confronted me to my face. 10 In his anger he has cast me down; he has gnashed his teeth upon me: the weapons of his robbershavefallenuponme. 11 He has attacked me with the keen glances of his eyes; with his sharp *spear* he has smitten me *down* upon my knees; and they have run upon me with one accord. 12 For the Lord has delivered me into the hands of unrighteous men, and thrown me upon the ungodly. 13 When I was at peace he distracted me: he took me by the hair of the head, and plucked it out: he set me up as a mark. 14 They surrounded me with spears, aiming at my reins: without sparing *me* they poured out my gall upon the ground. 15 They overthrew me with fall upon fall: they ran upon me in *their* might. 16 They sewed sackcloth upon my skin, and my strength has been spent on the ground. 17 My belly has been parched with wailing, and darkness is on my eyelids. 18 Yet there was no injustice in my hands, and my prayer is pure. 19 Earth, cover not over the blood of my flesh, and let my cry have no place. 20 And now, behold, my witness is in heaven, and my advocate is on high. 21 Let my supplication come to the Lord, and let mine eye weep before him. 22 Oh that a man might plead before the Lord, even *as* the son of man with his neighbor! 23 But my years are numbered and *their end* come, and I shall go by the way by which I shall not return.

Job.17 1 I perish, carried away by the wind, and I seek for burial, and obtain *it* not. 2 Weary I intreat; and what have I done? and strangers have stolen my goods. 3 Who is this? let him join hands with me. 4 For thou hast hid their heart from wisdom; therefore thou shalt not exalt them. 5 He shall promise mischief to *his* companions: but *their* eyes have failed for *their* children. 6 But thou has made me a byword amount the nations, and I am become a scorn to them. 7 For my eyes are dimmed through pain; I have been grievously beset by all. 8 Wonder has seized true men upon this; and let the just rise up against the transgressor. 9 But let the faithful hold on his own way, and let him that is pure of hands take courage. 10 Howbeit, do ye all strengthen *yourselves* and come now, for I do not find truth in you. 11 My days have passed in groaning, and my heart-strings are broken. 12 I have turned the night into day: the light is short because of darkness. 13 For if I remain, Hades is my habitation: and my bed has been made in darkness. 14 I have called upon death to be my father, and corruption *to be* my mother and sister. 15 Where then is yet my hope? or *where* shall I see my good? 16 Will they go down with me to Hades, or shall we go down together to the tomb?

Job.18 1 Then Baldad the Sauchite answered and said, 2 How long wilt thou continue? forbear, that we also may speak. 3 For wherefore have we been silent before thee like brutes? 4 Anger has possessed thee: for what if thou shouldest die; would *the earth* under heaven be desolate? or shall the mountains be overthrown from their foundations? 5 But the light of the ungodly shall be quenched, and their flame shall not go up. 6 His light *shall be* darkness in *his* habitation, and his lamp shall be put out with him. 7 Let the meanest of men spoil his goods, and let his counsel deceive *him*. 8 His foot also has been caught in a snare, *and* let it be entangled in a net. 9 And let snares come upon him: he shall strengthen those that thirst for his destruction. 10 His snare is hid in the earth, and that which shall take him is by the path. 11 Let pains destroy him round about, and let many *enemies* come about him, 12 *vex him* with distressing hunger: and a signal destruction has been prepared for him. 13 Let the soles of his feet be devoured: and death shall consume his beauty. 14 And let health be utterly banished from his tabernacle, and let distress seize upon him with a charge from the king. 15 It shall dwell in his tabernacle in his night: his excellency shall be sown with brimstone. 16 His roots shall be dried up from beneath, and his crop shall fall away from above. 17 Let his memorial perish out of the earth, and his name shall be publicly cast out. 18 Let *one* drive him from light into darkness. 19 He shall not be known among his people, nor his house preserved on the earth. 20 But strangers shall dwell in his possessions: the last groaned for him, and wonder seized the first. 21 These are the houses of the unrighteous, and this is the place of them that know not the Lord.

Job.19 1 Then Job answered and said, 2 How long will ye vex my soul, and destroy me with words? only know that the Lord has dealt with me thus. 3 Ye speak against me; ye do not feel for me, but bear hard upon me. 4 Yea verily, I have erred in truth, (but the error abides with myself) in having spoken words which it was not right *to speak*; and my words err, and are unreasonable. 5 But alas! for ye magnify yourselves against me, and insult me with reproach. 6 Know then that it is the Lord that has troubled *me*, and has raised his bulwark against me. 7 Behold, I laugh at reproach; I will not speak: *or* I will cry out, but *there is* nowhere judgment. 8 I am fenced round about, and can by no means escape: he has set darkness before my face. 9 And he has stripped me of my glory, and has taken the crown from my head. 10 He has torn me around about, and I am gone: and he has cut off my hope like a tree. 11 And he has dreadfully handled me in anger, and has counted me for an enemy. 12 His troops also came upon me with one accord, liars in wait compassed my ways. 13 My brethren have stood aloof from me; they have recognized strangers *rather* than me: and my friends have become pitiless. 14 My nearest of kin have not acknowledged me, and they that knew my name, have forgotten me. 15 *As for* my household, and my maid-servants, I was a stranger before them. 16 I called my servant, and he hearkened not; and my mouth intreated *him*.

17 And I besought my wife, and earnestly intreated the sons of my concubines. 18 But they rejected me for ever; whenever I rise up, they speak against me. 19 They that saw me abhorred me: the very persons whom I had loved, rose up against me. 20 My flesh is corrupt under my skin, and my bones are held in *my* teeth. 21 Pity me, pity me, O friends; for it is the hand of the Lord that has touched me. 22 Wherefore do ye persecute me as also the Lord *does*, and are not satisfied with my flesh? 23 For oh that my words were written, and that they were recorded in a book forever, 24 with an iron pen and lead, or graven in the rocks! 25 For I know that he is eternal who is about to deliver me, 26 *and* to raise up upon the earth my skin that endures these *sufferings*: for these things have been accomplished to me of the Lord; 27 which I am conscious of in myself, which mine eye has seen, and not another, but all have been fulfilled to me in *my* bosom. 28 But if ye shall also say, What shall we say before him, and *so* find the root of the matter in him? 29 Do ye also beware of deceit: for wrath will come upon transgressors; and then shall they know where their substance is.

Job.20 1 Then Sophar the Minaean answered and said, 2 I did not suppose that thou wouldest answer thus: neither do ye understand more than I. 3 I will hear my shameful reproach; and the spirit of my understanding answers me. 4 Hast thou *not* known these things of old, from the time that man was set upon the earth? 5 But the mirth of the ungodly is a signal downfall, and the joy of transgressors is destruction: 6 although his gifts should go up to heaven, and his sacrifice reach the clouds. 7 For when he shall seem to be now established, then he shall utterly perish: and they that knew him shall say, Where is he? 8 Like a dream that has fled away, he shall not be found; and he has fled like a vision of the night. 9 The eye has looked upon him, but shall not *see him* again; and his place shall no longer perceive him. 10 Let *his* inferiors destroy his children, and let his hands kindle the fire of sorrow. 11 His bones have been filled with *vigour of* his youth, and it shall lie down with him in the dust. 12 Though evil be sweet in his mouth, *though* he will hide it under his tongue; 13 though he will not spare it, and will not leave it, but will keep it in the midst of his throat: 14 yet he shall not at all be able to help himself; the gall of an asp is in his belly. 15 *His* wealth unjustly collected shall be vomited up; a messenger *of wrath* shall drag him out of his house. 16 And let him suck the poison of serpents, and let the serpent's tongue slay him. 17 Let him not see the milk of the pastures, nor the supplies of honey and butter. 18 He has laboured unprofitably and in vain, *for* wealth of which he shall not taste: *it is* as a lean thing, unfit for food, which he cannot swallow. 19 For he has broken down the houses of many mighty men: and he has plundered an habitation, though he built *it* not. 20 There is no security to his possessions; he shall not be saved by his desire. 21 There is nothing remaining of his provisions; therefore his goods shall not flourish. 22 But when he shall seem to be just satisfied, he shall be straitened; and all distress shall come upon him. 23 If by any means he would fill his belly, let *God* send upon him the fury of wrath; let him bring a torrent of pains upon him. 24 And he shall by no means escape from the power of the sword; let the brazen bow wound him. 25 And let the arrow pierce through his body; and let the stars be against his dwelling-place: let terrors come upon him. 26 And let all darkness wait for him: a fire that burns not out shall consume him; and let a stranger plague his house. 27 And let the heaven reveal his iniquities, and the earth rise up against him. 28 Let destruction bring his house to an end; let a day of wrath come upon him. 29 This is the portion of an ungodly man from the Lord, and the possession of his goods *appointed him* by the all-seeing *God.*

Job.21 1 But Job answered and said, 2 Hear ye, hear ye my words, that I may not have this consolation from you. 3 Raise me, and I will speak; then ye shall not laugh me to scorn. 4 What! is my reproof of man? and why should I not be angry? 5 Look upon me, and wonder, laying your hand upon your cheek. 6 For even when I remember, I am alarmed, and pains seize my flesh. 7 Wherefore do the ungodly live, and grow old even in wealth? 8 Their seed is according to *their* desire, and their children are in *their* sight. 9 Their houses are prosperous, neither *have they* any where *cause for* fear, neither is there a scourge from the Lord upon them. 10 Their cow does not cast her calf, and their *beast* with young is safe, and does not miscarry. 11 And they remain as an unfailing flock, and their children play before *them,* taking up the psaltery and harp; 12 and they rejoice at the voice of a song. 13 And they spend their days in wealth, and fall asleep in the rest of the grave. 14 Yet *such a man* says to the Lord, Depart from me; I desire not to know thy ways. 15 What is the Mighty One, that we should serve him? and what profit is there that we should approach him? 16 For their good things were in *their* hands, but he regards not the works of the ungodly. 17 Nevertheless, the lamp of the ungodly also shall be put out, and destruction shall come upon them, and pangs of vengeance shall seize them. 18 And they shall be as chaff before the wind, or as dust which the storm has taken up. 19 Let his substance fail *to supply* his children: *God* shall recompense him, and he shall know it. 20 Let his eyes see his own destruction, and let him not be saved by the Lord. 21 For his desire is in his house with him, and the number of his months has been suddenly cut off. 22 Is it not the Lord who teaches understanding and knowledge? and does not he judge murders? 23 One shall die in his perfect strength, and wholly at ease and prosperous; 24 and his inwards are full of fat, and his marrow is diffused *throughout him.* 25 And another dies in bitterness of soul, not eating any good thing. 26 But they lie down in the earth together, and corruption covers them. 27 So I know you, that ye presumptuously attack me: 28 so that ye will say, Where is the house of the prince? and where is the covering of the tabernacles of the ungodly? 29 Ask those that go by the way, and do not disown their tokens. 30 For the wicked hastens to the day of destruction: they shall be led away for the day of his vengeance. 31 Who will tell him his way to his face, whereas he has done *it?* who shall recompense him? 32 And he has been led away to the tombs, and he has watched over the heaps. 33 The stones of the valley have been sweet to him, and every man shall

depart after him, and *there are* innumerable *ones* before him. 34 How then do ye comfort me in vain? whereas I have no rest from your molestation.

Job.22 1 Then Eliphaz the Thaemanite answered and said, 2 Is it not the Lord that teaches understanding and knowledge? 3 For what matters it to the Lord, if thou wert blameless in *thy* works? or is it profitable that thou shouldest perfect thy way? 4 Wilt thou maintain and plead thine own cause? and will he enter into judgment with thee? 5 Is not thy wickedness abundant, and thy sins innumerable? 6 And thou hast taken security of thy brethren for nothing, and hast taken away the clothing of the naked. 7 Neither hast thou given water to the thirsty to drink, but hast taken away the morsel of the hungry. 8 And thou hast accepted the persons of some; and thou hast established those *that were already settled* on the earth. 9 But thou hast sent widows away empty, and has afflicted orphans. 10 Therefore snares have compassed thee, and disastrous war has troubled thee. 11 The light has proved darkness to thee, and water has covered thee on thy lying down. 12 Does not he that dwells in the high places observe? and has he not brought down the proud? 13 And thou has said, What does the Mighty One know? does he judge in the dark? 14 A cloud is his hiding-place, and he shall not be seen; and he passes through the circle of heaven. 15 Wilt thou *not* mark the old way, which righteous men have trodden? 16 who were seized before their time: their foundations *are as* an overflowing stream. 17 Who say, What will the Lord do to us? or what will the Almighty bring upon us? 18 Yet he filled their houses with good things: but the counsel for the wicked is far from him. 19 The righteous have seen *it,* and laughed, and the blameless one has derided *them.* 20 Verily their substance has been utterly destroyed, and the fire shall devour what is left of their *property.* 21 Be firm, I pray thee, if thou canst endure; then thy fruit shall prosper. 22 And receive a declaration from his mouth, and lay up his words in thine heart. 23 And if thou shalt turn and humble thyself before the Lord, thou hast *thus* removed unrighteousness far from thy habitation. 24 Thou shalt lay up for thyself *treasure* in a heap on the rock; and Sophir *shall be* as the rock of the torrent. 25 So the Almighty shall be thy helper from enemies, and he shall bring thee forth pure as silver that has been tried by fire. 26 Then shalt thou have boldness before the Lord, looking up cheerfully to heaven. 27 And he shall hear thee when thou prayest to him, and he shall grant thee *power* to pay thy vows. 28 And he shall establish to thee again a habitation of righteousness and there shall be light upon thy paths. 29 Because thou hast humbled thyself; and thou shalt say, *Man* has behaved proudly, but he shall save him that is of lowly eyes. 30 He shall deliver the innocent, and do thou save thyself by thy pure hands.

Job.23 1 Then Job answered and said, 2 Yea, I know that pleading is out of my reach; and his hand has been made heavy upon my groaning. 3 Who would then know that I might find him, and come to an end *of the matter?* 4 And I would plead my own cause, and he would fill my mouth with arguments. 5 And I would know the remedies which he would speak to me, and I would perceive what he would tell me. 6 Though he should come on me in *his* great strength, then he would not threaten me; 7 for truth and reproof are from him; and he would bring forth my judgment to an end. 8 For if I shall go first, and exist no longer, still what do I know *concerning* the latter end? 9 When he wrought on the left hand, then I observed *it* not: his right hand shall encompass me but I shall not see *it*. 10 For he knows already my way; and he has tried me as gold. 11 And I will go forth according to his commandments, for I have kept his ways; and I shall not turn aside from his commandments, 12 neither shall I transgress; but I have hid his words in my bosom. 13 And if too he has thus judged, who is he that has contradicted, for he has both willed *a thing* and done it. 14 For he performs what is appointed for me; and many such things are with him. 15 Therefore am I troubled at him; and when I was reproved, I thought of him. Therefore let me take good heed before him: I will consider, and be afraid of him. 16 But the Lord has softened my heart, and the Almighty has troubled me. 17 For I knew not that darkness would come upon me, and thick darkness has covered *me* before my face.

Job.24

1 But why have the seasons been hidden from the Lord, 2 while the ungodly have passed over the bound, carrying off the flock with the shepherd? 3 They have led away, the ass of the fatherless, and taken the widow's ox for a pledge. 4 They have turned aside the weak from the right way: and the meek of the earth have hidden themselves together. 5 And they have departed like asses in the field, having gone forth on my account according to their own order: his bread is sweet to *his* little ones. 6 They have reaped a field that was not their own before the time: the poor have laboured in the vineyards of the ungodly without pay and without food. 7 They have caused many naked to sleep without clothes, and they have taken away the covering of their body. 8 They are wet with the drops of the mountains: they have embraced the rock, because they had no shelter. 9 They have snatched the fatherless from the breast, and have afflicted the outcast. 10 And they have wrongfully caused *others* to sleep without clothing, and taken away the morsel of the hungry. 11 They have unrighteously laid wait in narrow places, and have not known the righteous way. 12 Who have cast forth *the* poor from the city and their own houses, and the soul of the children has groaned aloud. 13 Why then has he not visited these? forasmuch as they were upon the earth, and took no notice, and they knew not the way of righteousness, neither have they walked in their *appointed* paths? 14 But having known their works, he delivered them into darkness: and in the night one will be as a thief: 15 and the eye of the adulterer has watched *for* the darkness, saying, Eye shall not perceive me, and he puts a covering on his face. 16 In darkness he digs through houses: by day they conceal themselves securely: they know not the light. 17 For the morning is to them all *as* the shadow of death, for *each* will be conscious of the terror of the shadow of death. 18 He is swift on the face of the water: let his portion be cursed on the earth; and let their plants be laid bare. 19 *Let them be* withered upon the

earth; for they have plundered the sheaves of the fatherless. 20 Then is his sin brought to remembrance, and he vanishes like a vapour of dew: but let what he has done be recompensed to him, and let every unrighteous one be crushed like rotten wood. 21 For he has not treated the barren woman well, and has had no pity on a feeble woman. 22 And in wrath he has overthrown the helpless: therefore when he has arisen, *a man* will not feel secure of his own life. 23 When he has fallen sick, let him not hope to recover: but let him perish by disease. 24 For his exaltation has hurt many; but he has withered as mallows in the heat, or as an ear of corn falling off of itself from the stalk. 25 But if not, who is he that says I speak falsely, and will make my words of no account?

Job.25

1 Then Baldad the Sauchite answered and said, 2 What beginning or fear is his—even he that makes all things in the highest? 3 For let none think that there is a respite for robbers: and upon whom will there not come a snare from him? 4 For how shall a mortal be just before the Lord? or who that is born of a woman shall purify himself? 5 If he gives an order to the moon, then it shines not; and the stars are not pure before him. 6 But alas! man is corruption, and the son of man a worm.

Job.26

1 But Job answered and said, 2 To whom dost thou attach thyself, or whom art thou going to assist? is it not he that *has* much strength, and *he* who has a strong arm? 3 To whom hast thou given counsel? is it not to him who has all wisdom? whom wilt thou follow? is it not one who has the greatest power? 4 To whom hast thou uttered words? and whose breath is it that has come forth from thee? 5 Shall giants be born from under the water and the inhabitants thereof? 6 Hell is naked before him, and destruction has no covering. 7 He stretches out the north wind upon nothing, and he upon nothing hangs the earth; 8 binding water in his clouds, and the cloud is not rent under it. 9 He keeps back the face of his throne, stretching out his cloud upon it. 10 He has encompassed the face of the water by an appointed ordinance, until the end of light and darkness. 11 The pillars of heaven are prostrate and astonished at his rebuke. 12 He has calmed the sea with *his* might, and by *his* wisdom the whale has been overthrown. 13 And the barriers of heaven fear him, and by a command he has slain the apostate dragon. 14 Behold, these are parts of his way; and we will hearken to him at the least intimation of his word: but the strength of his thunder who knows, when he shall employ *it*?

Job.27

1 And Job further continued and said in his parable, 2 *As* God lives, who has thus judge me; and the Almighty, who has embittered my soul; 3 verily, while my breath is yet in *me*, and the breath of God which remains to me is in my nostrils, 4 my lips shall not speak evil words, neither shall my soul meditate unrighteous thoughts. 5 Far be it from me that I should justify you till I die; for I will not let go my innocence, 6 but keeping fast to *my* righteousness I will by no means let it go: for I am not conscious to myself of having done any thing amiss. 7 Nay rather, but let mine enemies be as the overthrow of the ungodly, and they that

rise up against me, as the destruction of transgressors. 8 For what is the hope of the ungodly, that he holds to it? will he indeed trust in the Lord *and* be saved? 9 Will God hear his prayer? or, when distress has come upon him, 10 has he any confidence before him? or will *God* hear him as he calls upon him? 11 Yet now I will tell you what is in the hand of the Lord: I will not lie concerning the things which are with the Almighty. 12 Behold, ye all know that ye are adding vanity to vanity. 13 This is the portion of an ungodly man from the Lord, and the possession of oppressors shall come upon them from the Almighty. 14 And if their children be many, they shall be for slaughter: and if they grow up, they shall beg. 15 And they that survive of him shall utterly perish, and no one shall pity their widows. 16 Even if he should gather silver as earth, and prepare gold as clay; 17 All these things shall the righteous gain, and the truehearted shall possess his wealth. 18 And his house is gone like moths, and like a spider's web. 19 The rich man shall lie down, and shall not continue: he has opened his eyes, and he is not. 20 Pains have come upon him as water, and darkness has carried him away by night. 21 And a burning wind shall catch him, and he shall depart, and it shall utterly drive him out of his place. 22 And *God* shall cast *trouble* upon him, and not spare: he would fain flee out of his hand. 23 He shall cause *men* to clap their hands against them, and shall hiss him out of his place.

Job.28 1 For there is a place for the silver, whence it comes, and a place for the gold, whence it is refined. 2 For iron comes out of the earth, and brass is hewn out like stone. 3 He has set a bound to darkness, and he searches out every limit: a stone *is* darkness, and the shadow of death. 4 There is a cutting off the torrent by reason of dust: so they that forget the right way are weakened; they are removed from *among* men. 5 *As for* the earth, out of it shall come bread: under it has been turned up as it were fire. 6 Her stones are the place of the sapphire: and *her* dust *supplies* man with gold. 7 *There is* a path, the fowl has not known it, neither has the eye of the vulture seen it: 8 neither have the sons of the proud trodden it, a lion has not passed upon it. 9 He has stretched forth his hand on the sharp *rock*, and turned up mountains by the roots: 10 and he has interrupted the whirlpools of rivers, and mine eye has seen every precious thing. 11 And he has laid bare the depths of rivers, and has brought his power to light. 12 But whence has wisdom been discovered? and what is the place of knowledge? 13 A mortal has not known its way, neither indeed has it been discovered among men. 14 The depth said, It is not in me: and the sea said, It is not with me. 15 One shall not give fine gold instead of it, neither shall silver be weighed in exchange for it. 16 Neither shall it be compared with gold of Sophir, with the precious onyx and sapphire. 17 Gold and crystal shall not be equalled to it, neither shall vessels of gold be its exchange. 18 Coral and fine pearl shall not be mentioned: but do thou esteem wisdom above the most precious things. 19 The topaz of Ethiopia shall not be equalled to it; it shall not be compared with pure gold. 20 Whence then is wisdom found? and of what kind is the place of understanding? 21 It has escaped the notice of every

man, and has been hidden from the birds of the sky. 22 Destruction and Death said, We have heard the report of it. 23 God has well ordered the way of it, and he knows the place of it. 24 For he surveys the whole *earth* under heaven, knowing the things in the earth: 25 all that he has made; the weight of the winds, the measures of the water. 26 When he made *them*, thus he saw and numbered them, and made a way for the pealing of the thunder. 27 Then he saw it, and declared it: he prepared it *and* traced it out. 28 And he said to man, Behold, godliness is wisdom: and to abstain from evil is understanding.

Job.29 1 And Job continued and said in his parable, 2 Oh that I were as in months past, wherein God preserved me! 3 As when his lamp shone over my head; when by his light I walked through darkness. 4 *As* when I steadfastly pursued my ways, when God took care of my house. 5 When I was very fruitful, and my children were about me; 6 when my ways were moistened with butter, and the mountains flowed for me with milk. 7 When I went forth early in the city, and the seat was placed for me in the streets. 8 The young men saw me, and hid themselves: and all the old men stood up. 9 And the great men ceased speaking, and laid their finger on their mouth. 10 And they that heard *me* blessed me, and their tongue clave to their throat. 11 For the ear heard, and blessed me; and the eye saw me, and turned aside. 12 For I saved the poor out of the hand of the oppressor, and helped the fatherless who had no helper. 13 Let the blessing of the perishing one come upon me; yea, the mouth of the widow has blessed me. 14 Also I put on righteousness, and clothed myself with judgment like a mantle. 15 I was the eye of the blind, and the foot of the lame. 16 I was the father of the helpless; and I searched out the cause which I knew not. 17 And I broke the jaw-teeth of the unrighteous; I plucked the spoil out of the midst of their teeth. 18 And I said, My age shall continue as the stem of a palm-tree; I shall live a long while. 19 *My* root was spread out by the water, and the dew would lodge on my crop. 20 My glory was fresh in me, and by bow prospered in his hand. 21 *Men* heard me, and gave heed, and they were silent at my counsel. 22 At my word they spoke not again, and they were very gland whenever I spoke to them. 23 As the thirsty earth expecting the rain, so they *waited for* my speech. 24 Were I to laugh on them, they would not believe *it*; and the light of my face has not failed. 25 I chose out their way, and sat chief, and dwelt as a king in the midst of warriors, as one comforting mourners.

Job.30 1 But now the youngest have laughed me to scorn, now they reprove me in *their* turn, whose fathers I set at nought; whom I did not deem worthy *to be with* my shepherd dogs. 2 Yea, why had I the strength of their hands? for them the full term *of life* was lost. 3 *One is* childless in want and famine, *such as* they that fled but lately the distress and misery of drought. 4 Who compass the salt places on the sounding *shore*, who had salt *herbs* for their food, and were dishonorable and of no repute, in want of every good thing; who also ate roots of trees by reason of great hunger. 5 Thieves have risen up against me, 6 whose houses were the caves of the rocks, who lived under the wild shrubs. 7 They will cry out among the rustling *bushes*. 8 *They are* sons of fools and vile men, *whose* name and glory *are* quenched from off the earth. 9 But now I am their music, and they have me for a by-word. 10 And they stood aloof and abhorred me, and spared not to spit in my face. 11 For he has opened his quiver and afflicted me: they also have cast off the restraint of my presence. 12 They have risen up against *me* on the right hand of *their* offspring; they have stretched out their foot, and directed against me the ways of their destruction. 13 My paths are ruined; for they have stripped off my raiment: he has shot at me with his weapons. 14 And he has pleaded against me as he will: I am overwhelmed with pains. 15 My pains return upon *me*; my hope is gone like the wind, and my safety as a cloud. 16 Even now my life shall be poured forth upon me; and days of anguish seize me. 17 And by night my bones are confounded; and my sinews are relaxed. 18 With great force *my disease* has taken hold of my garment: it has compassed me as the collar of my coat. 19 And thou hast counted me as clay; my portion in dust and ashes. 20 And I have cried to thee, but thou hearest me not: but they stood still, and observed me. 21 They attacked me also without mercy: thou hast scourged me with a strong hand. 22 And thou hast put me to grief, and hast cast me away from safety. 23 For I know that death will destroy me: for the earth is the house *appointed* for every mortal. 24 Oh then that I might lay hands upon myself, or at least ask another, and he should do this for me. 25 Yet I wept over every helpless man; I groaned when I saw a man in distress. 26 But I, when I waited for good things, behold, days of evils came the more upon me. 27 My belly boiled, and would not cease: the days of poverty prevented me. 28 I went mourning without restraint: and I have stood and cried out in the assembly. 29 I am become a brother of monsters, and a companion of ostriches. 30 And my skin has been greatly blackened, and my bones are burned with heat. 31 My harp also has been turned into mourning, and my song into my weeping.

Job.31 1 I made a covenant with mine eyes, and I will not think upon a virgin. 2 Now what portion has God given from above? and is there an inheritance *given* of the Mighty One from the highest? 3 Alas! destruction to the unrighteous, and rejection to them that do iniquity. 4 Will he not see my way, and number all my steps? 5 But if I had gone with scorners, and if too my foot has hasted to deceit: 6 (for I am weighed in a just balance, and the Lord knows my innocence:) 7 if my foot has turned aside out of the way, or if mine heart has followed mine eye, and if too I have touched gifts with my hands; 8 then let me sow, and let others eat; and let me be uprooted on the earth. 9 If my heart has gone forth after another man's wife, and if I laid wait at her doors; 10 then let my wife also please another, and let my children be brought low. 11 For the rage of anger is not to be controlled, *in the case* of defiling *another* man's wife. 12 For it is a fire burning on every side, and whomsoever it attacks, it utterly destroys. 13 And if too I despised the judgment of my servant or *my* handmaid, when they pleaded with me; 14 what then shall I do if the Lord should try me? and if also he should at all visit me,

can I make an answer? 15 Were not they too formed as I also was formed in the womb? yea, we were formed in the same womb. 16 But the helpless missed not whatever need they had, and I did not cause the eye of the widow to fail. 17 And if too I ate my morsel alone, and did not impart *of it* to the orphan; 18 (for I nourished *them* as a father from my youth and guided *them* from my mother's womb.) 19 And if too I overlooked the naked as he was perishing, and did not clothe him; 20 and if the poor did not bless me, and their shoulders were *not* warmed with the fleece of my lambs; 21 if I lifted my hand against an orphan, trusting that my strength was far superior *to his*. 22 let them my shoulder start from the blade-bone, and my arm be crushed off from the elbow. 23 For the fear of the Lord constrained me, and I cannot bear up by reason of his burden. 24 If I made gold my treasure, and if too I trusted the precious stone; 25 and if too I rejoiced when my wealth was abundant, and if too I laid my hand on innumerable *treasures*. 26 (do we not see the shining sun eclipsed, and the moon waning? for they have not *power to continue*:) 27 and if my heart was secretly deceived, and if I have laid my hand upon my mouth and kissed it: 28 let this also then be reckoned to me as the greatest iniquity: for I *should* have lied against the Lord Most High. 29 And if too I was glad at the fall of mine enemies, and mine heart said, Aha! 30 let then mine ear hear my curse, and let me be a byword among my people in my affliction. 31 And if too my handmaids have often said, Oh that we might be satisfied with his flesh; (whereas I was very kind: 32 for the stranger did not lodge without, and my door was opened to every one that came:) 33 or if too having sinned unintentionally, I hid my sin; 34 (for I did not stand in awe of a great multitude, so as not to declare boldly before them:) and if too I permitted a poor man to go out of my door with an empty bosom: 35 (Oh that I had a hearer,) and if I had not feared the hand of the Lord; and *as to* the written charge which I had against any one, 36 I would place *it* as a chaplet on my shoulders, and read it. 37 And if I did not read it and return it, having taken nothing from the debtor: 38 If at any time the land groaned against me, and if its furrows mourned together; 39 and if I ate its strength alone without price, and if I too grieved the heart of the owner of the soil, by taking *aught* from *him*. 40 then let the nettle come up to me instead of wheat, and a bramble instead of barley. And Job ceased speaking.

Job.32 1 And his three friends also ceased any longer to answer Job: for Job was righteous before them. 2 Then Elius the son of Barachiel, the Buzite, of the kindred of Ram, of the country of Ausis, was angered: and he was very angry with Job, because he justified himself before the Lord. 3 And he was also very angry with *his* three friends, because they were not able to return answers to Job, yet set him down for an ungodly man. 4 But Elius had forborne to give an answer to Job, because they were older than he. 5 And Elius saw that there was no answer in the mouth of the three men; and he was angered in his wrath. 6 And Elius the Buzite the son of Barachiel answered and said, I am younger in age, and ye are elder, wherefore I kept silence, fearing to declare to you my own knowledge. 7 And I said,

It is not time that speaks, though in many years *men* know wisdom: 8 but there is a spirit in mortals; and the inspiration of the Almighty is that which teaches. 9 The long-lived are not wise *as such*; neither do the aged know judgment. 10 Wherefore I said, Hear me, and I will tell you what I know. 11 Hearken to my words; for I will speak in your hearing, until ye shall have tried *the matter* with words: 12 and I shall understand as far as you; and, behold, there was no one of you that answered Job his words in argument, 13 lest ye should say, We have found that we have added wisdom to the Lord. 14 And ye have commissioned a man to speak such words. 15 They were afraid, they answered no longer; they gave up their speaking. 16 I waited, (for I had not spoken,) because they stood still, they answered not. 17 And Elius continued, and said, I will again speak, 18 for I am full of words, for the spirit of my belly destroys me. 19 And my belly is as a skin of sweet wine, bound up *and* ready to burst; or as a brazier's labouring bellows. 20 I will speak, that I may open my lips and relieve myself. 21 For truly I will not be awed because of man, nor indeed will I be confounded before a mortal. 22 For I know not how to respect persons: and if otherwise, even the moths would eat me.

Job.33

1 Howbeit hear, Job, my words, and hearken to my speech. 2 For behold, I have opened my mouth, and my tongue has spoken. 3 My heart *shall be found* pure by *my* words; and the understanding of my lips shall meditate purity. 4 The Divine Spirit is that which formed me, and the breath of the Almighty that which teaches me. 5 If thou canst, give me an answer: wait therefore; stand against me, and I *will stand* against thee. 6 Thou art formed out of the clay as also I: we have been formed out of the same *substance*. 7 My fear shall not terrify thee, neither shall my hand be heavy upon thee. 8 But thou hast said in mine ears, (I have heard the voice of thy words;)because thou sayest, I am pure, not having sinned; 9 I am blameless, for I have not transgressed. 10 Yet he has discovered a charge against me, and he has reckoned me as an adversary. 11 And he has put my foot in the stocks, and has watched all my ways. 12 For how sayest thou, I am righteous, yet he has not hearkened to me? for he that is above mortals is eternal. 13 But thou sayest, Why has he not heard every word of my cause? 14 For when the Lord speaks once, or a second time, 15 *sending* a dream, or in the meditation of the night; (as when a dreadful alarm happens to fall upon men, in slumberings on the bed:) 16 then opens he the understanding of men: he scares them with such fearful visions: 17 to turn a man from unrighteousness, and he delivers his body from a fall. 18 He spares also his soul from death, and *suffers* him not to fall in war. 19 And again, he chastens him with sickness on his bed, and the multitude of his bones is benumbed. 20 And he shall not be able to take any food, though his soul shall desire meat; 21 until his flesh shall be consumed, and he shall shew his bones bare. 22 His soul also draws nigh to death, and his life is in Hades. 23 Though there should be a thousand messengers of death, not one of them shall wound him: if he should purpose in his heart to turn to the Lord, and declare to man his fault, and shew his folly; 24 he will support him, that he should

not perish, and will restore his body as *fresh* plaster upon a wall; and he will fill his bones with marrow. 25 And he will make his flesh tender as that of a babe, and he will restore him among men in *his* full strength. 26 And he shall pray to the Lord, and his prayer shall be accepted of him; he shall enter with a cheerful countenance, with a full expression *of praise*: for he will render to men *their* due. 27 Even then a man shall blame himself, saying, What kind of things have I done? and he has not punished me according to the full amount of my sins. 28 Deliver my soul, that it may not go to destruction, and my life shall see the light. 29 Behold, all these things, the Mighty One works in a threefold manner with a man. 30 And he has delivered my soul from death, that my life may praise him in the light. 31 Hearken, Job, and hear me: be silent, and I will speak. 32 If thou hast words, answer me: speak, for I desire thee to be justified. 33 If not, do thou hear me: be silent, and I will teach thee.

Job.34

1 And Elius continued, and said, 2 Hear me, ye wise men; hearken, ye that have knowledge. 3 For the ear tries words, and the mouth tastes meat. 4 Let us choose judgment to ourselves: let us know amount ourselves what is right. 5 For Job has said, I am righteous: the Lord has removed my judgment. 6 And he has erred in my judgment: my wound is severe without unrighteousness *of mine*. 7 What man is as Job, drinking scorning like water? 8 *saying*, I have not sinned, nor committed ungodliness, nor had fellowship with workers of iniquity, to go with the ungodly. 9 For thou shouldest not say, There shall be no visitation of a man, whereas *there is* a visitation on him from the Lord. 10 Wherefore hear me, ye that are wise in heart: far be it from me to sin before the Lord, and to pervert righteousness before the almighty. 11 Yea, he renders to a man accordingly as each of them does, and in a man's path he will find him. 12 And thinkest thou that the Lord will do wrong, or will the Almighty who made the earth wrest judgment? 13 And who is he that made *the whole world* under heaven, and all things therein? 14 For if he would confine, and restrain his spirit with himself; 15 all flesh would die together, and every mortal would return to the earth, whence also he was formed. 16 Take heed lest he rebuke *thee*: hear this, hearken to the voice of words. 17 Behold then the one that hates iniquities, and that destroys the wicked, who is for ever just. 18 *He is* ungodly that says to a king, Thou art a transgressor, *that says* to princes, O most ungodly one. 19 *Such a one* as would not reverence the face of an honourable man, neither knows how to give honour to the great, so as that their persons should be respected. 20 But it shall turn out vanity to them, to cry and beseech a man; for they dealt unlawfully, the poor being turned aside *from their right*. 21 For he surveys the works of men, and nothing of what they do has escaped him. 22 Neither shall there be a place for the workers of iniquity to hide themselves. 23 For he will not lay upon a man more *than right*. 24 For the Lord looks down upon all men, who comprehends unsearchable things, glorious also and excellent things without number. 25 Who discovers their works, and will bring night about *upon them*, and they shall be brought low. 26 And he quite destroys the ungodly, for they are seen before him. 27 Because they

turned aside from the law of God, and did not regard his ordinances, 28 so as to bring before him the cry of the needy; for he will hear the cry of the poor. 29 And he will give quiet, and who will condemn? and he will hide his face, and who shall see him? whether *it be done* against a nation, or against a man also: 30 causing a hypocrite to be king, because of the waywardness of the people. 31 For *there is* one that says to the Mighty One, I have received *blessings*; I will not take a pledge: 32 I will see apart from myself: do thou shew me if I have done unrighteousness; I will not do *so* any more. 33 Will he take vengeance for it on thee, whereas thou wilt put *it* far *from thee*? for thou shalt choose, and not I; and what thou knowest, speak thou. 34 Because the wise in heart shall say this, and a wise man listens to my word. 35 But Job has not spoken with understanding, his words are not *uttered* with knowledge. 36 Howbeit do thou learn, Job: no longer make answer as the foolish: 37 that we add not to our sins: for iniquity will be reckoned against us, if *we* speak many words before the Lord.

Job.35 1 And Elius resumed and said, 2 What is this that thou thinkest to be according to right? who art thou that thou hast said, I am righteous before the Lord? 3 I will answer thee, and thy three friends. 4 Look up to the sky and see; and consider the clouds, how high *they are* above thee. 5 If thou hast sinned, what wilt thou do? 6 and if too thou hast transgressed much, what canst thou perform? 7 And suppose thou art righteous, what wilt thou give him? or what shall he receive of thy hand? 8 Thy ungodliness *may affect* a man who is like to thee; or thy righteousness a son of man. 9 They that are oppressed of a multitude will be ready to cry out; they will call for help because of the arm of many. 10 But none said, Where is God that made me, who appoints the night-watches; 11 who makes me to differ from the four-footed beasts of the earth, and from the birds of the sky? 12 There they shall cry, and none shall hearken, even because of the insolence of wicked men. 13 For the Lord desires not to look on error, for he is the Almighty One. 14 He beholds them that perform lawless deeds, and he will save me: and do thou plead before him, if thou canst praise him, as it is *possible* even now. 15 For he is not *now* regarding his wrath, nor has he noticed severely any trespass. 16 Yet Job vainly opens his mouth, in ignorance he multiplies words.

Job.36 1 And Elius further continued, and said, 2 Wait for me yet a little while, that I may teach thee: for there is yet speech in me. 3 Having fetched my knowledge from afar, and according to my works, 4 I will speak just things truly, and thou shalt not unjustly receive unjust words. 5 But know that the Lord will not cast off an innocent man: being mighty in strength of wisdom, 6 he will not by any means save alive the ungodly: and he will grant the judgment of the poor. 7 He will not turn away his eyes from the righteous, but *they shall be* with kings on the throne: and he will establish them in triumph, and they shall be exalted. 8 But they that are bound in fetters shall be holden in cords of poverty. 9 And he shall recount to them their works, and their transgressions, for such will act with violence. 10 But he will hearken to the righteous: and he has said that they

shall turn from unrighteousness. 11 If they should hear and serve *him*, they shall spend their days in prosperity, and their years in honour. 12 But he preserves not the ungodly; because they are not willing to know the Lord, and because when reproved they were disobedient. 13 And the hypocrites in heart will array wrath *against themselves*; they will not cry, because he has bound them. 14 Therefore let their soul die in youth, and their life be wounded by messengers *of death*. 15 Because they afflicted the weak and helpless: and he will vindicate the judgment of the meek. 16 And he has also enticed thee out of the mouth of the enemy: 17 *there is* a deep gulf *and* a rushing stream beneath it, and thy table came down full of fatness. Judgment shall not fail from the righteous; 18 but there shall be wrath upon the ungodly, by reason of the ungodliness of the bribes which they received for iniquities. 19 Let not *thy* mind willingly turn thee aside from the petition of the feeble that are in distress. 20 And draw not forth all the mighty *men* by night, so that the people should go up instead of them. 21 But take heed lest thou do that which is wrong: for of this thou has made choice because of poverty. 22 Behold, the Mighty One shall prevail by his strength: for who is powerful as he is? 23 And who is he that examines his works? or who can say, he has wrought injustice? 24 Remember that his works are great *beyond* those which men have attempted. 25 Every man has seen in himself, how many mortals are wounded. 26 Behold, the Mighty One is great, and we shall not know *him*: the number of his years is even infinite. 27 And the drops of rain are numbered by him, and shall be poured out in rain to form a cloud. 28 The ancient *heavens* shall flow, and the clouds overshadow innumerable mortals: he has fixed a time to cattle, and they know the order of rest. *Yet* by all these things thy understanding is not astonished, neither is thy mind disturbed in *thy* body. 29 And though one should understand the outspreadings of the clouds, *or* the measure of his tabernacle; 30 behold he will stretch his bow against him, and he covers the bottom of the sea. 31 For by them he will judge the nations: he will give food to him that has strength. 32 He has hidden the light in *his* hands, and given charge concerning it to the interposing *cloud*. 33 The Lord will declare concerning this *to* his friend: *but there is* a portion also for unrighteousness.

Job.37 1 At this also my heart is troubled, and moved out of its place. 2 Hear thou a report by the anger of the Lord's wrath, and a discourse shall come out of his mouth. 3 His dominion is under the whole heaven, and his light is at the extremities of the earth. 4 After him shall be a cry with a *loud* voice; he shall thunder with the voice of his excellency, yet he shall not cause men to pass away, for one shall hear his voice. 5 The Mighty One shall thunder wonderfully with his voice: for he has done great things which we knew not; 6 commanding the snow, Be thou upon the earth, and the stormy rain, and the storm of the showers of his might. 7 He seals up the hand of every man, that every man may know his own weakness. 8 And the wild beasts come in under the covert, and rest in *their* lair. 9 Troubles come on out of the secret chambers, and cold from the mountain-tops. 10 And from the breath of the Mighty One he will send frost; and he guides the water in whatever way he pleases. 11 And *if* a cloud obscures *what is* precious *to him*, his light will disperse the cloud. 12 And he will carry round the encircling *clouds* by his governance, to *perform* their works: whatsoever he shall command them, 13 this has been appointed by him on the earth, whether for correction, *or* for his land, or if he shall find him *an object* for mercy. 14 Hearken to this, O Job: stand still, and be admonished of the power of the Lord. 15 We know that god has disposed his works, having made light out of darkness. 16 And he knows the divisions of the clouds, and the signal overthrows of the ungodly. 17 But thy robe is warm, and there is quiet upon the land. 18 Wilt thou establish with him *foundations* for the ancient *heavens? they are* strong as a molten mirror. 19 Wherefore teach me, what shall we say to him? and let us cease from saying much. 20 Have I a book or a scribe my me, that I may stand and put man to silence? 21 But the light is not visible to all: it shines afar off in the heavens, as that which is from him in the clouds. 22 From the *north* come the clouds shining like gold: in these great are the glory and honour of the Almighty; 23 and we do not find another his equal in strength: *as for* him that judges justly, dost thou not think that he listens? 24 Wherefore men shall fear him; and the wise also in heart shall fear him.

Job.38

1 And after Elius had ceased from speaking, the Lord spoke to Job through the whirlwind and clouds, *saying,* 2 Who is this that hides counsel from me, and confines words in *his* heart, and thinks to conceal *them* from me? 3 Gird thy loins like a man; and I will ask thee, and do thou answer me. 4 Where wast thou when I founded the earth? tell me now, if thou hast knowledge, 5 who set the measures of it, if thou knowest? or who stretched a line upon it? 6 On what are its rings fastened? and who is he that laid the corner-stone upon it? 7 When the stars were made, all my angels praised me with a loud voice. 8 And I shut up the sea with gates, when it rushed out, coming forth out its mother's womb. 9 And I made a cloud its clothing, and swathed it in mist. 10 And I set bounds to it, surrounding it with bars and gates. 11 And I said to it, Hitherto shalt thou come, but thou shalt not go beyond, but thy waves shall be confined within thee. 12 Or did I order the morning light in thy time; and *did* the morning star *then first* see his appointed place; 13 to lay hold of the extremities of the earth, to cast out the ungodly out of it? 14 Or didst thou take clay of the ground, and form a living creature, and set it with the power of speech upon the earth? 15 And hast thou removed light from the ungodly, and crushed the arm of the proud? 16 Or hast thou gone to the source of the sea, and walked in the tracks of the deep? 17 And do the gates of death open to thee for fear; and did the porters of hell quake when they saw thee? 18 And hast thou been instructed in the breadth of the *whole earth* under heaven? tell me now, what is the extent of it? 19 And in what kind of a land does the light dwell? and of what kind is the place of darkness? 20 If thou couldest bring me to their *utmost* boundaries, and if also thou knowest their paths; 21 I know then that thou wert born at that time, and the number of thy years is great. 22

But hast thou gone to the treasures of snow? and hast thou seen the treasures of hail? 23 And is there a store *of them*, for thee against the time of *thine* enemies, for the day of wars and battle? 24 And whence proceeds the frost? or *whence* is the south wind dispersed over the *whole world* under heaven? 25 And who prepared a course for the violent rain, and a way for the thunders; 26 to rain upon the land where *there is* no man, the wilderness, where there is not a man in it; so as to feed the untrodden and uninhabited *land,* 27 and cause it to send forth a crop of green herbs? 28 Who is the rain's father? and who has generated the drops of dew? 29 And out of whose womb comes the ice? and who has produced the frost in the sky, 30 which descends like flowing water? who has terrified the face of the ungodly? 31 And dost thou understand the band of Pleias, and hast thou opened the barrier of Orion? 32 Or wilt thou reveal Mazuroth in his season, and the evening star with his rays? Wilt thou guide them? 33 And knowest thou the changes of heaven, or the events which take place together under heaven? 34 And wilt thou call a cloud with thy voice, and will it obey thee with a violent shower of much rain? 35 And wilt thou send lightnings, and they shall go? and shall they say to thee, What is *thy pleasure?* 36 And who has given to women skill in weaving, or knowledge of embroidery? 37 And who is he that numbers the clouds in wisdom, and has bowed the heaven *down* to the earth? 38 For it is spread out as dusty earth, and I have cemented it as one hewn stone to another. 39 And wilt thou hunt a prey for the lions? and satisfy the desires of the serpents? 40 For they fear in their lairs, and lying in wait couch in the woods. 41 And who has prepared food for the raven? for its young ones wander and cry to the Lord, in search of food.

Job.39

1 *Say* if thou knowest the time of the bringing forth of the wild goats of the rock, and *if* thou hast marked the calving of the hinds: 2 and *if* thou has hast numbered the full months of their being with young, and *if* thou hast relieved their pangs: 3 and hast reared their young without fear; and wilt thou loosen their pangs? 4 Their young will break forth; they will be multiplied with offspring: *their young* will go forth, and will not return to them. 5 And who is he that sent forth the wild ass free? and who loosed his bands? 6 whereas I made his habitation the wilderness, and the salt land his coverts. 7 He laughs to scorn the multitude of the city, and hears not the chiding of the tax-gatherer. 8 He will survey the mountains *as* his pasture, and he seeks after every green thing. 9 And will the unicorn be willing to serve thee, or to lie down at thy manger? 10 And wilt thou bind his yoke with thongs, or will he plough furrows for thee in the plain? 11 And dost thou trust him, because his strength is great? and wilt thou commit thy works to him? 12 And wilt thou believe that he will return to thee thy seed, and bring *it* in *to* thy threshing-floor? 13 The peacock has a beautiful wing: if the stork and the ostrich conceive, *it is worthy of notice,* 14 for *the ostrich* will leave her eggs in the ground, and warm them on the dust, 15 and has forgotten that the foot will scatter them, and the wild beasts of the field trample them. 16 She has hardened *herself* against her young ones, as though *she bereaved* not herself: she labours

in vain without fear. 17 For God has withholden wisdom from her, and not given her a portion in understanding. 18 In her season she will lift herself on high; she will scorn the horse and his rider. 19 Hast thou invested the horse with strength, and clothed his neck with terror? 20 And hast thou clad him in perfect armour, and made his breast glorious with courage? 21 He paws exulting in the plain, and goes forth in strength into the plain. 22 He laughs to scorn a king as he meets him, and will by no means turn back from the sword. 23 The bow and sword resound against him; and *his* rage will swallow up the ground: 24 and he will not believe until the trumpet sounds. 25 And when the trumpet sounds, he says, Aha! and afar off he smells the war with prancing and neighing. 26 And does the hawk remain steady by thy wisdom, having spread out her wings unmoved, looking toward the region of the south? 27 And does the eagle rise at thy command, and the vulture remain sitting over his nest, 28 on a crag of a rock, and in a secret *place*? 29 Thence he seeks food, his eyes observe from far. 30 And his young ones roll themselves in blood, and wherever the carcasses may be, immediately they are found. 31 And the Lord God answered Job, and said, 32 Will *any one* pervert judgment with the Mighty One? and he that reproves God, let him return it for answer.33 And Job answered and said to the Lord, 34 Why do I yet plead? being rebuked even while reproving the Lord: hearing such things, whereas I am nothing: and what shall I answer to these *arguments*? I will lay my hand upon my mouth. 35 I have spoken once; but I will not do so a second time.

Job.40 1 And the Lord yet again answered and spoke to Job out of the cloud, *saying,* 2 Nay, gird up now thy loins like a man; and I will ask thee, and do thou answer me. 3 Do not set aside my judgment: and dost thou think that I have dealt with thee in any other way, than that thou mightest appear to be righteous? 4 Hast thou an arm like the Lord's? or dost thou thunder with a voice like his? 5 Assume now a lofty bearing and power; and clothe thyself with glory and honour. 6 And send forth messengers with wrath; and lay low every haughty one. 7 Bring down also the proud man; and consume at once the ungodly. 8 And hide them together in the earth; and fill their faces with shame. 9 *Then* will I confess that thy right hand can save *thee.* 10 But now look at the wild beasts with thee; they eat grass like oxen. 11 Behold now, his strength is in his loins, and his force is in the navel of his belly. 12 He sets up his tail like a cypress; and his nerves are wrapped together. 13 His sides are sides of brass; and his backbone is *as* cast iron. 14 This is the chief of the creation of the Lord; made to be played with by his angels. 15 And when he has gone up to a steep mountain, he causes joy to the quadrupeds in the deep. 16 He lies under trees of every kind, by the papyrus, and reed, and bulrush. 17 And the great trees make a shadow over him with their branches, and *so do* the bushes of the field. 18 If there should be a flood, he will not perceive it; he trust that Jordan will rush up into his mouth. 19 *Yet one* shall take him in his sight; *one* shall catch *him* with a cord, and pierce his nose. 20 But wilt thou catch the serpent with a hook, and put a halter about his nose? 21 Or wilt thou fasten a ring in his nostril,

and bore his lip with a clasp? 22 Will he address thee with a petition? softly, with the voice of a suppliant? 23 And will he make a covenant with thee? and wilt thou take him for a perpetual servant? 24 And wilt thou play with him as with a bird? or bind him as a sparrow for a child? 25 And do the nations feed upon him, and the nations of the Phoenicians share him? 26 And all the ships come together would not be able to bear the mere skin of his tail; neither *shall they carry* his head in fishing-vessels. 27 But thou shalt lay thy hand upon him *once,* remembering the war that is waged by his mouth; and let it not be done any more.

Job.41 1 Hast thou not seen him? and hast thou not wondered at the things said *of him*? Dost thou not fear because preparation has been made by me? for who is there that resists me? 2 Or who will resist me, and abide, since the whole *world* under heaven is mine? 3 I will not be silent because of him: though because of his power *one* shall pity his antagonist. 4 Who will open the face of his garment? and who can enter within the fold of his breastplate? 5 Who will open the doors of his face? terror is round about his teeth. 6 His inwards are as brazen plates, and the texture of his *skin* as a smyrite stone. 7 One *part* cleaves fast to another, and the air cannot come between them. 8 They will remain united each to the other: they are closely joined, and cannot be separated. 9 At his sneezing a light shines, and his eyes are *as* the appearance of the morning star. 10 Out of his mouth proceed as it were burning lamps, and as it were hearths of fire are cast abroad. 11 Out of his nostrils proceeds smoke of a furnace burning with fire of coals. 12 His breath is *as* live coals, and a flame goes out of his mouth. 13 And power is lodged in his neck, before him destruction runs. 14 The flesh also of his body is joined together: *if one* pours *violence* upon him, he shall not be moved. 15 His heart is firm as a stone, and it stands like an unyielding anvil. 16 And when he turns, *he is* a terror to the four-footed wild beasts which leap upon the earth. 17 If spears should come against him, *men* will effect nothing, *either with* the spear or the breast-plate. 18 For he considers iron as chaff, and brass as rotten wood. 19 The bow of brass shall not would him, he deems a slinger as grass. 20 Mauls are counted as stubble; and he laughs to scorn the waving of the firebrand. 21 His lair is *formed of* sharp points; and all the gold of the sea under him is an immense *quantity of* clay. 22 He makes the deep boil like a brazen caldron; and he regards the sea as a pot of ointment, 23 and the lowest part of the deep as a captive: he reckons the deep as *his* range. 24 There is nothing upon the earth like to him, formed to be sported with by my angels. 25 He beholds every high thing: and he is king of all that are in the waters.

Job.42 1 Then Job answered and said to the Lord, 2 I know that thou canst do all things, and nothing is impossible with thee. 3 For who is he that hides counsel from thee? or who keeps back his words, and thinks to hide them from thee? and who will tell me what I knew not, great and wonderful things which I understood not? 4 But hear me, O Lord, that I also may speak: and I will ask thee, and do thou teach me. 5 I have heard the report of thee by the ear before; but now mine eye has seen thee. 6 Wherefore I have counted myself vile, and have fainted: and I esteem myself dust and ashes. 7 And it came to pass after the Lord had spoken all these words to Job, *that* the Lord said to Eliphaz the Thaemanite, Thou hast sinned, and thy two friends: for ye have not said anything true before me, as my servant Job *has*. 8 Now then take seven bullocks, and seven rams, and go to my servant Job, and he shall offer a burnt-offering for you. And my servant Job shall pray for you, for I will only accept him: for but his sake, I would have destroyed you, for ye have not spoken the truth against my servant Job. 9 So Eliphaz the Thaemanite, and Baldad the Sauchite, and Sophar the Minaean, went and did as the Lord commanded them: and he pardoned their sin for the sake of Job. 10 And the Lord prospered Job: and when he prayed also for his friends, he forgave them *their* sin: and the Lord gave Job twice as much, even the double of what he had before. 11 And all his brethren and his sisters heard all that had happened to him, and they came to him, and *so did* all that had known him from the first: and they ate and drank with him, and comforted him, and wondered at all that the Lord had brought upon him: and each one gave him a lamb, and four drachms' weight of gold, even of unstamped *gold*. 12 And the Lord blessed the latter end of Job, *more* than the beginning: and his cattle were fourteen thousand sheep, six thousand camels, a thousand yoke of oxen, a thousand she-asses of the pastures. 13 And there were born to him seven sons and three daughters. 14 And he called the first Day, and the second Casia, and the third Amalthaea's horn. 15 And there were not found in comparison with the daughters of Job, fairer *women* than they in all the world: and their father gave them an inheritance among their brethren. 16 And Job lived after *his* affliction a hundred and seventy years: and all the years he lived were two hundred and forty: and Job saw his sons and his sons' sons, the fourth generation. 17 And Job died, an old man and full of days: and it is written that he will rise again with those whom the Lord raises up. This man is described in the Syriac book *as* living in the land of Ausis, on the borders of Idumea and Arabia: and his name before was Jobab; and having taken an Arabian wife, he begot a son whose name was Ennon. And he himself was the son of his father Zare, one of the sons of Esau, and of his mother Bosorrha, so that he was the fifth from Abraam. And these were the kings who reigned in Edom, which country he also ruled over: first, Balac, the son of Beor, and the name of his city was Dennaba: but after Balac, Jobab, who is called Job, and after him Asom, who was governor out of the country of Thaeman: and after him Adad, the son of Barad, who destroyed Madiam in the plain of Moab; and the name of his city was Gethaim. And *his* friends who came to him were Eliphaz, of the children of Esau, king of the Thaemanites, Baldad sovereign the Sauchaeans, Sophar king of the Minaeans.

PSALMS

Ps.1 1 Blessed is the man who has not walked in the counsel of the ungodly, and has not stood in the way of sinners, and has not sat in the seat of evil men. 2 But his pleasure is in the law of the Lord; and in his law will he meditate day and night. 3 And he shall be as a tree planted by the brooks of waters, which shall yield its fruit in its season, and its leaf shall not fall off; and whatsoever he shall do shall be prospered. 4 Not so the ungodly;—not so: but rather as the chaff which the wind scatters away from the face of the earth. 5 Therefore the ungodly shall not rise in judgment, nor sinners in the counsel of the just. 6 For the Lord knows the way of the righteous; but the way of the ungodly shall perish.

Ps.2 1 Wherefore did the heathen rage, and the nations imagine vain things? 2 The kings of the earth stood up, and the rulers gathered themselves together, against the Lord, and against his Christ; 3 *saying*, Let us break through their bonds, and cast away their yoke from us. 4 He that dwells in the heavens shall laugh them to scorn, and the Lord shall mock them. 5 Then shall he speak to them in his anger, and trouble them in his fury. 6 But I have been made king by him on Sion his holy mountain, 7 declaring the ordinance of the Lord: the Lord said to me, Thou art my Son, to-day have I begotten thee. 8 Ask of me, and I will give thee the heathen *for* thine inheritance, and the ends of the earth *for* thy possession. 9 Thou shalt rule them with a rod of iron; thou shalt dash them in pieces as a potter's vessel. 10 Now therefore understand, ye kings: be instructed, all ye that judge the earth. 11 Serve the Lord with fear, and rejoice in him with trembling. 12 Accept correction, lest at any time the Lord be angry, and ye should perish from the righteous way: whensoever his wrath shall be suddenly kindled, blessed are all they that trust in him.

Ps.3 *A Psalm of David, when he fled from the presence of his son Abessalom.* 1 O Lord, why are they that afflict me multiplied? many rise up against me. 2 Many say concerning my soul, There is no deliverance for him in his God. Pause. 3 But thou, O Lord, art my helper: my glory, and the one that lifts up my head. 4 I cried to the Lord with my voice, and he heard me out of his holy mountain. Pause. 5 I lay down and slept; I awaked; for the Lord will help me. 6 I will not be afraid of ten thousands of people, who beset me round about. 7 Arise, Lord; deliver me, my God: for thou hast smitten all who were without cause mine enemies; thou hast broken the teeth of sinners. 8 Deliverance is the Lord's, and thy blessing is upon thy people.

Ps.4 *For the End, a Song of David among the Psalms.* 1 When I called upon *him*, the God of my righteousness heard me: thou hast made room for me in tribulation; pity me, and hearken to my prayer. 2 O ye sons on men, how long *will ye be* slow of heart? wherefore do ye love vanity, and seek falsehood? Pause. 3 But know ye that the Lord has done wondrous things for his holy one: the Lord will hear me when I cry to him. 4 Be ye angry, and sin not; feel compunction upon your beds for what ye say in your hearts. Pause. 5 Offer the sacrifice of righteousness, and trust in the Lord. 6 Many say, Who will shew us good things? the light of thy countenance, O Lord, has been manifested towards us. 7 Thou hast put gladness into my heart: they have been satisfied with the fruit of their corn and wine and oil. 8 I will both lie down in peace and sleep: for thou, Lord, only hast caused me to dwell securely.

Ps.5 *For the end, a Psalm of David, concerning her that inherits.* 1 Hearken to my words, O Lord, attend to my cry. 2 Attend to the voice of my supplication, my King, and my God: for to thee, O Lord, will I pray. 3 In the morning thou shalt hear my voice: in the morning will I wait upon thee, and will look up. 4 For thou art not a god that desires iniquity; neither shall the worker of wickedness dwell with thee. 5 Neither shall the transgressors continue in thy sight: thou hatest, O Lord, all them that work iniquity. 6 Thou wilt destroy all that speak falsehood: the Lord abhors the bloody and deceitful man. 7 But I will enter into thine house in the multitude of thy mercy: I will worship in thy fear toward thy holy temple. 8 Lead me, O Lord, in thy righteousness because of mine enemies; make my way plain before thy face. 9 For there is no truth in their mouth; their heart is vain; their throat is an open sepulchre; with their tongues they have used deceit. 10 Judge them, O God; let them fail of their counsels: cast them out according to the abundance of their ungodliness; for they have provoked thee, O Lord. 11 But let all that trust on thee be glad in thee: they shall exult for ever, and thou shalt dwell among them; and all that love thy name shall rejoice in thee. 12 For thou, Lord, shalt bless the righteous: thou hast compassed us as with a shield of favour.

Ps.6 *For the End, a Psalm of David among the Hymns for the eighth.* 1 O Lord, rebuke me not in thy wrath, neither chasten me in thine anger. 2 Pity me, O Lord; for I am weak: heal me, O Lord; for my bones are vexed. 3 My soul also is grievously vexed: but thou, O Lord, how long? 4 Return, O Lord, deliver my soul: save me for thy mercy's sake. 5 For in death no man remembers thee: and who will give thee thanks in Hades? 6 I am wearied with my groaning; I shall wash my bed every night; I shall water my couch with tears. 7 Mine eye is troubled because of my wrath; I am worn out because of all mine enemies. 8 Depart from me, all ye that work iniquity; for the Lord has heard the voice of my weeping. 9 The Lord has hearkened to my petition; the Lord has accepted my prayer. 10 Let all mine enemies be put to shame and sore troubled: let them be turned back and grievously put to shame speedily.

Ps.7 *A Psalm of David, which he sang to the Lord because of the words of Chusi the Benjamite.* 1 O Lord my God, in thee have I trusted: save me from all them that persecute me, and deliver me. 2 Lest at any time *the enemy* seize my soul as a lion, while there is none to ransom, nor to save. 3 O Lord my God, if I have done this; (if there is unrighteousness in my hands;) 4 if I have requited with evil those who requited me *with good*; may I then perish empty by means of my enemies. 5 Let the enemy persecute my soul, an take it; and let him trample my life on the ground, and lay my glory in the dust. Pause. 6 Arise, O Lord, in thy wrath; be exalted in the utmost boundaries of mine enemies: awake, O Lord my God, according to the decree which thou didst command. 7 And the congregation of the nations shall compass thee: and for this cause do thou return on high. 8 The Lord shall judge the nations: judge me, O Lord, according to my righteousness, and according to my innocence that is in me. 9 Oh let the wickedness of sinners come to an end; and *then*

thou shalt direct the righteous, O God that searchest the hearts and reins. 10 My help is righteous, *coming* from God who saves the upright in heart. 11 God is a righteous judge, and strong, and patient, not inflicting vengeance every day. 12 If ye will not repent, he will furbish his sword; he has bent his bow, and made it ready. 13 And on it he has fitted the instruments of death; he has completed his arrows for the raging ones. 14 Behold, he has travailed with unrighteousness, he has conceived trouble, and brought forth iniquity. 15 He has opened a pit, and dug it up, and he shall fall into the ditch which he has made. 16 His trouble shall return on his own head, and his unrighteousness shall come down on his own crown. 17 I will give thanks to the Lord according to his righteousness; I will sing to the name of the Lord most high.

Ps.8 *For the end, concerning the wine-presses, a Psalm of David.* 1 O Lord, our Lord, how wonderful is thy name in all the earth! for thy magnificence is exalted above the heavens. 2 Out of the mouth of babes and sucklings hast thou perfected praise, because of thine enemies; that thou mightest put down the enemy and avenger. 3 For I will regard the heavens, the work of thy fingers; the moon and stars, which thou hast established. 4 What is man, that thou art mindful of him? or the son of man, that thou visitest him? 5 Thou madest him a little less than angels, thou hast crowned him with glory and honour; 6 and thou hast set him over the works of thy hands: thou hast put all things under his feet: 7 sheep and all oxen, yea and the cattle of the field; 8 the birds of the sky, and the fish of the sea, the *creatures* passing through the paths of the sea. 9 O Lord our Lord, how wonderful is thy name in all the earth!

Ps.9 *For the end, a Psalm of David, concerning the secrets of the Son.* 1 I will give thanks to thee, O Lord, with my whole heart; I will recount all thy wonderful works. 2 I will be glad and exult in thee: I will sing to thy name, O thou Most High. 3 When mine enemies are turned back, they shall be feeble and perish at thy presence. 4 For thou hast maintained my cause and my right; thou satest on the throne, that judgest righteousness. 5 Thou hast rebuked the nations, and the ungodly one has perished; thou hast blotted out their name for ever, even for ever and ever. 6 The swords of the enemy have failed utterly; and thou hast destroyed cities: their memorial has been destroyed with a noise, 7 but the Lord endures for ever: he has prepared his throne for judgment. 8 And he will judge the world in righteousness, he will judge the nations in uprightness. 9 The Lord also is become a refuge for the poor, a seasonable help, in affliction. 10 And let them that know thy name hope in thee: for thou, O Lord, hast not failed them that diligently seek thee. 11 Sing praises to the Lord, who dwells in Sion: declare his dealings among the nations. 12 For he remembered them, *in* making inquisition for blood: he has not forgotten the supplication of the poor. 13 Have mercy upon me, O Lord; look upon my affliction *which I suffer* of mine enemies, thou that liftest me up from the gates of death: 14 that I may declare all thy praises in the gates of the daughter of Sion: I will exult in thy salvation. 15 The heathen are caught in the destruction which they planned: in the very snare which they hid is their foot taken. 16 The Lord is known as executing judgments: the sinner is taken in the works of his hands. A song of Pause. 17 Let sinners be driven away into Hades, *even* all the nations that forget God. 18 For the poor shall not be forgotten for ever: the patience of the needy ones shall not perish for ever. 19 Arise, O Lord, let not man prevail: let the heathen be judged before thee. 20 Appoint, O Lord, a lawgiver over them: let the heathen know that they are men. Pause.

Ps.10 1 Why standest thou afar off, O Lord? *why* dost thou overlook *us* in times of need, in affliction? 2 While the ungodly one acts proudly, the poor is hotly pursued: *the wicked* are taken in the crafty counsels which they imagine. 3 Because the sinner praises himself for the desires of his heart; and the unjust one blesses himself. 4 The sinner has provoked the Lord: according to the abundance of his pride he will not seek after *him*: God is not before him. 5 His ways are profane at all times; thy judgments are removed from before him: he will gain the mastery over all his enemies. 6 For he has said in his heart, I shall not be moved, *continuing* without evil from generation to generation. 7 Whose mouth is full of cursing, and bitterness, and fraud: under his tongue are trouble and pain. 8 He lies in wait with rich *men* in secret places, in order to slay the innocent: his eyes are set against the poor. 9 He lies in wait in secret as a lion in his den: he lies in wait to ravish the poor, to ravish the poor when he draws him *after him*: he will bring him down in his snare. 10 He will bow down and fall when he has mastered the poor. 11 For he has said in his heart, God has forgotten: he has turned away his face so as never to look. 12 Arise, O Lord God; let thy hand be lifted up: forget not the poor. 13 Wherefore, has the wicked provoked God? for he has said in his heart, He will not require *it*. 14 Thou seest *it*; for thou dost observe trouble and wrath, to deliver them into thy hands: the poor has been left to thee; thou wast a helper to the orphan. 15 Break thou the arm of the sinner and wicked man: his sin shall be sought for, and shall not be found. 16 The Lord shall reign for ever, even for ever and ever: ye Gentiles shall perish out his land. 17 The Lord has heard the desire of the poor: thine ear has inclined to the preparation of their heart; 18 to plead for the orphan and afflicted, that man may no more boast upon the earth.

Ps.11 *For the end, a Psalm of David.* 1 In the Lord I have put my trust: how will ye say to my soul, Flee to the mountains as a sparrow? 2 For behold the sinners have bent their *bow*, they have prepared their arrows for the quiver, to shoot privily at the upright in heart. 3 For they have pulled down what thou didst frame, but what has the righteous done? 4 The Lord is in his holy temple, as for the Lord, his throne is in heaven: his eyes look upon the poor, his eyelids try the sons of men. 5 The Lord tries the righteous and the ungodly: and he that loves unrighteousness hates his own soul. 6 He shall rain upon sinners snares, fire, and brimstone, and a stormy blast *shall be* the portion of their cup. 7 For the Lord *is* righteous, and loves righteousness; his face beholds uprightness.

Ps.12 *For the end, A Psalm of David, upon the eighth.* 1 Save me, O Lord; for the godly man has failed; for truth is diminished from among the children of men. 2 Every one has spoken vanity to his neighbour: their lips are deceitful, they have spoken with a double heart. 3 Let the Lord destroy all the deceitful lips, and the tongue that speaks great words: 4 who have said, We will magnify our tongue; our lips are our own: who is Lord of us? 5 Because of the misery of the poor, and because of the sighing of the needy, now will I arise, saith the Lord, I will set *them* in safety; I will speak *to them* thereof openly. 6 The oracles of the Lord are pure oracles; as silver tried in the fire, proved *in* a furnace of earth, purified seven times. 7 Thou, O Lord, shalt keep us, and shalt preserve us, from this generation, and for ever. 8 The ungodly walk around: according to thy greatness thou has greatly exalted the sons of men.

Ps.13 *For the end, a Psalm of David.* 1 How long, O Lord, wilt thou forget me? for ever? how long wilt thou turn away thy face from me? 2 How long shall I take counsel in my soul, *having* sorrows in my heart daily? how long shall my enemy be exalted over me? 3 Look on me, hearken to me, O Lord my God: lighten mine eyes, lest I sleep in death; 4 lest at any time mine enemy say, I have prevailed against him: my persecutors will exult if ever I should be moved. 5 But I have hoped in thy mercy; my heart shall exult in thy salvation. 6 I will sing to the Lord who has dealt bountifully with me, and I will sing psalms to the name of the Lord most high.

Ps.14 *For the end, Psalm of David.* 1 The fool has said in his heart, There is no God. They have corrupted *themselves*, and become abominable in their devices; there is none that does goodness, there is not even so much as one. 2 The Lord looked down from heaven upon the sons of men, to see if there were any that understood, or sought after god. 3 They are all gone out of the way, they are together become good for nothing, there is none that does good, no not one. Their throat is an open sepulchre; with their tongues they have used deceit; the poison of asps is under their lips: whose mouth is full of cursing and bitterness; their feet are swift to shed blood: destruction and misery are in their ways; and the way of peace they have not known: there is no fear of God before their eyes. 4 Will not all the workers of iniquity know, who eat up my people as they would eat bread? they have not called upon the Lord. 5 There were they alarmed with fear, where there was no fear; for God is in the righteous generation. 6 Ye have shamed the counsel of the poor, because the Lord is his hope. 7 Who will bring the salvation of Israel out of Sion? when the Lord brings back the captivity of his people, let Jacob exult, and Israel be glad.

Ps.15 *A Psalm of David.* 1 O Lord, who shall sojourn in thy tabernacle? And who shall dwell in thy holy mountain? 2 He that walks blameless, and works righteousness, who speaks truth in his heart. 3 Who has not spoken craftily with is tongue, neither has done evil to his neighbour, nor taken up a reproach against them that dwelt nearest to him. 4 In his sight an evil-worker is set at nought, but he honours them that fear the Lord. He swears to his neighbour, and disappoints *him* not. 5 He has not lent his money on usury, and has not received bribes against the innocent. He that does these things shall never be moved.

Ps.16 *A writing of David.* 1 Keep me, O Lord; for I have hoped in thee. 2 I said to the Lord, Thou art my Lord; for thou has no need of my goodness. 3 On behalf of the saints that are in his land, he has magnified all his pleasure in them. 4 Their weaknesses have been multiplied; afterward they hasted. I will by no means assemble their bloody meetings, neither will I make mention of their names with my lips. 5 The Lord is the portion of mine inheritance and of my cup: thou art he that restores my inheritance to me. 6 The lines have fallen to me in the best places, yea, I have a most excellent heritage. 7 I will bless the Lord who has instructed me; my reins too have chastened me even till night. 8 I foresaw the Lord always before my face; for he is on my right hand, that I should not be moved. 9 Therefore my heart rejoiced an my tongue exulted; moreover also my flesh shall rest in hope: 10 because thou wilt not leave my soul in hell, neither wilt thou suffer thine Holy One to see corruption. 11 Thou hast made known to me the ways of life; thou wilt fill me with joy with thy countenance: at thy right hand *there are* delights for ever.

Ps.17 *A prayer of David.* 1 Hearken, O Lord of my righteousness, attend to my petition; give ear to my prayer not *uttered* with deceitful lips. 2 Let my judgment come forth from thy presence; let mine eyes behold righteousness. 3 Thou has proved mine heart; thou hast visited *me* by night; thou hast tried me as with fire, and unrighteousness has not been found in me: *I am purposed* that my mouth shall not speak *amiss.* 4 As for the works of men, by the words of thy lips I have guarded *myself from* hard ways. 5 Direct my steps in thy paths, that my steps slip not. 6 I have cried, for thou heardest me, O God: incline thine ear to me, and hearken to my words. 7 Shew the marvels of thy mercies, thou that savest them that hope in thee. 8 Keep me as the apple of the eye from those that resist thy right hand: thou shalt screen me by the covering of thy wings, 9 from the face of the ungodly that have afflicted me: mine enemies have compassed about my soul. 10 They have enclosed *themselves with* their own fat: their mouth has spoken pride. 11 They have now cast me out and compassed me round about: they have set their eyes *so as* to bow them down to the ground. 12 They laid wait for me as a lion ready for prey, and like a lion's whelp dwelling in secret *places.* 13 Arise, O Lord, prevent them, and cast them down: deliver my soul from the ungodly: *draw* thy sword, 14 because of the enemies of thine hand: O Lord, destroy them from the earth; scatter them in their life, though their belly has been filled with thy hidden *treasures:* they have been satisfied with uncleanness, and have left the remnant *of their possessions* to their babes. 15 But I shall appear in righteousness before thy face: I shall be satisfied when thy glory appears.

Ps.18 *For the end, a Psalm of David, the servant of the Lord; the words which he spoke to the Lord, even the words of this Song, in the day in which the Lord delivered him out the hand of all his enemies,* *and out the hand of Saul: and he said:* 1 I will love thee, O Lord, my strength. 2 The Lord is my firm support, and my refuge, and my deliverer; my God is my helper, I will hope in him; *he is* my defender, and the horn of my salvation, and my helper. 3 I will call upon the Lord with praises, and I shall be saved from mine enemies. 4 The pangs of death compassed me, and the torrents of ungodliness troubled me exceedingly. 5 The pangs of hell came round about me: the snares of death prevented me. 6 And when I was afflicted I called upon the Lord, and cried to my God: he heard my voice out of this holy temple, and my cry shall enter before him, *even* into his ears. 7 Then the earth shook and quaked, and the foundations of the mountains were disturbed, and were shaken, because God was angry with them. 8 There went up a smoke in his wrath, and fire burst into a flame at his presence: coals were kindled at it. 9 And he bowed the heaven, and came down: and thick darkness was under his feet. 10 And he mounted on cherubs and flew: he flew on the wings of winds. 11 And he made darkness his secret place: round about him was his tabernacle, *even* dark water in the clouds of the air. 12 At the brightness before him the clouds passed, hail and coals of fire. 13 The Lord also thundered from heaven, and the Highest uttered his voice. 14 And he sent forth *his* weapons, and scattered them; and multiplied lightnings, and routed them. 15 And the springs of waters appeared, and the foundations of the world were exposed, at thy rebuke, O Lord, at the blasting of the breath of thy wrath. 16 He sent from on high and took me, he drew me to himself out of many waters. 17 He will deliver me from my mighty enemies, and from them that hate me; for they are stronger than I. 18 They prevented me in the day of mine affliction: but the Lord was my stay against *them.* 19 And he brought me out into a wide place: he will deliver me, because he has pleasure in me. 20 And the Lord will recompense me according to my righteousness; even according to the purity of my hands will he recompense me. 21 For I have kept the way of the Lord and have not wickedly departed from my God. 22 For all his judgments were before me, and his ordinances departed not from me. 23 And I shall be blameless with hem, and shall keep myself from mine iniquity. 24 And the Lord shall recompense me according to my righteousness, and according to the purity of my hands before his eyes. 25 With the holy thou wilt be holy; and with the innocent man thou wilt be innocent. 26 And with the excellent *man* thou wilt be excellent; and with the perverse thou wilt shew frowardness. 27 For thou wilt save the lowly people, and wilt humble the eyes of the proud. 28 For thou, O Lord, wilt light my lamp: my God, thou wilt lighten my darkness. 29 For by thee shall I be delivered from a troop; and by my God I will pass over a wall. 30 *As for* my God, his way is perfect: the oracles of the Lord are tried in the fire; he is a protector of all them that hope in him. 31 For who is God but the Lord? and who is a God except our God? 32 *It is* God that girds me with strength, and has made my way blameless: 33 who strengthens my feet as hart's feet, and sets me upon high places. 34 He instructs my hands for war: and thou hast made my arms *as* a brazen bow. 35 And thou hast made me secure in my salvation: and thy right hand has helped me, and thy correction has upheld me to the end; yea, thy correction itself shall instruct me. 36 Thou has made room for my goings under me, and by footsteps did not fail. 37 I will pursue mine enemies, and overtake them; and I will not turn back until they are consumed. 38 I will dash them to pieces and they shall not be able to stand: they shall fall under my feet. 39 For thou hast girded me with strength for war: thou hast beaten down under me all that rose up against me. 40 And thou has made mine enemies turn their backs before me; and thou hast destroyed them that hated me. 41 They cried, but there was no deliverer: *even* to the Lord, but he hearkened not to them. 42 I will grind them as the mud of the streets: and I will beat them small as dust before the wind. 43 Deliver me from the gain sayings of the people: thou shalt make me head of the Gentiles: a people whom I knew not served me, 44 at the hearing of the ear they obeyed me: the strange children lied to me. 45 The strange children waxed old, and fell away from their paths through lameness. 46 The Lord lives; and blessed *be* my God; and let the God of my salvation be exalted. 47 *It is* God that avenges me, and has subdued the nations under me; 48 my deliverer from angry enemies: thou shalt set me on high above them that rise up against me: thou shalt deliver me from the unrighteous man. 49 Therefore will I confess to thee, O Lord, among the Gentiles, and sing to thy name. 50 *God* magnifies the deliverances of his king; and deals mercifully with David his anointed, and his seed, for ever.

Ps.19 *For the end, a Psalm of David.*1 The heavens declare the glory of God; and the firmament proclaims the work of his hands. 2 Day to day utters speech, and night to night proclaims knowledge. 3 There are no speeches or words, in which their voices are not heard. 4 Their voice is gone out into all the earth, and their words to the ends of the world. 5 In the sun he has set his tabernacle; and he comes forth as a bridegroom out of his chamber: he will exult as a giant to run his course. 6 His going forth is from the extremity of heaven, and his circuit to the *other* end of heaven: and no one shall be hidden from his heat. 7 The law of the Lord is perfect, converting souls: the testimony of the Lord is faithful, instructing babes. 8 The ordinances of the Lord are right, rejoicing the heart: the commandment of the Lord is bright, enlightening the eyes. 9 The fear of the Lord is pure, enduring for ever and ever: the judgments of the Lord are true, *and* justified altogether. 10 To be desired more than gold, and much precious stone: sweeter also than honey and the honey-comb. 11 For thy servant keeps to them: in the keeping of them *there is* great reward. 12 Who will understand *his* transgressions? purge thou me from my secret *sins*. 13 And spare thy servant *the attack* of strangers: if they do not gain the dominion over me, then shall I be blameless, and I shall be clear from great sin. 14 So shall the sayings of my mouth, and the meditation of my heart, be pleasing continually before thee, O Lord my helper, and my redeemer.

Ps.20 *For the end, a Psalm of David.* 1 The Lord hear thee in the day of trouble; the name of the God of Jacob defend thee. 2 Send thee help from the sanctuary, and aid thee out of Sion. 3 Remember all thy sacrifice, and enrich thy whole-burnt-offering. Pause. 4 Grant thee according to thy heart, and fulfill all thy desire. 5 We will exult in thy salvation, and in the name of our God shall we be magnified: the Lord fulfil all thy petitions. 6 Now I know that the Lord has saved his Christ: he shall hear him from his holy heaven: the salvation of his right hand is mighty. 7 Some *glory* in chariots, and some in horses: but we will glory in the name of the Lord our God. 8 They are overthrown and fallen: but we are risen, and have been set upright. 9 O Lord, save the king: and hear us in whatever day we call upon thee.

Ps.21 *For the end, a Psalm of David.* 1 O Lord, the king shall rejoice in thy strength; and in thy salvation he shall greatly exult. 2 Thou hast granted him the desire of his soul, and hast not withheld from him the request of his lips. Pause. 3 For thou hast prevented him with blessings of goodness: thou has set upon his head a crown of precious stone. 4 He asked life of thee, and thou gavest him length of days for ever and ever. 5 His glory is great in thy salvation: thou wilt crown him with glory and majesty. 6 For thou wilt give him a blessing for ever and ever: thou wilt gladden him with joy with thy countenance. 7 For the king trusts in the Lord, and through the mercy of the Highest he shall not be moved. 8 Let thy hand be found by all thine enemies: let thy right hand find all that hate thee. 9 Thou shalt make them as a fiery oven at the time of thy presence: the Lord shall trouble them in his anger, and fire shall devour them. 10 Thou shalt destroy their fruit from the earth, and their seed from *among* the sons of men. 11 For they intended evils against thee; they imagined a device which they shall by no means be able to perform. 12 For thou shalt make them *turn their* back in thy latter end, thou wilt prepare their face. 13 Be thou exalted, O Lord, in thy strength: we will sing and praise thy mighty acts.

Ps.22 *For the end, concerning the morning aid, a Psalm of David.* 1 O God, my God, attend to me: why hast thou forsaken me? the account of my transgressions is far from my salvation. 2 O my God, I will cry to thee by day, but thou wilt not hear: and by night, and *it shall* not *be accounted* for folly to me. 3 But thou, the praise of Israel, dwellest in a sanctuary. 4 Our fathers hoped in thee; they hoped, and thou didst deliver them. 5 They cried to thee, and were saved: they hoped in thee, and were not ashamed. 6 But I am a worm, and not a man; a reproach of men, and scorn of the people. 7 All that saw me mocked me: they spoke with *their* lips, they shook the head, *saying*, 8 He hoped in the Lord: let him deliver him, let him save him, because he takes pleasure in him. 9 For thou art he that drew me out of the womb; my hope from my mother's breasts. 10 I was cast on thee from the womb: thou art my God from my mother's belly. 11 Stand not aloof from me; for affliction is near; for there is no helper. 12 Many bullocks have compassed me: fat bulls have beset me round. 13 They have opened their mouth against me, as a ravening and roaring lion. 14 I am poured out like water, and all my bones are loosened: my heart in the midst of my belly is become like melting wax. 15 My strength is dried up, like a potsherd; and my tongue is glued to my throat; and thou hast brought me down to the dust of death. 16 For many dogs have compassed me: the assembly of the wicked doers has beset me round: they pierced my hands and my feet. 17 They counted all my bones; and they observed and looked upon me. 18 They parted my garments *among* themselves, and cast lots upon my raiment. 19 But thou, O Lord, remove not my help afar off: be ready for mine aid. 20 Deliver my soul from the sword; my only-begotten one from the power of the dog. 21 Save me from the lion's mouth; and *regard* my lowliness from the horns of the unicorns. 22 I will declare thy name to my brethren: in the midst of the church will I sing praise to thee. 23 Ye that fear the Lord, praise him; all ye seed of Jacob, glorify him: let all the seed of Israel fear him. 24 For he has not despised nor been angry at the supplication of the poor; nor turned away his face from me; but when I cried to him, he heard me. 25 My praise is of thee in the great congregation: I will pay my vows before them that fear him. 26 The poor shall eat and be satisfied; and they shall praise the Lord that seek him: their heart shall live for ever. 27 All the ends of the earth shall remember and turn to the Lord: and all the kindreds of the nations shall worship before him. 28 For the kingdom is the Lord's; and he is the governor of the nations. 29 All the fat ones of the earth have eaten and worshipped: all that go down to the earth shall fall down before him: my soul also lives to him. 30 And my seed shall serve him: the generation that is coming shall be reported to the Lord. 31 And they shall report his righteousness to the people that shall be born, whom the Lord has made.

Ps.23 *A Psalm of David.* 1 The Lord tends me as a shepherd, and I shall want nothing. 2 In a place of green grass, there he has made me dwell: he has nourished me by the water of rest. 3 He has restored my soul: he has guided me into the paths of righteousness, for his name's sake. 4 Yea, even if I should walk in the midst of the shadow of death, I will not be afraid of evils: for thou art with me; thy rod and thy staff, these have comforted me. 5 Thou has prepared a table before me in presence of them that afflict me: thou hast thoroughly anointed my head with oil; and thy cup cheers me like the best *wine*. 6 Thy mercy also shall follow me all the days of my life: and my dwelling *shall be* in the house of the Lord for a very long time.

Ps.24 *A Psalm for David on the first day of the week.* 1 The earth is the Lord's and the fullness thereof; the world, and all that dwell in it. 2 He has founded it upon the seas, and prepared it upon the rivers. 3 Who shall go up to the mountain of the Lord, and who shall stand in his holy place? 4 He that is innocent in his hands and pure in his heart; who has not lifted up his soul to vanity, nor sworn deceitfully to his neighbour. 5 He shall receive a blessing from the Lord, and mercy from God his Saviour. 6 This is the generation of them that seek him, that seek the face of the God of Jacob. Pause. 7 Lift up your gates, ye princes, and be ye lifted up, ye everlasting doors; and the king of glory shall come in. 8 Who is this king of Glory? the Lord strong and mighty, the Lord mighty in battle. 9 Lift up your gates, ye princes; and be ye lift up, ye everlasting doors; and the king of glory shall come in. 10 Who is this king of glory? The Lord of hosts, he is this king of glory.

Ps.25 *A Psalm of David.* 1 To thee, O Lord, have I lifted up my soul. 2 O my God, I have trusted in thee: let me not be confounded, neither let mine enemies laugh me to scorn. 3 For none of them that wait on thee shall in any wise be ashamed: let them be ashamed that transgress without cause. 4 Shew me thy ways, O Lord; and teach me thy paths. 5 Lead me in thy truth, and teach me: for thou art God my Saviour: and I have waited on thee all the day. 6 Remember thy compassions, O Lord, and thy mercies, for they are from everlasting. 7 Remember not the sins of my youth, nor *my sins* of ignorance: remember me according to thy mercy, for thy goodness' sake, O Lord. 8 Good and upright is the Lord: therefore will he instruct sinners in *the* way. 9 The meek will he guide in judgment: the meek will he teach his ways. 10 All the ways of the Lord are mercy and truth to them that seek his covenant and his testimonies. 11 For thy name's sake, O Lord, do thou also be merciful to my sin; for it is great. 12 Who is the man that fears the Lord? he shall instruct him in the way which he has chosen. 13 His soul shall dwell in prosperity; and his seed shall inherit the earth. 14 The Lord is the strength of them that fear him; and his covenant is to manifest *truth* to them. 15 Mine eyes are continually to the Lord; for he shall draw my feet out of the snare. 16 Look upon me, and have mercy upon me; for I am an only child and poor. 17 The afflictions of my heart have been multiplied; deliver me from my distresses. 18 Look upon mine affliction and my trouble; and forgive all my sins. 19 Look upon mine enemies; for they have been multiplied; and they have hated me with unjust hatred. 20 Keep my soul, and deliver me: let me not be ashamed; for I have hoped in thee. 21 The harmless and upright joined themselves to me: for I waited for thee, O Lord. 22 Deliver Israel, O God, out of all his afflictions.

Ps.26 *A Psalm of David.* 1 Judge me, O Lord; for I have walked in my innocence: and hoping in the Lord I shall not be moved. 2 Prove me, O Lord, and try me; purify as with fire my reins and my heart. 3 For thy mercy is before mine eyes: and I am well pleased with thy truth. 4 I have not sat with the council of vanity, and will in nowise enter in with transgressors. 5 I have hated the assembly of wicked doers; and will not sit with ungodly *men*. 6 I will wash my hands in innocency, and compass thine altar, O Lord: 7 to hear the voice of praise, and to declare all thy wonderful works. 8 O Lord, I have loved the beauty of thy house, and the place of the tabernacle of thy glory. 9 Destroy not my soul together with the ungodly, nor my life with bloody men: 10 in whose hands *are* iniquities, *and* their right hand is filled with bribes. 11 But I have walked in my innocence: redeem me, and have mercy upon me. 12 My foot stands in an even place: in the congregations will I bless thee, O Lord.

Ps.27 *A Psalm of David, before he was anointed.* 1 The Lord is my light and my Saviour; whom shall I fear? the Lord is the defender of my life; of whom shall I be afraid? 2 When evil-doers drew nigh against me to eat up my flesh, my persecutors and mine enemies, they fainted and fell. 3 Though an army should set itself in array against me, my heart shall not be afraid: though war should rise up against me, in this am I confident. 4 One thing have I asked of the

Lord, this will I earnestly seek: that I should dwell in the house of the Lord, all the days of my life, that I should behold the fair beauty of the Lord, and survey his temple. 5 For in the day of mine afflictions he hid me in his tabernacle: he sheltered me in the secret of his tabernacle; he set me up on a rock. 6 And now, behold, he has lifted up mine head over mine enemies: I went round and offered in his tabernacle the sacrifice of joy; I will sing even sing psalms to the Lord. 7 Hear, O Lord, my voice which I have uttered aloud: pity me, and hearken to me. 8 My heart said to thee, I have diligently sought thy face: thy face, O Lord, I will seek. 9 Turn not thy face away from me, turn not thou away from thy servant in anger: be thou my helper, forsake me not; and, O God my Saviour, overlook me not. 10 For my father and my mother have forsaken me, but the Lord has taken me to himself. 11 Teach me, O Lord, in thy way, and guide me in a right path, because of mine enemies. 12 Deliver me not over to the desire of them that afflict me; for unjust witnesses have risen up against me, and injustice has lied within herself. 13 I believe that I shall see the goodness of the Lord in the land of the living. 14 Wait on the Lord: be of good courage, and let thy heart be strengthened: yea wait on the Lord.

Ps.28 *A Psalm of David.* 1 To thee, O Lord, have I cried; my God, be not silent toward me: lest thou be silent toward me, and so I should be likened to them that go down to the pit. 2 Hearken to the voice of my supplication, when I pray to thee, when I lift up my hands toward thy holy temple. 3 Draw not away my soul with sinners, and destroy me not with the workers of iniquity, who speak peace with their neighbours, but evils are in their hearts. 4 Give them according to their works, and according to the wickedness of their devices: give them according to the works of their hands; render their recompense unto them. 5 Because they have not attended to the works of the Lord, even to the works of his hands, thou shalt pull them down, and shalt not build them up. 6 Blessed be the Lord, for he has hearkened to the voice of my petition. 7 The Lord is my helper and my defender; my heart has hoped in him, and I am helped: my flesh has revived, and willingly will I give praise to him. 8 The Lord is the strength of his people, and the saving defender of his anointed. 9 Save thy people, and bless thine inheritance: and take care of them, and lift them up for ever.

Ps.29 *A Psalm of David on the occasion of the solemn assembly of the Tabernacle.* 1 Bring to the Lord, ye sons of God, bring to the Lord young rams; bring to the Lord glory and honour. 2 Bring to the Lord glory, *due* to his name; worship the lord in his holy court. 3 The voice of the Lord is upon the waters: the God of glory has thundered: the Lord is upon many waters. 4 The voice of the Lord is mighty; the voice of the Lord is full of majesty. 5 *There is* the voice of the Lord who breaks the cedars; the Lord will break the cedars of Libanus. 6 And he will beat them small, *even* Libanus itself, like a calf; and the beloved one is as a young unicorn. 7 *There is* a voice of the Lord who divides a flame of fire. 8 A voice of the Lord who shakes the wilderness; the Lord will shake the wilderness of Cades. 9 The voice of the Lord strengthens the hinds, and will uncover the thickets: and in his temple every one speaks *of his* glory. 10 The Lord will dwell on the waterflood: and the Lord will sit a king for ever. 11 The Lord will give strength to his people; the Lord will bless his people with peace.

Ps.30 *For the end, a Psalm and Song at the dedication of the house of David.* 1 I will exalt thee, O Lord; for thou hast lifted me up, and not caused mine enemies to rejoice over me. 2 O Lord my God, I cried to thee, and thou didst heal me. 3 O Lord, thou hast brought up my soul from Hades, thou hast delivered me from *among* them that go down to the pit. 4 Sing to the Lord, ye his saints, and give thanks for the remembrance of his holiness. 5 For anger is in his wrath, but life in his favour: weeping shall tarry for the evening, but joy shall be in the morning. 6 And I said in my prosperity, I shall never be moved. 7 O Lord, in thy good pleasure thou didst add strength to my beauty: but thou didst turn away thy face, and I was troubled. 8 To thee, O Lord, will I cry; and to my God will I make supplication. 9 What profit is there in my blood, when I go down to destruction? Shall the dust give praise to thee? or shall it declare thy truth? 10 The Lord heard, and had compassion upon me; the Lord is become my helper. 11 Thou hast turned my mourning into joy for me: thou hast rent off my sackcloth, and girded me with gladness; 12 that my glory may sing praise to thee, and I may not be pierced *with sorrow.* O Lord my God, I will give thanks to thee for ever.

Ps.31 *For the end, a Psalm of David, an utterance of extreme fear.* 1 O Lord, I have hoped in thee; let me never be ashamed: deliver me in thy righteousness and rescue me. 2 Incline thine ear to me; make haste to rescue me: be thou to me for a protecting God, and for a house of refuge to save me. 3 For thou art my strength and my refuge; and thou shalt guide me for thy name's sake, and maintain me. 4 Thou shalt bring me out of the snare which they have hidden for me; for thou, O Lord, art my defender. 5 Into thine hands I will commit my spirit: thou hast redeemed me, O Lord God of truth. 6 Thou has hated them that idly persist in vanities: but I have hoped in the Lord. 7 I will exult and be glad in thy mercy: for thou hast looked upon mine affliction; thou hast saved my soul from distresses. 8 And thou hast not shut me up into the hands of the enemy: thou hast set my feet in a wide place. 9 Pity me, O Lord, for I am afflicted: my eye is troubled with indignation, my soul and by belly. 10 For my life is spent with grief, and my years with groanings: my strength has been weakened through poverty, and my bones are troubled. 11 I became a reproach among all mine enemies, but exceedingly so to my neighbours, and a fear to mine acquaintance: they that saw me without fled from me. 12 I have been forgotten as a dead man out of mind: I am become as a broken vessel. 13 For I heard the slander of many that dwelt round about: when they were gathered together against me, they took counsel to take my life. 14 But I hoped in thee, O Lord: I said, Thou art my God. 15 My lots are in thy hands: deliver me from the hand of mine enemies, 16 and from them that persecute me. Make thy face to shine upon thy servant: save me in thy mercy. 17 O Lord, let me not be ashamed, for I have called upon thee: let the ungodly be ashamed, and brought down to Hades. 18 Let the deceitful lips become dumb, which speak iniquity against the righteous with pride and scorn. 19 How abundant is the multitude of thy goodness, O Lord, which thou hast laid up for them that fear thee! thou hast wrought *it* out for them that hope on thee, in the presence of the sons of men. 20 Thou wilt hide them in the secret of thy presence from the vexation of man: thou wilt screen them in a tabernacle from the contradiction of tongues. 21 Blessed be the Lord: for he has magnified his mercy in a fortified city. 22 But I said in my extreme fear, I am cast out from the sight of thine eyes: therefore thou didst hearken, O Lord, to the voice of my supplication when I cried to thee. 23 Love the Lord, all ye his saints: for the Lord seeks for truth, and renders *a reward* to them that deal very proudly. 24 Be of good courage, and let your heart be strengthened, all ye that hope in the Lord.

Ps.32 *A Psalm of instruction by David.* 1 Blessed *are they* whose transgressions are forgiven, and who sins are covered. 2 Blessed is the man to whom the Lord will not impute sin, and whose mouth there is no guile. 3 Because I kept silence, my bones waxed old, from my crying all the day. 4 For day and night thy hand was heavy upon me: I became thoroughly miserable while a thorn was fastened in *me.* Pause. 5 I acknowledged my sin, and hid not mine iniquity: I said, I will confess mine iniquity to the Lord against myself; and thou forgavest the ungodliness of my heart. Pause. 6 Therefore shall every holy one pray to thee in a fit time: only in the deluge of many waters they shall not come nigh to him. 7 Thou art my refuge from the affliction that encompasses me; my joy, to deliver me from them that have compassed me. Pause. 8 I will instruct thee and guide thee in this way wherein thou shalt go: I will fix mine eyes upon thee. 9 Be ye not as horse and mule, which have no understanding; *but thou must* constrain their jaws with bit and curb, lest they should come nigh to thee. 10 Many are the scourges of the sinner: but him that hopes in the Lord mercy shall compass about. 11 Be glad in the Lord, and exult, ye righteous: and glory, all ye that are upright in heart.

Ps.33 *A Psalm of David.* 1 Rejoice in the Lord, ye righteous; praise becomes the upright. 2 Praise the Lord on the harp; platy to him on a psaltery of ten strings. 3 Sing to him a new song; play skillfully with a loud noise. 4 For the word of the Lord is right; and all his works are faithful. 5 He loves mercy and judgment; the earth is full the mercy of the Lord. 6 By the word of the Lord the heavens were established; and all the host of them by the breath of his *mouth.* 7 Who gathers the waters of the sea as *in* a bottle; who lays up the deeps in treasuries. 8 Let all the earth fear the Lord; and let all that dwell in the world be moved because of him. 9 For he spoke, and they were made; he commanded, and they were created. 10 The Lord frustrates the counsels of the nations; he brings to nought also the reasonings of the peoples, and brings to nought the counsels of princes. 11 But the counsel of the Lord endures for ever, the thoughts of his heart from generation to generation. 12 Blessed is the nation whose God is the Lord; the people whom he has chosen for his own inheritance. 13 The Lord looks out of heaven; he

beholds all the sons of men. 14 He looks from his prepared habitation on all the dwellers on the earth; 15 who fashioned their hearts alone; who understands all their works. 16 A king is not saved by reason of a great host; and a giant shall not be delivered by the greatness of his strength. 17 A horse is vain for safety; neither shall he be delivered by the greatness of his power. 18 Behold, the eyes of the Lord are on them that fear him, those that hope in his mercy; 19 to deliver their souls from death, and to keep them alive in famine. 20 Our soul waits on the Lord; for he is our helper and defender. 21 For our heart shall rejoice in him, and we have hoped in his holy name. 22 Let thy mercy, O Lord, be upon us, according as we have hoped in thee.

Ps.31 *A Psalm of David, when he changed his countenance before Abimelech; and he let him go, and he departed.* 1 I will bless the Lord at all times: his praise shall be continually in my mouth. 2 My soul shall boast herself in the Lord: let the meek hear, and rejoice. 3 Magnify ye the Lord with me, and let us exalt his name together. 4 I sought the Lord diligently, and he hearkened to me, and delivered me from all my sojournings. 5 Draw near to him, and be enlightened: and your faces shall not *by any means* be ashamed. 6 This poor man cried, and the Lord hearkened to him, and delivered him out of all his afflictions. 7 The angel of the Lord will encamp round about them that fear him, and will deliver them. 8 Taste and see that the Lord is good: blessed is the man who hopes in him. 9 Fear the Lord, all ye his saints: for there is no want to them that fear him. 10 The rich have become poor and hungry: but they that seek the Lord diligently shall not want any good thing. Pause. 11 Come, ye children, hear me: I will teach you the fear of the Lord. 12 What man is there that desires life, loving to see good days? 13 Keep thy tongue from evil, and thy lips from speaking guile. 14 Turn away from evil, and do good; seek peace, and pursue it. 15 The eyes of the Lord are over the righteous, and his ears *are open* to their prayer: 16 but the face of the Lord is against them that do evil, to destroy their memorial from the earth. The righteous cried, and the Lord hearkened to them, 17 and delivered them out of all their afflictions. 18 The Lord is near to them that are of a contrite heart; and will save the lowly in spirit. 19 Many are the afflictions of the righteous: but out of them all Lord will deliver them. 20 He keeps all their bones: not one of them shall be broken. 21 The death of sinners is evil: and they that hate righteousness will go wrong. 22 The Lord will redeem the souls of his servants: and none of those that hope in him shall go wrong.

Ps.35 *A Psalm of David.* 1 Judge thou, O Lord, them that injure me, fight against them that fight against me. 2 Take hold of shield and buckler, and arise for my help. 3 Bring forth a sword, and stop *the way* against them that persecute me: say to my soul, I am thy salvation. 4 Let them that seek my soul be ashamed and confounded: let them that devise evils against me be turned back and put to shame. 5 Let them be as dust before the wind, and an angel of the Lord afflicting them. 6 Let their way be dark and slippery, and an angel of the Lord persecuting them. 7 For without cause they have hid for me their destructive snare: without a cause they have reproached my soul. 8 Let a snare which they know not come upon them; and the gin which they hid take them; and let them fall into the very same snare. 9 But my soul shall exult in the Lord: it shall delight in his salvation. 10 All my bones shall say, O Lord, who is like to thee? delivering the poor out of the hand of them that are stronger than he, yea, the poor and needy one from them that spoil him. 11 Unjust witnesses arose, and asked me of things I new not. 12 They rewarded me evil for good, and bereavement to my soul. 13 But I, when they troubled me, put on sackcloth, and humbled my soul with fasting: and my prayer shall return to my *own* bosom. 14 I behaved agreeably towards them as *if it had been* our neighbour *or* brother: I humbled myself as one mourning and sad of countenance. 15 Yet they rejoiced against me, and plagues were plentifully brought against me, and I knew *it* not: they were scattered, but repented not. 16 They tempted me, they sneered at me most contemptuously, they gnashed their teeth upon me. 17 O Lord, when wilt thou look upon me? Deliver my soul from their mischief, mine only- begotten one from the lions. 18 I will give thanks to thee even in a great congregation: in an abundant people I will praise thee. 19 Let not them that are mine enemies without a cause rejoice against me; who hate me for nothing, and wink with their eyes. 20 For to me they spoke peaceably, but imagined deceits in *their* anger. 21 And they opened wide their mouth upon me; they said Aha, aha, our eyes have seen *it*. 22 Thou hast seen *it*, O Lord: keep not silence: O Lord, withdraw not *thyself* from me. 23 Awake, O Lord, and attend to my judgment, *even* to my cause, my God and my Lord. 24 Judge me, O Lord, according to thy righteousness, O Lord my God; and let them not rejoice against me. 25 Let them not say in their hearts, Aha, aha, *it is pleasing* to our soul: neither let them say, We have devoured him. 26 Let them be confounded and ashamed together that rejoice at my afflictions: let them be clothed with shame and confusion that speak great swelling words against me. 27 Let them that rejoice in my righteousness exult and be glad: and let them say continually, The Lord be magnified, who desire the peace of his servant. 28 And my tongue shall meditate on thy righteousness, *and* on thy praise all the day.

Ps.36 *For the end, by David the servant of the Lord.* 1 The transgressor, that he may sin, says within himself, *that* there is no fear of God before his eyes. 2 For he has dealt craftily before him, to discover his iniquity and hate it. 3 The words of his mouth are transgression and deceit: he is not inclined to understand *how* to do good. 4 He devises iniquity on his bed; he gives himself to every evil way; and does not abhor evil. 5 O Lord, thy mercy is in the heaven; and thy truth *reaches* to the clouds. 6 Thy righteousness is as the mountains of God, thy judgments are as a great deep: O Lord, thou wilt preserve men and beasts. 7 How hast thou multiplied thy mercy, O God! so the children of men shall trust in the shelter of thy wings. 8 They shall be fully satisfied with the fatness of thine house; and thou shalt cause them to drink of the full stream of thy delights. 9 For with thee is the fountain of life: in thy light we shall see light. 10 Extend thy mercy to them that know thee; and thy righteousness to the

upright in heart. 11 Let not the foot of pride come against me, and let not the hand of sinners move me. 12 There have all the workers of iniquity fallen: they are cast out, and shall not be able to stand.

Ps.37 *A Psalm of David.* 1 Fret not thyself because of evil-doers, neither be envious of them that do iniquity. 2 For they shall soon be withered as the grass, and shall soon fall away as the green herbs. 3 Hope in the Lord, and do good; and dwell on the land, and thou shalt be fed with the wealth of it. 4 Delight *thyself* in the Lord; and he shall grant thee the requests of thine heart. 5 Disclose thy way to the Lord, and hope in him; and he shall bring *it* to pass. 6 And he shall bring forth thy righteousness as the light, and thy judgment as the noon-day. 7 Submit thyself to the Lord, and supplicate him: fret not thyself because of him that prospers in his way, at the man that does unlawful deeds. 8 ease from anger, and forsake wrath: fret not thyself so as to do evil. 9 For evil-doers shall be destroyed: but they that wait on the Lord, they shall inherit the land. 10 And yet a little while, and the sinner shall not be, and thou shalt seek for his place, and shalt not find *it*. 11 But the meek shall inherit the earth; and shall delight *themselves* in the abundance of peace. 12 The sinner will watch for the righteous, and gnash his teeth upon him. 13 But the Lord shall laugh at him: for he foresees that his day will come. 14 Sinners have drawn their swords, they have bent their bow, to cast down the poor and needy one, *and* to slay the upright in heart. 15 Let their sword enter into their *own* heart, and their bows be broken. 16 A little is better to the righteous than abundant wealth of sinners. 17 For the arms of sinners shall be broken; but the Lord supports the righteous. 18 The Lord knows the ways of the perfect; and their inheritance shall be for ever. 19 They shall not be ashamed in an evil time; and in days of famine they shall be satisfied. 20 For the sinners shall perish; and the enemies of the Lord at the moment of their being honoured and exalted have utterly vanished like smoke. 21 The sinner borrows, and will not pay again: but the righteous has compassion, and gives. 22 For they that bless him shall inherit the earth; and they that curse him shall be utterly destroyed. 23 The steps of a man are rightly ordered by the Lord: and he will take pleasure in his way. 24 When he falls, he shall not be ruined: for the Lord supports his hand. 25 I was *once* young, indeed I am now old; yet I have not seen the righteous forsaken, nor his seed seeking bread. 26 He is merciful, and lends continually; and his seed shall be blessed. 27 Turn aside from evil, and do good; and dwell for ever. 28 For the Lord loves judgment, and will not forsake his saints; they shall be preserved for ever: the blameless shall be avenged, but the seed of the ungodly shall be utterly destroyed. 29 But the righteous shall inherit the earth, and dwell upon it for ever. 30 The mouth of the righteous will meditate wisdom, and his tongue will speak of judgment. 31 The law of his God is in his heart; and his steps shall not slide. 32 The sinner watches the righteous, and seeks to slay him. 33 But the Lord will not leave him in his hands, nor by any means condemn him when he is judged. 34 Wait on the Lord, and keep his way, and he shall exalt thee to inherit the land:

when the wicked are destroyed, thou shalt see *it*. 35 I saw the ungodly very highly exalting himself, and lifting himself up like the cedars of Libanus. 36 Yet I passed by, and lo! he was not: and I sought him, but his place was not found. 37 Maintain innocence, and behold uprightness: for there is a remnant to the peaceable man. 38 But the transgressors shall be utterly destroyed together: the remnants of the ungodly shall be utterly destroyed. 39 But the salvation of the righteous is of the Lord; and he is their defender in the time of affliction. 40 And the Lord shall help them, and deliver them: and he shall rescue them from sinners, and save them, because they have hoped in him.

Ps.38 *A Psalm of David for remembrance concerning the Sabbath-day.* 1 O Lord, rebuke me not in thy wrath, neither chasten me in thine anger. 2 For thy weapons are fixed in me, and thou hast pressed thy hand heavily upon me. 3 For there is no health in my flesh because of thine anger; there is no peace to my bones because of my sins. 4 For my transgressions have gone over mine head: they have pressed heavily upon me like a weighty burden. 5 My bruises have become noisome and corrupt, because of my foolishness. 6 I have been wretched and bowed down continually: I went with a mourning countenance all the day. 7 For my soul is filled with mockings; and there is no health in my flesh. 8 I have been afflicted and brought down exceedingly: I have roared for the groaning of my heart. 9 But all my desire is before thee; and my groaning is not hidden from thee. 10 My heart is troubled, my strength has failed me; and the light of mine eyes is not with me. 11 My friends and my neighbours drew near before me, and stood still; and my nearest of kin stood afar off. 12 While they pressed hard upon me that sought my soul: and they that sought my hurt spoke vanities, and devised deceits all the day. 13 But I, as a deaf man, heard not; and was as a dumb man not opening his mouth. 14 And I was as a man that hears not, and who has no reproofs in his mouth. 15 For I hoped in thee, O Lord: thou wilt hear, O Lord my God. 16 For I said, Lest mine enemies rejoice against me: for when my feet were moved, they spoke boastingly against me. 17 For I am ready for plagues, and my grief is continually before me. 18 For I will declare mine iniquity, and be distressed for my sin. 19 But mine enemies live, and are mightier than I: and they that hate me unjustly are multiplied. 20 They that reward evil for good slandered me; because I followed righteousness. 21 Forsake me not, O Lord my God: depart not from me. 22 Draw nigh to my help, O Lord of my salvation.

Ps.39 *For the end, a Song of David, to Idithun.* 1 I said, I will take heed to my ways, that I sin not with my tongue: I set a guard on my mouth, while the sinner stood in my presence. 2 I was dumb, and humbled myself, and kept silence from good *words*; and my grief was renewed. 3 My heart grew hot within me, and a fire would kindle in my meditation: I spoke with my tongue, 4 O Lord, make me to know mine end, and the number of my days, what it is; that I may know what I lack. 5 Behold, thou hast made my days old; and my existence *is* as nothing before thee: nay, every man living *is* altogether vanity. Pause. 6 Surely man walks in a shadow;

nay, he is disquieted in vain: he lays up treasures, and knows not for whom he shall gather them. 7 And now what *is* my expectation? *is it* not the Lord? and my ground *of hope* is with thee. Pause. 8 Deliver me from all my transgressions: thou hast made me a reproach to the foolish. 9 I was dumb, and opened not my mouth; for thou art he that made me. 10 Remove thy scourges from me: I have fainted by reason of the strength of thine hand. 11 Thou chastenest man with rebukes for iniquity, and thou makest his life to consume away like a spider's web; nay, every man is disquieted in vain. Pause. 12 O Lord, hearken to my prayer and my supplication: attend to my tears: be not silent, for I am a sojourner in the land, and a stranger, as all my fathers *were*. 13 Spare me, that I may be refreshed, before I depart, and be no more.

Ps.40 *For the end, a Psalm of David.* 1 I waited patiently for the Lord; and he attended to me, and hearkened to my supplication. 2 And he brought me up out of a pit of misery, and from miry clay: and he set my feet on a rock, and ordered my goings aright. 3 And he put a new song into my mouth, *even* a hymn to our God: many shall see *it*, and fear, and shall hope in the Lord. 4 Blessed *is* the man whose hope is in the name of the Lord, and *who* has not regarded vanities and false frenzies. 5 O Lord my God, thou hast multiplied thy wonderful works, and in thy thoughts there is none who shall be likened to thee: I declared and spoke *of them*: they exceeded number. 6 Sacrifice and offering thou wouldest not; but a body hast thou prepared me: whole-burnt-offering and *sacrifice* for sin thou didst not require. 7 Then I said, Behold, I come: in the volume of the book it is written concerning me, 8 I desired to do thy will, O my God, and thy law in the midst of mine heart. 9 I have preached righteousness in the great congregation; lo! I will not refrain my lips; O Lord, thou knowest my righteousness. 10 I have not hid thy truth within my heart, and I have declared thy salvation; I have not hid thy mercy and thy truth from the great congregation. 11 But thou, Lord, remove not thy compassion far from me; thy mercy and thy truth have helped me continually. 12 For innumerable evils have encompassed me; my transgressions have taken hold of me, and I could not see; they are multiplied more than the hairs of my head; and my heart has failed me. 13 Be pleased, O Lord, to deliver me; O Lord, draw nigh to help me. 14 Let those that seek my soul, to destroy it, be ashamed and confounded together; let those that wish me evil be turned backward and put to shame. 15 Let those that say to me, Aha, aha, quickly receive shame for their reward. 16 Let all those that seek thee, O Lord, exult and rejoice in thee; and let them that love thy salvation say continually, The Lord be magnified. 17 But I am poor and needy; the Lord will take care of me; thou art my helper, and my defender, O my God, delay not.

Ps.41 *For the end, a Psalm of David.* 1 Blessed *is the man* who thinks, on the poor and needy: the Lord shall deliver him in an evil day. 2 May the Lord preserve him and keep him alive, and bless him on the earth, and not deliver him into the hands of his enemy. 3 May the Lord help him upon the bed of his pain; thou hast made all his bed in his sickness.

4 I said, O Lord, have mercy upon me; heal my soul; for I have sinned against thee. 5 Mine enemies have spoken evil against me, *saying*, When shall he die, and his name perish? 6 And if he came to see *me*, his heart spoke vainly; he gathered iniquity to himself; he went forth and spoke in like manner. 7 All my enemies whispered against me; against me they devised my hurt. 8 They denounced a wicked word against me, *saying*, Now that he lies, shall he not rise up again? 9 For even the man of my peace, in whom I trusted, who ate my bread, lifted up *his* heel against me. 10 But thou, O Lord, have compassion upon me, and raise me up, and I shall requite them. 11 By this I know that thou hast delighted in me, because mine enemy shall not rejoice over me. 12 But thou didst help me because of *mine* innocence, and hast established me before thee for ever. 13 Blessed *be* the Lord God of Israel from everlasting, and to everlasting. So be it, so be it.

Ps.42 *For the end, a Psalm for instruction, for the sons of Core.* 1 As the hart earnestly desires the fountains of water, so my soul earnestly longs for thee, O God. 2 My soul has thirsted for the living God: when shall I come and appear before God? 3 My tears have been bread to me day and night, while they daily said to me, Where is thy God? 4 I remembered these things, and poured out my soul in me, for I will go to the place of thy wondrous tabernacle, *even* to the house of God, with a voice of exultation and thanksgiving and of the sound of those who keep festival. 5 Wherefore art thou very sad, O my soul? and wherefore dost thou trouble me? hope in God; for I will give thanks to him; *he is* the salvation of my countenance. 6 O my God, my soul has been troubled within me: therefore will I remember thee from the land of Jordan, and of the Ermonites, from the little hill. 7 Deep calls to deep at the voice of thy cataracts: all thy billows and thy waves have gone over me. 8 By day the Lord will command his mercy, and manifest *it* by night: with me *is* prayer to the God of my life. 9 I will say to God, Thou art my helper; why hast thou forgotten me? wherefore do I go sad of countenance, while the enemy oppresses *me*? 10 While my bones were breaking, they that afflicted me reproached me; while they said to me daily, Where is thy God? 11 Wherefore art thou very sad, O my soul? and wherefore dost thou trouble me? hope in God; for I will give thanks to him; *he is* the health of my countenance, and my God.

Ps.43 *A Psalm of David.* 1 Judge me, o God, and plead my cause, against an ungodly nation: deliver me from the unjust and crafty man. 2 For thou, O God, art my strength: wherefore hast thou cast me off? and why do I go sad of countenance, while the enemy oppresses *me*? 3 Send forth thy light and thy truth: they have led me, and brought me to thy holy mountain, and to thy tabernacles. 4 And I will go in to the altar of God, to God who gladdens my youth: I will give thanks to thee on the harp, O God, my God. 5 Wherefore art thou very sad, O my soul? and wherefore dost thou trouble me? Hope in God; for I will give thanks to him, *who is* the health of my countenance, *and* my God.

Ps.44 *For the end, a Psalm for instruction, for the sons of Core.* 1 O God, we have heard with our ears, our fathers have told us, the work which thou wroughtest in their days, in the days of old. 2 Thine hand utterly destroyed the heathen, and thou didst plant them: thou didst afflict the nations, and cast them out. 3 For they inherited not the land by their *own* sword, and their *own* arm did not deliver them; but thy right hand, and thine arm, and the light of thy countenance, because thou wert well pleased in them. 4 Thou art indeed my King and my God, who commandest deliverances for Jacob. 5 In thee will we push down our enemies, and in thy name will we bring to nought them that rise up against us. 6 For I will not trust in my bow, and my sword shall not save me. 7 For thou hast saved us from them that afflicted us, and hast put to shame them that hated us. 8 In God will we make our boast all the day, and to thy name will we give thanks for ever. Pause. 9 But now thou hast cast off, and put us to shame; and thou wilt not go forth with our hosts. 10 Thou hast turned us back before our enemies; and they that hated us spoiled for themselves. 11 Thou madest us as sheep for meat; and thou scatteredst us among the nations. 12 Thou hast sold thy people without price, and there was no profit by their exchange. 13 Thou hast made us a reproach to our neighbours, a scorn and derision them that are round about us. 14 Thou hast made us a proverb among the Gentiles, a shaking of the head among the nations. 15 All the day my shame is before me, and the confusion of my face has covered me, 16 because of the voice of the slanderer and reviler; because of the enemy and avenger. 17 All these things are come upon us: but we have not forgotten thee, neither have we dealt unrighteously in thy covenant. 18 And our heart has not gone back; but thou hast turned aside our paths from thy way. 19 For thou hast laid us low in a place of affliction, and the shadow of death has covered us. 20 If we have forgotten the name of our God, and if we have spread out our hands to a strange god; shall not God search these things out? 21 for he knows the secrets of the heart. 22 For, for thy sake we are killed all the day long; we are counted as sheep for slaughter. 23 Awake, wherefore sleepest thou, O Lord? arise, and do not cast *us* off for ever. 24 Wherefore turnest thou thy face away, *and* forgettest our poverty and our affliction? 25 For our soul has been brought down to the dust; our belly has cleaved to the earth. 26 Arise, O Lord, help us, and redeem us for thy name's sake.

Ps.45 *For the end, for alternate strains by the sons of Core; for instruction, a Song concerning the beloved.* 1 My heart has uttered a good matter: I declare my works to the king: my tongue is the pen of a quick writer. 2 Thou art more beautiful than the sons of men: grace has been shed forth on thy lips: therefore God has blessed thee for ever. 3 Gird thy sword upon thy thigh, O Mighty One, in thy comeliness, and in thy beauty; 4 and bend *thy bow*, and prosper, and reign, because of truth and meekness and righteousness; and thy right hand shall guide thee wonderfully. 5 Thy weapons are sharpened, Mighty One, (the nations shall fall under thee) *they are* in the heart of the king's enemies. 6 Thy throne, O God, is for ever and ever: the sceptre of thy kingdom is a sceptre of righteousness. 7 Thou hast loved righteousness, and hated iniquity: therefore God, thy God, has anointed thee with the oil of gladness beyond thy fellows. 8 Myrrh, and stacte, and cassia *are exhaled* from thy garments, *and* out of the ivory palaces, 9 with which kings' daughters have gladdened thee for thine honour: the queen stood by on thy right hand, clothed in vesture wrought with gold, *and* arrayed in divers colours. 10 Hear, O daughter, and see, and incline thine ear; forget also thy people, and thy father's house. 11 Because the king has desired thy beauty; for he is thy Lord. 12 And the daughter of Tyre shall adore him with gifts; the rich of the people of the land shall supplicate thy favour. 13 All her glory *is that* of the daughter of the king of Esebon, robed *as she is* in golden fringed garments, 14 in embroidered *clothing*: virgins shall be brought to the king after her: her fellows shall be brought to thee. 15 They shall be brought with gladness and exultation: they shall be led into the king's temple. 16 Instead of thy fathers children are born to thee: thou shalt make them princes over all the earth. 17 They shall make mention of thy name from generation to generation: therefore shall the nations give thanks to thee for ever, even for ever and ever.

Ps.46 *For the end, for the sons of Core; a Psalm concerning secret things.* 1 God is our refuge and strength, a help in the afflictions that have come heavily upon us. 2 Therefore will we not fear when the earth is troubled, and the mountains are removed into the depths of the seas. 3 Their waters have roared and been troubled, the mountains have been troubled by his might. Pause. 4 The flowings of the river gladden the city of God: the Most High has sanctified his tabernacle. 5 God is in the midst of her; she shall not be moved: God shall help her with his countenance. 6 The nations were troubled, the kingdoms tottered: he uttered his voice, the earth shook. 7 The Lord of hosts is with us; the God of Jacob is our helper. Pause. 8 Come, and behold the works of the Lord, what wonders he has achieved on the earth. 9 Putting an end to wars as for the ends of the earth; he will crush the bow, and break in pieces the weapon, and burn the bucklers with fire. 10 Be still, and know that I am God: I will be exalted among the nations, I will be exalted in the earth. 11 The Lord of hosts is with us; the God of Jacob is our helper.

Ps.47 *For the end, a Psalm for the sons of Core.* 1 Clap your hands, all ye nations; shout to God with a voice of exultation. 2 For the Lord most high is terrible; *he is* a great king over all the earth. 3 He has subdued the peoples under us, and the nations under our feet. 4 He has chosen out his inheritance for us, the beauty of Jacob which he loved. Pause. 5 God is gone up with a shout, the Lord with a sound of a trumpet. 6 Sing praises to our God, sing praises: sing praises to our King, sing praises. 7 For God is king of all the earth: sing praises with understanding. 8 God reigns over the nations: God sits upon the throne of his holiness. 9 The rulers of the people are assembled with the God of Abraam: for God's mighty ones of the earth have been greatly exalted.

Ps.48 *A Psalm of praise for the sons of Core on the second day of the week.* 1 Great is the Lord, and greatly to be praised in the city of our God, in his holy mountain. 2 The city of the great King is well planted *on* the mountains of Sion, with the joy of the whole earth, *on* the sides of the north. 3 God is known in her palaces, when he undertakes to help her. 4 For, behold the kings of the earth were assembled, they came together. 5 They saw, and so they wondered: they were troubled, they were moved. 6 Trembling took hold on them: there were the pangs as of a woman in travail. 7 Thou wilt break the ships of Tharsis with a vehement wind. 8 As we have heard, so have we also seen, in the city of the Lord of hosts, in the city of our God: God has founded it for ever. Pause. 9 We have thought of thy mercy, O God, in the midst of thy people. 10 According to thy name, O God, so is also thy praise to the ends of the earth: thy right hand is full of righteousness. 11 Let mount Sion rejoice, let the daughters of Judaea exult, because of thy judgments, O Lord. 12 Go round about Sion, and encompass her: tell ye her towers. 13 Mark ye well her strength, and observe her palaces; that ye may tell the next generation. 14 For this is our God for ever and ever: he will be our guide for evermore.

Ps.49 *For the end, a Psalm for the sons of Core.* 1 Hear these words, all ye nations, hearken, all ye that dwell upon the earth: 2 both the sons of mean men, and sons of *great* men; the rich and poor *man* together. 3 My mouth shall speak of wisdom; and the meditation of my heart shall bring *forth* understanding. 4 I will incline mine ear to a parable: I will open my riddle on the harp. 5 Wherefore should I fear in the evil day? the iniquity of my heel shall compass me. 6 They that trust in their strength, and boast themselves in the multitude of their wealth— 7 A brother does not redeem, shall a man redeem? he shall not give to God a ransom for himself, 8 or the price of the redemption of his soul, though he labour for ever, 9 and live to the end, *so that* he should not see corruption. 10 When he shall see wise men dying, the fool and the senseless one shall perish together; and they shall leave their wealth to strangers. 11 And their sepulchres are their houses for ever, *even* their tabernacles to all generations: they have called their lands after their own names. 12 And man being in honour, understands not: he is compared to the senseless cattle, and is like to them. 13 This their way is an offence to them: yet afterwards men will commend their sayings. Pause. 14 They have laid *them* as sheep in Hades; death shall feed on them; and the upright shall have dominion over them in the morning, and their help shall fail in Hades from their glory. 15 But God shall deliver my soul from the power of Hades, when he shall receive me. Pause. 16 Fear not when a man is enriched, and when the glory of his house is increased. 17 For he shall take nothing when he dies; neither shall his glory descend with him. 18 For his soul shall be blessed in his life: he shall give thanks to thee when thou dost well to him. 19 *Yet* he shall go in to the generation of his fathers; he shall never see light. 20 Man that is in honour, understands not: he is compared to the senseless cattle, and is like them.

Ps.50 *A Psalm for Asaph.* 1 The God of gods, the Lord, has spoken, and called the earth from the rising of the sun to the going down *thereof.* 2 Out of Sion *comes* the excellence of his beauty. 3 God, our God, shall come manifestly, and shall not keep silence: a fire shall be kindled before him, and round about him there shall be a very great tempest. 4 He shall summon the heaven above, and the earth, that he may judge his people. 5 Assemble ye his saints to him, those that have engaged in a covenant with him upon sacrifices. 6 And the heavens shall declare his righteousness: for God is judge. Pause. 7 Hear, my people, and I will speak to thee, O Israel: and I will testify to thee: I am God, thy God. 8 I will not reprove thee on account of thy sacrifices; for thy whole-burnt-offerings are before me continually. 9 I will take no bullocks out of thine house, nor he-goats out of thy flocks. 10 For all the wild beasts of the thicket are mine, the cattle on the mountains, and oxen. 11 I know all the birds of the sky; and the beauty of the field is mine. 12 If I should be hungry, I will not tell thee: for the world is mine, and the fullness of it. 13 Will I eat the flesh of bulls, or drink the blood of goats? 14 Offer to God the sacrifice of praise; and pay thy vows to the Most High. 15 And call upon me in the day of affliction; and I will deliver thee, and thou shalt glorify me. Pause. 16 But to the sinner God has said, Why dost thou declare my ordinances, and take up my covenant in thy mouth? 17 Whereas thou hast hated instruction, and hast cast my words behind *thee.* 18 If thou sawest a thief, thou rannest along with him, and hast cast in thy lot with adulterers. 19 Thy mouth has multiplied wickedness, and thy tongue has framed deceit. 20 Thou didst sit and speak against thy brother, and didst scandalize thy mother's son. 21 These things thou didst, and I kept silence: thou thoughtest wickedly that I should be like thee, *but* I will reprove thee, and set *thine offences* before thee. 22 Now consider these things, ye that forget God, lest he rend *you,* and there is no deliverer. 23 The sacrifice of praise will glorify me: and that is the way wherein I will shew to him the salvation of God.

Ps.51 *For the end, a Psalm of David, when Nathan the prophet came to him, when he had gone to Bersabee.* 1 Have mercy upon me, O God, according to thy great mercy; and according to the multitude of thy compassions blot out my transgression. 2 Wash me thoroughly from mine iniquity, and cleanse me from my sin. 3 For I am conscious of mine iniquity; and my sin is continually before me. 4 Against thee only have I sinned, and done evil before thee: that thou mightest be justified in thy sayings, and mightest overcome when thou art judged. 5 For, behold, I was conceived in iniquities, and in sins did my mother conceive me. 6 For, behold, thou lovest truth: thou hast manifested to me the secret and hidden things of thy wisdom. 7 Thou shalt sprinkle me with hyssop, and I shall be purified: thou shalt wash me, and I shall be made whiter than snow. 8 Thou shalt cause me to hear gladness and joy: the afflicted bones shall rejoice. 9 Turn away thy face from my sins, and blot out all mine iniquities. 10 Create in me a clean heart, O God; and renew a right spirit in my inward parts. 11 Cast me not away from thy presence; and remove not thy holy Spirit from me. 12 Restore to me the joy of thy salvation: establish me with thy directing Spirit. 13 *Then* will I teach transgressors thy ways; and ungodly men shall turn to thee. 14 Deliver me from blood-guiltiness, O God, the God of my salvation: *and* my tongue shall joyfully declare thy righteousness. 15 O Lord, thou shalt open my lips; and my mouth shall declare thy praise. 16 For if thou desiredst sacrifice, I would have given *it*: thou wilt not take pleasure in whole-burnt -offerings. 17 Sacrifice to God is a broken spirit: a broken and humbled heart God will not despise. 18 Do good, O Lord, to Sion in thy good pleasure; and let the walls of Jerusalem be built. 19 Then shalt thou be pleased with a sacrifice of righteousness, offering, and whole-burnt- sacrifices: then shall they offer calves upon thine altar.

Ps.52 *For the end, a Psalm of instruction by David, when Doec the Idumean came and told Saul, and said to him, David is gone to the house of Abimelech.* 1 Why dost thou, O mighty man, boast of iniquity in *thy* mischief? All the day 2 thy tongue has devised unrighteousness; like a sharpened razor thou hast wrought deceit. 3 Thou hast loved wickedness more than goodness; unrighteousness better than to speak righteousness. Pause. 4 Thou has loved all words of destruction, *and* a deceitful tongue. 5 Therefore may God destroy thee for ever, may he pluck thee up and utterly remove thee from *thy* dwelling, and thy root from the land of the living. Pause. 6 And the righteous shall see, and fear, and shall laugh at him, and say, 7 Behold the man who made not God his help; but trusted in the abundance of his wealth, and strengthened himself in his vanity. 8 But I am as a fruitful olive in the house of God: I have trusted in the mercy of God for ever, even for evermore. 9 I will give thanks to thee for ever, for thou hast done *it*: and I will wait on thy name; for *it is* good before the saints.

Ps.53 *For the end, a Psalm of David upon Maeleth, of instruction.* 1 The fool has said in his heart, There is no God. They have corrupted *themselves*, and become abominable in iniquities: there is none that does good. 2 God looked down from heaven upon the sons of men, to see if there were any that understood, or sought after God. 3 They have all gone out of the way, they are together become unprofitable; there is none that does good, there is not even one. 4 Will none of the workers of iniquity know, who devour my people as they would eat bread? they have not called upon God. There were they greatly afraid, where there was no fear: 5 or God has scattered the bones of the men-pleasers; they were ashamed, for God despised them. 6 Who will bring the salvation of Israel out of Sion? When the Lord turns the captivity of his people, Jacob shall exult, and Israel shall be glad.

Ps.54 *For the end, among Hymns of instruction by David, when the Ziphites came and said to Saul, Lo, is not David hid with us?* 1 Save me, O God, by thy name, and judge me by thy might. 2 O God, hear my prayer; hearken to the words of my mouth. 3 For strangers have risen up against me, and mighty men have sought my life: they have not set God before them. Pause. 4 For lo! God assists me; and the Lord is the helper of my soul. 5 He shall return evil to mine enemies; utterly destroy them in thy truth. 6 I will willingly sacrifice to thee: I will give thanks to thy name, O Lord; for *it is* good. 7 For thou hast delivered me out of all affliction, and mine eye has seen *my desire* upon mine enemies.

Ps.55 *For the end, among Hymns of instruction by David.* 1 Hearken, O God, to my prayer; and disregard not my supplication. 2 Attend to me, and hearken to me: I was grieved in my meditation, and troubled; 3 because of the voice of the enemy, and because of the oppression of the sinner: for they brought iniquity against me, and were wrathfully angry with me. 4 My heart was troubled within me; and the fear of death fell upon me. 5 Fear and trembling came upon me, and darkness covered me. 6 And I said, O that I had wings as *those* of a dove! then would I flee away, and be at rest. 7 Lo! I have fled afar off, and lodged in the wilderness. Pause. 8 I waited for him that should deliver me from distress of spirit and tempest. 9 Destroy, O Lord, and divide their tongues: for I have seen iniquity and gain saying in the city. 10 Day and night he shall go round about it upon its walls: iniquity and sorrow and unrighteousness *are* in the midst of it; 11 and usury and craft have not failed from its streets. 12 For if an enemy had reproached me, I would have endured it; and if one who hated *me* had spoken vauntingly against me, I would have hid myself from him. 13 But thou, O man like minded, my guide, and my acquaintance, 14 who in companionship with me sweetened *our* food: we walked in the house of God in concord. 15 Let death come upon them, and let them go down alive into Hades, for iniquity is in their dwellings, in the midst of them. 16 I cried to God, and the Lord hearkened to me. 17 Evening, and morning, and at noon I will declare and make known *my wants*: and he shall hear my voice. 18 He shall deliver my soul in peace from them that draw nigh to me: for they were with me in many *cases*. 19 God shall hear, and bring them low, *even* he that has existed from eternity. Pause. For they suffer no reverse, and *therefore* they have not feared God. 20 He has reached forth his hand for retribution; they have profaned his covenant. 21 They were scattered at the anger of his countenance, and his heart drew nigh them. His words were smoother than oil, yet are they darts. 22 Cast thy care upon the Lord, and he shall sustain thee; he shall never suffer the righteous to be moved. 23 But thou, O God, shalt bring them down to the pit of destruction; bloody and crafty men shall not live out half their days; but I will hope in thee, O Lord.

Ps.56 *For the end, concerning the people that were removed from the sanctuary, by David for a memorial, when the Philistines caught him in Geth.* 1 Have mercy upon me, O God; for man has trodden me down; all the day long he warring has afflicted me. 2 Mine enemies have trodden me down all the day from the dawning of the day; for there are many warring against me. 3 They shall be afraid, but I will trust in thee. 4 In God I will praise my words; all the day have I hoped in God; I will not fear what flesh shall do to me. 5 All the day long they have abominated my words; all their devices *are* against me for evil. 6 They will dwell near and hide *themselves*; they will watch my steps, accordingly as I have waited patiently

in my soul. 7 Thou wilt on no account save them; thou wilt bring down the people in wrath. 8 O God, I have declared my life to thee; thou has set my tears before thee, even according to thy promise. 9 Mine enemies shall be turned back, in the day wherein I shall call upon thee; behold, I know that thou art my God. 10 In God, will I praise *his* word; in the Lord will I praise *his* saying. 11 I have hoped in God; I will not be afraid of what man shall do to me. 12 The vows of thy praise, O God, which I will pay, are upon me. 13 For thou hast delivered my soul from death, and my feet from sliding, that I should be well-pleasing before God in the land of the living.

Ps.57 *For the end. Destroy not: by David, for a memorial, when he fled from the presence of Saul to the cave.* 1 Have mercy, upon me, O God, have mercy upon me: for my soul has trusted in thee: and in the shadow of thy wings will I hope, until the iniquity have passed away. 2 I will cry to God most high; the God who has benefited me. Pause. 3 He sent from heaven and saved me; he gave to reproach them that trampled on me: God has sent forth his mercy and his truth; 4 and he has delivered my soul from the midst of *lions'* whelps: I lay down to sleep, *though* troubled. *As for* the sons of men, their teeth are arms and *missile* weapons, and their tongue a sharp sword. 5 Be thou exalted, O God, above the heavens; and thy glory above all the earth. 6 They have prepared snares for my feet, and have bowed down my soul: they have dug a pit before my face, and fallen into it *themselves*. Pause. 7 My heart, O God, *is* ready, my heart *is* ready: I will sing, yea will sing psalms. 8 Awake, my glory; awake, psaltery and harp: I will awake early. 9 O Lord, I will give thanks to thee among the nations: I will sing to thee among the Gentiles. 10 For thy mercy has been magnified even to the heavens, and thy truth to the clouds. 11 Be thou exalted, O God, above the heavens; and thy glory above all the earth.

Ps.58 *For the end. Destroy not: by David, for a memorial.* 1 If ye do indeed speak righteousness, *then* do ye judge rightly, ye sons of men. 2 For ye work iniquities in *your* hearts in the earth: your hands plot unrighteousness. 3 Sinners have gone astray from the womb: they go astray from the belly: they speak lies. 4 Their venom is like *that* of a serpent; as *that* of a deaf asp, and that stops her ears; 5 which will not hear the voice of charmers, nor *heed* the charm prepared skillfully by the wise. 6 God has crushed their teeth in their mouth: God has broken the cheek-teeth of the lions. 7 They shall utterly pass away like water running through: he shall bend his bow till they shall fail. 8 They shall be destroyed as melted wax: the fire has fallen and they have not seen the sun. 9 Before your thorns feel the white thorn, he shall swallow you up as living, as in his wrath. 10 The righteous shall rejoice when he sees the vengeance of the ungodly: he shall wash his hands in the blood of the sinner. 11 And a man shall say, Verily then there is a reward for the righteous: verily there is a God that judges them in the earth.

Ps.59 *For the end. Destroy not: by David for a memorial, when Saul sent, and watched his house to kill him.* 1 Deliver me from mine enemies, O God; and ransom me from those that rise up against me. 2 Deliver me from the workers of iniquity, and save me from bloody men. 3 For, behold, they have hunted after my soul; violent men have set upon me: neither *is it* my iniquity, nor my sin, O Lord. 4 Without iniquity I ran and directed *my course aright*: awake to help me, and behold. 5 And thou, Lord God of hosts, the God of Israel, draw nigh to visit all the heathen; pity not any that work iniquity. Pause. 6 They shall return at evening, and hunger like a dog, and go round about the city. 7 Behold, they shall utter a voice with their mouth, and a sword is in their lips; for who, *say they*, has heard? 8 But thou, Lord, wilt laugh them to scorn; thou wilt utterly set at nought all the heathen. 9 will keep my strength, *looking* to thee; for thou, O God, art my helper. 10 *As for* my God, his mercy shall go before me: my God will shew me *vengeance* on mine enemies. 11 Slay them not, lest they forget thy law; scatter them by thy power; and bring them down, O Lord, my defender. 12 *For* the sin of their mouth, *and* the word of their lips, let them be even taken in their pride. 13 And for *their* cursing and falsehood shall utter destruction be denounced: *they shall fall* by the wrath of utter destruction, and shall not be; so shall they know that the God of Jacob is Lord of the ends of the earth. Pause. 14 They shall return at evening, and be hungry as a dog, and go round about the city. 15 They shall be scattered hither and thither for meat; and if they be not satisfied, they shall even murmur. 16 But I will sing to thy strength, and in the morning will I exult *in* thy mercy; for thou hast been my supporter, and my refuge in the day of mine affliction. 17 *Thou art* my helper; to thee, my God, will I sing; thou art my supporter, O my God, *and* my mercy.

Ps.60 *For the end, for them that shall yet be changed; for an inscription by David for instruction, when he had burned Mesopotamia of Syria, and Syria Sobal, and Joab had returned and smitten in the valley of salt twelve thousand.* 1 O God, thou hast rejected and destroyed us; thou hast been angry, yet hast pitied us. 2 Thou hast shaken the earth, and troubled it; heal its breaches, for it has been shaken. 3 Thou hast shewn thy people hard things: thou has made us drink the wine of astonishment. 4 Thou hast given a token to them that fear thee, that they might flee from the bow. Pause. 5 That thy beloved ones may be delivered; save with thy right hand, and hear me. 6 God has spoken in his holiness; I will rejoice, and divide Sicima, and measure out the valley of tents. 7 Galaad is mine, and Manasse is mine; and Ephraim is the strength of my head; 8 Judas is my king; Moab is the caldron of my hope; over Idumea will I stretch out my shoe; the Philistines have been subjected to me. 9 Who will lead me into the fortified city? who will guide me as far a Idumea? 10 Wilt not thou, O God, who hast cast us off? and wilt not thou, O God, go forth with our forces? 11 Give us help from trouble: for vain is the deliverance of man. 12 In God will we do valiantly; and he shall bring to nought them that harass us.

Ps.61 *For the end, among the Hymns of David.* 1 O God, hearken to my petition; attend to my prayer. 2 From the ends of the earth have I cried to thee, when my heart was in trouble: thou liftedst me up on a rock thou didst guide me: 3 because thou wert my hope, a tower of strength from the face of the enemy. 4 I will dwell in thy tabernacle for ever; I will

shelter myself under the shadow of thy wings. Pause. 5 For thou, o God, hast heard my prayers; thou hast given an inheritance to them that fear thy name. 6 Thou shalt add days to the days of the king; *thou shalt lengthen* his years to all generations. 7 He shall endure for ever before God: which of them will seek out his mercy and truth? 8 So will I sing to thy name for ever and ever, that I may daily perform my vows.

Ps.62 *For the end, a Psalm of David for Idithun.* 1 Shall not my soul be subjected to God? for of him is my salvation. 2 For he is my God, and my saviour; my helper, I shall not be moved very much. 3 How long will ye assault a man? ye are all slaughtering as with a bowed wall and a broken hedge. 4 They only took counsel to set at nought mine honour: I ran in thirst: with their mouth they blessed, but with their heart they cursed. Pause. 5 Nevertheless do thou, my soul, be subjected to God; for of him *is* my patient hope. 6 For he *is* my God and my Saviour; my helper, I shall not be moved. 7 In God *is* my salvation and my glory: *he is* the God of my help, and my hope is in God. 8 Hope in him, all ye congregation of the people; pour out your hearts before him, for God is our helper. Pause. 9 But the sons of men are vain; the sons of men are false, so as to be deceitful in the balances; they are all alike *formed* out of vanity. 10 Trust not in unrighteousness, and lust not after robberies: if wealth should flow in, set not your heart upon it. 11 God has spoken once, *and* I have heard these two things, that power is of God; 12 and mercy is thine, O Lord; for thou wilt recompense every one according to his works.

Ps.63 *A Psalm of David, when he was in the wilderness of Idumea.* 1 O God, my God, I cry to thee early; my soul has thirsted for thee: how often has my flesh *longed* after thee, in a barren and trackless and dry land! 2 Thus have I appeared before thee in the sanctuary, that I might see thy power and thy glory. 3 For thy mercy is better than life: my lips shall praise thee. 4 Thus will I bless thee during my life: I will lift up my hands in thy name. 5 Let my soul be filled as with marrow and fatness; and *my* joyful lips shall praise thy name. 6 Forasmuch as I have remembered thee on my bed: in the early seasons I have meditated on thee. 7 For thou hast been my helper, and in the shelter of thy wings will I rejoice. 8 My soul has kept very close behind thee: thy right hand has upheld me. 9 But they vainly sought after my soul; they shall go into the lowest parts o the earth. 10 They shall be delivered up to the power of the sword; they shall be portions for foxes. 11 But the king shall rejoice in God; every one that swears by him shall be praised; for the mouth of them that speak unjust things has been stopped.

Ps.64 *For the end, a Psalm of David.* 1 Hear my prayer, O God, when I make my petition to thee; deliver my soul from fear of the enemy. 2 Thou hast sheltered me from the conspiracy of them that do wickedly; from the multitude of them that work iniquity; 3 who have sharpened their tongues as a sword; they have bent their bow maliciously; 4 to shoot in secret at the blameless; they will shoot him suddenly, and will not fear. 5 They have set up for themselves an evil matter, they have given counsel to hide snares; they have said, Who shall see them? 6 They have searched out iniquity; they have wearied themselves with searching diligently, a man shall approach and the heart is deep, 7 and God shall be exalted, their wounds were *caused by* the weapon of the foolish children, 8 and their tongues have set him at nought, all that saw them were troubled; 9 and every man was alarmed, and they related the works of God, and understood his deeds. 10 The righteous shall rejoice in the Lord, and hope on him, and all the upright in heart shall be praised.

Ps.65 *For the end, a Psalm and Song of David.* 1 Praise becomes thee, O God, in Sion; and to thee shall the vow be performed. 2 Hear my prayer; to thee all flesh shall come. 3 The words of transgressors have overpowered us; but do thou pardon our sins. 4 Blessed *is he* whom thou hast chosen and adopted; he shall dwell in thy courts; we shall be filled with the good things of thy house; thy temple is holy. 5 *Thou art* wonderful in righteousness. Hearken to us, O God our Saviour; the hope of all the ends of the earth, and of them *that are* on the sea afar off: 6 who dost establish the mountains in thy strength, being girded about with power; 7 who troublest the depth of the sea, the sounds of its waves. 8 The nations shall be troubled, and they that inhabit the ends *of the earth* shall be afraid of thy signs; thou wilt cause the outgoings of morning and evening to rejoice. 9 Thou hast visited the earth, and saturated it; thou hast abundantly enriched it. The river of God is filled with water; thou hast prepared their food, for thus is the preparation *of it.* 10 Saturate her furrows, multiply her fruits; *the crop* springing up shall rejoice in its drops. 11 Thou wilt bless the crown of the year *because* of thy goodness; and thy plains shall be filled with fatness. 12 The mountains of the wilderness shall be enriched; and the hills shall gird themselves with joy. 13 The rams of the flock are clothed *with wool,* and the valleys shall abound in corn; they shall cry aloud, yea they shall sing hymns.

Ps.66 *For the end, a Song of Psalm of resurrection.* 1 Shout unto God, all the earth. 2 O sing praises to his name; give glory to his praise. 3 Say unto God, How awful are thy works! through the greatness of thy power thine enemies shall lie to thee. 4 Let all the earth worship thee, and sing to thee; let them sing to thy name. Pause. 5 Come and behold the works of God; *he is* terrible in *his* counsels beyond the children of men. 6 Who turns the sea into dry land; they shall go through the river on foot; there shall we rejoice in him, 7 who by his power is Lord over the age, his eyes look upon the nations; let not them that provoke *him* be exalted in themselves. Pause. 8 Bless our God, ye Gentiles, and make the voice of his praise to be heard; 9 who quickens my soul in life, and does not suffer my feet to be moved. 10 For thou, O God, has proved us; thou hast tried us with fire as silver is tried. 11 Thou broughtest us into the snare; thou laidest afflictions on our back. 12 Thou didst mount men upon our heads; we went through the fire and water; but thou broughtest us out into *a place of* refreshment. 13 I will go into thine house with whole-burnt-offerings; I will pay thee my vows, 14 which my lips framed, and my mouth uttered in my affliction. 15 I will offer to thee whole-burnt-

sacrifices full of marrow, with incense and rams; I will sacrifice to thee oxen with goats. Pause. 16 Come, hear, and I will tell, all ye that fear God, how great things he has done for my soul. 17 I cried to him with my mouth, and exalted him with my tongue. 18 If I have regarded iniquity in my heart, let not the Lord hearken *to me.* 19 Therefore God has hearkened to me; he has attended to the voice of my prayer. 20 Blessed be God, who has not turned away my prayer, nor his mercy from me.

Ps.67 *For the end, a Psalm of David among the Hymns.* 1 God be merciful to us, and bless us; *and* cause his face to shine upon us. Pause. 2 That *men* may know thy way on the earth, thy salvation among all nations. 3 Let the nations, O God, give thanks to thee; let all the nations give thanks to thee. 4 Let the nations rejoice and exult, for thou shalt judge the peoples in equity, and shalt guide the nations on the earth. Pause. 5 Let the peoples, O God, give thanks to thee; let all the peoples give thanks to thee. 6 The earth has yielded her fruit; let God, our God bless us. 7 Let God bless us; and let all the ends of the earth fear him.

Ps.68 *For the end, a Psalm of a Song by David.* 1 Let God arise, and let his enemies be scattered; and let them that hate him flee from before him. 2 As smoke vanishes, let them vanish: as wax melts before the fire, so let the sinners perish from before God. 3 But let the righteous rejoice; let them exult before God: let them be delighted with joy. 4 Sing to God, sing praises to his name: make a way for him that rides upon the west (the Lord is his name) and exult before him. They shall be troubled before the face of him, 5 *who is* the father of the orphans, and judge of the widows: *such is* God in his holy place. 6 God settles the solitary in a house; leading forth prisoners mightily, also them that act provokingly, *even* them that dwell in tombs. 7 O God, when thou wentest forth before thy people, when thou wentest through the wilderness; Pause: 8 the earth quaked, yea, the heavens dropped *water* at the presence of the God of Sina, at the presence of the God of Israel. 9 O God, thou wilt grant to thine inheritance a gracious rain; for it was weary, but thou didst refresh it. 10 Thy creatures dwell in it: thou hast in thy goodness prepared for the poor. 11 The Lord God will give a word to them that preach *it* in a great company. 12 The king of the forces of the beloved, of the beloved, *will* even *grant them* for the beauty of the house to divide the spoils. 13 Even if ye should lie among the lots, *ye shall have* the wings of a dove covered with silver, and her breast with yellow gold. 14 When the heavenly One scatters kings upon it, they shall be made snow-white in Selmon. 15 The mountain of God is a rich mountain; a swelling mountain, a rich mountain. 16 Wherefore do ye conceive *evil,* ye swelling mountains? *this is* the mountain which God has delighted to dwell in; yea, the Lord will dwell *in it* for ever. 17 The chariots of God are ten thousand fold, thousands of rejoicing ones: the Lord is among them, in Sina, in the holy place. 18 Thou art gone up on high, thou hast led captivity captive, thou hast received gifts for man, yea, for *they were* rebellious, that thou mightest dwell among them. 19 Blessed be the Lord God, blessed be the Lord daily; and the God of our salvation shall prosper us. Pause.

20 Our God is the God of salvation; and to the Lord belong the issues from death. 21 But God shall crust the heads of his enemies; the hairy crown of them that go on in their trespasses. 22 The Lord said, I will bring again from Basan, I will bring *my people* again through the depths of the sea. 23 That thy foot may be dipped in blood, *and* the tongue of thy dogs *be stained* with that of *thine* enemies. 24 Thy goings, O God, have been seen; the goings of my God, the king, in the sanctuary. 25 The princes went first, next before the players on instruments, in the midst of damsels playing on timbrels. 26 Praise God in the congregations, the Lord from the fountains of Israel. 27 There is Benjamin the younger *one* in ecstasy, the princes of Juda their rulers, the princes of Zabulon, the princes of Nephthali. 28 O God, command thou thy strength: strengthen, O God, this which thou hast wrought in us. 29 Because of thy temple at Jerusalem shall kings bring presents to thee. 30 Rebuke the wild beasts of the reed: let the crowd of bulls with the heifers of the nations *be rebuked*, so that they who have been proved with silver may not be shut out: scatter thou the nations that wish for wars. 31 Ambassadors shall arrive out of Egypt; Ethiopia shall hasten *to stretch out* her hand readily to God. 32 Sing to God, ye kingdoms of the earth; sing psalms to the Lord. Pause. 33 Sing to God that rides on the heaven of heaven, eastward: lo, he will utter a mighty sound with his voice. 34 Give ye glory to God: his excellency is over Israel, and his power is in the clouds. 35 God is wonderful in his holy *places*, the God of Israel: he will give power and strength to his people: blessed be God.

Ps.69 *For the end, a Psalm of David, for alternate strains.* 1 Save me, O God; for the waters have come in to my soul. 2 I am stuck fast in deep mire, and there is no standing: I am come in to the depths of the sea, and a storm has overwhelmed me. 3 I am weary *of* crying, my throat has become hoarse; mine eyes have failed by my waiting on my God. 4 They that hate me without a cause are more than the hairs of my head: my enemies that persecute me unrighteously are strengthened: then I restored that which I took not away. 5 O God, thou knowest my foolishness; and my transgressions are not hidden from thee. 6 Let not them that wait on thee, O Lord of hosts, be ashamed on my account: let not them that seek thee, be ashamed on my account, O God of Israel. 7 For I have suffered reproach for thy sake; shame has covered my face. 8 I became strange to my brethren, and a stranger to my mother's children. 9 For the zeal of thine house has eaten me up; and the reproaches of them that reproached thee are fallen upon me. 10 And I bowed down my soul with fasting, and that was made my reproach. 11 And I put on sackcloth for my covering; and I became a proverb to them. 12 They that sit in the gate talked against me, and they that drank wine sang against me. 13 But I *will cry* to thee, O Lord, in my prayer; O God, it is a propitious time: in the multitude of thy mercy hear me, in the truth of thy salvation. 14 Save me from the mire, that I stick not *in it*: let me be delivered from them that hate me, and from the deep waters. 15 Let not the waterflood drown me, nor let the deep swallow me up; neither let the well shut its mouth upon me. 16 Hear me, O Lord; for thy mercy is good: according to the multitude of thy compassions look upon me. 17 And turn not away thy face from thy servant; for I am afflicted: hear me speedily. 18 Draw nigh to my soul and redeem it: deliver me because of mine enemies. 19 For thou knowest my reproach, and my shame, and my confusion; all that afflict me are before thee. 20 My soul has waited for reproach and misery; and I waited for one to grieve with me, but there was none; and for one to comfort me, but I found none. 21 They gave *me* also gall for my food, and made me drink vinegar for my thirst. 22 Let their table before them be for a snare, and for a recompense, and for a stumbling-block. 23 Let their eyes be darkened that they should not see; and bow down their back continually. 24 Pour out thy wrath upon them, and let the fury of thine anger take hold on them. 25 Let their habitation be made desolate; and let there be no inhabitant in their tents: 26 Because they persecuted him whom thou hast smitten; and they have added to the grief of my wounds. 27 Add iniquity to their iniquity; and let them not come into thy righteousness. 28 Let them be blotted out of the book of the living, and let them not be written with the righteous. 29 I am poor and sorrowful; but the salvation of thy countenance has helped me. 30 I will praise the name of my God with a song, I will magnify him with praise; 31 and *this* shall please God more than a young calf having horns and hoofs. 32 Let the poor see and rejoice; seek the Lord diligently, and ye shall live. 33 For the Lord hears the poor, and does not set at nought his fettered ones. 34 Let the heavens and the earth raise him, the sea, and all things moving in them. 35 For God will save Sion, and the cities of Judea shall be built; and *men* shall dwell there, and inherit it. 36 And the seed of his servants shall possess it, and they that love his name shall dwell therein.

Ps.70 *For the end, by David for a remembrance, that the Lord may save me.* 1 Draw nigh, O God, to my help. 2 Let them be ashamed and confounded that seek my soul: let them be turned backward and put to shame, that wish me evil. 3 Let them that say to me, Aha, aha, be turned back and put to shame immediately. 4 Let all that seek thee exult and be glad in thee: and let those that love thy salvation say continually, Let God be magnified. 5 But I am poor and needy; O God, help me: thou art my helper and deliverer, O Lord, delay not.

Ps.71 *By David, a Psalm sung by the sons of Jonadab, and the first that were taken captive.* 1 O Lord, I have hoped in thee: let me never be put to shame. 2 In thy righteousness deliver me and rescue me: incline thine ear to me, and save me. 3 Be to me a protecting God, and a strong hold to save me: for thou art my fortress and my refuge. 4 Deliver me, O my God, from the hand of the sinner, from the hand of the transgressor and unjust man. 5 For thou art my support, O Lord; O Lord, *thou art* my hope from my youth. 6 On thee have I been stayed from the womb: from the belly of my mother thou art my protector: of thee is my praise continually. 7 I am become as it were a wonder to many: but thou art *my* strong helper. 8 Let my mouth be filled with praise, that I may hymn thy glory, *and* thy majesty all the day. 9 Cast me not off at the time of old age; forsake me not when my strength fails. 10 For mine enemies have spoken against me; and they that lay wait for my soul have taken counsel together, 11 saying, God has forsaken him: persecute ye and take him; for there is none to deliver *him*. 12 O God, go not far from me, O my God, draw nigh to my help. 13 Let those that plot against my soul be ashamed and utterly fail: let those that seek my hurt be clothed with shame and dishonour. 14 But I will hope continually, and will praise thee more and more. 15 My mouth shall declare thy righteousness openly, *and* thy salvation all the day; for I am not acquainted with the affairs *of men*. 16 I will go on in the might of the Lord: O Lord, I will make mention of thy righteousness only. 17 O God, thou hast taught me from my youth, and until now will I declare thy wonders; 18 even until I am old and advanced in years. O God, forsake me not; until I shall have declared thine arm to all the generation that is to come: 19 even thy power and thy righteousness, O God, up to the highest *heavens, even* the mighty works which thou has done: O God, who is like to thee? 20 What afflictions many and sore hast thou shewed me! yet thou didst turn and quicken me, and broughtest me again from the depths of the earth. 21 Thou didst multiply thy righteousness, and didst turn and comfort me, and broughtest me again out of the depths of the earth. 22 I will also therefore give thanks to thee, O God, *because of* thy truth, on an instrument of psalmody: I will sing psalms to thee on the harp, O Holy One of Israel. 23 My lips shall rejoice when I sing to thee; and my soul, which thou hast redeemed. 24 Moreover also my tongue shall dwell all the day upon thy righteousness; when they shall be ashamed and confounded that seek my hurt.

Ps.72 *For Solomon.* 1 O God, give thy judgment to the king, and thy righteousness to the king's son; 2 *that he may* judge thy people with righteousness, and thy poor with judgment. 3 Let the mountains and the hills raise peace to thy people: 4 he shall judge the poor of the people in righteousness, and save the children of the needy; and shall bring low the false accuser. 5 And he shall continue as long as the sun, and before the moon for ever. 6 He shall come down as rain upon a fleece; and as drops falling upon the earth. 7 In his days shall righteousness spring up; and abundance of peace till the moon be removed. 8 And he shall have dominion from sea to sea, and from the river to the ends of the earth. 9 The Ethiopians shall fall down before him; and his enemies shall lick the dust. 10 The kings of Tharsis, and the isles, shall bring presents: the kings of the Arabians and Saba shall offer gifts. 11 And all kings shall worship him; all the Gentiles shall serve him. 12 For he has delivered the poor from the oppressor; and the needy who had no helper. 13 He shall spare the poor and needy, and shall deliver the souls of the needy. 14 He shall redeem their souls from usury and injustice: and their name *shall be* precious before him. 15 And he shall live, and there shall be given him of the gold of Arabia: and *men* shall pray for him continually; *and* all the day shall they praise him. 16 There shall be an establishment on the earth on the tops of the mountains: the fruit thereof shall be exalted above Libanus, and they of the city shall flourish as grass of the earth. 17

Let his name be blessed for ever: his name shall endure longer than the sun: and all the tribes of the earth shall be blessed in him: all nations shall call him blessed. 18 Blessed is the Lord God of Israel, who alone does wonders. 19 And blessed is his glorious name for ever, even for ever and ever: and all the earth shall be filled with his glory. So be it, so be it. 20 The hymns of David the son of Jessae are ended.

Ps.73 *A Psalm for Asaph.* 1 How good is God to Israel, to the upright in heart! 2 But my feet were almost overthrown; my goings very nearly slipped. 3 For I was jealous of the transgressors, beholding the tranquility of sinners. 4 For there is no sign of reluctance in their death: and *they have* firmness under their affliction. 5 They are not in the troubles of *other* men; and they shall not be scourged with *other* men. 6 Therefore pride has possessed them; they have clothed themselves with their injustice and ungodliness. 7 Their injustice shall go forth as out of fatness: they have fulfilled their intention. 8 They have taken counsel and spoken in wickedness: they have uttered unrighteousness loftily. 9 They have set their mouth against heaven, and their tongue has gone through upon the earth. 10 Therefore shall my people return hither: and full days shall be found with them. 11 And they said, How does God know? and is there knowledge in the Most High? 12 Behold, these *are* the sinners, and they that prosper always: they have possessed wealth. 13 And I said, Verily in vain have I justified my heart, and washed my hands in innocency. 14 For I was plagued all the day, and my reproof *was* every morning. 15 If I said, I will speak thus; behold, I *should* have broken covenant with the generation of thy children. 16 And I undertook to understand this, *but* it is too hard for me, 17 until I go into the sanctuary of God; *and so* understand the latter end. 18 Surely thou hast appointed *judgments* to them because of their crafty dealings: thou hast cast them down when they were lifted up. 19 How have they become desolate! suddenly they have failed: they have perished because of their iniquity. 20 As the dream of one awakening, O Lord, in thy city thou wilt despise their image. 21 For my heart has rejoiced, and my reins have been gladdened. 22 But I *was* vile and knew not: I became brutish before thee. 23 Yet I am continually with thee: thou hast holden my right hand. 24 Thou hast guided me by thy counsel, and thou hast taken me to thyself with glory. 25 For what have I in heaven *but thee*? and what have I desired upon the earth beside thee? 26 My heart and my flesh have failed: *but* God *is the strength* of my heart, and God is my portion for ever. 27 For, behold, they that remove themselves far from thee shall perish: thou hast destroyed every one that goes a whoring from thee. 28 But it is good for me to cleave close to God, to put my trust in the Lord; that I may proclaim all thy praises in the gates of the daughter of Sion.

Ps.74 *A Psalm of instruction for Asaph.* 1 Wherefore hast thou rejected *us*, O God, for ever? *wherefore* is thy wrath kindled against the sheep of thy pasture? 2 Remember thy congregation which thou hast purchased from the beginning; thou didst ransom the rod of thine inheritance; this mount Sion wherein thou hast dwelt. 3 Lift up thine hands against their pride continually; *because of* all that the enemy has done wickedly in thy holy places. 4 And they that hate thee have boasted in the midst of thy feast; they have set up their standards for signs, 5 ignorantly as it were in the entrance above; 6 they cut down its doors at once with axes as in a wood of trees; they have broken it down with hatchet and stone cutter. 7 They have burnt thy sanctuary with fire to the ground; they have profaned the habitation of thy name. 8 They have said in their heart, *even* all their kindred together, Come, let us abolish the feasts of the Lord from the earth. 9 We have not seen our signs; there is no longer a prophet; and *God* will not know us any more. 10 How long, O God, shall the enemy reproach? shall the enemy provoke thy name forever? 11 Wherefore turnest thou away thine hand, and thy right hand from the midst of thy bosom for ever? 12 But God is our King of old; he has wrought salvation in the midst of the earth. 13 Thou didst establish the sea, in thy might, thou didst break to pieces the heads of the dragons in the water. 14 Thou didst break to pieces the heads of the dragon; thou didst give him *for* meat to the Ethiopian nations. 15 Thou didst cleave fountains and torrents; thou driedst up mighty rivers. 16 The day is thine, and the night is thine; thou hast prepared the sun and the moon. 17 Thou hast made all the borders of the earth; thou hast made summer and spring. 18 Remember this thy creation: an enemy has reproached the Lord, and a foolish people has provoked thy name. 19 Deliver not to the wild beasts a soul that gives praise to thee: forget not for ever the souls of thy poor. 20 Look upon thy covenant: for the dark *places* of the earth are filled with the habitations of iniquity. 21 let not the afflicted and shamed one be rejected: the poor and needy shall praise thy name. 22 Arise, O God, plead thy cause: remember thy reproaches that come from the foolish one all the day. 23 Forget not the voice of thy suppliants: let the pride of them that hate thee continually ascend before thee.

Ps.75 *For the end, Destroy not, a Psalm of a Song for Asaph.* 1 We will give thanks to thee, O God, we will give thanks, and call upon thy name: I will declare all thy wonderful works. 2 When I shall take a set time, I will judge righteously. 3 The earth is dissolved, and all that dwell in it: I have strengthened its pillars. Pause. 4 I said unto the transgressors, Do not transgress; and to the sinners, Lift not up the horn. 5 Lift not up your horn on high; speak not unrighteousness against God. 6 For *good comes* neither from the east, nor from the west, nor from the desert mountains. 7 For God is the judge; he puts down one, and raises up another. 8 For *there is* a cup in the hand of the Lord, full of unmingled wine; and he has turned *it* from side to side, but its dregs have not been wholly poured out; all the sinners of the earth shall drink *them.* 9 But I will exult for ever: I will sing praises to the God of Jacob. 10 And I will break all the horns of sinners; but the horns of the righteous one shall be exalted.

Ps.76 *For the end, among the Hymns, a Psalm for Asaph; a Song for the Assyrian.* 1 God is known in Judea: his name is great in Israel. 2 And his place has been in peace, and his dwelling-place in Sion. 3 There he broke the power of the bows, the shield, and the sword, and the battle. Pause. 4

Thou dost wonderfully shine forth from the everlasting mountains. 5 All the simple ones in heart were troubled; all the men of wealth have slept their sleep, and have found nothing in their hands. 6 At thy rebuke, O God of Jacob, the riders on horses slumbered. 7 Thou art terrible; and who shall withstand thee, because of thine anger? 8 Thou didst cause judgment to be heard from heaven; the earth feared, and was still, 9 when God arose to judgment, to save all the meek in heart. Pause. 10 For the inward thought of man shall give thanks to thee: and the memorial of his inward thought shall keep a feast to thee. 11 Vow, and pay *your vows* to the Lord our God; all that are round about him shall bring gifts, *even* to him that is terrible, 12 and that takes away the spirits of princes; to him that is terrible among the kings of the earth.

Ps.77 *For the end, for Idithun, a Psalm of Asaph.* 1 I cried to the Lord with my voice, yea, my voice *was addressed* to God; and he gave heed to me. 2 In the day of mine affliction I earnestly sought the Lord; *even* with my hands by night before him, and I was not deceived; my soul refused to be comforted. 3 I remembered God, and rejoiced; I poured out my complaint, and my soul fainted. Pause. 4 All mine enemies set a watch *against me.* I was troubled, and spoke not. 5 I considered the days of old, and remembered ancient years. 6 And I meditated; I communed with my heart by night, and diligently searched my spirit, *saying,* 7 Will the Lord cast off for ever? and will he be well pleased no more? 8 Will he cut off his mercy for ever, even for ever and ever? 9 Will God forget to pity? or will he shut up his compassions in his wrath? Pause. 10 And I said, Now I have begun; this is the change of the right hand of the Most High. 11 I remembered the works of the Lord; for I will remember thy wonders from the beginning. 12 And I will meditate on all thy works, and will consider thy doings. 13 O God, thy way is in the sanctuary; who is a great God as our God? 14 Thou art the God that doest wonders; thou hast made known thy power among the nations. 15 Thou hast with thine arm redeemed thy people, the sons of Jacob and Joseph. Pause. 16 The waters saw thee, O God, the waters saw thee, and feared; and the depths were troubled. 17 *There was* an abundant sound of waters: the clouds uttered a voice; for thine arrows went abroad. 18 The voice of thy thunder was abroad, and around thy lightnings appeared to the world; the earth trembled a quaked. 19 Thy way is in the sea, and thy paths in many waters, and thy footsteps cannot be known. 20 Thou didst guide thy people as sheep by the hand of Moses and Aaron.

Ps.78 *A Psalm of instruction for Asaph.* 1 Give heed, O my people, to my law: incline your ear to the words of my mouth. 2 I will open my mouth in parables: I will utter dark sayings *which have been* from the beginning. 3 All which we have heard and known, and our fathers have declared to us. 4 They were not hid from their children to a second generations; *the fathers* declaring the praises of the Lord, and his mighty acts, and his wonders which he wrought. 5 And he raised up a testimony in Jacob, and appointed a law in Israel, which he commanded our fathers, to make it known to their children: 6 that another generation might know, even the sons which should be born; and they should arise and declare them to their children. 7 That they might set their hope on God, and not forget the works of God, but diligently seek his commandments. 8 That they should not be as their fathers, a perverse and provoking generation; a generation which set not its heart aright, and its spirit was not steadfast with God. 9 The children of Ephraim, bending and shooting *with* the bow, turned *back* in the day of battle. 10 They kept not the covenant of God, and would not walk in his law. 11 And they forgot his benefits, and his miracles which he *had* shewed them; 12 the miracles which he wrought before their fathers, in the land of Egypt, in the plain of Tanes. 13 He clave the sea, and led them through: he made the waters to stand as *in* a bottle. 14 And he guided them with a cloud by day, and all the night with a light of fire. 15 he clave a rock in the wilderness, and made them drink as in a great deep. 16 And he brought water out of the rock, and caused waters to flow down as rivers. 17 And they sinned yet more against him; they provoked the Most High in the wilderness. 18 And they tempted God in their hearts, in asking meat for *the desire of* their souls. 19 They spoke also against God, and said, Will God be able to prepare a table in the wilderness? 20 Forasmuch as he smote the rock, and the waters flowed, and the torrents ran abundantly; will he be able also to give bread, or prepare a table for his people? 21 Therefore the Lord heard, and was provoked: and fire was kindled in Jacob, and wrath went up against Israel. 22 Because they believed not in God, and trusted not in his salvation. 23 Yet he commanded the clouds from above, and opened the doors of heaven, 24 and rained upon them manna to eat, and gave them the bread of heaven. 25 Man ate angels' bread; he sent them provision to the full. 26 He removed the south wind from heaven; and by his might he brought in the south-west wind. 27 And he rained upon them flesh like dust, and feathered birds like the sand of the seas. 28 And they fell into the midst of their camp, round about their tents. 29 So they ate, and were completely filled; and he gave them their desire. 30 They were not disappointed of their desire: *but* when their food was yet in their mouth, 31 then the indignation of God rose up against them, and slew the fattest of them, and overthrew the choice men of Israel. 32 In the midst of all this they sinned yet more, and believed not his miracles. 33 And their days were consumed in vanity, and their years with anxiety. 34 When he slew them, they sought him: and they returned and called betimes upon God. 35 And they remembered that God was their helper, and the most high God was their redeemer. 36 Yet they loved him *only* with their mouth, and lied to him with their tongue. 37 For their heart *was* not right with him, neither were they steadfast in his covenant. 38 But he is compassionate, and will forgive their sins, and will not destroy *them*: yea, he will frequently turn away his wrath, and will not kindle all his anger. 39 And he remembered that they are flesh; a wind that passes away, and returns not. 40 How often did they provoke him in the wilderness, *and* anger him in a dry land! 41 Yea, they turned back, and tempted God, and provoked the Holy One of Israel. 42 They remembered not his hand, the day in which he delivered them from the hand of the oppressor. 43 How he had wrought his signs in Egypt, and his wonders in the field of Tanes: 44 and had changed their rivers into blood; and their streams, that they should not drink. 45 He sent against them the dog-fly, and it devoured them; and the frog, and it spoiled them. 46 And he gave their fruit to the canker worm, and their labours to the locust. 47 He killed their vines with hail, and their sycamores with frost. 48 And he gave up their cattle to hail, and their substance to the fire. 49 He sent out against them the fury of his anger, wrath, and indignation, and affliction, a message by evil angels. 50 He made a way for his wrath; he spared not their souls from death, but consigned their cattle to death; 51 and smote every first-born in the land of Egypt; the first-fruits of their labours in the tents of Cham. 52 And he removed his people like sheep; he led them as a flock in the wilderness. 53 And he guided them with hope, and they feared not: but the sea covered their enemies. 54 And he brought them in to the mountain of his sanctuary, this mountain which his right hand had purchased. 55 And he cast out the nations from before them, and made them to inherit by a line of inheritance, and made the tribes of Israel to dwell in their tents. 56 Yet they tempted and provoked the most high God, and kept not his testimonies. 57 And they turned back, and broke covenant, even as also their fathers: they became like a crooked bow. 58 And they provoked him with their high places, and moved him to jealousy with their graven images. 59 God heard and lightly regarded *them*, and greatly despised Israel. 60 And he rejected the tabernacle of Selom, his tent where he dwelt among men. 61 And he gave their strength into captivity, and their beauty into the enemy's hand. 62 And he gave his people to the sword; and disdained his inheritance. 63 Fire devoured their young men; and their virgins mourned not. 64 Their priests fell by the sword; and their widows shall not be wept for. 65 So the Lord awaked as one out of sleep, *and* as a mighty man who has been heated with wine. 66 And he smote his enemies in the hinder parts: he brought on them a perpetual reproach. 67 And he rejected the tabernacle of Joseph, and chose not the tribe of Ephraim; 68 but chose the tribe of Juda, the mount Sion which he loved. 69 And he built his sanctuary as *the place* of unicorns; he founded it for ever on the earth. 70 He chose David also his servant, and took him up from the flocks of sheep. 71 He took him from following the ewes great with young, to be the shepherd of Jacob his servant, and Israel his inheritance. 72 So he tended them in the innocency of his heart; and guided them by the skillfulness of his hands.

Ps.79 *A Psalm for Asaph.* 1 O God, the heathen are come into thine inheritance; they have polluted thy holy temple; they have made Jerusalem a storehouse of fruits. 2 They have given the dead bodies of thy servants *to be* food for the birds of the sky, the flesh of thy holy ones for the wild beasts of the earth. 3 They have shed their blood as water, round about Jerusalem; and there was none to bury *them*. 4 We are become a reproach to our neighbours, a scorn and derision to them *that are* round about us. 5 How long, O Lord? wilt thou be angry for ever? shall thy jealousy burn like fire? 6 Pour out thy wrath upon the heathen that have not known thee, and upon the kingdoms which have not called upon thy name. 7 For they have devoured Jacob, and laid his place waste. 8 Remember not our old transgressions; let thy tender mercies speedily prevent us; for we are greatly impoverished. 9 Help us, O God our Saviour; for the glory of thy name, O Lord, deliver us; and be merciful to our sins, for thy name's sake. 10 Lets haply they should say among the heathen, Where is their God? and let the avenging of thy servant's blood that has been shed be known among the heathen before our eyes. 11 Let the groaning of the prisoners come in before thee; according to the greatness of thine arm preserve the sons of the slain ones. 12 Repay to our neighbours sevenfold into their bosom their reproach, with which they have reproached thee, O Lord. 13 For we are thy people and the sheep of thy pasture; we will give thee thanks for ever; we will declare thy praise throughout all generations.

Ps.80 *For the end, for alternate strains, a testimony for Asaph, a Psalm concerning the Assyrian.* 1 Attend, O Shepherd of Israel, who guidest Joseph like a flock; thou who sittest upon the cherubs, manifest thyself; 2 before Ephraim and Benjamin and Manasse, stir up thy power, and come to deliver us. 3 Turn us, O God, and cause thy face to shine; and we shall be delivered. 4 O Lord God of hosts, how long art thou angry with the prayer of thy servant? 5 Thou wilt feed us with bread of tears; and wilt cause us to drink tears by measure. 6 Thou has made us a strife to our neighbours; and our enemies have mocked at us. 7 Turn us, O Lord God of hosts, and cause thy face to shine; and we shall be saved. Pause. 8 Thou hast transplanted a vine out of Egypt: thou hast cast out the heathen, and planted it. 9 Thou madest a way before it, and didst cause its roots to strike, and the land was filled *with it.* 10 Its shadow covered the mountains, and its shoots equalled the goodly cedars. 11 It sent forth its branches to the sea, and its shoots to the river. 12 Wherefore hast thou broken down its hedge, while all that pass by the way pluck it? 13 The boar out of the wood has laid it waste, and the wild beast has devoured it. 14 O God of hosts, turn, we pray thee: look on *us* from heaven, and behold and visit this vine; 15 and restore that which thy right hand has planted: and look on the son of man whom thou didst strengthen for thyself. 16 *It is* burnt with fire and dug up: they shall perish at the rebuke of thy presence. 17 Let thy hand be upon the man of thy right hand, and upon the son of man whom thou didst strengthen for thyself. 18 So will we not depart from thee: thou shalt quicken us, and we will call upon thy name. 19 Turn us, O Lord God of hosts, and make thy face to shine; and we shall be saved.

Ps.81 *For the end, a Psalm for Asaph, concerning the wine-presses.* 1 Rejoice ye in God our helper; shout aloud to the God of Jacob. 2 Take a psalm, and produce the timbrel, the pleasant psaltery with the harp. 3 Blow the trumpet at the new moon, in the glorious day of your feast. 4 For *this* is an ordinance for Israel, and a statute of the God of Jacob. 5 He made it *to be* a testimony in Joseph, when he came forth out of the land of Egypt: he heard a language which he understood not. 6 He removed his back from burdens: his hands slaved in making the baskets. 7 Thou didst call upon me in trouble, and I delivered thee; I heard thee in the secret place of the storm: I proved thee at the water of Strife. Pause. 8 Hear, my people, and I will speak to thee, O Israel; and I will testify to thee: if thou wilt hearken to me; 9 there shall be no new god in thee; neither shalt thou worship a strange god. 10 For I am the Lord thy God, that brought thee out of the land of Egypt: open thy mouth wide, and I will fill it. 11 But my people hearkened not to my voice; and Israel gave no heed to me. 12 So I let them go after the ways of their own hearts: they will go on in their own ways. 13 If my people had hearkened to me, if Israel had walked in my ways, 14 I should have put down their enemies very quickly, and should have laid my hand upon those that afflicted them. 15 The Lord's enemies *should have* lied to him: but their time shall be for ever. 16 And he fed them with the fat of wheat; and satisfied them with honey out of the rock.

Ps.82 *A Psalm for Asaph.* 1 God stands in the assembly of gods; and in the midst *of them* will judge gods. 2 How long will ye judge unrighteously, and accept the persons of sinners? Pause. 3 Judge the orphan and poor: do justice to the low and needy. 4 Rescue the needy, and deliver the poor out of the hand of the sinner. 5 They know not, nor understand; they walk on in darkness: all the foundations of the earth shall be shaken. 6 I have said, Ye are gods; and all *of you* children of the Most High. 7 But ye die as men, and fall as one of the princes. 8 Arise, O God, judge the earth: for thou shalt inherit all nations.

Ps.83 *A Song of a Psalm for Asaph.* 1 O God, who shall be compared to thee? be not silent, neither be still, O God. 2 For behold, thine enemies have made a noise; and they that hate thee have lifted up the head. 3 Against thy people they have craftily imagined a device, and have taken counsel against thy saints. 4 They have said, Come, and let us utterly destroy them out of the nation; and let the name of Israel be remembered no more at all. 5 For they have taken counsel together with one consent: they have made a confederacy against thee; 6 even the tents of the Idumeans, and the Ismaelites; Moab, and the Agarenes; 7 Gebal, and Ammon, and Amalec; the Philistines also, with them that dwell at Tyre. 8 Yea, Assur too is come with them: they have become a help to the children of Lot. Pause. 9 Do thou to them as to Madiam, and to Sisera; as to Jabin at the brook of Kison. 10 They were utterly destroyed at Aendor: they became as dung for the earth. 11 Make their princes as Oreb and Zeb, and Zebee and Salmana; *even* all their princes: 12 who said, let us take to ourselves the altar of God as an inheritance. 13 O my God, make them as a wheel; as stubble before the face of the wind. 14 As fire which shall burn up a wood, as the flame may consume the mountains; 15 so shalt thou persecute them with thy tempest, and trouble them in thine anger. 16 Fill their faces with dishonour; so shall they seek thy name, O Lord. 17 Let them be ashamed and troubled for evermore; yea, let them be confounded and destroyed. 18 And let them know that thy name is Lord; that thou alone art Most High over all the earth.

Ps.84 *For the end, a Psalm for the sons of Core, concerning the wine-presses.* 1 How amiable are thy tabernacles, O Lord of hosts! 2 My soul longs, and faints for the courts of the Lord: my heart and my flesh have exulted in the living god. 3 Yea, the sparrow has found himself a home, and the turtle-dove a nest for herself, where she may lay her young, *even* thine altars, O Lord of hosts, my King, and my God. 4 Blessed are they that dwell in thy house: they will praise thee evermore. Pause. 5 Blessed is the man whose help is of thee, O Lord; in his heart he has purposed to go up 6 the valley of weeping, to the place which he has appointed, for *there* the law-giver will grant blessings. 7 They shall go from strength to strength: the God of gods shall be seen in Sion. 8 O Lord God of hosts, hear my prayer: hearken, O God of Jacob. Pause. 9 Behold, O God our defender, and look upon the face of thine anointed. 10 For one day in thy courts is better than thousands. I would rather be an abject in the house of God, than dwell in the tents of sinners. 11 For the Lord loves mercy and truth: God will give grace and glory: the Lord will not withhold good things from them that walk in innocence. 12 O Lord of hosts, blessed is the man that trusts in thee.

Ps.85 *For the end, a Psalm for the sons of Core.* 1 O Lord, thou has taken pleasure in thy land: thou hast turned back the captivity of Jacob. 2 Thou hast forgiven thy people their transgressions; thou has covered all their sins. Pause. 3 Thou has caused all thy wrath to cease: thou hast turned from thy fierce anger. 4 Turn us, O God of our salvation, and turn thy anger away from us. 5 Wouldest thou be angry with us for ever? or wilt thou continue thy wrath from generation to generation? 6 O God, thou wilt turn and quicken us; and thy people shall rejoice in thee. 7 Shew us thy mercy, O Lord, and grant us thy salvation. 8 I will hear what the Lord God will say concerning me: for he shall speak peace to his people, and to his saints, and to those that turn their heart toward him. 9 Moreover his salvation is near them that fear him; that glory may dwell in our land. 10 Mercy and truth are met together: righteousness and peace have kissed *each other*. 11 Truth has sprung out of the earth; and righteousness has looked down from heaven. 12 For the Lord will give goodness; and our land shall yield her fruit. 13 Righteousness shall go before him; and shall set his steps in the way.

Ps.86 *A Prayer of David.* 1 O Lord, incline thine ear, and hearken to me; for I am poor and needy. 2 Preserve my soul, for I am holy; save thy servant, O God, who hopes in thee. 3 Pity me, O Lord: for to thee will I cry all the day. 4 Rejoice the sold of thy servant: for to thee, O Lord, have I lifted up my soul. 5 For thou, O Lord, art kind, and gentle; and plenteous in mercy to all that call upon thee. 6 Give ear to my prayer, o Lord; and attend to the voice of my supplication. 7 In the day of my trouble I cried to thee: for thou didst hear me. 8 There is none like to thee, O Lord, among the god; and there are no *works* like to thy works. 9 All nations whom thou hast made shall come, and shall worship before thee, O Lord; and shall glorify thy name. 10 For thou art great, and doest wonders: thou art the only *and* the great God. 11 Guide me, O Lord, in thy way, and I will walk in thy truth: let my heart rejoice, that I may fear thy name. 12 I will give thee thanks, O Lord my God, with all my heart; and I will glorify thy name for ever. 13 For thy mercy is great toward me; and thou hast delivered my soul from the lowest hell. 14 O God, transgressors have risen up against me, and an assembly of violent *men* have sought my life; and have not set thee before them. 15 But thou, O Lord God, art compassionate and merciful, long-suffering, and abundant in mercy and true. 16 Look thou upon me, and have mercy upon me: give thy strength to thy servant, and save the son of thine handmaid. 17 Establish with me a token for good; and let them that hate me see *it* and be ashamed; because thou, O Lord, hast helped me, and comforted me.

Ps.87 *A Psalm of a Song for the sons of Core.* 1 His foundations are in the holy mountains. 2 The Lord loves the gates of Sion, more than all the tabernacles of Jacob. 3 Glorious things have been spoken of thee, O city of God. Pause. 4 I will make mention of Raab and Babylon to them that know me: behold also the Philistines, and Tyre, and the people of the Ethiopians: these were born there. 5 A man shall say, Sion *is my* mother; and *such* a man was born in her; and the Highest himself has founded her. 6 The Lord shall recount *it* in the writing of the people, and of these princes that were born in her. 7 The dwelling of all within thee is *as the dwelling* of those that rejoice.

Ps.88 *A song of a Psalm for the sons of Core for the end, upon Maeleth for responsive strains, of instruction for Æman the Israelite.* 1 O Lord God of my salvation, I have cried by day and in the night before thee. 2 Let my prayer come in before thee; incline thine ear to my supplication, O Lord. 3 For my soul is filled with troubles, and my life has drawn nigh to Hades. 4 I have been reckoned with them that go down to the pit; I became as a man without help; 5 free among the dead, as the slain ones cast out, who sleep in the tomb; whom thou rememberest no more; and they are rejected from thy hand. 6 They laid me in the lowest pit, in dark *places*, and in the shadow of death. 7 Thy wrath has pressed heavily upon me, and thou hast brought upon me all thy billows. Pause. 8 Thou hast removed my acquaintance far from me; they have made me an abomination to themselves; I have been delivered up, and have not gone forth. 9 Mine eyes are dimmed from poverty; but I cried to thee, O Lord, all the day; I spread forth my hands to thee. 10 Wilt thou work wonders for the dead? or shall physicians raise *them* up, that they shall praise thee? 11 Shall any one declare thy mercy in the tomb? and thy truth in destruction? 12 Shall thy wonders be known in darkness? and thy righteousness in a forgotten land? 13 But I cried to thee, O Lord; and in the morning shall my prayer prevent thee. 14 Wherefore, O Lord, dost thou reject my prayer, *and* turn thy face away from me? 15 I am poor and in troubles from my youth; and having been exalted, I was brought low and into despair. 16 Thy wrath has passed over me; and thy terrors have greatly disquieted me. 17 They compassed me like water; all the day they beset me together. 18 Thou hast put far from me *every* friend, and mine acquaintances because of *my* wretchedness.

Ps.89 *A Psalm of instruction for Ætham the Israelite.* 1 I will sing of thy mercies, O Lord, for ever: I will declare thy truth with my mouth to all generations. 2 For thou hast said,

Mercy shall be built up for ever: thy truth shall be established in the heavens. 3 I made a covenant with my chosen ones, I sware unto David my servant. 4 I will establish thy seed for ever, and build up thy throne to all generations. Pause. 5 The heavens shall declare thy wonders, O Lord; and thy truth in the assembly of the saints. 6 For who in the heavens shall be compared to the Lord? and who shall be likened to the Lord among the sons of God? 7 God is glorified in the council of the saints; great and terrible toward all that are round about him. 8 O Lord God of hosts, who is like to thee? thou art mighty, O Lord, and thy truth is round about thee. 9 Thou rulest the power of the sea; and thou calmest the tumult of its waves. 10 Thou has brought down the proud as one that is slain; and with the arm of thy power thou has scattered thine enemies. 11 The heavens are thine, and the earth is thine: thou hast founded the world, and the fullness of it. 12 Thou hast created the north and the west: Thabor and Hermon shall rejoice in thy name. 13 Thine is the mighty arm: let thy hand be strengthened, let thy right hand be exalted. 14 Justice and judgment are the establishment of thy throne: mercy and truth shall go before thy face. 15 Blessed is the people that knows the joyful sound: they shall walk, O Lord, in the light of thy countenance. 16 And in thy name shall they rejoice all the day: and in thy righteousness shall they be exalted. 17 For thou art the boast of their strength; and in thy good pleasure shall our horn be exalted, 18 for *our* help is of the Lord; and of the Holy One of Israel, our king. 19 Then thou spokest in vision to thy children, and saidst, I have laid help on a mighty one; I have exalted one chosen out of my people. 20 I have found David my servant; I have anointed him by *my* holy mercy. 21 For my hand shall support him; and mine arm shall strengthen him. 22 The enemy shall have no advantage against him; and the son of transgression shall not hurt him again. 23 And I will hew down his foes before him, and put to flight those that hate him. 24 But my truth and my mercy shall be with him; and in my name shall his horn be exalted. 25 And I will set his hand in the sea, and his right hand in the rivers. 26 He shall call upon me, *saying,* Thou art my Father, my God, and the helper of my salvation. 27 And I will make him *my* first- born, higher than the kings of the earth. 28 I will keep my mercy for him for ever, and my covenant *shall be* firm with him. 29 And I will establish his seed for ever and ever, and his throne as the days of heaven. 30 If his children should forsake my law, and walk not in my judgments; 31 if they should profane my ordinances, and not keep my commandments; 32 I will visit their transgressions with a rod, and their sins with scourges. 33 But my mercy I will not utterly remove from him, nor wrong my truth. 34 Neither will I by any means profane my covenant; and I will not make void the things that proceed out of my lips. 35 Once have I sworn by my holiness, that I will not lie to David. 36 His see shall endure for ever, and his throne as the sun before me; 37 and as the moon *that is* established for ever, and as the faithful witness in heaven. Pause. 38 But thou hast cast off and set at nought, thou has rejected thine anointed. 39 Thou hast overthrown the covenant of thy servant; thou has profaned his sanctuary, *casting it* to the ground. 40 Thou hast broken down all his

hedges; thou hast made his strong holds a terror. 41 All that go by the way have spoiled him: he is become a reproach to his neighbours. 42 Thou hast exalted the right hand of his enemies; thou hast made all his enemies to rejoice. 43 Thou hast turned back the help of his sword, and hast not helped him in the battle. 44 Thou hast deprived him of glory: thou hast broken down his throne to the ground. 45 Thou hast shortened the days of his throne: thou hast poured shame upon him. Pause. 46 How long, O Lord, wilt thou turn away, for ever? shall thine anger flame out as fire? 47 Remember what my being is: for hast thou created all the sons of men in vain? 48 What man is there who shall live, and not see death? shall *any one* deliver his soul from the hand of Hades? Pause. 49 Where are thine ancient mercies, O Lord, which thou swarest to David in thy truth? 50 Remember, O Lord, the reproach of thy servants, which I have borne in my bosom, *even the reproach* of many nations; 51 wherewith thine enemies have reviled, O Lord: wherewith they have reviled the recompense of thine anointed. 52 Blessed be the Lord for ever. So be it, so be it.

Ps.90 *A Prayer of Moses the man of God.* 1 Lord, thou hast been our refuge in all generations. 2 Before the mountains existed, and *before* the earth and the world were formed, even from age to age, Thou art. 3 Turn not man back to *his* low place, whereas thou saidst, Return, ye sons of men? 4 For a thousand years in thy sight are as the yesterday which is past, and as a watch in the night. 5 Years shall be vanity to them: let the morning pass away as grass. 6 In the morning let it flower, and pass away: in the evening let it droop, let it be withered and dried up. 7 For we have perished in thine anger, and in thy wrath we have been troubled. 8 Thou hast set our transgressions before thee: our age is in the light of thy countenance. 9 For all our days are gone, and we have passed away in thy wrath: our years have spun out their tale as a spider. 10 *As for* the days of our years, in them are seventy years; and if *men should be* in strength, eighty years: and the greater part of them would be labour and trouble; for weakness overtakes us, and we shall be chastened. 11 Who knows the power of thy wrath? 12 and *who knows how* to number *his days* because of the fear of thy wrath? So manifest thy right hand, and those that are instructed in wisdom in the heart. 13 Return, O Lord, how long? and be intreated concerning thy servants. 14 We have been satisfied in the morning with thy mercy; and we did exult and rejoice: 15 let us rejoice in all our days, in return for the days wherein thou didst afflict us, the years wherein we saw evil. 16 And look upon thy servants, and upon thy works; and guide their children. 17 And let the brightness of the Lord our God be upon us: and do thou direct for us the works of our hands.

Ps.91 *Praise of a Song, by David.* 1 He that dwells in the help of the Highest, shall sojourn under the shelter of the God of heaven. 2 He shall say to the Lord, Thou art my helper and my refuge: my God; I will hope in him. 3 For he shall deliver thee from the snare of the hunters, from *every* troublesome matter. 4 He shall overshadow thee with his shoulders, and thou shalt trust under his wings: his truth shall cover thee with a shield. 5 Thou shalt not be afraid of terror by night; nor of the arrow flying by day; 6 *nor* of the *evil* thing that walks in darkness; *nor* of calamity, and the evil spirit at noon-day. 7 A thousand shall fall at thy side, and ten thousand at thy right hand; but it shall not come nigh thee. 8 Only with thine eyes shalt thou observe and see the reward of sinners. 9 For thou, O Lord, art my hope: thou, my soul, hast made the Most High thy refuge. 10 No evils shall come upon thee, and no scourge shall draw night to thy dwelling. 11 For he shall give his angels charge concerning thee, to keep thee in all thy ways. 12 They shall bear thee up on their hands, lest at any time thou dash thy foot against a stone. 13 Thou shalt tread on the asp and basilisk: and thou shalt trample on the lion and dragon. 14 For he has hoped in me, and I will deliver him: I will protect him, because he has known my name. 15 He shall call upon me, and I will hearken to him: I am with him in affliction; and I will deliver him, and glorify him. 16 I will satisfy him with length of days, and shew him my salvation.

Ps.92 *A Psalm of a Song for the Sabbath-day.* 1 It is a good thing to give thanks to the Lord, and to sing praises to thy name, O thou Most High; 2 to proclaim thy mercy in the morning, and thy truth by night, 3 on a psaltery of ten strings, with a song on the harp. 4 For thou, O Lord, hast made me glad with thy work: and in the operations of thy hands will I exult. 5 How have thy works been magnified, O Lord! thy thoughts are very deep. 6 A foolish man will not know, and a senseless man will not understand this. 7 When the sinners spring up as the grass, and all the workers of iniquity have watched; *it is* that they may be utterly destroyed for ever. 8 But thou, O Lord, art most high for ever. 9 For, behold, thine enemies shall perish; and all the workers of iniquity shall be scattered. 10 But my horn shall be exalted *as the horn* of a unicorn; and mine old age with rich mercy. 11 And mine eye has seen mine enemies, and mine ear shall hear the wicked that rise up against me. 12 The righteous shall flourish as a palm-tree: he shall be increased as the cedar in Libanus. 13 They that are planted in the house of the Lord shall flourish in the courts of our God. 14 Then shall they be increased in a fine old age; and they shall be prosperous; that they may declare 15 that the Lord my God is righteous, and there is no iniquity in him.

Ps.93 *For the day before the Sabbath, when the land was first inhabited, the praise of a Song by David.* 1 The Lord reigns; he has clothed himself with honour: the Lord has clothed and girded himself with strength; for he has established the world, which shall not be moved. 2 Thy throne is prepared of old: thou art from everlasting. 3 The rivers have lifted up, O Lord, the rivers have lifted up their voices, 4 at the voices of many waters: the billows of the sea are wonderful: the Lord is wonderful in high places. 5 Thy testimonies are made very sure: holiness becomes thine house, O Lord, for ever.

Ps.94 *A Psalm of David for the fourth day of the week.* 1 The Lord is a God of vengeance; the God of vengeance has declared himself. 2 Be thou exalted, thou that judgest the earth: render a reward to the proud. 3 How long shall sinners, O Lord, how long shall sinners boast? 4 They will utter and

speak unrighteousness; all the workers of iniquity will speak *so*. 5 They have afflicted thy people, O Lord, and hurt thine heritage. 6 They have slain the widow and fatherless, and murdered the stranger. 7 And they said, The Lord shall not see, neither shall the God of Jacob understand. 8 Understand now, ye simple among the people; and ye fools, at length be wise. 9 He that planted the ear, does he not hear? or he that formed the eye, does not he perceive? 10 He that chastises the heathen, shall not he punish, *even* he that teaches man knowledge? 11 The Lord knows the thoughts of men, that they are vain. 12 Blessed is the man whomsoever thou shalt chasten, O Lord, and shalt teach him out of thy law; 13 to give him rest from evil days, until a pit be digged for the sinful one. 14 For the Lord will not cast off his people, neither will he forsake his inheritance; 15 until righteousness return to judgment, and all the upright in heart shall follow it. Pause. 16 Who will rise up for me against the transgressors? or who will stand up with me against the workers of iniquity? 17 If the Lord had not helped me, my soul had almost sojourned in Hades. 18 If I said, My foot has been moved; 19 thy mercy, O Lord, helped me. O Lord, according to the multitude of my griefs within my heart, thy consolation have soothed my soul. 20 Shall the throne of iniquity have fellowship with thee, which frames mischief by an ordinance? 21 They will hunt for the soul of the righteous, and condemn innocent blood. 22 But the Lord was my refuge; and my God the helper of my hope. 23 And he will recompense to them their iniquity and their wickedness: the Lord our God shall utterly destroy them.

Ps.95 *The praise of a Song by David.* 1 Come, let us exult in the Lord; let us make a joyful noise to God our Saviour. 2 Let us come before his presence with thanksgiving, and make a joyful noise to him with psalms. 3 For the Lord is a great God, and a great king over all gods: for the Lord will not cast off his people. 4 For the ends of the earth are in his hands; and the heights of the mountains are his. 5 For the sea is his, and he made it: and is hands formed the dry land. 6 Come, let us worship and fall down before him; and weep before the Lord that made us. 7 For he is our God; and we are the people of his pasture, and the sheep of his hand. 8 To-day, if ye will hear his voice, harden not your hearts, as in the provocation, according to the day of irritation in the wilderness: 9 where your fathers tempted me, proved me, and saw my works. 10 Forty years was I grieved with this generation, and said, They do always err in their heart, and they have not known my ways. 11 So I sware in my wrath, They shall not enter into my rest.

Ps.96 *When the house was built after the Captivity, a Song of David.* 1 Sing to the Lord a new song; sing to the Lord, all the earth. 2 Sing to the Lord, bless his name: proclaim his salvation from day to day. 3 Publish his glory among the Gentiles, his wonderful works among all people. 4 For the Lord is great, and greatly to be praised: he is terrible above all gods. 5 For all the gods of the heathen are devils: but the Lord made the heavens. 6 Thanksgiving and beauty are before him: holiness and majesty are in his sanctuary. 7 Bring to the Lord, ye families of the Gentiles, bring to the Lord glory and honour. 8 Bring to the Lord the glory *becoming* his name: take offerings, and go into his courts. 9 Worship the Lord in his holy court: let all the earth tremble before him. 10 Say among the heathen, The Lord reigns: for he has established the world so that it shall not be moved: he shall judge the people in righteousness. 11 Let the heavens rejoice, and the earth exult; let the sea be moved, and the fullness of it. 12 The plains shall rejoice, and all things in them: then shall all the trees of the wood exult before the presence of the Lord: 13 for he comes, for he comes to judge the earth; he shall judge the world in righteousness, and the people with his truth.

Ps.97 *For David, when his land is established.* 1 The Lord reigns, let the earth exult, let many islands rejoice. 2 Cloud, and darkness are round about him; righteousness and judgment are the establishment of his throne. 3 Fire shall go before him, and burn up his enemies round about. 4 His lightnings appeared to the world; the earth saw, and trembled. 5 The mountains melted like wax at the presence of the Lord, at the presence of the Lord of the whole earth. 6 The heavens have declared his righteousness, and all the people have seen his glory. 7 Let all that worship graven images be ashamed, who boast of their idols; worship him, all ye his angels. 8 Sion heard and rejoiced; and the daughters of Judea exulted, because of thy judgments, O Lord. 9 For thou art Lord most high over all the earth; thou art greatly exalted above all gods. 10 Ye that love the Lord, hate evil; the Lord preserves the souls of his saints; he shall deliver them from the hand of sinners. 11 Light is sprung up for the righteous, and gladness for the upright in heart. 12 Rejoice in the Lord, ye righteous; and give thanks for a remembrance of his holiness.

Ps.98 *A Psalm of David.* 1 Sing to the Lord a new song; for the Lord has wrought wonderful works, his right hand, and his holy arm, have wrought salvation for him. 2 The Lord has made known his salvation, he has revealed his righteousness in the sight of the nations. 3 He has remembered his mercy to Jacob, and his truth to the house of Israel; all the ends of the earth have seen the salvation of our God. 4 Shout to God, all the earth; sing, and exult, and sing psalms. 5 Sing to the Lord with a harp, with a harp, and the voice of a psalm. 6 With trumpets of metal, and the sound of a trumpet of horn make a joyful noise to the Lord before the king. 7 Let the sea be moved, and the fullness of it; the world, and they that dwell in it. 8 The rivers shall clap their hands together; the mountains shall exult. 9 For he is come to judge the earth; he shall judge the world in righteousness, and the nations in uprightness.

Ps.99 *A Psalm of David.* 1 The Lord reigns; —let the people rage; *it is he* that sits upon the cherubs, let the earth be moved. 2 The Lord is great in Sion, and is high over all the people. 3 Let them give thanks to thy great name; for it is terrible and holy. 4 And the king's honour loves judgment; thou hast prepared equity, thou hast wrought judgment and justice in Jacob. 5 Exalt ye the Lord our God, and worship *at* his footstool; for he is holy. 6 Moses and Aaron among his priests, and Samuel among them that call upon his name; they called upon the Lord, and he heard them. 7 He

spoke to them in a pillar of cloud; they kept his testimonies, and the ordinances which he gave them. 8 O Lord our God, thou heardest them; O God, thou becamest propitious to them, though thou didst take vengeance on all their devices. 9 Exalt ye the Lord our God, and worship at his holy mountain; for the Lord our God is holy.

Ps.100 *A Psalm for Thanksgiving.* 1 Make a joyful noise to the Lord, all the earth. 2 Serve the Lord with gladness; come before his presence with exultation. 3 Know that the Lord he is God; he made us, and not we ourselves; *we are* his people, and the sheep of his pasture. 4 Enter into his gates with thanksgiving, and his courts with hymns; give thanks to him, praise his name. 5 For the Lord is good, his mercy is for ever; and his truth *endures* to generation and generation.

Ps.101 *A Psalm of David.* 1 I will sing to thee, O Lord, of mercy and judgment; I will sing a psalm, 2 and I will be wise in a blameless way. When wilt thou come to me? I walked in the innocence of my heart, in the midst of my house. 3 I have not set before mine eyes any unlawful ting; I have hated transgressors. 4 A perverse heart has not cleaved to me; I have not known an evil man, forasmuch as he turns away from me. 5 Him that privily speaks against his neighbour, him have I driven from *me*: he that is proud in look and insatiable in heart, —with him I have not eaten. 6 Mine eyes *shall be* upon the faithful of the land, that they may dwell with me: he that walked in a perfect way, the same ministered to me. 7 The proud doer dwelt not in the midst of my house; the unjust speaker prospered not in my sight. 8 Early did I slay all the sinners of the land, that I might destroy out of the city of the Lord all that work iniquity.

Ps.102 *A Prayer for the Poor; when he is deeply afflicted, and pours out his supplication before the Lord.* 1 Hear my prayer, O Lord, and let my cry come to thee. 2 Turn not away thy face from me: in the day *when* I am afflicted, incline thine ear to me: in the day *when* I shall call upon thee, speedily hear me. 3 For my days have vanished like smoke, and my bones have been parched like a stick. 4 I am blighted like grass, and my heart is dried up; for I have forgotten to eat my bread. 5 By reason of the voice of my groaning, my bone has cleaved to my flesh. 6 I have become like a pelican of the wilderness; 7 I have become like an owl in a ruined house. I have watched, and am become as a sparrow dwelling alone on a roof. 8 All the day long mine enemies have reproached me; and they that praised me have sworn against me. 9 For I have eaten ashes as it were bread, and mingled my drink with weeping; 10 because of thine anger and thy wrath: for thou hast lifted me up, and dashed me down. 11 My days have declined like a shadow; and I am withered like grass. 12 But thou, Lord, endurest for ever, and thy memorial to generation and generation. 13 Thou shalt arise, and have mercy upon Sion: for *it is* time to have mercy upon her, for the set time is come. 14 For thy servants have taken pleasure in her stones, and they shall pity her dust. 15 So the nations shall fear thy name, O Lord, and all kings thy glory. 16 For the Lord shall build up Sion, and shall appear in his glory.

17 He has had regard to the prayer of the lowly, and has not despised their petition. 18 Let this be written for another generation; and the people that shall be created shall praise the Lord. 19 For he has looked out from the height of his sanctuary; the Lord looked upon the earth from heaven; 20 to hear the groaning of the fettered ones, to loosen the sons of the slain; 21 to proclaim the name of the Lord in Sion, and his praise in Jerusalem; 22 when the people are gathered together, and the kings, to serve the Lord. 23 He answered him in the way of his strength: tell me the fewness of my days. 24 Take me not away in the midst of my days: thy years *are* through all generations. 25 In the beginning thou, O Lord, didst lay the foundation of the earth; and the heavens are the works of thine hands. 26 They shall perish, but thou remainest: and *they all* shall wax old as a garment; and as a vesture shalt thou fold them, and they shall be changed. 27 But thou art the same, and thy years shall not fail. 28 The children of thy servants shall dwell *securely*, and their seed shall prosper for ever.

Ps.103 *A Psalm of David.* 1 Bless the Lord, O my soul; and all *that is* within me, *bless* his holy name. 2 Bless the Lord, O my soul, and forget not all his praises: 3 who forgives all thy transgressions, who heals all thy diseases; 4 who redeems thy life from corruption; who crowns thee with mercy and compassion; 5 who satisfies thy desire with good things: *so that* thy youth shall be renewed like *that* of the eagle. 6 The Lord executes mercy and judgment for all that are injured. 7 He made known his ways to Moses, his will to the children of Israel. 8 The Lord is compassionate and pitiful, long-suffering, and full of mercy. 9 He will not be always angry; neither will he be wrathful for ever. 10 He has not dealt with us according to our sins, nor recompensed us according to our iniquities. 11 For as the heaven is high above the earth, the Lord has *so* increased his mercy toward them that fear him. 12 As far as the east is from the west, *so far* has he removed our transgressions from us. 13 As a father pities *his* children, the Lord pities them that fear him. 14 For he knows our frame: remember that we are dust. 15 *As for* man, his days are as grass; as a flower of the field, so shall he flourish. 16 For the wind passes over it, and it shall not be; and it shall know its place no more. 17 But the mercy of the Lord is from generation to generation upon them that fear him, and his righteousness to children's children; 18 to them that keep his covenant, and remember his commandments to do them. 19 The Lord has prepared his throne in the heaven; and his kingdom rules over all. 20 Bless the Lord, all ye his angels, mighty in strength, who perform his bidding, *ready* to hearken to the voice of his words. 21 Bless the Lord, all ye his hosts; *ye* ministers of his that do his will. 22 Bless the Lord, all his works, in every place of his dominion: bless the Lord, O my soul.

Ps.104 *A Psalm of David.* 1 Bless the Lord, O my soul. O Lord my God, thou art very great; thou hast clothed thyself with praise and honour: 2 who dost robe thyself with light as with a garment; spreading out the heaven as a curtain. 3 Who covers his chambers with waters; who makes the clouds his chariot; who walks on the wings of the wind. 4 Who makes his angels spirits, and his ministers a flaming fire. 5 Who establishes the earth on her sure foundation: it shall not be moved for ever. 6 The deep, as it were a garment, is his covering: the waters shall stand on the hills. 7 At thy rebuke they shall flee; at the voice of thy thunder they shall be alarmed. 8 They go up to the mountains, and down to the plains, to the place which thou hast founded for them. 9 Thou hast set a bound which they shall not pass, neither shall they turn again to cover the earth. 10 He sends forth his fountains among the valleys: the waters shall run between the mountains. 11 They shall give drink to all the wild beasts of the field: the wild asses shall take *of them* to *quench* their thirst. 12 By them shall the birds of the sky lodge: they shall utter a voice out of the midst of the rocks. 13 He waters the mountains from his chambers: the earth shall be satisfied with the fruit of thy works. 14 He makes grass to grow for the cattle, and green herb for the service of men, to bring bread out of the earth; 15 and wine makes glad the heart of man, to make his face cheerful with oil: and bread strengthens man's heart. 16 The trees of the plain shall be full *of sap; even* the cedars of Libanus which he has planted. 17 There the sparrows will build their nests; and the house of the heron takes the lead among them. 18 The high mountains are a refuge for the stags, *and* the rock for the rabbits. 19 He appointed the moon for seasons: the sun knows his going down. 20 Thou didst make darkness, and it was night; in it all the wild beasts of the forest will be abroad: 21 *even* young lions roaring for prey, and to seek meat for themselves from God. 22 The sun arises, and they shall be gathered together, and shall lie down in their dens. 23 Man shall go forth to his work, and to his labour till evening. 24 How great are thy works, O Lord! in wisdom hast thou wrought them all: the earth is filled with thy creation. 25 *So is* this great and wide sea: there are things creeping innumerable, small animals and great. 26 There go the ships; *and* this dragon whom thou hast made to play in it. 27 All wait upon thee, to give them *their* food in due season. 28 When thou hast given *it* them, they will gather *it*; and when thou hast opened thine hand, they shall all be filled with good. 29 But when thou hast turned away thy face, they shall be troubled: thou wilt take away their breath, and they shall fail, and return to their dust. 30 Thou shalt send forth thy Spirit, and they shall be created; and thou shalt renew the face of the earth. 31 Let the glory of the Lord be for ever: the Lord shall rejoice in his works; 32 who looks upon the earth, and makes it tremble; who touches the mountains, and they smoke. 33 I will sing to the Lord while I live; I will sing praise to my God while I exist. 34 Let my meditation be sweet to him: and I will rejoice in the Lord. 35 Let the sinners fail from off the earth, and transgressors, so that they shall be no more. Bless the Lord, O my soul.

Ps.105 *Alleluia.* 1 Give thanks to the Lord, and call upon his name; declare his works among the heathen. 2 Sing to him, yea, sing praises to him: tell forth all his wonderful works. 3 Glory in his holy name: let the heart of them that seek the Lord rejoice. 4 Seek ye the Lord, and be strengthened; seek his face continually. 5 Remember his wonderful works that he has done; his wonders, and the judgments of his mouth; 6 *ye* seed of Abraam, his servants, *ye* children of Jacob, his chosen ones. 7 He is the Lord our God; his judgments are in all the earth. 8 He has remembered his covenant for ever, the word which he commanded for a thousand generation: 9 which he established as a covenant to Abraam, and *he remembered* his oath to Isaac. 10 And he established it to Jacob for an ordinance, and to Israel for an everlasting covenant; 11 saying To thee will I give the land of Chanaan, the line of your inheritance: 12 when they were few in number, very few, and sojourners in it. 13 And they went from nation to nation, and from *one* kingdom to another people. 14 He suffered no man to wrong them; and he rebuked kings for their sakes: 15 *saying*, Touch not my anointed ones; and do my prophets no harm. 16 Moreover he called for a famine upon the land; he broke the whole support of bread. 17 He sent a man before them; Joseph was sold for a slave. 18 They hurt his feet with fetters; his soul passed into iron, 19 until the time that his cause came on; the word of the Lord tried him as fire. 20 The king sent and loosed him; *even* the prince of the people, and let him go free. 21 He made him Lord over his house, and ruler of all his substance; 22 to chastise his rulers at his pleasure, and to teach his elders wisdom. 23 Israel also came into Egypt, and Jacob sojourned in the land of Cham. 24 And he increased his people greatly, and made them stronger than their enemies. 25 And he turned their heart to hate his people, to deal craftily with his servants. 26 He sent fort Moses his servant, *and* Aaron whom he had chosen. 27 He established among them his signs, and *his* wonders in the land of Cham. 28 He sent forth darkness, and made it dark; yet they rebelled against his words. 29 He turned their waters into blood, and slew their fish. 30 Their land produced frogs abundantly, in the chambers of their kings. 31 He spoke, and the dog-fly came, and lice in all their coasts. 32 He turned their rain into hail, *and sent* flaming fire in their land. 33 And he smote their vines and their fig trees; and broke every tree of their coast. 34 He spoke, and the locust came, and caterpillars innumerable, 35 and devoured all the grass in their land, and devoured the fruit of the ground. 36 He smote also every first-born of their land, the first-fruits of all their labour. 37 And he brought them out with silver and gold; and there was not a feeble one among their tribes. 38 Egypt rejoiced at their departing; for the fear of them fell upon them. 39 He spread out a cloud for a covering to them, and fire to give them light by night. 40 They asked, and the quail came, and he satisfied them with the bread of heaven. 41 He clave the rock, and the waters flowed, rivers ran in dry places. 42 For he remembered his holy word, which *he promised* to Abraam his servant. 43 And he brought out his people with exultation, and his chosen with joy; 44 and gave them the lands of the heathen; and they inherited the labours of the people; 45 that they might keep his ordinances, and diligently seek his law.

Ps.106 *Alleluia.* 1 Give thanks to the Lord; for he is good: for his mercy *endures* for ever. 2 Who shall tell the mighty acts of the Lord? *who* shall cause all his praises to be heard? 3 Blessed are they that keep judgment, and do righteousness at all times. 4 Remember us, O Lord, with the favour *thou hast* to thy people: visit us with thy salvation; 5 that we may

behold the good of thine elect, that we may rejoice in the gladness of thy nation, that we may glory with thine inheritance. 6 We have sinned with our fathers, we have transgressed, we have done unrighteously. 7 Our fathers in Egypt understood not thy wonders, and remembered not the multitude of thy mercy; but provoked *him* as they went up by the Red Sea. 8 Yet he saved them for his name's sake, that he might cause his mighty power to be known. 9 And he rebuked the Red Sea, and it was dried up: so he led them through the deep as through the wilderness. 10 And he saved them out of the hand of them that hated *them*, and redeemed them out of the hand of the enemy. 11 The water covered those that oppressed them: there was not one of them left. 12 Then they believed his words, and celebrated his praise. 13 They made haste, they forgot his works; they waited not for his counsel. 14 And they lusted exceedingly in the wilderness, and tempted God in the dry *land*. 15 And he gave them their request, and sent fullness into their souls. 16 They provoked Moses also in the camp, and Aaron the holy one of the Lord. 17 The earth opened and swallowed up Dathan, and closed upon the congregation of Abiron. 18 And a fire was kindled in their congregation, and a flame burnt up the sinners. 19 And they made a calf in Choreb, and worshipped the graven image, 20 and they changed their glory into the similitude of a calf that feeds on grass. 21 They forgot God that saved them, who had wrought great deeds in Egypt; 22 wondrous *works* in the land of Cham, and terrible things at the Red Sea. 23 So he said that he would have destroyed them, had not Moses his chosen stood before him in the breach, to turn *him* away from the fierceness of his anger, so that he should not destroy them. 24 Moreover they set at nought the desirable land, and believed not his word. 25 And they murmured in their tents: they hearkened not to the voice of the Lord. 26 So he lifted up his hand against them, to cast them down in the wilderness; 27 and to cast down their seed among the nations, and to scatter them in the countries. 28 They were joined also to Beelphegor, and ate the sacrifices of the dead. And they provoked him with their devices; 29 and destruction, was multiplied among them. 30 Then Phinees stood up, and made atonement: and the plague ceased. 31 And it was counted to him for righteousness, to all generations for ever. 32 They provoked him also at the water of Strife, and Moses was hurt for their sakes; 33 for they provoked his spirit, and he spoke *unadvisedly* with his lips. 34 They destroyed not the nations which the Lord told them *to destroy*; 35 but were mingled with the heathen, and learned their works. 36 And they served their graven images; and it became an offence to them. 37 And they sacrificed their sons and their daughters to devils, 38 and shed innocent blood, the blood of their sons and daughters, whom they sacrificed to the idols of Chanaan; and the land was defiled with blood. 39 and was polluted with their works; and they went a whoring with their own devices. 40 So the Lord was very angry with his people, and he abhorred his inheritance. 41 And he delivered them into the hands of *their* enemies; and they that hated them ruled over them. 42 Ands their enemies oppressed them, and they were brought down under their hands. 43 Many a time he delivered them; but they provoked him by their counsel, and they were brought low by their iniquities. 44 Ye the Lord looked upon their affliction, when he heard their petition. 45 And he remembered his covenant, and repented according to the multitude of his mercy. 46 And he caused them to be pitied in the sight of all who carried them captive. 47 Save us, O Lord our God, and gather us from among the heathen, that we may give thanks to thy holy name, that we may glory in thy praise. 48 Blessed be the Lord God of Israel from everlasting and to everlasting; and all the people shall say, Amen, Amen.

Ps.107 *Alleluia.* 1 Give thanks to the Lord, for he is good; for his mercy *endures* for ever. 2 Let them say *so* who have been redeemed by the Lord, whom he has redeemed from the hand of the enemy; 3 and gathered them out of the countries, from the east, and west, and north, and south. 4 They wandered in the wilderness in a dry land; they found no way to a city of habitation. 5 Hungry and thirsty, their soul fainted in them. 6 Then they cried to the Lord in their affliction, and he delivered them out of their distresses. 7 And he guided them into a straight path, that they might go to a city of habitation. 8 Let them acknowledge to the Lord his mercies, and his wonderful works to the children of men. 9 For he satisfies the empty soul, and fills the hungry *soul* with good things, 10 *even* them that sit in darkness and the shadow of death, fettered in poverty and iron; 11 because they rebelled against the words of God, and provoked the counsel of the Most High. 12 So their heart was brought low with troubles; they were weak, and there was no helper. 13 Then they cried to the Lord in their affliction, and he saved them out of their distresses. 14 And he brought them out of darkness and the shadow of death, and broke their bonds asunder. 15 Let them acknowledge to the Lord his mercies, and his wonders to the children of men. 16 For he broke to pieces the brazen gates, and crushed the iron bars. 17 He helped them out of the way of their iniquity; for they were brought low because of their iniquities. 18 Their soul abhorred all meat; and they drew near to the gates of death. 19 Then they cried to the Lord in their affliction, and he saved them out of their distresses. 20 He sent his word, and healed them, and delivered them out of their destructions. 21 Let them acknowledge to the Lord his mercies, and his wonderful works to the children of men. 22 And let them offer to him the sacrifice of praise, and proclaim this works with exultation. 23 They that go down to the sea in ships, doing business in many waters; 24 these *men* have seen the works of the Lord, and his wonders in the deep. 25 He speaks, and the stormy wind arises, and its waves are lifted up. 26 They go up to the heavens, and go down to the depths; their soul melts because of troubles. 27 They are troubled, they stagger as a drunkard, and all their wisdom is swallowed up. 28 Then they cry to the Lord in their affliction, and he brings them out of their distresses. 29 And he commands the storm, and it is calmed into a gentle breeze, and its waves are still. 30 And they are glad, because they are quiet; and he guides them to their desire haven. 31 Let them acknowledge to the Lord his mercies, and his wonderful works to the children of men. 32 Let

them exalt him in the congregation of the people, and praise him in the seat of the elders. 33 He turns rivers into a desert, and streams of water into a dry land; 34 a fruitful land into saltness, for the wickedness of them that dwell in it. 35 He turns a wilderness into pools of water, and a dry land into streams of water. 36 And there he causes the hungry to dwell, and they establish for themselves cities of habitation. 37 And they sow fields, and plant vineyards, and they yield fruit of increase. 38 And he blesses them, and they multiply exceedingly, and he diminishes not the number of their cattle. 39 Again they become few, and are brought low, by the pressure of evils and pain. 40 Contempt is poured upon their princes, and he causes them to wander in a desert and trackless land. 41 But he helps the poor out of poverty, and makes *him* families as a flock. 42 The upright shall see and rejoice; and all iniquity shall stop her mouth. 43 Who is wise, and will observe these things, and understand the mercies of the Lord?

Ps.108 *Song of a Psalm by David.* 1 O God, my heart is ready, my heart is ready; I will sing and sing psalms with my glory. 2 Awake, psaltery and harp; I will awake early. 3 I will give thanks to thee, O Lord, among the people; I will sing praise to thee among the Gentiles. 4 For thy mercy is great above the heavens, and thy truth *reaches* to the clouds. 5 Be thou exalted, O God, above the heavens; and thy glory above all the earth. 6 That thy beloved *ones* may be delivered, save with thy right hand, and hear me. God has spoken in his sanctuary; 7 I will be exalted, and will divide Sicima, and will measure out the valley of tents. 8 Galaad is mine; and Manasses is mine; and Ephraim is the help of mine head; Judas is my king; 9 Moab is the caldron of my hope; over Idumea will I cast my sandal; the Philistines are made subject to me. 10 Who will bring me into the fortified city? or who will guide me to Idumea? 11 Wilt not thou, O God, who hast rejected us? and wilt not thou, O God, go forth with our hosts? 12 Give us help from tribulation: for vain is the help of man. 13 Through God we shall do valiantly; and he will bring to nought our enemies.

Ps.109 *For the end, a Psalm of David.* 1 O God, pass not over my praise in silence; 2 for the mouth of the sinner and the mouth of the crafty *man* have been opened against me: they have spoken against me with a crafty tongue. 3 And they have compassed me with words of hatred; and fought against me without a cause. 4 Instead of loving me, they falsely accused me: but I continued to pray. 5 And they rewarded me evil for good, and hatred for my love. 6 Set thou a sinner against him; and let the devil stand at his right hand. 7 When he is judged, let him go forth condemned: and let his prayer become sin. 8 Let his days be few: and let another take his office of overseer. 9 Let his children be orphans, and his wife a widow. 10 Let his children wander without a dwelling-place, and beg: let them be cast out of their habitations. 11 Let *his* creditor exact all that belongs to him: and let strangers spoil his labours. 12 Let him have no helper; neither let there be any one to have compassion on his fatherless children. 13 Let his children be *given up* to utter destruction: in one generation let his name be blotted out. 14 Let the iniquity of his fathers be remembered before the

Lord; and let not the sin of his mother be blotted out. 15 Let them be before the Lord continually; and let their memorial be blotted out from the earth. 16 Because he remembered not to shew mercy, but persecuted the needy and poor man, and *that* to slay him that was pricked in the heart. 17 He loved cursing also, and it shall come upon him; and he took not pleasure in blessing, so it shall be removed far from him. 18 Yea, he put on cursing as a garment, and it is come as water into his bowels, and as oil into his bones. 19 Let it be to him as a garment which he puts on, and as a girdle with which he girds himself continually. 20 This is the dealing of the Lord with those who falsely accuse me, and of them that speak evil against my soul. 21 But thou, O Lord, Lord, deal *mercifully* with me, for thy name's sake: for thy mercy is good. 22 Deliver me, for I am poor and needy; and my heart is troubled within me. 23 I am removed as a shadow in its going down: I am tossed up and down like locusts. 24 My knees are weakened through fasting, and my flesh is changed by reason of *the want of* oil. 25 I became also a reproach to them: *when* they saw me they shook their heads. 26 Help me, O Lord my God; and save me according to thy mercy. 27 And let them know that this is thy hand; and *that* thou, Lord, hast wrought it. 28 Let them curse, but thou shalt bless: let them that rise up against me be ashamed, but let thy servant rejoice. 29 Let those that falsely accuse me be clothed with shame, and let them cover themselves with their shame as with a mantle. 30 I will give thanks to the Lord abundantly with my mouth; and in the midst of many I will praise him. 31 For he stood on the right hand of the poor, to save *me* from them that persecute my soul.

Ps.110 *A Psalm of David.* 1 The Lord said to my Lord, Sit thou on my right hand, until I make thine enemies thy footstool. 2 The Lord shall send out a rod of power for thee out of Sion: rule thou in the midst of thine enemies. 3 With thee is dominion in the day of thy power, in the splendours of thy saints: I have begotten thee from the womb before the morning. 4 The Lord sware, and will not repent, Thou art a priest for ever, after the order of Melchisedec. 5 The Lord at thy right hand has dashed in pieces kings in the day of his wrath. 6 He shall judge among the nations, he shall fill up *the number of* corpses, he shall crush the heads of many on the earth. 7 He shall drink of the brook in the way; therefore shall he lift up the head.

Ps.111 *Alleluia.* 1 I will give thee thanks, O Lord, with my whole heart, in the council of the upright, and *in* the congregation. 2 The works of the Lord are great, sought out according to all his will. 3 His work is *worthy of* thanksgiving and honour: and his righteousness endures for ever and ever. 4 He has caused his wonderful works to be remembered: the Lord is merciful and compassionate. 5 He has given food to them that fear him: he will remember his covenant for ever. 6 He has declared to his people the power of his works, to give them the inheritance of the heathen. 7 The works of his hands are truth and judgment: all his commandments are sure: 8 established for ever and ever, done in truth and uprightness. 9 He sent redemption to his people: he commanded his covenant for ever: holy

and fearful is his name. 10 The fear of the Lord is the beginning of wisdom, and all that act accordingly have a good understanding; his praise endures for ever and ever.

Ps.112 *Alleluia.* 1 Blessed is the man that fears the Lord: he will delight greatly in his commandments. 2 His seed shall be mighty in the earth: the generation of the upright shall be blessed. 3 Glory and riches shall be in his house; and his righteousness endures for evermore. 4 To the upright light has sprung up in darkness: he is pitiful, and merciful, and righteous. 5 The good man is he that pities and lends: he will direct his affairs with judgment. 6 For he shall not be moved for ever; the righteous shall be in everlasting remembrance. 7 He shall not be afraid of *any* evil report: his heart is ready to trust in the Lord. 8 His heart is established, he shall not fear, till he shall see *his desire* upon his enemies. 9 He has dispersed abroad; he has given to the poor; his righteousness endures for evermore: his horn shall be exalted with honour. 10 The sinner shall see and be angry, he shall gnash his teeth, and consume away: the desire of the sinner shall perish.

Ps.113 *Alleluia.* 1 Praise the Lord, ye servants *of his*, praise, the name of the Lord. 2 Let the name of the Lord be blessed, from this present time and for ever. 3 From the rising of the sun to his setting, the name of the Lord is to be praised. 4 The Lord is high above all the nations; his glory is above the heavens. 5 Who is as the Lord our God? who dwells in the high places, 6 and *yet* looks upon the low things in heaven, and on the earth: 7 who lifts up the poor from the earth, and raises up the needy from the dunghill; 8 to set him with princes, *even* with the princes of his people: 9 who settles the barren *woman* in a house, *as* a mother rejoicing over children.

Ps.114 *Alleluia.* 1 At the going forth of Israel from Egypt, of the house of Jacob from a barbarous people, 2 Judea became his sanctuary, *and* Israel his dominion. 3 The sea saw and fled: Jordan was turned back. 4 The mountains skipped like rams, and the hills like lambs. 5 What *ailed* thee, O sea, that thou fleddest? and thou Jordan, that thou wast turned back? 6 *Ye* mountains, that ye skipped like rams, and *ye* hills, like lambs? 7 The earth trembled at the presence of the Lord, at the presence of the God of Jacob; 8 who turned the rock into pools of water, and the flint into fountains of water.

Ps.115 1 Not to us, O Lord, not to us, but to thy name give glory, because of thy mercy and thy truth; 2 lest at any time the nations should say, Where is their God? 3 But our God has done in heaven and on earth, whatsoever he has pleased. 4 The idols of the nations are silver and gold, the works of men's hands. 5 They have a mouth, but they cannot speak; they have eyes, but they cannot see: 6 they have ears, but they cannot hear; they have noses, but they cannot smell; 7 they have hands, but they cannot handle; they have feet, but they cannot walk: they cannot speak through their throat. 8 Let those that make them become like to them, and all who trust in them. 9 The house of Israel trusts in the Lord: he is their helper and defender. 10 The house of Aaron trusts in the Lord: he is their helper and defender. 11 They that fear the Lord trust in the Lord: he is their helper and defender. 12 The Lord has remembered us, and blessed us: he has blessed the house of Israel, he has blessed the house of Aaron. 13 He has blessed them that fear the Lord, both small and great. 14 The Lord add *blessings* to you and to your children. 15 Blessed are ye of the Lord, who made the heaven and the earth. 16 The heaven of heavens *belongs* to the Lord: but he has given the earth to the sons of men. 17 The dead shall not praise thee, O Lord, nor any that go down to Hades. 18 But we, the living, will bless the Lord, from henceforth and for ever.

Ps.116 *Alleluia.* 1 I am well pleased, because the Lord will hearken to the voice of my supplication. 2 Because he has inclined his ear to me, therefore will I call upon him while I live. 3 The pangs of death compassed me; the dangers of hell found me: I found affliction and sorrow. 4 Then I called on the name of the Lord: O Lord, deliver my soul. 5 The Lord is merciful and righteous; yea, our God has pity. 6 The Lord preserves the simple: I was brought low, and he delivered me. 7 Return to thy rest, O my soul; for the Lord has dealt bountifully with thee. 8 For he has delivered my soul from death, mine eyes from tears, and my feet from falling. 9 I shall be well- pleasing before the Lord in the land of the living. Alleluia: 10 I believed, wherefore I have spoken: but I was greatly afflicted. 11 And I said in mine amazement, Every man is a liar. 12 What shall I render to the Lord for all the things wherein he has rewarded me? 13 I will take the cup of salvation, and call upon the name of the Lord. 14 I will pay my vows to the Lord, in the presence of all his people. 15 Precious in the sight of the Lord is the death of his saints. 16 O Lord, I am thy servant; I am thy servant, and the son of thine handmaid: thou hast burst by bonds asunder. 17 I will offer to thee the sacrifice of praise, and will call upon the name of the Lord. 18 I will pay my vows unto the Lord, in the presence of all his people, 19 in the courts of the Lord's house, in the midst of thee, Jerusalem.

Ps.117 *Alleluia.* 1 Praise the Lord, all ye nations: praise him, all ye peoples. 2 For his mercy has been abundant toward us: and the truth of the Lord endures for ever.

Ps.118 *Alleluia.* 1 Give thanks to the Lord; for *he is* good: for his mercy *endures* for ever. 2 Let now the house of Israel say, that *he is* good: for his mercy *endures* for ever. 3 Let now the house of Aaron say, that *he is* good: for his mercy *endures* for ever. 4 Let now all that fear the Lord say, that *he is* good: for his mercy *endures* for ever. 5 I called on the Lord out of affliction: and he hearkened to me, *so as to bring me* into a wide place. 6 The Lord is my helper; and I will not fear what man shall do to me. 7 The Lord is my helper; and I shall see *my desire* upon mine enemies. 8 *It is* better to trust in the Lord than to trust in man. 9 *It is* better to hope in the Lord, than to hope in princes. 10 All nations compassed me about: but in the name of the Lord I repulsed them. 11 They completely compassed me about: but in the name of the Lord I repulsed them. 12 They compassed me about as bees *do* a honeycomb, and they burst into flame as fire among thorns: but in the name of the Lord I repulsed them. 13 I

was thrust, and sorely shaken, that I might fall: but the Lord helped me. 14 The Lord is my strength and my song, and is become my salvation. 15 The voice of exultation and salvation is in the tabernacles of the righteous: the right hand of the Lord has wrought mightily. 16 The right hand of the Lord has exalted me: the right hand of the Lord has wrought powerfully. 17 I shall not die, but live, and recount the works of the Lord. 18 The Lord has chastened me sore: but he has not given me up to death. 19 Open to me the gates of righteousness: I will go into them, and give praise to the Lord. 20 This is the gate of the Lord: the righteous shall enter by it. 21 I will give thanks to thee; because thou hast heard me, and art become my salvation. 22 The stone which the builders rejected, the same is become the head of the corner. 23 This has been done of the Lord; and it is wonderful in our eyes. 24 This is the day which the Lord has made: let us exult and rejoice in it. 25 O Lord, save now: O Lord, send now prosperity. 26 Blessed is he that comes in the name of the Lord: we have blessed you out of the house of the Lord. 27 God is the Lord, and he has shined upon us: celebrate the feast with thick *branches, binding the victims* even to the horns of the altar. 28 Thou art my God, and I will give thee thanks: thou art my God, and I will exalt thee. I will give thanks to thee, for thou hast heard me, and art become my salvation. 29 Give thanks to the Lord; for he is good: for his mercy *endures* for ever.

Ps.119 *Alleluia.* 1 Blessed are the blameless in the way, who walk in the law of the Lord. 2 Blessed are they that search out his testimonies: they will diligently seek him with the whole heart. 3 For they that work iniquity have not walked in his ways. 4 Thou hast commanded *us* diligently to keep thy precepts. 5 O that my ways were directed to keep thine ordinances. 6 Then shall I not be ashamed, when I have respect to all thy commandments. 7 I will give thee thanks with uprightness of heart, when I have learnt the judgments of thy righteousness. 8 I will keep thine ordinances: O forsake me not greatly. 9 Wherewith shall a young man direct his way? by keeping thy words. 10 With my whole heart have I diligently sought thee: cast me not away from thy commandments. 11 I have hidden thine oracles in my heart, that I might not sin against thee. 12 Blessed art thou, O Lord: teach me thine ordinances. 13 With my lips have I declared all the judgments of thy mouth. 14 I have delighted in the way of thy testimonies, *as much* as in all riches. 15 I will meditate on thy commandments, and consider thy ways. 16 I will meditate on thine ordinances: I will not forget thy words. 17 Render a recompense to thy servant: *so* shall I live, and keep thy words. 18 Unveil thou mine eyes, and I shall perceive wondrous things of thy law. 19 I am a stranger in the earth: hide not thy commandments from me. 20 My soul has longed exceedingly for thy judgments at all times. 21 Thou has rebuked the proud: cursed are they that turn aside from thy commandments. 22 Remove from me reproach and contempt; for I have sought out thy testimonies. 23 For princes sat and spoke against me: but thy servant was meditating on thine ordinances. 24 For thy testimonies are my meditation, and thine ordinances are my counsellors. 25 My soul has cleaved to the ground; quicken thou me according to thy word. 26 I declared my ways, and thou didst hear me: teach me thine ordinances. 27 Instruct me in the way of thine ordinances; and I will meditate on thy wondrous works. 28 My soul has slumbered for sorrow; strengthen thou me with thy words. 29 Remove from me the way of iniquity; and be merciful to me by thy law. 30 I have chosen the way of truth; and have not forgotten thy judgments. 31 I have cleaved to thy testimonies, O Lord; put me not to shame. 32 I ran the way of thy commandments, when thou didst enlarge my heart. 33 Teach me, O Lord, the way of thine ordinances, and I will seek it out continually. 34 Instruct me, and I will search out thy law, and will keep it with my whole heart. 35 Guide me in the path of thy commandments; for I have delighted in it. 36 Incline mine heart to thy testimonies, and not to covetousness. 37 Turn away mine eyes that I may not behold vanity: quicken thou me in thy way. 38 Confirm thine oracle to thy servant, that he may fear thee. 39 Take away my reproach which I have feared: for thy judgments are good. 40 Behold, I have desired thy commandments: quicken me in thy righteousness. 41 And let thy mercy come upon me, O Lord; *even* thy salvation, according to thy word. 42 And *so* I shall render an answer to them that reproach me: for I have trusted in thy words. 43 And take not the word of truth utterly out of my mouth; for I have hoped in thy judgments. So shall I keep thy law continually, for ever and ever. 45 I walked also at large: for I sought out thy commandments. 46 And I spoke of thy testimonies before kings, and was not ashamed. 47 And I meditated on thy commandments, which I loved exceedingly. 48 And I lifted up my hands to thy commandments which I loved; and I meditated in thine ordinances. 49 Remember thy words to thy servant, wherein thou hast made me hope. 50 This has comforted me in mine affliction: for thine oracle has quickened me. 51 The proud have transgressed exceedingly; but I swerved not from thy law. 52 I remembered thy judgments of old, O Lord; and was comforted. 53 Despair took hold upon me, because of the sinners who forsake thy law. 54 Thine ordinances were my songs in the place of my sojourning. 55 I remembered thy name, O Lord, in the night, and kept thy law. 56 This I had, because I diligently sought thine ordinances. 57 Thou art my portion, O Lord: I said that I would keep thy law. 58 I besought thy favour with my whole heart: have mercy upon me according to thy word. 59 I thought on thy ways, and turned my feet to thy testimonies. 60 I prepared myself, (and was not terrified,) to keep thy commandments. 61 The snares of sinners entangled me: but I forgot not thy law. 62 At midnight I arose, to give thanks to thee for the judgments of thy righteousness. 63 I am a companion of all them that fear thee, and of them that keep thy commandments. 64 O Lord, the earth is full of thy mercy: teach me thine ordinances. 65 Thou hast wrought kindly with thy servant, o Lord, according to thy word. 66 Teach me kindness, and instruction, and knowledge: for I have believed thy commandments. 67 Before I was afflicted, I transgressed; therefore have I kept thy word. 68 Good art thou, O Lord; therefore in thy goodness teach me thine ordinances. 69 The injustice of the proud has been multiplied against me: but I will search out thy commandments with all my heart. 70 Their heart has been curdled like milk; but I have meditated on thy law. 71 *It is* good for me that thou hast afflicted me; that I might learn thine ordinances. 72 The law of thy mouth is better to me than thousands of gold and silver. 73 Thy hands have made me, and fashioned me: instruct me, that I may learn thy commandments. 74 They that fear thee will see me and rejoice: for I have hoped in thy words. 75 I know, O Lord, that thy judgments are righteousness, and *that* thou in truthfulness hast afflicted me. 76 Let, I pray thee, thy mercy be to comfort me, according to thy word to thy servant. 77 Let thy compassions come to me, that I may live: for thy law is my meditation. 78 Let the proud be ashamed; for they transgressed against me unjustly: but I will meditate in thy commandments. 79 Let those that fear thee, and those that know thy testimonies, turn to me. 80 Let mine heart be blameless in thine ordinances, that I may not be ashamed. 81 My soul faints for thy salvation: I have hoped in thy words. 82 Mine eyes failed *in waiting* for thy word, saying, When wilt thou comfort me? 83 For I am become as a bottle in the frost: *yet* I have not forgotten thine ordinances. 84 How many are the days of thy servant? when wilt thou execute judgment for me on them that persecute me? 85 Transgressors told me *idle tales*; but not according to thy law, O Lord. 86 All thy commandments are truth; they persecuted me unjustly; help thou me. 87 They nearly made an end of me in the earth; but I forsook not thy commandments. 88 Quicken me according to thy mercy; so shall I keep the testimonies of thy mouth. 89 Thy word, O Lord, abides in heaven for ever. 90 Thy truth *endures* to all generations; thou hast founded the earth, and it abides. 91 The day continues by thy arrangement; for all things are thy servants. 92 Were it not that thy law is my meditation, then I should have perished in mine affliction. 93 I will never forget thine ordinances; for with them thou hast quickened me. 94 I am thine, save me; for I have sought out thine ordinances. 95 Sinners laid wait for me to destroy me; *but* I understood thy testimonies. 96 have seen an end of all perfection; *but* thy commandment is very broad. 97 How I have loved thy law, O Lord! it is my meditation all the day. 98 Thou hast made me wiser than mine enemies *in* thy commandment; for it is mine for ever. 99 I have more understanding than all my teachers; for thy testimonies are my medication. 100 I understand more that the aged; because I have sought out thy commandments. 101 I have kept back my feet from every evil way, that I might keep thy words. 102 I have not declined from thy judgments; for thou hast instructed me. 103 How sweet are thine oracles to my throat! more so than honey to my mouth! 104 I gain understanding by thy commandments: therefore I have hated every way of unrighteousness. 105 Thy law is a lamp to my feet, and a light to my paths. 106 I have sworn and determined to keep the judgments of thy righteousness. 107 I have been very greatly afflicted, O Lord: quicken me, according to thy word. 108 Accept, I pray thee, O Lord, the freewill-offerings of my mouth, and teach me thy judgments. 109 My soul is continually in thine hands; and I have not forgotten thy law. 110 Sinners spread a snare for me; but I erred not from thy commandments. 111 I have inherited thy testimonies for ever; for they are the joy of my heart. 112 I have inclined my heart to perform thine ordinances for ever, in return *for thy mercies*. 113 I have hated transgressors; but I have loved thy law. 114 Thou art my helper and my supporter; I have hoped in thy words. 115 Depart from me, ye evil-doers; for I will search out the commandments of my God. 116 Uphold me according to thy word, and quicken me; and make me not ashamed of my expectation. 117 Help me, and I shall be saved; and I will meditate in thine ordinances continually. 118 Thou hast brought to nought all that depart from thine ordinances; for their inward thought is unrighteous. 119 I have reckoned all the sinners of the earth as transgressors; therefore have I loved thy testimonies. 120 Penetrate my flesh with thy fear; for I am afraid of thy judgments. 121 I have done judgment and justice; deliver me not up to them that injure me. 122 Receive thy servant for good: let not the proud accuse me falsely. 123 Mine eyes have failed for thy salvation, and for the word of thy righteousness. 124 Deal with thy servant according to thy mercy, and teach me thine ordinances. 125 I am thy servant; instruct me, and I shall know thy testimonies. 126 *It is* time for the Lord to work: they have utterly broken thy law. 127 Therefore have I loved thy commandments more than gold, or the topaz. 128 Therefore I directed myself *according* to all thy commandments: I have hated every unjust way. 129 Thy testimonies are wonderful: therefore my soul has sought them out. 130 The manifestation of thy words will enlighten, and instruct the simple. 131 I opened my mouth, and drew breath: for I earnestly longed after thy commandments. 132 Look upon me and have mercy upon me, after the manner of them that love thy name. 133 Order my steps according to thy word: and let not any iniquity have dominion over me. 134 Deliver me from the false accusation of men: so will I keep thy commandments. 135 Cause thy face to shine upon thy servant: and teach me thine ordinances. 136 Mine eyes have been bathed in streams of water, because I kept not thy law. 137 Righteous art thou, O Lord, and upright are thy judgments. 138 Thou has commanded righteousness and perfect truth, *as* thy testimonies. 139 Thy zeal has quite wasted me: because mine enemies have forgotten thy words. 140 Thy word *has been* very fully tried; and thy servant loves it. 141 I am young and despised: *yet* I have not forgotten thine ordinances. 142 Thy righteousness is an everlasting righteousness, and thy law is truth. 143 Afflictions and distresses found me: *but* thy commandments *were* my meditation. 144 Thy testimonies *are* an everlasting righteousness: instruct me, and I shall live. 145 I cried with my whole heart; hear me, O Lord: I will search out thine ordinances. 146 I cried to thee; save me, and I will keep thy testimonies. 147 I arose before the dawn, and cried: I hoped in thy words. 148 Mine eyes prevented the dawn, that I might meditate on thine oracles. 149 Hear my voice, O Lord, according to thy mercy; quicken me according to thy judgment. 150 They have drawn nigh who persecuted me unlawfully; and they are far removed from thy law. 151 Thou art near, O Lord; and all thy ways are truth. 152 I have known of old concerning thy testimonies, that thou hast founded them for ever. 153 Look upon mine affliction, and rescue me; for I have not forgotten thy law. 154 Plead my cause, and ransom me: quicken me because of thy word. 155 Salvation is far from sinners: for they have not searched out thine ordinances. 156 Thy mercies, O Lord, are many: quicken me according to thy judgment. 157 Many are they that persecute me and oppress me: *but* I have not declined from thy testimonies. 158 I beheld men acting foolishly, and I pined away; for they kept not thine oracles. 159 Behold, I have loved thy commandments, O Lord: quicken me in thy mercy. 160 The beginning of thy words is truth; and all the judgments of thy righteousness *endure* for ever. 161 Princes persecuted me without a cause, but my heart feared because of thy words. 162 I will exult because of thine oracles, as one that finds much spoil. 163 I hate and abhor unrighteousness; but I love thy law. 164 Seven times in a day have I praised thee because of the judgments of thy righteousness. 165 Great peace have they that love thy law: and there is no stumbling-block to them. 166 I waited for thy salvation, O Lord, and have loved thy commandments. 167 My soul has kept thy testimonies, and loved them exceedingly. 168 I have kept thy commandments and thy testimonies; for all my ways are before thee, O Lord. 169 Let my supplication come near before thee, o Lord; instruct me according to thine oracle. 170 Let my petition come in before thee, O Lord; deliver me according to thine oracle. 171 Let my lips utter a hymn, when thou shalt have taught me thine ordinances. 172 Let my tongue utter thine oracles; for all thy commandments are righteous. 173 Let thine hand be *prompt* to save me; for I have chosen thy commandments. 174 I have longed after thy salvation, O Lord; and thy law is my meditation. 175 My soul shall live, and shall praise thee; and thy judgments shall help me. 176 I have gone astray like a lost sheep; seek thy servant; for I have not forgotten thy commandments.

Ps.120 *A Song of Degrees.* 1 In mine affliction I cried to the Lord, and he hearkened to me. 2 Deliver my soul, O Lord, from unjust lips, and from a deceitful tongue. 3 What should be given to thee, and what should be added to thee, for *thy* crafty tongue? 4 Sharpened weapons of the mighty, with coals of the desert. 5 Woe is me, that my sojourning is prolonged; I have tabernacled among the tents of Kedar. 6 My soul has long been a sojourner; 7 I was peaceable among them that hated peace; when I spoke to them, they warred against me without a cause.

Ps.121 *A Song of Degrees.* 1 I lifted up mine eyes to the mountains, whence my help shall come. 2 My help *shall come* from the Lord, who made the heaven and the earth. 3 Let not thy foot be moved; and let not thy keeper slumber. 4 Behold, he that keeps Israel shall not slumber nor sleep. 5 The Lord shall keep thee: the Lord is thy shelter upon thy right hand. 6 The sun shall not burn thee by day, neither the moon by night. 7 May the Lord preserve thee from all evil: the Lord shall keep thy soul. 8 The Lord shall keep thy coming in, and thy going out, from henceforth and even for ever.

Ps.122 *A Song of Degrees.* 1 I was glad when they said to me, Let us go into the house of the Lord. 2 Our feet stood in thy courts, O Jerusalem. 3 Jerusalem is built as a city whose fellowship is complete. 4 For thither the tribes went up, the tribes of the Lord, as a testimony for Israel, to give thanks unto the name of the Lord. 5 For there are set thrones for judgment, *even* thrones for the house of David. 6 Pray now for the peace of Jerusalem: and *let there be* prosperity to them that love thee. 7 Let peace, I pray, be within thine host, and prosperity in thy palaces. 8 For the sake of my brethren and my neighbours, I have indeed spoken peace concerning thee. 9 Because of the house of the Lord our God, I have diligently sought thy good.

Ps.123 *A Song of Degrees.* 1 Unto thee who dwellest in heaven have I lifted up mine eyes. 2 Behold, as the eyes of servants *are directed* to the hands of their masters, *and* as the eyes of a maidservant to the hands of her mistress; so our eyes *are directed* to the Lord our God, until he have mercy upon us. 3 Have pity upon us, O Lord, have pity upon us: for we are exceedingly filled with contempt. 4 *Yea,* our soul has been exceedingly filled *with it: let* the reproach *be* to them that are at ease, and contempt to the proud.

Ps.124 *A Song of Degrees.* 1 If it had not been that the Lord was among us, let Israel now say; 2 if it had not been that the Lord was among us, when men rose up against us; 3 verily they would have swallowed us up alive, when their wrath was kindled against us: 4 verily the water would have drowned us, our soul would have gone under the torrent. 5 Yea, our soul would have gone under the overwhelming water. 6 Blessed be the Lord, who has not given us for a prey to their teeth. 7 Our soul has been delivered as a sparrow from the snare of the fowlers: the snare is broken, and we are delivered. 8 Our help is in the name of the Lord, who made heaven and earth.

Ps.125 *A Song of Degrees.* 1 They that trust in the Lord *shall be* as mount Sion: he that dwells in Jerusalem shall never be moved. 2 The mountains are round about her, and *so* the Lord is round about his people, from henceforth and even for ever. 3 For the Lord will not allow the rod of sinners to be upon the lot of the righteous; lest the righteous should stretch forth their hands to iniquity. 4 Do good, O Lord, to them *that are* good, and to them *that are* upright in heart. 5 But them that turn aside to crooked ways the Lord will lead away with the workers of iniquity: *but* peace *shall be* upon Israel.

Ps.126 A Song of Degrees. 1 When the Lord turned the captivity of Sion, we became as comforted ones. 2 Then was our mouth filled with joy, and our tongue with exultation: then would they say among the Gentiles, 3 The Lord has done great things among them. The Lord has done great things for us, we became joyful. 4 Turn, O Lord, our captivity, as the steams in the south. 5 They that sow in tears shall reap in joy. 6 They went on and wept as they cast their seeds; but they shall surely come with exultation, bringing their sheaves *with them.*

Ps.127 *A Song of Degrees.* 1 Except the Lord build the house, they that build labour in vain: except the Lord keep the city, the watchman watches in vain. 2 It is vain for you to rise early: ye rise up after resting, ye that eat the bread of grief; while he gives sleep to his beloved. 3 Behold, the inheritance of the Lord, children, the reward of the fruit of the womb. 4 As arrows in the hand of a mighty man; so are the children of those who were outcasts. 5 Blessed is the man who shall satisfy his desire with them: they shall not be ashamed when they shall speak to their enemies in the gates.

Ps.128 *A Song of Degrees.* 1 Blessed are all they that fear the Lord; who walk in his ways. 2 Thou shalt eat the labours of thy hands: blessed art thou, and it shall be well with thee. 3 Thy wife shall be as a fruitful vine on the sides of thy house: thy children as young olive-plants round about thy table. 4 Behold, thus shall the man be blessed that fears the Lord. 5 May the Lord bless thee out of Sion; and mayest thou see the prosperity of Jerusalem all the days of thy life. 6 And mayest thou see thy children's children. Peace be upon Israel.

Ps.129 *A Song of Degrees.* 1 Many a time have they warred against me from my youth, let Israel now say: 2 Many a time have they warred against me from my youth: and yet they prevailed not against me. 3 The sinners wrought upon my back: they prolonged their iniquity. 4 The righteous Lord has cut asunder the necks of sinners. 5 Let all that hate Sion be put to shame and turned back. 6 Let them be as the grass of the house- tops, which withers before it is plucked up. 7 Wherewith the reaper fills not his hand, nor he that makes up the sheaves, his bosom. 8 Neither do they that go by say, The blessing of the Lord be upon you: we have blessed you in the name of the Lord.

Ps.130 *A Song of Degrees.* 1 Out of the depths have I cried to thee, O Lord. 2 O Lord, hearken to my voice; let thine ears be attentive to the voice of my supplication. 3 If thou, O Lord, shouldest mark iniquities, O Lord, who shall stand? 4 For with thee is forgiveness: for thy name's sake 5 have I waited for thee, O Lord, my soul has waited for thy word. 6 My soul has hoped in the Lord; from the morning watch till night. 7 Let Israel hope in the Lord: for with the Lord is mercy, and with him is plenteous redemption. 8 And he shall redeem Israel from all his iniquities.

Ps.131 *A Song of Degrees.* 1 O Lord, my heart is not exalted, neither have mine eyes been *haughtily* raised: neither have I exercised myself in great *matters,* nor in things too wonderful for me. 2 *I shall have sinned* if I have not been humble, but have exulted my soul: according to *the relation of* a weaned child to his mother, so wilt thou recompense my soul. 3 Let Israel hope in the Lord, from henceforth and for ever.

Ps.132 *A Song of Degrees.* 1 Lord, remember David, and all his meekness: 2 how he sware to the Lord, *and* vowed to the God of Jacob, *saying,* 3 I will not go into the tabernacle of my house; I will not go up to the couch of my bed; 4 I will not give sleep to mine eyes, nor slumber to mine eyelids, nor rest to my temples, 5 until I find a place for the Lord, a tabernacle for the God of Jacob. 6 Behold, we heard of it in Ephratha; we found it in the fields of the wood. 7 Let us enter into his tabernacles: let us worship at the place where his feet stood. 8 Arise, O Lord, into thy rest; thou, and the ark of thine holiness. 9 Thy priests shall clothe themselves with righteousness; and thy saints shall exult. 10 For the sake of thy servant David turn not away the face of thine anointed. 11 The Lord sware *in* truth to David, and he will not annul it, *saying*, Of the fruit of thy body will I set *a king* upon thy throne. 12 If thy children will deep my covenant, and these my testimonies which I shall teach them, their children also shall sit upon thy throne for ever. 13 For the Lord has elected Sion, he has chosen her for a habitation for himself, *saying*, 14 This is my rest for ever: here will I dwell; for I have chosen it. 15 I will surely bless her provision: I will satisfy her poor with bread. 16 I will clothe her priests with salvation; and her saints shall greatly exult. 17 There will I cause to spring up a horn to David: I have prepared a lamp for mine anointed. 18 His enemies will I clothe with a shame; but upon himself shall my holiness flourish.

Ps.133 *A Song of Degrees.* 1 See now! what is so good, or what so pleasant, as for brethren to dwell together? 2 *It is* as ointment on the head, that ran down to the beard, *even* the beard of Aaron; that ran down to the fringe of his clothing. 3 As the dew of Aermon, that comes down on the mountains of Sion: for there, the Lord commanded the blessing, even life for ever.

Ps.134 *A Song of Degrees.* 1 Behold now, bless ye the Lord, all the servants of the Lord, who stand in the house of the Lord, in the courts of the house of our God. 2 Lift up your hands by night in the sanctuaries, and bless the Lord. 3 May the Lord, who made heaven and earth, bless thee out of Sion.

Ps.135 *Alleluia.* 1 Praise ye the name of the Lord; praise the Lord, *ye his* servants, 2 who stand in the house of the Lord, in the courts of the house of our God. 3 Praise ye the Lord; for the Lord is good: sing praises to his name; for *it is* good. 4 For the Lord has chosen Jacob for himself, *and* Israel for his peculiar treasure. 5 For I know that the Lord is great, and our Lord is above all gods; 6 all that the Lord willed, he did in heaven, and on the earth, in the sea, and in all deeps. 7 Who brings up clouds from the extremity of the earth: he has made lightnings for the rain: he brings winds out of his treasures. 8 Who smote the first-born of Egypt, both of man and beast. 9 He sent signs and wonders into the midst of thee, O Egypt, on Pharao, and on all his servants. 10 Who smote many nations, and slew mighty kings; 11 Seon king of the Amorites, and Og king of Basan, and all the kingdoms of Chanaan: 12 and gave their land *for* an inheritance, an inheritance to Israel his people. 13 O Lord, thy name *endures* for ever, and thy memorial to all generations. 14 For the Lord shall judge his people, and comfort himself concerning his servants. 15 The idols of the heathen are silver and gold, the works of men's hands. 16 They have a mouth, but they cannot speak; they have eyes, but they cannot see; 17 they have ears, but they cannot hear; for there is no breath in their mouth. 18 Let those who make them be made like to them; and all those who trust in them. 19 O house of Israel, bless ye the Lord: O house of Aaron, bless ye the Lord: 20 O house of Levi, bless ye the Lord: ye that fear the Lord, bless the Lord. 21 Blessed in Sion be the Lord, who dwells in Jerusalem.

Ps.136 *Alleluia.* 1 Give thanks to the Lord: for he is good: for his mercy *endures* for ever. 2 Give thanks to the God of gods; for his mercy *endures* for ever. 3 Give thanks to the Lord of lords: for his mercy *endures* for ever. 4 To him who along has wrought great wonders: for his mercy *endures* for ever. 5 To him who made the heavens by understanding; for his mercy *endures* for ever. 6 To him who established the earth on the waters; for his mercy *endures* for ever. 7 To him who alone made great lights; for his mercy *endures* for ever. 8 The sun to rule by day; for his mercy *endures* for ever. 9 The moon and the stars to rule the night; for his mercy *endures* for ever. 10 To him who smote Egypt with their first-born; for his mercy *endures* for ever. 11 And brought Israel out of the midst of them; for his mercy *endures* for ever: 12 with a strong hand, and a high arm: for his mercy *endures* for ever. 13 To him who divided the Red Sea into parts: for his mercy *endures* for ever: 14 and brought Israel through the midst of it: for his mercy *endures* for ever: 15 and overthrew Pharao and his host in the Red Sea: for his mercy endures for ever. 16 To him who led his people through the wilderness: for his mercy *endures* for ever. 17 To him who smote great kings: for his mercy *endures* for ever: 18 and slew mighty kings: for his mercy *endures* for ever: 19 Seon king of the Amorites: for his mercy *endures* for ever: 20 and Og king of Basan: for his mercy *endures* for ever: 21 and gave their land *for* an inheritance: for his mercy *endures* for ever: 22 even an inheritance to Israel his servant: for his mercy *endures* for ever. 23 For the Lord remembered us in our low estate; for his mercy *endures* for ever: 24 and redeemed us from our enemies; for his mercy *endures* for ever. 25 Who gives food to all flesh; for his mercy *endures* for ever. 26 Give thanks to the God of heaven; for his mercy *endures* for ever.

Ps.137 *For David, a Psalm of Jeremias.* 1 By the rivers of Babylon, there we sat; and wept when we remembered Sion. 2 We hung our harps on the willows in the midst of it. 3 For there they that had taken us captive asked of us the words of a song; and they that had carried us away *asked* a hymn, *saying*, Sing us *one* of the songs of Sion. 4 How should we sing the Lord's song in a strange land? 5 If I forget thee, O Jerusalem, let my right hand forget *its skill.* 6 May my tongue cleave to my throat, if I do not remember thee; if I do not prefer Jerusalem as the chief of my joy. 7 Remember, O Lord, the children of Edom in the day of Jerusalem; who said, Rase *it*, rase *it*, even to its foundations. 8 Wretched daughter of Babylon! blessed *shall he be* who shall reward thee as thou hast rewarded us. 9 Blessed *shall he be* who shall seize and dash thine infants against the rock.

Ps.138 *A Psalm for David, of Aggaeus and Zacharias.* 1 I will give thee thanks, O Lord, with my whole heart; and I will sing psalms to thee before the angels; for thou hast heard all the words of my mouth. 2 I will worship toward thy holy temple, and give thanks to thy name, on account of thy mercy and thy truth; for thou hast magnified thy holy name above every thing. 3 In whatsoever day I shall call upon thee, hear me speedily; thou shalt abundantly provide me with thy power in my soul. 4 Let all the kings of the earth, o Lord, give thanks unto thee; for they have heard all the words of thy mouth. 5 And let them sing in the ways of the Lord; for great is the glory of the Lord. 6 For the Lord is high, and *yet* regards the lowly; and he knows high things from afar off. 7 Though I should walk in the midst of affliction, thou wilt quicken me; thou hast stretched forth thine hands against the wrath of mine enemies, and thy right hand has saved me. 8 O Lord, thou shalt recompense *them* on my behalf: thy mercy, O Lord, *endures* for ever: overlook not the works of thine hands.

Ps.139 *For the end, a Psalm of David.* 1 O Lord, thou hast proved me, and known me. 2 Thou knowest my down-sitting and mine up-rising: thou understandest my thoughts long before. 3 Thou hast traced my path and my bed, and hast foreseen all my ways. 4 For there is no unrighteous word in my tongue: behold, O Lord, thou hast known all things, 5 the last and the first: thou hast fashioned me, and laid thine hand upon me. 6 The knowledge of thee is too wonderful for me; it is very difficult, I cannot *attain* to it. 7 Whither shall I go from thy Spirit? and whither shall I flee from my presence? 8 If I should go up to heaven, thou art there: if I should go down to hell, thou art present. 9 If I should spread my wings *to fly* straight forward, and sojourn at the extremity of the sea, *it would be vain,* 10 for even there thy hand would guide me, and thy right hand would hold me. 11 When I said, Surely the darkness will cover me; even the night *was* light in my luxury. 12 For darkness will not be darkness with thee; but night will be light as day: as its darkness, so shall its light *be to thee.* 13 For thou, O Lord, hast possessed my reins; thou hast helped me from my mother's womb. 14 I will give thee thanks; for thou art fearfully wondrous; wondrous are thy works; and my soul knows *it* well. 15 My bones, which thou madest in secret were not hidden from thee, nor my substance, in the lowest parts of the earth. 16 Thine eyes saw my unwrought *substance,* and all *men* shall be written in thy book; they shall be formed by day, though *there should for a time* be no one among them. 17 But thy friends, O God, have been greatly honoured by me; their rule has been greatly strengthened. 18 I will number them, and they shall be multiplied beyond the sand; I awake, and am still with thee. 19 Oh that thou wouldest slay the wicked, O God; depart from me, ye men of blood. 20 For thou wilt say concerning *their* thought, *that* they shall take thy cities in vain. 21 Have I not hated them, O Lord, that hate thee? and wasted away because of thine enemies? 22 I have hated them with perfect hatred; they were counted my enemies. 23 Prove me, O God, and know my heart; examine me, and know my paths; 24 and see if *there is any* way of iniquity in me, and lead me in an everlasting way.

Ps.140 *For the end, a Psalm of David.* 1 Rescue me, O Lord, from the evil man; deliver me from the unjust man. 2 Who have devised injustice in their hearts; all the day they prepared war. 3 They have sharpened their tongue as *the tongue* of a serpent; the poison of asps is under their lips. Pause. 4 Keep me, O Lord, from the hand of the sinner; rescue me from unjust men; who have purposed to overthrow my goings. 5 The proud have hid a snare for me, and have stretched out ropes *for* snares for my feet; they set a stumbling-block for me near the path. Pause. 6 I said to the Lord, Thou art my God; hearken, O Lord, to the voice of my supplication. 7 O Lord God, the strength of my salvation; thou hast screened my head in the day of battle. 8 Deliver me not, O Lord, to the sinner, according to my desire: they have devised *mischief* against me; forsake me not, lest they should be exalted. Pause. 9 *As for* the head of them that compass me, the mischief of their lips shall cover them. 10 Coals of fire shall fall upon them on the earth; and thou shalt cast them down in afflictions: they shall not bear up *under them.* 11 A talkative man shall not prosper on the earth: evils shall hunt the unrighteous man to destruction. 12 I know that the Lord will maintain the cause of the poor, and the right of the needy ones. 13 Surely the righteous shall give thanks to thy name: the upright shall dwell in thy presence.

Ps.141 *A Psalm of David.* 1 O Lord, I have cried to thee; hear me: attend to the voice of my supplication, when I cry to thee. 2 Let my prayer be set forth before thee as incense; the lifting up of my hands *as* an evening sacrifice. 3 Set a watch, O Lord, on my mouth, and a strong door about by lips. 4 Incline not my heart to evil things, to employ pretexts for sins, with me who work iniquity: and let me not unite with their choice ones. 5 The righteous shall chasten me with mercy, and reprove me: but let not the oil of the sinner anoint my head: for yet shall my prayer also be in their pleasures. 6 Their mighty ones have been swallowed up near the rock: they shall hear my words, for they are sweet. 7 As a lump of earth is crushed upon the ground, our bones have been scattered by the *mouth of* the grave. 8 For mine eyes are to thee, O Lord God: I have hoped in thee; take not away my life. 9 Keep me from the snare which they have set for me, and from the stumbling blocks of them that work iniquity. 10 Sinners shall fall by their own net: I am alone until I shall escape.

Ps.142 *A Psalm of instruction for David, when he was in the cave, —a Prayer.* 1 I cried to the Lord with my voice; with my voice I made supplication to the Lord. 2 I will pour out before him my supplication: I will declare before him mine affliction. 3 When my spirit was fainting within me, then thou knewest my paths; in the very way wherein I was walking, they hid a snare for me. 4 I looked on *my* right hand, and behold, for there was none that noticed me; refuge failed me; and there was none that cared for my soul. 5 I cried unto thee, O Lord, and said, Thou art my hope, my portion in the land of the living. 6 Attend to my supplication, for I am brought very low; deliver me from them that persecute me; for they are stronger than I. 7 Bring my soul out of prison, that I may give thanks to thy name, O Lord; the righteous shall wait for me, until thou recompense me.

Ps.143 *A Psalm of David, when his son pursued him.* 1 O Lord, attend to my prayer: hearken to my supplication in thy truth; hear me in thy righteousness. 2 And enter not into judgment with thy servant, for in thy sight shall no *man* living be justified. 3 For the enemy has persecuted my soul; he has brought my life down to the ground; he has made me to dwell in a dark *place*, as those that have been long dead. 4 Therefore my spirit was grieved in me; my heart was troubled within me. 5 I remembered the days of old; and I meditated on all thy doings: *yea*, I meditated on the works of thine hands. 6 I spread forth my hands to thee; my soul *thirsts* for thee, as a dry land. Pause. 7 Hear me speedily, O Lord; my spirit has failed; turn not away thy face from me, else I shall be like to them that go down to the pit. 8 Cause me to hear thy mercy in the morning; for I have hoped in thee; make known to me, O Lord, the way wherein I should walk; for I have lifted up my soul to thee. 9 Deliver me from mine enemies, O Lord; for I have fled to thee for refuge. 10 Teach me to do thy will; for thou art my God; thy good Spirit shall guide me in the straight *way*. 11 Thou shalt quicken me, O Lord, for thy name's sake; in thy righteousness thou shalt bring my soul out of affliction. 12 And in thy mercy thou wilt destroy mine enemies, and wilt destroy all those that afflict my soul; for I am thy servant.

Ps.144 *A Psalm of David concerning Goliad.* 1 Blessed *be* the Lord my God, who instructs my hands for battle, *and* my fingers for war. 2 My mercy, and my refuge; my helper, and my deliverer; my protector, in whom I have trusted; who subdues my people under me. 3 Lord, what is man, that thou art made known to him? or the son of man, that thou takest account of him? 4 Man is like to vanity: his days pass as a shadow. 5 O Lord, bow thy heavens, and come down: touch the mountains, and they shall smoke. 6 Send lightning, and thou shalt scatter them: send forth thine arrows, and thou shalt discomfit them. 7 Send forth thine hand from on high; rescue me, and deliver me out of great waters, out of the hand of strange children; 8 whose mouth has spoken vanity, and their right hand is a right hand of iniquity. 9 O God, I will sing a new song to thee: I will play to thee on a psaltery of ten strings. 10 *Even* to him who gives salvation to kings: who redeems his servant David from the hurtful sword. 11 Deliver me, and rescue me from the hand of strange children, whose mouth has spoken vanity, and their right hand is a right hand of iniquity; 12 whose children are as plants, strengthened in their youth: their daughters are beautiful, sumptuously adorned after the similitude of a temple. 13 Their garners are full, and bursting with one kind of store after another; their sheep are prolific, multiplying in their streets. 14 Their oxen are fat: there is no falling down of a hedge, nor going out, nor cry in their folds. 15 Men bless the people to whom this lot belongs, *but* blessed is the people whose God is the Lord.

Ps.145 *David's Psalm of praise.* 1 I will exalt thee, my God, my king; and I will bless thy name for ever and ever. 2 Every day will I bless thee, and I will praise thy name for ever and ever. 3 The Lord is great, and greatly to be praised; and there is no end to his greatness. 4 Generation after generation shall praise thy works, and tell of thy power. 5 And they shall speak of the glorious majesty of thy holiness, and recount thy wonders. 6 And they shall speak of the power of thy terrible *acts*; and recount thy greatness. 7 They shall utter the memory of the abundance of thy goodness, and

shall exult in thy righteousness. 8 The Lord is compassionate, and merciful; long suffering, and abundant in mercy. 9 The Lord is good to those that wait *on him*; and his compassions are over all his works. 10 Let all thy works, O Lord, give thanks to thee; and let thy saints bless thee. 11 They shall speak of the glory of thy kingdom, and talk of thy dominion; 12 to make known to the sons of men thy power, and the glorious majesty of thy kingdom. 13 Thy kingdom is an everlasting kingdom, and thy dominion *endures* through all generations. The Lord is faithful in his words, and holy in all his works. 14 The Lord supports all that are falling, and sets up all that are broken down. 15 The eyes of all wait upon thee; and thou givest *them* their food in due season. 16 Thou openest thine hands, and fillest every living thing with pleasure. 17 The Lord is righteous in all his ways, and holy in all his works. 18 The Lord is near to all that call upon him, to all that call upon him in truth. 19 He will perform the desire of them that fear him: and he will hear their supplication, and save them. 20 The Lord preserves all that love him: but all sinners he will utterly destroy. 21 My mouth shall speak the praise of the Lord: and let all flesh bless his holy name for ever and ever.

Ps.146 *Alleluia, a Psalm of Aggaeus and Zacharias.* 1 My soul, praise the Lord. 2 While I live will I praise the Lord: I will sing praises to my God as long as I exist. 3 Trust not in princes, nor in the children of men, in whom there is no safety. 4 His breath shall go forth, and he shall return to his earth; in that day all his thoughts shall perish. 5 Blessed is he whose helper is the God of Jacob, whose hope is in the Lord his God: 6 who made heaven, and earth, the sea, and all things in them: who keeps truth for ever: 7 who executes judgment for the wronged: who gives food to the hungry. The Lord looses the fettered ones: 8 the Lord gives wisdom to the blind: The Lord sets up the broken down: the Lord loves the righteous: the Lord preserves the strangers; 9 he will relieve the orphan and widow: but will utterly remove the way of sinners. 10 The Lord shall reign for ever, *even* thy God, O Sion, to all generations.

Ps.147 *Alleluia, a Psalm of Aggaeus and Zacharias.* 1 Praise ye the Lord: for psalmody is a good thing; let praise be sweetly sung to our God. 2 The Lord builds up Jerusalem; and he will gather together the dispersed of Israel. 3 He heals the broken in heart, and binds up their wounds. 4 He numbers the multitudes of stars; and calls them all by names. 5 Great is our Lord, and great is his strength; and his understanding is infinite. 6 The Lord lifts up the meek; but brings sinners down to the ground. 7 Begin *the song* with thanksgiving to the Lord; sing praises on the harp to our God: 8 who covers the heaven with clouds, who prepares rain for the earth, who causes grass to spring up on the mountains, [and green herb for the service of men;] 9 and gives cattle their food, and to the young ravens that call upon him. 10 He will not take pleasure in the strength of a horse; neither is he well-pleased with the legs of a man. 11 The Lord takes pleasure in them that fear him, and in all that hope in his mercy. Alleluia, a Psalm of Aggaeus and Zacharias. 12 Praise the Lord, O Jerusalem; praise thy God, O Sion. 13 For he has strengthened the bars of thy gates; he has blessed thy children within thee. [14] He makes thy borders peaceful, and fills thee with the flour of wheat. [15] He sends his oracle to the earth: his word will run swiftly. [16] He gives snow like wool: he scatters the mist like ashes. [17] Casting *forth* his ice like morsels: who shall stand before his cold? [18] He shall send out his word, and melt them: he shall blow *with* his wind, and the waters shall flow. [19] He sends his word to Jacob, his ordinances and judgments to Israel. [20] He has not done so to any *other* nation; and he has not shewn them his judgments.

Ps.148 *Alleluia, a Psalm of Aggaeus and Zacharias.* [1] Praise ye the Lord from the heavens: praise him in the highest. [2] Praise ye him, all his angels: praise ye him, all his hosts. [3] Praise him, sun and moon; praise him, all ye stars and light. [4] Praise him, ye heavens of heavens, and the water that is above the heavens. [5] Let them praise the name of the Lord: for he spoke, and they were made; he commanded, and they were created. [6] He has established them for ever, even for ever and ever: he has made an ordinance, and it shall not pass away. [7] Praise the Lord from the earth, ye serpents, and all deeps. [8] Fire, hail, snow, ice, stormywind; the things that perform his word. [9] Mountains, and all hills; fruitful trees, and all cedars: [10] wild beasts, and all cattle; reptiles, and winged birds: [11] kings of the earth, and all peoples; princes, and all judges of the earth: [12] young men and virgins, old men with youths: [13] let them praise the name of the Lord: for his name only is exalted; his praise is above the earth and heaven, [14] and he shall exalt the horn of his people, *there is* a hymn for all his saints, *even* of the children of Israel, a people who draw near to him.

Ps.149 *Alleluia.* [1] Sing to the Lord a new song: his praise is in the assembly of the saints. [2] Let Israel rejoice in him that made him; and let the children of Sion exult in their king. [3] Let them praise his name in the dance: let them sings praises to him with timbrel and psaltery. [4] For the Lord takes pleasure in his people; and will exalt the meek with salvation. [5] The saints shall rejoice in glory; and shall exult on their beds. [6] The high praises of God shall be in their throat, and two-edged swords in their hands; [7] to execute vengeance on the nations, *and* punishments among the peoples; [8] to bind their kings with fetters, and their nobles with manacles of iron; [9] to execute on them the judgment written: this honour have all his saints.

Ps.150 *Alleluia.* [1] Praise God in his holy places: praise him in the firmament of his power. [2] Praise him on *account of* his mighty acts: praise him according to his abundant greatness. [3] Praise him with the sound of a trumpet: praise him with psaltery and harp. [4] Praise him with timbrel and dance: praise him with stringed instruments and the organ. [5] Praise him with melodious cymbals: praise him with loud cymbals. [6] Let every thing that has breath praise the Lord.

Ps.151 *This Psalm is a genuine one of David, though supernumerary, composed when he fought in single combat with Goliad.* [1] I was small among my brethren, and youngest in my father's house: I tended my father's sheep. [2] My hands formed a musical instrument, and my fingers tuned a psaltery. [3] And who shall tell my Lord? the Lord himself, he himself hears. [5] He

sent forth his angel, and took me from my father's sheep, and he anointed me with the oil of his anointing. [5] My brothers were handsome and tall; but the Lord did not take pleasure in them. [6] I went forth to meet the Philistine; and he cursed me by his idols. [7] But I drew his own sword, and beheaded him, and removed reproach from the children of Israel.

Ps.152 *Prayer of Manasses* [1] O Lord, Almighty God of our fathers, Abraham, Isaac, and Jacob, and of their righteous seed; [2] who hast made heaven and earth, with all the ornament thereof; [3] who hast bound the sea by the word of thy commandment; who hast shut up the deep, and sealed it by thy terrible and glorious name; [4] whom all men fear, and tremble before thy power; [5] for the majesty of thy glory cannot be borne, and thine angry threatening toward sinners is importable: [6] but thy merciful promise is unmeasurable and unsearchable; [7] for thou art the most high Lord, of great compassion, longsuffering, very merciful, and repentest of the evils of men. Thou, O Lord, according to thy great goodness hast promised repentance and forgiveness to them that have sinned against thee: and of thine infinite mercies hast appointed repentance unto sinners, that they may be saved. [8] Thou therefore, O Lord, that art the God of the just, hast not appointed repentance to the just, as to Abraham, and Isaac, and Jacob, which have not sinned against thee; but thou hast appointed repentance unto me that am a sinner: [9] for I have sinned above the number of the sands of the sea. My transgressions, O Lord, are multiplied: my transgressions are multiplied, and I am not worthy to behold and see the height of heaven for the multitude of mine iniquities. [10] I am bowed down with many iron bands, that I cannot lift up mine head, neither have any release: for I have provoked thy wrath, and done evil before thee: I did not thy will, neither kept I thy commandments: I have set up abominations, and have multiplied offences. [11] Now therefore I bow the knee of mine heart, beseeching thee of grace. [12] I have sinned, O Lord, I have sinned, and I acknowledge mine iniquities: [13] wherefore, I humbly beseech thee, forgive me, O Lord, forgive me, and destroy me not with mine iniquities. Be not angry with me for ever, by reserving evil for me; neither condemn me to the lower parts of the earth. For thou art the God, even the God of them that repent; [14] and in me thou wilt shew all thy goodness: for thou wilt save me, that am unworthy, according to thy great mercy. [15] Therefore I will praise thee for ever all the days of my life: for all the powers of the heavens do praise thee, and thine is the glory for ever and ever. Amen.

PROVERBS

Prov.1 [1] The Proverbs of Solomon son of David, who reigned in Israel; [2] to know wisdom and instruction, and to perceive words of understanding; [3] to receive also hard saying, and to understand true justice, and *how* to direct judgment; [4] that he might give subtlety to the simple, and to the young man discernment and understanding. [5] For by the hearing of these a wise man will be wiser, and man of understanding will gain direction; [6] and will understand a parable, and a dark speech; the saying of the wise also, and riddles. 7 The fear of the Lord is the beginning of wisdom; and *there is* good understanding to all that practise it: and piety toward God is the beginning of discernment; but the ungodly will set at nought wisdom and instruction. 8 Hear, *my* son, the instruction of thy father, and reject not the rules of thy mother. 9 For thou shalt receive for thine head a crown of graces, and a chain of gold round thy neck. 10 *My* son, let not ungodly men lead thee astray, neither consent thou *to them.* 11 If they should exhort thee, saying, Come with us, partake in blood, and let us unjustly hide the just man in the earth: 12 and let us swallow him alive, as Hades *would,* and remove the memorial of him from the earth: 13 let us seize on his valuable property, and let us fill our houses with spoils: 14 but do thou cast in thy lot with us, and let us all provide a common purse, and let us have one pouch: 15 go not in the way with them, but turn aside thy foot from their paths: 16 for their feet run to evil, and make haste to shed blood. 17 or nets are not without cause spread for birds. 18 For they that are concerned in murder store up evils for themselves; and the overthrow of transgressors is evil. 19 These are the ways of all that perform lawless deeds; for by ungodliness they destroy their own life. 20 Wisdom sings aloud in passages, and in the broad places speaks boldly. 21 And she makes proclamation on the top of the walls, and sits by the gates of princes; and at the gates of the city boldly says, 22 So long as the simple cleave to justice, they shall not be ashamed: but the foolish being lovers of haughtiness, having become ungodly have hated knowledge, and are become subject to reproofs. 23 Behold, I will bring forth to you the utterance of my breath, and I will instruct you in my speech. 24 Since I called, and ye did not hearken; and I spoke at length, and ye gave no heed; 25 but ye set at nought my counsels, and disregarded my reproofs; 26 therefore I also will laugh at your destruction; and I will rejoice against *you* when ruin comes upon you: 27 yea when dismay suddenly comes upon you, and *your* overthrow shall arrive like a tempest; and when tribulation and distress shall come upon you, or when ruin shall come upon you. 28 For it shall be that when ye call upon me, I will not hearken to you: wicked men shall seek me, but shall not find *me.* 29 For they hated wisdom, and did not choose the word of the Lord: 30 neither would they attend to my counsels, but derided my reproofs. 31 Therefore shall they eat the fruits of their own way, and shall be filled with their own ungodliness. 32 For because they wronged the simple, they shall be slain; and an inquisition shall ruin the ungodly. 33 But he that hearkens to me shall dwell in confidence, and shall rest securely from all evil.

Prov.2 1 *My* son, if thou wilt receive the utterance of my commandment, and hide it with thee; 2 thine ear shall hearken to wisdom; thou shalt also apply thine heart to understanding, and shalt apply it to the instruction of thy son. 3 For it thou shalt call to wisdom, and utter thy voice for understanding; 4 and if thou shalt seek it as silver, and search diligently for it as for treasures; 5 then shalt thou understand the fear of the Lord, and find the knowledge of God. 6 For the Lord gives wisdom; and from his presence *come* knowledge and understanding, 7 and he treasures up

salvation for them that walk uprightly: he will protect their way; 8 that he may guard the righteous ways: and he will preserve the way of them that fear him. 9 Then shalt thou understand righteousness, and judgment; and shalt direct all thy course aright. 10 For if wisdom shall come into thine understanding, and discernment shall seem pleasing to thy soul, 11 good counsel shall guard thee, and holy understanding shall keep thee; 12 to deliver thee from the evil way, and from the man that speaks nothing faithfully. 13 Alas *for those* who forsake right paths, to walk in ways of darkness; 14 who rejoice in evils, and delight in wicked perverseness; 15 whose paths are crooked, and their courses winding; 16 to remove thee far from the straight way, and to estrange thee from a righteous purpose. *My* son, let not evil counsel overtake thee, 17 *of her* who has forsaken the instruction of her youth, and forgotten the covenant of God. 18 For she has fixed her house near death, and *guided* her wheels near Hades with the giants. 19 None that go by her shall return, neither shall they take hold of right paths, for they are not apprehended of the years of life. 20 For had they gone in good paths, they would have found the paths of righteousness easy. 21 For the upright shall dwell in the earth, and the holy shall be left behind in it. 22 The paths of the ungodly shall perish out of the earth, and transgressors shall be driven away from it.

Prov.3 1 *My* son, forget not my laws; but let thine heart keep my words: 2 for length of existence, and years of life, and peace, shall they add to thee. 3 Let not mercy and truth forsake thee; but bind them about thy neck: 4 so shalt thou find favour: and do thou provide things honest in the sight of the Lord, and of men. 5 Trust in God with all thine heart; and be not exalted in thine own wisdom. 6 In all thy ways acquaint thyself with her, that she may rightly direct thy paths. 7 Be not wise in thine own conceit; but fear God, and depart from all evil. 8 Then shall there be health to thy body, and good keeping to thy bones. 9 Honour the Lord with thy just labours, and give him the first of thy fruits of righteousness: 10 that thy storehouses may be completely filled with corn, and that thy presses may burst forth with wine. 11 *My* son, despise not the chastening of the Lord; nor faint when thou art rebuked of him: 12 for whom the Lord loves, he rebukes, and scourges every son whom he receives. 13 Blessed is the man who has found wisdom, and the mortal who knows prudence. 14 For it is better to traffic for her, than for treasures of gold and silver. 15 And she is more valuable than precious stones: no evil thing shall resist her: she is well known to all that approach her, and no precious thing is equal to her in value. 16 For length of existence and years of life are in her right hand; and in her left hand are wealth and glory: out of her mouth proceeds righteousness, and she carries law and mercy upon her tongue. 17 Her ways are good ways, and all her paths are peaceful. 18 She is a tree of life to all that lay hold upon her; and she is *a* secure *help* to all that stay themselves on her, as on the Lord. 19 God by wisdom founded the earth, and by prudence he prepared the heavens. 20 By understanding were the depths broken up, and the clouds dropped water. 21 *My* son, let *them* not pass from *thee,* but keep my counsel and understanding: 22 that thy soul may live, and that there may be grace round thy neck; and it shall be health to thy flesh, and safety to thy bones: 23 that thou mayest go confidently in peace in all thy ways, and that thy foot may not stumble. 24 For if thou rest, thou shalt be undismayed; and if thou sleep, thou shalt slumber sweetly. 25 And thou shalt not be afraid of alarm coming upon thee, neither of approaching attacks of ungodly men. 26 For the Lord shall be over all thy ways, and shall establish thy foot that thou be not moved. 27 Forbear not to do good to the poor, whensoever thy hand may have *power* to help *him*. 28 Say not, Come back another time, to-morrow I will give; while thou art able to do *him* good: for thou knowest not what the next day will bring forth. 29 Devise not evil against thy friend, living near thee and trusting in thee. 30 Be not ready to quarrel with a man without a cause, lest he do thee some harm. 31 Procure not the reproaches of bad men, neither do thou covet their ways. 32 For every transgressor is unclean before the Lord; neither does he sit among the righteous. 33 The curse of God is in the houses of the ungodly; but the habitations of the just are blessed. 34 The Lord resists the proud; but he gives grace to the humble. 35 The wise shall inherit glory; but the ungodly have exalted *their own* dishonour.

Prov.4 1 Hear, ye children, the instruction of a father, and attend to know understanding. 2 For I give you a good gift; forsake ye not my law. 3 For I also was a son obedient to *my* father, and loved in the sight of *my* mother: 4 who spoke and instructed me, *saying*, Let our speech be fixed in thine heart, keep *our* commandments, forget them not: 5 and do not neglect the speech of my mouth. 6 And forsake it not, and it shall cleave to thee: love it, and it shall keep thee. 7 Wisdom is the principal thing; therefore get wisdom: and with all thy getting get understanding. 8 Secure it, and it shall exalt thee: honour it, that it may embrace thee; 9 that it may give unto thy head a crown of graces, and may cover thee with a crown of delight. 10 Hear, *my* son, and receive my words; and the years of thy life shall be increased, that the resources of thy life may be many. 11 For I teach thee the ways of wisdom; and I cause thee to go in right paths. 12 For when thou goest, thy steps shall not be straitened; and when thou runnest, thou shalt not be distressed. 13 Take hold of my instruction; let it not go, —but keep it for thyself for thy life. 14 Go not in the ways of the ungodly, neither covet the ways of transgressors. 15 In whatever place they shall pitch their camp, go not thither; but turn from them, and pass away. 16 For they cannot sleep, unless they have done evil: their sleep is taken away, and they rest not. 17 For these live upon the bread of ungodliness, and are drunken with wine of transgression. 18 But the ways of the righteous shine like light; they go on and shine, until the day be fully come. 19 But the ways of the ungodly are dark; they know not how they stumble. 20 *My* son, attend to my speech; and apply thine ear to my words: 21 that thy fountains may not fail thee; keep them in *thine* heart. 22 For they are life to those that find them, and health to all *their* flesh. 23 Keep thine heart with the utmost care; for out of these are the issues of life. 24 Remove from thee a froward mouth, and put far away from thee unjust lips. 25 Let thine eyes look right on, and let thine eyelids assent *to just things*. 26 Make straight paths for thy feet, and order thy ways aright. 27 Turn not aside to the right hand nor to the left, but turn away thy foot from an evil way: [for God knows the ways on the right hand, but those on the left are crooked:] and he will make thy ways straight, and will guide thy steps in peace.

Prov.5 1 *My* son, attend to my wisdom, and apply thine ear to my words; 2 that thou mayest keep good understanding, and the discretion of my lips gives thee a charge. Give no heed to a worthless woman; 3 for honey drops from the lips of a harlot, who for a season pleases thy palate: 4 but afterwards thou wilt find her more bitter than gall, and sharper than a two-edged sword. 5 For the feet of folly lead those who deal with her down to the grave with death; and her steps are not established. 6 For she goes not upon the paths of life; but her ways are slippery, and not easily known. 7 Now then, *my* son, hear me, and make not my words of none effect. 8 Remove thy way far from her; draw not near to the doors of her house: 9 lest thou give away thy life to others, and thy substance to the merciless: 10 lest strangers be filled with thy strength, and thy labours come into the houses of strangers; 11 And thou repent at last, when the flesh of thy body is consumed, 12 and thou shalt say, How have I hated instruction, and my heart avoided reproofs! 13 I heard not the voice of him that instructed me, and taught me, neither did I apply mine ear. 14 I was almost in all evil in the midst of the congregation and assembly. 15 Drink waters out of thine own vessels, and out of thine own springing wells. 16 Let not waters out of thy fountain be spilt by thee, but let thy waters go into thy streets. 17 Let them be only thine own, and let no stranger partake with thee. 18 Let thy fountain of water be *truly* thine own; and rejoice with the wife of thy youth. 19 Let *thy* loving hart and thy graceful colt company with thee, and let her be considered thine own, and be with thee at all times; for ravished with her love thou shalt be greatly increased. 20 Be not intimate with a strange woman, neither fold thyself in the arms of a woman not thine own. 21 For the ways of a man are before the eyes of God, and he looks on all his paths. 22 Iniquities ensnare a man, and every one is bound in the chains of his own sins. 23 Such a man dies with the uninstructed; and he is cast forth from the abundance of his own substance, and has perished through folly.

Prov.6 1 *My* son, if thou become surety for thy friend, thou shalt deliver thine hand to an enemy. 2 For a man's own lips become a strong snare to him, and he is caught with the lips of his own mouth. 3 *My* son, do what I command thee, and deliver thyself; for on thy friend's account thou art come into the power of evil *men*: faint not, but stir up even thy friend for whom thou art become surety. 4 Give not sleep to thine eyes, nor slumber with thine eyelids; 5 that thou mayest deliver thyself as a doe out of the toils, and as a bird out of a snare. 6 Go to the ant, O sluggard; and see, and emulate his ways, and become wiser than he. 7 For whereas he has no husbandry, nor any one to compel him, and is under no master, 8 he prepares food for himself in the summer, and lays by abundant store in harvest. Or go to the bee, and learn how diligent she is, and how earnestly she is engaged in her work; whose labours kings and private men use for health, and she is desired and respected by all: though weak in body, she is advanced by honouring wisdom. 9 How long wilt thou lie, O sluggard? and when wilt thou awake out of sleep? 10 Thou sleepest a little, and thou restest a little, and thou slumberest a short *time*, and thou foldest thine arms over thy breast a little. 11 Then poverty comes upon thee as an evil traveller, and want as a swift courier: but if thou be diligent, thine harvest shall arrive as a fountain, and poverty shall flee away as a bad courier. 12 A foolish man and a transgressor goes in ways that are not good. 13 And the same winks with the eye, and makes a sign with his foot, and teaches with the beckonings of his fingers. 14 *His* perverse heart devises evils: at all times such a one causes troubles to a city. 15 Therefore his destruction shall come suddenly; overthrow and irretrievable ruin. 16 For he rejoices in all things which God hates, and he is ruined by reason of impurity of soul. 17 The eye of the haughty, a tongue unjust, hands shedding the blood of the just; 18 and a heart devising evil thoughts, and feet hastening to do evil, —*are hateful to God*. 19 An unjust witness kindles falsehoods, and brings on quarrels between brethren. 20 *My* son, keep the laws of thy father, and reject not the ordinances of thy mother: 21 but bind them upon thy soul continually, and hang them as a chain about thy neck. 22 Whensoever thou walkest, lead this along and let it be with thee; that it may talk with thee when thou wakest. 23 For the commandment of the law is a lamp and a light; a way of life; reproof also and correction: 24 to keep thee continually from a married woman, and from the calumny of a strange tongue. 25 Let not the desire of beauty overcome thee, neither be thou caught by thine eyes, neither be captivated with her eyelids. 26 For the value of a harlot is as much as of one loaf; and a woman hunts for the precious souls of men. 27 Shall any one bind fire in his bosom, and not burn his garments? 28 or will any one walk on coals of fire, and not burn his feet? 29 So is he that goes in to a married woman; he shall not be held guiltless, neither any one that touches her. 30 It is not to be wondered at if one should be taken stealing, for he steals that when hungry he may satisfy his soul: 31 but if he should be taken, he shall repay sevenfold, and shall deliver himself by giving all his goods. 32 But the adulterer through want of sense procures destruction to his soul. 33 He endures both pain and disgrace, and his reproach shall never be wiped off. 34 For the soul of her husband is full of jealousy: he will not spare in the day of vengeance. 35 He will not forego *his* enmity for any ransom: neither will he be reconciled for many gifts.

Prov.7 1 *My* son, keep my words, and hide with thee my commandments. *My* son, honour the Lord, and thou shalt be strong; and fear none but him: 2 keep my commandments, and thou shalt live; and *keep* my words as the pupils of *thine* eyes. 3 And bind them on thy fingers, and write *them* on the table of thine heart. 4 Say that wisdom is thy sister, and gain prudence as an acquaintance for thyself; 5 that she may keep thee from the strange and wicked

woman, if she should assail thee with flattering words. 6 For she looks from a window out of her house into the streets, at one whom she may see of the senseless ones, a young man void of understanding, 7 passing by the corner in the passages near her house, 8 and speaking, in the dark of the evening, 9 when there happens *to be* the stillness of night and of darkness: 10 and the woman meets him having the appearance of a harlot, that causes the hearts of young men to flutter. 11 And she is fickle, and debauched, and her feet abide not at home. 12 For at one time she wanders without, and at *another* time she lies in wait in the streets, at every corner. 13 Then she caught him, and kissed him, and with an impudent face said to him, 14 I have a peace-offering; today I pay my vows: 15 therefore I came forth to meet thee, desiring thy face; *and* I have found thee. 16 I have spread my bed with sheets, and I have covered it with double tapestry from Egypt. 17 I have sprinkled my couch with saffron, and my house with cinnamon. 18 Come, and let us enjoy love until the morning; come, and let us embrace in love. 19 For my husband is not at home, but is gone on a long journey, 20 having taken in his hand a bundle of money: after many days he will return to his house. 21 So with much converse she prevailed on him to go astray, and with the snares of her lips forced him from *the right path*. 22 And he followed her, being gently led on, and *that* as an ox is led to the slaughter, and as a dog to bonds, or as a hart shot in the liver with an arrow: 23 and he hastens as a bird into a snare, not knowing that he is running for *his* life. 24 Now then, *my* son, hearken to me, and attend to the words of my mouth. 25 Let not thine heart turn aside to her ways: 26 for she has wounded and cast down many, and those whom she has slain are innumerable. 27 Her house is the way of hell, leading down to the chambers of death.

Prov.8 1 Thou shalt proclaim wisdom, that understanding may be obedient to thee. 2 For she is on lofty eminences, and stands in the midst of the ways. 3 For she sits by the gates of princes, and sings in the entrances, *saying*, 4 You, O men, I exhort; and utter my voice to the sons of men. 5 O ye simple, understand subtlety, and ye that are untaught, imbibe knowledge. 6 Hearken to me; for I will speak solemn *truths*; and will produce right *sayings* from my lips. 7 For my throat shall meditate truth; and false lips are an abomination before me. 8 All the words of my mouth are in righteousness; there is nothing in them wrong or perverse. 9 They are all evident to those that understand, and right to those that find knowledge. 10 Receive instruction, and not silver; and knowledge rather than tried gold. 11 For wisdom is better than precious stones; and no valuable substance is of equal worth with it. 12 I wisdom have dwelt *with* counsel and knowledge, and I have called upon understanding. 13 The fear of the Lord hates unrighteousness, and insolence, and pride, and the ways of wicked men; and I hate the perverse ways of bad men. 14 Counsel and safety are mine; prudence is mine, and strength is mine. 15 By me kings reign, and princes decree justice. 16 By me nobles become great, and monarchs by me rule over the earth. 17 I love those that love me; and they that seek me shall find *me*. 18 Wealth and glory belong to me; yea, abundant possessions and righteousness. 19 *It is* better to have my fruit than *to have* gold and precious stones; and my produce is better than choice silver. 20 I walk in ways of righteousness, and *am* conversant with the paths of judgment; 21 that I may divide substance to them that love me, and may fill their treasures with good things. If I declare to you the things that daily happen, I will remember *also* to recount the things of old. 22 The Lord made me the beginning of his ways for his works. 23 He established me before time *was* in the beginning, before he made the earth: 24 even before he made the depths; before the fountains of water came forth: 25 before the mountains were settled, and before all hills, he begets me. 26 The Lord made countries and uninhabited *tracks*, and the highest inhabited parts of the world. 27 When he prepared the heaven, I was present with him; and when he prepared his throne upon the winds: 28 and when he strengthened the clouds above; and when he secured the fountains of the earth: 29 and when he strengthened the foundations of the earth: 30 I was by him, suiting *myself to him*, I was that wherein he took delight; and daily I rejoiced in his presence continually. 31 For he rejoiced when he had completed the world, and rejoiced among the children of men. 32 Now then, *my* son, hear me: blessed is the man who shall hearken to me, and the mortal who shall keep my ways; 33 hear instruction, and be wise, and refuse it not. 34 watching daily at my doors, waiting at the posts of my entrances. 35 For my outgoings are the outgoings of life, and *in them* is prepared favour from the Lord. 36 But they that sin against me act wickedly against their own souls: and they that hate me love death.

Prov.9 1 Wisdom has built a house for herself, and set up seven pillars. 2 She has killed her beasts; she has mingled her wine in a bowl, and prepared her table. 3 She has sent forth her servants, calling with a loud proclamation to the feast, saying, 4 Whoso is foolish, let him turn aside to me: and to them that want understanding she says, 5 Come, eat of my bread, and drink wine which I have mingled for you. 6 Leave folly, that ye may reign for ever; and seek wisdom, and improve understanding by knowledge. 7 He that reproves evil *men* shall get dishonour to himself; and he that rebukes an ungodly *man* shall disgrace himself. 8 Rebuke not evil *men*, lest they should hate thee: rebuke a wise *man*, and he will love thee. 9 Give an opportunity to a wise *man*, and he will be wiser: instruct a just man, and he will receive more *instruction*. 10 The fear of the Lord is the beginning of wisdom, and the counsel of saints is understanding: for to know the law is *the character* of a sound mind. 11 For in this way thou shalt live long, and years of thy life shall be added to thee. 12 Son, if thou be wise for thyself, thou shalt also be wise for thy neighbours; and if thou shouldest prove wicked, thou alone wilt bear the evil. He that stays himself upon falsehoods, attempts to rule the winds, and the same will pursue birds in their fight: for he has forsaken the ways of his own vineyard, and he has caused the axles of his own husbandry to go astray; and he goes through a dry desert, and a *land* appointed to drought, and he gathers barrenness with his hands. 13 A foolish and bold woman, who knows not modesty, comes to want a morsel. 14 She sits at the

doors of her house, on a seat openly in the streets, 15 calling to passers by, and to those that are going right on their ways; 16 *saying*, Whoso is most senseless of you, let him turn aside to me; and I exhort those that want prudence, saying, 17 Take and enjoy secret bread, and the sweet water of theft. 18 But he knows that mighty men die by her, and he falls in with a snare of hell. But hasten away, delay not in the place, neither fix thine eye upon her: for thus shalt thou go through strange water; but do thou abstain from strange water, and drink not of a strange fountain, that thou mayest live long, and years of life may be added to thee.

Prov.10 1 A wise son makes *his* father glad: but a foolish son is a grief to his mother. 2 Treasures shall not profit the lawless: but righteousness shall deliver from death. 3 The Lord will not famish a righteous soul: but he will overthrow the life of the ungodly. 4 Poverty brings a man low: but the hands of the vigorous make rich. A son who is instructed shall be wise, and shall use the fool for a servant. 5 A wise son is saved from heat: but a lawless son is blighted of the winds in harvest. 6 The blessing of the Lord is upon the head of the just: but untimely grief shall cover the mouth of the ungodly. 7 The memory of the just is praised; but the name of the ungodly *man* is extinguished. 8 A wise man in heart will receive commandments; but he that is unguarded in his lips shall be overthrown in his perverseness. 9 He that walks simply, walks confidently; but he that perverts his ways shall be known. 10 He that winks with his eyes deceitfully, procures griefs for men; but he that reproves boldly is a peacemaker. 11 *There is* a fountain of life in the hand of a righteous man; but destruction shall cover the mouth of the ungodly. 12 Hatred stirs up strife; but affection covers all that do not love strife. 13 He that brings forth wisdom from his lips smites the fool with a rod. 14 The wise will hide discretion; but the mouth of the hasty draws near to ruin. 15 The wealth of rich men is a strong city; but poverty is the ruin of the ungodly. 16 The works of the righteous produce life; but the fruits of the ungodly *produce* sins. 17 Instruction keeps the right ways of life; but instruction unchastened goes astray. 18 Righteous lips cover enmity; but they that utter railings are most foolish. 19 By a multitude of words thou shalt not escape sin; but if thou refrain thy lips thou wilt be prudent. 20 The tongue of the just is tried silver; but the heart of the ungodly shall fail. 21 The lips of the righteous know sublime *truths*: but the foolish die in want. 22 The blessing of the Lord is upon the head of the righteous; it enriches *him*, and grief of heart shall not be added to *it*. 23 A fool does mischief in sport; but wisdom brings forth prudence for a man. 24 The ungodly is engulphed in destruction; but the desire of the righteous is acceptable. 25 When the storm passes by, the ungodly vanishes away; but the righteous turns aside and escapes for ever. 26 As a sour grape is hurtful to the teeth, and smoke to the eyes, so iniquity hurts those that practise it. 27 The fear of the Lord adds *length* of days: but the years of the ungodly shall be shortened. 28 Joy rests long with the righteous: but the hope of the ungodly shall perish. 29 The fear of the Lord is a strong hold of the saints: but ruin *comes* to them that work wickedness. 30 The righteous shall never fail: but the ungodly shall not dwell in the earth. 31 The mouth of the righteous drops wisdom: but the tongue of the unjust shall perish. 32 The lips of just men drop grace: but the mouth of the ungodly is perverse.

Prov.11 1 False balances are an abomination before the Lord: but a just weight is acceptable unto him. 2 Wherever pride enters, there will be also disgrace: but the mouth of the lowly meditates wisdom. 3 When a just man dies he leaves regret: but the destruction of the ungodly is speedy, and causes joy. 4 Riches profit not in the day of wrath: but righteousness delivers from death. 5 Righteousness traces out blameless paths: but ungodliness encounters unjust dealing. 6 The righteousness of upright men delivers them: but transgressors are caught in their own destruction. 7 At the death of a just man his hope does not perish: but the boast of the ungodly perishes. 8 A righteous man escapes from a snare, and the ungodly man is delivered up in his place. 9 In the mouth of ungodly men is a snare to citizens: but the understanding of righteous men is prosperous. 10 In the prosperity of righteous men a city prospers: 11 but by the mouth of ungodly men it is overthrown. 12 A man void of understanding sneers at *his fellow* citizens: but a sensible man is quiet. 13 A double-tongued man discloses the *secret* counsels of an assembly: but he that is faithful in spirit conceals matters. 14 They that have no guidance fall like leaves: but in much counsel there is safety. 15 A bad man does harm wherever he meets a just man: and he hates the sound of safety. 16 A gracious wife brings glory to her husband: but a woman hating righteousness is a theme of dishonour. The slothful come to want: but the diligent support themselves with wealth. 17 A merciful man does good to his own soul: but the merciless destroys his own body. 18 An ungodly man performs unrighteous works: but the seed of the righteous is a reward of truth. 19 A righteous son is born for life: but the persecution of the ungodly *ends* in death. 20 Perverse ways are an abomination to the Lord: but all they that are blameless in their ways are acceptable to him. 21 He that unjustly strikes hands shall not be unpunished: but he that sows righteousness he shall receive a faithful reward. 22 As an ornament in a swine's snout, so is beauty to an ill-minded women. 23 All the desire of the righteous is good: but the hope of the ungodly shall perish. 24 There are *some* who scatter their own, and make it more: and there are *some* also who gather, *yet* have less. 25 Every sincere soul is blessed: but a passionate man is not graceful. 26 May he that hoards corn leave it to the nation: but blessing be on the head of him that gives *it.* 27 He that devises good *counsels* seeks good favour: but *as for* him that seeks after evil, *evil* shall overtake him. 28 He that trusts in wealth shall fall; but he that helps righteous men shall rise. 29 He that deals not graciously with his own house shall inherit the wind; and the fool shall be servant to the wise man. 30 Out of the fruit of righteousness grows a tree of life; but the souls of transgressors are cut off before their time. 31 If the righteous scarcely be saved, where shall the ungodly and the sinner appear?

Prov.12 1 He that loves instruction loves sense, but he that hates reproofs is a fool. 2 He that has found favour with the Lord *is made* better; but a transgressor shall be passed over in silence. 3 A man shall not prosper by wickedness; but the roots of the righteous shall not be taken up. 4 A virtuous woman is a crown to her husband; but as a worm in wood, so a bad woman destroys her husband. 5 The thoughts of the righteous *are true* judgments; but ungodly men devise deceits. 6 The words of ungodly men are crafty; but the mouth of the upright shall deliver them. 7 When the ungodly is overthrown, he vanishes away; but the houses of the just remain. 8 The mouth of an understanding *man* is praised by a man; but he that is dull of heart is had in derision. 9 Better is a man in dishonour serving himself, than one honouring himself and wanting bread. 10 A righteous man has pity for the lives of his cattle; but the bowels of the ungodly are unmerciful. 11 He that tills his own land shall be satisfied with bread; but they that pursue vanities are void of understanding. He that enjoys himself in banquets of wine, shall leave dishonour in his own strong holds. 12 The desires of the ungodly are evil; but the roots of the godly are firmly set. 13 For the sin of *his* lips a sinner falls into snare; but a righteous man escapes from them. He whose looks are gentle shall be pitied, but he that contends in the gates will afflict souls. 14 The soul of a man shall be filled with good from the fruits of his mouth; and the recompence of his lips shall be given to him. 15 The ways of fools are right in their own eyes; but a wise man hearkens to counsels. 16 A fool declares his wrath the same day; but a prudent man hides his own disgrace. 17 A righteous man declares the open truth; but an unjust witness is deceitful. 18 Some wound as they speak, *like* swords; but the tongues of the wise heal. 19 True lips establish testimony; but a hasty witness has an unjust tongue. 20 *There is* deceit in the heart of him that imagines evil; but they that love peace shall rejoice. 21 No injustice will please a just man; but the ungodly will be filled with mischief. 22 Lying lips are a abomination to the Lord; but he that deals faithfully is accepted with him. 23 An understanding man is a throne of wisdom; but the heart of fools shall meet with curses. 24 The hand of chosen men shall easily obtain rule; but the deceitful shall be for a prey. 25 A terrible word troubles the heart of a righteous man; but a good message rejoices him. 26 A just arbitrator shall be his own friend; but mischief shall pursue sinners; and the way of ungodly men shall lead them astray. 27 A deceitful man shall catch no game; but a blameless man is a precious possession. 28 In the ways of righteousness is life; but the ways of those that remember injuries *lead* to death.

Prov.13 1 A wise son is obedient to his father: but a disobedient son will be destroyed. 2 A good *man* shall eat of the fruits of righteousness: but the lives of transgressors shall perish before their time. 3 He that keeps his own mouth keeps his own life: but he that is hasty with his lips shall bring terror upon himself. 4 Every slothful man desires, but the hands of the active are diligent. 5 A righteous man hates an unjust word: but an ungodly man is ashamed, and will have no confidence. 6 Righteousness keeps the blameless in the way: but wickedness overthrows the sinner. 7 There are *some* who, having nothing, enrich themselves: and there are *some* who bring themselves down in *the midst of* much wealth. 8 A man's own wealth is the ransom of his life: but the poor endures not threatening. 9 The righteous always have light: but the light of the ungodly is quenched. Crafty souls go astray in sins: but just men pity, and are merciful. 10 A bad man does evil with insolence: but they that are judges of themselves are wise. 11 Wealth gotten hastily with iniquity is diminished: but he that gathers for himself with godliness shall be increased. The righteous is merciful, and lends. 12 Better is he that begins to help heartily, than he that promises and leads *another* to hope: for a good desire is a tree of life. 13 He that slights a matter shall be slighted of it: but he that fears the commandment has health *of soul*. To a crafty son there shall be nothing good: but a wise servant shall have prosperous doings, and his way shall be directed aright. 14 The law of the wise is fountain of life: but the man void of understanding shall die by a snare. 15 Sound discretion gives favour, and to know the law is the part of a sound understanding: but the ways of scorners tend to destruction. 16 Every prudent man acts with knowledge: but the fool displays his own mischief. 17 A rash king shall fall into mischief: but a wise messenger shall deliver him. 18 Instruction removes poverty and disgrace: but he that attends to reproofs shall be honoured. 19 The desires of the godly gladden the soul, but the works of the ungodly are far from knowledge. 20 If thou walkest with wise men thou shalt be wise: but he that walks with fools shall be known. 21 Evil shall pursue sinners; but good shall overtake the righteous. 22 A good man shall inherit children's children; and the wealth of ungodly men is laid up for the just. 23 The righteous shall spend many years in wealth: but the unrighteous shall perish suddenly. 24 He that spares the rod hates his son: but he that loves, carefully chastens *him*. 25 A just *man* eats and satisfies his soul: but the souls of the ungodly are in want.

Prov.14 1 Wise women build houses: but a foolish one digs *hers* down with her hands. 2 He that walks uprightly fears the Lord; but he that is perverse in his ways shall be dishonoured. 3 Out of the mouth of fools *comes* a rod of pride; but the lips of the wise preserve them. 4 Where no oxen are, the cribs are clean; but where there is abundant produce, the strength of the ox is apparent. 5 A faithful witness does not lie; but an unjust witness kindles falsehoods. 6 Thou shalt seek wisdom with bad men, and shalt not find it; but discretion is easily available with the prudent. 7 All things are adverse to a foolish man; but wise lips are the weapons of discretion. 8 The wisdom of the prudent will understand their ways; but the folly of fools leads astray. 9 The houses of transgressors will need purification; but the houses of the just are acceptable. 10 *If* a man's mind is intelligent, his soul is sorrowful; and when he rejoices, he has no fellowship with pride. 11 The houses of ungodly men shall be utterly destroyed; but the tabernacles of them that walk uprightly shall stand. 12 There is a way which seems to be right with men, but the ends of it reach to the depths of hell. 13 Grief mingles not with mirth; and joy in the end comes to grief. 14 A stout-hearted *man* shall be filled with his own ways; and a good man with

his own thoughts. 15 The simple believes every word: but the prudent man betakes himself to after-thought. 16 A wise man fears, and departs from evil; but the fool trusts in himself, and joins himself with the transgressor. 17 A passionate man acts inconsiderately; but a sensible man bears up under many things. 18 Fools shall have mischief for their portion; but the prudent shall take fast hold of understanding. 19 Evil men shall fall before the good; and the ungodly shall attend at the gates of the righteous. 20 Friends will hate poor friends; but the friends of the rich are many. 21 He that dishonours the needy sins: but he that has pity on the poor is most blessed. 22 They that go astray devise evils: but the good devise mercy and truth. The framers of evil do not understand mercy and truth: but compassion and faithfulness are with the framers of good. 23 With every one *who is* careful there is abundance: but the pleasure-taking and indolent shall be in want. 24 A prudent man is the crown of the wise: but the occupation of fools is evil. 25 A faithful witness shall deliver a soul from evil: but a deceitful *man* kindles falsehoods. 26 In the fear of the Lord is strong confidence: and he leaves his children a support. 27 The commandment of the Lord is a fountain of life; and it causes *men* to turn aside from the snare of death. 28 In a populous nation is the glory of a king: but in the failure of people is the ruin of a prince. 29 A man slow to wrath abounds in wisdom: but a man of impatient spirit is very foolish. 30 A meek-spirited man is a healer of the heart: but a sensitive heart is a corruption of the bones. 31 He that oppresses the needy provokes his Maker: but he that honours him has pity upon the poor. 32 The ungodly shall be driven away in his wickedness: but he who is secure in his own holiness is just. 33 There is wisdom in the good heart of a man: but in the heart of fools it is not discerned. 34 Righteousness exalts a nation: but sins diminish tribes. 35 An understanding servant is acceptable to a king; and by his good behaviour he removes disgrace.

Prov.15 1 Anger slays even wise men; yet a submissive answer turns away wrath: but a grievous word stirs up anger. 2 The tongue of the wise knows what is good: but the mouth of the foolish tells out evil things. 3 The eyes of the Lord behold both the evil and the good in every place. 4 The wholesome tongue is a tree of life, and he that keeps it shall be filled with understanding. 5 A fool scorns his father's instruction; but he that keeps his commandments is more prudent. In abounding righteousness is great strength: but the ungodly shall utterly perish from the earth. 6 In the houses of the righteous is much strength: but the fruits of the ungodly shall perish. 7 The lips of the wise are bound by discretion: but the hearts of the foolish are not safe. 8 The sacrifices of the ungodly are an abomination to the Lord; but the prayers of them that walk honestly are acceptable with him. 9 The ways of an ungodly *man* are an abomination to the Lord; but he loves those that follow after righteousness. 10 The instruction of the simple is known by them that pass by; but they that hate reproofs die disgracefully. 11 Hell and destruction are manifest to the Lord; how shall not also be the hearts of men? 12 An uninstructed person will not love those that reprove him;

neither will he associate with the wise. 13 When the heart rejoices the countenance is cheerful; but when it is in sorrow, *the countenance* is sad. 14 An upright heart seeks discretion; but the mouth of the uninstructed will experience evils. 15 The eyes of the wicked are always looking for evil things; but the good are always quiet. 16 Better is a small portion with the fear of the Lord, than great treasures without the fear *of the Lord.* 17 Better is an entertainment of herbs with friendliness and kindness, than a feast of calves, with enmity. 18 A passionate man stirs up strife; but *he that is* slow to anger appeases even a rising one. A man slow to anger will extinguish quarrels; but an ungodly man rather stirs *them* up. 19 The ways of sluggards are strewn with thorns; but those of the diligent are made smooth. 20 A wise son gladdens *his* father; but a foolish son sneers at his mother. 21 The ways of a foolish man are void of sense; but a wise man proceeds on his way aright. 22 They that honour not councils put off deliberation; but counsel abides in the hearts of counsellors. 23 A bad man will by no means attend to counsel; neither will he say anything seasonable, or good for the common *weal.* 24 The thoughts of the wise are ways of life, that he may turn aside and escape from hell. 25 The Lord pulls down the houses of scorners; but he establishes the border of the widow. 26 An unrighteous thought is abomination to the Lord; but the sayings of the pure are held in honour. 27 A receiver of bribes destroys himself; but he that hates the receiving of bribes is safe. [By alms and by faithful dealings sins are purged away;] but by the fear of the Lord every one departs from evil. 28 The hearts of the righteous meditate faithfulness; but the mouth of the ungodly answers evil things. The ways of righteous men are acceptable with the Lord; and through them even enemies become friends. 29 God is far from the ungodly; but he hearkens to the prayers of the righteous. Better are small receipts with righteousness, than abundant fruits with unrighteousness. 30 Let the heart of a man think justly, that his steps may be rightly ordered of God. The eye that sees rightly rejoices the heart; and a good report fattens the bones. 31 32 He that rejects instruction hates himself; but he that mind reproofs loves his soul. 33 The fear of the Lord is instruction and wisdom; and the highest honour will correspond therewith.

Prov.16 2All the works of the humble *man* are manifest with God; but the ungodly shall perish in an evil day. 5 Every one that is proud in heart is unclean before God, and he that unjustly strikes hands with hand shall not be held guiltless. The beginning of a good way is to do justly; and it is more acceptable with God than to offer sacrifices. He that seeks the Lord shall find knowledge with righteousness: and they that rightly seek him shall find peace. All of the works of the Lord *are done* with righteousness; and the ungodly *man* is kept for the evil day. 10 *There is* an oracle upon the lips of a king; and his mouth shall not err in judgment. 11 The poise of the balance is righteousness with the Lord; and his works are righteous measures. 12 An evil-doer is an abomination to a king; for the throne of rule is established by righteousness. 13 Righteous lips are acceptable to a king; and he loves right words. 14 The anger of a king is a messenger

of death; but a wise man will pacify him. 15 The son of a king is in the light of life; and they that are in favour with him are as a cloud of latter rain. 16 The brood of wisdom is more to be chosen than gold, and the brood of prudence more to be chosen than silver. 17 The paths of life turn aside from evil; and the ways of righteousness are length of life. He that receives instruction shall be in prosperity; and he that regards reproofs shall be made wise. He that keeps his ways, preserves his own soul; and he that loves his life will spare his mouth. 18 Pride goes before destruction, and folly before a fall. 19 Better is a meek-spirited *man* with lowliness, than one who divides spoils with the proud. 20 *He who is* skillful in business finds good: but he that trusts in God is most blessed. 21 *Men* call the wise and understanding evil: but they that are pleasing in speech shall hear more. 22 Understanding is a fountain of life to its possessors; but the instruction of fools is evil. 23 The heart of the wise will discern the *things which proceed* from his own mouth; and on his lips he will wear knowledge. 24 Good words are honeycombs, and the sweetness thereof is a healing of the soul. 25 There are ways that seem to be right to a man, but the end of them looks to the depth of hell. 26 A man who labours, labours for himself, and drives from *him* his own ruin. 27 But the perverse bears destruction upon his own mouth: a foolish man digs up evil for himself, and treasures fire on his own lips. 28 A perverse man spreads mischief, and will kindle a torch of deceit with mischiefs; and he separates friends. 29 A transgressor tries *to ensnare* friends, and leads them in ways *that are* not good. 30 And the man that fixes his eyes devises perverse things, and marks out with his lips all evil: he is a furnace of wickedness. 31 Old age is a crown of honour, but it is found in the ways of righteousness. 32 A man slow to anger is better than a strong *man*; and he that governs *his* temper better than he that takes a city. 33 All *evils* come upon the ungodly into *their* bosoms; but all righteous things *come* of the Lord.

Prov.17 1 Better is a morsel with pleasure in peace, than a house *full* of many good things and unjust sacrifices, with strife. 2 A wise servant shall have rule over foolish masters, and shall divide portions among brethren. 3 As silver and gold are tried in a furnace, so are choice hearts with the Lord. 4 A bad man hearkens to the tongue of transgressors: but a righteous man attends not to false lips. 5 He that laughs at the poor provokes him that made him; and he that rejoices at the destruction of another shall not be held guiltless: but he that has compassion shall find mercy. 6 Children's children are the crown of old men; and their fathers are the glory of children. The faithful has the whole world full of wealth; but the faithless not even a farthing. 7 Faithful lips will not suit a fool; nor lying lips a just man. 8 Instruction is to them that use it a gracious reward; and whithersoever it may turn, it shall prosper. 9 He that conceals injuries seeks love; but he that hates to hide *them* separates friends and kindred. 10 A threat breaks down the heart of a wise man; but a fool, though scourged, understands not. 11 Every bad man stirs up strifes: but the Lord will send out against him an unmerciful messenger. 12 Care may befall a man of understanding; but fools will meditate evils. 13 Whoso rewards evil for good, evil shall not be removed from his house. 14 Rightful rule gives power to words; but sedition and strife precede poverty. 15 He that pronounces the unjust just, and the just unjust, is unclean and abominable with God. 16 Why has the fool wealth? for a senseless man will not be able to purchase wisdom. He that exalts his own house seeks ruin; and he that turns aside from instruction shall fall into mischief. 17 Have thou a friend for every time, and let brethren be useful in distress; for on this account are they born. 18 A foolish man applauds and rejoices over himself, *as he* also that becomes surety would make himself responsible for his own friends. 19 A lover of sin rejoices in strifes; 20 and the hard-hearted man comes not in for good. A man of a changeful tongue will fall into mischiefs; 21 and the heart of a fool is grief to its possessor. A father rejoices not over an uninstructed son; but a wise son gladdens his mother. 22 A glad heart promotes health; but the bones of a sorrowful man dry up. 23 The ways of a man who unjustly receives gifts in *his* bosom do not prosper; and an ungodly man perverts the ways of righteousness. 24 The countenance of a wise man is sensible; but the eyes of a fool *go* to the ends of the earth. 25 A foolish son *is a cause of* anger to his father, and grief to her that bore him. 26 *It is* not right to punish a righteous man, nor *is it* holy to plot against righteous princes. 27 He that forbears to utter a hard word is discreet, and a patient man is wise. 28 Wisdom shall be imputed to a fool who asks after wisdom: and he who holds his peace shall seem to be sensible.

Prov.18 1 A man who wishes to separate from friends seeks excuses; but at all times he will be liable to reproach. 2 A senseless man feels no need of wisdom, for he is rather led by folly. 3 When an ungodly man comes into a depth of evils, he despises *them*; but dishonour and reproach come upon him. 4 A word in the heart of a man is a deep water, and a river and fountain of life spring forth. 5 *It is* not good to accept the person of the ungodly, nor *is it* holy to pervert justice in judgment. 6 The lips of a fool bring *him* into troubles, and his bold mouth calls for death. 7 A fool's mouth is ruin to him, and his lips are a snare to his soul. 8 Fear casts down the slothful; and the souls of the effeminate shall hunger. 9 A man who helps not himself by his labour is brother of him that ruins himself. 10 The name of the Lord is of great strength; and the righteous running to it are exalted. 11 The wealth of a rich man is a strong city; and its glory casts a broad shadow. 12 Before ruin a man's heart is exalted, and before honour it is humble. 13 Whoso answers a word before he hears *a cause*, it is folly and reproach to him. 14 A wise servant calms a man's anger; but who can endure a faint-hearted man? 15 The heart of the sensible *man* purchases discretion; and the ears of the wise seek understanding. 16 A man's gift enlarges him, and seats him among princes. 17 A righteous man accuses himself at the beginning of his speech, but when he has entered upon the attack, the adversary is reproved. 18 A silent *man* quells strifes, and determines between great powers. 19 A brother helped by a brother is as a strong and high city; and is *as* strong as a *well*-founded palace. 20 A man fills his belly with

the fruits of his mouth; and he shall be satisfied with the fruits of his lips. 21 Life and death are in the power of the tongue; and they that rule it shall eat the fruits thereof. 22 He that has found a good wife has found favours, and has received gladness from God. [He that puts away a good wife, puts away a good thing, and he that keeps an adulteress is foolish and ungodly.]

Prov.19 1 The folly of a man spoils his ways: and he blames God in his heart. 4 Wealth acquires many friends; but the poor is deserted even of the friend he has. 5 A false witness shall not be unpunished, and he that accuses unjustly shall not escape. 6 Many court the favour of kings; but every bad man becomes a reproach to *another* man. 7 Every one who hates *his* poor brother shall also be far from friendship. Good understanding will draw near to them that know it, and a sensible man will find it. He that does much harm perfects mischief; and he that used provoking words shall not escape. 8 He that procures wisdom loves himself; and he that keeps wisdom shall find good. 9 A false witness shall not be unpunished; and whosoever shall kindle mischief shall perish by it. 10 Delight does not suit a fool, nor *is it seemly* if a servant should begin to rule with haughtiness. 11 A merciful man is long-suffering; and his triumph overtakes transgressors. 12 The threatening of a king is like the roaring of a lion; but as dew on the grass, so is his favour. 13 A foolish son is a disgrace to his father: vows *paid out* of the hire of a harlot are not pure. 14 Fathers divide house and substance to *their* children: but a wife is suited to a man by the Lord. 15 Cowardice possesses the effeminate *man*; and the soul of the sluggard shall hunger. 16 He that keeps the commandment keeps his own soul; but he that despises his ways shall perish. 17 He that has pity on the poor lends to the Lord; and he will recompense to him according to his gift. 18 Chasten thy son, for so he shall be hopeful; and be not exalted in thy soul to haughtiness. 19 A malicious man shall be severely punished, and if he commit injury, he shall also lose his life. 20 Hear, son, the instruction of thy father, that thou mayest be wise at thy latter end. 21 *There are* many thoughts in a man's heart; but the counsel of the Lord abides for ever. 22 Mercy is a fruit to a man: and a poor man is better than a rich liar. 23 The fear of the Lord is life to a man: and he shall lodge without fear in places where knowledge is not seen. 24 He that unjustly hides his hands in his bosom, will not even *bring* them up to his mouth. 25 When a pestilent character is scourged, a simple man is made wiser: and if thou reprove a wise man, he will understand discretion. 26 He that dishonours his father, and drives away his mother, shall be disgraced and shall be exposed to reproach. 27 A son who ceases to attend to the instruction of a father will cherish evil designs. 28 He that becomes surety for a foolish child will despise the ordinance: and the mouth of ungodly men shall drink down judgment. 29 Scourges are preparing for the intemperate, and punishments likewise for fools.

Prov.20 1 Wine is an intemperate thing, and strong drink full of violence: but every fool is entangled with them. 2 The threat of a king differs not from the rage of a lion; and he that provokes him sins against his own soul. 3 It is a glory to a man to turn aside from railing; but every fool is entangled with such matters. 4 A sluggard when reproached is not ashamed: so also he who borrows corn in harvest. 5 Counsel in a man's heart is deep water; but a prudent man will draw it out. 6 Most men will proclaim every one his own goodness: but a faithful man who can find? 7 The just man walks in his integrity: his children are blessed after him. 8 A king that sits in the throne of judgment scatters away all evil with his eyes. 9 Who can say, I have made my heart clean, I am pure from my sin? 10 Divers weights, and divers measures, both of them are alike abomination to the Lord. 11 Even a child is known by his doings, whether his work be pure, and whether it be right. 12 The hearing ear, and the seeing eye, the Lord has made even both of them. 13 Love not sleep, lest you come to poverty; open your eyes, and you shall be satisfied with bread. 14 It is naught, it is naught, says the buyer: but when he is gone his way, then he boasts. 15 There is gold, and a multitude of rubies: but the lips of knowledge are a precious jewel. 16 Take his garment that is surety for a stranger: and take a pledge of him for a strange woman. 17 Bread of deceit is sweet to a man; but afterwards his mouth shall be filled with gravel. 18 Every purpose is established by counsel: and with good advice make war. 19 He that goes about as a talebearer reveals secrets: therefore meddle not with him that flatters with his lips. 20 Whoso curses his father or his mother, his lamp shall be put out in obscure darkness. 21 An inheritance may be gotten hastily at the beginning; but the end thereof shall not be blessed. 22 Say not thou, I will recompense evil; but wait on the Lord, and he shall save thee. 23 Divers weights are an abomination unto the Lord; and a false balance is not good. 24 Man's goings are of the Lord; how can a man then understand his own way? 25 It is a snare to the man who devours that which is holy, and after vows to make inquiry. 26 A wise king scatters the wicked, and brings the wheel over them. 27 The spirit of man is the candle of the Lord, searching all the inward parts of the belly. 28 Mercy and truth preserve the king: and his throne is upheld by mercy. 29 The glory of young men is their strength: and the beauty of old men is the grey head. 30 The blueness of a wound cleanses away evil: so do stripes the inward parts of the belly.

Prov.21 1 As a rush of water, so is the king's heart in God's hand: he turns it whithersoever he may desire to point out. 2 Every man seems to himself righteous; but the Lord directs the hearts. 3 To do justly and to speak truth, are more pleasing to God than the blood of sacrifices. 4 A high-minded man is stout-hearted in *his* pride; and the lamp of the wicked is sin. 5 6 He that gathers treasures with a lying tongue pursues vanity *on* to the snares of death. 7 Destruction shall lodge with the ungodly; for they refuse to do justly. 8 To the froward God sends froward ways; for his works are pure and right. 9 *It is* better to dwell in a corner on the house-top, than in plastered *rooms* with unrighteousness, and in an open house. 10 The soul of the ungodly shall not be pitied by any man. 11 When an intemperate man is punished the simple becomes wiser: and a wise man understanding will receive knowledge. 12 A

righteous man understands the hearts of the ungodly: and despises the ungodly for their wickedness. 13 He that stops his ears from hearing the poor, himself also shall cry, and there shall be none to hear *him*. 14 A secret gift calms anger: but he that forbears to give stirs up strong wrath. 15 *It is* the joy of the righteous to do judgment: but a holy *man* is abominable with evil-doers. 16 A man that wanders out of the way of righteousness, shall rest in the congregation of giants. 17 A poor man loves mirth, loving wine and oil in abundance; 18 and a transgressor is the abomination of a righteous man. 19 *It is* better to dwell in a wilderness than with a quarrelsome and talkative and passionate woman. 20 A desirable treasure will rest on the mouth of the wise; but foolish men will swallow it up. 21 The way of righteousness and mercy will find life and glory. 22 A wise man assaults strong cities, and demolishes the fortress in which the ungodly trusted. 23 He that keeps his mouth and his tongue keeps his soul from trouble. 24 A bold and self-willed and insolent *man* is called a pest: and he that remembers injuries is a transgressor. 25 Desires kill the sluggard; for his hands do not choose to do anything. 26 An ungodly man entertains evil desires all the day: but the righteous is unsparingly merciful and compassionate. 27 The sacrifices of the ungodly are abomination to the Lord, for they offer them wickedly. 28 A false witness shall perish; but an obedient man will speak cautiously. 29 An ungodly man impudently withstands with his face; but the upright man himself understands his ways. 30 There is no wisdom, there is no courage, there is no counsel against the ungodly. 31 A horse is prepared for the day of battle; but help is of the Lord.

Prov.22 1 A fair name is better than much wealth, and good favour is above silver and gold. 2 The rich and the poor meet together; but the Lord made them both. 3 An intelligent man seeing a bad man severely punished is himself instructed, but fools pass by and are punished. 4 The fear of the Lord is the offspring of wisdom, and wealth, and glory, and life. 5 Thistles and snares are in perverse ways; but he that keeps his soul will refrain from them. 6 7 The rich will rule over the poor, and servants will lend to their own masters. 8 He that sows wickedness shall reap troubles; and shall fully receive the punishment of his deeds. God loves a cheerful and liberal man; but *a man* shall fully prove the folly of his works. 9 He that has pity on the poor shall himself be maintained; for he has given of his own bread to the poor. He that gives liberally secures victory an honour; but he takes away the life of them that posses *them*. 10 Cast out a pestilent person from the council, and strife shall go out with him; for when he sits in the council he dishonours all. 11 The Lord loves holy hearts, and all blameless persons are acceptable with him: a king rules with his lips. 12 But the eyes of the Lord preserve discretion; but the transgressor despises *wise* words. 13 The sluggard makes excuses, and says, *There is* a lion in the ways, and murderers in the streets. 14 The mouth of a transgressor is a deep pit; and he that is hated of the Lord shall fall into it. Evil ways are before a man, and he does not like to turn away from them; but it is needful to turn aside from a perverse and bad way. 15 Folly is attached to the heart of a child, but the rod and instruction are *then* far from him. 16 He that oppresses the poor, increases his own substance, yet gives to the rich so as to make it less. 17 Incline thine ear to the words of wise men: hear also my word, and apply thine heart, 18 that thou mayest know that they are good: and if thou lay them to heart, they shall also gladden thee on thy lips. 19 That thy hope may be in the Lord, and he may make thy way known to thee. 20 And do thou too repeatedly record them for thyself on the table of thine heart, for counsel and knowledge. 21 I therefore teach thee truth, and knowledge good to hear; that thou mayest answer words of truth to them that question thee. 22 Do no violence to the poor, for he is needy: neither dishonour the helpless *man* in the gates. 23 For the Lord will plead his cause, and thou shalt deliver thy soul in safety. 24 Be not companion to a furious man; neither lodge with a passionate man: 25 lest thou learn of his ways, and get snares to thy soul. 26 Become not surety from respect of a man's person. 27 For if those have not whence to give compensation, they will take the bed *that is* under thee. 28 Remove not the old landmarks, which thy fathers placed. 29 It is fit that an observant man and *one* diligent in his business should attend on kings, and not attend on slothful men.

Prov.23 1 If thou sit to sup at the table of a prince, consider attentively the things set before thee: 2 and apply thine hand, knowing that it behoves thee to prepare such *meats*: but if thou art very insatiable, 3 desire not his provisions; for these belong to a false life. 4 If thou art poor, measure not thyself with a rich man; but refrain thyself in thy wisdom. 5 If thou shouldest fix thine eye upon him, he will disappear; for wings like an eagle's are prepared for him, and he returns to the house of his master. 6 Sup not with an envious man, neither desire thou his meats: 7 so he eats and drinks as if any one should swallow a hair, and do not bring him in to thyself, nor eat thy morsel with him: 8 for he will vomit it up, and spoil thy fair words. 9 Say nothing in the ears of a fool, lest at any time he sneer at thy wise words. 10 Remove not the ancient landmarks; and enter not upon the possession of the fatherless: 11 for the Lord is their redeemer; he is mighty, and will plead their cause with thee. 12 Apply thine heart to instruction, and prepare thine ears for words of discretion. 13 Refrain not from chastening a child; for if thou beat him with the rod, he shall not die. 14 For thou shalt beat him with the rod, and shalt deliver his soul from death. 15 Son, if thy heart be wise, thou shalt also gladden my heart; 16 and thy lips shall converse with my lips, if they be right. 17 Let not thine heart envy sinners: but be thou in the fear of the Lord all the day. 18 For if thou shouldest keep these things, thou shalt have posterity; and thine hope shall not be removed. 19 Hear, *my* son, and be wise, and rightly direct the thoughts of thine heart. 20 Be not a wine- bibber, neither continue long at feasts, and purchases of flesh: 21 for every drunkard and whoremonger shall be poor; and every sluggard shall clothe himself with tatters and ragged garments. 22 Hearken, *my* son, to thy father which begot thee, and despise not *thy mother* because

she is grown old. 23 24 A righteous father brings up *his children* well; and his soul rejoices over a wise son. 25 Let thy father and thy mother rejoice over thee, and let her that bore thee be glad. 26 *My* son, give me thine heart, and let thine eyes observe my ways. 27 For a strange house is a vessel full of holes; and a strange well is narrow. 28 For such a one shall perish suddenly; and every transgressor shall be cut off. 29 Who *has* woe? who trouble? who *has* quarrels? and who vexations and disputes? who *has* bruises without a cause? whose eyes are livid? 30 Are not those of them that stay long at wine? *are* not *those* of them that haunt *the places* where banquets are? Be not drunk with wine; but converse with just men, and converse *with them* openly. 31 For if thou shouldest set thine eyes on bowls and cups, thou shalt afterwards go more naked than a pestle. 32 But at last *such a one* stretches himself out as one smitten by a serpent, and venom is diffused through him as by a horned serpent. 33 Whenever thine eyes shall behold a strange woman, then thy mouth shall speak perverse things. 34 And thou shalt lie as in the midst of the sea, and as a pilot in a great storm. 35 And thou shalt say, They smote me, and I was not pained; and they mocked me, and I knew it not: when will it be morning, that I may go and seek those with whom I may go in company?

Prov.24 1 *My* son, envy not bad men, nor desire to be with them. 2 For their heart meditates falsehoods, and their lips speak mischiefs. 3 A house is built by wisdom, and is set up by understanding. 4 By discretion the chambers are filled with all precious and excellent wealth. 5 A wise man is better than a strong man; and a man who has prudence than a large estate. 6 War is carried on with generalship, and aid is supplied to the heart of a counsellor. 7 Wisdom and good understanding are in the gates of the wise: the wise turn not aside from the mouth of the Lord, 8 but deliberate in council. Death befalls uninstructed *men*. 9 The fools also dies in sins; and uncleanness *attaches* to a pestilent man. 10 He shall be defiled in the evil day, and in the day of affliction, until he be utterly consumed. 11 Deliver them that are led away to death, and redeem them that are appointed to be slain; spare not *thy help*. 12 But if thou shouldest say, I know not this man; know that the Lord knows the hearts of all; and he that formed breath for all, he knows all things, who renders to every man according to his works. 13 *My* son, eat honey, for the honeycomb is good, that thy throat may be sweetened. 14 Thus shalt thou perceive wisdom in thy soul: for if thou find it, thine end shall be good, and hope shall not fail thee. 15 Bring not an ungodly man into the dwelling of the righteous: neither be deceived by the feeding of the belly. 16 For a righteous man will fall seven times, and rise *again*: but the ungodly shall be without strength in troubles. 17 If thine enemy should fall, rejoice not over him, neither be elated at his overthrow. 18 For the Lord will see *it*, and it will not please him, and he will turn away his wrath from him. 19 Rejoice not in evil-doers, neither be envious of sinners. 20 For the evil man shall have no posterity: and the light of the wicked shall be put out. 21 *My* son, fear God and the king; and do not disobey either of them. 22 For they will suddenly punish the ungodly, and who can know the vengeance *inflicted* by both? [A son that keeps the commandment shall escape destruction; for *such an one* has fully received it. Let no falsehood be spoken by the king from the tongue; yea, let no falsehood proceed from his tongue. The king's tongue is a sword, and not one of flesh; and whosoever shall be given up to *it* shall be destroyed: for if his wrath should be provoked, he destroys men with cords, and devours men's bones, and burns them up as a flame, so that they are not *even* fit to be eaten by the young eagles. *My* son, reverence my words, and receive them, and repent.]

Prov.25 1 These things says the man to them that trust in God; and I cease. 2 For I am the most simple of all men, and there is not in me the wisdom of men. 3 God has taught me wisdom, and I know the knowledge of the holy. 4 Who has gone up to heaven, and come down? who has gathered the winds in his bosom? who has wrapped up the waters in a garment? who has dominion of all the ends of the earth? what is his name? or what is the name of his children? 5 For all the words of God are tried in the fire, and he defends those that reverence him. 6 Add not unto his words, lest he reprove thee, and thou be made a liar. 7 Two things I ask of thee; take not favour from me before I die. 8 Remove far from me vanity and falsehood: and give me not wealth *or* poverty; but appoint me what is needful and sufficient: 9 lest I be filled and become false, and say, Who sees me? or be poor and steal, and swear *vainly* by the name of God. 10 Deliver not a servant into the hands of his master, lest he curse thee, and thou be utterly destroyed. 11 A wicked generation curse their father, and do not bless their mother. 12 A wicked generation judge themselves to be just, but do not cleanse their way. 13 A wicked generation have lofty eyes, and exalt themselves with their eyelids. 14 A wicked generation have swords *for* teeth and jaw-teeth *as* knives, so as to destroy and devour the lowly from the earth, and the poor of them from among men. 23 And this thing I say to you that are wise *for you* to learn: It is not good to have respect of persons in judgment. 24 He that says of the ungodly, He is righteous, shall be cursed by peoples, and hateful among the nations. 25 But they that reprove *him* shall appear more excellent, and blessing shall come upon them; 26 and *men* will kiss lips that answer well. 27 Prepare thy works for *thy* going forth, and prepare thyself for the field; and come after me, and thou shalt rebuild thine house. 28 Be not a false witness against thy *fellow* citizen, neither exaggerate with thy lips. 29 Say not, As he has treated me, so will I treat him, and I will avenge myself on him for that wherein he has injured me. 30 A foolish man is like a farm, and a senseless man is like a vineyard. 31 If thou let him alone, he will altogether remain barren and covered with weeds; and he becomes destitute, and his stone walls are broken down. 32 Afterwards I reflected, I looked that I might receive instruction. 33 *The sluggard says,* I slumber a little, and I sleep a little, and for a little while I fold my arms across *my* breast. 34 But if thou do this, thy poverty will come speedily; and thy want like a swift courier. 15 The horse-leech had three dearly-beloved daughters: and these three did not satisfy her; and the fourth was not contented so as to say, Enough. 16 The grave, and the love of a woman, and the earth not filled with water; water also and fire will not say, It is enough. 17 The eye that laughs to scorn a father, and dishonours the old age of a mother, let the ravens of the valleys pick it out, and let the young eagles devour it. 18 Moreover there are three things impossible for me to comprehend, and the fourth I know not: 19 the track of a flying eagle; and the ways of a serpent on a rock; and the paths of a ship passing through the sea; and the ways of a man in youth. 20 Such is the way of an adulterous woman, who having washed herself from what she has done, says she has done nothing amiss. 21 By three thing the earth is troubled, and the fourth it cannot bear: 22 if a servant reign; or a fool be filled with food; 23 or if a maid-servant should cast out her own mistress; and if a hateful woman should marry a good man. 24 And *there are* four very little things upon the earth, but these are wiser than the wise: 25 the ants which are weak, and *yet* prepare *their* food in summer; 26 the rabbits also *are* a feeble race, who make their houses in the rocks. 27 The locusts have no king, and *yet* march orderly at one command. 28 And the eft, which supports itself by *its* hands, and is easily taken, dwells in the fortresses of kings. 29 And there are three things which go well, and a fourth which passes along finely. 30 A lion's whelp, stronger than *all other* beasts, which turns not away, nor fears *any* beast; 31 and a cock walking in boldly among the hens, and the goat leading the herd; and a king publicly speaking before a nation. 32 If thou abandon thyself to mirth, and stretch forth thine hand in a quarrel, thou shalt be disgraced. 33 Milk out milk, and there shall be butter, and if thou wing *one's* nostrils there shall come out blood: so if thou extort words, there will come forth quarrels and strifes.

Prov.26 1 My words have been spoken by God—the oracular answer of a king, whom his mother instructed. 2 What wilt thou keep, my son, what? the words of God. My firstborn son, I speak to thee: what? son of my womb? what? son of my vows? 3 Give not thy wealth to women, nor thy mind and living to remorse. Do all things with counsel: drink wine with counsel. 4 Princes are prone to anger: let them then not drink wine: 5 lest they drink, and forget wisdom, and be not able to judge the poor rightly. 6 Give strong drink to those that are in sorrow, and the wine to drink to those in pain: 7 that they may forget their poverty, and may not remember their troubles any more. 8 Open thy mouth with the word of God, and judge all fairly. 9 Open thy mouth and judge justly, and plead the cause of the poor and weak.

Prov.27 1 These are the miscellaneous instructions of Solomon, which the friends of Ezekias king of Judea copied out. 2 The glory of God conceals a matter: but the glory of a king honours business. 3 Heaven is high, and earth is deep, and a king's heart is unsearchable. 4 Beat the drossy silver, and it shall be made entirely pure. 5 Slay the ungodly from before the king, and his throne shall prosper in righteousness. 6 Be not boastful in the presence of the king, and remain not in the places of princes; 7 for *it is* better for thee that it should be said, Come up to me, than that *one* should humble thee in the presence of the prince; speak of that which thine eyes have seen. 8 Get not suddenly into a quarrel, lest thou repent at last. 9 Whenever thy friend shall reproach thee, retreat backward, despise *him* not; 10 lest thy friend continue to reproach thee, so thy quarrel and enmity shall not depart, but shall be to thee like death. Favour and friendship set *a man* free, which do thou keep for thyself, lest thou be made liable to reproach; but take heed to thy ways peaceably. 11 *As* a golden apple in a necklace of sardius, so *is it* to speak a *wise* word. 12 In an earring of gold a precious sardius is also set; *so is* a wise word to an obedient ear. 13 As a fall of snow in the time of harvest is good against heat, so a faithful messenger *refreshes* those that send him; for he helps the souls of his employers. 14 As winds and clouds and rains are most evident *objects*, so is he that boasts of a false gift. 15 In long-suffering is prosperity to kings, and a soft tongue breaks the bones. 16 Having found honey, eat *only* what is enough, lest haply thou be filled, and vomit it up. 17 Enter sparingly into thy friend's house, lest he be satiated with thy company, and hate thee. 18 *As* a club, and a dagger, and a pointed arrow, so also is a man who bears false witness against his friend. 19 The way of the wicked and the foot of the transgressor shall perish in an evil day. 20 As vinegar is bad for a sore, so trouble befalling the body afflicts the heart. As a moth in a garment, and a worm in wood, so the grief of a man hurts the heart. 21 If thine enemy hunger, feed him; if he thirst, give him drink; 22 for so doing thou shalt heap coals of fire upon his head, and the Lord shall reward thee *with* good. 23 The north wind raises clouds; so an impudent face provokes the tongue. 24 *It is* better to dwell on a corner of the roof, than with a railing woman in an open house. 25 As cold water is agreeable to a thirsting soul, so is a good message from a land far off. 26 As if one should stop a well, and corrupt a spring of water, so *is it* unseemly for a righteous man to fall before an ungodly man. 27 *It is* not good to eat much honey; but it is right to honour venerable sayings. 28 As a city whose walls are broken down, and which is unfortified, so is a man who does anything without counsel.

Prov.28 1 As dew in harvest, and as rain in summer, so honour is not *seemly* for a fool. 2 As birds and sparrows fly, so a curse shall not come upon any one without a cause. 3 As a whip for a horse, and a goad for an ass, so *is* a rod for a simple nation. 4 Answer not a fool according to his folly, lest thou become like him. 5 Yet answer a fool according to his folly, lest he seem wise in his own conceit. 6 He that sends a message by a foolish messenger procures for himself a reproach from his own ways. 7 *As well* take away the motion of the legs, as transgression from the mouth of fools. 8 He that binds up a stone in a sling, is like one that gives glory to a fool. 9 Thorns grow in the hand of a drunkard, and servitude in the hand of fools. 10 All the flesh of fools endures much hardship; for their fury is brought to nought. 11 As when a dog goes to his own vomit, and becomes abominable, so is fool who returns in his wickedness to his own sin. [There is a shame that brings sin: and there is a shame *that is* glory and grace.] 12 I have seen a man who seemed to himself to be wise; but a fool had more hope than he. 13 A sluggard when sent on a journey says, *There is* a lion in the ways, and *there are* murderers in the streets. 14 As a door turns on the hinge, so does a sluggard on his bed. 15 A sluggard having hid his hand in his bosom, will not be able to bring it up to his mouth. 16 A sluggard seems to himself wiser than one who most satisfactorily brings back a message. 17 As he that lays hold of a dog's tail, so is he that makes himself the champion of another's cause. 18 As those who need correction put forth *fair* words to men, and he that first falls in with the proposal will be overthrown; 19 so are all that lay wait for their own friends, and when they are discovered, say, I did it in jest. 20 With much wood fire increases; but where there is not a double-minded man, strife ceases. 21 A hearth for coals, and wood for fire; and railing man for the tumult of strife. 22 The words of cunning knaves are soft; but they smite *even* to the inmost parts of the bowels. 23 Silver dishonestly given is to be considered as a potsherd: smooth lips cover a grievous heart. 24 A weeping enemy promises all things with his lips, but in his heart he contrives deceit. 25 Though *thine* enemy intreat thee with a loud voice, consent not: for there are seven abominations in his heart. 26 He that hides enmity frames deceit: but being easily discerned, exposes his own sins in the public assemblies. 27 He that digs a pit for his neighbour shall fall into it: and he that rolls a stone, rolls it upon himself. 28 A lying tongue hates the truth; and an unguarded mouth causes tumults.

Prov.29 1 Boast not of to-morrow; for thou knowest not what the next day shall bring forth. 2 Let thy neighbour, and not thine own mouth, praise thee; a stranger, and not thine own lips. 3 A stone is heavy, and sand cumbersome; but a fool's wrath is heavier than both. 4 Wrath is merciless, and anger sharp: but envy can bear nothing. 5 Open reproofs are better than secret love. 6 The wounds of a friend are more to be trusted than the spontaneous kisses of an enemy. 7 A full soul scorns honeycombs; but to a hungry soul even bitter things appear sweet. 8 As when a bird flies down from its own nest, so a man is brought into bondage whenever he estranges himself from his own place. 9 The heart delights in ointments and wines and perfumes: but the soul is broken by calamities. 10 Thine own friend, and thy father's friend, forsake not; and when thou art in distress go not into thy brother's house: better is a friend *that is* near than a brother living far off. 11 Son, be wise, that thy heart may rejoice; and remove thou from thyself reproachful words. 12 A wise man, when evils are approaching, hides himself; but fools pass on, and will be punished. 13 Take away the man's garment, (for a scorner has passed by) whoever lays waste another's goods. 14 Whosoever shall bless a friend in the morning with a loud voice, shall seem to differ nothing from one who curses *him*. 15 On a stormy day drops *of rain* drive a man out of his house; so also does a railing woman *drive a man* out of his own house. 16 The north wind is sharp, but it is called by name propitious. 17 Iron sharpens iron; and a man sharpens his friend's countenance. 18 He that plants a fig-tree shall eat the fruits of it: so he that waits on his own master shall be honoured. 19 As faces are not like *other* faces, so neither are the thoughts of men. 20 Hell and destruction are not filled; so also are the eyes of men insatiable. [He that fixes his eye is an abomination to the Lord; and the uninstructed do not restrain their tongue.] 21 Fire is the trial for silver and gold; and a man is tried by the mouth of them that praise him. The heart of the transgressor seeks after mischiefs; but an upright heart seeks knowledge. 22 Though thou scourge a fool, disgracing him in the midst of the council, thou wilt *still* in no wise remove his folly from him. 23 Do thou thoroughly know the number of thy flock, and pay attention to thine herds. 24 For a man *has* not strength and power for ever; neither does he transmit it from generation to generation. 25 Take care of the herbage in the field, and thou shalt cut grass, and gather the mountain hay; 26 that thou mayest have *wool of* sheep for clothing: pay attention to the land, that thou mayest have lambs. 27 *My* son, thou hast from me words very useful for thy life, and for the life of thy servants.

Prov.30 1 The ungodly *man* flees when no one pursues: but the righteous is confident as a lion. 2 By reason of the sins of ungodly men quarrels arise; but a wise man will quell them. 3 A bold man oppresses the poor by ungodly deeds. As an impetuous and profitable rain, 4 so they that forsake the law praise ungodliness; but they that love the law fortify themselves with a wall. 5 Evil men will not understand judgment: but they that seek the Lord will understand everything. 6 A poor man walking in truth is better than a rich liar. 7 A wise son keeps the law: but he that keeps up debauchery dishonours his father. 8 He that increases his wealth by usuries and *unjust* gains, gathers it for him that pities the poor. 9 He that turns away his ear from hearing the law, even he has made his prayer abominable. 10 He that causes upright men to err in an evil way, himself shall fall into destruction: transgressor also shall pass by prosperity, but shall not enter into it. 11 A rich man is wise in his own conceit; but an intelligent poor man will condemn him. 12 By reason of the help of righteous men great glory arises: but in the places of the ungodly men are caught. 13 He that covers his own ungodliness shall not prosper: but he that blames *himself* shall be loved. 14 Blessed is the man who religiously fears always: but the hard of heart shall fall into mischiefs. 15 A hungry lion and a thirsty wolf *is he*, who, being poor, rules over a poor nation. 16 A king in need of revenues is a great oppressor: but he that hates injustice shall live a long time. 17 He that becomes surety for a man charged with murder shall be an exile, and not in safety. Chasten thy son, and he shall love thee, and give honour to thy soul: he shall not obey a sinful nation. 18 He that walks justly is assisted: but he that walks in crooked ways shall be entangled *therein*. 19 He that tills his own land shall be satisfied with bread: but he that follows idleness shall have plenty of poverty. 20 A man worthy of credit shall be much blessed: but the wicked shall not be unpunished. 21 He that reverences not the persons of the just is not good: such a one will sell a man for a morsel of bread. 22 An envious man makes haste to be rich, and knows not that the merciful man will have the mastery over him. 23 He that reproves a man's ways shall have more favour than he that flatters with

the tongue. 24 He that casts off father or mother, and thinks he sins not; the same is partaker with an ungodly man. 25 An unbelieving man judges rashly: but he that trusts in the Lord will act carefully. 26 He that trusts to a bold heart, such an one is a fool: but he that walks in wisdom shall be safe. 27 He that gives to the poor shall not be in want: but he that turns away his eye *from him* shall be in great distress. 28 In the places of ungodly *men* the righteous mourn: but in their destruction the righteous shall be multiplied.

Prov.31 1 A reprover is better than a stiff-necked man: for when the latter is suddenly set on fire, there shall be no remedy. 2 When the righteous are praised, the people will rejoice: but when the ungodly rule, men mourn. 3 When a man loves wisdom, his father rejoices: but he that keeps harlots will waste wealth. 4 A righteous king establishes a country: but a transgressor destroys *it*. 5 He that prepares a net in the way of his own friend, entangles his own feet in it. 6 A great snare *is spread* for a sinner: but the righteous shall be in joy and gladness. 7 A righteous man knows how to judge for the poor: but the ungodly understands not knowledge; and the poor man has not an understanding mind. 8 Lawless men burn down a city: but wise men turn away wrath. 9 A wise man shall judge nations: but a worthless man being angry laughs and fears not. 10 Bloody men hate a holy *person*, but the upright will seek his soul. 11 A fool utters all is mind: but the wise reserves his in part. 12 When a king hearkens to unjust language, all his subjects are transgressors. 13 When the creditor and debtor meet together, the Lord oversees them both. 14 When a king judges the poor in truth, his throne shall be established for a testimony. 15 Stripes and reproofs give wisdom: but an erring child disgraces his parents. 16 When the ungodly abound, sins abound: but when they fall, the righteous are warned. 17 Chasten thy son, and he shall give thee rest; and he shall give honour to thy soul. 18 There shall be no interpreter to a sinful nation: but he that observes the law is blessed. 19 A stubborn servant will not be reproved by words: for even if he understands, still he will not obey. 20 If thou see a man hasty in *his* words, know that the fool has hope rather than he. 21 He that lives wantonly from a child, shall be a servant, and in the end shall grieve over himself. 22 A furious man stirs up strife, and a passionate man digs up sin. 23 Pride brings a man low, but the Lord upholds the humble-minded with honour. 24 He that shares with a thief, hates his own soul: and if any having heard an oath uttered tell not of it, 25 *they* fearing and reverencing men *unreasonably* have been overthrown, but he that trusts in the Lord shall rejoice. Ungodliness causes a man to stumble: but he that trusts in his master shall be safe. 26 Many wait on the favour of rulers; but justice comes to a man from the Lord. 27 A righteous man is an abomination to an unrighteous man, and the direct way is an abomination to the sinner. 10 Who shall find a virtuous woman? for such a one is more valuable than precious stones. 11 The heart of her husband trusts in her: such a one shall stand in no need of fine spoils. 12 For she employs all her living for her husband's good. 13 Gathering wool and flax, she makes it serviceable with her hands. 14 She is like a ship trading from a distance: so she procures her livelihood. 15 And she rises by night, and gives food to her household, and *appointed* tasks to her maidens. 16 She views a farm, and buys it: and with the fruit of her hands she plants and a possession. 17 She strongly girds her loins, and strengthens her arms for work. 18 And she finds by experience that working is good; and her candle goes not out all night. 19 She reaches forth her arms to needful *works*, and applies her hands to the spindle. 20 And she opens her hands to the needy, and reaches out fruit to the poor. 21 Her husband is not anxious about those at home when he tarries anywhere abroad: for all her household are clothed. 22 She makes for her husband clothes of double texture, and garments for herself of fine linen and scarlet. 23 And her husband becomes a distinguished *person* in the gates, when he sits in council with the old inhabitants of the land. 24 She makes fine linens, and sells girdles to the Chananites: she opens her mouth heedfully and with propriety, and controls her tongue. 25 She puts on strength and honour; and rejoices in the last days. 26 But she opens her mouth wisely, and according to law. 27 The ways of her household are careful, and she eats not the bread of idleness. 28 And *her* kindness to them sets up her children for them, and they grow rich, and her husband praises her. 29 Many daughters have obtained wealth, many have wrought valiantly; but thou hast exceeded, thou hast surpassed all. 30 Charms are false, and woman's beauty is vain: for it is a wise woman that is blessed, and let her praise the fear the Lord. 31 Give her of the fruit of her lips; and let her husband be praised in the gates.

ECCLESIASTES

Eccles.1 1 The words of the Preacher, the son of David, king of Israel in Jerusalem. 2 Vanity of vanities, said the Preacher, vanity of vanities; all is vanity. 3 What advantage *is there* to a man in all his labour that he takes under the sun? 4 A generation goes, and a generation comes: but the earth stands for ever. 5 And the sun arises, and the sun goes down and draws toward its place; 6 arising there it proceeds southward, and goes round toward the north. The wind goes round and round, and the wind returns to its circuits. 7 All the rivers run into the sea; and yet the sea is not filled: to the place whence the rivers come, thither they return again. 8 All things are full of labour; a man will not be able to speak *of them*: neither shall the eye be satisfied with seeing, neither shall the ear be filled with hearing. 9 What is that which has been? the very thing which shall be: and what is that which has been done? the very thing which shall be done: and there is no new thing under the sun. 10 *Who is he* that shall speak and say, Behold, this is new? it has already been in the ages that have passed before us. 11 There is no memorial to the first things; neither to the things that have been last shall their memorial be with them that shall at the last *time.* 12 I the Preacher was king over Israel in Jerusalem. 13 And I applied my heart to seek out and examine by wisdom concerning all things that are done under heaven, for God has given to the sons of men an evil trouble to be troubled therewith. 14 I beheld all the works that were wrought under the sun; and, beheld, all were vanity and waywardness of spirit. 15 That which is crooked cannot be made straight: and deficiency cannot be numbered. 16 I spoke in my heart, saying, Behold, I am increased, and have acquired wisdom beyond all who were before me in Jerusalem: also I applied my heart to know wisdom and knowledge. 17 And my heart knew much—wisdom, and knowledge, parables and understanding: I perceived that this also is waywardness of spirit. 18 For in the abundance of wisdom is abundance of knowledge; and he that increases knowledge will increase sorrow.

Eccles.2 1 I said in my heart, Come now, I will prove thee with mirth, and behold thou good: and, behold, this is also vanity. 2 I said to laughter, Madness: and to mirth, Why doest thou this? 3 And I examined whether my heart would excite my flesh as *with* wine, (though my heart guided *me* in wisdom,) and I *desired* to lay hold of mirth, until I should see of what kind is the good to the sons of men, which they should do under the sun all the days of their life. 4 I enlarged my work; I built me houses; I planted me vineyards. 5 I made me gardens and orchards, and planted in them every kind of fruit-tree. 6 I made me pools of water, to water from them the timber-bearing wood. 7 I got servants and maidens, and servants were born to me in the house: also I had abundant possession of flocks and herds, beyond all who were before me in Jerusalem. 8 Moreover I collected for myself both silver and gold also, and the peculiar treasures of kings and provinces: I procured me singing men and singing women, and delights of the sons of men, a butler and female cupbearers. 9 So I became great, and advanced beyond all that were before in Jerusalem: also my wisdom was established to me. 10 And whatever mine eyes desired, I withheld not from them, I withheld not my heart from all my mirth: for my heart rejoiced in all my labour; and this was my portion of all my labour. 11 And I looked on all my works which my hands had wrought, and on my labour which I laboured to perform: and behold, all was vanity and waywardness of spirit, and there is no advantage under the sun. 12 Then I looked on to see wisdom, and madness, and folly: for who is the man who will follow after counsel, in all things where in he employs it? 13 And I saw that wisdom excels folly, as much as light excels darkness. 14 The wise man's eyes are in his head; but the fool walks in darkness: and I perceived, even I, that one event shall happen to them all. 15 And I said in my heart, As the event of the fool is, so shall it be to me, even to me: and to what purpose have I gained wisdom? I said moreover in my heart, This is also vanity, because the fool speaks of his abundance. 16 For there is no remembrance of the wise man with the fool for ever; forasmuch as now *in* the coming days all things are forgotten: and how shall the wise man die with the fool? 17 So I hated life; because the work that was wrought under the sun was evil before me: for all is vanity and waywardness of spirit. 18 And I hated the whole of my labour which I took under the sun; because I must leave it to the man who will come after me. 19 And who knows whether he will be a wise *man* or a fool? and whether he will have power over all my labour in which I laboured, and wherein I grew wise under the sun? this is also vanity. 20 so I went about to dismiss from my heart all my labour wherein I had laboured under the sun. 21 For there is *such a* man that his labour is in wisdom, and in knowledge, and in fortitude; *yet* this man shall give his portion to one who has not laboured therein. This is also vanity and great evil. 22 For it happens to a man in all his labour, and in the purpose of his heart wherein he labours under the sun. 23 For all his days *are days* of sorrows, and vexation of spirit is his; in the night also his heart rests not. This is also vanity. 24 A man has nothing *really* good to eat, and to drink, and to shew his soul *as* good in his trouble. This also I saw, that it is from the hand of God. 25 For who shall eat, or who shall drink, without him? 26 For *God* has given to the man who is good in his sight, wisdom, and knowledge, and joy: but he has given to the sinner trouble, to add and to heap up, that he may give to him that is good before God; for this is also vanity and waywardness of spirit.

Eccles.3 1 To all things there is a time, and a season for every matter under heaven. 2 A time of birth, and a time to die; a time to plant, and a time to pluck up what has been planted; 3 a time to kill, and a time to heal; a time to pull down, and a time to build up; 4 a time to weep, and a time to laugh; a time to lament, and a time to dance; 5 a time to throw stones, and a time to gather stones together; a time to embrace, and a time to abstain from embracing; 6 a time to seek, and a time to lose; a time to keep, and a time to cast away; 7 a time to rend, and a time to sew; a time to be silent, and a time to speak; 8 a time to love, and a time to hate; a time of war, and a time of peace. 9 What advantage *has* he that works in those things wherein he labours? 10 I have seen all the trouble, which God has given to the sons of men to be troubled with. 11 All the things which he has made are beautiful in his time: he has also set the whole world in their heart, that man might not find out the work which God has wrought from the beginning even to the end. 12 I know that there is no good in them, except *for a man* to rejoice, and to do good in his life. 13 Also *in the case of* every man who shall eat and drink, and see good in all his labour, *this* is a gift of God. 14 I know that whatsoever things God has done, they shall be for ever: it is impossible to add to it, and it is impossible to take away from it: and God has done *it*, that *men* may fear before him. 15 That which has been is now; and whatever things *are appointed* to be have already been; and God will seek out that which is past. 16 And moreover I saw under the sun the place of judgment, there was the ungodly one; and the place of righteousness, there was the godly one. 17 And I said in my heart, God will judge the righteous and the ungodly: for there is a time there for every action and for every work. 18 I said in my heart, concerning the speech of the sons of man, God will judge them, and that to shew that they are breasts. 19 Also to them is the event of the sons of man, and the event of the brute; one event befalls them: as is the death of the one, so also the death of the other; and there is one breath to all: and what has the man more than the brute? nothing; for all is vanity. 20 All *go* to one place; all were formed of the dust, and all will return to dust. 21 And who has seen the spirit of the sons of man, whether it goes upward? and the spirit of the beast, whether it goes downward to the earth? 22 And I

saw that there was no good, but that wherein a man shall rejoice in his works, for it is his portion, for who shall bring him to see any thing of that which shall be after him?

Eccles.4 1 So I returned, and saw all the oppressions that were done under the sun: and behold the tear of the oppressed, and they had no comforter; and on the side of them that oppressed them was power; but they had no comforter: 2 and I praised all the dead that had already died more than the living, as many as are alive until now. 3 Better also than both these is he who has not yet been, who has not seen all the evil work that is done under the sun. 4 And I saw all labour, and all the diligent work, that this is a man's envy from his neighbour. This is also vanity and waywardness of spirit. 5 The fool folds his hands together, and eats his own flesh. 6 Better is a handful of rest than two handfuls of trouble and waywardness of spirit. 7 So I returned, and saw vanity under the sun. 8 There is one *alone*, and there is not a second; yea, he has neither son nor brother: yet there is no end to all his labour; neither is his eye satisfied with wealth; and for whom do I labour, and deprive my soul of good? this is also vanity, and an evil trouble. 9 Two *are* better than one, *seeing* they have a good reward for their labour. 10 For if they fall, the one will lift up his fellow: but woe to him that is alone when he falls, and there is not a second to lift him up. 11 Also if two should lie together, they also get heat: but how shall one be warmed *alone?* 12 And if one should prevail against *him*, the two shall withstand him; and a threefold cord shall not be quickly broken. 13 Better is a poor and wise child than an old and foolish king, who knows not how to take heed any longer. 14 For he shall come forth out of the house of the prisoners to reign, because *he* also that was in his kingdom has become poor. 15 I beheld all the living who were walking under the sun, with the second youth who shall stand up in each one's place. 16 There is no end to all the people, to all who were before them: and the last shall not rejoice in him: for this also is vanity and waywardness of spirit. 17 Keep thy foot, whensoever thou goest to the house of God; and *when thou art* near to hear, let thy sacrifice *be* better than the gift of fools: for they know not that they are doing evil.

Eccles.5 1 Be not hasty with thy mouth, and let not thine heart be swift to utter anything before God; for God is in heaven above, and thou upon earth: therefore let thy words be few. 2 For through the multitude of trial a dream comes; and a fool's voice is with a multitude of words. 3 Whenever thou shalt vow a vow to God, defer not to pay it; for *he has* no pleasure in fools: pay thou therefore whatsoever thou shalt have vowed. 4 *It is* better that thou shouldest not vow, than that thou shouldest vow and not pay. 5 Suffer not thy mouth to lead thy flesh to sin; and say not in the presence of God, It was an error: lest God be angry at thy voice, and destroy the works of thy hands. 6 For *there is evil* in a multitude of dreams and vanities and many words: but fear thou God. 7 If thou shouldest see the oppression of the poor, and the wresting of judgment and of justice in the land, wonder not at the matter: for *there is* a high one to watch over him that is high, and high ones over them. 8

Also the abundance of the earth is for every one: the king *is dependent on* the tilled field. 9 He that loves silver shall not be satisfied with silver: and who has loved gain, in the abundance thereof? this is also vanity. 10 In the multitude of good they are increased that eat it: and what virtue has the owner, but the right of beholding *it* with his eyes? 11 The sleep of a servant is sweet, whether he eat little or much: but to one who is satiated with wealth, there is none that suffers him to sleep. 12 There is an infirmity which I have seen under the sun, *namely*, wealth kept for its owner to his hurt. 13 And that wealth shall perish in an evil trouble: and *the man* begets a son, and there is nothing in his hand. 14 As he came forth naked from his mother's womb, he shall return back as he came, and he shall receive nothing for his labour, that it should go *with him* in his hand. 15 And this is also an evil infirmity: for as he came, so also shall he return: and what is his gain, for which he vainly labours? 16 Yea, all his days are in darkness, and in mourning, and much sorrow, and infirmity, and wrath. 17 Behold, I have seen good, that it is a fine thing *for a man* to eat and to drink, and to see good in all his labour in which he may labour under the sun, *all* the number of the days of his life which God has given to him: for it is his portion. 18 Yea, and *as for* every man to whom God has given wealth and possessions, and has given him power to eat thereof, and to receive his portion, and to rejoice in his labour; this is the gift of God. 19 For he shall not much remember the days of his life; for God troubles him in the mirth of his heart.

Eccles.6 1 There is an evil which I have seen under the sun, and it is abundant with man: 2 a man to whom God shall give wealth, and substance, and honour, and he wants nothing for his soul of all things that he shall desire, yet God shall not give him power to eat of it, for a stranger shall devour it: this is vanity, and an evil infirmity. 3 If a man beget a hundred *children*, and live many years, yea, however abundant the days of his years shall be, yet *if* his soul shall not be satisfied with good, and also he have no burial; I said, An untimely birth is better than he. 4 For he came in vanity, and departs in darkness, and his name shall be covered in darkness. 5 Moreover he has not seen the sun, nor known rest: there is *no more rest* to this one than another. 6 Though he has lived to the return of a thousand years, yet he has seen no good: do not all go to one place? 7 All the labour of a man is for his mouth, and yet the appetite shall not be satisfied. 8 For *what* advantage has the wise man over the fool, since *even* the poor knows how to walk in the direction of life? 9 The sight of the eyes is better than that which wanders in soul: this is also vanity, and waywardness of spirit. 10 If anything has been, its name has already been called: and it is known what man is; neither can he contend with him who is stronger than he. 11 For there are many things which increase vanity.

Eccles.7 1 What advantage has a man? for who knows *what is* good for a man in his life, *during* the number of the life of the days of his vanity? and he has spent them as a shadow; for who shall tell a man what shall be after him under the sun? 2 A good name is better than good oil; and the day of death than the day of birth. 3 *It is* better to go to the house

of mourning, than to go to the banquet house: since this is the end of every man; and the living man will apply good *warning* to his heart. 4 Sorrow is better than laughter: for by the sadness of the countenance the heart will be made better. 5 The heart of the wise is in the house of mourning; but the heart of fools is in the house of mirth. 6 *It is* better to hear a reproof of a wise man, than for a man to hear the song of fools. 7 As the sound of thorns under a caldron, so is the laughter of fools: this is also vanity. 8 for oppression makes a wise man mad, and destroys his noble heart. 9 The end of a matter is better than the beginning thereof: the patient is better than the high-minded. 10 Be not hasty in thy spirit to be angry: for anger will rest in the bosom of fools. 11 Say not, What has happened, that the former days were better than these? for thou dost not enquire in wisdom concerning this. 12 Wisdom is good with an inheritance: and *there is* an advantage *by it* to them that see the sun. 13 For wisdom in its shadow is as the shadow of silver: and the excellence of the knowledge of wisdom will give life to him that has it. 14 Behold the works of God: for who shall be able to straighten him whom God has made crooked? 15 In the day of prosperity live joyfully, and consider in the day of adversity: consider, *I say*, God also has caused the one to agree with the other for *this* reason, that man should find nothing after him. 16 I have seen all things in the days of my vanity: there is a just man perishing in his justice, and there is an ungodly man remaining in his wickedness. 17 Be not very just; neither be very wise: lest thou be confounded. 18 Be not very wicked; and be not stubborn: lest thou shouldest die before thy time. 19 It is well for thee to hold fast by this; also by this defile not thine hand: for to them that fear God all things shall come forth *well*. 20 Wisdom will help the wise man more than ten mighty men which are in the city. 21 For there is not a righteous man in the earth, who will do good, and not sin 22 Also take no heed to all the words which ungodly men shall speak; lest thou hear thy servant cursing thee. 23 For many times he shall trespass against thee, and repeatedly shall he afflict thine heart; for thus also hast thou cursed others. 24 All these things have I proved in wisdom: I said, I will be wise; but it was far from me. 25 *That which is* far beyond what was, and a great depth, who shall find it out? 26 I and my heart went round about to know, and to examine, and to seek wisdom, and the account *of things*, and to know the folly and trouble and madness of the ungodly man. 27 And I find her *to be*, and I will pronounce *to be* more bitter than death the woman which is a snare, and her heart nets, *who has* a band in her hands: *he that is* good in the sight of God shall be delivered from her; but the sinner shall be caught by her. 28 Behold, this have I found, said the Preacher, *seeking* by one at a time to find out the account, 29 which my soul sought after, but I found not: for I have found one man of a thousand; but a woman in all these I have not found. 30 But, behold, this have I found, that God made man upright; but they have sought out many devices.

Eccles.8 1 Who knows the wise? and who knows the interpretation of a saying? A man's wisdom will lighten his countenance; but a man of shameless countenance will be hated. 2 Observe the commandment of the king, and *that* because of the word of the oath of God. 3 Be not hasty; thou shalt go forth out of his presence: stand not in an evil matter; for he will do whatsoever he shall please, 4 even as a king having power: and who will say to him, What doest thou? 5 He that keeps the commandment shall not know an evil thing: and the heart of the wise knows the time of judgment. 6 For to every thing there is time and judgment; for the knowledge of a man is great to him. 7 For there is no one that knows what is going to be: for who shall tell him how it shall be? 8 There is no man that has power over the spirit to retain the spirit; and there is no power in the day of death: and there is no discharge in the day of the battle; neither shall ungodliness save her votary. 9 So I saw all this, and I applied my heart to every work that has been done under the sun; all the things wherein man has power over man to afflict him. 10 And then I saw the ungodly carried into the tombs, and *that* out of the holy place: and they departed, and were praised in the city, because they had done thus: this also is vanity. 11 Because there is no contradiction made on the part of those who do evil quickly, therefore the heart of the children of men is fully determined in them to do evil. 12 He that has sinned has done evil from that time, and long from beforehand: nevertheless I know, that it is well with them that fear God, that they may fear before him: 13 but it shall not be well with the ungodly, and he shall not prolong his days, *which are* as a shadow; forasmuch as he fears not before God. 14 There is a vanity which is done upon the earth; that there are righteous persons to whom it happens according to the doing of the ungodly; and there are ungodly men, to whom it happens according to the doing of the just: I said, This is also vanity. 15 Then I praised mirth, because there is no good for a man under the sun, but to eat, and drink, and be merry: and this shall attend him in his labour all the days of his life, which God has given him under the sun. 16 Whereupon I set my heart to know wisdom, and to perceive the trouble that was wrought upon the earth: for there is that neither by day nor night sees sleep with his eyes. 17 And I beheld all the works of God, that a man shall not be able to discover the work which is wrought under the sun; whatsoever things a man shall endeavour to seek, however a man may labour to seek it, yet he shall not find it; yea, how much soever a wise man may speak of knowing it, he shall not be able to find it: for I applied all this to my heart, and my heart has seen all this.

Eccles.9 1 *I saw* that the righteous, and the wise, and their works, are in the hand of God: yea, there is no man that knows either love or hatred, *though* all are before their face. 2 Vanity is in all: there is one event to the righteous, and to the wicked; to the good, and to the bad; both to the pure, and to the impure; both to him that sacrifices, and to him that sacrifice not: as is the good, so is the sinner: as is the swearer, even so is he that fears an oath. 3 There is this evil in all that is done under the sun, that there is one event to all: yea, the heart of the sons of men is filled with evil, and madness is in their heart during their life, and after that *they go* to the dead. 4 for who is he that has fellowship with all the living? there is hope *of him*: for a living dog is better than a dead lion. 5 For the living will know that they shall die: but the dead know nothing, and there is no longer any reward to them; for their memory is lost. 6 also their love, and their hatred, and their envy, have now perished; yea, there is no portion for them any more for ever in all that is done under the sun. 7 Go, eat thy bread with mirth, and drink thy wine with a joyful heart; for now God has favourably accepted thy works. 8 Let thy garments be always white; and let not oil be wanting on thine head. 9 And see life with the wife whom thou lovest all the days of the life of thy vanity, which are given thee under the sun: for that is thy portion in thy life, and in thy labour wherein thou labourest under the sun. 10 Whatsoever thine hand shall find to do, do with all thy might; for there is no work, nor device, nor knowledge, nor wisdom, in Hades wither thou goest. 11 I returned, and saw under the sun, that the race is not to the swift, nor the battle to the strong, nor yet bread to the wise, nor yet wealth to men of understanding, nor yet favour to men of knowledge; for time and chance will happen to them all. 12 For surely man also knows not his time: as fishes that are taken in an evil net, and as birds that are caught in a snare; even thus the sons of men are snared at an evil time, when it falls suddenly upon them. 13 This I also saw *to be* wisdom under the sun, and it is great before me: 14 *suppose there were* a little city, and few men in it; and there should come against it a great king, and surround it, and build great mounds against it; 15 and should find in it a poor wise man, and he should save the city through his wisdom: yet no man would remember that poor man. 16 And I said Wisdom is better than power: yet the wisdom of the poor man is set at nought, and his words not listened to. 17 The words of the wise are heard in quiet more than the cry of them that rule in folly. 18 Wisdom is better than weapons of war: and one sinner will destroy much good.

Eccles.10 1 Pestilent flies will corrupt a preparation of sweet ointment: *and* a little wisdom is more precious than great glory of folly. 2 A wise man's heart is at his right hand; but a fool's heart at his left. 3 Yea, and whenever a fool walks by the way, his heart will fail him, and all that he thinks of is folly. 4 If the spirit of the ruler rise up against thee, leave not thy place; for soothing will put an end to great offences. 5 There is an evil which I have seen under the sun, wherein an error has proceeded from the ruler. 6 The fool has been set in very high places, while rich men would sit in a low one. 7 I have seen servants upon horses, and princes walking as servants on the earth. 8 He that digs a pit shall fall into it; and him that breaks down a hedge a serpent shall bite. 9 He that removes stones shall be troubled thereby; he that cleaves wood shall be endangered thereby. 10 If the axe-head should fall off, then the man troubles his countenance, and he must put forth more strength: and *in that case* skill is of no advantage to a man. 11 If a serpent bite when there is no *charmer's* whisper, then there is no advantage to the charmer. 12 The words of a wise mouth are gracious: but the lips of a fool will swallow him up. 13 The beginning of the words of his mouth is folly: and the end of his talk mischievous madness. 14 A fool moreover multiplies words: man knows not what has been, nor what will be: who shall tell him what will come after him? 15 The labour of fools will afflict them, *as that of one* who knows not to go to the city. 16 Woe to thee, O city, whose king is young, and thy princes eat in the morning! 17 Blessed art thou, O land, whose king is a son of nobles, and whose princes shall eat seasonably, for strength, and shall not be ashamed. 18 By slothful neglect a building will be brought low: and by idleness of the hands the house will fall to pieces. 19 Men prepare bread for laughter, and wine and oil that the living should rejoice: but to money all things will humbly yield obedience. 20 Even in thy conscience, curse not the king; and curse not the rich in thy bedchamber: for a bird of the air shall carry thy voice, and that which has wings shall report thy speech.

Eccles.11 1 Send forth thy bread upon the face of the water: for thou shalt find it after many days. 2 Give a portion to seven, and also to eight; for thou knowest not what evil there shall be upon the earth. 3 If the clouds be filled with rain, they pour *it* out upon the earth: and if a tree fall southward, or if it fall northward, in the place where the tree shall fall, there it shall be. 4 He that observes the wind sows not; and he that looks at the clouds will not reap. 5 Among whom none knows what is the way of the wind: as the bones *are hid* in the womb of a pregnant *woman*, so thou shalt not know the works of God, *even* all things whatsoever he shall do. 6 In the morning sow thy seed, and in the evening let not thine hand be slack: for thou knowest not what sort shall prosper, whether this or that, or whether both shall be good alike. 7 Moreover the light is sweet, and it is good for the eyes to see the sun. 8 For even if a man should live many years, *and* rejoice in them all; yet let him remember the days of darkness; for they shall be many. All that comes is vanity. 9 Rejoice, O young man, in thy youth; and let thy heart cheer thee in the days of thy youth, and walk in the ways of thy heart blameless, but not in the sight of thine eyes: yet know that for all these things God will bring thee into judgment. 10 Therefore remove sorrow from thy heart, and put away evil from thy flesh: for youth and folly are vanity.

Eccles.12 1 And remember thy Creator in the days of thy youth, before the days of evil come, and the years overtake *thee* in which thou shalt say, I have no pleasure in them. 2 While the sun and light are not darkened, nor the moon and the stars; nor the clouds return after the rain: 3 in the day wherein the keepers of the house shall tremble, and the mighty men shall become bent, and the grinding *women* cease because they have become few, and the *women* looking out at the windows be dark; 4 and they shall shut the doors in the market-place, because of the weakness of the voice of her that grinds *at the mill*; and he shall rise up at the voice of the sparrow, and all the daughters of song shall be brought low; 5 and they shall look up, and fears *shall be* in the way, and the almond tree shall blossom, and the locust shall increase, and the caper shall be scattered: because man has gone to his eternal home, and the mourners have gone about the market: 6 before the silver cord be *let go*, or the choice gold be broken, or the pitcher be broken at the

fountain, or the wheel run down to the cistern; 7 *before* the dust also return to the earth as it was, and the spirit return to God who gave it. 8 Vanity of vanities, said the Preacher; all is vanity. 9 And because the Preacher was wise above *others, so it was* that he taught man excellent knowledge, and the ear will trace out the parables. 10 The Preacher sought diligently to find out acceptable words, and a correct writing, *even* words of truth. 11 The words of the wise are as goads, and as nails firmly fastened, which have been given from one shepherd by agreement. 12 AAnd moreover, my son, guard thyself by means of them: of making many books there is no end; and much study is a weariness of the flesh. 13 Hear the end of the matter, the sun: Fear God, and keep his commandments: for this is the whole man. 14 For God will bring every work into judgment, with everything that has been overlooked, whether *it be* good, or whether *it be* evil.

SONG OF SONGS (SONG OF SOLOMON)

Song.1 1 The Song of songs, which is Solomon's. 2 Let him kiss me with the kisses of his mouth: for thy breasts are better than wine. 3 And the smell of thine ointments is better than all spices: thy name is ointment poured forth; therefore do the young maidens love thee. 4 They have drawn thee: we will run after thee, for the smell of thine ointments: the king has brought me into closet: let us rejoice and be glad in thee; we will love thy breasts more than wine: righteousness loves thee. 5 I am black, but beautiful, ye daughters of Jerusalem, as the tents of Kedar, as the curtains of Solomon. 6 Look not upon me, because I am dark, because the sun has looked unfavourably upon me: my mother's sons strove with me; they made me keeper in the vineyards; I have not kept my own vineyard. 7 Tell me, *thou* whom my soul loves, where thou tendest thy flock, where thou causest *them* to rest at noon, lest I become as one that is veiled by the flocks of thy companions. 8 If thou know not thyself, thou fair one among women, go thou forth by the footsteps of the flocks, and feed thy kids by the shepherd's tents. 9 I have likened thee, my companion, to my horses in the chariots of Pharao. 10 How are thy cheeks beautiful as *those* of a dove, thy neck as chains! 11 We will make thee figures of gold with studs of silver. 12 So long as the king was at table, my spikenard gave forth its smell. 13 My kinsman is to me a bundle of myrrh; he shall lie between my breasts. 14 My kinsman is to me a cluster of camphor in the vineyards of Engaddi. 15 Behold, thou art fair, my companion; behold, thou art fair; thine eyes are doves. 16 Behold, thou art fair, my kinsman, yea, beautiful, overshadowing our bed. 17 The beams of our house are cedars, our ceilings are of cypress.

Song.2 1 I am a flower of the plain, a lily of the valleys. 2 As a lily among thorns, so is my companion among the daughters. 3 As the apple among the trees of the wood, so is my kinsman among the sons. I desired his shadow, and sat down, and his fruit was sweet in my throat. 4 Bring me into the wine house; set love before me. 5 Strengthen me with perfumes, stay me with apples: for I *am* wounded with love. 6 His left *hand shall be* under my head, and his right hand shall embrace me. 7 I have charged you, ye daughters of Jerusalem, by the powers and by the virtues of the field, that ye do not rouse or wake *my* love, until he please. 8 The voice of my kinsman! behold, he comes leaping over the mountains, bounding over the hills. 9 My kinsman is like a roe or a young hart on the mountains of Baethel: behold, he is behind our wall, looking through the windows, peeping through the lattices. 10 My kinsman answers, and says to me, Rise up, come, my companion, my fair one, my dove. 11 For, behold, the winter is past, the rain is gone, it has departed. 12 The flowers are seen in the land; the time of pruning has arrived; the voice of the turtle-dove has been heard in our land. 13 The fig-tree has put forth its young figs, the vines put forth the tender grape, they yield a smell: arise, come, my companion, my fair one, my dove; yea, come. 14 *Thou art* my dove, in the shelter of the rock, near the wall: shew me thy face, and cause me to hear thy voice; for thy voice is sweet, and thy countenance is beautiful. 15 Take us the little foxes that spoil the vines: for our vines put forth tender grapes. 16 My kinsman is mine, and I am his: he feeds *his flock* among the lilies. 17 Until the day dawn, and the shadows depart, turn, my kinsman, be thou like to a roe or young hart on the mountains of the ravines.

Song.3 1 By night on my bed I sought him whom my soul loves: I sought him, but found him not; I called him, but he hearkened not to me. 2 I will rise now, and go about in the city, in the market -places, and in the streets, and I will seek him whom my soul loves: I sought him, but I found him not. 3 The watchmen who go their rounds in the city found me. *I said*, Have ye seen him whom my soul loves? 4 *It was* as a little *while* after I parted from them, that I found him whom my soul loves: I held him, and did not let him go, until I brought him into my mother's house, and into the chamber of her that conceived me. 5 I have charged you, O daughters of Jerusalem, by the powers and by the virtues of the field, that ye rouse not nor awake *my* love, until he please. 6 Who is this that comes up from the wilderness as pillars of smoke, perfumed with myrrh and frankincense, with all powders of the perfumer? 7 Behold Solomon's bed; sixty mighty men of the mighty ones of Israel are round about it. 8 They all hold a sword, being expert in war: every man *has* his sword upon his thigh because of fear by night. 9 King Solomon made himself a litter of woods of Lebanon. 10 He made the pillars of it silver, the bottom of it gold, the covering of it scarlet, in the midst of it a pavement of love, for the daughters of Jerusalem. 11 Go forth, ye daughters of Sion, and behold king Solomon, with the crown wherewith his mother crowned him, in the day of his espousals, and in the day of the gladness of his heart.

Song.4 1 Behold, thou art fair, my companion; behold, thou art fair; thine eyes are doves, beside thy veil: thy hair is as flocks of goats, that have appeared from Galaad. 2 Thy teeth are as flocks of shorn *sheep*, that have gone up from the washing; all of them bearing twins, and there is not a barren one among them. 3 Thy lips are as a thread of scarlet, and thy speech is comely: like the rind of a pomegranate is thy cheek without thy veil. 4 Thy neck is as the tower of David, that was built for an armoury: a thousand shields hang upon it, *and* all darts of mighty men. 5 Thy two breasts are as two twin fawns, that feed among the lilies. 6 Until the day dawn, and the shadows depart, I will betake me to the mountain of myrrh, and to the hill of frankincense. 7 Thou art all fair, my companion, and there is no spot in thee. 8 Come from Libanus, *my* bride, come from Libanus: thou shalt come and pass from the top of Faith, from the top of Sanir and Hermon, from the lions' dens, from the mountains of the leopards. 9 My sister, *my* spouse, thou hast ravished my heart; thou hast ravished my heart with one of thine eyes, with one chain of thy neck. 10 How beautiful are thy breasts, my sister, my spouse! how much more beautiful are thy breasts than wine, and the smell of thy garments than all spices! 11 Thy lips drop honeycomb, my spouse: honey and milk are under thy tongue; and the smell of thy garments is as the smell of Libanus. 12 My sister, *my* spouse is a garden enclosed; a garden enclosed, a fountain sealed. 13 Thy shoots are a garden of pomegranates, with the fruit of choice berries; camphor, with spikenard: 14 spikenard and saffron, calamus and cinnamon; with all woods of Libanus, myrrh, aloes, with all chief spices: 15 a fountain of a garden, and a well of water springing and gurgling from Libanus. 16 Awake, O north wind; and come, O south; and blow through my garden, and let my spices flow out.

Song.5 1 Let my kinsman come down into his garden, and eat the fruit of his choice berries. I am come into my garden, my sister, *my* spouse: I have gathered my myrrh with my spices; I have eaten my bread with my honey; I have drunk my wine with my milk. Eat, O friends, and drink; yea, brethren, drink abundantly. 2 I sleep, but my heart is awake: the voice of my kinsman knocks at the door, *saying*, Open, open to me, my companion, my sister, my dove, my perfect one: for my head is filled with dew, and my locks with the drops of the night. 3 I have put off my coat; how shall I put it on? I have washed my feet, how shall I defile them? 4 My kinsman put forth his hand by the hole *of the door*, and my belly moved for him. 5 I rose up to open to my kinsman; my hands dropped myrrh, my fingers choice myrrh, on the handles of the lock. 6 I opened to my kinsman; my kinsman was gone: my soul failed at his speech: I sought him, but found him not; I called him, but he answered me not. 7 The watchman that go their rounds in the city found me, they smote me, they wounded me; the keepers of the walls took away my veil from me. 8 I have charged you, O daughters of Jerusalem, by the powers and the virtues of the field: if ye should find my kinsman, what are ye to say to him? That I am wounded with love. 9 What is thy kinsman *more* than *another* kinsman, O thou beautiful among women? what is thy kinsman *more* than *another* kinsman, that thou hast so charged us? 10 My kinsman is white and ruddy, chosen out from myriads. 11 His head is *as* very fine gold, his locks are flowing, black as a raven. 12 His eyes are as doves, by the pools of waters, washed with milk, sitting by the pools. 13 His cheeks are as bowls of spices pouring forth perfumes: his lips are lilies, dropping choice myrrh. 14 His hands are as turned gold set with beryl: his belly is an ivory tablet on a sapphire stone. 15 His legs are marble pillars set on golden sockets: his form is as Libanus, choice as the cedars. 16 His throat is most sweet, and altogether desirable. This is my kinsman, and this is my companion, O daughters of Jerusalem. 17 Whither is thy kinsman gone, thou beautiful among women? whither has thy kinsman turned aside? *tell us*, and we will seek him with thee.

Song.6 1 My kinsman is gone down to his garden, to the beds of spice, to feed *his flock* in the gardens, and to gather lilies. 2 I am my kinsman's, and my kinsman is mine, who feeds among the lilies. 3 Thou art fair, my companion, as Pleasure, beautiful as Jerusalem, terrible as *armies* set in array. 4 Turn away thine eyes from before me, for they have ravished me: thy hair is as flocks of goats which have appeared from Galaad. 5 Thy teeth are as flocks of shorn *sheep*, that have gone up from the washing, all of them bearing twins, and there is none barren among them: thy lips are as a thread of scarlet, and thy speech is comely. 6 Thy cheek is like the rind of a pomegranate, *being seen* without thy veil. 7 There are sixty queens, and eighty concubines, and maidens without number. 8 My dove, my perfect one is one; she is the *only* one of her mother; she is the choice of her that bore her. The daughters saw her, and the queens will pronounce her blessed, yea, and the concubines, and they will praise her. 9 Who is this that looks forth as the morning, fair as the moon, choice as the sun, terrible as *armies* set in array? 10 I went down to the garden of nuts, to look at the fruits of the valley, to see if the vine flowered, *if* the pomegranates blossomed. 11 There I will give thee my breasts: my soul knew *it* not: it made me as the chariots of Aminadab. 12 Return, return, O Sunamite; return, return, and we will look at thee. What will ye see in the Sunamite? She comes as bands of armies.

Song.7 1 Thy steps are beautiful in shoes, O daughter of the prince: the joints of *thy* thighs are like chains, the work of the craftsman. 2 Thy navel is *as* a turned bowl, not wanting liquor; thy belly is *as* a heap of wheat set about with lilies. 3 Thy two breasts are as two twin fawns. 4 Thy neck is as an ivory tower; thine eyes are as pools in Esebon, by the gates of the daughter of many: thy nose is as the tower of Libanus, looking toward Damascus. 5 Thy head upon thee is as Carmel, and the curls of thy hair like scarlet; the king is bound in the galleries. 6 How beautiful art thou, and how sweet art thou, *my* love! 7 This is thy greatness in thy delights: thou wast made like a palm tree, and thy breasts to cluster. 8 I said, I will go up to the palm tree, I will take hold of its high boughs: and now shall thy breasts be as clusters of the vine, and the smell of thy nose of apples; 9 and thy throat as good wine, going well with my kinsman, suiting my lips and teeth. 10 I am my kinsman's, and his desire is toward me. 11 Come, my kinsman, let us go forth into the field; let us lodge in the villages. 12 Let us go early into the vineyards; let us see if the vine has flowered, *if* the blossoms have appeared, if the pomegranates have blossomed; there will I give thee my breasts. 13 The mandrakes have given a smell, and at our doors *are* all kinds of choice fruits, new and old. O my kinsman, I have kept *them* for thee.

Song.8 1 I would that thou, O my kinsman, wert he that sucked the breasts of my mother; when I found thee without, I would kiss thee; yea, they should not despise me. 2 I would take thee, I would bring thee into my mother's house, and into the chamber of her that conceived me; I would make thee to drink of spiced wine, of the juice of my pomegranates. 3 His left hand *should be* under my head, and his right hand should embrace me. 4 I have charged you, ye daughters of Jerusalem, by the virtues of the field, that ye stir not up, nor awake *my* love, until he please. 5 Who is this that comes up all white, leaning on her kinsman? I raised thee up under an apple- tree; there thy mother brought thee forth; there she that bore thee brought thee forth. 6 Set me as a seal upon thy heart, as a seal upon thine arm; for love is strong as death; jealousy is cruel as the grave, her shafts are shafts of fire, *even* the flames thereof. 7 Much water will not be able to quench love, and rivers shall not drown it; if a man would give all his substance for love, *men* would utterly despise it. 8 Our sister is little, and has no breasts; what shall we do for our sister, in the day wherein she shall be spoken for? 9 If she is a wall, let us build upon her silver bulwarks; and if she is a door, let us carve for her cedar panels. 10 I am a wall, and my breasts are as towers; I was in their eyes as one that found peace. 11 Solomon had a vineyard in Beelamon; he let his vineyard to keepers; every one was to bring for its fruit a thousand *pieces* of silver. 12 My vineyard, even mine, is before me; Solomon *shall have* a thousand, and they that keep its fruit two hundred. 13 Thou that dwellest in the gardens, the companions hearken to thy voice: make me hear *it*. 14 Away, my kinsman, and be like a doe or a fawn on the mountains of spices.

WISDOM

Wis.1 1 Love righteousness, ye that be judges of the earth: think of the Lord with a good (heart,) and in simplicity of heart seek him. 2 For he will be found of them that tempt him not; and sheweth himself unto such as do not distrust him. 3 For froward thoughts separate from God: and his power, when it is tried, reproveth the unwise. 4 For into a malicious soul wisdom shall not enter; nor dwell in the body that is subject unto sin. 5 For the holy spirit of discipline will flee deceit, and remove from thoughts that are without understanding, and will not abide when unrighteousness cometh in. 6 For wisdom is a loving spirit; and will not acquit a blasphemer of his words: for God is witness of his reins, and a true beholder of his heart, and a hearer of his tongue. 7 For the Spirit of the Lord filleth the world: and that which containeth all things hath knowledge of the voice. 8 Therefore he that speaketh unrighteous things cannot be hid: neither shall vengeance, when it punisheth, pass by him. 9 For inquisition shall be made into the counsels of the ungodly: and the sound of his words shall come unto the Lord for the manifestation of his wicked deeds. 10 For the ear of jealousy heareth all things: and the noise of murmurings is not hid. 11 Therefore beware of murmuring, which is unprofitable; and refrain your tongue from backbiting: for there is no word so secret, that shall go for nought: and the mouth that belieth slayeth the soul. 12 Seek not death in the error of your life: and pull not upon yourselves destruction with the works of your hands. 13 For God made not death: neither hath he pleasure in the destruction of the living. 14 For he created all things, that they might have their being: and the generations of the world were healthful; and there is no poison of destruction in them, nor the kingdom of death upon the earth: 15 (For righteousness is immortal:) 16 But ungodly men with their works and words called it to them: for when they thought to have it their friend, they consumed to nought, and made a covenant with it, because they are worthy to take part with it.

Wis.2 1 For the ungodly said, reasoning with themselves, but not aright, Our life is short and tedious, and in the death of a man there is no remedy: neither was there any man known to have returned from the grave. 2 For we are born at all adventure: and we shall be hereafter as though we had never been: for the breath in our nostrils is as smoke, and a little spark in the moving of our heart: 3 Which being extinguished, our body shall be turned into ashes, and our spirit shall vanish as the soft air, 4 And our name shall be forgotten in time, and no man shall have our works in remembrance, and our life shall pass away as the trace of a cloud, and shall be dispersed as a mist, that is driven away with the beams of the sun, and overcome with the heat thereof. 5 For our time is a very shadow that passeth away; and after our end there is no returning: for it is fast sealed, so that no man cometh again. 6 Come on therefore, let us enjoy the good things that are present: and let us speedily use the creatures like as in youth. 7 Let us fill ourselves with costly wine and ointments: and let no flower of the spring pass by us: 8 Let us crown ourselves with rosebuds, before they be withered: 9 Let none of us go without his part of our voluptuousness: let us leave tokens of our joyfulness in every place: for this is our portion, and our lot is this. 10 Let us oppress the poor righteous man, let us not spare the widow, nor reverence the ancient gray hairs of the aged. 11 Let our strength be the law of justice: for that which is feeble is found to be nothing worth. 12 Therefore let us lie in wait for the righteous; because he is not for our turn, and he is clean contrary to our doings: he upbraideth us with our offending the law, and objecteth to our infamy the transgressings of our education. 13 He professeth to have the knowledge of God: and he calleth himself the child of the Lord. 14 He was made to reprove our thoughts. 15 He is grievous unto us even to behold: for his life is not like other men's, his ways are of another fashion. 16 We are esteemed of him as counterfeits: he abstaineth from our ways as from filthiness: he pronounceth the end of the just to be blessed, and maketh his boast that God is his father. 17 Let us see if his words be true: and let us prove what shall happen in the end of him. 18 For if the just man be the son of God, he will help him, and deliver him from the hand of his enemies. 19 Let us examine him with despitefulness and torture, that we may know his meekness, and prove his patience. 20 Let us condemn him with a shameful death: for by his own saying he shall be respected. 21 Such things they did imagine, and were deceived: for their own wickedness hath blinded them. 22 As for the mysteries of God, they knew them not:

neither hoped they for the wages of righteousness, nor discerned a reward for blameless souls. 23 For God created man to be immortal, and made him to be an image of his own eternity. 24 Nevertheless through envy of the devil came death into the world: and they that do hold of his side do find it.

Wis.3 1 But the souls of the righteous are in the hand of God, and there shall no torment touch them. 2 In the sight of the unwise they seemed to die: and their departure is taken for misery, 3 And their going from us to be utter destruction: but they are in peace. 4 For though they be punished in the sight of men, yet is their hope full of immortality. 5 And having been a little chastised, they shall be greatly rewarded: for God proved them, and found them worthy for himself. 6 As gold in the furnace hath he tried them, and received them as a burnt offering. 7 And in the time of their visitation they shall shine, and run to and fro like sparks among the stubble. 8 They shall judge the nations, and have dominion over the people, and their Lord shall reign for ever. 9 They that put their trust in him shall understand the truth: and such as be faithful in love shall abide with him: for grace and mercy is to his saints, and he hath care for his elect. 10 But the ungodly shall be punished according to their own imaginations, which have neglected the righteous, and forsaken the Lord. 11 For whoso despiseth wisdom and nurture, he is miserable, and their hope is vain, their labours unfruitful, and their works unprofitable: 12 Their wives are foolish, and their children wicked: 13 Their offspring is cursed. Wherefore blessed is the barren that is undefiled, which hath not known the sinful bed: she shall have fruit in the visitation of souls. 14 And blessed is the eunuch, which with his hands hath wrought no iniquity, nor imagined wicked things against God: for unto him shall be given the special gift of faith, and an inheritance in the temple of the Lord more acceptable to his mind. 15 For glorious is the fruit of good labours: and the root of wisdom shall never fall away. 16 As for the children of adulterers, they shall not come to their perfection, and the seed of an unrighteous bed shall be rooted out. 17 For though they live long, yet shall they be nothing regarded: and their last age shall be without honour. 18 Or, if they die quickly, they have no hope, neither comfort in the day of trial. 19 For horrible is the end of the unrighteous generation.

Wis.4 1 Better it is to have no children, and to have virtue: for the memorial thereof is immortal: because it is known with God, and with men. 2 When it is present, men take example at it; and when it is gone, they desire it: it weareth a crown, and triumpheth for ever, having gotten the victory, striving for undefiled rewards. 3 But the multiplying brood of the ungodly shall not thrive, nor take deep rooting from bastard slips, nor lay any fast foundation. 4 For though they flourish in branches for a time; yet standing not last, they shall be shaken with the wind, and through the force of winds they shall be rooted out. 5 The imperfect branches shall be broken off, their fruit unprofitable, not ripe to eat, yea, meet for nothing. 6 For children begotten of unlawful beds are witnesses of wickedness against their parents in their trial. 7 But though the righteous be prevented with death, yet shall he be in rest. 8 For honourable age is not that which standeth in length of time, nor that is measured by number of years. 9 But wisdom is the gray hair unto men, and an unspotted life is old age. 10 He pleased God, and was beloved of him: so that living among sinners he was translated. 11 Yea speedily was he taken away, lest that wickedness should alter his understanding, or deceit beguile his soul. 12 For the bewitching of naughtiness doth obscure things that are honest; and the wandering of concupiscence doth undermine the simple mind. 13 He, being made perfect in a short time, fulfilled a long time: 14 For his soul pleased the Lord: therefore hasted he to take him away from among the wicked. 15 This the people saw, and understood it not, neither laid they up this in their minds, That his grace and mercy is with his saints, and that he hath respect unto his chosen. 16 Thus the righteous that is dead shall condemn the ungodly which are living; and youth that is soon perfected the many years and old age of the unrighteous. 17 For they shall see the end of the wise, and shall not understand what God in his counsel hath decreed of him, and to what end the Lord hath set him in safety. 18 They shall see him, and despise him; but God shall laugh them to scorn: and they shall hereafter be a vile carcase, and a reproach among the dead for evermore. 19 For he shall rend them, and cast them down headlong, that they shall be speechless; and he shall shake them from the foundation; and they shall be utterly laid waste, and be in sorrow; and their memorial shall perish. 20 And when they cast up the accounts of their sins, they shall come with fear: and their own iniquities shall convince them to their face.

Wis.5 1 Then shall the righteous man stand in great boldness before the face of such as have afflicted him, and made no account of his labours. 2 When they see it, they shall be troubled with terrible fear, and shall be amazed at the strangeness of his salvation, so far beyond all that they looked for. 3 And they repenting and groaning for anguish of spirit shall say within themselves, This was he, whom we had sometimes in derision, and a proverb of reproach: 4 We fools accounted his life madness, and his end to be without honour: 5 How is he numbered among the children of God, and his lot is among the saints! 6 Therefore have we erred from the way of truth, and the light of righteousness hath not shined unto us, and the sun of righteousness rose not upon us. 7 We wearied ourselves in the way of wickedness and destruction: yea, we have gone through deserts, where there lay no way: but as for the way of the Lord, we have not known it. 8 What hath pride profited us? or what good hath riches with our vaunting brought us? 9 All those things are passed away like a shadow, and as a post that hasted by; 10 And as a ship that passeth over the waves of the water, which when it is gone by, the trace thereof cannot be found, neither the pathway of the keel in the waves; 11 Or as when a bird hath flown through the air, there is no token of her way to be found, but the light air being beaten with the stroke of her wings and parted with the violent noise and motion of them, is passed through, and therein afterwards no sign where she went is to be found; 12 Or like as when an arrow is shot at a mark, it parteth the air, which immediately cometh together again, so that a man cannot know where it went through: 13 Even so we in like manner, as soon as we were born, began to draw to our end, and had no sign of virtue to shew; but were consumed in our own wickedness. 14 For the hope of the ungodly is like dust that is blown away with the wind; like a thin froth that is driven away with the storm; like as the smoke which is dispersed here and there with a tempest, and passeth away as the remembrance of a guest that tarrieth but a day. 15 But the righteous live for evermore; their reward also is with the Lord, and the care of them is with the most High. 16 Therefore shall they receive a glorious kingdom, and a beautiful crown from the Lord's hand: for with his right hand shall he cover them, and with his arm shall he protect them. 17 He shall take to him his jealousy for complete armour, and make the creature his weapon for the revenge of his enemies. 18 He shall put on righteousness as a breastplate, and true judgment instead of an helmet. 19 He shall take holiness for an invincible shield. 20 His severe wrath shall he sharpen for a sword, and the world shall fight with him against the unwise. 21 Then shall the right aiming thunderbolts go abroad; and from the clouds, as from a well drawn bow, shall they fly to the mark. 22 And hailstones full of wrath shall be cast as out of a stone bow, and the water of the sea shall rage against them, and the floods shall cruelly drown them. 23 Yea, a mighty wind shall stand up against them, and like a storm shall blow them away: thus iniquity shall lay waste the whole earth, and ill dealing shall overthrow the thrones of the mighty.

Wis.6 1 Hear therefore, O ye kings, and understand; learn, ye that be judges of the ends of the earth. 2 Give ear, ye that rule the people, and glory in the multitude of nations. 3 For power is given you of the Lord, and sovereignty from the Highest, who shall try your works, and search out your counsels. 4 Because, being ministers of his kingdom, ye have not judged aright, nor kept the law, nor walked after the counsel of God; 5 Horribly and speedily shall he come upon you: for a sharp judgment shall be to them that be in high places. 6 For mercy will soon pardon the meanest: but mighty men shall be mightily tormented. 7 For he which is Lord over all shall fear no man's person, neither shall he stand in awe of any man's greatness: for he hath made the small and great, and careth for all alike. 8 But a sore trial shall come upon the mighty. 9 Unto you therefore, O kings, do I speak, that ye may learn wisdom, and not fall away. 10 For they that keep holiness holily shall be judged holy: and they that have learned such things shall find what to answer. 11 Wherefore set your affection upon my words; desire them, and ye shall be instructed. 12 Wisdom is glorious, and never fadeth away: yea, she is easily seen of them that love her, and found of such as seek her. 13 She preventeth them that desire her, in making herself first known unto them. 14 Whoso seeketh her early shall have no great travail: for he shall find her sitting at his doors. 15 To think therefore upon her is perfection of wisdom: and whoso watcheth for her shall quickly be without care. 16 For she goeth about seeking such as are worthy of her, sheweth herself favourably unto them in the ways, and meeteth them in every thought. 17 For the very true beginning of her is the desire of discipline; and the care of discipline is love; 18 And love is the keeping of her laws; and the giving heed unto her laws is the assurance of incorruption; 19 And incorruption maketh us near unto God: 20 Therefore the desire of wisdom bringeth to a kingdom. 21 If your delight be then in thrones and sceptres, O ye kings of the people, honour wisdom, that ye may reign for evermore. 22 As for wisdom, what she is, and how she came up, I will tell you, and will not hide mysteries from you: but will seek her out from the beginning of her nativity, and bring the knowledge of her into light, and will not pass over the truth. 23 Neither will I go with consuming envy; for such a man shall have no fellowship with wisdom. 24 But the multitude of the wise is the welfare of the world: and a wise king is the upholding of the people. 25 Receive therefore instruction through my words, and it shall do you good.

Wis.7 1 I myself also am a mortal man, like to all, and the offspring of him that was first made of the earth, 2 And in my mother's womb was fashioned to be flesh in the time of ten months, being compacted in blood, of the seed of man, and the pleasure that came with sleep. 3 And when I was born, I drew in the common air, and fell upon the earth, which is of like nature, and the first voice which I uttered was crying, as all others do. 4 I was nursed in swaddling clothes, and that with cares. 5 For there is no king that had any other beginning of birth. 6 For all men have one entrance into life, and the like going out. 7 Wherefore I prayed, and understanding was given me: I called upon God, and the spirit of wisdom came to me. 8 I preferred her before sceptres and thrones, and esteemed riches nothing in comparison of her. 9 Neither compared I unto her any precious stone, because all gold in respect of her is as a little sand, and silver shall be counted as clay before her. 10 I loved her above health and beauty, and chose to have her instead of light: for the light that cometh from her never goeth out. 11 All good things together came to me with her, and innumerable riches in her hands. 12 And I rejoiced in them all, because wisdom goeth before them: and I knew not that she was the mother of them. 13 I learned diligently, and do communicate her liberally: I do not hide her riches. 14 For she is a treasure unto men that never faileth: which they that use become the friends of God, being commended for the gifts that come from learning. 15 God hath granted me to speak as I would, and to conceive as is meet for the things that are given me: because it is he that leadeth unto wisdom, and directeth the wise. 16 For in his hand are both we and our words; all wisdom also, and knowledge of workmanship. 17 For he hath given me certain knowledge of the things that are, namely, to know how the world was made, and the operation of the elements: 18 The beginning, ending, and midst of the times: the alterations of the turning of the sun, and the change of seasons: 19 The circuits of years, and the positions of stars: 20 The natures of living creatures, and the furies of wild beasts: the violence of winds, and the reasonings of men: the diversities of plants and the virtues of roots: 21 And all

such things as are either secret or manifest, them I know. 22 For wisdom, which is the worker of all things, taught me: for in her is an understanding spirit holy, one only, manifold, subtil, lively, clear, undefiled, plain, not subject to hurt, loving the thing that is good quick, which cannot be letted, ready to do good, 23 Kind to man, steadfast, sure, free from care, having all power, overseeing all things, and going through all understanding, pure, and most subtil, spirits. 24 For wisdom is more moving than any motion: she passeth and goeth through all things by reason of her pureness. 25 For she is the breath of the power of God, and a pure influence flowing from the glory of the Almighty: therefore can no defiled thing fall into her. 26 For she is the brightness of the everlasting light, the unspotted mirror of the power of God, and the image of his goodness. 27 And being but one, she can do all things: and remaining in herself, she maketh all things new: and in all ages entering into holy souls, she maketh them friends of God, and prophets. 28 For God loveth none but him that dwelleth with wisdom. 29 For she is more beautiful than the sun, and above all the order of stars: being compared with the light, she is found before it. 30 For after this cometh night: but vice shall not prevail against wisdom.

Wis.8 1 *Wisdom* reacheth from one end to another mightily: and sweetly doth she order all things. 2 I loved her, and sought her out from my youth, I desired to make her my spouse, and I was a lover of her beauty. 3 In that she is conversant with God, she magnifieth her nobility: yea, the Lord of all things himself loved her. 4 For she is privy to the mysteries of the knowledge of God, and a lover of his works. 5 If riches be a possession to be desired in this life; what is richer than wisdom, that worketh all things? 6 And if prudence work; who of all that are is a more cunning workman than she? 7 And if a man love righteousness her labours are virtues: for she teacheth temperance and prudence, justice and fortitude: which are such things, as men can have nothing more profitable in their life. 8 If a man desire much experience, she knoweth things of old, and conjectureth aright what is to come: she knoweth the subtilties of speeches, and can expound dark sentences: she foreseeth signs and wonders, and the events of seasons and times. 9 Therefore I purposed to take her to me to live with me, knowing that she would be a counsellor of good things, and a comfort in cares and grief. 10 For her sake I shall have estimation among the multitude, and honour with the elders, though I be young. 11 I shall be found of a quick conceit in judgment, and shall be admired in the sight of great men. 12 When I hold my tongue, they shall bide my leisure, and when I speak, they shall give good ear unto me: if I talk much, they shall lay their hands upon their mouth. 13 Moreover by the means of her I shall obtain immortality, and leave behind me an everlasting memorial to them that come after me. 14 I shall set the people in order, and the nations shall be subject unto me. 15 Horrible tyrants shall be afraid, when they do but hear of me; I shall be found good among the multitude, and valiant in war. 16 After I am come into mine house, I will repose myself with her: for her conversation hath no bitterness; and to live with her hath no sorrow, but mirth and joy. 17 Now when I considered these things in myself, and pondered them in my heart, how that to be allied unto wisdom is immortality; 18 And great pleasure it is to have her friendship; and in the works of her hands are infinite riches; and in the exercise of conference with her, prudence; and in talking with her, a good report; I went about seeking how to take her to me. 19 For I was a witty child, and had a good spirit. 20 Yea rather, being good, I came into a body undefiled. 21 Nevertheless, when I perceived that I could not otherwise obtain her, except God gave her me; and that was a point of wisdom also to know whose gift she was; I prayed unto the Lord, and besought him, and with my whole heart I said,

Wis.9 1 O God of my fathers, and Lord of mercy, who hast made all things with thy word, 2 And ordained man through thy wisdom, that he should have dominion over the creatures which thou hast made, 3 And order the world according to equity and righteousness, and execute judgment with an upright heart: 4 Give me wisdom, that sitteth by thy throne; and reject me not from among thy children: 5 For I thy servant and son of thine handmaid am a feeble person, and of a short time, and too young for the understanding of judgment and laws. 6 For though a man be never so perfect among the children of men, yet if thy wisdom be not with him, he shall be nothing regarded. 7 Thou hast chosen me to be a king of thy people, and a judge of thy sons and daughters: 8 Thou hast commanded me to build a temple upon thy holy mount, and an altar in the city wherein thou dwellest, a resemblance of the holy tabernacle, which thou hast prepared from the beginning. 9 And wisdom was with thee: which knoweth thy works, and was present when thou madest the world, and knew what was acceptable in thy sight, and right in thy commandments. 10 O send her out of thy holy heavens, and from the throne of thy glory, that being present she may labour with me, that I may know what is pleasing unto thee. 11 For she knoweth and understandeth all things, and she shall lead me soberly in my doings, and preserve me in her power. 12 So shall my works be acceptable, and then shall I judge thy people righteously, and be worthy to sit in my father's seat. 13 For what man is he that can know the counsel of God? or who can think what the will of the Lord is? 14 For the thoughts of mortal men are miserable, and our devices are but uncertain. 15 For the corruptible body presseth down the soul, and the earthy tabernacle weigheth down the mind that museth upon many things. 16 And hardly do we guess aright at things that are upon earth, and with labour do we find the things that are before us: but the things that are in heaven who hath searched out? 17 And thy counsel who hath known, except thou give wisdom, and send thy Holy Spirit from above? 18 For so the ways of them which lived on the earth were reformed, and men were taught the things that are pleasing unto thee, and were saved through wisdom.

Wis.10 1 She preserved the first formed father of the world, that was created alone, and brought him out of his fall, 2 And gave him power to rule all things. 3 But when the unrighteous went away from her in his anger, he perished also in the fury wherewith he murdered his brother. 4 For whose cause the earth being drowned with the flood, wisdom again preserved it, and directed the course of the righteous in a piece of wood of small value. 5 Moreover, the nations in their wicked conspiracy being confounded, she found out the righteous, and preserved him blameless unto God, and kept him strong against his tender compassion toward his son. 6 When the ungodly perished, she delivered the righteous man, who fled from the fire which fell down upon the five cities. 7 Of whose wickedness even to this day the waste land that smoketh is a testimony, and plants bearing fruit that never come to ripeness: and a standing pillar of salt is a monument of an unbelieving soul. 8 For regarding not wisdom, they gat not only this hurt, that they knew not the things which were good; but also left behind them to the world a memorial of their foolishness: so that in the things wherein they offended they could not so much as be hid. 9 Rut wisdom delivered from pain those that attended upon her. 10 When the righteous fled from his brother's wrath she guided him in right paths, shewed him the kingdom of God, and gave him knowledge of holy things, made him rich in his travels, and multiplied the fruit of his labours. 11 In the covetousness of such as oppressed him she stood by him, and made him rich. 12 She defended him from his enemies, and kept him safe from those that lay in wait, and in a sore conflict she gave him the victory; that he might know that goodness is stronger than all. 13 When the righteous was sold, she forsook him not, but delivered him from sin: she went down with him into the pit, 14 And left him not in bonds, till she brought him the sceptre of the kingdom, and power against those that oppressed him: as for them that had accused him, she shewed them to be liars, and gave him perpetual glory. 15 She delivered the righteous people and blameless seed from the nation that oppressed them. 16 She entered into the soul of the servant of the Lord, and withstood dreadful kings in wonders and signs; 17 Rendered to the righteous a reward of their labours, guided them in a marvellous way, and was unto them for a cover by day, and a light of stars in the night season; 18 Brought them through the Red sea, and led them through much water: 19 But she drowned their enemies, and cast them up out of the bottom of the deep. 20 Therefore the righteous spoiled the ungodly, and praised thy holy name, O Lord, and magnified with one accord thine hand, that fought for them. 21 For wisdom opened the mouth of the dumb, and made the tongues of them that cannot speak eloquent.

Wis.11 1 She prospered their works in the hand of the holy prophet. 2 They went through the wilderness that was not inhabited, and pitched tents in places where there lay no way. 3 They stood against their enemies, and were avenged of their adversaries. 4 When they were thirsty, they called upon thee, and water was given them out of the flinty rock, and their thirst was quenched out of the hard stone. 5 For by what things their enemies were punished, by the same they in their need were benefited. 6 For instead of a fountain of a perpetual running river troubled with foul blood, 7 For a manifest reproof of that commandment, whereby the infants were slain, thou gavest unto them abundance of water by a means which they hoped not for: 8 Declaring by that thirst then how thou hadst punished their adversaries. 9 For when they were tried albeit but in mercy chastised, they knew how the ungodly were judged in wrath and tormented, thirsting in another manner than the just. 10 For these thou didst admonish and try, as a father: but the other, as a severe king, thou didst condemn and punish. 11 Whether they were absent or present, they were vexed alike. 12 For a double grief came upon them, and a groaning for the remembrance of things past. 13 For when they heard by their own punishments the other to be benefited, they had some feeling of the Lord. 14 For whom they respected with scorn, when he was long before thrown out at the casting forth of the infants, him in the end, when they saw what came to pass, they admired. 15 But for the foolish devices of their wickedness, wherewith being deceived they worshipped serpents void of reason, and vile beasts, thou didst send a multitude of unreasonable beasts upon them for vengeance; 16 That they might know, that wherewithal a man sinneth, by the same also shall he be punished. 17 For thy Almighty hand, that made the world of matter without form, wanted not means to send among them a multitude of bears or fierce lions, 18 Or unknown wild beasts, full of rage, newly created, breathing out either a fiery vapour, or filthy scents of scattered smoke, or shooting horrible sparkles out of their eyes: 19 Whereof not only the harm might dispatch them at once, but also the terrible sight utterly destroy them. 20 Yea, and without these might they have fallen down with one blast, being persecuted of vengeance, and scattered abroad through the breath of thy power: but thou hast ordered all things in measure and number and weight. 21 For thou canst shew thy great strength at all times when thou wilt; and who may withstand the power of thine arm? 22 For the whole world before thee is as a little grain of the balance, yea, as a drop of the morning dew that falleth down upon the earth. 23 But thou hast mercy upon all; for thou canst do all things, and winkest at the sins of men, because they should amend. 24 For thou lovest all the things that are, and abhorrest nothing which thou hast made: for never wouldest thou have made any thing, if thou hadst hated it. 25 And how could any thing have endured, if it had not been thy will? or been preserved, if not called by thee? 26 But thou sparest all: for they are thine, O Lord, thou lover of souls.

Wis.12 1 For thine incorruptible Spirit is in all things. 2 Therefore chastenest thou them by little and little that offend, and warnest them by putting them in remembrance wherein they have offended, that leaving their wickedness they may believe on thee, O Lord. 3 For it was thy will to destroy by the hands of our fathers both those old inhabitants of thy holy land, 4 Whom thou hatedst for doing most odious works of witchcrafts, and wicked sacrifices; 5 And also those merciless murderers of children, and devourers of man's flesh, and the feasts of blood, 6 With their priests out of the midst of their idolatrous crew, and the parents, that killed with their own hands souls destitute of help: 7 That the land, which thou esteemedst above all other, might receive a worthy colony of God's children. 8 Nevertheless even those thou sparedst as men, and didst send wasps, forerunners of thine host, to destroy them by little and little. 9 Not that thou wast unable to bring the ungodly under the hand of the righteous in battle, or to destroy them at once with cruel beasts, or with one rough word: 10 But executing thy judgments upon them by little and little, thou gavest them place of repentance, not being ignorant that they were a naughty generation, and that their malice was bred in them, and that their cogitation would never be changed. 11 For it was a cursed seed from the beginning; neither didst thou for fear of any man give them pardon for those things wherein they sinned. 12 For who shall say, What hast thou done? or who shall withstand thy judgment? or who shall accuse thee for the nations that perish, whom thou made? or who shall come to stand against thee, to be revenged for the unrighteous men? 13 For neither is there any God but thou that careth for all, to whom thou mightest shew that thy judgment is not unright. 14 Neither shall king or tyrant be able to set his face against thee for any whom thou hast punished. 15 Forsomuch then as thou art righteous thyself, thou orderest all things righteously: thinking it not agreeable with thy power to condemn him that hath not deserved to be punished. 16 For thy power is the beginning of righteousness, and because thou art the Lord of all, it maketh thee to be gracious unto all. 17 For when men will not believe that thou art of a full power, thou shewest thy strength, and among them that know it thou makest their boldness manifest. 18 But thou, mastering thy power, judgest with equity, and orderest us with great favour: for thou mayest use power when thou wilt. 19 But by such works hast thou taught thy people that the just man should be merciful, and hast made thy children to be of a good hope that thou givest repentance for sins. 20 For if thou didst punish the enemies of thy children, and the condemned to death, with such deliberation, giving them time and place, whereby they might be delivered from their malice: 21 With how great circumspection didst thou judge thine own sons, unto whose fathers thou hast sworn, and made covenants of good promises? 22 Therefore, whereas thou dost chasten us, thou scourgest our enemies a thousand times more, to the intent that, when we judge, we should carefully think of thy goodness, and when we ourselves are judged, we should look for mercy. 23 Wherefore, whereas men have lived dissolutely and unrighteously, thou hast tormented them with their own abominations. 24 For they went astray very far in the ways of error, and held them for gods, which even among the beasts of their enemies were despised, being deceived, as children of no understanding. 25 Therefore unto them, as to children without the use of reason, thou didst send a judgment to mock them. 26 But they that would not be reformed by that correction, wherein he dallied with them, shall feel a judgment worthy of God. 27 For, look, for what things they grudged, when they were punished, that is, for them whom they thought to be gods; *now* being punished in them, when they saw it, they acknowledged him to be the true God, whom before they denied to know: and therefore came extreme damnation upon them.

Wis.13 1 Surely vain are all men by nature, who are ignorant of God, and could not out of the good things that are seen know him that is: neither by considering the works did they acknowledge the workmaster; 2 But deemed either fire, or wind, or the swift air, or the circle of the stars, or the violent water, or the lights of heaven, to be the gods which govern the world. 3 With whose beauty if they being delighted took them to be gods; let them know how much better the Lord of them is: for the first author of beauty hath created them. 4 But if they were astonished at their power and virtue, let them understand by them, how much mightier he is that made them. 5 For by the greatness and beauty of the creatures proportionably the maker of them is seen. 6 But yet for this they are the less to be blamed: for they peradventure err, seeking God, and desirous to find him. 7 For being conversant in his works they search him diligently, and believe their sight: because the things are beautiful that are seen. 8 Howbeit neither are they to be pardoned. 9 For if they were able to know so much, that they could aim at the world; how did they not sooner find out the Lord thereof? 10 But miserable are they, and in dead things is their hope, who call them gods, which are the works of men's hands, gold and silver, to shew art in, and resemblances of beasts, or a stone good for nothing, the work of an ancient hand. 11 Now a carpenter that felleth timber, after he hath sawn down a tree meet for the purpose, and taken off all the bark skilfully round about, and hath wrought it handsomely, and made a vessel thereof fit for the service of man's life; 12 And after spending the refuse of his work to dress his meat, hath filled himself; 13 And taking the very refuse among those which served to no use, being a crooked piece of wood, and full of knots, hath carved it diligently, when he had nothing else to do, and formed it by the skill of his understanding, and fashioned it to the image of a man; 14 Or made it like some vile beast, laying it over with vermilion, and with paint colouring it red, and covering every spot therein; 15 And when he had made a convenient room for it, set it in a wall, and made it fast with iron: 16 For he provided for it that it might not fall, knowing that it was unable to help itself; for it is an image, and hath need of help: 17 Then maketh he prayer for his goods, for his wife and children, and is not ashamed to speak to that which hath no life. 18 For health he calleth upon that which is weak: for life prayeth to that which is dead; for aid humbly beseecheth that which hath least means to help: and for a good journey he asketh of that which cannot set a foot forward: 19 And for gaining and getting, and for good success of his hands, asketh ability to do of him, that is most unable to do any thing.

Wis.14 1 Again, one preparing himself to sail, and about to pass through the raging waves, calleth upon a piece of wood more rotten than the vessel that carrieth him. 2 For verily desire of gain devised that, and the workman built it by his skill. 3 But thy providence, O Father, governeth it: for thou hast made a way in the sea, and a safe path in the waves; 4 Shewing that thou canst save from all danger: yea, though a man went to sea without art. 5 Nevertheless thou wouldest not that the works of thy wisdom should be idle, and therefore do men commit their lives to a small piece of wood, and passing the rough sea in a weak vessel are saved. 6 For in the old time also, when the proud giants perished, the hope of the world governed by thy hand escaped in a weak vessel, and left to all ages a seed of generation. 7 For blessed is the wood whereby righteousness cometh. 8 But that which is made with hands is cursed, as well it, as he that made it: he, because he made it; and it, because, being corruptible, it was called god. 9 For the ungodly and his ungodliness are both alike hateful unto God. 10 For that which is made shall be punished together with him that made it. 11 Therefore even upon the idols of the Gentiles shall there be a visitation: because in the creature of God they are become an abomination, and stumblingblocks to the souls of men, and a snare to the feet of the unwise. 12 For the devising of idols was the beginning of spiritual fornication, and the invention of them the corruption of life. 13 For neither were they from the beginning, neither shall they be for ever. 14 For by the vain glory of men they entered into the world, and therefore shall they come shortly to an end. 15 For a father afflicted with untimely mourning, when he hath made an image of his child soon taken away, now honoured him as a god, which was then a dead man, and delivered to those that were under him ceremonies and sacrifices. 16 Thus in process of time an ungodly custom grown strong was kept as a law, and graven images were worshipped by the commandments of kings. 17 Whom men could not honour in presence, because they dwelt far off, they took the counterfeit of his visage from far, and made an express image of a king whom they honoured, to the end that by this their forwardness they might flatter him that was absent, as if he were present. 18 Also the singular diligence of the artificer did help to set forward the ignorant to more superstition. 19 For he, peradventure willing to please one in authority, forced all his skill to make the resemblance of the best fashion. 20 And so the multitude, allured by the grace of the work, took him now for a god, which a little before was but honoured. 21 And this was an occasion to deceive the world: for men, serving either calamity or tyranny, did ascribe unto stones and stocks the incommunicable name. 22 Moreover this was not enough for them, that they erred in the knowledge of God; but whereas they lived in the great war of ignorance, those so great plagues called they peace. 23 For whilst they slew their children in sacrifices, or used secret ceremonies, or made revellings of strange rites; 24 They kept neither lives nor marriages any longer undefiled: but either one slew another traitorously, or grieved him by adultery. 25 So that there reigned in all men without exception blood, manslaughter, theft, and dissimulation, corruption, unfaithfulness, tumults, perjury, 26 Disquieting of good men, forgetfulness of good turns, defiling of souls, changing of kind, disorder in marriages, adultery, and shameless uncleanness. 27 For the worshipping of idols not to be named is the beginning, the cause, and the end, of all evil. 28 For either they are mad when they be merry, or prophesy lies, or live unjustly, or else lightly forswear themselves. 29 For insomuch as their trust is in idols, which have no life; though they swear falsely, yet they look not to be hurt. 30 Howbeit for both causes shall they be justly punished: both because they thought not well of God, giving heed unto idols, and also unjustly swore in deceit, despising holiness. 31 For it is not the power of them by whom they swear: but it is the just vengeance of sinners, that punisheth always the offence of the ungodly.

Wis.15 1 But thou, O God, art gracious and true, longsuffering, and in mercy ordering all things, 2 For if we sin, we are thine, knowing thy power: but we will not sin, knowing that we are counted thine. 3 For to know thee is perfect righteousness: yea, to know thy power is the root of immortality. 4 For neither did the mischievous invention of men deceive us, nor an image spotted with divers colours, the painter's fruitless labour; 5 The sight whereof enticeth fools to lust after it, and so they desire the form of a dead image, that hath no breath. 6 Both they that make them, they that desire them, and they that worship them, are lovers of evil things, and are worthy to have such things to trust upon. 7 For the potter, tempering soft earth, fashioneth every vessel with much labour for our service: yea, of the same clay he maketh both the vessels that serve for clean uses, and likewise also all such as serve to the contrary: but what is the use of either sort, the potter himself is the judge. 8 And employing his labours lewdly, he maketh a vain god of the same clay, even he which a little before was made of earth himself, and within a little while after returneth to the same, out when his life which was lent him shall be demanded. 9 Notwithstanding his care is, not that he shall have much labour, nor that his life is short: but striveth to excel goldsmiths and silversmiths, and endeavoureth to do like the workers in brass, and counteth it his glory to make counterfeit things. 10 His heart is ashes, his hope is more vile than earth, and his life of less value than clay: 11 Forasmuch as he knew not his Maker, and him that inspired into him an active soul, and breathed in a living spirit. 12 But they counted our life a pastime, and our time here a market for gain: for, say they, we must be getting every way, though it be by evil means. 13 For this man, that of earthly matter maketh brittle vessels and graven images, knoweth himself to offend above all others. 14 And all the enemies of thy people, that hold them in subjection, are most foolish, and are more miserable than very babes. 15 For they counted all the idols of the heathen to be gods: which neither have the use of eyes to see, nor noses to draw breath, nor ears to hear, nor fingers of hands to handle; and as for their feet, they are slow to go. 16 For man made them, and he that borrowed his own spirit fashioned them: but no man can make a god like unto himself. 17 For being mortal, he worketh a dead thing with wicked hands: for he himself is better than the things which he worshippeth: whereas he lived once, but they never. 18 Yea, they worshipped those beasts also that are most hateful: for being compared together, some are worse than others. 19 Neither are they beautiful, so much as to be desired in respect of beasts: but they went without the praise of God and his blessing.

Wis.16 1 Therefore by the like were they punished worthily, and by the multitude of beasts tormented. 2 Instead of which punishment, dealing graciously with thine own people, thou preparedst for them meat of a strange taste, even quails to stir up their appetite: 3 To the end that they, desiring food, might for the ugly sight of the beasts sent among them lothe even that, which they must needs desire; but these, suffering penury for a short space, might be made partakers of a strange taste. 4 For it was requisite, that upon them exercising tyranny should come penury, which they could not avoid: but to these it should only be shewed how their enemies were tormented. 5 For when the horrible fierceness of beasts came upon these, and they perished with the stings of crooked serpents, thy wrath endured not for ever: 6 But they were troubled for a small season, that they might be admonished, having a sign of salvation, to put them in remembrance of the commandment of thy law. 7 For he that turned himself toward it was not saved by the thing that he saw, but by thee, that art the Saviour of all. 8 And in this thou madest thine enemies confess, that it is thou who deliverest from all evil: 9 For them the bitings of grasshoppers and flies killed, neither was there found any remedy for their life: for they were worthy to be punished by such. 10 But thy sons not the very teeth of venomous dragons overcame: for thy mercy was ever by them, and healed them. 11 For they were pricked, that they should remember thy words; and were quickly saved, that not falling into deep forgetfulness, they might be continually mindful of thy goodness. 12 For it was neither herb, nor mollifying plaister, that restored them to health: but thy word, O Lord, which healeth all things. 13 For thou hast power of life and death: thou leadest to the gates of hell, and bringest up again. 14 A man indeed killeth through his malice: and the spirit, when it is gone forth, returneth not; neither the soul received up cometh again. 15 But it is not possible to escape thine hand. 16 For the ungodly, that denied to know thee, were scourged by the strength of thine arm: with strange rains, hails, and showers, were they persecuted, that they could not avoid, and through fire were they consumed. 17 For, which is most to be wondered at, the fire had more force in the water, that quencheth all things: for the world fighteth for the righteous. 18 For sometime the flame was mitigated, that it might not burn up the beasts that were sent against the ungodly; but themselves might see and perceive that they were persecuted with the judgment of God. 19 And at another time it burneth even in the midst of water above the power of fire, that it might destroy the fruits of an unjust land. 20 Instead whereof thou feddest thine own people with angels' food, and didst send them from heaven bread prepared without their labour, able to content every man's delight, and agreeing to every taste. 21 For thy sustenance declared thy sweetness unto thy children, and serving to the appetite of the eater, tempered itself to every man's liking. 22 But snow and ice endured the fire, and melted not, that they might know that fire burning in the hail, and sparkling in the rain, did destroy the fruits of the enemies. 23 But this again did even forget his own strength, that the righteous might be nourished. 24 For the creature that serveth thee, who art the Maker increaseth his strength against the unrighteous for their punishment, and abateth his strength for the benefit of such as put their trust in thee. 25 Therefore even then was it altered into all fashions, and was obedient to thy grace, that nourisheth all things, according to the desire of them that had need: 26 That thy children, O Lord, whom thou lovest, might know, that it is not the growing of fruits that nourisheth man: but that it is thy word, which preserveth them that put their trust in thee. 27 For that which was not destroyed of the fire, being warmed with a little sunbeam, soon melted away: 28 That it might be known, that we must prevent the sun to give thee thanks, and at the dayspring pray unto thee. 29 For the hope of the unthankful shall melt away as the winter's hoar frost, and shall run away as unprofitable water.

Wis.17 1 For great are thy judgments, and cannot be expressed: therefore unnurtured souls have erred. 2 For when unrighteous men thought to oppress the holy nation; they being shut up in their houses, the prisoners of darkness, and fettered with the bonds of a long night, lay *there* exiled from the eternal providence. 3 For while they supposed to lie hid in their secret sins, they were scattered under a dark veil of forgetfulness, being horribly astonished, and troubled with *strange* apparitions. 4 For neither might the corner that held them keep them from fear: but noises *as of waters* falling down sounded about them, and sad visions appeared unto them with heavy countenances. 5 No power of the fire might give them light: neither could the bright flames of the stars endure to lighten that horrible night. 6 Only there appeared unto them a fire kindled of itself, very dreadful: for being much terrified, they thought the things which they saw to be worse than the sight they saw not. 7 As for the illusions of art magick, they were put down, and their vaunting in wisdom was reproved with disgrace. 8 For they, that promised to drive away terrors and troubles from a sick soul, were sick themselves of fear, worthy to be laughed at. 9 For though no terrible thing did fear them; yet being scared with beasts that passed by, and hissing of serpents, 10 They died for fear, denying that they saw the air, which could of no side be avoided. 11 For wickedness, condemned by her own witness, is very timorous, and being pressed with conscience, always forecasteth grievous things. 12 For fear is nothing else but a betraying of the succours which reason offereth. 13 And the expectation from within, being less, counteth the ignorance more than the cause which bringeth the torment. 14 But they sleeping the same sleep that night, which was indeed intolerable, and which came upon them out of the bottoms of inevitable hell, 15 Were partly vexed with monstrous apparitions, and partly fainted, their heart failing them: for a sudden fear, and not looked for, came upon them. 16 So then whosoever there fell down was straitly kept, shut up in a prison without iron bars, 17 For whether he were husbandman, or shepherd, or a labourer in the field, he was overtaken, and endured that necessity, which could not be avoided: for they were all bound with one chain of darkness. 18 Whether it were a whistling wind, or a melodious noise of birds among the spreading branches, or a pleasing fall of water running violently, 19 Or a terrible sound of stones cast down, or a running that could not be seen of skipping beasts, or a roaring voice of most savage wild beasts, or a rebounding echo from the hollow mountains; these things made them to swoon for fear. 20 For the whole world shined with clear light, and none were hindered in their labour: 21 Over them only was spread an heavy night, an image of that darkness which should afterward receive them: but yet were they unto themselves more grievous than the darkness.

Wis.18 1 Nevertheless thy saints had a very great light, whose voice they hearing, and not seeing their shape, because they also had not suffered the same things, they counted them happy. 2 But for that they did not hurt them now, of whom they had been wronged before, they thanked them, and besought them pardon for that they had been enemies. 3 Instead whereof thou gavest them a burning pillar of fire, both to be a guide of the unknown journey, and an harmless sun to entertain them honourably. 4 For they were worthy to be deprived of light and imprisoned in darkness, who had kept thy sons shut up, by whom the uncorrupt light of the law was to be given unto the world. 5 And when they had determined to slay the babes of the saints, one child being cast forth, and saved, to reprove them, thou tookest away the multitude of their children, and destroyedst them altogether in a mighty water. 6 Of that night were our fathers certified afore, that assuredly knowing unto what oaths they had given credence, they might afterwards be of good cheer. 7 So of thy people was accepted both the salvation of the righteous, and destruction of the enemies. 8 For wherewith thou didst punish our adversaries, by the same thou didst glorify us, whom thou hadst called. 9 For the righteous children of good men did sacrifice secretly, and with one consent made a holy law, that the saints should be like partakers of the same good and evil, the fathers now singing out the songs of praise. 10 But on the other side there sounded an ill according cry of the enemies, and a lamentable noise was carried abroad for children that were bewailed. 11 The master and the servant were punished after one manner; and like as the king, so suffered the common person. 12 So they all together had innumerable dead with one kind of death; neither were the living sufficient to bury them: for in one moment the noblest offspring of them was destroyed. 13 For whereas they would not believe any thing by reason of the enchantments; upon the destruction of the firstborn, they acknowledged this people to be the sons of God. 14 For while all things were in quiet silence, and that night was in the midst of her swift course, 15 Thine Almighty word leaped down from heaven out of thy royal throne, as a fierce man of war into the midst of a land of destruction, 16 And brought thine unfeigned commandment as a sharp sword, and standing up filled all things with death; and it touched the heaven, but it stood upon the earth. 17 Then suddenly visions of horrible dreams troubled them sore, and terrors came upon them unlooked for. 18 And one thrown here, and another there, half dead, shewed the cause of his death. 19 For the dreams that troubled them did foreshew this, lest they should perish, and not know why they were afflicted. 20 Yea, the tasting of death touched the righteous also, and there was a destruction of the multitude in the wilderness: but the wrath endured not long. 21 For then the blameless man made haste, and stood forth to defend them; and bringing the shield of his proper ministry, even prayer, and the propitiation of incense, set himself against the wrath, and so brought the calamity to an end, declaring that he was thy servant. 22 So he overcame the destroyer, not with strength of body, nor force of arms, but with a word subdued him that punished, alleging the oaths and covenants made with the fathers. 23 For when the dead were now fallen down by heaps one upon another, standing between, he stayed the wrath, and parted the way to the living. 24 For in the long garment was the whole world, and in the four rows of the stones was the glory of the fathers graven, and thy Majesty upon the diadem of his head. 25 Unto these the destroyer gave place, and was afraid of them: for it was enough that they only tasted of the wrath.

Wis.19 1 As for the ungodly, wrath came upon them without mercy unto the end: for he knew before what they would do; 2 How that having given them leave to depart, and sent them hastily away, they would repent and pursue them. 3 For whilst they were yet mourning and making lamentation at the graves of the dead, they added another foolish device, and pursued them as fugitives, whom they had intreated to be gone. 4 For the destiny, whereof they were worthy, drew them unto this end, and made them forget the things that had already happened, that they might fulfil the punishment which was wanting to their torments: 5 And that thy people might pass a wonderful way: but they might find a strange death. 6 For the whole creature in his proper kind was fashioned again anew, serving the peculiar commandments that were given unto them, that thy children might be kept without hurt: 7 As namely, a cloud shadowing the camp; and where water stood before, dry land appeared; and out of the Red sea a way without impediment; and out of the violent stream a green field: 8 Where through all the people went that were defended with thy hand, seeing thy marvellous strange wonders. 9 For they went at large like horses, and leaped like lambs, praising thee, O Lord, who hadst delivered them. 10 For they were yet mindful of the things that were done while they sojourned in the strange land, how the ground brought forth flies instead of cattle, and how the river cast up a multitude of frogs instead of fishes. 11 But afterwards they saw a new generation of fowls, when, being led with their appetite, they asked delicate meats. 12 For quails came up unto them from the sea for their contentment. 13 And punishments came upon the sinners not without former signs by the force of thunders: for they suffered justly according to their own wickedness, insomuch as they used a more hard and hateful behaviour toward strangers. 14 For the Sodomites did not receive those, whom they knew not when they came: but these brought friends into bondage, that had well deserved of them. 15 And not only so, but peradventure some respect shall be had of those, because they used strangers not friendly: 16 But these very grievously afflicted them, whom they had received with feastings, and were already made partakers of the same laws with them. 17 Therefore even with blindness were these stricken, as those were at the doors of the righteous man: when, being compassed about with horrible great darkness, every one sought the passage of his own doors. 18 For the elements were changed in themselves by a kind of harmony, like as in a psaltery notes change the name of the tune, and yet are always sounds; which may well be perceived by the sight of the things that have been done. 19 For earthly things were turned into watery, and the things, that before swam in the water, now went upon the ground. 20 The fire had power in the water, forgetting his own virtue: and the water forgat his own quenching nature. 21 On the other side, the flames wasted not the flesh of the corruptible living things, though they walked therein; neither melted they the icy kind of heavenly meat that was of nature apt to melt. 22 For in all things, O Lord, thou didst magnify thy people, and glorify them, neither didst thou lightly regard them: but didst assist them in every time and place.

SIRACH (ECCLESIASTICUS)

The Prologue to the Wisdom of Jesus the Son of Sirach.
Whereas many and great things have been delivered unto us by the law and the prophets, and by others that have followed their steps, for the which things Israel ought to be commended for learning and wisdom; and whereof not only the readers must needs become skilful themselves, but also they that desire to learn be able to profit them which are without, both by speaking and writing: my grandfather Jesus, when he had much given himself to the reading of the law, and the prophets, and other books of our fathers, and had gotten therein good judgment, was drawn on also himself to write something pertaining to learning and wisdom; to the intent that those which are desirous to learn, and are addicted to these things, might profit much more in living according to the law. Wherefore let me intreat you to read it with favour and attention, and to pardon us, wherein we may seem to come short of some words, which we have laboured to interpret. For the same things uttered in Hebrew, and translated into another tongue, have not the same force in them: and not only these things, but the law itself, and the prophets, and the rest of the books, have no small difference, when they are spoken in their own language. For in the eight and thirtieth year coming into Egypt, when Euergetes was king, and continuing there some time, I found a book of no small learning: therefore I thought it most necessary for me to bestow some diligence and travail to interpret it; using great watchfulness and skill in that space to bring the book to an end, and set it forth for them also, which in a strange country are willing to learn, being prepared before in manners to live after the law.

Sir.1 1 All wisdom *cometh* from the Lord, and is with him for ever. 2 Who can number the sand of the sea, and the drops of rain, and the days of eternity? 3 Who can find out the height of heaven, and the breadth of the earth, and the deep, and wisdom? 4 Wisdom hath been created before all things, and the understanding of prudence from everlasting. 5 The word of God most high is the fountain of wisdom; and her ways are everlasting commandments. 6 To whom hath the root of wisdom been revealed? or who hath known her wise counsels? 7 *Unto whom hath the knowledge of wisdom been made manifest? and who hath understood her great experience?* 8 There is one wise and greatly to be feared, the Lord sitting upon his throne. 9 He created her, and saw her, and numbered her, and poured her out upon all his works. 10 She is with all flesh according to his gift, and he hath given her to them that love him. 11 The fear of the Lord is honour, and glory, and gladness, and a crown of rejoicing. 12 The fear of the Lord maketh a merry heart, and giveth joy, and gladness, and a long life. 13 Whoso feareth the Lord, it shall go well with him at the last, and he shall find favour in the day of his death. 14 To fear the Lord is the beginning of wisdom: and it was created with the faithful in the womb. 15 She hath built an everlasting foundation with men, and she shall continue with their seed. 16 To fear the Lord is fulness of wisdom, and filleth men with her fruits. 17 She filleth all their house with things desirable, and the garners with her increase. 18 The fear of the Lord is a crown of wisdom, making peace and perfect health to flourish; both which are the gifts of God: and it enlargeth their rejoicing that love him. 19 Wisdom raineth down skill and knowledge of understanding standing, and exalteth them to honour that hold her fast. 20 The root of wisdom is to fear the Lord, and the branches thereof are long life. 21 The fear of the Lord driveth away sins: and where it is present, it turneth away wrath. 22 A furious man cannot be justified; for the sway of his fury shall be his destruction. 23 A patient man will tear for a time, and afterward joy shall spring up unto him. 24 He will hide his words for a time, and the lips of many shall declare his wisdom. 25 The parables of knowledge are in the treasures of wisdom: but godliness is an abomination to a sinner. 26 If thou desire wisdom, keep the commandments, and the Lord shall give her unto thee. 27 For the fear of the Lord is wisdom and instruction: and faith and meekness are his delight. 28 Distrust not the fear of the Lord when thou art poor: and come not unto him with a double heart. 29 Be not an hypocrite in the sight of men, and take good heed what thou speakest. 30 Exalt not thyself, lest thou fall, and bring dishonour upon thy soul, and so God discover thy secrets, and cast thee down in the midst of the congregation, because thou camest not in truth to the fear of the Lord, but thy heart is full of deceit.

Sir.2 1 My son, if thou come to serve the Lord, prepare thy soul for temptation. 2 Set thy heart aright, and constantly endure, and make not haste in time of trouble. 3 Cleave unto him, and depart not away, that thou mayest be increased at thy last end. 4 Whatsoever is brought upon thee take cheerfully, and be patient when thou art changed to a low estate. 5 For gold is tried in the fire, and acceptable men in the furnace of adversity. 6 Believe in him, and he will help thee; order thy way aright, and trust in him. 7 Ye that fear the Lord, wait for his mercy; and go not aside, lest ye fall. 8 Ye that fear the Lord, believe him; and your reward shall not fail. 9 Ye that fear the Lord, hope for good, and for

everlasting joy and mercy. 10 Look at the generations of old, and see; did ever any trust in the Lord, and was confounded? or did any abide in his fear, and was forsaken? or whom did he ever despise, that called upon him? 11 For the Lord is full of compassion and mercy, longsuffering, and very pitiful, and forgiveth sins, and saveth in time of affliction. 12 Woe be to fearful hearts, and faint hands, and the sinner that goeth two ways! 13 Woe unto him that is fainthearted! for he believeth not; therefore shall he not be defended. 14 Woe unto you that have lost patience! and what will ye do when the Lord shall visit you? 15 They that fear the Lord will not disobey his Word; and they that love him will keep his ways. 16 They that fear the Lord will seek that which is well, pleasing unto him; and they that love him shall be filled with the law. 17 They that fear the Lord will prepare their hearts, and humble their souls in his sight, 18 Saying, We will fall into the hands of the Lord, and not into the hands of men: for as his majesty is, so is his mercy.

Sir.3 1 Hear me your father, O children, and do thereafter, that ye may be safe. 2 For the Lord hath given the father honour over the children, and hath confirmed the authority of the mother over the sons. 3 Whoso honoureth his father maketh an atonement for his sins: 4 And he that honoureth his mother is as one that layeth up treasure. 5 Whoso honoureth his father shall have joy of his own children; and when he maketh his prayer, he shall be heard. 6 He that honoureth his father shall have a long life; and he that is obedient unto the Lord shall be a comfort to his mother. 7 He that feareth the Lord will honour his father, and will do service unto his parents, as to his masters. 8 Honour thy father and mother both in word and deed, that a blessing may come upon thee from them. 9 For the blessing of the father establisheth the houses of children; but the curse of the mother rooteth out foundations. 10 Glory not in the dishonour of thy father; for thy father's dishonour is no glory unto thee. 11 For the glory of a man is from the honour of his father; and a mother in dishonour is a reproach to the children. 12 My son, help thy father in his age, and grieve him not as long as he liveth. 13 And if his understanding fail, have patience with him; and despise him not when thou art in thy full strength. 14 For the relieving of thy father shall not be forgotten: and instead of sins it shall be added to build thee up. 15 In the day of thine affliction it shall be remembered; thy sins also shall melt away, as the ice in the fair warm weather. 16 He that forsaketh his father is as a blasphemer; and he that angereth his mother is cursed: of God. 17 My son, go on with thy business in meekness; so shalt thou be beloved of him that is approved. 18 The greater thou art, the more humble thyself, and thou shalt find favour before the Lord. 19 Many are in high place, and of renown: but mysteries are revealed unto the meek. 20 For the power of the Lord is great, and he is honoured of the lowly. 21 Seek not out things that are too hard for thee, neither search the things that are above thy strength. 22 But what is commanded thee, think thereupon with reverence, for it is not needful for thee to see with thine eyes the things that are in secret. 23 Be not curious in unnecessary matters: for more things are shewed unto thee than men understand. 24 For many are deceived by their own vain opinion; and an evil suspicion hath overthrown their judgment. 25 Without eyes thou shalt want light: profess not the knowledge therefore that thou hast not. 26 A stubborn heart shall fare evil at the last; and he that loveth danger shall perish therein. 27 An obstinate heart shall be laden with sorrows; and the wicked man shall heap sin upon sin. 28 In the punishment of the proud there is no remedy; for the plant of wickedness hath taken root in him. 29 The heart of the prudent will understand a parable; and an attentive ear is the desire of a wise man. 30 Water will quench a flaming fire; and alms maketh an atonement for sins. 31 And he that requiteth good turns is mindful of that which may come hereafter; and when he falleth, he shall find a stay.

Sir.4 1 My son, defraud not the poor of his living, and make not the needy eyes to wait long. 2 Make not an hungry soul sorrowful; neither provoke a man in his distress. 3 Add not more trouble to an heart that is vexed; and defer not to give to him that is in need. 4 Reject not the supplication of the afflicted; neither turn away thy face from a poor man. 5 Turn not away thine eye from the needy, and give him none occasion to curse thee: 6 For if he curse thee in the bitterness of his soul, his prayer shall be heard of him that made him. 7 Get thyself the love of the congregation, and bow thy head to a great man. 8 Let it not grieve thee to bow down thine ear to the poor, and give him a friendly answer with meekness. 9 Deliver him that suffereth wrong from the hand of the oppressor; and be not fainthearted when thou sittest in judgment. 10 Be as a father unto the fatherless, and instead of an husband unto their mother: so shalt thou be as the son of the most High, and he shall love thee more than thy mother doth. 11 Wisdom exalteth her children, and layeth hold of them that seek her. 12 He that loveth her loveth life; and they that seek to her early shall be filled with joy. 13 He that holdeth her fast shall inherit glory; and wheresoever she entereth, the Lord will bless. 14 They that serve her shall minister to the Holy One: and them that love her the Lord doth love. 15 Whoso giveth ear unto her shall judge the nations: and he that attendeth unto her shall dwell securely. 16 If a man commit himself unto her, he shall inherit her; and his generation shall hold her in possession. 17 For at the first she will walk with him by crooked ways, and bring fear and dread upon him, and torment him with her discipline, until she may trust his soul, and try him by her laws. 18 Then will she return the straight way unto him, and comfort him, and shew him her secrets. 19 But if he go wrong, she will forsake him, and give him over to his own ruin. 20 Observe the opportunity, and beware of evil; and be not ashamed when it concerneth thy soul. 21 For there is a shame that bringeth sin; and there is a shame which is glory and grace. 22 Accept no person against thy soul, and let not the reverence of any man cause thee to fall. 23 And refrain not to speak, when there is occasion to do good, and hide not thy wisdom in her beauty. 24 For by speech wisdom shall be known: and learning by the word of the tongue. 25 In no wise speak against the truth; but be abashed of the error of thine ignorance. 26 Be not ashamed to

confess thy sins; and force not the course of the river. 27 Make not thyself an underling to a foolish man; neither accept the person of the mighty. 28 Strive for the truth unto death, and the Lord shall fight for thee. 29 Be not hasty in thy tongue, and in thy deeds slack and remiss. 30 Be not as a lion in thy house, nor frantick among thy servants. 31 Let not thine hand be stretched out to receive, and shut when thou shouldest repay.

Sir.5 1 Set thy heart upon thy goods; and say not, I have enough for my life. 2 Follow not thine own mind and thy strength, to walk in the ways of thy heart: 3 And say not, Who shall control me for my works? for the Lord will surely revenge thy pride. 4 Say not, I have sinned, and what harm hath happened unto me? for the Lord is longsuffering, he will in no wise let thee go. 5 Concerning propitiation, be not without fear to add sin unto sin: 6 And say not His mercy is great; he will be pacified for the multitude of my sins: for mercy and wrath come from him, and his indignation resteth upon sinners. 7 Make no tarrying to turn to the Lord, and put not off from day to day: for suddenly shall the wrath of the Lord come forth, and in thy security thou shalt be destroyed, and perish in the day of vengeance. 8 Set not thine heart upon goods unjustly gotten, for they shall not profit thee in the day of calamity. 9 Winnow not with every wind, and go not into every way: for so doth the sinner that hath a double tongue. 10 Be stedfast in thy understanding; and let thy word be the same. 11 Be swift to hear; and let thy life be sincere; and with patience give answer. 12 If thou hast understanding, answer thy neighbour; if not, lay thy hand upon thy mouth. 13 Honour and shame is in talk: and the tongue of man is his fall. 14 Be not called a whisperer, and lie not in wait with thy tongue: for a foul shame is upon the thief, and an evil condemnation upon the double tongue. 15 Be not ignorant of any thing in a great matter or a small.

Sir.6 1 Instead of a friend become not an enemy; for *thereby* thou shalt inherit an ill name, shame, and reproach: even so shall a sinner that hath a double tongue. 2 Extol not thyself in the counsel of thine own heart; that thy soul be not torn in pieces as a bull *straying alone*. 3 Thou shalt eat up thy leaves, and lose thy fruit, and leave thyself as a dry tree. 4 A wicked soul shall destroy him that hath it, and shall make him to be laughed to scorn of his enemies. 5 Sweet language will multiply friends: and a fairspeaking tongue will increase kind greetings. 6 Be in peace with many: nevertheless have but one counsellor of a thousand. 7 If thou wouldest get a friend, prove him first and be not hasty to credit him. 8 For some man is a friend for his own occasion, and will not abide in the day of thy trouble. 9 And there is a friend, who being turned to enmity, and strife will discover thy reproach. 10 Again, some friend is a companion at the table, and will not continue in the day of thy affliction. 11 But in thy prosperity he will be as thyself, and will be bold over thy servants. 12 If thou be brought low, he will be against thee, and will hide himself from thy face. 13 Separate thyself from thine enemies, and take heed of thy friends. 14 A faithful friend is a strong defence: and he that hath found such an one hath found a treasure. 15 Nothing doth countervail a faithful friend, and his excellency is invaluable. 16 A faithful friend is the medicine of life; and they that fear the Lord shall find him. 17 Whoso feareth the Lord shall direct his friendship aright: for as he is, so shall his neighbour be also. 18 My son, gather instruction from thy youth up: so shalt thou find wisdom till thine old age. 19 Come unto her as one that ploweth and soweth, and wait for her good fruits: for thou shalt not toil much in labouring about her, but thou shalt eat of her fruits right soon. 20 She is very unpleasant to the unlearned: he that is without understanding will not remain with her. 21 She will lie upon him as a mighty stone of trial; and he will cast her from him ere it be long. 22 For wisdom is according to her name, and she is not manifest unto many. 23 Give ear, my son, receive my advice, and refuse not my counsel, 24 And put thy feet into her fetters, and thy neck into her chain. 25 Bow down thy shoulder, and bear her, and be not grieved with her bonds. 26 Come unto her with thy whole heart, and keep her ways with all thy power. 27 Search, and seek, and she shall be made known unto thee: and when thou hast got hold of her, let her not go. 28 For at the last thou shalt find her rest, and that shall be turned to thy joy. 29 Then shall her fetters be a strong defence for thee, and her chains a robe of glory. 30 For there is a golden ornament upon her, and her bands are purple lace. 31 Thou shalt put her on as a robe of honour, and shalt put her about thee as a crown of joy. 32 My son, if thou wilt, thou shalt be taught: and if thou wilt apply thy mind, thou shalt be prudent. 33 If thou love to hear, thou shalt receive understanding: and if thou bow thine ear, thou shalt be wise, 34 Stand in the multitude of the elders; and cleave unto him that is wise. 35 Be willing to hear every godly discourse; and let not the parables of understanding escape thee. 36 And if thou seest a man of understanding, get thee betimes unto him, and let thy foot wear the steps of his door. 37 Let thy mind be upon the ordinances of the Lord and meditate continually in his commandments: he shall establish thine heart, and give thee wisdom at thine owns desire.

Sir.7 1 Do no evil, so shall no harm come unto thee. 2 Depart from the unjust, and iniquity shall turn away from thee. 3 My son, sow not upon the furrows of unrighteousness, and thou shalt not reap them sevenfold. 4 Seek not of the Lord preeminence, neither of the king the seat of honour. 5 justify not thyself before the Lord; and boast not of thy wisdom before the king. 6 Seek not to be judge, being not able to take away iniquity; lest at any time thou fear the person of the mighty, an stumblingblock in the way of thy uprightness. 7 Offend not against the multitude of a city, and then thou shalt not cast thyself down among the people. 8 Bind not one sin upon another; for in one thou shalt not be unpunished. 9 Say not, God will look upon the multitude of my oblations, and when I offer to the most high God, he will accept it. 10 Be not fainthearted when thou makest thy prayer, and neglect not to give alms. 11 Laugh no man to scorn in the bitterness of his soul: for there is one which humbleth and exalteth. 12 Devise not a lie against thy brother; neither do the like to thy friend. 13 Use not to make any manner of lie: for the

custom thereof is not good. 14 Use not many words in a multitude of elders, and make not much babbling when thou prayest. 15 Hate not laborious work, neither husbandry, which the most High hath ordained. 16 Number not thyself among the multitude of sinners, but remember that wrath will not tarry long. 17 Humble thyself greatly: for the vengeance of the ungodly is fire and worms. 18 Change not a friend for any good by no means; neither a faithful brother for the gold of Ophir. 19 Forego not a wise and good woman: for her grace is above gold. 20 Whereas thy servant worketh truly, entreat him not evil. nor the hireling that bestoweth himself wholly for thee. 21 Let thy soul love a good servant, and defraud him not of liberty. 22 Hast thou cattle? have an eye to them: and if they be for thy profit, keep them with thee. 23 Hast thou children? instruct them, and bow down their neck from their youth. 24 Hast thou daughters? have a care of their body, and shew not thyself cheerful toward them. 25 Marry thy daughter, and so shalt thou have performed a weighty matter: but give her to a man of understanding. 26 Hast thou a wife after thy mind? forsake her not: but give not thyself over to a light woman. 27 Honour thy father with thy whole heart, and forget not the sorrows of thy mother. 28 Remember that thou wast begotten of them; and how canst thou recompense them the things that they have done for thee? 29 Fear the Lord with all thy soul, and reverence his priests. 30 Love him that made thee with all thy strength, and forsake not his ministers. 31 Fear the Lord, and honour the priest; and give him his portion, as it is commanded thee; the firstfruits, and the trespass offering, and the gift of the shoulders, and the sacrifice of sanctification, and the firstfruits of the holy things. 32 And stretch thine hand unto the poor, that thy blessing may be perfected. 33 A gift hath grace in the sight of every man living; and for the dead detain it not. 34 Fail not to be with them that weep, and mourn with them that mourn. 35 Be not slow to visit the sick: fir that shall make thee to be beloved. 36 Whatsoever thou takest in hand, remember the end, and thou shalt never do amiss.

Sir.8 1 Strive not with a mighty man' lest thou fall into his hands. 2 Be not at variance with a rich man, lest he overweigh thee: for gold hath destroyed many, and perverted the hearts of kings. 3 Strive not with a man that is full of tongue, and heap not wood upon his fire. 4 Jest not with a rude man, lest thy ancestors be disgraced. 5 Reproach not a man that turneth from sin, but remember that we are all worthy of punishment. 6 Dishonour not a man in his old age: for even some of us wax old. 7 Rejoice not over thy greatest enemy being dead, but remember that we die all. 8 Despise not the discourse of the wise, but acquaint thyself with their proverbs: for of them thou shalt learn instruction, and how to serve great men with ease. 9 Miss not the discourse of the elders: for they also learned of their fathers, and of them thou shalt learn understanding, and to give answer as need requireth. 10 Kindle not the coals of a sinner, lest thou be burnt with the flame of his fire. 11 Rise not up *in anger* at the presence of an injurious person, lest he lie in wait to entrap thee in thy words 12 Lend not unto him that is mightier than thyself; for if thou lendest him, count it but lost. 13 Be not surety above thy power: for if thou be surety, take care to pay it. 14 Go not to law with a judge; for they will judge for him according to his honour. 15 Travel not by the way with a bold fellow, lest he become grievous unto thee: for he will do according to his own will, and thou shalt perish with him through his folly. 16 Strive not with an angry man, and go not with him into a solitary place: for blood is as nothing in his sight, and where there is no help, he will overthrow thee. 17 Consult not with a fool; for he cannot keep counsel. 18 Do no secret thing before a stranger; for thou knowest not what he will bring forth. 19 Open not thine heart to every man, lest he requite thee with a shrewd turn.

Sir.9 1 Be not jealous over the wife of thy bosom, and teach her not an evil lesson against thyself. 2 Give not thy soul unto a woman to set her foot upon thy substance. 3 Meet not with an harlot, lest thou fall into her snares. 4 Use not much the company of a woman that is a singer, lest thou be taken with her attempts. 5 Gaze not on a maid, that thou fall not by those things that are precious in her. 6 Give not thy soul unto harlots, that thou lose not thine inheritance. 7 Look not round about thee in the streets of the city, neither wander thou in the solitary place thereof. 8 Turn away thine eye from a beautiful woman, and look not upon another's beauty; for many have been deceived by the beauty of a woman; for herewith love is kindled as a fire. 9 Sit not at all with another man's wife, nor sit down with her in thine arms, and spend not thy money with her at the wine; lest thine heart incline unto her, and so through thy desire thou fall into destruction. 10 Forsake not an old friend; for the new is not comparable to him: a new friend is as new wine; when it is old, thou shalt drink it with pleasure. 11 Envy not the glory of a sinner: for thou knowest not what shall be his end. 12 Delight not in the thing that the ungodly have pleasure in; but remember they shall not go unpunished unto their grave. 13 Keep thee far from the man that hath power to kill; so shalt thou not doubt the fear of death: and if thou come unto him, make no fault, lest he take away thy life presently: remember that thou goest in the midst of snares, and that thou walkest upon the battlements of the city. 14 As near as thou canst, guess at thy neighbour, and consult with the wise. 15 Let thy talk be with the wise, and all thy communication in the law of the most High. 16 And let just men eat and drink with thee; and let thy glorying be in the fear of the Lord. 17 For the hand of the artificer the work shall be commended: and the wise ruler of the people for his speech. 18 A man of an ill tongue is dangerous in his city; and he that is rash in his talk shall be hated.

Sir.10 1 A wise judge will instruct his people; and the government of a prudent man is well ordered. 2 As the judge of the people is himself, so are his officers; and what manner of man the ruler of the city is, such are all they that dwell therein. 3 An unwise king destroyeth his people; but through the prudence of them which are in authority the city shall be inhabited. 4 The power of the earth is in the hand of the Lord, and in due time he will set over it one that is profitable. 5 In the hand of God is the prosperity of man: and upon the person of the scribe shall he lay his honour. 6 Bear not hatred to thy neighbour for every wrong; and do nothing at all by injurious practices. 7 Pride is hateful before God and man: and by both doth one commit iniquity. 8 Because of unrighteous dealings, injuries, and riches got by deceit, the kingdom is translated from one people to another. 9 Why is earth and ashes proud? There is not a more wicked thing than a covetous man: for such an one setteth his own soul to sale; because while he liveth he casteth away his bowels. 10 The physician cutteth off a long disease; and he that is to day a king to morrow shall die. 11 For when a man is dead, he shall inherit creeping things, beasts, and worms. 12 The beginning of pride is when one departeth from God, and his heart is turned away from his Maker. 13 For pride is the beginning of sin, and he that hath it shall pour out abomination: and therefore the Lord brought upon them strange calamities, and overthrew them utterly. 14 The Lord hath cast down the thrones of proud princes, and set up the meek in their stead. 15 The Lord hath plucked up the roots of the proud nations, and planted the lowly in their place. 16 The Lord overthrew countries of the heathen, and destroyed them to the foundations of the earth. 17 He took some of them away, and destroyed them, and hath made their memorial to cease from the earth. 18 Pride was not made for men, nor furious anger for them that are born of a woman. 19 They that fear the Lord are a sure seed, and they that love him an honourable plant: they that regard not the law are a dishonourable seed; they that transgress the commandments are a deceivable seed. 20 Among brethren he that is chief is honourably; so are they that fear the Lord in his eyes. 21 The fear of the Lord goeth before the obtaining of authority: but roughness and pride is the losing thereof. 22 Whether he be rich, noble, or poor, their glory is the fear of the Lord. 23 It is not meet to despise the poor man that hath understanding; neither is it convenient to magnify a sinful man. 24 Great men, and judges, and potentates, shall be honoured; yet is there none of them greater than he that feareth the Lord. 25 Unto the servant that is wise shall they that are free do service: and he that hath knowledge will not grudge when he is reformed. 26 Be not overwise in doing thy business; and boast not thyself in the time of thy distress. 27 Better is he that laboureth, and aboundeth in all things, than he that boasteth himself, and wanteth bread. 28 My son, glorify thy soul in meekness, and give it honour according to the dignity thereof. 29 Who will justify him that sinneth against his own soul? and who will honour him that dishonoureth his own life? 30 The poor man is honoured for his skill, and the rich man is honoured for his riches. 31 He that is honoured in poverty, how much more in riches? and he that is dishonourable in riches, how much more in poverty?

Sir.11 1 Wisdom lifteth up the head of him that is of low degree, and maketh him to sit among great men. 2 Commend not a man for his beauty; neither abhor a man for his outward appearance. 3 The bee is little among such as fly; but her fruit is the chief of sweet things. 4 Boast not of thy clothing and raiment, and exalt not thyself in the day of honour: for the works of the Lord are wonderful, and his works among men are hidden. 5 Many kings have sat down upon the ground; and one that was never thought of hath worn the crown. 6 Many mighty men have been greatly disgraced; and the honourable delivered into other men's hands. 7 Blame not before thou hast examined the truth: understand first, and then rebuke. 8 Answer not before thou hast heard the cause: neither interrupt men in the midst of their talk. 9 Strive not in a matter that concerneth thee not; and sit not in judgment with sinners. 10 My son, meddle not with many matters: for if thou meddle much, thou shalt not be innocent; and if thou follow after, thou shalt not obtain, neither shalt thou escape by fleeing. 11 There is one that laboureth, and taketh pains, and maketh haste, and is so much the more behind. 12 Again, there is another that is slow, and hath need of help, wanting ability, and full of poverty; yet the eye of the Lord looked upon him for good, and set him up from his low estate, 13 And lifted up his head from misery; so that many that saw from him is peace over all the 14 Prosperity and adversity, life and death, poverty and riches, come of the Lord. 15 Wisdom, knowledge, and understanding of the law, are of the Lord: love, and the way of good works, are from him. 16 Error and darkness had their beginning together with sinners: and evil shall wax old with them that glory therein. 17 The gift of the Lord remaineth with the ungodly, and his favour bringeth prosperity for ever. 18 There is that waxeth rich by his wariness and pinching, and this his the portion of his reward: 19 Whereas he saith, I have found rest, and now will eat continually of my goods; and yet he knoweth not what time shall come upon him, and that he must leave those things to others, and die. 20 Be stedfast in thy covenant, and be conversant therein, and wax old in thy work. 21 Marvel not at the works of sinners; but trust in the Lord, and abide in thy labour: for it is an easy thing in the sight of the Lord on the sudden to make a poor man rich. 22 The blessing of the Lord is in the reward of the godly, and suddenly he maketh his blessing flourish. 23 Say not, What profit is there of my service? and what good things shall I have hereafter? 24 Again, say not, I have enough, and possess many things, and what evil shall I have hereafter? 25 In the day of prosperity there is a forgetfulness of affliction: and in the day of affliction there is no more remembrance of prosperity. 26 For it is an easy thing unto the Lord in the day of death to reward a man according to his ways. 27 The affliction of an hour maketh a man forget pleasure: and in his end his deeds shall be discovered. 28 Judge none blessed before his death: for a man shall be known in his children. 29 Bring not every man into thine house: for the deceitful man hath many trains. 30 Like as a partridge taken *and kept* in a cage, so is the heart of the proud; and like as a spy, watcheth he for thy fall: 31 For he lieth in wait, and turneth good into evil, and in things worthy praise will lay blame upon thee. 32 Of a spark of fire a heap of coals is kindled: and a sinful man layeth wait for blood. 33 Take heed of a mischievous man, for he worketh wickedness; lest he bring upon thee a perpetual blot. 34 Receive a stranger into thine house, and he will disturb thee, and turn thee out of thine own.

Sir.12 1 When thou wilt do good know to whom thou doest it; so shalt thou be thanked for thy benefits. 2 Do good to the godly man, and thou shalt find a recompence; and if not from him, yet from the most High. 3 There can no good come to him that is always occupied in evil, nor to him that giveth no alms. 4 Give to the godly man, and help not a sinner. 5 Do well unto him that is lowly, but give not to the ungodly: hold back thy bread, and give it not unto him, lest he overmaster thee thereby: for *else* thou shalt receive twice as much evil for all the good thou shalt have done unto him. 6 For the most High hateth sinners, and will repay vengeance unto the ungodly, and keepeth them against the mighty day of their punishment. 7 Give unto the good, and help not the sinner. 8 A friend cannot be known in prosperity: and an enemy cannot be hidden in adversity. 9 In the prosperity of a man enemies will be grieved: but in his adversity even a friend will depart. 10 Never trust thine enemy: for like as iron rusteth, so is his wickedness. 11 Though he humble himself, and go crouching, yet take good heed and beware of him, and thou shalt be unto him as if thou hadst wiped a lookingglass, and thou shalt know that his rust hath not been altogether wiped away. 12 Set him not by thee, lest, when he hath overthrown thee, he stand up in thy place; neither let him sit at thy right hand, lest he seek to take thy seat, and thou at the last remember my words, and be pricked therewith. 13 Who will pity a charmer that is bitten with a serpent, or any such as come nigh wild beasts? 14 So one that goeth to a sinner, and is defiled with him in his sins, who will pity? 15 For a while he will abide with thee, but if thou begin to fall, he will not tarry. 16 An enemy speaketh sweetly with his lips, but in his heart he imagineth how to throw thee into a pit: he will weep with his eyes, but if he find opportunity, he will not be satisfied with blood. 17 If adversity come upon thee, thou shalt find him there first; and though he pretend to help thee, yet shall he undermine thee. 18 He will shake his head, and clap his hands, and whisper much, and change his countenance.

Sir.13 1 He that toucheth pitch shall be defiled therewith; and he that hath fellowship with a proud man shall be like unto him. 2 Burden not thyself above thy power while thou livest; and have no fellowship with one that is mightier and richer than thyself: for how agree the kettle and the earthen pot together? for if the one be smitten against the other, it shall be broken. 3 The rich man hath done wrong, and yet he threateneth withal: the poor is wronged, and he must intreat also. 4 If thou be for his profit, he will use thee: but if thou have nothing, he will forsake thee. 5 If thou have any thing, he will live with thee: yea, he will make thee bare, and will not be sorry for it. 6 If he have need of thee, he will deceive thee, and smile upon thee, and put thee in hope; he will speak thee fair, and say, What wantest thou? 7 And he will shame thee by his meats, until he have drawn thee dry twice or thrice, and at the last he will laugh thee to scorn afterward, when he seeth thee, he will forsake thee, and shake his head at thee. 8 Beware that thou be not deceived and brought down in thy jollity. 9 If thou be invited of a mighty man, withdraw thyself, and so much the more will he invite thee. 10 Press thou not upon him, lest thou be put back; stand not far off, lest thou be forgotten. 11 Affect not to be made equal unto him in talk, and believe not his many words: for with much communication will he tempt thee, and smiling upon thee will get out thy secrets: 12 But cruelly he will lay up thy words, and will not spare to do thee hurt, and to put thee in prison. 13 Observe, and take good heed, for thou walkest in peril of thy overthrowing: when thou hearest these things, awake in thy sleep. 14 Love the Lord all thy life, and call upon him for thy salvation. 15 Every beast loveth his like, and every man loveth his neighbour. 16 All flesh consorteth according to kind, and a man will cleave to his like. 17 What fellowship hath the wolf with the lamb? so the sinner with the godly. 18 What agreement is there between the hyena and a dog? and what peace between the rich and the poor? 19 As the wild ass is the lion's prey in the wilderness: so the rich eat up the poor. 20 As the proud hate humility: so doth the rich abhor the poor. 21 A rich man beginning to fall is held up of his friends: but a poor man being down is thrust away by his friends. 22 When a rich man is fallen, he hath many helpers: he speaketh things not to be spoken, and yet men justify him: the poor man slipped, and yet they rebuked him too; he spake wisely, and could have no place. 23 When a rich man speaketh, every man holdeth his tongue, and, look, what he saith, they extol it to the clouds: but if the poor man speak, they say, What fellow is this? and if he stumble, they will help to overthrow him. 24 Riches are good unto him that hath no sin, and poverty is evil in the mouth of the ungodly. 25 The heart of a man changeth his countenance, whether it be for good or evil: and a merry heart maketh a cheerful countenance. 26 A cheerful countenance is a token of a heart that is in prosperity; and the finding out of parables is a wearisome labour of the mind.

Sir.14 1 Blessed is the man that hath not slipped with his mouth, and is not pricked with the multitude of sins. 2 Blessed is he whose conscience hath not condemned him, and who is not fallen from his hope in the Lord. 3 Riches are not comely for a niggard: and what should an envious man do with money? 4 He that gathereth by defrauding his own soul gathereth for others, that shall spend his goods riotously. 5 He that is evil to himself, to whom will he be good? he shall not take pleasure in his goods. 6 There is none worse than he that envieth himself; and this is a recompence of his wickedness. 7 And if he doeth good, he doeth it unwillingly; and at the last he will declare his wickedness. 8 The envious man hath a wicked eye; he turneth away his face, and despiseth men. 9 A covetous man's eye is not satisfied with his portion; and the iniquity of the wicked drieth up his soul. 10 A wicked eye envieth *his* bread, and he is a niggard at his table. 11 My son, according to thy ability do good to thyself, and give the Lord his due offering. 12 Remember that death will not be long in coming, and that the covenant of the grave is not shewed unto thee. 13 Do good unto thy friend before thou die, and according to thy ability stretch out thy hand and give to him. 14 Defraud not thyself of the good day, and let not the

part of a good desire overpass thee. 15 Shalt thou not leave thy travails unto another? and thy labours to be divided by lot? 16 Give, and take, and sanctify thy soul; for there is no seeking of dainties in the grave. 17 All flesh waxeth old as a garment: for the covenant from the beginning is, Thou shalt die the death. 18 As of the green leaves on a thick tree, some fall, and some grow; so is the generation of flesh and blood, one cometh to an end, and another is born. 19 Every work rotteth and consumeth away, and the worker thereof shall go withal. 20 Blessed is the man that doth meditate good things in wisdom, and that reasoneth of holy things by his understanding. 21 He that considereth her ways in his heart shall also have understanding in her secrets. 22 Go after her as one that traceth, and lie in wait in her ways. 23 He that prieth in at her windows shall also hearken at her doors. 24 He that doth lodge near her house shall also fasten a pin in her walls. 25 He shall pitch his tent nigh unto her, and shall lodge in a lodging where good things are. 26 He shall set his children under her shelter, and shall lodge under her branches. 27 By her he shall be covered from heat, and in her glory shall he dwell.

Sir.15 1 He that feareth the Lord will do good, and he that hath the knowledge of the law shall obtain her. 2 And as a mother shall she meet him, and receive him as a wife married of a virgin. 3 With the bread of understanding shall she feed him, and give him the water of wisdom to drink. 4 He shall be stayed upon her, and shall not be moved; and shall rely upon her, and shall not be confounded. 5 She shall exalt him above his neighbours, and in the midst of the congregation shall she open his mouth. 6 He shall find joy and a crown of gladness, and she shall cause him to inherit an everlasting name. 7 But foolish men shall not attain unto her, and sinners shall not see her. 8 For she is far from pride, and men that are liars cannot remember her. 9 Praise is not seemly in the mouth of a sinner, for it was not sent him of the Lord. 10 For praise shall be uttered in wisdom, and the Lord will prosper it. 11 Say not thou, It is through the Lord that I fell away: for thou oughtest not to do the things that he hateth. 12 Say not thou, He hath caused me to err: for he hath no need of the sinful man. 13 The Lord hateth all abomination; and they that fear God love it not. 14 He himself made man from the beginning, and left him in the hand of his counsel; 15 If thou wilt, to keep the commandments, and to perform acceptable faithfulness. 16 He hath set fire and water before thee: stretch forth thy hand unto whether thou wilt. 17 Before man is life and death; and whether him liketh shall be given him. 18 For the wisdom of the Lord is great, and he is mighty in power, and beholdeth all things: 19 And his eyes are upon them that fear him, and he knoweth every work of man. 20 He hath commanded no man to do wickedly, neither hath he given any man licence to sin.

Sir.16 1 Desire not a multitude of unprofitable children, neither delight in ungodly sons. 2 Though they multiply, rejoice not in them, except the fear of the Lord be with them. 3 Trust not thou in their life, neither respect their multitude: for one that is just is better than a thousand; and better it is to die without children, than to have them that are ungodly. 4 For by one that hath understanding shall the city be replenished: but the kindred of the wicked shall speedily become desolate. 5 Many such things have I seen with mine eyes, and mine ear hath heard greater things than these. 6 In the congregation of the ungodly shall a fire be kindled; and in a rebellious nation wrath is set on fire. 7 He was not pacified toward the old giants, who fell away in the strength of their foolishness. 8 Neither spared he the place where Lot sojourned, but abhorred them for their pride. 9 He pitied not the people of perdition, who were taken away in their sins: 10 Nor the six hundred thousand footmen, who were gathered together in the hardness of their hearts. 11 And if there be one stiffnecked among the people, it is marvel if he escape unpunished: for mercy and wrath are with him; he is mighty to forgive, and to pour out displeasure. 12 As his mercy is great, so is his correction also: he judgeth a man according to his works 13 The sinner shall not escape with his spoils: and the patience of the godly shall not be frustrate. 14 Make way for every work of mercy: for every man shall find according to his works. 15 The Lord hardened Pharaoh, that he should not know him, that his powerful works might be known to the world. 16 His mercy is manifest to every creature; and he hath separated his light from the darkness with an adamant. 17 Say not thou, I will hide myself from the Lord: shall any remember me from above? I shall not be remembered among so many people: for what is my soul among such an infinite number of creatures? 18 Behold, the heaven, and the heaven of heavens, the deep, and the earth, and all that therein is, shall be moved when he shall visit. 19 The mountains also and foundations of the earth be shaken with trembling, when the Lord looketh upon them. 20 No heart can think upon these things worthily: and who is able to conceive his ways? 21 It is a tempest which no man can see: for the most part of his works are hid. 22 Who can declare the works of his justice? or who can endure them? for his covenant is afar off, and the trial of all things is in the end. 23 He that wanteth understanding will think upon vain things: and a foolish man erring imagineth follies. 24 My son, hearken unto me, and learn knowledge, and mark my words with thy heart. 25 I will shew forth doctrine in weight, and declare his knowledge exactly. 26 The works of the Lord are done in judgment from the beginning: and from the time he made them he disposed the parts thereof. 27 He garnished his works for ever, and in his hand are the chief of them unto all generations: they neither labour, nor are weary, nor cease from their works. 28 None of them hindereth another, and they shall never disobey his word. 29 After this the Lord looked upon the earth, and filled it with his blessings. 30 With all manner of living things hath he covered the face thereof; and they shall return into it again.

Sir.17 1 The Lord created man of the earth, and turned him into it again. 2 He gave them few days, and a short time, and power also over the things therein. 3 He endued them with strength by themselves, and made them according to his image, 4 And put the fear of man upon all flesh, and gave him dominion over beasts and fowls. 5 *They received the use of the five operations of the Lord, and in the sixth place he imparted them understanding, and in the seventh speech, an interpreter of the cogitations thereof.* 6 Counsel, and a tongue, and eyes, ears, and a heart, gave he them to understand. 7 Withal he filled them with the knowledge of understanding, and shewed them good and evil. 8 He set his eye upon their hearts, that he might shew them the greatness of his works. 9 He gave them to glory in his marvellous acts for ever, that they might declare his works with understanding. 10 And the elect shall praise his holy name. 11 Beside this he gave them knowledge, and the law of life for an heritage. 12 He made an everlasting covenant with them, and shewed them his judgments. 13 Their eyes saw the majesty of his glory, and their ears heard his glorious voice. 14 And he said unto them, Beware of all unrighteousness; and he gave every man commandment concerning his neighbour. 15 Their ways are ever before him, and shall not be hid from his eyes. 16 Every man from his youth is given to evil; neither could they make to themselves fleshy hearts for stony. 17 For in the division of the nations of the whole earth he set a ruler over every people; but Israel is the Lord's portion: 18 Whom, being his firstborn, he nourisheth with discipline, and giving him the light of his love doth not forsake him. 19 Therefore all their works are as the sun before him, and his eyes are continually upon their ways. 20 None of their unrighteous deeds are hid from him, but all their sins are before the Lord 21 But the Lord being gracious and knowing his workmanship, neither left nor forsook them, but spared them. 22 The alms of a man is as a signet with him, and he will keep the good deeds of man as the apple of the eye, and give repentance to his sons and daughters. 23 Afterwards he will rise up and reward them, and render their recompence upon their heads. 24 But unto them that repent, he granted them return, and comforted those that failed in patience. 25 Return unto the Lord, and forsake thy sins, make thy prayer before his face, and offend less. 26 Turn again to the most High, and turn away from iniquity: for he will lead thee out of darkness into the light of health, and hate thou abomination vehemently. 27 Who shall praise the most High in the grave, instead of them which live and give thanks? 28 Thanksgiving perisheth from the dead, as from one that is not: the living and sound in heart shall praise the Lord. 29 How great is the lovingkindness of the Lord our God, and his compassion unto such as turn unto him in holiness! 30 For all things cannot be in men, because the son of man is not immortal. 31 What is brighter than the sun? yet the light thereof faileth; and flesh and blood will imagine evil. 32 He vieweth the power of the height of heaven; and all men are but earth and ashes.

Sir.18 1 He that liveth for ever Hath created all things in general. 2 The Lord only is righteous, and there is none other but he, 3 Who governeth the world with the palm of his hand, and all things obey his will: for he is the King of all, by his power dividing holy things among them from profane. 4 To whom hath he given power to declare his works? and who shall find out his noble acts? 5 Who shall number the strength of his majesty? and who shall also tell out his mercies? 6 As for the wondrous works of the Lord, there may nothing be taken from them, neither may any thing be put unto them, neither can the ground of them be found out. 7 When a man hath done, then he beginneth; and when he leaveth off, then he shall be doubtful. 8 What is man, and whereto serveth he? what is his good, and what is his evil? 9 The number of a man's days at the most are an hundred years. 10 As a drop of water unto the sea, and a gravelstone in comparison of the sand; so are a thousand years to the days of eternity. 11 Therefore is God patient with them, and poureth forth his mercy upon them. 12 He saw and perceived their end to be evil; therefore he multiplied his compassion. 13 The mercy of man is toward his neighbour; but the mercy of the Lord is upon all flesh: he reproveth, and nurtureth, and teacheth and bringeth again, as a shepherd his flock. 14 He hath mercy on them that receive discipline, and that diligently seek after his judgments. 15 My son, blemish not thy good deeds, neither use uncomfortable words when thou givest any thing. 16 Shall not the dew asswage the heat? so is a word better than a gift? 17 Lo, is not a word better than a gift? but both are with a gracious man. 18 A fool will upbraid churlishly, and a gift of the envious consumeth the eyes. 19 Learn before thou speak, and use physick or ever thou be sick. 20 Before judgment examine thyself, and in the day of visitation thou shalt find mercy. 21 Humble thyself before thou be sick, and in the time of sins shew repentance. 22 Let nothing hinder thee to pay thy vow in due time, and defer not until death to be justified. 23 Before thou prayest, prepare thyself; and be not as one that tempteth the Lord. 24 Think upon the wrath that shall be at the end, and the time of vengeance, when he shall turn away his face. 25 When thou hast enough, remember the time of hunger: and when thou art rich, think upon poverty and need. 26 From the morning until the evening the time is changed, and all things are soon done before the Lord. 27 A wise man will fear in every thing, and in the day of sinning he will beware of offence: but a fool will not observe time. 28 Every man of understanding knoweth wisdom, and will give praise unto him that found her. 29 They that were of understanding in sayings became also wise themselves, and poured forth exquisite parables. 30 Go not after thy lusts, but refrain thyself from thine appetites. 31 If thou givest thy soul the desires that please her, she will make thee a laughingstock to thine enemies that malign thee. 32 Take not pleasure in much good cheer, neither be tied to the expense thereof. 33 Be not made a beggar by banqueting upon borrowing, when thou hast nothing in thy purse: for thou shalt lie in wait for thine own life, and be talked on.

Sir.19 1 A labouring man that A is given to drunkenness shall not be rich: and he that contemneth small things shall fall by little and little. 2 Wine and women will make men of understanding to fall away: and he that cleaveth to harlots will become impudent. 3 Moths and worms shall have him to heritage, and a bold man shall be taken away. 4 He that is hasty to give credit is lightminded; and he that sinneth shall offend against his own soul. 5 Whoso taketh pleasure in wickedness shall be condemned: but he that resisteth pleasures crowneth his life. 6 He that can rule his tongue shall live without strife; and he that hateth babbling shall

have less evil. 7 Rehearse not unto another that which is told unto thee, and thou shalt fare never the worse. 8 Whether it be to friend or foe, talk not of other men's lives; and if thou canst without offence, reveal them not. 9 For he heard and observed thee, and when time cometh he will hate thee. 10 If thou hast heard a word, let it die with thee; and be bold, it will not burst thee. 11 A fool travaileth with a word, as a woman in labour of a child. 12 As an arrow that sticketh in a man's thigh, so is a word within a fool's belly. 13 Admonish a friend, it may be he hath not done it: and if he have done it, that he do it no more. 14 Admonish thy friend, it may be he hath not said it: and if he have, that he speak it not again. 15 Admonish a friend: for many times it is a slander, and believe not every tale. 16 There is one that slippeth in his speech, but not from his heart; and who is he that hath not offended with his tongue? 17 Admonish thy neighbour before thou threaten him; and not being angry, give place to the law of the most High. 18 The fear of the Lord is the first step to be accepted *of him,* and wisdom obtaineth his love. 19 The knowledge of the commandments of the Lord is the doctrine of life: and they that do things that please him shall receive the fruit of the tree of immortality. 20 The fear of the Lord is all wisdom; and in all wisdom is the performance of the law, and the knowledge of his omnipotency. 21 If a servant say to his master, I will not do as it pleaseth thee; though afterward he do it, he angereth him that nourisheth him. 22 The knowledge of wickedness is not wisdom, neither at any time the counsel of sinners prudence. 23 There is a wickedness, and the same an abomination; and there is a fool wanting in wisdom. 24 He that hath small understanding, and feareth God, is better than one that hath much wisdom, and transgresseth the law of the most High. 25 There is an exquisite subtilty, and the same is unjust; and there is one that turneth aside to make judgment appear; and there is a wise man that justifieth in judgment. 26 There is a wicked man that hangeth down his head sadly; but inwardly he is full of deceit, 27 Casting down his countenance, and making as if he heard not: where he is not known, he will do thee a mischief before thou be aware. 28 And if for want of power he be hindered from sinning, yet when he findeth opportunity he will do evil. 29 A man may be known by his look, and one that hath understanding by his countenance, when thou meetest him. 30 A man's attire, and excessive laughter, and gait, shew what he is.

Sir.20 1 There is a reproof that is not comely: again, some man holdeth his tongue, and he is wise. 2 It is much better to reprove, than to be angry secretly: and he that confesseth his fault shall be preserved from hurt. 3 How good is it, when thou art reproved, to shew repentance! for so shalt thou escape wilful sin. 4 As is the lust of an eunuch to deflower a virgin; so is he that executeth judgment with violence. 5 There is one that keepeth silence, and is found wise: and another by much babbling becometh hateful. 6 Some man holdeth his tongue, because he hath not to answer: and some keepeth silence, knowing his time. 7 A wise man will hold his tongue till he see opportunity: but a babbler and a fool will regard no time. 8 He that useth many words shall be abhorred; and he that taketh to himself authority therein shall be hated. 9 There is a sinner that hath good success in evil things; and there is a gain that turneth to loss. 10 There is a gift that shall not profit thee; and there is a gift whose recompence is double. 11 There is an abasement because of glory; and there is that lifteth up his head from a low estate. 12 There is that buyeth much for a little, and repayeth it sevenfold. 13 A wise man by his words maketh him beloved: but the graces of fools shall be poured out. 14 The gift of a fool shall do thee no good when thou hast it; neither yet of the envious for his necessity: for he looketh to receive many things for one. 15 He giveth little, and upbraideth much; he openeth his mouth like a crier; to day he lendeth, and to morrow will he ask it again: such an one is to be hated of God and man. 16 The fool saith, I have no friends, I have no thank for all my good deeds, and they that eat my bread speak evil of me. 17 How oft, and of how many shall he be laughed to scorn! for he knoweth not aright what it is to have; and it is all one unto him as if he had it not. 18 To slip upon a pavement is better than to slip with the tongue: so the fall of the wicked shall come speedily. 19 An unseasonable tale will always be in the mouth of the unwise. 20 A wise sentence shall be rejected when it cometh out of a fool's mouth; for he will not speak it in due season. 21 There is that is hindered from sinning through want: and when he taketh rest, he shall not be troubled. 22 There is that destroyeth his own soul through bashfulness, and by accepting of persons overthroweth himself. 23 There is that for bashfulness promiseth to his friend, and maketh him his enemy for nothing. 24 A lie is a foul blot in a man, yet it is continually in the mouth of the untaught. 25 A thief is better than a man that is accustomed to lie: but they both shall have destruction to heritage. 26 The disposition of a liar is dishonourable, and his shame is ever with him. 27 A wise man shall promote himself to honour with his words: and he that hath understanding will please great men. 28 He that tilleth his land shall increase his heap: and he that pleaseth great men shall get pardon for iniquity. 29 Presents and gifts blind the eyes of the wise, and stop up his mouth that he cannot reprove. 30 Wisdom that is hid, and treasure that is hoarded up, what profit is in them both? 31 Better is he that hideth his folly than a man that hideth his wisdom. 32 Necessary patience in seeking the Lord is better than he that leadeth his life without a guide.

Sir.21 1 My son, hast thou sinned? do so no more, but ask pardon for thy former sins. 2 Flee from sin as from the face of a serpent: for if thou comest too near it, it will bite thee: the teeth thereof are as the teeth of a lion, slaying the souls of men. 3 All iniquity is as a two edged sword, the wounds whereof cannot be healed. 4 To terrify and do wrong will waste riches: thus the house of proud men shall be made desolate. 5 A prayer out of a poor man's mouth reacheth to the ears of God, and his judgment cometh speedily. 6 He that hateth to be reproved is in the way of sinners: but he that feareth the Lord will repent from his heart. 7 An eloquent man is known far and near; but a man of understanding knoweth when he slippeth. 8 He that

buildeth his house with other men's money is like one that gathereth himself stones for the tomb of his burial. 9 The congregation of the wicked is like tow wrapped together: and the end of them is a flame of fire to destroy them. 10 The way of sinners is made plain with stones, but at the end thereof is the pit of hell. 11 He that keepeth the law of the Lord getteth the understanding thereof: and the perfection of the fear of the Lord is wisdom. 12 He that is not wise will not be taught: but there is a wisdom which multiplieth bitterness. 13 The knowledge of a wise man shall abound like a flood: and his counsel is like a pure fountain of life. 14 The inner parts of a fool are like a broken vessel, and he will hold no knowledge as long as he liveth. 15 If a skilful man hear a wise word, he will commend it, and add unto it: but as soon as one of no understanding heareth it, it displeaseth him, and he casteth it behind his back. 16 The talking of a fool is like a burden in the way: but grace shall be found in the lips of the wise. 17 They enquire at the mouth of the wise man in the congregation, and they shall ponder his words in their heart. 18 As is a house that is destroyed, so is wisdom to a fool: and the knowledge of the unwise is as talk without sense. 19 Doctrine unto fools is as fetters on the feet, and like manacles on the right hand. 20 A fool lifteth up his voice with laughter; but a wise man doth scarce smile a little. 21 Learning is unto a wise man as an ornament of gold, and like a bracelet upon his right arm. 22 A foolish man's foot is soon in his *neighbour's* house: but a man of experience is ashamed of him. 23 A fool will peep in at the door into the house: but he that is well nurtured will stand without. 24 It is the rudeness of a man to hearken at the door: but a wise man will be grieved with the disgrace. 25 The lips of talkers will be telling such things as pertain not unto them: but the words of such as have understanding are weighed in the balance. 26 The heart of fools is in their mouth: but the mouth of the wise is in their heart. 27 When the ungodly curseth Satan, he curseth his own soul. 28 A whisperer defileth his own soul, and is hated wheresoever he dwelleth.

Sir.22 1 A slothful man is compared to a filthy stone, and every one will hiss him out to his disgrace. 2 A slothful man is compared to the filth of a dunghill: every man that takes it up will shake his hand. 3 An evilnurtured man is the dishonour of his father that begat him: and a *foolish* daughter is born to his loss. 4 A wise daughter shall bring an inheritance to her husband: but she that liveth dishonestly is her father's heaviness. 5 She that is bold dishonoureth both her father and her husband, but they both shall despise her. 6 A tale out of season *is as* musick in mourning: but stripes and correction of wisdom are never out of time. 7 Whoso teacheth a fool is as one that glueth a potsherd together, and as he that waketh one from a sound sleep. 8 He that telleth a tale to a fool speaketh to one in a slumber: when he hath told his tale, he will say, What is the matter? 9 If children live honestly, and have wherewithal, they shall cover the baseness of their parents. 10 But children, being haughty, through disdain and want of nurture do stain the nobility of their kindred. 11 Weep for the dead, for he hath lost the light: and weep for the fool, for he wanteth understanding: make little weeping for the dead, for he is at rest: but the life of the fool is worse than death. 12 Seven days do men mourn for him that is dead; but for a fool and an ungodly man all the days of his life. 13 Talk not much with a fool, and go not to him that hath no understanding: beware of him, lest thou have trouble, and thou shalt never be defiled with his fooleries: depart from him, and thou shalt find rest, and never be disquieted with madness. 14 What is heavier than lead? and what is the name thereof, but a fool? 15 Sand, and salt, and a mass of iron, is easier to bear, than a man without understanding. 16 As timber girt and bound together in a building cannot be loosed with shaking: so the heart that is stablished by advised counsel shall fear at no time. 17 A heart settled upon a thought of understanding is as a fair plaistering on the wall of a gallery. 18 Pales set on an high place will never stand against the wind: so a fearful heart in the imagination of a fool cannot stand against any fear. 19 He that pricketh the eye will make tears to fall: and he that pricketh the heart maketh it to shew her knowledge. 20 Whoso casteth a stone at the birds frayeth them away: and he that upbraideth his friend breaketh friendship. 21 Though thou drewest a sword at thy friend, yet despair not: for there may be a returning *to favour*. 22 If thou hast opened thy mouth against thy friend, fear not; for there may be a reconciliation: except for upbraiding, or pride, or disclosing of secrets, or a treacherous wound: for for these things every friend will depart. 23 Be faithful to thy neighbour in his poverty, that thou mayest rejoice in his prosperity: abide stedfast unto him in the time of his trouble, that thou mayest be heir with him in his heritage: for a mean estate is not always to be contemned: nor the rich that is foolish to be had in admiration. 24 As the vapour and smoke of a furnace goeth before the fire; so reviling before blood. 25 I will not be ashamed to defend a friend; neither will I hide myself from him. 26 And if any evil happen unto me by him, every one that heareth it will beware of him. 27 Who shall set a watch before my mouth, and a seal of wisdom upon my lips, that I fall not suddenly by them, and that my tongue destroy me not?

Sir.23 1 O Lord, Father and Governor of all my whole life, leave me not to their counsels, and let me not fall by them. 2 Who will set scourges over my thoughts, and the discipline of wisdom over mine heart? that they spare me not for mine ignorances, and it pass not by my sins: 3 Lest mine ignorances increase, and my sins abound to my destruction, and I fall before mine adversaries, and mine enemy rejoice over me, whose hope is far from thy mercy. 4 O Lord, Father and God of my life, give me not a proud look, but turn away from thy servants always a haughty mind. 5 Turn away from me vain hopes and concupiscence, and thou shalt hold him up that is desirous always to serve thee. 6 Let not the greediness of the belly nor lust of the flesh take hold of me; and give not over me thy servant into an impudent mind. 7 Hear, O ye children, the discipline of the mouth: he that keepeth it shall never be taken in his lips. 8 The sinner shall be left in his foolishness: both the evil speaker and the proud shall fall thereby. 9 Accustom not thy mouth to swearing; neither use thyself to the naming of the Holy One. 10 For as a servant that is continually beaten shall not be without a blue mark: so he that sweareth and nameth God continually shall not be faultless. 11 A man that useth much swearing shall be filled with iniquity, and the plague shall never depart from his house: if he shall offend, his sin shall be upon him: and if he acknowledge not his sin, he maketh a double offence: and if he swear in vain, he shall not be innocent, but his house shall be full of calamities. 12 There is a word that is clothed about with death: God grant that it be not found in the heritage of Jacob; for all such things shall be far from the godly, and they shall not wallow in their sins. 13 Use not thy mouth to intemperate swearing, for therein is the word of sin. 14 Remember thy father and thy mother, when thou sittest among great men. Be not forgetful before them, and so thou by thy custom become a fool, and wish that thou hadst not been born, and curse they day of thy nativity. 15 The man that is accustomed to opprobrious words will never be reformed all the days of his life. 16 Two sorts of men multiply sin, and the third will bring wrath: a hot mind is as a burning fire, it will never be quenched till it be consumed: a fornicator in the body of his flesh will never cease till he hath kindled a fire. 17 All bread is sweet to a whoremonger, he will not leave off till he die. 18 A man that breaketh wedlock, saying thus in his heart, Who seeth me? I am compassed about with darkness, the walls cover me, and no body seeth me; what need I to fear? the most High will not remember my sins: 19 Such a man only feareth the eyes of men, and knoweth not that the eyes of the Lord are ten thousand times brighter than the sun, beholding all the ways of men, and considering the most secret parts. 20 He knew all things ere ever they were created; so also after they were perfected he looked upon them all. 21 This man shall be punished in the streets of the city, and where he suspecteth not he shall be taken. 22 Thus shall it go also with the wife that leaveth her husband, and bringeth in an heir by another. 23 For first, she hath disobeyed the law of the most High; and secondly, she hath trespassed against her own husband; and thirdly, she hath played the whore in adultery, and brought children by another man. 24 She shall be brought out into the congregation, and inquisition shall be made of her children. 25 Her children shall not take root, and her branches shall bring forth no fruit. 26 She shall leave her memory to be cursed, and her reproach shall not be blotted out. 27 And they that remain shall know that there is nothing better than the fear of the Lord, and that there is nothing sweeter than to take heed unto the commandments of the Lord. 28 It is great glory to follow the Lord, and to be received of him is long life.

Sir.24 1 Wisdom shall praise herself, and shall glory in the midst of her people. 2 In the congregation of the most High shall she open her mouth, and triumph before his power. 3 I came out of the mouth of the most High, and covered the earth as a cloud. 4 I dwelt in high places, and my throne is in a cloudy pillar. 5 I alone compassed the circuit of heaven, and walked in the bottom of the deep. 6 In the waves of the sea and in all the earth, and in every people and nation, I got a possession. 7 With all these I sought rest: and in whose inheritance shall I abide? 8 So the Creator of all things gave me a commandment, and he that made me caused my tabernacle to rest, and said, Let thy dwelling be in Jacob, and thine inheritance in Israel. 9 He created me from the beginning before the world, and I shall never fail. 10 In the holy tabernacle I served before him; and so was I established in Sion. 11 Likewise in the beloved city he gave me rest, and in Jerusalem was my power. 12 And I took root in an honourable people, even in the portion of the Lord's inheritance. 13 I was exalted like a cedar in Libanus, and as a cypress tree upon the mountains of Hermon. 14 I was exalted like a palm tree in En-gaddi, and as a rose plant in Jericho, as a fair olive tree in a pleasant field, and grew up as a plane tree by the water. 15 I gave a sweet smell like cinnamon and aspalathus, and I yielded a pleasant odour like the best myrrh, as galbanum, and onyx, and sweet storax, and as the fume of frankincense in the tabernacle. 16 As the turpentine tree I stretched out my branches, and my branches are the branches of honour and grace. 17 As the vine brought I forth pleasant savour, and my flowers are the fruit of honour and riches. 18 I am the mother of fair love, and fear, and knowledge, and holy hope: I therefore, being eternal, am given to all my children which are named of him. 19 Come unto me, all ye that be desirous of me, and fill yourselves with my fruits. 20 For my memorial is sweeter than honey, and mine inheritance than the honeycomb. 21 They that eat me shall yet be hungry, and they that drink me shall yet be thirsty. 22 He that obeyeth me shall never be confounded, and they that work by me shall not do amiss. 23 All these things are the book of the covenant of the most high God, even the law which Moses commanded for an heritage unto the congregations of Jacob. 24 Faint not to be strong in the Lord; that he may confirm you, cleave unto him: for the Lord Almighty is God alone, and beside him there is no other Saviour. 25 He filleth all things with his wisdom, as Phison and as Tigris in the time of the new fruits. 26 He maketh the understanding to abound like Euphrates, and as Jordan in the time of the harvest. 27 He maketh the doctrine of knowledge appear as the light, and as Geon in the time of vintage. 28 The first man knew her not perfectly: no more shall the last find her out. 29 For her thoughts are more than the sea, and her counsels profounder than the great deep. 30 I also came out as a brook from a river, and as a conduit into a garden. 31 I said, I will water my best garden, and will water abundantly my garden bed: and, lo, my brook became a river, and my river became a sea. 32 I will yet make doctrine to shine as the morning, and will send forth her light afar off. 33 I will yet pour out doctrine as prophecy, and leave it to all ages for ever. 34 Behold that I have not laboured for myself only, but for all them that seek wisdom.

Sir.25 1 In three things I was beautified, and stood up beautiful both before God and men: the unity of brethren, the love of neighbours, a man and a wife that agree together. 2 Three sorts of men my soul hateth, and I am greatly offended at their life: a poor man that is proud, a rich man that is a liar, and an old adulterer that doateth. 3 If thou hast gathered nothing in thy youth, how canst thou find any thing in thine age? 4 O how comely a thing is judgment for gray hairs, and for ancient men to know counsel! 5 O how comely is the wisdom of old men, and understanding and counsel to men of honour. 6 Much experience is the crown of old men, and the fear of God is their glory. 7 There be nine things which I have judged in mine heart to be happy, and the tenth I will utter with my tongue: A man that hath joy of his children; and he that liveth to see the fall of his enemy: 8 Well is him that dwelleth with a wife of understanding, and that hath not slipped with his tongue, and that hath not served a man more unworthy than himself: 9 Well is him that hath found prudence, and he that speaketh in the ears of them that will hear: 10 O how great is he that findeth wisdom! yet is there none above him that feareth the Lord. 11 But the love of the Lord passeth all things for illumination: he that holdeth it, whereto shall he be likened? 12 The fear of the Lord is the beginning of his love: and faith is the beginning of cleaving unto him. 13 *Give me* any plague, but the plague of the heart: and any wickedness, but the wickedness of a woman: 14 And any affliction, but the affliction from them that hate me: and any revenge, but the revenge of enemies. 15 There is no head above the head of a serpent; and there is no wrath above the wrath of an enemy. 16 I had rather dwell with a lion and a dragon, than to keep house with a wicked woman. 17 The wickedness of a woman changeth her face, and darkeneth her countenance like sackcloth. 18 Her husband shall sit among his neighbours; and when he heareth it shall sigh bitterly. 19 All wickedness is but little to the wickedness of a woman: let the portion of a sinner fall upon her. 20 As the climbing up a sandy way is to the feet of the aged, so is a wife full of words to a quiet man. 21 Stumble not at the beauty of a woman, and desire her not for pleasure. 22 A woman, if she maintain her husband, is full of anger, impudence, and much reproach. 23 A wicked woman abateth the courage, maketh an heavy countenance and a wounded heart: a woman that will not comfort her husband in distress maketh weak hands and feeble knees. 24 Of the woman came the beginning of sin, and through her we all die. 25 Give the water no passage; neither a wicked woman liberty to gad abroad. 26 If she go not as thou wouldest have her, cut her off from thy flesh, and give her a bill of divorce, and let her go.

Sir.26 1 Blessed is the man that hath a virtuous wife, for the number of his days shall be double. 2 A virtuous woman rejoiceth her husband, and he shall fulfil the years of his life in peace. 3 A good wife is a good portion, which shall be given in the portion of them that fear the Lord. 4 Whether a man be rich or poor, if he have a good heart toward the Lord, he shall at all times rejoice with a cheerful countenance. 5 There be three things that mine heart feareth; and for the fourth I was sore afraid: the slander of a city, the gathering together of an unruly multitude, and a false accusation: all these are worse than death. 6 But a grief of heart and sorrow is a woman that is jealous over another woman, and a scourge of the tongue which communicateth with all. 7 An evil wife is a yoke shaken to and fro: he that hath hold of her is as though he held a scorpion. 8 A drunken woman and a gadder abroad causeth great anger, and she will not cover her own shame. 9 The whoredom of a woman may be known in her haughty looks and eyelids. 10 If thy daughter be shameless, keep her in straitly, lest she abuse herself through overmuch liberty. 11 Watch over an impudent eye: and marvel not if she trespass against thee. 12 She will open her mouth, as a thirsty traveller when he hath found a fountain, and drink of every water near her: by every hedge will she sit down, and open her quiver against every arrow. 13 The grace of a wife delighteth her husband, and her discretion will fatten his bones. 14 A silent and loving woman is a gift of the Lord; and there is nothing so much worth as a mind well instructed. 15 A shamefaced and faithful woman is a double grace, and her continent mind cannot be valued. 16 As the sun when it ariseth in the high heaven; so is the beauty of a good wife in the ordering of her house. 17 As the clear light is upon the holy candlestick; so is the beauty of the face in ripe age. 18 As the golden pillars are upon the sockets of silver; so are the fair feet with a constant heart. 19 My son, keep the flower of thine age sound; and give not thy strength to strangers. 20 When thou hast gotten a fruitful possession through all the field, sow it with thine own seed, trusting in the goodness of thy stock. 21 So thy race which thou leavest shall be magnified, having the confidence of their good descent. 22 An harlot shall be accounted as spittle; but a married woman is a tower against death to her husband. 23 A wicked woman is given as a portion to a wicked man: but a godly woman is given to him that feareth the Lord. 24 A dishonest woman contemneth shame: but an honest woman will reverence her husband. 25 A shameless woman shall be counted as a dog; but she that is shamefaced will fear the Lord. 26 A woman that honoureth her husband shall be judged wise of all; but she that dishonoureth him in her pride shall be counted ungodly of all. 27 A loud crying woman and a scold shall be sought out to drive away the enemies. 28 There be two things that grieve my heart; and the third maketh me angry: a man of war that suffereth poverty; and men of understanding that are not set by; and one that returneth from righteousness to sin; the Lord prepareth such an one for the sword. 29 A merchant shall hardly keep himself from doing wrong; and an huckster shall not be freed from sin.

Sir.27 1 Many have sinned for a small matter; and he that seeketh for abundance will turn his eyes away. 2 As a nail sticketh fast between the joinings of the stones; so doth sin stick close between buying and selling. 3 Unless a man hold himself diligently in the fear of the Lord, his house shall soon be overthrown. 4 As when one sifteth with a sieve, the refuse remaineth; so the filth of man in his talk. 5 The furnace proveth the potter's vessels; so the trial of man is in his reasoning. 6 The fruit declareth if the tree have been dressed; so is the utterance of a conceit in the heart of man. 7 Praise no man before thou hearest him speak; for this is the trial of men. 8 If thou followest righteousness, thou shalt obtain her, and put her on, as a glorious long robe. 9 The birds will resort unto their like; so will truth return unto

them that practise in her. 10 As the lion lieth in wait for the prey; so sin for them that work iniquity. 11 The discourse of a godly man is always with wisdom; but a fool changeth as the moon. 12 If thou be among the indiscreet, observe the time; but be continually among men of understanding. 13 The discourse of fools is irksome, and their sport is the wantonness of sin. 14 The talk of him that sweareth much maketh the hair stand upright; and their brawls make one stop his ears. 15 The strife of the proud is bloodshedding, and their revilings are grievous to the ear. 16 Whoso discovereth secrets loseth his credit; and shall never find friend to his mind. 17 Love thy friend, and be faithful unto him: but if thou betrayest his secrets, follow no more after him. 18 For as a man hath destroyed his enemy; so hast thou lost the love of thy neighbour. 19 As one that letteth a bird go out of his hand, so hast thou let thy neighbour go, and shalt not get him again 20 Follow after him no more, for he is too far off; he is as a roe escaped out of the snare. 21 As for a wound, it may be bound up; and after reviling there may be reconcilement: but he that betrayeth secrets is without hope. 22 He that winketh with the eyes worketh evil: and he that knoweth him will depart from him. 23 When thou art present, he will speak sweetly, and will admire thy words: but at the last he will writhe his mouth, and slander thy sayings. 24 I have hated many things, but nothing like him; for the Lord will hate him. 25 Whoso casteth a stone on high casteth it on his own head; and a deceitful stroke shall make wounds. 26 Whoso diggeth a pit shall fall therein: and he that setteth a trap shall be taken therein. 27 He that worketh mischief, it shall fall upon him, and he shall not know whence it cometh. 28 Mockery and reproach are from the proud; but vengeance, as a lion, shall lie in wait for them. 29 They that rejoice at the fall of the righteous shall be taken in the snare; and anguish shall consume them before they die. 30 Malice and wrath, even these are abominations; and the sinful man shall have them both.

Sir.28 1 He that revengeth shall find vengeance from the Lord, and he will surely keep his sins *in remembrance.* 2 Forgive thy neighbour the hurt that he hath done unto thee, so shall thy sins also be forgiven when thou prayest. 3 One man beareth hatred against another, and doth he seek pardon from the Lord? 4 He sheweth no mercy to a man, which is like himself: and doth he ask forgiveness of his own sins? 5 If he that is but flesh nourish hatred, who will intreat for pardon of his sins? 6 Remember thy end, and let enmity cease; *remember* corruption and death, and abide in the commandments. 7 Remember the commandments, and bear no malice to thy neighbour: *remember* the covenant of the Highest, and wink at ignorance. 8 Abstain from strife, and thou shalt diminish thy sins: for a furious man will kindle strife, 9 A sinful man disquieteth friends, and maketh debate among them that be at peace. 10 As the matter of the fire is, so it burneth: and as a man's strength is, so is his wrath; and according to his riches his anger riseth; and the stronger they are which contend, the more they will be inflamed. 11 An hasty contention kindleth a fire: and an hasty fighting sheddeth blood. 12 If thou blow the spark, it shall burn: if thou spit upon it, it shall be quenched: and both these come out of thy mouth. 13 Curse the whisperer and doubletongued: for such have destroyed many that were at peace. 14 A backbiting tongue hath disquieted many, and driven them from nation to nation: strong cities hath it pulled down, and overthrown the houses of great men. 15 A backbiting tongue hath cast out virtuous women, and deprived them of their labours. 16 Whoso hearkeneth unto it shall never find rest, and never dwell quietly. 17 The stroke of the whip maketh marks in the flesh: but the stroke of the tongue breaketh the bones. 18 Many have fallen by the edge of the sword: but not so many as have fallen by the tongue. 19 Well is he that is defended through the venom thereof; who hath not drawn the yoke thereof, nor hath been bound in her bands. 20 For the yoke thereof is a yoke of iron, and the bands thereof are bands of brass. 21 The death thereof is an evil death, the grave were better than it. 22 It shall not have rule over them that fear God, neither shall they be burned with the flame thereof. 23 Such as forsake the Lord shall fall into it; and it shall burn in them, and not be quenched; it shall be sent upon them as a lion, and devour them as a leopard. 24 Look that thou hedge thy possession about with thorns, and bind up thy silver and gold, 25 And weigh thy words in a balance, and make a door and bar for thy mouth. 26 Beware thou slide not by it, lest thou fall before him that lieth in wait.

Sir.29 1 He that is merciful will lend unto his neighbour; and he that strengtheneth his hand keepeth the commandments. 2 Lend to thy neighbour in time of his need, and pay thou thy neighbour again in due season. 3 Keep thy word, and deal faithfully with him, and thou shalt always find the thing that is necessary for thee. 4 Many, when a thing was lent them, reckoned it to be found, and put them to trouble that helped them. 5 Till he hath received, he will kiss a man's hand; and for his neighbour's money he will speak submissly: but when he should repay, he will prolong the time, and return words of grief, and complain of the time. 6 If he prevail, he shall hardly receive the half, and he will count as if he had found it: if not, he hath deprived him of his money, and he hath gotten him an enemy without cause: he payeth him with cursings and railings; and for honour he will pay him disgrace. 7 Many therefore have refused to lend for other men's ill dealing, fearing to be defrauded. 8 Yet have thou patience with a man in poor estate, and delay not to shew him mercy. 9 Help the poor for the commandment's sake, and turn him not away because of his poverty. 10 Lose thy money for thy brother and thy friend, and let it not rust under a stone to be lost. 11 Lay up thy treasure according to the commandments of the most High, and it shall bring thee more profit than gold. 12 Shut up alms in thy storehouses: and it shall deliver thee from all affliction. 13 It shall fight for thee against thine enemies better than a mighty shield and strong spear. 14 An honest man is surety for his neighbour: but he that is impudent will forsake him. 15 Forget not the friendship of thy surety, for he hath given his life for thee. 16 A sinner will overthrow the good estate of his surety: 17 And he that is of an unthankful mind will

leave him *in danger* that delivered him. 18 Suretiship hath undone many of good estate, and shaken them as a wave of the sea: mighty men hath it driven from their houses, so that they wandered among strange nations. 19 A wicked man transgressing the commandments of the Lord shall fall into suretiship: and he that undertaketh and followeth other men's business for gain shall fall into suits. 20 Help thy neighbour according to thy power, and beware that thou thyself fall not into the same. 21 The chief thing for life is water, and bread, and clothing, and an house to cover shame. 22 Better is the life of a poor man in a mean cottage, than delicate fare in another man's house. 23 Be it little or much, hold thee contented, that thou hear not the reproach of thy house. 24 For it is a miserable life to go from house to house: for where thou art a stranger, thou darest not open thy mouth. 25 Thou shalt entertain, and feast, and have no thanks: moreover thou shalt hear bitter words: 26 Come, thou stranger, and furnish a table, and feed me of that thou hast ready. 27 Give place, thou stranger, to an honourable man; my brother cometh to be lodged, and I have need of mine house. 28 These things are grievous to a man of understanding; the upbraiding of houseroom, and reproaching of the lender.

Sir.30 1 He that loveth his son causeth him oft to feel the rod, that he may have joy of him in the end. 2 He that chastiseth his son shall have joy in him, and shall rejoice of him among his acquaintance. 3 He that teacheth his son grieveth the enemy: and before his friends he shall rejoice of him. 4 Though his father die, yet he is as though he were not dead: for he hath left one behind him that is like himself. 5 While he lived, he saw and rejoiced in him: and when he died, he was not sorrowful. 6 He left behind him an avenger against his enemies, and one that shall requite kindness to his friends. 7 He that maketh too much of his son shall bind up his wounds; and his bowels will be troubled at every cry. 8 An horse not broken becometh headstrong: and a child left to himself will be wilful. 9 Cocker thy child, and he shall make thee afraid: play with him, and he will bring thee to heaviness. 10 Laugh not with him, lest thou have sorrow with him, and lest thou gnash thy teeth in the end. 11 Give him no liberty in his youth, and wink not at his follies. 12 Bow down his neck while he is young, and beat him on the sides while he is a child, lest he wax stubborn, and be disobedient unto thee, and so bring sorrow to thine heart. 13 Chastise thy son, and hold him to labour, lest his lewd behaviour be an offence unto thee. 14 Better is the poor, being sound and strong of constitution, than a rich man that is afflicted in his body. 15 Health and good estate of body are above all gold, and a strong body above infinite wealth. 16 There is no riches above a sound body, and no joy above the joy of the heart. 17 Death is better than a bitter life or continual sickness. 18 Delicates poured upon a mouth shut up are as messes of meat set upon a grave. 19 What good doeth the offering unto an idol? for neither can it eat nor smell: so is he that is persecuted of the Lord. 20 He seeth with his eyes and groaneth, as an eunuch that embraceth a virgin and sigheth. 21 Give not over thy mind to heaviness, and afflict not thyself in thine own counsel. 22 The gladness of the heart is the life of man, and the joyfulness of a man prolongeth his days. 23 Love thine own soul, and comfort thy heart, remove sorrow far from thee: for sorrow hath killed many, and there is no profit therein. 24 Envy and wrath shorten the life, and carefulness bringeth age before the time. 16 I awaked up last of all, as one that gathereth after the grapegatherers: by the blessing of the Lord I profited, and filled my winepress like a gatherer of grapes. 17 Consider that I laboured not for myself only, but for all them that seek learning. 18 Hear me, O ye great men of the people, and hearken with your ears, ye rulers of the congregation. 19 Give not thy son and wife, thy brother and friend, power over thee while thou livest, and give not thy goods to another: lest it repent thee, and thou intreat for the same again. 20 As long as thou livest and hast breath in thee, give not thyself over to any. 21 For better it is that thy children should seek to thee, than that thou shouldest stand to their courtesy. 22 In all thy works keep to thyself the preeminence; leave not a stain in thine honour. 23 At the time when thou shalt end thy days, and finish thy life, distribute thine inheritance. 24 Fodder, a wand, and burdens, are for the ass; and bread, correction, and work, for a servant. 25 If thou set thy servant to labour, thou shalt find rest: but if thou let him go idle, he shall seek liberty. 26 A yoke and a collar do bow the neck: so are tortures and torments for an evil servant. 27 Send him to labour, that he be not idle; for idleness teacheth much evil. 28 Set him to work, as is fit for him: if he be not obedient, put on more heavy fetters. 29 But be not excessive toward any; and without discretion do nothing. 30 If thou have a servant, let him be unto thee as thyself, because thou hast bought him with a price. 31 If thou have a servant, entreat him as a brother: for thou hast need of him, as of thine own soul: if thou entreat him evil, and he run from thee, which way wilt thou go to seek him?

Sir.31 1 The hopes of a man void of understanding are vain and false: and dreams lift up fools. 2 Whoso regardeth dreams is like him that catcheth at a shadow, and followeth after the wind. 3 The vision of dreams is the resemblance of one thing to another, even as the likeness of a face to a face. 4 Of an unclean thing what can be cleansed? and from that thing which is false what truth can come? 5 Divinations, and soothsayings, and dreams, are vain: and the heart fancieth, as a woman's heart in travail. 6 If they be not sent from the most High in thy visitation, set not thy heart upon them. 7 For dreams have deceived many, and they have failed that put their trust in them. 8 The law shall be found perfect without lies: and wisdom is perfection to a faithful mouth. 9 A man that hath travelled knoweth many things; and he that hath much experience will declare wisdom. 10 He that hath no experience knoweth little: but he that hath travelled is full of prudence. 11 When I travelled, I saw many things; and I understand more than I can express. 12 I was ofttimes in danger of death: yet I was delivered because of these things. 13 The spirit of those that fear the Lord shall live; for their hope is in him that saveth them. 14 Whoso feareth the Lord shall not fear nor be afraid; for he is his hope. 15 Blessed is the soul of him that feareth the Lord: to whom

doth he look? and who is his strength? 16 For the eyes of the Lord are upon them that love him, he is their mighty protection and strong stay, a defence from heat, and a cover from the sun at noon, a preservation from stumbling, and an help from falling. 17 He raiseth up the soul, and lighteneth the eyes: he giveth health, life, and blessing. 18 He that sacrificeth of a thing wrongfully gotten, his offering is ridiculous; and the gifts of unjust men are not accepted. 19 The most High is not pleased with the offerings of the wicked; neither is he pacified for sin by the multitude of sacrifices. 20 Whoso bringeth an offering of the goods of the poor doeth as one that killeth the son before his father's eyes. 21 The bread of the needy is their life: he that defraudeth him thereof is a man of blood. 22 He that taketh away his neighbour's living slayeth him; and he that defraudeth the labourer of his hire is a bloodshedder. 23 When one buildeth, and another pulleth down, what profit have they then but labour? 24 When one prayeth, and another curseth, whose voice will the Lord hear? 25 He that washeth himself after the touching of a dead body, if he touch it again, what availeth his washing? 26 So is it with a man that fasteth for his sins, and goeth again, and doeth the same: who will hear his prayer? or what doth his humbling profit him?

Sir.32 1 He that keepeth the law bringeth offerings enough: he that taketh heed to the commandment offereth a peace offering. 2 He that requiteth a good turn offereth fine flour; and he that giveth alms sacrificeth praise. 3 To depart from wickedness is a thing pleasing to the Lord; and to forsake unrighteousness is a propitiation. 4 Thou shalt not appear empty before the Lord. 5 For all these things *are to be done* because of the commandment. 6 The offering of the righteous maketh the altar fat, and the sweet savour thereof is before the most High. 7 The sacrifice of a just man is acceptable. and the memorial thereof shall never be forgotten. 8 Give the Lord his honour with a good eye, and diminish not the firstfruits of thine hands. 9 In all thy gifts shew a cheerful countenance, and dedicate thy tithes with gladness. 10 Give unto the most High according as he hath enriched thee; and as thou hast gotten, give with a cheerful eye. 11 For the Lord recompenseth, and will give thee seven times as much. 12 Do not think to corrupt with gifts; for such he will not receive: and trust not to unrighteous sacrifices; for the Lord is judge, and with him is no respect of persons. 13 He will not accept any person against a poor man, but will hear the prayer of the oppressed. 14 He will not despise the supplication of the fatherless; nor the widow, when she poureth out her complaint. 15 Do not the tears run down the widow's cheeks? and is not her cry against him that causeth them to fall? 16 He that serveth the Lord shall be accepted with favour, and his prayer shall reach unto the clouds. 17 The prayer of the humble pierceth the clouds: and till it come nigh, he will not be comforted; and will not depart, till the most High shall behold to judge righteously, and execute judgment. 18 For the Lord will not be slack, neither will the Mighty be patient toward them, till he have smitten in sunder the loins of the unmerciful, and repayed vengeance to the heathen; till he have taken away the multitude of the proud, and broken the sceptre of the unrighteous; 19 Till he have rendered to every man according to his deeds, and to the works of men according to their devices; till he have judged the cause of his people, and made them to rejoice in his mercy. 20 Mercy is seasonable in the time of affliction, as clouds of rain in the time of drought.

Sir.33 1 Have mercy upon us, O Lord God of all, and behold us: 2 And send thy fear upon all the nations that seek not after thee. 3 Lift up thy hand against the strange nations, and let them see thy power. 4 As thou wast sanctified in us before them: so be thou magnified among them before us. 5 And let them know thee, as we have known thee, that there is no God but only thou, O God. 6 Shew new signs, and make other strange wonders: glorify thy hand and thy right arm, that they may set forth thy wondrous works. 7 Raise up indignation, and pour out wrath: take away the adversary, and destroy the enemy. 8 Sake the time short, remember the covenant, and let them declare thy wonderful works. 9 Let him that escapeth be consumed by the rage of the fire; and let them perish that oppress the people. 10 Smite in sunder the heads of the rulers of the heathen, that say, There is none other but we. 11 Gather all the tribes of Jacob together, and inherit thou them, as from the beginning. 12 A cheerful and good heart will have a care of his meat and diet.

Sir.34 1 Watching for riches consumeth the flesh, and the care thereof driveth away sleep. 2 Watching care will not let a man slumber, as a sore disease breaketh sleep, 3 The rich hath great labour in gathering riches together; and when he resteth, he is filled with his delicates. 4 The poor laboureth in his poor estate; and when he leaveth off, he is still needy. 5 He that loveth gold shall not be justified, and he that followeth corruption shall have enough thereof. 6 Gold hath been the ruin of many, and their destruction was present. 7 It is a stumblingblock unto them that sacrifice unto it, and every fool shall be taken therewith. 8 Blessed is the rich that is found without blemish, and hath not gone after gold. 9 Who is he? and we will call him blessed: for wonderful things hath he done among his people. 10 Who hath been tried thereby, and found perfect? then let him glory. Who might offend, and hath not offended? or done evil, and hath not done it? 11 His goods shall be established, and the congregation shall declare his alms. 12 If thou sit at a bountiful table, be not greedy upon it, and say not, There is much meat on it. 13 Remember that a wicked eye is an evil thing: and what is created more wicked than an eye? therefore it weepeth upon every occasion. 14 Stretch not thine hand whithersoever it looketh, and thrust it not with him into the dish. 15 Judge not thy neighbour by thyself: and be discreet in every point. 16 Eat as it becometh a man, those things which are set before thee; and devour note, lest thou be hated. 17 Leave off first for manners' sake; and be not unsatiable, lest thou offend. 18 When thou sittest among many, reach not thine hand out first of all. 19 A very little is sufficient for a man well nurtured, and he fetcheth not his wind short upon his bed. 20 Sound sleep cometh of moderate eating: he riseth early, and his wits are with him:

but the pain of watching, and choler, and pangs of the belly, are with an unsatiable man. 21 And if thou hast been forced to eat, arise, go forth, vomit, and thou shalt have rest. 22 My son, hear me, and despise me not, and at the last thou shalt find as I told thee: in all thy works be quick, so shall there no sickness come unto thee. 23 Whoso is liberal of his meat, men shall speak well of him; and the report of his good housekeeping will be believed. 24 But against him that is a niggard of his meat the whole city shall murmur; and the testimonies of his niggardness shall not be doubted of. 25 Shew not thy valiantness in wine; for wine hath destroyed many. 26 The furnace proveth the edge by dipping: so doth wine the hearts of the proud by drunkenness. 27 Wine is as good as life to a man, if it be drunk moderately: what life is then to a man that is without wine? for it was made to make men glad. 28 Wine measurably drunk and in season bringeth gladness of the heart, and cheerfulness of the mind: 29 But wine drunken with excess maketh bitterness of the mind, with brawling and quarrelling. 30 Drunkenness increaseth the rage of a fool till he offend: it diminisheth strength, and maketh wounds. 31 Rebuke not thy neighbour at the wine, and despise him not in his mirth: give him no despiteful words, and press not upon him with urging him *to drink.*

Sir.35 1 If thou be made the master *of a feast,* lift not thyself up, but be among them as one of the rest; take diligent care for them, and so sit down. 2 And when thou hast done all thy office, take thy place, that thou mayest be merry with them, and receive a crown for thy well ordering of the feast. 3 Speak, thou that art the elder, for it becometh thee, but with sound judgment; and hinder not musick. 4 Pour not out words where there is a musician, and shew not forth wisdom out of time. 5 A concert of musick in a banquet of wine is as a signet of carbuncle set in gold. 6 As a signet of an emerald set in a work of gold, so is the melody of musick with pleasant wine. 7 Speak, young man, if there be need of thee: and yet scarcely when thou art twice asked. 8 Let thy speech be short, comprehending much in few words; be as one that knoweth and yet holdeth his tongue. 9 If thou be among great men, make not thyself equal with them; and when ancient men are in place, use not many words. 10 Before the thunder goeth lightning; and before a shamefaced man shall go favour. 11 Rise up betimes, and be not the last; but get thee home without delay. 12 There take thy pastime, and do what thou wilt: but sin not by proud speech. 13 And for these things bless him that made thee, and hath replenished thee with his good things. 14 Whoso feareth the Lord will receive his discipline; and they that seek him early shall find favour. 15 He that seeketh the law shall be filled therewith: but the hypocrite will be offended thereat. 16 They that fear the Lord shall find judgment, and shall kindle justice as a light. 17 A sinful man will not be reproved, but findeth an excuse according to his will. 18 A man of counsel will be considerate; but a strange and proud man is not daunted with fear, even when of himself he hath done without counsel. 19 Do nothing without advice; and when thou hast once done, repent not. 20 Go not in a way wherein thou mayest fall, and stumble not among the stones. 21 Be not confident in a plain way. 22 And beware of thine own children. 23 In every good work trust thy own soul; for this is the keeping of the commandments. 24 He that believeth in the Lord taketh heed to the commandment; and he that trusteth in him shall fare never the worse.

Sir.36 1 There shall no evil happen unto him that feareth the Lord; but in temptation even again he will deliver him. 2 A wise man hateth not the law; but he that is an hypocrite therein is as a ship in a storm. 3 A man of understanding trusteth in the law; and the law is faithful unto him, as an oracle. 4 Prepare what to say, and so thou shalt be heard: and bind up instruction, and then make answer. 5 The heart of the foolish is like a cartwheel; and his thoughts are like a rolling axletree. 6 A stallion horse is as a mocking friend, he neigheth under every one that sitteth upon him. 7 Why doth one day excel another, when as all the light of every day in the year is of the sun? 8 By the knowledge of the Lord they were distinguished: and he altered seasons and feasts. 9 Some of them hath he made high days, and hallowed them, and some of them hath he made ordinary days. 10 And all men are from the ground, and Adam was created of earth: 11 In much knowledge the Lord hath divided them, and made their ways diverse. 12 Some of them hath he blessed and exalted and some of them he sanctified, and set near himself: but some of them hath he cursed and brought low, and turned out of their places. 13 As the clay is in the potter's hand, to fashion it at his pleasure: so man is in the hand of him that made him, to render to them as liketh him best. 14 Good is set against evil, and life against death: so is the godly against the sinner, and the sinner against the godly. 15 So look upon all the works of the most High; and there are two and two, one against another. 11 Though I was the last to wake up, yet I received their inheritance as from the beginning. 12 O Lord, have mercy upon the people that is called by thy name, and upon Israel, whom thou hast named thy firstborn. 13 O be merciful unto Jerusalem, thy holy city, the place of thy rest. 14 Fill Sion with thine unspeakable oracles, and thy people with thy glory: 15 Give testimony unto those that thou hast possessed from the beginning, and raise up prophets that have been in thy name. 16 Reward them that wait for thee, and let thy prophets be found faithful. 17 O Lord, hear the prayer of thy servants, according to the blessing of Aaron over thy people, that all they which dwell upon the earth may know that thou art the Lord, the eternal God. 18 The belly devoureth all meats, yet is one meat better than another. 19 As the palate tasteth divers kinds of venison: so doth an heart of understanding false speeches. 20 A froward heart causeth heaviness: but a man of experience will recompense him. 21 A woman will receive every man, yet is one daughter better than another. 22 The beauty of a woman cheereth the countenance, and a man loveth nothing better. 23 If there be kindness, meekness, and comfort, in her tongue, then is not her husband like other men. 24 He that getteth a wife beginneth a possession, a help like unto himself, and a pillar of rest. 25 Where no hedge is, there the possession is spoiled: and he that hath no wife will wander up and down mourning. 26 Who will trust a thief well appointed, that skippeth from city to city? so *who will believe* a man that hath no house, and lodgeth wheresoever the night taketh him?

Sir.37 1 Every friend saith, I am his friend also: but there is a friend, which is only a friend in name. 2 Is it not a grief unto death, when a companion and friend is turned to an enemy? 3 O wicked imagination, whence camest thou in to cover the earth with deceit? 4 There is a companion, which rejoiceth in the prosperity of a friend, but in the time of trouble will be against him. 5 There is a companion, which helpeth his friend for the belly, and taketh up the buckler against the enemy. 6 Forget not thy friend in thy mind, and be not unmindful of him in thy riches. 7 Every counsellor extolleth counsel; but there is some that counselleth for himself. 8 Beware of a counsellor, and know before what need he hath; for he will counsel for himself; lest he cast the lot upon thee, 9 And say unto thee, Thy way is good: and afterward he stand on the other side, to see what shall befall thee. 10 Consult not with one that suspecteth thee: and hide thy counsel from such as envy thee. 11 Neither consult with a woman touching her of whom she is jealous; neither with a coward in matters of war; nor with a merchant concerning exchange; nor with a buyer of selling; nor with an envious man of thankfulness; nor with an unmerciful man touching kindness; nor with the slothful for any work; nor with an hireling for a year of finishing work; nor with an idle servant of much business: hearken not unto these in any matter of counsel. 12 But be continually with a godly man, whom thou knowest to keep the commandments of the Lord, whose, mind is according to thy mind, and will sorrow with thee, if thou shalt miscarry. 13 And let the counsel of thine own heart stand: for there is no man more faithful unto thee than it. 14 For a man's mind is sometime wont to tell him more than seven watchmen, that sit above in an high tower. 15 And above all this pray to the most High, that he will direct thy way in truth. 16 Let reason go before every enterprise, and counsel before every action. 17 The countenance is a sign of changing of the heart. 18 Four manner of things appear: good and evil, life and death: but the tongue ruleth over them continually. 19 There is one that is wise and teacheth many, and yet is unprofitable to himself. 20 There is one that sheweth wisdom in words, and is hated: he shall be destitute of all food. 21 For grace is not given, him from the Lord, because he is deprived of all wisdom. 22 Another is wise to himself; and the fruits of understanding are commendable in his mouth. 23 A wise man instructeth his people; and the fruits of his understanding fail not. 24 A wise man shall be filled with blessing; and all they that see him shall count him happy. 25 The days of the life of man may be numbered: but the days of Israel are innumerable. 26 A wise man shall inherit glory among his people, and his name shall be perpetual. 27 My son, prove thy soul in thy life, and see what is evil for it, and give not that unto it. 28 For all things are not profitable for all men, neither hath every soul pleasure in every thing. 29 Be not unsatiable in any dainty thing, nor too greedy upon meats: 30 For excess of meats bringeth sickness, and surfeiting will turn into choler. 31 By surfeiting have many perished; but he that taketh heed prolongeth his life.

Sir.38 [1] Honour a physician with the honour due unto him for the uses which ye may have of him: for the Lord hath created him. [2] For of the most High cometh healing, and he shall receive honour of the king. [3] The skill of the physician shall lift up his head: and in the sight of great men he shall be in admiration. [4] The Lord hath created medicines out of the earth; and he that is wise will not abhor them. [5] Was not the water made sweet with wood, that the virtue thereof might be known? [6] And he hath given men skill, that he might be honoured in his marvellous works. [7] With such doth he heal *men,* and taketh away their pains. [8] Of such doth the apothecary make a confection; and of his works there is no end; and from him is peace over all the earth, [9] My son, in thy sickness be not negligent: but pray unto the Lord, and he will make thee whole. [10] Leave off from sin, and order thine hands aright, and cleanse thy heart from all wickedness. [11] Give a sweet savour, and a memorial of fine flour; and make a fat offering, as not being. [12] Then give place to the physician, for the Lord hath created him: let him not go from thee, for thou hast need of him. [13] There is a time when in their hands there is good success. [14] For they shall also pray unto the Lord, that he would prosper that, which they give for ease and remedy to prolong life. [15] He that sinneth before his Maker, let him fall into the hand of the physician. [16] My son, let tears fall down over the dead, and begin to lament, as if thou hadst suffered great harm thyself; and then cover his body according to the custom, and neglect not his burial. [17] Weep bitterly, and make great moan, and use lamentation, as he is worthy, and that a day or two, lest thou be evil spoken of: and then comfort thyself for thy heaviness. [18] For of heaviness cometh death, and the heaviness of the heart breaketh strength. [19] In affliction also sorrow remaineth: and the life of the poor is the curse of the heart. [20] Take no heaviness to heart: drive it away, and member the last end. [21] Forget it not, for there is no turning again: thou shalt not do him good, but hurt thyself. [22] Remember my judgment: for thine also shall be so; yesterday for me, and to day for thee. [23] When the dead is at rest, let his remembrance rest; and be comforted for him, when his Spirit is departed from him. [24] The wisdom of a learned man cometh by opportunity of leisure: and he that hath little business shall become wise. [25] How can he get wisdom that holdeth the plough, and that glorieth in the goad, that driveth oxen, and is occupied in their labours, and whose talk is of bullocks? [26] He giveth his mind to make furrows; and is diligent to give the kine fodder. [27] So every carpenter and workmaster, that laboureth night and day: and they that cut and grave seals, and are diligent to make great variety, and give themselves to counterfeit imagery, and watch to finish a work: [28] The smith also sitting by the anvil, and considering the iron work, the vapour of the fire wasteth his flesh, and he fighteth with the heat of the furnace: the noise of the hammer and the anvil is ever in his ears, and his eyes look still upon the pattern of the thing that he maketh; he setteth his mind to finish his work, and watcheth to polish it perfectly: [29] So doth the potter sitting at his work, and turning the wheel about with his feet, who is alway carefully set at his work, and maketh all his work by number; [30] He fashioneth the clay with his arm, and boweth down his strength before his feet; he applieth himself to lead it over; and he is diligent to make clean the furnace: [31] All these trust to their hands: and every one is wise in his work. [32] Without these cannot a city be inhabited: and they shall not dwell where they will, nor go up and down: [33] They shall not be sought for in publick counsel, nor sit high in the congregation: they shall not sit on the judges' seat, nor understand the sentence of judgment: they cannot declare justice and judgment; and they shall not be found where parables are spoken. [34] But they will maintain the state of the world, and *all* their desire is in the work of their craft.

Sir.39 [1] But he that giveth his mind to the law of the most High, and is occupied in the meditation thereof, will seek out the wisdom of all the ancient, and be occupied in prophecies. [2] He will keep the sayings of the renowned men: and where subtil parables are, he will be there also. [3] He will seek out the secrets of grave sentences, and be conversant in dark parables. [4] He shall serve among great men, and appear before princes: he will travel through strange countries; for he hath tried the good and the evil among men. [5] He will give his heart to resort early to the Lord that made him, and will pray before the most High, and will open his mouth in prayer, and make supplication for his sins. [6] When the great Lord will, he shall be filled with the spirit of understanding: he shall pour out wise sentences, and give thanks unto the Lord in his prayer. [7] He shall direct his counsel and knowledge, and in his secrets shall he meditate. [8] He shall shew forth that which he hath learned, and shall glory in the law of the covenant of the Lord. [9] Many shall commend his understanding; and so long as the world endureth, it shall not be blotted out; his memorial shall not depart away, and his name shall live from generation to generation. [10] Nations shall shew forth his wisdom, and the congregation shall declare his praise. [11] If he die, he shall leave a greater name than a thousand: and if he live, he shall increase it. [12] Yet have I more to say, which I have thought upon; for I am filled as the moon at the full. [13] Hearken unto me, ye holy children, and bud forth as a rose growing by the brook of the field: [14] And give ye a sweet savour as frankincense, and flourish as a lily, send forth a smell, and sing a song of praise, bless the Lord in all his works. [15] Magnify his name, and shew forth his praise with the songs of your lips, and with harps, and in praising him ye shall say after this manner: [16] All the works of the Lord are exceeding good, and whatsoever he commandeth shall be accomplished in due season. [17] And none may say, What is this? wherefore is that? for at time convenient they shall all be sought out: at his commandment the waters stood as an heap, and at the words of his mouth the receptacles of waters. [18] At his commandment is done whatsoever pleaseth him; and none can hinder, when he will save. [19] The works of all flesh are before him, and nothing can be hid from his eyes. [20] He seeth from everlasting to everlasting; and there is nothing wonderful before him. 21 A man need not to say, What is this? wherefore is that? for he hath made all things for their uses. 22 His blessing covered the dry land as a river, and watered it as a flood. 23 As he hath turned the waters into saltness: so shall the heathen inherit his wrath. 24 As his ways are plain unto the holy; so are they stumblingblocks unto the wicked. 25 For the good are good things created from the beginning: so evil things for sinners. 26 The principal things for the whole use of man's life are water, fire, iron, and salt, flour of wheat, honey, milk, and the blood of the grape, and oil, and clothing. 27 All these things are for good to the godly: so to the sinners they are turned into evil. 28 There be spirits that are created for vengeance, which in their fury lay on sore strokes; in the time of destruction they pour out their force, and appease the wrath of him that made them. 29 Fire, and hail, and famine, and death, all these were created for vengeance; 30 Teeth of wild beasts, and scorpions, serpents, and the sword punishing the wicked to destruction. 31 They shall rejoice in his commandment, and they shall be ready upon earth, when need is; and when their time is come, they shall not transgress his word. 32 Therefore from the beginning I was resolved, and thought upon these things, and have left them in writing. 33 All the works of the Lord are good: and he will give every needful thing in due season. 34 So that a man cannot say, This is worse than that: for in time they shall all be well approved. 35 And therefore praise ye the Lord with the whole heart and mouth, and bless the name of the Lord.

Sir.40 1 Great travail is created for every man, and an heavy yoke is upon the sons of Adam, from the day that they go out of their mother's womb, till the day that they return to the mother of all things. 2 Their imagination of things to come, and the day of death, *trouble* their thoughts, and *cause* fear of heart; 3 From him that sitteth on a throne of glory, unto him that is humbled in earth and ashes; 4 From him that weareth purple and a crown, unto him that is clothed with a linen frock. 5 Wrath, and envy, trouble, and unquietness, fear of death, and anger, and strife, and in the time of rest upon his bed his night sleep, do change his knowledge. 6 A little or nothing is his rest, and afterward he is in his sleep, as in a day of keeping watch, troubled in the vision of his heart, as if he were escaped out of a battle. 7 When all is safe, he awaketh, and marvelleth that the fear was nothing. 8 *Such things happen* unto all flesh, both man and beast, and that is sevenfold more upon sinners. 9 Death, and bloodshed, strife, and sword, calamities, famine, tribulation, and the scourge; 10 These things are created for the wicked, and for their sakes came the flood. 11 All things that are of the earth shall turn to the earth again: and that which is of the waters doth return into the sea. 12 All bribery and injustice shall be blotted out: but true dealing shall endure for ever. 13 The goods of the unjust shall be dried up like a river, and shall vanish with noise, like a great thunder in rain. 14 While he openeth his hand he shall rejoice: so shall transgressors come to nought. 15 The children of the ungodly shall not bring forth many branches: but are as unclean roots upon a hard rock. 16 The weed growing upon every water and bank of a river shall be pulled up before all grass. 17 Bountifulness is as a most fruitful garden, and mercifulness endureth for ever. 18 To labour, and to be content with that a man hath, is a sweet life: but he that findeth a treasure is above them both. 19 Children and the building of a city continue a man's name: but a blameless wife is counted above them both. 20 Wine and musick rejoice the heart: but the love of wisdom is above them both. 21 The pipe and the psaltery make sweet melody: but a pleasant tongue is above them both. 22 Thine eye desireth favour and beauty: but more than both corn while it is green. 23 A friend and companion never meet amiss: but above both is a wife with her husband. 24 Brethren and help are against time of trouble: but alms shall deliver more than them both. 25 Gold and silver make the foot stand sure: but counsel is esteemed above them both. 26 Riches and strength lift up the heart: but the fear of the Lord is above them both: there is no want in the fear of the Lord, and it needeth not to seek help. 27 The fear of the Lord is a fruitful garden, and covereth him above all glory. 28 My son, lead not a beggar's life; for better it is to die than to beg. 29 The life of him that dependeth on another man's table is not to be counted for a life; for he polluteth himself with other men's meat: but a wise man well nurtured will beware thereof. 30 Begging is sweet in the mouth of the shameless: but in his belly there shall burn a fire.

Sir.41 1 O death, how bitter is the remembrance of thee to a man that liveth at rest in his possessions, unto the man that hath nothing to vex him, and that hath prosperity in all things: yea, unto him that is yet able to receive meat! 2 O death, acceptable is thy sentence unto the needy, and unto him whose strength faileth, that is now in the last age, and is vexed with all things, and to him that despaireth, and hath lost patience! 3 Fear not the sentence of death, remember them that have been before thee, and that come after; for this is the sentence of the Lord over all flesh. 4 And why art thou against the pleasure of the most High? there is no inquisition in the grave, whether thou have lived ten, or an hundred, or a thousand years. 5 The children of sinners are abominable children, and they that are conversant in the dwelling of the ungodly. 6 The inheritance of sinners' children shall perish, and their posterity shall have a perpetual reproach. 7 The children will complain of an ungodly father, because they shall be reproached for his sake. 8 Woe be unto you, ungodly men, which have forsaken the law of the most high God! for if ye increase, it shall be to your destruction: 9 And if ye be born, ye shall be born to a curse: and if ye die, a curse shall be your portion. 10 All that are of the earth shall turn to earth again: so the ungodly shall go from a curse to destruction. 11 The mourning of men is about their bodies: but an ill name of sinners shall be blotted out. 12 Have regard to thy name; for that shall continue with thee above a thousand great treasures of gold. 13 A good life hath but few days: but a good name endureth for ever. 14 My children, keep discipline in peace: for wisdom that is hid, and a treasure that is not seen, what profit is in them both? 15 A man that hideth his foolishness is better than a man that hideth his wisdom. 16 Therefore be shamefaced according to my word: for it is not good to retain all shamefacedness; neither is it altogether approved in every thing. 17 Be ashamed of whoredom before father and mother: and of a lie before a prince and a mighty man; 18 Of an offence before a judge and ruler; of iniquity before a congregation and people; of unjust dealing before thy partner and friend; 19 And of theft in regard of the place where thou sojournest, and in regard of the truth of God and his covenant; and to lean with thine elbow upon the meat; and of scorning to give and take; 20 And of silence before them that salute thee; and to look upon an harlot; 21 And to turn away thy face from thy kinsman; or to take away a portion or a gift; or to gaze upon another man's wife. 22 Or to be overbusy with his maid, and come not near her bed; or of upbraiding speeches before friends; and after thou hast given, upbraid not;

Sir.42 1 Or of iterating and speaking again that which thou hast heard; and of revealing of secrets. So shalt thou be truly shamefaced and find favour before all men. Of these things be not thou ashamed, and accept no person to sin thereby: 2 Of the law of the most High, and his covenant; and of judgment to justify the ungodly; 3 Of reckoning with thy partners and travellers; or of the gift of the heritage of friends; 4 Of exactness of balance and weights; or of getting much or little; 5 And of merchants' indifferent selling; of much correction of children; and to make the side of an evil servant to bleed. 6 Sure keeping is good, where an evil wife is; and shut up, where many hands are. 7 Deliver all things in number and weight; and put all in writing that thou givest out, or receivest in. 8 Be not ashamed to inform the unwise and foolish, and the extreme aged that contendeth with those that are young: thus shalt thou be truly learned, and approved of all men living. 9 A daughter is a wakeful care to a father; and the care for her taketh away sleep: when she is young, lest she pass away the flower of her age; and being married, lest she should be hated: 10 In her virginity, lest she should be defiled and gotten with child in her father's house; and having an husband, lest she should misbehave herself; and when she is married, lest she should be barren. 11 Keep a sure watch over a shameless daughter, lest she make thee a laughingstock to thine enemies, and a byword in the city, and a reproach among the people, and make thee ashamed before the multitude. 12 Behold not every bodys beauty, and sit not in the midst of women. 13 For from garments cometh a moth, and from women wickedness. 14 Better is the churlishness of a man than a courteous woman, a woman, I say, which bringeth shame and reproach. 15 I will now remember the works of the Lord, and declare the things that I have seen: In the words of the Lord are his works. 16 The sun that giveth light looketh upon all things, and the work thereof is full of the glory of the Lord. 17 The Lord hath not given power to the saints to declare all his marvellous works, which the Almighty Lord firmly settled, that whatsoever is might be established for his glory. 18 He seeketh out the deep, and the heart, and considereth their crafty devices: for the Lord knoweth all that may be known, and he beholdeth the signs of the world. 19 He declareth the things that are past, and for to come, and revealeth the steps of hidden things. 20 No thought escapeth him, neither any word is hidden from him. 21 He hath garnished the excellent works of his wisdom, and he is from everlasting to everlasting: unto him may nothing be added, neither can he be diminished, and he hath no need of any counsellor. 22 Oh how desirable are all his works! and that a man may see even to a spark. 23 All these things live and remain for ever for all uses, and they are all obedient. 24 All things are double one against another: and he hath made nothing imperfect. 25 One thing establisheth the good or another: and who shall be filled with beholding his glory?

Sir.43 1 The pride of the height, the clear firmament, the beauty of heaven, with his glorious shew; 2 The sun when it appeareth, declaring at his rising a marvellous instrument, the work of the most High: 3 At noon it parcheth the country, and who can abide the burning heat thereof? 4 A man blowing a furnace is in works of heat, but the sun burneth the mountains three times more; breathing out fiery vapours, and sending forth bright beams, it dimmeth the eyes. 5 Great is the Lord that made it; and at his commandment runneth hastily. 6 He made the moon also to serve in her season for a declaration of times, and a sign of the world. 7 From the moon is the sign of feasts, a light that decreaseth in her perfection. 8 The month is called after her name, increasing wonderfully in her changing, being an instrument of the armies above, shining in the firmament of heaven; 9 The beauty of heaven, the glory of the stars, an ornament giving light in the highest places of the Lord. 10 At the commandment of the Holy One they will stand in their order, and never faint in their watches. 11 Look upon the rainbow, and praise him that made it; very beautiful it is in the brightness thereof. 12 It compasseth the heaven about with a glorious circle, and the hands of the most High have bended it. 13 By his commandment he maketh the snow to fall apace, and sendeth swiftly the lightnings of his judgment. 14 Through this the treasures are opened: and clouds fly forth as fowls. 15 By his great power he maketh the clouds firm, and the hailstones are broken small. 16 At his sight the mountains are shaken, and at his will the south wind bloweth. 17 The noise of the thunder maketh the earth to tremble: so doth the northern storm and the whirlwind: as birds flying he scattereth the snow, and the falling down thereof is as the lighting of grasshoppers: 18 The eye marvelleth at the beauty of the whiteness thereof, and the heart is astonished at the raining of it. 19 The hoarfrost also as salt he poureth on the earth, and being congealed, it lieth on the top of sharp stakes. 20 When the cold north wind bloweth, and the water is congealed into ice, it abideth upon every gathering together of water, and clotheth the water as with a breastplate. 21 It devoureth the mountains, and burneth the wilderness, and consumeth the grass as fire. 22 A present remedy of all is a mist coming speedily, a dew coming after heat refresheth. 23 By his counsel he appeaseth the deep, and planteth islands therein. 24 They that sail on the sea tell of the danger thereof; and when we hear it with our ears, we marvel thereat. 25 For therein be strange and wondrous works, variety of all kinds of beasts and whales created. 26 By him the end of them hath prosperous success, and by his word all things consist. 27 We may speak much, and yet come short: wherefore in sum, he is all. 28 How shall we be able to magnify him? for he is great above all his works. 29 The Lord is terrible and very great, and marvellous is his power. 30 When ye glorify the Lord, exalt him as much as ye can; for even yet will he far exceed: and when ye exalt him, put forth all your strength, and be not weary; for ye can never go far enough. 31 Who hath seen him, that he might tell us? and who can magnify him as he is? 32 There are yet hid greater things than these be, for we have seen but a few of his works. 33 For the Lord hath made all things; and to the godly hath he given wisdom.

Sir.44 1 Let us now praise famous men, and our fathers that begat us. 2 The Lord hath wrought great glory by them through his great power from the beginning. 3 Such as did bear rule in their kingdoms, men renowned for their power, giving counsel by their understanding, and declaring prophecies: 4 Leaders of the people by their counsels, and by their knowledge of learning meet for the people, wise and eloquent are their instructions: 5 Such as found out musical tunes, and recited verses in writing: 6 Rich men furnished with ability, living peaceably in their habitations: 7 All these were honoured in their generations, and were the glory of their times. 8 There be of them, that have left a name behind them, that their praises might be reported. 9 And some there be, which have no memorial; who are perished, as though they had never been; and are become as though they had never been born; and their children after them. 10 But these were merciful men, whose righteousness hath not been forgotten. 11 With their seed shall continually remain a good inheritance, and their children are within the covenant. 12 Their seed standeth fast, and their children for their sakes. 13 Their seed shall remain for ever, and their glory shall not be blotted out. 14 Their bodies are buried in peace; but their name liveth for evermore. 15 The people will tell of their wisdom, and the congregation will shew forth their praise. 16 Enoch pleased the Lord, and was translated, being an example of repentance to all generations. 17 Noah was found perfect and righteous; in the time of wrath he was taken in exchange *for the world;* therefore was he left as a remnant unto the earth, when the flood came. 18 An everlasting covenant was made with him, that all flesh should perish no more by the flood. 19 Abraham was a great father of many people: in glory was there none like unto him; 20 Who kept the law of the most High, and was in covenant with him: he established the covenant in his flesh; and when he was proved, he was found faithful. 21 Therefore he assured him by an oath, that he would bless the nations in his seed, and that he would multiply him as the dust of the earth, and exalt his seed as the stars, and cause them to inherit from sea to sea, and from the river unto the utmost part of the land. 22 With Isaac did he establish likewise *for Abraham his father's sake* the blessing of all men, and the covenant, 23 And made it rest upon the head of Jacob. He acknowledged him in his blessing, and gave him an heritage, and divided his portions; among the twelve tribes did he part them. 24 And he brought out of him a merciful man, which found favour in the sight of all flesh, even Moses, beloved of God and men, whose memorial is blessed.

Sir.45 1 2 He made him like to the glorious saints, and magnified him, so that his enemies stood in fear of him. 3 By his words he caused the wonders to cease, and he made him glorious in the sight of kings, and gave him a commandment for his people, and shewed him part of his glory. 4 He sanctified him in his faithfulness and meekness, and chose him out of all men. 5 He made him to hear his voice, and brought him into the dark cloud, and gave him commandments before his face, even the law of life and knowledge, that he might teach Jacob his covenants, and Israel his judgments. 6 He exalted Aaron, an holy man like unto him, even his brother, of the tribe of Levi. 7 An everlasting covenant he made with him and gave him the priesthood among the people; he beautified him with comely ornaments, and clothed him with a robe of glory. 8 He put upon him perfect glory; and strengthened him with rich garments, with breeches, with a long robe, and the ephod. 9 And he compassed him with pomegranates, and with many golden bells round about, that as he went there might be a sound, and a noise made that might be heard in the temple, for a memorial to the children of his people; 10 With an holy garment, with gold, and blue silk, and purple, the work of the embroiderer, with a breastplate of judgment, and with Urim and Thummim; 11 With twisted scarlet, the work of the cunning workman, with precious stones graven like seals, and set in gold, the work of the jeweller, with a writing engraved for a memorial, after the number of the tribes of Israel. 12 He set a crown of gold upon the mitre, wherein was engraved Holiness, an ornament of honour, a costly work, the desires of the eyes, goodly and beautiful. 13 Before him there were none such, neither did ever any stranger put them on, but only his children and his children's children perpetually. 14 Their sacrifices shall be wholly consumed every day twice continually. 15 Moses consecrated him, and anointed him with holy oil: this was appointed unto him by an everlasting covenant, and to his seed, so long as the heavens should remain, that they should minister unto him, and execute the office of the priesthood, and bless the people in his name. 16 He chose him out of all men living to offer sacrifices to the Lord, incense, and a sweet savour, for a memorial, to make reconciliation for his people. 17 He gave unto him his commandments, and authority in the statutes of judgments, that he should teach Jacob the testimonies, and inform Israel in his laws. 18 Strangers conspired together against him, and maligned him in the wilderness, even the men that were of Dathan's and Abiron's side, and the congregation of Core, with fury and wrath. 19 This the Lord saw, and it displeased him, and in his wrathful indignation were they consumed: he did wonders upon them, to consume them with the fiery flame. 20 But he made Aaron more honourable, and gave him an heritage, and divided unto him the firstfruits of the increase; especially he prepared bread in abundance: 21 For they eat of the sacrifices of the

Lord, which he gave unto him and his seed. 22 Howbeit in the land of the people he had no inheritance, neither had he any portion among the people: for the Lord himself is his portion and inheritance. 23 The third in glory is Phinees the son of Eleazar, because he had zeal in the fear of the Lord, and stood up with good courage of heart: when the people were turned back, and made reconciliation for Israel. 24 Therefore was there a covenant of peace made with him, that he should be the chief of the sanctuary and of his people, and that he and his posterity should have the dignity of the priesthood for ever: 25 According to the covenant made with David son of Jesse, of the tribe of Juda, that the inheritance of the king should be to his posterity alone: so the inheritance of Aaron should also be unto his seed. 26 God give you wisdom in your heart to judge his people in righteousness, that their good things be not abolished, and that their glory may endure for ever.

Sir.46 1 Jesus the son a Nave was valiant in the wars, and was the successor of Moses in prophecies, who according to his name was made great for the saving of the elect of God, and taking vengeance of the enemies that rose up against them, that he might set Israel in their inheritance. 2 How great glory gat he, when he did lift up his hands, and stretched out his sword against the cities! 3 Who before him so stood to it? for the Lord himself brought his enemies unto him. 4 Did not the sun go back by his means? and was not one day as long as two? 5 He called upon the most high Lord, when the enemies pressed upon him on every side; and the great Lord heard him. 6 And with hailstones of mighty power he made the battle to fall violently upon the nations, and in the descent *of Beth-horon* he destroyed them that resisted, that the nations might know all their strength, because he fought in the sight of the Lord, and he followed the Mighty One. 7 In the time of Moses also he did a work of mercy, he and Caleb the son of Jephunne, in that they withstood the congregation, and withheld the people from sin, and appeased the wicked murmuring. 8 And of six hundred thousand people on foot, they two were preserved to bring them in to the heritage, even unto the land that floweth with milk and honey. 9 The Lord gave strength also unto Caleb, which remained with him unto his old age: so that he entered upon the high places of the land, and his seed obtained it for an heritage: 10 That all the children of Israel might see that it is good to follow the Lord. 11 And concerning the judges, every one by name, whose heart went not a whoring, nor departed from the Lord, let their memory be blessed. 12 Let their bones flourish out of their place, and let the name of them that were honoured be continued upon their children. 13 Samuel, the prophet of the Lord, beloved of his Lord, established a kingdom, and anointed princes over his people. 14 By the law of the Lord he judged the congregation, and the Lord had respect unto Jacob. 15 By his faithfulness he was found a true prophet, and by his word he was known to be faithful in vision. 16 He called upon the mighty Lord, when his enemies pressed upon him on every side, when he offered the sucking lamb. 17 And the Lord thundered from heaven, and with a great noise made his voice to be heard. 18 And he destroyed the rulers of the Tyrians, and all the princes of the Philistines. 19 And before his long sleep he made protestations in the sight of the Lord and his anointed, I have not taken any man's goods, so much as a shoe: and no man did accuse him. 20 And after his death he prophesied, and shewed the king his end, and lifted up his voice from the earth in prophecy, to blot out the wickedness of the people.

Sir.47 1 And after him rose up Nathan to prophesy in the time of David. 2 As is the fat taken away from the peace offering, so was David chosen out of the children of Israel. 3 He played with lions as with kids, and with bears as with lambs. 4 Slew he not a giant, when he was yet but young? and did he not take away reproach from the people, when he lifted up his hand with the stone in the sling, and beat down the boasting of Goliath? 5 For he called upon the most high Lord; and he gave him strength in his right hand to slay that mighty warrior, and set up the horn of his people. 6 So the people honoured him with ten thousands, and praised him in the blessings of the Lord, in that he gave him a crown of glory. 7 For he destroyed the enemies on every side, and brought to nought the Philistines his adversaries, and brake their horn in sunder unto this day. 8 In all his works he praised the Holy One most high with words of glory; with his whole heart he sung songs, and loved him that made him. 9 He set singers also before the altar, that by their voices they might make sweet melody, and daily sing praises in their songs. 10 He beautified their feasts, and set in order the solemn times until the end, that they might praise his holy name, and that the temple might sound from morning. 11 The Lord took away his sins, and exalted his horn for ever: he gave him a covenant of kings, and a throne of glory in Israel. 12 After him rose up a wise son, and for his sake he dwelt at large. 13 Solomon reigned in a peaceable time, and was honoured; for God made all quiet round about him, that he might build an house in his name, and prepare his sanctuary for ever. 14 How wise wast thou in thy youth and, as a flood, filled with understanding! 15 Thy soul covered the whole earth, and thou filledst it with dark parables. 16 Thy name went far unto the islands; and for thy peace thou wast beloved. 17 The countries marvelled at thee for thy songs, and proverbs, and parables, and interpretations. 18 By the name of the Lord God, which is called the Lord God of Israel, thou didst gather gold as tin and didst multiply silver as lead. 19 Thou didst bow thy loins unto women, and by thy body thou wast brought into subjection. 20 Thou didst stain thy honour, and pollute thy seed: so that thou broughtest wrath upon thy children, and wast grieved for thy folly. 21 So the kingdom was divided, and out of Ephraim ruled a rebellious kingdom. 22 But the Lord will never leave off his mercy, neither shall any of his works perish, neither will he abolish the posterity of his elect, and the seed of him that loveth him he will not take away: wherefore he gave a remnant unto Jacob, and out of him a root unto David. 23 Thus rested Solomon with his fathers, and of his seed he left behind him Roboam, even the foolishness of the people, and one that had no understanding, who turned away the people through his counsel. There was also Jeroboam the son of Nebat, who caused Israel to sin, and shewed Ephraim the way of sin: 24 And their sins were multiplied exceedingly, that they were driven out of the land. 25 For they sought out all wickedness, till the vengeance came upon them.

Sir.48 1 Then stood up Elias the prophet as fire, and his word burned like a lamp. 2 He brought a sore famine upon them, and by his zeal he diminished their number. 3 By the word of the Lord he shut up the heaven, and also three times brought down fire. 4 O Elias, how wast thou honoured in thy wondrous deeds! and who may glory like unto thee! 5 Who didst raise up a dead man from death, and his soul from the place of the dead, by the word of the most High: 6 Who broughtest kings to destruction, and honourably men from their bed: 7 Who heardest the rebuke of the Lord in Sinai, and in Horeb the judgment of vengeance: 8 Who anointedst kings to take revenge, and prophets to succeed after him: 9 Who was taken up in a whirlwind of fire, and in a chariot of fiery horses: 10 Who wast ordained for reproofs in their times, to pacify the wrath of the Lord's judgment, before it brake forth into fury, and to turn the heart of the father unto the son, and to restore the tribes of Jacob. 11 Blessed are they that saw thee, and slept in love; for we shall surely live. 12 Elias it was, who was covered with a whirlwind: and Eliseus was filled with his spirit: whilst he lived, he was not moved with the presence of any prince, neither could any bring him into subjection. 13 No word could overcome him; and after his death his body prophesied. 14 He did wonders in his life, and at his death were his works marvellous. 15 For all this the people repented not, neither departed they from their sins, till they were spoiled and carried out of their land, and were scattered through all the earth: yet there remained a small people, and a ruler in the house of David: 16 Of whom some did that which was pleasing to God, and some multiplied sins. 17 Ezekias fortified his city, and brought in water into the midst thereof: he digged the hard rock with iron, and made wells for waters. 18 In his time Sennacherib came up, and sent Rabsaces, and lifted up his hand against Sion, and boasted proudly. 19 Then trembled their hearts and hands, and they were in pain, as women in travail. 20 But they called upon the Lord which is merciful, and stretched out their hands toward him: and immediately the Holy One heard them out of heaven, and delivered them by the ministry of Esay. 21 He smote the host of the Assyrians, and his angel destroyed them. 22 For Ezekias had done the thing that pleased the Lord, and was strong in the ways of David his father, as Esay the prophet, who was great and faithful in his vision, had commanded him. 23 In his time the sun went backward, and he lengthened the king's life. 24 He saw by an excellent spirit what should come to pass at the last, and he comforted them that mourned in Sion. 25 He shewed what should come to pass for ever, and secret things or ever they came.

Sir.49 1 The remembrance of Josias is like the composition of the perfume that is made by the art of the apothecary: it is sweet as honey in all mouths, and as musick at a banquet of wine. 2 He behaved himself uprightly in the conversion of the people, and took away the abominations of iniquity.

3 He directed his heart unto the Lord, and in the time of the ungodly he established the worship of God. 4 All, except David and Ezekias and Josias, were defective: for they forsook the law of the most High, even the kings of Juda failed. 5 Therefore he gave their power unto others, and their glory to a strange nation. 6 They burnt the chosen city of the sanctuary, and made the streets desolate, according to the prophecy of Jeremias. 7 For they entreated him evil, who nevertheless was a prophet, sanctified in his mother's womb, that he might root out, and afflict, and destroy; and that he might build up also, and plant. 8 It was Ezekiel who saw the glorious vision, which was shewed him upon the chariot of the cherubims. 9 For he made mention of the enemies under the figure of the rain, and directed them that went right. 10 And of the twelve prophets let the memorial be blessed, and let their bones flourish again out of their place: for they comforted Jacob, and delivered them by assured hope. 11 How shall we magnify Zorobabel? even he was as a signet on the right hand: 12 So was Jesus the son of Josedec: who in their time builded the house, and set up an holy temple to the Lord, which was prepared for everlasting glory. 13 And among the elect was Neemias, whose renown is great, who raised up for us the walls that were fallen, and set up the gates and the bars, and raised up our ruins again. 14 But upon the earth was no man created like Enoch; for he was taken from the earth. 15 Neither was there a young man born like Joseph, a governor of his brethren, a stay of the people, whose bones were regarded of the Lord. 16 Sem and Seth were in great honour among men, and so was Adam above every living thing in creation.

Sir.50 1 Simon the high priest, the son of Onias, who in his life repaired the house again, and in his days fortified the temple: 2 And by him was built from the foundation the double height, the high fortress of the wall about the temple: 3 In his days the cistern to receive water, being in compass as the sea, was covered with plates of brass: 4 He took care of the temple that it should not fall, and fortified the city against besieging: 5 How was he honoured in the midst of the people in his coming out of the sanctuary! 6 He was as the morning star in the midst of a cloud, and as the moon at the full: 7 As the sun shining upon the temple of the most High, and as the rainbow giving light in the bright clouds: 8 And as the flower of roses in the spring of the year, as lilies by the rivers of waters, and as the branches of the frankincense tree in the time of summer: 9 As fire and incense in the censer, and as a vessel of beaten gold set with all manner of precious stones: 10 And as a fair olive tree budding forth fruit, and as a cypress tree which groweth up to the clouds. 11 When he put on the robe of honour, and was clothed with the perfection of glory, when he went up to the holy altar, he made the garment of holiness honourable. 12 When he took the portions out of the priests' hands, he himself stood by the hearth of the altar, compassed about, as a young cedar in Libanus; and as palm trees compassed they him round about. 13 So were all the sons of Aaron in their glory, and the oblations of the Lord in their hands, before all the congregation of Israel. 14 And finishing the service at the altar, that he might adorn the offering of the most high Almighty, 15 He stretched out his hand to the cup, and poured of the blood of the grape, he poured out at the foot of the altar a sweetsmelling savour unto the most high King of all. 16 Then shouted the sons of Aaron, and sounded the silver trumpets, and made a great noise to be heard, for a remembrance before the most High. 17 Then all the people together hasted, and fell down to the earth upon their faces to worship their Lord God Almighty, the most High. 18 The singers also sang praises with their voices, with great variety of sounds was there made sweet melody. 19 And the people besought the Lord, the most High, by prayer before him that is merciful, till the solemnity of the Lord was ended, and they had finished his service. 20 Then he went down, and lifted up his hands over the whole congregation of the children of Israel, to give the blessing of the Lord with his lips, and to rejoice in his name. 21 And they bowed themselves down to worship the second time, that they might receive a blessing from the most High. 22 Now therefore bless ye the God of all, which only doeth wondrous things every where, which exalteth our days from the womb, and dealeth with us according to his mercy. 23 He grant us joyfulness of heart, and that peace may be in our days in Israel for ever: 24 That he would confirm his mercy with us, and deliver us at his time! 25 There be two manner of nations which my heart abhorreth, and the third is no nation: 26 They that sit upon the mountain of Samaria, and they that dwell among the Philistines, and that foolish people that dwell in Sichem. 27 Jesus the son of Sirach of Jerusalem hath written in this book the instruction of understanding and knowledge, who out of his heart poured forth wisdom. 28 Blessed is he that shall be exercised in these things; and he that layeth them up in his heart shall become wise. 29 For if he do them, he shall be strong to all things: for the light of the Lord leadeth him, who giveth wisdom to the godly. Blessed be the name of the Lord for ever. Amen, Amen.

Sir.51 1 I will thank thee, O Lord and King, and praise thee, O God my Saviour: I do give praise unto thy name: 2 For thou art my defender and helper, and has preserved my body from destruction, and from the snare of the slanderous tongue, and from the lips that forge lies, and has been mine helper against mine adversaries: 3 And hast delivered me, according to the multitude of they mercies and greatness of thy name, from the teeth of them that were ready to devour me, and out of the hands of such as sought after my life, and from the manifold afflictions which I had; 4 From the choking of fire on every side, and from the midst of the fire which I kindled not; 5 From the depth of the belly of hell, from an unclean tongue, and from lying words. 6 By an accusation to the king from an unrighteous tongue my soul drew near even unto death, my life was near to the hell beneath. 7 They compassed me on every side, and there was no man to help me: I looked for the succour of men, but there was none. 8 Then thought I upon thy mercy, O Lord, and upon thy acts of old, how thou deliverest such as wait for thee, and savest them out of the hands of the enemies. 9 Then lifted I up my supplications from the earth, and prayed for deliverance

from death. 10 I called upon the Lord, the Father of my Lord, that he would not leave me in the days of my trouble, and in the time of the proud, when there was no help. 11 I will praise thy name continually, and will sing praises with thanksgiving; and so my prayer was heard: 12 For thou savedst me from destruction, and deliveredst me from the evil time: therefore will I give thanks, and praise thee, and bless they name, O Lord. 13 When I was yet young, or ever I went abroad, I desired wisdom openly in my prayer. 14 I prayed for her before the temple, and will seek her out even to the end. 15 Even from the flower till the grape was ripe hath my heart delighted in her: my foot went the right way, from my youth up sought I after her. 16 I bowed down mine ear a little, and received her, and gat much learning. 17 I profited therein, therefore will I ascribe glory unto him that giveth me wisdom. 18 For I purposed to do after her, and earnestly I followed that which is good; so shall I not be confounded. 19 My soul hath wrestled with her, and in my doings I was exact: I stretched forth my hands to the heaven above, and bewailed my ignorances of her. 20 I directed my soul unto her, and I found her in pureness: I have had my heart joined with her from the beginning, therefore shall I not be forsaken. 21 My heart was troubled in seeking her: therefore have I gotten a good possession. 22 The Lord hath given me a tongue for my reward, and I will praise him therewith. 23 Draw near unto me, ye unlearned, and dwell in the house of learning. 24 Wherefore are ye slow, and what say ye to these things, seeing your souls are very thirsty? 25 I opened my mouth, and said, Buy her for yourselves without money. 26 Put your neck under the yoke, and let your soul receive instruction: she is hard at hand to find. 27 Behold with your eyes, how that I have but little labour, and have gotten unto me much rest. 28 Get learning with a great sum of money, and get much gold by her. 29 Let your soul rejoice in his mercy, and be not ashamed of his praise. 30 Work your work betimes, and in his time he will give you your reward.

ESAIAS (ISAIAH)

Isa.1 1 The vision which Esaias the son of Amos saw, which he saw against Juda, and against Jerusalem, in the reign of Ozias, and Joatham, and Achaz, and Ezekias, who reigned over Judea. 2 Hear, O heaven, and hearken, O earth: for the Lord has spoken, *saying*, I have begotten and reared up children, but they have rebelled against me. 3 The ox knows his owner, and the ass his master's crib: but Israel does not know me, and the people has not regarded me. 4 Ah sinful nation, a people full of sins, an evil seed, lawless children: ye have forsaken the Lord, and provoked the Holy One of Israel. 5 Why should ye be smitten *any* more, transgressing more and more? the whole head is pained, and the whole heart sad. 6 From the feet to the head, there is no soundness in them; neither wound, nor bruise, nor festering ulcer *are healed*: it is not possible to apply a plaister, nor oil, nor bandages. 7 Your land is desolate, your cities burned with fire: your land, strangers devour it in your presence, and it is made desolate, overthrown by strange nations. 8 The daughter of Sion shall be deserted as a tent in a vineyard, and as a storehouse of fruits in a garden of cucumbers, as a besieged city. 9 And if the Lord of Sabaoth had not left us a seed, we should have been as Sodom, and we should have been made like Gomorrha. 10 Hear the word of the Lord, ye rulers of Sodoma; attend to the law of God, thou people of Gomorrha. 11 Of what *value* to me is the abundance of your sacrifices? saith the Lord: I am full of whole-burnt-offerings of rams; and I delight not in the fat of lambs, and the blood of bulls and goats: 12 neither shall ye come *with these* to appear before me; for who has required these things at your hands? Ye shall no more tread my court. 13 Though ye bring fine flour, *it is* vain; incense is an abomination to me; I cannot bear your new moons, and your sabbaths, and the great day; 14 *your* fasting, and rest from work, your new moons also, and your feasts my soul hates: ye have become loathsome to me; I will no more pardon your sins. 15 When ye stretch forth your hands, I will turn away mine eyes from you: and though ye make many supplications, I will not hearken to you; for your hands are full of blood. 16 Wash you, be clean; remove your iniquities from your souls before mine eyes; cease from your iniquities; 17 learn to do well; diligently seek judgment, deliver him that is suffering wrong, plead for the orphan, and obtain justice for the widow. 18 And come, let us reason together, saith the Lord: and though your sins be as purple, I will make them white as snow; and though they be as scarlet, I will make *them* white as wool. 19 And if ye be willing, and hearken to me, ye shall eat the good of the land: 20 but if ye be not willing, nor hearken to me, a sword shall devour you: for the mouth of the Lord has spoken this. 21 How has the faithful city Sion, *once* full of judgment, become a harlot! wherein righteousness lodged, but now murderers. 22 Your silver is worthless, thy wine merchants mix the wine with water. 23 Thy princes are rebellious, companions of thieves, loving bribes, seeking after rewards; not pleading for orphans, and not heeding the cause of widows. 24 Therefore thus saith the Lord, the Lord of hosts, Woe to the mighty *men* of Israel; for my wrath shall not cease against mine adversaries, and I will execute judgment on mine enemies. 25 And I will bring my hand upon thee, and purge thee completely, and I will destroy the rebellious, and will take away from thee all transgressors. 26 And I will establish thy judges as before, and thy counsellors as at the beginning: and afterward thou shalt be called the city of righteousness, the faithful mother-city of Sion. 27 For her captives shall be saved with judgment, and with mercy. 28 And the transgressors and the sinners shall be crushed together, and they that forsake the Lord shall be utterly consumed. 29 For they shall be ashamed of their idols, which they delighted in, and they are made ashamed of the gardens which they coveted. 30 For they shall be as a turpentine tree that has cast its leaves, and as a garden that has no water. 31 And their strength shall be as a thread of tow, and their works as sparks, and the transgressors and the sinners shall be burnt up together, and there shall be none to quench *them*.

Isa.2 1 The word which came to Esaias the son of Amos concerning Judea, and concerning Jerusalem. 2 For in the last days the mountain of the Lord shall be glorious, and the house of God *shall be* on the top of the mountains, and it shall be exalted above the hills; and all nations shall come to it. 3 And many nations shall go and say, Come, and let us go up to the mountain of the Lord, and to the house of the God of Jacob; and he will tell us his way, and we will walk in it: for out of Sion shall go forth the law, and the word of the Lord out of Jerusalem. 4 And he shall judge among the nations, and shall rebuke many people: and they shall beat their swords into plow- shares, and their spears into sickles: and nation shall not take up sword against nation, neither shall they learn to war any more. 5 And now, O house of Jacob, come, *and* let us walk in the light of the Lord. 6 For he has forsaken his people the house of Israel, because their land is filled as at the beginning with divinations, as the *land* of the Philistines, and many strange children were born to them. 7 For their land is filled with silver and gold, and there was no number of their treasures; their land also is filled with horses, and there was no number of chariots. 8 And the land is filled with abominations, *even* the works of their hands; and they have worshipped *the works* which their fingers made. 9 And the mean man bowed down, and the great man was humbled: and I will not pardon them. 10 Now therefore enter ye into the rocks, and hide yourselves in the earth, for fear of the Lord, and by reason of the glory of his might, when he shall arise to strike terribly the earth. 11 For the eyes of the Lord are high, but man is low; and the haughtiness of men shall be brought low, and the Lord alone shall be exalted in that day. 12 For the day of the Lord of hosts shall be upon every one that is proud and haughty, and upon every one that is high and towering, and they shall be brought down; 13 and upon every cedar of Libanus, of them that are high and towering, and upon every oak of Basan, 14 and upon every high mountain, and upon every high hill, 15 and upon every high tower, and upon every high wall, 16 and upon every ship of the sea, and upon every display of fine ships. 17 And every man shall be brought low, and the pride of men shall fall: and the Lord alone shall be exalted in that day. 18 And they shall hide all *idols* made with hands, 19 having carried *them* into the caves, and into the clefts of the rocks, and into the caverns of the earth, for fear of the Lord, and by reason of the glory of his might, when he shall arise to strike terribly the earth. 20 For in that day a man shall cast forth his silver and gold abominations, which they made *in order* to worship vanities and bats; 21 to enter into the caverns of the solid rock, and into the clefts of the rocks, for fear of the Lord, and by reason of the glory of his might, when he shall arise to strike terribly the earth.

Isa.3 1 Behold now, the Lord, the Lord of hosts, will take away from Jerusalem and from Judea the mighty man and mighty woman, the strength of bread, and the strength of water, 2 the great and mighty man, the warrior and the judge, and the prophet, and the counsellor, and the elder, 3 the captain of fifty also, and the honourable counsellor, and the wise artificer, and the intelligent hearer. 4 And I will make youths their princes, and mockers shall have dominion over them. 5 And the people shall fall, man upon man, and *every* man upon his neighbor: the child shall insult the elder man, and the base the honourable. 6 For a man shall lay hold of his brother, as one of his father's household, saying, Thou hast raiment, be thou our ruler, and let my meat be under thee. 7 And he shall answer in that day, and say, I will not be thy ruler; for I have no bread in my house, nor raiment: I will not be the ruler of this people. 8 For Jerusalem is ruined, and Judea has fallen, and their tongues *have spoken* with iniquity, disobedient *as they are* towards the Lord. 9 Wherefore now their glory has been brought low, and the shame of their countenance has withstood them, and they have proclaimed their sin as Sodom, and made it manifest. 10 Woe to their soul, for they have devised an evil counsel against themselves, saying against themselves, Let us bind the just, for he is burdensome to us: therefore shall they eat the fruits of their works. 11 Woe to the transgressor! evils shall happen to him according to the works of his hands. 12 O my people, your exactors strip you, and extortioners rule over you: O my people, they that pronounce you blesses lead you astray, and pervert the path of your feet. 13 But now the Lord will stand up for judgment, and will enter into judgment with his people. 14 The Lord himself shall enter into judgment with the elders of the people, and with their rulers: but why have ye set my vineyard on fire, and *why is* the spoil of the poor in your houses? 15 Why do ye wrong my people, and shame the face of the poor? 16 Thus saith the Lord, Because the daughters of Sion are haughty, and have walked with an outstretched neck, and with winking of the eyes, and motion of the feet, at the same time drawing their garments in trains, and at the same time sporting with their feet: 17 therefore the Lord will humble the chief daughters of Sion, and the Lord will expose their form in that day; 18 and the Lord will take away the glory of their raiment, the curls and the fringes, and the crescents, 19 and the chains, and the ornaments of their faces, 20 and the array of glorious ornaments, and the armlets, and the bracelets, and the wreathed work, and the finger-rings, and the ornaments for the right hand, 21 22 23 and the ear-rings, and the garments with scarlet borders, and the garments with purple grounds, and the shawls to be worn in the house, and the Spartan transparent dresses, and those made of fine linen, and the purple *ones*, and the scarlet *ones*, and the fine linen, interwoven with gold and purple, and the light coverings for couches. 24 And there shall be instead of a sweet smell, dust; and instead of a girdle, thou shalt gird thyself with a rope; and instead of a golden ornament for the head, thou shalt have baldness on account of thy works; and instead of a tunic with a scarlet ground, thou shalt gird thyself with sackcloth. 25 And thy most beautiful son whom thou lovest shall fall by the sword; and your mighty men shall fall by the sword, and shall be brought low. 26 And the stores of your ornaments shall mourn, and thou shalt be left alone, and shalt be levelled with the ground.

Isa.4 1 And seven women shall take hold of one man, saying, We will eat our own bread, and wear our own raiment: only let thy name be called upon us, *and* take away our reproach. 2 And in that day God shall shine gloriously in counsel on the earth, to exalt and glorify the remnant of Israel. 3 And it shall be, *that* the remnant left in Sion, and the remnant left in Jerusalem, *even* all that are appointed to life in Jerusalem, shall be called holy. 4 For the Lord shall wash away the filth of the sons and daughters of Sion, and shall purge out the blood from the midst of them, with the spirit of judgment, and the spirit of burning. 5 And he shall come, and it shall be with regard to every place of mount Sion, yea, all the region round about it shall a cloud overshadow by day, and *there shall be* as it were the smoke and light of fire burning by night: and upon all the glory shall be a defence. 6 And it shall be for a shadow from the heat, and as a shelter and a hiding place from inclemency *of weather* and from rain.

Isa.5 1 Now I will sing to *my* beloved a song of my beloved concerning my vineyard. *My* beloved had a vineyard on a high hill in a fertile place. 2 And I made a hedge round it, and dug a trench, and planted a choice vine, and built a tower in the midst of it, and dug a place for the wine-vat in it: and I waited *for it* to bring forth grapes, and it brought forth thorns. 3 And now, ye dwellers in Jerusalem, and *every* man of Juda, judge between me and my vineyard. 4 What shall I do any more to my vineyard, that I have not done to it? Whereas I expected *it* to bring forth grapes, but it has brought forth thorns. 5 And now I will tell you what I will do to my vineyard: I will take away its hedge, and it shall be for a spoil; and I will pull down its walls, and it shall be *left* to be trodden down. 6 And I will forsake my vineyard; and it shall not be pruned, nor dug, and thorns shall come up upon it as on barren land; and I will command the clouds to rain no rain upon it. 7 For the vineyard of the Lord of hosts is the house of Israel, and the men of Juda *his* beloved plant: I expected *it* to bring forth judgment, and it brought forth iniquity; and not righteousness, but a cry. 8 Woe *to them* that join house to house, and add field to field, that they may take away something of their neighbor's: will ye dwell alone upon the land? 9 For these things have reached the ears of the Lord of hosts: for though many houses should be built, many and fair houses shall be desolate, and there shall be no inhabitants in them. 10 For where ten yoke of oxen plough *the land* shall yield one jar-full, and he that sows six homers shall produce three measures. 11 Woe *to them* that rise up in the morning, and follow strong drink; who wait *at it till* evening: for the wine shall inflame them. 12 For they drink wine with harp, and psaltery, and drums, and pipes: but they regard not the works of the Lord, and consider not the works of his hands. 13 Therefore my people have been taken captive, because they know not the Lord: and there has been a multitude of dead *bodies*, because of hunger and of thirst for water. 14 Therefore hell has enlarged its desire and opened its mouth without ceasing: and her glorious and great, and her rich and her pestilent men shall go down *into it*. 15 And the mean man shall be brought low, and the great man shall be disgraced, and the lofty eyes shall be brought low. 16 But the Lord of hosts shall be exalted in judgment, and the holy God shall be glorified in righteousness. 17 And they that were spoiled shall be fed as bulls, and lambs shall feed on the waste places of them that are taken away. 18 Woe *to them* that draw sins to them as with a long rope, and iniquities as with a thong of the heifer's yoke: ¹⁹ who say, Let him speedily hasten what he will do, that we may see *it*: and let the counsel of the Holy One of Israel come, that we may know *it*. ²⁰ Woe *to them* that call evil good, and good evil; who make darkness light, and light darkness; who make bitter sweet, and sweet bitter. ²¹ Woe *to them* that are wise in their own conceit, and knowing in their own sight. ²² Woe to the strong *ones* of you that drink wine, and the mighty *ones* that mingle strong drink: ²³ who justify the ungodly for rewards, and take away the righteousness of the righteous. ²⁴ Therefore as stubble shall be burnt by a coal of fire, and shall be consumed by a violent flame, their root shall be as chaff, and their flower shall go up as dust: for they rejected the law of the Lord of hosts, and insulted the word of the Holy One of Israel. ²⁵ Therefore the Lord of hosts was greatly angered against his people, and he reached forth his hand upon them, and smote them: and the mountains were troubled, and their carcasses were as dung in the midst of the way: yet for all this his anger has not been turned away, but his hand is yet raised. ²⁶ Therefore shall he lift up a signal to the nations that are afar, and shall hiss for them from the end of the earth; and, behold, they are coming very quickly. ²⁷ They shall not hunger nor be weary, neither shall they slumber nor sleep; neither shall they loose their girdles from their loins, neither shall their shoe-latchets be broken. ²⁸ Whose arrows are sharp, and their bows bent; their horses' hoofs are counted as solid rock: their chariot-wheels are as a storm. ²⁹ They rage as lions, and draw nigh as a lion's whelps: and he shall seize, and roar as a wild beast, and he shall cast *them* forth, and there shall be none to deliver them. ³⁰ And he shall roar on account of them in that day, as the sound of the swelling sea; and they shall look to the land, and, behold, *there shall be* thick darkness in their perplexity.

Isa.6 ¹ And it came to pass in the year in which king Ozias died, *that* I saw the Lord sitting on a high and exalted throne, and the house was full of his glory. ² And seraphs stood round about him: each one had six wings: and with two they covered *their* face, and with two they covered *their* feet, and with two they flew. ³ And one cried to the other, and they said, Holy, holy, holy *is the* Lord of hosts: the whole earth is full of his glory. ⁴ And the lintel shook at the voice they uttered, and the house was filled with smoke. ⁵ And I said, Woe is me, for I am pricked to the heart; for being a man, and having unclean lips, I dwell in the midst of a people having unclean lips; and I have seen with mine eyes the King, the Lord of hosts. ⁶ And there was sent to me one of the seraphs, and he had in his hand a coal, which he had taken off the altar with the tongs: ⁷ and he touched my mouth, and said, Behold, this has touched thy lips, and will take away thine iniquities, and will purge off thy sins. ⁸ And I heard the voice of the Lord, saying, Whom shall I send, and who will go to this people? And I said, behold, I am *here*, send me. And he said, Go, and say to this people, ⁹ Ye shall hear indeed, but ye shall not understand; and ye shall see indeed, but ye shall not perceive. ¹⁰ For the heart of this people has become gross, and their ears are dull of hearing, and their eyes have they closed; lest they should

see with their eyes, and hear with their ears, and understand with their heart, and be converted, and I should heal them. ¹¹ And I said, How long, O Lord? And he said, Until cities be deserted by reason of their not being inhabited, and the houses by reason of there being no men, and the land shall be left desolate. ¹² And after this God shall remove the men far off, and they that are left upon the land shall be multiplied. ¹³ And yet there shall be a tenth upon it, and again it shall be for a spoil, as a turpentine tree, and as an acorn when it falls out of its husk.

Isa.7 ¹ And it came to pass in the days of Achaz *the son* of Joatham, the son of Ozias, king of Juda, there came up Rasim king of Aram, and Phakee son of Romelias, king of Israel, against Jerusalem to war against it, but they could not take it. ² And a message was brought to the house of David, saying, Aram has conspired with Ephraim. And his soul was amazed, and the soul of his people, as in a wood a tree is moved by the wind. ³ And the Lord said to Esaias, Go forth to meet Achaz, thou, and thy son Jasub who is left, to the pool of the upper way of the fuller's field. ⁴ And thou shalt say to him, Take care to be quiet, and fear not, neither let thy soul be disheartened because of these two smoking firebrands: for when my fierce anger is over, I will heal again. ⁵ And *as for* the son of Aram, and the son of Romelias, forasmuch as they have devised an evil counsel, *saying,* ⁶ We will go up against Judea, and having conferred with them we will turn them away to our side, and we will make the son of Tabeel king of it; ⁷ thus saith the Lord of hosts, This counsel shall not abide, nor come to pass. ⁸ But the head of Aram is Damascus, and the head of Damascus, Rasim; and yet within sixty and five years the kingdom of Ephraim shall cease from *being* a people. ⁹ And the head of Ephraim is Somoron, and the head of Somoron the son of Romelias: but if ye believe not, neither will ye at all understand. ¹⁰ And the Lord again spoke to Achaz, saying, ¹¹ Ask for thyself a sign of the Lord thy God, in the depth or in the height. ¹² And Achaz said, I will not ask, neither will I tempt the Lord. ¹³ And he said, Hear ye now, O house of David; is it a little thing for you to contend with men? and how do ye contend against the Lord? ¹⁴ Therefore the Lord himself shall give you a sign; behold, a virgin shall conceive in the womb, and shall bring forth a son, and thou shalt call his name Emmanuel. ¹⁵ Butter and honey shall he eat, before he knows either to prefer evil *or* choose the good. ¹⁶ For before the child shall know good or evil, he refuses evil, to choose the good; and the land shall be forsaken which thou art afraid of because of the two kings. ¹⁷ But God shall bring upon thee, and upon thy people, and upon the house of thy father, days which have never come, from the day that Ephraim took away from Juda the king of the Assyrians. ¹⁸ And it shall come to pass in that day that the Lord shall hiss for the flies, which *insect* shall rule over a part of the river of Egypt, and for the bee which is in the land of the Assyrians. ¹⁹ And they all shall enter into the clefts of the land, and into the holes of the rocks, and into the caves, and into every ravine. ²⁰ In that day the Lord shall shave with the hired razor of the king of Assyria beyond the river the head, and the hairs of the feet, and will remove the beard. 21 And it shall come to pass in that day, *that* a man shall rear a heifer, and two sheep. 22 And it shall come to pass from their drinking an abundance of milk, *that* every one that is left on the land shall eat butter and honey. 23 And it shall come to pass in that day, *for* every place where there shall be a thousand vines at a thousand shekels, they shall become barren land and thorns. 24 *Men* shall enter thither with arrow and bow; for all the land shall be *barren* ground and thorns. 25 And every mountain shall be certainly ploughed: there shall no fear come thither: for there shall be from *among* the *barren* ground and thorns that whereon cattle shall feed and oxen shall tread.

Isa.8 1 And the Lord said to me, Take to thyself a volume of a great new *book*, and write in it with a man's pen concerning the making a rapid plunder of spoils; for it is near at hand. 2 And make me witnesses *of* faithful men, Urias, and Zacharias the son of Barachias. 3 And I went in to the prophetess; and she conceived, and bore a son. And the Lord said to me, Call his name, Spoil quickly, plunder speedily. 4 For before the child shall know *how* to call *his* father or *his* mother, *one* shall take the power of Damascus and the spoils of Samaria before the king of the Assyrians. 5 And the Lord spoke to me yet again, *saying,* 6 Because this people chooses not the water of Siloam that goes softly, but wills to have Rassin, and the son of Romelias *to be* king over you; 7 therefore, behold, the Lord brings up upon you the water of the river, strong and abundant, *even* the king of the Assyrians, and his glory: and he shall come up over every valley of yours, and shall walk over every wall of yours: 8 and he shall take away from Juda *every* man who shall be able to lift up his head, *and every one* able to accomplish anything; and his camp shall fill the breadth of thy land, O God with us. 9 Know, ye Gentiles, and be conquered; hearken ye, even to the extremity of the earth: be conquered, after ye strengthened yourselves; for even if ye should again strengthen yourselves, ye shall again be conquered. 10 And whatsoever counsel ye shall take, the Lord shall bring it to nought; and whatsoever word ye shall speak, it shall not stand among you: for God is with us. 11 Thus saith the Lord, With a strong hand they revolt from the course of the way of this people, saying, 12 Let them not say, *It is* hard, for whatsoever this people says, is hard: but fear not ye their fear, neither be dismayed. 13 Sanctify ye the Lord himself; and he shall be thy fear. 14 And if thou shalt trust in him, he shall be to thee for a sanctuary; and ye shall not come against *him* as against a stumbling-stone, neither as against the falling of a rock: but the houses of Jacob are in a snare, and the dwellers in Jerusalem in a pit. 15 Therefore many among them shall be weak, and fall, and be crushed; and they shall draw nigh, and men shall be taken securely. 16 Then shall those who seal themselves that they may not learn the law be made manifest. 17 And *one* shall say, I will wait for God, who has turned away his face from the house of Jacob, and I will trust in him. 18 Behold I and the children which God has given me: and they shall be *for* signs and wonders in the house of Israel from the Lord of hosts, who dwells in mount Sion. 19 And if they should say to you, Seek those who have in them a divining

spirit, and them that speak out of the earth, them that speak vain words, who speak out of their belly: shall not a nation diligently seek to their God? why do they seek to the dead concerning the living? 20 For he has given the law for a help, that they should not speak according to this word, concerning which there are no gifts to give for it. 21 And famine shall come sorely upon you, and it shall come to pass, *that* when ye shall be hungry, ye shall be grieved, and ye shall speak ill of the prince and your fathers' ordinances: and they shall look up to heaven above, 22 and they shall look on the earth below, and behold severe distress, and darkness, affliction, and anguish, and darkness so that *one cannot* see; and he that is in anguish shall not be distressed only for a time.

Isa.9 1 Drink this first. Act quickly, O land of Zabulon, land of Nephthalim, and the rest *inhabiting* the sea-coast, and *the land* beyond Jordan, Galilee of the Gentiles. 2 O people walking in darkness, behold a great light: ye that dwell in the region *and* shadow of death, a light shall shine upon you. 3 The multitude of the people which thou hast brought down in thy joy, they shall even rejoice before thee as they that rejoice in harvest, and as they that divide the spoil. 4 Because the yoke that was laid upon them has been taken away, and the rod that was on their neck: for he has broken the rod of the exactors, as in the day of Madiam. 5 For they shall compensate for every garment that has been acquired by deceit, and *all* raiment with restitution; and they shall be willing, *even* if they were burnt with fire. 6 For a child is born to us, and a son is given to us, whose government is upon his shoulder: and his name is called the Messenger of great counsel: for I will bring peace upon the princes, and health to him. 7 His government shall be great, and of his peace there is no end: *it shall be* upon the throne of David, and *upon* his kingdom, to establish it, and to support *it* with judgment and with righteousness, from henceforth and forever. The seal of the Lord of hosts shall perform this. 8 The Lord has sent death upon Jacob, and it has come upon Israel. 9 And all the people of Ephraim, and they that dwelt in Samaria shall know, who say in their pride and lofty heart, 10 The bricks are fallen down, but come, let us hew stones, and cut down sycamores and cedars, and let us build for ourselves a tower. 11 And God shall dash down them that rise up against him on mount Sion, and shall scatter his enemies; 12 *even* Syria from the rising of the sun, and the Greeks from the setting of the sun, who devour Israel with open mouth. For all this *his* anger is not turned away, but still *his* hand is exalted. 13 But the people turned not until they were smitten, and they sought not the Lord. 14 So the Lord took away from Israel the head and tail, great and small, in one day: 15 the old man, and them that respect persons, this is the head; and the prophet teaching unlawful things, he is the tail. 16 And they that pronounce this people blessed shall mislead them; and they mislead them that they may devour them. 17 Therefore the Lord shall not take pleasure in their young men, neither shall he have pity on their orphans or on their widows: for they are all transgressors and wicked, and every mouth speaks unjustly. For all this *his* anger is not turned away, but *his* hand is yet exalted. 18 And iniquity shall burn as fire, and shall be devoured by fire as dry grass: and it shall burn in the thickets of the wood, and shall devour all that is round about the hills. 19 The whole earth is set on fire because of the fierce anger of the Lord, and the people shall be as men burnt by fire: no man shall pity his brother. 20 But *one* shall turn aside to the right hand, for he shall be hungry; and shall eat on the left, and a man shall by no means be satisfied with eating the flesh of his own arm. 21 For Manasses shall eat *the flesh* of Ephraim, and Ephraim *the flesh* of Manasses; for they shall besiege Juda together. For all this *his* anger is not turned away, but *his* hand is yet exalted.

Isa.10 1 Woe to them that write wickedness; for when they write they do write wickedness, 2 perverting the cause of the poor, violently wresting the judgment of the needy ones of my people, that the widow may be a prey to them, and the orphan a spoil. 3 And what will they do in the day of visitation? for affliction shall come to you from afar: and to whom will ye flee for help? and where will ye leave your glory, 4 that ye may not fall into captivity? For all this *his* wrath is not turned away, but *his* hand is yet exalted. 5 Woe to the Assyrians; the rod of my wrath, and anger are in their hands. 6 I will send my wrath against a sinful nation, and I will charge my people to take plunder and spoil, and to trample the cities, and to make them dust. 7 But he meant not thus, neither did he devise thus in his soul: but his mind shall change, and *that* to destroy nations not a few. 8 And if they should say to him, Thou alone art ruler; 9 then shall he say, Have I not taken the country above Babylon and Chalanes, where the tower was built? and have I *not* taken Arabia, and Damascus, and Samaria? 10 As I have taken them, I will also take all the kingdoms: howl, ye idols in Jerusalem, and in Samaria. 11 For as I did to Samaria and her idols, so will I do also to Jerusalem and her idols. 12 And it shall come to pass, when the Lord shall have finished doing all things on Mount Sion and Jerusalem, *that* I will visit upon the proud heart, *even* upon the ruler of the Assyrians, and upon the boastful haughtiness of his eyes. 13 For he said, I will act in strength, and in the wisdom of *my* understanding I will remove the boundaries of nations, and will spoil their strength. 14 And I will shake the inhabited cities: and I will take with my hand all the world as a nest: and I will even take them as eggs that have been left; and there is none that shall escape me, or contradict me. 15 Shall the axe glorify itself without him that hews with it? or shall the saw lift up itself without him that uses it, as if one should lift a rod or staff? but it shall not be so; 16 but the Lord of hosts shall send dishonour upon thine honour, and burning fire shall be kindled upon thy glory. 17 And the light of Israel shall be for a fire, and he shall sanctify him with burning fire, and it shall devour the wood as grass. 18 In that day the mountains shall be consumed, and the hills, and the forests, and *fire* shall devour *both* soul and body: and he that flees shall be as one fleeing from burning flame. 19 And they that are left of them shall be a *small* number, and a child shall write them. 20 And it shall come to pass in that day *that* the remnant of Israel shall no more join themselves with, and the saved of Jacob shall no more trust in, them that

injured them; but they shall trust in the Holy God of Israel, in truth. 21 And the remnant of Jacob shall *trust* on the mighty God. 22 And though the people of Israel be as the sand of the sea, a remnant of them shall be saved. 23 He will finish the work, and cut it short in righteousness: because the Lord will make a short work in all the world. 24 Therefore thus saith the Lord of hosts, Be not afraid, my people who dwell in Sion, of the Assyrians, because he shall smite thee with a rod: for I am bringing a stroke upon thee, that *thou* mayest see the way of Egypt. 25 For yet a little while, and the indignation shall cease: but my wrath shall be against their council. 26 And God will stir up *enemies* against them, according to the stroke of Madiam in the place of affliction: and his wrath shall be by the way of the sea, *even* to the way that leads to Egypt. 27 And it shall come to pass in that day, *that* his yoke shall be taken away from thy shoulder, and his fear from thee, and the yoke shall be destroyed from off your shoulders. 28 For he shall arrive at the city of Angai, and shall pass on to Maggedo, and shall lay up his stores in Machmas. 29 And he shall pass by the valley, and shall arrive at Angai: fear shall seize upon Rama, the city of Saul. 30 The daughter of Gallim shall flee; Laisa shall hear; one shall hear in Anathoth. 31 Madebena also is amazed, and the inhabitants of Gibbir. 32 Exhort ye *them* to-day to remain in the way: exhort ye *beckoning* with the hand the mountain, the daughter of Sion, even ye hills that are in Jerusalem. 33 Behold, the Lord, the Lord of hosts, will mightily confound the glorious ones; and the haughty in pride shall be crushed, and the lofty shall be brought low: 34 and the lofty ones shall fall by the sword, and the Libanus shall fall with his lofty ones.

Isa.11 1 And there shall come forth a rod out of the root of Jesse, and a blossom shall come up from *his* root: 2 and the Spirit of God shall rest upon him, the spirit of wisdom and understanding, the spirit of counsel and strength, the spirit of knowledge and godliness shall fill him; 3 the spirit of the fear of God. He shall not judge according to appearance, nor reprove according to report: 4 but he shall judge the cause of the lowly, and shall reprove the lowly of the earth: and he shall smite the earth with the word of his mouth, and with the breath of his lips shall he destroy the ungodly one. 5 And he shall have his loins girt with righteousness, and his sides clothed with truth. 6 And the wolf shall feed with the lamb, and the leopard shall lie down with the kid; and the young calf and bull and lion shall feed together; and a little child shall lead them. 7 And the ox and bear shall feed together; and their young shall be together: and the lion shall eat straw like the ox. 8 And an infant shall put his hand on the holes of asps, and on the nest of young asps. 9 And they shall not hurt, nor shall they at all be able to destroy any one on my holy mountain: for the whole *world* is filled with the knowledge of the Lord, as much water covers the seas. 10 And in that day there shall be a root of Jesse, and he that shall arise to rule over the Gentiles; in him shall the Gentiles trust, and his rest shall be glorious. 11 And it shall be in that day, *that* the Lord shall again shew his hand, to be zealous for the remnant that is left of the people, which shall be left by the Assyrians, and *that* from Egypt, and from the country of Babylon, and from Ethiopia, and from the Elamites, and from the rising of the sun, and out of Arabia. 12 And he shall lift up a standard for the nations, and he shall gather the lost ones of Israel, and he shall gather the dispersed of Juda from the four corners of the earth. 13 And the envy of Ephraim shall be taken away, and the enemies of Juda shall perish: Ephraim shall not envy Juda, and Juda shall not afflict Ephraim. 14 And they shall fly in the ships of the Philistines: they shall at the same time spoil the sea, and them *that come* from the east, and Idumea: and they shall lay their hands on Moab first; but the children of Ammon shall first obey *them.* 15 And the Lord shall make desolate the sea of Egypt; and he shall lay his hand on the river with a strong wind, and he shall smite the seven channels, so that men shall pass through it dry- shod. 16 And there shall be a passage for my people that is left in Egypt: and it shall be to Israel as the day when he came forth out of the land of Egypt.

Isa.12 1 And in that day thou shalt say, I *will* bless thee, O Lord; for thou wast angry with me, but thou hast turned aside thy wrath, and hast pitied me. 2 Behold, my God is my Saviour; I will trust in him, and not be afraid: for the Lord is my glory and my praise, and is become my salvation. 3 Draw ye therefore water with joy out of the wells of salvation. 4 And in that day thou shalt say, sing to the Lord, call aloud upon his name, proclaim his glorious *deeds* among the Gentiles; make mention that his name is exalted. 5 Sing praise to the name of the Lord; for he has done great *things*: declare this in all the earth. 6 Exalt and rejoice, ye that dwell in Sion: for the Holy One of Israel is exalted in the midst of her.

Isa.13 1 THE VISION WHICH ESAIAS SON OF AMOS SAW AGAINST BABYLON. 2 Lift up a standard on the mountain of the plain, exalt the voice to them, beckon with the hand, open *the gates*, ye rulers. 3 I give command, and I bring them: giants are coming to fulfil my wrath, rejoicing at the same time and insulting. 4 A voice of many nations on the mountains, *even* like *to that* of many nations; a voice of kings and nations gathered together: the Lord of hosts has given command to a war-like nation, 5 to come from a land afar off, from the utmost foundation of heaven; the Lord and his warriors *are coming* to destroy all the world. 6 Howl ye, for the day of the Lord is near, and destruction from God shall arrive. 7 Therefore every hand shall become powerless, and every soul of man shall be dismayed. 8 The elders shall be troubled, and pangs shall seize them, as of a woman in travail: and they shall mourn one to another, and shall be amazed, and shall change their countenance as a flame. 9 For behold! the day of the Lord is coming which cannot be escaped, *a day* of wrath and anger, to make the world desolate, and to destroy sinners out of it. 10 For the stars of heaven, and Orion, and all the host of heaven, shall not give their light; and it shall be dark at sunrise, and the moon shall not give her light. 11 And I will command evils for the whole world, and *will visit* their sins on the ungodly: and I will destroy the pride of transgressors, and will bring low the pride of the haughty. 12 And they that are left shall be more precious than gold tried in the fire; and a man shall be more

precious than the stone that is in Suphir. 13 For the heaven shall be enraged, and the earth shall be shaken from her foundation, because of the fierce anger of the Lord of hosts, in the day in which his wrath shall come on. 14 And they that are left shall be as a fleeing fawn, and as a stray sheep, and there shall be none to gather *them*: so that a man shall turn back to his people, and a man shall flee to his own land. 15 For whosoever shall be taken shall be overcome; and they that are gathered together shall fall by the sword. 16 And they shall dash their children before their eyes; and they shall spoil their houses, and shall take their wives. 17 Behold, I will stir up against you the Medes, who do not regard silver, neither have they need of gold. 18 They shall break the bows of the young men; and they shall have no mercy on your children; nor shall their eyes spare thy children. 19 And Babylon, which is called glorious by the king of the Chaldeans, shall be as *when* God overthrew Sodoma, and Gomorrha. 20 It shall never be inhabited, neither shall any enter into it for many generations: neither shall the Arabians pass through it; nor shall shepherds at all rest in it. 21 But wild beasts shall rest there; and the houses shall be filled with howling; and monsters shall rest there, and devils shall dance there, 22 and satyrs shall dwell there; and hedgehogs shall make their nests in their houses. It will come soon, and will not tarry.

Isa.14 1 And the Lord will have mercy on Jacob, and will yet choose Israel, and they shall rest on their land: and the stranger shall be added to them, yea, shall be added to the house of Jacob. 2 And the Gentiles shall take them, and bring them into their place: and they shall inherit them, and they shall be multiplied upon the land for servants and handmaidens: and they that took them captives shall become captives *to them*; and they that had lordship over them shall be under *their* rule. 3 And it shall come to pass in that day, *that* the Lord shall give thee rest from thy sorrow and vexation, *and from* thy hard servitude wherein thou didst serve them. 4 And thou shalt take up this lamentation against the king of Babylon, How has the extortioner ceased, and the taskmaster ceased! 5 The Lord has broken the yoke of sinners, the yoke of princes. 6 Having smitten a nation in wrath, with an incurable plague, smiting a nation with a wrathful plague, which spared *them* not, he rested in quiet. 7 All the earth cries aloud with joy: 8 the trees also of Libanus rejoice against thee, and the cedar of Libanus, *saying*, From the time that thou hast been laid low, no one has come up to cut us down. 9 Hell from beneath is provoked to meet thee: all the great ones that have ruled over the earth have risen up together against thee, they that have raised up from their thrones all the kings of the nations. 10 All shall answer and say to thee, Thou also hast been taken, even as we; and thou art numbered amongst us. 11 Thy glory has come down to Hades, and thy great mirth: under thee they shall spread corruption, and the worm shall be thy covering. 12 How has Lucifer, that rose in the morning, fallen from heaven! He that sent *orders* to all the nations is crushed to the earth. 13 But thou saidst in thine heart, I will go up to heaven, I will set my throne above the stars of heaven: I will sit on a lofty mount, on the lofty mountains toward the north: ¹⁴ I will go up above the clouds: I will be like the Most High. ¹⁵ But now thou shalt go down to hell, even to the foundations of the earth. ¹⁶ They that see thee shall wonder at thee, and say, This is the man that troubled the earth, that made kings to shake; ¹⁷ that made the whole world desolate, and destroyed its cities; he loosed not those who were in captivity. ¹⁸ All the kings of the nations lie in honour, *every* man in his house. ¹⁹ But thou shalt be cast forth on the mountains, as a loathed carcase, with many dead who have been pierced with swords, going down to the grave. ²⁰ As a garment defiled with blood shall not be pure, so neither shalt thou be pure; because thou hast destroyed my land, and hast slain my people: thou shalt not endure for ever, —*thou* an evil seed. ²¹ Prepare thy children to be slain for the sins of their father; that they arise not, and inherit the earth, nor fill the earth with wars. ²² And I will rise up against them, saith the Lord of hosts, and I will destroy their name, and remnant, and seed: thus saith the Lord. ²³ And I will make the region of Babylon desert, so that hedgehogs shall dwell *there*, and it shall come to nothing: and I will make it a pit of clay for destruction. ²⁴ Thus saith the Lord of hosts, As I have said, so it shall be: and as I have purposed, so *the matter* shall remain: ²⁵ *even* to destroy the Assyrians upon my land, and upon my mountains: and they shall be for trampling; and their yoke shall be taken away from them, and their glory shall be taken away from their shoulders. ²⁶ This is the purpose which the Lord has purposed upon the whole earth: and this the hand that is uplifted against all the nations. ²⁷ For what the Holy God has purposed, who shall frustrate? and who shall turn back his uplifted hand? ²⁸ In the year in which king Achaz died this word came. ²⁹ Rejoice not, all ye Philistines, because the yoke of him that smote you is broken: for out of the seed of the serpent shall come forth the young asps, and their young shall come forth flying serpents, ³⁰ And the poor shall be fed by him, and poor men shall rest in peace: but he shall destroy thy seed with hunger, and shall destroy thy remnant. ³¹ Howl, ye gates of cities; let the cities be troubled and cry, *even* all the Philistines: for smoke is coming from the north, and there is no *possibility* of living. ³² And what shall the kings of the nations answer? That the Lord has founded Sion, and by him the poor of the people shall be saved.

Isa.15 ¹ THE WORD AGAINST THE LAND OF MOAB. By night the land of Moab shall be destroyed; for by night the wall of the land of Moab shall be destroyed. ² Grieve for yourselves; for even Debon, where your altar is, shall be destroyed: thither shall ye go up to weep, over Nabau of the land of Moab: howl ye: baldness shall be on every head, *and* all arms *shall be* wounded. ³ Gird yourselves with sackcloth in her streets: and lament upon her roofs, and in her streets, and in her ways; howl all of you with weeping. ⁴ For Esebon and Eleale have cried: their voice was heard to Jassa: therefore the loins of the region of Moab cry aloud; her soul shall know. ⁵ The heart of the region of Moab cries within her to Segor; for it is *as* a heifer of three years old: and on the ascent of Luith they shall go up to thee weeping by the way of Aroniim: she cries, Destruction,

and trembling. ⁶ The water of Nemerim shall be desolate, and the grass thereof shall fail: for there shall be no green grass. ⁷ Shall *Moab* even thus be delivered? for I *will* bring the Arabians upon the valley, and they shall take it. ⁸ For the cry has reached the border of the region of Moab, *even* of Agalim; and her howling *has gone* as far as the well of Ælim. ⁹ And the water of Dimon shall be filled with blood: for I will bring Arabians upon Dimon, and I will take away the seed of Moab, and Ariel, and the remnant of Adama.

Isa.16 ¹ I will send as it were reptiles on the land: is *not* the mount of the daughter of Sion a desolate rock? ² For thou shalt be as a young bird taken away from a bird that has flown: *even* thou shalt be *so*, daughter of Moab: and then do thou, O Arnon, ³ take farther counsel, and continually make thou a shelter from grief: they flee in darkness at mid-day; they are amazed; be not thou led captive. ⁴ The fugitives of Moab shall sojourn with thee; they shall be to you a shelter from the face of the pursuer: for thine alliance has been taken away, and the oppressing ruler has perished from off the earth. ⁵ And a throne shall be established with mercy; and one shall sit upon it with truth in the tabernacle of David, judging, and earnestly seeking judgments, and hasting righteousness. ⁶ We have heard of the pride of Moab; he is very proud. I have cut off his pride: thy prophecy shall not be thus, *no* not thus. ⁷ Moab shall howl; for all shall howl in the land of Moab: but thou shalt care for them that dwell in Seth, and thou shalt not be ashamed. ⁸ The plains of Esebon shall mourn, the vine of Sebama: swallowing up the nations, trample ye her vines, even to Jazer: ye shall not come together; wander ye in the desert: they that were sent are deserted, for they have gone over to the sea. ⁹ Therefore will I weep as with the weeping of Jazer for the vine of Sebama; Esebon and Eleale have cast down thy trees; for I will trample on thy harvest and on thy vintages, and all *thy plants* shall fall. ¹⁰ And gladness and rejoicing shall be taken away from the vineyards; and they shall not at all tread wine into the vats; for *the vintage* has ceased. ¹¹ Therefore my belly shall sound as a harp for Moab, and thou hast repaired my inward parts as a wall. ¹² And it shall be to thy shame, (for Moab is wearied at the altars,) that he shall go in to the idols thereof to pray, but they shall not be at all able to deliver him. ¹³ This is the word which the Lord spoke against Moab, when he spoke. ¹⁴ And now I say, in three years, of the years of an hireling, the glory of Moab shall be dishonoured *with* all his great wealth; and he shall be left few in number, and not honoured.

Isa.17 ¹ THE WORD AGAINST DAMASCUS. Behold, Damascus shall be taken away from among cities, and shall become a ruin; ² abandoned for ever, to *be* a fold and resting-place for flocks, and there shall be none to go after them. ³ And she shall no longer be a strong place for Ephraim to flee to, and there shall no longer be a kingdom in Damascus, or a remnant of Syrians; for thou art no better than the children of Israel, *even* than their glory; thus saith the Lord of hosts. ⁴ There shall be in that day a failure of the glory of Jacob, and the riches of his glory shall be shaken. ⁵ And it shall be as if one should gather standing corn, and reap the grain of the ears; and it shall be as if one should gather ears in a rich valley; 6 and *as if* there should be left stubble therein, or *as it were* the berries of an olive tree, two or three on the topmost bough, or *as if* four or five should be left on their branches; thus saith the Lord, the God of Israel. 7 In that day a man shall trust in him that made him, and his eyes shall have respect to the Holy One of Israel. 8 And they shall not at all trust in their altars, nor in the works of their hands, which their fingers made; and they shall not look to the trees, nor to their abominations. 9 In that day thy cities shall be deserted, as the Amorites and the Evaeans deserted *theirs*, because of the children of Israel; and they shall be desolate. 10 Because thou hast forsaken God thy Saviour, and hast not been mindful of the Lord thy helper; therefore shalt thou plant a false plant, and a false seed. 11 In the day wherein thou shalt plant thou shalt be deceived; but if thou sow in the morning, *the seed* shall spring up for a crop in the day wherein thou shalt obtain an inheritance, and as a man's father, thou shalt obtain an inheritance for thy sons. 12 Woe *to* the multitude of many nations, as the swelling sea, so shall ye be confounded; and the force of many nations shall sound like water; 13 many nations like much water, as when much water rushes violently: and they shall drive him away, and pursue him afar, as the dust of chaff when men winnow before the wind, and as a storm whirling the dust of the wheel. 14 Toward evening, and there shall be grief; before the morning, and he shall not be. This is the portion of them that spoiled you, and the inheritance to them that robbed you of your inheritance.

Isa.18 1 Woe to you, ye wings of the land of ships, beyond the rivers of Ethiopia. 2 He sends messengers by the sea, and paper letters on the water: for swift messengers shall go to a lofty nation, and to a strange and harsh people. Who is beyond it? a nation not looked for, and trodden down. 3 Now all the rivers of the land shall be inhabited as an inhabited country; their land shall be as when a signal is raised from a mountain; it shall be audible as the sound of a trumpet. 4 For thus said the Lord to me, There shall be security in my city, as the light of noonday heat, and it shall be as a cloud of dew in the day of harvest. 5 Before the reaping time, when the flower has been completely formed, and the unripe grape has put forth its flower and blossomed, then shall he take away the little clusters with pruning-hooks, and shall take away the small branches, and cut them off; 6 And he shall leave *them* together to the birds of the sky, and to the wild beasts of the earth: and the fowls of the sky shall be gathered upon them, and all the beasts of the land shall come upon him. 7 In that time shall presents be brought to the Lord of hosts from a people afflicted and peeled, and from a people great from henceforth and for ever; a nation hoping and *yet* trodden down, which is in a part of a river of his land, to the place where is the name of the Lord of hosts, the mount Sion.

Isa.19 1 THE VISION OF EGYPT. Behold, the Lord sits on a swift cloud, and shall come to Egypt: and the idols of Egypt shall be moved at his presence, and their heart shall faint within them. 2 And the Egyptians shall be stirred up against the Egyptians: and a man shall fight against his brother, and a man against his neighbor, city against city, and law against law. 3 And the spirit of the Egyptians shall be troubled within them; and I will frustrate their counsel: and they shall enquire of their gods and their images, and them that speak out of the earth, and them that have in them a divining spirit. 4 And I will deliver Egypt into the hands of men, of cruel lords; and cruel kings shall rule over them: thus saith the Lord of hosts. 5 And the Egyptians shall drink the water that is by the sea, but the river shall fail, and be dried up. 6 And the streams shall fail, and the canals of the river; and every reservoir of water shall be dried up, in every marsh also of reed and papyrus. 7 And all the green herbage round about the river, and everything sown by the side of the river, shall be blasted with the wind and dried up. 8 And the fishermen shall groan, and all that cast a hook into the river shall groan; they also that cast nets, and the anglers shall mourn. 9 And shame shall come upon them that work fine flax, and them that make fine linen. 10 And they that work at them shall be in pain, and all that make beer shall be grieved, and be pained in their souls. 11 And the princes of Tanis shall be fools: *as for* the king's wise counsellors, their counsel shall be turned into folly: how will ye say to the king, we are sons of wise men, sons of ancient kings? 12 Where are now thy wise men? and let them declare to thee, and say, What has the Lord of hosts purposed upon Egypt? 13 The princes of Tanis have failed, and the princes of Memphis are lifted up *with pride*, and they shall cause Egypt to wander by tribes. 14 For the Lord has prepared for them a spirit of error, and they have caused Egypt to err in all their works, as one staggers who is drunken and vomits also. 15 And there shall be no work to the Egyptians, which shall make head or tail, or beginning or end. 16 But in that day the Egyptians shall be as women, in fear and in trembling because of the hand of the Lord of hosts, which he shall bring upon them. 17 And the land of the Jews shall be for a terror to the Egyptians: whosoever shall name it to them, they shall fear, because of the counsel which the Lord of hosts has purposed concerning it. 18 In that day there shall be five cities in Egypt speaking the language of Chanaan, and swearing by the name of the Lord of hosts; one city shall be called the city of Asedec. 19 In that day there shall be an altar to the Lord in the land of the Egyptians, and a pillar to the Lord by its border. 20 And it shall be for a sign to the Lord for ever in the land of Egypt: for they shall presently cry to the Lord by reason of them that afflict them, and he shall send them a man who shall save them; he shall judge and save them. 21 And the Lord shall be known to the Egyptians, and the Egyptians shall know the Lord in that day; and they shall offer sacrifices, and shall vow vows to the Lord, and pay *them*. 22 And the Lord shall smite the Egyptians with a stroke, and shall completely heal them: and they shall return to the Lord, and he shall hear them, and thoroughly heal them. 23 In that day there shall be a way from Egypt to the Assyrians, and the Assyrians shall enter into Egypt, and the Egyptians shall go to the Assyrians, and the Egyptians shall serve the Assyrians. 24 In that day shall Israel be third with the Egyptians and the Assyrians, blessed in the land which the

Lord of hosts has blessed, 25 saying, Blessed be my people that is in Egypt, and that is among the Assyrians, and Israel mine inheritance.

Isa.20 1 In the year when Tanathan came to Azotus, when he was sent by Arna king of the Assyrians, and warred against Azotus, and took it; 2 then the Lord spoke to Esaias the son of Amos, saying, Go and take the sackcloth off thy loins, and loose thy sandals from off thy feet, and do thus, going naked and barefoot. 3 And the Lord said, As my servant Esaias has walked naked and barefoot three years, there shall be three years for signs and wonders to the Egyptians and Ethiopians; 4 for thus shall the king of the Assyrians lead the captivity of Egypt and the Ethiopians, young men and old, naked and barefoot, having the shame of Egypt exposed. 5 And the Egyptians being defeated shall be ashamed of the Ethiopians, in whom they had trusted; for they were their glory. 6 And they that dwell in this island shall say in that day, Behold, we trusted to flee to them for help, who could not save themselves from the king of the Assyrians: and how shall we be saved?

Isa.21 1 THE VISION OF THE DESERT. As though a whirlwind should pass through the desert, coming from a desert, *even* from such a land, 2 *so* a fearful and a grievous vision was declared to me: he that is treacherous deals treacherously, the transgressor transgresses. The Elamites are upon me, and the ambassadors of the Persians come against me: now will I groan and comfort myself. 3 Therefore are my loins filled with feebleness, and pangs have seized me as a travailing woman: I dealt wrongfully that I might not hear; I hasted that I might not see. 4 My heart wanders, and transgression overwhelms me; my soul is occupied with fear. 5 Prepare the table, eat, drink: arise, ye princes, and prepare *your* shields. 6 For thus said the Lord to me, Go and station a watchman for thyself, and declare whatever thou shalt see. 7 And I saw two mounted horsemen, and a rider on an ass, and a rider on a camel. 8 Hearken with great attention, and call thou Urias to the watch-tower: the Lord has spoken. I stood continually during the day, and I stood in the camp all night: 9 and, behold, he comes riding in a chariot and pair: and he answered and said, Babylon is fallen, is fallen; and all her images and her idols have been crushed to the ground. 10 Hear, ye that are left, and ye that are in pain, hear what things I have heard of the Lord of hosts *which* the God of Israel has declared to us. THE VISION OF IDUMEA. 11 Call to me out of Seir; guard ye the bulwarks. 12 I watch in the morning and the night: if thou wouldest enquire, enquire, and dwell by me. 13 Thou mayest lodge in the forest in the evening, or in the way of Daedan. 14 Ye that dwell in the country of Thaeman, bring water to meet him that is thirsty; 15 meet the fugitives with bread, because of the multitude of the slain, and because of the multitude of them that lose their way, and because of the multitude of swords, and because of the multitude of bent bows, and because of the multitude of them that have fallen in war. 16 For thus said the Lord to me, Yet a year, as the year of an hireling, *and* the glory of the sons of Kedar shall fail: 17 and the remnant of the strong bows of the sons of Kedar shall be small: for the Lord God of Israel has spoken *it*.

Isa.22 1 THE WORD OF THE VALLEY OF SION. What has happened to thee, that now ye are all gone up to the housetops which help you not? 2 The city is filled with shouting *men*: thy slain are not slain with swords, nor are thy dead those who have died in battle. 3 All thy princes have fled, and *thy* captives are tightly bound, and the mighty *men* in thee have fled far away. 4 Therefore I said, Let me alone, I will weep bitterly; labour not to comfort me for the breach of the daughter of my people. 5 For *it is* a day of trouble, and of destruction, and of treading down, and *there is* perplexity *sent* from the Lord of hosts: they wander in the valley of Sion; they wander from the least to the greatest on the mountains. 6 And the Elamites took *their* quivers, and *there were* men mounted on horses, and *there was* a gathering for battle. 7 And it shall be *that* thy choice valleys shall be filled with chariots, and horsemen shall block up thy gates. 8 And they shall uncover the gates of Juda, and they shall look in that day on the choice houses of the city. 9 And they shall uncover the secret places of the houses of the citadel of David: and they saw that they were many, and that one *had* turned the water of the old pool into the city; 10 and that they *had* pulled down the houses of Jerusalem, to fortify the wall of the city. 11 And ye procured to yourselves water between the two walls within the ancient pool: but ye looked not to him that made it from the beginning, and regarded not him that created it. 12 And the Lord, the Lord of hosts, called in that day for weeping, and lamentation, and baldness, and for girding with sackcloth: 13 but they engaged in joy and gladness, slaying calves, and killing sheep, so as to eat flesh, and drink wine; saying, Let us eat and drink; for to-morrow we die. 14 And these things are revealed in the ears of the Lord of hosts: for this sin shall not be forgiven you, until ye die. 15 Thus saith the Lord of hosts, Go into the chamber, to Somnas the treasurer, and say to him, Why art thou here? 16 and what hast thou to do here, that thou hast here hewn thyself a sepulchre, and madest thyself a sepulchre on high, and hast graven for thyself a dwelling in the rock? 17 Behold now, the Lord of hosts casts forth and will utterly destroy *such* a man, and will take away thy robe and thy glorious crown, 18 and will cast thee into a great and unmeasured land, and there thou shalt die: and he will bring thy fair chariot to shame, and the house of thy prince to be trodden down. 19 And thou shalt be removed from thy stewardship, and from thy place. 20 And it shall come to pass in that day, that I will call my servant Eliakim the son of Chelcias: 21 and I will put on him thy robe, and I will grant him thy crown with power, and I will give thy stewardship into his hands: and he shall be as a father to them that dwell in Jerusalem, and to them that dwell in Juda. 22 And I will give him the glory of David; and he shall rule, and there shall be none to speak against him: and I will give him the key of the house of David *upon* his shoulder; and he shall open, and there shall be none to shut; and he shall shut, and there shall be none to open. 23 And I will make him a ruler in a sure place, and he shall be for a glorious throne of his father's house. 24 And every one that is glorious in the house of his father shall trust in him, from the least to the greatest; and they shall depend upon him in that day. 25 Thus saith the Lord of hosts, The man that is fastened in the sure place shall be removed and be taken away, and shall fall; and the glory that is upon him shall be utterly destroyed: for the Lord has spoken it.

Isa.23 1 THE WORD CONCERNING TYRE. Howl, ye ships of Carthage; for she has perished, and *men* no longer arrive from the land of the Citians: she is led captive. 2 To whom are the dwellers in the island become like, the merchants of Phoenice, passing over the sea 3 in great waters, a generation of merchants? as when the harvest is gathered in, *so are* these traders with the nations. 4 Be ashamed, O Sidon: the sea has said, yea, the strength of the sea has said, I have not travailed, nor brought forth, nor have I brought up young men, nor reared virgins. 5 Moreover when it shall be heard in Egypt, sorrow shall seize them for Tyre. 6 Depart ye to Carthage; howl, ye that dwell in this island. 7 Was not this your pride from the beginning, before she was given up? 8 Who has devised this counsel against Tyre? Is she inferior? or has she no strength? her merchants were the glorious princes of the earth. 9 The Lord of hosts has purposed to bring down all the pride of the glorious ones, and to disgrace every glorious thing on the earth. 10 Till thy land; for ships no more come out of Carthage. 11 And thy hand prevails no more by sea, which troubled kings: the Lord of hosts has given a command concerning Chanaan, to destroy the strength thereof. 12 And *men* shall say, Ye shall no longer at all continue to insult and injure the daughter of Sidon: and if thou depart to the Citians, neither there shalt thou have rest. 13 And *if thou depart* to the land of the Chaldeans, this also is laid waste by the Assyrians, for her wall is fallen. 14 Howl, ye ships of Carthage: for your strong hold is destroyed. 15 And it shall come to pass in that day, *that* Tyre shall be left seventy years, as the time of a king, as the time of a man: and it shall come to pass after seventy years, *that* Tyre shall be as the song of a harlot. 16 Take a harp, go about, O city, thou harlot that hast been forgotten; play well on the harp, sing many *songs*, that thou mayest be remembered. 17 And it shall come to pass after the seventy years, *that* God will visit Tyre, and she shall be again restored to her primitive state, and she shall be a mart for all the kingdoms of the world on the face of the earth. 18 And her trade and her gain shall be holiness to the Lord: it shall not be gathered for them, but for those that dwell before the Lord, *even* all her trade, to eat and drink and be filled, and for a covenant *and* a memorial before the Lord.

Isa.24 1 Behold, the Lord is about to lay waste the world, and will make it desolate, and will lay bare the surface of it, and scatter them that dwell therein. 2 And the people shall be as the priest, and the servant as the lord, and the maid as the mistress; the buyer shall be as the seller, the lender as the borrower, and the debtor as his creditor. 3 The earth shall be completely laid waste, and the earth shall be utterly spoiled: for the mouth of the Lord has spoken these things. 4 The earth mourns, and the world is ruined, the lofty ones of the earth are mourning. 5 And she has sinned by reason of her inhabitants; because they have transgressed the law,

and changed the ordinances, *even* the everlasting covenant. 6 Therefore a curse shall consume the earth, because the inhabitants thereof have sinned: therefore the dwellers in the earth shall be poor, and few men shall be left. 7 The wine shall mourn, the vine shall mourn, all the merry-hearted shall sigh. 8 The mirth of timbrels has ceased, the sound of the harp has ceased. 9 They are ashamed, they have not drunk wine; strong drink has become bitter to them that drink *it*. 10 All the city has become desolate: one shall shut his house so that none shall enter. 11 There is a howling for the wine everywhere; all the mirth of the land has ceased, all the mirth of the land has departed. 12 And cities shall be left desolate, and houses being left shall fall to ruin. 13 All this shall be in the land in the midst of the nations, as if one should strip an olive tree, so shall they strip them; but when the vintage is done, 14 these shall cry aloud; and they that are left on the land shall rejoice together in the glory of the Lord: the water of the sea shall be troubled. 15 Therefore shall the glory of the Lord be in the isles of the sea; the name of the Lord shall be glorious. 16 O Lord God of Israel, from the ends of the earth we have heard wonderful things, *and there is* hope to the godly: but they shall say, Woe to the despisers, that despise the law. 17 Fear, and a pit, and a snare, are upon you that dwell on the earth. 18 And it shall come to pass, *that* he that flees from the fear shall fall into the pit; and he that comes up out of the pit shall be caught by the snare: for windows have been opened in heaven, and the foundations of the earth shall be shaken, 19 the earth shall be utterly confounded, and the earth shall be completely perplexed. 20 It reels as a drunkard and one oppressed with wine, and the earth shall be shaken as a storehouse of fruits; for iniquity has prevailed upon it, and it shall fall, and shall not be able to rise. 21 And God shall bring *his* hand upon the host of heaven, and upon the kings of the earth. 22 And they shall gather the multitude thereof into prisons, and they shall shut them into a strong hold: after many generations they shall be visited. 23 And the brick shall decay, and the wall shall fall; for the Lord shall reign from out of Sion, and out of Jerusalem, and shall be glorified before *his* elders.

Isa.25 1 O Lord God, I will glorify thee, I will sing to thy name; for thou hast done wonderful things, *even* an ancient *and* faithful counsel. So be it. 2 For thou hast made cities a heap, *even* cities *made* strong that their foundations should not fall: the city of ungodly men shall not be built for ever. 3 Therefore shall the poor people bless thee, and cities of injured men shall bless thee. 4 For thou hast been a helper to every lowly city, and a shelter to them that were disheartened by reason of poverty: thou shalt deliver them from wicked men: *thou hast been* a shelter of them that thirst, and a refreshing air to injured men. 5 *We were* as faint-hearted men thirsting in Sion, by reason of ungodly men to whom thou didst deliver us. 6 And the Lord of hosts shall make *a feast* for all the nations: on this mount they shall drink gladness, they shall drink wine: 7 they shall anoint themselves with ointment in this mountain. Impart thou all these things to the nations; for this is *God's* counsel upon all the nations. 8 Death has prevailed and swallowed *men* up;

but again the Lord God has taken away every tear from every face. He has taken away the reproach of *his* people from all the earth: for the mouth of the Lord has spoken it. 9 And in that day they shall say, behold our God in whom we have trusted, and he shall save us: this *is* the Lord; we have waited for him, and we have exulted, and will rejoice in our salvation. 10 God will give rest on this mountain, and the country of Moab shall be trodden down, as they tread the floor with waggons. 11 And he shall spread forth his hands, even as he also brings down *man* to destroy *him*: and he shall bring low his pride *in regard to the thing* on which he has laid his hands. 12 And he shall bring down the height of the refuge of the wall, and it shall come down even to the ground.

Isa.26 1 In that day they shall sing this song in the land of Judea; Behold a strong city; and he shall make salvation *its* wall and bulwark. 2 Open ye the gates, let the nation enter that keeps righteousness, and keeps truth, 3 supporting truth, and keeping peace: for on thee, O Lord, 4 they have trusted with confidence for ever, the great, the eternal God; 5 who hast humbled and brought down them that dwell on high, thou shalt cast down strong cities, and bring them to the ground. 6 And the feet of the meek and lowly shall trample them. 7 The way of the godly is made straight: the way of the godly is also prepared. 8 For the way of the Lord is judgment: we have hoped in thy name, and on the remembrance *of thee*, 9 which our soul longs for: my spirit seeks thee very early in the morning, O God, for thy commandments are a light on the earth: learn righteousness, ye that dwell upon the earth. 10 For the ungodly one is put down: no one who will not learn righteousness on the earth, shall be able to do the truth: let the ungodly be taken away, that he see not the glory of the Lord. 11 O Lord, thine arm is exalted, yet they knew it not: but when they know they shall be ashamed: jealousy shall seize upon an untaught nation, and now fire shall devour the adversaries. 12 O Lord our God, give us peace: for thou hast rendered to us all things. 13 O Lord our God, take possession of us: O Lord, we know not *any* other beside thee: we name thy name. 14 But the dead shall not see life, neither shall physicians by any means raise *them* up: therefore thou hast brought *wrath* upon *them*, and slain *them*, and hast taken away every male of them. Bring more evils upon them, O Lord; 15 bring more evils on the glorious ones of the earth. 16 Lord, in affliction I remembered thee; thy chastening was to us with small affliction. 17 And as a woman in travail draws nigh to be delivered, *and* cries out in her pain; so have we been to thy beloved. 18 We have conceived, O Lord, because of thy fear, and have been in pain, and have brought forth the breath of thy salvation, which we have wrought upon the earth: we shall not fall, but all that dwell upon the land shall fall. 19 The dead shall rise, and they that are in the tombs shall be raised, and they that are in the earth shall rejoice: for the dew from thee is healing to them: but the land of the ungodly shall perish. 20 Go, my people, enter into thy closets, shut thy door, hide thyself for a little season, until the anger of the Lord have passed away. 21 For, behold, the Lord is bringing wrath

from *his* holy place upon the dwellers on the earth: the earth also shall disclose her blood, and shall not cover her slain.

Isa.27 1 In that day God shall bring *his* holy and great and strong sword upon the dragon, even the serpent that flees, upon the dragon, the crooked serpent: he shall destroy the dragon. 2 In that day *there shall be* a fair vineyard, *and* a desire to commence *a song* concerning it. 3 I am a strong city, a city in a siege: in vain shall I water it; for it shall be taken by night, and by day the wall shall fall. 4 There is no woman that has not taken hold of it; who will set me to watch stubble in the field? because of this enemy I have set her aside; therefore on this account the Lord has done all that he appointed. 5 I am burnt up; they that dwell in her shall cry, Let us make peace with him, let us make peace, 6 they that are coming are the children of Jacob. Israel shall bud and blossom, and the world shall be filled with his fruit. 7 Shall he himself be thus smitten, even as he smote? and as he slew, shall he be thus slain? 8 Fighting and reproaching he will dismiss them; didst thou not meditate with a harsh spirit, to slay them with a wrathful spirit? 9 Therefore shall the iniquity of Jacob be taken away; and this is his blessing, when I shall have taken away his sin; when they shall have broken to pieces all the stones of the altars as fine dust, and their trees shall not remain, and their idols shall be cut off, as a thicket afar off. 10 The flock that dwelt *there* shall be left, as a deserted flock; and *the ground* shall be for a long time for pasture, and there shall flocks lie down to rest. 11 And after a time there shall be in it no green thing because of *the grass* being parched. Come hither, ye women that come from a sight; for it is a people of no understanding; therefore he that made them shall have no pity upon them, and he that formed them shall have no mercy *upon them*. 12 And it shall come to pass in that day *that* God shall fence *men* off from the channel of the river as far as Rhinocorura; but do ye gather one by one the children of Israel. 13 And it shall come to pass in that day *that* they shall blow the great trumpet, and the lost ones in the land of the Assyrians shall come, and the lost ones in Egypt, and shall worship the Lord on the holy mountain in Jerusalem.

Isa.28 1 Woe to the crown of pride, the hirelings of Ephraim, the flower that has fallen from the glory of the top of the fertile mountain, they that are drunken without wine. 2 Behold, the anger of the Lord is strong and severe, as descending hail where there is no shelter, violently descending; as a great body of water sweeping away the soil, he shall make rest for the land. 3 The crown of pride, the hirelings of Ephraim, shall be beaten down with the hands and with the feet. 4 And the fading flower of the glorious hope on the top of the high mountain shall be as the early fig; he that sees it, before he takes it into his hand, will desire to swallow it down. 5 In that day the Lord of hosts shall be the crown of hope, the woven *crown* of glory, to the remnant of the people. 6 They shall be left in the spirit of judgment for judgment, and for the strength of them that hinder slaying. 7 For these have trespassed through wine; they have erred through strong drink: the priest and the prophet are mad through strong drink, they are swallowed up by reason of wine, they have staggered through drunkenness; they have erred: this is *their* vision. 8 A curse shall devour this counsel, for this *is their* counsel for the sake of covetousness. 9 To whom have we reported evils? and to whom have we reported a message? *even to those* that are weaned from the milk, who are drawn from the breast. 10 Expect thou affliction on affliction, hope upon hope: yet a little, *and* yet a little, 11 by reason of the contemptuous *words* of the lips, by means of another language: for they shall speak to this people, saying to them, 12 This is the rest to him that is hungry, and this is the calamity: but they would not hear. 13 Therefore the oracle of God shall be to them affliction on affliction, hope on hope, yet a little, *and* yet a little, that they may go and fall backward; and they shall be crushed and shall be in danger, and shall be taken. 14 Therefore hear ye the word of the Lord, ye afflicted men, and ye princes of this people that is in Jerusalem. 15 Because ye have said, We have made a covenant with Hades, and agreements with death; if the rushing storm should pass, it shall not come upon us: we have made falsehood our hope, and by falsehood shall we be protected: 16 Therefore thus saith the Lord, *even* the Lord, Behold, I lay for the foundations of Sion a costly stone, a choice, a corner-stone, a precious *stone*, for its foundations; and he that believes *on him* shall by no means be ashamed. 17 And I will cause judgment *to be* for hope, and my compassion shall be for *just* measures, and ye that trust vainly in falsehood *shall fall*: for the storm shall by no means pass by you, 18 except it also take away your covenant of death, and your trust in Hades shall by no means stand: if the rushing storm should come upon you, ye shall be beaten down by it. 19 Whenever it shall pass by, it shall take you; morning by morning it shall pass by in the day, and in the night there shall be an evil hope. Learn to hear, 20 ye that are distressed; we cannot fight, but we are ourselves too weak for you to be gathered. 21 The Lord shall rise up as a mountain of ungodly *men*, and shall be in the valley of Gabaon; he shall perform his works with wrath, *even* a work of bitterness, and his wrath shall deal strangely, and his destruction shall be strange. 22 Therefore do not ye rejoice, neither let your bands be made strong; for I have heard of works finished and cut short by the Lord of hosts, which he will execute upon all the earth. 23 Hearken, and hear my voice; attend, and hear my words. 24 Will the ploughman plough all the day? or will he prepare the seed beforehand, before he tills the ground? 25 Does he not, when he has levelled the surface thereof, then sow the small black poppy, or cumin, and afterward sow wheat, and barley, and millet, and bread-corn in thy borders? 26 So thou shalt be chastened by the judgment of thy God, and shalt rejoice. 27 For the black poppy is not cleansed with harsh treatment, nor will a wagon-wheel pass over the cumin; but the black poppy is threshed with a rod, and the cumin shall be eaten with bread; 28 for I will not be wroth with you for ever, neither shall the voice of my anger crush you. 29 And these signs came forth from the Lord of hosts. Take counsel, exalt vain comfort.

Isa.29 1 Alas for the city of Ariel, which David besieged. Gather ye fruits year by year; eat ye, for ye shall eat with Moab. 2 For I will grievously afflict Ariel: and her strength and her wealth shall be mine. 3 And I will compass thee about like David, and will raise a mound about thee, and set up towers round thee. 4 And thy words shall be brought down to the earth, and thy words shall sink down to the earth, and thy voice shall be as they that speak out of the earth, and thy voice shall be lowered to the ground. 5 But the wealth of the ungodly shall be as dust from a wheel, and the multitude of them that oppress thee as flying chaff, and it shall be suddenly as a moment, 6 from the Lord of Hosts: for there shall be a visitation with thunder, and earthquake, and a loud noise, a rushing tempest, and devouring flame of fire. 7 And the wealth of all the nations together, as many as have fought against Ariel, and all they that war against Jerusalem, and all who are gathered against her, and they that distress her, shall be as one that dreams in sleep by night. 8 And as men drink and eat in sleep, and when they have arisen, the dream is vain: and as a thirsty man dreams as if he drank, and having arisen is still thirsty, and his soul has desired in vain: so shall be the wealth of all the nations, as many as have fought against the mount Sion. 9 Faint ye, and be amazed, and be overpowered, not with strong drink nor with wine. 10 For the Lord has made you to drink a spirit of deep sleep; and he shall close their eyes, and *the eyes* of their prophets and of their rulers, who see secret things. 11 And all these things shall be to you as the words of this sealed book, which if they shall give to a learned man, saying, Read this, he shall then say, I cannot read *it*, for it is sealed. 12 And this book shall be given into the hands of a man that is unlearned, and *one* shall say to him, Read this; and he shall say, I am not learned. 13 And the Lord has said, This people draw nigh to me with their mouth, and they honour me with their lips, but their heart is far from me: but in vain do they worship me, teaching the commandments and doctrines of men. 14 Therefore behold I will proceed to remove this people, and I will remove them: and I will destroy the wisdom of the wise, and will hide the understanding of the prudent. 15 Woe to them that deepen their counsel, and not by the Lord. Woe to them that take secret counsel, and whose works are in darkness, and they say, Who has seen us? and who shall know us, or what we do? 16 Shall ye not be counted as clay of the potter? Shall the thing formed say to him that formed it, Thou didst not form me? or the work to the maker, Thou hast not made me wisely? 17 *Is it* not yet a little while, and Libanus shall be changed as the mountains of Chermel, and Chermel shall be reckoned as a forest? 18 And in that day the deaf shall hear the words of the book, and they that are in darkness, and they that are in mist: the eyes of the blind shall see, 19 and the poor shall rejoice with joy because of the Lord, and they that had no hope among men shall be filled with joy. 20 The lawless man has come to nought, and the proud man has perished, and they that transgress mischievously have been utterly destroyed: 21 and they that cause men to sin by a word: and men shall make all that reprove in the gates an offence, because they have unjustly turned aside the righteous. 22 Therefore thus saith the Lord concerning the house of Jacob, whom he set apart from Abraam, Jacob shall not now be ashamed, neither shall he now change countenance. 23 But when their children shall have seen my works, they shall sanctify my name for my sake, and they sanctify the Holy One of Jacob, and shall fear the God of Israel. 24 And they that erred in spirit shall know understanding, and the murmurers shall learn obedience, and the stammering tongues shall learn to speak peace.

Isa.30 1 Woe to the apostate children, saith the Lord: ye have framed counsel, not by me, and covenants not by my Spirit, to add sins to sins: 2 *even* they that proceed to go down into Egypt, but they have not enquired of me, that they might be helped by Pharao, and protected by the Egyptians. 3 For the protection of Pharaoh shall be to you a disgrace, and *there shall be* a reproach to them that trust in Egypt. 4 For there are princes in Tanes, evil messengers. 5 In vain shall they labour *in seeking* to a people, which shall not profit them for help, but *shall be* for a shame and reproach. 6 THE VISION OF THE QUADRUPEDS IN THE DESERT. In affliction and distress, *where are* the lion and lion's whelp, thence *come* also asps, and the young of flying asps, *there shall they be* who bore their wealth on asses and camels to a nation which shall not profit them. 7 The Egyptians shall help you utterly in vain: tell them, This your consolation is vain. 8 Now then sit down and write these words on a tablet, and in a book; for these things shall be for *many long* days, and even for ever. 9 For the people is disobedient, false children, who would not hear the law of God: 10 who say to the prophets, Report not to us; and to them that see visions, Speak *them* not to us, but speak and report to us another error; 11 and turn us aside from this way; remove from us this path, and remove from us the oracle of Israel. 12 Therefore thus saith the Holy One of Israel, Because ye have refused to obey these words, and have trusted in falsehood; and because thou hast murmured, and been confident in this respect: 13 therefore shall this sin be to you as a wall suddenly falling when a strong city has been taken, of which the fall is very near at hand. 14 And the fall thereof shall be as the breaking of an earthen vessel, *as* small fragments of a pitcher, so that thou shouldest not find among them a sherd, with which thou mightest take up fire, and with which thou shouldest draw a little water. 15 Thus saith the Lord, the Holy Lord of Israel; When thou shalt turn and mourn, then thou shalt be saved; and thou shalt know where thou wast, when thou didst trust in vanities: *then* your strength became vain, yet ye would not hearken: 16 but ye said, We will flee upon horses; therefore shall ye flee: and, We will be aided by swift riders; therefore shall they that pursue you be swift. 17 A thousand shall flee because of the voice of one, and many shall flee on account of the voice of five; until ye be left as a signal-post upon a mountain, and as one bearing an ensign upon a hill. 18 And the Lord will again wait, that he may pity you, and will therefore be exalted that he may have mercy upon you: because the Lord your God is a judge: blessed are they that stay themselves upon him. 19 For the holy people shall dwell in Sion: and *whereas* Jerusalem has wept bitterly, *saying,* Pity me; he shall pity thee: when he perceived the voice of thy cry, he hearkened to thee. 20 And *though* the Lord shall give you the bread of affliction and scant water, yet they that cause thee to err shall no more at all draw nigh to thee; for thine eyes shall see those that cause thee to err, 21 and thine ears shall hear the words of them that went after thee to lead thee astray, who say, This *is* the way, let us walk in it, whether to the right or to the left. 22 And thou shalt pollute the plated idols, and thou shalt grind to powder the gilt ones, and shalt scatter them as the water of a removed *woman,* and thou shalt thrust them forth as dung. 23 Then shall there be rain to the seed of thy land; and the bread of the fruit of thy land shall be plenteous and rich: and thy cattle shall feed in that day in a fertile and spacious place. 24 Your bulls and your oxen that till the ground, shall eat chaff mixed with winnowed barley. 25 And there shall be upon every lofty mountain and upon every high hill, water running in that day, when many shall perish, and when the towers shall fall. 26 And the light of the moon shall be as the light of the sun, and the light of the sun shall be sevenfold in the day when the Lord shall heal the breach of his people, and shall heal the pain of thy wound. 27 Behold, the name of the Lord comes after a *long* time, burning wrath: the word of his lips is with glory, a word full of anger, and the anger of his wrath shall devour as fire. 28 And his breath, as rushing water in a valley, shall reach as far as the neck, and be divided, to confound the nations for *their* vain error: error also shall pursue them, and overtake them. 29 Must ye always rejoice, and go into my holy places continually, as they that keep a feast? and must ye go with a pipe, as those that rejoice, into the mountain of the Lord, to the God of Israel? 30 And the Lord shall make his glorious voice to be heard, and the wrath of his arm, to make a display with wrath and anger and devouring flame: he shall lighten terribly, and *his wrath shall be* as water and violent hail. 31 For by the voice of the Lord the Assyrians shall be overcome, *even* by the stroke wherewith he shall smite them. 32 And it shall happen to him from every side, *that* they from whom their hope of assistance was, in which he trusted, themselves shall war against him in turn with drums and with harp. 33 For thou shalt be required before *thy* time: has it been prepared for thee also to reign? nay, God has *prepared for thee* a deep trench, wood piled, fire and much wood: the wrath of the Lord *shall be* as a trench kindled with sulphur.

Isa.31 1 Woe to them that go down to Egypt for help, who trust in horses and chariots, for they are many; and in horses, *which are* a great multitude; and have not trusted in the Holy One of Israel, and have not sought the Lord. 2 Therefore he has wisely brought evils upon them, and his word shall not be frustrated; and he shall rise up against the houses of wicked men, and against their vain hope, 3 *even* an Egyptian, a man, and not God; the flesh of horses, and there is no help *in them:* but the Lord shall bring his hand upon them, and the helpers shall fail, and all shall perish together. 4 For thus said the Lord to me, As a lion would roar, or a lion's whelp over prey which he has taken, and cry over it, until the mountains are filled with his voice, and *the animals* are awe-struck and tremble at the fierceness of his wrath: so the Lord of hosts shall descend to fight upon the mount Sion, *even* upon her mountains. 5 As birds flying, so shall the Lord of hosts defend; he shall defend Jerusalem, and he shall rescue, and save and deliver. 6 Turn, ye children of Israel, who devise a deep and sinful counsel. 7 For in that day men shall renounce their silver idols and *their* golden idols, which their hands made. 8 And the Assyrian shall fall: not the sword of a great man, nor the sword of a mean man shall devour him; neither shall he flee from the face of the sword: but the young men shall be overthrown: 9 for they shall be compassed with rocks as with a trench, and shall be worsted; and he that flees shall be taken. Thus saith the Lord, Blesses is he that has a seed in Sion, and household friends in Jerusalem.

Isa.32 1 For, behold, a righteous king shall reign, and princes shall govern with judgment. 2 And a man shall hide his words, and be hidden, as from rushing water, and shall appear in Sion as a rushing river, glorious in a thirsty land. 3 And they shall no more trust in men, but they shall incline their ears to hear. 4 And the heart of the weak ones shall attend to hear, and the stammering tongues shall soon learn to speak peace. 5 And they shall no more at all tell a fool to rule, and thy servants shall no more at all say, Be silent. 6 For the fool shall speak foolish words, and his heart shall meditate vanities, and to perform lawless deeds and to speak error against the Lord, to scatter hungry souls, and he will cause the thirsty souls to be empty. 7 For the counsel of the wicked will devise iniquity, to destroy the poor with unjust words, and ruin the cause of the poor in judgment. 8 But the godly have devised wise *measures*, and this counsel shall stand. 9 Rise up, ye rich women, and hear my voice; ye confident daughters, hearken to my words. 10 Remember for a full year in pain, yet with hope: the vintage has been cut off; it has ceased, it shall by no means come again. 11 Be amazed, be pained, ye confident ones: strip you, bare yourselves, gird your loins; 12 and beat your breasts, because of the pleasant field, and the fruit of the vine. 13 *As for* the land of my people, the thorn and grass shall come upon *it,* and joy shall be removed from every house. 14 *As for* the rich city, the houses are deserted; they shall abandon the wealth of the city, *and* the pleasant houses: and the villages shall be caves for ever, the joy of wild asses, shepherds' pastures; 15 until the Spirit shall come upon you from on high, and Chermel shall be desert, and Chermel shall be counted for a forest. 16 Then judgment shall abide in the wilderness, and righteousness shall dwell in Carmel. 17 And the works of righteousness shall be peace; and righteousness shall ensure rest, and *the righteous* shall be confident for ever. 18 And his people shall inhabit a city of peace, and dwell in *it* in confidence, and they shall rest with wealth. 19 And if the hail should come down, it shall not come upon you; and they that dwell in the forests shall be in confidence, as those in the plain country. 20 Blessed are they that sow by every water, where the ox and ass tread.

Isa.33 1 Woe to them that afflict you; but no one makes you miserable: and he that deals perfidiously with you does not deal perfidiously: they that deal perfidiously shall be taken and given up, and as a moth on a garment, so shall they be spoiled. 2 Lord, have mercy upon us; for we have trusted in thee: the seed of the rebellious is gone to destruction, but our deliverance was in a time of affliction. 3 By reason of the terrible sound the nations were dismayed for fear of thee, and the heathen were scattered. 4 And now shall the spoils of your small and great be gathered: as if one should gather locusts, so shall they mock you. 5 The God who dwells on high is holy: Sion is filled with judgment and righteousness. 6 They shall be delivered up to the law: our salvation is our treasure: there are wisdom and knowledge and piety toward the Lord; these are the treasures of righteousness. 7 Behold now, these shall be terrified with fear of you: those whom ye feared shall cry out because of you: messengers shall be sent, bitterly weeping, entreating for peace. 8 For the ways of these shall be made desolate: the terror of the nations has been made to cease, and the covenant with these is taken away, and ye shall by no means deem them men. 9 The land mourns; Libanus is ashamed: Saron is become marshes; Galilee shall be laid bare, and Chermel. 10 Now will I arise, saith the Lord, now will I be glorified; now will I be exalted. 11 Now shall ye see, now shall ye perceive; the strength of your breath, shall be vain; fire shall devour you. 12 And the nations shall be burnt up; as a thorn in the field cast out and burnt up. 13 They that are afar off shall hear what I have done; they that draw nigh shall know my strength. 14 The sinners in Sion have departed; trembling shall seize the ungodly. Who will tell you that a fire is kindled? Who will tell you of the eternal place? 15 He that walks in righteousness, speaking rightly, hating transgression and iniquity, and shaking his hands from gifts, stopping his ears that he should not hear the judgment of blood, shutting his eyes that he should not see injustice. 16 he shall dwell in a high cave of a strong rock: bread shall be given him, and his water shall be sure. 17 Ye shall see a king with glory: your eyes shall behold a land from afar. 18 Your soul shall meditate terror. Where are the scribes? where are the counsellors, where is he that numbers them that are growing up, 19 *even* the small and great people? with whom he took not counsel, neither did he understand *a people* of deep speech, so that a despised people should not hear, and there is no understanding to him that hears. 20 Behold the city of Sion, our refuge: thine eyes shall behold Jerusalem, a rich city, tabernacles which shall not be shaken, neither shall the pins of her tabernacle be moved for ever, neither shall her cords be at all broken: 21 for the name of the Lord is great to you: ye shall have a place, *even* rivers and wide and spacious channels: thou shalt not go this way, neither a vessel with oars go *thereby.* 22 For my God is great: the Lord our judge shall not pass me by: the Lord is our prince, the Lord is our king; the Lord, he shall save us. 23 Thy cords are broken, for they had no strength: thy meat has given way, it shall not spread the sails, it shall not bear a signal, until it be given up for plunder; therefore shall many lame men take spoil. 24 And the people dwelling among them shall by no means say, I am in pain: for their sin shall be forgiven them.

Isa.34 1 Draw near, ye nations; and hearken, ye princes; let the earth hear, and they that are in it; the world, and the people that are therein. 2 For the wrath of the Lord is upon all nations, and *his* anger upon the number of them, to destroy them, and give them up to slaughter. ³ And their slain shall be cast forth, and their corpses; and their *ill* savour shall come up, and the mountains shall be made wet with their blood. ⁴ And all the powers of the heavens shall melt, and the sky shall be rolled up like a scroll: and all the stars shall fall like leaves from a vine, and as leaves fall from a fig-tree. ⁵ My sword has been made drunk in heaven: behold, it shall come down upon Idumea, and with judgment upon the people doomed to destruction. ⁶ The sword of the Lord is filled with blood, it is glutted with fat, with the blood of goats and lambs, and with the fat of goats and rams: for the Lord has a sacrifice in Bosor, and a great slaughter in Idumea. ⁷ And the mighty ones shall fall with them, and the rams and the bulls; and the land shall be soaked with blood, and shall be filled with their fat. ⁸ For it is the day of judgment of the Lord, and the year of the recompence of Sion in judgment. ⁹ And her valleys shall be turned into pitch, and her land into sulphur; and her land shall be as pitch burning night and day; ¹⁰ and it shall never be quenched, and her smoke shall go up: it shall be made desolate throughout her generations, ¹¹ and for a long time birds and hedgehogs, and ibises and ravens shall dwell in it: and the measuring line of desolation shall be cast over it, and satyrs shall dwell in it. ¹² Her princes shall be no more; for her kings and her great men shall be destroyed. ¹³ And thorns shall spring up in their cities, and in her strong holds: and they shall be habitations of monsters, and a court of ostriches. ¹⁴ And devils shall meet with satyrs, and they shall cry one to the other: there shall satyrs rest, having found for themselves *a place of* rest. ¹⁵ There has the hedgehog made its nest, and the earth has safely preserved its young: there have the deer met, and seen one another's faces. ¹⁶ They passed by in *full* number, and not one of them perished: they sought not one another; for the Lord commanded them, and his Spirit gathered them. ¹⁷ And he shall cast lots for them, and his hand has portioned out *their* pasture, *saying*, Ye shall inherit *the land* for ever: they shall rest on it *through* all generations.

Isa.35 ¹ Be glad, thou thirsty desert: let the wilderness exult, and flower as the lily. ² And the desert places of Jordan shall blossom and rejoice; the glory of Libanus has been given to it, and the honour of Carmel; and my people shall see the glory of the Lord, and the majesty of God. ³ Be strong, ye relaxed hands and palsied knees. ⁴ Comfort one another, ye fainthearted; be strong, fear not; behold, our God renders judgment, and he will render *it*; he will come and save us. ⁵ Then shall the eyes of the blind be opened, and the ears of the deaf shall hear. ⁶ Then shall the lame man leap as an hart, and the tongue of the stammerers shall speak plainly; for water has burst forth in the desert, and a channel *of water* in a thirsty land. ⁷ And the dry land shall become pools, and a fountain of water shall *be poured* into the thirsty land; there shall there be a joy of birds, ready habitations and marshes. ⁸ There shall be there a pure way, and it shall be called a holy way; and there shall not pass by there any unclean person, neither shall there be there an unclean way; but the dispersed shall walk on it, and they

shall not go astray. ⁹ And there shall be no lion there, neither shall any evil beast go up upon it, nor at all be found there; but the redeemed and gathered on the Lord's behalf, shall walk in it, ¹⁰ and shall return, and come to Sion with joy, and everlasting joy *shall be* over their head; for on their head *shall be* praise and exultation, and joy shall take possession of them: sorrow and pain, and groaning have fled away.

Isa.36 ¹ Now it came to pass in the fourteenth year of the reign of Ezekias, *that* Sennacherim, king of the Assyrians, came up against the strong cities of Judea, and took them. ² And the king of the Assyrians sent Rabsaces out of Laches to Jerusalem to king Ezekias with a large force: and he stood by the conduit of the upper pool in the way of the fuller's field. ³ And there went forth to him Heliakim the steward, the *son* of Chelcias, and Somnas the scribe, and Joach the *son* of Asaph, the recorder. ⁴ And Rabsaces said to them, Say to Ezekias, Thus says the great king, the king of the Assyrians, Why art thou secure? ⁵ Is war carried on with counsel and *mere* words of the lips? and now on whom dost thou trust, that thou rebellest against me? ⁶ Behold, thou trustest on this bruised staff of reed, on Egypt: *as soon* as a man leans upon it, it shall go into his hand, and pierce it: so is Pharao king of Egypt and all that trust in him. ⁷ But if ye say, We trust in the Lord our God; ⁸ yet now make an agreement with my lord the king of the Assyrians, and I will give you two thousand horses, if ye shall be able to set riders upon them. ⁹ And how can ye *then* turn to the face of the satraps? They that trust on the Egyptians for horse and rider, are *our* servants. ¹⁰ And now, Have we come up against this land to fight against it without the Lord? The Lord said to me, Go up against this land, and destroy it. ¹¹ Then Eliakim and Somnas and Joach said to him, Speak to thy servants in the Syrian tongue; for we understand *it*: and speak not to us in the Jewish tongue: and wherefore speakest thou in the ears of the men on the wall? ¹² And Rabsaces said to them, Has my lord sent me to your lord or to you, to speak these words? *has he* not *sent* me to the men that sit on the wall, that they may eat dung, and drink *their* water together with you? ¹³ And Rabsaces stood and cried with a loud voice in the Jewish language, and said, Hear ye the words of the great king, the king of the Assyrians: ¹⁴ thus says the king, Let not Ezekias deceive you with words: he will not be able to deliver you. ¹⁵ And let not Ezekias say to you, That God will deliver you, and this city will not at all be delivered into the hand of the king of the Assyrians. ¹⁶ Hearken not to Ezekias: thus says the king of the Assyrians, If ye wish to be blessed, come out to me: and ye shall eat every one *of* his vine and his fig-trees, and ye shall drink water out of your own cisterns: ¹⁷ until I come and take you to a land, like your own land, a land of corn and wine, and bread, and vineyards. ¹⁸ Let not Ezekias deceive you, saying, God will deliver you. Have the gods of the nations delivered each one his own land out of the hand of the king of the Assyrians? ¹⁹ Where is the god of Emath, and Arphath? and where is the god of Eppharuaim? have they been able to deliver Samaria out of my hand? ²⁰ Which is the god of all these nations, that has delivered his land out of my hand, that God should deliver Jerusalem out of my hand? 21 And they were silent, and none answered him a word; because the king had commanded that none should answer. 22 And Heliakim the *son* of Chelcias, the steward, and Somnas the military scribe, and Joach the *son* of Asaph, the recorder, came in to Ezekias, having their garments rent, and they reported to him the words of Rabsaces.

Isa.37 1 And it came to pass, when king Ezekias heard *it, that* he rent his clothes, and put on sackcloth, and went up to the house of the Lord. 2 And he sent Heliakim the steward, and Somnas the scribe, and the elders of the priests clothed with sackcloth, to Esaias the son of Amos, the prophet. And they said to him, Thus says Ezekias, 3 To-day is a day of affliction, and reproach, and rebuke, and anger: for the pangs are come upon the travailing *woman*, but she has not strength to bring forth. 4 May the Lord thy God hear the words of Rabsaces, which the king of the Assyrians has sent, to reproach the living God, even to reproach with the words which the Lord thy God has heard: therefore thou shalt pray to thy Lord for these that are left. 5 So the servants of king Ezekias came to Esaias. 6 And Esaias said to them, Thus shall ye say to your master, Thus saith the Lord, Be not thou afraid at the words which thou hast heard, wherewith the ambassadors of the king of the Assyrians have reproached me, 7 Behold, I *will* send a blast upon him, and he shall hear a report, and return to his own country, and he shall fall by the sword in his own land. 8 So Rabsaces returned, and found the king of the Assyrians besieging Lobna: for he had heard that he had departed from Lachis. 9 And Tharaca king of the Ethiopians went forth to attack him. And when he heard it, he turned aside, and sent messengers to Ezekias, saying, 10 Thus shall ye say to Ezekias king of Judea, Let not thy God, in whom thou trustest, deceive thee, saying, Jerusalem shall not be delivered into the hand of the king of the Assyrians. 11 Hast thou not heard what the kings of the Assyrians have done, how they have destroyed the whole earth? and shalt thou be delivered? 12 Have the gods of the nations which my fathers destroyed delivered them, both Gozan, and Charrhan, and Rapheth, which are in the land of Theemath? 13 Where are the kings of Emath? and where *is the king of* Arphath? and where *is the king* of the city of Eppharuaim, *and of* Anagugana? 14 And Ezekias received the letter from the messengers, and read it, and went up to the house of the Lord, and opened it before the Lord. 15 And Ezekias prayed to the Lord, saying, 16 O Lord of hosts, God of Israel, who sittest upon the cherubs, thou alone art the God of every kingdom of the world: thou hast made heaven and earth. 17 Incline thine ear, O Lord, hearken, O Lord; open thine eyes, O Lord, look, O Lord: and behold the words of Sennacherim, which he has sent to reproach the living God. 18 For of a truth, Lord, the kings of the Assyrians have laid waste the whole world, and the countries thereof, 19 and have cast their idols into the fire: for, they were no gods, but the work of men's hands, wood and stone; and they have cast them away. 20 But now, O Lord our God, deliver us from his hands, that every kingdom of the earth may know that thou art God alone.

21 And Esaias the son of Amos was sent to Ezekias, and said to him, Thus saith the Lord, the God of Israel, I have heard thy prayer to me concerning Sennacherim king of the Assyrians. 22 This is the word which God has spoken concerning him; The virgin daughter of Sion has despised thee, and mocked thee; the daughter of Jerusalem has shaken her head at thee. 23 Whom hast thou reproached and provoked? and against whom hast thou lifted up thy voice? and hast thou not lifted up thine eyes on high against the Holy One of Israel? 24 For thou hast reproached the Lord by messengers; for thou hast said, With the multitude of chariots have I ascended to the height of mountains, and to the sides of Libanus; and I have cropped the height of his cedars and the beauty of his cypresses; and I entered into the height of the forest region: 25 and I have made a bridge, and dried up the waters, and every pool of water. 26 Hast thou not heard of these things which I did of old? I appointed *them* from ancient times; but now have I manifested *my purpose* of desolating nations in *their* strong holds, and them that dwell in strong cities. 27 I weakened *their* hands, and they withered; and they became as dry grass on the house-tops, and as grass. 28 But now I know thy rest, and thy going out, and thy coming in. 29 And thy wrath wherewith thou hast been enraged, and thy rancour has come up to me; therefore I will put a hook in thy nose, and a bit in thy lips, and will turn thee back by the way by which thou camest. 30 And this shall be a sign to thee, Eat this year what thou hast sown; and the second year that which is left: and the third year sow, and reap, and plant vineyards, and eat the fruit of them. 31 And they that are left in Judea shall take root downward, and bear fruit upward: 32 for out of Jerusalem there shall be a remnant, and the saved ones out of mount Sion: the zeal of the Lord of hosts shall perform this. 33 Therefore thus saith the Lord concerning the king of the Assyrians, He shall not enter into this city, nor cast a weapon against it, nor bring a shield against it, nor make a rampart round it. 34 But by the way by which he came, by it shall he return, and shall not enter into this city: thus saith the Lord. 35 I will protect this city to save it for my own sake, and for my servant David's sake. 36 And the angel of the Lord went forth, and slew out of the camp of the Assyrians a hundred and eighty-five thousand: and they arose in the morning and found all *these* bodies dead. 37 And Sennacherim king of the Assyrians turned and departed, and dwelt in Nineve. 38 And while he was worshipping Nasarach his country's god in the house, Adramelech and Sarasar his sons smote him with swords; and they escaped into Armenia: and Asordan his son reigned in his stead.

Isa.38 1 And it came to pass at that time, *that* Ezekias was sick even to death. And Esaias the prophet the son of Amos came to him, and said to him, Thus saith the Lord, Give orders concerning thy house: for thou shalt die, and not live. 2 And Ezekias turned his face to the wall, and prayed to the Lord, saying, 3 Remember, O Lord, how I have walked before thee in truth, with a true heart, and have done that which was pleasing in thy sight. And Ezekias wept bitterly. 4 And the word of the Lord came to Esaias, saying, Go, and say to Ezekias, 5 Thus saith the Lord, the

God of David thy father, I have heard thy prayer, and seen thy tears: behold, I *will* add to thy time fifteen years. 6 And I will deliver thee and this city out of the hand of the king of the Assyrians: and I will defend this city. 7 And this *shall be* a sign to thee from the Lord, that God will do this thing; 8 behold, I will turn back the shadow of the degrees *of the dial* by which ten degrees on the house of thy father the sun has gone down—I will turn back the sun the ten degrees; so the sun went back the ten degrees by which the shadow had gone down. 9 THE PRAYER OF EZEKIAS KING OF JUDEA, WHEN HE HAD BEEN SICK, AND WAS RECOVERED FROM HIS SICKNESS. 10 I said in the end of my days, I shall go to the gates of the grave: I shall part with the remainder of my years. 11 I said, I shall no more at all see the salvation of God in the land of the living: I shall no more at all see the salvation of Israel on the earth: I shall no more at all see man. 12 *My life* has failed from among my kindred: I have parted with the remainder of my life: it has gone forth and departed from me, as one that having pitched a tent takes it down *again*: my breath was with me as a weaver's web, when she that weaves draws nigh to cut off *the* thread. 13 In that day I was given up as to a lion until the morning: so has he broken all my bones: for I was so given up from day *even* to night. 14 As a swallow, so will I cry, and as a dove, so do I mourn: for mine eyes have failed with looking to the height of heaven to the Lord, who has delivered me, and removed the sorrow of my soul. 16 *Yea*, O Lord, for it was told thee concerning this; and thou hast revived my breath; and I am comforted, and live. 17 For thou hast chosen my soul, that it should not perish: and thou hast cast all *my* sins behind me. 18 For they that are in the grave shall not praise thee, neither shall the dead bless thee, neither shall they that are in Hades hope for thy mercy. 19 The living shall bless thee, as I also *do*: for from this day shall I beget children, who shall declare thy righteousness, 20 O God of my salvation; and I will not cease blessing thee with the psaltery all the days of my life before the house of God. 21 Now Esaias had said to Ezekias; Take a cake of figs, and mash them, and apply them as a plaster, and thou shalt be well. 22 And Ezekias said, This is a sign to Ezekias, that I shall go up to the house of God.

Isa.39 1 At that time Marodach Baladan, the son of Baladan, the king of Babylonia, sent letters and ambassadors and gifts to Ezekias: for he had heard that he had been sick *even* to death, and was recovered. 2 And Ezekias was glad of their coming, and he shewed them the house of *his* spices, and of silver, and gold, and myrrh, and incense, and ointment, and all the houses of his treasures, and all that he had in his stores: and there was nothing in his house, nor in all his dominion, which Ezekias did not shew. 3 And Esaias the prophet came to king Ezekias, and said to him, What say these men? and whence came they to thee? and Ezekias said, They are come to me from a land afar off, from Babylon. 4 And Esaias said, What have they seen in thine house? and Ezekias said, They have seen everything in my house; and there is nothing in my house which they have not seen: yea, also the *possessions* in my treasuries. 5 And Esaias said to him, Hear the word of the Lord of hosts: 6 Behold, the days come, when they shall take all the *things that are* in thine house, and all that thy fathers have gathered until this day, shall go to Babylon; and they shall not leave anything at all: and God hath said, 7 that they shall take also of thy children whom thou shalt beget; and they shall make them eunuchs in the house of the king of the Babylonians. 8 And Ezekias said to Esaias, Good is the word of the Lord, which he hath spoken: let there, I pray, be peace and righteousness in my days.

Isa.40 1 Comfort ye, comfort ye my people, saith God. 2 Speak, ye priests, to the heart of Jerusalem; comfort her, for her humiliation is accomplished, her sin is put away: for she has received of the Lord's hand double *the amount of* her sins. 3 The voice of one crying in the wilderness, Prepare ye the way of the Lord, make straight the paths of our God. 4 Every valley shall be filled, and every mountain and hill shall be brought low: and all the crooked *ways* shall become straight, and the rough *places* plains. 5 And the glory of the Lord shall appear, and all flesh shall see the salvation of God: for the Lord has spoken *it*. 6 The voice of one saying, Cry; and I said, What shall I cry? All flesh is grass, and all the glory of man as the flower of grass: 7 8 The grass withers, and the flower fades: but the word of our God abides for ever. 9 O thou that bringest glad tidings to Zion, go up on the high mountain; lift up thy voice with strength, thou that bringest glad tidings to Jerusalem; lift it up, fear not; say unto the cities of Juda, Behold your God! 10 Behold the Lord! The Lord is coming with strength, and *his* arm is with power: behold, his reward is with him, and *his* work before him. 11 He shall tend his flock as a shepherd, and he shall gather the lambs with his arm, and shall soothe them that are with young. 12 Who has measured the water in his hand, and the heaven with a span, and all the earth in a handful? Who has weighed the mountains in scales, and the forests in a balance? 13 Who has known the mind of the Lord? and who has been his counsellor, to instruct him? 14 Or with whom has he taken counsel, and he has instructed him? or who has taught him judgment, or who has taught him the way of understanding; 15 since all the nations are counted as a drop from a bucket, and as the turning of a balance, *and* shall be counted as spittle? 16 And Libanus is not enough to burn, nor all beasts enough for a whole-burnt offering: 17 and all the nations are as nothing, and counted as nothing. 18 To whom have ye compared the Lord? and with what likeness have ye compared him? 19 Has not the artificer made an image, or the goldsmith having melted gold, gilt it over, *and* made it a similitude? 20 For the artificer chooses out a wood that will not rot, and will wisely enquire how he shall set up his image, and *that so* that it should not be moved. 21 Will ye not know? will ye not hear? has it not been told you of old? Have ye not known the foundations of the earth? 22 *It is* he that comprehends the circle of the earth, and the inhabitants in it are as grasshoppers; he that set up the heaven as a chamber, and stretched *it* out as a tent to dwell in: 23 he that appoints princes to rule as nothing, and has made the earth as nothing. 24 For they shall not plant, neither shall they sow, neither shall their root be fixed in the ground: he has blown upon them, and they are withered, and a storm shall carry them away like sticks. 25 Now then to whom have ye compared me, that I may be exalted? saith the Holy One. 26 Lift up your eyes on high, and see, who has displayed all these things? *even* he that brings forth his host by number: he shall call them all by name by *means of his* great glory, and by the power of his might: nothing has escaped thee. 27 For say not thou, O Jacob, and why hast thou spoken, Israel, *saying*, My way is hid from God, and my God has taken away *my* judgement, and has departed? 28 And now, hast thou not known? hast thou not heard? the eternal God, the God that formed the ends of the earth, shall not hunger, nor be weary, and there is no searching of his understanding. 29 He gives strength to the hungry, and sorrow to them that are not suffering. 30 For the young *men* shall hunger, and the youths shall be weary, and the choice *men* shall be powerless: 31 but they that wait on God shall renew *their* strength; they shall put forth new feathers like eagles; they shall run, and not be weary; they shall walk, and not hunger.

Isa.41 1 Hold a feast to me, ye islands: for the princes shall renew *their* strength: let them draw nigh and speak together: then let them declare judgment. 2 Who raised up righteousness from the east, *and* called it to his feet, so that it should go? shall appoint *it* an adversary of Gentiles, and shall dismay kings, and bury their swords in the earth, and cast forth their bows and arrows as sticks? 3 And he shall pursue them; the way of his feet shall proceed in peace. 4 Who has wrought and done these things? he has called it who called it from the generations of old; I God, the first and to *all* futurity, I AM. 5 The nations saw, and feared; the ends of the earth drew nigh, and came together, 6 every one judging for his neighbor and *that* to assist his brother: and one will say, 7 The artificer has become strong, and the coppersmith that smites with the hammer, *and* forges also: sometimes he will say, It is a piece well joined: they have fastened them with nails; they will fix them, and they shall not be moved. 8 But thou, Israel, art my servant Jacob, and he whom I have chosen, the seed of Abraam, whom I have loved: 9 whom I have taken hold of from the ends of the earth, and from the high places of it I have called thee, and said to thee, Thou art my servant; I have chosen thee, and I have not forsaken thee. 10 Fear not; for I am with thee: wander not; for I am thy God, who have strengthened thee; and I have helped thee, and have established thee with my just right hand. 11 Behold, all thine adversaries shall be ashamed and confounded; for they shall be as if they were not: and all thine opponents shall perish. 12 Thou shalt seek them, and thou shalt not find the men who shall insolently rage against thee: for they shall be as if they were not, and they that war against thee shall not be. 13 For I am thy God, who holdeth thy right hand, who saith to thee, 14 Fear not, Jacob, *and thou* Israel few in number; I have helped thee, saith thy God, he that redeems thee, O Israel. 15 Behold, I have made thee as new saw-shaped threshing wheels of a waggon; and thou shalt thresh the mountains, and beat the hills to powder, and make *them* as chaff: 16 and thou shalt winnow *them*, and the wind shall carry them away, and a tempest shall scatter them: but thou shalt rejoice in the holy ones of Israel. 17 And the poor and the needy shall exult; for *when* they shall seek water, and there shall be none, *and* their tongue is parched with thirst, I the Lord God, I the God of Israel will hear, and will not forsake them: 18 but I will open rivers on the mountains, and fountains in the midst of plains: I will make the desert pools of water, and a thirsty land watercourses. 19 I will plant in the dry land the cedar and box, the myrtle and cypress, and white poplar: 20 that they may see, and know, and perceive, and understand together, that the hand of the Lord has wrought these *works*, and the Holy One of Israel has displayed *them*. 21 Your judgment draws nigh, saith the Lord God; your counsels have drawn nigh, saith the King of Jacob. 22 Let them draw nigh, and declare to you what things shall come to pass; or tell *us* what things were of old, and we will apply *our* understanding, and we shall know what are the last and the future things: 23 tell us, declare ye to us the things that are coming on at the last *time*, and we shall know that ye are gods: do good, and do evil, and we shall wonder, and see at the same time 24 whence ye are, and whence is your works: they have chosen you an abomination out of the earth. 25 But I have raised up him that *comes* from the north, and him that *comes* from the rising of the sun: they shall be called by my name: let the princes come, and as potter's clay, and as a potter treading clay, so shall ye be trodden down. 26 For who will declare the things from the beginning, that we may know also the former things, and we will say that they are true? there is no one that speaks beforehand, nor anyone that hears your words. 27 I will give dominion to Sion, and will comfort Jerusalem by the way. 28 For from among the nations, behold, *there was* no one; and of their idols there was none to declare *anything*: and if I should ask them, Whence are ye? they could not answer me. 29 For *these* are your makers, *as ye think*, and they that cause you to err in vain.

Isa.42 1 Jacob is my servant, I will help him: Israel is my chosen, my soul has accepted him; I have put my Spirit upon him; he shall bring forth judgment to the Gentiles. 2 He shall not cry, nor lift up *his voice*, nor shall his voice be heard without. 3 A bruised reed shall he not break, and smoking flax shall he not quench; but he shall bring forth judgment to truth. 4 He shall shine out, and shall not be discouraged, until he have set judgment on the earth: and in his name shall the Gentiles trust. 5 Thus saith the Lord God, who made the heaven, and established it; who settled the earth, and the things in it, and gives breath to the people on it, and spirit to them that tread on it: 6 I the Lord God have called thee in righteousness, and will hold thine hand, and will strengthen thee: and I have given thee for the covenant of a race, for a light of the Gentiles: 7 to open the eyes of the blind, to bring the bound and them that sit in darkness out of bonds and the prison-house. 8 I am the Lord God: that is my name: I will not give my glory to another, nor my praises to graven images. 9 Behold, the ancient things have come to pass, and *so will* the new things which I tell you: yea, before I tell *them* they are made known to you. 10 Sing a new hymn to the Lord: ye *who are* his dominion, glorify his name from the end of the earth: ye that go down to the sea, and sail upon it; the islands, and they that dwell in them. 11 Rejoice, thou wilderness, and the villages thereof, the hamlets, and the dwellers in Kedar: the inhabitants of the rock shall rejoice, they shall shout from the top of the mountains. 12 They shall give glory to God, *and* shall proclaim his praises in the islands. 13 The Lord God of hosts shall go forth, and crush the war: he shall stir up jealousy, and shall shout mightily against his enemies. 14 I have been silent: shall I also always be silent and forbear: I have endured like a travailing *woman*: I will *now* amaze and wither at once. 15 I will make desolate mountains and hills, and will dry up all their grass; and I will make the rivers islands, and dry up the pools. 16 And I will bring the blind by a way that they knew not, and I will cause them to tread paths which they have not known: I will turn darkness into light for them, and crooked things into straight. These things will I do, and will not forsake them. 17 But they are turned back: be ye utterly ashamed that trust in graven *images*, who say to the molten *images*, Ye are our gods. 18 Hear, ye deaf, and look up, ye blind, to see. 19 And who is blind, but my servants? and deaf, but they that rule over them? yea, the servants of God have been made blind. 20 Ye have often seen, and have not taken heed; *your* ears have been opened, and ye have not heard. 21 The Lord God has taken counsel that he might be justified, and might magnify *his* praise. 22 And I beheld, and the people were spoiled and plundered: for *there is* a snare in the secret chambers everywhere, and in the houses also, where they have hidden them: they became a spoil, and there was no one that delivered the prey, and there was none who said, Restore. 23 Who *is there* among you that will give ear to these things? hearken ye to the things which are coming to pass. 24 For what did he give to Jacob up to spoil, and Israel to them that plundered him? Did not God *do it* against whom they sinned? *and* they would not walk in his ways, nor hearken to his law. 25 So he brought upon them the fury of his wrath; and the war, and those that burnt round about them, prevailed against them; yet no one of them knew *it*, neither did they lay *it* to heart.

Isa.43 1 And now thus saith the Lord God that made thee, O Jacob, and formed thee, O Israel, Fear not: for I have redeemed thee, I have called thee *by* thy name; thou art mine. 2 And if thou pass through water, I am with thee; and the rivers shall not overflow thee: and if thou go through fire, thou shalt not be burned; the flame shall not burn thee. 3 For I am the Lord thy God, the Holy One of Israel, that saves thee: I have made Egypt and Ethiopia thy ransom, and *given* Soene for thee. 4 Since thou becamest precious in my sight, thou hast become glorious, and I have loved thee: and I will give men for thee, and princes for thy life. 5 Fear not; for I am with thee: I will bring thy seed from the east, and will gather thee from the west. 6 I will say to the north, Bring; and to the south, Keep not back; bring my sons from the *land* afar off, and my daughters from the ends of the earth; 7 *even* all who are called by my name: for I have prepared him for my glory, and I have formed him, and have made him: 8 and I have brought forth the blind people;

for *their* eyes are alike blind, and they that have ears are deaf. 9 All the nations are gathered together, and princes shall be gathered out of them: who will declare these things? or who will declare to you things from the beginning? let them bring forth their witnesses, and be justified; and let them hear, and declare the truth. 10 Be ye my witnesses, and I *too am* a witness, saith the Lord God, and my servant whom I have chosen: that ye may know, and believe, and understand that I am *he*: before me there was no other God, and after me there shall be none. 11 I am God; and beside me there is no Saviour. 12 I have declared, and have saved; I have reproached, and there was no strange *god* among you: ye are my witnesses, and I am the Lord God, 13 even from the beginning; and there is none that can deliver out of my hands: I will work, and who shall turn it back? 14 Thus saith the Lord God that redeems you, the Holy One of Israel; for your sakes I will send to Babylon, and I will stir up all that flee, and the Chaldeans shall be bound in ships. 15 I am the Lord God, your Holy One, who have appointed for Israel your king. 16 Thus saith the Lord, who makes a way in the sea, and a path in the mighty water; 17 who brought forth chariots and horse, and a mighty multitude: but they have lain down, and shall not rise: they are extinct, as quenched flax. 18 Remember ye not the former things, and consider not the ancient things. 19 Behold, I *will* do new things, which shall presently spring forth, and ye shall know them: and I will make a way in the wilderness, and rivers in the dry land. 20 the beasts of the field shall bless me, the owls and young ostriches; for I have given water in the wilderness, and rivers in the dry land, to give drink to my chosen race, 21 my people whom I have preserved to tell forth my praises. 22 I have not now called thee, O Jacob; neither have I made thee weary, O Israel. 23 Thou hast not brought me the sheep of thy whole-burnt-offering; neither hast thou glorified me with thy sacrifices. I have not caused thee to serve with sacrifices, neither have I wearied thee with frankincense. 24 Neither hast thou purchased for me victims for silver, neither have I desired the fat of thy sacrifices: but thou didst stand before me in thy sins, and in thine iniquities. 25 I, *even* I, am he that blots out thy transgressions for mine own sake, and thy sins; and I will not remember *them*. 26 But do thou remember, and let us plead *together*: do thou first confess thy transgressions, that thou mayest be justified. 27 Your fathers first, and your princes have transgressed against me. 28 And the princes have defiled my sanctuaries: so I gave Jacob *to enemies* to destroy, and Israel to reproach.

Isa.44 1 But now hear, Jacob my servant; and Israel, whom I have chosen. 2 Thus saith the Lord God that made thee, and he that formed thee from the womb; Thou shalt yet be helped: fear not, my servant Jacob; and beloved Israel, whom I have chosen. 3 For I will give water to the thirsty that walk in a dry land: I will put my Spirit upon thy seed, and my blessings upon thy children: 4 and they shall spring up as grass between brooks, and as willows on *the banks of* running water. 5 One shall say, I am God's; and another shall call himself by the name of Jacob; and another shall write with his hand, I am God's, and shall call himself by the name of Israel. 6 Thus saith God the King of Israel, and the God of hosts that delivered him; I am the first, and I am hereafter: beside me there is no God. 7 Who is like me? let him stand, and call, and declare, and prepare for me from the time that I made man for ever; and let them tell you the things that are coming before they arrive. 8 Hide not yourselves, nor go astray: have ye not heard from the beginning, and *have not* I told you? ye are witnesses if there is a God beside me. 9 But they that framed *false gods* did not then hearken; and they that graved *images* are all vain, performing their own desires, which shall not profit them, but they shall be ashamed 10 that form a god, and all that grave worthless things: 11 and all by whom they were made are withered: yea, let all the deaf be gathered from *among* men, and let them stand together; and let them be ashamed and confounded together: 12 For the artificer sharpens the iron; he fashions *the idol* with an axe, and fixes it with an awl, and fashions it with the strength of his arm: and he will be hungry and weak, and will drink no water. 13 The artificer having chosen a piece of wood, marks it out with a rule, and fits it with glue, and makes it as the form of a man, and as the beauty of a man, to set it up in the house. 14 He cuts wood out of the forest, which the Lord planted, *even* a pine tree, and the rain made it grow, 15 that it might be for men to burn: and having taken part of it he warms himself; yea, they burn part of it, and bake loaves thereon; and *of* the rest they make for themselves gods, and they worship them. 16 Half thereof he burns in the fire, and with half of it he bakes loaves on the coals; and having roasted flesh on it he eats, and is satisfied, and having warmed himself he says, I am comfortable, for I have warmed myself, and have seen the fire. 17 And the rest he makes a graven god, and worships, and prays, saying, Deliver me; for thou art my God. 18 They have no understanding to perceive; for they have been blinded so that they should not see with their eyes, nor perceive with their heart. 19 And one has not considered in his mind, nor known in his understanding, that he has burnt up half of it in the fire, and baked loaves on the coals thereof and has roasted and eaten flesh, and of the rest of it he has made an abomination, and they worship it. 20 Know thou that their heart is ashes, and they err, and no one is able to deliver his soul: see, ye will not say, *There is a* lie in my right hand. 21 Remember these things, O Jacob and Israel; for thou art my servant; I have formed thee *to be* my servant: and do thou, Israel, not forget me. 22 For behold, I have blotted out as a cloud thy transgressions, and thy sin as darkness: turn to me, and I will redeem thee. 23 Rejoice, ye heavens; for God has had mercy upon Israel: sound the trumpet, ye foundations of the earth: ye mountains, shout *with* joy, ye hills, and all the trees therein: for God has redeemed Jacob, and Israel shall be glorified. 24 Thus saith the Lord that redeems thee, and who formed thee from the womb, I am the Lord that performs all things: I stretched out the heaven alone, and established the earth. 25 Who else will frustrate the tokens of those that have divining spirits, and prophecies from the heart of *man?* turning the wise back, and making their counsel foolishness; 26 and confirming the word of his servant, and verifying the counsel of his messengers: who says to

Jerusalem, Thou shalt be inhabited; and to the cities of Idumea, Ye shall be built, and her desert places shall spring forth. 27 Who says to the deep, Thou shalt be dried up, and I will dry up the rivers. 28 Who bids Cyrus be wise, and he shall perform all my will: who says to Jerusalem, Thou shalt be built, and I will lay the foundation of my holy house.

Isa.45 1 Thus saith the Lord God to my anointed Cyrus, whose right hand I have held, that nations might be obedient before him; and I will break through the strength of kings; I will open doors before him, and cities shall not be closed. 2 I will go before thee, and will level mountains: I will break to pieces brazen doors, and burst iron bars. 3 And I will give thee the treasures of darkness, I will open to thee hidden, unseen *treasures,* that thou mayest know that I, the Lord thy God, that call thee by name, am the God of Israel. 4 For the sake of my servant Jacob, and Israel mine elect, I will call thee by thy name, and accept thee: but thou hast not known me. 5 For I am the Lord God, and there is no other God beside me; I strengthened thee, and thou hast not known me. 6 That they that *come* from the east and they that *come* from the west may know that there is no God but me. I am the Lord God, and there is none beside. 7 I am he that prepared light, and formed darkness; who make peace, and create evil; I am the Lord God, that does all these things. 8 Let the heaven rejoice from above, and let the clouds rain righteousness: let the earth bring forth, and blossom *with* mercy, and bring forth righteousness likewise: I am the Lord that created thee. 9 What excellent thing have I prepared as clay of the potter? Will the ploughman plough the earth all day? shall the clay say to the potter, What art thou doing that thou dost not work, nor hast hands? shall the thing formed answer him that formed it? 10 As though one should say to *his* father, What wilt thou beget me? and to his mother, What art thou bringing forth? 11 For thus saith the Lord God, the Holy One of Israel, who has formed the things that are to come, Enquire of me concerning my sons, and concerning the works of my hands command me. 12 I have made the earth, and man upon it: I with my hand have established the heaven; I have given commandment to all the stars. 13 I have raised him up *to be* a king with righteousness, and all his ways are right: he shall build my city, and shall turn the captivity of my people, not for ransoms, nor for rewards, saith the Lord of hosts. 14 Thus saith the Lord of hosts, Egypt has laboured *for thee;* and the merchandise of the Ethiopians, and the Sabeans, men of stature, shall pass over to thee, and shall be thy servants; and they shall follow after thee bound in fetters, and shall pass over to thee, and shall do obeisance to thee, and make supplication to thee: because God is in thee; and there is no God beside thee, *O Lord.* 15 For thou art God, yet we knew *it* not, the God of Israel, the Saviour. 16 All that are opposed to him shall be ashamed and confounded, and shall walk in shame: ye isles, keep a feast to me. 17 Israel is saved by the Lord with an everlasting salvation: they shall not be ashamed nor confounded for evermore. 18 Thus saith the Lord that made the heaven, this God that created the earth, and made it; he marked it out, he made it not in vain, but formed it to be inhabited: I am the Lord, and there is none beside. 19 I have not spoken in secret, nor in a dark place of the earth: I said not to the seed of Jacob, Seek vanity: I, even I, am the Lord, speaking righteousness, and proclaiming truth. 20 Assemble yourselves and come; take counsel together, ye that escape of the nations: they that set up wood, *even* their graven image, have no knowledge, nor they who pray to gods that do not save. 21 If they will declare, let them draw nigh, that they may know together, who has caused these things to be heard from the beginning: then was it told you. I am God, and there is not another beside me; a just *God* and a Saviour; there is none but me. 22 Turn ye to me, and ye shall be saved, ye that *come* from the end of the earth: I am God, and there is none other. 23 By myself I swear, righteousness shall surely proceed out of my mouth; my words shall not be frustrated; that to me every knee shall bend, and every tongue shall swear by God, 24 saying, Righteousness and glory shall come to him: and all that remove them from their borders shall be ashamed. 25 By the Lord shall they be justified, and in God shall all the seed of the children of Israel be glorified.

Isa.46 1 Bel has fallen, Nabo is broken to pieces, their graven images are gone to the wild beasts and the cattle: ye take them packed up as a burden to the weary, exhausted, hungry, and *at the same time* helpless man; 2 who will not be able to save themselves from war, but they themselves are led *away* captive. 3 Hear me, O house of Jacob, and all the remnant of Israel, who are borne *by me* from the womb, and taught *by me* from infancy, *even* to old age: 4 I am *he*; and until ye shall have grown old, I am *he*: I bear you, I have made, and I will relieve, I will take up and save you. 5 To whom have ye compared me? see, consider, ye that go astray. 6 They that furnish gold out of a purse, and silver by weight, will weigh it in a scale, and they hire a goldsmith and make idols, and bow down, and worship them. 7 They bear it upon the shoulder, and go; and if they put it upon its place, it remains, it cannot move: and whosoever shall cry to it, it cannot hear; it cannot save him from trouble. 8 Remember ye these things, and groan: repent, ye that have gone astray, return in your heart; 9 and remember the former things *that were* of old: for I am God, and there is none other beside me, 10 telling beforehand the latter events before they come to pass, and they are accomplished together: and I said, all my counsel shall stand, and I will do all things that I have planned: 11 calling a bird from the east, and from a land afar off, for the things which I have planned: I have spoken, and brought *him*, I have created and made *him*, I have brought him, and prospered his way. 12 Hearken to me, ye senseless ones, that are far from righteousness: 13 I have brought near my righteousness, and I will not be slow with the salvation that is from me: I have given salvation in Sion to Israel for glory.

Isa.47 1 Come down, sit on the ground, O virgin daughter of Babylon: sit on the ground, O daughter of the Chaldeans: for thou shalt no more be called tender and luxurious. 2 Take a millstone, grind meal: remove thy veil, uncover thy white hairs, make bare the leg, pass through the rivers. 3 Thy shame shall be uncovered, thy reproaches

shall be brought to light: I will exact of thee due vengeance, I will no longer deliver thee to men. 4 Thy deliverer is the Lord of hosts, the Holy One of Israel is his name. 5 Sit thou down pierced with woe, go into darkness, O daughter of the Chaldeans: thou shalt no more be called the strength of a kingdom. 6 I have been provoked with my people; thou hast defiled mine inheritance: I gave them into thy hand, but thou didst not extend mercy to them: thou madest the yoke of the aged man very heavy, 7 and saidst, I shall be a princess for ever: thou didst not perceive these things in thine heart, nor didst thou remember the latter end. 8 But now hear these words, thou luxurious one, *who art* the one that sits *at ease*, that is secure, that says in her heart, I am, and there is not another; I shall not sit a widow, neither shall I know bereavement. 9 But now these two things shall come upon thee suddenly in one day, the loss of children and widowhood shall come suddenly upon thee, for thy sorcery, for the strength of thine enchantments, 10 for thy trusting in wickedness: for thou saidst, I am, and there is not another: know thou, the understanding of these things and thy harlotry shall be thy shame; for thou saidst in thy heart, I am, and there is not another. 11 And destruction shall come upon thee, and thou shalt not be aware; *there shall be a* pit, and thou shalt fall into it: and grief shall come upon thee, and thou shalt not be able to be clear; and destruction shall come suddenly upon thee, and thou shalt not know. 12 Stand now with thine enchantments, and with the abundance of thy sorcery, which thou hast learned from thy youth; if thou canst be profited. 13 Thou art wearied in thy counsels. Let now the astrologers of the heaven stand and deliver thee, let them that see the stars tell thee what is about to come upon thee. 14 Behold, they all shall be burnt up as sticks in the fire; neither shall they at all deliver their life from the flame. Because thou hast coals of fire, sit thou upon them; 15 these shall be thy help. Thou hast wearied thyself with traffic from thy youth: every man has wandered to his own home, but thou shalt have no deliverance.

Isa.48 1 Hear these *words*, ye house of Jacob, who are called by the name of Israel, and have come forth out of Juda, who swear by the name of the Lord God of Israel, making mention *of it, but* not with truth, nor with righteousness; 2 maintaining also the name of the holy city, and staying themselves on the God of Israel: the Lord of hosts is his name. The former things I have already declared; 3 and they that have proceeded out of my mouth, and it became well known; I wrought suddenly, and *the events* came to pass. 4 I know that thou art stubborn, and thy neck is an iron sinew, and thy forehead brazen. 5 And I told thee of old what *should be* before it came upon thee; I made it known to thee, lest thou shouldest say, *My* idols have done *it* for me; and shouldest say, *My* graven and molten images have commanded me. 6 Ye have heard all this, but ye have not known: yet I have made known to thee the new things from henceforth, which are coming to pass, and thou saidst not, 7 Now they come to pass, and not formerly: and thou heardest not of them in former days: say not thou, Yea, I know them. 8 Thou hast neither known, nor understood, neither from the beginning have I opened thine ears: for I knew that thou wouldest surely deal treacherously, and wouldest be called a transgressor even from the womb. 9 For mine own sake will I shew thee my wrath, and will bring before thee my glorious acts, that I may not utterly destroy thee. 10 Behold, I have sold thee, *but* not for silver; but I have rescued thee from the furnace of affliction. 11 For mine own sake I will do *this* for thee, because my name is profaned; and I will not give my glory to another. 12 Hear me, O Jacob, and Israel whom I call; I am the first, and I endure for ever. 13 My hand also has founded the earth, and my right hand has fixed the sky: I will call them, and they shall stand together. 14 And all shall be gathered, and shall hear: who has told them these things? Out of love to thee I have fulfilled thy desire on Babylon, to abolish the seed of the Chaldeans. 15 I have spoken, I have called, I have brought him, and made his way prosperous. 16 Draw nigh to me, and hear ye these words; I have not spoken in secret from the beginning: when it took place, there was I, and now the Lord, *even* the Lord, and his Spirit, hath sent me. 17 Thus saith the Lord that delivered thee, the Holy One of Israel; I am thy God, I have shewn thee how thou shouldest find the way wherein thou shouldest walk. 18 And if thou hadst hearkened to my commandments, *then* would thy peace have been like a river, and thy righteousness as a wave of the sea. 19 Thy seed also would have been as the sand, and the offspring of thy belly as the dust of the ground: neither now shalt thou by any means be utterly destroyed, neither shall thy name perish before me. 20 Go forth of Babylon, thou that fleest from the Chaldeans: utter aloud a voice of joy, and let this be made known, proclaim it to the end of the earth; say ye, The Lord hath delivered his servant Jacob. 21 And if they shall thirst, he shall lead them through the desert; he shall bring forth water to them out of the rock: the rock shall be cloven, and the water shall flow forth, and my people shall drink. 22 There is no joy, saith the Lord, to the ungodly.

Isa.49 1 Hearken to me, ye islands; and attend, ye Gentiles; after a long time it shall come to pass, saith the Lord: from my mother's womb he has called my name: 2 and he has made my mouth as a sharp sword, and he has hid me under the shadow of his hand; he has made me as a choice shaft, and he has hid me in his quiver; 3 and said to me, Thou art my servant, O Israel, and in thee I will be glorified. 4 Then I said, I have laboured in vain, I have given my strength for vanity and for nothing: therefore is my judgment with the Lord, and my labour before my God. 5 And now, thus saith the Lord that formed me from the womb to be his own servant, to gather Jacob to him and Israel. I shall be gathered and glorified before the Lord, and my God shall be my strength. 6 And he said to me, *It is* a great thing for thee to be called my servant, to establish the tribes of Jacob, and to recover the dispersion of Israel: behold, I have given thee for the covenant of a race, for a light of the Gentiles, that thou shouldest be for salvation to the end of the earth. 7 Thus saith the Lord that delivered thee, the God of Israel, Sanctify him that despises his life, him that is abhorred by the nations that are the servants of princes: kings shall behold him, and princes shall arise, and shall worship him,

for the Lord's sake: for the Holy One of Israel is faithful, and I have chosen thee. 8 Thus saith the Lord, In an acceptable time have I heard thee, and in a day of salvation have I succored thee: and I have formed thee, and given thee for a covenant of the nations, to establish the earth, and to cause to inherit the desert heritages: 9 saying to them that are in bonds, Go forth; and *bidding* them that are in darkness shew themselves. They shall be fed in all the ways, and in all the paths *shall be* their pasture. 10 They shall not hunger, neither shall they thirst; neither shall the heat nor the sun smite them; but he that has mercy on them shall comfort *them*, and by fountains of waters shall he lead them. 11 And I will make every mountain a way, and every path a pasture to them. 12 Behold, these shall come from far: *and* these from the north and the west, and others from the land of the Persians. 13 Rejoice, ye heavens; and let the earth be glad: let the mountains break forth *with* joy; for the Lord has had mercy on his people, and has comforted the lowly ones of his people. 14 But Sion said, The Lord has forsaken me, and, The Lord has forgotten me. 15 Will a woman forget her child, so as not to have compassion upon the offspring of her womb? but if a woman should even forget these, yet I will not forget thee, saith the Lord. 16 Behold, I have painted thy walls on my hands, and thou art continually before me. 17 And thou shalt soon be built by those by whom thou were destroyed, and they that made thee desolate shall go forth of thee. 18 Lift up thine eyes round about, and look on them all; behold, they are gathered together, and are come to thee. *As* I live, saith the Lord, thou shalt clothe thyself with them all as with an ornament, and put them on as a bride her attire. 19 For thy desert and marred and ruined *places* shall now be too narrow by reason of the inhabitants, and they that devoured thee shall be removed far from thee. 20 For thy sons whom thou hast lost shall say in thine ears, The place *is too* narrow for me: make room for me that I may dwell. 21 And thou shalt say in thine heart, Who has begotten me these? whereas I *was* childless, and a widow; but who has brought up these for me? and I was left alone; but whence came these to me? 22 Thus saith the Lord, *even* the Lord, Behold, I lift up mine hand to the nations, and I will lift up my signal to the islands: and they shall bring thy sons in *their* bosom, and shall bear thy daughters on *their* shoulders. 23 And kings shall be thy nursing fathers, and their princesses thy nurses, they shall bow down to thee on the face of the earth, and shall lick the dust of thy feet; and thou shalt know that I am the Lord, and they that wait on me shall not be ashamed. 24 Will any one take spoils from a giant? and if one should take *a man* captive unjustly, shall he be delivered? 25 For thus saith the Lord, If one should take a giant captive, he shall take spoils, and he who takes *them* from a mighty *man* shall be delivered: for I will plead thy cause, and I will deliver thy children. 26 And they that afflicted thee shall eat their own flesh; and they shall drink their own blood as new wine, and shall be drunken: and all flesh shall perceive that I am the Lord that delivers thee, and that upholds the strength of Jacob.

Isa.50 1 Thus saith the Lord, Of what kind is your mother's bill of divorcement, by which I put her away? or to which debtor have I sold you? Behold, ye are sold for your sins, and for your iniquities have I put your mother away. 2 Why did I come, and there was no man? *why* did I call, and there was none to hearken? Is not my hand strong to redeem? or can I not deliver? behold, by my rebuke I will dry up the sea, and make rivers a wilderness; and their fish shall be dried up because there is no water, and shall die for thirst. 3 I will clothe the sky with darkness, and will make its covering as sackcloth. 4 The Lord *even* God gives me the tongue of instruction, to know when it is fit to speak a word: he has appointed for me early, he has given me an ear to hear: 5 and the instruction of the Lord, even the Lord, opens mine ears, and I do not disobey, nor dispute. 6 I gave my back to scourges, and my cheeks to blows; and I turned not away my face from the shame of spitting: 7 but the Lord God became my helper; therefore I was not ashamed, but I set my face as a solid rock; and I know that I shall never be ashamed, 8 for he that has justified me draws near; who is he that pleads with me? let him stand up against me at the same time: yea, who is he that pleads with me? let him draw nigh to me. 9 Behold, the Lord, the Lord, will help me; who will hurt me? behold, all ye shall wax old as a garment, and a moth shall devour you. 10 Who is among you that fears the Lord? let him hearken to the voice of his servant: ye that walk in darkness, and have no light, trust in the name of the Lord, and stay upon God. 11 Behold, ye all kindle a fire, and feed a flame: walk in the light of your fire, and in the flame which ye have kindled. This has happened to you for my sake; ye shall lie down in sorrow.

Isa.51 1 Hearken to me, ye that follow after righteousness, and seek the Lord: look to the solid rock, which ye have hewn, and to the hole of the pit which ye have dug. 2 Look to Abraam your father, and to Sarrha that bore you: for he was alone when I called him, and blessed him, and loved him, and multiplied him. 3 And now I will comfort thee, O Sion: and I have comforted all her desert places; and I will make her desert places as a garden, and her western places as the garden of the Lord; they shall find in her gladness and exultation, thanksgiving and the voice of praise. 4 Hear me, hear me, my people; and ye kings, hearken to me: for a law shall proceed from me, and my judgment *shall be* for a light of the nations. 5 My righteousness speedily draws nigh, and my salvation shall go forth as light, and on mine arm shall the Gentiles trust: the isles shall wait for me, and on mine arm shall they trust. 6 Lift up your eyes to the sky, and look on the earth beneath: for the sky was darkened like smoke, and the earth shall wax old like a garment, and the inhabitants shall die in like manner: but my righteousness shall not fail. 7 Hear me, ye that know judgment, the people in whose heart is my law: fear not the reproach of men, and be not overcome by their contempt. 8 For as a garment will be devoured by time, and as wool will be devoured by a moth, *so shall they be consumed*; but my righteousness shall be for ever, and my salvation for all generations. 9 Awake, awake, O Jerusalem, and put on the strength of thine arm; awake as in the early time, as the ancient generation. 10 Art thou not it that dried the sea, the water, *even* the abundance of the deep; that made the depths of the sea a way of

passage for the delivered and redeemed? 11 for by *the help of* the Lord they shall return, and come to Sion with joy and everlasting exultation, for praise and joy shall come upon their head: pain, and grief, and groaning, have fled away. 12 I, *even* I, am he that comforts thee: consider who thou art, that thou wast afraid of mortal man, and of the son of man, who are withered as grass. 13 And thou hast forgotten God who made thee, who made the sky and founded the earth; and thou wert continually afraid because of the wrath of him that afflicted thee: for *whereas* he counselled to take thee away, yet now where is the wrath of him that afflicted thee? 14 For in thy deliverance he shall not halt, nor tarry; 15 for I am thy God, that troubles the sea, and causes the waves thereof to roar: the Lord of hosts is my name. 16 I will put my words into thy mouth, and I will shelter thee under the shadow of mine hand, with which I fixed the sky, and founded the earth: and *the Lord* shall say to Sion, Thou art my people. 17 Awake, awake, stand up, O Jerusalem, that hast drunk at the hand of the Lord the cup of his fury: for thou hast drunk out and drained the cup of calamity, the cup of wrath: 18 and there was none to comfort thee of all the children whom thou borest; and there was none to take hold of thine hand, not even of all the children whom thou has reared. 19 Wherefore these things are against thee; who shall sympathize with thee in thy grief? downfall, and destruction, famine, and sword: who shall comfort thee? 20 Thy sons are the perplexed ones, that sleep at the top of every street as a half-boiled beet; they that are full of the anger of the Lord, caused to faint by the Lord God. 21 Therefore hear, thou afflicted one, and drunken, *but* not with wine; 22 thus saith the Lord God that judges his people, Behold, I have taken out of thine hand the cup of calamity, the cup of my wrath; and thou shalt not drink it any more. 23 And I will give it into the hands of them that injured thee, and them that afflicted thee; who said to thy soul, Bow down, that we may pass over: and thou didst level thy body with the ground to them passing by without.

Isa.52 1 Awake, awake, Sion; put on thy strength, O Sion; and o thou put on thy glory, Jerusalem the holy city: there shall no more pass through thee, the uncircumcised and unclean. 2 Shake off the dust and arise; sit down, Jerusalem: put off the band of thy neck, captive daughter of Sion. 3 For thus saith the Lord, Ye have been sold for nought; and ye shall not be ransomed with silver. 4 Thus saith the Lord, My people went down before to Egypt to sojourn there; and were carried away forcibly to the Assyrians. 5 And now why are ye here? Thus saith the Lord, Because my people was taken for nothing, wonder ye and howl. Thus saith the Lord, On account of you my name is continually blasphemed among the Gentiles. 6 Therefore shall my people know my name in that day, for I am he that speaks: I am present, 7 as a season of beauty upon the mountains, as the feet of one preaching glad tidings of peace, as one preaching good news: for I will publish thy salvation, saying, O Sion, thy God shall reign. 8 For the voice of them that guard thee is exalted, and with the voice together they shall rejoice: for eyes shall look to eyes, when the Lord shall have mercy upon Sion. 9 Let the waste places of Jerusalem break forth *in* joy together, because the Lord has had mercy upon her, and has delivered Jerusalem. 10 And the Lord shall reveal his holy arm in the sight of all the nations; and all the ends of the earth shall see the salvation that *comes* from our God. 11 Depart ye, depart, go out from thence, and touch not the unclean thing; go ye out from the midst of her; separate yourselves, ye that bear the vessels of the Lord. 12 For ye shall not go forth with tumult, neither go by flight: for the Lord shall go first in advance of you; and the God of Israel shall be he that brings up your rear. 13 Behold, my servant shall understand, and be exalted, and glorified exceedingly. 14 As many shall be amazed at thee, so shall thy face be without glory from men, and thy glory *shall not be honoured* by the sons of men. 15 Thus shall many nations wonder at him; and kings shall keep their mouths shut: for they to whom no report was brought concerning him, shall see; and they who have not heard, shall consider.

Isa.53 1 O Lord, who has believed our report? and to whom has the arm of the Lord been revealed? 2 We brought a report as *of* a child before him; *he is* as a root in a thirsty land: he has no form nor comeliness; and we saw him, but he had no form nor beauty. 3 But his form was ignoble, and inferior to that of the children of men; *he was* a man in suffering, and acquainted with the bearing of sickness, for his face is turned from *us*: he was dishonoured, and not esteemed. 4 He bears our sins, and is pained for us: yet we accounted him to be in trouble, and in suffering, and in affliction. 5 But he was wounded on account of our sins, and was bruised because of our iniquities: the chastisement of our peace was upon him; *and* by his bruises we were healed. 6 All we as sheep have gone astray; every one has gone astray in his way; and the Lord gave him up for our sins. 7 And he, because of his affliction, opens not his mouth: he was led as a sheep to the slaughter, and as a lamb before the shearer is dumb, so he opens not his mouth. 8 In *his* humiliation his judgment was taken away: who shall declare his generation? for his life is taken away from the earth: because of the iniquities of my people he was led to death. 9 And I will give the wicked for his burial, and the rich for his death; for he practised no iniquity, nor craft with his mouth. 10 The Lord also is pleased to purge him from his stroke. If ye can give an offering for sin, your soul shall see a long-lived seed: 11 the Lord also is pleased to take away from the travail of his soul, to shew him light, and to form *him* with understanding; to justify the just one who serves many well; and he shall bear their sins. 12 Therefore he shall inherit many, and he shall divide the spoils of the mighty; because his soul was delivered to death: and he was numbered among the transgressors; and he bore the sins of many, and was delivered because of their iniquities.

Isa.54 1 Rejoice, thou barren that bearest not; break forth and cry, thou that dost not travail: for more are the children of the desolate than of her that has a husband: for the Lord has said, 2 Enlarge the place of thy tent, and of thy curtains: fix *the pins*, spare not, lengthen thy cords, and strengthen thy pins; 3 spread forth *thy tent* yet to the right and the left: for thy seed shall inherit the Gentiles, and thou shalt make the desolate cities to be inhabited. 4 Fear not, because thou has been put to shame, neither be confounded, because thou was reproached: for thou shalt forget thy former shame, and shalt no more at all remember the reproach of thy widowhood. 5 For *it is* the Lord that made thee; the Lord of hosts is his name: and he that delivered thee, he is the God of Israel, *and* shall be called *so* by the whole earth. 6 The Lord has not called thee as a deserted and faint-hearted woman, nor as a woman hated from *her* youth, saith thy God. 7 For a little while I left thee: but with great mercy will I have compassion upon thee. 8 In a little wrath I turned away my face from thee; but with everlasting mercy will I have compassion upon thee, saith the Lord that delivers thee. 9 From the time of the water of Noe this is my *purpose*: as I sware to him at that time, *saying* of the earth, I will no more be wroth with thee, neither when thou art threatened, 10 shall the mountains depart, nor shall thy hills be removed: so neither shall my mercy fail thee, nor shall the covenant of thy peace be at all removed: for the Lord *who is* gracious to thee has spoken *it*. 11 Afflicted and outcast thou has not been comforted: behold, I *will* prepare carbuncle *for* thy stones, and sapphire for thy foundations; 12 and I will make thy buttresses jasper, and thy gates crystal, and thy border precious stones. 13 And *I will cause* all thy sons *to be* taught of God, and thy children *to be* in great peace. 14 And thou shalt be built in righteousness: abstain from injustice, and thou shalt not fear; and trembling shall not come nigh thee. 15 Behold, strangers shall come to thee by me, and shall sojourn with thee, and shall run to thee for refuge. 16 Behold, I have created thee, not as the coppersmith blowing coals, and bringing out a vessel *fit* for work; but I have created thee, not for ruin, that *I* should destroy *thee*. 17 I will not suffer any weapon formed against thee to prosper; and every voice that shall rise up against thee for judgment, thou shalt vanquish them all; and thine adversaries shall be *condemned* thereby. There is an inheritance to them that serve the Lord, and ye shall be righteous before me, saith the Lord.

Isa.55 1 Ye that thirst, go to the water, and all that have no money, go *and* buy; and eat *and drink* wine and fat without money or price. 2 Wherefore do ye value at the price of money, and *give* your labour for that which will not satisfy? hearken to me, and ye shall eat that which is good, and your soul shall feast itself on good things. 3 Give heed with your ears, and follow my ways: hearken to me, and your soul shall live in prosperity; and I will make with you an everlasting covenant, the sure mercies of David. 4 Behold I have made him a testimony among the Gentiles, a prince and commander to the Gentiles. 5 Nations which know thee not, shall call upon thee, and peoples which are not acquainted with thee, shall flee to thee for refuge, for the sake of the Lord thy God, the Holy One of Israel; for he has glorified thee. 6 Seek ye the Lord, and when ye find him, call upon him; and when he shall draw nigh to you, 7 let the ungodly leave his ways, and the transgressor his counsels: and let him return to the Lord, and he shall find mercy; for he shall abundantly pardon your sins. 8 For my counsels are not as your counsels, nor are my ways as your ways, saith the Lord. 9 But as the heaven is distant from the earth, so is my way distant from your ways, and your thoughts from my mind. 10 For as rain shall come down, or snow, from heaven, and shall not return until it have saturated the earth, and it bring forth, and bud, and give seed to the sower, and bread for food: 11 so shall my word be, whatever shall proceed out of my mouth, it shall by no means turn back, until all the things which I willed shall have been accomplished; and I will make thy ways prosperous, and *will effect* my commands. 12 For ye shall go forth with joy, and shall be taught with gladness: for the mountains and the hills shall exult to welcome you with joy, and all the trees of the field shall applaud with their branches. 13 And instead of the bramble shall come up the cypress, and instead of the nettle shall come up the myrtle: and the Lord shall be for a name, and for an everlasting sign, and shall not fail.

Isa.56 1 Thus saith the Lord, Keep ye judgment, and do justice: for my salvation is near to come, and my mercy to be revealed. 2 Blessed is the man that does these things, and the man that holds by them, and keeps the sabbaths from profaning them, and keeps his hands from doing unrighteousness. 3 Let not the stranger who attaches himself to the Lord, say, Surely the Lord will separate me from his people: and let not the eunuch say, I am a dry tree. 4 Thus saith the Lord to the eunuchs, as many as shall keep my sabbaths, and choose the things which I take pleasure in, and take hold of my covenant; 5 I will give to them in my house and within my walls an honourable place, better than sons and daughters: I will give them an everlasting name, and it shall not fail. 6 And *I will give it* to the strangers that attach themselves to the Lord, to serve him, and to love the name of the Lord, to be to him servants and handmaids; and *as for* all that keep my sabbaths from profaning *them*, and that take hold of my covenant; 7 I will bring them to my holy mountain, and gladden them in my house of prayer: their whole-burnt-offerings and their sacrifices shall be acceptable upon mine altar; for my house shall be called a house of prayer for all nations, 8 saith the Lord that gathers the dispersed of Israel; for I will gather to him a congregation. 9 All ye beasts of the field, come, devour, all ye beasts of the forest. 10 See how they are all blinded: they have not known; *they are* dumb dogs *that* will not bark; dreaming of rest, loving to slumber. 11 Yea, they are insatiable dogs, that know not what it is to be filled, and they are wicked, having no understanding: all have followed their own ways, each according to his *will*.

Isa.57 1 See how the just man has perished, and no one lays *it* to heart: and righteous men are taken away, and no one considers: for the righteous has been removed out of the way of injustice. 2 His burial shall be in peace: he has been removed out of the way. 3 But draw ye near hither, ye lawless children, the seed of adulterers and the harlot. 4 Wherein have ye been rioting? and against whom have ye opened your mouth, and against whom have ye loosed your tongue? are ye not children of perdition? a lawless seed? 5 who call upon idols under the leafy trees, slaying your children in the valleys among the rocks? 6 That is thy portion, this is thy lot: and to them hast thou poured forth

drink-offerings, and to these hast thou offered meat-offerings. Shall I not therefore be angry for these things? 7 On a lofty and high mountain, there is thy bed, and thither thou carriedst up thy meat- offerings: 8 and behind the posts of thy door thou didst place thy memorials. Didst thou think that if thou shouldest depart from me, thou wouldest gain? thou hast loved those that lay with thee; 9 and thou hast multiplied thy whoredom with them, and thou hast increased the number of them that are far from thee, and hast sent ambassadors beyond thy borders, and hast been debased even to hell. 10 Thou has wearied thyself with thy many ways; yet thou saidst not, I will cease to strengthen myself: for thou has done these things; therefore thou has not supplicated me. 11 Through dread of whom hast thou feared, and lied against me, and has not remembered, nor considered me, nor regarded me, yea, though when I see thee I pass thee by, yet thou has not feared me. 12 And I will declare thy righteousness, and thy sins, which shall not profit thee. 13 When thou criest out, let them deliver thee in thine affliction: for all these the wind shall take, and the tempest shall carry *them* away: but they that cleave to me shall possess the land, and shall inherit my holy mountain. 14 And they shall say, Clear the ways before him, and take up the stumbling-blocks out of the way of my people. 15 Thus saith the Most High, who dwells on high for ever, Holy in the holies, is his name, the Most High resting in the holies, and giving patience to the faint-hearted, and giving life to the broken-hearted: 16 I will not take vengeance on you for ever, neither will I be always angry with you: for my Spirit shall go forth from me, and I have created all breath. 17 On account of sin for a little while I grieved him, and smote him, and turned away my face from him; and he was grieved, and he went on sorrowful in his ways. 18 I have seen his ways, and healed him, and comforted him, and given him true comfort; 19 peace upon peace to them that are far off, and to them that are nigh: and the Lord has said, I will heal them. 20 But the unrighteous shall be tossed as troubled waves, and shall not be able to rest. 21 There is no joy to the ungodly, said God.

Isa.58 1 Cry aloud, and spare not; lift up thy voice as with a trumpet, and declare to my people their sins, and to the house of Jacob their iniquities. 2 They seek me day by day, and desire to know my ways, as a people that had done righteousness, and had not forsaken the judgment of their God: they now ask of me righteous judgment, and desire to draw nigh to God, 3 saying, Why have we fasted, and thou regardest not? *why* have we afflicted our souls, and thou didst not know it? Nay, in the days of your fasts ye find your pleasures, and all them that are under your power ye wound. 4 If ye fast for quarrels and strifes, and smite the lowly with *your* fists, wherefore do ye fast to me as *ye do* this day, so that your voice may be heard in crying? 5 I have not chosen this fast, nor *such* a day for a man to afflict his soul; neither though thou shouldest bend down thy neck as a ring, and spread under thee sackcloth and ashes, neither thus shall ye call a fast acceptable. 6 I have not chosen such a fast, saith the Lord; but do thou loose every burden of iniquity, do thou untie the knots of hard bargains, set the bruised free, and cancel every unjust account. 7 Break thy bread to the hungry, and lead the unsheltered poor to thy house: if thou seest one naked, clothe *him*, and thou shalt not disregard the relations of thine own seed. 8 Then shall thy light break forth as the morning, and thy health shall speedily spring forth: and thy righteousness shall go before thee, and the glory of God shall compass thee. 9 Then shalt thou cry, and God shall hearken to thee; while thou art yet speaking he will say, Behold, I am here. If thou remove from thee the band, and the stretching forth of the hands, and murmuring speech; 10 and *if* thou give bread to the hungry from thy heart, and satisfy the afflicted soul; then shall thy light spring up in darkness, and thy darkness *shall be* as noon-day: 11 and thy God shall be with thee continually, and thou shalt be satisfied according as thy soul desires; and thy bones shall be made fat, and shall be as a well-watered garden, and as a fountain *from* which the water has not failed. 12 And thy old waste desert *places* shall be built up, and thy foundations shall last through all generations; and thou shalt be called a repairer of breaches, and thou shalt cause thy paths between to be in peace. 13 If thou turn away thy foot from the sabbath, so as not to do thy pleasure on the holy days, and shalt call the sabbaths delightful, holy to God; *if* thou shalt not lift up thy foot to work, nor speak a word in anger out of thy mouth, 14 then shalt thou trust on the Lord; and he shall bring thee up to the good places of the land, and feed thee with the heritage of Jacob thy father: for the mouth of the Lord has spoken this.

Isa.59 1 Has the hand of the Lord no power to save? or has he made his ear heavy, so that he should not hear? 2 Nay, your iniquities separate between you and God, and because of your sins has he turned away *his* face from you, so as not to have mercy *upon you.* 3 For your hands are defiled with blood, and your fingers with sins; your lips also have spoken iniquity, and your tongue meditates unrighteousness. 4 None speaks justly, neither is there true judgment: they trust in vanities, and speak empty *words;* for they conceive trouble, and bring forth iniquity. 5 They have hatched asps' eggs, and weave a spider's web: and he that is going to eat of their eggs, having crushed an addled egg, has found also in it a basilisk. 6 Their web shall not become a garment, nor shall they at all clothe themselves with their works; for their works are works of iniquity. 7 And their feet run to wickedness, swift to shed blood; their thoughts also are thoughts of murder; destruction and misery are in their ways; 8 and the way of peace they know not, neither is there judgment in their ways; for their paths by which they go are crooked, and they know not peace. 9 Therefore has judgment departed from them, and righteousness shall not overtake them: while they waited for light, darkness came upon them; while they waited for brightness, they walked in perplexity. 10 They shall feel for the wall as blind *men,* and shall feel *for it* as if they had no eyes: and they shall feel at noon-day as at midnight; they shall groan as dying men. 11 They shall proceed together as a bear and as a dove: we have waited for judgment, and there is no salvation, it is gone far from us. 12 For our iniquity is great before thee,

and our sins have risen up against us: for our iniquities are in us, and we know our unrighteous deeds. 13 We have sinned, and dealt falsely, and revolted from our God: we have spoken unrighteous words, and have been disobedient; we have conceived and uttered from our heart unrighteous words. 14 And we have turned judgment back, and righteousness has departed afar off: for truth is consumed in their ways, and they could not pass by a straight *path.* 15 And truth has been taken away, and they have turned aside *their* mind from understanding. And the Lord saw it, and it pleased him not that there was no judgment. 16 And he looked, and there was no man, and he observed, and there was none to help: so he defended them with his arm, and stablished *them* with *his* mercy. 17 And he put on righteousness as a breast-plate, and placed the helmet of salvation on his head; and he clothed himself with the garment of vengeance, and with his cloak, 18 as one about to render a recompence, *even* reproach to his adversaries. 19 So shall they of the west fear the name of the Lord, and they *that come* from the rising of the sun his glorious name: for the wrath of the Lord shall come as a mighty river, it shall come with fury. 20 And the deliverer shall come for Sion's sake, and shall turn away ungodliness from Jacob. 21 And this shall be my covenant with them, said the Lord; My Spirit which is upon thee, and the words which I have put in thy mouth, shall never fail from thy mouth, nor from the mouth of thy seed, for the Lord has spoken it, henceforth and for ever.

Isa.60 1 Be enlightened, be enlightened, O Jerusalem, for thy light is come, and the glory of the Lord is risen upon thee. 2 Behold, darkness shall cover the earth, and *there shall be* gross darkness on the nations: but the Lord shall appear upon thee, and his glory shall be seen upon thee. 3 And kings shall walk in thy light, and nations in thy brightness. 4 Lift up thine eyes round about, and behold thy children gathered: all thy sons have come from far, and thy daughters shall be borne on *men's* shoulders. 5 Then shalt thou see, and fear, and be amazed in thine heart; for the wealth of the sea shall come round to thee, and of nations and peoples; and herds of camels shall come to thee, 6 and the camels of Madiam and Gaepha shall cover thee: all from Saba shall come bearing gold, and shall bring frankincense, and they shall publish the salvation of the Lord. 7 And all the flocks of Kedar shall be gathered, and the rams of Nabaeoth shall come; and acceptable sacrifices shall be offered on my altar, and my house of prayer shall be glorified. 8 Who are these *that* fly as clouds, and as doves with young ones to me? 9 The isles have waited for me, and the ships of Tharsis among the first, to bring thy children from afar, and their silver and their gold with them, and *that* for the sake of the holy name of the Lord, and because the Holy One of Israel is glorified. 10 And strangers shall build thy walls, and their kings shall wait upon thee: for by reason of my wrath I smote thee, and by reason of mercy I loved thee. 11 And thy gates shall be opened continually; they shall not be shut day nor night; to bring in to thee the power of the Gentiles, and their kings as captives. 12 For the nations and the kings which will not serve thee shall perish; and those nations shall be made utterly desolate. 13 And the glory of Libanus shall come to thee, with the cypress, and pine, and cedar together, to glorify my holy place. 14 And the sons of them that afflicted thee, and of them that provoked thee, shall come to thee in fear; and thou shalt be called Sion, the city of the Holy One of Israel. 15 Because thou has become desolate and hated, and there was no helper, therefore I will make thee a perpetual gladness, a joy of many generations. 16 And thou shalt suck the milk of the Gentiles, and shalt eat the wealth of kings: and shalt know that I am the Lord that saves thee and delivers thee, the Holy One of Israel. 17 And for brass I will bring thee gold, and for iron I will bring thee silver, and instead of wood I will bring thee brass, and instead of stones, iron; and I will make thy princes peaceable, and thine overseers righteous. 18 And injustice shall no more be heard in thy land, nor destruction nor misery in thy coasts; but thy walls shall be called Salvation, and thy gates Sculptured Work. 19 And thou shalt no more have the sun for a light by day, nor shall the rising of the moon lighten thy night; but the Lord shall be thine everlasting light, and God thy glory. 20 For the sun shall no more set, nor shall the moon be eclipsed; for the Lord shall be thine everlasting light, and the days of thy mourning shall be completed. 21 Thy people also shall be all righteous; they shall inherit the land for ever, preserving that which they have planted, *even* the works of their hands, for glory. 22 The little one shall become thousands, and the least a great nation; I the Lord will gather them in *due* time.

Isa.61 1 The Spirit of the Lord is upon me, because he has anointed me; he has sent me to preach glad tidings to the poor, to heal the broken in heart, to proclaim liberty to the captives, and recovery of sight to the blind; 2 to declare the acceptable year of the Lord, and the day of recompence; to comfort all that mourn; 3 that there should be given to them that mourn in Sion glory instead of ashes, the oil of joy to the mourners, the garment of glory for the spirit of heaviness: and they shall be called generations of righteousness, the planting of the Lord for glory. 4 And they shall build the old waste places, they shall raise up those that were before made desolate, and shall renew the desert cities, *even* those that had been desolate for *many* generations. 5 And strangers shall come and feed thy flocks, and aliens *shall be thy* ploughmen and vine-dressers. 6 But ye shall be called priests of the Lord, the ministers of God: ye shall eat the strength of nations, and shall be admired because of their wealth. 7 Thus shall they inherit the land a second time, and everlasting joy shall be upon their head. 8 For I am the Lord who love righteousness, and hate robberies of injustice; and I will give their labour to the just, and will make an everlasting covenant with them. 9 And their seed shall be known among the Gentiles, and their offspring in the midst of peoples: every one that sees them shall take notice of them, that they are a seed blessed of God; 10 and they shall greatly rejoice in the Lord. Let my soul rejoice in the Lord; for he has clothed me with the robe of salvation, and the garment of joy: he has put a mitre on me as on a bridegroom, and adorned me with ornaments as a bride. 11 And as the earth putting forth her flowers, and

as a garden its seed; so shall the Lord, *even* the Lord, cause righteousness to spring forth, and exultation before all nations.

Isa.62 1 For Sion's sake I will not hold my peace, and for Jerusalem's sake I will not rest, until her righteousness go forth as light, and my salvation burn as a torch. 2 And the Gentiles shall see thy righteousness, and kings thy glory: and one shall call thee *by* a new name, which the Lord shall name. 3 And thou shalt be a crown of beauty in the hand of the Lord, and a royal diadem in the hand of thy God. 4 And thou shalt no more be called Forsaken; and thy land shall no more be called Desert: for thou shalt be called My Pleasure, and thy land Inhabited: for the Lord has taken pleasure in thee, and thy land shall be inhabited. 5 And as a young man lives with a virgin, so shall thy sons dwell in *thee*: and it shall come to pass *that* as a bridegroom will rejoice over a bride, so will the Lord rejoice over thee. 6 And on thy walls, O Jerusalem, have I set watchmen all day and all night, who shall never cease making mention of the Lord. 7 For there is none like you, when he shall have established, and made Jerusalem a praise on the earth. 8 For the Lord has sworn by his glory, and by the might of his arm, I will no more give thy corn and thy provisions to thine enemies; nor shall strangers any more drink thy wine, for which thou has laboured. 9 But they that have gathered them shall eat them, and they shall praise the Lord; and they that have gathered *the grapes* shall drink thereof in my holy courts. 10 Go through my gates, and make a way for my people; and cast the stones out of the way; lift up a standard for the Gentiles. 11 For behold, the Lord has proclaimed to the end of the earth, say ye to the daughter of Sion, Behold, thy Saviour has come to thee, having his reward and his work before his face. 12 And one shall call them the holy people, the redeemed of the Lord: and thou shalt be called a city sought out, and not forsaken.

Isa.63 1 Who is this that is come from Edom, *with* red garments from Bosor? thus fair in his apparel, with mighty strength? I speak of righteousness and saving judgment. 2 Wherefore are thy garments red, and thy raiment as *if fresh* from a trodden winepress? 3 I am full of trodden *grape*, and of the nations there is not a man with me; and I trampled them in my fury, and dashed them to pieces as earth, and brought down their blood to the earth. 4 For the day of recompence has come upon them, and the year of redemption is at hand. 5 And I looked, and there was no helper; and I observed, and none upheld: therefore my arm delivered them, and mine anger drew nigh. 6 And I trampled them in mine anger, and brought down their blood to the earth. 7 I remembered the mercy of the Lord, the praises of the Lord in all things wherein he recompenses us. The Lord is a good judge to the house of Israel; he deals with us according to his mercy, and according to the abundance of his righteousness. 8 And he said, Is it not my people? the children surely will not be rebellious: and he became to them deliverance 9 out of all their affliction: not an ambassador, nor a messenger, but himself saved them, because he loved them and spared them: he himself redeemed them, and took them up, and lifted them up all the days of old. 10 But they disobeyed, and provoked his Holy Spirit: so he turned to be an enemy, he himself contended against them. 11 Then he remembered the ancient days, *saying*, Where is he that brought up from the sea the shepherd of the sheep? where is he that put his Holy Spirit in them? 12 who led Moses with his right hand, the arm of his glory? he forced the water *to separate* from before him, to make himself an everlasting name. 13 He led them through the deep, as a horse through the wilderness, and they fainted not, 14 and as cattle through a plain: the Spirit came down from the Lord, and guided them: thus thou leddest thy people, to make thyself a glorious name. 15 Turn from heaven, and look from thy holy habitation and *from* thy glory: where is thy zeal and thy strength? where is the abundance of thy mercy and of thy compassions, that thou hast withholden thyself from us? 16 For thou art our Father; for *though* Abraham knew us not, and Israel did not acknowledge us, yet do thou, O Lord, our Father, deliver us: thy name has been upon us from the beginning. 17 Why hast thou caused us to err, O Lord, from thy way? *and* has hardened our hearts, that we should not fear thee? Return for thy servants' sake, for the sake of the tribes of thine inheritance, 18 that we may inherit a small part of thy holy mountain. 19 We are become as at the beginning, when thou didst not rule over us, and thy name was not called upon us.

Isa.64 1 If thou wouldest open the heaven, trembling will take hold upon the mountains from thee, and they shall melt, 2 as wax melts before the fire; and fire shall burn up the enemies, and thy name shall be manifest among the adversaries: at thy presence the nations shall be troubled, 3 whenever thou shalt work gloriously; trembling from thee shall take hold upon the mountains. 4 From of old we have not heard, neither have our eyes seen a God beside thee, and thy works which thou wilt perform to them that wait for mercy. 5 For *these blessings* shall happen to them that work righteousness, and they shall remember thy ways: behold, thou wast angry and we have sinned; therefore we have erred, 6 and we are all become as unclean, and all our righteousness as a filthy rag: and we have fallen as leaves because of our iniquities; thus the wind shall carry us *away*. 7 And there is none that calls upon thy name, or that remembers to take hold on thee: for thou hast turned thy face away from us, and hast delivered us up because of our sins. 8 And now, O Lord, thou art our Father, and we are clay, all *of us* the work of thine hands. 9 Be not very wroth with us, and remember not our sins for ever; but now look on *us*, for we are all thy people. 10 The city of thy holiness has become desolate, Sion has become as a wilderness, Jerusalem a curse. 11 The house, our sanctuary, and the glory which our fathers blessed, has been burnt with fire: and all our glorious things have gone to ruin. 12 And for all these things thou, O Lord, has withholden, thyself, and been silent, and hast brought us very low.

Isa.65 1 I became manifest to them that asked not for me; I was found of them that sought me not: I said, Behold, I am *here*, to a nation, who called not on my name. 2 I have stretched forth my hands all day to a disobedient and gainsaying people, to them that walked in a way that was not good, but after their sins. 3 This is the people that provokes me continually in my presence; they offer sacrifices in gardens, and burn incense on bricks to devils, which exist not. 4 They lie down to sleep in the tombs and in the caves for the sake of dreams, *even* they that eat swine's flesh, and the broth of *their* sacrifices: all their vessels are defiled: 5 who say, Depart from me, draw not nigh to me, for I am pure. This is the smoke of my wrath, a fire burns with it continually. 6 Behold, it is written before me: I will not be silent until I have recompensed into their bosom, 7 their sins and *the sins* of their fathers, saith the Lord, who have burnt incense on the mountains, and reproached me on the hills: I will recompense their works into their bosom. 8 Thus saith the Lord, As a grape-stone shall be found in the cluster, and they shall say, Destroy it not; for a blessing is in it: so will I do for the sake of him that serves me, for his sake I will not destroy *them* all. 9 And I will lead forth the seed *that came* of Jacob and of Juda, and they shall inherit my holy mountain: and mine elect and my servants shall inherit it, and shall dwell there. 10 And there shall be in the forest folds of flocks, and the valley of Achor *shall* be for a resting-place of herds for my people, who have sought me. 11 But ye are they that have left me, and forget my holy mountain, and prepare a table for the devil, and fill up the drink-offering to Fortune. 12 I will deliver you up to the sword, ye shall all fall by slaughter: for I called you, and ye hearkened not; I spoke, and ye refused to hear; and ye did evil in my sight, and chose the things wherein I delighted not. 13 Therefore thus saith the Lord, Behold, my servants shall eat, but ye shall hunger: behold, my servants shall drink, but ye shall thirst: behold, my servants shall rejoice, but ye shall be ashamed: 14 behold, my servants shall exult with joy, but ye shall cry for the sorrow of your heart, and shall howl for the vexation of your spirit. 15 For ye shall leave your name for a loathing to my chosen, and the Lord shall destroy you: but my servants shall be called by a new name, 16 which shall be blessed on the earth; for they shall bless the true God: and they that swear upon the earth shall swear by the true God; for they shall forget the former affliction, it shall not come into their mind. 17 For there shall be a new heaven and a new earth: and they shall not at all remember the former, neither shall they at all come into their mind. 18 But they shall find in her joy and exultation; for, behold, I make Jerusalem a rejoicing, and my people a joy. 19 And I will rejoice in Jerusalem, and will be glad in my people: and there shall no more be heard in her the voice of weeping, or the voice of crying. 20 Neither shall there be there any more a *child that dies* untimely, or an old man who shall not complete his time: for the youth shall be a hundred years *old*, and the sinner who dies at a hundred years shall also be accursed: 21 and they shall build houses, and themselves shall dwell in *them*; and they shall plant vineyards, and themselves shall eat the fruit thereof. 22 They shall by no means build, and others inhabit; and they shall by no means plant, and others eat: for as the days of the tree of life shall be the days of my people, they shall long enjoy the fruits of their labours. 23 My chosen shall not toil in vain, neither shall they beget children to be cursed;

for they are a seed blessed of God, and their offspring with them. 24 And it shall come to pass, *that* before they call, I will hearken to them; while they are yet speaking, I will say, What is it? 25 Then wolves and lambs shall feed together, and the lion shall eat chaff like the ox, and the serpent earth as bread. They shall not injure nor destroy in my holy mountain, saith the Lord.

Isa.66 1 Thus saith the Lord, Heaven is my throne, and the earth is my footstool: what kind of a house will ye build me? and of what kind *is to be* the place of my rest? 2 For all these things are mine, saith the Lord: and to whom will I have respect, but to the humble and meek, and the *man* that trembles *at* my words? 3 But the transgressor that sacrifices a calf to me, is as he that kills a dog; and he that offers fine flour, as *one that offers* swine's blood; he that gives frankincense for a memorial, is as a blasphemer. Yet they have chosen their own ways, and their soul has delighted in their abominations. 4 I also will choose their mockeries, and will recompense their sins upon them; because I called them, and they did not hearken to me; I spoke, and they heard not: and they did evil before me, and chose the things wherein I delighted not. 5 Hear the words of the Lord, ye that tremble at his word; speak ye, our brethren, to them that hate you and abominate you, that the name of the Lord may be glorified, and may appear their joy; but they shall be ashamed. 6 A voice of a cry from the city, a voice from the temple, a voice of the Lord rendering recompence to *his* adversaries. 7 Before she that travailed brought forth, before the travail-pain came on, she escaped *it* and brought forth a male. 8 Who has heard such a thing? and who has seen after this manner? Has the earth travailed in one day? or has even a nation been born at once, that Sion has travailed, and brought forth her children? 9 But I have raised this expectation, yet thou hast not remembered me, saith the Lord: behold, have not I made the bearing and barren woman? saith thy God. 10 Rejoice, O Jerusalem, and all ye that love her hold in her a general assembly: rejoice greatly with her, all that *now* mourn over her: 11 that ye may suck, and be satisfied with the breast of her consolation; that ye may milk out, and delight yourselves with the influx of her glory. 12 For thus saith the Lord, Behold, I turn toward them as a river of peace, and as a torrent bringing upon them in a flood the glory of the Gentiles: their children shall be borne upon the shoulders, and comforted on the knees. 13 As if his mother should comfort one, so will I also comfort you; and ye shall be comforted in Jerusalem. 14 And ye shall see, and your heart shall rejoice, and your bones shall thrive like grass: and the hand of the Lord shall be known to them that fear him, and he shall threaten the disobedient. 15 For, behold, the Lord will come as fire, and his chariots as a storm, to render his vengeance with wrath, and his rebuke with a flame of fire. 16 For with the fire of the Lord all the earth shall be judged, and all flesh with his sword: many shall be slain by the Lord. 17 They that sanctify themselves and purify themselves in the gardens, and eat swine's flesh in the porches, and the abominations, and the mouse, shall be consumed together, saith the Lord. 18 And I *know* their works and their imagination. I am going

to gather all nations and tongues; and they shall come, and see my glory. 19 And I will leave a sign upon them, and I will send forth them that have escaped of them to the nations, to Tharsis, and Phud, and Lud, and Mosoch, and to Thobel, and to Greece, and to the isles afar off, to those who have not heard my name, nor seen my glory; and they shall declare my glory among the Gentiles. 20 And they shall bring your brethren out of all nations for a gift to the Lord with horses, and chariots, in litters *drawn by* mules with awnings, to the holy city Jerusalem, said the Lord, as though the children of Israel should bring their sacrifices to me with psalms into the house of the Lord. 21 And I will take of them priests and Levites, saith the Lord. 22 For as the new heaven and the new earth, which I make, remain before me, saith the Lord, so shall your seed and your name continue. 23 And it shall come to pass from month to month, and from sabbath to sabbath, *that* all flesh shall come to worship before me in Jerusalem, saith the Lord. 24 And they shall go forth, and see the carcasses of the men that have transgressed against me: for their worm shall not die, and their fire shall not be quenched; and they shall be a spectacle to all flesh.

JEREMIAS (JEREMIAH)

Jer.1 1 The word of God which came to Jeremias the *son* of Chelcias, of the priests, who dwelt in Anathoth in the land of Benjamin: 2 *accordingly* as the word of God came to him in the days of Josias son of Amos king of Juda, in the thirteenth year of his reign. 3 And it was in the days of Joakim, son of Josias king of Juda, until the eleventh year of Sedekias king of Juda, *even* until the captivity of Jerusalem in the fifth month. 4 And the word of the Lord came to him, *saying,* 5 Before I formed thee in the belly, I knew thee; and before thou camest forth from the womb, I sanctified thee; I appointed thee a prophet to the nations. 6 And I said, O Lord, thou that art supreme Lord, behold, I know not *how* to speak, for I am a child. 7 And the Lord said to me, Say not, I am a child: for thou shalt go to all to whomsoever I shall send thee, and according to all *the words* that I shall command thee, thou shalt speak. 8 Be not afraid before them: for I am with thee to deliver thee, saith the Lord. 9 And the Lord stretched forth his hand to me, and touched my mouth: and the Lord said to me, Behold, I have put my words into thy mouth. 10 Behold, I have appointed thee this day over nations and over kingdoms, to root out, and to pull down, and to destroy, and to rebuild, and to plant. 11 And the word of the Lord came to me, saying, What seest thou? And I said, A rod of an almond tree. 12 And the Lord said to me, Thou hast well seen: for I have watched over my words to perform them. 13 And the word of the Lord came to me a second time, saying, What seest thou? And I said, A caldron on the fire; and the face of it is toward the north. 14 And the Lord said to me, From the north shall flame forth evils upon all the inhabitants of the land. 15 For, behold, I call together all the kingdoms of the earth from the north, saith the Lord; and they shall come, and shall set each one his throne at the entrance of the gates of Jerusalem, and against all the walls round about her, and against all the cities of Juda. 16 And I will speak to them in judgment, concerning all their iniquity, *forasmuch* as they have forsaken me, and sacrificed to strange gods, and worshipped the works of their own hands. 17 And do thou gird up thy loins, and stand up, and speak all *the words* that I shall command thee: be not afraid of their face, neither be thou alarmed before them; for I am with thee to deliver thee, saith the Lord. 18 Behold, I have made thee this day as a strong city, and as a brazen wall, strong *against* all the kings of Juda, and the princes thereof, and the people of the land. 19 And they shall fight against thee; but they shall by no means prevail against thee; because I am with thee, to deliver thee, saith the Lord.

Jer.2 1 And he said, Thus saith the Lord, 2 I remember the kindness of thy youth, and the love of thine espousals, 3 in following the Holy One of Israel, saith the Lord, Israel was the holy *people* to the Lord, *and* the first-fruits of his increase: all that devoured him shall offend; evils shall come upon them, saith the Lord. 4 Hear the word of the Lord, O house of Jacob, and every family of the house of Israel. 5 Thus saith the Lord, What trespass have your fathers found in me, that they have revolted far from me, and gone after vanities, and become vain? 6 And they said not, Where is the Lord, who brought us up out of the land of Egypt, who guided us in the wilderness, in an untried and trackless land, in a land which no man at all went through, and no man dwelt there? 7 And I brought you to Carmel, that ye should eat the fruits thereof, and the good thereof; and ye went in, and defiled my land, and made mine heritage an abomination. 8 The priests said not, Where is the Lord? and they that held by the law knew me not: the shepherds also sinned against me, and the prophets prophesied by Baal, and went after that which profited not. 9 Therefore I will yet plead with you, and will plead with your children's children. 10 For go to the isles of the Chettians, and se; and send to Kedar, and observe accurately, and see if such things have been done; 11 if the nations will change their gods, though they are not gods: but my people have changed their glory, *for that* from which they shall not be profited. 12 The heaven is amazed at this, and is very exceedingly horror-struck, saith the Lord. 13 For my people has committed two *faults*, and evil ones: they have forsaken me, the fountain of water of life, and hewn out for themselves broken cisterns, which will not be able to hold water. 14 Is Israel a servant, or a home-born slave? why has he become a spoil? 15 The lions roared upon him, and uttered their voice, which have made his land a wilderness: and his cities are broken down, that they should not be inhabited. 16 Also the children of Memphis and Taphnas have known thee, and mocked thee. 17 Has not thy forsaking me brought these things upon thee? saith the Lord thy God. 18 And now what hast thou to do with the way of Egypt, to drink the water of Geon? and what hast thou to do with the way of the Assyrians, to drink the water of rivers? 19 Thine apostasy shall correct thee, and thy wickedness shall reprove thee: know then, and see, that thy forsaking me *has been* bitter to thee, saith the Lord thy God; and I have taken no pleasure in thee, saith the Lord thy God. 20 For of old thou hast broken thy yoke, and plucked

asunder thy bands; and thou has said, I will not serve thee, but will go upon every high hill, and under every shady tree, there will I indulge in my fornication. 21 Yet I planted thee a fruitful vine, entirely of the right sort: how art thou a strange vine turned to bitterness! 22 Though thou shouldest wash thyself with nitre, and multiply to thyself soap, *still* thou art stained by thine iniquities before me, saith the Lord. 23 How wilt thou say, I am not polluted, and have not gone after Baal? behold thy ways in the burial-ground, and know what thou hast done: her voice has howled in the evening: 24 she has extended her ways over the waters of the desert; she was hurried along by the lusts of her soul; she is given up *to them*, who will turn her back? none that seek her shall be weary; at *the time of* her humiliation they shall find her. 25 Withdraw thy foot from a rough way, and thy throat from thirst: but she said I will strengthen myself: for she loved strangers, and went after them. 26 As is the shame of a thief when he is caught, so shall the children of Israel be ashamed; they, and their kings, and their princes, and their priests, and their prophets. 27 They said to a stock, Thou art my father; and to a stone, Thou has begotten me: and they have turned *their* backs to me, and not their faces: yet in the time of their afflictions they will say, Arise, and save us. 28 And where are thy gods, which thou madest for thyself? will they arise and save in the time of thine affliction? for according to the number of thy cities were thy gods, O Juda; and according to the number of the streets of Jerusalem they sacrificed to Baal. 29 Wherefore do ye speak unto me? ye all have been ungodly, and ye all have transgressed against me, saith the Lord. 30 In vain have I smitten your children; ye have not received correction: a sword has devoured your prophets as a destroying lion; yet ye feared not. 31 Hear ye the word of the Lord: thus saith the Lord, Have I been a wilderness or a dry land to Israel? wherefore has my people said, We will not be ruled over, and will not come to thee any more? 32 Will a bride forget her ornaments, or a virgin her girdle? but my people has forgotten me days without number. 33 What fair device wilt thou yet employ in thy ways, so as to seek love? *it shall* not *be* so; moreover thou has done wickedly in corrupting thy ways; 34 and in thine hands has been found the blood of innocent souls; I have not found them in holes, but on every oak. 35 Yet thou saidst, I am innocent: only let his wrath be turned away from me. Behold, I *will* plead with thee, whereas thou sayest, I have not sinned. 36 For thou has been so exceedingly contemptuous as to repeat thy ways; but thou shalt be ashamed of Egypt, as thou wast ashamed of Assur. 37 For thou shalt go forth thence also with thine hands upon thine head; for the Lord has rejected thine hope, and thou shalt not prosper in it.

Jer.3 1 If a man put away his wife, and she depart from him, and become another man's, shall she return to him any more at all? shall not that woman be utterly defiled? ye thou hast gone a- whoring with many shepherds, and hast returned to me, saith the Lord. 2 Lift up thine eyes *to look* straight forward, and see where thou hast not been utterly defiled. Thou hast sat for them by the wayside as a deserted crow, and hast defiled the land with thy fornications and thy wickedness. 3 And thou didst retain many shepherds for a stumbling-block to thyself: thou hadst a whore's face, thou didst become shameless toward all. 4 Hast thou not called me as it were a home, and the father and guide of thy virgin-time? 5 Will *God's anger* continue for ever, or be preserved to the end? Behold, thou hast spoken and done these bad things, and hadst power *to do them.* 6 And the Lord said to me in the days of Josias the king, Hast thou seen what things the house of Israel has done to me? they have gone on every high mountain, and under every shady tree, and have committed fornication there. 7 And I said after she had committed all these acts of fornication, Turn again to me. Yet she returned not. And faithless Juda saw her faithlessness. 8 And I saw that (for all the sins of which she was convicted, wherein the house of Israel committed adultery, and I put her away, and gave into her hands a bill of divorcement,) yet faithless Juda feared not, but went and herself also committed fornication. 9 And her fornication was nothing accounted of; and she committed adultery with wood and stone. 10 And for all these things faithless Juda turned not to me with all her heart, but falsely. 11 And the Lord said to me, Israel has justified himself more than faithless Juda. 12 Go and read these words toward the north, and thou shalt say, Return to me, O house of Israel, saith the Lord; and I will not set my face against you: for I am merciful, saith the Lord, and I will not be angry with you for ever. 13 Nevertheless, know thine iniquity, that thou hast sinned against the Lord thy God, and hast scattered thy ways to strangers under every shady tree, but thou didst not hearken to my voice, saith the Lord. 14 Turn, ye children that have revolted, saith the Lord; for I will rule over you: and I will take you one of a city, and two of a family, and I will bring you in to Sion: 15 and I will give you shepherds after my heart, and they shall certainly tend you with knowledge. 16 And it shall come to pass that when ye are multiplied and increased upon the land, saith the Lord, in those days they shall say no more, The ark of the covenant of the Holy One of Israel: it shall not come to mind; it shall not be named; neither shall it be visited; nor shall *this* be done any more. 17 In those days and at that time they shall call Jerusalem the throne of the Lord; and all the nations shall be gathered to it: and they shall not walk any more after the imaginations of their evil heart. 18 In those days the house of Juda, shall come together to the house of Israel, and they shall come, together, from the land of the north, and from all the countries, to the land, which I caused their fathers to inherit. 19 And I said, So be it, Lord, for *thou saidst* I will set thee among children, and will give thee a choice land, the inheritance of the Almighty God of the Gentiles: and I said, Ye shall call me Father; and ye shall not turn away from me. 20 But as a wife acts treacherously against her husband, so has the house of Israel dealt treacherously against me, saith the Lord. 21 A voice from the lips was heard, *even* of weeping and supplication of the children of Israel: for they have dealt unrighteously in their ways, they have forgotten God their Holy One. 22 Turn, ye children that are given to turning, and I will heal your bruises. Behold, we will be thy servants; for thou art the Lord our God. 23 Truly the hills and the strength of the mountains were a lying refuge: but by the Lord our God is the salvation of Israel. 24 But shame has consumed the labours of our fathers from our youth; their sheep and their calves, and their sons and their daughters. 25 We have lain down in our shame, and our disgrace has covered us: because we and our fathers have sinned before our God, from our youth until this day; and we have not hearkened to the voice of the Lord our God.

Jer.4 1 If Israel will return to me, saith the Lord, he shall return: and if he will remove his abominations out of his mouth, and fear before me, and swear, 2 The Lord lives, with truth, in judgment and righteousness, then shall nations bless by him, and by him they shall praise God in Jerusalem. 3 For thus saith the Lord to the men of Juda, and to the inhabitants of Jerusalem, Break up fresh ground for yourselves, and sow not among thorns. 4 Circumcise yourselves to your God, and circumcise your hardness of heart, ye men of Juda, and inhabitants of Jerusalem: lest my wrath go forth as fire, and burn, and there be none to quench it, because of the evil of your devices. 5 Declare ye in Juda, and let it be heard in Jerusalem: say ye, Sound the trumpet in the land; cry ye aloud: say ye, Gather yourselves together, and let us enter into the fortified cities. 6 Gather up *your wares* and flee to Sion: hasten, stay not: for I will bring evils from the north, and great destruction. 7 The lion is gone up from his lair, he has roused *himself* to the destruction of the nations, and has gone forth out of his place, to make the land desolate; and the cities shall be destroyed, so as to be without inhabitant. 8 For these things gird yourselves with sackclothes, and lament, and howl: for the anger of the Lord is not turned away from you. 9 And it shall come to pass in that day, saith the Lord, that the heart of the king shall perish, and the heart of the princes; and the priests shall be amazed, and the prophets shall wonder. 10 And I said, O sovereign Lord, verily thou hast deceived this people and Jerusalem, saying, There shall be peace; whereas behold, the sword has reached even to their soul. 11 At that time they shall say to this people and to Jerusalem, *There is* a spirit of error in the wilderness: the way of the daughter of my people is not to purity, nor to holiness. 12 *But* a spirit of full vengeance shall come upon me; and now I declare my judgments against them. 13 Behold, he shall come up as a cloud, and his chariots as a tempest: his horses are swifter than eagles. Woe unto us! for we are in misery. 14 Cleanse thine heart from wickedness, O Jerusalem, that thou mayest be saved: how long will thy grievous thoughts be within thee? 15 For a voice of one publishing from Dan shall come, and trouble out of mount Ephraim shall be heard of. 16 Remind ye the nations; behold, they are come: proclaim *it* in Jerusalem, that bands are approaching from a land afar off, and have uttered their voice against the cities of Juda. 17 As keepers of a field, they have surrounded her; because thou, saith the Lord, has neglected me. 18 Thy ways and thy devices have brought these things upon thee; this is thy wickedness, for *it is* bitter, for it has reached to thy heart. 19 I am pained in my bowels, my bowels, and the sensitive powers of my heart; my soul is in great commotion, my heart is torn: I will not be silent, for my soul has heard the sound of a trumpet, the cry of war, and of distress: it calls on destruction; 20 for all the land is distressed: suddenly *my* tabernacle is distressed, my curtains have been rent asunder. 21 How long shall I·see fugitives, and hear the sound of the trumpet? 22 For the princes of my people have not known me, they are foolish and unwise children: they are wise to do evil, but *how* to do good they have not known. 23 I looked upon the earth, and, behold, *it was* not; and to the sky, an there was no light in it. 24 I beheld the mountains, and they trembled, and *I saw* all the hills in commotion. 25 I looked, and behold, there was no man, and all the birds of the sky were scared. 26 I saw, and, behold, Carmel was desert, and all the cities were burnt with fire at the presence of the Lord, and at the presence of his fierce anger they were utterly destroyed. 27 Thus saith the Lord, The whole land shall be desolate; but I will not make a full end. 28 For these things let the earth mourn, and let the sky be dark above: for I have spoken, and I will not repent; I have purposed, and I will not turn back from it. 29 The whole land has recoiled from the noise of the horseman and the bent bow; they have gone into the caves, and have hidden themselves in the groves, and have gone up upon the rocks: every city was abandoned, no man dwelt in them. 30 And what wilt thou do? Though thou clothe thyself with scarlet, and adorn thyself with golden ornaments; though thou adorn thine eyes with stibium, thy beauty *will be* in vain: thy lovers have rejected thee, they seek thy life. 31 For I have heard thy groaning as the voice of a woman in travail, as of her that brings forth her first child; the voice of the daughter of Zion shall fail through weakness, and she shall lose the strength of her hands, *saying*, Woe is me! for my soul faints because of the slain.

Jer.5 1 Run ye about in the streets of Jerusalem, and see, and know, and seek in her broad places, if ye can find *one*, if there is any one that does judgment, and seeks faithfulness; and I will pardon them, saith the Lord. 2 The Lord lives, they say; do they not therefore swear falsely? 3 O Lord, thine eyes are upon faithfulness: thou hast scourged them, but they have not grieved; thou hast consumed them; but they would not receive correction: they have made their faces harder than a rock; and they would not return. 4 Then I said, It may be they are poor; for they are weak, for they know not the way of the Lord, or the judgment of God. 5 I will go to the rich men, and will speak to them; for they have known the way of the Lord, and the judgment of God: but, behold, with one consent they have broken the yoke, they have burst the bonds. 6 Therefore has a lion out of the forest smitten them, and a wolf has destroyed them even to *their* houses, and a leopard has watched against their cities: all that go forth from them shall be hunted: for they have multiplied their ungodliness, they have strengthened themselves in their revoltings. 7 In what *way* shall I forgive thee for these things? Thy sons have forsaken me, and sworn by them that are no gods: and I fed them to the full, and they committed adultery, and lodged in harlots' houses. 8 They became as wanton horses: they neighed each one after his neighbour's wife. 9 Shall I

not visit for these things? saith the Lord: and shall not my soul be avenged on such a nation as this. 10 Go up upon her battlements, and break *them* down; but make not a full end: leave her buttresses: for they are the Lord's. 11 For the house of Israel have indeed dealt treacherously against me, saith the Lord: the house of Juda also 12 have lied to their Lord, and they have said, These things are not so; no evils shall come upon us; and we shall not see sword or famine. 13 Our prophets became wind, and the word of the Lord was not in them. 14 Therefore thus saith the Lord Almighty, Because ye have spoken this word, behold, I have made my words in thy mouth fire, and this people wood, and it shall devour them. 15 Behold, I *will* bring upon you a nation from far, O house of Israel, saith the Lord; a nation the sound of whose language one shall not understand. 16 *They are* all mighty men: 17 and they shall devour your harvest, and your bread; and shall devour your sons, and your daughters; and they shall devour your sheep, and your calves, and devour your vineyards, and your fig-plantations, and your olive yards: and they shall utterly destroy your strong cities, wherein ye trusted, with the sword. 18 And it shall come to pass in those days, saith the Lord thy God, that I will not utterly destroy you. 19 And it shall come to pass, when ye shall say, Wherefore has the Lord our God done all these things to us? that thou shalt say to them, Because ye served strange gods in your land, so shall ye serve strangers in a land that is not yours. 20 Proclaim these things to the house of Jacob, and let them be heard in the house of Juda. 21 Hear ye now these things, O foolish and senseless people; who have eyes, and see not; and have ears, and hear not: 22 will ye not be afraid of me? saith the Lord; and will ye not fear before me, who have set the sand for a bound to the sea, *as* a perpetual ordinance, and it shall not pass it: yea, it shall rage, but not prevail; and its waves shall roar, but not pass over it. 23 But this people has a disobedient and rebellious heart; and they have turned aside and gone back: 24 and they have not said in their heart, Let us fear now the Lord our God, who gives us the early and latter rain, according to the season of the fulfillment of the ordinance of harvest, and has preserved *it* for us. 25 Your transgressions have turned away these things, and your sins have removed good things from you. 26 For among my people were found ungodly men; and they have set snares to destroy men, and have caught *them*. 27 As a snare which has been set is full of birds, so are their houses full of deceit: therefore have they grown great, and become rich: 28 and they have transgressed *the rule of* judgment; they have not judged the cause of the orphan, nor have they judged the cause of the widow. 29 Shall I not visit for these things? saith the Lord: and shall not my soul be avenged on such a nation as this? 30 Shocking and horrible deeds have been done on the land; 31 the prophets utter unrighteous prophecies, and the priests have clapped their hands: and my people has loved *to have it* thus: and what will ye do for the future.

Jer.6 1 Strengthen yourselves, ye children of Benjamin, *to flee* out of the midst of Jerusalem, and sound an alarm with the trumpet in Thecue, and set up a signal over Baethacharma: for evil threatens from the north, and a great destruction is coming. ² And *thy* pride, O daughter of Sion, shall be taken away. ³ The shepherds and their flocks shall come to her; and they shall pitch *their* tents against her round about, and shall feed *their flocks* each with his hand. ⁴ Prepare yourselves for war against her; rise up, and let us go up against her at noon. Woe to us! for the day has gone down, for the shadows of the day fail. ⁵ Rise, and let us go up against her by night, and destroy her foundations. ⁶ For thus saith the Lord, Hew down her trees, array a numerous force against Jerusalem. O false city; *there is* all oppression in her. ⁷ As a cistern cools water, so her wickedness cools her, ungodliness and misery shall be heard in her, *as* continually before her. ⁸ Thou shalt be chastened, O Jerusalem, with pain and the scourge, lest my soul depart from thee; lest I make thee a desert land, which shall not be inhabited. ⁹ For thus saith the Lord, Glean, glean thoroughly as a vine the remnant of Israel: turn back *your hands* as a grape-gatherer to his basket. ¹⁰ To whom shall I speak, and testify, that he may hearken? behold, thine ears are uncircumcised, and they shall not be able to hear: behold, the word of the Lord is become to them a reproach, they will not at all desire it. ¹¹ And I allowed my wrath to come to full, yet I kept *it* in, and did not utterly destroy them: I will pour it out on the children without, and on the assembly of young men together: for man and woman shall be taken together, the old man with him that is full of days. ¹² And their houses shall be turned to others, *with* their fields and their wives together: for I will stretch out my hand upon the inhabitants of this land, saith the Lord. ¹³ For from the least of them even to the greatest they have all committed iniquity; from the priest even to the false prophet they have all wrought falsely. ¹⁴ And they healed the breach of my people *imperfectly*, making light *of it*, and saying, Peace, peace, and where is peace? ¹⁵ They were ashamed because they failed; yet they were not ashamed as those who are *truly* ashamed, and they knew not their own disgrace: therefore shall they *utterly* fall when they do fall, and in the time of visitation shall they perish, said the Lord. ¹⁶ Thus saith the Lord, Stand ye in the ways, and see, and ask for the old paths of the Lord; and see what is the good way, and walk in it, and ye shall find purification for your souls. But they said, We will not walk *in them*. ¹⁷ I have set watchmen over you, *saying*, Hear ye the sound of the trumpet. But they said, We will not hear *it*. ¹⁸ Therefore have the nations heard, and they that feed their flocks. ¹⁹ Hear, O earth: behold, I will bring evils upon this people, *even* the fruit of their rebellions; for they have not heeded my words, and they have rejected my law. ²⁰ Wherefore do ye bring me frankincense from Saba, and cinnamon from a land afar off? your whole-burnt-offerings are not acceptable, and your sacrifices have not been pleasant to me. ²¹ Therefore thus saith the Lord, Behold, I *will* bring weakness upon this people, and the fathers and sons shall be weak together; the neighbour and his friend shall perish. ²² Thus saith the Lord, Behold, a people comes from the north, and nations shall be stirred up from the end of the earth. ²³ They shall lay hold on bow and spear; *the people* is fierce, and will have no mercy; their voice is as the roaring sea; they shall array themselves for war against thee as fire on horses and chariots, O daughter of Sion. ²⁴ We have heard the report of them: our hands are weakened: anguish has seized us, the pangs as of a woman in travail. ²⁵ Go not forth into the field, and walk not in the ways; for the sword of the enemy lingers round about. ²⁶ O daughter of my people, gird thyself with sackcloth: sprinkle *thyself* with ashes; make for thyself pitiable lamentation, *as* the mourning for a beloved *son*: for misery will come suddenly upon you. ²⁷ I have caused thee to be tried among tried nations, and thou shalt know me when I have tried their way. ²⁸ *They are* all disobedient, walking perversely: *they are* brass and iron; they are all corrupted. ²⁹ The bellows have failed from the fire, the lead has failed: the silversmith works at his trade in vain; their wickedness is not consumed. ³⁰ Call ye them reprobate silver, because the Lord has rejected them.

Jer.7 ¹ ² Hear ye the word of the Lord, all Judea. ³ Thus saith the Lord God of Israel, Correct your ways and your devices, and I will cause you to dwell in this place. ⁴ Trust not in yourselves with lying words, for they shall not profit you at all, saying, It is the temple of the Lord, the temple of the Lord. ⁵ For if ye thoroughly correct your ways and your practices, and do indeed execute judgment between a man and his neighbour; ⁶ and oppress not the stranger, and the orphan, and the widow, and shed not innocent blood in this place, and go not after strange gods to your hurt: ⁷ then will I cause you to dwell in this place, in the land which I gave to your fathers of old and for ever. ⁸ But whereas ye have trusted in lying words, whereby ye shall not be profited; ⁹ and ye murder, and commit adultery, and steal, and swear falsely, and burn incense to Baal, and are gone after strange gods whom ye know not, ¹⁰ so that it is evil with you; yet have ye come, and stood before me in the house, whereon my name is called, and ye have said, We have refrained from doing all these abominations. ¹¹ Is my house, whereon my name is called, a den of robbers in your eyes? And, behold, I have seen *it*, saith the Lord. ¹² For go ye to my place with is in Selo, where I caused my name to dwell before, and see what I did to it because of the wickedness of my people Israel. ¹³ And now, because ye have done all these deeds, and I spoke to you, but ye hearkened not to me; and I called you, but ye answered not; ¹⁴ therefore I also will do to the house whereon my name is called, wherein ye trust, and to the place which I gave to you and to your fathers, as I did to Selo. ¹⁵ And I will cast you out of my sight, as I cast away your brethren, all the seed of Ephraim. ¹⁶ Therefore pray not thou for this people, and intercede not for them to be pitied, yea, pray not, and approach me not for them: for I will not hearken *unto thee*. ¹⁷ Seest thou not what they do in the cities of Juda, and in the streets of Jerusalem? ¹⁸ Their children gather wood, and their fathers kindle a fire, and their women knead dough, to make cakes to the host of heaven; and they have poured out drink-offerings to strange gods, that they might provoke me to anger. ¹⁹ Do they provoke me to anger? saith the Lord: do they not *provoke* themselves, that their faces may be ashamed? ²⁰ Therefore thus saith the Lord; Behold, my anger and wrath shall be poured out upon this place, and upon the men, and upon the cattle, and upon every tree of their field, and upon the fruits of the land; and it shall burn, and not be quenched. 21 Thus saith the Lord, Gather your whole-burnt-offerings with your meat-offerings, and eat flesh. 22 For I spoke not to your fathers, and commanded them not in the day wherein I brought them up out of the land of Egypt, concerning whole-burnt-offerings and sacrifice: 23 but I commanded them this thing, saying, Hear ye my voice, and I will be to you a God, and ye shall be to me a people: and walk ye in all my ways which I shall command you, that it may be well with you. 24 But they hearkened not to me, and their ear gave no heed, but they walked in the imaginations of their evil heart, and went backward, and not forward; 25 from the day that their fathers went forth out of the land of Egypt, even until this day. And I sent to you all my servants, the prophets, by day and early in the morning: yea, I sent *them*, 26 but they hearkened not to me, and their ear gave no heed; and they made their neck harder than their fathers. 27 Therefore thou shalt speak this word to them; 28 This is the nation which has not hearkened to the voice of the Lord, nor received correction: truth has failed from their mouth. 29 Cut off thine hair, and cast it away, and take up a lamentation on thy lips; for the Lord has reprobated and rejected the generation that does these things. 30 For the children of Juda have wrought evil before me, saith the Lord; they have set their abominations in the house on which my name is called, to defile it. 31 And they have built the altar of Tapheth, which is in the valley of the son of Ennom, to burn their sons and their daughters with fire; which I did not command them *to do*, neither did I design it in my heart. 32 Therefore, behold, the days come, saith the Lord, when they shall no more say, The altar of Tapheth, and the valley of the son of Ennom, but, The valley of the slain; and they shall bury in Tapheth, for want of room. 33 And the dead bodies of this people shall be for food to the birds of the sky, and to the wild beasts of the earth; and there shall be none to drive *them* away. 34 And I will destroy out of the cities of Juda, and the streets of Jerusalem, the voice of them that make merry, and the voice of them that rejoice, the voice of the bridegroom, and the voice of the bride; for the whole land shall become a desolation.

Jer.8 1 At that time, saith the Lord, they shall bring out the bones of the kings of Juda, and the bones of his princes, and the bones of the priests, and the bones of the prophets, and the bones of the inhabitants of Jerusalem, out of their graves; 2 and they shall spread them out to the sun, and the moon, and to all the stars, and to all the host of heaven, which they have loved, and which they have served, and after which they have walked, and to which they have held, and which they have worshipped; they shall not be mourned for, neither shall they be buried; but they shall be for an example on the face of the earth, 3 because they chose death rather than life, even to all the remnant that are left of that family, in every place whither I shall drive them out. 4 For thus saith the Lord, Shall not he that falls arise? or he that turns away, shall he not turn back again? 5

Wherefore has this my people turned away with a shameless revolting, and strengthened themselves in their willfulness, and refused to return? 6 Hearken, I pray you, and hear: will they not speak thus, There is no man that repents of his wickedness, saying, What have I done? the runner has failed from his course, as a tired horse in his neighing. 7 Yea, the stork in the heaven knows her time, *also* the turtle-dove and wild swallow; the sparrows observe the times of their coming in; but this my people knows not the judgments of the Lord. 8 How will ye say, We are wise, and the law of the Lord is with us? In vain have the scribes used a false pen. 9 The wise men are ashamed, and alarmed, and taken; because they have rejected the word of the Lord; what wisdom is there in them? 10 Therefore will I give their wives to others, and their fields to *new* inheritors; and they shall gather their fruits, saith the Lord. 11 12 13 There are no grapes on the vines, and there are no figs on the fig-trees, and the leaves have fallen off. 14 Why do we sit still? assemble yourselves, and let us enter into the strong cities, and let us be cast out there: for God has cast us out, and made us drink water of gall, because we have sinned before him. 15 We assembled for peace, but there was no prosperity; for a time of healing, but behold anxiety. 16 We shall hear the neighing of his swift horses out of Dan: the whole land quaked at the sound of the neighing of his horses; and he shall come, and devour the land and the fullness of it; the city, and them that dwell in it. 17 For, behold, I send forth against you deadly serpents, which cannot be charmed, and they shall bite you 18 mortally with the pain of your distressed heart. 19 Behold, *there is* a sound of the cry of the daughter of my people from a land afar off: Is not the Lord in Sion? is there not a king there? because they have provoked me with their graven *images*, and with strange vanities. 20 The summer is gone, the harvest is past, and we are not saved. 21 For the breach of the daughter of my people I have been saddened: in my perplexity pangs have seized upon me as of a woman in travail. 22 And is there no balm in Galaad, or is there no physician there? why has not the healing of the daughter of my people taken place?

Jer.9 1 Who will give water to my head, and a fountain of tears to my eyes? then would I weep for this my people day and night, *even* for the slain of the daughter of my people. 2 Who would give me a most distant lodge in the wilderness, that I might leave my people, and depart from them? for they all commit adultery, an assembly of treacherous men. 3 And they have bent their tongue like a bow: falsehood and not faithfulness has prevailed upon the earth; for they have gone on from evil to evil, and have not known me, saith the Lord. 4 Beware ye each of his neighbour, and trust ye not in your brethren: for every one will surely supplant, and every friend will walk craftily. 5 Every one will mock his friend; they will not speak truth: their tongue has learned to speak falsehoods; they have committed iniquity, they ceased not, so as to return. 6 *There is* usury upon usury, and deceit upon deceit: they would not know me, saith the Lord. 7 Therefore thus saith the Lord, Behold, I will try them with fire, and prove them; for I will do *thus* because of the wickedness of the daughter of my people. 8 Their tongue is a wounding arrow; the words of their mouth are deceitful: *one* speaks peaceably to his neighbour, but in himself retains enmity. 9 Shall I not visit for these things? saith the Lord: and shall not my soul be avenged on such a people as this? 10 Take up a lamentation for the mountains, and a mournful dirge for the paths of the wilderness, for they are desolate for want of men; they heard not the sound of life from the birds of the sky, nor the cattle: they were amazed, they are gone. 11 And I will remove the inhabitants of Jerusalem, and make it a dwelling-place of dragons; and I will utterly waste the cities of Juda, so that they shall not be inhabited. 12 Who is the wise man, that he may understand this? and he that has the word of the mouth of the Lord *addressed* to him, let him tell you wherefore the land has been destroyed, has been ravaged by fire like a desert, so that no one passes through it. 13 And the Lord said to me, Because they have forsaken my law, which I set before them, and have not hearkened to my voice; 14 but went after the lusts of their evil heart, and after the idols which their fathers taught them *to worship*: 15 therefore thus saith the Lord God of Israel, Behold, I will feed them with trouble and will cause them to drink water of gall: 16 and I will scatter them among the nations, to them whom neither they nor their fathers knew; and I will send a sword upon them, until I have consumed them with it. 17 Thus saith the Lord, Call ye the mourning women, and let them come; and send to the wise women, and let them utter their voice; 18 and let them take up a lamentation for you, and let your eyes pour down tears, and your eyelids drop water. 19 For a voice of lamentation has been heard in Sion, How are we become wretched! we are greatly ashamed, for we have forsaken the land, and have abandoned our tabernacles! 20 Hear now, ye women, the word of God, and let your ears receive the words of his mouth, and teach your daughters lamentation, and *every* woman her neighbour a dirge. 21 For death has come up through your windows, it has entered into our land, to destroy the infants without, and the young men from the streets. 22 And the carcases of the men shall be for an example on the face of the field of your land, like grass after the mower, and there shall be none to gather *them*. 23 Thus saith the Lord, Let not the wise man boast in his wisdom, and let not the strong man boast in his strength, and let not the rich man boast in his wealth; 24 but let him that boasts boast in this, the understanding and knowing that I am the Lord that exercise mercy, and judgment, and righteousness, upon the earth; for in these things is my pleasure, saith the Lord. 25 Behold, the days come, saith the Lord, when I will visit upon all the circumcised their uncircumcision; 26 on Egypt, and on Idumea, and on Edom, and on the children of Ammon, and on the children of Moab, and on every one that shaves his face round about, *even* them that dwell in the wilderness; for all the Gentiles are uncircumcised in flesh, and all the house of Israel are uncircumcised *in* their hearts.

Jer.10 1 Hear ye the word of the Lord, which he has spoken to you, O house of Israel. 2 Thus saith the Lord, Learn ye not the ways of the heathen, and be not alarmed at the signs of the sky; for they are alarmed at them, *falling* on their faces. 3 For the customs of the nations are vain; it is a tree cut out of the forest, the work of the carpenter, or a molten image. 4 *They are* beautified with silver and gold, they fix them with hammers and nails; 5 they will set them up that they may not move; it is wrought silver, they will not walk, it is forged silver They must certainly be borne, for they cannot ride *of themselves*. Fear them not; for they cannot do any evil, and there is no good in them. 11 Thus shall ye say to them, Let the gods which have not made heaven and earth perish from off the earth, and from under this sky. 12 It is the Lord that made the earth by his strength, who set up the world by his wisdom, and by his understanding stretched out the sky, 13 and set abundance of waters in the sky, and brought up clouds from the ends of the earth; he made lightnings for the rain, and brought forth light out of his treasures. 14 Every man is deprived of knowledge, every goldsmith is confounded because of his graven images; for he has cast false gods, there is no breath in them. 15 They are vain works, wrought in mockery; in the time of their visitation they shall perish. 16 Such is not the portion of Jacob; for he that formed all things, he is his inheritance; the Lord is his name. 17 He has gathered thy substance from without the lodged in choice *vessels*. 18 For thus saith the Lord, Behold, I *will* overthrow the inhabitants of this land with affliction, that thy plague may be discovered. 19 Alas for thy ruin! thy plague is grievous: and I said, Surely this is thy wound, and it has overtaken thee. 20 Thy tabernacle is in a ruinous state, it has perished; and all thy curtains have been torn asunder: my children and my cattle are no more: there is no more any place for my tabernacle, *nor* place for my curtains. 21 For the shepherds have become foolish, and have not sought the Lord; therefore the whole pasture has failed, and *the sheep* have been scattered. 22 Behold, there comes a sound of a noise, and a great earthquake from the land of the north, to make the cities of Juda a desolation, and a resting-place for ostriches. 23 I know, O Lord, that man's way is not his own; neither shall a man go, and direct his going. 24 Chasten us, O Lord, but with judgment; and not in wrath, lest thou make us few. 25 Pour out thy wrath upon the nations that have not known thee, and upon the families that have not called upon thy name: for they have devoured Jacob, and consumed him, and have made his pasture desolate.

Jer.11 1 The word that came to Jeremias from the Lord, saying, 2 Hear ye the words of this covenant, and thou shalt speak to the men of Juda, and to the dwellers in Jerusalem; 3 and thou shalt say to them, Thus saith the Lord God of Israel, Cursed is the man, who shall not hearken to the words of this covenant, 4 which I commanded your fathers, in the day wherein I brought them up out of the land of Egypt, out of the iron furnace, saying, Hearken to my voice, and do all things that I shall command you; so shall ye be to me a people, and I will be to you a God; 5 that I may confirm mine oath, which I sware to your fathers, to give them a land flowing *with* milk and honey, as *it is* this day. Then I answered and said, So be it, O Lord. 6 And the Lord said to me, Read these words in the cities of Juda, and in the streets of Jerusalem, saying, Hear ye the words of this covenant, and do them. [7] [8] But they did *them* not. [9] And the Lord said to me, A conspiracy is found among the men of Juda, and among the dwellers in Jerusalem. [10] They are turned *aside* to the iniquities of their fathers that were of old, who would not hearken to my words: and, behold, they go after strange gods, to serve them: and the house of Israel and the house of Juda have broken my covenant, which I made with their fathers. [11] Therefore thus saith the Lord, Behold, I bring evils upon this people, out of which they shall not be able to come forth; and they shall presently cry to me, but I will not hearken to them. [12] And the cities of Juda and the dwellers in Jerusalem shall go, and cry to the gods to whom they burn incense; which shall not deliver them in the time of their troubles. [13] For according to the number of thy cities were thy gods, O Juda; and according to the number of the streets of Jerusalem have ye set up altars to burn incense to Baal. [14] And thou, pray not for this people, and intercede not for them in supplication and prayer: for I will not hear in the day in which they call upon me, in the day of their affliction. [15] Why has *my* beloved wrought abomination in my house? will prayers and holy offerings take away thy wickedness from thee, or shalt thou escape by these things? [16] The Lord called thy name a fair olive tree, of a goodly shade in appearance, at the noise of its being lopped, fire was kindled against it; great is the affliction *coming* upon thee: her branches are become good for nothing. [17] And the Lord that planted thee has pronounced evils against thee, because of the iniquity of the house of Israel and the house of Juda, whatsoever they have done against themselves to provoke me to anger by burning incense to Baal. [18] O Lord, teach me, and I shall know: then I saw their practices. [19] But I as an innocent lamb led to the slaughter, knew not: against me they devised an evil device, saying, Come and let us put wood into his bread, and let us utterly destroy him from off the land of the living, and let his name not be remembered any more. [20] O Lord, that judgest righteously, trying the reins and hearts, let me see thy vengeance *taken* upon them, for to thee I have declared my cause. [21] Therefore thus saith the Lord concerning the men of Anathoth, that seek my life, that say, Thou shalt not prophesy at all in the name of the Lord, but if thou dost, thou shalt die by our hands: [22] behold, I will visit them: their young men shall die by the sword; and their sons and their daughters shall die of famine: [23] and there shall be no remnant *left* of them; for I will bring evil upon the dwellers in Anathoth, in the year of their visitation.

Jer.12 [1] Righteous art thou, O Lord, that I may make my defence to thee, yea, I will speak to thee *of* judgments. Why *is it* that the way of ungodly *men* prospers? *that* all that deal very treacherously are flourishing? [2] Thou hast planted them, and they have taken root; they have begotten children, and become fruitful; thou art near to their mouth, and far from their reins. [3] But thou, Lord, knowest me; thou hast proved my heart before thee; purify them for the day of their slaughter. [4] How long shall the land mourn, and the grass of the field wither, for the wickedness of them, that

dwell in it? the beasts and birds are utterly destroyed; because *the people* said, God shall not see our ways. [5] Thy feet run, and they cause thee to faint; how wilt thou prepare *to ride* upon horses? and thou hast been confident in the land of thy peace? how wilt thou do in the roaring of Jordan? [6] For even thy brethren and the house of thy father, even these have dealt treacherously with thee; and they have cried out, they are gathered together in pursuit of thee; trust not thou in them, though they shall speak fair *words* to thee. [7] I have forsaken mine house, I have left mine heritage; I have given my beloved one into the hands of her enemies. [8] My inheritance has become to me as a lion in a forest; she has uttered her voice against me; therefore have I hated her. [9] Is not my inheritance to me a hyaena's cave, or a cave round about her? Go ye, gather together all the wild beasts of the field, and let them come to devour her. [10] Many shepherds have destroyed my vineyard, they have defiled my portion, they have made my desirable portion a trackless wilderness; [11] it is made a complete ruin: for my sake the whole land has been utterly ruined, because there is none that lays *the matter* to heart. [12] The ravagers are come to every passage in the wilderness: for the sword of the Lord will devour from one end of the land to the other: no flesh has any peace. [13] Sow wheat, and reap thorns; their portions shall not profit them: be ashamed of your boasting, because of reproach before the Lord. [14] For thus saith the Lord, concerning all the evil neighbours that touch mine inheritance, which I have divided to my people Israel; Behold, I *will* draw them away from their land, and I will cast out Juda from the midst of them. [15] And it shall come to pass, after I have cast them out, *that* I will return, and have mercy upon them, and will cause them to dwell every one in his inheritance, and every one in his land. [16] And it shall be, if they will indeed learn the way of my people, to swear by my name, *saying*, The Lord lives; as they taught my people to swear by Baal; then shall *that nation* be built in the midst of my people. [17] But if they will not return, then will I cut off that nation with utter ruin and destruction.

Jer.13 [1] Thus saith the Lord, Go and procure for thyself a linen girdle, and put it about thy loins, and let it not be put in water. [2] So I procured the girdle according to the word of the Lord, and put it about my loins. [3] And the word of the Lord came to me, saying, [4] Take the girdle that is upon thy loins, and arise, and go to the Euphrates, and hide it there in a hole of the rock. [5] So I went, and hid it by the Euphrates, as the Lord commanded me. [6] And it came to pass after many days, that the Lord said to me, Arise, go to the Euphrates, and take thence the girdle, which I commanded thee to hide there. [7] So I went to the river Euphrates, and dug, and took the girdle out of the place where I *had* buried it: and, behold, it was rotten, utterly good for nothing. [8] And the word of the Lord came to me, saying, Thus saith the Lord, [9] Thus will I mar the pride of Juda, and the pride of Jerusalem; [10] *even* this great pride *of the men* that will not hearken to my words, and have gone after strange gods, to serve them, and to worship them: and they shall be as this girdle, which can be used for nothing. [11] For as a girdle cleaves about the loins of a man, so have

I caused to cleave to myself the house of Israel, and the whole house of Juda; that they might be to me a famous people, and a praise, and a glory: but they did not hearken to me. 12 And thou shalt say to this people, Every bottle shall be filled with wine: and it shall come to pass, if they shall say to thee, Shall we not certainly know that every bottle shall be filled with wine? that thou shalt say to them, 13 Thus saith the Lord, Behold, I *will* fill the inhabitants of this land, and their kings the sons of David that sit upon their throne, and the priests, and the prophets, and Juda and all the dwellers in Jerusalem, with strong drink. 14 And I will scatter them a man and his brother, and their fathers and their sons together: I will not have compassion, saith the Lord, and I will not spare, neither will I pity *to save them* from destruction. 15 Hear ye, and give ear, and be not proud: for the Lord has spoken. 16 Give glory to the Lord your God, before he cause darkness, and before your feet stumble on the dark mountains, and ye shall wait for light, and behold the shadow of death, and they shall be brought into darkness. 17 But if ye will not hearken, your soul shall weep in secret because of pride, and your eyes shall pour down tears, because the Lord's flock is sorely bruised. 18 Say ye to the king and the princes, Humble yourselves, and sit down; for your crown of glory is removed from your head. 19 The cities toward the south were shut, and there was none to open *them.* Juda is removed *into captivity,* they have suffered a complete removal. 20 Lift up thine eyes, O Jerusalem, and behold them that come from the north; where is the flock that was given thee, the sheep of thy glory? 21 What wilt thou say when they shall visit thee, for thou didst teach them lessons for rule against thyself; shall not pangs seize thee as a woman in travail? 22 And if thou shouldest say in thine heart, Wherefore have these things happened to me? Because of the abundance of thine iniquity have thy skirts been discovered, that thine heels might be exposed. 23 If the Ethiopian shall change his skin, or the leopardess her spots, then shall ye be able to do good, having learnt evil. 24 So I scattered them as sticks carried by the wind into the wilderness. 25 Thus is thy lot, and the reward of your disobedience to me, saith the Lord; as thou didst forget me, and trust in lies, 26 I also will expose thy skirts upon thy face, and thy shame shall be seen; 27 thine adultery also, and thy neighing, and the looseness of thy fornication: on the hills and in the fields I have seen thine abominations. Woe to thee, O Jerusalem, for thou hast not been purified so as to follow me; how long yet *shall it be?*

Jer.14 1 AND THE WORD OF THE LORD CAME TO JEREMIAS CONCERNING THE DROUGHT. 2 Judea has mourned, and her gates are emptied, and are darkened upon the earth; and the cry of Jerusalem is gone up. 3 And her nobles have sent their little ones to the water: they came to the wells, and found no water: and brought back their vessels empty. 4 And the labours of the land failed, because there was no rain: the husbandmen were ashamed, they covered their heads. 5 And hinds calved in the field, and forsook *it,* because there was no grass. 6 The wild asses stood by the forests, and snuffed up the wind; their eyes failed, because there was no grass. 7 Our sins have risen up against us: O Lord, do thou for us for thine own sake; for our sins are many before thee; for we have sinned against thee. 8 O Lord, *thou art* the hope of Israel, and deliverest *us* in time of troubles; why art thou become as a sojourner upon the land, or as one born in the land, yet turning aside for a resting-place? 9 Wilt thou be as a man asleep, or as a *strong* man that cannot save? yet thou art among us, O Lord, and thy name is called upon us; forget us not. 10 Thus saith the Lord to this people, They have loved to wander, and they have not spared, therefore God has not prospered them; now will he remember their iniquity. 11 And the Lord said to me, Pray not for this people for *their* good: 12 for though they fast, I will not hear their supplication; and though they offer whole-burnt-offerings and sacrifices, I will take no pleasure in them: for I will consume them with sword, and with famine, and with pestilence. 13 And I said, O *ever* living Lord! behold, their prophets prophesy, and say, Ye shall not see a sword, nor shall famine be among you; for I will give truth and peace on the land, and in this place. 14 Then the Lord said to me, The prophets prophesy lies in my name: I sent them not, and I commanded them not, and I spoke not to them: for they prophesy to you false visions, and divinations, and auguries, and devices of their own heart. 15 Therefore thus saith the Lord concerning the prophets that prophesy lies in my name, and I sent them not, who say, Sword and famine shall not be upon this land; they shall die by a grievous death, and the prophets shall be consumed by famine. 16 And the people to whom they prophesy, they also shall be cast out in the streets of Jerusalem, because of the sword and famine; and there shall be none to bury them: their wives also, and their sons, and their daughters *shall die thus;* and I will pour out their wickedness upon them. 17 And thou shalt speak this word to them; Let your eyes shed tears day and night, and let them not cease: for the daughter of my people has been sorely bruised, and her plague is very grievous. 18 If I go forth into the plain, then behold the slain by the sword! and if I enter into the city, then behold the distress of famine! for priest and prophet have gone to a land which they knew not. 19 Hast thou utterly rejected Juda? and has thy soul departed from Sion? wherefore has thou smitten us, and there is no healing for us? we waited for peace, but there was no prosperity; for a time of healing, and behold trouble! 20 We know, O Lord, our sins, *and* the iniquities of our fathers: for we have sinned before thee. 21 Refrain for thy name's sake, destroy not the throne of thy glory: remember, break not thy covenant with us. 22 Is there any one among the idols of the Gentiles that can give rain? and will the sky yield his fulness *at their bidding?* Art not thou he? we will even wait on thee, O Lord: for thou hast made all these things.

Jer.15 1 And the Lord said to me, Though Moses and Samuel stood before my face, my soul could not be toward them: dismiss this people, and let them go forth. 2 And it shall be, if they say to thee, Whither shall we go forth? then thou shalt say to them, Thus saith the Lord; As many as are for death, to death; and as many as are for famine, to famine; and as many as are for the sword, to the sword; and as many as are for captivity, to captivity. 3 And I will punish them with four kinds *of death*, saith the Lord, the sword to slay, and the dogs to tear, and the wild beasts of the earth, and the birds of the sky to devour and destroy. 4 And I will deliver them up for distress to all the kingdoms of the earth, because of Manasses son of Ezekias king of Juda, for all that he did in Jerusalem. 5 Who will spare thee, O Jerusalem? and who will fear for thee? or who will turn back *to ask* for thy welfare? 6 Thou hast turned away from me, saith the Lord, thou wilt go back: therefore I will stretch out my hand, and will destroy thee, and will no more spare them. 7 And I will completely scatter them; in the gates of my people they are bereaved of children: they have destroyed my people because of their iniquities. 8 Their widows have been multiplied more than the sand of the sea: I have brought young men against the mother, *even* distress at noon-day: I have suddenly cast upon her trembling and anxiety. 9 She that bore seven is spent; her soul has fainted under trouble; her sun is gone down while it is yet noon; she is ashamed and disgraced: I will give the remnant of them to the sword before their enemies. 10 Woe is me, *my* mother! thou hast born me as some man of strife, and at variance with the whole earth; I have not helped *others*, nor has any one helped me; my strength has failed among them that curse me. 11 Be it so, Lord, in their prosperity; surely I stood before thee in the time of their calamities, and in the time of their affliction, for *their* good against the enemy. 12 Will iron be known? whereas thy strength is a brazen covering. 13 Yea, I will give thy treasures for a spoil as a recompence, because of all thy sins and *that* in all thy borders. 14 And I will enslave thee to thine enemies round about, in a land which thou hast not known; for a fire has been kindled out of my wrath; it shall burn upon you. 15 O Lord, remember me, and visit me, and vindicate me before them that persecute me; do not bear long with them; know how I have met with reproach for thy sake, from those who set at nought thy words; 16 consume them; and thy word shall be to me for the joy and gladness of my heart: for thy name has been called upon me, O Lord Almighty. 17 I have not sat in the assembly of them as they mocked, but I feared because of thy power: I sat alone, for I was filled with bitterness. 18 Why do they that grieve me prevail against me? my wound is severe; whence shall I be healed? it is indeed become to me as deceitful water, that has no faithfulness. 19 Therefore thus saith the Lord, If thou wilt return, then will I restore thee, and thou shalt stand before my face: and if thou wilt bring forth the precious from the worthless, thou shalt be as my mouth: and they shall return to thee; but thou shalt not return to them. 20 And I will make thee to this people as a strong brazen wall; and they shall fight against thee, but they shall by no means prevail against thee; 21 for I am with thee to save thee, and to deliver thee out of the hand of wicked *men*; and I will ransom thee out of the hand of pestilent *men*.

Jer.16 1 And thou shalt not take a wife, saith the Lord God of Israel: 2 and there shall be no son born to thee, nor daughter in this place. 3 For thus saith the Lord concerning the sons and concerning the daughters that are born in this place, and concerning their mothers that have born them, and concerning their fathers that have begotten them in this land; 4 They shall die of grievous death; they shall not be lamented, nor buried; they shall be for an example on the face of the earth; and they shall be for the wild beasts of the land, and for the birds of the sky: they shall fall by the sword, and shall be consumed with famine. 5 Thus saith the Lord, Enter not into their mourning feast, and go not to lament, and mourn not for them: for I have removed my peace from this people. 6 They shall not bewail them, nor make cuttings for them, and they shall not shave themselves *for them*: 7 and there shall be no bread broken in mourning for them for consolation over the dead: they shall not give one to drink a cup for consolation over his father or his mother. 8 Thou shalt not enter into the banquet-house, to sit with them to eat and to drink. 9 For thus saith the Lord God of Israel; Behold, I *will* make to cease out of this place before your eyes, and in your days, the voice of joy, and the voice of gladness, the voice of the bridegroom, and the voice of the bride. 10 And it shall come to pass, when thou shalt report to this people all these words, and they shall say to thee, Wherefore has the Lord pronounced against us all these evils? what is our unrighteousness? and what is our sin which we have sinned before the Lord our God? 11 Then thou shalt say to them, Because your fathers forsook me, saith the Lord, and went after strange gods and served them, and worshipped them, and forsook me, and kept not my law; 12 (and ye sinned worse than your fathers; for, behold, ye walk every one after the lusts of your own evil heart, so as not to hearken to me); 13 therefore I will cast you off from this good land into a land which neither ye nor your fathers have known; and ye shall serve their other gods, who shall have no mercy upon you. 14 Therefore, behold, the days come, saith the Lord, when they shall no more say, The Lord lives, that brought up the children of Israel out of the land of Egypt; 15 but, The Lord lives, who brought up the house of Israel from the land of the north, and from all countries whither they were thrust out: and I will restore them to their own land, which I gave to their fathers. 16 Behold, I *will* send many fishers, saith the Lord, and they shall fish them; and afterward I will send many hunters, and they shall hunt them upon every mountain, and upon every hill, and out of the holes of the rocks. 17 For mine eyes are upon all their ways; and their iniquities have not been hidden from mine eyes. 18 And I will recompense their mischiefs doubly, and their sins, whereby they have profaned my land with the carcases of their abominations, and with their iniquities, whereby they have trespassed against mine inheritance. 19 O Lord, thou art my strength, and mine help, and my refuge in days of evil: to thee the Gentiles shall come from the end of the earth, and shall say, How vain *were the* idols *which* our fathers procured to themselves, and there is no help in them. 20 Will a man make gods for himself, whereas these are no gods? 21 Therefore, behold, I will at this time manifest my hand to them, and will make known to them my power; and they shall know that my name is the Lord.

Jer.17 1 Cursed is the man who trusts in man, and will lean his arm of flesh upon him, while his heart departs from the Lord. 6 And he shall be as the wild tamarisk in the desert: he shall not see when good comes; but he shall dwell in barren *places*, and in the wilderness, in a salt land which is not inhabited. 7 But blessed is the man who trusts in the Lord, and whose hope the Lord shall be. 8 And he shall be as a thriving tree by the waters, and he shall cast forth his root toward a moist place: he shall not fear when heat comes, and there shall be upon him shady branches: he shall not fear in a year of drought, and he shall not fail to bear fruit. 9 The heart is deep beyond all things, and it is the man, and who can know him? 10 I the Lord try the hearts, and prove the reins, to give to every one according to his ways, and according to the fruits of his devices. 11 The partridge utters her voice, she gathers *eggs* which she did not lay; *so is a man* gaining his wealth unjustly; in the midst of his days *his riches* shall leave him, and at his latter end he will be a fool. 12 An exalted throne of glory is our sanctuary. 13 O Lord, the hope of Israel, let all that have left thee be ashamed, let them that have revolted be written on the earth, because they have forsaken the fountain of life, the Lord. 14 Heal me, O Lord, and I shall be healed; save me, and I shall be saved; for thou art my boast. 15 Behold, they say to me, Where is the word of the Lord? let it come. 16 But I have not been weary of following thee, nor have I desired the day of man; thou knowest; the *words* that proceed out of my lips are before thy face. 17 Be not to me a stranger, *but* spare me in the evil day. 18 Let them that persecute me be ashamed, but let me not be ashamed: let them be alarmed, but let me not be alarmed: bring upon them the evil day, crush them with double destruction. 19 Thus saith the Lord; Go and stand in the gates of the children of thy people, by which the kings of Juda enter, and by which they go out, and in all the gates of Jerusalem: 20 and thou shalt say to them, Hear the word of the Lord, ye kings of Juda, and all Judea, and all Jerusalem, *all* who go in at these gates: 21 thus saith the Lord; Take heed to your souls, and take up no burdens on the sabbath-day, and go not forth *through* the gates of Jerusalem; 22 and carry forth no burdens out of your houses on the sabbath-day, and ye shall do no work: sanctify the sabbath-day, as I commanded your fathers. 23 But they hearkened not, and inclined not their ear, but stiffened their neck more than their fathers *did*, so as not to hear me, and not to receive correction. 24 And it shall come to pass, if ye will hearken to me, saith the Lord, to carry in no burdens through the gates of this city on the sabbath-day, and to sanctify the sabbath-day, so as to do no work *upon it*, 25 that there shall enter through the gates of this city kings and princes sitting on the throne of David, and riding on their chariots and horses, they, and their princes, the men of Juda, and the dwellers in Jerusalem: and this city shall be inhabited for ever. 26 And *men* shall come out of the cities of Juda, and from round about Jerusalem, and out of the land of Benjamin, and out of the plain country, and from the hill country, and from the south *country*, bringing whole-burnt- offerings, and sacrifices, and incense, and manna, and frankincense, bringing praise to the house of the Lord. 27 But it shall come to pass, if ye will not hearken to me to sanctify the sabbath-day, to bear no burdens, nor go in *with them by* the gates of Jerusalem on the sabbath-day; then will I kindle a fire in the gates thereof, and it shall devour the streets of Jerusalem, and shall not be quenched.

Jer.18 1 The word that came from the Lord to 2 Jeremias, saying, Arise, and go down to the potter's house, and there thou shalt hear my words. 3 So I went down to the potter's house, and behold, he was making a vessel on the stones. 4 And the vessel which he was making with his hands fell: so he made it again another vessel, as it seemed good to him to make *it*. 5 And the word of the Lord came to me, saying, 6 Shall I not be able, O house of Israel, to do to you as this potter? behold, as the clay of the potter are ye in my hands. 7 *If* I shall pronounce a decree upon a nation, or upon a kingdom, to cut them off, and to destroy *them*, 8 and that nation turn from all their sins, then will I repent of the evils which I purposed to do to them. 9 And *if* I shall pronounce a decree upon a nation and kingdom, to rebuild and to plant *it*; 10 and they do evil before me, so as not to hearken to my voice, then will I repent of the good which I spoke of, to do it to them. 11 And now say to the men of Juda, and to the inhabitants of Jerusalem, Behold, I prepare evils against you, and devise a device against you: let every one turn now from his evil way, and amend your practices. 12 And they said, We will quit ourselves like men, for we will pursue our perverse ways, and we will perform each the lusts of his evil heart. 13 Therefore thus saith the Lord; Enquire now among the nations, who has heard such very horrible things as the virgin of Israel has done? 14 Will fertilising streams fail *to flow* from a rock, or snow *fail* from Libanus? will water violently impelled by the wind turn aside? 15 For my people have forgotten me, they have offered incense in vain, and they fail in their ways, *leaving* the ancient tracks, to enter upon impassable paths; 16 to make their land a desolation, and a perpetual hissing; all that go through it shall be amazed, and shall shake their heads. 17 I will scatter them before their enemies like an east wind; I will shew them the day of their destruction. 18 Then they said, Come, and let us devise a device against Jeremias; for the law shall not perish from the priest, nor counsel from the wise, nor the word from the prophet. Come, and let us smite him with the tongue, and we will hear all his words. 19 Hear me, O Lord, and hear the voice of my pleading. 20 Forasmuch as evil is rewarded for good; for they have spoken words against my soul, and they have hidden the punishment they *meant* for me; remember that I stood before thy face, to speak good for them, to turn away thy wrath from them. 21 Therefore do thou deliver their sons to famine, and gather them to the power of the sword: let their women be childless and widows; and let their men be cut off by death, and their young men fall by the sword in war. 22 Let there be a cry in their houses: thou shalt bring upon them robbers suddenly: for they have formed a plan to take me, and have hidden snares for me. 23 And thou, Lord, knowest all their deadly counsel against me: account not their iniquities guiltless, and blot not out their sins from before thee: let their weakness come before thee; deal with them in the time of thy wrath.

Jer.19 1 Then said the Lord to me, Go and get an earthen bottle, the work of the potter, and thou shalt bring *some* of the elders of the people, and of the priests; 2 and thou shalt go forth to the burial-place of the sons of their children, which is at the entrance of the gate of Charsith; and do thou read there all these words which I shall speak to thee: 3 and thou shalt say to them, Hear ye the word of the Lord, ye kings of Juda, and men of Juda, and the dwellers in Jerusalem, and they that enter in by these gates; thus saith the Lord God of Israel; Behold, I *will* bring evil upon this place, so that the ears of every one that hears it shall tingle. 4 Because they forsook me, and profaned this place, and burnt incense in it to strange gods, which they and their fathers knew not; and the kings of Juda have filled this place with innocent blood, 5 and built high places for Baal, to burn their children in the fire, which things I commanded not, neither did I design *them* in my heart: 6 Therefore, behold, the days come, saith the Lord, when this place shall no more be called, The fall and burial-place of the son of Ennom, but, The burial-place of slaughter. 7 And I will destroy the counsel of Juda and the counsel of Jerusalem in this place; and I will cast them down with the sword before their enemies, and by the hands of them that seek their lives: and I will give their dead bodies for food to the birds of the sky and to the wild beasts of the earth. 8 And I will bring this city to desolation and *make it* a hissing; every one that passes by it shall scowl, and hiss because of all her plague. 9 And they shall eat the flesh of their sons, and the flesh of their daughters; and they shall eat every one the flesh of his neighbour in the blockade, and in the siege wherewith their enemies shall besiege them. 10 And thou shalt break the bottle in the sight of the men that go forth with thee, 11 and thou shalt say, Thus saith the Lord, Thus will I break in pieces this people, and this city, even as an earthen vessel is broken in pieces which cannot be mended again. 12 Thus will I do, saith the Lord, to this place, and to the inhabitants of it, that this city may be given up, as one that is falling to ruin. 13 And the houses of Jerusalem, and the houses of the kings of Juda shall be as a ruinous place, because of their uncleannesses in all the houses, wherein they burnt incense upon their roofs to all the host of heaven, and poured drink-offerings to strange gods. 14 And Jeremias came from *the place* of the Fall, whither the Lord had sent him to prophesy; and he stood in the court of the Lord's house: and said to all the people, Thus saith the Lord; 15 Behold I bring upon this city, and upon all the cities belonging to it, and upon the villages of it, all the evils which I have spoken against it, because they have hardened their neck, *that they might not* hearken to my commands.

Jer.20 1 Now Paschor the son of Emmer, the priest, who also had been appointed chief of the house of the Lord, heard Jeremias prophesying these words. 2 And he smote him, and cast him into the dungeon which was by the gate of the upper house that was set apart, which was by the house of the Lord. 3 And Paschor brought Jeremias out of the dungeon: and Jeremias said to him, *The Lord* has not called thy name Paschor, but Exile. 4 For thus saith the Lord, Behold, I *will* give thee up to captivity with all thy friends: and they shall fall by the sword of their enemies, and thine eyes shall see *it*: and I will give thee and all Juda into the hands of the king of Babylon, and they shall carry them captives, and cut them in pieces with swords. 5 And I will give all the strength of this city, and all the labours of it, and all the treasures of the king of Juda, into the hands of his enemies, and they shall bring them to Babylon. 6 And thou and all the dwellers in thine house shall go into captivity: and thou shalt die in Babylon, and there thou and all thy friends shall be buried, to whom thou hast prophesied lies. 7 Thou hast deceived me, O Lord, and I have been deceived: thou hast been strong, and has prevailed: I am become a laughing-stock, I am continually mocked every day. 8 For I will laugh with my bitter speech, I will call upon rebellion and misery: for the word of the Lord is become a reproach to me and a mockery all my days. 9 Then I said, I will by no means name the name of the Lord, and I will no more at all speak in his name. But it was a burning fire flaming in my bones, and I am utterly weakened on all sides, and cannot bear *up*. 10 For I have heard the reproach of many gathering round, *saying*, Conspire ye, and let us conspire together against him, *even* all his friends: watch his intentions, if perhaps he shall be deceived, and we shall prevail against him, and we shall be avenged on him. 11 But the Lord was with me as a mighty man of war: therefore they persecuted *me*, but could not perceive *anything against me*; they were greatly confounded, for they perceived not their disgrace, which shall never be forgotten. 12 O Lord, that provest just *deeds*, understanding the reins and hearts, let me see thy vengeance upon them: for to thee I have revealed my cause. 13 Sing ye to the Lord, sing praise to him: for he has rescued the soul of the poor from the hand of evil-doers. 14 Cursed be the day wherein I was born: the day wherein my mother brought me forth, let it not be blessed. 15 Cursed be the man who brought the glad tidings to my father, saying, A male child is born to thee. 16 Let that man rejoice as the cities which the Lord overthrew in wrath, and repented not: let him hear crying in the morning, and loud lamentation at noon; 17 because he slew me not in the womb, and my mother became not my tomb, and her womb always great with me. 18 Why is it that I came forth of the womb to see troubles and distresses, and my days are spent in shame?

Jer.21 1 THE WORD THAT CAME FROM THE LORD TO JEREMIAS, WHEN KING SEDEKIAS SENT TO HIM PASCHOR THE SON OF MELCHIAS, AND SOPHONIAS SON OF BASAEAS, THE PRIEST, SAYING, 2 Enquire of the Lord for us; for the king of Babylon has risen up against us; if the Lord will do according to all his wonderful works, and *the king* shall depart from us. 3 And Jeremias said to them, Thus shall ye say to Sedekias king of Juda, 4 Thus saith the Lord; Behold, I *will* turn back the weapons of war wherewith ye fight against the Chaldeans that have besieged you from outside the wall, and I will gather them into the midst of this city. 5 And I will fight against you with an outstretched hand and with a strong arm, with wrath and great anger. 6 And I will smite all the dwellers in this city, *both* men and cattle, with grievous pestilence: and they shall die. 7 And after this, thus saith the Lord; I will give Sedekias king of Juda, and his servants, and the people that is left in this city from the pestilence, and from the famine, and from the sword, into the hands of their enemies, that seek their lives: and they shall cut them in pieces with the edge of the sword: I will not spare them, and I will not have compassion upon them. 8 And thou shalt say to this people, Thus saith the Lord; Behold, I have set before you the way of life, and the way of death. 9 He that remains in this city shall die by the sword, and by famine: but he that goes forth to advance to the Chaldeans that have besieged you, shall live, and his life shall be to him for a spoil, and he shall live. 10 For I have set my face against this city for evil, and not for good: it shall be delivered into the hands of the king of Babylon, and he shall consume it with fire. 11 O house of the king of Juda, hear ye the word of the Lord. 12 O house of David, thus saith the Lord; Judge judgment in the morning, and act rightly, and rescue the spoiled one from the hand of him that wrongs him, lest mine anger be kindled like fire, and it burn, and there be none to quench *it.* 13 Behold, I am against thee that dwellest in the valley of Sor; in the plain country, *even against* them that say, Who shall alarm us? or who shall enter into our habitation? 14 And I will kindle a fire in the forest thereof, and it shall devour all things round about it.

Jer.22 1 Thus saith the Lord; Go thou, and go down to the house of the king of Juda, and thou shalt speak there this word, 2 and thou shalt say, Hear the word of the Lord, O king of Juda, that sittest on the throne of David, thou, and thy house, and thy people, and they that go in at these gates: 3 thus saith the Lord; Execute ye judgment and justice, and rescue the spoiled out of the hand of him that wrongs him: and oppress not the stranger, and orphan, and widow, and sin not, and shed no innocent blood in this place. 4 For if ye will indeed perform this word, then shall there enter in by the gates of this house kings sitting upon the throne of David, and riding on chariots and horses, they, and their servants, and their people. 5 But if ye will not perform these words, by myself have I sworn, saith the Lord, that this house shall be *brought* to desolation. 6 For thus saith the Lord concerning the house of the king of Juda; Thou art Galaad to me, *and* the head of Libanus: *yet* surely I will make thee a desert, *even* cities that shall not be inhabited: 7 and I will bring upon thee a destroying man, and his axe: and they shall cut down thy choice cedars, and cast *them* into the fire. 8 And nations shall pass through this city, and each shall say to his neighbour, Why has the Lord done thus to this great city? 9 And they shall say, Because they forsook the covenant of the Lord their God, and worshipped strange gods, and served them. 10 Weep not for the dead, nor lament for him: weep bitterly for him that goes away: for he shall return no more, nor see his native land. 11 For thus saith the Lord concerning Sellem the son of Josias, who reigns in the place of Josias his father, who has gone forth out of this place; He shall not return thither any more: 12

but in that place whither I have carried him captive, there shall he die, and shall see this land no more. 13 He that builds his house not with justice, and his upper chambers not with judgment, who works by means of his neighbour for nothing, and will by no means give him his reward. 14 Thou hast built for thyself a well-proportioned house, airy chambers, fitted with windows, and wainscoted with cedar, and painted with vermilion. 15 Shalt thou reign, because thou art provoked with thy father Achaz? they shall not eat, and they shall not drink: it is better for thee to execute judgment and justice. 16 They understood not, they judged not the cause of the afflicted, nor the cause of the poor: is not this thy not knowing me? saith the Lord. 17 Behold, thine eyes are not good, nor thine heart, but *they go* after thy covetousness, and after the innocent blood to shed it, and after acts of injustice and slaughter, to commit them. 18 Therefore thus saith the Lord concerning Joakim son of Josias, king of Juda, even concerning this man; they shall not bewail him, *saying,* Ah brother! neither shall they at all weep for him, *saying,* Alas Lord. 19 He shall be buried with the burial of an ass; he shall be dragged roughly along and cast outside the gate of Jerusalem. 20 Go up to Libanus, and cry; and utter thy voice to Basan, and cry aloud to the extremity of the sea: for all thy lovers are destroyed. 21 I spoke to thee on *occasion of* thy trespass, but thou saidst, I will not hearken. This *has been* thy way from thy youth, thou hast not hearkened to my voice. 22 The wind shall tend all thy shepherds, and thy lovers shall go into captivity; for then shalt thou be ashamed and disgraced because of all thy lovers. 23 O thou that dwellest in Libanus, making thy nest in the cedars, thou shalt groan heavily, when pangs as of a travailing woman are come upon thee. 24 *As* I live, saith the Lord, though Jechonias son of Joakim king of Juda were indeed the seal upon my right hand, thence would I pluck thee; 25 and I will deliver thee into the hands of them that seek thy life, before whom thou art afraid, into the hands of the Chaldeans. 26 And I will cast forth thee, and thy mother that bore thee, into a land where thou wast not born; and there ye shall die. 27 But they shall by no means return to the land which they long for in their souls. 28 Jechonias is dishonoured as a good-for-nothing vessel; for he is thrown out and cast forth into a land which he knew not. 29 Land, land, hear the word of the Lord. 30 Write ye this man an outcast: for there shall none of his seed at all grow up to sit on the throne of David, *or as* a prince yet in Juda.

Jer.23 1 Woe to the shepherds that destroy and scatter the sheep of their pasture! 2 Therefore thus saith the Lord against them that tend my people; Ye have scattered my sheep, and driven them out, and ye have not visited them: behold, I *will* take vengeance upon you according to your evil practices. 3 And I will gather in the remnant of my people in every land, whither I have driven them out, and will set them in their pasture; and they shall increase and be multiplied. 4 And I will raise up shepherds to them, who shall feed them: and they shall fear no more, nor be alarmed, saith the Lord. 5 Behold, the days come, saith the Lord, when I will raise up to David a righteous branch, and a king shall reign and understand, and shall execute judgment and righteousness on the earth. 6 In his days both Juda shall be saved, and Israel shall dwell securely: and this is his name, which the Lord shall call him, Josedec among the prophets. 7 Therefore, behold, the days come, saith the Lord, when they shall no more say, The Lord lives, who brought up the house of Israel out of the land of Egypt; 8 but The Lord lives, who has gathered the whole seed of Israel from the north land, and from all the countries whither he *had* driven them out, and has restored them into their own land. 9 My heart is broken within me; all my bones are shaken: I am become as a broken-down man, and as a man overcome with wine, because of the Lord, and because of the excellence of his glory. 10 For because of these things the land mourns; the pastures of the wilderness are dried up; and their course is become evil, and so *also* their strength. 11 For priest and prophet are defiled; and I have seen their iniquities in my house. 12 Therefore let their way be to them slippery and dark: and they shall be tripped up and fall in it: for I will bring evils upon them, in the year of their visitation. 13 And in the prophets of Samaria I have seen lawless deeds; they prophesied by Baal, and led my people Israel astray. 14 Also in the prophets of Jerusalem I have seen horrible things: as they committed adultery, and walked in lies, and strengthened the hands of many, that they should not return each from his evil way: they are all become to me as Sodom, and the inhabitants thereof as Gomorrha. 15 Therefore thus saith the Lord; Behold, I will feed them with pain, and give them bitter water to drink: for from the prophets of Jerusalem has defilement gone forth *into* all the land. 16 Thus saith the Lord Almighty, Hearken not to the words of the prophets: for they frame a vain vision for themselves; they speak from their own heart, and not from the mouth of the Lord. 17 They say to them that reject the word of the Lord, There shall be peace to you; and to all that walk after their own lusts, and to everyone that walks in the error of his heart, they have said, No evil shall come upon thee. 18 For who has stood in the counsel of the Lord, and seen his word? who has hearkened, and heard? 19 Behold, *there is* an earthquake from the Lord, and anger proceeds to a convulsion, it shall come violently upon the ungodly. 20 And the Lord's wrath shall return no more, until he have accomplished it, and until he have established it, according to the purpose of his heart: at the end of the days they shall understand it. 21 I sent not the prophets, yet they ran: neither spoke I to them, yet they prophesied. 22 But if they had stood in my counsel, and if they had hearkened to my words, then would they have turned my people from their evil practices. 23 I am a God nigh at hand, saith the Lord, and not a God afar off. 24 Shall any one hide himself in secret places, and I not see him? Do I not fill heaven and earth? saith the Lord. 25 I have heard what the prophets say, what they prophesy in my name, saying falsely, I have seen a night vision. 26 How long shall *these things* be in the heart of the prophets that prophesy lies, when they prophesy the purposes of their own heart? 27 who devise that *men* may forget my law by their dreams, which they have told every one to his neighbour, as their fathers forgot my name in *the worship of*

Baal. 28 The prophet who has a dream, let him tell his dream; and *he* in whom is my word *spoken* to him, let him tell my word truly: what is the chaff to the corn? so are my words, saith the Lord. 29 Behold, are not my words as fire? saith the Lord; and as an axe cutting the rock? 30 Behold, I am therefore against the prophets, saith the Lord God, that steal my words every one from his neighbour. 31 Behold, I am against the prophets that put forth prophecies of mere words, and slumber their sleep. 32 Therefore, behold, I am against the prophets that prophesy false dreams, and have not told them *truly*, and have caused my people to err by their lies, and by their errors; yet I sent them not, and commanded them not; therefore, they shall not profit this people at all. 33 And if this people, or the priest, or the prophet, should ask, What is the burden of the Lord? then thou shalt say to them, Ye are the burden, and I will dash you down, saith the Lord. 34 *As for* the prophet, and the priests, and the people, who shall say, The burden of the Lord, I will even take vengeance on that man, and on his house. 35 Thus shall ye say every one to his neighbour, and every one to his brother, What has the Lord answered? and, what has the Lord said? 36 And do ye name no more the burden of the Lord; for his own word shall be a man's burden. 37 But wherefore, *say ye*, has the Lord our God spoken? 38 Therefore thus saith the Lord our God; Because ye have spoken this word, The burden of the Lord, and I sent to you, saying, ye shall not say, The burden of the Lord; 39 therefore, behold, I *will* seize, and dash down you and the city which I gave to you and your fathers. 40 And I will bring upon you an everlasting reproach, and everlasting disgrace, which shall not be forgotten. 7 Therefore, behold, the days come, saith the Lord, when they shall no more say, The Lord lives, who brought up the house of Israel out of the land of Egypt; 8 but The Lord lives, who has gathered the whole seed of Israel from the north land, and from all the countries whither he *had* driven them out, and has restored them into their own land.

Jer.24 1 The Lord shewed me two baskets of figs, lying in front of the temple of the Lord, after Nabuchodonosor king of Babylon had carried captive Jechonias son of Joakim king of Juda, and the princes, and the artificers, and the prisoners, and the rich men out of Jerusalem, and had brought them to Babylon. 2 The one basket was *full* of very good figs, as the early figs; and the other basket was *full* of very bad figs, which could not be eaten, for their badness. 3 And the Lord said to me, What seest thou, Jeremias? and I said, Figs; the good figs, very good; and the bad, very bad, which cannot be eaten, for their badness. 4 And the word of the Lord came to me, saying, 5 Thus saith the Lord, the God of Israel; As these good figs, so will I acknowledge the Jews that have been carried away captive, whom I have sent forth out of this place into the land of the Chaldeans for good. 6 And I will fix mine eyes upon them for good, and I will restore them into this land for good: and I will build them up, and not pull them down; and I will plant them, and not pluck them up. 7 And I will give them a heart to know me, that I am the Lord: and they shall be to me a people, and I will be to them a God: for they shall turn to me with all their heart. 8 And as the bad figs, which cannot be eaten, for their badness; thus saith the Lord, So will I deliver Sedekias king of Juda, and his nobles, and the remnant of Jerusalem, them that are left in this land, and the dwellers in Egypt. 9 And I will cause them to be dispersed into all the kingdoms of the earth, and they shall be for a reproach, and a proverb, and an *object of* hatred, and a curse, in every place whither I have driven them out. 10 And I will send against them famine, and pestilence, and the sword, until they are consumed from off the land which I gave them.

Jer.25 1 THE WORD THAT CAME TO JEREMIAS concerning all the people of Juda in the fourth year of Joakim, son of Josias, king of Juda; 2 which he spoke to all the people of Juda, and to the inhabitants of Jerusalem, saying, 3 In the thirteenth year of Josias, son of Amos, king of Juda, even until this day for three and twenty years, I have both spoken to you, rising early and speaking, 4 and I sent to you my servants the prophets, sending them early; (but ye hearkened not, and listened not with your ears;) saying, 5 Turn ye every one from his evil way, and from your evil practices, and ye shall dwell in the land which I gave to you and your fathers, of old and for ever. 6 Go ye not after strange gods, to serve them, and to worship them, that ye provoke me not by the works of your hands, to do you hurt. 7 But ye hearkened not to me. 8 Therefore thus saith the Lord; Since ye believed not my words, 9 behold I *will* send and take a family from the north, and will bring them against this land, and against the inhabitants of it, and against all the nations round about it, and I will make them utterly waste, and make them a desolation, and a hissing, and an everlasting reproach. 10 And I will destroy from *among* them the voice of joy, and the voice of gladness, the voice of the bridegroom, and the voice of the bride, the scent of ointment, and the light of a candle. 11 And all the land shall be a desolation; and they shall serve among the Gentiles seventy years. 12 And when the seventy years are fulfilled, I will take vengeance on that nation, and will make them a perpetual desolation. 13 And I will bring upon that land all my words which I have spoken against it, *even* all things that are written in this book. 34 THE PROPHECIES OF JEREMIAS AGAINST THE NATIONS OF ÆLAM. 35 Thus saith the Lord, The bow of Ælam is broken, *even* the chief of their power. 36 And I will bring upon Ælam the four winds from the four corners of heaven, and I will disperse them toward all these winds; and there shall be no nation *to* which they shall not come—*even* the outcasts of Ælam. 37 And I will put them in fear before their enemies that seek their life; and I will bring evils upon them according to my great anger; and I will send forth my sword after them, until I have utterly destroyed them. 38 And I will set my throne in Ælam, and will send forth thence king and rulers. 39 But it shall come to pass at the end of days, that I will turn the captivity of Ælam, saith the Lord.

Jer.26 1 In the beginning of the reign of king Sedekias, there came this word concerning Ælam. 2 FOR EGYPT, AGAINST THE POWER OF PHARAO NECHAO KING OF EGYPT, who was by the river Euphrates in Charmis, whom Nabuchodonosor king of Babylon smote in the fourth year of Joakim king of Juda. 3 Take up arms and spears, and draw nigh to battle; 4 and harness the horses: mount, ye horsemen, and stand ready in your helmets; advance the spears, and put on your breast-plates. 5 Why do they fear, and turn back? even because their mighty men shall be slain: they have utterly fled, and being hemmed in they have not rallied, saith the Lord. 6 Let not the swift flee, and let not the mighty man escape to the north: the *forces* at Euphrates are become feeble, and they have fallen. 7 Who is this *that* shall come up as a river, and as rivers roll *their* waves? 8 The waters of Egypt shall come up like a river: and he said, I will go up, and will cover the earth, and will destroy the dwellers in it. 9 Mount ye the horses, prepare the chariots; go forth, ye warriors of the Ethiopians, and Libyans armed with shields; and mount, ye Lydians, bend the bow. 10 And that day *shall be* to the Lord our God a day of vengeance, to take vengeance on his enemies: and the sword of the Lord shall devour, and be glutted, and be drunken with their blood: for the Lord *has* a sacrifice from the land of the north at the river Euphrates. 11 Go up to Galaad, and take balm for the virgin daughter of Egypt: in vain hast thou multiplied thy medicines; there is no help in thee. 12 The nations have heard thy voice, and the land has been filled with thy cry: for the warriors have fainted fighting one against another, *and* both are fallen together. 13 THE WORDS WHICH THE LORD SPOKE by Jeremias, concerning the coming of the king of Babylon to smite the land of Egypt. 14 Proclaim *it* at Magdol, and declare *it* at Memphis: say ye, Stand up, and prepare; for the sword has devoured thy yew-tree. 15 Wherefore has Apis fled from thee? thy choice calf has not remained; for the Lord has utterly weakened him. 16 And thy multitude has fainted and fallen; and each one said to his neighbour, Let us arise, and return into our country to our people, from the Grecian sword. 17 Call ye the name of Pharao Nechao king of Egypt, Saon esbeie moed. 18 *As* I live, saith the Lord God, he shall come as Itabyrion among the mountains, and as Carmel that is on the sea. 19 O daughter of Egypt dwelling *at home*, prepare thee stuff for removing: for Memphis shall be utterly desolate, and shall be called Woe, because there are no inhabitants in it. 20 Egypt is a fair heifer, *but* destruction from the north is come upon her. 21 Also her hired *soldiers* in the midst of her are as fatted calves fed in her; for they also have turned, and fled with one accord: they stood not, for the day of destruction was come upon them, and the time of their retribution. 22 Their voice is as *that* of a hissing serpent, for they go upon the sand; they shall come upon Egypt with axes, as men that cut wood. 23 They shall cut down her forest, saith the Lord, for *their number* cannot at all be conjectured, for it exceeds the locust in multitude, and they are innumerable. 24 The daughter of Egypt is confounded; she is delivered into the hands of a people from the north. 25 Behold, I *will* avenge Ammon her son upon Pharao, and upon them that trust in him. 26 27 But fear not thou, my servant Jacob, neither be thou alarmed, Israel: for, behold, I will save thee from afar, and thy seed from their captivity; and Jacob shall return, and be at ease, and sleep, and there shall be no one to trouble him. 28 Fear not thou, my servant Jacob, saith the Lord; for I am with thee: she *that was* without fear and in luxury, has been delivered up: for I will make a full end of every nation among whom I have thrust thee forth; but I will not cause thee to fail: yet will I chastise thee in the way of judgment, and will not hold thee entirely guiltless.

Jer.27 1 THE WORD OF THE LORD WHICH HE SPOKE AGAINST BABYLON. 2 Proclaim ye among the Gentiles, and cause the tidings to be heard, and suppress *them* not: say ye, Babylon is taken, Belus is confounded; the fearless, the luxurious Maerodach is delivered up. 3 For a nation has come up against her from the north, he shall utterly ravage her land, and there shall be none to dwell in it, neither man nor beast. 4 In those days, and at that time, the children of Israel shall come, they and the children of Juda together; they shall proceed, weeping as they go, seeking the Lord their God. 5 They shall ask the way till *they come to* Sion, for that way shall they set their face; and they shall come and flee for refuge to the Lord their God; for the everlasting covenant shall not be forgotten. 6 My people have been lost sheep: their shepherds thrust them out, they caused them to wander on the mountains: they went from mountain to hill, they forgot their resting-place. 7 All that found them consumed them: their enemies said, Let us not leave them alone, because they have sinned against the Lord: he that gathered their fathers *had* a pasture of righteousness. 8 Flee ye out of the midst of Babylon, and from the land of the Chaldeans, and go forth, and be as serpents before sleep. 9 For, behold, I stir up against Babylon the gatherings of nations out of the land of the north; and they shall set themselves in array against her: thence shall she be taken, as the dart of an expert warrior shall not return empty. 10 And Chaldea shall be a spoil: all that spoil her shall be satisfied. 11 Because ye rejoiced, and boasted, *while* plundering mine heritage; because ye exulted as calves in the grass, and pushed with the horn as bulls. 12 Your mother is greatly ashamed; your mother that bore you for prosperity is confounded: *she is* the last of the nations, desolate, 13 by reason of the Lord's anger: it shall not be inhabited, but it shall be all a desolation; and every one that passes through Babylon shall scowl, and they shall hiss at all her plague. 14 Set yourselves in array against Babylon round about, all ye that bend the bow; shoot at her, spare not your arrows, 15 and prevail against her: her hands are weakened, her bulwarks are fallen, and her wall is broken down: for it is vengeance from God: take vengeance upon her; as she has done, do to her. 16 Utterly destroy seed out of Babylon, *and* him that holds a sickle in time of harvest: for fear of the Grecian sword, they shall return every one to his people, and every one shall flee to his own land. 17 Israel is a wandering sheep; the lions have driven him out: the king of Assyria first devoured him, and afterward this king of Babylon *has gnawed* his bones. 18 Therefore thus saith the Lord; Behold, I *will* take vengeance on the king of Babylon, and upon his land, as I took vengeance on the king of Assyria. 19 And I will restore Israel to his pasture, and he shall feed on Carmel and on mount Ephraim and in Galaad, and his soul shall be satisfied. 20 In those days, and

at that time, they shall seek for the iniquity of Israel, and there shall be none; and for the sins of Juda, and they shall not be found: for I will be merciful to them that are left 21 on the land, saith the Lord. Go up against it roughly, and against them that dwell on it: avenge, O sword, and destroy utterly, saith the Lord, and do according to all that I command thee. 22 A sound of war, and great destruction in the land of the Chaldeans! 23 How is the hammer of the whole earth broken and crushed! How is Babylon become a desolation among the nations! 24 They shall come upon thee, and thou shalt not know it, Babylon, that thou wilt even be taken captive: thou art found and taken, because thou didst resist the Lord. 25 The Lord has opened his treasury, and brought forth the weapons of his anger: for the Lord God *has* a work in the land of the Chaldeans. 26 For her times are come: open ye her storehouses: search her as a cave, and utterly destroy her: let there be no remnant of her. 27 Dry ye up all her fruits, and let them go down to the slaughter: woe to them! for their day is come, and the time of their retribution. 28 A voice of men fleeing and escaping from the land of Babylon, to declare to Sion the vengeance *that comes* from the Lord our God. 29 Summon many against Babylon, *even* every one that bends the bow: camp against her round about; let no one of her *people* escape: render to her according to her works; according to all that she has done, do to her: for she has resisted the Lord, the Holy God of Israel. 30 Therefore shall her young men fall in the streets, and all her warriors shall be cast down, saith the Lord. 31 Behold, I am against thee the haughty one, saith the Lord: for thy day is come, and the time of thy retribution. 32 And thy pride shall fail, and fall, and there shall be no one to set it up again: and I will kindle a fire in her forest, and it shall devour all things round about her. 33 Thus saith the Lord; The children of Israel and the children of Juda have been oppressed: all they that have taken them captive have oppressed them together; for they would not let them go. 34 But their Redeemer is strong; the Lord Almighty is his name: he will enter into judgment with his adversaries, that he may destroy the earth; 35 and he will sharpen a sword against the Chaldeans, and against the inhabitants of Babylon, and upon her nobles and upon her wise men; 36 a sword upon her warriors, and they shall be weakened: a sword upon their horses, and upon their chariots: 37 a sword upon their warriors and upon the mixed people in the midst of her; and they shall be as women: a sword upon the treasures, and they shall be scattered upon her water, 38 and they shall be ashamed: for it is a land of graven *images*; and in the islands, where they boasted. 39 Therefore shall idols dwell in the islands, and the young of monsters shall dwell in it: it shall not be inhabited any more for ever. 40 As God overthrew Sodom and Gomorrha, and the cities bordering upon them, saith the Lord: no man shall dwell there, and no son of man shall sojourn there. 41 Behold, a people comes from the north, and a great nation, and many kings shall be stirred up from the end of the earth; holding bow and dagger: 42 *the people* is fierce, and will have no mercy: their voices shall sound as the sea, they shall ride upon horses, prepared for war, like fire, against thee, O daughter of Babylon. 43 The king of Babylon heard the sound of them, and his hands were enfeebled: anguish overcame him, pangs as of a woman in travail. 44 Behold, he shall come up as a lion from Jordan to Gaethan; for I will speedily drive them from her, and I will set all the youths against her: for who is like me? and who will resist me? and who is this shepherd who will stand before me? 45 Therefore hear ye the counsel of the Lord, which he has taken against Babylon; and his devices, which he has devised upon the Chaldeans inhabiting *it*: surely lambs of their flock shall be destroyed: surely pasture shall be cut off from them. 46 For at the sound of the taking of Babylon the earth shall quake, and a cry shall be heard among the nations.

Jer.28 1 Thus saith the Lord; Behold, I stir up against Babylon, and against the Chaldeans dwelling therein, a deadly burning wind. 2 And I will send forth against Babylon spoilers, and they shall spoil her, and shall ravage her land. Woe to Babylon round about *her* in the day of her affliction. 3 Let the archer bend his bow, and him that has armour put it on: and spare ye not her young men, but destroy ye all her host. 4 And slain men shall fall in the land of the Chaldeans, and *men* pierced through shall fall without it. 5 For Israel and Juda have not been forsaken of their God, of the Lord Almighty; whereas their land was filled with iniquity against the holy things of Israel. 6 Flee ye out of the midst of Babylon, and deliver every one his soul: and be not overthrown in her iniquity; for it is the time of her retribution from the Lord; he is rendering to her a recompence. 7 Babylon has been a golden cup in the Lord's hand, causing all the earth to be drunken: the nations have drunk of her wine; therefore they were shaken. 8 And Babylon is fallen suddenly, and is broken to pieces: lament for her; take balm for her deadly wound, if by any means she may be healed. 9 We tried to heal Babylon, but she was not healed: let us forsake her, and depart every one to his own country: for her judgment has reached to the heaven, it has mounted up to the stars. 10 The Lord has brought forth his judgment: come, and let us declare in Sion the works of the Lord our God. 11 Prepare the arrows; fill the quivers: the Lord has stirred up the spirit of the king of the Medes: for his wrath is against Babylon, to destroy it utterly; for it is the Lord's vengeance, it is the vengeance of his people. 12 Lift up a standard on the walls of Babylon, prepare the quivers, rouse the guards, prepare the weapons: for the Lord has taken *the work* in hand, and will execute what he has spoken against the inhabitants of Babylon, 13 dwelling on many waters, and amidst the abundance of her treasures; thine end is come verily into thy bowels. 14 For the Lord has sworn by his arm, *saying,* I will fill thee with men as with locusts; and they that come down shall cry against thee. 15 The Lord made the earth by his power, preparing the world by his wisdom, by his understanding he stretched out the heaven. 16 At *his* voice he makes a sound of water in the heaven, and brings up clouds from the extremity of the earth; he makes lightnings for rain, and brings light out of his treasures. 17 Every man has completely lost understanding; every goldsmith is confounded because of his graven *images*: for they have cast false *gods*, there is no breath in them. 18 They are vain works, objects of scorn; in the time of their visitation they shall perish. 19 Not such is Jacob's portion; for he that formed all things, he is his inheritance; the Lord is his name. 20 Thou scatterest for me the weapons of war: and I will scatter nations by thee, and will destroy kings by means of thee. 21 And by thee I will scatter the horse and his rider; and by thee I will scatter chariots and them that ride in them. 22 And by thee I will scatter youth and maid; and by thee I will scatter man and woman. 23 And by thee I will scatter the shepherd and his flock; and by thee I will scatter the husbandman and his husbandry; and by thee I will scatter leaders and the captains. 24 And I will recompense to Babylon and to all the Chaldeans that dwell *there* all their mischiefs that they have done to Sion before your eyes, saith the Lord. 25 Behold, I am against thee, the ruined mountain, that destroys the whole earth; and I will stretch out mine hand upon thee, and will roll thee down upon the rocks, and will make thee as a burnt mountain. 26 And they shall not take from thee a stone for a corner, nor a stone for a foundation: for thou shalt be a desolation for ever, saith the Lord. 27 Lift up a standard in the land, sound the trumpet among the nations, consecrate the nations against her, raise up kings against her by me, and *that* for the people of Achanaz; set against her engines of war; bring up against her horses as a multitude of locusts. 28 Bring up nations against her, *even* the king of the Medes and of the whole earth, his rulers, and all his captains. 29 The earth has quaked and been troubled, because the purpose of the Lord has risen up against Babylon, to make the land of Babylon a desolation, and uninhabitable. 30 The warrior of Babylon has failed to fight; they shall sit there in the siege; their power is broken; they are become like women; her tabernacles have been set on fire; her bars are broken. 31 One shall rush, running to meet *another* runner, and one *shall go* with tidings to meet *another* with tidings, to bring tidings to the king of Babylon, that his city is taken. 32 At the end of his passages they were taken, and his cisterns they have burnt with fire, and his warriors are going forth. 33 For thus saith the Lord, The houses of the king of Babylon shall be threshed as a floor in the season; yet a little while, and her harvest shall come. 34 He has devoured me, he has torn me asunder, airy darkness has come upon me; Nabuchodonosor king of Babylon has swallowed me up, as a dragon has he filled his belly with my delicacies. 35 My troubles and my distresses have driven me out into Babylon, shall she that dwells in Sion say; and my blood *shall be* upon the Chaldeans dwelling *there*, shall Jerusalem say. 36 Therefore thus saith the Lord, Behold, I will judge thine adversary, and I will execute vengeance for thee; and I will waste her sea, and dry up her fountain. 37 And Babylon shall be a desolation, and shall not be inhabited. 38 For they rose up together as lions, and as lions' whelps. 39 In their heat I will give them a draught, and make them drunk, that they may be stupified, and sleep an everlasting sleep, and not awake, saith the Lord. 40 And bring thou them down as lambs to the slaughter, and rams with kids. 41 How has the boast of all the earth been taken and caught in a snare! how has Babylon become a desolation among the nations! ⁴² The sea has come up upon Babylon with the sound of its waves, and she is covered. ⁴³ Her cities are become like a dry and trackless land; not so much as one *man* shall dwell in it, neither shall a son of man lodge in it. ⁴⁴ And I will take vengeance on Babylon, and bring forth out of her mouth what she has swallowed down, and the nations shall no more be gathered to her: ⁴⁵ ⁴⁶ ⁴⁷ ⁴⁸ ⁴⁹ and in Babylon the slain men of all the earth shall fall. ⁵⁰ Go forth of the land, ye that escape, and stay not; ye that are afar off, remember the Lord, and let Jerusalem come into your mind. ⁵¹ We are ashamed, because we have heard our reproach; disgrace has covered our face; aliens are come into our sanctuary, *even* into the house of the Lord. ⁵² Therefore, behold, the days come, saith the Lord, when I will take vengeance upon her graven *images*: and slain men shall fall in all her land. ⁵³ For though Babylon should go up as the heaven, and though she should strengthen her walls with her power, from me shall come they that shall destroy her, saith the Lord. ⁵⁴ A sound of a cry in Babylon, and great destruction in the land of the Chaldeans: ⁵⁵ for the Lord has utterly destroyed Babylon, and cut off from her the great voice sounding as many waters: he has consigned her voice to destruction. ⁵⁶ For distress has come upon Babylon, her warriors are taken, their bows are useless: for God recompenses them. ⁵⁷ The Lord recompenses, and will make her leaders and her wise men and her captains completely drunk, saith the King, the Lord Almighty is his name. ⁵⁸ Thus saith the Lord, The wall of Babylon was made broad, but it shall be completely broken down, and her high gates shall be burnt with fire; and the peoples shall not labour in vain, nor the nations fail in *their* rule. ⁵⁹ THE WORD WHICH THE LORD COMMANDED THE PROPHET JEREMIAS to say to Saraeas son of Nerias, son of Maasaeas, when he went from Sedekias king of Juda to Babylon, in the fourth year of his reign. And Saraeas was over the bounties. ⁶⁰ And Jeremias wrote in a book all the evils which should come upon Babylon, *even* all these words that are written against Babylon. ⁶¹ And Jeremias said to Saraeas, When thou art come to Babylon, and shalt see and read all these words; ⁶² then thou shalt say, O Lord God, thou hast spoken against this place, to destroy it, and that there should be none to dwell in it, neither man nor beast; for it shall be a desolation for ever. ⁶³ And it shall come to pass, when thou shalt cease from reading this book, that thou shalt bind a stone upon it, and cast it into the midst of Euphrates; ⁶⁴ and shalt say, Thus shall Babylon sink, and not rise, because of the evils which I bring upon it.

Jer.29 ¹ THUS SAITH THE LORD AGAINST THE PHILISTINES; ² Behold, waters come up from the north, and shall become a sweeping torrent, and it shall sweep away the land, and its fulness; the city, and them that dwell in it: and men shall cry and all that dwell in the land shall howl, ³ at the sound of his rushing, at *the sound of* his hoofs, and at the rattling of his chariots, at the noise of his wheels: the fathers turned not to their children because of the weakness of their hands, ⁴ in the day that is coming to destroy all the Philistines: and I will utterly destroy Tyre and Sidon and all the rest of their allies: for the Lord will destroy the remaining *inhabitants* of the islands. ⁵ Baldness is come upon Gaza; Ascalon is cast away, and the remnant of the Enakim. ⁶ How long wilt thou smite, O sword of the Lord? how long will it be ere thou art quiet? return into thy sheath, rest, and be removed. ⁷ How shall it be quiet, whereas the Lord has given it a commission against Ascalon, and against the regions on the sea-coast, to awake against the remaining *countries*! ⁷ CONCERNING IDUMEA, thus saith the Lord; There is no longer wisdom in Thaeman, counsel has perished from the wise ones, their wisdom is gone, ⁸ their place has been deceived. Dig deep for a dwelling, ye that inhabit Daedam, for he has wrought grievously: I brought trouble upon him in the time at which I visited him. ⁹ For grape-gatherers are come, who shall not leave thee a remnant; as thieves by night, they shall lay their hand upon *thy possessions.* ¹⁰ For I have stripped Esau, I have uncovered their secret places; they shall have no power to hide themselves, they have perished *each* by the hand of his brother, my neighbour, and it is impossible ¹¹ for thy fatherless one to be left to live, but I shall live, and the widows trust in me. ¹² For thus saith the Lord; They who were not appointed to drink the cup have drunk *it*; and thou shalt by no means be cleared: ¹³ for by myself I have sworn, saith the Lord, that thou shalt be in the midst of her an impassable *land*, and a reproach, and a curse; and all her cities shall be desert for ever. ¹⁴ I have heard a report from the Lord, and he has sent messengers to the nations, *saying*, Assemble yourselves, and come against her; rise ye up to war. ¹⁵ I have made thee small among the nations, utterly contemptible among men. ¹⁶ Thine insolence has risen up against thee, the fierceness of thine heart has burst the holes of the rocks, it has seized upon the strength of a lofty hill; for as an eagle he set his nest on high: thence will I bring thee down. ¹⁷ And Idumea shall be a desert: every one that passes by shall hiss at it. ¹⁸ As Sodom was overthrown and Gomorrha and they that sojourned in her, saith the Lord Almighty, no man shall dwell there, nor shall any son of man inhabit there. ¹⁹ Behold, he shall come up as a lion out of the midst of Jordan to the place of Ætham: for I will speedily drive them from it, and do ye set the young men against her: for who is like me? and who will withstand me? and who *is* this shepherd, who shall confront me? ²⁰ Therefore hear ye the counsel of the Lord, which he has framed against Idumea; and his device, which he has devised against the inhabitants of Thaeman: surely the least of the sheep shall be swept off; surely their dwelling shall be made desolate for them. ²¹ For at the sound of their fall the earth was scared, and the cry of the sea was not heard. ²² Behold, he shall look *upon her* as an eagle, and spread forth *his* wings over her strongholds; and the heart of the mighty men of Idumea shall be in that day as the heart of a woman in her pangs.

Jer.30 ¹ CONCERNING THE SONS OF AMMON thus saith the Lord, Are there no sons in Israel? or have they no one to succeed *them*? wherefore has Melchol inherited Galaad, and why shall their people dwell in their cities? ²

Therefore, behold, the days come, saith the Lord, when I will cause to be heard in Rabbath a tumult of wars; and they shall become a waste and ruined place, and her altars shall be burned with fire; then shall Israel succeed to his dominion. ³ Howl, O Esebon, for Gai has perished; cry, ye daughters of Rabbath, gird yourselves with sack -clothes, and lament; for Melchol shall go into banishment, his priests and his princes together. ⁴ Why do ye exult in the plains of the Enakim, thou haughty daughter, that trustest in *thy* treasures, that sayest, Who shall come in to me? ⁵ Behold, I *will* bring terror upon thee, saith the Lord, from all the country round about thee; and ye shall be scattered every one right before him, and there is none to gather you. ²⁸ CONCERNING KEDAR THE QUEEN OF THE PALACE, WHOM NABUCHODONOSOR KING OF BABYLON SMOTE, thus saith the Lord; Arise ye, and go up to Kedar, and fill the sons of Kedem. ²⁹ They shall take their tents and their sheep, they shall take for themselves their garments, and all their baggage and their camels; and summon ye destruction against them from every side. ³⁰ Flee ye, dig very deep for a dwelling-place, ye that dwell in the palace; for the king of Babylon has framed a counsel, and devised a device against you. ³¹ Rise up, and go up against a nation settled *and* dwelling at ease, who have no doors, nor bolts, nor bars, *who* dwell alone. ³² And their camels shall be a spoil, and the multitude of their cattle shall be destroyed: and I will scatter them as chaff with every wind, having their hair cut about their foreheads, I will bring on their overthrow from all sides, saith the Lord. ³³ And the palace shall be a resting-place for ostriches, and desolate for ever: no man shall abide there, and no son of man shall dwell there. ²³ CONCERNING DAMASCUS. Emath is brought to shame, and Arphath: for they have heard an evil report: they are amazed, they are angry, they shall be utterly unable to rest. ²⁴ Damascus is utterly weakened, she is put to flight; trembling has seized upon her. ²⁵ How has she not left my city, they have loved the village? ²⁶ Therefore shall the young men fall in thy streets, and all thy warriors shall fall, saith the Lord. ²⁷ And I will kindle a fire in the wall of Damascus, and it shall devour the streets of the son of Ader.

Jer.31 ¹ Thus has the Lord said concerning MOAB, Woe to Nabau! for it has perished: Cariathaim is taken: Amath and Agath are put to shame. ² There is no longer any healing for Moab, *nor* glorying in Esebon: he has devised evils against her: we have cut her off from *being* a nation, and she shall be completely still: after thee shall go a sword; ³ for *there is* a voice of *men* crying out of Oronaim, destruction and great ruin. ⁴ Moab is ruined, proclaim *it* to Zogora: ⁵ for Aloth is filled with weeping: one shall go up weeping by the way of Oronaim; ye have heard a cry of destruction. ⁶ Flee ye, and save your lives, and ye shall be as a wild ass in the desert. ⁷ Since thou hast trusted in thy strong-hold, therefore thou shalt be taken: and Chamos shall go forth into captivity, and his priests, and his princes together. ⁸ And destruction shall come upon every city, it shall by no means escape; the valley also shall perish, and the plain country shall be completely destroyed, as the Lord

has said. ⁹ Set marks upon Moab, for she shall be touched with a plague-spot, and all her cities shall become desolate; whence *shall there be* an inhabitant for her? ¹⁰ Cursed is the man that does the works of the Lord carelessly, keeping back his sword from blood. ¹¹ Moab has been at ease from a child, and trusted in his glory; he has not poured out *his liquor* from vessel to vessel, and has not gone into banishment, therefore his taste remained in him, and his smell departed not. ¹² Therefore, behold, his days come, saith the Lord, when I shall send upon him bad leaders, and they shall lead him astray, and they shall utterly break in pieces his possessions, and shall cut his horns asunder. ¹³ And Moab shall be ashamed of Chamos, as the house of Israel was ashamed of Baethel their hope, having trusted in them. ¹⁴ How will ye say, We are strong, and men strong for war? ¹⁵ Moab is ruined, *even* his city, and his choice young men have gone down to slaughter. ¹⁶ The day of Moab is near at hand, and his iniquity moves swiftly *to vengeance.* ¹⁷ Shake *the head* at him, all ye that are round about him; all *of you* utter his name; say ye, How is the glorious staff broken to pieces, the rod of magnificence! ¹⁸ Come down from *thy* glory, and sit down in a damp place: Daebon shall be broken, because Moab is destroyed: there has gone up against thee one to ravage thy strong-hold. ¹⁹ Stand by the way, and look, thou that dwellest in Arer; and ask him that is fleeing, and him that escapes, and say, What has happened? ²⁰ Moab is put to shame, because he is broken: howl and cry; proclaim in Arnon, that Moab has perished. ²¹ And judgment is coming against the land of Misor, upon Chelon, and Rephas, and Mophas, ²² and upon Daebon, and upon Nabau, and upon the house of Daethlathaim, ²³ and upon Cariathaim, and upon the house of Gaemol, and upon the house of Maon, ²⁴ and upon Carioth, and upon Bosor, and upon all the cities of Moab, far and near. ²⁵ The horn of Moab is broken, and his arm is crushed. ²⁶ Make ye him drunk; for he has magnified himself against the Lord: and Moab shall clap with his hand, and shall be also himself a laughing-stock. ²⁷ For surely Israel was to thee a laughing-stock, and was found among thy thefts, because thou didst fight against him. ²⁸ The inhabitants of Moab have left the cities, and dwelt in rocks; they have become as doves nestling in rocks, at the mouth of a cave. ²⁹ And I have heard of the pride of Moab, he has greatly heightened his pride and his haughtiness, and his heart has been lifted up. ³⁰ But I know his works: is it not enough for him? has he not done thus? ³¹ Therefore howl ye for Moab on all sides; cry out against the shorn men *in* a gloomy place. I will weep for thee, ³² O vine of Aserema, as with the weeping of Jazer: thy branches are gone over the sea, they reached the cities of Jazer: destruction has come upon thy fruits, *and* upon thy grape-gatherers. ³³ Joy and gladness have been utterly swept off the land of Moab: and *though* there was wine in thy presses, in the morning they trod it not, neither in the evening did they raise the cry of joy. ³⁴ From the cry of Esebon even to Ætam their cities uttered their voice, from Zogor to Oronaim, and their tidings *as* a heifer of three years old, for the water also of Nebrin shall be dried up. ³⁵ And I will destroy Moab, saith the Lord, as he comes up to the altar, and burns incense to his gods. ³⁶ Therefore the heart of Moab shall sound as pipes, my heart shall sound as a pipe for the shorn men; forasmuch as what *every* man has gained has perished from him. 37 They shall all have their heads shaved in every place, and every beard shall be shaved; and all hands shall beat *the breasts*, and on all loins shall be sackcloth. 38 And on all the housetops of Moab, and in his streets *shall be mourning*: for I have broken *him*, saith the Lord, as a vessel, which is useless. 39 How has he changed! how has Moab turned *his* back! Moab is put to shame, and become a laughing-stock, and an object of anger to all that are round about him. 40 For thus said the Lord; 41 Carioth is taken, and the strong-holds have been taken together. 42 And Moab shall perish from being a multitude, because he has magnified himself against the Lord. 43 A snare, and fear, and the pit, are upon thee, O inhabitant of Moab. 44 He that flees from the terror shall fall into the pit, and he that comes up out of the pit shall even be taken in the snare: for I will bring these things upon Moab in the year of their visitation.

Jer.32 15 Thus said the Lord God of Israel; Take the cup of this unmixed wine from mine hand, and thou shalt cause all the nations to drink, to whom I send thee. 16 And they shall drink, and vomit, and be mad, because of the sword which I send among them. 17 So I took the cup out of the Lord's hand, and caused the nations to whom the Lord sent me to drink: 18 Jerusalem, and the cities of Juda, and the kings of Juda, and his princes, to make them a desert place, a desolation, and a hissing; 19 and Pharao king of Egypt, and his servants, and his nobles, and all his people; 20 and all the mingled *people*, and all the kings of the Philistines, and Ascalon, and Gaza, and Accaron, and the remnant of Azotus, 21 and Idumea, and the land of Moab, and the children of Ammon, 22 and the kings of Tyre, and the kings of Sidon, and the kings in the *country* beyond the sea, 23 and Daedan, and Thaeman, and Ros, and every one that is shaved round about the face, 24 and all the mingled *people* lodging in the wilderness, 25 and all the kings of Ælam, and all the kings of the Persians, 26 and all the kings from the north, the far and the near, each one with his brother, and all the kingdom s which are on the face of the earth. 27 And thou shalt say to them, Thus said the Lord Almighty; Drink ye, be ye drunken; and ye shall vomit, and shall fall, and shall in nowise rise, because of the sword which I send among you. 28 And it shall come to pass, when they refuse to take the cup out of thine hand, to drink it, that thou shalt say, Thus said the Lord; Ye shall surely drink. 29 For I am beginning to afflict the city whereon my name is called, and ye shall by no means be held guiltless: for I am calling a sword upon all that dwell upon the earth. 30 And thou shalt prophesy against them these words, and shalt say, The Lord shall speak from on high, from his sanctuary he will utter his voice; he will pronounce a declaration on his place; and these shall answer like men gathering grapes: and destruction is coming on them that dwell on the earth, 31 *even* upon *the extreme* part of the earth; for the Lord *has* a controversy with the nations, he is pleading with all flesh, and the ungodly are given to the sword, saith the Lord. 32 Thus said the Lord; Behold, evils are proceeding from

nation to nation, and a great whirlwind goes forth from the end of the earth. 33 And the slain of the Lord shall be in the day of the Lord from *one* end of the earth even to the *other* end of the earth: they shall not be buried; they shall be as dung on the face of the earth. 34 Howl, ye shepherds, and cry; and lament, ye rams of the flock: for your days have been completed for slaughter, and ye shall fall as the choice rams. 35 And flight shall perish from the shepherds, and safety from the rams of the flock. 36 A voice of the crying of the shepherds, and a moaning of the sheep and the rams: for the Lord has destroyed their pastures. 37 And the peaceable abodes that remain shall be destroyed before the fierceness of my anger. 38 He has forsaken his lair, as a lion: for their land is become desolate before the great sword.

Jer.33 1 IN THE BEGINNING OF THE REIGN OF KING JOAKIM SON OF JOSIAS THERE CAME THIS WORD FROM THE LORD. 2 Thus said the Lord; Stand in the court of the Lord's house, and thou shalt declare to all the Jews, and to all that come to worship in the house of the Lord, all the words which I commanded thee to speak to them; abate not one word. 3 Peradventure they will hear, and turn every one from his evil way: then I will cease from the evils which I purpose to do to them, because of their evil practices. 4 And thou shalt say, Thus said the Lord; If ye will not hearken to me, to walk in my statutes which I set before you, 5 to hearken to the words of my servants the prophets, whom I send to you early in the morning; yea, I sent them, but ye hearkened not to me; 6 then will I make this house as Selo, and I will make *this* city a curse to all the nations of all the earth. 7 And the priests, and the false prophets, and all the people heard Jeremias speaking these words in the house of the Lord. 8 And it came to pass, when Jeremias had ceased speaking all that the Lord had ordered him to speak to all the people, that the priests and the false prophets and all the people took him, saying, 9 Thou shalt surely die, because thou hast prophesied in the name of the Lord, saying, This house shall be as Selo, and this city shall be made quite destitute of inhabitants. And all the people assembled against Jeremias in the house of the Lord. 10 And the princes of Juda heard this word, and they went up out of the house of the king to the house of the Lord, and sat in the entrance of the new gate. 11 Then the priests and the false prophets said to the princes and to all the people, The judgment of death *is due* to this man; because he has prophesied against this city, as ye have heard with your ears. 12 Then Jeremias spoke to the princes, and to all the people, saying, The Lord sent me to prophesy against this house and against this city, all the words which ye have heard. 13 And now amend your ways and your works, and hearken to the voice of the Lord; and the Lord shall cease from the evils which he has pronounced against you. 14 And behold, I am in your hands; do to me as is expedient, and as it is best for you. 15 But know for a certainty, that if ye slay me, ye bring innocent blood upon yourselves, and upon this city, and upon them that dwell in it; for in truth the Lord has sent me to you to speak in your ears all these words. 16 Then the princes and all the people said to the priests and to the false prophets; Judgment of death is not *due* to this man; for he has spoken to us in the name of the Lord our God. 17 And there rose up men of the elders of the land, and said to all the assembly of the people, 18 Michaeas the Morathite lived in the days of Ezekias king of Juda, and said to all the people of Juda, Thus saith the Lord; Sion shall be ploughed as a field, and Jerusalem shall become a desolation, and the mountain of the house shall be a thicket of trees. 19 Did Ezekias and all Juda in any way slay him? Was it not that they feared the Lord, and they made supplication before the Lord, and the Lord ceased from the evils which he *had* pronounced against them? whereas we have wrought great evil against our own souls. 20 And there was *another* man prophesying in the name of the Lord, Urias the son of Samaeas of Cariathiarim; and he prophesied concerning this land according to all the words of Jeremias. 21 And king Joakim and all the princes heard all his words, and sought to slay him; and Urias heard *it* and went into Egypt. 22 And the king sent men into Egypt; 23 and they brought him thence, and brought him into the king; and he smote him with the sword, and cast him into the sepulchre of the children of his people. 24 Nevertheless the hand of Achicam son of Saphan was with Jeremias, to prevent his being delivered into the hands of the people, or being killed.

Jer.34 1 Thus said the Lord; Make to thyself bonds and yokes, and put *them* about thy neck, 3 and thou shalt send them to the king of Idumea, and to the king of Moab, and to the king of the children of Ammon, and to the king of Tyre, and to the king of Sidon, by the hands of their messengers that come to meet them at Jerusalem to Sedekias king of Juda. 4 And thou shalt commission them to say to their lords, Thus said the Lord God of Israel; Thus shall ye say to your lords; 5 I have made the earth by my great power, and with my high arm, and I will give it to whomsoever it shall seem *good* in mine eyes. 6 I gave the earth to Nabuchodonosor king of Babylon to serve him, and the wild beasts of the field to labour for him. 7 8 And the nation and kingdom, all that shall not put their neck under the yoke of the king of Babylon, with sword and famine will I visit them, saith the Lord, until they are consumed by his hand. 9 And hearken ye not to your false prophets, nor to them that divine to you, nor to them that foretell events by dreams to you, nor to your auguries, nor your sorcerers, that say, Ye shall by no means work for the king of Babylon: 10 for they prophesy lies to you, to remove you far from your land. 11 But the nation which shall put its neck under the yoke of the king of Babylon, and serve him, I will even leave it upon its land, and it shall serve him, and dwell in it. 12 I spoke also to Sedekias king of Juda according to all these words, saying, Put your neck into *the yoke*, and serve the king of Babylon. 13 14 For they prophesy unrighteous *words* to you, 15 for I sent them not, saith the Lord; and they prophesy *in* my name unjustly, that I might destroy you, and ye should perish, and your prophets, who unrighteously prophesy lies to you. 16 I spoke to you, and to all this people, and to the priests, saying, Thus said the Lord; Hearken not to the words of the prophets that prophesy to you, saying, Behold, the vessels of the Lord's

house shall return from Babylon: for they prophesy to you unrighteous *words*. 17 I sent them not. 18 If they are prophets, and if the word of the Lord is in them, let them meet me, for thus has the Lord said. 19 And as for the remaining vessels, 20 which the king of Babylon took not, when he carried Jechonias prisoner out of Jerusalem, 21 22 they shall go into Babylon, saith the Lord.

Jer.35 1 And it came to pass in the fourth year of Sedekias king of Juda, in the fifth month, *that* Ananias the false prophet, the son of Azor, from Gabaon, spoke to me in the house of the Lord, in the sight of the priests and all the people, saying, 2 Thus saith the Lord; I have broken the yoke of the king of Babylon. 3 Yet two full years, and I will return into this place the vessels of the house of the Lord, 4 and Jechonias, and the captivity of Juda: for I will break the yoke of the king of Babylon. 5 Then Jeremias spoke to Ananias in the sight of all the people, and in the sight of the priests that stood in the house of the Lord, 6 and Jeremias said, May the Lord indeed do thus; may he confirm thy word which thou dost prophesy, to return the vessels of the house of the Lord, and all the captivity, out of Babylon to this place. 7 Nevertheless hear ye the word of the Lord which I speak in your ears, and in the ears of all the people. 8 The prophets that were before me and before you of old, also prophesied over much country, and against great kingdoms, concerning war. 9 *As for* the prophet that has prophesied for peace, when the word has come *to pass*, they shall know the prophet whom the Lord has sent them in truth. 10 Then Ananias took the yokes from the neck of Jeremias in the sight of all the people, and broke them to pieces. 11 And Ananias spoke in the presence of all the people, saying, Thus said the Lord; Thus will I break the yoke of the king of Babylon from the necks of all the nations. And Jeremias went his way. 12 And the word of the Lord came to Jeremias, after that Ananias had broken the yokes off his neck, saying, 13 Go and speak to Ananias, saying, Thus saith the Lord; Thou hast broken the yokes of wood; but I will make instead of them yokes of iron. 14 For thus said the Lord, I have put a yoke of iron on the neck of all the nations, that they may serve the king of Babylon. 15 And Jeremias said to Ananias, The Lord has not sent thee; and thou hast caused this people to trust in unrighteousness. 16 Therefore thus said the Lord: Behold, I *will* cast thee off from the face of the earth: this year thou shalt die. 17 So he died in the seventh month.

Jer.36 1 And these are the words of the book which Jeremias sent from Jerusalem to the elders of the captivity, and to the priests, and to the false prophets, even an epistle to Babylon for the captivity, and to all the people; 2 (after the departure of Jechonias the king and the queen, and the eunuchs, and every freeman, and bondman, and artificer, out of Jerusalem;) 3 by the hand of Eleasan son of Saphan, and Gamarias son of Chelcias, (whom Sedekias king of Juda sent to the king of Babylon to Babylon) saying, 4 Thus said the Lord God of Israel concerning the captivity which I caused to be carried away from Jerusalem; 5 Build ye houses, and inhabit *them*; and plant gardens, and eat the fruits thereof; 6 and take ye wives, and beget sons and daughters; and take wives for your sons, and give your daughters to husbands, and be multiplied, and be not diminished. 7 And seek the peace of the land into which I have carried you captive, and ye shall pray to the Lord for the people: for in its peace ye shall *have* peace. 8 For thus saith the Lord; Let not the false prophets that are among you persuade you, and let not your diviners persuade you, and hearken not to your dreams which ye dream. 9 For they prophesy to you unrighteous *words* in my name; and I sent them not. 10 For thus said the Lord; When seventy years shall be on the point of being accomplished at Babylon, I will visit you, and will confirm my words to you, to bring back your people to this place. 11 And I will devise for you a device of peace, and not evil, to bestow upon you these *good things.* 12 And do ye pray to me, and I will hearken to you: and do ye earnestly seek me, and ye shall find me; 13 for ye shall seek me with your whole heart. 14 And I will appear to you: 15 whereas ye said, The Lord has appointed for us prophets in Babylon: 21 Thus saith the Lord concerning Achiab, and concerning Sedekias; Behold, I *will* deliver them into the hands of the king of Babylon; and he shall smite them in your sight. 22 And they shall make of them a curse in all the captivity of Juda in Babylon, saying, The Lord do to thee as he did to Sedekias, and as he did to Achiab, whom the king of Babylon fried in the fire; 23 because of the iniquity which they wrought in Israel, and *because* they committed adultery with the wives of their fellow-citizens; and spoke a word in my name, which I did not command them *to speak,* and I am witness, saith the Lord. 24 And to Samaeas the Ælamite thou shalt say, 25 I sent thee not in my name: and to Sophonias the priest the son of Maasaeas say thou, 26 The Lord has made thee priest in the place of Jodae the priest, to be ruler in the house of the Lord over every prophet, and to every madman, and thou shalt put them in prison, and into the dungeon. 27 And now wherefore have ye reviled together Jeremias of Anathoth, who prophesied to you? 28 Did he not send for this purpose? for in the course of this month he sent to you to Babylon, saying, It is far off: build ye houses, and inhabit *them,* and plant gardens, and eat the fruit of them. 29 And Sophonias read the book in the ears of Jeremias. 30 Then the word of the Lord came to Jeremias, saying, 31 Send to the captivity, saying, Thus saith the Lord concerning Samaeas the Ælamite, Since Samaeas has prophesied to you, and I sent him not, and he has made you to trust in iniquity, 32 therefore thus saith the Lord; Behold, I will visit Samaeas, and his family: and there shall not be a man of them in the midst of you to see the good which I will do to you: they shall not see *it.*

Jer.37 1 THE WORD THAT CAME TO JEREMIAS FROM THE LORD, SAYING, 2 Thus speaks the Lord God of Israel, saying, Write all the words which I have spoken to thee in a book. 3 For, behold, the days come, saith the Lord, when I will bring back the captivity of my people Israel and Juda, said the Lord: and I will bring them back to the land which I gave to their fathers, and they shall be lords of it. 4 AND THESE ARE THE WORDS WHICH THE LORD SPOKE CONCERNING

ISRAEL AND JUDA; 5 Thus said the Lord: Ye shall hear a sound of fear, *there is* fear, and there is not peace. 6 Enquire, and see if a male has born a child? and *ask* concerning the fear, wherein they shall hold their loins, and *look for* safety: for I have seen every man, and his hands are on his loins; *their* faces are turned to paleness. 7 For that day is great, and there is not such *another,* and it is a time of straitness to Jacob; but he shall be saved out of it. 8 In that day, said the Lord, I will break the yoke off their neck, and will burst their bonds, and they shall no longer serve strangers: 9 but they shall serve the Lord their God; and I will raise up to them David their king. 10 11 12 Thus saith the Lord; I have brought on *thee* destruction; thy stroke is painful. 13 There is none to judge thy cause: thou hast been painfully treated for healing, there is no help for thee. 14 All thy friends have forgotten thee; they shall not ask *about thee* at all, for I have smitten thee with he stroke of an enemy, *even* severe correction: thy sins have abounded above all thine iniquity. 15 Thy sins have abounded beyond the multitude of thine iniquities, *therefore* they have done these things to thee. Therefore all that devour thee shall be eaten, and all thine enemies shall eat all their *own* flesh. 16 And they that spoil thee shall become a spoil, and I will give up to be plundered all that have plundered thee. 17 For I will bring about thy healing, I will heal thee of thy grievous wound, saith the Lord; for thou art called Dispersed: she is your prey, for no one seeks after her. 18 Thus said the Lord; Behold, I will turn the captivity of Jacob, and will have pity upon his prisoners; and the city shall be built upon her hill, and the people shall settle after their manner. 19 And there shall go forth from them singers, *even* the sound of men making merry: and I will multiply them, and they shall not at all be diminished. 20 And their sons shall go in as before, and their testimonies shall be established before me, and I will visit them that afflict them. 21 And their mighty ones shall be over them, and their prince shall proceed of themselves; and I will gather them, and they shall return to me: for who is this that has set his heart to return to me? saith the Lord. 23 For the wrathful anger of the lord has gone forth, *even* a whirlwind of anger has gone forth: it shall come upon the ungodly. 24 The fierce anger of the Lord shall not return, until he shall execute *it,* and until he shall establish the purpose of his heart: in the latter days ye shall know these things.

Jer.38 1 At that time, saith the Lord, I will be a God to the family of Israel, and they shall be to me a people. 2 Thus saith the Lord, I found him warm in the wilderness with them that were slain with the sword: go ye and destroy not Israel. 3 The Lord appeared to him from afar, *saying,* I have loved thee with an everlasting love: therefore have I drawn thee in compassion. 4 For I will build thee, and thou shalt be built, O virgin of Israel: thou shalt yet take thy timbrel, and go forth with the party of them that make merry. 5 For ye have planted vineyards on the mountains of Samaria: plant ye, and praise. 6 For it is a day when those that plead on the mountains of Ephraim shall call, *saying,* Arise ye, and go up to Sion to the Lord your God. 7 For thus saith the Lord to Jacob; Rejoice ye, and exult over the head of the nations: make proclamation, and praise ye: say, The Lord has delivered his people, the remnant of Israel. 8 Behold, I bring them from the north, and will gather them from the end of the earth to the feast of the passover: and *the people* shall beget a great multitude, and they shall return hither. 9 They went forth with weeping, and I will bring them back with consolation, causing them to lodge by the channels of waters in a straight way, and they shall not err in it: for I am become a father to Israel, and Ephraim is my first-born. 10 Hear the words of the Lord, ye nations, and proclaim *them* to the islands afar off; say, He that scattered Israel will also gather him, and keep him as one that feeds his flock. 11 For the Lord has ransomed Jacob, he has rescued him out of the hand of them *that were* stronger than he. 12 And they shall come, and shall rejoice in the mount of Sion, and shall come to the good things of the Lord, *even* to a land of corn, and wine, and fruits, and cattle, and sheep: and their soul shall be as a fruitful tree; and they shall hunger no more. 13 Then shall the virgins rejoice in the assembly of youth, and the old men shall rejoice; and I will turn their mourning into joy, and will make them merry. 14 I will expand and cheer with wine the soul of the priests the sons of Levi, and my people shall be satisfied with my good things: thus saith the Lord. 15 A voice was heard in Rama, of lamentation, and of weeping, and wailing; Rachel would not cease weeping for her children, because they are not. 16 Thus saith the Lord; Let thy voice cease from weeping, and thine eyes from thy tears: for their is a reward for thy works; and they shall return from the land of *thine* enemies. 17 *There shall be* an abiding *home* for thy children. 18 I have heard the sound of Ephraim lamenting, *and saying*, Thou hast chastened me, and I was chastened; I as a calf was not *willingly* taught: turn thou me, and I shall turn; for thou *art* the Lord my God. 19 For after my captivity I repented; and after I knew, I groaned for the day of shame, and shewed thee that I bore reproach from my youth. 20 Ephraim is a beloved son, a pleasing child to me: for because my words are in him, I will surely remember him: therefore I made haste *to help* him; I will surely have mercy upon him, saith the Lord. 21 Prepare thyself, O Sion; execute vengeance; look to thy ways: return, O virgin of Israel, by the way by which thou wentest, return mourning to thy cities. 22 How long, O disgraced daughter, wilt thou turn away? for the Lord has created safety for a new plantation: men shall go about in safety. 23 For thus saith the Lord; They shall yet speak this word in the land of Juda, and in the cities thereof, when I shall turn his captivity; blessed be the Lord on his righteous holy mountain! 24 And there shall be dwellers in the cities of Juda, and in all his land, together with the husbandman, and *the shepherd* shall go forth with the flock. 25 For I have saturated every thirsting soul, and filled every hungry soul. 26 Therefore I awake, and beheld; and my sleep was sweet to me. 27 Therefore, behold, the days come, saith the Lord, when I will sow the house of Israel and the house of Juda with the seed of man, and the seed of beast. 28 And it shall come to pass, that as I watched over them, to pull down, and to afflict, so will I watch over them, to build, and to plant, saith the Lord. 29 In those days they shall certainly not say, The fathers ate a sour grape, and the children's teeth

were set on edge. 30 But every one shall die in his own sin; and the teeth of him that eats the sour grape shall be set on edge. 31 Behold, the days come, saith the Lord, when I will make a new covenant with the house of Israel, and with the house of Juda: 32 not according to the covenant which I made with their fathers in the day when I took hold of their hand to bring them out of the land of Egypt; for they abode not in my covenant, and I disregarded them, saith the Lord. 33 For this is my covenant which I will make with the house of Israel; after those days, saith the Lord, I will surely put my laws into their mind, and write them on their hearts; and I will be to them a God, and they shall be to me a people. 34 And they shall not at all teach every one his *fellow* citizen, and every one his brother, saying, Know the Lord: for all shall know me, from the least of them to the greatest of them: for I will be merciful to their iniquities, and their sins I will remember no more. 35 Thus saith the Lord, who gives the sun for a light by day, the moon and the stars for a light by night, and *makes* a roaring in the sea, so that the waves thereof roar; the Lord Almighty is his name: 36 if these ordinances cease from before me, saith the Lord, then shall the family of Israel cease to be a nation before me forever. 37 Though the sky should be raised to a *greater* height, saith the Lord, and though the ground of the earth should be sunk *lower* beneath, yet I will not cast off the family of Israel, saith the Lord, for all that they have done. 38 Behold, the days come, saith the Lord, when the city shall be built to the Lord from the tower of Anameel to the gate of the corner. 39 And the measurement of it shall proceed in front of them as far as the hills of Gareb, and it shall be compassed with a circular wall of choice stones. 40 And all the Asaremoth even to Nachal Kedron, as far as the corner of the horse-gate eastward, shall be holiness to the Lord; and it shall not fail any more, and shall not be destroyed for ever.

Jer.39 1 The word that came from the Lord to Jeremias in the tenth year of king Sedekias, this is the eighteenth year of king Nabuchodonosor king of Babylon. 2 And the host of the king of Babylon had made a rampart against Jerusalem: and Jeremias was kept in the court of the prison, which is in the king's house; 3 in which king Sedekias *had* shut him up, saying, Wherefore dost thou prophesy, saying, Thus saith the Lord, Behold, I *will* give this city into the hands of the king of Babylon, and he shall take it; 4 and Sedekias shall by no means be delivered out of the hand of the Chaldeans, for he shall certainly be given up into the hands of the king of Babylon, and his mouth shall speak to his mouth, and his eyes shall look upon his eyes; 5 and Sedekias shall go into Babylon, and dwell there? 6 AND THE WORD OF THE LORD CAME TO JEREMIAS, SAYING, 7 Behold, Anameel the son of Salom thy father's brother is coming to thee, saying, Buy thee my field that is in Anathoth: for thou *hast* the right to take *it* as a purchase. 8 So Anameel the son of Salom my father's brother came to me into the court of the prison, and said, Buy thee my field that is in the land of Benjamin, in Anathoth: for thou *hast* a right to buy it, and thou art the elder. So I knew that it was the word of the Lord. 9 And I bought the field of

Anameel the son of my father's brother, and I weighed him seventeen shekels of silver. 10 And I wrote *it* in a book, and sealed *it*, and took the testimony of witnesses, and weighed the money in the balance. 11 And I took the book of the purchase that was sealed; 12 and I gave it to Baruch son of Nerias, son of Maasaeas, in the sight of Anameel my father's brother's son, and in the sight of the men that stood by and wrote in the book of the purchase, and in the sight of the Jews that were in the court of the prison. 13 And I charged Baruch in their presence, saying, Thus saith the Lord Almighty; 14 Take this book of the purchase, and the book that has been read; and thou shalt put it into an earthen vessel, that it may remain many days. 15 For thus saith the Lord; There shall yet be bought fields and houses and vineyards in this land. 16 And I prayed to the Lord after I had given the book of the purchase to Baruch the son of Nerias, saying, 17 O *ever* living Lord! thou hast made the heaven and the earth by thy great power, and with thy high and lofty arm: nothing can be hidden from thee. 18 Granting mercy to thousands, and recompensing the sins of the fathers into the bosoms of their children after them: the great, the strong God; 19 the Lord of great counsel, and mighty in deeds, the great Almighty God, and Lord of great name: thine eyes are upon the ways of the children of men, to give to every one according to his way: 20 who hast wrought signs and wonders in the land of Egypt even to this day, and in Israel, and among the inhabitants of the earth; and thou didst make for thyself a name, as at this day; 21 and thou didst bring out thy people Israel out of the land of Egypt with signs, and with wonders, with a mighty hand, and with a high arm, and with great sights; 22 and thou gavest them this land, which thou didst swear *to give* to their fathers, a land flowing with milk and honey; 23 and they went in, and took it; but they hearkened not to thy voice, and walked not in thine ordinances; they did none of the things which thou didst command them, and they caused all these calamities to happen to them. 24 Behold, a multitude is come against the city to take it; and the city is given into the hands of the Chaldeans that fight against it, by the power of the sword, and the famine: as thou hast spoken, so has it happened. 25 And thou sayest to me, Buy thee the field for money; and I wrote a book, and sealed *it*, and took the testimony of witnesses: and the city is given into the hands of the Chaldeans. 26 And the word of the Lord came to me, saying, 27 I am the Lord, the God of all flesh: shall anything be hidden from me! 28 Therefore thus saith the Lord God of Israel; This city shall certainly be delivered into the hands of the king of Babylon, and he shall take it: 29 and the Chaldeans shall come to war against this city, and they shall burn this city with fire, and shall burn down the houses wherein they burnt incense on the roofs thereof to Baal, and poured drink-offerings to other gods, to provoke me. 30 For the children of Israel and the children of Juda alone did evil in my sight from their youth. 31 For this city was *obnoxious* to my anger and my wrath, from the day that they built it even to this day; that I should remove it from my presence, 32 because of all the wickedness of the children of Israel and Juda, which they wrought to provoke me, they and their kings, and their princes, and their priests, and their prophets, the men of Juda, and the dwellers in Jerusalem. 33 And they turned the back to me, and not the face: whereas I taught them early in the morning, but they hearkened no more to receive instructions. 34 And they set their pollutions in the house, on which my name was called, by their uncleannesses. 35 And they built to Baal the altars that are in the valley of the son of Ennom, to offer their sons and their daughters to king Moloch; which things I commanded them not, neither came it into my mind that they should do this abomination, to cause Juda to sin. 36 And now thus has the Lord God of Israel said concerning this city, of which thou sayest, it shall be delivered into the hands of the king of Babylon by the sword, and by famine, and banishment. 37 Behold, I *will* gather them out of every land, where I have scattered them in my anger, and my wrath, and great fury; and I will bring them back into this place, and will cause them to dwell safely: 38 and they shall be to me a people, and I will be to them a god. 39 And I will give them another way, and another heart, to fear me continually, and *that* for good to them and their children after them. 40 And I will make with them an everlasting covenant, which I will by no means turn away from them, and I will put my fear into their heart, that they may not depart from me. 41 And I will visit *them* to do them good, and I will plant them in this land in faithfulness, and with all my heart, and with all *my* soul. 42 For thus saith the Lord; As I have brought upon this people all these great evils, so will I bring upon them all the good things which I pronounced upon them. 43 And there shall yet be fields bought in the land, of which thou sayest, it shall be destitute of man and beast; and they are delivered into the hands of the Chaldeans. 44 And they shall buy fields for money, and thou shalt write a book, and seal *it*, and shalt take the testimony of witnesses in the land of Benjamin, and round about Jerusalem, and in the cities of Juda, and in the cities of the mountain, and in the cities of the plain, and in the cities of the south: for I will turn their captivity.

Jer.40 1 And the word of the Lord came to Jeremias the second time, when he was yet bound in the court of the prison, saying, 2 Thus saith the Lord, who made the earth and formed it, to establish it; the Lord is his name; 3 Cry to me, and I will answer thee, and I will declare to thee great and mighty things, which thou knowest not. 4 For thus saith the Lord concerning the houses of this city, and concerning the houses of the king of Juda, which have been pulled down for mounds and fortifications, 5 to fight against the Chaldeans, and to fill it with the corpses of men, whom I smote in mine anger and my wrath, and turned away my face from them, for all their wickedness: 6 Behold, I bring upon her healing and cure, and I will show *myself* to them, and will heal her, and make both peace and security. 7 And I will turn the captivity of Juda, and the captivity of Israel, and will build them, even as before. 8 And I will cleanse them from all their iniquities, whereby they have sinned against me, and will not remember their sins, whereby they have sinned against me, and revolted from me. 9 And it shall be for joy and praise, and for glory to all the people of the earth, who shall hear all the good that I will do: and they shall fear and be provoked for all the good things and for all the peace which I will bring upon them. ¹⁰ Thus saith the Lord; There shall yet be heard in this place, of which ye say, it is destitute of men and cattle, in the cities of Juda, and in the streets of Jerusalem, *the places* that have been made desolate for want of men and cattle, ¹¹ the voice of gladness, and the voice of joy, the voice of the bridegroom, and the voice of the bride, the voice of men saying, Give thanks to the Lord Almighty: for the Lord is good; for his mercy *endures* fore ever: and they shall bring gifts into the house of the Lord; for I will turn all the captivity of that land as before, said the Lord. ¹² Thus saith the Lord of hosts; There shall yet be in this place, that is desert for want of man and beast, in all the cities thereof, resting-places for shepherds causing their flocks to lie down. ¹³ In the cities of the hill country, and in the cities of the valley, and in the cities of the south, and in the land of Benjamin, and in the *cities* round about Jerusalem, and in the cities of Juda, flocks shall yet pass under the hand of him that numbers *them*, saith the Lord.

Jer.41 ¹ The word that came to Jeremias from the Lord (now Nabuchodonosor king of Babylon, and all his army, and all the country of his dominion, were warring against Jerusalem, and against all the cities of Juda,) saying, ² Thus has the Lord said; Go to Sedekias king of Juda, and thou shalt say to him, Thus has the Lord said, This city shall certainly be delivered into the hands of the king of Babylon, and he shall take it, and shall burn it with fire: ³ and thou shalt not escape out of his hand, but shalt certainly be taken, and shalt be given into his hands; and thine eyes shall see his eyes, and thou shalt enter into Babylon. ⁴ But hear the word of the Lord, O Sedekias king of Juda; Thus saith the Lord, ⁵ Thou shalt die in peace: and as they wept for thy fathers that reigned before thee, they shall weep also for thee, *saying*, Ah lord! and they shall lament for thee down to the grave: for I have spoken the word, said the Lord. ⁶ And Jeremias spoke to king Sedekias all these words in Jerusalem. ⁷ And the host of the king of Babylon warred against Jerusalem, and against the cities of Juda, and against Lachis, and against Azeca: for these strong cities were left among the cities of Juda. ⁸ The word that came from the Lord to Jeremias, after king Sedekias had concluded a covenant with the people, to proclaim a release; ⁹ That every one should set at liberty his servant, and every one has handmaid, the Hebrew man and Hebrew woman, that no man of Juda should be a bondman. ¹⁰ Then all the nobles, and all the people who had entered into the covenant, *engaging* to set free every one his man-servant, and every one his maid, turned, ¹¹ and gave them over to be men-servants and maid-servants. ¹² And the word of the Lord came to Jeremias, saying, ¹³ Thus saith the Lord; I made a covenant with your fathers in the day wherein I took them out of the land of Egypt, out of the house of bondage, saying, ¹⁴ When six years are accomplished, thou shalt set free thy brother the Hebrew, who shall be sold to thee: for he shall serve thee six years, and *then* thou shalt let him go free: but they hearkened not to me, and inclined not their ear. ¹⁵ And this day they turned to do that which was

right in my sight, to proclaim every one the release of his neighbour; and they had concluded a covenant before me, in the house whereon my name is called. ¹⁶ But ye turned and profaned my name, to bring back every one his servant, and every one his handmaid, whom ye had sent forth free *and* at their own disposal, to be to you men- servants and maid-servants. ¹⁷ Therefore thus said the Lord; Ye have not hearkened to me, to proclaim a release every one to his neighbour: behold, I proclaim a release to you, to the sword, and to the pestilence, and to the famine; and I will give you up to dispersion *among* all the kingdoms of the earth. ¹⁸ And I will give the men that have transgressed my covenant, who have not kept my covenant, which they made before me, the calf which they prepared to sacrifice with it, ¹⁹ the princes of Juda, and the men in power, and the priests, and the people; ²⁰ I will even give them to their enemies, and their carcases shall be food for the birds of the sky and for the wild beasts of the earth. ²¹ And I will give Sedekias king of Judea, and their princes, into the hands of their enemies, and the host of the king of Babylon *shall come upon* them that run away from them. ²² Behold, I *will* give command, saith the Lord, and will bring them back to this land; and they shall fight against it, and take it, and burn it with fire, and the cities of Juda; and I will make them desolate without inhabitants.

Jer.42 ¹ THE WORD THAT CAME TO JEREMIAS from the Lord in the days of Joakim, king of Juda, saying, ² Go to the house of the Archabin, and thou shalt bring them to the house of the Lord, into one of the courts, and give them wine to drink. ³ So I brought forth Jechonias the son of Jeremin the son of Chabasin, and his brethren, and his sons, and all the family of the Archabin; ⁴ and I brought them into the house of the Lord, into the chamber of the sons of Joanan, the son of Ananias, the son of Godolias, a man of God, who dwells near the house of the princes that are over the house of Maasaeas the son of Selom, who kept the court. ⁵ And I set before them a jar of wine, and cups, and I said, Drink ye wine. ⁶ But they said, We will on no account drink wine, for our father Jonadab the son of Rechab commanded us, saying, Ye shall on no account drink wine, *neither* ye, nor your sons for ever: ⁷ nor shall ye at all build houses, nor sow any seed, nor shall ye have a vineyard: for ye shall dwell in tents all your days; that ye may live many days upon the land, in which ye sojourn. ⁸ And we hearkened to the voice of Jonadab our father, so as to drink no wine all our days, we, and our wives, and our sons, and our daughters; ⁹ and so as to build no houses to dwell in: and we have had no vineyard, nor field, nor seed: ¹⁰ but we have dwelt in tents, and have hearkened, and done according to all that Jonadab our father commanded us. ¹¹ And it came to pass, when Nabuchodonosor came up against the land, that we said we would come in; and we entered into Jerusalem, for fear of the host of the Chaldeans, and for fear of the host of the Assyrians: and we dwelt there. ¹² And the word of the Lord came to me, saying, ¹³ Thus saith the Lord, Go, and say to the men of Juda, and to them that dwell in Jerusalem, Will ye not receive correction to hearken to my words? ¹⁴ The sons of

Jonadab the son of Rechab have kept the word which he commanded his children, that they should drink no wine; and they have not drunk *it*: but I spoke to you early, and ye hearkened not. 15 And I sent to you my servants the prophets, saying, Turn ye every one from his evil way, and amend your practices, and go not after other gods to serve them, and ye shall dwell upon the land which I gave to you and to your fathers: but ye inclined not your ears, and hearkened not. 16 But the sons of Jonadab the son of Rechab have kept the command of their father; but this people has not hearkened to me. 17 Therefore thus saith the Lord; Behold, I *will* bring upon Juda and upon the inhabitants of Jerusalem all the evils which I pronounced against them. 18 Therefore thus saith the Lord; Since the sons of Jonadab the son of Rechab have hearkened to the command of their father, to do as their father commanded them: 19 there shall never be wanting a man of the sons of Jonadab the son of Rechab to stand before my face while the earth remains.

Jer.43 1 IN THE FOURTH YEAR OF JOAKIM son of Josias king of Juda, the word of the Lord came to me, saying, 2 Take thee a roll of a book, and write upon it all the words which I spoke to thee against Jerusalem, and against Juda, and against all the nations, from the day when I spoke to thee, from the days of Josias king of Juda, even to this day. 3 Perhaps the house of Juda will hear all the evils which I purpose to do to them; that they may turn from their evil way; and *so* I will be merciful to their iniquities and their sins. 4 So Jeremias called Baruch the son of Nerias: and he wrote from the mouth of Jeremias all the words of the Lord, which he had spoken to him, on a roll of a book. 5 And Jeremias commanded Baruch, saying, I am in prison; I cannot enter into the house of the Lord: 6 so thou shalt read in this roll in the ears of the people in the house of the Lord, on the fast day; and in the ears of all Juda that come out of their cities, thou shalt read to them. 7 Peradventure their supplication will come before the Lord, and they will turn from their evil way: for great is the wrath and the anger of the Lord, which he has pronounced against this people. 8 And Baruch did according to all that Jeremias commanded him—reading in the book the words of the Lord in the Lord's house. 9 And it came to pass in the eighth year of king Joakim, in the ninth month, all the people in Jerusalem, and the house of Juda, proclaimed a fast before the Lord. 10 And Baruch read in the book the words of Jeremias in the house of the Lord, in the house of Gamarias son of Saphan the scribe, in the upper court, in the entrance of the new gate of the house of the Lord, and in the ears of all the people. 11 And Michaeas the son of Gamarias the son of Saphan heard all the words of the Lord, out of the book. 12 And he went down to the king's house, into the house of the scribe: and, behold, there were sitting there all the princes, Elisama the scribe, and Dalaeas the son of Selemias, and Jonathan the son of Acchobor, and Gamarias the son of Saphan, and Sedekias the son of Ananias, and all the princes. 13 And Michaeas reported to them all the words which he had heard Baruch reading in the ears of the people. 14 And all the princes sent to Baruch son of Nerias

Judin the son of Nathanias, the son of Selemias, the son of Chusi, saying, Take in thine hand the roll in which thou readest in the ears of the people, and come. So Baruch took the roll, and went down to them. 15 And they said to him, Read *it* again in our ears. And Baruch read *it*. 16 And it came to pass, when they *had* heard all the words, *that* they took counsel each with his neighbour, and said, Let us by all means tell the king all these words. 17 And they asked Baruch, saying, Where didst thou write all these words? 18 And Baruch said, Jeremias told me from his *own* mouth all these words, and I wrote them in a book. 19 And they said to Baruch, Go, and hide, thou and Jeremias; let no man know where ye *are*. 20 And they went in to the king into the court, and gave the roll *to one* to keep in the house of Elisama; and they told the king all these words. 21 And the king sent Judin to fetch the roll: and he took it out of the house of Elisama: and Judin read in the ears of the king, and in the ears of all the princes who stood round the king. 22 Now the king was sitting in the winter house: and *there was* a fire on the hearth before him. 23 And it came to pass when Judin had read three or four leaves, he cut them off with a penknife, and cast *them* into the fire that was on the hearth, until the whole roll was consumed in the fire that was on the hearth. 24 And the king and his servants that heard all these words sought not *the Lord*, and rent not their garments. 25 But Elnathan and Godolias suggested to the king that he should burn the roll. 26 And the king commanded Jeremeel the king's son, and Saraeas the son of Esriel, to take Baruch and Jeremias: but they were hidden. 27 Then the word of the Lord came to Jeremias, after the king had burnt the roll, *even* all the words which Baruch wrote from the mouth of Jeremias, saying, 28 Again take thou another roll, and write all the words that were on the roll, which king Joakim has burnt. 29 And thou shalt say, Thus saith the Lord; Thou hast burnt this roll, saying, Why hast thou written therein, saying, The king of Babylon shall certainly come in, and destroy this land, and man and cattle shall fail from off it? 30 Therefore thus saith the Lord concerning Joakim king of Juda; He shall not have *a man* to sit on the throne of David: and his carcass shall be cast forth in the heat by day, and in the frost by night. 31 And I will visit him, and his family, and his servants: and I will bring upon him, and upon the inhabitants of Jerusalem, and upon the land of Juda, all the evils which I spoke of to them; and they hearkened not. 32 And Baruch took another roll, and wrote upon it from the mouth of Jeremias all the words of the book which Joakim had burnt: and there were yet more words added to it like the former.

Jer.44 1 And Sedekias the son of Josias reigned instead of Joakim, whom Nabuchodonosor appointed to reign over Juda. 2 And he and his servants and the people of the land hearkened not to the words of the Lord, which he spoke by Jeremias. 3 And king Sedekias sent Joachal son of Selemias and Sophonias the priest son of Maasaeas to Jeremias, saying, Pray now for us to the Lord. 4 Now Jeremias came and went through the midst of the city: for they *had* not put him into the house of the prison. 5 And the host of Pharao was come forth out of Egypt; and the

Chaldeans heard the report of them, and they went up from Jerusalem. 6 And the word of the Lord came to Jeremias, saying, 7 Thus said the Lord; Thus shalt thou say to the king of Juda who sent to thee, to seek me; Behold, the army of Pharao which is come forth to help you: they shall return to the land of Egypt: 8 and the Chaldeans themselves shall turn again, and fight against this city, and take it, and burn it with fire. 9 For thus saith the Lord; Suppose not in your hearts, saying, The Chaldeans will certainly depart from us: for they shall not depart. 10 And though ye should smite the whole host of the Chaldeans that fight against you, and there should be left a few wounded *men*, these should rise up each in his place, and burn this city with fire. 11 And it came to pass, when the host of the Chaldeans had gone up from Jerusalem for fear of the host of Pharao, 12 that Jeremias went forth from Jerusalem to go into the land of Benjamin, to buy thence *a property* in the midst of the people. 13 And he was in the gate of Benjamin, and *there was* there a man with whom he lodged, Saruia the son of Selemias, the son of Ananias; and he caught Jeremias, saying, Thou art fleeing to the Chaldeans. 14 And he said, *It is* false; I do not flee to the Chaldeans. But he hearkened not to him; and Saruia caught Jeremias, and brought him to the princes. 15 And the princes were very angry with Jeremias, and smote him, and sent him into the house of Jonathan the scribe: for they had made this a prison. 16 So Jeremias came into the dungeon, and into the cells, and he remained there many days. 17 Then Sedekias sent, and called him; and the king asked him secretly, saying, Is there a word from the Lord? and he said, There is: thou shalt be delivered into the hands of the king of Babylon. 18 And Jeremias said to the king, Wherein have I wronged thee, or thy servants, or this people, that thou puttest me in prison? 19 And where are your prophets who prophesied to you saying, The king of Babylon shall not come against this land? 20 Now therefore, my lord the king, let my supplication come before thy face: and why dost thou send me back to the house of Jonathan the scribe? and let me not on any account die there. 21 Then the king commanded, and they cast him into the prison, and gave him a loaf a day out of the place where they bake, until the bread failed out of the city. So Jeremias continued in the court of the prison.

Jer.45 1 And Saphanias the son of Nathan, and Godolias the son of Paschor, and Joachal the son of Semelias, heard the words which Jeremias spoke to the people, saying, 2 Thus saith the Lord; He that remains in this city shall die by the sword, and by the famine: but he that goes out to the Chaldeans shall live; and his soul shall be given him for a found treasure, and he shall live. 3 For thus saith the Lord; This city shall certainly be delivered into the hands of the host of the king of Babylon, and they shall take it. 4 And they said to the king, Let that man, we pray thee, be slain, for he weakens the hands of the fighting men that are left in the city, and the hands of all the people, speaking to them according to these words: for this man does not prophesy peace to this people, but evil. 5 Then the king said, Behold, he is in your hands. For the king could not resist them. 6 And they cast him into the dungeon of Melchias the king's

son, which was in the court of the prison; and they let him down into the pit: and there was no water in the pit, but mire: and he was in the mire. 7 And Abdemelech the Ethiopian heard, (now he was in the king's household,) that they *had* put Jeremias into the dungeon; and the king was in the gate of Benjamin: 8 and he went forth to him, and spoke to the king and said, 9 Thou hast done evil in what thou hast done to slay this man with hunger: for there is no more bread in the city. 10 And the king commanded Abdemelech, saying, Take with thee hence thirty men, and bring him up out of the dungeon, that he die not. 11 So Abdemelech took the men and went into the underground *part of the* king's house, and took thence old rags and old ropes, and threw them to Jeremias into the dungeon. 12 And he said, Put these under the ropes. And Jeremias did so. 13 And they drew him with the ropes, and lifted him out of the dungeon: and Jeremias remained in the court of the prison. 14 Then the king sent, and called him to himself into the house of Aselisel, which was in the house of the Lord: and the king said to him, I will ask thee a question, and I pray thee hide nothing from me. 15 And Jeremias said to the king, If I tell thee, wilt thou not certainly put me to death? and if I give thee counsel, thou wilt not at all hearken to me. 16 And the king swore to him, saying, *As* the Lord lives who gave us this soul, I will not slay thee, neither will I give thee into the hands of these men. 17 And Jeremias said to him, Thus saith the Lord; If thou wilt indeed go forth to the captains of the king of Babylon, thy soul shall live, and this city shall certainly not be burnt with fire; and thou shalt live, and thy house. 18 But if thou wilt not go forth this city shall be delivered into the hands of the Chaldeans, and they shall burn it with fire, and thou shalt by no means escape. 19 And the king said to Jeremias, I consider the Jews that have gone over to the Chaldeans, lest they deliver me into their hands, and they mock me. 20 And Jeremias said, They shall in no wise deliver thee up. Hear the word of the Lord which I speak to thee; and it shall be better for thee, and thy soul shall live. 21 But if thou wilt not go forth, this is the word which the Lord has shewn me. 22 And, behold, all the women that are left in the house of the king of Juda were brought forth to the princes of the king of Babylon; and they said, The men who were at peace with thee have deceived thee, and will prevail against thee; and they shall cause thy foot to slide and fail, they have turned back from thee. 23 And they shall bring forth thy wives and thy children to the Chaldeans: and thou shalt by no means escape, for thou shalt be taken by the hand of the king of Babylon, and this city shall be burnt. 24 Then the king said to him, Let no man know *any* of these words, and certainly thou shalt not die. 25 And if the princes shall hear that I have spoken to thee, and they come to thee, and say to thee, Tell us, what said the king to thee? hide *it* not from us, and we will in no wise slay thee, and what said the king to thee? 26 Then thou shalt say to them, I brought my supplication before the presence of the king, that he would not send me back into the house of Jonathan, that I should die there. 27 And all the princes came to Jeremias, and asked him: and he told them according to all these words, which the king had commanded him. And they were silent, because the word of the Lord was not heard. [28] And Jeremias remained in the court of the prison, until the time when Jerusalem was taken.

Jer.46 [1] And it came to pass in the ninth month of Sedekias king of Juda, *that* Nabuchodonosor king of Babylon came, and all his host, against Jerusalem, and they besieged it. [2] And in the eleventh year of Sedekiass, in the fourth month, on the ninth day of the month, the city was broken *up*. [3] And all the leaders of the king of Babylon went in, and sat in the middle gate, Marganasar, and Samagoth, and Nabusachar, and Nabusaris, Nagargas, Naserrabamath, and the rest of the leaders of the king of Babylon, [4 5 6 7 8 9 10 11 12 13 14] and they sent, and took Jeremias out of the court of the prison, and gave him *in charge* to Godolias the son of Achicam, the son of Saphan: and they brought him out, and he sat in the midst of the people. [15] And the word of the Lord came to Jeremias in the court of the prison, saying, [16] Go and say to Abdemelech the Ethiopian, Thus said the Lord God of Israel; Behold, I *will* bring my words upon this city for evil, and not for good. [17] But I will save thee in that day, and I will by no means deliver thee into the hands of the men before whom thou art afraid. [18] For I will surely save thee, and thou shalt by no means fall by the sword; and thou shalt find thy life, because thou didst trust in me, saith the Lord.

Jer.47 [1] The word that came from the Lord to Jeremias, after that Nabuzardan the captain of the guard had let him go out of Rama, when he had taken him in manacles in the midst of the captivity of Juda, *even* those who were carried to Babylon. [2] And the chief captain of the guard took him, and said to him, The Lord thy God has pronounced all these evils upon this place: [3] and the Lord has done it; because ye sinned against him, and hearkened not to his voice. [4] Behold, I have loosed thee from the manacles that were upon thine hands. If it seem good to thee to go with me to Babylon, then will I set mine eyes upon thee. [5] But if not, depart; return to Godolias the son of Achicam, the son of Saphan, whom the king of Babylon has appointed governor in the land of Juda, and dwell with him in the midst of the people in the land of Juda: to whatsoever places it seems good in thine eyes to go, do thou even go. And the captain of the guard made him presents, and let him go. [6] And he came to Godolias to Massepha, and dwelt in the midst of his people that was left in the land. [7] And all the leaders of the host that was in the country, they and their men, heard that the king of Babylon had appointed Godolias *governor* in the land, and they committed to him the men and their wives, whom *Nabuchodonosor had* not removed to Babylon. [8] And there came to Godolias to Massepha Ismael the son of Nathanias, and Joanan son of Caree, and Saraeas the son of Thanaemeth, and the sons of Jophe the Netophathite, and Ezonias son of the Mochathite, they and their men. [9] And Godolias swore to them and to their men, saying, Be not afraid before the children of the Chaldeans: dwell in the land, and serve the king of Babylon, and it shall be better for you. [10] And, behold, I dwell in your presence at Massepha, to stand before the Chaldeans who shall come against you: and do

ye gather grapes, and fruits, and oil, and put *them* into your vessels, and dwell in the cities which ye have obtained possession of. [11] And all the Jews that were in Moab, and among the children of Ammon, and those *that were* in Idumea, and those *that were* in all *the rest of* the country, heard that the king of Babylon *had* granted a remnant to Juda, and that he had appointed over them Godolias the son of Achicam. [12] And they came to Godolias into the land of Juda, to Massepha, and gathered grapes, and very much summer fruit, and oil. [13] And Joanan the son of Caree, and all the leaders of the host, who were in the fields, came to Godolias to Massepha, [14] and said to him, Dost thou indeed know that king Beleissa son of Ammon has sent Ismael to thee to slay thee? But Godolias believed them not. [15] And Joanan said to Godolias secretly in Massepha, I will go now and smite Ismael, and let no man know *it*; lest he slay thee, and all the Jews that are gathered to thee be dispersed, and the remnant of Juda perish. [16] But Godolias said to Joanan, Do not the thing, for thou speakest lies concerning Ismael.

Jer.48 [1] Now it came to pass in the seventh month that Ismael the son of Nathanias the son of Eleasa of the seed royal, came, and ten men with him, to Godolias to Massepha: and they ate bread there together. [2] And Ismael rose up, and the ten men that were with him, and smote Godolias, whom the king of Babylon had appointed *governor* over the land, [3] and all the Jews that were with him in Massepha, and all the Chaldeans that were found there. [4] And it came to pass on the second day after he had smitten Godolias, and no man knew *of it*, [5] that there came men from Sychem, and from Salem, and from Samaria, *even* eighty men, having their beards shaven, and their clothes rent, and beating their breasts, and *they had* manna and frankincense in their hands, to bring *them* into the house of the Lord. [6] And Ismael went out to meet them; *and* they went on and wept: and he said to them, Come in to Godolias. [7] And it came to pass, when they had entered into the midst of the city, *that* he slew them *and cast them* into a pit. [8] But ten men were found there, and they said to Ismael, Slay us not: for we have treasures in the field, wheat and barley, honey and oil. So he passed by, and slew them not in the midst of their brethren. [9] Now the pit into which Ismael cast all whom he smote, is the great pit, which king Asa had made for fear of Baasa king of Israel: *even* this Ismael filled with slain men. [10] And Ismael brought back all the people that were left in Massepha, and the king's daughter, whom the captain of the guard had committed in charge to Godolias the son of Achicam: and he went away beyond the children of Ammon. [11] And Joanan the son of Caree, and all the leaders of the host that were with him, heard of all the evil deeds which Ismael had done. [12] And they brought all their army, and went to fight against him, and found him near much water in Gabaon. [13] And it came to pass, when all the people that was with Ismael saw Joanan, and the leaders of the host that was with him, [14] that they returned to Joanan. [15] But Ismael escaped with eight men and went to the children of Ammon. [16] And Joanan, and all the leaders of the host that were with him, took all the remnant of the people, whom he *had* brought back from Ismael, mighty men in war, and the women, and the other *property*, and the eunuchs, whom they *had* brought back from Gabaon: 17 and they departed, and dwelt in Gaberoch-amaa, that is by Bethleem, to go into Egypt, for fear of the Chaldeans: 18 for they were afraid of them, because Ismael had smitten Godolias, whom the king of Babylon made *governor* in the land.

Jer.49 1 Then came all the leaders of the host, and Joanan, and Azarias the son of Maasaeas, and all the people great and small, 2 to Jeremias the prophet, and said to him, Let now our supplication come before thy face, and pray thou to the Lord thy God for this remnant; for we are left few out of many, as thine eyes see. 3 And let the Lord thy God declare to us the way wherein we should walk, and the thing which we should do. 4 And Jeremias said to them, I have heard *you*; behold, I will pray for you to the Lord our God, according to your words; and it shall come to pass, *that* whatsoever word the Lord God shall answer, I will declare *it* to you; I will not hide anything from you. 5 And they said to Jeremias, Let the Lord be between us for a just and faithful witness, if we do not according to every word which the Lord shall send to us. 6 And whether *it be* good, or whether *it be* evil, we will hearken to the voice of the Lord our God, to whom we send thee; that it may be well with us, because we shall hearken to the voice of the Lord our God. 7 And it came to pass after ten days, *that* the word of the Lord came to Jeremias. 8 And he called Joanan, and the leaders of the host, and all the people from the least even to the greatest, 9 and he said to them, Thus saith the Lord; 10 If ye will indeed dwell in this land, I will build you, and will not pull *you* down, but will plant you, and in no wise pluck you up: for I have ceased from the calamities which I brought upon you. 11 Be not afraid of the king of Babylon, of whom ye are afraid; be not afraid of him, saith the Lord: for I am with you, to deliver you, and save you out of their hand. 12 And I will grant you mercy, and pity you, and will restore you to your land. 13 But if ye say, We will not dwell in this land, that we may not hearken to the voice of the Lord; 14 for we will go into the land of Egypt, and we shall see no war, and shall not hear the sound of a trumpet, and we shall not hunger for bread; and there we will dwell: 15 then hear the word of the Lord; thus saith the Lord; 16 If ye set your face toward Egypt, and go in there to dwell; then it shall be, *that* the sword which ye fear shall find you in the land of Egypt, and the famine to which ye have regard, shall overtake you, *coming* after you in Egypt; and there ye shall die. 17 And all the men, and all the strangers who have set their face toward the land of Egypt to dwell there, shall be consumed by the sword, and by the famine: and there shall not one of them escape from the evils which I bring upon them. 18 For thus saith the Lord; As my wrath has dropped upon the inhabitants of Jerusalem, so shall my wrath drop upon you, when ye have entered into Egypt: and ye shall be a desolation, and under the power of others, and a curse and a reproach: and ye shall no more see this place. 19 *These are the words* which the Lord has spoken concerning you the remnant of Juda; Enter ye not into Egypt: and now know ye for a certainty, 20 that ye have wrought wickedness in your hearts, when ye sent me, saying, Pray thou for us to the Lord; and according to all that the Lord shall speak to thee we will do. 21 And ye have not hearkened to the voice of the Lord, with which he sent me to you. 22 Now therefore ye shall perish by sword and by famine, in the place which ye desire to go into to dwell there.

Jer.50 1 And it came to pass, when Jeremias ceased speaking to the people all the words of the Lord, *for* which the Lord had sent him to them, *even* all these words, 2 that Azarias son of Maasaeas spoke, and Joanan, the son of Caree, and all the men who had spoken to Jeremias, saying, *It is* false: the Lord has not sent thee to us, saying, Enter not into Egypt to dwell there: 3 but Baruch the son of Nerias sets thee against us, that thou mayest deliver us into the hands of the Chaldeans, to kill us, and that we should be carried away captives to Babylon. 4 So Joanan, and all the leaders of the host, and all the people, refused to hearken to the voice of the Lord, to dwell in the land of Juda. 5 And Joanan, and all the leaders of the host, took all the remnant of Juda, who had returned to dwell in the land; 6 the mighty men, and the women, and the children that were left, and the daughters of the king, and the souls which Nabuzardan had left with Godolias the son of Achicam and Jeremias the prophet, and Baruch the son of Nerias. 7 And they came into Egypt: for they hearkened not to the voice of the Lord: and they entered into Taphnas. 8 And the word of the Lord came to Jeremias in Taphnas, saying, 9 Take thee great stones, and hide them in the entrance, at the gate of the house of Pharao in Taphnas, in the sight of the men of Juda: 10 and thou shalt say, Thus has the Lord said; Behold, I *will* send, and will bring Nabuchodonosor king of Babylon, and he shall place his throne upon these stones which thou hast hidden, and he shall lift up weapons against them. 11 And he shall enter in, and smite the land of Egypt, *delivering* some for death to death; and some for captivity to captivity; and some for the sword to the sword. 12 And he shall kindle a fire in the houses of their gods, and shall burn them, and shall carry them away captives: and shall search the land of Egypt, as a shepherd searches his garment; and he shall go forth in peace. 13 And he shall break to pieces the pillars of Heliopolis that are in On, and shall burn their houses with fire.

Jer.51 1 THE WORD THAT CAME TO JEREMIAS for all the Jews dwelling in the land of Egypt, and for those settled in Magdolo and in Taphnas, and in the land of Pathura, saying, 2 Thus has the Lord God of Israel said; Ye have seen all the evils which I have brought upon Jerusalem, and upon the cities of Juda; and, behold, they are desolate without inhabitants, 3 because of their wickedness, which they have wrought to provoke me, *by* going to burn incense to other gods, whom ye knew not. 4 yet I sent to you my servants the prophets early in the morning, and I sent, saying, Do not ye this abominable thing which I hate. 5 But they hearkened not to me, and inclined not their ear to turn from their wickedness, so as not to burn incense to strange gods. 6 So mine anger and my wrath dropped *upon them*, and was kindled in the gates of Juda, and in the streets of Jerusalem; and they became a desolation and a waste, as at this day. 7 And now thus has the Lord Almighty said, Wherefore do ye commit *these* great evils against your souls? to cut off man and woman of you, infant and suckling from the midst of Juda, to the end that not one of you should be left; 8 by provoking me with the works of your hands, to burn incense to other gods in the land of Egypt, into which ye entered to dwell there, that ye might be cut off, and that ye might become a curse and a reproach among all the nations of the earth? 9 Have ye forgotten the sins of your fathers, and the sins of the kings of Juda, and the sins of your princes, and the sins of your wives, which they wrought in the land of Juda, and in the streets of Jerusalem? 10 And have not ceased even to this day, and they have not kept to my ordinances, which I set before their fathers. 11 Therefore thus saith the Lord; Behold I do set my face against *you* 12 to destroy all the remnant that are in Egypt; and they shall fall by the sword, and by famine, and shall be consumed small and great: and they shall be for reproach, and for destruction, and for a curse. 13 And I will visit them that dwell in the land of Egypt, as I have visited Jerusalem, with sword and with famine: 14 and there shall not one be preserved of the remnant of Juda that sojourn in the land of Egypt, to return to the land of Juda, to which they hope in their hearts to return: they shall not return, but only they that escape. 15 Then all the men that knew that their wives burned incense, and all the women, a great multitude, and all the people that dwelt in the land of Egypt, in Pathura, answered Jeremias, saying, 16 *As for* the word which thou hast spoken to us in the name of the Lord, we will not hearken to thee. 17 For we will surely perform every word that shall proceed out of our mouth, to burn incense to the queen of heaven, and to pour drink-offerings to her, as we and our fathers have done, and our kings and princes, in the cities of Juda, and in the streets of Jerusalem: and *so* we were filled with bread, and were well, and saw no evils. 18 But since we left off to burn incense to the queen of heaven, we have all been brought low, and have been consumed by sword and by famine. 19 And whereas we burned incense to the queen of heaven, and poured drink- offerings to her, did we make cakes to her, and pour drink-offerings to her, without our husbands? 20 Then Jeremias answered all the people, the mighty men, and the women, and all the people that returned him *these* words for answer, saying, 21 Did not the Lord remember the incense which ye burned in the cities of Juda, and in the streets of Jerusalem, ye, and your fathers, and your kings, and your princes, and the people of the land? and came it not into his heart? 22 And the Lord could no longer bear *you*, because of the wickedness of your doings, and because of your abominations which ye wrought; and so your land became a desolation and a waste, and a curse, as at this day; 23 because of your burning incense, and *because* of the things wherein ye sinned against the Lord: and ye have not hearkened to the voice of the Lord, and have not walked in his ordinances, and in his law, and in his testimonies; and so these evils have come upon you. 24 And Jeremias said to the people, and to the women, Hear ye the word of the Lord. 25 Thus has the Lord God of Israel said; Ye women have spoken with your mouth, and ye fulfilled *it* with your hands, saying, We will surely perform our vows that we have vowed, to burn incense to the queen of heaven, and to pour drink-offerings to her: full well did ye keep to your vows, and ye have indeed performed *them*. 26 Therefore hear ye the word of the Lord, all Jews dwelling in the land of Egypt; Behold, I have sworn by my great name, saith the Lord, my name shall no longer be in the mouth of every Jew to say, The Lord lives, in all the land of Egypt. 27 For I have watched over them, to hurt them, and not to do them good: and all the Jews dwelling in the land of Egypt shall perish by sword and by famine, until they are utterly consumed. 28 And they that escape the sword shall return to the land of Juda few in number, and the remnant of Juda, who have continued in the land *of* Egypt to dwell there, shall know whose word shall stand. 29 And this *shall be* a sign to you, that I will visit you for evil. 30 Thus said the Lord; Behold, I *will* give Uaphres king of Egypt into the hands of his enemy, and into the hands of one that seeks his life; as I gave Sedekias king of Juda into the hands of Nabuchodonosor king of Babylon, his enemy, and who sought his life.

Jer.52 1 THE WORD WHICH JEREMIAS THE PROPHET spoke to Baruch son of Nerias, when he wrote these words in the book from the mouth of Jeremias, in the fourth year of Joakim the son of Josias king of Juda. 2 Thus has the Lord said to thee, O Baruch. 3 Whereas thou hast said, Alas! alas! for the Lord has laid a grievous trouble upon me; I lay down in groaning, I found no rest; 4 say thou to him, Thus saith the Lord; Behold, I pull down those whom I have built up, and I pluck up those whom I have planted. 5 And wilt thou seek great things for thyself? seek *them* not: for, behold, I bring evil upon all flesh, saith the Lord: but I will give *to thee* thy life for a spoil in every place whither thou shalt go. It was the twenty-first year of Sedekias, when he began to reign, and he reigned eleven years in Jerusalem. And his mother's name was Amitaal, the daughter of Jeremias, of Lobena. 4 And it came to pass in the ninth year of his reign, in the ninth month, on the tenth day of the month, *that* Nabuchodonosor king of Babylon came, and all his host, against Jerusalem, and they made a rampart round it, and built a wall round about it with large stones. 5 So the city was besieged, until the eleventh year of king Sedekias, 6 on the ninth day of the month, and *then* the famine was severe in the city, and there was no bread for the people of the land. 7 And the city was broken up, and all the men of war went out by night by the way of the gate, between the wall and the outworks, which were by the king's garden; and the Chaldeans were by the city round about; and they went by the way *leading* to the wilderness. 8 But the host of the Chaldeans pursued after the king, and overtook him in the *country* beyond Jericho; and all his servants were dispersed from *about* him. 9 And they took the king, and brought him to the king of Babylon to Deblatha, and he judged him. 10 And the king of Babylon slew the sons of Sedekias before his eyes; and he slew all the princes of Juda in Deblatha. 11 And he put out the eyes of Sedekias, and bound him in fetters; and the king of

Babylon brought him to Babylon, and put him into the grinding-house, until the day when he died. 12 And in the fifth month, on the tenth day of the month, Nabuzardan the captain of the guard, who waited on the king of Babylon, came to Jerusalem; 13 and he burnt the house of the Lord, and the king's house; and all the houses of the city, and every great house he burnt with fire. 14 And the host of the Chaldeans that was with the captain of the guard pulled down all the wall of Jerusalem round about. 15 16 But the captain of the guard left the remnant of the people to be vinedressers and husbandmen. 17 And the Chaldeans broke in pieces the brazen pillars that were in the house of the Lord, and the bases, and the brazen sea that was in the house of the Lord, and they took the brass thereof, and carried it away to Babylon. 18 Also the rim, and the bowls, and the flesh-hooks, and all the brazen vessels, wherewith they ministered; 19 and the basons, and the snuffers, and the oil- funnels, and the candlesticks, and the censers, and the cups, the golden, of gold, and the silver, of silver, the captain of the guard took away. 20 And the two pillars, and the one sea, and the twelve brazen oxen under the sea, which *things* king Solomon made for the house of the Lord; the brass of which *articles* was without weight. 21 And as for the pillars, the height of one pillar was thirty-five cubits; and a line of twelve cubits compassed it round; and the thickness of it *all* round was four fingers. 22 And *there was* a brazen chapiter upon them, and the length was five cubits, *even* the height of one chapiter; and *there were* on the chapiter round about network and pomegranates, all of brass: and correspondingly the second pillar *had* eight pomegranates to a cubit for the twelve cubits. 23 And the pomegranates were ninety-six on a side; and all the pomegranates on the network round about were a hundred. 24 And the captain of the guard took the chief priest, and the second priest, and those that kept the way; 25 and one eunuch, who was over the men of war, and seven men of renown, who were in the king's presence that were found in the city; and the scribe of the forces, who did the part of a scribe to the people of the land; and sixty men of the people of the land, who were found in the midst of the city. 26 And Nabuzardan the captain of the king's guard took them, and brought them to the king of Babylon to Deblatha. 27 And the king of Babylon smote them in Deblatha, in the land of Æmath. 28 29 30 31 And it came to pass in the thirty-seventh year after that Joakim king of Juda had been carried away captive, in the twelfth month, on the four and twentieth *day* of the month, *that* Ulaemadachar king of Babylon, in the year in which he began to reign, raised the head of Joakim king of Juda, and shaved him, and brought him out of the house where he was kept, 32 and spoke kindly to him, and set his throne above the kings that were with him in Babylon, 33 and changed his prison garments: and he ate bread continually before him all the days that he lived. 34 And his appointed portion was given him continually by the king of Babylon from day to day, until the day when he died.

LAMENTATIONS

Lam.1 And it came to pass, after Israel was taken captive, and Jerusalem made desolate, *that* Jeremias sat weeping, and lamented *with* this lamentation over Jerusalem, and said, 1:1 ALEPH. How does the city that was filled with people sit solitary! she is become as a widow: she that was magnified among the nations, *and* princess among the provinces, has become tributary. 2 BETH. She weeps sore in the night, and her tears are on her cheeks; and there is none of all her lovers to comfort her: all that were her friends have dealt deceitfully with her, they are become her enemies. 3 GIMEL. Judea is gone into captivity by reason of her affliction, and by reason of the abundance of her servitude: she dwells among the nations, she has not found rest: all her pursuers have overtaken her between her oppressors. 4 DALETH. The ways of Sion mourn, because there are none that come to the feast: all her gates are ruined: her priests groan, her virgins are led captive, and she is in bitterness in herself. 5 HE. Her oppressors are become the head, and her enemies have prospered; for the Lord has afflicted her because of the multitude of her sins: her young children are gone into captivity before the face of the oppressor. 6 VAU. And all her beauty has been taken away from the daughter of Sion: her princes were as rams finding no pasture, and are gone *away* in weakness before the face of the pursuer. 7 ZAIN. Jerusalem remembered the days of her affliction, and her rejection; *she thought on* all her desirable things which were from the days of old, when her people fell into the hands of the oppressor, and there was none to help her: when her enemies saw *it* they laughed at her habitation. 8 HETH. Jerusalem has sinned a *great* sin; therefore has she come into tribulation, all that used to honour her have afflicted her, for they have seen her shame: yea, she herself groaned, and turned backward. 9 TETH. Her uncleanness is before her feet; she remembered not her last end; she has lowered her boasting *tone*, there is none to comfort her. Behold, O Lord, my affliction: for the enemy has magnified himself. 10 JOD. The oppressor has stretched out his hand on all her desirable things: for she has seen the Gentiles entering into her sanctuary, *concerning* whom thou didst command that they should not enter into thy congregation. 11 CHAPH. All her people groan, seeking bread: they have given their desirable things for meat, to restore their soul: behold, Lord, and look; for she is become dishonoured. 12 LAMED. All ye that pass by the way, turn, and see if there is sorrow like to my sorrow, which has happened *to me*. The Lord who spoke by me has afflicted me in the day of his fierce anger. 13 MEM. He has sent fire from his lofty habitation, he has brought it into my bones: he has spread a net for my feet, he has turned me back: he has made me desolate *and* mourning all the day. 14 NUN. He has watched over my sins, they are twined about my hands, they have come up on my neck: my strength has failed; for the Lord has laid pains on my hands, I shall not be able to stand. 15 SAMECH. The Lord has cut off all my strong men from the midst of me: he has summoned against me a time for crushing my choice men: the Lord has trodden a wine-press for the virgin daughter of Juda: for these things I weep. 16

AIN. Mine eye has poured out water, because he that should comfort me, that should restore my soul, has been removed far from me: my sons have been destroyed, because the enemy has prevailed. 17 PHE. Sion has spread out her hand, *and* there is none to comfort her: the Lord has commanded *concerning* Jacob, his oppressors are round about him: Jerusalem has become among them as a removed woman. 18 TSADE. The Lord is righteous; for I have provoked his mouth: hear, I pray you, all people, and behold my grief: my virgins and my young men are gone into captivity. 19 KOPH. I called my lovers, but they deceived me: my priests and my elders failed in the city; for they sought meat that they might restore their souls, and found *it* not. 20 RHECHS. Behold, O Lord; for I am afflicted: my belly is troubled, and my heart is turned within me; for I have been grievously rebellious: abroad the sword has bereaved me, even as death at home. 21 CHSEN. Hear, I pray you, for I groan: there is none to comfort me: all mine enemies have heard *of* mine afflictions, and rejoice because thou hast done *it*: thou hast brought on the day, thou hast called the time: they are become like to me. 22 THAU. Let all their wickedness come before thy face; and strip them, as they have made a gleaning for all my sins: for my groans are many, and my heart is grieved.

Lam.2 1 ALEPH. How has the Lord darkened in his wrath the daughter of Sion! he has cast down the glory of Israel from heaven to earth, and has not remembered his footstool. 2 BETH. In the day of his wrath the Lord has overwhelmed *her* as in the sea, *and* not spared: he has brought down in his fury all the beautiful things of Jacob; he has brought down to the ground the strong-holds of the daughter of Juda; he has profaned her kings and her princes. 3 GIMEL. He has broken in his fierce anger all the horn of Israel: he has turned back his right hand from the face of the enemy, and has kindled a flame in Jacob as a fire, and it has devoured all things round about. 4 DALETH. He has bent his bow as an opposing enemy: he has strengthened his right hand as an adversary, and has destroyed all the desirable things of my eyes in the tabernacle of the daughter of Sion: he has poured forth his anger as fire. 5 HE. The Lord is become as an enemy: he has overwhelmed Israel as in the sea, he has overwhelmed her palaces: he has destroyed her strong-holds, and has multiplied the afflicted and humbled ones to the daughter of Juda. 6 VAU. And he has scattered his tabernacle as a vine, he has marred his feast: the Lord has forgotten the feast and the sabbath which he appointed in Sion, and in the fury of his wrath has vexed the king, and priest, and prince. 7 ZAIN. The Lord has rejected his altar, he has cast off his sanctuary, he has broken by the hand of the enemy the wall of her palaces; they have uttered their voice in the house of the Lord as on a feast day. 8 HETH. And he has turned to destroy the wall of the daughter of Sion: he has stretched out the measuring line, he has not turned back his hand from afflicting *her*: therefore the bulwark mourned, and the wall was weakened with it. 9 TETH. Her gates are sunk into the ground: he has destroyed and broken to pieces her bars, *and* her king and her prince among the

Gentiles: there is no law, nay, her prophets have seen no vision from the Lord. 10 JOD. The elders of the daughter of Sion have sat upon the ground, they have kept silence: they have cast up dust upon their heads; they have girded themselves with sackcloths: they have brought down to the ground the chief virgins in Jerusalem. 11 CHAPH. Mine eyes have failed with tears, my heart is troubled, my glory is cast down to the ground, for the destruction of the daughter of my people; while the infant and suckling swoon in the streets of the city. 12 LAMED. They said to their mothers, Where is corn and wine? while they fainted like wounded men in the streets of the city, while their souls were poured out into their mother's bosom. 13 MEM. What shall I testify to thee, or what shall I compare to thee, O daughter of Jerusalem? who shall save and comfort thee, O virgin daughter of Sion? for the cup of thy destruction is enlarged: who shall heal thee? 14 NUN. Thy prophets have seen for thee vanities and folly: and they have not discovered thine iniquity, to turn back thy captivity; but they have seen for thee vain burdens, and worthless visions. 15 SAMECH. All that go by the way have clapped their hands at thee; they have hissed and shaken their head at the daughter of Jerusalem. Is this the city, they say, the crown of joy of all the earth? 16 AIN. All thine enemies have opened their mouth against thee: they have hissed and gnashed their teeth, and said, We have swallowed her up: moreover this is the day which we looked for; we have found it, we have seen it. 17 PHE. The Lord has done that which he purposed; he has accomplished his word, *even* the things which he commanded from the ancient days: he has thrown down, and has not spared: and he has caused the enemy to rejoice over thee, he has exalted the horn of him that afflicted thee. 18 TSADE. Their heart cried to the Lord, Ye walls of Sion, pour down tears like torrents day and night: give thyself no rest; let not the apple of thine eyes cease. 19 KOPH. Arise, rejoice in the night at the beginning of thy watch: pour out thy heart as water before the face of the Lord; lift up thy hands to him for the life of thine infants, who faint for hunger at the top of all the streets. 20 RHECHS. Behold, O Lord, and see for whom thou has gathered thus. Shall the women eat the fruit of their womb? the cook has made a gathering: shall the infants sucking at the breasts be slain? wilt thou slay the priest and prophet in the sanctuary of the Lord? 21 CHSEN. The child and old man have lain down in the street: my virgins and my young men are gone into captivity: thou hast slain *them* with the sword and with famine; in the day of thy wrath thou hast mangled *them*, thou has not spared. 22 THAU. He has called my sojourners round about to a solemn day, and there was not in the day of the wrath of the Lord any one that escaped or was left; whereas I have strengthened and multiplied all mine enemies.

Lam.3 1 ALEPH. I am the man that sees poverty, through the rod of his wrath upon me. 2 He has taken me, and led me away into darkness, and not *into* light. 3 Nay, against me has he turned his hand all the day. 4 He has made old my flesh and my skin; he has broken my bones. 5 BETH. He has built against me, and compassed my head, and brought travail *upon me*. 6 He has set me in dark places, as them that have long been dead. 7 He has builded against me, and I cannot come forth: he has made my brazen *chain* heavy. 8 GIMEL. Yea, *though* I cry and shout, he shuts out my prayer. 9 DALETH. He has built up my ways, he has hedged my paths; 10 he has troubled me, *as* a she- bear lying in wait: he is to me *as* a lion in secret places. 11 He pursued *me* after I departed, and brought me to a stand: he has utterly ruined me. 12 HE. He has bent his bow, and set me as a mark for the arrow. 13 He has caused the arrows of his quiver to enter into my reins. 14 I became a laughing-stock to all my people; and their song all the day. 15 VAU. He has filled me with bitterness, he has drenched me with gall. 16 And he has dashed out my teeth with gravel, he has fed me with ashes. 17 He has also removed my soul from peace: I forgot prosperity. 18 Therefore my success has perished, and my hope from the Lord. 19 ZAIN. I remembered by reason of my poverty, and because of persecution my bitterness and gall shall be remembered; 20 and my soul shall meditate with me. 21 This will I lay up in my heart, therefore I will endure. 22 HETH. *It is* the mercies of the Lord, that he has not failed me, because his compassions are not exhausted. Pity *us*, O Lord, early *every* month: for we are not brought to an end, because his compassions are not exhausted. 23 *They are* new every morning: great is thy faithfulness. 24 The Lord is my portion, says my soul; therefore will I wait for him. 25 TETH. The Lord is good to them that wait for him: the soul which shall seek him 26 *is* good, and shall wait for, and quietly expect salvation of the Lord. 27 TETH. *It is* good for a man when he bears a yoke in his youth. 28 He will sit alone, and be silent, because he has borne *it* upon him. 29 30 JOD. He will give *his* cheek to him that smites him: he will be filled full with reproaches. 31 For the Lord will not reject for ever. 32 CHAPH. For he that has brought down will pity, and *that* according to the abundance of his mercy. 33 He has not answered *in anger* from his heart, though he has brought low the children of a man. 34 LAMED. To bring down under his feet all the prisoners of the earth, 35 to turn aside the judgment of a man before the face of the Most High, 36 to condemn a man *unjustly* in his judgment, the Lord has not given commandment. 37 Who has thus spoken, and it has come to pass? the Lord has not commanded it. 38 Out of the mouth of the Most High there shall not come forth evil and good. 39 MEM. Why should a living man complain, a man concerning his sin? 40 NUN. Our way has been searched out and examined, and we will turn to the Lord. 41 Let us lift up our hearts with *our* hand to the lofty One in heaven. 42 We have sinned, we have transgressed; and thou hast not pardoned. 43 SAMECH. Thou has visited *us* in wrath, and driven us away: thou has slain, thou has not pitied. 44 Thou hast veiled thyself with a cloud because of prayer, that I might be blind, 45 and be cast off. AIN. Thou hast set us *alone* in the midst of the nations. 46 All our enemies have opened their mouth against us. 47 Fear and wrath are come upon us, suspense and destruction. 48 Mine eye shall pour down torrents of water, for the destruction of the daughter of my people. 49 PHE. Mine eye is drowned *with tears*, and I will not be silent, so that there shall be no rest, 50 until the Lord look down, and behold from heaven. 51 Mine eye shall prey upon my soul, because of all the daughters of the city. 52 TSADE. The fowlers chased me as a sparrow, all mine enemies destroyed my life in a pit without cause, 53 and laid a stone upon me. 54 Water flowed over my head: I said, I am cut off. 55 KOPH. I called upon thy name, O Lord, out of the lowest dungeon. 56 Thou heardest my voice: close not thine ears to my supplication. 57 Thou drewest nigh to my help: in the day wherein I called upon thee thou saidst to me, Fear not. 58 RECHS. O Lord, thou has pleaded the causes of my soul; thou has redeemed my life. 59 Thou hast seen, O Lord, my troubles: thou hast judged my cause. 60 Thou hast seen all their vengeance, *thou hast looked* on all their devices against me. 61 CHSEN. Thou hast heard their reproach *and* all their devices against me; 62 the lips of them that rose up against me, and their plots against me all the day; 63 their sitting down and their rising up: look thou upon their eyes. 64 Thou wilt render them a recompense, O Lord, according to the works of their hands. 65 THAU. Thou wilt give them *as* a covering, the grief of my heart. 66 Thou wilt persecute them in anger, and wilt consume them from under the heaven, O Lord.

Lam.4 1 ALEPH. How will the gold be tarnished, *and* the fine silver changed! the sacred stones have been poured forth at the top of all the streets. 2 BETH. The precious sons of Zion, who were equalled in value with gold, how are they counted as earthen vessels, the works of the hands of the potter! 3 GIMEL. Nay, serpents have drawn out the breasts, they give suck to their young, the daughters of my people are incurably cruel, as an ostrich in a desert. 4 DALETH. The tongue of the sucking child cleaves to the roof of its mouth for thirst: the little children ask for bread, *and* there is none to break *it* to them. 5 HE. They that feed on dainties are desolate in the streets: they that used to be nursed in scarlet have clothed themselves with dung. 6 VAU. And the iniquity of the daughter of my people has been increased beyond the iniquities of Sodoma, *the city* that was overthrown very suddenly, and none laboured against her *with their* hands. 7 ZAIN. Her Nazarites were made purer than snow, they were whiter than milk, they were purified *as* with fire, their polishing was superior to sapphire stone. 8 HETH. Their countenance is become blacker than smoke; they are not known in the streets: their skin has cleaved to their bones; they are withered, they are become as a stick. 9 TETH. The slain with the sword were better than they that were slain with hunger: they have departed, pierced through from *want of* the fruits of the field. 10 JOD. The hands of tender-hearted women have sodden their own children: they became meat for them in the destruction of the daughter of my people. 11 CHAPH. The Lord has accomplished his wrath; he has poured out fierce anger, and has kindled a fire in Sion, and it has devoured her foundations. 12 LAMED. The kings of the earth, *even all* that dwell in the world, believed not that an enemy and oppressor would enter through the gates of Jerusalem. 13 MEM. For the sins of her prophets, *and* iniquities of her priests, who shed righteous blood in the midst of her, 14 NUN. her watchmen staggered in the streets, they were defiled with blood in their weakness, they touched their raiment *with it*. 15 SAMECH. Depart ye from the unclean ones: call ye them: depart, depart, touch *them* not: for they are on fire, yea, they stagger: say ye among the nations, They shall no more sojourn *there*. 16 AIN. The presence of the Lord *was* their portion; *but* he will not again look upon them: they regarded not the person of the priests, they pitied not the prophets. 17 PHE. While we yet lived our eyes failed, while we looked in vain for our help. TSADE. We looked to a nation that could not save. 18 We have hunted *for* our little ones, that they should not walk in our streets. KOPH. Our time has drawn nigh, our days are fulfilled, our time is come. 19 Our pursuers were swifter than the eagles of the sky, they flew on the mountains, in the wilderness they laid wait for us. 20 RECHS. The breath of our nostrils, *our* anointed Lord, was taken in their destructive snares, of whom we said, In his shadow we shall live among the Gentiles. 21 CHSEN. Rejoice and be glad, O daughter of Idumea, that dwellest in the land: yet the cup of the Lord shall pass through to thee: thou shalt be drunken, and pour forth. 22 THAU. O daughter of Sion, thine iniquity has come to an end; he shall no more carry thee captive: he has visited thine iniquities, O daughter of Edom; he has discovered thy sins.

Lam.5 1 Remember, O Lord, what has happened to us: behold, and look on our reproach. 2 Our inheritance has been turned away to aliens, our houses to strangers: 3 we are become orphans, we have no father, our mothers are as widows. 4 We have drunk our water for money; our wood is sold to us *for a burden* on our neck: 5 we have been persecuted, we have laboured, we have had no rest. 6 Egypt gave the hand *to us*, Assur to their own satisfaction. 7 Our fathers sinned, *and* are not: we have borne their iniquities. 8 Servants have ruled over us: there is none to ransom *us* out of their hand. 9 We shall bring in our bread with *danger of* our lives, because of the sword of the wilderness. 10 Our skin is blackened like an oven; they are convulsed, because of the storms of famine. 11 They humbled the women in Sion, the virgins in the cities of Juda. 12 Princes were hanged up by their hands: the elders were not honoured. 13 The chosen men lifted up *the voice in* weeping, and the youths fainted under the wood. 14 And the elders ceased from the gate, the chosen men ceased from their music. 15 The joy of our heart has ceased; our dance is turned into mourning. 16 The crown has fallen *from* our head: yea, woe to us! for we have sinned. 17 For this has grief come; our heart is sorrowful: for this our eyes are darkened. 18 Over the mountain of Sion, because it is made desolate, foxes have walked therein. 19 But thou, O Lord, shalt dwell for ever; thy throne *shall endure* to generation and generation. 20 Wherefore wilt thou utterly forget us, and abandon us a long time? 21 Turn us, O Lord, to thee, and we shall be turned; and renew our days as before. 22 For thou hast indeed rejected us; thou hast been very wroth against us.

BARUCH

Bar.1 1 And these are the words of the book, which Baruch the son of Nerias, the son of Maasias, the son of Sedecias, the son of Asadias, the son of Chelcias, wrote in Babylon, 2 In the fifth year, and in the seventh day of the month, what time as the Chaldeans took Jerusalem, and burnt it with fire. 3 And Baruch did read the words of this book in the hearing of Jechonias the son of Joachim king of Juda, and in the ears of all the people that came to hear the book, 4 And in the hearing of the nobles, and of the king's sons, and in the hearing of the elders, and of all the people, from the lowest unto the highest, even of all them that dwelt at Babylon by the river Sud. 5 Whereupon they wept, fasted, and prayed before the Lord. 6 They made also a collection of money according to every man's power: 7 And they sent it to Jerusalem unto Joachim the high priest, the son of Chelcias, son of Salom, and to the priests, and to all the people which were found with him at Jerusalem, 8 At the same time when he received the vessels of the house of the Lord, that were carried out of the temple, to return them into the land of Juda, the tenth day of the month Sivan, namely, silver vessels, which Sedecias the son of Josias king of Jada had made, 9 After that Nabuchodonosor king of Babylon had carried away Jechonias, and the princes, and the captives, and the mighty men, and the people of the land, from Jerusalem, and brought them unto Babylon. 10 And they said, Behold, we have sent you money to buy you burnt offerings, and sin offerings, and incense, and prepare ye manna, and offer upon the altar of the Lord our God; 11 And pray for the life of Nabuchodonosor king of Babylon, and for the life of Balthasar his son, that their days may be upon earth as the days of heaven: 12 And the Lord will give us strength, and lighten our eyes, and we shall live under the shadow of Nabuchodonosor king of Babylon, and under the shadow of Balthasar his son, and we shall serve them many days, and find favour in their sight. 13 Pray for us also unto the Lord our God, for we have sinned against the Lord our God; and unto this day the fury of the Lord and his wrath is not turned from us. 14 And ye shall read this book which we have sent unto you, to make confession in the house of the Lord, upon the feasts and solemn days. 15 And ye shall say, To the Lord our God belongeth righteousness, but unto us the confusion of faces, as it is come to pass this day, unto them of Juda, and to the inhabitants of Jerusalem, 16 And to our kings, and to our princes, and to our priests, and to our prophets, and to our fathers: 17 For we have sinned before the Lord, 18 And disobeyed him, and have not hearkened unto the voice of the Lord our God, to walk in the commandments that he gave us openly: 19 Since the day that the Lord brought our forefathers out of the land of Egypt, unto this present day, we have been disobedient unto the Lord our God, and have been negligent in not hearing his voice. 20 Wherefore the evils cleaved unto us, and the curse, which the Lord appointed by Moses his servant at the time that he brought our fathers out of the land of Egypt, to give us a land that floweth with milk and honey, like as it is to see this day. 21 Nevertheless we have not hearkened unto the voice of the Lord our God, according unto all the words of the prophets, whom he sent unto us: 22 But every man followed the imagination of his own wicked heart, to serve strange gods, and to do evil in the sight of the Lord our God.

Bar.2 1 Therefore the Lord hath made good his word, which he pronounced against us, and against our judges that judged Israel, and against our kings, and against our princes, and against the men of Israel and Juda, 2 To bring upon us great plagues, such as never happened under the whole heaven, as it came to pass in Jerusalem, according to the things that were written in the law of Moses; 3 That a man should eat the flesh of his own son, and the flesh of his own daughter. 4 Moreover he hath delivered them to be in subjection to all the kingdoms that are round about us, to be as a reproach and desolation among all the people round about, where the Lord hath scattered them. 5 Thus we were cast down, and not exalted, because we have sinned against the Lord our God, and have not been obedient unto his voice. 6 To the Lord our God appertaineth righteousness: but unto us and to our fathers open shame, as appeareth this day. 7 For all these plagues are come upon us, which the Lord hath pronounced against us 8 Yet have we not prayed before the Lord, that we might turn every one from the imaginations of his wicked heart. 9 Wherefore the Lord watched over us for evil, and the Lord hath brought it upon us: for the Lord is righteous in all his works which he hath commanded us. 10 Yet we have not hearkened unto his voice, to walk in the commandments of the Lord, that he hath set before us. 11 And now, O Lord God of Israel, that hast brought thy people out of the land of Egypt with a mighty hand, and high arm, and with signs, and with wonders, and with great power, and hast gotten thyself a name, as appeareth this day: 12 O Lord our God, we have sinned, we have done ungodly, we have dealt unrighteously in all thine ordinances. 13 Let thy wrath turn from us: for we are but a few left among the heathen, where thou hast scattered us. 14 Hear our prayers, O Lord, and our petitions, and deliver us for thine own sake, and give us favour in the sight of them which have led us away: 15 That all the earth may know that thou art the Lord our God, because Israel and his posterity is called by thy name. 16 O Lord, look down from thine holy house, and consider us: bow down thine ear, O Lord, to hear us. 17 Open thine eyes, and behold; for the dead that are in the graves, whose souls are taken from their bodies, will give unto the Lord neither praise nor righteousness: 18 But the soul that is greatly vexed, which goeth stooping and feeble, and the eyes that fail, and the hungry soul, will give thee praise and righteousness, O Lord. 19 Therefore we do not make our humble supplication before thee, O Lord our God, for the righteousness of our fathers, and of our kings. 20 For thou hast sent out thy wrath and indignation upon us, as thou hast spoken by thy servants the prophets, saying, 21 Thus saith the Lord, Bow down your shoulders to serve the king of Babylon: so shall ye remain in the land that I gave unto your fathers. 22 But if ye will not hear the voice of the Lord, to serve the king of Babylon, 23 I will cause to cease out of the cites of Judah, and from without Jerusalem, the voice of mirth, and the voice of joy, the voice of the bridegroom, and the voice of the bride: and the whole land shall be desolate of inhabitants. 24 But we would not hearken unto thy voice, to serve the king of Babylon: therefore hast thou made good the words that thou spakest by thy servants the

prophets, namely, that the bones of our kings, and the bones of our fathers, should be taken out of their place. 25 And, lo, they are cast out to the heat of the day, and to the frost of the night, and they died in great miseries by famine, by sword, and by pestilence. 26 And the house which is called by thy name hast thou laid waste, as it is to be seen this day, for the wickedness of the house of Israel and the house of Juda. 27 O Lord our God, thou hast dealt with us after all thy goodness, and according to all that great mercy of thine, 28 As thou spakest by thy servant Moses in the day when thou didst command him to write the law before the children of Israel, saying, 29 If ye will not hear my voice, surely this very great multitude shall be turned into a small number among the nations, where I will scatter them. 30 For I knew that they would not hear me, because it is a stiffnecked people: but in the land of their captivities they shall remember themselves. 31 And shall know that I am the Lord their God: for I will give them an heart, and ears to hear: 32 And they shall praise me in the land of their captivity, and think upon my name, 33 And return from their stiff neck, and from their wicked deeds: for they shall remember the way of their fathers, which sinned before the Lord. 34 And I will bring them again into the land which I promised with an oath unto their fathers, Abraham, Isaac, and Jacob, and they shall be lords of it: and I will increase them, and they shall not be diminished. 35 And I will make an everlasting covenant with them to be their God, and they shall be my people: and I will no more drive my people of Israel out of the land that I have given them.

Bar.3 1 O Lord Almighty, God of Israel, the soul in anguish the troubled spirit, crieth unto thee. 2 Hear, O Lord, and have mercy; ar thou art merciful: and have pity upon us, because we have sinned before thee. 3 For thou endurest for ever, and we perish utterly. 4 O Lord Almighty, thou God of Israel, hear now the prayers of the dead Israelites, and of their children, which have sinned before thee, and not hearkened unto the voice of thee their God: for the which cause these plagues cleave unto us. 5 Remember not the iniquities of our forefathers: but think upon thy power and thy name now at this time. 6 For thou art the Lord our God, and thee, O Lord, will we praise. 7 And for this cause thou hast put thy fear in our hearts, to the intent that we should call upon thy name, and praise thee in our captivity: for we have called to mind all the iniquity of our forefathers, that sinned before thee. 8 Behold, we are yet this day in our captivity, where thou hast scattered us, for a reproach and a curse, and to be subject to payments, according to all the iniquities of our fathers, which departed from the Lord our God. 9 Hear, Israel, the commandments of life: give ear to understand wisdom. 10 How happeneth it Israel, that thou art in thine enemies' land, that thou art waxen old in a strange country, that thou art defiled with the dead, 11 That thou art counted with them that go down into the grave? 12 Thou hast forsaken the fountain of wisdom. 13 For if thou hadst walked in the way of God, thou shouldest have dwelled in peace for ever. 14 Learn where is wisdom, where is strength, where is understanding; that thou mayest know also where is length of days, and life, where is the light of the eyes, and peace. 15 Who hath found out her place? or who hath come into her treasures? 16 Where are the princes of the heathen become, and such as ruled the beasts upon the earth; 17 They that had their pastime with the fowls of the air, and they that hoarded up silver and gold, wherein men trust, and made no end of their getting? 18 For they that wrought in silver, and were so careful, and whose works are unsearchable, 19 They are vanished and gone down to the grave, and others are come up in their steads. 20 Young men have seen light, and dwelt upon the earth: but the way of knowledge have they not known, 21 Nor understood the paths thereof, nor laid hold of it: their children were far off from that way. 22 It hath not been heard of in Chanaan, neither hath it been seen in Theman. 23 The Agarenes that seek wisdom upon earth, the merchants of Meran and of Theman, the authors of fables, and searchers out of understanding; none of these have known the way of wisdom, or remember her paths. 24 O Israel, how great is the house of God! and how large is the place of his possession! 25 Great, and hath none end; high, and unmeasurable. 26 There were the giants famous from the beginning, that were of so great stature, and so expert in war. 27 Those did not the Lord choose, neither gave he the way of knowledge unto them: 28 But they were destroyed, because they had no wisdom, and perished through their own foolishness. 29 Who hath gone up into heaven, and taken her, and brought her down from the clouds? 30 Who hath gone over the sea, and found her, and will bring her for pure gold? 31 No man knoweth her way, nor thinketh of her path. 32 But he that knoweth all things knoweth her, and hath found her out with his understanding: he that prepared the earth for evermore hath filled it with fourfooted beasts: 33 He that sendeth forth light, and it goeth, calleth it again, and it obeyeth him with fear. 34 The stars shined in their watches, and rejoiced: when he calleth them, they say, Here we be; and so with cheerfulness they shewed light unto him that made them. 35 This is our God, and there shall none other be accounted of in comparison of him 36 He hath found out all the way of knowledge, and hath given it unto Jacob his servant, and to Israel his beloved. 37 Afterward did he shew himself upon earth, and conversed with men.

Bar.4 1 This is the book of the commandments of God, and the law that endureth for ever: all they that keep it shall come to life; but such as leave it shall die. 2 Turn thee, O Jacob, and take hold of it: walk in the presence of the light thereof, that thou mayest be illuminated. 3 Give not thine honour to another, nor the things that are profitable unto thee to a strange nation. 4 O Israel, happy are we: for things that are pleasing to God are made known unto us. 5 Be of good cheer, my people, the memorial of Israel. 6 Ye were sold to the nations, not for *your* destruction: but because ye moved God to wrath, ye were delivered unto the enemies. 7 For ye provoked him that made you by sacrificing unto devils, and not to God. 8 Ye have forgotten the everlasting God, that brought you up; and ye have grieved Jerusalem, that nursed you. 9 For when she saw the wrath of God coming upon you, she said, Hearken, O ye that dwell about Sion: God hath brought upon me great mourning; 10 For I saw the captivity of my sons and daughters, which the Everlasting brought upon them. 11 With joy did I nourish them; but sent them away with weeping and mourning. 12 Let no man rejoice over me, a widow, and forsaken of many, who for the sins of my children am left desolate; because they departed from the law of God. 13 They knew not his statutes, nor walked in the ways of his commandments, nor trod in the paths of discipline in his righteousness. 14 Let them that dwell about Sion come, and remember ye the captivity of my sons and daughters, which the Everlasting hath brought upon them. 15 For he hath brought a nation upon them from far, a shameless nation, and of a strange language, who neither reverenced old man, nor pitied child. 16 These have carried away the dear beloved children of the widow, and left her that was alone desolate without daughters. 17 But what can I help you? 18 For he that brought these plagues upon you will deliver you from the hands of your enemies. 19 Go your way, O my children, go your way: for I am left desolate. 20 I have put off the clothing of peace, and put upon me the sackcloth of my prayer: I will cry unto the Everlasting in my days. 21 Be of good cheer, O my children, cry unto the Lord, and he will deliver you from the power and hand of the enemies. 22 For my hope is in the Everlasting, that he will save you; and joy is come unto me from the Holy One, because of the mercy which shall soon come unto you from the Everlasting our Saviour. 23 For I sent you out with mourning and weeping: but God will give you to me again with joy and gladness for ever. 24 Like as now the neighbours of Sion have seen your captivity: so shall they see shortly your salvation from our God which shall come upon you with great glory, and brightness of the Everlasting. 25 My children, suffer patiently the wrath that is come upon you from God: for thine enemy hath persecuted thee; but shortly thou shalt see his destruction, and shalt tread upon his neck. 26 My delicate ones have gone rough ways, and were taken away as a flock caught of the enemies. 27 Be of good comfort, O my children, and cry unto God: for ye shall be remembered of him that brought these things upon you. 28 For as it was your mind to go astray from God: so, being returned, seek him ten times more. 29 For he that hath brought these plagues upon you shall bring you everlasting joy with your salvation. 30 Take a good heart, O Jerusalem: for he that gave thee that name will comfort thee. 31 Miserable are they that afflicted thee, and rejoiced at thy fall. 32 Miserable are the cities which thy children served: miserable is she that received thy sons. 33 For as she rejoiced at thy ruin, and was glad of thy fall: so shall she be grieved for her own desolation. 34 For I will take away the rejoicing of her great multitude, and her pride shall be turned into mourning. 35 For fire shall come upon her from the Everlasting, long to endure; and she shall be inhabited of devils for a great time. 36 O Jerusalem, look about thee toward the east, and behold the joy that cometh unto thee from God. 37 Lo, thy sons come, whom thou sentest away, they come gathered together from the east to the west by the word of the Holy One, rejoicing in the glory of God.

Bar.5 1 Put off, O Jerusalem, the garment of mourning and affliction, and put on the comeliness of the glory that cometh from God for ever. 2 Cast about thee a double garment of the righteousness which cometh from God; and set a diadem on thine head of the glory of the Everlasting. 3 For God will shew thy brightness unto every country under heaven. 4 For thy name shall be called of God for ever The peace of righteousness, and The glory of God's worship. 5 Arise, O Jerusalem, and stand on high, and look about toward the east, and behold thy children gathered from the west unto the east by the word of the Holy One, rejoicing in the remembrance of God. 6 For they departed from thee on foot, and were led away of their enemies: but God bringeth them unto thee exalted with glory, as children of the kingdom. 7 For God hath appointed that every high hill, and banks of long continuance, should be cast down, and valleys filled up, to make even the ground, that Israel may go safely in the glory of God, 8 Moreover even the woods and every sweet smelling tree shall overshadow Israel by the commandment of God. 9 For God shall lead Israel with joy in the light of his glory with the mercy and righteousness that cometh from him.

Bar.6 1 A copy of an epistle, which Jeremy sent unto them which were to be led captives into Babylon by the king of the Babylonians, to certify them, as it was commanded him of God. 2 Because of the sins which ye have committed before God, ye shall be led away captives into Babylon by Nabuchodonosor king of the Babylonians. 3 So when ye be come unto Babylon, ye shall remain there many years, and for a long season, namely, seven generations: and after that I will bring you away peaceably from thence. 4 Now shall ye see in Babylon gods of silver, and of gold, and of wood, borne upon shoulders, which cause the nations to fear. 5 Beware therefore that ye in no wise be like to strangers, neither be ye and of them, when ye see the multitude before them and behind them, worshipping them. 6 But say ye in your hearts, O Lord, we must worship thee. 7 For mine angel is with you, and I myself caring for your souls. 8 As for their tongue, it is polished by the workman, and they themselves are gilded and laid over with silver; yet are they but false, and cannot speak. 9 And taking gold, as it were for a virgin that loveth to go gay, they make crowns for the heads of their gods. 10 Sometimes also the priests convey from their gods gold and silver, and bestow it upon themselves. 11 Yea, they will give thereof to the common harlots, and deck them as men with garments, *being* gods of silver, and gods of gold, and wood. 12 Yet cannot these gods save themselves from rust and moth, though they be covered with purple raiment. 13 They wipe their faces because of the dust of the temple, when there is much upon them. 14 And he that cannot put to death one that offendeth him holdeth a scepter, as though he were a judge of the country. 15 He hath also in his right hand a dagger and an axe: but cannot deliver himself from war and thieves. 16 Whereby they are known not to be gods: therefore fear them not. 17 For like as a vessel that a man useth is nothing

worth when it is broken; even so it is with their gods: when they be set up in the temple, their eyes be full of dust through the feet of them that come in. 18 And as the doors are made sure on every side upon him that offendeth the king, as being committed to suffer death: even so the priests make fast their temples with doors, with locks, and bars, lest their gods be spoiled with robbers. 19 They light them candles, yea, more than for themselves, whereof they cannot see one. 20 They are as one of the beams of the temple, yet they say their hearts are gnawed upon by things creeping out of the earth; and when they eat them and their clothes, they feel it not. 21 Their faces are blacked through the smoke that cometh out of the temple. 22 Upon their bodies and heads sit bats, swallows, and birds, and the cats also. 23 By this ye may know that they are no gods: therefore fear them not. 24 Notwithstanding the gold that is about them to make them beautiful, except they wipe off the rust, they will not shine: for neither when they were molten did they feel it. 25 The things wherein there is no breath are bought for a most high price. 26 They are borne upon shoulders, having no feet whereby they declare unto men that they be nothing worth. 27 They also that serve them are ashamed: for if they fall to the ground at any time, they cannot rise up again of themselves: neither, if one set them upright, can they move of themselves: neither, if they be bowed down, can they make themselves straight: but they set gifts before them as unto dead men. 28 As for the things that are sacrificed unto them, their priests sell and abuse; in like manner their wives lay up part thereof in salt; but unto the poor and impotent they give nothing of it. 29 Menstruous women and women in childbed eat their sacrifices: by these things ye may know that they are no gods: fear them not. 30 For how can they be called gods? because women set meat before the gods of silver, gold, and wood. 31 And the priests sit in their temples, having their clothes rent, and their heads and beards shaven, and nothing upon their heads. 32 They roar and cry before their gods, as men do at the feast when one is dead. 33 The priests also take off their garments, and clothe their wives and children. 34 Whether it be evil that one doeth unto them, or good, they are not able to recompense it: they can neither set up a king, nor put him down. 35 In like manner, they can neither give riches nor money: though a man make a vow unto them, and keep it not, they will not require it. 36 They can save no man from death, neither deliver the weak from the mighty. 37 They cannot restore a blind man to his sight, nor help any man in his distress. 38 They can shew no mercy to the widow, nor do good to the fatherless. 39 Their gods of wood, and which are overlaid with gold and silver, are like the stones that be hewn out of the mountain: they that worship them shall be confounded. 40 How should a man then think and say that they are gods, when even the Chaldeans themselves dishonour them? 41 Who if they shall see one dumb that cannot speak, they bring him, and intreat Bel that he may speak, as though he were able to understand. 42 Yet they cannot understand this themselves, and leave them: for they have no knowledge. 43 The women also with cords about them, sitting in the ways, burn bran for perfume: but if any of them, drawn by some that passeth by, lie with him, she reproacheth her fellow, that she was not thought as worthy as herself, nor her cord broken. 44 Whatsoever is done among them is false: how may it then be thought or said that they are gods? 45 They are made of carpenters and goldsmiths: they can be nothing else than the workmen will have them to be. 46 And they themselves that made them can never continue long; how should then the things that are made of them be gods? 47 For they left lies and reproaches to them that come after. 48 For when there cometh any war or plague upon them, the priests consult with themselves, where they may be hidden with them. 49 How then cannot men perceive that they be no gods, which can neither save themselves from war, nor from plague? 50 For seeing they be but of wood, and overlaid with silver and gold, it shall be known hereafter that they are false: 51 And it shall manifestly appear to all nations and kings that they are no gods, but the works of men's hands, and that there is no work of God in them. 52 Who then may not know that they are no gods? 53 For neither can they set up a king in the land, nor give rain unto men. 54 Neither can they judge their own cause, nor redress a wrong, being unable: for they are as crows between heaven and earth. 55 Whereupon when fire falleth upon the house of gods of wood, or laid over with gold or silver, their priests will flee away, and escape; but they themselves shall be burned asunder like beams. 56 Moreover they cannot withstand any king or enemies: how can it then be thought or said that they be gods? 57 Neither are those gods of wood, and laid over with silver or gold, able to escape either from thieves or robbers. 58 Whose gold, and silver, and garments wherewith they are clothed, they that are strong take, and go away withal: neither are they able to help themselves. 59 Therefore it is better to be a king that sheweth his power, or else a profitable vessel in an house, which the owner shall have use of, than such false gods; or to be a door in an house, to keep such things therein, than such false gods. or a pillar of wood in a palace, than such false gods. 60 For sun, moon, and stars, being bright and sent to do their offices, are obedient. 61 In like manner the lightning when it breaketh forth is easy to be seen; and after the same manner the wind bloweth in every country. 62 And when God commandeth the clouds to go over the whole world, they do as they are bidden. 63 And the fire sent from above to consume hills and woods doeth as it is commanded: but these are like unto them neither in shew nor power. 64 Wherefore it is neither to be supposed nor said that they are gods, seeing, they are able neither to judge causes, nor to do good unto men. 65 Knowing therefore that they are no gods, fear them not, 66 For they can neither curse nor bless kings: 67 Neither can they shew signs in the heavens among the heathen, nor shine as the sun, nor give light as the moon. 68 The beasts are better than they: for they can get under a cover and help themselves. 69 It is then by no means manifest unto us that they are gods: therefore fear them not. 70 For as a scarecrow in a garden of cucumbers keepeth nothing: so are their gods of wood, and laid over with silver and gold. 71 And likewise their gods of wood, and laid over with silver and gold, are like to a white thorn in an orchard, that every bird sitteth upon; as also to a dead body, that is cast into the dark. 72 And ye shall know them to be no gods by the bright purple that rotteth upon them: and they themselves afterward shall be eaten, and shall be a reproach in the country. 73 Better therefore is the just man that hath none idols: for he shall be far from reproach.

JEZEKIEL (EZEKIEL)

Ezek.1 1 Now it came to pass in the thirtieth year, in the fourth month, on the fifth day of the month, that I was in the midst of the captivity by the river of Chobar; and the heavens were opened, and I saw visions of God. 2 On the fifth day of the month; this was the fifth year of the captivity of king Joakim. 3 And the word of the Lord came to Jezekiel the priest, the son of Buzi, in the land of the Chaldeans, by the river of Chobar; and the hand of the Lord was upon me. 4 And I looked, and, behold, a sweeping wind came from the north, and a great cloud on it, and *there was* brightness round about it, and gleaming fire, and in the midst of it as it were the appearance of amber in the midst of the fire, and brightness in it. 5 And in the midst as it were the likeness of four living creatures. And this was their appearance; the likeness of a man was upon them. 6 And each one *had* four faces, and each one *had* four wings. 7 And their legs were straight; and their feet were winged, and *there were* sparks, like gleaming brass, and their wings were light. 8 And the hand of a man was under their wings on their four sides. 9 And the faces of them four turned not when they went; they went everyone straight forward. 10 And the likeness of their faces was the face of a man, and the face of a lion on the right of the four; and the face of a calf on the left of the four; and the face of an eagle to the four. 11 And the four had their wings spread out above; each one *had* two joined to one another, and two covered their bodies. 12 And each one went straight forward: wherever the spirit was going they went, and turned not back. 13 And in the midst of the living creatures *there was* an appearance as of burning coals of fire, as an appearance of lamps turning among the living creatures; and the brightness of fire, and out of the fire came forth lightning. 14 15 And I looked, and, behold, the four *had each* one wheel on the ground near the living creatures. 16 And the appearance of the wheels was as the appearance of beryl: and the four had one likeness: and their work was as it were a wheel in a wheel. 17 They went on their four sides: they turned not as they went; 18 neither did their backs *turn*: and they were high: and I beheld them, and the backs of them four were full of eyes round about. 19 And when the living creatures went, the wheels went by them: and when the living creatures lifted themselves off the earth, the wheels were lifted off. 20 Wherever the cloud happened to be, there was the spirit ready to go: the wheels went and were lifted up with them; because the spirit of life was in the wheels. 21 When those went, *the wheels* went; and when those stood, *the wheels* stood; and when those lifted themselves off the earth, they were lifted off with them: for the spirit of life was in the wheels. 22 And the likeness over the heads of the living creatures was as a firmament, as the appearance of crystal, spread out over their wings above. 23 And their wings were spread out under the firmament, reaching one to the other; two *wings* to each, covering their bodies. 24 And I heard the sound of their wings when they went, as the sound of much water: and when they stood, their wings were let down. 25 And lo! a voice from above the firmament 26 that was over their head, *there was* as the appearance of a sapphire stone, *and* the likeness of a throne upon it: and upon the likeness of the throne was the likeness as an appearance of a man above. 27 And I saw as it were the resemblance of amber from the appearance of the loins and upwards, and from the appearance of the loins and under I saw an appearance of fire, and the brightness thereof round about. 28 As the appearance of the bow when it is in the cloud in days of rain, so was the form of brightness round about.

Ezek.2 1 This was the appearance of the likeness of the glory of the Lord. And I saw and fell upon my face, and heard the voice of one speaking: and he said to me, Son of man, stand upon thy feet, and I will speak to thee. 2 And the Spirit came upon me, and took me up, and raised me, and set me on my feet: and I heard him speaking to me. 3 And he said to me, Son of Man, I send thee forth to the house of Israel, them that provoke me; who have provoked me, they and their fathers to this day. 4 And thou shalt say to them, Thus saith the Lord. 5 Whether then indeed they shall hear or fear, (for it is a provoking house,) yet they shall know that thou art a prophet in the midst of them. 6 And thou, son of man, fear them not, nor be dismayed at their face; (for they will madden and will rise up against thee round about, and thou dwellest in the midst of scorpions): be not afraid of their words, nor be dismayed at their countenance, for it is a provoking house. 7 And thou shalt speak my words to them, whether they will hear or fear: for it is a provoking house. 8 And thou, son of man, hear him that speaks to thee; be not thou provoking, as the provoking house: open thy mouth, and eat what I give thee. 9 And I looked, and behold, a hand stretched out to me, and in it a volume of a book. 10 And he unrolled it before me: and in it the front and the back were written *upon*: and there was written *in it* Lamentation, and mournful song, and woe.

Ezek.3 1 And he said to me, Son of Man, eat this volume, and go and speak to the children of Israel. 2 So he opened my mouth, and caused me to eat the volume. And he said to me, Son of man, 3 thy mouth shall eat, and thy belly shall be filled with this volume that is given to thee. So I ate it; and it was in my mouth as sweet as honey. 4 And he said to me, Son of man, go thy way, and go in to the house of Israel, and speak my words to them. 5 For thou art not sent to a people of hard speech, *but* to the house of Israel; 6 neither to many nations of other speech and other tongues, nor of harsh language, whose words thou wouldest not understand: although if I *had* sent thee to such, they would have hearkened to thee. 7 But the house of Israel will not be willing to hearken to thee; for they will not hearken to me: for all the house of Israel are stubborn and hardhearted. 8 And, behold, I have made thy face strong against their faces, and I will strengthen thy power against their

power. 9 And it shall be continually stronger than a rock: be not afraid of them, neither be dismayed at their faces, because it is a provoking house. 10 And he said to me, Son of man, receive into thine heart all the words that I have spoken to thee, and hear *them* with thine ears. 11 And go thy way, go in to the captivity, to the children of thy people, and thou shalt speak to them, and say to them, Thus saith the Lord; whether they will hear, *or* whether they will forbear. 12 Then the Spirit took me up, and I heard behind me the voice *as* of a great earthquake, *saying*, Blessed *be* the glory of the Lord from his place. 13 And I perceived the sound of the wings of the living creatures clapping one to the other, and the sound of the wheels was near them, and the sound of the earthquake. 14 And the Spirit lifted me, and took me up, and I went in the impulse of my spirit; and the hand of the Lord was mighty upon me. 15 Then I passed through the air and came into the captivity, and went round *to* them that dwelt by the river of Chobar who were there; and I sat there seven days, conversant in the midst of them. 16 And after the seven days the word of the Lord came to me, saying, Son of man, 17 I have made thee a watchman to the house of Israel; and thou shalt hear a word of my mouth, and shalt threaten them from me. 18 When I say to the wicked, Thou shalt surely die; and thou hast not warned him, to give warning to the wicked, to turn from his ways, that he should live; that wicked man shall die in his iniquity; but his blood will I require at thy hand. 19 But if thou warn the wicked, and he turn not from his wickedness, and from his way, that wicked man shall die in his iniquity, and thou shalt deliver thy soul. 20 And when the righteous turns away from his righteousness, and commits a trespass, and I shall bring punishment before him, he shall die, because thou didst not warn him: he shall even die in his sins, because his righteousness shall not be remembered; but his blood will I require at thine hand. 21 But if thou warn the righteous not to sin, and he sin not, the righteous shall surely live, because thou hast warned him; and thou shalt deliver thine own soul. 22 And the hand of the Lord came upon me; and he said to me, Arise, and go forth into the plain, and there shalt thou be spoken to. 23 And I arose, and went forth to the plain: and, behold, the glory of the Lord stood there, according to the vision, and according to the glory of the Lord, which I saw by the river of Chobar: and I fell on my face. 24 Then the Spirit came upon me, and set me on my feet, and spoke to me, and said to me, Go in, and shut thyself up in the midst of thine house. 25 And thou, son of man, behold, bonds are prepared for thee, and they shall bind thee with them, and thou shalt not come forth of the midst of them. 26 Also I will bind thy tongue, and thou shalt be dumb, and shalt not be to them a reprover: because it is a provoking house. 27 But when I speak to thee, I will open thy mouth, and thou shalt say to them, Thus saith the Lord, He that hears, let him hear; and he that is disobedient, let him be disobedient: because it is a provoking house.

Ezek.4 1 And thou, son of man, take thee a brick, and thou shalt set it before thy face, and shalt portray on it the city, *even* Jerusalem. 2 And thou shalt besiege it, and build works against it, and throw up a mound round about it, and pitch camps against it, and set up engines round about. 3 And take thou to thyself an iron pan, and thou shalt set it *for* an iron wall between thee and the city: and thou shalt set thy face against it, and it shall be in a siege, and thou shalt besiege it. This is a sign to the children of Israel. 4 And thou shalt lie upon thy left side, and lay the iniquities of the house of Israel upon it, according to the number of the hundred and fifty days *during* which thou shalt lie upon it: and thou shalt bear their iniquities. 5 For I have appointed thee their iniquities for a number of days, for a hundred and ninety days: so thou shalt bear the iniquities of the house of Israel. 6 And thou shalt accomplish this, and *then* shalt lie on thy right side, and shalt bear the iniquities of the house of Juda forty days: I have appointed thee a day for a year. 7 So thou shalt set thy face to the siege of Jerusalem, and shalt strengthen thine arm, and shalt prophesy against it. 8 And, behold, I have prepared bonds for thee, land thou mayest not turn from thy one side to the other, until the days of thy siege shall be accomplished. 9 Take thou also to thee wheat, and barley, and beans, and lentils, and millet, and bread-corn; and thou shalt cast them into one earthen vessel, and shalt make them into loaves for thyself; and thou shalt eat them a hundred and ninety days, according to the number of the days *during* which thou sleepest on thy side. 10 And thou shalt eat thy food by weight, twenty shekels a day: from time to time shalt thou eat them. 11 And thou shalt drink water by measure, even from time to time thou shalt drink the sixth part of a hin. 12 And thou shalt eat them *as* a barley cake: thou shalt bake them before their eyes in man's dung. 13 And thou shalt say, Thus saith the Lord God of Israel; Thus shall the children of Israel eat unclean things among the Gentiles. 14 Then I said, Not so, Lord God of Israel: surely my soul has not been defiled with uncleanness; nor have I eaten, that which died of itself or was torn of beasts from my birth until now; neither has any corrupt flesh entered into my mouth. 15 And he said to me, Behold, I have given thee dung of oxen instead of man's dung, and thou shalt prepare thy loaves upon it. 16 And he said to me, Son of man, behold, I break the support of bread in Jerusalem: and they shall eat bread by weight and in want; and shall drink water by measure, and in a state of ruin: 17 that they may want bread and water; and a man and his brother shall be brought to ruin, and they shall pine away in their iniquities.

Ezek.5 1 And thou, son of man, take thee a sword sharper than a barber's razor; thou shalt procure it for thyself, and shalt bring it upon thine head, and upon thy beard: and thou shalt take a pair of scales, and shalt separate the hair. 2 A fourth part thou shalt burn in the fire in the midst of the city, at the fulfillment of the days of the siege: and thou shalt take a fourth part, and burn it up in the midst of it: and a fourth part thou shalt cut with a sword round about it: and a fourth part thou shalt scatter to the wind; and I will draw out a sword after them. 3 And thou shalt take thence a few in number, and shalt wrap them in the fold of thy garment. 4 And thou shalt take of these again, and cast them into the midst of the fire, and burn them up with fire: from thence shall come forth fire; and thou shalt say to the whole

house of Israel, 5 Thus saith the Lord; This is Jerusalem: I have set her and the countries round about her in the midst of the nations. 6 And thou shalt declare mine ordinances to the lawless one from out of the nations; and my statutes *to the sinful one* of the countries round about her: because they have rejected mine ordinances, and have not walked in my statutes. 7 Therefore thus saith the Lord, Because your occasion *for sin has been taken* from the nations round about you, and ye have not walked in my statutes, nor kept mine ordinances, nay, ye have not even done according to the ordinances of the nations round about you; therefore thus saith the Lord; 8 Behold, I am against thee, and I will execute judgment in the midst of thee in the sight of the nations. 9 And I will do in thee things which I have not done, and the like of which I will not do again, for all thine abominations. 10 Therefore the fathers shall eat *their* children in the midst of thee, and children shall eat *their* fathers; and I will execute judgments in thee, and I will scatter all that are left of thee to every wind. 11 Therefore, *as* I live, saith the Lord; surely, because thou hast defiled my holy things with all thine abominations, I also will reject thee; mine eye shall not spare, and I will have no mercy. 12 A fourth part of thee shall be cut off by pestilence, and a fourth part of thee shall be consumed in the midst of thee with famine: and *as for another* fourth part of thee, I will scatter them to every wind; and a fourth part of thee shall fall by sword round about thee, and I will draw out a sword after them. 13 And my wrath and mine anger shall be accomplished upon them: and thou shalt know that I the Lord have spoken in my jealousy, when I have accomplished mine anger upon them. 14 And I will make thee desolate, and thy daughters round about thee, in the sight of every one that passes through. 15 And thou shalt be mourned over and miserable among the nations round about thee, when I have executed judgments in thee in the vengeance of my wrath. I the Lord have spoken. 16 And when I have sent against them shafts of famine, then they shall be consumed, and I will break the strength of thy bread. 17 So I will send forth against thee famine and evil beasts, and I will take vengeance upon thee; and pestilence and blood shall pass through upon thee; and I will bring a sword upon thee round about. I the Lord have spoken.

Ezek.6 1 And the word of the Lord came to me, saying, 2 Son of man, set thy face against the mountains of Israel, and prophesy against them; 3 and thou shalt say, Ye mountains of Israel, hear the word of the Lord; thus saith the Lord to the mountains, and to the hills, and to the valleys, and to the forests; Behold, I bring a sword upon you, and your high places shall be utterly destroyed. 4 And your altars shall be broken to pieces, and your consecrated plats; and I will cast down your slain *men* before your idols. 5 And I will scatter your bones round about your altars, 6 and in all your habitations: the cities shall be made desolate, and the high places utterly laid waste; that your altars may be destroyed, and your idols be broken to pieces, and your consecrated plats be abolished. 7 And slain *men* shall fall in the midst of you, and ye shall know that I am the Lord. 8 When there are *some* of you escaping from the sword among the Gentiles, and when ye are scattered in the countries; 9 then they of you that escape among the nations whither they were carried captive shall remember me; (I have sworn *an oath* against their heart that goes a- whoring from me, and their eyes that go a-whoring after their practices;) and they shall mourn over themselves for all their abominations. 10 And they shall know that I the Lord have spoken. 11 Thus saith the Lord; Clap with *thy* hand, and stamp with *thy* foot and say, Aha, aha! for all the abominations of the house of Israel: they shall fall by the sword, and by pestilence, and by famine. 12 He that is near shall fall by the sword; and he that is far off shall die by the pestilence; and he that is in the siege shall be consumed with famine: and I will accomplish mine anger upon them. 13 Then ye shall know that I am the Lord, when your slain are in the midst of your idols round about your altars, on every high hill, and under *every* shady tree, where they offered a sweet savour to all their idols. 14 And I will stretch out my hand against them, and I will make the land desolate and ruined from the wilderness of Deblatha, in all their habitations: *and* ye shall know that I am the Lord.

Ezek.7 1 Moreover the word of the Lord came to me, saying, Also, thou, son of man, say, 2 Thus saith the Lord; An end is come to the land of Israel, the end is come on the four corners of the land. 3 The end is come on thee, 7 the inhabitant of the land: the time is come, the day has drawn nigh, not with tumult, nor with pangs. 8 Now I will pour out my anger upon thee near at hand, and I will accomplish my wrath on thee: and I will judge thee for thy ways, and recompense upon thee all thine abominations. 9 Mine eye shall not spare, nor will I have any mercy: for I will recompense thy ways upon thee, and thine abominations shall be in the midst of thee; and thou shalt know that I am the Lord that smite *thee*. 7 Now the end *is come* to thee, and I will send *judgment* upon thee: and I will take vengeance on thy ways, and will recompense all thine abominations upon thee. 4 Mine eye shall not spare, nor will I have any mercy: for I will recompense thy way upon thee, and thine abominations shall be in the midst of thee; and thou shalt know that I am the Lord. 5 For thus saith the Lord; Behold, the end is come. 10 Behold, the day of the Lord! although the rod has blossomed, 11 pride has sprung up, and will break the staff of the wicked one, and *that* not with tumult, nor with haste. 12 The time is come, behold the day: let not the buyer rejoice, and let not the seller mourn. 13 For the buyer shall never again return to the seller, neither shall a man cleave with the eye *of hope* to his life. 14 Sound ye the trumpet, and pass sentence on all together. 15 *There shall be* war with the sword without, and famine and pestilence within: he that is in the field shall die by the sword; and famine and pestilence shall destroy them that are in the city. 16 But they that escape of them shall be delivered, and shall be upon the mountains: and I will slay all *the rest*, every one for his iniquities. 17 All hands shall be completely weakened, and all thighs shall be defiled with moisture. 18 And they shall gird themselves with sackcloth, and amazement shall cover them; and shame shall be upon them, *even* upon every face, and baldness upon every head.

19 Their silver shall be cast forth in the streets, and their gold shall be despised: their souls shall not be satisfied, and their bellies shall not be filled: for it was the punishment of their iniquities. 20 *As for* their choice ornaments, they employed them for pride, and they made of them images of their abominations: therefore have I made them uncleanness to them. 21 And I will deliver them into the hands of strangers to make them a prey, and to the pests of the earth for a spoil; and they shall profane them. 22 And I will turn away my face from them, and they shall defile my charge, and shall go in to them unguardedly, and profane them. 23 And they shall work uncleanness: because the land is full of strange nations, and the city is full of iniquity. 24 And I will turn back the boasting of their strength; and their holy things shall be defiled. 25 And *though* propitiation shall come, and *one* shall seek peace, yet there shall be none. 26 There shall be woe upon woe, and there shall be message upon message; and a vision shall be sought from a prophet; but the law shall perish from the priest, and counsel from the elders. 27 The prince shall clothe himself with desolation, and the hands of the people of the land shall be made feeble: I will do to them according to their ways, and according to their judgments will I punish them; and they shall know that I am the Lord.

Ezek.8 1 And it came to pass in the sixth year, in the fifth month, on the fifth *day* of the month, I was sitting in the house, and the elders of Juda were sitting before me: and the hand of the Lord came upon me. 2 And I looked, and, behold, the likeness of a man: from his loins and downwards *there was* fire, and from his loins upwards *there was* as the appearance of amber. 3 And he stretched forth the likeness of a hand, and took me by the crown of my head; and the Spirit lifted me up between the earth and sky, and brought me to Jerusalem in a vision of God, to the porch of the gate that looks to the north, where was the pillar of the Purchaser. 4 And, behold, the glory of the Lord God of Israel was there, according to the vision which I saw in the plain. 5 And he said to me, Son of man, lift up thine eyes toward the north. So I lifted up mine eyes toward the north, and, behold, *I looked* from the north toward the eastern gate. 6 And he said to me, Son of man, hast thou seen what these do? They commit great abominations here so that I should keep away from my sanctuary: and thou shalt see yet greater iniquities. 7 And he brought me to the porch of the court. 8 And he said to me, Son of man, dig: so I dug, and behold a door. 9 And he said to me, Go in, and behold the iniquities which they practise here. 10 So I went in and looked; and beheld vain abominations, and all the idols of the house of Israel, portrayed upon them round about. 11 And seventy men of the elders of the house of Israel, and Jechonias the son of Saphan stood in their presence in the midst of them, and each one held his censer in his hand; and the smoke of the incense went up. 12 And he said to me, Thou hast seen, son of man, what the elders of the house of Israel do, each one of them in their secret chamber: because they have said, The Lord see not; The Lord has forsaken the earth. 13 And he said to me, Thou shalt see yet greater iniquities which these do. 14 And he brought me in to the porch of the house of the Lord that looks to the north; and, behold *there were* women sitting there lamenting for Thammuz. 15 And he said to me, Son of man, thou hast seen; but thou shalt yet see *evil* practices greater then these. 16 And he brought me into the inner court of the house of the Lord, and at the entrance of the temple of the Lord, between the porch and the altar, were about twenty men, with their back parts toward the temple of the Lord, and their faces *turned* the opposite way; and these were worshipping the sun. 17 And he said to me, Son of man, thou hast seen this. *Is it* a little thing to the house of Juda to practise the iniquities which they have practised here? for they have filled the land with iniquity: and, behold, these are as scorners. 18 Therefore will I deal with them in wrath: mine eye shall not spare, nor will I have any mercy.

Ezek.9 1 And he cried in mine ears with a loud voice, saying, The judgment of the city has drawn nigh; and each had the weapons of destruction in his hand. 2 And, behold, six men came from the way of the high gate that looks toward the north, and each one's axe was in his hand; and there was one man in the midst of them clothed with a long robe down to the feet, and a sapphire girdle was on his loins: and they came in and stood near the brazen altar. 3 And the glory of the God of Israel, that was upon them, went up from the cherubs to the porch of the house. And he called the man that was clothed with the long robe, who had the girdle on his loins; 4 And said to him, Go through the midst of Jerusalem, and set a mark on the foreheads of the men that groan and that grieve for all the iniquities that are done in the midst of them. 5 And he said to the first in my hearing, Go after him into the city, and smite: and let not your eyes spare, and have no mercy. 6 Slay utterly old man and youth, and virgin, and infants, and women: but go ye not nigh any on whom is the mark: begin at my sanctuary. So they began with the elder men who were within in the house. 7 And he said to them, Defile the house, and go out and fill the ways with dead bodies, and smite. 8 And it came to pass as they were smiting, that I fell upon my face, and cried out, and said, Alas, O Lord! wilt thou destroy the remnant of Israel, in pouring out thy wrath upon Jerusalem? 9 Then said he to me, The iniquity of the house of Israel and Juda is become very exceedingly great: for the land is filled with many nations, and the city is filled with iniquity and uncleanness: because they have said, The Lord has forsaken the earth, The Lord looks not upon *it*. 10 Therefore mine eye shall not spare, neither will I have any mercy: I have recompensed their ways upon their heads. 11 And, behold, the man clothed with the long robe, and girt with the girdle about his loins, answered and said, I have done as thou didst command me.

Ezek.10 1 Then I looked, and, behold, over the firmament that was above the head of the cherubs *there was* a likeness of a throne over them, as a sapphire stone. 2 And he said to the man clothed with the *long* robe, Go in between the wheels that are under the cherubs, and fill thine hands with coals of fire from between the cherubs, and scatter *them* over the city. And he went in my sight. 3 And the cherubs stood on the right hand of the house, as the man went in;

and the cloud filled the inner court. 4 Then the glory of the Lord departed from the cherubs to the porch of the house; and the cloud filled the house, and the court was filled with the brightness of the glory of the Lord. 5 And the sound of the cherubs' wings was heard as far as the outer court, as the voice of the Almighty God speaking. 6 And it came to pass, when he gave a charge to the man clothed with the sacred robe, saying, Take fire from between the wheels from between the cherubs, that he went in, and stood near the wheels. 7 And he stretched forth his hand into the midst of the fire that was between the cherubs, and took *thereof*, and put *it* into the hands of the man clothed with the sacred robe: and he took *it*, and went out. 8 And I saw the cherubs *having* the likeness of men's hands under their wings. 9 And I saw, and behold, four wheels stood by the cherubs, one wheel by each cherub: and the appearance of the wheels was as the appearance of a carbuncle stone. 10 And *as for* their appearance, *there was* one likeness to the four, as if there should be a wheel in the midst of a wheel. 11 When they went, they went on their four sides; they turned not when they went, for whichever way the first head looked, they went; and they turned not as they went. 12 And their backs, and their hands, and their wings, and the wheels, were full of eyes round about the four wheels. 13 And these wheels were called Gelgel in my hearing. 14 15 And the cherubs were the same living creature which I saw by the river of Chobar. 16 And when the cherubs went, the wheels went, and they were close to them: and when the cherubs lifted up their wings to mount up from the earth, their wheels turned not. 17 When they stood, *the wheels* stood; and when they mounted up, *the wheels* mounted up with them: because the spirit of life was in them. 18 Then the glory of the Lord departed from the house, and went up on the cherubs. 19 And the cherubs lifted up their wings, and mounted up from the earth in my sight: when they went forth, the wheels were also beside them, and they stood at the entrance of the front gate of the house of the Lord; and the glory of the God of Israel was upon them above. 20 This is the living creature which I saw under the God of Israel by the river of Chobar; and I knew that they were cherubs. 21 Each one *had* four faces, and each one *had* eight wings; and under their wings was the likeness of men's hands. 22 And *as for* the likeness of their faces, these are the *same* faces which I saw under the glory of the God of Israel by the river of Chobar: and they went each straight forward.

Ezek.11 1 Moreover the Spirit took me up, and brought me to the front gate of the house of the Lord, that looks eastward: and behold at the entrance of the gate were about five and twenty men; and I saw in the midst of them Jechonias the son of Ezer, and Phaltias the son of Banaeas, the leaders of the people. 2 And the Lord said to me, Son of man, these are the men that devise vanities, and take evil counsel in this city: 3 who say, Have not the houses been newly built? This is the caldron, and we are the flesh. 4 Therefore prophesy against them, prophesy, son of man. 5 And the Spirit of the Lord fell upon me, and said to me, say; Thus saith the Lord; Thus have ye said, O house of Israel: and I know the devices of your spirit. 6 Ye have multiplied your dead in this city, and ye have filled your ways with slain men. 7 Therefore thus saith the Lord; Your dead whom ye have smitten in the midst of it, these are the flesh, and this *city* is the caldron: but I will bring you forth out of the midst of it. 8 Ye fear the sword; and I will bring a sword upon you, saith the Lord. 9 And I will bring you forth out of the midst of it, and will deliver you into the hands of strangers, and will execute judgments among you. 10 Ye shall fall by the sword; I will judge you on the mountains of Israel; and ye shall know that I am the Lord. 11 And it came to pass, while I was prophesying, that Phaltias the son of Banaeas died. And I fell upon my face, and cried with a loud voice, and said, Alas, alas, O Lord! wilt thou utterly destroy the remnant of Israel? 14 And the word of the Lord came to me, saying, 15 Son of man, thy brethren, and the men of thy captivity, and all the house of Israel are come to the full, to whom the inhabitants of Jerusalem said, Keep ye far away from the Lord: the land is given to us for an inheritance. 16 Therefore say thou, Thus saith the Lord; I will cast them off among the nations, and will disperse them into every land, yet will I be to them for a little sanctuary in the countries which they shall enter. 17 Therefore say thou, Thus saith the Lord; I will also take them from the heathen, and gather them out of the lands wherein I have scattered them, and will give them the land of Israel. 18 And they shall enter in there, and shall remove all the abominations of it, and all its iniquities from it. 19 And I will give them another heart, and will put a new spirit within them; and will extract the heart of stone from their flesh, and give them a heart of flesh: 20 that they may walk in my commandments, and keep mine ordinances, and do them: and they shall be to me a people, and I will be to them a God. 21 And as for the heart *set upon* their abominations and their iniquities, as their heart went *after them*, I have recompensed their ways on their heads, saith the Lord. 22 Then the cherubs lifted up their wings, and the wheels beside them; and the glory of the God of Israel was over them above. 23 And the glory of the Lord went up from the midst of the city, and stood on the mountain which was in front of the city. 24 And the Spirit took me up, and brought me to the land of the Chaldeans, to the captivity, in a vision by the Spirit of God: and I went up after the vision which I saw. 25 And I spoke to the captivity all the words of the Lord which he had shewed me.

Ezek.12 1 And the word of the Lord came to me, saying, 2 Son of man, thou dwellest in the midst of the iniquities of those, who have eyes to see, and see not; and have ears to hear, and hear not: because it is a provoking house. 3 Thou therefore, son of man, prepare thyself baggage for going into captivity by day in their sight; and thou shalt be led into captivity from thy place into another place in their sight; that they may see that it is a provoking house. 4 And thou shalt carry forth thy baggage, baggage for captivity, by day before their eyes: and thou shalt go forth at even, as a captive goes forth, in their sight. 5 Dig for thyself into the wall *of the house*, and thou shalt pass through it in their sight: 6 thou shalt be lifted up on *men's* shoulders, and shalt go forth in secret: thou shalt cover thy face, and shalt not see

the ground: because I have made thee a sign to the house of Israel. 7 And I did thus according to all that he commanded me; and I carried forth my baggage for captivity by day, and in the evening I dug through the wall for myself, and went out secretly; I was taken up on *men's* shoulders before them. 8 And the word of the Lord came to me in the morning, saying, 9 Son of man, have not the house of Israel, the provoking house, said to thee, What doest thou? 10 Say to them, Thus saith the Lord God, the Prince and the Ruler in Israel, even to all the house of Israel who are in the midst of them: 11 say, I am performing signs: as I have done, so shall it be to him: they shall go into banishment and captivity. 12 And the prince in the midst of them shall be borne upon shoulders, and shall go forth in secret through the wall, and shall dig so that he may go forth thereby: he shall cover his face, that he may not be seen by *any* eye, and he himself shall not see the ground. 13 And I will spread out my net upon him, and he shall be caught in my toils: and I will bring him to Babylon to the land of the Chaldeans; but he shall not see it, though he shall die there. 14 And I will scatter to every wind all his assistants round about him, and all that help him; and I will draw out a sword after them; 15 And they shall know that I am the Lord, when I have scattered them among the nations; and I will disperse them in the countries. 16 And I will leave of them *a few* men in number *spared* from the sword, and from famine, and pestilence; that they may declare all their iniquities among the nations whither they have gone; and they shall know that I am the Lord. 17 And the word of the Lord came to me, saying, 18 Son of man, eat thy bread with sorrow, and drink *thy* water with torment and affliction. 19 And thou shalt say to the people of the land, Thus saith the Lord to the inhabitants of Jerusalem, on the land of Israel; They shall eat their bread in scarcity, and shall drink their water in desolation, that the land may be desolate with all that it contains: for all that dwell in it are ungodly. 20 And their inhabited cities shall be laid utterly waste, and the land shall be desolate; and ye shall know that I am the Lord. 21 And the word of the Lord came to me, saying, 22 Son of man, what is your parable on the land of Israel, that ye say, The days are long, the vision has perished? 23 Therefore say to them, Thus saith the Lord; I will even set aside this parable, and the house of Israel shall no more at all use this parable: for thou shalt say to them, The days are at hand, and the import of every vision. 24 For there shall no more be any false vision, nor any one prophesying flatteries in the midst of the children of Israel. 25 For I the Lord will speak my words; I will speak and perform *them*, and will no more delay, for in your days, O provoking house, I will speak the word, and will perform *it*, saith the Lord. 26 Moreover the word of the Lord came to me, saying, 27 Son of man, behold, the provoking house of Israel boldly say, The vision which this man sees is for many days, and he prophesies for times afar off. 28 Therefore say to them, Thus saith the Lord; Henceforth none of my words shall linger, which I shall speak: I will speak and do, saith the Lord.

Ezek.13 1 And the word of the Lord came to me, saying, 2 Son of man, prophesy against the prophets of Israel, and thou shalt prophesy, and shalt say to them, Hear ye the word of the Lord: 3 Thus saith the Lord, Woe to them that prophesy out of their own heart, and who see nothing at all. 4 Thy prophets, O Israel, are like foxes in the deserts. 5 They have not continued steadfast, and they have gathered flocks against the house of Israel, they that say, 6 In the day of the Lord, have not stood, seeing false *visions*, prophesying vanities, who say, The Lord saith, and the Lord has not sent them, and they began *to try* to confirm the word. 7 Have ye not seen a false vision? and spoken vain prophecies? 8 And therefore say, Thus saith the Lord; Because your words are false, and your prophecies are vain, therefore, behold, I am against you, saith the Lord. 9 And I will stretch forth my hand against the prophets that see false *visions*, and those that utter vanities: they shall not partake of the instruction of my people, neither shall they be written in the roll of the house of Israel, and they shall not enter into the land of Israel; and they shall know that I am the Lord. 10 Because they have caused my people to err, saying, Peace; and there is no peace; and one builds a wall, and they plaster it, —it shall fall. 11 Say to them that plaster *it*, It shall fall; and there shall be a flooding rain; and I will send great stones upon their joinings, and they shall fall; and there shall be a sweeping wind, and it shall be broken. 12 And lo! the wall has fallen; and will they not say to you, Where is your plaster wherewith ye plastered *it*? 13 Therefore thus saith the Lord; I will even cause to burst forth a sweeping blast with fury, and there shall be a flooding rain in my wrath; and in *my* fury I will bring on great stones for complete destruction. 14 And I will break down the wall which ye have plastered, and it shall fall; and I will lay it on the ground, and its foundations shall be discovered, and it shall fall; and ye shall be consumed with rebukes: and ye shall know that I am the Lord. 15 And I will accomplish my wrath upon the wall, and upon them that plaster it; it shall fall: and I said to you, The wall is not, nor they that plaster it, 16 even the prophets of Israel, who prophesy concerning Jerusalem, and who see *visions of* peace for her, and there is no peace, saith the Lord. 17 And thou, son of man, set thy face firmly against the daughters of thy people, that prophesy out of their own heart; and prophesy against them. 18 And thou shalt say, Thus saith the Lord, Woe to the *women* that sew pillows under every elbow, and make kerchiefs on the head of every stature to pervert souls! The souls of my people are perverted, and they have saved souls alive. 19 And they have dishonoured me before my people for a handful of barley, and for pieces of bread, to slay the souls which should not die, and to save alive the souls which should not live, while ye speak to a people hearing vain speeches. 20 Therefore thus saith the Lord God, Behold, I am against your pillows, whereby ye there confound souls, and I will tear them away from your arms, and will set at liberty their souls which ye pervert to scatter them. 21 And I will tear your kerchiefs, and will rescue my people out of your hands, and they shall no longer be in your hands to be confounded; and ye shall know that I am the Lord. 22 Because ye have perverted the heart of the righteous, whereas I perverted him not, and *that* in order to strengthen the hands of the wicked, that he should not at all turn from his evil way and live: 23 therefore ye shall not see false *visions*, and ye shall no more utter prophecies: but I will deliver my people out of your hand; and ye shall know that I am the Lord.

Ezek.14 1 And there came to me men of the people of Israel, of the elders, and sat before me. 2 And the word of the Lord came to me, saying, 3 Son of man, these men have conceived their devices in their hearts, and have set before their faces the punishment of their iniquities: shall I indeed answer them? 4 Therefore speak to them, and thou shalt say to them, Thus saith the Lord; Any man of the house of Israel, who shall conceive his devices in his heart, and shall set the punishment of his iniquity before his face, and shall come to the prophet; I the Lord will answer him *according to the things* in which his mind is entangled, 5 that he should turn aside the house of Israel, according to their hearts that are estranged from me in their thoughts. 6 Therefore say to the house of Israel, Thus saith the Lord God, Be converted, and turn from your *evil* practices, and from all your sins, and turn your faces back again. 7 For any man of the house of Israel, or of the strangers that sojourn in Israel, who shall separate himself from me, and conceive his imaginations in his heart, and set before his face the punishment of his iniquity, and come to the prophet to enquire of him concerning me; I the Lord will answer him, *according to the things* wherein he is entangled. 8 And I will set my face against that man, and will make him desolate and ruined, and will cut him off from the midst of my people; and ye shall know that I am the Lord. 9 And if a prophet should cause to err and should speak, I the Lord have caused that prophet to err, and will stretch out my hand upon him, and will utterly destroy him from the midst of my people Israel. 10 And they shall bear their iniquity according to the trespass of him that asks; and it shall be in like manner to the prophet according to the trespass: 11 that the house of Israel may no more go astray from me, and that they may no more defile themselves with any of their transgressions: so shall they be my people, and I will be their God, saith the Lord. 12 And the word of the Lord came to me, saying, 13 Son of man, if a land shall sin against me by committing a trespass, then will I stretch out my hand upon it, and will break its staff of bread, and will send forth famine upon it, and cut off from it man and beast. 14 And though these three men should be in the midst of it, Noe, and Daniel, and Job, they *alone* should be delivered by their righteousness, saith the Lord. 15 If again I bring evil beasts upon the land, and take vengeance upon it, and it be ruined, and there be no one to pass through for fear of the wild beasts: 16 and *if* these three men should be in the midst of it, *as* I live, saith the Lord, neither sons nor daughters shall be saved, but these only shall be saved, and the land shall be destroyed. 17 Or again if I bring a sword upon that land, and say, Let the sword go through the land; and I cut off from them man and beast: 18 though these three men were in the midst of it, as I live, saith the Lord, they shall not deliver sons or daughters, but they only shall be saved themselves. 19 Or *if* again I send pestilence upon that land, and pour out my wrath upon it in blood, to destroy from off it man and beast: 20 and should Noe, and Daniel, and Job, be in the midst of it, *as* I live, saith the Lord, there shall be left *them* neither sons nor daughters; *only* they by their righteousness shall deliver their souls. 21 Thus saith the Lord, And if I even send upon Jerusalem my four sore judgments, sword, and famine, and evil beasts, and pestilence, to destroy from out of it man and beast; 22 yet, behold, *there shall be* men left in it, the escaped thereof, who *shall* lead forth of it sons and daughters: behold, they *shall* go forth to you, and ye shall see their ways and their thoughts: and ye shall mourn over the evils which I have brought upon Jerusalem, *even* all the evils which I have brought upon it. 23 And they shall comfort you, because ye shall see their ways and their thoughts: and ye shall know that I have not done in vain all that I have done in it, saith the Lord.

Ezek.15 1 And the word of the Lord came to me, saying, 2 And thou, son of man—of all the wood, of the branches that are among the trees of the forest, what shall be made of the wood of the vine? 3 Will they take wood of it to make *it fit* for work? will they take of it a peg to hang any vessel upon it? 4 It is only given to the fire to be consumed; the fire consumes that which is yearly pruned of it, and it is utterly gone. Will it be useful for *any* work? 5 Not even while it is yet whole will it be *useful* for *any* work: if the fire shall have utterly consumed it, will it still be *fit* for work? 6 Therefore say, Thus saith the Lord, As the vine-tree among the trees of the forest, which I have given up to the fire to be consumed, so have I given up the inhabitants of Jerusalem. 7 And I will set my face against them; they shall go forth of the fire, and *yet* fire shall devour them; and they shall know that I am the Lord, when I have set my face against them. 8 And I will give up the land to ruin, because they have utterly transgressed, saith the Lord.

Ezek.16 1 Moreover the word of the Lord came to me, saying, 2 Son of man, testify to Jerusalem *of* her iniquities; 3 and thou shalt say, Thus saith the Lord to Jerusalem; Thy root and thy birth are of the land of Chanaan: thy father was an Amorite, and thy mother a Chettite. 4 And *as for* thy birth in the day wherein thou wast born, thou didst not bind thy breasts, and thou wast not washed in water, neither wast thou salted with salt, neither wast thou swathed in swaddling- bands. 5 Nor did mine eye pity thee, to do for thee one of all these things, to feel at all for thee; but thou wast cast out on the face of the field, because of the deformity of thy person, in the day wherein thou wast born. 6 And I passed by to thee, and saw thee polluted in thy blood; and I said to thee, *Let there be* life out of thy blood: 7 increase; I have made thee as the springing grass of the field. So thou didst increase and grow, and didst enter into great cities: thy breasts were set, and thy hair grew, whereas thou wast naked and bare. 8 And I passed by thee and saw thee, and, behold, *it was* thy time and a time of resting; and I spread my wings over thee, and covered thy shame, and swear to thee: and I entered into covenant with thee, saith the Lord, and thou becamest mine. 9 And I

washed thee in water, and washed thy blood from thee, and anointed thee with oil. 10 And I clothed thee with embroidered *garments*, and clothed thee beneath with purple, and girded thee with fine linen, and clothed thee with silk, 11 and decked thee also with ornaments, and put bracelets on thine hands, and a necklace on thy neck. 12 And I put a pendant on thy nostril, and rings in thine ears, and a crown of glory on thine head. 13 So thou wast adorned with gold and silver; and thy raiment was of fine linen, and silk, and variegated work: thou didst eat fine flour, and oil, and honey, and didst become extremely beautiful. 14 And thy name went forth among the nations for thy beauty: because it was perfected with elegance, *and* in the comeliness which I put upon thee, saith the Lord. 15 Thou didst trust in thy beauty, and didst go a-whoring because of thy renown, and didst pour out thy fornication on every passer by. 16 And thou didst take of thy garments, and madest to thyself idols of needlework, and didst go a-whoring after them; therefore thou shalt never come in, nor shall *the like* take place. 17 And thou tookest thy fair ornaments of my gold and of my silver, of what I gave thee, and thou madest to thyself male images, and thou didst commit whoredom with them. 18 And thou didst take thy variegated apparel and didst clothe them, and thou didst set before them mine oil and mine incense. 19 And *thou tookest* my bread which I gave thee, (*yea* I fed thee with fine flour and oil and honey) and didst set them before them for a sweet-smelling savour: yea, it was so, saith the Lord. 20 And thou tookest thy sons and thy daughters, whom thou borest, and didst sacrifice *these* to them to be destroyed. Thou didst go a-whoring as *if that were* little, 21 and didst slay thy children, and gavest them up in offering them to them for an expiation. 22 This is beyond all thy fornication, and thou didst not remember thine infancy, when thou wast naked and bare, *and* didst live *though* defiled in thy blood. 23 And it came to pass after all thy wickedness, saith the Lord, 24 that thou didst build thyself a house of fornication, and didst make thyself a public place in every street; 25 and on the head of every way thou didst set up thy fornications, and didst defile thy beauty, and didst open thy feet to every passer by, and didst multiply thy fornication. 26 And thou didst go a-whoring after the children of Egypt thy neighbors, great of flesh; and didst go a-whoring, often to provoke me to anger. 27 And if I stretch out my hand against thee, then will I abolish thy statutes, and deliver *thee* up to the wills of them that hate thee, *even to* the daughters of the Philistines that turned thee aside from the way wherein thou sinned. 28 And thou didst go a-whoring to the daughters of Assur, and not even thus wast thou satisfied; yea, thou didst go a-whoring, and wast not satisfied. 29 And thou didst multiply thy covenants with the land of the Chaldeans; and not even with these wast thou satisfied. 30 Why should I make a covenant with thy daughter, saith the Lord, while thou doest all these things, the works of a harlot? and thou hast gone a-whoring in a threefold degree with thy daughters. 31 Thou hast built a house of harlotry in every top of a way, and hast set up thine high place in every street; and thou didst become as a harlot gathering hires. 32 An adulteress resembles thee, taking rewards of her husband. 33 She has even given rewards to all that went a-whoring after her, and thou hast given rewards to all thy lovers, yea, thou didst load them with rewards, that they should come to thee from every side for thy fornication. 34 And there has happened in thee perverseness in thy fornication beyond *other* women, and they have committed fornication with thee, in that thou givest hires over and above, and hires were not given to thee; and *thus* perverseness happened in thee. 35 Therefore, harlot, hear the word of the Lord: 36 Thus saith the Lord, Because thou hast poured forth thy money, therefore thy shame shall be discovered in thy harlotry with thy lovers, and *with* regard to all the imaginations of thine iniquities, and for the blood of thy children which thou hast given to them. 37 Therefore, behold, I *will* gather all thy lovers with whom thou hast consorted, and all whom thou hast loved, with all whom thou didst hate; and I will gather them against thee round about, and will expose thy wickedness to them, and they shall see all thy shame. 38 And I will be avenged on thee with the vengeance of an adulteress, and I will bring upon thee blood of fury and jealousy. 39 And I will deliver thee into their hands, and they shall break down thy house of harlotry, and destroy thine high place; and they shall strip thee of thy garments, and shall take thy proud ornaments, and leave thee naked and bare. 40 And they shall bring multitudes upon thee, and they shall stone thee with stones, and pierce thee with their swords. 41 And they shall burn thine houses with fire, and shall execute vengeance on thee in the sight of many women: and I will turn thee back from harlotry, and I will no more give *thee* rewards. 42 So will I slacken my fury against thee, and my jealousy shall be removed from thee, and I will rest, and be no more careful *for thee*. 43 Because thou didst not remember thine infancy, and thou didst grieve me in all these things; therefore, behold, I have recompensed thy ways upon thine head, saith the Lord: for thus hast thou wrought ungodliness above all thine *other* iniquities. 44 These are all the things they have spoken against thee in a proverb, saying, 45 As is the mother, so is thy mother's daughter: thou art she that has rejected her husband and her children; and the sisters of thy sisters have rejected their husbands and their children: your mother was a Chettite, and *your* father an Amorite. 46 Your elder sister who dwells on thy left hand is Samaria, she and her daughters: and thy younger sister, that dwells on the right hand, is Sodom and her daughters. 47 Yet notwithstanding thou hast not walked in their ways, neither hast thou done according to their iniquities within a little, but thou hast exceeded them in all thy ways. 48 *As* I live, saith the Lord, this Sodom and her daughters have not done as thou and thy daughters have done. 49 Moreover this was the sin of thy sister Sodom, pride: she and her daughters lived in pleasure, in fullness of bread *and* in abundance: this belonged to her and her daughters, and they helped not the hand of the poor and needy. 50 And they boasted, and wrought iniquities before me: so I cut them off as I saw *fit*. 51 Also Samaria has not sinned according to half of thy sins; but thou hast multiplied thine iniquities beyond them, and thou hast justified thy sisters in all thine iniquities which thou hast committed. 52 Thou therefore bear thy punishment, for that thou hast corrupted thy sisters by thy sins which thou hast committed beyond them; and thou hast made them *appear* more righteous than thyself: thou therefore be ashamed, and bear thy dishonour, in that thou hast justified thy sisters. 53 And I will turn their captivity, *even* the captivity of Sodom and her daughters; and I will turn the captivity of Samaria and her daughters; and I will turn thy captivity in the midst of them: 54 that thou mayest bear thy punishment, and be dishonoured for all that thou hast done in provoking me to anger. 55 And thy sister Sodom and her daughters shall be restored as they were at the beginning, and thou and thy daughters shall be restored as ye were at the beginning. 56 And surely thy sister Sodom was not mentioned by thy mouth in the days of thy pride: 57 before thy wickedness was discovered, even now thou art the reproach of the daughters of Syria, and of all that are round about her, *even* of the daughters of the Philistines that compass thee round about. 58 *As for* thine ungodliness and thine iniquities, thou hast borne them, saith the Lord. 59 Thus saith the Lord; I will even do to thee as thou hast done, as thou hast dealt shamefully in these things to transgress my covenant. 60 And I will remember my covenant *made* with thee in the days of thine infancy, and I will establish to thee an everlasting covenant. 61 Then thou shalt remember thy way, and shalt be utterly dishonoured when thou receivest thine elder sisters with thy younger ones: and I will give them to thee for building up, but not by thy covenant. 62 And I will establish my covenant with thee; and thou shalt know that I am the Lord: 63 that thou mayest remember, and be ashamed, and mayest no more be able to open thy mouth for thy shame, when I am reconciled to thee for all that thou hast done, saith the Lord.

Ezek.17 1 And the word of the Lord came to me, saying, 2 Son of man, relate a tale, and speak a parable to the house of Israel: 3 and thou shalt say, Thus saith the Lord; A great eagle with large wings, spreading them out very far, with many claws, which has the design of entering into Libanus—and he took the choice *branches* of the cedar: 4 he cropped off the ends of the tender twigs, and brought them into the land of Chanaan; he laid them up in a walled city. 5 And he took of the seed of the land, and sowed it in a field planted by much water; he set it in a conspicuous place. 6 And it sprang up, and became a weak and little vine, so that the branches thereof appeared *upon* it, and its roots were under it: and it became a vine, and put forth shoots, and sent forth its tendrils. 7 And there was another great eagle, with great wings and many claws: and, behold, this vine bent itself round toward him, and her roots *were turned* towards him, and she sent forth her branches towards him, that *he* might water her together with the growth of her plantation. 8 She thrives in a fair field by much water, to produce shoots and bear fruit, that she might become a great vine. 9 Therefore say, Thus saith the Lord; Shall it prosper? shall not the roots of her tender stem and her fruit be blighted? yea, all her early shoots shall be dried up, and *that* not by a mighty arm, nor by many people, to tear her up from her roots. 10 And, behold, it thrives: shall it prosper? shall it not wither as soon as the east wind touches it? it shall be withered together with the growth of its shoots. 11 Moreover the word of the Lord came to me saying, 12 Son of man, say now to the provoking house, Know ye not what these things were? say *to them*, Whenever the king of Babylon shall come against Jerusalem, then he shall take her king and her princes, and shall take them home to Babylon. 13 And he shall take of the seed royal, and shall make a covenant with him, and shall bind him with an oath: and he shall take the princes of the land: 14 that it may become a weak kingdom, so as never to lift itself up, that he may keep his covenant, and establish it. 15 And *if* he shall revolt from him, to send his messengers into Egypt, that *they* may give him horses and much people; shall he prosper? shall he that acts as an adversary be preserved? and shall he that transgresses the covenant be preserved? 16 *As* I live, saith the Lord, verily in *the* place where the king is that made him king, who dishonoured my oath, and who broke my covenant, shall he die with him in the midst of Babylon. 17 And Pharaoh shall make war upon him not with a large force or great multitude, in throwing up a mound, and in building of forts, to cut off souls. 18 Whereas he has profaned the oath so as to break the covenant, when, behold, I engage his hand, and he has done all these things to him, he shall not escape. 19 Therefore say, Thus saith the Lord; *As* I live, surely mine oath which he has profaned, and my covenant which he has transgressed, I will even recompense it upon his head. 20 And I will spread a net upon him, and he shall be caught in its snare. 21 In every battle of his they shall fall by the sword, and I will scatter *his* remnant to every wind: and ye shall know that I the Lord have spoken it. 22 For thus saith the Lord; I will even take of the choice *branches* of the cedar from the top *thereof*, I will crop off their hearts, and I will plant it on a high mountain: 23 and I will hang it on a lofty mountain of Israel: yea, I will plant it, and it shall put forth shoots, and shall bear fruit, and it shall be a great cedar: and every bird shall rest beneath it, even every fowl shall rest under its shadow: its branches shall be restored. 24 And all the trees of the field shall know that I am the Lord that bring low the high tree, and exalt the low tree, and wither the green tree, and cause the dry tree to flourish: I the Lord have spoken, and will do *it*.

Ezek.18 1 And the word of the Lord came to me, saying, 2 Son of man, what mean ye by this parable among the children of Israel, saying, The fathers have eaten unripe grapes, and the children's teeth have been set on edge? 3 *As* I live, saith the Lord, surely this parable shall no more be spoken in Israel. 4 For all souls are mine; as the soul of the father, so also the soul of the son, they are mine: the soul that sins, it shall die. 5 But the man who shall be just, who executes judgment and righteousness, 6 who shall not eat upon the mountains, and shall not at all lift up his eyes to the devices of the house of Israel, and shall not defile his neighbor's wife, and shall not draw nigh to her that is removed, 7 and shall not oppress any man, *but* shall return the pledge of the debtor, and shall be guilty of no plunder, shall give his bread to the hungry, and clothe the naked; 8

and shall not lend his money upon usury, and shall not receive usurious increase, and shall turn back his hand from injustice, shall execute righteous judgment between a man and his neighbor, 9 and has walked in my commandments and kept mine ordinances, to do them; he is righteous, he shall surely live, saith the Lord. 10 And if he beget a mischievous son, shedding blood and committing sins, 11 who has not walked in the way of his righteous father, but has even eaten upon the mountains, and has defiled his neighbor's wife, 12 and has oppressed the poor and needy, and has committed robbery, and not restored a pledge, and has set his eyes upon idols, has wrought iniquities, 13 has lent upon usury, and taken usurious increase; he shall by no means live: he has wrought all these iniquities; he shall surely die; his blood shall be upon him. 14 And if he beget a son, and *the son* see all his father's sins which he has wrought, and fear, and not do according to them, 15 and *if* he has not eaten on the mountains, and has not set his eyes on the devices of the house of Israel, and has not defiled his neighbor's wife, 16 and has not oppressed a man, and has not retained the pledge, nor committed robbery, has given his bread to the hungry, and has clothed the naked, 17 and has turned back his hand from unrighteousness, has not received interest or usurious increase, has wrought righteousness, and walked in mine ordinances; he shall not die for the iniquities of his father, he shall surely live. 18 But if his father grievously afflict, or plunder, he has wrought enmity in the midst of my people, and shall die in his iniquity. 19 But ye will say, Why has not the son borne the iniquity of the father? Because the son has wrought judgment and mercy, has kept all my statues, and done them, he shall surely live. 20 But the soul that sins shall die: and the son shall not bear the iniquity of the father, nor shall the father bear the iniquity of the son: the righteousness of the righteous shall be upon him, and the iniquity of the transgressor shall be upon him. 21 And if the transgressor turn away from all his iniquities which he has committed, and keep all my commandments, and do justice and mercy, he shall surely live, and shall by no means die. 22 None of his trespasses which he has committed shall be remembers: in his righteousness which he has done he shall live. 23 Shall I at all desire death of the sinner, saith the Lord, as I *desire* that he should turn from *his* evil way, and live? 24 But when the righteous man turns away from his righteousness, and commits iniquity, according to all the transgressions which the transgressor has wrought, none of his righteousness which he has wrought shall be at all remembered: in his trespass wherein he has trespassed, and in his sins wherein he has sinned, in them shall he die. 25 Yet ye have said, The way of the Lord is not straight. Hear now, all the house of Israel; will not my way be straight? Is your way straight? 26 When the righteous turns away from his righteousness and commits a trespass, and dies in the trespass he has committed, he shall *even* die in it. 27 And when the wicked man turns away from his wickedness that he has committed, and shall do judgment and justice, he has kept his soul, 28 and has turned away from all his ungodliness which he has committed: he shall surely live, he shall not die. 29 Yet the house of Israel say, The way of the Lord is not right. Is not my way right, O house of Israel? is not your way wrong? 30 I will judge you, O house of Israel, saith the Lord, each one according to his way: be converted, and turn from all your ungodliness, and it shall not become to you the punishment of iniquity. 31 Cast away from yourselves all your ungodliness wherein ye have sinned against me; and make to yourselves a new heart and a new spirit: for why should ye die, O house of Israel? 32 For I desire not the death of him that dies, saith the Lord.

Ezek.19 1 Moreover do thou take up a lamentation for the prince of Israel, 2 and say, Why is thy mother become a whelp in the midst of lions? in the midst of lions she has multiplied her whelps. 3 And one of her whelps sprang forth; he became a lion, and learned to take prey, he devoured men. 4 And the nations heard a report of him; he was caught in their pit, and they brought him into the land of Egypt in chains. 5 And she saw that he was driven away from her, *and* her hope *of him* perished, and she took another of her whelps; she made him a lion. 6 And he went up and down in the midst of lions, he became a lion, and learned to take prey, he devoured men. 7 And he prowled in his boldness and laid waste their cities, and made the land desolate, and the fullness of it, by the voice of his roaring. 8 Then the nations set upon him from the countries round about, and they spread their nets upon him: he was taken in their pit. 9 And they put him in chains and in a cage, *and* he came to the king of Babylon; and he cast him into prison, that his voice should not be heard on the mountains of Israel. 10 Thy mother was as a vine and as a blossom on a pomegranate tree, planted by water: her fruit and her shoot abounded by reason of much water. 11 And she became a rod for a tribe of princes, and was elevated in her bulk in the midst of *other* trees, and she saw her bulk in the multitude of her branches. 12 But she was broken down in wrath, she was cast upon the ground, and the east wind dried up her choice *branches*: vengeance came upon them, and the rod of her strength was withered; fire consumed it. 13 And now they have planted her in the wilderness, in a dry land. 14 And fire is gone out of a rod of her choice *boughs*, and has devoured her; and there was no rod of strength in her. Her race is become a parable of lamentation, and it shall be for a lamentation.

Ezek.20 1 And it came to pass in the seventh year, on the fifteenth day of the month, there came men of the elders of the house of Israel to enquire of the Lord, and they sat before me. 2 And the word of the Lord came to me, saying, 3 Son of man, speak to the elders of the house of Israel, and thou shalt say to them, Thus saith the Lord; Are ye come to enquire of me? *As* I live, I will not be enquired of by you, saith the Lord. 4 Shall I utterly take vengeance on them, son of man? testify to them of the iniquities of their fathers: 5 and thou shalt say to them, Thus saith the Lord; From the day that I chose the house of Israel, and became known to the seed of the house of Jacob, and was known to them in the land of Egypt, and helped them with my hand, saying, I am the Lord your God; 6 in that day I helped them with my hand, to bring them out of the land of Egypt into the land which I prepared for them, a land flowing with milk and honey, it is abundant beyond every land. 7 And I said to them, Let every one cast away the abominations of his eyes, and defile not yourselves with the devices of Egypt: I am the Lord your God. 8 But they revolted from me, and would not hearken to me: they cast not away the abominations of their eyes, and forsook not the devices of Egypt: then I said that I would pour out my wrath upon them, to accomplish my wrath upon them in the midst of Egypt. 9 But I wrought *so* that my name should not be at all profaned in the sight of the Gentiles, in the midst of whom they are, among whom I was made known to them in their sight, to bring them out of the land of Egypt. 10 And I brought them into the wilderness. 11 And I gave them my commandments, and made known to them mine ordinances, all which *if* a man shall do, he shall even live in them. 12 And I gave them my sabbaths, that they should be for a sign between me and them, that they should know that I am the Lord that sanctify them. 13 And I said to the house of Israel in the wilderness, Walk ye in my commandments: but they walked not *in them*, and they rejected mine ordinances, which *if* a man shall do, he shall even live in them; and they grievously profaned my sabbaths: and I said that I would pour out my wrath upon them in the wilderness, to consume them. 14 But I wrought *so* that my name should not be at all profaned before the Gentiles, before whose eyes I brought them out. 15 But I lifted up my hand against them in the wilderness once for all, that I would not bring them into the land which I gave them, a land flowing with milk and honey, it is sweeter than all lands: 16 because they rejected mine ordinances, and walked not in my commandments, but profaned my sabbaths, and went after the imaginations of their hearts. 17 Yet mine eyes spared them, so as *not* to destroy them utterly, and I did not make an end of them in the wilderness. 18 And I said to their children in the wilderness, Walk not ye in the customs of your fathers, and keep not their ordinances, and have no fellowship with their practices, nor defile yourselves *with them*. 19 I *am* the Lord your God; walk in my commandments, and keep mine ordinances, and do them; 20 and hallow my sabbaths, and let them be a sign between me and you, that ye may know that I am the Lord your God. 21 But they provoked me, and their children walked not in my commandments, and they took no heed to mine ordinances to do them, which *if* a man shall do, he shall even live in them, and they profaned my sabbaths: then I said that I would pour out my wrath upon them in the wilderness, to accomplish mine anger upon them. 22 But I wrought so that my name might not be at all profaned before the Gentiles; and I brought them out in their sight. 23 I lifted up my hand against them in the wilderness, that I would scatter them among the Gentiles, *and* disperse them in the countries; 24 because they kept not mine ordinances, and rejected my commandments, and profaned my sabbaths, and their eyes went after the imaginations of their fathers. 25 So I gave them commandments *that were* not good, and ordinances in which they should not live. 26 And I will defile them by their *own* decrees, when I pass through upon every one that opens the womb, that I may destroy them. 27 Therefore, son of man, speak to the house of Israel, and thou shalt say to them, Thus saith the Lord: Hitherto have your fathers provoked me in their trespasses in which they transgressed against me. 28 Whereas I brought them into the land concerning which I lifted up mine hand to give it them; and they looked upon every high hill, and every shady tree, and they sacrificed there to their gods, and offered there sweet-smelling savour, and there they poured out their drink-offerings. 29 And I said to them, What is Abama, that ye go in thither? and they called its name Abama, until this day. 30 Therefore say to the house of Israel, Thus saith the Lord, Do ye pollute yourselves with the iniquities of your fathers, and do ye go a-whoring after their abominations, 31 and *do ye pollute yourselves* with the first-fruits of your gifts, in the offerings wherewith ye pollute yourselves in all your imaginations, until this day; and shall I answer you, O house of Israel? *As* I live, saith the Lord, I will not answer you, neither shall this thing come upon your spirit. 32 And it shall not be as ye say, We will be as the nations, and as the tribes of the earth, to worship stocks and stones. 33 Therefore, *as* I live, saith the Lord, I will reign over you with a strong hand, and with a high arm, and with outpoured wrath: 34 I will bring you out from the nations, and will take you out of the lands wherein ye were dispersed, with a strong hand, and with a high arm, and with outpoured wrath. 35 And I will bring you into the wilderness of the nations, and will plead with you there face to face. 36 As I pleaded with your fathers in the wilderness of the land of Egypt, so will I judge you, saith the Lord. 37 And I will cause you to pass under my rod, and I will bring you in by number. 38 And I will separate from among you the ungodly and the revolters; for I will lead them forth out of their place of sojourning, and they shall not enter into the land of Israel: and ye shall know that I am the Lord, *even* the Lord. 39 And *as to* you, O house of Israel, thus saith the Lord, *even* the Lord; Put away each one his *evil* practices, and hereafter if ye hearken to me, then shall ye no more profane my holy name by your gifts and by devices. 40 For upon my holy mountain, on the high mountain, saith the Lord, *even* the Lord, there shall all the house of Israel serve me for ever: and there will I accept *you*, and there will I have respect to your first-fruits, and the first-fruits of your offerings, in all your holy things. 41 I will accept you with a sweet-smelling savour, when I bring you out from the nations, and take you out of the countries wherein ye have been dispersed; and I will be sanctified among you in the sight of the nations. 42 And ye shall know that I am the Lord, when I have brought you into the land of Israel, into the land concerning which I lifted up my hand to give it to your fathers. 43 And ye shall there remember your ways, and your devices wherewith ye defiled yourselves; and ye shall bewail yourselves for all your wickedness. 44 And ye shall know that I am the Lord, when I have done thus to you, that my name may not be profaned in your evil ways, and in your corrupt devices, saith the Lord. 45 And the word of the Lord came to me, saying, 46 Son of man, set thy face against Thaeman, and look toward Darom, and prophesy against the chief forest of Nageb, 47 and thou shalt say to the forest of Nageb, Hear the word of the Lord; thus saith the Lord, *even* the Lord;

Behold, I *will* kindle a fire in thee, and it shall devour in thee every green tree, and every dry tree: the flame that is kindled shall not be quenched, and every face shall be scorched with it from the south to the north. 48 And all flesh shall know that I the Lord have kindled it: it shall not be quenched. 49 And I said, Not so, O Lord God! they say to me, Is not this that is spoken a parable?

Ezek.21 1 And the word of the Lord came to me, saying, 2 Therefore prophesy, son of man, set thy face steadfastly toward Jerusalem, and look toward their holy places, and thou shalt prophesy against the land of Israel, 3 and thou shalt say to the land of Israel, Thus saith the Lord; Behold, I am against thee, and I will draw forth my sword out of its sheath, and I will destroy out of thee the transgressor and unrighteous. 4 Because I will destroy out of thee the unrighteous and the transgressor, *therefore* so shall my sword come forth out of its sheath against all flesh from the south to the north: 5 and all flesh shall know that I the Lord have drawn forth my sword out of its sheath: it shall not return any more. 6 And thou, son of man, groan with the breaking of thy loins; thou shalt even groan heavily in their sight. 7 And it shall come to pass, if they shall say to thee, Wherefore dost thou groan? that thou shalt say, For the report; because it comes: and every heart shall break, and all hands shall become feeble, and all flesh and every spirit shall faint, and all thighs shall be defiled with moisture: behold, it comes, saith the Lord. 8 And the word of the Lord came to me, saying, 9 Son of man, prophesy, and thou shalt say, Thus saith the Lord; Say, Sword, sword, be sharpened and rage, 10 that thou mayest slay victims; be sharpened that thou mayest be bright, ready for slaughter, slay, set at nought, despise every tree. 11 And he made it ready for his hand to hold: the sword is sharpened, it is ready to put into the hand of the slayer. 12 Cry out and howl, son of man: for this *sword* is come upon my people, this *sword is come* upon all the princes of Israel: they shall be as strangers: *judgment* with the sword is come upon my people: therefore clap thine hands, for sentence has been passed: 13 and what if even the tribe be rejected? it shall not be, saith the Lord God. 14 And thou, son of man, prophesy, and clap thine hands, and take a second sword: the third sword is *the sword* of the slain, the great sword of the slain: and thou shalt strike them with amazement, lest the heart should faint 15 and the weak ones be multiplied at every gate—they are given up to the slaughter of the sword: it is well fitted for slaughter, it is well fitted for glittering. 16 And do thou go on, sharpen thyself on the right and on the left whithersoever thy face may set itself. 17 And I also will clap my hands, and let loose my fury: I the Lord have spoken *it*. 18 And the word of the Lord came to me, saying, 19 and thou, son of man, appoint thee two ways, that the sword of the king of Babylon may enter in: the two shall go forth of one country; and *there shall be* a force at the top of the way of the city, thou shalt set *it* at the top of the way, 20 that the sword may enter in upon Rabbath of the children of Ammon, and upon Judea, and upon Jerusalem in the midst thereof. 21 For the king of Babylon shall stand on the old way, at the head of the two ways, to use divination, to make bright the arrow, and to enquire of the graven images, and to examine *the victims*. 22 On his right was the divination against Jerusalem, to cast a mound, to open the mouth in shouting, to lift up the voice with crying, to cast a mound against her gates, to cast up a heap, and to build forts. 23 And he was to them as one using divination before them, and he himself recounting his iniquities, that they might be borne in mind. 24 Therefore thus saith the Lord, Because ye have caused your iniquities to be remembered, in the discovery of your wickedness, so that your sins should be seen, in all your wickedness and in your *evil* practices; because ye have caused remembrance *of them*, in these shall ye be taken. 25 And thou profane wicked prince of Israel, whose day, *even* an end, is come in a sea of iniquity, thus saith the Lord; 26 Thou hast taken off the mitre and put on the crown, it shall not have such *another* after it: thou hast abased that which was high, and exalted that which was low. 27 Injustice, injustice, injustice, will I make it: woe to it: such shall it be until he comes to whom it belongs; and I will deliver *it* to him. 28 And thou, son of man, prophesy, and thou shalt say, Thus saith the Lord, concerning the children of Ammon, and concerning their reproach; and thou shalt say, O sword, sword, drawn for slaughter, and drawn for destruction, awake, that thou mayest gleam. 29 While thou art seeing vain *visions*, and while thou art prophesying falsehoods, to bring thyself upon the necks of ungodly transgressors, the day is come, *even* an end, in a season of iniquity. 30 Turn, rest not in this place wherein thou wert born: in thine own land will I judge thee. 31 And I will pour out my wrath upon thee, I will blow upon thee with the fire of my wrath, and I will deliver thee into the hands of barbarians skilled in working destruction. 32 Thou shalt be fuel for fire; thy blood shall be in the midst of thy land; there shall be no remembrance at all of thee: for I the Lord have spoken *it*.

Ezek.22 1 And the word of the Lord came to me, saying, 2 And thou, son of man, wilt thou judge the bloody city? yea, declare thou to her all her iniquities. 3 And thou shalt say, Thus saith the Lord God: O city that sheds blood in the midst of her, so that her time should come, and that forms devices against herself, to defile herself; 4 in their blood which thou hast shed, thou hast transgressed; and in thy devices which thou hast formed, thou hast polluted thyself; and thou hast brought nigh thy days, and hast brought on the time of thy years: therefore have I made thee a reproach to the Gentiles, and a mockery to all the countries, 5 to those near thee, and to those far distant from thee; and they shall mock thee, *thou that art* notoriously unclean, and abundant in iniquities. 6 Behold, the princes of the house of Israel have conspired in thee each one with his kindred, that they might shed blood. 7 In thee they have reviled father and mother; and in thee they have behaved unjustly toward the stranger: they have oppressed the orphan and widow. 8 And they have set at nought my holy things, and in thee they have profaned my sabbaths. 9 *There are* robbers in thee, to shed blood in thee; and in thee they have eaten upon the mountains: they have wrought ungodliness in the midst of thee. 10 In thee they have uncovered the father's shame; and

in thee they have humbled her that was set apart for uncleanness. 11 They have dealt unlawfully each one with his neighbor's wife; and each one in ungodliness has defiled his daughter-in-law: and in thee they have humbled each one his sister, the daughter of his father. 12 In thee they have received gifts to shed blood; they have received in thee interest and usurious increase; and by oppression thou hast brought thy wickedness to the full, and hast forgotten me, saith the Lord. 13 And if I shall smite my hand at *thine iniquities* which thou hast accomplished, which thou hast wrought, and at thy blood that has been shed in the midst of thee, 14 shall thy heart endure? shall thine hands be strong in the days which I bring upon thee? I the Lord have spoken, and will do *it*. 15 And I will scatter thee among the nations, and disperse thee in the countries, and thy uncleanness shall be removed out of thee. 16 And I will give heritages in thee in the sight of the nations, and ye shall know that I am the Lord. 17 And the word of the Lord came to me, saying, 18 Son of man, behold, the house of Israel are all become to me *as it were* mixed with brass, and iron, and tin, and lead; they are mixed up in the midst of the silver. 19 Therefore say, Thus saith the Lord God; Because ye have become one mixture, therefore I will gather you into the midst of Jerusalem. 20 As silver, and brass, and iron, and tin, and lead, are gathered into the midst of the furnace, to blow fire into it, that they may be melted: so will I take *you* in my wrath, and I will gather and melt you. 21 And I will blow upon you in the fire of my wrath, and ye shall be melted in the midst thereof. 22 As silver is melted in the midst of a furnace, so shall ye be melted in the midst thereof; and ye shall know that I the Lord have poured out my wrath upon you. 23 And the word of the Lord came to me, saying, 24 Son of man, say to her, Thou art the land that is not rained upon, neither has rain come upon thee in the day of wrath; 25 whose princes in the midst of her are as roaring lions seizing prey, devouring souls by oppression, and taking bribes; and thy widows are multiplied in the midst of thee. 26 Her priests also have set at nought my law, and profaned my holy things: they have not distinguished between the holy and profane, nor have they distinguished between the unclean and the clean, and have hid their eyes from my sabbaths, and I was profaned in the midst of them. 27 Her princes in the midst of her are as wolves ravening to shed blood, that they may get dishonest gain. 28 And her prophets that daub them shall fall, that see vanities, that prophesy falsehoods, saying, Thus saith the Lord, when the Lord has not spoken. 29 That sorely oppress the people of the land with injustice, and commit robbery; oppressing the poor and needy, and not dealing justly with the stranger. 30 And I sought from among them a man behaving uprightly, and standing before me perfectly in the time of wrath, so that I should not utterly destroy her: but I found *him* not. 31 So I have poured out my wrath upon her in the fury of mine anger, to accomplish *it*. I have recompensed their ways on their own heads, saith the Lord God.

Ezek.23 1 And the word of the Lord came to me, saying, 2 Son of man, there were two women, daughters of one mother: 3 and they went a-whoring in Egypt in their youth:

there their breasts fell, there they lost their virginity. 4 And their names were Oola the elder, and Ooliba her sister: and they were mine, and bore sons and daughters: and *as for* their names, Samaria was Oola, and Jerusalem was Ooliba. 5 And Oola went a-whoring from me, and doted on her lovers, on the Assyrians that were her neighbors, 6 clothed with purple, princes and captains; *they were* young men and choice, all horseman riding on horses. 7 And she bestowed her fornication upon them; all were choice sons of the Assyrians: and on whomsoever she doted herself, with them she defiled herself in all *their* devices. 8 And she forsook not her fornication with the Egyptians: for in her youth they committed fornication with her, and they deflowered her, and poured out their fornication upon her. 9 Therefore I delivered her into the hands of her lovers, into the hands of the children of the Assyrians, on whom she doted. 10 They uncovered her shame: they took her sons and daughters, and slew her with the sword: and she became a byword among women: and they wrought vengeance in her for the sake of the daughters. 11 And her sister Ooliba saw *it*, and she indulged in her fondness more corruptly than she, and in her fornication more than the fornication of her sister. 12 She doted upon the sons of the Assyrian, princes and captains, her neighbours, clothed with fine linen, horsemen riding on horses; *they were* all choice young men. 13 And I saw that they were defiled, *that* the two *had* one way. 14 And she increased her fornication, and she saw men painted on the wall, likenesses of the Chaldeans painted with a pencil, 15 having variegated girdles on their loins, having also richly dyed *attire* upon their heads; all had a princely appearance, the likeness of the children of the Chaldeans, of their native land. 16 And she doted upon them as soon as she saw them, and sent forth messengers to them into the land of the Chaldeans. 17 And the sons of Babylon came to her, into the bed of rest, and they defiled her in her fornication, and she was defiled by them, and her soul was alienated from them. 18 And she exposed her fornication, and exposed her shame: and my soul was alienated from her, even as my soul was alienated from her sister. 19 And thou didst multiply thy fornication, so as to call to remembrance the days of thy youth, wherein thou didst commit whoredom in Egypt, 20 and thou didst dote upon the Chaldeans, whose flesh is as the flesh of the asses, and their members *as* the members of horses. 21 And thou didst look upon the iniquity of thy youth, *the things* which thou wroughtest in Egypt in thy lodgings, where were the breasts of thy youth. 22 Therefore, Ooliba, thus saith the Lord; Behold, I *will* stir up thy lovers against thee, from whom thy soul is alienated, and I will bring them upon thee round about, 23 the children of Babylon, and all the Chaldeans, Phacuc, and Sue, and Hychue, and all the sons of the Assyrians with them; choice young men, governors and captains, all princes and renowned, riding on horses. 24 And they all shall come upon thee from the north, chariots and wheels, with a multitude of nations, shields and targets; and *the enemy* shall set a watch against thee round about: and I will set judgment before them, and they shall take vengeance on thee with their judgments. 25 And I will bring upon thee my jealousy, and they shall deal with thee in great wrath: they shall take away thy nose and thine ears; and shall cast down thy remnant with the sword: they shall take thy sons and thy daughters; and thy remnant fire shall devour. 26 And they shall strip thee of thy raiment, and take *away* thine ornaments. 27 So I will turn back thine ungodliness from thee, and thy fornication from the land of Egypt: and thou shalt not lift up thine eyes upon them, and shalt no more remember Egypt. 28 Wherefore thus saith the Lord God; Behold, I *will* deliver thee into the hands of those whom thou hatest, from whom thy soul is alienated. 29 And they shall deal with thee in hatred, and shall take all *the fruits* of thy labours and thy toils, and thou shalt be naked and bare: and the shame of thy fornication shall be exposed: and thy ungodliness and thy fornication 30 brought this upon thee, in that thou wentest a-whoring after the nations, and didst defile thyself with their devices. 31 Thou didst walk in the way of thy sister; and I will put her cup into thine hands. 32 Thus saith the Lord; Drink thy sister's cup, deep and large, and full, to cause complete drunkenness. 33 And thou shalt be thoroughly weakened; and the cup of destruction, the cup of thy sister Samaria, 34 drink thou it, and I will take away her feasts and her new moons: for I have spoken *it*, saith the Lord. 35 Therefore thus saith the Lord; Because thou has forgotten me, and cast me behind thy back, therefore receive thou *the reward* of thine ungodliness and thy fornication. 36 And the Lord said to me, Son of man, wilt thou not judge Oola and Ooliba? and declare to them their iniquities? 37 For they have committed adultery, and blood was in their hands, they committed adultery with their devices, and they passed through the fire to them their children which they bore to me. 38 So long too as they did these things to me, they defiled my sanctuary, and profaned my sabbaths. 39 And when they sacrificed their children to their idols, they also went into my sanctuary to profane it: and whereas they did thus in the midst of my house; 40 and whereas they did thus to the men that came from afar, to whom they sent messengers, and as soon as they came, immediately thou didst wash thyself, and didst paint thine eyes and adorn thyself with ornaments, 41 and satest on a prepared bed, and before it *there was* a table set out, and *as for* mine incense and mine oil, they rejoiced in them, 42 and they raised a sound of music, and *that* with men coming from the wilderness out of a multitude of men, and they put bracelets on their hands, and a crown of glory on their heads; 43 Therefore I said, Do they not commit adultery with these? and has she also gone a-whoring *after* the manner of a harlot? 44 And they went in to her, as *men* go in to a harlot; so they went in to Oola and to Ooliba to work iniquity. 45 And they are just men, and shall take vengeance on them with the judgment of an adulteress and the judgment of blood: for they are adulteresses, and blood is in their hands. 46 Thus saith the Lord God, Bring up a multitude upon them, and send trouble and plunder into the midst of them. 47 And stone them with the stones of a multitude, and pierce them with their swords: they shall slay their sons and their daughters, and shall burn up their houses. 48 And I will remove ungodliness out of the land, and all the women shall be instructed, and shall not do according to their ungodliness.

49 And your ungodliness shall be recompensed upon you, and ye shall bear the guilt of your devices: and ye shall know that I am the Lord.

Ezek.24 1 And the word of the Lord came to me, in the ninth year, in the tenth month, on the tenth *day* of the month, saying, 2 Son of man, write for thyself daily from this day, on which the king of Babylon set himself against Jerusalem, *even* from this day. 3 And speak a parable to the provoking house, and thou shalt say to them, Thus saith the Lord; Set on the caldron, and pour water into it: 4 and put the pieces into it, every prime piece, the leg and shoulder taken off from the bones, 5 *which are* taken from choice cattle, and burn the bones under them: her bones are boiled and cooked in the midst of her. 6 Therefore thus saith the Lord; O bloody city, the caldron in which there is scum, and the scum has not gone out of, she has brought it forth piece by piece, no lot has fallen upon it. 7 For her blood is in the midst of her; I have set it upon a smooth rock: I have not poured it out upon the earth, so that the earth should cover it; 8 that my wrath should come up for complete vengeance to be taken: I set her blood upon a smooth rock, so as not to cover it. 9 Therefore thus saith the Lord, I will also make the firebrand great, 10 and I will multiply the wood, and kindle the fire, that the flesh may be consumed, and the liquor boiled away; 11 and that *it* may stand upon the coals, that her brass may be thoroughly heated, and be melted in the midst of her filthiness, and her scum may be consumed, 12 and her abundant scum may not come forth of her. 13 Her scum shall become shameful, because thou didst defile thyself: and what if thou shalt be purged no more until I have accomplished my wrath? 14 I the Lord have spoken; and it shall come, and I will do *it*; I will not delay, neither will I have any mercy: I will judge thee, saith the Lord, according to thy ways, and according to thy devices: therefore will I judge thee according to thy bloodshed, and according to thy devices will I judge thee, thou unclean, notorious, and abundantly provoking one. 15 And the word of the Lord came to me, saying, 16 Son of man, behold I take from thee the desire of thine eyes by violence: thou shalt not lament, neither shalt thou weep. 17 Thou shalt groan for blood, and have mourning upon thy loins; thy hair shall not be braided upon thee, and thy sandals *shall be* on thy feet; thou shalt in no wise be comforted by their lips, and thou shalt not eat the bread of men. 18 And I spoke to the people in the morning, as he commanded me in the evening, and I did in the morning as it was commanded me. 19 And the people said to me, Wilt thou not tell us what these things are that thou doest? 20 Then I said to them, The word of the Lord came to me, saying, 21 Say to the house of Israel, Thus saith the Lord; Behold, I *will* profane my sanctuary, the boast of your strength, the desire of your eyes, and for which your souls are concerned; and your sons and your daughters, whom ye have left, shall fall by the sword. 22 And ye shall do as I have done: ye shall not be comforted at their mouth, and ye shall not eat the bread of men. 23 And your hair *shall be* upon your head, and your shoes on your feet: neither shall ye at all lament or weep; but ye shall pine away in your

iniquities, and shall comfort every one his brother. 24 And Jezekiel shall be for a sign to you: according to all that I have done shall ye do, when these things shall come; and ye shall know that I am the Lord. 25 And thou, son of man, *shall it* not *be* in the day when I take their strength from them, the pride of their boasting, the desires of their eyes, and the pride of their soul, their sons and their daughters, 26 that in that day he that escapes shall come to thee, to tell *it* thee in thine ears? 27 In that day thy mouth shall be opened to him that escapes; thou shalt speak, and shalt be no longer dumb: and thou shalt be for a sign to them, and they shall know that I am the Lord.

Ezek.25 1 And the word of the Lord came to me, saying, 2 Son of man, set thy face steadfastly against the children of Ammon, and prophesy against them; 3 and thou shalt say to the children of Ammon, Hear ye the word of the Lord; thus saith the Lord; Forasmuch as ye have rejoiced against my sanctuary, because it was profaned; and against the land of Israel, because it was laid waste; and against the house of Juda, because they went into captivity; 4 therefore, behold, I *will* deliver you to the children of Kedem for an inheritance, and they shall lodge in thee with their stuff, and they shall pitch their tents in thee: they shall eat thy fruits, and they shall drink thy milk. 5 And I will give up the city of Ammon for camels' pastures, and the children of Ammon for a pasture of sheep: and ye shall know that I am the Lord. 6 For thus saith the Lord; Because thou hast clapped thine hands, and stamped with thy foot, and heartily rejoiced against the land of Israel; 7 therefore I will stretch out my hand against thee, and I will make thee a spoil to the nations; and I will utterly destroy thee from among the peoples, and I will completely cut thee off from out of the countries: and thou shalt know that I am the Lord. 8 Thus saith the Lord; Because Moab has said, Behold, are not the house of Israel and Juda like all the *other* nations? 9 Therefore, behold, I will weaken the shoulder of Moab from his frontier cities, *even* the choice land, the house of Bethasimuth above the fountain of the city, by the sea -side. 10 I have given him the children of Kedem in addition to the children of Ammon for an inheritance, that there may be no remembrance of the children of Ammon. 11 And I will execute vengeance on Moab; and they shall know that I am the Lord. 12 Thus saith the Lord; Because of what the Idumeans have done in taking vengeance on the house of Juda, and *because they* have remembered injuries, and have exacted full recompense; 13 therefore thus saith the Lord; I will also stretch out my hand upon Idumea, and will utterly destroy out of it man and beast; and will make it desolate; and they that are pursued out of Thaeman shall fall by the sword. 14 And I will execute my vengeance on Idumea by the hand of my people Israel: and they shall deal in Idumea according to mine anger and according to my wrath, and they shall know my vengeance, saith the Lord. 15 Therefore thus saith the Lord, Because the Philistines have wrought revengefully, and raised up vengeance rejoicing from their heart to destroy *the Israelites* to a man; 16 therefore thus saith the Lord; Behold, I *will* stretch out my hand upon the Philistines, and will utterly destroy the Cretans, and will cut off the remnant that dwell by the sea-coast. 17 And I will execute great vengeance upon them; and they shall know that I am the Lord, when I have brought my vengeance upon them.

Ezek.26 1 And it came to pass in the eleventh year, on the first *day* of the month, *that* the word of the Lord came to me, saying, 2 Son of man, because Sor has said against Jerusalem, Aha, she is crushed: the nations are destroyed: she is turned to me: she that was full is made desolate: 3 therefore thus saith the Lord; Behold, I am against thee, O Sor, and I will bring up many nations against thee, as the sea comes up with its waves. 4 And they shall cast down the walls of Sor, and shall cast down thy towers: and I will scrape her dust from off her, and make her a bare rock. 5 She shall be in the midst of the sea a place for repairing nets: for I have spoken *it*, saith the Lord: and it shall be a spoil for the nations. 6 And her daughters *which are* in the field shall be slain with the sword, and they shall know that I am the Lord. 7 For thus saith the Lord; Behold, I *will* bring up against thee, O Sor, Nabuchodonosor king of Babylon from the north: he is a king of kings, with horses, and chariots, and horsemen, and a concourse of very many nations. 8 He shall slay thy daughters that are in the field with the sword, and shall set a watch against thee, and build forts around thee, and carry a rampart round against thee, and set up warlike works, and array his spears against thee. 9 He shall cast down with his swords thy walls and thy towers. 10 By reason of thy multitude of his horses their dust shall cover thee, and by reason of the sound of his horsemen and the wheels of his chariots the walls shall be shaken, when he enters into thy gates, as one entering into a city from the plain. 11 With the hoofs of his horses they shall trample all thy streets: he shall slay thy people with the sword, and shall bring down to the ground the support of thy strength. 12 And he shall prey upon thy power, and plunder thy substance, and shall cast down thy walls, and break down thy pleasant houses: and he shall cast thy stones and thy timber and thy dust into the midst of thy sea. 13 And he shall destroy the multitude of thy musicians, and the sound of thy psalteries shall be heard no more. 14 And I will make thee a bare rock: thou shalt be a place to spread nets upon; thou shalt be built no more: for I the Lord have spoken *it*, saith the Lord. 15 For thus saith the Lord God to Sor; Shall not the isles shake at the sound of thy fall, while the wounded are groaning, while they have drawn a sword in the midst of thee? 16 And all the princes of the nations of the sea shall come down from their thrones, and shall take off their crowns from their heads, and shall take off their embroidered raiment: they shall be utterly amazed; they shall sit upon the ground, and fear their *own* destruction, and shall groan over thee. 17 And they shall take up a lamentation for thee, and shall say to thee, How art thou destroyed from out of the sea, the renowned city, that brought her terror upon all her inhabitants. 18 And the isles shall be alarmed at the day of thy fall. 19 For thus saith the Lord God; When I shall make the city desolate, as the cities that shall not be inhabited, when I have brought the deep up upon thee, 20 and great waters shall cover thee;

and I shall bring thee down to them that go down to the pit, to the people of old time, and shall cause thee to dwell in the depths of the earth, as in everlasting desolation, with them that go down to the pit, that thou mayest not be inhabited, nor stand upon the land of life; 21 I will make thee a destruction, and thou shalt be no more for ever, saith the Lord God.

Ezek.27 1 And the word of the Lord came to me saying, 2 And thou, son of man, take up a lamentation against Sor; 3 and thou shalt say to Sor that dwells at the entrance of the sea, to the mart of the nations coming from many islands, Thus saith the Lord to Sor; Thou hast said, I have clothed myself with my beauty. 4 In the heart of the sea thy sons have put beauty upon thee for Beelim. 5 Cedar in Senir was employed for thee in building: boards of cypress timber were taken out of Libanus, and wood to make thee masts of fir. 6 They made thine oars *of wood* out of the land of Basan; thy sacred utensils they made of ivory, thy shady houses of wood from the isles of Chetiim. 7 Fine linen with embroidery from Egypt supplied the couch, to put honour upon thee, and to clothe thee with blue and purple from the isles of Elisai; and they became thy coverings. 8 And thy princes were the dwellers in Sidon, and the Aradians were thy rowers: thy wise men, O Sor, who were in thee, these were thy pilots. 9 The elders of the Biblians, and their wise men, who were in thee, these helped thy counsel: and all the ships of the sea and their rowers traded for thee to the utmost west. 10 Persians and Lydians and Libyans were in thine army: thy warriors hung in thee shields and helmets; these gave *thee* thy glory. 11 The sons of the Aradians and thine army were upon the walls; there were guards in thy towers: they hung their quivers on thy battlements round about; these completed thy beauty. 12 The Carthaginians were thy merchants because of the abundance of all thy strength; they furnished thy market with silver, and gold, and iron, and tin, and lead. 13 Greece, both the whole *world*, and the adjacent coasts, these traded with thee in the persons of men, and they gave *as* thy merchandise vessels of brass. 14 Out of the house of Thogarma horses and horsemen furnished the market. 15 The sons of the Rhodians were thy merchants; from the islands they multiplied thy merchandise, *even* elephants' teeth: and to them that came in thou didst return thy prices, 16 *even* men *as* thy merchandise, from the multitude of thy trading *population*, myrrh and embroidered works from Tharsis: Ramoth also and Chorchor furnished thy market. 17 Juda and the children of Israel, these were thy merchants; in the sale of corn and ointments and cassia: and they gave the best honey, and oil, and resin, to thy trading *population*. 18 *The people of* Damascus were thy merchants by reason of the abundance of all thy power; wine out of Chelbon, and wool from Miletus; and they brought wine into thy market. 19 Out of Asel *came* wrought iron, and there is the sound of wheels among thy trading *population*. 20 *The people of* Daedan were thy merchants, with choice cattle for chariots. 21 Arabia and all the princes of Kedar, these were thy traders with thee, *bringing* camels, and lambs, and rams, in which they trade with thee. 22 The merchants of Sabba and

Ramma, these were thy merchants, with choice spices, and precious stones: and they brought gold to thy market. 23 Charra, and Chanaa, these were thy merchants: Assur, and Charman, were thy merchants: 24 bringing *for* merchandise blue, and choice stores bound with cords, and cypress wood. 25 Ships were thy merchants, in abundance, with thy trading *population*: and thou wast filled and very heavily loaded in the heart of the sea. 26 Thy rowers have brought thee into great waters: the south wind has broken thee in the heart of the sea. 27 Thy forces, and thy gain, and that of thy traders, and thy rowers, and thy pilots, and thy counselors, and they that traffic with thee, and all thy warriors that are in thee: and all thy company in the midst of thee shall perish in the heart of the sea, in the day of thy fall. 28 At the cry of thy voice thy pilots shall be greatly terrified. 29 And all the rowers and the mariners shall come down from the ships, and the pilots of the sea shall stand on the land. 30 And they shall wail over thee with their voice, and cry bitterly, and put earth on their heads, and spread ashes under them. 31,32 And their sons shall take up a *lament* for thee, even a lamentation for Sor, *saying*, 33 How large a reward hast thou gained from the sea? thou hast filled nations out of thine abundance; and out of thy mixed merchandise thou hast enriched all the kings of the earth. 34 Now art thou broken in the sea, thy traders are in the deep water, and all thy company in the midst of thee: all thy rowers have fallen. 35 All the dwellers in the islands have mourned over thee, and their kings have been utterly amazed, and their countenance has wept. 36 Merchants from the nations have hissed at thee; thou art utterly destroyed, and shalt not be any more for ever.

Ezek.28 1 And the word of the Lord came to me, saying, 2 And thou, son of man, say to the prince of Tyrus, Thus saith the Lord; Because thine heart has been exalted, and thou hast said, I am God, I have inhabited the dwelling of God in the heart of the sea; yet thou art man and not God, though thou hast set thine heart as the heart of God: 3 art thou wiser than Daniel? or have not the wise instructed thee with their knowledge? 4 Hast thou gained power for thyself by thine *own* knowledge or thine *own* prudence, and *gotten* gold and silver in thy treasures? 5 By thy abundant knowledge and thy traffic thou hast multiplied thy power; thy heart has been lifted up by thy power. 6 Therefore thus saith the Lord; Since thou hast set thine heart as the hart of God; 7 because of this, behold, I *will* bring on thee strange plagues from the nations; and they shall draw their swords against thee, and against the beauty of thy knowledge, 8 and they shall bring down thy beauty to destruction. And they shall bring thee down; and thou shalt die the death of the slain in the heart of the sea. 9 Wilt thou indeed say, I am God, before them that slay thee? whereas thou art man, and not God. 10 Thou shalt perish by the hands of strangers among the multitude of the uncircumcised: for I have spoken it, saith the Lord. 11 And the word of the Lord came to me, saying, 12 Son of man, take up a lamentation for the prince of Tyre, and say to him, Thus saith the Lord God; Thou art a seal of resemblance, and crown of beauty. 13 Thou wast in the delight of the paradise of God; thou hast

bound upon thee every precious stone, the sardius, and topaz, and emerald, and carbuncle, and sapphire, and jasper, and silver, and gold, and ligure, and agate, and amethyst, and chrysolite, and beryl, and onyx: and thou hast filled thy treasures and thy stores in thee with gold. 14 From the day that thou wast created thou *wast* with the cherub: I set thee on the holy mount of God; thou wast in the midst of the stones of fire. 15 Thou wast faultless in thy days, from the day that thou wast created, until iniquity was found in thee. 16 Of the abundance of thy merchandise thou hast filled thy storehouses with iniquity, and hast sinned: therefore thou hast been cast down wounded from the mount of God, and the cherub has brought thee out of the midst of the stones of fire. 17 Thy heart has been lifted up because of thy beauty; thy knowledge has been corrupted with thy beauty: because of the multitude of thy sins I have cast thee to the ground, I have caused thee to be put to open shame before kings. 18 Because of the multitude of thy sins and the iniquities of thy merchandise, I have profaned thy sacred things; and I will bring fire out of the midst of thee, this shall devour thee; and I will make thee *to be* ashes upon thy land before all that see thee. 19 And all that know thee among the nations shall groan over thee: thou art gone to destruction, and thou shalt not exist any more. 20 And the word of the Lord came to me, saying, 21 Son of man, set thy face against Sidon, and prophesy against it, 22 and say, Thus saith the Lord; Behold, I am against thee, O Sidon; and I will be glorified in thee; and thou shalt know that I am the Lord, when I have wrought judgments in thee, and I will be sanctified in thee. 23 Blood and death *shall be* in thy streets; and *men* wounded with swords shall fall in thee and on every side of thee; and they shall know that I am the Lord. 24 And there shall no more be in the house of Israel a thorn of bitterness and a pricking briar proceeding from them that are round about them, who dishonoured them; and they shall know that I am the Lord. 25 Thus saith the Lord God; I will also gather Israel from the nations, among whom they have been scattered, and I will be sanctified among them, and before the peoples and nations: and they shall dwell upon their land, which I gave to my servant Jacob. 26 Yea, they shall dwell upon it safely, and they shall build houses, and plant vineyards, and dwell securely, when I shall execute judgment on all that have dishonoured them, *even* on those *that are* round about them; and they shall know that I am the Lord their God, and the God of their fathers.

Ezek.29 1 In the twelfth year, in the tenth month, on the first *day* of the month, the word of the Lord came to me, saying, 2 Son of man, set thy face against Pharao king of Egypt, and prophesy against him, and against the whole of Egypt: 3 and say, Thus saith the Lord; Behold, I am against Pharao, the great dragon that lies in the midst of his rivers, that says, The rivers are mine, and I made them. 4 And I will put hooks in thy jaws, and I will cause the fish of thy river to stick to thy sides, and I will bring thee up out of the midst of thy river: 5 and I will quickly cast down thee and all the fish of thy river: thou shalt fall on the face of the plain, and shalt by no means be gathered, and shalt not be brought together: I have given thee for food to the wild beasts of the earth and to the fowls of the sky. 6 And all the dwellers in Egypt shall know that I am the Lord, because thou hast been a staff of reed to the house of Israel. 7 When they took hold of thee with their hand, thou didst break: and when every hand was clapped against them, and when they leaned on thee, thou wast utterly broken, and didst crush the loins of them all. 8 Therefore thus saith the Lord; Behold, I *will* bring a sword upon thee, and will cut off from thee man and beast; 9 and the land of Egypt shall be ruined and desert; and they shall know that I am the Lord; because thou sayest, The rivers are mine, and I made them. 10 Therefore, behold, I am against thee, and against all thy rivers, and I will give up the land of Egypt to desolation, and the sword, and destruction, from Magdol and Syene even to the borders of the Ethiopians. 11 No foot of man shall pass through it, and no foot of beast shall pass through it, and it shall not be inhabited for forty years. 12 And I will cause her land to be utterly destroyed in the midst of a land that is desolate, and her cities shall be *desolate* forty years in the midst of cities that are desolate: and I will disperse Egypt among the nations, and will utterly scatter them into the countries. 13 Thus saith the Lord; After forty years I will gather the Egyptians from the nations among whom they have been scattered; 14 and I will turn the captivity of the Egyptians, and will cause them to dwell in the land of Phathore, in the land whence they were taken; 15 and it shall be a base kingdom beyond all *other* kingdoms; it shall not any more be exalted over the nations; and I will make them few in number, that they may not be *great* among the nations. 16 And they shall no more be to the house of Israel a confidence bringing iniquity to remembrance, when they follow after them; and they shall know that I am the Lord. 17 And it came to pass in the twenty-seventh year, on the first *day* of the month, the word of the Lord came to me, saying, 18 Son of man, Nabuchodonosor king of Babylon caused his army to serve a great service against Tyre; every head was bald, and every shoulder peeled; yet there was no reward to him or to his army *serving* against Tyre, nor for the service wherewith they served against it. 19 Thus saith the Lord God; Behold, I *will* give to Nabuchodonosor king of Babylon the land of Egypt, and he shall take the plunder thereof, and seize the spoils thereof; and *it* shall be a reward for his army. 20 In return for his service wherewith he served against Tyre, I have given him the land of Egypt; thus saith the Lord God: 21 In that day shall a horn spring forth for all the house of Israel, and I will give thee an open mouth in the midst of them; and they shall know that I am the Lord.

Ezek.30 1 And the word of the Lord came to me, saying, 2 Son of man, prophesy, and say, Thus saith the Lord; Woe, woe *worth* the day! 3 For the day of the Lord is nigh, a day of cloud; it shall be the end of the nations. 4 And the sword shall come upon the Egyptians, and there shall be tumult in Ethiopia, and in Egypt *men* shall fall down slain together, and her foundations shall fall. 5 Persians, and Cretans, and Lydians, and Libyans, and all the mixed multitude, and they of the children of my covenant, shall fall by the sword

therein. 6 And the supports of Egypt shall fall; and the pride of her strength shall come down from Magdol to Syene: they shall fall by the sword in it, saith the Lord. 7 And it shall be made desolate in the midst of desolate countries, and their cities shall be *desolate* in the midst of desolate cities: 8 and they shall know that I am the Lord, when I shall send fire upon Egypt, and *when* all that help her shall be broken. 9 In that day shall messengers go forth hasting to destroy Ethiopia utterly, and there shall be tumult among them in the day of Egypt: for, behold it comes. 10 Thus saith the Lord God; I will also destroy the multitude of the Egyptians by the hand of Nabuchodonosor king of Babylon, 11 his *hand* and his people's; *they are* plagues sent forth from the nations to destroy the land: and they all shall unsheath their swords against Egypt, and the land shall be filled with slain. 12 And I will make their rivers desolate, and will destroy the land and the fulness of it by the hands of strangers: I the Lord have spoken. 13 For thus saith the Lord God; I will also destroy the nobles from Memphis, and the princes of Memphis out of the land of Egypt; and they shall be no more. 14 And I will destroy the land of Phathore, and will send fire upon Tanis, and will execute vengeance on Diospolis. 15 And I will pour out my wrath upon Sais the strength of Egypt, and will destroy the multitude of Memphis. 16 And I will send fire upon Egypt; and Syene shall be sorely troubled; and there shall be a breaking in Diospolis, and waters shall be poured out. 17 The youths of Heliopolis and Bubastum shall fall by the sword, and the women shall go into captivity. 18 And the day shall be darkened in Taphnae, when I have broken there the scepters of Egypt: and the pride of her strength shall perish there: and a cloud shall cover her, and her daughters shall be taken prisoners. 19 And I will execute judgment on Egypt; and they shall know that I am the Lord. 20 And it came to pass in the eleventh year, in the first month, on the seventh *day* of the month, the word of the Lord came to me, saying, 21 Son of man, I have broken the arms of Pharao, king of Egypt; and, behold, it has not been bound up to be healed, to have a plaster put upon it, *or* to be strengthened to lay hold of the sword. 22 Therefore thus saith the Lord God; Behold, I am against Pharao king of Egypt, and I will break his strong and outstretched arms, and will smite down his sword out of his hand. 23 And I will disperse the Egyptians among the nations, and will utterly scatter them among the countries. 24 And I will strengthen the arms of the king of Babylon, and put my sword into his hand: and he shall bring it upon Egypt, and shall take her plunder and seize her spoils. 25 Yea, I will strengthen the arms of the king of Babylon, and the arms of Pharao shall fail: and they shall know that I am the Lord, when I have put my sword into the hands of the king of Babylon, and he shall stretch it out over the land of Egypt. 26 And I will disperse the Egyptians among the nations, and utterly scatter them among the countries; and they all shall know that I am the Lord.

Ezek.31 1 And it came to pass in the eleventh year, in the third month, on the first *day* of the month, the word of the Lord came to me, saying, 2 Son of man, say to Pharao king of Egypt, and to his multitude; To whom hast thou compared thyself in thy haughtiness? 3 Behold, the Assyrian was a cypress in Libanus, and was fair in shoots, and high in stature: his top reached to the midst of the clouds. 4 The water nourished him, the depth made him grow tall; she led her rivers round about his plants, and she sent forth her streams to all the trees of the field. 5 Therefore was his stature exalted above all the trees of the field, and his branches spread far by the help of much water. 6 All the birds of the sky made their nests in his boughs, and under his branches all the wild beasts of the field bred; the whole multitude of nations dwelt under his shadow. 7 And he was fair in his height by reason of the multitude of his branches: for his roots were amidst much water. 8 And such cypresses *as this* were in the paradise of God; and there were no pines like his shoots, and there were no firs like his branches: no tree in the paradise of God was like him in his beauty, 9 because of the multitude of his branches: and the trees of God's paradise of delight envied him. 10 Therefore thus saith the Lord; Because thou art grown great, and hast set thy top in the midst of the clouds, and I saw when he was exalted; 11 therefore I delivered him into the hands of the prince of the nations, and he wrought his destruction. 12 And ravaging strangers from the nations have destroyed him, and have cast him down upon the mountains: his branches fell in all the valleys, and his boughs were broken in every field of the land; and all the people of the nations are gone down from their shelter, and have laid him low. 13 All the birds of the sky have settled on his fallen trunk, and all the wild beasts of the field came upon his boughs: 14 in order that none of the trees by the water should exalt themselves by reason of their size: whereas they set their top in the midst of the clouds, yet they continued not in their high state in their place, all that drank water, all were consigned to death, to the depth of the earth, in the midst of the children of men, with them that go down to the pit. 15 Thus saith the Lord God; In the day wherein he went down to Hades, the deep mourned for him: and I stayed her floods, and restrained her abundance of water: and Libanus saddened for him, all the trees of the field fainted for him. 16 At the sound of his fall the nations quaked, when I brought him down to Hades with them that go down to the pit: and all the trees of Delight comforted him in the heart, and the choice of *plants* of Libanus, all that drink water. 17 For they went down to hell with him among the slain with the sword; and his seed, *even* they that dwelt under his shadow, perished in the midst of their life. 18 To whom art thou compared? descend, and be thou debased with the trees of paradise to the depth of the earth: thou shalt lie in the midst of the uncircumcised with them that are slain by the sword. Thus shall Pharao be, and the multitude of his host, saith the Lord God.

Ezek.32 1 And it came to pass in the twelfth year, in the tenth month, on the first *day* of the month, *that* the word of the Lord came to me, saying, 2 Son of man, take up a lamentation for Pharao king of Egypt, and say to him, Thou art become like a lion of the nations, and as a serpent that is in the sea: and thou didst make assaults with thy rivers, and didst disturb the water with thy feet, and didst trample thy rivers. 3 Thus saith the Lord; I will also cast over thee the nets of many nations, and will bring thee up with my hook: 4 and I will stretch thee upon the earth: the fields shall be covered *with thee*, and I will cause all the birds of the sky to settle upon thee, and I will fill *with thee* all the wild beasts of the earth. 5 And I will cast thy flesh upon the mountains, and will saturate *them* with thy blood. 6 And the land shall be drenched with thy dung, because of thy multitude upon the mountains: I will fill the valleys with thee. 7 And I will veil the heavens when thou art extinguished, and will darken the stars thereof; I will cover the sun with a cloud, and the moon shall not give her light. 8 All the *bodies* that give light in the sky, shall be darkened over thee, and I will bring darkness upon the earth, saith the Lord God. 9 And I will provoke to anger the heart of many people, when I shall lead thee captive among the nations, to a land which thou hast not known. 10 And many nations shall mourn over thee, and their kings shall be utterly amazed, when my sword flies in their faces, as they wait for their *own* fall from the day of thy fall. 11 For thus saith the Lord God; The sword of the king of Babylon shall come upon thee, 12 with the swords of mighty men; and I will cast down thy strength: *they are* all destroying ones from the nations, and they shall destroy the pride of Egypt, and all her strength shall be crushed. 13 And I will destroy all her cattle from *beside* the great water; and the foot of man shall not trouble it any more, and the step of cattle shall no more trample it. 14 Thus shall their waters then be at rest, and their rivers shall flow like oil, saith the Lord, 15 when I shall give up Egypt to destruction, and the land shall be made desolate with the fullness thereof; when I shall scatter all that dwell in it, and they shall know that I am the Lord. 16 There is a lamentation, and thou shalt utter it; and the daughters of the nations shall utter it, *even* for Egypt, and they shall mourn for it over all the strength thereof, saith the Lord God. 17 And it came to pass in the twelfth year, in the first month, on the fifteenth *day* of the month, the word of the Lord came to me, saying, 18 Son of man, lament over the strength of Egypt, for the nations shall bring down her daughters dead to the depth of the earth, to them that go down to the pit. 19 20 They shall fall with him in the midst of them *that are* slain with the sword, and all his strength shall perish: the giants also shall say to thee, 21 Be thou in the depth of the pit: to whom art thou superior? yea, go down, and lie with the uncircumcised, in the midst of them *that are* slain with the sword. 22 There are Assur and all his company: all *his* slain have been laid there: 23 and their burial is in the depth of the pit, and his company are set around about his tomb: all the slain that fell by the sword, who had caused the fear of them *to be* upon the land of the living. 24 There is Ælam and all his host round about his tomb: all the slain that fell by the sword, and the uncircumcised that go down to the deep of the earth, who caused their fear to be upon the land of the living: and they have received their punishment with them that go down to the pit, 25 in the midst of the slain. 26 There were laid Mosoch, and Thobel, and all his strength round about his tomb: all his slain men, all the uncircumcised, slain with the sword, who caused their fear to be in the land of the living. 27 And they are laid with the giants that fell of old, who went down to Hades with *their* weapons of war: and they laid their swords under their heads, but their iniquities were upon their bones, because they terrified all men during their life. 28 And thou shalt lie in the midst of the uncircumcised, with them that have been slain by the sword. 29 There are laid the princes of Assur, who yielded their strength to a wound of the sword: these are laid with the slain, with them that go down to the pit. 30 There are the princes of the north, *even* all the captains of Assur, who go down slain *to Hades*: they lie uncircumcised among the slain with the sword together with their terror and their strength, and they have received their punishment with them that go down to the pit. 31 King Pharao shall see them, and shall be comforted over all their force, saith the Lord God. 32 For I have caused his fear to be upon the land of the living yet he shall lie in the midst of the uncircumcised with them that are slain with the sword, *even* Pharao, and all his multitude with him, saith the Lord God.

Ezek.33 1 And the word of the Lord came to me, saying, 2 Son of man, speak to the children of thy people, and thou shalt say to them, On whatsoever land I shall bring a sword, and the people of the land take one man of them, and set him for their watchman: 3 and he shall see the sword coming upon the land, and blow the trumpet, and sound an alarm to the people; 4 and he that hears the sound of the trumpet shall hear *indeed*, and *yet* not take heed, and the sword shall come upon him, and overtake him, his blood shall be upon his *own* head. 5 Because he heard the sound of the trumpet, and took no heed, his blood shall be upon him: but the other, because he took heed, has delivered his soul. 6 But if the watchman see the sword coming, and do not sound the trumpet, and the people do not watch; and the sword come, and take a soul from among them, that *soul* is taken because of its iniquity; but the blood *thereof* will I require at the watchman's hand. 7 And thou, son of man, I have set thee *as* a watchman to the house of Israel, and thou shalt hear a word from my mouth. 8 When I say to the sinner, Thou shalt surely die; *if* thou speak not to warn the wicked from his way, the wicked himself shall die in his iniquity; but his blood will I require at thine hand. 9 But if thou forewarn the wicked of his way to turn from it, and he turn not from his way, he shall die in his ungodliness; but thou hast delivered thine own soul. 10 And thou, son of man, say to the house of Israel; Thus have ye spoken, saying, Our errors, and our iniquities weigh upon us, and we pine away in them, and how then shall we live? 11 Say to them, Thus saith the Lord; *As* I live, I desire not the death of the ungodly, as that the ungodly should turn from his way and live: turn ye heartily from your way; for why will ye die, O house of Israel? 12 Say to the children of thy people, The righteousness of the righteous shall not deliver him, in the day wherein he errs: and the iniquity of the ungodly shall not harm him, in the day wherein he turns from his iniquity, but the righteous *erring* shall not be able to deliver himself. 13 When I say to the righteous, *Thou shalt live; and* he trusts in his righteousness, and shall commit iniquity, none of his righteousnesses shall be remembered; in his unrighteousness which he has wrought, in it shall he die. 14 And when I say to the ungodly, Thou shalt surely die; and he shall turn from his sin, and do judgment and justice, 15 and return the pledge, and repay that which he has robbed, *and* walk in the ordinances of life, so as to do no wrong; he shall surely live, and shall not die. 16 None of his sins which he has committed shall be remembered: because he has wrought judgment and righteousness; by them shall he live. 17 Yet the children of thy people will say, The way of the Lord is not straight: whereas this their way is not straight. 18 When the righteous turns away from his righteousness, and shall commit iniquities, then shall he die in them. 19 And when the sinner turns from his iniquity, and shall do judgment and righteousness, he shall live by them. 20 And this is that which ye said, The way of the Lord is *not* straight. I will judge you, O house of Israel, every one for his ways. 21 And it came to pass in the tenth year of our captivity, in the twelfth month, on the fifth *day* of the month, *that* one that had escaped from Jerusalem came to me, saying, The city is taken. 22 Now the hand of the Lord had come upon me in the evening, before he came; and he opened my mouth, when he came to me in the morning: and my mouth was open, it was no longer kept closed. 23 And the word of the Lord came to me, saying, 24 Son of man, they that inhabit the desolate *places* on the land of Israel say, Abram was one, and he possessed the land: and we are more numerous; to us the land is given for a possession. 25,26,27 Therefore say to them, Thus saith the Lord God, *As* I live, surely they that are in the desolate places shall fall by swords and they that are in the open plain shall be given for food to the wild beasts of the field, and them that are in the fortified *cities* and them that are in the caves I will slay with pestilence. 28 And I will make the land desert, and the pride of her strength shall perish; and the mountains of Israel shall be made desolate by reason of no man passing through. 29 And they shall know that I am the Lord; and I will make their land desert, and it shall be made desolate because of all their abominations which they have wrought. 30 And *as for* thee, son of man, the children of thy people are they that speak concerning thee by the walls, and in the porches of the houses, and they talk one to another, saying, Let us come together, and let us hear the *words* that proceed from the Lord. 31 They approach thee as a people comes together, and sit before thee, and hear thy words, but they will not do them: for *there is* falsehood in their mouth, and their heart *goes* after their pollutions. 32 And thou art to them as a sound of a sweet, well-tuned psaltery, and they will hear thy words, but they will not do them. 33 But whenever it shall come *to pass*, they will say, Behold, it is come: and they shall know that there was a prophet in the midst of them.

Ezek.34 1 And the word of the Lord came to me, saying, 2 Son of man, prophesy against the shepherds of Israel, prophesy, and say to the shepherds, Thus saith the Lord God; O shepherds of Israel, do shepherds feed themselves? do not the shepherds feed the sheep? 3 Behold, ye feed on the milk, and clothe yourselves with the wool, and slay the fat: but ye feed not my sheep. 4 The weak one ye have not strengthened, and the sick ye have not cherished, and the bruised ye have not bound up, and the stray one ye have not turned back, and the lost ye have not sought; and the strong ye have wearied with labour. 5 And my sheep were scattered, because there were no shepherds: and they became meat to all the wild beasts of the field. 6 And my sheep were scattered on every mountain, and on every high hill: yea, they were scattered on the face of the earth, and there was none to seek them out, nor to bring them back. 7 Therefore, ye shepherds, hear the word of the Lord. 8 *As* I live, saith the Lord God, surely because my sheep became a prey, and my sheep became meat to all the wild beasts of the field, because there were no shepherds, and the shepherds sought not out my sheep, and the shepherds fed themselves, but fed not my sheep. 9 For this cause, O shepherds, 10 thus saith the Lord God, Behold, I am against the shepherds; and I will require my sheep at their hands, and will turn them back that they shall not feed my sheep, and the shepherds shall no longer feed them; and I will deliver my sheep out of their mouth, and they shall no longer be meat for them. 11 For thus saith the Lord God, Behold, I will seek out my sheep, and will visit them. 12 As the shepherd seeks his flock, in the day when there is darkness and cloud, in the midst of the sheep that are separated: so will I seek out my sheep, and will bring them back from every place where they were scattered in the day of cloud and darkness. 13 And I will bring them out from the Gentiles, and will gather them from the countries, and will bring them into their own land, and will feed them upon the mountains of Israel, and in the valleys, and in every inhabited place of the land. 14 I will feed them in a good pasture, on a high mountain of Israel: and their folds shall be there, and they shall lie down, and there shall they rest in perfect prosperity, and they shall feed in a fat pasture on the mountains of Israel. 15 I will feed my sheep, and I will cause them to rest; and they shall know that I am the Lord: thus saith the Lord God. 16 I will seek that which is lost, and I will recover the stray one, and will bind up that which was broken, and will strengthen the fainting, and will guard the strong, and will feed them with judgment. 17 And *as for* you, ye sheep, thus saith the Lord God, Behold, I will distinguish between sheep and sheep, *between* rams and he-goats. 18 And *is it* not enough for you that ye fed on the good pasture, that ye trampled with your feet the remnant of your pasture? and *that* ye drank the standing water, *that* ye disturbed the residue with your feet? 19 So my sheep fed on that which ye had trampled with your feet; and they drank the water that had been disturbed by your feet. 20 Therefore thus saith the Lord God; Behold, I will separate between the strong sheep and the weak sheep. 21 Ye did thrust with your sides and shoulders, and pushed with your horns, and ye cruelly treated all the sick. 22 Therefore I will save my sheep, and they shall not be any more for a prey; and will judge between ram and ram. 23 And I will raise up one shepherd over them, and he shall tend them, *even* my servant David, and he shall be their shepherd; 24 and I the Lord will be to them a God, and David a prince in the midst of them; I the Lord have spoken it. 25 And I will make with David a covenant of peace and I will utterly destroy evil beasts from off the land; and they shall dwell in the wilderness, and sleep in the forests. 26 And I will settle them round about my mountain; and I will give you the rain, the rain of blessing. 27 And the trees that are in the field shall yield their fruit, and the earth shall yield her strength, and they shall dwell in the confidence of peace on their land, and they shall know that I am the Lord, when I have broken their yoke; and I will deliver them out of the hand of those that enslaved them. 28 And they shall no more be a spoil to the nations, and the wild beasts of the land shall no more at all devour them; and they shall dwell safely, and there shall be none to make them afraid. 29 And I will raise up for them a plant of peace, and they shall no more perish with hunger upon the land, and they shall no more bear the reproach of the nations. 30 And they shall know that I am the Lord their God, and they my people. O house of Israel, saith the Lord God, 31 ye are my sheep, even the sheep of my flock, and I am the Lord your God, saith the Lord God.

Ezek.35 1 And the word of the Lord came to me, saying, 2 Son of man, set thy face against mount Seir, and prophesy against it, 3 and say to it, Thus saith the Lord God; Behold, I am against thee, O mount Seir, and I will stretch out my hand against thee, and will make thee a waste, and thou shalt be made desolate. 4 And I will cause desolation in thy cities, and thou shalt be desolate, and thou shalt know that I am the Lord. 5 Because thou hast been a perpetual enemy, and hast laid wait craftily for the house of Israel, with the hand of enemies with a sword, in the time of injustice, at the last: 6 Therefore, as I live, saith the Lord God, verily thou hast sinned even to blood, therefore blood shall pursue thee. 7 And I will make mount Seir a waste, and desolate, and I will destroy from off it men and cattle: 8 and I will fill thy hills and thy valleys with slain men, and in all thy plains there shall fall in thee men slain with the sword. 9 I will make thee a perpetual desolation, and thy cities shall not be inhabited any more: and thou shalt know that I am the Lord. 10 Because thou saidst, The two nations and the two countries shall be mine, and I shall inherit them; whereas the Lord is there: 11 therefore, *as* I live, saith the Lord, I will even deal with thee according to thine enmity, and I will be made known to thee when I shall judge thee: 12 and thou shalt know that I am the Lord. I have heard the voice of thy blasphemies, whereas thou hast said, The desert mountains of Israel are given to us for food; 13 and thou hast spoken swelling words against me with thy mouth: I have heard *them*. 14 Thus saith the Lord; When all the earth is rejoicing, I will make thee desert. 15 Thou shalt be desert, O mount Seir, and all Idumea; and it shall be utterly consumed: and thou shalt know that I am the Lord their God.

Ezek.36 1 And thou, son of man, prophesy to the mountains of Israel, and say to the mountains of Israel, Hear ye the word of the Lord: 2 Thus saith the Lord God; Because the enemy has said against you, Aha, the old waste places are become a possession for us: 3 therefore prophesy, and say, Thus saith the Lord God; Because ye have been dishonoured, and hated by those round about you, that ye might be a possession to the remainder of the nations, and ye became a by-word, and a reproach to the nations: 4 therefore, ye mountains of Israel, hear the word of the Lord; Thus saith the Lord to the mountains, and to the hills, and to the streams, and to the valleys, and to *the places* that have been made desolate and destroyed, and to the cities that have been deserted, and have become a spoil and a trampling to the nations that were left round about; 5 therefore, thus saith the Lord; Verily in the fire of my wrath have I spoken against the rest of the nations, and against all Idumea, because they have appropriated my land to themselves for a possession with joy, disregarding the lives *of the inhabitants*, to destroy *it* by plunder: 6 therefore prophesy concerning the land of Israel, and say to the mountains, and to the hills, and to the valleys, and to the forests, Thus saith the Lord; Behold, I have spoken in my jealousy and in my wrath, because ye have borne the reproaches of the heathen: 7 therefore I will lift up my hand against the nations that are round about you; they shall bear their reproach. 8 But your grapes and your fruits, O mountains of Israel, shall my people eat; for they are hoping to come. 9 For, behold, I am toward you, and I will have respect to you, and ye shall be tilled and sown: 10 and I will multiply men upon you, *even* all the house of Israel to the end: and the cities shall be inhabited, and the desolate land shall be built upon. 11 And I will multiply men and cattle upon you; and I will cause you to dwell as at the beginning, and will treat you well, as in your former *times*: and ye shall know that I am the Lord. 12 And I will increase men upon you, *even* my people Israel; and they shall inherit you, and ye shall be to them for a possession; and ye shall no more be bereaved of them. 13 Thus saith the Lord God: Because they said to thee, Thou *land* devourest men, and hast been bereaved of thy nation; 14 therefore thou shalt no more devour men, and thou shalt no more bereave thy nation, saith the Lord God. 15 And there shall no more be heard against you the reproach of the nations, and ye shall no more bear the revilings of the peoples, saith the Lord God. 16 And the word of the Lord came to me, saying, 17 Son of man, the house of Israel dwelt upon their land, and defiled it by their way, and with their idols, and with their uncleannesses; and their way was before me like the uncleanness of a removed woman. 18 So I poured out my wrath upon them: 19 and I dispersed them among the nations, and utterly scattered them through the countries: I judged them according to their way and according to their sin. 20 And they went in among the nations, among which they went, and they profaned my holy name, while it was said of them, These are the people of the Lord, and they came forth out of his land. 21 But I spared them for the sake of my holy name, which the house of Israel profaned among the nations, among whom they went. 22 Therefore say to the house of Israel, Thus saith the Lord; I do not this, O house of Israel, for your sakes, but because of my holy name, which ye have profaned among the nations, among whom ye went. 23 And I will sanctify my great name, which was profaned among the nations, which ye profaned in the midst of them; and the nations shall know that I am the Lord, when I am sanctified among you before their eyes. 24 And I will take you out from the nations, and will gather you out of all the lands, and will bring you into your own land: 25 and I will sprinkle clean water upon you, and ye shall be purged from all your uncleannesses, and from all your idols, and I will cleanse you. 26 And I will give you a new heart, and will put a new spirit in you: and I will take away the heart of stone out of your flesh, and will give you a heart of flesh. 27 And I will put my Spirit in you, and will cause you to walk in mine ordinances, and to keep my judgments, and do *them*. 28 And ye shall dwell upon the land which I gave to your fathers; and ye shall be to me a people, and I will be to you a God. 29 And I will save you from all your uncleannesses: and I will call for the corn, and multiply it, and will not bring famine upon you. 30 And I will multiply the fruit of the trees, and the produce of the field, that ye may not bear the reproach of famine among the nations. 31 And ye shall remember your evil ways and your practices that were not good, and ye shall be hateful in your own sight for your transgressions and for your abominations. 32 Not for your sakes do I *this*, saith the Lord God, *as* it is known to you: be ye ashamed and confounded for your ways, O house of Israel. 33 Thus saith the Lord God; In the day wherein I shall cleanse you from all your iniquities I will also cause the cities to be inhabited, and the waste *places* shall be built upon: 34 and the desolate land shall be cultivated, whereas it was desolate in the eyes of every one that passed by. 35 And they shall say, That desolate land is become like a garden of delight; and the waste and desolate and ruined cities are inhabited. 36 And the nations, as many as shall have been left round about you, shall know that I the Lord have built the ruined *cities* and planted the waste *lands*: I the Lord have spoken, and will do *it*. 37 Thus saith the Lord God; Yet *for* this will I be sought by the house of Israel, to establish them; I will multiply them *even* men as sheep; 38 as holy sheep, as the sheep of Jerusalem in her feasts; thus shall the desert cities be full of flocks of men: and they shall know that I *am* the Lord.

Ezek.37 1 And the hand of the Lord came upon me, and the Lord brought me forth by the Spirit, and set me in the midst of the plain, and it was full of human bones. 2 And he led me round about them every way: and, behold, *there were* very many on the face of the plain, very dry. 3 And he said to me, Son of man, will these bones live? and I said, O Lord God, thou knowest this. 4 And he said to me, Prophesy upon these bones, and thou shalt say to them, Ye dry bones, hear the word of the Lord. 5 Thus saith the Lord to these bones; Behold, I *will* bring upon you the breath of life: 6 and I will lay sinews upon you, and will bring up flesh upon you, and will spread skin upon you, and will put my Spirit into you, and ye shall live; and ye shall know that I am the Lord. 7 So I prophesied as *the Lord* commanded me: and it came to pass while I was prophesying, that, behold, *there was* a shaking, and the bones approached each one to his joint. 8 And I looked, and behold, sinews and flesh grew upon them, and skin came upon them above: but there was not breath in them. 9 And he said to me, Prophesy to the wind, prophesy, son of man, and say to the wind, Thus saith the Lord; Come from the four winds, and breathe upon these dead *men*, and let them live. ¹⁰ So I prophesied as he commanded me, and the breath entered into them, and they lived, and stood upon their feet, a very great congregation. ¹¹ And the Lord spoke to me, saying, Son of man, these bones are the whole house of Israel: and they say, Our bones are become dry, our hope has perished, we are quite spent. ¹² Therefore prophesy and say, Thus saith the Lord; Behold, I *will* open your tombs, and will bring you up out of your tombs, and will bring you into the land of Israel. ¹³ And ye shall know that I am the Lord, when I have opened your graves, that I may bring up my people from *their* graves. ¹⁴ And I will put my Spirit within you, and ye shall live, and I will place you upon your own land: and ye shall know that I *am* the Lord; I have spoken, and will do *it*, saith the Lord. ¹⁵ And the word of the Lord came to me, saying, ¹⁶ Son of man, take for thyself a rod, and write upon it, Juda, and the children of Israel his adherents; and thou shalt take for thyself another rod, and thou shalt inscribe it for Joseph, the rod of Ephraim, and all the children of Israel that belong to him. ¹⁷ And thou shalt joint them together for thyself, so as that they should bind themselves into one stick; and they shall be in thine hand. ¹⁸ And it shall come to pass, when the children of thy people shall say to thee, Wilt thou not tell us what thou meanest by these things? ¹⁹ Then shalt thou say to them, Thus saith the Lord; behold, I will take the tribe of Joseph, which is in the hand of Ephraim, and the tribes of Israel that belong to him, and I will add them to the tribe of Juda, and they shall become one rod in the hand of Juda. ²⁰ And the rods on which thou didst write shall be in thine hand in their presence. ²¹ And thou shalt say to them, Thus saith the Lord God; Behold, I *will* take the whole house of Israel out of the midst of the nations, among whom they have gone, and I will gather them from all that are round about them, and I will bring them into the land of Israel. ²² And I will make them a nation in my land, even on the mountains of Israel; and they shall have one prince: and they shall be no more two nations, neither shall they be divided any more at all into two kingdoms: ²³ that they may no more defile themselves with their idols; and I will deliver them from all their transgressions whereby they have sinned, and will cleanse them; and they shall be to me a people, and I the Lord will be to them a God. ²⁴ And my servant David *shall be* a prince in the midst of them: there shall be one shepherd of *them* all; for they shall walk in mine ordinances, and keep my judgments, and do them. ²⁵ And they shall dwell in their land, which I have given to my servant Jacob, where their fathers dwelt; and they shall dwell upon it: and David my servant *shall be their* prince forever. ²⁶ And I will make with them a covenant of peace; it shall be an everlasting covenant with them; and I will establish my sanctuary in the midst of them for ever. ²⁷ And my tabernacle shall be among them; and I will be to them a God, and they shall be my people. ²⁸ And the nations shall know that I am the Lord that sanctifies them, when my sanctuary is in the midst of them for ever.

Ezek.38 ¹ And the word of the Lord came to me, saying, ² Son of man, set thy face against Gog, and the land of Magog, Rhos, prince of Mesoch and Thobel, and prophesy against him, ³ and say to him, Thus saith the Lord God; Behold, I am against thee, Rhos prince of Mesoch and Thobel: ⁴ and I will gather thee, and all thine host, horses and horsemen, all wearing breast-plates, with a great multitude, shields and helmets and swords: ⁵ Persians, and Ethiopians, and Libyans; all with helmets and shields. ⁶ Gomer, and all belonging to him; the house of Thorgama, from the end of the north, and all belonging to him; and many nations with thee. ⁷ Be thou prepared, prepare thyself, thou, and all thy multitude that is assembled with thee, and thou shalt be to me for a guard. ⁸ He shall be prepared after many days, and he shall come at the end of years, and shall come to a land that is brought back from the sword, when *the people* are gathered from many nations against the land of Israel, which was entirely desolate: and he is come forth out of the nations, and they shall all dwell securely. ⁹ And thou shalt go up as rain, and shalt arrive as a cloud to cover the land, and there shall be thou, and all that are about thee, and many nations with thee. ¹⁰ Thus saith the Lord God; It shall also come to pass in that day, that thoughts shall come up into thine heart, and thou shalt devise evil devices. ¹¹ And thou shalt say, I will go up to the rejected land; I will come upon them that are at ease in tranquility, and dwelling in peace, all inhabiting a land in which there is no wall, nor bars, nor have they doors; ¹² to seize plunder, and to take their spoil; to turn my hands against the desolate land that is *now* inhabited, and against a nation that is gathered from many nations, that have acquired property, dwelling in the midst of the land. ¹³ Sabba, and Daedan, and Carthaginian merchants, and all their villages shall say to thee, Thou art come for plunder to take a prey, and to get spoils: thou hast gathered thy multitude to take silver and gold, to carry off property, to take spoils. ¹⁴ Therefore prophesy, son of man, and say to Gog, Thus saith the Lord; Wilt thou not arise in that day, when my people Israel are dwelling securely, ¹⁵ and come out of thy place from the farthest north, and many nations with thee? all of them mounted on horses, a great gathering, and a large force? ¹⁶ And thou shalt come up upon my people Israel as a cloud to cover the land; it shall come to pass in the last days, that I will bring thee up upon my land, that all the nations may know me, when I am sanctified in thee before them. ¹⁷ Thus saith the Lord God, to Gog; Thou art *he* concerning whom I spoke in former times, by the hand of my servants the prophets of Israel, in those days and years, that I would bring thee up against them. ¹⁸ And it shall come to pass in that day, in the day when Gog shall come against the land of Israel, saith the Lord God, ¹⁹ *that* my wrath and my jealousy shall arise, I have spoken in the fire of mine anger, verily in that day there shall be a great shaking in the land of Israel; ²⁰ and the fish of the sea shall quake at the presence of the Lord, and the birds of the sky and the wild beasts of the field, and all the reptiles that creep upon the earth, and all the men that are on the face of the earth; and the mountains shall be rent, and the valleys shall fall, and every wall on the land shall fall. ²¹ And I will summon against it even every fear, saith the Lord: the sword of *every* man shall be against his brother. ²² And I will judge him with pestilence, and blood, and sweeping rain, and hailstones; and I will rain upon him fire and brimstone, and upon all that are with him, and upon many nations with him. 23 And I will be magnified, and sanctified, and glorified; and I will be known in the presence of many nations, and they shall know that I am the Lord.

Ezek.39 1 And thou, son of man, prophesy against Gog, and say, Thus saith the Lord; Behold, I am against thee, O Gog, Rhos prince of Mesoch and Thobel: 2 and I will assemble thee, and guide thee, and raise thee up on the extremity of the north, and I will bring thee up upon the mountains of Israel. 3 And I will destroy the bow out of thy left hand, and thine arrows out of thy right hand, and I will cast thee down on the mountains of Israel; 4 and thou and all that belong to thee shall fall, and the nations that are with thee shall be given to multitudes of birds, *even* to every fowl, and I have given thee to all the wild beasts of the field to be devoured. 5 Thou shalt fall on the face of the field: for I have spoken *it*, saith the Lord. 6 And I will send a fire upon Gog, and the islands shall be securely inhabited: and they shall know that I am the Lord. 7 And my holy name shall be known in the midst of my people Israel; and my holy name shall no more be profaned: and the nations shall know that I am the Lord, the Holy *One* in Israel. 8 Behold it is come, and thou shalt know that it shall be, saith the Lord God; this is the day concerning which I have spoken. 9 And they that inhabit the cities of Israel shall come forth, and make a fire with the arms, the shields and the spears, and bows and arrows, and hand-staves, and lances, and they shall keep fire burning with them for seven years: 10 and they shall not take any wood out of the field, neither shall they cut any out of the forests, but they shall burn the weapons with fire: and they shall plunder those that plundered them, and spoil those that spoiled them, saith the Lord. 11 And it shall come to pass *that* in that day I will give to Gog a place of renown, a tomb in Israel, the burial-place of them that approach the sea: and they shall build round about the outlet of the valley, and there they shall bury Gog and all his multitude: and *the place* shall then be called the burial-place of Gog. 12 And the house of Israel shall bury them, that the land may be cleansed in the space of seven months. 13 Yea, all the people of the land shall bury them; and it shall be to them a *place* of renown in the day wherein it was glorified, saith the Lord. 14 And they shall appoint men continually to go over the land, to bury them that have been left on the face of the earth, to cleanse it after the space of seven months, and they shall seek *them* out. 15 And every one that goes through the land, and sees a man's bone, shall set up a mark by it, until the buriers shall have buried it in the valley, the burial place of Gog. 16 For the name of the city *shall be* Burial-place: so shall the land be cleansed. 17 And thou, son of man, say, Thus saith the Lord; Say to every winged bird, and to all the wild beasts of the field, Gather yourselves, and come; gather yourselves from all *places* round about to my sacrifice, which I have made for you, *even* a great sacrifice on the mountains of Israel, and ye shall eat flesh, and drink blood. 18 Ye shall eat the flesh of mighty men, and ye shall drink the blood of

princes of the earth, rams, and calves and goats, and they are all fatted calves. 19 And ye shall eat fat till ye are full, and shall drink wine till ye are drunken, of my sacrifice which I have prepared for you. 20 And ye shall be filled at my table, *eating* horse, and rider, and mighty man, and every warrior, saith the Lord. 21 And I will set my glory among you, and all the nations shall see my judgment which I have wrought, and my hand which I have brought upon them. 22 And the house of Israel shall know that I am the Lord their God, from this day and onwards. 23 And all the nations shall know that the house of Israel were led captive because of their sins, because they rebelled against me, and I turned away my face from them, and delivered them into the hands of their enemies, and they all fell by the sword. 24 According to their uncleannesses and according to their transgressions did I deal with them, and I turned away my face from them. 25 Therefore thus saith the Lord God, Now will I turn back captivity in Jacob, and will have mercy on the house of Israel, and will be jealous for the sake of my holy name. 26 And they shall bear their reproach, and the iniquity which they committed when they dwelt upon their land in peace. Yet there shall be none to terrify *them* 27 when I have brought them back from the nations, and gathered them out of the countries of the nations: and I will be sanctified among them in the presence of the nations. 28 And they shall know that I am the Lord their God, when I have been manifested to them among the nations. 29 And I will no more turn away my face from them, because I have poured out my wrath upon the house of Israel, saith the Lord God.

Ezek.40 1 And it came to pass in the twenty-fifth year of our captivity, in the first month, on the tenth *day* of the month, in the fourteenth year after the taking of the city, in that day the hand of the Lord was upon me, and brought me 2 in a vision of God into the land of Israel, and set me on a very high mountain, and upon it *there was* as it were the frame of a city before *me*. 3 And he brought me in thither, and, behold, *there was* a man, and the appearance of him was as the appearance of shining brass, and in his hand was a builder's line, and a measuring reed; and he stood at the gate. 4 And the man said to me, Look with thine eyes at him whom thou hast seen, son of man, and hear with thine ears, and lay up in thine heart all things that I show thee; for thou hast come in hither that *I* might show thee, and thou shalt show all things that thou seest to the house of Israel. 5 And behold a wall round about the house without, and in the man's hand a reed, the measure *of it was* six cubits by the cubit, and a span: and he measured across the front wall; the breadth was equal to the reed, and the length of it equal to the reed. 6 And he entered by seven steps into the gate that looks eastward, and he measured across the porch of the gate equal to the reed. 7 And the chamber was equal in length to the reed, and equal in breadth to the reed; and the porch between the chambers six cubits; and the second chamber equal in breadth to the reed, and equal in length to the reed, and the porch five cubits. 8 And the third chamber equal in length to the reed, and equal in breadth to the reed. 9 And the porch of the gateway (near the porch of the gate) eight cubits; and the posts there of two cubits; and the porch of the gate was inward: 10 and the chambers of the gate of the chamber in front *were* three on one side and three on the other, and *there was* one measure to the three: *there was* one measure to the porches on this side and on that. 11 And he measured the breadth of the door of the gateway, ten cubits; and the breadth of the gateway thirteen cubits. 12 And the space before the chambers was narrowed to a cubit in front of the chambers on this side and on that side: and the chamber was six cubits this way, and six cubits that way. 13 And he measured the gate from the wall of one chamber to the wall of the other chamber: the breadth was twenty-five cubits, the one gate over against the other gate. 14 And the open space of the porch of the gate without, was twenty cubits to the chambers round about the gate. 15 And the open space of the gate without to the open space of the porch of the gate within was fifty cubits. 16 And *there were* secret windows to the chambers, and to the porches within the gate of the court round about, and in the same manner windows to the porches round about within: and on the porch *there were* palm-trees on this side and on that side. 17 And he brought me into the inner court, and, behold, *there were* chambers, and peristyles round about the court; thirty chambers within the ranges of columns. 18 And the porticos were behind the gates; according to the length of the gates, was the lower peristyle. 19 And he measured the breadth of the court, from the open space of the outer gate inwards to the open space of the gate looking outwards: a hundred cubits *was the distance to the place* of the gate looking eastward: and he brought me to the north; 20 and behold a gate looking northwards *belonging to* the outer court, and he measured it, both the length of it and the breadth; 21 and the chambers, three on this side and three on that; and the posts, and the porches, and the palm- trees thereof: and they were according to the measures of the gate that looks eastward: the length thereof was fifty cubits, and the breadth thereof was twenty-five cubits. 22 And its windows, and its porches, and its palm-trees, were according to *the dimensions of* the gate looking eastward; and they went up to it by seven steps; and the porches were within. 23 And *there was* a gate to the inner court looking toward the north gate, after the manner of the gate looking toward the east; and he measured the court from gate to gate, a hundred cubits. 24 And he brought me to the south side, and behold a gate looking southwards: and he measured it, and its chambers, and its posts, and its porches, according to these dimensions. 25 And its windows and its porches round about were according to the windows of the porch: the length thereof was fifty cubits, and the breadth thereof was five and twenty cubits. 26 And it had seven steps, and porches within: and it *had* palm-trees on the posts, one on one side, and one on the other side. 27 And *there was* a gate opposite the gate of the inner court southward: and he measured the court from gate to gate, a hundred cubits in breadth southward. 28 And he brought me into the inner court of the south gate: and he measured the gate according to these measures; 29 and the chambers, and the posts, 30 and the porches, according to these measures: and *there were* windows to it and to the porches round about: its length

was fifty cubits, and *its* breadth twenty-five cubits, 31 from the porch to the outer court: and *there were* palm-trees to the post *thereof,* and eight steps. 32 And he brought me in at the gate that looks eastward: and he measured it according to these measures: 33 and the chambers, and the posts, and the porches according to these measures: and *there were* windows to it, and porches round about: the length of it was fifty cubits, and the breadth of it twenty-five cubits. 34 And *there were* porches *opening* into the inner court, and palm-trees on the posts on this side and on that side: and it *had* eight steps. 35 And he brought me in at the northern gate, and measured *it* according to these measures; 36 and the chambers, and the posts, and the porches: and it *had* windows round about, and *it had* its porches: the length of it was fifty cubits, and the breadth twenty-five cubits. 37 And its porches were toward the inner court; and *there were* palm-trees to the posts on this side and on that side: and it *had* eight steps. 38 Its chambers and its door-ways, and its porches at the second gate *served as* a drain, 39 that they might slay in it the sin-offerings, and the trespass-offerings. 40 And behind the drain for the whole-burnt-offerings at the north *gate,* two tables eastward behind the second gate; and *behind* the porch of the gate two tables eastward. 41 Four on one side and four on the other side behind the gate; upon them they kill the victims, in front of the eight tables of sacrifices. 42 And *there were* four tables of hewn stone for whole-burnt-offerings, the breadth *of them was* a cubit and a half, and the length *of them* two cubits *and* a half, and *their* height was a cubit: on them they shall place the instruments with which they slay there the whole-burnt-offerings and the victims. 43 And they shall have within a border of hewn stone round about of a span broad, and over the tables above screens for covering *them* from the wet and from the heat. 44 And he brought me into the inner court, and behold *there were* two chambers in the inner court, one behind the gate looking to the north, turning southward, and one behind the southern gate, but which looks to the north. 45 And he said to me, This chamber that looks to the south, is for the priests that keep the charge of the house. 46 And the chamber that looks to the north is for the priests that keep the charge of the altar: they are the sons of Sadduc, those of the tribe of Levi who draw near to the Lord to serve him. 47 And he measured the court, the length *whereof was* a hundred cubits, and the breadth a hundred cubits, on its four sides; and the altar in front of the house. 48 And he brought me into the porch of the house; and he measured the post of the porch, the breadth was five cubits on one side and five cubits on the other side; and the breadth of the door *was* fourteen cubits, and the side-pieces of the door of the porch *were* three cubits on one side, and three cubits on the other side. 49 And the length of the porch was twenty cubits, and the breadth twelve cubits; and they went up to it by ten steps; and *there were* pillars to the porch, one on this side and one on that side.

Ezek.41 1 And he brought me into the temple, the porch of which he measured, six cubits the breadth on one side, and six cubits the breadth of the porch on the other side. 2 And the breadth of the gateway was ten cubits, and the side-pieces of the gateway were five cubits on this side, and five cubits on that side: and he measured the length of it, forty cubits, and the breadth, twenty cubits. 3 And he went into the inner court, and measured the post of the door, two cubits; and the door, six cubits; and the side-pieces of the door, seven cubits on one side, and seven cubits on the other side. 4 And he measured the length of the doors, forty cubits; and the breadth, twenty cubits, in front of the temple: and he said, This is the holy of holies. 5 And he measured the wall of the house, six cubits: and the breadth of *each* side, four cubits round about. 6 And the sides were twice ninety, side against side; and *there was* a space in the wall of the house at the sides round about, that they should be for them that take hold of them to see, that they should not at all touch the walls of the house. 7 And the breadth of the upper side *was made* according to the projection out of the wall, against the upper one round about the house, that it might be enlarged above, and that *men* might go up to the upper chambers from those below, and from the ground-sills to the third story. 8 And as for the height of the house round about, *each* space between the sides was equal to a reed of six cubits; 9 and the breadth of the wall of each side without was five cubits; and the spaces that were left between the sides of the house, 10 and between the chambers, were a width of twenty cubits, the circumference of the house. 11 And the doors of the chambers were toward the space left by the one door that looked northward, and *there was* one door southward; and the breadth of the remaining open space *was* five cubits in extent round about. 12 And the partition *wall* in front of the remaining space, toward the west, was seventy cubits in breadth; the breadth of the partition wall was five cubits round about, and the length of it ninety cubits. 13 And he measured in front of the house a length of a hundred cubits, and the remaining spaces and the partitions; and the walls thereof were in length a hundred cubits. 14 And the breadth in front of the house, and the remaining *spaces* before *it were* a hundred cubits. 15 And he measured the length of the partition in front of the space left by the back parts of that house; and the *spaces* left on this side and on that side were in length a hundred cubits: and the temple and the corners and the outer porch were ceiled. 16 And the windows were latticed, *giving* light round about to the three *stories*, so as to look through: and the house and the parts adjoining were planked round about, and *so was* the floor, and from the floor up to the windows, and the window *shutters* folded back in three parts for one to look through. 17 And almost all the way to the inner, and close to the outer *side*, and upon all the wall round about within and without, 18 were carved cherubs and palm-trees between the cherubs, *and each* cherub *had* two faces. 19 The face of a man was toward one palm-tree on this side and on that side, and the face of a lion toward another palm-tree on this side and on that side: the house was carved all round. 20 From the floor to the ceiling were cherubs and palm-trees carved. 21 And the holy place and the temple opened on four sides; in front of the holy places the appearance was as the look of 22 a wooden altar, the height of it three cubits, and the length two cubits, and the breadth two cubits; and it had

horns, and the base of it and the sides of it were of wood: and he said to me, This is the table, which is before the face of the Lord. 23 And the temple *had* two doors, and the sanctuary *had* two doors, with two turning leaves *apiece;* 24 two leaves to the one, and two leaves to the other door. 25 And *there was* carved work upon them, and cherubs on the doors of the temple, and palm-trees according to the carving of the sanctuary; and *there were* stout planks in front of the porch without. 26 And *there were* secret windows; and he measured from side to side, to the roofing of the porch; and the sides of the house were closely planked.

Ezek.42 1 And he brought me into the inner court eastward, opposite the northern gate: and he brought me in, and behold five chambers near the vacant space, and near the northern partition, 2 a hundred cubits in length toward the north, and in breadth fifty, 3 ornamented accordingly as the gates of the inner court, and arranged accordingly as the peristyles of the outer court, *with* triple porticos fronting one another. 4 And in front of the chambers was a walk ten cubits in breadth, the length *reaching* to a hundred cubits; and their doors were northward. 5 And the upper walks were in like manner: for the peristyle projected from it, *even* from the range of columns below, and *there was* a space between; so *were there* a peristyle and a space between, and so *were there* two porticos. 6 For they were triple, and they had not pillars like the pillars of the outer ones: therefore they projected from the lower ones and the middle ones from the ground. 7 And *there was* light without, corresponding to the chambers of the outer court looking toward the front of the northern chambers; the length *of them was* fifty cubits. 8 For the length of the chambers looking toward the inner court was fifty cubits, and these are the ones that front the others; the whole was a hundred cubits. 9 And *there were* doors of these chambers for an outlet toward the east, so that one should go through them out of the outer court, 10 by the opening of the walk at the corner; and the south parts were toward the south, toward the remaining space, and toward the partition, and *so were* the chambers. 11 And the walk was in front of them, according to the measures of the chambers toward the north, both according to the length of them, and according to the breadth of them, and according to all their openings, an according to all their turnings, and according to their lights, and according to their doors. 12 *So were the measures* of the chambers toward the south, and according to the doors at the entrance of the walk, as it were the distance of a reed for light, and eastward as one went in by them. 13 And he said to me, The chambers toward the north, and the chambers toward the south, in front of the void spaces, these are the chambers of the sanctuary, wherein the priests the sons of Sadduc, who draw night to the Lord, shall eat the most holy things: and there shall they lay the most holy things, and the meat-offering, and the sin-offerings, and the trespass-offerings; because the place is holy. 14 None shall go in thither except the priests, *and* they shall not go forth of the holy place into the outer court, that they that draw nigh *to me* may be continually holy, and may not touch their garments in which they minister, *with* *defilement*, for they are holy; and they shall put on other garments whenever they come in contact with the people. 15 So the measurement of the house within was accomplished: and he brought me forth by the way of the gate that looks eastward, and measured the plan of the house round about in order. 16 And he stood behind the gate looking eastward, and measured five hundred *cubits* with the measuring reed. 17 And he turned to the north and measured in front of the north *side* five hundred cubits with the measuring reed. 18 And he turned to the west, and measured in front of the west side, five hundred *cubits* with the measuring reed. 19 And he turned to the south, and measured in front of the south side, five hundred *cubits* by the measuring reed. 20 The *four sides he measured* by the same reed, and he marked out the house and the circumference of the parts round about, *a space* of five hundred *cubits* eastward, and a breadth of five hundred cubits, to make a division between the sanctuary and the outer wall, that *belonged to* the design of the house.

Ezek.43 1 Moreover he brought me to the gate looking eastward, and led me forth. 2 And, behold, the glory of the God of Israel came by the eastern way; and *there was* a voice of an army, as the sound of many redoubling *their shouts*, and the earth shone like light from the glory round about. 3 And the vision which I saw was like the vision which I saw when I went in to anoint the city: and the vision of the chariot which I saw was like the vision which I saw at the river Chobar; and I fell upon my face. 4 And the glory of the Lord came into the house, by the way of the gate looking eastward. 5 And the Spirit took me up, and brought me into the inner court; and, behold, the house of the Lord was full of glory. 6 And I stood, and behold *there was* a voice out of the house of one speaking to me, and a man stood near me, 7 and he said to me, Son of man, thou hast seen the place of my throne, and the place of the soles of my feet, in which my name shall dwell in the midst of the house of Israel for ever; and the house of Israel shall no more profane my holy name, they and their princes, by their fornication, or by the murders of *their* princes in the midst of them; 8 when they set my door-way by their door-way, and my thresholds near to their thresholds: and they made my wall as it were joining myself and them, and they profaned my holy name with their iniquities which they wrought: and I destroyed them in my wrath and with slaughter. 9 And now let them put away from me their fornication, and the murders of their princes, and I will dwell in the midst of them forever. 10 And thou, son of man, shew the house to the house of Israel, that they may cease from their sins; and *shew* its aspect and the arrangement of it. 11 And they shall bear their punishment for all the things that they have done: and thou shalt describe the house, and its entrances, and the plan thereof, and all its ordinances, and thou shalt make known to them all the regulations of it, and describe *them* before them: and they shall keep all my commandments, and all my ordinances, and do them. 12 And thou shalt shew the plan of the house on the top of the mountain: all its limits round about *shall be* most holy. 13 And these are the measures of the altar by the cubit of a cubit and a span, the cavity *shall be* a cubit deep, and a cubit shall be the breadth, and the border on the rim of it round about shall be a span: and this *shall be* the height of the altar 14 from the bottom at the commencement of the hollow part to this great mercy-seat, from beneath was two cubits, and the breadth was a cubit; and from the little mercy-seat to the great mercy-seat, four cubits, and the breadth was a cubit. 15 And the altar *shall be* four cubits; and from the altar and above the horns a cubit. 16 And the altar *shall be* of the length of twelve cubits, by twelve cubits *in breadth*, square upon its four sides. 17 And the mercy-seat *shall be* fourteen cubits in length, by fourteen cubits in breadth on its four sides; and *there shall be* a border to it carried round about it of half a cubit; and the rim of it *shall be* a cubit round about; and the steps thereof looking eastward. 18 And he said to me, Son of man, thus saith the Lord God of Israel; These are the ordinances of the altar in the day of its being made, to offer upon it whole-burnt-offerings, and to pour blood upon it. 19 And thou shalt appoint to the priests the Levites of the seed of Sadduc, that draw nigh to me, saith the Lord God, to minister to me, a calf of the herd for a sin-offering. 20 And they shall take of its blood, and shall put *it* on the four horns of the altar, and upon the four corners of the propitiatory, and upon the base round about, and they shall make atonement for it. 21 And they shall take the calf of the sin-offering, and it shall be consumed by fire in the separate place of the house, outside the sanctuary. 22 And on the second day they shall take two kids of the goats without blemish for a sin-offering; and they shall make atonement for the altar, as they made atonement with the calf. 23 And after they have finished the atonement, they shall bring an unblemished calf of the herd, and an unblemished ram of the flock. 24 And ye shall offer *them* before the Lord, and the priests shall sprinkle salt upon them, and shall offer them up *as* whole-burnt-offerings to the Lord. 25 Seven days shalt thou offer a kid daily for a sin-offering, and a calf of the herd, and a ram out of the flock: they shall sacrifice them unblemished for seven days: 26 and they shall make atonement for the altar, and shall purge it; and they shall consecrate themselves. 27 And it shall come to pass from the eighth day and onward, *that* the priests shall offer your whole-burnt-offerings on the altar, and your peace-offerings; and I will accept you, saith the Lord.

Ezek.44 1 Then he brought me back by the way of the outer gate of the sanctuary that looks eastward; and it was shut. 2 And the Lord said to me, This gate shall be shut, it shall not be opened, and no one shall pass through it; for the Lord God of Israel shall enter by it, and it shall be shut. 3 For the prince, he shall sit in it, to eat bread before the Lord; he shall go in by the way of the porch of the gate, and shall go forth by the way of the same. 4 And he brought me in by the way of the gate that looks northward, in front of the house: and I looked, and, behold, the house was full of the glory of the Lord: and I fell upon my face. 5 And the Lord said to me, Son of man, attend with thine heart, and see with *thine* eyes, and hear with thine ears all that I say to thee, according to all the ordinances of the house of the

Lord, and all the regulations thereof; and thou shalt attend well to the entrance of the house, according to all its outlets, in all the holy things. 6 And thou shalt say to the provoking house, *even* to the house of Israel, Thus saith the Lord God; Let it suffice you *to have committed* all your iniquities, O house of Israel! 7 that ye have brought in aliens, uncircumcised in heart, and uncircumcised in flesh, to be in my sanctuary, and to profane it, when ye offered bread, flesh, and blood; and ye transgressed my covenant by all your iniquities; 8 and ye appointed *others* to keep the charges in my sanctuary. 9 Therefore thus saith the Lord God; No alien, uncircumcised in heart or uncircumcised in flesh, shall enter into my sanctuary, of all the children of strangers that are in the midst of the house of Israel. 10 But as for the Levites who departed far from me when Israel went astray from me after their imaginations, they shall even bear their iniquity. 11 yet they shall minister in my sanctuary, *being* porters at the gates of the house, and serving the house: they shall slay the victims and the whole-burnt-offerings for the people, and they shall stand before the people to minister to them. 12 Because they ministered to them before their idols, and it became to the house of Israel a punishment of iniquity; therefore have I lifted up my hand against them, saith the Lord God. 13 And they shall not draw nigh to me to minister to me in the priests' office, nor to approach the holy things of the children of Israel, nor *to approach* my holy of holies: but they shall bear their reproach for the error wherein they erred. 14 They shall bring them to keep the charges of the house, for all the service of it, and for all that they shall do. 15 The priests the Levites, the sons of Sadduc, who kept the charges of my sanctuary when the house of Israel went astray from me, these shall draw night to me to minister to me, and shall stand before my face, to offer sacrifice to me, the fat and the blood, saith the Lord God. 16 These shall enter into my sanctuary, and these shall approach my table, to minister to me, and they shall keep my charges. 17 And it shall come to pass when they enter the gates of the inner court, *that* they shall put on linen robes; and they shall not put on woollen garments when they minister at the gate of the inner court. 18 And they shall have linen mitres upon their heads, and shall have linen drawers upon their loins; and they shall not tightly gird themselves. 19 And when they go out into the outer court to the people, they shall put off their robes, in which they minister; and they shall lay them up in the chambers of the sanctuary, and shall put on other robes, and they shall not sanctify the people with their robes. 20 And they shall not shave their heads, nor shall they pluck off their hair; they shall carefully cover their heads. 21 And no priest shall drink any wine, when they go into the inner court. 22 Neither shall they take to themselves to wife a widow, or one that is put away, but a virgin of the seed of Israel: but if there should happen to be a priest's widow, they shall take *her*. 23 And they shall teach my people *to distinguish* between holy and profane, and they shall make known to them *the difference* between unclean and clean. 24 And these shall attend at a judgment of blood to decide it: they shall rightly observe my ordinances, and judge my judgments, and keep my statutes and my commandments in all my feasts; and they shall hallow my sabbaths. 25 And they shall not go in to the dead body of a man to defile themselves: only *a priest* may defile himself for a father, or for a mother, or for a son, or for a daughter, or for a brother, or for his sister, who has not been married. 26 And after he has been cleansed, let him number to himself seven days. 27 And on whatsoever day they shall enter into the inner court to minister in the holy place, they shall bring a propitiation, saith the Lord God. 28 And it shall be to them for an inheritance: I am their inheritance: and no possession shall be given them among the children of Israel; for I am their possession. 29 And these shall eat the meat-offerings, and the sin-offerings, and the trespass-offerings; and every special offering in Israel shall be theirs. 30 *And* the first-fruits of all things, and the first-born of all *animals* and all offerings, of all your first-fruits there shall be *a share* for the priests; and ye shall give your earliest produce to the priest, to bring your blessings upon your houses. 31 And the priests shall eat no bird or beast that dies of itself, or is taken of wild beasts.

Ezek.45 1 And when ye measure the land for inheritance, ye shall set apart first-fruits to the Lord, a holy space of the land, in length twenty and five thousand *reeds*, and in breadth twenty thousand; it shall be holy in all the borders thereof round about. 2 And there shall be a sanctuary out of this, five hundred *reeds in length* by five hundred in breadth, a square round about; and *there shall be* a vacant space *beyond* this of fifty cubits round about. 3 And out of this measurement shalt thou measure the length five and twenty thousand, and the breadth twenty thousand: and in it shall be the holy of holies. 4 Of the land shall be *a portion* for the priests that minister in the holy place, and it shall be for them that draw nigh to minister to the Lord: and it shall be to them a place for houses set apart for their sacred office; 5 the length *shall be* twenty-five thousand, and the breadth twenty thousand: and the Levites that attend the house, they shall have cities to dwell in for a possession. 6 And ye shall appoint *for* the possession of the city five thousand in breadth, and in length twenty-five thousand: after the manner of the first-fruits of the holy portion, they shall be for all the house of Israel. 7 And the prince *shall have a portion* out of this, and out of this *there shall be a portion* for the first-fruits of the sanctuary, *and* for the possession of the city, in front of the first-fruits of the sanctuary, and in front of the possession of the city westward, and from the western parts eastward: and the length *shall be* equal to one of the parts of the western borders, and the length *shall be* to the eastern borders of the land. 8 And he shall have it for a possession in Israel: and the princes of Israel shall no more oppress my people; but the house of Israel shall inherit the land according to their tribes. 9 Thus saith the Lord God; Let it suffice you, ye princes of Israel: remove injustice and misery, execute judgment and justice; take away oppression from my people, saith the Lord God. 10 Ye shall have a just balance, and a just measure, and a just choenix for measure. 11 And in like manner there shall be one choenix as a measure of capacity; the tenth of the gomor *shall be* the choenix, and the tenth of the gomor shall be in fair proportion to the gomor. 12 And the weights *shall be* twenty oboli, your pound shall be five shekels, fifteen shekels and fifty shekels. 13 And these are the first-fruits which ye shall offer; a sixth part of a gomor of wheat, and the sixth part of it *shall consist* of an ephah of a core of barley. 14 And *ye shall give as* the appointed measure of oil one bath of oil out of ten baths; for ten baths are a gomor. 15 And one sheep from the flock out of ten, as an oblation from all the tribes of Israel, for sacrifices, and for whole-burnt-offerings, and for peace-offerings, to make atonement for you, saith the Lord God. 16 And all the people shall give these first-fruits to the prince of Israel. 17 And through the prince shall be *offered* the whole-burnt-offerings and the meat-offerings, and the drink-offerings in the feasts, and at the new moons, and on the sabbaths; and in all the feasts of the house of Israel: he shall offer the sin-offerings, and the meat-offering, and the whole-burnt-offerings, and the peace-offerings, to make atonement for the house of Israel. 18 Thus saith the Lord God; In the first month, on the first *day* of the month, ye shall take a calf without blemish out of the herd, to make atonement for the holy place. 19 And the priest shall take of the blood of the atonement, and put it on the thresholds of the house, and upon the four corners of the temple, and upon the altar, and upon the thresholds of the gate of the inner court. 20 And thus shalt thou do in the seventh month; on the first *day* of the month thou shalt take a rate from each one; and ye shall make atonement for the house. 21 And in the first *month*, on the fourteenth *day* of the month, ye shall have the feast of the passover; seven days shall ye eat unleavened bread. 22 And the prince shall offer in that day a calf for a sin-offering for himself, and the house, and for all the people of the land. 23 And for the seven days of the feast he shall offer as whole-burnt-offerings to the Lord seven calves and seven rams without blemish daily for the seven days; and a kid of the goats daily for a sin- offering, and a meat-offering. 24 And thou shalt prepare a cake for the calf, and cakes for the ram, and a hin of oil for the cake. 25 And in the seventh month, on the fifteenth *day* of the month, thou shalt sacrifice in the feast in the same way seven days, as *they sacrificed* the sin-offerings, and the whole-burnt-offerings, and the freewill-offering, and the oil.

Ezek.46 1 Thus saith the Lord God; The gate that is in the inner court, that looks eastward, shall be shut the six working days; *but* let it be opened on the sabbath-day, and it shall be opened on the day of the new moon. 2 And the prince shall enter by the way of the porch of the inner gate, and shall stand at the entrance of the gate, and the priests shall prepare his whole-burnt-offerings and his peace-offerings, and he shall worship at the entrance of the gate: then shall he come forth; but the gate shall not be shut till evening. 3 And the people of the land shall worship at the entrance of that gate, both on the sabbaths and at the new moons, before the Lord. 4 And the prince shall offer whole-burnt-offerings to the Lord on the sabbath-day, six lambs without blemish, and a ram without blemish; 5 and a freewill-offering, a meat-offering for the ram, and a meat-offering for the lambs, the gift of his hand, and a hin of oil

for the meat- offering. 6 And on the day of the new moon a calf without blemish, and six lambs, and there shall be a ram without blemish; 7 and a meat-offering for the ram, and there shall be a meat- offering for the calf as a freewill-offering, and for the lambs, according as his hand can furnish, and *there shall be* a hin of oil for the cake. 8 And when the prince goes in, he shall go in by the way of the porch of the gate, and he shall go forth by the way of the gate. 9 And whenever the people of the land shall go in before the Lord at the feasts, he that goes in by the way of the north gate to worship shall go forth by the way of the south gate; and he that goes in by the way of the south gate shall go forth by the way of the north gate: he shall not return by the gate by which he entered, but he shall go forth opposite it. 10 And the prince shall enter with them in the midst of them when they go in; and when they go forth, he shall go forth. 11 And in the feasts and in the general assemblies the freewill oblation shall be a meat-offering for the calf, and a meat-offering for the ram, and for the lambs, as his hand can furnish, and a hin of oil for the meat-offering. 12 And if the prince should prepare *as* a thanksgiving a whole- burnt-peace-offering to the Lord, and should open for himself the gate looking eastward, and offer his whole-burnt-offering, and his peace-offerings, as he does on the sabbath-day; then shall he go out, and shall shut the doors after he has gone out. 13 And he shall prepare daily as a whole-burnt-offering to the Lord a lamb of a year old without blemish: in the morning shall he prepare it. 14 And he shall prepare a freewill-offering for it in the morning, the sixth part of a measure *of flour*, and a third part of a hin of oil to mix *therewith* the fine flour, *as* a freewill-offering to the Lord, a perpetual ordinance. 15 Ye shall prepare the lamb, and the freewill-offering, and the oil in the morning, *for* a perpetual whole- burnt-sacrifice. 16 Thus saith the Lord God; If the prince shall give a gift to one of his sons out of his inheritance, this shall be to his sons a possession *as* an inheritance. 17 But if he give a gift to one of his servants, then it shall belong to him until the year of release; and *then* he shall restore *it* to the prince: but of the inheritance of his sons *the possession* shall continue to them. 18 And the prince shall by no means take of the inheritance of the people, to oppress them: he shall give an inheritance to his sons out of his *own* possession: that my people be not scattered, every one from his possession. 19 And he brought me into the entrance of the *place* behind the gate, into the chamber of the sanctuary belonging to the priests, that looks toward the north: and, behold, there was a place set apart. 20 And he said to me, This is the place where the priests shall boil the trespass- offerings and the sin-offerings, and there shall they bake the meat-offering always; so as not to carry *them* out into the outer court, to sanctify the people. 21 And he brought me into the outer court, and led me round upon the four sides of the court; and, behold, there was a court on *each of* the sides of the court, 22 on *every* side a court, *even* a court for all the four *sides*, and *each* little court belonging to the court was in length forty cubits, and *in* breadth thirty cubits, *there was* one measure to the four. 23 And *there were* chambers in them round about, round about the four, and cooking-places formed under the chambers round about.

24 And he said to me, These are the cooks' houses, where they that serve the house shall boil the sacrifices of the people.

Ezek.47 1 And he brought me to the entrance of the house; and, behold, water issued from under the porch eastward, for the front of the house looked eastward; and the water came down from the right side, from the south to the altar. 2 And he brought me out by the way of the northern gate, and he led me round by the way outside to the gate of the court that looks eastward; and, behold, water came down from the right side, 3 in *the direction* in which a man went forth opposite; and *there was* a measuring line in his hand, and he measured a thousand *cubits* with the measure; 4 and he passed through the water; *it was* water of a fountain: and *again* he measured a thousand, and passed through the water; and the water was up to the thighs: and *again* he measured a thousand; and he passed through water up to the loins. 5 and *again* he measured a thousand; and he could not pass through: for *the water* rose as of a torrent which *men* cannot pass over. 6 And he said to me, Hast thou seen *this*, son of man? Then he brought me, and led me back to the brink of the river 7 as I returned; and, behold, on the brink of the river *there were* very many trees on this side and on that side. 8 And he said to me, This is the water that goes forth to Galilee that lies eastward, and it is gone down to Arabia, and has reached as far as to the sea to the outlet of the water: and it shall heal the waters. 9 And it shall come to pass, *that* every animal of living *and* moving creatures, all on which the river shall come, shall live: and there shall be there very many fish; for this water shall go thither, and it shall heal *them*, and they shall live: everything on which the river shall come shall live. 10 And fishers shall stand there from Ingadin to Enagallim; it shall be a place to spread out nets upon; it shall be distinct; and the fishes thereof *shall be* as the fishes of the great sea, a very great multitude. 11 But at the outlet of the water, and the turn of it, and where it overflows *its banks*, they shall not heal at all; they are given to salt. 12 And every fruit tree shall grow by the river, *even* on the bank of it on this side and on that side: they shall not decay upon it, neither shall their fruit fail: they shall bring forth the first-fruit of their early crop, for these their waters come forth of the sanctuary: and their fruit shall be for meat, and their foliage for health. 13 Thus saith the Lord God; Ye shall inherit these borders of the land; *they are* given by lot to the twelve tribes of the children of Israel. 14 And ye shall inherit it, each according to his brother's portion, *even the land* concerning which I lifted up my hand to give *it* to your fathers: and this land shall fall to you by lot. 15 And these are the borders of the land that lies northward, from the great sea that comes down, and divides the entrance of Emaseldam; 16 Maabthera, Ebrameliam, between the coasts of Damascus and the coasts of Emathi, the habitation of Saunan, which *places* are above the coasts of Auranitis. 17 These are the borders from the sea, from the habitations of Ænan, the coasts of Damascus, and the northern *coasts*. 18 And the eastern coasts between Loranitis, and Damascus, and the land of Galaad, and the land of Israel, the Jordan divides to the sea that is east of the city of palm-trees. These

are the eastern *coasts*. 19 And the southern and south-western *coasts are* from Thaeman and the city of palm-trees, to the water of Marimoth Cadem, reaching forth to the great sea. This part is the south and south-west. 20 This part of the great sea forms a border, till *one comes* opposite the entrance of Emath, *even* as far as the entrance thereof. These are the parts west of Emath. 21 So ye shall divide this land to them, *even* to the tribes of Israel. 22 Ye shall cast the lot upon it, for yourselves and the strangers that sojourn in the midst of you, who have begotten children in the midst of you: and they shall be to you as natives among the children of Israel; they shall eat with you in *their* inheritance in the midst of the tribes of Israel. 23 And they shall be in the tribe of proselytes among the proselytes that are with them: there shall ye give them an inheritance, saith the Lord God.

Ezek.48 1 And these are the names of the tribes from the northern corner, on the side of the descent that draws a line to the entrance of Emath the palace of Ælam, the border of Damascus northward on the side of Emath the palace; and they shall have the eastern parts as far as the sea, for Dan, one *portion*. 2 And from the borders of Dan eastward as far as the west sea-coast, for Asser, one. 3 And from the borders of Asser, from the eastern parts as far as the west coasts, for Nephthalim, one. 4 And from the borders of Nephthalim, from the east as far as the west coasts, for Manasse, one. 5 And from the borders of Manasse, from the eastern parts as far as the west coasts, for Ephraim, one. 6 And from the borders of Ephraim, from the eastern parts to the west coasts, for Ruben, one. 7 And from the borders of Ruben, from the eastern parts as far as the west coasts, for Juda, one. 8 And from the borders of Juda, from the eastern parts shall be the offering of first-fruits, in the breadth twenty-five thousand *reeds*, and in length as one of the portions *measured* from the east even to the western parts: and the sanctuary shall be in the midst of them. 9 *As for* the first-fruits which they shall offer to the Lord, *it shall be* in length twenty-five thousand, and in breadth twenty-five thousand. 10 Out of this shall be the first-fruits of the holy things to the priests, northward, five and twenty-thousand, and towards the west, ten thousand, and southward, five and twenty thousand: and the mountain of the sanctuary, shall be in the midst of it, 11 for the priests, for the consecrated sons of Sadduc, who keep the charges of the house, who erred not in the error of the children of Israel, as the Levites erred. 12 And the first-fruits shall be given to them out of the first-fruits of the land, *even* a most holy portion from the borders of the Levites. 13 And the Levites *shall have* the *part*, next to the borders of the priests, in length twenty-five thousand, and in breadth ten thousand: the whole length *shall be* five and twenty thousand, and the breadth twenty thousand. 14 No *part* of it shall be sold, nor measured *as for sale*, neither shall the first-fruits of the land be taken away: for they are holy to the Lord. 15 But *concerning* the five thousand that remain in the breadth in the five and twenty thousand, they shall be a suburb to the city for dwelling, and for a space before it: and the city shall be in the midst thereof. 16 And these *shall* *be* its dimensions; from the northern side four thousand and five hundred, and from the southern side four thousand and five hundred, and from the eastern side four thousand and five hundred, and from the western side *they shall measure* four thousand five hundred. 17 And there shall be a space to the city northward two hundred and fifty, and southward two hundred and fifty, and eastward two hundred and fifty, and westward two hundred and fifty. 18 And the remainder of the length that is next to the first-fruits of the holy *portion shall be* ten thousand eastward, and ten thousand westward: and they shall be the first-fruits of the sanctuary; and the fruits thereof shall be for bread to them that labour for the city. 19 And they that labour for the city shall labour for it out of all the tribes of Israel. 20 The whole offering *shall be* a square of twenty-five thousand by twenty-five thousand: ye shall separate *again part* of it, the first-fruits of the sanctuary, from the possession of the city. 21 And the prince *shall have* the remainder on this side and on that side from the first-fruits of the sanctuary, and *there shall be* a possession of the city, for five and twenty thousand cubits in length, to the eastern and western borders, for five and twenty thousand to the western borders, next to the portions of the prince; and the first-fruits of the holy things and the sanctuary of the house *shall be* in the midst of it. 22 And there shall be *a portion taken* from the Levites, from the possession of the city in the midst of the princes between the borders of Juda and the borders of Benjamin, and it shall be *the portion* of the princes. 23 And *as for* the rest of the tribes, from the eastern parts as far as the western, Benjamin *shall have* one *portion*. 24 And from the borders of Benjamin, from the eastern parts to the western, Symeon, one. 25 And from the borders of Symeon, from the eastern parts to the western, Issachar, one. 26 And from the borders of Issachar, from the eastern parts to the western, Zabulon, one. 27 And from the borders of Zabulon, from the east to the western parts, Gad, one. 28 And from the borders of Gad, from the eastern parts to the south-western parts; his coasts shall even be from Thaeman, and the water of Barimoth Cades, for an inheritance, unto the great sea. 29 This is the land, which ye shall divide by lot to the tribes of Israel, and these are their portions, saith the Lord God. 30 And these are the goings out of the city northward, four thousand and five hundred by measure. 31 And the gates of the city *shall be* after the names of the tribes of Israel: three gates northward; the gate of Ruben, one, and the gate of Juda, one, and the gate of Levi, one. 32 And eastward four thousand and five hundred: and three gates; the gate of Joseph, one, and the gate of Benjamin, one, and the gate of Dan, one. 33 And southward, four thousand and five hundred by measure: and three gates; the gate of Symeon, one, and the gate of Issachar, one, and the gate of Zabulon, one. 34 And westward, four thousand and five hundred by measure: *and* three gates; the gate of Gad, one, and the gate of Asser, one, and the gate of Nephthalim, one. 35 The circumference, eighteen thousand *measures*: and the name of the city, from the day that it shall be finished, shall be the name thereof.

DANIEL

Dan.1 1 In the third year of the reign of Joakim king of Juda, came Nabuchodonosor king of Babylon to Jerusalem, and besieged it. 2 And the Lord gave into his hand Joakim king of Juda, and part of the vessels of the house of God: and he brought them into the land of Sennaar to the house of his god; and he brought the vessels into the treasure-house of his god. 3 And the king told Asphanez his chief eunuch, to bring in some of the captive children of Israel, and of the seed of the kingdom, and of the princes; 4 young men in whom was no blemish, and beautiful in appearance, and skilled in all wisdom, and possessing knowledge, and acquainted with prudence, and who had ability to stand in the house before the king, and the king gave commandment to teach them the learning and language of the Chaldeans. 5 And the king appointed them a daily portion from the king's table, and from the wine which he drank; and *gave orders* to nourish them three years, and *that* afterwards they should stand before the king. 6 Now these were among them of the children of Juda, Daniel, and Ananias, and Azarias, and Misael. 7 And the chief of the eunuchs gave them names: to Daniel, Baltasar; and to Ananias, Sedrach; and to Misael, Misach; and to Azarias, Abdenago. 8 And Daniel purposed in his heart, that he would not defile himself with the king's table, nor with the wine of his drink: and he intreated the chief of the eunuchs that he might not defile himself. 9 Now God *had* brought Daniel into favour and compassion with the chief of the eunuchs. 10 And the chief of the eunuchs said to Daniel, I fear my lord the king, who has appointed your meat and your drink, lest he see your countenances gloomy in comparison of the young men your equals; also shall ye endanger my head to the king. 11 And Daniel said to Amelsad, whom the chief of the eunuchs had appointed over Daniel, Ananias, Misael, *and* Azarias. 12 Prove now thy servants ten days; and let them give us pulse, and let us eat, and let us drink water: 13 And let our countenances be seen by thee, and the countenances of the children that eat *at* the king's table; and deal with thy servants according as thou shalt see. 14 And he hearkened to them, and proved them ten days. 15 And at the end of the ten days their countenances appeared fairer and stouter in flesh, than the children that fed at the king's table. 16 So Amelsad took away their supper and the wine of their drink, and gave them pulse. 17 And *as for* these four children, God gave them understanding and prudence in all learning and wisdom: and Daniel had understanding in all visions and dreams. 18 And at the end of the days, *after* which the king had given orders to bring them in, then the chief of the eunuchs brought them in before Nabuchodonosor. 19 And the king spoke with them; and there were not found out of them all any like Daniel, and Ananias and Misael, and Azarias: and they stood before the king. 20 And in every matter of wisdom and knowledge wherein the king questioned them, he found them ten times wiser than all the enchanters and sorcerers that were in all his kingdom. 21 And Daniel continued till the first year of king Cyrus.

Dan.2 1 In the second year of *his* reign Nabuchodonosor dreamed a dream, and his spirit was amazed, and his sleep departed from him. 2 And the king gave orders to call the enchanters, and the magicians, and the sorcerers, and the Chaldeans, to declare to the king his dreams. And they came and stood before the king. 3 And the king said to them, I have dreamed, and my spirit was troubled to know the dream. 4 And the Chaldeans spoke to the king in the Syrian language, *saying*, O king, live for ever: do thou tell the dream to thy servants, and we will declare the interpretation. 5 The king answered the Chaldeans, The thing has departed from me: if ye do not make known to me the dream and the interpretation, ye shall be destroyed, and your houses shall be spoiled. 6 But if ye make known to me the dream, and the interpretation thereof, ye shall receive of me gifts and presents and much honour: only tell me the dream, and the interpretation thereof. 7 They answered the second time, and said, Let the king tell the dream to his servants, and we will declare the interpretation. 8 And the king answered and said, I verily know that ye are trying to gain time, because ye see that the thing has gone from me. 9 If then ye do not tell me the dream, I know that ye have concerted to utter before me a false and corrupt tale, until the time shall have past: tell me my dream, and I shall know that ye will also declare to me the interpretation thereof. 10 The Chaldeans answered before the king, and said, There is no man upon the earth, who shall be able to make known the king's matter: forasmuch as no great king or ruler asks such a question of an enchanter, magician, or Chaldean. 11 For the question which the king asks is difficult, and there is no one else who shall answer it before the king, but the gods, whose dwelling is not with any flesh. 12 Then the king in rage and anger commanded to destroy all the wise men of Babylon. 13 So the decree went forth, and they began to slay the wise men; and they sought Daniel and his fellows to slay *them*. 14 Then Daniel answered *with* counsel and prudence to Arioch the captain of the royal guard, who was gone forth to kill the wise men of Babylon; *saying*, 15 Chief magistrate of the king, wherefore has the preemptory command proceeded from the king? So Arioch made known the matter to Daniel. 16 And Daniel intreated the king to give him time, and that he might *thus* declare to the king the interpretation of it. 17 So Daniel went into his house, and made known the matter to Ananias, and Misael, and Azarias, his friends. 18 And they sought mercies from the God of heaven concerning this mystery; that Daniel and his friends might not perish with the rest of the wise men of Babylon. 19 Then the mystery was revealed to Daniel in a vision of the night; and Daniel blessed the God of heaven, and said, 20 May the name of God be blessed from everlasting and to everlasting: for wisdom and understanding are his. 21 And he changes times and seasons: he appoints kings, and removes *them*, giving wisdom to the wise, and prudence to them that have understanding: 22 he reveals deep and secret *matters*; knowing what is in darkness, and the light is with him. 23 I give thanks to thee, and praise *thee*, O God of my fathers, for thou has given me wisdom and power, and has made known to me the things which we asked of thee; and

thou has made known to me the king's vision. 24 And Daniel came to Arioch, whom the king had appointed to destroy the wise men of Babylon, and said to him; Destroy not the wise men of Babylon, but bring me in before the king, and I will declare the interpretation to the king. 25 Then Arioch in haste brought in Daniel before the king, and said to him, I have found a man of the children of the captivity of Judea, who will declare the interpretation to the king. 26 And the king answered and said to Daniel, whose name was Baltasar, Canst thou declare to me the dream which I saw, and the interpretation thereof? 27 And Daniel answered before the king, and said, The mystery which the king asks *the explanation of* is not *in the power* of the wise men, magicians, enchanters, *or* soothsayers to declare to the king. 28 But there is a God in heaven revealing mysteries, and he has made known to king Nabuchodonosor what things must come to pass in the last days. Thy dream, and the visions of thy head upon thy bed, are as follows, 29 O king: thy thoughts upon thy bed arose *as to* what must come to pass hereafter: and he that reveals mysteries has made known to thee what must come to pass. 30 Moreover, this mystery has not been revealed to me by reason of wisdom which is in me beyond all *others* living, but for the sake of making known the interpretation to the king, that thou mightest know the thoughts of thine heart. 31 Thou, O king, sawest, and behold an image: that image was great, and the appearance of it excellent, standing before thy face; and the form of it was terrible. 32 *It was* an image, the head of which was of fine gold, its hands and breast and arms of silver, *its* belly and thighs of brass, 33 its legs of iron, its feet, part of iron and part of earthenware. 34 Thou sawest until a stone was cut out of a mountain without hands, and it smote the image upon its feet of iron and earthenware, and utterly reduced them to powder. 35 Then once for all the earthenware, the iron, the brass, the silver, the gold, were ground to powder, and became as chaff from the summer threshingfloor; and the violence of the wind carried them away, and no place was found for them: and the stone which had smitten the image became a great mountain, and filled all the earth. 36 This is the dream; and we will tell the interpretation thereof before the king. 37 Thou, O king, art a king of kings, to whom the God of heaven has given a powerful and strong and honourable kingdom, 38 in every place where the children of men dwell: and he has given into thine hand the wild beasts of the field, and the birds of the sky and the fish of the sea, and he has made thee lord of all. 39 Thou art the head of gold. And after thee shall arise another kingdom inferior to thee, an a third kingdom which is the brass, which shall have dominion over all the earth; 40 and a fourth kingdom, which shall be strong as iron: as iron beats to powder and subdues all things, so shall it beat to powder and subdue. 41 And whereas thou sawest the feet and the toes, part of earthenware and part of iron, the kingdom shall be divided; yet there shall be in it of the strength of iron, as thou sawest the iron mixed with earthenware. 42 And *whereas* the toes of the feet were part of iron and part of earthenware, part of the kingdom shall be strong, and *part* of it shall be broken. 43 Whereas thou sawest the iron mixed with earthenware, they shall be mingled with the seed of men: but they shall not cleave together, as the iron does not mix itself with earthenware. 44 And in the days of those kings the God of heaven shall set up a kingdom which shall never be destroyed: and his kingdom shall not be left to another people, *but* it shall beat to pieces and grind to powder all *other* kingdoms, and it shall stand for ever. 45 Whereas thou sawest that a stone was cut out of a mountain without hands, and it beat to pieces the earthenware, the iron, the brass, the silver, the gold; the great God has made known to the king what must happen hereafter: and the dream is true, and the interpretation thereof sure. 46 Then king Nabuchodonosor fell upon his face, and worshipped Daniel, and gave orders to offer to him gifts and incense. 47 And the king answered and said to Daniel, Of a truth your God is a God of gods, and Lord of kings, who reveals mysteries; for thou has been able to reveal this mystery. 48 And the king promoted Daniel, and gave him great and abundant gifts, and set him over the whole province of Babylon, and *made him* chief satrap over all the wise men of Babylon. 49 And Daniel asked of the king, and he appointed Sedrach, Misach, and Abdenago, over the affairs of the province of Babylon: but Daniel was in the king's palace.

Dan.3 1 In *his* eighteenth year Nabuchodonosor the king made a golden image, its height was sixty cubits, its breadth six cubits: and he set it up in the plain of Deira, in the province of Babylon. 2 And he sent forth to gather the governors, and the captains, and the heads of provinces, chiefs, and princes, and those who were in authority, and all the rulers of districts, to come to the dedication of the image. 3 So the heads of provinces, the governors, the captains, the chiefs, the great princes, those who were in authority, and all the rulers of districts, were gathered to the dedication of the image which king Nabuchodonosor had set up; and they stood before the image. 4 Then a herald cried aloud, To you it is commanded, ye peoples, tribes, *and* languages, 5 at what hour ye shall hear the sound of the trumpet, and pipe, and harp, and sackbut, and psaltery, and every kind of music, ye shall fall down and worship the golden image which king Nabuchodonosor has set up. 6 And whosoever shall not fall down and worship, in the same hour he shall be cast into the burning fiery furnace. 7 And it came to pass when the nations heard the sound of the trumpet, and pipe, and harp, and sackbut, and psaltery, and all kinds of music, all the nations, tribes, *and* languages, fell down and worshipped the golden image which king Nabuchodonosor had set up. 8 Then came near *certain* Chaldeans, and accused the Jews to the king, *saying,* 9 O king, live for ever. 10 Thou, O king, has made a decree that every man who shall hear the sound of the trumpet, and pipe, and harp, sackbut, and psaltery, and all kinds of music, 11 and shall not fall down and worship the golden image, shall be cast into the burning fiery furnace. 12 There are *certain* Jews whom thou has appointed over the affairs of the province of Babylon, Sedrach, Misach, *and* Abdenago, who have not obeyed thy decree, O king: they serve not thy gods, and worship not the golden image which thou hast set up. 13 Then Nabuchodonosor in wrath and anger commanded to bring Sedrach, Misach, and Abdenago: and they were brought before the king. 14 And Nabuchodonosor answered and said to them, Is it true, Sedrach, Misach, *and* Abdenago, that ye serve not my gods, and worship not the golden image which I have set up? 15 Now then if ye be ready, whensoever ye shall hear the sound of the trumpet, and pipe, and harp, and sackbut, and psaltery, and harmony, and every kind of music, to fall down and worship the golden image which I have made; *well:* but if ye worship not, in the same hour ye shall be cast into the burning fiery furnace; and who is the God that shall deliver you out of my hand? 16 Then answered Sedrach, Misach *and* Abdenago and said to king Nabuchodonosor, We have no need to answer thee concerning this matter. 17 For our God whom we serve is in the heavens, able to deliver us from the burning fiery furnace, and he will rescue us from thy hands, O king. 18 But if not, be it known to thee, O king, that we *will* not serve thy gods, nor worship the image which thou hast set up. 19 Then Nabuchodonosor was filled with wrath, and the form of his countenance was changed toward Sedrach, Misach, and Abdenago: and he gave orders to heat the furnace seven times *more than usual,* until it should burn to the uttermost. 20 And he commanded mighty men to bind Sedrach, Misach, and Abdenago, and to cast *them* into the burning fiery furnace. 21 Then those men were bound with their coats, and caps, and hose, and were cast into the midst of the burning fiery furnace, 22 forasmuch as the king's word prevailed; and the furnace was made exceeding hot. 23 Then these three men, Sedrach, Misach, and Abdenago, fell bound into the midst of the burning furnace, and walked in the midst of the flame, singing praise to God, and blessing the Lord.

Song of the Three Children 1 Then Azarias stood up, and prayed on this manner; and opening his mouth in the midst of the fire said, 2 Blessed art thou, O Lord God of our fathers: thy name is worthy to be praised and glorified for evermore: 3 For thou art righteous in all the things that thou hast done to us: yea, true are all thy works, thy ways are right, and all thy judgments truth. 4 In all the things that thou hast brought upon us, and upon the holy city of our fathers, even Jerusalem, thou hast executed true judgment: for according to truth and judgment didst thou bring all these things upon us because of our sins. 5 For we have sinned and committed iniquity, departing from thee. 6 In all things have we trespassed, and not obeyed thy commandments, nor kept them, neither done as thou hast commanded us, that it might go well with us. 7 Wherefore all that thou hast brought upon us, and every thing that thou hast done to us, thou hast done in true judgment. 8 And thou didst deliver us into the hands of lawless enemies, most hateful forsakers of God, and to an unjust king, and the most wicked in all the world. 9 And now we cannot open our mouths, we are become a shame and reproach to thy servants; and to them that worship thee. 10 Yet deliver us not up wholly, for thy name's sake, neither disannul thou thy covenant: 11 And cause not thy mercy to depart from us, for thy beloved Abraham's sake, for thy servant Isaac's sake, and for thy holy Israel's sake; 12 To whom thou hast spoken and promised, that thou wouldest multiply their seed as the stars of heaven, and as the sand that lieth upon the seashore. 13 For we, O Lord, are become less than any nation, and be kept under this day in all the world because of our sins. 14 Neither is there at this time prince, or prophet, or leader, or burnt offering, or sacrifice, or oblation, or incense, or place to sacrifice before thee, and to find mercy. 15 Nevertheless in a contrite heart and an humble spirit let us be accepted. 16 Like as in the burnt offerings of rams and bullocks, and like as in ten thousands of fat lambs: so let our sacrifice be in thy sight this day, and grant that we may wholly go after thee: for they shall not be confounded that put their trust in thee. 17 And now we follow thee with all our heart, we fear thee, and seek thy face. 18 Put us not to shame: but deal with us after thy lovingkindness, and according to the multitude of thy mercies. 19 Deliver us also according to thy marvellous works, and give glory to thy name, O Lord: and let all them that do thy servants hurt be ashamed; 20 And let them be confounded in all their power and might, and let their strength be broken; 21 And let them know that thou art God, the only God, and glorious over the whole world. 22 And the king's servants, that put them in, ceased not to make the oven hot with rosin, pitch, tow, and small wood; 23 So that the flame streamed forth above the furnace forty and nine cubits. 24 And it passed through, and burned those Chaldeans it found about the furnace. 25 But the angel of the Lord came down into the oven together with Azarias and his fellows, and smote the flame of the fire out of the oven; 26 And made the midst of the furnace as it had been a moist whistling wind, so that the fire touched them not at all, neither hurt nor troubled them. 27 Then the three, as out of one mouth, praised, glorified, and blessed, God in the furnace, saying, 28 Blessed art thou, O Lord God of our fathers: and to be praised and exalted above all for ever. 29 And blessed is thy glorious and holy name: and to be praised and exalted above all for ever. 30 Blessed art thou in the temple of thine holy glory: and to be praised and glorified above all for ever. 31 Blessed art thou that beholdest the depths, and sittest upon the cherubims: and to be praised and exalted above all for ever. 32 Blessed art thou on the glorious throne of thy kingdom: and to be praised and glorified above all for ever. 33 Blessed art thou in the firmament of heaven: and above all to be praised and glorified for ever. 34 O all ye works of the Lord, bless ye the Lord: praise and exalt him above all for ever, 35 O ye heavens, bless ye the Lord: praise and exalt him above all for ever. 36 O ye angels of the Lord, bless ye the Lord: praise and exalt him above all for ever. 37 O all ye waters that be above the heaven, bless ye the Lord: praise and exalt him above all for ever. 38 O all ye powers of the Lord, bless ye the Lord: praise and exalt him above all for ever. 39 O ye sun and moon, bless ye the Lord: praise and exalt him above all for ever. 40 O ye stars of heaven, bless ye the Lord: praise and exalt him above all for ever. 41 O every shower and dew, bless ye the Lord: praise and exalt him above all for ever. 42 O all ye winds, bless ye the Lord: praise and exalt him above all for ever, 43 O ye fire and heat, bless ye the Lord: praise and exalt him above all for ever. 44 O ye winter and summer, bless ye the Lord: praise and exalt him above all for ever. 45 O ye dews and storms of snow, bless ye the Lord: praise and exalt him above all for ever. 46 O ye nights and days, bless ye the Lord: bless and exalt him above all for ever. 47 O ye light and darkness, bless ye the Lord: praise and exalt him above all for ever. 48 O ye ice and cold, bless ye the Lord: praise and exalt him above all for ever. 49 O ye frost and snow, bless ye the Lord: praise and exalt him above all for ever. 50 O ye lightnings and clouds, bless ye the Lord: praise and exalt him above all for ever. 51 O let the earth bless the Lord: praise and exalt him above all for ever. 52 O ye mountains and little hills, bless ye the Lord: praise and exalt him above all for ever. 53 O all ye things that grow in the earth, bless ye the Lord: praise and exalt him above all for ever. 54 O ye mountains, bless ye the Lord: Praise and exalt him above all for ever. 55 O ye seas and rivers, bless ye the Lord: praise and exalt him above all for ever. 56 O ye whales, and all that move in the waters, bless ye the Lord: praise and exalt him above all for ever. 57 O all ye fowls of the air, bless ye the Lord: praise and exalt him above all for ever. 58 O all ye beasts and cattle, bless ye the Lord: praise and exalt him above all for ever. 59 O ye children of men, bless ye the Lord: praise and exalt him above all for ever. 60 O Israel, bless ye the Lord: praise and exalt him above all for ever. 61 O ye priests of the Lord, bless ye the Lord: praise and exalt him above all for ever. 62 O ye servants of the Lord, bless ye the Lord: praise and exalt him above all for ever. 63 O ye spirits and souls of the righteous, bless ye the Lord: praise and exalt him above all for ever. 64 O ye holy and humble men of heart, bless ye the Lord: praise and exalt him above all for ever. 65 O Ananias, Azarias, and Misael, bless ye the Lord: praise and exalt him above all for ever: for he hath delivered us from hell, and saved us from the hand of death, and delivered us out of the midst of the furnace and burning flame: even out of the midst of the fire hath he delivered us. 66 O give thanks unto the Lord, because he is gracious: for his mercy endureth for ever. 67 O all ye that worship the Lord, bless the God of gods, praise him, and give him thanks: for his mercy endureth for ever. 24 And Nabuchodonosor heard them singing praises; and he wondered, and rose up in haste, and said to his nobles, Did we not cast three men bound into the midst of the fire? and they said to the king, Yes, O king. 25 And the king said, But I see four men loose, and walking in the midst of the fire, and there has no harm happened to them; and the appearance of the fourth is like the Son of God. 26 Then Nabuchodonosor drew near to the door of the burning fiery furnace, and said, Sedrach, Misach, *and* Abdenago, ye servants of the most high God, proceed forth, and come hither. So Sedrach, Misach, *and* Abdenago, came forth out of the midst of the fire. 27 Then were assembled the satraps, and captains, and heads of provinces, and the royal princes; and they saw the men, *and perceived* that the fire had not had power against their bodies, and the hair of their head was not burnt, and their coats were not scorched, nor was the smell of fire upon them. 28 And king Nabuchodonosor answered and said, Blessed be the God of Sedrach, Misach, *and* Abdenago, who has sent his angel, and delivered his servants, because they trusted in him; and they have changed the king's word, and delivered their bodies to be burnt, that they might not serve nor worship any god, except their own God. 29 Wherefore I publish a decree: Every people, tribe, *or* language, that shall speak reproachfully against the God of Sedrach, Misach, *and* Abdenago shall be destroyed, and their houses shall be plundered: because there is no other God who shall be able to deliver thus. 30 Then the king promoted Sedrach, Misach, *and* Abdenago, in the province of Babylon, and advanced them, and gave them authority to rule over all the Jews who were in his kingdom. 31 King Nabuchodonosor to all nations, tribes, and tongues, who dwell in all the earth; Peace be multiplied to you. 32 It seemed good to me to declare to you the signs and wonders which the most high God has wrought with me, 33 how great and mighty *they are*: his kingdom is an everlasting kingdom, and his power to all generations.

Dan.4 1 I Nabuchodonosor was thriving in my house, and prospering. 2 I saw a vision, and it terrified me, and I was troubled on my bed, and the visions of my head troubled me. 3 And I made a decree to bring in before me all the wise men of Babylon, that they might make known to me the interpretation of the dream. 4 So the enchanters, magicians, soothsayers, *and* Chaldeans came in: and I told the dream before them; but they did not make known to me the interpretation thereof; 5 until Daniel came, whose name is Baltasar, according to the name of my God, who has within him the Holy Spirit of God; to whom I said, 6 O Baltasar, chief of the enchanters, of whom I know that the Holy Spirit of God is in thee, and no mystery is too hard for thee, hear the vision of my dream which I had, and tell me the interpretation of it. 7 I had a vision upon my bed; and behold a tree in the midst of the earth, and its height was great. 8 The tree grew large and strong, and its height reached to the sky, and its extent to the extremity of the whole earth: 9 its leaves were fair, and its fruit abundant, and in it was meat for all; and under it the wild beasts of the field took shelter, and the birds of the sky lodged in the branches of it, and all flesh was fed of it. 10 I beheld in the night vision upon my bed, and, behold, a watcher and an holy one came down from heaven and cried aloud, and thus he said, 11 Cut down the tree, and pluck off its branches, and shake off its leaves, and scatter its fruit: let the wild beasts be removed from under it, and the birds from its branches. 12 Only leave the stump of its roots in the earth, and *bind it* with an iron and brass band; and it shall lie in the grass that is without and in the dew of heaven, and its portion *shall be* with the wild beasts in the grass of the field. 13 His heart shall be changed from that of man, and the heart of a wild beast shall be given to him; and seven times shall pass over him. 14 The matter is by the decree of the watcher, and the demand is a word of the holy ones; that the living may known that the Lord is most high *over* the kingdom of men, and he will give it to whomsoever he shall please, and will set up over it that which is set at nought of men. 15 This is the vision which I king Nabuchodonosor saw: and do thou, Baltasar, declare the interpretation, for

none of the wise men of my kingdom are able to shew me the interpretation of it: but thou, Daniel, art able; for the Holy Spirit of God is in thee. 16 Then Daniel, whose name is Baltasar, was amazed about one hour, and his thoughts troubled him. And Baltasar answered and said, *My* lord, let the dream be to them that hate thee, and the interpretation of it to thine enemies. 17 The tree which thou sawest, that grew large and strong, whose height reached to the sky and its extent to all the earth; 18 and whose leaves were flourishing, and its fruit abundant, (and it was meat for all; under it the wild beasts lodged, and the birds of the sky took shelter in its branches:) 19 is thyself, O king; for thou art grown great and powerful, and thy greatness has increased and reached to heaven, and thy dominion to the ends of the earth. 20 And whereas the king saw a watcher and a holy one coming down from heaven, and he said, Strip the tree, and destroy it; only leave the stump of its roots in the ground, and *bind it* with a band of iron and brass; and it shall lie in the grass that is without, and in the dew of heaven, and its portion shall be with wild beasts, until seven times have passed over it; 21 this is the interpretation of it, O king, and it is a decree of the Most High, which has come upon my lord the king. 22 And they shall drive thee forth from men, and thy dwelling shall be with wild beasts, and they shall feed thee with grass as an ox, and thou shall have thy lodging under the dew of heaven, and seven times shall pass over thee, until thou known that the Most High is Lord of the kingdom of men, and will give it to whom he shall please. 23 And whereas they said, Leave the stumps of the roots of the tree; thy kingdom abides *sure* to thee from the time that thou shalt know the power of the heavens. 24 Therefore, O king, let my counsel please thee, and atone for thy sins by alms, and *thine* iniquities by compassion on the poor: it may be God will be long-suffering to thy trespasses. 25 All these things came upon king Nabuchodonosor. 26 After a twelvemonth, as he walked in his palace in Babylon, 27 the king answered and said, Is not this great Babylon, which I have built for a royal residence, by the might of my power, for the honour of my glory? 28 While the word was yet in the king's mouth, there came a voice from heaven, *saying*, To thee, king Nabuchodonosor, they say, The kingdom has departed from thee. 29 And they *shall* drive thee from men, and thy dwelling shall be with the wild beasts of the field, and they shall feed thee with grass as an ox: and seven times shall pass over thee, until thou know that the Most High is Lord of the kingdom of men, and he will give it to whomsoever he shall please. 30 In the same hour the word was fulfilled upon Nabuchodonosor: and he was driven forth from men, and he ate grass as an ox, and his body was bathed with the dew of heaven, until his hairs were grown like lions' *hairs*, and his nails as birds' *claws*. 31 And at the end of the time I Nabuchodonosor lifted up mine eyes to heaven, and my reason returned to me, and I blessed the Most High, and praised him that lives for ever, and gave *him* glory; for his dominion is an everlasting dominion, and his kingdom *lasts* to all generations: 32 and all the inhabitants of the earth are reputed as nothing: and he does according to his will in the army of heaven, and among the inhabitants of the earth: and there is none who shall withstand his power, and say to him, What has thou done? 33 At the same time my reason returned to me, and I came to the honour of my kingdom; and my *natural* form returned to me, and my princes, and my nobles, sought me, and I was established in my kingdom, and more abundant majesty was added to me. 34 Now therefore I Nabuchodonosor praise and greatly exalt and glorify the King of heaven; for all his works are true, and his paths are judgment: and all that walk in pride he is able to abase.

Dan.5 1 Baltasar the king made a great supper for his thousand nobles, and *there was* wine before the thousand. 2 And Baltasar drinking gave orders as he tasted the wine that they should bring the gold and silver vessels, which Nabuchodonosor his father had brought forth from the temple in Jerusalem; that the king, and his nobles, and his mistresses, and his concubines, should drink out of them. 3 So the gold and silver vessels were brought which *Nabuchodonosor* had taken out of the temple of God in Jerusalem; and the king, and his nobles, and his mistresses, and his concubines, drank out of them. 4 They drank wine, and praised the gods of gold, and of silver, and of brass, and of iron, and of wood, and of stone. 5 In the same hour came forth fingers of a man's hand, and wrote in front of the lamp on the plaster of the wall of the king's house: and the king saw the knuckles of the hand that wrote. 6 Then the king's countenance changed, and his thoughts troubled him, and the joints of his loins were loosed, and his knees smote one another. 7 And the king cried aloud to bring in the magicians, Chaldeans, *and* soothsayers; and he said to the wise men of Babylon, Whosoever shall read this writing, and make known to me the interpretation, shall be clothed with scarlet, and *there shall be* a golden chain upon his neck, and he shall be the third ruler in my kingdom. 8 Then came in all the king's wise men: but they could not read the writing, nor make known the interpretation to the king. 9 And king Baltasar was troubled, and his countenance changed upon him, and his nobles were troubled with him. 10 Then the queen came into the banquet house, and said, O king, live for ever: let not thy thoughts trouble thee, and let not thy countenance be changed. 11 There is a man in thy kingdom, in whom is the Spirit of God; and in the days of thy father watchfulness and understanding were found in him; and king Nabuchodonosor thy father made him chief of the enchanters, magicians, Chaldeans, *and* soothsayers. 12 For *there is* an excellent spirit in him, and sense and understanding in him, interpreting dreams *as he does*, and answering hard *questions*, and solving difficulties: *it is* Daniel, and the king gave him the name of Baltasar: now then let him be called, and he shall tell thee the interpretation of the writing. 13 Then Daniel was brought in before the king: and the king said to Daniel, Art thou Daniel, of the children of the captivity of Judea, which the king my father brought? 14 I have heard concerning thee, that the Spirit of God is in thee, and *that* watchfulness and understanding and excellent wisdom have been found in thee. 15 And now, the wise men, magicians, *and* soothsayers, have come in before me, to read the writing, and make

known to me the interpretation: but they could not tell it me. 16 And I have heard concerning thee, that thou art able to make interpretations: now then if thou shalt be able to read the writing, and to make known to me the interpretation of it, thou shalt be clothed with purple, and there shall be a golden chain upon thy neck, and thou shalt be third ruler in my kingdom. 17 And Daniel said, before the king, Let thy gifts be to thyself, and give the present of thine house to another; but I will read the writing, and will make known to thee the interpretation of it. 18 O king, the most high God gave to thy father Nabuchodonosor a kingdom, and majesty, and honour, and glory: 19 and by reason of the majesty which he gave to him, all nations, tribes, *and* languages trembled and feared before him: whom he would he slew; and whom he would he smote; and whom he would he exalted; and whom he would he abased. 20 But when his heart was lifted up, and his spirit was emboldened to act proudly, he was deposed from his royal throne, and *his* honour was taken from him. 21 And he was driven forth from men; and his heart was given him after the nature of wild beasts, and his dwelling was with the wild asses; and they fed him with grass as an ox, and his body was bathed with the dew of heaven; until he knew that the most high God is Lord of the kingdom of men, and will give it to whomsoever he shall please. 22 And thou accordingly, his son, O Baltasar, has not humbled thine heart before God: knowest thou not all this? 23 And thou has been exalted against the Lord God of heaven; and they have brought before thee the vessels of his house, and thou, and thy nobles, and thy mistresses, and thy concubines, have drunk wine out of them; and thou has praised the gods of gold, and silver, and brass, and iron, and wood, and stone, which see not, and which hear not, and know not: and the God in whose hand are thy breath, and all thy ways has thou not glorified. 24 Therefore from his presence has been sent forth the knuckle of a hand; and he has ordered the writing. 25 And this is the ordered writing, Mane, Thekel, Phares. 26 This is the interpretation of the sentence: Mane; God has measured thy kingdom, and finished it. 27 Thekel; it has been weighed in the balance, and found wanting. 28 Phares; thy kingdom is divided, and given to the Medes and Persians. 29 Then Baltasar commanded, and they clothed Daniel with scarlet, and put the golden chain about his neck, and proclaimed concerning him that he was the third ruler in the kingdom. 30 In the same night was Baltasar the Chaldean king slain. 31 And Darius the Mede succeeded to the kingdom, being sixty-two years *old*.

Dan.6 1 And it pleased Darius, and he set over the kingdom a hundred and twenty satraps, to be in all his kingdom; 2 and over them three governors, of whom one was, Daniel; for the satraps to give account to them, that the king should not be troubled. 3 And Daniel was over them, for *there was* an excellent spirit in him; and the king set him over all his kingdom. 4 Then the governors and satraps sought to find occasion against Daniel; but they found against him no occasion, nor trespass, nor error, because he was faithful. 5 And the governors said, We shall not find occasion against

Daniel, except in the ordinances of his God. 6 Then the governors and satraps stood by the king, and said to him, King Darius, live for ever. 7 All who preside over thy kingdom, captains and satraps, chiefs and local governors, have taken counsel together, to establish by a royal statue and to confirm a decree, that whosoever shall ask a petition of any god or man for thirty days, save of thee, O king, shall be cast into the den of lions. 8 Now then, O king, establish the decree, and publish a writ, that the decree of the Persians and Medes be not changed. 9 Then king Darius commanded the decree to be written. 10 And when Daniel knew that the decree was ordered, he went into his house; and his windows were opened in his chambers toward Jerusalem, and three times in the day he knelt upon his knees, and prayed and gave thanks before his God, as he used to do before. 11 Then these men watched, and found Daniel praying and supplicating to his God. 12 And they came and said to the king, O king, has thou not made a decree, that whatsoever man shall ask a petition of any god or man for thirty days, but of thee, O king, shall be cast into the den of lions? And the king said, The word is true, and the decree of the Medes and Persians shall not pass. 13 Then they answered and said before the king, Daniel of the children of the captivity of Judea, has not submitted to thy decree; and three times in the day he makes his requests of his God. 14 Then the king, when he heard the saying, was much grieved for Daniel and he greatly exerted himself for Daniel to deliver him: and he exerted himself till evening to deliver him. 15 Then those men said to the king, Know, O king, that the law of the Medes and Persians is that we must not change any decree of statue which the king shall make. 16 Then the king commanded, and they brought Daniel, and cast him into the den of lions. But the king said to Daniel, Thy God whom thou servest continually, he will deliver thee. 17 And they brought a stone, and put it on the mouth of the den; and the king sealed *it* with his ring, and with the ring of his nobles; that the case might not be altered with regard to Daniel. 18 And the king departed to his house, and lay down fasting, and they brought him no food; and his sleep departed from him. But God shut the mouths of the lions, and they not molest Daniel. 19 Then the king arose very early in the morning, and came in hast to the den of lions. 20 And when he drew near to the den, he cried with a loud voice, Daniel, servant of the living God, has thy God, whom thou servest continually, been able to deliver thee from the lion's mouth? 21 And Daniel said to the king, O king, live for ever. 22 My God has sent his angel, and stopped the lions' mouths, and they have not hurt me: for uprightness was found in me before him; and moreover before thee, O king, I have committed no trespass. 23 Then the king was very glad for him, and he commanded to bring Daniel out of the den. So Daniel was brought out of the den, and there was found no hurt upon him, because he believed in his God. 24 And the king commanded, and they brought the men that had accused Daniel, and they were cast into the den of lions, they, and their children, and their wives: and they reached not the bottom of the den before the lions had the mastery of them, and utterly broke to pieces all their bones. 25 Then king Darius wrote to all nations, tribes, *and* languages, who dwell in all the earth, *saying,* Peace be multiplied to you. 26 This decree has been set forth by me in every dominion of my kingdom, that *men* tremble and fear before the God of Daniel: for he is the living and eternal God, and his kingdom shall not be destroyed, and his dominion is for ever. 27 He helps and delivers, and works signs and wonders in the heaven and on the earth, who has rescued Daniel from the power of the lions. 28 And Daniel prospered in the reign of Darius, and in the reign of Cyrus the Persian.

Dan.7 1 In the first year of Baltasar, king of the Chaldeans Daniel had a dream, and visions of his head upon his bed: and he wrote his dream. 2 I Daniel beheld, and, lo, the four winds of heaven blew violently upon the great sea. 3 And there came up four great beasts out of the sea, differing from one another. 4 The first *was* as a lioness, and her wings as an eagle's; I beheld until her wings were plucked, ands she was lifted off from the earth, and she stood on human feet, and a man's heart was given to her. 5 And, behold, a second beast like a bear, and it supported itself on one side, and there were three ribs in its mouth, between its teeth: and thus they said to it, Arise, devour much flesh. 6 After this one I looked, and behold another wild beast as a leopard, and it had four wings of a bird upon it: and the wild beast had four heads, and power was given to it. 7 After this one I looked, and behold a fourth beast, dreadful and terrible, and exceedingly strong, and its teeth were of iron; devouring and crushing to atoms, and it trampled the remainder with its feet: and it was altogether different from the beasts that were before it; and it *had* ten hours. 8 I noticed his horns, and behold, another little horn came up in the midst of them, and before it three of the former horns were rooted out: and, behold, *there were* eyes as the eyes of a man in this horn, and a mouth speaking great things. 9 I beheld until the thrones were set, and the Ancient of days sat; and his raiment was white as snow, and the hair of his head, as pure wool: his throne was a flame of fire, *and* his wheels burning fire. 10 A stream of fire rushed forth before him: thousand thousands ministered to him, and ten thousands of myriads, attended upon him: the judgment sat, and the books were opened. 11 I beheld then because of the voice of the great words which that horn spoke, until the wild beast was slain and destroyed, and his body given to be burnt with fire. 12 And the dominion of the rest of the wild beasts was taken away; but a prolonging of life was given them for certain times. 13 I beheld in the night vision, and, lo, *one* coming with the clouds of heaven as the Son of man, and he came on to the Ancient of days, and was brought near to him. 14 And to him was given the dominion, and the honour, and the kingdom; and all nations, tribes, and languages, shall serve him: his dominion is an everlasting dominion, which shall not pass away, and his kingdom shall not be destroyed. 15 *As for* me Daniel, my spirit in my body trembled, and the visions of my head troubled me. 16 And I drew near to one of them that stood by, and I sought to learn of him the truth of all these things: and he told me the truth, and made known to me the interpretation of the things. 17 These four beasts are four kingdoms *that* shall rise up on the earth: 18 which shall be taken away; and the saints of the Most High shall take the kingdom, and possess it for ever and ever. 19 Then I enquired carefully concerning the fourth beast; for it differed from every *other* beast, exceeding dreadful: its teeth were of iron, and its claws of brass, devouring, and utterly breaking to pieces, and it trampled the remainder with its feet: 20 and concerning it ten horns that were in its head, and the other that came up, and rooted up *some* of the former, which had eyes, and a mouth speaking great things, and his look was bolder than the rest. 21 I beheld, and that horn made war with the saints, and prevailed against them; 22 until the Ancient of days came, and he gave judgment to the saints of the Most High; and the time came on, and the saints possessed the kingdom. 23 And he said, The fourth beast shall be the fourth kingdom on the earth, which shall excel all *other* kingdoms, and shall devour the whole earth, and trample and destroy it. 24 And his ten horns are ten kings *that* shall arise: and after them shall arise another, who shall exceed all the former ones in wickedness and he shall subdue three kings. 25 And he shall speak words against the Most High, and shall wear out the saints of the Most High, and shall think to change times and law: and *power* shall be given into his hand for a time and times and half a time. 26 And the judgment has sat, and they shall remove *his* dominion to abolish it, and to destroy it utterly. 27 And the kingdom and the power and the greatness of the kings that are under the whole heaven were given to the saints of the Most High; and his kingdom is an everlasting kingdom, and all powers shall serve and obey him. 28 Hitherto is the end of the matter. As for me Daniel, my thoughts greatly troubled me, and my countenance was changed: but I kept the matter in my heart.

Dan.8 1 In the third year of the reign of king Baltasar a vision appeared to me, *even* to me Daniel, after that which appeared to me at the first. 2 And I was in Susa the palace, which is in the land of Ælam, and I was on the *bank of* Ubal. 3 And I lifted up mine eyes, and saw, and, behold, a ram standing in front of the Ubal; and he had high horns; and one was higher than the other, and the high one came up last. 4 And I saw the ram butting westward, and northward, and southward; and no beast could stand before him, and there was none that could deliver out of his hand; and he did according to his will, and became great. 5 And I was considering, and, behold, a he-goat came from the south-west on the face of the whole earth, and touched not the earth: and the goat *had* a horn between his eyes. 6 And he came to the ram that had the horns, which I had seen standing in front of the Ubal, and he ran at him with the violence of his strength. 7 And I saw him coming up close to the ram, and he was furiously enraged against him, and he smote the ram, and broke both his horns: and there was no strength in the ram to stand before him, but he cast him on the ground, and trampled on him; and there was none that could deliver the ram out of his hand. 8 And the he-goat grew exceedingly great: and when he was strong, his great horn was broken; and four other *horns* rose up in its place toward the four winds of heaven. 9 And out of one of

them came forth one strong horn, and it grew very great toward the south, and toward the host: 10 and it magnified itself to the host of heaven; and there fell to the earth *some* of the host of heaven and of the stars, and they trampled on them. 11 And *this shall be* until the chief captain shall have delivered the captivity: and by reason of him the sacrifice was disturbed, and he prospered; and the holy place shall be made desolate. 12 And a sin-offering was given for the sacrifice, and righteousness was cast down to the ground; and it practised, and prospered. 13 And I heard one saint speaking, and a saint said to a certain one speaking, How long shall the vision continue, *even* the removal of the sacrifice, and the bringing in of the sin of desolation; and *how long* shall the sanctuary and host be trampled? 14 And he said to him, Evening and morning *there shall be* two thousand and four hundred days; and *then* the sanctuary shall be cleansed. 15 And it came to pass, as I, *even* I Daniel, saw the vision, and sought to understand it, that, behold, there stood before me as the appearance of a man. 16 And I heard the voice of a man between *the banks of* the Ubal; and he called, and said, Gabriel, cause that man to understand the vision. 17 And he came and stood near where I stood: and when he came, I was struck with awe, and fell upon my face: but he said to me, Understand, son of man: for yet the vision is for an appointed time. 18 And while he spoke with me, I fell upon my face to the earth: and he touched me, and set me on my feet. 19 And he said, Behold, I make thee know the things that shall come to pass at the end of the wrath: for the vision *is* yet for an appointed time. 20 The ram which thou sawest that had the horns is the king of the Medes and Persians. 21 The he-goat is the King of the Greeks: and the great horn which was between his eyes, he is the first king. 22 And *as for* the one that was broken, in whose place there stood up four horns, four kings shall arise out of his nation, but not in their *own* strength. 23 And at the latter time of their kingdom, when their sins are coming to the full, there shall arise a king bold in countenance, and understanding riddles. 24 And his power *shall be* great, and he shall destroy wonderfully, and prosper, and practise, and shall destroy mighty men, and the holy people. 25 And the yoke of his chain shall prosper: *there is* craft in his hand; and he shall magnify himself in his heart, and by craft shall destroy many, and he shall stand up for the destruction of many, and shall crush them as eggs in his hand. 26 And the vision of the evening and morning that was mentioned is true: and do thou seal the vision; for *it is* for many days. 27 And I Daniel fell asleep, and was sick: then I arose, and did the king's business; and I wondered at the vision, and there was none that understood *it*.

Dan.9 1 In the first year of Darius the son of Assuerus, of the seed of the Medes, who reigned over the kingdom of the Chaldeans, 2 I Daniel understood by books the number of the years which was the word of the Lord to the prophet Jeremias, *even* seventy years for the accomplishment of the desolation of Jerusalem. 3 And I set my face toward the Lord God, to seek *him* diligently by prayer and supplications, with fastings and sackcloth. 4 And I prayed to the Lord my God, and confessed, and said, O Lord, the great and wonderful God, keeping thy covenant and thy mercy to them that love thee, and to them that keep thy commandments; we have sinned, 5 we have done iniquity, we have transgressed, and we have departed and turned aside from thy commandments and from thy judgments: 6 and we have not hearkened to thy servants the prophets, who spoke in thy name to our kings, and our princes, and our fathers, and to all the people of the land. 7 To thee, O Lord, *belongs* righteousness, an to us confusion of face, as at this day; to the men of Juda, and to the dwellers in Jerusalem, and to all Israel, to them that are near, and to them that are far off in all the earth, wherever thou has scattered them, for the sin which they committed. 8 In thee, O Lord, is our righteousness, and to us *belongs* confusion of faced, and to our kings, and to our princes, and to our fathers, forasmuch as we have sinned. 9 To thee, the Lord our God, *belong* compassions and forgivenesses, whereas we have departed *from thee*; 10 neither have we hearkened to the voice of the Lord our God, to walk in his laws, which he set before us by the hands of his servants the prophets. 11 Moreover all Israel have transgressed thy law, and have refused to hearken to thy voice; so the curse has come upon us, and the oath that is written in the law of Moses the servant of God, because we have sinned against him. 12 And he has confirmed his words, which he spoke against us, and against our judges who judged us, *by* bringing upon us great evils, such as have not happened under the whole heaven, according to what has happened in Jerusalem. 13 As it is written in the law of Moses, all these evils have come upon us: yet we have not besought the Lord our God, that we might turn away from our iniquities, and have understanding in all thy truth. 14 The Lord also has watched, and brought the evils upon us: for the Lord our God is righteous in all his work which he has executed, but we have not hearkened to his voice. 15 And now, O Lord our God, who broughtest thy people out of the land of Egypt with a mighty hand, and madest to thyself a name, as *at* this day; we have sinned, we have transgressed. 16 O Lord, thy mercy is over all: let, I pray thee, thy wrath turn away, and thine anger from thy city Jerusalem, *even* thy holy mountain: for we have sinned, and because of our iniquities, and those of our fathers, Jerusalem and thy people are become a reproach among all that are round about us. 17 And now, O lord our God, hearken to the prayer of thy servant, and his supplications, and cause thy face to shine on thy desolate sanctuary, for thine *own* sake, O Lord. 18 Incline thine ear, O my God, and hear; open thine eyes and behold our desolation, and that of thy city on which thy name is called: for we do not bring our pitiful case before thee on *the ground of* our righteousness, but on *the ground of* thy manifold compassions, O Lord. 19 Hearken, O Lord; be propitious, O Lord; attend, O Lord; delay not, O my God, for thine own sake: for thy name is called upon thy city and upon thy people. 20 And while I was yet speaking, and praying, and confessing my sins and the sins of my people Israel, and bringing my pitiful case before the Lord my God concerning the holy mountain; 21 yea, while I was yet speaking in prayer, behold the man Gabriel, whom I had seen in the vision at the beginning, *came* flying, and he touched me about the hour of the evening sacrifice. 22 And he instructed me, and spoke with me, and said, O Daniel, I am now come forth to impart to thee understanding. 23 At the beginning of thy supplication the word came forth, and I am come to tell thee; for thou art a man much beloved: therefore consider the matter, understand the vision. 24 Seventy weeks have been determined upon thy people, and upon the holy city, for sin to be ended, and to seal up transgressions, and to blot out the iniquities, and to make atonement for iniquities, and to bring in everlasting righteousness, and to seal the vision and the prophet, and to anoint the Most Holy. 25 And thou shalt know and understand, that from the going forth of the command for the answer and for the building of Jerusalem until Christ the prince *there shall be* seven weeks, and sixty-two weeks; and then *the time* shall return, and the street shall be built, and the wall, and the times shall be exhausted. 26 And after the sixty-two weeks, the anointed one shall be destroyed, and there is no judgment in him: and he shall destroy the city and the sanctuary with the prince that is coming: they shall be cut off with a flood, and to the end of the war which is rapidly completed he shall appoint *the city* to desolations. 27 And one week shall establish the covenant with many: and in the midst of the week my sacrifice and drink-offering shall be taken away: and on the temple *shall be* the abomination of desolations; and at the end of time an end shall be put to the desolation.

Dan.10 1 In the third year of Cyrus king of the Persians a thing was revealed to Daniel, whose name was called Baltasar; and the thing was true, and great power and understanding in the vision was given to him. 2 In those days I Daniel was mourning three full weeks. 3 I ate no pleasant bread, and no flesh or wine entered into my mouth, neither did I anoint myself with oil, until three whole weeks were accomplished. 4 On the twenty-fourth day of the first month, I was near the great river, which is Tigris Eddekel. 5 And I lifted up mine eyes, and looked, and behold a man clothed in linen, and his loins were girt with gold of Ophaz: 6 and his body was as Tharsis, and his face was a the appearance of lightning, and his eyes as lamps of fire, and his arms and his legs as the appearance of shining brass, and the voice of his words as the voice of a multitude. 7 And I Daniel only saw the vision: and the men that were with me saw not the vision; but a great amazement fell upon them, and they fled in fear. 8 So I was left alone, and saw this great vision, and there was no strength left in me, and my glory was turned into corruption, and I retained no strength. 9 Yet I heard the voice of his words: and when I heard him I was pricked *in the heart*, and *I fell with* my face to the earth. 10 And, behold, a hand touched me, and it raised me on my knees. 11 And he said to me, O Daniel, man greatly beloved, understand the words which I speak to thee, and stand upright: for I am now sent to thee. And when he had spoken to me this word, I stood trembling. 12 And he said to me, Fear not, Daniel: for from the first day that thou didst set thine heart to understand, and to afflict thyself before the Lord thy God, they words were heard, and I am come because of thy words. 13 But the prince of the kingdom of the Persians withstood me twenty-one days: and behold, Michael, one of the princes, came to help me; and I left him there with the chief of the kingdom of the Persians: 14 and I have come to inform thee of all that shall befall thy people in the last days: for the vision is yet for *many* days. 15 And when he had spoken with me according to these words, I turned my face to the ground, and was pricked *in the heart.* 16 And, behold, as it were the likeness of a son of man touched my lips; and I opened my mouth, and spoke, and said to him that stood before me, O *my* lord, at the sight of thee my bowels were turned within me, and I had no strength. 17 And how shall thy servant be able, O *my* lord, to speak with this my lord? and as for me, from henceforth strength will not remain in me, and there is no breath left in me. 18 And there touched me again as it were the appearance of a man, and he strengthened me, 19 and said to me, Fear not, man greatly beloved: peace be to thee, quit thyself like a man, and be strong. And when he had spoken with me, I received strength, and said, Let my lord speak; for thou hast strengthened me. 20 And he said, Knowest thou, wherefore I am come to thee? and now I will return to fight with the prince of the Persians: and I was going in, and the prince of the Greeks came. 21 But I will tell thee that which is ordained in the scripture of truth: and there is no one that holds with me in these matters but Michael your prince.

Dan.11 1 And I in the first year of Cyrus stood to strengthen and confirm *him.* 2 And now I will tell thee the truth. Behold, there shall yet rise up three kings in Persia: and the fourth shall be very far richer than all: and after that he is master of his wealth, he shall rise up against all the kingdoms of the Greeks. 3 An there shall rise up a mighty king, and he shall be lord of a great empire, and shall do according to his will. 4 And when his kingdom shall stand up, it shall be broken, and shall be divided to the four winds of heaven; but not to his posterity, nor according to his dominion which he ruled over: for his kingdom shall be plucked up, and *given* to others beside these. 5 And the king of the south shall be strong; and one of their princes shall prevail against him, and shall obtain a great dominion. 6 And after his years they shall associate; and the daughter of the king of the south shall come to the king of the north, to make agreements with him: but she shall not retain power of arm; neither shall his seed stand: and she shall be delivered up, and they that brought her, and the maiden, and he that strengthened her in these times. 7 *But* out of the flower of her root there shall arise *one on* his place, and shall come against the host, and shall enter into the strongholds of the king of the north, and shall fight against them, and prevail. 8 Yea, he shall carry with a body of captives into Egypt their gods with their molten *images, and* all their precious vessels of silver and gold; and he shall last longer than the king of the north. 9 And he shall enter into the kingdom of the king of the south, and shall return to his own land. 10 And his sons shall gather a multitude among many: and one shall certainly come, and overflow, and pass through, and he shall rest, and collect his strength. 11 And the king of the south shall be greatly enraged, and shall

come forth, and shall war with the king of the north: and he shall raise a great multitude; but the multitude shall be delivered into his hand. 12 And he shall take the multitude, and his heart shall be exalted; and he shall cast down many thousands; but he shall not prevail. 13 For the king of the north shall return, and bring a multitude greater than the former, and at the end of the times of years an invading army shall come with a great force, and with much substance. 14 And in those times many shall rise up against the king of the south; and the children of the spoilers of thy people shall exalt themselves to establish the vision; and they shall fail. 15 And the king of the north shall come in, and cast up a mound, and take strong cities: and the arms of the king of the south shall withstand, and his chosen ones shall rise up, but there shall be no strength to stand. 16 And he that comes in against him shall do according to his will, and there is no one to stand before him: and he shall stand in the land of beauty, and it shall be consumed by his hand. 17 And he shall set his face to come in with the force of his whole kingdom, and shall cause everything to prosper with him: and he shall give him the daughter of women to corrupt her: but she shall not continue, neither be on his side. 18 And he shall turn his face to the islands, and shall take many, and cause princes to cease from their reproach: nevertheless his own reproach shall return to him. 19 Then he shall turn back his face to the strength of his own land: but he shall become weak, and fall, and not be found. 20 And there shall arise out of his root one that shall cause a plant of the kingdom to pass over his place, earning kingly glory: and yet in those days shall he be broken, yet not openly, nor in war. 21 *One* shall stand on his place, *who* has been set a nought, and they have not put upon him the honour of the kingdom: but he shall come in prosperously, and obtain the kingdom by deceitful ways. 22 And the arms of him that overflows shall be washed away as with a flood from before him, and shall be broken, and *so shall be* the head of the covenant. 23 And because of the leagues made with him he shall work deceit: and he shall come up, and overpower them with a small nation. 24 And he shall enter with prosperity, and *that* into fertile districts; and he shall do what his fathers and his fathers' fathers have not done; he shall scatter among them plunder, and spoils, and wealth; and he shall devise plans against Egypt, even for a time. 25 And his strength and his heart shall be stirred up against the king of the south with a great force; and the king of the south shall engage in war with a great and very strong force; but *his forces* shall not stand, for they shall devise plans against him: 26 and they shall eat his provisions, and shall crush him, and he shall carry away armies as with a flood, and many shall fall down slain. 27 And *as for* both the kings, their hearts *are set* upon mischief, and they shall speak lies at one table; but it shall not prosper; for yet the end is for a *fixed* time. 28 And he shall return to his land with much substance; and his heart *shall be* against the holy covenant; and he shall perform *great deeds*, and return to his own land. 29 At the *set* time he shall return, and shall come into the south, but the last *expedition* shall *not* be as the first. 30 For the Citians issuing forth shall come against him, and he shall be brought low, and shall return, and shall be incensed against the holy covenant: and he shall do *thus*, and shall return, and have intelligence with them that have forsaken the holy covenant. 31 And seeds shall spring up out of him, and they shall profane the sanctuary of strength, and they shall remove the perpetual *sacrifice*, and make the abomination desolate. 32 And the transgressors shall bring about a covenant by deceitful ways: but a people knowing their God shall prevail, and do *valiantly*. 33 And the intelligent of the people shall understand much: yet they shall fall by the sword, and by flame, and by captivity, and by spoil of *many* days. 34 And when they are weak they shall be helped with a little help: but many shall attach themselves to them with treachery. 35 And *some* of them that understand shall fall, to try them as with fire, and to test *them*, and that they may be manifested at the time of the end, for the matter *is* yet for a *set* time. 36 And he shall do according to his will, and the king shall exalt and magnify himself against every god, and shall speak great swelling words, and shall prosper until the indignation shall be accomplished: for it is coming to an end. 37 And he shall not regard any gods of his fathers, nor the desire of women, neither shall he regard any deity: for he shall magnify himself above all. 38 And he shall honour the god of forces on his place: and a god whom his fathers knew not he shall honour with gold, and silver, and precious stones, and desirable things. 39 And he shall do *thus* in the strong places of refuge with a strange god, and shall increase his glory: and he shall subject many to them, and shall distribute the land in gifts. 40 And at the end of the time he shall conflict with the king of the south: and the king of the north shall come against him with chariots, and with horsemen, and with many ships; and they shall enter into the land: and he shall break in pieces, and pass on: 41 and he shall enter into the land of beauty, and many shall fail: but these shall escape out of his hand, Edom, and Moab, and the chief of the children of Ammon. 42 And he shall stretch forth *his* hand over the land; and the land of Egypt shall not escape. 43 And he shall have the mastery over the secret *treasures* of gold and silver, and over all the desirable *possessions* of Egypt, and of the Libyans and Ethiopians in their strongholds. 44 But rumors and anxieties out of the east and from the north shall trouble him; and he shall come with great wrath to destroy many. 45 And he shall pitch the tabernacle of his palace between the seas in the holy mountain of beauty: *but* he shall come to his portion, and there is none to deliver him.

Dan.12 1 And at that time Michael the great prince shall stand up, that stands over the children of thy people: and there shall be a time of tribulation, such tribulation as has not been from the time that there was a nation on the earth until that time: at that time thy people shall be delivered, *even* every one that is written in the book. 2 And many of them that sleep in the dust of the earth shall awake, some to everlasting life, and some to reproach and everlasting shame. 3 And the wise shall shine as the brightness of the firmament, and *some* of the many righteous as the stars for ever and ever. 4 And thou, Daniel, close the words, and seal the book to the time of the end; until many are taught, and knowledge is increased. 5 And I Daniel saw, and, behold, two others stood, on one side of the bank of the river, and the other on the other side of the bank of the river. 6 And *one* said to the man clothed in linen, who was over the water of the river, When *will be* the end of the wonders which thou has mentioned? 7 And I heard the man clothed in linen, who was over the water of the river, and he lifted up his right hand and his left hand to heaven, and sware by him that lives for ever, that *it should be* for a time of times and half a time: when the dispersion is ended they shall know all these things. 8 And I heard, but I understood not: and I said, O Lord, what *will be* the end of these things? 9 And he said, Go, Daniel: for the words are closed and sealed up to the time of the end. 10 Many must be tested, and thoroughly whitened, and tried with fire, and sanctified; but the transgressors shall transgress: and none of the transgressors shall understand; but the wise shall understand. 11 And from the time of the removal of the perpetual sacrifice, when the abomination of desolation shall be set up, *there shall be* a thousand two hundred and ninety days. 12 Blessed is he that waits, and comes to the thousand three hundred and thirty-five days. 13 But go thou, and rest; for *there are* yet days and seasons to the fulfillment of the end; and thou shalt stand in thy lot at the end of the days.

Dan.13 History of Susanna 1 There dwelt a man in Babylon, called Joacim: 2 And he took a wife, whose name was Susanna, the daughter of Chelcias, a very fair woman, and one that feared the Lord. 3 Her parents also were righteous, and taught their daughter according to the law of Moses. 4 Now Joacim was a great rich man, and had a fair garden joining unto his house: and to him resorted the Jews; because he was more honourable than all others. 5 The same year were appointed two of the ancients of the people to be judges, such as the Lord spake of, that wickedness came from Babylon from ancient judges, who seemed to govern the people. 6 These kept much at Joacim's house: and all that had any suits in law came unto them. 7 Now when the people departed away at noon, Susanna went into her husband's garden to walk. 8 And the two elders saw her going in every day, and walking; so that their lust was inflamed toward her. 9 And they perverted their own mind, and turned away their eyes, that they might not look unto heaven, nor remember just judgments. 10 And albeit they both were wounded with her love, yet durst not one shew another his grief. 11 For they were ashamed to declare their lust, that they desired to have to do with her. 12 Yet they watched diligently from day to day to see her. 13 And the one said to the other, Let us now go home: for it is dinner time. 14 So when they were gone out, they parted the one from the other, and turning back again they came to the same place; and after that they had asked one another the cause, they acknowledged their lust: then appointed they a time both together, when they might find her alone. 15 And it fell out, as they watched a fit time, she went in as before with two maids only, and she was desirous to wash herself in the garden: for it was hot. 16 And there was no body there save the two elders, that had hid themselves, and watched her. 17 Then she said to her maids, Bring me oil and washing balls, and shut the garden doors, that I may wash me. 18 And they did as she bade them, and shut the garden doors, and went out themselves at privy doors to fetch the things that she had commanded them: but they saw not the elders, because they were hid. 19 Now when the maids were gone forth, the two elders rose up, and ran unto her, saying, 20 Behold, the garden doors are shut, that no man can see us, and we are in love with thee; therefore consent unto us, and lie with us. 21 If thou wilt not, we will bear witness against thee, that a young man was with thee: and therefore thou didst send away thy maids from thee. 22 Then Susanna sighed, and said, I am straitened on every side: for if I do this thing, it is death unto me: and if I do it not I cannot escape your hands. 23 It is better for me to fall into your hands, and not do it, than to sin in the sight of the Lord. 24 With that Susanna cried with a loud voice: and the two elders cried out against her. 25 Then ran the one, and opened the garden door. 26 So when the servants of the house heard the cry in the garden, they rushed in at the privy door, to see what was done unto her. 27 But when the elders had declared their matter, the servants were greatly ashamed: for there was never such a report made of Susanna. 28 And it came to pass the next day, when the people were assembled to her husband Joacim, the two elders came also full of mischievous imagination against Susanna to put her to death; 29 And said before the people, Send for Susanna, the daughter of Chelcias, Joacim's wife. And so they sent. 30 So she came with her father and mother, her children, and all her kindred. 31 Now Susanna was a very delicate woman, and beauteous to behold. 32 And these wicked men commanded to uncover her face, (for she was covered) that they might be filled with her beauty. 33 Therefore her friends and all that saw her wept. 34 Then the two elders stood up in the midst of the people, and laid their hands upon her head. 35 And she weeping looked up toward heaven: for her heart trusted in the Lord. 36 And the elders said, As we walked in the garden alone, this woman came in with two maids, and shut the garden doors, and sent the maids away. 37 Then a young man, who there was hid, came unto her, and lay with her. 38 Then we that stood in a corner of the garden, seeing this wickedness, ran unto them. 39 And when we saw them together, the man we could not hold: for he was stronger than we, and opened the door, and leaped out. 40 But having taken this woman, we asked who the young man was, but she would not tell us: these things do we testify. 41 Then the assembly believed them as those that were the elders and judges of the people: so they condemned her to death. 42 Then Susanna cried out with a loud voice, and said, O everlasting God, that knowest the secrets, and knowest all things before they be: 43 Thou knowest that they have borne false witness against me, and, behold, I must die; whereas I never did such things as these men have maliciously invented against me. 44 And the Lord heard her voice. 45 Therefore when she was led to be put to death, the Lord raised up the holy spirit of a young youth whose name was Daniel: 46 Who cried with a loud voice, I am clear from the blood of this woman. 47 Then all the people turned them toward him, and said, What mean these words that thou hast spoken? 48 So he standing in the midst of them said, Are ye such fools, ye sons of Israel, that without examination or knowledge of the truth ye have condemned a daughter of Israel? 49 Return again to the place of judgment: for they have borne false witness against her. 50 Wherefore all the people turned again in haste, and the elders said unto him, Come, sit down among us, and shew it us, seeing God hath given thee the honour of an elder. 51 Then said Daniel unto them, Put these two aside one far from another, and I will examine them. 52 So when they were put asunder one from another, he called one of them, and said unto him, O thou that art waxen old in wickedness, now thy sins which thou hast committed aforetime are come to light. 53 For thou hast pronounced false judgment and hast condemned the innocent and hast let the guilty go free; albeit the Lord saith, The innocent and righteous shalt thou not slay. 54 Now then, if thou hast seen her, tell me, Under what tree sawest thou them companying together? Who answered, Under a mastick tree. 55 And Daniel said, Very well; thou hast lied against thine own head; for even now the angel of God hath received the sentence of God to cut thee in two. 56 So he put him aside, and commanded to bring the other, and said unto him, O thou seed of Chanaan, and not of Juda, beauty hath deceived thee, and lust hath perverted thine heart. 57 Thus have ye dealt with the daughters of Israel, and they for fear companied with you: but the daughter of Juda would not abide your wickedness. 58 Now therefore tell me, Under what tree didst thou take them companying together? Who answered, Under an holm tree. 59 Then said Daniel unto him, Well; thou hast also lied against thine own head: for the angel of God waiteth with the sword to cut thee in two, that he may destroy you. 60 With that all the assembly cried out with a loud voice, and praised God, who saveth them that trust in him. 61 And they arose against the two elders, for Daniel had convicted them of false witness by their own mouth: 62 And according to the law of Moses they did unto them in such sort as they maliciously intended to do to their neighbour: and they put them to death. Thus the innocent blood was saved the same day. 63 Therefore Chelcias and his wife praised God for their daughter Susanna, with Joacim her husband, and all the kindred, because there was no dishonesty found in her. 64 From that day forth was Daniel had in great reputation in the sight of the people.

Dan.14 Bel and the Dragon 1 And king Astyages was gathered to his fathers, and Cyrus of Persia received his kingdom. 2 And Daniel conversed with the king, and was honoured above all his friends. 3 Now the Babylonians had an idol, called Bel, and there were spent upon him every day twelve great measures of fine flour, and forty sheep, and six vessels of wine. 4 And the king worshipped it and went daily to adore it: but Daniel worshipped his own God. And the king said unto him, Why dost not thou worship Bel? 5 Who answered and said, Because I may not worship idols made with hands, but the living God, who hath created the heaven and the earth, and hath sovereignty over all flesh. 6 Then said the king unto him, Thinkest thou not that Bel is a living God? seest thou not how much he eateth and drinketh every day? 7 Then Daniel smiled, and said, O king, be not deceived: for this is but clay within, and brass without, and did never eat or drink any thing. 8 So the king was wroth, and called for his priests, and said unto them, If ye tell me not who this is that devoureth these expenses, ye shall die. 9 But if ye can certify me that Bel devoureth them, then Daniel shall die: for he hath spoken blasphemy against Bel. And Daniel said unto the king, Let it be according to thy word. 10 Now the priests of Bel were threescore and ten, beside their wives and children. And the king went with Daniel into the temple of Bel. 11 So Bel's priests said, Lo, we go out: but thou, O king, set on the meat, and make ready the wine, and shut the door fast and seal it with thine own signet; 12 And to morrow when thou comest in, if thou findest not that Bel hath eaten up all, we will suffer death: or else Daniel, that speaketh falsely against us. 13 And they little regarded it: for under the table they had made a privy entrance, whereby they entered in continually, and consumed those things. 14 So when they were gone forth, the king set meats before Bel. Now Daniel had commanded his servants to bring ashes, and those they strewed throughout all the temple in the presence of the king alone: then went they out, and shut the door, and sealed it with the king's signet, and so departed. 15 Now in the night came the priests with their wives and children, as they were wont to do, and did eat and drink up all. 16 In the morning betime the king arose, and Daniel with him. 17 And the king said, Daniel, are the seals whole? And he said, Yea, O king, they be whole. 18 And as soon as he had opened the dour, the king looked upon the table, and cried with a loud voice, Great art thou, O Bel, and with thee is no deceit at all. 19 Then laughed Daniel, and held the king that he should not go in, and said, Behold now the pavement, and mark well whose footsteps are these. 20 And the king said, I see the footsteps of men, women, and children. And then the king was angry, 21 And took the priests with their wives and children, who shewed him the privy doors, where they came in, and consumed such things as were upon the table. 22 Therefore the king slew them, and delivered Bel into Daniel's power, who destroyed him and his temple. 23 And in that same place there was a great dragon, which they of Babylon worshipped. 24 And the king said unto Daniel, Wilt thou also say that this is of brass? lo, he liveth, he eateth and drinketh; thou canst not say that he is no living god: therefore worship him. 25 Then said Daniel unto the king, I will worship the Lord my God: for he is the living God. 26 But give me leave, O king, and I shall slay this dragon without sword or staff. The king said, I give thee leave. 27 Then Daniel took pitch, and fat, and hair, and did seethe them together, and made lumps thereof: this he put in the dragon's mouth, and so the dragon burst in sunder: and Daniel said, Lo, these are the gods ye worship. 28 When they of Babylon heard that, they took great indignation, and conspired against the king, saying, The king is become a Jew, and he hath destroyed Bel, he hath slain the dragon, and put the priests to death. 29 So they came to the king, and said, Deliver us Daniel, or else we will destroy thee and thine house. 30 Now when the king saw that they pressed him sore, being constrained, he delivered Daniel unto them: 31 Who cast him into the lions' den: where he was six days. 32 And in the den there were seven lions, and they had given them every day two carcases, and two sheep: which then were not given to them, to the intent they might devour Daniel. 33 Now there was in Jewry a prophet, called Habbacuc, who had made pottage, and had broken bread in a bowl, and was going into the field, for to bring it to the reapers. 34 But the angel of the Lord said unto Habbacuc, Go, carry the dinner that thou hast into Babylon unto Daniel, who is in the lions' den. 35 And Habbacuc said, Lord, I never saw Babylon; neither do I know where the den is. 36 Then the angel of the Lord took him by the crown, and bare him by the hair of his head, and through the vehemency of his spirit set him in Babylon over the den. 37 And Habbacuc cried, saying, O Daniel, Daniel, take the dinner which God hath sent thee. 38 And Daniel said, Thou hast remembered me, O God: neither hast thou forsaken them that seek thee and love thee. 39 So Daniel arose, and did eat: and the angel of the Lord set Habbacuc in his own place again immediately. 40 Upon the seventh day the king went to bewail Daniel: and when he came to the den, he looked in, and behold, Daniel was sitting. 41 Then cried the king with a loud voice, saying, Great art Lord God of Daniel, and there is none other beside thee. 42 And he drew him out, and cast those that were the cause of his destruction into the den: and they were devoured in a moment before his face.

OSEE (HOSEA)

Hos.1 1 The word of the Lord which came to Osee the son of Beeri, in the days of Ozias, and Joatham, and Achaz, and Ezekias, kings of Juda, and in the days of Jeroboam son of Joas, king of Israel. 2 The beginning of the word of the Lord by Osee. And the Lord said to Osee, Go, take to thyself a wife of fornication, and children of fornication: for the land will surely go a-whoring in departing from the Lord. 3 So he went and took Gomer, daughter of Debelaim; and she conceived, and bore him a son. 4 And the Lord said to him, Call his name Jezrael; for yet a little *while*, and I will avenge the blood of Jezrael on the house of Juda, and will make to cease the kingdom of the house of Israel. 5 And it shall be, in that day, *that* I will break the bow of Israel in the valley of Jezrael. 6 And she conceived again, and bore a daughter. And he said to him, Call her name, Unpitied: for I will no more have mercy on the house of Israel, but will surely set myself in array against them. 7 But I will have mercy on the house of Juda, and will save them by the Lord their God, and will not save them with bow, nor with sword, nor by war, nor by horses, nor by horsemen. 8 And she weaned Unpitied; and she conceived again, and bore a son. 9 And he said, Call his name, Not my people: for ye are not my people, and I am not your *God*. 10 Yet the number of the children of Israel was as the sand of the sea, which shall not be measured nor numbered: and it shall come to pass, *that* in the place where it was said to them, Ye are not my people, even they shall be called the sons of the living God. 11 And the children of Juda shall be gathered, and the children of Israel together, and shall appoint themselves one head, and shall come up out of the land: for great *shall be* the day of Jezrael.

Hos.2 1 Say to your brother, My people, and to your sister, Pitied. 2 Plead with your mother, plead: for she is not my wife, and I am not her husband: and I will remove her fornication out of my presence, and her adultery from between her breasts: 3 that I may strip her naked, and make her again as she was at the day of her birth: and I will make her desolate, and make her as a dry land, and will kill her with thirst. 4 And I will not have mercy upon her children; for they are children of fornication. 5 And their mother went a-whoring: she that bore them disgraced *them*: for she said, I will go after my lovers, that give me my bread and my water, and my garments, and my linen clothes, my oil and my necessaries. 6 Therefore, behold, I hedge up her way with thorns, and I will stop the ways, and she shall not find her path. 7 And she shall follow after her lovers, and shall not overtake them; and she shall seek them, but shall not find them: and she shall say, I will go, and return to my former husband; for it was better with me than now. 8 And she knew not that I gave her her corn, and wine, and oil, and multiplied silver to her: but she made silver and gold *images* for Baal. 9 Therefore I will return, and take away my corn in its season, and my wine in its time; and I will take away my raiment and my linen clothes, so that she shall not cover her nakedness. 10 And now I will expose her uncleanness before her lovers, and no one shall by any means deliver her out of my hand. 11 And I will take away all her gladness, her feasts, and her festivals at the new moon, and her sabbaths, and all her solemn assemblies. 12 And I will utterly destroy her vines, and her fig-trees, all things of which she said, These are my hire which my lovers have given me: and I will make them a testimony, and the wild beasts of the field, and the birds of the sky, and the reptiles of the earth shall devour them. 13 And I will recompense on her the days of Baalim, wherein she sacrificed to them, and put on her ear-rings, and her necklaces, and went after her lovers, and forgot me, saith the Lord. 14 Therefore, behold, I *will* cause her to err, and will make her as desolate, and will speak comfortably to her. 15 And I will giver her possessions from thence, and the valley of Achor to open her understanding: and she shall be afflicted there according to the days of her infancy, and according to the days of her coming up out of the land of Egypt. 16 And it shall come to pass in that day, saith the Lord, *that* she shall call me, My husband, and shall no longer call me Baalim. 17 And I will take away the names of Baalim out of her mouth, and their names shall be remembered no more at all. 18 And I will make for them in that day a covenant with the wild beasts of the field, and with the birds of the sky, and with the reptiles of the earth: and I will break the bow and the sword and the battle from off the earth, and will cause thee to dwell safely. 19 And I will betroth thee to myself for ever; yea, I will betroth thee to myself in righteousness, and in judgment, and in mercy, and in tender compassions; 20 and I will betroth thee to myself in faithfulness: and thou shalt know the Lord. 21 And it shall come to pass in that day, saith the Lord, I will hearken to the heaven, and it shall hearken to the earth; 22 and the earth shall hearken to the corn, and the wine, and the oil; and they shall hearken to Jezrael. 23 And I will sow her to me on the earth; and will love her that was not loved, and will say to that which was not my people, Thou art my people; and they shall say, Thou art the Lord my God.

Hos.3 1 And the Lord said to me, Go yet, and love a woman that loves evil things, an adulteress, even as the Lord loves the children of Israel, and they have respect to strange gods, and love cakes of dried grapes. 2 So I hired *her* to myself for fifteen *pieces* of silver, and a homer of barley, and a flagon of wine. 3 And I said unto her, Thou shalt wait for me many days; and thou shalt not commit fornication, neither shalt thou be for *another* man; and I *will be* for thee. 4 For the children of Israel shall abide many days without a king, and without a prince, and without a sacrifice, and without an altar, and without a priesthood, and without manifestations. 5 And afterward shall the children of Israel return, and shall seek the Lord their God, and David their king; and shall be amazed at the Lord and at his goodness in the latter days.

Hos.4 1 Hear the word of the Lord, ye children of Israel: for the Lord *has* a controversy with the inhabitants of the land, because there is no truth, nor mercy, nor knowledge of God in the land. 2 Cursing, and lying, and murder, and theft, and adultery abound in the land, and they mingle blood with blood. 3 Therefore shall the land mourn, and shall be diminished with all that dwell in it, with the wild beasts of the field, and the reptiles of the earth, and with the birds of the sky, and the fish of the sea shall fail: 4 that neither any one may plead, nor any one reprove *another*; but my people are as a priest spoken against. 5 Therefore they shall fall by day, and the prophet with thee shall fall: I have compared thy mother unto night. 6 My people are like as if they had no knowledge: because thou hast rejected knowledge, I will also reject thee, that thou shalt not minister as priest to me: and *as* thou has forgotten the law of thy God, I also will forget thy children. 7 According to their multitude, so they sinned against me: I will turn their glory into shame. 8 They will devour the sins of my people, and will set their hearts on their iniquities. 9 And the priest shall be as the people: and I will avenge on them their ways, and I will recompense to them their counscls. 10 And they shall eat, and shall not be satisfied: they have gone a-whoring, and shall by no means prosper: because they have left off to take heed to the Lord. 11 The heart of my people has gladly engaged in fornication and wine and strong drink. 12 They asked counsel by *means of* signs, and they reported answer to them by their staves: they have gone astray in a spirit of whoredom, and gone grievously a-whoring from their God. 13 They have sacrificed on the tops of the mountains, and on the hills they have sacrificed under the oak and poplar, and under the shady tree, because the shade was good: therefore your daughters shall go a-whoring, and your daughters-in-law shall commit adultery. 14 And I will not visit upon your daughters when they shall commit fornication, nor your daughters-in-law when they shall commit adultery: for they themselves mingled themselves with harlots, and sacrificed with polluted ones, and the people that understood not entangled itself with a harlot. 15 But thou, O Israel, be not ignorant, and go ye not, *men of* Juda, to Galgala; and go not up to the house of On, and swear not by the living Lord. 16 For Israel was maddened like a mad heifer: now the Lord will feed them as a lamb in a wide place. 17 Ephraim, joined with idols, has laid stumbling-blocks in his own way. 18 He has chosen the Chananites: they have grievously gone a-whoring: they have loved dishonour through her insolence. 19 Thou art a blast of wind in her wings, and they shall be ashamed because of their altars.

Hos.5 1 Hear these things, ye priests; and attend, O house of Israel; and hearken, O house of the king; for the controversy is with you, because ye have been a snare in Scopia, and as a net spread on Itabyrium, 2 which they that hunt the prey have fixed: but I will correct you. 3 I know Ephraim, and Israel is not far from me: for now Ephraim has gone grievously a-whoring, Israel is defiled. 4 They have not framed their counsels to return to their God, for the spirit of fornication is in them, and they have not known the Lord. 5 And the pride of Israel shall be brought low before his face; and Israel and Ephraim shall fall in their iniquities; and Judas also shall fall with them. 6 They shall go with sheep and calves diligently to seek the Lord; but they shall not find him, for he has withdrawn himself from them. 7 For they have forsaken the Lord; for strange children have been born to them: now shall the cankerworm devour them and their heritages. 8 Blow ye the trumpet on the hills, sound aloud on the heights: proclaim in the house of On, Benjamin is amazed. 9 Ephraim has come to nought in the days of reproof: in the tribes of Israel I have shown faithful *dealings*. 10 The princes of Juda became as they that removed the bounds: I will pour out upon them my fury as water. 11 Ephraim altogether prevailed against his adversary, he trod judgment under foot, for he began to go after vanities. 12 Therefore I *will be* as consternation to Ephraim, and as a goad to the house of Juda. 13 And Ephraim saw his disease, and Judas his pain; then Ephraim went to the Assyrians, and sent ambassadors to king Jarim: but he could not heal you, and your pain shall in nowise cease from you. 14 Wherefore I am as a panther to Ephraim, and as a lion to the house of Juda: and I will tear, and go away; and I will take, and there shall be none to deliver. 15 I will go and return to my place, until they are brought to nought, and *then* shall they seek my face.

Hos.6 1 In their affliction they will seek me early, saying, Let us go, and return to the Lord our God; for he has torn, and will heal us; 2 he will smite, and bind us up. 3 After two days he will heal us: in the third day we shall arise, and live before him, and shall know *him*. 4 let us follow on to know the Lord: we shall find him ready as the morning, and he will come to us as the early and latter rain to the earth. 5 What shall I do unto thee, Ephraim? What shall I do to thee, Juda? whereas your mercy is as a morning cloud, and as the early dew that goes away. 6 Therefore have I mown down your prophets; I have slain them with the word of my mouth: and my judgment shall go forth as the light. 7

For I will *have* mercy rather than sacrifice, and the knowledge of God rather than whole -burnt-offerings. 8 But they are as a man transgressing a covenant: 9 there the city Galaad despised me, working vanity, troubling water. 10 And thy strength *is that* of a robber: the priests have hid the way, they have murdered *the people of* Sicima; for they have wrought iniquity in the house of Israel. 11 I have seen horrible *things* there, *even* the fornication of Ephraim: Israel and Juda are defiled; 12 begin together grapes for thyself, when I turn the captivity of my people.

Hos.7 1 When I have healed Israel, then shall the iniquity of Ephraim be revealed, and the wickedness of Samaria; for they have wrought falsehood: and a thief shall come in to him, *even* a robber spoiling in his way; 2 that they may concert together as *men* singing in their heart: I remember all their wickedness: now have their own counsels compassed them about; they came before my face. 3 They gladdened kings with their wickedness, and princes with their lies. 4 They are all adulterers, as an oven glowing with flame for hot-baking, on account of the kneading of the dough, until it is leavened. 5 *In* the days of our kings, the princes began to be inflamed with wine: he stretched out his hand with pestilent fellows. 6 Wherefore their hearts are inflamed as an oven, while they rage all the night: Ephraim is satisfied with sleep; the morning is come; he is burnt up as a flame of fire. 7 They are all heated like an oven, and have devoured their judges: all their kings are fallen; there was not among them one that called on me. 8 Ephraim is mixed among his people; Ephraim became a cake not turned. 9 Strangers devoured his strength, and he knew *it* not; and grey hairs came upon him, and he knew *it* not. 10 And the pride of Israel shall be brought down before his face: yet they have not returned to the Lord their God, neither have they diligently sought him for all this. 11 And Ephraim was as a silly dove, not having a heart: he called to Egypt, and they went to the Assyrians. 12 Whenever they shall go, I will cast my net upon them; I will bring them down as the birds of the sky, I will chasten them with the rumor of their *coming* affliction. 13 Woe to them! for they have started aside from me: they are cowards; for they have sinned against me: yet I redeemed them, but they spoke falsehoods against me. 14 And their hearts did not cry to me, but they howled on their beds: they pined for oil and wine. 15 They were instructed by me, and I strengthened their arms; and they devised evils against me. 16 They turned aside to that which is not, they became as a bent bow: their princes shall fall by the sword, by reason of the unbridled state of their tongue: this is their setting at nought in the land of Egypt.

Hos.8 1 *He shall come* into their midst as the land, as an eagle against the house of the Lord, because they have transgressed my covenant, and have sinned against my law. 2 They shall soon cry out to me, *saying*, O God, we know thee. 3 For Israel has turned away from good things; they have pursued an enemy. 4 They have made kings for themselves, but not by me: they have ruled, but they did not make it known to me: *of* their silver and their gold they have made images to themselves, that they might be destroyed. 5 Cast off thy calf, O Samaria; mine anger is kindled against them: how long will they be unable to purge themselves in Israel? 6 Whereas the workman made it, and it is not God; wherefore thy calf, Samaria, was a deceiver: 7 for they sowed blighted *seed*, and their destruction shall await them, a sheaf of corn that avails not to make meal; and even if it should produce it, strangers shall devour it. 8 Israel is swallowed up: now is he become among the nations as a worthless vessel. 9 For they have gone up to the Assyrians: Ephraim has been strengthened against himself; they loved gifts. 10 Therefore shall they be delivered to the nations: now I will receive them, and they shall cease a little to anoint a king and princes. 11 Because Ephraim has multiplied altars, *his* beloved altars are become sins to him. 12 I will write down a multitude *of commands* for him; but his statutes are accounted strange things, *even* the beloved altars. 13 For if they should offer a sacrifice, and eat flesh, the lord will not accept them: now will he remember their iniquities, and will take vengeance on their sins: they have returned to Egypt, and they shall eat unclean things among the Assyrians. 14 And Israel has forgotten him that made him, and they have built fanes, and Juda has multiplied walled cities: but I will send fire on his cities, and it shall devour their foundations.

Hos.9 1 Rejoice not, O Israel, neither make merry, as *other* nations: for thou hast gone a-whoring from thy God; thou hast loved gifts upon every threshing-floor. 2 The threshing-floor and wine- press knew them not, and the wine disappointed them. 3 They dwelt not in the Lord's land: Ephraim dwelt in Egypt, and they shall eat unclean things among the Assyrians. 4 They have not offered wine to the Lord, neither have their sacrifices been sweet to him, *but* as the bread of mourning to them; all that eat them shall be defiled; for their bread for their soul shall not enter into the house of the Lord. 5 What will ye do in the day of the general assembly, and in the day of the feast of the Lord? 6 Therefore, behold, they go forth from the trouble of Egypt, and Memphis shall receive them, and Machmas shall bury them: *as for* their silver, destruction shall inherit it; thorns *shall be* in their tents. 7 The days of vengeance are come, the days of thy recompense are come; and Israel shall be afflicted as the prophet that is mad, as a man deranged: by reason of the multitude of thine iniquities thy madness has abounded. 8 The watchman of Ephraim *was* with God: the prophet is a crooked snare in all his ways: they have established madness in the house of God. 9 They have corrupted themselves according to the days of the hill: he will remember their iniquities, he will take vengeance on their sins. 10 I found Israel as grapes in the wilderness, and I saw their fathers as an early watchman in a fig-tree: they went in to Beel-phegor, and were shamefully estranged, and the abominable became as the beloved. 11 Ephraim has flown away as a bird; their glories from the birth, and the travail, and the conception. 12 For even if they should rear their children, yet shall they be utterly bereaved: wherefore also there is woe to them, *though* my flesh is of them. 13 Ephraim, *even* as I saw, gave their children for a prey; yea, Ephraim *was ready* to bring out his children to slaughter. 14

Give them, O Lord: what wilt thou give them? a miscarrying womb, and dry breasts. 15 All their wickedness is in Galgal: for there I hated them: because of the wickedness of their practices, I will cast them out of my house, I will not love them any more: all their princes are disobedient. 16 Ephraim is sick, he is dried up at his roots, he shall in no wise any more bear fruit: wherefore even if they should beget *children*, I will kill the desired *fruit* of their womb. 17 God shall reject them, because they have not hearkened to him: and they shall be wanderers among the nations.

Hos.10 1 Israel is a vine with goodly branches, her fruit is abundant: according to the multitude of her fruits she has multiplied *her* altars; according to the wealth of his land, he has set up pillars. 2 They have divided their hearts; now shall they be utterly destroyed: he shall dig down their altars, their pillars shall mourn. 3 Because now they shall say, We have no king, because we feared not the Lord: 4 and what should a king do for us, speaking false professions *as his* words? he will make a covenant: judgment shall spring up as a weed on the soil of the field. 5 The inhabitants of Samaria shall dwell near the calf of the house of On; for the people of it mourned for it: and as they provoked him, they shall rejoice at his glory, because he has departed from them. 6 And having bound it for the Assyrians, they carried it away as presents to king Jarim: Ephraim shall receive a gift, and Israel shall be ashamed of his counsel. 7 Samaria has cast off her king as a twig on the surface of the water. 8 And the altars of On, the sins of Israel, shall be taken away: thorns and thistles shall come up on their altars; and they shall say to the mountains, Cover us; and to the hills, Fall on us. 9 From the time the hills *existed* Israel has sinned: there they stood: war *waged* against the children of iniquity 10 to chastise them shall not overtake them on the hill, the nations shall be gathered against them, when they are chastened for their two sins, 11 Ephraim is a heifer taught to love victory, but I will come upon the fairest part of her neck: I will mount Ephraim; I will pass over Juda in silence; Jacob shall prevail against him. 12 Sow to yourselves for righteousness, gather in for the fruit of life: light ye for yourselves the light of knowledge; seek the Lord till the fruits of righteousness come upon you. 13 Wherefore have ye passed over ungodliness in silence, and reaped the sins of it? ye have eaten false fruit; for thou has trusted in thy sins, in the abundance of thy power. 14 Therefore shall destruction rise up among thy people, and all thy strong places shall be ruined: as a prince Solomon *departed* out of the house of Jeroboam, in the days of battle they dashed the mother to the ground upon the children, 15 thus will I do to you, O house of Israel, because of the unrighteousness of your sins.

Hos.11 1 Early in the morning were they cast off, the king of Israel has been cast off: for Israel is a child, and I loved him, and out of Egypt have I called his children. 2 As I called them, so they departed from my presence: they sacrificed to Baalim, and burnt incense to graven images. 3 Yet I bound the feet of Ephraim, I took him on my arm; but they knew not that I healed them. 4 When men were destroyed, I drew them with the bands of my love: and I will be to them as a man smiting *another* on his cheek: and I will have respect to him, I will prevail with him. 5 Ephraim dwelt in Egypt; and *as for* the Assyrian, he was his king, because he would not return. 6 And in his cities he prevailed not with the sword, and he ceased *to war* with his hands: and they shall eat *of the fruit* of their own devices: 7 and his people *shall* cleave fondly to their habitation; but God shall be angry with his precious things, and shall not at all exalt him. 8 How shall I deal with thee, Ephraim? *how* shall I protect thee, Israel? what shall I do with thee? I will make thee as Adama, and as Seboim; my heart is turned at once, my repentance is powerfully excited. 9 I will not act according to the fury of my wrath, I will not abandon Ephraim to be utterly destroyed: for I am God, and not man; the Holy One within thee: and I will not enter into the city. 10 I will go after the Lord: he shall utter *his voice* as a lion: for he shall roar, and the children of the waters shall be amazed. 11 They shall be amazed *and fly* as a bird out of Egypt, and as a dove out of the land of the Assyrians: and I will restore them to their houses, saith the Lord. 12 Ephraim has compassed me with falsehood, and the house of Israel and Juda with ungodliness: *but* now God knows them, and they shall be called God's holy people.

Hos.12 1 But Ephraim is an evil spirit, he has chased the east wind all the day: he has multiplied empty and vain things, and made a covenant with the Assyrians, and oil has gone in the way of traffic into Egypt. 2 And the Lord *has* a controversy with Juda, in order to punish Jacob: according to his ways and according to his practices will he recompense him. 3 He took his brother by the heel in the womb, and in his labours he had power with God. 4 And he prevailed with the angel and was strong: they wept, and intreated me: they found me in the house of On, and there *a word* was spoken to them. 5 But the Lord God Almighty shall be his memorial. 6 Thou therefore shalt return to thy God: keep thou mercy and judgment, and draw nigh to thy God continually. 7 *As for* Chanaan, in his hand is a balance of unrighteousness: he has loved to tyrannize. 8 And Ephraim said, Nevertheless I am rich, I have found refreshment to myself. None of his labours shall be found *available* to him, by reason of the sins which he has committed. 9 But I the Lord thy God brought thee up out of the land of Egypt: I will yet cause thee to dwell in tabernacles, according to the days of the feast. 10 And I will speak to the prophets, and I have multiplied visions, and by the means of the prophets I was represented. 11 If Galaad exists not, then the chiefs in Galaad when they sacrificed were false, and their altars were as heaps on the ground of the field. 12 And Jacob retreated into the plain of Syria, and Israel served for a wife, and waited for a wife. 13 And the Lord brought Israel out of the land of Egypt by a prophet, and by a prophet was he preserve. 14 Ephraim was angry and excited, therefore his blood shall be poured out upon him, and the Lord shall recompense to him his reproach.

Hos.13 1 According to the word of Ephraim he adopted ordinances for himself in Israel; and he established them for Baal, and died. 2 And now they have sinned increasingly, and have made for themselves a molten image of their silver, according to the fashion of idols, the work of artificers accomplished for them: they say, Sacrifice men, for the calves have come to an end. 3 Therefore shall they be as a morning cloud, and as the early dew that passes away, as chaff blown away from the threshing-floor, and as a vapor from tears. 4 But I am the Lord thy God that establishes the heaven, and creates the earth, whose hands have framed the whole host of heaven: but I shewed them not to thee that thou shouldest go after them: and I brought thee up out of the land of Egypt, and thou shalt know no God but me; and there is no Saviour beside me. 5 I tended thee as a shepherd in the wilderness, in an uninhabited land. 6 According to their pastures, so they were completely filled; and their hearts were exalted; therefore they forgot me. 7 And I will be to them as a panther, and as a leopard. 8 I will meet them by the way of the Assyrians, as a she-bear excited, and I will rend the caul of their heart, and the lions' whelps of the thicket shall devour them there; the wild beasts of the field shall rend them in pieces. 9 O Israel, who will aid *thee* in thy destruction? 10 Where is this thy king? let him even save thee in all thy cities: let him judge thee, of whom thou saidst, Give me a king and a prince. 11 And I gave thee a king in mine anger, and kept *him* back in my wrath. 12 Ephraim *has framed* a conspiracy of unrighteousness, his sin is hidden. 13 Pains as of a woman in travail shall come upon him: he is thy wise son, because he shall not stay in the destruction of *thy* children. 14 I will deliver *them* out of the power of Hades, and will redeem them from death: where is thy penalty, O death? O Hades, where is thy sting? comfort is hidden from mine eyes. 15 Forasmuch as he will cause a division among *his* brethren, the Lord shall bring upon him an east wind from the desert, and shall dry up his veins *and* quite drain his fountains: he shall dry up his land, and *spoil* all his precious vessels.

Hos.14 1 Samaria shall be utterly destroyed: for she has resisted her God; they shall fall by the sword, and their sucklings shall be dashed against the ground, and their women with child ripped up. 2 Return, O Israel, to the Lord thy God; for the people have fallen through thine iniquities. 3 Take with you words, and turn to the Lord your God: speak to him, that ye may not receive *the reward of* unrighteousness, but that ye may receive good things: and we will render in return the fruit of our lips. 4 Assur shall never save us; we will not mount on horseback; we will no longer say to the works of our hands, Our gods. He who is in thee shall pity the orphan. 5 I will restore their dwellings, I will love them truly: for he has turned away my wrath from him. 6 I will be as dew to Israel: he shall bloom as the lily, and cast forth his roots as Libanus. 7 His branches shall spread, and he shall be as a fruitful olive, and his smell shall be as *the smell* of Libanus. 8 They shall return, and dwell under his shadow: they shall live and be satisfied with corn, and he shall flower as a vine: his memorial shall be to Ephraim as the wine of Libanus. 9 What *has* he to do any more with idols? I have afflicted him, and I will strengthen him: I am as a leafy juniper tree. From me is thy fruit found. 10 Who is wise, and will understand these things? or prudent, and will know them? for the ways of the Lord are straight, and the righteous shall walk in them: but the ungodly shall fall therein.

JOEL

Joel.1 1 The word of the Lord which came to Joel the son of Bathuel. 2 Hear these *words*, ye elders, and hearken all ye that inhabit the land. Have such things happen in your days, or in the days of your fathers? 3 Tell your children concerning them, and *let* your children *tell* their children, and their children another generation. 4 The leavings of the caterpillar has the locust eaten, and the leavings of the locust has the palmerworm eaten, and the leavings of the palmerworm has the cankerworm eaten. 5 Awake, ye drunkards, from your wine, and weep: mourn, all ye that drink wine to drunkenness: for joy and gladness and removed are from your mouth. 6 For a strong and innumerable nation is come up against my land, their teeth are lion's teeth, and their back teeth those of a *lion's* whelp. 7 He has ruined my vine, and utterly broken my fig-trees: he has utterly searched *my vine*, and cast it down; he has peeled its branches. 8 Lament to me more than a virgin girded with sackcloth for the husband of her youth. 9 The meat-offering and drink-offering are removed from the house of the Lord: mourn, ye priests that serve at the altar of the Lord. 10 For the plains languish: let the land mourn, for the corn languishes; the wine is dried up, the oil becomes scarce; 11 the husbandmen are consumed: mourn your property on account of the wheat and barley; for the harvest has perished from off the field. 12 The vine is dried up, and the fig-trees are become few; the pomegranate, and palm- tree, and apple, and all trees of the field are dried up: for the sons of men have have abolished joy. 13 Gird yourselves *with sackcloth*, and lament, ye priests: mourn, ye that serve at the altar: go in, sleep in sackcloths, ye that minister to God: for the meat-offering and drink-offering are withheld from the house of your God. 14 Sanctify a fast, proclaim a *solemn* service, gather the elders *and* all the inhabitants of the land into the house of your God, and cry earnestly to the Lord, 15 Alas, Alas, Alas for the day! for the day of the Lord is nigh, and it will come as trouble upon trouble. 16 *Your* meat has been destroyed before your eyes, joy and gladness from out of the house of your God. 17 The heifers have started at their mangers, the treasures are abolished, the wine-presses are broken down; for the corn is withered. 18 What shall we store up for ourselves? the herds of cattle have mourned, because they had no pasture; and the flocks of sheep have been utterly destroyed. 19 To thee, O Lord, will I cry: for fire has devoured the fair places of the wilderness, and a flame has burnt up all the trees of the field. 20 And the cattle of the field have looked up to thee: for the fountains of waters have been dried up, and fire has devoured the fair places of the wilderness.

Joel.2 1 Sound the trumpet in Sion, make a proclamation in my holy mountain, and let all the inhabitants of the land be confounded: for the day of the Lord is near; 2 for a day of darkness and gloominess is near, a day of cloud and mist: a numerous and strong people shall be spread upon the mountains as the morning; there has not been from the beginning one like it, and after it there shall not be again even to the years of many generations. 3 Before them is a consuming fire, and behind them is a flame kindled: the land before them is as a paradise of delight, and behind them a desolate plain: and there shall none of them escape. 4 Their appearance is as the appearance of horses; and as horsemen, so shall they pursue. 5 As the sound of chariots on the tops of mountains shall they leap, and as the sound of a flame of fire devouring stubble, and as a numerous and strong people setting themselves in array for battle. 6 Before them shall the people be crushed: every face *shall be* as the blackness of a caldron. 7 As warriors shall they run, and as men of war shall they mount on the walls; and each shall move in his *right* path, and they shall not turn aside from their tracks: 8 and not one shall stand aloof from his brother: they shall go on weighed down with their arms, and they fall upon their weapons, yet shall they in no wise be destroyed. 9 They shall seize upon the city, and run upon the walls, and go up upon the houses, and enter in through the windows as thieves. 10 Before them the earth shall be confounded, and the sky shall be shaken: the sun and the moon shall be darkened, and the stars shall withdraw their light. 11 And the Lord shall utter his voice before his host: for his camp is very great: for the execution of his words is mighty: for the day of the Lord is great, very glorious, and who shall be able to *resist* it? 12 Now therefore, saith the Lord your God, turn to me with all your heart, and with fasting, and with weeping, and with lamentation: 13 and rend your hearts, and not your garments, and turn to the Lord your God: for he is merciful and compassionate, long-suffering, and plenteous in mercy, and repents of evils. 14 Who knows if he will return, and repent, and leave a blessing behind him, even a meat-offering and a drink-offering to the Lord your God? 15 Sound the trumpet in Sion, sanctify a fast, proclaim a *solemn* service: 16 gather the people, sanctify the congregation, assemble the elders, gather the infants at the breast: let the bridegroom go forth of his chamber, and the bride out of her closet. 17 Between the porch and the altar let the priests that minister to the Lord weep, and say, Spare thy people, O Lord, and give not thine heritage to reproach, that the heathen should rule over them, lest they should say among the heathen, Where is their God? 18 But the Lord was jealous of his land, and spared his people. 19 And the Lord answered and said to his people, Behold, I *will* send you corn, and wine, and oil, and ye shall be satisfied with them: and I will no longer make you a reproach among the Gentiles. 20 And I will chase away from you the northern *adversary*, and will drive him away into a dry land, and I will sink his face in the former sea, and his back parts in the latter sea, and his ill savour shall come up, and his stink come up, because he has wrought great things. 21 Be of good courage, O land; rejoice and be glad: for the Lord has done great things. 22 Be of good courage, ye beasts of the plain, for the plains of the wilderness have budded, for the trees have borne their fruit, the fig tree and the vine have yielded their strength. 23 Rejoice then and be glad, ye children of Sion, in the Lord your God: for he has given you food fully, and he will rain on you the early and the latter rain, as before. 24 And the floors shall be filled with corn, and the presses shall overflow with wine and oil. 25 And I will recompense you for the years which the locust, and the caterpillar, and the palmerworm, and the cankerworm have eaten, *even* my great army, which I sent against you. 26 And ye shall eat abundantly, and be satisfied, and shall praise the name of the Lord your God *for the things* which he has wrought wonderfully with you: and my people shall not be ashamed for ever. 27 And ye shall know that I am in the midst of Israel, and *that* I am the Lord your God, and *that* there is none else beside me; and my people shall no more be ashamed for ever. 28 And it shall come to pass afterward, that I will pour out of my Spirit upon all flesh; and your sons and your daughters shall prophesy, and your old men shall dream dreams, and your young men shall see visions. 29 And on my servants and on *my* handmaids in those days will I pour out of my Spirit. 30 And I will shew wonders in heaven, and upon the earth, blood, and fire, and vapor of smoke. 31 The sun shall be turned into darkness, and the moon into blood, before the great and glorious day of the Lord come. 32 And it shall come to pass *that* whosoever shall call on the name of the Lord shall be saved: for in mount Sion and in Jerusalem shall the saved one be as the Lord has said, and they that have glad tidings preached to them, whom the Lord has called.

Joel.3 1 For, behold, in those days and at that time, when I shall have turned the captivity of Juda and Jerusalem, 2 I will also gather all the Gentiles, and bring them down to the valley of Josaphat, and will plead with them there for my people and my heritage Israel, who have been dispersed among the Gentiles; and *these Gentiles* have divided my land, 3 and cast lots over my people, and have given *their* boys to harlots, and sold *their* girls for wine, and have drunk. 4 And what have ye to do with me, O Tyre, and Sidon, and all Galilee of the Gentiles? do ye render me a recompense? or do ye bear malice against me? quickly and speedily will I return your recompense on your own heads: 5 because ye have taken my silver and my gold, and ye have brought my choice ornaments into your temples; 6 and ye have sold the children of Juda and the children of Jerusalem to the children of the Greeks, that ye might expel them from their coasts. 7 Therefore, behold, I *will* raise them up out of the place whither ye have sold them, and I will return your recompense on your own heads. 8 And I will sell your sons and your daughters into the hands of the children of Juda, and they shall sell them into captivity to a far distant nation: for the Lord has spoken *it.* 9 Proclaim these things among the Gentiles; declare war, arouse the warriors, draw near and go up, all ye men of war. 10 Beat your ploughshares into swords, and your sickles into spears: let the weak say, I am strong. 11 Gather yourselves together, and go in, all ye nations round about, and gather yourselves there; let the timid become a warrior. 12 Let them be aroused, let all the nations go up to the valley of Josaphat: for there will I sit to judge all the Gentiles round about. 13 Bring forth the sickles, for the vintage is come: go in, tread *the grapes,* for the press is full: cause the vats to overflow; for their wickedness is multiplied. 14 Noises have resounded in the valley of judgment: for the day of the Lord is near in the valley of judgment. 15 The sun and the moon shall be darkened, and the stars shall withdraw their light. 16 And the Lord shall cry out of Sion, and shall utter his voice from Jerusalem; and the heaven and the earth shall be shaken, but the Lord shall spare his people, and shall strengthen the children of Israel. 17 And ye shall know that I am the Lord your God, who dwell in Sion my holy mountain: and Jerusalem shall be holy, and strangers shall not pass through her anymore. 18 And it shall come to pass in that day *that* the mountains shall drop sweet wine, and the hills shall flow with milk, and all the fountains of Juda shall flow with water, and a fountain shall go forth of the house of the Lord, and water the valley of flags. 19 Egypt shall be a desolation, and Idumea shall be a desolate plain, because of the wrongs of the children of Juda, because they have shed righteous blood in their land. 20 But Judea shall be inhabited for ever, and Jerusalem to all generations. 21 And I will make inquisition for their blood, and will by no means leave it unavenged: and the Lord shall dwell in Sion.

AMOS

Amos.1 1 The words of Amos which came *to him* in Accarim out of Thecue, which he saw concerning Jerusalem, in the days of Ozias king of Juda, and in the days of Jeroboam the son of Joas king of Israel, two years before the earthquake. 2 And he said, The Lord has spoken out of Sion, and has uttered his voice out of Jerusalem; and the pastures of the shepherds have mourned, and the top of Carmel is dried up. 3 And the Lord said, For three sins of Damascus, and for four, I will not turn away from it; because they sawed with iron saws the women with child of the Galaadites. 4 And I will send a fire on the house of Azael, and it shall devour the foundations of the son of Ader. 5 And I will break to pieces the bars of Damascus, and will destroy the inhabitants out of the plain of On, and will cut in pieces a tribe out of the men of Charrhan: and the famous people of Syria shall be led captive, saith the Lord. 6 Thus saith the Lord; For three sins of Gaza, and for four, I will not turn away from them; because they took prisoners the captivity of Solomon, to shut *them* up into Idumea. 7 And I will send forth a fire on the walls of Gaza, and it shall devour its foundations. 8 And I will destroy the inhabitants out of Azotus, and a tribe shall be cut off from Ascalon, and I will stretch out my hand upon Accaron: and the remnant of the Philistines shall perish, saith the Lord. 9 Thus saith the Lord; For three transgressions of Tyre, and for four, I will not turn away from it; because they shut up the prisoners of Solomon into Idumea, and remembered not the covenant of brethren. 10 And I will send forth a fire on the walls of Tyre, and it shall devour the foundations of it. 11 Thus saith the Lord; For three sins of Idumea, and for four, I will not turn away from them; because they pursued their brother with the sword, and destroyed the mother upon the earth, and summoned up his anger for a testimony, and kept up his fury to the end. 12 And I will send forth a fire upon Thaman, and it shall devour the foundations of her walls. 13 Thus saith the Lord; For three sins of the children of Ammon, and for four, I will not turn away from him; because they ripped up the women with child of the Galaadites, that they might widen their coasts. ¹⁴ And I will kindle a fire on the walls of Rabbath, and it shall devour her foundations with shouting in the day of war, and she shall be shaken in the days of her destruction: ¹⁵ and her kings shall go into captivity, their priests and their rulers together, saith the Lord.

Amos.2 ¹ Thus saith the Lord; For three sins of Moab, and for four, I will not turn away from it; because they burnt the bones of the king of Idumea to lime. ² But I will send forth a fire on Moab, and it shall devour the foundations of its cities: and Moab shall perish in weakness, with a shout, and with the sound of a trumpet. ³ And I will destroy the judge out of her, and slay all her princes with him, saith the Lord. ⁴ Thus saith the Lord; For three sins of the children of Judah, and for four, I will not turn away from him; because they have rejected the law of the Lord, and have not kept his ordinances, and their vain *idols* which they made, which their fathers followed, caused them to err. ⁵ And I will send a fire on Juda, and it shall devour the foundations of Jerusalem. ⁶ Thus saith the Lord; for three sins of Israel, and for four, I will not turn away from him; because they sold the righteous for silver, and the poor for sandals, ⁷ wherewith to tread on the dust of the earth, and they have smitten upon the heads of the poor, and have perverted the way of the lowly: and a son and his father have gone into the same maid, that they might profane the name of their God. ⁸ And binding their clothes with cords they have made them curtains near the altar, and they have drunk wine gained by extortion in the house of their God. ⁹ Nevertheless I cut off the Amorite from before them, whose height was as the height of a cedar, and he was strong as an oak; and I dried up his fruit from above, and his roots from beneath. ¹⁰ And I brought you up out of the land of Egypt, and led you about in the desert forty years, that ye should inherit the land of the Amorites. ¹¹ And I took of your sons for prophets, and of your young men for consecration. Are not these things so, ye sons of Israel? saith the Lord. ¹² But ye gave the consecrated ones wine to drink; and ye commanded the prophets, saying, Prophesy not. ¹³ Therefore, behold, I roll under you, as a waggon full of straw is rolled. ¹⁴ And flight shall perish from the runner, and the strong shall not hold fast his strength, and the warrior shall not save his life: ¹⁵ and the archer shall not withstand, and he that is swift of foot shall in no wise escape; and the horseman shall not save his life. ¹⁶ And the strong shall find no confidence in power: the naked shall flee away in that day, saith the Lord.

Amos.3 ¹ Hear ye this word, O house of Israel, which the Lord has spoken concerning you, and against the whole family whom I brought up out of the land of Egypt, saying, ² You especially have I known out of all the families of the earth: therefore will I take vengeance upon you for all your sins. ³ Shall two walk together at all, if they do not know one another? ⁴ Will a lion roar out of his thicket if he has no prey? will a *lion's* whelp utter his voice at all out of his lair, if he have taken nothing? ⁵ Will a bird fall on the earth without a fowler? will a snare be taken up from the earth

without having taken anything? ⁶ Shall the trumpet sound in the city, and the people not be alarmed? shall there be evil in a city which the Lord has not wrought? ⁷ For the Lord God will do nothing, without revealing instruction to his servants the prophets. ⁸ A lion shall roar, and who will not be alarmed? the Lord God has spoken, and who will not prophesy? ⁹ Proclaim it to the regions among the Assyrians, and to the regions of Egypt, and say, Gather yourselves to the mountain of Samaria, and behold many wonderful things in the midst of it, and the oppression that is in it. ¹⁰ And she knew not what things would come against her, saith the Lord, *even* those that store up wrong and misery in their countries. ¹¹ Therefore thus saith the Lord God; O Tyre, thy land shall be made desolate round about *thee*; and he shall bring down thy strength out of thee, and thy countries shall be spoiled. ¹² Thus saith the Lord; As when a shepherd rescues from the mouth of a lion two legs or a piece of an ear, so shall be drawn forth the children of Israel who dwell in Samaria in the presence of *a foreign* tribe, and in Damascus. ¹³ Hear, O ye priests, and testify to the house of Jacob, saith the Lord God Almighty. ¹⁴ For in the day wherein I shall take vengeance of the sins of Israel upon him, I will also take vengeance on the altars of Bethel: and the horns of the altar shall be broken down, and they shall fall upon the ground. ¹⁵ I will crush and smite the turreted-house upon the summer-house; and the ivory-houses shall be destroyed, and many other houses also, saith the Lord.

Amos.4 ¹ Hear ye this word, ye heifers of the land of Basan that are in the mountain of Samaria, that oppress the poor, and trample on the needy, which say to their masters, Give us that we may drink. ² The Lord swears by his holiness, that, behold, the days come upon you, when they shall take you with weapons, and fiery destroyers shall cast those with you into boiling caldrons. ³ And ye shall be brought forth naked in the presence of each other; and ye shall be cast forth on the mountain Romman, saith the Lord. ⁴ Ye went into Bethel, and sinned, and ye multiplied sin at Galgala; and ye brought your meat- offerings in the morning, *and* your tithes every third day. ⁵ And they read the law without, and called for public professions: proclaim aloud that the children of Israel have loved these things, saith the Lord. ⁶ And I will give you dulness of teeth in all your cities, and want of bread in all your places: yet ye returned not to me, saith the Lord. ⁷ Also I withheld from you the rain three months before the harvest: and I will rain upon one city, and on another city I will not rain: one part shall be rained upon, and the part on which I shall not rain shall be dried up. ⁸ And *the inhabitants of* two or three cities shall be gathered to one city to drink water, and they shall not be satisfied: yet ye have not returned to me, saith the Lord. ⁹ I smote you with parching, and with blight: ye multiplied your gardens, your vineyards, and your fig-grounds, and the cankerworm devoured your olive-yards: yet not *even* thus did ye return to me, saith the Lord. ¹⁰ I sent pestilence among you by the way of Egypt, and slew your young men with the sword, together with thy horses that were taken captive; and in my wrath against you I set fire to your camps: yet not even thus did ye return to me, saith the Lord. 11 I overthrew you, as God overthrew Sodoma and Gomorrha, and ye became as a brand plucked out of the fire: yet not even thus did ye return to me, saith the Lord. 12 Therefore thus will I do to thee, O Israel: nay because I will do thus to thee, prepare to call on thy God, O Israel. 13 For, behold, I am he that strengthens the thunder, and creates the wind, and proclaims to men his Christ, forming the morning and the darkness, and mounting on the high places of the earth, The Lord God Almighty is his name.

Amos.5 1 Hear ye this word of the Lord, even a lamentation, which I take up against you. The house of Israel is fallen; it shall no more rise. 2 The virgin of Israel has fallen upon his land; there is none that shall raise her up. 3 Therefore thus saith the Lord God; The city out of which there went forth a thousand, *in it* there shall be left a hundred, and *in that* out of which there went forth a hundred, there shall be left ten to the house of Israel. 4 Wherefore thus saith the Lord to the house of Israel, Seek ye me, and ye shall live. 5 But seek not Bethel, and go not into Galgala, and cross not over to the Well of the Oath: for Galgala shall surely go into captivity, and Bethel shall be as that which is not. 6 Seek ye the Lord, and ye shall live; lest the house of Joseph blaze as fire, and it devour him, and there shall be none to quench it for the house of Israel. 7 *It is he* that executes judgment in the height *above*, and he has established justice on the earth: 8 who makes all things, and changes *them*, and turns darkness into the morning, and darkens the day into night: who calls for the water of the sea, and pours it out on the face of the earth: the Lord is his name: 9 who dispenses ruin to strength, and brings distress upon the fortress. 10 They hated him that reproved in the gates, and abhorred holy speech. 11 Therefore because they have smitten the poor with their fists, and ye have received of them choice gifts; ye have built polished houses, but ye shall not dwell in them; ye have planted desirable vineyards, but ye shall not drink the wine of them. 12 For I know your many transgressions, and your sins are great, trampling on the just, taking bribes, and turning aside *the judgment of* the poor in the gates. 13 Therefore the prudent shall be silent at that time; for it is a time of evils. 14 Seek good, and not evil, that ye may live: and so the Lord God Almighty shall be with you, as ye have said, 15 We have hated evil, and loved good: and restore ye judgment in the gates; that the Lord God Almighty may have mercy on the remnant of Joseph. 16 Therefore thus saith the Lord God Almighty; In all the streets *shall be* lamentations; and in all the ways shall it be said, Woe, woe! the husbandman shall be called to mourning and lamentation, and to them that are skilled in complaining. 17 And *there shall be* lamentation in all the ways; because I will pass through the midst of thee, saith the Lord. 18 Woe to you that desire the day of the Lord! what is this day of the Lord to you? whereas it is darkness, and not light. 19 As if a man should flee from the face of a lion, and a bear should meet him; and he should spring into his house, and lean his hands upon the wall, and a serpent should bite him. 20 Is not the day of the Lord darkness, and not light? and is not this *day* gloom without

brightness? 21 I hate, I reject your feasts, and I will not smell *your* meat-offerings in your general assemblies. 22 Wherefore if ye should bring me your whole-burnt-sacrifices and meat-offerings, I will not accept *them*: neither will I have respect to your grand peace-offerings. 23 Remove from me the sound of thy songs, and I will not hear the music of thine instruments. 24 But let judgment roll down as water, and righteousness as an impassable torrent. 25 Have ye offered to me victims and sacrifices, O house of Israel, forty years in the wilderness? 26 Yea, ye took up the tabernacle of Moloch, and the star of your god Raephan, the images of them which ye made for yourselves. 27 And I will carry you away beyond Damascus, saith the Lord, the Almighty God is his name.

Amos.6 1 Woe to them that set at nought Sion, and that trust in the mountain of Samaria: they have gathered *the harvest of* the heads of the nations, and they have gone in themselves. 2 O house of Israel, pass by all *of you*, and see; and pass by thence to Ematrabba; and thence descend to Geth of the Philistines, the chief of all these kingdoms, *see* if their coasts are greater than your coasts. 3 Ye who are approaching the evil day, who are drawing near and adopting false sabbaths; 4 who sleep upon beds of ivory, and live delicately on their couches, and eat kids out of the flocks, and sucking calves out of the midst of the stalls; 5 who excel in the sound of musical instruments; they have regarded them as abiding, not as fleeting *pleasures*; 6 who drink strained wine, and anoint themselves with the best ointment; and have suffered nothing on occasion of the calamity of Joseph. 7 Therefore now shall they depart into captivity from the dominion of princes, and the neighing of horses shall be cut off from Ephraim. 8 For the Lord has sworn by himself, *saying*, Because I abhor all the pride of Jacob, I do also hate his countries, and I will cut off *his* city with all who inhabit it. 9 And it shall come to pass, if there be ten men left in one house, that they shall die. 10 But a remnant shall be left behind, and their relations shall take them, and shall strenuously endeavor to carry forth their bones from the house: and one shall say to the heads of the house, Is there yet *any one* else with thee? 11 And he shall say, No *one* else. And *the other* shall say, Be silent, that thou name not the name of the Lord. 12 For, behold, the Lord commands, and he will smite the great house with breaches, and the little house with rents. 13 Will horses run upon rocks? will they refrain from neighing at mares? for ye have turned judgment into poison, and the fruit of righteousness into bitterness: 14 ye who rejoice at vanity, who say, Have we not possessed horns by our own strength? 15 For behold, O house of Israel, I will raise up against you a nation, saith the Lord of hosts; and they shall afflict you so that ye shall not enter into Æmath, and as it were *from* the river of the wilderness.

Amos.7 1 Thus has the Lord God shewed me; and, behold, a swarm of locusts coming from the east; and, behold, one caterpillar, king Gog. 2 And it came to pass when he had finished devouring the grass of the land, that I said, Lord God, be merciful; who shall raise up Jacob? for he is small in number. 3 Repent, O Lord, for this. And this shall not be, saith the Lord. 4 Thus has the Lord shewed me; and, behold, the Lord called for judgment by fire, and it devoured the great deep, and devoured the Lord's portion. 5 Then I said, O Lord, cease, I pray thee: who shall raise up Jacob? for he is small in number. Repent, O Lord, for this. 6 This also shall not be, saith the Lord. 7 Thus the Lord shewed me; and behold, he stood upon a wall of adamant, and in his hand *was* an adamant. 8 And the Lord said to me, What seest thou, Amos? And I said, An adamant. And the Lord said to me, Behold, I appoint an adamant in the midst of my people Israel: I will not pass by them any more. 9 And the joyful altars shall be abolished, and the sacrifices of Israel shall be set aside; and I will rise up against the house of Jeroboam with the sword. 10 Then Amasias the priest of Bethel sent to Jeroboam king of Israel, saying, Amos is forming conspiracies against thee in the midst of the house of Israel: the land will be utterly unable to bear all his words. 11 For thus says Amos, Jeroboam shall die by the sword, and Israel shall be led away captive from his land. 12 And Amasias said to Amos, Go, seer, remove thou into the land of Juda, and live there, and thou shalt prophesy there: 13 but thou shalt no longer prophesy at Bethel: for it is the king's sanctuary, and it is the royal house. 14 And Amos answered, and said to Amasias, I was not a prophet, nor the son of a prophet; but I was a herdman, and a gatherer of sycamore fruits. 15 And the Lord took me from the sheep, and the Lord said to me, Go, and prophesy to my people Israel. 16 And now hear the word of the Lord: Thou sayest, Prophesy not to Israel, and raise not a tumult against the house of Jacob. 17 Therefore thus saith the Lord; Thy wife shall be a harlot in the city, and thy sons and thy daughters shall fall by the sword, and thy land shall be measured with the line; and thou shalt die in an unclean land; and Israel shall be led captive out of his land. Thus has the Lord God shewed me.

Amos.8 1 And behold a fowler's basket. 2 And he said, What seest thou, Amos? And I said, A fowler's basket. And the Lord said to me, The end is come upon my people Israel; I will not pass by them any more. 3 And the ceilings of the temple shall howl in that day, saith the Lord God: *there shall be* many a fallen one in every place; I will bring silence upon *them*. 4 Hear now this, ye that oppress the poor in the morning, and drive the needy ones by tyranny from the earth, 5 saying, When will the month pass away, and we shall sell, and the sabbath, and we shall open the treasure, to make the measure small, and to enlarge the weight, and make the balance unfair? 6 That we may buy the poor for silver, and the needy for shoes; and we will trade in every kind of fruit. 7 The Lord swears against the pride of Jacob, None of your works shall ever be forgotten. 8 And shall not the land be troubled for these things, and shall not every one who dwells in it mourn? whereas destruction shall come up as a river, and shall descend as the river of Egypt. 9 And it shall come to pass in that day, saith the Lord God, *that* the sun shall go down at noon, and the light shall be darkened on the earth by day: 10 and I will turn your feasts into mourning, and all your songs into lamentation; and I will bring up sackcloth on all loins, and baldness on every head; and I will make them as the mourning of a beloved *friend*, and those with them as a day of grief. 11 Behold, the days come, saith the Lord, that I will send forth a famine on the land, not a famine of bread, nor a thirst for water, but a famine of hearing the word of the Lord. 12 And the waters shall be troubled from sea to sea, and from the north to the east shall *men* run hither and thither, seeking the word of the Lord, and they shall not find *it*. 13 In that day shall the fair virgins and the young men faint for thirst; 14 they who swear by the propitiation of Samaria, and who say, Thy god, O Dan, lives; and, Thy god, O Bersabee, lives; and they shall fall, and shall no more rise again.

Amos.9 1 I saw the Lord standing on the altar: and he said, Smite the mercy-seat, and the porch shall be shaken: and cut through into the heads of all; and I will slay the remnant of them with the sword: no one of them fleeing shall escape, and no one of them, striving to save himself shall be delivered. 2 Though they hid themselves in hell, thence shall my hand drag them forth; and though they go up to heaven, thence will I bring them down. 3 If they hide themselves in the top of Carmel, thence will I search *them* out and take them; and if they should go down from my presence into the depths of the sea, there will I command the serpent, and he shall bite them. 4 And if they should go into captivity before the face of their enemies, there will I command the sword, and it shall slay them: and I will set mine eyes against them for evil, and not for good. 5 And the Lord, the Lord God Almighty, *is he* that takes hold of the land, and causes it to shake, and all that inhabit it shall mourn; and its destruction shall go up as a river, and shall descend as the river of Egypt. 6 *It is he* that builds his ascent up to the sky, and establishes his promise on the earth; who calls the water of the sea, and pours it out on the face of the earth; the Lord Almighty is his name. 7 Are not ye to me as the sons of the Ethiopians, O children of Israel? saith the Lord. Did I not bring Israel up out of the land of Egypt, and the Philistines from Cappadocia, and the Syrians out of the deep? 8 Behold, the eyes of the Lord God are upon the kingdom of sinners, and I will cut it off from the face of the earth; only I will not utterly cut off the house of Jacob, saith the Lord. 9 For I *will* give commandment, and sift the house of Israel among all the Gentiles, as *corn* is sifted in a sieve, and *yet* a fragment shall not in any wise fall upon the earth. 10 All the sinners of my people shall die by the sword, who say, Calamities shall certainly not draw near, nor come upon us. 11 In that day I will raise up the tabernacle of David that is fallen, and will rebuild the ruins of it, and will set up the parts thereof that have been broken down, and will build it up as in the ancient days: 12 that the remnant of men, and all the Gentiles upon whom my name is called, may earnestly seek *me*, saith the Lord who does all these things. 13 Behold, the days come, saith the Lord, when the harvest shall overtake the vintage, and the grapes shall ripen at seedtime; and the mountains shall drop sweet wine, and all the hills shall be planted. 14 And I will turn the captivity of my people Israel, and they shall rebuild the ruined cities, and shall inhabit *them*; and they shall plant vineyards, and shall drink the wine from them; and they shall form gardens, and eat the fruit of them. 15 And I will plant them on their land, and they shall no more be plucked up from the land which I have given them, saith the Lord God Almighty.

OBDIAS (OBADIAH)

Obad.1 1 The vision of Obdias. Thus saith the Lord God to Idumea; I have heard a report from the Lord, and he has sent forth a message to the nations. 2 Arise ye, and let us rise up against her to war. 3 Behold, I have made thee small among the Gentiles: thou art greatly dishonoured. The pride of thine heart has elated thee, dwelling *as thou dost* in the holes of the rocks, *as one that* exalts his habitation, saying in his heart, Who will bring me down to the ground? 4 If thou shouldest mount up as the eagle, and if thou shouldest make thy nest among the stars, thence will I bring thee down, saith the Lord. 5 If thieves came in to thee, or robbers by night, where wouldest thou have been cast away? would they not have stolen *just* enough for themselves? and if grape-gatherers went in to thee, would they not leave a gleaning? 6 How has Esau been searched out, and *how* have his hidden things been detected? 7 They sent thee to thy coasts: all the men of thy covenant have withstood thee; thine allies have prevailed against thee, they have set snares under thee: they have no understanding. 8 In that day, saith the Lord, I will destroy the wise men out of Idumea, and understanding out of the mount of Esau. 9 And thy warriors from Thaeman shall be dismayed, to the end that man may be cut off from the mount of Esau. 10 Because of the slaughter and the sin *committed against* thy brother Jacob, shame shall cover thee, and thou shalt be cut off for ever. 11 From the day that thou stoodest in opposition *to him*, in the days when foreigners were taking captive his forces, and strangers entered into his gates, and cast lots on Jerusalem, thou also wast as one of them. 12 And thou shouldest not have looked on the day of thy brother in the day of strangers; nor shouldest thou have rejoiced against the children of Juda in the day of their destruction; neither shouldest thou have boasted in the day of *their* affliction. 13 Neither shouldest thou have gone into the gates of the people in the day of their troubles; nor yet shouldest thou have looked upon their gathering in the day of their destruction, nor shouldest thou have attacked their host in the day of their perishing. 14 Neither shouldest thou have stood at the opening of their passages, to destroy utterly those of them that were escaping; neither shouldest thou have shut up his fugitives in the day of affliction. 15 For the day of the Lord is near upon all the Gentiles: as thou have done, so shall it be *done* to thee: thy recompense shall be returned on thine *own* head. 16 For as thou hast drunk upon my holy mountain, *so* shall all the nations drink wine; they shall drink, and go down, and be as if they were not. 17 But on mount Sion there shall be deliverance, and there shall be a sanctuary; and the house of Jacob shall take for an inheritance those that took them for an inheritance. 18 And the house of Jacob shall be fire, and the house of Joseph a flame, and the house of Esau *shall be* for stubble; and *Israel* shall flame forth against them, and shall devour them, and there shall not be a corn-field *left* to the house of Esau; because the Lord has spoken. 19 And they *that dwell* in the south shall inherit the mount of Esau, and they in the plain the Philistines: and they shall inherit the mount of Ephraim, and the plain of Samaria, and Benjamin, and the land of Galaad. 20 And this *shall be* the domain of the captivity of the children of Israel, the land of the Chananites as far as Sarepta; and the captives of Jerusalem *shall inherit* as far as Ephratha; they shall inherit the cities of the south. 21 And they that escape shall come up from mount Sion, to take vengeance on the mount of Esau; and the kingdom shall be the Lord's.

JONAS (JONAH)

Jonah.1 1 Now the word of the Lord came to Jonas the son of Amathi, saying, 2 Rise, and go to Nineve, the great city, and preach in it; for the cry of its wickedness is come up to me. 3 But Jonas rose up to flee to Tharsis from the presence of the Lord. And he went down to Joppa, and found a ship going to Tharsis: and he paid his fare, and went up into it, to sail with them to Tharsis from the presence of the Lord. 4 And the Lord raised up a wind on the sea; and there was a great storm on the sea, and the ship was in danger of being broken. 5 And the sailors were alarmed, and cried every one to his god, and cast out the wares that were in the ship into the sea, that it might be lightened of them. But Jonas was gone down into the hold of the ship, and was asleep, and snored. 6 And the shipmaster came to him, and said to him, Why snorest thou? arise, and call upon thy God, that God may save us, and we perish not. 7 And each man said to his neighbour, Come, let us cast lots, and find out for whose sake this mischief is upon us. So they cast lots, and the lot fell upon Jonas. 8 And they said to him, Tell us what is thine occupation, and whence comest thou, and of what country and what people art thou? 9 And he said to them, I am a servant of the Lord; and I worship the Lord God of heaven, who made the sea, and the dry *land*. 10 Then the men feared exceedingly, and said to him, What is this *that* thou hast done? for the men knew that he was fleeing from the face of the Lord, because he had told them. 11 And they said to him, What shall we do to thee, that the sea may be calm to us? for the sea rose, and lifted its wave exceedingly. 12 And Jonas said to them, Take me up, and cast me into the sea, and the sea shall be calm to you: for I know that for my sake this great tempest is upon you. 13 And the men tried hard to return to the land, and were not able: for the sea rose and grew more and more tempestuous against them. 14 And they cried to the Lord, and said, Forbid it, Lord: let us not perish for the sake of this man's life, and bring not righteous blood upon us: for thou, Lord, hast done as thou wouldest. 15 So they took Jonas, and cast him out into the sea: and the sea ceased from its raging. 16 And the men feared the Lord very greatly, and offered a sacrifice to the Lord, and vowed vows.

Jonah.2 1 Now the Lord had commanded a great whale to swallow up Jonas: and Jonas was in the belly of the whale three days and three nights. 2 And Jonas prayed to the Lord his God out of the belly of the whale, 3 and said, I cried in my affliction to the Lord my God, and he hearkened to me, *even* to my cry out of the belly of hell: thou heardest my voice. 4 Thou didst cast me into the depths of the heart of the sea, and the floods compassed me: all thy billows and thy waves have passed upon me. 5 And I said, I am cast out of thy presence: shall I indeed look again toward thy holy temple? 6 Water was poured around me to the soul: the lowest deep compassed me, my head went down 7 to the clefts of the mountains; I went down into the earth, whose bars are the everlasting barriers: yet, O Lord my God, let my ruined life be restored. 8 When my soul was failing me, I remembered the Lord; and may my prayer come to thee into thy holy temple. 9 They that observe vanities and lies have forsaken their own mercy. 10 But I will sacrifice to thee with the voice of praise and thanksgiving: all that I have vowed I will pay to thee, the Lord of *my* salvation. 11 And the whale was commanded by the Lord, and it cast up Jonas on the dry *land*.

Jonah.3 1 And the word of the Lord came to Jonas the second time, saying, 2 Rise, go to Nineve, the great city, and preach in it according to the former preaching which I spoke to thee of. 3 And Jonas arose, and went to Nineve, as the Lord had spoken. Now Nineve was an exceeding great city, of about three days' journey. 4 And Jonas began to enter into the city about a day's journey, and he proclaimed, and said, Yet three days, and Nineve shall be overthrown. 5 And the men of Nineve believed God, and proclaimed a fast, and put on sackcloths, from the greatest of them to the least of them. 6 And the word reached the king of Nineve, and he arose from off his throne, and took off his raiment from him, and put on sackcloth, and sat on ashes. 7 And proclamation was made, and it was commanded in Nineve by the king an by his great men, saying, Let not men, or cattle, or oxen, or sheep, taste *any thing*, nor feed, nor drink water. 8 So men and cattle were clothed with sackcloths, and cried earnestly to God; and they turned every one from their evil way, and from the iniquity that was in their hands, saying, 9 Who knows if God will repent, and turn from his fierce anger, and *so* we shall not perish? 10 And God saw their works, that they turned from their evil ways; and God repented of the evil which he had said he would do to them; and he did *it* not.

Jonah.4 1 But Jonas was very deeply grieved, and he was confounded. 2 And he prayed to the Lord, and said, O Lord, were not these my words when I was yet in my land? therefore I made haste to flee to Tharsis; because I knew that thou are merciful and compassionate, long-suffering, and abundant in kindness, and repentest of evil. 3 And now, Lord God, take my life from me; for *it is* better for me to die than to live. 4 And the Lord said to Jonas, Art thou very much grieved? 5 And Jonas went out from the city, and sat over against the city; and he made for himself there a booth, and he sat under it, until he should perceive what would become of the city. 6 And the Lord God commanded a gourd, and it came up over the head of Jonas, to be a shadow over his head, to shade him from his calamities: and Jonas rejoiced with great joy for the gourd. 7 And God commanded a worm the next morning, and it smote the gourd, and it withered away. 8 And it came to pass at the rising of the sun, that God commanded a burning east wind; and the sun smote on the head of Jonas, and he

fainted, and despaired of his life, and said, *It is* better for me to die than to live. 9 And God said to Jonas, Art thou very much grieved for the gourd? And he said, I am very much grieved, even to death. 10 And the Lord said, Thou hadst pity on the gourd, for which thou has not suffered, neither didst thou rear it; which came up before night, and perished before *another* night: 11 and shall not I spare Nineve, the great city, in which dwell more than twelve myriads of human beings, who do not know their right hand or their left hand; and *also* much cattle?

MICHAEAS (MICAH)

Mic.1 1 And the word of the Lord came to Michaeas the son of Morasthi, in the days of Joatham, and Achaz, and Ezekias, kings of Juda, concerning what he saw regarding Samaria and Jerusalem. 2 Hear *these* words, ye people; and let the earth give heed, and all that are in it: and the Lord God shall be among you for a testimony, the Lord out of his holy habitation. 3 For, behold, the Lord comes forth out of his place, and will come down, and will go upon the high places of the earth. 4 And the mountains shall be shaken under him, and the valleys shall melt like wax before the fire, and as water rushing down a declivity. 5 All these *calamities are* for the transgression of Jacob, and for the sin of the house of Israel. What is the transgression of Jacob? *is it* not Samaria? and what is the sin of the house of Juda? *is it* not Jerusalem? 6 Therefore I will make Samaria *as* a store-house of the fruits of the field, and *as* a planting of a vineyard: and I will utterly demolish her stones, and I will expose her foundations. 7 And they shall cut in pieces all the graven images, and all that she has hired they shall burn with fire, and I will utterly destroy all her idols: because she has gathered of the hires of fornication, and of the hires of fornication has she amassed *wealth*. 8 Therefore shall she lament and wail, she shall go barefooted, and *being* naked she shall make lamentation as *that* of serpents, and mourning as of the daughters of sirens. 9 For her plague has become grievous; for it has come even to Juda; and has reached to the gate of my people, even to Jerusalem. 10 Ye that are in Geth, exalt not yourselves, and ye Enakim, do not rebuild from *the ruins of* the house in derision: sprinkle dust *in the place of* your laughter. 11 The inhabitant of Sennaar, fairly inhabiting her cities, came not forth to mourn for the house next to her: she shall receive of you the stroke of grief. 12 Who has begun *to act* for good to her that dwells in sorrow? for calamities have come down from the Lord upon the gates of Jerusalem, 13 *even* a sound of chariots and horsemen: the inhabitants of Lachis, she is the leader of sin to the daughter of Sion: for in thee were found the transgressions of Israel. 14 Therefore shall he cause men to be sent forth as far as the inheritance of Geth, *even* vain houses; they are become vanity to the kings of Israel; 15 until they bring the heirs, O inhabitant of Lachis: the inheritance shall reach to Odollam, *even* the glory of the daughter of Israel. 16 Shave thine hair, and make thyself bald for thy delicate children; increase thy widowhood as an eagle; for *thy people* are gone into captivity from thee.

Mic.2 1 They meditated troubles, and wrought wickedness on their beds, and they put it in execution with the daylight;

for they have not lifted up their hands to God. 2 And they desired fields, and plundered orphans, and oppressed families, and spoiled a man and his house, even a man and his inheritance. 3 Therefore thus saith the Lord; Behold, I devise evils against this family, out of which ye shall not lift up your necks, neither shall ye walk upright speedily: for the time is evil. 4 In that day shall a parable be taken up against you, and a plaintive lamentation shall be uttered, saying, We are thoroughly miserable: the portion of my people has been measured out with a line, and there was none to hinder him so as to turn him back; your fields have been divided. 5 Therefore thou shalt have no one to cast a line for the lot. 6 Weep not with tears in the assembly of the Lord, neither let *any* weep for these things; for he shall not remove the reproaches, 7 who says, The house of Jacob has provoked the Spirit of the Lord; are not these his practices? Are not the Lord's words right with him? and have they not proceeded correctly? 8 Even beforetime my people withstood *him* as an enemy against his peace; they have stripped off his skin to remove hope *in* the conflict of war. 9 The leaders of my people shall be cast forth from their luxurious houses; they are rejected because of their evil practices; draw ye near to the everlasting mountains. 10 Arise thou, and depart; for this is not thy rest because of uncleanness: ye have been utterly destroyed; 11 ye have fled, no one pursuing *you: thy* spirit has framed falsehood, it has dropped on thee for wine and strong drink. But it shall come to pass, *that* out of the dropping of this people, 12 Jacob shall be completely gathered with all *his people:* I will surely receive the remnant of Israel; I will cause them to return together, as sheep in trouble, as a flock in the midst of their fold: they shall rush forth from among men through the breach made before them: 13 they have broken through, and passed the gate, and gone out by it: and their king has gone out before them, and the Lord shall lead them.

Mic.3 1 And he shall say, Hear now these words, ye heads of the house of Jacob, and ye remnant of the house of Israel; is it not for you to know judgment? 2 *who* hate good, and seek evil; *who* tear their skins off them, and their flesh off their bones: 3 even as they devoured the flesh of my people, and stripped their skins off them, and broke their bones, and divided *them* as flesh for the caldron, and as meat for the pot, 4 thus they shall cry to the Lord, but he shall not hearken to them; and he shall turn away his face from them at that time, because they have done wickedly in their practices against themselves. 5 Thus saith the Lord concerning the prophets that lead my people astray, that bit with their teeth, and proclaim peace to them; and *when* nothing was put into their mouth, they raised up war against them: 6 therefore there shall be night to you instead of a vision, and there shall be to you darkness instead of prophecy; and the sun shall go down upon the prophets, and the day shall be dark upon them. 7 And the seers of night-visions shall be ashamed, and the prophets shall be laughed to scorn: and all the people shall speak against them, because there shall be none to hearken to them. 8 Surely I will strengthen myself with the Spirit of the Lord,

and of judgment, and of power, to declare to Jacob his transgressions, and to Israel his sins. 9 Hear now these words, ye chiefs of the house of Jacob, and the remnant of the house of Israel, who hate judgment, and pervert all righteousness; 10 who build up Sion with blood, and Jerusalem with iniquity. 11 The heads thereof have judged for gifts, and the priests thereof have answered for hire, and her prophets have divined for silver: and *yet* they have rested on the Lord, saying, Is not the Lord among us? no evil shall come upon us. 12 Therefore on your account Sion shall be ploughed as a field, and Jerusalem shall be as a storehouse of fruits, and the mountain of the house as a grove of the forest.

Mic.4 1 And at the last days the mountain of the Lord shall be manifest, established on the tops of the mountains, and it shall be exalted above the hills; and the peoples shall hasten to it. 2 And many nations shall go, and say, Come, let us go up to the mountain of the Lord, and to the house of the God of Jacob; and they shall shew us his way, and we will walk in his paths: for out of Sion shall go forth a law, and the word of the Lord from Jerusalem. 3 And he shall judge among many peoples, and shall rebuke strong nations afar off; and they shall beat their swords into ploughshares, and their spears into sickles; and nation shall no more lift up sword against nation, neither shall they learn to war any more. 4 And every one shall rest under his vine, and every one under his fig-tree; and there shall be none to alarm *them*: for the mouth of the Lord Almighty has spoken these *words*. 5 For all *other* nations shall walk everyone in his own way, but we will walk in the name of the Lord our God for ever and ever. 6 In that day, saith the Lord, I will gather her that is bruised, and will receive her that is cast out, and those whom I rejected. 7 And I will make her that was bruised a remnant, and her that was rejected a mighty nation: and the Lord shall reign over them in mount Sion from henceforth, even for ever. 8 And thou, dark tower of the flock, daughter of Sion, on thee the dominion shall come and enter in, *even* the first kingdom from Babylon to the daughter of Jerusalem. 9 And now, why hast thou known calamities? was there not a king to thee? or has thy counsel perished that pangs as of a woman in travail have seized upon thee? 10 Be in pain, and strengthen thyself, and draw near, O daughter of Sion, as a woman in travail: for now thou shalt go forth out of the city, and shalt lodge in the plain, and shalt reach even to Babylon: thence shall the Lord thy God deliver thee, and thence shall he redeem thee out of the hand of thine enemies. 11 And now have many nations gathered against thee, saying, We will rejoice, and our eyes shall look upon Sion. 12 But they know not the thought of the Lord, and have not understood his counsel: for he has gathered them as sheaves of the floor. 13 Arise, and thresh them, O daughter of Sion: for I will make thine horns iron, and I will make thine hoofs brass: and thou shalt utterly destroy many nations, and shalt consecrate their abundance to the Lord, and their strength to the Lord of all the earth.

Mic.5 1 Now shall the daughter *of Sion* be completely hedged in: he has laid siege against us: they shall smite the tribes of Israel with a rod upon the cheek. 2 And thou, Bethleem, house of Ephratha, art few in number to be *reckoned* among the thousands of Juda; *yet* out of thee shall one come forth to me, to be a ruler of Israel; and his goings forth were from the beginning, *even* from eternity. 3 Therefore shall he appoint them *to wait* till the time of her that travails: she shall bring forth, and *then* the remnant of their brethren shall return to the children of Israel. 4 And the Lord shall stand, and see, and feed his flock with power, and they shall dwell in the glory of the name of the Lord their God: for now shall they be magnified to the ends of the earth. 5 And she shall have peace when Assur shall come into your land, and when he shall come up upon your country; and there shall be raised up against him seven shepherds, and eight attacks of men. 6 And they shall tend the Assyrian with a sword, and the land of Nebrod with her trench: and he shall deliver *you* from the Assyrian, when he shall come upon your land, and when he shall invade your coasts. 7 And the remnant of Jacob shall be among the Gentiles in the midst of many peoples, as dew falling from the Lord, and as lambs on the grass; that none may assemble nor resist among the sons of men. 8 And the remnant of Jacob shall be among the Gentiles in the midst of many nations, as a lion in the forest among cattle, and as a *lion's* whelp among the flocks of sheep, even as when he goes through, and selects, and carries off *his prey*, and there is none to deliver. 9 Thine hand shall be lifted up against them that afflict thee, and all thine enemies shall be utterly destroyed. 10 And it shall come to pass in that day, saith the Lord, *that* I will utterly destroy the horses out of the midst of thee, and destroy thy chariots; 11 and I will utterly destroy the cities of thy land, and demolish all thy strong-holds: 12 and I will utterly destroy thy sorceries out of thine hands; and there shall be no soothsayers in thee. 13 And I will utterly destroy thy graven images, and thy statues out of the midst of thee; and thou shalt never any more worship the works of thine hands. 14 And I will cut off the groves out of the midst of thee, and I will abolish thy cities. 15 and I will execute vengeance on the heathen in anger and wrath, because they hearkened not.

Mic.6 1 Hear now a word: the Lord God has said; Arise, plead with the mountains, and let the hills hear thy voice. 2 Hear ye, O mountains, the controversy of the Lord, and *ye* valleys *even* the foundations of the earth: for the Lord *has* a controversy with his people, and will plead with Israel. 3 O my people, what have I done to thee? or wherein have I grieved thee? or wherein have I troubled thee? answer me. 4 For I brought tee up out of the land of Egypt, and redeemed thee out of the house of bondage, and sent before thee Moses, and Aaron, and Mariam. 5 O my people, remember now, what counsel Balac king of Moab took against thee, and what Balaam the son of Beor answered him, from the reeds to Galgal; that the righteousness of the Lord might be known. 6 Wherewithal shall I reach the Lord, *and* lay hold of my God most high? shall I reach him by whole-burnt-offerings, by calves of a year old? 7 Will the Lord accept thousands of rams, or ten thousands of fat goats? should I give my first-born for ungodliness, the fruit of my body for the sin of my soul? 8 Has it *not* been told thee, O man, what *is* good? or what does the Lord require of thee, but to do justice, and love mercy, and be ready to walk with the Lord thy God? 9 The Lord's voice shall be proclaimed in the city, and he shall save those that fear his name: hear, O tribe; and who shall order the city? 10 *Is there* not fire, and the house of the wicked heaping up wicked treasures, and *that* with the pride of unrighteousness? 11 Shall the wicked be justified by the balanced, or deceitful weights in the bag, 12 whereby they have accumulated their ungodly wealth, and they that dwell in the city have uttered falsehoods, and their tongue has been exalted in their mouth? 13 Therefore will I begin to smite thee; I will destroy thee in thy sins. 14 Thou shalt eat, and shalt not be satisfied; and there shall be darkness upon thee; and he shall depart from *thee*, and thou shalt not escape; and all that shall escape shall be delivered over to the sword. 15 Thou shalt sow, but thou shalt not reap; thou shalt press the olive, but thou shalt not anoint thyself with oil; and *shalt make* wine, but ye shall drink no wine: and the ordinances of my people shall be utterly abolished. 16 For thou hast kept the statues of Zambri, and *done* all the works of the house of Achaab; and ye have walked in their ways, that I might deliver thee to utter destruction, and those that inhabit the city to hissing: and ye shall bear the reproach of nations.

Mic.7 1 Alas for me! for I am become as one gathering straw in harvest, and as *one gathering* grape- gleanings in the vintage, when there is no cluster for me to eat the first-ripe fruit: alas my soul! 2 For the godly is perished from the earth; and there is none among men that orders *his way* aright: they all quarrel even to blood: they grievously afflict every one his neighbour: 3 they prepare their hands for mischief, the prince asks *a reward*, and the judge speaks flattering words; it is the desire of their soul: 4 therefore I will take away their goods as a devouring moth, and as one who acts by a *rigid* rule in a day of visitation. Woe, woe, thy times of vengeance are come; now shall be their lamentations. 5 Trust not in friends, and confide not in guides: beware of thy wife, so as not to commit anything to her. 6 For the son dishonours his father, the daughter will rise up against her mother, the daughter-in-law against her mother-in- law: those in his house *shall be* all a man's enemies. 7 But I will look to the Lord; I will wait upon God my Saviour: my God will hearken to me. 8 Rejoice not against me, mine enemy; for I have fallen *yet* shall arise; for though I should sit in darkness, the Lord shall be a light to me. 9 I will bear the indignation of the Lord, because I have sinned against him, until he make good my cause: he also shall maintain my right, and shall bring me out to the light, *and* I shall behold his righteousness. 10 And she that is mine enemy shall see it, and shall clothe herself with shame, who says, Where *is* the Lord thy God? mine eyes shall look upon her: now shall she be for trampling as mire in the ways. 11 *It is* the day of making of brick; that day shall be thine utter destruction, and that day shall utterly abolish thine ordinances. 12 And thy cities shall be levelled, and parted among the Assyrians; and thy strong cities shall be parted from Tyre to the river, and from sea to sea, and from mountain to mountain. 13 And the land shall be utterly desolate together with them that inhabit it, because of the fruit of their doings. 14 Tend thy people with thy rod, the sheep of thine inheritance, those that inhabit by themselves the thicket in the midst of Carmel: they shall feed in the land of Basan, and in the land of Galaad, as in the days of old. 15 And according to the days of thy departure out of Egypt shall ye see marvellous *things*. 16 The nations shall see and be ashamed; and at all their might they shall lay their hands upon their mouth, their ears shall be deafened. 17 They shall lick the dust as serpents crawling on the earth, they shall be confounded in their holes; they shall be amazed at the Lord our God, and will be afraid of thee. 18 Who is a God like thee, cancelling iniquities, and passing over the sins of the remnant of his inheritance? and he has not kept his anger for a testimony, for he delights in mercy. 19 He will return and have mercy upon us; he will sink our iniquities, and they shall be cast into the depth of the sea, *even* all our sins. 20 He shall give blessings truly to Jacob, and mercy to Abraam, as thou swarest to our fathers, according to the former days.

NAUM (NAHUM)

Nah.1 1 The burden of Nineve: the book of the vision of Naum the Elkesite. 2 God is jealous, and the Lord avenges; the Lord avenges with wrath; the Lord takes vengeance on his adversaries, and he cuts off his enemies. 3 The Lord is long-suffering, and his power is great, and the Lord will not hold any guiltless: his way is in destruction and in the whirlwind, and the clouds are the dust of his feet. 4 He threatens the sea, and dries it up, and exhausts all the rivers: the land of Basan, and Carmel are brought low, and the flourishing *trees* of Libanus have come to nought. 5 The mountains quake at him, and the hills are shaken, and the earth recoils at his presence, *even* the world, and all that dwell in it. 6 Who shall stand before his anger? and who shall withstand in the anger of his wrath? his wrath brings to nought kingdoms, and the rocks are burst asunder by him. 7 The Lord is good to them that wait on him in the day of affliction; and he knows them that reverence him. 8 But with an overrunning flood he will make an utter end: darkness shall pursue those that rise up against *him* and his enemies. 9 What do ye devise against the Lord? he will make a complete end: he will not take vengeance by affliction twice at the same time. 10 For *the enemy* shall be laid bare even to the foundation, and shall be devoured as twisted yew, and as stubble fully dry. 11 Out of thee shall proceed a device against the Lord, counselling evil things hostile *to him*. 12 Thus saith the Lord who rules over many waters, Even thus shall they be sent away, and the report of thee shall not be heard any more. 13 And now will I break his rod from off thee, and will burst *thy* bonds. 14 And the Lord shall give a command concerning thee; there shall no more of thy name be scattered: I will utterly destroy the graven *images* out of the house of thy god, and the molten *images*: I will make thy grave; for *they are* swift. 15 Behold upon the mountains the feet of him that brings glad tidings, and publishes peace! O Juda, keep thy feasts, pay thy vows: for they shall no more pass through thee to *thy* decay.

Nah.2 1 It is all over with him, he has been removed, *one* who has been delivered from affliction has come up panting into thy presence, watch the way, strengthen *thy* loins, be very valiant in *thy* strength. 2 For the Lord has turned aside the pride of Jacob, as the pride of Israel: for they have utterly rejected them, and have destroyed their branches. 3 *They have destroyed* the arms of their power from among men, their mighty men sporting with fire: the reins of their chariots *shall be destroyed* in the day of his preparation, and the horsemen shall be thrown into confusion 4 in the ways, and the chariots shall clash together, and shall be entangled in each other in the broad ways: their appearance is as lamps of fire, and as gleaming lightnings. 5 And their mighty men shall bethink themselves and flee by day; and they shall be weak as they go; and they shall hasten to her walls, and shall prepare their defences. 6 The gates of the cities have been opened, and the palaces have fallen into ruin, 7 and the foundation has been exposed; and she has gone up, and her maid-servants were led *away* as doves moaning in their hearts. 8 And *as for* Nineve, her waters *shall be* as a pool of water: and they fled, and staid not, and there was none to look back. 9 They plundered the silver, they plundered the gold, and there was no end of their adorning; they were loaded *with it* upon all their pleasant vessels. 10 *There is* thrusting forth, and shaking, and tumult, and heart-breaking, and loosing of knees, and pangs on all loins; and the faces of all *are* as the blackening of a pot. 11 Where is the dwelling-place of the lions, and the pasture that belonged to the whelps? where did the lion go, that the lion's whelp should enter in there, and there was none to scare *him* away? 12 The lion seized enough prey for his whelps, and strangled for his *young* lions, and filled his lair with prey, and his dwelling-place with spoil. 13 Behold, I am against thee, saith the Lord Almighty, and I will burn up thy multitude in the smoke, and the sword shall devour thy lions; and I will utterly destroy thy prey from off the land, and thy deeds shall no more at all be heard of.

Nah.3 1 O city of blood, wholly false, full of unrighteousness; the prey shall not be handled. 2 The noise of whips, and the noise of the rumbling of wheels, and of the pursuing horse, and of the bounding chariot, 3 and of the mounting rider, and of the glittering sword, and of the gleaming arms, and of a multitude of slain, and of heavy falling: and there was no end to her nations, but they shall be weak in their bodies 4 because of the abundance of fornication: *she is* a fair harlot, and well-favoured, skilled in sorcery, that sells the nations by her fornication, and peoples by her sorceries. 5 Behold, I am against thee, saith the Lord God Almighty, and I will uncover thy skirts in thy presence, and I will shew the nations thy shame, and the kingdoms thy disgrace. 6 And I will cast abominable filth upon thee according to thine unclean ways, and will make thee a public example. 7 And it shall be *that* every one that sees thee shall go down from thee, and shall say, Wretched Nineve! who shall lament for her? whence shall I seek comfort for her? 8 Prepare thee a portion, tune the chord, prepare a portion for Ammon: she that dwells among the rivers, water is round about her, whose dominion is the sea, and whose walls are water. 9 And Ethiopia is her strength, and Egypt; and there was no limit of the flight *of her enemies*; and the Libyans became her helpers. 10 Yet she shall go as a prisoner into captivity, and they shall dash her infants against the ground at the top of all her ways: and they shall cast lots upon all her glorious *possessions*, and all her nobles shall be bound in chains. 11 And thou shalt be drunken, and shalt be overlooked; and thou shalt seek for thyself strength because of *thine* enemies. 12 All thy strong-holds are as fig-trees having watchers: if they be shaken, they shall fall into the mouth of the eater. 13 Behold, thy people within thee are as women: the gates of thy land shall surely be opened to thine enemies: the fire shall devour thy bars. 14 Draw thee water for a siege, and well secure thy strong-holds: enter into the clay, and be thou trodden in the chaff, make *the fortifications* stronger than brick. 15 There the fire shall devour thee; the sword shall utterly destroy thee, it shall devour thee as the locust, and thou shalt be pressed down as a palmerworm. 16 Thou hast multiplied thy merchandise beyond the stars of heaven: the palmerworm has attacked *it*, and has flown away. 17 Thy mixed *multitude* has suddenly departed as the grasshopper, as the locust perched on a hedge in a frosty day; the sun arises, and it flies off, and knows not its place: woe to them! 18 Thy shepherds have slumbered, the Assyrian king has laid low thy mighty men: thy people departed to the mountains, and there was none to receive *them*. 19 There is no healing for thy bruise; thy wound has rankled: all that hear the report of thee shall clap their hands against thee; for upon whom has not thy wickedness passed continually?

AMBACUM (HABAKKUK)

Hab.1 1 The burden which the prophet Ambacum saw. 2 How long, O Lord, shall I cry out, and thou wilt not hearken? *how long* shall I cry out to thee being injured, and thou wilt not save? 3 Wherefore hast thou shown me troubles and griefs to look upon, misery and ungodliness? judgment is before me, and the judge receives a reward. 4 Therefore the law is frustrated, and judgment proceeds not effectually, for the ungodly *man* prevails over the just; therefore perverse judgment will proceed. 5 Behold, ye despisers, and look, and wonder marvelously, and vanish: for I work a work in your days, which ye will in no wise believe, though a man declare *it to you*. 6 Wherefore, behold, I stir up the Chaldeans, the bitter and hasty nation, that walks upon the breadth of the earth, to inherit tabernacles not his own. 7 He is terrible and famous; his judgment shall proceed of himself, and his dignity shall come out of himself. 8 And his horses shall bound *more swiftly* than leopards, and *they are* fiercer than the wolves of Arabia: and his horsemen shall ride forth, and shall rush from far; and they shall fly as an eagle hasting to eat. 9 Destruction shall come upon ungodly men, resisting with their adverse front, and he shall gather the captivity as the sand. 10 And he shall be at his ease with kings, and princes are his toys, and he shall mock at every strong-hold, and shall cast a mound, and take possession of it. 11 Then shall he change his spirit, and he shall pass through, and make an atonement, *saying*, This strength *belongs* to my god. 12 *Art* not thou from the

beginning, O Lord God, my Holy One? and surely we shall not die. O Lord, thou hast established it for judgment, and he has formed me to chasten *with* his correction. 13 *His* eye is too pure to behold evil *doings*, and to look upon grievous afflictions: wherefore dost thou look upon despisers? wilt thou be silent when the ungodly swallows up the just? 14 And wilt thou make men as the fishes of the sea, and as the reptiles which have no guide? 15 He has brought up destruction with a hook, and drawn one with a casting net, and caught another in his drags: therefore shall his heart rejoice and be glad. 16 Therefore will he sacrifice to his drag, and burn incense to his casting-net, because by them he has made his portion fat, and his meats choice. 17 Therefore will he cast his net, and will not spare to slay the nations continually.

Hab.2 1 I will stand upon my watch, and mount upon the rock, and watch to see what he will say by me, and what I shall answer when I am reproved. 2 And the Lord answered me and said, Write the vision, and *that* plainly on a tablet, that he that reads it may run. 3 For the vision *is* yet for a time, and it shall shoot forth at the end, and not in vain: though he should tarry, wait for him; for he will surely come, and will not tarry. 4 If he should draw back, my soul has no pleasure in him: but the just shall live by my faith. 5 But the arrogant man and the scorner, the boastful man, shall not finish anything; who has enlarged his desire as the grave, and like death he is never satisfied, and he will gather to himself all the nations, and will receive to himself all the peoples. 6 Shall not all these take up a parable against him? and a proverb to tell against him? and they shall say, Woe to him that multiplies to himself the possessions which are not his! how long? and who heavily loads his yoke. 7 For suddenly there shall arise up those that bite him, and they that plot against thee shall awake, and thou shalt be a plunder to them. 8 Because thou hast spoiled many nations, all the nations that are left shall spoil *thee*, because of the blood of men, and the sins of the land and city, and of all that dwell in it. 9 Woe to him that covets an evil covetousness to his house, that he may set his nest on high, that he may be delivered from the power of evils. 10 Thou hast devised shame to thy house, thou hast utterly destroyed many nations, and thy soul has sinned. 11 For the stone shall cry out of the wall, and the beetle out of the timber shall speak. 12 Woe to him that builds a city with blood, and establishes a city by unrighteousness. 13 Are not these things of the Lord Almighty? surely many people have been exhausted in the fire, and many nations have fainted. 14 For the earth shall be filled with the knowledge of the glory of the Lord; it shall cover them as water. 15 Woe to him that gives his neighbour to drink the thick lees *of wine*, and intoxicates *him*, that he may look upon their secret parts. 16 Drink thou also *thy* fill of disgrace instead of glory: shake, O heart, and quake, the cup of the right hand of the Lord has come round upon thee, and dishonour has gathered upon thy glory. 17 For the ungodliness of Libanus shall cover thee, and distress because of wild beasts shall dismay thee, because of the blood of men, and the sins of the land and city, and of all that dwell in it. 18 What profit it the graven image, that they have graven it? *one* has made it a molten work, a false image; for the maker has trusted in his work, to make dumb idols. 19 Woe to him that says to the wood, Awake, arise; and to the stone, Be thou exalted! whereas it is an image, and this is a casting of gold and silver, and there is no breath in it. 20 But the Lord is in his holy temple: let all the earth fear before him.

Hab.3 1 A PRAYER OF THE PROPHET AMBACUM, WITH A SONG.

2 O Lord, I have heard thy report, and was afraid: I considered thy works, and was amazed: thou shalt be known between the two living creatures, thou shalt be acknowledged when the years draw nigh; thou shalt be manifested when the time is come; when my soul is troubled, thou wilt in wrath remember mercy. 3 God shall come from Thaeman, and the Holy One from the dark shady mount Pharan. Pause. 4 His excellence covered the heavens, and the earth was full of his praise. And his brightness shall be as light; *there were* horns in his hands, and he caused a mighty love of his strength. 5 Before his face shall go a report, and it shall go forth into the plains, 6 the earth stood at his feet and trembled: he beheld, and the nations melted away: the mountains were violently burst through, the everlasting hills melted at his everlasting going forth. 7 Because of troubles I looked upon the tents of the Ethiopians: the tabernacles also of the land of Madiam shall be dismayed. 8 Wast thou angry, O Lord, with the rivers? or *was* thy wrath against the rivers, or thine anger against the sea? for thou wilt mount on thine horses, and thy chariots are salvation. 9 Surely thou didst bend they bow at scepters, saith the Lord. Pause. The land of rivers shall be torn asunder. 10 The nations shall see thee and be in pain, *as thou dost* divide the moving waters: the deep uttered her voice, and raised her form on high. 11 The sun was exalted, and the moon stood still in her course: thy darts shall go forth at the light, at the brightness of the gleaming of thine arms. 12 Thou wilt bring low the land with threatening, and in wrath thou wilt break down the nations. 13 Thou wentest forth for the salvation of thy people, to save thine anointed: thou shalt bring death on the heads of transgressors; thou has brought bands upon *their* neck. Pause. 14 Thou didst cut asunder the heads of princes with amazement, they shall tremble in it; they shall burst their bridles, *they shall be* as a poor man devouring in secret. 15 And thou dost cause thine horses to enter the sea, disturbing much water. 16 I watched, and my belly trembled at the sound of the prayer of my lips, and trembling entered into my bones, and my frame was troubled within me; I will rest in the day of affliction, from going up to the people of my sojourning. 17 For *though* the fig-tree shall bear no fruit, and there shall be no produce on the vines; the labour of the olive shall fail, and the fields shall produce no food: the sheep have failed from the pasture, and there are no oxen at the cribs; 18 yet I will exult in the Lord, I will joy in God my Saviour. 19 The Lord God is my strength, and he will perfectly strengthen my feet; he mounts me upon high places, that I may conquer by his song.

SOPHONIAS (ZEPHANIAH)

Zeph.1 1 The word of the Lord which came to Sophonias the son of Chusi, the son of Godolias, the son of Amorias, the son of Ezekias, in the days of Josias son of Amon, king of Juda. 2 Let there be an utter cutting off from the face of the land, saith the Lord. 3 Let man and cattle be cut off; let the birds of the air and the fishes of the sea be cut off; and the ungodly shall fail, and I will take away the transgressors from the face of the land, saith the Lord. 4 And I will stretch out mine hand upon Juda, and upon all the inhabitants of Jerusalem; and I will remove the names of Baal out of this place, and the names of the priests; 5 and them that worship the host of heaven upon the house-tops; and them that worship and swear by the Lord, and them that swear by their king; 6 and them that turn aside from the Lord, and them that seek not the Lord, and them that cleave not to the Lord. 7 Fear ye before the Lord God; for the day of the Lord is near; for the Lord has prepared his sacrifice, and has sanctified his guests. 8 And it shall come to pass in the day of the Lord's sacrifice, that I will take vengeance on the princes, and on the king's house, and upon all that wear strange apparel. 9 And I will openly take vengeance on the porches in that day, *on the men* that fill the house of the Lord their God with ungodliness and deceit. 10 And there shall be in that day, saith the Lord, the sound of a cry from the gate of men slaying, and a howling from the second *gate*, and a great crashing from the hills. 11 Lament, ye that inhabit the *city* that has been broken down, for all the people has become like Chanaan; and all that were exalted by silver have been utterly destroyed. 12 And it shall come to pass in that day, *that* I will search Jerusalem with a candle, and will take vengeance on the men that despise the things committed to them; but they say in their hearts, The Lord will not do any good, neither will he do any evil. 13 And their power shall be for a spoil, and their houses for utter desolation; and they shall build houses, but shall not dwell in them; and they shall plant vineyards, but shall not drink the wine of them. 14 For the great day of the Lord *is* near, *it is* near, and very speedy; the sound of the day of the Lord is made bitter and harsh. 15 A mighty day of wrath is that day, a day of affliction and distress, a day of desolation and destruction, a day of gloominess and darkness, a day of cloud and vapour, 16 a day of the trumpet and cry against the strong cities, and against the high towers. 17 And I will greatly afflict the men, and they shall walk as blind men, because they have sinned against the Lord; therefore he shall pour out their blood as dust, and their flesh as dung. 18 And their silver and their gold shall in nowise be able to rescue them in the day of the Lord's wrath; but the whole land shall be devoured by the fire of his jealously; for he will bring a speedy destruction on all them that inhabit the land.

Zeph.2 1 Be ye gathered and closely joined together, O unchastened nation; 2 before ye become as the flower that passes away, before the anger of the Lord come upon you, before the day of the wrath of the Lord come upon you. 3 Seek ye the Lord, all ye meek of the earth; do judgment, and seek justice, and answer accordingly; that ye may be hid in the day of the wrath of the Lord. 4 For Gaza shall be utterly spoiled, and Ascalon shall be destroyed; and Azotus shall be cast forth at noon-day, and Accaron shall be rooted up. 5 Woe to them that dwell on the border of the sea, neighbours of the Cretans! the word of the Lord is against you, O Chanaan, land of the Philistines, and I will destroy you out of *your* dwelling-place. 6 And Crete shall be a pasture of flocks, and a fold of sheep. 7 And the sea cost shall be for the remnant of the house of Juda; they shall pasture upon them in the houses of Ascalon; they shall rest in the evening because of the children of Juda; for the Lord their God has visited them, and he will turn away their captivity. 8 I have heard the revilings of Moab, and the insults of the children of Ammon, wherewith they have reviled my people, and magnified themselves against my coasts. 9 Therefore, *as* I live, saith the Lord of hosts, the God of Israel, Moab shall be as Sodoma, and the children of Ammon as Gomorrha; and Damascus *shall be* left as a heap of the threshing-floor, and desolate for ever: and the remnant of my people shall plunder them, and the remnant of my nations shall inherit them. 10 This is their punishment in return for their haughtiness, because they have reproached and magnified themselves against the Lord Almighty. 11 The Lord shall appear against them, and shall utterly destroy all the gods of the nations of the earth; and they shall worship him every one from his place, *even* all the islands of the nations. 12 Ye Ethiopians also are the slain of my sword. 13 And he shall stretch forth his hand against the north and destroy the Assyrian, and make Nineve a dry wilderness, *even* as a desert. 14 And flocks, and all the wild beasts of the land, and chameleons shall feed in the midst thereof: and hedgehogs shall lodge in the ceilings thereof; and wild beasts shall cry in the breaches thereof, and ravens in her porches, whereas her loftiness was *as* as cedar.

Zeph.3 1 This is the scornful city that dwells securely, that says in her heart, I am, and there is no longer any *to be* after me: how is she become desolate, a habitation of wild beasts! every one that passes through her shall hiss, and shake his hands. Alas the glorious and ransomed city. 2 The dove hearkened not to the voice; she received not correction; she trusted not in the Lord, and she drew not near to her God. 3 Her princes within her were as roaring lions, her judges as the wolves of Arabia; they remained not till the morrow. 4 Her prophets are light *and* scornful men: her priests profane the holy things, and sinfully transgress the law. 5 But the just Lord is in the midst of her, and he will never do an unjust thing: morning by morning he will bring out his judgment to the light, and it is not hidden, and he knows not injustice by extortion, nor injustice in strife. 6 I have brought down the proud with destruction; their corners are destroyed: I will make their ways completely waste, so that none shall go through: their cities are come to an end, by reason of no man living or dwelling *in them*. 7 I said, But do ye fear me, and receive instruction, and ye shall not be cut off from the face of the land *for* all the vengeance I have brought upon her: prepare thou, rise early: all their produce is spoilt. 8 Therefore wait upon me, saith the Lord, until the day when I rise up for a witness: because my judgment *shall be* on the

gatherings of the nations, to draw to me kings, to pour out upon them all *my* fierce anger: for the whole earth shall be consumed with the fire of my jealousy. 9 For then will I turn to the peoples a tongue for her generation, that all may call on the name of the Lord, to serve him under one yoke. 10 From the boundaries of the rivers of Ethiopia will I receive my dispersed ones; they shall offer sacrifices to me. 11 In that day thou shalt not be ashamed of all thy practices, wherein thou hast transgressed against me: for then will I take away from thee thy disdainful pride, and thou shalt no more magnify thyself upon my holy mountain. 12 And I will leave in thee a meek and lowly people; 13 and the remnant of Israel shall fear the name of the Lord, and shall do no iniquity, neither shall they speak vanity; neither shall a deceitful tongue be found in their mouth: for they shall feed, and lie down, and there shall be none to terrify them. 14 Rejoice, O daughter of Sion; cry aloud, O daughter of Jerusalem; rejoice and delight thyself with all thine heart, O daughter of Jerusalem. 15 The Lord has taken away thine iniquities, he has ransomed thee from the hand of thine enemies: the Lord, the King of Israel, is in the midst of thee: thou shalt not see evil any more. 16 At that time the Lord shall say to Jerusalem, Be of good courage, Sion; let not thine hands be slack. 17 The Lord thy God is in thee; the Mighty One shall save thee: he shall bring joy upon thee, and shall refresh thee with his love; and he shall rejoice over thee with delight as in a day of feasting. 18 And I will gather thine afflicted ones. Alas! who has taken up a reproach against her? 19 Behold, I *will* work in thee for thy sake at that time, saith the Lord: and I will save her that was oppressed, and receive her that was rejected; and I will make them a praise, and honoured in all the earth. 20 And *their enemies* shall be ashamed at that time, when I shall deal well with you, and at the time when I shall receive you: for I will make you honoured and a praise among all the nations of the earth, when I turn back your captivity before you, saith the Lord.

AGGAEUS (HAGGAI)

Hag.1 1 In the second year of Darius the king, in the sixth month, on the firs *day* of the month, the word of the Lord came by the hand of the prophet Aggaeus, saying, Speak to Zorobabel the son of Salathiel, of the tribe of Juda, and to Jesus the son of Josedec, the high priest, saying, 2 Thus saith the Lord Almighty, saying, This people say, The time is not come to build the house of the Lord. 3 And the word of the Lord came by the hand of the prophet Aggaeus, saying, 4 Is it time for you to dwell in your ceiled houses, whereas our house is desolate? 5 And now thus saith the Lord Almighty; Consider your ways, I pray you. 6 Ye have sown much, but brought in little; ye have eaten, and are not satisfied; ye have drunk, and are not satisfied with drink, ye have clothed yourselves, and have not become warm thereby: and he that earns wages has gathered *them* into a bag full of holes. 7 Thus saith the Lord Almighty; Consider your ways. 8 Go up to the mountain, and cut timber; build the house, and I will take pleasure in it, and be glorified, saith the Lord. 9 Ye looked for much, and there came little; and it was brought into the house, and I blew it away. Therefore thus saith the

Lord Almighty, Because my house is desolate, and ye run everyone into his own house; 10 therefore shall the sky withhold dew, and the earth shall keep back her produce. 11 And I will bring a sword upon the land, and upon the mountains, and upon the corn, and upon the wine, and upon the oil, and all that the earth produces, and upon the men, and upon the cattle, and upon all the labours of their hands. 12 And Zorobabel the son of Salathiel, of the tribe of Juda, and Jesus the son of Josedec, the high priest, and all the remnant of the people, hearkened to the voice of the Lord their God, and the words of the prophet Aggaeus, according as the Lord their God had sent him to them, and the people feared before the Lord. 13 And Aggaeus the Lord's messenger spoke among the messengers of the Lord to the people, *saying*, I am with you, saith the Lord. 14 And the Lord stirred up the spirit of Zorobabel the son of Salathiel, of the tribe of Juda, and the spirit of Jesus the son of Josedec, the high priest, and the spirit of the remnant of all the people; and they went in, and wrought in the house of the Lord Almighty their God, 15 on the four and twentieth *day* of the sixth month, in the second year of Darius the king.

Hag.2 1,2 In the seventh month, on the twenty-first *day* of the month, the Lord spoke by Aggaeus the prophet, saying, 3 Speak now to Zorobabel the son of Salathiel, of the tribe of Juda, and to Jesus the son of Josedec, the high priest, and to all the remnant of the people, saying, 4 Who *is there* of you that saw this house in her former glory? and how do ye now look upon it, as it were nothing before your eyes? 5 Yet now be strong, O Zorobabel, saith the Lord; and strengthen thyself, O Jesus the high priest, the son of Josedec; and let all the people of the land strengthen themselves, saith the Lord, and work, for I am with you, saith the Lord Almighty; 6 and my Spirit remains in the midst of you; be of good courage. 7 For thus saith the Lord Almighty; Yet once I will shake the heaven, and the earth, and the sea, and the dry *land*; 8 and I will shake all nations, and the choice *portions* of all the nations shall come: and I will fill this house with glory, saith the Lord Almighty. 9 Mine is the silver, and mine the gold, saith the Lord Almighty. 10 For the glory of this house shall be great, the latter more than the former, saith the Lord Almighty: and in this place will I give peace, saith the Lord Almighty, even peace of soul for a possession to every one that builds, to raise up this temple. 11 On the four and twentieth *day* of the ninth month, in the second year of Darius, the word of the Lord came to Aggaeus the prophet, saying, 12 Thus saith the Lord Almighty; Inquire now of the priest *concerning* the law, saying, 13 If a man should take holy flesh in the skirt of his garment, and the skirt of his garment should touch bread, or pottage, or wine, or oil, or any meat, shall it be holy? And the priests answered and said, No. 14 And Aggaeus said, If a defiled person who is unclean by reason of a dead body, touch any of these, shall it be defiled? And the priests answered and said, It shall be defiled. 15 And Aggaeus answered and said, So is this people, and so is this nation before me, saith the Lord; and so are all the works of their hands: and whosoever shall approach them, shall

be defiled [because of their early burdens: they shall be pained because of their toils; and ye have hated him that reproved in the gates]. 16 And now consider, I pray you, from this day and beforetime, before they laid a stone on a stone in the temple of the Lord, what manner of men ye were. 17 When ye cast into the corn-bin twenty measures of barley, and there were *only* ten measures of barley: and ye went to the vat to draw out fifty measures, and there were *but* twenty. 18 I smote you with barrenness, and with blasting, and all the works of your hands with hail; yet ye returned not to me, saith the Lord. 19 Set your hearts now *to think* from this day and upward, from the four and twentieth *day* of the ninth month, even from the day when the foundation of the temple of the Lord was laid; 20 consider in your hearts, whether *this* shall be known on the corn-floor, and whether yet the vine, and the fig-tree, and the pomegranate, and the olive-trees that bear no fruit *are with you*: from this day will I bless *you*. 21 And the word of the Lord came the second time to Aggaeus the prophet, on the four and twentieth *day* of the month, saying, 22 Speak to Zorobabel the son of Salathiel, of the tribe of Juda, saying, I shake the heaven, and the earth, and the sea, and the dry *land*; 23 and I will overthrow the thrones of kings, and I will destroy the power of the kings of the nations; and I will overthrow chariots and riders; and the horses and their riders shall come down, every one by the sword striving against his brother. 24 In that day, saith the Lord Almighty, I will take thee, O Zorobabel, the son of Salathiel, my servant, saith the Lord, and will make thee as a seal: for I have chosen thee, saith the Lord Almighty.

ZACHARIAS (ZECHARIAH)

Zech.1 1 In the eighth month, in the second year of *the reign of* Darius, the word of the Lord came to Zacharias, the son of Barachias, the son of Addo, the prophet, saying, 2 The Lord has been very angry with your fathers. 3 And thou shalt say to them, Thus saith the Lord Almighty: Turn to me, saith the Lord of hosts, and I will turn to you, saith the Lord of hosts. 4 And be ye not as your fathers, whom the prophets before charged, saying, Thus saith the Lord Almighty: Turn ye from your evil ways, and from your evil practices: but they hearkened not, and attended not to hearken to me, saith the Lord. 5 Where are your fathers, and the prophets? Will they live for ever? 6 But do ye receive my words and mine ordinances, all that I command by my Spirit to my servants the prophets, who lived in the days of your fathers; and they answered and said, As the Lord Almighty determined to do to us, according to our ways, and according to our practices, so has he done to us. 7 On the twenty-fourth *day* in the eleventh month, this is the month Sabat, in the second year of *the reign of* Darius, the word of the Lord came to Zacharias, the son of Barachias, the son of Addo, the prophet, saying, 8 I saw by night, and behold a man mounted on a red horse, and he stood between the shady mountains; and behind him were red horses, and grey, and piebald, and white. 9 And I said, What are these, *my* lord? And the angel spoke with me said to me, I will shew thee what these *things* are. 10 And the man that stood between the mountains answered, and said to me,

These are *they* whom the Lord has sent forth to go round the earth. 11 And they answered the angel of the Lord that stood between the mountains, and said, We have gone round all the earth, and, behold, all the earth is inhabited, and is at rest. 12 Then the angel of the Lord answered and said, O Lord Almighty, how long wilt thou have no mercy on Jerusalem, and the cities of Juda, which thou has disregarded these seventy years? 13 And the Lord Almighty answered the angel that spoke with me good words and consolatory sayings. 14 And the angel that spoke with me said to me, Cry out and say, Thus saith the Lord Almighty; I have been jealous for Jerusalem and Sion with great jealousy. 15 And I am very angry with the heathen that combine to attack *her*: forasmuch as I indeed was a little angry, but they combined to attack *her* for evil. 16 Therefore thus saith the Lord: I will return to Jerusalem with compassion; and my house shall be rebuilt in her, saith the Lord Almighty, and a measuring line shall yet be stretched out over Jerusalem. 17 And the angel that spoke with me said to me, Cry yet, and say, Thus saith the Lord Almighty; Yet shall cities be spread abroad through prosperity; and the Lord shall yet have mercy upon Sion, and shall choose Jerusalem. 18 And I lifted up mine eyes and looked, and behold four horns. 19 And I said to the angel that spoke with me, What are these things, *my* lord? And he said to me, These are the horns that have scattered Juda, and Israel, and Jerusalem. 20 And the Lord shewed me four artificers. 21 And I said, What are these coming to do? And he said, These are the horns that scattered Juda, and they broke Israel in pieces, and none of them lifted up his head: and these are come forth to sharpen them for their hands, *even* the four horns, the nations that lifted up the horn against the land of the Lord to scatter it.

Zech.2 1 And I lifted up mine eyes, and looked, and behold a man, and in his hand a measuring line. 2 And I said to him, Whither goest thou? And he said to me, To measure Jerusalem, to see what is the breadth of it, and what is the length of it. 3 And, behold, the angel that spoke with me stood *by*, and another angel went forth to meet him, 4 and spoke to him, saying, Run and speak to that young man, saying, Jerusalem shall be fully inhabited by reason of the abundance of men and cattle in the midst of her. 5 And I will be to her, saith the Lord, a wall of fire round about, and I will be for a glory in the midst of her. 6 Ho, ho, flee from the land of the north, saith the Lord: for I will gather you from the four winds of heaven, saith the Lord, 7 *even* to Sion: deliver yourselves, ye that dwell *with* the daughter of Babylon. 8 For thus saith the Lord Almighty; After the glory has he sent me to the nations that spoiled you: for he that touches you is as one that touches the apple of his eye. 9 For, behold, I bring my hand upon them, and they shall be a spoil to them that serve them: and ye shall know that the Lord Almighty has sent me. 10 Rejoice and be glad, O daughter of Sion: for, behold, I come, and will dwell in the midst of thee, saith the Lord. 11 And many nations shall flee for refuge to the Lord in that day, and they shall be for a people to him, and they shall dwell in the midst of thee: and thou shalt know that the Lord Almighty has sent me to

thee. 12 And the Lord shall inherit Juda his portion in the holy *land*, and he will yet choose Jerusalem. 13 Let all flesh fear before the Lord: for he has risen up from his holy clouds.

Zech.3 1 And the Lord shewed me Jesus the high priest standing before the angel of the Lord, and the Devil stood on his right hand to resist him. 2 And the Lords said to the Devil, 3 The Lord rebuke thee, O Devil, even the Lord that has chosen Jerusalem rebuke thee: behold! is not this as a brand plucked from the fire? 4 Now Jesus was clothed in filthy raiment, and stood before the angel. 5 And *the Lord* answered and spoke to those who stood before him, saying, Take away the filthy raiment from him: and he said to him, Behold, I have taken away thine iniquities: and clothe ye him with a long robe, 6 and place a pure mitre upon his head. So they placed a pure mitre upon his head, and clothed him with garments: and the angel of the Lord stood *by*. 7 And the angel of the Lord testified to Jesus, saying, 8 Thus saith the Lord Almighty; If thou wilt walk in my ways, and take heed to my charges, then shalt thou judge my house: and if thou wilt diligently keep my court, then will I give thee men to walk in the midst of these that stand *here*. 9 Hear now, Jesus the high priest, thou, and thy neighbours that are sitting before *thee*: for they are diviners, for, behold, I bring forth my servant The Branch. 10 For *as for* the stone which I have set before the face of Jesus, on the one stone are seven eyes: behold, I am digging a trench, saith the Lord Almighty, and I will search out all the iniquity of that land in one day. 11 In that day, saith the Lord Almighty, ye shall call together every man his neighbour under the vine and under the fig-tree.

Zech.4 1 And the angel that talked with me returned, and awakened me, as when a man is awakened out of his sleep. 2 And he said to me, What seest thou? And I said, I have seen, and behold a candlestick all of gold, and its bowl upon it, and seven lamps upon it, and seven oil funnels to the lamps upon it: 3 and two olive-trees above it, one on the right of the bowl, and one on the left. 4 And I inquired, and spoke to the angel that talked with me, saying, What are these things, *my* lord? 5 And the angel that talked with me answered, and spoke to me, saying, Knowest thou not what these things are? And I said, No, *my* lord. 6 And he answered and spoke to me, saying, This is the word of the Lord to Zorobabel, saying, Not by mighty power, nor by strength, but by my Spirit, saith the Lord Almighty. 7 Who art thou, the great mountain before Zorobabel, that thou shouldest prosper? whereas I will bring out the stone of the inheritance, the grace of it the equal of *my* grace. 8 And the word of the Lord came to me, saying, 9 The hands of Zorobabel have laid the foundation of this house, and his hands shall finish it: and thou shalt know that the Lord Almighty has sent me to thee. 10 For who has despised the small days? surely they shall rejoice, and shall see the plummet of tin in the hand of Zorobabel: these are the seven eyes that look upon all the earth. 11 And I answered, and said to him, What are these two olive-trees, which are on the right and left hand of the candlestick? 12 And I asked the second time, and said to him, What are the two branches of the olive-trees that are by the side of the two golden pipes that pour into and communicate with the golden oil funnels? 13 And he said to me, Knowest thou not what these are? and I said, No, *my* lord. 14 And he said, These are the two anointed ones *that* stand by the Lord of the whole earth.

Zech.5 1 And I turned, and lifted up mine eyes, and looked and behold a flying sickle. 2 And he said to me, What seest thou? And I said, I see a flying sickle, of the length of twenty cubits, and of the breadth of ten cubits. 3 And he said to me, This is the curse that goes forth over the face of the whole earth: for every thief shall be punished with death on this side, and every false swearer shall be punished on that side. 4 And I will bring it forth, saith the Lord Almighty, and it shall enter into the house of the thief, and into the house of him that swears falsely by my name: and it shall rest in the midst of his house, and shall consume it, and the timber of it, and the stones of it. 5 And the angel that talked with me went forth, and said to me, Lift up thine eyes, and see this that goes forth. 6 And I said, What is it? And he said, This is the measure that goes forth. And he said, This is their iniquity in all the earth. 7 And behold a talent of lead lifted up: and behold a woman sat in the midst of the measure. 8 And he said, This is iniquity. And he cast it into the midst of the measure, and cast the weight of lead on the mouth of it. 9 And I lifted up mine eyes, and saw, and, behold, two women coming forth, and the wind was in their wings; and they had stork's wings: and they lifted up the measure between the earth and the sky. 10 And I said to the angel that spoke with me, Whither do these carry away the measure? 11 And he said to me, To build it a house in the land of Babylon, and to prepare *a place for it*; and they shall set it there on its own base.

Zech.6 1 And I turned, and lifted up mine eyes, and looked, and, behold, four chariots coming out from between two mountains; and the mountains were brazen mountains. 2 In the first chariot *were* red horses; and in the second chariot black horses; 3 and in the third chariot white horses; and in the fourth chariot piebald *and* ash-coloured horses. 4 And I answered and said to the angel that talked with me, What are these, my Lord? 5 And the angel that talked with me answered and said, These are the four winds of heaven, *and* they are going forth to stand before the Lord of all the earth. 6 *As for the chariot* in which were the black horses, they went out to the land of the north; and the white went out after them; and the piebald went out to the land of the south. 7 And the ash-coloured went out, and looked to go and compass the earth: and he said, Go, and compass the earth. And they compassed the earth. 8 And he cried out and spoke to me, saying, Behold, these go out to the land of the north, and they have quieted mine anger in the land of the north. 9 And the word of the Lord came to me, saying, 10 Take the things of the captivity from the chief men, and from the useful men of it, and from them that have understood it; and thou shalt enter in that day into the house of Josias the son of Sophonias that came out of Babylon. 11 And thou shalt take silver and gold, and make crowns, and thou shalt put *them* upon the head of Jesus the son of Josedec the high priest; 12 and thou shalt say to him, Thus saith the Lord Almighty; Behold the man whose name is The Branch; and he shall spring up from his stem, and build the house of the Lord. 13 And he shall receive power, and shall sit and rule upon his throne; and there shall be a priest on his right hand, and a peaceable counsel shall be between *them* both. 14 And the crown shall be to them that wait patiently, and to the useful men of the captivity, and to them that have known it, and for the favour of the son of Sophonias, and for a psalm in the house of the Lord. 15 And they *that are* far from them shall come and build in the house of the Lord, and ye shall know that the Lord Almighty has sent me to you: and *this* shall come to pass, if ye will diligently hearken to the voice of the Lord your God.

Zech.7 7:1 And it came to pass in the fourth year of Darius the king, *that* the word of the Lord came to Zacharias on the fourth *day* of the ninth month, which is Chaseleu. 2 And Sarasar and Arbeseer the king and his men sent to Bethel, and *that* to propitiate the Lord, 3 speaking to the priests that were in the house of the Lord Almighty, and to the prophets, saying, The holy offering has come in hither in the fifth month, as it has done already many years. 4 And the word of the Lord of hosts came to me, saying, 5 Speak to the whole people of the land, and to the priests, saying, Though ye fasted or lamented in the fifth or seventh *months* (yea, behold, these seventy years) have ye at all fasted to me? 6 And if ye eat or drink, do ye not eat and drink for yourselves? 7 Are not these the words which the Lord spoke by the former prophets, when Jerusalem was inhabited and in prosperity, and her cities round about her, and the hill country and the low country was inhabited? 8 And the word of the Lord came to Zacharias, saying, 9 Thus saith the Lord Almighty; Judge righteous judgment, and deal mercifully and compassionately every one with his brother: 10 and oppress not the widow, or the fatherless, or the stranger, or the poor; and let not one of you remember in his heart the injury of his brother. 11 But they refused to attend, and madly turned their back, and made their ears heavy, so that they should not hear. 12 And they made their heart disobedient, so as not to hearken to my law, and the words which the Lord Almighty sent forth by his Spirit by the former prophets: so there was great wrath from the Lord Almighty. 13 And it shall come to pass, *that* as he spoke, and they hearkened not, so they shall cry, and I will not hearken, saith the Lord Almighty. 14 And I will cast them out among all the nations, whom they know not; and the land behind them shall be made utterly destitute of any going through or returning: yea they have made the choice land a desolation.

Zech.8 1 And the word of the Lord Almighty came, saying, 2 Thus saith the Lord Almighty; I have been jealous for Jerusalem and for Sion with great jealousy, and I have been jealous for her with great fury. 3 Thus saith the Lord; I will return to Sion, and dwell in the midst of Jerusalem: and Jerusalem shall be called a true city, and the mountain of the Lord Almighty a holy mountain. 4 Thus saith the Lord Almighty; There shall yet dwell old men and old women in the streets of Jerusalem, every one holding his staff in his hand for age. 5 And the broad places of the city shall be filled with boys and girls playing in the streets thereof. 6 Thus saith the Lord Almighty; If it shall be impossible in the sight of the remnant of this people in those days, shall it also be impossible in my sight? saith the Lord Almighty. 7 Thus saith the Lord Almighty; Behold, I *will* save my people from the east country, and the west country; 8 and I will bring them in, and cause *them* to dwell in the midst of Jerusalem: and they shall be to me a people, and I will be to them a God, in truth and in righteousness. 9 Thus saith the Lord Almighty; Let your hands be strong, *ye that* hear in these days these words out of the mouth of the prophets, from the day that the house of the Lord Almighty was founded, and from the time that the temple was built. 10 For before those days the wages of men could not be profitable, and there could be no hire of cattle, and there could be no peace by reason of the affliction to him that went out or to him that came in: for I would have let loose all men, every one against his neighbour. 11 But now I *will* not do to the remnant of this people according to the former days, saith the Lord Almighty. 12 But I will shew peace: the vine shall yield her fruit, and the land shall yield her produce, and the heaven shall give its dew: and I will give as an inheritance all these things to the remnant of my people. 13 And it shall come to pass, as ye were a curse among the nations, O house of Juda, and house of Israel; so will I save you, and ye shall be a blessing: be of good courage, and strengthen your hands. 14 For thus saith the Lord Almighty; As I took counsel to afflict you when your fathers provoked me, saith the Lord Almighty, and I repented not: 15 so have I prepared and taken counsel in these days to do good to Jerusalem and to the house of Juda: be ye of good courage. 16 These *are* the things which ye shall do; speak truth every one with his neighbour; judge truth and peaceable judgment in your gates: 17 and let none of you devise evil in his heart against his neighbour; and love not a false oath: for all these things I hate, saith the Lord Almighty. 18 And the word of the Lord Almighty came to me, saying, 19 Thus saith the Lord Almighty, The fourth fast, and the fifth fast, and the seventh fast, and the tenth fast, shall be to the house of Juda for joy and gladness, and for good feasts; and ye shall rejoice; and love ye the truth and peace. 20 Thus saith the Lord Almighty; Yet shall many peoples come, and the inhabitants of many cities; 21 and the inhabitants of five cities shall come together to one city, saying, Let us go to make supplication to the Lord, and to seek the face of the Lord Almighty; I will go also. 22 And many peoples and many nations shall come to seek earnestly the face of the Lord Almighty in Jerusalem, and to obtain favour of the Lord. 23 Thus saith the Lord Almighty; In those days *my word shall be fulfilled* if ten men of all the languages of the nations should take hold—even take hold of the hem of a Jew, saying, We will go with thee; for we have heard that God is with you.

Zech.9 1 The burden of the word of the Lord, in the land of Sedrach, and his sacrifice *shall be* in Damascus; for the Lord looks upon men, and upon all the tribes of Israel. 2

And in Emath, *even* in her coasts, *are* Tyre and Sidon, because they were very wise. 3 And Tyrus built strong-holds for herself, and heaped up silver as dust, and gathered gold as the mire of the ways. 4 And therefore the Lord will take them for a possession, and will smite her power in the sea; and she shall be consumed with fire. 5 Ascalon shall see, and fear; Gaza also, and shall be greatly pained, and Accaron; for she is ashamed at her trespass; and the king shall perish from Gaza, and Ascalon shall not be inhabited. 6 And aliens shall dwell in Azotus, and I will bring down the pride of the Philistines. 7 And I will take their blood out of their mouth, and their abominations from between their teeth; and these also shall be left to our God, and they shall be as a captain of a thousand in Juda, and Accaron as a Jebusite. 8 And I will set up a defence for my house, that they may not pass through, nor turn back, neither shall there any more come upon them one to drive them away: for now have I seen with mine eyes. 9 Rejoice greatly, O daughter of Sion; proclaim *it* aloud, O daughter of Jerusalem; behold, the King is coming to thee, just, and a Saviour; he is meek and riding on an ass, and a young foal. 10 And he shall destroy the chariots out of Ephraim, and the horse out of Jerusalem, and the bow of war shall be utterly destroyed; and *there shall be* abundance and peace out of the nations; and he shall rule over the waters as far as the sea, and the rivers *to* the ends of the earth. 11 And thou by the blood of thy covenant has sent forth thy prisoners out of the pit that has no water. 12 Ye shall dwell in strongholds, ye prisoners of the congregation: and for one day of thy captivity I will recompense thee double. 13 For I have bent thee, O Juda, for myself *as* a bow, I have filled Ephraim; and I will raise up thy children, O Sion, against the children of the Greeks, and I will handle thee as the sword of a warrior. 14 And the Lord shall be over them, and *his* arrow shall go forth as lightning: and the Lord Almighty shall blow with the trumpet; and shall proceed with the tumult of his threatening. 15 The Lord Almighty shall protect them, and they shall destroy them, and overwhelm them with sling-stones; and they shall swallow them down as wine, and fill the bowls as the altar. 16 And the Lord their God shall save them in that day, *even* his people as a flock; for holy stones are rolled upon his land. 17 For if he has anything good, and if he has anything fair, the young *men* shall have corn, and *there shall be* fragrant wine to the virgins.

Zech.10 1 Ask ye of the Lord rain in season, the early and the latter: the Lord has given bright signs, and will give them abundant rain, to every one grass in the field. 2 For the speakers have uttered grievous things, and the diviners *have seen* false visions, and they have spoken false dreams, they have given vain comfort: therefore have they fallen away like sheep, and been afflicted, because there was no healing. 3 Mine anger was kindled against the shepherds, and I will visit the lambs; and the Lord God Almighty shall visit his flock, the house of Juda, and he shall make them as his goodly horse in war. 4 And from him he looked, and from him he set *the battle in order*, and from him *came* the bow in anger, *and* from him shall come forth every oppressor together. 5 And they shall be as warriors treading clay in the ways in war; and they shall set the battle in array, because the Lord is with them, and the riders on horses shall be put to shame. 6 And I will strengthen the house of Juda, and save the house of Joseph, and I will settle them; because I have loved them: and they shall be as *if* I had not cast them off: for I am the Lord their God, and I will hear them. 7 And they shall be as the warriors of Ephraim, and their heart shall rejoice as with wine: and their children also shall see *it*, and be glad; and their heart shall rejoice in the Lord. 8 I will make a sign to them, and gather them in; for I will redeem them, and they shall be multiplied according to their number before. 9 And I will sow them among the people; and they that are afar off shall remember me: they shall nourish their children, and they shall return. 10 And I will bring them again from the land of Egypt, and I will gather them in from among the Assyrians; and I will bring them into the land of Galaad and to Libanus; and there shall not even one of them be left behind. 11 And they shall pass through a narrow sea, they shall smite the waves in the sea, and all the deep places of the rivers shall be dried up: and all the pride of the Assyrians shall be taken away, and the sceptre of Egypt shall be removed. 12 And I will strengthen them in the Lord their God; and they shall boast in his name, saith the Lord.

Zech.11 1 Open thy doors, O Libanus, and let the fire devour thy cedars. 2 Let the pine howl, because the cedar has fallen; for the mighty men have been greatly afflicted: howl, ye oaks of the land of Basan; for the thickly planted forest has been torn down. 3 *There is* a voice of the shepherds mourning; for their greatness is brought low: a voice of roaring lions; for the pride of Jordan is brought down. 4 Thus saith the Lord Almighty, Feed the sheep of the slaughter; 5 which their possessors have slain, and have not repented: and they that sold them said, Blessed be the Lord; for we have become rich: and their shepherds have suffered no sorrow for them. 6 Therefore I will no longer have mercy upon the inhabitants of the land, saith the Lord: but, behold, I will deliver up the men every one into the hand of his neighbour, and into the hand of his king; and they shall destroy the land, and I will not rescue out of their hand. 7 And I will tend the flock of slaughter in the land of Chanaan: and I will take for myself two rods; the one I called Beauty, and the other I called Line; and I will tend the flock. 8 And I will cut off three shepherds in one month; and my soul shall grieve over them, for their souls cried out against me. 9 And I said, I will not tend you: that which dies, let it die; and that which falls off, let it fall off; and let the rest eat every one the flesh of his neighbour. 10 And I will take my beautiful staff, and cast it away, that I may break my covenant which I made with all the people. 11 And it shall be broken in that day; and the Chananites, the sheep that are kept for me, shall know that it is the word of the Lord. 12 And I will say to them, If it be good in your eyes, give *me* my price, or refuse it. And they weighed for my price thirty pieces of silver. 13 And the Lord said to me, Drop them into the furnace, and I will see if it is good *metal*, as I was proved for their sakes. And I took the thirty pieces of silver, and cast them into the furnace in the house of the Lord. 14 And I cast away *my* second rod, *even* Line, that I might break the possession between Juda and Israel. 15 And the Lord said to me, Take yet to thee shepherd's implements belonging to an unskillful shepherd. 16 For, behold, I *will* raise up a shepherd against the land: he shall not visit that which is perishing, and he shall not seek that which is scattered, and he shall not heal that which is bruised, nor guide that which is whole: but he shall devour the flesh of the choice *ones*, and shall dislocate the joints *of their necks*. 17 Alas for the vain shepherds that have forsaken the sheep! the sword *shall be* upon the arms of such a one, and upon his right eye: his arm shall be completely withered, and his right eye shall be utterly darkened.

Zech.12 1 The burden of the word of the Lord for Israel; saith the Lord, that stretches out the sky, and lays the foundation of the earth, and forms the spirit of man within him. 2 Behold, I *will* make Jerusalem as trembling doorposts to all the nations round about, and in Judea there shall be a siege against Jerusalem. 3 And it shall come to pass in that day *that* I will make Jerusalem a trodden stone to all the nations: every one that tramples on it shall utterly mock at *it*, and all the nations of the earth shall be gathered together against it. 4 In that day, saith the Lord Almighty, I will smite every horse with amazement, and his rider with madness: but I will open mine eyes upon the house of Juda, and I will smite all the horses of the nations with blindness. 5 And the captains of thousands of Juda shall say in their hearts, We shall find for ourselves the inhabitants of Jerusalem in the Lord Almighty their God. 6 In that day I will make the captains of thousands of Juda as a firebrand among wood, and as a torch of fire in stubble; and they shall devour on the right hand and on the left all the nations round about: and Jerusalem shall dwell again by herself, *even* in Jerusalem. 7 And the Lord shall save the tabernacles of Juda as at the beginning, that the boast of the house of David, and the pride of the inhabitants of Jerusalem, may not magnify themselves against Juda. 8 And it shall come to pass in that day, *that* the Lord shall defend the inhabitants of Jerusalem; and the weak one among them in that day shall be as David, and the house of David as the house of God, as the angel of the Lord before them. 9 And it shall come to pass in that day, *that* I will seek to destroy all the nations that come against Jerusalem. 10 And I will pour upon the house of David, and upon the inhabitants of Jerusalem, the spirit of grace and compassion: and they shall look upon me, because they have mocked *me*, and they shall make lamentation for him, as for a beloved *friend*, and they shall grieve intensely, as for a firstborn *son*. 11 In that day the lamentation in Jerusalem shall be very great, as the mourning for the pomegranate grove cut down in the plain. 12 And the land shall lament in separate families, the family of the house of David by itself, and their wives by themselves; the family of the house of Nathan by itself, and their wives by themselves; 13 the family of the house of Levi by itself, and their wives by themselves; the family of Symeon by itself, and their wives by themselves; 14 all the families that are left, each family by itself, and their wives by themselves.

Zech.13 1 In that day every place shall be opened to the house of David and to the inhabitants of Jerusalem for removal and for separation. 2 And it shall come to pass in that day, saith the Lord of hosts, *that* I will utterly destroy the names of the idols from off the land, and there shall be no longer *any* remembrance of them: and I will cut off the false prophets and the evil spirit from the land. 3 And it shall come to pass, if a man will yet prophesy, that his father and his mother which gave birth to him shall say to him, Thou shalt not live; for thou has spoken lies in the name of the Lord: and his father and his mother who gave him birth shall bind him as he is prophesying. 4 And it shall come to pass in that day, *that* the prophets shall be ashamed every one of his vision when he prophesies; and they shall clothe themselves with a garment of hair, because they have lied. 5 And *one* shall say, I am not a prophet, for I am a tiller of the ground, for a man brought me up *thus* from my youth. 6 And I will say to him, What are these wounds between thine hands? and he shall say, *Those* with which I was wounded in my beloved house. 7 Awake, O sword, against my shepherds, and against the man *who is* my citizen, saith the Lord Almighty: smite the shepherds, and draw out the sheep: and I will bring mine hand upon the little ones. 8 And it shall come to pass, *that* in all the land, saith the Lord, two parts thereof shall be cut off and perish; but the third shall be left therein. 9 And I will bring the third *part* through the fire, and I will try them as silver is tried, and I will prove them as gold is proved: they shall call upon my name, and I will hear them, and say, This is my people: and they shall say, The Lord *is* my God.

Zech.14 1 Behold, the days of the Lord come, and thy spoils shall be divided in thee. 2 And I will gather all the Gentiles to Jerusalem to war, and the city shall be taken, and the houses plundered, and the women ravished; and half of the city shall go forth into captivity, but the rest of my people shall not be utterly cut off from the city. 3 And the Lord shall go forth, and fight with those Gentiles as when he fought in the day of war. 4 And his feet shall stand in that day on the mount of Olives, which is before Jerusalem on the east, and the mount of Olives shall cleave asunder, half of it toward the east and the west, a very great division; and half the mountain shall lean to the north, and half of it to the south. 5 And the valley of my mountains shall be closed up, and the valley of the mountains shall be joined on to Jasod, and shall be blocked up as it was blocked up in the days of the earthquake, in the days of Ozias king of Juda; and the Lord my God shall come, and all the saints with him. 6 And it shall come to pass in that day that there shall be no light, 7 and there shall be for one day cold and frost, and that day *shall be* known to the Lord, and *it shall* not *be* day nor night: but towards evening it shall be light. 8 And in that day living water shall come forth out of Jerusalem; half of it toward the former sea, and half of it toward the latter sea: and so shall it be in summer and spring. 9 And the Lord shall be king over all the earth: in that day there shall be one Lord, and his name one, 10 compassing all the earth, and the wilderness from Gabe unto Remmon south of Jerusalem. And Rama shall remain in its place. From the gate of Benjamin to the place of the first gate, to the gate of the corners, and to the tower of Anameel, as far as the king's winepresses, 11 they shall dwell in the city; and there shall be no more any curse, and Jerusalem shall dwell securely. 12 And this shall be the overthrow with which the Lord will smite all the nations, as many as have fought against Jerusalem; their flesh shall consume away while they are standing upon their feet, and their eyes shall melt out of their holes, and their tongue shall consume away in their mouth. 13 And there shall be in that day a great panic from the Lord upon them; and they shall lay hold every man of the hand of his neighbour, and his hand shall be clasped with the hand of his neighbour. 14 Juda also shall fight in Jerusalem; and *God* shall gather the strength of all the nations round about, gold, and silver, and apparel, in great abundance. 15 And this shall be the overthrow of the horses, and mules, and camels, and asses, and all the beasts that are in those camps, according to this overthrow. 16 And it shall come to pass, *that* whosoever shall be left of all the nations that came against Jerusalem, shall even come up every year to worship the king, the Lord Almighty, and to keep the feast of tabernacles. 17 And it shall come to pass, *that* whosoever of all the families of the earth shall not come up to Jerusalem to worship the king, the Lord Almighty, even these shall be added to the others. 18 And if the family of Egypt shall not go up, nor come; then upon them shall be the overthrow with which the Lord shall smite all the nations, whichever of them shall not come up to keep the feast of tabernacles. 19 This shall be the sin of Egypt, and the sin of all the nations, whosoever shall not come up to keep the feast of tabernacles. 20 In that day there shall be upon the bridle of every horse Holiness to the Lord Almighty; and the caldrons in the house of the Lord shall be as bowls before the altar. 21 And every pot in Jerusalem and in Juda shall be holy to the Lord Almighty: and all that sacrifice shall come and take of them, and shall seethe *meat* in them: and in that day there shall be no more the Chananite in the house of the Lord Almighty.

MALACHIAS (MALACHI)

Mal.1 1 The burden of the word of the Lord to Israel by the hand of his messenger. Lay *it*, I pray you, to heart. 2 I have loved you, saith the Lord. And ye said, Wherein hast thou loved us? Was not Esau Jacob's brother? saith the Lord: yet I loved Jacob, 3 and hated Esau and laid waste his borders, and made his heritage as dwellings of the wilderness? 4 Because one will say, Idumea has been overthrown, but let us return and rebuild the desolate places; thus saith the Lord Almighty, They shall build, but I will throw down; and they shall be called The borders of wickedness, and, The people against whom the Lord has set himself for ever. 5 And your eyes shall see, and ye shall say, The Lord has been magnified upon the borders of Israel. 6 A son honours *his* father, and a servant his master: if then I am a father, where is mine honour? and if I am a master, where is my fear? saith the Lord Almighty. Ye the priests are they that despise my name: yet ye said, Wherein have we despised thy name? 7 In that ye bring to mine altar polluted bread; and ye said, Wherein have we polluted it? In that ye say, The table of the Lord is polluted, and that which was set thereon ye have despised. 8 For if ye bring a blind *victim* for sacrifices, *is it* not evil? and if ye bring the lame or the sick, *is it* not evil? offer it now to thy ruler, *and see* if he will receive thee, if he will accept thy person, saith the Lord Almighty. 9 And now intreat the face of your God, and make supplication to him. These things have been done by your hands; shall I accept you? saith the Lord Almighty. 10 Because even among you the doors shall be shut, and *one* will not kindle *the fire of* mine altar for nothing, I have no pleasure in you, saith the Lord Almighty, and I will not accept a sacrifice at your hands. 11 For from the rising of the sun even to the going down *thereof* my name has been glorified among the Gentiles; and in every place incense is offered to my name, and a pure offering: for my name is great among the Gentiles, saith the Lord Almighty. 12 But ye profane it, in that ye say, The table of the Lord is polluted, and his meats set thereon are despised. 13 And ye said, These *services* are troublesome: therefore I have utterly rejected them with scorn, saith the Lord Almighty: and ye brought in torn victims, and lame, and sick: if then ye should bring an offering, shall I accept them at your hands? saith the Lord Almighty. 14 And cursed *is the man* who had the power, and possessed a male in his flock, and whose vow is upon him, and who sacrifices a corrupt thing to the Lord: for I am a great King, saith the Lord Almighty, and my name is glorious among the nations.

Mal.2 1 And now, O priests, this commandment is to you. 2 If ye will not hearken, and if ye will not lay *it* to heart, to give glory to my name, saith the Lord Almighty, then I will send forth the curse upon you, and I will bring a curse upon your blessing: yea, I will curse it, and I will scatter your blessing, and it shall not exist among you, because ye lay not this to heart. 3 Behold, I turn my back upon you, and I will scatter dung upon your faces, the dung of your feasts, and I will carry you away at the same time. 4 And ye shall know that I have sent this commandment to you, that my covenant might be with the sons of Levi, saith the Lord Almighty. 5 My covenant of life and peace was with him, and I gave *it* him that he might reverently fear me, and that he might be awe-struck at my name. 6 The law of truth was in his mouth, and iniquity was not found in his lips: he walked before me directing *his way* in peace, and he turned many from unrighteousness. 7 For the priest's lips should keep knowledge, and they should seek the law at his mouth: for he is the messenger of the Lord Almighty. 8 But ye have turned aside from the way, and caused many to fail in *following* the law: ye have corrupted the covenant of Levi, saith the Lord Almighty. 9 And I have made you despised and cast out among all the people, because ye have not kept my ways, but have been partial in the law. 10 Have ye not all one father? Did not one God create you? why have ye forsaken every man his brother, to profane the covenant of your fathers? 11 Juda has been forsaken, and an abomination has been committed in Israel and in Jerusalem; for Juda has profaned the holy things of the Lord, which he delighted in, and has gone after other gods. 12 The Lord will utterly destroy the man that does these

things, until he be even cast down from out of the tabernacles of Jacob, and from among them that offer sacrifice to the Lord Almighty. 13 And these things which I hated, ye did: ye covered with tears the altar of the Lord, and with weeping and groaning because of troubles: *is it* meet *for me* to have respect to your sacrifice, or to receive *anything* from your hands *as* welcome? 14 Yet ye said, Wherefore? Because the Lord has borne witness between thee and the wife of thy youth, whom thou has forsaken, and *yet* she was thy partner, and the wife of thy covenant. 15 And did he not do well? and *there was* the residue of his spirit. But ye said, What does God seek but a seed? But take ye heed to your spirit, and forsake not the wife of thy youth. 16 But if thou shouldest hate *thy wife* and put her away, saith the Lord God of Israel, then ungodliness shall cover thy thoughts, saith the Lord Almighty: therefore take ye heed to your spirit, and forsake *them* not, 17 ye that have provoked God with your words. But ye said, Wherein have we provoked him? In that ye say, Every one that does evil is a pleasing *object* in the sight of the Lord, and he takes pleasure in such; and where is the God of justice?

Mal.3 1 Behold, I send forth my messenger, and he shall survey the way before me: and the Lord, whom ye seek, shall suddenly come into his temple, even the angel of the covenant, whom ye take pleasure in: behold, he is coming, saith the Lord Almighty. 2 And who will abide the day of his coming? or who will withstand at his appearing? for he is coming in as the fire of a furnace and as the herb of fullers. 3 He shall sit to melt and purify as it were silver, and as it were gold: and he shall purify the sons of Levi, and refine them as gold and silver, and they shall offer to the Lord an offering in righteousness. 4 And the sacrifice of Juda and Jerusalem shall be pleasing to the Lord, according to the former days, and according to the former years. 5 And I will draw near to you in judgment; and I will be a sift witness against the witches, and against the adulteresses, and against them that swear falsely by my name, and against them that keep back the hireling's wages, and them that oppress the widow, and afflict orphans, and that wrest the judgment of the stranger, and fear not me, saith the Lord Almighty. 6 For I am the Lord your God, and I am not changed: 7 but ye, the sons of Jacob, have not refrained from the iniquities of your fathers: ye have perverted my statutes, and have not kept them. Return to me, and I will return to you, saith the Lord Almighty. But ye said, Wherein shall we return? 8 Will a man insult God? for ye insult me. But ye say, Wherein have we insulted thee? In that the tithes and first-fruits are with you *still*. 9 And ye do surely look off from me, and ye insult me. 10 The year is completed, and ye have brought all the produce into the storehouses; but there shall be the plunder thereof in its house: return now on this behalf, saith the Lord Almighty, *see* if I will not open to you the torrents of heaven, and pour out my blessing upon you, until ye are satisfied. 11 And I will appoint food for you, and I will not destroy the fruit of your land; and your vine in the field shall not fail, saith the Lord Almighty. 12 And all nations shall call you blessed: for ye shall be a desirable land, saith the Lord Almighty. 13 Ye have spoken grievous words against me, saith the Lord. Yet ye said, Wherein have we spoken against thee? 14 Ye said, He that serves God labours in vain: and what have we gained in that we have kept his ordinances, and in that we have walked as suppliants before the face of the Lord Almighty? 15 And now we pronounce strangers blessed; and all they who act unlawfully are built up; and they have resisted God, and *yet* have been delivered. 16 Thus spoke they that feared the Lord, every one to his neighbour: and the Lord gave heed, and hearkened, and he wrote a book of remembrance before him for them that feared the Lord and reverenced his name. 17 And they shall be mine, saith the Lord Almighty, in the day which I appoint for a peculiar possession; and I will make choice of them, as a man makes choice of his son that serves him. 18 Then shall ye return, and discern between the righteous and the wicked, and between him that serves God, and him that serves *him* not.

Mal.4 1 For, behold, a day comes burning as an oven, and it shall consume them; and all the aliens, and all that do wickedly, shall be stubble: and the day that is coming shall set them on fire, saith the Lord Almighty, and there shall not be left of them root or branch. 2 But to you that fear my name shall the Sun of righteousness arise, and healing *shall be* in his wings: and ye shall go forth, and bound as young calves let loose from bonds. 3 And ye shall trample the wicked; for they shall be ashes underneath your feet in the day which I appoint, saith the Lord Almighty. 5 And, behold, I will send to you Elias the Thesbite, before the great and glorious day of the Lord comes; 6 who shall turn again the heart of the father to the son, and the heart of a man to his neighbour, lest I come and smite the earth grievously. Remember the law of my servant Moses, accordingly as I charged him *with it* in Choreb for all Israel, *even* the commandments and ordinances.

Made in the USA
Columbia, SC
21 June 2025

59692868R00328